Great Britain

David Else, Oliver Berry, Nicky Crowther, Fionn Davenport, Martin Hughes,
Sam Martin, Etain O'Carroll, Becky Ohlsen, Andy Symington

Contents

Highlands & Northern Islands p869

Central Scotland p813

Edinburgh p743

Southern Scotland p771

Northeast England p610

Cumbria & the Lakes p583

Yorkshire p491

Northwest England p548

North Wales p709

The Midlands p394

Mid-Wales p685

The Marches p368

Eastern England p446

South Wales p655

Cardiff p639

London p100

Southwest England p229

Southeast England p172

Oxfordshire, Gloucestershire & the Cotswolds p336

The Channel Islands p938

Destination Britain

Britain is a banquet, a feast of delights to make your mouth water. It's hard to believe that Scotland's snowcapped mountains, the azure waters on Cornwall's sandy beaches, the tranquil village pubs of Wales or the high-energy clubs of Manchester are all in the same country – a country in which it takes just 12 hours to drive end-to-end.

This combination of stunning scenery, amazing variety and compact geography is Britain's unique drawcard. It also provides a tangible link to the island's extraordinary history, making a journey through Britain a trip through 30 centuries: you can follow Roman footsteps on Hadrian's Wall, go mystic at Stonehenge, visit *Braveheart* battlefields, immerse yourself in royal intrigue at Warwick Castle, and recall the legend of King Arthur as you hike up Mount Snowdon. Then shift the pace up a gear, and experience Britain's world-class cities. London overflows with spectacle, and the gems of Oxford, Bath, York and Edinburgh never fail to impress. Together they tempt with stunning new buildings, superlative attractions, and truly excellent museums. After dark, fine restaurants, top-class theatre, stylish bars and cutting-edge venues provide a string of nights to remember (or to forget – depending how hard you party).

For us it was a hard job picking the best to include in this book So mix our pointers with your own discoveries. See the world-famous sights, but get off the beaten track, too. Whether you're aged 17 or 70, Britain is yours for the taking. The beauty of the country, the diversity of the attractions and the hospitality of the people together ensure Britain's place as one of the world's most popular destinations.

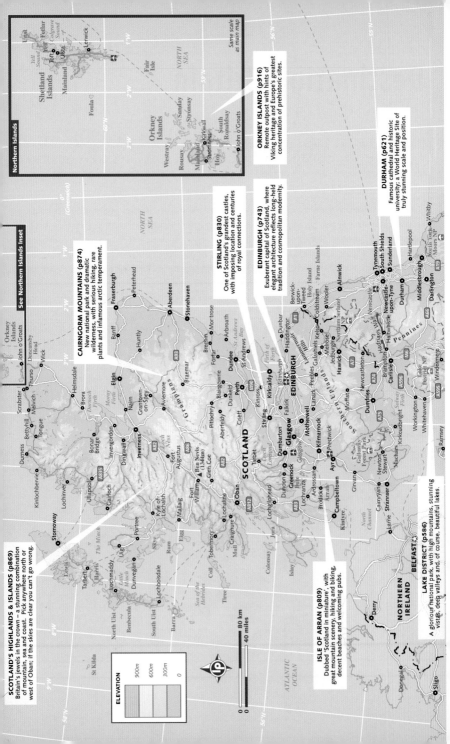

Northern Islands

Same scale as main map

See Northern Islands Inset

ORKNEY ISLANDS (p916)
Remote outpost with hints of Viking heritage and Europe's greatest concentration of prehistoric sites.

DURHAM (p621)
Famous cathedral and historic university; a World Heritage Site of truly stunning scale and position.

CAIRNGORM MOUNTAINS (p874)
New national park and dramatic wilderness, with serious hiking, rare plants and infamous arctic temperament.

STIRLING (p830)
One of Scotland's grandest castles, with imposing location and centuries of royal connections.

EDINBURGH (p743)
Exuberant capital of Scotland, where elegant architecture reflects long-held tradition and cosmopolitan modernity.

SCOTLAND'S HIGHLANDS & ISLANDS (p869)
Britain's jewels in the crown – a stunning combination of mountain, sea and coast. Pick anywhere north or west of Oban; if the skies are clear you can't go wrong.

ISLE OF ARRAN (p809)
Dubbed 'Scotland in miniature', with great mountain scenery, hiking and biking, decent beaches and welcoming pubs.

LAKE DISTRICT (p586)
A glorious national park, with high mountains, stunning vistas, deep valleys and, of course, beautiful lakes.

ELEVATION
900m
600m
300m
0

0   80 km
0   40 miles

NORTH SEA

ATLANTIC OCEAN

SCOTLAND

NORTHERN IRELAND

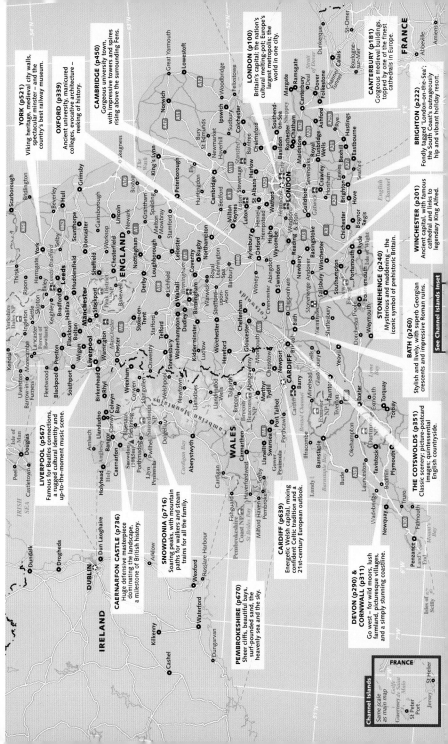

YORK (p521)
Viking heritage, medieval city walls, spectacular minster – and the country's best railway museum.

OXFORD (p339)
Ancient university, manicured colleges, evocative architecture – reeking of history.

CAMBRIDGE (p450)
Gorgeous university town, with impressive towers and spires rising above the surrounding Fens.

LONDON (p100)
Britain's capital; the nation's cultural melting-pot; Europe's largest metropolis; the world in one city.

CANTERBURY (p181)
Gorgeous medieval buildings, topped by one of the finest cathedrals in Europe.

BRIGHTON (p222)
Fondly tagged 'London-on-the-Sea'; the South Coast's outrageously hip and vibrant holiday resort.

LIVERPOOL (p567)
Famous for Beatles connections, a rugged cultural identity and up-to-the-moment music scene.

CAERNARFON CASTLE (p736)
Huge defensive masterpiece dominating the landscape, a milestone of British history.

SNOWDONIA (p716)
Soaring peaks, with mountain paths for walkers and steam trains for all the family.

PEMBROKESHIRE (p670)
Sheer cliffs, beautiful bays, surf-pounded sand, the heavenly sea and the sky.

CARDIFF (p639)
Energetic Welsh capital, mixing a confident Celtic tradition and a 21st-century European outlook.

DEVON (p290) & CORNWALL (p311)
Go west – for wild moors, lush farmland, picturesque villages, and a simply stunning coastline.

THE COTSWOLDS (p351)
Classic scenery; picture-postcard images; quintessential English countryside.

WINCHESTER (p201)
Ancient capital, with famous cathedral and links to legendary King Alfred.

STONEHENGE (p240)
Mysterious and maddening – the iconic symbol of prehistoric Britain.

BATH (p260)
Stylish and lively, with superb Georgian crescents and impressive Roman ruins.

See Channel Islands inset

Channel Islands
Same scale as main map

Everyone knows **Windsor** (p196), but don't miss **Warwick** (p409), **Stirling** (p831), **Glamis** (p867), **Caernarfon** (p736), **Conwy** (p733) and **Chepstow** (p660). If cathedrals inspire, head for **Canterbury** (p182), **Salisbury** (p235) and **Winchester** (p201). Or search for legendary King Arthur at **Tintagel** (p330), **Glastonbury** (p270) and **Mt Snowdon** (p705). **Bath** (p260) has Roman remains, while **Durham** (p621), **Oxford** (p340) and **Cambridge** (p451) are university towns with evocative architecture. Travel back to **Stonehenge** (p240), see the ancient tomb of **Pentre Ifan** (p683), wander among Bronze Age ruins on **Dartmoor** (p304) or reach the remote **Orkney Islands** (p916) for Europe's greatest concentration of prehistoric sites.

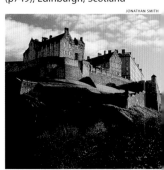

Experience the commanding presence of Edinburgh Castle (p749), Edinburgh, Scotland

JONATHAN SMITH

DAVID WALL

Visit the impressive collections at the Natural History Museum (p138), London, England

Tour the technically progressive fortifications of Beaumaris Castle (p738), Beaumaris, England

ANDERS BLOMQVIST

GREG GAWLOWSKI

Get mystical at the eerie Callanish Standing Stones (p913), Lewis, Scotland

GLENN BEANLAND

Be impressed with the largest medieval cathedral in Great Britain, York Minster (p523), York, England

Take in the excellent views from the walkways of Tower Bridge (p135), London, England

MARTIN MOOS

Britain's cities are confident and cutting-it. **Bristol** (p249) is a hotbed of musical innovation, **Brighton** (p222) is a hip seaside resort and **Birmingham** (p397) has big-name clubs and top theatre. **Manchester** (p551) is renowned for night-time activities, **Liverpool** (p567) is famous for Beatles connections and a rugged cultural identity, while **Leeds** (p500) has sleek entertainment and shopping to die for. **Cardiff** (p639) combines defiant Celtic tradition and a 21st-century European outlook, to produce enticing cuisine, stunning architecture, vibrant venues and world-class rock bands.

NEIL SETCHFIELD

Shop till you drop at fashionable Liberty (p166), London, England

Check out the interesting armadillo-shaped Clyde Auditorium (p789), Glasgow, Scotland

MARTIN MOOS

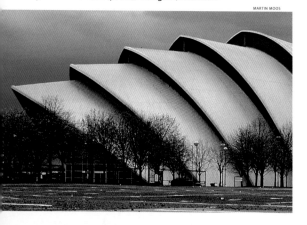

NEIL SETCHFIELD

Become a reader at the controversial British Library (p141), London, England

Drink yourself dry at the popular bar of Beluga (p765), Edinburgh, Scotland

JONATHAN SMITH

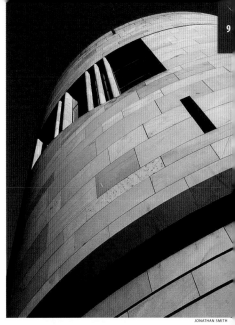

JONATHAN SMITH

Explore Scottish heritage at the Museum of Scotland (p755), Edinburgh, Scotland

Sample the shopping delights of Ocean Terminal (p768), Edinburgh, Scotland

JONATHAN SMITH

While away the hours at a chic café in Soho (p154), London, England

NEIL SETCHFIELD

For classic British scenery try **Devon** (p290), **Cornwall** (p311) and **Pembrokeshire** (p655). Stroll down the limestone dales of **Derbyshire** (p430), along the beaches of **Suffolk** (p462) or through the heath of **New Forest** (p209). For mountains head for **Snowdonia** (p716), **Ben Nevis** (p880) or the **Brecon Beacons** (p689). Or experience the high hills of **Northumberland** (p635), **Mid Wales** (p613) or the **Cairngorms** (p874). But for paradise on earth it has to be the highlands and islands of **Northwest Scotland** (p895), a stunning mix of rock and water where mountains plunge into the sea and crystal-clear lochs cut deep inland.

SIMON ROWE

Witness charming architectural traditions in the Cotswolds (p351), England

Breathe in the mountain air walking over Buachaille Etive Mor in Glen Coe (p883), Scotland

GARETH MCCORMACK

ANDREW MACCOLL

Gaze across the picturesque rural pastures of the Peak District National Park (p435), England

Stroll along the spectacular cliffs of the 100-mile-long South Downs Way (p175), England

Ponder the tranquility of the Lake District National Park (p586), Scotland

Ramble through beautiful Pembrokeshire Coast National Park (p670), Wales

Hurrah for gastro-pubs and comfortable country inns. Our favourites: Crickhowell's **Bear Hotel** (p697), offering Welsh cuisine and traditional hospitality; Great Tew's **Falkland Arms** (p356), with snuff, wet dogs and honest fare; Corscombe's **Fox Inn** (p289), an idyllic rose-clad pub serving rustic food; Titley's **Stagg Inn** (p380), gastronomy without pretension; Castleton's **George** (p442), with great grub and fine beer; the **Moulin Hotel** (p851), near Pitlochry, comes with ambience and filling haggis; and the **Ferry Inn** (p922) near Stromness.

CHARLOTTE HINDLE

Down a pint at one of England's oldest pubs, Ye Olde Fighting Cocks (p177), St Albans, England

SIMON BRACKEN

Look inside a traditional favourite, the Westminster Arms (p161), London, England

Have a 'wee swallie' at any one of a plethora of Scottish pubs in Edinburgh (p764), Scotland

JONATHAN SMITH

Getting Started

Here's a handy slogan to keep in mind while planning your trip: Britain is a breeze. Travel here is simple compared to many other parts of the world, and in this compact country you're never far from the next town, the next national park, the next pub, or the next impressive castle on your hit-list of highlights.

WHEN TO GO

It won't take long to appreciate the British obsession with weather. Generally, temperatures are mild and rain can fall any time, but the key word is *changeable* – conditions can be bad one minute, great the next.

Summer (June to August) normally gets the most sunshine, but there are cloudy days too. Conversely, winter (November to February) may enjoy fantastic clear spells between bouts of snow, while spring (March to May) or autumn (September to October) sometimes produce the best weather of the year. There are also variations over distance: southern England might be chilly, while Scotland enjoys a heat wave. Or vice versa. Be prepared for anything and you won't get a surprise.

With that in mind, May to September is undoubtedly the best period to travel in Britain, although July and August are busy (it's school-holiday time) in coastal towns, national parks and historic cities like Oxford, Bath, Edinburgh and York. April and October are marginal, but can be good for avoiding crowds, although some Tourist Information Centres (TICs), hotels and attractions close from mid-October to Easter.

Overall, the least hospitable months for visitors are November to February. It's pretty cold in the south, very cold in the north, and days are short. In Scotland, north Wales and the hills of northern England, roads can sometimes be closed by snow. Reaching the islands can also be a problem as high winds disrupt ferries.

For winter visits, London and the big cities are an exception; they're busy all the time, and there's such a lot to see that the weather is immaterial. Besides, you're almost as likely to have a damp day in June as you are in January.

COSTS & MONEY

If you're a global traveller, whatever your budget, you'll know that Britain is expensive compared to many other countries. But don't let that put you off. If funds are tight you'll still have a great trip with some

For more facts and figures, see the climate charts on p952.

Take only what you need. In this throwaway age, it's cheaper to buy a new pair of socks from a market or bargain shop than have your old ones washed in hotel laundry.

DON'T LEAVE HOME WITHOUT...

Travel in Britain is not like crossing the Sahara or exploring the Amazon. Anything can be bought as you go (including Vegemite), so our advice is to take only what you absolutely need, which may include:

- a rain jacket
- comfortable shoes (the sort your granny would call 'stout')
- a small day-pack for sightseeing (and for carrying that rain jacket when the sun shines)
- a taste for beer that isn't icy cold
- listening skills and a sense of humour

forward planning, a bit of shopping around and a modicum of common sense. There's a lot of stuff that's cheap or good value, and a lot that's completely free. The following will give you some guidelines; for more details see the Directory and Transport chapters.

If you're on a tight budget, take this tip: Spend less time in London and more around the country. You'll save cash and get a broader view of Britain, too.

Backpackers in London need £40 a day for survival. Dorm beds cost around £15, basic sustenance £10 per day, and transport around town £5 unless you hoof it. If your purse-strings aren't so short, budget London hotels charge about £50 to £75 per person. Past that price-range are more choices: around £100 gets you something pretty decent. On top of food and bed, extras might include a pint in a pub (£2.75), entrance to a club (£5 to £10, up to £20 at weekends), and admission to museums and galleries (£15 a day, though many don't charge).

Out of London, shoestringers need around £30 per day to cover hostels and food. Mid-rangers will be fine on £50 to £75, based on around £20 to £30 for a B&B; £10 to £15 for lunch, snacks and drinks; £10 to £20 for evening meals. Admission fees are the same for everyone – work on £10 per day.

The Transport chapter, p963, has a lot more information on travel costs.

Travel costs depend on your transport. Train travel costs about £25 per 100 miles. Long-distance buses about half that. The pricing structure for public transport can be quite complicated, see p967 for some helpful information. Drivers should allow £10 per 100 miles for fuel, plus extra for parking (and hire charges).

TRAVEL LITERATURE

There's nothing like a decent travelogue to set the mood for your own trip. The choice of books about travel in Britain can be daunting, so here's a list of our favourites to inspire you, add an extra dimension to your planning, or help you dig under the British skin a little when you're on the road.

- *Notes from a Small Island,* by Bill Bryson, is incisive and perceptive. This American author really captures the spirit of Britain. When he pokes fun, he's spot on, so the locals don't mind.
- *The Kingdom by the Sea,* by Paul Theroux, provides more keen observations from another cousin across the pond, although without Bryson's sense of fondness. It was published 20 years ago, but still worth a read.
- *Lights Out for the Territory,* by Iain Sinclair, is a darkly humorous, entertaining and acerbic exploration of 1990s London, taking in – among other things – Jeffrey Archer's penthouse and an East End gangster funeral.
- *Park and Ride,* by Miranda Sawyer, is a wry and minutely observed 2001 sojourn through British suburbia, the land of never-ending home improvements and keeping up appearances.

- *Two Degrees West,* by Nicholas Crane, describes a walk from the northeastern tip of England to the Dorset coast in a perfectly straight line (two degrees west of the Greenwich meridian), wading rivers, cutting through towns, sleeping in fields, and meeting an astounding selection of real people along the way.
- *Native Stranger,* by Alistair Scott, describes the author's journey through Scotland, a homeland he hardly knew after decades of globetrotting journalism. Slightly dated, but it remains incisive and deep.
- *On Borrow's Trail,* by Hugh Oliff, retraces the journeys through Wales made by 19th-century writer George Borrow, combining a rich synopsis of the original observations with modern photos and colour illustrations.

■ *Crap Towns,* edited by Sam Jordison, and Dan Kieran catalogues the 50 worst places to live in Britain – as voted by their own long-suffering residents. This book is vitriolic, and darkly funny. There are some surprising nominations too – Brighton, Winchester and Liverpool, for example – but presumably that's because some towns that are unpleasant for locals are still great for visitors. Maybe it's best read *after* your trip.

TOP TENS

Must-See Movies

Predeparture planning is no chore if it includes a trip to the cinema or a night on the sofa with a DVD and a bowl of popcorn. Our parameters for a 'British' film? Anything about Britain. Anything which gives a taste of history, scenery or peculiar cultural traits. For reviews of these and other cinematic gems, see p63.

■ *Brief Encounter* (1945)
Director: David Lean

■ *Braveheart* (1995)
Director: Mel Gibson

■ *Brassed Off* (1996)
Director: Mark Herman

■ *The Full Monty* (1997)
Director: Pater Cattaneo

■ *Shakespeare in Love* (1999)
Director: John Madden

■ *Passport to Pimlico* (1949)
Director: Henry Cornelius

■ *Sense & Sensibility* (1996)
Director: Ang Lee

■ *Trainspotting* (1996)
Director: Danny Boil

■ *East is East* (1999)
Director: Damien O'Donnell

■ *Billy Elliot* (2000)
Director: Stephen Daldry

Rave Reads

Travel broadens the mind. Especially if you read before you go. For a taste of life in Britain, try a few of these novels – from past classics to contemporary milestones. For more details on these and other great books, see p60.

■ *Pride & Prejudice* (1813) Jane Austen

■ *The Trumpet Major* (1895) Thomas Hardy

■ *How Green Was My Valley* (1939)
Richard Llewellyn

■ *Waterland* (1983) Graham Swift

■ *High Fidelity* (1995) Nick Hornby

■ *Kidnapped!* (1886) Robert Louis Stevenson

■ *The Rainbow* (1915) DH Lawrence

■ *The Prime of Miss Jean Brodie* (1962)
Muriel Spark

■ *Trainspotting* (1993) Irvine Welsh

■ *White Teeth (2000)* Zadie Smith

Fave Festivals

For entertainment or sheer fun to weave your travels around, here's a list of our 10 favourite festivals. For more ideas, see p954:

■ Jorvik Viking Festival – York, February

■ Bath International Music Festival – Bath, May

■ Mardi Gras Pride in the Park Gay & Lesbian Festival – London, June/July

■ International Eisteddfod – Llangollen, July

■ Reading Festival – Reading, August

■ Brighton Arts Festival – Brighton, May

■ Glastonbury Festival – Somerset, June

■ Edinburgh International Arts Festival – Edinburgh, August

■ T in the Park – Kinross, July

■ Notting Hill Carnival – London, August

HALF-PRICE FOR KIDS

Most museums and historic sites in Britain charge about half-price for children. Throughout this book, if a child price is not given it is about half the specified adult rate. Where children pay significantly higher or lower than half the adult price both adult and child rates are given. Likewise, we quote just adult rates for hostels and campsites; children usually pay about 50% to 75%. In hotels, children get similar discounts – and may even go free-of-charge if sharing a parent's room.

INTERNET RESOURCES

The Internet is a wonderful planning tool for travellers, and there are millions of sites about Britain. Before plunging into the cyber-maze, try these for starters:

192.com (www.192.com) Database of phone numbers and locations of people and businesses.

Able to Go (www.abletogo.com) Excellent listings for visitors with mobility difficulties.

Backpax (www.backpaxmag.com) Cheerful info on budget travel, visas, activities and work.

BBC (www.bbc.co.uk) Immense and invaluable site from the world's best broadcaster.

i-UK (www.i-uk.com) Official site for all UK matters - business, education, travel and more.

Independent Hostels (www.independenthostelguide.co.uk) Hostels in Britain and beyond.

Lonely Planet (www.lonelyplanet.com) Travel news, merchandise, and the legendary Thorn Tree bulletin board.

UK Student Life (www.ukstudentlife.com) Language schools and courses, plus where to go outside study time.

VisitBritain (www.visitbritain.com) A great first port of call for all national tourist information.

Yell (www.yell.com) Yellow pages online, great for locating shops and services across Britain.

Itineraries

CLASSIC ROUTES

CAPITAL HIGHLIGHTS
One to two weeks / London to Stirling Castle

Start in **London** (p100), the capital of Britain, brimming with spectacle, energy and choice. Go west to **Winchester** (p201), ancient capital of King Alfred, before continuing via **Stonehenge** (p240), Britain's famous pre-historic site, and **Bath** (p260), renowned for architecture and Roman remains.

Cross Severn Bridge to **Cardiff** (p639), the capital of Wales and a cultural hub. Then travel north to **Caernarfon Castle** (p736), the seat of government for Edward I's subjugation of Wales.

Next, a cross-country epic takes you via **Ironbridge Gorge** (p386), a celebration of the heritage of Britain's industrial growth, and **Manchester** (p551), modern-day capital of northern England, to **York** (p521), capital for the Vikings who controlled the same area a millennium ago.

Then head for **Edinburgh** (p743), exuberant capital of the newly devolved Scotland, where the elegant architecture reflects long-held tradition and cosmopolitan modernity. Finish at the dramatic **Stirling Castle** (p831), ancient royal seat and scene of *Braveheart* battles.

Without stopping much you could do this 900-mile journey in a week. But pause to drink in the culture and history, not to mention the occasional beer in a country pub, and two weeks becomes a much better option.

PASTORAL PLEASURES Three to four weeks / New Forest to Outer Hebrides

Britain may be small, and crowded in places, but there are some beautiful national parks and rural areas to enjoy.

First stop, the **New Forest** (p209) for a spot of walking, cycling or horse-riding, or simply relaxing, then to **Devon** (p290) and **Cornwall** (p311), which tempt with wild moors, grassy hills, and a beautiful coast of cliffs and sandy beaches.

The **Cotswolds** (p351) promise quintessential English countryside, with neat fields, clear rivers and endless pretty villages of honey-coloured stone – all glowing contentedly whenever the sun is out.

Head west again, to Wales, through the rolling hills of the **Brecon Beacons** (p689), and down to the heavenly sea and sky of **Pembrokeshire** (p670). Then go north to scale the stunning peaks of **Snowdonia** (p716) with mountains for walkers and steam trains for all the family.

Then it's back to England, through the valleys of the **Yorkshire Dales** (p510) and over the mountains of the **Lake District** (p586), to Scotland where two new national parks await: the glorious combination of **Loch Lomond and the Trossachs** (p818), and the mountain wilderness of the **Cairngorms** (p874).

That may be wonder enough, but Britain's pastoral pleasures are crowned by Northwest Scotland, the famous Highlands and Islands, where jewels in the crown include peaks like **Ben Nevis** (p880) and **Torridon** (p902), while out to sea the lovely islands (take your pick) – **Arran** (p809), **Skye** (p904), **Mull** (p827), **Islay** (p821), **Jura** (p824), **North Uist** (p914), **South Uist** (p915), **Lewis** (p911) and all – bask in the afternoon sun…

This is a tour to recharge your batteries, replenish your soul and fill your lungs with fresh air. The main route is around 1300 miles, plus another 300 miles if you visit all the islands. Allow three weeks, or a month if you don't rush. Do lots of walking or cycling, and it might be double again.

THE GRAND TOUR One to two months / London to Cambridge (the long way)

This is a trip for those with time, or an urge to see everything. So brace yourself, and let's be off.

From **London** (p100), aim for **Winchester** (p201), **Salisbury** (p235) and the **New Forest** (p209). Or sample hip **Brighton** (p222) and marvel at historic **Canterbury Cathedral** (p182), before tracking across-country via **Stonehenge** (p240) to reach **Bath** (p260) and **Bristol** (p249).

Then to Wales, via stunning **Chepstow Castle** (p660) and energetic **Cardiff** (p639), to the coastal paradise of **Pembrokeshire** (p670). Retrace to the **Brecon Beacons** (p689) and through book-mad **Hay-on-Wye** (p698), to reach the **Cotswolds** (p351), charming **Oxford** (p339), spectacular **Warwick Castle** (p409), and Shakespeare's birthplace **Stratford-upon-Avon** (p411).

Continue north to **Chester** (p563), then divert into North Wales for the grand castles at **Conwy** (p733) and **Caernarfon** (p736), and the equally stunning mountains of **Snowdonia** (p716). Then ferry across the Mersey to **Liverpool** (p567) and **Manchester** (p551) for a taste of city life, followed by a complete change of scenery in the **Lake District** (p586), and a journey back in time along **Hadrian's Wall** (p626).

Hop across the border to Scotland, via the tranquil **Southern Uplands** (p794), to good-time **Glasgow** (p773). Then trek to **Ben Nevis** (p880), from where it's easy to reach for **Skye** (p904).

Time to head south again, via **Stirling Castle** (p831) to **Edinburgh** (p743), through the border abbey towns of **Kelso** (p798) and **Jedburgh** (p800), to reach World Heritage site **Durham** (p621) and the ancient Viking capital of **York** (p521), ending with a final flourish in beautiful **Cambridge** (p450).

This energetic pack-it-in loop is about 2100 miles. If you don't want to hurry, just leave out a few places. With even more time, you could expand the trip to include Devon and Cornwall, Norfolk and Suffolk, Mid Wales or the East Coast of Scotland.

ROADS LESS TRAVELLED

URBAN ODYSSEY

One to two weeks / Bristol to Manchester

If you want to dig under Britain's skin a little, take this ride through some of the country's less well-known cities.

Kick off in **Bristol** (p249), once a poor cousin to neighbour Bath, today a city with fierce pride, a rich historic legacy and a music scene that rivals cool northern outposts. Next stop, **Birmingham** (p397), a city that oozes transformation, with a renovated waterside, energised museums and a space-age shopping centre. Nearby is **Nottingham** (p425), forever associated with Robin Hood, but renowned today for some very merry nightlife. If hitting the dance-floor isn't your thing, relax in the city's great pubs.

But don't dawdle. Down your pint. We're off again – to culturally restyled and famously to-the-hilt party town **Newcastle-upon-Tyne** (p614).

Still want more? It's got to be **Glasgow** (p773). Sign up here for pubs and clubs, some truly electric venues, fabulous galleries and – only in Scotland – unpretentious bars.

Pausing only for coffee and toast, head next for **Liverpool** (p567). The Beatles may be done to death, but there's a rich and genuine musical heritage here plus a rather famous football team.

Finish in **Manchester** (p551), England's second city and a long-time hotbed of musical endeavour, with thriving arts and club scenes, galleries a go-go, dramatic new architecture and a rather well-known football team.

In theory you could do this 725-mile urban odyssey in a week, but England's cities may tempt you to linger longer. Better to allow at least 10 days. Two weeks would be even better. Don't say we didn't warn you...

CINDERELLA BRITAIN   Two to three weeks / Suffolk to Fife

Some of Britain's best-known national parks and natural beauties are mentioned under Classic Routes. This fabulous jaunt takes you through slightly less frequented (but no less scenic) countryside.

Surprisingly near London sit the tranquil counties of **Suffolk** (p462) and **Norfolk** (p471), their coastline dotted with picturesque harbours, shingle beaches, salt marshes, bird reserves and the occasional old-fashioned seaside resort. Inland lie rivers and lakes, pretty villages and endless miles of flat countryside perfect for gentle cycling.

Between England and Wales lie **The Marches** (p368), and over the border loom the **Cambrian Mountains** (p686) – big, wild, remote and rarely on tourist itineraries. Put them on yours!

Go north again to the **North York Moors** (p538), with heather-covered hills and delightful dales. Inland sit the **North Pennines** (p626), 'England's backbone' between the Yorkshire Dales and Hadrian's Wall, perfect for dramatic hiking or enjoying old pubs in sturdy hill-country towns.

Head further north to the wild and empty big-sky landscapes of the **Cheviot Hills** (p635), blending into the undulating hills, green valleys, stately homes and ruined abbeys of Scotland's **Southern Uplands** (p794).

If time's on your side, take in the **Northumberland Coast** (p631), famous for empty beaches, dramatic castles and delicious crab sandwiches.

For a final fling, cross the Firth of Forth to reach the 'kingdom' of **Fife** (p839), with lush rolling farmland ideal for cycling, and a delightful coastline peppered with quaint harbours, perfect for a postlunch stroll.

If you don't stop much, you could see these 'hidden' areas in two weeks, covering about 900 miles. Allow three weeks or more if you plan to wear your hiking boots, or want to relax over tea and cake, and catch a little local flavour off the beaten track.

TAILORED TRIPS

BRITAIN FOR KIDS

'Are we there yet?' Follow this suggested route, and you soon will be.

Start at **Origins** (p473) in Norwich, an interactive museum that includes big-screen historic panoramas, and hands-on opportunities to flood the Fens. Then to **London** (p100), where the scope of child-friendly attractions is mesmerising, and across to Bristol to the interactive science museum **Explore** (p252), and on to Cardiff for fairy-tale **castles** (p642) and up-to-the-moment **Techniquest** (p645).

Touch down at the **National Space Centre** (p423) near Leicester, where highlights include interplanetary displays, zero-gravity toilets and germ-devouring underpants. We know why kids love it. And it *is* rocket science.

Hungry after crossing the galaxy? No problem. Next stop is **Cadbury World** (p407) near Birmingham, a lip-smacking exploration of chocolate production and consumption. Make sure those samples settle in tiny tummies before riding the rollercoaster at **Alton Towers** (p418).

Then turn north to Glasgow's ultramodern **Science Centre** (p779), complete with IMAX cinema and interactive science mall, a bounty of discovery. From here, it's a hop to Dundee and **Sensation** (p865), for more hands-on, and heads-in, activity.

Finish at **Our Dynamic Earth** (p754) in Edinburgh, a special-effects marvel recreating the planet's history from the Big Bang to tea-time.

SLOWLY FLOWS THE THAMES

This route follows Britain's best-known river from picture-postcard countryside to the pumping heart of the capital. Travel by car, train or bike, or walk the whole way on the Thames Path long-distance trail, perhaps sampling a few sections by boat.

Start at the source of the Thames, a damp patch in a field near the town of **Cirencester** (p352), once the second-largest city in Roman Britain. Follow the Thames through the **Cotswolds** (p351) to **Oxford** (p339), famous for its university, and a good place to hire a boat.

Continue downstream via the leafy **Chiltern Hills** (p175) to charming **Henley-on-Thames** (p350), site of the nation's favourite regatta.

The Thames runs past **Windsor Castle** (p196), a royal residence since 850 AD, **Runnymede** (p200), where the Magna Carta was signed, and **Hampton Court Palace** (p145), home to Henry VIII, before reaching **London** (p100). Following the riverside paths as the Thames weaves through neighbourhoods both grotty and smart is a great way to see all sides of the capital. **Tower Bridge** (p135) makes a stunning end to your trip.

WELSH WANDERER

Many visitors to Wales are attracted (understandably) to the lively cities or stunning beaches of the coast. This inland journey shows you a different side of the country.

Start at **Brecon** (p693). If it's jazz you like, come for the August festival, but for the rest of the year this town is an excellent base for trips by horse, bike or foot into the **Brecon Beacons National Park** (p689).

Then go northwest to **Llanwrtyd Wells** (p701), a sleepy spa town set in tranquil countryside, regularly enlivened by its calendar of whacky competitions, including the world bog-snorkelling championships. Or go northeast to **Hay-on-Wye** (p698), a global centre of second-hand books.

Rejoin again at **Llandrindod Wells** (p702), a well-preserved spa town oozing an air of gentility. For air of a different sort, you can fill your lungs on a walk in the hills around **Knighton** (p702) or marvel at the red kites in the bird reserves near **Rhayader** (p701).

Keep heading north through peaceful farm-land to reach the country town of **Welshpool** (p702), where you can admire venerable **Powis Castle** (p703), or more modern structures at the **Andrew Logan Museum of Sculpture** (p703).

Take in the fabulous castle at **Chirk** (p716), then finish at **Llangollen** (p714), home to a host of Welsh treasures, including stately Plas Newydd, ruined Valle Crucis Abbey and stunning Pontcysyllte Aqueduct.

WHISKY GALORE

If any produce is linked to Scotland, it's whisky. This trip takes you to the homes of some of the most famous, or simply the finest, names in the whisky world. In all, about 40 distilleries open their doors to visitors. It's not all about malts and barrels though. Between distilleries, you'll pass through some of the country's most beautiful scenery.

Start in the valley of the silvery River Spey. Stop off in **Dufftown** (p861), then head out to the numerous Speyside distilleries, including Macallan, Glenfiddich, Benromach, Cardhu, Dallas Dhu, Glen Grant, Glenlivet and Strathisla.Loop round the top of Loch Ness (after all those tastings, your best chance of seeing the monster?), through **Inverness** (p887) and on again to **Tain** (p892), home of the Glenmorangie Distillery.

Aficionados could go to the ends of the earth – well, at least to the end of the mainland – and cross to the **Orkney Islands** (p916), where the distinctive Highland Park is made. Alternatively, head over the sea to **Skye** (p904) where the Talisker malts await your pleasure at Carbost.

Finish your journey on the isle of **Islay** (p821), where the fine drams of Ardbeg, Bowmore, Bunnahabhain, Bruichladdich, Caol Ila, Laga-vulin and Laphroaig are produced, and su-perbly accompanied by fresh local shellfish – a perfect finale to a hard day's sightseeing.

24

The Authors

DAVID ELSE — Coordinating Author

David's knowledge of Britain comes from a lifetime of travel around the country, often by foot and bike – a passion which started at university, when heading for the hills was always more attractive than visiting the library. Originally from London, David slowly trekked northwards, via Wiltshire, Bristol and Derbyshire – interspersed with exile in Wales and long spells in Africa – to his present base in Yorkshire. A full-time travel writer, David is the author of previous editions of Lonely Planet's *England* and *Britain*, as well as about 20 other guidebooks, including *Walking in Britain*.

My Favourite Day
It's 7am. I drink a cup of tea – English Breakfast, naturally – then go straight down to the River Thames. This is my favourite time in London; early in the morning on a sunny day. I cross Westminster Bridge to the South Bank, and walk past 1000-year-old Lambeth Palace and new-millennium symbol The London Eye, later getting views of St Paul's Cathedral and the Tower of London. Icons, I love 'em. Next, a boat down to Greenwich and a long lunch in an old pub near the *Cutty Sark,* before walking it off with a mooch around the National Maritime Museum and a stroll through two hemispheres. Just before rush hour, the Docklands Light Railway gives a bargain-priced bird's-eye view of London and a quick ride back to the heart of the city.

OLIVER BERRY — Cumbria & The Lakes; Southwest England

Oliver graduated from University College London with a degree in English and now works as a freelance writer. Having moved to Cornwall at the tender age of one, he has spent the last twenty-six years trying to find excuses for wandering along the county's beaches and clifftops; writing a guidebook is the best one yet. Oliver has received several awards for his writing including *The Guardian* Young Travel Writer of the Year.

NICKY CROWTHER — Wales

Being British and a cyclist, Nicky explored as much of the rest of the world as possible, before returning home for a proper look at her own country while working on Lonely Planet's *Cycling in Britain*. Following a glorious summer pedalling the lanes of the English shires she realised she was hooked, and has been thrilled ever since to explore Britain's wilder parts and diverse identities, found in abundance in Wales. Her favourite regions of this nation-within-a-nation are the Vale of Usk for its beauty and cooking, Mid Wales for its great, green emptiness, and the mountains of southern Snowdonia.

FIONN DAVENPORT
Northeast England, Northwest England, Yorkshire

Dublin born and bred, Fionn was separated from England by little more than a polluted puddle, but for years had no clue what England was like. He thought Ireland had the monopoly on wild scenery and friendliness, and England was essentially London and its suburbs. When he crossed the puddle to write the first edition, he wasn't expecting much. He was wrong. He's worked on every edition since and returns to Ireland preaching England's stunning beauty to the wholly surprised. Maybe that puddle is bigger than he thought.

MARTIN HUGHES
London

Martin Hughes was born and bred in Dublin where, as an adult, he dithered for five years between journalism and public relations before ditching both and shifting to the brighter lights of London. After a year of very odd jobs, he took off on a three-year Grand Tour of the world, popping back to London each summer to raise funds. He eventually settled in Melbourne, Australia, where he works as a freelance journalist and travel writer. He still earns a crust from London, where he returns at least twice a year for cultural catch-ups and assignments.

SAM MARTIN
Southeast England

Sam first encountered England as a two-year-old, when he moved with his family to London from the US. He lived there for five years before returning to the States and settling in Texas. There he quickly lost his English accent under the withering criticism of his fellow eight-year-olds. Sam has travelled to and through England many times since. He now lives in Austin, Texas, with his wife and two sons. Sam works as a full-time writer and has contributed to Lonely Planet's *USA* and *San Antonio, Austin & The Hill Country*.

ETAIN O'CARROLL
The Marches, Oxfordshire, Gloucestershire & the Cotswolds; Southwest England

Etain's childhood trips to England consisted of seemingly endless tours of stately homes and castle ruins. These tours sowed the seeds of a deep appreciation of the wonderful buildings and countryside in southern England, and work on this edition led back to many old haunts in glorious villages and winding country lanes. Etain now lives and works in Oxford as a travel writer and photographer and has published with a variety of magazines and papers.

BECKY OHLSEN The Midlands; Eastern England

Becky has studied and practised the English language for 32 years, though her accent remains stubbornly American. After roughly a decade strapped to her desk as a copy editor in the alternative press, she was seized with the urge to ramble, and ramble she did, spending a year backpacking on a quest to explore every nook and cranny of Europe. Given her fondness for warm beer, green hills, yellow journalism and tiny cars, it's no surprise Becky got hooked on England almost instantly. Several visits later, she's decided the Peak District is her favourite part, with London a close second.

ANDY SYMINGTON Scotland

Born in Britain but raised in Australia, Andy wound up in Scotland after several dubious adventures. Settling in Edinburgh's portside district of Leith, he cunningly found work selling whisky to the Scots, inspiring in him a passion which resulted in much random roaming of the country and glazed eyes seeking the next distillery in the Highland mist. Around the same time someone suggested Andy as a likely candidate to review pubs, and thus he embarked on a writing career. Since then he has written several guidebooks and articles. Andy is currently based in northern Spain.

Snapshot

At the start of the 21st century, Britain has the feel of a country punching above its weight. What's this little nation on the edge of Europe doing? What's it all about, this getting into bed with American presidents, this swaggering around the planet, this invading Iraq? The British Empire is gone, say the cynics, and we should all remember that.

True, say the optimists, the colonial days are over, but Britain still stands comfortably on the international stage. Coal mines and shipyards no longer form the backbone of Britain's economy, but it's still the fourth-largest in the world. And Britain is a major player at the UN. When the British Prime Minister speaks, the other head honchos listen. Well, most of them.

But for the Brits themselves, the citizens on the street, interest in global politics is not exactly all-consuming. So what else do they talk about? At the time of going to press, what hot topics are being discussed at dinner parties, on the bus or in the pub?

For some people, wars overseas are overshadowed by conflict closer to home: yes, the great British fox-hunting debate. On one side, hunting opponents (mostly city-dwellers) are concerned about animal welfare; they say hounds tearing apart a fox isn't a pastime that befits today's Britain. On the other side, hunt campaigners (mostly country folk) say it's a rural tradition representing a way of life outsiders don't understand. True, many urbanites perceive hunters as a privileged elite – although wrong, it's a perception re-inforced by some hunt campaigners – and their antihunt stance is as much a pop at the nobs as it is a concern for wildlife. So as well as the urban-rural split, there's a class war too (both divides are far more complex than that), and it's clear some townies derive pleasure from the country folks' shock at finding themselves a victimised minority, perhaps for the first time in history. In reality, there are many serious issues in rural Britain today – unemployment, low wages, high house-prices, diminishing services – not to mention important events elsewhere in the world – but these get over-looked while fox-hunting frequently grabs the headlines.

After several years of debate, during which time members of Parliament voted against hunting half-a-dozen times, the Labour government in November 2004 forced through a law that banned hunting. The Countryside Alliance, the main prohunt lobby, vowed to carry on hunting and threat-ened a campaign of civil disobedience through 2005. The Conservatives (Labour's traditional foe) promised to repeal the law should they be elected to government, but as this book was in production the Liberal-Democrats, Britain's third-largest party, enjoyed more support in the polls and may yet be the main opposition in future. With the next general election on the ho-rizon at the time of going to press, all parties were gearing up for battle.

And what will they argue about? Britain in Europe, for one. Suspicion of matters 'continental' is a particularly English trait, while the Welsh and Scots are notably more pro-European, but nearly everyone has opinions on the European Parliament, the European currency, or the European Union (EU). For many people, they're all lumped under the same diaboli-cal banner anyway. A fact not missed by the fledgling UK Independence Party; their main policy to withdraw Britain from the EU earned them a whole lot of votes at the 2004 European elections.

Back at the bars and dinner parties, discussion about Euro-expansion rolls into concerns about foreigners. Asylum seekers, economic migrants, refugees, terrorists – they're all the same, according to some newspapers,

FAST FACTS

Population: 60 million

Size: 88,500 sq miles (230,000 sq km)

Inflation: 2.7%

Unemployment: 2.3%

Number of years Britain ruled by Queen Elizabeth II: 54

Number of ships launched by Queen Elizabeth II: 16

Average household weekly cost of alcohol consumed at home: £6

Average household weekly cost of fruit and vegetables: £5.50

Number of fish and chip shops: 8500

Proportion of British adults overweight: 66%

where a regular dose of xenophobia ('outsiders destroy the British way of life, and must be kept out') helps sell millions of copies each day.

Britain's immigration law is less emotional than rabble-rousing newsprint, but it's increasingly stringent. If you're escaping a brutal government there's a chance you can stay; if you come to Britain illegally because you're poor, you'll be sent packing pretty soon.

Meanwhile, on the home front, other big issues in Britain include the condition of public services – especially health and education. Politicians from both the Labour and Conservative sides claim their policies mean more choice. But they miss the point: the punters don't want to choose between Hospital A and Hospital B. They want to go to a place nearby, and they simply want it to be good.

As an increasing number of Brits think the politicians are out of touch, so election turnouts have dropped steadily since the 1960s. (Although postal ballots in 2004 pushed figures up again in some areas.) It's a telling indictment when more people vote in TV talent shows than for their own political leaders, and it's also symptomatic of Britain's ever-growing obsession with fame and the famous.

The popular newspapers feature celebrities on a daily basis, while dedicated magazines such as *Hello* and *Heat* sell half-a-million copies every week. And we all lap up the endless stories and pictures of these perfectly tanned people – even though their skills seem limited to singing a jolly tune, being related to the Queen, or looking good in tight trousers.

Why are celebs everywhere? Maybe it's because the great unwashed were stealing their limelight. The trend started with the genuinely ground-breaking *Big Brother,* which spawned a thousand more reality TV shows where ordinary folks exchanged houses and partners, had their gardens replanted, or attempted an assault course in the jungle. So the celebs fought back, and now the schedules are crammed with the likes of Celebrity Fat Club. In truth, 'reality' TV– with celebs or proles – is so contrived it makes the soaps look ad-libbed. Whatever, millions of us still tune in, and watch to see what happens next.

And, of course, that brings us back to Iraq. There's considerable resentment among most British people about the government's part in the invasion, the postwar anarchy, the kidnappings and the death toll among service personnel and innocent civilians – not to mention disquiet about prisoners, including some Britons, still held in Guantanamo Bay. While we might agree that Saddam Hussein was an evil dictator and a threat to world peace, if that's reason enough to march into countries and depose leaders, there's surely a long list of other candidates due the same treatment. And has the 'war against terrorism' made Britain, or the world, a safer place? We're not sure…

BRITAIN? ENGLAND? WHAT'S IN A NAME?

The state of Great Britain consists of three separate countries – England, Wales and Scotland. Three countries in one might seem a strange setup, and visitors are sometimes confused about the difference between England and Britain – as are a lot of English people. But getting a grip on this basic principle will ease your understanding of British history and culture, and make your travel more enjoyable too.

For the record, the UK consists of Great Britain, Northern Ireland and some semiautonomous islands such as the Isle of Man. The island of Ireland consists of Northern Ireland and the Republic of Ireland (also called Eire). And for you scholars, the British Isles is a *geographical* term for the whole group of islands that make up the UK and the Republic of Ireland. Got all that? Good.

History

It may be a small island on the edge of Europe, but Britain was never on the sidelines of history. For thousands of years, invaders and other incomers have arrived, settled and made their mark. The result is a fascinating mix of landscape, culture and language – a dynamic pattern that shaped the nation and continues to evolve today.

For many visitors, this rich historic legacy is Britain's main attraction: everything from Stonehenge to Glen Coe, via Hadrian's Wall, Canterbury Cathedral, Caernarfon Castle, the Tower of London, hundreds of palaces and stately homes, and endless lines of kings and queens. Even if you're not big on dates and dynasties, British history will dominate your travels – the bare essentials in this chapter will just as certainly help you enjoy it.

FIRST ARRIVALS

Human habitation in Britain stretches back at least 400,000 years, although exact dates depend on your definition of 'human'. Things got a little more definite as the centuries rolled on. Ice Ages came and went, sea levels rose and fell, and the island now called Britain was frequently joined to the European mainland. Hunter-gatherers crossed the land bridge, moving north as the ice melted and retreating to warmer climes when the glaciers advanced again.

Around 4000 BC a new group of migrants arrived from Europe. What made them different was their use of stone tools, and this allowed a pivotal switch from nomadic hunting to a settled agricultural lifestyle. They farmed in patches of open landscape between the forests, most notably in the chalky hill areas of England such as the South Downs and Salisbury Plain, and soon spread across the rest of the island.

Alongside the fields, Britain's Stone Age people used rocks and turf to build massive burial mounds, and many of these can still be seen today, including the West Kennet Long Barrow in Wiltshire (p249), the stone frame of the *cromlech* (burial chamber) of Pentre Ifan in Pembrokeshire (p683), and the great passage grave at Maes Howe, Orkney (p923).

But perhaps the most enduring, and certainly the most impressive, legacy left by these nascent Britons are the great stone circles such as Callanish on Lewis (p913), and – most famously – the elaborate and enigmatic sites of Avebury (p246) and Stonehenge (p240) in southern England.

IRON & CELTS

Move on a millennium or two, and it's the Iron Age. The population expanded and began to divide into specific groups or tribes. Across the whole island the forests were cleared with increasing efficiency as more land was turned to farming. This led to a patchwork pattern of fields, woods and small villages that still exists in many parts of rural lowland Britain. As the population grew, territorial defence became an issue, so the Iron Age people left another legacy – the great 'earthworks' of southern England, stone forts in northern England, and the *brochs* (defensive towers) in Wales and Scotland.

A History of Britain by TV star Simon Schama is an incisive and highly accessible three-volume set, putting events from 3000 BC to AD 2000 in a modern context.

The Isles: A History by Norman Davies provides much-acclaimed and highly readable coverage of the past 10,000 years in Britain.

A Brief History of British Kings & Queens by Mike Ashley is a great overview: a concise, comprehensive rundown with timelines, lists, biographies and family trees. Good for pub-quiz training too.

TIMELINE	4000 BC	500 BC
	Neolithic migrants arrive from Europe. Great stone circles – Callanish and Stonehenge – built	Celts settled in Britain

As landscapes altered, this was also a time of cultural change. The Celts, a people who originally migrated from Central Europe, had settled across much of the island of Britain by around 500 BC. Absorbing the indigenous inhabitants, a Celtic-British population developed – sometimes known as the 'Ancient Britons' – divided into about 20 different tribes, including the Cantiaci (in today's county of Kent), the Iceni (today's Norfolk) the Brigantes (northwest England), the Picts and Caledonii (Scotland), the Ordivices (parts of Wales), and the Scotti (much of Ireland). You noticed the Latin-sounding names? That's because the tribal tags were first handed out by the next arrivals on Britain's shores…

ENTER THE ROMANS

Think of the Romans, and you think of legions, centurions and aqueducts. They were all here, as Britain and much of Europe came under the power (or the yoke, for those on the receiving end) of the Classical Period's greatest military empire.

Julius Caesar, the emperor everyone remembers, made forays into Britain from what is now France in 55 BC. But the real Roman invasion happened a century later when Emperor Claudius led a ruthless campaign that resulted in the Romans controlling pretty much everywhere in southern England by AD 50.

Much of the occupation was straightforward: several Celtic-British tribal kings realised collaboration was more profitable than battle. For example, King Togidbnus of the Regnenses tribe changed his name to Tiberius Cogidumnus and built a Roman-style villa, which can still be seen today at Fishbourne near the town of Chichester; and a historian called Nennius suggests in his *Historia Britonum* (written around AD 800) that the people of Wales revered their Roman governors so much that one governor, Magnus Maximus, was transformed into a mythical hero called Maxen Wledig.

It wasn't all plain sailing, though: some locals decided to battle for their independence. The most famous freedom fighter was warrior-queen Boudicca, who led an army as far as Londinium, the Roman port on the present site of London.

But overall, opposition was sporadic and no real threat to the legions' military might. By around AD 80 the new province of Britannia (much of today's England and Wales) was firmly under Roman rule. And although it's tempting to imagine noble natives battling courageously against occupying forces, in reality Roman control and stability were probably welcomed by the general population, tired of feuding chiefs and insecure tribal territories.

HADRIAN DRAWS A LINE

North of Britannia was the land the Romans called Caledonia (one day to become Scotland). This proved a harder place to find a fan club. In AD 80, Governor Julius Agricola spent four years trying to subdue the wild tribes called the Picts (from the Latin *pictus,* meaning 'painted'), all to no avail. So in AD 122 Emperor Hadrian decided that rather than conquer the Picts, he'd settle for keeping them at bay. So a barricade was built across northern England – between today's cities of Carlisle and

55 BC	AD 43
Roman invaders under Julius Caesar make forays into southern England	Full Roman invasion of Britain led by Emperor Claudius

Newcastle. For nearly 300 years it marked the northernmost limit of the Roman Empire, and today Hadrian's Wall is one of Britain's best-known historic sites (see p626).

EXIT THE ROMANS

Settlement by the Romans in Britain lasted almost four centuries, and intermarriage was common between locals and incomers (many from other parts of the empire – today's Belgium, Spain and Syria – rather than Rome itself) so that a Romano-British population evolved. This was particularly so in the towns, while indigenous Celtic culture remained in rural areas.

Along with stability and wealth, the Romans introduced another cultural facet to Britain – a new religion called Christianity, after it was recognised by Emperor Constantine in AD 313. But by this time, although Romano-British culture was thriving, back in its Mediterranean heartland the Empire was already in decline.

It was an untidy finale. The Romans were not driven out by the Ancient Britons; in reality Britannia was simply dumped by the rulers in Rome and slowly fizzled out of existence as a colony. On the ground, though, it's likely that the population noticed little difference. By this time Romano-British culture was well established, and regional governors probably remained in place – along with their laws and administration systems – for several decades at least. But historians are neat folk, and the end of Roman power in Britain is generally dated at AD 410.

THE EMERGENCE OF ENGLAND

With the empire ended, coins were no longer minted in Britain, so the use of money dwindled and long-distance trade declined. Some Romano-British towns in England and Wales were abandoned (most of Scotland had escaped Roman control in the first place), and some rural areas became no-go zones as former regional governors became local warlords and fought over fiefdoms. Compared with other periods of history, little is known about the period following the end of Roman rule, and this era is often dubbed the Dark Ages.

Britain's post-Roman vacuum didn't go unnoticed, and once again a bunch of pesky continentals invaded. This time Angles and Saxons – Teutonic tribes from northern Europe – advanced across the former

London is another epic from Edward Rutherford, or rather around 50 separate mininovels, each set in a key historical era – from the Roman invasion to the Blitz of WWII. Exhaustive and exhausting, but great for a sense of each period.

DID YOU KNOW?

The Romans were settled in Britain for almost 400 years. That's longer than European settlement in Australia or North America in our own era.

LEGACY OF THE LEGIONS

To control the territory they'd occupied, the Romans built castles and garrisons, and many of these developed into towns, later to be called 'chesters' and today remembered by names such as Winchester, Manchester and Colchester. The Romans are also well known for the roads they built – initially so the legions could march quickly from place to place, and later so that trade could develop. Wherever possible the roads were built in straight lines (because it was efficient, not – as the old joke goes – to stop the Ancient Britons hiding round corners), and included Ermine St between London and York, Watling St between London and Chester, and the Fosse Way between Exeter and Lincoln. Many ruler-straight Roman roads are still followed by modern highways today, and in a land better known for old lanes and turnpike routes winding through the landscape, they clearly stand out on the atlas.

122
Hadrian's Wall built

410
End of Roman rule in Britain

Roman turf. They moved fast, and quickly overcame the Celts and what remained of Romano-British culture, so that by the late 6th century the country now called England was predominantly Anglo-Saxon. So thorough was the invasion that even today much of the English language is Anglo-Saxon in origin, many place-names have Anglo-Saxon roots, and the very term 'Anglo-Saxon' has become a (much abused and factually incorrect) byword for 'purely English'.

It was during the Dark Ages that a particularly powerful leader came to prominence, whose name just may have been Arthur. He may have been a Romano-Briton, he may have been a Celt. He may have come from southern England, or was maybe born in Wales. He might have fought against the Anglo-Saxons. In truth, virtually nothing is known about this mythical figure from the mists of time, but King Arthur has nevertheless become the focus of many legends. Along with Merlin the magician and the Knights of the Round Table, Arthur inspired a huge body of literature, not least by the Welsh in the epic tale *Mabinogion,* and by Thomas Malory in his masterpiece *Morte d'Arthur.* Numerous sites in Britain, from Cornwall to Snowdonia, via Glastonbury and Pembrokeshire, claim Arthurian links that you'll undoubtedly come across as you travel around Britain today. For more tales see the boxed text, p705. Meanwhile, back in reality, Northumbria was initially the dominant Anglo-Saxon kingdom, covering much of today's northern England and extending its power into Scotland. In the 8th century, the kingdom of Mercia became stronger and its ruler, King Offa, marked a clear border between England and Wales – a defensive ditch called Offa's Dyke that can still be seen today. A century later, at the top of the league was the kingdom Wessex covering today's southern England, ruled by King Egbert, grandfather of the future King Alfred.

On the religious front, the Anglo-Saxons were pagans, and their invasion forced Celtic culture and the Christian religion to the edges of the British Isles – to Wales, Scotland and Ireland. The pope of the time, Gregory, decided this was a poor show, and in 597 sent missionaries to Britain to revive interest in Christianity. One holy pioneer was St Augustine, who successfully converted Angles in Kent, and some good-looking specimens were sent to Rome as proof – giving rise to Pope Gregory's famous quip about Angles looking like angels.

Meanwhile in central and northern England another missionary called St Aidan was even more successful. With faith and fervour, he converted the entire populations of Mercia and Northumbria, and still had time to establish a monastery at Lindisfarne that can still be seen today (see p633).

THE WAKING OF WALES

Meanwhile, away from the kingdoms of England, the Celts on the outer fringes of Britain (and particularly in Ireland) had kept alive their own distinct yet Roman-influenced culture, along with the ideals of Christianity. And while the Anglo-Saxons took advantage of the post-Roman void in eastern Britain, towards the end of the 5th century others played the same game on the west side of the island: the Scotti people (from today's Ireland) invaded the home of the Picts (today's Wales and Scotland).

In response to the invasion, people from the kingdom of Gododdin (in today's Scotland) came to northwest Wales. Their initial plan was to drive

London – The Biography by Peter Ackroyd is an absorbing and original 'warts-and-all' treatment of the capital as a living organism, approaching its history through intriguing themes such as drinking and crime. In fact, it's mainly warts.

Missionary St Augustine revives interest in Christianity among the Anglo-Saxons

Vikings conquer and occupy east and northeast England, making Yorvik their capital (today's York)

out the invaders, but they stayed and settled in the area, which became the kingdom of Gwynedd. (The modern county in northern Wales still proudly bears this name.)

The struggle between Welsh settlers and Irish raiders along the coast carried on for the rest of the Dark Ages. At the same time, more settlers came to Wales from today's Cornwall and western France, and Christian missionaries arrived from Ireland in the 6th and 7th centuries.

While these newcomers arrived from the west and south, the people of Wales were also under pressure to the east – harassed by the Anglo-Saxons of England pretty much constantly for hundreds of years. In response, by the 8th century the disparate tribes of Wales had started to band together and sow the seeds of nationhood. They called themselves Cymry (fellow countrymen), and today Cymru is the Welsh word for Wales.

THE STIRRING OF SCOTLAND

While Wales was becoming established in the west of Britain, similar events were taking place to the north, in the land the Romans had called Caledonia. The Picts (who called their kingdom Alba) were the region's dominant indigenous tribe.

In the power vacuum that followed the fizzle-out of Roman rule in Britannia, Alba was invaded from two sides: First, towards the end of the 5th century, the Scotti crossed the sea from today's Ireland and established the kingdom of Dalriada (in today's Argyll). Then in the 7th century Anglo-Saxons from the expanding kingdom of Northumbria in England moved in to colonise southeast Alba. But by this time the Scotti were well dug in alongside the Picts, foreshadowing the time when yet another name – Scotland – would be applied to northern Britain.

THE VIKING ERA

Just as the new territories of England, Wales and Scotland were becoming established, Britain was once again invaded from the European mainland. This time, Vikings appeared on the scene.

It's another classic historical image: blonde Scandinavians, horned helmets, big swords, square-sailed longboats, raping and pillaging. School history books give the impression that Vikings turned up, killed everyone, took everything and left. There's *some* truth in that, but in reality many

---

WHOSE PATRON SAINT IS THIS?

Along the coast of Wales, the struggle between settlers and raiding Irish pirates was a major feature of life during the Dark Ages. Even St Patrick, the patron saint of Ireland, is reputed to have been a Welshman, captured by brigands and taken to Ireland as a slave.

At around the same time, other visitors from Ireland to Wales were Christian missionaries. Among them was a monk named Dewi, who became known as David, and later became patron saint of Wales.

So in a fair swap, the patron saint of Wales was an Irishman, while the patron saint of Ireland could well have been Welsh. It seems odd, but then the patron saint of England, St George, was a Turk, and the patron saint of Scotland, St Andrew, was a Palestinian, so maybe in the British Isles it's all par for the course.

927	**1066**
Athelstan, grandson of King Alfred the Great, crowned first King of England	Battle of Hastings; William the Conqueror of Normandy invades; one in the eye for King Harold

Vikings settled here for good, and their legacy is still evident in parts of Scotland and northern England – in the form of place names, local dialect and even the traces of Nordic DNA in some of today's inhabitants.

DID YOU KNOW?

King Knut is better known as King Canute, famous for reputedly giving his regal power a test too far. He was carried to a beach and commanded the tide not to roll in. He got his feet wet.

There were two main waves of Viking invaders, the first from the country now called Norway, who attacked northern Scotland and the parts of northern England now called Cumbria and Lancashire. By around 850 a second wave from Denmark had conquered and occupied east and northeast England, making the city of Yorvik (now York) their capital.

From their northern territories, the Vikings then spread across central England until they were confronted by Anglo-Saxon armies coming from the south led by the new king of Wessex, Alfred the Great. The battles that followed were seminal to the foundation of the nation-state of England, but they didn't all go Alfred's way. For a few months he was on the run, wading through swamps, hiding in peasant hovels, and famously burning cakes. It was the stuff of legend, which is just what you need when the chips are down. By 886, Alfred had garnered his forces and pushed the Vikings back to the north.

Thus England was divided in two: north and east was Viking 'Danelaw', while south and west was Anglo-Saxon territory. Alfred was hailed as king of the English – the first time the Anglo-Saxons truly regarded themselves as a united people.

Alfred's son and successor was Edward the Elder. After more battles, Edward gained control of Danelaw, and thus the whole of England. His son, Athelstan, took the process a stage further and was specifically crowned King of England in 927. But it was hardly cause for celebration: the Vikings were still around, and later in the 10th century more raids from Scandinavia threatened this fledgling English unity. Over the following decades, control swung from Saxon (King Edgar), to Dane (King Knut), and back to Saxon again (King Edward the Confessor). As England came to the end of the first millennium AD, the future was anything but certain.

The Year 1000 by Robert Lacey and Danny Danzinger looks hard and deep at British life a millennium ago. Apparently, it was cold and damp then too.

HIGHS & LOWS IN WALES

Meanwhile, as England fought off the Viking threat, Wales was also dealing with the Nordic intruders. Building on the initial cooperation forced upon them by Anglo-Saxon oppression, in the 9th and 10th centuries the small kingdoms of Wales began cooperating, through necessity, to repel the Vikings.

King Rhodri Mawr (who died in 878) defeated a Viking force off Anglesey and began the unification process. His grandson Hywel the Good is thought to have been responsible for drawing up a unified set of laws between the disparate Welsh tribes. Things were going well, but just as Wales was becoming a recognisable entity, the young country was faced with more destructive onslaughts than it could handle, and in 927 the Welsh kings recognised the Anglo-Saxon King Athelstan as their overlord in exchange for an anti-Viking alliance.

SCOTLAND BECOMES A KINGDOM

While the Welsh were forming their own nation, similar events were being played out in Alba. In the 9th century, the king of the Scotti of Dalriada was one Kenneth MacAilpin (usually anglicised to MacAlpin). His father was a Scotti, but his mother was a Pict princess, so MacAlpin took advantage of the Pictish custom of matrilineal succession to declare himself ruler of both the Scots and the Picts, and therefore king of all Alba.

In a surprisingly short time, the Scots gained cultural and political ascendancy. The Picts were absorbed, and Pictish culture simply – and quite suddenly – came to an end, while Alba became known as Scotia.

In the 11th century, Scottish nation-building was further consolidated by King Malcolm III (whose most famous act was the 1057 murder of Macbeth – as immortalised by William Shakespeare). With his English queen, Margaret, he founded the Canmore dynasty that would rule Scotland for the next two centuries.

1066 & ALL THAT

While Wales and Scotland laid the foundations of nationhood, back in England things were unsettled, as the royal pendulum was still swinging between Saxon and Danish-Viking monarchs. When King Edward the Confessor died, the crown passed to Harold, his brother-in-law. That should've settled things, but Edward had a cousin in Normandy called William, who thought *he* should have succeeded to the throne of England.

The end result was the Battle of Hastings in 1066, the most memorable of dates for anyone who's studied British history – or for anyone who hasn't. William sailed from France with an army of Norman soldiers, the Saxons were defeated, and Harold was killed – by an arrow in the eye, according to tradition. (For more details see p221.)

NORMAN LAW & ORDER

William became king of England, earning himself the prestigious title of William the Conqueror. It was no idle nickname. To control the Anglo-Saxons, the Norman invaders built numerous castles, and by 1085–86 the Domesday Book provided a census of the country's current stock and future potential.

William the Conqueror was followed by William II, who was mysteriously assassinated during a hunting trip and succeeded by Henry I, another Norman ruler, and the first of a long line of kings called Henry.

In the years after the invasion, the French-speaking Normans and the English-speaking Saxon inhabitants kept pretty much to themselves. A strict hierarchy of class developed, known as the feudal system. At the top was the monarch, below that the nobles (barons, bishops, dukes and

Medieval Women by Henrietta Leyser looks through a female lens at the period from AD 500 to 1500: a life of work, marriage, sex and children (not necessarily in that order).

LOOKING SOUTH

The arrival of William the Conqueror was a seminal event, as it marked the end of Britain's century-old ties to the Nordic countries (only in Orkney and Shetland did the Viking presence continue until the 15th century). The mainland's perspective turned to France, Western Europe and the Mediterranean, giving rise to massive cultural implications that were to last into our own time. In addition, the Norman landing capped an era of armed invasion. Since 1066, in the near-on thousand years to the present day, Britain has never again been seriously invaded by a foreign power.

1240	1290
King Llywelyn of Wales ('Llywelyn the Great') dies; his grandson 'Llywelyn the Last' becomes the first Prince (not King) of Wales	Robert Bruce crowned King of Scotland

earls), then knights and lords, and at the bottom peasants or 'serfs', effectively slaves.

The feudal system may have established the basis of a class system that still exists in Britain today, but intermarriage was not completely unknown. Henry himself married a Saxon princess. Nonetheless, such unifying moves stood for nothing after Henry's death: a bitter struggle for succession followed, finally won by Henry II who took the throne as the first king of the House – or dynasty – of Plantagenet.

NORMAN EFFECT ON WALES & SCOTLAND

By the time the Normans arrived in England, the Welsh no longer needed anti-Viking protection and had returned to their independent ways. Not if William the Conqueror had anything to do with it. To secure his new kingdom, and keep the Welsh in theirs, William built castles (see the boxed text, p36) and appointed feudal barons along the border. The Lords Marcher, as they were known, became massively rich and powerful, and the parts of western England along the Welsh border are still called the Marches today.

In Scotland, King Malcolm III and Queen Margaret were more accommodating to Norman ways – or, at least, they liked the way Normans ran a country. Malcolm's successor, David I (1124–53), was impressed too, and adopted the Norman feudal system, as well as granting land to great Norman families. By 1212, a courtier called Walter of Coventry remarked that the Scottish court was 'French in race and manner of life, in speech and culture'.

But while the French impression of the Normans changed England and lowland Scotland over the following centuries, further north the Highland clans remained inaccessible in their glens – a law unto themselves for another 600 years.

ROYAL & HOLY SQUABBLING

Back at the heart of things, the king of England, Henry II, was flexing his muscles. The church, also very powerful, pushed back. Things came to a head in 1170 when Henry had 'turbulent priest' Thomas Becket murdered in Canterbury Cathedral – still a site of Christian pilgrimage (see p182).

Perhaps the next king, Richard I, wanted to make amends for his forebears' unholy sentiments, so he launched a Crusade against Muslim

---

DOMINATING THE LANDSCAPE

If you're travelling through Wales, it won't take you long to notice the country's most striking architectural asset: castles. There are around 600 in all, giving Wales the dubious honour of being Europe's most densely fortified country. Most were built in medieval times, first by William the Conqueror, then by other Anglo-Norman kings, to keep a lid on the Welsh. In the late 13th century, Edward I built the spectacular castles at Caernarfon, Harlech, Conwy and Beaumaris – now jointly listed as a Unesco World Heritage Site. Other castles to see include Rhuddlan, Denbigh, Cricceith, Raglan, Pembroke, Kidwelly, Chepstow and Caerphilly. Great for visitors, of course, but a sore point for patriotic Welsh; the writer Thomas Pennant called them 'the magnificent badge of our subjection'.

1296	1297
King Edward I invades Scotland	Battle of Stirling Bridge; England defeated by a Scots army under the leadership of William Wallace

'infidels' in today's Middle East – then called The Holy Land. Unfortunately, he was too busy crusading to bother about governing England (although his bravery earned him the Richard Lionheart sobriquet), and after his brother John became king things got even worse. According to legend, it was during this time that a nobleman called Robert of Loxley, better known as Robin Hood, took to hiding in forests and energetically engaging in a spot of wealth redistribution. For more on this story see the boxed text, p428.

KING JOHN CALLED TO BOOK

By 1215 the barons had found King John's erratic rule increasingly hard to swallow, and forced him to sign a document called the Magna Carta, limiting the monarch's power for the first time in British history. Although originally intended as a set of handy ground rules, the Magna Carta was a fledgling bill of human rights that eventually led to the creation of Parliament – a body to rule the country, independent of the throne. The signing took place at Runnymede, near Windsor, and you can still visit the site today (see p200).

EDWARD MAKES HIS MARK

Next king along was Henry III, followed in 1272 by Edward I – a skilled ruler and ambitious general. During a 56-year reign, Edward expounded English nationalism and was unashamedly expansionist in his outlook, leading ruthless campaigns into Wales and Scotland.

Some decades earlier, the Welsh king Llywelyn the Great (who died in 1240) had attempted to set up a state in Wales along the lines of the new feudal system in England, and his grandson Llywelyn ('Llywelyn the Last') was recognised by Henry III as the first Prince (but not King) of Wales. But Edward I had no time for such niceties, and descended on Wales in a bloody invasion that lasted much of the 1270s. In the end, Wales became a dependent principality, owing allegiance to England. There were no more Welsh kings, and just to make it clear who was boss, Edward made his own son Prince of Wales. Ever since, the British sovereign's eldest son has been automatically given the title. (Most recently, in 1969, Prince Charles was formally proclaimed Prince of Wales at Caernarfon Castle.)

Edward I then looked north. For the past 200 years, Scotland had been ruled by the Canmores, but the dynasty effectively ended in 1286 with the death of Alexander III. He was succeeded by his four-year-old grand-daughter, Margaret ('the Maid of Norway'), who was engaged to the son of Edward I, but she died in 1290 before the wedding could take place.

There followed a dispute for the Scottish throne for which there were 13 *tanists* (contestants), but in the end it came down to two: John Balliol and Robert Bruce of Annandale. Arbitration was needed, and Edward I was called in; he chose Balliol. But having finished the job, Edward then sought to formalise his feudal overlordship and travelled the country forcing clan leaders to swear allegiance. In a final blow to Scottish pride, Edward removed the Stone of Scone, on which the kings of Scotland had been crowned for centuries, and sent it to London (see the boxed text, p749).

That was just too much. In response, Balliol got in touch with Edward's old enemy, France, and arranged a treaty of cooperation – the start of an

Myths and Legends of the British Isles by Richard Barber is ideal if you want a break from historical facts. Gen up on King Arthur and the Knights of the Round Table, plus lots more from the mists of time.

1314	**1337**
Battle of Bannockburn; England defeated by Scots under Robert Bruce	Start of the Hundred Years' War with France

anti-English partnership ('the Auld Alliance') that was to last for many centuries – and to the present day when it comes to rugby or football.

But Edward wasn't the sort of bloke to brook opposition. His ruthless retaliation earned him the title 'Hammer of the Scots', and in 1296 the English army defeated Balliol, forcing the Scottish barons to accept Edward's rule. But the Scottish people thought otherwise: in 1297, at the Battle of Stirling Bridge, the English were defeated by a Scots army under the leadership of William Wallace. Almost 700 years later, Wallace is still remembered as the epitome of patriotic Scots (see p833).

The story of William Wallace is told in the Mel Gibson epic *Braveheart*. In devolution debates of the 1990s, the patriotic pride engendered by this movie did more for Scottish nationalism than any politician's speech.

PLANTAGENET GLOOM

Back in England, Edward I was succeeded by Edward II, but the new model lacked the military success of his forebear, and his favouring of personal friends over barons didn't help. Edward apparently failed in the marriage department too, and his rule came to a grisly end when his wife, Isabella, and her lover, Roger Mortimer, had him murdered in Berkeley Castle.

By this time, Robert the Bruce (grandson of Robert Bruce of Annandale) had crowned himself king of Scotland (1290), been beaten in battle, gone on the run, and while hiding in a cave been famously inspired to renew his efforts by a spider persistently spinning its web. Bruce's army went on to defeat Edward II and the English at the Battle of Bannockburn in 1314, another milestone in Scotland's long fight to remain independent.

Next in line was Edward III. Notable events during his reign included the start of the Hundred Years' War with France in 1337 and the arrival of the Black Death (bubonic plague) about a decade later, which eventually carried off 1.5 million people – more than a third of the country's population. Nothing to be proud of, but another change of king didn't improve things much either. Richard II had barely taken the throne when the Peasants' Revolt erupted in 1381. This attempt by commoners to overthrow the feudal system was brutally suppressed, further injuring an already deeply divided country.

STEWARTS ENTER THE SCENE

While the Hundred Years' War raged (or rather, rumbled) between England and France, things weren't much better in Scotland. After the death of Robert the Bruce in 1329, the country was ravaged by endless civil disputes and plague epidemics.

Bruce's son became David II of Scotland, but he was soon caught up in battles against fellow Scots disaffected by his father and aided by England's Edward III. So when David died in 1371, the Scots quickly crowned Robert Stewart (Robert the Bruce's grandson) as king, marking the start of the House of Stewart, which was to crop up again in England a bit later down the line.

HOUSES OF YORK & LANCASTER

The ineffectual Richard II was ousted in 1399 by a powerful baron called Henry Bolingbroke, who became Henry IV – the first monarch of the House of Lancaster. Less than a year later, his rule was disrupted by a final cry of resistance from the downtrodden Welsh, led by royal-descendant Owain Glyndwr (Owen Glendower to the English). It wasn't a good result for Wales. The rebellion was crushed, vast areas of farmland were destroyed, Glyndwr died an outlaw, and the Welsh elite were barred from public life for many years.

Henry IV was followed, neatly, by Henry V, who decided it was time to stir up the dormant Hundred Years' War. From his point of view, it was worth it; he defeated France at the Battle of Agincourt and the patriotic tear-jerker speech he was given by Shakespeare ('cry God for Harry, England and St George') has ensured his pole position among the most famous English kings of all time.

Still keeping things neat, Henry V was followed by Henry VI. His main claim to fame was overseeing the building of great places of worship (King's College Chapel in Cambridge, Eton Chapel near Windsor), interspersed with great bouts of insanity.

When the Hundred Years' War finally ground to a halt in 1453, you'd have thought things would be calm for a while. But no. The English forces returning from France threw their energies into another battle – a civil conflict dubbed the War of the Roses.

Briefly, it went like this: Henry VI of the House of Lancaster (whose emblem was a red rose) was challenged by Richard, Duke of York (proud holder of a white-rose flag). Henry was weak and it was almost a walkover for Richard, but Henry's wife, Margaret of Anjou, was made of sterner stuff and her forces defeated the challenger. But it didn't rest there. Richard's son Edward entered the scene with an army, turned the tables, drove out Henry, and became King Edward IV – the first monarch of the House of York.

But life was never easy for the guy at the top. Edward IV hardly had time to catch his breath before facing a challenger to his own throne. Enter scheming Richard Neville, Earl of Warwick, who liked to be billed as 'the kingmaker'. In 1470 he teamed up with the energetic Margaret of Anjou to banish Edward into exile and return the throne to Henry VI. But a year later Edward IV came bouncing back – to kill Warwick, capture Margaret, and have Henry snuffed out in the Tower of London.

DARK DEEDS IN THE TOWER

Although Edward IV's position seemed secure, he ruled for only a decade before being succeeded by his 12-year-old son, now Edward V. But the boy-king's rule was even shorter than his dad's. In 1483 he was mysteriously murdered, along with his brother, and once again the Tower of London was the scene of the crime.

With the 'little princes' dispatched, the throne was left open for their dear uncle Richard. Whether he was the princes' killer is still the subject of debate, but his rule as Richard III was short-lived. Despite another famous Shakespearean soundbite ('A horse, a horse, my kingdom for a horse'), few tears were shed when he was tumbled from rule in 1485 by Henry Tudor.

MOVES TOWARDS UNITY

There hadn't been a Henry on the throne for a while, and this new incumbent, Henry VII, harked back to the days of his namesakes with a skilful

Shakespeare's *Henry V* was filmed most recently in 1989 – a superb modern epic, staring English cinema darling Kenneth Branagh. A 1944 film of the same name, staring Laurence Olivier, filmed as a patriotic rallying cry in the dark days of WWII, is also worth catching.

DID YOU KNOW?
Today, 600 years after the War of the Roses, Yorkshire's symbol is still a white rose, while Lancashire's is still a red rose, and rivalry between the people of these two counties is still very strong – especially when it comes to cricket or football.

1400	1459–71
Owain Glyndwr leads Welsh rebels against English army	War of the Roses

reign. After the York-vs-Lancaster War of the Roses, his Tudor neutrality was important. He also diligently mended fences with his northern neighbours by marrying off his daughter to James IV of Scotland, thereby linking the Tudor and Stewart lines. On top of his family links with Scotland, Henry was also half-Welsh. He withdrew many of the anti-Welsh restrictions imposed after the Glyndwr uprising, and his countrymen were only too grateful to enjoy new-found preferential treatment at the English court and career opportunities in English public life.

Matrimony may have been more useful than warfare for Henry VI, but the multiple marriages of his successor, Henry VIII, were a very different story. Fathering a male heir was his problem – hence the famous six wives – but the Pope's disapproval of divorce and remarriage led to a split with the Catholic Church. Parliament made Henry the head of the Protestant Church of England – the beginning of a pivotal division between Catholics and Protestants that still exists in some areas of Britain.

In 1536 Henry VIII 'dissolved' the smaller monasteries in Britain and Ireland, a blatant takeover of their land and wealth and another stage in the struggle between church and state. The populace felt little sympathy for the wealthy and often corrupt monasteries, and in 1539–40 another monastic land grab swallowed the larger ones as well. At the same time, Henry signed the Acts of Union (1536–43), formally uniting England and Wales. This was welcomed by the aspiring Welsh gentry, as it meant English law and parliamentary representation for Wales, plus plenty of trade opportunities. The Welsh language, however, ceased to be recognised in the law courts.

In Scotland, James IV had been succeeded by James V, who died in 1542, broken-hearted, it is said, after yet another defeat at the hands of the English. His baby daughter, Mary, became queen and Scotland was ruled by Regents, who rejected Henry VIII's plan that Mary should marry his son. Not forgetting the Auld Alliance, she was sent to France instead. Henry was furious and his armies ravaged southern Scotland and sacked Edinburgh in a failed attempt to force agreement to the wedding – the Rough Wooing, as it was called with typical Scottish irony and understatement.

THE ELIZABETHAN AGE

Henry VIII died in 1547, and was succeeded by his son Edward VI, then by daughter Mary I, but their reigns were short. So, unexpectedly, the third child, Elizabeth, came to the throne.

As Elizabeth I, she inherited a nasty mess of religious strife and divided loyalties, but after an uncertain start she gained confidence and turned the country around. Refusing marriage, she borrowed from biblical imagery and became known as the Virgin Queen – perhaps the first British monarch to create a cult image. It paid off. Her 45-year reign was a period of boundless English optimism characterised by the writings of Shakespeare and Christopher Marlow, the defeat of the Spanish Armada, the expansion of trade, and the global explorations of English seafarers Walter Raleigh and Francis Drake.

MARY QUEEN OF SCOTS

Meanwhile, Elizabeth's cousin Mary (the daughter of Scottish King James V who'd been sent to France to evade the attention of Henry VIII) had

---

The 1955 film version of Shakespeare's *Richard III*, starring Laurence Olivier and John Gielgud, is now available on DVD; a great choice for the award-winning drama of its time, and for a view on this turbulent period in history.

Six Wives: the Queens of Henry VIII by David Starky is an accessible modern study of this turbulent period, based on a popular TV history series.

1509–47

Rule of Henry VIII; marries six times and dissolves monasteries

1536–43

Acts of Union, formally uniting England and Wales

become known as Mary Queen of Scots. In France she'd married the French dauphin (crown prince), thereby becoming queen of France as well. After her husband's death, Mary returned to Scotland, and claimed the English throne as well – on the grounds that Elizabeth I was illegitimate. But Mary's plans failed; in Scotland she was imprisoned and forced to abdicate in favour of her son – who became James VI of Scotland.

Mary escaped to England and appealed to Elizabeth for help. Bad move. It could have been a rookie error; she might have been advised by courtiers with their own agenda. Either way, Mary was not surprisingly seen as a security risk and imprisoned once again. In an uncharacteristic display of indecision, before finally ordering her execution, Elizabeth held Mary under arrest for 19 years, moving her frequently from house to house, so that today England has many stately homes (and even a few pubs) claiming 'Mary Queen of Scots slept here'.

UNITED & DISUNITED BRITAIN

Despite a bountiful reign, one thing the Virgin Queen failed to provide was an heir. When Elizabeth died in 1603, she was succeeded by her closest relative, James, the son of the murdered Mary. He became James I of England and VI of Scotland, the first monarch in England of the House of Stuart (Mary's time in France had Gallicised the Stewart name). Most importantly, James united England, Wales and Scotland into one kingdom for the first time in history. It was another step towards British unity – at least on paper.

James was Protestant, but eager to smooth relations with Catholics (who had suffered since the days of Henry VIII's falling out with Rome). His ecumenical plans were foiled by the anti-Catholic outcry that followed the infamous Guy Fawkes Gunpowder Plot, a terrorist attempt to blow up Parliament in 1605. (An event still celebrated every 5 November, with fireworks, bonfires and burning effigies of Guy himself.)

Along with the Catholic–Protestant rift, the divide between king and parliament continued to smoulder. The power struggle worsened during the reign of the next king, Charles I, and eventually degenerated into the Civil War of 1644–49. The antiroyalist forces were led by Oliver Cromwell, a Puritan who preached against the excesses of the monarch and the established church. Cromwell's army of parliamentarians (Roundheads) was pitched against the king's forces (the Cavaliers) in a war that tore England apart – although fortunately for the last time in history. The war ended with victory for the Roundheads, with the king executed and England declared a republic – and Cromwell hailed as 'Protector'.

The civil war had been a bitter conflict, but failed to exhaust Cromwell's appetite for mayhem; a devastating rampage to gain control of Ireland – the first British colony – followed quickly in its wake. Meanwhile, the Scots suffered their own parallel civil war between the royalists and radical 'Covenanters' who sought freedom from state interference in church government.

THE RETURN OF THE KING

By 1653 Cromwell was finding parliament too restricting and he assumed dictatorial powers, much to his supporters' dismay. On his death, he was

This time the Bard gets his own movie. *Shakespeare in Love* is unashamedly romantic, undoubtedly modern and unrepentantly funny: a fabulous romp through backstage Elizabethan London, especially enthralling if you know a few lines from the plays. The Norfolk coast has a cameo role too.

Elizabeth, directed by Shekhar Kapur and starring Cate Blanchett, covers the early years of the Virgin Queen's rule – as she moves from novice princess to commanding monarch – a time of forbidden love, unwanted suitors, assassination attempts, intrigue and death.

Elizabeth I comes to throne: enter playwright William Shakespeare, exit due west explorers Walter Raleigh and Francis Drake

English Civil War between king's royalists forces (Cavaliers) and Oliver Cromwell's parliamentarians (Roundheads)

followed half-heartedly by his son, but in 1660 parliament decided to re-establish the monarchy – because republican alternatives were proving far worse.

DID YOU KNOW?

Charles I wore two shirts on the day of his execution, to avoid shivering and being thought cowardly.

So Charles II (the exiled son of Charles I) came to the throne, and his rule, 'the Restoration', saw scientific and cultural activity bursting forth after the strait-laced ethics of Cromwell's time. Exploration and expansion were also on the agenda. Backed by the army and navy (modernised, ironically, by Cromwell), colonies stretched down the American coast, while the East India Company set up headquarters in Bombay (now Mumbai), laying foundations for what was to become the British Empire.

The next king, James II of England (and VII of Scotland), had a harder time. Attempts to ease restrictive laws on Catholics ended with his defeat at the Battle of the Boyne by William III, the Protestant king of Holland, better known as William of Orange. Ironically, William was married to James' own daughter Mary, but it didn't stop him doing the dirty on his father-in-law.

With James ousted into exile, William and Mary both had equal rights to the throne and their joint accession in 1688 was known as the Glorious Revolution. It's lucky they were married, or there might have been *another* civil war.

KILLIECRANKIE & GLEN COE

What the Tudors & Stuarts Did For Us by TV presenter and historian Adam Hart-Davis covers great achievements and innovations in this key period of history.

In Scotland, things weren't quite so glorious. Anti-English (essentially anti-William) and Jacobite (pro-James) feelings ran high. In 1689, a Jacobite leader called Graham of Claverhouse, better-known as 'Bonnie Dundee', raised a Highlander army and routed the English troops at Killiecrankie. Then in 1692 came the infamous Glen Coe Massacre, when on English government orders members of the Campbell clan killed most of the MacDonald clan for failing to swear allegiance to William. (For more details see the boxed text, p883) The massacre was a dark day for Scotland, and further tightened the grip of English domination on the island of Britain, although Jacobite sentiment enjoyed a swansong (albeit doomed) before finally succumbing to history – see the boxed text, p43.

FULL FINAL UNITY

In 1694 Mary died, leaving just William. He died a few years later, and was followed by his sister-in-law Anne (the second daughter of James II). In 1707, during Anne's reign, the Act of Union was passed, bringing an end to the independent Scottish Parliament, and finally linking the countries of England, Wales and Scotland under one parliament (based in London) for the first time. The nation of Britain was now established as a single state, with a bigger, better and more powerful parliament, and a constitutional monarchy with clear limits on the power of the king or queen.

The new-look parliament didn't wait long to flex its muscles. On the side, the Act of Union banned any Catholic, or anyone married to a Catholic, from ascending the throne – a rule still in force today. And although the Glorious Revolution was relatively painless in Britain, the impact on Ireland (where the Protestant ascendancy dates from William's victory over James) laid the seeds for the troubles that have continued into our own time.

1688	1692
Joint accession of William of Orange and Mary; known as the Glorious Revolution	Glen Coe Massacre; Campbell clan members kill MacDonald clan members for not swearing allegiance to King William

THE JACOBITE REBELLIONS

Despite, or perhaps because of, the Act of Union, anti-English feeling in Scotland refused to disappear. The Jacobite rebellions, most notably those of 1715 and 1745, were attempts to overthrow the Hanoverian monarchy, and bring back the Stuarts. Although these are iconic events in Scottish history, in reality there was never much support for the Jacobite cause outside the Highlands: the people of the Lowlands were mainly Protestant, and feared a return to the Catholicism, which the Stuarts represented.

The 1715 rebellion was led by James Edward Stuart (the Old Pretender), the son of the exiled James II of England and VII of Scotland. When the attempt failed, he fled to France, and to impose control on the Highlands, the English military (under the notorious General Wade) constructed roads into previously inaccessible glens.

In 1745, James' son Charles Edward Stuart (Bonnie Prince Charlie, the Young Pretender) landed in Scotland to claim the crown for his father. He was successful initially, moving south into England as far as Derby, but the prince and his Highland supporters suffered a catastrophic defeat at the Battle of Culloden in 1746. For more details see p891. His legendary escape to the Western Isles is eternally remembered in the *Skye Boat Song*. And in a different way, General Wade is remembered too – many of the roads his troops built are still in use today.

In 1714 Anne died without leaving an heir, marking the end of the Stuart line. The throne was then passed to distant (but still safely Protestant) German relatives – the House of Hanover.

THE EMPIRE STRIKES OUT

By the mid-18th century, struggles for the British throne seemed a thing of the past, and the Hanoverian kings increasingly relied on parliament to govern the country. As part of the process, from 1721 to 1742 a senior parliamentarian called Sir Robert Walpole effectively became Britain's first prime minister.

Stronger control over the British Isles was mirrored by even greater expansion abroad. The British Empire – which, despite its official title, was predominantly an *English* entity – continued to grow in America, Canada and India. The first claims were made to Australia after Captain James Cook's epic voyage in 1768.

The Empire's first major reverse came when the American colonies won the War of Independence (1776–83). This setback forced Britain to withdraw from the world stage for a while, a gap not missed by French ruler Napoleon. He threatened to invade Britain and hinder the power of the British overseas, before his ambitions were curtailed by navy hero Viscount Horatio Nelson and military hero the Duke of Wellington at the famous battles of Trafalgar (1805) and Waterloo (1815).

THE INDUSTRIAL AGE

While the Empire expanded abroad, at home Britain had become the crucible of the Industrial Revolution. Steam power (patented by James Watt in 1781) and steam trains (launched by George Stephenson in 1830), transformed methods of production and transport. The towns of the English Midlands became the first industrial cities – and a hitherto predominantly rural populace came in search of work.

DID YOU KNOW?

Cook's voyage to the southern hemisphere was primarily a scientific expedition. His objectives included monitoring the transit of Venus, an astronomical event that happens only twice every 180 years or so (most recently in 2004). 'Discovering' Australia was just a sideline.

This population shift was mirrored in Scotland. From about 1750 onwards, much of Scotland's Highlands region had been emptied of people, as landowners casually expelled entire farms and villages to make way for more profitable sheep farming, a seminal event in Scotland's history known as The Clearances (see p894). Industrialisation just about finished off the job. Although many of the dispossessed left for the New World, others came from the glens to the burgeoning factories of the Lowlands. The tobacco trade with America boomed, and then gave way to textile and engineering industries, as the cotton mills of Lanarkshire and the Clyde shipyards around Glasgow expanded rapidly.

The same happened in Wales. By the early 19th century, copper, iron and slate were being extracted in the Merthyr Tydfil and Monmouth areas. The 1860s saw the Rhondda valleys opened up for coal mining, and Wales soon became a major exporter of coal, as well as the world's leading producer of tin plate.

Across Britain, industrialisation meant people were on the move as never before. Farmers left the land and villages their families had occupied for generations. Often they went to the nearest factory, but not always. Scots and English workers both settled in South Wales, for example. The rapid change from rural to urban society caused great dislocation, and although knowledge of science and medicine also improved alongside industrial advances, for many people poverty and deprivation were the adverse side effects of Britain's economic blossoming.

Nevertheless, by the time Queen Victoria took the throne in 1837, Britain's fleets dominated the seas, and Britain's factories dominated world trade. The rest of the 19th century was seen as Britain's Golden Age (for some people, it still is) – a period of confidence not seen since the days of the last great queen, Elizabeth I.

Victoria ruled a proud nation at home, and many territories abroad – including Canada, the Caribbean, Australia, New Zealand and much of Africa and India – trumpeted as 'the Empire where the sun never sets'. In a final move of PR genius, the Queen's chief spin doctor and most effective prime minister, Benjamin Disraeli, had Victoria crowned Empress of India. She'd never even been there, but the British people loved the idea.

The times were optimistic, but it wasn't all tub-thumping jingoism. Disraeli and his successor William Gladstone also introduced social reforms to address the worst excesses of the Industrial Revolution. Education became universal, trade unions were legalised, and the right to vote was extended to commoners. Well, to male commoners. Women didn't get the vote for another few decades. Disraeli and Gladstone may have been enlightened gentlemen, but there *were* limits.

WORLD WAR I

Queen Victoria died in 1901 and ever-expanding Britain died with her. But at the dawn of the 20th century, when Edward VII ushered in the relaxed new Edwardian era, it wasn't evident that a long period of decline was about to set in.

In continental Europe, things were far from calm. Four restless military powers (Russia, Austro-Hungary, Turkey and Germany) focused their sabre rattling on the Balkan states, and the assassination of Archduke Fer-

---

1746

Battle of Culloden; the end of the Jacobite Rebellions

1750

Start of Britain's Industrial Age

dinand at Sarajevo in 1914 finally sparked a clash that became the Great War – WWI. When German forces entered Belgium, on their way to invade France, soldiers from Britain and allied countries were drawn into a vicious conflict of stalemate and horrendous slaughter – most infamously on the killing fields of Flanders and the beaches of Gallipoli.

By the war's weary end in 1918 over a million Britons had died (not to mention millions more from many other countries) and there was hardly a street or village untouched by death, as the sobering lists of names on war memorials all over Britain still show. The conflict added 'trench warfare' to the dictionary, and further deepened the huge gulf that had existed between ruling and working classes since the days of the Norman feudal system.

DISILLUSION & DEPRESSION

For the soldiers who did return from WWI, disillusion led to questioning of the social order. A new political force – the Labour Party, to represent the working class – upset the balance long enjoyed by the Liberal and Conservative parties since the days of Walpole. The first Labour leader was Keir Hardie, a Scottish politician representing a Welsh constituency (the coal-mining town of Merthyr Tydfil) in the London-based parliament.

The Labour Party won for the first time in the 1923 election, in coalition with the Liberals; James Ramsay MacDonald was the first Labour prime minister. A year later the Conservatives regained power, but the rankling 'them-and-us' mistrust, fertilised by soaring unemployment, led to the 1926 General Strike. When half a million workers marched through the streets, the government sent in the army – setting the stage for industrial unrest that was to plague Britain for the next 50 years.

Unrest at home was mirrored by unrest abroad – in Ireland, Britain's oldest colony. WWI was no sooner over than Britain was involved in the bitter Anglo-Irish War, which ended in mid-1921, with most of Ireland achieving full independence (although six counties in the north remained British). The new political entity may have been billed as the United Kingdom of Great Britain and Northern Ireland, but the decision to divide the island of Ireland in two was to have long-term repercussions that still dominate political agendas in both the UK and the Republic of Ireland today.

The unrest of the 1920s worsened in the '30s as the world economy slumped and the Great Depression took hold – a decade of misery and political upheaval. Even the royal family took a knock when Edward VIII abdicated in 1936 so he could marry a woman who was twice divorced and, horror of horrors, American. The ensuing scandal was good for newspaper sales and hinted at the prolonged 'trial by media' suffered by royals in more recent times.

The throne was taken by Edward's less-than-charismatic brother George VI and Britain dithered through the rest of the decade, with mediocre and visionless government failing to confront the country's problems.

WORLD WAR II

Meanwhile in mainland Europe, there was nothing mediocre about the rise of Adolf Hitler, leader of the German Nazi party. Many British people feared another Great War, but Prime Minister Neville Chamberlain met

Birdsong by Sebastian Faulks is partly set in the trenches of WWI. Understated, perfectly paced and severely moving, it tells of love, passion, fear, waste and death, as well as incompetent generals and the poor bloody infantry.

DID YOU KNOW?

In the election after WWI, men over 21 years, and women over 30 could vote. It wasn't until 1928 that women were granted the same rights as men – despite the opposition of an up-and-coming politician called Winston Churchill.

1799	1805
Start of Napoleonic Wars	Battles of Trafalgar and Waterloo, end of Napoleonic Wars

Hitler in 1938 and promised Britain 'peace in our time'. Unfortunately, he was wrong, and the following year Hitler invaded Poland. Two days later Britain was once again at war with Germany.

The German army moved with astonishing speed, swept west through France, and pushed back British forces to the beaches of Dunkirk in June 1940. An extraordinary flotilla of rescue vessels turned total disaster into a brave defeat – and Dunkirk Day is still remembered with pride and sadness in Britain every year.

By mid-1940 most of Europe was controlled by Germany. In Russia, Joseph Stalin had negotiated a peace agreement. The USA was neutral,

RULING BRITANNIA

A glance at Britain's tempestuous history clearly shows that life was never dull for the folk at the top of the tree. Despite immense power and privilege, the position of monarch (or, perhaps worse, *potential* monarch) probably ranks as one of history's least safe occupations.

English kings have been beheaded (Charles I), murdered by a wicked uncle (Edward V) or knocked off by their queen (Edward II) – to mention just a few unintentional exits. Similarly, life was just as uncertain for the rulers of Wales and Scotland; threats came from ambitious clan chiefs – you only have to think of Shakespeare's *Macbeth* – and often from the English king next door.

Below is a brief overview of the last millennium or so, showing English monarchs since 1066, plus key Welsh and Scottish rulers of the period (with dates of their reigns). As you visit the castles and battlefields of Britain, this basic picture of who ruled when should make your visit much more rewarding.

England

Normans

William I (the Conqueror) 1066–87
William II 1087–1100
Henry I 1100–35
Stephen 1135–54

House of Plantagenet

Henry II 1154–89
Richard I (Lionheart) 1189–99
John 1199–1216
Henry III 1216–72
Edward I 1272–1307
Edward II 1307–27
Edward III 1327–77
Richard II 1377–99

House of Lancaster

Henry IV (Bolingbroke) 1399–1413
Henry V 1413–22
Henry VI 1422–61 & 1470–71

House of York

Edward IV 1461–70 & 1471–83
Edward V 1483
Richard III 1483–85

House of Tudor

Henry VII 1485–1509
Henry VIII 1509–47
Edward VI 1547–53
Mary I 1553–58
Elizabeth I 1558–1603

House of Stuart

James I 1603–25
Charles I 1625–49

Protectorate (Republic)

Oliver Cromwell 1649–58
Richard Cromwell 1658–59

leaving Britain virtually isolated. Neville Chamberlain, reviled for his earlier 'appeasement', stood aside to let Winston Churchill lead a coalition government.

Hitler had expected an easy victory, but Churchill's extraordinary dedication (not to mention his radio speeches) inspired the country to resist, and between July and October 1940 Britain's Royal Air Force withstood Germany's aerial raids to win what became known as the Battle of Britain – a major turning point in the war, and a chance for land forces to rebuild their strength. The pendulum swung further as the USA entered the war to support Britain, while Japan mobilised behind

Restoration

Charles II 1660–85
James II 1685–88
William III (of Orange) 1688–1702
Mary II 1688–94
Anne 1702–14

House of Hanover

George I 1714–27
George II 1727–60
George III 1760–1820
George IV 1820–30
William IV 1830–37
Victoria 1837–1901

Houses of Saxe-Coburg & Windsor

Edward VII 1901–10
George V 1910–36
Edward VIII 1936
George VI 1936–52
Elizabeth II 1952–

Scotland
House of MacAilpin

Kenneth (king of Alba – Picts and Scots) 840–58
Donald II (first king of Scotland) 889–900
Malcolm I 943–54
Malcolm II 1005–34
Duncan 1034–1040
Macbeth 1040–57

House of Canmore

Malcolm III 1058–93
Donald III 1093–97
Alexander I 1107–24

David I 1124–53
Malcolm IV 1153–65
William 1165–1214
Alexander II 1214–49
Alexander III 1249–86
Margaret (Maid of Norway) 1286–90

Interregnum (period between monarchs)

John Balliol 1292–96
William Wallace 1297–98

House of Bruce

Robert (the Bruce) 1 1306–29
David II 1329–71

House of Stewart

Robert II 1371–90
Robert III 1390–1406
James I 1406–37
James II 1437–60
James III 1460–88
James IV 1488–1513
James V 1513–42
Mary (Queen of Scots) 1542–67
James VI of Scotland (& James I of England) 1567–1625

Wales
Rulers of Gwynedd (main Welsh kingdom)

Rhodri ap Merfyn (Rhodri Mawr, the Great) 844–78
Gruffydd ap Llywelyn (first king of all Wales) 1039–63
Owain Gwynedd 1137–70
Dafydd ap Owain 1170–95
Llywelyn (the Great) 1195–1240
Dafydd ap Llywelyn 1240–46
Llywelyn (the Last) 1246–82

1916	1926
Welsh politician David Lloyd George becomes prime minister of Britain	General Strike

Germany, and by late 1941 Germany was bogged down on the 'eastern front' fighting Russia.

DID YOU KNOW?

The Normandy Landings was the largest military armada in history; involving over 5000 ships, with hundreds of thousands of troops landing in about four days. Many thousands (soldiers and French civilians) were killed, but the invasion was successful. June 2004 marked its 60th anniversary.

In 1942 German forces were defeated in North Africa, and by 1944 Germany was in retreat. Britain and the USA controlled the skies, Russia's Red Army pushed back from the east, and the Allies were once again on the beaches of France as the Normandy Landings (D-Day, as it's better remembered) marked the start of the liberation of Europe from the west, and in Churchill's words 'the beginning of the end of the war'. By 1945 Hitler was dead, and Germany a smoking ruin. Two atomic bombs forced the surrender of Japan and finally brought WWII to a dramatic and terrible close.

SWINGING & SLIDING

In Britain, despite the war victory, there was an unexpected swing on the political front. An electorate tired of war and hungry for change tumbled Churchill's Conservatives, and voted in the Labour Party, led by Clement Attlee. This was the dawn of the 'welfare state'; the National Health Service was founded and key industries (such as steel, coal and railways) were nationalised. But rebuilding Britain was a slow process: peacetime boosted reproduction rates, meaning postwar 'baby boomers' experienced food rationing well into the 1950s.

Windrush – The Irresistible Rise of Multi-Racial Britain by Mike and Trevor Phillips traces the history of Britain's West Indian immigrants, from the first arrivals in 1949 (on the merchant ship *Empire Windrush*) to their modern-day descendants.

The effects of depleted reserves were felt overseas too, as one by one the colonies became independent, including India and Pakistan in 1947, Malaya in 1957 and Kenya in 1963. People from these ex-colonies – and especially from the Caribbean – were drawn to the mother country through the 1960s. In many cases they were specifically invited, as additional labour was needed to help rebuild postwar Britain. In the 1970s many immigrants of Asian origin arrived, having been forced out of Uganda by dictator Idi Amin.

In the Empire the sun was setting, but Britain's royal family was still going strong. In 1952 George VI was succeeded by his daughter Elizabeth II. Following the trend set by earlier queens Elizabeth I and Victoria, she has remained on the throne for over 50 years (2002 was her Golden Jubilee), like them overseeing a period of massive social and economic change.

The Queen's Story by Marcus Kiggell is a royal biography far more studied and serious, and far less gushing, than many titles similarly covering the current monarch's happy and glorious rule.

By the late 1950s, recovery was strong enough for Prime Minister Harold Macmillan to famously remind the British people that they'd 'never had it so good'. Some saw this as a boast for a confident future, others as a warning about difficult times ahead. However, most probably forgot all about it because by this time the 1960s had started and grey old Britain was suddenly more fun and lively than it had been for generations – especially if you were over 10 and under 30 years old. There was the music of the Beatles, the Rolling Stones, Cliff Richard and the Shadows, while cinema audiences flocked to see Michael Caine, Peter Sellers and Glenda Jackson.

Alongside the glamour, business seemed to be swinging too, but the 1970s brought inflation, the oil crisis and international competition – a deadly combination quickly revealing everything that was weak about Britain's economy, and a lot that was rotten in British society, too. The struggle between disgruntled working classes and inept ruling classes

1939–45	**1948**
WWII; Britain at war with Germany, again	National Health Service founded

was brought to the boil once again; the rest of the decade was marked by industrial disputes, three-day weeks and general all-round gloom – especially when the electricity was cut, as power stations went short of fuel or labour.

Even when Britain discovered 'local' oil and gas in the North Sea, east of Scotland, things improved only slightly. Prosperity came to the Aberdeen area and the Shetland Islands, but most of the revenue was siphoned off back to England. This, along with takeovers of many Scottish companies by English ones, fuelled increasing nationalist sentiment in Scotland.

Neither the Conservatives under Edward Heath, nor Labour under Harold Wilson and Jim Callaghan, proved capable of controlling the strife. The British public had had enough, and the elections of 1979 returned the Conservatives led by a little-known politician called Margaret Thatcher.

Small Island by Andrea Levy is a novel (and 2004 Orange Prize winner) about a Caribbean couple who settle in 1950s London. The author is of Jamaican origin, and draws on rich family memories of the time.

THE THATCHER YEARS

Soon everyone had heard of Mrs Thatcher. Love her or hate her, no-one could argue that her methods weren't dramatic. British workers were Luddites? She fired them. British industries inefficient? She shut them down. Nationalised companies a mistake? She sold them off – with a sense of purpose that made Henry VIII's dissolution of the monasteries seem like a Sunday-school picnic.

And just in case there was any doubt about Mrs Thatcher's patriotism, in 1982 she led Britain into war against Argentina in a dispute over the Falkland Islands, leading to a bout of public flag-waving that hadn't been seen since WWII, or probably since Agincourt.

Against this background, Mrs Thatcher also waged a relentless assault on the power of trade unions, fronted by the closure of 'uneconomic' coal mines throughout Britain. In response, the nationwide strike by miners in the early 1980s was one of the most bitter disputes in British history, but Mrs Thatcher was victorious: since 1984 around 140 coal pits have closed, meaning a quarter of a million jobs lost, and communities destroyed across the country.

The social costs of Thatcherism were enormous and questionable, but, in line with a global upswing, by the late 1990s the British economy was in better shape than it had been for years. In two decades, the economic base has shifted away from heavy industry, and today the majority of Britons are employed in less labour-intensive light engineering, high-tech and electronic fields (including computers and telecommunications), finance, retail and the service sectors.

But the new, competitive Britain was also a greatly polarised Britain. Once again a trench formed, but not between the classes; this time it was between the people who gained from the prosperous wave of Thatcherism and those left drowning in its wake – not only jobless, but jobless in a harsh environment. Even Thatcher fans were unhappy about the brutal and uncompromising methods favoured by the 'iron lady', but by 1988 she was the longest serving British prime minister of the 20th century. However, her repeated electoral victories were helped in no small way by the Labour Party's total incompetence and destructive internal struggles.

DID YOU KNOW?
Other key areas of the British economy today include agriculture and fisheries – Scotland alone catches over two-thirds of the UK's fish haul. Tourism is also a major economic force – it's Scotland's largest single industry and provides 10% of jobs in Wales.

1952	1963
Queen Elizabeth II ascends the throne of Britain	Members of the Beatles become household names; outbreak of incurable 'Beatlemania'

STAND DOWN MARGARET

When any leader believes they're invincible, it's time to go. In 1990 Mrs Thatcher was finally dumped when her introduction of the hugely unpopular 'poll tax' breached even the Conservatives' limits of tolerance. The voters regarded Labour with even more suspicion, however, allowing new Conservative leader John Major to unexpectedly win the 1992 election.

Another half-decade of political stalemate followed, as the Conservatives imploded and Labour was rebuilt on the sidelines. It all came to a head in 1997 when 'New' Labour swept to power with a record parliamentary majority. After nearly 18 years of Conservative rule, it really seemed that Labour's victory call ('things can only get better') was true – and some people literally danced in the streets when the results were announced.

Under Prime Minister Tony Blair, the government disappointed old socialist stalwarts who expected a swing back to the left. New Labour was a more centrist force, adopting many market reforms favoured by moderate Conservatives. Ministers kept a tight rein on public spending – much to the pleasure of financial institutions. In turn, this sometimes blurred the distinction between Labour and the Liberal-Democrats, and forced the Conservatives to take a sizable jump to the right.

As well as fiscal prudence, major constitutional reforms were introduced in other areas. Devolution of government, at least in part, was granted to Scotland and Wales, with a Scottish Parliament established in Edinburgh, and Cardiff seeing the arrival of the Welsh Assembly, reversing some of the centuries-old unification laws introduced by rulers as far back as Edward I, Henry VII and William and Mary. (See the Edinburgh chapter p754, and p646 of the Cardiff chapter for more devolution details.)

NEW LABOUR, NEW MILLENNIUM

A general election was called in 2001, and although the opposition parties (Conservatives, Liberal-Democrats and the nationalist parties in Wales and Scotland) regained some seats, it was still pretty much a walkover for Tony Blair and the Labour party.

On the opposition benches, the Conservatives replaced John Major with William Hague, a little-loved leader who tried to soften his staid image by wearing a baseball cap. It didn't work and he was soon followed by Ian Duncan-Smith, a more serious contender from the 'Euro-sceptic' right of the party. His rule was short-lived too, and in 2004 the experienced hardliner Michael Howard became Conservative leader.

Meanwhile, Tony Blair remained at the helm of government (2004 was his 10th year as party leader, and seventh as prime minister), if not always in total control, as Labour's rule since the turn of the millennium proved remarkably eventful and frequently doused in controversy. Hot topics included House of Lords reform, where the government's apparent favouritism in the appointment of members led to cries of 'Tony's cronies', and the ongoing issues of economic migrants and asylum seekers – the latter addressed by a raft of new rules from the increasingly tough (some would say rough) Home Secretary David Blunkett.

One of Us: A Biography of Mrs Thatcher by respected journalist and commentator Hugo Young covers the early life of the 'iron lady' and her time in power – showing that her grip on events, and on her own party, wasn't as steely as it seemed.

Things Can Only Get Better by John O'Farrell is a witty, self-deprecating story of politics in the 1980s and early '90s – the era of Thatcher and Conservative domination – from a struggling Labour viewpoint. As well as comedy, the author also wrote speeches for Chancellor Gordon Brown.

1979	1982
Conservatives win election; Margaret Thatcher becomes prime minister	Britain at war with Argentina over the Falkland Islands

Of even greater significance was Britain's role in Iraq. Initially, not-withstanding a massive peace campaign, there was considerable – if grudging – support from the opposition Conservatives in Parliament and a significant proportion of the public for Tony Blair's decision to back the American invasion. But when weapons of mass destruction (the central premise for the war) were not discovered, and when it became apparent that secret reports indicating this nonexistence were ignored by the government (or not passed to those responsible), then the positions of ministers and the prime minister himself were seriously called into question.

As the Iraq war continued to backfire, newspapers carried reports that Tony Blair had considered resignation (leaving the door open for Chancellor of the Exchequer Gordon Brown – so long the PM-in-waiting – to finally go for the top job) but was persuaded to stay on by loyal ministers. This led to a new-found resolve at the top, which translated into mixed success in the local council and European Parliament elections of June

---

DRINKING IN HISTORY

As you travel around Britain, you can't fail to notice the splendid selection of pub names, often illustrated with attractive signboards, and most with strong historic links.

The most popular is the Red Lion, with over 500 pubs in England alone bearing this title. It dates from the early 17th century, when King James VI of Scotland became King James I of England. Lest the populace forget his origin, he ordered that the lion, his heraldic symbol, be displayed in public places.

The second-most-popular pub name is the Crown, which has more obvious royal connections, while the third-most-popular name, the Royal Oak, recalls the days of the Civil War when King Charles escaped Cromwell's army by hiding in a tree. (Look hard at most Royal Oak pub signs and you'll see his face peeping out from between the leaves.)

The King's Arms is another pub name with clear royal connections, as is the Queen's Head, the Prince of Wales, and so on. Less obvious is the White Hart – the heraldic symbol of Richard II, who in 1393 decreed that every pub should display a sign to distinguish it from other buildings. The decree rounded off by saying anyone failing in this duty 'shall forfeit his ale', so many landlords chose the White Hart as a sign of allegiance, and an insurance against stock loss.

Another common pub name is the Rose and Crown. Again, the regal links are obvious, but look carefully at the colour of the rose painted on those signs, especially if you're in the north of England. West of the Pennine Hills it should be the red rose of the House of Lancaster; east of the Pennines it's the white rose depicting the House of York. Woe betide any pub sign that is sporting the wrong colour!

While some pub names crop up in their hundreds, others are far from common, although many still have links to history. Nottingham's most famous pub, Ye Olde Trip to Jerusalem (see Drinking, p429), commemorates knights and soldiers departing for crusades in the Holy Land in the 12th century. Pub names such as the George and Dragon may date from the same era – as a story brought back from the east by returning crusaders. Move on several centuries and pub names such as the Spitfire, the Lancaster or the Churchill recall the days of WWII.

For a more local perspective, the Nobody Inn near Exeter in Devon is said to recall a mix-up over a coffin, the Hit or Miss near Chippenham in Wiltshire recalls a close-run game of village cricket, while the Quiet Woman near Buxton in Derbyshire, with a sign of a headless female, is a reminder of more chauvinistic times.

1997	1999
'New' Labour win general election, ending 18 years of Conservative party rule	Devolution of power to Scottish Parliament and Welsh Assembly

2004: Labour lost some seats, as the public used their vote to register their unhappiness, and the Conservatives and Liberal-Democrats made gains – the latter benefiting in no small way from their consistent antiwar stance. But this election also saw the rise of a new force: the UK Independence Party (UKIP), whose primary aim is to withdraw the country from the European Union, ironically just as a European constitution is launched and a referendum in Britain to accept it (or not) finally becomes a reality.

Despite the gloom and numerous controversies, opinion polls in mid-2004 showed that Labour was still the most popular party in Britain, and the party most people trusted (or, at least, the one they distrusted least). Polls also showed more public support for the Liberal-Democrats than the Conservatives. But more than this, polls also revealed that the people of Britain were unanimous in their desire for major improvements in the social sectors of health and education. In response, in July 2004, Chancellor Gordon Brown rolled out a major 'spending review', pledging a massive increase in funds for schools and hospitals, and for other areas such as transport and housing. How would this increase be paid for? Partly by cutting over 100,000 jobs in the civil service, said Mr Brown, and rechannelling a saving of over £20 billion. The Conservatives counter-claimed they would spend even more than Labour on public services, without diminishing the civil service and without increasing tax. Comments from some observers included the words 'rabbits' and 'hats'.

With all these promises in mind, during the third quarter of 2004 (as the final parts of this book were being written), the eyes and minds of politicians, newspaper editors and the British public – well, probably about half of them – were focused on the next general election, tipped to happen in 2005. It remains to be seen if the voters thought Labour's improvements were sufficient, or simply too little too late.

Walks Through Britain's History (published by AA) guides you through castles and battlefields, and hundreds of other locations with a link to the past. Take the air. Breathe history!

2002

Queen Elizabeth II celebrates her Golden Jubilee

2004

Tony Blair celebrates 10 years as Labour party leader and seven as prime minister

The Culture

THE NATIONAL PSYCHE

It's difficult to generalise about a British national psyche or homogenous cultural trait – mainly because there isn't one! Even the words 'Britain' and 'British' were invented less than 200 years ago. Not surprisingly, Britishness combines aspects of the cultures of England, Wales and Scotland, as well as the island of Ireland. On top of this home mix, 'indigenous' British culture has also been greatly influenced by peoples from all over the world – the French, Russians, West Indians and Somalis, to name but a few – who have immigrated here over the centuries. Despite the claims of ethnic supremacists and excitable newspapers, the British are a mongrel race – and many are happy to revel in this diversity.

Although the national psyche may be hard to pin down, for many visitors there's still a preconception that the British are reserved, inhibited and stiflingly polite. But it's important here not to confuse British culture with English culture (for more on these differences see the boxed text, p28), and while these characteristics may indeed apply in some parts of England (notably in the south and southeast), in general, across the whole country, they simply don't. Anywhere in Britain, if you visit a pub, a nightclub, a football match, a seaside resort or simply go walking in city parks or wild open hills, you'll soon come across other British characteristics – they're uninhibited, tolerant, exhibitionist, passionate, aggressive, sentimental, hospitable and friendly. It hits you like a breath of fresh air.

Having said all that, a major factor still running through British – and especially English – culture and society, even in these egalitarian days, is class. Although the days of peasants doffing their caps to the lord of the manor may be gone, some Brits still judge others by their school, accent or family wealth (and how long they've had it), rather than by their skills, intelligence and personality.

On a more positive note, another cultural trait that runs though British society is an obsession with hobbies and pastimes. We're not talking about obvious things like football and cricket (although fanatical supporters number in their millions), but about bird-watchers, train spotters, model makers, home improvers, pigeon fanciers, royal observers, antique hoarders, teapot collectors, ramblers, anglers, gardeners, caravanners and crossword fans. The list goes on, with many participants verging on the edge of complete madness. But it's all great, and Britain just wouldn't be the same without them.

The English: A Portrait of a People by Jeremy Paxman is an incisive exploration of the English psyche, as you'd expect from one of toughest interviewers on the airwaves.

QUEUING FOR BRITAIN

The British are notoriously addicted to queues – for buses, train tickets, or to pay at the supermarket. The order is sacrosanct and woe betide any foreigner who gets this wrong! Few things are more calculated to spark an outburst of tutting – about as publicly cross as most British get – than 'pushing in' at a queue.

The same applies to escalators. If you want to stand still, then keep to the right, so that people can pass you on the left. There's a definite convention here and recalcitrants have been hung, drawn and quartered (well, it's at least provoked more tutting) for blocking the path of folk in a hurry.

LIFESTYLE

When it comes to family life, many British people regard the 'Victorian values' of the late 19th century as an idyllic benchmark – a time of perfect morals and harmonious nuclear families, a high point from which the country has been sliding ever since. As recently as the 1960s, only 2% of couples would 'live in sin' before getting married, whereas by 2004 'cohabiting' (there's still not a proper word for it) was perfectly acceptable in most circles; around 60% of couples who marry are already living together, and at any given time about a third of all couples living together are unmarried.

In line with this, the number of unmarried couples having children has also increased in the last 40 years; whereas 'illegitimate' children were comparatively rare and a social stigma in the 1960s, about 40% of births in the UK each year are to unmarried couples today. The 'pro-family' lobby argues that married couples provide more stability and a better environment for children. But marriage apparently provides no guarantees: currently about one in three British marriages ends in divorce.

All we've said on marriage so far relates to heterosexual marriage. In Britain, it's still not legal for gay or lesbian couples to get hitched. To be precise, it's not illegal either – it's just that gay weddings aren't recognised. This makes it tricky when dealing with matters like pensions and inheritance (as is the case for unmarried straight couples), although the legal situation in England and Wales will change in 2005 when the Civil Partnership Act comes into force (Scotland has its own legal system). However, there's still a way to go before total tolerance and full equality is reached.

It's a similar situation when it comes to race. In most parts of Britain general tolerance prevails, with commercial organisations and official bodies such as the police trying hard to stamp out discrimination. But bigotry can still lurk close to the surface: far-right political parties won several seats in the council elections of 2004, and it's not unusual to hear people openly discuss other races in quite unpleasant terms – in smart country pubs as well as in rough city bars. And while it's no longer OK for comedians to tell racist jokes on prime-time TV (as it was until the 1980s), this type of humour still goes down well in some quarters.

Along with race, health is another major issue in Britain. Obesity, especially in the young, is the number-one hot topic on everyone's lips. In a mid-2004 radio interview, former Conservative minister Norman

GOING TO THE DOGS

The British are notorious for their love of animals, and this passion extends especially to pets. Foreigners may notice that while striking up a conversation with a stranger is unusual, many locals are quite happy to talk to another person's dog.

This special affection means dogs can get away with anything. On city streets, pet dogs on leads obstruct pedestrians and crap all over the footpaths. In the countryside, pet dogs chase sheep, disturb wildlife and – you guessed it – crap all over the footpaths. Of course, we can't blame the dogs, it's the owners who are at fault. Although pooper scoopers have made a big impact in recent years, the antisocial habits of many pet dogs are tolerated to an incredible degree by most Brits.

Such is the tolerance that many dog owners let their pets run around in blatant disregard of the 'Keep Dogs on Lead' signs. If you're terrified by the unwanted attentions of a giant muddy hound while you're out walking in a park or the countryside, be prepared for the usual response – 'Don't worry, he's only being friendly'.

Tebbit famously managed to make it a moral issue, linking it, incongruously, with homosexuality (or as he put it, 'buggery'). Smoking has moved down to number two on the list; although it's still a major cause of disease, recent studies showed that about 75% of the population do not smoke – the lowest figures since records began. And another study in mid-2004 showed that about 80% of the population would support a total ban on smoking in public places (including pubs and restaurants), hot on the heels of a similar ban in Ireland. What's even more interesting is that 60% of the smokers in the study wanted the ban. Obviously these people want to be told they should stop.

SCOTTISH CULTURAL ICONS

Of the three separate nations that make of the state of Great Britain, perhaps Scotland has some the finest and most easily recognised cultural icons that you'll come across on your travels.

Bagpipes

Bagpipes define Scotland and Scottishness in the minds of many visitors (and many Scots), and the sounds of pipes and drums certainly stir the spirit. It's therefore no surprise that pipers have accompanied Scottish troops into many battles over the centuries, from Stirling Bridge to the Somme.

Different forms of bagpipe have been used for thousands of years, and in many parts of the world from Ireland to India. Indeed, the Romans used bagpipes in their armies and early Caledonian tribes fighting off invaders may first have heard the instrument's unique sound from their enemy's side rather than their own.

The key feature of all bagpipes is that the air to produce the sound comes from a bellows-like bag rather than the musician's mouth. Scottish (Highland) bagpipes comprise a leather bag and four pipes. The bag is covered with tartan cloth, held under the arm and inflated by a blowpipe. By squeezing the bag, the piper sends air through the pipes; three of these are appropriately known as 'drones', which play all the time (without being touched by the piper) and produce the pipes' unique background sound. The fourth pipe (the 'chanter') has holes on which the piper's fingers produce the tune.

Here are two tips to endear you to the Scots: refer to bagpipes simply as 'the pipes', and be ready to agree that the music they produce is indeed the very sound of heaven.

Kilts & Tartans

A kilt is a skirt that's made from heavy woollen material and is worn by men. Every Scottish man worth his sporran will have a kilt tucked away in the wardrobe to bring out at special occasions like weddings, graduations or football matches. And if they haven't got their own, no problem – kilt hire is a major industry north of the border.

Tartan is a pattern of horizontal and vertical lines, today popular the world over, and made into everything from bedspreads to scarfs as well as, of course, kilts. Although tartans have existed for millennia, particular setts (patterns) weren't associated with certain clans until the 17th century. Today every clan (indeed, every football team) has its own distinctive tartan.

Although assumed to have a long-standing heritage, the kilt is actually a relatively modern invention. For centuries the everyday garment of choice for Highland men was the plaid, a long length of material that formed a kilt and also a covering around the chest and shoulders. The wearing of Highland dress was banned after the Jacobite rebellions but interest was revived by novelist, poet and dedicated patriot Sir Walter Scott in the 19th century, and even by royal patronage – King George IV and his English courtiers donned kilts for their visit to Scotland in 1822. By then, however, many of the old setts had been forgotten, so some tartans are actually Victorian creations, and the cut of the modern kilt was reputedly invented by Thomas Rawlinson – an Englishman!

POPULATION

Britain's population is around 57 million, and growth has been virtually static in recent years (if you don't count the annual influx of about 25 million tourists). The highest concentration is in England, which has a population of 49 million, with London the largest city in the country. The other main centres are Birmingham (Britain's second-largest city), Manchester and Sheffield (ranking third and fourth in size), with Liverpool and Leeds not far away – in distance and size.

Wales has around three million people, with the population concentrated along the coast between Cardiff (the Welsh capital) and Swansea and in the former mining valleys running north from there. Scotland has around five million people, with the population concentrated in and around the cities of Glasgow, Edinburgh, Aberdeen and Dundee. Scotland's Highland region is Britain's most sparsely populated area, with an average of just 20 people per sq mile, a legacy of the notorious Clearances (see p894).

A major characteristic of Britain's population is the so-called 'north–south divide', in reality a split between wealthy Southeast England and the rest of the UK. For example, around London there are towns where high-tech jobs are on the rise and there's less than 1% unemployment. In sharp contrast, economic depression is a major issue in parts of the Midlands, northern England, South and North Wales and many parts of urban and rural Scotland – an 'archipelago of deprivation' according to one report.

However, this split is oversimplified, and across the country there are pockets of affluence in 'poor' areas, and zones of poverty just a few blocks from Millionaires' Row. But, overall, even though the cost of living in London and the Southeast is much higher than elsewhere (double the price for a beer, 10 times more for a house), and despite government efforts to relocate public- and private-sector jobs to 'the regions', people – and the work opportunities that attract them – still seem relentlessly drawn to the capital and its environs.

To check the dates and details of football, cricket, horse racing and numerous other events in Britain tomorrow, next week or next month, a great start is the sports pages of www.whatson when.com.

Meanwhile, and contrary to expectations, an even more significant migration is under way. In the last decade, over one million people in Britain have moved from urban to rural areas. A 2004 report from the Countryside Agency says this is four times more than the number moving from north to south. The new country-dwellers seek a better standard of living, and many can work from home via phone and the Internet. Others use their skills to set up small businesses, providing new employment opportunities for the locals – especially valuable in rural areas where traditional jobs such as farming are on the wane. But there are downsides, too, most notably the rise in rural house prices. This is pushing property beyond the reach of local inhabitants and forcing them to move to the towns that the incomers have just vacated.

SPORT

The British invented – or at least laid down the modern rules for – many of the world's most popular spectator sports including cricket, tennis, rugby and football. Trouble is, the national teams aren't always so good at playing them (as the newspapers continually like to remind us), although recent years have seen some notable success stories. But a mixed result doesn't dull enthusiasm for the fans. Every weekend, thousands of people turn out to cheer their favourite team, and sporting highlights such as Wimbledon or the Derby keep the entire nation enthralled.

This section gives an overview of spectator sports you might see as part of your travels; the regional chapters have more details. For information on participation sports, see Outdoor Activities (p74) and Directory (p945).

Football (Soccer)

The English football league has some of the finest teams and players in the world. They're the richest too, with multimillion-pound sponsorship deals regularly clinched by powerful agents. The elite English Premier League is for the country's top 20 clubs – including globally renowned Manchester United, Arsenal and Liverpool. Seventy-two other clubs play in the Championship, League One and League Two (renamed from Divisions 1, 2 and 3 in 2004 – an attempt, say cynics, to make them seem more exciting). The Scottish Premier League is dominated by Glasgow Rangers and Glasgow Celtic (see the boxed text, p790). In Wales, football is comparatively less popular, although some of the bigger teams such as Wrexham, Cardiff City and Swansea City play in lower English leagues.

The football season lasts from August to May, so seeing a match can easily be tied into most visitors' itineraries. But tickets for the major games are like gold-dust, and cost £20 to £50 even if you're lucky enough to find one. (Your best bet is an agency such as www.ticketmaster.co.uk.) If you can't get in to see the big names, tickets for lower division matches are cheaper and often available on the spot at grounds.

Of the national sides, England has enjoyed mixed fortunes in the last couple of years, although since qualifying for the World Cup of 2002 and European Championships of 2004 support for the team has never been so strong.

Rugby

A wit once said that football was a gentlemen's game played by hooligans, while rugby was the other way around. Whatever the truth of this quip, rugby is very popular in Britain, and it's worth catching a game for the fun atmosphere on the terraces. Tickets cost around £15 to £40 depending on the club's status and fortunes.

There are two variants of the game – rugby union is played in southern England, Wales and Scotland, while rugby league is the main sport in northern England, although there's a lot of crossover. In England, Leicester, Bath and Gloucester are among the better rugby union clubs, while London has a host of good-quality teams (including Wasps and Saracens). In Scotland, rugby union teams from the Scottish Borders including Hawick,

DID YOU KNOW?

The word 'soccer' (the favoured term in countries where 'football' means another game) is derived from 'Association'. The sport is still officially called Association Football, to distinguish it from Rugby Football.

DID YOU KNOW?

At one time, British football was associated with fan violence, but through the 1990s this problem has been tackled seriously. Every now and then hooliganism raises its head at club and international matches, but most football grounds are good for a family day out.

THE SWEET FA CUP

The Football Association (FA) held its first interclub knockout tournament in 1871. Fifteen clubs took part, playing for a nice piece of silverware called the FA Cup – then worth about £20.

Nowadays, around 600 clubs compete for this legendary and priceless trophy. It differs from many other competitions in that every team – from the lowest-ranking part-timers to the stars of the Premier League – is in with a chance. The preliminary rounds begin in August, and the world-famous Cup Final is held in May. It's been staged at Wembley for decades, although the current venue is Cardiff's Millennium Stadium while Wembley undergoes extensive refurbishment.

Manchester United has won the most FA Cup Finals, with 10 victories. But the British have an affection for the underdog, so public attention always goes to 'giant-killers' – minor clubs who claw their way up through the rounds, unexpectedly beating higher-ranking competitors. The best-known giant-killing event occurred in 1992, when Wrexham, then ranked 24th in Division 3, famously beat league champions Arsenal.

In recent years, the FA Cup has become one competition among many. The Premier League and Champion's League (against European teams) have a higher profile, bigger kudos, and – simply – more money to play with. Perhaps the FA Cup will one day be consigned to history – but what a sweet and glorious history it's been!

Kelso and Melrose are among the better teams. In Wales, the most success-ful club sides are Cardiff, Swansea, Neath and Llanelli. Rugby league teams to watch include the Wigan Warriors, Bradford Bulls and Leeds Rhinos.

The main season for club matches is roughly September to Easter, while the international Rugby Union calendar is dominated by the annual Six Nations Championship (England, Scotland, Wales, Ireland, France and Italy) between January and April. Currently, England is one of the strongest national teams (it also won the Rugby World Cup in 2004), which means the fans of Wales and Scotland are even more pas-sionate about the performance of their own sides. It's usual for the Scots to support Wales, or vice versa, when either team is playing 'old enemy' England. Scots will enthusiastically support France too – keeping alive memories of the Auld Alliance (see p37), but it's all good natured really. However, just to keep the English in their place, from August to Febru-ary the Celtic League brings together club teams from Scotland, Wales and Eire. Only.

www.sportstoursinter national.co.uk – offers packages (tickets plus extras) for major football games

Cricket

The rules and terminology of cricket appear arcane, but for aficionados the game provides 'resolute and graceful confrontations within an in-tricate and psychologically thrilling framework'. OK, this quote is from a cricket fan. Nonetheless, at least one cricket match should feature in your travels around Britain, although the game remains a predominantly English phenomenon with only a few teams in Wales and Scotland.

One-day games and five-day Test Matches are played against sides such as Australia and the West Indies at landmark grounds like Lords in London, Edgbaston in Birmingham and Headingley in Leeds. Test match tickets cost £25 to £100 and tend to go fast. County championships usually charge £10 to £15 per adult – local games even less – and rarely sell out.

Golf

Details on playing golf are given in the Directory chapter, but if you want to watch men hit little white balls with sticks (and it is mostly men's golf that draws the crowds), the main event is the British Open, known to all as simply 'The Open'. It's played every July in rotation on nine courses around the country. In 2005 it will be held at St Andrews in Scotland ('the birthplace of golf' – see p841 for more details), then Liverpool in 2006 and Carnoustie in 2007. Other important competitions include the Brit-ish Amateur Championship and the Welsh Open (at Celtic Manor Hotel near Newport, South Wales). Spectator tickets start at about £10, going up to £75 for a good position at the major events. British interest in golf was higher than usual in late 2004, following Europe's significant defeat of the USA in the Ryder Cup, helped by some skilful putting on the part of Brit-ain's Colin Montgomerie and Lee Westwood. Let's hope they can keep up the form until 2010, when the Ryder Cup will be played at Celtic Manor.

Leap the net to www .wimbledon.org – for everything you need to know on the grassy drama of the All England Championships.

Tennis

Tennis is widely played at club and regional levels, but the best-known tournament is the All England Championships – known to all as Wim-bledon. For this, tennis fever sweeps through the country for the last week of June and the first week of July every year. Britain's current top player is Tim Henman, who's the cause of another disease – Henmania. In between matches, the crowds traditionally feast on strawberries and cream. That's 28 tonnes of strawberries and 7000 litres of cream annu-ally, to be precise.

Tickets for Wimbledon are sold through a public ballot. Send a stamped addressed envelope (or International Reply Coupon) to: PO Box 98, London SW18 5AE, between August and December. Those in luck are contacted in March. If you want to take your chance on the spot, about 6000 tickets are sold each day (but not in the last four days). Queuing from around 7am should get you into the ground, though not a seat at Centre Court.

Horse Racing

There's a horse race somewhere in Britain pretty much every day, but the top event in the calendar is Royal Ascot in mid-June, when even the Queen turns up to put a fiver each way on Lucky Boy in the 3.15. (Actually, she know her nags, this lady, with 19 Ascot winners to date from the monarchic stables.)

Other highlights include the Grand National steeplechase at Aintree in early April, and the Derby, run at Epsom on the first Saturday in June. The latter is especially popular with the masses so, unlike Ascot, you won't see so many morning suits and outrageous hats.

MEDIA

Breakfast need never be boring in Britain. For such a small country, there's an amazing range of daily newspapers to read over your corn-flakes. (For information on the broadcast media, see p959.)

The bottom end of the market is occupied by easy-to-read tabloids, full of sensational 'exclusives' and simplistic political coverage. The *Sun* is a national institution, with mean-spirited contents and headlines based on outrageous puns. Apparently this is a good combination, as the *Sun* is Britain's biggest-selling paper, with a circulation of around three million and a readership three times that. The *Mirror* was once the 'paper of the workers', then it tried to compete head-on with the Sun for a while, and then it rediscovered its left-of-centre, pro-Labour heritage. The *Sport* takes bad taste to the ultimate, with stories of aliens and celebrities (sometimes in the same report), and pictures of semi-naked women of improbable proportions.

The *Daily Mail* and *Daily Express* bill themselves as middle-market, but are little different to the tabloids – both are thunderously right of centre with a steady stream of crime and scare stories about threatening immigrants and rampant homosexuals. Some may find this diet distaste-ful, but about eight million readers don't.

At the upper end of the market are the broadsheets: the *Daily Telegraph* is right of centre and easily outsells its rivals; the *Times* is conservative, Murdoch-owned, thorough and influential; the *Guardian* is left of centre and innovative; and the *Independent* lives up to its title. 'Tabloid' and 'broadsheet' have always referred more to substance than actual dimen-sions, but the distinction is now totally content-based as several serious papers are also issued in handy-to-carry sizes.

Most dailies have Sunday stable mates (*Sunday Mirror*, *Sunday Express*, *Sunday Telegraph* and so on) and there's also the long-standing, liberal-slanted *Observer*. The broadsheets are filled more with comment and analysis than hot news, and on their day of rest the British settle in arm-chairs to plough through endless supplements; the *Sunday Times* alone comes in 12 different parts, and must destroy a rainforest every issue.

Most of the papers mentioned here are available all over Britain, but can have an English bias, so Scotland maintains a flock of homegrown dailies. These include the *Scotsman* – aligned with the Liberal Democrats – and

Private Eye is a weekly no-frills satirical publica-tion, with stories to make you laugh (pompous 'pseuds') and cry (govern-ment corruption), well worth reading along with more mainstream publications.

Want to scan the papers online? Find them at:

Daily Express – www .express.co.uk

Daily Telegraph – www .telegraph.co.uk

Guardian – www .guardianunlimited.co.uk

Independent – www .independent.co.uk

Mirror – www.mirror .co.uk

Sun – www.the-sun .co.uk

Times – www.the-times .co.uk

the popular tabloid *Daily Record*. The *Herald*, founded in 1783, is the oldest daily in the English-speaking world, and the *Sunday Post* is a best-seller. In Wales, the *Western Mail* is the national daily, with *Wales on Sunday* taking over at weekends.

There are also local and regional papers throughout Britain. These range from London's commuter favourite, the *Evening Standard*, and quaintly home-spun country-town weeklies, to city dailies like the *Manchester News* or *Swansea Evening Post* – the latter famous as the paper where Dylan Thomas cut his journalistic teeth.

RELIGION

The Church of England (Anglican Church) became independent of Rome in the 16th century at the behest of Henry VIII, and today remains large, wealthy and influential – even in these increasingly secular times. Although the vast majority of English people write 'C of E' when filling in forms, only about a million attend Sunday services. The Church of England is traditionally conservative, and predominantly Conservative (it has been called 'the Tory Party at prayer'); it's only since 1994 that women have been ordained as priests. The debate has now moved on to the rights and wrongs of gay clergy.

Across Britain, about 10% of people consider themselves Roman Catholic. There are also sizable groups of Methodists, Baptists and other nonconformists – most notably in Wales, where the Anglican Church ceased to be the established church way back in the 1920s, and the Church–Chapel divide (ie between the Protestant and nonconformist faiths) is still clearly evident. In Scotland, you'll find the (Presbyterian) Church of Scotland with its spin-off minorities, the United Free Presbyterians and the Free Church of Scotland (known as the Wee Frees). Generally, attendances across Britain in the mainstream churches are down; evangelical and charismatic churches are the only ones attracting growing congregations.

There are around 1.5 million Muslims in Britain – about 3% of the total population. Those of other faiths include Sikhs, Hindus and Jews (and those druids at Stonehenge). Numbers may be small, but nowadays more non-Christians in Britain regularly visit their places of worship than do all the Anglicans, Catholics, Methodists and Baptists combined.

ARTS
Literature

Modern English literature – poetry and prose – starts around 1387 (yes, that's modern in history-soaked Britain) with Geoffrey Chaucer's classic *The Canterbury Tales*. It's a collection of fables, stories and morality tales using a mixed bag of travelling pilgrims – the Knight, the Wife of Bath, the Nun's Priest, and so on – as a narrative hook. For more background see the boxed text, p184.

Two centuries later, William Shakespeare entered the scene. He's still Britain's best-known playwright (as discussed under Theatre on p72), although he was pretty good at poems, too. The famous line 'Shall I compare thee to a summer's day?' comes from 'Sonnet No 18'. He penned over 150 sonnets in all.

If you studied Eng Lit at school you'll remember the Metaphysical poets of the early 17th century; their vivid imagery and far-fetched conceits (comparisons) daringly pushed the boundaries. In *A Valediction: Forbidding Mourning*, for instance, John Donne compares two lovers with the points of a compass. Racy stuff in its day.

For a literary lowdown while on the road the *Oxford Literary Guide to Great Britain and Ireland* gives details of writers who immortalised towns, villages and countryside.

Nick Hornby is easily lumped in the lad-lit bracket, but his *Fever Pitch* (about football and relationships) and *High Fidelity* (about music and relationships) are spot-on studies of young bloke-ishness.

YDACH CHI YN GALLU SIARAD CYMRAEG?

That means 'Can you speak Welsh?', and it's the widespread survival of Welsh as a national living language that marks out Wales so distinctly from the rest of Britain. Other indigenous British languages include Scots Gaelic (spoken by around 80,000 people in the Highlands and islands), Manx (on the Isle of Man) and Cornish (Cornwall), but as a tourist in Britain, it's Welsh you're most likely to come across.

The origins of Welsh go back thousands of years. It's an Indo-European language, with the same root as English (despite its weird-looking double Ls and strings of consecutive consonants), but its history is quite different. When the Act of Union in 1536 formally linked Wales and England (see p41) officials had to speak English as well as Welsh. In other circumstances, Welsh may have started to fade, but Bishop Morgan's translation of the Bible in 1588 played an important part in keeping the language alive, and during the 17th and 18th centuries, the nonconformist faiths that made such headway in Wales also supported the native language.

The rot set in during the Industrial Revolution of the 19th century, when a whole new ruling class of landlords and employers came from England, and from then on the number of Welsh speakers went into steep decline. In 1801, about 80% of the population spoke Welsh; by 1901 this had sunk to 50%. Through the following decades numbers continued to fall, and it wasn't until the 1960s that Welsh speakers started to make a determined fightback.

The first victory was the 1967 Welsh Language Act that ensured that Welsh speakers could use their own language in court. Then, in the 1980s and '90s, things really took off, with a much-revived interest across Wales, not least among incomers. In 1982, Channel 4 set up Sianel Pedwar Cymru (S4C – Channel 4 Wales), which still broadcasts Welsh TV programmes daily, and in 1988 a Welsh Language Board was set up to advise the secretary of state for Wales on everything to do with the language. In 1994 a new Welsh Language Act gave equal validity to Welsh as a language for use in public-sector businesses.

Today about 20% of people in Wales speak Welsh as a first language, and for many more it's a strong second tongue. As you travel around, you'll notice all road signs are bilingual – although don't be surprised if the English words have been daubed out in green paint, a sign that nationalist feelings still remain strong in some areas.

Perhaps you're more familiar with 'Auld Lang Syne', traditionally sung at New Year throughout Britain. It was penned by prolific 18th-century poet and lyricist Robert Burns. His more unusual 'Address to a Haggis' plays an important part of 'Burn's Night', a Scottish celebration held on 25 January. For more on this celebration see p802.

Moving on a little, the stars of the 19th century were the Romantic poets. John Keats, Percy Bysshe Shelley and Lord Byron wrote with emotion, exulting the senses and power of imagination, and were particularly passionate about nature. The best-known Romantic, William Wordsworth, lived in the Lake District, and his famous line from *Daffodils*, 'I wandered lonely as a cloud', was inspired by a hike in the hills.

The Romantic movement produced a genre called 'literary Gothic', exemplified by Mary Shelley's *Frankenstein*, which she originally penned for a private ghost-story competition with her husband Percy. This was satirised in *Northanger Abbey* by Jane Austen, who is still one of Britain's best-known and best-loved novelists.

Next came the reign of Queen Victoria and the era of industrial expansion. Novels of the time often took social and political issues as subject matter: in *Oliver Twist*, Charles Dickens captures the lives of young thieves in the London slums; in *Hard Times* he paints a brutal picture of capitalism. Meanwhile, Thomas Hardy's classic *Tess of the d'Urbervilles* deals with the decline of the peasantry, and his *The Trumpet Major* paints a picture of idyllic English country life changed by war and encroaching modernity.

Another well-known (though perhaps little-read) poem of the 17th century is John Milton's epic *Paradise Lost*, on the downfall of Adam and Eve. It can be hard-going for mortals, but is worth dipping into for a taste of the rich language.

North of the border, Sir Walter Scott produced the classic Scottish novel *Waverley*, set in the time of the 1745 Jacobite rebellion. For more on Sir Walter, see p798. Other major figures from the 19th century are the Brontë sisters – Charlotte Brontë's *Jane Eyre* and Anne Brontë's *The Tennant of Wildfell Hall* are classics of passion, mystery and love. Fans still flock to Haworth (p508), their former home, perched on the edge of the wild Pennine moors that inspired so many books.

Also popular at this time were two Scottish novelists: Robert Louis Stevenson, best known for his children's books *Treasure Island* and *Kidnapped*; and Sir Arthur Conan Doyle, inventor of detective Sherlock Holmes who, with sidekick Watson, starred in a string of murder mysteries.

In the 20th century, the pace of British writing increased. A landmark was the 1908 success of Welsh poet WH Davies, whose *The Autobiography of a Super-Tramp* contained the immortal words 'What is this life if, full of care/We have no time to stand and stare?'.

A few years later, WWI made heroes of English poets Rupert Brooke and Wilfred Owen. Brooke's 'The Soldier' is romantic and idealistic but Owen's 'Dulce et Decorum Est' is harshly cynical about the 'glory' of war. Meanwhile, DH Lawrence produced *Sons and Lovers* and *The Rainbow*, novels set in the English Midlands, following the lives and loves of generations as the country changes from 19th-century idyll to the modern world. In 1928, Lawrence pushed his explorations of sexuality further in *Lady Chatterley's Lover*, which was initially banned as pornographic. Torrid affairs are no great shakes today, but the quality of the writing still shines.

Other highlights of the interwar years included EM Forster's *A Passage to India*, about the hopelessness of British colonial rule, and Daphne du Maurier's romantic suspense novel *Rebecca*, set on the Cornish coast. Evelyn Waugh gave us *Brideshead Revisited* and Richard Llewellyn wrote the Welsh classic *How Green Was My Valley*. In a different world entirely, JRR Tolkien published *The Hobbit*, trumping it some 20 years later with his awesome trilogy, *The Lord of the Rings*.

After WWII, Compton Mackenzie lifted post-war spirits with *Whisky Galore*, a comic novel about a cargo of booze washed up from a sinking ship onto a Scottish island. Elsewhere, a less whimsical breed of writer emerged. George Orwell wrote *Animal Farm* and *Nineteen Eighty-Four*, his closely observed studies of totalitarian rule, while the Cold War inspired Graham Greene's *Our Man in Havana*, in which a secret agent studies the workings of a vacuum cleaner to inspire fictitious spying reports.

Another spook of that period was full-blooded hero James Bond. He first appeared in 1953 in Ian Fleming's novel *Casino Royale*, then swashbuckled through numerous thrillers for another decade. Meanwhile, TH White's *The Once and Future King* covered battles of a different time – the magical world of King Arthur and the Knights of the Round Table.

The 20th century was also a great time for poets. Big names: WH Auden ('Funeral Blues' is his most popular work, thanks to a role in the movie *Four Weddings and a Funeral*) and TS Eliot, who penned the epic *Waste Land*. However, Eliot is better known for *Old Possum's Book of Practical Cats* (later turned into the musical *Cats* by Andrew Lloyd Webber). Roger McGough and friends determined to make art relevant to daily life; their first publication – *The Mersey Sound* – was landmark pop poetry for the streets.

Different again was the harsh, gritty verse of Ted Hughes, sometimes renowned as much for the stormy relationship with his wife (American poet Sylvia Plath) as for his works, although in 1984 he became Poet Laureate. Meanwhile, Dylan Thomas, also known for his energetic social diary, came to the fore with *Portrait of The Artist As A Young Dog*, although his

---

Jane Austen's favoured subjects were the provincial middle classes. Intrigues and passions boiling under the stilted preserve of social convention are beautifully portrayed in *Emma* and *Pride and Prejudice*.

Helen Fielding's *Bridget Jones's Diary*, a fond look at the heartache of a modern single girl's blundering search for love, epitomised the late-1990s 'chick-lit' genre.

Of the Brontë family's prodigious output, Emily Brontë's *Wuthering Heights* is the best known; it's a tale of obsession and revenge, where the moody landscape plays a role as great as any human character.

most celebrated work is a radio play *Under Milk Wood* (1954), exposing the tensions of small-town Wales. For more Dylan details see p663.

Then came the swinging '60s and '70s. New writers included Muriel Spark, who introduced the world to a highly unusual Edinburgh school mistress in *The Prime of Miss Jean Brodie*, and Martin Amis, who was just 24 in 1973 when he wrote *The Rachel Papers*, a witty, minutely observed story of sexual obsession in puberty. Since then Amis has published many books, including *London Fields* and *The Information*, all greeted with critical acclaim and high sales. Similarly, Ian McEwan was one of Britain's angriest young novelists, earning the nickname Ian Macabre for his early work like *The Cement Garden* and *The Comfort of Strangers*, but in 1998 he cracked the establishment and became a Booker Prize winner with *Amsterdam*.

In contrast, two authors who struggled for recognition initially then hit the jackpot with later works were Sebastian Faulks and Louis de Bernières. Their respective novels *Birdsong*, a perfect study of passion and the horrors of WWI, and *Captain Corelli's Mandolin*, a tale of love, war and life on a Greek island, were massive sellers in the 1990s.

Contemporary novels in a different vein include 1993's *Trainspotting* by Irvine Welsh, a deep, dark look at the rawness of Edinburgh's drug culture, and the start of a new genre coined 'Tartan Noir'. Other successful modern Scottish novelists include Iain Banks (who also writes sci-fi under the cunning pseudonym of Iain M Banks) and Ian Rankin, whose Detective Inspector Rebus novels are always eagerly awaited.

For many readers, the best-known British author of the last five years or so is JK Rowling, author of the Harry Potter epics, some of the highest-selling titles in history. Other hot names of the early 21st century include Zadie Smith, whose novel *White Teeth* topped bestseller lists in 2000. She followed it up with the equally hyped, and almost as good, *The Autograph Man*. Another star is Hari Kunzru, who received one of the largest advances in publishing history in 2002 for his debut *The Impressionist*. His second novel, *Transmission*, was published in June 2004, rewarded with (mostly) critical acclaim and high sales in the bookstores.

Perhaps the most talked-about titles of 2004 were The *No 1 Ladies Detective Agency* series by Alexander McCall Smith, billed as 'Jean Brodie in Botswana', which brought other works (such as *Heavenly Date and Other Flirtations*) of this hitherto-unknown novelist to international attention, and Mark Haddon's *The Curious Incident of the Dog in the Night-time*, a murder mystery narrated by a boy with a form of autism, which provides unique and unexpected results.

Cinema

In the early years of the 20th century, silent movies from Britain, many filmed in Wales, gave the Americans a run for their money. *Blackmail* by Alfred Hitchcock – Hitchcock is still one of Britain's best-known film directors – launched the British film industry's era of sound production in 1929, before moving to the US in 1939.

How Green Was My Valley, a tale of everyday life in the coal-mining villages of Wales, was made in 1941. Still perhaps the best-known Welsh film of all time, it also annoys more Welsh people than any other, as it features stereotypical characters and no Welsh actors, and was shot in a Hollywood studio. It is worth a watch, though, for a taste of the period.

After a decline in film output during WWII, British film recovered in the 1940s and '50s, led by Ealing Studios with a series of eccentric ('very English') comedies such as *Kind Hearts* and *Coronets*, starring Alec Guinness. More serious box-office hits of the time included *Hamlet*, starring

As the Pennine moors haunt Brontë novels, so the marshy Cambridgeshire Fens dominate *Waterland* by Graham Swift – a tale of personal and national history, betrayal and compassion, and rated a milestone work of the 1980s.

White Teeth, the best-selling debut novel by Zadie Smith, is a story about families living in North London. It's also a moving and witty book about friendship, marriage, race, class, immigration and different generations. Despite the hype that surrounds the Booker Prize, this novel was a deserving winner.

Man and Boy by Tony Parsons is considered a key 'lad-lit' title: it's about a son and his single-parent father, both growing up fast. Follow-on titles are *Man and Wife* and *One for My Baby*. Continuing familiar themes, Parson's latest novel is *The Family Way*.

Passport to Pimlico is an Ealing Studios' film classic; it's the story of a London suburb declaring independence from the rest of the country.

Laurence Olivier (the first British film to win an Oscar in the Best Picture category) and Carol Reed's *The Third Man*. An absolute classic of the era is *Brief Encounter*, directed by David Lean, who went on to make *Lawrence of Arabia* and *Doctor Zhivago*.

Super-sleuth James Bond arrived on the big screen in 1962, with *Dr No* starring Scotland's very own Sean Connery. Since then about 20 Bond movies have been made, and Bond has been played by other British actors including Roger Moore and Timothy Dalton. More recent producers have brought a somewhat misogynistic Bond into the modern age, with the enlightened casting of Dame Judi Dench as Bond's boss, 'M'.

By the end of the 1960s, British film production had declined again and didn't really pick up until David Puttnam's *Chariots of Fire* won four Oscars in 1981. Perhaps inspired by this success, TV company Channel 4 began financing films for the large and small screen, one of the first being *My Beautiful Laundrette* – a story of multicultural life and love in Mrs Thatcher's Britain. The following year, Richard Attenborough's big-budget epic *Gandhi* carried off eight Oscars including Best Director and Best Picture, while another classic of the 1980s was *Withnail and I*, starring Richard E Grant and Paul McGann.

Chariots of Fire is an inspiring dramatisation of a true story: the progress of two athletes from university to the 1924 Olympics, their friendship and rivalry, and – for one of them – the conflict of sport with faith. When receiving his Oscars, the director boasted: 'the British are coming'.

Things were quiet again until the mid-1990s, which saw another mini-renaissance in British film-making, ushered in by *Four Weddings and a Funeral*. This featured US star Andie MacDowell, and introduced Hugh Grant as a likable and self-deprecating Englishman. This movie spearheaded a genre of quirky low-budget 'Brit flicks', including *Bhaji on the Beach*, a East-meets-West-meets-Blackpool road movie, *Brassed Off*, a gritty northern drama centred around pit closures and music competitions, *Secrets and Lies*, about reunited families (winner of the Palme d'Or at Cannes), *The Full Monty*, which became Britain's most successful film ever, *The Englishman Who Went Up a Hill and Came Down a Mountain*, an affectionate story about a peak in North Wales that was too short, and *Trainspotting*, a hard-hitting film about Edinburgh's drugged-out underbelly. *Trainspotting* launched the careers of Scottish actors Ewan McGregor and Robert Carlyle, now frequently seen in Hollywood these days, along with their Welsh thespian colleagues Anthony Hopkins and Catherine Zeta Jones.

Other great films of the 1990s include London gangster flick *Lock, Stock and Two Smoking Barrels* – which went on to spawn a host of geezer copycats, and incidentally launched the acting career of former footballer Vinnie Jones (more recently seen, but not heard, in *Gone in 60 Seconds*).

Brief Encounter is frequently cited as a milestone in British cinema – a film where the drama comes from the acting (Trevor Howard and Celia Johnstone) rather than the set (uninspiring suburbs and railway-station buffets). It's a story of unexpected love and smouldering sexual attraction that can never be fulfilled.

In a very different tone, *East is East* is a beautifully understated study of the clash between first- and second-generation Pakistanis in 1970s Manchester, while *Breaking the Waves* is a perfect study of culture clash in 1970s Scotland, and *Human Traffic* is an edgy romp through Cardiff's clubland. A very popular movie that decade was *Notting Hill*, set in a London bookshop and starring Julia Roberts, with Hugh Grant as …a likable and self-deprecating Englishman. Much more enjoyable was *Sense and Sensibility*, with English doyens Emma Thompson (who also wrote the fabulous screenplay) and Kate Winslet as the Dashwood sisters, and Hugh Grant as (you guessed it) a likable and self-deprecating Englishman.

Award-winning Welsh-language films of the 1990s include *Hedd Wynn*, a heartbreaking story of a poet killed in WWI, and *Soloman and Gaenor*, a passionate tale of forbidden love at the turn of the 20th century.

A great success of 2000, and a classic of the Brit-flick genre, was *Billy Elliott*, while 2001 saw the release of internationally hyped *Harry Potter and the Philosopher's Stone* and perfectly understated *Last Orders* – both with near-exclusive British casts. A year later, critical acclaim was dished

BRITAIN ON LOCATION

Still movie-hungry? Here's a short list of some classic films set in Britain's towns, cities or countryside. To search for more British film locations, see www.visitbritain.com/moviemap.

■ **The 39 Steps** (1935) A classic Hitchcock spy thriller set in Scotland, including a famous scene on the Forth Rail Bridge.

■ **Whisky Galore** (1949) A comedy set in the Outer Hebrides about a shipwrecked cargo of whisky.

■ **Under Milk Wood** (1973) An adaptation of the Dylan Thomas radio play filmed on the west coast of Wales staring Welsh heart-throb Richard Burton.

■ **Gregory's Girl** (1981) The trials and tribulations of teenage love, set in and around Cumbernauld near Glasgow.

■ **Local Hero** (1983) The story of an oil magnate turned conservationist, filmed at Scotland's Pennan in Aberdeenshire, and Camusdarrach in Morar.

■ **Rob Roy** (1995) The rollicking adventures of this famous 18th-century Highlander were filmed at Glen Nevis and at several castles in Perthshire.

■ **The Full Monty** (1997) A comedy about a group of unemployed steelworkers turned strippers, set in Sheffield, Yorkshire.

■ **Little Voice** (1998) The story of an odd but talented singer, filmed in Scarborough, Yorkshire.

■ **Last Orders** (2001) Four buddies take a trip down memory lane to scatter their friend's ashes, with scenes at Canterbury Cathedral, the Chatham War Memorial, Eastbourne and Margate Pier.

■ **Harry Potter and the Chamber of Secrets** (2002) The schoolboy wizard returns to locations used in the first Harry Potter movie – Gloucester Cathedral, Alnwick Castle, and Goathland in North Yorkshire – with additional sets at Fort William and the Glenfinnan Viaduct in Scotland.

■ **24 Hour Party People** (2002) Manchester's streets and a lovingly re-created Hacienda Club was the set for this tale of '80s pop excess.

■ **Calendar Girls** (2003) Local ladies of the parish pose nude for a calendar, while the villages and valleys of the Yorkshire Dales make a suitably stunning set.

■ **Tomb Raider 2** (2003) Some of Lara Croft's unfeasibly epic adventures were shot in Snowdonia.

out to *Iris*, a heart-wrenching dramatisation of Iris Murdoch's descent into Alzheimer's, with a winning combination of Dame Judi Dench, Jim Broadbent and Kate Winslet – darlings of the British film industry. In contrast, *About a Boy* was a feel-good movie about a dating ploy leading unexpectedly to true romance and fatherly responsibilities, starring the ever-popular Hugh Grant as (who'd have thought) a likable and self-deprecating Englishman. Meanwhile, surprise hit *Bend It Like Beckham* addressed more fundamental themes: growing up, first love, sex, class, race – and football.

Notable British films of the last couple of years include *Love Actually*, in which Hugh Grant plays (yep) a likable and self-deprecating prime minister who falls in love with the tea lady at No 10 Downing St, and *Shaun of the Dead*, a great horror spoof where the main character fails to notice the walking corpses because most of his neighbours are zombies at the best of times. A return from death (this time for real) is the topic of *Touching the Void*, about British mountaineer Joe Simpson's survival of an appalling accident in the Andes. This won the UK movie industry's 2004 award for Best British Film. Other British films of note in 2004 include *Vera Drake*, from highly respected Brit film-maker Mike Leigh, staring Imelda Staunton; *Dead Man's Shoes*, described as 'melancholy, with dark humour – a Brit version of High Plains Drifter'; and *Trauma*, staring Colin Firth, which is so much better than the silly Bridget Jones sequel in which he also starred.

Billy Elliot is yet another film with Britain's declining industry as a backdrop, but also about people rising above it: particularly a boy – the son of a hardened coalminer – who strives to becomes a ballet dancer.

The Full Monty centres on a group of unemployed steel-workers who turn to stripping on stage to raise cash. It's a great film, but the hard truth (six blokes getting their kit off can't solve an economic slump) is heavily glossed over.

In 2005, films to look out for include: *Hitch-hikers Guide to the Galaxy* – already an British cult book and radio series – staring Bill Nighy as Slatibartfast and Mos Def as Ford Prefect; *Pride & Prejudice*, a high-profile remake of the Jane Austen classic with Donald Sutherland and British stars Dame Judi Dench, Brenda Blethyn, Mathew Macfadyen and Keira Knightley (best known for her recent *Pirates of the Caribbean* role); and *Bride & Prejudice* – another Austen-inspired movie, but this time with singing, dancing and outrageous Bollywood panache.

Music

In Britain you're never short of choice for live music. London has several world-class venues for pop, rock, jazz and classical, while most other cities have concert halls and stadiums for the big names. For live music on a smaller scale, local folk singers or grungy garage bands thrive all over the country. Once again, London has the largest choice, but you can hear great sounds (and some really dire stuff) in pubs and clubs everywhere. Options are more restricted in the countryside – but then you're in the wrong place for bright lights anyway.

POP & ROCK

A film about love, betrayal, brass bands, coal-mine closures and the breakdown of society in 1980s Britain, *Brassed Off* makes you laugh then cry, and shouldn't be missed.

Since the dawn of the swinging '60s, Britain has been firmly on the main stage of pop and rock music. The first big exports were the Beatles, the Rolling Stones, the Who, the Kinks and Welsh soul man Tom Jones. They were followed in the 1970s by stardust-speckled heroes like the Bay City Rollers, Marc Bolan and David Bowie. Other artists of the time included Cream (featuring Eric Clapton), the Faces (starring Rod Stewart), Genesis (initially fronted by Peter Gabriel and later by Phil Collins), Roxy Music (featuring last-word-in-suave Brian Ferry and, for a while, the highly influential Brian Eno), as well as Pink Floyd, Deep Purple, Led Zeppelin, Queen and Elton John; all very different, but all globally renowned, and some – such as Bowie – still delivering decent material today.

In the late '70s and early '80s, self-indulgent dinosaur bands were left floundering in the wake of punk music. It was energetic and anarchic ('here's three chords, now form a band'), and frequently tuneless, but punk was great fun and returned pop to grassroots level, at least for a while. The Sex Pistols produced one album and a clutch of mostly banned singles, while more prolific were the Clash, the Damned, the Buzzcocks, the Stranglers, the Exploited and the UK Subs. Then punk begat 'New Wave' (ie everything that was a bit punky), with leading exponents including the Jam, the Tourists and Elvis Costello, and this crossed over with the brief ska revival of the 1980s led by the Specials and tapped into by the Beat and Madness. Meanwhile, a punk-and-reggae-influenced trio called the Police – fronted by bassist Sting – became one of the biggest names of the decade.

The website of the British Film Institute – www .screenonline.org.uk – has complete coverage of Britain's film and TV industry.

Around this time, heavy metal enjoyed an upsurge, with bands such as Black Sabbath (featuring the currently once-again-famous Ozzy Osbourne) and Judas Priest exporting soulful melodies and intriguing interpretations of established religion to concert halls worldwide.

The ever-changing music of the 1980s also experienced a surge of electronica with the likes of Depeche Mode, Cabaret Voltaire and Human League, which overlapped into the 'New Romantic' bands such as Spandau Ballet, Duran Duran and Culture Club – all frills and fringes, and a definite swing of pop's pendulum away from untidy punks.

Other big names of that decade included the Eurythmics, Texas, Joy Division (later becoming New Order), Wham! (a two-piece boy band headed by a bright young fellow called George Michael), the Stone Roses

BUT IF WE DID...

In this music section we've focused on pop and rock, and you might wonder why we haven't mentioned Britain's other rich musical genres – jazz, folk, roots, fusion, house, bhangra, techno, chill-out, drum'n'bass, dance, dub, gospel, urban, hip-hop and eski, to name a few. It's simply because we don't have space to discuss them in full. But if we did, here are some names we would mention: Basement Jaxx, Faithless, Prodigy, Roots Manuva, LTJ Bukem, Roni Size, Goldie, Craig David, Massive Attack, Zero 7, Portishead, Leftfield, Underworld, Fila Brazillia, the Chemical Brothers, Fatboy Slim, Dillinja, Total Science, Kathryn Williams, Goldfrapp, Paul Oakenfold, Jesus & Mary Chain, Panjabi MC, Rae & Christian, Cassius Henry, Gerard Presencer, Courtney Pine, Jamie Cullum, Lostprophets, PJ Harvey, Special D, Tricky, Goldie Lookin Chain, Funeral for a Friend, Gorky's Zygotic Mynci, Zabrinski, McClusky, Shy FX, Andrew Weatherall, EZ Rollers, Lemon Jelly, Carl Cox, Tom Middleton, Jah Wobble, Morcheeba, Raghav, Talvin Singh, Nitin Sawhney, Shooglenifty, Kate Rusby, the Levellers, Runrig, Wolfstone, Martin Bennet, Peatbog Faeries, Nick Drake, Eliza Carthy, Martyn Joseph, Billy Bragg, Jools Holland...

By the time this book is published, new names (and even new genres) will have undoubtedly stepped into the limelight, as the great British musical scene never fails to grow and develop at a brain-boggling pace.

and the Happy Mondays (the latter two epitomising the late '80s/early '90s scene in Manchester, England's second city and musical hotbed), and the painfully morose but curiously engaging Smiths, fronted by Morrissey (also currently enjoying a comeback). These artists were all very different, but were all quintessentially British, and all had worldwide followings.

The '90s saw the renaissance of indie bands, where the likes of Blur, Elastica, Suede, Supergrass, Ocean Colour Scene, Manic Street Preachers, the Verve, Pulp, Travis, Feeder, Super Furry Animals, Stereophonics, Catatonia, Radiohead and, above all, Oasis revived the flagging guitar-based format. Heralded as the Britpop revolution, it's largely thanks to these bands that the indie guitar sound remains such a major feature of music today – as exemplified by Franz Ferdinand, Badly Drawn Boy, Gomez, Snow Patrol, Razorlight, British Sea Power and The Libertines, while Coldplay, Starsailor and Muse tend towards the more soulful side of the genre.

Halfway through first decade of the 21st century, British pop seems dominated by the likes of faux-indies Busted and ex–Pop Idol Will Young. The Darkness makes glam rock cool again, and bands like the Zutons and Keane show that even genuine indie music is also going through a retro phase. On the solo songstress front, Dido remains massively popular, with Amy Winehouse, Amy Wadge and the very soulful Joss Stone the rising stars of 2004. Meanwhile, despite some quiet periods, leading dance, R&B, hip-hop and garage acts like Fatboy Slim, Ty, Ms Dynamite, Jamelia, Mis-Teeq, The Streets, Dizzee Rascal and Groove Armada fight the good fight against a relentless onslaught of US imports. Going the other way, however, should we be proud that Britain's biggest export of recent times is ex–Take That crooner and Sinatra wannabe Robbie Williams?

24 Hour Party People is a totally irreverent, suitably chaotic film about the 1990s Manchester music scene – the Hacienda, Factory Records, Joy Division, Happy Mondays, the lot.

CLASSICAL MUSIC & OPERA

The country that gave you the Beatles, Rod Stewart and the Manic Street Preachers is also a hive of classical music, with several professional symphony orchestras, dozens of amateur orchestras, and an active National Association of Youth Orchestras. Such enthusiasm is all the more remarkable given Britain's small number of well-known classical composers, especially compared with countries such as Austria, Germany

ACE CLUBS

If clubbing floats your boat, the major cities of Britain have some of the best clubs and late bars in the world, with DJs and theme nights that bring in eager punters from miles around. Of course, London is indisputably the top spot, but Brighton, Bristol, Cardiff, Nottingham, Glasgow, Manchester, Sheffield, Swansea, Edinburgh, Leeds and Liverpool all have large and ecstatic club scenes. Whatever your taste when it comes to clubs or any other kind of entertainment, the best way to find out who's who and what's hot is to check out posters, pick up flyers, or scan the local listing magazines (which are mentioned throughout this book). Then go out and enjoy!

and Italy. In fact, the only significant British composer before the 20th century was Henry Purcell, who flourished in the Restoration period.

In more recent times, key English composers include: Thomas Arne, best known for the patriotic anthem *Rule Britannia*; Edward Elgar, famous for his *Enigma Variations*; Gustav Holtz, from Cheltenham, who wrote *The Planets* (everyone knows the Mars, Bringer of War bit); Vaughan Williams, whose *London Symphony* ends with chimes from Big Ben; and Benjamin Britten, best known for the *Young Person's Guide to the Orchestra* and the opera *Peter Grimes*. Also of note are Welsh composers William Mathias, Alun Hoddinott and Karl Jenkins; and Scotland's Alexander Campbell Mackenzie and Oliver Knussen. On the international stage, the works of Sir Michael Tippett, John Tavener, Peter Maxwell Davies and Harrison Birtwhistle have found fame, while the music of composer William Lloyd Webber has been brought to public attention by his sons Julian and Andrew.

See www.bbc.co.uk/proms for full details of dates, tickets and when to sing 'Land of Hope and Glory'.

Best known of all British classic-music concert programmes is the Proms (short for 'promenade' – because people used to walk about, or stand, while they listened). It's one of the world's greatest music festivals, held from mid-July to mid-September each year at the Royal Albert Hall in London, and widely broadcast on TV and radio.

England, Wales and Scotland each have a national opera company, and the recent multimillion-pound renovation at the Royal Opera House in London's Covent Garden is bringing in the crowds. English National Opera's (ENO) zenith of 2004 was a stunning performance of Wagner's Ring Trilogy, with *Valkyrie* right up there in the list of top London attractions. Later that year, ENO performed Act Three of the opera, which includes Ride of the Valkyries (you know, the bit from *Apocalypse Now*), at the Glastonbury festival (p272) – fittingly under gathering storm clouds – proudly sharing the bill with Morrissey and James Brown.

Architecture

One of the many good reasons to visit Britain is to savour its rich architectural heritage; everything from 5000-year-old Bronze Age burial mounds to the stunning steel-and-glass constructions of the 21st century.

Perhaps the best-known construction of prehistoric times is the mysterious stone circle of Stonehenge (p240) – top of the highlight hit-list for many visitors – although the Callanish Standing Stones on Scotland's Isle of Lewis are even older. The Scottish islands also hold many of Europe's best surviving remains of Bronze Age and Iron Age times, such as the stone villages of Skara Brae in Orkney (p924) and Jarlshof in Shetland (p930).

Moving on a few millennia, the Roman occupation of Britain around 2000 years ago also left an impressive legacy, including grand Fishbourne Palace in West Sussex and the well-preserved swimming pools and saunas that gave the city of Bath (p260) its name – another major highlight for many visitors.

In much of the 1000 years or so leading up to our own time, British architecture was dominated by two aspects: worship and defence. This gave us the incredibly diverse and truly magnificent collection of cathedrals, minsters, abbeys and monasteries dotted across the country, and an equally diverse collection of forts and castles. These range from evocative ruins such as Dunstanburgh on the coast of Northumberland, via the dramatic battlements of castles such as Stirling (p831) in Scotland and Conwy (p733) in Wales, to England's iconic Tower of London (p134), with walls, moats, battlements and ramparts from every century since the Norman Conquest.

Castles were good for keeping out the enemy, but there were few other benefits of living in a large, damp pile of stones. As times grew more peaceful from around the 16th century, the landed gentry started to build fine residences, known simply as country houses. There was a particular boom in England, Wales and parts of Scotland in the 18th and 19th centuries, and one of the most distinctive features of the British countryside today is the sheer number (not to mention the sheer size) of these grand and beautiful structures.

But it's not all about big houses. Alongside the stately homes, ordinary domestic architecture – often centuries old – can also still be seen in rural areas. Black-and-white 'half-timbered' houses still characterise counties such as Worcestershire, while brick-and-flint cottages pepper Suffolk and Sussex, and hardy centuries-old farms built with slate or local gritstone are a feature of areas such as Derbyshire, North Wales and the Lake District.

In our own era, the rebuilding that followed WWII showed scant regard for the overall 'feel' of the cities, and for the lives of the people who lived in them. This has left us with legacies such as tower-block inner-city housing estates and the 'brutalist' concrete structures of London's South Bank Centre (p165). Perhaps this is why, generally speaking, the British are conservative in their architectural tastes, and often resent ambitious or experimental designs. This is especially so when such designs are applied to public buildings, or when form appears more important than function. But a familiar pattern often unfolds: after a few years of resentment, first comes a nickname (London's new near-spherical City Hall was called 'Livingstone's Ball' by some, after the capital's well-known mayor), then grudging acceptance, and finally – once the locals have got used to it – pride in and affection for the new building. The British just don't like to be rushed, that's all.

DID YOU KNOW

As well as a host of grand cathedrals, England has over 12,000 parish churches noted for historic or architectural significance; Wales and Scotland have many too.

SOUNDS OF SUMMER

If you're a fan of the performing arts, some fine productions are staged outdoors from May to September. Many stately homes put on open-air plays (*Macbeth* at dusk is magic) while purpose-built places such as Regents Park Theatre in London and cliff-edge Minack Theatre in Cornwall (p322) always pull in crowds. The best-known music event is Glyndebourne – a programme of world-class opera in the spectacular setting of a country-house garden.

Summertime also inspires villages, towns and cities across the country to stage arts festivals. You can visit everything from small-scale weekend shows to massive spectaculars like the Bath International Music Festival (p263), via specialist events like the Three Choirs Festival – held once every three years on rotation at the cathedrals of Gloucester (p361), Hereford (p377) and Worcester (p372) – Buxton Opera Festival (p438), Edinburgh Jazz & Blues Festival (p759), or Brecon Jazz festival (p694). And don't forget pop and rock extravaganzas such as the Leeds Festival (p502); Glastonbury Festival (p272); or T in the Park in Kinross; the colourful Womad global music gathering in Reading; and the unashamedly good-time-hunting Sesiwn Fawr (it means simply 'big session'), a three-day bash of rock, folk and beer in the mid-Wales town of Dolgellau (p728).

BUILDING ON SUCCESS

Two men have dominated modern British architecture for the last 30 years: Sir Norman Foster and Lord Richard Rogers.

Foster favours clean designs with flowing lines. Key works include the sinuous and sensuous glass roof for the Great Court of the British Museum (p131); try to visit on a sunny day to catch the crisscross of shadows. And don't miss the Millennium Bridge (p137) between St Paul's and the Tate Modern in London – it's almost organic in form. The Sage concert hall (p619) in Gateshead, Newcastle-upon-Tyne, is another splendid recent example of his work. Foster was also one of the architects shortlisted to design a building to replace the World Trade Center in New York.

In contrast, the work of Rogers is technical and intricate. Perhaps his best-known work is the Millennium Dome (p144), a tent-like structure with vast curving white fields held aloft by cables and spindly yellow towers. A more recent work is the massive Paddington Basin complex, near the London train station of the same name. Rogers has also worked for Ken Livingstone, mayor of London, on 20,000 new homes.

Meanwhile, Foster's latest project for Mayor Ken is City Hall, which opened in July 2002. It looks like a tilted beehive, and the glass walls mean you can see everyone inside, hard at work – a deliberate symbol of local government transparency – while at the top there's the spectacular Londoner's Lounge where you can admire the panoramic views and buy a traditional British cappuccino.

With this attitude in mind, British architecture has started to redeem itself over the last 15 years or so, and many big cities now have contemporary buildings that their residents can enjoy. Highlights in London include the spiky MI6 HQ in Vauxhall and the bulging cone of the SwissRE building (already dubbed 'the gherkin') that dominates the financial district. Architecture also continues to become more internationalised, as British architects design airports in Germany or South-East Asia, and overseas architects head for Britain – for example a Spanish architect designed the new Scottish Parliament in Edinburgh (p753).

Outside of London, contemporary architecture is epitomised by Manchester's theatrically stunning Imperial War Museum North (p556), the soaring wood-and-glass arcs of Sheffield's Winter Gardens (p496), the chic new Bullring (p397) in Birmingham, the Deep aquarium (p518) in Hull, the Welsh National Assembly building and the Wales Millennium Centre, both on the Cardiff waterfront (p643), the interlocking arches of the Glasgow's Scottish Exhibition & Conference Centre (p788; already affectionately called 'the armadillo') and the Sage concert hall (p619) in Gateshead.

Painting & Sculpture

In the days before cameras, portrait-painting was a reliable if unadventurous mainstay for most working artists in Britain, as for the rest of Europe. Styles changed over the centuries, but generally British artists were influenced by the great European movements, rather than being world leaders themselves. Two of Britain's best-known portrait artists are Sir Joshua Reynolds, whose portraits in the 'grand style' include Lady Anstruther (seen today in London's Tate Britain gallery, p127) and his rival, Thomas Gainsborough, who produced informal works with subjects at ease in a landscape, such as Mr & Mrs Andrews (National Portrait Gallery, p125).

In the 18th century William Hogarth proved to be a breakaway figure from the comfortable world of portraits, producing a series of paintings that highlighted social issues of the day (such as Gin Lane), satirised politicians (such as Canvassing for Votes), or told a moral story (such as A Rake's Progress, which can be seen today at Soane's Museum (p132), London.

DID YOU KNOW?

William Hogarth helped form the Royal Academy of Arts in 1768, along with Sir Joshua Reynolds (who became its first president). The Royal Academy is still at the forefront of the British artistic establishment today.

Two other key figures of 18th-century British art were Joseph Wright, whose interest in science inspired the oddly titled but beautifully executed *An Experiment on a Bird in the Air Pump*, and George Stubbs, whose passion for animal anatomy (particularly of horses), is evident in many works at Tate Britain and in countless prints on countless country pub walls.

Gainsborough's English landscape tradition was continued by John Constable, who painted mainly in Suffolk (still billed as 'Constable Country' by the local tourist board). His most famous work is *The Haywain* (National Gallery, p124) – an idyllic rural scene.

Constable's contemporaries include poet, painter and visionary William Blake, and JMW Turner, whose works increasingly subordinated picture details to the effects of light and colour. By the 1840s, Turner's compositions became almost entirely abstract and were widely vilified. Both artists have rooms dedicated to their work at Tate Britain, and the Turner collection at Petworth House in West Sussex (p218) is exquisite.

In 1848 Sir John Everett Millais, William Holman Hunt and Dante Gabriel Rossetti formed the Pre-Raphaelite Brotherhood, which combined the simplicity of early Italian art with a closely observed realism. Millais' *Ophelia*, showing the damsel picturesquely drowned in a pool, is an excellent example of their style, and can be seen the Tate Britain gallery. However, one of the best collections of Pre-Raphaelite art is in the Birmingham Museum and Art Gallery (p400).

A good friend of the Pre-Raphaelites was William Morris; he saw late 19th century furniture and interior design as increasingly vulgar, and with Rossetti and Edward Burne-Jones founded the Arts and Crafts movement. This movement encouraged the revival of a decorative approach to features such as wallpaper, tapestries and windows. Many of his designs are still used today.

North of the border, Charles Rennie Mackintosh, fresh from the Glasgow School of Art, fast became a renowned artist, designer and architect. He is still Scotland's greatest Art Nouveau exponent, and much of his work remains in this city (see p781 for more details). Mackintosh influenced a group of artists from the 1890s called the Glasgow Boys, among them James Guthrie and EA Walton, who were also much taken with French impressionism. Perhaps inevitably, another group of decorative artists and designers emerged called the Glasgow Girls.

In the 20th century, the place of British art in the international arena was ensured by the monumental sculptures of Henry Moore and Barbara Hepworth, Francis Bacon's contorted paintings, David Hockney's highly representational images of – among other things – swimming pools and dachshunds, and the works of a group known as the Scottish Colourists – Francis Cadell, SJ Peploe, Leslie Hunter and JD Ferguson. Much of Hockney's work can be seen at the Salt's Mill gallery in Bradford (his hometown; see p505). Hepworth is forever associated with St Ives in Cornwall (p323), while the seascapes of Peploe and Cadell have been turned into the type of prints and postcards favoured by Scottish souvenir shops.

Paul Nash, an official war artist in WWI and WWII, and Graham Sutherland, Nash's counterpart in WWII, followed in the Romantic and visionary tradition of Blake and Turner. Between the wars, Welsh sister-and-brother artists Gwen and Augustus John flourished; Gwen John painted gentle, introspective portraits of women friends, cats and nuns – and famously became the model and lover of French artist August Rodin. Augustus was Britain's leading portrait painter, with such famous sitters as Thomas Hardy and George Bernard Shaw. One place to admire works by the Johns is at the Glynn Vivian Art Gallery in Swansea (see p665 for information).

DID YOU KNOW?

Standing beside the busy A1 highway, the *Angel of the North* is passed by thousands of cars per hour, meaning millions of drivers each year can't help but marvel at this huge and impressive sculpture. See www.gateshead.gov.uk/angel for more.

For more on the metal guru Anthony Caro, see www.anthonycaro.org.

The Scottish Colourists were followed in the interwar years by a group known as the Edinburgh School. This group included William MacTaggart, who was much influenced by the French expressionists and went on to become one of Scotland's best-known painters. His rich and colourful landscapes can be seen in the National Gallery, and in Hunterian Art Gallery in Glasgow (p780).

After WWII, Howard Hodgkin and Patrick Heron developed a British version of American abstract expressionism. At the same time, but in great contrast, Manchester artist LS Lowry painted his much-loved 'matchstick men' figures set in an urban landscape of narrow streets and smoky factories. A good place to see his work is in the Lowry (p556), Manchester.

In 1956, a young artist called Richard Hamilton created a photomontage called *Just what is it that makes today's homes so different, so appealing?* as a poster for the Whitechapel Art Gallery in London. It launched the pop-art movement in England, which culminated with record covers such as Peter Blake's psychedelic *Sergeant Pepper's Lonely Hearts Club Band* for the Beatles. This influenced Scottish artists Alan Davie and Sir Eduardo Paolozzi, who became leading figures in the world of pop art and abstract expressionism. Their works can be seen in Edinburgh's Dean Gallery.

The Whitechapel Art Gallery also helped launch the career of Anthony Caro, a sculptor who works mainly in steel and bronze, with a groundbreaking exhibition in 1963. Since then, Caro has become an influential figure, and is considered by many to be Britain's greatest living sculptor.

Jumping forward a few decades, the contemporary art scene is dominated by the 'Brit pack', a group of artists championed by advertising tycoon Charles Saatchi. These include Rachel Whiteread, who casts commonplace objects in resin; Damien Hirst, whose use of animals, alive and dead, caused outrage; and Tracey Emin, still most famous for *My Bed*, a combination of soiled sheets and – as one reviewer put it – 'sluttish detritus'.

Key sculptors of today include Antony Gormley, whose *Angel Of The North* overlooks the city of Gateshead near Newcastle; it's a massive steel construction of a human figure with wings outstretched – although these wings would be more fitting on a 747 than on a heavenly being. Initially derided by the locals, it is now a proud symbol of the northeast, and one of the most viewed works of art in the world.

Theatre

However you budget your time and money, make sure that you see some British theatre as you travel around the country. It easily lives up to its reputation as the finest in the world, and London's West End is the international centre for performing arts – whatever New Yorkers say.

But first, let's set the stage with some history. Britain's best-known theatrical name is, of course, William Shakespeare, whose plays were first performed in the 16th century at the Globe Theatre. His brilliant plots and sharp prose, and the sheer size of his canon of work (including *Hamlet* and *Romeo and Juliet*), have turned him into a national icon. The Globe has now been rebuilt (see p136), and today you can see the Bard's plays performed in Elizabethan style – in the round, with no roof, and with 'groundlings' down the front heckling and joining in the bits they know. In Stratford-upon-Avon (p411), Shakespeare's birthplace, you can see more Shakespeare plays performed, and a whole load more of everything to do with Shakespeare!

Theatres were great fun, and therefore firmly closed as dens of iniquity in Oliver Cromwell's day. But when Charles II returned from exile in 1660 he opened the doors again, and encouraged radical Continental practices such as female actors (roles for women had previously been played by

---

Click on www.saatchi
-gallery.co.uk for details
of artists, works and
exhibitions at one of
London's most high-
profile galleries of
contemporary art.

DID YOU KNOW?

Britain's first theatre was
built in 1576 on the northern outskirts of London
and was called – rather
unimaginatively – 'The
Theatre'. Shakespeare's
famous Globe Theatre
came a little later.

For a sample of Restora-
tion comedy, try to see
William Congreve's *The
Way of the World* – or at
least read a few pages.
Full of adultery, gossip
and intrigue, it was a
huge hit in 1700.

boys) – an innovation that London audiences loved. They also loved the humorous plays known as Restoration comedies, which delighted in bawdy word play and mockery of the upper classes. The leading lady of the day was Nell Gwyn, and to underline Charles II's passion for theatre, she also became his mistress.

In the 18th century, theatres were built in the larger British cities. The Bristol Old Vic (p258) and The Grand in Lancaster date from this time, along with plays such as Oliver Goldsmith's uproarious *She Stoops to Conquer*. Top of the bill was actor David Garrick, who later gave his name to one of London's leading theatres.

The innovation of gas lighting at London's Drury Lane and Covent Garden theatres set the 19th-century stage for some wonderful shows, including the brilliant comedies of Oscar Wilde – everyone's heard of *The Importance of Being Earnest* (even if they haven't seen it). The quality continued into the 20th century, with the 1950s a particularly rich era, when Laurence Olivier, John Gielgud and Peggy Ashcroft were at their peak.

The post-war years also marked the emergence of new playwrights with new freedoms. One was John Osborne, whose best-known work is *Look Back in Anger*. A contemporary was Harold Pinter, who developed a new dramatic style and perfectly captured the stuttering illogical diction of real-life conversation. In the 1960s and 1970s, plays by Tom Stoppard *(Rosencrantz and Guildenstern are Dead)*, Peter Shaffer *(Amadeus)*, Michael Frayn *(Noises Off)* and Alan Ayckbourn *(The Norman Conquests)* took the country by storm – and famous British actors such as Helen Mirren, Glenda Jackson, Judi Dench and Tom Courtenay did them justice on stage.

In the 1990s and early years of the 21st century, big names in English theatre included (and still include) Brenda Blethyn, Charles Dance, Dame Judi Dench (yes, still!), Ian McKellen, Anthony Sher, Simon Callow, Toby Stephens, Jane Horrocks and Ralph Fiennes, although most perform in stage productions only once or twice a year, combining this with more regular (and more lucrative) appearances on the small or silver screen. In London, other stars of the stage these days are the directors, especially Nicholas Hytner at the National, or the writers, like Conor McPherson. Meanwhile, the native actors are sometimes joined by visitors from over the pond – the likes of Madonna, Nicole Kidman, Gwyneth Paltrow, Matthew Perry, Molly Ringwald, Aaron Eckhart, Julia Stiles, Macaulay Culkin and Kevin Spacey have performed in London productions in recent years, exchanging pay cuts for the genuine cred that only treading West End boards can bestow. Spacey is now based in London as artistic director at the prestigious Old Vic Theatre. Another recent arrival is Christian Slater, to star in *One Flew Over the Cuckoo's Nest* at the Gielgud Theatre. Some more cues about the capital's current drama scene are given on p163.

While there's often an urge among producers to stick with the big names and safe (profitable) productions, the risk and innovation normally associated more with fringe events sometimes filters through at places like Cardiff's Sherman Theatre and London's Donmar Warehouse. This makes British theatre more innovative and exciting than it's been probably since the Restoration, and certainly – according to some critics – since the angry post-war era of Osborne and co.

However, for many visitors, the theatres of the West End mean one thing: musicals. These ranged from *Jesus Christ Superstar* in the 1970s to *Billy Elliot* in 2004, through to *Cats, Les Mis, Phantom* and the rest. Many of today's shows are based on the pop lexicon, with a host of family-friendly singalongs from 'We Will Rock You' to 'Tonight's the Night' proving that – as in Shakespeare's day – we all just like to join in really.

Look Back in Anger launched the career of playwright John Osborne and actor Alan Bates, with rebellious lead character Jimmy Porter perfectly capturing the spirit of an unhappy and frustrated post-war generation.

Harold Pinter wrote numerous plays, but is probably still best known for his landmark work, *The Birthday Party* – a study of sinister figures and shady pasts.

DID YOU KNOW?

A London tradition is the 'long run' – plays that are performed season after season. The record holder is *The Mousetrap* by Agatha Christie; the play has been running at London's St Martin's Theatre for more than 50 years.

Outdoor Activities

As you travel around Britain, pursuing an outdoor activity is an ideal way to get beyond the beaten track and escape the veneer of major tourist sites. Fresh air is good for your body and soul, of course, and becoming actively involved in the country's way of life is much more rewarding than staring at it through a camera lens or car window.

This chapter concentrates on walking and cycling (the most popular and accessible outdoor activities for Brits and visitors alike), and also touches on surfing and rock climbing. More formal or organised activities, such as golf and fishing, are covered on p948.

For walkers and cyclists especially, the options are endless, and open up some of the most beautiful corners of the country. You can go on a short ramble or major expedition, conquer mountains or cruise across plains – there's something for young and old, and it's often perfect for families. Whatever your budget, a walk or ride through the British countryside will almost certainly be a highlight of your trip.

The first stop for outdoor fans should be www.visit britain.com/uk/outdoor britain – with excellent sections on walking, cycling and other activities, including details about routes, maps, tours and the annual walking festivals promoted by towns around the country.

INFORMATION

Numerous local walks and cycle rides are described in this book, and the start of each regional chapter gives an overview of the best outdoor activities in that area. For more details and inspiration, your first stop should always be a Tourist Information Centre (TIC). These have racks of free leaflets on local walks and rides, and also sell booklets (for a nominal fee) plus detailed books and maps (around £5) describing everything from half-hour strolls to week-long treks. TICs can also tell you where to arrange local guides, hire bikes, find repair shops and so on. In rural areas, books and maps are also available in local newsagents. Outdoor-equipment shops are another good source of information – especially in areas where rock-climbing or surfing is a big draw; the tanned outdoor types that work in the shop almost certainly hit the rock or the waves on their day off.

WALKING

Perhaps because Britain is such a crowded place, open spaces are highly valued, and every weekend millions of British people get their boots on and take to the countryside. You could do a lot worse than join them!

Every village and town is surrounded by a web of footpaths, while most patches of open country are crossed by paths and tracks. You can walk from place to place in true backpacking style, or base yourself in one interesting spot for a week or so, and go out on day walks to explore the surrounding countryside.

For more details on where to roam in England see www.countrysideaccess .gov.uk. For Wales, see www.ccw.gov.uk and for Scotland, see www.snh .org.uk.

The joy of walking in Britain is due in no small part to the 'right of way' network – public paths and tracks across private property. Nearly all land (including in national parks) in Britain is privately owned, but if there's a right of way, you can follow it through fields, woods, even farmhouse yards, as long as you keep to the route and do no damage.

The main types of right of way are footpaths and bridleways (the latter open to horse riders and mountain bikers', too). There are also byways, mainly old tracks which due to a quirk of history are open to all traffic, so don't be surprised if your peaceful day is disturbed by off-road driving fanatics.

Thanks to recent landmark legislation, walkers (not bikers and drivers) in England can now leave rights of way in some areas – mostly in 'open country' (ie mountains and moorlands). In enclosed fields or cultivated areas you still must stick to the path. New signboards and maps show Access Land – ie areas where you can leave the rights of way. It's part of a massive nationwide project that should be complete by early 2006.

In Wales, new rights of access are due to be introduced in May 2005. Scotland has a different legal system to England and Wales, with fewer rights of way, but a tradition of relatively free access in mountain and moorland areas (although there are restrictions during the grouse- and deer-hunting seasons).

WHERE TO WALK

Here's a quick rundown of some great walking areas, with everything from gentle hills to high peaks.

Southern & Eastern England

You might be hard pressed to think of any empty, wild and high landscape in southern England, but Dartmoor (p304) has all this, plus granite outcrops called 'tors' – looking for all the world like abstract sculptures – and valleys full of Bronze Age sites and other ancient remains. Good places to base yourself for walks include Buckfastleigh on the south side of Dartmoor, or Sticklepath in the north.

Also good is Exmoor (p274), with grassy and heather-covered hills, cut by deep valleys and edged by spectacular cliffs, great beaches, quiet villages and busy seaside resorts. The walking opportunities are immense. Good bases include Exford (p277) and Simonsbath, or Lynton (p277) and Lynmouth (p277) on the coast.

In the deep south lies the New Forest (p209). Visitors to Britain love this name, – the area is over a thousand years old and there aren't *that* many trees – it's mainly conifer plantation and great open areas of gorse and heath. But apart from these minor details, it's a wonderful place for easy strolls, and the towns of Lyndhurst (p210) or Lymington (p211) make good bases.

And just over the water is the Isle of Wight (p212). If you're new to walking in Britain, or simply not looking for high peaks and wilderness, this is a great first choice. The local authorities have put a lot of effort into footpaths and trails; most are linear and can be done in a day, and you can always get back to your starting point using the island's excellent bus service.

Other good areas are the North Downs in Surrey (p194) and Kent (p181), the South Downs in Sussex (p215) and the coast of Norfolk (p471).

Central England

The gem of central England is the Cotswold Hills (p351). This is classic English countryside, with gentle paths through neat fields and mature

---

THERE'S COLD IN THEM THERE HILLS

The British countryside often looks gentle and welcoming but the weather can turn nasty at any time of year, especially on the high hills or open moors. If you're walking in these areas, it's vital that you're well equipped. You should carry (and know how to use) good maps and a compass. If you're really going off the beaten track, leave details of your route with someone. Wear decent footwear. Carry warm and waterproof clothing (even in summer). Make sure you've got some drink, food and high-energy stuff like chocolate. Carrying a whistle and torch – in case of emergency – is not a bad idea either.

woodland, past clear rivers flowing down grassy valleys, or pretty villages with churches, farms and cottages of honey-coloured stone. The marvellously named towns of Moreton-in-Marsh (p358), Stow-on-the-Wold (p357) and Bourton-on-the-Water (p357) all make ideal bases.

Northern England

The Lake District (p586) is the heart and soul of walking in England – a wonderful area of soaring peaks, endless views, deep valleys and, of course, beautiful lakes. There's a great selection of country hotels, B&Bs and campsites, while good bases include Ambleside (p593), Keswick (p600) and Patterdale (p603).

Further north, keen walkers love the starkly beautiful hills of Northumberland National Park (p635), where good bases include Wooler and Bellingham. The Northumberland coast is less daunting but just as dramatic; head for Alnmouth, east of Alnwick (p631), or Bamburgh (p633), where your backdrop is a spectacular castle.

For something a little gentler, the rolling hills of the Yorkshire Dales is one of the most popular walking areas in England. Good bases for walks include the villages of Grassington (p512) and Malham (p513). Further north, the dramatic valleys of Wensleydale (p515) and Swaledale (p517) provide more options.

South & Mid-Wales

The Brecon Beacons (p689) is a large group of mountains, forming a natural border between the central and southern parts of Wales. There are few pointed peaks; this is a range of gigantic rolling whalebacks, with broad ridges and table-top summits, cut by deep valleys where sides fall so steeply the grass has often given up the ghost and exposed large areas of bare rock. There's a fantastic choice of walks for all abilities, with ideal bases including Crickhowell (p695), Abergavenny (p695) and Brecon (p693).

Out in the wild west of Wales is Pembrokeshire (p670). It's a gem of an area, with one of the most beautiful stretches of coastline in Britain – a wonderful array of beaches, cliffs, rock arches, stacks, buttresses, islands, coves and harbours. You have to go to Cornwall to get anything like this and to northwest Scotland for anything better. The relatively mild climate means you can walk here year-round, although the coast gets hammered by some spectacular gales, especially in winter.

North Wales

For walkers, North Wales is Snowdonia (p719), where the remains of ancient, eroded volcanoes bequeath a striking landscape of jagged peaks, sharp ridges and steep cliffs. There are challenging walks on Snowdon itself – at 1085m, the highest peak in England and Wales – and many more on the surrounding Glyders or Carneddau ranges. Ideal bases include the towns of Llanberis (p720), Beddgelert (p722) or Betws-y-Coed (p723). In the southern part of the park, aim for Dolgellau (p728).

Southern & Central Scotland

The extensive region between Crianlarich and the lowland plains, and from the west coast to the edge of Glasgow, embraces several areas just perfect for keen walkers, including Ben Lomond (p818), the best-known peak in the area, the Arrochar 'Alps' on the west of Loch Lomond (p818), the nearby Trossachs range (p836), and the higher peaks around Ben More (p827). Also here is the splendid Isle of Arran (p810) – 'Scotland in miniature' – with a great choice of coastal rambles and high mountain hikes.

The Ramblers' Association's annually published *RA Yearbook* is an invaluable publication for all walkers – it outlines routes and walking areas, and has handy lists of walker-friendly B&Bs and hostels all over Britain.

For inspiration before you go, or memories after your trip, a great series of full-colour books covering national parks and other wild or scenic areas is published by Halsgrove (www.halsgrove.co.uk). Places covered include the Yorkshire Dales, South Downs, Peak District, Cheviot Hills, Dorset Coast, Lake District and Dartmoor.

For comprehensive coverage of a selection of walking routes and areas, we recommend Lonely Planet's *Walking in Britain*, which also covers places to stay and eat along several long-distance walks and in popular walking areas, plus detailed information on what to take and what to see along the way.

North & West Scotland

Two of Scotland's most famous place names, Glen Coe (p883) and Ben Nevis (at 1343m, Britain's highest mountain), are at the heart of a truly excellent walking area, where complex geology and the forces of nature have created scenery that really lives up to the postcard images. This is the gateway to heaven for serious walkers, and there are plenty of places for easy strolls too. A good base for starters is the town of Fort William (p880).

Off the west coast lies the Isle of Skye (p904), and some of the most impressive mountains in Britain, including the spectacular jagged ridges of the Black Cuillin (p908). Most of these airy peaks are the domain of adventurous walkers with rock-scrambling skills and a head for heights,

---

BEST OF BRITAIN – WALKING

Still undecided? Here's our own list of favourites.

Best Coastline Walk

The rollercoaster cliffs of Cornwall and Pembrokeshire are hard to beat. This is the place for secluded beaches, traditional fishing villages, wildflowers, birds, seals and fantastic views. For a wilder edge go for Scotland's western coast and islands.

Best High Walk

Dartmoor and the North Pennines have high moors, while Snowdonia and the Lake District provide wonderful airy walking among proper mountains. Most serious, and most rewarding, are the wild Scottish highlands.

Best Weekend Walk

Take your pick: Hunstanton to Wells-next-the-Sea on the North Norfolk Coast, Chepstow to Monmouth on Offa's Dyke Path, the Limestone Way in the Peak District, the Coniston to Keswick section of the Cumbria Way in the Lake District, or Crianlarich to Kinlochleven on the West Highland Way.

Best Wilderness Walk

Without a doubt, northwest Scotland is best. It's remote, with unpredictable weather, and you need sound navigation skills, but it's unrivalled in beauty. Easier to reach are Rannoch Moor in central Scotland, the North Pennines and parts of Dartmoor in England, and sections of the Owain Glyndwr path through Mid Wales.

Best River Walk

The Thames Path is a long-distance riverside classic, with a lot of variation from countryside to city centre. A five-day option is the Dales Way, which follows the beautiful River Wharfe through Yorkshire. In Scotland, the Speyside Way is simply stunning. You can do these routes end-to-end, or just dip your toe in the water and follow them for a day or two.

Best Bird Walk

The Northumberland coast is a must for keen bird-watchers, with a side trip to the nearby Farne Islands, home to thousands of seabirds. The Norfolk coast also has several excellent bird reserves.

Best Ancient Culture Walk

Dartmoor has a wealth of standing stones, burial mounds and Bronze Age settlements. You can also walk The Ridgeway from England's largest stone circle, past Neolithic long barrows and mysterious figures carved in chalk hillsides. Pembrokeshire is peppered with history and mystery, while in Scotland head for the northern islands for stunning reminders of the past.

but there are a few places here, and on the more rounded tops of the neighbouring Red Cuillin, where experienced walkers can still get a 'Skye high' experience. And should the cloud be down, or you just want a rest, the island's glens and coast offers great low-level walking.

Keep going north and west, and things just keep getting better. You're through the gateway. For serious and experienced mountain walkers, Scotland's northwest Highlands region *is* sheer paradise: a remote and starkly beautiful area, sparsely populated, with scenic glens and lochs, and some of the finest mountains in Britain – some say in Europe – plus a host of Munros to bag (see the boxed text, p79). Good places to base yourself before setting off into the wilds of the Wester Ross NSA (National Scenic Area) include the villages of Torridon (p902), Gairloch (p902) or Poolewe (p902), while further north the charming port of Ullapool (p900) is a jumping-off point for the stark and rugged landscapes of Assynt Coigach and Sutherland NSAs.

LONG-DISTANCE WALKS

Many walkers savour the chance of completing one of Britain's famous long-distance walking trails or routes. There are hundreds, 19 of which are official National Trails (in England and Wales) or Long Distance Routes (in Scotland), with better signposting and maintenance – so they're ideal for beginners or visitors – and together offering over 3000 miles of top-notch walking. Other long walks such as the Dales Way are not national trails, but are just as popular. You don't have to do these long routes end-to-end; you can walk just a section for a day or two, or use the trail as a basis for shorter loops exploring the surrounding area. Here's a short list of our favourites to get you started:

Coast to Coast Walk (190 miles) England's No 1 favourite, through the Lake District, Yorkshire Dales and North York Moors national parks, with spectacular scenery, sea-cliffs, mountains and moors. It can be busy, but don't let that stop you.

Cotswold Way (100 miles) A fascinating walk through central England's classic picture-postcard countryside.

Cumbria Way (68 miles) A perfect introduction to the Lake District, sticking mainly to valleys, with top-quality mountain views.

Dales Way (84 miles) A great walk through the farmland and valleys of the Yorkshire Dales, leading into the Lake District.

Glyndwr's Way (132 miles) A long loop through the beautiful and surprisingly remote rolling hills of mid-Wales, the land of 15th-century Welsh freedom fighter Owain Glyndwr.

Great Glen Way (70 miles) A nonarduous route along the geological fault that splits Scotland, including a section beside famous Loch Ness.

Hadrian's Wall Path (84 miles) In the footsteps of the legions, following the Roman Wall as it strides across northern England.

Offa's Dyke Path (177 miles; see p659) A historical hike along the ancient defensive ditch marking the border between England and Wales, through a tremendous range of scenery.

Pembrokeshire Coast Path (186 miles; see p672) An awe-inspiring walk along one of the finest coastlines in Britain, and best-loved long route in Wales.

Pennine Way (256 miles) The grand-daddy of them all, along the mountainous spine of northern England and over the border to Scotland.

South West Coast Path (610 miles; see p231) A seaside rollercoaster epic past beaches, bays, shipwrecks, fishing villages, busy resorts and clifftop castles.

Southern Upland Way (212 miles; see p773) Striding through the heart of Scotland's Southern Uplands, an extremely remote and challenging route, with some very long daily sections.

Speyside Way (84 miles; see p861) Billed as a walk that 'captures the spirit of Scotland', this scenic riverside route links the Cairngorm foothills to the sea – and it also passes several whisky distilleries.

Stroll over to www .nationaltrail.co.uk for full details on options in England and Wales. For more information and inspiration see the 'get active' pages of www .visitbritain.com, which include Scotland.

DID YOU KNOW?

If you like the idea of a trip along one of Britain's long-distance walks, but don't want to lug heavy gear, many routes are served by baggage-carrying services. For about £5 to £10 per day, your pack will be delivered to your next B&B by dedicated van or local taxi. For starters, see www.carrylite.com, www.cumbria.com/pack horse and www.pikedaw .freeserve.co.uk/walks.

The movie *Arthur's Dyke* follows the progress of a mismatched group of hikers along the Offa's Dyke Path. Frankly, it's silly, but the Welsh landscape provides a beautiful backdrop.

Thames Path (173 miles; see p338) A journey of contrasts beside Britain's best-known river, from rural Gloucestershire to the heart of London.

West Highland Way (95 miles; see p815) Scotland's – and Britain's – most popular long-distance path, leading walkers from the outskirts of Glasgow to Fort William in the highlands, past mountains, lochs and fast-flowing rivers.

CYCLING

A bike is the perfect transport for exploring back-road Britain. Once you escape the busy main highways, there's a vast network of quiet country lanes leading through fields and peaceful villages, ideal for touring on a road bike or mountain bike. Off-road riders can go further into the wilds on the many tracks and bridleways that cross Britain's farmlands, forests and high moors.

The opportunities are endless. Depending on your energy and enthusiasm you can amble round flat lanes, taking it easy and stopping for cream teas, or thrash all day through hilly areas, revelling in steep ascents and swooping downhill sections. You can cycle from place to place, camping

---

THE ANCIENT ART OF MUNRO-BAGGING

In 1891 an eager hill-walker and member of the recently founded Scottish Mountaineering Club, Sir Hugh Munro, published a list of about 500 Scottish mountains measuring over 3000ft – a height at which he felt they gained particular significance (although the measurement loses some mystique when converted to the metric equivalent of 914m). With great diligence, Sir Hugh differentiated between 'mountains in their own right' (usually those with a significant drop on all sides or some other distinguishing feature such as 'peculiarity of formation'), and the surrounding peaks, which he regarded as mere satellites of the main summits.

Little did Sir Hugh know that a century later his name would be used to describe any main mountain over the magic 3000ft line, and that it would be the object (some say obsession) of many keen walkers to 'bag' (reach the summit of) as many Munros as possible. The satellite peaks are called 'tops' and are often bagged at the same time.

In fact, the peculiar practice of Munro-bagging started soon after the list was first published, because by 1901 another eager walker, one Reverend AE Robertson, had reached the lot. In our own era, Munro baggers keep their own Munro tick-list, and attempt to add to it in the same way golfers try to get their handicap down. Between 1901 and 1981, only 250 people had bagged all the Munros, but by 2001 the number of officially declared 'Munroists' had topped 2600.

These days there are all sorts of additional records: oldest person to bag all Munros, first person to bag them all in a single trip, fastest person to do them all (66 days), first person to do them all in a kilt and so on. There have been people who bagged them strictly in order of south to north, strictly in order of height (from lowest to highest), and rumours of aficionados doing them in alphabetical order, or even in order of length of name (starting with the likes of Ben Lui and finishing with wonders such as Braigh Coire Chruinn-bhalgain). Madness it may be, but even for the sane, Munros offer wonderful walking and some great views; there's no reason why any reasonably fit and well-equipped hiker shouldn't bag a few during a Scottish visit.

Note, however, that the final tally of Munros is not fixed. For some decades the figure was 277, but a more recent list puts it at 284, and it continues to change as increasingly accurate surveys move mountain peaks just over or under that magical 3000ft level.

Some people say that arguments are pointless, and that Munros should be those on Sir Hugh's original list (whatever his errors) with no additions or removals, while revisionists believe passionately in keeping the list up to date, adding new Munros when appropriate or mercilessly scrubbing pretenders that don't quite make the grade. Other people wryly note that the continuing debate does little more than provide material for men with beards to rant about in pubs and bothies.

or staying in B&Bs (many are 'cyclist friendly'), or you can stay in one place for a few days and go out on rides in different directions.

ACCESS & RULES

Visit the website of the Cyclists' Touring Club (☎ 0870 873 0060; www.ctc.org.uk), the UK's leading recreational cycling and campaigning body, for information (free to members) about cycling in Britain, lists of suggested routes, local contacts, cyclist-friendly accommodation, organised holidays, cycle-hire directory and mail-order service for maps and books.

Bikes aren't allowed on motorways, but you can cycle on all other public roads, although main roads (A-roads) tend to be very busy and should be avoided. Many B-roads suffer heavy motor traffic too, so the best places for cycling are the small C-roads and unclassified roads ('lanes') covering rural Britain, especially in lowland areas, meandering through quiet countryside and linking small, picturesque villages. In northern Scotland, A-roads are sometimes the only option, but traffic is light, and cyclists can enjoy stunning scenery in a fume-free environment.

Cycling is *not* allowed on footpaths, but mountain bikers can ride on any unmade road or bridleway that is a public right of way. For mountain biking it's often worth seeking out forestry areas; among the vast plantations, signposted routes of varying difficulty have been specially developed for single-track fans.

WHERE TO CYCLE

While you can cycle anywhere in Britain, some areas are better than others, although the popular areas attract drivers too, so car traffic can be a problem on summer weekends. This section gives a brief overview of the best places. With a map and a sense of adventure, the rest is up to you!

Southern & Eastern England

Norfolk (p471), Suffolk (p462) and parts of Lincolnshire (p481) are generally low-lying, and great for easy pedalling, with lanes winding through farmland and picturesque villages, past rivers, lakes and welcoming country pubs. Cornwall (p311) and Devon (p290) are beautiful, but the rugged landscape makes for a harder day in the saddle. Somerset (p267), Dorset (p279) and Wiltshire (p234) have more gentle hills (plus a few steep valleys to keep you on your toes) and a beautiful network of quiet lanes, perfect for leisurely cycle touring. In Hampshire, the ancient woodland and open heath of the New Forest (p209) is especially good for on-road and off-road rides, while the South Downs region of Sussex (p175) area has numerous mountain-bike options.

Anyone planning a cycle tour in Britain should visit www.sustrans.org.uk, site of Sustrans (☎ 0845 113 0065), originators of the National Cycle Network; as well as providing general information, cycling tips and useful contacts, it has a shop area (also available as a printed catalogue) with a huge range of dedicated cycling maps and guidebooks.

Central England

Derbyshire's Peak District (p435) is a very popular cycling area, although the hills are quite steep in places. More leisurely options are the excellent cycle routes cutting through the landscape along disused railways – dramatic and effortless at the same time. The Cotswolds area (p352) is another good place, with lanes through farmland and quaint villages. From the western side of the hills you get fantastic views over the Severn Valley, but you wouldn't want to go up and down this escarpment too often! The Marches region (p371), where England borders Wales, is a rural delight, with good quiet lanes and some off-road options in the hills.

Northern England

One of the best areas for cycle touring is the Yorkshire Dales (p510), the part of the Pennine Hills between Skipton in the south and Swaledale in the north. Some routes can be strenuous though (it's no accident that many of England's top racing cyclists come from this area) but the scenery is superb, and well worth the effort. Also good for touring, and with some exhilarating off-road rides, is the North York Moors (p538).

Wales

The varied Welsh landscape, crossed by a wonderful network of lanes and forest tracks, makes an excellent place to cycle, although much of it is hilly, so low gears will often be the order of the day.

In the north, the rugged peaks of the Snowdonia mountains (p718) provide a dramatic backdrop to any cycling trip, although some ascents can be stiff. An easier option is the nearby Isle of Anglesey (p737).

In mid-Wales, the Cambrian mountains (p703) offer quiet cycling in a scenic and surprisingly little-visited region, while around the Brecon Beacons (the border between mid and south Wales; p690) the area is popular for tourists and off-roaders. Finally, out to the west, lovely Pembrokeshire (p671) is also excellent on a bike – although the hills go all the way to the sea!

A good starting point for cycle touring is the *Guide to the National Cycle Network* (£10.99) published by Sustrans, describing 30 one-day rides throughout Britain. For off-roading, get *Where to Mountain Bike in Britain* (£9.50) published by Open Air Books, or see www.wheretoMTB.com.

Scotland

The Scottish Borders (p794) is an excellent area for touring by bike. It offers a combination of rolling farmland, lochs, glens and hills, all easily accessible, with a peaceful, intimate charm. For off-road fans, there's a fantastic range of specially constructed routes in the Galloway Forest Park in Dumfries and Galloway (p801) and several other sites across the southern part of the country. See www.7stanes.gov.uk for more details.

Cyclists in search of the wild and remote will love Scotland's far northwest. It's especially good north of the Great Glen (p880), and totally stunning beyond Ullapool (see p902). There are not many roads in this part of Scotland, but their surfaces are smooth and traffic is light. As you pass majestic mountains, beautiful lochs and coasts with views of mystical islands, it won't just be the pedalling that takes your breath away.

If you really want to get away from traffic, head for the islands. Ferries (which carry bikes) go from the mainland to the Western Isles (p910) – wonderful getaway options for two-wheeled travel.

DID YOU KNOW?

The Cyclists Touring Club is the oldest cycling organisation in Britain. It was founded in 1878, when the bike of choice was the 'penny-farthing', and the national scandal of the day was 'lady bicyclists' wearing trousers.

SPREADING THE NET

Anyone riding a bike through Britain today will almost certainly come across the National Cycle Network, a web of roads and paths that spreads across Britain, on target to cover 10,000 miles by 2005. Strands of the network pass through the heart of busy cities and are aimed at commuters or school kids, while other sections follow some of the most remote roads in the country – simply perfect for touring.

The whole scheme is the brainchild of Sustrans (derived from 'sustainable transport'), a campaign group barely taken seriously in 1978 when the network idea was first announced. But the growth of cycling, coupled with near-terminal car congestion, has earned the scheme lots of attention – not to mention a £40 million wedge of government funding. The eventual goal is to have the network pass within 2 miles of half the homes in Britain.

Most of the network keeps to quiet country lanes, while traffic-free sections make use of old roads and former railways, as well as purpose-built cycle paths. Where the network follows city streets, cyclists normally have their own lane, separate from motor traffic.

Several long-distance touring routes have been designed using the most scenic sections of the National Cycle Network (and a few less-that-scenic sections through some towns, it has to be said). Other features include a great selection of sculptures and works of art to admire along the way. In fact, the network is billed as the country's largest outdoor sculpture gallery. The whole scheme is a resounding success, and a credit to the visionaries who persevered against inertia all those year ago.

ROCK CLIMBING & MOUNTAINEERING

One of the many outdoor activities pioneered in Britain over a century ago was rock climbing, and today this is a rapidly growing and internationally recognised sport. There are numerous indoor-climbing competitions in various venues around Britain, but this section concentrates on the outdoor, noncompetitive side.

For online info, see www .thebmc.co.uk, home of the British Mountaineering Council. In Scotland, the main bodies are the Scottish Mountaineering Club (www.smc.org.uk) and the Mountaineering Council of Scotland (www.mountaineering -scotland.org.uk).

WHERE TO CLIMB

Areas for mountaineering in Britain include, naturally enough, the high mountains of Scotland (especially the northwest), with favourite spots including Glen Coe (p883), the Ben Nevis area (p880) and the Cuillin Ridge on Skye (p904). In Wales, Snowdonia (p720) offers long and short routes, while England's main centre for long routes is the Lake District (p585), and there are some fine short routes here as well. From the websites of Britain's climbing organisations you can learn about more options, guidebooks, competitions, indoor climbing walls and outdoor access rules – remember, *all* mountains and rock outcrops are privately owned, even in national parks (see p87).

For short or single-pitch rock climbing, popular areas include the Peak District (p435), where climbers come from miles around to test themselves on the world-famous gritstone 'edges' of Stanage and Froggat. There's high-quality limestone in the Yorkshire Dales (p510), and in southern England, good climbing areas include Cheddar Gorge (p269) and the tors (rocky outcrops) of Dartmoor (p306). Britain also offers the sheer exhilaration of sea-cliff climbing, from the Land's End area (p322) in Cornwall, through Pembrokeshire, to the classic Old Man of Storr rock tower (p909) in Scotland. Nothing makes you concentrate more on finding that next hold than crashing waves 30m below!

Hang ten, take five, whatever – take a look at www.britsurf.co.uk, the official site of the British Surfing Association, with news on approved instruction centres, courses, competitions and so on. Also handy is www.britsurf.org, with comprehensive links and reports from around Britain.

SURFING

For all you tanned and sexy surfers out there, Britain may not be renowned as a place for a beach holiday, and there are good reasons for this, not least the climate and the water temperature. But Britain has some truly magnificent stretches of coastline with long, flat, sandy beaches and some wonderful breaks when conditions are right.

If you've come from the other side of the world, you'll be delighted to learn that summer water temperatures in England are roughly equivalent to winter temperatures in southern Australia (approximately 13°C). But thanks to the Gulf Stream bringing warm water from the tropics, and as

---

SCRAMBLING

Scrambling seems to be another outdoor activity invented in Britain – covering the twilight zone between serious hiking and real rock climbing. Scrambling definitely involves using your hands, as well as your feet – and often involves a little rush of adrenaline now and again too. While experienced climbers may cruise effortlessly up a scramble, someone new to the game may need a rope and a lot of encouragement. Classic scrambles in Britain include Bristly Ridge and Crib Coch in Snowdonia, Jack's Rake and Striding Edge in the Lake District, and the Aonach Eagach Ridge in Scotland's Glen Coe. Local guidebooks can suggest many more. It's great fun, as long as you know what you're doing.

COASTEERING

As if scrambling wasn't enough, the Brits then went and invented another crazy outdoor activity. This time it's coasteering. It's like mountaineering, although instead of going up, you go sideways – along the coast, using a mix of climbing, scrambling, jumping and swimming. Required equipment includes a wetsuit, a buoyancy jacket, a helmet and old training shoes. Other requirements are an experienced guide, a yen for adventure and a big sense of fun. The main centre for coasteering is Pembrokeshire, and several outdoor centres offer outings, from a few hours to a weekend (the latter combined with other watery activities such as kayaking). See p672 for details.

long as you've got a wetsuit, it's no problem. Britain's huge tidal range means there's often a completely different set of breaks at low and high tides, so you'll never be bored either.

WHERE TO SURF

Beaches that have been awarded 'blue flags' means the local town authority is taking sea (and sand) cleanliness seriously. Good beaches for surfing, with the best chance of some sun and the genuine possibility of luring you into the water, are in Cornwall (p311) and Devon (p290). The entire western coast here is exposed to the Atlantic and there is a string of surf spots from Land's End all the way to Ilfracombe. The shallow continental shelf, however, means the waves rarely get over 2.5m. Newquay (p328) in Cornwall is the capital of British surfing and home to the main competitions. There's a plethora of surf shops and all the trappings, from Kombis to bleached hair. The boards and wetsuits sold are good quality and competitively priced in international terms.

Elsewhere in England, the east coast of Yorkshire has a small surf scene, notably on the beaches around Scarborough (p536), noted for its more relaxed and less pretentious atmosphere compared to things 'down south'.

Southwest Wales has many good surfing spots, including Manorbier (p674), Newgale and Whitesands near St David's (to name a few; see p671). It's easy to hire boards and gear, or arrange lessons. In the south, conditions at Porthcawl are also very good and the Gower Peninsula has a lively scene, especially at Llangennith (p668) on Rhossili Bay.

Scotland's west coast is mainly sheltered by islands, and on the east coast the swells are unreliable, so in the north, particularly around Thurso (p896), which has outstanding world-class possibilities, and a surprisingly large and lively surf scene. Although the air is colder than in southern Britain, water temperatures drop only marginally, so a visit should be high on the list for surf fiends.

For something a bit different, experienced surfers could consider riding the Severn Bore, a wave that comes *up* the River Severn in certain tide conditions, often for several miles. See www.boreriders.com or www.severn-bore.co.uk for more details

Every surfer looking for pointers needs *Surf UK* by Wayne Alderson, a comprehensive guidebook covering almost 400 breaks around the country.

Surfers Against Sewage (www.sas.org.uk) is an active campaign group whose name says it all. Although the situation is improving, some British towns still discharge a fair amount of crap into the sea.

Environment

The island of Britain consists of three nations: England in the south and centre, Scotland to the north and Wales to the west. Further west lies the island of Ireland. Looking southeast, France is just 20 miles away.

THE LAND

Ever wondered about the origin of Hastings, Stratford or Thorpeness? *Place Names in the Landscape* by Margaret Gelling is a fascinating study of the geographical roots of Britain's town and village titles.

Geologically at least, Britain is part of Europe. It's on the edge of the Eurasian landmass, separated from the mother continent by the shallow English Channel. (The French are not so proprietorial, and call it La Manche – the sleeve.) About 10,000 years ago, Britain was *physically* part of Europe, but then sea levels rose and created the island we know today. Only in more recent times has there been a reconnection, in the form of the Channel Tunnel.

When it comes to topology, Britain is not a place of extremes. There are no Himalayas or Lake Baikals here. But there's plenty to keep you enthralled, and even a short journey can take you through a surprising mix of landscapes.

Southern England is dotted with small hills and covered in a mix of countryside, towns and cities. East Anglia is almost entirely low and flat, while the Southwest Peninsula has wild moors, granite outcrops and rich pastures (Devon's cream is world famous), plus a rugged coast with sheltered beaches, making it a favourite holiday destination.

In the north of England, farmland is interspersed with towns and cities, but the landscape here is bumpier than in the south. A line of large hills called the Pennines (fondly tagged 'the backbone of England') runs from Derbyshire to the Scottish border, and includes the peaty plateaus of the Peak District, the wild moors around Haworth (immortalised in Brontë novels), the delightful valleys of the Yorkshire Dales and the frequently windswept but ruggedly beautiful hills of Northumberland. In northwest England is the Lake District, a small but spectacular cluster of mountains, where Scaféll Pike (a towering 978m) is England's highest peak.

Wild Britain: A Traveller's Guide by Douglas Botting describes the geography, geology, flora and fauna in over 150 wilderness areas across the country.

The landscape of Wales is also defined by hills and mountains: notably the rounded Black Mountains and Brecon Beacons in the south, and the spiky peaks of Snowdonia in the north, with Snowdon (1085m) the highest peak in Wales. In between lie the wild rolling hills and farmland of mid-Wales, ending on the west coast in spectacular cliffs and shimmering river estuaries.

For real mountains, though, you've got to go to Scotland, especially the relatively remote and thinly populated northwest Highlands. Separated from the rest of the country by a diagonal gash in the earth's crust (the

---

COMPARING COVERAGE

Statistics can be boring, but these approximate area measurements may be handy for planning or perspective as you travel around:

- Wales 8000 sq miles
- England 50,000 sq miles
- UK 95,000 sq miles
- Scotland 30,500 sq miles
- Britain 88,500 sq miles
- British Isles 123,000 sq miles

If you want comparisons, France is about 210,000 sq miles, Texas 260,000 sq miles, Australia nearly three million sq miles and the USA over 3½ million sq miles. When Britain is compared with these giants, it's amazing that such a small island can make so much noise.

Boundary Fault), the Highlands is an area of peaks and mountains, and some of the wildest landscape in Europe. The Highlands are further enhanced by the vast cluster of beautiful islands that lie off the loch-indented west coast. Ben Nevis (1343m) is Scotland's – and Britain's – highest mountain, but there are many more to choose from.

South of the Scottish Highlands is a relatively flat area called the Central Lowlands, home to the bulk of Scotland's population. Further south, down to the border with England, things get hillier again; this is the Southern Uplands, a fertile farming area.

WILDLIFE

Britain is a small country, and some native plant and animal species are hidden away. However, there are undoubted gems, from woods carpeted in shimmering bluebells to a stately herd of deer in the mountains. This wildlife is part of the fabric of Britain, and having a closer look will enhance your trip enormously.

Animals

When strolling through farmland and woodland areas, you'll easily spot birds such as the robin, with its red breast and cheerful whistle, and the yellowhammer, with its 'little-bit-of-bread-and-no-cheese' song. You might also hear the warbling cry of a skylark as it flutters high over the fields – a classic, but now threatened, sound of the British countryside.

Between the fields, hedges provide cover for flocks of finches, but these seedeaters must watch out for sparrowhawks – birds of prey that come from nowhere at tremendous speed. Other predators include barn owls, a wonderful sight as they fly silently along hedgerows listening for the faint rustle of a vole or shrew. In rural Wales or Scotland you may see a buzzard, Britain's most common large raptor.

Also in fields, look out for the brown hare, another increasingly rare mammal species; they're related to rabbits but are much larger, with longer legs and ears. Males who battle for territory in early spring are, of course, as 'mad as a March hare'.

A classic British mammal is the red fox. You may only see one in the countryside, but these wily beasts adapt well to any situation, so you're just as likely to see them scavenging in towns, and even in city suburbs.

Another well-known British mammal is the black-and-white striped badger. You'll probably only see the burrows of this nocturnal animal, but if you're driving at night you might catch sight of 'old Brock' in your headlights. Farmers believe badgers spread tuberculosis to cattle, although the evidence is inconclusive, and the debate rumbles on between the agricultural and environmental lobbies.

In woodland areas, mammals include the small white-spotted fallow deer and the even smaller roe deer. You're much more likely to see grey squirrels; this species was introduced from North America and has proved so adaptable that native British red squirrels are severely endangered (see the boxed text, p86). Much larger than squirrels are pine martens, which are seen in some forested regions, especially in Scotland. With beautiful brown coats, they were once hunted for their fur, but are now fully protected.

Out of the trees and up in the moors, birds you might see include the red grouse, and the curlew with its elegant curved bill. Golden plovers are beautifully camouflaged so you have to look hard, but you can't miss the show-off lapwings with their spectacular aerial displays.

The most visible moorland mammal is the red deer. Herds survive on Exmoor and Dartmoor, in the Lake District, and in larger numbers in

Wildlife Walks by Malcolm Tait suggests over 500 days out on foot in an astounding collection of nature reserves and other wildlife areas throughout Britain.

If you want a single, handy volume covering common mammals, birds, fish, plants, snakes, insects and even fungi, the *Complete Guide to British Wildlife* by N Arlott, R Fitter and A Fitter is highly recommended.

As the name implies, the Woodland Trust (www .woodland-trust.org) is concerned with the protection, creation and public understanding of native woodland. The Trust publishes several guidebooks to areas of woodland throughout Britain.

Scotland. The males are most spectacular after June, when their antlers have grown ready for the rutting season. The stags keep their antlers through the winter and then shed them again in February.

Mountain birds include red kites (in Wales there has been a successful project to reintroduce these spectacular fork-tailed raptors – see the boxed text, p701), while on the high peaks of Scotland you may see the grouse's northern cousin, the ptarmigan, dappled brown in the summer but white in the winter. Also in the Scottish mountains, keep an eye peeled for golden eagles, Britain's largest birds of prey, as they glide and soar along ridges.

The Royal Society for the Protection of Birds (www.RSPB.org.uk) is a major conservation body, working in the UK and overseas – 'for birds, for people, for ever'.

If there is water nearby you have a chance of spotting an osprey; one of the best places in Britain to see this magnificent bird catch fish is Rutland Water (in the Midlands – see p425). You could also look along the riverbanks for signs of water voles, endearing rodents that were once very common but are now all but wiped out by wild mink, another American immigrant (first introduced to stock fur farms).

In contrast to water voles, the formerly rare otters are beginning to make a comeback after suffering from polluted water, habitat destruction and persecution by anglers. In southern Britain they inhabit the banks of rivers and lakes, and in Scotland they frequently live on the coast. Although their numbers are growing, they are mainly nocturnal and hard to see, but keep your eyes peeled and you might be lucky.

On the coasts of Britain, particularly in Cornwall, Pembrokeshire and northwest Scotland, the dramatic cliffs are a marvellous sight in early summer (around May), when they are home to hundreds of thousands of breeding seabirds. Guillemots, razorbills and kittiwakes, among others, fight for space on impossibly crowded rock ledges. The sheer numbers of birds makes this one of Britain's finest wildlife spectacles, as the cliffs become white with droppings and the air is filled with their shrill calls.

The Birdwatchers Pocket Guide by Peter Hayman is highly rated, and frequently carried, by keen (as opposed to obsessive) bird-watchers; it's slim, light, and designed for speedy reference on the move, with clear illustrations and good notes.

Another bird to look out for in coastal areas is the comical puffin (especially common in Shetland), with its distinctive rainbow beak and 'nests' burrowed in sandy soil. In total contrast, gannets are one of the largest seabirds and make dramatic dives for fish, often from a great height.

And finally, the sea mammals. There are two species of seal that frequent British coasts; the larger grey seal is more often seen than the (misnamed) common seal. Dolphins, porpoises, minke whales and basking sharks can all be seen off the west coast, particularly off Scotland, and especially from May to September when viewing conditions are better. Whale-watching trips (which are also good for seeing other marine wild-

SEEING RED

The red squirrel used to be commonplace in many parts of woodland Britain, but it's now one of the country's most endangered mammal species. Where they once numbered in millions, populations have declined significantly over the last 50 years to about 150,000 – confined mainly to Scotland, with isolated groups in the Lake District, Norfolk and the Isle of Wight. The simple reason for this is the arrival of larger grey squirrels from America.

The problem isn't that grey squirrels attack their red cousins. The problem is food. Greys can eat hazelnuts and acorns when they are still tough, whereas reds can only eat these nuts when they're soft and ripe. So the greys get their fill first, and there's not much left for the reds. So thorough are the greys in cleaning up, that once they arrive in an area the reds are usually gone within about 15 years.

One place where reds can do well is pine plantations, as they are more adept than greys at getting the seeds out of pine cones. However, even this advantage is threatened, as in recent years the indomitable and adaptable greys have started learning the cone seed-popping technique.

life) are available from several Scottish harbour towns, and we give details of these trips throughout this book.

Plants

In any part of Britain, the best places to see wildflowers are in areas that evade large-scale farming. For example, in the chalky hill country of southern England and the limestone areas further north (such as the Peak District and Yorkshire Dales), many fields erupt with great profusions of cowslips and primroses in April and May. Some flowers prefer woodland, and the best time to visit these areas is also April and May. This is because the leaf canopy of the woods has at that time not fully developed, and this allows sunlight to break through to encourage plants such as bluebells (a beautiful and internationally rare species).

Another classic British plant is gorse – you can't miss the swathes of this spiky bush in heath areas, most notably in the New Forest in southern England. Legend says that it's the season for kissing when gorse blooms. Luckily, its vivid yellow flowers show year-round.

In contrast, the blooming season for heather is quite short. On the Scottish mountains, the Pennine moors of northern England, and Dartmoor in the south, the wild hill-country is covered in a riot of purple in August and September.

Although the tree you're most likely to see as you travel through Britain is the pine, most pines are non-native and recently planted, harbouring little in the way of wildlife. In some parts of Scotland, stands of indigenous Caledonian can still be seen, while across Britain natural deciduous trees include oak, ash, hazel and rowan. The New Forest in southern England and the Forest of Dean on the Wales–England border are examples of this type of habitat. The seeds and leaves of these trees support a vast range of insects and birds, and fortunately for biodiversity more of these species are planted these days, instead of the somewhat ugly Scandinavian conifers.

NATIONAL PARKS

Way back in 1810, poet and outdoor lover William Wordsworth suggested that the Lake District should be 'a sort of national property, in which every man has a right'. More than a century later, the Lake District became a

www.wildlifetrusts.org
.uk – site for numerous
local trusts which make
up the national Wildlife
Trusts organisation,
whose key aims include
habitat conservation and
environmental education
for young people.

A great series of handy
wildlife guides (*Trees,
Birds, Wild Flowers,
Insects* etc) is produced
by the Wildlife Trusts
(www.wildlifetrusts.org
.uk). Proceeds from sales
support environmental
and educational
campaigns.

BRITAIN'S WORLD HERITAGE SITES

Unesco's World Heritage Sites are places of great environmental or cultural significance. There are around 700 sites globally. Twenty-five are in the UK and its overseas territories. Britain's include:

Bath Georgian city (p260)
Blaenavon Industrial Landscape (p861)
Blenheim Palace (p349)
Canterbury Cathedral sites (p182)
Caernarfon (p736), **Conwy** (p733),
Beaumaris (p738) **& Harlech Castles** (p727)
Derwent Valley Mills
Dorset & East Devon Coast (p279)
Durham Castle (p623) and Cathedral (p622)
Edinburgh Old (p749) and New Towns (p755)
New Lanark (p793)
Greenwich Maritime sites (p143)

Hadrian's Wall (p626)
Ironbridge Gorge (p386)
Kew Royal Botanic Gardens (p145)
Liverpool Commercial Centre & Waterfront (p570)
Orkney Neolithic sites (p916)
Saltaire (p506)
St Kilda (island west of Scotland)
Stonehenge (p240) **& Avebury** (p246)
Studley Royal Park & Fountains Abbey
(p532)
Tower of London (p134)
Westminster Palace & Westminster Abbey
(p126)

Whenever you visit a national park in England and Wales, look out for the excellent series of *Official National Park Guides*, published by Pevensey Press (David & Charles), celebrating the landscape and history with stunning photos and informative text.

national park (although quite different from Wordsworth's vision), along with the Brecon Beacons, Cairngorms, Dartmoor, Exmoor, Loch Lomond and the Trossachs, New Forest, Norfolk and Suffolk Broads, Northumberland, North York Moors, Peak District, Pembrokeshire Coast, Snowdonia and Yorkshire Dales. The South Downs in southern England is set to become Britain's next national park, due for completion in 2006.

Combined, Britain's national parks now cover over 10% of the country. It's an impressive total, but the term 'national park' can cause confusion. First, these areas are not state owned: nearly all land is private, belonging to farmers, companies, estates and conservation organisations. Second, they are not total wilderness areas, as in many other countries. In Britain's national parks you'll see roads, railways, villages and even towns. Development is strictly controlled, but about 250,000 people live and work inside national-park boundaries. Some of them work in industries such as quarrying, which ironically does great damage to these supposedly protected landscapes. On the flip side, these industries provide vital jobs (although sometimes for people outside the park), and several wildlife reserves have been established on former quarry sites.

Despite these apparent anomalies, national parks still contain vast tracts of wild mountains and moorland, rolling downs and river valleys, and other areas of quiet countryside, all ideal for long walks, cycle rides, easy rambles, sightseeing or just lounging around. To help you get the best from the parks, they all have information centres, and all provide

National Park	Features	Activities	Best Time to Visit	Page
Brecon Beacons	great green ridgelines, waterfalls; Welsh mountain ponies, red kites, buzzards, peregrine falcons, otters, kingfishers, dinosaurs	horse riding, cycling, caving, canoeing, hang-gliding	Mar & Apr – spring lambs shaking their tails	p689
Cairngorms	soaring snowy peaks, pine forests: ospreys, pine martens, wildcats, grouse, capercaillies	skiing, bird-watching, walking	Feb – for the snow	p874
Dartmoor	wild heath, marshy moorland: Dartmoor ponies, deer, otters, badgers, rabbits, buzzards, peregrine falcons, sheep	walking, horse riding	May & Jun – wildflowers in full bloom	p304
Exmoor	craggy sea cliffs, sweeping moors; native, wild red deer, Exmoor ponies, horned sheep	horse riding, walking	Sep – heather in bloom	p274
Lake District	majestic fells, rugged mountains, glassy lakes: ospreys, red squirrels, waterfowl, sparrowhawks, sheep, England's only golden eagles	walking, cycling, water sports	Sep & Oct – autumn colours abound, and summer crowds have left	p586
Loch Lomond & Trossachs	sparkling lochs, brooding mountains: deer, squirrels, badgers, foxes, buzzards, otters	climbing, walking, cycling	Sep & Oct – after the summer rush	p818
New Forest	woodlands and heath: wild ponies, otter, owl, Dartford warbler, southern damselfly	walking, cycling, horse riding	Apr-Sep – wild ponies are grazing	p209

various recreational facilities (trails, car parks, campsites etc) for visitors. It's worth noting also that there are many beautiful parts of Britain that are not national parks (such as mid-Wales, the North Pennines and many parts of Scotland). These can be just as good for outdoor activities or simply exploring by car or foot, and are often less crowded than the popular national parks.

ENVIRONMENTAL ISSUES

With Britain's long history of human occupation, it's not surprising that the land's appearance is almost totally the result of people's interactions with the environment. Ever since Neolithic farmers learnt how to make axes, trees have been cleared so that crops could be planted – a trend that has continued into our own time. In Scotland particularly, the Clearances of the 18th century (see p894) meant that people were moved off the land to make room for sheep, who nibbled to death any saplings brave enough to try growing on the mountainsides. Today, the Highlands is undoubtedly a wilderness, a place of stunning and rugged beauty, but don't be under any impression that it's 'natural' or 'unspoilt'.

Even more dramatic environmental changes hit rural areas after WWII, especially in England, when a drive to be self-reliant in food meant new farming methods. This changed the landscape from a patchwork of small fields to a scene of vast prairies – walls were demolished, trees felled, ponds filled, wetlands drained and, most notably, hedgerows ripped out.

DID YOU KNOW?

Although national parks are not owned by the state, large sections of several national parks are owned by the National Trust (NT) – one of the largest charities in Britain – but the NT has no formal link with national park administrative bodies.

National Park	Features	Activities	Best Time to Visit	Page
Norfolk & Suffolk Broads	expansive shallow lakes and marshlands: water lilies, wildfowl, otters	walking, boating most active	Apr & May – birds	p476
Northumberland	high and wild moors of heather and gorse: black grouse, red squirrels, sheep	walking, climbing, cycling	spring – lambs & Sep – heather in bloom	p635
North York Moors	heather-clad moors and deep green valleys with lonely farms and isolated villages: curlews, golden plovers	walking, cycling heather in bloom	Aug & Sep – purple	p538
Peak District	rolling hills, limestone caverns: jackdaws, kestrels, grouse, rabbits, foxes, badgers, and – of course – sheep	walking, cycling, hang-gliding	Apr & May – newborn lambs everywhere	p435
Pembrokeshire Coast	wave-ravaged shoreline of cliffs and beaches: puffin, fulmar, shearwater, grey seal, dolphin, porpoise	walking, kayaking, coasteering, mountain biking, horse riding	Apr & May – spring flowers clinging to clifftops	p670
Snowdonia	major mountain ranges, lakes and estuaries: wild goats, choughs, red kites, curlews, Snowdon lilies, buzzards, polecats	walking, cycling, canoeing, sailing, horse riding	May-Sep – summit temperatures mellow out	p716
Yorkshire Dales	limestone hills and lush valleys (dales) cut through by rugged stone walls and spotted with the faded, spectral grandeur of monastic ruins	walking, cycling	Apr & May	p510

In most cases, hedgerows were a few metres wide, a dense network of bushes, shrubs and trees that stretched across the countryside protecting fields from erosion, supporting a varied range of flowers and providing shelter for numerous insects, birds and small mammals. But in the rush to improve farm yields, thousands of miles of hedgerow have been destroyed since 1950. And the destruction continues – from 1984 to 2002, another 25% disappeared. However, farmers are now encouraged to 'set aside' hedges and other uncultivated areas as havens for wildlife, so the tide might be turning – albeit very slowly.

Ironically, despite this farming development, the food produced is often of dubious quality, as simple realities like tasteless carrots or national emergencies like the 'mad cow' disease of the 1990s clearly show. But you can't blame the farmers – well, not all of them. They have a living to earn, and are often encouraged to act in environmentally irresponsible ways by misguided directives (and vast subsidies) from the UK government and the EU.

Naturally enough, environmental issues are not exclusive to rural areas. In Britain's town and cities, topics such as air pollution, light pollution, levels of car use, road building, airport construction, public-transport provision, household waste recycling and so on are never far from the political agenda. Some might say they're not near enough to the top of the list, and the main political parties certainly show a lack of real engagement. However, apathy abounds in most areas; for example, the Green Party enjoyed only modest increased support in the council elections of 2004.

Meanwhile, back in rural Britain, hot environmental issues include farming methods such as irrigation, monocropping, pesticide use and the intensive rearing of cows, sheep and other stock. The result: rivers run dry, fish are poisoned by runoff, food quality is questionable, and vast fields consist of one type of grass, with not another plant to be seen. These 'green deserts' support no insects, which in turn means populations of some wild bird species dropped by an incredible 70% from 1970 to 1990. This is not a case of old wizened peasants recalling the idyllic days of their forebears; you only have to be over 30 in Britain to remember a countryside where birds such as skylarks or lapwings were visibly much more numerous.

But all is not lost. In the face of apparently overwhelming odds, Britain still boasts a great biodiversity, and some of the best wildlife habitats are protected to a greater or lesser extent, thanks to the creation of national parks and similar conservation zones – often within areas privately owned by conservation campaign groups. These groups include the Wildlife Trusts, Woodland Trust, National Trust and Royal Society for the Protection of Birds. Many of these areas are open to the public – they're ideal spots for walking, bird-watching or simply enjoying the peace and beauty of the countryside.

Also on the plus side, and especially important for an island such as Britain, sea protection is better than it's ever been. Major efforts been made to stem the flow of sewage into the sea. Oil spills still occur, but the clean-up process is quick and efficient. While some coastal areas may still be dirty and polluted, there are many other areas (around Southwest England, and much of Wales and Scotland, for example) where the water is clear and many popular holiday beaches are proud holders of 'blue flag' awards. These awards show they meet international standards of cleanliness – on the sand and in the waves. The birds and whales like clean water too, the tourists are happy, the locals make some money and the scenery is stunning. Everybody wins!

Food & Drink

Britain once boasted a cuisine so undesirable that there was no equivalent term in the language for *bon appétit*, but these days it's easy to find decent food. For every greasy spoon and fast-food joint, there's a pub or restaurant serving up enticing local specialities – and even if you're travelling in Britain on a tight budget, tasty eating definitely won't break the bank.

Having said that, Britain's culinary heritage of ready-sliced white bread, fatty meats and veg boiled to death, all washed down by tea with four sugars, remains firmly in place in many parts of the country. And that's before we get on to treats like pork scratchings and deep-fried Mars bars. (The latter gourmet offering was invented in Glasgow, so perhaps it's no surprise that Scotland, with the help of high cigarette and alcohol consumption, has one of the worst rates of heart disease in Europe.)

But to a large extent, food in Britain is changing for the better, and it's largely thanks to outside influences. Chinese and Indian restaurants have been around since the 1960s, and in more recent times dishes from Thailand and other countries east of Suez have become available, too. Closer to home, pastas, pizzas and Mediterranean specialities are commonplace in restaurants, but also in everyday pubs and cafés.

The overall effect of these influences has been the introduction of new techniques (like steaming) and revolutionary ingredients (like crisp, fresh vegetables) in British restaurants. We've also seen the creation of 'modern British cuisine', where even humble bangers and mash rise to new heights when handmade thyme-flavoured sausages are paired with lightly chopped fennel and organic new potatoes.

And finally – it's official – vegetarianism is no longer weird. Many restaurants have at least a token vegetarian dish (another meat-free lasagne, anyone?) but better places offer more-imaginative choices. Vegans will find the going tough, except at dedicated vegetarian-vegan restaurants – where possible we recommend good options throughout this book.

www.deliaonline.com is the site of Delia Smith – leading kitchen guru of the 1980s and '90s, and still going strong today. Come here for Yorkshire pudding recipes, ingredient advice and cooking tips.

Nigella Lawson snatched the culinary crown from Delia some time around the turn of the millennium, thanks to a no-nonsense style and outright seduction with recipes like chicken in Coca-Cola. See www.nigella.com.

STAPLES & SPECIALITIES

In the view of many outsiders, a typical British dinner is a plate of roast beef. There's some truth in this, but it's more of an English tradition than a British one (and is also why the French call English people *'les rosbif'*). Meat consumption took a bit of a knock in 2000 and 2001 following 'mad cow' scares and the foot-and-mouth outbreak, but good-quality roasts from well-reared cattle now grace menus everywhere from Cornwall to the Highlands, and are well worth sampling. Perhaps the most famous beef of all comes from Scotland's Aberdeen Angus cattle, while the best-known food from Wales is lamb (however, a lowly vegetable, the leek, is a national emblem – along with the daffodil). For a change from beef and lamb, try venison (usually from red deer); it's readily available in Scotland, as well as in parts of Wales and England – most notably in the New Forest.

The traditional accompaniment for beef is Yorkshire pudding. It's simply roast batter, but very tasty when properly cooked. In many pubs and cafés, especially in northern England, you can buy a big bowl-shaped Yorkshire pudding, filled with meat stew, beans, vegetables or – in these multicultural days – curry. Another local speciality in northern England is Cumberland sausage – a tasty mix of minced meat and herbs so large it has to be spiralled to fit on your plate. Cook sausage and Yorkshire pud together and you have another classic British dish: toad-in-the-hole.

DID YOU KNOW?
In Yorkshire, the eponymous pudding is traditionally eaten *before* the main meal, usually with gravy. This harks back to days of yore, when food was scarce. The pudding was a stomach-filler, so you then didn't mind so much about the tiny piece of meat on your platter.

DID YOU KNOW?

Although top-notch fish and chips can be found in many places, the best you can say about some other 'chippies' is that they provide cheap piles of stodge. Perhaps that's why curry is now Britain's most popular takeaway.

A most popular meal, all across Britain, is fish and chips. It's served in pubs and cafés and is available from takeaways. Sometimes it's greasy and tasteless (especially once you get far from the sea), but at towns with salt in the air this deep-fried delight is always worth trying. Other seafood specialities include Norfolk crab, Northumberland kippers, and jellied eels in London, while restaurants in Scotland, West Wales and Southwest England regularly conjure up prawns, lobsters, oysters, mussels and scallops.

A British lunch-time speciality – especially in pubs – is the ploughman's lunch. Originally a lump of cheese and a lump of bread, this meal has been smartened up to include butter, salad, pickled onion, dressings and a selection of cheeses. You'll also find other variations – farmer's lunch (bread and chicken), stockman's lunch (bread and ham), Frenchman's lunch (brie and baguette) and fisherman's lunch (you guessed it, bread and fish).

Feel like something more straightforward, more fundamental, more earthy to spread on your toast? Look out for Marmite – a dark and pungent yeast extract that generations of little Britons either hated with a passion or thrived on through childhood. For some, it stays a favourite through adulthood too: Marmite on toast is popular at breakfast and especially great for late-night munchies.

Like the taste of meat, but don't like the idea of battery pens? Click on www.farmgatedirect .com – a list of lamb, veal, beef, chicken and salmon producers approved by the RSPCA.

For cheese and bread in a different combination, try Welsh rarebit (originally called Welsh rabbit) – a sophisticated variation of cheese on toast, seasoned and flavoured with butter, milk and sometimes a little beer. Other traditional Welsh dishes include *bara brith* (spicy fruit loaf), *cawl* (a thick vegetable broth, often flavoured with meat) and *laverbread* – not a bread at all, but seaweed that is often served mixed up with oatmeal and bacon on toast, a surprisingly tasty combination.

In Scotland, instead of toast (or fried bread) at breakfast, you might get oatcakes – in sweet and salty varieties. Scones are larger, and Scottish bakeries usually offer milk scones, tattie scones and griddle scones as well as plain varieties. *Bannocks* (a cross between scones and pancakes), shortbread (a sweet biscuit) and Dundee cake (a rich fruit mix topped with almonds) are highly recommended. Also look out for Scotch broth (a thick soup made with barley, lentils and mutton stock), sometimes offered as a starter, but filling enough as a meal in itself. Another sturdy Scottish soup is cock-a-leekie, made from chicken and leeks.

Of course, the Scottish food that everyone knows is haggis. It was traditionally a poor man's sausage, made from a sheep's stomach filled with

---

BRITISH BREAKFASTS

If you stay in B&Bs or visit cafés during your visit to Britain, as you surely will, you'll just as surely come across the phenomenon known as the 'full breakfast'. This usually consists of bacon, sausages, eggs, tomatoes, mushrooms, baked beans and fried bread. In B&Bs it's preceded by cereals, served with tea or coffee, and followed by toast, butter, jam and marmalade. In northern Britain (if you're really lucky) you might also be served black pudding – a mixture of meat, blood and fat, served in slices.

If you don't feel like eating half a farmyard, it's quite OK to ask for just the eggs and tomatoes. In Scotland, you might get oatcakes instead of fried bread, and porridge instead of Cocopops – although you'll have to order it the night before (good porridge can't be rushed). Some B&Bs and hotels offer other alternatives such as kippers (smoked fish) or a 'continental breakfast', which completely omits the cooked stuff and may add something really exotic like croissants or fresh fruit.

> **NAME THAT PASTY**
>
> The Cornish pasty – a mix of cooked vegetables wrapped in pastry – is now available everywhere in Britain, far beyond its original homeland of Cornwall. It's often available in meat varieties too, much to the chagrin of Cornish purists. Invented long before Tupperware, the pasty was an all-in-one-lunch pack that tin miners could carry underground and leave on a ledge ready for mealtime. So that pasties weren't mixed up, they were marked with owners' initials – always at one end, so the miner could eat half and safely leave the rest to snack on later, without it mistakenly disappearing into the mouth of a workmate. And before going back to the surface, the miners traditionally left the last corner of the pasty as a gift for the spirits of the mine (who were known as 'knockers'), to ensure a safe shift the next day.

minced meat, oatmeal and various other bits of the sheep, then roasted. Some pubs and restaurants in Scotland serve very good haggis, and it's also available deep-fried with chips at takeaways. For more juicy details see the boxed text, p764.

Scottish salmon is well known, and available everywhere in Britain smoked or poached, but there's a big difference between bland and fatty farmed salmon and the lean and tasty wild version. The latter is more expensive, but as well as the taste, there are also sound environmental reasons for preferring the nonfarmed variety.

Kippers are another Scottish dish, and you may also find Arbroath smokies (lightly smoked fresh haddock) on the menu north of the border. Other fishy flavours include herrings in oatmeal, which is good if you don't mind the bones. If you're feeling really brave, try *krappin heit* – cod's head stuffed with oatmeal and fish livers.

DRINKS

A nice cup of tea might be the favourite British drink, but a nice pint of beer isn't far behind. Brands like Fosters and Budweiser have a major hold on the market, so foreigners can at least be assured of familiar tipples, but as you travel around Britain it's definitely worth exploring beyond the easily recognised names and trying some of the local brew.

British beer is usually brown in colour and often called 'ale' or 'bitter' (the yellow-coloured beer found in most other parts of the world is usually called 'lager' to distinguish it from the native variety), and beer made and served by traditional methods is known as 'real ale'. This is the stuff you should try. But be ready! Your first taste may come as a shock – a warm, flat and expensive shock. This is partly to do with Britain's climate, and partly with the beer being served by hand-pump rather than gas-pressure. But after a few mouthfuls you'll notice the most important feature: the integral flavour. British beer fans savour the complex tastes and aromas of regional varieties in the same way wine buffs love to sample a good Shiraz or Chardonnay. And the flavour is why traditional British real ale *doesn't need* to be chilled or fizzed. Drink a cheap lager that has sat in its glass for an hour and you'll find it has very little actual taste.

A final key feature of real ale is that it must be looked after (that's why many pubs don't serve it), so beware of pubs where staff give the barrels as much care as they give the cigarette machine. There's nothing worse than a bad pint of real ale – you might as well have a bottle of Bud.

The average price of a pint of beer is around £2.25. You'll pay under £2 in some areas (northwest England enjoys the cheapest booze in the country) and up to £3 in smarter pubs in London and southeast England.

Rick Stein is a TV chef, energetic restaurateur and real-food evangelist. His book, *Food Heroes*, praises the numerous small-scale producers around the country, their produce ranging from organic veg to sausages made from free-roaming wild boar.

Tipplers' favourite tomes include the annual *Good Beer Guide to Great Britain* (produced by the Campaign for Real Ale), which steers you to the best beers and the pubs that serve them.

Due to demand, lagers tend to cost about 10% more. If bitter or lager doesn't tickle your palate, try cider – available in sweet and dry 'scrumpy' varieties. On hot summer days, go for shandy – a mix of bitter or lager and lemonade.

Many foreigners (and many Brits) are surprised to learn that over 250 vineyards exist in Britain– the vast majority are in England, and many of these are very small concerns – but it's rare to find English wine in pubs. (We're talking about wine made from grapes here – there's a number of places across Britain making and selling great wines made from ingredients like elderflower or fruit.) The best places to find English wine (or, in a few instances, Welsh wine) are large supermarkets or specialist wine shops. Avoid at all costs 'British' wine – this is an industrial concoction made in factories from French grape concentrate. For more details see www.english-wine.com. The largest and best-known vineyard is Denbies; their highly rated produce is found in fine restaurants and gets snapped up for home consumption by savvy mail-order customers.

The usual arrays of gin, vodka, rum and so on are served in pubs and bars (in 35mL shots), but the spirit most visitors associate with Britain – and especially Scotland – is whisky (spelt without an 'e' if it's Scottish). Over 2000 brands are produced, but the two main kinds are single malt, made from malted barley; and blended whisky, from unmalted grain blended with malts. Single malts are rarer (there are only about 100 brands) and more expensive.

When ordering a dram in Scotland remember to ask for whisky – only the English and other foreigners say 'Scotch' (what else would you be served in Scotland?). And if you're bemused by the wide choice, ask to try a local whisky – although if your budget is low, you might want to check the price first. A measure of blended whisky will cost around £1.50 to £2.50, and a straightforward single malt around £3, while a rare classic could be £10 or more.

WHERE TO EAT & DRINK

There's a huge choice of places to eat in Britain, and this section outlines just some of your options. For details on opening times see Business Hours on p951. The tricky issue of tipping is covered under Money on p958, while some pointers on restaurants' attitudes to kids are under Children on p952.

For picnics or self-catering, markets can be a great place for food bargains – everything from dented tins of tomatoes for 1p (mmm) to home-baked cakes and organic goats' cheese. Farmers' markets are a great way for producers to sell good wholesome food direct to consumers, with both sides avoiding supermarkets.

Cafés & Teashops

The traditional British café is nothing like its Continental European namesake. Most are basic places serving basic food. And the usual café accent is often omitted too; it's pronounced 'caffy', or shortened to 'caff'. Meals like meat pie or omelette with chips cost around £3. Sandwiches, cakes and other snacks are £1 to £2.

Some cafés definitely earn their 'greasy spoon' handle, while others are neat and friendly. Smarter cafés are called teashops, and you might pay a bit more for extras like tablecloths, twee décor and table service. In country areas, cafés cater for tourists, walkers, cyclists and so on, and in summer they're open every day. Like B&Bs, good cafés are a wonderful institution and always worth a stop.

The *Good Pub Guide* details thousands of establishments across the country, rated for the quality of their drinks, food, service and atmosphere – from the finest country inns to humble local watering holes.

The Campaign for Real Ale (www.camra.org.uk) promotes the understanding of traditional British beer – and recommends good pubs that serve it. Look for endorsement stickers on pub windows.

DID YOU KNOW?

Denbies' wine originates from the same chalky soil as that found in the Champagne region of France. Thanks to strata dipping under the English Channel, and happily for tipplers, this means top-class wine-growing conditions in both countries. For more corking facts see www .denbiesvineyard.co.uk

In most cities and towns you'll find American-flavoured coffee shops and Euro-style café-bars serving decent lattes and espressos, and bagels or ciabattas rather than beans on toast. Some of these places even have outside chairs and tables – brave considering the narrow pavements and inclement weather much of Britain enjoys.

Restaurants

There are many excellent restaurants in Britain. London has scores of eateries that could hold their own in major cities worldwide, while places in Bath, Cardiff, Leeds, Manchester and Edinburgh give the capital a fair run for its money (actually, often for rather less money). We've taken great pleasure in seeking out some of the best and best-value restaurants in Britain, and in recommending a small selection throughout this book.

Prices vary considerably across the country, with a main course in a straightforward restaurant costing around £7 to £10, rising to £15 or £20 at good-quality places. Utterly excellent food, service and surroundings can be enjoyed for £30 to £50.

It's worth noting that many – but not all – restaurants these days have no-smoking areas. So if you don't want your meal ruined by someone else's smoke, choose carefully.

Pubs & Bars

The pub is one of Britain's finest social institutions, although the rise in popularity of both dinner parties and DVD mean Brits increasingly drink at home these days.

Britain has scores of splendid pubs, although in recent years many traditional favourites have been turned into chain outlets with infantile names (the Slug & Lettuce, the Floozy & Firkin), or fake Irish or Australian watering holes (O'Neill's, Walkabout Inns). But despite this disquieting move, many independent pubs survive and thrive, and we take great pleasure in listing some good ones throughout this book. From a charming rural pub in Devon to a classic Edwardian drinking palace in Edinburgh, you'll find many memorable places in which to enjoy a pint or two.

The difference between pubs and bars is sometimes vague, but generally bars are smarter, larger and louder than pubs, with a younger crowd. Drinks are more expensive too, unless there's a gallon-of-vodka-and-Red-Bull-for-a-fiver promotion – which there often is.

Farmers' markets are not a rural thing – there are almost 20 in London alone. Find the one nearest you at www.farmersmarkets.net.

The Wines of Britain & Ireland by Stephen Skelton, a handy paperback published in 2001, is by far the best guide available by the acknowledged expert on the subject.

THE OLDEST PUB

Studious drinkers are often surprised to learn that the word 'pub', although apparently steeped in history, dates only from the 19th century. But places selling beer have been around for much longer, and the 'oldest pub in the country' is a hotly contested title. In Scotland old pubs include Stirling's Settle Inn (p835) and the Inn at Lathones (St Andrews), both around 400 years old, while the Blue Anchor, at Aberthaw, west of Cardiff, claims to be the oldest pub in Wales, dating from the 14th century. But it's in England where the competition is most serious.

One of England's oldest pubs, with the paperwork to prove it, is Ye Olde Trip to Jerusalem (p429) in Nottingham, which was serving ale to departing Crusaders in the 12th century. Other contenders sniff at this newcomer: Ye Olde Fighting Cocks (see p177) in St Albans (Hertfordshire) apparently dates back to the 8th century – although the 13th is more likely, while a fine old hotel called the Eagle & Child (p358) in Stow-on-the-Wold (Gloucestershire) claims to have been selling beer since AD 950.

But then back comes Ye Olde Trip with a counterclaim: one of its bars is in a cave that's hollowed out of living rock – and that's more than a million years old.

Perhaps the biggest difference is when it comes to food. In recent years, pubs in Britain have become a good-value option whether you're looking for a toasted sandwich or a three-course meal. Some began to specialise in excellent food, while maintaining their informal atmosphere – and bingo, the gastro-pub was born.

What makes a good pub? It's often hard to pin down. Friendly staff and a welcoming ambience are two important features – and this is the type of pub that we have often recommended in this book. But nothing beats the fun of doing your own research, so here are a few more things to look for:

- A good menu of snacks and meals, cooked on the premises, not shipped in by the truck-full and de-frozen in the microwave by untrained staff.
- Hand-pulled pumps to serve the beer. This means real ale, and a willingness on the part of the landlord to put in extra effort, which often indicates extra effort on food, atmosphere, cleanliness and so on.
- A choice of beers from local brewers. Classic names include the following: Adnams (eastern England), Aarkells (south and southwest England), Belhaven (Scotland), Black Sheep (north England), Caledonian (Scotland and north England), Fullers (southeast England), Greene King (east, central and south England), Hardys & Hansons (central England), Hook Norton (south England and Midlands), Jennings (northwest England), Marstons (south, central and north England), Orkney Brewery (Scotland), St Austell (Southwest England), Shepherd Neam (southeast England), Timothy Taylor (north England), Wadworth (west and south England), Youngs (southeast England). We're thirsty already.

England

ENGLAND

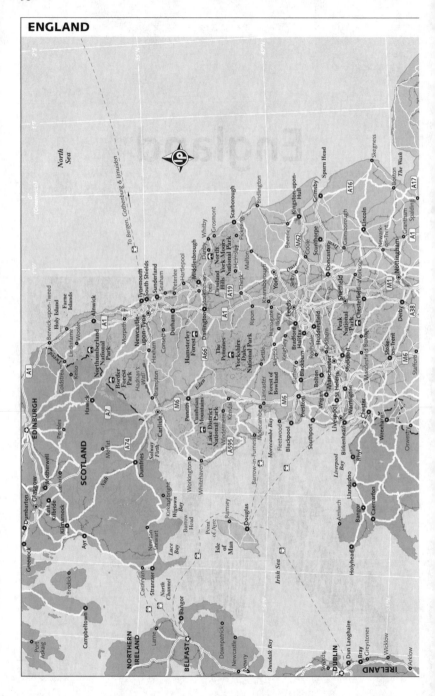

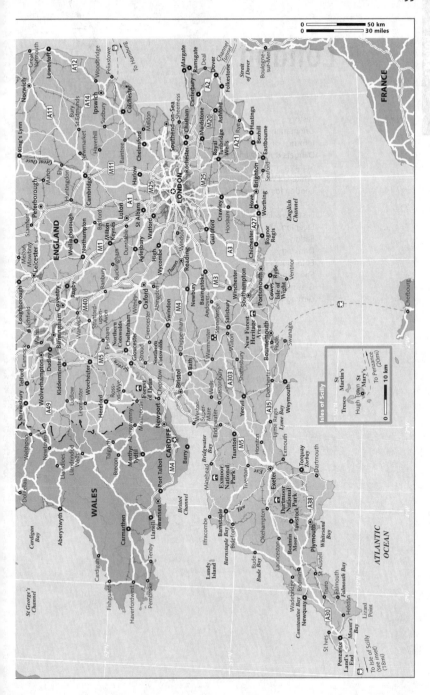

LONDON

London

CONTENTS

Britain abounds in enticing cities, towns, villages and hamlets but you won't fully appreciate any of them until you've got a handle on its colossal capital. London can be different things to different people but it will never leave you indifferent; whether you're fleeing its concrete immensity or dazzling in its lights, it's the essential reference for a trip to this island.

A rite of passage for Britons from every corner, London is also a cradle of multiculturalism. It is home to some seven million people representing 40 different ethnic groups speaking 300 languages. It's a kaleidoscope of different cultures, more fascinating with every twist.

It can feel dirty, polluted and overcrowded but don't let your first impressions colour your whole experience. Whatever you're after you'll find lots of it here. If history rings your bell you'll marvel at the gravitas of Westminster and Greenwich. Several of the world's finest museums and galleries compete for your attention with the icons of old-money London such as Harrods, Mayfair and the Ritz. Royal London beckons with airs, graces and traditions – but you might prefer to just soak up the atmosphere in a venerable old pub, atop a red double-decker bus or on a walking tour of your own.

Far from resting on its considerable laurels, London is the dynamo for some of the best and most progressive music, theatre, visual arts, fashion and gastronomy; you can indulge yourself with world-class events and experiences any night of the week. It might not swagger with the technicoloured exuberance of the 'swinging '60s' but it has long since got its mojo back.

HIGHLIGHTS

- Exploring almost a millennium of art at the **National Gallery** (p124)
- Soaking in the gravitas of **Westminster** (p126)
- Going to see **live bands** (p164)
- Being astonished at the **British Museum** (p131)
- Getting tipsy in a traditional **West End pub** (p160)

LONDON
★

■ TELEPHONE CODE: 020   ■ POPULATION: 7.2 MILLION   ■ AREA: 607 SQ MILES

LONDON

HISTORY

Celts first established themselves around a ford across the River Thames. However, it was the Romans who developed the square mile now known as the City of London (which lies within today's Greater London city – note the small 'c') with a crossing, near today's London Bridge, that served as the hub of their road system. By the end of the 3rd century AD 'Londinium' was almost as multicultural as it is today with 30,000 people of various ethnic groups (albeit all Roman citizens, of course) and temples dedicated to a large number of cults. Parts of London like Aldgate and Ludgate get their names from the gates of the original city walls built by the Romans. Internal strife and relentless barbarian attacks took their toll on the Romans, who abandoned Britain in the 5th century, reducing the conurbation to a sparsely populated backwater.

The Saxons then moved in, establishing farmsteads and villages, and their 'Lundenwic' prospered, becoming a large, well-organised town divided into 20 different wards. As the city grew in importance, it caught the eye of Danish Vikings who launched many invasions and razed the city in the 9th century. The Saxons held on until, finally beaten down in 1016, they were forced to accept the Danish leader Knut (Canute) as King of England, after which London replaced Winchester as its capital. In 1042 the throne reverted to the Saxon Edward the Confessor, whose main contribution to the city was the building of Westminster Abbey.

A dispute over his successor led to what's known as the Norman Conquest (Normans broadly being Vikings with shorter beards). When William the Conqueror won the watershed Battle of Hastings in 1066, he and his forces marched into London where he was crowned king. He built the White Tower (the core of the Tower of London), negotiated taxes with the merchants, and affirmed the city's independence and right to self-government.

The throne passed through various houses in the millennium or so since (the House of Windsor has warmed its cushion since 1910), but royal power has been concentrated in London since the 12th century.

From the 12th century to the late 15th century, London politics were largely taken up by a three-way power struggle between the monarchy, the church and city guilds.

The greatest threat to the burgeoning city was that of disease caused by unsanitary living conditions and impure drinking water. In 1348 rats on ships from Europe brought the bubonic plague, which wiped out a third of London's population of 100,000 over the following year.

Violence became commonplace in the hard times that followed. In 1381, miscalculating or just disregarding the mood of the nation, the king tried to impose a poll tax on everyone in the realm. Tens of thousands of peasants marched on London. Several ministers were murdered and many buildings razed before the so-called Peasants' Revolt ran its course. The ringleaders were executed, but there was no more mention of a poll tax (until Margaret Thatcher, not heeding the lessons of history, tried to introduce it in the 1980s).

Despite these setbacks, London was consolidated as the seat of law and government in the kingdom during the 14th century. An uneasy political compromise was reached between the factions, and the city expanded rapidly under the House of Tudor. The first recorded map of London was published in 1558, and John Stow produced the first comprehensive history of the capital in 1598.

The 'Great Plague' struck in 1665 and 100,000 Londoners perished by the time the winter cold arrested the epidemic. Just as the population considered a sigh of relief, another disaster struck.

The mother of all blazes, the Great Fire of 1666, virtually razed the place, destroying most of its medieval, Tudor and Jacobean architecture. One plus was that it created a blank canvas upon which master architect Christopher Wren could build his magnificent churches.

London's growth continued unabated and by 1700 it was Europe's largest city with 600,000 people. An influx of foreign workers brought expansion to the east and south, while those who could afford it headed to the more salubrious environs of the north and west, divisions that still largely shape London today.

Georgian London saw a great surge in creativity in architecture, music and art with the likes of Dr Johnson, Handel, Gainsborough and Reynolds enriching the city's culture while Georgian architects fashioned an elegant new metropolis. At the same time the gap between the rich and poor grew ever wider, and lawlessness was rife.

In 1837 18-year-old Victoria ascended the throne. During her reign (1837–1901), London became the fulcrum of the British Empire, which covered a quarter of the earth's surface. The Industrial Revolution saw the building of new docks and railways (including the first underground line in 1863), while the Great Exhibition of 1851 showcased London to the world. The city's population mushroomed from just over two million to 6.6 million during Victoria's reign.

Road transport was revolutionised in the early 20th century when the first motor buses were introduced and replaced the horse-drawn versions that had trotted their trade since 1829.

Although London suffered relatively minor damage during WWI, it was devastated by the Luftwaffe in WWII when huge swathes of the centre and East End were totally flattened and 32,000 people were killed. Ugly housing and low-cost developments were hastily erected in postwar London, and immigrants from around the world flocked to the city and changed its character forever.

The latest major disaster to beset the capital was the great smog on 6 December 1952, when a lethal combination of fog, smoke and pollution descended on the city and killed some 4000 people.

Prosperity gradually returned, and the creative energy that had been bottled up in the postwar years was suddenly unleashed. London became the capital of cool in fashion and music in the 'swinging '60s'.

The party didn't last long, however, and London returned to the doldrums in the harsh economic climate of the 1970s. Recovery began – for the business community at least – under the iron fist of Margaret Thatcher, elected Britain's first woman prime minister in 1979. Her monetarist policy and determination to crush socialism sent unemployment skyrocketing and her term was marked by civil unrest.

London got its first true mayor in 2000 when feisty 'Red' Ken Livingstone swept to victory on the promise that he would lock horns with the central government when it came to doing what was best for London.

TOP FIVE – OLD-FASHIONED LONDON
- **Ritz** (p148)
- **Fortnum & Mason** (p166)
- **Wallace Collection** (p140)
- **Buckingham Palace** (p128)
- **Inns of Court** (p132)

His big plan has been to improve public transport and reduce traffic congestion. Londoners voted for it but weren't too happy when he made moves to fix it. However, even the most cynical locals concede that Ken's controversial 'congestion tax' on vehicles entering central London has reduced the traffic jams, and the mayor has also followed through on his word to get the buses running on time.

ORIENTATION

The city's main geographical feature is the murky Thames, a river that was sufficiently deep (for anchorage) and narrow (for bridging) to attract the Romans here in the first place. It divides the city roughly into north and south.

The 'square mile' of the City of London – the capital's financial district – is counted as one of London's 33 council-run boroughs and is referred to simply as 'the City' (look for the capital 'C'). The M25 ring road encompasses the 607 sq miles that is broadly regarded as Greater London.

London's Underground railway ('the tube') makes this enormous city relatively accessible. The Underground map – now a London icon – is easy to use although geographically confounding. Most of the important sights, theatres, restaurants and even affordable places to stay lie within a reasonably compact rectangle formed by the tube's Circle Line (colour-coded yellow), which encircles central London just north of the river.

Londoners commonly refer to areas by their postcode. The letters correspond to compass directions from the centre of London, approximately St Paul's Cathedral. EC means East Central, W means West and so on. The numbering system after the letters is less helpful: 1 is the centre of the zone but after that it gets confusing.

LONDON IN...

Two Days

Start your express tour with a walk around **Westminster** (p126) and its sights. You don't need to visit the sights to soak up the atmosphere. Head to grandiose **Trafalgar Square** (p124), and the **National Gallery** (p124) for a squiz at its sensational collection. Catch a Routemaster open-backed bus into the heart of the West End and lunch in **Chinatown** (p130). Wander around **Soho** (p130) and **Covent Garden** (p130). On your way to **St Paul's Cathedral** (p133), have a look at **Somerset House** (p131) and stop for a cup of tea on its back terrace. Pull into the first traditional-looking pub you come across, peruse the listings and go to see a band.

Four Days

Visit the **British Museum** (p131), undergo some retail therapy, go to a football match and retire. Head 'sarf' of the river, have a go on the giant wheel, visit Charles Saatchi's 'Trophy Room' of contemporary Britart at the **Saatchi Gallery** (p137) and compare his collection with the fabulous **Tate Modern** (p136). Imagine Shakespeare at the **Globe Theatre** (p136). Get a big dollop of old London at **Borough Market** (p167) before heading to the hulking **Tower of London** (p134) for a history lesson. A riverside pub would be nice.

One Week

With the luxury of a week, go with the flow but try to see the following. **South Kensington** (p138) has three world-class museums and the inimitable **Harrods** (p166). The Victorian Valhalla of **Highgate Cemetery** (p141) is in north London but worth the trip. Don't miss **Portobello Rd Market** (p167) on the weekend. A day out in Greenwich – at the **National Maritime Museum** (p143) and on board **Cutty Sark** (p143) – will be well spent. You don't have to pay the exorbitant admission prices to get a feel for Royal London. Wander over to **Buckingham Palace** (p128) and **Kensington Palace** (p139), and around **St James's Park** (p128) and **Kensington Gardens** (p139). Marvel at outstanding smaller sights like **Sir John Soane's Museum** (p132) and the **Wallace Collection** (p140).

Maps

The *London A–Z* series produce a range of excellent maps and hand-held street atlases. Lonely Planet also publishes a *London City Map*. Stanfords' bookshop (right) is one of the best travel shops in the world.

INFORMATION
Bookshops

Books for Cooks (Map pp110-1; ☎ 7221 1992; 4 Blenheim Cres W11; ☻ Ladbroke Grove) What the label says.

Borders (Map pp118-20; ☎ 7292 1600; 203 Oxford St W1; ☻ Oxford Circus) Flagship of the huge nonunionising chain.

Forbidden Planet (Map pp118-20; ☎ 7836 4179; 179 Shaftesbury Ave; ☻ Leicester Square or Covent Garden) A trove of comics, sci-fi, horror and fantasy literature.

Foyle's (Map pp118-20; ☎ 7437 5660; 113-119 Charing Cross Rd WC2; ☻ Tottenham Court Road) Venerable and respected independent store with a broad range and a version of the old women's books specialist Silver Moon on the top floor.

Gay's the Word (Map pp108-9; ☎ 7278 7654; 66 Marchmont St WC1; ☻ Russell Square) Everything from advice on coming out to queer and lesbian literature.

Grant & Cutler (Map pp118-20; ☎ 7734 2012; 55-57 Great Marlborough St W1; ☻ Oxford Circus) The best foreign language store in town.

Helter Skelter (Map pp118-20; ☎ 7836 1151; 4 Denmark St WC2; ☻ Oxford Circus) Biographies, fanzines and rock literature.

Sportspages (Map pp118-20; ☎ 7240 9604; 94-96 Charing Cross Rd WC2; ☻ Leicester Square or Tottenham Court Road) For the inside track on sporting heroes, heroics and help on how to.

Stanfords (Map pp118-20; ☎ 7836 1321; 12-14 Long Acre W C2; ☻ Covent Garden) The grandaddy of travel bookstores.

Travel Bookshop (Map pp110-1; ☎ 7229 5260; 13 Blenheim Cres W11; ☻ Ladbroke Grove) This shop stocks the latest guidebooks, travel literature and antiquarian gems.

Waterstone's (Map pp118-20; ☎ 7851 2400; 203-206 Piccadilly W1; ☻ Piccadilly Circus) The best of this book-purveying giant.

Zwemmer Art & Architecture (Map pp118-20; ☎ 7240 4158; 24 Litchfield St WC2; ☻ Tottenham Court Road) Tomes of fine art here and photography and cinema across the road.

LONDON

Cultural Centres

Alliance Française (Map pp110-1; ☎ 7723 6439;
1 Dorset Sq NW1; ⊖ Marylebone) Organises French-
language classes, and social and cultural events.
British Council (Map pp118-20; ☎ 7930 8466;
10 Spring Gardens SW1; ⊖ Charing Cross) Can advise
foreign students on educational opportunities in Britain.

Emergency

Police/Fire/Ambulance (☎ 999)
Samaritans (☎ 08457 909 090)
Rape & Sexual Abuse Support Centre (☎ 8683 3300)

Internet Access

Cyberia (Map pp114-6; ☎ 7681 4223; 39 Whitfield St
W1; ⊖ Goodge Street)
easyEverything Victoria (Map p121; ☎ 7233 8456; 9-13
Wilton Rd SW1; ⊖ Victoria); Tottenham Court Road (Map
pp118-20; 9-16 Tottenham Court Rd; ⊖ Tottenham
Court Road) A chain with branches throughout central
London.
Internet Exchange (Map pp118-20; ☎ 7836 8636; 37
The Market WC2; ⊖ Covent Garden) Another ubiquitous
chain.
Internet Lounge (Map pp112-3; ☎ 7370 5742;
24a Earl's Court Gardens SW5; ⊖ Earl's Court)

Internet Resources

The Lonely Planet website (www.lonely
planet.com) offers a speedy link to many
of London's websites. You can also try the
following:
BBC London (www.bbc.co.uk/London/whereyoulive)
Evening Standard (www.thisislondon.co.uk)
Time Out (www.timeout.com)
UK Weather (www.met-office.gov.uk)

Laundry

Many hostels and some hotels have self-
service washing machines and dryers, and
nearly every main street has a laundrette.
The average cost of washing and drying a
single load of laundry is £3. Your lodging
will be able to guide you to the nearest
laundrette.

Media

The only true London paper is the *Evening
Standard*. This is a jingoistic tabloid that
hits the streets in early and late editions
throughout the day. *Metro* is a morning
freebie from the same publishing stable,
while *Time Out* (£2.20) is the local listing
guide par excellence – it's published every
Wednesday.

Medical Services

To find a local doctor or hospital, consult
the local telephone directory or call ☎ 100
(toll free). There is always one local chemist that opens 24 hours (see local newspapers or notices in chemist windows).
In the event of a dental crisis, phone the
Dental Emergency Care Service (☎ 7955 2186)
weekdays between 8.45am and 3.30pm, or
call into **Eastman Dental Hospital** (Map pp108-9;
☎ 7915 1000; 256 Gray's Inn Rd WC1; ⊖ King's Cross
St Pancras).

The following hospitals, among others,
have 24-hour accident and emergency units
should you need them:
Guy's Hospital (Map p117; ☎ 7955 5000; St Thomas St
SE1; ⊖ London Bridge)
Royal Free Hospital (Map pp106-7; ☎ 7794 0500;
Pond St NW3; ⊖ Belsize Park)
University College Hospital (Map pp108-9;
☎ 7387 9300; Grafton Way WC1; ⊖ Euston Square)

Money

There is a plentiful spread of banks and
ATMs across central London. Most of them
are linked to the international money systems such as Cirrus and Maestro. If you're
carrying cash (besides asking for trouble),
you won't have a problem changing it over
because banks, bureaux de change and
travel agents are tripping over themselves
to get your business. If you use bureaux de
change, make sure to check commission
rates *and* exchange rates, because some
can be extortionate.

There are 24-hour bureaus in Heathrow
Terminals 1, 3 and 4 (the one in Terminal
2 opens 6am to 11pm), in Gatwick's South
and North Terminals, and at Stansted. The
airport bureaus are good value; they charge
less than most high-street banks – usually
about 1.5% of the transaction value, with
a £3 minimum. The following are reliable
bureaus (both have outlets at Victoria train
station):
American Express (AmEx; Map pp118-20; ☎ 7930 4411;
6 Haymarket SW1; currency exchange 🕐 9am-6pm Mon-
Sat, 10am-5pm Sun; ⊖ Piccadilly Circus) Has branches all
around town.
Thomas Cook (Map pp114-6; ☎ 7853 6400;
30 St James's St SW1; 🕐 9am-5.30pm Mon, Tue, Thu &
Fri, 10am-5.30pm Wed, 9am-4pm Sat; ⊖ Green Park)
Also has branches around London.

(Continued on page 123)

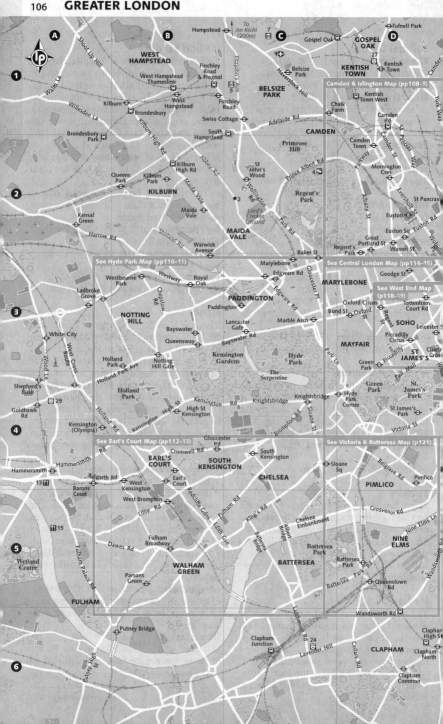

0 — 1 km
0 — 0.5 miles

INFORMATION
Royal Free Hospital.....................1 C1

SIGHTS & ACTIVITIES (pp124–46)
Abbey Rd Zebra Crossing.............2 C2
Design Museum..........................3 F4
Entrance to London Zoo..............4 C2
Freud Museum............................5 C1
Geffrye Museum.........................6 F2
Keat's House..............................7 C1
Tate Britain................................8 D4

SLEEPING (pp147–53)
Rotherhithe YHA Hostel..............9 G3

EATING (pp153–60)
Blue Print Café....................(see 3)
Brick Lane Beigel Bake..............10 F2
Bug Bar Restaurant & Lounge.....11 E6
Fifteen.....................................12 F2
Gate..13 A4
Real Greek................................14 F2
River Café................................15 A5

DRINKING (pp160–2)
Brixtonian Havana Club.............16 E6
Cantaloupe...............................17 F2
Captain Kidd............................18 G4
Dragon Bar...............................19 F2
Prospect of Whitby....................20 G3
Sosho......................................21 F2

ENTERTAINMENT (pp163–6)
333...22 F2
AMP Oval Cricket Ground.........23 E5
Battersea Arts Centre................24 C6
Brixton Academy.......................25 E6
Cargo......................................26 F2
Forum......................................27 D1
Hackney Ocean........................28 G1
Shepherd's Bush Empire............29 A4

SHOPPING (pp166–7)
Brick Lane Market.....................30 F2
Brixton Market..........................31 E6

0   500 m
0   0.25 miles

E   **F**   **G**   **H**

Caledonian Rd

Mackenzie Rd
Gough Rd
Westbourne Rd
Sheringham Rd
Furlong Rd
Highbury Corner
Highbury Pl
Hamilton Pl
St Paul's Rd **1**

BARNSBURY

Bride St
Ellington St
Highbury & Islington
Compton Rd
Cosser St

Caledonian Park

Brewery Rd
Roman Way
Arundel Sq
Arundel Pl
Highbury Station Rd
Laycock St
Upper St
Compton Ave
Canonbury Sq
Canonbury Rd
Alwyne Villas

Market Rd
Blundell St

Pentonville Prison
Caledonian Rd & Barnsbury

Orford Rd
Halton Rd
Scaton Rd

Belitha Villas
Barnsbury Park
Islington Park St
2
20

Huntingdon St
Thornhill Square
Bridgeman Rd
Barnsbury Square
Thornhill Rd
Bewdley St
Brooksby St
Lofting Rd
Barnsbury St
College Cross
Liverpool Rd
Florence St
Hawes St

Pembroke St
Carnoustie Drve
Ripplevale Gve.
ISLINGTON
Milner Sq
11 16
Almeida St
22
Essex Rd

Bingfield St
Benecroft Rd
Twyford St
Matilda St
Hemingford Rd
Richmond Ave
Gibson Sq
Theberton St
Gaskin St
Cross St
Packington St
Britannia Row **3**

Havelock St
Copenhagen St
KING'S CROSS
Barnard Park
Cloudesley Rd
Cloudesley St
Islington Green
24

Charlotte Tce
Cloudesley Pl
Batchelor St
Camden Passage
Charlton Pl
10
St Peter's St
Cruden St
Chantry St
Gerrard Rd
Noel Rd
Duncton St
Danbury St

Grand Union Canal

Carnegie St
Muriel St
Wynford Rd
Dewey Rd
Ritchie St
Tolpuddle St
Parkfield St
Duncan St
Vincent Tce
Ella St
Graham St

Wharfdale Rd
Chapel Market
Chapel Market
Islington High St
Angel **4**

King's Cross Station
York Way
Caledonia St
Killick St
Northdown St
Coller St
Cumming St
Donegal St
Rodney St
Cynthia St
Baron St
White Lion St
PENTONVILLE
Duncan Tce

St Pancras Station

King's Cross St Pancras
King's Cross Thameslink
Pentonville Rd
Penton Rise
Western Rise
Claremont Sq
Myddelton Sq
Chadwell St
Owen St
City Rd
Wakley St
Hall St
Moreland St **5**

Cheney Rd

Leeke St
Britannia St
Wicklow St
Lemon Rise
Percy Circus
Gt. Percy St
Amwell St
River St
Myddelton St
27
Rawstorne St
Spencer St
City University
Goswell Rd

St Chad's St
Swinton St
Acton St
Frederick St
Wharton St
Lloyd Sq
Lloyd Baker St
FINSBURY
Hardwick St
Percival St

Argyle St
Tonbridge St
Cromer St
Harrison St
Regent Sq
Sidmouth St
Ampton St
Margery St
Rosebery Ave
Skinner St
Myddelton St
Gloucester Way
Compton St
Aylesbury St
St John St
Dallington St
Sekforde St

17
6
St George's Gardens
Handel St
Heathcote St
Gray's Inn Rd
Calthorpe St
St. Andrew's Gardens
Guilt St
Wren St
Easton St
Exmouth Market
Spa Fields
Corporation Row
Northampton Row
Bowling Green
Hayward's Pl

St Pancras Coram's Fields
2
ST PANCRAS
St. George's Gardens
1
St. Andrew's Gardens
CLERKENWELL
Mount Pleasant (Postal Sorting Office)
14
Warner St
Bowling Green
In Porter St
Clerkenwell Rd
9
Gt. Sutton St
Northburgh St **6**

Brunswick Centre
Bernard St
Handel St
Guildford St
Doughty St
Roger St
Elm St
Millman St
Phoenix Pl
Mt Pleasant
Eyre St Hill
Back Hill
Herbal Hill
Farringdon La
Farringdon Rd

Russell Sq
Hospital for Sick Children

Bernard St

See Central London Map (pp114-15)

See Earl's Court Map (pp112–13)▶

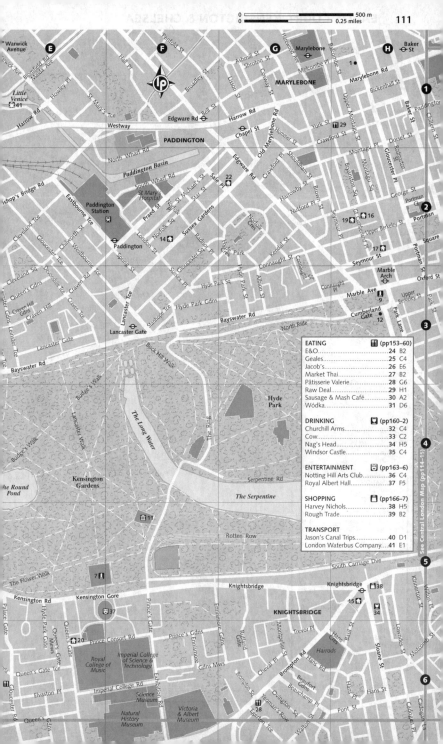

EATING 🍴 (pp153–60)
E&O.................................24 B2
Geales..............................25 C4
Jacob's.............................26 E6
Market Thai.......................27 B2
Pâtisserie Valerie...............28 G6
Raw Deal..........................29 H1
Sausage & Mash Café.........30 A2
Wódka.............................31 D6

DRINKING 🍷 (pp160–2)
Churchill Arms...................32 C4
Cow..................................33 C2
Nag's Head........................34 H5
Windsor Castle...................35 C4

ENTERTAINMENT 🎭 (pp163–6)
Notting Hill Arts Club..........36 C4
Royal Albert Hall................37 F5

SHOPPING 🛍 (pp166–7)
Harvey Nichols...................38 H5
Rough Trade.......................39 B2

TRANSPORT
Jason's Canal Trips..............40 D1
London Waterbus Company....41 E1

See Central London Map (pp114-15)

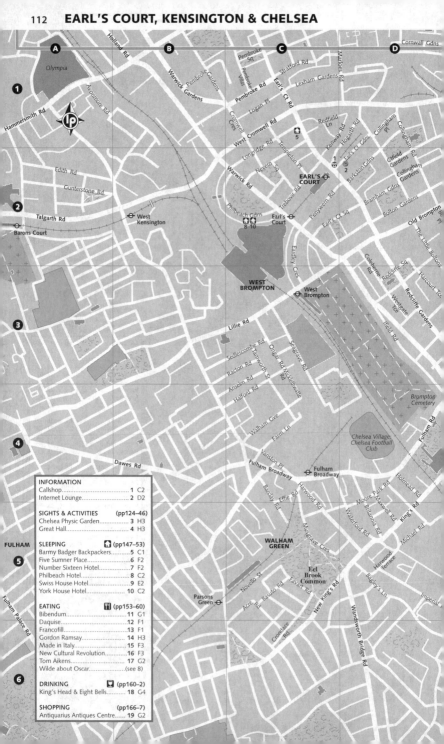

0   500 m
0   0.3 miles

See Hyde Park Map (pp110–11)

E Queen's Gdns

F Victoria & Albert Museum

G

H

Pont St

Cadogan Pl

Cheltenham

Natural History Museum

Gloucester Rd

Cromwell Rd

Thurloe Pl

Egerton Gdns

Egerton Terrace

Ovington St

Lennox Gdns

Clabon Rd

Cadogan Gdns

Cadogan Sq

Pavilion Rd

Sloane St

1

Ellis St

Sloane Tce

Cliveden

Gloucester Rd

Ctfield Rd

Gloucester Rd

arrington Gdns

Stanhope Gdns

Queen's Pway

Harrington Rd

Gre Pl

Thurloe St

Thurloe Sq

South Terrace

Walton St

Fitst St

Hasker St

Milner St

Moore St

Halsey St

Cadogan St

Sloane Sq

Lower Sloane St

Sloane Sq

12

South Kensington

Pelham St

Mossop St

Denyer St

Rawlings St

13

Draycott Ave

Sumner Pl

Onslow Sq

Pond St

Lucan Pl

Elystan Pl

Pelwyard

Sloane Ave

Whitehead's Gve

Draycott Pl

SOUTH KENSINGTON

6 **7**

Cale St

St Luke's St

Jubilee Pl

Markham St

Elystan Pl

Cheltenham Tce

Walpole St

Turks Row

Burton's Court

9

The Boltons

Drayton Gardens

Roland Gardens

Cranley Gdns

Neville St

Foulis Tce

Onslow Gdns

Fulham Rd

South Pde

Chelsea Sq

Manresa Rd

Dovehouse St

Sydney St

Britten St

Markham St

Radnor Walk

Shawfield St

17

CHELSEA

11

Ixworth Pl

Elystan St

Maxham St

Royal Ave

St Leonard's Tce

Ranelagh Gardens

2

Gunter Rd

Priory Wlk

Gilston Rd

Evelyn Gdns

Elm Park Gardens

Old Church St

Clyde St

Bramerton St

Glebe St

Flood Walk

Chelsea Manor St

Aloha Pl

Redburn St

Christchurch St

Royal Hospital Rd

West Rd

The St

19

3

Hollywood Rd

Cathcart Rd

Redcliffe Rd

Park Walk

Limerston St

Chelsea Gdns

Chelsea Park

Elm Park Gardens

Mulford St

Paultons Sq

Upper Cheyne Row

Phene St

Cheyne Gdns

Flood St

Swan Walk

Dilke St

14

Chelsea Embankment

3

15

16

Gertrude St

Lamont Rd

Langton St

The Vale

Paultons Sq

Upper Row

18

Beaufort St

King's Rd

See Victoria & Battersea Map (p121)

Cremorne Rd

Ann Ln

Cheyne Walk

Albert Bridge

Cheyne Walk

The Pde

4

Fernshaw Rd

Blantyre St

Edith Gve

Gunter Gve

Ashburnham Rd

Uverdale Rd

Tadema Rd

Battersea Church Rd

Battersea Bridge

Hester Rd

Anhalt Rd

Parkgate Rd

Carriage Dve West

Children's Zoo

4

Lost Rd

Chelsea Creek

Harbour Ave

Battersea Bridge Rd

Edro St

Ebbo St

Juer St

Worfield St

Parkgate Rd

Albert Bridge Rd

Battersea Park

Boating Lake

Telcot Rd

Westbridge Rd

Petworth St

BATTERSEA

Carriage Dve South

Prince of Wales Dve

Warriner Gardens

5

Parkham Surrey Ln

Obel St

Octavia St

Ursula St

Edna St

Camb Rd

Brynmaer Rd

Battersea Park Rd

Latchmore Rd

6

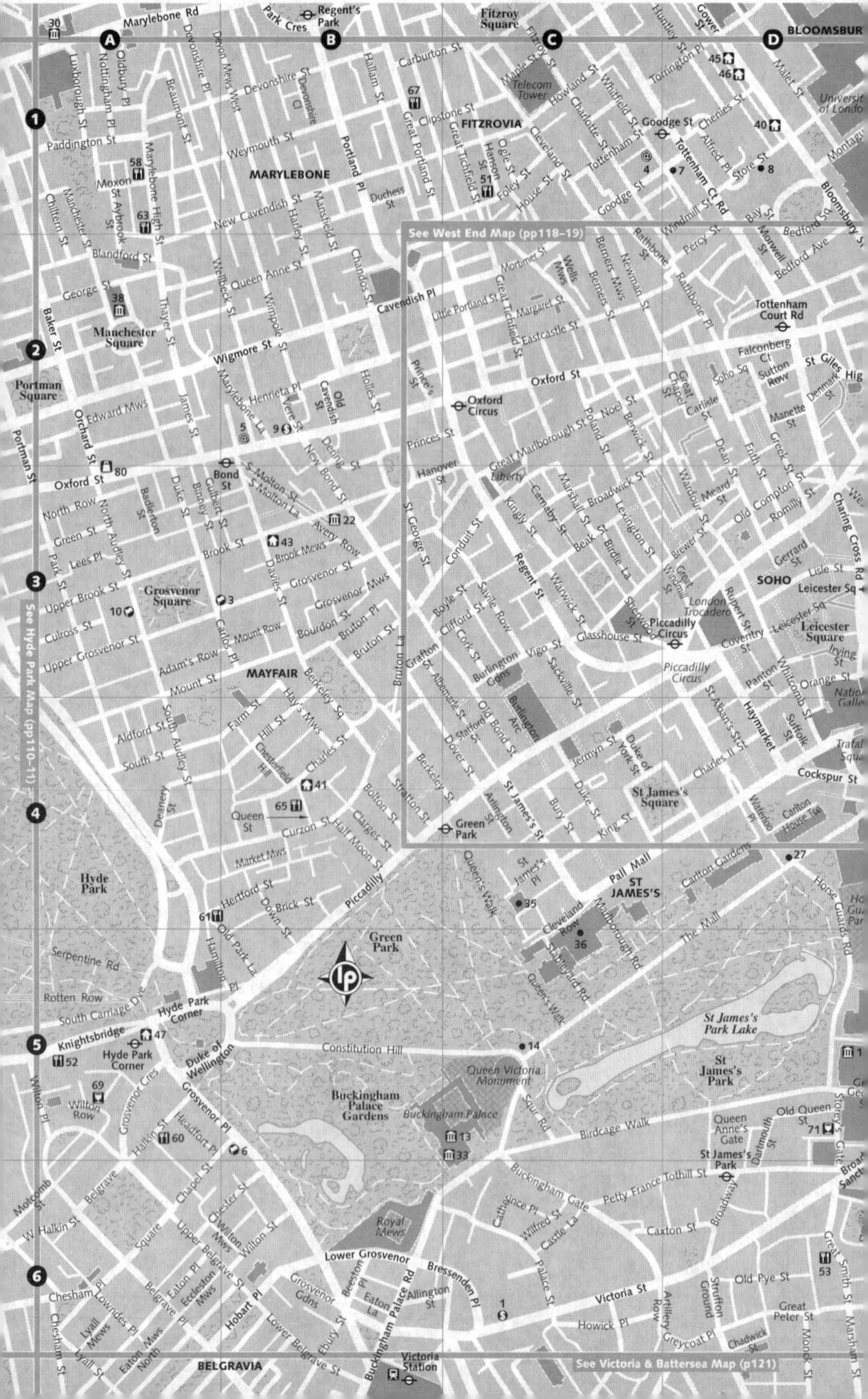

A
B
C
D
1
2
3
4
5
6
BLOOMSBURY
FITZROVIA
MARYLEBONE
MAYFAIR
SOHO
ST JAMES'S
BELGRAVIA
Fitzroy Square
Telecom Tower
Manchester Square
Portman Square
Grosvenor Square
Leicester Square
St James's Square
Hyde Park
Green Park
St James's Park
St James's Park Lake
Buckingham Palace Gardens
Buckingham Palace
Queen Victoria Monument
Royal Mews
Liberty
London Trocadero
Burlington Arc
Regent's Park
Goodge St
Tottenham Court Rd
Oxford Circus
Bond St
Piccadilly Circus
Green Park
Hyde Park Corner
St James's Park
Victoria Station
See West End Map (pp118–19)
See Hyde Park Map (pp110–11)
See Victoria & Battersea Map (p121)
Marylebone Rd
Park Cres
Devonshire Pl
Devon Mews West
Devonshire St
Carburton St
Hallam St
Great Portland St
Clipstone St
Great Titchfield St
Hanson St
Ogle St
Foley St
Howland St
Maple St
Charlotte St
Whitfield St
Cleveland St
Tottenham St
Goodge St
Tottenham Ct Rd
Chenies St
Alfred Pl
Store St
Torrington Pl
Huntley St
Gower St
Malet St
Montague
Bloomsbury St
Bedford Sq
Bedford Ave
Bay St
Morwell St
Windmill St
Percy St
Rathbone St
Rathbone Pl
Newman St
Berners Mws
Berners St
Wells Mws
Mortimer St
Margaret St
Eastcastle St
Little Portland St
Cavendish Pl
Chandos St
Duchess St
Portland Pl
Mansfield St
Harley St
Weymouth St
New Cavendish St
Queen Anne St
Wimpole St
Welbeck St
Wigmore St
Thayer St
Beaumont St
Marylebone High St
Nottingham Pl
Oldbury Pl
Luxborough St
Paddington St
Moxon St
Aybrook St
Manchester St
Chiltern St
Blandford St
George St
Baker St
Edward Mws
Orchard St
Portman St
Oxford St
Marylebone La
Henrietta Pl
Vere St
Old Cavendish St
Holles St
Dering St
New Bond St
James St
Duke St
Binney St
Gilbert St
S Molton St
S Molton La
Avery Row
Brook St
Brook Mews
Grosvenor St
Grosvenor Mws
Bourdon St
Bruton Pl
Bruton St
Bruton La
Davies St
Carlos Pl
Mount Row
Adam's Row
Mount St
Berkeley Sq
Hay's Mws
Farm St
Hill St
Chesterfield Hill
Charles St
Bolton St
Clarges St
Half Moon St
Curzon St
Queen St
Market Mws
Hertford St
Brick St
Down St
Old Park La
Hamilton Pl
Piccadilly
Stratton St
South Audley St
Aldford St
South St
Deanery St
North Row
Green St
North Audley St
Lees Pl
Park St
Upper Brook St
Culross St
Upper Grosvenor St
Balderton St
Prince's St
Princes St
Hanover St
St George St
Great Marlborough St
Conduit St
Regent St
Boyle St
Savile Row
Clifford St
Cork St
Grafton St
Albemarle St
Dover St
Stafford St
Old Bond St
Burlington Gdns
Vigo St
Sackville St
Kingly St
Carnaby St
Marshall St
Beak St
Broadwick St
Lexington St
Poland St
Noel St
Berwick St
Warwick St
Glasshouse St
Sherwood St
Great Windmill St
Brewer St
Wardour St
Dean St
Meard St
Frith St
Greek St
Old Compton St
Romilly St
Soho Sq
Carlisle St
Great Chapel St
Falconberg Ct
Sutton Row
St Giles High
Denmark St
Manette St
Charing Cross Rd
Gerrard St
Lisle St
Leicester Sq
Rupert St
Coventry St
Irving St
Panton St
Whitcomb St
Orange St
Haymarket
Suffolk St
St Alban's St
Charles II St
Cockspur St
Waterloo Pl
Carlton House Tce
Jermyn St
Duke of York St
Duke St
Bury St
King St
St James's St
Arlington St
Berkeley St
St James's Pl
Pall Mall
Carlton Gardens
Horse Guards Rd
Cleveland Row
Marlborough Rd
Stable Yard Rd
Queen's Walk
The Mall
Constitution Hill
Serpentine Rd
Rotten Row
South Carriage Dve
Knightsbridge
Duke of Wellington Pl
Grosvenor Pl
Grosvenor Cres
Wilton Pl
Wilton Row
Halkin St
Headfort Pl
Chapel St
Chester St
Belgrave Sq
Motcomb St
W Halkin St
Upper Belgrave St
Wilton Mws
Wilton St
Eaton Pl
Eccleston Mws
Chesham Pl
Chesham St
Lowndes Pl
Lyall Mews
Lyall St
Eaton Mws North
Belgrave Pl
Hobart Pl
Lower Grosvenor Pl
Grosvenor Gdns
Beeston Pl
Eaton La
Allington St
Bressenden Pl
Buckingham Palace Rd
Lower Belgrave St
Ebury St
Spur Rd
Birdcage Walk
Buckingham Gate
Catherine Pl
Wilfred St
Castle La
Palace St
Petty France
Tothill St
Caxton St
Victoria St
Howick Pl
Artillery Row
Greycoat Pl
Strutton Ground
Old Pye St
Great Peter St
Chadwick St
Broadway
Dartmouth St
Queen Anne's Gate
Old Queen St
Storey's Gate
Broad Sanctuary
Great Smith St
Marsham St
Monck St
University of London
National Gallery
Trafalgar Square
Horse Guards Parade

0 |————| 500 m
0 |————| 0.25 miles

Russell Sq

See Camden & Islington Map (pp108–9)

Clerkenwell Rd

CLERKENWELL

Farringdon Station 49 56

Gray's Inn Court

Leather Lane Market

Farringdon

64 48 54

Chancery La

Charterhouse

Smithfield Market

73 68

West Smithfield

Hosier La Cock La Bartholomew's Hospital

Snow Hill

HOLBORN 79

Holborn High Holborn

Lincoln's Inn Fields Lincoln's Inn Court

Holborn Viaduct

Newgate St

COVENT GARDEN

17 Amen Ct

18 72 City Thameslink Pilgrim St Ludgate Hill

34 Fleet St

42 55 Puddle Dock Queen Victoria St

37

Royal Opera House Covent Garden Theatre Museum

Aldwych India House

21

Temple

Blackfriars

Upper Thames St White Lion Hill

Victoria Embankment

Thames

62

See City Map (p117)

Tate Modern

Charing Cross Embankment Victoria Embankment Gardens

Charing Cross Station

Golden Jubilee Bridge

Waterloo Bridge

Upper Ground

78 75 76 23 77

SOUTHWARK

Waterloo East Southwark

Horse Guards Ave

11

32 20 16 70

31 Westminster 12

Parliament Square

39 24

Jubilee Gardens 29

County Hall 44 28

SOUTH BANK

Waterloo International (Eurostar)

Waterloo

57 66 59 The Cut

BOROUGH

Westminster Pier

Westminster Bridge St

Westminster Bridge

19

St Thomas's Hospital

Lambeth North

Lambeth Palace Rd

Archbishop's Park

LAMBETH

Westminster Bridge Rd

St George's Rd

Lambeth Rd

Borough Rd

25

Elephant & Castle

CITY (p117)

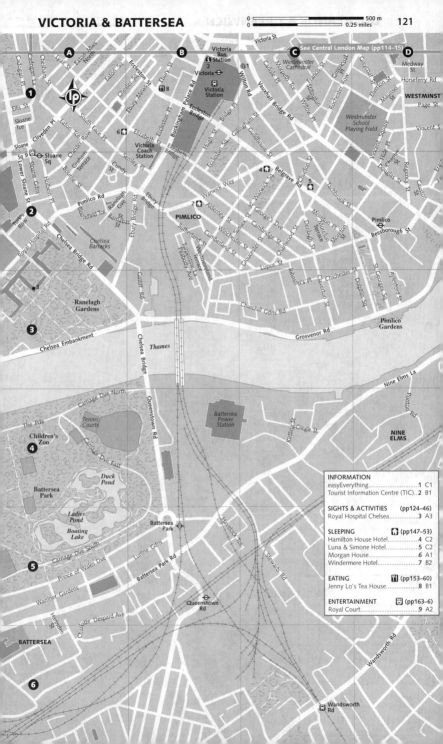

0   500 m
0   0.25 miles

INFORMATION
easyEverything.............................1 C1
Tourist Information Centre (TIC)..2 B1

SIGHTS & ACTIVITIES (pp124–46)
Royal Hospital Chelsea.................3 A3

SLEEPING (pp147–53)
Hamilton House Hotel...................4 C2
Luna & Simone Hotel.....................5 C2
Morgan House................................6 A1
Windermere Hotel.........................7 B2

EATING (pp153–60)
Jenny Lo's Tea House.....................8 B1

ENTERTAINMENT (pp163–6)
Royal Court....................................9 A2

0 —————— 500 m
0 —————— 0.25 miles

POPLAR

A   B   C   Blackwell DLR   D

West India Quay DLR   Poplar DLR

Canary Wharf DLR   Canary Wharf   Poplar Dock

Canary Wharf DLR

Heron Quay's DLR   Blackwall Basin

West India Docks   Blackwall Tunnel (New) Southbound

Blackwall Tunnel (Old Northbound)

South Quay DLR   5 ● Millennium Dome

North Greenwich

ISLE OF DOGS

Millwall Inner Dock

4

Crossharbour & London Arena DLR

Millwall Outer Dock

Mudchute Park

MILLWALL

Mudchute DLR   Millwall Park

Thames

DEPTFORD

Manchester Rd   Saunders Ness Rd   Island Gardens DLR   Pelton Rd

Greenwich Foot Tunnel

13   Old Woolwich Rd   Tuska St

8   Park Row   Trafalgar Rd   Maze Hill

2 ●   ℹ 1   University of Greenwich   9

Creek Rd   12   Cutty Sark DLR   Romney Rd   10   Park Vista

Bardsley Ln   7   King William Wk

Roan St   Greenwich Park

Norman Rd   GREENWICH

Tarves Way   Straightsmouth St   3   11   The Ave   Blackheath

Greenwich & Greenwich DLR   Circus   Hyde Vale

Greenwich High Rd   Ashburnham Pl   Ashburnham Gve   Egerton Dve   Circus St

See Greater London Map (pp106–7)

(Continued from page 105)

Post

London post offices usually open from 8.30am or 9am to 5pm or 5.30pm Monday to Friday. Some main ones also open 9am to noon or 1pm Saturday. The **Trafalgar Square post office** (Map pp118-20; GPO/Poste Restante; actually on William IV St) opens 8.30am to 6.30pm Monday to Friday, as well as 9am to 5.30pm Saturday.

Telephone

CallShop (Map pp112-3; ☎ 7390 4549; ☒ 9am-noon) Earl's Court Rd (181a Earl's Court Rd SW5; ⊖ Earl's Court); Edgware Rd (189 Edgware Rd; ⊖ Edgware Road) A private company with cheaper international calls than British Telecom (BT). You can also send and receive faxes.

Tourist Information

Britain Visitor Centre (Map pp118-20; www.visit britain.com; 1 Regent St SW1; ☒ 9am-6.30pm Mon-Fri year-round; 10am-4pm Sat & Sun Oct-late Jun; 9am-5pm Sat, 10am-4pm Sun late Jun-Sep; ⊖ Piccadilly Circus) A comprehensive information and booking centre with a map and guidebook shop, accommodation desk, entertainment and transport ticket desks, a bureau de change, international telephones and computer terminals for accessing tourist information on the Internet. It handles walk-in inquirers only, but there's lots of good information on its website. You can also get the lowdown on the rest of the British Isles here.

Corporation of London information centre (☎ 7332 1456; www.cityoflondon.gov.uk; ☒ 9.30am-5pm daily Apr-Sep, 9.30am-5pm Mon-Fri, 9.30am-2pm Sat the rest of the year; ⊖ St Paul's) In St Paul's Churchyard EC4, opposite St Paul's Cathedral.

London Line (☎ 09068 663344; per min 60p) A telephone service that will give you the lowdown on events and attractions.

London Tourist Board & Convention Bureau (www .londontown.com; Glen House, Stag Pl, London SW1E 5LT) Send written inquiries here.

Tourist Information Centre (TIC) Victoria train station (Map p121; ☒ 8am-8pm Mon-Sat, 8am-6pm Sun Apr-Oct; 8am-7pm Mon-Sat, 8am-6pm Sun Nov-Mar; ⊖ Victoria); Waterloo International Terminal (Map pp114-6; ☒ 8.30am-10.30pm; ⊖ Waterloo); Liverpool Street station (Map p117; ☒ 8am-6pm; ⊖ Liverpool St); Heathrow Terminals 1, 2 & 3 (☒ 8am-6pm) The Victoria train station branch is London's main TIC and handles accommodation bookings. Be warned: it can get positively mobbed in the peak season. TICs are also at Gatwick, Stansted, Luton and London City airports. You'll also find information desks at Paddington train station and Victoria coach station.

Travel Agencies

STA Travel Old Brompton Rd (Map pp112-3; European inquiries ☎ 7361 6161, worldwide inquiries ☎ 7361 6262, tours, accommodation, car hire or insurance ☎ 7361 6160; www.statravel.co.uk; 86 Old Brompton Rd SW7; ⊖ South Kensington); Euston Rd (Map pp108-9; 117 Euston Rd NW1; ⊖ Euston) Long-standing and reliable.

Trailfinders (Map pp110-1; long-haul travel ☎ 7938 3939, 1st- & business-class flights ☎ 7938 3444; www.trail finders.com; 194 Kensington High St W8; ☒ 9am-5pm Mon-Wed & Fri, 9am-6pm Thu, 10am-5.15pm Sat; ⊖ High Street Kensington) A visa and passport service (☎ 7938 3848), immunisation centre (☎ 7938 3999), foreign exchange (☎ 7938 3836) and information centre (☎ 7938 3303).

DANGERS & ANNOYANCES

The greatest danger of robbery is during daylight hours in tourist areas. However, considering its size and the disparities in wealth of its inhabitants, London is remarkably safe. That said, don't take anything for granted and don't let your guard down too low, particularly in heavily touristed areas.

Take particular care at night. When travelling by tube, choose a carriage with other people in it and avoid deserted suburban stations. Solo women travellers should avoid unlicensed minicabs at night. The drivers are often unreliable and occasionally dangerous.

Scams

Wherever tourists congregate, you're always going to get a few scallies trying to part them from their money, although London's not nearly as bad as many other capitals. Scams come and go. At the time of research, card-cloning was becoming a problem. Cards can be copied at ATM cashpoints, and if someone can see your PIN they can take off with a cloned copy of your card. So guard your PIN details carefully.

Hotel and hostel touts descend on backpackers at popular tube and main-line stations. Don't accept lifts from them unless you know exactly where you are going. In general, if an offer appears too good to be true, then it probably is.

Some Soho strip clubs and hostess bars are dodgy, and people should be especially wary of those that tout for business on the street.

SIGHTS

It's difficult to get your bearings in vast and sprawling London, and only more difficult if you're using the geographically nonsensical tube to get around. Your best bet is to start in the tourist heart, the West End, which incorporates familiar names like Soho, Covent Garden and Bloomsbury. It's around here you'll find many of London's finest galleries and museums, its main-stream entertainment, its funkiest shopping and its steepest prices. West of here you enter what you might picture as old-money London, incorporating the la-di-da neigh-bourhoods of Mayfair, St James's and Ken-sington. This is where royalty resides and the cashed-up play. It's also where you will find some outstanding museums. It gets groovier as you head north into the likes of Marylebone and Notting Hill, while to the south is Westminster, Whitehall and the cradle of British democracy.

Across the river from the West End, con-veniently called the South Bank, is an area that has been regenerated in the last decade or so and is now home to some of London's most popular attractions, including the Lon-don Eye, the Tate Modern and the Saatchi Gallery. Heading anticlockwise over the river again is Britain's financial cockpit, a square mile known simply as the City (note the capital 'C'). St Paul's Cathedral is the main draw for you here. Continuing the loop you'll come upon the reclaimed areas of Hoxton and Shoreditch, new centres of London cool, and then on to Camden and Islington, the ones they replaced.

Trafalgar Square

In many ways Trafalgar Sq is the centre of London, where great rallies and marches have taken place, and the New Year is ush-ered in by tens of thousands of revellers. It's also here that Londoners congregate to celebrate anything from football victories to the ousting of political leaders. While neglected for many decades, when it was ringed with gnarling traffic and invaded by pesky pigeons, it has undergone a remark-able transformation in recent years and stakes a claim to being one of the world's grandest public places.

It's now easier to appreciate not only the square but also the splendid buildings flank-ing it: the National Gallery, the National

Portrait Gallery and the eye-catching church of St Martin-in-the-Fields. The ceremonial **Pall Mall** runs southwest from the top of the square. To the southwest stands **Admiralty Arch** (erected in honour of Queen Victoria in 1910), beyond which the Mall leads to Buckingham Palace. The 43.5m-high **Nelson's Column** – upon which the admiral surveys his fleet of ships to the southwest – has stood in the centre of the square since 1843 and com-memorates Nelson's victory over Napoleon off Cape Trafalgar in Spain in 1805.

NATIONAL GALLERY

There's an astonishing collection of Euro-pean paintings at the **National Gallery** (Map pp118-20; ☎ 7747 2885; www.nationalgallery.org.uk; Tra-falgar Sq WC2; admission free, temporary exhibition prices vary; ☯ 10am-6pm Thu-Tue, 10am-9pm Wed; ✆ Charing Cross), one of the finest galleries in the world and a destination for some five million visi-tors each year.

More than 2000 paintings form a con-tinuous time-line, from the Old Masters (1260–1510) in the Sainsbury addition and the Renaissance-influenced West Wing (1510–1600) to the Dutch and Italian-focused North Wing (1600–1700) and East Wing (1700–1900).

The highlights listed in the boxed text (p125) show the cream of the gallery's ex-hibits, but if you want to know a lot more borrow an audio guide (contribution sug-gested) from the central hall and simply punch in the number of each painting that catches your eye. Free one-hour guided tours introduce you to a manageable half-dozen paintings at a time, and leave at 11.30am and 2.30pm on weekdays and at 2pm and 3.30pm on Saturday (additional tour at 6.30pm on Wednesday). A **Micro Gallery**

(🕑 10am-5.30pm Thu-Tue, 10am-8.30pm Wed), on the 1st floor of the Sainsbury Wing, has interactive screens providing a visual encyclopaedia of the collection. The gallery provides activity sheets for kids.

NATIONAL PORTRAIT GALLERY

As much about history as about art, this **gallery** (Map pp118-20; ☎ 7306 0055; www.npg.org .uk; St Martin's Cres WC2; admission free; 🕑 10am-6pm Sat-Wed, 10am-9pm Thu & Fri; ⊖ Charing Cross) provides a great opportunity to put faces to the famous and infamous names of Britain's past. There is an imaginative calendar of temporary exhibitions, which helps the gallery overcome what used to be a rather staid atmosphere.

Founded in 1856, the gallery houses a primary collection of some 10,000 works from different media (ranging from water colours to electronic art) spread out over five floors. The pictures are displayed roughly in chronological order, starting with the early Tudors on the top floor and descending to contemporary figures on the ground floor, where it seems some of the artists have begun to think that they are more important than the subjects. No court in the land would prosecute fashion designer Zandra Rhodes if she took a sledgehammer to the bust that some chancer made of her.

NATIONAL GALLERY HIGHLIGHTS

- *The Arnolfini Portrait* – van Eyck
- *Rokeby Venus* – Velázquez
- *The Wilton Diptych Bathers* – Cézanne
- *Venus and Mars* – Botticelli
- *The Virgin of the Rocks* – da Vinci
- *The Virgin and Child with St Anne and St John the Baptist* – da Vinci
- *The Battle of San Romano* – Uccello
- *The Ambassadors* – Holbein the Younger
- *Equestrian Portrait of Charles I* – Van Dyck
- *Le Chapeau de Paille* – Rubens
- *The Hay Wain* – Constable
- *Sunflowers* – Van Gogh
- *The Water-Lily Pond* – Monet
- *The Fighting Temeraire* – Turner

Since the 1990s the gallery has seen a major revamp with expansions to exhibition spaces and the creation of a café and shop in the basement, while escalators in the new Ondaatje Wing can whisk you up to the **Portrait Restaurant** on the top floor and a splendid view. An **IT Gallery** on the mezzanine above the information desk lets you examine the entire collection digitally. June to September is when to see the entrants in the prestigious national Portrait Award.

Whitehall

Whitehall is the administrative heart of the country and is best explored on foot (see the Whitehall Walking Tour p146).

BANQUETING HOUSE

The **Banqueting House** (Map pp114-6; ☎ 7930 4179; www.hrp.org.uk/webcode/banquet_home.asp; Whitehall; adult/child £4/3; 🕑 10am-5pm Mon-Sat; ⊖ Charing Cross) is the only surviving part of the Tudor Whitehall Palace, which once stretched most of the way along Whitehall but burnt down in 1698. Designed by Inigo Jones in 1622, this was England's first purely Renaissance building and looked like no other building in the country at the time. The highlight is the ceiling of the 1st-floor ceremonial hall, which features nine panels painted by Rubens in 1634. A bust outside commemorates 30 January 1649 when Charles I, accused by Cromwell of treason, was executed on a scaffold built against a 1st-floor window here. There's a video account of the house's history.

FOREIGN & COMMONWEALTH OFFICE

The Foreign & Commonwealth Office (FCO) was built in 1872 and restored by Sir George Gilbert Scott and Matthew Digby Wyatt. If you're interested in how Britain projects itself through global diplomacy, there's a **visitor centre** (Map pp114-6; ☎ 7270 1500; Parliament St; admission free; 🕑 10am-4.30pm Mon-Fri; ⊖ Westminster) with audio and visual exhibitions as well as an information technology centre.

CABINET WAR ROOMS

The **Cabinet War Rooms** (Map pp114-6; ☎ 7930 6961; www.iwm.org.uk; King Charles St; adult/child £7/5.50; 🕑 9.30am-6pm May-Sep, 10am-6pm Oct-Apr; ⊖ Westminster) are the bunkers in which the British government took refuge during the hairier moments of WWII. It's a wonderfully evocative and atmospheric museum that has captured the drama and sense of the time with restored and preserved rooms, and an entertaining audio guide. A new **Churchill Museum** was slated to open in 2005 to coincide with the 40th anniversary of the wartime PM's death.

Westminster, Victoria & Pimlico

While the City of London (known simply as 'the City') has always concerned itself with the business of making money, Westminster has been the centre of political power for over a millennium and most of its interesting places are linked with the monarchy, parliament or the Church of England. The area is a remarkable spectacle, a picture of rare architectural cohesion and an awesome display of power, gravitas and historical import.

Pimlico, to the south and southwest, is unfortunate to be clumped with these. It is, by comparison, mind-numbingly bland and would probably disappear in an X-ray. Its only redeeming features are Tate Britain and the view it affords across the river to Battersea Power Station.

Victoria has little to recommend it – there are no attractions and it's best known for coming and going via its huge train and coach stations.

WESTMINSTER ABBEY

One of the most visited churches in Christendom, **Westminster Abbey** (Map pp114-6; ☎ 7222 5152; www.westminster-abbey.org; Dean's Yard SW1; adult/child £7.50/5; ☽ 9am-4.45pm Mon-Fri, 9am-2.45pm Sat, services Sun; ☉ Westminster) is one of the most sacred and symbolic sites in England and has played an enormous role in the history of the country and the Anglican Church. Apart from Edward V and Edward VIII, every sovereign has been crowned here since William the Conqueror in 1066, and most of the monarchs from Henry III (died 1272) to George II (1760) were also buried here. As well as being the well from which the Anglican Church draws its inspiration, the abbey is also where the nation commemorates its political and artistic idols. It's difficult to imagine its equivalent anywhere else in the world.

The abbey is a magnificent, arresting sight. Though a mixture of architectural styles, it is considered the finest example of Early Eng-

lish Gothic (1180–1280) in existence. The original church was built during the Dark Ages by the King (later St) Edward the Confessor in the 11th century, who is buried in the chapel behind the main altar. Henry III (r 1216–72) began work on the new building but didn't complete it; the French Gothic nave was finished in 1388. Henry VII's huge and magnificent chapel was added in 1519. Unlike St Paul's, Westminster Abbey has never been a cathedral. It is what is called a 'royal peculiar' and is administered directly by the Crown.

Without in any way belittling its architectural achievements, the abbey is probably more impressive from the outside than within. The interior is chock-a-block with small chapels, elaborate tombs of monarchy and monuments to various luminaries from down the ages. As you might expect, it can get intolerably busy in here and the combination of clutter and crowds can make you wish you were still outside looking in.

That said, there are many highlights inside, including the incongruously ordinary-looking **Coronation Chair**, upon which almost every monarch is said to have been crowned since the late 13th century. The **Henry VII Chapel** is an outstanding example of late perpendicular architecture (a variation of English Gothic) with spectacular circular vaulting on the ceiling. In the **Royal Air Force (RAF) Chapel**, beneath a stained-glass window commemorating the force's finest hour, the Battle of Britain, a plaque marks the spot where Oliver Cromwell's body lay for two years until the Restoration, when it was disinterred, hanged and beheaded.

The octagonal **Chapter House** (adult with/without abbey ticket £1/2.50; ☽ 9.30am-5pm Apr-Sep, 10am-5pm Oct, 10am-4pm Nov-Mar) has one of Europe's best-preserved medieval tile floors. Separate museums include the formal royal treasury, the **Pyx Chamber** (adult with/without abbey ticket £1/2.50) and the **Abbey Museum** where you'll find the death masks of generations of royalty.

There are free lunch-time concerts from 12.30pm to 2pm on Thursday in July and August in the 900-year-old **College Garden** (☽ 10am-6pm Tue-Thu Apr-Sep, 10am-4pm Tue-Thu Oct-Mar), the oldest in England, and accessed through Dean's Yard.

There are 1½-hour **guided tours** (☎ 7222 7110; adult £4; Mon-Sat), leaving several times each day, and limited **audio tours** (£3). One of the best ways to visit the abbey is to attend a service (evensong 5pm weekdays, 3pm at weekends). Sunday Eucharist is at 11am.

HOUSES OF PARLIAMENT

Comprising the House of Commons and the House of Lords, the **Houses of Parliament** (Map pp114-6; ☎ 7219 4272; www.parliament.uk; Parliament Sq SW1; ⊖ Westminster) are in the Palace of Westminster, built by Sir Charles Barry and Augustus Pugin in 1840 when neo-Gothic style was all the rage. A recent cleaning has revealed the soft golden brilliance of the original.

The most famous feature outside the palace is the clock tower, commonly known as **Big Ben**. The real Ben, a bell named after Benjamin Hall, who was commissioner of works when the tower was completed in 1858, hangs inside. If you're very keen, you can apply in writing for a free tour of the clock tower (see the website). Thirteen-ton Ben has rung in the New Year since 1924, and gets its hands and face washed by abseiling cleaners once every five years. The best view of the whole complex is from the eastern side of Lambeth Bridge.

The House of Commons is where members of parliament (MPs) meet to propose and discuss new legislation. Although the national assembly comprises 659 MPs, the chamber has seating for only 437 of them.

When Parliament is in session, visitors are admitted to the **House of Commons Visitors' Gallery**. Expect to queue for at least an hour if you haven't already organised a ticket through your local British embassy. Parliamentary recesses (ie holidays) last for three months over the summer, and a couple of weeks over Easter and Christmas, so it's best to ring in advance to check whether Parliament is in session. Bags and cameras must be checked at a cloakroom before you enter the gallery, and no large suitcases or backpacks are allowed through the airport-style security gate. The **House of Lords Visitors' Gallery** (☎ 7219 3107; admission free; ⏰ from 2.30pm Mon-Wed, from 3pm Thu, from 11am Fri) is also open to outsiders and is as good a place as any for an afternoon nap along with the peers.

The roof of **Westminster Hall**, added between 1394 and 1401, is the earliest known example of a hammer-beam roof and has been called 'the greatest surviving achievement of medieval English carpentry'.

When parliament is in recess, there are guided **summer tours** (☎ 0870 906 3773; www.parliament.uk; from St Stephen's Entrance, St Margaret St; 75-min tours £7/5; times change, so telephone or check website) of both chambers and other historic buildings.

WESTMINSTER CATHEDRAL

Completed in 1903, **Westminster Cathedral** (Map p121; ☎ 7798 9064; Victoria St SW1; admission free, donation suggested; ⏰ 7am-7pm; ⊖ Victoria) is the headquarters of the Roman Catholic Church in Britain and the only good example of neo-Byzantine architecture in London. Its distinctive candy-striped redbrick and white-stone tower features prominently on the west London skyline.

The interior is part splendid marble and mosaic and part bare brick; funds dried up and the cathedral was never completed. It features the highly regarded stone carvings of the 14 **Stations of the Cross** (1918) by Eric Gill. For £2 you can take a lift up to the 83m tower of the **Campanile Bell** for splendid panoramic views of London, or take an **audio guide** (£2.50).

TATE BRITAIN

The place to see, appreciate and interpret British art from the 16th century to the present, **Tate Britain** (Map pp106-7; ☎ 7887 8008; www.tate.org.uk; Millbank SW1; admission free, temporary exhibitions vary; ⏰ 10am-5.50pm; ⊖ Pimlico) has been spruced up, expanded and rearranged in broadly chronological order. It features works by notables such as William Blake, the Hogarths, Gainsborough, Whistler, Spencer and many more. Adjoining the main building is the quirky **Clore Gallery**, where the bulk of JMW Turner's paintings can be found.

TATE-A-TATE

If you wish to see both of London's Tate galleries, Britain and Modern, you can easily get between the two in style. The **Tate-to-Tate ferries** – one of which sports a Damien Hirst dot painting – will whisk you from the Millennium Pier at Tate Britain to the Bankside Pier at Tate Modern, stopping en route at the London Eye. Services run 10am to 6pm daily at 40-minute intervals. A three-stop ticket (purchased on board) costs £4.50 (discounts available).

There are free one-hour guided tours, a general tour at 11.30am weekdays, one on Turner and his contemporaries at 2.30pm and 3.30pm weekdays, and a Tate Highlights tour at 3pm Saturday. There are also children's activities throughout the week. The immensely popular **Tate Restaurant** (☎ 7887 8825; mains £9-17.50; ☻ noon-3pm Mon-Sat, noon-4pm Sun), with an impressive Rex Whistler mural, is open for lunch only.

St James's & Mayfair

Mayfair is where high society high fives. Its defining features are silver spoons and old-fashioned razzmatazz. As any Monopoly player knows, it's the most expensive place in London, and if you land here you could go bankrupt. St James's is a mixture of exclusive gentlemen's clubs (the Army and Navy sort as opposed to lap-dancing), historic shops and elegant buildings; indeed, there are some 150 historically noteworthy buildings within its 36 hectares. Despite a lot of commercial development, its matter-of-fact elitism remains pretty much intact.

INSTITUTE FOR CONTEMPORARY ARTS

Renowned for being at the cutting edge is the **Institute for Contemporary Arts** (ICA; Map pp114-6; ☎ 7930 3647; www.ica.org.uk; the Mall SW1; admission varies; ☻ noon-7.30pm; ✆ Charing Cross). In any given week you might see art-house films, dance, photography, art, theatre, music, lectures, multimedia works or book readings. The complex includes a bookshop, gallery, cinema, bar, theatre and café.

ST JAMES'S PARK & ST JAMES'S PALACE

The neatest and most royal of London's royal parks, **St James's Park** (Map pp114-6; The Mall SW1; ✆ St James's Park or Charing Cross) also has the best vistas, including Westminster, Buckingham Palace and St James's Palace. The

---

TOP FIVE GREEN SPACES

- ■ **Hyde Park** (p140)
- ■ **St James's Park** (p128)
- ■ **Hampstead Heath** (p141)
- ■ **Regent's Park** (p140)
- ■ **Kew Gardens** (p145)

---

flowerbeds are spectacular in summer, but it's the lake and waterfowl that make a stroll or a lounge in here so special.

The striking Tudor gatehouse of St James's Palace, the only surviving part of a building initiated by the palace-mad Henry VIII in 1530, is best approached from St James's St to the north of the park. This was the residence of Prince Charles and his sons until they shifted next door to the former residence of the Queen Mother **Clarence House** (1828) after she died in 2002 (and the future king spent £4.6 million reshaping the house to his own design).

SPENCER HOUSE

The ancestral home of Princess Diana's family, **Spencer House** (Map pp114-6; ☎ 7499 8620; www.spencerhouse.co.uk; 27 St James's Pl SW1; adult/child £6/5; ☻ 10.30am-5.45pm Sun Feb-Jul & Sep-Dec; ✆ Green Park) was built in the Palladian style between 1756 and 1766. Although the Spencers moved out in 1927 and the house became offices, an £18 million restoration project returned it to its former glory in the 1980s. Visits through the house are by guided tour only. The restored gardens (£3.50) are opened just a few days each summer.

BUCKINGHAM PALACE

The official residence of Queen Elizabeth II, **Buckingham Palace** (Map pp114-6; ☎ 7830 4832; credit-card bookings ☎ 7321 2233; adult £12.50; ☻ 9.30am-4.30pm daily early Aug-late Sep; ✆ St James's Park or Victoria) is at the southwestern end of the Mall.

Built in 1803 for the Duke of Buckingham, it has been the royal family's London home since 1837 when St James's Palace was judged too old-fashioned and unimpressive. Nineteen lavishly furnished staterooms, used by the royals to meet and greet, are open to visitors during part of the summer when HRH takes her holidays in Scotland. The tour includes **Queen Victoria's Picture Gallery** (a full 76.5m long, with works by Rembrandt, Van Dyck, Canaletto, Poussin and Vermeer) and the **Throne Room**, with his-and-hers pink chairs initialled 'ER' and 'P' sitting smugly under what looks like a theatre arch. The Queen has also swung open the gates to part of her backyard, although many people still find the visit distinctly underwhelming.

Changing of the Guard

London's quintessential tourist attraction takes place when the old guard (Foot Guards of the Household Regiment) comes off duty to be replaced by the new guard in the forecourt of Buckingham Palace. If you're dedicated to pomp – and arrive early to get a good vantage point by the rails – you can gape at the soldiers' bright-red uniforms and bearskin hats as they shout and march in one of the world's most famous displays of pageantry. Otherwise, you'll see little more than the backs of heads. The **ceremony** (☎ 0839-123411) takes place at 11.30am daily from April until the end of July and on alternate days for the rest of the year, weather permitting.

Queen's Gallery

This **gallery** (adult £6.50; ⊙ 10am-5.30pm) houses changing displays from the extensive Royal Collection of art and treasures, shaped by the tastes of monarchs through the centuries. It was originally designed by John Nash as a conservatory and blown to smithereens by the Luftwaffe in 1940 before being reopened as a gallery in 1962. The exhibition space was greatly expanded in a £20 million renovation project and reopened for the Queen's Golden Jubilee in 2002.

Royal Mews

The **Royal Mews** (Buckingham Palace Rd SW1; adult £5.50; ⊙ 11am-4pm Apr-Oct; ❸ Victoria) provides shelter for the immaculately groomed royal horses and the opulent vehicles the monarchy uses for getting from A to B, including the stunning gold coach of 1762, which has been used for every coronation since that of George III, and the Glass Coach of 1910, used for royal weddings.

HANDEL HOUSE MUSEUM

The house where George Frideric Handel lived and wrote some of his greatest works, including *Messiah*, is now a **museum** (Map pp114-6; ☎ 7495 1685; www.handelhouse.org; 25 Brook St W1K; adult £4.50; ⊙ 10am-6pm Tue, Wed, Fri & Sat, 10am-8pm Thu, noon-6pm Sun; ❸ Bond Street). It has been restored to how it would have looked when the composer lived here – for 36 years until his death in 1759. Visitors can wander through the rooms, see personal belongings and hear recitals of his music.

GREEN PARK

Green Park is less manicured than the adjoining St James's Park, and has trees and open space, sunshine and shade. It was once a duelling ground and served as a vegetable garden during WWII.

West End – Soho to the Strand

No two Londoners ever agree on the exact borders of the West End (more a cultural term than a geographical one), but let's just say it takes in Piccadilly Circus and Trafalgar Sq to the south, Oxford St and Tottenham Court Rd to the north, Regent St to the west and Covent Garden and the Strand to the east. A heady mixture of consumerism and culture, the West End is where outstanding museums, galleries, historic buildings and entertainment venues rub shoulders with tacky tourist traps.

PICCADILLY CIRCUS

Piccadilly Circus is home to the popular landmark the **Eros statue** and was named after the stiff collars ('picadils') that were the sartorial staple of a 17th-century tailor who lived nearby. It is a ridiculously busy hub characterised by gaudy neon advertising hoarding (billboards), choking fumes and reliable Tower Records (p167).

London Trocadero

Basically just a huge indoor amusement arcade, the **Trocadero** (Map pp118-20; ☎ 09068-881100; www.londontrocadero.com; 1 Piccadilly Circus W1; ⊙ 10am-midnight Sun-Thu, 10am-1am Fri & Sat; ❸ Piccadilly Circus) has six levels of high-tech, high-cost fun for youngsters, and cinemas, US-themed restaurants and bars for anyone else with nothing better to do. Each ride costs from £3, but you can get discounts on multiple tickets.

PICCADILLY

Piccadilly is home to the quintessential London icons of the Ritz Hotel and Fortnum & Mason department store.

Royal Academy of Arts

Britain's first art school, the **Royal Academy of Arts** (Map pp118-20; ☎ 7300 8000; www.royalacademy .org.uk; Burlington House, Piccadilly W1; admission varies; ⊙ 10am-6pm Sat-Thu, 10am-10pm Fri; ❸ Green Park), used to play second fiddle to the Hayward Gallery (p137). It has created a storm in recent years, however, with perfectly pitched shows ranging from the art of the Aztecs to its popular Summer Exhibitions showcasing the work of contemporary British artists.

Burlington Arcade

Flanking the Royal Academy of Arts, you'll find the curious **Burlington Arcade** (Map pp118-20; 51 Piccadilly W1; ⊖ Green Park), built in 1819 and today a shopping precinct for the well heeled. It is most famous for the Burlington Berties, uniformed guards who patrol the area keeping an eye out for punishable offences such as running, chewing gum or whatever else might lower the arcade's tone.

REGENT STREET

Distinguished by elegant shop fronts, Regent St is where you'll find Hamley's, London's premier toy and game store, and the upmarket department store Liberty (p166).

OXFORD STREET

Oxford St is the zenith of High St shopping, a must or a miss depending on your retail persuasion and eye for style. West towards Marble Arch, you'll find many famous department stores including the incomparable Selfridges (p166).

SOHO

One of the liveliest corners of London, this is the place to come for fun and games after dark. A decade ago it was known mostly for strip clubs and peepshows. The sleaze is still there, of course, but these days it blends with some of London's trendiest clubs, bars and restaurants. West of Soho proper is **Carnaby St**, the epicentre of London's 'swinging '60s'. It subsequently descended into tourist tack, but has lately regained some of its cred.

LEICESTER SQUARE

Pedestrianised Leicester (*les*-ter) Sq is usually heaving with tourists – and inevitably buskers – but it essentially feels like somewhere you pass through on the way elsewhere.

CHINATOWN

Lisle and Gerrard Sts form the heart of Chinatown, which is full of verve and unfairly hip Japanese youngsters. Street signs are bilingual and the streets themselves are lined with Asian restaurants. If you're in town in late January or early February, don't miss the sparkles and crackles of Chinese New Year.

COVENT GARDEN

This elegant **piazza** (Map pp118-20; ⊖ Covent Garden), London's first planned square, is a tourist mecca where chain restaurants, souvenir shops, balconied bars and street entertainers vie for the punters' pound. It positively heaves with activity in summer, especially weekends, yet seems unfettered by the fickleness of fashion. It's also one of the few parts of London where pedestrians rule.

In the 1630s Inigo Jones converted the former vegetable field into a graceful square that at first contained the fruit and vegetable market immortalised in the film *My Fair Lady*. The area eventually slumped and became home to brothels and coffee houses, but the market was shifted in the 1980s and Covent Garden was transformed into one of the city's grooviest hubs.

London Transport Museum

Tucked into a corner of Covent Garden, this **museum** (Map pp118-20; ☎ 7836 8557; www .ltmuseum.co.uk; Covent Garden Piazza WC2; adult £5.95; ⊙ 10am-6pm Sat-Thu, 11am-6pm Fri; ⊖ Covent Garden) is an unexpected delight, exploring how London made the transition from streets choked with horse-drawn carriages to streets choked with horse-powered cars.

Theatre Museum

This **museum** (Map pp118-20; ☎ 7836 7891; Russell St WC2; admission free; ⊙ 10am-6pm Tue-Sun; ⊖ Covent Garden) is a branch of the Victoria & Albert Museum and displays costumes, artefacts and curiosities relating to the history of British theatre. There are regular programmes and activities for kids.

THE STRAND

Described by Benjamin Disraeli in the 19th century as Europe's finest street, this 'beach' of the Thames – which was built to connect Westminster (the seat of political power) and the City (the commercial centre) – has since lost much of its lustre. It still boasts a few classy hotels and theatres, but today is as well known for the homeless who sleep in its doorways.

Somerset House

The splendid Palladian masterpiece of **Somerset House** (Map pp114-6; www.somerset-house.org.uk; the Strand WC2; ⊖ Temple) was designed by William Chambers in 1775 and contains three fabulous galleries: the Courtauld Gallery, the Gilbert Collection and the Hermitage Rooms. Its expansive central courtyard – a car park for civil servants only a few years ago – was returned to its former glory in a millennial make-over and is now one of the most elegant spaces in London, with dancing water fountains, outside tables and all the panache of Paree. It hosts a summer programme of open-air events from music to theatre. Out the back there's a wonderful terrace and café overlooking the Thames, while the Admiralty restaurant (p155) is a little bit special.

The **Courtauld Gallery** (Map pp118-20; ☎ 7848 2526; adult/child £5/free, admission free 10am-2pm Mon; ⊗ 10am-6pm) displays some of the Courtauld Institute's marvellous collection of paintings in grand surroundings. There's a wealth of 14th- to 20th-century works, including a roomful of Rubens and Impressionist and post-Impressionist works by Van Gogh, Renoir and Toulouse-Lautrec.

The **Gilbert Collection** (Map pp114-6; ☎ 7240 5782; adult/child £5/free, admission free after 4.30pm; ⊗ 10am-6pm) includes such treasures as European silverware, gold snuffboxes and Italian mosaics bequeathed to the nation by London-born American businessman Arthur Gilbert.

The **Hermitage Rooms** (Map pp114-6; ☎ 7845 4630; www.hermitagerooms.co.uk; adult/child £6/free; ⊗ 10am-6pm) displays diverse and rotating exhibitions from St Petersburg's renowned (and underfunded) State Hermitage Museum, to which goes a slice of your admission fee.

Royal Courts of Justice

Designed in 1874, the gargantuan melange of Gothic spires, pinnacles and burnished Portland stone of the **Royal Courts of Justice** (Map pp114-6; ☎ 7936 6000; 460 the Strand; ⊗ 9am-4.30pm Mon-Fri; ⊖ Temple) is where civil, and usually rather dry, cases are heard.

Bloomsbury

Largely nonresidential, Bloomsbury is a genteel blend of the University of London, beautiful Georgian squares, the British Museum and literary history. **Russell Square**, its very heart, was laid out in 1800 and is London's largest.

Between the World Wars these pleasant streets were colonised by a group of artists and intellectuals known collectively as the Bloomsbury Group, which included the novelists Virginia Woolf and EM Forster, and the economist John Maynard Keynes.

BRITISH MUSEUM

London's most visited attraction – with more than six million punters each year – the **British Museum** (Map pp114-6; ☎ 7636 1555; www .thebritishmuseum.ac.uk; Great Russell St WC1; admission free; ⊗ 10am-5pm Mon-Sat, noon-6pm Sun; ⊖ Tottenham Court Road or Russell Square) is the largest in the country and one of the oldest and finest in the world, boasting vast Egyptian, Etruscan, Greek, Oriental and Roman galleries among many others. It was started in 1749 in the form of a 'cabinet of curiosities' belonging to Dr Hans Sloane (one of the royal physicians), which he later bequeathed to the country, and has been augmented over the years partly through the plundering of the empire (see Britain & Greece Squabble Over Marbles, p132).

You'll need multiple visits to savour even the highlights here, which include a spectacular glass-and-steel roof designed by Norman Foster and opened to the public as the **Great Court** in late 2000. From here, there are nine 50-minute **'eye opener' tours** (tours free; ⊗ 11am-3pm Mon-Sat, 1-4pm Sun) to help you decide which part of the collection you want to focus on. Other tours include the 1½-hour **highlights tour** (adult/child £8/5; ⊗ 10.30am, 1pm & 3pm Mon-Sat) and a range of **audio guides** (£3.50). The back entrance at Montague Pl is usually quieter than the porticoed main one off Great Russell St. Also, you should calmly consider a guided tour before starting your exploration because the museum's size and scope really are mind-boggling.

Among the many must-sees are the **Rosetta Stone**, discovered in 1799 and the key to deciphering Egyptian hieroglyphics; the controversial **Parthenon Marbles**, which once adorned the walls of the Parthenon in Athens; the stunning **Oxus Treasure** of 7th- to 4th-century BC Persian gold; and the Anglo-Saxon **Sutton Hoo Ship Burial** site. In the centre of the Great Court is the **Reading Room**, where Karl Marx wrote *The Communist Manifesto*.

BRITAIN & GREECE SQUABBLE OVER MARBLES

Wonderful though it is, the British Museum can sometimes feel like one vast repository for stolen booty. Much of what's on display wasn't just 'picked up' along the way by Victorian travellers and explorers, but stolen, or purchased under dubious circumstances.

Restive foreign governments occasionally pop their heads over the parapet to demand the return of their property. The British Museum says 'no' and the problem goes away until the next time. Not the Greeks, however. They have been kicking up a stink demanding the return of the so-called Parthenon Marbles, the ancient marble sculptures that once adorned the Parthenon. The British Museum, and successive British governments, steadfastly refuse to hand over the priceless works that were removed from the Parthenon and shipped to England by the British ambassador to the Ottoman Empire, the Earl of Elgin, in 1806. (When Elgin blew all his dough, he sold the marbles to the government.) The diplomatic spat continues. Only time will tell who blinks first.

Along with the Great Court, the most recent additions to the museum are the **Sainsbury African Galleries**, the restored **King's Library** and the new **Wellcome Gallery of Ethnography**.

Holborn & Clerkenwell

Holborn's most distinctive features are the wonderful Sir John Soane's Museum and the atmospheric Inns of Court, built here to symbolise the law's role as mediator in the traditional power struggle between Westminster and the City. The little pocket of Clerkenwell was for most of the 19th and 20th centuries a dilapidated, working-class area of no interest to anyone but its inhabitants. In the 1980s property developers realised the value of such central, tourist-free real estate and Clerkenwell has since been transformed into a glaringly trendy corner of the capital, replete with new pubs, restaurants and clubs.

SIR JOHN SOANE'S MUSEUM

One of the most charming London sights, this ridiculously under-visited **museum** (Map pp118-20; ☎ 7405 2107; www.soane.org; 13 Lincoln's Inn Fields WC2; admission free, tour 2.30pm Sat £3; ☺ 10am-5pm Tue-Sat, 6-9pm 1st Tue of month; ⊖ Holborn) is partly a beautiful, bewitching house and partly a small museum representing the taste of celebrated architect and collector extraordinaire Sir John Soane (1753–1837).

The house is largely as it was when Sir John was taken out in a box. It has a glass dome that brings light right down to the basement, a lantern room filled with statuary, rooms within rooms and a picture gallery where each painting folds away when pressed and reveals another one behind. Among his eclectic acquisitions are an Egyp-

tian sarcophagus, ancient vases and works of arts, and the original *A Rake's Progress*, William Hogarth's set of cartoon caricatures of late-18th-century London lowlife.

The tour is well worth catching should you be in the neighbourhood on Saturday afternoon; tickets are sold at the museum from 2pm.

INNS OF COURT

Clustered around Holborn to the south of Fleet St are the Inns of Court whose alleys, atmosphere and open spaces provide an urban oasis. All London barristers work from within one of the four Inns, and a roll call of former members would include the likes of Oliver Cromwell and Charles Dickens to Mahatma Gandhi and Margaret Thatcher. It would take a lifetime working here to grasp the intricacies of the arcane protocols of the Inns – they're similar to the Freemasons, and both are 13th-century creations. It's best just to soak up the dreamy atmosphere, relax, and thank your lucky stars you're not one of the bewigged and deadly serious barristers scurrying about.

Lincoln's Inn (Map pp114-6; ☎ 7405 1393; Lincoln's Inn Fields WC2; ☺ grounds 9am-6pm Mon-Fri, chapel 12.30-2.30pm Mon-Fri; ⊖ Holborn), largely intact with several original 15th-century buildings, is the most attractive of the bunch with a chapel and pretty landscaped gardens. **Gray's Inn** (Map pp114-6; ☎ 7458 7800; Gray's Inn Rd WC1; ☺ grounds 10am-4pm Mon-Fri, chapel 10am-6pm Mon-Fri; ⊖ Chancery Lane) was largely rebuilt after the Luftwaffe levelled it. **Middle Temple** (Map pp114-6; ☎ 7427 4800; Middle Temple Lane EC4; ☺ grounds 10-11.30am & 3-4pm Mon-Fri; ⊖ Temple) and **Inner Temple** (Map pp114-6; ☎ 7797 8250; King's Bench Walk EC4; ☺ grounds 10am-4pm Mon-Fri; ⊖ Temple), the former being the best preserved, are both part of the Temple complex between Fleet St and Victoria Embankment (see also Temple Church p143).

The City
The City of London, the commercial heart of the capital, is 'the square mile' on the northern bank of the Thames where the Romans first built their walled community two millennia ago. Its boundaries have changed little since, and you can always tell when you're within them because the Corporation of London's coat of arms appears on the street signs.

Less than 10,000 people actually live here, although some 300,000 descend on it each weekday, where they generate almost three-quarters of Britain's entire GDP before nicking back off to wherever it is they live.

St Paul's Cathedral and the Tower of London are also here and a quiet weekend stroll offers a unique opportunity to explore the area's architectural richness, including the many atmospheric alleyways snaking between the modern office towers.

FLEET ST
Twentieth-century London's 'Street of Shame', **Fleet St** (Map pp114-6; ⊖ Blackfriars) was synonymous with the UK's scurrilous tabloids until the mid-1980s when the press barons embraced computer technology, ditched a load of staff and largely relocated to the Docklands. It was here in 1850 that Reuters news agency, the last media outlet to stick with Fleet St, began its service with a loft of carrier pigeons.

CENTRAL CRIMINAL COURT (OLD BAILEY)
Many of Britain's most notorious criminals – and a few Irishmen who were in the wrong place at the wrong time – have been convicted at the Central Criminal Court, better known as the Old Bailey after the street on which it stands. Look up at the great copper dome and you'll see the figure of justice holding a sword and scales in her hands. Oddly, she is *not* blindfolded, which has sparked many a sarcastic comment from those being brought in here.

You can visit the court's **public gallery** (Map pp114-6; ☎ 7248 3277; Newgate St; ⌚ 10.30am-1pm & 2-4pm Mon-Fri).

DR JOHNSON'S HOUSE
Where Samuel Johnson and his assistants compiled the first English dictionary between 1748 and 1759, **Dr Johnson's House** (Map pp114-6; ☎ 7353 3745; www.drjh.dircon.co.uk; 17 Gough Sq EC4; adult/concession £4/3; ⌚ 11am-5.30pm Mon-Sat May-Sep, 11am-5pm Oct-Apr; ⊖ Chancery Lane) is a well-preserved, Georgian building. It's full of prints and portraits of friends and intimates, including Johnson's Jamaican servant, to whom he bequeathed the house.

ST PAUL'S CATHEDRAL
Dominating the City with a dome second in size only to St Peter's in Rome, **St Paul's Cathedral** (Map p117; ☎ 7236 4128; www.stpauls.co.uk; adult £6; ⌚ 8.30am-4pm Mon-Sat; ⊖ St Paul's) was built between 1675 and 1710 by Sir Christopher Wren after the Great Fire of 1666. Four other cathedrals on this site, the first dating from 604, preceded it.

The dome is renowned for somehow dodging the bombs during the Blitz of WWII and became an icon of the resilience shown in the capital during the crisis. Outside the cathedral, to the north, is a **monument to the people of London**, a simple and elegant memorial to the 32,000 Londoners who weren't so lucky.

Inside, some 30m above the main paved area, is the first of three domes (actually a dome inside a cone, inside a dome) supported by eight huge columns. The walkway round its base is called the **Whispering Gallery**, because if you talk close to the wall your words will carry to the opposite side 32m away.

This, the **Stone Gallery** and the **Golden Gallery** can be reached by a staircase on the western side of the scrubbed-up southern transept. It is 530 lung-busting steps to the Golden Gallery at the very top, and an unforgettable view of London. But even if that's too much, you can still get terrific city vistas from the lower galleries.

The **Crypt** has memorials to up to 300 military demigods, including Wellington, Kitchener and Nelson, whose body lies below the dome. But the most poignant memorial is to Sir Christopher Wren himself. On a simple slab bearing his name a Latin inscription translates as: 'If you seek his memorial, look about you'.

Audio tours lasting 45 minutes are available for £3.50. **Guided tours** (adult/child £2.50/2) leave the tour desk at 11am, 11.30am, 1.30pm and 2pm (90 minutes). There are organ concerts at St Paul's at 5pm most Sundays. Evensong takes place at 5pm most weekdays and at 3.15pm on Sunday.

GUILDHALL

The **Guildhall** (Map p117; ☎ 7606 3030; Basinghall St EC2; admission free; ✆ 10am-5pm Mon-Sat, 10am-4pm Sun May-Sep; 10am-5pm daily Oct-Apr; ⊖ Bank) sits exactly in the centre of the sq mile and has been the seat of the City's local government for eight centuries. The present building dates from the early 15th century.

You can see the **Great Hall** where the mayor is still elected, a vast empty space with ecclesiastical-style monuments and the shields and banners of London's 12 principal livery companies, which emerged from the guilds of the Middle Ages. Beneath it is London's largest **medieval crypt** (☎ 7606 3030, ext 1463; visited by free guided tour only) with 19 stained-glass windows showing the livery companies' coats of arms.

The **Guildhall Art Gallery** (adult £2.50) holds more than 4000 artworks, primarily of historical import. Only 250 or so are displayed at any one time.

BARBICAN

Tucked into a corner of the City of London where a watchtower (or 'barbican') once stood, the **Barbican** (Map p117; ☎ 7638 4141; Silk St EC2; ⊖ Barbican or Moorgate) is a prime example of a local council making a pig's ear of development.

The plan was to create an ultramodern complex for offices, residences and the arts on a vast bomb site provided by WWII. The result – which was only completed in the early 1980s, by which time the ultramodern plans should have been museum pieces – is a forbidding series of wind tunnels and gloomy high-rise apartments, with an enormous cultural centre hidden somewhere in the middle.

The **Barbican Centre** is the home of the Royal Shakespeare Company (RSC), the London Symphony Orchestra and the London Classical Orchestra. It also houses the Museum of London and the wonderful **Barbican Art Gallery** (☎ 7588 9023; adult £4.50; ✆ 10am-6pm Mon-Sat, noon-6pm Sun) on Level 3, with some of the best photographic exhibits in London. The programmes are generally

first-rate, but it's a hassle finding the complex in the first place, never mind reaching the right spot at the right time.

MUSEUM OF LONDON

Despite its unprepossessing setting in the Barbican (look for gate 7), the **Museum of London** (Map p117; ☎ 7600 0807; www.museumoflondon .org.uk; London Wall EC2; admission free; ✆ 10am-5.50pm Mon-Sat, noon-5.50pm Sun; ⊖ Barbican) is one of the city's finest, and is expanding its exhibitions depicting the city's evolution from the ice age to the Internet. Among more than one million objects is a 2000-year-old plaque engraved with the Latin word 'Londiniensium'. It was only discovered in late 2002 and is the earliest – known physical proof of the capital's original Roman name.

TOWER OF LONDON

Despite the heaving crowds and all the marketing claptrap, the **Tower of London** (Map p117; ☎ 7680 9004; www.hrp.org.uk; Tower Hill EC3; adult/child £12.50/8; ✆ 9am-6pm Mon-Sat, 10am-6pm Sun Apr-Oct; 9am-5pm Mon-Sat, 10am-5pm Sun Nov-Mar; ⊖ Tower Hill) is one of the most essential sights to see in London, and a window into a gruesome, fascinating history. It is also one of the city's three World Heritage Sites (joining Westminster Abbey and Maritime Greenwich). Well over two million people visit each year and, even in winter, you should arrive early to commandeer enough space to savour the experience.

To help get your bearings, take the hugely entertaining and free guided tour with any of the Tudor-garbed Beefeaters. Hour-long tours leave every 30 minutes from the Middle Tower between 9am and 3pm Monday to Saturday and from 10am Sunday.

In 1078 William the Conqueror laid the first stone of the White Tower to replace the timber-and-earth castle he'd already built here. By 1285 two walls with towers and a moat were built around it and the medieval defences have barely been altered since. A former royal residence, treasury, mint and arsenal, it became most famous as a prison when Henry VIII moved to Whitehall Palace in 1529 and started dishing out his preferred brand of punishment.

The most striking building is the huge **White Tower**, in the centre of the courtyard, with its solid Romanesque architecture and four turrets, which today houses a collection from the Royal Armouries. On the 2nd floor is the **Chapel of St John the Evangelist**, dating from 1080 and therefore the oldest church in London.

On the green at the front of the church stood the **scaffold**, set up during Henry VIII's reign, where seven people were beheaded, among them Anne Boleyn and her cousin Catherine Howard (his second and fifth wives).

Facing the White Tower to the north is the **Waterloo Barracks**, which now contains the Crown Jewels. On a busy day, you'll be whisked past with hardly time to blink.

On the far side of the White Tower from here is the **Bloody Tower**, where the 12-year-old Edward V and his little brother were held 'for their own safety' and later murdered, probably by their uncle, the future Richard III. Sir Walter Raleigh did a 13-year stretch here, when he wrote his *History of the World*, a copy of which is on display.

On the patch of green between the Wakefield and White Towers you'll find the latest in the tower's long line of famous ravens, which legend says could cause the White Tower to collapse should they leave. Their wings have been clipped just in case they get any ideas.

TOWER BRIDGE

When it was built in 1894, London was still a thriving port and Tower Bridge was designed to rise and allow ships to pass through. It is raised electronically these days but you can still see the original steam engines. There are excellent views from the walkways.

For the **Tower Bridge Exhibition** (Map p117; ☎ 7378 1928; www.towerbridge.org.uk; adult £5.50; ⊗ 10am-6.30pm Apr-Oct, 9.30am-6pm Nov-Mar; ⊖ Tower Hill), a lift takes you up from the modern visitors' facility in the northern tower where the story of its building is recounted with videos and animatronics.

BANK OF ENGLAND MUSEUM

Guardian of the country's financial system, the Bank of England was established in 1694 when the government needed to raise some cash to support a war with France. It was moved here in 1734 and largely renovated by Sir John Soane. The **museum** (Map p117; ☎ 7601 5545; www.bankofengland.co.uk; Bartholomew Lane EC2; admission free; ⊗ 10am-5pm Mon-

Fri; ⊖ Bank) traces the history of the bank and bank notes with various interactive technology, and isn't quite as dry as it sounds.

THE MONUMENT

Designed by Christopher Wren to commemorate the Great Fire of 1666, the **Monument** (Map p117; ☎ 7626 2717; Monument St; adult/child £1.50/50p; ⊗ 10am-5.40pm; ⊖ Monument) is 60.6m high, the exact distance from its base to the bakery on Pudding Lane east where the blaze began. If you're up to it, 311 tight steps lead to a balcony beneath the gilded bronze urn at the top and a splendid view.

South of the Thames

A little over a decade ago, the southern part of central London was the city's forgotten underside – run-down, neglected and offering little for foreign visitors. All that has changed in recent years and even north Londoners are venturing 'sarf' of the river for play and stimulation. Although parts of Bermondsey still look a bit dejected, there are pockets of refurbishment and revitalisation, such as the Design Museum and the brand new Zandra Rhodes' Fashion & Textile Museum. (See also To Market, to Market, p167.)

BERMONDSEY
Design Museum

The gleaming white **Design Museum** (Map pp106-7; ☎ 7403 6933; www.designmuseum.org; 28 Shad Thames SE1; adult/child £6/4; ⊗ 10am-5.45pm; ⊖ Tower Hill) is a must for anyone interested in the evolution of design and all its applications. The 1st floor is dedicated to innovation from around the world, the 2nd concentrates on the practicalities of design, while a relatively new gallery focuses on contemporary design.

Fashion & Textile Museum

Kooky British designer Zandra Rhodes' **Fashion & Textile Museum** (Map p117; ☎ 7403 0222; www.ftmlondon.org; 83 Bermondsey St SE1; adult/child £6/4; ⊖ London Bridge) showcases the best of vintage and modern, local and international fashion plus textile design (as well as thousands of her own pieces, of course) in a cool Mediterranean building.

SOUTHWARK

An important thoroughfare during the Middle Ages, Southwark (suth-erk) is in a transition period, retaining at least some of its working-class gritty edge while a slew of sights and attractions – such as the magnificent Tate Modern – open up along the Thames in Bankside.

HMS Belfast

Launched in 1938, the **HMS Belfast** (Map p117; ☎ 7407 6328; Morgan's Lane, Tooley St SE1; adult/child £6/free; ☽ 10am-6pm Mar-Oct, 10am-5pm Nov-Feb; ⊖ London Bridge) is a large, light cruiser with 16 six-inch guns. It saw much action during WWII and is hugely popular with little boys.

London Dungeon

The **London Dungeon** (Map p117; ☎ 7403 7221; www.thedungeons.com; 28-34 Tooley St SE1; adult/child £14.50/9.75; ☽ 10am-6.30pm Apr-Jun & Sep, 10am-9pm Jul & Aug; ⊖ London Bridge) is long on gore and short on substance. Kids, of course, love it. Beware of touts selling fake tickets.

Britain at War Experience

Designed to educate future generations about the hardships endured, and spirit exemplified, during WWII, the **Britain at War Experience** (Map p117; ☎ 7403 3171; www.britainatwar .co.uk; 64-66 Tooley St SE1; adult £8.50; ☽ 10am-5.30pm Apr-Sep, 10am-4.30pm Oct-Mar) is crammed with fascinating memorabilia from a bombarded London.

Old Operating Theatre Museum & Herb Garret

One of London's most genuinely gruesome attractions is the **Old Operating Theatre Museum** (Map p117; ☎ 7955 4791; www.thegarret .org.uk; 9a St Thomas St SE1; adult £4; ☽ 10.30am-5pm; ⊖ London Bridge). The primitive surgical tools of the 19th century are terrifying.

There's also an apothecary where medicinal herbs were once stored; it now houses a medical museum hung with bunches of herbs.

Southwark Cathedral

Although the central tower dates from 1520 and the choir from the 13th century, **Southwark Cathedral** (Map p117; ☎ 7367 6722; Montague Close SE1; admission by donation; ☽ 8am-6pm; ⊖ London Bridge) is largely Victorian. It's been scrubbed up in recent years and has a new visitors centre. Inside are monuments and details galore and it's worth picking up

one of the small guides. Catch Evensong at 5.30pm on Tuesday and Friday, 4pm on Saturday and 3pm on Sunday.

Shakespeare's Globe & Exhibition

The rebuilt **Globe Theatre** (Map p117; ☎ 7401 9919; www.shakespeares-globe.org; 21 New Globe Walk SE1; adult/child £8/5.50; ☽ 10am-5pm; ⊖ London Bridge) offers the opportunity to see Shakespeare as it was originally performed in this faithful replica of the original 'Wooden O' under a thatched roof and surrounded by standing and often unruly punters.

The original Globe was erected in 1599, burnt down in 1613 and immediately rebuilt. The Puritans, who regarded theatres as dreadful dens of iniquity, eventually closed it down in 1642. Beneath it, an exhibition focuses on Elizabethan London and the struggle by American actor and director Sam Wanamaker to get the theatre rebuilt.

Visits include a guided tour of the theatre itself, although in summer there are usually matinee performances and tours take place in the morning only.

Tate Modern

This former power station is home to the wonderful **Tate Modern** (Map p117; information ☎ 7887 8008; www.tate.org.uk; Queen's Walk SE1; admission free; ☽ 10am-6pm Sun-Thu, 10am-10pm Fri & Sat; ⊖ Blackfriars or London Bridge), Europe's most successful contemporary art gallery and London's number-one attraction.

Enter through the vast and dramatic Turbine Hall and lick your lips. The collection is spread over five floors and encompasses art in all its forms from the beginning of the 20th century. The works are displayed thematically rather than chronologically and some of the early stuff gets a little lost compared with the bolder contemporary works. Although the displays change regularly, you're certain to clap eyes on pieces by Monet, Picasso, Dali, Pollock, Warhol and Rothko as well as various members of '90s brat pack (including Damien Hirst and Tracey Emin).

However, it's with its temporary exhibitions (for which there are always admission fees) that the Tate really shines (check listings for details). Another attraction is the view from the top-floor **restaurant** and **café**. The **audio guides** (£1) are worthwhile for their descriptions of selected works.

Millennium Bridge

Although it nowadays provides a smooth river crossing, the Millennium Bridge will long be known to Londoners as the 'wobbly bridge'. Designed by Norman Foster and Anthony Caro, its low-slung frame looks pretty spectacular, particularly when it's lit up at night with fibre-optics – the so-called 'blade of light' effect. But it's hard to forget this footbridge's abortive opening in June 2000. It was closed after just three days, when it began to sway alarmingly under the weight and movement of pedestrian traffic. A year and a half, plus £5 million worth of dampeners, later, it reopened and has since conveyed crowds, without incident, between Peter's Hill (in front of St Paul's) on the Thames' northern bank and Tate Modern and Bankside south of the river.

SOUTH BANK

Twentieth-century planners weren't too kind to the area south of Waterloo Bridge. Although presenting the South Bank with a wealth – and a labyrinth – of cultural and arts venues like the Royal National Theatre and the National Film Theatre, the architecture in which they were housed is indescribably ugly. But they've gone a long way towards making amends. The South Bank is now home to the cherished London Eye, the Saatchi Gallery, extended Jubilee Gardens and the latest Norman Foster landmark, a futuristic glass egg designed to house the Greater London Authority (GLA) headquarters.

Saatchi Gallery

The greatest hits of the '90s Britart, or Young British Art (YBA) movement – from Damien Hirst's sheep in formaldehyde to Tracy Emin's bed – are to be found here, in the rather incongruous Edwardian setting of the former County Hall. Now the **Saatchi Gallery** (☎ 0870 1160 278; www.saatchi-gallery.co.uk; County Hall, Westminster Bridge Rd SE1; adult £8.75; 🕑 10am-8pm Sun-Thu, 10am-10pm Fri & Sat; ⊖ Westminster or Waterloo), it's filled with works that became world famous in the twilight of the 20th century when Britannia's artists famously and controversially waived the rules.

Hayward Gallery

New foyer notwithstanding, the trick with the monolithic **Hayward Gallery** (Map pp114-6; ☎ 7928 3144; www.hayward-gallery.org.uk; Belvedere Rd SE1; admission prices vary; ⊖ Waterloo) is to get inside quick – away from the ugly concrete exterior into the roomy, modernist interiors that provide a perfect backdrop to the leading international exhibitions of contemporary art held here.

London Eye

Right on the Thames, the British Airways' **London Eye** (Map pp114-6; ☎ 0870 500 0600; www .ba-londoneye.com; adult £11.50; 🕑 9.30am-8pm Mon-Fri Oct-Apr, 9.30am-8pm daily May, 9.30am-9pm daily Jun & Sep, 9.30am-10pm daily Jul & Aug; ⊖ Waterloo) is the world's largest sightseeing wheel. (For all sorts of technical reasons it can't be called a Ferris wheel.) It's certainly the most fondly regarded of all London's millennium projects.

It is a thrilling experience to be in one of the 32 enclosed glass gondolas, enjoying views of some 25 miles (on clear days) across the capital. The 135m-tall wheel takes 30 minutes to rotate completely and it's best experienced at dusk.

Such is the wheel's popularity that, even though the opening hours keep extending, if you turn up without a ticket you might not get on; phone ahead or book online. To rock up and ride, you either have to arrive before opening to nab one of the few same-day tickets or run the gauntlet of the touts.

London Aquarium

One of the largest in Europe, the **London Aquarium** (Map pp114-6; ☎ 7967 8000; www.london aquarium.co.uk; County Hall, Westminster Bridge Rd SE1; adult/child £8.75/5.25; 🕑 10am-6pm; ⊖ Westminster or Waterloo) has three levels of fish organised by geographical origin, none of which you'll see during school holidays when the place is stuffed to the gills with kiddies.

LAMBETH

Lambeth is the district just south of Westminster Bridge, home to a few interesting museums and Lambeth Palace, the official residence to successive archbishops of Canterbury since the 12th century.

Imperial War Museum

Even pacifists appreciate the **Imperial War Museum** (Map pp106-7; ☎ 7416 5000; www.iwm. org.uk; Lambeth Rd SE1; admission free; 🕑 10am-6pm; ⊖ Lambeth North) because, alongside its famous collection of planes, tanks and other military hardware, it provides a telling lesson in modern history. Highlights included a recreated WWI trench, recreated WWII bomb shelter and a **Holocaust Exhibition**.

Florence Nightingale Museum

Attached to St Thomas's Hospital and celebrating the achievements of social campaigner and the world's most famous nurse is the **Florence Nightingale Museum** (Map p114-6; ☎ 7620 0374; www.florence-nightingale .co.uk; 2 Lambeth Palace Rd SE1; adult/child £5.80/4.20; ☯ 10am-5pm Mon-Fri, 11.30am-4.30pm Sat & Sun, last admission 1hr before closing; ⊖ Westminster or Waterloo), which recounts the story of 'the lady with the lamp' who led a team of nurses tending to the injured during the Crimean War. Upon returning to London she established a training school for nurses at this hospital in 1859. The small and thoughtful museum contains displays of personal mementos and other belongings.

Chelsea, South Kensington & Earl's Court

Much of west London could be classed as uptown. The residents of Kensington and Chelsea have the highest incomes of any London borough (shops and restaurants will presume you do too) and the area, like the Chelsea football team, is thoroughly cosmopolitan chic. Thanks to the 1851 Great Exhibition, South Kensington is first and foremost museum land, boasting the Natural History, Science and Victoria & Albert Museums all on one road.

Further west, Earl's Court is lively and cosmopolitan, although less prosperous. It's particularly popular with travelling antipodeans and was once known as Kangaroo Valley.

VICTORIA & ALBERT MUSEUM

A vast, rambling and wonderful museum of decorative art and design, the **Victoria & Albert (V&A) Museum** (Map pp110-1; ☎ 7942 2000; www.vam.ac.uk; Cromwell Rd SW7; admission free; ☯ 10am-5.45pm Thu-Tue, 6.30-9.30pm Wed; ⊖ South Kensington) is part of Prince Albert's legacy to Londoners in the wake of the successful Great Exhibition of 1851.

It's a bit like the nation's attic, comprising four million objects collected over the years from Britain and around the globe. Spread over nearly 150 galleries, it houses the world's greatest collection of decorative arts, including ancient Chinese ceramics, modernist architectural drawings, Korean bronze and Japanese swords, samples from William Morris' 19th-century Arts and Crafts movement, cartoons by Raphael, spellbinding Asian and Islamic art, Rodin sculptures, Elizabethan gowns, dresses straight from this year's Paris fashion shows, ancient jewellery, a 1930s' wireless set, an all-wooden Frank Lloyd Wright study, and a pair of Doc Martens. Yes, you'll need to plan. Alternatively, take an introductory hour-long **guided tours** (admission free; ☯ 10.30am-4.30pm).

NATURAL HISTORY MUSEUM

Kids – and most adults – will lose their minds at the **Natural History Museum** (Map pp110-1; ☎ 7938 9123; www.nhm.ac.uk; Cromwell Rd SW7; admission free; ☯ 10am-5.50pm Mon-Sat, 11am-5.50pm Sun; ⊖ South Kensington), where the main collections are divided between adjoining Life and Earth Galleries. Where once the former was full of dusty glass cases of butterflies and stick insects, there are now wonderful interactive displays on themes such as Human Biology and Creepy Crawlies. Plus there's the crowd-pulling exhibition on mammals and dinosaurs, which includes animatronic movers and shakers such as the 4m-high Tyrannosaurus Rex. The Earth Galleries are equally impressive. An escalator slithers up and into a hollowed-out globe where two main ex-

---

CRYSTAL PALACE & THE GREAT EXHIBITION

In 1851 Queen Victoria's consort, the German-born Prince Albert, organised a huge celebration of global technology in Hyde Park. The so-called Great Exhibition was held in a 7.5-hectare revolutionary iron-and-glass hothouse, a 'Crystal Palace' designed by gardener and architect Joseph Paxton. So successful was the exhibition – more than two million people flocked to see its more than 100,000 exhibits – that Albert arranged for the profits to be ploughed into building two permanent exhibitions, which today house the Science Museum and the Victoria & Albert Museum. The Crystal Palace itself was moved to Sydenham, where it burnt down in 1936.

hibits – Earthquake and the Restless Surface – explain how wind, water, ice, gravity and life itself impact on the earth.

The **Darwin Centre**, a vast new education centre, houses some 22 million zoological exhibits, which can be visited by tour.

SCIENCE MUSEUM

With seven floors of interactive and educational exhibits, the **Science Museum** (Map pp110-1; ☎ 7942 4455; www.sciencemuseum.org.uk; Exhibition Rd SW7; admission free; ⓨ 10am-6pm; ⊖ South Kensington) helps you discover everything from the history of the Industrial Revolution to the exploration of space. There is something for all ages from vintage cars, old trains and antique aeroplanes to labour-saving devices for the home, a wind tunnel and flight simulator. The even more high-tech extension, the **Wellcome Wing**, focuses on contemporary science and makes presentations on recent breakthroughs. There's also a 450-seat **IMAX cinema**.

CHELSEA PHYSIC GARDEN

Established in 1673 to provide a means for students to study medicinal plants and healing, this peaceful **garden** (Map pp112-3; ☎ 7352 5646; www.chelseaphysicgarden.co.uk; 66 Royal Hospital Rd SW3; adult £5; ⓨ noon-5pm Wed Apr-Oct, noon-5pm Mon-Fri, 2-6pm Sun during Chelsea Flower Show in May; ⊖ Sloane Square) is one of the oldest botanical gardens in Europe and contains many rare trees and plants.

ROYAL HOSPITAL CHELSEA

Designed by Christopher Wren, the **Royal Hospital Chelsea** (Map p121; ☎ 7881 5204; Royal Hospital Rd SW3; admission free; ⓨ 10am-noon & 2-4pm Mon-Sat, 2-4pm Sun; ⊖ Sloane Square) is a superb structure that was built in 1692 to provide shelter for ex-servicemen. Today it houses hundreds of war veterans known as Chelsea Pensioners, who are fondly regarded as a national treasure. As you wander around the grounds or inspect the elegant chapel you may see them in their winter blue coats or summer reds. The Chelsea Flower Show takes place in the hospital grounds in May.

Knightsbridge & Kensington

These are among London's poshest precincts and of particular interest to shoppers with black credit cards. Knightsbridge is where you'll find some of London's best-known department stores, including Harrods and Harvey Nichols, while Kensington High St has a lively mix of chains and boutiques.

KENSINGTON PALACE

Dating from 1605, **Kensington Palace** (Map pp110-1; ☎ 7937 9561; www.hrp.org.uk; Kensington Gardens W8; adult/child £10.80/7; ⓨ 10am-5pm; ⊖ High Street Kensington) was the birthplace of Queen Victoria in 1819 but is best known today as the last home of Princess Diana. Hour-long tours take you around the surprisingly small **Staterooms**. A collection of Princess Di's dresses is on permanent display along with frocks and ceremonial gowns from HRH and her predecessors. There's an **audio tour**, included in the entry fee, if you want to explore on your own.

KENSINGTON GARDENS

These **royal gardens** (Map pp110-1; ⓨ dawn until dusk) are part of Kensington Palace but blend in almost seamlessly with Hyde Park. There's a splendid, contemporary art space, the **Serpentine Gallery** (Map pp110-1; ☎ 7402 6075; www.serpentinegallery.org; admission free; ⓨ 10am-6pm; ⊖ Knightsbridge or Lancaster Gate), beautifully located south of the lake. The **Sunken Garden**, near the palace, is at its prettiest in summer, while tea in the **Orangery** is a treat.

On the southern edge of the gardens, opposite the Royal Albert Hall, is the restored **Albert Memorial** (⊖ South Kensington or Gloucester Road), as over-the-top as the subject, Queen Victoria's German husband Albert (1819–61), was purportedly humble. It was designed by George Gilbert Scott in 1872.

On the far side of the gardens is **Diana, Princess of Wales Memorial Playground**, an elaborate amusement park your kids will love.

Notting Hill

The status of the Notting Hill Carnival (in late August) reflects the multicultural appeal of this part of West London, into which West Indian immigrants moved in the 1950s. After decades of exploitation and strife, the community took off in the 1980s and the area is now a thriving, vibrant corner of central London that is retaining its charm despite steady gentrification.

Bayswater, to the east, was neglected for centuries, but is now mainly a fairly well-to-do residential area with Queensway as its main thoroughfare.

Hyde Park

At 145 hectares, **Hyde Park** (Map pp110-1; 5.30am-midnight) is central London's largest open space. Henry VIII expropriated it from the Church in 1536, when it became a hunting ground and later a venue for duels, executions and horse-racing. The 1851 Great Exhibition was held here and during WWII it became an enormous potato field. These days, it serves as an occasional concert venue and a full-time green space for fun and frolics. There's boating on the Serpentine for the physically energetic or, near Marble Arch, there's **Speaker's Corner** for oratorical acrobats. These days, it's largely nutters and religious fanatics who maintain the tradition begun in 1872 as a response to rioting.

A plaque on the traffic island at Marble Arch indicates the spot where the infamous Tyburn Tree, a three-legged gallows, once stood. It is estimated that up to 50,000 people were executed here between 1300 and 1783, many having been dragged from the Tower of London.

A more soothing structure, in memory of Princess Diana – a meandering stream that splits at the top, flows gently downhill and reassembles in a pool at the bottom – was unveiled here in mid-2004 with inevitable debate over matters of taste and gravitas.

MARBLE ARCH

London's grandest bedsit – with a one-room flat inside – **Marble Arch** (Map pp110-1; Marble Arch) was designed by John Nash in 1827 as the entrance to Buckingham Palace. However, it was too small and unimposing for the job so was moved here in 1851.

Marylebone

Increasingly hip Marylebone is home to several attractions, from London's primo tourist trap Madame Tussaud's to the artistic treasure trove that is the oft overlooked Wallace Collection.

WALLACE COLLECTION

Arguably London's finest small gallery, the **Wallace Collection** (Map pp114-6; 7935 0687; www.the-wallace-collection.org.uk; Hertford House, Manchester Sq W1; admission free; 10am-5pm Mon-Sat, 2-5pm Sun; Bond Street) comprises a wealth of 17th- and 18th-century European artefacts and art including works by Rubens, Titian, Rembrandt and Gainsborough, all housed

---

> ### TOP FIVE – MULTI-ETHNIC LONDON
>
> - Dancing at the **Notting Hill Carnival** (p147)
> - Eating in **Brick Lane** (p156)
> - Hanging out in **Brixton** (p144)
> - Gigging in **Hackney** (p164)
> - Walking through **Chinatown** (p130)

---

in a splendid and sumptuously restored Italianate mansion. Free guided tours take place daily; phone for the exact times.

MADAME TUSSAUD'S

This toweringly tedious **waxworks collection** (Map pp114-6; 0870 400 3000; www.madame-tussauds.com; Marylebone Rd NW1; prices vary according to time of year & entry, adult/child incl Planetarium £12-22/£7-16; 10am-5.30pm Mon-Fri, 9.30am-5.30pm Sat & Sun; Baker Street) is still living off the name it made for itself in Victorian times and attracts almost three million punters every year. If you want to join them you'd better reserve your ticket and arrive early in the morning or late in the afternoon to avoid the long queues (particularly in summer).

LONDON PLANETARIUM

Attached to Madame Tussaud's (and included in the admission charge), the **London Planetarium** (Map pp114-6; www.madame-tussauds.com; adult £3; 10am-5.30pm Mon-Fri, 9.30am-5.30pm Sat & Sun) presents a 15-minute star show projected onto the dome ceiling. It has galactic bits and bobs in the foyer to occupy the kids while you wait for the next screening.

Regent's Park

A former royal hunting ground, **Regent's Park** (Map pp108-9; Baker Street or Regent's Park) was designed by John Nash early in the 19th century, although what was actually laid out is only a fraction of the celebrated architect's grand plan. Nevertheless, it's a lovely space in the middle of the city – at once lively and serene, cosmopolitan and local – with football pitches, tennis courts and a boating lake. **Queen Mary's Gardens**, towards the south of the park, are the prettiest part of the gardens with spectacular roses in summer when the **open-air theatre** (7486 7905) hosts performances of Shakespeare.

LONDON ZOO

Established in 1828 and one of the world's oldest, **London Zoo** (Map pp108-9; ☎ 7722 3333; www .londonzoo.co.uk; Regent's Park NW1; adult/child £13/9.75; ☗ 10am-5.30pm Mar-Oct, 10am-4pm Nov-Feb; ⊖ Camden Town) got into hot water because its historical buildings weren't conducive to animal comforts. Smarting from the criticism, the zoo embarked on a 10-year, £21 million project focusing on conservation, education and breeding programmes. All the same, you'll find this zoo as thrilling or upsetting as any other. Feeding times, reptile handling and the petting zoo are always popular.

North London

The northern reaches of central London stretch from St John's Wood in the west to Islington in the east. Camden Market and Hampstead Heath are among North London's most popular attractions, while Islington is awash with lively pubs and eateries. Upper St is particularly worth a wander.

EUSTON & KING'S CROSS

These aren't especially inviting areas and will be most familiar to users of the tube and anyone taking a train to the north of England. If you're due to pass through King's Cross St Pancras, rise to the surface and check out St Pancras station, the pinnacle of the neo-Gothic revival architecture.

British Library

Colin St John's new **British Library** (Map pp108-9; ☎ 7412 7000; www.bl.uk; 96 Euston Rd NW1; admission free; ☗ 9.30am-6pm Mon & Wed-Fri, 9.30am-8pm Tue, 9.30am-5pm Sat, 11am-5pm Sun; ⊖ King's Cross St Pancras), which opened in 1998, has copped flak for its façade, but its interior is superb. Only members can use the collection, but historical documents, including the Magna Carta, are on public display.

ST JOHN'S WOOD

Posh St John's Wood is where you'll find Lord's, the home of cricket. You'll also find 3 Abbey Rd, where the Beatles recorded most of their albums, including *Abbey Road* (1969) itself, with its cover shot taken on the zebra crossing outside.

MCC Museum & Lord's Tour

The next best thing to watching a test at **Lord's Cricket Ground** (Map pp106-7; ☎ 7432 1033; www.lords.org; St John's Wood Rd NW8; adult/child £7.50/5.50; tours 10am, noon & 2pm Apr-Sep, noon & 2pm Oct-Mar when there's no play; ⊖ St John's Wood) is the absorbingly anecdotal 90-minute tour of the ground and facilities, which takes in the famous (members only) Long Room and a museum featuring evocative memorabilia.

CAMDEN

Camden's popularity has grown out of all proportion in recent years, largely propelled by **Camden Market** (see the boxed text, p167), now London's most popular 'unticketed' tourist attraction with an estimated 10 million visitors a year. This was a working-class Irish and Greek enclave just two decades ago but has been largely gentrified since. There are a few outstanding pubs, restaurants and music venues, but it's the Camden vibe people swear by.

HAMPSTEAD & HIGHGATE

These quaint and well-heeled villages, perched on hills above central London, are home to an inordinate number of celebrities and intelligentsia. The villages are largely as they were laid out in the 18th century and boast close proximity to the vast Hampstead Heath, where it's as easy to forget you're in a big city as it is to get completely lost.

Hampstead Heath

With its rolling woodlands and meadows, **Hampstead Heath** (Map pp106-7; ⊖ Hampstead, Gospel Oak or Hampstead Heath main-line station) is a million miles away – well approximately four – from the city of London. A walk up Parliament Hill affords one of the most spectacular views of the city.

Kenwood House (Map pp106-7; ☎ 8348 1286; Hampstead Lane NW3; admission free, tour adult £3.50; ☗ 10am-6pm Apr-Sep, 10am-5pm Mar & Oct, 10am-4pm Nov-Feb; ⊖ Archway or Golders Green) is a magnificent neoclassical mansion on the northern side of the heath, and houses a small collection of paintings by European masters. From the station catch bus No 210.

The Heath also has several swimming ponds – for the strong and hardy – with separate ponds for single-sex and mixed bathing. Once you've worked up a thirst, that's *after* your swim, there are several good pubs in the vicinity (see p162).

Highgate Cemetery

Most famous as the final resting place of Karl Marx and other notable mortals, **Highgate Cemetery** (Map pp106-7; ☎ 8340 1834; Swain's Lane N6; adult £2; eastern section 🕑 10am-5pm Mon-Fri, 11am-5pm Sat & Sun Apr-Oct; 10am-4pm Mon-Fri, 11am-4pm Sat & Sun rest of yr; ⊖ Highgate) is set in 20 wonderfully wild and atmospheric hectares with absurdly overdecorated Victorian graves and sombre tombs.

The cemetery is divided into two parts. You can visit Marx on the maintained east side on your own, but to visit the vine-covered western section of this Victorian Valhalla you'll have to take a **tour** (adult/child £3/1; 🕑 noon Mon-Fri, on the hr 11am-4pm Sat & Sun Apr-Oct; on the hr 11am-3pm Sat & Sun Nov-Mar).

Keats House

The golden boy of the Romantic poets lived in this elegant Regency **house** (Map pp106-7; ☎ 7435 2062; Wentworth Pl, Keats Grove NW3; adult/child £3/free; 🕑 noon-4pm Tue-Sun Nov-late Mar, noon-5pm Tue-Sun Mar-Oct; tours by appointment; ⊖ Hampstead) from 1818 to 1820 – until doctors advised him to move to sunnier climes – and penned some of his most famous works here. In the secluded garden, under a tree that has long since been replaced, he wrote *Ode to a Nightingale*. Among the personal mementos are love letters and old manuscripts. Restorations are scheduled to take place, so ring ahead.

Freud Museum

After fleeing Nazi-occupied Vienna in 1938, Sigmund Freud came to this house where he lived the last 18 months of his life. The **Freud Museum** (Map pp106-7; ☎ 7435 2002; www.freud.org.uk; 20 Maresfield Gardens NW3; adult/child £4/free; 🕑 noon-5pm Wed-Sun) contains the psychoanalyst's original couch, his books and his Greek and Asian artefacts.

East London

The eastern reaches of central London are taken up by the East End – the London of old Hollywood films and Christmas pantomimes – and the sprawl of the Docklands, where the brand new sits alongside the old and decaying.

EAST END

The East End districts of Shoreditch, Hoxton, Spitalfields and Whitechapel may lie within walking distance of the City, but the change of pace and style is extraordinary. Traditionally, this was working-class London, settled by different waves of immigrants all of whom have left their mark. Run down and neglected by the early 1980s, it is now looking up and pockets of it, like Hoxton, have become centres of cool. There are no major attractions to drag you into the East End, but it's a good place to immerse yourself in modern, multicultural London.

Geffrye Museum

With a sequence of recreated domestic interiors, running chronologically from Elizabethan times to the end of the 20th century along 14 interconnected 18th-century almshouses, the **Geffrye Museum** (Map pp106-7; ☎ 7739 9893; www.geffrye-museum.org.uk; 136 Kingsland Rd E2; admission free; 🕑 10am-5pm Tue-Sat, noon-5pm Sun; ⊖ Old Street, then bus No 243) provides a delightfully engaging peek at British domestic style. There's a lovely walled herb garden, a design centre, shop and restaurant.

DOCKLANDS

The Port of London was once the world's greatest port, the hub of the British Empire and its enormous global trade. Since being pummelled by the Luftwaffe in WWII its fortunes have been topsy-turvy, but new development and infrastructure have seen people and tenants return in recent years.

The new **Museum in Docklands** (Map p122; ☎ 7515 1162; www.museumindocklands.org.uk; Hertsmere Rd, West India Quay E17; adult/child £5/free; 🕑 10am-5.30pm), housed in a heritage-listed warehouse, uses artefacts and multimedia displays to chart the history of the Docklands from Roman trading to its renewal in the twilight of the 20th century. It's a fascinating look through the Docklands window into Britain's past.

South London

Glamorous Greenwich is the main attraction south of London's centre but you will also have fun exploring Brixton's colourful market or visiting the excellent Horniman Museum in Forest Hill.

GREENWICH

Quaint and village-like, Greenwich (*gren-*itch) is a delightful place with a recharg-

LONDON'S OTHER CHURCHES

St Bartholomew-the-Great (Map p117; West Smithfield; ✆ Barbican) is one of London's oldest and most atmospheric churches. It featured in the film *Four Weddings and a Funeral* and has Norman arches encasing a dimly lit interior.

St Martin-in-the-Fields (Map pp118-20; Trafalgar Sq; brass-rubbing ☎ 7766 1199; ✆ Charing Cross) is an early 18th-century masterpiece by James Gibbs that contributes to one of London's greatest vistas. The curious and ancient activity of 'brass-rubbing' is practised in the crypt, but perhaps the biggest draw at this acoustically gifted church, where Handel and Mozart once jammed, is the calendar of classical concerts throughout the year and the evensong at 5pm each Sunday.

St Mary-le-Bow (Map p117; Cheapside EC2; ✆ Bank or St Paul's) is another famous Wren (1673). Its bells dictate who is – and who isn't – a cockney; if you were born within the sound of their peal, you're the genuine article. The delicate steeple is particularly impressive.

Temple Church (Map pp114-6; King's Bench Walk, Inner Temple EC4; ✆ Temple) is London's only church with a round interior in London, and was built by the secretive Knights Templar in 1185. Its frequently shifting opening times are just as mysterious as its founders, so ring ahead.

St Paul's Church (Map pp118-20; Bedford St WC2; ✆ Covent Garden) is known as the 'actors' church' because of its long association with theatre and thespians. Interior walls are lined with memorials to actors such as Charlie Chaplin and Vivien Leigh. The first recorded Punch and Judy show took place under the church's portico in 1662.

ing sense of space, splendid architecture and strong connections with the sea, science, sovereigns and time. It has earned its place on Unesco's list of World Heritage Sites and you should allow a full day to do your visit justice. All the great architects of the Enlightenment made their mark here, largely due to royal patronage, and there's an extraordinary cluster of classical buildings to explore.

The **TIC** (Map p122; ☎ 0870 608 2000; fax 8853 4607; 2 Cutty Sark Gardens SE10; Docklands Light Rail (DLR) Cutty Sark; ⏱ 10am-5pm) has all the information you need on the area and sells the **Greenwich Passport ticket** (adult/child £12/2.50), which covers admission to the *Cutty Sark*, National Maritime Museum and Royal Observatory.

Cutty Sark

A famous Greenwich landmark, this **clipper** (Map p122; ☎ 8858 3445; www.cuttysark.org.uk; King William Walk; adult/child £4/3; ⏱ 10am-5pm) was the fastest ship in the world when it was launched in 1869. You can stroll on its decks, admire the beautiful and ongoing restoration and descend into the hold to inspect maritime prints, paintings and the world's largest collection of ship figureheads.

Old Royal Naval College

Walk south along King William Walk and you'll see the **Old Royal Naval College** (Map p122;

☎ 8858 2154; www.greenwichfoundation.org.uk), designed by Wren and a magnificent example of monumental classical architecture. Now used by the University of Greenwich, you can still view the **chapel** and the fabulous **Painted Hall** (adult/child £5/free; ⏱ 10am-5pm Mon-Sat, 12.30-5pm Sun), which took artist Sir James Thornhill 19 years of hard graft to complete.

National Maritime Museum

Further south along King William Walk, you'll come to the **National Maritime Museum** (Map p122; ☎ 8312 6565; www.nmm.ac.uk; Romney Rd SE10; admission free; ⏱ 10am-5pm), a magnificent neoclassical building by Inigo Jones, which houses a massive collection of marine paraphernalia recounting Britain's seafaring history. Exhibits range from interactive displays to old-fashioned humdingers like Nelson's tunic complete with a hole from the bullet that killed him.

Queen's House

Attached to the National Maritime Museum on its eastern side, the **Palladian Queen's House** (Map p122; ☎ 8858 4422; admission free; ⏱ 10am-5pm) has been restored to something resembling Inigo Jones' intention when he designed the place in 1616. It is a spectacular exhibition venue, focusing on illustrious seafarers and historic Greenwich.

Royal Observatory

Charles II had the **Royal Observatory** (Map p122; ☎ 8858 4422; www.rog.nmm.ac.uk; admission free; ⊙ 10am-5pm) built here in 1865 to help solve the riddle of longitude. Success was confirmed in 1884 when Greenwich was designated as the prime meridian of the world, and Greenwich Mean Time (GMT) became the universal measurement of standard time. On this spot you can stand with your feet straddling the western and eastern hemispheres.

If you arrive just before lunch time, you will see a bright red ball climb the observatory's northeastern turret at 12.58pm and drop at 1pm – as it has every day since 1833, when it was introduced to allow the ships on the Thames to set their clocks. If you arrive just *after* lunch time, you can console yourself with superb views across London or a visit to the atmospheric preserved rooms containing the actual timepieces described in Dava Sobel's *Longitude*, the bestselling book about the fascinating quest to measure longitude.

Fan Museum

Apart from things nautical, Greenwich also provides the engaging **Fan Museum** (Map p122; ☎ 8305 1441; www.fan-museum.org; 12 Croom's Hill SE10; DLR Greenwich; adult/child £3.50/2.50; ⊙ 11am-5pm Tue-Sat, noon-5pm Sun), housed in an 18th-century Georgian house and one of only two of its kind in the world. Only a fraction of the hand-held folding fans, collected from around the world and dating back to the 17th century, are on display at any one time, although there's always enough to stoke your enthusiasm and you'll find yourself eagerly exploring the history.

Getting There & Away

Greenwich is now most easily reached on the DLR; Cutty Sark is the station closest to the TIC and most of the sights. There are fast, cheap trains from Charing Cross to Greenwich station (preferably Maze Hill) about every 15 minutes.

Alternatively, to get yourself in the mood, come by boat. **Thames River Services** (☎ 7930 4097; www.westminsterpier.co.uk) departs hourly from Westminster Pier (Map pp114–6) and Greenwich, and the trip takes approximately 50 minutes (return £8.25).

AROUND GREENWICH
Millennium Dome

The public never took to the **dome** (Map p122), the centrepiece of Britain's millennium celebrations. And it gobbled up millions of pounds as the government held on, waiting for a white knight to save its white elephant. Help eventually came from a multinational consortium, which took out a 999-year lease on the dome in 2002. It is being transformed into a 20,000-seater sports and entertainment arena, surrounded by shops, restaurants and affordable housing. It won't be completed before spring 2007.

BRIXTON

West Indian immigrants flocked to Brixton after WWII and infused the ramshackle area with a Caribbean flavour. A generation or so later, economic decline, Margaret Thatcher and hostility between the

---

A DICKIE BIRD ABOUT COCKNEY

Cockneys are generally regarded as the cheeky, chappy, salt-of-the-earth, working-class East Enders born within earshot of the church bells of St Mary-le-Bow. Cockney rhyming slang was possibly developed by rogues here in the 19th century as a code to evade the attention of the newly formed police force.

The true cockney language replaces common nouns and verbs with rhyming phrases, whereby wife becomes 'trouble and strife' and so on. With familiarity, the actual rhyming word in some phrases gets dropped so the wife simply becomes trouble, 'loaf' (of bread) is used instead of the word head, 'china' (plate) means mate, 'on the dog' (and bone) is on the phone, while 'syrup' (of fig) is a wig.

You'll still hear conversations peppered with cockney phrases, although the slang has evolved considerably, often ridiculously, since its East End origins. You wouldn't Adam and Eve the number of new versions and sometimes even the locals don't have a Danny La Rue what's being said – and that's no word of a pork pie.

police and black residents (who accounted for less than a third of the local population at the time) sparked several serious riots, which earned Brixton world notoriety. The mood is decidedly more upbeat these days, and the streets are full of vitality and verve. Despite gradual gentrification, it retains its edge, and the partying is hardcore. (See the boxed text on the Brixton Market, p167.)

FOREST HILL
Horniman Museum
This extraordinary museum, specialising in African art and sculpture, would be a major draw if it weren't so far out of town. Set in an Art Nouveau building with a clock tower and mosaics, **Horniman Museum** (Map pp106-7; ☎ 8699 1872; www.horniman.ac.uk; 100 London Rd SE23; admission free; ☼ 10.30am-5.30pm Mon-Sat, 2-5.30pm Sun; ✆ Forest Hill) has an assorted jumble of exhibits that were collected by the Victorian tea-merchant Frederick John Horniman. There's everything from Africa's largest masks to a superb collection of musical instruments.

Turn left out of Forest Hill station along Devonshire Rd, then right along London Rd, and you'll see the Horniman on your right.

West London
KEW GARDENS
In 1759 botanists began rummaging around the world's gardens for specimens they could plant in the three-hectare plot known as the **Royal Botanic Gardens at Kew** (☎ 8332 5000, recorded message ☎ 8940 1171; www.rbgkew.org.uk; Kew Rd, Kew; adult £5; ☼ 9.30am-6.30pm Mon-Fri, 9.30am-7.30pm Sat & Sun; ✆ Kew Gardens). They never stopped collecting, and now the gardens, which have bloomed to 120 hectares, provide the most comprehensive botanical collection on earth as well as a delightful pleasure garden for the people of London.

Any time is a good time to visit although the gardens are at their most picturesque in spring and summer, when weekends are normally chock-a-block. First-time visitors should board the **Kew Explorer** (adult/child £3.50/1.50), a hop-on hop-off road train that leaves from Victoria Gate – where you will enter from if you get the tube – and takes you around the gardens' main sights.

Its wonderful plants and trees aside – including the world's largest collection of

orchids – Kew has all sorts of charms within its borders. Highlights include the enormous **Palm House**, a hothouse of metal and curved sheets of glass; the stunning **Princess of Wales Conservatory**; the red-brick, 17th-century **Kew Palace** (1631); the celebrated **Great Pagoda** designed by William Chambers in 1762; and the **Temperate House**, which is the world's largest ornamental glasshouse and home to its biggest indoor plant, the 18m Chilean Wine Palmand.

The gardens are easily reached by tube but, during summer, you might prefer to cadge a lift on a riverboat from the **Westminster Passenger Services Association** (☎ 7930 2062; www.wpsa.co.uk; 1½hr), which runs boats several times daily departing from Westminster Pier from April to September (return £15).

HAMPTON COURT PALACE
Built by Cardinal Thomas Wolsey in 1514, but coaxed out of him by Henry VIII just before the chancellor fell from favour, **Hampton Court Palace** (☎ 8781 9500; www.hrp.org.uk; Hampton Court station; adult £11.80; ☼ 9.30am-6pm Tue-Sun, 10.15am-6pm Mon mid-Mar–Oct; 9.30am-4.30pm Tue-Sun, 10.15am-4.30pm Mon Nov–mid-Mar) is the largest and grandest Tudor structure in England. It was already one of the most sophisticated palaces in Europe when, in the 17th century, Christopher Wren was commissioned to build an extension. The result is a beautiful blend of Tudor and 'restrained baroque' architecture.

Steeped in history, the palace makes for an enthralling visit and you should set aside the best part of a day to savour it. At the ticket office by the main Trophy Gate, pick up a leaflet listing schedules for the themed guided tours led by historians bedecked in period clobber.

If you're in a rush, or have an aversion to guided tours, highlights include **Henry VIII's State Apartments**, including the Great Hall with its spectacular hammer-beamed roof; the **Tudor Kitchens**, staffed by 'servants'; and the **Renaissance Picture Gallery**. Spend some time in the superb gardens and get lost in the 300-year-old **maze**.

Hampton Court Palace is 13 miles southwest of central London and is easily reached by train from Waterloo via Hampton Court station. Alternatively, you can take the 3½-hour riverboat journey from Westminster Pier (p145).

LONDON

RICHMOND PARK

London's wildest park spans more than 1000 hectares and is home to all sorts of wildlife, most notably herds of red and fallow deer. It's a terrific place for bird-watching, rambling and cycling.

To get there from the Richmond tube station, turn left along George St, then left at the fork that leads up Richmond Hill until you come to the main entrance of Richmond Gate.

WHITEHALL WALKING TOUR

Lined with government buildings, statues, monuments and other historical sights, Whitehall (⊖ Charing Cross or Westminster), and its extension, Parliament St, is the wide avenue that connects Trafalgar Sq with Parliament Sq. Whitehall was once the administrative heart of the British Empire and is still the focal point for British government.

The best way to take it all in is with the following short and leisurely stroll.

Start at the southern end of Trafalgar Sq as it leads into Whitehall. As you start walk-ing south, on the right you'll see 1910 **Admiralty Arch** (**1**; p124) and the **Old Admiralty** (**2**).

Further along on the left is the **Ministry of Defence** (**3**), on the far side of which you'll find the **Banqueting House** (**4**; p125).

On the other side of Whitehall is **Horse Guards Parade** (**5**; ⏲ 11am Mon-Sat, 10am Sun), where the mounted troopers of the Household Cavalry are changed in a ceremony you'll find more accessible than the one outside Buckingham Palace.

The next intersection south of Horse Guards Parade brings you to **Downing St** (**6**), site of the British prime minister's official residence since 1732, when George II presented No 10 to Robert Walpole. Tony Blair and his family actually now live in the larger apartments at No 11.

Whitehall becomes Parliament St and, on your left, you'll see the **Cenotaph** (**7**; Greek for 'empty tomb'), a memorial to Commonwealth citizens killed in the two world wars.

On your right is the **Foreign & Commonwealth Office** (**8**; p125).

A right turn down King Charles St will bring you to the **Cabinet War Rooms** (**9**; p125).

Whitehall ends at **Parliament Square** (**10**), watched over by statues of past prime ministers. Left along Bridge St is the ultramodern **New Parliament Building** (**11**).

LONDON FOR CHILDREN

Although getting around with small children can be difficult here, London offers a cornucopia of sights and museums that will get your kids as excited about their trip as you are. Apart from the obvious destinations such as the London Dungeon, the London Zoo, Madame Tussaud's, the Science Museum, the Tower of London, the London Aquarium, the *Cutty Sark* and the London Eye, there are many green spaces with playground facilities throughout the centre and children are widely welcomed and catered for everywhere – with the exception of pubs.

All top-range hotels offer an in-house babysitting service. Prices vary enormously from hotel to hotel, so ask the concierge. You might also like to try www.babysitter.co.uk – membership costs £49 plus VAT, then sitters cost as little as £5.20 per hour.

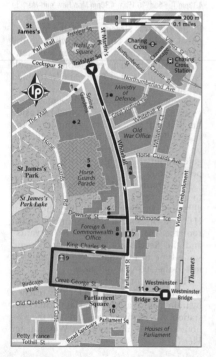

TOURS

If you're short on time and big on company, the **Original London Sightseeing Tour** (☎ 8877 1722), the **Big Bus Company** (☎ 7233 9533) and **London Pride Sightseeing** (☎ 7520 2050) offer tours of the main sights on hop-on hop-off, double-decker buses, which you'll see trundling through town. They cost adult/child £15/10 for the day, but are only worth getting if you're in town for a short stopover. London Pride Sightseeing includes Docklands and Greenwich in one of its tours.

Citisights (☎ 8806 4325; www.chr.org.uk/cswalks .htm), **Historical Tours** (☎ 8668 4019), **London Walks** (☎ 7624 3978; www.walks.com) and **Mystery Tours** (☎ 8558 9446; mysterywalks@hotmail.com) offer a variety of themed walking tours.

More imaginative and rewarding tours include the following:

Black Taxi Tours of London (☎ 7935 9363; www.black taxitours.co.uk; 8am-6pm £75, 6pm-midnight £85) Takes you on a two-hour spin past the major sights with a chatty cabbie as your guide.

Cabair Helicopters (☎ 8953 4411; www.cabair.com; Elstree Aerodrome, Borehamwood, Herts; tours £129) Offers 30-minute helicopter 'flight-seeing' tours over London every Sunday.

City Cruises (☎ 7740 0400; www.citycruises.com; Westminster Pier SW1; cruises £8.70; ⊙ 10am-4.30pm, later in Jun-Aug, fewer sailings Nov-Mar) Operates a year-round ferry service from Westminster Pier to Tower Pier and Tower Pier to Greenwich in a continuous loop that allows passengers to jump on and off at various stops. Boats depart every 20 to 40 minutes, with later departures in summer, fewer in winter.

London Bicycle Tour Company (☎ 7928 6838; www .londonbicycle.com; 1a Gabriel's Wharf, 56 Upper Ground SE1; £14.95 incl bike) Offers themed cycle tours of the 'East', 'Royal West' and 'Middle London'.

London Duck Tours (☎ 7928 3132; www.londonduck tours.co.uk; departing from County Hall; adult/child £16.50/11; ⊙ 10am-6pm) Uses the same sort of amphibious landing craft used on D-Day in WWII. You cruise the streets of central London before making a dramatic plunge into the Thames.

FESTIVALS & EVENTS

Although not renowned as a festival city, London has a few events that might influence your plans or give you advance warning of when and where it will be busy.

London Art Fair (www.londonartfair.co.uk; ☎ 0870 739 9500 for tickets; Business Design Centre, Islington; admission £12 with unlimited access) Held in January, this fair sees over 100 major galleries participating in what is now one of the largest contemporary art fairs in Europe.

Chinese New Year (www.chinatown-online.co.uk; Chinatown) Late January or early February sees Chinatown snap, crackle and pop with a colourful street parade and eating aplenty.

Chelsea Flower Show (www.rhs.org.uk; Royal Hospital Chelsea) Held in May, this is the world's most renowned horticultural show and attracts green fingers from near and far.

Royal Academy Summer Exhibition (www.royal academy.org.uk; Royal Academy of Arts) Beginning in June and running through August, this is an annual showcase of works submitted by artists from all over Britain, gratefully distilled to a thousand or so pieces.

Wimbledon Lawn Tennis Championships Held at the end of June, the world's most splendid tennis event is as much about strawberries, cream and tradition as smashing balls.

Pride Parade In July, this is London's gay and lesbian community's opportunity to paint the town pink, with a parade and a huge party in Hyde Park.

Notting Hill Carnival (www.thecarnival.tv) Held in August, this is Europe's largest and London's most vibrant outdoor carnival, which celebrates its Caribbean community with music, dancing, costumes and a little street crime over the summer bank holiday weekend.

SLEEPING

Wherever you choose to lay your head, the cost may well put a serious dent in your travel budget. Weigh up your options very carefully and decide what order of centrality, comfort and affordability should be in your plans.

At the lower end of the market, it's worth booking at least a couple of nights' lodgings before you arrive, particularly in July and August. Anything below £55 for a double is pretty much 'budget' in London.

Earl's Court is one of your safest bets for budget beds, while Bloomsbury and the area around the more upmarket South Kensington have lots of mid-range places to stay. You can forget about staying in or around the West End or the 'old money' London of Mayfair unless you've got money to burn. That said, there's a reasonable spread of accommodation options and you should try to park yourself close to where you intend spending most of your time.

West End – Soho to the Strand

You can't get more central than this so, naturally, accommodation here comes at a price. It specialises in deluxe hotels, many of which are tourist attractions in their own right.

BOOKING SERVICES

It's possible to make same-day accommodation bookings for free at most of the TICs, and **Visit London** (☎ 08456 443 010; www .visitlondonoffers.com) also has good deals.

At Home in London (☎ 8748 1943; www .athomeinlondon.co.uk) Can arrange B&B accommodation and charges percentage booking fees.

British Hotel Reservation Centre (☎ 0800 282888; www.bhronline.com; Victoria train station; per reservation £3; ⏰ 24hr)

First Option (£5 per booking) There are kiosks at the Britain Visitor Centre, Euston (☎ 7388 7435); King's Cross (☎ 7837 5681), Victoria (☎ 7828 4646) and Gatwick Airport (☎ 01293-529372) train stations; and South Kensington tube station (☎ 7581 9766).

London Homestead Services (☎ 8949 4455; www.lhslondon.com; Coombe Wood Rd, Kingston-upon-Thames KT2 7JY) Takes bookings for a minimum of three days and charges £5 per person.

Youth Hostels Association (YHA; ☎ 0870 870 8808; lonres@yha.org.uk) Operates its own central reservations service provided you can give them at least two weeks' notice.

BUDGET

Oxford St YHA (Map pp118-20; ☎ 0870 770 5984; oxfordst@yha.org.uk; 14 Noel St W1; 3- or 4-bed dm £22, tw per person £22; ⊖ Oxford Circus) The most central of the hostels, it's basic, clean and welcoming. There's a large kitchen but no meals are served apart from a packed breakfast. Most of the 75 beds are twins.

MID-RANGE

Regent Palace Hotel (Map pp118-20; ☎ 0870 400 8703; fax 7734 6435; Piccadilly Circus, cnr Glasshouse St W1; s with shared facilities/ en suite d from £50/80; ⊖ Piccadilly) In Piccadilly Circus, this place is ideally located but a little too busy. Serving some 1000 rooms, the hotel lobby is frenetic and the whole place feels rather impersonal.

Harlingford Hotel (Map pp108-9; ☎ 7387 1551; www.harlingfordhotel.com; 61 Cartwright Gardens WC1; d from £75, f £110; ⊖ Russell Square) This jolly good hotel comprises three 19th-century town houses and a bewitching chain of halls and stairways. The further up the stairs you go, the bigger and brighter the rooms generally get, although bathrooms are small whichever level you're on.

Fielding Hotel (Map pp118-20; ☎ 7836 8305; www .the-fielding-hotel.co.uk; 4 Broad Ct, Bow St WC2; s/d from £80/110; ⊖ Covent Garden) On a pedestrianised street a block away from the Royal Opera House. Space is at a premium and the décor is shop-bought but there's no better place to be located if you want to take in a lot of London in just a few days.

TOP END

Hazlitt's (Map pp118-20; ☎ 7434 1771; www.hazlittshotel .com; 6 Frith St W1; d from £205, ste £300; ⊖ Tottenham Court Road) The former abode of author William Hazlitt is a charming Georgian house and one of central London's finest hotels. There are 23 individually decorated rooms, each brimming with character.

St Martin's Lane (Map pp118-20; ☎ 7300 5500, 0800 634 5500; www.ianschragerhotels.com; 45 St Martin's Lane; r from £195; ⊖ Leicester Square) A joint effort between international hotelier Ian Schrager and French designer Philippe Starck, and is so cool that you would hardly notice it was there. The rooms have floor-to-ceiling windows affording sweeping views of the West End. The public rooms are bustling meeting points and everything – and everyone – is beautiful.

DELUXE

Brown's Hotel (Map pp118-20; ☎ 7493 6020; www .brownshotel.com; 30 Albemarle St W1; s/d from £320/370; ⊖ Green Park) A stunning hotel that opened in 1837 and the first in London to have a lift, telephone and electric lighting. Service is tip top and the atmosphere quintessentially English.

Covent Garden Hotel (Map pp118-20; ☎ 7806 1000; www.firmdale.com; 10 Monmouth St WC2; d/ste £210/350; ⊖ Covent Garden) Combines gorgeous fabrics and a theatrical theme to stake out its individuality among the deluxe boutiques (although it's really the location you pay for).

One Aldwych (Map pp118-20; ☎ 7300 1000; www .onealdwych.com; 1 Aldwych WC2; d/ste from £370/570; ⊖ Covent Garden) Luxurious and trendy, with (mostly) spacious rooms and lots of modern art. The highly regarded **Axis Restaurant & Bar** is the place to be seen and hosts food and live jazz evenings on Tuesday and Wednesday.

Ritz (Map pp118-20; ☎ 7493 8181; www.theritzhotel .co.uk; 150 Piccadilly W1; d/ste from £320/600; ⊖ Green Park) London's most celebrated hotel. After lending its name to the English lexicon, you might expect this most ritzy of establishments to rest on its laurels, don some slippers and fade out. Not so. While it's still the royal family's home away from home, such is the Ritz's unyielding cred that even the new generation of cultural elite are taking to it. The rooms are expectedly opulent while the restaurant is decked out like a rococo boudoir.

Trafalgar (Map pp118-20; ☎ 7870 2900; www.the trafalgar.hilton.com; 2 Spring Gardens SW1; d from £340; ⊖ Charing Cross) This is where the young, hip and fashionable come to savour tasteful minimalism and some spectacular views of the square.

Westminster & Victoria

Victoria isn't the most attractive part of town although you'll be close to the action and the budget accommodation is generally better value than in Earl's Court. Pimlico is more residential and is convenient for Tate Britain at Millbank.

BUDGET

Luna & Simone Hotel (Map p121; ☎ 7834 5897; www .lunasimonehotel.com; 47-49 Belgrave Rd SW1; standard s/ d from £35/50; en suite d £80; ⊖ Victoria) A central, spotlessly clean and comfortable place, the best among many on this street. A full English breakfast is included and there are free storage facilities if you want to leave bags while travelling. If all of London's budget hotels were like this, we'd probably stay longer.

MID-RANGE

Hamilton House Hotel (Map p121; ☎ 7821 7113; www .hamiltonhousehotel.com; 60 Warwick Way SW1; basic/en suite d £65/90; ⊖ Victoria) Friendly and close to Victoria's transport options. Although a little small, the 40 rooms are bright and cheerful.

Morgan House (Map p121; ☎ 7730 2384; www .morganhouse.co.uk; 120 Ebury St SW1; d from £90, ste £125; ⊖ Victoria) Alongside the British Museum, Morgan House is one of the best mid-priced hotels in London. The warmth and hospitality more than make up for the slightly cramped guest quarters.

Windermere Hotel (Map p121; ☎ 7834 5163; www .windermere-hotel.co.uk; 142-144 Warwick Way SW1; d from £84; ⊖ Victoria) The Windermere is an award-winning hotel, with 22 small, distinctive rooms housed in a sparkling-white, mid-Victorian town house.

St James's & Mayfair

This is the top end of town, 'old money' London, and you shouldn't even read the listings unless money's no object.

TOP END

Chesterfield (Map pp114-6; ☎ 7491 2622; www.red carnationhotels.com; 35 Charles St W1; d from £100; ⊖ Green Park) Comprises five floors of refinement and lustre hidden behind a fairly plain Georgian town house. It has moulding ceilings, marble floors and period-style furnishing as you'd expect from a grande dame of London digs.

DELUXE

Claridges (Map pp114-6; ☎ 7629 8860; www.savoy -group.co.uk/claridges; Brook St W1; d from £370; ⊖ Bond Street) One of the greatest of London's five-star hotels, a leftover from a bygone era and *the* place to sip martinis whether you're a paying guest or not. Many of the Art Deco features of the public areas and suites were designed in the late 1920s.

Lanesborough (Map pp114-6; ☎ 7259 5599; www .lanesborough.com; Hyde Park Corner; r from £320; ⊖ Hyde Park Corner) Where visiting divas doze and Regency opulence meets state-of-the-art technology.

Bloomsbury & Fitzrovia

Bloomsbury is very convenient, especially for the West End and the British Museum, and there are lots of places – of varying quality – on Gower and North Gower Sts. This one-time bohemian enclave of Fitzrovia is off the tourist map, yet within easy walking distance of Soho and lots of good restaurants. Tucked away in leafy Cartwright Gardens to the north of Russell Sq, you'll find some of London's best-value hotels.

TOP FIVE – ROMANTIC LONDON

- Kissing in the back of a black cab
- A squeeze on top of the **London Eye** (p137)
- Jumping hand-in-hand across puddles
- Walking back from the pub together just *before* closing time
- Canoodling on, or by, a canal

BUDGET

Generator (Map pp108-9; ☎ 7388 7666; www.the
-generator.co.uk; Compton Pl, 37 Tavistock Pl WC1; dm
£12.50-17, s £37; ⊖ Russell Square) One of the
liveliest budget options in central London.
The futuristic décor looks like an updated
set from Terry Gilliam's film *Brazil*. Along
with 207 rooms (830 beds), it has flirtatious
staff and a bar that stays open until 2am –
but the two don't necessarily go together.
There's also a pool, Internet access, safe-
deposit boxes and a large eating area but no
kitchen. All prices include breakfast.

MID-RANGE

Hotel Cavendish (Map pp108-9; ☎ 7636 9079; www
.hotelcavendish.com; 75 Gower St WC1; basic s/d from
£38/48; ⊖ Goodge Street) Spick, span and run
by an amiable family, this hotel can be a
budget option if you don't mind sharing
bathroom facilities. Rates include breakfast,
and the purple and burgundy rooms are
simply furnished and comfy. If the Cavendish is full, you'll be referred to its sister
hotel **Jesmond Hotel**, nearby, where rates and
standards are similar.

Crescent Hotel (Map pp108-9; ☎ 7387 1515; www
.crescenthoteloflondon.com; 49-50 Cartwright Gardens WC1;
standard s from £46, en suite d from £89; ⊖ Russell Square)
Built in 1810, it has a mix of rooms rang-
ing from poky singles without facilities, to
relatively spacious doubles with en suites.
The staff are hospitable either way.

Jenkins Hotel (Map pp108-9; ☎ 7387 2067; www
.jenkinshotel.demon.co.uk; 45 Cartwright Gardens WC1;
standard s £52, en suite s/d from £85; ⊖ Russell Square)
A smoke-free zone and has pretty rooms
with washbasin, TV, phone and fridge. The
rooms are small but the welcome is huge.

Ridgemount Hotel (Map pp114-6; ☎ 7636 1141;
www.ridgemounthotel.co.uk; 65-67 Gower St WC1; basic/
en suite d from £50/65; ⊖ Goodge Street) An old-
fashioned place, it offers a warmth and consideration seldom found in the city.

St Margaret's Hotel (Map pp114-6; ☎ 7636 4277;
www.stmargaretshotel.co.uk; 26 Bedford Pl WC1; basic/en
suite d from £63/98; ⊖ Russell Square or Holborn) An
exceedingly friendly Italian family-run
hotel in a classic Georgian town house, with
bright and comfy public and guest rooms
and a lovely garden.

TOP END

Charlotte Street Hotel (Map pp118-20; ☎ 7806 2000;
www.firmdale.com; 15 Charlotte St W1; d from £220;

⊖ Goodge Street) A fave with visiting media
types, this is where Laura Ashley goes postmodern and comes up smelling of roses.

Holborn & Clerkenwell

The availability of accommodation hasn't
kept pace with Clerkenwell's revival although things are quickly changing, and
this central area is becoming an increasingly good choice to lay your head.

MID-RANGE

Malmaison (Map pp114-6; ☎ 7012 3700; www.mal
maison.com; Charterhouse Sq EC1; weekday/weekend d
from £165/99; ⊖ Farringdon) One of a modern
Scottish boutique chain providing value
for money in trendy Clerkenwell. Suave,
sophisticated and refreshingly understated.

Zetter Hotel (Map pp108-9; ☎ 7324 4455; www
.thezetter.com; 86-88 Clerkenwell Rd EC1; d from £145;
⊖ Farringdon) A stylish, 21st-century conversion of a 19th-century warehouse. The furnishings are an enticing blend of old and
new, and the facilities cutting edge.

TOP END

Rookery (Map pp114-6; ☎ 7336 0931; www.rookery
hotel.com; Peter's Lane, Cowcross St EC1; s/d from £215/245;
⊖ Farringdon) Occupies a row of once-derelict
18th-century Georgian houses and provides
a luxurious hideaway in fashionable Clerkenwell. Rooms have period furniture including Victorian baths, showers and toilets.

The City

Obviously very central, the City can offer
good deals on weekends when the workers
are back in the suburbs tending to their gardens. But be mindful – you'll be swamped
with them during the week, and there's very
little action at night.

BUDGET

City of London YHA (Map pp114-6; ☎ 0870 5764;
city@yha.org.uk; 36 Carter Lane EC4; dm £15-26; ⊖ St
Paul's) An excellent facility (193 beds in
three- to 15-bed dorms) that stands in the
shadow of St Paul's Cathedral. There's a
licensed cafeteria but no kitchen. Although
right in the centre of London, it's pretty
quiet around here outside business hours.

TOP END

Great Eastern Hotel (Map p121; ☎ 7618 5010; www
.great-eastern-hotel.co.uk; Liverpool St EC2; s/d from

£225/265; ⊖ Liverpool Street) Just the right mix of hip and classic, without any unnecessary attitude.

Borough & Southwark

Just south of the river is good if you want to immerse yourself in workaday London, still be central and get fairly modest, non-descript accommodation (that doesn't cost the earth) in the numerous chain hotels that have sprung up here in recent years.

BUDGET

St Christopher's Village (Map p117; ☎ 7407 1856; www.st-christophers.co.uk; 163 Borough High St SE1; dm £15-19, tw £45; ⊖ Borough) The flagship of a chain of hostels that has gained a reputation for being cheap and reliable, fun and relaxed. The empire is expanding and it now has hostels in Camden, Shepherd's Bush and Greenwich, plus three along this street in Southbank. Facilities here include a sauna, solarium and hot tub.

MID-RANGE

County Hall Travel Inn Capital (Map pp114-6; ☎ 7902 1600; www.travelinn.co.uk; Belvedere Rd SE1; r £85; ⊖ Waterloo) Fairly bare bones, but the rooms are large and reasonable. If you can't get in here, there are about a dozen Travel Inns throughout London.

Chelsea, South Kensington & Knightsbridge

Classy Chelsea and 'South Ken' offer easy access to the museums and fashion retailers. The prices are reasonable for the neighbourhood and there's a relaxing villagey vibe.

BUDGET

Holland House (Map pp110-1; ☎ 0870 770 5866; hollandhouse@yha.org.uk; Holland Walk W8; dm £22; ⊖ High Street Kensington) With 201 beds, it's built into the Jacobean wing of Holland House and overlooks Holland Park. Though large, very busy and rather institutional, the position can't be beaten. There's a café and kitchen, and breakfast is included.

MID-RANGE

Abbey House (Map pp110-1; ☎ 7727 2594; www.abbeyhousekensington.com; 11 Vicarage Gate W8; standard s/d from £45/74; ⊖ High Street Kensington) A humble but pleasant abode near Kensington Palace. The floral motif may not be to everybody's

taste, but the rooms are undeniably cosy and the price is right. There's a rustic breakfast room and a kitchen where guests can make tea and coffee.

Five Sumner Place (Map pp112-3; ☎ 7584 7586; www.sumnerplace.com; 5 Sumner Pl SW7; s/d from £85/130; ⊖ South Kensington) On a quiet leafy road just off Old Brompton Rd, this place is restful, refined and elegant. It has 13 well-equipped rooms (any room with a drinks cabinet is 'well equipped') and there's an attractive conservatory and courtyard garden.

Swiss House Hotel (Map pp112-3; ☎ 7373 2769; www.swiss-hh.demon.co.uk; 171 Old Brompton Rd SW5; standard s £51, en suite s/d from £71/89; ⊖ Gloucester Road) An outstanding place for the price. It's set in a Victorian terrace house that's festooned with flowers, the staff are gracious and welcoming, and the amply sized rooms are cosily shabby chic. Rooms at the rear look out over a pleasant garden and don't get any noise from the street.

TOP END

Basil St Hotel (Map pp110-1; ☎ 581 3311; www.thebasil.com; Basil St SW3; d from £145; ⊖ Knightsbridge) A lovely, antique-stuffed hideaway in Knightsbridge. It's decidedly low-tech – baths instead of showers, no lifts etc – but it's a delightful vision of little England in big London.

Gore (Map pp110-1; ☎ 7584 6601; www.gorehotel.com; 189 Queen's Gate SW7; d from £190; ⊖ High Street Kensington or Gloucester Road) Features include lots of polished mahogany, Turkish carpets, antique-style bathrooms, aspidistras, thousands of portraits and prints, and a great bar.

Number Sixteen Hotel (Map pp112-3; ☎ 7589 5232; www.numbersixteenhotel.co.uk; 16 Sumner Pl SW7; d from £165; ⊖ South Kensington) A gorgeous spot, with bright and muted rooms, embroidered bedspreads, relaxing guest lounges and a tree-filled garden and conservatory.

Earl's Court

Although not really within walking distance of many places of interest, Earl's Court is the centre of inexpensive digs and the tube station is a busy tourist interchange with an infectious holiday atmosphere.

BUDGET

Barmy Badger Backpackers (Map pp112-3; ☎ /fax 7370 5213; barmy_badger.b@virgin.net; 17 Longridge Rd SW5; dm from £16; ⊖ Earl's Court) A basic hostel with dorm beds; rates include breakfast. There's a big kitchen and safe-deposit boxes. (There's also a YHA hostel nearby.)

York House Hotel (Map pp112-3; ☎ 7373 7519; yorkhh@aol.com; 27-28 Philbeach Gardens SW5; basic s/d from £35/55, en suite r from £48/73; ⊖ Earl's Court) Situated on a pretty, unassuming Earl's Court crescent, this small place has seen better days, but is good value, particularly if you are happy to share facilities.

MID-RANGE

Philbeach Hotel (Map pp112-3; ☎ 7373 1244; www .philbeachhotel.freeserve.co.uk; 30-31 Philbeach Gardens; en suite s/d £65/90; ⊖ Earl's Court) In a pleasant, quiet side street, this is one of London's few gay hotels, and its interiors are suitably stylish and unique. The garden restaurant Wilde about Oscar and Jimmy's bar on the ground floor are popular with the local gay crowd.

Notting Hill, Bayswater & Paddington

Bayswater is an extremely convenient location though some of the streets immediately to the west of Queensway, which has a decent selection of restaurants, are pretty grim. Scruffy Paddington has lots of cheap hotels and is a handy transit point. Notting

---

Hill is expensive in comparison, but has lots of good bars and restaurants.

BUDGET

Balmoral House Hotel (Map pp110-1; ☎ 7723 7445; fax 7402 0118; 156-157 Sussex Gardens W2; basic/en suite d £48/68; ⊖ Paddington) Immaculate and comfortable, although they've gone totally over the top with the room décor (not for light sleepers). There are two properties directly opposite one another on a street lined with small hotels and, unfortunately, lots of traffic.

Garden Court Hotel (Map pp110-1; ☎ 7229 2553; www.gardencourthotel.co.uk; 30-31 Kensington Gardens Sq W2; standard s/d £39/58, en suite s/d £58/88; ⊖ Bayswater) It barely squeezes into this category, but this is one of London's best budget options. It's cobbled from two 19th-century town houses and overlooks a pretty Victorian square. The same friendly family has run it for aeons. All 34 rooms have a phone and TV.

MID-RANGE

Pavilion Hotel (Map pp110-1; ☎ 7262 0905; www .msi.com.mt/pavilion; 34-36 Sussex Gardens W2; d from £100; ⊖ Paddington) Has 'Fashion, Glam & Rock 'n' Roll' as the motto and 30 singularly themed rooms which are fun and good value although definitely B-list.

TOP END

Portobello Hotel (Map pp110-1; ☎ 7727 2777; www .portobello-hotel.co.uk; 22 Stanley Gardens W11; d from £160; ⊖ Notting Hill Gate) A firm favourite with rock and rollers and movie stars down the years. Rooms and furnishing are eccentric in a funky, haphazard way, and there's a 24-hour bar to fuel guests on their merry way. The most coveted room is number 16, featuring a round bed which has seen action from the likes of Johnny Depp and Kate Moss.

Marylebone

Increasingly hip and groovy Marylebone is central and characterised by graceful Georgian squares and bustling High Sts. It's within walking distance of Hyde Park, staggering distance of West End nightlife and, for our money, one of the best neighbourhoods to stay.

BUDGET

Glynne Court Hotel (Map pp110-1; ☎ 7723 4613; fax 7724 2071; 41 Great Cumberland Pl W1; s/d from £50/60; ⊖ Marble Arch) Fairly typical for this price

---

AIRPORT HOTELS

Europa Hotel Gatwick (☎ 01293 886666; Balcombe Rd, Maidenbower, Crawley, West Sussex RH10 7ZR; d from £84) As good as any other mid-range airport hotel, and it has half-hourly transfers to the airport.

Hotel Ibis Heathrow Airport (☎ 8759 4888; fax 8564 7894; 112-114 Bath Rd, Hayes UB3 5AL; d from £65) It has clean, serviceable rooms and a restaurant.

Radisson SAS Hotel Stansted Airport (☎ 0127 966 1012; Stansted Airport; d from £105) A five-minute walk from the terminal.

range and location, it has 15 rooms, all with TV and phone.

MID-RANGE

Bryanston Court Hotel (Map pp110-1; ☎ 7262 3141; www.bryanstonhotel.com; 56-60 Great Cumberland Pl W1; standard d from £120; ⊖ Marble Arch) Open fireplaces, leather armchairs, creaky floors and oil paintings give it a hushed and traditional English atmosphere. There are 60 pleasantly furnished rooms, although the ones at the back are quieter and brighter.

Edward Lear Hotel (Map pp110-1; ☎ 7402 5401; www.edlear.com; 28-30 Seymour St W1; basic/en suite d from £70/93; ⊖ Marble Arch) In a terrific location just a short walk from Hyde Park Corner. You can eat a full English breakfast, with meat provided by HRH's traditional butcher. Rooms and furnishings are a little threadbare and there are four floors and no lifts.

Outside Central London

Staying outside the centre and commuting can be a drag, but these places are handy for great attractions on the outskirts.

BUDGET

Hampstead Heath YHA (☎ 0870 770 5846; hampstead@yha.org.uk; 4 Wellgarth Rd NW11; dm £22; ⊖ Golders Green) With 200 beds it's perfect if you want easy access to the centre of London but value fresh air at the same time. There's a well-kept garden, the dormitories are comfortable and each room has a washbasin. There's a licensed café and a kitchen.

Rotherhithe YHA (Map pp106-7; ☎ 0870 770 6010; rotherhithe@yha.org.uk; 20 Salter Rd SE16; dm £24, tw £55; ⊖ Rotherhithe) YHA's flagship London hostel is right by the River Thames and the perfect choice for anyone who's keen on spending time in historical Greenwich but doesn't mind being a little isolated. There are 320 rooms, most of which have four or six beds, though there are also 22 doubles (four of them adapted for disabled visitors); all have an en suite. There's a bar and restaurant, as well as kitchen facilities and a laundry. Rates include breakfast.

MID-RANGE

Hampstead Village Guesthouse (☎ 7439 8679; www.hampsteadguesthouse.com; 2 Kemplay Rd NW3; standard s/d £54/72, en suite s/d £66/84; ⊖ Hampstead) Only 20 minutes by tube to the centre of London, it has rustic, antique décor and furnishings,

comfy beds and a delightful back garden in which you can enjoy a cooked breakfast (if you pay the extra £7). There's also a studio flat, which can accommodate up to five people.

EATING

There has been an astonishing growth in the number and type of restaurants in London over the last decade or so, and dining out has become so fashionable that you can hardly open a menu without banging into some celebrity chef or restaurateur. Unfortunately, this new status doesn't automatically guarantee quality. Food and restaurants can be hit and miss no matter how much you spend. In this section, we steer you towards restaurants and cafés distinguished by their location, value for money, unique features, original settings and, of course, good food.

Opening hours vary. Many restaurants in Soho close Sunday, those in the City for the whole weekend. We've tried to note where places stray from the standard 'open daily for lunch and dinner' (standard business hours are outlined on p951), but it's always safest to call and check.

'Gastro-pubs' are hugely popular here, so you should also check the pub section for options. Vegetarians needn't worry. London has a host of dedicated meat-free joints, while most other restaurants offer vegetarian options.

West End – Soho to the Strand

Soho is the gastronomic heart of London, with stacks of restaurants and cuisines to choose from. The liveliest streets tend to be Greek, Frith, Old Compton and Dean Sts. Gerrard and Lisle Sts are chock-ablock with Chinese eateries. Bear in mind, though, that the phrase 'West End prices' is well known to Londoners.

MEAL COSTS

Our pricing categories for London are per person for a two-course dinner and a drink. You'll pay much less for lunch.

■ Budget – under £15

■ Mid-range – £15–£40

■ Top end – over £40

BUDGET

Café in the Crypt (Map pp118-20; ☎ 7839 4342; St Martin-in-the-Fields, Duncannon St WC2; mains £5-7, 'quick meals' from £3.95; ✷ closed Sun; ✦ Charing Cross) An atmospheric crypt in which to rest weary bones and enjoy good food from soups to casseroles. Lunch time is frantic.

Food for Thought (Map pp118-20; ☎ 7836 0239; 31 Neal St WC2; mains under £5) A classic old vegetarian joint that's big on sociability and flavour but small on price and space. Food ranges from soups to traditional Indian *thalis* (all-you-can-eat mixed plates).

Wong Kei (Map pp118-20; ☎ 7437 3071; 41-43 Wardour St W1; mains £4.50-7.50, set menus from £6; ✦ Leicester Square) Legendary for its rude waiters, although they're really not that bad (or good, depending on what you're after). The Cantonese food is a little stodgy but as good value as you'll find on a (plastic) plate.

MID-RANGE

Kettners (Map pp118-20; ☎ 7734 6112; 29 Romilly St W1; mains £9-16; ✦ Leicester Square) A gem, serving mouth-watering pizzas and burgers, which you can wash down with champagne while soaking in the gently fading grandeur with a piano tinkling softly in the background.

Gay Hussar (Map pp118-20; ☎ 7437 0973; 2 Greek St W1; mains £12.50-20; ✦ Tottenham Court Road) An old-style, Hungarian eatery and Soho institution that's hardly changed in more than half a century. The menu is rich, authentic and meaty, and the portions are colossal.

Tokyo Diner (Map pp118-20; ☎ 7287 8777; 2 Newport Pl WC2; mains £8-10; ✦ Leicester Square) Does everyday Japanese food at everyday prices. It's great for a quick and hassle-free bowl of noodles or plate of sushi to launch you into the night, or a set bento box on the run.

Mildred's (Map pp118-20; ☎ 494 1634; 45 Lexington St W1; mains £5-7; ✦ Piccadilly Circus) The best veggie restaurant in central London and a treat for carnivores and herbivores alike. Don't be shy about sharing a table or you'll miss out on excellent and hugely portioned wholesome veggie fare from stir-fries to beanburgers.

Neal's Yard Bakery & Tearoom (Map pp118-20; ☎ 7836 5199; 6 Neal's Yard WC2; snacks £2.50-4.50; ✷ lunch only) A great vegetarian café – relaxed upstairs, hectic below – with terrific filled rolls, burgers and soups. There is a cluster of veggie places nearby.

Ozer (Map pp118-20; ☎ 7323 0505; 5 Langham Pl W1; mains £7.50-13; ✷ closes 11.30pm Mon-Sat; ✦ Oxford Circus) Does 'Ottoman cuisine' that is lighter and more refined than the Turkish norm, as local workers and shoppers fully appreciate. Its Ankara sibling is supposed to be one of the best restaurants in Turkey.

Back to Basics (Map pp118-20; ☎ 7436 2181; 2a Foley St W1; mains £14-16; ✦ Oxford Circus) There are other options on the menu but fish is the focus at this superb corner restaurant, which you'll find cosy or cramped, loud or just lively depending on your mood.

Rasa Samudra (Map pp118-20; ☎ 7637 0222; 5 Charlotte St W1; mains £9-12; ✦ Goodge Street) Rasa Samudra is one of many restaurants on Goodge St, but its tantalising South Indian vegetarian cuisine and Keralan seafood set it apart from the rest. It's just north of Oxford St.

Rock & Sole Plaice (Map pp118-20; ☎ 7836 3785; 47 Endell St WC2; fish & chips £8-13) A classic, central chippy with restaurant, outdoor tables and takeaway. It's a model for modern British

---

SOHO CAFÉS

Soho's cafés are great for whiling away the hours inside or, weather permitting, on underused street furniture. These are a few stand-outs.

Bar Italia (☎ 7437 4520; 22 Frith St W1; ✦ Leicester Square) A great favourite with slumming celebrities lapping up the reviving juices and hunky paninis amid cool 1950s décor. It's always packed and buzzing but you can normally get a seat – after 1am.

Maison Bertaux (☎ 7437 6007; 28 Greek St W1; ✦ Tottenham Court Road) Has exquisite confections, unhurried service, a French bohemian vibe and 130 years of history.

Monmouth Coffee House (☎ 7836 5272; 27 Monmouth St WC2; ✦ Covent Garden) Brews beans sourced from all over the coffee-growing world. It's essentially a shop but has a few seats upon which you can slowly savour the magnificent blends.

Old Compton Café (☎ 7439 3309; 34 Old Compton St; ✷ 24hr) A friendly, often frantic place with cheap snacks, and the epicentre of gay Soho.

Pâtisserie Valerie (☎ 7437 3466; 44 Old Compton St W1; ✦ Tottenham Court Road or Leicester Square) A sweet Soho institution with delicious, delicate pastries, stylish sandwiches and strictly no phones *le mobile*.

cuisine (ie traditional foods, even mushy peas, cooked the right way).

Saigon (Map pp118-20; ☎ 7437 7109; 45 Frith St W1; mains around £11; ✆ Leicester Square) Saigon is required dining for anyone on a gastronomic tour of Asia, via Chinatown. While London isn't particularly well endowed with Vietnamese eateries, this one manages to satisfy body and soul with authentic tastes and furnishings.

Spiga (Map pp118-20; ☎ 7734 3444; 84-86 Wardour St W1; mains £9-14; ✆ Tottenham Court Road) One of a small, upmarket chain specialising in feisty pizzas, perky pastas and excellent vegetarian antipasto in sleek, casual surroundings.

Wagamama (Map pp118-20; ☎ 7292 0990; 10a Lexington St W1; mains £5-8; ✆ Leicester Square) This (or any of its dozen or so central London branches) is the place to throw back a bowl of Japanese noodles while sitting at a long communal table listening to anything but your own thoughts (which you won't be able to hear). Queuing seems *de rigueur*.

Woodlands (Map pp118-20; ☎ 7839 7258; 37 Panton St SW1; thalis £7-9; ✆ Leicester Square) One of an Indian chain that in India is only so-so but here…wow. Superb *thalis* are a highlight as is anything from the South Indian menu.

Zipangu (Map pp118-20; ☎ 7437 5042; 8 Little Newport St WC2; set menus £10-14; ✆ Leicester Square) Though not much to look at, it's got three storeys of outstandingly tasty, constantly fresh, exceedingly good food and graceful service.

TOP END

Admiralty (Map pp118-20; ☎ 7845 4646; Somerset House, the Strand WC2; set lunches £25; ✆ Embankment) The flagship restaurant of the restored Somerset House, it has a traditional interior and modern French food. There's a lovely terrace outside overlooking the Thames. The degustation menus – including vegetarian – are sublime.

J Sheekey (Map pp118-20; ☎ 7240 2565; 28-32 St Martin's Ct WC2; mains £10-25; ✆ Leicester Square) A jewel of the local scene. It is incredibly smart and has four discreet rooms in which to savour the riches of the sea, cooked simply and exquisitely. Waiters are tall and handsome while the menu is short and select.

Rules (Map pp118-20; ☎ 7836 5314; 35 Maiden Lane; mains £18-24) Established in 1798, this is London's oldest restaurant and specialises in classic game cookery, serving some 18,000

birds a year. Despite the history, it's not a museum piece and its sustained vitality attracts locals as well as the tourist masses.

Sketch (Map pp118-20; ☎ 0870 777 4488; 9 Conduit St W1; Lecture Room mains £50-75; Gallery mains from £10; ✆ Oxford Circus) A design enthusiast's wildest dream, with shimmering white rooms, designer Tulip chairs and toilet cubicles shaped like eggs. And that's just the downstairs video art gallery, which becomes a buzzy restaurant at night, then a funky club after midnight. Upstairs in the Lecture Room is the most expensive eatery in London with starters going for £65.

Wolseley (Map pp118-20; ☎ 7499 6996; 160 Piccadilly W1; afternoon tea £15; ✆ Piccadilly) Occupies a grand 1920s building that once served as a showroom for Wolseley cars. These days, it's a classic Viennese café serving everything from emergency quick croissants to a slow trot around a global menu.

Westminster & Pimlico

There's very little action around these parts at night, although the following restaurants are worth a short detour in themselves.

BUDGET

Jenny Lo's Tea House (Map p121; ☎ 7259 0399; 14 Eccleston St SW1; mains £5-7; ✆ Victoria) A simple, friendly Asian place that serves soups and rice dishes, but specialises in noodles and other wok-based specials.

TOP END

Cinnamon Club (Map pp114-6; ☎ 7222 2555; Old Westminster Library, 30 Great Smith St W1; mains £10-18; ✆ St James's Park) Has domed skylights, high ceilings, parquet flooring and a book-lined mezzanine that evokes an atmosphere reminiscent of when this place was the Westminster Library. Hushed, eager-to-please waiters hover like anxious footmen although they really have no need to be concerned because the Indian food here is fit for a rajah.

Tamarind (Map pp114-6; ☎ 7629 3561; 20 Queen St W1; mains £10-30; ✆ Green Park) One of those places where you're passed along a chain of assorted staff before sitting down – à la Bobby de Niro in *Goodfellas*. The slightly older crowd is froufrou, in keeping with the beautiful restaurant and neighbourhood, while the food – a cavalcade of Indian classics – is out of this world.

East End & the City

It can be difficult to find a decent, affordable restaurant that stays open after office hours in the City. Meanwhile, from the hit-and-miss Indian and Bangladeshi restaurants of Brick Lane to the trendy eateries of Hoxton and Shoreditch, the East End has finally made it onto London's culinary map.

BUDGET

Arkansas Café (Map p117; ☎ 7377 6999; Unit 12, Spitalfields Market, 107b Commercial St E1; mains £4-12.50; ☺ noon-2.30pm Mon-Fri, noon-4pm Sun; ⊖ Liverpool Street or Aldgate East) Serves good ole, down-home country cookin' on the unprepossessing edges of Spitalfield markets. Not for vegetarians.

Brick Lane Beigel Bake (Map pp106-7; ☎ 7729 0616; 159 Brick Lane E2; most bagels less than £1; ☺ 24hr; ⊖ Shoreditch) A relic of London's Jewish East End, it's more of a delicatessen than a café and sells the cheapest bagels anywhere in London. You only get what you pay for, but they're a good snack on a bellyful of booze.

Crussh (Map p117; ☎ 7626 2175; 48 Cornhill EC3; ⊖ Bank) The perfect place to pep up, with a range of juices and light, healthy snacks.

Dim Sum (Map p117; ☎ 7236 1114; 5-6 Deans Ct EC4; mains £4-7; ☺ Mon-Fri; ⊖ St Paul's) A budget traveller's delight and convenient for St Paul's and the City of London YHA hostel. It serves Peking and Sichuan dishes and has an all-you-can-eat buffet (minimum four people) in the evening from Monday to Friday.

Le Taj (Map p117; ☎ 7247 4210; 134 Brick Lane E1; mains £4-8; ⊖ Liverpoool Street or Shoreditch) A modestly dressed Bengali favourite, it's one of the better restaurants on this strip.

Place Below (Map p117; ☎ 7329 0789; St Mary-le-Bow Church, Cheapside EC2; light meals £6-8; ☺ lunch only, closed weekend; ⊖ St Paul's or Mansion House) A vegetarian café in a church crypt that's free of pinstripes and serves decent salads, pastas and quiches.

MID-RANGE

Real Greek (Map pp106-7; ☎ 7739 8212; 15 Hoxton Market N1; meze £9, mains £14-17; ☺ closed Sun; ⊖ Old Street) Set in Hoxton Market, London's trendy area du jour. This popular restaurant, in an old pub, specialises in innovative Greek cuisine, and if you think it looks familiar, you're thinking of the fight scene from the film *Bridget Jones's Diary*.

Sweeting's (Map p117; ☎ 7248 3062; 39 Queen Victoria St EC4; mains £9-20; ⊖ Mansion House) An old-fashioned place with a mosaic floor and waiters in white aprons standing behind narrow counters serving up a cavalcade of fresh and seasonal seafood.

TOP END

Fifteen (Map pp106-7; ☎ 7251 1515; 15 Westland Pl N1; mains £11-26; ☺ booking line 9.30am-5.30pm Mon-Fri, restaurant noon-3pm & 7-10pm Mon-Fri, 7-10pm Sat; ⊖ Old Street) Jamie Oliver's not-for-profit venture to train and employ young, disadvantaged kids. Reviews are mixed but people like to visit for a glimpse of the cheeky chappy himself, so you'll need to book ahead.

Southwark, Bermondsey & Lambeth

This part of south London is not immediately attractive as somewhere to eat out, although there are several good places and they are better value than the ones across the river.

BUDGET

Konditor & Cook (Map p117; ☎ 7620 2700; 10 Stoney St SE1; most dishes under £3; ⊖ London Bridge) The original location of arguably the best bakery in London, it serves excellent hot and cold lunches. There's not much space but everything is yours to take away.

Manze's (Map p117; ☎ 7407 2985; 87 Tower Bridge Rd SE1; pie & mash £2.50; ⊖ London Bridge) One of London's oldest and prettiest pie shops, it's been doling out the working-class staples of jellied eels and pie and mash for over a century.

MID-RANGE

Delfina (Map p117; ☎ 7357 0244; 50 Bermondsey St SE1; mains £9.95-14; ☺ noon-3pm Mon-Fri; ⊖ London Bridge) A chic artists' cooperative canteen that serves mean and modern international cuisine.

Blue Print Café (Map pp106-7; ☎ 7378 7031; Design Museum, Butlers Wharf, Shad Thames SE1; starters £5-6.50, mains £11-16.50; ⊖ Tower Hill) A restaurant by Sir Terence Conran, the man who first put London on the gastronomic map, this place serves an everchanging cavalcade of modern international seasonal fare. There are spectacular views of the river from here and the Design Museum is next door.

Fish! (Map p117; ☎ 7836 3236; Cathedral St SE1; mains £9-18; ⊖ London Bridge) Situated in an all-glass

London Eye (p137), London, England

Tyrannosauraus Rex, Natural History Museum (p138), London, England

Speaker's Corner (p140), London, England

Canary Wharf, London, England

LONDON UNDERGROUND

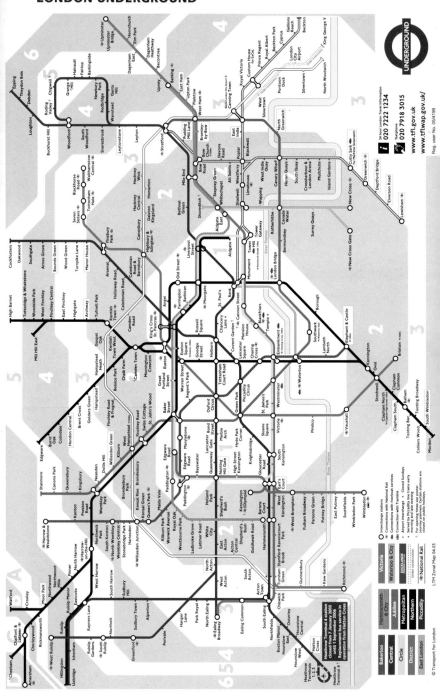

05/4199

Victorian pavilion overlooking Borough Market and Southwark Cathedral, it's part of a fast-breeding chain serving fresher-than-fresh fish and seafood prepared simply: steamed or grilled. Noisy!

Mesón Don Felipe (Map pp114-6; ☎ 7928 3237; 53 The Cut SE1; tapas £2.50-5; ⊖ Waterloo) Tops for tapas and authentic Spanish atmosphere, helped along by classical Spanish guitar in the evenings. There are about half a dozen vegetarian options, more than you get in Spain.

Tas (Map pp114-6; ☎ 7928 1444; 33 The Cut SE1; mains £5-15; ⊖ Southwark) An outstanding Turkish place with plush surroundings, fab kebabs and an unusually large range of vegetarian fare. There's also a café attached.

TOP END

Oxo Tower Restaurant & Brasserie (Map pp114-6; ☎ 7803 3888; Barge House St SE1; mains around £17; ⊖ Waterloo) Offers good grub – a bit Mediterranean, a bit French, some Pacific Rim – and is all about special-event dining. There are splendid views over the Thames and St Paul's Cathedral. This price guide is for the slightly cheaper brasserie.

Chelsea, South Kensington & Knightsbridge

These three areas boast an incredible array of eateries to suit all budgets, ranging from Michelin-starred indulgence to reliable caffs. There is such a concentration of French people in South Kensington that it's sometimes referred to as 'Little France'. You'll find a lot of French-operated businesses just southwest of South Kensington tube station.

BUDGET

New Cultural Revolution (Map pp112-3; ☎ 7352 9281; 305 King's Rd SW3; mains around £6; ⊖ Sloane Square) A trendy, good-value dumpling and noodle bar.

MID-RANGE

Francofill (Map pp112-3; ☎ 7584 0087; 1 Old Brompton Rd SW7; meals around £10) Around the corner from Bute St, it's a delightful café-restaurant.

Made in Italy (Map pp112-3; ☎ 7352 1880; 249 King's Rd SW3; mains £6-15; ⊖ Sloane Square) Family run and convivial, with the best pizzas for miles, it's as close as you'll get to southern Italy without packing a bag.

Boxwood Café (Map pp114-6; ☎ 7235 1010; Berkeley Hotel, Wilton Pl SW1; mains £13-16; ⊖ Knightsbridge) A

New York–style café set up by super-chef Gordon Ramsay in a valiant attempt to kick back with young folk and make fine dining in London 'a little bit more relaxed'. The décor is a little dreary but the food first rate.

Daquise (Map pp112-3; ☎ 7589 6117; 20 Thurloe St SW7; mains £5.50-12.50; ⊖ South Kensington) An attractively dowdy Polish diner and as charming a place as you're likely to find this close to the centre. The menu has lots of vegetarian as well as meat options; and the borscht (beetroot and bean soup) is a stand-out.

Wódka (Map pp110-1; ☎ 7937 6513; 12 St Alban's Grove W8; mains £11-14; ⊖ High Street Kensington) An authentic Polish joint providing Kraków-chic on a quiet residential strip not far from Kensington High St. Specialities include *blinis* (filled pancakes), fishcakes and eye-popping vodkas.

TOP END

Bibendum (Map pp112-3; ☎ 7581 5817; 81 Fulham Rd SW3; full meals with wine around £60; ⊖ South Kensington) Another Sir Terence Conran establishment, it's in one of London's finest settings for a restaurant – the Art Nouveau Michelin House (1911). The popular **Bibendum Oyster Bar** (half-dozen oysters £3.60-10.20) is on the ground floor, where you really feel at the heart of the architectural finery. Upstairs is lighter and brighter.

Gordon Ramsay (Map pp112-3; ☎ 7352 4441; 68-69 Royal Hospital Rd SW3; set lunch/dinner £35/65; ⊖ Sloane Square) One of Britain's finest restaurants and the only one in the capital with three Michelin stars. The food is, of course, blissful and perfect for a luxurious treat. The only quibble is that you don't get time to linger. Bookings are made in specific eat-it-and-beat-it time slots and, if you've seen the chef on TV, you won't argue.

Nahm (Map pp114-6; ☎ 7333 1234; Halkin Hotel, Halkin St SW1; mains £25-30; ⊖ Hyde Park Corner) A hotel restaurant serving up scandalously good tucker prepared by Aussie chef David Thompson. It's the only Thai eatery outside the kingdom to have a Michelin star.

Nobu (Map pp114-6; ☎ 7447 4747; Metropolitan Hotel, 19 Old Park Lane W1; mains £5-28; ⊖ Hyde Park Corner) A London designer's idea of a Japanese restaurant, this is, nonetheless, a strong contender for the best Asian food in town. Comfortably minimalist, anonymously efficient and out of this frikkin' world when it comes to exquisitely prepared and presented sushi and sashimi.

Tom Aikens (Map pp112-3; ☎ 7584 2003; 43 Elystan St SW3; set lunch menu £25, average à la carte without drinks £75; ⊖ South Kensington) Tom Aikens is the name of the notorious kitchen firebrand who runs this wonderful modern European restaurant where the setting is handsome and the food fab.

Notting Hill, Bayswater & Marylebone

Notting Hill teems with good places to eat, from cheap takeaways to atmospheric pubs (see p162) and restaurants worthy of the fine-dining tag.

BUDGET

Geales (Map pp110-1; ☎ 7727 7528; 2 Farmer St W8; fish & chips £10; ⊖ Notting Hill Gate) A popular fish restaurant that's more expensive than your average chippy (prices vary according to weight and season), but worth every penny.

Jacob's (Map pp110-1; ☎ 7581 9292; 20 Gloucester Rd SW7; meals around £10; ⊖ Gloucester Road) A charismatic Armenian joint serving salads, falafel and kebabs that are a treat for your palate and a relief to your purse.

Raw Deal (Map pp110-1; ☎ 7262 4841; 65 York St W1; main & 2 salads £6.50; ⊖ Baker Street) Occupies a glass corner of a Marylebone backstreet, and feels like the café on a Victorian railway platform where trains never come. Kooky and compelling, it's run by friendly South American smoothies who dish up robust and hearty salads along with pre-made hot dishes that never disappoint.

Sausage & Mash Café (Map pp110-1; ☎ 8968 8898; 268 Portobello Rd W10; mains £5-7; ⊖ Ladbroke Grove) Takes the British favourite of bangers and mash to new levels. There is not just a choice of different sausages, as you'd expect, but also variations of creamy mounds of mash and even gravy in this S&M club that won't give your wallet a spanking.

MID-RANGE

La Fromagerie Café (Map pp114-6; ☎ 7935 0341; 2-4 Moxon St W1; mains £6.50-9.50; ⊖ Baker Street or Bond Street) It's like celebrated food writer and owner Patricia Michelson's own kitchen, with bowls of delectable salads, antipasto, peppers and beans scattered about the communal table. Huge slabs of bread invite you to tuck in, and all the while the heavenly

waft from the cheese room beckons. Sensational food, smiley service, sensible prices.

Villandry (Map pp114-6; ☎ 7631 3131; 170 Great Portland St W1; mains £10-20; ⊖ Great Portland Street) Enter through a shop stocked with tempting goodies into this simple, stylish dining room where you can enjoy terrific modern European dishes like white bean stew with black truffle shavings.

Market Thai (Map pp110-1; ☎ 7460 8320; 240 Portobello Rd; mains £5-8; ⊖ Ladbroke Grove) is a delightful restaurant with dripping white candles, carved arches and wrought iron chairs. It occupies the 1st floor of the Market Bar but feels way, way, way beyond the market crowds. Hospitable staff and fresh, delicately spiced Thai cuisine make this place a little money very well spent.

Providores (Map pp114-6; ☎ 7935 6175; 109 Marylebone High St W1; tapas £2-10, mains £10-15; ⊖ Baker Street or Bond Street) A sassy, sociable and sexy restaurant that is split into two levels, with tapas tempting grazers on the ground floor and full meals along the same broadly Spanish lines in the elegant and understated dining room above.

TOP END

E&O (Map pp110-1; ☎ 7229 5454; 14 Blenheim Cres W11; mains £6-20; ⊖ Notting Hill Gate or Ladbrooke Grove) A Notting Hill hotspot and one of the best in a notable neighbourhood. E&O presents fusion fare that usually starts with an Asian base and pirouettes into something resembling Pacific Rim. The décor is stark and minimalist, but you're better off appreciating it at lunch because the evenings are mentally busy. You can dim sum at the bar.

Bloomsbury, Holborn & Clerkenwell

Holborn and Bloomsbury have relatively few good restaurants and nightspots to tempt you after dark while Clerkenwell has truly arrived on/as the scene.

BUDGET

Greenery (Map pp114-6; ☎ 7490 4870; 5 Cowcross St EC1; light meals £2-7; ⊖ Farringdon) A salt-of-the-earth veggie café, surviving for the moment amid the gentrification of Clerkenwell.

St John (Map pp114-6; ☎ 7251 0848; 26 St John St EC1; ⊖ Farringdon) Next to Smithfield Market, it offers an intrepid romp through ye olde English staples such as pigs' trotters, smoked eel and an awful lot of offal.

MID-RANGE

Abeno (Map pp118-20; ☎ 7405 3211; 47 Museum St WC1; mains £5-25; ⊖ Tottenham Court Road) An understated restaurant specialising in *okonomi-yaki*, a Japanese savoury pancake combined with the ingredients of your choice (there are over 20 varieties, with anything from sliced meat, vegetables, egg, noodles and cheese). It's all cooked in front of you on the hotplate that makes up most of your table.

Eagle (Map pp108-9; ☎ 7837 1353; 159 Farringdon Rd EC1; mains £5-12.50; ⊖ Farringdon) Small and vivacious, it doesn't try to be too clever despite its trendy appeal and status as London's first gastro-pub. Menus are seasonal, creative and Mediterranean-influenced.

North Sea Fish Restaurant (Map pp108-9; ☎ 7387 5892; 7-8 Leigh St WC1; mains £8-17; ⊖ Russell Square) This restaurant cooks fresh fish and potatoes – a simple ambition that it realises with aplomb. Look forward to jumbo-sized plaice or halibut steaks, deep-fried or grilled, and a huge serving of chips. The setting is characterless, but the charismatic staff amply compensate.

TOP END

Club Gascon (Map pp114-6; ☎ 7796 0600; 57 West Smithfield EC1; mains from £30; ⊖ Farringdon) Right next to glorious St Bartholomew's-the-Great, it has a Michelin star and exquisite food from southwest France. Dishes are served tapas-style in multiple portions.

Hakkasan (Map pp118-20; ☎ 7907 1888; 8 Hanway Pl W1; meals £6-30; ⊖ Tottenham Court Road) Hidden down a lane like all the most fashionable haunts need to be, it combines celebrity status, a stunning design, persuasive cocktails and surprisingly sophisticated Chinese food. It was the first Chinese restaurant to get a Michelin star.

Camden & Islington

There are plenty of decent places to eat on and around Camden High St and Upper St in Islington. There are far fewer worthwhile stops in Euston and King's Cross in between.

BUDGET

Afghan Kitchen (Map pp108-9; ☎ 7359 8019; 35 Islington Green N1; mains around £5; 🕑 closed Sun & Mon; ⊖ Angel) Small, laid-back and perpetually hip, this place serves simple, tasty Afghan fare – half vegetarian, half with meat – and the prices are charitable.

Diwana (Map pp108-9; ☎ 7387 5556; 121 Drummond St; mains £3-6.50; ⊖ King's Cross) The first of its kind on the street – and still the best according to many. It specialises in Bombay-style *bel poori* (a sweet and sour, soft and crunchy 'party mix' snack) and *dosas* (filled pancakes). There's an all-you-can-eat lunchtime buffet for £5.80.

MID-RANGE

Almeida (Map pp108-9; ☎ 7354 477730; Almeida St N1; mains £11-20; ⊖ Angel) Has trolleys of pâtés and terrines for starters, classic French mains, and tarts for desserts. It's a Sir Terence Conran and it's a winner.

Café Delancey (Map pp108-9; ☎ 7387 1985; 3 Delancey St NW1; mains £7-15; ⊖ Camden Town) The grandaddy of French-style brasseries in London, it offers the chance to get a decent cup of coffee with a snack or full meal in relaxed, European-style surroundings complete with newspapers. The bickering staff and Charles Aznavour soundtrack are suitably Parisian.

Le Mercury (Map pp108-9; ☎ 7354 4088; 140a Upper St N1; mains £5.95, specials £7-12; ⊖ Highbury or Islington) A cosy Gaelic haunt ideal for a romantic tête-à-tête. Sunday lunch by the open fire upstairs is a treat although you'll have to book.

Engineer (Map pp108-9; ☎ 7722 0950; 65 Gloucester Ave NW1; mains £10-15; ⊖ Chalk Farm) One of London's first gastro-pubs, it serves up good international cuisine to hip north Londoners. There are a good selection of wines and beers, and a splendid garden.

Fulham

Fulham Rd is a good place for a meal and a night out. These two are London standouts.

Gate (Map pp106-7; ☎ 8748 6932; 51 Queen Caroline St W6; mains £8-12; ⊖ Hammersmith) This place alone is enough reason to include a Fulham section. It's one of London's best restaurants. Taste, service and presentation are paramount but never get in the way of fun and friendliness. And it's vegetarian too.

River Café (Map pp106-7; ☎ 7386 4200; Thames Wharf, Rainville Rd W6; mains £20-30; ⊖ Hammersmith) A see-and-be-seen Italian eatery that owes its fame as much to the cookbooks it has spawned as to the food actually served here, which is based on the very best ingredients cooked simply.

Outside Central London

If you're visiting the sights in Brixton, Greenwich, Hampstead, Kew or Richmond consider a meal at any of the following restaurants and save yourself having to bolt back to the centre of town.

BRIXTON

Bug Bar Restaurant & Lounge (Map pp106-7; ☎ 7738 3366; St Matthew's Church, Brixton Hill SW2; mains £7.50-10.50; ❤ 5-11pm Mon-Thu, 5-11.30pm Fri & Sat, 11am-11pm Sun; ⊖ Brixton) Situated in the crypt of St Matthew's Church. Arches, candles and gilt mirrors all create an ecclesiastical flavour, but it's Bug's organic, vegetarian or free-range meat cuisine that will be most memorable.

GREENWICH

Goddards Ye Olde Pie Shop (Map p122; ☎ 8293 9312; 45 Greenwich Church St SE10; meals under £3.50; ❤ Tue-Sun lunch only) This is truly a step back into the past. A real London caff, with wooden benches and meals such as steak and kidney pie with liquor and mash, and shepherd's pie with beans and a rich brown gravy.

HAMPSTEAD

Jin Kichi (Map pp106-7; ☎ 7794 6158; 73 Heath St NW3; mains £5.50-13; ⊖ Hampstead) One of the best Japanese restaurants in north London. It's small and slightly shabby but so popular with London's Japanese that you won't be able to enjoy its grilled meats and other Oriental flavours unless you book.

KEW

Glasshouse (☎ 8940 6777; 14 Station Parade W9; set lunch/dinner £17.50/30; ⊖ Kew Gardens) Virtually next door to the tube station, this restaurant specialises in modern British cuisine and is a fabulous way to round off a visit to the gardens. The menus are set, but there are a wide range of dishes to choose from. The flavours will be etched on your palate all the way home.

Newens Maids of Honour (☎ 8940 2752; 288 Kew Rd; set teas £5.45; ❤ Tue-Sun; ⊖ Kew Gardens) An old-fashioned tearoom famed for its 'maid of honour', a dessert supposedly concocted by Henry VIII's second wife, the ill-fated Anne Boleyn. You'll find it a short distance north of Victoria Gate, the main entrance to Kew Gardens.

RICHMOND

Chez Lindsay (☎ 8948 7473; 11 Hill Rise; 3-course set dinner £15; ⊖ Richmond) A gregarious Breton hideaway renowned for its seafood as well as sweet and savoury crêpes chased down with cider.

DRINKING

The pub is the social focus of London life and savouring pub life is one of the pleasures of any visit. From ancient atmospheric taverns to slick DJ bars, London has a lot to offer the discerning tippler no matter how hard the themed and chain bars try to take over.

West End – Soho to the Strand

Coach & Horses (Map pp118-20; 29 Greek St W1; ⊖ Leicester Square) Sample the splendidly seedy atmosphere of this Soho institution made famous by writer and newspaper columnist Jeffrey Bernard who, more or less, drank himself to death here.

Freedom Brewing Company (Map pp118-20; 41 Earlham St WC2; ⊖ Covent Garden) London's primo microbrewery, although it might be a little expensive for the casual drinker.

Intrepid Fox (Map pp118-20; 99 Wardour St W1; ⊖ Leicester Square or Piccadilly Circus) It's so not Soho. This loud, arrestingly unaffected rock 'n' goth pub will be recognisable by the demented gargoyle above the door, the fake spiders and bats along the walls and the motley human assembly of Goths, punks and metal-heads with indoor complexions and impressive cleavages. The music is loud, the toilets grubby, the beer inexpensive and the bullshit barred.

Lamb & Flag (Map pp118-20; 33 Rose St WC2; ⊖ Covent Garden) A popular historic pub and everyone's Covent Garden 'find', so it's frequently jampacked. It was built in 1623 and was formerly called the 'Bucket of Blood'.

Punch & Judy (Map pp118-20; 40 The Market WC2; ⊖ Covent Garden) Inside Covent Garden's central market hall itself, it's a very busy and touristy two-level boozer. However, it has a balcony that lets you look down on St Paul's Church and the buskers, and is great on a sunny afternoon.

Scruffy Murphy's (Map pp118-20; 15 Denman St W1; ⊖ Piccadilly Circus) The most authentic of the Irish bars in Soho, short on ceremony and tall on tales.

Westminster & Pimlico

Red Lion (Map pp114-6; 48 Parliament St SW1; ⊖ Westminster) A classic, late-19th-century pub with polished mahogany and etched glassware. The pub's TV shows parliamentary broadcasts just in case a sitting kicks off in the house and the MPs have to hurry back.

Westminster Arms (Map pp114-6; 9 Storey's Gate SW1; ⊖ Westminster) A pleasant, atmospheric place just around the corner from Big Ben so it gets its fair share of politicians. It's great for a rejuvenating half pint after a tour of Westminster Abbey (think of the convenience).

Bloomsbury, Holborn, Hoxton & Clerkenwell

Cantaloupe (Map pp106-7; 35-43 Charlotte Rd EC2; ⊖ Old Street or Shoreditch) Was one of the pioneers of the Shoreditch warehouse conversion scene and is still a popular gastro-pub, although not nearly as fashionable (thankfully).

Cock Tavern (Map pp114-6; East Poultry Ave EC1; ⊖ Farringdon) A legendary pub where you can top up between 6.30am and 10.30am when it feeds and waters the workers from Smithfield Market.

Dragon Bar (Map pp106-7; ☎ 7490 7110; 5 Leonard St N1; ⊖ Old Street) Super cool in that louche, moody (as opposed to overtly posey) Hoxton way. It's easy to miss as the name is only embossed on the entrance stairs, but once inside it's all exposed brick, Chinese lanterns, velvet curtains and no suits.

Museum Tavern (Map pp118-20; 49 Great Russell St WC1; ⊖ Tottenham Court Road) Where Karl Marx used to retire to for a sup after a hard day in the British Museum Reading Room. If it was good enough for him...

Princess Louise (Map pp118-20; ☎ 7405 8816; 208 High Holborn WC1; ⊖ Holborn) Ww-oW! We may have used the word 'gem' before, but we take all of the other instances back. This late-19th-century Victorian boozer is spectacularly decorated with a riot of fine tiles, etched mirrors, plasterwork and a stunning central horseshoe bar. There are invariably more bums than seats until the after-workers split.

Sosho (Map pp106-7; 2 Tabernacle St EC2; ⊖ Moorgate) Sexy, glamorous and off limits if you're not feeling either of the above; although the cocktails could soon get you in the mood.

East End & the City

Captain Kidd (Map pp106-7; 108 Wapping High St E1; ⊖ Wapping) A great little pub on the Thames, it has large windows, a fine beer garden and a mock scaffold recalling the hanging of the eponymous pirate in 1701.

Jamaica Wine House (Map p117; 12 St Michael's Alley EC3; ⊖ Bank) It stands on the spot of London's first coffee house and is actually a traditional Victorian pub, not a wine bar.

Prospect of Whitby (Map pp106-7; 57 Wapping Wall E1; ⊖ Wapping) Dating from 1520 – last remodelled in the 18th century – it's one of London's oldest boozers. It's firmly on the tourist trail but there's a terrace overlooking the Thames, a decent restaurant upstairs and open fires in winter.

Ye Olde Cheshire Cheese (Map pp114-6; Wine Office Ct EC4; ⊖ Blackfriars) Rebuilt six years after the Great Fire, it was popular with Dr Johnson, Thackeray, Dickens and the visiting Mark Twain. Touristy but always atmospheric and enjoyable for a pub meal (mains around £7).

Ye Olde Mitre (Map pp114-6; 1 Ely Ct EC1; ⊖ Chancery Lane) An 18th-century treasure hidden down an alley. Just finding it makes you feel like claiming it as your local.

Borough, Southwark & Bermondsey

Anchor (Map p117; 34 Park St SE1; ⊖ London Bridge) An 18th-century boozer just east of the Globe Theatre, it has a terrace offering superb views over the Thames. Dr Johnson is said to have written some of his dictionary here.

George Inn (Map p117; Talbot Yard, 77 Borough High St SE1; ⊖ London Bridge or Borough) Tucked away in a cobbled courtyard not far from the Thames, this is London's last surviving galleried coaching inn and dates from 1676. Charles Dickens used to frequent the Middle Bar.

Market Porter (Map p117; 9 Stoney St SE1; ⊖ London Bridge) Across the road from Borough Market, this pub has a good range of beers and a diverse crowd.

Chelsea, South Kensington & Knightsbridge

Grenadier (Map pp114-6; 18 Wilton Row SW1; ⊖ Hyde Park Corner) Down a quiet and rather exclusive mews, the Grenadier is as pretty as a picture from the outside and welcoming within (despite the sabres and bayonets on the walls).

King's Head & Eight Bells (Map pp112-3; 50 Cheyne Walk SW3; ⊖ Sloane Square) An attractive corner pub pleasantly hung with flower baskets during summer. It was a favourite of the painter Whistler and the writer Carlyle.

Nag's Head (Map pp110-1; 53 Kinnerton St SW1; ⊖ Knightsbridge) In a serene mews not far from bustling Knightsbridge, this terrific early-19th-century drinking den has eccentric décor, a sunken bar and no mobile phones.

Notting Hill, Bayswater & Marylebone

Churchill Arms (Map pp110-1; 119 Kensington Church St W8; ⊖ Notting Hill Gate) A lovely, traditional tavern stuffed with Winston memorabilia and bric-a-brac. There's an excellent Thai restaurant upstairs (mains around £7) and a pleasant conservatory out the back.

Cow (Map pp110-1; ☎ 7221 5400; 89 Westbourne Park Rd W2; ⊖ Westbourne Park or Royal Oak) A superb gastro-pub with outstanding food and a jovial pub-is-a-pub atmosphere. Seafood is a speciality and the staff are much friendlier than you'd expect from somewhere so perpetually hip.

Mash (Map pp118-20; ☎ 7637 5555; 19-21 Great Portland St W1; ☾ closes 2am Mon-Sat; ⊖ Oxford Circus) Has a microbrewery and café so it's an all-day and all-week affair, although the main, huge and high-ceilinged bar requires a crowd to take off and is probably best kept for the weekend. It's a futuristic setting in an old car showroom, and the mechanics make mean mojitos.

Windsor Castle (Map pp110-1; 114 Campden Hill Rd W11; ⊖ Notting Hill Gate) A memorable pub with oak partitions separating the original bars. The panels have tiny doors so big drinkers will have trouble getting past the front bar. It also has one of the loveliest walled gardens (with heaters in winter) of any pub in London.

Camden & Islington

Bar Vinyl (Map pp108-9; 6 Inverness St NW1; ⊖ Camden Town) With loud music and groovy clientele, it's an earful of the Camden scene.

Crown & Goose (Map pp108-9; 100 Arlington Rd NW1; ⊖ Camden Town) One of our favourite London pubs. The square room has a central wooden bar between British Racing Green Walls studded with gilt-framed mirrors and illuminated by big shuttered windows. More importantly, the Crown & Goose combines

a good-looking crowd, easy conviviality, top tucker and good beer. What else could you possibly need?

Medicine Bar (Map pp108-9; 181 Upper St N1; ⊖ Highbury or Islington) Coolly unpretentious, it plays good music from funk to disco and stays open until 2am at the weekend. This place is members only at weekends. It also has a sister bar in Shoreditch.

Pembroke Castle (Map pp108-9; 150 Gloucester Ave NW1; ⊖ Chalk Farm) A light, airy retro place where you can feel just as comfortable supping wine as ale.

Outside Central London

BRIXTON

Brixtonian Havana Club (Map pp106-7; 11 Beehive Pl SW9; ⊖ Brixton) As laid-back as you might expect a bar with hundreds of different kinds of rum to be. Cocktails are the speciality and DJs set the mood.

GREENWICH

Trafalgar Tavern (Map p122; Park Row SE10; DLR Cutty Sark) A Regency-style pub that was built in 1837 and stands above the site of the old Placentia Palace where Henry VIII was born. It is the former drinking den of Dickens, Gladstone and Disraeli.

HAMPSTEAD

Hollybush (22 Holly Mount, above Heath St, reached via Holly Bush Steps, NW3; ⊖ Hampstead) A beautiful pub that makes you envy the privileged residents of Hampstead. It has an antique Victorian interior, a lovely secluded hilltop location, open fires in winter and a knack for making you stay longer than you had intended any time of the year.

Old Bull & Bush (North End Way NW3; ⊖ Hampstead) Has origins dating back to Charles I. One of London's most celebrated pubs, it was immortalised in the old music hall song *Down by the Old Bull and Bush*.

Spaniard's Inn (Spaniard's Rd NW3; ⊖ Hampstead, then bus No 21) A marvellous tavern that dates from 1585 and has more character than a West End musical. Dick Turpin, the dandy highwayman (or was that Adam Ant?), was born here and used it as a hangout in his later years, while more savoury literary sorts like Dickens, Shelley, Keats and Byron also availed themselves of its charms. Come here for the big, blissful garden and good food.

ENTERTAINMENT

If you've come to the capital to be entertained, you won't be disappointed. Whatever you want – from cutting-edge clubs and international bands to Hollywood stars doing theatre turns and the world's best footballers strutting their stuff – you'd need a lifetime to exhaust the opportunities for fun. This list only scratches the surface; make sure to check the listings (see p105) for what's going on.

Theatre

London is a world capital for theatre and there's a lot more than mammoth musicals to tempt you into the West End. The term 'West End' – as with Broadway – generally refers to the big-money productions like musicals, but also includes such heavyweights as the **Royal Court** (Map pp112-3; ☎ 7565 5000; Sloane Sq SW1; ⊖ Sloane Square), the patron of new British writing; the **Royal National Theatre** (Map pp114-6; ☎ 7452 3000; South Bank; ⊖ Waterloo), which has three auditoriums and hosts classic and contemporary plays from some of the world's best companies; and the **Royal Shakespeare Company** (RSC; ☎ 7638 8891), which hosts productions of the Bard's classics as well as stuff he might have been interested in. Unfortunately, at the time of writing, the esteemed RSC is without a permanent home and is staging performances at various West End theatres.

On performance days you can buy half-price tickets for West End productions (cash only) from the **Leicester Square Half-Price Ticket Booth** (Map pp118-20; Leicester Sq; ⊙ noon-6.30pm; ⊖ Leicester Square), on the south side of Leicester Sq. The booth is the one with the clock tower – beware of touts selling dodgy tickets. It charges £2 commission for each ticket.

Off West End – where you'll generally find the most original works – includes venues like the recently refurbished **Almeida** (Map pp108-9; ☎ 7359 4404; www.almeida.co.uk; Almeida St N1), **Battersea Arts Centre** (Map pp106-7; Lavender Hill SW1) and the **Young Vic** (Map pp114-6; 66 The Cut, Waterloo Rd SE1). The next rung down is known as the fringe. These shows take place anywhere there's a stage.

For a comprehensive look at what's being staged where, consult *Time Out*, pick up a copy of the free pamphlet *The Official London Theatre Guide* or visit www.official londontheatre.co.uk.

Clubs

This clubbers' capital has been propping up the vanguard of dance music since the term 'recreational party drugs' was coined. From low-key DJ bars to warehouses and 'superclubs', the city has a simply astonishing range of venues offering everything from sexy R&B to thumping garage to, well, you name it. Some venues have several different rooms, while others change the tempo according to the night. Admission prices vary from £3 to £10 Sunday to Thursday, but on Friday and Saturday can be as much as £20.

Astoria (Map pp118-20; ☎ 7434 9592; www.g-a-y .co.uk; 157-165 Charing Cross Rd WC2) This dark, sweaty and atmospheric club has a G-A-Y night Saturday, a cheap Pink Pounder Monday and a disco-orientated Camp Attach Friday. There are good views of the stage and a huge dance floor.

Bar Rumba (Map pp118-20; ☎ 7287 2715; 36 Shaftesbury Ave W1; ⊖ Piccadilly Circus) Along a Soho backstreet, it's a small club with a big reputation. There's a different style each night – from Latin and jazz to deep house and garage – but everyone's a winner.

Cargo (Map pp106-7; ☎ 7739 3440; 83 Rivington St EC2; adult £5-10; ⊖ Old Street) A hugely popular club with local and international DJs and a courtyard where you can simultaneously enjoy big sounds and the great outdoors. The music policy is particularly innovative, but you can usually rely on Latin house, Nu jazz and rare grooves.

GAY & LESBIAN LONDON

London's gay scene has exploded in recent years and there are gay – and to a lesser extent lesbian – venues all over the city. It is rare to encounter any problems with couples sharing rooms or holding hands on the street. In the gay cafés, bars and clubs listed (see Old Compton Café, Astoria, Heaven, Ghetto, Madame Jo Jos, Gay's the Word and the Philbeach Hotel), you should find the political *Pink Paper* (free) or, for listings, *Gay Times* (£3.10), *Boyz* (free) or the lesbian *Diva* (£2.65). The gay sections of *Time Out* and the *Evening Standard's Metro Life* are also useful, as are the websites www.rainbownetwork .com for men and www.gingerbeer.co.uk for women.

Cross (Map pp108-9; ☎ 7837 0828; Goods Way Depot, York Way N1; ⊖ King's Cross St Pancras) Out of the way in the King's Cross wastelands, this is one of London's leading clubs serving up a Continental-style beat to a convivial crowd.

End (Map pp118-20; ☎ 7419 9199; 16a West Central St WC1; adult £5-15; ⊖ Holborn) Has industrial décor and a big sound. It's the best venue around the West End for serious clubbers who like their music hard.

Fabric (Map pp114-6; ☎ 7490 0444; 77a Charterhouse St EC1; adult £10-15; ⊖ Farringdon) The latest feather in Clerkenwell's well-plumed cap and boasts three dance floors in a converted meat cold-store. Residences have included Sasha and Groove Armada. Expect to queue.

Ghetto (Map pp118-20; ☎ 7287 3726; 5-6 Falconberg Ct W1; ⊖ Tottenham Court Road) London's gay venue du jour. Hosts not only the celebrity-attended, mixed-evening Nag, Nag, Nag on Wednesday, but also Friday's electro/pop the Cock, among others. It's popular with Muscle Marys, trannies, punks and polysexual fashionistas.

Heaven (Map pp118-20; ☎ 7930 2020; The Arches, Villiers St WC2; ⊖ Charing Cross) One of the world's best-known gay clubs. It has three rooms; some nights are mixed but it positively fizzes with party boys on Saturday night, while there are cheap drinks and no pretension at Monday's Popcorn.

Madame Jo Jo's (Map pp118-20; ☎ 7734 3040; 8 Brewer St W1; ⊖ Leicester Square or Piccadilly Circus) A renowned transvestite cabaret, which is sleazy, fun and kitsch. It gives way to a deep house/Nu jazz club night on Saturday and a 'Deep Funk' night on Friday.

Ministry of Sound (Map p117; ☎ 7378 6528; www .ministryofsound.co.uk; 103 Gaunt St SE1; adult £12-15; ⏰ until 8am; ⊖ Elephant & Castle) Where the global brand started. Naturally, it lost a little of its edge over time, but it sharpened up its act with a major refurbishment in late 2003. It's London's most famous club and continues to pack in a diverse crew with big local and international names.

Notting Hill Arts Club (Map pp110-1; ☎ 7460 4459, 21 Notting Hill Gate W11; ⏰ 6pm-1am Tue-Thu, 6pm-2am Fri & Sat, 4-11pm Sun; ⊖ Notting Hill Gate) A laid-back, funky basement club that attracts an eclectic crowd and has indie music celebrity residences.

333 (Map pp106-7; ☎ 7739 5949; 333 Old St EC1; ⏰ 10pm-5am Fri, 10pm-4am Sat & Sun) A Hoxton old-timer with three different shambling levels of breakbeats, techno to funk, and a determinedly down-to-earth vibe.

Live Music
ROCK
London's live music scene is fantastic, and any night of the week you can catch bands and performances that would be the envy of any other gig-goer around the world.

Barfly @ the Monarch (Map pp108-9; ☎ 7691 4244, 7691 4245; www.barflyclub.com; Monarch pub, 49 Chalk Farm Rd NW1; ⊖ Chalk Farm or Camden Town) Pleasantly grungy, and the place to see the best upcoming bands.

Borderline (Map pp118-20; ☎ 7734 2095; www .borderline.co.uk; Orange Yard W1; ⊖ Tottenham Court Road) A small, relaxed venue, hosting bands on the verge of the mainstream. It's also your best bet to see big-name acts performing under pseudonyms.

Brixton Academy (Map pp106-7; ☎ 7771 2000; www .brixton-academy.co.uk; 211 Stockwell Rd SW9; ⊖ Brixton) A huge, user-friendly place with a sloping floor that allows you to see the band no matter how far back you are. Great bands and always thrumming with bonhomie.

Garage (Map pp108-9; ☎ 7607 1818; www.mean fiddler.com; 20-22 Highbury Corner N5; ⊖ Highbury or Islington) A good, medium-sized venue that hosts local and visiting indie bands. It can be ridiculously hot and sweaty in summer.

Forum (Map pp106-7; ☎ 7344 0044; 9-17 Highgate Road NW5; ⊖ Kentish Town) A grand old theatre and one of London's best large venues.

Hackney Ocean (Map pp106-7; ☎ 8986 5336; 270 Mare St E8; ⊖ Bethnal Green) Has sensational acoustics and hosts the usual headliners, but adds a strong line in world music, reflecting the multiculturalism of Hackney.

Jazz Café (Map pp108-9; ☎ 7344 0044; 5 Parkway NW1; ⊖ Camden Town) A rather swanky restaurant venue. While you don't have to eat, it's better to book a table when the big names are in town.

Ronnie Scott's (Map pp118-20; ☎ 7439 0747; 47 Frith St W1; ⊖ Leicester Square) Familiar to aficionados as the best jazz club in London. The food, atmosphere and acts are always spot-on.

Shepherd's Bush Empire (Map pp106-7; ☎ 7771 2000; www.shepherds-bush-empire.co.uk; Shepherd's Bush Green W12; ⊖ Shepherd's Bush) A slightly dishevelled, mid-size theatre that hosts some terrific bands watched by laid-back punters.

100 Club (Map pp118-20; ☎ 7636 0933; 100 Oxford St W1; ⊖ Oxford Circus) This legendary London venue once showcased the Stones and was at the centre of the punk revolution. It now divides its time between jazz, rock and even a little swing.

CLASSICAL

With four world-class symphony orchestras, two opera companies, various smaller ensembles, brilliant venues, reasonable prices and high standards of performance, London is a capital for classical.

South Bank Centre (Map pp114-6; ☎ 7960 4242; South Bank; ⊖ Embankment) has three premier venues in the **Royal Festival Hall** and the smaller **Queen Elizabeth Hall** and **Purcell Room**, which host classical, opera, jazz and choral music. It has a range of cafés and restaurants. There are free recitals in the foyer.

The **Barbican Centre** (Map p117; ☎ 7638 8891; www.barbican.org.uk; Silk St EC2; ⊖ Barbican) may be aesthetically challenged, but its acoustics are sound and it is home to the London Symphony Orchestra, which plays some 80 concerts here every year.

The **Royal Albert Hall** (Map pp110-1; ☎ 7589 8212; www.royalalberthall.com; Kensington Gore SW7; ⊖ South Kensington) is a splendid Victorian arena that often hosts classical concerts, but is best known as the venue for the Proms.

Opera & Dance

The once starchy and now gleaming **Royal Opera House** (Map pp118-20; ☎ 7304 4000; www.royaloperahouse.org; Royal Opera House, Bow St WC2; tickets £6-150, midweek matinees £6.50-50; ⊖ Covent Garden) has been attracting a young, wealthy audience since its £213 million millennium redevelopment, which seems to have breathed new life into programming. The home of the progressive **English National Opera** is the **Coliseum** (Map pp118-20; ☎ 7632 8300; St Martin's Lane WC1; ⊖ Leicester Square).

The **Royal Ballet** (☎ 7304 4000; www.royalballet.com; Royal Opera House, Bow St WC2; tickets £4-80; ⊖ Covent Garden), the best classical-ballet company in the land, is also based at the Royal Opera House, while there are four other major dance companies and a host of small and experimental ones. **Sadler's Wells** (Map pp108-9; ☎ 7863 8000; www.sadlers-wells.com; Rosebery Ave EC1; tickets £10-40; ⊖ Angel) is a glittering modern venue that was in fact first established in the 17th century. It has been given much credit in recent years for bringing modern dance to the mainstream.

TOP FIVE VIEWS OF LONDON

- Of Buckingham Palace from the footbridge over **St James's Park lake** (p128)
- From the **London Eye** (p137)
- From **Marble Arch viewing platform** (p140)
- From **Waterloo Bridge** (preferably at sunset)
- From the gardens of **Royal Hospital Chelsea** (p139) across the Thames to Battersea Power Station

---

Cinemas

High-profile British premieres take place in Leicester Sq, usually at the mega, near-2000-seat Odeon. Blockbusters apart, London is an outstanding place to catch a range of films that might not even make it to a cinema near you at home, although mainstream films are often released later here for some reason. *Time Out* is indispensable.

National Film Theatre (Map pp114-6; ☎ 7928 3232; South Bank Centre; ⊖ Waterloo) A film-lover's dream, it screens some 2000 flicks a year, ranging from vintage classics to foreign art-house.

Sport

As the capital of a sports-mad nation, you can expect London to be brimming over with sporting spectacles throughout the year. As always, the entertainment weekly *Time Out* is the best source of information on fixtures, times, venues and ticket prices.

FOOTBALL

Tickets for Premier League football matches are ridiculously hard to come by for casual fans these days, and London's top-flight clubs play to full stadiums most weeks. But if you want to try your luck, the telephone numbers for the Premiership clubs are listed here:

Arsenal	☎ 7704 4040
Charlton	☎ 8333 4010
Chelsea	☎ 7386 7799
Crystal Palace	☎ 8771 8841
Fulham	☎ 7893 8383
Tottenham Hotspur	☎ 0870 112222

RUGBY
Twickenham (☎ 8892 2000; Rugby Rd, Twickenham; tickets around £30; ✈ Hounslow East, then bus No 281 or Twickenham main-line station) is the home of English rugby union, but as with football, tickets for internationals are difficult to get unless you have contacts. The ground also boasts the state-of-the-art **Museum of Rugby** (adult incl stadium tour £8; ⏰ 10am-5pm Tue-Sat, 2-5pm Sun).

CRICKET
Despite a so-so England team, cricket remains popular in the land of its origin. Test matches take place at two venerable grounds: **Lord's Cricket Ground** (Map pp106-7; ☎ 7432 1066; St John's Wood Rd NW8; ✈ St John's Wood) and the **AMP Oval Cricket Ground** (Map pp106-7; ☎ 7582 7764; Kennington Oval SE11; ✈ Oval). Tickets are from £15 to £50, but if you're a fan you'll know it's worth it.

SHOPPING
From famous department stores to quirky backstreet retailers, London is a mecca for shoppers with an eye for style and a card to exercise. If you're looking for something distinctly 'British', eschew the Union Jack–emblazoned kitsch of the tourist thoroughfares and fill your bags with Duffer layers, Burberry accessories, Tiffany sparkles, Ben Sherman shirts, Royal Doulton china or a Saville Row suit. Everything will seem more prestigious if it's in a Harrods bag.

Fashion
If there's a label worth having, you'll find it in central London. Shopping options are well scattered, although some streets are renowned for their specialities. Oxford St is the place for High St fashion, while the chains of Regent St crank it up a notch. Kensington High St has a nice mix of chains and boutiques, while the streets around Covent Garden are crammed with groovy street labels and alternative boutiques. Mayfair's South Molton St is the strip for local and international urban chic, while Bond St is the fat end of the high-fashion wedge. Knightsbridge draws the hordes with quintessentially English department stores.

DEPARTMENT STORES
It's hard to resist the lure of London's famous department stores, even if you don't intend to spree.

Harrods (Map pp110-1; ☎ 7730 1234; 87 Brompton Rd SW1; ✈ Knightsbridge) Like a theme park for fans of the British establishment, Harrods is always crowded with slow tourists. There are more rules than at an army boot camp but even the toilets will impress.

Harvey Nichols (Map pp110-1; ☎ 7235 5000; 109-125 Knightsbridge SW1; ✈ Knightsbridge) London's temple of high fashion. The jewellery and perfume departments are worth a short prison sentence.

Fortnum & Mason (Map pp118-20; ☎ 7734 8040; 181 Piccadilly W1; ✈ Piccadilly Circus) The byword for quality and service from a bygone area, steeped as it is in 300 years of tradition. It is especially noted for its old-world ground-floor food hall where Britain's elite come for their cornflakes and bananas.

Selfridges (Map pp114-6; ☎ 7629 1234; 400 Oxford St W1; ✈ Bond Street) The funkiest and most vital of London's one-stop shops where fashion runs the gamut from street to formal. The food hall is unparalleled and the cosmetics hall the largest in Europe.

Liberty (Map pp118-20; ☎ 7734 1234; 214-220 Regent St W1; ✈ Oxford Circus) An irresistible blend of contemporary styles in an old-fashioned atmosphere. You can't leave London without some 'Liberty Florals' (printed fabrics).

Antiques
Curios, baubles and period pieces abound along Camden Passage, Bermondsey Market, the Saturday market at Portobello and along Islington's Upper St from Angel towards Highbury Corner (see To Market, to Market opposite for market details).

Antiquarius Antiques Centre (Map pp112-3; ☎ 7969 1500; 131 King's Rd SW3; ⊖ Sloane Square) Packed with 120 stalls and dealers selling everything from top hats and corkscrews to old luggage and jewellery.

London Silver Vaults (Map pp114-6; ☎ 7242 3844; 53-63 Chancery Lane WC2; ⊖ Chancery Lane) Has 72 subterranean shops forming the world's largest collection of silver under one roof.

Music

If it's been recorded, you can buy it in London. For the biggest general collections of CDs and tapes, take on the West End giants of **Tower Records** (Map pp118-20; ☎ 7439 2500; 1 Piccadilly Circus W1; ⊗ until midnight Mon-Sat; ⊖ Piccadilly Circus), **HMV** (Map pp118-20; ☎ 7631 3423; 150 Oxford St W1; ⊗ until 8pm Mon-Fri; ⊖ Oxford Circus) and **Virgin Megastore** (Map pp118-20; ☎ 7631 1234; 14-30 Oxford St W1; ⊗ until 9pm Mon-Sat; ⊖ Tottenham Court Road).

For personality, visit the following:

Rough Trade Neal's Yard (Map pp118-20; ☎ 7240 0105; 16 Neal's Yard WC2; ⊖ Covent Garden); Talbot Rd (☎ 7229 8541; 130 Talbot Rd W11; ⊖ Ladbroke Grove) In the basement of Slam City Skates, it's the most central outlet of this famous store that was at the forefront of the punk explosion in the 1970s. This – and its original store in Notting Hill – is the best place to come for underground specials, vintage rarities and pretty much anything of an indie or alternative bent.

Ray's Jazz Shop (Map pp118-20; ☎ 7240 3969; 180 Shaftesbury Ave WC2; ⊖ Tottenham Court Road) Where aficionados will find those elusive back catalogues from their favourite jazz and blues artists.

Black Market Records (Map pp118-20; ☎ 7437 0478; 25 D'Arblay St W1; ⊖ Oxford Circus) Your best bet for dance, and if they haven't got what you're after, they'll know who has.

TO MARKET, TO MARKET

London has more than 350 markets selling everything from antiques and curios to flowers and fish. Some, such as Camden and Portobello Rd, are well known to tourists, while others exist just for the locals and have everything from dinner to underwear for sale in the stalls. Here's a sample.

Bermondsey Market (Map p117; ☎ 7351 5353; Bermondsey Sq SE1; ⊗ 5am-1pm Fri; ⊖ Borough) The place to come if you're after old opera glasses, bowling balls, hatpins, costume jewellery, porcelain or other curios. The main market is outdoors on the square, although adjacent warehouses shelter the more vulnerable furnishings and bric-a-brac.

Borough Market (Map p117; cnr Borough High & Stoney Sts SE1; ⊗ 9am-6pm Fri, 9am-4pm Sat; ⊖ London Bridge) A farmers market sometimes called London's Larder, it has been here in some form since the 13th century. It's a wonderfully atmospheric food market, where you'll find everything from organic falafel to a boar's head.

Brick Lane Market (Map pp106-7; Brick Lane E1; ⊗ 8.30am-1pm Sat; ⊖ Shoreditch or Aldgate East) This is an East End pearl, a sprawling bazaar featuring everything from fruit and veggies to paintings and bric-a-brac.

Brixton Market (Map pp106-7; Electric Ave & Granville Arcade; ⊗ 8am-5.30pm Mon-Sat, 8am-1pm only Wed; ⊖ Brixton) A cosmopolitan treat that mixes everything from the Body Shop and reggae to slick Muslim preachers, South American butcher shops and exotic fruits. On Electric Ave and in the covered Granville Arcade you can buy wigs, unusual foods and spices, and homeopathic root cures.

Camden Market (Map pp108-9; Camden High St NW1; ⊗ 9am-5pm Thu-Sun; ⊖ Camden Town) One of London's most popular tourist attractions although it stopped being cutting edge a long time ago. It's positively mobbed at the weekend.

Petticoat Lane Market (Map p117; Middlesex St E1; ⊗ 8am-2pm Sun; ⊖ Aldgate, Aldgate East or Liverpool Street) A cherished East End institution overflowing with cheap consumer durables of little interest to tourists (although you'll see a hell of a lot of them).

Portobello Rd Market (Map pp110-1; Portobello Rd W10; ⊖ Notting Hill Gate, Ladbroke Grove or Westbourne Park) One of London's most famous (and crowded) street markets, that has taken over from Camden in the hip stakes. New and vintage clothes are its main attraction.

Spitalfields Market (Map p117; Commercial St E1; ⊗ 9.30am-5.30pm Sun, organic market 9.30am-5pm Fri; ⊖ Liverpool Street) In a Victorian warehouse, with a great mix of arts and crafts, clothes, books, food and *joie de vivre*.

GETTING THERE & AWAY

London is the major gateway to Britain, so further transport information can be found in the main Transport chapter.

Air

For information on flying to/from London via the main airports of Heathrow and Gatwick, see p963 in the Transport chapter. The following are London's smaller airports.

STANSTED

London's third-busiest airport, **Stansted** (STN; ☎ 0870 000 0303; www.baa.com/main/airports/stansted) is 35 miles northeast of the centre. It is Europe's fastest growing airport thanks to the success of no-frills carriers **Ryanair** (www.ryanair.com) and **EasyJet** (☎ 0870 600 0000; www.easyjet .com).

LONDON CITY

London City Airport (LCY; ☎ 7646 0000; www.londoncityairport.com), 6 miles east of central London in the Docklands, is largely used for business travellers and serves 22 Continental European and eight national destinations.

LUTON

A small airport some 35 miles north of central London, **Luton** (LTN; ☎ 01582 405100; www .london-luton.co.uk) is the main base of low-cost airline EasyJet and smaller charter flights.

Bus

Most long-distance coaches leave London from **Victoria coach station** (Map p121; ☎ 7730 3466; 164 Buckingham Palace Rd SW1; ⊖ Victoria, then about a 10-min walk), a lovely 1930s-style building. The arrivals terminal is in a separate building across Elizabeth St from the main coach station.

Car

See p968 of the Transport chapter for reservation numbers of the main car-hire firms, all of which have airport and various city locations.

Train

London has 10 main-line terminals, all linked by the tube and each serving a different geographical area of the UK.
Charing Cross (Map pp118-20) Southeast England
Euston (Map pp108-9) Northern and northwest England, Scotland

King's Cross (Map pp108-9) North London, Hertfordshire, Cambridgeshire, northern and northeast England, Scotland
Liverpool Street (Map p117) East and northeast London, Stansted airport, East Anglia
London Bridge (Map p117) Southeast England
Marylebone (Map pp110-1) Northwest London, the Chilterns
Paddington (Map pp110-1) South Wales, western and southwest England, south Midlands, Heathrow airport
St Pancras (Map pp108-9) East Midlands, southern Yorkshire
Victoria (Map p121) Southern and southeast England, Gatwick airport, Channel ferry ports
Waterloo (Map pp114-6) Southwest London, southern and southwest England

Most stations now have left-luggage facilities (around £4) and lockers, toilets (a 20p coin) with showers (around £3), newsstands and bookshops, and a range of eating and drinking outlets. Victoria and Liverpool Street stations have shopping centres attached.

GETTING AROUND
To/From the Airports
HEATHROW

The airport is accessible by bus, the Underground (between 5am and 11pm), mainline train and taxi. The fastest way to and from central London is on the **Heathrow Express** (☎ 0845 600 1515; www.heathrowexpress .co.uk), an ultramodern train to and from Paddington station (adult/child one way £6/11.50, return £13/25, 15 minutes, every 15 minutes 5.10am to 11.30pm). You can purchase tickets on board (£2 extra), online or from self-service machines (cash and credit cards accepted) at both terminals. The cheapest way between Heathrow and central London is on London Underground's Piccadilly line (£3.80, one hour, departing every five to 10 minutes 5.30am to 11.45pm), accessed from all terminals. The **Airbus A2** (☎ 08705 747777) links King's Cross station and Heathrow (one way/return £8/15, 1½ hours, departing 5.30am to 10pm from Heathrow, every 30 minutes during peak times). A black cab to the centre of London will cost you around £50, a minicab around £30.

GATWICK

The **Gatwick Express train** (☎ 0870 530 1530; www .gatwickexpress.co.uk) runs nonstop between Victoria train station and the South Terminal (adult return £21.50, 30 minutes, departing every 15 minutes 5.50am to 1.35am, with an earlier train at 5.20am). The normal train service is slower but cheaper. **Airbus No 025** (☎ 08705 747777; www.nationalexpress.com) operates from Victoria coach station to Gatwick (one way/return £5/10, 18 daily 6am to 11pm to Gatwick, 4.15am to 9.15pm to London). A black cab to/from central London costs around £80 to £85.

STANSTED

The **Stansted Express** (☎ 0845 748 4950; www.stansted express.com) connects with Liverpool Street station (one way/return £13.80/24, 45 minutes, departing every 15 minutes 8am to 5.30pm, otherwise every 30 minutes). The **Airbus A6** (☎ 08705 747777) links with Victoria coach station (one way/return £6/15, departing every 20 minutes 5.30am to midnight). A black cab to/from central London costs about £100 to £105.

LONDON CITY

The blue airport **Shuttlebus** (☎ 7646 0088; www .londoncityairport.com/shuttlebus) connects with Liverpool Street train station (one way/return £6/12, 25 minutes), departing every 10 minutes 6.50am (11am Sunday) to 10pm (1.15pm Saturday). From Liverpool Street station, the first bus leaves at 9pm weekdays (12.45pm Saturday); the last departs at 9.08pm weekdays (12.40pm Saturday and 8.50pm Sunday). The journey takes eight minutes from Canary Wharf. The green airport **Shuttlebus** (☎ 7646 0088; www.londoncity airport.com/shuttlebus) links London City and Canning Town station (adult/child £2/1, five minutes), departing every 10 minutes 6am (10.05am Sunday) to 10.20pm (1.15pm Saturday), which is on the Jubilee tube, the DLR and Silverlink lines. A black taxi costs around £20 to/from central London.

LUTON

Thameslink (☎ 0845 748 4950; www.thameslink.co.uk) runs trains from King's Cross and other central London stations to Luton Airport Parkway station (adult/child one way £9.50/4.75, 35 minutes, departing every five to 15 minutes 7am to 10pm), from where a shuttle bus will get you to the airport within eight minutes. A black taxi costs around £75 to/from central London.

Car

Driving in London is the perfect way to ruin a good holiday. Traffic is very heavy, parking is a nightmare and wheel-clampers are very busy. If you bring your car into central London from 7am to 6.30pm on a weekday, you'll need to pay a £5 per day **congestion charge** (☎ 0845 900 1234; www.cclondon.com to register) or face a fine.

Public Transport

Transport for London (TfL; www.transportforlondon .gov.uk/tfl) is an organisation that aims to integrate the entire London transport network. Its website is very handy for information on all modes of transport in the capital.

As you might imagine, servicing a city this large is a logistical nightmare for planners who get no end of criticism from locals. But amazingly, the system works pretty well, especially since Mayor Ken Livingstone has made it his cause célèbre. Trains, tube lines, day and night buses, cabs and even shuttle boats work in tandem to fill the gaps and make it possible to navigate the behemoth (unless you're trying to get out of Soho on a weekend night, of course).

A Travelcard (see p170) can be used on all forms of public transport: the tube, suburban trains, the Docklands Light Rail (DLR), day and night buses, and for discounts on boats. The relatively new prepay

---

THE TUBE – FUN FACTS TO KNOW & TELL

The tube is the world's oldest (1863), most extensive (253 miles of track) and busiest (785 million journeys a year) underground transport system in the world. With breakdowns every 16 minutes on average, it is also the most unreliable, and for the journey between Covent Garden and Leicester Sq (£1.60 for 250m), the per-kilometre price makes taking the tube more expensive than it is to take a stretch limo.

The London Underground map, used by millions of people every day, is so familiar that it's often used as a symbol for the city itself. It was created in 1931 by Henry Beck, an engineering draughtsman, who received five guineas (£5.25) for his efforts.

Oystercard (www.oystercard.com) can also be used throughout the public transport network and is particularly handy if you're going to be in London for an extended period.

BOAT

There is a myriad of boat services on the Thames, with more being announced all the time. Travelling by boat allows you to avoid the traffic while enjoying great views. Travelcard holders get one-third off all fares.

City Cruises (☎ 7740 0400; www.citycruises.com) operates year-round from Westminster Pier (for more details see p147).

Westminster Passenger Services Association (☎ 7930 2062; www.wpsa.co.uk) is the only company that operates a schedule service upriver from Westminster. It takes in Kew Gardens and Hampton Park (for prices see Kew Gardens p145).

The **London Waterbus Company** (☎ 7482 2660) runs trips between Camden Lock and Little Venice, or try **Jason's Canal Trips** (☎ 7286 3428; www.jasons.co.uk) at Little Venice. London has some 40 miles of inner-city canals, mostly built in the 19th century and in the process of renewal.

BUS

Travelling round London by double-decker bus is an enjoyable way to explore the city and get a feel for its districts and size. For short journeys it's often more efficient to take a bus than the tube. The free *Central London Bus Guide Map* is an essential planning tool, and is available from most TICs and tube stations. Make sure to catch one of the open-backed Routemasters before they're phased out. A recommended 'scenic' route is No 24, which runs from Victoria to Hampstead Heath through the West End.

Buses run regularly between 7am and midnight. Single-journey bus tickets (valid for two hours) cost adult/child £1/40p, day passes are adult/child £2.50/1. In central London, at stops with yellow signs it's important to buy your ticket from the automatic machine *before* boarding. Otherwise, buy it as you board.

Less-frequent night buses (prefixed with the letter 'N') wheel into action when the tube stops. They stop on request, so clearly signal the driver with an outstretched arm. Trafalgar Sq, Tottenham Court Rd and Oxford Circus are the main terminals for them.

Stationlink buses (☎ 7941 4600) have a driver-operated ramp for wheelchair access and follow a similar route to the Underground Circle Line, joining up all the main-line stations. People with mobility problems and those with heavy luggage may find this easier to use than the tube, although it only operates once an hour. From Paddington there are services clockwise (the SL1) from 8.15am to 7.15pm, and anticlockwise (the SL2) from 8.40am to 6.40pm.

DLR & TRAIN

The independent, driverless **Docklands Light Railway** (DLR; ☎ 7363 9700; www.dlr.co.uk) links the City at Bank and Tower Gateway with Canary Wharf, Greenwich and Stratford. It provides good views of development at this end of town. The fares operate in the same way as those on the tube.

Several rail companies also operate suburban rail services in and around London. These are especially important south of the river where there are few tube lines. Once again, fares operate in the same way as those on the tube.

LONDON UNDERGROUND

The 12 lines of the 'tube' extend as far as Buckinghamshire, Essex and Heathrow. There are Underground travel info centres at all Heathrow terminals, a half-dozen major tube stations and at larger main-line train stations. Services run from 5.30am to roughly midnight (from 7am on Sunday).

SOME HAVE THE KNOWLEDGE – OTHERS HAVEN'T A CLUE

Once you've been around the block a few times with a hackney cab driver – during which the car's broken down, he's consulted the *London A–Z* twice and telephoned base for directions – you'll begin to appreciate the more expensive black cabs. To get an all-London licence, 'cabbies' must pass a rigorous test, which requires them to memorise up to 25,000 streets within a 6-mile radius of Charing Cross and know all the points of interest from hotels to churches. It's a feat that can sometimes take years to achieve, and ensures, according to the Public Carriage Office, that only the most committed join the noble trade.

The Underground is divided into six concentric zones. The basic fare for Zone 1 is adult/child £2/60p; to cross all six zones (eg, to/from Heathrow) costs £3.80/1.50. A carnet of 10 tickets for Zone 1 costs £15/5. These tickets can be bought from machines or from counters at the entrance to each station.

If you're travelling through a couple of zones or several times in one day, consider a Travelcard. One-day Travelcards can be used after 9.30am weekdays (any time at weekends) on all transport – tubes, main-line trains, the DLR and buses (including night buses). Most visitors find a one-day Travelcard for Zones 1 and 2 (adult/child £4.30/2) is sufficient. Before 9.30am Monday to Friday, you need a Peak Travelcard (£5.30/2.60 for Zones 1 and 2). A weekly for Zones 1 and 2, valid any time of day, costs £20.20/8.20. A Weekend Travelcard, valid Saturday and Sunday in Zones 1 and 2, costs £6.40/3. Family Travelcards are also available.

Taxi

Drivers of licensed black cabs have undergone extensive training to obtain 'the knowledge' of every central London street, so you're sure to arrive at your destination. Cabs are available for hire when the yellow light above the windscreen is lit. Fares are metered, with flag fall at £1.60 and each successive kilometre costing 90p. To order a black cab by phone, try **Dial-a-Cab** (☎ 7253 5000); you must pay by credit card and will be charged a premium.

Minicabs, some of which are now licensed, are cheaper competitors to cabs. However, they can only be hired by phone or from a minicab office; every neighbourhood and High St has one. Some minicab drivers also have a limited idea of how to get around efficiently – or safely. Minicabs can carry up to four people and don't have meters, so get a quote before you start. Bargaining is sometimes acceptable. Small companies are based in particular areas. Try a large **24-hour operator** (☎ 7387 8888, 7272 2222, 7272 3322 or 8888 4444).

Be aware that there have been many reports of assault by unlicensed minicab drivers. Solo female travellers should be very wary of jumping into a minicab unaccompanied.

Southeast England

CONTENTS

Both blessed and cursed because of their proximity to London, the five 'Home Counties' adjoining the city, which include Hertfordshire, Berkshire and Surrey, may be home to commuter hubs and business communities but there's also some important historic sites and a slower pace of life. Windsor and Eton and the great Windsor Castle in Berkshire often make visitors' top-ten lists (as they should). But for those looking to escape the summertime crowds, the outlying areas have plenty of out-of-the-way country pubs, quaint cafés and family-sized B&Bs.

The rest of the Southeast includes Essex, Kent, East and West Sussex and Hampshire, where you'll find a rich repository of English history, a bustling nightlife and some of the natural beauty that makes England unique. There is the magnificent Canterbury Cathedral, the picturesque medieval town of Rye, the poetic white cliffs of Dover and Brighton – the hip and happening town nicknamed London-by-the-Sea.

The summertime crowds in this part of England are unrelenting and because of that many towns have recobbled their streets, blocked off the car traffic and restored shop fronts to their medieval splendour. But behind the quaintness lies a sophisticated dynamism that belies its 'old-style' appearance. Here you'll find a highly developed and elaborate tourist infrastructure created to capitalise on the enormous numbers of visitors. Inside sloping, half-timbered Tudor buildings you may find an Internet café with high-speed connections, a trendy Asian-fusion restaurant or a hip, boutique hotel with the latest wallpaper.

SOUTHEAST ENGLAND

HIGHLIGHTS

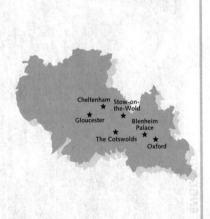

- Drinking and dining on **Brighton beach** (p222) in summer and shopping its North Laine

- Braving a peek down the 500ft chalk cliffs at **Beachy Head** (p222)

- Spending a weekend in the romantic village of **Arundel** (p215) in West Sussex

- Strolling the poetic heights of the **white cliffs of Dover** (p192) on a clear day

- Drinking a pint of hand-pulled real ale in **Canterbury** (p181) after visiting the cathedral

- Ambling alongside **Whitstable's** colourful beach huts (p187) and dining on the fresh sea fare

- Exploring the magnificent and ancient **Winchester Cathedral** (p201)

- Enjoying a pint at **Ye Olde Fighting Cocks** (p177) in St Albans, one of England's oldest pubs

- Visiting the grand **Windsor Castle** (p196) for a peek at royal living

POPULATION: 9,294,300	AREA: 9784 SQ MILES

SOUTHEAST ENGLAND

SOUTHEAST ENGLAND

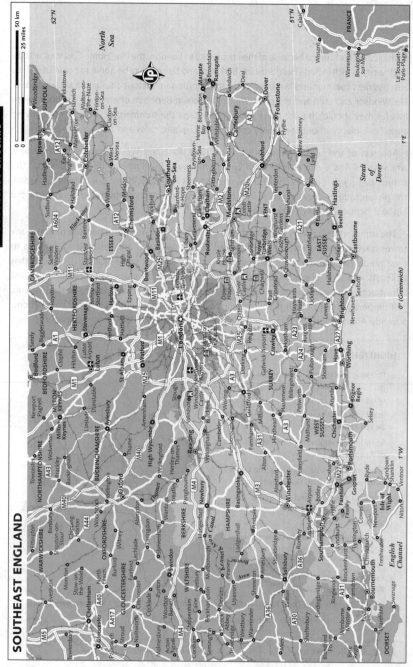

51°N

FRANCE

North Sea

Strait of Dover

English Channel

50 km
25 miles

0° (Greenwich)

Information

Southeast England is a heavily visited region, with fantastic tourist information centres (TICs) offering brochures, maps, booking services and helpful local advice. Accommodation is plentiful, with the possible exception of the more remote regions of Hertfordshire, Berkshire and Surrey. It is always recommended to book in advance to beat the summer tourist rush, especially along the coast. Youth hostels often host a surprising number of adults and seniors and also make travelling with a family more affordable. Because of the brisk business that's done in the areas immediately surrounding London, the hotels there tend to be higher priced. Banks abound so you'll have no trouble getting cash to spend at the largely available post offices and Internet café's. For loads more information, check out **Tourism South East** (www.seetb.org.uk), the country's official website for south and southeast England.

Activities

Southeast England may be the most crowded corner of Britain, but there are still many opportunities for enjoying the great outdoors. This section gives a quick rundown of the options. More information is given in Outdoor Activities (p74, and suggestions for shorter walks and rides are given throughout this chapter. Regional tourism websites all contain walking and cycling information, and TICs all stock leaflets (free) plus maps and guides (usually £1 to £5) covering walking, cycling and other activities.

CYCLING

Seeking out quiet roads for cycle touring can take persistence in southeast England, but some good routes definitely exist here.

Garden of England Cycle Route (170 miles) London to Dover, and then Hastings and part of the National Cycle Network (see p81).

Downs & Weald Cycle Route (150 miles) Hastings to London.

South Downs Way National Trail (100 miles) Mountain bikes can legally ride it end to end. Hard nuts do it in two days. Four would be more enjoyable.

The **North Downs** has lanes that are good for touring, and some good tracks for off-road riding. The **Chiltern Hills** also have a good selection of quiet country lanes and bridleways, including the dedicated mountain-bike venue of Aston Woods at Wendover, while the **New Forest** has a wonderfully vast network of tracks, ideal for gentle or beginner mountain biking, and also offers a week of organised cycling tours every July.

WALKING

The southeast region is well endowed with long-distance national trails, which all make a great focus for walking, even if it's just for a few hours, a day or a weekend.

1066 Country Walk (31 miles) Historic walk through the East Sussex countryside. Links Rye, Battle and Pevensey and joins the South Downs Way.

North Downs Way (157 miles) The path starts in Farnham and goes to Dorking before heading east to Ashford and Dover.

South Downs Way (100 miles) A roller-coaster walk between Winchester, the ancient capital of England, and Eastbourne.

Thames Path (173 miles) Follows Britain's best-known river from its source.

Thanet Coastal Path (20 miles) Hugs the far eastern shore from Margate to Pegwell Bay via Broadstairs and Ramsgate.

For shorter walks, Box Hill and the Devil's Punchbowl in Surrey offer excellent views, sloping grasslands and some wooded areas. This is also a good area to come for mountain biking as there are a number of bridleways. On top of the hill is a **visitor information centre** (☎ 01306-885502; ☺ 11am-dusk), where you'll find information on guided walks, self-guided walk leaflets, maps and an ice-cream kiosk. Shorter walks can also be found in the **South Downs**, the **Chiltern Hills** and the **New Forest**. Off the south coast, the **Isle of Wight** is especially walker-friendly, with a good network of paths and some fine stretches of coastline.

Getting There & Around

All the places mentioned in throughout this chapter are quite easy to reach by train or bus, and all could be visited in a day trip from London. Renting a car is also a great option, but watch for the commuter traffic around the rush hours from 6am to 9.30am and 4pm to 7pm, especially in counties close to the capital city. The **National Traveline** (☎ 0870 608 2608) provides information on all public transport throughout the region.

BUS

Explorer tickets (adult/child £5.50/4) provide day-long unlimited travel on most buses throughout the region; buy them at bus stations or on your first bus.

Country Rover tickets (adult/child £5/2.50) are valid after 9am Monday to Friday and all day weekends.

Diamond Rover tickets (adult/child £7/5) are good for Green Line services any time and day, excluding service into London before 9am Monday to Friday.

Arriva (☎ 01279-426349) offers a variety of daily, weekly and monthly passes and has good deals for families travelling in Buckinghamshire, Hertfordshire, Essex, Kent, Surrey and Sussex.

Stagecoach Coastline (www.stagecoachbus.com) serves the coastline, East Kent and East Sussex. Travellers can buy an unlimited day (£5) or week (£20) Solent Travel Card good on 10 bus lines along the Hampshire coast.

TRAIN

For general rail information, phone ☎ 08457 484950. The BritRail SouthEast Pass allows unlimited rail travel for three or four days in eight or seven days in fifteen and must be purchased outside the UK (p972).

The **Network Railcard** (☎ 08457 225 225; www .railcard.co.uk/network/network.htm; per yr £20) is a discount card available for visitors travelling in London, the Home Counties and South England. Passengers get a 34% discount (children ride for £1), but they have to travel at off-peak times.

HERTFORDSHIRE

There's not a whole lot to do in sleepy Hertfordshire, which is entirely to your benefit if you're looking for relief from the crowds. Most of the county is pastoral farmland though if you want bustle, head to the lovely market town of St Albans, a wonderfully preserved Georgian town with a rich Roman past and a predilection for real-ale pubs. Hatfield House, one of Britain's most important stately homes, is the county's top attraction.

ST ALBANS

☎ 01727 / pop 82,429

The lovely town of St Albans is one of the best and most popular towns to visit in any of the Home Counties. Its short distance from London (25 minutes by train) makes it a perfect day trip.

Founded by the Romans as Verulamium after their invasion of AD 43, St Albans was renamed in the 3rd century after a Roman soldier, Alban, who had made the error of sheltering a Christian priest in 209. His Samaritan instincts cost him his head, but he was England's first Christian martyr and the town soon became a centre for pilgrimage.

Visitors with more earthly concerns will find St Albans worth a stop for its magnificent cathedral, outstanding Roman museum and the town's aesthetically pleasing mix of Tudor and Georgian architecture. They also take their beer seriously here and have the real-ale pubs and the festivals to prove it.

Orientation & Information

St Peter's St, 10 minutes' walk west of the train station on Stanhope Rd, is the focus of the town. East of St Peters, St George St turns into Fishpool St, a lovely neighbourhood lane that winds its way past country pubs to Verulamium Park.

The **Tourist Information Centre** (TIC; ☎ 864511; tic@stalbans.gov.uk; Market Pl; 9.30am-5.30pm Mon-Sat Easter-Oct & Mon-Sat 10am-4pm Nov-Easter) is in the town hall in the town's bustling marketplace. It sells the useful *Discover St Albans* town trail (£1). The *Official Visitors Guide* is free and features a detailed town walk covering all the sights. There are free guided walks of the town at 11.15am and 3pm on Sunday, Easter to September – meet at the **Clocktower** (High St). On Wednesday and Saturday mornings the central marketplace comes alive.

All the major banks and ATMs are on St Peter's St, near the TIC. The main **post office** (St Peter's St; 9.30am-5pm Mon-Sat) is also in the town centre. Internet access is free in the **library** (☎ 737333; Malting Shopping Centre).

Paton Books (34 Holywell Hill) is a marvellous bookshop full of new titles and dusty old ones (including those hard-to-find ones) housed in an elegant 17th-century building.

There's a **laundrette** (13 Catherine St) off St Peter's St.

Sights

ST ALBANS CATHEDRAL

In the 8th century, King Offa of Mercia founded a Benedictine abbey on the site of Alban's martyrdom, but the actual **cathedral**

(☎ 860780; ☻ 8am-5.45pm) you see today dates from 1077, when the first Norman abbot, Paul, ordered a new one to be constructed, albeit incorporating elements of the earlier Saxon building – you can see parts of a Saxon archway in the southern aisle alongside the presbytery. Many Roman bricks were used and they sit conspicuously in the central tower. Restoration took place in 1877.

There are **guided tours** (☻ 11.30am & 2.30pm Mon-Fri, 11.30am & 2pm Sat, 2.30pm Sun) of the cathedral. In the southern aisle you can watch a free audiovisual account of the cathedral's history. Admission is by donation.

VERULAMIUM MUSEUM & ROMAN RUINS

Nowhere in England can you learn more about everyday life under the Romans than at this excellent **museum** (☎ 751810; St Michael's St; adult £3.30; ☻ 10am-5pm Mon-Sat, 2-5pm Sun). There are interactive and audiovisual displays as well as recreations of how rooms would have looked in a Roman house. Most impressive is the Mosaic Room, where five outstanding floors uncovered between 1930 and 1955 are laid out.

Tickets allow you a return visit on the same day. You can take a free guided walk of the 'city' of Verulamium – essentially the grassed-over area where it once stood – from the museum at 3pm every Sunday.

In adjacent **Verulamium Park** you can inspect remains of a basilica, bathhouse and parts of the city wall.

CLOCK TOWER

The medieval **clock tower** (High St; admission 30p; ☻ 10.30am-5pm Sat, Sun & bank holidays Apr-Oct) was built between 1403 and 1412. It's the only medieval belfry in England and the original bell (called 'Gabriel') is still there. You can climb the 93 steps to the top for great views over the town.

Sleeping

Mrs Thomas (☎ 858939; 8 Hall Place Gardens; s/d £20/40) This small, lovely spot has spacious rooms and garden views with shared bathrooms.

Wren Lodge (☎ 855540; 24 Beaconsfield Rd; s/d £35/60) An elegant Edwardian home where you will be looked after with care, 10 minutes' walk from the town centre.

White Hart (☎ 853624; fax 840237; 25 Holywell Hill; s/d from £40/55, family r £75; ☒) A charming half-timbered hotel with exposed beams and

creaky floors just a couple of minutes' walk from the centre. A full English breakfast is £5.50 extra.

Eating

Waffle House (☎ 853502; St Michael's St; mains £3-6; ☻ 10am-6pm Mon-Sat, 11am-5pm Sun; ☒) While the speciality is Belgian waffles, this popular eatery inside the Saxon-era Kingsbury Water Mill also serves dishes such as sweet-potato coconut soup and lamb moussaka.

Claude's Creperie (☎ 846424; 15 Holywell Hill; mains £6-9.50; ☻ 10.30am-6pm Tue-Fri, 10.30am-11pm Sat & Sun; ☒) Long a local hangout, Claude's Creperie is so cosy it's almost communal dining. It serves French and Italian regional cooking.

Thai Rack (☎ 850055; 13 George St; mains £5-10; ☻ lunch & dinner) This peaceful and small restaurant has a meditative outdoor patio and excellent curry.

Drinking

St Albans has one of the best collections of pubs in South England.

Ye Olde Fighting Cocks (☎ 865830; 16 Abbey Mill Lane) This ancient and charming spot is loaded with dark wood and cosy nooks and is supposedly one of the oldest pubs in England. Beer has been poured here since the 13th century.

Rose & Crown (☎ 851903; 10 St Michael's St) This charming spot, with a beautiful beer garden, features live music Monday at 9pm and Irish music on Thursday at 8pm.

Goat (☎ 833934; 37 Sopwell Lane) Tucked away on a residential lane, this nice old pub in a Tudor-style building is popular with the locals.

Also recommended:

Black Lion Inn (☎ 851786; 198 Fishpool St) Roman malting ovens were found here. Probably the least atmospheric of all St Albans pubs.

Lower Red Lion Freehouse (☎ 855669; 36 Fishpool St) A little rough around the edges, but there's a charming outdoor beer garden and regular beer festivals.

Six Bells (☎ 856945; 16-18 St Michael's St) Next door to the Rose & Crown, this popular, low-ceilinged spot has a cosy fireplace and good pub food.

Getting There & Away

Rail is the most direct way to get to St Albans, although if you are coming from Heathrow you can catch Green Line bus No 724 which leaves hourly and takes an hour.

SOUTHEAST ENGLAND

St Albans station is on Stanhope Rd, a 10-minute walk east of St Peter's St. Thameslink trains depart every 15 minutes from London King's Cross to St Albans station (£7.40, 23 minutes).

AROUND ST ALBANS
Hatfield House

England's most magnificent Jacobean mansion, **Hatfield House** (☎ 01707-262823; adult £7.50 Sat-Thu, £10.50 Fri, park only £2; ☼ noon-4pm, gardens 11am-4pm Easter-Sep) was built between 1607 and 1611 for Robert Cecil, first earl of Salisbury and secretary of state to both Elizabeth I and James I.

Inside you'll find a grand marble hall, famous portraits and a magnificent oak staircase decorated with carved figures, including one of John Tradescant, the 17th-century botanist responsible for the gardens.

Hatfield House can only be visited by guided tour on weekdays; they depart as soon as a large enough group gathers. The house is opposite Hatfield train station, and there are numerous trains from London King's Cross station (£7, 25 minutes). **Green Line** (☎ 02087 608 7261) runs bus No 797 from London to Hatfield hourly, and bus No 724 between St Albans and Hatfield every hour.

Shaw's Corner

This **Victorian villa** (☎ 01438 820307; Ayot St Lawrence; adult £3.80; ☼ 1-4.30pm Wed-Sun Apr-Oct) is where the playwright George Bernard Shaw died in 1950. It has been preserved much as he left it. In the garden is the revolving summerhouse (revolving to catch the sun) where he wrote several works including *Pygmalion*, the play on which the film *My Fair Lady* was based.

Bus No 304 from St Albans drops you at Gustardwood, 1¼ miles from Ayot St Lawrence.

TOP FIVE SIGHTS

- **Canterbury Cathedral** (p182)
- **Winchester Cathedral** (p201)
- **Windsor Castle** (p196)
- **Dover Castle** (p191)
- **Royal Pavilion Brighton** (p223)

ESSEX

If you spend any amount of time in England, you'll start to hear joke about Essex, long the butt of many an English punch line. Its inhabitants are routinely made fun of for their unique accents, white trainers, gold chains and promiscuous attitudes. And when you do get past the jokes, the only town anyone ever mentions in Essex is Southend-on-Sea, a tacky seaside resort that is one of the country's most popular. So if you're ever inclined not to read a book by its cover, this is the time to do it. Essex is home to Britain's oldest town as well as a number of exquisite medieval villages and some stunning countryside that inspired the painter John Constable.

SOUTHEND-ON-SEA

☎ 01702 / pop 269,415

Southend is more pugnacious and brash than some of England's other fun-by-the-sea destinations and unless you're after tacky seaside arcades, flash amusement rides or sleazy nightspots, there's not much to do in Essex's largest town and most popular seaside resort. Still, if you're after a day trip fuelled by rock candy and fish and chips, look no further. Southend is less than 50 miles from London and was pegged as an out-of-town retreat at the turn of the 19th century when the Prince Regent brought his wife Princess Caroline here to enjoy healthier climes, while he disappeared off to Brighton to indulge himself.

Information

The **TIC** (☎ 215120; marketing@southend.gov.uk; Western Esplanade; ☼ 8am-6pm Mon-Fri & 8am-8pm Sat & Sun May, 8am-10pm Mon-Fri & 8am-8pm Sat & Sun Jun-Sep, 8am-4pm Oct-Apr) is at the entrance to the pier. Banks and the shops run along the High St.

Sights & Activities

Southend action seems to pool along the coast to each side of its 1.3-mile-long **pier** (adult £2.20; ☼ 8am-10pm Apr-Oct, 8am-5pm Mon-Fri & 8am-7pm Sat & Sun Nov-Mar), supposedly the longest in the world.

The free trip on the old and cramped **Pier Railway** isn't all that great, especially considering that the walk to the end of the pier is mercifully quiet.

If you have kids, the **Sealife Adventure** (☎ 442200; Eastern Esplanade; adult/child £5.50/4;

10am-7pm), about half a mile east of the pier, has the usual aquatic suspects behind glass, including a couple of sharks. The same company also runs **Adventure Island** (☎ 443400; Western Esplanade; ☺ daily Apr-Aug, Sat & Sun Sep-Mar), an amusement park near the pier. There are plenty of rides at about £2 each.

Sleeping & Eating

For those who can't get their fill of candy floss and bingo in one day, Southend has a number of B&Bs.

Mayflower Hotel (☎ 340489; www.themayflower hotel.co.uk; 6 Royal Tce; s/d/tr from £28.20/42.30/56.40; ☒) This charming Victorian row-house B&B has flower-lined, wrought-iron balconies and pier-and-beach views.

Gleneagles Hotel (☎ 333635; www.thegleneagles hotel.co.uk; 5 Clifftown Pde; s/d £39.50/50; ☒) Close to the High St and pier, this crisp B&B has lovely patio and front rooms overlooking a conservation garden and the sea.

Despite the tackiness of its seafront, Southend offers a surprising number of stylish restaurants.

Bailey's Fry Inn (☎ 467680; 20 Eastern Esplanade; mains £3-4; ☺ lunch & dinner Mon-Fri, 11.45am-10pm Sat & Sun) Front and centre on the seafront, this is a fabulously greasy fish-and-chips dive with timeless, local charm.

For eats away from the glitter of the seaside, walk up the hill to **Singapore Sling** (☎ 431313; 12 Clifftown Pde; mains £4-10; ☺ lunch & dinner Tue-Sun; ☒), an Asian bistro with Thai, Japanese and Vietnamese fare. Nearby is **Fleur de Provence** (☎ 532987; 54 Alexandra St; mains £16-18; ☺ lunch & dinner Mon-Fri, dinner Sat; ☒), an elegant French restaurant with blonde-wood floors and white tablecloths all set up for a special night out. A three-course prix fixe lunch is £15.

Getting There & Around

From London, **Green Line** (☎ 0870 608 7261) bus No X1 departs at 9am, noon and 4.30pm from London Victoria to Victoria Station in Southend (£5.50, 2½ hours).

There's several hourly trains from either London Liverpool St to Southend Victoria station or from London Fenchurch St to Southend Central station (£10, 55 minutes).

The seafront is a 15-minute walk from the train station and getting around town on foot is easy.

If you need a taxi try **Southend Six Seater** (☎ 304848) or **Southend Radio Cars** (☎ 345678).

COLCHESTER
☎ 01206 / pop 104,390
Most visitors to Essex tend to overlook Colchester but they shouldn't. This charming place is England's oldest city with a recorded settlement dating back to the 5th century BC, hundreds of years before the Romans arrived in AD 43 to make Colchester their Northern capital. Back then, the city was known as Camulodunum. Today, it's possible to see the evidence of Roman life at the town's main feature – the impressive Norman castle built by William the Conqueror atop the ruins of an old Roman fortress. Apart from the rich history, Colchester is an easy-going place perfect for a day trip from London.

Orientation & Information
There are two train stations, but most services stop at North station, about half a mile north of the town centre. The **bus and coach station** (☎ 282645) is in the centre of town, near the TIC and the castle. A **First Day ticket** (adult £2.20) allows unlimited bus service in the Colchester area.

The **TIC** (☎ 282920; www.visitcolchester.com; 1 Queen St; ☎ 9.30am-6pm Mon-Sat, 11am-4pm Sun) is opposite the castle.

There are a couple of **post offices** (North Hill & Longe Wyre St) in town. Banks and ATMs can be found on Culver St West and on the High St.

Sights & Activities
Situated at the edge of a beautiful park across from the TIC, **Colchester Castle** (☎ 282939; adult £4.50; ☺ 10am-5pm Mon-Sat, 11am-4.30pm Sun) is a great place to linger. It was built by William I on the foundations of a Roman fort, the walls of which are still visible just outside the front door. Construction began in 1076 and was completed in 1125. It boasts the largest castle keep in Europe – bigger than the Tower of London. The museum contains Roman mosaics and statues. For another £1.50 you can take a guided tour of the Roman vaults, the Norman chapel on the roof of the castle and the top of the castle walls.

In Tymperleys – a magnificent, restored 15th-century building about 100m east of the castle just off the High St – is the **Clock Museum** (☎ 282931; admission free; ☺ 10am-1pm & 2-5pm Mon-Sat Apr-Oct), with one of the largest collections of clocks in Britain. It's also interesting to walk around the **Dutch Quarter**, just north of High St, which was established in the 16th century by Protestant refugee weavers from Holland.

Opposite the castle, the **Natural History Museum** (☎ 282932; High St; ☯ 10am-5pm Mon-Sat, 11am-5pm Sun) has exhibits devoted to the local area, with hands-on displays, live animals and a small nature reserve.

About 5 miles northeast of town is **Colchester Zoo** (☎ 331292; Maldon Rd, Stanway; adult £11.99; ☯ 9.30am-6pm Easter-Jun, Sep & Oct, 9.30am-6.30pm Jul & Aug, 9.30am-dusk Oct-Mar), one of the best zoos in Europe, with a huge selection of animals. It's very modern and extremely well organised.

Eastern National bus No 75 to Tiptree stops at the zoo. It leaves on the hour from stand 17 at the bus station.

Tours

The TIC has a variety of themed, guided **walking tours** (£2.50; ☯ Apr-Oct) of the town at 11.30am several days of the week. Call ahead to ask for details. The TIC also sells tickets for **open-top bus tours** (£5.75; ☯ mid-Jul–Sep).

Sleeping

Most accommodation in Colchester is in the mid-range category, though you can definitely splurge if you want to.

Peveril Hotel (☎ /fax 574001; 51 North Hill; s/d from £30/42; ✗) Conveniently located on the road to the train station, this 17-room hotel is good value. Most rooms share bathrooms.

Old Manse (☎ 545154; www.doveuk.com/oldmanse; 15 Roman Rd; s/d £34/53; ✗) This wonderful Victorian home is only a few minutes' walk from the centre and is a run by a lovely, engaging couple. It doesn't cater for children. Part of the Roman wall is at the bottom of the garden.

Red Lion (☎ 577986; www.redlion@brook-hotels .co.uk; High St; s/d from £55/65; Ⓟ ✗) This well-preserved Tudor hotel has comfortable rooms furnished with period-style antiques. The restaurant serves steak-and-kidney pie and other takes on traditional English fare.

Rose & Crown Hotel (☎ 866677; www.rose-and -crown.com; East St; s/d from £66/76; Ⓟ ☐ ✗) The Rose & Crown may be the oldest hotel in town, but it features a sharp, modern wing. All 30 rooms have an en suite and are loaded with amusing distractions.

George (☎ 578494; www.londonandedinburghinns .com/ColchesterGeorge; 116 High St; s/d from £85/95; ✗)

Don't let the charming sloped floors in this gorgeous 15th-century inn fool you. The rooms here are clean with modern amenities; smoking rooms can be a bit musty.

Eating

Garden Café at the Minories Art Gallery (☎ 500169; 74 High St; mains £4-6; ☯ 10am-4.30 Mon-Sat; ✗) This is an eclectic, artsy and airy café with an enormous garden. If they've run out of main dishes (they're cooked fresh daily and served until 3pm), go for the amaretto bombe. The café is housed in a gallery that shows local, national and international travelling exhibits of contemporary art.

Franco (☎ 549080; Balkerne Passage off North Hill; mains £5-15; ☯ lunch & dinner Tue-Fri, dinner Sat; ✗) Look no further for sophisticated but traditional Italian country dishes such as risotto, mussels, and melon with figs. The atmosphere is colourful and lively.

Lemon Tree (☎ 767337; 48 St John's St; mains £9-13; ☯ 10.30am-9.30pm Mon-Sat; ✗) This place seems a bit plain until you notice part of an original Roman wall and cavern in the corner. It's the only place to sit for good upscale French cuisine or even a simple pot of tea.

Getting There & Away

Colchester is 62 miles from London. There are daily National Express buses from London Victoria (£9) and rail services every half hour or so from London Liverpool St (£16.90, 45 minutes).

AROUND COLCHESTER
Dedham Vale

Known to the locals as Constable country, Dedham Vale in the Stour Valley, near the border with Suffolk, was an oft-used subject for early–19th-century painter John Constable. His landscapes depicting country lanes, springtime fields and babbling creeks may have been romantic visions of times past but there's no doubt that the charm of the local countryside still exists. The Vale centres on the villages of Dedham, East Bergholt (in Suffolk, where the painter was born) and Flatford. The area is best explored in your own car but there are bus and train services.

Bridge Cottage (☎ 01206-298260; admission free; ☯ 10am-5.30pm May-Sep, 11am-4.30pm Oct, 11am-5pm Wed-Sun Mar-Apr & Nov-Dec, 11am-3.30pm Sat & Sun Jan-Feb) has Constable landscapes on display as well as a tea garden, boat hire and access to National Trust land. When guided tours are not available, audio tapes can be hired (tours/tapes £2).

Several bus companies operate services from Colchester to East Bergholt. It's better to come by train (get off at Manningtree), as you get a pleasant 1¾-mile walk along footpaths through Constable country. If you are in Manningtree, make a quick diversion and walk up the hill to the town of Mistly for a wonderful view over the estuary of the River Stour. The TIC in Colchester sells cycling maps of Dedham Vale.

KENT

If you're looking for beach towns and cathedrals, it doesn't get much better than Kent. Home to Dover's famous white cliffs as well as several classic 19th-century English beach resorts (complete with Punch and Judy puppet shows and cheap fish-and-chip shops) and Canterbury Cathedral, one of the world's greatest religious buildings, Kent offers an array of picture-postcard destinations. Plus, inside its ocean-lined borders, you'll find rolling farmland pocked with farm stores, country estates, Scottish cattle and, most important of all, the world-renowned Kent hops, the main ingredient in some of England's (and the world's) finest ales.

Unfortunately, Kent is by no means a well-kept secret. Its popularity as a holiday destination began with the construction of the railway in the 19th century and the crowds haven't abated since. The county's close proximity to London also means that many of the small towns are within commuting distance, thereby clogging the main routes to and from the city during the rush hours.

Trails along the North and South Downs (p175) attract walkers from all over the world. Between the North and South Downs lies an area known as the Weald, much of it designated an Area of Outstanding Natural Beauty (AONB).

CANTERBURY

☎ 01227 / pop 45,055

Most people have heard of Canterbury's great cathedral and rightly so. It's one of Europe's (and some say the world's) finest examples of Gothic religious architecture.

But if you come to town only to see the beautiful buildings (and there are many), then you'll miss out on a vibrant scene in its own right. In addition to a very rich history, Canterbury is a youthful university town with some great pubs, excellent restaurants and an easy, laid-back atmosphere all set in a gorgeous medieval centre that has retained much of its original character. Plus, this is a great place to base yourself while visiting the nearby coastal towns. Any time you come to Canterbury, it's essential to book ahead for hotels and some of the nicer restaurants. The crowds of visitors that descend on the city year-round are not to be underestimated.

History

Canterbury's past is as rich as it comes. From AD 200 there was a Roman town called Durovernum Cantiacorum here, which later became the capital of the Saxon kingdom of Kent. When St Augustine arrived in England in 597 to carry the Christian message to the pagan hordes, he chose Canterbury as his *cathedra*, or primary see, and set about building an abbey on the town outskirts. Following the martyrdom of Thomas Becket (see the boxed text, p182), Canterbury became northern Europe's most important centre of pilgrimage, which in turn led to Geoffrey Chaucer's *The Canterbury Tales*, one of the most outstanding poetic works in English literature (see the boxed text, p184).

Blasphemous murders and rampant tourism aside, Canterbury remains the primary see for the Church of England.

Orientation

The old town of Canterbury is enclosed by a medieval city wall and a modern ring road. Most streets in the Old Town are closed to cars, but there is parking inside the wall, and meandering down the streets is an added attraction.

Information
BOOKSHOPS
Chaucer Bookshop (Beer Cart Lane) A wonderful, well-stocked used-book shop.
Waterstone's (☎ 456343; 20-21 St Margaret's St)

INTERNET ACCESS
Main library (☎ 452747; High St; ⊙ Mon-Sat) Free Internet access. Located inside the Royal Museum & Art Gallery.

MEDIA

Two free magazines, *What, Where & When* and *Great Days Out*, have details of what's on in Canterbury and Kent. They're both available from the TIC.

MEDICAL SERVICES

Canterbury Health Centre (☎ 452444; 26 Old Dover Rd) For general medical consultations.

Kent & Canterbury Hospital (☎ 766877; Etherbert Rd) Has an emergency room and is a mile from the centre.

MONEY

ATMs and most major banks are on High St, near the corner of St Margaret's St.

Lloyd's TSB (28 St Margaret's St) Has a bureau de change.

POST

Main post office (cnr St Peter's & Stour Sts; ☷ 9.30am-5.30pm Mon-Sat)

TOURIST OFFICES

TIC (☎ 378100; www.canterbury.co.uk; 12 Sun St; ☷ 9.30am-5.30pm Mon-Sat, 10am-4pm Sun) Across from the cathedral gate.

Sights

There are some great things to see in Canterbury, headed up of course by the great cathedral.

CANTERBURY CATHEDRAL

The Church of England could not have a more splendid and imposing mother church. This extraordinary **cathedral complex** (☎ 762862; adult/child £4.50/3.50; ☷ 9am-6.30pm Mon-Fri May-Aug, 9am-5pm Mon-Fri Sep-Apr, 9am-2.30pm & 4.30-5.30pm Sunday year-round) is undoubtedly worth the few hours you can spend visiting. The sheer wealth of detail, treasure and stories

associated with the cathedral is worthwhile, so we recommend you join a **tour** (adult/child £3.50/1.50; ☷ 10.30am, noon & 2.30pm Mon-Fri, 10.30am, noon & 1.30pm Sat), or you can take a 30-minute **self-guided audio tour** (adult/child £2.95/1.95). At the very least, pick up a free leaflet that briefly points out the many sights. There is an additional charge (£4) to take photographs inside the cathedral during your visit.

The first church built here was badly damaged by fire in 1067. A replacement cathedral was begun in 1070 but only fragments of this remain today, as a second fire in 1174 destroyed most of the eastern half of the building. Thankfully, the magnificent crypt beneath the choir survived.

Following the martyrdom of Thomas Becket (see the boxed text, below), the cathedral's fortunes increased dramatically. Pilgrims began appearing in droves and a new cathedral, created by William of Sens, was constructed to reflect the town's growing importance. It was the first major Gothic construction in England, built in a style now known as 'Early English'. In 1988 Unesco declared the cathedral – along with St Augustine's Abbey and St Martin's Church – a World Heritage Site.

The spot where Becket was murdered is in the northwest transept, marked by a lit candle. The original **Altar of Sword's Point** – the final destination of millions of pilgrims over the last 1000 years – was replaced by a modern version of the same in 1982, when Pope John Paul II came here.

MUSEUMS

The first three museums listed here can all be visited with one ticket (adult/child £5/3). Individual admission costs are given below.

KEEP YOUR ENEMIES CLOSE...

In 1162 King Henry II did what every good monarch should do. He appointed his good mate Thomas Becket to the highest clerical office in the land in the hope that a friendly archbishop could force the increasingly vocal religious lobby to toe the royal line. But Henry didn't count on Thomas taking his job as seriously as he did, and by 1170 Henry had become exasperated with his former favourite's penchant for disagreeing with virtually everything the king said or did. He sulked and raged for a while, then late in the year 'suggested' to four of his knights that Thomas was a little too much to bear. The dirty deed was done on December 29. Becket's martyrdom – and canonisation in double-quick time (1173) – catapulted the cathedral to the top spot in northern Europe's top 10 pilgrimage sites. Mindful of the growing opprobrium at his role in Becket's murder, Henry arrived here in 1174 for a dramatic *mea culpa*, and after allowing himself to be whipped and scolded was granted absolution.

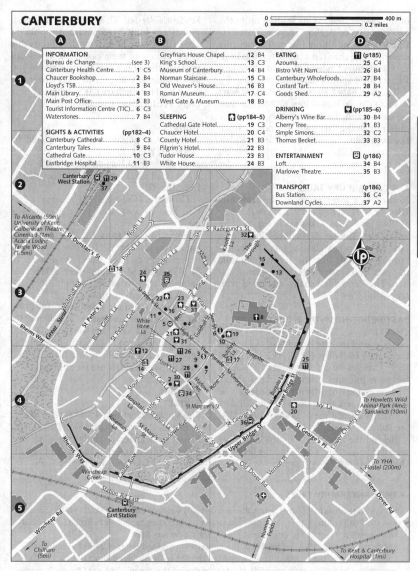

CANTERBURY

SOUTHEAST ENGLAND

An excellent place to visit, the **Roman Museum** (☎ 785575; Butchery Lane; adult £2.80; ☺ 10am-5pm Mon-Sat year-round, 1.30-5pm Sun Jun-Oct) is one of the few museums of this kind where you are allowed to actually touch old stuff. And not only can you handle original artefacts uncovered in the remains of a Roman town house lying below the museum, you can also walk around a reconstructed kitchen (smelling the odours) and check out the extensive remains of a mosaic floor.

Once the Poor Priests' Hospital, the **Museum of Canterbury** (☎ 452747; Stour St; adult/child £3.10/2.10; ☺ 10.30am-5pm Mon-Sat year-round, 1.30-5pm Sun Jun-Oct) has wonderful exhibitions and artefacts including a visual breakdown of the people and events leading up to the assassination of Becket. There's also a new Rupert Bear addition (Mary Tourtel, the creator of the children's character, was born in Canterbury) where the kids can join Rupert for a spot of tea or time travel.

The **West Gate & Museum** (☎ 452747; St Peter's St; adult £1.10; ☒ 11am-12.30pm & 1.30-3.30pm Mon-Sat) dates from the 14th century and is the only remaining city gate. It's now a small museum featuring arms and armour. Kids – and some adults – might enjoy trying on the replica armour.

THE CANTERBURY TALES

Housed in a former church, the **Canterbury Tales** (☎ 479227; St Margaret's St; adult/child £6.95/5.25; ☒ 10am-5pm Mar-Jun, 9.30am-5pm Jul-Aug, 10am-5pm Sep-Oct, 10am-4.30pm Nov-Feb) is a three-dimensional take on Chaucer's classic story. It's entertaining enough but the jerky, hydraulic puppets don't do the historic stories justice. The centre is usually crammed with schoolchildren.

EASTBRIDGE HOSPITAL & GREYFRIARS CHAPEL

Founded in 1180, the Hospital of St Thomas the Martyr **Eastbridge** (☎ 462395; 25 High St; adult £1; ☒ 10am-5pm Mon-Sat) was built as a hospice for poor pilgrims visiting Becket's shrine (the recessions in which they slept can be found between the pillars in the Undercroft). Its almshouses (dating from 1584) are still in use today.

Behind the hospital in a surprisingly serene garden setting, you'll find the **Greyfriars Chapel** (☎ 471688; 25 High St; admission free; ☒ 2-4pm Mon-Sat mid-May–Sep). This was the first English monastery built by Franciscan monks in 1267 (they were known as Grey Friars due to the colour of their cassocks). The small upstairs chapel is a serene place where you can recharge your spirit away from the crowds. The Eucharist is celebrated here every Wednesday at 12.30pm.

Tours

A variety of guided walks are offered by **Canterbury Walks** (☎ 459779; www.canterbury-walks .co.uk; £3.75; ☒ 11.30am daily Apr-Oct, Mon-Sat Jul & Aug). Call ahead to book. Walks depart from the TIC.

Cross the footbridge at Canterbury Station East to walk atop the city's **medieval walls**.

Popular **ghost tours** (☎ 575831; www.green bard.8m.com; adult/child £5/£4) of the Old Town depart from outside Alberry's wine bar in St Margaret's St at 8pm every Friday and Saturday all year in all weather. Bookings are only needed for groups.

Canterbury Historic River Tours (☎ 07790-534744; www.canterburyrivertours.co.uk; adult/child £5/4; ☒ 10am-5pm Mon-Sat & 11am-5pm Sun Apr-Sep) will take you on a rowing-boat tour including (prebooked) candlelit tours, from behind the Old Weaver's House on St Peter's St.

Sleeping
BUDGET

Kipp's Independent Hostel (☎ 786121; info@kipps -hostel.com; 40 Nunnery Fields; dm from £11; ☒) This bright and cheery, family-run place has clean facilities, Internet access (£1 per half-hour), and a lovable dog named Cuba.

THE CANTERBURY TALES

If English literature has a father figure, then it is certainly Geoffrey Chaucer (1342/3–1400). Chaucer was the first English writer to introduce characters – rather than 'types' – into fiction, and he did so to greatest effect in his most popular work, *The Canterbury Tales*.

Written between 1387 and his death, the *Tales* is an unfinished series of 24 stories supposedly told by a party of pilgrims on their journey from London to the shrine of Thomas Becket at Canterbury and back. Chaucer successfully created the illusion that the pilgrims, not Chaucer (though he appears in the tales as himself), are telling the stories, which allowed him unprecedented freedom as an author to explore the rich fictive possibilities of a number of genres.

Chaucer's achievement remains a high point of European literature, but it was also the first time that English came to match Latin (the language of the Church) and French (spoken by the Norman court) as a language of high literature. *The Canterbury Tales*, summed up by Dryden as 'God's Plenty', remains one of the pillars of the literary canon, even if contemporary modern readers would probably enjoy a modern transliteration more than the original Old English version.

YHA Hostel (☎ 0870 770 5744; www.yha.org.uk; 54 New Dover Rd; dm beds £16.40; ⊙ Feb–late Dec; P ✕ ▣) Staying in a fine Victorian Gothic villa was never so affordable. Amenities include a bureau de change and a large garden. Located 1¼ miles southeast of the centre.

MID-RANGE

White House (☎ 761836; www.canterburybreaks.co.uk; 6 St Peter's Lane; s/d from £35/55; ▣ ✕) A gorgeous Regency townhouse that was owned by the Church of England until 1979 with spacious, comfortable rooms and unparalleled service.

Cathedral Gate Hotel (☎ 464381; cgate@cgate .demon.co.uk; 36 Burgate; s/d with shared bathroom from £35/50, with private bathroom from £60/90, cots extra £8.50; ✕) Although the floors slope, the walls are thin and it's above a – gasp! – Starbucks, the rooms at this spot next door to the Cathedral Gate are very comfortable and the views of the cathedral are stunning.

Pilgrim's Hotel (☎ 464531; pilgrimshotel@netscape online.co.uk; 18 The Friars; s/d £50/70; P ✕) Exit stage left from the Marlowe Theatre and find yourself on the doorstep of this fine Tudor hotel, with its clean, conservative rooms appointed with country-style antiques.

Tudor House (☎ 765650; 6 Best Lane, s/d £22/46; ⊙ Apr–Oct; ✕) This quaint, family-run spot is right on the river near the High St. Rooms are standard but clean.

Other recommendations:

Acacia Lodge & Tanglewood Cottage (☎ 769955; www.acacialodge.com; 39 London Rd; s/d from £30/38; P ✕)

Alicante (☎ /fax 766277; 4 Roper Rd; s/d £35/65; ✕)

TOP END

County Hotel (☎ 766266; www.macdonaldhotels .co.uk; 30 High St; s/d £112/122; P ✕) Located just across from the striking Royal Museum & Art Gallery on the High St, the rooms in this wonderful building are laden with antiques. This hotel is pet friendly.

Chaucer Hotel (☎ 464427; www.swallowhotels.com; 63 Ivy Lane; s/d from £60/90; P ✕) Once a Georgian house, this top-class hotel has been substantially altered to create a comfortable and modern place to stay. Breakfast is extra.

Eating

There's a good range of eateries in Canterbury. Bookings are recommended for the pricier spots, especially at weekends.

Custard Tart (☎ 785178; 35a St Margaret's St; mains £3-4.50; ⊙ lunch & dinner; ✕) Start your morning with a fresh and heavenly sugar-dusted chocolate donut (55p) from the takeaway counter. The lunch-time sandwiches in the upstairs café are very popular.

Bistro Viêt Nam (☎ 760022; The Old Linen Store, White Horse Lane; mains £5-10; ⊙ lunch & dinner; ✕) The modern southeast Asian menu features a range of well-presented dishes including a superb Vietnamese tapas menu. It is simply fabulous.

Azouma (☎ 760076; www.azouma.co.uk; 4 Church St; mains £8-11; ⊙ lunch & dinner) Follow the smell of roasted couscous, raisins and paprika for an inventive Middle Eastern experience in a beautifully lush and authentic setting.

For self-catering, **Canterbury Wholefoods** (☎ 464623; 1-2 Jewry Lane; ⊙ 9am-6pm Mon-Sat, 11am-5pm Sun) is a wholefood shop with postings for political events, yoga classes, gay and lesbian gatherings and the like.

Drinking

Canterbury has a lively student population, so there are plenty of nightlife options.

Thomas Becket (☎ 464384; 21 Best Lane; mains £6-9) As good as it gets for English pubs. A cosy fireplace, copper pots and bushels of Kent hops hang from the ceiling. The cool jazz on the sound system give the place a timeless charm. Better-than-average pub fare.

Simple Simons (☎ 762355; 3-9 Church Lane) If you've come to England to sample the beer look no further. This wonderfully woody 14th-century building serves at least six different hand-pulled real ales and it has the expert drinkers to prove it.

Cherry Tree (☎ 451266; White Horse Lane) This back-alley pub is quiet and friendly with dark wood and smoky nooks and crannies.

Entertainment
NIGHTCLUBS

Loft (☎ 456515; 516 St Margaret's St) Chill out to cool electronic beats in a modern setting with one extremely long couch, a black granite bar and DJs spinning from Thursday to Saturday. The crowd is sophisticated and international.

Alberry's Wine Bar (☎ 452378; www.alberrys.co.uk; St Margaret's St) Situated across the street from the Loft, this hot after-hours jazz bar is the place to be for Canterbury's young professionals. DJs and live music on Monday and Thursday play smooth jazz and hip-hop.

THEATRE

Marlowe Theatre (☎ 787787; www.marlowetheatre.com; The Friars) This newly remodelled building brings in some truly wonderful events year-round, including plays, dances, concerts and musicals.

Gulbenkian Theatre (☎ 769075; www.kent.ac.uk/gulbenkian; University of Kent) Located on the university campus, this long-time performance venue is larger than the Marlowe with fewer frills. They put on serious contemporary plays, modern dance and great live music.

Getting There & Away

Canterbury is 58 miles from London and is 15 miles from Margate and Dover.

BUS

The bus station is just within the city walls at the eastern end of High St.

There are frequent buses from London Victoria to Canterbury (bus No 20, £10.50, one hour 50 minutes, hourly). Buses from Canterbury go to Dover (No 5, 45 minutes, every 20 minutes). Bus Nos 8, 8A and 88 travel from Canterbury to Margate (45 minutes, half hourly), to Broadstairs (one hour) and to Ramsgate (one hour 20 minutes).

TRAIN

There are two train stations: Canterbury East (for the YHA hostel), accessible from London Victoria; and Canterbury West, accessible from London's Charing Cross, Victoria and Waterloo stations.

London to Canterbury trains leave frequently (£17.30, 1½ hours, every ½ hour), as do Canterbury East to Dover Priory trains (30 minutes, every ½ hour).

Getting Around

Cars are not permitted to enter the centre of town. There are car parks at various points along and just within the walls. Parking vouchers cost £3.60 for 24 hours or £1 from 6pm to 10am.

For a taxi, try **Laser Taxis** (☎ 464422) or **Cabwise** (☎ 712929).

Downland Cycles (☎ 479643) is based at Canterbury West station. Mountain bikes cost £10/50 per day/week with a £25 deposit.

AROUND CANTERBURY
Howlett's Wild Animal Park

The world's largest collection of Lowland gorillas can be observed at this 28-hectare **park** (☎ 1303 264647; www.howletts.net; Bekesbourne; adult £11.95; ☼ 10am-dusk). You'll also see elephants, monkeys, wolves, small wild cats and tigers. Save 20% with tickets purchased in advance.

The park is 4 miles east of Canterbury. By car, take the A257 and turn right at the sign for Bekesbourne, then follow the signs to

---

WORTH THE TRIP

You wouldn't know Polish nobleman and auto enthusiast Count Louis Vorrow Zborowski (1895–1923), except by the name of his car. In 1921 Zborowski custom built his beloved Chitty Chitty Bang Bang out of a Mercedes and an airplane engine. It never flew, but the imaginations of children around the world did when Ian Fleming (of James Bond fame) wrote a book based on the car in 1964. It was later made into a movie and the rest is history.

Zborowski built Chitty Chitty Bang Bang at **Higham Park** (☎ 01227-830830; admission garden £3, house tour only £2; ☼ 11am-6pm Sun-Thu Apr-Oct), a magnificent Palladian mansion with superb Italianate gardens about 3 miles south of Canterbury off the A2. From Canterbury, bus Nos 16 and 17 to Folkestone stop nearby (£1, 10 minutes).

the Animal Park. From the main bus station you can catch Stagecoach bus No 111/211 or 611–14 to Littlebourne, from where it's an eight-minute walk to the park.

Chilham

Five miles southwest of Canterbury on the A252, Chilham is one of the best examples of a medieval village you'll see anywhere on your travels through England. Built in true feudal fashion around the small square at the front of a castle, the village consists of a 13th-century Norman church (added to in the 15th century) and a collection of Tudor and Jacobean timber-framed houses.

Chilham lies on the North Downs Way (p175) and would make a pleasant day's walk from Canterbury. Alternatively, bus No 652 from Canterbury makes the trip in 24 minutes and departs hourly.

WHITSTABLE

☎ 01227 / pop 30,195

Compared with Margate, Broadstairs and Ramsgate, Whitstable has more of a remote, unspoilt charm, which may be why it's known as the 'Pearl of Kent'. A quiet fishing village with street names such as Squeeze Gut Alley and Skinner's Alley, the town is known for its superb seafood – particularly the oysters – as well as its collection of somewhat odd multicoloured beach huts lining the Tankerton Slopes east of town. Higher up on the lawn-edged cliffs of the Slopes you can also get a perfect view of the Street, a narrow shingle ridge stretching half a mile out to sea (but only visible at low tide).

The TIC (☎ 275482; 7 Oxford St; ❧ 10am-5pm Mon-Sat Jul & Aug, 10am-4pm Mon-Sat Sep-Jun) runs a free accommodation booking service.

There are plenty of art galleries that you can wander into for a look. Most of the best ones line Harbour St, on the seafront.

July hosts the Whitstable Oyster Festival (www.whitstableoysterfestival.co.uk), an arts and music extravaganza where you can wash down oysters with pints of Guinness or glasses of champagne. The programme of events is varied and interesting, featuring everything from how-to demonstrations of various crafts to jazz bands and classical quartets. The whole town lends a hand and it's the highlight of the summer. For info on upcoming events, contact the TIC.

Sleeping

As Whitstable is popular with weekenders and day-trippers from all over southeast England, there are plenty of B&Bs.

Hotel Continental (☎ 280280; www.hotelcontinental.co.uk; 29 Beach Walk; s/d/huts from £50/55/100; ✗) This Art Deco building on the seafront has elegantly appointed rooms as well as eight converted Fisherman's Huts on the beach that are just plain charming, if a little close together. Room rates increase at weekends, July and August.

Rooms at both the Duke of Cumberland (☎ 280617; www.thedukeinwhitstable.co.uk; High St; d from £60; ✗) and the Marine (☎ 272672; www.shepherd-neame.co.uk; 33 Marine Pde; s/d £55/75; ✗) are above bright, spacious and tastefully appointed pubs. Outdoor seating at the Marine comes with a sea view.

Eating

Fish is the speciality here. Oysters are the real treat, but all restaurants serve up quite a varied seafood menu.

Wheeler's Oyster Bar (☎ 273311; 8 High St; mains £13.50-18.75; ❧ 1-7.30pm Thu-Sat, Mon & Tue, 1-7pm Sun; ✗) Sit up front at the bar at this one-of-a-kind find, or duck into the tiny and rustic Oyster Parlour for an elegant meal surrounded by old photos and seafaring paraphernalia. The staff are wonderful.

More great seafood can be had at Pearson's Crab & Oyster House (☎ 272005; The Horse bridge; mains $12-16; ❧ lunch & dinner; ✗), another great atmospheric stop, and at the Whitstable Oyster Fishery Co Restaurant (☎ 276856; 17-20 Sea St; mains £12.50-25; ❧ lunch & dinner; ✗), where the whole roasted sea bass with garlic and rosemary is delectable.

Getting There & Away

Stagecoach bus Nos 4, 4A, 4B or 4C leave Canterbury every 15 minutes for the 30-minute trip to Whitstable.

ISLE OF THANET

No, that's not a typo – nor is this peninsula at the far eastern tip of the country an island, at least not anymore. It lost that distinction sometime during the first millennium when the Watsun Channel, as it was known, started to dry up. When Thanet was surrounded by water, the Romans used it as a base in the first century AD. It was here that Augustine landed in AD 597 to kick off his Conversion of Pagan England Tour. Your reason for coming, however, is to visit a couple of pretty seaside towns. And if you fancy some exercise, try the **Thanet Coastal Path**, a 20-mile trail that hugs the far eastern shore from Margate to Pegwell Bay via Broadstairs and Ramsgate.

Margate
☎ 01843 / pop 58,465
Because of its proximity to London and its nice sandy beach, Margate was one of the first seaside resorts to be developed in England. It remains very popular and much of its Victorian glamour is still intact. Here you'll find painted, striped beach huts, period architecture, Punch-and-Judy puppet shows and tasty fish and chips.

The **TIC** (☎ 583333; 12-13 The Parade; ☯ 9.15am-1pm & 1.45-4.45pm Mon-Fri, 10am-4pm Sat & Sun) will tell you all you need to know about the town.

Margate's most famous attraction is the **Shell Grotto** (☎ 220008; Grotto Hill; adult £2; ☯ 10am-5pm daily Easter-Oct, 11am-4pm Sat & Sun Nov-April), discovered in 1835 and lined with elaborate shell mosaics. It's truly a unique adventure and well worth the visit.

SLEEPING & EATING
Walpole Bay Hotel (☎ 221703; 5th Ave, Cliftonville; s/d from £40/60; ☒) A couple of miles from the centre, in the suburb of Cliftonville, this superb hotel is a slice of Victorian heaven. Not only are the rooms furnished with period antiques but most of the hotel is an actual museum with glass-cased displays showing off the owner's collection of memorabilia from the 1800s. Wraparound porches overlook the sea and a stately bowling green.

Elonville Hotel B&B (☎ 298635; 70-72 Harold, Cliftonville; s/d £26/52; ☒) The hostess at this clean and cosy guesthouse goes out of her way to serve you. Dinner and breakfast costs an additional £31.

For budget accommodation, there's a good **YHA Hostel** (☎ 0870 770 5956; margate@yha.org.uk; The Beachcomber, 3-4 Royal Esplanade; dm £11.50; ☯ mid-Apr–Oct; ☒) on the water's edge by the beach. Families welcome. You must book 48 hours in advance.

Eating in Margate leaves a lot to be desired. Nevertheless, for a simple but refined atmosphere with country French cuisine, try **Newbys Wine Bar & Brasserie** (☎ 292888; 1 Market St, Old Town; mains £8-12; ☯ dinner Thu, lunch

& dinner Fri & Sat). Also, **La galleria** (☎ 229900; 2-14 High St; mains £5.25-16.95; ☯ lunch & dinner) is an Italian bistro with a chic preclub downstairs that's open from 8pm to 1am.

GETTING THERE & AWAY
Buses to Margate leave from London Victoria (£10.50, 2¼ hours, five daily). From Canterbury take bus No 8 or 88 (45 minutes, half hourly).

Trains run hourly to Margate from London Victoria or Charing Cross, costing £20.40 and taking an hour and 40 minutes.

Broadstairs
☎ 01843 / pop 22,712
While Margate and Ramsgate have embraced the casinos and seaside arcades that populate much of the English seaside, Broadstairs seems to have resisted. Because of that, this quaint and pretty village has retained a nostalgic Victorian atmosphere that will remind many of childhood summers filled with sandy beaches, buckets and spades and rock candy. Of course, Victorian nostalgia wouldn't be complete without Charles Dickens, who holidayed here regularly, as the TIC and several other establishments in town are proud to remind you. Behind the scenes is Broadstairs' long history of smuggling and shipbuilding.

The **TIC** (☎ 862242; fax 865650; 6b High St; ☯ 9.15am-4.45pm Mon-Fri, 10am-4pm Sat) has all the information you'll need, including details of the annual, week-long **Dickens Festival** in June which culminates in a ball in Victorian dress.

Dickens wrote parts of *Bleak House* and *David Copperfield* in the cliff-top house above the pier between 1837 and 1859. Now a museum, the appositely named **Bleak House** (☎ 862224; adult/child £3/2.80; ☯ 10am-6pm Mar-June & Sep-Dec, 10am-9pm Jul & Aug) has three rooms arranged pretty much as they were when Dickens rented it. They're quite interesting, but what makes this place worth visiting are the displays on local shipwrecks and a terrific room devoted to smuggling.

The **Dickens House Museum** (☎ 861232; 2 Victoria Pde; adult £2.30; ☯ 2-5pm Apr-Oct) wasn't actually his house but the home of Mary Pearson Strong, on whom he based Betsey Trotwood in *David Copperfield*. Dickensiana on display includes personal possessions and letters.

Stonehenge (p240), England

Hot-air balloons, International Balloon Fiesta (p255), Bristol, England

Sunbathers near the palace pier (p223), Brighton, England

Royal Crescent (p262), Bath, England

TONY WHEELER

Warwick Castle (p409), Warwick,
England

Gloucester Cathedral (p361), Gloucester,
England

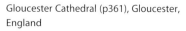

JON DAVISON

NICHOLAS R

Symonds Yat (p380),
Herefordshire, England

Oxford (p339), Oxfordshire, England

DOUG MCKE

THE CINQUE PORT POMP REMAINS

Due to their proximity to Europe, the coastal towns of southeast England were the frontline against Viking raids and invasions during Anglo-Saxon times. In the absence of a professional army and navy, these towns were frequently called upon to defend themselves, and the kingdom, at land and sea.

In 1278, King Edward I formalised this already ancient arrangement by legally defining the Confederation of Cinque (pronounced sink, meaning five) Ports. The five head ports – Sandwich, Dover, Hythe, Romney (now New Romney) and Hastings – were granted numerous privileges in exchange for providing the king with ships. The number of Cinque Ports gradually expanded to include about 30 coastal towns and villages.

By the end of the 15th century, most of the Cinque Ports' harbours had become largely unusable thanks to the shifting coastline, and a professional navy was based at Portsmouth.

Although their real importance and power have evaporated, the pomp and ceremony remains. The Lord Warden of the Cinque Ports is a prestigious post now given to faithful servants of the crown. The most recent warden was the Queen Mother, while previous incumbents included the Duke of Wellington, Sir Winston Churchill and Sir Robert Menzies, former prime minister of Australia.

SOUTHEAST ENGLAND

SLEEPING & EATING

There are a few lovely places to stay in Broadstairs, most of them only a stone's throw from the beach.

Royal Albion Hotel (☎ 868071; www.albionbroadstairs.co.uk; 6-12 Albion St; s/d from £60/78 Sep-Jun, £70/105 Jul-Aug) This is the town's top spot, but unless you're willing to shell out for one of the two Dickens suites, you'll have to make do with slightly small, albeit elegantly appointed rooms. Sea-facing rooms are more expensive.

YHA Hostel (☎ 0870 770 5730; broadstairs@yha.org.uk; Thistle Lodge, 3 Osborne Rd; dm £10.60; ✗) A great spot near the town centre with small rooms and a small garden and sun room.

Thai Four Two (☎ 862925; 42 York St; mains £4-6; ☾ dinner Mon-Sat; ✗) Highly recommended, this small and cosy restaurant has the best home-cooked Thai food this side of the Hindu Kush.

Marchesi Brothers (☎ 862481; www.marchesi.co.uk; 18 Albion St; mains £10-14; ☾ lunch & dinner Tue-Sun) For well-constructed and elegant Italian fare, this spot near the beach is Broadstairs' fanciest restaurant.

GETTING THERE & AWAY

A bus timetable for the area is available from the TIC.

Stagecoach bus Nos 100, 101, 200 and 201 all run hourly from Broadstairs to Margate, Ramsgate, Sandwich, Deal and Dover. Bus Nos 100 and 200 also go to Canterbury. A National Express bus leaves from the top of the hill next to the war memorial for London Victoria via Hempstead Valley shopping centre at 10.30am, 2pm and 5pm daily. The trip takes 2½ hours and costs £10.50.

Trains from London Victoria, London Bridge or Charing Cross make the 2½-hour trip to Broadstairs every hour for £21.50. You may have to change at Ramsgate.

DOVER

☎ 01304 / pop 39,078

If you took away Dover Castle and the white cliffs, the only thing the bland town of Dover would have going for it would be its port. For it is here that you can catch ferries to Europe (Calais in France is a mere 20 miles over the English Channel). Still, history buffs should find plenty to hold their interest as Dover has been an important strategic location since Roman times. And anyone interested in castles should not miss Dover's. Built by the Normans and modified right up through WWII, this hilltop fortress is, with good reason, Dover's premier tourist attraction, along with the spectacular white cliffs. Otherwise, the town is a bit too run down and noisy to offer any charm, and a bit too small to offer very many restaurants that you haven't seen before.

Orientation

Dover Castle dominates the town from a high promontory to the east of town, above the famous white cliffs. The town itself runs back from the sea along a valley formed by

SOUTHEAST ENGLAND

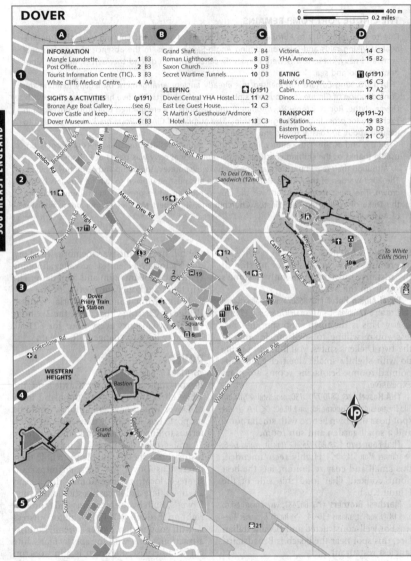

DOVER

INFORMATION	
Mangle Laundrette	**1** B3
Post Office	**2** B3
Tourist Information Centre (TIC)	**3** B3
White Cliffs Medical Centre	**4** A4

SIGHTS & ACTIVITIES	(p191)
Bronze Age Boat Gallery	(see 6)
Dover Castle and keep	**5** C2
Dover Museum	**6** B3

Grand Shaft	**7** B4
Roman Lighthouse	**8** D3
Saxon Church	**9** D3
Secret Wartime Tunnels	**10** D3

SLEEPING	(p191)
Dover Central YHA Hostel	**11** A2
East Lee Guest House	**12** C3
St Martin's Guesthouse/Ardmore Hotel	**13** C3

Victoria	**14** C3
YHA Annexe	**15** B2

EATING	(p191)
Blake's of Dover	**16** C3
Cabin	**17** A2
Dinos	**18** C3

TRANSPORT	(pp191–2)
Bus Station	**19** B3
Eastern Docks	**20** D3
Hoverport	**21** C5

the unimpressive River Dour. Ferry departures are from the Eastern Docks (accessible by bus) southeast of the castle, but the Hoverport is below the Western Heights. Dover Priory train station is a short walk to the west of the town centre. The bus station is closer to the centre of things on Pencester Rd.

Information

Banks and ATMs are located on Market Sq.
Mangle laundrette (Worthington St; ☺ 9am-4pm Mon-Fri, 9am-1pm Sat & Sun) Around £3 a load.
Post office (Pencester Rd; ☺ 9am-5.30pm Mon-Sat)
TIC (☎ 205108; www.whitecliffscountry.org.uk; Biggin St; ☺ 9am-5.30pm Mon-Fri, 10am-4pm Sat & Sun) Has accommodation and ferry-booking services (both free).

White Cliffs Medical Centre (☎ 201705; 143 Folkestone Rd) Five minutes' walk from the centre of Dover.
William Harvey Hospital (☎ 01233-633331;
Kennington Rd, Wilesborough) Accident and Emergency Department; in Ashford, 20 miles west of Dover.

Sights & Activities
DOVER CASTLE

The virtually impregnable **Dover Castle** (EH; ☎ 211067; adult £8.50; ⓨ daily Feb-Oct, Thu-Mon Nov-Jan) is one of the most impressive castles in Britain; it's a mighty fortress commanding a superb view of the English Channel and the township below. On the vast grounds there is a restored **Saxon church** and, interestingly, the remains of a **Roman lighthouse**, which dates from AD 50 and is quite possibly the oldest standing building in all of Britain.

Henry II's mighty **keep** is a striking sight (the keep's walls are 7m thick in places) but it is the series of **secret wartime tunnels** under Dover Castle that are the most interesting attraction here. The first tunnel was dug during the Napoleonic Wars and they were expanded in WWII to act as a command post. The highly entertaining 50-minute tour is included in the general admission price.

Bus Nos 90, 91 and 111 run from Dover Priory station to the castle.

OTHER SIGHTS AND ACTIVITIES

The small **Dover Museum** (☎ 201066; Market Sq; adult £2; ⓨ 10am-5.30pm Mon-Sat) covers Dover's prehistoric past. The displays won't hold your interest for long. The best thing here is the second-floor, award-winning **Bronze Age Boat Gallery**, which features a 3600-year-old boat discovered off the Dover Coast in 1992. It is the world's oldest known seagoing vessel and measures a pretty impressive 9.5m by 2.4m.

Beginning at Snargate St, the **Grand Shaft** (adult £1; ⓨ 2-5pm Tue-Sun Jul & Aug) is worth a quick peek. This 43m triple staircase was cut into the white cliffs as a shortcut to town for troops stationed on the Western Heights during the Napoleonic Wars.

Sleeping
If you want a sea view, be prepared to pay for it.

Dover Central YHA Hostel (☎ 0870 770 5798; fax 202236; 306 London Rd; dm £14.90; ✗ ▣ ▢) The old

Georgian building is a little far from the town centre (though it is close to the train station) and its exterior is a little worse for wear. Still, it's friendly, clean and includes breakfast. The hostel annexe in Godwyne Rd is more convenient.

St Martin's Guesthouse/Ardmore Hotel (☎ 20 5938; www.stmartinsgh.co.uk; 17 Castle Hill Rd; s/d £24/48; ✗) This friendly spot (the two hotels are basically one) has good-sized, spotless and cosy rooms.

Victoria (☎ 205140; wham101496@aol.com; 1 Laureston Pl; s/d from £28/40; ✗) Run by an extremely friendly elderly couple, the Victoria is a highly attractive home with four large and comfortable rooms.

Also recommended:
East Lee Guest House (☎ 210176; www.eastlee.co.uk; 108 Maison Dieu Rd; s/d £35/48; ✗) Good value with vegetarian breakfasts.

Eating
Cabin (☎ 206118; 91 High St; mains £9-12; ⓨ dinner Tue-Sat; ✗) Aside from the shabby exterior and the busy street out front, this is a fine place to dine on wild rabbit and other English delicacies. Be sure to try one of the dozen puddings on the ever-changing menu.

Dino's (☎ 204678; 58 Castle Hill Rd; mains £6-13; ⓨ dinner Tue-Sun) Join the locals for some good family Italian at this tucked-away spot.

Blake's of Dover (☎ 202194; www.blakesofdover.com; 52 Castle St; mains £9-16; ⓨ lunch & dinner Mon-Fri, dinner only Sat; ✗) Surround yourself with dark wood and candlelight and sample one of 52 malt whiskeys in this upmarket English restaurant.

Getting There & Away
Dover is 75 miles from London and 15 miles from Canterbury.

BOAT

Ferries depart from the Eastern Docks (p192), below the castle and accessible by bus. **P&O Stena** (☎ 0870 600 0600; www.poferries.com) ferries leave for Calais every 30 minutes. **Seafrance** (☎ 0870 571 1711; www.seafrance.com) ferries leave hourly. The **Hoverspeed** (☎ 0870 240 8070; www.hoverspeed.com) hoverport is below the Western Heights; the Seacat (one hour) to Calais leaves hourly. Fares vary according to season and advance purchase. See the websites for specials.

BUS

Dover's **bus station** (☎ 240024; Pencester Rd) is in the heart of town. Stagecoach East Kent has a Canterbury to Dover service (45 minutes, every 20 minutes). National Express coaches leave half-hourly from London Victoria (£10.50, two hours 25 minutes).

Buses from Dover go to Brighton, Hastings (£5.50, three hours 20 minutes, every hour and a half), Canterbury (45 minutes, every 30 minutes) and Sandwich (one hour 10 minutes, hourly).

CHANNEL TUNNEL

The Channel Tunnel begins its descent into the English Channel 9 miles west of Dover, just off the M20 between London and Dover. The nearest station foot passengers can board the **Eurostar** (☎ 0870 518 6186) train is at Ashford. From Dover, it's easier if you have a car: take junction 11A for the Channel Tunnel (it's very well signposted). To cross the channel via the **Eurotunnel** (☎ 0870 535 3535; www.eurotunnel.com) can cost anywhere from £50 to £200 depending on specials and how far ahead you book (see p965).

TRAIN

There are more than 40 trains daily from London Victoria and Charing Cross stations to Dover Priory via Ashford and Sevenoaks (£20.70, two hours).

Getting Around

The ferry companies run complimentary buses between the docks and the train station as they're a long walk apart. On local buses a trip from one side of town to the other costs about £1.70.

Heritage (☎ 204420) and **Central Taxis** (☎ 240 441) both have 24-hour services. You could also try **Star Taxis** (☎ 228822). A one-way trip to Deal costs about £11; to Sandwich it's about £17.

AROUND DOVER
The White Cliffs

The world-famous white cliffs extend for 10 miles on either side of Dover, but it is the 6-mile stretch east of town – properly known as the Langdon Cliffs – that has captivated visitors for centuries. Once you visit, you'll see why.

The chalk here is about 250m deep, and the cliffs about half a million years old, formed when the melting waters from the giant icecap that covered all of northern Europe forced a channel through the landmass that was then France and England, creating at once the English Channel and the cliffs.

You can appreciate their majesty – and get in some decent exercise – by walking along the path that snakes its way for 2 miles along the top from the car park (£1.60 per car). It's a pretty bracing walk so be sure to wear appropriate footwear. On the eastern side is the **South Foreland Lighthouse** (☎ 202756; adult £2; ☼ 1-5pm Thu-Mon), built in 1843. It was from here, on 24 December 1898, that Guglielmo Marconi made the world's first shore-to-ship and international radio transmission.

The Langdon Cliffs are managed by the National Trust, which has recently opened a **visitors centre** (☎ 01304-202756; admission free; ☼ 10am-5pm Mar-Oct, 11am-4pm Nov-Feb) on the western side of this section.

The cliffs are at the end of Upper Rd, 2 miles east of Dover along Castle Hill Rd and the A258 road to Deal. Bus No 113 from Dover stops near the main entrance. City Sightseeing Guide includes the cliffs as part of their hop-on, hop-off town tours. First departure is from Market Sq in Dover at 10am; last departure from the car park at the cliffs is at 4.40pm.

If you fancy seeing the cliffs from the sea, **White Cliffs Boat Tours** (☎ 01303-271388; www .whitecliffsboattours.co.uk; adult/child £5/3; ☼ 10am-5pm daily Jun-Aug, Sat & Sun Apr-May & Sep-Oct) run water tours aboard the 70-seater *Southern Queen*. Trips run hourly from De Bradelei Wharf at the Eastern Docks and children are welcome to take the helm.

THE KENT WEALD

The Weald, as it's known locally, is really an area covering part of Kent and some of East Sussex with the town of Royal Tunbridge Wells pretty much at its centre. Its name comes from the Old German world *wald*, meaning forest, though the only trees you'll find are the oft-pruned ones in the many well-manicured gardens in the area; most of the timber here was harvested long ago. Instead, you'll find pretty rolling hills, country lanes and well-to-do villages that house some of England's wealthiest citizens. It's also home to three extraordinary castles and two much-visited manor houses.

Sevenoaks

☎ 01732 / pop 26,99

Very near to the M25, and therefore very much the home of choice for many a London commuter, Sevenoaks has become somewhat homogenised over the years. Even the trees that gave the town its name are gone, knocked over in a freak storm in 1987. That said, the reason to visit is to see the country estate Knole House; you won't be disappointed.

SIGHTS

Located at the southern end of High St, **Knole House** (☎ 450608; adult £6; ☻ 11am-4pm Wed-Sun Apr-Oct) is one of the most treasured houses in England. The estate has existed since the 12th century, but in 1456 the Archbishop of Canterbury, Thomas Bouchier, bought the whole property for just £266 and set about rebuilding the lot to make it 'fit for the Princes of the Church'. The result is very impressive indeed, and is curiously designed to match the Gregorian calendar, so there are seven courtyards, 52 staircases and 365 rooms. You can also pay a visit to the Knole House **gardens** (adult £2; ☻ 1st Wed of month May-Sep).

The house is about 1½ miles from Sevenoaks train station and less than one mile from the bus station.

There are no direct bus services from London to Sevenoaks so you're better off catching the train. From nearby Tonbridge, however, there is a bus to Sevenoaks.

The station is on London Rd. Trains leave three times an hour from London Charing Cross (£7, 35 minutes) and continue to Tunbridge Wells (£6, 20 minutes) and Hastings (£14, one hour 10 minutes).

Chartwell

Six miles southeast of Sevenoaks is **Chartwell** (☎ 01732-868381; Westerham; adult £7, garden & studio only £3.50; ☻ 11am-5pm Wed-Sun Apr-Jun, 11am-5pm Tue-Sun Jul & Aug, 11am-5pm Wed-Sun Sep–early-Nov), Sir Winston Churchill's home from 1924 until his death in 1965. Architecturally unremarkable, this much-altered Tudor house is nevertheless a fascinating place, as well as being one of the most visited of all NT-owned properties.

The rooms and gardens are pretty much as Winnie left them, full of pictures, books, personal mementos and plenty of maps. Churchill was also an artist of considerable talent, and the interesting collection of sketches and watercolours in the garden studio display a softer side of the cigar-chomping bombast of popular perception.

The Chartwell Explorer bus runs six times a day between Sevenoaks train/bus stations and Chartwell on the weekend and bank holidays from mid-May to mid-September, and Wednesday to Friday during July and August. The trip takes 30 minutes and the ticket (adult/child £4.50/3) includes a pot of tea at Chartwell. A combined ticket, including return rail travel from London to Sevenoaks, bus transfer to Chartwell and admission costs £15/7.50; inquire at Charing Cross train station.

Hever Castle

Idyllic **Hever Castle** (☎ 01732-865224; adult £8.80, gardens only £7; ☻ noon-5pm Mar-Oct, noon-4pm Nov), near Edenbridge, a few miles west of Tonbridge, was the childhood home of Anne Boleyn, mistress to Henry VIII and then his doomed queen. Walking through the main gate into the courtyard of Hever is

---

OAST HOUSES

Oast houses were basically giant, housed kilns for drying hops, a key ingredient in the brewing of beer, introduced to the region in the early 15th century.

An oast house is made up of four rooms: the kiln (oven), the drying room (located above the kiln), the cooling room and the storage room where hops were pressed and baled, ready to go to the local inn brewery. The cone-shaped roof was necessary to create a draught for the fire. The bits sticking out from the top of the cone are cowls. They could be moved to regulate the airflow to the fire.

Many oast houses have been converted into homes, and are increasingly sought after as prime real estate. Oast house B&Bs are becoming more and more common throughout the county; check with the various tourist information centres for information on local possibilities or call the **Kent Tourism Alliance** (☎ 01622-696165), which will locate a B&B in your area.

like stepping onto the set of a period film. It's beautiful.

The moated castle dates from 1270, with the Tudor house added in 1505 by the Bullen (Boleyn) family, who bought the castle in 1462. Although the castle was home to two queens – Anne Boleyn and, later, Anne of Cleves – it fell into disrepair until 1903, when it was bought by the American multimillionaire William Waldorf Astor. The exterior is unchanged from Tudor times, but the interior now has superb Edwardian carved wooden panelling.

Hever is a great place to bring the kids. There are hedge and water mazes, playgrounds and other childhood delights that will keep children of all ages occupied for hours.

From London Victoria, trains go to Hever (change at Oxted), a 1-mile walk from the castle (£7, 50 minutes, hourly). Alternatively, you could take the train to Edenbridge, from where it's a 4-mile taxi ride. A nice idea is to hire a bicycle in Edenbridge and ride to Hever. From Edenbridge High St the route to Hever is signposted.

Leeds Castle

Just to the east of Maidstone, **Leeds Castle** (EH; ☎ 01622-765400; adult/child Mar-Oct £12.50/9, Nov-Feb £10.50/7; ⊗ 10am-5pm Apr-Oct, 10am-3pm Nov-Mar) is one of the most famous and most visited castles in the world. It stands on two small islands in a lake surrounded by a huge estate that contains woodlands, an aviary and a really weird grotto that can only be entered once you've successfully negotiated your way through a hedge maze.

The building dates from the 9th century. Henry VIII transformed it from a fortress into a palace, and it was privately owned until 1974 when Lady Billie, the castle's last owner, died. Paintings, furniture and other décor in the castle date from the last eight centuries.

A private trust now manages the property and some of the rooms are used for conferences and other events. This creates a problem for the visitor in that some of the rooms are closed to the public quite regularly. If you want to be sure you can see all the rooms and get your money's worth, ring ahead. Another problem is the sheer number of people to be negotiated – at weekends it's the families, during the week it's the school groups.

National Express runs one direct bus daily from London Victoria coach station, leaving at 9am and returning at 3.05pm (£11, 1½ hours). It must be prebooked.

Sissinghurst Castle Garden

One of England's loveliest and most famous gardens, **Sissinghurst Castle Garden** (☎ 01580-710700; Sissinghurst, near Cranbrook; adult £7; ⊗ 11am-5.30pm Fri-Tue Apr-Oct) is a spectacular example of planned landscaping. The castle itself dates back to the 12th century, but the romantic gardens were crafted by Vita Sackville-West and her husband Harold Nicolson after they bought the estate in 1930. Highlights include the rose garden and the White Garden, where all the blooms are, yes, white. Sissinghurst is 2 miles northeast of Cranbrook and one mile east of Sissinghurst village off the A262.

SURREY

Much of Surrey is the commuter base for a good chunk of London's more wealthy workers, which is why many people call this county an extension of the M25. Even so, as you get further from the large motorways, the landscape spreads out into some inspiring settings made famous by authors Sir Author Conan Doyle, Sir Walter Scott and Jane Austen, all of whom cherished the gentle rolling hills and lush pastures Surrey has to offer. For Londoners this is a nearby place to come breathe some fresh country air and for travellers, it's a good introduction to the famous English countryside.

FARNHAM

☎ 01252 / pop 36,298

Farnham is Surrey's most attractive market town. The reason to come here is to check out the exquisite Georgian homes and to shop – you'll find anything you might need short of a Paul Smith suit. There's also some winding cobblestone lanes to get lost in as well as a few arts-and-crafts shops, an award-winning museum and one of Surrey's only intact castles. Farnham is also home to the Surrey Institute of Art & Design. The town makes for a good day trip from London.

Orientation & Information

Farnham is easily explored on foot. The most interesting part of Farnham is its historical

centre, where East, West, South and Castle
Sts meet.

The train station is at the southern end
of South St (Station Hill).

The friendly **TIC** (☎ 715109; itourist@waverley
.gov.uk; South St; ⏰ 9.30am-5.15pm Mon-Thu, 9.30am-
4.45pm Fri, 9am-noon Sat) has free maps of the
town and surrounding countryside and the
free *Farnham Heritage Trail*. You can use
the Internet across the hall in the public
library, also gratis.

You'll find an ATM on the Borough, near
the corner of Castle St (where banks can be
found). The main post office and a bureau
de change are on West St, which is the continuation of The Borough.

Guided walks (☎ 712014; adult/child £2/50p) run
at 3pm on the first Sunday of every month
between April and October. Meet at the
entrance of the Wagon Yard Car Park at
the southern end of Downing St. Tours last
approximately 1½ hours.

Sights

Run by English Heritage (EH), **Farnham Castle**
(☎ 2522013; adult £2.50; ⏰ 10am-5pm Apr-Sep) consists of a castle keep and a residential palace
house. The palace house was built in the
13th century for the bishops of Winchester
as a stopover on London journeys; from
1926 to the 1950s it was taken over by the
bishops of Guildford and is now a Centre
for International Briefing.

The excellent **Farnham museum** (☎ 715094; 38
West St; admission free; ⏰ 10am-5pm Tue-Sat) is located
in the splendid Willmer House, a Georgian
townhouse built in 1718. Since it opened
in 1962, the museum has won a number of
awards, including the European Museum of
the Year Award.

The museum's permanent exhibits include a timeline of Farnham from prehistory
through Saxon and Norman times to today.
Next to it is an extraordinary **doll's house**,
built in the 1780s for the Manwaring children who lived next door at No 39. Lucky
kids. The **Art & Architecture Room** features exhibits on the town's architectural heritage.

Sleeping & Eating

Because Farnham is a business centre, accommodation is on the higher end though
rates drop significantly on weekends.

Sandiway (☎ 710721; 24 Shortheath Rd; r per person
£25-45; P ✗) This spot is about a 15-minute

walk from town in a 1920s house with a
pleasant garden.

Bishop's Table (☎ 710222; welcome@bishopstable
.com; 27 West St; s/d Mon-Fri £95/110, Sat & Sun £70/95)
Here you'll find a beautiful and very well-
kept Georgian hotel with 15 rooms right in
the town centre.

Downing St is home to a number of excellent eateries and several mid-range chain
restaurants.

Stirling Sandwich Shop (☎ 711602; 49a Downing
St; ⏰ 8am-4pm Mon-Sat; mains £1.50-2.90 ✗) This
place makes scrumptious (takeaway only)
sandwiches and has such a loyal clientele
that at lunch the queue stretches the length
of Downing St.

Nelson Arms (☎ 716078; 50 Castle St; ⏰ 11am-
11pm; lunch mains £6-10, dinner £8-16) No longer a
grubby pub, the Nelson is now a gastro-pub,
popular with the locals for its modern chic,
tranquil electronic tunes and home-cooked
à la carte food.

Food is also the draw (though the décor
is nothing special) at the **Banaras** (☎ 734081; 40
Downing St; ⏰ noon-2pm & 6-11pm; mains £5-11; ✗),
a traditional Indian restaurant with happy
staff, lots of vegetarian options and a Sunday buffet.

Getting There & Away

Half-hourly train services run from London
Waterloo (50 minutes). From Winchester,
trains depart every 45 minutes for Woking
(30 minutes). Change there for half-hourly
trains to Farnham (25 minutes). The train
station is at the end of South St, on the other
side of the A31 from the old town centre.

Stagecoach (☎ 01256-464501) bus No X64
runs from Winchester at 10 minutes past
the hour for a 70-minute trip to Farnham.
The stop is on The Borough.

AROUND FARNHAM
Waverley Abbey

The inspiration for Sir Walter Scott's eponymous novel, the Waverley Abbey ruins sit
almost forlornly on the banks of the River
Wey about 2 miles southeast of Farnham.

This was the first Cistercian abbey built
in England (construction began in 1128)
and, like Beaulieu Abbey in the New Forest
(see p211), was based on a parent abbey at
Citeaux in France.

Across the Wey is the impressive **Waverley Abbey House** (closed to the public), built

in 1783 using bricks from the demolished abbey. In the 19th century it was owned by Florence Nightingale's brother-in-law, and the famous nurse was a regular visitor. Fittingly, the house was used as a military hospital in WWI. Since 1973, it has been the headquarters of the Crusade for World Revival (CWR), a Christian charity.

The abbey and house are off the B3001.

Hindhead

The tiny hamlet of Hindhead, 8 miles south of Farnham off the A287, lies in the middle of the largest area of open heath in Surrey. During the 19th century a number of prominent Victorians bought up property in the area, including Sir Arthur Conan Doyle (1859–1930), creator of Sherlock Holmes.

The most beautiful part of the area is to the northeast, where you'll find a natural depression known as the **Devil's Punchbowl**. Here there are a number of excellent trails and bridle-paths that make for a most enjoyable walk. To get the best view of the surrounding area, we suggest that you make for Gibbet Hill (280m), once an execution ground. It is well signposted.

The **Hindhead YHA Hostel** (☎ 01428-604285; www.yha.org.uk; Devil's Punchbowl, Thursley; dm £10.60) is a beautiful, completely secluded cottage on the northern edge of the Punchbowl, about a mile from Hindhead, run by the National Trust. It's a great place for walkers since the nearest bus stop and car park are a half-mile away.

The **Undershaw Hotel** (☎ 01428-604039; Portsmouth Rd; s/d £35/40) is the former home of Sir Arthur himself. The rooms are comfortable and well appointed. Breakfast is an additional £5.

Bus No 19 runs every hour (£2.30, 20 minutes).

BERKSHIRE

Posh and prosperous Berkshire has long had the distinction of being home to some of the country's most important figures including past prime ministers (Winston Churchill was born here) and the Queen herself, who often spends time at the mighty and wonderful Windsor Castle. Plus, the county is full of exquisitely maintained villages and fabulous countryside.

WINDSOR & ETON

☎ 01753 / pop 30,568

You might not see the Queen at her favourite castle, but that's not a reason to stay away. Windsor and the adjacent college town of Eton, separated only by a narrow footbridge across the River Thames, are two of the country's most visited places, mainly because of the great Windsor Castle. It is a stunning display of royal wealth and power that dates back nearly 1000 years. Eton too is an excellent town to see. Home to the country's most famous (and most exclusive) public school, this quaint village has great bookshops, excellent pubs and fine restaurants.

Orientation

The town of Windsor sits beside the River Thames, dwarfed by Windsor Castle. Skirting the castle are Thames St and High St, but the town's main drag is pedestrianised Peascod St. The village of Eton is on the far side of a small pedestrian bridge spanning the swan-filled Thames.

Information

The **TIC** (☎ 743900; www.windsor.gov.uk; 24 High St; 🕙 10am-5pm daily Apr-Sep, 10am-4pm Mon-Fri Oct-Mar) is an agent for the National Express bus service and sells tickets to some local attractions. It also offers a B&B booking service (£5).

Both the TIC and post office have bureaux de change. There are plenty of ATMs along High and Thames Sts.

The **post office** (🕙 9am-5.30pm Mon-Sat) is in Peascod St. High-speed Internet is free (with a beverage) at **Café Puccinos** (Peascod St, nr High St).

The **Eton Bridge Book Store** (77 High St) is an excellent choice, with all the latest titles. There are also a number of second-hand bookstores – with a mix of academic tomes and classic works of fiction – along Peascod St in Windsor.

Sights

WINDSOR CASTLE

Standing on chalk bluffs overlooking the Thames, **Windsor Castle** (☎ 831118; adult £12; 🕙 9.45am-4pm Mar-Oct, 9.45am-3pm Nov-Feb) is the largest and oldest occupied fortress in the world. In fact, there has been a royal residence here since the 9th century, but the existing structure owes its beginnings to

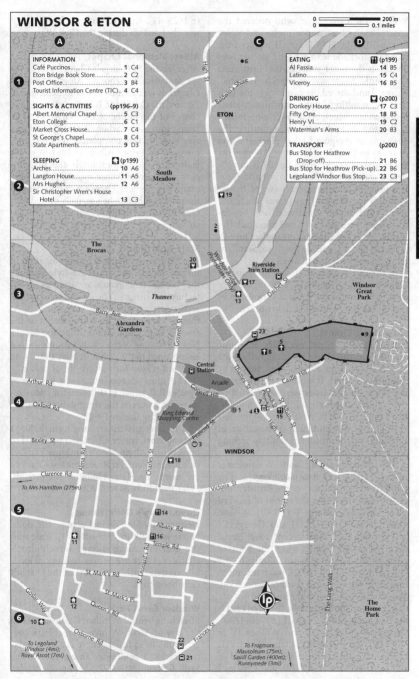

WINDSOR & ETON

SOUTHEAST ENGLAND

William the Conqueror, who ordered the construction of a wooden motte and bailey fort in 1070. In 1165 Henry II replaced the wooden stockade with a round stone tower and built the outer walls to the north, east and south. Successive monarchs tinkered, enlarged and altered the castle up to the 19th century, resulting in the gargantuan affair visible today, which occupies five hectares.

Weather and other events permitting, the changing of the guard takes place at 11am Monday to Saturday. The State Apartments are closed when the royal family is in residence, traditionally during April and June. It is thought that the queen has a particular fondness for Windsor, as it was where she spent much of her childhood, and she returns whenever she can. The Union Jack flying over the castle doesn't mean the Queen's at home; instead look for the Royal Standard flying from the Round Tower.

St George's Chapel closes on Sunday. Guided tours of the State Apartments take about 45 minutes and leave at various times during the day; ask at the ticket office.

St George's Chapel

One of Britain's finest examples of Gothic architecture, this chapel was designed for the Order of the Garter and was commenced by Edward IV in 1475. It was built in two stages: the choir and the aisles were completed by 1483, but the stone vaulting was not finished until 1528. The nave is one of the best examples of perpendicular architecture in England, with beautiful fan vaulting arching out from the pillars.

The chapel – along with Westminster Abbey – serves as a **royal mausoleum**, and its tombs read like a history of the British monarchy. Here you'll find the tombs of Edward VI (r 1461–83), George V (r 1910–36) and Queen Mary (1867–1953) and George VI (r 1936–52). The most recent royal burial occurred in April 2002, when the body of George VI's widow, Queen Elizabeth, the Queen Mother (1900–2002), was transported here in a splendid and sombre procession. She is buried alongside her husband.

In between the **garter stalls**, the **Royal Vault** is the burial place of George III (r 1760–1820), George IV (r 1820–30) and William IV (r 1830–37). Another **vault** contains Henry VIII (r 1509–47), his favourite wife (the third of six) Jane Seymour (1509–37), and Charles I (r 1625–49), reunited with his head after it was chopped off during the Civil War.

Albert Memorial Chapel

After leaving St George's Chapel, don't miss the fantastically elaborate Albert Memorial Chapel. It was built in 1240 and dedicated to Edward the Confessor. It became the original chapel of the Order of the Garter in 1350, falling into disuse when St George's Chapel was built. It was completely restored after the death of Prince Albert in 1861. A major feature of the restoration is the magnificent vaulted roof whose mosaic pieces were crafted in Venice. There's a monument to the prince, although he's actually buried with Queen Victoria in the Frogmore Royal Mausoleum not far from the castle grounds.

State Apartments

The State Apartments are a combination of formal rooms and museum-style exhibits that house some exquisite paintings, architecture and history. The guided tours of this section are excellent and well worth it. At the very least, pick up a free leaflet at the front desk to guide you through the details. Note that some of the smaller rooms are not always open to the public at busy times – an excellent reason for visiting out of season!

The most impressive room here is **St George's Hall**, which is still used for state dinners and incurred the most damage during a devastating fire in 1992.

Also don't miss the art hanging in the **King's Dressing Room**, where Charles II preferred to bunk down. Alongside Sir Anthony Van Dyck's magnificent *Triple Portrait of Charles I* are works by Hans Holbein, Rembrandt, Peter Paul Rubens and Albrecht Dürer.

Queen Mary's Dolls' House

Designed by Sir Edwin Lutyens, the dolls' house was built in 1923 on a 1:12 scale with the aim of raising money for children's charities. There are occasional special exhibitions here, such as displays of the Queen's childhood toys.

Windsor Great Park

Stretching behind Windsor Castle almost all the way to Ascot, Windsor Great Park covers about 40 sq miles. There is a lake, walking tracks, a bridleway and gardens. The **Savill Garden** (☎ 860222; ⏱ 10am-6pm Mar-Oct,

10am-4pm Nov-Feb) is particularly lovely. Admission ranges from £3.50 to £5.50 depending on the time of year.

The **Long Walk** is a three-mile walk along a tree-lined path from King George IV Gate to the Copper Horse statue (of George III) on Snow Hill, the highest point of the park. There are some great views of the castle along here. Locals have informed us that the queen occasionally drives herself down the Long Walk, accompanied by a bodyguard. The walk is signposted from the town centre.

ETON COLLEGE

Cross the Thames by the pedestrian Windsor Bridge to arrive at another enduring symbol of England's class system. **Eton College** (☎ 671177; adult/child £3.80/3; ☟ 10.30am-4.30pm Apr-Aug, 2-4.30pm Sep-Mar) is the largest and most famous public (meaning very private) school in England, founded by Henry VI in 1440–41 with a view towards educating 70 highly qualified boys awarded a scholarship from a fund endowed by the king. Every year since, 70 King's Scholars have been chosen based on the results of a highly competitive exam for boys aged 12 to 14 – known as Oppidans, they are housed in separate quarters from the rest of the 1000 or so other students.

While the King's Scholars are chosen exclusively on the basis of exam results, Oppidans usually come from Britain's wealthiest and most aristocratic families, the only ones who can afford the £15,000-per-annum fees. Eton prides itself on educating the cream of the crop (rich and thick, scoff their detractors) and counts no fewer than 18 prime ministers among its alumni, as well as a few royals, including Prince William.

The college has one-hour **guided tours** (☟ 2.15pm & 3.15pm; adult/child £4.90/4).

LEGOLAND WINDSOR

Windsor's other great attraction – at least for the four to 12s – is the elaborate mix of model masterpieces and white-knuckle rides at **Legoland** (☎ 0870 504 0404; www.lego.com; adult/child £23/20; ☟ 10am-7pm mid-Jul–Aug, 10am-5pm mid-Mar–mid-Jul, Sep & Oct). The idea is family fun, but you'll have to dig deep to entertain everyone. Child admission is for children aged three to 15. If you prebook online you save about £2.

Buses run from Thames St to Legoland between 10am and 5.15pm.

Tours

Open-top double-decker bus tours of the town are run from Windsor Castle by **City Sightseeing Tours** (adult/child £6/2.50; ☟ every 30mins daily Mar-Sep, Sat & Sun Nov & Dec).

Sleeping

Windsor has a good selection of quality hotels and B&Bs. Since the YHA hostel burned down in 2004 there are few budget options.

Arches (☎ 869268; thearches.windsor@virgin.net; 9 York Rd; s/d from £25/40; P ☒) This family-run B&B is a bargain for Windsor.

Mrs Hughes (☎ 866036; 62 Queens Rd; s with kitchenette £35, d £55, f per adult/child £25/15) The family room here sleeps six and all rooms have fridges and en-suite bathrooms.

Mrs Hamilton (☎ 865775; 22 York Ave; s/d £35/58; P) Large, bright rooms and very friendly service make this an extremely comfortable place to stay.

Langton House (☎ 858299; www.langtonhouse .com; 46 Alma Rd; s/d £60/75; P ☒) Langton House is the pick of lodgings in Windsor. The house's four elegant rooms with en suite are superb, and its friendly owners are always on hand to fill you in with local information.

SOMETHING SPECIAL

Sir Christopher Wren's House Hotel (☎ 86 1354; www.sirchristopherwren.co.uk; Thames St; s/d £170/213; P) Built by the famous architect in 1676, this magnificent 90-room hotel overlooking the Thames has luxurious amenities including gym and spa facilities.

Eating

Al Fassia (☎ 855370; 27 St Leonard's Rd; mains £8-12; ☟ lunch & dinner Mon-Sat; ☒) This excellent Moroccan restaurant is considered to be as good as – if not better than – the top Moroccan eateries in London.

Viceroy (☎ 858005; 49-51 St Leonard's Rd; mains £7-9; ☟ lunch & dinner) This is probably the best Indian restaurant in town, with lots of vegetarian options.

Latino (☎ 857711; 3 Church Lane; mains £7-11) Have an intimate dinner at this family-run Greek restaurant or join the traditional dancers and wiggle to live music on Friday and Saturday nights.

Drinking

Windsor and Eton are simply packed with pubs, although most of them cater to the tourist trade. The following have a more local appeal.

Donkey House (☎ 620003; 10 Thames St) A riverside pub and a terrific place to have a drink on a warm summer's evening.

Henry VI (☎ 866051; 37 High St, Eton) A great pub in which to sip an afternoon pint and discuss poetry. On Friday and Saturday evenings, rock out to live pop music.

Waterman's Arms (☎ 861001; Brocas St, Eton) A perfect olde Englishe pub with numerous rooms to wile away the day in. It is popular with rowers.

Fifty One (☎ 755950; 51 Peascod St) Some sophisticated drinking goes on at this artsy and cool gastro-pub. Upscale pub food ranges from £8 to £14.

WORTH THE TRIP

Anyone with an elementary knowledge of horse racing will have heard of **Royal Ascot**, a four-day festival that takes place at the Ascot racecourse in the middle of June. The race attracts royals and commoners alike. Men wear black ties and tails and women spend enormous amounts of time and money trying to see who can wear the most outrageous hat. Book tickets well in advance. In 2004 tickets for the Grandstand and Paddock were £49 per day, though there are cheaper, less sought-after tickets for 'commoners' as well as more expensive seats in the Royal Enclosure. Call ☎ 01344-876876 for information, or check the website at www.ascot.co.uk.

Getting There & Away

Windsor is 21 miles west of central London and only about 15 minutes by car from Heathrow airport.

BUS

Green Line bus No 702 goes to Windsor and Legoland from London Victoria coach station hourly (two hourly on Sunday, £6.80, 1¼ hours). Bus Nos 192 (Monday to Saturday), 190 and 191 (Sunday) connect Windsor with Heathrow airport from Windsor High St opposite the Parish Church to Heathrow Central Station. For details, call ☎ 524144.

TRAIN

There are two Windsor and Eton train stations – Central station on Thames St, opposite Windsor Castle, and Riverside station near the bridge to Eton.

From London Waterloo, trains run to Riverside station every half-hour (hourly on Sunday). Some services from London Paddington to Central station require a change at Slough, five minutes from Windsor, but take about the same time with a similar fare (£6.50, 50 minutes).

AROUND WINDSOR & ETON
Runnymede

In June 1215 King John met his barons and bishops in a large field 3 miles southeast of Windsor, and over the next few days they hammered out an agreement on a basic charter of rights guaranteeing the liberties of the king's subjects and restricting the monarch's absolute power. The document they signed, of course, was the Magna Carta, the world's first constitution.

Runnymede – from the Anglo-Saxon words *ruinige* (take council) and *moed* (meadow) – was chosen because it was the largest piece of open land between the king's residence at Windsor and the bishop's palace at Staines. Today the field remains pretty much as it was, except now it features two lodges (1930) designed by Sir Edward Lutyens. In the woods behind the field are two **memorials**, the first to the Magna Carta designed by Sir Edward Maufe (1957). The second is to John F Kennedy, and was built by Geoffrey Jellicoe in 1965 on an acre of land granted in perpetuity to the US government following Kennedy's assassination in 1963.

Bus No 43 stops near here on the Windsor to Slough route.

HAMPSHIRE

Hampshire's golden age may be past, but its history is intact and well worth seeing. This is the former location of the once great Kingdom of Wessex (along with parts of Wiltshire and Dorset), where King Alfred ruled. The kingdom's former capital was the city of Wessex – now Winchester – and its splendour is still largely on display, especially at Winchester Cathedral. The town should make anyone's top ten list. Also, anyone with an interest in maritime history will relish a trip to the coast to Portsmouth, the long-time home of the once-powerful Royal Navy, as well as to the Isle of Wight. Otherwise, Hampshire is mostly an agricultural area with thatched-roof farm houses and lovely country lanes.

The county is well served by bus. The *Public Transport Map of Hampshire* is very useful and stocked by TICs. For information on all public transport in the county phone ☎ 01962-846992.

WINCHESTER
☎ 01962 / pop 41,420

Easily reached from London, the beautiful cathedral city of Winchester makes for a superb weekend away. Nestled in a valley of the River Itchen, this ancient capital city for many a Saxon king has a rich history that is evident in the bronze statues of past heroes, the cobbled streets and the magnificent church that dominates the centre. The town is also home to a vibrant collection of bars and restaurants, reflecting the youthful tastes of Winchester's growing University College and its new £6 million Performing Arts and Conference Centre.

History

The Romans built the town of Venta Bulgarum, later giving way to a Saxon settlement, but Winchester really took off in AD 670 when the powerful West Saxon bishops moved their Episcopal see here from Dorchester. Thereafter, Winchester was the most important town in the powerful kingdom of Wessex. King Alfred the Great (r 871–99) made it his capital, and it remained so under Knut (r 1016–35) and the Danish kings. After the Norman invasion of 1066, William the Conqueror arrived here to claim the throne of England, and in 1086 he commissioned local monks to write the all-important *Domesday Book* (pronounced 'doomsday'), an administrative survey of the whole country that ranks as the most important clerical accomplishment of the Middle Ages. Winchester thrived until the 12th century, when a fire gutted most of the city, after which it was superseded in importance by London. A long slump lasted until the 18th century, when the town was largely rebuilt and found new life as a prosperous market town.

Orientation

The city centre is compact and easily managed on foot. Partly pedestrianised High St and Buttercross run from west to east through the town, and most of the sights are on or just off them. The bus and coach station is smack in the middle of town opposite the Guildhall and TIC, while the train station is five minutes' walk northwest. Jewry St borders the western side of the centre and was once part of the city's Jewish quarter – today it is where you'll find a chunk of the town's nightlife.

Information

The **TIC** (☎ 840500; www.winchester.gov.uk; ⏰ 9.30am-5.30pm Mon-Sat & 11am-4pm Sun May-Sep, 10am-5pm Mon-Sat Oct-Apr) is in the Guildhall on Broadway.

There is a **post office** (⏰ 9.30am-6pm Mon-Sat) on Middle Brook St. Internet access can be had at the **Byte Internet Café** (⏰ 863235; Parchment St; ⏰ 9am-5pm Mon-Fri). There are plenty of banks and ATMs on High St.

Sights
WINCHESTER CATHEDRAL

Winchester's main attraction is one of the world's great buildings, a magnificent testament to English architecture, more than 900 years old and one of the finest examples of the Gothic perpendicular style to be found anywhere.

The present-day **cathedral** (☎ 853137; admission donation £3.50; ⏰ 8.30am-6pm) is just south of the town's original minster church built by King Cenwalh in 643. In 1070 the first Norman bishop, Walkelin, decided to replace the old church (even then the largest in the country) with a new one built in the Romanesque style. The new cathedral, completed in 1093, featured a nave that was 164m long and was 14m wider than the current building.

Soggy ground and poor workmanship did not augur well for the church, and the collapse of the central tower in 1107 was just one of several problems the authorities had to deal with. Floors are still wavy due to settling of the gravel bed underneath in the last 800 years.

Near the entrance in the northern aisle is the grave of Jane Austen, who died a stone's throw from the cathedral in 1817 at **Jane Austen's House** (College St), where the writer lived for the last six weeks of her life; it's now a private residence. The transepts are the most original parts of the cathedral. Note the early Norman rounded arches and painted wooden ceiling.

Tours of the crypt are often suspended due to flooding, although you can still access the first part of the crypt, where the powerful sculpture by Anthony Gormley – of *Angel of the North* fame (see p621) is on display.

Tours (recommended donation £3; every hr 10am-3pm Mon-Sat) of the Cathedral are run by enthusiastic volunteers. There are also **tower and roof tours** (£3; 2.15pm Wed, 11.30am & 2.15pm Sat Jan-May, 2.15pm Tue, Wed & Fri, 11.30am or 2.15pm Sat Jun-Sep). Photography is permitted inside. Sunday services take place at 8am, 10am and 11.15am, with Evensong at 3.30pm. Evensong is also held at 5.30pm Monday to Saturday.

MUSEUMS

City Museum (863064; The Square; admission free; 10am-5pm Mon-Fri, 10am-1pm Sat & 2-5pm Sat & Sun Apr-Sep, 10am-5pm Tue-Fri, 10am-1pm Sat & 2-5pm Sat & Sun Oct-Mar) has interesting displays on Roman ruins, a collection of Winchester shop fronts and tells the story of Saxon and Norman Winchester.

Located in the old medieval gateway, **Westgate Museum** (848269; High St; admission free; 10am-5pm Mon-Sat, noon-5pm Sun Apr-Oct, 10am-4pm Tue-Sat, noon-4pm Sun Feb & Mar) is a one-time debtors' prison with a macabre set of gibbeting irons last used to display the body of an executed criminal in 1777. You can also see graffiti carved into the walls by prisoners.

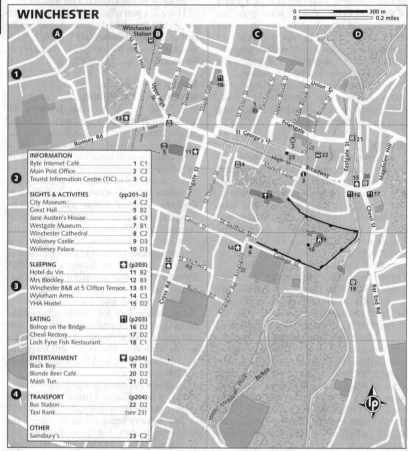

WINCHESTER

0 _____ 300 m
0 _____ 0.2 miles

INFORMATION	
Byte Internet Café	1 C1
Main Post Office	2 C2
Tourist Information Centre (TIC)	3 C2

SIGHTS & ACTIVITIES	(pp201–3)
City Museum	4 C2
Great Hall	5 B2
Jane Austen's House	6 C3
Westgate Museum	7 B1
Winchester Cathedral	8 C2
Wolvesey Castle	9 D3
Wolvesey Palace	10 D3

SLEEPING	(p203)
Hotel du Vin	11 B2
Mrs Blockley	12 B3
Winchester B&B at 5 Clifton Terrace	13 B1
Wykeham Arms	14 C3
YHA Hostel	15 D2

EATING	(p203)
Bishop on the Bridge	16 D2
Chesil Rectory	17 D2
Loch Fyne Fish Restaurant	18 C1

ENTERTAINMENT	(p204)
Black Boy	19 D3
Blonde Beer Café	20 D2
Mash Tun	21 D2

TRANSPORT	(p204)
Bus Station	22 D2
Taxi Rank	(see 23)

OTHER	
Sainsbury's	23 C2

Great Hall (☎ 846476; admission free; ⊗ 10am-5pm) was the only part of Winchester Castle that Oliver Cromwell did not destroy. The castle was begun by William the Conqueror in 1067 and was added to and fortified by many successive kings of England. It was the site of a number of dramatic moments in English history, including the trial of Sir Walter Raleigh in 1603. It was last used as a court from 1938 to 1978.

The Great Hall long claimed to house King Arthur's Round Table, but don't get too excited: it's a 600-year-old fake. The wonderful steel gates were made in 1981 to commemorate the wedding of Charles and Diana. Part of the Roman wall, built around AD 200, can be seen in an enclosure near the entrance to the Great Hall.

WOLVESEY CASTLE & PALACE
Wolvesey Castle (☎ 854766; admission free; ⊗ 10am-5pm Apr-Sep) owes its name to a Saxon king's demand for an annual payment of 300 wolves' heads, or so the story goes. Work began on the castle in 1107, and was completed more than half a century later by Henry de Blois, grandson of William the Conqueror. In the medieval era it was the residence of the bishop of Winchester. Queen Mary I and Philip of Spain had their wedding breakfast here. It was largely demolished in the 1680s and today the bishop lives in the adjacent Wolvesey Palace.

Walking
From the Wolvesey Castle entrance, the **Water Meadows Walk** goes for a mile to the St Cross Hospital. The **Riverside Walk** runs from the castle along the bank of the River Itchen to High St. The walk up to **St Giles' Hill** is rewarded by great views over the city. It's at the top of East Hill, half a mile from the castle, and is signposted.

Tours
There are 1½-hour **guided walks** (adult/under 16 £3/free; ⊗ 11.30am & 2.30pm Mon-Sat & 11.30am only Sun May-Sep, 11.30am & 2.30pm Sat Oct-Apr) from the Wolvesey Castle entrance.

If you prefer you can take the **Phantasm Ghostwalk** (☎ 07990-876217), which leaves from outside the cathedral at sunset each day and lasts for one hour. You'll need to book ahead.

Sleeping
B&Bs in Winchester tend not to hang signs out the front. The TIC, however, has a complete list.

YHA Hostel (☎ 0870 770 6092; City Mill, 1 Water Lane; dm £10.60; ✗) Located in the beautiful 18th-century water mill on the river, this basic accommodation is a great place to stay.

Mrs Blockley (☎ 852073; mcblockley@tcp.co.uk; 54 St Cross Rd; s/d £26/45; ✗ P) The rooms are well appointed in this charming Edwardian house. The service is friendly and it's only a short walk from the cathedral.

Winchester B&B at 5 Clifton Terrace (☎ 1962 890053; 5 Clifton Tce; s/d/family £50/60/80) On a proper terrace that could be in Bath, this elegant two-room B&B, in a balconied Georgian townhouse, has a charming and friendly proprietor who is a great cook.

Wykeham Arms (☎ 853834; 75 Kingsgate St; s/d £80/90, r with shared bathroom from £55; ✗) This place has the best character in town so book ahead. The pub and restaurant are very welcoming and popular with the locals (see below).

Hotel du Vin (☎ 841414; admin@winchester.hoteldu vin.co.uk; Southgate St; rooms £105-185) This luxurious, modern hotel is the most fashionable spot in town. Relax on Egyptian linen and use your minibar, VCR and CD player all at the same time.

Eating
Bishop on the Bridge (☎ 855111; 1 High St; mains £7-10) The upscale bar food is as good as the beer and is best enjoyed on the secluded outdoor seating area overlooking the river.

Wykeham Arms (☎ 853834; 75 Kingsgate St; mains £9-13) This is an excellent place to eat (and drink), with a cheaper bar menu, although no food is served on Sunday. With school desks as tables and tankards hanging from the ceiling the look is very olde Englishe.

Loch Fyne Fish Restaurant (☎ 853566; www.loch fyne.com; 18 Jewry St; mains £9-15; ⊗ 9am-10pm Mon-Thu, 9am-11pm Fri, 10am-11pm Sat, 9am-9.30pm Sun; ✗) There are fireplaces throughout this beautiful Tudor building. The atmosphere can be both lively and romantic.

Chesil Rectory (☎ 851555; 1 Chesil St; 2-/3-course lunch £30/35, 3-course dinner £45; ⊗ lunch & dinner Sat, dinner only Tue-Sat; ✗) Here you'll find a romantic, refined setting inside Winchester's oldest house (1450). Dinner is complete with white tablecloths and smiling, sombre wait staff.

Drinking

Mash Tun (60 Eastgate St) Strictly for the young bohemian set, this is one of the nicest places in town to chill out and enjoy a drink in the riverside garden.

Blonde Beer Café (5 Bridge St) Suede bar stools, elegant chrome light fixtures and a beautiful fireplace make for a modern cool interior at this bar. The food is an upscale version of pub grub.

On the other side of the river from The Wykeham Arms, the **Black Boy** (1 Wharf Hill) has the atmosphere of an art-house pub. Bookshelves line the walls and there is an outdoor terrace.

Getting There & Away

Winchester is 65 miles from London and 15 miles from Southampton.

BUS

National Express has several direct buses to Winchester from London Victoria Bus Station (£11, one hour 55 minutes).

Stagecoach Hampshire (☎ 01256-464501) has a good network of services linking Salisbury, Southampton, Portsmouth and Brighton. **Explorer tickets** (adult/child £5.70/4.10) are good on most Wilts & Dorset buses, which serve the region to the west, including New Forest.

TRAIN

There are fast links with London Waterloo, the Midlands and south coast. Trains leave about every 15 minutes from London (£20, one hour), Southampton (£5.50, 20 minutes) and Portsmouth (£9, one hour).

Getting Around

Your feet are the best form of transport. There's plenty of day parking within five minutes' walk of the centre or you can use the park-and-ride service which costs £1.50.

If you want a taxi, try the rank outside Sainsbury's on Middle Brook St or phone **Wintax Taxis** (☎ 854838 or 866208) or **Wessex Cars** (☎ 853000).

PORTSMOUTH

☎ 023 / pop 442,252

Anyone interested in maritime history should flag this page. Not only is Portsmouth home to Lord Nelson's 18th-century warship, the HMS Victory, which led the charge at Trafalgar in 1805, but it is also the principal port of Britain's Royal Navy, whose ships once exported the empire to the far-flung corners of the world and now sit in ominous grey readiness. Though the city was heavily bombed during WWII, the areas around The Point and The Hard still manage to evoke an atmosphere of salty dogs and scurvy scallywags, especially if you can manage a visit during cold rainy weather, which shouldn't be too difficult. The rest of the city is fairly bland and boring with the exception of the edgy suburb of Southsea where you'll find some good beaches, bars, restaurants and places to sleep.

Orientation

Your first stop in town should be the quay known as The Hard, which is where you'll find the TIC, the entrance to the Naval Heritage Area, the Portsmouth Harbour train station and the passenger ferry terminal for the Isle of Wight. About a mile east along the water is Old Portsmouth and The Point, a cluster of sea-worn, atmospheric buildings around the old harbour, called The Camber.

Southsea, where the beaches are, plus most of the accommodation and restaurants, is about 2 miles south of the harbour.

The rest of the city has a number of interesting museums, but most of your sightseeing and activities are likely to be concentrated along the water's edge.

Information

The **Main TIC** (☎ 9282 6722; tic@portsmouthcc.gov.uk; The Hard; ☼ 9.30am-5.45pm) provides guided tours and an accommodation service. Next to the Blue Reef Aquarium in Southsea is a **TIC branch** (☎ 9283 2464; fax 9282 7519; Clarence Esplanade; ☼ 9.30am-5.45pm May-Sep).

There's a **post office** (42 Broad St) in Old Portsmouth and another **post office** (Palmerston Rd) in Southsea. Both are open 9am to 5.30pm Monday to Saturday. There are ATMs on Osbourne Rd, Southsea, as well as a laundrette.

Internet access is available at **Southsea Backpackers Lodge** (☎ 239 28324954; Clarence Rd, Southsea; per 30 mins £2). You don't have to be a guest to use it.

Sights & Activities

FLAGSHIP PORTSMOUTH (NAVAL HERITAGE AREA)

The **Naval Heritage Area** (☎ 9286 1512; 3-for-2 ticket adult/child £13.75/11, all-inclusive attraction ticket £15.50/

SOUTHEAST ENGLAND

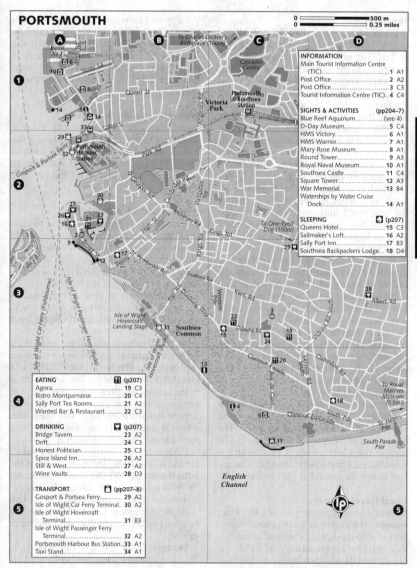

PORTSMOUTH

0 —————— 500 m
0 —————— 0.25 miles

INFORMATION	
Main Tourist Information Centre	
(TIC).......................................1	A1
Post Office...................................2	A2
Post Office...................................3	C3
Tourist Information Centre (TIC)...4	C4

SIGHTS & ACTIVITIES	(pp204–7)
Blue Reef Aquarium..............(see 4)	
D-Day Museum...........................5	C4
HMS Victory................................6	A1
HMS Warrior...............................7	A1
Mary Rose Museum.....................8	A1
Round Tower..............................9	A3
Royal Naval Museum.................10	A1
Southsea Castle........................11	C4
Square Tower............................12	A3
War Memorial...........................13	B4
Waterships by Water Cruise	
Dock.....................................14	A1

SLEEPING	(p207)
Queens Hotel............................15	C3
Sailmaker's Loft........................16	A2
Sally Port Inn............................17	B3
Southsea Backpackers Lodge... 18	D4

EATING	(p207)
Agora.......................................19	C3
Bistro Montparnasse.................20	C4
Sally Port Tea Rooms.................21	A2
Wanted Bar & Restaurant.........22	C3

DRINKING	(p207)
Bridge Tavern...........................23	A2
Drift..24	C3
Honest Politician......................25	C3
Spice Island Inn........................26	A2
Still & West..............................27	A2
Wine Vaults.............................28	D3

TRANSPORT	(pp207–8)
Gosport & Portsea Ferry............29	A2
Isle of Wight Car Ferry Terminal.. 30	A2
Isle of Wight Hovercraft	
Terminal................................31	B3
Isle of Wight Passenger Ferry	
Terminal................................32	A2
Portsmouth Harbour Bus Station.33	A1
Taxi Stand...............................34	A1

English Channel

12.50, season ticket £28/23.50; 10am-5.30pm Apr-Oct, 10am-5pm Nov-Mar) is the city's main draw, and it's a humdinger. Three classic ships and excellent museums form the core of England's tribute to the historical might of the Royal Navy, on the edge of the country's most important naval port. Even the most devoted landlubber should find this a good day out.

And it is indeed a full day out. There are individual admission costs for each ship. To see more than one attraction, we recommend the all-inclusive ticket, which covers single admissions to all of the ships and museums. The season ticket offers unlimited entry to all the attractions for two years and a subscription to the *Semaphore* newsletter.

The Ships

The main attraction is **HMS Victory** (adult/child £9.50/8), Lord Nelson's flagship at the Battle of Trafalgar in 1805. This remarkable ship carried up to 900 crew and had a top speed of 10mph when she led the British fleet at Trafalgar, which resulted in victory against the French but cost Nelson his life. The ship limped into harbour and out of active duty in 1922, where it was fully refurbished and converted into a museum, although incredibly it remains in commission and as such is subject to military regulations, which basically means no photography.

Which is a shame, because the pretimed, 40-minute tours of the ship are one of the best you'll find anywhere. Conducted at breakneck speed but with liberal doses of great humour, the tours are as close as you'll get to a step back in time.

Nearby are the remains of the **Mary Rose** (adult/child £9.70/8). Built in 1509 under the orders of Henry VIII, the 700-tonne ship sank in shallow water off Portsmouth in 1545. There was much speculation about why she sank. At the time it was put down to 'human folly and bad luck'. The ship and her time-capsule contents were raised to the surface in 1982, after 437 years under water. Finds from the ship are displayed in the Mary Rose Museum (see below).

Dating from 1860, and at the cutting edge of the technology of the time, **HMS Warrior** (adult/child £9.70/8) was a transition ship, as wood was forsaken for iron and sail for steam. The four decks of the ship illustrate life in the navy in the Victorian era. It's not nearly as impressive as the others, though. You are free to wander around at your leisure.

Royal Naval Museum

Housed in five separate galleries, this huge **museum** (adult £3.75) has an extensive collection of ship models, dioramas of naval battles, exhibits on the history of the Royal Navy, medals and paintings. Audiovisual displays recreate the Battle of Trafalgar and one even lets you take command of a battleship – see if you can cure the scurvy and avoid mutiny and execution.

Mary Rose Museum

A massive salvage operation that began in 1965 resulted in the raising of the *Mary Rose*, and you discover all there is to know about the ship and its recovery at this fascinating **museum** (adult/child £9.70/8) through exhibits, audiovisuals and great sound effects. It also recounts the failed salvage attempt made in the late 16th century by two hopeful Venetians. The ticket also covers admission to the ship itself (see The Ships, left).

Waterships by Water Cruises

To be able to see all the ships, old and new, from a different angle you can take a 40-minute guided cruise around the harbour for £3.50/2 per adult/child. If you have an all-inclusive attraction ticket the cruise is included.

OTHER SIGHTS & ACTIVITIES

One of the more pleasant spots in town is the **Point**, along the cobbled streets of Old Portsmouth, which has a few atmospheric old pubs that, on a sunny day, are ideal spots to sit and watch the ferries and navy ships go in and out of the harbour.

Immediately south of Old Portsmouth is the **Round Tower**, originally built by Henry V, a stretch of old fort walls and the **Square Tower** of 1494.

At the Southsea end of the waterfront there's a cluster of attractions on Clarence Esplanade. The **Blue Reef Aquarium** (☎ 9287 5222; adult £5.95; 9.30am-5pm Mar-Oct, 10am-3pm Nov-Feb) is more interesting than most other sea-life centres in that the attractions – including a huge walk-through aquarium filled with coloured corals and plenty of different fish – have a much more hands-on feel.

Portsmouth was a major departure poinzt for the Allied D-Day forces in 1944 and the **D-Day Museum** (☎ 9282 7261; Clarence Esplanade; adult £5; ☙ 10am-5.30pm Apr-Oct, 10am-5pm Nov-Mar) recounts the story of the Normandy landing with the 83m-long Overlord Embroidery (inspired by the Bayeux Tapestry) and other exhibits.

Southsea Castle (☎ 9282 7261; adult £2.50; ☙ 10am-5.30pm Apr-Oct) was built by Henry VIII to protect the town against French invasion. It was altered in the early 19th century to accommodate more guns and soldiers and a tunnel under the moat. It's said that Henry VIII watched the *Mary Rose* sink from the castle.

The **Royal Marines Museum** (☎ 9281 9385; Barracks Rd; adult £4.75; ☙ 10am-4pm Jun-Aug, 10am-3.30pm Sep-May) tells the story of the navy's elite force, while an assault course outside puts the kids through their paces.

Charles Dickens' Birthplace (☎ 9282 7261; 393 Old Commercial Rd; adult £2.50; ⏰ 10am-5.30pm Apr-Oct) is furnished in a style appropriate to 1812, the year of Dickens' birth, but the only genuine piece of Dickens' furniture is the couch on which he died in 1870!

Sleeping

The hotels and B&Bs in Portsmouth could use a thorough updating. That said, some of the better B&Bs are near The Point in Old Portsmouth, though you'll find a bed in Southsea as well. Rooms fill up quickly so book in advance.

Southsea Backpackers Lodge (☎ 9283 2495; 4 Florence Rd, Southsea; dm/d £10/25) The friendly owners have made this place homely and comfortable.

Sailmaker's Loft (☎ 9282 3045; sailmakersloft@aol.com; 5 Bath Sq; s/d £25/54) This is so close to the sea you can hear the ferry boats coming in.

Queens Hotel (☎ 9282 2466; www.bw-queenshotel.co.uk; Clarence Pde, Southsea; s/d from £40/80; **P**) Join a somewhat elderly clientele in this stately mansion with views of the water. The lobby is packed with marble columns and ceiling murals. It may be the best place in town.

Sally Port Inn (☎ 9282 1860; fax 9282 1293; High St; s/d from £40/60, f £75) This 16th-century inn is a bit musty and old, which is one way of saying it's historic. There are no en suite facilities but doubles have showers in the room.

Eating

Southsea offers a variety of dining options, many of which are quite tasty.

Sally Port Tea Rooms (☎ 9281 6265; 35 Broad St; breakfasts £3.75-5.25, lunch £3-5; ⏰ 10am-5pm; ✗) As spry as she ever was, the 75-year-old proprietor serves up traditional tearoom delights such as a smoked mackerel and horseradish baguette while you enjoy the 1940s jazz.

Wanted Bar and Restaurant (☎ 9282 6858; 39 Osborne Rd; mains £4-10; ⏰ 11am-11pm; ✗) An eclectic and inventive menu accompanies soul jazz in this high-style bar and restaurant, serving steak, mussels and gnocchi.

Agora (☎ 9282 2617; 9 Clarendon Rd; mains £7-10; ⏰ 9am-4pm & 5.30-11.30pm; ✗) This Turkish hookah bar is tucked into an English Tudor building with exposed beams on the ceiling

and tasty Greek and Turkish food on the plates. There's a children's menu.

Bistro Montparnasse (☎ 9281 6754; 103 Palmerstown Rd; 2-/3-course lunch £13/16, dinner £20/25; ⏰ lunch & dinner Tue-Sat; ✗) This cosy but feisty bistro serves inventive French cuisine with an English flavour amid bright orange walls and old wood floors.

Drinking

A few pubs on The Point are good for a summer's evening drink, but the real action is to be found in Southsea.

Drift (78 Palmerston Rd) This is a very atmospheric and hip London-style bar and lounge with DJs on the weekends. Be sure to visit the unusual bathrooms.

Honest Politician (47 Elm Grove) This wonderfully mellow bar is perfect for an afternoon's drink over the newspaper.

Wine Vaults (43-47 Albert Rd) This is another great bar that is very popular with the local intelligentsia.

Popular bars on The Point include **Bridge Tavern** (54 East St), whose fireplace makes for a cosy afternoon drinking companion on a rainy day, **Still & West** (2 Bath Sq), with an upscale sea-dog's look about it, and **Spice Island Inn** (65 Broad St), with nice wooden booths to sip a pint in.

Getting There & Away

Portsmouth is about 75 miles southwest of London.

BOAT

There are a number of ways of getting to the Isle of Wight from Portsmouth (see p214).

Condor Ferries (☎ 0105-761555) runs a car-and-passenger service from Portsmouth to Jersey and Guernsey (6½ hours) from £55 one way. **P&O Ferries** (☎ 0870 242 4999) sails twice a week to Bilbao in Spain and daily to Cherbourg (five to six hours, two hours longer at night) and Le Havre in France. **Brittany Ferries** (☎ 0870 901 2400; www.brittanyferries.co.uk) has overnight services to St Malo, Caen (six hours) and Cherbourg in France. The continental Ferryport is north of Flagship Portsmouth.

BUS

There are National Express buses every hour or so from London (£12, 2¼ hours), some via Heathrow airport (£12, 2¾ hours) and Southampton (£2.75, 50 minutes). Between Brighton and Portsmouth a bus leaves every half-hour (£3.20, 3½ hours).

Stagecoach Coastline bus No 700 also runs between Brighton and Portsmouth and on to Southampton via Chichester (half-hourly Monday to Saturday, hourly on Sunday). No 69 runs to Winchester (one hour 50 minutes, hourly).

TRAIN

There are trains every 10 minutes or so from London Victoria (£17.50, two hours 20 minutes) and Waterloo stations (£21, 1½ hours).

Trains from Portsmouth go to Brighton (£12.80, one hour 40 minutes, hourly), Winchester (£7.30, one hour, hourly) and Chichester (£4.90, 40 minutes, three hourly).

For the ships at Flagship Portsmouth get off at the final stop, Portsmouth Harbour.

Getting Around

Local bus No 6 operates between the Portsmouth Harbour bus station, right beside the train station, and South Parade Pier in Southsea. Bus No 17 or 6 will take you from the station to Old Portsmouth.

Ferries shuttle back and forth between The Hard and Gosport (£1.60 return, bicycles travel free) every few minutes Monday to Saturday (every 15 minutes on Sunday). For a taxi try **MPS Taxis** (☎ 8261 1111) in Southsea. There's also a taxi stand near the TIC in Flagship Portsmouth.

SOUTHAMPTON

☎ 023 / pop 304,400

Frankly, there isn't much to see or do in Southampton, but it wasn't always the case. Its strategic location on the Solent – an 8-mile inlet into which flow the Itchen and Test Rivers – made it one of England's most important medieval trading centres, doing roaring business with France and other continental countries. Even when trade declined, Southampton turned its efforts to large-scale shipbuilding, and made a good job of it too (the *Queen Mary* was built here). This is also where the *Titanic* set sail on its doomed voyage in 1912; 600 local residents (mostly crew members) were killed in the tragedy. In addition, the city ran a profitable sideline in aircraft manufacturing, but during WWII its industries were the targets of a concerted

bombing effort: over two nights alone, more than 30,000 bombs rained down on factories and virtually everything else as well.

The **TIC** (☎ 8083 3333; 9 Civic Centre Rd; 8.30am-5.30pm Mon, Tue & Thu-Sat, 10am-5.30pm Wed) offers free **guided walks** (10.30am Sun & bank holidays year-round, 10.30am & 2.30pm daily late-Jun–mid-Sep) of the old town. Meet at Bargate on High St.

Directly opposite the TIC is the massive Civic Centre, which houses the excellent **Southampton Art Gallery** (☎ 8083 2277; admission free; 10am-5pm Tue-Sat, 1-4pm Sun). The permanent collection features the best of 20th-century British art, including work by Sir Stanley Spencer, Matthew Smith and Philip Wilson Steer.

The tragic story of the *Titanic*, as well as the history of Southampton's port since 1838, is told in detail at the **Maritime Museum** (☎ 8022 3941; The Wool House, Town Quay; admission free; 10am-5pm Tue-Sat & 2-5pm Sun Apr-Oct, 10am-4pm Tue-Sat & 1-4pm Sun Nov-Mar).

Getting There & Away

AIR

The ultramodern **Southampton International Airport** (☎ 0870 040 0009) has flights to Brussels, Paris, Zurich, Amsterdam, Dublin and major holiday resorts in Spain. Bus 101 leaves regularly from the airport to the city centre. There are four trains hourly between the airport and the main train station (£2, seven minutes).

BOAT

Ferries run by **Red Funnel** (☎ 8033 4010; www.red funnel.co.uk) go to the Isle of Wight and there is a ferry service to Hythe in the New Forest (p210). **Channel Hoppers** (☎ 01481-728680; info@channelhoppers.com) has a ferry service between Southampton and the Channel Islands and France.

BUS

National Express coaches run to Southampton from London and Heathrow hourly (£12, 2½ hours). National Express also runs a 6.45pm bus to Lymington (40 minutes) via Lyndhurst (20 minutes) in the New Forest.

Stagecoach Bus No 700 runs between Portsmouth and Southampton. Nos 47 and 29 go between Southampton and Winchester (£2.40, 40 minutes) half hourly with reduced services on Sunday. Wilts & Dorset bus No 56/56A goes to all main towns in the New Forest hourly (every two hours on Sunday). Explorer tickets are valid on these routes.

TRAIN

Trains from Portsmouth run three times an hour (£6.45, 45 minutes). Trains for Winchester (£4, 17 minutes) leave about every 15 minutes.

NEW FOREST

New Forest gained national park recognition in 2004 and with good reason. Home to wild ponies and several unique species of birds, this 150-sq-mile swathe of woodland and wild heaths is the largest area of relatively natural vegetation in England. The Forest is also home to a network of very prosperous villages with upper-crust prep schools and well-preserved traditions dating back 1000 years (see the boxed text, p210).

To really get a feel for this wildlife-filled landscape, it's best to rent a car. Better still, get off the roads and onto some of the excellent cycling and walking tracks. The New Forest is a popular destination for campers, but make sure you pitch your tent in a proper campsite; the TIC in Lyndhurst has a brochure with details. For more general information go to www.thenewforest.co.uk.

Activities
CYCLING

The New Forest is a great place to cycle and there are several rental shops. You will need to pay a deposit (usually £20) and provide one or two forms of identification. You can pick up cycle route maps from TICs and bicycle shops.

AA Bike Hire (☎ 8028 3349; www.aabikehirenewforest .co.uk; Fern Glen, Gosport Lane, Lyndhurst; ½/full day £6/10)

Cyclexperience (☎ 01590-624204; www.cyclex.co.uk; Brookley Rd, Brockenhurst)

Forest Leisure Cycling (☎ 01425-403584; www.forest leisurecycling.co.uk; The Cross, Village Centre, Burley; per day from £10)

HORSE RIDING

This is a great way to explore the New Forest but we're not talking about saddling up

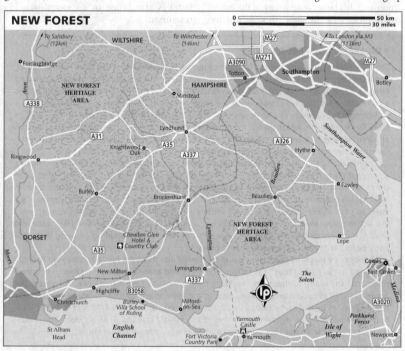

NEW FOREST

one of the wild ponies here. There are a couple of trail-riding set-ups where you can arrange a pleasant one- or two-hour ride. Both places welcome beginners.

Sandy Balls (☎ 01425-653042; www.sandy-balls.co.uk) (honestly!) is at Godshill in Fordingbridge.

Burley Villa School of Riding (☎ 01425-610278) is off the B3058, just south of New Milton and has Western riding, English riding and forest hacking.

Getting There & Around

Southampton and Bournemouth bracket the New Forest and there are regular bus services from both.

Busabout tickets offer unlimited travel on main bus lines for seven days and £21/12 (adult/child). The Solent Blue line X1 service goes through New Forest taking the Bournemouth-Burley-Lyndhurst-Southampton route.

LYNDHURST

☎ 023 / pop 2281

The clean, well-to-do town of Lyndhurst is a pleasant stopover on your way through the woodland. It's larger than many of the other small villages in the area (though not by much) and it has a couple of good local pubs and restaurants. Lyndhurst would make a good base for exploring the surrounding countryside.

The **TIC** (☎ 8028 2269; www.thenewforest.co.uk; High St; ☉ 10am-5pm), next to the library, sells a wide variety of information on the New Forest including cycling maps (£2 to £3.50), a map showing walking tracks (£1.50), a more comprehensive Collins map (£5.99) and a free camping and caravanning guide.

Sleeping & Eating

South View (☎ 8028 2224; Gosport Lane; per person with shared bathroom £20, s/d with private bathroom £30/50; ✗) This eight-room B&B has a friendly atmosphere and a lovely dog.

Primrose Cottage (☎ 1300 341352; 29 The Street; r per person £23; ✗) This cob-and-thatched-roof cottage has an Inglenook fireplace with wood stove, but modern amenities in the rooms.

Le Poussin at Parkhill (☎ 8028 2944; www.lepoussin atparkhill.co.uk; Beaulieu Rd; r from £65; 2-course lunch £15, 4-course dinner from £35; ✗) One of Hampshire's finest hotels, Le Poussin has sumptuous rooms overlooking its private park. The hotel is also home to an award-winning restaurant.

VERDERERS, AGISTERS & PONIES

The New Forest is the only area of England to remain relatively untouched since Norman times, thanks in large part to its unsuitability as agricultural land. If the presence of so much unfenced territory is remarkable enough, what is truly fascinating about the New Forest is that it still retains a code of law first handed down during the reign of William the Conqueror.

Although the presence of wild ponies was recorded by King Knut's Forest Law of 1016, William officially declared the whole area a royal hunting preserve in 1079, thereby protecting it from any form of development. The crown still owns 100 sq miles of the New Forest, though it is the Forestry Commission that has been responsible for its maintenance since 1924.

The remaining 50 sq miles are owned by verderers, or commoners, who in the preautomobile age reared the ponies as work horses. Today they are either reared as riding ponies or left to graze the land at will. The verderers' status is protected by the Commoners' Charter, first laid down in 1077, which guaranteed them six basic rights, the most important of which is the 'common' (or right) to pasture. Every year, the 300-odd verderers that still exercise their rights gather to elect five agisters, who are responsible for the daily management of the 3000 ponies, 1800 cattle and smaller numbers of donkeys, pigs and sheep in the New Forest, including ensuring that each pony bears the brand of the verderer who owns it.

Outsiders are more than welcome to wander freely throughout the forest, but they are strongly requested not to feed or touch the ponies. These are wild animals, and feeding them will attract them onto the roads; furthermore they have been known to have a nasty bite. To protect the ponies, as well as cyclists and walkers, there is a 40mph speed limit on unfenced roads. If you come across an injured pony, phone Lyndhurst Police on ☎ 023-8028 2813 and state the location and, if possible, the registration number of any vehicle involved in an accident. You should try to stay with the animal (but don't touch it) to protect it from further injury.

Mad Hatter Tea Rooms (☎ 8028 2341; 10 High St; mains £4-6; ✆ 10am-5pm; ✗) You can get a delicious breakfast, ploughman's lunch and rarebits at this beautiful café. A children's menu is available.

La Pergola Ristorante & Wine Bar (☎ 8028 4184; Southampton Rd; mains £8-15; ✆ lunch & dinner Tue-Sun; ✗) It is decidedly lively, but there are some romantic corners in this old pub that serves pizza, pasta, antipasto, steak, veal and other classic Italian fare.

Getting There & Away

Wilts & Dorset bus Nos 56 and 56a run twice hourly from Southampton to Lyndhurst (£2.70/4.50 one-way/return) daily except Sunday.

Lyndhurst has no train station and the nearest stop is Brockenhurst, 8 miles south. Trains run every half-hour from London Waterloo station via Brockenhurst (£25.60, 1½ hours) to Bournemouth, Poole and Weymouth.

White Horse Ferries (☎ 8084 0722) operates a service from Southampton to Hythe, 13 miles southwest of Lyndhurst, every half-hour (£3.90 return, 12 minutes).

AROUND LYNDHURST
Beaulieu & National Motor Museum

The New Forest's most impressive and most visited (non-natural) attraction is a tourist complex, **Beaulieu** (☎ 01590-612345; adult £14; ✆ 10am-6pm May-Sep, 10am-5pm Oct-Apr), pronounced 'bewley'. Once the site of England's most important Cistercian monastery, it was founded in 1204 by order of King John as an act of contrition after he ordered that a group of monks be trampled to death. The 3200-hectare abbey was dissolved following Henry VIII's monastic land-grab of 1536 and sold to the ancestors of the Montague family in 1538.

Lord Montague's **National Motor Museum** is the biggest attraction. There are 250 vehicles on show, including buses, cars and motorcycles, spanning the whole history of motor transport. As well as classics, you can run your hands along a £650,000 McLaren F1 and the jet-powered *Bluebird*, which broke the land-speed record (403mph) in 1964 (see p586). There's also a ride-through display giving you the low-down on car history. Rev-heads will love it, but you don't need to be one to enjoy it.

Beaulieu's **Palace House** (✆ 11am-6pm May-Sep, 11am-5pm Oct-Easter) was once the abbey gatehouse and is an odd combination of 14th-century Gothic and 19th-century Scottish Baronial architecture, as converted by Baron Montague in the 1860s. Unlike other manor homes you might visit, this place really feels like a home and exudes a certain warmth.

The 13th-century **abbey** has an excellent exhibit on everyday life in the monastery. If you're into ghosts, the abbey is supposed to be one of England's most haunted places.

Bus No 49 runs to Beaulieu from Brockenhurst Station at 11.05am, 12.35pm, 2.05pm and 3.35pm (45 minutes). You can also get here from Southampton by taking a ferry to Hythe and catching bus No 112 or X9. Solent Blue Line buses also run here from various towns in New Forest.

Trains from London Waterloo run to Brockenhurst (p211), from where it's a short taxi ride.

LYMINGTON
☎ 01590 / pop 14,227

With a bustling High St full of book shops, old inns and restaurants, the quaint harbour and market town of Lymington is a great base for visits to both the New Forest and the Isle of Wight. Lymington was once a centre for salt manufacture and it has long been a yachting centre, still reflected in its two marinas and the occasional yacht race. It was also known as a smugglers port.

The **TIC** (☎ 689000; www.thenewforest.co.uk; New St; ✆ 10am-5pm) is a block off the High St next to the St Barbe Museum and sells walking tours of town (25p) as well as a variety of information on the New Forest in general. It will also help you find accommodation.

Free Internet can be had at the Lymington **library** (☎ 673050; North Close; ✆ 9.30am-5pm Mon-Sat), a few blocks from Lymington Town train station.

ATMs, banks and a variety of shops are on the Georgian and Victorian High St. The bus station is behind the optometrists on the High St and there's a post office at the end of the High St near St Thomas Church. There are also train links to Southampton and destinations onward.

Sleeping & Eating

Angel Inn (☎ 672050; angelinn.lymingont@eldridge-pope.co.uk; 108 High St; s/d from £35/70; ✗ ℗) This highly recommended eclectic boutique hotel is housed in a newly remodelled Georgian coach inn and features clean, modern rooms and an imaginative bistro downstairs. All rooms have an en suite and rates are £10 less during the week.

Café Uno (☎ 688689; 118 High St; mains £5-14; ☉ lunch & dinner; ☒) For a fun but elegant atmosphere with brick-oven pizza and Italian cooking, try this colourful spot. With rustic wood tables, yellow ceilings and orange walls, the casual, cool restaurant promotes a lively chatter at the weekend. Children are welcome.

Getting There & Away

Lymington has two train stations: Lymington Town and Lymington Pier, which is where the Isle of Wight ferry drops off and picks up. Trains to Southampton leave roughly every half-hour, take 40 minutes and cost £7.20.

Wightlink Ferries (☎ 0990 827744; www.wight link.co.uk) connects Lymington to Yarmouth on the Isle of Wight every half-hour for about £9.

SOMETHING SPECIAL

A mile north of the pretty little village of New Milton, just on the southern outskirts of the New Forest, you'll find **Chewton Glen Hotel & Country Club** (☎ 01425-275341; www.chewtonglen.com; r £250-720), a spot that *Gourmet* magazine calls 'the best country house hotel in the world'. The service at this resort is unsurpassed with every comfort provided for, including full spa treatments and a range of outdoor activities including golf and croquet clinics. For those looking to unwind in style look no further.

ISLE OF WIGHT

While summer crowds jam the motorways and beaches of the mainland, only a couple of miles offshore is the Isle of Wight, a peaceful and still largely secluded getaway that has been a holiday spot for yachtsmen, cyclists, ramblers and beach goers for over a hundred years. Here you'll find grazing cattle and sheep on lush green hills that roll down to 25 miles of clean and unspoilt beaches. In

fact, over a third of the island is an Area of Outstanding Natural Beauty (AONB). Plus, the weather here is milder than anywhere else in Britain, which all adds up to a great place to come and enjoy the outdoors. Although most visitors are day trippers, there's enough here to warrant staying at least a couple of days, particularly if you set about exploring the lovely coastal towns.

Also, every year in June, the quiet Victorian atmosphere is crashed with the sounds of thousands of young rockers who ship over for the Isle of Wight festival, a massive rock concert that first brought fame to the sheltered Isle in 1969.

For good online information, check out the website at www.islandbreaks.co.uk.

Activities

CYCLING

The island is a cyclist's paradise. There is a 62-mile cycleway, and in 2002 a Cycling Festival was inaugurated; check with the TICs for details. Enthusiasts should also check out the *Cyclist's Guide to the Isle of Wight* (£3.50) by Ron Crick and the two-volume *Cycling Wight* by John Goodwin and Ian Williams (£3 each), all sold at **Offshore Sports** (☎ 866269; www.offshore-sports.co.uk; 19 Orchardleigh Rd, Shanklin or ☎ 290514; 2-4 Birmingham Rd, Cowes).

Bike rentals are available in Cowes, Freshwater Bay, Ryde, Sandown, Shanklin, Ventnor and Yarmouth. **Wavells** (☎ 760738; The Square, Yarmouth; half-day/day £7/12, deluxe £10/15) has free helmets and locks.

WALKING

There are 500 miles of well-marked walking paths and bridleways, which make the island one of the best places in southern England for less strenuous walks and gentle rambling. They are so serious about their walking here that there is an annual **Walking Festival** (☎ 813818), which takes place over two weeks in May. In 2004 the festival offered 160 different guided walks over more than 500 miles of trails. The event draws walkers from around the world.

COWES

☎ 01983 / pop 19,110 (including Northwood)

Located at the northern tip of the island, Cowes is a hilly, Georgian harbour town. This is a major yachting centre and the late-July/early-August **Cowes Week** is an important international yachting event. The town has a **maritime museum** (☎ 01983 293394; Beckford Rd; admission free; 🕑 9.30am-4.30pm Mon-Wed, Fri & Sat).

Since its appearance in the film *Mrs Brown*, **Osborne House** (EH; ☎ 200022; adult £8.50; 🕑 10am-6pm Apr-Sep) has become English Heritage's most visited attraction. The house was built between 1845 and 1851, and Queen Victoria died here in 1901. Osborne House has an antipodean connection: the Australian state of Victoria's Government House, is a copy, built in 1872. The house is in East Cowes, separated from the rest of the town by the River Medina and linked by a chain ferry. From October to March, it opens from 10am to 4pm Sunday through Thursday for guided tours only (£5.50/3.50 per adult/child).

Sleeping & Eating

Doghouse (☎ 293677; Crossways Rd, East Cowes; s/d £25/35) This four-diamond rated guesthouse has two gorgeous rooms, impeccable service and is anything but punishment.

Fountain (☎ 292397; High St; mains around £7) Here you'll find a wonderful, traditional old pub that serves filling meals and a good pint.

RYDE

☎ 01983 / pop 22,806

Most visitors to the island land at Ryde, and then move on very quickly. It has a handful of elegant Victorian buildings, but it's the least pretty of the island's towns.

There is a **TIC** (☎ 813818; 81-83 Union St). At **St Cecilia's Abbey** (Appley Rise) you can hear Gregorian chants by Benedictine nuns during Mass at 9.15am daily (10am Sunday).

Seahaven Hotel (☎ 563069; seahaven@netguides .co.uk; St Thomas St; s/d £29/50) is a comfortable Victorian house with great views of the sea – provided you ask for a room at the front.

VENTNOR

☎ 01983 / pop 6257

Of the island's larger towns, Ventnor is easily the most pleasant, probably because it's chilled out and doesn't seem to notice whether visitors are around or not.

The **TIC** (☎ 813818; 34 High St) is near the bus stop in a beautiful stone building high on a bluff with coastal views, good displays on the island's geography, free town maps and cheery staff.

SOUTHEAST ENGLAND

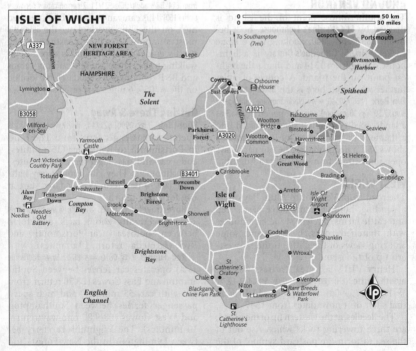

One mile south of the town, off the A3055, is the **Rare Breeds & Waterfowl Park** (☎ 852649; Undercliffe Dr; adult/child £3.90/3; ☺ 10am-5.30pm Apr-Sep, 11am-4pm Oct), home to a large array of rare and not-so-rare farm animals including llamas, African cattle and Falabella miniature horses. Bus Nos 7, 7A and 31 will get you there from Ryde or Ventnor.

Ventnor Guided Walks (☎ 856647) organises a mixed bag of walks, including ghost walks, rock-pool rambles and explorations of smugglers' caves. They run on Tuesday and Thursday from June to September and cost £3/1 (adult/child).

The **Spy Glass Inn** (☎ 855338; The Esplanade; 2-person flats £60) provides accommodation in self-contained flats (no kids, no dogs) situated above the beach with great views of the town. The atmosphere in the pub below is charged and friendly and there's live music.

Choose between Thai curries, Chinese noodles and Vietnamese spring rolls in a fun, bright and irreverent atmosphere at **Shanghai Lil's** (☎ 856825; 7 Belgrave Rd; mains £5-7; ☺ dinner Mon-Sat).

AROUND VENTNOR

The southernmost point of the island is marked by **St Catherine's Lighthouse**, built between 1837 and 1840. Looking like a stone rocket ship, **St Catherine's Oratory** is a lighthouse dating from 1314 and marks the highest point on the island. A couple of miles further west from here is the **Blackgang Chine Fun Park** (☎ 730330; www.blackgangchine.com; ages 4 & up £7.50; ☺ 10am-5pm), which opened in 1843 as a landscaped garden but slowly evolved into a theme park with water gardens, animated shows and a hedge maze. The fun park stays open until 10pm from mid-July to August.

WEST WIGHT

The road from Ventnor to Alum Bay offers a winding, bumpy scenic drive past sheep and cattle farms, ancient stone farmhouses with thatched roofs, beaches and some amazing views of the cliffs off the far western tip of the island.

Henry VIII's last great fortress was **Yarmouth Castle** (EH; ☎ 760678; Quay St; adult £2.30; ☺ 10am-6pm Apr-Oct). Its façade, which is all that's left of it now, dates from 1547.

The **Needles**, at the western tip of the island, are three towering rocks which rise out of the sea to form the postcard symbol of the island. At one time there was another rock, a 37m-high spire which really was needle-like, but it collapsed into the sea in 1764.

Needles Park at Alum Bay (☎ 458 0022; admission free; ☺ 10am-dusk Apr-Nov) has a range of attractions (about £2 each) including kiddie rides, crazy golf, a motion simulator, boat rides and a chairlift down to the beach. Our favourite is the sweet factory, where you can watch how those teeth-rotters are actually made.

A walking path leads a mile from Alum Bay to the **Needles Old Battery** (☎ 754772; adult £3.60; ☺ 10.30am-5pm Sun-Thu Apr-Jun, Sep & Oct, 10.30am-5pm daily Jul & Aug), a fort established in 1862 and used as an observation post during WWII. There's a 60m tunnel leading down through the cliff to a searchlight lookout. Buses run between Alum Bay and the battery hourly (every half-hour in peak season).

Sleeping

Totland Bay Youth Hostel (☎ 0870 770 6070; Hirst Hill, Totland; dm £11.80) A marvellous Victorian house overlooking the water.

Brighstone Holiday Centre (☎ 740244; www.brighstone-holidays.co.uk; 2-/4-person tent sites £7/12, caravans from £14, B&B adult/child £21/11, 2-person cabins per week from £160) This caravan park and B&B, perched high on the cliffs overlooking the island's most stunning stretch of coastline, is the most scenic place to stay and is also close to walking trails. There are self-catering cabins and B&B (continental breakfast). It's located on the A3055, 6 miles east of Freshwater.

Getting There & Away

Wightlink (☎ 0990 827744; www.wightlink.co.uk) operates a passenger ferry from The Hard in Portsmouth to Ryde pier (15 minutes) and a car-and-passenger ferry (35 minutes) to Fishbourne. They run about every half-hour (£9.90 day return). Car fares start at £49 for a day return.

Hovertravel (☎ 01983-811000; www.hovertravel.co.uk) hovercrafts zoom back and forth between Southsea (near Portsmouth) and Ryde (£8.60 day return, 10 minutes).

Red Funnel (☎ 0870 444 8898; www.redfunnel.co.uk) operates car ferries between Southampton and East Cowes (£8.70 return, from £51 with car, 55 minutes) and high-speed passenger ferries between Southampton and West Cowes (£8/9.80 one way/return, 10 minutes). The Wightlink car ferry between Lymington (in the New Forest) and

Yarmouth costs £7.50 for passengers and £49.50 for cars. The trip takes half an hour and ferries run every half-hour. Children travel for half price on all these services.

Getting Around
Southern Vectis (☎ 827005; 32 High St, Cowes) operates buses around the island. Buses circumnavigate the island hourly and run between the towns on the eastern side of the island about every 30 minutes. Trains run twice hourly from Ryde to Shanklin and the Isle of Wight Steam Railway branches off from this line at Havenstreet and goes to Wootton.

Rover Tickets give you unlimited use of buses and trains for £6.50 for a day, £10.50 for two days and £27 for a week.

WEST SUSSEX

Slow and easy West Sussex is less crowded than many parts of the Southeast, making it a welcome respite for many travellers. The countryside is dominated by the manicured rolling hills of the South Downs, which is slated to become England's next national park. A great place to base yourself is beautiful Arundel, home of the Duke of Norfolk and his castle on the hill.

ARUNDEL
☎ 01903 / pop 3297
Arundel is one of West Sussex's prettiest towns, sitting comfortable atop a hill beneath the stunning 700-year-old castle that is the seat of the dukes of Norfolk. Here you'll find a surprising number of excellent restaurants, some great antique stores and plenty of personable locals. Despite its medieval appearance and long history, most of the town dates from Victorian times.

Information
The **TIC** (☎ 882268; fax 882419; 61 High St; ✆ 10am-6pm Mon-Sat, 10am-1pm & 1.30-4pm Sun Easter-Oct, 10am-3pm daily Nov-Easter) has *A Walk Around Arundel* (40p), although everything to see in the town is pretty well signposted.

Sights & Activities
Arundel Castle (☎ 882173; adult £9.50; ✆ noon-5pm Sun-Fri Apr-Oct) is a great sight and well worth the entry fee. It was originally built in the 11th century, but it was thoroughly ruined

during the Civil War. Most of what you see today is the result of enthusiastic reconstruction by the eighth, 11th and 15th dukes (the current duke still lives in part of the castle). The building's highlight is the massive Great Hall and the library, which has paintings by Gainsborough and Holbein among others.

The town's other architectural landmark is the 19th-century **cathedral** (☎ 882297; ✆ 9am-6pm summer, 9am-dusk winter), built in the French Gothic style by Henry, the 15th duke. Inside are the remains of the fourth duke's son, St Philip Howard, a Catholic martyr who made the grievous error of being caught praying for a Spanish victory against the English in 1588. He died in the Tower of London and was canonised in 1970.

You can hire a boat to Littlehampton (an out-of-the-way fishing village on the coast) or cruise the River Arun with the swans while you dine on an **evening buffet** (☎ 07814 183824; 12 person min, per person £20). Trips depart from the Town Quay at the foot of the High St.

An excellent collection of antique stores lines the High St.

Sleeping
Arundel YHA (☎ 0870 770 5676; www.yha.org.uk /hostel/hostelpages/154.html; Warning Camp; dm £13.40; ✖ ▣) Catering to South Downs walkers and families, this large Georgian house isn't as warm a hostel as some, but its facilities are superb. It's on a pleasant country lane about a 20-minute walk from the town centre off the A27 (call ahead for directions).

St Mary's Gate Inn (☎ 883145; www.stmarysgate .co.uk; London Rd; r £39; mains from £10) This lovely country-style inn next door to the cathedral has a wonderful local atmosphere and family-run feeling. The restaurant and pub are both worth a visit.

Town House (☎ 883847; www.thetownhouse.co.uk; 65 High St; s/d from £50/60; ✖) This elegant, beautifully furnished boutique hotel is simply marvellous, with a welcoming atmosphere and top-notch service. The restaurant downstairs is equally exquisite.

Eating
Town House (☎ 883847; www.thetownhouse.co.uk; 65 High St; mains £14-18; ✖) The gold-and-walnut ceiling is as immaculate as the cuisine in this cosy, special-night-out spot. The jaunty proprietor adds to the bubbly, champagne-like spirit. Book ahead.

SOUTHEAST ENGLAND

Papperdelle Ristorante (☎ 882025; 41a High St; mains £7-12; ♥ lunch &dinner Tue-Sat, dinner only Mon; ✗) Vines cling to the hand-painted walls of this romantic Italian restaurant. Fresh, authentic dishes are served by professional and knowledgeable staff. Ask for the bay-window seat overlooking High St.

Pallant of Arundel (☎ 882288; 17 High St) Set yourself up for an English picnic with a selection of local cheese, fresh bread, pâté, wine and other upmarket delicatessen treats from this superb speciality shop. Juicy spit-roasted chickens are available next door at the butcher.

Getting There & Away

Rail is the best way of getting to/from Arundel. There are trains to Arundel from London Victoria (£17.40, 1½ hours, twice hourly), Brighton (£7, 57 minutes, twice hourly) and Chichester (£3.80, 21 minutes, twice hourly).

AROUND ARUNDEL
Bignor Roman Villa

In 1811 farmer George Tupper was doing a little ploughing when he struck a large stone. After digging around a bit, Tupper realised that he had discovered something quite out of the ordinary.

Much excavation later, it was realised that the plough had struck the remains of a **Roman villa** (☎ 869259; adult £3.65; ♥ 10am-6pm daily Jun-Sep, 10am-5pm daily May & Oct, 10am-5pm Tue-Sun Mar-Apr) built around AD 190. Unfortunately, only the mosaic floors and hypocaust (Roman duct heating) remain, but the mosaics are simply fantastic. New findings are still being made; the most recent was the complete skeleton of a child dating from the 4th century.

Bignor is 6 miles north of Arundel off the A29, but it's a devil of a place to get to unless you have your own car. A terribly slow bus (one hour) from Chichester stops 300m from the entrance, but it only runs twice daily.

CHICHESTER
☎ 01243 / pop 27,477

Situated on the flat meadows between the South Downs and the sea, Chichester is home to a great theatre-and-arts festival each July as well as some good Roman ruins. Otherwise, it's a fairly uninspiring, though bustling Georgian market town that serves as the administrative capital of West Sussex.

Orientation & Information

The Market Cross, built in 1501 to shelter marketgoers, is the centre of town. The streets around it are pedestrianised and everything you'd want to see is within walking distance. The town is surrounded by walls, around which is a ring road.

There is a **TIC** (☎ 775888; chitic@chichester.gov.uk; 29a South St; ♥ 9.15am-5.15pm Mon-Sat year-round, 11am-3.30pm Sun Apr-Sep) and a **post office** (cnr Chapel & West Sts) in town.

Sights

The elegant **Chichester cathedral** (☎ 782595; donation £3; ♥ 7.15am-7pm Jun-Aug, 7.15am-6.30pm Sep-May) is one of the few Romanesque churches not to have undergone major restructuring. Begun in 1075, it burnt down and was rebuilt in the 13th century and only cosmetically altered since then. The only major changes were the construction of the freestanding church tower in the 15th century and the addition of a 19th-century spire. Inside is a marvellous stained-glass window by Marc Chagall.

Guided tours operate at 11am and 2.15pm Monday to Saturday, Easter to October and the cathedral choir sings daily at **evensong** (♥ 5.30pm Mon-Sat, 3.30pm Sun).

Of the many fine Georgian houses in town, **Pallant House Gallery** (☎ 774557; 9 North Pallant; adult/child £4/free; ♥ 10am-5pm Tue-Sat, 12.30-5pm Sun) is outstanding. It was built by a wealthy wine merchant who spared no expense. It has since been carefully restored and now houses an excellent collection of 20th-century, mainly British, art in the form of paintings, furniture, sculpture and porcelain. Among them are works by Picasso, Moore, Sutherland and Cézanne. There are also a lot of works by a German artist named Feibusch who escaped the Nazis in Germany in 1933. He died in London in 1998 and left the contents of his studio to Pallant House.

Festivals & Events

Chichester Festivities (☎ 780192; www.chifest.org.uk) is a three-week festival that includes arts and music but specialises in great theatre. It has been held every June and July since 1974.

Sleeping & Eating

Travellers on a budget won't find much accommodation to suit their needs. Most places are mid-range.

Litten House (☎ 774503; www.littenho.demon.co.uk; 148 St Pancras St; d from £48; ✗) Home-made bread and jams are served in the garden or conservatory at this comfortable and centrally located B&B with spacious rooms.

George & Dragon (☎ 775525; www.georgeand dragoninn.co.uk; 51 North St; s/d £50/85) Sleep in a converted barn at the back of this pub with worn wooden floors and quiet window seats. The 10 rooms are thoroughly modern and quite charming.

Shepherd's Tea Rooms (☎ 774761; 35 Little London; ☉ 9.15am-5pm Mon-Fri, 10am-4pm Sun) Down a small lane off East St, this three-time winner of Chichester's 'Top Tea Place of the Year' award serves a range of sandwiches and rarebits with home-made white-milk bread.

Saddlers (☎ 774765; 1 Saddler's Walk, 41 East St; mains £8-13; ☉ 11am-11pm Mon-Sat) This cool and rustic restaurant with a sophisticated air has outdoor seating in the large garden. It's a nice place to relax over dinner, with steak, pasta and tapas.

Drinking & Entertainment

Chichester Festival Theatre (☎ 781312; www.cft.org .uk; Oakland's Park; tickets £9-35) This modern playhouse was built in 1962 and has a long and distinguished history. Sir Laurence Olivier was the theatre's first director and Ingrid Bergman, Sir John Gielgud, Maggie Smith and Sir Anthony Hopkins are a few of the other famous names to have played here.

SOUTHEAST ENGLAND

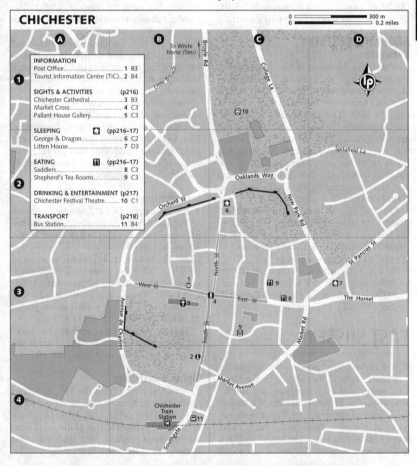

CHICHESTER

0 — 300 m
0 — 0.2 miles

INFORMATION
Post Office..................................1 B3
Tourist Information Centre (TIC)..2 B4

SIGHTS & ACTIVITIES (p216)
Chichester Cathedral...................3 B3
Market Cross................................4 C3
Pallant House Gallery...................5 C3

SLEEPING (pp216-17)
George & Dragon.........................6 C2
Litten House.................................7 D3

EATING (pp216-17)
Saddlers.......................................8 C3
Shepherd's Tea Rooms................9 C3

DRINKING & ENTERTAINMENT (p217)
Chichester Festival Theatre.........10 C1

TRANSPORT (p218)
Bus Station.................................11 B4

Getting There & Away

Chichester is 60 miles from London and 18 miles from Portsmouth.

BUS

Chichester is served by bus No 700, which runs every half hour (hourly on Sunday) between Brighton (2½ hours) and Portsmouth (one hour). National Express has a rather protracted daily service from London Victoria (£12.20, five hours 12 minutes).

TRAIN

Chichester can be reached easily from London Victoria (£17.40, 1½ hours, half-hourly) via Gatwick airport and Arundel. It's also on the coast line between Brighton (£8.20, 45 minutes) and Portsmouth (£5.10, 25 minutes). Trains run every half-hour.

AROUND CHICHESTER
Petworth

Twelve miles northeast of Chichester is the pleasant village of Petworth. On the outskirts is **Petworth House** (☎ 01798-342207; adult £7; ⊙ 11am-5.30pm Sat-Wed Apr-Oct), a stately home built in 1688. The architecture is impressive (especially the western front), but the art collection is extraordinary. JMW Turner was a regular visitor and the house is still home to the largest collection (20) of his paintings outside the Tate Gallery. There are also many paintings by Van Dyck, Reynolds, Gainsborough, Titian and Blake.

Petworth is most famous for **Petworth Park** (adult/child £1.50/free; ⊙ 8am-sunset), regarded as the supreme achievement of Lancelot 'Capability' Brown's natural-landscape theory. It's also home to herds of deer.

Petworth is 6 miles from the train station at Pulborough. There's a limited bus service (No 1/1A) from the station to Petworth Square (Monday to Saturday).

EAST SUSSEX

If you choose any two counties to visit in Southeast England, they should be Kent and East Sussex and even then you may not be able to take in all the sights. Like the rest of this corner of country, East Sussex is dominated by gorgeous countryside. But it's also home to Brighton, where the superb nightlife and beach scene makes this one of the coolest

cities in all of England, save perhaps London. Further afield you'll find the cobblestone streets of ancient Rye, a picturesque medieval village, the historically important Battle, where William the Conqueror first engaged the Saxons in 1066, and the breathtaking white cliffs of Beachy Head, near Eastbourne. Anywhere you turn, this part of England is one of the most popular for tourists and weekending Londoners winding down.

RYE
☎ 01797 / pop 4195

If you've come to England to find a medieval village, look no further than Rye. Once a Cinque Port, this exquisite town looks like it has been preserved in historical formaldehyde. Not even the most talented Hollywood set designers could have come up with a better representation of Ye Olde Englishe Village: the half-timbered Tudor buildings, cobbled streets, abundant flowerpots and strong literary associations should be enough to temper even the most hard-bitten cynic's weariness of the made-for-tourism look.

Inevitably, such beauty *has* made it a tourist magnet, but thankfully most wander about the town in almost muted appreciation, lest their gasps of surprise disturb the air of genuine tranquillity that pervades the place. If you do visit – and you absolutely should – avoid summer weekends.

Information

There is a helpful **TIC** (☎ 226696; ryetic@rother.gov.uk; Strand Quay; ⊙ 9.30am-5pm Mar-Oct, 10am-4pm Nov-Feb) where you can view the Rye Town Model Sound & Light Show, a visual history, for £2.50. The town is easily covered on foot and the TIC sells the *Rye Town Walk* map, which gives a detailed history of the town's buildings for £1. There's also a self-guided audio tour costing £2.50. For guided walks, phone ☎ 01424-882343 or ☎ 01424-882466.

There are several pay-and-display parking lots around town. The one closest to the centre is across the river from the TIC.

Sights & Activities

Around the corner from the TIC, in Strand Quay, are a number of antique shops selling all kinds of wonderful junk. From here walk up cobbled **Mermaid St**, one of the most famous streets in England, with timber-framed houses dating from the 15th century.

Turn right at the T-junction for the Georgian **Lamb House** (☎ 224982; West St; adult £2.75; 2-6pm Wed & Sat Apr-Oct), mostly dating from 1722. It was the home of American writer Henry James from 1898 to 1916; he wrote *The Wings of the Dove* here.

Continue around the dogleg until you come out at Church Sq. This square is surrounded by some attractive houses, including the **Friars of the Sack** on its south side at No 40. Now a private residence, it was once part of a 13th-century Augustinian friary. The **Church of St Mary the Virgin** incorporates a mixture of ecclesiastical styles. The turret clock is the oldest in England (1561) and still works with its original pendulum mechanism. There are great views from the **church tower** (adult £2).

Turn right at the square's east corner for **Ypres Tower** (adult £1.90; 10.30am-1pm & 2-5pm Mon & Thu-Sun Apr-Oct, 10.30am-3pm Sat & Sun Nov-Mar), pronounced 'wipers', part of a 13th-century fort with views over Romney Marsh and Rye Bay. It now houses one part of the **Rye Castle Museum** (☎ 226728; 3 East St; adult £1.90; 10.30am-1pm & 2-5pm Thu-Mon Apr-Oct, 10.30am-3.30pm Nov-Mar tower only), home to loot from the city's past.

At the northeastern edge of the village is **Landgate**. Built in 1329 to fortify the town, it's the only remaining gate out of four.

If you're up for a longer historic walk, the 31-mile **1066 Country Walk** takes you through the East Sussex countryside from Rye to Battle and Pevensey where it joins the South Downs Way.

Festivals & Events

The town celebrates its medieval heritage with a two-day festival each August, and in September there is the two-week **Festival of Music and the Arts** (www.ryefestival.co.uk).

Sleeping

Accommodation is plentiful and of a very high standard.

Mermaid Inn (☎ 223065; www.mermaidinn.com; Mermaid St; s/d £80/160) This marvellously atmospheric hostelry has been around since 1420, but the site dates back to 1156 and comes complete with a resident ghost.

Old Borough Arms (☎ 222128; www.oldborough arms.co.uk; The Strand; s/d £40/70;) A former smugglers' inn, this truly lovely guesthouse has

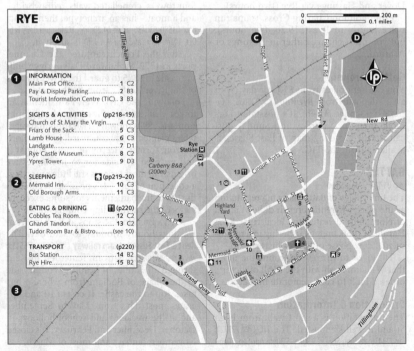

RYE

0		200 m
0		0.1 miles

INFORMATION
Main Post Office...................................1 C2
Pay & Display Parking..........................2 B3
Tourist Information Centre (TIC)..3 B3

SIGHTS & ACTIVITIES (pp218–19)
Church of St Mary the Virgin.......4 C3
Friars of the Sack..................................5 C3
Lamb House...6 C3
Landgate...7 D1
Rye Castle Museum.............................8 C2
Ypres Tower...9 D3

SLEEPING (pp219–20)
Mermaid Inn..10 C3
Old Borough Arms..............................11 C3

EATING & DRINKING (p220)
Cobbles Tea Room...............................12 C2
Ghandi Tandori....................................13 C2
Tudor Room Bar & Bistro.........(see 10)

TRANSPORT (p220)
Bus Station..14 B2
Rye Hire...15 B2

spacious and clean neo-rustic rooms complete with four-poster beds. The downstairs café serves sandwiches and cream teas.

Carberry (☎ 223740; dave@rotherplus.com; 40 Udimore Rd; s/d £25/55; P ✗) The owners are very welcoming at this thoughtfully appointed B&B. Family rooms are available.

Eating & Drinking

Cobbles Tea Room (☎ 225962; 1 Highland Yard; mains £4-7; ☽ 10am-5pm Wed-Mon; ✗) Ladies in white aprons serve the tea and cakes (breakfast, too) at this home-style tearoom.

Ghandi's Tandoori (☎ 223091; Cinque Ports St; mains £4-8; ☽ lunch & dinner) Eat here not only for the name but for inexpensive curries, biryanis and other south-Indian specialities.

Tudor Room Bar & Bistro (☎ 223065; Mermaid St; mains £14.50-18, 3-/4-course lunch £19.50/35, 4-course dinner £36.50; ☽ lunch & dinner) This restaurant at the Mermaid Inn is worthy of the ancient building housing it. Try delights such as smoked-quail salad and rump of English lamb.

Getting There & Away

Stagecoach Bus No 711 runs hourly between Dover and Hastings via Rye (two hours).

From London Charing Cross, trains run twice hourly to Rye (£19.20, two hours), but you must change either in Hastings or Ashford.

Getting Around

You can rent bikes from £10 per day (with a £25 deposit) from **Rye Hire** (☎ 223033; 1 Cyprus Pl; ☽ 8am-5pm Mon-Fri). It's possible to arrange hires for Saturday and Sunday; just call ahead. A cycling map of East Sussex is available from the TIC.

BATTLE

☎ 01424 / pop 5190

The tiny village of Battle has a big reputation as the place where the French duke William of Normandy defeated the local ruler King Harold in 1066, thereby ushering in a monumental new phase of British history.

The lovely town grew up around the abbey that William, flush with the thrill of victory, ordered built to commemorate his success.

Orientation & Information

The train station is a short walk from High St and is well signposted. The **TIC** (☎ 773721; fax 773436; 88 High St; ☽ 9.30am-5.30pm Apr-Sep, 10am-

5pm Oct, 10am-4pm Nov-Mar) is in the Battle Abbey Gatehouse, along with a wonderful gift shop that can supply you with chain mail and Christian crusader outfits for the kids. The post office and ATMs are also on High St.

Sights

BATTLEFIELD & BATTLE ABBEY

Battle Abbey (☎ 773792; adult £4.50; ☽ 10am-dusk Apr-Oct, 10am-4pm Nov-Mar) is a pretty interesting place, but more for its unique location, built smack in the middle of the actual battlefield, so your visit should be steeped in historical significance. The guided walk – courtesy of a free audio unit – gives blow-by-blow descriptions of the battle.

Construction of the abbey began in 1070. It was occupied by Benedictines until the dissolution of the monasteries in 1536 (p39). Only the foundations of the church can now be seen and the altar's position is marked by a plaque, but quite a few monastic buildings survive and the scene is very painterly.

BODIAM CASTLE

If the castle of childhood imagination – four towers, crenellated walls, a drawbridge and a moat – has an archetype, then **Bodiam** (☎ 01580-830436; adult £4.20; ☽ 10am-6pm daily Feb-Oct, 10am-4pm Sat & Sun Nov-Jan) is surely it.

After the French captured the Channel ports in 1372, Sir Edward Dalyngrigge built the castle in 1385 to guard the lower reaches of the River Rother from further attack.

Following the Civil War, Parliamentarian forces deliberately ruined it; photographs from the 1890s show ivy-clad ruins and vegetables planted in the courtyard. In 1917 Lord Curzon, former Viceroy of India, bought it and restored the exterior to its impressive origins, but the interior is still little more than a collection of ruins. It's possible to climb to the top of the battlements for some excellent views of the surrounding countryside.

Arriva Bus No 254 stops at Bodiam from Hastings hourly Monday to Saturday. The **Kent & East Sussex steam railway** (☎ 01580-765155; www.kesr.org.uk) runs from Tenterden in Kent through 10½ miles of beautiful countryside to the village of Bodiam from where a bus takes you to the castle. It costs £10 and operates most days from May to September and at the weekend and school holidays in October, December and February. It's closed November, January and most of March.

Sleeping & Eating

Abbey Hotel (☎ 772755; 84 High St; s/d from £28/56)
The pub rooms, located opposite the abbey,
come with easy access to a pint.

Beauport Park Hotel (☎ 851222; www.beauport
parkhotel.co.uk; Battle Rd; nr Battle; s/d £65/130; ⊠) After
spending with a number of pleasant diver-
sions, sit back and enjoy a flambé dish in
the restaurant overlooking an Italian garden.
This elegant country house has everything
you could want from an upscale retreat.

Pilgrim's Restaurant (☎ 772314; 1 High St; mains
£11-22; ⏰ 10.30am-9.30pm; ⊠) Modern beats
play gently over the clink of wine glasses and
fine silver in a 16th-century Tudor set up for
a special night out. The expertly thought out
menu of seafood and local meat dishes represent new English cuisine at its best. Open for
lunch, afternoon tea, cocktails and dinner.

Getting There & Away

National Express bus Nos 023 and 024
from London to Hastings pass through
Battle twice daily (£9.25, 2¼ hours), and
Eastbourne Buses No 22 service runs from
Eastbourne to Battle on weekdays (three
daily). From Battle you can reach Pevensey
(45 minutes) and Bodiam (20 minutes) on
the irregular No 19 service. Local Rider bus
No 4/5 runs hourly to Hastings.

Trains run to and from London Charing
Cross every half-hour (£17, 1½ hours), via
Hastings (£2.30, 20 minutes).

AROUND BATTLE
Bateman's

About half a mile south of the town of Bur-
wash along the A259 is **Bateman's** (☎ 01435-
882302; adult £5.50; ⏰ 11am-5pm Sat-Wed Apr-Oct), the
home of Rudyard Kipling from 1902 until
his death in 1936. Inside this beautiful Jacobean home built in 1634, everything is pretty
much just as the writer would have left it,
down to the blotting paper on the desk. The
furnishings reflect Kipling's love of the East,
and there are plenty of oriental rugs and Indian artefacts. This is a great side trip.

A small path leads down to the River Dud-
well, where the writer converted a watermill
to generate electricity. These days, the mill
grinds corn every Saturday at 2pm. Also on
display is the Rolls Royce Kipling kept to
explore the Sussex countryside.

EASTBOURNE
☎ 01323 / pop 106,562

Long a favourite south-coast resort for octo-
genarians, Eastbourne is a lovely Victorian
seaside town that your bold and artsy aunt
might enjoy. Its pier is well kept and the seafront has manicured gardens rather than the
tacky casinos that plague much of the southeast coast. If you're looking for nightlife, head
up the coast to Brighton. But if you're looking for a relaxed time eating Mr Softy by the
seashore, you've come to the right place.

The **TIC** (☎ 411400; eastbournetic@btclick.com;
Cornfield Rd; ⏰ 9.30am-5.30pm Mon-Fri, 9.30am-5pm Sat
Apr-Sep) has a number of helpful leaflets and
will find you accommodation for £3.

Sleeping & Eating

Lindau Lodge (☎ 640792; 71 Royal Pde; per person
from £18) This homey and clean B&B is five
minutes' walk west of the centre along the
seafront and is the best choice of places

THE LAST INVASION OF ENGLAND

The Battle of Hastings in 1066 was a dramatic event. Harold's army arrived on the scene on 14 October and created a three-ring defence consisting of archers, cavalry, and infantry. William marched
north from Hastings and took up a position about 400m south of Harold and his troops. He tried to
break the English cordon, but Harold's men held fast. William's knights then feigned retreat, drawing
some of Harold's troops after them. It was a fatal mistake. Seeing the gap in the English wall, William
ordered his remaining troops to charge through, and the battle was as good as won. Among the
English casualties was King Harold who, according to events depicted in the Bayeux Tapestry, was
hit in or near the eye by an arrow. While he tried to pull the arrow from his head he was struck by
Norman knights. At the news of his death the last of the English resistance collapsed.

In their wonderfully irreverent *1066 And All That*, published in 1930, WC Sellar and RJ Yeat-
man suggest that 'the Norman conquest was a Good Thing, as from this time onward England
stopped being conquered and thus was able to become top nation…' When you consider that
England hasn't been successfully invaded since, it's hard to disagree.

around here. A three-course evening meal costs £10.

Alexandra Hotel (☎ 720131; www.alexandrahotel .mistral.co.uk; King Edward's Pde; per person £28) In a grand, white Victorian on the seafront, this (small) dog-friendly hotel also has special terms for children. For a sea view, rates increase by £4 per person.

Nessa's Plaice (☎ 258-260 Terminus Rd; ☺ 10am-7pm) Classic fish and chips (from a fry vat a block long) can be had at this old favourite across from the sea.

Lamb (☎ 720545; cnr High St & Ocklynge Rd; mains £5-8) For standard hearty pub fare in the Old Town, the Lamb is the place to go.

Getting There & Away

National Express runs one bus a day to Eastbourne from London Victoria, departing at 3pm (£10.50, 2¾ hours), plus an 8.45am bus from Eastbourne to Brighton (£3.25, 55 minutes). The slower No 712 runs three times an hour (twice hourly on Sunday) to Brighton (one hour 20 minutes). Bus No 711 runs hourly (every two hours on Sunday) from Dover to Eastbourne (£5.20, 2¾ hours).

Trains from London Victoria leave every half-hour for Eastbourne (£18.50, 1½ hours), and there are half-hourly trains (20 minutes) between Eastbourne and Brighton.

AROUND EASTBOURNE
Beachy Head

The chalk cliffs at Beachy Head are the highest point of the Seven Sisters Cliffs that mark this rugged stretch of coast at the southern end of the South Downs. The sheer, 175m-high coastal cliffs are awe-inspiring enough, but when they're chalk white and backed by emerald-green turf they're breathtaking.

A few miles along the coast past Beachy Head is the seaside village (more like a collection of houses) of Burling Gap. Here you'll find the **Thatched Bar** (☎ 01323-423197; ☺ 11am-11pm Mon-Sat, noon-11pm Sun) at the Burling Gap Hotel, a country pub with good food and ice cream. You can access the rocky beach below the stupendous pub by a set of metal stairs riveted to the side of the cliff, and it's possible to make the several-mile walk all the way back to the lighthouse. Just watch the tide.

If you're coming by car, Beachy Head is off the B2103, from the A259 between Eastbourne and Newhaven. Follow the road along the cliffs until you reach Burling Gap.

THE LONG MAN

If you're travelling along the A27 between Eastbourne and Lewes, be sure to look southwards out the window, just east of the town of Wilmington, to see the stick-figure-like **Long Man of Wilmington**. No-one really knows how this 70m-high man got here. The original markings in the grass have been replaced by white concrete blocks to preserve the image.

There is a turn-off for the Long Man at the town of Wilmington from where you can get a better view. Wilmington is 7 miles west of Eastbourne. If you're walking this section of the South Downs, you will pass him and get a close-up view.

BRIGHTON & HOVE
☎ 01273 / pop 206,648

With its retro boutique shops, cool bars, fabulous restaurants, art galleries and vibrant, diverse crowds, the coastal city of Brighton is making a strong play as one of England's most happening places to visit. Without doubt, this should be a highlight of any visit to this part of the country. In December of 2000, Brighton Town merged with its less well-known neighbour Hove to become Brighton & Hove, though the locals most always leave off the Hove.

The great thing about Brighton is its diversity. You'll find beef-eating urban jetsetters rubbing elbows with vegetarian dread-locked hippies as well as transvestites in six-inch heels strolling past young mums and their push carts. Throw this mix into a laid-back seaside atmosphere with a large (but rocky) beach front and crowds of sunbathing beauties and there's nowhere else you could be but Brighton. Whatever you're into, there's a spot for you here.

Brighton's wonderful eccentricity can be traced to the beginning of the 19th century when the Prince Regent came to town to party. For more formal good times George eventually built The Royal Pavilion, now a showpiece museum that's well worth a visit. These days, if it's nightlife you're after Brighton is – relative to its size – easily a match for London and Manchester. It also has some of the best cafés and restaurants south of the M25, though you won't run into London-style prices.

Orientation

Old Steine (steen) is the major road running from the pier to the city centre. To the west is the warren of pedestrian-only streets known as The Lanes, full of good restaurants and boutiques. Immediately north is the North Laine, full of quirky shops and lovely cafés that define the city's more bohemian character. The train station is half a mile north of the beach. The tiny bus station is in Poole Valley. Hove lies to the west.

Brighton's vibrant gay scene thrives in Kemptown, which is east of Old Steine along St James' St.

Information

BOOKSHOPS

Borders Books (☎ 731122; Churchill Square Shopping Centre) CDs, a café and the occasional live event.
Brighton Books (☎ 693845; 18 Kensington Gardens) Second-hand and specialist bookshop.

INTERNET ACCESS

Curve Internet (☎ 603031; 44-47 Gardner St; per hr £1.50; ☺ 10am-11pm) Next door to Komedia Theatre.

LAUNDRY

Bubbles Laundrette (75 Preston St)

MEDICAL SERVICES

Royal Sussex County Hospital (☎ 696955; Eastern Rd) Has an accident and emergency department 2 miles east of the centre.
Wiston's Clinic (☎ 506263; 138 Dyke Rd) For general medical consultations; located under a mile from the centre.

MONEY

American Express (☎ 712906; 82 North St) Has a bureau de change.
NatWest (Castle Sq) Has an ATM near the entrance to the Royal Pavilion.
Thomas Cook (☎ 329872; 153 North St)

POST

Main post office (Ship St; ☺ 9.30am-5.30pm Mon-Sat) There is a smaller branch on Western Rd.

TOURIST INFORMATION

TIC (☎ 292599; www.visitbrighton.co.uk; 10 Bartholomew Sq; ☺ 9am-5pm Mon-Fri, 10am-4pm Sun Easter-Sep, 9am-5pm Mon-Sat Sep-Easter) Has a 24-hour-accessible computer with resources for accommodations, restaurants and sights.

Sights

ROYAL PAVILION

The **Royal Pavilion** (☎ 290900; adult £5.95; ☺ 10am-4.30pm Oct-Mar, 9.30am-5pm Apr-Sep) is an absolute highlight of any trip to southern England. This lavish fantasy is one of the most sumptuously hedonistic buildings you'll see anywhere in England and is a fitting symbol of Brighton's 'un-English' decadence. Unlike so many of the country's grand but slightly dreary stately homes, the Pavilion does not disappoint. In fact, the stunning Moorish and Indian-styled exterior is merely a prelude to the flamboyant, no-expense-spared décor of the rooms inside. This is one hell of a holiday cottage (see the boxed text, p225).

A free visitors' guide is available to take you through the place, room by room, but we strongly recommend that you take one of the guided tours, which take place at 11.30am and 2.30pm daily.

BRIGHTON MUSEUM & ART GALLERY

Aside from its good collection of 20th-century art and design (including a Salvador Dali sofa in the shape of Mae West's lips), **Brighton Museum & Art Gallery** (☎ 290 900; Royal Pavilion Gardens; admission free; ☺ 10am-7pm Tue, 10am-5pm Wed-Sat, 2-5pm Sun) has a fascinating exhibit on world art, including a Hindu shrine created in collaboration with the local Gujerati community. Also worth checking out is the Images of Brighton exhibit, featuring a collection of revealing oral histories of the city.

PALACE PIER

With the Royal Pavilion, this **pier** (admission free) is Brighton's most distinctive landmark and the epitome of seaside tackiness. It's got the usual selection of fairground rides (including the Helter Skelter made famous by the Beatles' song), dingy amusement arcades and food stalls, where you can buy a stick of the famous Brighton Rock. It's cheesy, but because it's the only part of Brighton to bear any resemblance to a typical British seaside resort, it's terrific fun.

On the far side of the beach, you'll notice the remains of the **West Pier** whose middle collapsed late in 2002. Once a Victorian splendour, it now serves as a charred eyesore.

BOOTH MUSEUM OF NATURAL HISTORY

This **museum** (☎ 292777; 194 Dyke Rd; admission free; ☺ 10am-5pm Mon-Sat, 2-5pm Sun) is a Victorian

BRIGHTON & HOVE

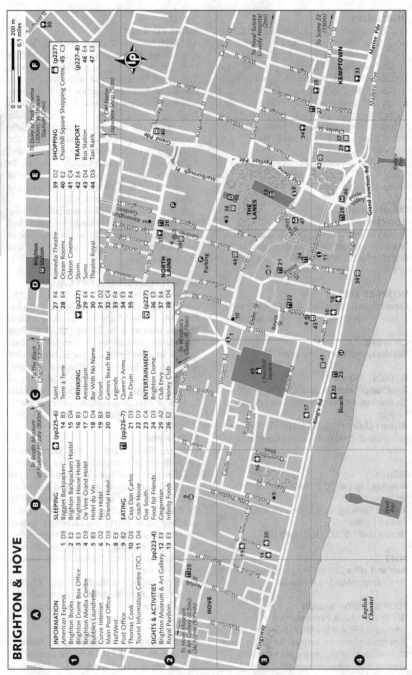

INFORMATION
American Express................1 D3
Brighton Books...................2 E2
Brighton Dome Box Office......3 E3
Brighton Media Centre..........4 D3
Bubbles Laundrette...............5 B3
Curve Internet.....................6 D2
Main Post Office..................7 D3
NatWest.............................8 E3
Post Office.........................9 B2
Thomas Cook....................10 D3
Tourist Information Centre (TIC)..11 D4

SIGHTS & ACTIVITIES (pp223–4)
Brighton Museum & Art Gallery..12 E3
Royal Pavilion....................13 E3

SLEEPING (pp225–6)
Baggies Backpackers............14 B3
Brighton Backpackers Hostel..15 D4
Brighton House Hotel..........16 B3
De Vere Grand Hotel...........17 C3
Hotel du Vin.....................18 D4
Neo Hotel........................19 B3
Oriental Hotel...................20 B3

EATING (pp226–7)
Casa Don Carlos................21 D3
Coach House.....................22 D3
Due South........................23 C4
Food for Friends................24 D3
Gingerman.......................25 A2
Infinity Foods...................26 E2

Saint..............................27 F4
Terre à Terre....................28 E4

DRINKING (p227)
Amsterdam.......................29 E4
Bar With No Name..............30 F1
Dorset............................31 D2
Gemini Beach Bar..............32 C4
Legends..........................33 F4
Queen's Arms...................34 E3
Tin Drum........................35 F4

ENTERTAINMENT (p227)
Brighton Dome..................36 E3
Club Envy........................37 D4
Honey Club......................38 D4

Komedia Theatre................39 D2
Ocean Rooms...................40 E2
Odeon Cinema..................41 C4
Storm.............................42 E4
Sumo.............................43 D4
Theatre Royal...................44 D3

SHOPPING (p227)
Churchill Square Shopping Centre..45 C3

TRANSPORT (pp227–8)
Bus Station......................46 E4
Taxi Rank........................47 E3

To Booth Museum
of Natural History (800m)

To The Black
Chapati (650m)

To Duke of York Cinema
(300m); Withdean
Stadium (2mi)

To Oki Nami
Japanese Shop (150m)

To Royal Sussex
County Hospital (2mi)

To Winston's Church
Clinic (0.75mi)

To Hove Museum
& Art Gallery (0.5mi);
Oki Nami (500yds)

English
Channel

West
Pier

Palace
Pier

HOVE

KEMPTOWN

THE
LANES

NORTH
LAINE

Churchill
Square

'dead zoo' with more than 500,000 specimens. The bird room is particularly creepy, especially if you've seen Hitchcock's classic movie, *The Birds*. The museum is about half a mile north of the train station. Buses 27 and 27A stop nearby on Dyke Rd from where it's a short walk.

HOVE MUSEUM & ART GALLERY

You may be surprised to know that Hove is the birthplace of British cinema, with the first short film shot in 1898. You can see it, along with other fantastic attractions, at this Victorian villa, built in the 1870s, which houses the **museum and art gallery** (☎ 290200; 19 New Church Rd; ☼ 10am-5pm Tue-Sat, 2-5pm Sun). The children's room lights up with fairy lights when you enter and exhibits include old zoetropes, a magic lantern and a small cupboard with a periscope inside. Highlights also include the Toy Gallery and interactive Film Gallery. Take bus No 1, 1A, 6, 6A or 49.

Tours

Guided tours covering a range of interests can be booked through the TIC. They cost around £4 and take about one hour.

Guide Friday (☎ 746205) open-top buses stop on either side of the Palace Pier and take you around the main sights of Brighton. You can hop on and off as much as you like. Tickets are available from the driver and cost £6.70/2.70 per adult/child.

Brighton Walks (☎ 888596; www.brightonwalks.com; £6) offers a range of standard and offbeat themes including the Quadrophenia Tour (£8), Gay's The Word and Ghost Walk. Call to book and to find out where to meet.

Festivals & Events

The three-week-long **Brighton Festival** (☎ 2929 61, 709709; www.brighton-festival.org.uk) is the largest arts festival in Britain after Edinburgh. Held in May, it has a packed programme of theatre, dance and music drawing performers from all over the world. The programme is available months in advance from the TIC.

Sleeping

There's plenty of choice for accommodation in Brighton, though prices are generally higher than in some surrounding towns. You should book ahead for weekends in summer and during the Brighton Festival.

THE PRINCE, THE PALACE & THE PISS-UP

The young Prince George (1762–1830), eldest son of George III, was not your typical wayward kid. By the age of 17, he was drinking with abandon and enjoying the pleasures of women. But he was the king's heir, and daddy was none too impressed. The elder George's displeasure turned to contempt when his son began hanging out with his dissolute uncle the Duke of Cumberland, who was enjoying himself royally by the sea in Brighton.

George loved the town so much that in 1787 he commissioned Henry Holland (1745–1806) to design a neoclassical villa where he could party. The elegant result, known as the Marine Pavilion, was George's personal pleasure palace. In the years he waited to accede to the throne (when his father was declared officially insane in 1810, he was sworn in as Prince Regent), George spent the bulk of his time organising extravagant piss-ups for himself, his mistresses and his aristocratic mates, which included the day's most notorious dandy and arbiter of fashion, Beau Brummell.

Ever conscious of what was trendy and what was not, George decided in 1815 to convert the Marine Pavilion so as to reflect the current fascination with all things Eastern. He engaged the services of John Nash (1752–1835), who laboured for eight years to create a Mogul Indian–style palace, complete with the most lavish Chinese interior imaginable.

George finally had a palace suited to his outlandish tastes, and to boot he was now the king. He continued to throw parties, but the boundless energy of his youth was fast disappearing, and he last visited Brighton in 1827. Three years later, he died of respiratory problems.

His brother and successor, William IV (1765–1837), also used the pavilion as a royal residence, as did William's niece Victoria (1819-1901) when she became queen in 1837. But the conservative queen didn't quite take to the place in the manner of her uncles and in 1850 she sold it to the town, but not before stripping it of every piece of furniture – 143 wagons were needed to transport the contents. Thankfully, many of the original items were later returned by the queen and successive monarchs, and today the house has been almost fully restored to its former elegance.

BUDGET

Brighton's independent hostels are a genuinely relaxed bunch, although some might say a little too much so. What they lack in tidiness, they make up for in atmosphere.

Baggies Backpackers (☎ 733740; 33 Oriental Pl; dm/d £13/35) The best hostel in town. Close to the seafront, it has good facilities, general cleanliness and easygoing atmosphere. There's a £5 room-key deposit.

Brighton Backpackers Hostel (☎ 777717; www .brightonbackpackers.com; 75-76 Middle St; dm per night/week £13/70, in seafront annexe £15/80; ☐) Colourful borders on psychedelic here. It's rough around the edges but has friendly staff.

MID-RANGE

There are a lot of good mid-range hotels in Brighton. Our favourites are among the more expensive. There are loads of moderately priced guest houses just off Regency Sq.

Neo Hotel (☎ 711104; 19 Oriental Pl; s/d £50/100; ✗) This highly recommended bright boutique hotel offers very sleek and modern décor including bamboo wallpaper and cutting-edge art. The hotel does not cater to kids.

Oriental Hotel (☎ 205050; www.orientalhotel.co.uk; 9 Oriental Pl; d with shared bathroom £35, with private bathroom Sun-Thu £55, Fri & Sat £80; ☐ ✗) Stylishly decorated in mint and rouge with a cool atmosphere, its groovy interior is Brighton to a tee.

Brighton House Hotel (☎ 323282; www.brighton househotel.co.uk; 52 Regency Sq; s/d from £35/50; ✗) The proprietor is lovely and helpful at this luxurious Regency hotel on Regency Sq. The rooms are immaculate and breakfast is refreshingly healthy. Sorry, no children.

TOP END

De Vere Grand Hotel (☎ 224300; www.grandbrighton .co.uk; King's Rd; s/d from £170/250; P) The IRA tried to kill Margaret Thatcher and her cabinet here in 1983 by exploding a huge bomb. Now it's all comfort, with luxurious facilities.

Hotel du Vin (☎ 718588; www.hotelduvin.com; Ship St; rooms from £125; ✗) Housed in a collection of Gothic buildings near the seafront, this lovely hotel has attentive staff and a wonderful bistro with an extensive wine list. Rooms are thoroughly modern and elegant.

Eating

Brighton has the best dining options on the south coast. Wander around the Lanes and North Laine or walk along Preston St,

which runs back from the seafront near West Pier, and you'll uncover a wide selection of cafés, diners and restaurants.

BUDGET

Food For Friends (☎ 202310; 17a Prince Albert St; mains £4-8; 🕙 11.30am-10pm) The very inventive vegetarian food is complemented by a bright interior and staff. With organic beer.

Coach House (☎ 719000; www.coachhousebrighton .com; 59a Middle St; mains £8-11; 🕙 lunch & dinner) The eclectic menu at this bright and stylish former coach house includes Italian and Moroccan as well as the Sunday roast. Sip a cappuccino or bar drink by the courtyard fountain.

For a Zen moment amid the bustle, meditate on the Japanese cuisine at **Oki Nami** (☎ 773777; www.okinami.com; 208 New Church Rd, Hove; mains £8.95-15.95; 🕙 lunch Wed-Sun, dinner Mon-Sun), an intimate spot. Or snatch a *bento* box (£2.50 to £4.40) and a Hello Kitty purse at **Oki Nami Japanese Shop** (☎ 677702; 12 York Pl; 🕙 8.30am-6.30pm) across from St Peter's Church and head back into the fray.

Infinity Foods (25 North Rd; 🕙 9.30am-6pm Mon-Sat, 11am-4pm Sun) is a natural and organic grocery co-op on the North Laine.

MID-RANGE

Saint (☎ 607835; 22 St James' St; mains £8-11; 🕙 lunch & dinner Tue-Sun) The Italian and Spanish bistro cuisine, such as Lamb Navarin with leek pomme purée (the menu changes weekly), is popular so book ahead at weekends.

Casa Don Carlos (☎ 327177, 303274; 5 Union St, The Lanes; tapas £3-6; 🕙 lunch & dinner Mon-Sun; ✗) Tables spill out onto a brick pedestrian lane in this fabulous tapas spot that captures the rustic, casual elegance of Spain.

Terre á Terre (☎ 729051; 71 East St; mains £10-15; 🕙 lunch & dinner Wed-Sun) Orange walls hold large oil paintings and a Colour Field mural in this refined and well-known vegetarian restaurant. The staff are very professional.

Due South (☎ 821218; 139 Kings Rd Arches; mains £11-14; 🕙 lunch & dinner) Only local and organic ingredients are used in the English and French fare. Look out for the open-arched windows of the upstairs dining room or sit near the promenade for refined beachfront dining.

De Vere Grand (☎ 224300; King's Rd; afternoon tea £13.50) This is *the* place to go for that most English of afternoon activities. Sit in the conservatory and discover the delights of cucumber sandwiches washed town with tea. Afternoon tea is served from 3pm to 6pm.

Gingerman (☎ 326688; 21a Norfolk Sq, Hove; 2-/3-course £15.95/18.95) You could make a meal out of several of the inventive starters here, although the classic French dishes are also solid and savoury.

Drinking

Brighton's nightlife is on a par with London's so you won't have any trouble finding cool places to wet your whistle in style.

Bar With No Name (☎ 601419; 58 Southover St) The epitome of a Brighton bar, this traditional pub is popular with local artists, clubbers and those simply looking for a good pint and a chat.

Dorset (☎ 605423; 28 North Rd) The laid-back atmosphere is perfect for morning coffee or an evening pint, in the heart of North Laine district. In good weather the doors and windows are open wide.

Tin Drum (☎ 777575; 43 St James' St) This place is known for its East European theme and wide selection of vodka. It gets pretty full on weekend nights, but it's a nice and relaxing spot for Sunday brunch.

Gemini Beach Bar (☎ 327888; 127 King's Rd Arches) On a nice summer's day, there's nowhere better to sit and watch the weird-and-wonderful parade down the promenade than at this perfect beach bar.

Entertainment

Brighton has the best choice of entertainment on the south coast, with a selection of clubs better than you'll find anywhere else outside of London or Manchester. As with anywhere, what's hot and what's not comes and goes with the tide, so keep an eye out for *This is Brighton, The Brighton Latest, The List* or *The Source* to keep on top.

NIGHTCLUBS

If Britain's top DJs aren't spending their summers playing in Ibiza, you'll most likely find them in Brighton. All clubs open until at least 2am, some as late as 5am.

Sumo (☎ 749469; 9-11 Middle St; adult £2) DJs spin the latest in cool R&B and club tunes in this dim lounge with red lighting and hip art.

Honey Club (☎ 07000-446639; www.thehoneyclub .co.uk; 214 Kings Rd Arches; adult £5-12) The crowd is young and out to party at this trendy spot

right on the beach promenade, where cyber and flamboyant dress is encouraged.

Ocean Rooms (☎ 699069; 1 Morley St; adult £1-10) Sumptuously decorated in red – red sofas, red drapes and red cushioned walls – this spot is a favourite with the late-20s/early-30s crowd, who come here at weekends for the excellent soul, funk and disco.

CINEMA

The multiscreen **Odeon Cinema** (☎ 244007; cnr King's Rd & West St) shows mainstream films. The **Duke of York** (☎ 602503; Preston Circus), about a mile north of North Rd, generally runs a programme of art-house films and old classics.

THEATRE

Brighton Dome (☎ 709709; www.brighton-dome.org .uk; 29 New Rd) Once the stables and exercise yard of King George IV, this complex houses three theatre venues within the Royal Pavilion estate. The box office is on New Rd.

Theatre Royal (☎ 328488; Bond St) Built by decree of the Prince of Wales in 1806, this venue hosts plays, musicals and operas.

Komedia Theatre (☎ 467100; www.komedia.co.uk; Gardner St) A former Tesco supermarket, now a stylish fringe theatre and cabaret space in the centre of Brighton.

Shopping

The **Lanes** is Brighton's most popular shopping district, a confusing maze of small streets and tiny alleyways that are chock-a-block with shops and boutiques selling everything from 17th-century rifles to the latest fashions. There's less of a touristy, upmarket feel in **North Laine** – a series of streets northwest of The Lanes, including Bond, Gardner, Kensington and Sydney Sts – which abound with retro-cool boutiques, record and CD stalls, Asian import shops and craft outlets.

Getting There & Away

Brighton is 53 miles from London and bus and train services are fast and frequent.

BUS

National Express has an office at the bus station and tickets can also be bought at the TIC. Coaches leave hourly from London Victoria to Brighton (£9, two hours 10 minutes).

Stagecoach Buses leave Brighton for Arundel (two hours, half-hourly); Chichester (2½ hours, half-hourly); Portsmouth

GAY & LESBIAN BRIGHTON

Perhaps it's Brighton's long-time association with the theatre, but for over 100 years the city has been a gay haven. Gay icons Noel Coward and Ivor Novello were visitors, but in those days the scene was furtive and separate. From the 1960s onwards, it really began to open up, especially in the Kemptown area and around Old Steine. Today, with more than 25,000 gay men and 10,000 to 15,000 lesbians living here, it is the most vibrant queer community in the country outside London.

Kemptown (aka Camptown), on and off St James' St, is where it's all at. In recent years the old Brunswick Town area of Hove has emerged as a quieter alternative to the traditionally cruisy (and sometimes seedy) Kemptown, but the community here has responded by branching out from the usual pubs that served as nightly pick-up joints. Now you will find a rank of gay-owned businesses, from cafés and hotels to bookshops as well as the more obvious bars, clubs and saunas. There's even a Gay's The Word walking tour (see p225).

For up-to-date information on what's going on in Gay Brighton, check out www.gay.brighton .co.uk or www.realbrighton.com.

For dining...
St James' St has plenty of cafés and restaurants to suit your every taste.
Scene 22 (129 St James' St; snacks £2-3) Is where you should go to get the latest word on everything going on in town, make hotel bookings, collect tickets for shows and leave messages on the bulletin board. There is free wireless Internet use with refreshment purchase.

For drinking...
Brighton's gay pubs are generally raucous, no-holds-barred kind of places, but there are a number of cooler, more reserved bars.
Amsterdam (11-12 Marine Pde) Is a European-style hotel, sauna and bar on the seafront that attracts a mixed crowd.
Legends (31-32 Marine Pde) Is modern and cool, with live entertainment and karaoke.
Queen's Arms (7 George St) Has our favourite sign in town: 'A friendly welcome greets you in the Queen's Arms'. There is plenty of camp in the cabaret and karaoke acts, making it a definite stop on the Brighton Sunday trail.

For dancing...
Bars and pubs may be fun, but the real action takes place on and off the dance floor.
Club Envy (8-9 Marine Pde) Is upstairs from Charles St. Cool, sophisticated and trendy, it still gets down and dirty when it's full.
Storm (5 Steine St) Has a more relaxed and friendly feeling as well as the legendary Electro Homo Disco Freakshow on Sunday.

(3¾ hours, half-hourly); Lewes (45 minutes, every 15 minutes) and Eastbourne (one hour 20 minutes, every 15 minutes). Tickets can be purchased from the driver.

Airlinks (☎ 0870 575 7747) is a daily coach service to/from all London airports.

TRAIN
There are twice-hourly services to Brighton from London Victoria and King's Cross stations (£15.90, 50 minutes). For £1.50 on top of the rail fare, you can have unlimited travel on Brighton & Hove buses for the day. There are hourly services to Portsmouth (£13.90, one hour 20 minutes) and frequent services to Eastbourne, Hastings, Canterbury and Dover.

Getting Around
Brighton is spread out, though you'll be able to cover all the sights mentioned on foot.

The local bus company is **Brighton & Hove** (☎ 886200). A day ticket costs £2.70 from the driver.

Parking in Brighton can be a nightmare. To park in any street space, you will need a voucher. They can be purchased from garages and various shops around town and cost about £1 per half-hour but prices do vary.

If you need a cab, **Brighton Streamline Taxis** (☎ 747474), **Yellow Cab Company** (☎ 884488) or **Radio Cars** (☎ 414141) are all worth a try. There is a taxi rank at the junction of East and Market Sts.

Southwest England

SOUTHWEST ENGLAND

Britain is a nation made of many lands, and nowhere is this more obvious than in the southwest of England. From big cities and bustling towns to sleepy villages and countryside hamlets, and from wild heath to windswept cliff the southwest of England has a completely unique character. The old Great Western Railway from London to the southwest – one of Britain's classic train journeys – makes an ideal introduction to the region.

Though the old kingdom of Wessex has long since disappeared (except in the novels of Thomas Hardy), its legacy remains in the present-day counties of Wiltshire, Somerset and Dorset. It's an area rich in heritage and history, home to the ancient stone circles of Avebury and Stonehenge, as well as the upstanding chalk figure of the Cerne Giant, and the supposed burial place of King Arthur at Glastonbury. More-recent history can be found along the stately streets of Roman and Georgian Bath, and in the medieval cathedrals of Salisbury and Wells, but if it's urban thrills you're after, Bristol is the place to head for.

Further west, the counties of Devon and Cornwall – collectively known as the Westcountry – couldn't be more different from each other. Devon boasts miles of unspoiled coast and countryside. Much of its centre is taken up by the rugged tors and rocky outcrops of Dartmoor. Jutting out into the Atlantic west of Devon is the ancient land of Cornwall, once an independent nation with its own language, now best known for its stunning beaches and clifftops. Both counties are steeped in history, dotted with tumbledown castles and lavish country houses, but ground-breaking projects such as the National Marine Aquarium in Plymouth and the Eden Project near St Austell ensures one eye is always on the world of tomorrow.

Southwest England

HIGHLIGHTS

- Admiring the architecture in regal **Bath** (p260)
- Hitting the town in buzzy **Bristol** (p258)
- Climbing the tors and walking the trails of **Dartmoor National Park** (p304)
- Marvelling at the medieval cathedrals of **Salisbury** (p235), **Wells** (p267) and **Exeter** (p292)
- Staring down the centuries at **Avebury** (p246) and **Stonehenge** (p242)
- Hitting the waves off **Cornwall's north coast** (p326)
- Global gardening in the biomes of the **Eden Project** (p315)
- Catching a show at the clifftop **Minack Theatre** (p322) in West Cornwall
- Getting away from it all on the **Isles of Scilly** (p332)

- POPULATION: 2,505,800
- AREA: 7517 SQ MILES

Orientation & Information

The chalk downs centred on Salisbury Plain run right across Wiltshire and through central Dorset to the coast. The granite plateau of Dartmoor and Exmoor dominate much of the Devon landscape, and the central part of North Cornwall is taken up by the largely uninhabited Bodmin Moor.

The railways converge on Bristol and Exeter before cutting south towards the coast, skirting the edge of Dartmoor and continuing west all the way to Truro and Penzance. The main road through the region is the M5, which runs into the A30 just west of Exeter and continues on into Cornwall. Another main route is the A303, which cuts across Salisbury Plain past Stonehenge on its way towards Exeter and Plymouth, before joining the A38 into Cornwall.

The **South West Tourist Board** (www.visitsouthwest .co.uk) covers a huge area from Gloucestershire and Dorset down to the Isles of Scilly. Its website has useful information such as driving itineraries and weather trends, plus links to local sites such as www.cornwall-devon .com, with accommodation listed by town.

Pick up the free monthly magazine *twenty4-seven* (www.twenty4-seven.co.uk) from Tourist Information Centres (TICs), bars and restaurants for previews and listings of events, bars, gigs and clubs.

ACTIVITIES

With such wonderful countryside, from rugged moorland to sweeping bays, it's no surprise that the southwest of England is a haven for outdoorw activities. Regional tourism websites contain walking and cycling information on a variety of routes around the region, and TICs stock leaflets (free) plus maps and guides (usually £1 to £5) covering walking, cycling and other activities.

CYCLING

Gentle gradients and a network of quiet country lanes make Wessex ideal cycling country. Wiltshire is particularly good and the 160-mile circular Wiltshire Cycleway provides a good basis for longer or shorter rides.

Devon and Cornwall make for spectacular cycling, but you'll need legs and lungs of steel. Areas such as Dartmoor and Exmoor are surprisingly hilly, and the coastal routes can be very tiring. Of the long-distance cycle

routes in this region, the West Country Way is one of the most popular – a 250-mile jaunt from Bristol to Padstow via Glastonbury, Taunton and Barnstaple. The shorter Devon Coast to Coast Cycle Route travels for 100 miles through Exmoor and Dartmoor.

For off-road riding, the best areas are Dartmoor and Exmoor, which have many tracks and bridleways, plus some old railways that have been converted for two-wheel use. Other scenic former-railways include the Camel Trail (named after a river – not your form of transport) from Padstow and the Tarka Trail (named after a fictitious but famous otter) around Barnstaple. Bikes can be hired in most major regional centres, including Exeter, Plymouth, Penzance, Padstow and Barnstaple.

WALKING

If you're a mile-eater, look no further than the South West Coast Path; at over 600 miles, it's Britain's longest national trail. Only the hardiest walkers do it all in one go, but following a small section is very popular – the 14-day loop from Padstow to Falmouth is the most scenic stretch and gets the most visitors.

At the opposite end of the region, in northeast Wiltshire, the Ridgeway national trail (www.nationaltrails.gov.uk) starts near Avebury and winds 44 miles (three days) east through chalk hills to meet the River Thames at Goring. The trail then continues another 41 miles (another three days) through the Chiltern Hills (see p175).

As with all long routes, you can use national trails as a focus for short walks of a few hours or several days. Stretches of longer trails that are ideal for short or long walks wind their way along the coastline, and through Exmoor (p275), the Mendip Hills (p270) and the Quantock Hills (p272). Another excellent walking area is the national park of Dartmoor (p304). Larger and wilder than neighbouring Exmoor, Dartmoor has some of the highest hills in southern England and is crossed by several routes, including the popular Two Moors Way, which also crosses through part of Exmoor.

OTHER ACTIVITIES

Other activities include horse and pony riding, especially in Exmoor and Dartmoor; rock climbing on the tors (rocky outcrops)

SOUTHWEST ENGLAND

WALES

To Rosslare (Ireland)
Porthgain
St David's
Newgale
Whitesands Bay
Haverfordwest
A40
Narberth
To Cork
Carew Castle
Pembroke
Freshwater West
Manorbier
Tenby
Pembrokeshire Coast National Park
Carmarthen
Llandeilo
St Clears
A40
Laugharne
Amroth
Llanelli
Rhossili
Gower Peninsula
Swansea
Swansea Airport
Neath
Port Talbot
Black Mountains
Ammanford
Porthcawl

Bristol Channel

Lundy Island

ATLANTIC OCEAN

Isles of Scilly
Tresco
St Martin's
Hugh Town
St Mary's
St
To Penzance (38mi)
0 — 10 km

Ilfracombe
Woolacombe
Croyde Bay
Croyde
Saunton Sands
Barnstaple Bay
Appledore
Westward Ho!
Northam
Clovelly
Bideford
Hartland Abbey
Braunton
Barnstaple
Combe Martin
Lynton
A39
Exmoor National Park
Dunkery Beacon (519m)
Hawkridge
South Molton
A361
Chulmleigh
Witheridge
A377
DEVON
Crediton
Kilkhampton
Bude
Bude Bay
Stratton
Holsworthy
A39
A338
A386
Hatherleigh
A3072
Great Torrington
Okehampton
A3072
CORNWALL
Boscastle
Tintagel
Rough Torn (400m)
Port Isaac
Padstow
Rock
Camelford
Davidstow
Henfort
Launceston
A30
▲ **Brown Willy (419m)**
Bolventor
Jamaica Inn
Bodmin Moor
Bridestowe
Lydford
Milton Abbot
Callington
Tavistock
Cotehele
Calstock
Dartmoor National Park
Merrivale
Dartmeet
Teign
Dewey
Buckfast Abbey
Buckfastleigh
Newton Abbot
Wadebridge
Constantine Bay
Newquay
A39
Bodmin
Lanhydrock House
A30
Trerice
Eden Project
St Austell
Liskeard
Restormel Castle
Lostwithiel
Bodinnick
Buckland Abbey
Lopwell
Saltash
Plymouth
A38
Ivybridge
Compton Castle
Totnes
Dartmouth
St Agnes Head
Perranporth
St Agnes
Mithian
Porthtowan
Portreath
Redruth
Truro
Tregony
Veryan
Portloe
St-Just-in-Roseland
Roseland Peninsula
St Mawes
Charlestown
St Austell Bay
Par
Fowey
Polruan
Polperro
Whitsand Bay
Looe
Torpoint
Modbury
Kingsbridge
Stockenham
Salcombe
South West Coast Path
St Ives
St Ives Bay
St Just-in-Penwith
Land's End
Minack Theatre
Penzance
Hayle
Camborne
Penryn
A394
Helston
Gweek
Falmouth Bay
Falmouth
Helford
Mount's Bay
Porthleven
Mullion
The Lizard
Coverack
St Keverne
Cadgwith
Lizard Point
To Isle of Scilly (see inset) (28mi)
Penzance
St Just-in-Penwith
Portreath
Camborne

SOUTHWEST ENGLAND

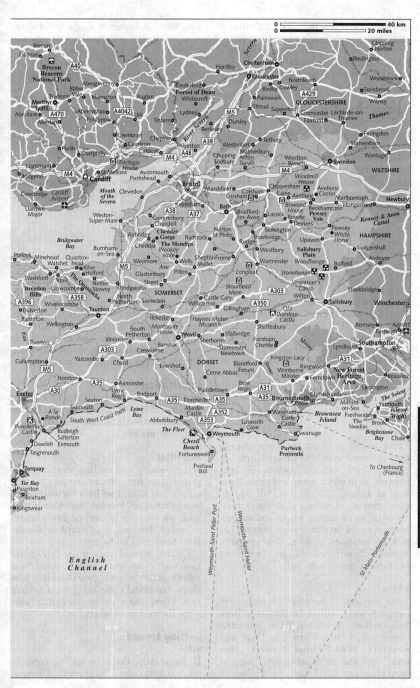

of Dartmoor or on the cliffs of Cornwall; and surfing along the spectacular coastline of Devon and Cornwall. Diving is also a popular activity, especially around Lundy Island, the Isles of Scilly and the many shipwrecks along Cornwall's coastline.

Getting Around

BUS

National Express provides frequent connections to the main towns and cities. Local bus services cover most other areas, though in parts of the Southwest services can be extremely sketchy, and timetables can change without warning out of season. Transport around Dartmoor is skimpy in summer, and virtually nonexistent at other times; the same is true for most of west Cornwall and rural Wiltshire. For regional timetables, call ☎ 01202-673555 in Wiltshire and Dorset, ☎ 01392-382800 in Devon or ☎ 01872-322142 in Cornwall, or contact **Traveline** (☎ 0870 608 2608).

The **First** (www.firstgroup.com) group of companies provides the majority of the region's bus services. The First Bus & Rail Card (adult £10) allows unlimited travel on First Great Western trains and most First buses throughout Devon and Cornwall. The pass can be bought from bus drivers and train conductors, or at Totnes and Plymouth railway stations. Other First passes cover specific areas within the southwest.

CAR

There are plenty of car-hire companies in the region, and most international firms (including Hertz, National, Avis and Budget) have offices in major towns and cities. Rates start at around £35 per day, but bear in mind that short-term and one-way rentals often incur higher prices and one-off surcharges. **UK Car Hire** (www.uk-carhire.net) has pick-up locations in Bath, Bournemouth, Bristol, Salisbury, Swindon and Yeovil, and offers some good deals.

TRAIN

Train services in the west are reasonably comprehensive, with main-line trains from London linking Bristol, Bath, Salisbury, Weymouth, Exeter, Plymouth, Truro and Penzance. Branch lines connect other areas with the main southwest line, but rural areas can usually only be reached by bus. Beyond Exeter, a single line follows the coast as far as Penzance, with spurs to Barnstaple, Paignton, Gunnislake, Looe, Falmouth, St Ives and Newquay. The line from Exeter to Penzance is one of England's most scenic routes.

Several regional rail passes are available, including the Freedom of the South-West Rover pass, which allows eight days' unlimited travel over 15 days in an area west of (and including) Salisbury, Bath, Bristol and Weymouth (adult £61).

For more information on train travel in the region, contact **National Rail Enquiries** (☎ 0845 748 4950; www.nationalrail.co.uk).

WILTSHIRE

Predominantly rural and strewn with relics from the past, Wiltshire is an excellent candidate for roaming. Its rolling chalk downs feature some of Britain's most important prehistoric sites, among them the mystifying stone circles of Stonehenge and Avebury, the spectacular cathedral at Salisbury, a host of sturdy castles and elegant stately homes, and a smattering of stunning stone villages such as Lacock and Castle Combe.

Information

In addition to town and district TICs, **Visit Wiltshire** (☎ 0870 240 5599) and **Wiltshire Tourism** (www.wiltshiretourism.co.uk) have general countywide information.

Activities

Some walking and cycling ideas are suggested in the Activities section on p231. For a historical slant, **Foot Trails** (☎ 01747-861851; www.foottrails.co.uk; 2 Underdown Mead, White Rd, Mere) leads various walks around Stonehenge, Salisbury, Purbeck, Old Wardour Castle, Stourhead and Old Sarum.

Cyclists should pick up the *Wiltshire Cycleway* leaflet from TICs. It details this route and its various options, and lists bike shops and rental outlets. *Off-Road Cycling in Wiltshire* (£6) is a waterproof guide, with maps for mountain bikers.

Getting Around

BUS

Unfortunately, there are gaping holes in the bus coverage of Northwest Wiltshire, so either use your own wheels or be prepared for long waits.

First Travel (☎ 01934-620122; www.firstbadgerline.co
.uk) Has services in the far west of the county.

Wilts & Dorset Buses (☎ 01722-336855; www.wdbus
.co.uk) Covers most destinations.

Wiltshire Bus Line (☎ 0845 709 0899) The Wiltshire
Day Rover pass (adult/child £6.50/4.50) is valid with most
bus operators in the county, and can be bought from bus
drivers.

TRAIN

Rail lines run from London to Salisbury and beyond to Exeter and Plymouth, branching off north to Bradford-on-Avon, Bath and Bristol. Trains from London Paddington to Bath stop at Chippenham, the largest town and transport hub in the county's northwest, which is otherwise uninspiring. Chippenham is a useful jumping-off point for Lacock and Castle Combe.

Unless you're going to Salisbury or Bradford, train travel isn't really useful within the county. The rail coverage isn't good, there aren't many lines, and those that pass through the area stop only at the main centres.

SALISBURY

☎ 01722 / pop 43,335

Centred on a glorious towering cathedral, the gracious market town of Salisbury is a fantastic base for touring the area. It has a host of excellent museums, some wonderful historic buildings and a good selection of accommodation. Despite being a popular spot with tourists, the city retains a remarkably authentic air, the bustling market square providing a keen contrast to the tranquillity of the cathedral close.

Orientation

Salisbury's compact town centre revolves around Market Sq, which is dominated by its impressive guildhall. The train station is a 10-minute walk to the west, while the bus station is just 90m north up Endless St.

Information

Lloyds TSB (☎ 413443; 38 Blue Boar Row)
Main post office (cnr Castle St & Chipper Lane)
NatWest (☎ 0845 610 1234; 48 Blue Boar Row)
Starlight InterNetGate (☎ 349359; 1 Endless St; Net
access per 15min £1; ☼ 9.30am-8pm Mon-Sat, 9.30am-
4.30pm Sun)

TIC (☎ 334956; www.visitsalisbury.com; Fish Row;
☼ 9.30am-5pm Mon-Sat Oct-May, 9.30am-6pm Mon-Sat
Jun-Sep, plus 10.30am-4.30pm Sun May-Sep) Stocks the
useful *Walk Around Salisbury* guide (80p).

Washing Well Laundrette (☎ 421874; 28 Chipper
Lane; ☼ 7.30am-8.30pm)

Sights
SALISBURY CATHEDRAL

A masterpiece of the Early English Gothic style, **Salisbury Cathedral** (Cathedral Church of the Blessed Virgin Mary; ☎ 555100; www.salisburycathedral.org
.uk; requested donation adult/child £3.80/2; ☼ 7.15am-6.15pm Sep–mid-Jun, 7.15am-7.15pm mid-Jun–Aug) is one of the most beautiful churches in Britain. It was built between 1220 and 1258 with showcase pointed arches and flying buttresses, and a feeling of austerity. Little subsequent work was done to interfere with the uniform style apart from the addition of the magnificent spire later in the century. At 123m, it is the highest spire in Britain.

The main entrance is by the highly decorative **West Front**, which is graced by scores of statues. A small door leads into the beautiful cloister passage and on into the soaring 70m-long nave. Lined with handsome Purbeck marble piers, the nave is rather bare, the interior elements having been 'tidied up' by James Wyatt between 1789 and 1792. Look out for a fascinating old **clock** from 1386 in the north aisle, probably the oldest working clock in the world. In the south aisle a **model** shows the cathedral's elaborate construction.

Monuments and tombs neatly line the walls, including that of **William Longespée**, son of Henry II and half-brother of King John. At the eastern end of the ambulatory the magnificent vivid blue **Prisoners of Conscience** stained-glass window (1980) lords over the grandiose **tomb of Edward Seymour** (1539–1621) and **Lady Catherine Grey**. Also at the eastern end is **Trinity Chapel**, the first part of the cathedral to be built. It was completed in 1225 and has beautiful Purbeck marble pillars.

The cathedral's most impressive feature, though, is its soaring **spire**. Added well after the completion of the main building, the additional weight has visibly bent the four central piers of the nave. Flying buttresses were later added externally to support the four corners of the original tower, while buttresses and **scissor arches** at the openings to the eastern transepts reinforced the interior. A **brass plate** in the floor of the nave

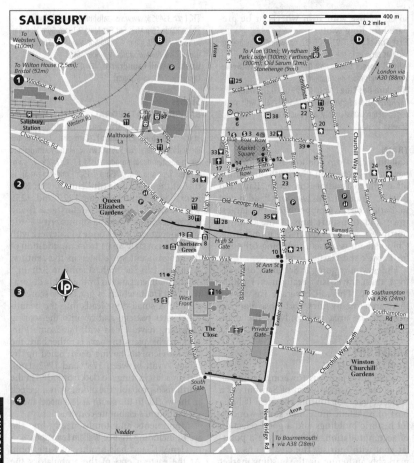

SALISBURY

is used to measure any shift, and reinforcement work on the notoriously 'wonky spire' continues to this day.

You can take a 1½-hour **tower tour** (adult/child £4/3; 11.15am & 2.15pm Mar & Oct, 11.15am, 2.15pm & 3.15pm Apr-Sep, plus 5pm Mon-Sat Jun-Aug).

Before leaving make sure you visit the beautiful Gothic **Chapter House** (9.30am-5.30pm Mon-Sat Sep–mid-Jun, 9.30am-7.15pm Mon-Sat mid-Jun–Aug, noon-5.30pm Sun year-round), which houses one of the four surviving original versions of the **Magna Carta** – the agreement made between King John and his barons in 1215. The delicate fan-vaulted ceiling is supported by a single central column while a medieval, carved frieze around the room recounts Old Testament tales.

CATHEDRAL CLOSE

Salisbury Cathedral has England's largest, and arguably most beautiful, cathedral close. Many of the buildings were erected at the same time as the cathedral, and in 1333 the close was actually walled in, physically separating it from the town. The cathedral at Old Sarum (p240) was a source of building material. To this day it remains an elite enclave, with the wall gates still locked every night.

The close has several museums and houses open to visitors.

The **Salisbury & South Wiltshire Museum** (332151; www.salisburymuseum.org.uk; 65 The Close; adult/child £4/1.50; 10am-5pm Mon-Sat year-round, plus 2-5pm Sun Jul & Aug), in the heritage-listed King's House, contains a very impressive collection, including exhibits from Old Sarum; an interactive Stonehenge gallery; and watercolours of the town by JMW Turner.

In the magnificent, 13th-century **Medieval Hall** (☎ 412472; www.medieval-hall.co.uk; West Walk, The Close; adult/child £2.25/1.75; ⏰ 11am-5pm), a 40-minute audiovisual presentation – *Discover Salisbury* – describes the city's history.

Home to the **Redcoats military museum**, the **Wardrobe** (☎ 414536; www.thewardrobe.org.uk; 58 The Close; adult/child £2.75/75p; ⏰ 10am-5pm daily Apr-Oct, Tue-Sun Feb-Nov) – another impressive 13th-century building – tells the story of a soldier's life over 250 years.

Built in 1701, **Mompesson House** (National Trust (NT); ☎ 335659; The Close; adult/child £4/2; ⏰ 11am-5pm Sat-Wed Easter-Sep) is a fine Queen Anne house with magnificent plasterwork ceilings, exceptional period furnishings, a wonderful carved staircase and a peaceful walled garden.

Other notable buildings include **Malmesbury House**, originally a 13th-century canonry that sports a façade by Christopher Wren; the **College of Matrons** (38 The Close) founded in 1682 for widows and unmarried daughters of clergymen; and the **Bishop's Palace** (now the Cathedral School), parts of which date back to 1220.

ST THOMAS'S CHURCH
In any other town, the splendid **St Thomas's Church** would attract a lot of attention, but it's overshadowed by the cathedral and so is saved from hordes of tourists. Originally built for cathedral workmen in 1219 and named, unusually, after St Thomas Becket (the archbishop murdered in Canterbury Cathedral), the light, airy edifice seen today dates mainly from the 15th century. It's renowned for the superb 'doom' – a **judgement-day painting** – that spreads up and over the chancel arch. It was painted around 1470 and shows Christ sitting in judgement astride a rainbow, surrounded by scenes of heaven and hell.

MARKET SQUARE
Markets were first held here in 1219, and since 1361 the hustle and bustle of cheerful trading has engulfed the square every Tuesday and Saturday. The narrow lanes that surround the square reveal their medieval specialities in names like Oatmeal Row, Fish Row or Silver St, but today the action is confined to the square where you can pick up anything from fresh fish to dodgy digital watches.

The square is dominated by the lovely late-18th-century **guildhall** and, facing it, two **medieval houses**. Immediately behind Market Sq look out for **Fish Row**, with some fine old houses; there is also a 15th-century **Poultry Cross**.

Activities
CYCLING
The ride to Stonehenge along the Woodford Valley is popular – see Getting Around on p239 for bike hire information.

Sleeping
BUDGET
Salisbury YHA Hostel (☎ 0870 770 6018; salisbury@yha .org.uk; Milford Hill; dm £14.90; Ⓟ ☒) In a lovely 200-year-old building in secluded grounds, this hostel has comfortable but basic rooms and is just a short walk from town. The dormitories are pretty big, but there are some smaller dorms available at a slightly higher price.

Matt & Tiggy's (☎ 327443; 51 Salt Lane; dm £11-16) Small and basic, but comfortable, the rooms here are good value and the atmosphere is very laid-back. It's convenient for the bus station and town centre and a good option if you want something more homely than the YHA.

MID-RANGE

Castle Rd has a wide choice of B&Bs between the ring road and Old Sarum.

Websters (☎ 339779; www.websters-bed-breakfast .com; 11 Hartington Rd; s/d £38/48; P X ; wheelchair access) This quiet house in a colourful Victorian terrace is an excellent choice, with fantastic service and attention to detail. The rooms are bright and cheerful with subtle floral décor. Vegan and vegetarian breakfasts are available.

Griffin Cottage (☎ 328259; mark@brandonasoc .demon.co.uk; 10 St Edmunds Church St; d £45-49; X) This largely 17th-century cottage is an atmospheric place to stay with its mix of antique furniture, beamed rooms and modern comforts. Lavender-scented beds, a roaring fire and home-baked bread make it feel very cosy and welcoming.

Farthings (☎ 330749; www.farthingsbandb.co.uk; 9 Swayne's Close; s/d £25/46; P X) Tucked into a beautiful quiet close, Farthings is a distinctive Victorian house with an attractive garden and wonderful views of the cathedral. The spacious rooms have colourful patchwork quilts and simple décor. The cheaper rooms have shared bathrooms.

Wyndham Park Lodge (☎ 416517; www.wyndham parklodge.co.uk; 51 Wyndham Road; s/d £39/49; X P) This classically elegant place has large rooms with coordinating wallpaper and fabrics and period antiques, but it's not too over the top. The house has a lovely garden and is set on a quiet road within easy walking distance of the centre.

Also recommended:

94 Milford Hill (☎ 322454; 94 Milford Hill; s/d £22/44; X) A quiet 17th-century town house with simple but comfortable rooms and pleasant décor.

TOP END

Red Lion Hotel (☎ 323334; www.the-redlion.co.uk; Milford St; s/d £94/122; P X) Much nicer and more atmospheric than the somewhat tacky façade suggests, this 13th-century place was originally built to house cathedral draughtsmen. Pretty, traditional-style rooms with period features and antique furniture surround the charming creeper-clad courtyard.

King's Arms Hotel (☎ 327629; kingsarmshotelsalis bury@fsmail.net; 9-11 St John St; s/d £79/99; P X) Creaky sloping floors, tilting ceilings, crooked beams and plenty of charm make this character-filled old place an excellent choice. The rooms are decorated in a very traditional style but aren't over the top on floral patterns or frills.

Eating
BUDGET

Prezzo (☎ 341333; 52-54 High St; mains £7-9; lunch & dinner) A sleek, modern place with giant windows streaming light into the wood- and leather-bound interior. This Italian stands out from the pizza-pasta norm with some interesting specialities and a cool but unpretentious atmosphere.

Lemon Tree (☎ 333471; 92 Crane St; mains £7.50-9.50; lunch & dinner) This small but light and airy place has a fresh look and a lovely garden and conservatory dining area. The excellent food spans the globe, there are plenty of veg choices and children are welcome.

Thai Café (☎ 414778; 58a Fisherton St; mains £7-8; lunch & dinner, closed Sun) Tucked away above a laundrette, this tiny Thai place uses plenty of fresh ingredients, has a no-MSG policy and very good prices. The food is fantastic and not altered for Western palates, so beware when you order that curry.

MID-RANGE

Afon (☎ 552366; Millstream Approach; mains lunch £5-9, 2-/3-course dinner £15/18; lunch & dinner) A modern brasserie-bar ideal for warm summer suppers. This stylish place has a relaxed and friendly attitude and dishes up innovative international cuisine. The fantastic riverside location is a real plus, and on summer evenings there's an Aussie-style barbecue.

Café Med (☎ 328402; 68 Castle St; 2-course set menu £19; lunch & dinner) A cosy, rustic-style place serving up an eclectic mix of English and Continental (modern and highly traditional), from its buzzing kitchen. There's good seafood, and plenty of vegetarian options.

Mojito (☎ 417999; 2 Salt Lane; mains £6-16; lunch & dinner) This fun, ultramodern bistro has an open kitchen dishing up great modern Mediterranean dishes and interesting tapas (£2.20 to £5.95). The staff also sell a range of Cuban cigars.

SOUTHWEST ENGLAND

Gallery (☎ 500200; 108 Fisherton St; 2-course dinner £15; ☉ lunch Tue-Sat, dinner Thu-Sat) Set in a stylishly restored, 17th-century grain mill, this place has a wonderful outside seating area and a creative menu featuring global cuisine. Specials feature anything from chicken and noodle laksa with coconut and coriander to tomato, fennel and potato stew.

TOP END
LXIX (☎ 340000; 67-69 New St; mains £9-19; ☉ lunch & dinner Mon-Sat) Cool, trendy and exclusive, Salisbury's hottest restaurant serves up creative modern British cuisine in sleek and stylish surroundings. The **Aprés LXIX** (☎ 320000; mains £5-13) bistro next door is more relaxed and cheaper, but equally good.

Drinking
Haunch of Venison (☎ 322024; 1-5 Minster St) A medieval pub with lots of little nooks and crannies. This wonderful bar serves more than 50 malt whiskies. It also has excellent food in its top-floor restaurant (mains £5 to £14) ranging from wraps and salads to venison steak and aubergine caviar.

Escoba (☎ 329608; 5-7 Winchester St) A modern, funky Spanish bar with big comfy seats, giant windows and a good range of tasty tapas (£3 to £6). It serves a young bubbly crowd who throng the place at weekends.

Moloko (☎ 507050; 5 Bridge St) A hip and happening little joint with passionate red décor and some wannabe-trendy clientele. Moloko is a late night haunt with DJs at weekends and an alarming array of flavoured vodkas.

Spirit (☎ 338387; 46 Catherine St) A trendy bar-club with DJs, cocktails and a range of tunes from live music on Wednesday night to Thursday hip-hop, weekend house and Sunday night mellow vibes. This place generally acts as a pre-club venue for sister act NN Bar next door.

Entertainment
Classical concerts take place regularly at many venues around town. Visit www.music insalisbury.org for up-to-date listings and information.

Salisbury Arts Centre (☎ 321744; www.salisbury artscentre.co.uk; Bedwin St) is one of the best in the south and has an interesting programme of contemporary music and theatre performances. Alternatively, you'll find highbrow classical dramas, musicals, comedy and new writing at the **Salisbury Playhouse** (☎ 320333; www.salisburyplayhouse.com; Malthouse Lane).

Getting There & Away
BUS
Three National Express coaches run daily to London via Heathrow (£13, three hours). There is only one service to Bath (£7.75, 1½ hours) and Bristol (£7.75, two hours).

Local bus X4 runs hourly via Wilton (10 minutes) to Warminster (one hour), from where there are immediate connections on buses X5 and X6 to Bath (two hours) via Bradford-on-Avon (1½ hours). Bus X3 runs to Bournemouth (1¼ hours) and Poole (1½ hours) hourly Monday to Saturday (every two hours on Sunday).

TRAIN
Trains run half-hourly from London's Waterloo station (£24.20, 1½ hours) and hourly from Salisbury on to Exeter (£21, 1¾ hours). A second line runs from Portsmouth (£11.60, 1½ hours, hourly) or Brighton (£21.60, 2½ hours, hourly) via Southampton (£6.40, 30 minutes, half-hourly) and on to Bradford-on-Avon (£7.50, 45 minutes, hourly), Bath (£10.40, 50 minutes, half-hourly) and Bristol (£12.60, 1¼ hours, half-hourly).

Getting Around
You can easily get around Salisbury on foot. Bikes can be hired from **Hayball Cycle Shop** (☎ 411378; 26-30 Winchester St; per day £10, £25 deposit).

AROUND SALISBURY

Old Sarum

The massive, Iron-Age hill-fort of **Old Sarum** (☎ 01722-335398; adult/child £2.50/1.30; ⌚ 10am-6pm Apr-Sep, 10am-5pm Oct, 10am-4pm Nov-Mar) was home to successive generations from the Romans right through to the Normans. Today the impressive 22-hectare earthworks includes Norman ramparts and ruins of a castle, cathedral and bishop's palace.

The first cathedral on the site was completed in 1092, and although Old Sarum flourished in medieval times, the pope granted permission in 1217 to move the cathedral to a better location. The action immediately shifted to Salisbury (see p235) and Old Sarum was abandoned. By 1331 the cathedral had been demolished to provide building material for the walls of the new cathedral close. A scale model of 12th-century Old Sarum in Salisbury Cathedral provides a good impression of how the site once looked.

There are free guided tours at 2.30pm on Monday, Wednesday and Friday in July and August.

Old Sarum is 2 miles north of Salisbury; between them, bus Nos 3, 5, 6, 8 and 9 run every 15 minutes (10 minutes, hourly on Sunday).

Wilton House

One of the finest stately homes in the country, **Wilton House** (☎ 01722-746729; www.wilton house.com; house & gardens adult/child £9.75/5.50, gardens only £4.50/3.50; ⌚ 10.30am-5.30pm Tue-Sat Apr-Oct; wheelchair access) has been home to the Earls of Pembroke since 1542. The house has marvellous art and furniture collections, and the wonderful grounds have 17th-century landscaping and fantastic water features.

The majestic rooms of Wilton House have attracted plenty of filmmakers; the Single and Double Cube Rooms designed by Inigo Jones with their magnificent painted ceilings, elaborate plasterwork and paintings by Sir Anthony Van Dyck are of particular interest. You can also see the famous Pembroke Palace dolls house (1907) and works by Rembrandt van Rijn, Pieter Brueghel the Elder and Sir Joshua Reynolds.

Wilton House is 2½ miles west of Salisbury on the A30; bus Nos 60, 60A and 61 run from New Canal in Salisbury (10 minutes, every 15 minutes). Last admission is at 4.30pm.

STONEHENGE

A mystical and magical place and one of England's most popular attractions, the 5000-year-old stone circle at **Stonehenge** (EH/NT; ☎ 01980-624715; www.nationaltrust.org.uk/main/news/stonehenge.htm; adult/child £5.20/2.60; ⌚ 9.30am-6pm mid-Mar–May & Sep–mid-Oct, 9am-7pm Jun-Aug, 9.30am-dusk mid-Oct–mid-Mar) is Europe's most famous prehistoric site. The complex still baffles archaeologists, who cannot agree whether it was a gargantuan astronomical calendar or a place of sun worship and ritual sacrifice.

The Site

Construction at Stonehenge started around 3000 BC when the outer circular bank and ditch were erected. A thousand years later an inner circle of granite stones, known as bluestones from their original colouring, was added. Incredibly, these four-ton mammoths had been hauled 250 miles from the Preseli Hills in South Wales.

Around 1500 BC, the huge stones that make Stonehenge instantly recognisable were dragged to the site, erected in a circle and topped by equally massive lintels to make the trilithons (two vertical stones topped by a horizontal one). The sarsen (a type of sandstone) stones were cut from an extremely hard rock found on the Marlborough Downs about 20 miles from the site. It's estimated that dragging one of these 50-ton stones across the countryside to Stonehenge would require about 600 people.

Also around this time, the bluestones from 500 years earlier were rearranged as an **inner horseshoe** with an **altar stone** (a name given for no scientific reason) at the centre. Outside this a **second horseshoe** of five trilithons was erected. Three of these are intact; the other two have just a single upright. Then came the **major circle** of 30 massive vertical stones, of which 17 uprights and six lintels remain.

Much further out was **another circle** delineated by the 58 Aubrey Holes, named after John Aubrey who discovered them in the 1600s. Inside are the **South and North Barrows**, each originally topped by a stone. Between them are two other stones, though not quite on the east–west axis. Surrounding all this is a bank and then a ditch.

The inner horseshoes are aligned along the sun's axis on rising in midsummer and setting in midwinter, but little is really known about the significance of this and Stonehenge's pur-

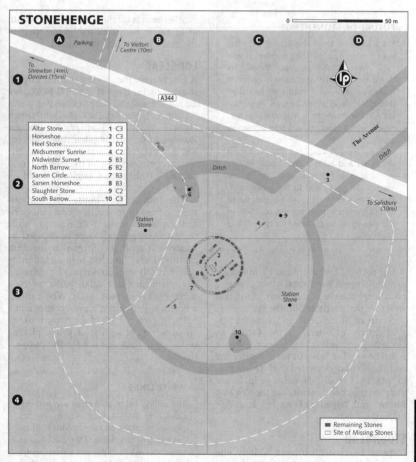

STONEHENGE

Altar Stone	1	C3
Horseshoe	2	C3
Heel Stone	3	D2
Midsummer Sunrise	4	C2
Midwinter Sunset	5	B3
North Barrow	6	B2
Sarsen Circle	7	B3
Sarsen Horseshoe	8	B3
Slaughter Stone	9	C2
South Barrow	10	C3

■ Remaining Stones
□ Site of Missing Stones

pose. Leading out from the site is the **Avenue**, with the entrance to the circle marked by the **Slaughter Stone** (another 18th-century name tag). Further out is the **Heel Stone** on one side. Recent excavations suggest that there may have been a second heel stone.

Admission includes an audio tour but once in, you are kept at some distance from the stones. Private views can be arranged with **English Heritage** (EH; ☎ 01980-626267) if you apply well in advance.

Getting There & Away
Buses leave Salisbury bus station for Stonehenge (40 minutes, nine times daily in summer). They pick up at the train station, from 10am.

There are several companies offering organised tours to the site, including **City Sightseeing** (☎ 01789-294466; adult/child £15/7.50; 3 tours daily Apr-Oct), which runs two-hour tours from Salisbury train station to Stonehenge via Old Sarum. The price of the tour includes admission to the site.

AROUND STONEHENGE
A collection of much-less-visited prehistoric sites surrounds Stonehenge, adding to the mystery of the entire area. The *Stonehenge Estate Archaeological Walks* leaflet details walks round the sites within the NT boundaries. Other prehistoric sites are on private property and are not available to the public.

SOUTHWEST ENGLAND

FUTURE OF STONEHENGE

For a relatively small site, Stonehenge has always received a daunting number of visitors – over 800,000 per year. Despite its World Heritage status, the site is hemmed in by busy roads, and visitors are funnelled through a tunnel under the road. They then stare at the stones from behind a wire barricade, with a constant backdrop of roaring traffic.

There are well-advanced plans to tunnel the roads and build a brand new visitors centre 2 miles from the site, from where visitors will be bussed to the monument. The visitors centre should be completed by 2006 and the road tunnels by 2008. In the meantime, be prepared for crowds and road noise.

Just north of Amesbury and 1½ miles east of Stonehenge is **Woodhenge**, where concrete posts mark the site of a concentric wooden structure that predates Stonehenge.

North of Stonehenge and running approximately east–west is the **Cursus**, an elongated embanked oval whose purpose is unknown. The **Lesser Cursus** looks like the end of a similar elongated oval. Other prehistoric sites around Stonehenge include a number of burial mounds, like the **New King Barrows** and **Vespasian's Camp** (an Iron-Age hillfort).

STOURHEAD

Inspired by classical images of Italy, the estate of **Stourhead** (NT; ☎ 01747-841152; Stourton; house & garden adult £9.40, garden or house £5.40; ☼ house 11am-5pm Fri-Tue mid-Mar–Oct, garden 9am-7pm/sunset year-round) is landscape gardening at its finest. Although the Palladian house itself has some fine Chippendale furniture and paintings by Gaspard Poussin and Claude Lorrain, for most visitors these are sideshows to the magnificent garden.

The garden spreads across the valley beside the house and features stunning vistas, rare plants, magnificent trees and ornate temples. A lovely 2-mile circuit takes you past the most ornate follies, with a 3½-mile side trip to **King Alfred's Tower** (adult/child £2/1; ☼ noon-5pm mid-Mar–Oct), which is a 50m-high folly with wonderful views of the surrounding countryside.

Stourhead is off the B3092, 8 miles south of Frome in Somerset; public transport to the house is virtually nonexistent.

LONGLEAT

A far cry from the sobriety of most English stately homes, **Longleat** (☎ 01985-844400; www .longleat.co.uk; adult/child house & grounds £9/6, grounds & gardens £3/2, safari park £10/7, all-inclusive passport £18/14; ☼ house 10am-5.30pm Easter-Sep, safari park 10am-4pm Apr-Oct, other attractions 11am-5.30pm Apr-Nov) is spectacular if you can see past the blatant commercialism of its extensive franchising, gift shops and 'family-fun' add-on attractions.

The 16th-century house has sumptuously furnished rooms that boast magnificent tapestries and ornate ceilings, while the extensive grounds were landscaped by Lancelot 'Capability' Brown in the 18th century. Today Longleat is run a tad more commercially than Brown may have originally intended with a safari park, mazes, a narrow-gauge railway, a Dr Who exhibit, a Postman Pat village, a pets' corner and a butterfly garden. Each of the attractions has an admission charge, so if you're planing to see more than one opt for the passport ticket.

WHITE LINES

The rolling fields of Wessex are a green cloak over a chalk substructure, and the practice of cutting pictures into the hillsides has a long history. Some of the chalk figures may date back to prehistoric times, though the history of the oldest is uncertain. While Wiltshire has more chalk figures than any other county, the best are probably the 55m-tall Cerne Abbas Giant (with his even more notable 12m penis; p285) in Dorset and the 110m-long Uffington White Horse in Oxfordshire (p350).

Horses were a particularly popular subject in the 18th century, and in more recent times regimental badges and even a giant kiwi have been cut into the hillsides. Kate Bergamar's *Discovering Hill Figures* (Shire Publications) gives the complete lowdown on England's chalky personalities, or pick up the excellent *Wiltshire's White Horse Trail* booklet (£6.50) at Tourist Information Centres (TICs).

Longleat is off the A362 between Frome and Warminster. It's about 3 miles from both towns and has no public transport.

BRADFORD-ON-AVON

☎ 01225 / pop 8800

The narrow and winding streets of honey-coloured Bradford slither down a hillside to the banks of the Avon. Graceful buildings, elegant town houses and wonderful old churches line the streets of this lovely little town, while a huge tithe barn gives a clue to its importance in times past.

The **TIC** (☎ 865797; www.bradfordonavon.com; 50 St Margaret's St; ⏰ 10am-5pm Apr-Dec, 10am-4pm Jan-Mar) sells numerous leaflets (30p each) on attractions and themed walks.

At Cottage Co-op (see p244), Internet access costs £1 for 15 minutes.

Sights & Activities

Bradford is great for rambling around and admiring architecture. A few Saxon buildings bear testament to its earlier history, but it was the growth of the weaving industry in the 17th and 18th centuries that brought wealth to Bradford. The superb factories and grand houses were the showpieces of the town's clothing entrepreneurs.

Start at the TIC and nip into the **Bradford-on-Avon Museum** (☎ 863280; Bridge St; admission free; ⏰ 10.30am-12.30pm & 2-4pm Wed-Sat, 2-4pm Sun Easter-Oct, 2-4pm Nov-Easter) for some local history.

Around the corner is graceful **Westbury House** and the **Town Bridge**. The unusual room jutting out from the bridge was originally a chapel but later became a jail.

Ramble up to **The Shambles**, the original marketplace, and check out the lovely **Coppice Hill** before wandering up Market St and beyond to the attractive terrace houses of **Middle Rank** and **Tory**. The restored **St Mary's Tory** was built as a hermitage chapel in the late 15th century.

Follow the hill down to the 12th-century **Holy Trinity Church**, now almost completely submerged beneath 14th-century extensions and 15th- and 19th-century rebuilding. Just opposite is one of Britain's finest Saxon churches, tiny **St Laurence**, which dates from around 1001.

From here, cross the bridge and take the riverside path to the 14th-century **Tithe Barn** (EH; admission free; ⏰ 10.30am-4pm) on the edge of the bank of the Kennet and Avon Canal. The

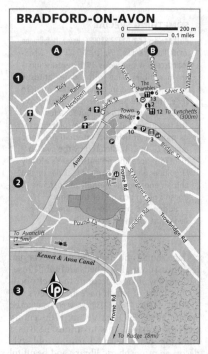

BRADFORD-ON-AVON

imposing 51m-long barn was used to store tithes (taxes in kind) in the Middle Ages.

If you're feeling energetic there's a pleasant 1½-mile walk or cycle ride along the canal to neighbouring Avoncliff, with its impressive Victorian aqueduct.

Sleeping & Eating

Lynchetts (☎ 866400; www.lynchetts.co.uk; 15 Woolley St; s/d £40/60; 🅿 ✗) This 18th-century town house has a charming mix of beamed

---

SOMETHING SPECIAL

Full Moon (☎ 01373 830936; www.thefullmoon
.co.uk; Rudge; s/d £45/69; **P** 🗶 🖥 🛋 ; wheelchair access) A gorgeous 17th-century inn –
an incredible place with some fantastic
rooms decorated in a classic but modern
style. There are also some self-catering cottages if you'd like to chill out for a few days.
The restaurant has a loyal local following for
its modern British and international food
(mains £8 to £14), dictated by the availability of fresh local ingredients. There's a lovely
large beer garden, plenty of real ales on tap
and an endearingly friendly atmosphere. It
doesn't get much better than this.

Rudge is 6 miles south of Bradford-on-
Avon, just off the A36.

---

cottage rooms and high-ceilinged Georgian
reception rooms. Brass beds and subtle rose-
patterned wallpaper decorate the pretty bedrooms, most of which have great views.

Priory Steps (☎ 862230; www.priorysteps.co.uk;
Newtown; s/d £65/85) Originally six 17th-century
weavers' cottages, this luxurious B&B is a
stunning place with charming old-style
décor, an atmospheric library and beautiful
rooms. The views from its hillside garden are
wonderful and children are very welcome.

Cottage Co-op (☎ 867444; 33 Silver St; mains £4-6;
🕙 10am-5.30pm Mon-Sat) This miniature, 17th-
century cottage serves top-notch vegetarian
and organic goodies made with fair-trade
ingredients. There's a retro lounge upstairs
with patchwork cushions, wicker furniture
and Internet access.

Le Mangetout (☎ 863111; Silver St; mains £6-17;
🕙 lunch & dinner) The best place to eat in town,
this light-filled brasserie-bar has few airs
and graces but an excellent modern British
and French menu served up in some style
in the relaxed conservatory.

Getting There & Around

Bath is only 8 miles away from Bradford-
on-Avon, making a day trip an easy option.
Bus Nos X4, X5 and X6 run from Bath (30
minutes, half-hourly, every two hours on
Sunday), continuing to Warminster for an
easy connection with bus No X4 to Salisbury (1½ hours, hourly).

Trains go roughly hourly from Bath (15
minutes).

MALMESBURY
☎ 01666 / pop 6094

The delightful hilltop town of Malmesbury
is somewhat marred by its sprawling suburbs, but persevere and you'll reach the ancient cottages, superb semi-ruined abbey
church and late-15th-century market cross
that mark the centre of town.

The **TIC** (☎ 823748; www.malmesbury.gov.uk;
Market Lane; 🕙 9am-4.50pm Mon-Thu, 9am-4.20pm Fri,
10am-4pm Sat) is in the town hall.

Malmesbury Abbey

A wonderful blend of ruin and living church,
Malmesbury Abbey (☎ 826666; donation requested;
🕙 10am-5pm Mon-Sat mid-Mar–Oct, 10am-4pm Mon-
Sat Nov–mid-Mar) is an evocative place with an
eventful history. The abbey started out as a
7th-century monastery, later replaced by a
Norman church. By the 14th century a massive edifice 100m long had been built, with
a tower at the western end and a tower and
spire at the crossing. It didn't last long. In
1479 a storm toppled the tower and spire,
destroying the crossing and the eastern
end of the church. The west tower followed
suit in 1662, destroying much of the nave.
This left today's church, about a third of the
original, framed by ruins at either end.

The church is entered via the stunning
south porch, its Norman doorway covered
with stone carvings illustrating Bible stories.
The huge **Apostles** are some of the finest
Romanesque carvings in Britain. Steps lead
up to a small room above the porch containing books, including a four-volume, il-
luminated-manuscript Bible from 1407. A
window at the western end of the church
shows Elmer the Flying Monk who, in 1010,
strapped on wings and jumped from the
tower. Although he broke both legs he survived and became a local hero.

Sleeping & Eating

Old Bell Inn (☎ 822344; www.oldbellhotel.com; Abbey
Row; s/d £85/110-170; **P** 🗶) Reputed to be the
oldest hotel in England (c 1220), this luxurious place is a mix of styles from medieval
and Edwardian in the main building to a
Japanese theme in the coach house. It's a
family-friendly place with lots of character,
restrained traditional rooms and an elegant
restaurant (mains £9 to £15).

Whole Hog (☎ 825845; 8 Market Cross; mains £6-12;
🕙 lunch & dinner) This café–cum–wine bar has

a clutter of old, mottled enamel signs on the exposed stone walls, and giant windows letting in a swathe of light. You can choose from a reasonable range of pasta, seafood and steaks or go for the house speciality: hogburgers.

Getting There & Away
Bus No 31 runs to Swindon (45 minutes, hourly Monday to Saturday), while No 92 heads to Chippenham (35 minutes, hourly Monday to Saturday). There are no buses after 7pm or on Sunday.

CASTLE COMBE
☎ 01249
An idyllic English village, Castle Combe claims to be the prettiest in the country and, frankly, this is hard to dispute. With the medieval castle long gone, the charms of this town fall squarely in the hands of the flower-strewn stone cottages of the main street, the gorgeous weavers' cottages by the packhorse bridge and the 13th-century **market cross**.

The beautiful medieval **Church of St Andrew** is central to the village and contains a remarkable 13th-century monument of Sir Walter de Dunstanville, lord of the manor, in chain mail. Bizarrely, there's also a motor-racing track nearby and the whine of engines punctures the peace on still days.

If you want to stay, the atmospheric 12th-century **Castle Inn** (☎ 783030; www.castle-inn.info; s/d £76/100; ✗) has traditional-style rooms complete with exposed beams (and whirlpool baths in many rooms). The restaurant has a good reputation and dishes up a mix of traditional and modern British food (lunch mains £7 to £9, dinner mains around £15).

The people's choice for food is the **White Hart** (☎ 782295; mains £6-12), a homely inn with friendly charm, good sambos (£4) and a traditional pub meals (£7 to £12).

Between them, bus Nos 35, 635 and 75 go to Chippenham bus station (30 minutes) six times daily Monday to Friday and four times on Saturday. On Wednesday bus No 76a makes one trip direct to and from Bath (one hour).

LACOCK
☎ 01249
There are no TV aerials, no yellow lines and no overhead cables in this gorgeous medieval village where most buildings date

from before 1800 – it's almost a surprise to see electric light in the windows. It's a really lovely place, used as a set for the BBC's acclaimed production of *Pride and Prejudice* and, more recently, parts of the *Harry Potter* films. It's well worth a detour here if you're in the area. The NT produces a free *Lacock Abbey* leaflet plotting a route around the most interesting buildings.

Lacock Abbey
Established as a nunnery in 1232, **Lacock Abbey** (NT; ☎ 730227; abbey, museum, cloisters & grounds adult/child £7/3.50, abbey, cloisters & grounds £5.60/2.80; ☻ abbey 1-5.30pm Wed-Mon Apr-Oct; wheelchair access) passed into the hands of Sir William Sharington in 1539. He converted the nunnery into an elaborate home, and the wonderful Gothic entrance hall is lined with many bizarre terracotta figures. Some of the original 13th-century structure is evident in the cloisters and there are traces of medieval wall paintings. The recently restored botanic garden is also worth a visit.

In the early 19th century, William Henry Fox Talbot (1800–77), a prolific inventor, conducted crucial experiments in the development of photography here. Inside the entrance to the abbey, the **Fox Talbot Museum of Photography** (☎ 730459; museum, cloisters & grounds only adult/child £4.40/2.20; ☻ 11am-5.30pm Mar-Oct) details his pioneering work to produce a photographic negative in the 1830s. His grave can be seen in the village cemetery.

Sleeping & Eating
Staying overnight allows you to enjoy the charm of the ancient village once the coaches have gone.

Old Rectory (☎ 730335; www.oldrectorylacock.co .uk; Cantax Hill; s/d £30/50; Ⓟ ✗) This gorgeous neo-Gothic house, just two minutes' stroll from the village, has mullioned windows, creeper-clad walls and great-value rooms. The décor is firmly traditional and there's a quintessentially English croquet lawn and tennis court in the grounds.

King John's Hunting Lodge (☎ 730313; kingjohns@ amserve.com; 21 Church St; s/d £50/75; Ⓟ ✗) Dating partly from the 13th century, this is the oldest house in the village. It's an extremely friendly place with requisite old beams, antique furniture and roaring fires. The rooms are traditional but not over the top and there's a lovely garden for children to play in.

SOMETHING SPECIAL

George & Dragon (☎ 01380-723053; Rowde; mains £9-16; ☽ lunch & dinner) It's food first, beer later at this renowned gastro-pub just outside Devizes. The 17th-century inn is a charming place with low ceilings and outside loos – and a passion for fresh fish. The décor is fish-themed and the daily changing menu on the blackboard relies strongly on its frequent deliveries from Cornwall's shores. Skate with capers and black butter or roast hake with aïoli and red peppers have the punters coming from miles around.

Rowde is 2 miles northwest of Devizes on the A342.

Sign of the Angel (☎ 730230; angel@lacock.co.uk; 6 Church St; s/d £75/100-150; **P**) The oak panelling, log fires and creaky floorboards create a charming and very authentic old-world feel in this 15th-century place. Choose from an antique-filled bedroom in the main house or a rustic cottage across the stream. The beamed dining room serves simple but stylish English food (mains £9 to £17).

Getting There & Away

Bus No 234 operates roughly hourly from Chippenham (Monday to Saturday, 20 minutes) and on to Frome (one hour).

DEVIZES

☎ 01380 / pop 14,379

Centred on its grand marketplace, Devizes is north Wiltshire's largest town and home to some elegant Georgian houses, medieval remains and an excellent museum. It also has its own brewery with shire horses that are still used to deliver beer to local pubs on weekday mornings.

The **TIC** (☎ 729408; www.kennet.gov.uk; Cromwell House, Market Pl; ☽ 9.30am-5pm Mon-Sat) provides the free *Medieval Town Trail* leaflet, and houses a small visitors centre with interactive displays.

Between St John's St and High St, **St John's Alley** has a wonderful collection of Elizabethan houses, with their upper storeys cantilevered over the street. **St John's Church**, on Market Pl, displays elements of its original Norman construction, particularly in the solid crossing tower. Other interesting buildings include the **Corn Exchange**, topped by a figure of Ceres – goddess of agriculture – and the **Old Town Hall** of 1750–52.

There are outstanding prehistory sections with Avebury and Stonehenge artefacts at the **Wiltshire Heritage Museum, Library & Gallery** (☎ 727369; www.wiltshireheritage.org.uk; 41 Long St; adult/child £1/free Tue-Sat, free Sun & Mon; ☽ museum 10am-5pm Mon-Sat, noon-4pm Sun). The museum also has social-history displays and a sizable art collection relating to the county.

Just north of the town centre the **Kennet & Avon Canal Museum** (☎ 729489; The Wharf; adult/child £1.50/50p; ☽ 10am-4.30pm Easter-Sep, 10am-4pm Oct-Dec & Feb-Easter) has displays detailing the conception, construction, restoration and everyday use of the canal. On the western outskirts of Devizes the **Caen Hill** flight of 29 successive locks raises the water level 72m in 2½ miles.

The **Bear Hotel** (☎ 722444; www.thebearhotel .net; Market Pl; s/d £50/75; **P** ✕) in the centre of town dates from the 16th century and combines old world beams with elegant period furnishings. The spacious rooms are traditional in style but not too frilly.

If you're in need of some sustenance, **Healthy Life** (☎ 725558; 4 Little Britox; lunch mains £4-6, dinner 3-course set menu £19.95; ☽ 10am-4pm Tue-Sat) is a sophisticated health-food shop and bistro specialising in sublime organic, fair-trade and vegetarian delicacies.

Bus No 49 serves Avebury (25 minutes, hourly Monday to Saturday, five on Sunday), while bus No 2 runs from Salisbury (1¼ hours, eight daily Monday to Saturday).

AVEBURY

☎ 01672

The massive stone circle at Avebury – bigger, older and quieter than Stonehenge – is an awe-inspiring sight. Although the stones are not as gargantuan as at its more famous neighbour, you can ramble freely between them and even on the busiest days there are none of the overwhelming crowds. Large enough to encompass a whole village, the circle then creeps across the surrounding fields into a complex of ceremonial sites, ancient avenues and burial chambers.

Avebury is also the western end of the Ridgeway national trail.

Orientation & Information

Avebury village has narrow, dead-end streets with no parking. Take advantage of the car park on the A4361 – it's only a short stroll from the circle.

The **TIC** (☎ 539425; allatic@kennet.gov.uk; Chapel Centre, Green St; ✆ 9.30am-5pm Wed-Sun) is right in the centre of the ring.

Sights
STONE CIRCLE

The massive stone circle dates from around 2500–2200 BC, between the first and second phase of construction at Stonehenge. With a diameter of about 348m, it's one of the largest stone circles in Britain. The site originally consisted of an outer circle of 98 standing stones from 3m to 6m in length, many weighing up to 20 tons. These had been selected for their size and shape, but had not been worked to shape like those at Stonehenge. The stones were surrounded by another circle formed by a giant earth bank and an enormous ditch. Inside were smaller stone circles to the north and south.

The circles remained largely intact through the Roman period, and later a Saxon settlement grew up inside the circle. In medieval times, when the church's power was strong and fear of paganism was even stronger, many of the stones were deliberately buried. Later, as the town expanded, some stones were used as building material.

In 1934 Alexander Keiller supervised the re-erection of the buried stones and the placing of markers to indicate those that had disappeared. The wealthy Keiller eventually

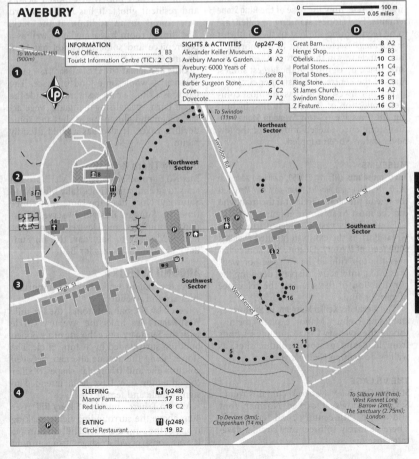

AVEBURY

0 ——— 100 m
0 ——— 0.05 miles

INFORMATION
Post Office......................................1 B3
Tourist Information Centre (TIC)..2 C3

SIGHTS & ACTIVITIES (pp247–8)
Alexander Keiller Museum........3 A2
Avebury Manor & Garden.........4 A2
Avebury: 6000 Years of
Mystery...................................(see 8)
Barber Surgeon Stone...............5 C4
Cove..6 C2
Dovecote......................................7 A2

Great Barn...................................8 A2
Henge Shop.................................9 B3
Obelisk.......................................10 C3
Portal Stones.............................11 C4
Portal Stones.............................12 C4
Ring Stone.................................13 C3
St James Church.......................14 A2
Swindon Stone..........................15 B1
Z Feature...................................16 C3

SLEEPING ⌂ (p248)
Manor Farm.............................17 B3
Red Lion...................................18 C2

EATING ⍓ (p248)
Circle Restaurant....................19 B2

SOUTHWEST ENGLAND

To Windmill Hill (900m)
To Swindon (11mi)
Northeast Sector
Northwest Sector
Swindon Rd
Green St
Southeast Sector
Southwest Sector
West Kennet Ave
High St
To Devizes (9mi); Chippenham (14 mi)
To Silbury Hill (1mi); West Kennet Long Barrow (2mi); The Sanctuary (2.75mi); London

bought Avebury in order to restore 'the outstanding archaeological disgrace of Britain'.

Modern roads into Avebury neatly dissect the circle into four sectors. Start from High St, near the Henge Shop, and walk around the circle in an anticlockwise direction. There are 11 standing stones in the southwest sector, one of them known as the **Barber Surgeon Stone**, after the skeleton of a man found under it. The equipment buried with him suggested he was a medieval travelling barber-surgeon.

The southeast sector starts with the huge **portal stones** that mark the entry to the circle from West Kennet Ave. The **southern inner circle** stood in this sector and within this circle was the **Obelisk** and a group of stones known as the **Z Feature**. Just outside this smaller circle, only the base of the **Ring Stone** remains. Few stones, standing or fallen, are to be seen around the rest of the southeast or northeast sectors. Most of the northern inner circle was in the northeast sector. The **Cove**, made up of three of the largest stones, marked the centre of this smaller circle.

The northwest sector has the most complete collection of standing stones, including the massive 65-ton **Swindon Stone**, the first stone encountered and one of the few never to have been toppled.

MUSEUMS

Two **museums** (NT; ☎ 539250; combined admission £4.20; ⏰ 10am-6pm Apr-Oct, 10am-4pm Nov-Mar) tell the tale of the stone circle and the man who did the most to solve the enigmas.

Housed in the vast, 17th-century thatched Great Barn is the exhibition called **Avebury: 6000 Years of Mystery**. Despite the somewhat over-the-top title, it has a series of well-presented, interactive displays detailing the construction of the site and the relevance of various finds.

The **Alexander Keiller Museum**, in the former stables of Avebury Manor, explains the history of the Avebury Circle and houses finds from here and nearby Neolithic sites, as well as describing Keiller's work.

THE VILLAGE

St James Church (⏰ 10am-dusk) contains round Saxon windows, a carved Norman font and a rare 15th-century rood (cross) loft. There's a lovely 16th-century circular **dovecote** close by.

Graceful **Avebury Manor** (NT; ☎ 539250; manor & gardens adult £3.80, garden only £2.90; ⏰ manor 2-4.30pm Sun-Tue, gardens 11am-5.30pm Fri-Tue) dates back to the 16th century but has Queen Anne and Edwardian alterations; visits are by timed tour only, every 40 minutes between 2pm and 4.40pm. The garden features elegant topiary, and medieval walls.

Sleeping & Eating

Manor Farm (☎ 539294; High St; s/d £40/60; Ⓟ ✗) The only real B&B in the village, this comfortable 18th-century farmhouse has spacious rooms with en suite, pretty, traditional décor and warm, friendly service.

Red Lion (☎ 539266; redlion.avebury@whitbread .com; High St; s/d £40/60; Ⓟ ✗) A creaky, well-worn, thatched pub with exposed beams and resident ghost. It has fairly standard new rooms in an addition at the back. The dining room has a medieval well as a centrepiece and some upmarket bar food (mains £6 to £12).

Circle Restaurant (☎ 539514; High St; mains £5-6; ⏰ lunch) A wholesome kind of place. The Circle is a simple café-restaurant beside the Great Barn, specialising in organic, vegetarian, vegan and gluten-free dishes and some devilish cakes. It also has a child-friendly menu.

Getting There & Away

Bus No 5 from Salisbury and Marlborough runs to Avebury five times daily Monday to Saturday. No 6 does the same route times on Sunday. Bus No 49 serves Swindon (40 minutes) and Devizes (25 minutes, hourly Monday to Saturday, five on Sunday); change at Devizes for Bath.

AROUND AVEBURY

Several excellent walks link the important sites around Avebury.

Lined by 100 pairs of stones, the 1½-mile **West Kennet Ave** links the Avebury Circle with the **Sanctuary**, once the site of a wooden building surrounded by a stone circle. The stones along the avenue alternate between column-like and triangular shapes. Keiller thought they may have been intended to signify male and female.

West of here, massive **Silbury Hill** rises 40m above the surrounding fields, making it one of the largest artificial hills in Europe. It was constructed in stages from around

2500 BC but its purpose is a mystery. Due to erosion, access is now forbidden; you can view the hill from a car park on the A4.

Across the fields south of Silbury Hill stands **West Kennet Long Barrow**, England's finest burial mound, dating from around 3500 BC. Its entrance is guarded by huge sarsens and its roof is constructed of gigantic overlapping capstones. About 50 skeletons were found when it was excavated and finds are on display at the Wiltshire Heritage Museum, Library & Gallery in Devizes (p246).

Northwest of the Avebury Circle you'll find **Windmill Hill**, a Neolithic enclosure or 'camp' dating from about 3700 BC. It's the earliest site in the area.

BRISTOL

☎ 0117 / pop 551,066

Bristol is buzzing. It's an artistic incubator and aeronautical hub, combining hip street culture with cutting-edge technology to make it one of Britain's hotbeds of innovation. Financial success has seen crumbling docks and warehouses rescued and transformed into a host of excellent museums, galleries and interactive attractions. At the same time, the edgy cool of Bristol's youth and the strong tradition of musical creativity means the city is also hip and happening with trendy shops and an endless choice of excellent restaurants, bars and clubs lining the streets.

But there is more to Bristol than its uber-cool image. At one end the genteel suburb of Clifton echoes the elegance of nearby Bath while at the other, massive housing developments battle with serious social problems. Bristol is an evolving city, full of contrasts but riding a wave of prosperity and on the cusp of even greater things to come.

HISTORY

A small Saxon village at the confluence of the Rivers Frome and Avon became the thriving medieval Brigstow (later Bristol), due to its developing trade in cloth and wine with mainland Europe. Religious houses were established on high ground (now the district of Temple) above the marshes and it was from here that celebrated 'local hero'

BRISTOL IN TWO DAYS

Kick-start your tour with a visit to **@tBristol** (p252) before strolling along the waterfront and across to the **Industrial Museum** (p252) for the lowdown on Bristol's history. Grab some lunch at **riverstation** (see Eating, p257) and then hop onto the **Bristol Harbour Railway** (p252) or the **ferry** (p259) and cruise down to the **SS Great Britain** (p253). Return to town and check in to the slick **Hotel du Vin** (see p256) before heading up the Whiteladies Rd for some top nosh and buzzing nightlife. In the morning head up to the **British Empire & Commonwealth Museum** (p252) or stroll down to the beautiful **St Mary Redcliffe Church** (p254). Hop onto bus No 8 or 9 to Clifton for brunch at the **Primrose Café** (p256) or **Clifton Sausage** (p253) and stroll around the leafy streets of Regency grandeur before watching the sun set from the incredible **suspension bridge** (p253).

John Cabot (actually a Genoese sailor called Giovanni Caboto) sailed to discover Newfoundland in 1497. Soon Bristol's wealth was dependent on the triangular trade in slaves, cocoa, sugar and tobacco with Africa and the New World.

By the 18th century the city was suffering from competition, from Liverpool in particular. With large ships having difficulty reaching the city-centre docks, trade moved to new ports at Avonmouth and Portishead instead. Bristol was losing ground fast. To compensate, the city developed a range of manufacturing industries, making it a target for WWII bombing that devastated the centre. Much reconstruction was unfortunate and it is only in the last decade that Bristol has regained its prosperity thanks mainly to the aerospace industry, communications and design.

ORIENTATION

The city centre, north of the river, is easy to get around on foot but is very hilly. The central area revolves around the narrow streets by the markets and Corn Exchange and around the newly developed docklands. Park St is lined with trendy shops and cafés while a strip of Whiteladies Rd, west of the centre, is the hub of bar and restaurant

BRISTOL

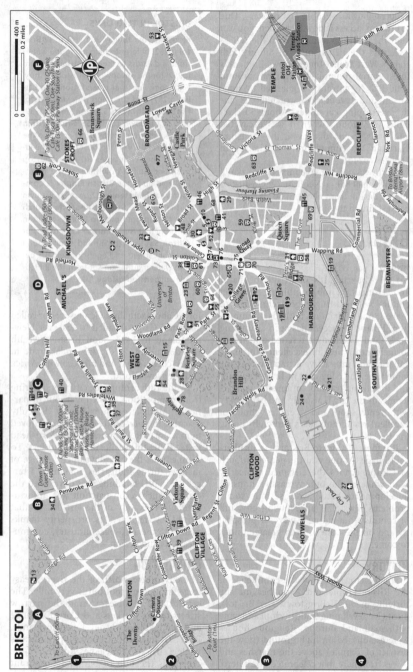

life. The refined suburb of Clifton, with its Georgian terraces and boutique shops, is a short bus ride west of the centre.

The suburb of St Paul's, just northeast of the centre, remains a run-down part of town with a heavy drug scene. It's best not visited alone at night.

The main train station is Temple Meads, a mile southeast of the centre. Some trains use Parkway station, 5 miles to the north. The bus station is on Marlborough St, northeast of the city centre. The airport is 8 miles southwest of town, and the **Bristol International Flyer** runs buses (single/return £5/7, 30 minutes, half-hourly 5am to 11pm) to the airport from Marlborough St bus station and Temple Meads train station. A taxi to the airport costs around £20.

INFORMATION

Bookshops

Blackwell's/George's (☎ 927 6602; 89 Park St) Vast new, used and academic bookshop; if you want it, it's here.
Waterstone's (☎ 925 2274; Galleries Shopping Centre, Broadmead) Good general bookshop in the shopping centre.

Emergency

Police (☎ 927 7777; Nelson St)

Internet Access

BristolLife.co.uk (☎ 945 9926; 27-29 Baldwin St; per hr £2-4; 10am-8pm Mon-Fri, 11am-8pm Sat)

Internet Café (☎ 973 6323; 140 Whiteladies Rd, Clifton; Net access per first half-hr £3, per subsequent half-hr £1.50; 10.30am-7pm Mon-Fri, 11am-6pm Sat, 11am-4pm Sun)

Internet Resources

This is Bristol (www.thisisbristol.com) News, information and what's on at the online version of the *Bristol Evening Post*.
Venue (www.venue.co.uk) Comprehensive details of what's on in Bristol with reviews of restaurants, bars and pubs.
Visit Bristol (www.visitbristol.co.uk) Official tourism website with attractions, events, accommodation and restaurant listings.

Laundry

Alma Laundrette (☎ 973 4121; 78 Alma Rd, Clifton; 7am-9pm)
Redland (☎ 970 6537; Chandos Rd, Clifton; 8am-8pm)

Medical Services

Bristol Royal Infirmary (☎ 923 0000; 2 Marlborough St)

Money

If you're strapped for cash, you'll find all the principal banks along Corn St, including Barclays at No 40, Lloyds at No 55, and NatWest at No 32.

Post

Post office (Upper Maudlin St & The Galleries, Broadmead)

SOUTHWEST ENGLAND

Tourist Information

i-plus points Free touch-screen kiosks scattered around the city providing tourist information.

TIC (☎ 0906 711 2191; www.visitbristol.co.uk; The Annexe, Wildscreen Walk, Harbourside; ☼ 10am-6pm Mar-Oct & 10am-5pm Mon-Sat, 11am-4pm Sun Nov-Feb) Stocks the *Slave Trade Trail* leaflet (£1.60), as well as mini leaflets on literary and maritime walks.

Travel Agencies

STA Travel (☎ 929 4399; 43 Queen's Rd)
Trailfinders (☎ 929 9000; 48 Corn St; ☼ 9am-6pm)

SIGHTS
@tBristol

Next to the TIC in Millennium Sq there's an award-winning complex of attractions, **@tBristol** (☎ 0845 345 1235; www.at-bristol.org.uk; Harbourside; combined tickets: Explore & Wildwalk or Explore & IMAX adult/child £12/8.20, Wildwalk & IMAX £11/7.75, all three £16.50/11.45; ☼ 10am-6pm).

Explore @tBristol (adult/child £7.50/4.95) is Bristol's impressive, interactive science museum. It has four themed zones: brainpower; global communication; the history of technology; and the Curiosity Zone – the latter features fascinating bits and pieces about the planet that aren't covered in the other three sections. There are loads of hands-on exhibits and lots of action for children, who will love this place.

The emphasis at **Wildwalk @tBristol** (adult/child £6.50/4.50) is on the natural world, spanning the breadth of biology from DNA to dinosaurs, with a healthy dollop of enviro-info and a walk-through rainforest.

IMAX (adult/child £6.50/4.50) is a 3-D cinema with a monstrous screen; the eye-popping films tend to relate to the other @tBristol attractions.

Look out for **Cary Grant** (born Archibald Leach in Bristol in 1904) among the many statues in Millennium Sq.

Municipal Museums

The city's municipal **museums** (www.bristol-city.gov.uk/museums) are free and, unless otherwise stated, open 10am to 5pm Saturday to Wednesday from April to October.

The **City Museum & Art Gallery** (☎ 922 3571; Queen's Rd) is a rambling old place with interesting local ceramics and archaeological relics. There are also collections of British and French paintings, and good touring exhibitions. The building itself is beautiful

and there's plenty to keep children occupied, with toddler steps and quiz sheets.

The gritty **Industrial Museum** (☎ 925 1470; Princes Wharf, Wapping Rd; ☼ 10am-5pm Sat-Wed Apr-Oct, 10am-5pm Sat & Sun Nov-Mar), illustrating the city's maritime, rail and aeronautical heritage, has a large collection of model trains and a mock-up of Concorde's cockpit (the supersonic airliner was developed in Bristol). There are also examples of Bristol-built cars, buses and bikes. The steam-driven **Bristol Harbour Railway** (single/return £1/60p) runs along the wharf from outside the museum to SS *Great Britain* (p253); the service operates several times every second weekend from March to October.

The 18th-century **Georgian House** (☎ 921 1362; 7 Great George St) is immaculately presented, complete with period fixtures and fittings; the breakfast room and kitchen are particularly interesting. The house shows life above and below stairs and has some horrific mementos of the slave trade.

The Elizabethan **Red Lodge** (☎ 921 1360; Park Row) was built in 1590 but was much remodelled in 1730; it's now furnished in keeping with both periods. It houses fine, 17th-century French engravings and boasts an attractive Tudor-style knot garden, but the highlight is the Oak Room, with superb carved panels, doorframes and fireplace.

In the northern suburb of Henbury lies **Blaise Castle House Museum** (☎ 950 6789; Henbury Rd), a late-18th-century house and social history museum. Displays include an array of vintage toys, costumes, wonderful paintings and general Victoriana. Across the road is **Blaise Hamlet**, a cluster of picturesque thatched cottages designed for estate servants by John Nash in 1811.

Bus No 43 (45 minutes, every 15 minutes) passes the castle from Colston Ave; bus No 1 (20 minutes, every 10 minutes) from St Augustine's Pde doesn't stop quite as close, but is quicker and more frequent.

British Empire & Commonwealth Museum

Isambard Kingdom Brunel's marvellous old train station at Temple Meads houses the **British Empire & Commonwealth Museum** (☎ 925 9480; www.empiremuseum.co.uk; Clock Tower Yard; adult/child £6.50/3.95; ☼ 10am-5pm; wheelchair access), which tells the story of 500 years of British exploration, trade and conquest. There's everything here

---

THE KINGDOM, THE (STEAM) POWER & THE GLORY

Bristol was home to the Victorian engineering genius Isambard Kingdom Brunel (1806–59), known for, among many other things, the Clifton Suspension Bridge. Brunel was seriously injured while resident engineer on the Thames Tunnel in London: the tunnel breached in 1827 and 1828 and he made daring rescue descents in a diving bell to free trapped workers. While recovering, he entered a competition to design a bridge over the Avon at Clifton. Although his first submission by rejected, his second was chosen as the best option, though he didn't live to see it completed.

Brunel's other achievements were numerous and lauded: he built more than 1000 miles of railway lines; designed the first great transatlantic steamship, the *Great Western*; constructed the first iron-hulled, screw-propeller vessel, the SS *Great Britain* (p253); and the world's largest passenger vessel SS *Great Eastern*.

By any standards he was a workaholic but Brunel also had a lighter side. He sometimes entertained children with conjuring tricks (although he once almost died when a coin lodged in his throat during such a trick!).

---

from old films to Inuit whalebone sunglasses and a Hawaiian feather cape. The museum confronts all the gruesome faces of empire, including slavery, exploitation and disrespect for indigenous culture. A series of fascinating oral histories from across the globe and from Bristol's own multiracial population helps puts everything in context.

SS Great Britain

In 1843 Brunel designed the mighty ocean-going **SS Great Britain** (☎ 929 1843; www.ss-great-britain.com; Great Western Dockyard, Gas Ferry Rd), the first large iron ship to be driven by a screw propeller. For 43 years the ship served as a cargo vessel and a liner, carrying passengers as far as Australia before being damaged in 1886 near the Falkland Islands. The owners sold it for storage and the ship remained in the Falklands for decades, forgotten and rusted, before it was towed to Bristol in 1970. Since then it has been undergoing restoration in the dry dock where it was originally built. Works should be complete by mid-2005.

Moored nearby is a replica of John Cabot's ship *Matthew*, which undertook the journey from Bristol to Newfoundland in 1497.

Entrance is via the informative **Maritime Heritage Centre** (☎ 927 9856; Great Western Dockyard, Gas Ferry Rd; adult £6.25; ☺ 10am-5.30pm Apr-Oct, 10am-4.30pm Nov-Mar), which celebrates Bristol's shipbuilding past.

Clifton & the Suspension Bridge

The genteel suburb of Clifton is often compared to Bath. It too boasts some splendid Georgian architecture, including **Cornwallis Cres** and **Royal York Cres**. The area effectively stretches from Whiteladies Rd to Clifton Village and the river; the further west you go, the posher the houses become. Clifton Village is full of wonderful delis, traditional barbers, interior designers and upmarket shoe shops.

The frequently photographed, 75m-high **Clifton Suspension Bridge** (www.clifton-suspension-bridge.org.uk), designed by Brunel, spans a dramatic stretch of the Avon Gorge and is both elegant and intriguing, with elements seemingly inspired by ancient Egyptian structures. Work on the bridge began in 1836 but wasn't completed until 1864, after Brunel's death. The bridge is an inevitable magnet for stunt artists and, more poignantly, suicides. In 1885 Sarah Ann Hedley jumped from the bridge after a lovers' tiff, but her voluminous petticoats parachuted her safely to earth and she lived to be 85.

A new Clifton Suspension Bridge visitors centre will open in late summer 2005. In the meantime, **guided tours** (☎ 9744665; visitinfo@clifton-suspension-bridge.org.uk) are available by arrangement.

Nearby is **Bristol Zoo Gardens** (☎ 973 8951; www.bristolzoo.org.uk; Clifton Down, Clifton; adult/child £9.50/6; ☺ 9am-5.30pm summer, 9am-4.30pm winter), a facility that aims to promote conservation as well as to entertain. Attractions include a group of West African gorillas, underwater walkways for viewing seals and penguins, and a Brazilian rainforest section where you can get up close and personal with agouti, capybara and golden lion tamarins.

Bus Nos 8 and 9 (10 minutes, eight hourly) run to Clifton and the zoo from St Augustine's Pde; add another 10 minutes from Temple Meads.

Bristol Cathedral

Founded as the church of an Augustinian monastery in 1140, **Bristol Cathedral** (☎ 926 4879; www.bristol-cathedral.co.uk; College Green; ⊙ 8am-6pm) has a remarkably fine Norman chapter house and gate, while the attractive lady chapels have eccentric carvings and fine heraldic glass. Although much of the nave and the west towers date from the 19th century, the 14th-century choir has fascinating misericords depicting apes in hell, quarrelling couples and dancing bears. The south transept shelters a rare Saxon carving of the 'Harrowing of Hell', discovered under the chapter-house floor after a 19th-century fire.

St Mary Redcliffe Church

Once described by Queen Elizabeth I as 'the fairest, goodliest and most famous parish church in England', **St Mary Redcliffe** (☎ 929 1487; www.stmaryredcliffe.co.uk; Redcliffe Way; ⊙ 8.30am-5pm Mon-Sat) is a stunning piece of perpendicular architecture with a soaring, 89m-high spire and a grand hexagonal porch that easily outdoes the cathedral in splendour. The extraordinary, 14th-century south porch is carved with intricate birds and animals, while inside, the beautiful vaulted ceiling has fine gilt bosses. At the entrance to the America Chapel there is a the whale rib presented to the church by John Cabot as a souvenir of his pioneering trip to Nova Scotia and Newfoundland in 1497.

Lord Mayor's Chapel

Once the chapel of St Mark's Hospital, the **Lord Mayor's Chapel** (☎ 929 4350; College Green; ⊙ 10am-noon & 1-4pm Tue-Sun) is a medieval gem squeezed in between shops. It's opposite the cathedral and is packed with 16th-century stained-glass windows, medieval monuments and ancient tiles. Church-loving poet laureate John Betjeman (1906–84) dubbed it 'for its size one of the very best churches in England'.

BRISTOL FOR CHILDREN

Bristol is an excellent city for entertaining children, with loads of hands-on activities and interesting events. On the whole, cafés and all but the most exclusive restaurants are quite tolerant of little people and many have highchairs available. Nearly all hotels

and some B&Bs can rustle up a baby cot or heat up a bottle; confirm when you make your booking. Baby-changing facilities are available in most supermarkets, department stores and shopping centres and at the major attractions.

The city doesn't have a huge variety of playgrounds, but most green areas will at least have some swings and a slide. More formal attractions are numerous, too, though: **@tBristol** (p252) has loads to keep the little ones enthralled; you can become a deck detective on the **SS Great Britain** (p253); **Bristol Zoo Gardens** (p253) has an excellent programme of children's events as well as a really good well-thought-out play area; and the **British Empire & Commonwealth Museum** (p252) and **City Museum & Art Gallery** (p252) have done a lot of work to make their collections relevant to their younger visitors. The **Pirate Walk** (☎ 07950 566483; adult/child £3.50/2.50; ⊙ 6.15pm Tue, Thu & Sat Apr-Sep), a two-hour trail of piracy geared towards children, is also a good bet. If you're visiting in July look out for information on the Bristol Children's Festival.

Most hotels will help to organise a babysitter or you could try one of the following agencies:

Park Lane Nannies (☎ 373 0003; www.parklane nannies.com)

Tinies (☎ 3005630; bristol@tinieschildcare.co.uk)

TOURS

Bristol Tour Guides (☎ 968 4638; studytours@aol.com; tours £3; ⊙ 11am & 2pm Apr-Sep) runs themed walks including Bristol Highlights, Maritime Bristol, Brunel Tours, Bristol Merchants and the Slave Trade, and High Society Clifton. Tours start from the TIC.

City Sightseeing (☎ 926 0767; www.citysightseeing .co.uk; adult/child £7.50/6.50; ⊙ 10am-4pm Easter-Sep) has a hop-on, hop-off open-top bus that visits all the major attractions. Buses leave St Augustine's Pde hourly (every 30 minutes July to September).

Bristol Packet Boat Trips (☎ 926 8157; www.bristol packet.co.uk; adult/child £4/2.50; ⊙ Mar-Oct) is one of a number of companies that runs boat trips (with commentary) around the historic harbour. Cruises last about 45 minutes and depart from the harbour next to the Watershed seven times daily. It also runs several other cruises including a day trip to Bath (adult/child £17.50/13).

GAY & LESBIAN BRISTOL

Bristol has a fairly vibrant gay scene, with the biggest selection of venues clustered in the area behind the Hippodrome. There's no specific gay publication in the city but *Venue* magazine (www .venue.co.uk; £1.20) is a good source for up-to-date listings. Another good bet for information is www.pridewest.co.uk/bristol.

For local advice, information or help try the **Bristol Gay and Lesbian Switchboard** (☎ 942 0842; ⏰ 8pm-10pm).

Following are some of the best-loved spots for a night on the town.

Queen's Shilling (0/-; ☎ 926 4342; 9 Frogmore St) Arguably the city's most popular gay bar, this trendy place with wall-to-wall mirrors lures a young, attractive crowd. It has a late licence and some serious dancing DJs at weekends.

Fusion (☎ 925 6969; 7-9 St Nicholas St) You'll find a mixed but mostly gay crowd at this kicking club with the usual bingo and karaoke nights, live music on Thursday, funk on Saturday and house and tribal sounds on Sunday.

Justwins (☎ 955 9269; 23-25 West St; admission free-£5) There's a strict dress code at this renowned place, but if you're into a wild night out with guys dressed in leather and uniforms then this is the only place to go.

Vibes (☎ 934 9076; 3 Frog Lane; admission free-£4) A popular gay club with a friendly atmosphere, plenty of cheesy retro disco and party pop sounds, and pretty people dancing their socks off.

FESTIVALS & EVENTS

Bristol has a lively annual programme of events. For full details ask at the TIC or try www.visitbristol.co.uk. In April the **bristolive** (www.bristolive.co.uk) international festival for amateur ensembles attracts the crowds, but the real action takes place in July. It starts with the street spectacle of **St Paul's Carnival** (☎ 944 4176) on the first Saturday and follows up with the **Ashton Court Festival** (www .ashtoncourtfestival.co.uk) featuring the best music, theatre and arts from the Bristol area. Also in July is the **Bristol Harbour Festival** (☎ 922 3148), the city's biggest waterside event. In August there's the **International Balloon Fiesta** (☎ 953 5884; www.bristolfiesta.co.uk), when hundreds of hot-air balloons take to the skies, followed by September's **International Kite Festival** (☎ 977 2002; www.kite-festival.org).

SLEEPING

Accommodation in Bristol tends to be far from inspiring in the mid-range bracket. As a given, expect old-fashioned style and service. Pick up a copy of the free *Visit Bristol* for accommodation listings and a handy map.

Budget

Bristol YHA Hostel (☎ 0870 770 5726; bristol@yha .org.uk; Hayman House, 14 Narrow Quay; dm/d £16.40/30; ✗) This restored warehouse makes an ideal base if you're on a budget and is a much better bet than most of the reasonably priced B&Bs. It has all the usual facilities and is at the heart of the Waterfront nightlife area.

Bristol Backpackers (☎ 925 7900; www.bristolback packers.co.uk; 17 St Stephen's St; dm/d £14/35; ✗ ⌨) Another good choice in the centre of town, but slightly more grungy than the YHA. This lively eco-friendly hostel has standard dorm rooms and fairly decent private accommodation. There's cheap Internet access, a bar and discounts on many attractions.

Baltic Wharf Caravan Club Site (☎ 926 8030; Cumberland Rd; tent sites £4-7) A lovely riverside spot just 1½ miles southwest of the centre. This caravan site has only a few tent sites so get in early. To get here take the Baltic Wharf Loop Bus (see p259) or the ferry (see p259).

Mid-Range

Sunderland Guest House (☎ 973 7249; sunderland .gh@blueyonder.co.uk; 4 Sunderland Pl, Clifton; s/d £30/40; P ✗) A great-value choice in posh Clifton, tucked away off Whiteladies Rd and offering simple tidy rooms with restrained décor and vegetarian breakfasts.

Toad Lodge (☎ 924 7080; www.toadlodge.com; 12 Cotham Park, Cotham; s/d £25/35; P) This elegant Georgian house is an excellent-value option, with bright simple rooms, a lovely garden and a friendly atmosphere. It's a little out of the city centre but has regular bus connections.

SOUTHWEST ENGLAND

Tyndall's Park Hotel (☎ 973 5407; www.tyndalls parkhotel.co.uk; 4 Tyndall's Park Rd, Clifton; s/d £48/58; ☒) An elegant Victorian house with period style and grace – this is one of the best places in the Whiteladies Rd enclave. The rooms are traditional in style but are a good size and have understated décor.

Washington Hotel (☎ 973 3980; washington@ cliftonhotels.co.uk; St Paul's Rd, Clifton; s £35-49, d £59-64; P ☒) The simplest and most reasonable of the row on St Paul's Rd. The cheaper rooms share bathrooms but are otherwise great value. The rooms are recently refurbished with a colourful, simple décor and period furnishings.

Naseby House Hotel (☎ 973 7859; www.nasebyhouse hotel.co.uk; 105 Pembroke Rd, Clifton; s/d £45/65; P) Many original Victorian architectural features have been retained at this plush B&B. The charming rooms are bathed in light and decorated in traditional style.

Other recommendations:

Channings Hotel (☎ 973 3970; 20 Pembroke Rd, Clifton; s/d £50/60) Grand but old-fashioned place with decent rooms.

Downs View Guest House (☎ 973 7046; www.downs viewguesthouse.co.uk; 38 Upper Belgrave Rd, Clifton; s/d £40/60; P ☒) Classic-style rooms with period features and fantastic views.

Top End

Hotel du Vin (☎ 925 5577; www.hotelduvin.com; Narrow Lewins Mead; s £125-160; P ☒) Six heritage-listed warehouses have been superbly converted into this designer emporium. The spacious, sleek rooms make the most of the simple elegance of their industrial past and feature wonderful beds, walk-through showers and oversized baths. The New York–style lofts are fantastic.

Berkeley Square Hotel (☎ 925 4000; berkeley@ cliftonhotels.com; 15 Berkeley Sq; s £54-106, d £90-127; P ☒ ▢) Set on an elegant square, this lovely hotel has a mix of classic features (think swag curtains and antiques) in the public rooms and sleek contemporary furnishings in the restaurant and bedrooms. The comfortable rooms have big windows and wide-screen TVs, as well as a complimentary decanter of sherry.

Brigstow Hotel (☎ 929 1030; www.brigstowhotel .com; Welsh Back; d £89-186; P ☒ ▨ ▢) Another designer joint; the Brigstow is all clean modern lines and low lighting. The rooms are stylish but fairly compact and feature

plasma-screen TVs in the bathrooms. It's a fantastic waterside location and ideal if you plan some late-night revelling.

EATING

Eating out in Bristol is a real pleasure, with excellent options in every price category.

Budget

RESTAURANTS

Budokan (☎ 914 1488; 31 Colston St; mains £7-10; ☒ lunch & dinner Mon-Sat) This trendy joint has floor-to-ceiling windows, and contemporary, pan-Asian food served up at communal tables. The flexible menu means you can fuel up on a selection of snacks, plunge for one main course or go for the bargain rapid-refuel menus (£5 to £6.50).

One Stop Thali Café (☎ 942 6687; 12a York Rd, Stokes Croft; set meal £6.50; ☒ lunch) This Bristol institution serves good, honest Asian street food in slightly kitsch surroundings with a jumble of furniture, silk cushions and some rather strange mannequins. There's no menu, just the daily set thali (a combination of six vegetarian dishes) served with rice and salad.

Primrose Café (☎ 946 6577; 1 Boyces Ave, Clifton; mains £4-6; ☒ lunch) Soups, sandwiches, hot snacks and home-made ice cream pull in shoppers and families to this funky little café in the wonderful Clifton Arcade. From Thursday to Saturday evenings it also doubles as a BYO bistro (three-course menu £17.95) specialising in fish dishes.

Mr Wolf (☎ 927 3221; 33 St Stephen's St; mains £4-6; ☒ closed Sun) A real gem that's great when you're in a hurry. This funky noodle bar has colourful décor, a chilled atmosphere and a great selection of Asian classics. It also serves beer and opens late (to 2am) on Friday and Saturday nights.

QUICK EATS

St Nicholas Market (Corn St; ☒ 9.30am-5pm Mon-Sat) Classics such as bangers and beans, jacket spuds and toasties can be found in this warren of stalls, as well as deli breads and cheeses, imaginative sambos at Royce Rolls and sublime goat's cheese and walnut crepes (£1.50 to £2.50) at Crêperie.

SELF-CATERING

Papadeli (☎ 973 6569; 84 Alma Rd, Clifton) Tapas-style takeaways draw the crowds to this haven of edible goodies, which stocks all sorts of delicacies from artichokes soaked in garlic to a fantastic selection of fresh hummus and other dips.

Chandos Deli (☎ 9706565; 121 Whiteladies Rd, Clifton) Queues filter out the door at lunch time at this popular deli. It has an incredible sandwich bar and shelves of fresh sushi, tapas, hand-made tapenade and artisanal chocolate. There are several branches throughout the city.

Mid Range

Clifton Sausage (☎ 973 11192; 7-9 Portland St, Clifton; mains £8.50-14; ☼ lunch & dinner) Church candles, oak furniture and flagstone floors set the atmosphere at this rustic gastro-pub. It's sausage central here, with eight varieties of bangers from which to choose. There's also plenty of classic comfort foods, from potato cakes and black pudding to steak and mussels.

riverstation (☎ 914 4434; The Grove; mains £14; ☼ lunch & dinner) Sleek and chic, riverstation plays host to the city's uber-cool with its adventurous menu and buzzy atmosphere. There's a bright and airy deli and espresso bar on the ground floor and innovative cooking served on the waterside balconies above.

One30 (☎ 944 2442; 130 Cheltenham Rd, Stokes Croft; mains £11-16; ☼ lunch & dinner) New kid on the block – One30 has striped floors, brick walls, leather sofas and a modern bar. Tapas is available during the day but by night it's the delicate flavours of Catalan seafood stew and spider crab on bruschetta that draw the crowds.

Touareg (☎ 904 4488; 77 Whiteladies Rd, Clifton; mains £15.50-17; ☼ lunch & dinner) Sultry North African surrounds with carved woodwork, twinkling lanterns and secluded alcoves make this atmospheric restaurant an excellent choice for an intimate dinner. Tagine, couscous and lamb dominate the menu, though there's also a good choice of meze.

Bells Diner (☎ 924 0357; 1-3 York Rd, Stokes Croft; mains £10-18; ☼ lunch & dinner) This converted '50s grocery shop–turned–bistro dishes up smart contemporary cooking from an array of tempting local organic produce. The creative cooking blends classic flavours with wild ingredients and boasts a loyal following among those in the know.

Top End

Quartier Vert (☎ 973 4482; 84 Whiteladies Rd, Clifton; mains £10.50-18.50; ☼ lunch & dinner) Deceptively simple cooking rules at this impeccable modern restaurant that serves up fantastic rustic Mediterranean food. You can stay in the bar with some tapas (£5 to £7) and a jug of sangria or go the whole hog and book well in advance for a table in the restaurant.

Deason's (☎ 973 6230; 43 Whiteladies Rd, Clifton; mains £13-20; ☼ closed Sun dinner) Stylish minimalist décor, modern artwork and epic flower arrangements set the scene at this ultra-smart restaurant that's frequented by the rich and the beautiful. The food is largely modern British though some Continental and Asian influences manage to sneak in.

DRINKING

The fortnightly listings magazine *Venue* (www.venue.co.uk; £1.20) gives the lowdown on what's on in Bristol and Bath with details of theatre, music, exhibitions, bars, clubs and anything else in the entertainment field. The more upmarket and style-oriented freebie mag *Folio* is published monthly.

Mall (☎ 974 5318; 66 The Mall, Clifton) Deep leather sofas, giant floor-to-ceiling windows and a traditional style make this relaxed but stylish bar an excellent spot for a quiet drink or lazy afternoon. A good range of snacks (£3 to £5) is available including flat breads, pizzas and mussels.

Arc (☎ 922 6456; 27 Broad St) This dark, slightly kitschy little disco bar pulls in the crowds at weekends for a mix of funk, hip-hop soul and disco. The dance floor is tiny, though, so don't plan any big moves.

Cornubia (☎ 925 4415; 142 Temple St) If you're looking for some old-world charm then come straight to this secluded bar. It has a fine selection of real ales and is a great place to meet the local beer lovers and debate the merits of genuine brews.

Elbow Room (☎ 930 0242; 64 Park St) With big windows opening out onto the street this bar/club/pool-hall is a great place for cool, edgy types to hang out on a fine day. There's a contemporary lounge upstairs with jazz, funk and R & B at weekends.

Park (☎ 940 6101; 37 Triangle West) Pre club bar and bohemian hang-out, this stylish place mixes funky beats with classic boogie on Wednesday and Thursday. It also hosts monthly residencies with some of Bristol's finest DJs on Friday and Saturday nights.

Other recommendations:

E-shed (☎ 907 4287; Canon's Rd, Waterside) Funky red hang-out playing hip-hop, house, R & B and drum'n'bass.

Z Bar (☎ 973 7225; 96 Whiteladies Rd, Clifton) Killer cocktails fuel a young and beautiful crowd.

ENTERTAINMENT
Nightclubs

Trendy nightspots come and go with alarming frequency, but there's always something going down along Canon's Rd and at Stokes Croft, though the latter isn't the best place to go wandering after dark.

Lakota (☎ 942 6208; 6 Upper York St; admission free–£15) Long-time Bristol favourite attracting big-name DJs, live acts and elaborate theme nights. Entertainment can feature anything from circus acts and giant projections to hard trance, hardcore, techno and nu-skool.

Thekla (☎ 929 3301; The Grove; admission £5-7) On this moored trawler, the finest funky house music vies with heavy drum'n'bass for the attentions of the young clubbers and vodka-heads on a serious night out.

Hatchet (☎ 941 1808; Frogmore St; admission £3) A 1st-floor youth hang-out with serious attitude and music ranging from garage rock, punk and new wave to electronic '80s and industrial.

Level (☎ 902 2001; 24 Park Row; admission £4) Cool student haunt in a space designed to resemble a '70s airport lounge. Funk, disco, alternative, commercial hip-hop and plenty of booze promotions keep punters happy.

Carling Academy (☎ 0870 711 2000; Frogmore St; admission £6-10) A Bristol institution and happening venue featuring big-name acts and serious DJs.

Theatre

Arnolfini Arts Centre (☎ 929 9191; www.arnolfini.org .uk; 16 Narrow Quay) About to reopen (summer 2005) after a major overhaul, this avant-garde arts centre stages performance art and contemporary dance, as well as housing an exhibition space and one of the city's art-house cinemas.

Bristol Old Vic (☎ 987 7877; www.bristol-old-vic .co.uk; King St) This well-respected theatre sticks with classic and contemporary drama, with occasional forays into comedy and dance.

Hippodrome (☎ 0870 607 7500; St Augustine's Pde) Bristol's giant auditorium, featuring block-

---

BRISTOL'S LIVE-MUSIC SCENE by Julian Owen

There's a fundamental key to understanding the current Bristol music scene: it probably doesn't sound like you think it does. Yes, the shadow of Portishead, Massive Attack et al was a large one – and for too long straightforward rock bands with DJs bolted onto the side hoped to mirror that sound – but Bristol has moved on.

Today, it's ambition – as opposed to coat-tail-hanging – that's driving the scene. Not ambition in the sense of minting a major label deal, but of playing whatever seems right for any given act and to hell with whether anyone else 'gets' it. And, almost despite itself, the resultant, wholly divergent music is increasingly beginning to make waves on a national level. The wonderfully dark, claustrophobic and extraordinary anti-folk of Gravenhurst, for example, has been snapped up by Warp, while the poppy glitch-rock of Chikinki now resides at Island, and War Against Sleep's twisted torch songs have found a home at Fire. Such successes have clearly stirred capital-based A&R bods into action, with increasing numbers heading down the M4 to inquire about – and witness first-hand – the gloriously melodic, harmony-heavy sounds of Valley Forge, the inspired inventiveness of Termites, the brutal onslaught of Ivory Springer, and many more besides.

The other crucial change is the increasing willingness of bands to stage their own shows, and, consequently, a host of venues – including Croft (p259), **Bar Unlimited** (☎ 904 8523; 209 Gloucester Rd), **Polish Club** (☎ 973 6244; 50 St Paul's Rd) and **Seymour's** (☎ 929 0093; 47-49 Barton Vale, St Phillips) – have joined the long-standing Fleece & Firkin (p259) and **Louisiana** (☎ 926 5978; Wapping Rd, Bathurst Tce) as staples of the live scene, with larger touring acts still ably housed in Carling Academy (p258), Colston Hall (p259) and **Anson Rooms** (☎ 954 5810; Students' Union, Queens Rd).

Confidence, in short, is high. And getting higher.

Julian Owen is music editor of Venue *magazine.*

buster musicals, large touring shows and a smattering of opera, ballet and concerts.

Colston Hall (☎ 922 3686; www.colstonhall.org; Colston St) An eclectic mix of opera, comedy, world music and pop.

Watershed (☎ 927 5100; www.watershed.co.uk; 1 Canon's Rd, Harbourside) This art-house cinema has a steady diet of foreign and left-of-centre films.

Live Music

Big names tend to play at Carling Academy (see p258), while a host of smaller venues feature the wave of up-and-coming Bristol bands and smaller tours.

Fleece & Firkin (☎ 945 0996; St Thomas' St) Regular live-music slots from cover bands to aspiring punk rockers.

Croft (☎ 987 4144; 117-119 Stokes Croft) Chilled club-bar and live-music venue with a policy of supporting new music of every style, especially local talent.

Tantric Jazz (☎ 940 2304; 39 St Nicholas St) Live jazz and world music every night of the week at this shabby but chic retro joint that has a loyal local following and a laid-back air.

GETTING THERE & AWAY
Air

Bristol International Airport (☎ 0870 121 2747; www .bristolairport.co.uk) is 8 miles southwest of town. Most flights are holiday charters but there's also a limited number of scheduled flights to European destinations. **EasyJet** (☎ 0870 600 0000; www.easyjet.com) and **British Airways** (☎ 0845 773 3377; www.ba.com) fly domestic routes to Glasgow and Edinburgh. EasyJet also flies to Newcastle, and **Air Southwest** (☎ 0870 241 6830; www.airsouthwest.com) flies to Plymouth.

Bus

National Express coaches travel to London (£14.50, 2½ hours, at least hourly), Cardiff (£6, 1¼ hours, four daily), Birmingham (£15.50, two hours, nine daily) and Exeter (£10.75, two hours, four daily). There's also one bus a day each to Nottingham (£23, 4¾ hours), Oxford (£14.50, three hours) and Stratford-upon-Avon (£15, 2½ hours).

Bus Nos X39 and 337, 338 and 339 run to Bath (50 minutes) several times an hour. Bus No 376 and 377 goes to Wells (one hour, hourly), and No 673 runs to Cheddar

(£3.75, 1½ hours, roughly hourly). You'll need to change in Wells or Bath for most destinations in Somerset and Wiltshire.

Train

Bristol is an important rail hub, with regular connections to London (£34, 1¾ hours, half-hourly). Bath makes an easy day trip (single £4.80, 11 minutes, four per hour). There are also frequent links to Cardiff (£7.20, 45 minutes, hourly), Oxford (£12.40, one hour and 10 minutes, hourly) and Birmingham (£26, 1½ hours, half-hourly).

GETTING AROUND
Bicycle

Hilly though Bristol is, masochists might want to hire bikes at **Blackboy Hill Cycles** (☎ 973 1420; 180 Whiteladies Rd; per day £9; ☯ 9am-5.30pm Mon-Sat).

Boat

The nicest way to get around is to use **Bristol Ferry Boat Co** (☎ 927 3416; www.bristolferryboat.co.uk) boats that ply the Floating Harbour every 20 minutes from April to September (weekends only in winter), stopping at the SS *Great Britain*, Hotwells, Baltic Wharf, the centre (by Watershed), Bristol Bridge, Castle Park and Temple Meads. A short hop is £1.20, or you can pay £5 for a day's unlimited travel.

Bus

Buses run from Parkway Station to the centre every 15 minutes, taking 30 minutes. Bus Nos 8 and 9 run every 15 minutes to Clifton (10 minutes) from St Augustine's Pde; add another 10 minutes from Temple Meads station. The Baltic Wharf Loop Bus (No 500; 10 minutes, half-hourly Monday to Saturday) runs from Temple Meads and St Augustine's Pde.

FirstDay tickets (adult/child/family £3.20/2.30/5.50) are valid on all buses for one day in the Greater Bristol area. Most bus numbers are prefaced by 50 outside peak hours; hence, bus No 8 becomes No 508.

Car & Motorcycle

Bristol's one-way systems seem designed to confuse, and parking can be a problem. **Park-and-ride** (☎ 922 2910; return £2.50, every 10min Mon-Sat) services operate at Portway, Bath Rd, Tollgate and Long Ashton. They're well signed on routes into the city.

BATH

☎ 01225 / pop 90,144

Oh so grand and oh so proud of it, Bath is a tourist's dream and nightmare rolled into one. The city is an architectural gem and the elegant Georgian terraces, grand façades and glorious honey-coloured buildings lining its magnificent streets attract visitors in droves. In the peak season the city is overwhelmed, accommodation is expensive and difficult to find and queues for the main attractions can be long and tiring. Despite this, the Unesco World Heritage city is a must, home to the only hot springs in the country, Roman baths, excellent museums and the languid air of exclusivity that made it the fashionable haunt of 18th-century English society.

HISTORY

Prehistoric peoples probably knew about the hot springs, and legend has it that King Bladud, father of King Lear, founded the town some 2800 years ago; he was supposedly cured of leprosy by a bath in the muddy swamps. The Romans established the town of Aquae Sulis in AD 44 and built the extensive baths complex and a temple to the goddess Sulis-Minerva.

Much later the Anglo-Saxons arrived and in 944 a monastery was founded on the site of the present abbey. Throughout the Middle Ages, Bath was an ecclesiastical centre and a wool-trading town, and it wasn't until the early 18th century that Allen and Richard 'Beau' Nash made Bath the centre of fashionable society.

As the 18th century wore on, sea bathing started to draw visitors away from Bath; by the mid-19th century the city was thoroughly out of fashion. Fortunately for us, most of Bath's grand architecture has been preserved.

ORIENTATION

Like Rome, Bath is famed for its seven hills, and although the city centre is compact it will test your legs. Most street signs are carved into the golden stone of the buildings.

The train and bus stations are both south of the TIC at the end of Manvers St. The most obvious landmark is the abbey, across from the Roman Baths and Pump Room.

INFORMATION
Internet Access
Click (☎ 481008; 13a Manvers St; per 20min £1; ⊗ 10am-10pm)
Retailer Internet Manvers St (☎ 443181; 12 Manvers St; per 30 min £1.50; ⊗ 9am-9pm Mon-Sat, 3-9pm Sun); Walcot St (☎ 445999; 128 Walcot St; per 30min £1.50; ⊗ 10.30am-7.30pm Mon-Sat)

Internet Resources
Bath Quarterly (www.bathquarterly.com) Guide to sights, accommodation, restaurants and events in the city.
What's On (www.whatsonbath.co.uk) Up-to-date listing on the city's events and nightlife.

Laundry
Laundrette (4 St Margaret's Bldgs; per load £2; ⊗ 6am-9pm)

Medical Services
Royal United Hospital (☎ 428331; Combe Park)

Post
Main post office (☎ 0845 722 3344; 25 New Bond St)

Tourist Information
i-plus points Free touch-screen kiosks providing tourist information, scattered around the city.
TIC (☎ 0906 711 2000 (50p per min); www.visitbath.co .uk; Abbey Churchyard; ⊗ 9.30am-6pm Mon-Sat, 10am-4pm Sun) Has a range of leaflets, including the free *Jane Austen Bath Walk*, and can help with accommodation bookings for a £5 fee.

SIGHTS
Baths

The city's steaming soul is the bath-and-temple complex built from the 1st century AD by the Romans, over one of Bath's three natural hot springs. The buildings were left to decay after the Romans departed and it wasn't until the end of the 17th century that the numbers of those coming to 'take the cure' in Bath began to rise again. In 1702 the visit of Queen Anne set the seal on the trend, and a few years later Ralph Allen started his town expansion programme.

The **Roman Baths Museum** (☎ 477785; www .romanbaths.co.uk; Abbey Churchyard; adult/child £9/5, incl Museum of Costume £12/7; ⊗ 9am-5pm Mar-Jun, Sep & Oct, 9am-9pm Jul & Aug, 9.30am-4.30pm Nov-Feb) is one of Britain's most popular attractions and can be overrun in summer. Ideally, visit early on a midweek morning and allow at least an hour to fully appreciate it.

BATH

The monumental remains are some of the best preserved in Britain and your first sight is that of the **Great Bath** from the Victorian gallery terrace. Head down to water level and along the raised walkway to see the Roman paving and lead base. A series of excavated passages and chambers beneath street level lead off in several directions and let you inspect the remains of other smaller baths and hypocaust (heating) systems, while an audio guide explains the details. One of the most picturesque corners of the complex is the 12th-century **King's Bath**, built around the original sacred spring. You can see the ruins of the vast 2000-year-old **Temple of Sulis-Minerva** under the Pump Room, and recent excavations of the **East Baths** give an insight into its 4th-century form.

Outside on Bath St, convenient arcading allowed bathers to walk between the town's three sets of baths without getting wet. At the end of Bath St stands the **Cross Bath** and just opposite is the **Hot Bath**. These two historic sites have been restored and, together with the Hetling Pump Room, are now part of the **Thermae Bath Spa** (☎ 331234; www.thermaebathspa.com; Hot Bath St). Massively over budget and beset by numerous legal problems, Bath's privately run and superbly designed complex was due to open in 2002 but has yet to actually let any bathers in the door. Promises of top-class treatments and a stunning rooftop pool have customers eagerly awaiting the final go-ahead.

Bath Abbey

Edgar, the first king of united England, was crowned in a church in Abbey Courtyard in 973, but the present **Bath Abbey** (☎ 422462; off Cheap St; requested donation £2.50; ☺ 9am-6pm Mon-Sat Easter-Oct, 9am-4.30pm Nov-Easter, afternoons only Sun) – more glass than stone – was built between 1499 and 1616, making it the last great medieval church raised in England. The nave's wonderful fan vaulting was erected in the 19th century.

The most striking feature of the abbey's exterior is the west façade, where angels climb up and down stone ladders, commemorating a dream of the abbey's founder, Bishop Oliver King. The abbey boasts the second-largest collection of wall monuments after Westminster Abbey. Among those buried here are Sir Isaac Pitman, who devised the Pitman method of shorthand,

and Beau Nash. Also worth a look are the choir stalls, carved with mythical beasts.

On the abbey's southern side, steps lead down to a vault in which the small **Heritage Vaults Museum** (adult £2.50; ☺ 10am-4pm Mon-Sat; wheelchair access) describes the abbey's history and its links with the baths and fashionable Georgian society. It also contains wonderful stone bosses, robes and other artefacts.

Royal Crescent & The Circus

The crowning glory of Georgian Bath and the city's most prestigious address, Royal Crescent, is a semicircular terrace of magnificent houses built between 1767 and 1775. Originally, wealthy socialites would have rented the houses by the season.

The grand Palladian town house **No 1 Royal Crescent** (☎ 428126; www.bath-preservation-trust.org .uk; adult/child £4/3.50; ☺ 10.30am-5pm Tue-Sun mid-Feb–Oct, 10.30am-4pm Nov) is superbly restored to the minutest detail of its 1770 magnificence, and is well worth visiting to see how people lived during Bath's glory days; staff dressed in period costume complete the effect.

A walk along Brock St from Royal Crescent leads to **The Circus**, a magnificent circle of 30 houses. Plaques on the houses commemorate famous residents such as Thomas Gainsborough, Clive of India and David Livingstone. To the south is the restored 18th-century **Georgian Garden**, with gravel taking the place of grass to protect women's long dresses from staining.

Assembly Rooms & Museum of Costume

In the 18th century, fashionable Bath visitors gathered to play cards, dance and listen to music in the **Assembly Rooms** (☎ 477785; www .museumofcostume.co.uk; Bennett St; ☺ 11am-5pm Mar-Oct, 11am-4pm Nov-Feb). You can wander around the rooms for free, taking in the grand décor and engravings, but most people head for the basement **Museum of Costume** (adult/child £6/4, incl Roman Baths Museum £12/7). The museum displays costumes worn from the 16th to late 20th centuries, including alarming crinolines that would have forced women to approach doorways side-on. There's an audio guide to talk you through the fickle vagaries of fashion.

Jane Austen Centre

For devotees, a visit to the **Jane Austen Centre** (☎ 443000; www.janeausten.co.uk; 40 Gay St; adult/child

£4.45/2.45; ⏰ 10am-5.30pm Mon-Sat, 10.30am-5.30pm Sun; wheelchair access) is a must. Displays include period costume, contemporary prints of the city and exhibits relating to the author's personal life, family and homes. It's a mecca for fans and insightful for everyone else.

Also of interest is a **plaque** at No 4 Sydney Pl, opposite the Holburne Museum. The plaque commemorates Jane Austen, who lived here for three (not particularly happy) years. She wrote parts of *Persuasion* and *Northanger Abbey* here; both vividly describe fashionable life in the city around 1800.

Other Museums

The splendid 18th-century **Holburne Museum** (☎ 466669; Great Pulteney St; adult £4; ⏰ 10am-5pm Tue-Sat mid-Feb–mid-Dec) houses the booty of Sir William Holburne, a 19th-century Bath resident who brought together an outstanding collection of porcelain, antiques and paintings by great 18th-century artists such as Gainsborough, Turner and Francesco Guardi.

Housed in an 18th-century Gothic chapel, the **Building of Bath Museum** (☎ 333895; www.bath-preservation-trust.org.uk; The Vineyards, The Paragon; adult £4; ⏰ 10.30am-5pm Tue-Sun mid-Feb–Nov) details how Bath's Georgian splendour came into being.

In 1781 William Herschel discovered the planet Uranus from the garden of his home, which now houses the **William Herschel Museum** (☎ 311342; www.bath-preservation-trust.org.uk; 19 New King St; adult £3.50; ⏰ 1-5pm Mon, Tue, Thu & Fri & 11am-5pm Sat & Sun mid-Jan–mid-Dec). The house is decorated as it would have been in the 18th century.

The municipal **Victoria Art Gallery** (☎ 477233; www.victoriagal.org.uk; Pulteney Bridge; admission free; ⏰ 10am-5.30pm Tue-Fri, 10am-5pm Sat, 2-5pm Sun) has changing exhibitions of mostly modern art, and permanent collections of elegant ceramics, Flemish masters and English paintings by Gainsborough and Turner.

The **Museum of East Asian Art** (☎ 464640; www.meaa.org.uk; 12 Bennett St; adult £3.50; ⏰ 10am-5pm Tue-Sat, noon-5pm Sun) contains more than 500 jade, bamboo, porcelain and bronze objects from Cambodia, Korea and Thailand, and substantial Chinese and Japanese carvings, ceramics and lacquerware.

TOURS

Free two-hour **walking tours** (☎ 477411; www.thecityofbath.co.uk) of the city leave from outside the Roman Baths' Pump Room at 10.30am and 2pm Sunday to Friday and at 10.30am on Saturday. From May to September there are additional tours at 7pm on Tuesday, Friday and Saturday.

Guides proudly declare their lack of cultural and historical knowledge on **Bizarre Bath Comedy Walks** (☎ 335124; www.bizarrebath.co.uk; adult/child £5/4.50; ⏰ 8pm Mar-Sep), but these tours offer a hilarious and irreverent look at the city. They leave from outside the Huntsman Inn on North Parade Passage and last about 1½ hours.

Jane Austen's Bath (☎ 443000; adult/child £3.50/2.50) traces the footsteps of the author, on tours leaving the KC Change in Abbey Churchyard at 1.30pm daily in July and August, Saturday and Sunday only September to June. Tours last 1½ hours.

Several companies, including **Classic Citytour** (☎ 07721 559686; adult/child £6.50/2) and **City Sightseeing** (☎ 330444; www.city-sightseeing.co.uk; tours £8; ⏰ Mar-Nov, Sat & Sun only Dec-Feb), offer hop-on, hop-off bus tours around the city operating from about 9am to 6pm every 20 minutes. The tours can be picked up at numerous points around the city centre.

The following Bath-based tours go to Wessex's top attractions. A one-day tour costs about £18.

Danwood Tours (☎ 465965) One-day City Safari tour taking in the Cotswolds, Avebury, Stonehenge, Salisbury and Longleat.

Mad Max Tours (☎ 325900; www.madmaxtours.com) One-day tours visiting Stonehenge, Avebury, Lacock and Castle Combe; and full-day tours of the Cotswolds.

FESTIVALS & EVENTS

The annual **Bath Literature Festival** (☎ 463362; www.bathlitfest.org.uk) takes place in early March and attracts the world of words.

From mid-May to early June the **Bath International Music Festival** (www.bathmusicfest.org.uk) is in full swing with events in all the town's venues. This festival focuses on classical music and opera, although there are also world music and jazz weekends.

Running concurrently with the music festival is the **Bath Fringe Festival** (www.bathfringe.co.uk), the biggest fringe festival in England, involving a blend of comedy, drama, performance art and world music.

Bookings for all events are handled by the **Bath Festivals box office** (☎ 463362; www.bathfestivals.org.uk; 2 Church St; ⏰ 9.30am-5.30pm Mon-Sat).

SOUTHWEST ENGLAND

SLEEPING

Finding somewhere to stay during busy periods can be tough. The TIC will book rooms for a £5 booking fee plus a deposit of 10% of the first night's accommodation. It also sells a brochure, *Bath & Beyond* (£1), with comprehensive listings.

Budget

YMCA (☎ 325900; reservations@ymcabath.co.uk; International House, Broad St Pl; dm/s/d £14/20/32) An excellent option right in the centre of town. The rooms here are immaculately kept and modern but lacking in character. There's a great health suite and a cheap restaurant, and reduced rates for stays of a week or more.

Bath YHA Hostel (☎ 465674; bath@yha.org.uk; dm/s/d £11.80/24/38; P ✗) If you're looking for some cheap crumbling grandeur, this hostel is set in a wonderful old Italianate mansion. It's a steep climb uphill (or a short hop on bus No 18) from the city centre, but the views are magnificent.

St Christopher's Inn (☎ 481444; www.st-christophers.co.uk; 9 Green St; dm/d per person £12/25; ▯) Right in the heart of the city, this new place has comfortable modern dorms and private rooms. It's a bit anonymous but perfectly placed for late night revelling, with discounts available in the pub below.

Mid-Range

Central B&Bs in the guise of 'hotels' tend to be overpriced and nothing special. It's worth moving slightly out of the centre for a much better deal.

Roban House (☎ 445390; www.bathholidayrooms.co.uk; 26 Lower Oldfield Park; s/d £25/40-62; ✗ ▯) A cross between university rooms and a hotel, this cheerful modern place has simple contemporary rooms. Although it doesn't have much character, it's an excellent deal and you get a fridge and DVD player in your room and free broadband access.

Koryu (☎ 337642; japanesekoryu@aol.com; 7 Pulteney Gardens; s/d £40/50; P ✗) Newly refurbished and extolling the values of simple living, this Anglo-Japanese guesthouse is a real treat. The great-value rooms are bright and minimalist and the service is very friendly.

Dorian House (☎ 426336; www.dorianhouse.co.uk; 1 Upper Oldfield Park; s/d from £42/55; P ✗) Pick of the crop in this price bracket, this excellent-value choice has luxurious rooms that blend Victorian elegance and contempo-

rary Italian style. Rooms are furnished with Asian antiques and fine art from around the world. The Stradivari and Elgar rooms have terrific views.

Beckford's (☎ 334959; www.beckford-house.com; 59 Upper Oldfield Park; s/d £48/65; P ✗) The lovely large rooms here are bright and beautiful with king-size beds, oversized showers and lots of books and magazines. Victorian features blend wonderfully with contemporary design and rooms have a pair of binoculars for you to admire the view.

Athole House (☎ 320009; www.atholehouse.co.uk; 33 Upper Oldfield Park; s/d £48/78; P ▯) Sleek, modern and without a hint of chintz, this large Victorian home is set in lovely gardens and has sleek and stylish rooms with good bathrooms. The owners are happy to pick you up from, or drop you off at, the station.

Top End

Bath has some classy hotels and if you're planning to splash out, this is the place to do it.

Royal Crescent Hotel (☎ 823333; www.royalcrescent.co.uk; 16 Royal Cres; d £207-837; P ✗ ❋) Oozing charm and style, Bath's top place to stay is on the grandest of grand crescents and has an understated air of refinement. There's a gorgeous secret garden and the period rooms are simply stunning. Pampering comes extra in the striking hotel spa with its numerous holistic treatments and therapies.

Queensberry Hotel (☎ 447928; enquiries@bath queensberry.com; Russell St; s £100-140, d £100-285; P ✗) Four marvellous Georgian town houses make up this wonderful hotel with secluded terraced gardens and chic décor. The bedrooms blend period character with contemporary style, gorgeous colours and sumptuous fabrics. The hotel is home to the classy Olive Tree Restaurant (p265).

EATING
Budget
RESTAURANTS

Pastiche Bistro (☎ 442323; 16 Argyle St; 2 courses £10; ☯ lunch & dinner) This trendy joint just over Pulteney Bridge has a great choice of international dishes including moussaka meatballs and swordfish on *sag aloo* (sauce of spinach and potato) with mint dressing. The service is as slick as the décor and the food really should cost a lot more.

Walrus & the Carpenter (☎ 314864; 28 Barton St; mains £5-8; ☻ lunch & dinner) There's a warren of rooms at this fun and funky place that dishes up top-notch home-made global cuisine with a heavy vegetarian bias. It does brilliant burgers and some killer Walrus cocktails.

Las Iguanas (☎ 36666; 12 Seven Dials, Saw Close; mains £5-8; ☻ lunch & dinner) Salsa music, vibrant colours and cool lighting set the mood at this lively Latino place, with a good choice of tapas in the bar and everything from *xinxim* (chicken in peanut, crayfish and lemon sauce) to sizzling fajitas in the restaurant. The early-bird menus are brilliant value at £7 for three courses.

CAFÉS
Café Retro (☎ 339347; 18 York St; mains £5-11; ☻ lunch & dinner) This hip, boho hang-out is a bit of a cult classic with café-style dining downstairs and a rush for the window seats upstairs. There's a good choice of paninis, burgers and salads as well as more-substantial fare to go with the super-chilled atmosphere.

Octagon Café (☎ 447991; 43 Milsom St; mains £3-6; ☻ 10am-5pm Mon-Fri) Photos line the walls of this café-cum-brasserie, with a creative menu of delicacies such as warm puy lentil salad with grilled goat's cheese, and almond profiteroles with praline cream. When you're done, scoot upstairs to see the exhibits at the Royal Photographic Society Gallery.

QUICK EATS
Boston Tea Party (☎ 313901; 19 Kingsmead Sq; ☻ lunch & dinner Mon-Sat) Gourmet sambos, soups and smoothies attract the crowds to this trendy joint. Just try making it out the door without giving in to those brownies, too.

F-east (☎ 333500; 27 High St; mains £6-8; ☻ lunch & dinner) For a quick but substantial bite head for this oriental emporium serving a selection of modern pan-Asian food in swish contemporary surroundings.

Mid-Range
Moon & Sixpence (☎ 460962; 6a Broad St; mains £10-15; ☻ lunch & dinner) Tucked away in a courtyard, this classy but relaxed diner serves fusion food in a stylish, understated space. You can sit outside in summer, but otherwise opt for the ground floor as it's much more atmospheric than upstairs.

Ring O'Bells (☎ 448870; 10 Widcombe Pde; mains £8-12; ☻ lunch & dinner) This unassuming little place is actually an excellent gastro-pub with a simple but sophisticated menu featuring jazzed-up old favourites. The interior is light-filled and fresh, with modern design and old-world character mixing seamlessly.

No 5 (☎ 444499; 5 Argyle St; mains £14.50-15.80; ☻ lunch & dinner) Classic French bistro–style food with a hint of the Mediterranean draws the crowds to this informal but stylish place. The food is expertly prepared with subtle flavours and beautiful presentation. Go for the veal kidneys if you can handle the guilt.

Wife of Bath (☎ 461745; 12 Pierrepont St; mains £10-15; ☻ lunch & dinner) Be prepared for giant portions at this warren of Georgian cellar rooms. The rooms feature alcoves with booth-style seating. The food spans the globe, featuring dishes from as far apart as Australia and the Caribbean, with a classic European touch thrown in.

Hop Pole (☎ 446327; 7 Albion Bldgs, Upper Bristol Rd; mains £8-16; ☻ lunch & dinner) This unassuming country-style pub with exposed beams and bright and airy rooms isn't quite what you'd expect in this city, but the juicy Sunday roasts and steaming steak and ale pies are famous round town.

Top End
Olive Tree Restaurant (☎ 447928; Russell St; 2-/3-course lunch £13.50/15.50, 3-course dinner £26; ☻ lunch & dinner) Chic and sleek, and one of the finest restaurants in town, this understated place with oak floors and dark leather furniture serves up a first-class menu of simple modern British and French cuisine.

Hole in the Wall (☎ 425242; 16 George St; mains £13-17; ☻ lunch & dinner) A top-notch joint serving modern British cooking rich with organic ingredients and a healthy dose of fish and vegetarian choices. The interior is wonderful with natural stone floors, a giant hearth and dazzling white linen.

DRINKING
Pulp (☎ 466411; 38 Monmouth St) A hip café-bar with street-side tables and good cocktails, this retro-chic place is ultra-cool but still manages to be really friendly. It has a vast cocktail list and trendy clientele and is a great place to just people-watch.

Bath Tap (☎ 404344; 19-20 St James's Pde; admission £2.50) One of Bath's top gay bars with a lively programme of cabaret, dance and karaoke. This place is also a good pre-club venue with plenty of cheesy tracks, a wicked wild side and a good mixed crowd.

DYMK? (Does Your Mother Know?; ☎ 330470; 11-12 Westgate Bldg; admission £1.50) Bath's hottest new gay venue packs punters in for the usual mix of drag, cabaret, karaoke and bingo. However, it's bigger and brassier than most and is a welcoming place for punters of any persuasion.

ENTERTAINMENT

Venue magazine (www.venue.co.uk; £1.20) has comprehensive listings with details of theatre, music, gigs – the works, basically – for Bristol and Bath. Pick up a copy at any newsagent.

Nightclubs

Cadillacs (☎ 464241; 90b Walcot St; admission £4-6) A popular late-night haunt. This place hosts the city's most popular salsa night on Monday, student booze-fest on Tuesday and a mix of chart, dance, R & B and soul into the weekend.

Moles (☎ 404445; 14 George St; admission £4-5) The best alternative club and live-music venue in town. It's a good place to see Bath's up-and-coming bands playing everything from reggae and ska to hard rock. Club nights feature lots of hip-hop.

Babylon (☎ 465002; Kingston Rd; admission £3-5) Bath's foremost late night out. Babylon is a glitzy dance spot featuring anything from Wednesday's boozy students' night with major drinks promotions and serious cheese, to Thursday's alternative rock, indie and punk, to the weekend's R & B, drum'n'bass and '70s and '80s funk.

Theatre & Cinema

Theatre Royal (☎ 448844; www.theatreroyal.org.uk; Saw Close) This sumptuous venue features drama, opera, ballet, comedy and world music on its eclectic programme at the main theatre, and more-experimental and student productions at its smaller Ustinov Studio.

Rondo Theatre (☎ 463362; www.rondotheatre.co.uk; St Saviours Rd, Larkhall) This adventurous rep theatre mixes professional, amateur and community work in a varied programme of comedy, panto, music and drama.

Little Theatre (☎ 466822; St Michael's Pl) Bath's art-house cinema, screening mostly fringe and foreign-language films.

Classical Music

At Bath Abbey (p262) there's a regular programme of lunch-time recitals, while the **Bath Spa University Concert Series** (☎ 463362; Michael Tippett Centre) has a mix of classical music, world music and sonic art.

GETTING THERE & AWAY

Bus

National Express coaches travel to London (£14.50, 3½ hours, 11 daily) via Heathrow (£14.50, 2½ hours), and to Manchester (£29, 6½ to 10½ hours, eight daily) and Oxford (£29.50, 2¼ hours, one daily).

Bus Nos X39 and 337, 338 and 339 run to Bristol (50 minutes) several times an hour. Other useful services include bus Nos X5 and X6 to Bradford-on-Avon (30 minutes, half-hourly), Nos X71 and X72 to Devizes (one hour, hourly) and Nos 173 and 773 to Wells (1¼ hours, hourly).

Map-timetables for individual routes are available from the **bus station office** (☎ 464446; Manvers St; ☉ 8am-5.30pm Mon-Sat).

Train

There are half-hourly trains to London Paddington (£28.50, 1½ hours) and Cardiff (£11.90, 1¼ hours), and several each hour to Bristol (£4.80, 11 minutes). There are trains to Oxford roughly hourly (£9.80, 1¼ hours) and trains every two hours to Weymouth (£10.80, two hours) via Bradford-on-Avon (£2.80, 15 minutes) and Dorchester West (£10.50, two hours). Hourly services head to Portsmouth (£13, 2½ hours) via Salisbury (£10.40, 50 minutes).

GETTING AROUND

Bicycle

Bikes can be hired from **Avon Valley Cycles** (☎ 461880; www.bikeshop.uk.com; Arch 37; half-/full-day £10/15). Cyclists can use the 12-mile Bristol and Bath Railway Path that follows a disused railway line.

Boat

Various companies run half-hourly passenger boats from Pulteney Bridge to Bathampton (£5, 50 minutes). Alternatively, you can hire canoes, punts or rowing boats to propel yourself along the Avon from £6 per hour; try **Bath Boating Station** (☎ 312900; Forester Rd; 🕙 Mar-Oct).

Bus

Bus No 18 runs from the bus station, High St and Great Pulteney St up Bathwick Hill past the YHA to the university every 10 minutes. Bus No 4 runs every 20 minutes to Bathampton from the same places. A First Day Pass for unlimited bus travel in the city costs £3/2.50 per adult/child.

Car

Bath has a bad traffic problem and an infuriating one-way system. **Park-and-ride services** (☎ 464446; return £1.60) operate at Lansdown to the north, Newbridge to the west and Odd Down to the south. The service runs to the centre every 10 to 15 minutes from 7.15am to 7.30pm, taking 10 minutes.

AROUND BATH
Prior Park

The beautiful 18th-century **Prior Park** (NT; ☎ 833422; adult £4.10; Ralph Allen Dr; 🕙 11am-5.30pm Wed-Mon Feb-Nov, Fri-Sun Dec & Jan; wheelchair access) is a landscaping glory created by Capability Brown. The gardens are set in a small sweeping valley and have spectacular views of Bath, a famous Palladian bridge and cascading lakes. Prior Park is 1 mile south of the centre but it's only accessible by bus (No 2 or 4, every 10 minutes) or on foot. There's a £1 discount if you show your bus ticket.

SOMERSET

Renowned as a slow-moving, slow-talking kind of place, drowsy, agricultural Somerset is an evocative remnant of rural life in times past. It's not all quiet charm, though – there's also excellent walking and cycling between the picturesque villages that pepper the hills, a magnificent gorge at Cheddar, the bohemian swing of Glastonbury and the wonderful cathedral city of Wells.

Orientation & Information

Somerset nestles around the elbow of the Bristol Channel. The Mendips, a range of low hills, follow a line below Bristol, just north of Wells and Cheddar, while the Quantocks sit just east of Exmoor. Most

places of interest are in northern Somerset. Bath or Wells make good bases to the east, as do Lynton and Lynmouth to the west.

Most towns have TICs and there's a central **Somerset visitors centre** (☎ 01934-750833; somersetvisitorcentre@somerset.gov.uk; Sedgemoor Services M5 South, Axbridge, Somerset BS26 2UF) for general information. Try www.somerset.gov.uk /celebratingsomerset for more information.

Getting Around

Bus services in Somerset are split between **First Travel** (☎ 0117-955 8211; www.firstbadgerline.co .uk) north of Bridgwater, including Bath and Bristol, and **First Southern National** (☎ 01823-366100; www.firstsouthernnational.co.uk) to the south, with other local operators chipping in.

The county council produces area-specific timetables that are available at bus stations and most TICs.

WELLS
☎ 01749 / pop 10,406

Almost perfectly preserved and brimful of character, the medieval cathedral city of Wells makes an excellent base for touring the nearby Mendip Hills, Cheddar Gorge and boho Glastonbury. It's a dignified place and one of England's finest and smallest cities. The magnificent cathedral is hidden until the last moment when it is dramatically revealed in all its glory. Nearby is the imposing Bishop's Palace (still surrounded by the spring water that gives the city its name) and a cluster of handsome medieval buildings.

Information

The **TIC** (☎ 672552; www.wells.gov.uk; Market Pl; 🕙 9.30am-5.30pm Apr-Oct, 10am-4pm Nov-Mar) stocks the *Wells City Trail* leaflet (30p) and has information on nearby walking and cycling routes. Wednesday and Saturday are market days.

Wells Laundrette (☎ 01458-830409; 39 St Cuthbert St; 🕙 8am-8pm) is opposite St Cuthbert's Church.

Sights
WELLS CATHEDRAL

Set in a marvellous close, the **Wells Cathedral** (Cathedral Church of St Andrew; ☎ 674483; Chain Gate, Cathedral Green; requested donation adult/child £4.50/1.50; 🕙 7am-7pm Sep-Jun, 7am-8.30pm Jul & Aug) is a majestic place that was built in stages between

1180 and 1508. The building incorporates several Gothic styles, but its most famous asset is the wonderful **west front**, an immense sculpture gallery with over 300 figures, built in the 13th century and restored to its original splendour in 1986.

Inside, the most striking feature is the pair of **scissor arches** separating the nave from the choir, a brilliant solution to the problem posed by the subsidence of the central tower. High up in the north transept is a wonderful **mechanical clock** dating from 1392 – the second-oldest surviving in England after the one in Salisbury Cathedral (p235). The clock shows the position of the planets and also the phases of the moon.

Other highlights are the elegant **lady chapel** (1326) at the eastern end and the seven **effigies** of Anglo-Saxon bishops ringing the choir. The 15th-century **chained library** houses books and manuscripts dating back to 1472. Access is from the **reading room** (adult 50p; 2.30-4.30pm Fri & Sat Apr-Oct) upstairs from the south transept.

From the north transept follow the worn steps to the glorious **Chapter House** (1306), with its delicate ceiling ribs sprouting like a palm from a central column. Externally, look out for the **Chain Bridge** built from the northern side of the cathedral to Vicars' Close to enable clerics to reach the cathedral without getting wet. The **cloisters** on the southern side surround a pretty courtyard.

Guided tours (10am, 11am, 1pm, 2pm & 3pm Mon-Sat) of the cathedral are free.

CATHEDRAL CLOSE
Wells Cathedral is the focal point of a cluster of buildings whose histories are inextricably linked. Facing the west front, on the left are the 15th-century **Old Deanery** and a salmon-coloured building housing **Wells Museum** (673477; 8 Cathedral Green; wellsmuseum@ukonline .co.uk; adult £3; 10am-5.30pm Easter-Oct, 10am-8pm Aug, 11am-4pm Wed-Mon Nov-Easter), with exhibits on local life, cathedral architecture and the infamous Witch of Wookey Hole.

Further along on the left, **Vicars' Close** is a stunning cobbled street of uniform houses dating back to the 14th century with a chapel at the end; members of the cathedral choir still live here. It is thought to be the oldest complete medieval street in Europe. Passing under the Chain Bridge,

inspect the outside of the lady chapel and a lovely medieval house called The Rib, before emerging at a main road called The Liberty.

Penniless Porch, a corner gate leading onto Market Sq and built by Bishop Bekynton around 1450, is so-called because beggars asked for alms here.

BISHOP'S PALACE
Beyond the cathedral is the moated 13th-century **Bishop's Palace** (678691; www.bishops palacewells.co.uk; adult/child £4/3; 10.30am-5pm Tue-Fri, 1-5pm Sun Apr-Oct), purportedly the oldest inhabited building in England. Set in a quad and surrounded by a huge wall, it is an incredible place with fine Italian Gothic state rooms, an imposing Great Hall and beautiful gardens. The springs that give the town its name bubble and babble here, feeding the moat. The swans in the moat have been trained to ring a bell outside one of the windows when they want to be fed.

Sleeping
Infield House (670989; www.infieldhouse.co.uk; 36 Portway; s/d £36/52; P) This beautifully restored Victorian town house has classical rooms with period furnishings and portraits, original fireplaces, bay windows and small bathrooms. Single rooms are £10 cheaper in the low season.

Old Farmhouse (675058; www.plus44.com/old farmhouse; 62 Chamberlain St; s/d £40/60;) Set right in the city in a beautiful walled garden, this 17th-century former farmhouse has lovely, warm cottage-style rooms with large beds, subtle floral patterns and period charm.

Beryl (678738; www.beryl-wells.co.uk; Hawkers Lane; s/d £55/75; P) If you fancy a bit of grand Victoriana, try this small but stunning neo-Gothic mansion set in extensive parklands just a mile outside town. The luxurious rooms are full of character with period furnishings, antiques, and family portraits on the walls.

Ancient Gate House Hotel (672029; www.ancient gatehouse.co.uk; Browne's Gate; s/d £63/78;) Actually part of the Great West Gate of Cathedral Close, this charming old place has little passages running to the warren of atmospheric rooms that have period character, four-poster or half-tester beds and rich fabrics.

Other recommendations:

Bay Tree House (☎ 677933; www.baytree-house.co.uk; 85 Portway; s/d £28/42; **P** ✖) A stylish 1930s house with bright, pleasant rooms and rural décor.

Swan Hotel (☎ 836300; swan@bhere.co.uk; Sadler St; s/d £89/125; **P** ✖) Elegant, 15th-century coaching inn with swanky rooms.

Eating

Le Café Bleu (☎ 677772; 9 Heritage Courtyard; mains £4-6; ☯ lunch & dinner) This hip and happening place, tucked off Sadler St, has a good range of sambos, salads and hot bakes, a chilled at-mosphere and a mellow soundtrack. There's lots of outdoor seating for fine weather, and live music every other Friday night.

Fountain Inn & Boxers (☎ 672317; 1 St Thomas St; mains £8-14; ☯ lunch & dinner) This appealing gastro-pub and restaurant is the local fa-vourite for its relaxed atmosphere and won-derful food. Fish and game feature heavily but there's also a good choice of vegetarian dishes and a children's menu.

Rugantino (☎ 672029; Brown's Gate; 3-course dinner £16.90; ☯ dinner) Part of the atmospheric An-cient Gate House (p268), this rustic Italian restaurant serves a great selection of trad-itional regional fare. The excellent-value set menu features a good range of interesting pastas and classic meat dishes.

Ritchers (☎ 679085; 5 Sadler St; 2-/3-course meals £19.50/23; ☯ lunch & dinner) This smart little res-taurant knocks up the city's finest modern French and British cuisine. Expect the likes of steamed lamb pudding with a prune and Armagnac jus, or chargrilled sea bass.

Getting There & Around

National Express runs to London once a day (£16.50, 4½ hours), but connecting services run from Bristol (Bus Nos 376 and 377; one hour, hourly) and Bath (Nos 173 and 403; 1¼ hours). Bus No 163 runs hourly to Glastonbury (15 minutes). Bus Nos 126 and 826 travel hourly (every two hours on Sunday) to Cheddar (20 minutes). There's no train station in Wells.

Bike City (☎ 671711; 31 Broad St; ☯ 9am-5.30pm Mon-Sat) charges £12 per day for bike hire. Except for visiting sights outside town, it's easy to navigate compact Wells on foot.

WOOKEY HOLE

On the southern edge of the Mendips, the River Axe has carved out a whole se-ries of caves, which are known as **Wookey Hole** (☎ 01749-672243; www.wookey.co.uk; adult/child £8.80/5.50; ☯ 10am-5pm Apr-Oct, 10.30am-4.30pm Nov-Mar). The caves contain a spectacular lake and some fascinating stalagmites, one of which gave rise to the legend of the Witch of Wookey Hole, an evil woman living in the caves who brought misfortune on the girls of the town. She was eventually turned to stone when the Abbot of Glastonbury sprinkled holy water over her.

Various Iron Age finds are displayed in the small museum, but the caves are now run as a 'family attraction', with an ancient hand made–paper mill, an Edwardian fair-ground, a maze of mirrors and an arcade of vintage amusement machines.

The **Wookey Hole Inn** (☎ 01749-676677; www .wookeyholeinn.com; s/d £50/75-90) has some really homely rooms, with plenty of knick-knacks strewn around, a cult video library, wide-screen TVs, Japanese-style king-size beds and lots of CDs. The inn also does a great menu of classic food (£6 to £15) and draught Belgian beers.

Bus No 171 runs hourly from Wells (10 minutes). A 3-mile walk to Wookey Hole is signposted from New St in Wells. Note that the village of Wookey just west of Wells is not the same as Wookey Hole.

CHEDDAR GORGE

☎ 01934

Dramatic Cheddar Gorge, with its steep stone cliffs, cuts a mile-long swathe through the southern side of the Mendips. At some points the cliff walls tower 138m above the winding narrow road that lies at its base. A signposted 3-mile round walk follows the cliffs along the most spectacular parts of the gorge.

The more or less natural attractions of the gorge have been incorporated into **Cheddar Caves & Gorge** (☎ 742343; www.cheddarcaves.co.uk; Explorer Ticket adult/child £9.50/6.50; ☯ 10am-5.30pm Jul & Aug, 10am-5pm Sep-Jun), a 'family' day out – expect tearooms, fish-and-chip outlets, gift shops and big crowds in summer.

Cox's and Gough's caves are filled with stalactites and stalagmites, and are indis-putably very impressive; a 40,000-year-old skeleton (imaginatively named Cheddar Man) was discovered in the latter. Add-on features include an open-top bus tour (Easter to September only), lookout tower and Crystal Quest theme cave for kids.

There's a **TIC** (☎ 744071; cheddar.tic@sedgemoor .gov.uk; ☼ 10am-5pm Easter-Sep, 10.30am-4.30pm Oct, 11am-4pm Sun Nov-Easter) in the gorge.

Cheddar village, southwest of the gorge, has an elegant church and an ancient market cross but is otherwise disappointing. A mile southwest of the caves on the western side of the village is the **Cheddar YHA Hostel** (☎ 0870 770 5760; cheddar@yha.org.uk; Hillfield; dm £11.80).

Bus Nos 126 and 826 run to Wells (25 minutes) hourly from Monday to Saturday and every two hours on Sunday. Bus Nos 672, 673 and 674 run from Bristol to Cheddar (1½ hours, six times Monday to Friday, five on Saturday, four on Sunday).

MENDIP HILLS

The Mendips are a ridge of limestone hills stretching from the coast near Weston-Super-Mare to Frome in eastern Somerset. Their highest point is Black Down (326m) to the northwest – but because they rise sharply, there are panoramic views towards Exmoor and across northwest Wiltshire.

Historically, the area has seen its share of action, and Neolithic earthworks, Bronze Age barrows and Iron-Age forts can be found scattered over the hills. More recently, lead and coal mining have left their mark, with remains of mines dotting the area around Radstock and Midsomer Norton. Quarrying for stone is an important (and controversial) industry to this day.

Until the Middle Ages, large tracts of land lay beneath swampy meadows, and the remaining wetlands provide an important habitat for wildlife and flora. The marshland hid relics too, including a Lake Village excavated at the turn of the 20th century (see p272).

The landscape is dotted with pretty villages and isolated pubs that once served the thirsty miners. The villages are home to some delightful timbered houses, and several have fine perpendicular church towers. Local TICs stock leaflets with information on walking and cycling in the area.

The A371 skirts the southern side of the Mendip Hills, and any of the towns along it make good touring bases, though Wells has the best range of facilities.

Getting There & Away

Bus Nos 126 and 826 run between Wells and Cheddar (hourly Monday to Saturday, every two hours on Sunday). Bus No 173

runs from Bath to Radstock (30 minutes), Midsomer Norton (40 minutes) and Wells (1¼ hours, hourly Monday to Saturday, four on Sunday).

GLASTONBURY

☎ 01458 / pop 8429

Unruly Glastonbury, with its bohemian attitude and ancient relics, is a fascinating stop for both the hippie and the history buff. Thanks to its mystical associations, convergence of ley lines and renowned music festival, Glastonbury is now a centre of New Age culture, where spiritual enlightenment of one kind or another is offered wherever you go. Incense, crystals, aromatherapy oils, stripy pants and comfy shoes are now the greatest commodities in the town that claims to be both the birthplace of English Christianity and the burial place of King Arthur and Queen Guinevere.

Information

Glastonbury's **TIC** (☎ 832954; www.glastonburytic .co.uk; The Tribunal, 9 High St; ☼ 10am-5pm Apr-Sep, 10am-4pm Oct-Mar) stocks free maps and accommodation lists, and sells leaflets describing local walks and the *Glastonbury Millennium Trail* (60p).

There is Internet access at Café Galatea (see p272) for £5 per hour.

Sights
GLASTONBURY ABBEY

Legend suggests that Joseph of Arimathea, great-uncle of Jesus, owned mines in this area. It's said he returned here with the Holy Grail (the chalice from the Last Supper) after the death of Christ and founded the first church here. However, the earliest evidence of Christianity is from the 7th century when King Ine gave a charter to a monastery. In 1184 the church was destroyed by fire and reconstruction began in the reign of Henry II.

In 1191 monks claimed to have had visions confirming hints in old manuscripts that the 6th-century warrior-king Arthur and his wife Guinevere were buried in the grounds. Excavations uncovered a tomb, and the couple was reinterred in front of the high altar of the new church in 1278. The tomb survived until 1539 when Henry VIII dissolved the monasteries and had

SOUTHWEST ENGLAND

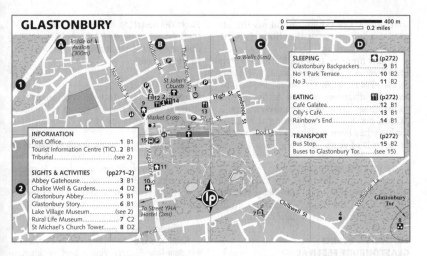

the last abbot hung, drawn and quartered on the tor. After that, the abbey complex gradually collapsed, its parts scavenged to provide building materials.

The ruins you see at Glastonbury today are mainly of the church built after the 1184 fire. They include: some nave walls; parts of the crossing arches, which may have been scissor-shaped like those in Wells Cathedral (p267); some medieval tiles; remains of the choir; and the St Mary's or lady chapel with an elaborately carved doorway. The site of the supposed tomb of Arthur and Guinevere is marked in the grass.

An award-winning **museum** explores the site's history and contains a model showing what the abbey would have looked like in its heyday. Entrance to the abbey is through the **Abbey Gatehouse** (☎ 832267; www.glastonburyabbey .com; Magdalene St; adult/child £3.50/1.50; ❤ 9.30am-6pm Mar-May & Sep-Nov, 9am-6pm Jun-Aug, 10am-dusk Dec-Feb).

GLASTONBURY TOR

Considered a sacred site by many and thought to be home of Gwyn ap Nudd (King of the Underworld), Glastonbury Tor is an exhilarating place with fantastic views over the surrounding countryside. *Tor* is a Celtic word used to describe a hill, and this 160m-high summit was a place of pilgrimage for many years. All that remains of the medieval church of **St Michael** is the tower, silhouetted by sunrise and sunset and visible for miles around.

It takes three-quarters of an hour to walk up and back down the tor. Parking is not permitted nearby so take the Tor Bus (£1) from Dunstan's car park near the abbey. It runs to the tor and back every 30 minutes from 9.30am to 5pm April to September and also stops at Chalice Well and the Rural Life Museum.

CHALICE WELL & GARDENS

Mysticism and mythology have long surrounded the **Chalice Well & Gardens** (☎ 831154; www.chalicewell.org.uk; Chilkwell St; adult £2.70; ❤ 10am-6pm Apr-Oct, 11am-5pm Feb, Mar & Nov, noon-4pm Dec & Jan), supposedly the hiding place of the Holy Grail. The iron-red water of the spring may have begun the myth: the Holy Grail was supposed to have been used to catch the blood from Christ's wounds while he was on the cross. However, the spring was probably used by Celts long before Christ or the 800-year-old well. Its water has traditions of healing. You can drink as it pours out through a lion's-head spout, or rest your feet in basins surrounded by flowers. Mysticism aside, the gardens and meadows are beautiful, peaceful spots in which to relax or picnic.

MUSEUMS

Artefacts associated with farming, cider-making, cheese-making and other aspects of Somerset country life are displayed at the interesting **Rural Life Museum** (☎ 831197; Abbey Farm, Chilkwell St; admission free; ❤ 10am-5pm Tue-Fri, 2-6pm Sat & Sun Easter-Oct, 10am-5pm Tue-Sat

Nov-Easter). A key exhibition follows the life of a Victorian farm worker through birth, school and marriage.

A new museum tells the **Glastonbury Story** (☎ 831666; www.glastonburystory.org.uk; 11-12 St John's Sq; adult/child £2.95/1.50; ☺ 11am-5pm late-Mar–Oct), from the discovery of King Arthur's grave in the abbey grounds to the present day. It does a good job of explaining why Glastonbury has been a place of pilgrimage for thousands of years.

LAKE VILLAGE MUSEUM
Upstairs from Glastonbury's TIC, in the medieval courthouse, the **Lake Village Museum** (EH; ☎ 832954; High St; adult £2) displays finds from a prehistoric bog village nearby.

Festivals & Events
GLASTONBURY FESTIVAL
This massive music festival is a renowned, three-day summer extravaganza held each year in late June. **Glastonbury Festival** (www.glastonburyfestivals.co.uk) is *the* summer music event in Britain, revered by musicians and punters alike for its unique atmosphere and wild carnival fringe. Around the main stages a huge alternative carnival involving world music, theatre, circus acts and natural healing takes place. The whole event is based at Worthy Farm in Pilton, 8 miles east of Glastonbury. Admission is by advance ticket only (about £112 for the whole festival).

Sleeping
Many of Glastonbury's B&Bs offer aromatherapy, muesli breakfasts, vegetarian meals and so on. The TIC has a complete list.

Glastonbury Backpackers (☎ 833353; www.glastonburybackpackers.com; 4 Market Pl; dm/d £10/35; P) A lively hostel with excellent-value private rooms. This popular place also has a good bar with live bands, a courtyard area and a funky café that serves noodles, salads and burritos (£5 to £6.50).

No 1 Park Terrace (☎ 835845; www.no1parkterrace .co.uk; Park Tce; s/d £25/40; P ⬛) This spacious Victorian house has good-value rooms decorated in period style with heritage colours, antique furniture and pretty but subtle florals. It's central and very friendly.

Other recommendations:
No 3 (☎ 832129; www.numberthree.co.uk; 3 Magdalene St; s/d £75/100; P ✗) A luxury B&B with really spacious and cheerful rooms.

Street YHA Hostel (☎ 0870 770 6056; www.yha.org.uk; The Chalet, Ivythorn Hill; dm £10.60; P ✗) A simple chalet hostel about 4 miles south of town. Take hourly bus No 376 (15 minutes).

Eating
Glastonbury is perfect for vegetarians, because it's one of the few places in England where nut roasts are more common than pot roasts.

Café Galatea (☎ 834284; 5a High St; mains £7.50; ☺ 11am-4pm Mon, 11am-9pm Wed-Sun; ✗) This lovely gallery café has a globally inspired and predominantly vegetarian menu, with everything from enchiladas to cannelloni to stir-fries. You can check your email here, wander the sculpture gallery or catch some live music at weekends.

Rainbow's End (☎ 833896; 17a High St; mains £4-6; ☺ 10am-4pm) Hearty vegan and vegetarian food is on offer at Glastonbury's legendary café. Great hot bakes, casseroles and salads supplement the huge chunks of chocolate cake and excellent coffee.

Olly's Café (☎ 834521; 52 High St; mains £5-8; ☺ Mon-Sat) This lively new café has a good choice of Mediterranean meat dishes as well as local vegetarian favourites. It has a lovely enclosed courtyard and hosts live music in the evenings.

Getting There & Away
There's one early morning National Express service to Bath (£5.25, 1½ hours) that goes on to London (£17.50, 4¼ hours), but more services connect through Wells (bus Nos 376 and 377, hourly, 15 minutes) and Bristol (bus Nos 376 and 377, hourly, 1½ hours). Bus Nos 29 and 929 go to Taunton (one hour) every two hours.

There is no train station.

AROUND GLASTONBURY
Quantock Hills
A ridge of red sandstone hills, the Quantocks (from a Celtic word meaning rim), runs for 12 miles down to the sea at Quantoxhead in western Somerset. The hills are about 3 miles wide, and at their highest only 385m, but they can be wild and bleak at times and make enjoyable walking country.

Some of the most attractive country is owned by the National Trust, including the Beacon and Bicknoller Hills, which offer views of the Bristol Channel and Exmoor to the northwest. In 1861 red deer were introduced to these hills from Exmoor and there's a local tradition of stag hunting.

The Quantock Hills have been designated an Area of Outstanding Natural Beauty (AONB). The **AONB Service** (☎ 01278-732845; www .quantockhills.com; Castle St, Nether Stowey), in the library at Nether Stowey, offers guided walks.

NETHER STOWEY & HOLFORD
The attractive village of **Nether Stowey** has plenty of old-world charm and the remains of an 11th-century castle topping a nearby hill. Poet Samuel Taylor Coleridge wrote *The Rime of the Ancient Mariner* while living in the village's **Coleridge Cottage** (NT; ☎ 01278-732662; 35 Lime St; adult £3.20; ☽ 2-5pm Thu-Sun Apr-Sep) in the village from 1797 to 1800.

Coleridge's friend William Wordsworth, and Wordsworth's sister Dorothy, spent 1797 at Alfoxden House in nearby **Holford**, a pretty village near a wooded valley. *Lyrical Ballads* (1798) was the joint product of Coleridge's and Wordsworth's sojourns.

If you'd like to stay in Nether Stowey, the **Manse** (☎ 01278-732917; Lime St; d £40; ☽ Easter-Sep; **P**) is a well-furnished B&B in an early-19th-century house opposite Coleridge Cottage. Alternatively, the **Old Cider House** (☎ 01278-732228; www.oldciderhouse.co.uk; 25 Castle St; s/d £35/50; **P** ☒) is an elegant Edwardian house with simple bright rooms with country-house styling. It also serves classic home cooking (three-course dinner £16.50) with vegetables from its organic garden.

Set in a wooded area 1½ miles west of Holford is the **Quantock Hills YHA Hostel** (☎ 0870 770 6006; www.yha.org.uk; Sevenacres; dm £10.60; **P** ☒). It's often booked out so call ahead. Bus Nos 15 and 615 from Bridgwater get you to Holford or Kilve (50 minutes, six daily), and No 23 from Taunton (one hour, five daily) will drop you at Kilve; in either case it's then a 1½-mile walk.

CROWCOMBE
One of the prettiest Quantock villages, Crowcombe still has cottages made of stone and cob (a mixture of mud and straw), many with thatched roofs. The ancient **Church of the Holy Ghost** has wonderful carved 16th-century bench ends with surprisingly pagan themes (the Green Man is common). The spire was struck by lightning in 1725, and part of it still stands in the churchyard.

There aren't many accommodation or eating options in Crowcombe – Nether Stowey (see left) has more facilities.

The **Crowcombe YHA Hostel** (☎ 0870 770 5782; www.yha.org.uk; Heathfield; dm £10.60; **P** ☒) is about 2 miles southeast of the village and just half a mile from Crowcombe station. It's a 7-mile walk over the Quantocks from the hostel in Holford.

In nearby Triscombe you'll find the **Blue Ball Inn** (☎ 01984-618242; mains £8-14), an unspoilt 18th-century thatched pub offering imaginative pub food and a friendly atmosphere. It's a popular choice for walkers as well as locals and has a blackboard menu changing daily.

GETTING THERE & AWAY
The Quantocks' lanes and villages are best enjoyed by avoiding crowded day-tripper weekends. Hourly trains from Bristol call at Taunton (£7.90, 45 minutes); from there, you really need your own wheels because buses are limited. Half-hourly bus No 28 runs from Taunton to Minehead but stops at Crowcombe (30 minutes) only once daily. Bus No 302 runs between Crowcombe and Taunton once on Tuesday and four times on Saturday. Bus No 23 runs between Taunton and Nether Stowey (30 minutes, three daily Monday to Friday).

TAUNTON
☎ 01823 / pop 58,241
There's little in Somerset's administrative capital to detain you but it's a good transport hub and gateway to the Quantocks. The most famous landmark is the **Church of St Mary Magdalene** (☽ 10am-4pm Mon-Fri, 10am-1pm Sat), with its 50m-high tower carved from red Quantock rock.

Battered **Taunton Castle**, sections of which date from the 12th century, hosts the **Somerset County & Military Museum** (☎ 320201; www .somerset.gov.uk/museums; Castle Green; admission free; ☽ 10am-5pm Tue-Sat Apr-Oct, 10am-3pm Tue-Sat Nov-Mar) in the Great Hall where Judge Jeffreys held one of his bloodiest assizes in 1685 (see the boxed text, p284).

The **TIC** (☎ 336344; tautic@somerset.gov.uk; Paul St; ☽ 9.30am-5.30pm Mon-Fri, 9.30am-5pm Sat) is in the library.

If you need to stay in Taunton, B&Bs are concentrated along Wellington Rd and Staplegrove. Try **Brookfield House** (☎ 272786; www .brookfieldguesthouse.uk.com; 16 Wellington Rd; s/d from

£30/50; (P) (X)), a pleasant Georgian house near the centre with simple but stylish traditional rooms.

National Express coaches run to London (£14.50, four hours, six daily), Bristol (£5.75, 1½ hours, four daily) and Exeter (£5.25, 45 minutes, six daily). Hourly buses Nos 28 (Monday to Saturday) and 928 (Sunday, every two hours) cross the Quantocks to Minehead (1¼ hours). Bus Nos 29 (Monday to Saturday) and 929 (Sunday) run to Glastonbury (one hour) and Wells (one hour) every two hours.

Trains run to London (£35, two hours, every two hours), Exeter (£7.60, 30 minutes, half-hourly) and Plymouth (£20, 1½ hours, half-hourly).

MONTACUTE

The ancient village of Montacute, named after the pointed hill originally called Mons Acutus, is home to one of England's finest Elizabethan mansions – **Montacute House** (NT; ☎ 01935-823289; montacute@ntrust.org.uk; house & garden adult £6.90, garden only £3.70; ☾ house 11am-5pm Wed-Mon Apr-Oct, garden 11am-4pm Wed-Sun Nov-Mar). The house boasts remarkable interior plasterwork, fine chimneypieces, magnificent tapestries and carved parapets. Built in the 1590s for Sir Edward Phelips, a Speaker of the House of Commons, its state rooms display Tudor and Jacobean portraits on loan from London's National Portrait Gallery (p125). Formal gardens and a landscaped park surround the house.

Bus No 681 from Yeovil (20 minutes, hourly Monday to Saturday) to South Petherton passes close by.

EXMOOR NATIONAL PARK

Small but breathtaking, Exmoor manages to pack verdant wooded valleys, bleak rolling moorland, stunning villages and a diverse selection of wildlife into its 265 sq miles. It's a forbidding place when shrouded by its notorious sea mists but on a clear day the shimmering heather, dramatic coastal cliffs and idyllic villages make it a haven for driving, cycling, and above all, walking.

More than 600 miles of public paths and bridleways crisscross the park from west-

ern Somerset into North Devon, passing the magnificent hidden valleys, wooded dells and fast-flowing streams that inspired Blackmore's swashbuckling romance, *Lorna Doone*. The park is also home to England's largest herd of wild red deer and an ancient stock of Exmoor ponies.

Orientation

The park is only about 21 miles wide from west to east and just 12 miles from north to south. Waymarked paths traverse the park and a dramatic section of the South West Coast Path runs from Minehead, just outside the northeastern boundary of the park, to Padstow in Cornwall.

Information

For the best maps, books and advice, contact one of the following five National Park Authority (NPA) visitors centres (all open 10am to 5pm Easter to October, with limited hours from November to Easter):

Combe Martin (☎ 01271-883319; Cross St)

County Gate (☎ 01598-741321; A39 Countisbury)

Dulverton (☎ 01398-323841; dulvertonvc@exmoor -nationalpark.gov.uk; 7-9 Fore St)

Dunster (☎ 01643-821835; Dunster Steep)

Exmoor NPA Administrative Offices (☎ 01398-323665; info@exmoor-nationalpark.gov.uk; Exmoor House, Dulverton)

Lynmouth (☎ 01598-752509; The Esplanade)

The *Exmoor Visitor* is a free annual newspaper listing useful addresses, accommodation and a programme of guided walks and bike rides. Most of the villages on Exmoor are tiny, so ATMs are few and far between – get cash in Dulverton, Lynton or Minehead, or bring plenty.

There are three comprehensive websites covering Exmoor:

Exmoor National Park (www.exmoor-nationalpark.gov .uk) The official NPA site.

Exmoor Tourist Association (www.exmoor.com) Lists details on accommodation and activities.

What's On Exmoor (www.whatsonexmoor.com) Local listings and information.

Activities
ADVENTURE SPORTS

You can sail, surf and kayak at **Wimbleball Lake Watersports Centre** (☎ 01398-371460; 2-hr session £26), while **Exmoor Adventure** (☎ 01271-830628; www.exmooradventure.co.uk; half/full day

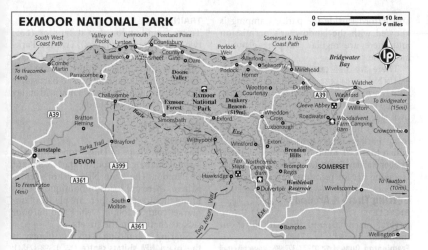

EXMOOR NATIONAL PARK

£74/152) can help arrange rock climbing and abseiling.

CYCLING

Official areas for cyclists include a coastal route; along the old Barnstaple railway line; parts of the Tarka Trail; the Brendon Hills; and the Crown Estate woodland. The West Country Way runs through Exmoor from Padstow to Bristol.

NPA visitors centres sell leaflets (75p each) describing routes through areas where cycling is permitted.

MOORLAND SAFARIS

Several companies offer 4WD safari trips – some tracking wild red deer – costing around £18 for three hours.

Barle Valley Safaris (☎ 01643-851386; www.exmoor -barlevalley-safaris.co.uk; Dulverton & Minehead)

Discovery Safaris (☎ 01643-863080; www.discovery safaris.com; Porlock)

Exmoor Safari (☎ 01643-831229; www.exmoor -hospitality-inns.co.uk; Exford)

PONY TREKKING & HORSE RIDING

Exmoor is popular riding country and stables around the park offer trips of a few hours to a full day; *Exmoor Visitor* has contact information for many. Charges start at about £12 per hour. Wet-weather gear is recommended, as it can turn cold and wet very quickly.

Some recommended operators:

Burrowhayes Farm (☎ 01643-862 463; www.burrow hayes.co.uk; Porlock)

Outovercott Stables (☎ 01598-753341; www.outover cott.co.uk; Lynton)

West Anstey Farm (☎ 01398-341354; Dulverton)

WALKING

Although a large percentage of Exmoor is privately owned, there are numerous way-marked paths. However, the park is prone to sudden blankets of sea mist, heavy rain and high winds, so be prepared for sudden changes in conditions.

The best-known routes are the **Somerset & North Devon Coast Path** (part of the South West Coast Path) and the Exmoor section of the **Two Moors Way**, which starts in Lynmouth and follows the River Barle through Withypool and on to Dartmoor.

Part of the 180-mile **Tarka Trail** (based on the countryside that inspired Henry Williamson's *Tarka the Otter*) is in the park. Join it in Combe Martin and walk to Lynton/Lynmouth, then inland to Brayford and Barnstaple.

Exmoor's walking centres are Lynton, Porlock, County Gate, Oare, Horner, Exford, Simonsbath, Withypool and Dulverton. Walks led by the NPA or similar go nearly daily in summer; they cost £3/5 for walks of under/over four hours' duration. Details are in *Exmoor Visitor*, or pick up information leaflets from NPA centres.

Sleeping & Eating

There are YHA hostels in Minehead and Ilfracombe (outside the park), and Lynton and Exford (inside the park). Camping is allowed with the landowner's permission and there are regular camping grounds along the coast.

There are also **camping barns** (☎ 0870 770 6113 for bookings; per person about £4.50) at Woodadvent Farm (near Roadwater) and Northcombe (a mile from Dulverton). Bring your own sleeping bag.

There's no shortage of B&Bs and hotels in the park and there are plenty of places at which to eat. If you'd like to hire a cottage, **Exmoor Holiday Group** (www.exmoor-holidays.co.uk) is a good bet for recommendations.

Getting There & Around
BICYCLE
Several places around the park hire out mountain bikes.

Fremington Quay (☎ 01271-372586; www.biketrail .co.uk; Fremington; per day £6.50-14.50)

Tarka Trail (☎ 01271-324202; Train Station, Barnstaple; per day £6-9.50)

BUS
National Express runs from London to Barnstaple (£25, 5½ hours, three daily) and Ilfracombe (£25, 6½ hours, one daily), and from Bristol to Barnstaple (£16.50, three hours, one daily).

Bus services are limited, and virtually nonexistent in the west of the park. The *Exmoor & West Somerset Public Transport Guide*, free from TICs, is invaluable. From Ilfracombe, bus No 300 runs to Lynton (one hour) and Porlock (1¾ hours) three times daily from Easter to October (weekends only November to Easter).

From Minehead, bus No 38 runs to Porlock (20 minutes, nine daily Monday to Saturday) and Porlock Weir (25 minutes, seven daily Monday to Saturday) via Selworthy. Nos 28 and 39 run to Dunster (15 minutes, every 30 minutes Monday to Saturday), while No 928 runs on Sunday (every two hours).

From Tiverton, No 398 runs to Dulverton (30 minutes) and Dunster (1½ hours) six times daily Monday to Saturday, occasionally diverting to Exford.

From Barnstaple, No 307 goes to Dulverton (1¼ hours, every two hours Monday to Saturday) and on to Taunton (1¼ hours from Dulverton), while Nos 309 and 310 run to Lynton (one hour, hourly).

TRAIN
Trains from London stop at Taunton (£35, two hours, every two hours), Tiverton Parkway (£36, 2½ hours, hourly) and Exeter (£42, 2½ hours, at least hourly). From Exeter, the scenic Tarka Line runs to Barnstaple (£10.10, one hour, every two hours Monday to Saturday, four on Sunday).

DULVERTON
☎ 01398
The sleepy village of Dulverton is the local 'capital' and a good spot to start your tour of Exmoor. The main NPA visitors centre is here, there are loads of boutiquey shops lining the streets and there are plenty of upmarket country folk in wellies and Barbour jackets chatting in the streets.

Sharing a building with the library is the main **NPA visitors centre** (☎ 01398-323841; dulvertonvc@exmoor-nationalpark.gov.uk; 7-9 Fore St; 🕙 10am-5pm Easter-Oct).

For more information visit the community website of www.dulverton.com.

Activities
WALKING
There's a stunning 12-mile circular walk along the river from Dulverton to Tarr Steps – an ancient stone clapper bridge haphazardly placed across the River Barle and shaded by gnarled old trees. The bridge was supposedly built by the devil for sunbathing. It's a four- to five-hour trek for the average walker. You can add another three or four hours to the walk by continuing from Tarr Steps up Winsford Hill for distant views over Devon.

Sleeping & Eating
Town Mills (☎ 323124; www.townmillsdulverton.co .uk; High St; s/d £35/56; ✕) This Georgian mill house has charming rooms with crackling open fires, rustic antique furniture and plenty of brightly coloured florals. It's the only really central B&B and offers breakfast in bed as the norm.

Winsbere House (☎ 323278; www.winsbere.co.uk; 64 Battleton; s/d £20/40; Ⓟ ✕) Just a mile outside town, this cosy, traditionally decorated farmhouse set in large gardens has pretty rooms with a floral frieze and bedspreads, and country furniture.

Archiamma (☎ 323397; 26 High St; lunch mains £6.50-10.50, dinner mains £9.50-17; 🕙 lunch Wed-Sat, dinner

Tue-Sat) This smart, modern bistro has an attractive vine-decked garden for summer days and a cosy but stylish interior. The British/ Mediterranean menu is strong on local produce, including Exmoor beef and fish.

Woods (☎ 324007; 4 Bank Sq; mains £9-14; ⚬ lunch & dinner) Dulverton's newest asset is this rustic restaurant and bar with big old benches and a good choice of cask ale. Choose from the imaginative tapas menu in the bar or the more formal, modern international cuisine in the dining area.

EXFORD
☎ 01643
Straddling the River Exe, the hamlet of Exford is one of the area's most photogenic villages. It has a good choice of accommodation and makes a popular base for walking, especially to Dunkery Beacon (519m), the highest point on Exmoor, 4 miles northeast.

Sleeping & Eating
Exford YHA Hostel (☎ 0870 770 5828; www.yha.org .uk; Exe Mead; dm £11.80; Ⓟ ✗) This lovely Victorian house is set right on the banks of the River Exe in the centre of the village, and is just steps from the pub. Dorms are fairly basic but atmospheric.

Exford Bridge (☎ 831304; www.exfordbridge.co.uk; Chapel St; s/d £40/60; ✗) If you fancy a break from chintz and florals, this lovely B&B offers sleek, stylish, contemporary rooms with deep-coloured walls, white bedspreads, power showers and DVD players. The restaurant (mains £9.50 to £13) offers a good selection of traditional British and modern international cuisine.

Crown Hotel (☎ 831554; www.crownhotelexmoor .co.uk; Chapel St; s/d £55/95; Ⓟ ✗) This wonderful old coaching inn has been completely overhauled and has a selection of luxurious rooms with tasteful traditional décor, complete with swags and florals. There's a great bar serving pub grub and a good selection of fine-dining choices in the restaurant (mains £10 to £15).

Getting There & Away
Over the moor, it's a 7-mile walk to Exford from Porlock, 10 miles from Minehead YHA Hostel, 12 miles from Dunster and 15 miles from Lynton.

See p276 for bus details.

LYNTON & LYNMOUTH
☎ 01598
Rocky Lynmouth – a picture-postcard smuggler's harbour – nestles below high cliffs in a steeply wooded gorge. Towering above it is the refined Victorian resort of Lynton, accessible by an incredible water-operated cliff railway. The coast on either side of town is spectacular and offers fantastic walking opportunities.

The **TIC** (☎ 0845 660 3232; info@lyntourism.co.uk; Lynton Town Hall, Lee Rd; ⚬ 9.30am-5pm Apr-Oct, 10am-4pm Nov-Mar) provides the *Lynton & Lynmouth Scene* (www.lyntonandlynmouthscene.co.uk), a free newspaper with accommodation, eating and activities listings.

Down by Lynmouth harbour there's an **NPA visitors centre** (☎ 752509; The Esplanade; ⚬ 10am-5pm Apr-Jun, Sep & Oct, 10am-9pm Jul & Aug).

Sights
In 1952 storms caused the East and West Lyn rivers to flood, sending a cascading mudslide down the cliffs. This destroyed 98 houses and claimed the lives of 34 people. The disaster is recorded at the **Lyn & Exmoor Museum** (☎ 752317; St Vincent's Cottage, Market St, Lynton; adult/child £1/20p; ⚬ 10am-12.30pm & 2-5pm Mon-Fri & 2-5pm Sun late-Mar–late Oct), along with varied collections of tools, paintings and local curios.

The **Cliff Railway** (☎ 753486; www.cliffrailway lynton.co.uk; one way adult/child £1.50/1; ⚬ 8.45am-7pm Easter-Nov) is a simple piece of environmentally friendly Victorian engineering. Two cars linked by a steel cable descend or ascend the slope according to the amount of water in their tanks. It's the best way to get between the two villages and the views across to the Exmoor cliffs are incredible.

From the Lynmouth crossroads, follow signs 200m to **Glen Lyn Gorge** (☎ 753207; adult/ child £3.50/2; ⚬ Easter-Oct). There are pleasant riverside walks and a small **exhibition centre** housing a collection of steam engines and exhibits on hydroelectric power.

Activities
WALKING
Lynton TIC and the NPA visitors centre have information about the many local walks. The South West Coast Path and the Tarka Trail pass through the villages, and the Two Moors Way, linking Exmoor with Dartmoor, starts in Lynmouth.

The **Valley of the Rocks**, which is believed to be where the River Lyn originally flowed, was described by the poet Robert Southey as, 'rock reeling upon rock, stone piled upon stone, a huge terrifying reeling mass'. It's just over a mile west of Lynton; the short walk along the coastal footpath is rewarded with fantastic views. East of Lynmouth, the lighthouse at **Foreland Point** is another good focus for a walk.

The walk to the confluence of two rivers at **Watersmeet**, 2 miles along the river from Lynmouth, is also popular.

Sleeping & Eating

There are loads of accommodation options in Lynton. with a whole bank of B&Bs along Lee Rd.

Lynton YHA Hostel (☎ 0870 770 5942; www.yha .org.uk; Lynbridge; dm £10.60; P ✗) This large Victorian house set right in the gorge has standard dorms but a welcoming atmosphere. The hostel is a steep 500m walk south of town.

Sea View Villa (☎ 753460; www.seaviewvilla.co.uk; 6 Summer House Path, Lynmouth; s £40, d £50-90; ✗) This gorgeous Georgian house is one of the best places to stay in town with its luxuriously elegant rooms, stylish but restrained classical décor and effortless charm. It's a world away from the standard B&Bs and is well worth a visit.

Rising Sun (☎ 753223; www.risingsunlynmouth.co .uk; Harbourside, Lynmouth; s/d £49/79) This atmospheric, 14th-century thatched smugglers' inn sits on Lynmouth harbour. It has a good choice of simple, contemporary, standard rooms or old-world ones with frills and four-posters. The oak-panelled restaurant (mains £18 to £24) serves up ambitious meat and game dishes.

Mad Hatters Bistro (☎ 753614; Church Steps, Lynton; mains £7.50-13; ✗ dinner Mon-Sat) This relaxed, cosy eatery serves up hearty portions of traditional local fare, including a good range of tasty fish and vegetarian dishes as well as venison and local free-range duck.

Getting There & Away

Driving between Lynton and Porlock, note that Countisbury Hill and Porlock Hill are notoriously steep; there are two alternative toll roads (£2) that avoid Porlock Hill (both are scenic and less drastic).

For bus information, see p276.

PORLOCK & AROUND
☎ 01643

Porlock is a picturesque village of thatched cottages and winding streets that can get overwhelmed with visitors on summer weekends, but at other times it's a wonderful place to visit. Just west of town is the charming little harbour of **Porlock Weir**, while to the east is the pretty NT-owned, cob-and-thatch village of **Selworthy**.

Porlock's helpful **visitors centre** (☎ 863150; www.porlock.co.uk; West End, High St; ☑ 10am-1pm & 2-5pm Mon-Sat & 10am-1pm Sun Apr-Oct, 10.15am-1pm Mon-Fri & 10am-2pm Sat Nov-Mar) offers a free accommodation booking service and has a small exhibition on Exmoor and Porlock life.

Sleeping & Eating

Myrtle Cottage (☎ 862978; www.smoothhound.co .uk/hotels/myrtle.html; High St; s/d £30/50; P ✗) This delightful, 16th-century thatched cottage has beautiful, cosy rooms with subtle modern décor and pretty fabrics. It's ideally located in the heart of the village and has a lovely small garden.

Porlock Vale House (☎ 862338; www.porlockvale .co.uk; West Porlock; s/d £65/100; P ✗) A stunning property. This old hunting lodge is an informal place with lovely rooms furnished with period pieces and traditional style. Chintz sofas, Persian rugs, shelves of books and sporting prints abound, and there's a glorious garden outside.

Andrew's on the Weir (☎ 863300; Porlock Weir; d £75; mains £18; ☑ lunch & dinner) This elegant Georgian restaurant with accommodation overlooking the weir is renowned for its exquisite traditional fish dishes and a smattering of local beef and lamb. All rooms are luxurious but chintzy , have antiques galore and great views of the waterfront.

DUNSTER
☎ 01643

Gorgeous old buildings and beautiful cottages flank Dunster's charming, winding streets, while a dramatic clifftop castle lords over all from on high. The village can get choked with visitors but it is undeniably pretty and well worth a visit.

The main attraction is the castle but Dunster also boasts a 16th-century stone dovecote, a 17th-century octagonal yarn market and a wonderful old packhorse bridge. The church, **St George's**, dates mostly from the

15th century and boasts a wonderfully carved fan-vaulted rood screen. Down the road is a working 18th-century **water mill** (☎ 821759; Mill Lane; adult £2.40; ☉ 11am-5pm Apr-Oct).

The **NPA visitors centre** (☎ 821835; Dunster Steep; ☉ 10am-5pm Easter-Oct) is in the main car park.

Dunster Castle
Heavily restored to the Victorian ideal of how castles should look – turrets, crenulations and all – **Dunster Castle** (NT; ☎ 821314; adult/child castle, garden & park £6.80/3.40, garden & park only £3.70/1.60; ☉ 11am-5pm Sat-Wed late-Mar–late-Oct) dates back to Norman times, although only the 13th-century gateway of the original structure survives. Inside are Tudor furnishings, stunning 17th-century plasterwork and portraits of the Luttrell family, including a bizarre 16th-century portrait of Sir John skinny-dipping. The surrounding terraced gardens and park are open most of the year.

Sleeping & Eating
Old Priory (☎ 821540; Priory Green; s/d £35/65) A huge stone fireplace and uneven floors give this amazing 12th-century house a wonderful uncontrived charm. It's set in walled gardens opposite the dovecote and has pretty rooms oozing grace and character.

Higher Orchard (☎ 821915; 30 St Georges St; s/d £25/40; ✗) This charming Victorian house is set in lovely gardens on a hill behind the church. The cottage-style rooms are bright and simple, if a little compact, the welcome is warm and it's handy for the village.

Luttrell Arms (☎ 851555; www.bhere.co.uk; 32-36 High St; s £65-105, d £95-140; ✗) The top spot in town is this medieval guesthouse, replete with 15th-century ambience. The rooms vary enormously from stunning high-ceilinged affairs to garish rooms, so look before you book. The restaurant serves classic British cuisine (mains £11 to £17) while the bar has more-modest fare (£4 to £6).

Hathaways Restaurant (☎ 821725; 5-8 West St; mains £9-11; ☉ lunch & dinner) This quaint, 16th-century building with low ceilings and rustic décor houses a good eating option, with an emphasis on pasta, poultry and steaks. The dishes are predominantly traditional, but there are a few modern twists thrown in.

Getting There & Away
See p276 for bus details.

DORSET

Dorset is a pleasure-filled but largely rural and underexposed county. It boasts beautiful beaches and ruddy-cheeked resorts along its sweeping Unesco Heritage Site coast as well as wonderful ancient remains and picturesque market towns inland. Apart from brassy Bournemouth, coastal Dorset is made up of charming bucket-and-spade resorts and fantastic cliffs and beaches, all linked by the spectacular Dorset Coast Path. Inland, low rolling hills shelter impossibly quaint villages such as Cerne Abbas (home to one of England's best-known chalk figures); bustling market towns such as Thomas Hardy's Dorchester; and a cluster of stately homes and Iron-Age remains.

Orientation & Information
Dorset stretches along the south coast from Lyme Regis on the western (Devon) border to Christchurch abutting Hampshire on the east. Dorchester, the county town, sits in-between and is the most central base for exploring, but Lyme Regis or Weymouth will suit those who prefer to hang out on the coast.

Dorset has a good web presence. For more information try:

Dorset County Council (www.dorset-cc.gov.uk)
Rural Dorset (www.ruraldorset.com)
West Dorset (www.westdorset.com)
Visit East Dorset (www.visiteastdorset.co.uk)

Getting Around
There are two slow railway lines running from Bristol and Bath through Dorchester West to Weymouth; and from London and Southampton to Bournemouth and Poole.

For buses your best bet is to pick up a free copy of *Dorset & South West Hampshire Bus Times* from TICs or bus stations. It has comprehensive listings of routes and timetables across the county. Otherwise, call **Traveline** (☎ 0870 608 2608; www.traveline.org.uk).

The main operator in east and central Dorset is **Wilts and Dorset** (☎ 01202-673555; www.wdbus .co.uk). For western Dorset and on to Devon and southern Somerset, **First Southern National** (☎ 01305-783645; www.firstsouthernnational.co.uk) is the main operator.

SOUTHWEST ENGLAND

BOURNEMOUTH

☎ 01202 / pop 167,527

An elegant haven for the blue rinse brigade by day and a brassy resort for boozy stags by night. What was once a terribly British seaside resort is now a contradictory place, attempting to shore up the traditional guesthouse and variety show trade while satisfying the hedonistic desires of hard-core party people. Property prices are soaring, though, and plans are underway for an artificial surf reef to reinforce and broaden its youth appeal. In the meantime that 7-mile stretch of glorious, golden sand can't fail to impress.

Orientation & Information

Bournemouth is a sprawling town that spreads along the coast towards Poole to the west and Christchurch to the east. The pier marks the central seafront area, and northeast from there is the town centre and train station.

Cyber Place (☎ 290099; 25 St Peter's Rd; per hr £2; ♥ 9.30am-midnight) There's a second branch at 132 Charminster Rd.

TIC (☎ 451700; www.bournemouth.co.uk; Westover Rd; ♥ 9.30am-5.30pm Mon-Sat year-round, 10.30am-5pm Sun May-Sep) Beside the Winter Gardens.

Sights & Activities

Bournemouth is noted for its beautiful *chines* (sharp-sided valleys running down to the sea), most of which are lined with villas.

An interesting mix of Italianate villa and Scottish baronial pile, the **Russell-Cotes Art Gallery & Museum** (☎ 451800; www.russell-cotes.bournemouth.gov.uk; Russell-Cotes Rd; admission free; ♥ 10am-5pm Tue-Sun) is a fascinating place looking out to sea near Bournemouth Pier. It hosts changing exhibitions as well as Victorian paintings by the likes of DG Rossetti, and an exquisite collection of Japanese pieces.

Right next to Bournemouth Pier, **Oceanarium** (☎ 311933; www.oceanarium.co.uk; adult £6.50; ♥ 10am-6pm) is a glitzy aquarium with themed areas housing sea and river life from around the world. There are flesh-eating piranhas to scare the kids and an underwater tunnel for close-ups of sharks, turtles and stingrays.

Sleeping

Bournemouth is plastered with B&Bs and hotels (many of them with one foot firmly in the past), but they fill up quickly in the summer. The TIC makes free bookings (accommodation line only ☎ 451700).

Bournemouth Backpackers (☎ 299491; www.bournemouthbackpackers.co.uk; 3 Frances Rd; dm/d £15/36) This friendly hostel near the bus and train stations has small dorms with basic but comfortable facilities and a few private rooms. Reception hours are limited so call ahead or be prepared to wait.

Tudor Grange (☎ 291472; www.tudorgrangehotel.co.uk; 31 Gervis Rd; s/d £45/60; Ⓟ) This lovely old half-timbered house is set in pleasant gardens and has loads of character. The public rooms are all oak-panelled and a fantastic staircase brings you up to the pretty, traditional-style rooms that have subtle floral patterns and antique furniture.

Langtry Manor (☎ 553887; www.langtrymanor.com; Derby Rd, East Cliff; s/d £70/140; Ⓟ ⓡ) This gorgeous house was given to socialite and actress Lillie Langtry by her lover, who was later to become King Edward VII. Nowadays, it endeavours to create an air of romance with four-posters, stylish period décor and a six-course Edwardian banquet (£34.75) on Saturday night.

Eating

Coriander (☎ 552202; 22 Richmond Hill; mains £6.50-11; ♥ lunch & dinner) Cacti, sombreros and colourful stripy blankets set the scene at this fun Mexican restaurant. The menu has excellent combos of all the reliables and there are high chairs and children's menus so that you can enjoy the jugs of margaritas without a mutiny on your hands.

CH2 (☎ 296296; 37 Exeter Rd; mains £6-18; ♥ lunch & dinner) There's a young trendy crowd at this modern minimalist place, with a strange mix of vivid artwork, light woods and Formica tables. The creative menu features plenty of fish and steaks – the swordfish with spinach and salsa is excellent.

Westbeach (☎ 587785; Pier Approach; 2-/3-course set lunch £14.95/16.95, 2-/3-course set dinner £21.95/24.95) This swanky place is bathed in light from the giant windows overlooking the beach. The modern British menu features simple but sophisticated dishes focusing strongly on fish, and on Thursday night crowds pack in for live jazz sessions.

Entertainment

Finding a pub (and not a chain boozer or a café-bar) in the centre of town is very nearly impossible and long queues are the norm for most clubs at the weekend. Wander along Firvale Rd, St Peter's Rd or Old Christchurch Rd for action.

Elements (☎ 311178; Firvale Rd) This is Bournemouth's biggest club, with four floors of fairly middle-of-the-road music.

Opera House (☎ 399922; 570 Christchurch Rd) This incredible converted theatre is Bournemouth's answer to the superclub. The omnipresent Slinky franchise has sunk its teeth in here, playing crowd-pleasing choons from Monday's Bak to Skool night through to Saturday cheese.

Getting There & Away

National Express runs from London (£16, 2½ hours, hourly) and Oxford (£16.50, three hours, three daily). Bus No X3 runs hourly from Salisbury (1¼ hours) and on to Poole (20 minutes), while the No X33 comes from Southampton (one hour, 10 Monday to Saturday). There's a multitude of buses between Bournemouth and Poole (20 minutes).

Trains run every half-hour from London Waterloo (£22.50, two hours); half of these continue on to Poole (£2.50, 10 minutes), Dorchester South (£7.70, 45 minutes) and Weymouth (£9.70, one hour).

POOLE

☎ 01202 / pop 144,800

Marketed as the 'Palm Beach of Britain', Europe's largest natural harbour plays host to B-list celebs and supposedly has the fourth-highest property prices in the world! The town has a lovely old harbour surrounded by narrow winding streets and attractive 18th-century buildings while the up-and-coming district of Sandbanks has a blue-flag beach, lots of water sports and a clutch of upmarket eateries.

The **TIC** (☎ 253253; www.pooletourism.com; Poole Quay; ⊙ 10am-5pm Mon-Sat, noon-5pm Sun) is on the quay. Nearby is the **Waterfront Museum** (☎ 262600; Old High St; admission free; ⊙ 10am-5pm Mon-Sat, noon-5pm Sun Apr-Oct, noon-3pm daily Nov-Mar), which recounts the town's history.

Deep-sea fishing and mackerel fishing are popular in Poole; half-day trips with **Sea Fishing** (☎ 679666; www.seafishingpoole.co.uk; The Quay) start at around £15.

Out at Sandbanks, windsurfing lessons start at £79 per day, with hire from £10 per hour. **Poole Harbour Boardsailing** (☎ 700503; www .pooleharbour.co.uk; 284 Sandbanks Rd) also offers one-/two-day kitesurfing courses for £95/165. **Cool Cats** (☎ 701100; www.coolcatswatersports.com) hires out kayaks (£10 per hour) and bikes (£10 to £19 per day), as well as offering windsurfing and catamaran sailing lessons (from £149 for two days).

For something more cultural, the dynamic arts centre **Poole Lighthouse** (☎ 685222; www.lighthousepoole.co.uk; 21 Kingland Rd) hosts a lively events calendar including live music, theatre, film and exhibitions.

There are plenty of accommodation options, such as **Laurel Cottages** (☎ 730894; laurel .cottages@btopenworld.com; 41 Foxholes Rd; s/d £30/50; ⊠ ⊒), a good-value choice slightly out of town. It has traditional-style rooms and an outdoor heated pool. Alternatively, try **Mansion House** (☎ 685666; www.themansionhouse .co.uk; Thames St; s/d £75/130; P ⊠), a gorgeous Georgian house with beautiful, themed rooms. The excellent restaurant (a two-/three-course set menu costs £21/27) focuses on fish, seafood and game. Another good option for food is **Storm** (☎ 674970; 16 High St; mains £12.50-16; ⊙ dinner), a rustic place serving some of the best seafood in town.

Countless buses cover the 20-minute trip to Bournemouth. Bus No 152 goes from Poole to Sandbanks (15 minutes, hourly). National Express runs hourly to London (£16, three hours). Train connections are as for Bournemouth (left), which is just 13 minutes closer to London Waterloo (£25.30).

WIMBORNE MINSTER

☎ 01202 / pop 14,844

Dominated by its impressive old minster, sleepy Wimborne is a dignified old town with a cluster of picturesque buildings and narrow rambling streets.

The **Wimborne Minster** (☎ 884753; www.wimborne minster.org.uk; ⊙ 9.30am-5.30pm), founded around 1050, was considerably enlarged in Decorated style in the 14th century and became the parish church in 1537 when Henry VIII dissolved the monasteries. The nave columns, the piers of the central tower and the north and south transepts are the main Norman survivors. Traces of 13th- to 15th-century painted murals can be seen in a Norman altar recess in the north transept. Other highlights include the impressive 15th-century perpendicular tower, a remarkable 14th-century astronomical clock and tessellated Roman mosaic tiles that can be seen in the nave. There's a wonderful **chained library** (10.30am-12.30pm & 2-4pm Mon-Thu, 10.30am-12.30pm Fri Easter-Oct) above the choir vestry.

Just 2 miles west of Wimborne is one of the country's finest 17th-century houses, **Kingston Lacy** (NT; 01202-883402; adult house, park & garden £7.20, park & garden only £3.60; house 11am-5pm Wed-Sun, grounds 10.30am-6pm Easter-Oct), left much as it was when the last occupant departed in 1981 without selling a thing. The house is dense with furniture and art, much of it collected by William Bankes, who was responsible for major renovations in the 1830s. The extensive 18th-century landscaped gardens and estate encompass the Iron-Age hill-fort of **Badbury Rings**.

Bus Nos 132 and 133 run between Bournemouth (45 minutes) and Poole (40 minutes) via Wimborne every half-hour Monday to Saturday (every two hours on Sunday). Bus Nos 182 and 183 run to Bournemouth and, more frequently, to Shaftesbury (1¼ hours, hourly, Monday to Saturday).

Sleeping & Eating

Beechleas (841684; 17 Poole Rd; s/d £69/79; ; wheelchair access) This delightful B&B is set in a beautifully restored Georgian house with a lovely walled garden. The restored coach house has cosy rooms with beamed ceilings, while rooms in the main house retain their period character and elegance.

King's Head (880101; www.thekingsheadhotel .com; The Square; s/d £75/95) This traditional Georgian coaching inn has been recently refurbished, but the large rooms are a little soulless with corporate-style features and little character. The bar and restaurant have retained period features and do decent but predictable food (mains £6 to £13).

Shapwick House Hotel (01458-210321; Monks Dr, Shapwick; s/d £85/100-160; 2-/3-course dinner £20/24.50;) This wonderful Tudor country house has huge rooms with eclectic décor, and a great restaurant serving traditional English classics and more-imaginative modern fare. Shapwick is 4 miles northwest of Wimborne off the A350.

Getting There & Away

Bus Nos 132 and 133 run between Bournemouth (45 minutes) and Poole (40 minutes) via Wimborne every half-hour Monday to

Saturday (every two hours on Sunday). Bus Nos 182 and 183 run to Bournemouth and, more frequently, to Shaftesbury (1¼ hours, hourly, Monday to Saturday).

SOUTHEAST DORSET

Pretty thatched villages, winding country lanes, crumbling ruins and a spectacular coastline make the Purbeck Peninsula of Southeast Dorset a fantastic place to ramble. Walkers shouldn't miss the towering cliffs and tranquil coves of this section of the Dorset Coast Path.

Wareham

 01929 / pop 2568

The charming town of Wareham on the River Frome has a lovely quay, remarkable remains of Saxon town walls and an impressive church dating from the same period. It also has a string of Lawrence of Arabia connections. Lawrence was an enigmatic figure renowned for his heroic achievements in WWI and his immense book *Seven Pillars of Wisdom*. His life was immortalised in David Lean's epic film *Lawrence of Arabia*.

Purbeck TIC (552740; www.purbeck-dc.gov.uk; Holy Trinity Church, South St; 9.30am-5pm Mon-Sat & 10am-1pm & 1.45-4pm Sun Apr-Sep, 10am-3pm Mon-Sat Oct-Mar) stocks an excellent free guide and walking-tour map.

The bijou **Wareham Museum** (553448; East St; admission free; 10am-4pm Easter-Oct) has an interesting Lawrence of Arabia collection as well as local items.

On the wall beside North St is the tiny but delightful Saxon **St Martin's Church**, which dates from about 1020. Although the porch and bell tower are later additions, and larger windows have been added over the centuries, the basic structure is unchanged. Inside there's a 12th-century fresco on the northern wall and a marble effigy of Lawrence of Arabia.

You'll find more Lawrence memorabilia at his tiny, austere former home, **Clouds Hill** (NT; 405616; adult £3.10; noon-5pm Thu-Sun Apr-Oct), still much as he would have left it after his death in 1935.

Lawrence was stationed at Bovington Camp, which is now a **Tank Museum** (405096; www.tankmuseum.org; adult/child £8/6; 10am-5pm; wheelchair access), 6 miles from Wareham. He died at Bovington Military Hospital six days after a nearby motorcycle accident.

Bus Nos 142, 143 and 144 run between Poole (35 minutes) and Wareham hourly (every two hours on Sunday). Bus Nos 101, 102, 103 and 104 run between Wareham (15 minutes) and Dorchester (one hour, hourly Monday to Saturday). Clouds Hill is a 1-mile walk from the nearest stop.

Corfe Castle
☎ 01929
The magnificent ruins of **Corfe Castle** (NT; ☎ 01929-481294; adult £4.70; ✆ 10am-6pm Apr-Oct, 10am-5pm Mar, 10am-4pm Nov-Feb) tower above the gorgeous stone village of the same name, offering wonderful views of the countryside. Even by English standards, the 1000-year-old castle has a dramatic history, with royal poisonings, treacherous stabbings and Civil War sieges. Elements of early Norman brickwork are still evident, but it's the fractured grandeur of the scene that draws the crowds.

The village has several pubs and B&Bs, and there are campsites nearby.

Bus Nos 142, 143 and 144 run hourly from Poole (50 minutes) through Wareham (15 minutes) to Swanage (20 minutes) via Corfe Castle.

Blue Pool
Designated a Site of Special Scientific Interest (SSSI), the **Blue Pool** (☎ 01929-551408; www .bluepooluk.com; Furzebrook; adult £3.80; ✆ grounds 9.30am-5pm Mar-Nov, closes later in summer) has water with a chameleonlike tendency to change colour. The grounds are home to rare wildlife including green sand lizards and Dartford warblers. The pool is signposted from the A351; hourly bus Nos 142, 143 and 144 from Wareham (10 minutes) stop nearby.

Lulworth Cove & the Coast
☎ 01929
The coastline between Swanage and Weymouth is simply stunning, with a fantastic drive across the moors from Corfe Castle to Lulworth and spectacular clifftop walks. There are some excellent beaches around **Durdle Door**, where a natural arch is formed by folding rock. At Lulworth Cove, a mile to the east, towering cliffs enclose an almost perfectly circular bay.

Stumpy **Lulworth Castle** (☎ 400352; www.lul worth.com; East Lulworth; adult £7; ✆ 10.30am-6pm Apr-Oct, 10.30am-4pm Nov-Mar) is in a picturesque

village about 3 miles inland. The castle is 'modern' compared with many in England and was built as a hunting lodge in 1608. It contains exhibits about its history and has a children's adventure playground outside. You can see jousting shows here throughout August.

There are lots of places to stay around Lulworth. Campers should head for **Durdle Door Holiday Park** (☎ 400200; durdle.door@lulworth .com; tent sites £11-16; ✆ Mar-Oct), spectacularly situated on the fields above the cliffs. In the lovely village of West Lulworth you'll find a small, simple **YHA Hostel** (☎ 0870 770 5940; www.yha.org.uk; School Lane; dm £10.60; ✆ Mar-Oct) and the Victorian **Graybank** (☎ 400256; West Lulworth; s/d £20/36; **P** ✖), an excellent-value B&B set in a Purbeck stone house with modest, traditional-style rooms.

Bus No 103 runs from Dorchester (40 minutes, five Monday to Saturday) to Lulworth Cove.

DORCHESTER
☎ 01305 / pop 16,171
A core of elegant 17th-century and Georgian buildings make up the heart of what was once Thomas Hardy's home and the centre of his fictional Wessex. It's a pleasant place, home to a lively Wednesday market and to the Poundbury development (Prince Charles' experiment in ideal town planning). Not content with its humble charms, the town also hosts a clutch of bizarre museums that exploit the tourist market.

Orientation & Information
Most of Dorchester's action takes place along South St, which runs north into pedestrianised Cornhill and then emerges in High St.

The **TIC** (☎ 267992; dorchester.tic@westdorset-dc .gov.uk; Antelope Walk; ✆ 9am-5pm Mon-Sat & 10am-3pm Sun Apr-Oct, 9am-4pm Mon-Sat Nov-Mar) stocks the *All About Dorchester* (£1) guide, with interesting walks around town. There's also lots of Hardy literature, including a set of leaflets (50p each) tracing the scenes of individual novels.

Sights
The foundations of a 1st-century **Roman town house** are behind the town hall on Northern Hay. The layout of the house is clearly visible and the remains of the main

THE BLOODY ASSIZES

In 1685 the Duke of Monmouth (illegitimate son of Charles II) landed at Lyme Regis intending to supplant James II and become king. His rebellion ended in defeat at the Battle of Sedgemoor in Somerset. The duke was beheaded in the Tower of London – it took four swings of the axe to sever his head. Judge Jeffreys, the chief justice, tried the rebels in Dorchester in a barbaric trial known as the Bloody Assizes.

Over 300 rebels were hanged and their gruesome drawn-and-quartered remains were displayed in towns and villages all over the region. Nearly 1000 more rebels were transported to Barbados and many others were imprisoned, fined or flogged.

building, housed within a glass structure, boast remarkable mosaic floors. To the northern end of town is **Poundbury Village**, HRH Prince Charles' vision of a model development for 21st-century communities.

The Hardy memorabilia at **Dorset County Museum** (☎ 262735; High West St; adult/child £3.50/ 1.70; ☻ 10am-5pm daily May-Oct, Mon-Sat Nov-Apr), featuring the novelist's study, is only part of a wide-ranging general collection that includes relics from the archaeological excavations at Maiden Castle, fossil finds from Lyme Regis and artefacts from the Roman town house.

The **Tutankhamun Exhibition** (☎ 269571; www .tutankhamun-exhibition.co.uk; High West St; adult/child £6/4.50; ☻ 9.30am-5.30pm) explores the discovery of the tomb, and its contents have been recreated in montages, complete with sounds and smells.

You can see more exotic displays at the **Terracotta Warriors Museum** (☎ 266040; www.terra cottawarriors.co.uk; East High St; adult/child £5/3; ☻ 10am-5.30pm), where eight full-size reconstructions of the 2m-high clay warriors found in Xi An are on show.

Other museums include the **Keep Military Museum** (☎ 264066; www.keepmilitarymuseum.org; Bridport Rd; adult/child £3/2; ☻ 9.30am-5pm Mon-Sat Apr-Sep & 10am-4pm Sun Jul & Aug, 9.30am-5pm Tue-Sat Oct-Mar), which traces Dorset and Devon military valour overseas, and the **Dinosaur Museum** (☎ 269880; Icen Way; adult/child £6/4.50; ☻ 9.30am-5.30pm), featuring fossils and life-size reconstructed beasts.

THOMAS HARDY SITES

The TIC has a free leaflet called *The Hardy Trail*, with information on Hardy connections around the town and surrounding area.

Designed by Thomas Hardy, **Max Gate** (NT; ☎ 262538; Alington Ave; adult £2.60; ☻ 2-5pm Mon, Wed & Sun Apr-Sep) was Hardy's home from 1885 until his death in 1928. It contains pieces of his furniture, but otherwise there's not exactly a wealth of memorabilia. Here he wrote several of his most famous works, including *Tess of the d'Urbervilles* and *Jude the Obscure*. It's a mile east of the town centre on the A352.

Similarly, the small cob-and-thatch **Hardy's Cottage** (NT; ☎ 01305-262366; adult £3; ☻ 11am-5pm Thu-Mon Apr-Oct), where Hardy was born, is furnished in appropriately simple style, but is unremarkable. It's at Higher Bockhampton, about 3 miles northeast of Dorchester and reached by a 10-minute walk from the car park.

Sleeping & Eating

Dorchester is blessed with some beautiful hotels and excellent restaurants, and makes a great base for the surrounding area.

Casterbridge Hotel (☎ 264043; www.casterbridge hotel.co.uk; 49 High East St; s £48-64, d £80-98; wheel-chair access) This lovely upmarket Georgian guesthouse has a choice of period rooms with traditional flowers and frills or contemporary rooms with neutral colours. The Casterbridge Hotel has a lovely courtyard garden and, despite the refined air, children are very welcome.

Yalbury Cottage (☎ 262382; www.yalburycottage .com; Lower Brockhampton; s/d £59/94; 3-course dinner £30; P ☒) A gorgeous, 17th-century thatched cottage near Thomas Hardy's birthplace. This charming place has rooms with exposed beams and rustic, period furnishings. The restaurant serves excellent contemporary food.

Potters Bistro & Café (☎ 260312; 19 Durngate St; lunch mains £4-6, dinner mains £7-14; ☻ breakfast, lunch & dinner) This beautifully renovated property blends traditional features with clean modern design. The daytime menu has gourmet sandwiches, stunning home-made soups and interesting salads and pastas. In the evening it steps up a level with tempting dishes such as marinated Balmoral venison or pan-fried fillet of wild sea bass.

Sienna (☎ 250022; 36 High West St; 2-course set lunch/dinner £13/24; ☺ lunch & dinner Tue-Sat) This tiny modern restaurant offers top-notch cuisine. Go for lemon sole fillets with tiger prawn tortellini, or pot-roasted quail with wild mushrooms and a puy lentil sauce, and follow it up with the wicked bitter chocolate mousse.

Getting There & Around

National Express coaches run from London (£17.50, four hours, once daily). Bus No 31 runs from Weymouth (30 minutes) and on to Lyme Regis (1¼ hours) hourly (every two hours on Sunday); No 10 also serves Weymouth every 20 minutes (every two hours on Sunday). Bus No 184 goes to Salisbury (1¾ hours, six daily Monday to Saturday, three on Sunday).

There are two train stations, Dorchester South and Dorchester West, both southwest of the town centre. Trains run hourly from Weymouth (£2.70, 11 minutes) to London (saver return £31, 2½ hours) via Dorchester South, Bournemouth (£7.70, 45 minutes) and Southampton (£15, 1¼ hours). Dorchester West has connections with Bath (£10.50, 1¾ hours) and Bristol (£11.40, two hours).

Dorchester Cycles (☎ 268787; 31 Great Western Rd; per day £10) hires bikes. Dorchester is a good town for cycling and you can also get around on foot easily.

AROUND DORCHESTER
Cerne Abbas & the Cerne Giant

The gorgeous village of Cerne Abbas, with its beautiful 16th-century houses, is an idyllic place to stroll and admire the wonderful buildings and quiet lanes. You'll see rare medieval frescoes and impish gargoyles in the 14th-century **St Mary's Church**, but the real attraction is the **Cerne Giant**, one of Britain's best-known chalk figures.

The giant stands 55m tall, wields a 37m-long club and is estimated to be anything between a few hundred and a couple of thousand years old. One thing is obvious – this old man has no need of Viagra! The poor fellow only regained his manhood last century after the prudish Victorians allowed grass to grow over his vital parts.

For refreshment visit the thatched **Royal Oak** (☎ 01300-341797; Long St; mains £5-8; ☺ lunch & dinner), a gorgeous pub just dripping with

character and good cheer. It serves some excellent pub grub in its low, beamed bar.

Bus No 216 runs to Dorchester (20 minutes, six times Monday to Saturday).

WEYMOUTH
☎ 01305 / pop 48,279

Afternoon teas, donkey rides and buckets and spades are the summer staples in the traditional family resort of Weymouth. The golden beach is flanked by old-style boarding houses and hotels while the old harbour is a more charming place, with a couple of engaging museums and pretty coloured cottages lining the narrow winding streets.

Orientation & Information

Central Weymouth is only a few blocks wide with The Esplanade following the seafront and the old harbour at the west end.

The **TIC** (☎ 785747; tic@weymouth.gov.uk; The Esplanade; ☺ 9.30am-5pm Apr-Oct, 10am-4pm Nov-Mar) is opposite the vivid statue of King George III, patron saint of Weymouth tourism. If you're planning to visit any of the attractions in Weymouth or Abbotsbury you can buy your tickets from the TIC at a substantial discount.

You can check your email at **Cobwebs** (☎ 779688; 28 St Thomas St; per 20min £1; ☺ 9.45am-9.30pm Mon-Fri, 10am-6pm Sat, noon-6pm Sun).

Sights & Activities

Over in the old part of town, Brewer's Quay has a shopping centre and plentiful attractions, including the excellent **Timewalk** (☎ 777622; Hope Sq; adult/child £4.50/3.25; ☺ 10am-5.30pm), a series of historical tableaux depicting the town's early history as a trading port, the disaster of the Black Death, the drama of the Spanish Armada and the development of Weymouth as a resort.

Also in Brewer's Quay is the fascinating **Weymouth Museum** (admission free; ☺ 10am-5pm), uncovering the town's maritime heritage.

Nearby, there's the wonderful **Tudor House** (☎ 812341; 3 Trinity St; adult/child £2.50/50p; ☺ 11am-3.45pm Tue-Fri Jun-Sep, 2-4pm 1st Sun of the month Oct-May) dating from around 1600. It's furnished in Tudor style and admission includes a guided tour delving into the everyday life of those days.

Don't be put off by the 'family fun' tag and gift-shop entrance at **Deep Sea Adventure** (☎ 0871 222 5760; www.deepsea-adventure.co.uk;

9 Custom House Quay; adult/child £4/3; ☺ 9.30am-7pm Sep-Jun, 9.30am-8pm Jul & Aug) – it's actually an absorbing examination of the history of diving, with exhibits on local shipwrecks and the *Titanic*. Last entry is 1½ hours before closing time.

Perched on the end of the promontory, 19th-century **Nothe Fort** (☎ 766465; Barrack Rd; adult/child £4.50/free; ☺ 10.30am-5.30pm daily May-Sep, 2.30-4.30pm Sun Oct-Apr) houses a museum that focuses on life in the fort for soldiers over the years. It's a substantial affair, with extensive collections of weapons and great views of the harbour and coast.

If you'd rather get wet, there are excellent wreck and drift dive sites near Weymouth. **Old Harbour Dive School** (☎ 861000; www.oldharbour diveschool.co.uk; 2 Coastguard Cottages, Grove Point, Portland) organises trips to the best sites from £40 per day, plus £45 to hire equipment.

For windsurfing lessons (from £50 for three hours) and hire (£10 to £25 per hour), contact **Windtek** (☎ 787900; www.windtek.co.uk; 109 Portland Rd). It also offers a beginners' kitesurfing course for £95.

Sleeping & Eating

Weymouth has a colossal number of guesthouses and hotels; most are pretty standard affairs with little character. If you're camping, there are plenty of sites near Chesil Beach and Weymouth Bay.

Chatsworth (☎ 785012; www.thechatsworth.co.uk; 14 The Esplanade; s/d £33/70; ℗) There's a range of rooms with views of the Old Harbour and the bay at this smart guesthouse so take a look at a few before deciding. The modern Mediterranean-style brasserie (mains £8 to £14) is strong on locally caught fish but also does a good range of meat dishes.

Oaklands Edwardian Guesthouse (☎ 767081; www.oaklands-guesthouse.co.uk; 1 Glendinning Ave; s/d £40/50; ℗ ✗ ; wheelchair access) This lovely Edwardian house is in a quiet area but within an easy stroll of the beach. The ground floor is elaborately restored with painted plaster mouldings and stained glass, but the bedrooms are modern with simple, light décor.

Yako (☎ 780888; 97 St Mary St; mains £4.80; ☺ lunch & dinner) This excellent Japanese noodle bar has a great selection of traditional dishes ranging from sushi to soba to bento boxes. The portions are generous, making it excellent value.

Isobar (☎ 750666; 19 Trinity Rd; mains £12.95-15.50; ☺ dinner) A lush, baroque bar-restaurant, this funky place offers modern British and international cuisine with plenty of seafood, game and local meats. It has welcoming velvet sofas and is a tempting spot to loll for the evening with a long drink.

Other recommendations:

Perry's (☎ 785799; 4 Trinity Rd; mains £12.95-15.95; ☺ dinner daily, lunch Tue-Fri & Sun) Classic style and excellent food overlooking the old harbour.

Victoria Hotel (☎ 761438; www.victoriaweymouth.com; 56-57 The Esplanade; s/d £26.50/45; ℗ ✗) Great-value rooms on the waterfront.

Getting There & Away

National Express coaches run to London (£17.50, 4¾ hours, six daily). Bus Nos 10, 31, 101, 102, 103 and 104 between them serve Dorchester (30 minutes) at least every 20 minutes. Bus No 31 goes on to Lyme Regis (1¾ hours, hourly), as does No X53 (six daily, Monday to Saturday – on Sundays three times between Lyme Regis and Weymouth), which continues to Exeter (three hours). Bus No 184 runs to Salisbury (1¾ hours, six daily Monday to Saturday, three on Sunday). First Explorer all-day travel tickets cost £2.50 and cover Weymouth, Portland and Dorchester.

From Dorchester West trains run hourly to London (£36.30, 2¾ hours) via Dorchester South (£2.70, 11 minutes), Bournemouth (£9.70, one hour) and Southampton (£15.90, 1¾ hours) and every two hours to Bath (£10.80, two hours) and Bristol (£12, 2¼ hours).

AROUND WEYMOUTH
Portland

Renowned as the source of the eponymous hard limestone, quarried here for centuries, Portland is essentially an island joined to the mainland by the long sweep of Chesil Beach. There are incredible views from the top of the craggy outcrop and it's a popular place for climbing and bird-watching. The clear waters surrounding it are also good for windsurfing and diving.

For superb views across the channel make for the **lighthouse** (☎ 01305-861233; ☺ 11am-5pm Apr-Sep), which houses the summer-only **TIC** (☎ 01305-861233), at the end of Portland Bill. It costs £2.50/1.50 per adult/child to climb the 41m-high tower.

Sturdy **Portland Castle** (EH; ☎ 820539; adult £3.50; ⏰ 10am-6pm Apr-Sep, to 5pm Oct, to 4pm Fri-Sun Nov-Mar) is one of the finest examples of the defensive castles constructed during Henry VIII's castle-building spree, spurred by fear of an attack from France. You can try on period armour and get great views over Portland harbour.

Portland Museum (☎ 01305-821804; 217 Wakeham St; adult/child £2.30/free; ⏰ 10.30am-5pm Fri-Tue Easter-Oct) has varied displays on local history, smuggling and literary connections, as well as some huge ammonites (fossils).

There are excellent wreck and drift dive sites around Portland and Weymouth. **Old Harbour Dive School** (☎ 861000; www.oldharbourdiveschool.co.uk; 2 Coastguard Cottages, Grove Point) organises trips to the best sites from £40 per day, plus £45 to hire equipment.

Weymouth & Portland National Sailing Academy (☎ 860101; www.wpsa.org.uk; Osprey Quay) runs two-day sailing courses for £150.

Bus No 1 runs to Portland from Weymouth every 10 minutes, while No 501 goes every 30 minutes.

Chesil Beach

A massive expanse of pebbles stretches along the coast for 10 miles between Portland and Abbotsbury, at times reaching up to 15m high. It's an incredible sight and encloses Fleet Lagoon, a haven for water birds. The stones vary from pebble size at Abbotsbury in the west to around 15cm in diameter at Portland. The **Chesil Beach Centre** (☎ 01305-760579; Ferrybridge; ⏰ 11am-6pm Apr-Sep, 11am-4pm Oct-Mar) provides information, and organises talks and guided walks.

Abbotsbury

☎ 01305

This gorgeous little village was once the site of a medieval abbey, but only scant remains of its devout past endure. However, the village in itself is a great ramble and with three popular attractions it is well worth a detour.

The huge, 83m-long tithe barn houses **Smuggler's Barn** (☎ 871817; adult/child £5.20/3.80; ⏰ 10am-6pm Easter-Oct), a children's farm and play area with a smidgen of smuggling lore. Traces of Abbotsbury's Benedictine monastery can be found by the barn.

On the coast is **Abbotsbury Swannery** (☎ 871858; New Barn Rd; adult/child £6.50/3.50; ⏰ 10am-6pm mid-Mar-Oct), founded by the monks of Abbotsbury's monastery, about 600 years ago. The colony of swans can number up to 600, plus cygnets, and the self-guided walk through will tell you all you ever wanted to know about swans. The energetic can walk up to 14th-century **St Catherine's Chapel** for superb views of the swannery, the village and Chesil Beach.

Laid out in 1765 as a kitchen garden, **Abbotsbury Subtropical Gardens** (☎ 871387; adult/child £6.50/3.80; ⏰ 10am-6pm Mar-Oct, 10am-4pm Nov-Feb) are now lush with camellias, hydrangeas and rhododendrons. Last admission is one hour before closing.

Joint tickets to Smuggler's Barn and either the Swannery or the Subtropical Gardens costs £10/6 per adult/child; see www.abbotsbury-tourism.com.

Bus No X53 runs from Weymouth (30 minutes) to Lyme Regis (one hour) via Abbotsbury six times daily Monday to Saturday (three on Sunday).

LYME REGIS

☎ 01297 / pop 4406

Perched right on the edge of Dorset, Lyme Regis manages to maintain its graceful air while still attracting the bucket-and-spade crowd. The charming narrow streets nestle around an old fishing village – prime material for Jane Austen, who wrote *Persuasion* here, and it was also used as a film set for *The French Lieutenant's Woman*. Some of the first dinosaur skeletons in the world were discovered in the fossil-rich limestone cliffs flanking the town.

Lyme Regis' **TIC** (☎ 442138; lyme.tic@westdorset-dc.gov.uk; Guildhall Cottage, Church St; ⏰ 10am-5pm Mon-Sat & 10am-4pm Sun Apr-Oct, 10am-3pm Mon-Sat Nov-Mar) is on the corner of Church and Bridge Sts.

The excellent **Philpot Museum** (☎ 443370; www.lymeregismuseum.co.uk; Bridge St; adult/child £2/free; ⏰ 10am-5pm Mon-Sat & 11am-5pm Sun Apr-Oct, 11am-5pm Sat & Sun Nov-Mar) is in a quirky building with displays of paintings and other artefacts relating to local history and literary connections. It contains a good fossil collection and displays on the life and finds of Mary Anning, a world-famous Lyme Regis palaeontologist.

If your own fossil-hunting happens to be unsuccessful, head to **Dinosaurland** (☎ 443541; www.dinosaurland.co.uk; Coombe St; adult/child £4/3;

SOUTHWEST ENGLAND

☺ 10am-5pm), where you'll see extensive fossil displays and reconstructed dinosaurs.

At the end of the **Cobb**, a 13th-century jetty-cum-breakwater, is the pleasantly low-tech **Marine Aquarium** (☎ 443678; adult/child £2.50/1.50p; ☺ 10am-5pm Apr-Oct, extended hrs in peak season) , with tanks housing local underwater life.

There's an abundance of accommodation in town. **Armada House** (☎ 445785; penny@lymeregis.com; 8 Coombe St; s/d £30/48; P ✗) is a pretty little courtyard cottage tucked away in old Lyme, with spacious rooms, king-size beds, subtle décor and large bathrooms with power showers. It's a charming place with a warm welcome and just a short stroll from the sea. On the waterfront, the **Cobb Arms** (☎ 443242; Marine Pde; s/d £40/60; P ✗) has a few excellent rooms with modern décor and simple colour schemes. The friendly bar serves a good range of snacks as well as decent pub grub (mains £5 to £10).

The 17th-century **Mariners Hotel** (☎ 442753; www.hotellymeregis.co.uk; Silver St; s/d £60/90; P ✗) has bright, spacious rooms with subtle modern features, and an excellent restaurant serving three-course dinners (£20.50) that features fresh local fish.

Another good bet for food is **Café Clemence** (☎ 445757; Mill Lane; mains £10-13; ☺ lunch & dinner), a snug little bistro in the atmospheric old-mill complex. It serves a good range of modern Mediterranean cuisine with a healthy dose of fish and seafood dishes.

Bus No 31 runs to Dorchester (1¼ hours) and Weymouth (1¾ hours) hourly Monday to Saturday (every two hours on Sunday). Bus No X53 goes west to Exeter (1¾ hours) and east to Weymouth (1½ hours) six times daily Monday to Saturday, and on Sundays three times daily between Lyme Regis and Weymouth.

SHERBORNE
☎ 01935 / pop 9350

The mellow stone village of Sherborne is today a peaceful country town, but its marvellous abbey and two magnificent castles, defiantly placed at either side of Sherborne Lake, give clues to its former importance and glory as capital of Wessex.

Sherborne's **TIC** (☎ 815341; sherborne.tic@west dorset-dc.ov.uk; Digby Rd; ☺ 9am-5pm Mon-Sat Apr-Oct, 10am-3pm Mon-Sat Nov-Mar) stocks the free *All About Sherborne* leaflet, which includes a map and town trail.

Sights

SHERBORNE ABBEY

Established early in the 8th century, the **Sherborne Abbey** (Abbey Church of St Mary the Virgin; ☎ 812452; suggested donation £2; ☺ 8.30am-6pm late Mar–late Oct, 8.30am-4pm Nov–mid-Mar) became a Benedictine abbey in 998 and functioned as a cathedral until 1075. The church boasts the oldest fan vaulting in the country, and the monks' choir stalls feature interesting misericords. Solid Saxon-Norman piers support the abbey's soaring central tower and the main entrance has a sturdy Norman porch that was built in 1180. On the edge of the abbey close are the cloistered 1437 **St Johns' Almshouses** (adult £1.50; ☺ 2-4pm Tue & Thu-Sat May-Sep), containing a medieval chapel.

OLD CASTLE

East of the town centre stand the ruins of the **Old Castle** (EH; ☎ 812730; adult £2.30; ☺ 10am-6pm Apr-Sep, 10am-5pm Oct), originally constructed from 1107 by Roger, Bishop of Salisbury. Sir Walter Raleigh acquired it (with the help of Elizabeth I) in the late 16th century, and spent large sums of money modernising the castle before deciding it wasn't worth the effort and moving across the River Yeo to start work on his new castle. Oliver Cromwell destroyed the 'malicious and mischievous castle' after a 16-day siege in 1645, leaving behind the evocative ruins you see today.

SHERBORNE CASTLE

Sir Walter Raleigh commenced building his **New Castle** (☎ 813182; www.sherbornecastle.com; castle & gardens adult/child £7/free, gardens only £3.50/free; ☺ 11am-4.30pm Tue-Thu & Sun, 2.30-4.30pm Sat Easter-Oct) – really a splendid manor house – in 1594. However, by 1608 he was back in prison, this time at the hands of James I, who eventually sold the castle to Sir John Digby, the Earl of Bristol, in 1617. It's been the Digby family residence ever since, and contains extensive collections of art, furniture and porcelain, as well as grounds landscaped by Capability Brown.

SHERBORNE MUSEUM

This **museum** (☎ 812252; Church Lane; adult/child £1/free; ☺ 10.30am-4.30pm Tue-Sat, 2.30pm-4.30pm Sun Apr-Oct) features local history and prehistory and a scale model of the Old Castle.

Fox Inn (☎ 01935-891330; http://heavenly
hotels.co.uk/fox-inn.html; Corscombe; s/d £50/70;
mains £8-18) This idyllic, rose-clad 17th-
century pub is pretty much unspoilt, with
beamed ceilings, flagstone floors, slate-
topped counters and hunting prints on the
walls. Blue gingham cloths cover the rustic
tables that are tucked away in nooks and
crannies, and the menu features imaginative pub food such as rabbit braised in cider,
and more-exotic dishes such as lamb tagine
with couscous, or monkfish with red pepper salsa. Wash it all down with ale tapped
from the cask or the pub's own sloe gin and
you'll soon be retiring to one of the charming cottage bedrooms, tucked beneath the
thatch, to sleep it all off.

Corscombe is 13 miles northwest of
Dorchester on the A356.

Sleeping & Eating

Eastbury Hotel (☎ 813131; www.theeastburyhotel
.co.uk; Long St; s/d £44/80; P ✗) This charming
Georgian hotel set in walled gardens has
traditionally decorated spacious rooms, with
subtle floral patterns and neutral colours.
The conservatory restaurant has a good selection of seafood, meat and vegetarian dishes
(mains £9 to £14).

Little Barwick House (☎ 01935-423902; www.little
barwickhouse.co.uk; Barwick; s/d £65/120; P ✗) This
stunning place oozes true charm and style.
The rooms are luxurious, and decorated
in an elegant but informal contemporary
style with big beds, beautiful light-coloured
fabrics and fresh flowers. The restaurant
(lunch £15.50, dinner £28.50) is equally
stylish and serves excellent modern British
fare. Barwick is 5 miles southwest of Sherborne off the A37.

Green (☎ 813821; 3 The Green; lunch mains £8.95-
13.50, dinner mains £17; ✆ Tue-Sat) This chic little bistro, with antique wooden tables and
chairs, starched linen and modern décor,
serves an excellent range of tempting dishes
prepared with local fish, meat and game.

Getting There & Away

Nearby Yeovil is a handy transport hub. Bus
No 57 runs hourly from Yeovil (30 minutes,
Monday to Saturday), as does the quicker
No 58 (12 minutes, every two hours Mon-

day to Saturday), which sometimes continues on to Shaftesbury (1½ hours). Bus No
216 runs to Dorchester (one hour, six daily
Monday to Saturday) via Cerne Abbas (30
minutes).

Trains run from Exeter (£12.20, 1¼
hours) to London (£32.30, 2¼ hours) via
Salisbury (£8.50, 45 minutes) roughly
hourly.

SHAFTESBURY
☎ 01747 / pop 6665

Old-fashioned, old-world Shaftesbury sits
on top of a sandstone outcrop and commands excellent views over the surrounding countryside. The town is also home to
the remains of an ancient abbey and the
charming Gold Hill.

The **TIC** (☎ 853514; www.shaftesburydorset.com; 8
Bell St; ✆ 10am-5pm daily Apr-Sep, 10am-3pm Mon-Sat
Oct-Mar) is by the Bleke St car park.

Situated on top of the 240m-high ridge,
Shaftesbury Abbey (☎ 852910; www.shaftesburyabbey
.co.uk; Park Walk; adult/child £2/60p; ✆ 10am-5pm
Apr-Oct) was founded in 888 by Alfred the
Great and was at one time England's richest
nunnery. Henry VIII's gentle attentions finished it off in 1539. Today, you can wander
around the foundations with a well-devised
audio guide, and visit the museum, which
tells the abbey's history.

The steep, picturesque cobbled **Gold Hill**
tumbles down the ridge from beside the
abbey ruins, offering great views of the surrounding plains. Its photogenic qualities
have been exploited by postcard-makers
and advertising companies alike.

The small **Shaftesbury Museum** (☎ 852157;
Sun & Moon Cottage, Gold Hill; adult/child £1.50/free;
✆ 10.30am-4.30pm Thu-Tue) is worth visiting to
see the Shaftesbury Hoard of coins, some
dating from 871, as well as a collection of
local buttons for which the town was once
famous.

Just west of town is the unique six-sided
Old Wardour Castle (EH; ☎ 01747-870487; adult £2.60;
✆ 10am-6pm Apr-Sep, 10am-5pm Oct, 10am-4pm Wed-
Sun Nov-Mar), which was built around 1393
and suffered severe damage during the Civil
War, leaving the magnificent remains you
see today. It's an ideal spot for a picnic and
there are fantastic views from the upper
levels.

Bus No 26 runs from Shaftesbury (four
daily Monday to Friday), 4 miles west.

Sleeping & Eating

Cobwebbs (☎ 853505; www.cobwebbs.me.uk; 14 Gold Hill; s/d £30/50; ✗) This white thatched cottage right on picturesque Gold Hill has beautiful bright and airy rustic rooms, an oak-beamed sitting room and a lovely garden terrace with great views over the surrounding countryside.

La Fleur de Lys (☎ 853717; www.lafleurdelys.co.uk; Bleke St; s/d £50/75; P ✗ ⬚ ; wheelchair access) You'll find old-world luxury mixed with modern comforts at this restaurant that also has accommodation. It's a charming place with attractive rooms and an excellent choice of ambitious food (mains £16.50 to £20) at its intimate restaurant. Traditional ingredients such as roe venison and veal sweetbreads feature strongly but in an innovative, modern way.

Ship Inn (☎ 853219; Bleke St; mains £6.50-9) For an excellent lunch or something more informal try this pleasant old stone pub, with its good selection of traditional pub grub, renowned pie and mash and a varied choice of real ales.

Getting There & Away

Bus Nos 182 and 183 run to Blandford Forum (40 minutes, eight daily Monday to Saturday); some go on to Bournemouth (two hours) though most require a change. Bus Nos 26 and 27 run from Salisbury (1¼ hours, four daily Monday to Saturday).

DEVON

With miles of unspoiled coastline, countless picture-postcard villages and some of the most beautiful countryside anywhere in England, Devon has long been one of Britain's most popular holiday spots. But there's more to the region than country walks and cream teas. The twin coastlines are markedly different from each other – along the bustling southern coast you'll find the popular tourist resorts of the English Riviera (Torquay, Paignton and Brixham) and the maritime port of Plymouth. However, the quieter northern coast is dotted with sleepy villages, quaint cottages and sweeping bays, which make ideal places to escape the summertime crowds. Most of the central part of Devon is taken up by the wild heathland and jagged tors of Dartmoor

National Park, one of the best destinations in the southwest for backcountry walking and cycling.

Orientation

Devon is bounded to the east by Somerset and Dorset, with the border skirting the southern edge of Exmoor and hitting the coast west of Lyme Regis. The border with Cornwall follows the River Tamar from its source near the north Devon coast to the estuary at Plymouth. Dartmoor claims much of the inland area between Plymouth and Exeter.

Getting Around

Contact the **Devon County Public Transport Help Line** (☎ 01392-382800; www.devon.gov.uk/devon bus; ⊙ 9am-5pm Mon-Fri) for information and timetables. It also provides the invaluable *Devon Public Transport Map* and the *Discovery Guide to Dartmoor*. **First Western National** (☎ 01271-376524; www.firstgroup.com) serves most of north Devon and much of the south and east, including most Dartmoor services.

Stagecoach Devon (☎ 01392-427711; www.stage coachbus.com) operates mostly local services and buses from Plymouth to Exeter or Totnes. Timetables are available to download from the website. The **Explorer Day Pass** (adult £6) allows one day of unlimited travel on Stagecoach Devon buses; for longer periods the **Goldrider Pass** (one week £16) offers the best value.

The main Great Western train line from London to the southwest skirts along the south Devon coast, passing through Exeter and Plymouth en route to Cornwall. There are many picturesque stretches where the line hugs the seashore, especially around Lyme Bay, Dawlish and Teignmouth. The **Devon Rover** allows three days' train travel in a week (adult £24) or eight days' travel in 15 days (adult £39.50).

EXETER

☎ 01392 / pop 106,780

With a touch of buzzy, big city atmosphere, a large student population and a thriving arts scene, Exeter is one of the liveliest cities in the southwest. The city was originally settled by Celts and later occupied by the Romans (who knew it as Dumnonii); by the time of the Norman conquest, Exeter had grown into an important commercial centre, and became rich from the wool trade during the years of Tudor rule. Although

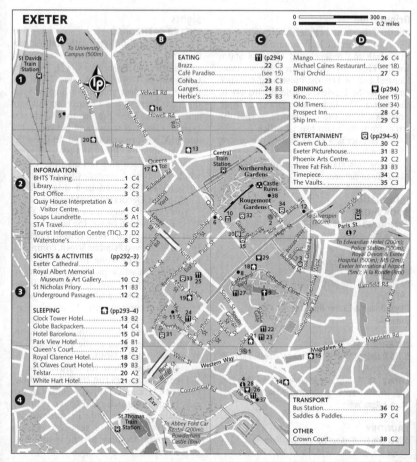

EXETER

INFORMATION
BHTS Training	**1** C4
Library	**2** C2
Post Office	**3** C3
Quay House Interpretation & Visitor Centre	**4** C4
Soaps Laundrette	**5** A1
STA Travel	**6** C2
Tourist Information Centre (TIC)	**7** D2
Waterstone's	**8** C3

SIGHTS & ACTIVITIES (pp292–3)
Exeter Cathedral	**9** C3
Royal Albert Memorial Museum & Art Gallery	**10** C2
St Nicholas Priory	**11** B3
Underground Passages	**12** C2

SLEEPING (pp293–4)
Clock Tower Hotel	**13** B2
Globe Backpackers	**14** C4
Hotel Barcelona	**15** D4
Park View Hotel	**16** B1
Queen's Court	**17** B2
Royal Clarence Hotel	**18** C3
St Olaves Court Hotel	**19** B3
Telstar	**20** A2
White Hart Hotel	**21** C3

EATING (p294)
Brazz	**22** C3
Café Paradiso	(see 15)
Cohiba	**23** C3
Ganges	**24** B3
Herbie's	**25** B3
Mango	**26** C4
Michael Caines Restaurant	(see 18)
Thai Orchid	**27** C3

DRINKING (p294)
Kino	(see 15)
Old Timers	(see 34)
Prospect Inn	**28** C4
Ship Inn	**29** C3

ENTERTAINMENT (pp294–5)
Cavern Club	**30** C2
Exeter Picturehouse	**31** B3
Phoenix Arts Centre	**32** C2
Three Fat Fish	**33** B3
Timepiece	**34** C2
The Vaults	**35** C3

TRANSPORT
Bus Station	**36** D2
Saddles & Paddles	**37** C4

OTHER
Crown Court	**38** C2

Exeter was heavily bombed during WWII, the historic centre survived largely intact, and the cathedral is one of the finest examples of late medieval architecture in Britain. The city's long heritage means there are plenty of monuments and historical attractions to occupy at least a day's sightseeing, and the excellent selection of funky bars, cafés and restaurants make Exeter a vibrant place to be after dark.

History
Exeter was founded by the Romans around AD 50 as the administrative capital for the Dumnonii of Devon and Cornwall, although an earlier settlement existed on the banks of the River Exe. By the 3rd century the city, which became an important Saxon settlement, was surrounded by a thick wall, parts of which can still be seen. Its fortifications were battered by Danish invaders and then by the Normans: in 1068 William the Conqueror took 18 days to break through the walls. He appointed a Norman seigneur (feudal lord) to construct a castle, the ruins of which can still be seen in Rougemont and Northernhay Gardens.

Exeter was a major trading port until a weir was built across the river in 1290, halting river traffic. It wasn't until 1563, when the first ship canal in Britain was dug to bypass the weir, that the city began to reestablish itself, especially through the wool and cloth trades.

Orientation

South of the ruined castle, the city centre radiates out from the leafy square around the cathedral; the redeveloped Quay is 500m south. There are two main train stations, Central and St Davids; most long-distance trains use St Davids, a mile northwest of the centre. The bus station is a short walk northeast from the city centre, across the street from the main tourist office.

The airport is 5 miles east of the centre, off the A30. Bus No 56 runs to the airport from the bus station (20 minutes, hourly Monday to Saturday).

Information

BOOKSHOPS

Waterstone's (☎ 218392; 48-49 High St; 🕘 9am-5.30pm Mon-Fri, 9am-6pm Sat, 10am-4.30pm Sun) Main branch of this large chain bookshop.

EMERGENCY

Police station (☎ 08452 777444; Heavitree Rd; 🕘 24hr)
Royal Devon & Exeter Hospital (☎ 411611; Barrack Rd)

INTERNET ACCESS

BHTS Training (☎ 678940; 8 Coombe St; per half-hr £1.25; 🕘 8.30am-6pm Mon-Sat)
Library (☎ 384201; Castle St; per hr £3; 🕘 9.30am-7pm Mon, Tue, Thu & Fri, 10am-5pm Wed, 9.30am-4pm Sat, 11am-2.30pm Sun)

LAUNDRY

Silverspin (12 Blackboy Rd; 🕘 8am-10pm)
Soaps (Isambard Pde; 🕘 8.15am-7.45pm Mon-Sat, 9.15am-5.45pm Sun) Beside St Davids train station.

MEDIA

The List is a free magazine detailing events, bars, restaurants and nightlife in the Exeter area.

POST

Main post office (☎ 223344; Bedford St; 🕘 9am-5.30pm Mon-Sat)

TOURIST INFORMATION

Quay House Interpretation & Visitors Centre (☎ 265213; The Quay; 🕘 10am-5pm Easter-Oct, weekends only Nov-Easter) Offers tourist information and displays on the Quay's history.
TIC (☎ 265700; tic@exeter.gov.uk; Paris St; 🕘 9am-5pm Mon-Sat)

Sights

EXETER CATHEDRAL

The magnificent **Exeter Cathedral** (Cathedral Church of St Peter; ☎ 255573; www.exeter-cathedral.org.uk; Cathedral Close; suggested donation £3; 🕘 7.30am-6.30pm Mon-Fri, 11.30am-5pm Sat, 8am-7.30pm Sun) is one of the most graceful of England's cathedrals. There's been a church on this spot since 932; in 1050 the Saxon church was granted cathedral status, and between 1112 and 1133 a Norman cathedral replaced the original building. In 1270 Bishop Bronescombe instigated the remodelling of the whole building, a process that took about 90 years and resulted in a mix of Early English and Decorated Gothic styles.

You enter through the impressive Great West Front, which boasts the largest collection of 14th-century sculpture in England. Inside, the carved **Pulpitum Screen**, completed in 1325, features some marvellous 17th-century ecclesiastical paintings. Nearby, the huge oak canopy over the **Bishop's Throne** was carved in 1312, and the **minstrels' gallery** (1350) is decorated with 12 angels playing musical instruments. The cathedral's most celebrated features include the 14th-century stained glass of the East and West Windows and the Gothic rib-vaulting (the world's longest) above the central nave.

Free guided tours run from April to October at 11am and 2.30pm Monday to Friday, 11am on Saturday and 4pm on Sunday. Extra tours are available in summer. It's also worth attending a service: evensong is at 5.30pm Monday to Friday and 3pm on Sunday.

UNDERGROUND PASSAGES

The medieval maintenance passages for the subterranean 14th-century lead water pipes still survive. They're dark, dank and definitely not for claustrophobics, but the **guided tours** (☎ 665887; £3.75; 🕘 2-5pm Tue-Fri & 10am-5pm Sat Oct-Jun, 10am-5.30pm Mon-Sat Jul-Sep) are surprisingly interesting. The entrance is in the alleyway beside Boots on High St.

ROYAL ALBERT MEMORIAL MUSEUM & ART GALLERY

This multipurpose **museum** (☎ 665858; Queen St; admission free; 🕘 10am-5pm Mon-Sat) has exhibitions ranging from prehistory to the present; highlights include some Roman artefacts and a reconstructed town house from the late 16th century. There are also good ethnography collections with costumes from around the globe. The gallery has a programme of changing exhibitions, emphasising local artists.

ST NICHOLAS PRIORY

Built as accommodation for overnight visitors, the guest wing of the 900-year-old Benedictine **St Nicholas Priory** (☎ 665858; The Mint; adult 50p; ☼ 2-4.30pm Apr-Oct) became the house of a wealthy Elizabethan cloth merchant. It looks just as it might have done when inhabited by the merchant and his family, with period furniture, wood-panelled rooms and plaster ceilings.

Tours

Free guided tours led by volunteer Exeter 'Redcoats' last 1½ to two hours and cover a range of subjects, from medieval themes to ghost walks to catacomb visits. Tours leave from the Royal Clarence Hotel or Quay House several times a day in summer. Ask at the TIC or contact ☎ 265203 or guidedtours@exeter.gov.uk for details.

Sleeping

BUDGET

Exeter YHA Hostel (☎ 0870 770 5826; exeter@yha.org .uk; 47 Countess Wear Rd; dm £13.40) Occupying a large house that overlooks the River Exe, this hostel is 2 miles southeast of the city towards Topsham. Catch bus No K or T from High St, or No 57 or 85 from the bus station to Countess Wear post office, from where it's half a mile.

Globe Backpackers (☎ 215521; caroline@globeback packers.freeserve.co.uk; 71 Holloway St; dm £10, 7th night free; ▫) Near the Quay, this busy, reader-recommended hostel is a short walk from the city centre. Facilities include Internet access, bike hire and a large kitchen and dining area.

Telstar (☎ 272466; www.telstar-hotel.co.uk; 75-77 St David's Hill; s £25-35, d £45-60; ✗) One of a string of B&Bs along the hill towards St Davids station, with a small private garden and comfortable, unremarkable rooms.

MID-RANGE

Clock Tower Hotel (☎ 424545; www.clocktowerhotel .co.uk; 16 New North Rd; s £40, d £45-65; P ✗) A good, central city hotel, decorated with plain colours and modern furnishings. Parking

permits are available for the street outside, or there's an off-site covered car park.

Queens Court (☎ 272709; www.queenscourt-hotel .co.uk; 6-8 Bystock Tce; s/d £59/64) This refurbished hotel, occupying a grand gabled building near New North Rd, offers 18 deluxe rooms decorated in muted shades of beige and magnolia; downstairs, the Olive Tree restaurant serves Mediterranean-influenced cuisine.

White Hart Hotel (☎ 279897; 66 South St; s £49-59, d £69-99; P ✗) Horse-drawn coaches once clattered through the cobbled courtyard of this 15th-century inn. Though the hotel retains much of its old-fashioned character (wood-panelled walls, faded carpets and rambling public bars), the bedrooms have been thoroughly modernised, with warm colours, contemporary furnishings and en-suite bathrooms.

Also recommended:

Edwardian (☎ 276102; www.edwardianexeter.co.uk; 30-32 Heavitree Rd; s/d £40/56; P ✗) Beautiful Edwardian house with period-style rooms.

Park View Hotel (☎ 271772; www.parkviewhotel .freeserve.co.uk; 8 Howell Rd; s/d from £24/45; P ✗) An end of terrace town house 10 minutes from the centre.

TOP END

St Olaves Court Hotel (☎ 217736; www.olaves.co.uk; Mary Arches St; d £105-155; P ✗) This lavish period hotel, housed in a heritage-listed Georgian

---

SOMETHING SPECIAL

Hotel Barcelona (☎ 281000; www.hotel barcelona-uk.com; Magdalen St; s/d £85/95; P ✗) Quite simply one of the hippest hotels in Britain. The old Eye Infirmary has been converted into the Barcelona with wit, style and enormous imagination. Sixties' furniture and abstract art sit alongside original cornicing and marble fireplaces; movie posters and mono prints cover the walls; and the hotel is dotted with medical paraphernalia, from the original gurney lift to wheelchairs on the stairway. The bedrooms are just as stylish, with colourful bedspreads, anglepoise lamps and retro furniture – you can even sleep in the old operating theatre. And if that's not enough, there's also an Italian-style marquee-cum-bistro, Café Paradiso, and a baroque-noir cellar bar, Kino. Drop-dead cool.

SOUTHWEST ENGLAND

mansion, could be a country hotel in the heart of rural Devon. Set around a quiet courtyard and private gardens, all the bedrooms are decorated with country prints and traditional furniture.

Royal Clarence Hotel (☎ 319955; www.royalclarence hotel.co.uk; Cathedral Yard; s/d £105/130) Exeter's oldest top-end hotel dates back to the 14th century and overlooks the cathedral square; former guests include Lord Nelson and Tsar Nicholas I. The handsome whitewashed façade and chic rooms are set to undergo a complete refurbishment in 2005. The hotel also houses the Michael Caines restaurant (below).

Eating

Mango (☎ 438538; The Quay; lunch dishes £2.50-6; 10am-6pm Sep-Jun, 10am-10pm Jul & Aug) A funky waterside café serving wraps, salads and paninis on the outside terrace or in the barrel-ceilinged interior.

Herbies (☎ 258473; 15 North St; mains £5-8; lunch Mon-Sat, dinner Tue-Sat) A homely, popular vegetarian restaurant that attracts a devoted local crowd; tuck into nutburgers, homity pie and vegetarian chilli, or plump for the best carrot cake in town.

Thai Orchid (☎ 214215; Cathedral Yard; mains £7-10) A top-notch Thai restaurant with possibly the largest menu you'll ever see (the owners compare it to *War and Peace*). The dining room is decorated with gilt Buddhas and musical instruments, and the cuisine is as authentic as it gets this side of Bangkok.

Brazz (☎ 252525; 10-12 Palace Gate; mains £5.50-15; lunch & dinner) Look no further for brasserie food in Exeter – Brazz has got the market cornered. Choose your aperitif at the bar, and head into the split-level dining room for pan-fried sea bream, classic Niçoise salad and Tuscan chicken – and don't forget to check out the fibre-optic ceiling and cylindrical fish tanks.

Michael Caines Restaurant (☎ 310031; www .michaelcaines.com; Cathedral Yard; mains from £16.95) This restaurant at the Royal Clarence Hotel (see above) has nothing to do with everyone's favourite Cockney actor. In fact, it's the flagship restaurant of Exeter's most renowned chef – serving modern European and British cuisine based on local produce.

Also recommended:

Cohiba (☎ 678445; South St; tapas £3-7, mains £8-13; lunch & dinner) Hispanic dishes and modern tapas in a sleek, neutral space.

Ganges (☎ 272630; 156 Fore St; mains £5-12; dinner) Great Indian restaurant specialising in regional dishes.

Zizzi (☎ 274737; 21-22 Gandy St; mains £6-8; lunch & dinner) Pizza and pasta served in an open-plan dining room.

Drinking

Ship Inn (☎ 272040; Martin's Lane) In the alley between High St and the cathedral, this old tavern is said to have been Sir Francis Drake's favourite local; expect wood beams, crazy ceilings, and nooks and crannies aplenty.

Prospect Inn (☎ 273152; The Quay) A cosy 17th-century pub down on the redeveloped Quay. There's live jazz, and it's a great place to sit outside on a summer evening.

Old Timers (☎ 477704; Little Castle St) Next door to Timepiece (below), this great drinking hole is covered in battered signs, stickers, placards and plaster statues, and makes an atmospheric place for an evening pint and pub grub.

Kino (Magdalen St; members & guests only after 10pm) A fabulous, film noir–style bar in the cellar of the Hotel Barcelona (p293), decked out with Chinese screens and moody lighting – there's live funk, blues, jazz or comedy most nights, and a late-night club at weekends. Nonmembers welcome up to 10pm.

Entertainment

NIGHTCLUBS

Three Fat Fish (☎ 424628; www.threefatfish.co.uk; 1 Mary Arches St) Exeter's newest bar and live-music venue, with regular nights devoted to DJs, bands, comedy and retro-music extravaganzas.

Cavern Club (☎ 495370; www.cavernclub.co.uk; 83-84 Queen St) Another excellent subterranean venue with live music or DJs each night; luminaries such as Coldplay and Groove Armada have gigged here, and the Cavern has a reputation for breaking new bands.

Timepiece (☎ 493096; www.timepiecenightclub.co .uk; Little Castle St) Arguably the best club in town – Latin night (Tuesday) and indie night (Friday) are always jam-packed.

Other clubs include **The Vaults** (☎ 203939; 8 Gandy St) – a friendly basement bar – and **Casbar** (☎ 275623; 53 Bartholomew St West), a popular gay club with top nights on Friday and Saturday.

THEATRE & CINEMAS

Phoenix Arts Centre (☎ 667080; www.exeterphoenix .org.uk; Gandy St) An excellent arts complex hosting dance, theatre, films, DJs and live music. The café-bar's pretty hip, too.

Exeter Picturehouse (☎ 435522; Bartholomew St West) Screens a mix of mainstream and art-house flicks.

Getting There & Away

AIR
Scheduled services connect **Exeter International Airport** (☎ 367433; www.exeter-airport.co.uk) and Dublin, the Channel Islands and the Isles of Scilly; chartered services go as far afield as the Algarve and Canada.

BUS
Bus No X38 runs to Plymouth (1¼ hours, every 90 minutes Monday to Saturday, every two hours Sunday); bus Nos 39 and X39 are slower (1¾ hours, at least every two hours) but stop at Buckfastleigh on the edge of Dartmoor. Bus No X46 runs to Torquay (£4.50, one hour, hourly Monday to Saturday, every 90 minutes Sunday).

National Express runs regular coaches to Bath (£12.85, three hours, four daily), Birmingham (£30.50, four hours, four daily), Bristol (£10.75, two hours, four daily), London (£20, 4½ hours, eight daily) and Penzance (£20.50, five hours, two daily).

TRAIN
The fastest trains between London and Exeter St Davids use Paddington station and take 2½ hours (£42, hourly). There are also hourly connections with Bristol (£16.20, one hour) and Penzance (£19.90, three hours).

The 39-mile Tarka Line between Exeter Central and Barnstaple (£10.10, 1¼ hours, every two hours Monday to Friday, four on Sunday) follows the valleys of the Rivers Yeo and Taw and gives good views of the countryside with its deep-sunken lanes.

Getting Around

BICYCLE & CANOE
Saddles & Paddles (☎ 424241; www.sadpad.com; 4 Kings Wharf, The Quay) rents out bikes (adult per day £13) and canoes (single kayaks per hour/day £5/15). It also organises 'paddling parties' to a nearby pub, plus canoeing weekends and cycling tours.

BUS
Exeter is well served by public transport. The one-day **Dayrider pass** (£3) gives un-

limited transport on Stagecoach's Exeter buses. Bus No N links St Davids and Central train stations and passes near the bus station.

CAR
The TIC provides a list of car-rental offices; try **Abbey Ford Car Rental** (☎ 254037; www .abbeyfordcarhire.co.uk; 30 Edwin Rd) for cheap rates.

Parking in the centre can be troublesome. Useful Park & Ride services run between Sowton and Matford via the centre (bus No PR1, at least every 10 minutes), and from Honiton Rd to the city (bus No N, every 30 minutes).

TAXI
Taxi ranks are located outside the train stations. Alternatively, you could try **Capital Taxis** (☎ 433433).

AROUND EXETER

Powderham Castle
Built in 1391 and later modified, **Powderham** (☎ 01626-890243; www.powderham.co.uk; adult £7.20, child £4.10; ⏰ 10am-5.30pm Apr-Oct) was the former home of the 18th Earl of Devon. Guided tours explore the state rooms, the wood-panelled great hall, and the collections of French china and Stuart and Regency furniture. Powderham is 8 miles south of Exeter. Catch bus No 85A (20 minutes, every 15 minutes Monday to Saturday, every 30 minutes Sunday).

À la Ronde
Having returned from their European Grand Tour, sisters Jane and Mary Parminter planned to combine the magnificence of the Church of San Vitale, which they'd visited in Ravenna, with the homeliness of a country cottage to create the perfect home. The result, completed around 1796, is an intriguing 16-sided **house** (NT; ☎ 01395-265514; Summer Lane, Exmouth; adult £4.20; ⏰ Sun-Thu Mar-Oct). It has a bizarre interior décor that includes a shell-encrusted room, a frieze of feathers, and sand and seaweed collages.

It's 2 miles north of Exmouth on the A376. En route to Exeter (30 minutes, at least every 30 minutes) Stagecoach Devon bus No 57 stops on the outskirts of Exmouth, from where it's an easy walk to À la Ronde.

SOUTH DEVON COAST
Torquay & Paignton
☎ 01803 / pop 110,370

The three Torbay towns (Torquay, Paignton and Brixham) collectively make up the area known – rather optimistically – as the English Riviera. Torquay is the classic South Devon seaside resort, a curious mix of old-world Victorian elegance and mass-market tourism. From the grand seafront promenade, the town climbs into a grid of streets lined with traditional tearooms, gift shops and endless hotels (one of which was run by the deranged hotelier, Basil Fawlty, in the classic British TV comedy *Fawlty Towers*). Around the bay to the south, Paignton is effectively the 'family fun' suburb of Torquay, big on coloured lights and fairy floss, less on sophistication.

In Torquay, the **TIC** (☎ 0906-680126; torbay.tic@ torbay.gov.uk; Vaughan Pde; ⊙ 9.30am-6pm Mon-Sat & 10am-6pm Sun Jun-Sep, 9.30am-5pm Mon-Sat Oct-May) sells discounted tickets for local attractions.

SIGHTS & ACTIVITIES
Agatha Christie was born in Torquay, and the **Torquay Museum** (☎ 293975; 529 Babbacombe Rd; adult £3; ⊙ 10am-5pm Mon-Sat & 1.30-5pm Sun summer, 10am-5pm Mon-Fri & 1.30-4pm Sun winter) and **Torre Abbey** (☎ 293593; Torre Abbey Meadows; adult £3.50; ⊙ 9.30am-6pm Apr-Nov), an 18th-century house in the grounds of a ruined abbey, display Christie memorabilia.

Pretty **Babbacombe Beach** is about 2 miles north of the centre; it's a delightful three-hour walk around the coast from the eastern end of the Esplanade, away from the lights and arcades.

SLEEPING
There are hundreds of B&Bs and hotels in Torquay, with a dense cluster around the Avenue Rd and Bridge Rd area. Most offer similar standards of accommodation and décor.

Torquay International Backpackers (☎ 299924; jane@torquaybackpackers.co.uk; 119 Abbey Rd; dm £12) The friendly owner of this hostel sometimes organises beach barbecues, trips to Dartmoor and, more often, hops to the pub.

Norwood Hotel (☎ 294236; www.norwoodhotel torquay.co.uk; 60 Belgrave Rd; d £44-50; ⊠) A classy B&B with some very spacious and surprisingly chic bedrooms; the luxury rooms are worth the higher price.

Cranbourne Hotel (☎ 292766; 58 Belgrave Rd; s/d from £30/60; ⊠) Right next door to Norwood Hotel, the Cranbourne is another superior choice. It's decorated in pale cream and lemon yellow, and most of the bedrooms have large windows and tasteful furnishings.

Palace Hotel (☎ 200200; www.palacetorquay.co.uk; Babbacombe Rd; d £71-140; P ⊠ ⬛ ⬛ ⬛) A class act – a huge hotel set in 25 acres of grounds, boasting tennis courts, saunas, snooker rooms and a private golf course.

Everglades Hotel (☎ 295389; www.evergladeshotel .co.uk; 32 St Marychurch Rd; d £50-56; P ⊠) A detached hotel with an elevated sundeck and modern sea-view rooms.

EATING & DRINKING
Mojo (☎ 294881; The Seafront, Torbay Rd; mains £6.50-10) Looks like a brash seaside bar but it's surprisingly mellow, with DJs Friday and Saturday, and decent fish and pasta.

Steps Bistro (☎ 201774; 1a Fleet St; mains £11-14) A tiny gem tucked away up some steps from Fleet St; worth seeking out for exceptional fresh fish and seafood.

Hole in the Wall (☎ 298020; 6 Park Lane; mains £4-10) Allegedly the oldest pub in Torquay, with good local beer and top-notch pub grub in a largely grockle-(tourist) free zone.

GETTING THERE & AWAY
The No X46 express bus service runs hourly from Exeter to Torquay and Paignton (£4.50, one hour). Bus No 120 runs from Torquay and Paignton to Kingswear for the Dartmouth ferry (£5.30 return, 45 minutes, six daily Monday to Friday).

A branch railway line runs from Exeter via Torquay (45 minutes) to Paignton (50 minutes). The **Paignton & Dartmouth Steam Railway** (☎ 555872; www.paignton-steamrailway.co.uk) runs from Paignton on the scenic 7-mile trip to Kingswear on the River Dart, linked by ferry (six minutes) to Dartmouth; a combined ticket costs £8.50 return per adult. You can add on a river cruise (£13) or a Round Robin boat trip to Totnes and back to Paignton by bus (£13.50).

Brixham
☎ 01803 / pop 17,460
In the mid-19th century Brixham was the country's busiest fishing port and it's still the place to come for a fishing expedition; with its attractive harbour, it's also the most

appealing (if the quietest) of the Torbay resorts.

The **TIC** (☎ 0906-680126; brixham.tic@torbay.org .uk; Old Market House, The Quay; ☼ 9.30am-6pm Mon-Sat Jun-Sep, 9.30am-5pm Mon-Fri Oct-May) is right on the harbour.

Brixham Heritage Museum (☎ 856267; www .brixhamheritage.org.uk; Bolton Cross; adult £1.50; ☼ 10am-5pm Mon-Fri, 10am-1pm Sat) explores the town's history and its connection to the sea, and contains reconstructions of Victorian rooms and shops.

Anchored in the harbour is a replica of the **Golden Hind** (☎ 856223; adult £2; ☼ 9am-5.30pm Mar-Sep), Drake's surprisingly small globe-circling ship.

It costs around £20 for a half-day trip to fish for conger, ling and coalfish around the wrecks in the bay. Head for the kiosks lining the quay – try **Boy Richard** (☎ 529147) for mackerel or **Our Jenny** (☎ 854444) for wreck fishing.

Bus No 12 runs at least every 20 minutes along the coast from Torquay (30 minutes) to Paignton (15 minutes) and Brixham.

Dartmouth

☎ 01803 / pop 5520

Dartmouth, an appealing town dotted with Georgian houses, medieval buildings and attractive streets winding down to the Dart estuary, has been an important port since Norman times. The Pilgrim Fathers sheltered here in 1620 on their way to Plymouth, and D-Day landing craft sailed for France from here in 1944; the town is still home to one of the oldest naval colleges in Britain. Today, the harbour is mostly filled with yachts and pleasure boats, and the historic town draws sizable crowds.

The **TIC** (☎ 834224; www.discoverdartmouth.com; Mayor's Ave; ☼ 9.30am-5pm Mon-Sat year-round, plus 10am-4pm Sun Apr-Oct) offers free accommodation booking and houses the Newcomen Engine, an early (1712) steam engine.

SIGHTS & ACTIVITIES

The hands-on exhibits at **Dartmouth Castle** (EH; ☎ 833588; adult £3.50; ☼ 10am-6pm Jul & Aug, 10am-5pm Apr-Jun & Sep, 10am-4pm Oct, 10am-4pm Sat & Sun Nov-Mar) bring its 600-year history to life. With its companion castle at Kingswear, the fortress was designed so that a chain could be drawn across the estuary, blocking sea vessels from entering the harbour.

There's a ferry along the estuary to the castle (three-quarters of a mile outside the town) from South Embankment every 15 minutes from 10am to 4.45pm (adult/child £1.20/70p one way).

In the centre, the **Butterwalk** is a row of 17th-century timber-framed houses, reconstructed following bomb damage sustained during WWII. Inside, the **Dartmouth Museum** (☎ 832923; Duke St; adult £1.50; ☼ 10am-4.30pm Mon-Sat Apr-Oct, noon-3pm Mon-Sat Nov-Mar) features exhibits on local and maritime history; check out the fine collection of ships in bottles.

SLEEPING

Little Admiral Hotel (☎ 832572; www.little-admiral .co.uk; 29 Victoria Rd; s £60-75, d £105-140; P ✗) This designer hotel is gaining a reputation as one of the best places to stay in South Devon. The individual rooms range from contemporary (magnolia walls and terracotta-tiled bathrooms) to old-fashioned (four-poster beds, goose-down pillows and Regency-style furniture). There's a funky mauve-walled foyer and guest lounge; and a great restaurant serving tapas and Mediterranean cuisine.

Hill View House (☎ 839372; www.hillviewdart mouth.co.uk; 76 Victoria Rd; d £55-82; ✗) This stylish, modern B&B near the town centre has rooms decorated with pale furnishings, pine furniture and anglepoise lamps. Fruit smoothies and fresh orange juice are included with the organic breakfasts.

Captain's House (☎ 832133; 18 Clarence St; d £53-68; ✗) A heritage-listed whitewashed Georgian town house with character-filled rooms.

EATING & DRINKING

Café Alf Resco (☎ 835880; Lower St; mains £5; ☼ lunch & dinner Wed-Sun) This excellent Mediterranean-flavoured brasserie wouldn't look out of place on the chic streets of Milan; shuttered windows, distressed paintwork and a great terrace all add to the effect. Look out for the flaming torch above the gateway.

New Angel (☎ 839425; 2 South Embankment; mains £10-20) Run by a celebrity TV chef, this super-modern bistro is a new addition to Dartmouth's quayside. It serves bold modern British cuisine in a muted interior, with an open-plan kitchen and plate-glass windows overlooking the harbour.

Strutt's Bistro (☎ 832491; 10 Fairfax Pl; mains £8-14; ☼ lunch & dinner Wed-Sat, lunch Sun) Global seafood served in a bright, pastel-shaded dining room.

RB's Diner (☎ 832882; 33 Lower St; mains £9-22; ☽ dinner) Another urban-styled diner, serving char-grilled tuna, baked Whitby cod and steak measured by the inch.

Cherub Inn (☎ 832571; 13 Higher St) Allegedly the oldest pub in the town.

GETTING THERE & AWAY

The best way to approach Dartmouth is by boat, either on the ferry from Kingswear (car/pedestrian £3/1, every six minutes) or downstream from Totnes (adult £8 return, 1¼ hours). **River Link** (☎ 834488; www.riverlink .co.uk) is one operator. From Exeter, take a train to Totnes and a boat or bus No 111 (40 minutes, at least five daily) from there.

For details of the popular Paignton & Dartmouth Steam Railway, see p296.

Totnes

☎ 01803 / pop 7930

Medieval legend has it that Totnes was where Trojan prince Brutus founded Britain in 1170 BC. Whatever the truth of the story, Totnes became rich by trading Dartmoor tin in Tudor times, and a walk up the High St reveals fine Elizabethan houses and museums; Totnes has a higher percentage of heritage-listed buildings than any other town in Britain. It's now a busy market town with a thriving arts scene (thanks to the nearby arts college) and a large new-age community.

The **TIC** (☎ 863168; www.totnesinformation.co.uk; Coronation Rd; ☽ 9.30am-5pm Mon-Sat) is housed in the town's old mill.

SIGHTS

Totnes Elizabethan Museum (☎ 863821; 70 Fore St; adult £1.75; ☽ 10.30am-5pm Mon-Fri Apr-Oct) was built in the 16th century and still retains many Tudor and Elizabethan features. Its displays explore the history of Totnes, and there's a room dedicated to the mathematician Charles Babbage, father of the modern computer.

The **Guildhall** (☎ 862147; Ramparts Walk; adult 75p; ☽ 10am-4pm Mon-Fri Apr-Oct) was once the refectory of a Benedictine priory, and was later used as the town's council chamber, courtroom and jailhouse.

The **Devonshire Collection of Period Costume** (High St; adult £2; ☽ 11am-5pm Mon-Fri May-Sep) features annually changing selections from the extensive costume collection, one of the finest in Britain.

Totnes Castle (EH; ☎ 864406; adult £2; ☽ 10am-6pm Jul & Aug, 10am-5pm Apr-Jun & Sep, 10am-4pm Oct) occupies a commanding position on a grassy hilltop above town. Little remains of the original Norman motte-and-bailey fortress, but the outer keep is still standing, and the views from the hilltop are fantastic.

SLEEPING

Dartington YHA Hostel (☎ 0870 770 5788; dm £10.60; ☽ mid-Apr–Aug) Two miles northwest of Totnes off the A385 near Week. Bus No X80 from Plymouth to Totnes stops hourly nearby at Shinners Bridge.

Old Forge at Totnes (☎ 862174; www.oldforge totnes.com; Seymour Pl; s/d from £46/56; P ✗) This 600-year old forge has been impeccably converted to provide the best bedrooms in Totnes, complete with fluffy pillows, huge beds and en suites. There's a private garden and a large dining room, and you can even see the old jailhouse.

EATING

Willow Vegetarian Restaurant (☎ 862605; 87 High St; mains £4-5.50; ☽ lunch Mon-Sat, dinner Wed, Fri & Sat) This rustic vegetarian restaurant is a great spot for organic meals, freshly baked bread, hearty soups and chillis, and live music at weekends.

Rumours (☎ 864682; 30 Fore St; mains £8.50-14.50; ☽ 10am-11pm Mon-Sat, 6-10.30pm Sun) The most popular restaurant in Totnes has stripped wood floors and local art on the walls; the daily changing menu includes pasta, pizza and lots of blackboard specials.

Bistro 57 (☎ 862604; 67 Fore St; mains £6.50-9; ☽ Mon-Sat) Another good choice for global cuisine – this sunny restaurant has a menu ranging through pine-nut fritters, fajitas, Moroccan meatballs and chilli-beef nachos.

GETTING THERE & AWAY

Bus No X64 runs to Exeter (£4.70 return, one hour, eight daily Monday to Saturday, two Sunday) and bus No X80 goes to Plymouth (1¼ hours, hourly). National Express coaches also run to Exeter (£6.50 economy return, 1½ hours, twice daily) and Plymouth (£3.25, 40 minutes, daily).

Frequent trains run to Exeter (£12.30 saver return, 45 minutes, several daily) and

Buckfast Abbey (☎ 01364-645500; www .buckfast.org.uk; admission free) The abbey was founded two miles north of Buckfastleigh in 1016 and flourished on wool money in the Middle Ages, but was abandoned after the dissolution of the monasteries in 1539. In 1806 the ruins were levelled and a mock-Gothic mansion erected; the house was purchased in 1882 by exiled French Benedictine monks, who rebuilt the abbey church to its original design between 1906 and 1938.

The abbey is now a popular tourist attraction, and the attached shop sells various gifts and souvenirs, including the famous Buckfast Tonic Wine.

The abbey is outside Buckfastleigh on the A38 between Exeter and Plymouth. Bus X38 runs regularly through Buckfastleigh on its way from Exeter to Plymouth.

Plymouth (£10.40, 25 minutes, hourly). The train station is half a mile from the centre.

A short walk from Totnes main-line train station, steam trains of the private **South Devon Railway Trust** (☎ 0845 345 1420; www.south devonrailway.org) run to Buckfastleigh (adult return £8, at least four daily Easter to October) on the edge of Dartmoor.

There are river cruises with frequent departures to Dartmouth in summer (p298).

PLYMOUTH
☎ 01752 / pop 243,800

There's no ignoring Plymouth's long maritime history, enlivened by characters such as the bowls-playing Sir Francis Drake and the Pilgrim Fathers. However, you'd be forgiven for not finding much evidence of old Plymouth; the city was levelled during the air raids of WWII, and just a few vestiges of the old town remain. Consequently, Devon's largest city is mainly comprised of modern suburbs and a bland commercial centre, but the well-preserved Barbican area – the largely Tudor quarter by the harbour – is steadily reinventing itself as one of the best eating and drinking spots in the city.

History
Plymouth really expanded in the 15th century with the development of larger vessels;

Plymouth Sound provided a perfect anchorage for warships. Local hero Sir Francis Drake, who achieved his knighthood through an epic voyage around the world, set out from Plymouth in 1577 in the *Golden Hind*, returning three years later.

In 1588 Drake played a major part in the defeat of the Spanish Armada (the fleet sent to invade England by Philip II), who wanted to restore Catholicism to the country. Whether Drake really was playing bowls on the Hoe at the time of the Spanish attack is debatable, but the English fleet certainly did set sail from Plymouth. Drake led the chase to Calais; the English then attacked the fleet with fire ships. Many of the Spanish vessels escaped but were wrecked off the Scottish coast. Total losses: England nil, Spain 51.

The royal dockyard was established at Devonport beside the River Tamar in 1690 and is still a large naval base.

Orientation
Plymouth has three main sections. The pedestrianised centre is south of the train station, and contains the city's main shopping streets. Further south is the headland Hoe area, packed with guesthouses and B&Bs, and east of the Hoe is the regenerated Barbican, with some fine harbour-front cafés, bars and restaurants.

Information
Hoegate Laundromat (☎ 223031; 55 Notte St; ☷ 8am-6pm Mon-Fri, 9am-5pm Sat)
Plymouth Internet Café (☎ 221777; 32 Frankfort Gate; per hr £5; ☷ 9am-5pm Mon-Sat)
Police station (Charles Cross; ☷ 24hr)
TIC (☎ 304849; www.visitplymouth.co.uk; 3-5 The Barbican; ☷ 9am-5pm Mon-Sat, 10am-4pm Sun May-Sep, 10am-4pm Mon-Sat Oct-Apr) Housed inside the Plymouth Mayflower building.
University Bookseller (☎ 660428; 42 Drake Circus; ☷ 9am-5.30pm Mon-Sat)
West Hoe Laundrette (☎ 667373; 1 Pier St; ☷ 9.15am-8pm Mon-Fri, 9am-6pm Sat, 10am-5pm Sun)

Sights & Activities
PLYMOUTH HOE
This famous promenade gives wonderful, breezy views over Plymouth Sound. In one corner there's a bowling green – **Drake's statue** now stands on the green on which he supposedly finished his game.

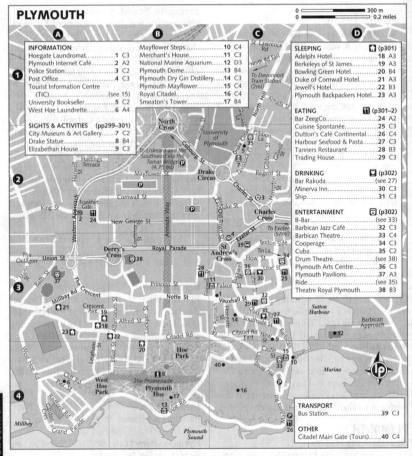

PLYMOUTH

0 ————— 300 m
0 ————— 0.2 miles

INFORMATION	
Hoegate Laundromat	**1** C3
Plymouth Internet Café	**2** A2
Police Station	**3** C2
Post Office	**4** C3
Tourist Information Centre	
(TIC)	(see 15)
University Bookseller	**5** C2
West Hoe Laundrette	**6** A4

SIGHTS & ACTIVITIES (pp299–301)	
City Museum & Art Gallery	**7** C2
Drake Statue	**8** B4
Elizabethan House	**9** C3

Mayflower Steps	**10** C4
Merchant's House	**11** C3
National Marine Aquarium	**12** D3
Plymouth Dome	**13** B4
Plymouth Dry Gin Distillery	**14** C3
Plymouth Mayflower	**15** C4
Royal Citadel	**16** C4
Smeaton's Tower	**17** B4

SLEEPING 🏠 (p301)	
Adelphi Hotel	**18** A3
Berkeleys of St James	**19** A3
Bowling Green Hotel	**20** B4
Duke of Cornwall Hotel	**21** A3
Jewell's Hotel	**22** B3
Plymouth Backpackers Hotel	**23** A3

EATING 🍴 (p301–2)	
Bar ZeegCo	**24** A2
Cuisine Spontanée	**25** C3
Dutton's Café Continental	**26** C4
Harbour Seafood & Pasta	**27** C3
Tanners Restaurant	**28** B3
Trading House	**29** C3

DRINKING 🍸 (p302)	
Bar Rakuda	(see 27)
Minerva Inn	**30** C3
Ship	**31** C3

ENTERTAINMENT 🎭 (p302)	
B-Bar	(see 33)
Barbican Jazz Café	**32** C3
Barbican Theatre	**33** C4
Cooperage	**34** C3
Cuba	**35** C2
Drum Theatre	(see 38)
Plymouth Arts Centre	**36** C3
Plymouth Pavilions	**37** A3
Ride	(see 35)
Theatre Royal Plymouth	**38** B3

TRANSPORT	
Bus Station	**39** C3

OTHER	
Citadel Main Gate (Tours)	**40** C4

Red-and-white-striped **Smeaton's Tower** (The Hoe; adult £2; 🕙 10am-4pm daily Apr-Oct, 10am-4pm Tue-Sat Nov-Mar) was built on the Eddystone Rocks in 1759, then rebuilt here in 1882. You can climb the 93 steps for great views and an insight into the history of the Eddystone lighthouses.

The take on history in **Plymouth Dome** (🕿 603300; The Hoe; adult £4.50; 🕙 10am-5pm Easter-Oct, 10am-4pm Oct-Easter) is both high-tech and theatrical, with audiovisual shows and a Tudor street complete with rowdy locals. A harbour observation deck with interactive computers and radar brings it up to the minute.

East of the Hoe is the **Royal Citadel**, built by Charles II in 1670 and still in military use. There are guided **tours** (🕿 0117-975 0700; adult £3; 🕙 2.30pm Tue May-Sep).

BARBICAN

To get an idea of what old Plymouth was like before the Luftwaffe redesigned it, head for the Barbican, with its many Tudor and Jacobean buildings (now converted into galleries, craft shops and restaurants).

The Pilgrim Fathers' famous vessel *Mayflower* set sail for America from the Barbican on 16 September 1620. At the **Mayflower Steps** a sign lists the passengers and marks the point of departure. Another famous voyage was led by Captain James Cook, who set out from the Barbican in 1768 in search of a southern continent.

Plymouth Mayflower (☎ 306330; 3-5 The Barbican; adult £4; ⌚ 10am-6pm Apr-Oct, 10am-5pm Nov-Mar) provides another high-tech rundown on Plymouth's nautical heritage, with the background on the Pilgrim Fathers' trip and plenty of interactive gizmos and multi-sensory displays.

The **Elizabethan House** (☎ 304774; 32 New St; adult £1.25; ⌚ 10am-5pm Tue-Sat Apr-Nov) is the former residence of an Elizabethan sea captain, housing 16th-century furniture and other period artefacts.

The **Plymouth Dry Gin distillery** (☎ 665292; www.plymouthgin.com; 60 Southside St; tours adult £5) is the oldest of its type in England and has been working since 1793. Tours run between 10.30am and 4.30pm daily in summer; phone ahead at other times.

OTHER SIGHTS & ACTIVITIES
Between the Barbican and the centre is the 17th-century **Merchant's House** (☎ 304774; 33 St Andrews St; adult £1.25; ⌚ 10am-5.30pm Tue-Fri & 10am-5pm Sat year-round, closed 1-2pm Apr-Oct), a timber-fronted Jacobean building featuring models, pictures, local curiosities (including truncheons and manacles) and replicas of a Victorian schoolroom and apothecary's shop.

The **National Marine Aquarium** (☎ 220084; Rope Walk, Coxside; www.national-aquarium.co.uk; adult £8.75, child £5.25; ⌚ 10am-6pm Apr-Oct, 10am-5pm Nov-Mar) is housed in an impressive building on Sutton Harbour. Visitors can explore a range of cleverly reproduced habitats: moorland stream, river estuary, shallow sea and deep reef – look out for the aquarium's four enormous sand tiger sharks.

The **City Museum & Art Gallery** (☎ 304774; Drake Circus; admission free; ⌚ 10am-5.30pm Mon-Fri, 10am-5pm Sat) hosts collections of local history, porcelain and naval art. The Cottonian Collection includes paintings by artists including Joshua Reynolds.

Sleeping
BUDGET
Plymouth Backpackers Hotel (☎ 225158; plymback@hotmail.com; 172 Citadel Rd; dm/d £11/28) A large hostel in an old town house on the Hoe, with a games room, large lounge, and comfortable dorms and double rooms.

MID-RANGE
The northwest corner of the Hoe around Citadel Rd is packed with B&Bs and hotels.

Jewell's Hotel (☎ 254760; 220 Citadel Rd; s/d £25/35-45; ✗) This excellent B&B has been decorated to an extremely high standard, with immaculate bedrooms and sparkling bathrooms.

Bowling Green Hotel (☎ 209090; www.bowlinggreenhotel.co.uk; 9-10 Osborne Pl, Lockyer St, The Hoe; d £58; **P** ✗) Another good-value B&B on the Hoe, opposite Drake's famous bowling green. The 12 pleasant, simple bedrooms are decorated with tasteful pictures and floral bedspreads, and all have en-suite showerrooms or porcelain baths.

Berkeleys of St James (☎ 221654; 4 St James Pl East; s/d £25/40-50; ✗) A small, quality guesthouse in a quiet side street, distinguished by its friendly owners and organic breakfasts.

Adelphi Hotel (☎ 225520; 59 Citadel Rd; s/d £35/48; **P** ✗) Former naval officer's town house with large lounge, pleasant rooms and a small rear terrace.

TOP END
Duke of Cornwall Hotel (☎ 275850; Millbay Rd; s/d £94/104-160) This striking neo-Gothic hotel is one of the oldest in Plymouth, built in 1863. The dramatic frontage, decorated with balconies, gables and an elegant circular turret, should give you some idea of what to expect inside; think fruit baskets, champagne and four-poster beds for the top rooms.

Eating
RESTAURANTS
Cuisine Spontanée (☎ 673757; Century Quay; mains £13.95-16.95; ⌚ lunch & dinner Mon-Sat) This exciting glass-fronted bistro serves global food with a twist – pick your ingredients (meat, fish or vegetables) and the chefs will cook them at your table in the flavour of your choosing (French, Thai, Mexican, Italian etc).

Trading House (☎ 257345; 8 The Parade; mains £10-17; ⌚ dinner) Sophisticated seafood served in a refined atmosphere is available on the top floor of this respected restaurant; downstairs, there's a relaxed bar and outside terrace for tapas and cold beer.

Tanners Restaurant (☎ 252001; www.tannersrestaurant.com; Prysten House, Finewell St; 2-/3-course dinner £23/29; ⌚ lunch & dinner Tue-Sat) The city's finest French and British cuisine can be found in Plymouth's oldest house (1498) – head for one of the stone-walled dining rooms or the medieval courtyard for alfresco eating in summer.

CAFÉS

Dutton's Café Continental (☎ 255245; Madeira Rd; mains £7-8.50; ⚘ 9.30am-5.30pm) Housed in an 1847 cannon room below the citadel (the gun holes are now windows), this café does good lunch-time snacks and afternoon cakes, as well as more-substantial meals.

Harbour Seafood & Pasta (☎ 260717; 10 Quay Rd; ⚘ lunch & dinner) A bustling brasserie next door to Bar Rakuda (below), with outside seating and an intimate dining room inside. The fresh scallops, huge seafood salads and the generous pasta dishes all come highly recommended.

Bar ZeegCo (☎ 664754; Frankfort Gate; mains £4.25-15) Bright, modern café, serving good Mediterranean and Middle Eastern food near the shopping centre.

Drinking

Plymouth has a buzzing nightlife, but the main club strip, Union St, has a reputation for trouble at kicking-out time. The area around the Barbican is wall-to-wall pubs and bars.

Bar Rakuda (☎ 221155; 11 Quay Rd; ⚘ 9am-11pm) This funky, modern café-bar is right on the waterfront and has a great selection of coffees, beers and cocktails.

Ship (☎ 667604; Quay Rd) Just along the quay, this historical tavern is another popular boozer in the Barbican.

Minerva Inn (☎ 223047; 31 Looe St) Reputedly the oldest pub in Plymouth, and once home of the naval press gangs; these days it's a low-ceilinged, smoky local, with live music at weekends.

Entertainment

BARS & NIGHTCLUBS

Barbican Jazz Café (☎ 672127; 11 The Parade; admission Fri & Sat £2; ⚘ noon-2am Mon-Sat, noon-midnight Sun) This cavernous, barrel-ceilinged club has nightly jazz and a livelier vibe than you might expect.

B-Bar (☎ 242021; Castle St) The in-house café-bar of the Barbican Theatre; B-Bar hosts live music, DJs, cabaret and comedy.

Cooperage (☎ 229275; www.thecooperage.co.uk; 134 Vauxhall St) This is the live-music venue of choice for new bands.

Ride (☎ 226655; 2 Sherwell Arcade) and **Cuba** (☎ 201520; 1 Sherwell Arcade) are popular student hang-outs aimed at the shooters-and-mixers crowd.

THEATRE & CINEMAS

Theatre Royal Plymouth (☎ 267222; www.theatreroyal.com; Royal Pde) Plymouth's main theatre puts on West End musicals and dance productions, while its Drum Theatre stages fringe plays.

Plymouth Pavilions (☎ 229922; www.plymouthpavilions.com; Millbay Rd) This large entertainment complex stages everything from Tom Jones to the Bolshoi Ballet.

Barbican Theatre (☎ 267131; www.barbicantheatre.co.uk; Castle St) Plymouth's foremost arts venue staging exhibitions and small-scale theatre and dance.

Plymouth Arts Centre (☎ 206114; www.plymouthac.org.uk; 38 Looe St) An excellent art-house cinema and gallery; there's also a good vegetarian restaurant.

Getting There & Away

BUS

Express bus No X38 runs to Exeter (1¼ hours, every 90 minutes Monday to Saturday, every two hours Sunday). Another useful service is bus No 86 (roughly hourly Monday to Saturday, two on Sunday), which runs to Okehampton (1¾ hours) via Tavistock (55 minutes) and Lydford (1½ hours), sometimes going on to Barnstaple (£5.50 return, three hours).

National Express has direct connections to numerous cities, including London (£25, five hours, eight daily), Bristol (£23, three to four hours, five daily) and Birmingham (£38, five hours, five daily).

TRAIN

Services run to London (£63.20, 3½ hours, hourly), Bristol (£37, two hours, at least hourly), Exeter (£10.70, one hour, hourly) and Penzance (£10.70, two hours, hourly).

NORTH DEVON
Braunton & Croyde

☎ 01271 / pop 8420

Croyde Bay and the nearby beach at Saunton Sands are Devon's most popular surfing spots; Croyde is also a pleasant seaside village, with good campsites, B&Bs and pubs. Check the north Devon **Surfcall** (☎ 0906 800 7007) for surfing conditions; calls cost 60p per minute.

Both towns have numerous surf-hire shops, charging around £10 per day for board and wetsuit. In Croyde, try **Le Sport** (☎ 890147; Hobbs Hill; 🕑 9am-9pm Apr-Sep) or, for lessons, **Surf South West** (☎ 890400; www.surf southwest.com; per half-/full-day £20/40).

SLEEPING & EATING

Campsites are plentiful but you should still book ahead. **Mitchum's Campsites** (☎ 890233; guy@croydebay.co.uk) has several locations; call for details and prices. **Bay View Farm** (☎ 890501; www.bayviewfarm.co.uk; tent sites £14), on the road from Braunton, is another good spot.

Chapel Farm (☎ 890429; www.chapelfarmcroyde .co.uk; Hobbs Hill; s/d from £25/50; P 🗶) A lovely old thatched farmhouse with beamed rooms, rustic furniture and an inglenook fireplace; you can also cook for yourself in the old smithy behind the house.

Thatch (☎ 890349; www.thethatch.com; 14 Hobbs Hill; d £50-60) Legendary among surfers for its great pub atmosphere and hearty food; the upstairs rooms are fine, but the nightlife can get a little rowdy.

Billy Budd's (☎ 890606; Hobbs Hill; mains £4-10) Another popular surfer's hang-out, serving jacket potatoes, chilli, nachos and huge sandwiches, as well as more-substantial main meals and local ales.

Ilfracombe
☎ 01271 / pop 10,510

Ilfracombe is north Devon's largest sea-side resort. Steep hills frame its attractive little harbour, although the best beaches are 5 miles west at Woolacombe. With its grand promenade, faded Victorian build-ings and classic seashore character, it makes an atmospheric place to stay in summer – though it can feel like the end of the earth on a wet winter's afternoon.

The **TIC** (☎ 863001; www.ilfracombe-tourism.co.uk; The Landmark, The Seafront; 🕑 10am-5pm Jun-Sep, 10am-5pm Mon-Fri & 10am-4pm Sat & Sun Oct-May) is in the striking twin-towered Landmark Theatre.

SLEEPING

Ilfracombe YHA Hostel (☎ 0870 770 5878; ilfracombe@ yha.org.uk; 1 Hillsborough Tce; dm/tw £10.25/23.50; 🕑 Easter-Nov) Decent hostel reached via a steep walk from the harbour.

Ocean Backpackers (☎ 867835; www.oceanback packers.co.uk; 29 St James Pl; dm £11) An excellent, lively hostel opposite the bus station.

Wellington's Retreat (☎ 864178; www.wellingtons retreat.co.uk; 28 Fore St; d £56-70; 🗶) A charming B&B in a heritage-listed Georgian build-ing, right in the centre of old Ilfracombe. The priciest room is positively regal, with a huge canopied bed and views across the harbour, but the others are very pleasant too, decorated with gingham bedcovers and neutral colours.

Also recommended:
Beechwood Hotel (☎ 863800; Torrs Park; r £55-60; P 🗶) A handsome detached house in Torrs Park, with elegant bedrooms and an antique-filled drawing room.
Norbury House Hotel (☎ 863888; Torrs Park; s/d from £20/45; P 🗶) Fine Victorian gentleman's residence on the west side of town.

EATING

Atlantis Restaurant (☎ 867835; mains £5-12; 🕑 dinner Wed-Sat) A simple, reliable restaurant with world music, quirky décor and global dishes (ranging from Thai red duck to Louisiana chicken).

WORTH THE TRIP

Ten miles offshore in the Bristol Channel, **Lundy Island** is just 3 miles long and half a mile wide. There's a resident population of 18 people, one pub, one church and no roads. Visitors come to climb the cliffs, watch the birds, explore the marine nature reserve (one of the top dive sites in Britain) or just escape from the outside world for a few days.

Interesting properties that can be rented include the lighthouse, the castle and a converted pigsty, but they need to be reserved months in advance. You can also camp for £4 to £8 per person. The **Lundy Shore Office** (☎ 01271-863636; www.lundyisland.co.uk) handles ferry bookings, camping and short stays. The **Landmark Trust** (☎ 01628-825925), which looks after the island on behalf of the National Trust, handles property bookings.

You can take a day trip from Ilfracombe on the **MS Oldenburg** (day return adult/child £28/14; 2hr; 2-5 sailings per wk Mar-Dec). Book through the Lundy Shore Office. You can also make day trips from Clovelly: the **Jessica Hettie** (☎ 01237-431042; www.clovelly-charters.ukf.net; return adult/child £25/22.50) departs Wednesday or Thursday from April to October.

Terrace (☎ 863482; Fore St; tapas £4-6, mains from £8; ☽ dinner) Authentic Spanish tapas is served at this popular brasserie, including griddled king prawns, char-grilled skewers and *jamon serrano* (mountain ham).

Pier Tavern (☎ 866225; The Quay; mains £4-10) A seafront pub with fresh seafood, a chatty crowd and live music on Sunday.

GETTING THERE & AWAY

National Express coaches run from London (£25, six hours, two daily). Bus Nos 3 and 30 (40 minutes, every half-hour Monday to Friday, hourly Sunday) run to Barnstaple. Bus No 300 heads to Lynton (one hour) and Minehead (two hours) three times daily.

Clovelly
☎ 01237

Clovelly's impossibly picturesque (but cruelly steep) cobbled street, lined with the cutest cottages, becomes thronged with tourists looking to take the perfect picture of the quaint harbour. The ancient fishing village dates back to before the 11th century - it's even mentioned in the Domesday Book. For centuries life revolved around the tides and the daily catch, which was brought up from the harbour on donkey-drawn sledges. At the **Kingsley Museum** (Providence House; admission free; ☽ 9.15am-5pm summer, 10.30am-3.30pm winter) you can see Charles Kingsley's study (he wrote *Westward Ho!* here), then squeeze your way around the tiny old **Fisherman's Cottage** behind.

To some extent, Clovelly has turned itself into a living museum. During the day, it costs £4 to park your car and enter via the **visitors centre** (☎ 431781), where there's a video presentation (and the obligatory gift shops); this also includes entry to the Kingsley Museum. From Easter to October, Land Rovers regularly ferry visitors up and down the slope for £2 between 10am and 5.45pm.

SLEEPING & EATING

There are only a few privately run B&Bs in the village; the visitors centre plugs the two hotels but has a list of other options.

Donkey Shoe Cottage (☎ 431601; 21 High St; d from £40) A friendly, flower-covered B&B halfway up the hill; bathrooms are shared.

New Inn (☎ 431303; newinn@clovelly.co.uk; High St; d £76.50-94; ✗) A classic old cob-walled pub with beautiful bedrooms refurbished in the style of William Morris, including embroidered tapestries, period furniture and *objets d'art*. Most rooms have balconies overlooking the cobbled street, and the downstairs pub is a great spot for pub grub and a pint.

Red Lion Hotel (☎ 431237; redlion@clovelly.co.uk; Harbour; d £93.50-115; ✗) If possible, this beautiful old-world inn is even more picturesque than the New Inn. The nautical-themed rooms look out onto the sea or the ancient harbour, and the downstairs restaurant serves hearty meals in one of the prettiest settings you could wish for.

GETTING THERE & AWAY

Bus No 319 runs five times daily to Bideford (40 minutes) and Barnstaple (one hour).

DARTMOOR NATIONAL PARK

Some 280 million years ago, large volumes of molten rock formed a granite mass stretching from the Isles of Scilly to eastern Devon, and it's at Dartmoor that the largest area (about 365 sq miles) has been exposed. Why the geology lesson? To illustrate why Dartmoor is so remarkably rugged: it's essentially a huge granite plateau covered by a thin layer of peaty soil. Vegetation is sparse; purple heather and gorse cover most of the high ground, with green, marshy mire in lowland areas and a few oak woods remaining in the coombs (sheltered valleys). Sheep, cattle and semi-wild Dartmoor ponies graze the land, which is interrupted by tors (rock pillars or hills sculpted into strange forms by the wind and weather).

Dartmoor is named after the River Dart, which has its source here; the West and East Dart merge at Dartmeet. Most of the park is around 600m high – the highest spot is High Willhays (621m) near Okehampton. About 40% of Dartmoor is common land but 15% (the northwestern section, including High Willhays and Yes Tor) is leased to the Ministry of Defence (MOD) and is closed for firing practice for part of the year.

Dartmoor encloses some of the wildest, bleakest country in England: suitable terrain for the Hound of the Baskervilles (one of Sherlock Holmes' more notorious foes). The landscape and weather can make this

SOUTHWEST ENGLAND

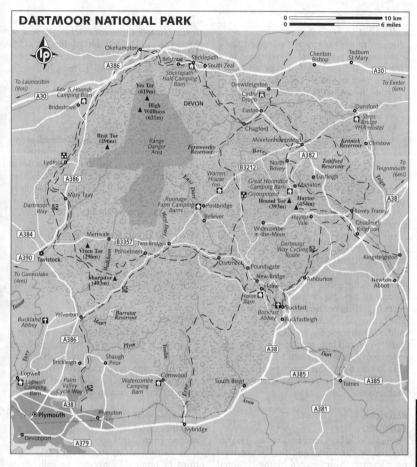

DARTMOOR NATIONAL PARK

an extremely eerie place; try not to think of *An American Werewolf in London* on a dark, foggy night. With its wild, open landscape and scattered prehistoric remains, it's magnificent walking country, but bring a good map: it's easy to get lost, particularly when the mist rolls in.

Orientation

Dartmoor is 6 miles from Exeter and 7 miles from Plymouth. It's ringed by a number of small market towns and villages, including Ashburton, Buckfastleigh, Tavistock and Okehampton. Buses link these towns with Princetown, Postbridge and Moretonhampstead on the moor itself. The two main roads across the moor meet near Princetown, the only village of any size on Dartmoor.

Postbridge, with its medieval clapper bridge, is the focal point for car and coach visitors, and can be crowded in summer. Most sights are on the eastern side; the western part is mainly for serious walkers.

Information

There's information about Dartmoor at the TICs in Exeter (p292) and Plymouth (p299), and visitors centres at Okehampton, Tavistock, Ivybridge, Ashburton, Buckfastleigh and Bovey Tracey; alternatively, head for the website of the **Dartmoor Tourist Association** (www.dartmoor-guide.co.uk). The **National Park Authority** (NPA; www.dartmoor-npa.gov.uk)

runs the High Moorland Visitors Centre in Princetown (p308), which is the best place to gather information.

The other national park visitors centres, generally open from 10am to 5pm daily, April to October, are at **Haytor** (☎ 01364-661520), **Postbridge** (☎ 01822-880272) and **Newbridge** (☎ 01364-631303).

These centres provide lots of useful literature, including the free *Dartmoor Visitor*, an annual newspaper that covers most aspects of getting out and about on the moor. The centres also stock walking and cycling guides, Ordnance Survey (OS) maps, and leaflets on walking, care of the moor and letterboxing (see the boxed text, p308).

Don't feed the Dartmoor ponies as this encourages them to move dangerously near to the roads.

Activities
CLIMBING
Popular climbing areas are at Haytor (owned by the NPA) and the Dewerstone near Shaugh Prior (owned by the National Trust). Groups need to book in advance. Ask at a national park visitors centre or TIC for details.

CYCLING
Cycling is only allowed on public roads, byways, public bridleways and Forestry Commission roads.

The **Plym Valley Cycle Way** follows the disused Great Western Railway between Plymouth and Yelverton, on the edge of the moor. **The Dartmoor Way** (see the boxed text, p307) is also the name of a 90-mile circular cycling route through Okehampton, Chagford, Buckfastleigh, Princetown and Tavistock. Cyclists can also follow the **Tarka Trail**.

Bikes can be hired in Exeter (p295) and from **Tavistock Cycles** (☎ 01822-617630; Brook St, Tavistock; per day £12). **Dartmoor Cycle Hire** (☎ 01822-618189; 6 Atlas House, West Devon Business Park), also in Tavistock, charges £6/12 for a half-/full-day; staff will deliver bikes to a number of hotels and guesthouses in Dartmoor.

FISHING
You can fish on certain stretches of the East and West Dart with a **Duchy of Cornwall permit** (☎ 01822-890205). Fishing is also permitted on seven reservoirs in the park; contact **South West Lakes Trust** (☎ 01837-871565). For fishing on the Rivers Tavy, Walkham, Plym, Meavy and Teign, a permit is usually needed; contact the **Environment Agency** (☎ 01925-653999).

PONY TREKKING & HORSE RIDING
There are riding stables spread all over the park, including **Shilstone Rocks Riding Centre** (☎ 01364-621281; www.dartmoor-riding.com; Widecombe-in-the-Moor). *Dartmoor Visitor* has full details.

WALKING
Dartmoor is excellent walking country. Postbridge, Princetown and Chagford are all good centres, and south of Okehampton there is a high, wild area around Yes Tor and High Willhays (inside the MOD firing range). Haytor is also a popular walking destination.

Guided walks focusing on wildlife, birdwatching, archaeology or folklore are arranged from April to October; they start from various points around the park. Some must be booked in advance by calling the **High Moorland Visitors Centre** (☎ 01822-890414). Prices range from £3 for two hours to £5 for six hours; to encourage use of public transport in the park, bus travellers can join the walk free of charge. Details appear in *Dartmoor Visitor*.

There are several waymarked walking routes on Dartmoor. The **Abbot's Way** runs along an ancient 14-mile route from Buckfast to Princetown. The **West Devon Way** is a 14-mile walk between Tavistock and Okehampton along old tracks and through pretty villages along the western edge of Dartmoor. YHA hostels are conveniently placed a day's walk apart across the moor, so a five-day circuit from either Exeter or Plymouth is possible.

DARTMOOR WALKS

The **Templer Way** is an 18-mile walk from Teignmouth to Haytor, following the route originally used to transport Dartmoor granite down to the docks.

The **Two Moors Way** is a longer option, running from Ivybridge, on the southern edge of Dartmoor, 103 miles across Dartmoor and Exmoor to Lynmouth on the north Devon coast.

The **Dartmoor Way** is a 90-mile circular route, stretching from Buckfastleigh in the south, through Moretonhampstead, northwest to Okehampton and south through Lydford to Tavistock. The *Dartmoor Way* pack (£7.95) includes a book and 1:25,000 scale map, and is available from TICs and National Park Authority centres. For further information, call ☎ 0870 241 1817 or check www.dartmoorway.org.uk.

The **Tarka Trail** circles north Devon and links with Dartmoor, south of Okehampton; *The Tarka Trail: A Walkers' Guide* can be purchased for £6.45.

It's always wise to carry a map, compass and rain gear since the weather can change very quickly and not all walks are waymarked. OS OL Explorer Map No 28 (1:50,000; £6.99) is the most comprehensive map, showing the park boundaries and Ministry of Defence firing-range areas.

Sleeping & Eating

Park authorities and owners of unenclosed moorland don't usually object to campers who keep to a simple code: don't camp on moorland enclosed by walls or within sight of roads or houses; don't stay on one site for more than two nights; don't light fires; and do leave the site exactly as you found it. Bear in mind that there are also specific areas that are entirely out of bounds; check with the NPA. With large tents, you can only camp in designated campsites. There are several camping and caravan parks around the area, many of which are located on farms.

There are YHA hostels at Postbridge (Bellever) and Steps Bridge, as well as at Okehampton, Exeter and Dartington. There are six YHA camping barns in Dartmoor National Park, plus some independent barns and bunkhouses. Cooking and shower facilities and a wood burner are provided. You sleep on the floor or a bunk bed; make sure you bring your own bedding. Charges are from £3.75 per person. For bookings, telephone ☎ 01200-420102, or visit www.yha.org.uk.

The larger towns on the edge of the park (such as Okehampton and Tavistock) have plentiful B&Bs and hotels. There are several country-house hotels within the park itself, but you'll need to book ahead in summer.

Based above the High Moor Visitors Centre in Princetown, the **Dartmoor Tourist Association** (☎ 01822-890567; www.discoverdartmoor.com) produces an annual *Dartmoor Guide*, with accommodation listings. There's a charge of £2.75 if you book rooms through any of the visitors centres.

Getting There & Around

The best starting points for the park are Exeter and Plymouth. National Express has coach services between London and Exeter, Newton Abbot, Okehampton and Plymouth.

Before you start planning, get a copy of the *Discovery Guide to Dartmoor*, free from most Devon TICs and the NPA offices. It has details of bus and train services around the park.

The **Dartmoor Sunday Rover ticket** (adult £5; ♻ Jun-Sep) entitles you to unlimited travel on most bus routes, and to rail travel on the Tamar Valley Line from Plymouth to Gunnislake. Buy your ticket from bus drivers or at Plymouth train station.

The most useful bus across Dartmoor is No 82 – the Transmoor Link – running between Exeter and Plymouth via Moretonhampstead, Warren House Inn, Postbridge, Princetown and Yelverton (three daily Monday to Saturday, five Sunday, weekends only in winter).

There are four trains between Okehampton and Exeter on Sunday (£5.50 Day Rover, 40 minutes). The only other train stations near the park are at Ivybridge and South Brent on the Exeter–Plymouth line. Ivybridge (from Exeter: £12.90 saver return, 50 minutes, every two hours) marks the start of the Two Moors Way (see the boxed text above).

LETTERBOXING

If you see a walker acting furtively and slipping an old Tupperware box into a tree stump or under a rock, you may be witnessing someone in the act of letterboxing. This wacky pastime has more than 10,000 addicts and involves a never-ending treasure hunt for several thousand 'letterboxes' hidden all over Dartmoor.

In 1844 the railway line reached Exeter, and Dartmoor started to receive visitors, who imagined themselves as great explorers here. One guide for these intrepid Victorian gentlefolk was James Perrott of Chagford. In 1854 he had the idea of getting them to leave their calling cards in a glass jar at Cranmere Pool, the most remote part of the moor accessible at that time. In 1938 a second 'box' was established, and the idea really took off after WWII. Originally, people left their card with a stamped addressed envelope and if someone found it they would send it back.

There are now about 4000 boxes, each with a visitors book for you to sign and a stamp and ink pad (if they haven't been stolen) to stamp your record book. Although it's technically illegal to leave a 'letterbox' (because in effect you're leaving rubbish on the moor), as long as the boxes are unobtrusive, most landowners tolerate them. Now there are even German, French, Belgian and American boxers, not to mention 'mobile boxers', odd characters who wander the moors waiting for a fellow letterboxer to approach them with the words 'Are you a travelling stamp?'!

Once you've collected 100 stamps, you can apply to join the '100 Club', whereupon you'll be sent a clue book with map references for other boxes. Contact **Godfrey Swinscow** (☎ 015488-21325; Cross Farm, Diptford, Totnes, Devon TQ9 7NU) for more information.

Inevitably, as more people go letterboxing, problems arise. A code of conduct now prohibits letterboxers from disturbing rocks, vegetation or archaeological sites in their zeal. Even so, there have been mutterings about the disturbance caused to nesting golden plovers and ring ouzels.

PRINCETOWN

☎ 01822

Perched on a bleak rise of moorland 8 miles east of Tavistock, Princetown is England's highest town, but it's best known as the location of **Dartmoor Prison**. The prison was built in 1809 to house French and American prisoners of war, and it's now one of Britain's most infamous high-security jails.

The **Dartmoor Prison Museum** (☎ 890305; adult £2; ⏱ 9.30am-4.30pm Tue-Sat), on the Tavistock road, gives an insight into the jail's early days, and sells crafts (mainly benches and garden gnomes) made by current prisoners.

The **High Moorland Visitors Centre** (☎ 890414; hmvc@dartmoor-npa.gov.uk; Old Duchy Hotel, Tavistock Rd; ⏱ 10am-5pm) has displays on Dartmoor and an information centre that stocks maps, guides and books. It's also the place to book guided walking tours.

Sleeping & Eating

Both of the village pubs have basic B&B rooms, including the **Plume of Feathers Inn** (☎ 890240; The Square; campsite from £3, bunkhouse from £5.50, d £55), and the **Railway Inn** (☎ 890232; railwayinnpl20@aol.com; Two Bridges Rd; d £40-50; **P**).

Getting There & Away

Bus No 82 (the Transmoor Link) runs to Princetown from Exeter (one hour and 40 minutes) and Plymouth (50 minutes).

POSTBRIDGE

☎ 01822

Postbridge, a tiny village in the middle of the park, is a popular walking centre. Little more than a few houses strung along the road, it's known for its granite clapper bridge across the East Dart, dating from the 13th century and made of large granite slabs supported by stone pillars.

Local legend tells of an 18th-century temperance-house landlady who took to serving alcohol, much to the horror of her husband, who poured it in the river. A dog that paused to quench its thirst was driven mad by the potent mixture and died. Its tormented spirit is still said to haunt Dartmoor – one version of the story gave Conan Doyle the idea for *The Hound of the Baskervilles*.

From April to October, there's an **NPA centre** (☎ 01822-880272) in the car park, generally open from morning until early afternoon. There's also a **post office** and **shop** in the village.

Sleeping & Eating

Bellever YHA Hostel (☎ 0870 770 5692; bellever@yha .org.uk; dm £11.80; ☯ Mar-Oct) Housed in former farm buildings, this rural walking hostel is a mile south of Postbridge. Bus No 98 runs from Tavistock (40 minutes, daily Monday to Saturday) and Princetown (20 minutes).

Runnage Farm Camping Barns (☎ 880222; www .runnagecampingbarns.co.uk; camping from £4, bunk beds £4) This farm has two YHA camping barns. Each sleeps up to 15 people and is kitted out with a stove, kettle, microwave oven, hot water, and gas heating. Toilets and showers are nearby. Take the small road off the B3212 towards Moretonhampstead just after Postbridge.

Lydgate House Hotel (☎ 880209; www.lydgate house.co.uk; s/d from £50/90; ℗ ✗) A lovely country hotel a quarter of a mile from Postbridge, overlooking a sheltered river valley and rolling moorland. The rooms are all named after Dartmoor birds, and are decorated in a homely, rustic style – choose from rooms with private lounges, Victorian bathrooms or a granite fireplace.

Warren House Inn (☎ 880208; mains £6-12) Two miles northeast of Postbridge, along the B3212 towards Moretonhampstead, this terrific country pub stands in an isolated spot surrounded by windswept moorland. There's real ale, pub food (from ploughman's lunches to home-made rabbit pie), and you can warm yourself by a fire that has allegedly been burning nonstop since 1845.

Getting There & Away

Bus No 82 runs through Postbridge between Plymouth (one hour) and Exeter (1½ hours). Bus No 98 runs to Tavistock daily (40 minutes).

WIDECOMBE-IN-THE-MOOR

☎ 01364

With its village green, quaint cottages, tea-shops and 14th-century granite church (known as the Cathedral in the Moor), Widecombe is one of the prettiest of Dartmoor's villages. The village is commemo-rated in the traditional English folk song of Widdicombe Fair; the fair still takes place every year on the second Tuesday of September.

There's a visitor information point at Sexton's Cottage, adjacent to the Church House. Built in 1537 as a brewhouse, the Church House is now the village hall.

Sleeping & Eating

Manor Cottage (☎ 621218; d from £40; ℗ ✗) Found beside the village post office, this snug little cottage is ideally situated for the nearby pubs and shops.

Old Rectory (☎ 621231; d from £40; ☯ Apr-Oct; ℗ ✗) Once the home of the village vicar, this gorgeous little slate-roofed house makes a fine spot for a night's stay, with sweet, simple rooms and a lovely private garden.

Old Inn (☎ 621207; mains £5-10) One of the most renowned pubs in Dartmoor. This fine old country inn has hearty meals, great beer and a pond garden.

Rugglestone Inn (☎ 621327; mains from £4) Just outside the village, this stone-walled pub is covered in geraniums and hanging baskets in summer, and pulls a fine pint of ale.

Also recommended:

Cockingford Farm Campsite (☎ 621258; campsites £3-8; ☯ mid-Mar–Nov) Found 1½ miles south of Widecombe.

Dartmoor Expedition Centre (☎ 621249; www .dartmoorbase.co.uk; Rowden; campsites from £3, bunk-house £7.50, d £18) Located 1½ miles west of Widecombe. Private rooms, bunkhouses, and a range of organised activities.

Getting There & Away

Many buses only stop at Widecombe on Sunday during the summer. These services include the No 170 between Exeter and Plymouth and the No 174 between Totnes and Okehampton. The No 172 (two daily Monday to Saturday July to August, four daily Sunday May to September) runs via Tavistock, Princetown, Newton Abbot and Totnes.

Bus No 672 runs from Newton Abbot and Buckfastleigh via Widecombe once daily on Wednesday and Friday.

MORETONHAMPSTEAD

☎ 01647

With its unusual two-storey almshouses, traditional shops and gabled Georgian houses, the sleepy market town of More-tonhampstead is another place in Dartmoor where time seems to have stood still. It's mainly of interest as an accommodation centre and gateway to the eastern moor.

Bus No 82 runs from Moretonhampstead to Princetown (40 minutes), Plymouth (1½ hours) and Exeter (50 minutes). Bus No 359 also goes to Exeter (six daily Monday to Saturday).

Sleeping & Eating

Steps Bridge YHA Hostel (☎ 0870 770 6048; dm adult/child £7.20/4.95; ☯ Apr-Sep) About 4½ miles northeast of Moretonhampstead along the B3212. Bus Nos 82 and 359 run to Moretonhampstead (15 minutes) and Exeter (40 minutes).

Sparrowhawk Backpackers (☎ 440318; 45 Ford St; dm/r £11/30) This excellent family-run, eco-friendly hostel has a nicely converted barn dorm, solar-powered showers and a pleasant outside courtyard.

Cookshayes (☎ 440374; cookshayes@eurobell.co.uk; 33 Court St; s £19, d from £38; P ⊠) Near the village centre, this whitewashed Victorian house boasts rooms with en suite; most have views over the large private garden.

White Hart Hotel (☎ 441340; The Square; mains £10-13; d £90; ☯ lunch & dinner; P ⊠) This newly refurbished pub has a great restaurant serving local dishes including Brixham cod, king scallops and corn-fed chicken; the upstairs rooms are comfortable and contemporary.

OKEHAMPTON

☎ 01837 / pop 5850

Off the A30 just north of the national park, busy little Okehampton was once a prosperous wool-trading town, and now makes a good base for walks in the northern part of the moor. This region is within the MOD's firing area; phone ahead to check whether the area is open.

The **TIC** (☎ 53020; oketic@visit.org.uk; Museum Courtyard, 3 West St; ☯ 10am-5pm Mon-Sat Easter-Oct, hrs vary in low season) can help with local accommodation and walks.

Sights & Activities

A Norman motte and ruined keep is all that remains of Devon's largest **castle** (EH; ☎ 52844; adult £2.80; ☯ 10am-5pm Apr-Jun & Sep, 10am-6pm Jul & Aug); a free audio guide fills in the missing parts.

It's a pleasant three- to four-hour walk along the Tarka Trail from Okehampton to Sticklepath, where the **Finch Foundry** (NT; ☎ 840046; adult £3; ☯ 11am-5.30pm Wed-Mon Apr-Oct) has three working water wheels. Bus

Nos X9 and X10 link Sticklepath with Okehampton (10 minutes).

Sleeping & Eating

Okehampton YHA Hostel (☎ 0870 770 5978; okehampton@yha.org.uk; Klondyke Rd; dm £13.40; ☯ Feb-Nov; P ⊠) One of the YHA's flagship Dartmoor hostels, housed in a converted goods shed beside the train station. It's also an activity centre with its own climbing wall.

Heathfield House (☎ 54211; Klondyke Rd; d £40-50; P ⊠ ☎) This smart Victorian house offers lovely rooms, a guest conservatory and an outside swimming pool in summer.

Fountain Hotel (☎ 53900; s/d £45/60; P ⊠) A refurbished 15th-century coaching inn with stylish rooms and an in-house restaurant.

Meadowlea (☎ 53200; 65 Station Rd; d from £45; ⊠) A simple B&B on the hill towards the train station.

Yertiz Caravan & Camping Park (☎ 52281; yertiz@dial.pipex.com; Exeter Rd; tent sites £4-8) This site is three-quarters of a mile east of Okehampton on the B3260.

Getting There & Away

National Express coaches run from London (£25, five hours, daily).

Bus No X9 runs to Bude (one hour), while No X10 goes to Boscastle (45 minutes); both also run to Exeter (one hour). Buses are roughly hourly Monday to Saturday; on Sunday No X9 runs four times each way. Bus No 86 runs to Plymouth (1¾ hours, hourly Monday to Saturday) and Barnstaple (1½ hours, every two hours Monday to Saturday, two on Sunday).

Four trains run from Exeter Central to Okehampton on Sunday (£5.50 Day Rover, 45 minutes). More interesting is the steam **Dartmoor Railway** (☎ 55637; www.dartmoor railway.co.uk) that runs between Meldon and Sampford Courtenay. The train runs from Meldon to Okehampton and from Okehampton to Sampford Courtenay (£2.50 single; five daily Saturday and Sunday, four daily Tuesday mid-September to mid-July, five daily school summer holidays). You can also travel from Meldon to Sampford Courtenay via Okehampton (£4 single; three daily Saturday and Sunday mid-September to mid-July, four to five daily school summer holidays). Return tickets from Meldon to Sampford Courtenay cost £6, or a day pass costs £10. Timetables change regularly; phone ahead for details or check the website.

LYDFORD
☎ 01822

A secluded village on the western edge of the moor, Lydford has evidence of both Celtic and Saxon settlements and the remains of a square Norman **castle keep** (EH; admission free), which later acted as the Stannary courthouse and jail.

Lydford is best known for the 1½-mile **Lydford Gorge** (NT; ☎ 820320; adult £4; ☽ 10am-5.30pm Apr-Sep, 10am-4pm Oct, 10.30am-3pm Nov-Mar). A riverside walk leads to the 28m-high White Lady waterfall past a series of bubbling whirlpools, including the Devil's Cauldron. Alternatively, you can drive to the car park at the other end of the track, near the waterfall itself.

A 5-mile walk leads to one of Dartmoor's best-known monuments, the **Widgery Cross** on Brat Tor, erected for Queen Victoria's golden jubilee in 1887. The scenery along the way is classic Dartmoor, rugged and windswept.

Bus No 86 runs to Okehampton (20 minutes), Barnstaple (1½ hours) and Plymouth (1½ hours), at least every two hours Monday to Saturday (only twice Sunday). Bus Nos 118 and 187 go to Tavistock (25 minutes) and Okehampton (30 minutes) six times a day on Sunday in the summer; No 118 is usually a vintage 1960s double-decker with conductor.

CORNWALL

For many centuries, the kingdom of Cornwall existed as an autonomous nation, governed by its own laws and language, and the defiantly independent Cornish spirit survives to this day. Even with the advantages of modern transport, Britain's westernmost county still feels a long way from the rest of the country. The Cornish coastline is arguably the most breathtaking in Britain, pockmarked by secret coves, shimmering bays and plummeting cliffs. The county's beaches and coast keep visitors returning year after year – but Cornwall has more to offer than awe-inspiring views. The abandoned mines and wheelhouses dotted across the Cornish landscape are ghostly

reminders of the county's industrial past. It is also steeped in tales of smuggling and shipwrecks – over the centuries, thousands of vessels have foundered along Cornwall's perilous coastline, and the sunken wrecks now provide some world-class diving. Whether it's surfing the north coast waves around Newquay and Perranporth, exploring the subtropical gardens of Trebah and Glendurgan, or marvelling at the futuristic biomes of the Eden Project, you'll discover that Cornwall is one of the most memorable regions in Britain. It's an ancient land rich in mystery, heritage and legend that stays with you long after you leave for home.

Unsurprisingly, as one of Britain's favourite domestic holiday spots, Cornwall is usually packed with visitors in summer, and space is at a premium. A secluded strip of sand or an empty hotel room can be almost impossible to find, and you're unlikely to be able to appreciate the county properly. Far better to visit during the shoulder months, when the roads and beaches are quieter, and most of the troublesome 'emmets' (a Cornish word for ant, ironically and not entirely affectionately applied these days to tourists) have left for home.

Orientation & Information

Cornwall is a little over 50 miles wide at its broadest (near the Devon border), and it's only 77 miles from Penzance to Plymouth (just across the Tamar from Cornwall), so you're never far from the coast and the main attractions.

In addition to TICs, tourism is coordinated by districts, most of which publish handy brochures with accommodation listings. The website of the **Cornwall Tourist Board** (www.cornwalltouristboard.co.uk) has accommodation information and themed guides (beaches, festivals, gardens, heritage and so on). **Cornwall Guide** (www.cata.co.uk) lists details of the county's visitor attractions, divided into categories such as industrial heritage and maritime attractions. **Cornwall Online** (www.cornwall-online.co.uk) is another good planning resource.

Getting Around

For more information about buses, there's an efficient **helpline** (☎ 01872-322142). The main bus operator is **First Western National** (☎ 01209-719988).

If you're taking the train, phone **rail information** (☎ 0845 748 4950). The main route from London ends in Penzance but there are branch lines to St Ives, Falmouth, Newquay and Looe. The **Cornish Rail Rover pass** (3-day pass £25.50 mid-May–mid-Sep, £18 mid-Sep–mid-May; 8-day pass £40.50 mid-May–mid-Sep, £33 mid-Sep–mid-May) allows three days' travel in a week or eight days' travel in 15 days; there's a 34% discount for children and railcard holders.

TICs stock the free annual *Public Transport Timetable* (with a map), listing all the air, bus, rail and ferry options in Cornwall.

TRURO

☎ 01872 / pop 20,920

Truro is Cornwall's administrative and commercial centre, a busy provincial city filled with modern shops, pubs, bars and cafés. The present-day town grew up around a hilltop castle (no longer standing) built by Richard Lucy, a minister of Henry II. From the 14th century onwards, Truro was an important port, but the shipping trade was lost to the deep-water harbour at Falmouth, and the town's docks at Lemon Quay (in front of the Hall for Cornwall) were covered over. Truro instead became wealthy from the distribution of Cornish tin and copper, and the town is littered with reminders of its prosperous past, including a collection of fine Georgian town houses along Lemon St and Walsingham Pl. The city's most obvious landmark is its three-spired cathedral; built in the late 19th century, it was the first new cathedral to be built in England since St Paul's.

Information

Library (☎ 279205; Union Pl; Net access per hr £3; ☑ 9am-6pm Mon-Fri, 9am-4pm Sat)
Post office (High Cross; 9am-5.30pm Mon-Sat)
TIC (☎ 274555; tic@truro.gov.uk; Boscawen St; ☑ 9am-5.30pm Mon-Fri, 9am-5pm Sat)

Sights

The **Royal Cornwall Museum** (☎ 272205; www .royalcornwallmuseum.org.uk; River St; admission free; ☑ 10am-5pm Mon-Sat) is the county's main museum, and has some excellent exhibits on Cornish history and archaeology, as well as displays of ceramics, minerals and local art. Its fine-art collection includes pieces by John Constable, Caravaggio and William Blake.

The foundations of **Truro Cathedral** (☎ 276 782; www.trurocathedral.org.uk; High Cross; suggested donation £4) were laid in 1880 on the site of a 16th-century parish church, but the building wasn't completed until 1903. Built in soaring Gothic Revival style by the architect John Loughborough Pearson, Cornwall's only cathedral contains an impressive high-vaulted nave, some fine examples of Victorian stained glass and the famous Father Willis Organ.

The recently refurbished **Lemon Street Market** (Lemon St) houses craft shops, cafés, delicatessens and an upstairs art gallery.

Guided tours (☎ 271257; adult/child £3/1.50) of the town depart from the TIC at 11am every Wednesday.

Sleeping

Carlton Hotel (☎ 223938; www.carltonhotel.co.uk; 49 Falmouth Rd; s/d from £40/57.50; **P** ✗) An old Victorian merchant's house uphill from town, fronted with wrought-iron balconies and window boxes in summer. The interior has been converted to provide light, simply furnished rooms, some with skylights and garden views.

Royal Hotel (☎ 270345; www.royalhotelcornwall .co.uk; Lemon St; s £59, d from £80; **P** ✗ 🖳) Despite the grand Georgian front, the interior of this centrally positioned hotel is chic and contemporary, with individually styled rooms all offering big beds, power-showers and CD players. The hotel also offers a range of award-winning 'aparthotels' (£110 to £150).

Alverton Manor (☎ 276633; Tregolls Rd; d £109-189; **P** ✗) An upmarket hotel in a converted convent surrounded by landscaped gardens, just outside the city centre. Large, elegant bedrooms, a good restaurant and a luxurious location make this the pick of the places to stay in the city.

Other B&Bs:

Fieldings (☎ 262783; averil@fieldingsintruro.com; 35 Treyew Rd; s/d £18/32) Pleasant Edwardian house with good views over town.
Townhouse (☎ 277374; www.trurohotels.com; 20 Falmouth Rd; s/d £25/55-65; **P** ✗) Efficient city-style B&B with a communal kitchen-breakfast room, complete with fridge and microwave.

Eating & Drinking

Mannings Restaurant (☎ 247900; www.trurorestaurants.co.uk; Lemon St; mains £7-18; ☑ lunch & dinner)

This popular restaurant, attached to the Manning's Hotel, offers an eclectic menu ranging from local seafood to rib-eye steaks, with coffee and technicolour cocktails on offer in the foyer bar.

Café Citron (☎ 274145; www.cafecitron.co.uk; 76 Lemon St; mains £6-12; ☺ lunch & dinner) A buzzy brasserie that does great morning coffee (cappuccinos, mochas), light lunches (ciabattas, smoked chicken salad) and evening meals (roast sea bass, oven-baked monkfish), all served in an informal Mediterranean-tinted dining room.

Indaba (☎ 274700; Tabernacle St; mains £5-12; ☺ lunch & dinner Mon-Sat) A contemporary café-bar with sleek tables, industrial piping and plate-glass windows, serving sandwiches and salads for lunch and fusion food in the evening. Daily specials include local seafood and a 'Cornish plate'.

MI Bar (☎ 277214; Lemon Quay) A voguish café-bar with stark walls, stripped-wood floors, a large cocktail menu and terrace seating in summertime. Local DJs sometimes play guest spots.

Heron (☎ 272773; Malpas; ☺ lunch & dinner Mon-Sat, dinner Sun) Two miles from the city along the river estuary, in the tiny village of Malpas, this pastel-coloured pub serves excellent food and good beer in a gorgeous creek-side setting.

Getting There & Away

BUS

Many National Express services change at Plymouth, bound for Truro. There are direct coaches to London (£33, seven hours, four daily), Penzance (£4.25, 1½ hours, five daily) and St Ives (£3.50, one hour, two daily).

TRAIN

Truro is on the main rail line between London Paddington (£79, five hours, hourly) and Penzance (£6.60, 45 minutes, hourly). There's a branch line to Falmouth (£2.90, 20 minutes, hourly Monday to Saturday).

SOUTHEAST CORNWALL

With its mild climate, traditional fishing villages and gentle fields, southeast Cornwall has a mellower atmosphere than the north and west coasts, although the coastal villages get packed in summer. Naturally verdant and with wonderful flowers in spring, the area is home to several stunning gardens and many plants that thrive nowhere else in England. TICs stock the free *Gardens of Cornwall* map and guide with full details.

Cotehele

One of the finest Tudor manor houses in Britain, **Cotehele** (NT; ☎ 01579-351346; St Dominick; adult £7, garden & mill only £4; ☺ 11am-5pm Sat-Thu Apr-Oct) was built between 1485 and 1627 by the Edgcumbe family. The main hall is particularly impressive, and many rooms are hung with fine tapestries. Look out for some medieval suits of armour, and keep an eye open for the ghostly figures said to wander through the house, accompanied by music and a peculiar herbal smell.

Outside, the gardens include a Victorian summerhouse, medieval dovecote, working quay and small museum. The restored **Cotehele Mill** is a 15-minute walk away.

Cotehele is 7 miles southwest of Tavistock on the western bank of the Tamar. You can get to Calstock, 1 mile from Cotehele, from Tavistock on bus No 79.

East & West Looe

☎ 01503 / pop 5280

Like so many of Cornwall's coastal communities, the twin villages of Looe are inextricably bound up with the sea. Looe has long been one of the county's busiest fishing and ship-building centres, but during the 19th century the town became a popular Victorian holiday spot and tourism has been an important part of the local economy ever since. Linked by a seven-arched Victorian bridge, the two villages occupy opposite sides of the river estuary, and the narrow streets are dotted with tourist shops, fishermen's cottages, gabled buildings and quaint pubs – all of which attract visitors in their droves in summer. There are **boat trips** from

SOUTHWEST ENGLAND

WORTH THE TRIP

At the head of the Fal estuary, 4 miles south of Truro, **Trelissick Garden** (NT; ☎ 01872-862090; Feock; adult £4.80; ☺ 10.30am-5.30pm daily mid-Feb–Oct, 11am-4pm daily Nov-Dec, 11am-4pm Thu-Sun Jan–mid-Feb) has panoramic views and superb landscaped gardens, particularly renowned for the rhododendrons and hydrangeas.

the quay to Looe Island (an offshore nature reserve) and to Fowey and Polperro.

The **TIC** (☎ 262072; www.southeastcornwall.co.uk; Fore St; ☼ 10am-5pm Easter-Oct, noon-5pm Mon-Fri & 10am-5pm Sat & Sun Oct-Easter) is in the Guildhall.

The **South East Cornwall Discovery Centre** (☎ 262777; West Looe; admission free; ☼ 10am-6pm Jul-Sep, 10am-4pm Oct-Jun) houses the Oceana exhibition, an interactive insight into the Cornish coastline.

Monkey Sanctuary (☎ 262532; www.monkey sanctuary.org; St Martins; adult £5; ☼ 11am-4.30pm Sun-Thu Easter-Sep), a popular attraction half a mile west of Looe, is home to a colony of unfeasibly cute woolly monkeys and a colony of rare horseshoe bats.

An excellent 5-mile walk (part of the South West Coast Path) links Looe to Polperro via beaches, cliffs and the old smuggling village of Talland; allow around two hours, and take a picnic.

SLEEPING

Trehaven Manor Hotel (☎ 262028; www.trehavenhotel .co.uk; Station Rd; d £60-90; **P** ✗) This traditional 19th-century manor house is a short walk from town. The country-style rooms are all beautifully decorated, and most have period features including original fireplaces and bay windows (some overlooking the river).

Beach House (☎ 262598; www.thebeachhouselooe .com; Hannafore Point; d £56-80; **P** ✗) A stunning, modern B&B out on Hannafore Point. All the rooms are named after Cornish beaches – the best is Fistral, which offers picture windows and a private balcony with gorgeous sea views.

Tidal Court (☎ 263695; 3 Church St, West Looe; d from £36; **P** ✗) An old-fashioned B&B in a slate-roofed gabled house.

St Aubyn's (☎ 264351; www.staubyns.co.uk; Marine Dr, Hannafore Point, West Looe; s £30-32, d £56-78; **P** ✗) An imposing pebble-dash Victorian house overlooking Hannafore Point.

GETTING THERE & AWAY

Trains travel the scenic Looe Valley Line from Liskeard (£2.40, 30 minutes, eight daily Monday to Saturday).

Polperro
☎ 01503

Polperro is another ancient fishing village, a picturesque jumble of narrow lanes and fishing cottages set around a tiny harbour,

best approached along the coastal path from Looe or Talland. It's always jammed with day-trippers and coach tours in summer, so arrive in the evening or out of season if possible.

Polperro was once heavily involved in pilchard fishing by day and smuggling by night; the small **Heritage Museum** (☎ 272423; The Warren; adult £1; ☼ 10am-6pm Easter-Oct) features some fascinating smuggling memorabilia and tells some interesting tales.

Fowey
☎ 01726 / pop 2070

With its graceful pastel-coloured terraces and tiny alleyways teetering over a broad, tree-lined river estuary, Fowey (pronounced foy) is one of the prettiest towns in south Cornwall. It has a long maritime history, and in the 14th century raids on French and Spanish coastal towns were conducted from here. This led to a Spanish attack on Fowey in 1380; for defence, Henry VIII constructed **St Catherine's Castle** (EH; admission free), the remains of which overlook Readymoney Beach, south of town. The town later prospered by shipping Cornish china clay, although its harbour is mainly filled with yachts these days. Stop to check out the fine Norman front of **St Fimbarrus Church**, founded in the 6th century but upgraded in 1336 and 1460.

The **TIC** (☎ 833616; www.fowey.co.uk; 5 South St; ☼ 9am-5.30pm Mon-Sat, 10am-5pm Sun) shares a building, phone and opening hours with the Daphne du Maurier Literary Centre.

Fowey is at the southern end of the Saints' Way, a 26-mile waymarked trail running to Padstow on the northern coast. **Ferries** (car/pedestrian £2/80p; ☼ year round, in summer last ferry 8.50pm) cross the river to Bodinnick every few minutes to access the 4-mile Hall Walk to Polruan, from where ferries sail back to Fowey.

SLEEPING & EATING

Golant YHA Hostel (☎ 0870 770 5832; golant@yha .org.uk; Penquite House; dm £13.40; ☼ Feb-Nov) A substantial Georgian house overlooking the estuary 4 miles north of Fowey. Organised activities include walking on Bodmin Moor (p331) and night-time badger-watching.

Globe Posting House Hotel (☎ 833322; 19 Fore St; s/d £22.50/40-75; ✗) This tiny little B&B is tucked away on the main street, and offers a rabbit warren of snug rooms, all with low ceilings and solid stone walls. The downstairs café is a good spot for tapas or a lunch-time salad.

Marina Hotel (☎ 833315; www.themarinahotel.co.uk; The Esplanade; d £100-188) A gorgeous boutique hotel in a converted town house, right above the river. The neutral-toned rooms are decorated with grace; the priciest have private balconies, patio tables and views to die for. The attached **Waterside Restaurant** (mains £18-23) is the best place for fish and seafood in town.

Also recommended:

King of Prussia (☎ 627208; www.smallandfriendly.co.uk; Town Quay; d £55-65) Atmospheric pub on Town Quay, named after a notorious local smuggler.

Ship Inn (☎ 839431; Trafalgar Square; d £50-60) Another local drinking hole, built in 1570 by John Rashleigh, cousin to Francis Drake and Walter Raleigh.

GETTING THERE & AWAY
Bus No 24 from St Austell (45 minutes, every 30 minutes) runs to Fowey via Par, which has the closest train station.

IN SEARCH OF MANDERLEY

Fowey's most famous resident was the British thriller writer **Daphne du Maurier** (1907–1989), who lived most of her life in a house at nearby Polridmouth Cove (used as the model for Manderley in *Rebecca*). Many of her books were inspired by Cornish landscapes and locations – the real **Frenchman's Creek** (p317) can be found along the Helford estuary, and the original **Jamaica Inn** (p331) stands in a wild, desolate spot on Bodmin Moor. Every May, Fowey hosts the **Daphne du Maurier Literary Festival** in honour of her work; find out more at www.dumaurier.org.

Restormel Castle
Perched on a hilltop overlooking the River Fowey, 1½ miles north of Lostwithiel, the circular Norman keep of this ruined 13th-century **castle** (☎ 01208-872687; adult £2.20; ☺ 10am-6pm Jul & Aug, 10am-5pm Apr-Jun & Sep, 10am-4pm Oct) gives spectacular views over the countryside; you can see why Edward, the Black Prince, chose it as his home.

Eden Project
The three biomes of the **Eden Project** (☎ 01726-811911; www.edenproject.com; Bodelva; adult £12; ☺ 10am-6pm Apr-Oct, 10am-4.30pm Nov-Mar) – the largest greenhouses in the world – were raised from the dust of an abandoned china clay pit near St Austell in 2000, and have become one of Britain's great success stories. Tropical, temperate and desert environments have been recreated inside the biomes with flora and fauna from around the globe.

It's impressive and immensely popular: crowds (and queues) can be large, so avoid peak times if possible, especially during summer. Eden is about 3 miles northeast of St Austell. Shuttle buses run from St Austell, Newquay, Helston, Falmouth and Truro; you can buy a combined bus and admission ticket on the bus. Contact Truronian buses on ☎ 01872-273453 for details.

Lost Gardens of Heligan
Discovered in 1991 by Tim Smit, the entrepreneur behind the Eden Project, **Heligan** (☎ 01726-845100; www.heligan.com; Pentewan, St Austell; adult/child £7.50/£2.50; ☺ 10am-6pm summer, 10am-5pm winter) was once one of Britain's finest Victorian landscaped gardens. It fell into disrepair during WWI, when most of its staff were killed. The lost gardens are now regaining something of their former glory: formal terraces, flower gardens, a working kitchen garden and a spectacular jungle walk through the 'Lost Valley' are just some of Heligan's secrets.

Roseland Peninsula
South of Truro, this beautiful rural peninsula gets its name not from flowers (although there are plenty) but from the Cornish word *ros*, meaning promontory. Highlights include the coastal villages of **Portloe** – a wreckers' hang-out on the South West Coast Path – and **Veryan**, awash with daffodils in spring and entered between two thatched roundhouses. Nearby are the beaches of **Carne** and **Pendower**, which join at low tide to form one of the best stretches of sand on Cornwall's south coast.

St Mawes has an unusual clover leaf–plan **castle** (EH; ☎ 01326-270526; adult £3.20; ☺ 10am-6pm Jul & Aug, 10am-5pm Apr-Jun & Sep, 10am-4pm Oct, 10am-4pm Fri-Mon Nov-Mar), the best preserved of Henry VIII's coastal fortresses. Across the Fal estuary is Pendennis Castle (p316); together the two fortresses were designed to protect the crucial waterway from Spanish and French invasion.

SOUTHWEST ENGLAND

SOMETHING SPECIAL

Tresanton Hotel (☎ 01326-270055; www.tres
anton.com; 27 Lower Castle Rd, St Mawes; d £165-
225; P ✗) One of Cornwall's most desirable destinations, and a hotel that brings a
distinctly Mediterranean chic to the pretty
seafront of St Mawes. Created as a yachts-
man's club in the 1940s, later a swish '60s
hotel, the Tresanton has been completely
redesigned with glamorous bedrooms, private sea-view terraces, antique furniture
and even a private cinema.

St Mawes is 12 miles south of Truro, and
can be reached via the A3078 from Tregony,
or the much quicker route along the B3289
from the King Harry Ferry, which crosses
the Fal River near Trelissick Gardens.

Bus No 50 from Truro (one hour, four
to six daily, except Sunday) travels to St
Mawes via Tregony.

St-Just-in-Roseland boasts one of the most
beautiful churchyards in the country, full of
flowers and tumbling down to a creek that
has boats and wading birds.

SOUTHWEST CORNWALL
Falmouth
☎ 01326 / pop 28,800
Falmouth is a seaside resort, a working
dock and a student town, and these three
elements combine well: there's a lively atmosphere and plenty to see and do. The
port came to prominence in the 17th century as the terminal for the Post Office
Packet boats taking mail to America, and
the dockyard is still important for repairs
and shipbuilding.

The **TIC** (☎ 312300; falmouthtic@yahoo.co.uk; 28
Killigrew St; ☉ 9.30am-5.15pm Mon-Sat Apr-Sep, 9.30am-
5.15pm Mon-Fri Oct-Mar & 10am-2pm Sun Jul & Aug) is
opposite the bus terminal.

SIGHTS
On the end of the promontory is the largest fortress in Cornwall, **Pendennis Castle** (EH;
☎ 316594; adult £4.50; ☉ 10am-6pm Jul & Aug, 10am-
5pm Apr-Jun & Sep, 10am-4pm Oct-Mar), which at the
behest of Henry VIII was contructed on
the opposite side of the estuary as the sister
fortress to St Mawes (p315). The hands-on
Discovery Centre explores the castle's 450-
year history, while the sights and sounds of

battle are recreated in the gun tower, with
cannons firing and gun-smoke billowing.

The **National Maritime Museum** (☎ 313388;
www.nmmc.co.uk; Discovery Quay; adult £6.50; ☉ 10am-
5pm), housed in an award-winning building
by Falmouth Docks, contains vessels and
exhibitions exploring Britain's seafaring
heritage through the ages. The Flotilla Gallery houses more than 40 boats from the
national collection.

ACTIVITIES
In summer, **boat trips** set out from the
Prince of Wales pier to the Helford River
and Frenchman's Creek (£8 return); a 500-
year-old smuggler's cottage upriver (£6.50
return); and Truro (£8 return, one hour).
The pier is lined with boat companies'
booths; try **Enterprise Boats** (☎ 374241) or **Cornish Belle** (☎ 01872-580309).

Passenger ferries cross to St Mawes and
Flushing from the pier hourly in summer.

The nearest beach to town is busy **Gyllyng-
vase**, a short walk from the town centre.
Further along the headland, Swanpool and
Maenporth are usually quieter.

SLEEPING
B&Bs and small hotels line Melvill Rd and
Avenue Rd near the train station.

Dolvean Hotel (☎ 313658; www.dolvean.co.uk;
50 Melvill Rd; s/d £35/70-80; P ✗) The best (and
frilliest) B&B in Falmouth. Enjoy the little
touches such as complimentary umbrellas,
and chocolates by your bed.

Chellowdene (☎ 314950; Gyllyngvase Hill; d from £42)
An unusually shaped gabled house within
easy reach of Falmouth Bay and Gyllyngvase
Beach, offering prim, plain rooms.

Green Lawns Hotel (☎ 312734; www.greenlawns
hotel.com; Western Tce; s £60-110, d £110-120; P ✗
🐾 🖥) This ivy-covered chateau-style hotel
is one of the best hotels in Falmouth. Upstairs from the grand Georgian lobby and
the fine-dining restaurant you'll discover
a selection of top-notch rooms, the best
of which boast antique furniture, sunken
Jacuzzis and four-poster beds.

Other recommendations:
Rosemary Hotel (☎ 314669; www.rosemaryhotel.co.uk;
22 Gyllyngvase Tce; s/d from £28/56; P ✗) Small sea-
view hotel near Gyllyngvase Beach.
Rosemullion Hotel (☎ 314690; gail@rosemullionhotel
.demon.co.uk; Gyllyngvase Hill; d £45-55; P ✗) Impressive Tudor-style hotel split over three floors.

EATING & DRINKING

De Wynn's (☎ 219259; Church St; ⏱ 10am-5pm Mon-Sat, plus 11am-4pm Sun in summer) A traditional teashop on the main street: the house speciality is the 'thunder and lightning' cream tea, which comes with treacle instead of jam.

No 33 (☎ 211914; 33 High St; mains £11-15; ⏱ dinner Mon-Sat) The best place for seafood in Falmouth – a relaxed and rustic restaurant offering huge plates of local mussels, whole-roasted flounder and Provençal fish soup. Highly recommended.

Hunky Dory (☎ 212997; 46 Arwenack St; mains £12-25; ⏱ dinner) A smart restaurant with low timber ceilings, simple wooden tables and local art on the walls. It serves fresh fusion dishes including sushi, giant Mozambique prawns, baked Newlyn cod and five-spice roast duck.

Falmouth's best pubs are the **Quayside** (☎ 312113; Arwenack St), with outside seating on the harbour, and the nautical-themed **Chain Locker** (☎ 311685; Quay St) for that genuine fishing-town feel.

ENTERTAINMENT

Falmouth Arts Centre (☎ 314566; www.falmoutharts .org; Church St) A good arts venue with programmes of theatre, music and cinema, which also hosts the **Cornwall Film Festival** (www.cornwall -film-festival.co.uk) in November.

GETTING THERE & AWAY

National Express coaches run to London (£41 economy return, eight hours, daily) and Penzance (£4.75, one hour, daily).

Bus No 2 runs to Penzance (every 30 minutes). Bus No T8 runs to Truro (1¼ hours, five daily Monday to Saturday).

Falmouth is at the end of the branch railway line from Truro (£2.90 single, 20 minutes, hourly Monday to Saturday).

SOMETHING SPECIAL

Pandora Inn (☎ 01326-372678; Restronguet Creek, Mylor Bridge, Falmouth; mains £4-12) One of Cornwall's oldest pubs, in a beautiful riverside setting on the Fal estuary – expect great pub food, rustic character and weekend saints in abundance. Hardy souls can sample some of the Pandora's fabled smuggler's rum: at 80% proof, though, you might need to arrange for a taxi home.

The Lizard
☎ 01326

The wild, sea-pounded coastline along the Lizard peninsula – Britain's most southerly point – has historically been one of Cornwall's most treacherous. Hundreds of ships have foundered on the rocks and hidden reefs around the Lizard's shores over the centuries, including several within living memory. Staring out from the clifftops at the rolling Atlantic waves, it's not difficult to imagine how the ships came to grief. Much of the coastline is owned by the NT, and in spring the cliffs and headland blaze with wildflowers, heather and gorse: keep an eye out for seals and dolphins offshore.

HELSTON

The gateway to the Lizard, Helston is most famous for the **Furry Dance**, the last remnant of an old pagan festival commemorating the coming of spring and the passing of winter.

Helston Folk Museum (☎ 564027; Church St; adult/child £2/50p; ⏱ 10am-1pm Mon-Sat, 10am-4pm Mon-Sat summer holidays), housed in the old butter market, explores the history of the Furry Dance and displays a mishmash of heritage artefacts, including a 5½-ton cider press from 1750.

The **TIC** (☎ 565431; info@helstontic.demon.co.uk; 79 Meneage St; ⏱ 10am-1pm & 2-4.30pm Mon-Fri, 10am-1pm Sat & 1-4pm Sat Aug) has visitor information.

GOONHILLY EARTH STATION

In 1901 Guglielmo Marconi transmitted the first transatlantic radio signals from the tiny cove of Poldhu. The Lizard is still associated with telecommunications – somewhat surprisingly, the huge satellite dishes of the **Goonhilly Earth Station** (☎ 0800 679 593; www .goonhilly.bt.com; adult £5; ⏱ varying – check website or call) make up the largest satellite station on the planet. The multimedia visitors centre documents the history of international communications.

HELFORD RIVER

Across the north of the Lizard flows the **Helford River**, lined with overhanging oaks and hidden inlets: the perfect smugglers' hideaway. **Frenchman's Creek**, the inspiration for Daphne du Maurier's novel of the same name, can be reached on foot from the car park in **Helford** village.

On the northern bank of the river is **Trebah** (☎ 250448; www.trebahgarden.co.uk; adult £5 Mar-Oct, £2.50 Nov-Feb; 🕙 10.30am-5pm), one of Cornwall's finest subtropical gardens, dramatically situated in a steep ravine filled with giant rhododendrons, huge Brazilian rhubarb plants and jungle ferns.

Just to the east are the gardens of **Glendurgan** (☎ 250906; glendurgan@ntrust.org.uk; adult £4.20; 🕙 10.30am-5.30pm Tue-Sat Feb-Oct), established in the 18th century by the Fox family. There are stunning views of the Helford River, and there's also a 19th-century maze and a secluded beach near Durgan village.

Near Gweek, 6 miles from Helston, is the **National Seal Sanctuary** (☎ 221361; www.seal sanctuary.co.uk/corn1.html; adult/child £7.50/5.50; 🕙 10am-5pm May-Sep, 9am-4pm Oct-Apr), which cares for sick, injured and orphaned seals before returning them to the wild.

LIZARD POINT & AROUND

Three miles southwest of Helston is **Porthleven**, another quaint fishing port with beaches nearby. **Lizard Point** is a 3½-mile walk along the South West Coast Path. **Cadgwith**, further east around the coast, is the quintessential Cornish fishing village, with thatched, whitewashed cottages and a small harbour.

At the peninsula's tip is the **Lizard Lighthouse** (☎ 290065), which was built in 1751 and now entirely automated. Lizard Point is one of the most treacherous coastal areas in Cornwall.

Below the lighthouse, a rough track leads down to the disused lifeboat station and a shingle cove. A little way inland, you'll find the small village of **The Lizard** and a smattering of giftshops and tearooms – as well as one of the county's best-known pasty shops.

A mile west of Lizard Point is the beautiful National Trust beach of **Kynance Cove**, overlooked by towering cliffs and flower-covered headland. Much of the red-green serpentine rock fashionable during the Victorian era was mined here.

SLEEPING

Lizard YHA Hostel (☎ 0870 770 5780; lizard@yha.org.uk; dm £13.40; 🕙 Apr-Oct) A wonderful hostel housed in a former Victorian hotel beside the Lizard Lighthouse – the views have to be seen to be believed.

Coverack YHA Hostel (☎ 0870 770 5780; coverack@ yha.org.uk; Coverack; dm £11.80; 🕙 Mar-Oct) A period country house above the pretty harbour of Coverack.

Housel Bay Hotel (☎ 01326-290417; www.houselbay .com; The Lizard; d £56-150; **P** ✗) This historic hotel commands a stunning position overlooking secluded Housel Bay, a short walk from Lizard Point. Constructed by a group of Victorian entrepreneurs at the end of the 19th century, the gabled building boasts a smart table d'hôte restaurant, endearingly old-world furnishings and a range of elegant rooms, many with sea views to die for. George Bernard Shaw, King George V and GK Chesterton are just some of the famous names to be found in the hotel's guestbook.

Polurrian Hotel (☎ 01326-240421; www.polurrian hotel.com; Polurrian Rd, Mullion; d £128-260; **P** ✗ 🐾) There are hundreds of holiday cottages dotted throughout the Lizard peninsula (some villages, like the tiny fishing port of Cadgwith, have nothing else), but the Polurrian Hotel is one of the smartest places to stay, with an unrivalled clifftop position, grand Edwardian-style rooms, and easy access to the beach at Polurrian Cove below.

GETTING THERE & AWAY

The Lizard's transportation hub is Helston, served by **Truronian buses** (☎ 01872-273453; www .truronian.co.uk). Bus No T1 runs from Truro via Helston (45 minutes) to Lizard village (1½ hours, 14 daily, four Sunday).

Bus No T2 runs from Helston to Goonhilly (20 minutes), Coverack (25 minutes) and St Keverne (40 minutes, around 10 daily Monday to Saturday).

Bus No T4 runs from Helston to Falmouth (70 minutes) via Gweek (25 minutes) and Trebah (45 minutes, every two hours Monday to Saturday, four Sunday).

TOP FIVE GARDENS

- **Glendurgan** (p317; Helford River)
- **Heligan** (p315; near St Austell)
- **Lanhydrock** (p331; near Bodmin)
- **Trebah** (p317; Helford River)
- **Trelissick** (p313; near Truro)

A Day Rover ticket valid on all Truronian buses costs £5.

St Michael's Mount

Perched on a rocky island and cut off from the mainland at high tide, **St Michael's Mount** (NT; ☎ 01736-710507; adult £5.20; ⏰ 10.30am-5.30pm daily Jun-Sep, 10.30am-5.30pm Sun-Fri Mar-Jun & Oct; last admission 4.45pm) is one of Cornwall's most famous landmarks. Named after a fisherman's vision of the archangel Michael, in 1070 the mount was bequeathed to the monks who built Mont St Michel off the Normandy coast, and it quickly became an important place of medieval pilgrimage. Since 1659 the mount has been the home of the St Aubyn family. The lavish interior features a rococo Gothic drawing room, an armoury and a fascinating 14th-century priory church. There are also subtropical **hanging gardens** (adult £2.50).

At low tide, you can walk across from Marazion but at high tide in summer there's a **ferry** (☎ 01736-710265; per adult £1).

Bus No 2 passes Marazion as it travels from Penzance to Falmouth.

WEST CORNWALL

West Cornwall contains some of the county's wildest scenery, a classic Cornish landscape of sea-battered cliffs, churning surf, crumbling mine-workings and wheeling gulls. The West Penwith area was one of the oldest Celtic settlements in Cornwall, and the area is littered with prehistoric sites, including the **Mên-an-Tol** stone near Madron, and the Iron-Age village of Chysauster (see the boxed text, p323).

Penzance

☎ 01736 / pop 20,260

The far-westerly town of Penzance has always had a peculiar end-of-the-line feel: as the last stop on the railway from London, it's the last decent-sized town between mainland Britain and the great grey expanse of the Atlantic Ocean. Once a busy shipping port and an important railway terminus, the town now has a mix of characters; it's part hippy hang-out, part artistic haven and part commercial centre. Dotted with craft shops, galleries, restaurants and B&Bs, as well as plenty of mainstream

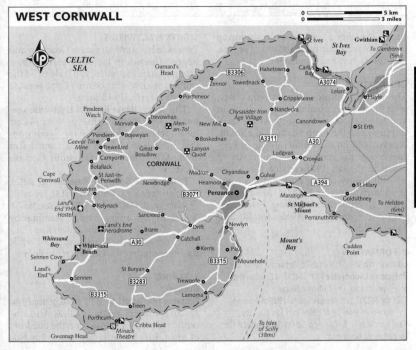

WEST CORNWALL

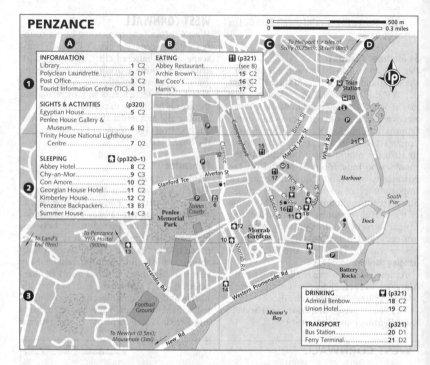

shops, it makes a great base for exploring the rest of west Cornwall, including St Ives, Zennor, St Just and Land's End.

ORIENTATION
The harbour spreads along Mount's Bay, with the ferry terminal to the east, the train and bus stations to the north of the ferry terminal and the main beach to the south. Newlyn, out on the southern edge of Penzance, was the centre of a community of artists in the late 19th century; these days it's still a busy fishing port and has some good restaurants and B&Bs. Most of the B&Bs are concentrated along Penzance's Western Promenade, Alexandra Rd and Morrab Rd.

INFORMATION
Library (☎ 363954; Morrab Rd; Net access per hr £3)
Polyclean Laundrette (☎ 364815; 4 East Tce; Net access per min 5p; ⏰ 7.30am-7.30pm)
TIC (☎ 362207; pztic@penwith.gov.uk; Station Approach; ⏰ 9am-6pm Mon-Sat & 10am-1pm Sun May-Sep, 9am-6pm Mon-Fri & 10am-1pm Sat Oct-Apr) Located in the car park by the bus station.

SIGHTS & ACTIVITIES
Penzance has some attractive Georgian and Regency houses in the older part of town around Chapel St, where you'll also find the exuberant early–19th century **Egyptian House** with its bizarre, florid front.

The **Trinity House National Lighthouse Centre** (☎ 360077; Wharf Rd; adult £3; ⏰ 10.30am-4.30pm Apr-Oct) relates the history of the lighthouses that have helped keep ships from harm along this stretch of treacherous Cornish coastline.

Penlee House Gallery & Museum (☎ 363625; www.penleehouse.org.uk; Morrab Rd; adult £2, free on Sat; ⏰ 10am-5pm Mon-Sat May-Sep, 10.30am-4.30pm Mon-Sat Oct-Apr) displays a fine range of paintings by artists of the Newlyn School, including Stanhope Forbes (see the boxed text, p326), while the museum devotes itself to archaeology.

SLEEPING
Budget
Penzance YHA Hostel (☎ 0870 770 5992; penzance@yha .org.uk; Castle Horneck, Alverton; dm £11.60) An 18th-century Georgian mansion on the outskirts of town, with fantastic bay views. Bus Nos

5B, 6B and 10B run from the train station; it's a 500m walk from the bus stop.

Penzance Backpackers (☎ 363836; pzbackpack@ndirect.co.uk; Alexandra Rd; dm/d £10/24) A cheery, comfortable hostel in a converted town house. Bus Nos 1, 1A, 5A and 6A travel from the bus station.

Con Amore (☎ 363423; www.con-amore.co.uk; 38 Morrab Rd; d £28-38; ✗) Popular B&B with country-style rooms, near the town centre.

Kimberley House (☎ 362727; 10 Morrab Rd; s/d from £25/40) Family-run B&B in a smart Cornish-stone house.

Mid-Range & Top End

Summer House (☎ 363744; www.summerhouse-cornwall .com; Cornwall Tce; s/d £70/75-95; ✗ closed Nov-Mar; P ✗) This grand Regency house was once an artist's studio, but it's now been transformed into one of Penzance's best places to stay. The bedrooms have been converted with lashings of style: huge beds, sunny colours and pinstripes on the walls, wood floors, cornicing and cast-iron fireplaces. There's also an in-house Mediterranean restaurant.

Abbey Hotel (☎ 366906; www.theabbeyonline.com; Abbey St; d £120-190) The best hotel in Penzance – an extravagant 17th-century town house that still retains its period character, from an oak-panelled dining room to the stately drawing room and walled garden. Most of the sumptuous bedrooms have bay views, and the bathrooms are huge.

Chy-an-Mor (☎ 363441; www.chyanmor.co.uk; 15 Regent Tce; d £56-68; P ✗) A highly recommended B&B, with a range of individually styled rooms near the seafront.

Georgian House Hotel (☎ 365664; 20 Chapel St; s/d £28/52; ✗) A comfortable, old-world B&B in the former mayor's residence.

EATING

Archie Brown's (☎ 362828; Bread St; mains £3-6; ✗ 9.30am-5pm Mon-Sat) A colourful vegetarian/vegan café furnished with sofas, wooden tables and potted plants. Try the homity pie (£5), huge sandwiches (£3 to £6) or freshly baked cakes, crumbles and puddings.

Bar Coco's (☎ 350222; 13 Chapel St; tapas £2-5; ✗ breakfast, lunch & dinner Mon-Sat, closed Sun) This popular Spanish-style café-bar serves decent tapas and Mediterranean dishes, but most come for the *cerveza* (beer).

Harris's (☎ 364408; 46 New St; mains £14.95-19.95; ✗ lunch & dinner Tue-Sat) This much-respected

restaurant is the place to head for seriously classy seafood. Steamed John Dory, goujons of sole and Falmouth bay scallops are some of the fine-dining delights on offer.

Abbey Restaurant (☎ 330680; Abbey St; 3 courses £19; ✗ lunch Fri & Sat, dinner Tue-Sat) Run by the owners of the Abbey Hotel (left), this modern restaurant is the most imaginative (and acclaimed) in Penzance. Upstairs, the light, bright restaurant experiments with classic French and British cuisine; downstairs, there's a scarlet-walled cellar bar with sofas and big chairs for post-dinner drinks.

DRINKING

Chapel St hosts a couple of well-known pubs.

Admiral Benbow (☎ 363448; 46 Chapel St) A super-kitsch pub covered with ship's wheels, tankards and plaster statues, all with a salty sea-dog theme.

Union Hotel (☎ 362951; Chapel St) Once the centre of Georgian Penzance (housing both the assembly rooms and town theatre), this venerable old inn has a couple of snug bars to choose from – ask at the bar about why there's a figure of Nelson in the doorway.

GETTING THERE & AWAY

Bus

National Express coaches run direct to London (£33, nine hours, six daily), Bristol (£34.50, 6½ hours, two daily), Exeter (£20.50, five hours, two daily), Plymouth (£6, 3½ hours, seven daily), Truro (£4.25, 1½ hours, five daily) and St Ives (£2.75, 25 minutes, five daily).

There are daily First Western National services to Land's End (one hour) on bus No 1, leaving hourly during the week but less frequently at the weekend.

Train

There are regular services to Penzance from London Paddington (£79, six hours, eight daily). There are a few direct trains from Penzance to St Ives (£2.90, 20 minutes, hourly), with connections at St Erth.

Mousehole

☎ 01736

Once a bustling pilchard-fishing port, and now a popular spot for second-homers, the pretty village of Mousehole (pronounced mowsel) is centred on the cluster of stone cottages around the old harbour. Described by Dylan Thomas as 'the loveliest village in England', it's certainly beautiful, but it's always packed in summer and in December, when the town switches on its famous Christmas lights.

Old Coastguard Hotel (☎ 731222; www.oldcoast guardhotel.co.uk; s £35-48, d £75-110) is a smart, modernised hotel, with a pleasant bar-diner overlooking the sea.

The cosy **Ship Inn** (☎ 731234; South Cliff; s/d £32.50/55), nestled down by the harbour, serves good seafood and fresh fish.

Bus Nos 5A/5B and 6A/6B run the 20-minute journey to Penzance every half-hour.

Minack Theatre

Surely the world's most spectacularly located theatre, the **Minack** (☎ 01736-810181; www.minack.com; tickets from £7.50) is carved into the cliffs overlooking Porthcurno Bay. The **visitors centre** (adult £3; ☯ 9.30am-5.30pm Apr-Sep, 10am-4pm Oct-Mar) recounts the story of Rowena Cade, the indomitable local woman who conceived and oversaw the theatre until her death in 1983. The theatre's 17-week season runs from mid-May to mid-September – you'll need to book well ahead.

Bus No 1 from Penzance to Land's End makes a stop at Porthcurno from Monday to Saturday.

Land's End

The coast on either side of Land's End is some of the most spectacular in England. Standing at the last promontory of the English mainland, gazing out over the vast expanse of the Atlantic Ocean, is quite a magical experience.

At least, it was until the **Legendary Land's End** (☎ 0870 458 0099; www.landsend-landmark.co.uk; adult/child £10/6; ☯ 10am-5pm summer, 10am-3pm winter) theme park began drawing in the hordes. The 'attractions' include a sweet factory, restored farm and several half-hearted multimedia shows, but you'll do better skipping the complex entirely. A short walk along the headland, the last rocky outcrops of Britain crumble into the pounding waves. On a clear day, it's possible to see all the way to the Isles of Scilly, 28 miles out to sea.

Land's End is 9 miles from Penzance and 874 miles from John O'Groats in Scotland

THE LOST LANDS OF LYONESSE

Legend tells that Land's End was once joined to the Isles of Scilly by the land of Lyonesse, which was engulfed by the sea around 900 years ago. The sole survivor was a man named Trevilian, who foresaw the disaster and outrode the advancing waves on a swift white horse, taking refuge in a cave near Marazion. The older fisherman around Mount's Bay still say that submerged buildings can sometimes be seen around the Seven Stones Lighthouse.

(p895). Bus No 300, usually open-topped in summer, runs along the coast to St Ives (1½ hours, four daily), and bus Nos 1, 1A and 1C (one hour) run hourly from Penzance.

Westward Airways (☎ 788771) offers sightseeing flights over Land's End from the airfield at St Just; a seven-minute hop costs from £18.

St Just-in-Penwith
☎ 01736 / pop 1890

The stern, grey-granite town of St-Just-in-Penwith (known as St Just), 6 miles north of Land's End, was formerly a centre for tin and copper mining. **Geevor Tin Mine** (☎ 788662; www.geevor.com; adult/child £6.50/4; ☯ 9am-5pm Sun-Fri Easter-Oct, 9am-3pm Sun-Fri Nov-Easter) at Pendeen, north of St Just, finally closed in 1990 and is now open to visitors. Claustrophobics should beware of the tours of the 18th-century mineshafts, which take place every hour in summer.

Land's End YHA Hostel (☎ 0870 770 5906; Letcha Vean; dm £11.80) is a remote hostel about half a mile south of St Just; it's tricky to find (call for directions) but wonderfully isolated, near the coast path.

Bus No 15 runs regularly from St Ives (one hour, four daily), while bus Nos 10, 10A, 10B and 11A go from Penzance (30 minutes, every 30 minutes).

Zennor
☎ 01736

A stunning 6-mile stretch of the South West Coast Path runs from St Ives to the windswept village of Zennor, where DH Lawrence wrote much of *Women in Love*. Zennor's **St Senara's Church** dates from at least 1150. Look for the church's carved

Mermaid Chair; legend tells of a beautiful, mysterious woman who lured a chorister into the sea at Mermaid's Cove, where you can still hear them singing.

Wayside Folk Museum (☎ 796945; adult £2.75; ☼ 10.30am-5.30pm Easter-Oct) is the oldest private museum in Britain. It houses an eclectic mix of local-interest exhibits, including displays on tin mining, fishing, farming and archaeology. Look out for the two water-powered mill wheels in the garden.

Old Chapel Backpackers Hostel (☎ 798307; dm/d £12/40; P) is a great hostel with comfortable dorms in a smartly converted Methodist chapel. It's perfectly placed for exploring the coast path, and there's an excellent café downstairs.

Tinner's Arms (☎ 792697; ploughman's lunch £5.50) is a perfect stop for pub food and a fortifying pint. It's a slate-roofed country inn where DH Lawrence lived before moving into an isolated farmhouse nearby. The pub remained a favoured drinking spot during Lawrence's year-and-a-half-long sojourn on the Zennor coastline.

From St Ives, catch Bus No 300 (20 minutes, five daily) or No 343 (20 minutes, six daily).

St Ives
☎ 01736 / pop 9870

Nestled into the cliffs west of Carbis Bay, St Ives was once one of Cornwall's busiest fishing ports and later became a centre of 20th-century art, but now it's better known as a thriving holiday town. From the granite harbour front, the town climbs into a warren of cobbled streets, where slate-roofed cottages, old pubs and tumbledown chapels jostle for space with tourist shops, trendy

restaurants, galleries and holiday homes. It's an intriguing blend of old and new worlds, where heritage and commerce collide head-on. Every year thousands of visitors are attracted to its vibrant art scene, atmospheric architecture and bustling cafés and bars, not to mention its beautiful seaside setting.

ORIENTATION
St Ives lies on the west side of St Ives Bay. The main road into town starts as Trelyon Ave, which becomes The Terrace near the bus and train stations and Tregenna Pl further downhill into town. It is lined with B&Bs and hotels, and passes the bus and train stations above Porthminster Beach, before joining the main shopping streets of Tregenna Pl, the High St and Fore St. The best restaurants and cafés are along the harbour, while most of the art galleries are west of Fore St.

INFORMATION
Library (☎ 795377; 1 Gabriel St; Net access per hr £3)
Post office (☎ 795004; Tregenna Pl; ☼ 9am-5.30pm Mon-Fri, 9am-12.30pm Sat)
stives-cornwall.co.uk Official town website with accommodation and activity guides.
TIC (☎ 796297; ivtic@penwith.gov.uk; Street-an-Pol; ☼ 9am-6pm Mon-Sat Easter-Sep, 10am-1pm Sun Easter-Jun & Sep, 10am-4pm Sun Jul & Aug, 9am-5pm Mon-Fri, 10am-1pm Sat Oct-Easter) Inside the Guildhall.

SIGHTS & ACTIVITIES
Tate St Ives
The streets of St Ives are dotted with art galleries, but the most impressive collection is held at **Tate St Ives** (☎ 796226; www .tate.org.uk/stives; Porthmeor Beach; adult £5.50, joint ticket with Barbara Hepworth museum £8.50; ☼ 10am-5.30pm daily Mar-Oct, 10am-4.30pm Tue-Sun Nov-Feb). Built in 1993 above Porthmeor Beach, and designed to echo its surroundings in glass, stone and white concrete, the building is almost a work of art in itself. The gallery contains work by celebrated local artists, including Terry Frost, Patrick Heron and Barbara Hepworth, along with commissioned pieces and special exhibitions. On the top floor there is a stylish café-bar with the best sea views in town.

Barbara Hepworth Museum & Sculpture Garden
The Tate also oversees this **museum** (☎ 796226; Barnoon Hill; adult £4.50, joint ticket with Tate St Ives £8.50;

ANCIENT CORNWALL
The area between St Just and St Ives is littered with standing stones and other ancient remains. If prehistory is your thing, track down **Lanyon Quoit** (a table-shaped dolmen between Madron and Morvah), the **Mên-an-Tol stone** (a ring-shaped stone near Madron) and **Chysauster Iron Age Village** (☎ 07831-757934; adult £2; ☼ 10am-6pm Jul & Aug, 10am-5pm Apr-Jun & Sep, 10am-4pm Oct), the most complete prehistoric settlement in Cornwall.

ST IVES

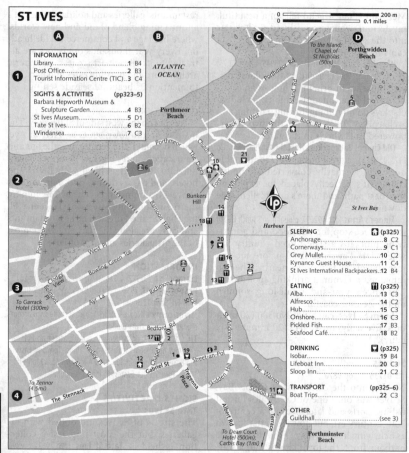

INFORMATION
Library.....................................1 B4
Post Office..............................2 B3
Tourist Information Centre (TIC)...3 C4

SIGHTS & ACTIVITIES (pp323–5)
Barbara Hepworth Museum &
  Sculpture Garden..................4 B3
St Ives Museum.........................5 D1
Tate St Ives...............................6 B2
Windansea................................7 C3

SLEEPING (p325)
Anchorage.................................8 C2
Cornerways...............................9 C1
Grey Mullet.............................10 C2
Kynance Guest House.............11 C4
St Ives International Backpackers..12 B4

EATING (p325)
Alba.......................................13 C3
Alfresco..................................14 C3
Hub..15 C3
Onshore..................................16 C3
Pickled Fish.............................17 B3
Seafood Café...........................18 B2

DRINKING (p325)
Isobar.....................................19 B4
Lifeboat Inn............................20 C3
Sloop Inn................................21 C2

TRANSPORT (pp325–6)
Boat Trips...............................22 C3

OTHER
Guildhall.............................(see 3)

10am-5.30pm daily Mar-Oct, 10am-4.30pm Tue-Sun Nov-Feb), in Barbara Hepworth's house and studio on Barnoon Hill. Hepworth was one of the leading sculptors of the 20th century, and a key figure in the St Ives art scene. The museum and gallery contains an archive of her letters and belongings, while the adjoining garden contains some of her famous sculptures. The studio has remained untouched since her death in a fire in 1975. Hepworth's work is scattered throughout St Ives; look for her sculptures outside the Guildhall and inside the 15th-century parish church of St Ia.

St Ives Museum
Housed in a pier-side building previously used over the years as a pilchard-packing factory, laundry, cinema, sailor's mission and copper mine, the **St Ives Museum** (Heritage Museum; ☎ 796005; adult £1.50; 10am-5pm Mon-Fri & 10am-4pm Sat Mar-Oct) contains local artefacts relating to blacksmithery, fishing and shipwrecks.

Beaches
The largest town beaches are **Porthmeor** and **Porthminster**, but the tiny cove of **Porthgwidden** is also popular. Nearby, the pre-14th-century **Chapel of St Nicholas** (St Nicholas was the patron saint of children and sailors) is the oldest church in St Ives, and with only one room, certainly the smallest. **Carbis Bay**, 1 mile to the southeast of town, is also worth seeking out.

SOUTHWEST ENGLAND

Several places on Porthmeor Beach and Fore St rent out wetsuits and surfboards; try **Windansea** (☎ 794830; 25 Fore St).

SLEEPING
Budget
St Ives International Backpackers (☎ 799444; www.backpackers.co.uk/st-ives; The Stennack; dm £10-16, d £30-35; 🖳) Housed inside an old Wesleyan chapel school, this sprawling hostel has grungy character (mismatched décor, colourful wall murals), but the rooms are cramped and very basic. You have to stay for at least a week in July and August.

Anchorage (☎ 797135; 5 Bunkers Hill; s/d from £27/55; ✗) One of the best B&Bs in old St Ives. The 18th-century cob-walled house has bags of rustic charm with original oak beams, granite fireplace and exposed stonework. The rooms are small, but some have harbour views.

Grey Mullet (☎ 796635; greymulletguesthouse@line one.net; 2 Bunkers Hill; s/d £25/48-52; ✗) Housed in a flower-covered building dating from 1776, this traditional B&B is full of old-world appeal, with photographs, sketches and period prints on the walls, and snug rooms overlooking the cobbled street or the harbour.

Mid-Range & Top End
Cornerways (☎ 796706; Bethesda Pl; d from £65) In the quiet Downalong quarter of St Ives, this attractive house hosted Daphne du Maurier during the 1940s; it's been updated since then but still has an air of elegance and understated style.

Kynance Guest House (☎ 796636; www.kynance .com; 24 The Warren; d £50-58; ✓ Mar-Oct; P ✗) An attractive B&B in an old tin-miners' cottage, along a quiet backstreet near Porthminster Beach. The wood-beamed dining room and lounge are decorated with local art, and there's a patio garden reached from the 2nd floor.

Dean Court Hotel (☎ 796023; www.deancourthotel .com; Trelyon Ave; d £70-102; P) A smart mid-range hotel in a double-fronted Victorian town house on the main avenue into St Ives. The rooms are impeccably furnished in neutral tones, and the best have bay windows overlooking St Ives.

Garrack Hotel (☎ 796199; www.garrack.com; Burthallen Lane; s/d from £68/114; P ✗ 🖳) One of several upmarket establishments in St Ives, this ivy-covered hotel feels like an exclusive country club, with landscaped grounds, an indoor swimming pool and huge, smartly decorated rooms, some with four-poster beds and antique furniture.

EATING
Alba (☎ 797222; Old Lifeboat House; mains £12-17; ✓ lunch & dinner) This renowned split-level restaurant offers superb seafood in a sleek, contemporary setting, with starched white tablecloths, modern furniture and picture windows overlooking the harbour.

Onshore (☎ 796000; The Wharf; ✓ lunch & dinner) Further along the wharf, this chrome-styled restaurant serves pasta and award-winning pizzas cooked in a roaring wood-fired oven.

Alfresco (☎ 793737; The Wharf; mains £10-14; ✓ lunch & dinner) Stylish fish and seafood with a Mediterranean flavour are served in a beautiful location on the waterfront, with sliding doors that open onto the wharfside terrace in summer.

Pickled Fish (☎ 795100; 3 Chapel St; mains £13-18; ✓ dinner Mon-Sat) The owner-chef of this tiny restaurant started out at the Dorchester Hotel, and now serves up some of St Ives' best food, based on local produce and top-quality ingredients.

Seafood Café (☎ 794004; 45 Fore St; mains £8.95-15.95; ✓ lunch & dinner) Buzzy, informal bistro offering gourmet burgers, bouillabaisse, huge ciabattas, and mussels for under £10.

Hub (☎ 799099; The Wharf; mains £6-10; ✓ 10am-11pm) Metropolitan-style café-bar with good coffee, lunch-time sandwiches and lively night-time drinking.

DRINKING
Isobar (☎ 796042; Tregenna Pl; ✓ 10am-2am) St Ives' most popular nightspot. There's a buzzy cocktail and café-bar on the ground floor, and a club with regular house/techno nights upstairs.

Sloop Inn (☎ 796584; The Wharf) The walls of this 14th-century inn are hung with paintings by local artists, but on summer evenings most people ignore them and drink out by the harbour.

Lifeboat Inn (☎ 794123; The Wharf) On the other side of the harbour, this place has a warm, welcoming atmosphere and a good selection of Cornish ales.

GETTING THERE & AWAY
National Express operates coaches to London (£33, 8½ hours, three daily), Plymouth

ST IVES & THE ARTS

Ever since JMW Turner sketched the town in 1811, St Ives has been a focal point for British art. During the 19th century, St Ives was linked with the Newlyn School, a group of figurative painters headed by Stanhope Forbes, who found ideal subjects among the rustic characters and landscapes of Cornwall. James Whistler and Walter Sickert made regular visits, and by the beginning of the 20th century there were scores of artists working in and around St Ives. In the 1930s and '40s, the work of abstract painters like Peter Lanyon, Henry Moore and Ben Nicholson, and Nicholson's wife, the sculptor Barbara Hepworth, led to the formation of the Penwith Society of Artists in 1949. Their avant-garde techniques inspired a third wave of St Ives artists in the 1960s and '70s, including Terry Frost, Patrick Heron and Roger Hilton. Today, St Ives continues to hold an enduring fascination – the Penwith area supports more working artists than almost anywhere else in Britain.

(£6, three hours, four daily), Exeter (£20.50, five hours, one daily) and most local towns.

Local First buses No 16/16B, 17A and 17B regularly connect St Ives with Penzance; Bus No 300 travels to Land's End en route. Most bus services stop at Zennor, Sennen and St Just. There are also direct services to Truro (£3.50, one hour, two daily).

St Ives is on a scenic branch railway line from St Erth (£2.90, 20 minutes, hourly), on the main London–Penzance line.

A Park & Ride train service operates from the Lelant Saltings Rail Halt 2 miles south of town.

NORTH CORNWALL COAST

Overlooking the vast expanse of the Atlantic Ocean, the north coast is, for many people, the quintessential Cornish landscape. There's a wild mix of granite rocks, craggy clifftops and booming surf, beloved by surfers, cyclists, walkers and beach-bums alike.

The coastline is dotted with sandy bays and secluded coves, but the best beaches are near Hayle at **Gwithian** and **Godrevy**. At low tide, 3 miles of sand are revealed by the receding tide; strong winds make this a popular spot for kite-boarders and surfers, though the swell can be powerful and unpredictable, so take care.

Further north, beyond the little harbour of **Portreath**, the beaches around **Porthtowan** and **St Agnes** are popular with surfers and holiday-makers, especially the tiny National Trust cove of **Chapel Porth**, from where the coast path leads up to the abandoned mine workings of **Wheal Coates**. North of St Agnes is the busy seaside town of **Perranporth**, where there's another excellent beach

and plenty of accommodation and summer nightlife.

Northwards along the coast towards Newquay are several more stunning beaches, including **Crantock** and **Holywell Bay**. Most dramatic of all are the stately rock towers of **Bedruthan Steps**, 7 miles north of Newquay.

Sleeping

Rose-in-Vale Hotel (☎ 01872-552202; www.rose-in-vale -hotel.co.uk; Mithian; d from £120; P ☒ ☲) A gorgeous country hotel inside an ivy-covered Georgian manor house, 2 miles from St Agnes. The hotel has landscaped grounds, renovated rooms, and a sauna, outdoor pool and summerhouse.

Driftwood Spars (☎ 01872-552428; www.driftwood spars.com; Trevaunance Cove; d £74-84; P ☒) A popular spot with Cornwall's surfing community, moments from the beach at Trevaunance Cove near St Agnes. Nautical-themed B&B rooms with sea views can be found above the 17th-century pub.

Penkerris (☎ 01872-552262; www.penkerris.co.uk; St Agnes; d £30-70; P ☒) A creeper-covered house on the edge of St Agnes village.

Seiners Arms (☎ 01872-573118; www.seinersarms .com; Perranporth; d £54-72; P ☒) Modern pub and hotel overlooking Perranporth Beach.

Eating & Drinking

Watering Hole (☎ 01872-572888; Perranporth Beach) A relaxed bar-restaurant on Perranporth Beach with outside decking and a buzzy surf-shack vibe. Regular bands play at weekends and throughout the summer.

Blue Bar (☎ 01209-890329; www.blue-bar.co.uk; Porthtowan; ☽ lunch & dinner Thu-Sun) A great café-brasserie overlooking Porthtowan beach, with a bright surf-style interior and a gorgeous sea-view patio. There's live music, parties and DJs at weekends.

Getting There & Away

Bus No 301 travels up and down the North Coast from Newquay four times daily in July and August, stopping at Perranporth (40 minutes), St Agnes (50 minutes), Hayle (80 minutes) and Penzance (two hours).

NEWQUAY

☎ 01637 / pop 19,570

Newquay is the kind of place that you either love or loathe. Scattered across the clifftops above the broad beaches of Fistral and Towan, it's indisputably one of the most famous surfing spots in all of England, and has an attitude to match. More recently, Newquay has also gained a reputation as Cornwall's biggest party town, with countless nightspots ranging from the ultra-tacky to the pseudo-chic, and throughout the summer the evening streets are jammed with clubbers, surfers and late-night drinkers.

Much of Newquay is relentlessly modern, but on the cliff north of Towan Beach stands the 14th-century **Huer's House**, a lookout for approaching pilchard shoals (these shoals were enormous until they were fished out early in the 20th century: one catch from 1868 netted a record 16.5 million fish). Every Cornish fishing village once had such a watchtower.

Look out for the annual **Run to the Sun Festival** (☎ 01637 851 851; www.runtothesun.co.uk), which takes place over one long weekend at the end of May at the Trevelgue Holiday Park, near Porth. What started out as a modest bash for Britain's devoted band of Volkswagen owners has now morphed into one of the town's biggest and brashest summer festivals, with bands, beer and more Beetles than you could possibly wish for.

Unsurprisingly, space is at a premium during the weekend, and the traffic is a real party-killer. Most of the town's hostels and B&Bs will be crammed to the rafters, so book well ahead – and watch out for any dodgy substances being sprayed from super-soakers.

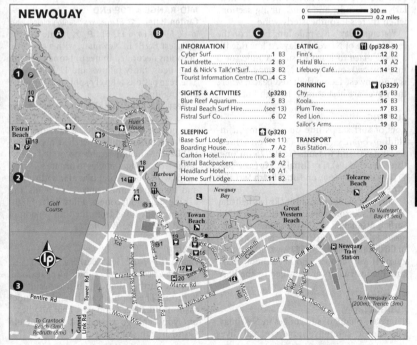

NEWQUAY

INFORMATION	
Cyber Surf	1 B3
Laundrette	2 B3
Tad & Nick's Talk'n'Surf	3 B2
Tourist Information Centre (TIC)	4 C3

SIGHTS & ACTIVITIES	(p328)
Blue Reef Aquarium	5 B3
Fistral Beach Surf Hire	(see 13)
Fistral Surf Co	6 D2

SLEEPING	(p328)
Base Surf Lodge	(see 11)
Boarding House	7 A2
Carlton Hotel	8 B2
Fistral Backpackers	9 A2
Headland Hotel	10 A1
Home Surf Lodge	11 B2

EATING	(pp328–9)
Finn's	12 B2
Fistral Blu	13 A2
Lifebuoy Café	14 B2

DRINKING	(p329)
Chy	15 B3
Koola	16 B3
Plum Tree	17 B3
Red Lion	18 B2
Sailor's Arms	19 B3

TRANSPORT	
Bus Station	20 B3

SOUTHWEST ENGLAND

Information

Cyber Surf (☎ 875497; 2 Broad St; Net access per min 7p; 🕙 10am-late)

Laundrette (☎ 875901; 1 Beach Pde, Beach Rd)

Tad & Nick's Talk'n'Surf (☎ 874868; 72 Fore St; Net access per hr £3; 🕙 10am-6pm)

TIC (☎ 854020; www.newquay.co.uk; Marcus Hill; 🕙 9.30am-5.30pm Mon-Sat & 9am-3.30pm Sun Jun-Sep, 9.30am-4.30pm Mon-Fri & 9.30am-12.30pm Sat Oct-May)

Sights & Activities

Blue Reef Aquarium (☎ 878134; www.bluereefaquar ium.co.uk; Towan Promenade; adult £5.95; 🕙 10am-5pm), right on Towan beach, has a good selection of weird and wonderful underwater characters, including local species, a great tropical tank and a predator's gallery.

Newquay Zoo (☎ 873342; www.newquayzoo.co.uk; Trenance Gardens; adult £6.95, child £4.45; 🕙 9.30am-6pm Apr-Nov, 10am-5pm Dec–mid-Mar) is big on cute beasties (meerkats, penguins, tamarins) and has some big cats and macaques, too.

BEACHES

Fistral Beach, west of town round Towan Head, is England's most famous surfing beach. There are fast hollow waves, particularly at low tide, and good tubing sections when there's a southeasterly wind.

Watergate Bay is a 2-mile-long beach on the eastern side of Newquay Bay. At low tide it's a good place to learn to surf. A mile (or 3 miles by car) southwest of Newquay, **Crantock** is a northwest-facing sheltered beach, where the waves are best at mid- to high tide.

SURFING

Lots of surf shops hire out equipment, including boards (£10/25/45 for one/three/seven days) and wetsuits (£5/12/25 for one/three/seven days). Try **Fistral Surf Co** (☎ 850808; 19 Cliff Rd; 🕙 9am-6pm) or **Fistral Beach Surf Hire** (☎ 850584; Fistral Beach).

Surf schools abound; all-inclusive, half-day beginner's lessons cost £20 to £25. Try **British Surfing Association** (BSA; www.nationalsurfingcentre .com) Fistral Beach (☎ 850737) Tolcarne Beach (☎ 851487) or **Offshore Extreme** (☎ 877083; www.offshore-extreme .co.uk). If you choose another school, make sure the instructors are certified by the BSA.

Sleeping

BUDGET

There are plenty of surf lodges in Newquay, but choose carefully; some are real dives catering mainly for beer-boys and stag parties. The best lodges have secure board storage and links with local surf schools.

Boarding House (☎ 873258; www.theboardinghouse .co.uk; 32 Headland Rd; dm £17.50-20; P 🖳) By far the best surf lodge in town, in a fantastic position 50m from Fistral Beach. Wood floors, tropical plants and a funky downstairs café-bar with an outside sundeck make this feel more like a boutique hotel than a hostel; upstairs, there are dorms and rooms with en suite, TVs and board lockers.

Home Surf Lodge (☎ 873387; www.homesurflodge .co.uk; 18 Tower Rd; dm £15-20; 🖳) A lively, friendly spot, with free Internet access and a bar, though the dorms are pretty cramped.

Base Surf Lodge (☎ 874852; www.basesurflodge .com; 20 Tower Rd; dm £10-20) Right next door to Home Surf Lodge this is a spotless hostel with a licensed bar and reasonably spacious dorms (but no kitchen).

Fistral Backpackers (☎ 873146; www.fistralback packers.co.uk; 18 Headland Rd; dm £7-15.50) Large and chaotic, but positioned right on Fistral Beach; facilities include a pool room, movie lounge, kitchen and basic dorms and doubles.

MID-RANGE & TOP END

Carlton Hotel (☎ 872658; www.carltonhotelnewquay .co.uk; 6 Dane Rd; d £52-60; P 🗙) One of the smartest B&Bs in Newquay, with a selection of rooms decorated in neutral tones, all with huge beds, fluffy pillows and DVD players. The rear patio is a lovely spot for a summer evening tipple.

Headland Hotel (☎ 872211; www.headlandhotel .co.uk; Fistral Beach; d £77-270; P 🗙 🗙 🖳 🕾) Newquay's grandest hotel, a fabulous red-brick Victorian edifice perched above Fistral Beach. The impeccably decorated rooms range from budget singles to ornate sea-view suites with balconies and luxury bathrooms, and there are tennis courts, two pools and a nine-hole golf course. Film buffs might recognise the hotel from the film version of Roald Dahl's *The Witches*.

Eating

Finn's (☎ 874062; South Quay Hill; mains £15-30; 🕙 lunch & dinner) If you're after local seafood, look no further than this bistro beside the harbour. The sophisticated menu includes sashimi tuna steak and pad Thai noodles – but you can't go wrong with a good old Cornish crab sandwich.

Fistral Blu (☎ 879444; www.fistral-blu.co.uk; Fistral Beach; mains £12-20; ☽ lunch & dinner) Newquay's newest, trendiest restaurant, housed in the recently opened shopping complex on Fistral Beach. Fusion flavours are served in the glass-fronted restaurant; downstairs, there's an informal café for sandwiches and lunchtime salads.

Lifebuoy Café (☎ 878076; Lower Tower Rd; mains £4.50-12) This colourful café is an ideal spot for lunch, offering jacket potatoes, baguettes, huge burgers and Cajun dishes.

Drinking

Newquay is crammed with pubs, bars and (mostly dodgy) clubs.

Chy (☎ 873415; www.the-chy.co.uk; 12 Beach Rd) This stylish, loft-style café-bar makes a welcome change from most of Newquay's drinking spots, with a huge chrome-fronted bar, designer seats, stainless-steel fittings and a fabulous terrace above the beach.

Koola (☎ 873415; www.thekoola.com; 12 Beach Rd) Underneath the Chy, the Koola is still the hippest venue in town, with a reputation for breaking new acts and underground tunes.

Central (☎ 878310; 11 Central Sq) One of the most popular pubs in the town centre, with a rowdy outdoor terrace that's always jammed at weekends.

Red Lion (☎ 872195; North Quay Hill) This rambling pub is the traditional surfers' hangout. Stick around for live bands on Friday and Saturday.

Plum Tree (☎ 872814; 19 Bank St) The latest pre-club option, with DJs, tangerine walls and a lethal cocktail menu.

Sailor's Arms (☎ 872838; Fore St) Shamelessly downmarket pub-club playing cheesy house and chunky choons.

Getting There & Away

National Express has direct buses to London (£41 economy return, seven hours, three

---

daily), Exeter (£16.50, 3½ hours, two daily), Plymouth (£6, 1½ hours, four daily), Penzance (£5.50, 1¾ hours, three daily) and St Ives (£5.50, 1¼ hours, three daily).

There are four trains daily between Newquay and Par (£4.30 single, 45 minutes), on the main London–Penzance line.

AROUND NEWQUAY
Trerice

Escape the cultural void of Newquay at **Trerice** (NT; ☎ 01637-875404; adult £4.70; ☽ 11am-5.30pm Sun-Fri Jul-Sep; 11.30am-5.30pm Sun, Mon & Wed-Fri Mar-Jun & Oct), a charming Elizabethan manor. Built in 1571, much of the structure and elaborate plasterwork is original, including the barrel-vaulted ceiling of the great chamber. There's also some fine oak and walnut furniture from the 17th and 18th centuries. An oddity is the lawnmower museum in the barn, with over 100 grasscutters going back over a century.

Trerice is 3 miles southeast of Newquay. During summer, bus No 50 runs directly here several times a day.

PADSTOW
☎ 01841 / pop 2450

Gourmet capital of Cornwall, Padstow is a popular fishing village on the Camel estuary, famous for its raucous May Day Festival. There are some wonderful stone cottages, a pretty harbour and some excellent accommodation, although these days TV chef Rick Stein has the place pretty much sewn up – the town is often known these days by its alternative name of 'Pad-stein'.

The **TIC** (☎ 533449; www.padstowlive.com; North Quay; ☽ 9.30am-5pm Mon-Sat & 9.30am-4pm Sun Easter-Oct, 9am-4pm Mon-Fri & 9am-noon Sat Nov-Easter) charges £3 to book accommodation.

Above the village is **Prideaux Place** (☎ 532411; adult £6; ☽ 12.30-4pm Sun-Thu Easter Sun–mid-Apr & mid-May–Oct), a lavish manor house built in 1592 by the Prideaux-Brune family (who still reside here), purported descendants of William the Conqueror. Its grand plasterwork ceilings and stately grandeur have been used as the setting for numerous period dramas.

The **Camel Trail** is a disused railway line, and now makes one of Cornwall's most popular cycling tracks. The trail starts in Padstow and runs east through Wadebridge (5¾ miles), Bodmin (11 miles) and beyond. Bicycles can be hired from **Padstow Cycle Hire**

TOP FIVE BEACHES

■ **Gwithian** (p326; near St Ives)

■ **Holywell Bay** (p326; near Newquay)

■ **Perranporth** (p326; north of St Agnes)

■ **Carne** (p315; Roseland Peninsula)

■ **Fistral** (p328; Newquay)

(☎ 533533; South Quay; ◔ 9am-5pm) for around £8 per day and **Brinhams** (☎ 532594; South Quay; ◔ 9am-5pm) for a similar price.

Sleeping

Treyarnon Bay YHA Hostel (☎ 0870 770 6076; Tregonnan; dm £11.80; Ⓟ ✗) A refurbished hostel and café in a fantastic headland position above Treyarnon Bay, 4½ miles west of Padstow. Bus No 55 from Padstow stops at nearby Constantine Bay.

Althea Library (☎ 532717; www.althealibrary.co.uk; 27 High St; d £64-72; Ⓟ ✗) A delightful, heritage-listed cottage offering vegan and vegetarian breakfasts. Choose from three colour-themed rooms (green, yellow or ivory), all with large beds and pine furniture, and relax in the gorgeous A-framed lounge.

St Petroc's Hotel & Bistro (☎ 532700; www.rickstein.com; 4 New St; mains £13.50-14.50; d £110-180; Ⓟ ✗) Boutique chic hits Padstow at this beautifully converted town house, part of the Rick Stein stable. Behind the neatly clipped hedges and clematis-covered front of the whitewashed house, you'll find a range of smart, contemporary rooms, complete with designer bedding and wrought-iron bedsteads.

Tregea Hotel (☎ 532455; www.tregea.co.uk; 16-18 High St; d £82-98; Ⓟ ✗) This ivy-clad hotel is another excellent choice, with warm-toned bedrooms and a designer lounge and dining room.

Dennis Cove Camping (☎ 532349; tent sites £10-14; ◔ May-Sep) A small, well-appointed site overlooking the estuary.

Eating

Seafood Restaurant (☎ 532700; www.rickstein.com; Riverside; mains £16.50-28; ◔ lunch & dinner) There's no denying the calibre of the cuisine at Rick Stein's sleek flagship restaurant – undoubtedly among the very best in Britain – but his fame ensures you'll need to book months in advance.

Rick Stein's Café (☎ 532700; www.rickstein.com; Middle St; mains £8-14; ◔ lunch & dinner) A stripped-down version of the Seafood's menu is available at this bistro – various concoctions of fish, steak, chicken and salads are all on the menu, which changes daily.

Stein's Fish & Chips (www.rickstein.com; South Quay; mains £4-8; ◔ noon-2.30pm & 5-9pm Mon-Tue & Thu-Sat, noon-6pm Sun) If all else fails, you can always try the latest addition to the Stein menu –

an upmarket fish-and-chip shop down by the quay.

Also recommended:

London Inn (☎ 532554; 6/8 Lanadwell St; mains £6-13) Cosy local with good Cornish beers and daily fish specials.

Rojano's (☎ 532796; 9 Mill Sq; mains £5-10; ◔ lunch & dinner Tue-Sun) Bright, buzzy pizza and pasta joint with outside tables.

Getting There & Away

Bus No 55 runs to Bodmin Parkway (50 minutes) and the Eden Project (1½ hours) hourly till 6pm. Bus No 555 goes to Truro (1¾ hours, four daily Monday to Saturday), while bus No 556 serves Newquay (1¼ hours, five daily Monday to Saturday, four Sunday).

TINTAGEL
☎ 01840

The mostly modern village of Tintagel sprawls inland from the clifftops and has little to offer beyond chintzy tearooms and souvenir shops. The real attraction lies closer to the coast. The ruins of **Tintagel Castle** (EH; ☎ 770328; adult £3.70; ◔ 10am-6pm Apr-Sep, 10am-5pm Oct, 10am-4pm Nov-Mar) are scattered across the rocky cliffs around Tintagel Head, reached down a steep track from the village. The present-day ruins mostly date from the 13th century, but were built on the site of a much earlier fortress – local legend has it that this was the birthplace of King Arthur. Whatever the truth of the legend, the views from the castle and clifftops are stunning and should not be missed. Part of the stronghold stands on a rock tower that's cut off from the mainland, accessed via a bridge and steep steps; bring a head for heights.

Back in the village, the **Old Post Office** (NT; ☎ 770024; Fore St; adult £2.40; ◔ 11am-5.30pm Apr-Sep, 11am-4pm Oct) is a fascinating 14th-century manor house that served as a post office in the 19th century.

The **TIC** (☎ 779084; tintagelvc@btconnect.com; Bossiney Rd; ◔ 10am-5pm Mar-Oct, 10.30am-4pm Nov-Feb) has small exhibits exploring local history and the Arthur legend.

Sleeping & Eating

Tintagel YHA Hostel (☎ 0870 770 6068; tintagel@yha .org.uk; Dunderhole Point; dm £10.60; ◔ Mar-Oct) A tiny whitewashed cottage in a spectacular clifftop setting on the South West Coast Path, three-quarters of a mile south of the village.

Old Borough House (☎ 770475; www.tintagelhotel
.co.uk; Bossiney Rd; d £70-78; P ☒) A beautiful
ivy-clad 16th-century Cornish mansion,
once owned by JB Priestley, with wonderfully converted rooms making use of the
original ceiling beams and exposed stonework. The more expensive rooms have fine
views and private sitting rooms.

Ye Olde Malthouse Inn (☎ 770461; d £46-50;
P ☒) A 14th-century slate-roofed pub
with good Cornish beer and bar food.

Old Millfloor (☎ 770234; Trebarwith Strand; d £50;
P ☒) Delightful 17th-century mill cot-
tage in a brookside dell, 3 miles west of
Tintagel.

Getting There & Away
Bus No 122/124 runs from Wadebridge (1¼
hours, eight daily Monday to Friday) and
No X10 comes from Exeter (2¼ hours, four
daily Monday to Saturday); both go on to
Boscastle (10 minutes).

BODMIN MOOR
Cornwall's 'roof' is a high heath pockmarked
with bogs and high tors, including Brown
Willy (419m) and Rough Tor (pronounced
row-tor with 'row' rhyming with 'how';
400m). It's a desolate place that works on
the imagination; the Beast of Bodmin, a
large, black, catlike creature, has been seen
regularly for many years.

Bodmin's **TIC** (☎ 01208-76616; www.bodminlive
.com; Mount Folly, Bodmin; ☒ 10am-5pm Mon-Sat) has
leaflets on exploring the moor; the small
Town Museum (☎ 01208-77067; Mount Folly, Bodmin;
admission free; ☒ 10.30am-4.30pm Mon-Sat Apr-Sep) is
opposite. The bizarre **Bodmin Jail** (☎ 01208-
76292; Berrycombe Rd, Bodmin; adult £4; ☒ 10am-6pm
Mon-Fri & Sun, 11am-6pm Sat) exhibition is in the
18th-century county prison; its tales of true
crimes of old are amateurish but strangely
enthralling.

The A30 cuts across the centre of the
moor from **Launceston**, which has a ruined
11th-century **castle** (EH; ☎ 01566-772365; adult £2;
☒ 10am-6pm Jul & Aug, 10am-5pm Apr-Jun & Sep, 10am-
4pm Oct), and a granite **church** with extensive
carvings.

Jamaica Inn (☎ 01566-86250; www.jamaicainn
.co.uk; s/d £40/60; P ☒), out on the desolate
Bodmin Moor near Bolventor, was made
famous by Daphne du Maurier's novel of
the same name. On a misty winter's night
the place still feels hugely atmospheric; the
inn also contains a small smuggling museum and a room devoted entirely to du
Maurier.

About a mile south is **Dozmary Pool**, said to
have been where Arthur's sword, Excalibur,
was thrown after his death. It's a 4-mile walk
northwest of Jamaica Inn to Brown Willy.

Bodmin has bus connections with St
Austell (No 29, one hour, hourly Monday
to Saturday), as well as Bodmin Parkway
(No 56, 15 minutes, hourly Monday to Saturday), a station on the London–Penzance
line. Bus No 76/X76 runs from Launceston
to Plymouth (1½ hours, hourly Monday to
Saturday).

Lanhydrock House
Set in 900 acres of private grounds above the
River Fowey, **Lanhydrock** (NT; ☎ 01208-73320;
house & gardens £7.50, gardens only £4.20; ☒ house
11am-5.30pm Tue-Sun late-Mar–Sep, 11am-5pm Tue-Sun
Oct, gardens 10am-6pm year-round) was a substantial
16th-century manor devastated by fire in
1881. It was later rebuilt in lavish style.

A magnificent plaster ceiling in the 17th-
century Long Gallery depicts Old Testament scenes. The gallery survived the fire,
but the house is principally of interest for
its insight into *Upstairs Downstairs* life in
Victorian England. The kitchens are particularly fascinating, complete with gadgets
that were mod-cons 100 years ago. Outside, the beautiful gardens are particularly
renowned for their magnolias, rhododendrons and camellias.

Lanhydrock is 2½ miles southeast of
Bodmin. To get there, take the A30 to
Bodmin or the A38 from St Austell. Al-
ternatively, bus No 55 runs from Bodmin
Parkway train station, which is 1¾ miles
from Lanhydrock.

BUDE
☎ 01288 / pop 5980
Just this side of the Cornwall–Devon border, Bude is a popular bucket-and-spade
resort with great surf. Crooklets Beach is
the main surfing area, just north of town.
Nearby Sandymouth is good for beginners,
and Duckpool is also popular. Summerleaze,
in the centre of Bude, is a family beach.

Bude visitors centre (☎ 354240; www.visitbude
.info; The Crescent; ☒ 10am-5pm Mon-Sat, plus 10am-
4pm Sun in summer) is a little way south of the
town centre.

SOUTHWEST ENGLAND

There are plenty of surf schools; try **Outdoor Adventure** (☎ 361312; www.outdooradventure .co.uk; Atlantic Ct; per half-/full-day lesson £16/30).

One of the best B&Bs in Bude is **Fairway House** (☎ 355059; www.fairwayguesthouse.co.uk; 8 Downs View; d £40-50; P ⊠), a Victorian terraced house near the town centre. It has comfortable rooms (all named after famous golf courses) and quilted bedspreads.

Life's a Beach (☎ 355222; Summerleaze Beach; mains £5-16; ⊠ lunch & dinner Mon-Sat) is a beachside café that turns from snack stop to snazzy seafood bistro at night, while **JJ's Bar** (☎ 352555; The Headland) is a popular pub on the headland behind Summerleaze Beach.

National Express coaches run from Exeter (£7.80 economy return, 1¾ hours, five daily), as does local bus No X9 (two hours, six daily).

ISLES OF SCILLY
☎ 01720

Legend has it that the Isles of Scilly, 28 miles southwest of mainland Cornwall, are the last remains of the fabled lost lands of Lyonesse. Whatever the truth of the legend, there's no doubt that the islands seem rooted in another age. Of the 140 islands, only five are inhabited: St Mary's is by far the largest and busiest island, closely followed by Tresco, while Bryher, St Martin's and St Agnes are home to tiny resident populations. Traditional crafts such as fishing, farming and flower growing are still important local industries, though tourism has become the islands' main source of income. It's not hard to see what keeps drawing back the holiday-makers year after year: broad, sandy beaches, sparkling bays and hidden inlets, rugged coastal scenery, world-class gardens, excellent diving, and a unique community atmosphere. With few roads, few residents and even fewer cars, the Scilly Isles is a place where it's truly possible to escape from the hustle and bustle of the outside world.

Information
The **Isles of Scilly Tourist Board** (☎ 422536; tic@scilly.gov.uk; Hugh Town, St Mary's; ⊠ 8.30am-5.30pm Mon-Thu, 8.30am-5pm Fri & Sat Easter-Oct, plus 10am-noon Sun Jun-Sep; closes noon Sat Nov-Dec, closed all day Sat & Sun Jan-Easter) is on St Mary's. The

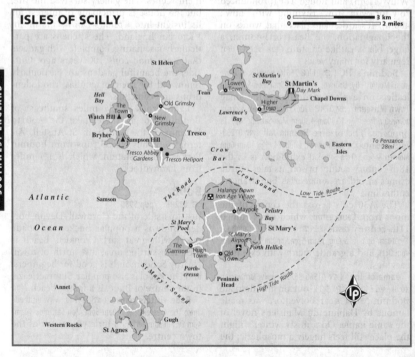

Standard Guidebook, Isles of Scilly (£3) is a good fold-out map with explanatory text.

A commercial website (www.scillyonline .co.uk) provides background information, while the TIC website (www.simplyscilly .co.uk) helps with listings of places to stay.

Accommodation should be booked well in advance. Many places close between November and May. All the islands, except Tresco, have a simple, reasonable campsite. There are plenty of self-catering options; the biggest operator is **Island Properties** (☎ 422211), whose flats start at around £200 per week. Every Friday evening you can watch gig racing, with traditional six-oar boats (some over 100 years old) originally used to race out to wrecked ships.

St Mary's

The largest island in the chain, and the most populated, St Mary's is the first port of call for most visitors. This is because it's the point of arrival for the *Scillonian III* ferry and flights from the mainland. With miles of breathtaking coastline, secluded beaches and bays, and many fine walking trails, it's little wonder that St Mary's gets crowded in summer; like the rest of the Scillys, the best time to visit is in spring or autumn, when the high season holiday-makers have left for home.

About a mile west of the airport is the main settlement of **Hugh Town**, where you'll find most of the island's hotels and guesthouses, and the **Isles of Scilly Museum** (☎ 422337; Church St; adult/child £2/50p; 10am-noon & 1.30-4.30pm Mon-Sat, plus 7.30-9pm Mon, Tue & Thu-Sat May-Sep, 2-4pm Wed Oct-Apr, or by arrangement), which explores the islands' history and houses some intriguing displays on Bronze Age burial finds and local shipwrecks.

A little way east of Hugh Town is **Old Town**, once the island's main harbour, but now home to a few small cafés, a village pub and a pleasant beach. Look out for the minuscule Old Town Church, where the services are still conducted by candlelight.

There are lots of small inlets scattered around the island's coastline, best reached on foot or by bike: Porth Hellick, Watermill Cove and the relatively remote Pelistry Bay are worth seeking out. St Mary's also has some unique ancient sites, notably the Iron-Age village at Halangy Down, a mile north of Hugh Town, and the barrows at Bant's Carn and Porth Hellick.

Scilly Walks (☎ 423326; www.scillywalks.co.uk) leads three-hour archaeological tours, costing £4/2 per adult/child, as well as visits to other offshore islands.

There are two accredited diving operations on St Mary's: **Isles of Scilly Underwater Centre** (☎ 422595) and **Underwater Island Safaris** (☎ 422732; Old Town). Both offer dives to nearby wrecks and reefs with or without your own equipment.

SLEEPING & EATING

Campsite (☎ 422670; tedmoulson@cs.com; Tower Cottage, Garrison Farm; tent sites £4.50-8) West of Hugh Town.

Evergreen Cottage (☎ 422711; The Parade; d £45-60) A charming 300-year-old cottage originally built for a sea captain, complete with whitewashed cob walls, slate roof and small, cosy rooms.

Wheelhouse (☎ 422719; Porthcressa; s/d from £33.50/77;) This smart B&B is an excellent base for exploring the rest of the island. The spacious rooms and brilliant location near Porthcressa Beach make it very popular, so you'll need to book ahead.

Star Castle Hotel (☎ 422317; www.star-castle.co .uk; The Garrison; d £98-260;) Built as part of a fort in 1593, this is now St Mary's top hotel, boasting quirky rooms, solid granite walls and elegant furnishings, as well as two award-winning restaurants, tennis courts and a heated swimming pool.

Wingletang (☎ 422381; The Parade, Hugh Town; s/d £37/74; May-Oct;) A pretty, traditional granite house in the centre of Hugh Town.

St Mary's Hall Hotel (☎ 422316; www.stmaryshall hotel.co.uk; d £128-188;) A stunningly refurbished mansion, originally built for an Italian nobleman in 1938.

Mermaid (☎ 422701; mains £6-10; lunch & dinner) Next to the harbour in Hugh Town, the nautically themed Mermaid is the place to head for a lively pint and fine pub grub.

Tresco

Once owned by Tavistock Abbey, Tresco is the second-largest island, and the second-most visited after St Mary's. The main attraction is the **Abbey Garden** (☎ 424105; www .tresco.co.uk/the_abbey_garden; adult £8.50; 9.30am-4pm), first laid out in 1834 on the site of a 10th-century Benedictine abbey. The terraced gardens feature more than 5000 subtropical plants, including species from

Brazil, New Zealand and South Africa, and the intriguing Valhalla collection, made up of figureheads and nameplates salvaged from the many ships that have come to grief off Tresco's shores.

There are only two places to stay on the island. The **New Inn** (☎ 422844; newinn@tresco.co .uk; d £82-115 depending on season; mains £6-16; ✗) is a comfortable pub with a selection of small, pleasant rooms upstairs, some with sea views over the Tresco channel and the nearby island of Bryher.

The swish **Island Hotel** (☎ 422883; islandhotel@ tresco.co.uk; d half-board £117-283; ✗ ✗ ✗) occupies a stunning position overlooking Old Grimsby Sound. The bedrooms are spread across several wings, and most have sweeping views and luxurious interiors; the best have private balconies and access to the gardens and private beach.

Bryher & Samson

Home to approximately 70 people, Bryher is the smallest and wildest inhabited island in the Scillys. Much of the landscape is covered by rough bracken and heather, and the coast often takes the full force of the Atlantic weather; Hell Bay in a winter gale is a powerful sight. There are good views over the islands from the top of Watch Hill, and Rushy Bay is one of the finest beaches in the Scillys. From the quay, occasional boats visit local seal and bird colonies and deserted Samson Island, where abandoned settlers' cottages tell a story of hard subsistence living.

The **campsite** (☎ 422886; tent sites £4.50-8) is near the quay.

Hell Bay Hotel (☎ 422947; hellbay@aol.com; d £180-400; ✗ ✗) is a beautiful hotel that consists entirely of upmarket, impeccably finished suites, most of which boast sleek, contemporary décor, a sitting room and private balcony.

St Martin's

Renowned for its beautiful beaches, St Martin's is the most northerly of the main islands. The largest settlement is **Higher Town**, where you'll find a small village shop and the **Isles of Scilly Dive School** (☎ 422848; www .scillydiving.com; Higher Town; dives from £36). A short way to the northwest is **Lower Town**, home to a cluster of tightly huddled cottages and the island's only hotel.

There are several small art galleries scattered across the island, as well as a tiny vineyard and a flower farm.

On the island's southern shore is Lawrence's Bay, which reveals a broad sweep of sandy flats at low tide. Along the northern side is Great Bay, arguably the finest beach in the Scillys; from the western end, you can cross to White Island at low tide. A walk east along the windswept northern cliffs leads to the Day Mark, a red-and-white candy-striped landmark built in 1687, and the secluded cove of Perpitch.

The **campsite** (☎ 422888; chris@stmartinscampsite .freeserve.co.uk; Middle Town; tent sites £4-8) is near Lawrence's Bay at the western end of the island.

Polreath (☎ 422046; Higher Town; s/d from £40/70; ✗) is a traditional cottage and one of the few B&Bs on the island. Rooms are snug and cosy, and it's handy for the island bakery and post office.

St Martin's on the Isle (☎ 422090; www.stmartins hotel.co.uk; d £115-215; ✗ ✗) is the only hotel on St Martin's, and said to be one of the best in the Scillys, with landscaped grounds, an indoor swimming pool and a private quay. The 30 bedrooms have a choice of sea or garden views, and there are several upmarket suites with private sitting rooms. The in-house restaurant is renowned throughout the islands.

St Agnes

Britain's most southerly community somehow transcends the tranquillity of even the other islands; it's an ideal spot to stroll, unwind and reflect, with lots of cloistered coves, coastal walks and a scattering of prehistoric sites. Visitors disembark at **Porth Conger**, near the decommissioned **Old Lighthouse** (one of the oldest in Britain). Other points of interest include the tiny **Troy Town Maze**, and the historic inlets of Periglis Cove and St Warna's Cove (dedicated to the patron saint of shipwrecks). At low tide you can cross to the island of **Gugh**, where there are some intriguing Bronze-Age remains and standing stones.

The **campsite** (☎ 422360; Troy Town Farm; tent sites £4-8) is at the southwestern corner of the island.

The little stone-walled **Covean Cottage** (☎ 422620; d £23.50-30.50) is the perfect location for getting away from the crowds; it offers four pleasant, good-value rooms and serves excellent cream teas, light meals and sticky treats during the day.

The most southwesterly pub in Britain, the **Turk's Head** (☎ 422434; mains £6-10; ⊘ lunch & dinner) is a real treat, with fine views, excellent beers, good pub grub and a hearty island atmosphere.

Getting There & Away

There's no transport to or from the islands on a Sunday.

AIR

The **Isles of Scilly Skybus** (☎ 0845 710 5555; www .ios-travel.co.uk) flies between St Mary's and Land's End (£108.50, 15 minutes) and Newquay (£125, 30 minutes) up to five times daily, Monday to Saturday year-round. Cheaper saver fares are available for travel from Monday to Friday after 3pm or before 11am. Flights also connect with Exeter (£119, 50 minutes) and Bristol (£245, 70 minutes).

British International (☎ 01736-363871; www.isles ofscillyhelicopter.com) helicopters fly to St Mary's (20 minutes, 17 daily Monday to Saturday April to October, five daily Monday to Saturday November to March) and Tresco (20 minutes, six daily Monday to Saturday April to October, four daily November to March) from Penzance heliport. Adult/ child return fares are £130/65. Cheaper short-break and day-return fares are also available. Parking at Penzance heliport costs £5 per day, and a minibus from Penzance train station connects with flights (£1.25 single, 10 minutes).

BOAT

The **Isles of Scilly Steamship** (☎ 0845 710 5555; www.ios-travel.co.uk) *Scillonian III* sails between Penzance and St Mary's (£78 return, two hours and 40 minutes, once daily Monday to Saturday). Children under 12 years pay half-price.

Getting Around

Boats sail from St Mary's harbour daily in summer, several times daily to Tresco. A return trip to most offshore islands costs around £6.40, while a triangular return (eg St Mary's–Tresco–Bryher–St Mary's) costs around £8. Fares to the uninhabited islands vary but are usually between £6 and £8.

The **airport bus service** (£2.50) departs from The Strand in Hugh Town 40 minutes before each flight. A circular bus service runs around St Mary's several times daily in summer (£1 to all destinations). There are tours of St Mary's by vintage 1948 **bus** (☎ 422387; £5) or 1929 Riley open-top **car** (☎ 422479; per 2/3/4 people £15/20/22).

Bikes are available at **Buccabu Hire** (☎ 422289; Porthcressa, Hugh Town; per day £6) and **Tresco Bicycle Hire** (☎ 422807; per day £8).

SOUTHWEST ENGLAND

Oxfordshire, Gloucestershire & the Cotswolds

Shaped by the prosperous medieval wool trade, centuries of academic achievement and the elegance of Regency society, this area oozes undeniable charm and offers visitors a chance to experience the romantic ideal of picture-postcard Britain.

A swathe of lush, rolling hills soaked in history and sprinkled with incredibly picturesque honey-coloured stone villages washes across the region, attracting moneyed commuters and visitors in their droves. Many towns shamelessly peddle nostalgia and are seemingly consumed by tourism but it's not difficult to get away from the crowds if you're willing to wander a little.

The area is home to some fine walking and cycling country, and by striking off on your own path on foot or by bike it's easy to get off the beaten track and lost in the timeless charm of country lanes and villages, oblivious to the passing of time. Although the smallest towns have few specific sights, the languid bucolic air, gorgeous flower-strewn cottages and humble churches are a draw on their own.

For more heady delights, the incredible architecture, fascinating museums and buzzing student nightlife make Oxford an ideal base. Just north of here Woodstock is home to the extraordinary Churchill pile of Blenheim Palace. Heading west the chocolate-box villages of Stow, the Slaughters and Bourton draw the crowds while chichi shoppers and racing fanatics will find plenty to do in genteel Regency Cheltenham. Nearby Gloucester boasts a magnificent Gothic cathedral and higgledy-piggledy Tewksbury has buckets of Tudor charm.

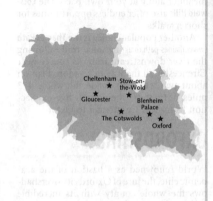

HIGHLIGHTS

- Admiring the overwhelming beauty of **Oxford University** (p342)
- Visiting **Blenheim Palace** (p349) and its superb gardens
- Appreciating the muted elegance of Regency **Cheltenham** (p364)
- Exploring **Gloucester Cathedral** (p361) and its magnificent cloisters
- Seeing the honey-stone villages of the **Cotswolds** (p351), particularly **Stow-on-the-Wold** (p357)
- Checking out the **National Hunt Festival** (p365) in Cheltenham in March, a highlight of the social and racing calendar

Cheltenham ★ Stow-on-the-Wold ★
Gloucester ★ ★ Blenheim Palace
The Cotswolds ★ ★ Oxford

- POPULATION: 1.2 MILLION
- AREA: 2222 SQ MILES

Activities

The Cotswold counties are inundated with visitors in peak season, but an ideal way to get away from the hordes and really appreciate the area is to get out and do some walking or cycling. For more information see the Outdoor Activities chapter or specific suggestions for walks and rides throughout this chapter.

CYCLING

Dedicated cycle ways, quiet country lanes, gated roads and gentle gradients make the Cotswold counties ideal for cycling. The Cotswold Hills are especially scenic, although the steep western escarpment can be a bit of a shock for the unprepared.

Waymarked, long-distance routes in the region include the **Thames Valley Cycle Way**, part of the National Cycle Network (see boxed text, p81), which starts in Oxford and leads eventually to London.

The **Cotswolds** and **Chilterns** both have many bridleways open to mountain bikers, and in the west of the region, the **Forest of Dean** has many dirt-track options, and some dedicated mountain-bike trails.

WALKING

The most popular long-distance route in this region is the **Cotswold Way** (www.cotswold -way.co.uk), an absolute classic covering 102 miles from Bath to Chipping Campden. The full trail takes about a week to walk. Alternatively, choose a section of it and meander along at your own pace. The **Cotswold Hills** also offer endless opportunities for shorter walks.

Another popular choice is the **Thames Path** (www.thames-path.co.uk) national trail following the river downstream from its source near Cirencester all the way to London. Plan on about two weeks to tackle the whole 173 miles, or try the very enjoyable five-day section from near Cirencester to Oxford.

OXFORDSHIRE

World renowned as a bastion of the academic elite, the lure of Oxford city overshadows the whole county with its incredible architecture, air of refinement and international reputation. There's a lot more to Oxfordshire than gowned cyclists and ivy-clad

quads though: affluent commuters people the picturesque villages to the northwest and the prosperous towns along the meandering River Thames; manor houses dot the landscape, peaking in Blenheim Palace, the spectacular birthplace of Sir Winston Churchill; and the mysterious giant White Horse of Uffington baffles archaeologists and visitors alike thousands of years after it was carved from the limestone hills to the south.

Activities

In addition to the national trails, other lengthy walking routes in this county include the **Oxfordshire Way** – a 65-mile waymarked trail running from Bourton-on-the-Water to Henley-on-Thames. Leaflets available from local TICs divide the route into 16 walks of between 2 and 8 miles in length.

Oxfordshire is also prime cycling country, because it's beribboned with many quiet roads and has few extreme gradients. If you don't have your own wheels, Oxford is the best bet for bike rental (see Getting Around, p348). Cycling routes through the county include the **Oxfordshire Cycleway**, which takes in Woodstock, Burford and Henley.

Getting Around

TICs stock bus and train timetables that detail routes and give contact telephone numbers for each operator. Oxford and Banbury are the main train stations, and provide services to London Paddington and Euston, Hereford, Birmingham, Bristol and Scotland.

The main bus operators offer day and weeklong bus passes that can be a good deal if you plan on doing a lot of bus travelling. See p967 for details.

Cotswold Roaming (☎ 308300; tours@cotswold -roaming.co.uk) Runs guided bus tours from Oxford between April and October. Half-day tours run to Blenheim Palace (adult/child £16/10), full-day tours go to Bath and Castle Combe (£30/18), and the Cotswolds (£32.50/20).

National Rail Enquiries (☎ 08457 484950)

Oxford Bus Company (☎ 01865 – 785400; www.oxford bus.co.uk)

Stagecoach (☎ 01865-772250; www.stagecoach-oxford .co.uk)

Traveline (☎ 0870 608 2608; www.traveline.org.uk) for all public-transport information.

OXFORDSHIRE & GLOUCESTERSHIRE

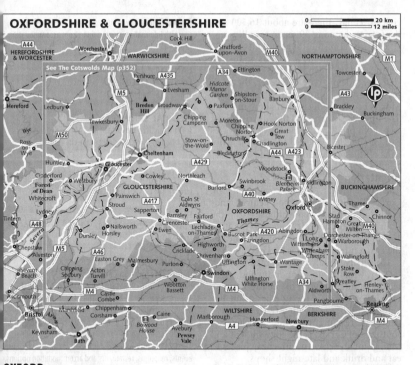

OXFORD

☎ 01865 / pop 143,016

The weight of academic achievement seeps from the walls of the beautiful buildings that house Britain's oldest and most famous university. Class distinction, received pronunciation and effortlessly polite but unyielding doormen firmly divide the academic elite from Oxford's working-class majority though; students and townspeople rarely mix, and for visitors access to the colleges is strictly controlled.

Tourists flock here in summer: the crowds of language learners and the glut of tour buses can be frustrating. However, the stunning vistas, world-class museums and buzzing nightlife rarely disappoint, and once you've seen the highlights you can pilot a teetering punt or wander the winding passages that lead to tiny drinking holes unchanged since the time of Tolkien, Auden and Elliott.

History

Strategically placed at the confluence of the River Cherwell and the Thames (called the Isis here, from the Latin name *Tamesis*), Oxford was a key Saxon town but its importance grew dramatically after 1167, when all Anglo-Norman students were expelled from the Sorbonne in Paris. Oxford's Augustinian abbey attracted students in droves but they managed to create a lasting enmity between themselves and the local townspeople, culminating in the St Scholastica's Day Massacre in 1355 (see boxed text, p343), after which the university was broken up into colleges.

The first colleges were built in the 13th century. At least three more were added in each of the following three centuries. The newer colleges, such as Keble, were added in the 19th and 20th centuries to cater for an expanding student population. So many brains in one place didn't necessarily bring enlightenment though: lecturers weren't allowed to marry until 1877 and women weren't admitted to until a year later. Even then, it took another 42 years before women would be granted a degree for their four years of hard labour. St Hilda's clings on doggedly as the last remaining all-female college. Today, there are about 16,500 students spread among 39 separate colleges.

The arrival of the canal system in 1790 created a link with the Midlands' industrial centres and the town began to expand outside its academic core. However, the city's real industrial boom came when William Morris began producing cars here in 1912. The Bullnose Morris and the Morris Minor were both produced in the Cowley factories east of the city, where BMW's new Mini runs off the production line today.

Orientation

The city centre can easily be covered on foot. Carfax Tower makes a good central landmark and there are frequent buses from the train station to the west. Alternatively, it's a 15-minute walk. The bus station is nearer the city centre, off Gloucester Green.

University buildings are spread through the city, with the most important and architecturally interesting in the centre. Jericho, in the northwest, is the upmarket but bohemian end of town with a range of trendy bars and restaurants, while Cowley Rd, southeast of Carfax, is the edgy student and immigrant area packed with cheap places to eat and drink and late-night shops.

Information

BOOKSHOPS

Blackwell's (☎ 792792; 48-51 Broad St) Stocks any book you could ever need and has a vast basement worth a visit in itself.

Little Bookshop (☎ 559176; Covered Market) Tiny shop bursting with first editions and rare books.

EMERGENCY

Police (☎ 266000; St Aldate's)

INTERNET ACCESS

Mices (☎ 726364; 118 High St; per 30min £1; ⏰ 9am-11pm Mon-Sat, 10am-11pm Sun) There's another branch on Gloucester Green.

Virgin (☎ 723906; 18 Cornmarket St; per 30min before noon £1, after noon £3; ⏰ 9am-7pm Mon-Sat, 11am-5pm Sun)

INTERNET RESOURCES

Daily Info (www.dailyinfo.co.uk) Everything you need to know about gigs, cinema, theatre and exhibitions.

Oxford City (www.oxfordcity.co.uk) Extensive accommodation and restaurant listings as well as entertainment and shopping.

Oxford Online (www.visitoxford.org) Tourism Oxford's site with information on everything from accommodation to activities.

LAUNDRY

Coin Wash (127 Cowley Rd; per load £2.60; ⏰ 9.15am-1pm & 3.15-7pm Mon-Sat)

MEDICAL SERVICES

John Radcliffe Hospital (☎ 741166; Headley Way, Headington) Three miles east of the city centre.

MONEY

Every major bank and ATM is represented on or near Cornmarket St.

POST

Post office (☎ 223344; 102 St Aldate's; ⏰ 9am-6pm Mon-Sat)

TOURIST INFORMATION

Oxford Information Centre (☎ 726871; www.visit oxford.org; 15-16 Broad St; ⏰ 9.30am-5pm Mon-Sat, 10am-3.30pm Sun Easter-Oct) The TIC stocks a *Welcome to Oxford* brochure (£1), which has a walking tour with college opening times, as well as the *University of Oxford* leaflet and *Oxford Accessible Guide* for travellers with disabilities. Also look out for two free publications: *In Oxford*, which lists events, museums, restaurants and accommodation options, and the less useful *WOW (What's on Where)*. The centre can book accommodation for a £3 fee plus a 10% deposit.

UNIVERSITIES

Oxford Brookes (☎ 741111; www.brookes.ac.uk) Oxford's lesser-known university.

Oxford University (☎ 270000; www.ox.ac.uk)

Sights

UNIVERSITY & PITT RIVERS MUSEUMS

Many would say there are plenty of dinosaurs lurking around Oxford, but you can see the real thing at the **University Museum** (☎ 272950; www.oum.ox.ac.uk; Parks Rd; admission free; ⏰ noon-5pm), housed in a superb Victorian Gothic structure worth a visit for its architecture alone. Inside, a glorious fantasy space of slender, cast-iron columns and ornate capitals lead to a soaring glass roof. The museum is devoted to natural science and has a whopping collection of over five million exhibits ranging from exotic insects and fossils to a towering T-Rex skeleton.

At the back of the museum a door leads into the half light of an Aladdin's cave of treasures: the **Pitt Rivers Museum** (☎ 270927;

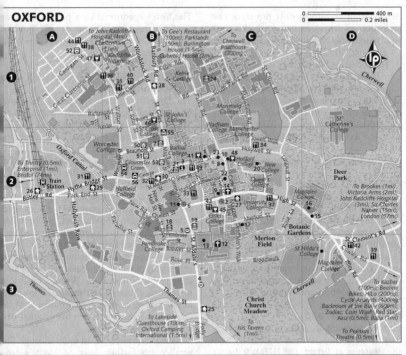

OXFORD

INFORMATION		
Blackwell's	1	C2
Bookshop	(see 33)	
Mic@s	(see 54)	
Mic@s	2	C2
Oxford Information Centre	3	B2
Police Station	4	B3
Post Office	5	B2
Virgin	6	B2

SIGHTS & ACTIVITIES	(pp340–4)	
Ashmolean Museum	7	B2
Bodleian Library	8	C2
Brasenose College	9	C2
Bridge of Sighs	10	C2
Carfax Tower	11	B2
Christ Church Cathedral	12	C3
Christ Church College	13	C3
Church of St Mary the Virgin	14	C2
Howard C & Sons Punts	15	D2
Magdalen College	16	D2
Merton College	17	C2
Modern Art Oxford	18	B2
Museum of Oxford	19	B2
New College	20	C2

Oxford Story	21	B2
Radcliffe Camera	22	C2
Salter Bros	(see 25)	
Sheldonian Theatre	23	C2
University Museum & Pitt Rivers Museum	24	C1

SLEEPING	(pp344–5)	
Head of the River	25	C3
New Oxford YHA Hostel	26	A2
Old Bank Hotel	27	C2
Old Parsonage Hotel	28	B1
Oxford Backpackers	29	A2
St Michael's Guesthouse	30	B2

EATING	(pp345–7)	
Bangkok House	31	A2
Chutneys	32	C3
Covered Market	33	B2
Edamame	34	C2
Felson's Baguette Bar	35	B1
Gluttons Deli	36	B1
Grand Café	37	C2
Jericho Café	38	A1
Joe's	39	D3

La Plaza Tapas	40	B1
Morton's	41	B2
Moya	42	D3
Quod	43	C2
Sip	44	A1
SoJo	(see 29)	

DRINKING	(p347)	
Baby Love	45	C2
Eagle & Child	46	B1
Frevd	47	A1
Turf Tavern	48	C2
White Horse	49	B2

ENTERTAINMENT	(pp347–8)	
Burton Taylor Theatre	50	B2
Oxford Playhouse	51	B2
Phoenix Picturehouse	52	A1
Po Na Na	53	B2

TRANSPORT	(p348)	
Gloucester Green Bus/Coach Station	54	B2
Taxi Rank	55	B2
Taxi Rank	(see 11)	
Taxi Rank	56	B2

www.prm.ox.ac.uk; admission free, audio tour £1; ☉ noon-4.30pm Mon-Sat, 2-4.30pm Sun). Feathered cloaks, necklaces of teeth, blowpipes, mummies magic charms and head-hunters' trophies including scalps and shrunken heads bulge out of cabinets and glass cases and should be enough to satisfy every armchair adventurer's wildest dreams. The museum also runs an excellent series of workshops for children (usually the first Saturday of the month).

ASHMOLEAN MUSEUM
England's oldest museum, the mammoth **Ashmolean** (☎ 278000; www.ashmol.ox.ac.uk; Beaumont St; admission free; ☉ 10am-5pm Tue-Sat, 2-5pm Sun) occupies one of Britain's best examples of

neo-Grecian architecture. It houses a vast collection of treasures based on the stash squirrelled away by John Tradescant, Charles I's gardener, and Dr Elias Ashmole.

The collection is so vast it's difficult to take it in. It's bursting with Egyptian, Islamic and Chinese art; rare porcelain, tapestries and silverware; priceless musical instruments; and large displays of European art (including works by Raphael and Michelangelo). You'd be well advised to study the floor plan so that you can plot a course through the sumptuous rooms and hallways.

MODERN ART OXFORD

An antidote to the musty hallways of history, **Modern Art Oxford** (☎ 722733; www.modernartoxford .org.uk; 30 Pembroke St; admission free; ⊙ 10am-5pm Tue-Sat, noon-5pm Sun) is one of the best contemporary-art museums outside London. It has a wonderful gallery space, excellent touring exhibitions and plenty of activities for children. The focus is on 20th-century painting, sculpture and photography.

MUSEUM OF OXFORD

For an excellent introduction to the history behind the city and university visit the **Museum of Oxford** (☎ 252761; St Aldate's; adult/child £2/50p; ⊙ 10am-4pm Tue-Fri, 10am-5pm Sat, noon-4pm Sun). Exhibits range from a mammoth's tooth and an Elizabethan pavement of cattle bones, to a series of rooms from different eras and a Morris Minor used to illustrate car production's huge part in the city's manufacturing boom.

OXFORD STORY

More fanfare and less information is on offer at the **Oxford Story** (☎ 728822; www.oxford story.co.uk; 6 Broad St; adult/child £6.95/5.25; ⊙ 9.30am-5pm Jul-Aug, 10am-4.30pm Mon-Sat & 11am-4.30pm Sun Sep-Jun), which is incredibly popular with tourists, but derided by locals and students. Basically, it's a 25-minute ride through the 900 years of university history in carriages designed to look like college desks.

CARFAX TOWER

The sole reminder of medieval St Martin's Church, **Carfax Tower** (☎ 792653; admission £1.40; ⊙ 10am-5.30pm Mon-Sat & 11am-5pm Sun May-Oct, 10am-3.30pm Nov-Apr) stands at the junction of four streets and derived its name from the Latin *quadri furcus*, meaning 'four forks'.

The tower is adorned by a pair of quarterboys (figures who hammer out the quarter hours on bells) and there's a good view over the city centre from the top.

UNIVERSITY BUILDINGS & COLLEGES
Christ Church College

The largest and most spectacular of all of Oxford's colleges, **Christ Church** (☎ 286573; www .visitchristchurch.net; St Aldate's; adult/child £4/3; ⊙ 9am-5.30pm Mon-Sat, noon-5.30pm Sun) is also its most popular. The college was founded in 1525 by Cardinal Thomas Wolsey – who suppressed 22 monasteries to acquire the funds.

Thirteen British prime ministers were educated here as well as Albert Einstein, philosopher John Locke, poet WH Auden and Charles Dodgson (the real name of storyteller Lewis Carroll). More recently it was used as a location for the Harry Potter films.

The main entrance is below **Tom Tower**, the upper part of which was designed by former student Sir Christopher Wren. The 7-ton tower bell chimes 101 times each evening at 9.05pm (Oxford is five minutes west of Greenwich), the time when the original 101 students were called in.

Visitors, however, must enter through the smaller gate further down St Aldate's. Immediately inside the main entrance to the left is the 15th-century cloister, a relic of the ancient Priory of St Frideswide whose shrine was a focus of pilgrimage. From here you go up to the magnificent **Great Hall**, the college's dining room on the south side of **Tom Quad**, the largest quadrangle in Oxford.

From the quad you enter **Christ Church Cathedral**, the smallest cathedral in the country, with brawny Norman columns topped by elegant vaulting and some beautiful stained-glass windows including a rare depiction of the murder of Thomas Becket.

You can also explore another two quads and the **Picture Gallery**, with its modest collection of Renaissance art. Leave the college by the south entrance to stroll the leafy lanes of **Christchurch Meadow**.

Merton College

Small, smart and affluent, **Merton College** (☎ 276310; www.merton.ox.ac.uk; Merton St; admission free; ⊙ 2-4pm Mon-Fri, 10am-4pm Sat & Sun) was one of the original three colleges founded in 1264 and represents the earliest form of collegiate planning.

The charming 14th-century **Mob Quad** was the first of the college quads. The **Old Library** leading off it is the oldest medieval library in use. JRR Tolkien (who taught here) undoubtedly spent many a day leafing through the dusty tomes in search of arcane runes and old Saxon words that helped shape *The Lord of the Rings*. Another literary giant associated with the college is TS Eliot.

If you're visiting in summer don't miss the wonderful candlelit concerts in the chapel in the evening. If it is a normal church-service concert, entrance is free.

Magdalen College

Oxford's wealthiest and probably most beautiful college, **Magdalen** (mawd-len; ☎ 276000; www.magd.ox.ac.uk; High St; adult/child £3/2; ⌚ noon-6pm Jul-Sep, 1pm-dusk Oct-Jun) even has its own herd of deer.

The medieval chapel, with its 43m bell tower, is well worth a visit as is the stunning cloister with its strange gargoyles and carved figures, said to have inspired CS Lewis' stone statues in the *Chronicles of Narnia*. Oscar Wilde, poet laureate Sir John Betjeman and actor Dudley Moore were students.

The college also boasts a fine choir that sings every May Day from the top of Magdalen Tower at 6am. For most students this event now marks the culmination of a solid night of drinking prior to gathering in their glad rags on Magdalen Bridge to listen to the madrigals.

Opposite Magdalen are the beautiful **Botanic Gardens** (☎ 286690; www.botanic-garden.ox.ac.uk; adult/child £2.50/free; ⌚ 9am-6pm May-Sep, 9am-4.30pm Oct-Apr) that sweep along the banks of the River Cherwell. The gardens are the oldest in Britain and were founded in 1621 for the study of medicinal plants.

Radcliffe Camera

The quintessential Oxford landmark and one of the city's most photographed buildings, the **Radcliffe Camera** (Radcliffe Sq) is a spectacular circular library built in 1748 in the Palladian style. It's closed to the public.

For superb views of the Radcliffe Camera climb the 14th-century tower in the beautiful **Church of Saint Mary the Virgin** (☎ 279111; cnr High & Catte Sts; tower admission £2/1; ⌚ 9am-7pm Jul-Aug, 9am-5pm Mon-Sat & noon-5pm Sun Sep-Jun).

Brasenose College

More enchanting than the larger colleges, 16th-century **Brasenose College** (☎ 277830; admission £1; ⌚ 2-4.30pm) has a charm and elegance lacking in its more famous neighbours. The college takes its name from an 11th-century snout-like door knocker stolen in 1334 by students from Stamford College, Lincolnshire. In 1890 Brasenose bought the whole of Stamford College to reacquire the door knocker. It now hangs in the dining hall. Next to it is a portrait of Alexander Nowell, a college principal, whose claim to fame is the 'invention' of bottled beer.

ST SCHOLASTICA'S DAY MASSACRE

Ever since the arrival of the first students in Oxford tension brewed with the locals. Name-calling often erupted into full-scale violence and in 1209 and 1330 battered scholars abandoned Oxford and established universities in Cambridge and Stamford respectively. What happened on February 10 and 11 1355, however, made previous riots seem like an innocent pillowfight.

Celebrations for St Scholastica's Day grew nasty when two drunken students started a fist fight with a tavern landlord. The fight spilled out into the street where students and townspeople soon took to each other's throats and hundreds of others rushed to join the brawl. By the end of the day the students had claimed victory and an uneasy truce was established. The next morning, however, the furious townspeople returned with the help of local villagers armed with pickaxes, shovels and pikes. By the end of the day 63 students and 30 townspeople were dead. King Edward III ordered troops to quell the riot, and eventually decided to bring the town under the control of the university.

On the anniversary of the riot each year the mayor and burgesses (citizens) were ordered to attend a service and pay the vice-chancellor a penny for every student killed. The practice continued until 1825 when the mayor flatly refused to pay the fine, as did his successors until 1955 when the university eventually extended the olive branch and awarded a Doctorate of Civil Law to Mayor William Richard Gowers.

New College

Stroll under the **Bridge of Sighs**, a 1914 copy of the famous bridge in Venice, to **New College** (☎ 279555; cnr Holywell St & New College Lane; adult/child £2/1 Easter-Sep, free Oct-Easter; ☻ 11am-5pm Easter-Sep, 2-4pm Oct-Easter), founded in 1379. The college is a fine example of the perpendicular style and has a chapel full of treasures. If you're visiting during term time it is well worth stopping in for Evensong at 6pm.

Former college warden William Spooner gave rise to the term 'spoonerism' after his habit of transposing the first consonants of words. It's claimed he once reprimanded a student by saying 'You have deliberately tasted two worms and can leave Oxford by the town drain'.

Sheldonian Theatre

The university's main public building, the **Sheldonian Theatre** (☎ 277299; www.sheldon.ox.ac.uk; Broad St; adult/child £1.50/1; ☻ 10am-12.30pm & 2-4.30pm Mon-Sat) was the first major work of Christopher Wren, at that time Professor of Astronomy. It's used for college ceremonies and public concerts and the ceiling of the main hall has a fine 17th-century painting of the triumph of truth over ignorance. There are good views from the cupola.

Bodleian Library

One of England's three copyright libraries, the **Bodleian Library** (☎ 277224; www.bodley.ox.ac.uk; cnr Broad St & Parks Rd; ☻ 9am-4.45pm Mon-Fri, 9am-12.30pm Sat; tours £4; no children under 14) is one of the oldest public libraries in the world. The building is accessed via the stunning Jacobean-period **Old Schools Quadrangle.** Tours take place at 10.30am, 11.30am, 2pm and 3pm, and show off the mysterious Duke Humfrey's library (1488).

Also not to be missed is the **Divinity School** (admission free), the oldest teaching room in the university. It is renowned as a masterpiece of 15th-century English Gothic architecture and has a superb fan-vaulted ceiling.

Activities

A trip to Oxford wouldn't be quite complete without an attempt at **punting**; it's one of the best ways of soaking up some local atmosphere. The secret to controlling these flat-bottomed boats is to push *gently* on the pole to get the punt moving and then use it as a rudder to keep on course.

You can punt on both the Cherwell and the Isis from Easter to September. A punt holding five people including the punter costs £12 per hour.

The most central location to rent punts is on the Isis at Magdalen Bridge from **Howard C & Sons** (☎ 202643; www.oxfordpunting.com; High St; deposit £30). Far better, though, is the **Cherwell Boat House** (☎ 515978; www.cherwellboathouse.co.uk; Bardwell Rd; deposit £60) for a countryside amble to the busy boozer the **Victoria Arms** (☎ 241382; Mill Lane). To get to the boathouse take bus No 2 or 7 from Magdalen St to Bardwell Rd and walk five minutes.

Tours

Blackwell's (☎ 333606; oxford@blackwell.co.uk; 53 Broad St) runs tours from April to October. Literary tours (adult/child £6/5.50) run at 2pm Tuesday, 11am Thursday and noon on Saturday, Inklings tours (£7/6.50) are at 11.45am on Wednesday, and Alice in Wonderland tours (£7/6) run on Friday at 2pm. The cost includes admission to Christchurch.

City Sightseeing (☎ 790522; www.citysightseeing oxford.com; adult/child £9/3) and **Full Circle Tours** (☎ 01789-720 002; www.fullcircletours.co.uk; adult/child £8/3) run hop-on, hop-off city bus tours every 15 to 20 minutes from 9.30am to 6pm between April and October, and less often in winter. Both leave from the train station.

Oxford Information Centre (see p340) runs a guided walking tour (adult/child £6.50/3) at 11am and 2pm. Inspector Morse tours (£7/3.50) follow the trail of the fictional Oxford sleuth every Saturday at 1.30pm, and ghost tours (£5/3) depart at 7.45pm on Friday and Saturday, June to September.

Sleeping

Accommodation in Oxford in general favours floral patterns over cutting-edge design. Between May and September beds fill up very quickly, so book in advance or join the queue at the TIC and pay £3 for help.

Good bus services to areas just outside Oxford's centre mean you can save on accommodation costs without missing any action.

BUDGET

New Oxford YHA Hostel (☎ 727275; oxford@yha.org.uk; 2a Botley Rd; dm/d £19.50/46; Ⓟ ☒ 🖳 ; wheelchair access) This friendly hostel has the best budget beds in town and is well worth considering for a double room over some of the city's grotty B&Bs. Rooms are bright and airy, if functional. Facilities include bike storage, luggage lockers and laundry.

Oxford Backpackers (☎ 721761; 9 Hythe Bridge St; dm £13; ☒ ☐) Convenient for town, this grungy hostel has bright murals, ancient armchairs and its own bar, which mean things can get a bit loud at weekends. It's a little dingy and dorms can have as many as 18 beds but plenty of visitors stay long term and take advantage of the £60 weekly rate.

Oxford Camping International (☎ 244088; 426 Abingdon Rd; camping per person £8.85) This large, well-serviced campsite is 1½ miles south of the city centre. It's a very popular spot and gets booked out well in advance.

MID-RANGE

Burlington House (☎ 513513; www.burlington-house .co.uk; 374 Banbury Rd; s/d from £58/80; P ☒) A top-notch option, this lovingly maintained, Victorian merchant house is simply but elegantly decorated. Rooms are bright and cheerful and the generous breakfast will keep you going for most of the day.

Parklands (☎ 554374; stay@parklandsoxford.co.uk; 100 Banbury Rd; s/d £59/89; P ☒) Bright modern rooms with understated décor and neutral tones make this Victorian town house worth a visit. Less than a mile from town, it is a good compromise option and children are very welcome.

Head of the River (☎ 721600; headofhteriver@fullers .co.uk; Folly Bridge; s/d £75/85) Go punting in your pyjamas from this surprisingly good hotel above a large pub. The comfortable, taste-fully decorated rooms are good value and in a beautiful location overlooking the Isis.

St Michael's Guesthouse (☎ 242101; 26 St Michael's St; s/d £35/50; ☒) Ideally located on a quiet street in the heart of the city, this friendly B&B has modest but comfortable rooms and is often booked out well ahead.

Cotswold House (☎ 310558; www.cotswoldhouse .co.uk; 363 Banbury Rd; s/d £50/75; P ☒) Bright, comfortable rooms with traditional décor, a warm welcome and a great breakfast make this excellent B&B, about 2 miles north of the city centre, well worth the effort.

TOP END

Old Parsonage Hotel (☎ 310210; www.oldparsonage -hotel.co.uk; 1 Banbury Rd; s £125, d £135-195; P ☒) Once home to Oscar Wilde and now Ox-

ford's best hotel, this place oozes charm and character from its 17th-century walls and individually furnished rooms. The creaky floors, antique furniture and floral patterns won't suit everyone, but the newer rooms at the back are more contemporary and just as luxurious.

Old Bank Hotel (☎ 799599; www.oldbank-hotel .co.uk; 92 High St; s/d from £140/160; P ☒ ☒ ☐) A haven of slick modern design in a city of tradition, the Old Bank Hotel combines clean lines and ur ban chic in its stylishly sleek rooms in muted natural tones. Most rooms have stunning views of Oxford's roof-line and all have large screen TVs and CD players.

Eating

Oxford has loads of choice when it comes to getting a bite to eat but there are plenty of joints serving up mediocre meals and will-ing to relieve gormless tourists and wealthy parents of their cash, so beware. For cheap-and-cheerful meals head for the student strip on Cowley Rd.

BUDGET

Edamame (☎ 246916; 15 Holywell St; mains £6-7.50; ☽ lunch & dinner) Look out for the queue half-way down Holywell St and you've found tiny Edamame where simple but delicious Japanese home cooking gets dished up to the lucky ones who made it inside. They don't take bookings but it's well worth the wait. Thursday night is sushi (£2 to £3.50) night.

La Plaza Tapas (☎ 516688; 11 Little Clarendon St; mains £8-11, tapas £3.20-4.50; ☾ lunch & dinner) Set in a beautiful narrow building with warm walls and a lovely bar. It's easy to pass a few hours here nibbling on the great tapas or settling in for the long haul with a traditional Spanish meal of salt cod or paella.

SoJo (☎ 202888; 6-9 Hythe Bridge St; mains £6-9; ☾ lunch & dinner) This chic, sultry new place has incredible-value meals and an extensive menu ranging from dim sum and hot pots to a Mongolian buffet (one visit £4.50) where you can pile up the meat and veg and see it cooked in front of you. Wash it all down with a SoJo MoJo and you'll be set for the night.

Joe's (☎ 201120; 21 Cowley Rd; mains £6-9; ☾ lunch & dinner) Serving what are possibly the best breakfasts in town, with or without a cocktail on the side, tiny Joe's dishes up a simple but delicious menu to everyone from those looking for a hangover cure to the hip brunch crew. Lunch and dinner specials make it worth a visit later on too.

Jericho Café (☎ 310840; 112 Walton St; mains £5-7; ☾ lunch & dinner) This cool, laid-back café is a great spot to refuel on healthy goodies, from tasty bruschettas and interesting salads to imaginative pizzas. Linger over a latte mid-afternoon, or drop in for a bite before a late show at the Phoenix Picturehouse.

MID-RANGE

Chutneys (☎ 724241; 36 St Michael's St; mains £7.50-10.50; ☾ lunch & dinner) Great food and chilled ambience lure the crowds to this fantastic bright and airy Indian. The menu always delivers something delicious, just don't go wild on the poppadums or you'll have no room for the succulent main courses.

Moya (☎ 200111; 97 St Clements; mains £9-11; ☾ lunch & dinner) Crisp, contemporary and minimalist, Moya serves up some weird but wonderful Slovak dishes like the incredible devil's toast (sausage, chilli and goat's cheese). The service is faultless and the cocktails (£4.50) alone make it worth a visit.

Grand Café (☎ 204463; 84 High St; high tea £13.50; ☾ lunch) Oxford's most elegant coffee house. Dine on cucumber sandwiches, scones, strawberries and truffles in opulent surroundings. The service is charming.

Bangkok House (☎ 200705; 42a Hythe Bridge St; mains £9-12; ☾ lunch & dinner) Sink into an enormous carved chair for what is simply the best Thai food in town. Delicious, coconut-based

---

SOMETHING SPECIAL

Sir Charles Napier (☎ 01494-483011; Sprigg's Alley, Chinnor; mains £11.50-17.50, 2-course menu £16.50) A veritable legend in food terms, the Sir Charles Napier is renowned for its excellent food, lavish gardens, stunning views and eclectic artwork. The unmatched chairs, junk-shop clutter and bold sculptures all add to the charm of this laid-back gourmet pad. The menu is Anglo-Mediterranean, with wild local game being the winter speciality and Cornish lobster drawing the crowds in summer. The wine list is well chosen, and the food – nothing less than divine.

Chinnor is located about 15 miles east of Oxford.

---

curries, sublime mushroom-and-galangal soup, faultless service and moderate prices make this place an excellent choice for a special night out.

Sip (☎ 311322; 102 Walton St; dishes £3-6.50; ☾ lunch & dinner) Seriously stylish and packed with trend-conscious cocktail drinkers, this minimalist restaurant serves up a tapas-style menu of Asian and fusion foods. The nosh is excellent, but by the time you've filled your belly your Prada purse will be quite a bit lighter.

TOP END

Quod (☎ 202505; 92 High St; mains £9-17; ☾ lunch & dinner) Popular with a trendy young crowd and the merely moneyed, Quod dishes up thoroughly good Mediterranean brasserie-style food. The place is buzzing every night and in summer the cool terrace with trickling water features is a real draw. Bright modern art adorns the walls inside and the stylish bar is a good place to sip cocktails and eye up the clientele.

Gee's Restaurant (☎ 553540; 61 Banbury Rd; mains £11-20; ☾ lunch & dinner) Set in a Victorian conservatory that was once a flower shop, this swanky restaurant dishes up an innovative feast of modern European food. It's a great place for a special evening out, but a bit stuffy for a night on the town.

QUICK EATS

If you're doing a whirlwind tour of the city and just can't stop for lunch, try some of these options for a quick but hearty sandwich (£2 to £4).

Felson's Baguette Bar (☎ 316631; 32 Little Clarendon St) Tiny place dishing up great takeaway treats.

Mortons (☎ 200867; 103 Covered Market & 22 Broad St) An Oxford institution and perennially popular for its great sandwiches.

SELF-CATERING

As soon as you walk into the **Covered Market** (Market St) you're hit with the smell of food wafting through the air – from the freshly baked cookies at one end to the traditional pies and fresh fruit at the other. You can pick up anything from Sicilian sausage to a pork-and-apricot pie, freshly made sandwiches, luscious fruit and excellent olives.

You'll also find old-style barbers and cobblers, funky clothes stalls and traditional butchers. If you're in Oxford at Christmas the displays of freshly hung deer, wild boar, ostrich and turkey are quite amazing.

Drinking

Oxford is overrun with watering holes, from the faithfully traditional where famous writers, politicians and scholars have debated their ideas for centuries, to the slick, modern bars for the urbane cool.

Turf Tavern (☎ 243235; 4 Bath Pl) One of the best-loved pubs in town, the Turf is hidden down a tiny alley near the Bridge of Sighs. It does a stunning array of ales and is filled with a mix of locals, students and tourists, spilling out of the snug low-ceilinged bar into the three courtyards outside.

Eagle & Child (☎ 310154; 49 St Giles') The cosy cubbyholes of this 17th-century place were a favourite haunt of JRR Tolkien, CS Lewis and their literary friends. The wonderful atmosphere can get spoiled by the hordes of tourists, but if you're lucky you'll just have to contend with a few dusty academics.

White Horse (☎ 721860; 52 Broad St) More a large cupboard than an actual pub, this tiny place plays host to an eclectic mix of dons and bookish students. It was a favourite retreat for TV detective Inspector Morse and gets crowded easily so come early, if not mid-afternoon.

Kazbar (☎ 202920; 25-27 Cowley Rd) A cavernous place with a Moroccan theme, it's easy to lose yourself for a few hours under the low lighting and the influence of several cocktails. The clientele is cool but laid-back and the Spanish and North African tapas (£2.50 to £4.50) are excellent.

Baby Love (☎ 200011; 3 King Edwards St) This place is packed most nights with hip young things sipping cocktails and you'll have to vie for space on the dance floor downstairs – unless you volunteer for some pole dancing in the corner. Watch out for the glass floor as you walk in the door, and don't bother apologising for entering the wrong loo – they're unisex.

Frevd (☎ 311171; 119 Walton St) Entombed in a converted neoclassical church complete with stained-glass windows, this crumbling café-bar is one of the best-loved spots in town. It's popular with a young style-conscious clientele nibbling on pizzas (£5 to £7) at lunch and throbbing with cocktail-sipping luvvies by night.

Entertainment
NIGHTCLUBS

Po Na Na (☎ 249171; 13-15 Magdalen St; admission up to £6) The best club in town, this is one of the originals of the Po Na Na Moroccan-style chain. Cavelike and very hip, its playlist features soulful Latin jazz, funk, hip-hop and the very best boogie choons in town.

Zodiac (☎ 420042; 190 Cowley Rd; admission up to £5) An Oxford institution and the city's best live-music venue, the Zodiac oozes a flirty alternative vibe and is generally packed with an eclectic and seriously unpretentious crowd intent on having a good time. Live gigs range from guitar-thrashing bands kicking off their England tours to jazz instrumentalists, while club nights feature anything from drum'n'bass to trashy disco.

Backroom at the Bully (☎ 244516; 162 Cowley Rd; admission up to £5) A regular student favourite, the Bullingdon Arms hosts everything from jazz and acoustic gigs to cheesy '70s disco, trance and occasional techno nights. Check the listings for the latest offerings.

THEATRE & CLASSICAL MUSIC

The **Oxford Playhouse** (☎ 305305; www.oxfordplayhouse.com; Beaumont St; wheelchair access) is the city's main stage for drama, and hosts an impressive selection of touring productions of theatre, music and dance.

Just around the corner the **Burton Taylor Theatre** (☎ 798600; Gloucester St) goes for more offbeat student productions while the **Pegasus Theatre** (☎ 722851; www.pegasustheatre.org.uk; Magdalen Rd; wheelchair access) is popular for its low-budget, independent productions.

Many venues around town host classical concerts throughout the year. Keep an eye out for posters around town or visit www .musicatoxford.com.

Getting There & Away

BUS

Competition on the bus route to London is fierce, with three companies serving the route. **Oxford Tube** (☎ 772250; www.oxfordtube .com; return £11; 1½hr) runs to London's Victoria coach station every 12 to 20 minutes 24 hours a day and leaves from Gloucester Green bus station. **London Espress** (☎ 785400; www.oxfordbus.co.uk; return £11; 1½hr) runs the same route as the Oxford Tube, at similar times. Board at Gloucester Green bus station. **Megabus** (www.megabus.com; one way from £1; 1¾ hr) is an Internet booking agent that runs coaches from Oxpens Coach Park to Gloucester Pl in London six times a day.

The Heathrow Express (three-month return £17, 70 minutes) runs half-hourly 7am to 11pm, hourly 11pm to 7am, while the Gatwick Express (three-month return £24, two hours) runs hourly 7am to 10pm and every two hours 10pm to 6am.

National Express has five buses to Birmingham (£9.25, two hours), one service to Bath (£10.50, two hours) and Bristol (£14, 2¼ hours), and two to Gloucester (£8.50, 1½ hours).

Stagecoach serves most of the small towns in Oxfordshire. If you're planning a lot of bus journeys it's worth buying a Megarider Plus Pass allowing unlimited bus travel in Oxfordshire for seven days. It costs £9.

The multi-operator pass known as the Plus Pass costs £5/14/40 for one day/week/ month.

CAR & MOTORCYCLE

Oxford has a serious traffic problem and parking is a nightmare. Five Park & Ride car parks surround the town. Parking costs 60p and a return bus journey to town (10 to 15 minutes, every 10 minutes) costs £1.80.

TRAIN

There are half-hourly services to London Paddington (one way £14.90, one hour); and hourly trains to Coventry (£15, one hour), Birmingham (£18, 1½ hours), Worcester (£11.50, 80 minutes) and Hereford (£14.70, two hours).

To connect with trains to the southwest you have to change at Didcot Parkway (one way £3.80, 15 minutes). There are plenty of connections to Bath (one way £9.80, 1½ hours).

Getting Around

BICYCLE

The *Cycle into Oxford* map, available from the TIC, shows all local cycle routes. Bikes can be hired from **Beeline Bikes** (☎ 246615; 61-63 Cowley Rd; per day/week £12/20, deposit £50) which dabbles in Hybrid and mountain bikes, and **Cycle Analysts** (☎ 424444; 150 Cowley Rd; per day/week £10/18, deposit £100) which hires Hybrid bikes, locks and lights.

BOAT

Salter Bros (☎ 243421; www.salterbros.co.uk) offers several interesting jaunts from Folly Bridge from May to September.

BUS

You can walk almost everywhere in Oxford's centre, but if you're feeling less than energetic bus Nos 1 and 5 serve Cowley Rd from Carfax, Nos 2 and 7 go along Banbury Rd from Magdalen St and Nos 31 and 35 run along Abingdon Rd from St Aldates.

TAXI

There are taxis outside the train station and near the bus station, as well as on St Giles' and at Carfax. Be prepared to join a long queue after closing time. A taxi to Blenheim Palace costs around £20.

WOODSTOCK
☎ 01993 / pop 2389

Steeped in history and oozing charm, the lovely village of Woodstock is home to a fine collection of 17th- and 18th-century buildings and the glorious country pile of the Churchill family, Blenheim Palace. Also worth a look are the town hall, built at the Duke of Marlborough's expense in 1766, and the church, which has an 18th-century tower tacked onto a medieval interior.

Opposite the church, Fletcher's House accommodates the **Oxfordshire Museum** (☎ 811456; Park St; admission free; ◷ 10am-5pm Tue-Sat, 2-5pm Sun), which has displays and dioramas on local history, art, archaeology and the environment. The **TIC** (☎ 813276; Park St; ◷ 9.30am-5.30pm Mon-Sat, 1-5pm Sun) is attached to the museum.

Blenheim Palace

Queen Anne's relief was so great after the defeat of the French at the Battle of Blenheim that she awarded cash to John Churchill, Duke of Marlborough, as thanks for his role in the victory. The result was the extravagant **Blenheim Palace** (☎ 08700 60 20 80; www .blenheimpalace.com; admission £11, park & garden only £6; ⏰ 10.30am-5.30pm mid-Feb–Oct, park open year-round), now a Unesco World Heritage Site. The palace is one of Europe's largest and was designed by Sir John Vanbrugh and Nicholas Hawksmoor between 1705 and 1722. Today, it is home of the 11th duke and duchess.

The interior of this remarkable baroque fantasy palace is stuffed with a variety of paintings, antiques, carvings and tapestries, but the crowds and the heady pace of the free guided tour make it hard to appreciate. First up is the **Great Hall**, which has 20m-high ceilings adorned with images of the first duke at the battle that earned him the house.

You proceed to the **Churchill Exhibition**, four rooms devoted to the life, work and writings of Sir Winston, who was born at Blenheim in 1874. According to a notice on the wall he was born prematurely, but historians have long since discounted this as a necessary lie – it seems Winnie's folks got a little ahead of themselves and couldn't wait until the wedding day. Churchill and his wife, Lady Clementine Spencer-Churchill, are buried in nearby Bladon Church; its spire is visible from the Great Hall.

On your way to the drawing rooms you'll pass the **China Cabinet**, which has entire collections of Meissen (Dresden) and Sèvres porcelain. Though the other rooms in the house are all magnificent, the most impressive of all is the 55m **Long Library**, with books collected by the 9th duke.

The extensive grounds are large enough that you can lose most of the crowds if you're willing to walk a little. Parts were landscaped by Lancelot 'Capability' Brown and are simply stunning. Just north of the house a dramatic artificial lake boasts a beautiful bridge by Vanbrugh.

Sleeping & Eating

It's top-end hotels only in Woodstock so plan a day trip if you're travelling on a budget.

Kings Arms Hotel (☎ 813636; www.kings-hotel -woodstock.co.uk; 19 Market St; s/d £70/130; ✗) Sleek, simple rooms with contemporary furnishings allow you to flee the chintz in style at this Georgian hotel. The bright brasserie (mains £8 to £14) serves up surprisingly good modern British fare in the large atrium area and the clutter-free bar.

Feathers Hotel (☎ 812291; www.feathers.co.uk; Market St; s £99, d £135-225; P ✗ ⌨) This hotel with winding staircases and hidden rooms just drips with character. The luxurious rooms are tastefully decorated with rich fabrics, antiques and beds to wallow in while the restaurant serves up fine French food (mains £19 to £23), which it takes *very* seriously, announcing every dish as it arrives.

Zaki's Deli (☎ 811535; 31 Oxford St; ⏰ lunch) If you need a quick snack or supplies for a palatial picnic on Blenheim lawn, Zaki's will stock you up with everything from fine cheeses and olives to choice meats and local Cotswold smoked salmon. Alternatively, you can eat in and refuel on delicious sambos (£3 to £4), coffee and cake.

Getting There & Away

Stagecoach bus No 20 runs every half hour (hourly on Sunday) from Oxford bus station (20 minutes, £2.60 one-way, £4.30 return). **Cotswold Roaming** (☎ 308300; www.cotswold-roaming .co.uk) offers organised excursions to Blenheim from Oxford, departing at 10am and returning at 1.50pm. The cost is £16/10 per adult/child, and includes admission to Blenheim.

TOP FIVE PUBS FOR SUNDAY LUNCH

- **Churchill Arms** (p359; Paxford) Honest gourmet fare in a seriously unpretentious setting.

- **Crooked Billet** (p351; Stoke Row) Temple of gastronomy in the one-time hangout of highwayman Dick Turpin.

- **Falkland Arms** (p356; Great Tew) Authentic, old-world charm in a stunning Cotswold village.

- **Kings Head** (p358; Bledington) Timeless, 16th-century inn with fine menu featuring local produce.

- **Sir Charles Napier** (p346; Chinnor) A culinary Oxford institution renowned for its food and eclectic artwork.

UFFINGTON WHITE HORSE

About 20 miles southwest of Oxford, near Wantage, the stylised image of a white horse is cut into a hillside. Along with Stonehenge, it's one of the most remarkable and mysterious of England's ancient sites. This chalk figure, which measures 114m long and 49m wide, was carved into the turf about 3000 years ago, and the lines of perspective are such that the horse is best·viewed from a distance. What exactly it is supposed to represent remains anyone's guess.

Just below the figure is **Dragon Hill**, so-called because it is believed that St George slew the dragon here. Above the chalk figure are the grass-covered earthworks of **Uffington Castle**.

Thomas Hughes, author of *Tom Brown's Schooldays*, was born in Uffington village. His house is now **Uffington Museum** (☎ 01376-820259; www.uffington.net/museum; Broad St; adult/child 60/30p; ۞ 2-5pm Sat & Sun Easter-Oct).

You can stay at the 17th-century thatched farmhouse, the **Craven** (☎ 01367-820449; www.thecraven.co.uk; Fernham Rd; s from £28, d £55-85), which has pretty rooms with hand-embroidered bed linen.

HENLEY-ON-THAMES

☎ 01491 / pop 10,513

Well bred and well heeled, conservative Henley is a sleepy but elegant place with a clutch of pretty stone houses, a few traces of Tudor grace and a large collection of chichi shops. The town sits firmly in the commuter belt and ambles along for most of the year but bursts into action during the first week of July with its world-famous regatta, a quintessentially English celebration of rowing, the rich and the beautiful.

The **TIC** (☎ 578034; The Barn, King's Rd; ۞ 9.30am-5pm Mon-Sat & 11am-4pm Sun May-Sep, 10am-4pm Oct-Apr) is next to the handsome town hall.

Sights & Activities

Henley's impressive **River & Rowing Museum** (☎ 415600; www.rrm.co.uk; Mill Meadows; adult/child £6/4; ۞ 10am-6pm Mon-Sat, 10.30am-6pm Sun; wheelchair access) documents the town's obsession with boating and the people, wildlife and culture of the River Thames. Interesting multimedia displays liven up proceedings for younger visitors. The *Wind in the Willows* exhibition brings Kenneth Grahame's stories of Ratty, Mole, Badger and Toad to life.

St Mary's Church, which dates back to the 13th century, dominates Hart St. On the graceful Georgian bridge across the river are **sculptures** of Isis and Father Thames. Two fine coaching inns, the **Red Lion** and the **Angel**, are at the Hart St end of the bridge.

Henley is the perfect place to indulge in a bit of messing about on the river. On summer Sundays, **Hobbs & Son** (☎ 572035; www.hobbs-of-henley.com) organises jazz cruises (£17) and short river trips (adult/child £5/4). You can also hire five-seater rowing boats (£10 per hour) or a four-seater motorboat (£20 per hour).

Festivals & Events

HENLEY ROYAL REGATTA

In 1839 English society descended on Henley to watch the first Oxford and Cambridge boat race. Soon the one-day event became a five-day spectacle and Henley's place in boating history was secured.

Today, corporate entertainment reaches its pinnacle at this weeklong pompous picnic. Although rowers of the highest calibre compete, for most spectators hanging out on the lawn swilling champagne and looking rich and beautiful is the main event.

The regatta is held in the first week of July. Access to the public enclosure is £8 on Wednesday and Thursday, £12 on Friday and Saturday and £10 for the Sunday final.

For more information visit www.hrr.co.uk.

HENLEY FESTIVAL

Surprisingly for such a conservative town, the **Henley Festival** (☎ 843404; www.henley-festival.co.uk) features a vibrant and diverse programme, ranging from opera to avant-garde French percussionists, jazz, rock, poetry and theatre. It's held at a variety of venues all over town in the week following the regatta, though the main events take place on a floating stage on the Thames. Tickets range from £7 for the car park to £87 for the front row of the grandstand – although the latter tend to be block-booked by corporate sharks long before the event.

Sleeping

During regatta and festival weeks, rooms here are impossible to find, so book well in advance.

Alftrudis (☎ 573099; www.alftrudis.co.uk; 8 Norman Ave; s/d £45/55; P ✗) Close to the centre of town, yet extremely quiet, this beautiful Victorian house offers elegant accommodation at a great price. The pretty, traditional-style rooms have floral curtains and cosy beds but steer clear of being too fussy.

Falaise House (☎ 573388; www.falaisehouse.com; 37 Market Pl; s/d £50/65; 🖳) This Georgian town house in the centre of town offers traditional luxury B&B. The rooms are bright and airy and have a balanced mix of country-cottage chintz and modern restraint.

Thamesmeade House Hotel (☎ 574745; www .thamesmeadhousehotel.co.uk; Remenham Lane; s/d £105/125; P ✕ 🖳) Overlooking the town's cricket green, this posh boutique hotel is an exercise in restraint. The rooms feature uncluttered Scandinavian design merged with classic style, rich fabrics and hand-painted furniture. Children are very welcome.

Eating

Good food is surprisingly hard to come by in Henley. There are a few good pubs, but most eateries are predictable chain restaurants.

Victoria (☎ 575628; 48 Market Pl; mains £4.50-8.50; ☾ lunch & dinner) This stylish café bar offers a decent assortment of baguettes, panini and ciabattas and some wood-fired pizzas. The décor mixes exposed beams with deep leather sofas. There's a decked garden at the back and live acoustic music on Friday and Saturday nights.

Loch Fyne (☎ 845780; Market Pl; mains £7.95-13.95; ☾ lunch & dinner) Part of the successful Loch Fyne seafood brigade, this wonderful light-filled restaurant has plenty of good choices

---

SOMETHING SPECIAL

Crooked Billet (☎ 01491-681048; www.the crookedbillet.co.uk; Stoke Row; mains £12-19) Drawing the crowds from miles around, the Crooked Billet, one-time hideout of highwayman Dick Turpin, is a 17th-century inn turned gastro-pub. The place is full of romance with an inglenook fireplace, hop bine–adorned windows, low beams and a charming atmosphere. The seasonal menus have a strong emphasis on carefully prepared local produce and include delicacies such as roast loin of Oxfordshire pork with crackling, apple sauce and roast potatoes. The set Sunday lunch (£16.95 for three courses) is very popular, so arrive early.

---

for fish lovers. There's a paved garden outside and the two-course set lunch is an excellent deal at £9.95.

Kathmando (☎ 574422; 34 Reading Rd; mains £6.95-11.95; ☾ lunch & dinner) All clean lines and streaming light, the minimalist chic of this trendy Nepalese restaurant stands in glorious contrast to the hearty portions of contemporary Nepalese curries and Asian classics served up by the friendly staff.

Getting There & Around

Bus No 139 links Henley and Abingdon (30 minutes, hourly) from where frequent buses run to Oxford. Trains to London Paddington take about one hour (£10.50, hourly).

THE COTSWOLDS

Just made for picture postcards, chocolate boxes and jigsaws, the Cotswolds are one of Britain's best-loved treasures: lush, rolling hills sheltering countless implausibly picturesque villages of thatched honey-stone cottages, beautiful old mansions, rambling lanes and secluded churches. The area really is that romantic ideal of quintessential English charm and should be high on any traveller's itinerary. Although the most popular villages such as Stow-on-the-Wold, the Slaughters and Bourton-on-the-Water get choked with traffic and tourists, it's not difficult to get off the beaten track and find your own little oasis of undisturbed medieval splendour. Take to the hills on foot or by bike or just throw away your map and walk aimlessly for the best possible introduction to this stunning region of Britain.

Orientation & Information

The Cotswolds extend across a narrow band of land east of the M5, stretching almost as far as Oxford at their widest point. The region can be separated into two distinct areas: the southern and northern Cotswolds roughly divided by the sweep of the A40.

For online information on attractions, accommodation and events in the Cotswalds try the following:

Cotswolds Calling (www.cotswolds-calling.com)
Cotswolds Tourism (www.cotswolds.gov.uk/tourism)
Oxfordshire Cotswolds (www.oxfordshirecotswolds.org)

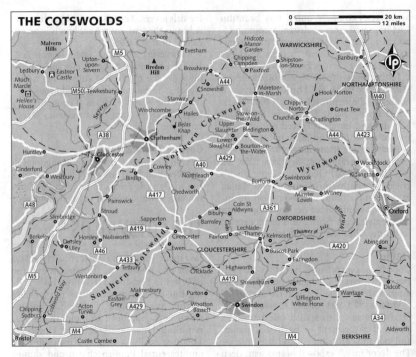

THE COTSWOLDS

Activities

The gentle, rolling hills of the Cotswolds are perfect for walking, and the 102-mile **Cotswold Way** makes a wonderful starting point. The route meanders gently from Chipping Campden to Bath, and has no major climbs or difficult stretches. Several companies offer guided or unguided walking tours. Try, for example, **Cotswold Walking Holidays** (☎ 01242-254353; www.cotswoldwalks.com; Cheltenham).

Cycling around the Cotswolds is an equally popular option for locals and visitors alike. **Cotswold Country Cycles** (☎ 01386-438706; www.cotswoldcountrycycles.com; Chipping Campden) rents out bicycles for £12 a day.

Getting Around

There are only limited bus services through the Cotswolds (particularly in the north) and the rail network only skims the northern and southern borders. **Traveline** (☎ 0870 608 2608) has travel information for all public transport.

Car hire can be arranged in most major centres (see p968).

CIRENCESTER

☎ 01285 / pop 15,861

Affluent yet unpretentious, steeped in history yet remarkably untouched by the tourist hordes, sleepy Cirencester has a definite old-time atmosphere despite being the largest settlement in the southern Cotswolds. The imposing townhouses of wealthy wool merchants flank the main streets and a fine perpendicular church lords it over the elegant market place. In Roman times Cirencester was second only to London in terms of its size and importance but little remains today from this golden era except the grassed-over ruins of one of the largest amphitheatres in the country.

You'll find the church and **TIC** (☎ 654180; Corn Hall; ⏰ 9.30am-5.30pm Apr-Dec, 9.30am-5pm Jan-Mar) on Market Sq where, appropriately enough, lively markets still take place every Monday and Friday. You can walk through the magnificent grounds of Cirencester House (closed to the public) from the entrance on Cecily Hill. The amphitheatre is on Cotswold Ave.

Sights

One of England's largest churches, the **Church of St John the Baptist** seems more like a cathedral with its soaring arches, magnificent fan vaulting and wild flying buttresses. The interior is bathed in light and plays host to a 15th-century painted stone pulpit and memorial brasses recording the matrimonial histories of important wool merchants. The east window contains fine medieval stained glass, while a wall safe displays the Boleyn Cup, made for Anne Boleyn, second wife of Henry VIII, in 1535. The superb perpendicular-style tower dominates the exterior, but it is the majestic three-storey south porch, which faces the square, that is the real highlight. Built as an office by late-15th-century abbots, it subsequently became the medieval town hall.

Impressive displays from the Roman era can be seen at the **Corinium Museum** (☎ 655611; www.cotswolds.gov.uk/museum; Park St; adult/child £3.50/2; 10am-5pm Mon-Sat, 2-5pm Sun), recently renovated to show off one of the largest collections of Roman artefacts in Britain. Highlights include the beautiful Hunting Dogs and Four Seasons floor mosaics, a reconstructed Roman kitchen and butcher's shop, and a dramatic new Anglo-Saxon gallery.

Sleeping & Eating

Victoria Rd has a string of B&Bs and guesthouses to choose from.

Corner House (☎ 641958; www.thecornerhouse.info; 101a Victoria Rd; s/d £32/40; P ✗) Large, bright rooms and tastefully restrained décor make this good value and a cut above many others along this strip. Children are welcome and there's a garden for outdoor games.

No 12 (☎ 640232; www.no12cirencester.co.uk; 12 Park St; d £70; ✗) One of the best choices in town, this elegant Georgian town house successfully combines antiques with a contemporary ambience. The spacious rooms are simple and sleek with great beds, feather pillows, merino-wool blankets and fine bed linen.

1651 (☎ 658507; Market Pl; mains £9.95-11.95; lunch & dinner) A cross between a wine bar and a brasserie, this stylish place at the Fleece Hotel have deep-red walls and stripped floors and serves an excellent selection of modern British and international cuisine. There are plenty of vegetarian options and very sensible prices.

Mackenzies Café Bar (☎ 656567; 34 Castle St; mains £5.75-8.95; lunch & dinner) Trendy young things flock here by night but by day the bright, modern surroundings and quiet atmosphere make it a good choice for lunch. The surprisingly good menu offers up everything from reliable old favourites such as wraps and nachos to more interesting pasta, meat and fish dishes.

Getting There & Away

National Express buses run roughly hourly from Cirencester to London (£14.50, 2½ hours), Cheltenham Spa (40 minutes) and Gloucester (one hour). Stagecoach bus No 51 also runs to Cheltenham hourly (40 minutes).

PAINSWICK

☎ 01452 / pop 1666

The 'Queen of the Cotswolds', Painswick is a rare delight; a gorgeous, unspoiled village seldom overrun by tourists. The tiny narrow streets lined with picture-perfect cottages and medieval inns seem genuinely lost in time.

In early July the town celebrates a Victorian market day. Ask at the **TIC** (☎ 813552; library, Stroud St; 10am-4.30pm Tue-Fri, 10am-1pm Sat & Sun Easter-Oct) for details. The **Cotswold Way** footpath runs through the village and is an excellent starting point for walks in the surrounding area.

Sights

St Mary's Church dominates the village and has some wonderful tabletop tombs of wealthy wool merchants in its graveyard. For many centuries 99 yew trees graced the grounds and legend has it that should the hundredth be allowed to grow, the devil would appear and shrivel it. To celebrate the millennium, however, they went ahead and planted the hundredth tree anyway – so far, no sign of the Wicked One. The streets behind the church are lined with handsome merchants' houses.

Half a mile to the north of town, the flamboyant pleasure gardens of **Painswick House** (☎ 813204; www.rococogarden.co.uk; adult/child £4/2; 11am-5pm Jan-Oct) are a restored version of original rococo gardens designed in the 1740s by Benjamin Hyett. They're laid out with geometrical precision, allowing stunning vistas of the many architectural features.

OXFORDSHIRE, GLOUCESTERSHIRE & THE COTSWOLDS

Sleeping & Eating

Hambutts Mynd (☎ 812352; ewarland@aol.com; Edge Rd; s/d £27/50; P ✗) This converted, early–18th-century corn mill has retained most of its original characteristics with old beams and crackling fires giving a warm welcome to weary hikers. The rooms are simple but tasteful.

Painswick Hotel (☎ 812160; www.painswickhotel .com; Kemps Lane; s/d from £75/125; P) The top spot in town, this former Georgian rectory has luxurious rooms with lovely antiques and rich fabrics. The restaurant (mains £12 to £19) serves delicacies such as wild venison. A good venue for a special night out.

March Hare (☎ 813452; Tibbiwell St; set dinner £23.50) Two tiny rooms with stone walls and wooden floors get packed out with happy diners digging into the terrific Thai food at this cosy place. The set, six-course dinner is excellent value and guaranteed to have you rolling out the door.

Getting There & Around

Bus No 46 connects Cheltenham (30 minutes) and Stroud (10 minutes) with Painswick hourly (four on Sunday).

TETBURY

☎ 01666 / pop 5250

The charming town of Tetbury, about 15 miles south of Gloucester, features a feast of timeless old buildings and almost as many antique shops. Once a prosperous wool-trading centre, the market square features a lovely, 17th-century **Market House**, and close by you'll find the Georgian Gothic **Church of St Mary the Virgin** with its graceful towering spire and wonderful interior.

The friendly **TIC** (☎ 503552; www.tetbury.com; 33 Church St; ☒ 9.30am-4.30pm Mon-Sat Mar-Oct, 10am-1pm Mon-Sat Nov-Feb) has plenty of information on the town.

The **Westonbirt Arboretum** (☎ 880220; www .forestry.gov.uk/westonbirt; adult/child £6/1; ☒ 10am-dusk), 2.5 miles southwest of town, boasts a superb selection of temperate trees and is famed for its autumn colour. It's wonderful for walking – ask at the TIC for a trail guide.

If you fancy staying overnight in Tetbury, **No 65** (☎ 503346; www.number65.co.uk; 65 Long St; s/d £25/45; ✗) is an excellent-value place with a couple of bright, comfortable rooms with simple, country-style décor. It also has a very good restaurant serving classic and modern English food (set three-course menu £24).

Other options for food include **Blue Zucchini** (☎ 505852; Church St; mains £5-8; ☒ lunch & dinner), a modern bistro-bar with a mostly Mediterranean menu, or **Trouble House** (☎ 502206; Cirencester Rd; mains £12-15; ☒ lunch & dinner), a fantastic place with a wonderfully informal, lived-in feel and exceptional modern British fare.

Bus No 92 serves Tetbury every two hours from Stroud (30 minutes) before transforming itself into No 620 and proceeding toward Bath (1¼ hours), making a stop at the Westonbirt Arboretum en route.

LECHLADE-ON-THAMES

☎ 01367 / pop 2415

A lovely Cotswold town about 25 miles west of Oxford, Lechlade is dominated by the graceful spire of **St Lawrence's Church**. Originally a wool church, it was rededicated to the Spanish saint by Catherine of Aragon.

The gorgeous Tudor pile **Kelmscott Manor** (☎ 252486; www.kelmscottmanor.co.uk; adult/child £8.50/ 4.25; ☒ 11am-5pm Wed Apr-Sep & selected summer Sats), once home to William Morris, the poet, artist and founder of the Arts and Crafts movement, is 3 miles east of Lechlade. The house displays fabrics and furniture designed by Morris as well as exotic, lacquered work introduced by Rossetti.

Another worthwhile side trip from Lechlade is **Buscot Park** (NT; ☎ 240786; www.buscot-park .com; adult/grounds only £6.50/4.50; ☒ 2-6pm Wed-Fri, grounds only Mon & Tue Apr-Sep & selected weekends), a Palladian mansion that is home to the Faringdon art collection, which includes paintings by Rembrandt, Reynolds, Rubens, Van Dyck and Murillo. The house is run by the National Trust (NT) and is 2½ miles southeast of Lechlade on the Faringdon road.

There are four buses, Monday to Saturday, from Lechlade to Cirencester (40 minutes).

BURFORD

☎ 01993

Slithering downhill to the medieval bridge over the River Windrush, Burford's High St is a picturesque medley of fine Cotswold stone houses, specialist boutiques and antique shops peddling flowery china and nostalgia. The town, about 20 miles west of Oxford, attracts visitors in their droves and can be frustratingly busy in midsummer. However, the lovely side streets are quieter and the gorgeous **Church of St John** is a peaceful oasis at any time.

You'll find the **TIC** (☎ 823558; Sheep St; ☽ 9.30am-5.30pm Mon-Sat Mar-Oct, 10am-4.30pm Mon-Sat Nov-Feb) by the Lamb Inn. Nearby, the 16th-century **Toll House** (Tolsey Museum; High St; admission by donation; ☽ 2-5pm Tue-Fri & Sun Apr-Oct) perches on pillars and houses a small museum on Burford's history.

For younger visitors, the excellent **Cotswold Wildlife Park** (☎ 823006; www.cotswoldwildlife park.co.uk; adult/child £8/5.50; ☽ 10am-4.30pm Mar-Sep, 10am-3.30pm Oct-Feb) is home to everything from ants to white rhinos and giant cats as well as an adventure playground. The park is 2 miles south of Burford on the A361.

If you have the time it's worth the effort to walk east along the river to the untouched and rarely visited village of **Swinbrook** (3 miles) where the beautiful church has some remarkable tombs including that of the Fettiplace family, with its comical carvings.

Sleeping & Eating

Priory (☎ 823249; 35 High St; s/d £15/40) The cheapest option in town, this basic place has small functional rooms around a little courtyard. Newer and better rooms (with private bathroom) at the back cost £50, although they're far from spacious. The café out front serves a decent selection of baguettes, salads and roasts (£4.95 to £7.95).

Lamb Inn (☎ 823155; www.lambinn-burford.co.uk; Sheep St; s £80-120, d £130-200; P) Dating from the 15th century, Burford's oldest pub is now a gorgeous place to stay with beamed ceilings, flagged floors, creaking stairs and a charming, laid-back atmosphere. The bright, period rooms are a tasteful mix of antique and chintz.

Jonathan's at the Angel (☎ 822714; www.theangel -uk.com; s/d £70/90, mains £14-19; ☽ lunch & dinner) This informal, country brasserie occupies a 16th-century coaching inn and serves up an excellent selection of modern British and European food. Three themed bedrooms offer luxury B&B in classic style.

Getting There & Away

From Oxford, Swanbrook runs four buses a day (two on Sunday) to Burford (45 minutes) via Witney. Stagecoach bus Nos 233 and X3 run between Witney and Burford nine times a day, Monday to Saturday only (20 minutes).

WITNEY
☎ 01993 / pop 22,765

An attractive market town, Witney built its fortunes on the production of blankets, and the baroque, 18th-century Blanket Hall dominates genteel High St. A cluster of beautiful, old buildings surround the central green, while the 17th-century Buttercross, originally a covered market, stands in Market Sq.

The **TIC** (☎ 775802; witney.tic@westoxon.gov.uk; 26a Market Sq; ☽ 9.30am-5.30pm Mon-Sat Mar-Sep, 10am-4.30pm Mon-Sat Oct-Feb) provides information on local attractions, though the only real one of note is **Cogges Manor Farm Museum** (☎ 772602; www.cogges.org; adult/child £4.40/2.30; ☽ 10.30am-5.30pm Tue-Fri, noon-5.30pm Sat & Sun late Mar-Nov), a 13th-century manor house reconstructed as a working farm. The real draw for children, however, is the domestic farm animals roaming the grounds.

If you'd like to stay, the **Fleece** (☎ 892270; thefleece@peachpubs.com; 11 Church Green; s/d £75/85; P ✗ ; wheelchair access) has sleek, stylish rooms with modern furnishings and muted colours – a joy for anyone seeking a little designer style in the land of floral patterns. The spacious brasserie downstairs offers a good choice of pizza, pasta and modern meat dishes (mains £7 to £13.50).

Swanbrook runs four buses Monday to Saturday (two on Sunday) between Cheltenham (one hour) and Oxford (30 minutes) via Witney. This service also goes to Gloucester (£6.20, 1½ hours) and serves a number of Cotswold towns along the way, including Northleach, Minster Lovell and Burford.

Stagecoach bus No 100 runs from Oxford to Witney every 20 minutes from Monday to Saturday (45 minutes).

MINSTER LOVELL
☎ 01993

Skirting a bend in the meandering River Windrush, a couple of miles west of Witney, this gorgeous little village was one of William Morris' favourite spots in the Cotswolds, and it's not hard to see why. It's an idyllic spot and a wonderful place to start a valley walk.

On the village outskirts are the ruins of **Minster Lovell Hall**, the family home of Viscount Francis Lovell, whose skeletal remains were found inside a secret vault in the house in 1708.

The village makes a very pleasant overnight base, with charming rooms available at **The Mill & Old Swan** (☎ 774441; www.millandold swan-isc.co.uk; s/d £40/60; ℗ ▣), a beautiful stone place on the banks of the river. The Old Swan has creaking old stairs and narrow corridors leading up to charming rooms, while the adjacent Mill is a vast modern conversion decked out in Scandinavian design. You can get decent pub food (£6 to £9) at the Old Swan.

Swanbrook coaches stop here on the Oxford to Cheltenham run (see p355). Stagecoach bus Nos 233 and X3 between Witney and Burford stop here nine times a day, Monday to Saturday (10 minutes each way).

CHIPPING NORTON & AROUND

☎ 01608 / pop 5688

A once-prosperous wool town, Chipping Norton is a sleepy but attractive place with a beautiful market square surrounded by handsome stone houses and half-timbered inns. The secluded **Church of St Mary** has a stunning setting just past a row of beautiful almshouses on Church St. The church itself is a classic example of Cotswold wool churches and has a wonderful 15th-century perpendicular nave. On the outskirts of town on the road to Moreton-in-Marsh, the **Bliss Tweed Mill** is a striking monument to the industrial architecture of the 19th century.

Five miles north of town you'll find the **Hook Norton Brewery** (☎ 737210; www.hooky.co.uk; adult/child £2/1; ☺ 9am-5pm Mon-Fri), an independent family-run Victorian tower brewery still churning out old-fashioned ale with a fascinating 25-horsepower steam engine.

There's plenty of accommodation in the area, including the **Forge** (☎ 658173; theforge@ rushbrooke.co.uk; B4450, Churchill; s/d £45/55; ℗ ✕), a lovely, 200-year-old country house offering top-notch B&B.

For scrumptious food head for the **Tite Inn** (☎ 676475; Mill End, Chadlington; mains £9-14), a beautiful, 17th-century village pub serving an inspired menu and plenty of real ale.

Worth's (☎ 677322; www.worthscoaches.co.uk) bus Nos 70 and 71 run from Oxford to Chipping Norton (one hour) six times a day. Stagecoach No 20 runs every hour Monday to Saturday (80 minutes); on Sunday the X50 does the same route four times (45 minutes).

SOMETHING SPECIAL

Falkland Arms (☎ 01608-683653; www.falkland arms.org.uk; Great Tew; s £65, d £70-80) Time has stood still in the gorgeous village of Great Tew, where a cluster of stunning thatched buildings gathers round the green. The village's 16th-century tavern is no exception and the low ceilings are rippled with oak beams hung with an assortment of mugs and jugs. The floor is original flagstone, the toilet is down the road and there's an atmospheric inglenook fireplace where the smoke masks the smell of wet dogs and wellies. Extensive ranges of real ales and whiskies are on offer as well as such essentials as clay pipes and snuff. Food ranges from interesting baguettes (£4.25) to full Sunday roasts (£8.50). Upstairs the comfortable rooms are set out in period style with exposed beams and iron-frame beds. It doesn't get much more genuine than this.

NORTHLEACH

☎ 01451 / pop 1923

A stunning market town, Northleach is a wonderful mix of architectural styles with a series of late-medieval cottages clustered around the gorgeous market square. The town has perhaps the finest of the wool churches, a masterpiece of the Cotswold perpendicular style, with an unrivalled collection of medieval memorial brasses.

The **TIC** (☎ 860715; Fosse Way), is in the old Northleach House of Correction, once a model 19th-century prison. Also here is the **Cotswold Heritage Centre** (☎ 860715; adult/child £2.50/1; ☺ 10.30am-5pm Mon-Sat, noon-5pm Sun Apr-Oct), fronted by a superb collection of old carts and shepherds' vans. Inside, you can watch some wonderful local films from the 1930s.

Near the square is Oak House, a 17th-century wool house that contains **Keith Harding's World of Mechanical Music** (☎ 860181; www .mechanicalmusic.co.uk; adult/child £5/2.50; ☺ 10am-6pm), where you can hear Rachmaninoff played on a piano roll.

About 4 miles southwest of Northleach is **Chedworth Roman Villa** (NT; ☎ 01242-890256; Yanworth; adult/child £4.10/2; ☺ 10am-5pm Tue-Sun Apr-Oct, 11am-4pm Feb-Mar & Nov), one of the best-exposed Roman villas in England. Built around AD 120 for a wealthy landowner, it contains some wonderful mosaics illustrating the seasons.

If you fancy staying overnight, the 17th-century **Prospect Cottage** (☎ 860875; www.prospect cottage.co.uk; West End; s/d £45/60; ✗) has bright, airy rooms with exposed beams, pine furniture and light linens.

The best bets for sustenance, solid or liquid, are the **Sherborne Arms**, the **Red Lion** and the **Wheatsheaf**, all around Market Sq.

Swanbrook runs four buses Monday to Saturday (two on Sunday) between Cheltenham (30 minutes) and Oxford (one hour) via Northleach.

BOURTON-ON-THE-WATER

☎ 01451 / pop 3093

Exceptionally beautiful and thoroughly over-exposed, Bourton is a tourist trap best seen in the evening when the coachloads have moved on. On a quiet day it's gorgeous, with the River Windrush passing beneath a series of low bridges in the village centre and an array of handsome houses in Cotswold stone lining the narrow lanes.

Not content to let the beauty of the village speak for itself, a series of 'attractions', including a model railway and village, perfume exhibition, maze and motor museum, has opened in town. The most interesting of the lot is **Birdland** (☎ 820480; adult/child £4.85/2.85; ⊙ 10am-5pm Apr-Oct, 10am-3pm Nov-Mar), a serious bird-conservation project.

One of the best-value accommodation options in town is **Trevone** (☎ 805250; www.the -mad-hatter-tearoom.co.uk; Moore Rd; s/d £20/40; Ⓟ), a Cotswold-stone house just a short hop from the village centre with beautiful, bright simple rooms.

For something much more classy head for **Dial House** (☎ 822244; www.dialhousehotel.com; High St; s/d £55/88; ✗), which offers pure luxury at incredible rates. It's one of the best places to stay in the Cotswolds. The rooms are bright and modern and subtly mix traditional, hand-painted wallpaper with contemporary design features, big comfy beds and luxurious linens. The restaurant (lunch mains £8 to £10, dinner mains £16 to £19) should be your first port of call for food and serves up excellent-value modern British cuisine.

Bus Nos 1 & 55 run to Moreton-in-Marsh roughly every 90 minutes between them (Monday to Saturday, 20 minutes).

THE SLAUGHTERS

☎ 01451 / pop 400

Despite their gruesome names these two villages are among the most famously picturesque in the Cotswolds. Every building is worth a photo, but unfortunately they have become a real bottleneck of tourists. If you can, come late in the day and experience the area as it should be in the evening quiet. The villages' names aren't as forbidding as they sound – they derive from the old English 'sloughre', meaning slough.

The best way to get here is to walk from Bourton, just over a mile away. The walk takes roughly an hour along winding paths though meadows to get to Lower Slaughter. If you continue on past the **Victorian flour mill** (adult/child £2/1; ⊙ 10am-6pm Mar-Oct) for another mile (about three quarters of an hour's walk) you'll get to Upper Slaughter.

Accommodation in the Slaughters is exclusive. The 17th-century **Lower Slaughter Manor** (☎ 820456; www.lowerslaughter.co.uk; s £95, d £220-400; Ⓟ ✗) is the kind of place where a decanter of sherry lies waiting for you in your room. Bursting with antique furniture, gilded frames, rich fabrics, log fires and stucco ceilings, it is unashamedly traditional in a frilly kind of way.

In Upper Slaughter the **Lords of the Manor** (☎ 820243; www.lordsofthemanor.com; s £100, d £160-200; Ⓟ ✗) is a 17th-century rectory with secluded gardens (complete with croquet lawn), individual bedrooms and wonderful views. Antique beds, oil paintings, chess sets, antiquarian books, freestanding cast-iron baths and roaring fires make the rooms snug and inviting, while the restaurant overlooking the wonderful grounds serves up more contemporary cuisine (mains £12 to £26).

STOW-ON-THE-WOLD

☎ 01451 / pop 2074

A genuinely elegant town, Stow-on-the-Wold is home to a plethora of antique shops lining the steep-walled alleyways that once funnelled sheep into the handsome market square. Craft shops, teashops and galleries take up any remaining space and sell beautiful and expensive trinkets to the crowds of visitors. A medieval cross at the south of the square was built to remind traders to be honest when brokering deals.

The **TIC** (☎ 831082; Hollis House; ⊙ 10-5pm Mon-Sat) is on Market Sq.

Sleeping & Eating

Stow-on-the-Wold YHA Hostel (☎ 0870 770 6050; www.yha.org.uk; Market Sq; dm £13.40; ☺ Apr-Sep, Fri & Sat only Nov-Feb; ℗ ⌧) Ideally located right in the centre of town, this beautiful 16th-century town house has top-class hostel accommodation in four- to eight-bed dorms. Children are very welcome and there's a play area in the garden.

King's Arms (☎ 830364; www.kingsarms-stow thewold.co.uk; Market St; d £90; ℗ ⌧) A former coaching inn, this 500-year-old hotel is a charming place with exposed stone walls and beams offsetting the contemporary furnishings, CD players and widescreen TVs. The bistro-style restaurant is usually buzzing with punters who come for the imaginative modern dishes (£6 to £12).

Hamiltons Brasserie (☎ 831700; Park St; mains £12-15; ☺ lunch & dinner) Cool urban chic has made it to Stow in the shape of this modern British brasserie with an enviable local reputation. The deep-blue seats, modern art and light tiles give the place sharp, clean lines while the chef turns out excellent specials such as blue-fin tuna with sautéed radicchio and roast artichoke with saffron sauce.

Eagle & Child (☎ 830670; Digbeth St; mains £9.95-12.75; ☺ lunch & dinner) Supposedly the oldest inn in the country, the Eagle and Child and adjoining restaurant, named 947AD, are all exposed beams, polished floors, real ales and old-world charm. The service is wonderful, and the deceptively simple menu, featuring lots of local meat and game, comes up trumps again and again.

SOMETHING SPECIAL

Nestled into a crook in a river, the **Kings Head** (☎ 01608-658365; www.kingsheadinn .net; Bledington; d £ 70-100; ℗) is a gorgeous, timeless 16th-century English inn. The sumptuous rooms are tastefully decorated with light colours, big comfortable beds and period features. The real draw, however, is the food in the traditional bar. Meat and game are sourced locally. Fish arrives daily from Cornwall. The menu (mains £9 to £15) features a fine collection of modern British dishes, good vegetarian options and a serious selection of local and foreign cheeses.

Bledington is on the B4450 5 miles southeast of Stow-on-the-Wold.

Getting There & Away

Pulhams Coaches and Beaumont Travel link Stow with Moreton-in-Marsh (15 minutes, every 90 minutes) Monday to Saturday.

The nearest train stations are 4 miles away at Kingham and Moreton-in-Marsh.

MORETON-IN-MARSH
☎ 01608 / pop 3198

Less assuming and more worklike than other Cotswold towns, Moreton has the best transport connections of the area. On Tuesdays the weekly market overtakes the town in a lively flurry of trading from the 200 or so stalls selling everything from fresh organic produce to fascinating junk.

About 1.5 miles west of Moreton is the spectacular, Mogul-style **Sezincote House** (admission house £6.50, garden adult/child £4.25/1.25; ☺ house 2.30-6pm Thu & Fri May-Jul & Sep, garden 2-6pm Thu-Fri Jan-Nov), built in 1810 by Charles Cockerell and thought to have inspired Brighton Pavilion. Children are not admitted to the house.

If you get stuck overnight the cosy **Acacia** (☎ 650130; 2 New Rd; s/d £25/40; ⌧) is good value, offering homely B&B in a charming Cotswold-stone house. It has simple but comfortable rooms, most with shared bathroom, overlooking a quiet garden.

Getting There & Away

Pulhams Coaches run between Moreton and Cheltenham (12 Monday to Saturday, two on Sunday May to September only, one hour) via Stow-on-the-Wold (15 minutes) and Bourton-on-the-Water (20 minutes).

There are trains roughly every hour to Moreton from London Paddington (£21.20, 1¾ hours) via Oxford (£8.20, 30 minutes) and on to Worcester (£8.90, 40 minutes) and Hereford (£12, 1¼ hours).

CHIPPING CAMPDEN
☎ 01386 / pop 1943

Relatively unspoiled by the tourist hordes, the gently curving main street of Chipping Campden is a real delight. Flanked by a succession of golden-hued terraced houses, each subtly different from the next, it stands in contrast to the equally stunning thatched roofs, clipped hedges and gorgeous gardens of the cottages off the main drag.

The **TIC** (☎ 841206; www.chippingcampden.co.uk; Noel Arms Courtyard; ☺ 10am-5pm Mon-Fri) is off High St. Across the road, the gabled **Market Hall** dates

Churchill Arms (☎ 01386-594000; www.the churchillarms.com; Paxford; s/d £40/70; P) Honest to the core, the Churchill is a seriously unpretentious place with a few very pretty rooms and a passion for good food. There's a motley collection of chairs and tables in the main dining room, menus scrawled on blackboards and a roaring fire in the hearth. The pasta is made in-house, and many dishes successfully team meat or fish with fruit, such as the crispy duck leg confit with roast pears and artichoke purée. Get there early as there is a no-bookings policy.

Paxford is on the B4479 about 5 miles northwest of Moreton-in-Marsh.

from 1627. At the western end is **St James**, a very fine Cotswold wool church with some splendid 17th-century monuments. Nearby are the Jacobean lodges and gateways of the vanished manor house, and a remarkable row of **almshouses**.

Above the town, Dover's Hill is the site of the **Cotswolds Olimpicks**, one of the most entertaining and bizarre sporting competitions in England. Founded in 1612 and reinstated in 1951, the competition includes events such as welly wanging (throwing), the sack race and climbing a slippery pole. The games are held at the beginning of June and run over the spring bank holiday.

Sleeping & Eating

Eight Bells (☎ 840371; www.eightbellsinn.co.uk; Church St; s/d £45/70; ✕) This friendly, 14th-century inn has bright rooms with tasteful décor. The excellent restaurant serves a British and Continental menu (mains £8) in rustic settings with diners spilling out into the sunny courtyard and garden in warm weather.

Kings Arms (☎ 840256; www.thekingsarmshotel .com; The Square; s/d £70/85; P) The good-value rooms at this 300-year-old hotel are bright and spacious, blending the contemporary with period touches. Mood lighting and antique furniture mix with the decidedly modern British fare (mains £9) at the stylish brasserie downstairs.

Cotswold House Hotel (☎ 840330; www.cotswold house.com; The Square; s/d from £110/125; P ✕) Contemporary style reigns at this Regency town house. The classic-chic bedrooms are

luxuriously kitted out with cashmere throws, aromatic sleep sprays and massive bathrooms. The indulgence overflows into Hick's Brasserie downstairs where the slick décor complements the ambitious and highly successful menu (mains £11 to £15).

Getting There & Around

Bus Nos 21, 22 and 522 run hourly to Stratford or Moreton. If you're feeling energetic you can hire a bike from **Cotswold Country Cycles** (☎ 438706; Longlands Farm Cottage; per day/week £12/60).

BROADWAY
☎ 01386 / pop 2496

Villages just don't get much more picturesque than this, and Broadway has inspired writers, artists and composers with its gorgeous buildings and graceful air. Tourists descend upon the place in droves and the village facilitates their cravings for old England with plenty of boutiques, antique shops and overpriced galleries.

The **TIC** (☎ 852937; 1 Cotswold Ct; ☺ 11am-1pm & 2-5pm Mon-Sat) is in a shopping arcade off the northern end of High St.

The lovely, medieval **Church of St Eadburgha** is a signposted 30-minute walk from town. For a longer walk (an uphill 2 miles), take the footpath opposite the church that leads up to **Broadway Tower** (☎ 852390; adult/child £3/2; ☺ 10.30am-5.30pm Apr-Oct, 11am-3pm Sat & Sun Nov-Mar), a crenulated, 18th-century Gothic folly on the crest of an escarpment. It has a small William Morris exhibition on one floor and stunning views from the top.

There's plenty of accommodation in Broadway, though all of it tends to be on the frilly side. Bright, airy rooms make **Milestone House** (☎ 853432; www.milestone-broadway.co .uk; High St; s/d £45/80; P ✕) a good option. The rooms in this 17th-century coaching inn have giant beds, exposed beams and subtle floral décor. Breakfast is particularly generous and children are very welcome.

For something extravagant, you should try the **Lygon Arms** (☎ 852255; www.thelygonarms .com; High St; s £119-159, d £179-495; P ☐ ☒ ; wheelchair access), probably the top hotel in all of the Cotswolds. The antique-strewn bedrooms and barrel-vaulted Great Hall dining room just ooze character and if you're in need of some pampering you can opt for hot stone therapy at the hotel's elegant spa.

There are plenty of teashops serving light snacks around town and most of the pubs serve up innocuous meals. For something slightly better, **Garford's** (☎ 858522; High St; mains £6.50) is a popular option for filling pies and bakes.

Getting There & Away

Bus Nos 21, 21A and 22 go to Moreton-in-Marsh (four daily Monday to Saturday, 20 minutes) and bus No 606 goes to Cheltenham (six daily, Monday to Saturday, 1½ hours).

WINCHCOMBE
☎ 01242

The most important town in the Cotswolds until the Middle Ages, Winchcombe was also the capital of the Saxon kingdom of Mercia. The town has gorgeous old houses, most notably those on Dents Tce and Vineyard St, and the evocative remains of a **Benedictine abbey**, once one of the country's main pilgrimage centres. Also look out for the fine gargoyles on the lovely **St Peter's Church**.

The town's main attraction is **Sudeley Castle** (☎ 604357; www.sudeleycastle.co.uk; adult/child £6.85/3.85; ☼ 10.30am-5.30pm Easter-Oct), once a retreat for Tudor and Stuart monarchs. The chapel houses the tomb of Catherine Parr, Henry VIII's last wife, while the house contains an interesting exhibition on Antarctic explorer Ernest Shackleton as well as paintings by Constable and Turner. Outside, the Queen's Garden is especially beautiful.

The local **TIC** (☎ 602925; www.winchcombe.co.uk; ☼ 10am-5pm Mon-Sat, 10am-4pm Sun Apr-Oct) is on High St.

Sleeping & Eating

White Hart Inn (☎ 602359; www.the-white-hart-inn .com; d £65-125; ✕) Sleek, stylish rooms at this old inn vary in style from warm Moroccan to rustic French Provencal and cool New England. To top off the international theme the restaurant dishes up traditional Swedish food (mains £14 to £17), while the basement pizzeria serves more humble classics for around £8.

Wesley House (☎ 602366; www.wesleyhouse.co.uk; High St; s/d £90/150) This beautiful half-timbered Tudor building has sympathetic rooms with a mix of antique furniture and contemporary furnishings. The restaurant has fantastic mullioned windows with views of Sudeley Castle and serves an excellent three-course French dinner for £35.

5 North St (☎ 604566; 5 North St; 2-course lunch £15.50, 2-course dinner £23.50) This small Michelin-starred establishment has deep-red walls, fine table settings and a winningly unpretentious air. The chef serves up an ambitious selection of classic French and modern British cuisine such as braised pig cheek with parsley mash and sage onion confit.

Getting There & Away

Buses run hourly Monday to Saturday (two on Sunday), from Winchcombe to Cheltenham (25 minutes) or Broadway (40 minutes).

GLOUCESTERSHIRE

Ruddy-cheeked and verdant, pastoral Gloucestershire oozes a mellow, unhurried charm and is much less trampled than many parts of the Cotswolds. Glorious stone villages adorn the rolling hills while elegant Regency townhouses line the graceful streets of sophisticated Cheltenham and a magnificent cathedral soars above the county capital, Gloucester. Further west lies the River Severn and on the border with Wales, the gorgeous Forest of Dean is an excellent area for cycling and walking.

Information

For online information on attractions, accommodation and events see www.visit-glos .org.uk.

Activities

Gloucestershire is perfect for walking and cycling, with plenty of footpaths and quiet roads, gentle gradients and fine pubs for refreshment. TICs stock walking guides and a useful pack called *Cycle Touring Routes in Gloucestershire*.

Compass Holidays (☎ 250642; www.compass-holidays .com) has bicycles for hire for £34 for two days and £64 for a week from Cheltenham train station, and also offers a bag-drop service (£6) and guided cycling tours of the area.

Getting Around

Most TICs stock local bus timetables, or you can phone **Traveline** (☎ 0870 608 2608).

GLOUCESTER

☎ 01452 / pop 123,205

For centuries Gloucester (*glos*-ter) played a strategic role in local history, first as a prestigious retirement home for Roman centurions, then as an important Saxon and Norman town, and in the Middle Ages as a place of pilgrimage after Edward II was buried here. Gloucester's glory days are long gone however, and years of decline have taken their toll. Today it is a rather downmarket town trying to shake off its dowdy image with a new dockland development of bars and restaurants. The real reason for visiting is the magnificent Norman cathedral and exquisite cloister, one of the most stunningly beautiful you'll see anywhere in England.

Orientation & Information

The city centre is based on a medieval cruciform pattern with Northgate, Southgate, Eastgate and Westgate Sts converging on The Cross. The **TIC** (☎ 396572; 28 Southgate St; ☒ 10am-5pm Mon-Sat year-round, plus 11am-3pm Sun Jul-Aug) runs 1½-hour **guided walks** (£2.50; ☒ 2.30pm mid-Jun–mid-Sep) of the historic centre.

Gloucester Library (☎ 426973; Brunswick Rd; ☒ 9.30am-7.30pm Mon, Tue & Thu, 9.30am-5pm Wed & Fri, 9.30am-4pm Sat) has free Internet access.

Sights

GLOUCESTER CATHEDRAL

The city's crowning glory is the magnificent Gothic **Gloucester Cathedral** (☎ 528095; www.gloucestercathedral.org.uk; College Green; admission

£3 donation; ☒ 7.30am-6pm, 7.30am-5pm Sat & Sun), an outstanding example of the English perpendicular style. Originally the site of a Saxon abbey, a church was added by a group of Benedictine monks in the 12th century.

Edward II was buried here after his murder in 1327, and his tomb proved so popular that Gloucester became a centre of pilgrimage. Income generated as a result the church's conversion into the magnificent building visible today.

Inside, the cathedral skilfully combines the best of Norman and Gothic design. The nave has retained much of its original character, from the sturdy columns that lend it an air of gracious solidity, to the wonderful Norman arcading, draped with beautiful mouldings. From the elaborate 14th-century wooden choir stalls, you can view the imposing eastern window, the largest in England. The window commemorates local participation in the Battle of Crecy.

You can take a closer look from the tribune gallery, where there is an **exhibition** (admission £2; ☒ 10.30am-4pm Mon-Fri, 10.30am-3pm Sat) on the cathedral's history and the making of the window. Here you'll also hear the wonderful effects of the whispering gallery: you can hear even the quietest of murmurs across the wonderfully elaborate lierne vaulting that spiders across the ceiling. Beneath the window in the northern ambulatory is Edward II's magnificent tomb. Nearby the late–15th-century **lady chapel** is a glorious patchwork of stained glass.

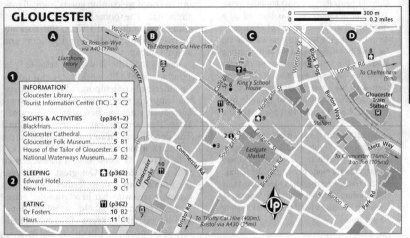

GLOUCESTER

0 — 300 m
0 — 0.2 miles

INFORMATION
Gloucester Library..................1 C2
Tourist Information Centre (TIC)..2 C2

SIGHTS & ACTIVITIES (pp361–2)
Blackfriars.............................3 C2
Gloucester Cathedral................4 C1
Gloucester Folk Museum............5 B1
House of the Tailor of Gloucester.6 C1
National Waterways Museum.....7 B2

SLEEPING (p362)
Edward Hotel..........................8 D1
New Inn.................................9 C2

EATING (p362)
Dr Fosters..............................10 B2
Haus....................................11 C1

To Ross-on-Wye via A40 (17mi)
To Enterprise Car Hire (1mi)
Llanthony Priory
Westgate St
Severn
King's School House
College Green
Westgate St
Worcester St
Black Dog Way
London Rd
To Cheltenham (9mi)
Gloucester Train Station
Northgate St
Burton Way
Bus Station
Eastgate St
Eastgate Market
Commercial Rd
Southgate St
Brunswick Rd
Metz Way
To Cirencester (16mi); London (105mi)
Gloucester Docks
Bristol Rd
To Thrifty Car Hire (400m); Bristol via A430 (35mi)
Barton St
Park Rd

The **Great Cloister**, which was completed in 1367, is the first example of fan vaulting in England and is only matched in beauty by Henry VIII's Chapel at Westminster Abbey. You (or your children) might recognise the cloister from the Harry Potter films: it was used in the corridor scenes at Hogwart's School.

You can get fabulous views of Gloucester from the 225ft **tower** (tours adult/child £2.50/1; ☽ 2.30pm Wed-Fri, 1.30pm & 2.30pm Sat & bank holidays). There are free guided **tours** (☽ 10.30am-4pm Mon-Sat, noon-2.30pm Sun) of the cathedral.

OTHER SIGHTS

Once Britain's largest inland port, **Gloucester Docks** (www.glosdocks.co.uk) lay derelict for many years, but now many of the beautiful Victorian warehouses have been restored and refurbished.

The most interesting of these is Llanthony, the largest warehouse. It houses the excellent **National Waterways Museum** (☎ 318054; www.nwm.org.uk; adult/child £5/4; ☽ 10am-5pm), which charts the history of the local waterways and has a varied collection of historic vessels.

Another worthwhile attraction is the **Gloucester Folk Museum** (☎ 396467; 99 Westgate St; admission £2; ☽ 10am-5pm Tue-Sat), housed in a series of wonderful Tudor and Jacobean timber-framed buildings that date from the 16th and 17th centuries. The museum

---

THE TAILOR OF GLOUCESTER

One of Beatrix Potter's most famous stories, *The Tailor of Gloucester*, was inspired by a real-life tailor, John Prichard of Gloucester. As in her tale, the waistcoat he was making for the city's mayor was only at the cutting stage on the Saturday before the Monday when the garment was due. When he returned to the shop on Monday, he found the waistcoat complete, bar a single buttonhole. A note pinned to it read, 'No more twist'.

Mystified (but commercially minded), he placed a note in his window encouraging people to come in and see the place where 'waistcoats are made at night by the fairies'. It later transpired that the tailor's assistants had finished the waistcoat after kipping in the shop because they'd stayed out too late to get home.

---

showcases local history, domestic life, crafts and industries from 1500 to the present.

Also worth a look is **Blackfriars** (Ladybellgate St; admission free; ☽ tours 3pm Sun Jul & Aug), Britain's finest surviving example of a 13th-century Dominican priory.

Fans of Beatrix Potter will love the **House of the Tailor of Gloucester** (☎ 422856; www.hop-skip-jump.com; admission £1; ☽ 10am-5pm Mon-Sat Apr-Oct, 10am-4pm Nov-Mar), off Westgate St, established in the shop that inspired the story of the same name.

Festivals & Events

The **Three Choirs Festival** (www.3choirs.org), an event shared with Hereford and Worcester Cathedrals, is held at the cathedral every three years. Gloucester is the 2007 festival host.

Sleeping & Eating

Gloucester has a dismal choice of hotels and you may want to consider staying in Cheltenham instead.

Edward Hotel (☎ 525865; www.edwardhotel-gloucester.co.uk; 88-92 London Rd; s/d £40/60; P ✗) This Victorian town house near the train station is one of the best options in town, with bright, newly renovated rooms. The décor mixes the old with the new and manages to avoid being too fussy. Children are very welcome.

New Inn (☎ 522177; www.newinnglos.com; 16 Northgate St; s/d £45/80; ✗) One of the most atmospheric places in town, this medieval galleried inn has been welcoming guests from all over since 1455. The rooms have dark-wood panelling and traditional styling, but go a little over the top on the floral patterns and stripy wallpaper.

Haus (☎ 525359; 56 Westgate; mains £8.50-16; ☽ lunch & dinner) This sleek restaurant does a fine menu of contemporary European cuisine featuring specialities such as Gressingham duck with poached pear and caramel, as well as some Asian-influenced dishes. The décor is all clean lines, sultry leathers and dark wood.

Dr Fosters (☎ 300990; Kimberly Warehouse; mains £9-15; ☽ lunch & dinner) Get great views over the docks from a deep leather sofa at this brasserie and wine bar in a renovated warehouse. The menu dabbles in international fusion food but also keeps a firm eye on traditional European and British favourites.

Getting There & Away

National Express has buses every two hours to London (£14.50, 3½ hours) and four times daily to Monmouth (£3, 1½ hours) on the Welsh border. Buses to Chepstow and Cardiff run via Bristol. Bus No 94 runs to Cheltenham every 10 minutes (30 minutes), but the quickest way to get there is by train (every 20 minutes, 10 minutes).

FOREST OF DEAN
☎ 01594

An undisturbed backwater, the lovely Forest of Dean was the first National Forest Park in England. Formerly a royal hunting ground and centre of iron and coal mining, this tract of forest covers a 42-sq-mile swathe between Gloucester, Ross-on-Wye and Chepstow. JRR Tolkien was a regular visitor and the forest is said to have inspired the setting for *The Lord of the Rings*. A web of well-maintained trails now covers the area and makes it an excellent place for walking and cycling.

Coleford is the Forest of Dean's main town, with good bus connections to Gloucester making it a convenient base for touring the area. In the south the magnificent youth hostel near Lydney makes a fantastic base, with regular trains back to the city from nearby Lydney Junction.

The main **TIC** (☎ 812388; www.forestofdean.gov.uk; High St, Coleford; ☯ 10am-4pm Mon-Fri, 10am-2pm Sat) stocks walking and cycling guides and also books accommodation (free). If you're driving, pick up a copy of the *Royal Forest Route*, a leaflet describing the 20-mile circular drive passing forest highlights.

Sights & Activities

Your first stop in the area should be the **Dean Heritage Centre** (☎ 822170; www.deanheritage museum.com; Camp Mill, Soudley; admission £4.50; ☯ 10am-5.30pm Apr-Sep, 10am-4pm Feb, Mar & Oct) near Cinderford. The museum tells the history of the forest and its free miners from medieval times to the industrial age of iron and coal.

In contrast to the museum, **Puzzle Wood** (☎ 833187; adult/child £3.25/2.25; ☯ 11am-5.30pm Tue-Sun Mar-Sep, 11am-4pm Feb & Oct) is a pre-Roman, open-cast ore mine which has been allowed to grow over. It is an extraordinary area with a maze of paths, eerie passageways through moss-covered rocks, hidden dead ends, weird rock formations, tangled vines and gorgeous untamed scenery. It's a brilliant place for children. Puzzle Wood is 1 mile south of Coleford on the B4228.

Mined since the Iron Age, **Clearwell Caves** (☎ 832535; www.clearwellcaves.com; adult/child £4/2.50; ☯ 10am-5pm Mar-Oct) is a warren of dank, spooky caves littered with vestiges of the mining era as well as shimmering pools and wonderful rock formations. Special events take place at major holiday periods with an underground rave at Halloween followed by a magical grotto in time for Christmas. The caves are signposted off the B4228 a mile south of Coleford.

The pretty village of **Newland** is worth a visit to see the 13th-century **All Saints,** the so-called 'Cathedral of the Forest'. It was restored and partially rebuilt in the 19th century and houses some fine stained-glass windows as well as a unique brass depicting a miner with a *nelly* (tallow candle) in his mouth, a pick in his hand and a *billy* (backpack) on his back.

Sleeping & Eating

St Briavels Castle YHA Hostel (☎ 0870 770 6040; www.yha.org.uk; Lydney; dm £11.80; P ☒) Probably the most impressive youth hostel in the country, this imposing, moated place was once a hunting lodge used by King John. The dorms have four to eight beds and are pretty unique. If you're around in August it's well worth staying for a medieval banquet (Wednesday and Saturday).

Forest House Hotel (☎ 832424; www.forest-house-hotel.co.uk; Cinder Hill, Coleford; s/d £40/70; P ☒) Beautiful, bright, modern rooms and excellent food (mains £8 to £12) make this restored 18th-century house a good option. The rooms are spacious and chintz-free, with colourful furnishings and good bathrooms.

Cider Press (☎ 54472; The Cross, Drybrook; mains £9-17; ☯ lunch Fri-Sun, dinner Wed-Sat) A gourmet oasis, this popular restaurant is an elegant, intimate place just north of Cinderford. The chef serves up delicious seafood, game and organic meats from a classic French menu with some contemporary twists. You need to book ahead.

Getting There & Around

From Gloucester, bus No 31 runs to Coleford every 15 minutes (one hour) and trains run to Lydney Junction (20 minutes) eight times daily. The **Dean Forest Railway** (☎ 843423; www.deanforestrailway.co.uk) runs steam trains from Lydney to Whitecroft (adult/child return £6.50/4.50) from March to October. Call or check the website for days of service.

You can hire bikes, buy maps and get advice on cycling routes at **Pedalabikeaway** (☎ 860065; www.pedalabikeaway.com; Cannop Valley, nr Coleford; bikes per day £12).

CHELTENHAM

☎ 01242 / pop 98,875

Elegant, refined and exclusive, Britain's most popular spa town revels in its gracious air and period charm and makes a stylish base from which to investigate the surrounding area. It's an undeniably lovely and sophisticated place with beautifully proportioned terraces, wrought-iron balconies and leafy crescents sheltering expensive boutiques and gourmet restaurants. Despite its grand and conservative air, the nightlife is good and an increasing number of festivals give it some cosmopolitan flavour.

History

Cheltenham was just another Cotswolds town until 1716, when it was discovered that pecking pigeons were eating salt crystals from a spring. It quickly developed into the definitive spa, a rival to its more illustrious sibling Bath. The town began attracting the sick and hypochondriac in ever-increasing numbers but a visit by George III in 1788 sealed the spa's future and new wells were built, as well as houses to accommodate the many visitors, among them Handel and Jane Austen.

Orientation

Cheltenham train station is out on a limb to the west; bus D or E will transport you to the town centre for 90p. The bus station is behind the Promenade in the town centre.

Central Cheltenham is easily walkable. The High St runs roughly east–west; south from it is the Promenade, a more elegant shopping area, which extends into Montpellier, the most exclusive part of town. Pittville Park and the old Pump Room are approximately a mile north of High St.

Information

All the major banks and the main post office can be found on High St.

Cheltenham Main Library (☎ 532688; Clarence St; ⌚ 9.30am-7pm Mon, Wed & Fri, 9.30am-5.30pm Tue & Thu, 9.30am-4pm Sat) Free Internet access.

Cheltenham Spa (www.visitcheltenham.info) The city's tourism website with information on everything from accommodation to attractions.

Equals (☎ 237292; 287 High St; Internet access per 30 min £2)

TIC (☎ 522878; 77 Promenade; ⌚ 9.30am-5.15pm Mon-Sat) Stocks Cotswold walking and cycling guides, as well as *The Romantic Road*, a guide to a 30-mile circular driving tour of the southern Cotswolds. It also runs a free accommodation service.

Sights

THE PROMENADE

The Promenade is the heart of Cheltenham and is at its best in summer, when its hanging baskets are full of flowers. The **municipal offices**, built as private residences in 1825, are among the best features of one of Britain's most beautiful thoroughfares. Following the Promenade towards Montpellier, you come to the **Imperial Gardens**, built to service the Imperial Spa.

PITTVILLE PUMP ROOM

Set in a delightful area of villas and parkland a mile from the town centre, the **Pittville Pump Room** (☎ 523852; Pittville Park; admission free; ⌚ 11am-4pm Wed-Mon) is the town's finest Regency building. Built between 1825 and 1830, it was constructed as a spa and social centre for Joseph Pitt's new estate. Upstairs there are occasional art exhibitions and downstairs (where you can still taste the spa water if you wish) the former ballroom is now used for concerts. The park itself is also used for Sunday concerts throughout the summer.

ART GALLERY & MUSEUM

Cheltenham's history is imaginatively displayed at the **Art Gallery & Museum** (☎ 237431; www.cheltenhammuseum.org.uk; Clarence St; admission free; ⌚ 10am-5.20pm Mon-Sat), which has excellent sections covering Edward Wilson William Morris and the Arts and Crafts movement, not to mention Dutch and British art as well. There is a temporary exhibition gallery located on the museum's ground floor.

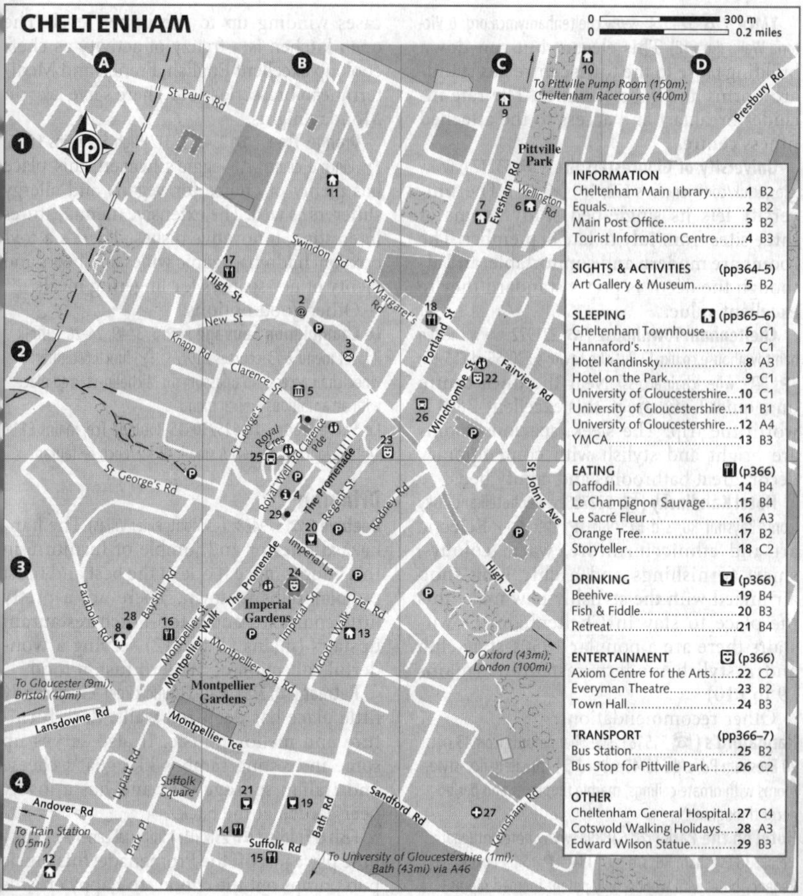
CHELTENHAM
0 300 m
0 0.2 miles
A
B
C
D
1
2
3
4
To Pittville Pump Room (150m); Cheltenham Racecourse (400m)
Prestbury Rd
St Paul's Rd
Pittville Park
Evesham Rd
Wellington Rd
Swindon Rd
High St
New St
Knapp Rd
Clarence St
St Margaret's Rd
Portland St
Fairview Rd
Winchcombe St
St George's Pl
Royal Cres
Royal Well Rd
Clarence Pde
The Promenade
Regent St
Rodney Rd
St George's Rd
St John's Ave
Imperial La
Imperial Gardens
Imperial Sq
Oriel Rd
High St
Parabola Rd
Bayshill Rd
Montpellier St
Montpellier Walk
Montpellier Spa Rd
Victoria Walk
To Oxford (43mi); London (100mi)
To Gloucester (9mi); Bristol (40mi)
Montpellier Gardens
Lansdowne Rd
Montpellier Tce
Lypiatt Rd
Suffolk Square
Andover Rd
To Train Station (0.5mi)
Park Pl
Suffolk Rd
Bath Rd
Sandford Rd
Keynsham Rd
To University of Gloucestershire (1mi); Bath (43mi) via A46
INFORMATION
Cheltenham Main Library 1 B2
Equals 2 B2
Main Post Office 3 B2
Tourist Information Centre 4 B3
SIGHTS & ACTIVITIES (pp364–5)
Art Gallery & Museum 5 B2
SLEEPING (pp365–6)
Cheltenham Townhouse 6 C1
Hannaford's 7 C1
Hotel Kandinsky 8 A3
Hotel on the Park 9 C1
University of Gloucestershire 10 C1
University of Gloucestershire 11 B1
University of Gloucestershire 12 A4
YMCA 13 B3
EATING (p366)
Daffodil 14 B4
Le Champignon Sauvage 15 B4
Le Sacré Fleur 16 A3
Orange Tree 17 B2
Storyteller 18 C2
DRINKING (p366)
Beehive 19 B4
Fish & Fiddle 20 B3
Retreat 21 B4
ENTERTAINMENT (p366)
Axiom Centre for the Arts 22 C2
Everyman Theatre 23 B2
Town Hall 24 B3
TRANSPORT (pp366–7)
Bus Station 25 B2
Bus Stop for Pittville Park 26 C2
OTHER
Cheltenham General Hospital 27 C4
Cotswold Walking Holidays 28 A3
Edward Wilson Statue 29 B3

CHELTENHAM RACECOURSE

On Cheltenham's northern outskirts is one of the country's top courses, which attracts 40,000 punters a day in March for an event known simply as The Festival (see below). At other times it's worth a trip for the **Hall of Fame museum** (☎ 513014; admission free; 🕑 8.30am-5.30pm Mon-Fri), which charts the history of steeplechasing since 1819.

Festivals & Events

The Festival is the highlight of the National Hunt racing calendar. For five days in March half of Ireland decamps to Cheltenham and thousands of race enthusiasts turn out for England's premier steeplechase event. Even if you're not prone to a flutter on the gee gees, it's well worth experiencing the passion and atmosphere of a big day at The Festival. Tickets (about £25) can be booked by calling ☎ 226226.

Cheltenham also hosts a **jazz festival** in late April and early May. Bookworms come out in October for the **literature festival**.

Tours

Walking tours (£2.50; 1¼ hr; 🕑 11am Jun-Sep) of Regency Cheltenham depart from the TIC.

Sleeping

Cheltenham has a good choice of hotels but book early if you're coming for any of the festivals. Montpellier, southwest of the town centre, is the best spot for good B&Bs.

YMCA (☎ 524024; www.cheltenhamymca.org; 6 Victoria Walk; dm £18) This elegant but run-down building close to the town centre has standard dorms and good facilities. The rate includes breakfast and access to the attached fitness centre.

University of Gloucestershire (☎ 532774; www .glos.ac.uk/conferences; s £22; P ✗ ▢) The university lets its single-bed study rooms at three sites from July to late September. The rooms are modern and comfortable, and although the décor is pretty standard they're excellent value.

Cheltenham Townhouse (☎ 221922; www.chelten hamtownhouse.co.uk; 12 Pittville Lawn; s £30-55, d £55-95; P ▢ ; wheelchair access) Near the town centre on a quiet leafy street, this excellent B&B is worth the trip. The sleek, spacious rooms are bright and stylish with contemporary décor, great bathrooms and comfy beds.

Hotel Kandinsky (☎ 527788; www.hotelkandinsky .com; Bayshill Rd; s/d £75/90; P ✗ ▣) Eclectic art and ethnic furniture, warm colours, smart furnishings and a chic junk-shop air mixed with the stylishly new make this *the* place to stay in Cheltenham. Downstairs there are a popular 1950s-style club and a stylish modern restaurant (mains £9 to £10).

Other recommendations:

Hannaford's (☎ 515181; sue@hannafords.icom43.net; 20 Evesham Rd; s/d £40/45; P ✗) True Regency-style rooms with ornate ceilings, marble fireplaces and period décor throughout.

Hotel on the Park (☎ 518898; www.hotelonthepark .co.uk; 38 Evesham Rd; s/d £97/134; P ✗) Luxurious Regency hotel with wonderfully potent themed rooms featuring extravagant décor.

Eating

Cheltenham has an excellent range of places to eat and something to suit everyone's taste and budget.

Storyteller (☎ 250343; 11 North Pl; mains £6-15; ☽ lunch & dinner) This buzzing eatery has a small restaurant area and a large heated conservatory and serves up an extensive menu of hearty meals to the masses. The food spans the globe, from Californian kitchen to Mexican, Mediterranean and Asian dishes including seafood, pastas and game.

Daffodil (☎ 700055; 18-20 Suffolk Pde; mains £12-20, 2-course lunch £10; ☽ lunch & dinner; wheelchair access) This former cinema now houses a dramatic Art Deco restaurant with two elegant staircases winding up to the upper level. The open kitchen is a frenzy of activity as chefs cook up excellent English, French and Mediterranean brasserie food. There's live jazz on Monday nights.

Orange Tree (☎ 234232; 317 High St; mains £8-15; ☽ lunch & dinner) A veggie's heaven, this place has plenty of choice for vegans and allergy sufferers as well. The extensive menu features interesting, innovative dishes. There's a toybox for children, organic wines and beers and plenty of newspapers for lingering meals.

Other good options:

Le Champignon Sauvage (☎ 573449; 24-26 Suffolk Rd; set menu 2-/3-courses £19/23; ☽ lunch & dinner; wheelchair access) An unassuming Michelin-starred place with an ambitious French menu.

Le Sacré Fleur (☎ 525230; 15 Rotunda Tce; mains £11-14; ☽ lunch & dinner) A small, slick French restaurant.

Drinking

Beehive (☎ 579443; 1-3 Montpellier Villas) The haphazard interior and jumble of furniture in this boozer make it one of the best and most popular pubs in town. There are a pretty little courtyard and a top-notch restaurant upstairs (mains £8 to £12) serving a wonderful collection of modern fusion food.

Retreat (☎ 235436; 10-11 Suffolk Pde) This trendy little place has deep-red walls, dark furniture and mellow music. It also serves up some interesting sambos like goat's cheese and Italian sausage (£6) and has a lovely beer garden at the back.

Fish & Fiddle (☎ 238001; 1 Imperial Lane) A funky little place just off the Promenade, this music pub pumps out the choons to happy crowds who pour in at weekends. Friday night is a mix of drum'n'bass and hip-hop, and on Saturday night it's funk, soul and jazz.

Entertainment

Everyman Theatre (☎ 572573; Regent St) stages anything from comedy and panto to Shakespeare. The **Pittville Pump Room** often hosts classical-music concerts, while the **Town Hall** (☎ 227979; Imperial Sq) offers the more popular stuff. The **Axiom Centre for the Arts** (☎ 690243; 57 Winchcombe St) has a regular programme of less mainstream theatrical events and music.

Getting There & Away
BUS

National Express runs bus services to London roughly hourly (£14.50, three hours).

Swanbrook Coaches has three buses to Oxford Monday to Saturday and one on Sunday (£6.20, 1½ hours).

Bus No 94 runs to Gloucester every 10 minutes (30 minutes) Monday to Saturday, and every 20 minutes on Sunday. Bus No 51 goes to Cirencester hourly (30 minutes).

Pulhams P1 bus runs to Moreton (one hour) via Bourton and Stow six times daily Monday to Saturday. Castleways Coaches run regularly to Broadway (45 minutes) via Winchcombe (20 minutes), Monday to Saturday. Stagecoach bus No 164 does the same journey four times on Sunday.

TRAIN

Cheltenham has hourly trains to London (£32, 2½ hours), Bristol (£7.50, 45 minutes), Bath (£11.50, one hour), and regular departures for Gloucester (£2.60, 10 minutes).

Getting Around

Compass Holidays (☎ 250642; www.compass-holidays .com; per day £17) has bicycles for hire at the train station.

TEWKESBURY

☎ 01684 / pop 9978

Buckled, timber-framed buildings line the main street and wonderful alleys of Tudor-heavy Tewkesbury, an attractive but depressed town that can get choked with traffic. Church St, Mill St and Mill Bank are particularly worth exploring.

The **TIC** (☎ 295027; www.tewkesburybc.gov.uk; Barton St; 9.30am-5pm Mon-Sat, 9.30-4pm Sun) has lots of information and a small museum upstairs. If you're visiting at the end of May ask about the Coopers Hill cheese-rolling competition, a 200-year-old tradition that sees locals chase seven-pound blocks of Double Gloucester cheese down the hill.

The town's focal point is the magnificent **Tewkesbury Abbey** (☎ 850959; www.tewkesburyabbey .org.uk; admission £2 donation; 7.30am-6pm), one of Britain's largest churches and the last of the monasteries to be dissolved by Henry VIII. Begun in the 12th century, the cathedral has a massive 40m-high tower and some spectacular Norman pillars lining the nave. Other highlights include the 14th-century stained glass above the choir and an organ dating from 1631. The magnificent tombs of the wealthy wool traders are also worth a look, as is that of John Wakeman, the last abbot, who is shown as a vermin-ridden skeleton. A **visitors centre** (10am-4pm Mon-Sat), by the gate, houses an exhibition on the abbey's history.

If you'd like to stay, **Carrant Brook House** (☎ 290355; www.carrantbrookhouse.co.uk; 3 Rope Walk; s/d £30/50; P) has good-value, simple, bright rooms and a lovely patio area. Alternatively, the **Royal Hop Pole** (☎ 293236; www .corushotels.com; Church St; s/d £75/100; P), one of the oldest inns in town, has elegant period-style rooms, and a delightful garden leading down to the river. The restaurant serves up a decent array of traditional and modern British food (mains £11 to £15).

Another good bet for food is **Aubergine** (☎ 292703; 73 Church St; mains £7.95-10.95; lunch & dinner), an elegant café bar serving new-world fusion cuisine – a welcome respite from the Tewkesbury norm.

Getting There & Away

Bus No X94 from Gloucester goes to Tewkesbury hourly (30 minutes). The nearest train station is at Ashchurch, 3 miles away.

The Marches

CONTENTS

Lush hills, rolling farmland and the simple pleasures of country living characterise life on the edge of England, although it was once the battleground of ferocious warriors and brutal landlords. This strip of country flanking the Wales–England border is alive with history, and littered with castles and ruins.

In medieval times trade across the border helped build handsome market towns such as the Tudor gem of Shrewsbury in Shropshire, while further south a gorgeous string of black-and-white villages was taking shape in Herefordshire. Impressive cathedrals shot up in Worcester and Hereford, the latter most famous for the marvellous 13th-century Mappa Mundi. By the 18th century manufacturing quotas had replaced religious fervour, and Ironbridge Gorge was forging its way as the birthplace of the Industrial Revolution.

But you needn't be a history buff to appreciate this area: pretty towns and villages are scattered throughout the hills from the genteel Victorian resort of Great Malvern to the gourmet hub of Ludlow. Outside the main centres the timeless rural scenery has a wonderful understated charm and a fascinating blend of Welsh and English character.

Despite the wealth of attractions, the Marches are squarely off the beaten track, the pace of life is unhurried, and in many places time and tourism seem to have passed by unnoticed. One of the greatest pleasures of this region is just to meander along the country lanes, visit the cider orchards and take a peek at authentic rural life in modern Britain. For the more energetic, the placid peaks of the south Shropshire and Malvern Hills make excellent walking and cycling territory and to the south the stunning scenery along the River Wye makes it ideal for canoeing.

HIGHLIGHTS

- Strolling around the atmospheric streetscapes of **Shrewsbury** (p383), England's most picturesque Tudor town

- Stepping back through time at **Ironbridge Gorge** (p385), the cradle of the Industrial Revolution

- Rambling through the gentle hills and tranquil valleys of Shropshire's **Long Mynd** (p390)

- Navigating the extraordinary 13th-century **Mappa Mundi** (p377) at Hereford Cathedral

- Taking in the stunning views and water adventures on the River Wye at **Symonds Yat** (p380)

- Dining in style in the Marches' gourmet capital, **Ludlow** (p392)

- Admiring the soaring nave, medieval manuscripts and tower views of **Worcester Cathedral** (p372)

- POPULATION: 1 MILLION
- AREA: 2541 SQ MILES

THE MARCHES

THE MARCHES

0 _____ 20 km
0 _____ 12 miles

Clwydian Ranges
Mold
Buckley
Tarporley
CHESHIRE
Sandbach
To Manchester
Congleton
A523
Leek
Ruthin
Chirk Castle
Farndon
Broxton
Crewe
M6
A34
Brymbo
Wrexham
Nantwich
Newcastle-under-Lyme
Stoke-on-Trent
Longton
Cheadle
Ashbourne
Eglwyseg
Erddig
Dee
A41
Audlem
DERBYSHIRE
Glyndyfrdwy
Ruabon
Whitchurch
M6
Uttoxeter
Llangollen
Froncysyllte
Chirk
Stone
A50
Chirk Castle
Ellesmere
Market Drayton
Eccleshall
STAFFORDSHIRE
Rhydycroesau
Oswestry
Llangollen Canal
Hawkstone Park
Tern Hill
Wollerton
Gnosall
To Burton-upon-Trent
Burlton
Wem
Hodnet Hall
Stafford
Yoxall
Tanat
Cain
A5
Harmerhill
Perry
Roden
Newport
Penkridge
Colwich
A38
Vyrnwy
Meifod
Severn
Battlefield
A518
A41
Gailey
Cannock
Lichfield
Welshpool
Shrewsbury
Telford
A5
Tamworth
Museum of Sculpture
Stiperstones
Atcham
Wroxeter
Ironbridge Gorge
Albrighton
M6
Berriew
Much Wenlock
Norton
Wolverhampton
Walsall
Montgomery
Church Stoke
The Long Mynd
Worfield
Himley
Dudley
Sutton Coldfield
Lydham
All Stretton
Church Stretton
Longville-in-the-Dale
Bridgnorth
Birmingham
Coleshill
Marshbrook
Wenlock Edge
Stourbridge
Birmingham Airport
Llanfair Waterdine
Clun
Craven Arms
Stokesay Castle
Cleobury Mortimer
Bewdley
Kidderminster
Halesowen
Shirley
Solihull
M42
Knighton
Ludlow
SHROPSHIRE
Stourport-on-Severn
Bromsgrove
Hockley Heath
M40
Elton
Tenbury Wells
Great Witley
Ombersley
Droitwich Spa
Redditch
Henley
To Banbury
Aymestry
Croft Castle
Tome
Witley Court
Droitwich
M5
Cook Hill
Titley
Eardisland
Pudleston
HEREFORDSHIRE & WORCESTER
Broadheath Common
A422
Stratford-upon-Avon
Pembridge
Leominster
A44
Bromyard
Worcester
WARWICKSHIRE
Kington
Ullingswick
Great Malvern
Kempsey
Pershore
Evesham
Willersley
Malvern Hills
Upton-upon-Severn
A38
Chipping Campden
Hay-on-Wye
A4103
Broadway
Llanigon
Dore
Golden Valley
Hereford
Ledbury
Eastnor Castle
M50
Tewkesbury
Moreton
Olasbury
Talgarth
Kilpeck
Much Marcle
Hellen's House
Waun Fach
Llanthony
Pontrilas
Wye
Ross-on-Wye
A40
Stow-on-the-Wold
Brecon Beacons National Park
Sugar Loaf
Llanfihangel Crucorney
Goodrich
Mitcheldean
Huntley
Gloucester
A40
Tretower
Llandewi Skirrid
Symonds Yat
Westbury
A40
North Leach
Crickhowell
Brecon Canal
Abergavenny
Cinderford
Newnham
Painswick
GLOUCESTERSHIRE
Govilon
Monmouth
Usk
Ebbw Vale
Raglan Castle
Raglan
Stroud
Tredegar
Lydney
M5
Cirencester
Fairford
Abertillery
Tintern Abbey
Severn
Nailsworth
Lechlade
Rhymney
Bargoed
Pontypool
Tintern
To Worcester
Blackwood

THE MARCHES

History

Territorial scuffles and all-out battles raged for centuries between feuding kingdoms along what is now the England–Wales border. In the 8th century, the Anglo-Saxon king Offa of Mercia built an earthwork barricade along the border to try to quell the tension. It was known as Offa's Dyke, and much of it is still traceable as a popular walking route today (see Walking, below).

In an effort to subdue the Welsh and secure his new kingdom, William the Conqueror set up feudal barons along the border. They were called Lords Marcher after the Anglo-Saxon word *mearc,* meaning boundary. From here they repeatedly raided Wales, taking as much territory as possible under their control. Ten centuries later, the counties of Shropshire, Herefordshire and Worcestershire are still known as the Marches.

Activities

The Marches region is perfect for gentle walking, cycling and other outdoor activities, with hundreds of miles of paths and tracks snaking through pastoral idylls, wooded valleys and gentle hills. This section provides a few ideas; see Outdoor Activities (p74) for more information.

CYCLING

Many parts of the Marches make good cycling country. Shropshire is ideal for touring, and you can rent bikes in Shrewsbury, Church Stretton, Ludlow and Ledbury. *Cycling for Pleasure in the Marches,* available from Tourist Information Centres (TICs), has comprehensive route maps and notes.

Off-road riding areas include the woods of Hopton near Ludlow, and Eastridge near Shrewsbury. High-level riding on the Long Mynd above Church Stretton (p390) is also rewarding. In Herefordshire, the **Ledbury Loop** is a 17-mile rural circuit based on the town of Ledbury.

WALKING

The best-known long-distance walk in this region is **Offa's Dyke**, a 177-mile national trail that follows the ancient border defence. Running south–north from Chepstow (south Wales) to Prestatyn (north Wales), it passes through some of the most spectacular scenery in Britain, but it's not for the inexperienced or unfit.

A more gentle option is the 107-mile **Wye Valley Walk**, which also starts in Chepstow and follows the River Wye upstream to Rhayader in Wales. Other favourites include the 100-mile **Three Choirs Way**, which links the cathedral cities of Hereford, Worcester and Gloucester, and the **Severn Way** route, through Worcester and Upton-upon-Severn.

Areas ideal for shorter walks include the Shropshire Hills, with the well-known ridges of Wenlock Edge (p390) and the lovely Long Mynd (p390) taken in by the 136-mile **Shropshire Way**, which loops from Shrewsbury south to Ludlow. The region's other main walking area is the **Malvern Hills** (see p375), which straddle the boundary between Worcestershire and Herefordshire, offering easy paths and breathtaking views.

OTHER ACTIVITIES

Symonds Yat on the River Wye makes a perfect base for canoeing (either easy-grade white-water, or longer river trips), while rocky buttresses above the river mean rock climbing is also popular. Further north, the Long Mynd is a renowned area for gliding and paragliding.

Getting Around

Without your own transport, getting around the Marches can be infuriating. Exploring rural attractions needs time, planning and patience. TICs stock timetables for most rural routes, or call **Traveline** (☎ 0870 608 2608; www.traveline.org.uk).

Railway lines radiate from Shrewsbury, Hereford and Worcester, but they only serve the largest towns.

The main bus operators:

Arriva (☎ 08701 201 088) An Arriva day ticket (£3.75) gives one day of unlimited travel.

First Travel (☎ 01905-359393) A First Tourist ticket (adult/child £4.60/3.10) offers the same deal as Arriva but on the First network.

WORCESTERSHIRE

A county of remarkable contrasts, Worcestershire marks the faultline between the bucolic idyll of rural England and the industrial sprawl of the Midlands. The flat plains of the north and east of the county offer little in the way of attractions, but the beauty of the undulating Malvern Hills to the south was enough to inspire Sir Edward Elgar's *Enigma Variations*. The hills offer wonderful walking opportunities and are home to the genteel Victorian resort of Great Malvern. Right in the centre is the regional capital, Worcester, with a magnificent cathedral and some beautiful Elizabethan and Tudor architecture.

Information

For online countywide information try www .worcestershire-tourism.co.uk.

Activities

The **Severn Way** walking route winds its way through Worcestershire, passing through Worcester and Upton-upon-Severn, while the **Three Choirs Way** links Worcester to Hereford and Gloucester.

Cyclists should pick up the handy leaflet *Elgar Ride Variations* (35p) from TICs. It has a choice of routes around the Malverns.

Getting Around

Regular train links are thin on the ground. Kidderminster is the southern railhead of the popular Severn Valley Railway.

The **Wye Valley Wanderer** (☎ 01432-260948) links Pershore and Worcester with Ledbury, Ross-on-Wye and Hereford on summer Sundays and bank-holiday Mondays.

WORCESTER

☎ 01905 / pop 94,050

Smothered by modern architectural blunders and possessed of a rather soulless centre, you do have to make an effort to find the finer charms of Worcester (*woos*-ter). However, underneath the ugly façade lies some stunning Tudor and Georgian architecture and a magnificent cathedral. The city is also home to the factory works of the world-renowned Royal Worcester Porcelain Works.

Orientation & Information

The centre of town lies to the east of the River Severn, with the cathedral dominating the city. Most of the city's action takes place along the beautiful thoroughfare of Friar and New Sts, where the best pubs and restaurants are clustered.

The **TIC** (☎ 726311; www.cityofworcester.gov.uk; Guildhall, High St; ☺ 9.30am-5pm Mon-Sat) organises 1½-hour **walking tours** (adult £3; ☺ 11am Mon-Fri & 2.30pm Wed May-Sep).

Sights

WORCESTER CATHEDRAL

Dominating the centre of the city, **Worcester Cathedral** (☎ 28854; www.worcestercathedral.org.uk; requested donation £3; ☺ 7.30am-6pm) encapsulates a medley of different styles that displays renovators' skills down through the ages. Begun in 1084 by Bishop – later Saint – Wulfstan, the cathedral boasts the largest Norman crypt in the country and a beautiful choir and lady chapel in 13th-century Early English style. Other highlights include an impressive 12th-century circular chapterhouse (one of the first of its kind) and some splendid Victorian stained glass.

Wicked King John of Magna Carta fame is buried in the choir (apart from his thumb, which was nicked as a souvenir). Knowing he stood only the flimsiest chance of making it through the Pearly Gates, the dying king asked to be buried disguised as a monk.

If you're fit and fond of a view, there are tours up the 249 steps (60m) of the tower for £1.50. To really appreciate the splendour of the cathedral, come for evensong; it's held at 5.30pm Monday to Wednesday, Friday and Saturday, and at 4pm Sunday.

COMMANDERY CIVIL WAR CENTRE

Not far from the cathedral, the **Commandery** (☎ 361821; www.worcestercitymuseums.org.uk; adult/child £3.95/2.95; ☺ 10am-5pm Mon-Sat, 1.30-5pm Sun) is a splendid Tudor building currently undergoing a major overhaul. Improvements to the building, new exhibits and restoration of the painted chamber that contains important frescoes from the 15th century should be complete by 2006. Meanwhile, exhibits detailing the ins and outs of the Civil War and battles in 17th-century England are still on view.

ROYAL WORCESTER PORCELAIN WORKS

In 1751 Dr John Warne and his buddies began making ornate bone china as a hobby; the result is the longest continuous production of any porcelain company in England. The firm was granted a royal warrant in 1789 and still supplies HRH with some of her preferred crockery.

The **Royal Worcester Porcelain Works** (☎ 746000; www.royal-worcester.co.uk; Severn St; factory tours £5; ☺ 9am-5.30pm Mon-Sat, 11am-5pm Sun) has an entire visitors complex, with tours, shops, a restaurant and a museum.

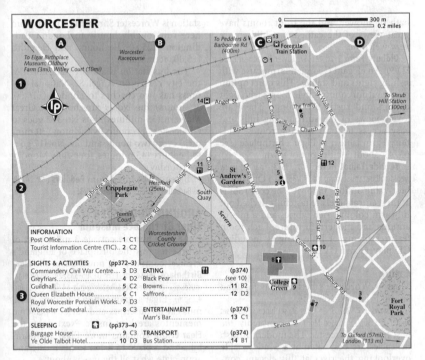

WORCESTER

0 — 300 m
0 — 0.2 miles

To Elgar Birthplace Museum; Oldbury Farm (3mi); Witley Court (10mi)

Worcester Racecourse

To Peddlers & Barbourne Rd (400m)

Foregate Train Station

To Shrub Hill Station (300m)

Angel St

The Cross
Swithun's
Church St
Broad St

The Trinity

City Walls Rd

Quay St
Bridge St
St Andrew's Gardens
Dean Way
High St
New St

To Hereford (25mi)

Cripplegate Park

Tennis Court

Worcestershire County Cricket Ground

South Quay

Severn

New Rd

Friar St
College St
City Walls Rd

College Green

Sidbury Rd

Fort Royal Park

Severn St

To Oxford (57mi); London (113 mi)

INFORMATION
Post Office.................................1 C1
Tourist Information Centre (TIC)..2 C2

SIGHTS & ACTIVITIES (pp372-3)
Commandery Civil War Centre....3 D3
Greyfriars.....................................4 D2
Guildhall.....................................5 C2
Queen Elizabeth House...............6 C1
Royal Worcester Porcelain Works..7 D3
Worcester Cathedral....................8 C3

SLEEPING (pp373-4)
Burgage House.............................9 C3
Ye Olde Talbot Hotel..................10 D3

EATING (p374)
Black Pear............................(see 10)
Browns.....................................11 B2
Saffrons....................................12 D2

ENTERTAINMENT (p374)
Marr's Bar.................................13 C1

TRANSPORT (p374)
Bus Station...............................14 B1

The **visitors centre** (adult/child £2.25/1.75) gives you an impression of the life of a 19th-century potter and details the history of the company, while the **museum** (adult/child £3/2.25; 9.30am-5pm Mon-Fri, 10am-5pm Sat) tells the factory's story through an intricate and extravagant collection of works, from the company's very first pieces to its most recent creations. A ticket for everything (tour, visitors centre and museum) costs £8/6.75 per adult/child, a significant saving if you're a real fan.

HISTORIC PROPERTIES
For an impression of what Worcester looked like before modern planners got their filthy paws on it, stroll down New and Friar Sts, both flanked by fine Tudor and Elizabethan buildings.

Built in 1480 and run by the National Trust (NT), **Greyfriars** (23571; Friar St; admission £3.20; 1-5pm Wed-Sat Apr-Oct) is an attractively restored, timber-framed Tudor merchant house, full of textiles and furnishings, with a pretty walled garden.

The splendid **Guildhall** (High St) is a Queen Anne building of 1722, designed by Thomas

White (a pupil of Sir Christopher Wren), who died in poverty after the city dragged its heels on paying him his dues. The period decoration inside is exceptional.

Originally a hospital almshouse, **Queen Elizabeth House** (The Trinity) is a beautiful, 15th-century, galleried timber-framed building. Local legend claims that Queen Elizabeth I addressed the people of Worcester from the balcony in 1575.

Festivals & Events
The **Three Choirs Festival** (www.3choirs.org), an event shared with Gloucester and Hereford Cathedrals, is held at the cathedral every three years. Worcester is the August 2005 host.

Sleeping
Due to business travel, lodgings in Worcester can be hard to come by midweek – there's a fairly grim bunch of B&Bs on Barbourne Rd if you're stuck.

Burgage House (25396; 4 College Precincts; s/d £30/50;) Far and away the best B&B in town. This lovely place on a quiet cobbled street has huge and comfortable rooms with bath or shower, and the front rooms have great views of the cathedral. Children are very welcome.

Oldbury Farm (☎ 421357; Lower Broadheath; s/d £30/50) An elegant Georgian farmhouse with fishing rights and stables. This quiet option has beautiful country-style rooms with light colours and rustic furnishings. There are lovely views of the surrounding hills and easy access to local walking routes. Oldbury Farm is next to Elgar's birthplace (see p374), about 3 miles out of town.

Ye Olde Talbot Hotel (☎ 23573; Friar St; www .yeoldetalbot.tablesir.com; s/d £70/86; 🖳) One of the best-value options in town. The cosy rooms at this central hotel are tastefully decked out in warm colours, rich fabrics and a mix of antique and modern furniture. Each room features plenty of little gadgets including CD players and DVDs.

Eating

Most of Worcester's best options for food are on Friar and New Sts.

Browns (☎ 26263; 24 Quay St; set lunch £20.50, set dinner £38.50; 🕐 closed Mon) Undoubtedly *the* best food in Worcester. The modern British delicacies are best eaten at a window table overlooking the river at this elegant converted cornmill.

Black Pear (☎ 23573; Friar St; mains £7-13; 🕐 lunch & dinner) Good-quality bistro-style pub grub ranging from steaks and salads to more adventurous Mediterranean and Asian fare is served at this low-ceilinged place, with its modern furniture and deep leather chairs.

Saffrons (☎ 610505; 15 New St; meals £14-16; 🕐 lunch & dinner) Scarlet walls and wooden tables give this colourful bistro a cheerful and relaxed atmosphere. The modern British food is confidently put together and beautifully presented but gloriously free from airs and graces.

Entertainment

Marr's Bar (☎ 613336; 12 Pierpoint St) A former dance studio turned live-music venue. This place has gigs almost every night, and sprung floors, making it a perfect spot to dance your socks off. Bands range from hard rock to world music and folk so check listings.

Getting There & Around

Worcester has two train stations but most services run to Worcester Foregate (the other station is Worcester Shrub Hill). Trains from here run roughly hourly to London Paddington (£25.80, 2¼ hours) and Hereford (£5.80, 45 minutes).

The bus station is a short walk north of the city centre on Angel St. National Express has two coaches to London (£16.50, 3½ hours). Bus No 44 runs hourly to Great Malvern (35 minutes), bus No 372 goes to Gloucester (1½ hours) via Upton (30 minutes) every two hours, and bus No 417 goes to Ledbury (45 minutes, four daily Monday to Saturday).

Bikes can be hired from **Peddlers** (☎ 24238; 46 Barbourne Rd; per day/week £10/35).

AROUND WORCESTER
Elgar Birthplace Museum

In 1857, a humble cottage 3 miles west of Worcester was the birthplace of England's greatest composer. It now houses the **Elgar Birthplace Museum** (☎ 01905-333224; www.elgar museum.org; Lower Broadheath; adult £4.50; 🕐 11am-4.15pm). Elgar's gramophone, writing desk, musical manuscripts and various personal mementos are kept inside. Next door, the **Elgar Centre** contains more Elgar memorabilia and a place to listen to his music and appreciate what all the fuss is about.

Bus Nos 311 and 317 go from Worcester to Broadheath Common (15 minutes, three times Monday to Saturday), a short walk away from the museum.

Witley Court

Run by English Heritage (EH) and arguably the most venerable and romantic ruin in England, **Witley Court** (☎ 01299-896636; Great Witley; adult £4.90; 🕐 10am-5pm daily Mar-Oct, 10am-4pm Thu-Mon Nov-Feb) was one of Britain's most extravagant private homes when it was built in the mid-19th century. It was sadly neglected over the years, but, even derelict, the house is stunning and the gardens are well on their way back to their former Victorian glory. The fountains, in particular, are spectacular.

The adjacent **Great Witley Church** is widely considered to be one of the finest baroque churches in England. Its simple exterior belies a sumptuous interior featuring paintings by the likes of Antonio Bellucci and some exceptionally ornate carving and glasswork.

Bus No 758 from Worcester or Kidderminster to Tenbury Wells passes this way infrequently.

GREAT MALVERN

☎ 01684 / pop 35,600

Great Malvern is at the centre of a cluster of towns and villages along the slopes of the Malvern Hills, whose humble peaks lord over the flat plains of Worcestershire below. The medicinal waters of the hills brought fame and fortune to the sleepy town, which became a popular resort in Victorian times. A languid air of sophistication still pervades the elegant streets, which gracefully tumble down the steep slopes, lofty gas lamps illuminating the grand façades by night.

The **TIC** (☎ 892289; www.malvernhills.gov.uk; 21 Church St; ⏰ 10am-5pm Mon-Sat, 10am-4pm Sun) has all you need to know. Guided tours of Victorian Great Malvern leave here at 10.30am on Saturday (£2, 1½ hours).

In early June the town hosts the bi-annual **Elgar Festival** (☎ 892277; www.elgar-festival.com), celebrating the life and works of the composer who lived nearby at Malvern Link.

Sights

The town's most important sight is **Malvern Priory** (☎ 561020; www.greatmalvernpriory.org.uk; Church St; admission free; ⏰ 9am-6.30pm Apr-Oct, 9am-4.30pm Nov-Mar), a Norman church founded in 1085. A shop inside the priory has a handy pamphlet pointing out the features of interest. Highlights include a wonderful collection of 15th-century stained glass, the oldest and finest collection of medieval tiles in Britain and many fine 14th and 15th-century misericords.

For the story of the town, visit the fascinating **Malvern Museum of Local History** (☎ 567811; adult/child £1.50/1; ⏰ 10.30am-5pm Easter-Oct, closed Wed during school term), housed in the impressive 15th-century gatehouse of the town's former Benedictine abbey. Located on a dead-end street off Abbey Rd, the museum tells the story of everything from the geology of the Malvern Hills to Victorian water cures and modern enterprise in the area.

Walking

The **Malvern Hills** are made up of 18 named peaks straddling the boundary between Worcestershire and Herefordshire. The highest point is Worcestershire Beacon (419m). The hills are crisscrossed by more than 100 miles of paths; trail guides (£1.75) and maps are available at the TIC. More than 70 springs and fountains pouring out

the famous medicinal waters are dotted around the hills. The TIC has a guide (£3.95) that will lead you to them.

Entertainment

One of Britain's leading provincial theatres, **Malvern Theatre** (☎ 892277; www.malvern-theatres .co.uk; Grange Rd) hosts a lively programme of classical concerts, dance, comedy, drama, opera and cinema.

Sleeping

There's lots of excellent accommodation in Great Malvern but it tends to be pricey. Head to the smaller villages for cheaper options.

Como House (☎ 561486; kevin@como-house.free serve.co.uk; Como Rd; s/d £25/45; P ✕ ; wheelchair access) This beautiful 19th-century Malvern-stone house is a good-value option for its comfortable, tastefully decorated rooms and quiet location. There's a large garden and the owner will gladly pick you up from the station or drop you off at walking points.

Cowleigh Park Farm (☎ 01684-566750; www.cow leighparkfarm.co.uk; Cowleigh Rd; s/d £40/60; P ✕) This early–13th-century farmhouse (a black-and-white timber-framed place) is an atmospheric option with smart rooms and a tranquil setting. The rooms are tastefully done with period furnishings and restrained traditional style.

Bredon House Hotel (☎ 566990; suereeves@bredon househotel.co.uk; 34 Worcester Rd; s/d £45/70; P ▯) Nestled high on a hill, this lovely 19th-century house has fantastic views over the area. Its elegant rooms are excellent value and are decorated in a subtle modern style with brass beds and rustic furniture.

Eating

Malvern's restaurants seem to come and go at an alarming rate but one perennial option is the doily and tea-cosy brigade: the town's many teashops.

St Ann's Well Café (☎ 560285; St Ann's Well; ⏰ lunch) This vegetarian place is the pick of this bunch, in Victorian premises at the top of a steep climb. You can wash down your wholesome salads or delicious cake with a glass of fresh springwater that's bubbling into a basin by the door.

Anupam (☎ 573814; 85 Church St; mains £8-9.50; ⏰ lunch & dinner) Probably the best place in town is this modern Indian restaurant just off the main drag. The décor is stylish and

---

SOMETHING SPECIAL

Walter de Cantelupe Inn (☎ 01905-820572; www.walterdecantelupeinn.com; Main Rd, Kempsey; mains £6-12, s £35, d £40-60; **P** ; wheelchair access) This small but wonderful spot is an ancient inn with great character and its own beer festivals. Plenty of real ales line up behind the bar, Morris dancers congregate here on bank-holiday weekends, and the kitchen cooks up fantastic traditional British food from locally sourced produce.

It's a warm, welcoming place with no pretension, a lovely beer garden and some simple, character-filled rooms if you just can't pull yourself away.

Kempsey is 4 miles south of Worcester on the A38.

---

contemporary and the menu features some outstanding specials such as *masala ma murg ka salan* – a subtle but flavoursome chicken dish featuring lime, fenugreek and coconut.

Rendezvous (☎ 290357; 78 Church St; mains £11-16; ☾ lunch & dinner) Another popular option. This refined place dishes up excellent modern British cuisine in its lovely atmospheric restaurant, cellar and walled garden. Although meat and fish feature strongly on the menu there are always some vegetarian options.

Getting There & Away

There are trains roughly hourly to Worcester (15 minutes) and Hereford (30 minutes).

National Express runs one bus daily to London (£17, 4½ hours) via Worcester – ask at the post office for details. Bus No 44 connects Worcester (35 minutes) with Great Malvern hourly, while bus No 675 runs every two hours to Ledbury (20 minutes, Monday to Saturday).

UPTON-UPON-SEVERN

☎ 01684 / pop 1800

A gorgeous little town with narrow winding streets flanked by a jumble of Tudor and Georgian architecture, Upton is well worth a stopover or a visit for the **Oliver Cromwell jazz festival** at the end of June.

The **TIC** (☎ 594200; upton.tic@malvernhills.gov.uk; ☾ 10am-5pm Mon-Sat, 10am-4pm Sun) is on High St. Map enthusiasts should head for the **Map**

Shop (☎ 593146; www.themapshop.co.uk; 15 High St), which has one of the best selections outside London.

The town's oldest building, the Pepperpot, now houses the **Heritage Centre** (☎ 92679; Church St; admission free; ☾ 1.30-4.30pm May-Sep), where displays detail the development of the town. Also worth a visit is **Tudor House** (☎ 592447; 16 Church St; adult £1; ☾ 2-5pm Apr-Oct), now a museum of local life and history.

Sleeping & Eating

Star Inn (☎ 592300; www.starinnupton.co.uk; s/d £40/55; **P**) This 17th-century hotel near the waterfront is one of the best options in town, with bright simple rooms and the odd exposed beam for character. The bar downstairs does good but traditional pub grub (mains £6 to £13) and often has live music.

White Lion (☎ 592551; www.whitelionhotel.biz; 21 High St; s/d £55/80; **P** **X**) A former 16th-century coaching inn, this old-fashioned place has some charming old-style rooms with plenty of frills and newer, more modern and functional rooms. The **Pepperpot Brasserie** (mains £12-14) is a lovely, oak-beamed restaurant downstairs serving little portions at big prices.

Getting There & Away

Bus No 372 runs between Upton and Worcester (30 minutes) every two hours from Monday to Saturday (fewer on Sunday).

HEREFORDSHIRE

Sleepy, pastoral Herefordshire receives few tourists. However, it shelters a series of worthy ports of call and a charming, unhurried way of life that's long lost in many other parts of Britain.

The collage of fields and hedgerows, cider orchards and pretty villages makes fantastic driving, walking or cycling territory, while the gorgeous black-and-white trail ambles though half-timbered villages lost in time. For the more adventurous the scenic River Wye provides ample opportunity for various water sports. Although most of Herefordshire's allure is rural, the county capital of Hereford hosts the area's most prized possession, the magnificent medieval Mappa Mundi.

Information

For online countywide information on attractions, accommodation and events:

Herefordshire Council (www.herefordshire.gov.uk)
Herefordshire Tourism (www.herefordshire-tourism
.org.uk)
Visit Heart of England (www.visitheartofengland.com)

Activities

Several long-distance walking paths pass
through this area. The **Offa's Dyke** path runs
along the western border with Wales, while
the 107-mile **Wye Valley Walk** begins in Chepstow (Wales) and follows the river's course
upstream into Herefordshire. The **Three
Choirs Way** is a 100-mile route connecting
the cathedrals of Hereford, Worcester and
Gloucester, where the music festival of the
same name has been celebrated for more
than three centuries.

Getting Around

There are railway stations at Hereford,
Leominster and Ledbury with good links to
the major English cities.

Numerous local and national bus companies provide services around the county
but you can pick up a free *Public Transport Map & Guide* from TICs and bus stations. Alternatively, try the **National Traveline**
(☎ 0870 608 2608).

HEREFORD

☎ 01432 / pop 56,400

Despite being the county town, with plenty
of shops and good transport connections,
drowsy Hereford has an air of inertia, lost

in time and only slowly catching up with
the rest of the country. Famed for its cider
and cattle, this rural backwater has an unusual cathedral that's home to the magnificent Mappa Mundi, a chart of the medieval
world.

Orientation & Information

The triangular, pedestrianised High Town
is the heart of the city, just north of the
River Wye. The cathedral is close to the
river while the bus and train stations lie to
the northeast, off Commercial Rd.

The **TIC** (☎ 268430; www.visitherefordshire.co.uk;
1 King St; ⏰ 9am-5pm Mon-Sat) is opposite the
cathedral. You can access the Internet for
free at the **library** (Broad St; ⏰ 9.30am-6pm Tue-Thu,
9.30am-8pm Fri, 9.30am-4pm Sat).

Hereford Cathedral

After the Welsh torched the town's original
cathedral, the **Hereford Cathedral** (☎ 374200;
www.herefordcathedral.co.uk; 5 College Cloisters; ⏰ 7.30am-
8pm) was rebuilt on the same site in the 11th
century. The building has evolved into a
well-packaged lesson on the entire history
of English architecture: the sturdy south
transept is Norman but it holds a 16th-
century triptych; the exquisite north transept with its great soaring windows dates
from the 13th century; the choir and the
tower date from the 14th century; while
the Victorian influence is visible almost
everywhere.

However, the cathedral is best known
for two ancient treasures, the most famous
being the magnificent **Mappa Mundi** (☎ 374209;
adult/child £4.50/3.50; ⏰ 10am-4.15pm Mon-Sat & 11am-
3.15pm Sun May-Sep, 10am-3.15pm Mon-Sat Oct-Apr), a
vellum map from the late 13th century that
records how scholars of the time saw the
world in spiritual and geographical terms.
It is the largest and best-preserved example
of this type of cartography and a fascinating
pictorial encyclopaedia of the times.

On the same ticket you can visit the largest surviving **chained library** in the world,
containing a unique collection of rare books
and manuscripts. The oldest book in the
collection – and the oldest artefact in the
cathedral – is the *Hereford Gospels,* created
in the 8th century.

You can catch evensong in the cathedral
at 5.30pm Monday to Saturday and at 2.30pm
on Sunday.

THE MARCHES

Other Sights

Marooned in the middle of High Town, the **Old House** (☎ 260694; admission free; ☒ 10am-5pm Tue-Sat year-round, plus 10am-4pm Sun Apr-Sep) is a marvellous black-and-white, three-storey wooden house, built in 1621 and fitted with 17th-century wooden furnishings showing the typical domestic arrangements of the time.

Hereford Cider Museum & King Offa Distillery (☎ 354207; www.cidermuseum.co.uk; 21 Ryelands St; adult/child £3/2; ☒ 10am-5pm daily Apr-Oct, 11am-3pm Tue-Sun Nov-Mar) explores the history of cider making, with a reconstructed farm cider house and 19th-century bottling machinery. The museum is just off the A438 to Brecon, or a dreary 10-minute walk from the centre of town.

The lively **Hereford Museum & Art Gallery** (☎ 260692; Broad St; admission free; ☒ 10am-5pm Tue-Sat year-round, plus 10am-4pm Sun Apr-Sep) displays a diverse range of exhibits from Roman antiquities and English watercolours to Saxon combs and a hive of bees. There's also a wonderful dressing-up box to keep younger visitors amused.

Festivals & Events

The **Three Choirs Festival** (www.3choirs.org), an event shared with Gloucester and Worcester Cathedrals, is held at the cathedral every three years. Hereford is the 2006 host.

Sleeping

Montgomery House (☎ 351454; lizforbes@lineone.net; 12 St Owens St; s/d £45/60; P ☒) A lovely Georgian town house with a touch of finesse. This place has elegant but restrained rooms with big comfy beds, Egyptian cotton sheets and blankets, and plenty of little extras.

Castle House (☎ 356321; www.castlehse.co.uk; Castle St; s £95, d £165-215; P ; wheelchair access) Once the bishop's residence, this elegant hotel is Hereford's most elegant option. The luxurious rooms have stylish but classical décor and the seriously sophisticated La Rive restaurant (mains £12 to £19) offers fine dining of the rich, classical sort.

Eating

Hereford isn't exactly blessed when it comes to eating out and you may be best off with some of the ubiquitous chain restaurants.

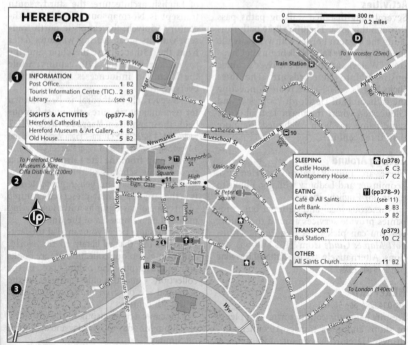

HEREFORD

0 — 300 m
0 — 0.2 miles

INFORMATION
Post Office...................................1 B2
Tourist Information Centre (TIC)..2 B3
Library.................................(see 4)

SIGHTS & ACTIVITIES (pp377-8)
Hereford Cathedral......................3 B3
Hereford Museum & Art Gallery...4 B2
Old House...................................5 B2

To Hereford Cider Museum & King Offa Distillery (200m)

To Worcester (25mi)
Train Station

SLEEPING (p378)
Castle House................................6 C3
Montgomery House.......................7 C2

EATING (pp378-9)
Café @ All Saints......................(see 11)
Left Bank....................................8 B3
Saxtys..9 B2

TRANSPORT (p379)
Bus Station................................10 C2

OTHER
All Saints Church........................11 B2

To London (140mi)

THE MARCHES

Café @ All Saints (☎ 370415; High St; mains £5-6; ☽ lunch) *The* most atmospheric place to eat in town – you can sit within spitting distance of the altar at this working church. The design is sleek and stylish and the menu features wholesome and mostly vegetarian fare. Look out for the medieval carving of a mooning gentleman.

Saxtys (☎ 357872; 33 Widemarsh St; mains £8-12; ☽ lunch & dinner Mon-Sat) A 30-something café-bar that is laid-back, mellow and modern, European beers and an excellent evening menu.

Left Bank (☎ 340200; Bridge St; ☽ lunch & dinner) Left Bank is the slick but soulless home to Floodgates Brasserie (mains £12 to £16) and the Charles Cocktail Bar (small/large tapas £3.45/6.25).

Getting There & Away

There are hourly trains to London (£30, three hours) via Worcester (£5.80, 45 minutes), and to Birmingham (£8.50, 1½ hours) and Abergavenny in Wales (22 minutes). National Express goes to London (£14.50, four hours, three daily) via Heathrow, Gloucester and Ross-on-Wye or Ledbury and once daily to Abergavenny (40 minutes).

From St Peter's Sq bus Nos 419 and 420 run hourly to Worcester Monday to Saturday (45 minutes, three on Sunday). From the bus station on Commercial Rd you can catch No 38 to Gloucester (50 min-

utes, hourly) via Ross-on-Wye (30 minutes, hourly Monday to Saturday, six on Sunday), No 476 to Ledbury (30 minutes, hourly Monday to Saturday, five on Sunday) and No 416 to Monmouth (50 minutes, seven daily).

AROUND HEREFORD
Golden Valley

The Golden Valley, at the foot of the Black Mountains, was made famous by the author CS Lewis and the film *Shadowlands*. It follows the course of the meandering River Dore and boasts beautiful unspoilt rural vistas, studded by historical ruins evoking the border valley's tumultuous past. *This* is why you brought the car.

Kilpeck

Deep within lush Herefordshire countryside is the tiny hamlet of Kilpeck, where you'll find an astonishing church that remains practically unchanged since the 12th century. Inside, remarkable corbels and original carvings ring the building. They range from the profound to the comical and include a famous sheila-na-gig (a Celtic fertility figure) on the south side.

Just 9 miles from Hereford, Kilpeck is less than 2 miles off the A465 and well worth a detour.

ROSS-ON-WYE

☎ 01989 / pop 10,100

Perched on a bluff above a bend in the river, picturesque Ross-on-Wye is a sleepy town unchanged by modern times, a pleasant base for exploring the lovely surrounding countryside. The town comes alive in mid-August when the **International Festival** brings on fireworks, live music and street theatre.

The 17th-century Market House hosts a **Heritage Centre** (☎ 260675; Market Pl; 10am-4pm Mon-Sat) and local history museum. The **TIC** (☎ 562768; Edde Cross St; ☽ 9.30am-4.30pm Mon-Sat) can help with information on activities and walks. You can hire bikes from **Revolutions** (☎ 562639; 48 Broad St) from £12 per day.

For good-value accommodation try **Linden House** (☎ 565373; www.lindenhouse.wyenet.co.uk; 14 Church St; s/d £30/50; ℗ ✄), a lovely brick house right in the centre of town with comfortable rooms that have exposed beams and brass beds. The décor is cheerful with warm hues and simple modern furnishings.

SOMETHING SPECIAL

Riverside Inn (☎ 01568-708440; www.theriversideinn.org; Aymestry; s/d £40/65, mains £11-16; ℗) This 16th-century half-timbered inn on the River Lugg is dripping with character and has some lovely rooms with low ceilings, oak beams and thick uneven walls. However, as beautiful as the accommodation is, it's the food that really draws the crowds; you can choose from simple bar food to fine dining in the cosy restaurant with hop-strewn beams and red lamps. The ambitious menu is mainly modern British with an emphasis on local ingredients. If you're a walker this place is mid-point on the Mortimer Trail and makes a wonderful stopover.

Aymestry is on the A4110, 15 miles north of Hereford.

For something more upmarket **Glewstone Court** (☎ 770367; www.glewstonecourt.com; Glewstone; s/d from £50/80; P) is a lovingly restored Georgian house chock-full of antiques, comfy sofas, period memorabilia and crackling open fires. The rooms have polished wooden floors, Eastern rugs and very traditional décor. The hotel is about 3 miles south of Ross just off the A40.

For food, your best option is **Pheasant at Ross** (☎ 565751; 52 Edde Cross St; mains £15; ☺ lunch & dinner Thu-Sat), famed for its extensive wine list and excellent nosh. It's an intimate wood-beamed place with an unpretentious attitude and a focus on rare-breed meats and succulent local game.

You'll find cheaper grub at **Riverside Inn** (☎ 564688; Wye St; mains £5-8; P), a lively pub with a popular restaurant.

Bus Nos 38 and 33 run hourly Monday to Saturday (six on Sunday) to and from Hereford and Gloucester respectively (30 minutes each way).

AROUND ROSS-ON-WYE
Goodrich

From the roof of the keep at **Goodrich Castle** (EH; ☎ 01600-890538; admission £4; ☺ 10am-5pm Mar-Oct, 10am-4pm Thu-Mon Nov-Feb) you get spectacular views of the Wye Valley and can appreciate how important – and impenetrable – this sandstone fortress would have been when it was built as a border stronghold in the 12th century. Even after a four-month siege by Oliver Cromwell's troops during the Civil War, it is still one of the most complete medieval castles in Britain.

From the village, it's a steep 1½-mile hill-hugging climb up to **Welsh Bicknor YHA Hostel** (☎ 0870 770 6086; welshbicknor@yha.org.uk; dm £11.80; ☺ daily Apr-Oct, Fri & Sat Nov-Mar; P ✗), a Victorian rectory standing in 10 hectares of gorgeous riverside grounds.

Goodrich is 5 miles south of Ross off the A40. Bus No 34 stops here every couple of hours on its route between Ross and Monmouth.

Symonds Yat
☎ 01600

In a gorgeous spot on the River Wye, Symonds Yat gets crammed with visitors on sunny Sundays and bank holidays, but is well worth a visit at quieter times. An ancient hand ferry (60p) joins the two pretty villages on either bank. Above Symonds Yat West you'll find a big, tacky fairground (summer only) with kiss-me-quick hats and an entirely different vibe.

The village is a centre for water sports, but the river is not as flat as it looks – it has a strong current and is not suitable for swimming.

ACTIVITIES
This area is renowned for canoeing and rock climbing, and there's good walking in the nearby Forest of Dean. The **Wyedean Canoe and Adventure Centre** (☎ 01594-833238; www.wyedean.co.uk) rents canoes and kayaks

---

BLACK-&-WHITE VILLAGES

A triangle of Tudor England survives almost untouched in northwest Herefordshire, where higgledy-piggledy black-and-white villages cluster round idyllic greens, seemingly oblivious to the modern world. The area makes for a wonderful drive, and a 40-mile circular route (the **Black & White Village Trail**) meanders through the most popular spots. It takes in handsome timber-framed buildings, old churches, convivial pubs and tranquil villages. You can pick up a guide from any TIC for £1 (or £4.99 for the cassette or CD version).

Eardisland is a real gem, as is **Pembridge**, with its huddle of classic houses and the useful **Black & White Villages Centre** (☎ 01544-388761; ☺ 9am-6pm) with TIC, tearooms, gift shop and cycle hire. The village makes a good base for touring the area, with lots of circular walks radiating from town and the **Mortimer Trail** (see p392) just north of the village.

For stunning food head for the **Stagg Inn** (☎ 01544-230221; www.thestagg.co.uk; Titley; mains £11-16; ☺ closed Sun evening & Mon), set in yet another picturesque village. It's a traditional country inn with roaring fires and antiques, and was the first pub to be awarded a Michelin star for its modern British menu. It also has a few very comfortable rooms (s/d £50/70).

The 3-mile **Titley Loop Walk** begins here and winds through gorgeous countryside, making it a good way to work up an appetite.

for £17 for a half-day and also organises multiday kayaking trips, white-water trips, caving and climbing.

From Symonds Yat East, it's a steep but easy walk – at least on a dry day – up 504m to the crown of the region, **Symonds Yat Rock**, which provides tremendous views of the river and valley. Two pairs of rare peregrine falcons nest in the cliffs opposite but there's a 90m drop over the harmless-looking wall, so keep an eye on children and dogs.

SLEEPING & EATING

There is a string of accommodation and feeding options on the east side of the river.

Old Court Hotel (☎ 890367; fax 890964; s/d £50/90; **P** **⊠**) This 15th-century manor house set in great gardens has excellent-value rooms with exposed beams, uneven floorboards and traditional but not-too-frilly décor. The Tudor restaurant serves up good food (mains £8 to £14) and cheaper bar snacks to feed the children.

Walnut Tree Cottage (☎ 890828; www.walnuttree hotel.co.uk; Symonds Yat West; s/d £45/70; **P** **⊠**) Set high above the river, this good-value option has simple, bright rooms with fantastic views, rustic furniture and light floral patterns. You can also have dinner here (set menu £20) but the food doesn't hold any surprises.

Saracen's Head (☎ 890435; www.saracensheadinn .co.uk; s/d £45/64) This popular, traditional inn by the river has some standard rooms and two new luxury suites in the boathouse that only cost a few pounds extra. You can dig into some decent bar food (£5 to £8) or choose from the more refined restaurant menu (mains £8 to £14).

GETTING THERE & AWAY

Bus No 53 goes to Symonds Yat West from Ross-on-Wye (25 minutes) on Friday only. Bus No 34 can drop you on the main road 1½ miles from the village on other days.

LEDBURY

☎ 01531 / pop 8500

A lovely little town with a wealth of historical architecture and plenty of antique shops, Ledbury makes a good day trip or an enjoyable stopover. The best way to enjoy the town is just to ramble the narrow lanes of crooked black-and-white buildings radiating from the main street.

TOP FIVE PUBS FOR SUNDAY LUNCH

- **Riverside Inn** (p397; Aymestry) Charming 16th-century inn just dripping with character

- **Stagg Inn** (opposite; Titley) Michelin-starred food with a down-to-earth attitude

- **Sun Inn** (p396; Marton) Where the locals come to play darts and the discerning come to dine

- **Three Crowns Inn** (p377; Ullingswick) Simple but sophisticated food at incredible prices

- **Walter de Cantelupe Inn** (p376; Kempsey) Small but ancient inn frequented by Morris dancers

---

The helpful **TIC** (☎ 636147; tic-ledbury@here fordshire.gov.uk; 3 The Homend; ☼ 10am-5pm Mon-Sat) has maps of the Ledbury Loop, a lovely 17-mile circular ride along secondary roads through rural Herefordshire.

Sights

Ledbury's centrepiece is the delightfully dainty **Market House** (Market Sq; admission free; ☼ 11am-1pm & 2-4pm Mon-Fri, 2-5pm Sun), a 17th-century, black-and-white timber-framed structure on oak columns. From here, you can wander up the creaky and cobbled **Church Lane**, chock-a-block with notable architecture, including the **Painted Room** (admission free; ☼ 11am-3pm Mon-Fri), with its 16th-century floral frescoes.

Still in Church Lane, the **Butcher's Row House** (☎ 632942; Church Lane; admission free; ☼ 11am-5pm Easter-Sep) is an engaging folk museum. It has displays ranging from 19th-century school clothing to a remarkable 18th-century communal 'boot' bath that used to be carted from door to door for the poor to scrub in.

At the far end of the lane is the 12th-century parish church of **St Michael and All Angels**, with its splendid 60m spire and tower, which are separate from the church. The spire was a 1733 addition to the Norman core.

Sleeping & Eating

Talbot Hotel (☎ 632963; www.visitledbury.co.uk/talbot; New St; s/d £32.50/60; **P**) The best-value option in town. This historic place has compact but comfortable rooms in period style and an amazing dining room with incredible oak panelling and rich traditional food (mains £8 to £15). Breakfast (£8.50) is not included in the room price.

Feathers Hotel (☎ 635266; www.feathers-ledbury .co.uk; High St; s/d £74.50/95.50; **P** **⌖**) Charming rooms with rich colours and modern styling are the order of the day at this homey Tudor establishment where there's also a small gym and pool. Fuggles restaurant downstairs (named after a locally grown hop) serves modern British brasserie-style food (mains £8 to £14).

Ceci Paolo (☎ 632976; www.cecipaolo.com; 21 High St; mains £6-7; ⌖ lunch) This food emporium combines city chic with country portions and has become a Ledbury institution. The top-notch cuisine features wholesome delicacies such as the Italian platter of tasty morsels. Downstairs there's a deli, and a kitchen and wine shop.

Getting There & Around

There are hourly trains to Hereford (15 minutes), Great Malvern (10 minutes), Worcester (20 minutes) and Birmingham (£7.40, one hour).

Bus No 476 runs to Hereford hourly Monday to Saturday (30 minutes, six on Sunday), bus No 132 runs to Gloucester (45 minutes, six daily Monday to Saturday), and No 675 runs to Great Malvern (20 minutes, every two hours Monday to Saturday).

The town is quite small and, considering the narrow medieval streets, you're much better off on foot than in a car.

You can hire bikes at **Saddle Bound Cycles** (☎ 633433; 3 The Southend; per day £8).

AROUND LEDBURY
Eastnor Castle

Straight out of the pages of a fairy tale, **Eastnor Castle** (☎ 01531-633160; www.eastnorcastle .com; castle & grounds adult/child £7/4, grounds only £5/3; ⌖ 11am-5pm Sun-Fri Jul & Aug, Sun & bank holidays Apr–early Oct) is an immaculate romantic Gothic folly. The interior is sumptuously designed with richly decorative Gothic and Italianate features, heavy tapestries and oodles of antiques. Even when the castle is closed, the extensive grounds – which include a deer park, maze, adventure playground and arboretum of rare trees – are worth a look.

The castle is just over 2 miles east of Ledbury on the A438.

Much Marcle

The village of Much Marcle is a tiny and remarkable place, home to two of the most impressive tourist attractions in the Marches.

First up is the enthralling historical house of **Hellens** (☎ 01531-660504; www.hellensmanor.com; adult/child £5/2.50; ⌖ tours 2pm, 3pm & 4pm Wed, Sat & Sun Apr-Sep), one of the oldest houses in Britain and still occasionally inhabited by descendants of the family who built it in the 13th century. The largely 17th-century interior has been almost perfectly preserved through benign neglect. Admission is by tour only but it's a mesmerising journey through the house and its history. You can also walk through the lovely garden to the charming brick dovecote.

You're deep in cider country here and can celebrate the fact with a visit to **Westons Cider Mills** (☎ 01531-660233; www.westons-cider.co .uk; The Bounds). Tours of the mill (£3.50, 1½ hours) are at 2.30pm Monday to Friday. Admission to the Edwardian-style garden and museum is free.

Bus No 45 passes through Much Marcle four times daily Monday to Saturday on its run between Ross-on-Wye and Ledbury.

SHROPSHIRE

The jewel in the Marches' crown, Shropshire boasts a wealth of attractions and some seriously beautiful and sparsely populated countryside. The county capital, Shrewsbury, is a wonderfully buckled Tudor town while close by is Ironbridge Gorge, the hotbed of industrial revolution. Although the north of the county is rather flat and unexceptional, the Shropshire Hills to the south are stunningly beautiful and littered with picturesque villages. In the far south is the historic town of Ludlow, strewn with wonderful buildings and famous for its passion for gourmet food.

Information

For online countywide information:
Shropshire Tourism (www.shropshiretourism.info)
South Shropshire (www.southshropshire.org.uk)
Virtual Shropshire (www.virtual-shropshire.co.uk)

Getting Around

There are useful rail services from Shrewsbury to Church Stretton, Craven Arms and

Ludlow. The invaluable *Shropshire Bus & Train Map*, available free from TICs, shows all bus routes.

SHREWSBURY

☎ 01743 / pop 67,150

Cradled in a horseshoe loop of the River Severn, Shrewsbury has been a strategic defence point since Saxon times. The town was key to keeping the Welsh at bay, and as border scuffles settled and trade prospered Shrewsbury grew rich on the wool trade. The meandering river has protected the town from development and today the higgledy-piggledy charms of its ancient half-timbered buildings make it Britain's finest Tudor town. Buckled black-and-white houses line the winding passageways and lanes and are perfect for aimless wandering.

Orientation

Shrewsbury's near-island status helps preserve the Tudor and Jacobean streetscapes of its centre and has prevented unattractive urban sprawl. The train station is a five-minute walk northeast of the centre and is as far as you'll need to venture.

Information

Library (☎ 255300; Castle Gates; 9.30am-5pm Mon, Wed, Fri & Sat, 9.30am-8pm Tue & Thu) Free Internet access.

Powney's Bookshop (☎ 369165; www.powneysbookshop .demon.co.uk; 4-5 Alkmund's Pl) A good source for walking maps.

Royal Shrewsbury Hospital (☎ 261000; Mytton Oak Rd)

TIC (☎ 281200; www.shrewsburytourism.co.uk; Music Hall, The Square; 9.30am-5.30pm Mon-Sat & 10am-4pm Sun May-Sep, 9.30am-5pm Mon-Sat Oct-Apr) Guided walking tours (adult £3, 1½ hours) leave the TIC at 2.30pm daily from May to September and at 2.30pm Saturday only from November to April.

Sights

The large red-sandstone **Shrewsbury Abbey** (☎ 232723; www.shrewsburyabbey.com; Abbey Foregate; admission £2 donation; 10am-4.45pm Easter-Oct, 10.30am-3pm Nov-Easter) is what's left of a Benedictine monastery founded in 1083. The architecture is in three different styles – Norman, Early English and Victorian – but its finest feature is the huge 14th-century west window of heraldic glass. You can also see the controversial sculpture of a crucified and decomposing Jesus, *The Naked Christ* by local artist Michelle Coxon. The

abbey is renowned for its acoustics and a noticeboard inside provides information on recitals.

Housed in beautifully restored 16th- and 17th-century buildings, the **Shrewsbury Museum** (☎ 361196; www.shrewsburymuseums.com; Barker St; admission free; 10am-4pm Tue-Sat Oct-May, 10am-5pm Tue-Sat & 10am-4pm Sun Jun-Sep) exhibits many Roman finds from Wroxeter (see p386) and has displays on local life. The **art gallery** here has a mixed bag of contemporary art.

Walking Tour

Starting from the TIC, the 16th-century **Market Hall** (☎ 351067; The Square), the centre of the historic wool trade, is in front of you across the road. Look out for the holes on the insides of the pillars, which were used to record the number of fleeces sold.

On your right at the junction with High St is the most impressive of Shrewsbury's timber-framed buildings, **Ireland's Mansion**. Cross over High St into narrow **Grope Lane** with its overhanging buildings and you'll end up in lovely Fish St before going up the steps to the restored 14th-century **Bear Steps Hall** (10am-4pm). There are several more atmospheric black-and-white houses along Butcher Row.

From here head for medieval **St Mary's Church** (St Mary's St), about 100m away, with its magnificent spire – one of the highest in England. Inside the great Jesse window is made from rare mid–14th-century English glass.

Pass the 17th-century **St Mary's Cottage** and cross Church St into Water Lane and head back down into Castle St. At the far end, about 150m away, is **Shrewsbury Castle**, which houses the **Shropshire Regimental Museum** (☎ 358516; adult/child £2/1; 10am-5pm Tue-Sat, 10am-4pm Sun & Mon May-Sep, 10am-4pm Wed-Sat Feb-Apr), although the view from the castle walls is more worthwhile than the collection.

Down the alley near the entrance is the Jacobean-style **Council House Gatehouse**, dating from 1620, and the **Old Council House**, where the Council of the Welsh Marches used to meet.

Across the road from the castle is the elaborate **library** with a **statue of Charles Darwin**, Shrewsbury's famous son who rocked the world with his theory of evolution. Returning to St Mary's St, follow it for 100m

THE MARCHES

into Dogpole and turn right into Wyle Cop, Welsh for 'hilltop'. Henry VII is said to have stayed in the **Henry Tudor House** before the Battle of Bosworth.

Head down Wyle Cop for 100m and turn left, and you'll reach the graceful 18th-century **English Bridge**, offering magnificent views of the town's skyline. **Shrewsbury Abbey** (p384) is 200m ahead of you.

Double back over the bridge and stroll west along the river to the manicured gardens of **Quarry Park**. Finally, wander up to the impressive **St Chad's Church**, built in 1792.

Sleeping

There's plenty of hotels in the centre and B&Bs clustered around Abbey Foregate.

164 (☎ 367750; www.164bedandbreakfast.co.uk; 164 Abbey Foregate; s/d £35/50; P ✗) An escape from the chintz brigade, this contemporary B&B has sleek, modern rooms in a lovely 16th-century property. There are colourful pictures on the walls and good bathrooms, and as an extra treat breakfast is served in bed.

Tudor House (☎ 351735; www.tudorhouseshrewsbury.com; 2 Fish St; s/d from £35/74; ✗) If nostalgia is your thing, this medieval masterpiece has buckets of character with pretty oak-beamed rooms decorated in light neutral colours. It's slap bang in the centre of town but on a really quiet street, and provides organic cooked breakfasts.

Cromwell's (☎ 361440; www.cromwellsinn.com; 11 Dogpole; s/d £55/60; ✗) Tudor chic combines

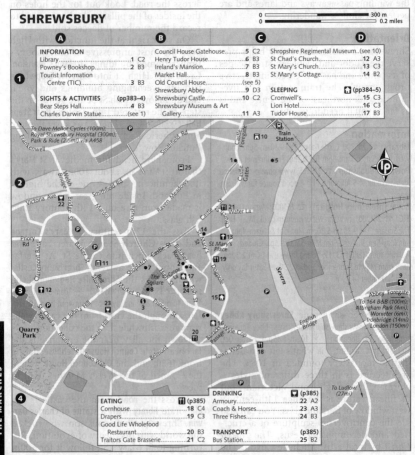

SHREWSBURY

| | | 0 ———— 300 m |
| | | 0 ———— 0.2 miles |

INFORMATION		Council House Gatehouse..........5 C2	Shropshire Regimental Museum..(see 10)
Library..........................1 C2		Henry Tudor House..................6 B3	St Chad's Church.................12 A3
Powney's Bookshop..........2 B3		Ireland's Mansion....................7 B3	St Mary's Church.................13 C3
Tourist Information		Market Hall............................8 B3	St Mary's Cottage................14 B2
Centre (TIC)................3 B3		Old Council House..............(see 5)	
		Shrewsbury Abbey..................9 D3	SLEEPING 🏠 (pp384–5)
SIGHTS & ACTIVITIES (pp383–4)		Shrewsbury Castle..................10 C2	Cromwell's..........................15 C3
Bear Steps Hall..................4 B3		Shrewsbury Museum & Art	Lion Hotel...........................16 C3
Charles Darwin Statue..........(see 1)		Gallery..............................11 A3	Tudor House.......................17 B3

EATING 🍴 (p385)		DRINKING 🍷 (p385)
Cornhouse........................18 C4		Armoury............................22 A2
Drapers...........................19 C3		Coach & Horses.................23 A3
Good Life Wholefood		Three Fishes......................24 B3
Restaurant.....................20 B3		
Traitors Gate Brasserie..........21 C2		TRANSPORT (p385)
		Bus Station........................25 B2

with modern styling at this frill-free modern guesthouse. The rooms have period features but contemporary furnishings, and the oak-panelled restaurant downstairs has a wonderful modern British menu (mains £11 to £17).

Lion Hotel (☎ 0870 609 6167; www.corushotels.com/thelion; Wyle Cop; s/d from £76/82; **P**) A classic 17th-century coaching inn, the Lion has played host to many a passing luminary. If you can, take the more expensive rooms as the standard rooms have an unexceptional corporate style and lack any real character. The suites, however, are the real McCoy and are furnished with stunning period antiques.

Eating

Traitors Gate Brasserie (☎ 249152; www.traitorsgate.co.uk; Castle St; mains £9-15; ✣ lunch & dinner) A warren of little cellars and intimate alcoves; the warm stone walls, soft lighting and rustic décor are a perfect setting for the ambitious Continental cuisine. Try the pan-fried venison with crushed juniper berries or the baked breast of chicken with blue cheese.

Cornhouse (☎ 231991; 59a Wyle Cop; mains £8-13; ✣ lunch & dinner) Excellent seasonal British food is served up in this cosy retreat, with an eclectic range of artwork, and interesting décor. The restaurant is dominated by a superb cast-iron spiral staircase; live piano music tinkles in the background; and there's blues on Sunday, just in time for brunch.

Good Life Wholefood Restaurant (☎ 350455; Barracks Passage; mains £4-6.50; ✣ lunch) Good honest meals and a pious glow emanate from this cosy little wholefood nook off Wyle Cop. It's a fantastic place for healthy, hearty and delicious fare, from sturdy salads to hot bakes and gorgeous desserts.

Drapers (☎ 344679; Drapers Hall, St Mary's Pl; mains £9.50-15.50; ✣ lunch & dinner) Expertly prepared classic French and English dishes are served up at this 16th-century hall that features an elegant Elizabethan façade. The restaurant has a giant open fireplace, oak-panelled walls and simply stunning food. For more relaxed dining try the Yellow Room (mains £6.50 to £9).

Drinking

Three Fishes (☎ 344793; 4 Fish St) Smoke-free and gloriously creaky, this fine Tudor alehouse has a reputation for good bar food

(£8 to £12) and a mellow clientele. There are plenty of real ales on tap at surprisingly good prices.

Coach & Horses (☎ 365661; Swan Hill) This wonderful old inn is one of the best in town with a lively atmosphere and friendly punters. It does a brilliant game roast and other hearty fare (£9 to £13) under the ageing beams and low lighting.

Armoury (☎ 340525; Welsh Bridge) Housed in a converted warehouse overlooking the river, this huge open shell of a pub features subtle lighting and a successful mix of old pictures and antiques lining the walls. It also serves a good range of modern British food (£7 to £10).

Getting There & Around
BICYCLE

You can hire a bicycle at **Dave Mellor Cycles** (☎ 366662; 9 New St) from £10 a day.

BUS

National Express has two direct buses to London (£15.50, 4½ hours) and two more via Birmingham (£15.50, 5½ hours). One bus a day goes to Welshpool (45 minutes). Bus No 96 serves Ironbridge (30 minutes) every second hour Monday to Saturday. Bus No 435 travels to Ludlow (1¼ hours) via Church Stretton (45 minutes) six times daily and bus No 553 heads to Bishop's Castle (one hour) six times daily.

The centre of town is very small and the streets are narrow, so there's no need for local bus use other than those mentioned here.

TRAIN

There are no direct trains connecting Shrewsbury and London – you must change at Wolverhampton and journey times to London vary from three to 6½ hours (£34.10). There are hourly trains to Ludlow (£7.10, 30 minutes) and seven trains daily to Welshpool (22 minutes) and on to Machynlleth in Wales (£11, one hour).

Shrewsbury is a popular starting point for two scenic routes into Wales: one loop takes in Shrewsbury, northern Wales and Chester; the other, **Heart of Wales Line** (☎ 01597-822053; www.heart-of-wales.co.uk), runs southwest to Swansea (£15.80, 3¾ hours, six daily) and connects with the Cardiff to Fishguard main line.

AROUND SHREWSBURY

Attingham Park

The grandest of Shropshire's stately homes, the late–18th-century mansion **Attingham Park** (NT; ☎ 01743-708123; house & grounds adult £5.50, grounds only adult £2.70; ☼ house noon-5pm Fri-Tue mid-Mar–Oct, grounds 10am-dusk Mar-Oct) combines elegance and ostentation in equal measures. Behind its imposing neoclassical façade, you'll find a picture gallery by John Nash and magnificent Regency interiors containing impressive collections of silver and lavish Italian furniture. The landscaped grounds shelter a herd of deer and a sculpture trail, and provide pleasant walks along the River Tern.

Attingham Park is 4 miles southeast of Shrewsbury at Atcham. Bus No 81 runs five times Monday to Friday, less on weekends.

Wroxeter

The remains of Roman Britain's fourth-largest city, Viroconium, can be viewed at **Wroxeter** (EH; ☎ 01743-761330; adult £4; ☼ 10am-5pm Mar-Oct, 10am-4pm Nov-Feb). Remote-sensing techniques show a city as large as Pompeii lying under the lush farmland, but the costs of excavation are prohibitive. For the time being at least, you'll need a strong imagination and have to make do with the extensive remains of the public baths and a few archaeological finds in the small **museum**.

Wroxeter is 6 miles southeast of Shrewsbury, off the B4380. Bus Nos 81 and 96 stop nearby, and run five times daily Monday to Friday, with fewer on weekends.

SOMETHING SPECIAL

Sun Inn (☎ 01938-561211; Marton; mains £11.50-13.50; wheelchair access) This unpretentious country pub does a very rare thing by providing a top-notch menu in a proper traditional bar. It's the kind of place where the locals come to dine – and play darts! The simple menu focuses on fresh ingredients from local farms and can feature anything from roast monkfish teamed with baby squid to plump beef cooked to perfection. Each dish is lovingly prepared and immaculately presented and will leave you sighing in contentment. Marton is 12 miles southwest of Shrewsbury on the B4386.

IRONBRIDGE GORGE

☎ 01952 / pop 1560

The Silicon Valley of the 18th century, Ironbridge Gorge is actually a cluster of picturesque little villages that are famed as the birthplace of the Industrial Revolution and which are now fully recognised as a World Heritage Site. The eponymous bridge is the centrepiece of the pretty main village while 10 fascinating museums in the surrounding area explain the history of the region and its importance in transforming industrial processes.

Ironbridge owes much of its success to the remarkable achievements of three generations of the Darby family. Abraham Darby made history when he pioneered the technique of smelting iron ore with coke in 1709, paving the way for local factories to begin mass production of iron wheels, rails and locomotives. Abraham Darby II invented the forging process that allowed for the production of single beams of iron, making it possible for Abraham Darby III to blaze a trail with the world's first iron bridge, constructed in Ironbridge Gorge in 1779.

Orientation & Information

The museums are scattered along the gorge and having your own wheels to get to these makes life a lot easier. See Getting Around (p389) for public-transport options.

The enthusiastic **TIC** (☎ 884391; www.ironbridge .org.uk, www.visitironbridge.co.uk; Tollhouse; ☼ 9am-5pm Mon-Fri, 10am-5pm Sat & Sun) is by the bridge. You can buy a **Passport Ticket** (adult £13.25) here that will admit you to all the sites.

Sights & Activities

The museums open from 10am to 5pm unless stated otherwise.

MUSEUM OF THE GORGE

A good way to begin your tour of the area is with a visit to the **Museum of the Gorge** (The Wharfage; adult £2.20), housed in a Gothic warehouse by the river. A small exhibition covers the history of the gorge, with an absorbing video setting the museum in its historical context. The displays provide an overview of the Industrial Revolution and look at the environmental consequences of industrialisation. Allow about 45 minutes for a visit.

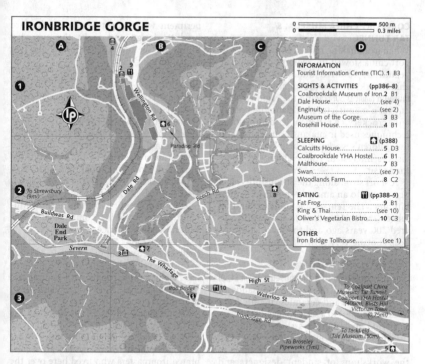

IRONBRIDGE GORGE

INFORMATION
Tourist Information Centre (TIC)..**1** B3

SIGHTS & ACTIVITIES   (pp386–8)
Coalbrookdale Museum of Iron.**2** B1
Dale House.........................(see 4)
Enginuity...........................(see 2)
Museum of the Gorge............**3** B3
Rosehill House......................**4** B1

SLEEPING   (p388)
Calcutts House......................**5** D3
Coalbrookdale YHA Hostel.....**6** B1
Malthouse............................**7** B3
Swan...................................(see 7)
Woodlands Farm....................**8** C2

EATING   (pp388–9)
Fat Frog.............................**9** B1
King & Thai........................(see 10)
Oliver's Vegetarian Bistro.......**10** C3

OTHER
Iron Bridge Tollhouse..............(see 1)

COALBROOKDALE MUSEUM OF IRON & DARBY HOUSES

The early industrial settlement of Coalbrookdale has survived almost intact with workers cottages, chapels and a church all undisturbed. A small army of local men and boys worked at the iron foundry, now converted into the **museum of iron** (adult £4.50). In its heyday in the 19th century, the foundry churned out heavy-duty iron equipment and delicate castings and it was here that the first Abraham Darby succeeded in smelting iron ore with coke. The museum charts the history of the company and houses some extraordinary products of iron making.

Just up the hill from the museum you can visit the beautifully restored 18th-century **Rosehill House** (☎ 433522; adult £3.10; ☒ closed Nov–Mar). Next door is **Dale House** and the office where the third Darby pored over his designs for the bridge. Combined admission to the museum and houses is £5.30.

IRON BRIDGE & TOLLHOUSE

The graceful arching bridge that also gives the area its name was a symbol of the success of the iron industry and the pioneering achievements of this Shropshire town. As well as providing a crossing over the river, Abraham Darby III's world-first iron bridge promoted the area and his technological prowess, ensuring the village's place in history as well as employment for all.

The former **tollhouse** (admission free) now houses an exhibition about the bridge's history.

BLISTS HILL VICTORIAN TOWN

A vast open-air Victorian theme park, **Blists Hill** (☎ 433522; Legges Way, Madeley; adult £8.50) is a complete reconstructed village with everything from a working foundry to sweet shops, a bank, grocer and chemist. Costumed staff explain the displays, craftspeople demonstrate skills, and there are special events such as Victorian weddings. If it all gets too much, exchange some cash for shillings and grab yourself a stiff drink at the Victorian pub. Allow three to four hours and a healthy dose of patience to get round all the exhibits. Call ahead for winter opening hours.

THE MARCHES

COALPORT CHINA MUSEUM & TAR TUNNEL

When iron making moved elsewhere, Coalport china slowed the region's decline. The beautifully restored buildings of the old china works now house an absorbing **china museum** (adult £4.50) tracing the region's glory days as a manufacturer of elaborate pottery and crockery. Craftspeople demonstrate techniques used in making bone china, and the children's workshops help keep younger visitors interested. Allow about 1½ hours for a visit.

A short stroll along the Shropshire Canal brings you to an amazing source of natural bitumen. The remarkable underground **tar tunnel** (adult £1.20; ⊙ closed Oct-Apr) was discovered 200 years ago and the black stuff just keeps oozing very slowly from the walls.

JACKFIELD TILE MUSEUM

Newly reopened, this **tile museum** (adult £4.50) has a wonderful display of thousands of decorative tiles and ceramics (mainly from Victorian times) in a series of gas-lit galleries in period style. Displays show the tiles in use in suburban villas, country churches, shops and tube stations. You can drop in to the workshops of student designers and manufacturers and see the 'Great Rock Sandwich' geological exhibition in the museum. Allow about an hour for a visit.

BROSELEY PIPEWORKS

A wonderfully preserved time capsule, the **Broseley Pipeworks** (adult £3.10; ⊙ 1-5pm May-Sep) charts the history of smoking in what was once Britain's most prolific pipe manufacturer. Production of the famous clay pipes came to a halt in 1957 and the factory's doors were closed, sealing 350 years of tradition. The building is largely as it was when the last worker turned out the lights. It's a captivating place and well worth an hour's visit.

ENGINUITY

Interactive design and technology centre **Enginuity** (adult £5.30) champions Ironbridge's pioneering spirit and celebrates the area's engineering and technological achievements. The hands-on, feet-on, full-on exploration of design and engineering in modern life allows you to become an apprentice engineer for a day. You get to ex-

periment with gadgets and gear that are used to design and make the everyday things we see and use. Allow about two hours for your visit.

Sleeping

There are YHA hostels at either end of Ironbridge Gorge.

Coalport YHA Hostel (☎ 0870 770 5882; ironbridge@yha.org.uk; High St, Coalport; dm £13.40; Ⓟ ✕) Housed in the old china factory, this hostel has a stunning setting by the canal but the rooms are more functional than historic.

Coalbrookdale YHA Hostel (Paradise Rd, Coalbrookdale; dm £11.50; Ⓟ ✕) In the 19th-century Literary and Scientific Institute near the Museum of Iron, offering comfortable rooms within walking distance of town.

Woodlands Farm (☎ 432741; www.woodlandsfarmguesthouse.co.uk; Beech Rd; s/d £22.50/48; Ⓟ ✕) One of the best-value places in town. Woodlands has bright, simple rooms with neutral and pastel furnishings. Most rooms have views over the garden, and a digital TV.

Calcutts House (☎ 882631; www.calcuttshouse.co.uk; Calcutts Rd; s/d £30/50; Ⓟ ✕) Tucked away from the relative hubbub, this 18th-century pad has opulent rooms named after celebrated ironmasters who lived here over the years. The styling is very traditional but tastefully done. The Alexander Brodie room is particularly pretty.

Malthouse (☎ 433712; The Wharfage; s/d £59/69; Ⓟ) and **Swan** (☎ 433712; The Wharfage; s/d £59/69; Ⓟ) are sister establishments in the centre of town. These two places offer beautiful beamed rooms with contemporary style – each room is different so it's worth looking at a few. You can also grab a bite at Malthouse (p389).

Eating

Oliver's Vegetarian Bistro (☎ 433086; 33 High St; mains £8.95; ⊙ lunch & dinner) Small and stylish, this place has modern artwork and music, top-notch dishes at great prices and a vast menu. Delicacies include cashew nut and carrot roast, and wild mushroom and sundried tomato sausage.

King & Thai (☎ 433913; 33a High St; mains £8-11; ⊙ dinner) Found above Oliver's, this split-level Thai emporium serves up generous portions of hot and spicy Thai food untamed for the English market. It's an unpretentious and extremely friendly place with some seriously good food.

Malthouse (☎ 433712; The Wharfage; mains £9-15; ☽ lunch & dinner) Try fasting before dining out here: the portions are enormous and the food is so good you won't want to leave any behind. The vibrant restaurant dishes up traditional favourites with a modern twist and there's live music in the bar from Wednesday to Saturday.

Fat Frog (☎ 433269; Wellington Rd; Coalbrookdale; mains £13-19; ☽ lunch & dinner) This French restaurant has whitewashed walls, red gingham tablecloths and battered wooden chairs, giving it the rustic charm of Provence. The food is excellent, there's a choice of traditional ales at the bar and there are frogs everywhere.

Getting There & Away

The nearest train station is 5 miles away at Telford. Bus No 96 runs every two hours (Monday to Saturday) between Shrewsbury (30 minutes) and Telford (10 minutes).

Getting Around

Bus WH1 connects the museums roughly every half-hour on weekends and bank holidays only. The WH2 and WH3 run to Much Wenlock four times on Saturday and once on Sunday. Midweek your only options are to walk or hire a bike from **Cycle Adventures** (☎ 07947-131349; www.cycleadventures .co.uk; half/full day £9/14), who will deliver bikes to you.

MUCH WENLOCK

☎ 01952 / pop 2650

Narrow winding streets, a patchwork of historical buildings from Tudor to Geor-

gian times, a beautiful timbered guildhall and the evocative ruins of a 12th-century priory make this little town a real treasure. Bizarrely, it also has strong claims to being the birthplace of the modern Olympics (see the boxed text, below).

The **TIC** (☎ 727679; The Square; ☽ 10.30am-1pm & 2-5pm Mon-Sat Apr-Oct, plus Sun Jun-Aug) provides a free map of the town's sights of historic interest, as well as copies of *The Olympian Trail*, a pleasant 1½-mile walking tour of the town that explores the link between the village and the modern Olympics.

The main sight of interest is the enchanting ruins of the 12th-century **Much Wenlock Priory** (EH; ☎ 727466; adult £3; ☽ 10am-4pm Thu-Mon Mar-May & Sep-Oct, 10am-6pm Jun-Aug, 10am-4pm Fri-Sun Nov-Feb), set in beautiful grounds studded with pine and cherry trees. An audio tour (included in the admission price) gives a monk's impression of life at the priory. There's also a display of kooky Victorian topiary including squirrels and teddy bears.

If you fancy staying, **Stokes Bunkhouse Barn** (☎ 727293; www.stokesbarn.co.uk; Newton House Farm; dm £7; (P) ☒) has cheap dorm beds in a beautifully converted 19th-century threshing barn with a magnificent dining area.

For something a little more luxurious, **Talbot Inn** (☎ 727077; www.the-talbot-inn.com; 13 High St; s/d £38/75; (P) ☒) is a wonderfully atmospheric old place with colossal beams and cavernous fireplaces. The rooms here have retained some period features and rustic furniture but the décor is generally bright and contemporary. The restaurant (mains £10 to £15) serves a fine French menu.

GRANDADDY OF THE MODERN OLYMPICS

Local doctor and sports enthusiast William Penny Brookes fused his knowledge of the ancient Olympics and rural British pastimes to launch the Much Wenlock Olympic Games in 1850. Begun as a distraction for the beer-swilling local youth, the games soon became an annual event and pricked the interest of Baron Pierre Coubertin, who came to Much Wenlock in 1890 to see them for himself.

He and Brookes became firm friends, with the shared dream of reviving the ancient Olympics. Coubertin went on to launch the modern Olympics in Athens in 1896; the games featured many of the events he had seen in Much Wenlock (although chasing a greased pig around town never really caught on). Brookes was invited to the event but he died, aged 86, before the games opened.

The good doctor never really got his share of the Olympic limelight until almost a century later, when International Olympic Committee President JA Samaranch visited his grave to 'pay tribute and homage to Dr Brookes, who really was the founder of the Modern Olympic Games'. The Much Wenlock Olympics are still held every July.

Other possibilities for food include **Edge** (☎ 727977; 14a High St; mains £9-13; ☺ lunch & dinner Tue-Sat), an innovative place serving simple lunches (£4 to £6) and stylish evening meals with plenty of local and organic ingredients.

Bus No 436 runs from Shrewsbury (40 minutes) via Much Wenlock to Bridgnorth (20 minutes) approximately every two hours Monday to Saturday (five on Sunday).

AROUND MUCH WENLOCK
Wenlock Edge
This steep limestone escarpment stretches 15 miles from Much Wenlock to Craven Arms and provides terrific walking with superb views. The National Trust owns much of the ridge, and there are many waymarked trails starting from car parks along the B4371.

A good accommodation option is **Wilderhope Manor YHA Hostel** (☎ 08707706090; wilderhope@yha.org.uk; Longville-in-the-Dale; dm £11.80; ☺ Feb-Oct; P ✗), a grand, gabled Elizabethan manor house set deep in lush countryside. The 16th-century pile has oak spiral staircases and a grand dining hall, making it a really atmospheric place to stay.

For food try the **Wenlock Edge Inn** (☎ 01746-785678; Hilltop; s/d £50/70), an award-winning pub loved by locals. It's quite an ordinary place with a relaxed atmosphere and unassuming décor, serving up home-made comfort food (mains £7 to £8). The pub is about 4½ miles southwest of Much Wenlock on the B4371.

You can catch buses from Ludlow and Bridgnorth to Shipton, a half-mile walk from Wilderhope. The Wenlock Wanderer runs from Church Stretton to Much Wenlock via Wenlock Edge five times on Saturday and Sunday, but you'll need your own transport midweek.

CHURCH STRETTON & AROUND
☎ 01694 / pop 3850
Church Stretton is a picturesque settlement in a deep valley that is formed by the Long Mynd and the Caradoc Hills. Apart from the lack of a decent boozer, it makes a terrific base for exploring the surrounding hills and has quite a few interesting old buildings, including an early–12th-century Norman church with a rare sheila-na-gig over the north doorway.

The **TIC** (☎ 723133; Church St; ☺ 10am-1pm & 2-5pm Mon-Sat Apr-Sep) has lots of useful walking information.

Walking
The **Long Mynd** is the most famous of Shropshire's hills and one of the best walking areas in the Marches. The Victorians called the area Little Switzerland, promoting it as a health resort, and the entire heathlands are webbed with walking trails that have memorable views.

Just a 10-minute walk from Church Stretton, the **Carding Mill Valley** trail leads up to the 517m summit of the Long Mynd. This trail can get very busy at weekends and in summer, so you might prefer to pick your own peak or cross the A49 and climb towards the 459m summit of Caer Caradoc.

The Long Mynd Shuttle bus (return trip £2, weekends only April to October) runs up the Carding Mill Valley from Beaumont Rd or the station.

Sleeping & Eating
Bridges Long Mynd YHA Hostel (☎ 01588-650656; www.yha.org.uk; Ratlinghope; dm £9.30; P ✗) This old village school now houses basic but comfortable dorms and provides easy access to the Shropshire Way, Long Mynd and Stiperstones walks. Boulton's bus No 551 comes here from Shrewsbury on Tuesday only. At weekends from April to October the Long Mynd shuttle runs hourly to Church Stretton.

Jinlye Guest House (☎ 723243; www.jinlye.co.uk; Castle Hill, All Stretton; s/d £45/60; P ✗) Perched on the Long Mynd, this 16th-century property is an excellent choice with lots of character and beautifully furnished rooms. Old beams, log fires and leaded windows feature in the public rooms while the beautiful bedrooms are furnished with a combination of antiques and delicate floral fabrics.

Berry's Coffee House (☎ 724452; 17 High St; meals £5-7; ☺ lunch; ▢) Organic free-range products rule the roost at this wonderful café off the main street. There's plenty of hearty and wholesome dishes to choose from and desserts to make your knees wobble. You can also check your email for free while you wait.

Studio (☎ 722672; 59 High St; meals £13-15; ☺ dinner only Tue-Sat, lunch Sun) This former artist's studio has been converted into an intimate restaurant that serves modern British and traditional French food. Local meats and game feature strongly on the menu, as do the fish specials.

For delicious snacks to take on a walk make a beeline for **Van Doesburg's Deli** (High St).

Getting There & Around

There are about a dozen trains to Shrewsbury (20 minutes), and bus No 435, which runs between Shrewsbury and Ludlow six times daily, stops here.

You can hire mountain bikes and tandems from **Shropshire Hills Bike Hire** (☎ 723302; 6 Castle Hill, All Stretton; mountain bikes/tandems per day £12/24); bikes can be delivered and collected for an extra charge.

BISHOP'S CASTLE

☎ 01588 / pop 1630

Although the eponymous castle no longer exists, this pretty little border town has an appealing collection of crooked half-timbered houses, second-hand bookshops and eclectic boutiques. At the centre of the town is the tiny Georgian **Town Hall** and nearby the picturesque 16th-century **House on Crutches** (☎ 630007; admission 50p; ☼ noon-4pm Sat & Sun), housing the town's museum. Tourist information is available from the beguilingly batty **Old Time** (☎ 638467; www.bishopscastle.co.uk; 29 High St; ☼ 10am-10pm Mon-Sat, 10am-2pm Sun).

The town is famed for its pub breweries. The locals' choice is the **Six Bells Inn** (☎ 630144; Church St; mains £6-12), a 17th-century coaching inn still producing its own ales in the adjoining brewery. The pub also has a reputation for good traditional food. Just around the corner, the **Three Tuns** (☎ 638797; Salop St) is one of Shropshire's most famous, if quite ordinary, pubs. Brewing has moved elsewhere but you can still sample the house brews at the bar.

If you're feeling energetic you can walk off your indulgences along the **Shropshire Way**, which runs through the town and joins up with the **Offa's Dyke** path to the south; the **Kerry Ridgeway** to the south; or head north and risk the forbidding ridges of the **Stiperstones**, where Satan is said to hold court.

If you fancy staying overnight, **Poppy House** (☎ 638443; www.poppyhouse.co.uk; 20 Market Sq; s/d £40/70; ✖) has some wonderful rooms with deep-red bedspreads and lots of little extras. The restaurant downstairs features an interesting menu (£5 to £8) with good vegetarian options.

The best bet for a light meal is **Capricho Café** (☎ 638181; 39 High St; mains £4-6; ☼ lunch Mon, Tue & Thu-Sat). This modern café and deli serves wonderful home-made soups, great sambos, Mediterranean deli snacks and delicious cakes, all with an emphasis on organic and fair-trade products.

Bus No 553 runs to and from Shrewsbury (one hour) six times daily.

LUDLOW

☎ 01584 / pop 9550

A treat for history buffs and food lovers alike, glorious Ludlow is the queen of the Marches, with an irresistible mix of historic architecture and gourmet passion. It's the kind of town made for wandering and grazing. The ruins of a Norman castle dominate the centre while the rambling sidestreets are lined with warped half-timbered Jacobean buildings, elegant Georgian town houses and Michelin-starred restaurants, and independent butchers, bakers and cheesemongers. Despite all this it doesn't receive many tourists, which makes it a fantastic base for the wonderful Shropshire hills.

Ludlow's **TIC** (☎ 875053; ludlow.tourism@shropshire-cc.gov.uk; Castle St; ☼ 10am-5pm) is in the 19th-century **assembly rooms** (☎ 878141; www.ludlowassemblyrooms.co.uk), now a lively arts and community centre with plenty of exhibitions and a good programme of live shows. There's also a small **museum** here.

There is a busy calendar of festivals throughout the year, the biggest being the **Ludlow Festival** (☎ 872150; www.ludlowfestival.co.uk), a fortnight of theatre and music that takes place in June and July. The **Ludlow Marches Food & Drink Festival** (www.foodfestival.co.uk) is promoted as Britain's foremost such festival, and takes place over a long weekend in September. Accommodation can be almost impossible to find during these festivals.

Sights & Activities

Ludlow is best enjoyed by just rambling the lovely streets and exploring the winding lanes that are lined with antique dealers and specialist food shops.

The town's biggest sight is the impressive **Ludlow Castle** (☎ 873355; www.ludlowcastle.com; Castle Sq; adult £3.50; ☼ 10am-4pm Sat & Sun Jan, 10am-4pm daily Feb & Mar & Oct-Dec, 10am-5pm daily Apr-Jul & Sep, 10am-7pm daily Aug), one of a line of fortifications built along the Marches to ward off the marauding Welsh. Built around 1090, the sturdy Norman keep has wonderful views over the surrounding hills and the rivers below. The castle was transformed into a palace by Roger Mortimer in

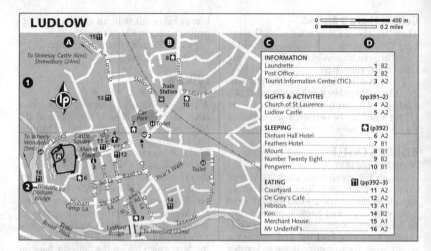

LUDLOW

| | 0 ——— 400 m |
| | 0 ——— 0.2 miles |

INFORMATION	
Laundrette......................................	**1** B2
Post Office.....................................	**2** B2
Tourist Information Centre (TIC)...........	**3** A2

SIGHTS & ACTIVITIES	(pp391–2)
Church of St Laurence......................	**4** A2
Ludlow Castle..................................	**5** A2

SLEEPING	(p392)
Dinham Hall Hotel............................	**6** A2
Feathers Hotel.................................	**7** B1
Mount..	**8** B1
Number Twenty Eight........................	**9** B2
Pengwern.......................................	**10** B1

EATING	(pp392–3)
Courtyard.......................................	**11** A2
De Grey's Café................................	**12** A2
Hibiscus...	**13** A1
Koo...	**14** B2
Merchant House................................	**15** A1
Mr Underhill's..................................	**16** A2

the 14th century but its chequered history is reflected in its different architectural styles. The round chapel in the inner bailey was built in 1120 and is one of few surviving round chapels in Britain. There is a wonderfully evocative audio tour (free), and the castle grounds provide an attractive setting during the Ludlow Festival.

The waymarked 30-mile **Mortimer Trail** to Kington starts just outside the castle entrance. The TIC can provide information on the trail.

The **Church of St Laurence** (King St), one of the largest parish churches in Britain, was extensively rebuilt in the 15th century but has some original Early English features. It also has a lofty tower, fine stained glass and some extraordinary, ornate medieval misericords ranging from the pious to the seemingly profane.

Guided walks run from April to October, leaving the cannon in Castle Sq at 2.30pm on Saturday and Sunday (£1.50). You can also take the **ghost walk** (adult £3.50; ☉ 8pm Fri) from the Buttercross.

Sleeping

In Ludlow accommodation can be a little expensive.

Mount (☎ 874084; rooms@themountludlow.co.uk; 61 Gravel Hill; s/d £30/50; P ☒) A good bet – this large Georgian house has airy, spacious rooms with simple, modern décor and a lovely garden. It's perched high on a hill and has great views of the town and countryside.

Number Twenty Eight (☎ 876996; info@lud lowno28.com; 28 Lower Broad St; d £75-120; ☒ ; wheelchair access) Right in the centre of town, this refined group of small period houses has charming rooms and several self-contained apartments. The mixture of period features and modern luxury makes it a very popular choice.

Feathers Hotel (☎ 875261; www.feathersatludlow .co.uk; Bull Ring; s/d £70/90) This stunningly picturesque timber-framed Jacobean property is the most atmospheric place to stay in town. It has magnificent public rooms and luxurious guest quarters, but ask for a room in the original building, as the newer bedrooms are more frilly than fascinating.

Other recommendations:

Dinham Hall Hotel (☎ 876464; www.dinhamhall.co.uk; s/d from £75/150; P ☒) Located by the castle, with sumptuous rooms, period design and a world-class restaurant (three-course dinner £35).

Pengwern (☎ 874635; www.pengwern.org.uk; 5 St Julians Ave; s/d £35/55; ☒) A large Edwardian house with bright modern rooms.

Eating

Courtyard (☎ 878080; Quality Sq; mains £5-7; ☉ lunch) Baked crab with lime and ginger or pheasant in red wine are some of the delicacies on offer at this wonderful lunch spot. Tucked away in a pretty courtyard, it has a loyal local following for its excellent-value food and simple snacks.

Koo (☎ 878462; 127 Old St; 4-course set menu £22.50; ☉ lunch & dinner Tue-Sat) This tiny Japanese place makes dinner a cultural experience, with a Japanese language lesson and tips on table etiquette thrown in. The minimalist décor reflects the traditional style of the food, which really is exquisite. A full option of vegetarian choices is also available.

Merchant House (☎ 875438; 62 Lower Corve St; set menu £33; ☺ lunch & dinner) Legendary in food terms yet totally unpretentious, this small and unassuming place has an international reputation. Creaky floors, low beams and rather old-style décor complement the classic European dishes that are done to absolute perfection. Plan ahead, though – this place is often booked up weeks in advance.

De Grey's Café (☎ 872764; 5-6 Broad St; mains £11-14; ☺ 9am-5pm Mon-Thu, 9am-5.30pm & 7-9pm Fri-Sat, 11am-5pm Sun; wheelchair access) A Ludlow institution, this unashamedly traditional tearoom with doily-and-antimacassar-style décor serves tea and decorated cakes by day and a classic European menu by night. The portions are generous and the cooking laudable if you're in the mood for traditional food.

Other recommendations:

Hibiscus (☎ 872325; 17 Corve St; set dinner menu £35; ☺ lunch & dinner) Contemporary Michelin-starred cuisine with a strong French accent and a fling with fusion.

Mr Underhill's (☎ 874431; Dinham Weir; set menu £32; ☺ lunch & dinner) In a wonderful riverside setting; serves incredible modern British food.

Getting There & Around

Trains go almost every hour to Shrewsbury (£7.10, 30 minutes), Church Stretton (£3.90, 15 minutes) and Hereford (£5.50, 25 minutes). Bus routes radiate to Hereford (No 492, one hour, six daily), Birmingham (No 192, 2¼ hours, nine daily Monday to Saturday, five on Sunday) and Shrewsbury (No 435, 1¼ hours, six daily). The town is very small and the sights are quite central, so your feet can easily take you where you want to go.

You can hire bikes from **Wheely Wonderful** (☎ 01568-770755; www.wheelywonderfulcycling.co.uk; Petchfield Farm, Elton), 5 miles west of Ludlow, for £12 to £15 per day. The company also organises cycling holidays in the area.

The Midlands

Anyone looking to find the 'real' England – not the typically pastoral scenes of postcards and tourist brochures, but the England where people actually live and labour – would be hard pressed to name a better region to search than the Midlands. If that sounds unglamorous, it shouldn't. The Midlands has some of the country's most gorgeous natural landscapes, particularly in the Peak District; several important castles (at Kenilworth and Warwick) and cathedrals (Lichfield, Southwell); and energetic urban centres with the kind of rollicking nightlife that naturally follows a hard day's work (Birmingham, Nottingham, Leicester). There are also the subtle charms of the ubiquitous market towns of England's industrial heartland, whose well-preserved half-timbered streets are seldom clogged with throngs of tourists. And, lest we forget, this is also the birthplace of Shakespeare.

Still, as England's manufacturing powerhouse, the Midlands are home to some fairly grim industrial settlements barricaded by mind-numbing ring roads. To make matters worse, several of the historic town centres that might have survived the Industrial Revolution were later bombed into aesthetic limbo during WWII. So, once you've checked off the unmissable sights, the best way to enjoy this region is to get right out of town. The hinterlands of most Midlands towns are delightful. From Birmingham you can hop on a narrow boat and wend your way west along the peaceful canals that once supplied the lifeblood of English industry. Ten miles outside Nottingham you can meander along gently winding roads through charming villages. and mere minutes from Derby, a busy transportation hub and industrial centre, you'll find yourself smack in the middle of prime wilderness area, seemingly a million miles from anything resembling a ring road.

HIGHLIGHTS

- Wandering hill and dale from pub to pub in the **Peak District National Park** (p435)
- Following in the footsteps of the Virgin Queen on a visit to the red ruins of **Kenilworth Castle** (p410)
- Checking out one of England's gloomiest – and loveliest – cathedrals in the pretty market town of **Lichfield** (p416)
- Taking a peek into the bedroom of Lord Byron, where all sorts of decadence went down, at **Newstead Abbey** (p429)
- Launching yourself into the stratosphere at Leicester's **National Space Centre** (p423)
- Trying out torture devices and dodging rats in the dungeons of **Warwick Castle** (p409)

- POPULATION: East Midlands 4,172,200; West Midlands 5,267,300
- AREA: 7193 SQ MILES

Orientation

It's perhaps appropriate that it's easiest to orientate yourself here by motorways. The M1 winds north from London, demarcating the eastern third of the region (which is bounded to the east by the A1) and running parallel with a line of the east Midlands' major towns: Bedford, Northampton, Leicester, Derby and Nottingham, in that order. The M40 does the same for the south and west Midlands, passing Stratford-upon-Avon and Warwick on its way to the M42 and Birmingham, in the middle of the region. Routes spider out from Birmingham, the M6 running east towards Coventry and the M1, and northwest up towards Wolverhampton, Stafford and Stoke-on-Trent; the M54 splits off at Wolverhampton to head over to Telford and Shrewsbury. The Peak District is midway between the M1 and the M6.

Information

The **Heart of England Tourist Board** (☎ 01905 761100; www.visitheartofengland.com) has centralised tourist information for the region and is a good place to start your planning.

Activities

Many parts of the Midlands are predominantly urban, and the opportunities for outdoor activities among the factories and streets are fairly limited. But out in those hinterlands, conditions are good for walking, cycling and water sports.

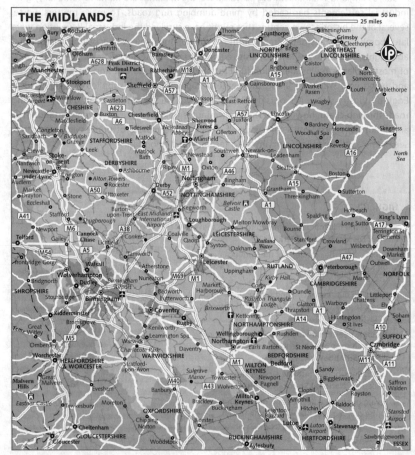

The Midlands

The Peak District National Park is one of the finest areas in England for walking and cycling – more details are given in the introduction to the Peak District section (p435). It's also home to the start of the Pennine Way national trail, which leads keen walkers for 256 miles through Yorkshire and Northumberland into Scotland. Under development, but with new sections opening all the time, the Pennine Bridleway runs roughly parallel to the walking route and is designed for horse riding and off-road cycling.

But these long-distance epics are the tip of the iceberg; the Peak District is crisscrossed with a vast network of paths for walkers, country lanes for touring cyclists, and tracks and bridleways for mountain bikers, and these include something for every level of ability, from mile-eating rides to gentle strolls. Ideal bases include the villages and small towns of Matlock Bath, Edale and Castleton, or the national park centre at Fairholmes on the Derwent Reservoirs. Bikes can be hired at Fairholmes and various other points around the Peak District, especially in the areas where old railway lines have been converted into delightful walking and cycling tracks.

In the south of the Midlands region, other good places for gentle walking and cycling include Cannock Chase and the National Forest – an ongoing project to plant 30 million trees across this part of central England. The main centre (called Conkers) is near Ashby-de-la-Zouch in Leicestershire.

Rutland Water, a large lake surrounded by cycling and walking trails, is also a great place for water sports such as sailing and windsurfing.

More information is given in Outdoor Activities (p74).

Getting There & Around

National Express (☎ 08705 808080; www.national express.com) provides extensive coach services in the Midlands. Birmingham is a major hub. For regional bus timetables, consult **SCB East Midlands Travel & Leisure** (www.scbeastmidstravel .co.uk). Regional bus services are provided by **Stagecoach** (☎ 01788 535555; Explorer tickets £5.99). A comprehensive network of bus services around the west Midlands is provided by **Travel West Midlands** (www.travelwm.co.uk). **Centro** (☎ 0121-200 2700; www.centro.org.uk), the transport

authority for the Birmingham and Coventry area, provides general travel advice and a comprehensive guide to getting around the west Midlands for those with mobility difficulties.

BIRMINGHAM

☎ 0121 / pop 970,900

Birmingham isn't what it once was. England's second-largest city – known colloquially as Brum, the inhabitants as Brummies and the dialect as Brummie – has long held a reputation as an industrial wasteland, an aesthetically challenged pit of crime and grime, the furthest thing from a tourist hotspot. While that bad rap may once have been somewhat justified, things have changed.

The most obvious difference to the visitor is architectural. A series of urban renewal projects has turned formerly dismal industrial parts of town into remarkably chic commercial areas; crumbling old warehouses have been renovated into experimental developments such as the Mailbox and the Bullring – sleek, shining outposts of fashionable shops and restaurants. At the same time, the city and its outlying areas have preserved several older cultural and architectural joys. The arts, culture and nightlife here are among the most vibrant in this part of the country, and a healthy manufacturing industry keeps the city's lifeblood flowing. In short, a visit to the new, improved Birmingham is mandatory for anyone who clings to an outdated impression of the place.

HISTORY

One of the great centres of the Industrial Revolution, Birmingham has been the birthplace of several inventions; it was home to steam pioneers James Watt (1736–1819) and Matthew Boulton (1728–1809) and chemist Joseph Priestley (1733–1804), to name a few. By the mid-19th century, though, the 'workshop of the world' exemplified everything that was bad about industrial development. It wasn't until later, under enlightened mayors such as Joseph Chamberlain (1836–1914), that the city first became a trendsetter in civic regeneration. But WWII air raids undid such leaders' good work, and post-war town planners completed the vandalism by

BIRMINGHAM

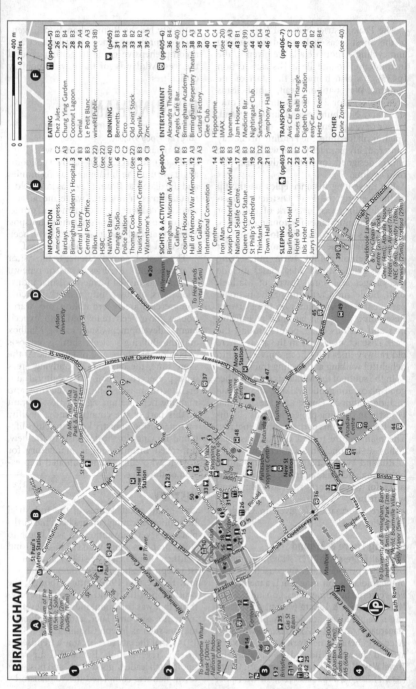

designing ring roads and motorways that virtually obliterated the old city centre, bar a few gems.

Fortunately, recently the city's leadership has once again devoted itself to ground-breaking civic revitalisation, creating developments such as the award-winning Brindleyplace, the Mailbox, Millennium Point and, most recently, the Bullring in formerly grim and often dangerous urban wastelands.

ORIENTATION

The one aspect of Birmingham that's still indisputably a nightmare is driving in it. The endless ring roads, roundabouts and underpasses make it particularly confusing for motorists to navigate. It's wise to park somewhere and explore the city on foot until you get your bearings.

The city centre is the pedestrian precinct in front of the huge Council House. Head west from here to Centenary Sq, the International Convention Centre and Symphony Hall, and the development at Gas St Basin and Brindleyplace.

Southeast of Council House, most of Birmingham's shops can be found along pedestrianised New St and in the modern City Plaza, Pallasades and Pavilions Shopping Centres; the latter is overlooked by the landmark Rotunda office block. Between New St station and Digbeth coach station is a much-ballyhooed new development called the Bullring, once a potentially scary eyesore and now a sleek, architecturally inventive shopping complex (see www.bullring .co.uk). See Tourist Information (right) for information about maps, and p406 for details on getting to/from the airport.

INFORMATION

Bookshops

Bonds Books (☎ 427 9343; 97a High Street, Harborne)
Dillons (☎ 631 4333; 128 New St)
Waterstone's (☎ 633 4353; Pavilions Shopping Centre, 24 High St)

Emergency

Police station (☎ 626 6000; Steelhouse Lane)
West Midlands Police (☎ 0845 113 5000)

Internet Access

Central Library (☎ 303 4511; Chamberlain Sq; ✆ 9am-8pm Mon-Fri, 9am-5pm Sat) Internet access is free by reservation.

Orange Studio (☎ 0800 790 0909; www.orangestudio .co.uk; 7 Cannon St; per hr £3; ✆ 8.30am-6.30pm Mon-Fri, 10am-6.30pm Sat) This hip 'chat café' off New St has DJs and a nightclub feel in the upstairs restaurant.

Internet Resources

Birmingham Museums & Art Gallery (www.bmag .org.uk) Information on most of the city's museums and galleries, including opening hours, admission costs and forthcoming exhibitions.
Itchy Birmingham (www.itchybirmingham.co.uk) An irreverent web guide to arts and culture.

Left Luggage

New Street Station (Station St; ✆ 6.45am-9.45pm Mon-Sat, 11.15am-6.45pm Sun)

Media

Free magazines litter hotels, bars and restaurants, providing updates on exhibitions, the best eateries, and the hippest bars and clubs. Pick of the bunch is the fortnightly *What's On* – free at some bars and at the Tourist Information Centre (TIC), elsewhere 80p.

Medical Services

Birmingham Children's Hospital (☎ 333 9999; Steelhouse Lane)
Heartlands Hospital (☎ 766 6611; Bordesley Green E) About 1.5 miles east of the centre; catch bus No 15, 17, 96, 97 or 99.

Money

American Express (☎ 644 5555; Bank House, Cherry St)
Barclays (Brindleyplace)
HSBC Bank & Thomas Cook Exchange (☎ 643 5057; 130 New St)
NatWest Bank (Arcadian Centre)

Post

Central post office (1 Pinfold St, Victoria Sq; ✆ 9am-5.30pm Mon-Fri, 9am-6pm Sat)

Tourist Information

TIC (www.birmingham.org.uk) Main branch (☎ 643 2514; 2 City Arcade; ✆ 9.30am-5.30pm Mon-Sat); National Exhibition Centre office (☎ 780 4321; piazza@bmp.org.uk; ✆ 9am-5.15pm Mon-Fri) The main branch has a wide range of maps, including themed leaflets; many are available as free downloads from the website. The National Exhibition Centre office is near Birmingham airport.

DANGERS & ANNOYANCES

What once were the scariest parts of Birmingham – the area around the Bullring, for example – have been transformed by the city's dramatic refurbishment efforts and are much less threatening than in days past. and the city's vibrant nightlife means there's as much activity on the busier streets at 2am as there is at 2pm. Still, as in most large cities, it's wise to avoid walking alone late at night in unlit areas, particularly for women.

SIGHTS & ACTIVITIES
Town Centre
The central pedestrian precinct of Victoria and Chamberlain Sqs features a **statue of Queen Victoria**, a fountain, a **memorial to Joseph Chamberlain** and some of Birmingham's most eye-catching architecture. The imposing **Council House** forms the northeastern face of the precinct. Its northwestern corner is formed by the modernist **Central Library**, reminiscent of an inverted ziggurat, with the Paradise Forum shop and café complex next to it.

To the south stands the **Town Hall**, designed by Joseph Hansom (creator of the hansom cab, forerunner to London's black taxis) in 1834 to look like the Temple of Castor and Pollux in Rome. For those who

won't make it to Gateshead to see Antony Gormley's *Angel of the North* statue (p621), his wingless **Iron Man** (1993), on Victoria Sq, is a step in the same direction.

West of the precinct, Centenary Sq is another pedestrian square, which is closed off at the western end by the **International Convention Centre** and the Symphony Hall, and overlooked by the Repertory Theatre. Inside Centenary Sq is the **Hall of Memory War Memorial**.

The **Birmingham Museum & Art Gallery** (☎ 303 2834; Chamberlain Sq; admission free; ☼ 10am-5pm Mon-Thu & Sat, 10.30am-5pm Fri, 12.30-5pm Sun) houses displays of local and natural history, fine archaeology and ethnography exhibits, and a renowned collection of Pre-Raphaelite paintings. Other highlights include works by Hilaire-Germain-Edgar Degas, Georges Braque, Pierre-Auguste Renoir and Antonio Canaletto. The charming Edwardian tearoom provides cake and coffee, too.

England's smallest cathedral, **St Philip's** (☎ 236 4333; Colmore Row; donations requested; ☼ 7am-7pm Mon-Fri, 9am-5pm Sat & Sun), was built in neoclassical style between 1709 and 1715. The Pre-Raphaelite artist Edward Burne-Jones

---

BIRMINGHAM IN...

Two Days
Spend your first day in Birmingham exploring the core of the city centre; wander through the pedestrian areas around Victoria, Chamberlain and Centenary Sqs, where the best of the city's historic buildings are preserved. Then delve into the **Birmingham Museum & Art Gallery** (p400). That evening, hit the Mailbox and Brindleyplace for dinner and nightlife. On day two, head for the **Jewellery Quarter** (p401) for good souvenir shopping and, at the museum, a fascinating lesson in the history of British industry.

Four Days
Follow the two-day itinerary, adding a meal at a balti joint to sample Birmingham's contribution to British cuisine. Next morning, make a pilgrimage to the **Barber Institute** (p401) and **Aston Hall** (p401) to see the region's most outstanding art collections. Spend day four on a narrowboat **cruise** (p403) of Birmingham's vast network of canals and waterways, then take the kids to **Cadbury World** (p407) for a sweet finale to your trip.

One Week
Follow the four-day schedule, then use the extra days to visit outlying areas. **Lichfield** (p416), with its marvellous three-spired cathedral, is only 14 miles to the northeast along the A38. The **Black Country Living Museum** (p407) in Dudley is also within easy reach for a day or half-day trip. Twenty miles east of Birmingham is Coventry, worth a stop for Sir Basil Spence's fantastic post-war **St Michael's Cathedral** (p415), which towers alongside the still-standing walls of the bombed-out old cathedral. Alternatively, for a longer jaunt, dash up to the **Peak District** (p435) for three days of long walks and cosy pubs.

was responsible for the magnificent stained-glass windows: the *Last Judgement* at the western end, and the *Nativity, Crucifixion* and *Ascension* at the eastern end.

Gas St, Brindleyplace & the Mailbox

Birmingham sits on the hub of England's canal network (the city actually has more canals than Venice), and visiting narrow boats can moor in the Gas St Basin right in the heart of the city. Nearby Brindleyplace, a waterfront development of trendy shops, restaurants and bars created during the 1990s, has transformed the area west of Centenary Sq into a buzzing nightlife scene. A similar development to the southeast, the Mailbox, is even more style-conscious, bristling with designer boutiques and sleek eateries.

The stylish **Ikon Gallery** (☎ 248 0708; www.ikon-gallery.co.uk; 1 Oozells Sq, Brindleyplace; admission free; ☼ 11am-6pm Tue-Sun & national holidays) is an airy, white space divided into several tiny rooms that feature changing exhibitions of modern art, ranging from the sublime to the ridiculous depending on one's taste. The attached café and coffee shop offers excellent food and even better trend-watching.

The **National Sealife Centre** (☎ 633 4700; www.sealife.co.uk; 3a Brindleyplace; adult £9.95; ☼ 10am-4pm Mon-Fri, 10am-5pm Sat & Sun), a state-of-the-art facility designed by Sir Norman Foster, is the largest inland aquarium in Britain; it swarms with exotic marine life. A seahorse breeding facility has recently been added; if you're lucky you might get a rare glimpse of a male seahorse delivering his thousand babies. The otter sanctuary is also a favourite with kids.

Jewellery Quarter

Birmingham has long been a major jewellery production centre, and the Jewellery Quarter is packed with manufacturers and showrooms. The TIC provides a free guide to the area, which includes background information about the industry and details of two walking trails around the district.

In the **Museum of the Jewellery Quarter** (☎ 554 3598; 75-79 Vyse St; admission free; ☼ 11.30am-4pm Tue-Sun Apr-Oct), the Smith & Pepper jewellery factory is preserved as it was on the day it closed in 1981 after 80 years of operation. You can explore the history of jewellery-making in Birmingham since the Middle Ages and watch demonstrations of the art.

The Jewellery Quarter is about three-quarters of a mile northwest of the centre; catch one of a host of buses (No 101 is the easiest), or take the metro from Snow Hill or the train from Moor St to Jewellery Quarter station.

Within walking distance of the Jewellery Quarter is **Soho House** (☎ 554 9122; Soho Ave, Handsworth; admission free; ☼ 11.30am-4pm Tue-Sun Apr-Oct), where the industrialist Matthew Boulton lived from 1766 to 1809. It has been painstakingly restored to reflect the styles of Boulton's era, and features displays on the great man's life and associates, including James Watt. Bus Nos 74, 78 and 79 pass nearby, or take the metro to Benson Rd station from Snow Hill.

Outlying Areas

East of the centre, the Millennium Point development was conceived as a way to bring technology to the people on a practical level. The focal point is **Thinktank** (☎ 202 2222; www.thinktank.ac; Curzon St; adult/child £6.95/4.95; ☼ 10am-5pm), a substantial and ambitious attempt to make science accessible (primarily to kids). Interactive displays cover topics such as the body and medicine, science in everyday life, nature, future technology, and industrial history.

A visit to the **Barber Institute** (☎ 414 7333; www.barber.org.uk; admission free; ☼ 10am-5pm Mon-Sat, noon-5pm Sun) is, for art lovers, the highlight of a visit to Birmingham. The collection takes in Renaissance masterpieces, paintings by old masters such as Peter Paul Rubens and Anthony van Dyck, British greats including Thomas Gainsborough, Joshua Reynolds and JMW Turner, an array of impressionist pieces and modern classics by the likes of Picasso and Schiele. The Barber Institute is at the University of Birmingham, 2½ miles south of the city centre. Take bus No 61, 62 or 63, or the train from New St to University station.

Aston Hall (☎ 327 0062; Trinity Rd, Aston; admission free; ☼ 11.30am-4pm Tue-Sun Easter-Oct), a Jacobean mansion built between 1618 and 1635, boasts some impressive friezes and ceilings, and houses a good portion of the furniture, paintings and textiles from the Birmingham Museum's collections. It's about 3 miles north of the city centre. Get here on bus No 65 or 104, or take a train to Aston station from New St Station.

WALKING TOUR

Birmingham's nickname – 'the Venice of the north' – feels a lot more apt at night, when the lights from the city's lively bars and clubs glimmer across the water of the canals. This tour meanders through some of the city's best nightlife quarters, stopping in at a few clubs and pubs along the way. Of course, you can do the tour in broad daylight as well, but these areas really shine at night.

The tour begins at the **Arcadian Centre (1)**, where there's a convenient underground car park, an ATM, and a small collection of techno-pumping clubs and bars that feature mood lighting and cocktails in vivid primary colours. You can stand in the central courtyard and pick one at random, but we like **Angels Café Bar** (p406).

> ### WALKING TOUR: BRUM NIGHTLIFE
>
> **Distance**: 1.5 miles
> **Duration**: 2–4 hours, depending on number of stops

Refreshed, continue northwest along Queensway until you reach the **Mailbox (2)**, a former mail-sorting factory and the latest of Birmingham's desiccated industrial skeletons to be turned into a trendy, attractive shopping-eating-clubbing complex. You can walk right through the building; go up the steps and inside, then take escalators to the balcony at the top, where you can stand and gaze out over one small vision of Birmingham's future. There are multiple opportunities for snacks and drinks up here.

From this vantage point, take the pedestrian bridge down to **Gas St (3)**, and follow the route of the narrow canal boats. Cross Broad St to explore **Brindleyplace (4)**, a mecca of cool modern architecture blended with industrial scraps and dotted with restaurants, bars and galleries. Don't miss **Ipanema** (p405), the **Ikon Gallery** (p401) or **Le Petit Blanc** (p404).

Wander up and down Broad St to look at the sparkly people in sparkly clubs, and hope you pass muster with at least one of the bouncers. When you're tired of that, follow Broad St back up past Centenary Sq

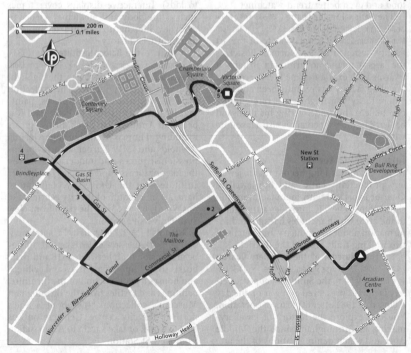

(stopping in at **wineREPublic**, p405, if you're still thirsty), through Paradise Circus and the spooky-at-night Chamberlain Sq, and into the centrally located **Victoria Sq (5)**, near the TIC, where our tour ends.

BIRMINGHAM FOR CHILDREN

Birmingham and the surrounding areas offer a few key attractions that'll keep the kids entertained. The most obvious is the **National Sealife Centre** (p401), where the playful otters entrance everyone, but especially the little ones. There's plenty to explore at **Thinktank** (p401), a gigantic attraction whose goal is to make science exciting and accessible, particularly at child level. Just outside of town, there's **Cadbury World** (p407), which is probably as much a guilty pleasure for parents as it is fun for their offspring. Finally, now that everyone has got a sugar high, try a family-friendly **cruise** down one of Birmingham's many narrow canals (p403).

TOURS

Second City Canal Cruises (☎ 236 9811; www.2nd citycboats.co.uk; adult/child £3/2) Tours leave by arrangement from the Canalside Souvenir Shop in Gas St Basin.

Sherborne Wharf (☎ 455 6163; www.sherbornewharf .co.uk; Sherborne St; ⏰ trips at 11.30am, 1pm, 2.30pm & 4pm daily mid-Apr–Oct, Sat & Sun year-round; adult/child £4.25/3.25) Canal cruises leave from the International Convention Centre, quayside.

FESTIVALS & EVENTS

Birmingham is a substantial and diverse enough city to support a number of interesting cultural festivals throughout the year, many focusing on its ever-growing arts scene. For a detailed and updated list, visit www.bbc.co.uk/birmingham. Following are some of the highlights:

Artsfest (Sep; www.artsfest.org.uk) The UK's largest free arts festival features visual arts, dance and musical performances in various venues across the city.

Collide (May-Jun; ☎ 303 2434) Birmingham City Council runs this ambitious, ground-breaking arts festival dedicated to showcasing the work of local up-and-coming black and Asian artists.

Crufts Dog Show (Mar; www.the-kennel-club.org.uk) The world's largest dog show, with 20,000 canines on parade.

Heritage Open Days (Sep; ☎ 8702 405 251; www .heritageopendays.org) This unique event allows visitors free access to historic properties that are not usually open or that normally charge an entrance fee, including 18 properties in and around Birmingham.

GAY & LESBIAN BIRMINGHAM

A comparatively strong appreciation for queer culture goes hand-in-hand with Birmingham's shiny new urban-chic image, thriving underground arts scene and party-all-night dance-club action. For dancing, the **Nightingale Club** (p405) is the biggest and best gay club; **Angels Café Bar** (p406) is a more casual gay-and-lesbian, straight-friendly hang-out in the heart of the gay club scene at the Arcadian Centre. **Clone Zone** (☎ 666 6640; 84 Hurst St; ⏰ 11am-9pm Mon-Sat, noon-7pm Sun) sells all kinds of fun sex toys, accessories and clothing aimed at a gay audience.

Resources include **B-Glad** (☎ 622 6589), a social support group for gays and lesbians suffering from depression; **Healthy Gay Life** (☎ 446 1085), an all-around information resource for gay and bisexual men; and the **Lesbian & Gay Switchboard** (☎ 622 6589; www.gaymidlands.org; ⏰ operators 7pm-10pm, recorded info at other times), a help and crisis line.

Horse of the Year Show (Oct; www.equine-world.co.uk) Top show-jumping equestrian event.

Latin American Festival (Jul; www.abslatin.co.uk) This annual festival celebrates the Latin-American community and culture in Birmingham.

SLEEPING

Central hotels court business visitors and can be at the higher end of the price spectrum, but they usually reduce their rates at the weekend. Check online or ask about specials at the TIC, which also makes accommodation bookings. Few B&Bs are central, but many lie within a 3-mile radius of the centre. Acocks Green (to the southeast) and the area stretching from Edgbaston to Selly Oak are popular areas.

Budget

Ashdale House Hotel (☎ 706 3598; www.ashdale house.co.uk; 39 Broad Rd, Acocks Green; s/d £25/46; P) This large, family-run place in a Victorian house overlooking a park is noted for its excellent vegetarian and organic breakfasts.

Mid-Range

Most of the mid-range options in the city centre are basic, rather unexciting chain hotels, but they do tend to offer parking and a great location from which to explore the Brindleyplace nightlife.

Ibis Hotel (☎ 622 6010; fax 622 6020; Arcadian Centre, Ladywell Walk; r Mon-Thu/Fri-Sun £65/55; **P**) There's nothing particularly remarkable about this chain hotel except that it's sparklingly modern (with all the fixings) and in a great location: inside the Arcadian Centre next to bars, cafés and Chinatown eateries aplenty. Parking costs £10 per night.

Awentsbury Hotel (☎ 472 1258; www.awentsbury .com; 21 Serpentine Rd, Selly Park; s/d from £40/63; **P**) In a cool Victorian house in Selly Park, close to the university, this friendly and cosy B&B boasts a private vintage car collection, which, if you're nice, the owners might show you.

Travelodge (☎ 191 4564; 230 Broad St; r Mon-Thu/ Fri-Sun £52.95/49.95; **P**) A Travelodge is a Travelodge, but this one is ideally positioned for exploring Brindleyplace's nightlife. It fills up fast, so be sure to book ahead.

Top End

Burlington Hotel (☎ 643 9191; www.burlingtonhotel .com; Burlington Arcade, 126 New St; s/d Sun-Thu £130/160, Fri & Sat £88/108; **P**) The Burlington is grand and classy, one of the best of the central options; its 112 rooms have all the mod cons but are painstakingly designed to create the feel of a much smaller boutique hotel. There's also a noted restaurant.

Hotel du Vin (☎ 236 0559; info@birmingham.hotel duvin.com; Church St; d from £110) This place, part of a highly reputable chain, is a former Victorian eye hospital converted into the sleekest boutique hotel in town, with a fine bistro, a health spa, a humidor and an amazing *cave du vin* (wine cellar).

Jurys Inn (☎ 606 9000; www.jurysdoyle.com; 245 Broad St; s/d from £59/99; **P**) Also right in among the pulsating throngs mobbing Brindleyplace, Jurys Inn has plush rooms and topnotch service, with a lobby that looks like a glowing shopping-mall entrance; weekend and online discounts are usually available here.

EATING

Birmingham's contribution to cuisine is the balti, a Pakistani dish that has been adopted by curry houses across the country. The heartland is the Birmingham Balti Triangle in Sparkbrook, 2 miles south of the centre.

Pick up a complete listings leaflet in the TIC (or see www.thebaltiguide.com) and head out on bus No 4, 5 or 6 from Corporation St.

Al Frash (☎ 753 3120; www.alfrash.com; 186 Ladypool Rd, Sparkbrook; mains £3-8; 🕑 5pm-midnight Sun-Thu, 5pm-1am Fri & Sat; **P**) If you only get to try one balti joint, this is it – it's one of the best, consistently winning awards for its baltis and scoring points for having more tasteful décor than the average.

Bank (☎ 633 4466; 4 Brindleyplace; 3-course meal £12.50, mains £9.50-20; 🕑 breakfast, lunch & dinner Mon-Fri, lunch & dinner Sat & Sun; **P**) Bank – as in where all your money goes? – is a classy restaurant that serves complicated mod-Brit dishes fit for the pretheatre crowd in a sophisticated atmosphere.

Chez Jules (☎ 633 4664; 5a Ethel St; mains £8.50-13, 2-course lunch £6.50; 🕑 lunch & dinner, closes 6pm Sun) It may be French, but this is a refreshingly unpretentious, faux-rustic place where bistro standards like steamed mussels are served on long, communal tables. Good prices on house wine seal the deal.

Chung Ying Garden (☎ 666 6622; 17 Thorp St; mains £7.50-13; 🕑 lunch & dinner) If you're anywhere near the Arcadian Centre, you'd be crazy to overlook tshis flagship of Birmingham's Chinatown, known for cooking up excellent Cantonese cuisine and turning out 70 varieties of dim sum.

Coconut Lagoon (☎ 643 3045; www.coconutlagoon .com; 12 Bennetts Hill; mains £10-14; 🕑 lunch & dinner) The inventive South Indian cuisine served at this branch of the small, award-winning regional chain has earned it the title of 'Best Indian Restaurant in the Midlands' in the *Good Curry Guide* for 2003–04.

Denial (☎ 643 3080; 120-122 Wharfside St; mains lunch/dinner £8.50/14.95, set 2-/3-course menu £12/13; 🕑 lunch & dinner Mon-Sat, breakfast & lunch Sun) Follow your ears to this canalside eatery in the Mailbox – the sleek restaurant-bar is notorious for pumping out the loud beats all day, but what draws the evening crowds is its highly rated modern British cuisine with a Mediterranean slant.

Le Petit Blanc (☎ 633 7333; 9 Brindleyplace; 2-/3-course set menu £12.50/15.50, mains £8.50-15.75; 🕑 lunch & dinner; **P**) Serious foodies will enjoy a pilgrimage here to sample chef Raymond Blanc's cuisine, with traditional Francophile favourites such as duck cooked in armagnac, and a substantial wine list. Reservations are recommended.

wineREPublic (☎ 644 6464; Centenary Sq; bar menu £4-7, mains £8-14; ☯ lunch & dinner Mon-Sat; P) The Rep theatre's restaurant is bright, sharp and airy, and the food comes in for plenty of praise. Everything on the extensive wine list can be bought by the glass or the bottle, so oenophiles can sample to their heart's content. Reservations are recommended.

DRINKING

As with the dining scene in Birmingham, the world of drinking and dancing is constantly changing. Keep an eye on the magazines and flyers in bars for the latest news. Chain bars are the norm here; finding an honest-to-god 'pub' in the centre is tricky, but there are many places worth checking out, including two impressive banks-turned-boozers.

Bennetts (☎ 643 9293; 8 Bennetts Hill) A plush bar in a former bank, Bennetts is a massive space, like the interior of a regency hall; there's a mellow 'library' area if the grand surroundings get too much.

Circo (☎ 643 1400; 6 Holloway Circus) An alternative to the pub scene, this modern bar is a student hang-out midweek, there's a preclub scene at the weekend, boasting some excellent guest DJs and stomach-lining tapas.

Old Joint Stock (☎ 200 1892; 4 Temple Row West) A vast, high-ceilinged cathedral of beer, this awesome venue in a former bank glitters with gilt mouldings and a glass dome, and serves fine Fuller's ales to a cheerful crowd.

Sputnik (☎ 643 7510; Upper Temple St) If hygiene isn't your first priority, this is the place: it has that grungy feel licked, with a basement bar displaying B-movie posters and varied tunes (reggae, drum'n'bass, funk and house), plus good beers and a friendly vibe.

Zinc (☎ 200 0620; Regency Wharf, Gas St Basin) Though it's probably obvious from the name, this is a Conran bar-diner; there's an enticing menu, and the cool, relaxed space lends itself to chilling to the jazz and funk soundtrack.

ENTERTAINMENT

There's no lack of things to do for fun in Birmingham. Tickets for most events can be purchased through the national **TicketWeb** (☎ 0870 771 2000; www.ticketweb.co.uk).

There's a range of entertainment options at the **Custard Factory** (☎ 604 7777; www.custard factory.com; Gibb St, Digbeth). So named because the building was constructed a century ago by custard magnate Sir Alfred Bird, this cool venue is a good place to start if you're looking for the motherlode of underground culture in Birmingham. Once a sprawling industrial site, the remarkable and ever-expanding arts and media centre has taken the city by storm; it houses a gallery, arts and recording studios, dance and theatre spaces, bars, cafés…you name it.

Cinemas

Imax (☎ 202 2222; www.imax.ac; Curzon St; adult/child £4.50/2.50) Birmingham's first IMAX cinema, with a five-storey screen, is at Millennium Point.

Live Music

National Exhibition Centre (NEC; ☎ 909 4133) This giant venue, located near the airport, hosts major rock and pop acts, as does its sister venue, the **National Indoor Arena** (☎ 909 4144; King Edwards Rd) behind Brindleyplace.

Jam House (☎ 200 3030; www.thejamhouse.com; 1 St Paul's Sq) This well-known and very classy music bar features live swing, jazz, R & B and rock & roll. The top-floor restaurant is noted for serving global cuisine that far surpasses what you'd expect from a music club.

Acts that don't come through Birmingham usually play the **Civic & Wulfrun Halls** in Wolverhampton (p407).

Other recommendations:

Birmingham Academy (☎ 262 3000; www.birmingham -academy.co.uk; 52-54 Dale End) The best rock and pop venue in town.

Symphony Hall (☎ 780 3333; Broad St; tickets from £7.50) For classical music, including performances by the City of Birmingham Symphony Orchestra.

Nightclubs

Medicine Bar (☎ 693 6001; Custard Factory, Gibb St, Digbeth) The night-time hotspot within the Custard Factory, this is where the hip and the curious drink till late to the sounds of the region's up-and-coming DJs.

Ipanema (☎ 643 5577; 9 Brindleyplace) In an airy space reminiscent of a tremendously chic lighting store, this restaurant/dance club doles out tapas, a mellow vibe, guest DJs and the chance to brush up on your salsa skills.

Nightingale Club (☎ 622 1718; Essex House, Kent St) Birmingham's oldest and largest gay club, the Nightingale rocks on three levels (including a restaurant); it's an always-hopping, see-and-be seen kind of place.

Angels Café Bar (☎ 244 2626; 127-131 Hurst St) A great place for a preclub drink and snack, this Arcadian Centre club has a varied, gay- and lesbian-friendly crowd and is more casual than many of the other way-chic bars in the area.

Sanctuary (☎ 246 1010; 78 Digbeth High St) With the closure of the legendary Que club, this large electronica venue has absorbed a fair share of the techno-loving crowd, with drum'n'bass a speciality.

Glee Club (☎ 0870 241 5093; www.glee.co.uk; Arcadian Centre) The region's primary comedy club hosts stand-up comedians several nights a week.

Sport
Villa Park (☎ 327 5353; www.avfc.co.uk; tickets adult/child from £5/15) Aston Villa football club plays in this arena north of the city centre.

Warwickshire County Cricket Club (☎ 446 5506; www.wccc.co.uk; County Ground, Edgbaston; tickets from £12) Tickets for international test matches sell out early, but local matches are usually available.

Theatre
Hippodrome (☎ 0870 730 1234; www.birmingham-hippodrome.co.uk; Hurst St) This place, Brum's primary venue for major theatrical events, hosts the Birmingham Royal Ballet as well as touring musicals of the *Jesus Christ Superstar* calibre.

Alexandra Theatre (☎ 08706077544; Suffolk St) This venue, near the train station, offers everything from *Aida* to *Annie* and seems particularly fond of talks by TV personalities.

Birmingham Repertory Theatre (☎ 236 4455; www.birmingham-rep.co.uk; Centenary Sq, Broad St) In two venues, the Main House and the more experimental Door, the Rep presents serious drama from around the UK and new plays straight from London's best theatres.

SHOPPING
Jewellery Quarter (www.the-quarter.com) Northwest of the centre, this is the obvious place for unique local shopping in Birmingham. In this region, where most of the jewellery manufactured in England comes from, more than a hundred shops sell traditional handcrafted gold and silver jewellery, watches, clocks and more. The Museum of the Jewellery Quarter (p401) has leaflets detailing notable retail outlets and artisans.

GETTING THERE & AWAY
Air
Birmingham has an increasingly busy **international airport** (☎ 767 5511; www.bhx.co.uk) with flights to numerous European destinations and New York. It's on the outskirts of Birmingham, about 7 miles east of the centre.

Bus
National Express (☎ 0990 808080) runs coaches between Digbeth coach station and destinations around England including London (£13 single, 2¾ hours, hourly), Oxford (£14.65 single, 1½ hours, five daily) and Manchester (£10.25 single, 2½ hours, 11 daily). Bus X20 runs to Stratford-upon-Avon hourly on weekdays (1¼ hours).

Train
Most national trains run from New St Station, beneath the Pallasades shopping centre, including those to and from London (£24.90 cheap day single, 1¾ hours, every 30 minutes) and Manchester (£22 single, 1¾ hours, every 30 minutes).

Other services, such as those heading to Stratford-upon-Avon (£4.95 single, 50 minutes, hourly), run from Snow Hill and Moor St stations.

In July and August, the **Shakespeare Express steam train** (☎ 707 4696; www.vintagetrains.co.uk; standard return £15) runs between Birmingham Snow Hill and Stratford-upon-Avon twice each Sunday. Journeys take one hour.

GETTING AROUND
To/From the Airport
Bus No 900 runs to the airport (45 minutes, every 20 minutes). Trains for the airport run between New St and Birmingham International station (45 minutes, every 10 minutes). A **taxi** (☎ 782 3744) from the airport to the centre costs about £18.

Bus
Centro (☎ 200 2700) is the agency that runs public transport in Birmingham; contact them for timetables, route information and ticket purchasing.

Car
The major players in town are **Avis** (☎ 782 6183; 7-9 Park St), **easyCar** (☎ 0906 333 3333; www.easycar.co.uk; Horse Fair Car Park, Bristol St), and **Hertz** (☎ 782 5158; Suffolk St).

Public Transport

Centro (☎ 200 2700; www.centro.org.uk) offers a **Daytripper ticket** (adult/child £4.10/2.60) for all-day travel on buses and trains after 9.30am; if you need to start earlier, buy a **Centrocard** (£5.20). Tickets are available from the **Central Travel Information Centre** (New St Station).

Local trains operate from Moor St station, which is only a few minutes' walk from New St – follow the red line on the footpath.

Birmingham's tram system, the **Metro** (www .travelmetro.co.uk), runs from Snow Hill to Wolverhampton via the Jewellery Quarter, West Bromwich and Dudley. Fares start at 60p and rise to £2.20 for the full length. A day pass costs £3.50.

Black cabs (☎ 782 3744) ideally should be reserved in advance.

AROUND BIRMINGHAM

CADBURY WORLD & BOURNVILLE VILLAGE

A lip-smacking exploration into the production, marketing and (naturally) consumption of chocolate, **Cadbury World** (☎ 0121-451 4159; www.cadburyworld.co.uk; Linden Rd; adult/child £9/6.80) comes complete with interactive gizmos and plenty to keep kids entertained. Ride a beanmobile or take a wander down Cocoa Rd, paved with 'talking chocolate splodges'. You must book ahead by phone. Opening hours are complicated; it's closed for much of December and January and open from 10am to 3pm or 10am to 4pm for most of the rest of the year (phone or check the website).

Cadbury World is part of pretty Bournville village, designed for early-20th-century factory workers by the Cadbury family. **Selly Manor** (☎ 0121-472 0199; Maple Rd; adult/child £2/50p; ☼ 10am-5pm Tue-Fri year-round, plus 2-5pm Sat & Sun Apr-Sep), dating from at least 1327, was carefully taken apart and reconstructed by George Cadbury in order to save it from destruction. It now houses 18th-century furnishings and has a Tudor garden.

To get to Bournville take a train from Birmingham New St, or bus No 83, 84 or 85.

THE BLACK COUNTRY

The industrial region west of Birmingham is known as the Black Country, a 19th-century epithet bestowed because of the smoke from its foundries and factories. It's since been cleaned up, and anyone interested in how industry shapes a country should make a stop. The **Black Country Living Museum** (☎ 0121-557 9643; www.bclm.co.uk; Tipton Rd, Dudley; adult/child £9.95/5.75; ☼ 10am-5pm Mar-Oct, 10am-4pm Wed-Sun Nov-Feb) features a coal mine, village and fairground, re-created as they would have been in the industrial heyday of the 19th century. It's a great place for a day out, with a full programme of mine trips, Charlie Chaplin films, and opportunities to watch glasscutters and sweet-makers in action.

To get here from Birmingham's city centre, take bus No 126 from Corporation St and ask to be let off at Tipton Rd. It's a 10-minute walk to the museum, or you can catch bus No 311 or 313. Alternatively, take the train from Birmingham New St to Tipton, 1 mile from the museum. A Daytripper ticket will cover the entire bus or train journey.

Wolverhampton

☎ 01902 / pop 251,000

If you thought Brummies sounded funny, wait'll you get to Wolverhampton. Situated just west of Birmingham, this town has an accent unique even in the west Midlands.

For information on the area, visit the **TIC** (☎ 556110; www.wolverhampton.tic.dial.pipex.com; 18 Queen Sq; ☼ 9.30am-5pm Mon-Sat Apr-Sep, 9.30am-4pm Mon-Sat Oct-Mar).

Along with the **Wolverhampton Art Gallery** (☎ 552055; Lichfield St; admission free; ☼ 10am-5pm Mon-Sat), boasting fine collections of pop art and 18th- and 19th-century landscape paintings, this town is also home to **Wightwick Manor** (☎ 761400; Wightwick Bank; adult £6; ☼ 1.30-5pm Thu, Sat & bank hols Mar-Dec). Run by the National Trust (NT), it is an Arts-and-Crafts masterpiece, complete with original William Morris wallpaper and fabrics, Kempe glass and de Morgan tiling.

The **Civic & Wulfrun Halls** (☎ 552121; www.wolves civic.co.uk; North St) draw fans from all across the west Midlands for rock, pop and alternative music concerts. Check out the website for upcoming gigs.

Wolverhampton is approximately 20km northwest of Birmingham along the A41. The train station is northeast of the city centre, just beyond the ring road. The bus station is at the end of Lichfield Street. Trains, buses and the downtown Metro Line all go to and from Birmingham several times daily (35 to 45 minutes).

WARWICKSHIRE

Home to two of England's best and most popular tourist attractions – the impressive Warwick Castle and the birthplace of William Shakespeare in Stratford-upon-Avon – Warwickshire would have been a lovely place to visit even without these essential sites. Full of lush, green river valleys and the cobblestone alleys and half-timbered houses typical of small English market towns, it's an ideal place for a country drive. For history and drama, it's hard to beat the picturesquely devastated Kenilworth Castle, and there's scarcely a better example of that old English stiff upper lip than the stunning modern cathedral lurking over the bombed-out shell of its sister at Coventry.

Orientation & Information

Warwickshire is roughly kidney-shaped, with Coventry sitting between the lobes. Kenilworth, Leamington Spa and Warwick lie in the line running south from Coventry; Stratford-upon-Avon sits on the other side of the M40 motorway that bisects the southern lobe.

Shakespeare Country tourism (www.shakespeare-country.co.uk) has information on the whole region.

Getting Around

Warwickshire transport (www.warwickshire.gov.uk/transport) has details of local bus and train services, as well as news on roads. Coventry is a major transport hub, with rail connections to London Euston, Birmingham New St and Leicester.

A good ticket option is the **Shakespeare Country Explorer** (adult one day £25, three days £30), which allows return train travel from London Marylebone or Paddington to Stratford, Warwick or Leamington Spa, plus unlimited travel between these towns for the duration of the ticket, and discounted admission to attractions.

WARWICK

☎ 01926 / pop 23,350

The obvious reason to visit Warwick is its outstanding castle, an all-day event that'll

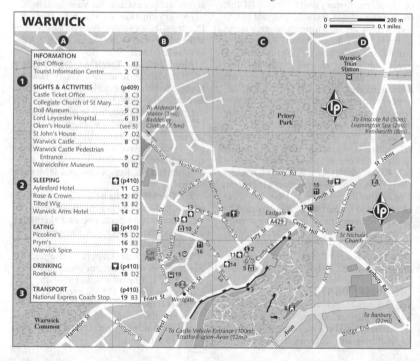

WARWICK

INFORMATION	
Post Office	1 B3
Tourist Information Centre	2 C3

SIGHTS & ACTIVITIES	(p409)
Castle Ticket Office	3 C3
Collegiate Church of St Mary	4 C2
Doll Museum	5 C3
Lord Leycester Hospital	6 B3
Oken's House	(see 5)
St John's House	7 D2
Warwick Castle	8 C3
Warwick Castle Pedestrian Entrance	9 C2
Warwickshire Museum	10 B2

SLEEPING	(p410)
Aylesford Hotel	11 C3
Rose & Crown	12 B2
Tilted Wig	13 B2
Warwick Arms Hotel	14 C3

EATING	(p410)
Piccolino's	15 D2
Prym's	16 B3
Warwick Spice	17 C2

DRINKING	(p410)
Roebuck	18 D2

TRANSPORT	(p410)
National Express Coach Stop	19 B3

impress parents and entrance kids. But don't rush off afterwards; despite a devastating fire in 1694, the quiet county town has several well-preserved historic buildings, many of which house interesting small museums, and it has a welcoming feel that invites casual strolling.

Orientation & Information

Warwick is simple to navigate; the A429 runs right through the centre with Westgate at one end and Eastgate at the other. The old town centre lies just north of this axis, the castle just south.

The TIC (☎ 492212; www.warwick-uk.co.uk; Court House, Jury St; ☒ 9.30am-4.30pm), near the junction with Castle St, sells the informative *Warwick Town Trail* leaflet (50p).

Sights

WARWICK CASTLE

Even without its sis-boom-bah presentation and eerily lifelike wax inhabitants, **Warwick Castle** (☎ 0870 442 2000; www.warwick-castle.co.uk; adult/child £13.50/8.25, peak dates £14.50/8.75; ☒ 10am-6pm Mon-Fri, 10am-7pm Sat & Sun Aug, 10am-6pm daily Apr-Jul & Sep, 10am-5pm daily Oct-Mar; **P**) would be a stunner. For starters, it's incredibly well preserved: the walls decaying just enough to be picturesque and the rest of it solid enough to climb around. Warwick, with its strategic position, has been the site of fortifications since the 10th century. William the Conqueror ordered the construction of a wooden motte-and-bailey fort here in 1068, but the magnificent medieval castle is largely the 14th-century work of Thomas de Beauchamp, with 17th- to 19th-century interior embellishments. Lancelot 'Capability' Brown landscaped the splendid grounds in 1753. The result is one of the most substantial and impressive castles in England: be prepared to spend hours wandering and wondering (and, in summer, queuing; it's very popular, though the crowds are well shepherded).

The castle is owned by Tussauds, and that influence is evident in the waxwork figures that populate the private apartments, displayed as a late-19th-century weekend party. The packaging and sheen don't mask the highlights, though: the superb furnishings and sheer splendour of the interior are fascinating, and a walk around the ramparts rewards with panoramic views. Kids love

the arrays of weighty armour, the dungeons (with torture chamber) and the 'ghost tower', while the 19th-century mill house offers an insight into early power generation.

COLLEGIATE CHURCH OF ST MARY

Originally built in 1123, this fine **church** (☎ 403940; Old Sq; requested donation £1; ☒ 10am-6pm Apr-Oct, 10am-4.30pm Nov-Mar) was badly damaged by the Great Fire of Warwick in 1694 and rebuilt in a mishmash of styles. The remarkable perpendicular Beauchamp Chapel (built 1442–60 at a cost of £2400, a huge sum for the time) survived the fire, and the magnificent bronze effigy of Richard Beauchamp, 13th earl of Warwick, graces the centre of the chapel. The sinister-looking figure on the corner of the tomb is Richard 'Kingmaker' Neville, who also figures prominently in the displays at Warwick Castle. Don't miss the 12th-century crypt with remnants of a medieval dunking stool, used to drench scolding wives.

LORD LEYCESTER HOSPITAL

At the Westgate end of the town, the road cuts through a sandstone cliff, above which perches the impressive **Lord Leycester Hospital** (☎ 491422; High St; adult £3.20, garden only £1.50; hospital ☒ 10am-5pm Tue-Sun Apr-Sep, 10am-4pm Tue-Sun Oct-Mar), which was turned into an almshouse in 1571 by Robert Dudley, earl of Leicester and favourite of Queen Elizabeth I. Housed in a group of 14th-century timber-framed buildings, it has a beautiful courtyard, a fine chapel and a guildhall built by Kingmaker Neville.

OTHER SIGHTS

Interesting sights include the **Warwickshire Museum** (☎ 412500; Market Pl; admission free; ☒ 10am-5pm Tue-Sat year-round, plus 11.30am-5pm Sun Apr-Sep), in the 17th-century market building, with displays on the natural history and archaeology of the region. The **Doll Museum** (☎ 495546; Castle St; adult/child £1/75p; ☒ 10am-5pm Tue-Sat, 11.30am-5pm Sun Apr-Sep, 10am-4pm Sat Oct-Mar), in the half-timbered medieval **Oken's House** – a worthy spectacle in its own right – contains a fine collection of early dolls and toys. **St John's House** (☎ 412132; St John's; admission free; ☒ 10am-5pm Tue-Sat year-round, plus 2.30-5pm Sun Apr-Sep), a charming Jacobean mansion, features reconstructed Victorian rooms and a regimental museum.

Sleeping

The nearest hostel is in Stratford-upon-Avon (see p414). Mid-range B&Bs line Emscote Rd, the eastern end of the main road through Warwick that heads for Leamington Spa.

Warwick Arms Hotel (☎ 492759; fax 410587; 17 High St; s/d £55/65; P) This plush hotel in an early-18th-century coaching inn has history and comfort galore.

Rose & Crown (☎ 411117; www.peachpubs.com; 30 Market Pl; r £65) Most of the rooms in this lively pub overlook the market square and are equipped with business-friendly gadgets.

Aylesford Hotel (☎ 492799; www.aylesfordhotel .co.uk; 1 High St; s/d £55/65) This first-class establishment opposite the TIC has great rooms (some with four-poster beds), a casual bistro and a medieval-styled cellar restaurant.

Tilted Wig (☎ 410466; tiltedwig@tiscali.co.uk; 11 Market Pl; s/d from £30/60; ✗) This pleasant old pub in the town centre, with views onto the market square, has four nonsmoking rooms, good pub food and an outdoor area for summer dining.

Eating & Drinking

Piccolino's (☎ 491020; 31 Smith St; pizza & pasta £5-7.50; ✤ lunch & dinner) This family-run Italian hangout is deservedly popular, with a real trattoria atmosphere and a really delicious seafood pasta.

Prym's (☎ 439504; 48 Brook St; mains £10-16; ✤ lunch & dinner Mon-Sat, lunch Sun) Although it looks like a simple café, this local favourite serves up fine, game-heavy specialities such as guinea fowl and venison.

Warwick Spice (☎ 491736; 24 Smith St; mains £4.50-10; ✤ dinner) Whether you're on a budget or willing to splurge, you'll find something to suit your taste at this relaxed place serving up Indian and Bangladeshi dishes.

Roebuck (☎ 494900; Smith St; ✤ lunch & dinner) Justifiably plugging itself as an 'ale shrine', this is a friendly, snug pub with a selection of good cask beers and photos of old Warwick.

Getting There & Away

National Express coaches operate from Puckerings Lane on Old Sq. Local bus Nos X16 and X18 run to Coventry (every 55 minutes), Stratford-upon-Avon (20 minutes) and Leamington Spa (15 minutes) from Market Sq (hourly Monday to Saturday, every two hours Sunday).

Trains run to Birmingham (30 minutes, every half-hour), Stratford-upon-Avon (20 minutes, hourly) and London (1½ hours, hourly).

KENILWORTH

☎ 01926 / pop 22,200

Kenilworth is best known for its medieval castle, famously visited by Elizabeth I and now falling attractively to pieces on its hilltop. The tiny old town is within easy walking distance and worth seeking out for its pretty streets lined with saggy-roofed pubs and antique shops. The modern section of town is pleasant enough and a good source of accommodation and eateries.

Information

TIC (☎ 852595; Library, 11 Smalley Pl; ✤ 9am-7pm Mon, Tue, Thu & Fri, 9.30am-4pm Sat) Local tourist information.

Sights

The dramatic, red-sandstone **Kenilworth Castle** (☎ 852078; adult £4.80; ✤ 10am-5pm Mar-May, Sep & Oct, 10am-6pm Jun-Aug, 10am-4pm Nov-Feb), run by the English Heritage (EH), was founded around 1120 and enlarged in the 14th and 16th centuries. It's been owned and inhabited by an array of powerful men, including John of Gaunt, Simon de Montfort and Robert Dudley, favourite of Elizabeth I, whose visits here were accompanied by gossip, intrigue and tremendous fanfare. The castle was partly dismantled and its vast lake drained in 1644 after the Civil War, but the huge 12th-century keep and extensive Norman walls remain. Don't skip the audio tour, which brings history to life as you wander around the atmospheric ruins. Various events and performances take place here throughout the year; call for details.

The impressive Georgian abbey-mansion **Stoneleigh Abbey** (☎ 858535; www.stoneleighabbey .org; adult £6; ✤ tours 11am, 2pm & 3pm Tue-Thu & Sun Easter-Oct), founded in 1154, was undergoing restoration at the time of research, but a large chunk is open to the public. The splendid Palladian West Wing, completed in 1726, contains richly detailed plasterwork ceilings and panelled rooms; the medieval gatehouse, dating from 1346, is also interesting, as are the grounds, landscaped by Repton and Nessfield. Stoneleigh is about 2 miles east of Kenilworth town centre, off the B4115.

Sleeping & Eating

Castle Laurels Hotel (☎ 856179; www.castlelaurels hotel.co.uk; Castle Rd; s/d £40/60) This superior B&B near the castle is much more like a small, exclusive hotel.

Virgins & Castle (☎ 853737; 7 High St; pub food £4-6, Filipino meals £8-9, spring rolls £4.50) This comfortably worn old pub is a homely, sprawling place full of nooks and crannies, with a room for every mood (there's even a balcony) and a menu that's filled with Filipino specialities.

Clarendon Arms (☎ 852017; 44 Castle Hill; pub food £4-8, dinners £8-13) This pub, opposite the castle, is renowned for its food and has a garden and courtyard for summer supping. For local flavour try the Godiva burger (served 'with nothing on').

Getting There & Away

Bus No X16 or X18 runs hourly to/from Stratford-upon-Avon (50 minutes), Warwick (20 minutes), Coventry (25 minutes) or Leamington Spa (15 minutes).

STRATFORD-UPON-AVON

☎ 01789 / pop 22,200

There is a lot more to Stratford-upon-Avon than Shakespeare-emblazoned T-shirts and keychains, although there are, of course, plenty of those things to be had. The Bard is ubiquitous in this town, and during the summer months the streets here are thronged with fans making pilgrimages. It can be a little overwhelming, but do not let the commercialism put you off. Stratford's irresistible appeal – it is an undeniably pretty town, full of historic buildings, half-timbered houses and thatched roofs – is sure to erase any Bard-sick cynicism. Stratford-upon-Avon is also a handy base for exploring the surrounding areas, particularly if you avoid the high tourism season when accommodation can be very hard to come by. Stratford is convenient to Coventry, Warwick and Kenilworth Castles, and the Cotswolds, and there's a wealth of dining and entertainment options.

Orientation

Arriving by coach or train, you'll find yourself within walking distance of the town centre, which is easy to explore on foot. Transport is only really essential for visiting Mary Arden's House.

Information

Cyber Junction (☎ 263400; 28 Greenhill St; ⊙ 10am-5.30pm Mon-Thu & Sat, 10am-6pm Fri, 10am-5pm Sun; per 30min/1 hour £5/3) Internet access and game play.

Guided walks (☎ 412602; ⊙ 10.30am Sat year-round, plus Sun Jul-Sep) Free two-hour walks depart from outside the TIC at 10.30am.

Sparklean Laundrette (☎ 269075; 74 Bull St; ⊙ 8am-9pm)

TIC (☎ 293127; stratfordtic@shake speare-country.co.uk; ⊙ 9am-6pm Mon-Sat, 10.30am-4.30pm Sun Apr-Oct, 9am-5pm Mon-Sat, 10am-3pm Sun Nov-Mar) Helpful, but frantically busy in summer.

Sights & Activities

THE SHAKESPEARE HOUSES

The best approach to the Bard is to purchase a combination ticket to all five Shakespeare properties and make a day of it. Managed by the **Shakespeare Birthplace Trust** (☎ 204016; www.shakespeare.org.uk; all 5 properties £13, 3 in-town houses £10; ⊙ generally 9am-5pm Mon-Sat, 10am-5pm Sun Jun-Aug, variable at other times), three of the houses are central, one is a short bus ride away, and the fifth a drive or bike ride out. Opening times are complicated and vary during the off season (check the website for details). In summer, crowds pack the small Tudor houses; a visit out of season is much more enjoyable. Note that wheelchair access to the properties is restricted.

The main attraction, **Shakespeare's Birthplace** (Henley St), has a modern exterior, but inside it is very much 'olde'. It has been a tourist hotspot for three centuries, famous 19th-century visitor-vandals have scratched their names on one of the windows, and the guest book bears the signatures of some big-time literati. Family rooms have been re-created in the style of Shakespeare's time, and there is a 'virtual reality' display downstairs for visitors unable to gain access to the upper areas. A ticket includes admission to the adjacent **Shakespeare Exhibition**, where well-devised interpretive displays give the lowdown on Stratford-upon-Avon's most famous son.

Displays in **Nash's House**, where Shakespeare's granddaughter Elizabeth lived, describe the town's history and contain a collection of 17th-century oak furniture and tapestries. The Elizabethan garden next door occupies part of the grounds of a (now demolished) house Shakespeare bought when he retired.

Shakespeare's daughter Susanna married the eminent doctor John Hall, and their fine Elizabethan town house, **Hall's Croft** (Old Town), now contains a fascinating insight into medical practice in Shakespeare's time.

Before their marriage, Shakespeare's wife lived in Shottery, a mile west of the centre, in a thatched farmhouse now known as **Anne Hathaway's Cottage**. A footpath (no bikes allowed) leads to Shottery from Evesham Pl, or catch a **bus** (☎ 404984) from the NatWest bank on Wood St to the end of Cottage Lane.

Mary Arden was Shakespeare's mother, and a **house** at Wilmcote, 3 miles west of Stratford, was her childhood home. If you cycle there via Anne Hathaway's Cottage,

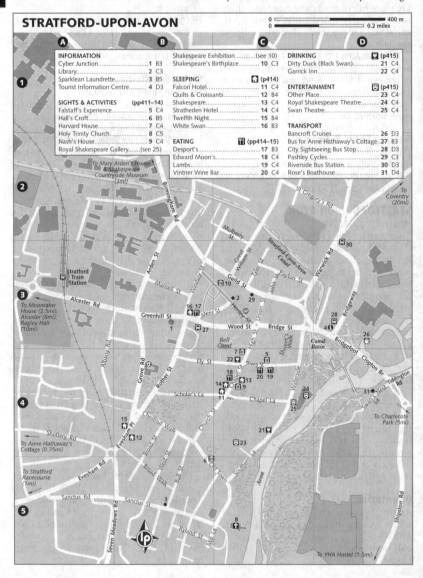

STRATFORD-UPON-AVON

0 — 400 m
0 — 0.2 miles

INFORMATION
Cyber Junction...........................1 B3
Library......................................2 C3
Sparklean Laundrette................3 B5
Tourist Information Centre........4 D3

SIGHTS & ACTIVITIES   (pp411-14)
Falstaff's Experience..................5 C4
Hall's Croft...............................6 B5
Harvard House..........................7 C4
Holy Trinity Church...................8 C5
Nash's House.............................9 C4
Royal Shakespeare Gallery.......(see 25)

Shakespeare Exhibition............(see 10)
Shakespeare's Birthplace.........10 C3

SLEEPING   ⌂ (p414)
Falcon Hotel...........................11 C4
Quilts & Croissants..................12 B4
Shakespeare...........................13 C4
Stratheden Hotel.....................14 C4
Twelfth Night..........................15 B4
White Swan.............................16 B3

EATING   🍴 (pp414-15)
Desport's.................................17 B3
Edward Moon's.......................18 C4
Lambs.....................................19 C4
Vintner Wine Bar....................20 C4

DRINKING   🍷 (p415)
Dirty Duck (Black Swan)..........21 C4
Garrick Inn.............................22 C4

ENTERTAINMENT   🎭 (p415)
Other Place.............................23 C4
Royal Shakespeare Theatre......24 C4
Swan Theatre..........................25 C4

TRANSPORT
Bancroft Cruises......................26 D3
Bus for Anne Hathaway's Cottage..27 B3
City Sightseeing Bus Stop........28 D3
Pashley Cycles.........................29 C3
Riverside Bus Station...............30 D3
Rose's Boathouse....................31 D4

follow the Stratford-upon-Avon Canal towpath to Wilmcote rather than retracing your route or riding back along the busy A3400. The easiest way to get here otherwise is on a bus tour (see Getting Around, p416).

The home of William's mother now houses the **Shakespeare Countryside Museum**, with exhibits tracing local country life over the past four centuries. Plan to spend more time here than at the other properties to appreciate its unique collection of rare farm animals and a turn-of-the-20th-century farmhouse.

OTHER SIGHTS & ACTIVITIES

Holy Trinity Church (☎ 266316; Old Town; suggested donation for chancel £1; ⊙ 8.30am-6pm Mon-Sat & 12.30-5pm Sun Apr-Oct, 9am-4pm Mon-Sat & 12.30-5pm Sun Nov-Mar) has transepts from the mid-13th century and many later additions (the spire dates from 1763), but it's the Bard connections that draw crowds. In the chancel are photocopies of Shakespeare's baptism and burial records, the graves of Will and his wife, and a bust created seven years after Shakespeare's death but before his wife's and thus assumed to be a good likeness.

The exuberantly carved **Harvard House** (☎ 204016; High St; adult £2.50, free with Shakespeare Houses ticket; ⊙ noon-5pm Wed-Sun Jul-Sep; Wed, Sat & Sun May, Jun & Sep-Nov) was home to the mother of John Harvard, after whom Harvard University in the USA was named in the 17th century. It now houses a **Museum of British Pewter**.

The **Royal Shakespeare Company Gallery** (RSC; ☎ 412617; adult £2; ⊙ 1.30pm-6.30pm Mon-Fri, 10.30am-6.30pm Sat, 10.30-4.30pm Sun), inside the Swan Theatre, features changing displays of the RSC's collection of props, costumes and theatrical paraphernalia. **Theatre tours** (☎ 403405; adult/child incl admission to RSC Gallery £5/4; ⊙ 1.30pm & 5.30pm Mon-Sat, 11am & 5.30pm matinee days, noon, 1pm, 2pm & 3pm Sun) offer a fascinating glimpse behind the scenes of a working theatre.

Falstaff's Experience (☎ 298070; www.falstaffs experience.co.uk; 40 Sheep St; adult £4.25; ⊙ 10am-5.30pm), an old timbered building housing re-creations of a witches' glade and a plague

---

ABOUT A BARD

William Shakespeare was born in Stratford-upon-Avon in 1564, the son of a local glovemaker. At 18 he married Anne Hathaway, eight years his senior, and their first daughter, Susanna, was born about six months later. Boy and girl twins, Hamnet and Judith, followed two years later.

Did the sheen of domestic bliss wear thin then? Around this time Shakespeare moved to London and began to write for the Lord Chamberlain's Company. This successful ensemble boasted the finest theatre (the Globe) and the best actors. It wasn't until the 1590s that Shakespeare's name appeared on his plays; before that, the company's name was regarded as more important than the dramatist's.

Shakespeare's 37 plays made novel and inventive use of the English language, often to ribald comic effect (although generations of schoolchildren would doubtless disagree), and boasted superb plot structures and deep insights into human nature – characteristics that have ensured not only their survival over the centuries but also their popularity in other languages. Early writings included comedies such as The Comedy of Errors, historical accounts such as Henry VI and Richard III, and tragedies including Romeo & Juliet. The new century saw the appearance of his great tragedies: Hamlet, Othello, King Lear and Macbeth.

Around 1610 Shakespeare retired and moved back to Stratford. He lived in comfortable circumstances until his death in 1616, whereupon his body (and a legacy of mass tourism) was conferred on the parish church. His wife outlived him by seven years.

Despite Shakespeare's prodigious output of plays, no letters or other personal writing have survived, and the little that is known about him and his family has been pieced together from birth, death and marriage files and other official records (including the will in which he left his wife his 'second-best bed'!). This paucity of information has bred theories that Shakespeare didn't actually write the plays. Since none have survived in manuscript form, there's no handwriting evidence to prove they're his. Some nonbelievers speculate that Shakespeare's origins and education were too humble to have provided the background, experience and knowledge to write the plays. Their favourites for the 'real' Shakespeare include the earl of Derby, the earl of Oxford and Will's fellow playwright Christopher Marlowe.

cottage, is like an extended, stationary ghost train with some history thrown in; morbid kids (and grown-ups) will absolutely love this experience.

Sleeping

Stratford's big hotels tend to be geared towards group travel, so they're often out of the price range of many independent travellers, and they fill up fast. B&Bs are plentiful, though, and generally offer good-quality accommodation in attractive Victorian houses. Prime hunting grounds are Evesham Pl, Grove Rd, Broad Walk and Alcester Rd. Accommodation can be hard to find during summer; if you're stuck, the TIC charges £3 plus 10% deposit to find something.

BUDGET
Stratford-upon-Avon YHA Hostel (☎ 0870 770 6052; stratford@yha.org.uk; Hemmingford House, Alveston; dm £12-17; **P**) The youth hostel is in a large, 200-year-old mansion 1½ miles east of the town centre along Tiddington Rd. Bus Nos X18 and 77 run to Alveston from Bridge St.

Quilts & Croissants (☎ 267629; rooms@quilt-croissants .demon.co.uk; 33 Evesham Pl; s/d £18/40; **P**) The owners of this cute B&B have travelled widely themselves; they're extremely amiable and go far to make you comfortable.

MID-RANGE
Moonraker House (☎ 267115; www.moonrakerhouse .com; 40 Alcester Rd; s/d from £40/55; **P**) B&Bs don't come much classier than this pristine yet luxuriously comfortable home. It's done up like an outsized doll's house, with canopied beds and flowers everywhere, and it's just five minutes' walk from the train station. The owners make you feel like you are at the Ritz, and the gorgeous breakfast includes organic, vegetarian and heart-healthy options.

Stratheden Hotel (☎ 297119; richard@stratheden .fsnet.co.uk; 5 Chapel St; r from £35) An old building (parts c1673) in the thick of the Shakespeare action, this hotel is tastefully furnished, very friendly and good value for the location.

Twelfth Night (☎ 414595; reservations@twelfth night.co.uk; 13 Evesham Pl; s/d from £35/42) An elegant confection of flowers and lace, this sweetly feminine B&B scores points with classy details, such as breakfast served on Wedgwood china.

TOP END
White Swan (☎ 297022; whiteswan@work.gb.com; Rother St; s/d from £60/80; **P**) Stratford's most character-drenched hotel has oak panelling and heavy wooden beams in its pub-style lobby and restaurant, and a choice between modern rooms and old-fashioned ones, some with brick fireplaces and four-poster beds. It's just a few steps from the Birthplace.

Shakespeare (☎ 0870 400 8182; shakespeare@mac donald-hotels.co.uk; Chapel St; r from £120; **P**) A conglomeration of beautiful historic buildings, this place is a four-star establishment; its labyrinthine warren of rooms and suites are named after Shakespearean characters. By necessity, they're a mishmash of different shapes and sizes, but all are beautifully antique-furnished and updated with fancy new bathrooms. Some have four-poster beds.

Falcon Hotel (☎ 279953; www.corushotels.com/the falcon; Chapel St; s/d £105/125; breakfast extra £7-10; **P**) You can choose between antique luxury and ultramodern luxury at this charming place, with beautifully timeworn rooms in an old timber-framed building and hip designer rooms in a newer wing. Special deals are sometimes available.

Eating

Shakespeare clearly makes you hungry: there's no shortage of eateries. Sheep St is chock-full with restaurants, most with a refined but relaxed ambience ideal for a pretheatre meal. Mains typically cost between £8 (vegetarian) and £16 (steak or seafood).

Desport's (☎ 269304; booking@desports.co.uk; 13-14 Meer St; ☽ Tue-Sat) Named one of the best restaurants outside London, chef Paul Desport's small restaurant in a 16th-century building creates international cuisine with Asian and Mediterranean influences, and there's a well-thought-out wine list to boot. The deli downstairs is a good option for lunch or picnic treats.

Lambs (☎ 292554; www.lambsrestaurant.co.uk; 12 Sheep St; ☽ lunch daily, dinner Wed-Sat) Where the locals take their in-laws to impress, this highly regarded restaurant has an eclectic menu of interesting takes on classic dishes, and an extensive wine list.

Vintner Wine Bar (☎ 297259; 5 Sheep St; ☽ lunch from 10am & dinner) A great spot for tapas, wine and pretheatre street theatre, thanks to its picture windows. The menu includes many inventive vegetarian options.

Edward Moon's (☎ 267069; 9 Chapel St; ☽ lunch & dinner) This long-standing favourite has the feel of a classy, upmarket pub, with a tasty menu from around the globe and sinful desserts, including a tempting sticky-toffee pudding.

Drinking

Dirty Duck (☎ 297312; Waterside) Officially called the Black Swan, this pretty, riverside cubby-hole of a pub is an essential Stratford experience for thespians and theatre-goers alike. From its small terrace you can watch school groups harass each other in rented boats along the canal.

Garrick Inn (☎ 292186; 25 High St) Steeped in history and stooping with age, the Garrick is worth visiting just to marvel at the low ceilings, dark wood beams and leaded windows. It's also one of the few nonsmoking pubs around.

Entertainment

Royal Shakespeare Company (☎ 0870 609 1110; www.rsc.org.uk; box office inside Royal Shakespeare Theatre; tickets £6-42; ☽ 9.30am-8pm Mon-Sat) Seeing an RSC production is a must; some major stars have graced the stage here, and your chances of seeing truly high-calibre theatre are good. Performances include the Bard's classics as well as contemporary offerings, and take place in the main Royal Shakespeare Theatre, the adjacent Swan Theatre or the nearby Other Place. Ticket prices depend on the performance and venue, but there's a bewildering range of offers for under-25s, students, seniors and other selected groups, plus discounts for previews; it's best to call or to check the website for details. For good seats, you'll want to book ahead, but there are always a few tickets sold on the day of the performance, which are available only to personal callers.

Getting There & Away

National Express destinations from Stratford's Riverside Bus Station include Birmingham (1¼ hours, daily), Oxford (1¼ hours, daily) and London Victoria (£16.50, 3½ hours, three daily).

The train station is a few minutes' walk west of the town centre. There are only a few direct services from London Paddington (two hours), but some services from Marylebone that require a change at Banbury or Leamington Spa are almost as quick.

WORTH THE TRIP

Though Coventry itself isn't terribly alluring, its spectacular pair of **cathedrals**, one new and one ruined, make it a worthwhile day trip from Stratford, Warwick or Birmingham. Founded in the 12th century and rebuilt from 1373, **St Michael's** was one of England's largest parish churches when it became a cathedral in 1918, its spire topped only by those of Salisbury and Norwich cathedrals. Then, in 1940, a Luftwaffe raid gutted the cathedral, leaving only the outer walls and the spire standing amid the ruins.

After the war the ruins were left as a reminder. Immediately next to them, a **new St Michael's Cathedral** (☎ 024 7622 7597; www.coventrycathedral.org; requested donation £3) was built between 1955 and 1962. Designed by Sir Basil Spence, it's one of the few examples of post-war British architecture to inspire popular affection. It's noted for the soaring etched-glass screen wall at the western end, for the Graham Sutherland tapestry above the altar, for John Piper's lovely stained glass and for Sir Jacob Epstein's sculpture of St Michael subduing the devil beside the entrance steps.

The **old cathedral spire** (☎ 024 7626 7070; adult £1.50) still looks down over the ruins; its 180 steps lead up to magnificent views. Opening hours are irregular, so call to check. The **Priory Visitors Centre** (☎ 7655 2242; Priory Row; admission free; ☽ 10am-5.30pm Mon-Sat, noon-4pm Sun) highlights the history of the original cathedral and priory, founded by the omnipresent Leofric a thousand years ago, with artefacts and computer-generated reconstructions.

National Express coaches go to London (2½ hours, nine daily) and Oxford (1¾ hours, two daily). Bus services are run by **Centro** (Hotline ☎ 01203 559559, ☎ 024 7655 9559). Bus Nos 157 (every 30 minutes) and X67 (hourly) run to Leicester (one hour), while bus Nos X16 and X18 run to Kenilworth (25 minutes), Leamington (40 minutes), Warwick (55 minutes) and Stratford (1¼ hours) from Trinity St hourly. The train station is just across the ring road, south of the centre. Birmingham (every 10 minutes) is less than 30 minutes away.

The **Shakespeare Express steam train** (☎ 0121-707 4696; www.vintagetrains.co.uk; s adult/child £10/3, return £15/5) operates between Birmingham Snow Hill and Stratford station twice each Sunday in July and August, taking one hour.

Getting Around
BICYCLE
Stratford is small enough to explore on foot, but a bicycle is good for getting out to the surrounding countryside or the rural Shakespeare properties. The canal towpath offers a fine route to Wilmcote. **Warwickshire County Council** (☎ 01827-872660; Shire Hall, Warwick; ☺ 9am-5.30pm Mon-Thu, 9am-4.30pm Fri) produces leaflets detailing cycling routes.

Pashley Cycles (☎ 205057; Guild St; per half-/full day from £5/10) hires out bikes.

BOAT
Punts, canoes and rowing boats are available from **Rose's Boathouse** (☎ 267073; rowboats/punts per hr £3/2) by Clopton Bridge. **Bancroft Cruises** (☎ 269669; www.bancroftcruises.co.uk) runs 45-minute trips (adult £4, daily April to October) leaving from the Moat House Hotel pier.

BUS
Open-top buses of **City Sightseeing** (☎ 299123; www.city-sightseeing.com; adult/child £8/3.50; ☺ every 15min Apr-Sep, fewer in winter) circuit past the TIC and the five Shakespeare properties. They operate on a jump-on-jump-off basis, so you can spend as long as you like at each attraction, and are a convenient way of getting to the out-of-town houses.

STAFFORDSHIRE

Nobody would expect to find a secret stash of wilderness tucked between the sprawling metropolises of Birmingham and Manchester, but that's just what Staffordshire offers. The prickly spine of the Peak District known as the Roaches cuts through the middle, and walking and cycling paths link remote villages and quiet little market towns. Stafford and Leek are two of the prettiest villages you'll find, with historic centres full of cream-coloured stone cottages and winding alleyways. Other unmissable highlights include Lichfield's gorgeous,

gloomy triple-spired cathedral and – for something completely different – the wild rides at Alton Towers.

Orientation
Staffordshire's attractions are spread fairly evenly around the county: Stoke to the northwest; the Peak District and Leek northeast, with Alton Towers just south; Lichfield to the southeast; and Stafford just southwest of the centre.

Information
Staffordshire Tourism (☎ 0870 500 4444; www .staffordshire.gov.uk/tourism) Distributes the *Canal County* leaflet on boating, cycling or walking along the county's waterways.

Getting There & Around
Busline (☎ 01782-206608) is the number to call for transport information, **Moorlands Traveller 21** (☎ 01538-386888) offer a flexible bus service linking the northeastern moorland villages with Leek. **Virgin Trains** (☎ 0845 722 2333; www .virgin.com/trains) operate through the area.

LICHFIELD
☎ 01543 / pop 28,400
This pretty town, all cobblestones and courtyard gardens, is home to one of England's most beautiful cathedrals, its three spires visible from miles away. It's also been something of a thinktank in its time: famed wit and lexicographer Samuel Johnson was born here, and Erasmus Darwin (Charles' grandfather) lived and studied here for years.

Information
TIC (☎ 308209; www.lichfield-tourist.co.uk; Donegal House, Bore St; ☺ 9am-5pm Mon-Fri & 9am-4.30pm Sat Apr-Sep, 9am-4.45pm Mon-Fri & 9am-2pm Sat Oct-Mar) Local tourist information.

Sights
LICHFIELD CATHEDRAL
The fine **cathedral** (☎ 306100; requested donation £4; ☺ 7.30am-6.15pm) is instantly recognisable by its three spires. It boasts a fine Gothic west front adorned with exquisitely carved statues of the kings of England from Edgar to Henry I, and the major saints. Its blackened façade is stunning, especially as you approach from the Minster Pond. Most of what you see dates from the various rebuildings of the Norman cathedral between

1200 and 1350. The gold-leafed skull of St Chad, the first bishop of Lichfield, was once kept in St Chad's Head Chapel, just to the west of the south transept.

A superb illuminated manuscript from AD 730, the *Lichfield Gospels*, is displayed in the beautifully vaulted mid-13th-century chapterhouse. You shouldn't miss the effigy of George Augustus Selwyn, first bishop of New Zealand in 1841, in the lady chapel (which boasts 16th-century Flemish stained glass), or Sir Francis Chantrey's *Sleeping Children* at the eastern end of the south aisle, a poignant memorial to two young girls who died in tragic circumstances.

A stroll round **Cathedral Close**, which is ringed with imposing 17th- and 18th-century houses, is also rewarding.

OTHER SIGHTS

The **Samuel Johnson Birthplace Museum** (☎ 264 972; www.lichfield.gov.uk/sjmuseum; Breadmarket St; adult £2.20; ⏲ 10.30am-4.30pm Apr-Sep, noon-4.30pm Oct-Mar) is in the house where the pioneering lexicographer was born in 1709. His dictionary, together with the biography written by his close friend James Boswell *(The Life of Samuel Johnson)*, established him as one of the great scholars, critics and wits of the English language. You can inspect the famous dictionary using the computer in the bookshop in the lobby, and learn about his life and work through the museum's exhibits and videos.

Grandfather of the more famous Charles, Erasmus Darwin was himself a remarkable autodidact, doctor, inventor, philosopher and poet, influencing the Romantics. The **Erasmus Darwin Centre** (☎ 306260; www.erasmus darwin.org; Beacon St; adult £2.50; ⏲ 10am-4.30pm Thu-Sat, noon-4.30pm Sun), in the house where he lived from 1756 to 1781, commemorates his life with a video, pictures and personal items. Exhibits and displays illustrate his varied work and association with luminaries such as Josiah Wedgwood, Matthew Boulton and James Watt.

The **Heritage Centre & Treasury** (☎ 256611; St Mary's Centre; adult/child £3.50/1; ⏲ 10am-5pm), on Market Sq, houses an audiovisual presentation covering 1300 years of Lichfield history; the treasury exhibits a small but attractive display of civic, ecclesiastical and regimental silverware. Climb the tower (admission £2) for fine views of the city.

Festivals & Events

The **Lichfield Festival** (☎ 306543; www.lichfield festival.org), held in the first half of July, features classical and world music, cinema and theatre in a variety of venues around town.

Sleeping

No 8 (☎ 418483; www.ldb.co.uk/accommodation.htm; 8 The Close; s/d from £28/48) Smack in front of the cathedral, No 8 is a heritage-listed town house with three rooms, some with a great view of the cathedral face; its owners pride themselves on it being a home, not a hotel, so there's no sign; call in advance to make arrangements.

George Hotel (☎ 414822; www.bw-george-lichfield .co.uk; 12-14 Bird St; s/d Mon-Thu from £106/120, Fri-Sun £59/98) An 18th-century coaching inn right in the heart of the city, the George Hotel (now part of the Best Western chain) achieves an effortless blend of old-fashioned atmosphere and modern luxury. Four-poster beds and business-traveller accommodation are also available.

Eating & Drinking

Cathedral Coffee Shop (☎ 306125; 19 The Close; sandwiches £1.70-3; ⏲ 9.30am-4.45pm Mon-Sat, noon-4.45pm Sun) Set in a charming 18th-century house, this café beloved by local pensioners is a good place for a snack or a full Sunday lunch (1-/2-/3-course meals for £6.75/9/11).

Samuel Johnson described Lichfield folk as 'the most sober, decent people in England' – but that was 250 years ago, and there are pubs aplenty these days. The **King's Head** (☎ 256822; 21 Bird St) is a good traditional one, with a conservatory area and a courtyard for sunbathing while supping.

Getting There & Away

Bus No 112 runs to Birmingham, while No 825 serves Stafford (both £2.50 single, 1¼ hours, hourly). Trains run to/from Birmingham New St station (30 minutes, every 15 minutes).

STOKE-ON-TRENT

☎ 01782 / pop 259,250

Staffordshire's industrial heart, though historically important in the production of pottery, holds limited appeal to the visitor, except in one department: porcelain. You could visit on a day trip from any of six or seven nearby towns, though you'd want a whole day to really explore the potteries. For a preview, check out Arnold Bennett's memorable descriptions of the area in its industrial heyday in his novels *Clayhanger* and *Anna of the Five Towns* (something of a misnomer, as Stoke actually consists of six towns).

Orientation

Stoke-on-Trent is made up of Tunstall, Burslem, Hanley, Stoke, Fenton and Longton, together often called the Potteries. Hanley is the official 'city centre'. Stoke-on-Trent train station is south of Hanley, but buses from outside the main entrance run here in minutes. The bus station is in the centre of Hanley.

Information

TIC (☎ 236000; stoke.tic@virgin.net; Quadrant Rd, Potteries shopping centre, Hanley; ☉ 9.15am-5.15pm Mon-Sat) Ask for a map with the locations of the various showrooms, factory shops and visitors centres.

Sights

It may sound unlikely, but one of the most exciting attractions in this part of the country is a bone china factory. The **Wedgwood Story visitors centre** (☎ 204218; www.thewedgwood story.com; Barlaston; adult weekday/weekend £8.25/7.50, with coalport tour £9.25; ☉ 9am-5pm Mon-Fri, 10am-5pm Sat & Sun) offers a fascinating insight into the production process, with an extensive collection of historic pieces to gawp at, artisans who calmly paint freehand designs onto china while you watch, and best of all, a troupe of Star Wars–esque anthropomorphic robots that dutifully churn out perfect plates and mugs with the Wedgwood stamp. Equally interesting are the film and displays on the life of founder Josiah Wedgwood (1730–95). An innovative potter whose consuming passion makes the quest for the perfect vase seem as exciting as the World Cup, he was also a driving force behind the construction of England's canal system and the abolition of slavery – altogether a remarkable man.

The **Potteries Museum & Art Gallery** (☎ 232323; Bethesda St, Hanley; admission free; ☉ 10am-5pm Mon-Sat & 2-5pm Sun Mar-Oct, 10am-4pm Mon-Sat & 1-4pm Sun Nov-Feb) covers the history of the Potteries and houses an extensive ceramics display as well as a surprisingly impressive collection of fine art (Picasso, Degas) and high-profile touring exhibitions.

Constructed around Stoke's last remaining bottle kiln and its yard, the wonderful **Gladstone Pottery Museum** (☎ 319232; Uttoxeter Rd, Longton; adult/child £4.95/3.50; ☉ 10am-5pm) is an evocative reconstruction of a typical small pottery in the early 20th century. A highlight for those of scatological bent is the Flushed With Pride exhibition, charting the story of the toilet from chamber pots and shared privy holes (with smell effects!) to modern hi-tech conveniences. Bus Nos 6, 7 and 8 serve Longton from Hanley.

Getting There & Away

National Express coaches run to/from London (four hours, five daily) and Manchester (1½ hours, eight daily). Bus No 101 runs to Stafford (1¼ hours) every 30 minutes. Trains run hourly to London (1¾ hours).

AROUND STOKE-ON-TRENT
Little Moreton Hall

England's most spectacular black-and-white timber-framed house (☎ 01260-272018; adult £5; ☉ 11.30am-5pm Wed-Sun late-Mar–Oct, 11.30am-4pm Sat & Sun Nov–late-Dec) dates back to the 16th century; within its over-the-top exterior are a series of important wall paintings and an indefinable sense of romance. Little Moreton is off the A34 south of Congleton.

Alton Towers

If you can look past the incredible commercialism, **Alton Towers** (☎ 0870 500 1100; www .altontowers.com; adult/child standard ticket £27/21; ☉ 9.30am-5pm Oct–mid-Mar, longer hrs mid-Mar–Sep) is an absolute must for white-knuckle fiends and is deservedly England's most popular theme park. There are more than 100 rides, including vertical drops, flying roller coasters, log flumes and more; trying to pinpoint the biggest buzz is all part of the fun – new thrills are introduced frequently. Prices vary depending on arcane 'seasons', and are at their highest during school holidays.

There's a hotel within the park, but most opt to stay in nearby villages; the park's website features a list of options. Alton itself is an attractive village with several B&Bs. **Old School House** (☎ 01538-702151; old_school_house@talk21.com; Castle Hill Rd, Alton; d £56) is an exceptional B&B in a heritage-listed school building dating from 1845. **Dimmingsdale YHA Hostel** (☎ 01538-702304; Oakamoor; dm £10.60) is 2 miles northwest of the park.

Alton Towers is east of Cheadle off the B5032. Public transport is sketchy, but various train companies periodically offer all-in-one packages from London and other cities; check the website for current details.

LEEK

☎ 01538 / pop 18,800

Gateway to the Staffordshire moorlands, especially the spectacular and climb-hungry Roaches, Leek is an attractive market town that makes a convenient base for visiting the Potteries and the Peak District.

The **TIC** (☎ 483741; tourism.smdc@staffordshire.gov.uk; 1 Market Pl; 🕑 9.30am-5pm Mon-Fri, 10am-4pm Sat) provides information on attractions and accommodation and will book rooms for a £3 fee.

St Edward's Church (Church St; 🕑 10am-4pm Wed, 10am-noon Fri & Sat), completed in 1306, has a beautiful rose window by William Morris.

Described by John Betjeman as 'one of the finest churches in Britain', **All Saints Church** (☎ 370786; Compton; 🕑 11am-4pm Wed & Sat) features Morris & Co stained glass windows at the eastern end from designs by Edward Burne-Jones, and ornate Arts & Crafts wallpainting.

Brindley Mill (☎ 381446; Mill St; adult £2; 🕑 2-5pm Mon-Wed mid-Jul–Aug, 2-5pm Sat & Sun Easter-Sep) was built in 1752 by canal pioneer James Brindley. It's beautifully restored and once again mills corn; inside the Brindley Mill is a small museum dedicated to Brindley and the art of millwrighting.

The **Peak Weavers Hotel** (☎ 383729; www.peak weavershotel.com; 21 King St; s/d from £30/60) has plush doll's house–style rooms and a fine restaurant that's turned out like a very upscale old-fashioned ice-cream parlour.

For liquid refreshment, try the **Roebuck** (☎ 372179; 18 Derby St), a traditional smoky pub that dates back to 1626, although some say it was originally built in Shrewsbury and moved to Leek later.

Bus Nos 16 and 18 run to Leek from Hanley (Stoke-on-Trent).

STAFFORD

☎ 01785 / pop 63,700

The county town of Staffordshire, once considered a crossroads for travellers, is a pleasant although fairly anonymous place, with a couple of attractions worth a look on your way through.

The **TIC** (☎ 619619; Market St; 🕑 9.30am-5pm Mon-Fri, 10am-5pm Sat) is behind the town hall.

The **Ancient High House** (☎ 619619; Greengate St; admission free; 🕑 10am-5pm Mon-Sat) is the largest timber-framed town house in the country and has period rooms containing displays on the history of the house since it was constructed in 1595.

There are only ruins left of **Stafford Castle** (☎ 257698; Newport Rd; admission free; visitors centre 🕑 10am-5pm Tue-Sun Apr-Oct, 10am-4pm Nov-Mar), built by William the Conqueror, but it's in a gorgeous setting atop a hill that affords sweeping views. The castle hosts various special events throughout the summer. There's a small visitors centre (closed Monday, but you can still wander the grounds) and a 'medieval herb garden', as well as a small network of forested trails that are ideal for a post-picnic wander.

Bus No 101 travels between Stafford and Stoke-on-Trent (1¼ hours, every 30 minutes).

NORTHAMPTONSHIRE

The lack of one obvious blockbuster tourist attraction in Northamptonshire has its advantages. The county is wonderful for easy drives through the countryside, from one cluster of honey-coloured villages to the next, and it's largely free of mass tourism. If aimless rambling isn't your style, there are stately homes and Saxon churches aplenty to seek out. Fans of Princess Diana make pilgrimages to her ancestral home at Althorp, and Doc Martens devotees come here to buy their shoes at the source.

Orientation & Information

Northamptonshire is roughly 50 miles long and 20 miles wide, running southwest to northeast. The M1 cuts diagonally across the county just below Northampton, which is located in the middle; attractions are scattered widely.

For general information about the county, check the website www.visitnorthampton shire.co.uk. Northampton's TIC stocks plenty of information about the whole county.

Getting Around

Driving is the way to see the most of the county; turning a corner on a winding country lane and coming across a sleepy village is one of the region's joys. All the major car-hire companies have branches in Northampton.

Both **Stagecoach** (www.stagecoachbus.com) and **Traveline** (☎ 0870 608 2608) buses run to most places of interest from Northampton and other nearby towns; some services run only a few times daily, so it's best to check times with the operator.

NORTHAMPTON
☎ 01604 / pop 197,200

Most will find they have Northampton pretty much to themselves, and it's not an unpleasant discovery. A modern town with pockets of history, it's an inviting place to shop at or just wander around, mingling with the locals in cafés or pubs. The casual observer might not guess it, but Northampton was among the most important cities in England during Saxon days. Thomas Becket was tried for fraud in Northampton Castle in 1164 (although there's not much to see now). These days it's the home of Doc Martens shoes and, more obscurely, comic-book genius Alan Moore, whose *Voice of the Fire* offers an unusual look at the place.

Orientation

The town is centred on Market Sq, with the main pedestrianised shopping route, Abington St, running east from it. From here it becomes the Kettering Rd, with its hotels and bars. To the south of Market Sq is the Guildhall and TIC, and the bus station is to the north.

Information

TIC (☎ 622677; www.northampton.gov.uk/tourism; Guildhall Rd; ☺ 10am-5pm Mon-Sat, 2-5pm Sun, 10am-2pm bank hols) Inside the Central Museum; the free *Historic Town Trail* leaflet describes a walking tour of the town's hidden treasures.

Sights

Foot fetishists won't be the only ones fascinated by the **Central Museum & Art Gallery** (☎ 639415; Guildhall Rd; admission free; ☺ 10am-5pm Mon-Sat, 2-5pm Sun). Alongside its huge, well-presented collection of shoes from the 14th century to the present, there are some fine paintings and changing special exhibitions.

St Peter's Church (Mayfair) is a marvellous Norman edifice built in 1150 and restored in the 19th century by Gilbert Scott. The detail on the original capitals is outstanding. For rock nuts: William Smith, known as the father of modern geology, is buried

here. Get the key from the Black Lion pub next door.

The **Church of the Holy Sepulchre** (☎ 754782) is one of only four round churches in England; founded after the first earl of Northampton returned from the Crusades in 1100, it's a near facsimile of its namesake in Jerusalem. Hours vary – call for details.

Sleeping & Eating

Lime Trees Hotel (☎ 632188; info@limetreeshotel.co.uk; 8 Langham Pl; s/d from £50/75; ℗) This is a fine accommodation option, an attractive Georgian house about half a mile north of the centre with a pretty courtyard at the back.

Malt Shovel (☎ 234212; 121 Bridge St; ℗) A Campaign for Real Ale (Camra) favourite, this place at the edge of the town centre has good solid pub food and offers a taste of local spirit with its chalkboard advertising 'up to 13 real ales!' There are always guest beers as well as a huge international selection of bottled beers.

Joe's Diner (☎ 620022; 104a Abington St; mains £6.75-16.95; ☺ Mon-Sat) A place breaking the mould of the American-theme eatery, Joe's gets it right with a huge range of quality burgers, friendly staff and a healthy dearth of tacky 'memorabilia'.

Entertainment

Picturedrome (☎ 230777; www.thepicturedrome.com; 222 Kettering Rd) This stylish, buzzing bar hosts fortnightly comedy nights, live music and other events.

Roadmender (☎ 604222; www.roadmender.org; 1 Lady's Lane) A local landmark, this is a uniquely versatile venue that features up-and-coming bands, theatre, comedy and club nights.

Derngate and the **Royal Theatre** (☎ 624811; www.northamptontheatres.com; Guildhall Rd) are managed cooperatively. The former is Northampton's arts centre and hosts anything from Tom Jones to Tom Thumb; the latter is a Victorian structure staging local theatre and quality West End productions.

Getting There & Away

National Express coaches run to London (£10.50 economy single, two hours, five daily), Nottingham (£9.50, 2½ hours, daily) and Birmingham (£5, 1½ hours, two daily).

Northampton has excellent rail links with Birmingham (one hour, hourly) and London Euston (one hour, at least every 30 minutes).

AROUND NORTHAMPTON
Althorp
The late Diana, Princess of Wales, is commemorated in a memorial and museum in the grounds of her ancestral home, **Althorp Park** (bookings ☎ 0870 167 9000; www.althorp.com; adult £11.50, plus £2.50 access to upstairs of house; ☻ 11am-5pm Jul-Sep). The 16th-century mansion itself boasts works by Rubens, Gainsborough and Van Dyck. Profits from ticket sales go to the Princess Diana Memorial Fund. The limited number of tickets must be booked by phone or on the website. Incidentally, Althorp should be pronounced 'altrup'.

Althorp is off the A428 northwest of Northampton. There are four buses daily linking Althorp with Northampton train station.

Rushton Triangular Lodge
To call the **Rushton Triangular lodge** (☎ 01536-710761; adult £2; ☻ 10am-5pm Thu-Mon Apr-Sep) a folly is to underestimate the power of faith on the mind of Sir Thomas Tresham. He designed a number of buildings in the area (and was imprisoned more than once for expressing his Catholic beliefs). With three of everything, from sides to floors to gables, the lodge is Tresham's enduring symbol of the trinity, built at the end of the 16th century. Mysterious, esoteric inscriptions and a magical setting among rapeseed fields give the place a surprising impact.

The lodge is 4 miles northwest of Kettering. Bus No 19 from Kettering stops in Desborough, 2 miles away (20 minutes, every 30 minutes Monday to Saturday, every two hours on Sunday). Kettering is 15 miles northeast of Northampton along the A43.

Kirby Hall
Once one of the finest Elizabethan mansions, known as the 'Jewel of the English Renaissance', **Kirby Hall** (☎ 01604-735400; adult £4; ☻ 10am-5pm Thu-Mon Apr-Jun, 10am-6pm daily Jul & Aug, 10am-5pm Thu-Mon Sep & Oct, 10am-4pm Thu-Mon Nov-Mar) was begun in 1570, and additions were made up to the 19th century. Abandoned and fallen into disrepair, it's still a remarkable, atmospheric site – it was used as the location for the 1999 film of Jane Austen's *Mansfield Park* – with fine filigree stonework, ravens cawing in the empty halls and peacocks roaming its restored formal parterre gardens.

Kirby Hall is 4 miles northeast of Corby; Corby is 9 miles north of Kettering along the A43.

LEICESTERSHIRE & RUTLAND

Anchored by Leicester – one of the most diverse and vibrant cultural centres in the region – the county of Leicestershire has charming villages and key historic sites. Two sights to aim for are the magnificent Gothic confection that is Belvoir Castle and the ruins of the castle at Ashby-de-la-Zouch.

Tiny Rutland was merged with Leicestershire in 1974, but in April 1997 regained its 'independence' as a county. With magnificent Rutland Water and charming settlements, it's a natural favourite among lovers of water sports and quaint villages.

Orientation & Information
Leicestershire and Rutland together look like an upside-down map of Australia. Leicester is virtually bang in the centre of its county, with the M1 motorway running north–south just to the west, dividing the largely industrial towns and National Forest of the west from the more rural east, including Belvoir Castle. Rutland's little solar system, east of Leicester and tucked away between four counties, revolves around central Rutland Water.

For general county-wide information, contact **Leicestershire Tourism** (☎ 0116-265 7302; tourism@leics.gov.uk).

Getting There & Around
Traveline (☎ 0870 608 2608) have transport information for the area, and **Arriva Fox County** (☎ 0116-264 400) operate Leicestershire bus services.

LEICESTER
☎ 0116 / pop 441,200
Victim to a barrage of aesthetic crimes perpetrated by everyone from the Luftwaffe to city planners, Leicester's appeal doesn't owe much to quaint physical charm. Instead, what draws people to this city is its palpable sense of excitement, largely a result of the diverse mix of ethnicities and cultures here. Leicester has overcome a rough past to turn itself into a socially and environmentally

progressive melting pot that has a few things to teach other, larger cities. Modern Leicester has a substantial and vibrant Asian community, with Hindu, Muslim, Jain and Sikh temples plenty of. Many of the city's most interesting events are staged around festivals such as Holi, Diwali and Eid-ul-Fitr, and the nightlife options give neighbouring Nottingham a run for its money.

Orientation

Leicester is initially difficult to navigate as there are few landmarks, but the pedestrianised central area around the market and clock tower makes things a little simpler. For drivers, it's plagued by the usual maze of one-way streets and forbidden turns. Although

there isn't a ring road as such, the A594 does almost a whole circuit and most attractions flank it or are contained within it.

The centre of the Asian community, Belgrave Rd (the 'Golden Mile') is about a mile northeast of the centre. Castle Park, with many of the historic attractions, lies immediately west of the centre, beside De Montfort University.

Information

CyberCuts (☎ 285 6661; 122 Granby St; Internet access per hr £1; ☻ 7am-9pm Mon-Sat, 10am-9pm Sun) A barber's shop where you surf while you await your trim.
TIC (☎ 299 8888; www.discoverleicester.com; 7-9 Every St; ☻ 9am-5.30pm Mon-Wed & Fri, 10am-5.30pm Thu, 10am-5pm Sat)

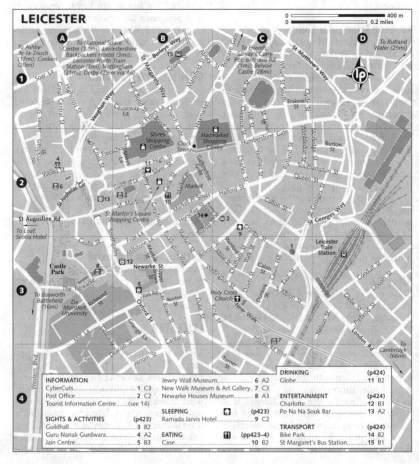

LEICESTER

0 ————— 400 m
0 ————— 0.2 miles

INFORMATION	
CyberCuts	1 C3
Post Office	2 C2
Tourist Information Centre	(see 14)

SIGHTS & ACTIVITIES	(p423)
Guildhall	3 B2
Guru Nanak Gurdwara	4 A2
Jain Centre	5 B3

Jewry Wall Museum	6 A2
New Walk Museum & Art Gallery	7 C3
Newarke Houses Museum	8 A3

SLEEPING 🏠	(p423)
Ramada Jarvis Hotel	9 C2

EATING 🍴	(pp423-4)
Case	10 B2

DRINKING	(p424)
Globe	11 B2

ENTERTAINMENT	(p424)
Charlotte	12 B3
Po Na Na Souk Bar	13 A2

TRANSPORT	(p424)
Bike Park	14 B2
St Margaret's Bus Station	15 B1

Sights
JEWRY WALL & MUSEUMS
All Leicester's **museums** (www.leicestermuseums
.ac.uk; ☺ 10am-5pm Mon-Sat & 1-5pm Sun Apr-Sep,
10am-4pm daily Oct-Mar) are free and all have the
same opening hours.

Despite its name, **Jewry Wall** is one of England's largest Roman civil structures and has
nothing to do with Judaism. You can walk
among excavated remains of the Roman public baths (around AD 150), of which the wall
was part. Notwithstanding its grim external
appearance, the **Jewry Wall Museum** (☎ 247 3021;
St Nicholas Circle) contains wonderful Roman
mosaics and frescoes, as well as an interactive
exhibition (The Making of Leicester), with
lots of artefacts and models.

New Walk Museum & Art Gallery (☎ 255 4100;
New Walk) houses a collection of fine Victorian,
German and decorative art as well as Egyptian mummies, natural history displays and
changing exhibitions.

Newarke Houses Museum (☎ 247 3222; The Newarke) contains a surprisingly varied collection
in two 16th-century buildings. There are
some reconstructed period shops, displays
of various oddities (an extensive selection
of truncheon covers 1796–1886) and exhibitions on two of Leicester's best-known
citizens: the mammoth Daniel Lambert
(see p486) and Thomas Cook, the package-
holiday pioneer.

In the late-14th-century **Guildhall** (☎ 253
2569; Guildhall Lane), reputedly the most haunted
building in Leicester, you can peer into old
police cells and inspect a copy of the last gibbet used to expose the body of an executed
murderer. There are also small temporary
exhibitions.

NATIONAL SPACE CENTRE
This **centre** (☎ 0870 607 7223; www.spacecentre.co
.uk; Exploration Dr; adult/child £8.95/6.95; ☺ 9.30am-
6pm Tue-Sun, plus Mon during Leicester school holidays,
last entry 4.30pm) is a spectacular and successful
attempt to bring space science to us ordinary mortals. Interactive displays cover
cosmic myths, the history of astronomy
and the development of space travel; in
the Space Now! area you can check on the
status of all current space missions. Films
in the domed Space Theatre (included in
the admission price) launch you to the far
reaches of the galaxy, and you can come
back to earth with a coffee in Boosters café,

sitting beneath huge booster rockets. Don't
miss the displays on zero-gravity toilets and
the amazing germ-devouring underpants.

The centre is off the A6 about 1½ miles
north of the city centre. Take bus No 54 from
Charles St or No 61 from Haymarket bus
station.

TEMPLES
Materials were shipped in from India to convert a disused church into a **Jain Centre** (☎ 254
3091; www.jaincentre.com; 32 Oxford St; ☺ 8.30am-8.30pm
Mon-Sat, 8.30am-6.30pm Sun). The building is faced
with marble, and the temple – the first constructed outside the subcontinent and the
only one in Europe – boasts a forest of beautifully carved pillars inside. The Jainism faith
evolved in India at around the same time as
Buddhism.

Close to the Jewry Wall is the Sikh **Guru
Nanak Gurdwara** (☎ 262 8606; 9 Holy Bones; ☺ 1-4pm
Thu or by arrangement). There is a small museum,
which contains an impressive model of the
Golden Temple in Amritsar.

Sleeping
Leicestershire Backpackers Hostel (☎ 267 3107; 157
Wanlip Lane, Birstall; tent sites £5, dm per night/week £10/48;
P) This odd little place 3 miles north of the
centre takes under-26 travellers only; cooking is communal, and rates include a basic
breakfast. Bus services are variable; phone
the hostel for details.

Ramada Jarvis Hotel (☎ 255 5599; sales.leicester@
ramadajarvis.com; Granby St; s/d Sun-Thu from £110/124,
B&B Fri-Sun £49/78; P) At the opposite end of
the spectrum is this listed establishment,
the city's top option in a central location.

Eating
The Golden Mile on Belgrave Rd, a mile to
the north of the centre (take bus No 22 or 37
from Haymarket bus station), is noted for its
fine Indian and vegetarian restaurants.

Friends (☎ 266 8809; 41-43 Belgrave Rd; mains £5-12;
☺ lunch Mon-Sat, dinner daily) An award-winning
tandoori eatery in the Golden Mile, this place
serves excellent North Indian food, with a
range of fish and vegetarian dishes.

Sanjay's Curry Pot (☎ 253 8256; mail@thecurrypot.co
.uk; 78-80 Belgrave Rd; mains £5-13; ☺ Mon-Sat) Outside
of Goa it's hard to find a place that specialises in both Indian and Portuguese cuisines,
but that's exactly what's on the menu in this
bright, funky place.

Case (☎ 251 7675; 4-6 Hotel St; mains £7-16; ⏲ Mon-Sat) This standby epitomises stylish contemporary dining, in a bright, airy 1st-floor space. The food is fashionable (pan-fried calf liver, wild boar sausages, scallops) and competent; the basement Champagne Bar serves cheaper snacks.

Drinking

Leicester has a thriving nightlife, due partly to the huge student population at Leicester and De Montfort Universities. Places come and go by the month; check www.leicester guide.co.uk/bars for up-to-the-minute tips. The centre has some good boozers and a few hip bars, as well as the inevitable rash of chain pubs. The left bank of the canal has been buzzing more recently; Braunstone Gate, Narborough Rd and Hinckley Rd are chock-a-block with bars and eateries.

Globe (☎ 262 9819; 43 Silver St) At last, here's that rare beast, a traditional old pub (built 1720) in a city centre with fine draught ales, a warm atmosphere and decent bar snacks.

Loaf (☎ 299 9424; 58-64 Braunstone Gate) Newspapers, bottled beers and the immortal motto 'it is better to have loafed and lost, than never to have loafed at all' – what more could you want in a bar? It's west of Castle Park.

Entertainment

Charlotte (☎ 255 3956; www.thecharlotte.co.uk; 8 Oxford St) Leicester's legendary venue has played host to all the biggies, including Oasis and Blur, before they became international megastars. It's a small place with a late licence and regular club nights.

Po Na Na Souk Bar (☎ 253 8190; 24 Careys Cl) Along with sister lounge bar Bam Bu Da, this outlet of the red-hot regional chain of clubs packs them in with danceable funk and house.

Getting There & Away

The **Great Central Railway** (☎ 01509-230726; www .gcrailway.co.uk; return ticket £10) runs steam locomotives between Leicester North station and Loughborough Central, the 8-mile route along which Thomas Cook ran his original package tour in 1841. The trains run daily from May to August and every weekend the rest of the year. Take bus No 37, 61 or 61A from Haymarket bus station.

National Express bus No 777 runs to Nottingham (one hour, eight daily Monday to Saturday), while Nos X67 (one hour, hourly) and 157 (every 30 minutes) run to Coventry.

Trains run to/from London St Pancras (1½ hours, every 30 minutes) and to/from Birmingham (one hour, every 30 minutes).

Getting Around

Central Leicester is fairly flat and easy to get around on foot. As an alternative to local buses, **Discover Leicester** (☎ 299 8888; adult/child under 15 £5/3; ⏲ 10am-4pm Jun-Sep on the hr) runs a jump-on-jump-off bus around the city and up to Belgrave Rd, the Great Central Railway and the National Space Centre. The main stop is at the Haymarket bus station.

Bike Park (☎ 299 1234; Town Hall Sq; ⏲ 8am-6.30pm Mon-Fri, 8.30am-6pm Sat; bike hire per day £8, bike parking per hr/day 50p/£1, showers 65p) offers great services, including bike hire, parking, cycle maps and information.

AROUND LEICESTER
Ashby-de-la-Zouch
☎ 01530 / pop 11,400

The excitingly named Ashby-de-la-Zouch is a likeable market town, but its real attraction is the **castle** (☎ 413343; adult £3.20; ⏲ 10am-6pm Apr-Sep, 10am-5pm Oct, 10am-4pm Wed-Sun Nov-Mar). Built in Norman times and owned by the Zouch family until 1399, it was extended in the 14th and 15th centuries and then reduced to its present picturesquely ruined state in 1648 after the Civil War; a lively audio guide introduces the characters and details the history. Bring a torch to explore the underground passageway connecting the tower with the kitchen.

For accommodation, contact the **TIC** (☎ 411767; North St; ⏲ 10am-5pm Mon-Fri, 10am-3pm Sat). Ashby is on the A511 about 15 miles northwest of Leicester. Bus No 118 (No 218 Sunday) runs hourly from St Margaret's bus station in Leicester.

Belvoir Castle

In the wilds of the county is **Belvoir Castle** (☎ 01476-870262; www.belvoircastle.com; adult/child £8/6; ⏲ 11am-5pm Tue-Thu, Sat & Sun May-Sep, 11am-5pm Sun Apr & Oct), pronounced *bee*-ver, a magnificent baroque and Gothic fantasy rebuilt in the 19th century after suffering serious damage during the Civil War. It's also home to the duke of Rutland. A hefty portion of the sumptuous interior is open to the public, and collections of weaponry, medals and art (including masterpieces by Reynolds, Gainsborough, Hans Holbein and Rubens) are highlights. There are marvellous views across the countryside, and peacocks roam the delightful gardens.

Belvoir is 6 miles west of Grantham, off the A1; Grantham is about 25 miles east of Nottingham along the A52.

RUTLAND

Tucked into a tiny niche between Leicestershire and Cambridgeshire, Rutland is England's smallest county. Its motto is 'Multum in Parvo' ('so much in so little'), and it lives up to the name. Rutland Water, a vast reservoir, takes up much of the county, making it an attractive playground for anyone interested in water sports and outdoor pursuits including climbing, bird-watching and sailing.

Information

Oakham TIC (☎ 01572-724329; 34 High St; ❧ 10am-4pm Tue-Sat)

Rutland Water TIC (☎ 01572-653026; Sykes Lane, Empingham; ❧ 10am-4pm Tue-Sat)

Sights & Activities

In Rutland Water, the **Rutland Belle** (☎ 01572-787630; www.rutlandwatercruises.com; the Harbour, Whitwell Park; adult/child £5/4) offers pleasure cruises every afternoon from May to September.

The **Watersports Centre** (☎ 01780-460154; Whitwell) organises sailing, windsurfing and canoeing. **Rutland Sailing School** (☎ 01780-721999; www .rutlandsailingschool.co.uk; Edith Weston) offers tuition to sailors of all abilities.

For bike hire, contact **Rutland Water Cycling** (☎ 01780-460705; www.rutlandcycling.co.uk; Whitwell Car Park).

The sleepy county town of **Oakham** has a famous school and **Oakham Castle** (admission free; ❧ 10am-1pm & 1.30-5pm Mon-Sat, 1-5pm Sun Mar-Oct, shorter hr Nov-Feb), really the Great Hall and sole standing remnant of a Norman structure.

Approximately 8 miles south of Oakham along the A6003 is the village of Lyddington, home to the **Bede House** (☎ 01572-822438; adult £3.20; ❧ 10am-6pm Apr-Sep, 10am-5pm Oct). Originally a wing of the medieval rural palace of the bishops of Lincoln, in 1600 it was converted into almshouses. Although the interior is sparsely furnished now, fine interpretative displays and an excellent free audio guide fill in the gaps.

Getting There & Away

Bus No 2 runs from Nottingham to Oakham in Rutland (1¼ hours, hourly); trains travel roughly hourly from Leicester and Peterborough.

NOTTINGHAMSHIRE

Merry men in tights, from thieves to poets, have made Nottinghamshire a place of pilgrimage. Home to the legendary Robin Hood, it's also the birthplace of provocative writer DH Lawrence and was the occasional retreat of decadent bad-boy poet Lord Byron. The city of Nottingham itself draws movers and shakers from all over the region, in business as well as in clubbing; it's a modern place, but still draped in myth and mystery, even down to its pubs.

Orientation & Information

Nottinghamshire is tall and thin, spreading a surprising distance north of Nottingham to finish level with Sheffield, though most of the county's attractions are in the southern half, with Newstead and Eastwood just north of Nottingham, Sherwood Forest in the county's centre and Newark-on-Trent and Southwell to the east.

Find county-wide information at www .nottinghamshiretourism.co.uk.

Getting Around

Useful journey planners with details of bus transport around the county can be found at www.ukbus.co.uk and www.itsnottingham .info. **Sherwood Forester buses** (☎ 0115-977 4268; Ranger ticket £5; ❧ Sun & bank hols Jun-Aug) operate to tourist attractions all over Nottinghamshire, with tickets giving discounted admission to some attractions.

NOTTINGHAM

☎ 0115 / pop 666,358

Nottingham is a city built on lace. The core of the old town, still called the Lace Market, is a warren of former lace shops and factories converted into clubs, restaurants and antiques stores. The lace trade peaked in the 19th century, but declined in the 1890s and was virtually killed off by WWI. Today it's largely the tourist industry that supports the remaining small-scale lace production, and the old manufacturing base of the city

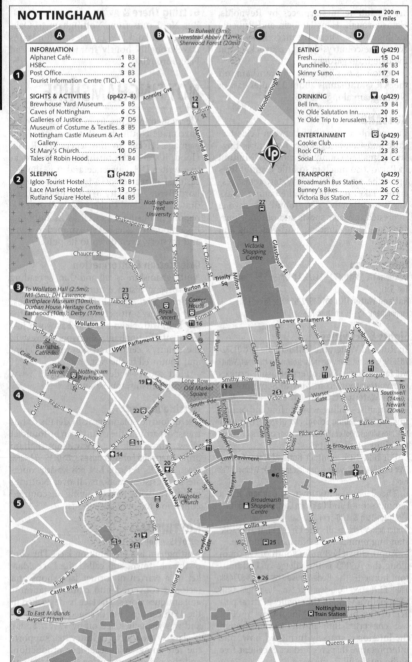

NOTTINGHAM

0 — 200 m
0 — 0.1 miles

INFORMATION
Alphanet Café.................................1 B3
HSBC...2 C4
Post Office......................................3 B3
Tourist Information Centre (TIC).4 C4

SIGHTS & ACTIVITIES   (pp427–8)
Brewhouse Yard Museum...............5 B5
Caves of Nottingham.....................6 C5
Galleries of Justice........................7 D5
Museum of Costume & Textiles....8 B5
Nottingham Castle Museum & Art
   Gallery..9 B5
St Mary's Church..........................10 D5
Tales of Robin Hood.....................11 B4

SLEEPING   (p428)
Igloo Tourist Hostel.....................12 B1
Lace Market Hotel........................13 D5
Rutland Square Hotel...................14 B5

EATING   (p429)
Fresh..15 D4
Punchinello....................................16 B3
Skinny Sumo.................................17 D4
V1..18 B4

DRINKING   (p429)
Bell Inn..19 B4
Ye Olde Salutation Inn.................20 B5
Ye Olde Trip to Jerusalem............21 B5

ENTERTAINMENT   (p429)
Cookie Club...................................22 B4
Rock City.......................................23 B3
Social...24 C4

TRANSPORT   (p429)
Broadmarsh Bus Station...............25 C5
Bunney's Bikes..............................26 C6
Victoria Bus Station......................27 C2

To Bulwell (3mi);
Newstead Abbey (12mi);
Sherwood Forest (20mi)

Woodborough St

Annesley Gve

Mansfield Rd

N Sherwood St

Bluecoat
St

Nottingham
Trent
University

Shakespeare St

Chaucer St

Goldsmith St

S Sherwood St

N Church St

Trinity
Sq

Milton St

Glasshouse St

Victoria
Shopping
Centre

To Wollaton Hall (2.5mi);
M1 (5mi); DH Lawrence
Birthplace Museum (10mi);
Durban House Heritage Centre,
Eastwood (10mi); Derby (17mi)

Talbot St

Burton St

Corner
House

Forman St

Royal
Concert
Hall

Wollaton St

Lower Parliament St

Cranbrook St

Derby
Rd

Barnabas
Cathedral

College
St

Sky
Mirror

Nottingham
Playhouse

Chapel Bar

Upper Parliament St

Market St

King St

Clinton St

Heathcote St

George St

Broad St

Regent St

Circus
St

St James's St

Angel
Row

Long Row

Old Market
Square

Smithy Row

Pelham St

Victoria St

Carlton St

Goosegate

Woolpack La

To
Southwell
(14mi);
Newark
(20mi)

St James St

St James Tce

Friar La

Wheeler
Gate

South Pde

Exchange
Walk

St Peter's Gate

Bridlesmith
Gate

Weekday
Cross

Warser
Gate

Stoney St

Barker Gate

Bellar Gate

St Mary's Gate

Plumptre St

Plumptre Gate

Low Pavement

High Pavement

Cliff Rd

Hounds Gate

Spaniel Row

Maid Marian Way

Castle Gate

Stanford St

St Nicholas'
Church

Middle Hill

Broadmarsh
Shopping
Centre

Lenton Rd

Peveril Dve

Castle Rd

Collin St

Canal St

Crofthall
Gate

Carrington St

Popham St

Hope Dve

Castle Blvd

Wilford St

Trent St

To East Midlands
Airport (13mi)

Nottingham
Train Station

Queens Rd

has shrunk. Phlegmatically known as Snotingham in Saxon days, the city now has a more cultural than industrial buzz. Fashion designer Paul Smith is a leading light on the scene, the clubs and bars are some of the liveliest, and Trent Bridge remains a major attraction for cricket fans. Nottingham is also an inviting mecca for shopaholics.

Nottingham's famed Goose Fair dates back to the Middle Ages; these days it's an outsized funfair that takes place in the Forest Recreation Ground every October.

Orientation

Like other Midlands cities, Nottingham is chopped into pieces by an inner ring road enclosing most of the attractions, eateries and bars. The train station is south of the canal on the southern edge of the centre. There are two bus stations: Victoria bus station is hidden away behind the Victoria shopping centre, just north of the city centre, while Broadmarsh bus station is behind the Broadmarsh shopping centre to the south.

Information

Alphanet Café (☎ 956 6988; 4 Queen St; 10am-6pm; Internet access per 30min £2)

TIC (☎ 915 5330; www.visitnottingham.com; 1-4 Smithy Row; 9am-5.30pm Mon-Fri, 9am-5pm Sat, 11am-3pm Sun May-Sep) Ask about discount combination tickets for major attractions.

Sights & Activities

NOTTINGHAM CASTLE MUSEUM & ART GALLERY

Nottingham Castle was demolished after the Civil War and replaced with a mansion in 1674. The **museum** (☎ 915 3700; adult £2 Sat & Sun, free Mon-Fri; 8am-5pm Mar-Oct, 10am-4pm Sat-Thu Nov-Feb) opened inside the castle shell in 1875. It vividly describes Nottingham's history and displays some of the medieval alabaster carvings for which Nottingham was noted. Upstairs there's an art gallery with changing exhibitions and some fine permanent pieces (LS Lowry, Delacroix and Dante Gabriel Rossetti). There's a stylish café and shop.

An underground passageway, known as **Mortimer's Hole** (tours £2; 2pm & 3pm Mon-Fri) leads from the castle to Brewhouse Yard. Roger Mortimer, who arranged Edward II's murder, is said to have been captured by supporters of Edward III who entered via this passage.

CAVES OF NOTTINGHAM

Nottingham stands on a plug of Sherwood sandstone riddled with artificial caves dating back to medieval times. Rather surprisingly, the entrance to the most fascinating, readily accessible **caves** (☎ 924 1424; adult £3.75; 10am-5pm Mon-Sat, 11am-5pm Sun) is inside Broadmarsh shopping centre. These contain an air-raid shelter, a medieval underground tannery, several pub cellars and a mock-up of a Victorian slum dwelling.

TALES OF ROBIN HOOD

The **tales** (☎ 948 3284; www.robinhood.uk.com; 30-38 Maid Marian Way; adult/child £6.95/4.95; 10am-6pm May-Sep, 10am-5.30pm Oct-Apr) is a silly but fun ride through models of Nottingham Castle and Sherwood Forest in the days when Robin was battling it out with the sheriff. After the dramatised version, you can find out more about the reality behind the legend. Look out for events like falconry days and jester workshops.

WOLLATON HALL

Built in 1588 by Sir Francis Willoughby, a land- and coal-mine owner, **Wollaton Hall** (☎ 915 3900; Wollaton Park, Derby Rd; admission free Mon-Fri, £1.50 Sat & Sun; 11am-5pm Apr-Oct, 11am-4pm Nov-Mar) is a fine example of Tudor architecture at its most extravagant. Architect Robert Smythson was also responsible for the equally avant-garde Longleat in Wessex (p424). The hall now houses a decent natural history museum.

The **Industrial Museum** (admission free Mon-Fri, £1.50, or £2 for combined ticket, Sat & Sun; 10am-5pm Apr-Oct), in the 18th-century stable block, displays lace-making equipment, Raleigh bicycles, a gigantic 1858 beam engine and oddities such as a locally invented, 1963 video recorder that never got off the ground.

Wollaton Hall is on the western edge of the city, 2½ miles from the centre; get here on bus No 35, 36 or 37. Wollaton Park, surrounding the hall, is a popular picnic spot.

BREWHOUSE YARD MUSEUM

Housed in five 17th-century cottages virtually below the castle, this **museum** (☎ 915 3600; Castle Blvd; admission free Mon-Fri, £1.50 Sat & Sun; 10am-4.30pm) re-creates daily life in Nottingham over the past 300 years (with particularly fine reconstructions of traditional shops) and hosts good temporary exhibitions.

MUSEUM OF COSTUME & TEXTILES

Arranged in period rooms, this intriguing **museum** (☎ 915 3500; Castle Gate; admission free; ☺ 10am-4pm Wed-Sun & bank hols) displays costumes from 1790 to the mid-20th century, as well as tapestries and lace. It's housed in a row of 17th- and 18th-century houses and is worth a look even if needlework isn't your bag.

GALLERIES OF JUSTICE

In the impressive Shire Hall building on High Pavement, the **Galleries of Justice** (☎ 952 0555; www.galleriesofjustice.org.uk; High Pavement; adult/child £6.95/5.25, £1 discount if booked at TIC; ☺ 10am-5pm Tue-Sun Apr-Oct, 10am-4pm Tue-Sun Nov-Mar) takes you through the history of the judicial system from medieval ordeals by water or hot iron to modern crime detection. You are guided through much of the action by 'jailers' and 'prisoners', and it's highly interactive: you may find yourself sentenced to death in a Victorian courtroom!

Tours

Nottingham Experience (☎ 911 5005; www.visit nottingham.com/tours.asp; tour 30min; tickets £4) Knowledgeable guides whisk visitors from the castle gatehouse on a rapid tour of the city, recounting the stories behind the sights. Longer, themed group tours are also available.

Original Nottingham Ghost Walk (☎ 01773-769300; www.ghost-walks.co.uk; tickets £4; ☺ 7pm Sat Jan-Nov) Departs from Ye Olde Salutation Inn (see Drinking, opposite) to explore the spooky underbelly of the city's past.

Festivals & Events

Events including a **Shakespeare Festival** (late July/early August) and **Robin Hood Pageant** (late October) are held at the Nottingham Castle Museum & Art Gallery (p427); call for details.

Sleeping

Rutland Square Hotel (☎ 941 1114; rutlandsquare@ zoffanyhotels.co.uk; St James St; s/d from £95/110) This central business-class hotel has style and good service, as well as serious discounts at the weekend.

Lace Market Hotel (☎ 852 3232; reservations@ lacemarkethotel.co.uk; 29-31 High Pavement; s/d £89/99) The Lace Market is a gorgeous old hotel in an atmospheric part of town; this exclusive boutique hotel sometimes offers reduced weekend rates.

Igloo Tourist Hostel (☎ 947 5250; www.igloohostel .co.uk; 110 Mansfield Rd; dm £12, breakfast extra) A favourite of backpackers, this 36-bed independent hostel is a short walk north of Victoria bus station. The hotel's entrance is on Fulforth St.

THE LEGEND OF ROBIN HOOD

In the Middle Ages most of Nottinghamshire was covered in forest, the stomping ground (legend has it) of Robin Hood and his merry men, who were trying to stymie the wicked Sheriff of Nottingham in the name of absentee 'good' King Richard I.

Sites associated with Robin abound. Nottingham Castle obviously played a key role, as did St Mary's Church in the Lace Market. Robin is said to have married Maid Marian in Edwinstowe church, while Fountaindale, near Blidworth, is the supposed site of his battle with Friar Tuck.

But did Robin ever really exist? As long ago as 1377 William Langland made fleeting reference to him in his poem *Piers Plowman*, but it was only in the early 16th century that the story began to be fleshed out, most notably in the ballad *A Geste of Robyn Hoode*. In 1795 Joseph Ritson collected all the known accounts of Robin into one volume, and since then innumerable authors (including Sir Walter Scott and Alfred, Lord Tennyson) have produced torrid novels and poems, while heart-throbs such as Errol Flynn, Kevin Costner and, um, Jason Connery have portrayed the robber-of-the-rich on silver and square screens.

Disappointingly, dedicated researchers have failed to turn up any hard evidence that the outlaw actually existed. Robin is, for example, said to have been born in Lockesley in Yorkshire or Nottinghamshire, but no such place appears on any map. Optimists point to a Loxley in Staffordshire where Robin Hood's father supposedly owned land, and even the suburb of Loxley in Sheffield – a fragile link that means the new regional airport (Sheffield Doncaster Robin Hood) is named after the 'local' lad. But it is more than likely that 'Robin' is no more than a jumbled memory of ancient ideas about forest fairies, or a character made up to give voice to medieval resentments.

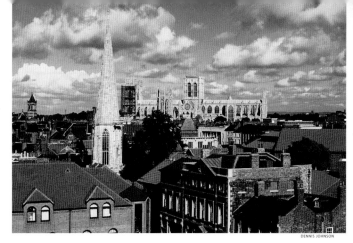
York Minster (p523), York, England

King's College Chapel (p452), Cambridge, England

Whitby Abbey (p543), Whitby, England
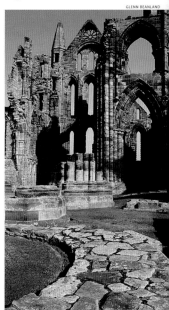

Thurne Windmill, Norfolk Broads (p476), Norfolk, England

MARK DAFFEY

Amusement ride, Pleasure Beach (p577),
Blackpool, England

NICHOLAS REUSS

Guillemot (p86; *Uria aalge*)

Hadrian's Wall (p626), England

CHRIS MELLOR

Boat cruise, Derwent Water
(p586), Lake District, England

DAVID

Eating

The area around Carlton St to the east of the centre is the eating (and drinking) hub. Good news for vegetarians: choices now range from burgers to haute cuisine.

V1 (☎ 941 5121; www.v-1.co.uk; Hounds Gate; meals £3.90-4.90; ❤ breakfast, lunch & dinner Mon-Sat, lunch Sun) This could be the future of fast food. It's just like any burger chain – fast, cheap and delicious – but without the meat.

Skinny Sumo (☎ 952 0188; 11-13 Carlton St; sushi platters from £8, rolls £1.50-3.50; ❤ lunch & dinner Tue-Sun) This inventively named restaurant has a sushi-bar conveyor belt and a variety of authentic Japanese dishes; look out for speciality nights (curry, noodles) during the week.

Punchinello (☎ 941 1965; 35 Forman St; mains £7.50-13; ❤ lunch & dinner) Allegedly Nottingham's oldest restaurant, this charming place has been pleasing diners with Med-influenced fare for decades.

Fresh (☎ 924 3336; 15 Goose Gate; dinner mains £9-12; ❤ 8am-5.30pm Mon & Tue, 8am-9pm Wed-Fri, 9am-9pm Sat) Bright and confident, Fresh serves world cuisine all day and good snacks at lunch time. There are tasty vegetarian and fish selections.

Drinking

Ye Olde Trip to Jerusalem (☎ 947 3171; Brewhouse Yard, Castle Rd) Tucked into the cliff below the castle, this is one of Britain's best (and oldest) pubs; it supposedly slaked the thirst of Crusaders predeparture. Inevitably, a fair number of tourists pop their heads in for a look, but there are enough nooks and crannies cut into the rock in the upstairs bar that the crowds generally don't interfere with the atmosphere.

Bell Inn (☎ 947 5241; 18 Angel Row) A favourite with locals, the ever-popular Bell is one of the few places right in the centre where you can get a decent beer and relax on a weekend night. Neither trendy nor quaint, it's just a great pub.

Ye Olde Salutation Inn (☎ 988 1948; Maid Marian Way) Near the Trip to Jerusalem in location, atmosphere and era, this is another comfortable, unpretentious oldie (c1240).

Entertainment

Sometimes it seems as if the whole of the Lace Market area is one huge, hyper-hip café-bar. They come and go, and some are cooler than others, but they all tend to follow the same pattern: brown leather sofas for lounging, subdued lighting for smooching and smooth talking, sleek food for feeding, an unspoken dress code and DJs for added cred.

Social (☎ 950 5078; 23 Pelham St) Sibling of the equally cool London joint, this standout place has DJs and live guests and is one of *the* places to be seen.

Cookie Club (☎ 950 5892; 22 St James St; ❤ 11pm-2am Wed-Sat) Just west of Market Sq, this is a friendly little club with alternative nights and fair prices. It's a nice reprieve from the prevailing brown-couch scene.

Rock City (☎ 941 2544; www.rock-city.co.uk; 8 Talbot St) The major live venue for bands, Rock City has popular indie, rock and student club nights.

Getting There & Away

East Midlands Airport (☎ 01332-852852; www.east Midlandsairport.com) is southwest of the city centre. Daily flights to Belfast, Dublin, Edinburgh, Glasgow, Guernsey and various continental European cities.

Dunn Line Buses (☎ 08700 121212) bus No 777 goes several times daily to/from Leicester (one hour).

Trent Buses (☎ 01773-712265; www.trentbuses.co .uk) Buses depart from Broadmarsh and Victoria bus stations to Derby (35 minutes), Chesterfield (90 minutes), and the also Peak District. All-day Zig Zag tickets cost £3.50.

Getting Around

For information on buses within Nottingham, call **Nottingham City Buses** (☎ 950 3665; www.nctx.co .uk). A Day Rider ticket gives you unlimited travel for £2.20.

A new **tram system** (www.thetram.net; s/all-day from 80p/£2) runs from Bulwell through the centre and Hockley to the train station.

Bunney's Bikes (☎ 947 2713; 97 Carrington St; bike hire per day from £8) is near the train station.

AROUND NOTTINGHAM
Newstead Abbey

With its attractive gardens, romantic lakeside ruins and notable connections with scoundrel poet Lord Byron (1788–1824), whose owned this country pile, **Newstead Abbey** (☎ 01623-455900; www.newsteadabbey.org.uk; house & park adult £5, gardens only £2.50; ❤ house noon-5pm Apr-Sep, garden 9am-dusk year-round) is a popular weekend destination for tourists and local families alike. Founded as an Augustinian priory around 1170, it was converted into a home after the dissolution of the monasteries in 1539. Beside the still-imposing façade of the priory church are the remains of the manor. It now houses some interesting Byron memorabilia – you can peek into his bedroom and toilet, which might have amused him – and Victorian paintings and furnishings in the extant chambers.

The house is 12 miles north of Nottingham, off the A60. The Sherwood Forester bus runs right here on summer Sundays. Bus Nos 737, 747 and 757 run from Nottingham's Victoria bus station (25 minutes, every 20 minutes, hourly on Sunday) to the abbey gates.

DH Lawrence Sites

The **DH Lawrence Birthplace Museum** (☎ 01773-717353; 8a Victoria St, Eastwood; admission free Mon-Fri, £2 Sat & Sun; ✆ 10am-5pm Apr-Oct, 10am-4pm Nov-Mar), former home of Nottingham's controversial author (1885–1930), has been reconstructed as it would have been in Lawrence's childhood, with period furnishings. Down the road, the **Durban House Heritage Centre** (☎ 01773-717353; Mansfield Rd; adult £2, or £3.50 for both sites; ✆ 10am-5pm Apr-Oct, 10am-4pm Nov-Mar) sheds light on the background to Lawrence's books by re-creating the life of the mining community at the turn of the 20th century.

Eastwood is about 10 miles northwest of the city; take Trent Buses service No 1.

Sherwood Forest Country Park

Don't expect to lose yourself like an outlaw: there are more tourists than trees in today's Sherwood Forest, although there are still peaceful spots to be found. The **Sherwood Forest visitors centre** (☎ 01623-823202; www.sherwoodforest.org.uk; admission free; ✆ 10.30am-5pm Apr-Oct, 10am-4.30pm Nov-Mar) houses 'Robyn Hode's Sherwode', a cute but corny exhibition describing the lifestyles of bandits, kings, peasants and friars in radical Rob's day. A major attraction is the Major Oak, where Robin is supposed to have hidden; these days it's more likely he'd have to hold it up, not hide in it. The Robin Hood Festival is a massive medieval re-enactment that takes place here every August.

Sherwood Forest YHA Hostel (☎ 0870 770 6026; sherwood@yha.org.uk; Forest Corner, Edwinstowe; dm £12.75) is a modern hostel with comfortable dorms located just a short distance from the visitors centre.

Sherwood Forester buses run the 20 miles to the park from Nottingham on Sunday; catch bus No 33 from Nottingham Monday to Saturday.

SOUTHWELL
☎ 01636 / pop 6290

One of those archetypal sleepy market towns bursting with tearooms and antique shops, Southwell is a key stop for another reason: **Southwell Minster** (☎ 812649; suggested donation £2; ✆ 8am-7pm May-Sep, 8am-dusk Oct-Apr) is a Gothic cathedral unlike any other in Britain, its two heavy, square front towers belying the treats within. The nave dates from the 12th century, although there is evidence of an earlier Saxon church floor, itself made with mosaics from a Roman villa. A highlight of the building is the chapterhouse, filled with incredible naturalistic 13th-century carvings of leaves, pigs, dogs and rabbits. The library is also a fascinating place, housing illuminated manuscripts and heavy tomes from the 16th century and earlier.

A visit to **Southwell Workhouse** (☎ 817250; Upton Rd; adult £4.40; ✆ noon-5pm Thu-Mon Mar-Jul, Sep & Oct, 11am-5pm Thu-Mon Aug) is a sobering but fascinating experience. An audio guide, narrated by 'inmates' and 'officials', describes the life of paupers in the mid-19th century to good (if grim) effect, despite the fact that most of the rooms are empty.

Bus Nos 101 and 201 run from Nottingham (40 minutes, every 20 minutes, hourly on Sunday) and on to Newark-on-Trent (25 minutes, hourly, every two hours on Sunday).

DERBYSHIRE

Hills and dales, sheep and pheasants, sturdy stone fences lining skinny country roads, Derbyshire has all the ingredients of picture-postcard rural England, and it's an outdoor enthusiast's dream. Part of the county is within the Peak District National Park, the starting point for some of the country's best walks. The parts of Derbyshire beyond the national park's boundary are also packed with attractions: the misplaced seaside resort of Matlock Bath, the twisted spire of Chesterfield church, and some wonderful stately homes – including the dishevelled Calke Abbey and the unforgettable Chatsworth. Derbyshire is one of the most visited and popular counties in all of England, and justifiably so.

Activities

Outdoor activities in Derbyshire include walking, cycling, rock climbing, caving and paragliding, to name but a few. Many of these activities take place inside the Peak District National Park (p435).

Getting There & Around

Derbyshire Wayfarer (☎ 0870 608 2608, Traveline; www.derbysbus.net; day pass adult/family £7.50/12) covers buses and trains throughout the county and beyond (eg to Manchester and Sheffield), while **Trent Buses** (☎ 01773-712265; www.trentbuses .co.uk; day ticket £3.50) is the award-winning operator of the TransPeak bus service.

DERBY

☎ 01332 / pop 236,740

The Industrial Revolution made a major manufacturing centre out of this once-sedate market town. First silk, then china, then railways made its fortunes, and finally Rolls-Royce aircraft engines. It may not demand an overnight stay, but it's a good day trip for those interested in the history of English engineering and the bone china industry. The TIC (☎ 255802; Market Pl) is in the attractive old-town district.

Sights

The town's 18th-century **cathedral** (Queen St) boasts a 64m-high tower and magnificent wrought-iron screens. Fairly new for an English cathedral, it has an unusually light, airy interior thanks to its creamy white plasterwork and large windows. Notice the huge tomb of Bess of Hardwick, one of Derbyshire's most formidable residents in days gone by; for more about Bess, see Hardwick Hall (p434).

The factory of **Royal Crown Derby** (☎ 712841; Osmaston Rd; ☒ 9am-5pm Mon-Sat, 10am-4pm Sun) turns out some of the finest bone china in England. There's no charge to visit the demonstration area to see workers skilfully make delicate china flowers, using little more than a hat-pin, spoon handle and – naturally – a head-lice comb. There's also a shop, piled high with teapots, collectable paperweights and various bargains (watch your elbows!), and a café. The factory tour (four daily from

Monday to Friday, £4.95) is fascinating even if china isn't your cup of tea; you'll see the entire process, from vats of raw powder and bone-mix through to the final touches of liquid gold decoration.

The **Derby Industrial Museum** (☎ 255308; Silk Mill Lane; admission free; ☒ 11am-5pm Mon, 10am-5pm Tue-Sat, 2-5pm Sun & bank hols), in a former Silk Mill, is heaven for train lovers and fans of aero-engines.

Eating & Drinking

Near the cathedral there's the traditional and intimate (OK, cramped) **Ye Olde Dolphin Inne** (Queen St; snacks & meals £2-5), with four little bars and good pub grub. Nearby, **Vida** (Queen St; mains £4-6) is a small café-bar with a good view of the cathedral. Near the train station, the award-winning **Brunswick Inn** (Railway Tce) brews its own beer on-site; its ambience is both crisply modern and appealingly old-fashioned, with blonde wood in one room and finely carved wooden wall panels in another.

Getting There & Away

TransPeak buses run to/from Manchester via Matlock Bath (1¼ hours), Bakewell (one hour) and Buxton (1½ hours, eight daily). There are trains to/from Matlock Bath (40 minutes), Sheffield (45 minutes, several daily) and London St Pancras (around two hours, several daily).

AROUND DERBY
Kedleston Hall

Sitting proudly in vast landscaped parkland, the superb neoclassical mansion of **Kedleston Hall** (☎ 01332-842191; adult £5.80; ☒ noon-4pm Sat-Wed Easter-Oct) is a must for fans of stately homes. The Curzon family has lived here since the 12th century; Sir Nathaniel Curzon tore down an earlier house in 1758 so this stunning masterpiece could be built. Meanwhile, the poor old peasants in Kedleston village had their humble dwellings moved a mile down the road, as they interfered with the view!

Highlights include the breathtaking Marble Hall, with its massive alabaster columns and statues of Greek deities, and a circular saloon with a domed roof, modelled on the Pantheon in Rome.

Kedleston Hall is 5 miles northwest of Derby. By bus, service No 109 between Derby and Ashbourne goes within about 1½ miles of Kedleston Hall (20 minutes, seven daily Monday to Saturday, five on Sunday), and on sunny days walking the rest is no hardship. On Sundays and bank holidays the bus loops right up to the house.

Calke Abbey

Looking like an enormous, long-neglected cabinet of wonders, **Calke Abbey** (☎ 01332-863822; adult £5.90; ⊗ 1-5.30pm Sat-Wed Apr-Oct) is not your usual glitzy, wealth-encrusted stately home. Built around 1703, it's been passed down among a dynasty of eccentric and reclusive baronets, so little has changed – especially since about 1880. It's a ramshackle maze of rooms crammed with unkemp furniture, mountains of taxidermied animal heads, random stacks of dusty books, thousands of stuffed birds and endless piles of bric-a-brac from the last three centuries. Some rooms are in fabulous condition, while others are deliberately untouched, complete with crumbling plaster and mouldy wallpaper.

Calke is 10 miles south of Derby. Visitors coming by car must enter via the village of Ticknall. Bus Nos 68 and 69 from Derby to Swadlincote stop at Ticknall (40 minutes, hourly) and from there it's a 2-mile walk through the park.

Ashbourne
☎ 01335

In the thriving little market town of Ashbourne, about 15 miles northwest of Derby, fine old buildings line the marketplace and precariously slanted main street. Most are now antique shops drawing crowds of eager browsers at weekends.

The **TIC** (☎ 343666; ⊗ 9.30am-5pm Mon-Sat, 10am-4pm Sun) is in the market place, which is also the site of the annual Shrovetide Football game (see the boxed text, below).

Ashbourne is famous for its gingerbread; get a sample at the **Gingerbread Shop** (St John's St), a bakery and tearoom in a half-timbered building. **Smith's Tavern** (St John's St) and the **Horns** (Victoria Sq), are both fine old pubs on the square.

Ashbourne is the southern terminus of the **Tissington Trail**, a former railway line and now a wonderful easy-gradient path cutting through fine west Derbyshire countryside. The trail takes you north towards Buxton and connects with the High Peak Trail running south towards Matlock Bath – for more details on circular route possibilities see Activities in the Peak District National Park section (p435).

About a mile outside town along Mapleton Lane, **Ashbourne Cycle Hire** (☎ 343156) is on the Tissington Trail, with a huge stock

---

ANCIENT CUSTOMS

Shrove Tuesday comes before Ash Wednesday, the first day of Lent – the Christian time of fasting – so Shrove Tuesday is the day to use up all your rich and fattening food. This led to the quaint tradition of Pancake Day in England and the rather less staid Mardi Gras festival elsewhere in the world.

On Shrove Tuesday, various English towns celebrate with pancake races, but in Ashbourne they go for something much more energetic. Here they play **Shrovetide Football** – but it's nothing like the football most people are used to. For a start, the goals are 3 miles apart, the 'pitch' is a huge patch of countryside, and the game lasts all afternoon and evening (then starts again the day after). There are two teams, but hundreds of participants, and very few rules indeed. A large leather ball is fought over voraciously as players maul their way through fields and gardens, along the river, and up the main street – where shop windows are specially boarded over for the occasion. Visitors come from far and wide to watch, but only the brave should take part!

About 8 miles up the road from Ashbourne, in the Staffordshire village of Wetton, another 'traditional' event takes place on an early weekend each June – the **World Toe Wrestling Championship**. It started in 1976, when talk at Ye Olde Royal Oak Inn turned to sport. Depressed at England's inability to dominate in any global event, regulars decided to invent a sport that the home country would always win (because nobody else knew about it). One year later a random Canadian strolled in and beat the local champion. Game over. Resurrected in 1990, the annual event now pulls in hefty crowds (and serious money for charity), with men and women sitting on a 'toedium' attempting to force their opponent's toe onto the side of the 'toesrack'.

of bikes and trailers for all ages, and free leaflets showing the route with pubs and teashops along the way.

There are numerous services from Derby; the trip takes 30 to 45 minutes. Direct buses include No 107 (hourly Monday to Saturday), No 111 (three per day on Sunday and bank holidays), and No X1 (five daily Monday to Friday, four daily Saturday and Sunday), which continues to Manchester.

MATLOCK BATH

☎ 01629 / pop 2200

Unashamedly brash and delightfully tacky, Matlock Bath is like a lost seaside resort, complete with a promenade of amusement arcades, an aquarium, cafés, pubs and souvenir shops – some with stock that seems left over since Victorian times. Roughly in the centre of Derbyshire, on the southeastern edge of the national park, it sits next to the pleasant town of Matlock, which has little in the way of sights but is a handy gateway to the scenic dales on this side of the park.

Every weekend – and all through the summer – groups of local lads and lasses, couples, families, kids and grannies come here from miles around, and there's a totally no-frills buzz about the place. At weekends, Matlock Bath is also especially popular with motorcyclists (the A6 is an irresistibly smooth, twisty road), so the buzz is sometimes a roar, but the throb of engines and parading leather-clad enthusiasts only adds to the general good-time atmosphere.

Orientation & Information

Matlock Bath is 2 miles south of Matlock. Everything revolves around North Pde and South Pde, a line of seaside-style shops, attractions and eateries along one side of the main road through town (the A6), with the River Derwent on the other side, standing in for the sea.

Matlock Bath's **TIC** (☎ 55082; www.derbyshire .gov.uk; the Pavilion; ⏱ 9.30am-5pm Mar-Oct, 9.30am-5pm Sat & Sun Nov-Feb) has friendly staff and plenty of leaflets and local guidebooks.

Sights & Activities

The first thing to do in Matlock Bath is relax: buy some candyfloss and just stroll around. Then cross the river to stroll some more in the park; if you're ambitious, climb up the hill for great clifftop viewpoints. A lazier way to

get those views is via the **Heights of Abraham** (☎ 582365; adult/child £8.50/5.50; ⏱ 10am-5pm Mar-Oct, 10am-5pm Sat & Sun Feb-Mar), a wholesome family attraction with underground caverns, playground, nature trails and an audiovisual show. The price includes a spectacular cable-car ride up from the valley floor.

From the cable-car base, walking trails lead up to airy viewpoints on top of **High Tor**; you can see down to Matlock Bath and over to **Riber Castle**, a Victorian folly.

At the **Mining Museum** (☎ 583834; the Pavilion; adult £3; ⏱ 10am-5pm) you can clamber through shafts and tunnels, and for £1.50 extra go down **Temple Mine** and try panning for 'gold'.

A mile south of Matlock Bath is **Masson Mill** (☎ 581001; adult/child £2.50/1.50; ⏱ 10am-4pm Mon-Sat, 11am-4pm Sun), built in 1783 for pioneering industrialist Sir Richard Arkwright and acknowledged as a masterpiece of the era. Today it's a working museum, with renovated looms and weaving machines, and the world's largest collection of bobbins.

From late August to October, don't miss the **Matlock Illuminations** (Pavilion Gardens; evenings from dusk Fri-Sun), when occasional fireworks displays and endless streams of outrageously decorated boats light up the river.

Sleeping

Matlock Bath has several B&Bs in the heart of things on North Pde and South Pde, and a few places just out of the centre. There are also more choices in nearby Matlock.

Hodgkinson's Hotel & Restaurant (☎ 582170; www.hodgkinsons-hotel.co.uk; 150 South Pde; s £38, d £68-88; P) More a wonder cabinet than ordinary hotel, this towering place has bizarrely shaped rooms, showers tucked into cupboards and stuffed animals glowering out from under antique chairs. The warmly Victorian décor and welcoming staff make it instantly cosy.

Temple Hotel (☎ 583911; Temple Rd; s/d £47/80; P) With its slightly dated seaside guesthouse feel – perfect for Matlock Bath – this hillside hotel makes a nice perch from which to gaze at the surroundings. The downstairs bar does good beer and pub food.

Matlock YHA Hostel (☎ 0870 770 5960; matlock@ yha.org.uk; 40 Bank Rd; dm £11, r from £39) This big, efficient housing block 2 miles from Matlock Bath has a convivial atmosphere and makes a great base to explore the entire area, but be sure to book ahead as it's very popular with youth groups.

Eating & Drinking

North Pde and South Pde are lined end-to-end with cafés, teashops and takeaways, all serving standards like chocolate cake, fish and chips, fried chicken, pies, and burgers – hear those arteries scream!

Of the pubs, the **Princess Victoria** (South Pde) is lively, the **County & Station** (Dale Rd) is relatively quiet, and the **Fishpond** (South Pde) has great live music and a patio that showcases the biker parade. Up on the hillside, the bar at the Temple Hotel (see Sleeping, p433) does good pub food, and the terrace outside is a great place to watch the firework displays that tie in with the Matlock Illuminations (late August to October).

Getting There & Away

The Peak District is extremely well-served by public transport, and Matlock is a hub. Bus Nos 210, 213 and 214 go to and from Sheffield several times a day. There are hourly buses to and from Derby (1¼ hours) and Chesterfield (35 minutes). Several trains a day serve Derby (40 minutes). For detailed travel planning information, go to www.derbysbus.net.

CHESTERFIELD

☎ 01246 / pop 100,880

The 'capital' of northeast Derbyshire, Chesterfield is best known for the remarkable crooked spire of **St Mary & All Saints Church** that overlooks the town. Dating from 1360, the spire twists and leans like something dreamed up by goth filmmaker Tim Burton. It's a giant corkscrew 68m high and 3m out of true – and no-one is really sure why (see the boxed text, right).

The church can be visited at any time, but if you want to go inside the spire, tours (£2.50) are available most days; just ask the verger if he's got time to show you around.

Right next to the church is Chesterfield's **Museum & Art Gallery** (St Mary's Gate; admission free; ◷ 10am-4pm Mon-Tue & Thu-Sat). Pride of place goes to a huge medieval winding wheel used to build the famous spire long before the days of tower-cranes, while a builder's mug that sat forgotten on a beam for 250 years is a reminder of the human touch.

It's worth linking a visit to the large and lively **market** (High St) held every Monday, Friday and Saturday (as it has been since the 12th century). Thursday sees a huge flea

market of antiques and oddities. The **TIC** (☎ 345777; Low Pavement) is nearby.

The easiest way to get here is by train; Chesterfield is between Nottingham/Derby (20 minutes) and Sheffield (10 minutes), with services about hourly.

AROUND CHESTERFIELD
Hardwick

If you're weighing up which stately homes to see, **Hardwick Hall** (☎ 01246-850430; adult £6.80; ◷ noon-4.30pm Wed-Thu, Sat & Sun Apr-Oct) should be high on your list. Home to the 16th century's second most famous woman, Elizabeth, countess of Shrewsbury – known to us all as Bess of Hardwick. Unashamedly modelling herself on the era's *most* famous woman, Queen Elizabeth I, Bess gained power and wealth by marrying four times, upwards each time.

When her fourth husband died in 1590, Bess had a huge fortune to play with, and built Hardwick Hall with the very best designs of the time. Glass was a status symbol, so she went all-out on the windows; a contemporary ditty quipped 'Hardwick Hall – more glass than wall'. Also astounding are the magnificent High Great Chamber and Long Gallery; these and many other rooms and broad stairways are decorated with fabulous large and detailed tapestries.

This place is special because after Bess died her descendants rarely used Hardwick Hall, and over the centuries it escaped the modern-

---

CHESTERFIELD'S CROOKED SPIRE

Why is the church spire at Chesterfield twisted and bent? Reasons given for this ecclesiastical anomaly include the following:

- it's because the devil once flew by and got his tail caught;

- it's because a virgin once got married here and the spire was so surprised it bent down to have a look;

- it's because many craftsmen were killed off by the Black Death, and cowboy builders did the job;

- it's because heavy lead tiles were fixed over a poorly seasoned timber frame.

Whatever the real reason, the people of Chesterfield prefer version two, and say that when another virgin gets married here, the spire will straighten up again.

isation that befell many other grand houses. The interior may not be as immediately sparkling as in some other stately homes, but what you see is truly Elizabethan.

Next door is **Hardwick Old Hall** (adult £3, joint ticket £9.20; 🕙 11am-6pm Mon, Wed, Thu, Sat & Sun Apr-Sep, 11am-5pm Mon, Wed, Thu, Sat & Sun Oct), Bess's first house, now a romantic ruin.

Also fascinating are the formal gardens, again virtually unchanged for centuries, and around the hall spreads the great expanse of **Hardwick Park** with short and long walking trails leading across fields and through woods. Pick up a (free) map at the ticket office. A point to aim for is the **Hardwick Inn**, which has a great sunny patio and does good pub food. You can also bring a picnic. All in all it's a great day out.

Hardwick Hall is 10 miles southeast of Chesterfield, just off the M1. A special historic coach runs from Chesterfield (Sunday only June to August, tickets £5, with half-price entry at Hardwick), out in the morning, back in the afternoon, giving about three hours at Hardwick. The bus also passes **Stainsby Mill** – a quaint working flour-mill dating from 1245 – and ends at **Bolsover Castle**, yet another stately home. For details, contact the Chesterfield TIC, or see www.cosycoach.co.uk.

PEAK DISTRICT NATIONAL PARK

For walkers, cyclists and nature lovers, the Peak District National Park is the undisputed highlight of a visit to the Midlands. It's named after an early British tribe that once lived here, not after the hills – they're actually more rounded than pointy, ideal for long, easy rambles or gentle bicycling trips. You'll find some of the wildest, most beautiful scenery in England here, from imposing stately homes to cute blond villages to green hills dotted with sheep. A matrix of small country lanes and squat stone fences line the district, and underground lurks a network of limestone caves, many of which are open to the public. This is the busiest national park in Europe, and the second-busiest in the world (after Mount Fuji), but with a bit of effort it's relatively easy to escape the crowds.

Orientation & Information

The Peak District is principally in Derbyshire but spills into five adjoining counties (including Yorkshire, Staffordshire and Cheshire) and is one of the largest national parks in England. This 555-sq-mile protected area is divided into two distinct zones: the harsher, higher, wilder Dark Peak to the north, characterised by peaty moors and dramatic gritstone cliffs called 'edges'; and the lower, prettier, more pastoral White Peak to the south, with green fields marked by dry-stone walls, and divided by deep-cut dales.

There are TICs (those that are run by the national park are called visitors centres) in Buxton, Bakewell, Castleton, Edale and in other locations, all overflowing with maps, guidebooks and leaflets that provide details of walks, cycle rides and other ideas to keep you occupied for a while. If you're looking for general information, the free *Peak District* newspaper and the official park website at www.peakdistrict.org cover transport, activities, local events, guided walks and so on.

Activities

CAVING

The Peak District limestone is riddled with caves and caverns – including 'showcaves' open to the public in Castleton, Buxton and Matlock Bath (described in each of those sections). For serious caving (or pot-holing) trips, TICs can provide a list of accredited outdoor centres, and if you know what you're doing, Castleton makes a great base.

For guidebooks, gear (to buy or hire) and a mine of local information, contact **Hitch n Hike** (☎ 01433-651013; www.hitchnhike.co.uk; Mytham Bridge, North Bamford, Hope Valley, Derbyshire), a specialist caving and outdoor activity shop in Bamford, near Castleton. The website also has more info about caving in the area.

CYCLING

The Peak District is a very popular cycling area, especially the White Peak and the parts of Derbyshire south of here around Matlock and Ashbourne. In the Dark Peak there are fewer roads, and they are quite busy with traffic, although there are some good off-road routes. A good place to start any cycling ride is a TIC – all stock maps, books and leaflets for cyclists and mountain bikers.

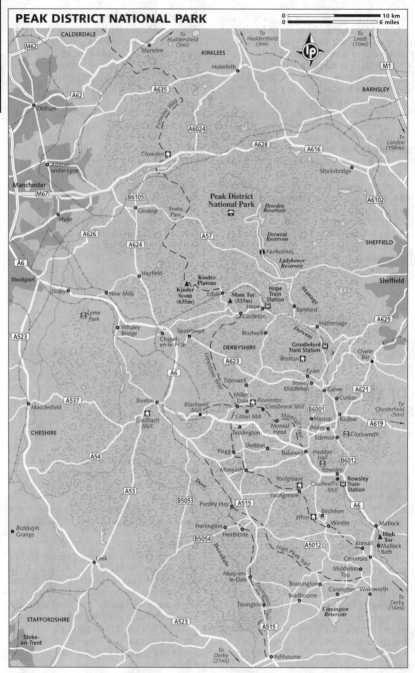

PEAK DISTRICT NATIONAL PARK

| 0 | 10 km |
| 0 | 6 miles |

In the Dark Peak, Edale is a popular starting point for mountain bikers. In the White Peak, all the villages mentioned in this section make good bases for cycle tours.

For easy traffic-free riding, head for the 17½-mile **High Peak Trail**, a route for cyclists and walkers on the mostly flat track of an old railway. You can join the trail at Cromford, near Matlock Bath, but it starts with a very steep incline, so if you prefer easy gradients a better start is Middleton Top, a mile or so south. The trail winds beautifully through hills and farmland to a village called Parsley Hay, and continues on for a few more miles towards Buxton. At Parsley Hay the **Tissington Trail** heads south for 13 miles to Ashbourne. You can go out and back as far as you like, or make it a triangular circuit, following quiet lanes through Bradbourne and Brassington.

There are several cycle hire centres in the Peak District, including **Parsley Hay** (☎ 01298-84493) and **Middleton Top** (☎ 01629-823204) near the Tissington and High Peak Trails. TICs have a leaflet detailing all hire centres, rates and opening times; plan on £10 to £15 a day for adults' bikes (deposit and ID required).

WALKING
The Peak District is one of the most popular walking areas in Britain, crossed by a vast network of footpaths and tracks – especially in the White Peak – and you can easily find a walk of a few miles or longer, depending on your energy and interests. If you want to explore the higher realms of the Dark Peak, which often involves the local art of 'bog trotting', make sure your boots are waterproof and be prepared for wind and rain, even if the sun is shining when you set off.

The Peak's most famous walking trail is the **Pennine Way**, with its southern end at Edale and its northern end over 250 miles away in Scotland. If you don't have a spare three weeks to cover this route, from Edale you can follow the trail north across wild hills and moors for just a day or two.

The 46-mile **Limestone Way** winds through the Derbyshire countryside from Castleton to Rocester in Staffordshire on a mix of footpaths, tracks and quiet lanes. The northern section of this route, through the White Peak between Castleton and Matlock, is 26 miles, and hardy folk can do it over a long summer day, but two days is better.

The route goes via Miller's Dale, Monyash, Youlgreave and Bonsall, with YHA hostels and B&Bs along the way, and ample pubs and cafés. TICs have a detailed leaflet.

TICs and YHAs have pamphlets detailing various walking routes. Shorter walks are described throughout this section.

Sleeping
TICs have lists of hotels, B&Bs and campsites – whatever suits your budget. Walkers may appreciate the 13 **camping barns** (per person from £3.50) dotted around the Peak. Usually owned by farmers, they are booked centrally through the **YHA** (☎ 0870 870 8808). Otherwise, pick up a *Camping Barns in England* leaflet at TICs.

Getting There & Around
The Peak District authorities are trying hard to wean visitors off their cars, and TICs stock the excellent *Peak District Timetable* (60p) covering local buses and trains. For more details, see p431.

BUXTON
☎ 01298 / pop 20,840
With its grand Georgian architecture, leafy parks and busy tourist ambience, Buxton is frequently compared to Bath, and just like Bath, Buxton also has a natural warm-water spring discovered by the Romans. The town's heyday was in the 18th century when 'taking the waters' was highly fashionable. It may not be as pristine as its sister city, but in the past couple of years a batch of restoration projects has brought back the gleam to Buxton. Away from the historical sights, it's just like many other north-country market towns, although none the worse for that.

Every Tuesday and Saturday, Market Pl is full of colourful stalls and has a great atmosphere. Around town, there's also a vast selection of shops selling crafts, books and antiques, perfect for a day of idle browsing.

Situated just outside the border of the Peak District National Park, Buxton makes a handy gateway for travel to the northern and western areas.

Orientation & Information
Buxton has two centres: the historical area, with the Crescent, Opera House and Pavilion; and Market Pl, surrounded by pubs and restaurants. There are several banks with

ATMs on the Quadrant. Other useful places include:

Northwest Computers (11 Bridge St; Internet access per hr 50p; ☉ 9am-5pm Mon-Sat)

Post office (Spring Gardens; ☉ 9am-6pm Mon-Fri, 9am-3pm Sat)

TIC (☎ 25106; www.peakdistrict-tourism.gov.uk; the Crescent) Sells useful leaflets on walks in the area.

Sights & Activities

The town's gorgeously restored **Opera House** (☎ 0845 127 2190; www.buxton-opera.co.uk; tours £2), which is a century-old jewel of a building, is the centre for the town's famous **Opera Festival** (which is held every July, and is the largest of its kind in all of England). Tours of the Opera House's auditorium and

backstage areas are available at 11am most Saturday mornings.

Nearby is the **Pavilion**, a giant palace of glass built in 1871, which overlooks **Pavilion Gardens** – a pleasant park with lawns, ponds and a miniature train. **Broad Walk** is a traffic-free road alongside the edge of the gardens, ideal for an evening perambulation – it's also lined with comfortable B&Bs.

Perhaps the grandest construction is the **Crescent**, a graceful curve of houses modelled on the Royal Crescent in Bath. Just east of here is **Cavendish Arcade**, formerly a thermal bathhouse (you can still see the chair used for lowering the infirm into the restorative waters) with several craft shops and book-shops, and a striking coloured-glass ceiling.

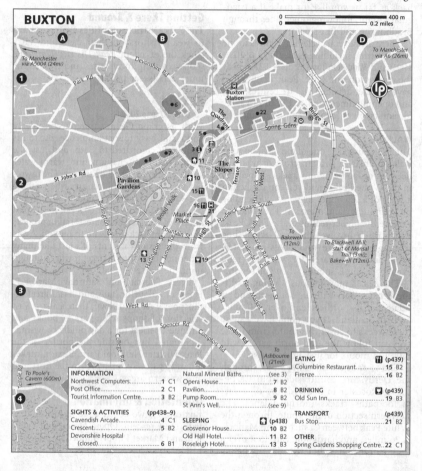

BUXTON

INFORMATION		Natural Mineral Baths...............(see 3)	EATING	(p439)
Northwest Computers................1 C1		Opera House.....................7 B2	Columbine Restaurant................15 B2
Post Office............................2 C1		Pavilion.............................8 B2	Firenze..............................16 B2
Tourist Information Centre.........3 B2		Pump Room.........................9 B2	
		St Ann's Well....................(see 9)	DRINKING	(p439)
SIGHTS & ACTIVITIES (pp438–9)			Old Sun Inn.........................19 B3
Cavendish Arcade.....................4 C1		SLEEPING (p438)	
Crescent..............................5 B2		Grosvenor House....................10 B2	TRANSPORT (p439)
Devonshire Hospital		Old Hall Hotel.....................11 B2	Bus Stop.............................21 B2
(closed)............................6 B1		Roseleigh Hotel....................13 B3	OTHER
			Spring Gardens Shopping Centre..22 C1

The TIC is in the old **Natural Mineral Baths**, where you can still see the source of the mineral water – now Buxton's most famous export. A small display tells the full story.

Across from the TIC, the **Pump Room**, which dispensed Buxton's spring water for nearly a century, now hosts temporary art exhibitions. Just outside is **St Ann's Well**, a fountain where you can fill up on free mineral water.

Buxton's most eye-catching edifice is the **Devonshire Hospital**, complete with towers and a massive dome; it's being converted into a new campus for the University of Derby.

Poole's Cavern (☎ 26978; www.poolescavern.co.uk; adult £5.50; ⊙ 10am-5pm Mar-Oct) is a splendid showcave about a mile from the centre. Amiable guides will take you deep underground to see an impressive selection of stalactites (including the longest in England) and stalagmites. In spring and autumn, running water makes the cave even more dramatic.

Sleeping

There are hundreds of hotels in Buxton, many dating from the Georgian and Victorian heydays. Around Pavilion Gardens and along Broad Walk are several particularly fine atmospheric places.

Old Hall Hotel (☎ 22841; the Square; s/d £65/96) Walking through the heavy doors and down the wood-panelled hallway of this grand establishment, which claims to be the oldest hotel in England, is as close as one gets to genuine time travel. Former guests include Mary, Queen of Scots, and Daniel Defoe.

Roseleigh Hotel (☎ 24904; www.roseleighhotel.co.uk; 19 Broad Walk; s/d from £25/55; ⓟ) This charming B&B, with a comfortable lounge full of travel guide books and deep leather armchairs, is run by a couple who are themselves seasoned travellers and adventure-tour guides.

Grosvenor House (☎ 72439; grosvenor.buxton@bt openworld.com; 1 Broad Walk; s/d from £25/50; ⓟ ⌨) A friendly family-run hotel with a budget café downstairs.

Eating & Drinking

The Market Pl and High St area has good cafés, pubs, restaurants and takeaways, and is definitely the place to be in the evening.

Columbine Restaurant (☎ 78752; Hall Bank; lunches around £5, dinner mains £10-12; ⊙ lunch Thu-Sat, dinner Mon-Sat) A local favourite, the Columbine serves fine food, including a full vegetarian menu, in calm and intimate surroundings.

Firenze (☎ 72203; Market Pl; pastas £5-6, mains £8-10) Another popular spot, this casual Italian eatery dishes out food such as pizzas, pastas and Mediterranean-style dishes in intimate (read: slightly cramped) surrounds.

Old Sun Inn (High St) Of the many watering holes this is our favourite – it could just be the perfect pub, with a friendly atmosphere, a warren of cosy rooms, a good menu of fine and affordable food and a range of well-kept beer to go with it.

Getting There & Away

Buxton is well served by public transport. Buses go to Derby (1½ hours, twice hourly), Chesterfield (1¼ hours, several daily) and Sheffield (65 minutes, twice hourly). Trains run hourly to and from Manchester (50 minutes).

EDALE
☎ 01433

Tiny Edale, nestled in the Edale Valley dividing the White and Dark Peak areas, is as much a point of departure as it is a village. Most famous as the southern terminus of the Pennine Way, it is a good place to start walks of varying difficulty in just about any direction.

Heading south, a great walk from Edale takes you up to **Hollins Cross**, a point on the ridge that runs south of the valley. From here, you can aim west to the top of spectacular **Mam Tor** and watch the hang-gliders swoop around above. Or go east along the ridge, with great views on both sides, past the cliffs of **Back Tor** to reach Lose Hill (which, naturally, faces Win Hill). Or you can continue south, down to the village of Castleton (described on p441).

From Edale you can also walk north onto the **Kinder Plateau** – dark and brooding in the mist, gloriously open and high when the sun's out. Weather permitting, a fine circular walk starts by following the Pennine Way through fields to **Upper Booth**, then up a path called Jacobs Ladder and along the southern edge of Kinder, before dropping down to Edale via the steep rocky valley of Grindsbrook Clough, or the ridge of Ringing Roger.

The **TIC** (☎ 670207; www.edale-valley.co.uk; ⊙ 10am-5pm) has a small exhibition about the park, and can supply all the leaflets, maps and guides you'll need.

Sleeping

The TIC can provide details on the many accommodation options available in farms and remote cottages in the surrounding area.

Edale YHA Hostel (☎ 0870 770 5808; edale@yha.org.uk; dm £11; **P**) A large and lively hostel in an old country house 1½ miles east of the village centre, this place is also an activity centre and popular with youth groups as well as walkers.

Old Parsonage (☎ 670232; Grindsbrook; B&B per person from £16; **P**) This place, a longtime favourite with walkers, is simple and straightforward but clean and tidy.

Mam Tor House (☎ 670253; Grindsbrook; B&B per person around £18; **P**) A good mid-range place

right next to the church and close to the train station, Mam Tor is another walkers' favourite with comfortable rooms and a great location inches from several trailheads. If it's full, the owners can direct you to other B&Bs.

Eating & Drinking

For filling no-frills food, head for **Cooper's Café** (near Cooper's Camp), or the café at the train station; both are open from breakfast-time to 5pm.

The township of Edale has two pubs, **Ye Old Nag's Head**, which is cosy and inviting, and actively courts walkers, and the **Rambler Inn**, which also does B&B; both serve passable pub grub (£4.95 to £6.95).

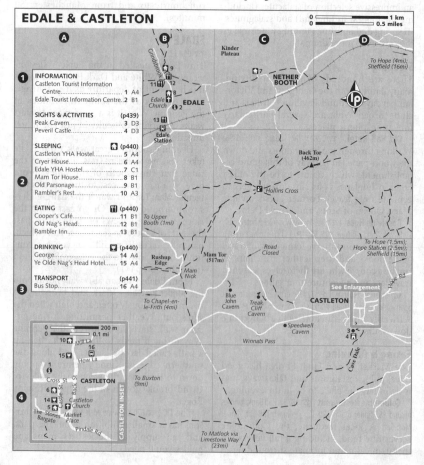

EDALE & CASTLETON

INFORMATION	
Castleton Tourist Information Centre	1 A4
Edale Tourist Information Centre	2 B1
SIGHTS & ACTIVITIES	**(p439)**
Peak Cavern	3 D3
Peveril Castle	4 D3
SLEEPING	**(p440)**
Castleton YHA Hostel	5 A4
Cryer House	6 A4
Edale YHA Hostel	7 C1
Mam Tor House	8 B1
Old Parsonage	9 B1
Rambler's Rest	10 A3
EATING	**(p440)**
Cooper's Café	11 B1
Old Nag's Head	12 B1
Rambler Inn	13 B1
DRINKING	**(p440)**
George	14 A4
Ye Olde Nag's Head Hotel	15 A4
TRANSPORT	**(p441)**
Bus Stop	16 A4

Getting There & Away

Edale is on the train line between Sheffield and Manchester (about eight per day Monday to Friday, five Saturday and Sunday). Trains also stop at several other Peak villages.

CASTLETON

☎ 01433

Nestled in the shadow of 517m-high Mam Tor and crowned by the ruins of Peveril Castle, the neat little settlement of Castleton has a central square (more of a triangle, actually), a couple of narrow lanes with sturdy gritstone houses and colourful gardens, and a good collection of cosy country pubs. Oh yes – and about a million tourists on summer weekends. But don't let that put you off. Come here at a quieter time to enjoy good walks in the surrounding area, and marvel at the famous 'showcaves', where a semiprecious stone called Blue John has been mined for centuries.

Orientation & Information

Castleton stands at the western end of the Hope Valley. The main route through the village (Cross St, the A6187) used to switchback up the side of notoriously unstable Mam Tor, but frequent landslips destroyed the road, and traffic now goes up the narrow, spectacular (and much older) Winnats Pass. On or just off Cross St are pubs, shops, cafés, B&Bs, the YHA hostel, and the sleek, modern **TIC** (☎ 620679; 🕑 10am-5.30pm Easter-Oct, Sat & Sun Oct-Apr).

Sights

Crowning the hill above Castleton is ruined **Peveril Castle** (☎ 620613; adult/child £2.70/1.40; 🕑 10am-6pm May-Jul, 10am-7pm daily Aug, 10am-5pm Sep-Oct, 10am-4pm Thu-Mon Nov-Mar, 10am-5pm Apr), well worth the steep walk up from the village. William Peveril, son of William the Conqueror, built it originally, and Henry II added the central keep in 1176. The ruins are interesting, but the real attraction is the setting, with its stunning view over the Hope Valley, straight down to Castleton's medieval street grid and north to Mam Tor with the Dark Peak beyond.

The area around Castleton is riddled with caves, and four are open to the public. Although mostly natural, they have been extensively mined for Blue John, lead and silver, and so have been enlarged over the centuries. The most convenient of these, **Peak Cavern** (☎ 620285; adult £5; 🕑 10am-4pm Apr-Oct, 10am-4pm Sat & Sun Nov-Mar), is easily reached by a pretty streamside walk from the village centre. The cave entrance is the largest in Britain, known (not so prettily) as the Devil's Arse. Visits are by hourly guided tour only.

The claustrophobic should avoid **Speedwell Cavern** (☎ 620512; 🕑 10am-4.30pm May-Sep, 10am-3pm Oct-Apr), but everyone else will get a thrill out of this former mineshaft near Winnats Pass. It's a unique flooded tunnel you travel along by boat to reach an underground lake called the 'bottomless pit'. The excellent guides have clearly practised their routines, but not to the point of boredom.

Walking

Castleton is the northern terminus of the Limestone Way (see p437), which includes narrow, rocky Cave Dale, far below the east wall of the castle.

If you feel like a shorter walk, you can follow the Limestone Way up Cave Dale for a few miles, then loop round on paths and tracks to the west of Rowter Farm to meet the Buxton Rd. Go straight (north) on a path crossing fields and another road to eventually reach Mam Nick, where the road to Edale passes through a gap in the ridge. Go up steps here to reach the summit of Mam Tor, for spectacular views along the Hope Valley. (You can also see the fractured remains of the old main road.) The path then aims northwest along the ridge to another gap called Hollins Cross, from where paths and tracks lead back down to Castleton. This 6-mile circuit takes three to four hours; maps are available at the TIC.

A shorter option from Castleton is to take the path direct to Hollins Cross, then go to Mam Tor, and return by the same route (about 4 miles, two to three hours). From Hollins Cross, extend any walk by dropping down to Edale, or you can walk direct from Castleton to Edale via Hollins Cross.

Sleeping

Rambler's Rest (☎ 620125; Mill Bridge; s/d from £20/35; 🅿) As the name implies, this attractive stone cottage offers a special welcome to walkers. It also has a large en-suite room with three or four beds (£22 per person), ideal for small groups or people with children. Some rooms have shared bathrooms.

Cryer House (☎ 620244; Castle St; r from £25; **P**) A long-standing favourite, this comfortable little B&B with affable hosts has a popular garden tearoom out the front.

Castleton YHA Hostel (☎ 0870 770 5758; castleton@ yha.org.uk; Castle St; dm £11.80, r from £40) Large and often full of school groups, this hostel is a great source of information even if you're not staying here, with knowledgeable staff who also conduct guided walks.

Eating & Drinking

Ye Olde Nag's Head Hotel (☎ 620451; How Lane; bar meals £7-9, mains £17.95, B&B per person £30; ☺ breakfast, lunch & dinner) The Nag's has both sass and class – the dining room serves romantic candlelit suppers and Sunday lunches, while the bar is a late-night hotspot, the place where everybody in town winds up eventually (and they do get pretty wound up). There are comfy B&B rooms upstairs, though they're not ideal for light sleepers.

George (☎ 620238; Castle St; mains around £7) Having grown out of a recent awkward phase, the George is thriving again under new proprietor Richard Symonds, whose outsized personality has made the place a mandatory stop on the village's busy pub circuit. An impressive menu and flagstone floor (to match the original) give the place a sophisticated air, but only until about 9pm, after which things get weird and rowdy in the way only a great small-town pub can.

Getting There & Away

You can get to Castleton from Bakewell on bus No 173 (45 minutes, five per day Monday to Friday, three per day Saturday and Sunday), via Hope and Tideswell.

The nearest train station is Hope, about 1 mile east of Hope village (a total of 3 miles east of Castleton) on the line between Sheffield and Manchester. At summer weekends a bus runs between Hope station and Castleton tying in with the trains, although it's not a bad walk in good weather.

DERWENT RESERVOIRS

In the centre of the Peak, three huge artificial lakes – Ladybower, Derwent and Howden, together known as the Derwent Reservoirs – collect water for the cities of Derbyshire and the Midlands. The lakes are also focal points for walking and mountain biking.

The place to aim for is **Fairholmes**, a national park centre that has a TIC (☎ 01433-650953), a car park, a snack bar and cycle hire. Numerous walks start here, from gentle strolls along the lakeside to more-serious outings on the moors above the valley. For cycling, a lane leads up the west side of Derwent and Howden reservoirs (closed to car traffic at weekends), and a dirt track comes down the east side, making a good 12-mile circuit, while challenging off-road routes lead deeper into the hills. The TIC stocks a very good range of route leaflets, maps and guidebooks.

Fairholmes is 2 miles north of the A57, the main road between Sheffield and Manchester. Bus No 257 runs from Sheffield to Fairholmes (every 30 minutes Saturday and Sunday from April to October) and continues up to the end of the road on the west side of Howden Reservoir – an excellent way to reach the high hills and one of the wildest parts of the Peak District.

EYAM

☎ 01433 / pop 900

The village of Eyam (pronounced ee-em, or eem) is a quaint little spot with a morbidly touching history. In 1665, a consignment of cloth from London delivered to a local tailor carried with it the dreaded disease known simply as the plague. What could have been a widespread disaster remained a localised tragedy: as the plague spread through Eyam, the rector convinced its inhabitants to quarantine themselves rather than transmit it further. Selflessly, they did so; by the time the plague ended in late 1666, around 250 of the village's 800 inhabitants had died, while people in surrounding villages remained relatively unscathed. Even independently of this poignant story, Eyam is well worth a visit; its sloping streets of old cottages backed by rolling green hills form a classic postcard view of the Peak District.

Sights

The **church** dates from Saxon times and has many reminders of the plague, including a cupboard said to be made from the box that carried the infected cloth to Eyam. More sobering is the plague register, recording those who died. Many plague victims were buried in the churchyard, but only two headstones from the time exist – one for Catherine Mompesson, the rector's wife.

Also in the churchyard, but from a much earlier era, the 8th-century **Celtic cross** is one of the finest in England. Before leaving, check your watch against the **sundial** on the church wall.

In the church you can buy the *Eyam Map* (£2.50), and smaller leaflets (20p), which describe the village's history and all the sites associated with the plague. You can also find a leaflet describing some of the monuments and headstones in the churchyard.

Around the village, many buildings have information plaques attached; these include the **plague cottages**, where the tailor lived, next to the church.

Eyam Hall (☎ 631976; adult £4.25; ☺ 11am-4pm Wed, Thu & Sun Jun-Aug) is a fine old 17th-century manor house, and the courtyard contains a tearoom and numerous craft workshops.

Eyam Museum (www.eyammuseum.demon.co.uk; adult/ child £1.75/1.25; ☺ 10am-4.30pm Tue-Sun Easter-Oct) naturally digs into the stories behind Eyam's plague experience, but there are also neat little exhibits on geology, Saxon history and the village's time as a lead-mining and silk-weaving centre.

Look out too for the **stocks** on the village green – somewhere handy to leave the kids, perhaps, while you look at the church?

Walking

Eyam makes a great base for walking and cycling in the surrounding White Peak area. A short walk for starters will lead you up Water Lane from the village square, then up through fields and a patch of woodland where you'll meet another lane running between Eyam and Grindleford; turn right here and keep going uphill, past another junction to **Mompesson's Well**, where food and other supplies were left during the plague time for Eyam folk by friends from other villages. The Eyam people paid for the goods using coins sterilised in vinegar. You can retrace your steps back down the lane, then take a path that leads directly to the church. This 2-mile circuit takes about 1½ hours.

Sleeping & Eating

Eyam YHA Hostel (☎ 0870 770 5830; eyam@yha.org.uk; Hawkhill Rd; dm £11.80, r from £45) is in a fine old Victorian house on the village edge. If it's full, **Bretton YHA Hostel** (☎ 0870 770 5720; Hope Valley) is only 1½ miles away.

Getting There & Away

Eyam is 7 miles north of Bakewell and 12 miles east of Buxton. Regular buses from Bakewell towards Sheffield or Chesterfield go to Calver, from where you can walk along the main road to Stoney Middleton, then take a path up the steep valley side to Eyam (2 miles). From Buxton, bus No 65 runs about six times a day to/from Calver, via Eyam.

BAKEWELL

☎ 01629 / pop 3676

After Buxton, this is the largest town in the Peak District (though it's hardly a metropolis) and a good base for walking, cycling or touring. It's also a notorious traffic bottleneck on summer weekends, but at quieter times it's worth a stop to see some interesting sights. and everyone should do their part to help settle the debate over which of the Bakewell pudding shops in town actually invented the famous dessert (see the boxed text, p445).

Orientation & Information

The centre of town is Rutland Sq, from where roads radiate to Matlock, Buxton and Sheffield. The **TIC** (☎ 813227; Bridge St; ☺ 10am-5pm), in the old Market Hall, has racks of leaflets and books about Bakewell and the national park.

Sights & Activities

Bakewell's weekly market is on Monday, when the square behind the TIC is very lively. On the hill above Rutland Sq, **All Saints Church** has some ancient Norman features, and even older Saxon stonework remains, including a tall cross in the churchyard, which sadly has suffered at the hands of time.

Near the church, **Old House Museum** (Cunningham Pl; adult £2.50; ☺ 1.30-4pm Easter-Jun & Oct, 11am-4pm Jul-Sep) displays local miscellany, including a Tudor loo.

A stroll from Rutland Sq down Bridge St brings you – not surprisingly – to the pretty **medieval bridge** over the River Wye, from where riverside walks lead in both directions. Go upstream through the water meadows, and then along Holme Lane to reach **Holme Bridge**, an ancient stone structure used by Peak District packhorses for centuries.

On the northern edge of Bakewell, a former railway line has been converted to a walking and cycling track called the

THE MIDLANDS

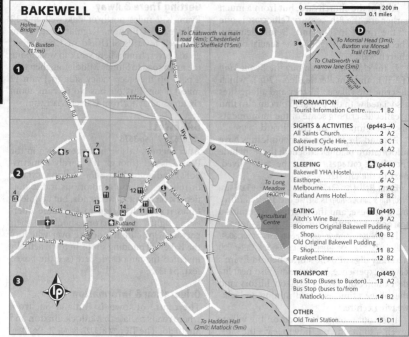

BAKEWELL

0 ———— 200 m
0 ———— 0.1 miles

INFORMATION
Tourist Information Centre........**1** B2

SIGHTS & ACTIVITIES   (pp443–4)
All Saints Church......................**2** A2
Bakewell Cycle Hire..................**3** C1
Old House Museum....................**4** A2

SLEEPING   (p444)
Bakewell YHA Hostel.................**5** A2
Easthorpe................................**6** A2
Melbourne...............................**7** A2
Rutland Arms Hotel...................**8** B2

EATING   (p445)
Aitch's Wine Bar.......................**9** A2
Bloomers Original Bakewell Pudding
  Shop...................................**10** B2
Old Original Bakewell Pudding
  Shop...................................**11** B2
Parakeet Diner.........................**12** B2

TRANSPORT   (p445)
Bus Stop (Buses to Buxton)......**13** A2
Bus Stop (buses to/from
  Matlock).............................**14** B2

OTHER
Old Train Station.....................**15** D1

Monsal Trail. From Bakewell you can cycle about 3 miles north and 1 mile south on the old railway itself – and there are numerous other tracks and country lanes nearby. **Bakewell Cycle Hire** (☎ 814004) at the old station has mountain bikes for about £10 per day; opening times depend on the weather, so phone ahead if possible.

Walkers on the Monsal Trail follow alternate sections of the old railway and pretty footpaths through fields and beside rivers. From Bakewell, an excellent out-and-back walk (3 miles each way) goes to the dramatic viewpoint at **Monsal Head** – where there's a good pub and a friendly café. Allow three hours for the round trip.

If you're out for the day, from Monsal Head you can keep following the Monsal Trail northwest towards Buxton. A good point to aim for is Miller's Dale, where impressive viaducts cross the steep-sided valley (and there's another good café), or you can go all the way to Blackwell Mill (3 miles east of Buxton) – a total distance of about 9 miles – and get a bus back. Alternatively, get a bus to Buxton, and walk back to Bakewell. The TICs at Bakewell

and Buxton have a *Monsal Trail* leaflet with all the details.

Other walking routes go to the stately homes of Haddon Hall (p445) and Chatsworth House (p445). You could take a bus or taxi there and walk back, so you don't put mud on the duke's carpet.

Sleeping

Bakewell YHA Hostel (☎ 0870 770 5682; Fly Hill; dm £10) A modern building just out of the centre at the top of a very steep hill. It's in a quiet residential area; curfew is 11pm. There are no laundry facilities or Internet access, but it's a very comfortable, friendly place and a great base for walking in the area.

Rutland Arms Hotel (☎ 812812; rutland@bakewell .demon.co.uk; Rutland Sq; r from £45; **P**) This venerable establishment, cashing in on its history (see the boxed text, opposite), is especially popular with coach tour groups. Front rooms overlook the square but can be noisy.

Easthorpe and **Melbourne** (☎ 815357; Buxton Rd; r from £23; **P**) are run as one unit on either side of a busy road, with plenty of rooms and friendly service.

WHICH BAKEWELL PUDDING?

Bakewell blundered into the recipe books around 1860 when a cook at the Rutland Arms Hotel made strawberry tart, but mistakenly (some stories say drunkenly) spread the egg mixture on top of the jam instead of stirring it into the pastry, thus creating the Bakewell pudding (pudding, mark you, not tart). It now features regularly on local dessert menus and is worth sampling.

Two of Bakewell's many pudding-selling establishments are locked in battle over whose is the original recipe, and both have records dating back to 1889. **Bloomers Original Bakewell Pudding Shop** (Water St) insists it's 'the first and only', while the **Old Original Bakewell Pudding Shop** (Bridge St) is adamant that its recipe is older. The latter certainly pulls in more trade, thanks to its position on the main thoroughfare.

History dictates that you should visit them both and do a comparison. It's good for fair play, if not for your waistline.

Eating & Drinking

The streets are lined with cute teashops and bakeries, most with 'pudding' in the name and all selling the town's eponymous cake. There are several fish-and-chip shops, too.

Parakeet Diner (Anchor Sq; breakfast, lunch & dinner) is a straightforward café, popular with walkers, offering snacks, meals and fry-up breakfasts. **Aitch's Wine Bar** (813895; Buxton Rd; lunches £5-7, evening mains £11-15; lunch & dinner) is a long-standing place with a highly rated and imaginative menu: 'around the world in eighty plates'.

Getting There & Away

Buses serve Bakewell from Derby (most 90 minutes but there are some faster buses, twice hourly) and Chesterfield (45 minutes, hourly).

AROUND BAKEWELL
Haddon Hall

Described as a medieval masterpiece, **Haddon Hall** (01629-812855; www.haddonhall.co.uk; adult/child £7.25/3.25; 10.30am-4.30pm Apr-Sep, 10.30am-4pm Thu-Sun Oct) was originally owned by William Peveril, son of William the Conqueror, and what you see today dates mainly from the 14th to 16th centuries. Haddon Hall was abandoned right through the 18th and 19th centuries, so it escaped the 'modernisation' experienced by so many other country houses. Highlights include the Chapel; the Long Gallery, stunningly bathed by natural light; and the vast Banqueting Hall, virtually unchanged since the days of Henry VIII. The popular film about Henry's daughter, *Elizabeth*, was shot here, and, not surprisingly, Haddon Hall made a perfect backdrop. Outside are beautiful gardens and courtyards.

The house is 2 miles south of Bakewell on the A6. You can get here on any bus heading for Matlock (about hourly) or walk along the footpath through the fields mostly on the east side of the river.

Chatsworth

The great stately home, manicured gardens and perfectly landscaped park of Chatsworth form a major highlight for visitors to England. **Chatsworth House** (01246-582204; www.chatsworth-house.co.uk; adult/child £9/3.50, Christmas season from 6 Nov additional £1/50p; 11am-4.30pm Easter-Oct, shorter hrs & days Nov & Dec), known as the 'Palace of the Peak', has been occupied by the dukes of Devonshire for centuries. The original house started in 1551 by the inimitable Bess of Hardwick; Mary, Queen of Scots, was imprisoned here between 1570 and 1581 at the behest of Elizabeth I. The house was extensively altered 1686 to 1707, and again enlarged and improved in the 1820s – much of it dates from these periods. Among the prime attractions are the painted and decorated ceilings, the 30 or so rooms are treasure-troves of splendid furniture and magnificent artworks. The house is surrounded by 40 sq km of **gardens** (adult £4.50), complete with a fountain so high it can be seen from the hills of the Dark Peak. Beyond that is another 400 hectares of parkland, originally landscaped by Capability Brown, open to the public for walking and picnicking.

Chatsworth is 3 miles northeast of Bakewell. If driving, it's £1 to park. Bus No 179 runs twice daily (Monday to Saturday) and No 211 four times daily (Sunday) from Bakewell. Virgin Trains runs a bus between Macclesfield, Buxton and Bakewell (two daily) extending to Chatsworth from June to September.

Eastern England

From the carnival air of seaside resorts like Great Yarmouth to the stately fortress of knowledge that is Cambridge, eastern England is nothing if not varied. The region consists of four counties – Cambridgeshire, Lincolnshire, Norfolk and Suffolk – each with its own distinct personality. Beyond its famed university, Cambridgeshire consists of the lush agricultural land known as the Fens, reclaimed from the sea. Lincolnshire, known for its remarkably well-preserved parish churches, has one of the friendliest county towns in England. Norfolk boasts the wide-open marshlands of the Broads, a bird-watcher's paradise, and some unusual landscapes along the coastline. And the meadows of Suffolk are dotted with 'wool churches' and distinctive houses decorated with plasterwork typical to the county.

Many of the settlements in eastern England were once economic powerhouses, driving and benefiting from industry in the heartland of the country. The wool trade prospered here centuries ago, and evidence of those glory days can be found in places like the Lincoln and Ely cathedrals and the historic cores of medieval market towns.

Certain areas of eastern England are becoming popular destinations for weekend breaks, which means travellers here will find new standards of quality in the boutique hotels and top-flight restaurants. For the most part, though, this region is mercifully free of mass tourism.

EASTERN ENGLAND

HIGHLIGHTS

- Walking the Norfolk Coastal Path in delightful **Burnham Deepdale** (p478)
- Strolling the regal streets of beautifully preserved **Stamford** (p486)
- Pondering the masses of brainpower that have passed through **Cambridge** (p450)
- Wondering at the gorgeous façades of **Lincoln Cathedral** (p483)
- Taking a cruise through the wilds of the **Norfolk Broads** (p476)
- Cooing over little pink thatch-roofed houses in **Lavenham** (p465))

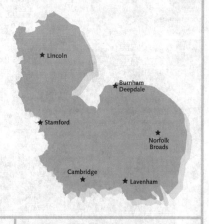

★ Lincoln

★ Burnham Deepdale

★ Stamford

★ Norfolk Broads

Cambridge ★

★ Lavenham

■ POPULATION: 5.4 million

■ AREA: 19,000 SQ MILES

EASTERN ENGLAND

History

East Anglia was a major Saxon kingdom, consisting of the northern people (Norfolk) and the southern ones (Suffolk). Raedwald, who died sometime between AD 616 and 628, was the first East Anglian king of whom anything is known, but the discovery of the Sutton Hoo ship (see p463) and all its treasures in 1939 suggested that he and his ilk knew something of the good life.

From the early Middle Ages, East Anglia became a major centre for wool and the manufacture of woollen products. Then, in the 14th century, Edward III invited Flemish weavers to settle in the area, and for the next four centuries Norwich was England's most important weaving town. Evidence

of the region's links with the Netherlands and Belgium is visible throughout eastern England; long drainage canals, windmills and the architecture (particularly in King's Lynn) have more than a hint of Dutch influence about them. The wealth brought by this connection built scores of churches and helped subsidise the development of Cambridge.

By the 17th century the emergence of a work-happy urban bourgeoisie growing ever richer on successful trade with Continental Europe, coupled with a fairly strong sense of religious duty, resulted in the twin principles of parliamentarianism and Puritanism that would climax in the Civil War. Oliver Cromwell, the uncrowned king of

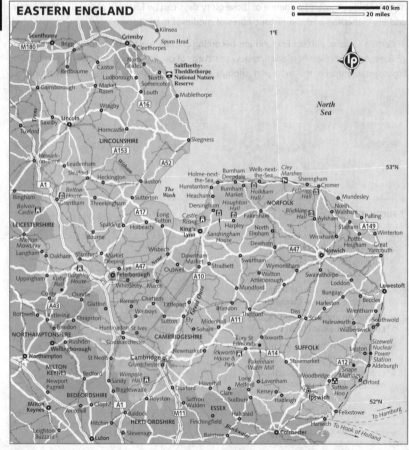

the parliamentarians, was a small-time merchant residing in Ely when he answered God's call to take up arms against the fattened and corrupt monarchy of Charles I.

By the middle of the 18th century, however, eastern England's fortunes were on the wane. The Industrial Revolution had begun in earnest, but it was all happening in the northwest.

While Manchester was building enormous mills to process Indian calico for sale in Europe and the American colonies, the cottage industries of East Anglia slowly began to go out of business. By the end of the 19th century, the only weaving done in the region was on a tiny, specialist scale.

Today, the region's economy is predominantly rural, though crops – especially barley – have replaced sheep as the mainstay. Market gardening is also a major earner, and most of the towns have developed some form of light industry.

Information

Consult the **East of England Tourist Board** (☎ 01473-822922; www.visiteastofengland.com) for regional tourist information.

Activities

Regional tourism websites all contain walking, cycling and sailing information, and Tourist Information Centres (TICs) all stock leaflets, maps and guides that cover walking, cycling and other outdoor activities.

CYCLING

With a long history of human settlement but little in the way of urbanisation, Norfolk, Suffolk, Lincolnshire and Cambridgeshire all have networks of quiet country lanes. Eastern England is also famous for being flat, and thus makes perfect country for gentle cycle-touring – as long as the wind is minimal or behind you. If you head east into cold winds you'll realise there are no hills to deflect them between here and the Urals. But with an eye on the weather, and judicious use of the cycle-friendly local train service, you can have a great time on two wheels.

There's gorgeous riding along the Suffolk and Norfolk coastlines, and in the Fens. In the northern part of the region, King's Lynn and Hunstanton make good bases, and bike hire is available. In the south of the region,

Cambridge is an excellent base for cycle tours, and bikes can be hired here, too.

For mountain bikers, Thetford Forest, near Thetford, is an ideal place to start. Much of Peddars Way (mentioned in the Walking section, p449) consists of lanes and bridlepaths that are also open to cyclists, and makes a mixed on- and off-road route. (The contiguous Norfolk Coast Path is strictly for walkers only.)

WALKING

Eastern England is not classic walking country. To put it bluntly, there aren't enough hills. But if that's not a worry, then the area is perfect for easy rambles through gentle farmland, or alongside rivers and small lakes in the Norfolk Broads. For more-saltwatery flavours, the coasts of Norfolk and Suffolk are both followed by footpaths.

The region's best-known long-distance walk is the **Peddars Way and Norfolk Coast Path**, a six-day, 88-mile national trail linking Cromer on the coast with Knettishall Heath near Thetford. It follows an ancient Roman road for its first half, then meanders along the beaches, sea walls, salt marshes and fishing villages of the coast for the second half. Any part of the route can be done just as a day or weekend option; this is much easier on the coast section, and especially rewarding if you're into bird-watching as there are some top-quality nature reserves along this stretch.

Further south, the 50-mile **Suffolk Coast and Heaths Path** runs between Felixstowe and Lowestoft, via Snape Maltings, Aldeburgh, Dunwich and Southwold. As with all long routes, even if you don't want to go the whole way, it makes the perfect focus for shorter walks and rambles.

OTHER ACTIVITIES

On the coast and Norfolk Broads, **sailing** is popular; there are several sailing centres where you can hire boats or arrange lessons. Alternatively, many people tour the Broads in **motorboats** these days. At towns like Wroxham you can hire boats – anything from large cabin cruisers for a week to little craft with phut-phut outboards for a couple of hours' gentle messing about on the river. More watery fun is available in Cambridge, where a visit is incomplete without a spot of **punting**. If you want to keep your feet dry, **land-yachting** takes place on some of the long, wide and frequently empty beaches of the Norfolk coast.

Getting There & Around

This region is well served by public transport – both rail and coach. For transport information on specific locales, see individual TICs listed throughout the chapter. Contact **One Anglia** (☎ 08457-484950; www.oneanglia.com; Anglia Plus pass 1/3 days in 7 £9/20) for regional rail information. For national bus timetable information, contact **Traveline** (☎ 0870 608 2608).

CAMBRIDGESHIRE

Cambridgeshire sits on a once-submerged area known as the Fens; flat and fertile, this land was stolen out from under the sea to become lush agricultural fields. The area rewards leisurely exploration on a bicycle, and easy footpaths wend through the landscape, although seasoned hill-walkers won't really find many challenges here. The tourist office in Cambridge stocks a number of useful guides, including *Walks in South Cambridgeshire*.

What Cambridgeshire is best known for, of course, is its world-famous university. Cambridge has a vibrant cultural life thanks to its student population, but even without that, the county town would merit a stop simply for its sheer beauty. An interesting way to see a good chunk of the county is to follow the 15-mile-long towpath from Cambridge to Ely, where the superb cathedral known as the 'Ship of the Fens' floats above the surrounding plains on a slight hill. For those visitors with a more modern agenda, Peterborough is known as England's shopping capital; it also has a fine cathedral.

Getting Around

Public transport centres on Cambridge, which is only 55 minutes by rail from London. This line continues north through Ely to terminate at King's Lynn in Norfolk. From Ely, branch lines run east through Norwich, southeast into Suffolk, and northwest to Peterborough and into Lincolnshire. The useful *Cambridgeshire and Peterborough Passenger Transport Map* is available at all TICs.

The primary services:
Cambridge Coach Services (☎ 01223-423900)
Cambridge to Norwich.
Stagecoach Cambus (☎ 01223-423554) Links Cambridge, Bury St Edmunds and Ely.
Stagecoach United Counties (☎ 01604-620077)
Cambridge to Huntingdon and Peterborough.

CAMBRIDGE

☎ 01223 / pop 131,465
Smaller and prettier than Oxford (referred to here as 'the other place'), Cambridge is undeniably a university town, but its appeal is by no means limited to what you'll find on campus. The capital's pristine core is at once immaculately preserved – its elegantly curving alleyways, moss-strewn courtyards and ornate gateways seem to have been sculpted all of a piece – and bustling with activity. The cobblestone streets are pleasantly thronged with locals and visitors alike, shopping, cycling, wandering around, punting on the peaceful River Cam or just relaxing at a quayside pub.

As for the sights, the university's King's College Chapel is a mandatory stop – it's indisputably among the highlights of any trip to England. Another campus treat is the 'Backs', where the river meanders along in the parklike strip behind the colleges. It's ideal for a picnic or just an afternoon stroll. There are upscale shopping streets lined with highbrow boutiques, a few happening nightclubs, countless historic pubs and a respectable selection of trendy restaurants. Still, although it has all the modern advantages, Cambridge has a tranquil, ageless beauty that can't be found anywhere else.

History

At first a Roman fort and later a small Saxon settlement, Cambridge was just a tiny rural backwater until 1209, when the university town of Oxford exploded in a riot between scholars and townspeople. This forced a group of students to quit while their heads were still intact and move up to Cambridge to found a new university. The facts surrounding the foundation are a little hazy, undoubtedly due to another riot in 1261 between 'town and gown', when the university records were burnt. At the rioters' trial the judges ruled in favour of the students, setting a precedent that would last for centuries. The new university had found favour with the law and began to establish a firm footing within the town.

The collegiate system, unique to Oxford and Cambridge, came into being gradually. The first Cambridge college, Peterhouse, was founded in 1284 by Hugo de Balsham (later Bishop of Ely). The plan was for tutors and students to live together in a community, much as they would in a monastery.

From the 14th century on, a number of colleges were founded by royalty, nobility, leading church figures, statesmen, academics and trade guilds – all for men only. In 1869 and 1871, however, women were finally accorded the right to study here with the founding of women-only Girton and Newnham colleges – although they had to wait until 1948 before they were allowed to graduate.

The honour roll of famous graduates reads like an international who's who of high achievers, and a list of their accomplishments in a wide variety of fields could fill a couple of thick volumes. So far, the university has produced 78 Nobel Prize winners (29 from Trinity College alone), 13 British prime ministers, nine archbishops of Canterbury, an immense number of scientists, and a healthy host of poets and other scribblers...and this is but a limited selection. Today the university remains at the top of the research league in British universities. It owns a prestigious publishing firm and a world-renowned examination syndicate; it is the leading centre for astronomy in Britain; its Fitzwilliam Museum contains an outstanding art collection; and its library is used by scholars from around the world.

Orientation

The colleges and university buildings comprise the centre of the city. The central area, lying in a wide bend of the River Cam, is easy to get around on foot or by bike. The best-known section of the Cam is the Backs, which combines lush river scenery with superb views of six colleges, and King's College Chapel. The other 25 colleges are scattered throughout the city.

The bus station is central on Drummer St, but the train station is a 20-minute walk to the south. Sidney St becomes St Andrew's St to the south and Bridge St then Magdalene St to the north, and is the main shopping street.

Information

BOOKSHOPS

Dillons (☎ 351688; 22 Sidney St)
Galloway & Porter (☎ 367876; 30 Sidney St) Mostly remaindered and damaged stock.
Heffers (☎ 568582; 20 Trinity St) Best for academic books.
Heffers Children's Bookshop (☎ 568551; 29-30 Trinity St)
Heffers Music (☎ 568562; 19 Trinity St) Excellent selection of classical CDs.
WH Smith (☎ 311313; 26 Lion Yard)

EMERGENCY

Police station (☎ 358966; Parkside)

INTERNET ACCESS

CB1 (☎ 576306; 32 Mill Rd; per hr £3.25; ☷ 10am-8pm)
International Telecom Centre (☎ 357358; 2 Wheeler St; per hr 99p; ☷ 9am-10pm)

LAUNDRY

Cleanomat Dry Cleaners (☎ 464719; 10 Victoria Ave)

MEDICAL SERVICES

Addenbrooke's Hospital (☎ 245151)
Boots (☎ 350213; 28 Petty Cury)
Vantage Pharmacy (☎ 353002; 66 Bridge St)

MONEY

Abbey National (☎ 350495; 60 St Andrew's St)
American Express (☎ 345203; 25 Sidney St)
HSBC (☎ 314822; 75 Regent St)
Thomas Cook (☎ 543100; 8 St Andrew's St)

POST

Main post office (☎ 323325; 9-11 St Andrew's St; ☷ 9am-5.30pm Mon-Sat)

TOURIST INFORMATION

TIC (☎ 322640; www.cambridge.gov.uk; Wheeler St; ☷ 10am-6pm Mon-Fri, 10am-5pm Sat, 11am-4pm Sun Apr-Oct, 10am-5.30pm Mon-Sat Nov-Mar)

Sights

CAMBRIDGE UNIVERSITY

Five of the colleges within the **university** (King's, Queen's, Clare, Trinity and St John's) charge admission for tourists (£1.50 to £4). You may also find that tourists are now denied admission at some of the colleges described in this section; each year more colleges decide that the tourist bandwagon is just too disruptive. Most colleges are closed to visitors for the Easter term and all are closed for exams from mid-May to mid-June. The precise details of opening hours vary from college to college and year to year, so contact the TIC or the university's **central information service** (☎ 337733) for updates.

King's College Chapel

One of the finest examples of Gothic architecture in England, **King's College Chapel** (☎ 331100) is supreme in its grandeur and comparable with Chartres cathedral in France. Henry VI conceived it as an act of piety, dedicated to the Virgin Mary; the king laid its foundation stone in 1446, and building was completed around 1516. Services are led by its choir, originally choristers from Eton College, another of Henry VI's foundations.

The choir's Festival of the Nine Lessons and Carols on Christmas Eve is broadcast all over the world.

The stained-glass windows are original. Cromwell's soldiers destroyed many church windows in East Anglia, but their leader, having been a Cambridge student, apparently had a soft spot for King's. Despite the stained glass, the atmosphere inside is light. The stunning interior of 12 bays is about 11m wide, 22m high and 80m long, the largest expanse in the world canopied by fan vaulting. The work of John Wastell, it reportedly prompted Christopher Wren to say, when he saw it, that he could have built it himself, but only if someone had shown him where to set the first stone.

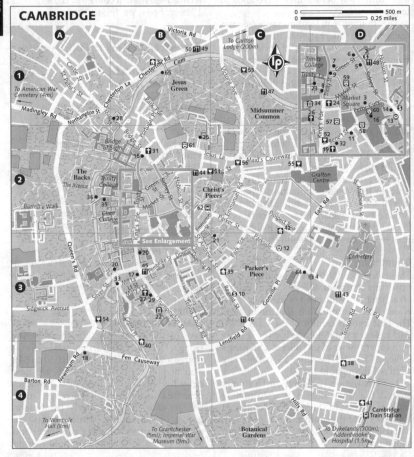

The antechapel and the choir are divided by the superbly carved **wooden screen**, a gift from Henry VIII. Designed and executed by the king's master carver Peter Stockton, the screen bears Henry's initials entwined with those of Anne Boleyn, who supposedly inspired Henry's act of generosity. Almost concealed by the mythical beasts and symbolic flowers is one angry human face: Stockton's miniature rebellion, perhaps.

Originally constructed between 1686 and 1688, the magnificent organ has been rebuilt and developed over the years. The **high altar** is framed by Peter Paul Rubens' *Adoration of the Magi* and the magnificent east window.

In the **Chapel Exhibition** (adult £4) you can see the stages and methods of building the chapel set against the historical panorama, from inception to completion. The chapel comes alive when the choir sings; even the most pagan heavy-metal fan will find **Choral Evensong** (5.30pm Tue-Sat, 10.30am & 3.30pm Sun mid-Jan–mid-Mar, mid-Apr–mid-Jun, mid-late Jul, Oct–early Dec & Dec 24 & 25) an extraordinary experience.

Trinity College

Henry VIII founded **Trinity College** (338400; Trinity St; adult £1.75) in 1546, but it was left to Dr Nevile, Master of Trinity (1593–1615) in Elizabeth's reign, to fulfil his wishes, as Henry died six weeks after founding the college.

As you walk through the impressive brick gateway (1535), have a look at the statue of Henry that adorns it. His left hand holds a golden orb, while his right grips a table

leg, put there by students who removed the golden sceptre years ago. As you enter the **Great Court**, scholastic humour gives way to a gaping sense of awe, for it is the largest of its kind in the world. The place is dripping with history: to the right of the entrance is a small tree, planted in the 1950s and reputed to be a descendant of the apple tree made famous by Trinity alumnus Sir Isaac Newton.

The court is also the scene of the run made famous by the film *Chariots of Fire* – 350m in 43 seconds (the time it takes the clock to strike 12). Although plenty of students have a go, Harold Abrahams (the hero of the film) never actually attempted it, and his fictional run wasn't even filmed here. If you fancy your chances remember that you'll need Olympian speed to even come close to making it in time.

The Gothic antechapel to the right of the gate is full of huge statues of famous Trinity men, such as Alfred, Lord Tennyson and Sir Isaac Newton. The vast hall has a hammer-beam roof and lantern. Beyond the hall are the cloisters of Nevile's Court and the dignified **Wren Library** (noon-2pm Mon-Fri year-round, 10am-6pm Mon-Fri & 10.30am-12.30pm Sat during term). It contains 55,000 books printed before 1820 and more than 2500 manuscripts, including AA Milne's original *Winnie the Pooh*. Both Milne and his son, Christopher Robin, were graduates.

The Backs

Two notable bridges cross the canal in the parklike area behind the colleges known as the **Backs**: the **Bridge of Sighs** (built in 1831, a replica of the original in Venice) and the bridge at **Clare College**. The latter is ornamented with decorative balls and is the oldest (1639), most interesting bridge on the Backs. Its architect was paid a grand total of 15p for his design so, feeling aggrieved at such a measly fee, he cut a slice out of one of the balls adorning the balustrade (the next to last one on the left), thus ensuring that the bridge would never be complete. Or so the story goes.

Great St Mary's Church

This university **church** (☎ 741716; Senate House Hill), built between 1478 and 1519 in the late-Gothic perpendicular style, has a feeling of space and light inside, thanks to its clerestory, wide arch and woodcarving. The traditional termly university sermons are preached here. To get your bearings, climb the 123 steps of the **tower** (adult £2) for a good view of the city. The building across King's Pde, on the right-hand side of the square, is the **Senate House**, designed in 1730 by James Gibbs. It's the most beautiful example of pure classical architecture in the city; graduations are held here.

Gonville & Caius

This fascinating old **college** (☎ 332400; Trinity St) was founded twice, first by a priest called Gonville, in 1348, and then again by Dr Caius (pronounced keys), a brilliant physician and scholar, in 1557. Of special interest here are the three gates: Virtue, Humility and Honour. They symbolise the progress of the good student, since the third gate (the *Porta Honoris,* a fascinating confection with a quirky dome and sundials) leads to the Senate House and thus graduation.

Trinity Hall College

This is a delightfully small **college** (☎ 332500; Trinity Lane), wedged among the great and the famous. Despite the name, it has nothing to do with Trinity College. It was founded in 1350 as a refuge for lawyers and clerics escaping the ravages of the Black Death, thus earning it the nickname of the 'Lawyers' College'. You enter through the newest court, which overlooks the river on one side and has a lovely fellows' garden on another. Walking into the next court, you pass the 16th-century library, which has original

Jacobean reading desks, and books chained to the shelves to prevent their permanent removal – the 16th century's equivalent of electronic bar codes.

Just outside the first court is a tall, historic gate, which gets little attention. It's the entry to Old Schools, the administrative centre of the university. The lower part dates back to 1441 and the upper part was added in the 1860s.

Jesus College

The approach (via the long 'chimney') to **Jesus** (☎ 339339; Jesus Lane), founded in 1496, is impressive – as is the main gate, which is under a rebus of the founder, Bishop Alcock. A rebus is a heraldic device suggesting the name of its owner: the bishop's consists of several cockerels. The spacious First Court, with its redbrick ranges, is open on the western side – an unusual feature.

Be sure to look at the tiny, intimate cloister court to your right, and the chapel, which dates back to the St Radegund nunnery originally on the site. The bishop closed the nunnery, expelled the nuns for misbehaving and founded the new college in its place. The inspiring chapel reflects the college's development over the centuries. It has a Norman arched gallery from the nunnery building, a 13th-century chancel and beautiful restoration work, and Art Nouveau features by Pugin, Morris (ceilings), Burne-Jones (stained glass) and Madox Brown.

Magdalene College

Originally a Benedictine hostel, the **college** (☎ 332100; Magdalene St) was refounded in 1542 by Lord Audley. It has the dubious honour of being the last college to allow women students; when they were finally admitted in 1988, male students wore black armbands and flew the college flag at half-mast.

Its river setting gives it a certain appeal, but its greatest asset is the Pepys Library, housing the magnificent collection of books the famous diarist Samuel Pepys bequeathed to his old college – he was a student here between 1650 and 1653.

Corpus Christi College

At **Corpus Christi** (☎ 338000; Trumpington St), an entrance leads into Old Court, which has been retained in its medieval form and still exudes a monastic atmosphere. The door to the chapel is flanked by two statues; on the right is Matthew Parker, who was college master in 1544 and Archbishop of Canterbury for much of the reign of Elizabeth I. A pretty bright lad, Mr Parker was known for his curiosity; his endless questioning gave us the term 'nosy parker'. Playwright Christopher Marlowe (1564–93), author of *Dr Faustus* and *Tamburlaine*, was a Corpus man – as a plaque, next to a fascinating sundial, bears out. New Court, beyond, is a 19th-century creation.

The college library has the finest collection of Anglo-Saxon manuscripts in the world. With other valuable books, they were preserved from destruction at the time of Henry VIII's dissolution of the monasteries.

Queen's College
One of the Backs' colleges, **Queens'** (☎ 335511; Silver St; adult £1.20) was the first Cambridge college to charge admission. This was initiated to pay for soundproofing its vulnerable site on this busy street. It takes its name from the two queens who founded it – Margaret of Anjou (wife of Henry VI) and Elizabeth of Woodville (wife of Edward IV), in 1448 and 1465 respectively – yet a conscientious rector of St Botolph's Church was its real creator.

The main entrance of the college is off Queens' Lane. The redbrick gate tower and Old Court, which immediately capture your attention, are part of the medieval college. So is Cloister Court, the next court, with its impressive cloister and picturesque, half-timbered President's Lodge ('president' is the name for the master). The famous Dutch scholar and reformer Desiderius Erasmus lodged in the tower from 1510 to 1514. He wasn't particularly enamoured of Cambridge: he thought that the wine tasted like vinegar, that the beer was slop and that the place was too expensive, but he did write that the local women were good kissers.

Peterhouse College
Founded in 1284 by Hugo de Balsham, later Bishop of Ely, **Peterhouse** (☎ 338200; Trumpington St) is the oldest and smallest of the colleges. It stands to the west of Trumpington St, just south of the Church of St Mary the Less (more tactfully known as **Little St Mary's**). The church's original odd-sounding name was St Peter's-without-Trumpington-Gate (be-

cause it stood outside, or 'without', the old gate) and it gave the college its name. Inside is a memorial to Godfrey Washington, an alumnus of the college and a great-uncle of George Washington. His family coat of arms was the stars and stripes, the inspiration for the US flag. A walk through Peterhouse gives you a clear picture of the 'community' structure of a Cambridge college though, unusually, the master's house is opposite the college, not within it. The college's list of notable alumni includes the poet Thomas Gray, who came up in 1742, and Henry Cavendish, the first person to measure the density of water. He also calculated the weight of the planet: if you must know, the earth weighs 6000 million million tonnes.

First Court, the oldest court, is small, neat and bright, with hanging baskets and window boxes. The 17th-century chapel is on the right, built in a mix of styles that blend well. Inside, luminous 19th-century stained-glass windows contrast with the older eastern window. The Burrough range, on the right, is 18th century and the hall, on the left, a restored, late-13th-century gem. Beyond the hall are sweeping grounds extending to the Fitzwilliam Museum.

Emmanuel College
Founded in 1584, this medium-sized **college** (☎ 334200; St Andrew's St) comprises some 600 people. If you stand in Front Court, one of the architectural gems of Cambridge faces you – the Wren chapel, cloister and gallery, completed in 1677. To the left is the hall; inside, the refectory-type tables are set at right angles to the high table. The next court, New Court, is around the corner. It has a quaint herb garden reminiscent of the old Dominican priory that preceded the college.

There are a few remnants of the priory in the *clunch* (chalk) core of the walls of the Old Library. Turn right to re-enter Front Court and go into the chapel. It has interesting windows, a high ceiling and a painting by Jacopo Amigoni. Near the side door is a plaque to a famous scholar, John Harvard (BA 1632), who was among 30 Emmanuel men who settled in New England. He left money to found the university that bears his name in the Massachusetts town of Cambridge. His portrait also features in one of the stained-glass windows – but, as the artist had no likeness of Harvard from which to work, he used the face of John Milton, a contemporary of Harvard's at the college.

ROUND CHURCH

Built by the mysterious Knights Templar in 1130 to commemorate its namesake in Jerusalem, the amazing **Round Church** (Church of the Holy Sepulchre; Bridge St; ☎ 518219) is one of only four of its type in England. It is strikingly unusual, with chunky, round Norman pillars that encircle the small nave. The rest of the church was added later in a different style; the conical roof dates from just the 19th century. No longer a parish church, it's now a **brass-rubbing centre** (☎ 871621; ☼ 10am-6pm summer, 1-4pm winter; costs £5 to £24 depending on size of brass).

CHURCH OF ST BENE'T

The **Saxon tower** of this Franciscan **church** (☎ 353903; Bene't St), built in 1025, is the oldest structure in Cambridgeshire. The rest of the church is newer but full of interesting features. The round holes above the belfry windows were designed to offer owls nesting privileges; owls were valued as mouse killers. It was here in 1670 that parish clerk Fabian Stedman invented change-ringing (the ringing of bells with different peals in a sequential order). The church also has a Bible that belonged to Thomas Hobson, owner of a nearby livery stable, who told customers they could hire any horse they liked as long as it was the one nearest the door – hence the term 'Hobson's choice', meaning no choice at all.

FITZWILLIAM MUSEUM

This massive **museum** (☎ 332900; Trumpington St; admission free; ☼ 10am-5pm Tue-Sat, 2.15-5pm Sun; tours 2.30pm Sun) is a neoclassical edifice, taking its name from the seventh Viscount Fitzwilliam, who bequeathed his fabulous art treasures to his old university in 1816. The building in which they are stored was begun by George Basevi in 1837, but he did not live to see its completion in 1848: while working on Ely Cathedral he stepped back to admire his handiwork, slipped and fell to his death. The Fitzwilliam was one of the first public art museums in Britain.

In the lower galleries are ancient Egyptian sarcophagi, Greek and Roman art, Chinese ceramics, English glass, and illuminated manuscripts. The upper galleries contain a wide range of paintings, including works by Titian, Rubens, the French Impressionists, Thomas Gainsborough, George Stubbs and John Constable, right up to Paul Cézanne and Pablo Picasso. It also has fine antique furniture.

Activities

PUNTING

Taking a punt along the Backs is sublime, though it can also be a wet and hectic experience, especially on a busy weekend (a punt is a flat-bottomed boat that's pushed through the water with a pole). If you wimp out, you can always opt for a chauffeured punt, and if the water doesn't attract you at all, the Backs are also perfect for a walk or a picnic.

Granta (Newnham Rd; per hr £10) A pub that hires punts on the side.

Scudamore's (☎ 359750; Silver St; per hr £12, chauffeured £40)

Trinity Punts (☎ 338483; behind Trinity College; per hr £8)

WALKING & CYCLING

One of the prettiest walks in the whole region is the 3-mile walk to Grantchester from Cambridge along the River Cam. More of a gentle stroll than a serious walk, the route simply follows the meandering river as it winds its way southwest. In fine weather the river is full of punts.

For tootling around town by bike, the flat topography makes things easy, although beyond the city the scenery can get a bit monotonous. The Cambridge TIC stocks several useful guides including *Cycle Routes and the Cambridge Green Belt Area*, and the *Cambridge Cycle Route Map*.

Tours

Guide Friday/City Sightseeing (☎ 362444; adult/child £7.50/3) Hop-on hop-off tour buses, starting from the railway station. However, you can get on or off at points along the route, including Fitzwilliam Museum and the Round Church.

Riverboat Georgina (☎ 500111; day/evening £7/8.50) Two-hour cruises from the river at Jesus Lock.

Walking tours (☼ 1.30pm daily year-round, extra tours 10.30am, 11.30am and 2.30pm May-Sep; tickets £7.25) The TIC arranges these as well as other theme tours; book in advance.

Sleeping

BUDGET

Cambridge YHA Hostel (☎ 0870 770 5742; fax 312780; 97 Tenison Rd; dm £12.75; P) This popular hostel near the train station has small dormitories, all the basic facilities (lockers, laundry) and a restaurant.

MID-RANGE

Warkworth House (☎ 363682; Warkworth Tce; s/d from £40/58) This beautiful Victorian terraced house just off Parkside has comfortable rooms, a delicious breakfast and extremely friendly owners; it's popular with students from overseas.

Dykelands (☎ 244300; dykelands@fsbdial.co.uk; 157 Mowbray Rd; s/d from £30/38; P) An excellent choice, albeit a little far from the action, just south of the train station. The rooms, all furnished in pine, are extremely comfortable. Its location will be no problem for cyclists.

Sleeperz (☎ 304050; info@sleeperz.com; Station Rd; s/d from £30/45) Right outside the train station, this is an attractively converted railway warehouse that almost always has vacancies for desperate late arrivals. Rooms are spartan and spotless with comfortable futon-style beds; those with double beds are larger – all others have cabin-style bunk beds.

TOP END

De Vere University Arms Hotel (☎ 351241; devere .uniarms@airtime.co.uk; Regent St; s/d from £80/130, specials often available; P) The top choice in Cambridge, this huge Victorian mansion overlooking Parker's Piece has elegant rooms, even the smallest of which have carefully chosen design flourishes. First-class service, conveniences for business travellers and a breakfast buffet served in a gorgeous annexe overlooking the park sweeten the deal. Look out for the enormous, creaky cage lift from 1927.

Arundel House Hotel (☎ 367701; info@arundel househotels.co.uk; 53 Chesterton Rd; s/d from £68/85) A large Victorian terrace overlooking the Cam, this refined place has beautiful rooms, many with views of the water.

Garden House (Moat House; ☎ 259988; Granta Pl, Mill Lane; s/d £169/200; P) More like something you'd find on an exclusive golf course, this posh, resorty hotel is right on the Cam and has its own private garden. It's an imposing, modern building with 117 luxurious bedrooms. Rates exclude breakfast. Look out for serious discounts on weekend rates.

Eating

Midsummer House (☎ 369299; set menu lunch £30, dinner £46; ☺ lunch Tue-Fri & Sun, dinner Tue-Sat) Overlooking the river on Midsummer Common is this smart, sophisticated place with a superb menu, said to have one of the most comprehensive wine lists outside Paris. It's a good idea to book several weeks in advance.

Twenty-Two (☎ 351880; 22 Chesterton Rd; set menu dinner £29.95) Cleverly disguised among a row of B&Bs is probably the best restaurant in town, with an outstanding gourmet menu (mostly French) that sends serious foodies straight to heaven. The service here is also top-notch.

Fitzbillies (☎ 352500; 52 Trumpington St) An institution in town, this is a brilliant bakery-café by day – the Chelsea buns (85p) are an outrageous experience and so is the chocolate cake, beloved by generations of students – and an elegant, classy restaurant by night. It's a good place to stock up on supplies before punting. Cakes and buns are also available by mail order.

Al Casbah (☎ 579500; 62 Mill Rd; mains £6-9) This tasty Algerian restaurant has a really good couscous for £8.95; the food is cooked on an indoor barbecue.

Gulshan (☎ 302330; 106 Regent St; mains from £5.95) This place has Indian food you will dream about for months afterwards – especially the curry.

Tatties (☎ 323399; 11 Sussex St; potatoes £1-4) A long-time budget favourite, Tatties specialises not only in baked potatoes stuffed with a variety of tempting fillings but also in breakfasts, filled baguettes, salads and cakes.

Clowns (☎ 355711; 54 King St; sandwiches around £2.50) A great spot for reading the newspaper, this café is full of well-dressed old men, dark wood and a pleasantly weighty sense of time. Gelato is available.

Drinking

Punting is a big deal in Cambridge, at least with a certain section of the university population. Even though members of that segment have earned themselves something of a reputation for being rowdy in the pub after a day's rowing, the punting pubs – where rowers hang out and tourists can rent punts – are definitely worth checking out. Away from the Cam, Cambridge has plenty of atmospheric pubs and trendy bars.

EASTERN ENGLAND

Fort St George (Midsummer Common) Said to be the oldest pub on the Cam, dating from the 16th century. The location is perfect – on the river at the north end of Midsummer Common – which means it's a popular spot, particularly in summer. You can rent punts from here.

Eagle (Bene't St) Nobel Prize–winning scientists Francis Crick and James Watson spent equal time in the laboratory and here, so perhaps Greene King, the Suffolk brewers, played a part in the discovery of the structure of DNA. This 16th-century pub was also popular with American airmen in WWII; they left their signatures on the ceiling.

St Radegund (127 King St) This ancient, priceless little pub in what looks like a fortress has burlap curtains, sagging walls and endless character; it's understandably popular with locals.

Champion of the Thames (68 King St) Despite the name, this place is not remotely connected with punting. It's just an old-style traditional pub, with live music on Tuesday, and it's a wonderful spot for a pint of ale.

Granta (Newnham Rd) Serving double duty as a place for punt hire, the Granta is a popular riverside rowers' pub.

Boathouse (14 Chesterton Rd) Taking the punt-to-the-pub idea even further, the Boathouse has its own mooring place.

Sophbeck Sessions (14 Tredgold Lane) A Cajun-style bar in the northeast of town – this is a popular place with students and visitors alike for a drink and some live jazz and soul.

Entertainment

NIGHTCLUBS

Fez (☎ 519224; 15 Market Passage; admission £2-7, free before 9pm Mon & Wed; 🕑 8pm-2am Mon-Sat) The place to go if clubbing is your thing, with queues most nights and the music loud and thumping. Admission prices vary depending on the night.

Po Na Na Souk Bar (☎ 323880; 7b Jesus Lane; admission £1.50; 🕑 to 2am) Part of a classy, well-designed regional chain, this terrific bar and club is in the basement of a neoclassical building. The style is Moroccan kasbah, and the DJs spin a mix of Latin, house and other funky rhythms.

Fifth Avenue (☎ 364222; Heidelburg Gardens, Lion Yard; admission £5-7) This popular place is a bit

of a meat market, but shopping can be good fun. It's a slice of Ibiza in Cambridge.

THEATRE

Corn Exchange (☎ 357851) Near the TIC, this interesting building is the city's main centre for arts and entertainment, attracting the top names in pop and rock as well as more-classical artists, such as the English National Ballet.

Arts Theatre (☎ 503333; 6 St Edward's Passage) Cambridge's only real theatre puts on everything from pantomime to serious dramatic works.

Getting There & Away

Cambridge can easily be visited as a day trip from London (although it's worth staying at least a night) or en route north. It's well served by trains, though not so well by bus.

Trains run every 30 minutes from London's King's Cross and Liverpool St stations (55 minutes). There are also hourly connections to Bury St Edmunds (45 minutes), Ely (15 minutes) and King's Lynn (50 minutes).

Airlink/Jetlink (☎ 0870 575 7747) runs an Inter-Varsity Link via Stansted airport, and buses to Heathrow and Gatwick airports, from Drummer St bus station.

Getting Around

BICYCLE

It's easy enough to get around Cambridge on foot, but if you're staying out of the centre or plan to explore the Fens, a bicycle can be useful. You don't need a flash mountain bike, because there are few hills; most places rent three-speeds. Good places to check out are **Ben Hayward Cycles** (☎ 355229; www.benhaywardcycles.com; 69 Trumpington St; per day £12), **Cambridge Recycles** (☎ 506035; 61 Newnham Rd; per day £8-10), **Geoff's Bike Hire** (☎ 365629; 65 Devonshire Rd; per day/week £8/16) and **Mike's Bikes** (☎ 312591; 28 Mill Rd; per day £8).

BUS

A free gas-powered shuttle stops at Emmanuel St in the centre of town. Four bus lines (85p to £1.50) run around town from Drummer St bus station, including bus No 3 from the train station to the town centre. Dayrider passes (£3) offer unlimited travel on all buses within Cambridge for one day; Megarider passes (£7) are valid for one week.

CAMBRIDGE, AKA...

It seems ironic that, in a city renowned for its academic excellence and the superior quality of its scholarly research, there is still doubt over how exactly Cambridge got its name. One thing, however, is certain: at the heart of the matter are two rivers, the Cam and its tributary the Granta. Until at least AD 1000 it was the latter that was deemed more important. Britain's first historian, the Venerable Bede, made reference to the settlement of *Grantacaestir* in around AD 730, while 15 years later Felix of Crowland wrote of *Grontricc*. In 875 the *Anglo-Saxon Chronicle* mentioned *Grantebrycge*, but from 1107 the town was known variously as *Caumbrigge, Caumbregge, Caumberage* and *Cantabrigia*. The first line of Chaucer's *Reeve's Tale*, written at the end of the 14th century, reads: 'At Trumpington, not fer fro Cantebrigge'. But still the town's name continued to change. In 1478 it was Camebrygge, finally becoming Cambridge during Elizabethan times.

CAR

Most vehicles are now banned from the centre of Cambridge. It's best to use the well-signposted park-and-ride car parks (£1.25) on the outskirts of town. Shuttle buses run between the centre and the car parks between 7am and 7pm daily.

TAXI

Contact **Cabco** (☎ 312444) for a taxi.

AROUND CAMBRIDGE

Grantchester

The poet Rupert Brooke, a student at King's before WWI, captured Grantchester's quintessential Englishness in the immortal lines: '...oh! yet/Stands the Church clock at 10 to three?/And is there honey still for tea?'. Three miles southeast of Cambridge, Grantchester is a delightful village of thatched cottages and flower-filled meadows beside the River Granta. Its most famous resident is the novelist Jeffrey Archer, who purchased the Old Vicarage shortly before being jailed for perjury (he's out now and presumably back to keeping Grantchester literary).

There are teashops, some attractive pubs and the Orchard tea garden, where cream teas are served in comfortable lawn chairs under apple trees. The best of the pubs is the Red Lion, near the river, which has a very pleasant garden and a lot of nooks and crannies in which to squirrel yourself away with a post-punt pint.

Walking here via the signposted towpath makes a wonderful afternoon stroll from Cambridge (see Walking & Cycling, p456).

American War Cemetery

Four miles west of Cambridge, at Madingley, is a very moving **cemetery** (☎ 01954-210350;

🕑 8am-5.30pm mid-Apr–Sep, 8am-5pm Oct–mid-Apr), which has neat rows of white-marble crosses stretching down the sloping site to commemorate 3811 Americans killed in battle (while based in Britain). You can visit the cemetery as part of a City Sightseeing tour (see Tours, p456).

Imperial War Museum

Military hardware enthusiasts should head directly to this **war museum** (☎ 835000; adult £10; 🕑 10am-6pm mid-Mar–Sep, 10am-4pm Oct–mid-Mar) in Duxford, 9 miles south of Cambridge right by the motorway. The museum is housed at an airfield that played a significant role in WWII, especially during the Battle of Britain. It was the home of the famous Dambuster squadron of Lancasters, and today is home to the Royal Air Force's Red Arrows squadron, which performs all kinds of celestial trickery at air shows throughout the world. You'll find Europe's biggest collection of historic aircraft, ranging from WWI biplanes to jets, including the Concorde. The **American Air Museum**, designed by Norman Foster, is also on the site. It has the largest collection of American civil and military aircraft outside the US. Air shows are frequently held here, and battlefield scenes are displayed in the land warfare hall, where you can check out WWII tanks and artillery. Kids will enjoy the adventure playground and the flight simulator.

The museum runs courtesy buses (the journey is included in the admission price) from Cambridge train station every 40 to 50 minutes between 9.40am and 3.40pm (until 2.20pm October to mid-March); they also stop outside the Crowne Plaza Hotel by the Lion Yard.

ELY

☎ 01353 / pop 13,954

Until recently a quiet little market town, Ely (ee-lee) is becoming ever more popular as a retreat for locals looking to get away from the big city. Its neat Georgian houses, river port and great cathedrals make it eminently worthy of a visit. The town also has a bizarrely interesting history: today it stands in the centre of the Fens, but at one time it was an island, and derived its name from the eels that swam in the surrounding waters.

Information

The **TIC** (☎ 662062; fax 668518; 29 St Mary's St; ⌚ 10am-5.30pm Apr-Sep, 10am-5pm Mon-Sat, 11.15am-4pm Sun Oct-Mar), inside Oliver Cromwell's house, has details about the 'passport to Ely', a combined ticket (£11) for the main sights – Ely Cathedral, the Stained Glass Museum, Ely Museum and Oliver Cromwell's House. It also books accommodation and has information about the busy farmers market, held in Market Pl from 8.30am to 3.30pm on Saturday twice a month.

The police station is at the corner of Egremont St and Lynn Rd, and there's a branch of Lloyd's TSB bank, with ATM, on High St.

Ely Cathedral

The origins of **Ely Cathedral** (☎ 667735; adult £4.80; ⌚ 7am-7pm Easter-Aug, 7.30am-6pm Mon-Sat, 7.30am-5pm Sun Sep-Easter), whose imposing silhouette dominates the town, lie with a remarkable queen of Northumbria, Etheldreda. She had married twice but was determined to pursue her vocation to become a nun. She founded an abbey in 673 and, for her good works, was canonised after her death. The abbey soon became a pilgrimage centre.

A Norman bishop, Simeon, first began the task of building the cathedral. It was completed in 1189 and remains a splendid example of the Norman Romanesque style. In 1322 – after the collapse of the central tower – the octagon and lantern, for which the cathedral is famous, were built. Other features of special interest include the gorgeous lady chapel, the largest of its kind in England, which was added in the 14th century. The niches were rifled by iconoclasts, but the delicate tracery and carving remain intact. There's an amazing view from just inside the western door – right down the nave, through the choir stalls and on to the glorious eastern window. There is no clutter, just a sublime sense of space, light and spirituality.

Ely was the first cathedral in the country to charge admission and, with funds gathered since 1986, it has managed to restore the octagon and lantern tower. There are free guided tours of the cathedral, and an octagon and roof tour (£4). There's a **stained glass museum** (adult/child £3.50/2.50) in the south triforium. Choral Sunday service is at 10.30am and evensong is at 5.30pm Monday to Saturday, and 3.45pm on Sunday.

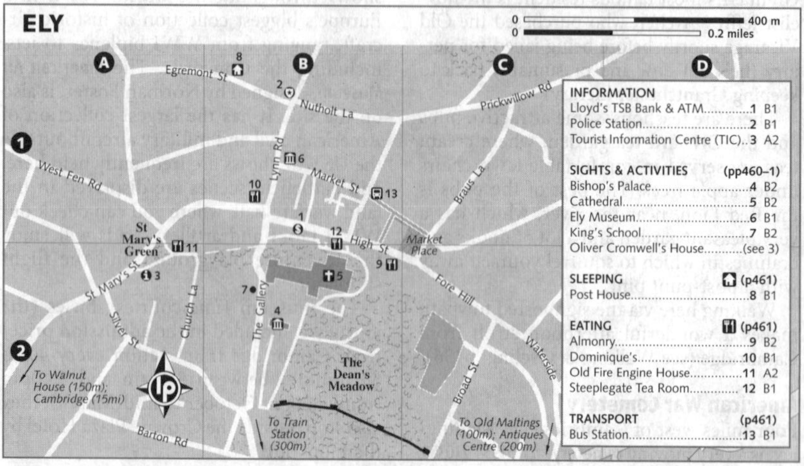
ELY
0 400 m
0 0.2 miles
A
B
C
D
1
2
Egremont St
Nutholt La
Prickwillow Rd
West Fen Rd
Lynn Rd
Market St
Braus La
High St
Market Place
St Mary's Green
St Mary's St
Church La
Silver St
The Gallery
Fore Hill
Waterside
Broad St
Barton Rd
The Dean's Meadow
To Walnut House (150m); Cambridge (15mi)
To Train Station (300m)
To Old Maltings (100m); Antiques Centre (200m)
INFORMATION
Lloyd's TSB Bank & ATM 1 B1
Police Station 2 B1
Tourist Information Centre (TIC) 3 A2
SIGHTS & ACTIVITIES (pp460–1)
Bishop's Palace 4 B2
Cathedral 5 B2
Ely Museum 6 B1
King's School 7 B2
Oliver Cromwell's House (see 3)
SLEEPING (p461)
Post House 8 B1
EATING (p461)
Almonry 9 B2
Dominique's 10 B1
Old Fire Engine House 11 A2
Steeplegate Tea Room 12 B1
TRANSPORT (p461)
Bus Station 13 B1

EOIN CLARKE

Hikers, Snowdonia National Park (p716), Wales

Millennium Stadium (p642), Cardiff, Wales

NEIL SETCHFIELD

Caernarfon Castle (p736), Caernarfon, Wales

ANN CECIL

Old College (p706),
Aberystwyth, Wales

Mawddach Estuary (p728), Snowdonia
National Park, Wales

Strumble Head, Pembrokeshire Coast National
Park (p670), Wales

Rhossili Bay (p668), Gower Peninsula, Wales

Other Sights & Activities

The area around the cathedral is historically and architecturally interesting. There's the former **Bishop's Palace**, now used as a nursing home, and **King's School**, which supplies the cathedral with choristers.

Oliver Cromwell's House (☎ 662062; adult £3.75) stands to the west, across St Mary's Green. Cromwell lived with his family in this attractive, half-timbered 14th-century house from 1636 to 1646, when he was the tithe collector of Ely. The TIC, occupying the front room of the house, offers an audiovisual presentation and an interesting tour of the rooms.

The history of the town is further described in **Ely Museum** (☎ 666655; cnr Lynn Rd & Market St; adult £2; ⏰ 10.30am-5.30pm Sun-Fri, 1-5pm Sun May-Oct, 10.30am-4pm Wed-Mon Nov-Apr), in the Old Gaol House.

Signs lead down to the river on a nice stroll to an interesting **antiques centre**. The **Old Maltings** (☎ 662633; Ship Lane), which stages exhibitions and has a café, is nearby.

River Great Ouse is a busy thoroughfare – swans and ducks compete with boats for river space. The towpath winds up- and downstream: for a quiet walk, turn left; for the pub and tea garden, turn right. If you continue along this path you'll see the Fens stretching to the horizon.

Sleeping

Post House (☎ 667184; 12a Egremont St; s/d from £20/40; **P**) Unmissable with the Union flag raised outside, this elegant building has plain but comfortable rooms and an ideal location.

Walnut House (☎ 661793; walnuthouse1@aol.com; 1 Houghton Gardens; s/d £25/50; **P**) Large and gorgeous with beautifully appointed rooms, this is another top choice for accommodation, southwest of the centre.

Eating

Not too surprisingly, eels are a local delicacy, served in several of the restaurants.

Old Fire Engine House (☎ 662582; St Mary's St; mains about £12; ⏰ lunch & dinner Mon-Sat) Ely's best restaurant – a good place to sample eels. It's more like the comfortable house of a friend than a restaurant, with excellent food.

Dominiques (☎ 665011; St Mary's St; mains around £5; ⏰ lunch & dinner; ✖) This restaurant, famed for its variety of vegetarian choices, serves cream teas, lunches and set dinners.

Steeplegate Tea Room (☎ 664731; 16 High St; snacks from £2.50) Right beside the cathedral, upstairs from a craft shop, this tearoom does light lunches and filling snacks such as baked potatoes.

Almonry (☎ 666360) To the left of the lady chapel, virtually within the cathedral grounds, this attractive garden restaurant has a wide range of teas and coffees.

Getting There & Away

Ely is on the A10, 15 miles northeast of Cambridge and an easy day trip from it. Following the Fen Rivers Way (map available from TICs), it's a 17-mile walk.

Bus Nos X11 and X12 run every half-hour from Cambridge's Drummer St bus station (one hour). The X8, which runs hourly to King's Lynn from Cambridge, is quicker, taking 45 minutes to reach Ely.

There are hourly trains from Cambridge (15 minutes). From Ely, there are hourly trains to Peterborough (35 minutes), and half-hourly trains to King's Lynn (1½ hours) and Norwich (55 minutes).

PETERBOROUGH

☎ 01733 / pop 136,292

There are two big reasons to visit Peterborough: shopping and church. It's a classic example of a retail mecca, which might not be too exciting to those already familiar with British shopping centres and high-street chain stores. But Peterborough is also home to a wonderful cathedral, and it's an easy day trip from Cambridge.

The cathedral precinct is an extension of the bustling Cowgate, Bridge St and Queensgate. The **TIC** (☎ 452336; tic@peterborough.gov.uk; 45 Bridge St; ⏰ 8.45am-5pm Mon-Wed & Fri, 10am-5pm Thu, 10am-4pm Sat) is nearby. The bus and train stations are within walking distance of the TIC, just west of the city centre.

Peterborough Cathedral

In Anglo-Saxon times, when the region was part of the kingdom of Mercia, King Peada, a recent convert to Christianity, founded a monastic church here in 655. This was sacked and gutted by the Danes in 870. In 1118 the Benedictine abbot John de Sais founded the present **cathedral** (☎ 343342; requested donation £3; ⏰ 9am-6.15pm) as the monastic church of the Benedictine abbey. It was finally consecrated in 1237.

As you enter the precinct from Cathedral Sq you get a breathtaking view of the early-13th-century western front, one of the most impressive of any cathedral in Britain. On entering the building, you're struck by the height of the nave and the lightness, which derives not only from the mellow Barnack stone (quarried close by and transported via the River Nene) but also from the clerestory windows. The nave, with its three storeys, is an impressive example of Norman architecture. Its unique timber ceiling is one of the earliest of its kind in Britain (possibly in Europe), and its original painted decoration has been preserved. The Gothic tower replaced the original Norman one but had to be taken down and carefully reconstructed after it began to crack in the late 19th century.

In the northern choir aisle is the tombstone of Henry VIII's first wife, the tragic Catherine of Aragon, buried here in 1536. Her divorce, engineered by the king because she could not produce a male heir, led to the Reformation in England. Her only child (a daughter) was not even allowed to attend her funeral. Every 29 January there is a procession in the cathedral to commemorate her death.

In the southern aisle, two standards mark what was the grave of Mary, Queen of Scots. On the accession of her son, James, to the throne, her body was moved to Westminster Abbey.

The eastern end of the cathedral, known as the New Building, was added in the 15th century. It has superb fan vaulting, probably the work of master mason John Wastell, who worked on King's College Chapel in Cambridge.

Getting There & Away

Stagecoach United Counties (☎ 01604-620077) runs buses from Cambridge.

SUFFOLK

The magnificent parish churches that dot the Suffolk landscape have their origins in a humble source: sheep. The county was an important wool-trading centre until the 16th century, producing enough wealth to establish still-beautiful villages and elaborate churches now beloved by film crews for their value as period-piece backdrops. These days, economics have stanched the cash flow and Suffolk has settled into its role as a charmingly rural backwater.

The flat, bike-friendly landscape here has a serene beauty, praised by the painter John Constable for its 'gentle declivities, its woods and rivers, its luxuriant meadow flats sprinkled with flocks and herds, and its well-cultivated uplands, with numerous scattered villages and churches, farms and picturesque cottages.'

Keep an eye out for the stucco plasterwork called pargeting that traditionally decorates buildings in Suffolk villages.

Getting Around

Contact **Suffolk County Tourism** (☎ 0845 958 3358) for local transport information.

IPSWICH

☎ 01473 / pop 141,658

Once a principal player in the Saxon world and a major trading centre during the Middle Ages, modern Ipswich barely registers on the list of England's most important towns. Yet the county capital is still an important commercial and shopping centre, as well as the county's transport hub. The town centre is a compact and relatively pleasant warren of small streets where you'll find a couple of beautiful examples of the Tudor style (Ancient House and Christchurch Mansion). Also worth checking out is the Wet Dock quayside, which is a thoughtful modern development.

The **TIC** (☎ 258070; tourist@ipswich.gov.uk; 🕑 9am-5pm Mon-Sat) is in St Stephen's Church, off St Stephen's Lane, close to the bus station and Ancient House. It organises 90-minute guided **tours** (☎ 462721 for reservations; adult/child £2/1.50) of the town at 2.15pm on Tuesday and Thursday, and guided ghost tours at 8pm on the first Thursday of every month.

Ipswich's attractions for the visitor don't necessarily merit an overnight stay, but if you do need accommodation, contact the TIC.

The train station is a 15-minute walk southwest of the TIC along Princes St and across the roundabout.

Sights

In the 17th-century **Ancient House** (☎ 214144; 40 Buttermarket; 🕑 9am-5.30pm Mon-Sat), now oddly enough a branch of Lakeland kitchen out-fitters, you can take a look at the exquisite hammer-beam roof on the 1st floor. The external décor, completed around 1670, is an extravagant example of the Restoration style, with plenty of stucco and some of the finest examples of pargeting in the country. The house is about 50m north of the TIC, just off St Stephen's Lane.

The **Unitarian Meeting House** (☎ 218217; Friars St; admission free; ☯ noon-4pm Tue-Thu & 10am-4pm Sat May-Sep) is a Grade I–listed building, erected in 1699 and known as one of the finest Dissenting Meeting Houses in the country.

The **Ipswich Museum** (☎ 433550; High St; admission free; ☯ 10am-5pm Tue-Sat) has exhibits on natural history, geology and archaeology, and a particularly good collection of British birds.

Set in a 26-hectare park around 300m north of town, **Christchurch Mansion** (☎ 433554; Soane St; admission free; ☯ mansion & gallery 10am-5pm Tue-Sat, 2.30-4.30pm Sun Mar-Sep, 10am-4pm Tue-Sat, 2.30-4.30pm Sun Oct-Feb) is a fine Tudor mansion which was built between 1548 and 1550. The mansion's exterior is festooned with Dutch-style gables, while the enormous interior is decorated with period furniture and the walls are adorned with an extensive collection of works by Constable and Gainsborough. The Wolsey Art Gallery hosts contemporary art exhibitions at the mansion. To get here, walk north from the TIC along St Stephen's Lane, which becomes Tower St. Turn right onto St Margaret's St and then take a left at the fork onto Soane St.

Getting There & Away

There are half-hourly trains to London's Liverpool St station (£25, 1¼ hours) and Norwich (£15, 50 minutes), and 12 trains daily to Bury St Edmunds (£5, 30 minutes).

Beestons (☎ 823243) run bus services every half-hour to Sudbury and **Chambers** (☎ 01787-227233) offers a Sunday bus service to Sudbury.

AROUND IPSWICH
Sutton Hoo

In 1939 archaeologists digging in and near a group of burial mounds close to the River Deben, 2 miles east of Woodbridge and 6 miles northeast of Ipswich, uncovered the hull of an Anglo-Saxon ship and a haul of other Saxon artefacts that together must be regarded as one of the most important discoveries in British history. In March 2002 a new **exhibition hall** (NT; ☎ 01394-389700; www.suttonhoo.org; Woodbridge; adult £4, discounts for those arriving on foot or bicycle; ☯ 10am-5pm Jun-Sep, 10am-5pm Wed-Sun Easter-May & Oct, Sat only Nov-Easter) opened to display these extraordinary finds, which include a full-scale reconstruction of King Raedwald's burial chamber and the Sutton Hoo ship. Other treasures recovered at the site, including a warrior's helmet and shield, gold ornaments and Byzantine silver, are on display in London's British Museum (p131).

There is a video introduction and a guided tour of the burial site. First Eastern Counties runs 12 buses to Woodbridge, Monday to Saturday (50p, 10 minutes); ask the driver to stop at Sutton Hoo.

Located in Woodbridge itself is **Seckford Hall** (☎ 01394-385678; reception@seckford.co.uk; s/d from £80/120), a lavish Tudor country house set in 14 hectares of woodland. The rooms are luxurious, and it has an indoor pool and an adjacent 18-hole golf course.

STOUR VALLEY

Running along the border between Suffolk and Essex, the River Stour flows through a soft, pastoral landscape that has inspired numerous painters, the most famous being Constable and Gainsborough. The beautiful houses and elegant churches of some of the sedate villages along the Stour are reminders of a time when these places thrived as part of the medieval weaving trade. By the end of the 15th century the Stour Valley was producing more cloth than anywhere else in England.

Within 100 years, production had shifted to the bigger towns like Colchester, Ipswich and Norwich, and the villages receded into industrial obscurity. By the end of the 19th century the Stour Valley was a rural backwater, ignored by the Industrial Revolution and virtually everyone else – not so great for locals, but a godsend for today's visitors looking for a genuine experience of the gentle English countryside. While the more famously picturesque towns, notably Lavenham and Sudbury, attract significant numbers of visitors, the area is still quiet enough to ensure that you will be able to explore it in peace.

Long Melford
☎ 01787 / pop 2734

Known for its 2-mile-long High St (the longest in England, locals say) and the lovely timber-framed buildings that line it, Long Melford has a magnificent church with some fine stained-glass windows, two stately homes and the obligatory antique shops.

Built in 1578, **Melford Hall** (☎ 880286; adult £4.50; ⊙ 2-5.30pm Wed-Sun May-Sep, 2-5.30pm Sat & Sun Apr & Oct, phone for other times) is a turreted Tudor mansion in the centre of the village. There's an 18th-century drawing room, a Regency library and a Victorian bedroom. There's also a display of paintings by Beatrix Potter, who was a relative of the Parker family – the family owned the house from 1786 to 1960, when it passed into the hands of the Treasury as part-payment of death duties.

On the edge of the village, at the end of a tree-lined avenue, lies **Kentwell Hall** (☎ 310207; www.kentwell.co.uk; adult £6.95; ⊙ noon-5pm Apr-Oct), another redbrick Tudor mansion, but one that's privately owned and makes much more of its origins. Once described in *Country Life* magazine as 'the epitome of many people's image of an Elizabethan house', this is not a museum but a house where the furnishings and décor have been meticulously restored over the past 30 years. It has received the Heritage Building of the Year award, given by the *Good Britain Guide*. The house is surrounded by a moat, and there's a brick-paved Tudor rose maze and a rare-breeds farm.

Although the house is a delight to visit at any time of year, the real treat occurs between mid-June and mid-July, when more than 200 Tudor enthusiasts abandon their contemporary cynicism and don their traditional hose and velvet jackets to re-create and live out a certain year in the Tudor calendar. Admission is more expensive during the historical re-enactment period.

The **Great Church of the Holy Trinity** (☎ 281836) has lunch-time recitals at 1.10pm every Wednesday from mid-May to mid-September.

SLEEPING & EATING
High Street Farm House (☎ 375765; anroy@lineone .net; s/d from £38/60) Large and salmon-coloured, this 16th-century building dominates the northern end of town. The rooms are large and comfortable, and an excellent breakfast is served in the oak-beamed dining room.

Black Lion Hotel & Restaurant (☎ 312356; fax 374557; the Green; s/d from £75/95) Right on the village green, the Black Lion has simply gorgeous rooms and an excellent restaurant (mains around £8).

Scutcher's Bistro (☎ 310200; Westgate St; mains £12.90-15) Not just the top dining spot in town, but one of the most renowned restaurants in the Stour Valley. The exquisite menu features classic British cuisine with Continental touches. It's just west of the green, near the Black Lion.

GETTING THERE & AWAY
Chambers Buses runs 12 buses from Monday to Saturday between Long Melford and Bury St Edmunds (one hour) calling at Sudbury (£1, five minutes). It also runs a circular bus route between Long Melford and Sudbury (10 minutes) at 10 and 40 minutes past the hour from Monday to Saturday.

Sudbury
☎ 01787 / pop 20,188

Re-created by Charles Dickens as Eatanswill in *The Pickwick Papers* (1836–37), Sudbury is the largest town in the western half of the Stour Valley. The groundwork for its success was laid in the Middle Ages, when the town went from strength to strength on the back of the roaring trade in wool. As in the rest of East Anglia, sheep have given way to crops, but Sudbury maintains a key link with the manufacture of cloth, especially silk weaving. Most visitors also drop in to visit the birthplace of the town's most famous son, portrait and landscape painter Thomas Gainsborough (1727–88), although Sudbury is a nice place to while away an afternoon even if you're not particularly interested in Gainsborough's work.

The **TIC** (☎ 881320; sudburytic@babergh.gov.uk; ⊙ 9am-5pm Mon-Fri year-round, plus 10am-4.45pm Sat Apr-Sep, 10am-2.45pm Sat Oct-Mar) is in the town hall.

The birthplace of one of England's most celebrated artists, **Gainsborough's House** (☎ 372958; 46 Gainsborough St; www.gainsborough.org; adult £3.50; ⊙ 10am-5pm Tue-Sat, 2-5pm Sun) has been preserved as a shrine and is now a museum with the largest collection of his work in the country. The house features a Georgian façade built by Gainsborough's father, while the mulberry tree in the garden features in some of the son's paintings. Inside,

EASTERN ENGLAND

the extensive collection features his earliest known work, *A Boy and a Girl in a Landscape*, now in two separate parts (the author of the separation is unknown), a portrait of *Reverend Tobias Rustat* and the exquisite *Lady Tracy*. This last work is particularly beautiful in its delicate portrayal of drapery. Gainsborough's studio features original furniture as well as his walking stick and pocket watch. In the parlour is a statue of a horse, the only known sculpture the artist ever produced.

The Gallery and the Weaving Room are home to constantly changing exhibits of modern art, while in summer the garden hosts sculpture exhibitions.

The **Old Bull Hotel** (☎ 374120; fax 379044; Church St; s/d from £45/55) is a family-run hotel in a 16th-century building with nine rooms, all decorated differently. **Boathouse Hotel** (☎ /fax 379090; Ballingdon Bridge; s/d from £40/50) is on the water, and the hotel rents out rowing boats.

GETTING THERE & AWAY

Bus travel in and out of Sudbury can be tricky. Beestons runs eight buses daily, Monday to Friday (seven on Saturday), to Ipswich (£3, one hour). To get just about anywhere else involves a few changes.

In addition Sudbury has a train station with an hourly service to London (£24.80, 1¼ hours).

Lavenham
☎ 01787

Lavenham is the prettiest village in Suffolk, at least the parts of it you can see peeking out from behind the tour buses. It's a beautifully preserved example of a medieval wool town, with more than 300 listed buildings. Some are timber-framed, others decorated with pargeting. There are cosy, pink thatched cottages, crooked houses, antique shops, art galleries, quaint tearooms and ancient inns. When the wool industry moved to the west and north of England in the late 17th century, none of Lavenham's inhabitants could afford to build anything more modern – too bad for them; lucky for modern-day visitors.

The **TIC** (☎ 248207; lavenham@babergh.gov.uk; Lady St; ☼ 10am-4.45pm Apr-Oct, 11am-3pm Sat & Sun Mar & Nov) offers guided walks (£3) around the village departing at 2.30pm Saturday and 11am and 2.30pm Sunday.

SIGHTS

Market Pl, which runs off High St, is dominated by a handsome **guildhall** (☎ 247646; adult £3.25; ☼ 11am-5pm Apr-Oct, 11am-4pm Sat & Sun Mar-Nov), a superb example of a close-studded, timber-framed building, dating back to the early 16th century. It's now a local history museum, with displays on the wool trade.

Little Hall (High St; adult £2; ☼ 2-5.30pm Wed, Thu, Sat & Sun Apr-Oct), which has soft ochre plastering and grey timber, is a private house – once belonging to a successful wool merchant – that is open to the public.

At the southern end of the village, opposite the car park, is the **Church of St Peter & St Paul**. Its soaring steeple is visible for miles around. The church bears witness to Lavenham's past prosperity as a centre of the local wool trade.

SLEEPING & EATING

Lavenham Priory (☎ 247404; www.lavenhampriory .co.uk; Water St; s/d from £70/90) Once the home of Benedictine monks, then medieval cloth merchants, the priory is now an upmarket B&B and is easily the most attractive sleeping option in town.

Swan Hotel (☎ 247477; fax 248286; High St; s/d from £80/160) One of the county's best-known hotels, the Swan is housed in a late medieval building that has been exquisitely restored and updated with modern amenities.

Angel (☎ 247388; Market Pl; mains around £14) Lavenham's top restaurant serves excellent modern British cuisine, with smoked fish the speciality of the house.

GETTING THERE & AWAY

Chambers Buses connects Lavenham with Bury St Edmunds (£1.70, 30 minutes) and Sudbury (£1.50, 20 minutes), with an hourly bus (until 6pm Monday to Saturday, no service on Sunday) from Bury St Edmunds to Colchester via Sudbury and Lavenham. There are no direct buses from Cambridge; you must go via Sudbury, also the location of the nearest train station.

Kersey
☎ 01473

If Lavenham has a rival for the title of most photogenic village in Suffolk, Kersey is it, although 'village' is an exaggeration; it's little more than a one-street hamlet. Many of the handsome Tudor-style, timber-framed houses have been bought up by city folk looking for a weekend getaway in Merrie Olde Englande, and they've paid handsomely for the privilege. Kersey is genuinely charming, but there is little to do here save admire the architecture and marvel at the fact that the village's only street (appositely named the Street) dips and disappears into a shallow ford (known as the Water Splash) before reappearing on the other side.

Kersey Pottery (☎ 822092; the Street; ⊗ 10am-5.30pm Tue-Sat & 11am-5pm Sun) is a well-respected potter's studio and shop where you can browse, and buy handmade stoneware.

The 14th-century, oak-timbered **Bell Inn** (☎ 823229) and the **White Horse** (☎ 824418) are good spots for a pint or a bit of pub grub.

Kersey is 8 miles southeast of Lavenham off the A1141. There are three buses daily between Kersey and Ipswich (one hour) from Monday to Saturday. The twice-daily Sunday service also serves Sudbury (£1.50, 20 minutes). From Lavenham, the only way to get here is by car or taxi; **Granger's Cars** (☎ 01787-247456, 0589 409237) charges around £8. The trip takes about 20 minutes.

Hadleigh
☎ 01473 / pop 7124

During the Middle Ages, Hadleigh was one of the largest wool and market towns in eastern England, outranked only by Ipswich and Bury St Edmunds. Today, the town remains relatively prosperous, but its heyday is long gone and it has to content itself with being an attractive, largish town with a rich architectural heritage.

At the centre of it all is the wonderful 15th-century **guildhall** (☎ 827752; adult £1.50; ⊗ 2-5pm Thu & Sun Jun-Sep), topped by a splendid crown-post roof. The building has been managed by the Hadleigh Market Feoffment (elected management committee) continuously since 1432. Admission includes a guided tour. In good weather, tea and scones are served in the guildhall garden.

Next door, the soaring **St Mary's Church** (Church St) is one of the largest parish churches in East Anglia, and its features date from the late-12th-century tower to the nave altar, which was completed in 1971.

To the west of the church is the **Deanery Tower** (not open to the public), built in 1495 by Archdeacon William Pykenham as a gatehouse for a projected mansion nearer the

river (he died before it could be built). The battlements and machicolation over the oriel window are purely ornamental, but they're a little incongruous, considering this was basically a clergyman's house. The building is also where the Oxford Movement, which sought to reassert Catholic teaching within the Church of England, was launched in 1833.

Hadleigh is also the headquarters of the **East of England Tourist Board** (☎ 822922; eastofenglandtouristboard@compuserve.com; Toppesfield Hall), just off the High St. It is not a walk-in office, so all inquiries should be by phone or email. It provides comprehensive lists of what to see and do in the region, as well as where to stay and eat.

Hadleigh is 2 miles southeast of Kersey. There are hourly buses from Ipswich (£1.80, 30 minutes) and Sudbury (£1.50, 35 minutes).

BURY ST EDMUNDS
☎ 01284 / pop 36,218

Straddling the Rivers Lark and Linnet amid gently rolling farmland, Bury St Edmunds has a mysterious appeal – maybe it's the architecture, maybe it's the beer (Greene King, the famous Suffolk brewer, is based here). Bury's distinct Georgian flavour, with street upon street of handsome, 18th-century façades that hark back to a period of great prosperity, make it Suffolk's most attractive large town. It's now a busy agricultural centre, and cattle, vegetable and fruit markets are held at Angel Hill every Wednesday and Saturday.

Centrally placed, Bury is a convenient point from which to explore western Suffolk. Don't miss the ruined abbey, set in a beautiful garden. There's also a fascinating clock museum and guided tours of the brewery.

History
Bury's motto, 'Shrine of a King, Cradle of the Law', recalls the two most memorable events in its history. The Danes decapitated Edmund, a Christian prince from Saxony who was destined to be the last king of East Anglia, in 855, and his body was brought here for reburial in 903. The shrine to this king (who later became a saint) was to be the focal point of a new Benedictine monastery called St Edmundsbury, around which the

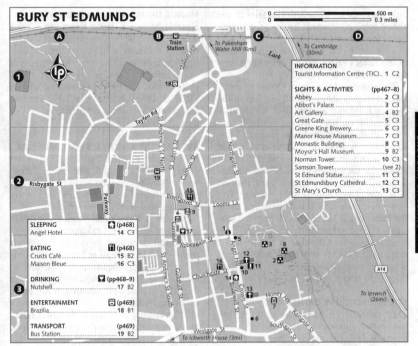

BURY ST EDMUNDS

	0	500 m
	0	0.3 miles

To Pakenham
Water Mill (6mi)

To Cambridge
(30mi)

Lark

**Train
Station**

Station Hill

INFORMATION
Tourist Information Centre (TIC)...... **1** C2

SIGHTS & ACTIVITIES (pp467–8)
Abbey... **2** C3
Abbot's Palace.............................. **3** C3
Art Gallery.................................... **4** B2
Great Gate................................... **5** C3
Greene King Brewery.................... **6** C3
Manor House Museum.................. **7** C3
Monastic Buildings....................... **8** C3
Moyse's Hall Museum................... **9** B2
Norman Tower............................. **10** C3
Samson Tower........................(see 2)
St Edmund Statue........................ **11** C3
St Edmundsbury Cathedral........... **12** C3
St Mary's Church......................... **13** C3

Tayfen Rd

St Andrew's St North

St John's St

Clifton St

Northgate St

Risbygate St

Parkway

Brentgovel St

Looms La

SLEEPING (p468)
Angel Hotel.................................. **14** C3

EATING (p468)
Crusts Café.................................. **15** B2
Maison Bleue................................ **16** C3

DRINKING (pp468–9)
Nutshell....................................... **17** B2

ENTERTAINMENT (p469)
Brazilia.. **18** B1

TRANSPORT (p469)
Bus Station................................... **19** B2

Cornhill

Abbeygate St

St Andrew's St South

Guildhall St

Churchgate St

Bridewell St

Crown St

Angel Hill

Honey Hill

Raingate St

Westgate St

Southgate St

A14

To Ipswich
(26mi)

To Ickworth House (3mi)

---

town grew. The abbey, now ruined, became one of the most famous pilgrimage centres in the country and, until the dissolution of the monasteries in 1536, was the wealthiest in the country.

The second memorable episode in Bury's early history took place at the abbey. In 1214, at St Edmund's Altar, the English barons drew up the petition that formed the basis of the Magna Carta.

Orientation & Information

Bury St Edmunds is an easy place to find your way around because it has preserved Abbot Baldwin's 11th-century grid layout. The train station is about a quarter of a mile north of the town centre; there are regular bus connections to the centre (50p). The **bus station** (St Andrew's St N) is located right in the heart of town.

The **TIC** (☎ 764667; tic@stedsbc.gov.uk; 6 Angel Hill; ☒ 9am-5.30pm Easter-Oct, 9am-5.30pm Mon-Sat Nov-Easter) has plenty of information on the town and is also the starting point for guided walking tours (£3) that depart at 2.30pm Monday to Saturday, Easter to September.

Tours of the Greene King Brewery (see p468) are popular, so you'll want to book ahead.

Sights

ABBEY & PARK

Although the **abbey** (admission free; ☒ sunrise to sunset) is very much a ruin, it's a spectacular one, set in a beautiful **garden**. After the dissolution of the monasteries, the townspeople made off with much of the stone – even St Edmund's grave and bones have disappeared.

You can enter the abbey grounds through the main **Great Gate**, built sometime between 1327 and 1346, or further up along Angel Hill via the older **Norman Tower**, built between 1120 and 1148 and designed to serve as the belfry for the adjacent church of St James (now St Edmundsbury Cathedral). These are the best-preserved buildings of the whole complex and give an impression of how imposing the whole pile must have been.

Just inside the Great Gate is the **Great Court**, which was once completely surrounded by buildings where the practical affairs of the abbey were conducted. Today it is an elegant formal garden. Just beyond the court is a dovecote that marks the only remains of the **Abbot's Palace**; his gardens have been transformed into a bowling green.

The most solid remains of the once powerful and mighty abbey church are part of the western front and **Samson Tower**, which since the dissolution have had houses built into them. In the small garden in front of Samson Tower is a beautiful **statue of St Edmund** by Elizabeth Frink (1976). The rest of the abbey church spreads eastward like a fallen skeleton, with bits of stonework and the odd pillar giving a clue to its immense size. You can guide yourself around the ruins using the information boards, which help to show what a large community this must have been; just north of the church lie the ruined remains of a cluster of **monastic buildings** that at one time served as a dormitory, a lavatory, the prior's house and an infirmary.

ST EDMUNDSBURY CATHEDRAL
This **cathedral** (8.30am-8pm Apr-Oct, 8.30am-7pm Nov-Mar), also known as St James', dates from the 16th century, but the eastern end was added between 1945 and 1960, and the northern side was not completed until 1990. It was made a cathedral in 1914.

The architecture of the entrance porch has a strong Spanish influence, a latter-day tribute to the devotion of Abbot Anselm (1121–48), who instead of making a pilgrimage to Santiago de Compostela in Galicia chose to stay and build a church dedicated to St James (Santiago in Spanish) on the abbey grounds.

The interior is light and lofty with a gorgeous painted hammer-beam roof. The Spanish theme continues in the lady chapel in the south transept, while the north transept houses a particularly beautiful sculpture of *Christ Crucified* by Elizabeth Frink. The cathedral has recently undergone massive restoration, thanks to an award of £8 million from the Millennium Commission.

ST MARY'S CHURCH
Built around 1430, **St Mary's** contains the tomb of Mary Tudor (Henry VIII's sister and a one-time queen of France). A bell is still rung to mark curfew, as it was in the Middle Ages.

MANOR HOUSE MUSEUM & BREWERY
Near St Mary's is **Manor House** (757072; 5 Honey Hill; adult £2.50;   10am-5pm Tue-Sun), a magnificent museum of horology, art and costume housed in a Georgian building. It is worth being here around noon, when all the clocks strike. The nearby **Greene King Brewery** (763222; Crown St; day/evening £6/7;   2.30pm Mon-Thu) is worth visiting while you're in this part of the town.

ART GALLERY & MOYSE'S HALL MUSEUM
In a Grade I–listed building, Bury's **art gallery** (762081; Cornhill; adult £1;   10.30am-5pm Tue-Sat) was designed in 1774 by Robert Adam, originally as a theatre. Inside are rotating exhibitions of contemporary art.

Nearby is **Moyse's Hall Museum** (706183; Cornhill; admission free;   9am-5.30pm Mon-Sat), with an exhibit dedicated to the Suffolk Regiment – its history, feats of bravery, and uniforms. The rest of the museum is devoted to local archaeology, complete with interactive displays. At least as interesting, if not more so, is the building itself, which dates from the 12th century and is probably East Anglia's oldest domestic building.

Sleeping
Saxon House (755547; 37 Southgate St; s/d from £40/60) This fully restored, 15th-century timber-frame building, once an almshouse, has two gorgeously appointed bedrooms. One has exposed beams and candlelight, the other overlooks a courtyard and herb garden.

Angel Hotel (753926; sales@theangel.co.uk; 3 Angel Hill; s/d from £69/89) This crown jewel in the centre of Bury once lodged Charles Dickens and is where Mr Pickwick enjoyed an 'excellent roast dinner'.

Eating
Maison Bleue (760623; 31 Churchgate St; mains £9-17.50, set menu £19.95;   lunch & dinner Mon-Sat) This local fave is a highly recommended seafood restaurant, with creative preparations of brill, sea bass and monkfish.

Crusts Café (763293; 13 Brentgovel St; mains around £4;   breakfast, lunch & dinner) This lovely café serves a wide range of dishes, from lasagne to steak and kidney pie.

Drinking & Entertainment
Nutshell (the Traverse) The best-known pub in Bury – claiming to be Britain's smallest – is

indeed tiny, with cheerful yellow walls and big windows ideal for people-watching.

Brazilia (☎ 769655; Station Hill; admission £4-7; ☿ Thu-Sat) At weekends the kids flock to this dance club, which features a popular mix of '70s disco and commercial house and trance. Dress up, as jeans and trainers will leave you in the cold.

Getting There & Away

There's a daily National Express bus to London (£12, two hours and 20 minutes). From Cambridge, Stagecoach Cambus runs buses to Bury (35 minutes) hourly from Monday to Saturday. First Eastern Counties runs buses every 30 minutes to Ipswich (1¼ hours).

Bury is on the Ipswich (20 minutes) to Ely (30 minutes) railway line, so trains to London (1¾ hours) go via these towns virtually every hour. From Cambridge, there are trains every two hours to Bury (45 minutes).

AROUND BURY ST EDMUNDS
Ickworth House & Park

Three miles southwest of Bury on the A143, **Ickworth House** (☎ 735270; adult house & park £6.40, park only £3; ☿ house 1-5pm mid-Mar-Oct, park 7am-7pm year-round) is the eccentric creation of Frederick Hervey (1730-1803), who was the fourth Earl of Bristol and the Bishop of Derry – see the boxed text, below. It's an amazing structure, with an immense oval rotunda dating back to 1795. It contains a fine collection of furniture, silver and paintings (by Titian, Gainsborough and Diego Velasquez). Outside, there's an unusual Italian garden and a park designed by Lancelot

'Capability' Brown, with waymarked trails, a deer enclosure and a hide.

First Eastern Counties runs a bus service (£1.50) at 12.35pm and 4.10pm daily, bound for Garboldisham (No 304), leaving from outside Bury train station.

Pakenham Water Mill

England's only remaining parish water mill and **windmill** (☎ 01359-230275; adult £2; ☿ 2-5.30pm Wed, Sat & Sun Good Friday–Sep) still in operation is in the small village of Pakenham, 6 miles northeast of Bury St Edmunds along the A143. Corn has been ground here for over 900 years, and the mill makes an appearance in the Domesday Book. The mill ceased production in 1974, but it was taken over four years later by the Suffolk Preservation Society, who sponsored a painstaking restoration. During the restoration a Tudor mill was uncovered on the site of the present building, which dates from the late 18th century. Visitors get a guided tour of the building and can observe the grinding process from start to finish; you can also buy ground corn produced on the premises.

There are four buses daily from the Bury St Edmunds bus station from 1.05pm (No 337 to Thetford), Monday to Friday, and three on Saturday (20 minutes). The bus stops in front of the Fox pub; the mill is just up the street.

ALDEBURGH
☎ 01728 / pop 2654

So cute that it has to be seen to be believed, diminutive Aldeburgh has a pretty shingle

---

THE ECCENTRIC EARL

The Hervey family had such a reputation for eccentricity that it was said of them that when 'God created the human race he made men, women and Herveys'. Perhaps the biggest weirdo of them all was the creator of Ickworth House, Frederick, the third son of the third Earl of Bristol. As Bishop of Derry (Ireland) he was renowned not for his piety but for his agnosticism, vanity and oddity: he would force his clergymen to race each other through peat bogs in the middle of the night, sprinkle flour on the floor of his house to catch night-time adulterers, champion the cause of Catholic emancipation (he was, after all, a Protestant bishop) and earn himself the sobriquet of 'wicked prelate' from George III.

Not content with his life in Ireland, in later years Frederick took to travelling around Europe, where he indulged each and every one of his passions: women, wine, art and intrigue. He tried to pass himself off as a spy in France, and for his trouble he was rewarded with a nine-month prison sentence in a Napoleonic jail. While in Italy, he horrified visiting English aristocrats with his dress sense and manners; he often dressed in military garb and once chucked a bowl of pasta onto a religious procession because he hated the sound of tinkling bells.

beach and a picturesque town centre. The sea is closing in on the village; the beach is now only yards away. Moot Hall, a 16th-century building, was once in the centre of town; now it's on the seashore. It's a shame to imagine the pretty little seaside town being gradually overtaken by salt water, as it's one of the nicest in the country. Poet George Crabbe and composer Benjamin Britten both lived here; Britten founded the widely popular annual **Aldeburgh Festival** (☎ 453543; www.aldeburgh.co.uk), East Anglia's primary arts and music festival, which takes place in June.

The **TIC** (☎ 453637; atic@suffolkcoastal.gov.uk; High St; ✆ 9am-5.15pm Easter-Oct, 10am-4pm Mon-Sat Nov-Easter) can help with information.

Walking

The Suffolk Coast and Heaths Path passes through Aldeburgh. You can follow it north beside the ocean for a few miles and enjoy the salty sea air. Alternatively, from Aldeburgh follow the path inland for a lovely 3-mile walk through some pleasant wooded areas and fields towards the village of Snape. Just south of Snape, where a road crosses the River Alde, are the large buildings of the Maltings.

Sleeping

White Lion Hotel (☎ 452720; Market Cross Pl; s/d from £75/115) Aldeburgh's oldest hotel overlooks the shingle beach and has recently received a 21st-century facelift. Sea-facing rooms are the best; they cost £10 extra.

Ocean House (☎ 452094; fax 453909; 25 Crag Path; s/d from £40/65, sea-facing r extra £5) This delightful guesthouse overlooking the sea in the middle of town has rooms all outfitted in period style.

Eating

Café 152 (☎ 454152; 152 High St; mains £10-14; ✆ closed Mon & Tue Nov-Mar) Seafood is the order of the day here, be it char-grilled squid on a bed of salad leaves or a less exotic (but equally delicious) grilled sole.

Captain's Cabin (☎ 452520; 170-172 High St; mains around £7) This cosy waterfront restaurant serves a mix of dishes from breaded plaice fillet to sausages and mash. Again, seafood is the obvious choice.

Lighthouse (☎ 453377; 77 High St; mains £8-10) A celebrated Aldeburgh eatery, Lighthouse is supremely popular with visiting London-ers. The imaginative menu features a wide range of eclectic dishes, with a particular emphasis on – what else? – fish.

SOUTHWOLD
☎ 01502 / pop 3858

Southwold may have seen better days as a trading centre, but it's among the prettiest of resort towns on this stretch of coastline. It has also triumphed by being perched safely atop a cliff, where it prospered as a fishing town in the middle of the 16th century while many of its neighbours began to disappear into the ocean. Its gorgeous sandy beach is a perennial Blue Flag (ie clean beach) award winner.

The **TIC** (☎ 724729; 69 High St; ✆ 10am-5.30pm Mon-Sat, 11am-4pm Sun Apr-Sep, 10.30am-5pm Mon-Fri, 10.30am-5.30pm Sat Oct-Mar) is right in the heart of town.

The town's most interesting architectural landmark is the **Church of St Edmund** (Church St; admission free; ✆ 9am-6pm Jun-Aug, 9am-4pm Sep-May), a 15th-century building with a superbly proportioned nave.

The **Southwold Museum** (☎ 07890-300532; Victoria St; admission free; ✆ 10.30am-noon Aug & 2-4pm Apr-Oct) has a good display on the town's history, with a particular emphasis on the Battle of Solebay (1672), fought between the English, French and Dutch fleets just off the coast. There were 132 ships and 50,000 troops involved, so it must've been one hell of a fight.

And of course there is the **pier**, originally built in 1899. It hasn't had the luckiest of histories: it was badly damaged by storms in 1934, 1955 and 1979 before eventually closing in 1998 for safety reasons. It has since reopened after a complete renovation and now boasts the requisite selection of bars, fast-food outlets and amusement arcades.

Sleeping & Eating

Saxon House (☎ 723651; 86 Pier Ave; s/d from £45/60) This mock-Tudor house has bright, airy rooms that are clean and comfortable. It is about 100m from the pier.

Victoria House (☎ 722317; 9 Dunwich Rd; s/d £25/50) This homely, family-run place has spacious rooms that feel lived-in; the south-facing double has a balcony with sea views.

Dutch Barn (☎ 723172; 53 Ferry Rd; mains around £9; ✆ lunch & dinner, closed Mon) A former factory that fronts the beach and marshlands, this friendly place is a good spot for lunch or dinner (fish is recommended) or a pint at the elaborately carved wooden bar.

Red Lion (South Green) Southwold is home to the Adnams Brewery, and you should try some of its creamy ales in one of the town's pubs – this is a favourite.

Getting There & Away
First Eastern Counties buses stop here on the Ipswich to Great Yarmouth run.

NORFOLK

Norfolk thrived as an important economic centre during the Middle Ages, but things are quite a bit calmer these days – the county is more a haven for bird-watchers than businessmen. There are long, unspoilt stretches of coastline that beckon city-weary travellers to get away from it all, a distinct change from the over-the-top fun frenzies of other coastal resort areas. The famous Norfolk Broads, a series of waterways spread diagonally across the county, invite relaxing boating holidays and other outdoor activities.

On the other hand, the county town of Norwich is a lively urban centre, with a large student population – the University of East Anglia is here – and a hopping nightlife scene. The whole area is easily accessible from Cambridge.

Information
For a comprehensive guide to what's on in Norfolk, consult www.visitnorfolk.co.uk. See www.norfolkcoast.co.uk for information about visiting the coast. **Independent Traveller's Norfolk** (www.itnorfolk.co.uk) produces a free leaflet covering activities, hostels, campsites and local transport.

Activities
Several waymarked walking trails cross the county, the best known being the **Peddars Way** and **Norfolk Coast Path** national trail, mentioned under Activities, p449. Other long routes include the **Weavers Way**, a 57-mile walk from Cromer to Great Yarmouth via Blickling and Stalham, and the **Angles Way**, which follows the valleys of the Rivers Waveney and Little Ouse for 70 miles.

The **Around Norfolk Walk** is a 220-mile circuit that combines the Peddars Way and

Norfolk Coast Path, the Weavers Way and the Angles Way. Any of these routes can be followed for just an hour or two or a day or two, and TICs have leaflets, route maps and other inspirational literature for walkers – and even more material for cyclists.

Getting Around
Two places to call for information are the **County public transport phone line** (☎ 08453-006116) and the **Norfolk Bus Information Centre** (NORBIC; ☎ 01603-285007).

NORWICH
☎ 01603 / pop 194,839
Norfolk's county town (pronounced nor-ritch), once England's largest outside London, is an attractive and energetic urban centre, with cobbled streets dashing up and down among pubs, castles and cathedrals. There's always something interesting to see at the open-air market in the centre square, and the University of East Anglia campus provides a core of youth culture and budget-friendly eating and drinking. Today, the urban landscape demonstrates an appreciation for Norwich's historic relics combined with an understanding that time must move on – witness the shopping mall and modern art gallery grafted onto the Norwich Castle Museum.

History
The East Angles built the village of Northwic on a gravel terrace above the River Wensum, and by the time a bunch of marauding Danes sacked the new-and-improved town of Norwich in 1004, it was already an important market centre. Shortly after their invasion in 1066, the Normans built the splendid castle keep, now the best-preserved example in the country. In 1336 Edward III encouraged Flemish weavers to settle here; their arrival helped establish the wool industry that would ensure Norwich's provincial importance until the end of the 18th century, when it was overtaken by the growing industrial cities of the north.

Norwich's links with the Low Countries were further strengthened in the 16th century, when mass immigration flooded the town with more weavers and textile workers. In 1579 more than a third of the town's 16,000 citizens were foreigners (of a staunch

EASTERN ENGLAND

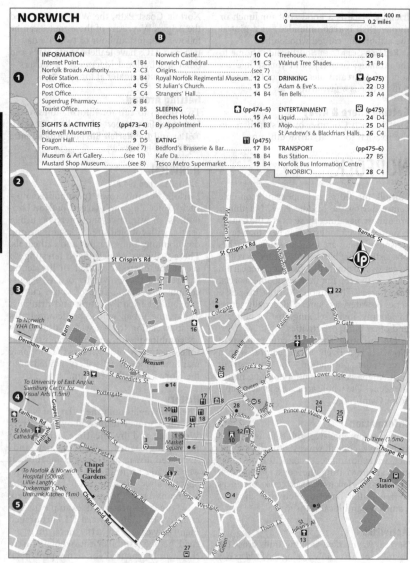

NORWICH

0 _____ 400 m
0 _____ 0.2 miles

INFORMATION	
Internet Point	1 B4
Norfolk Broads Authority	2 C3
Police Station	3 B4
Post Office	4 C5
Post Office	5 C4
Superdrug Pharmacy	6 B4
Tourist Office	7 B5

SIGHTS & ACTIVITIES	(pp473–4)
Bridewell Museum	8 C4
Dragon Hall	9 D5
Forum	(see 7)
Museum & Art Gallery	(see 10)
Mustard Shop Museum	(see 8)

Norwich Castle	10 C4
Norwich Cathedral	11 C3
Origins	(see 7)
Royal Norfolk Regimental Museum	12 C4
St Julian's Church	13 C5
Strangers' Hall	14 B4

SLEEPING	(pp474–5)
Beeches Hotel	15 A4
By Appointment	16 B3

EATING	(p475)
Bedford's Brasserie & Bar	17 B4
Kafe Da	18 B4
Tesco Metro Supermarket	19 B4

Treehouse	20 B4
Walnut Tree Shades	21 B4

DRINKING	(p475)
Adam & Eve's	22 D3
Ten Bells	23 A4

ENTERTAINMENT	(p475)
Liquid	24 D4
Mojo	25 D4
St Andrew's & Blackfriars Halls	26 C4

TRANSPORT	(pp475–6)
Bus Station	27 B5
Norfolk Bus Information Centre (NORBIC)	28 C4

Protestant stock, which proved beneficial during the Civil War, as the town's close ties with the parliamentary cause ensured that Norwich saw virtually no strife).

Modern Norwich remains one of England's most important centres of footwear manufacturing, and one of the country's largest agricultural and livestock markets.

Orientation

The castle is in the centre of Norwich. Below the castle lies what has been described as the most complete remaining medieval English city. Clustered around the castle and the Anglican cathedral, within the circle of river and city walls, are more than 30 parish churches. The Roman

Catholic cathedral lies to the west of the centre.

At the heart of the city is the **market** (Market Sq; ☺ around 8am-4.30pm), a patchwork of stall awnings known as tilts. This is one of the biggest and longest-running markets in the country. It was moved here 900 years ago from its original site in Tombland by what is now the Anglican cathedral.

Information
Internet Point (☎ 760808; Row B of the market; per 15min £1)
Norfolk & Norwich Hospital (☎ 286286; Wessex St)
Police station (☎ 768769; Bethel St)
Post office Central (☎ 220228; 13-17 Bank Plain); City South (☎ 761635; 84-85 Castle Mall)
Superdrug Pharmacy (☎ 619179; 25 Gentleman's Walk; ☺ 8.30am-6pm Mon-Sat)
TIC (☎ 727927; www.norwich.gov.uk; ☺ 10am-6pm Mon-Sat & 10.30am-4pm Sun Apr-Oct, 10am-5.30pm Mon-Sat Nov-Mar) Just inside the Forum on Millennium Plain.

Sights
NORWICH CASTLE MUSEUM & ART GALLERY
The massive Norman castle keep was built in about 1160 and measures 28m square by 21m high – a solid sentinel on the hill overlooking the medieval and modern cities. It's the best surviving example of Norman military architecture after the Tower of London and has worn pretty well, although it was refaced in 1834.

Bizarrely, **Norwich castle** (☎ 493636; castle & museum adult £3.50, art gallery & natural history exhibit £3, castle, museum & art gallery £5.25; ☺ 10.30am-6.30pm Mon-Sat Jun-Sep, 10.30am-4.30pm Oct-May) has had a gigantic shopping centre grafted onto it, an embodiment of Norwich's quirky blend of modern and historic. A major refurbishment to the historic side of things did wonders for the castle's **museum** and **art gallery**.

You have a choice of what to see: you can buy one ticket that grants you access to the castle keep and the museum – which has well-presented and documented exhibits of natural history and Norfolk archaeology – or you can opt for the art gallery and the bit of the museum devoted to natural history. We recommend the latter, partly because the gallery houses the paintings of the Norwich School. Founded by John Crome in the early 19th century, this group painted local landscapes and won acclaim throughout Europe.

Also on the premises, more specifically in the Shirehall (entrance opposite the Anglia TV station), is the **Royal Norfolk Regimental Museum** (☎ 493649; adult £2; ☺ 10am-5pm Mon-Sat, 2-5pm Sun), detailing the history of the local regiment since 1830.

THE FORUM & ORIGINS
Built with funds obtained from the National Lottery, the extraordinary all-glass, horseshoe-shaped **Forum** (Millennium Plain) is the most impressive building to hit Norwich's skyline in many decades. It is three storeys high and home to Norfolk's largest library, a number of cafés, the TIC and a couple of shops.

Origins (☎ 727920; adult £5; ☺ 10am-6pm Mon-Sat, 10.30am-4.30pm Sun), in the same building as the Forum, is an interactive museum devoted to 2000 years of Norfolk and Norwich history, where kids get to try their hand at speaking the original Norfolk dialect (not easy) and flooding the Norfolk Fens. A 40m-long, two-storey-high screen shows 180-degree images of the area's past, a particularly enthralling experience for children. It's not an in-depth look at the area's history, but it's a lot of fun and sure to impress.

ELM HILL
Thanks to an imaginative restoration, this **street** has retained its medieval charm and atmosphere and is, appropriately enough, the centre of the local antique business. It's one of the most attractive parts of the city. From here walk down Wensum St to Tombland, where the market was originally located. 'Tomb' is an old Norse word for 'empty' – hence space for a market.

NORWICH CATHEDRAL
The focal point of the city, the Anglican **cathedral** (☎ 764385; admission free; ☺ 7.30am-7pm May-Sep, 7.30am-6pm Oct-Apr) has retained the appearance and characteristics of a great Anglo-Norman abbey church more than any other English cathedral except Durham (p622).

The foundation stone was laid in 1096, and the building took 40 years to complete. In 1463 it was made fireproof by means of a magnificent stone lierne vault (a kind of inside roof) that, with its sculpted bosses, is one of the finest achievements of English medieval masonry.

As you enter the cathedral through the western door, the first thing that strikes you is the length of the nave. Its 14 bays are constructed in yellow-beige stone. Above, on the amazing vault, stories from the Old and New Testament are carved into the bosses. Beyond the tower, which is richly patterned, is probably the most beautiful part of the cathedral – the eastern section.

At the eastern end, outside the War Memorial Chapel, is the grave of Edith Cavell, a Norfolk nurse who was shot by the Germans in Belgium during WWI for helping POWs to escape.

The cathedral close contains some handsome houses and the old chapel of the King Edward VI School (where Admiral Horatio Nelson was educated). Its current students make up the choir, which usually performs in at least one of the three services held daily here.

ST JULIAN'S CHURCH
Tucked away in a tiny alley is **St Julian's Church** (☎ 624738; St Julian's Alley; admission free; ☯ 7.30am-5.30pm Apr-Sep, 7.30am-4pm Oct-Mar), where a shrine to Julian of Norwich is a centre for pilgrimage. Julian (also known as Juliana, 1342–c1416) wrote down her religious visions in a collection called *The Revelations of Divine Love*, which is unparalleled in English literature for its clarity and depth of perception. Although she was never beatified, she is still considered a saint. This is because when she once questioned her place in the world, God supposedly appeared to her and spoke the words 'All shall be well'. Pilgrims have been visiting her shrine for centuries, though the cell where she wrote the book was torn down during the Reformation, and pilgrims have had to content themselves with a small chapel that was built after WWII.

OTHER MUSEUMS
About 200m north of the castle are three museums in the same area. The **Mustard Shop museum** (☎ 627889; 15 Royal Arcade; admission free; ☯ 9.30am-5pm Mon-Sat, 11am-4pm bank holidays, closed Sun) tells the story of Colman's Mustard, a famous local product.

Nearby is **Bridewell Museum** (☎ 667227; Bridewell Alley; adult £4.95; ☯ 10am-5pm Mon-Sat), which has surprisingly interesting displays of local industries throughout the past 200

years. Formerly a merchant's house, in the 14th century it served as an open prison for vagrants (a bridewell).

Strangers' Hall (☎ 629127; adult £2.50; ☯ 9am-5pm Mon-Sat) is 250m west of Bridewell Museum, along St Andrew's St and Charing Cross. It's a medieval town house with rooms furnished in period styles from Tudor to Victorian. Highlights include the stone vaulted undercroft, dating from 1320, the fine Georgian dining room and the Tudor great hall with its stone-mullioned window and screen. Tours take a maximum of 15 people and run at 11am, 1pm and 3pm Wednesday and Saturday (adult £2.50).

Dragon Hall (☎ 663922; www.dragonhall.org; 115-123 King St; adult £2.50; ☯ 10am-4pm Mon-Sat Apr-Oct, 10am-4pm Mon-Fri Nov-Mar) is another medieval town house with a superb crown-post roof and an impressive, timber-framed great hall. It's named for the intricately carved dragon that roars down from its ceiling beams.

SAINSBURY CENTRE FOR VISUAL ARTS
To the west of the city, on the university campus (a 20-minute bus trip from Castle Meadow), the **Sainsbury Centre** (www.uea.ac.uk/scva; adult £2; ☯ 11am-5pm Tue-Sun) is remarkable both for the building itself and for the art it contains. It was designed by Norman Foster and is filled with an eclectic collection of works by Picasso, Henry Moore, Francis Bacon and Alberto Giacometti, displayed beside art from Africa, the Pacific and the Americas. At the time of writing, the centre was undergoing restoration and was due to reopen in late 2005.

Sleeping
Most of the B&Bs and cheaper hotels are outside the ring road, along Earlham and Unthank Rds to the west, and around the train station. The closer the B&Bs along Earlham Rd are to the town centre, the more expensive they are.

By Appointment (☎ 630730; 25-29 St George's St; s/d from £70/95) One of our favourite hotels in all of eastern England, By Appointment may have an odd name, but the 15th-century heritage-listed building has some of the most beautifully appointed rooms you'll find anywhere in the region. Lodgings are above the restaurant – just *try* to resist the aromas in the kitchen. It's a small and well-loved place, so book ahead.

Beeches Hotel (☎ 621167; reception@beeches.co.uk; 2-6 Earlham Rd; s/d from £65/85; **P**) Luxury accommodation in three separate Grade II–listed Victorian houses, collectively known as the Beeches. They're all terrific, but try to get a room in the Plantation, if only because of its wonderful garden.

Norwich YHA Hostel (☎ 08707705976; norwich@yha .org.uk; 112 Turner Rd; dm from £10; ☺ Apr-Oct) Two miles from the train station on the edge of the city, this hostel runs the Rent-a-Hostel scheme from November to March, which caters to large groups only; phone for information. In addition to dorm beds, there are family rooms with two to six beds.

Georgian House Hotel (☎ 615655; reception@ georgian-hotel.co.uk; 32-34 Unthank Rd; s/d from £55/80; **P**) In a sprawling, elegant Victorian house opposite St John's Roman Catholic Cathedral, this 28-room boutique hotel features clean-lined, modern design in the rooms and a tree-lined hilltop location. The award-winning restaurant emphasises ecofriendly ingredients.

Eating

CAFÉS & RESTAURANTS

Walnut Tree Shades (☎ 620166; Old Post Office Ct) This fabulous little restaurant in the city centre specialises in all things beefy; the steak Diane (£12.50) will have carnivores drooling.

Treehouse (☎ 763258; 14 Dove St; mains around £5-6.50; ☺ Mon-Sat) Nut-and-moonbeam pâté is but one of the quirky delicacies served at this excellent vegetarian restaurant, located above a health-food shop. Main courses come in two sizes at two prices.

Kafe Da (☎ 622836; 18 Bedford St; dishes £4.50-7) A trendy café themed around international espionage – the subs are named after Bond movies, the sandwiches after Russian leaders – it turns into a cool bar at night.

Bedford's Brasserie & Bar (☎ 666869; 1 Old Post Office Yard; mains £6-7) Almost opposite Kafe Da, Bedford's menu features sautéed king prawns with chilli jam in a light puff pastry – not exactly your run-of-the-mill pub grub!

QUICK EATS & SELF-CATERING

There's a convenient **Tesco Metro supermarket** (Market Sq) for self-catering. **Zuckerman's Deli** (Unthank Rd) is also excellent for takeaway items – the sausage rolls are legendary.

Next door, the Unthank Kitchen does an incredible hangover-curing English breakfast (£3 to £5).

Drinking

Adam & Eve's (Bishop Gate) This sunken-floored cute, tiny, stone pub is a haven for serious beer drinkers.

Ten Bells (76 St Benedict's St) This student-friendly pub has an instantly comfortable worn-in feel, with its ratty red velvet, eclectic signs and red phone booth in the corner.

Lillie Langtry (Unthank Rd) Another lively student hang-out, this pub is one of several lined up in a funky little alternative neighbourhood near the university.

Entertainment

NIGHTCLUBS

Norwich's club scene is the only one in East Anglia to rival Cambridge. All nightclubs run from 9pm or 10pm to at least 2am.

Time (☎ 767649; Riverside; admission £2-5) About a mile west of town on the Yare is the biggest club in Norwich, with a capacity of 1700. The music is hard house and crowd-pleasing dance anthems. Admission varies depending on the night. Trainers and jeans are no-nos.

Several clubs line Prince of Wales Rd, including **Liquid** (☎ 611113; Prince of Wales Rd; admission £5), with a suitable soundtrack of techno and hard house, and **Mojo** (☎ 622533; 62 Prince of Wales Rd; admission £4), which features soul, break-beats, hip-hop and R&B.

THEATRE

St Andrew's & Blackfriars' Halls (☎ 628477; St Andrew's Plain) Once home to Dominican Blackfriars, this spookily Gothic-looking complex now serves as an impressive civic centre where concerts, antique and craft markets, the Music and Arts Festival and even the annual beer festival are held; there's also a café in the crypt.

Getting There & Away

National Express has a daily bus to London (£15, three hours). First Eastern Counties runs hourly buses to King's Lynn (1½ hours) and Peterborough (two hours and 40 minutes); and half-hourly buses to Cromer (one hour). There are five buses daily to Bury St Edmunds (1½ hours) and an hourly service to Great Yarmouth (45 minutes).

EASTERN ENGLAND

There are hourly rail services to King's Lynn (45 minutes) and Ely (1¼ hours). To get to Cambridge you'll need to go via Ely.

NORFOLK BROADS

Bird-watchers and river rats will find paradise in the vast network of navigable rivers, lakes and marshes of the Norfolk Broads. Home to several wildlife reserves and bird sanctuaries, the Broads are a protected area of 117 sq miles in eastern Norfolk. Its wide-open, arguably desolate wilderness makes it ideal for bird-watching – not a lot can get between your binoculars and your feathered friends. Fans of water sports will find a variety of activities, from slow river cruises to freshwater lakes to bogs and marshes, along with an array of wildlife that inhabits them.

One of the top bird-watching places in Britain is here, at Cley Marshes, between Cromer and Wells. It boasts more than 300 recorded species of birds. The **visitors centre** (☎ 740008) is built on high ground for good views. But the best spot for bird-watching is among the reeds, where there are some excellent hides.

Orientation

The Broads form a triangle, with the Norwich–Cromer road, the Norwich–Lowestoft road and the coastline as the three sides.

Wroxham, on the A1151 from Norwich, and Potter Heigham, on the A1062 from Wroxham, are the main centres. Along the way there are plenty of waterside pubs, villages and market towns where you can stock up on provisions, and stretches of river where you can feel you are the only person around.

Information

The **Broads Authority** (☎ 01603-610734; www.broads -authority.gov.uk; Thomas Harvey House, 18 Colegate, Norwich NR3 1BQ) has details on conservation centres and Royal Society for the Protection of Birds bird-watching hides at Berney Marshes, Bure Marshes, Cockshoot Broad, Hickling Broad, Horsey Mere, How Hill, Ranworth, Strumpshaw Fen and Surlingham Church Marsh.

Getting Around

Two companies that operate boating holidays are **Blakes** (☎ 01603-782911; www.blakes.co.uk) and **Hoseasons** (☎ 01502-501010; www.hose asons.co .uk). Costs depend on the boat size, the time of year and the length of the holiday. A boat for two to four people costs £525 to £850 (depending on the season and type of boat) for a week including fuel and insurance. Short breaks (three to four days) during the off season are much cheaper.

Many boat yards (particularly in the Wroxham and Potter Heigham areas) have a variety of boats for hire by the hour, half-day or full day. These include the traditional flat-bottomed boats known as wherries. Charges still vary according to the season and the size of the boat, but they start from £12 for one hour, £32 for four hours and £50 for one day.

No previous experience is necessary to use the boats, but remember to stay on the right-hand side of the river, that the rivers are tidal, and to stick to the speed limit – you can be prosecuted for speeding.

If you don't feel like piloting your own boat, **Broads Tours** Wroxham (☎ 01603-782207; the

---

THE ORIGIN OF THE BROADS

For many years the origin of the Norfolk Broads was unclear. The rivers were undoubtedly natural, and many thought the lakes were, too – it's hard to believe they're not when you see them – but no-one could explain how they were formed.

The mystery was solved when records were discovered in the remains of St Benet's Abbey (on the River Bure). They showed that from the 12th century certain parts of land in Hoveton Parish were used for peat digging. The area had little woodland, and the only source of fuel was peat. Since East Anglia was well populated and prosperous, peat digging became a major industry.

Over a period of about 200 years approximately 1040 hectares were dug up. However, water gradually seeped through, causing marshes, and later lakes, to develop. The first broad to be mentioned in records is Ranworth Broad in 1275. Eventually, the amount of water made it extremely difficult for the diggers, and the peat-cutting industry died out. In no other area of England has human effort changed the natural landscape so dramatically.

Bridge); Potter Heigham (☎ 01692-670711; Herbert Woods) runs 1½-hour **pleasure trips** (adult/child £5.80/4.20) from April to September, with a commentary.

GREAT YARMOUTH
☎ 01493 / pop 66,788

You'll either love or despise Great Yarmouth, and it won't take you long to make up your mind. Norfolk's most popular seaside resort has gone the way of so many others – it's packed with amusement arcades, greasy spoon cafés and cheap B&Bs, and rivers of holiday-makers flow through its main streets towards the beach. If that spells 'ideal holiday' to you, you'll be in heaven; the vast beaches and long boardwalk demand strolling around with an ice-cream cone, checking out the scene. There is also a number of interesting buildings in the old town, and near the train station is a handy entry point to the Weaver's Way, a highly recommended walk that cuts through the Broads along the River Yare to Acle and then Potter Heigham. To find it, go around behind the train station and follow the tracks to the highway underpass; there's a bird-watching point and the beginning of the path just beyond it. The TIC sells a detailed map (75p).

The **TIC** (☎ 846345; ❤ 9am-5pm Mon-Fri) is in the town hall in the centre of town. There's also another **TIC** (☎ 842195; Marine Pde; ❤ 9.30am-5.30pm Easter–end Sep).

The **Elizabethan House Museum** (☎ 745526; South Quay; adult £2.70; ❤ 10am-5pm Sun-Fri) was a merchant's house and now contains a display of 19th-century domestic life. The **Tolhouse Museum** (☎ 858900; Tolhouse St; adult £1.50; ❤ 10am-5pm Mon-Fri, 1.15-5pm Sat & Sun) was once the town's courthouse and jail; prison cells can be seen, and there's a display covering the town's history. There's also a small **maritime museum** (Marine Pde) near the TIC. It has the same opening hours and admission prices as the Tolhouse.

The **Norfolk Nelson Museum** (☎ 850698; 26 South Quay; adult £2.50; ❤ 10am-5pm Mon-Fri) opened in 2002 to celebrate the life and times of the one-eyed hero of Trafalgar, who was a regular visitor to Great Yarmouth (the town seems proud of having erected their statue, on the South Denes, in 1819 – beating London by 24 years).

Also worth checking out is the **Maritime Festival**, which takes place on the sensitively restored South Quay in September. Celebrating the town's rich seafaring heritage, it is a weekend-long shindig of music, crafts and visiting vessels.

There are numerous B&Bs up and down Trafalgar St, and **Great Yarmouth Youth Hostel** (☎ 0870 770 5840; fax 856600; 2 Sandown Rd; dm £10.25) is three-quarters of a mile from the train station, near the beach.

Great Yarmouth has bus and rail connections to Norwich: First Eastern Counties runs an hourly bus service (£2.85, 45 minutes); Wherry Lines runs trains roughly every half-hour (£4.30, 25 minutes) daily except Sunday, when there are hourly departures between 8.20am and 5.20pm only.

CROMER
☎ 01263

Seeming much more remote than Yarmouth, Cromer was the most fashionable resort on the coast during the late Victorian and Edwardian eras. It's now somewhat rundown, but attractively so. With its elevated seafront, long sandy beach and scenic coastal walks, it's well worth visiting. Cromer has long been famous for its crabs, and they're still caught and sold here.

If you hear strange noises while you're strolling by the seaside, there's an explanation. During the 14th century the nearby village of Shipden was washed into the sea. In stormy weather, locals say, you can still hear the bells ringing from the submerged tower of the Church of St Peters.

The **TIC** (☎ 512497; ❤ 9.30am-6pm Mon-Sat, 9.30am-5pm Sun mid-Jul–Aug, 10am-5pm Mon-Sat Sep–mid-Jul) is by the bus station.

Two miles southwest of Cromer, **Felbrigg Hall** (☎ 837444; adult £6.30; ❤ 1-5pm Sat-Wed Mar-Oct) is one of the finest 17th-century houses in Norfolk. It contains a collection of 18th-century furniture; outside is an orangery walled garden, and landscaped park.

The TIC can point you to local accommodation, but one top choice is the **White Cottage** (☎ 512728; 9 Cliff Dr; s/d from £30/60), a family-run B&B just a short walk from the town centre, up the hill along the coastal path between the pier and the lighthouse. Rooms are plush, and the panoramic views are tremendous.

Cromer is one of the few coastal resorts with a train station linked to Norwich. There's 13 trains daily Monday to Saturday and six on Sunday (£3.40, 45 minutes). First Eastern Counties has a half-hourly bus from Norwich (one hour).

BURNHAM DEEPDALE
☎ 01485

This gorgeous place actually consists of two villages – it includes the hamlet of Brancaster Staithe, which frequently causes some confusion. There's not much to either of the villages – it takes longer to say their names than to drive through them lengthwise. But that's not to say there's nothing to see. The area's stunningly beautiful and there's plenty to do, including all kinds of water sports, walking and cycling. Topping that, one of England's best backpacker hostels is here.

Picking up the Norfolk Coastal Path just across the main road from the Deepdale Granary (see p478), you can go either east or west for as long as you like. If you head west, you'll soon reach **Northshore Sports & Leisure** (☎ 210236; the Boatyard, Brancaster Staithe), which can fulfil all your equipment needs, from kayaking to windsurfing.

The **TIC** (☎ 210256; 10am-4pm Thu-Mon) has plenty of information on activities and places to visit in the surrounding area, and also runs a free accommodation booking service. For information on the area, go to www.burn hamdeepdale.co.uk or www.itnorfolk.co.uk.

The big event in town is the **Deepdale Jazz Festival** (☎ 210256; www.deepdalejazzfestival.co.uk; tickets £7-10), at the time of research being held annually in mid-June, featuring regional bands, beer and barbecue, among other things.

Marsh Barn (☎ 210036) is half a mile east of town, just off the A149 coast road. The four barns are used for a variety of local events, including art exhibitions and lectures.

A hostel and a half, **Deepdale Granary** (☎ 210 256; deepdaleinformation@deepdalefarm.co.uk; dm weekday/ weekend £10.50/12.50) is a marvellous place spread across converted 17th-century stables and a barn. There's a good little coffee shop attached, camping in an adjoining field, a laundry, lounges, a library, picnic tables and Internet access (£1 per hour). The management runs a wide variety of tours and is a good source of local information; it's worth popping in to the office for reconnaissance, whether you're staying at the hostel or not.

There are two pubs, both in Brancaster along the main road heading west: the **White Horse** (☎ 210262; www.whitehorsebrancaster.co.uk) is a

more sedate, upscale place with a fine-food menu, while the **Jolly Sailors** (www.jollysailors.co .uk) is a more vivacious, late-night-drinking kind of pub, with a great outdoor patio and a small TV room for children.

The nearest train station is King's Lynn. Bus No 411 runs here (£1.40, 15 minutes) from Cromer.

KING'S LYNN
☎ 01553 / pop 40,921

Grown out of an unlikely combination of staunchly pious citizens and wild-and-woolly sailors, King's Lynn was once among England's most important medieval ports. Its location, about 3 miles from the sea on the River Great Ouse, made it a handy base for fishing fleets, and the number of religious devotees among its residents kept the fishing crews from getting out of hand. The old town is still a fascinating mixture of these elements, and Lynn is still a port today, though much less busy than it once was.

There are three market days a week: Tuesday (the major market, with everything from clothing to bric-a-brac to fish), Friday (with a limited selection of flowers and vegetables) and Saturday (a food market selling fish, fruit, flowers and vegetables). The Tuesday market takes place in the suitably named Tuesday Market Pl, while the Friday and Saturday markets are held in Saturday Market Pl, in front of St Margaret's Church. The markets open by 8am and usually run until 4pm, depending on the weather. In July there's the popular King's Lynn Festival of Music and the Arts.

Orientation
The old town lies along the eastern bank of the river. The train station is on the eastern side of the town. Uninspiring modern King's Lynn and the bus station are between them.

Information
Jai Chemists (☎ 772828; 68 High St; 9am-5.30pm Mon-Sat)
Police station (☎ 691211; St James Rd)
Post office (☎ 692185; Baxter's Plain; 9am-5.30pm Mon-Fri, 9am-12.30pm Sat)
Queen Elizabeth Hospital (☎ 613613; Gayton Rd)
TIC (☎ 819440; kings-lynn.tic@west-norfolk.gov.uk; 9.15am-5pm Mon-Sat & 10am-5pm Sun Apr-Oct, 10.30am-4pm daily Nov-Mar) In the Custom House (Purfleet Quay).

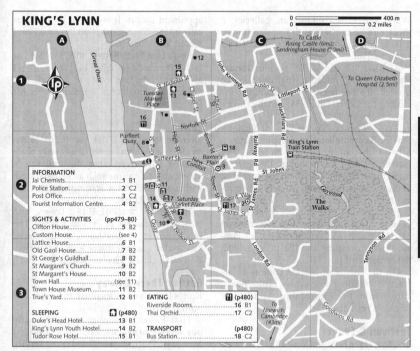

KING'S LYNN

0 — 400 m
0 — 0.2 miles

To Castle
Rising Castle (6mi);
Sandringham House (10mi)

To Queen Elizabeth
Hospital (2.5mi)

King's Lynn
Train Station

Tuesday
Market
Place

Purfleet
Quay

The
Walks

To
Norwich;
Cambridge
(43mi)

INFORMATION
Jai Chemists.................................**1** B1
Police Station...............................**2** C2
Post Office...................................**3** C2
Tourist Information Centre............**4** B2

SIGHTS & ACTIVITIES   (pp479–80)
Clifton House...............................**5** B2
Custom House.........................(see 4)
Lattice House..............................**6** B1
Old Gaol House...........................**7** B2
St George's Guildhall....................**8** B2
St Margaret's Church....................**9** B2
St Margaret's House....................**10** B2
Town Hall...............................(see 11)
Town House Museum..................**11** B2
True's Yard................................**12** B1

SLEEPING   (p480)
Duke's Head Hotel......................**13** B1
King's Lynn Youth Hostel............**14** B2
Tudor Rose Hotel........................**15** B1

EATING   (p480)
Riverside Rooms.........................**16** B1
Thai Orchid...............................**17** C2

TRANSPORT   (p480)
Bus Station................................**18** C2

EASTERN ENGLAND

Sights

Little remains of the original buildings, but
St Margaret's Church, founded in 1100 with
a Benedictine priory, is impressive for its
size (72m long) and contains two Flemish
brasses that are among the best examples
in the country. By the west door there are
flood-level marks – 1976 was the highest,
but the 1953 flood claimed more lives.

On the corner of St Margaret's Lane,
and dating back to the 15th century, is a
restored building that was once the warehouse or 'steelyard' of the Hanseatic League
(the Northern European merchants' group).
Now known as **St Margaret's House**, it is home
to a number of civic offices. In theory, access is restricted to those offices alone, but
you can wander in and have a look at the
interior. If there's a group of you, you're
better off seeking permission by calling the
Education League (☎ 669200).

Across Queen St is the **town hall**, dating
back to 1421. Next to it is the **Town House
Museum** (☎ 773450; 46 Queen St; adult £2; ☼ 10am-
5pm Mon-Sat, 2-5pm Sun May-Sep, 10am-4pm Mon-Sat
Oct-Apr). Inside you'll find exhibits charting

life in the town from the Middle Ages up
to the 1950s.

Next door, the **Old Gaol House** (☎ 774297;
adult £2; ☼ 10am-5pm Mon-Sat & 2-5pm Sun Easter-Oct,
10am-6pm daily Nov-Easter) has been converted
into a tourist attraction with self-guided
audio tours. The town's priceless civic
treasures, including the 650-year-old King
John Cup, can be seen in the basement. Last
entry is at 4.15pm.

Further down Queen St is **Clifton House**,
with its quirky barley-sugar columns and
waterfront tower, which was used by merchants to scan the river for returning ships.
Its interior is in dire need of restoration,
so access is restricted to groups organised
by the TIC.

Opposite the market square is **Purfleet
Quay**, in its heyday the principal harbour.
The quaint building with the lantern tower
is the **Custom House** (housing the TIC), which
dates back to 1683.

St George's Guildhall (☎ 767557) is the largest surviving 15th-century guildhall in England. It has served as a warehouse, theatre,
courthouse and armoury (during the Civil

War), and now contains art galleries, a theatre, a restaurant and a coffee house. This is the focal point of the annual King's Lynn festival.

At King St's end is the spacious **Tuesday Market Pl**, which fulfils its original role once a week. It's bordered by old buildings, including the Corn Hall (1854) and the Duke's Head Hotel (1689).

Across Tuesday Market Pl on St Nicholas St is the **Tudor Rose Hotel** (see Sleeping, below), a late-15th-century house with some very interesting features, including the original main door. North of here, on the corner of St Ann's St, is **True's Yard**, where the two remaining cottages of the 19th-century fishing community that used to be here have been restored and now house a **folk museum** (☎ 770479; adult £2.50; 🕙 10am-5pm Apr-Sep, 10am-4pm Oct-Mar) detailing the life of a shellfish fisherman around 1850.

On the corner of Market Lane is an attractive building known as **Lattice House**, dating from the 15th century, which now houses a restaurant.

Festivals & Events

The **King's Lynn Festival of Music & the Arts** – East Anglia's most important cultural gathering – was the brainchild of Lady Ruth Fermoy and offers a diverse programme of concerts and recitals of all kinds of 'serious' music, from medieval ballads to Jamaican jazz.

It usually takes place in the last week of July. There are also lectures and plays (Molière featured in the 2002 festival). Since 2001 the main festival has been preceded by the **Festival Too**, which usually takes place in and around Tuesday Market Pl and puts the spotlight squarely on rock and pop music.

For information on programmed events, contact the **administrative office** (☎ 767557; enquiries@klfestival.freeserve.co.uk) or the **box office** (☎ 764864).

Sleeping

Duke's Head Hotel (☎ 774996; Tuesday Market Pl; s/d from £55/95) This fine classical building overlooking the market is the town's top hotel. It has classy parlour sitting rooms, all of which are furnished in antiques.

Tudor Rose Hotel (☎ 762824; kltudorrose@aol.com; St Nicholas St; s/d from £30/60) Tucked away just off the market square is this 15th-century house, which comes with modern, well-

appointed rooms. It is located in a historically interesting building that has a well-preserved lobby/bar area.

King's Lynn Youth Hostel (☎ 0870 770 5902; fax 764312; Thoresby College, College Lane; dm £9.25; 🕙 1 Jul–31 Aug & varied times rest of year) is excellently located. Call to check opening times for September to June.

Eating

Riverside Rooms (☎ 773134; lunch £8.25-13.95, dinner £14.95-18; 🕙 lunch & dinner) This classy place right by the river, near the undercroft, serves upscale cuisine such as sea bass, lamb with apricots, and a scrumptious tomato and mozzarella tart.

Thai Orchid (☎ 767013; 33-39 St James St; lunch £6.95, dinner mains from £6; 🕙 lunch & dinner) The lunch buffet at this huge, atmospheric, kitsch-clad place features a rotating selection of 15 classic Thai dishes.

Getting There & Away

King's Lynn is 43 miles north of Cambridge on the A10.

First Eastern Counties runs an hourly bus service to Norwich (£4.85, 1½ hours) Monday to Saturday; on Sunday the service runs every two hours from 8.25am, with the last bus at 6.55pm.

There are hourly trains from Cambridge (£13.80, 50 minutes) and Norwich (£14.50, 45 minutes) to King's Lynn station.

AROUND KING'S LYNN
Castle Rising Castle

The amazingly well-preserved keep of this **castle** (☎ 631330; adult £3.75; 🕙 10am-6pm Apr-Oct, 10am-4pm Nov-Mar), built between 1138 and 1140, is set in the middle of a massive earthwork. It was once the home of Queen Isabella, who arranged the gruesome murder of her husband, Edward II, at Berkeley Castle in Gloucestershire. Watching the castle walls come into view as you pass through the stone gateway is genuinely transportive.

Bus No 411 runs here (£1.50, 19 minutes) every hour from King's Lynn bus station, 6 miles to the south.

Sandringham House

The Queen's country pile **Sandringham House** (☎ 772675; house, grounds & museum adult/child £6.50/4, grounds & museum only £4.50/2.50; 🕙 11am-

4.45pm Apr-Sep unless royal family is in residence) is set in 25 hectares of landscaped gardens and lakes, and it's open to the hoi polloi when the court is not at home.

Queen Victoria bought the house and an 8000-hectare estate in 1862 so as to give her son, the Prince of Wales (later Edward VII), somewhere to call his official residence, but he wasn't altogether happy with the Georgian building. Over the next eight years, the house was redesigned in the style that would eventually bear his name.

The current crop of royals spends about three weeks a year here from mid-July to the first week in August, but they don't have the run of the whole estate. About half of the remaining 7975 hectares is leased out to farm tenants (a royal living doesn't pay for itself, you know), while the remaining hectares are managed by the Crown Estate as forestry.

The house itself is home to a museum that contains a collection of vintage cars, photographs from the last 100 years and other royal memorabilia. There are guided tours of the formal gardens on Friday and Saturday at 2pm.

There is also a yearly programme of special events, including a craft fair in September. Check with the office for details of upcoming events or write to Sandringham House, the Estate Office, Sandringham, Norfolk PE35 6EN.

First Eastern Counties bus No 411 (which also goes to Castle Rising Castle) runs here from King's Lynn bus station (£1.80, 25 minutes), 10 miles to the southwest.

LINCOLNSHIRE

Lincolnshire boasts one of the most welcoming and attractive county towns in England. It has a fine Gothic cathedral that dramatically crowns a steep hilltop, and is surrounded by a medieval core of shops, cafés and serpentine cobblestone streets. Dotted across the rest of the county are smaller versions of the capital, historic villages whose beautiful parish churches and well-maintained centres are clear evidence of Lincolnshire's former status as an economic leader in the wool trade.

The landscape of Lincolnshire varies considerably, from salt marshes in the east to the rolling hills of the Lincolnshire Wolds, garnished with small, pretty market towns. To the southeast are the flat Lincolnshire Fens, fertile agricultural land reclaimed from the sea. A network of rivers criss-crosses the whole area, making it a good place for water sports enthusiasts. The coastline to the east offers vast beaches, sand dunes and salt marshes. Throughout the county, Lincolnshire's trademark stone houses with their red-tiled roofs are a favourite among film companies looking for period settings. A bonus for walkers and cyclists: Lincolnshire receives only half the national average of rainfall, a fact that earned it the slogan 'the drier side of Britain'.

Activities

Lincolnshire is not renowned as a walking area, but if you want a long route from the sea to the Midlands in the footsteps of history, try the **Viking Way**, a 140-mile way-marked trail that runs from the Humber Bridge through the Lincolnshire Wolds to Oakham in Leicestershire. For a taster, you can focus on the section in the Lincolnshire Wolds and use the route as a base for a day walk.

Renting a bike in Lincoln, or bringing one with you, is an excellent idea. TICs stock sets of leaflets entitled *Lincolnshire Cycle Trails*.

Getting There & Away

Stamford and Lincoln are easily reached by bus from London. However, Lincolnshire is not quite on the well-trodden transport trail, and your best bet for getting here from the south is probably by train, although if you're planning to visit the county from Cambridge you'll most likely have to change in Peterborough.

Getting Around

For regional travel information, contact **Traveline** (☎ 0870 608 2608). Press option four.

LINCOLN

☎ 01522 / pop 104,221

Lincoln is buffered by some fairly drab modern suburbs, but it's worth making the effort to get to the historic centre's network of twisting cobblestone streets and half-timbered houses. The fine cathedral, massive and regal at the top of a hill, is

EASTERN ENGLAND

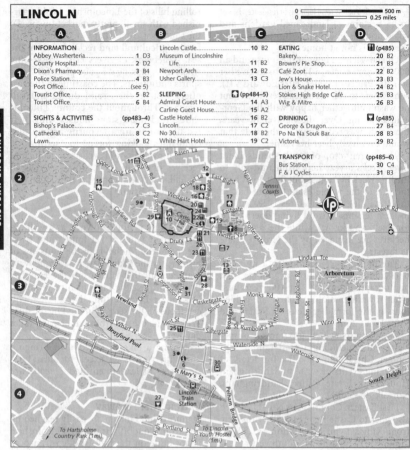

LINCOLN

0 ———— 500 m
0 ———— 0.25 miles

INFORMATION
Abbey Washerteria................ 1 D3
County Hospital.................... 2 D2
Dixon's Pharmacy.................. 3 B4
Police Station....................... 4 B3
Post Office.......................(see 5)
Tourist Office...................... 5 B2
Tourist Office...................... 6 B4

SIGHTS & ACTIVITIES (pp483–4)
Bishop's Palace..................... 7 C3
Cathedral............................ 8 C2
Lawn................................... 9 B2

Lincoln Castle....................... 10 B2
Museum of Lincolnshire
Life.................................. 11 B2
Newport Arch....................... 12 B2
Usher Gallery........................ 13 C3

SLEEPING (pp484–5)
Admiral Guest House............... 14 A3
Carline Guest House................ 15 A2
Castle Hotel......................... 16 B2
Lincoln................................ 17 C2
No 30................................. 18 B2
White Hart Hotel................... 19 C2

EATING (p485)
Bakery................................ 20 B2
Brown's Pie Shop................... 21 B3
Café Zoot............................ 22 B2
Jew's House.......................... 23 B3
Lion & Snake Hotel................. 24 B2
Stokes High Bridge Café........... 25 B3
Wig & Mitre......................... 26 B3

DRINKING (p485)
George & Dragon.................... 27 B4
Po Na Na Souk Bar.................. 28 B3
Victoria.............................. 29 B2

TRANSPORT (pp485–6)
Bus Station.......................... 30 C4
F & J Cycles.......................... 31 B3

900 years old and the third largest in England. Stretching from the cathedral down to the modern shopping district, and lined with some wonderful Tudor buildings, is one of the steepest urban climbs this side of San Francisco. The city's nightlife is vibrant, thanks to a youthful population and the presence of a university. But the nicest thing about spending time in Lincoln is that, perhaps because they aren't constantly overrun by tourists, the locals are consistently friendly and welcoming.

History
For the last 2000 years, most of Britain's invaders have recognised the potential of this site and made their mark. Lincoln's hill was of immense strategic importance, giving views for miles across the surrounding plain. Communications were found to be excellent – below it is the River Witham, navigable to the sea.

The Romans established a garrison and a town here that they called Lindum. In AD 71 it was given the status of a colonia (chartered town) – Lindum Colonia; hence Lincoln. Gracious public buildings were constructed, and Lincoln became a popular place for old soldiers past their prime to spend their twilight years.

The Normans began work on the castle in 1068 and the cathedral in 1072. In the 12th century the wool trade developed, and wealthy merchants established themselves.

The city was famous for the cloth known as Lincoln green, said to have been worn by Robin Hood. Many of the wealthiest merchants were Jews but, following the murder of a nine-year-old boy in 1255 for which one of their number was accused, they were mercilessly persecuted, and many were driven out.

During the Civil War the city passed from Royalist to Parliamentarian and back again, but it began to prosper as an agricultural centre in the 18th century. In the following century, after the arrival of the railway, Lincoln's engineering industry was established. Heavy machinery produced here included the world's first tank, which saw action in WWI.

Orientation

The cathedral stands imperiously on top of the hill in the centre of the old part of the city, with the castle and most of the other attractions located conveniently nearby. Three-quarters of a mile down from the cathedral (a 15-minute walk) lies the new town, and the bus and train stations. Joining the two is the appositely named Steep Hill, and believe us, they're not kidding. Even locals stop to catch their breath.

Information

Abbey Washeteria (☎ 530272; 197 Monks Rd; per load £5.50)

County hospital (☎ 573103) Found off Greetwell Rd, half a mile east of the visitors centre.

Dixon's Pharmacy (☎ 524821; 194 High St)

Police station (☎ 882222; West Pde)

Post office (☎ 526031; 90 Bailgate) Located next to the TIC.

TIC (tourism@lincoln.gov.uk) Main branch (☎ 873213; 9 Castle Hill; ⏰ 9am-5.30pm Mon-Fri & 10am-5pm Sat & Sun); Cornhill branch (☎ 873256; 21 the Cornhill; ⏰ 10am-5pm Mon-Sat)

Sights

LINCOLN CATHEDRAL

The county's greatest attraction is this superb **cathedral** (☎ 544544; www.lincolncathedral.com; adult £4; ⏰ 7.15am-8pm Mon-Sat, 7.15am-6pm Sun Jun-Aug, 7.15am-6pm Mon-Sat, 7.15am-5pm Sun Sep-May). Its three great towers dominate the city and can be seen from miles around. The central tower stands 81m high, which makes it the third highest in the country after Salisbury Cathedral (123m) and Liverpool's Anglican

Cathedral (101m). While this is impressive enough, imagine it twice as high, which it was until toppled by a storm in 1547.

Lincoln Cathedral was built on the orders of William the Conqueror, and construction began in 1072. It took only 20 years to complete the original building, which was 99m long with two western towers, but in 1185 an earthquake caused severe damage. Only the western front of the old cathedral survived. Rebuilding began under Bishop Hugh of Avalon (St Hugh), and most of the current building dates from the late 12th to late 13th centuries, in the Early English style.

The entrance is below the famous mid-12th-century frieze on the western front. Emerging into the nave, most people are surprised to find a substantial part of the cathedral empty, but this is actually how it would have looked back in 1250 when it was completed. Medieval cathedrals and churches, like mosques and Hindu temples today, did not have pews. This open area is now used for concerts and plays; services take place in St Hugh's choir. The stained glass in the nave is mostly Victorian, but the Belgian marble font dates back to the 11th century.

There are interesting stained-glass windows at each end of the transepts. The Dean's Eye contains glass that has been here since the 13th century; the glass in the Bishop's Eye dates from the 14th century. High above in the central tower, Great Tom is a 270kg bell that still sounds the hours.

St Hugh's Choir was the first section of the church to be rebuilt. The vaulting above is arranged at odd angles, but the canopied stalls of the choir are beautifully carved and over 600 years old.

The Angel Choir, named after the 28 angels carved high up the walls under the highest windows, was built as a shrine to St Hugh. Modern pilgrims search for the famous Lincoln Imp, a stonemason's joke that has become the city's emblem. The legend goes that this malevolent being was caught trying to chat up one of the angels and was turned to stone.

There are free one-hour tours of the cathedral at least twice a day; there are also less frequent tours of the tower (£4). You can listen to evensong in the cathedral daily except Wednesday at 5.15pm (3.45pm on Sunday), and Sung Eucharist at 9.30am on Sunday.

BISHOPS' PALACE

Just south of the cathedral are the impressive ruins of the medieval **Bishops' Palace** (☎ 527468; adult £3.50; ☺ 10am-6pm Apr-Sep, 10am-5pm Oct-Mar), which, had it not been gutted by parliamentary forces during the Civil War, would still be one of Lincoln's most imposing structures. It was begun in 1150 and in its day was the administrative centre of the largest diocese in England. The East Hall range, with its superb vaulted undercroft, was built by Bishop St Hugh around 1200 as his private residence. The walled terrace garden is part of English Heritage's Contemporary Heritage Gardens scheme, and affords lovely views of the town below.

LINCOLN CASTLE

Begun in 1068, just four years before the cathedral, **Lincoln Castle** (☎ 511068; adult/child £3.50/2; ☺ 9.30am-5.30pm Mon-Sat & 11am-5.30pm Sun Apr-Sep, 11am-4pm daily Oct-Mar) was built over the original Roman town and incorporates some of the old Roman walls. As well as the usual views from the battlements that you expect from a castle, the old prison is particularly interesting. Public executions used to draw crowds of up to 20,000 people, and took place in front of Cobb Hall, a horseshoe-shaped tower in the northeastern corner that served as the city's prison for centuries. The redbrick building on the eastern side replaced it and was used until 1878.

In the same building as the chapel, Lincoln's copy of the **Magna Carta** is on display. There are free tours of the castle at 11am and 2pm daily from April to September.

OTHER SIGHTS

The **Lawn** (☎ 873622; Union Rd; ☺ 9am-5pm Mon-Fri, 10am-5.30pm Sat & Sun Mar-Oct; shorter hrs Nov-Feb) is a former lunatic asylum that now houses a concert hall and several exhibition areas. The **Sir Joseph Banks Conservatory**, in this complex, is a tropical glasshouse containing descendants of some of the plants brought back by this Lincoln explorer who accompanied Captain James Cook to Australia.

A short walk up Burton Rd is the **Museum of Lincolnshire Life** (☎ 528448; adult/child £2/1.20; ☺ 10am-5.30pm May-Sep, 2-5.30pm Mon-Sat Oct-Apr). It's a fairly interesting museum of local social history – displays include everything from an Edwardian nursery to a WWI tank built here.

Newport Arch (Bailgate), built by the Romans, is the oldest arch in Britain that still has traffic passing through it.

In addition to the black-and-white **Tudor buildings** on Steep Hill, **Jew's House** is of particular interest, being one of the best examples of 12th-century domestic architecture in Britain. It's now an upmarket restaurant (see Eating, opposite).

Located one block east of Jew's House is the **Usher Gallery** (☎ 527980; Lindum Rd; admission free; ☺ 10am-5.30pm Mon-Sat, 2.30-5pm Sun), the city's art gallery. Inside, the main focus is on the paintings and drawings of Peter de Wint (1784–1849) and on memorabilia associated with Lincolnshire-born poet laureate, Alfred, Lord Tennyson (1809–92). There are also temporary exhibitions and displays geared towards children.

Tours

Guided walking tours (adult £3, 1½ hours) from the TIC in Castle Hill take place at 11am and 2.15pm daily from June to September, and at weekends in June, September and October. Also leaving from the TIC is a 1¼-hour ghost walk (adult/child £3/2) at 7pm Wednesday, Friday and Saturday. **Guide Friday bus tours** (☎ 01789-294466; adult/child £6/2.50) explore the town daily from April to September.

Sleeping

BUDGET

Hartsholme Country Park (☎ 873577; Skellingthorpe Rd; tent site & 2 people £4-8; ☺ 31 Mar–31 Oct) This camping area is about 3 miles southwest of the train station. Take the R66 bus from the main bus station in the direction of Birchwood Estate; ask the driver to drop you off (it's about a 20-minute ride).

Lincoln Youth Hostel (☎ 0870 770 5918; fax 567 424; 77 South Park Ave; dm £11, d £19; ☺ Feb-Oct, Fri & Sat Nov & Dec) This hostel provides good budget accommodation in various sized rooms.

MID-RANGE

Lincoln (☎ 530422; Eastgate; s/d from £60; ℗) Talk about wild juxtapositions: directly across the street from the cathedral is this ultrachic, ultramodern 72-room hotel. Its amenity-jammed rooms have huge windows; ask for one that faces the cathedral. Don't be alarmed as the disco lights flash on and off when you walk up and down the hallway.

No 30 (☎ 521417; 30 Bailgate; s/d £25/45) There are just two rooms in this beautiful Georgian town house that's about 250m from the cathedral. It's an excellent choice, but be sure to book as early as possible, as it's always full.

Carline Guest House (☎ 530422; 1-3 Carline Rd; s/d £30/44) A bit more upmarket than No 30, this place has 12 individually appointed rooms, all with a private bathroom.

Admiral Guest House (☎ 544467; 16-18 Nelson St; s/d £25/38) One of several B&Bs just off Carholme Rd, this lovely 100-year-old house has really comfortable facilities. Unusually, smokers can puff away in their rooms.

TOP END

White Hart Hotel (☎ 526222; heritagehotels-lincoln .white-hart@forte-hotels.com; Bailgate; d £115; P) Near the cathedral, the White Hart is Lincoln's top hotel. It's a luxurious place with 48 beautifully appointed rooms.

Castle Hotel (☎ 538801; fax 575457; Westgate; s/d from £62/84; P) Directly across from the TIC, the fancy and comfortable Castle is in a restored 19th-century building.

Eating

Lincoln has a number of excellent restaurants with fine gourmet menus, but cheaper cafés are also in plentiful supply. There's also a good **bakery** (cnr Westgate & Bailgate; ☽ breakfast & lunch).

Jew's House (☎ 524851; Steep Hill; mains £9-12; ☽ lunch & dinner) Occupying a 12th-century building that's an attraction in its own right (opposite), this is Lincoln's top restaurant, serving astounding little installations of food sculpture that send foodies to the moon.

Brown's Pie Shop (☎ 527330; 33 Steep Hill; pies £8-12) Close to the cathedral and popular with tourists, this is the place to try out the Lincolnshire speciality – pies, with every filling you can imagine and then a few more. Rabbit pie with Dorset scrumpy costs £9, but there are cheaper options.

Lion & Snake Hotel (☎ 523770; Bailgate; burgers & pub food £2-5) Founded in 1640, the Lion & Snake is Lincoln's oldest pub. It's known for its real ale and inexpensive but really good home-made bar food.

Stokes High Bridge Café (☎ 513825; 207 High St; ☽ 9am-5pm Mon-Sat) This teashop is hard to miss, as it's in a 16th-century half-timbered building on the bridge over the River Witham, directly above the main shopping corridor. In other words, it's an ideal place to people-watch or gaze over the water. Lunches and teas are available.

Café Zoot (☎ 536663; 5 Bailgate; mains £4.95, specials £8) This sleek, techno-style café near the TIC serves creative, affordable lunches and excellent Continental cuisine, with a healthy number of vegetarian options.

Wig & Mitre (☎ 535190; 29 Steep Hill; mains around £13) Though it's nominally a pub, the Wig, near Brown's Pie Shop, behaves more like an upscale restaurant, with ambitious meals, a good wine list and a sophisticated candlelit atmosphere.

Drinking

Victoria (6 Union Rd) Lincoln's most famous public house doesn't disappoint: it's a terrific bar with a huge selection of beers and just enough historic-pub bric-a-brac to seem warm, but not overdone or artificial. Every guided tour makes a stop at (or at least acknowledges) this historic place.

George & Dragon (100 High St) One of the more popular pubs in town, what it lacks in original character it more than makes up for in friendly ambience – though it can get very crowded at weekends.

Po Na Na Souk Bar (☎ 525828; 280-281 High St) Part of a vastly successful chain of clubs, Po Na Na is more serious about dancing than drinking. The tunes are deep, with a good mix of soulful house, eclectic funk and other esoteric sounds, set nicely against the place's vaguely Moroccan theme.

Getting There & Away

Lincoln is 142 miles from London, 94 miles from Cambridge and 81 miles from York.

National Express runs a direct service between Lincoln and London (£17.50, 4½ hours) daily. Buses also run from Lincoln to Birmingham (£10.75, 2¾ hours) and Cambridge (£16.25, three hours; change at Peterborough).

Travelling to and from Lincoln usually means changing trains. There are hourly trains to Boston (£13.30, 1¼ hours) and Skegness (£15.60, two hours); change at Sleaford. Hourly trains to Cambridge (£30.10, 2½ hours) also run; change at Peterborough and Ely. Trains to Grantham (£8.70, 40 minutes) run 20 times daily.

Getting Around

BICYCLE

You can rent everything from a three-speed to a mountain bike at **F&J Cycles** (☎ 545311; 41 Hungate), but 21 speeds are hardly an essential requirement for cycling in this flat county. An 18-speed costs £8 to £10 per day and up to £30 per week.

BUS

From the bus and train stations, bus No 51 runs past the youth hostel and Nos 7 and 8 link the cathedral area with the lower town (60p).

GRANTHAM

☎ 01476 / pop 34,592

Anyone old enough to remember the eventful reign of Lady Margaret Thatcher, who served as British prime minister from 1979 to 1990, will find a good example of her vision for Britain in the pleasant red-brick town where she was born. Baroness Thatcher lived at 2 North Pde, above her father's grocery store; today it's a chiropractor's clinic. Another noteworthy inhabitant of Grantham was Sir Isaac Newton, who received his early education here. There's a statue of him in front of the guildhall – we're still waiting on the statue of the former Conservative prime minister.

The **TIC** (☎ 406166; Ave Rd; 🕑 9.30am-5pm Mon-Sat) is near the guildhall.

Until that commemorative statue comes around, the Iron Lady will have to content herself with a section devoted to her in the town's **museum** (St Peter's Hill; admission free; 🕑 10am-5pm Mon-Sat). Another section is devoted to Newton and frankly, unless you really want to see the famous handbag with which the former prime minister saluted the press after her 1979 electoral victory, it is by far the more interesting.

Grantham possesses an interesting parish church, **St Wulfram's**, with an 85m-high spire, the sixth-highest in England. It dates from the late 13th century. Inside there's a chained library, which Isaac Newton used while studying there.

Three miles northeast of Grantham on the A607 is **Belton House** (☎ 566116; adult £5.50; 🕑 1-5pm Wed-Sun Apr-Oct), one of the finest examples of Restoration country-house architecture. Built in 1688 for Sir John Brownlow, and set in a 400-hectare park, the house is known for its ornate plasterwork ceilings and woodcarvings attributed to the Dutch carver Grinling Gibbons. To get here take bus No 601 or 609.

Sleeping & Eating

Coach House (☎ 573636; coachhousenn@cwcom.net; per person £25; ✖) Just outside Belton House, this hotel is in a heritage-listed building with a large, pleasant garden – smokers will no doubt make use of it.

Beehive (☎ 404554; Castlegate) The Beehive pub is best known for its sign – a real beehive full of live South African bees! The bees have been here since 1830, which makes them one of the oldest populations of bees in the world. Good, cheap lunches are available here, and the bees stay away from the customers.

Getting There & Away

Grantham is 25 miles south of Lincoln. Lincolnshire Roadcar runs buses every hour between the two Monday to Saturday and four times on Sunday (£2.80, one hour and 10 minutes, four daily Monday to Saturday). It also runs a service to Stamford (£2.60, 1½ hours); National Express runs one bus daily Monday to Saturday.

By train (£8.70, 40 minutes), you'll need to change at Newark to get to Lincoln. There is at least one train per hour throughout the day. Direct trains run from London King's Cross to Grantham (£30, 1¼ hours) hourly throughout the day.

STAMFORD

☎ 01780 / pop 19,525

This beautiful town of stone buildings and cobbled streets was made into a conservation area in 1967 and is one of the finest stone towns in the country. Its winding streets of medieval and Georgian houses slope gently down from the top of the hill to a riverside park that's ideal for a picnic.

The **TIC** (☎ 755611; 27 St Mary's St; 🕑 9.30am-5pm Mon-Sat year-round, plus 10am-3pm Sun Apr-Oct) is in the Stamford Arts Centre.

It's best to simply wander around town, but the **Stamford Museum** (☎ 766317; Broad St; admission free; 🕑 10am-5pm Mon-Sat year-round, plus 2-5pm Sun Apr-Sep) is certainly worth visiting. As well as displays charting the history of the town, there's a clothed model of local heavyweight Daniel Lambert, who tipped the scales at 336kg before his death in 1809. After his death his suits were displayed in a local pub where Charles Stratton, better known as Tom Thumb, would put on a show by fitting into the suit's armholes. Hilarious, apparently.

Sleeping & Eating

George (☎ 750750; georgehotelofstamford@btInternet .com; 71 St Martin's St; s/d from £85/120) Nestled at the bottom of a hill where an elegant stone bridge crosses the river, the George is the top place to stay and is worth peeking inside even if it's out of your price range. It's a wonderful old coaching inn where the Burghley crowd used to rack up astronomical bills; parts of the building date back a thousand years. There's a cobbled courtyard and luxurious rooms with first-class amenities. There's also an excellent restaurant divided into several rooms; if you want anything fancier than upmarket pub grub, expect to pay at least £20.

St George's B&B (☎ 482099; 16 St George's Sq; s/d from £25/40) Not to be confused with the George hotel, this is a gorgeous 19th-century house with Victorian fireplaces and antiques. It also has a private garden.

Martin's (☎ 752106; fax 482691; 20 St Martin's Rd; s/d from £35/55) Another stellar B&B, Martin's is just beyond the bridge over the River Welland, only a couple of minutes' walk from the centre of town.

There are a number of historic pubs that also offer accommodation, including the beautiful, lace-curtained **Bull & Swann Inn** (☎ 763558; High St; s/d £35/45); good meals and real ale are available here, too.

Getting There & Away

Stamford is 46 miles from Lincoln and 21 miles south of Grantham.

National Express serves Stamford from London (£9.75, 2¾ hours) via Lincoln (£7.75, 1½ hours). Lincolnshire Roadcar operates four buses daily Monday to Saturday between Stamford and Grantham (£2.60, 1½ hours). National Express also runs one bus daily.

There are 15 trains daily to Cambridge (£13.90, 1¼ hours) and Ely (£8.70, 55 minutes). Norwich (£15.20, one hour and 50 minutes) is on the same line, but there are fewer direct trains; you will most likely have to change at Ely.

AROUND STAMFORD
Burghley House

Just a mile south of Stamford, immensely grand **Burghley House** (bur-lee; ☎ 752451; www .burghley.co.uk; adult/child £7.80/3.50, 1 child free per paying adult; ⏰ 11am-5pm Apr–early Oct), a Tudor mansion, is the home of the Cecil family. It was built between 1565 and 1587 by William Cecil, Queen Elizabeth I's adviser.

It's an impressive place with 18 magnificent staterooms. The Heaven Room was painted by Antonio Verrio in the 17th century, and features floor-to-ceiling gods and goddesses disporting among the columns; on the flip side, there's the stairway to Hell, with an equally fascinating painting depicting Satan as a giant cat-eyed uterus devouring the world. There are over 300 paintings, including works by Gainsborough and Pieter Brueghel; state bedchambers, including the four-poster that Queen Victoria slept in; and cavernous Tudor kitchens. An exhibit in one of the lower hallways details the career of David Cecil, the Lord Burghley who was an Olympic athlete and part of the inspiration for the film *Chariots of Fire*.

It's a pleasant 15-minute walk through the park from Stamford train station. The **Burghley Horse Trials** take place here over three days in early September and are of international significance.

BOSTON
☎ 01205 / pop 35,124

A major port in the Middle Ages, Boston lies near the mouth of the River Witham, in the bay known as the Wash. By the end of the 13th century the town was one of the most important wool-trading centres in the country, exporting the fleeces of three million sheep annually. Boston's other claim to fame came in the 17th century, when it temporarily imprisoned a group of religious separatists looking to settle in the virtually unknown territories of the New World. These later became known as the Pilgrim Fathers, the first white settlers of the US. Word of their success made it back to the English Boston, whereupon a crowd of locals decided to sail across the Atlantic; there they founded a namesake town in the new colony of Massachusetts.

Today the Boston in Massachusetts wouldn't recognise its namesake; the English town is but a shadow of its former self.

THE FENS

The Fens were strange marshlands that stretched from Cambridge north to the Wash and beyond into Lincolnshire. They were home to people who led an isolated existence fishing, hunting, and farming scraps of arable land among a maze of waterways. In the 17th century, however, the Duke of Bedford and a group of speculators brought in Dutch engineer Sir Cornelius Vermuyden to drain the Fens, and the flat, open plains with their rich, black soil were created. The region is the setting for Graham Swift's excellent novel *Waterland*.

As the world's weather pattern changes and the sea level rises, the Fens are beginning to disappear under water again. It's estimated that by the year 2030 up to 400,000 hectares could be lost.

But it has retained much of its medieval appearance, down to the street grid, whereby the two main streets flank both sides of the river and are linked by small footbridges. It's an easy place to wander about in, and has a number of interesting sites.

The **TIC** (☎ 356656; Market Pl; 9am-5pm Mon-Sat) is under the Assembly Rooms. Market days are Wednesday and Saturday; you can buy pretty much everything from a fish to a bicycle.

As you walk around the town, be sure to check out **Shodfriars Hall** (South St; not open to the public), a marvellous Tudor building that has been faithfully restored.

St Botolph's Church

In keeping with its high-flying status, the town ordered the construction of an impressive church in 1309: the result was **St Botolph's** (☎ 362864; church free, tower £2; 9am-4.30pm Mon-Sat, btwn services Sun) and its 88m-high tower – known as the Boston Stump because it doesn't come to a point. The fenland on which it's built was not firm enough to support a thin spire, hence the sturdy tower. Climb the 365 steps to the top to see (on a clear day) Lincoln, 30 miles away.

Inside there is a splendid 17th-century **pulpit** from which John Cotton, the fiery vicar of St Botolph's, delivered five-hour catechisms and two-hour sermons during the 1630s. By all accounts, it was he who convinced his parishioners to follow in the footsteps of the Pilgrim Fathers and emigrate.

Guildhall

It was from Boston that the Pilgrim Fathers made their first break for the freedom of the New World in 1607. They were imprisoned in the **guildhall** (☎ 365954; adult £1.50; 10am-5pm Mon-Sat & 1.30-5pm Sun May-Sep), where the cells that held them are now a fairly extensive visitors centre, with multimedia exhibits on the town's history and a eulogising display on the struggles of the Pilgrim Fathers.

Sleeping & Eating

Bramley House (☎ /fax 354538; bramleyhouse@ic24 .net; 267 Sleaford Rd; s/d from £20/40) An old 18th-century farmstead, Bramley House is about half a mile west of town along Sleaford Rd. It has nine comfortable rooms and also does pub grub.

There are many eateries dotted about town, but we recommend you check out **Maud's Tea Rooms** (☎ 352188; Maud Foster Windmill, Willoughby Rd; mains £5-8), about half a mile northeast of Market Pl. This is a fully functional mill, and the tearooms serve good vegetarian dishes. You can also buy the local produce (organic flour – not exactly your typical souvenir).

Getting There & Away

From Lincoln it's easier to get to Boston by train than by bus, but even that involves a change at Sleaford. Trains run from Lincoln hourly (1¼ hours).

SKEGNESS

☎ 01754 / pop 16,806

Places like 'Skeggy' are engineered to cure a particular craving. It's a hankering for candyfloss, fried foods, penny arcades and cheap funfair rides, for thousands of pasty optimists doing brave impressions of sunbathing regardless of the weather, for ice-cream-faced kids with kites and sandcastles. In other words, it's absolutely everything you want in a classic English seaside resort. Tens of thousands of Britons holiday here every year, mostly because it's cheaper than going to Spain, it's by the sea, and every night offers the chance for some brand of wild abandon – whether it's disco, bingo or bad cabaret. Virtually every inch of the

Grand Pde, which skirts the 6-mile-long beach, is covered in amusement arcades, fish-and-chip shops, pubs and B&Bs.

The **TIC** (☎ 764821; Grand Pde; ☼ 9.30am-5pm Apr-Sep, 10am-4pm Mon-Fri Oct-Mar) is directly opposite the **Embassy Centre** (☎ 768333), home of Skeggy's cabaret scene and the place to watch your favourite Abba tribute band in all its glory; shows usually kick off at around 7.30pm. From July to September, this stretch of beach is anointed with 25,000 light bulbs, which come on in the evening to celebrate the Skegness Illuminations.

B&Bs are not hard to find and are generally quite cheap, starting from around £18 per person. The TIC will help you find a room if you need one.

Skegness is pretty easy to get to by either bus or train. From Boston, Lincolnshire Roadcar runs five buses daily, Monday to Saturday (1¼ hours). **Brylaine Travel** (☎ 01205-364087) runs three daily along the same route. Tickets, however, are only valid on the service provided by the issuing company. From Lincoln, Lincolnshire Roadcar buses run hourly Monday to Saturday and five times on Sunday (1¾ hours).

There are 15 trains daily Monday to Saturday and eight on Sunday between Skegness and Boston (35 minutes).

LOUTH
☎ 01507 / pop 15,930

The largely Georgian Louth – east Lincolnshire's largest market town – sits on the banks of the River Lud between the Wolds to the west and the marshes of the Lincoln-

shire coast. A curious fact about Louth is that it has two hemispheres – east and west – as the zero longitude line cuts right through the town.

Dominating the town is the soaring spire of **St James' Church** (☼ 10am-4.30pm Easter-Christmas), added to the medieval church between 1500 and 1515. The dramatic buttresses and battlements of the church exterior – described by Sir John Betjeman as 'one of the last great medieval Gothic masterpieces' – belie a fairly inconsequential interior; however, the lovely wooden roof, built in the early 19th century, is undoubtedly a feature. You can climb the tower (£1.50) for marvellous views of the town and surrounding countryside.

The **TIC** (☎ /fax 609289; New Market Hall, ☼ 9am-5pm Mon-Sat), off Cornmarket, has all the information you'll need.

The most elegant street in town is Westgate, which is lined with Georgian houses. The mid-17th-century **church precincts** at No 47 and the grander No 45 are particularly handsome. Just opposite is Westgate Pl, and through the archway you'll find a row of terraced houses, one of which bears a plaque commemorating Tennyson's residence here between 1816 and 1820.

Sleeping & Eating
Priory (☎ 602930; fax 609767; Eastgate; s/d £45/69) In a magnificent building from 1818 is this simply gorgeous hotel, an all-white half-castle, half-residence – it's easily the top spot in town. For an extra £15 you can get dinner at the excellent restaurant.

THE PILGRIMAGE OF GRACE

The revolt against Henry VIII's reformation of the church began in Louth in 1536. Deeply annoyed by Henry's plans to dissolve all of the monasteries and appoint new bishops to every diocese, northerners were pushed over the edge by Henry's minister Thomas Cromwell, who at the same time decided to pursue some fairly radical land-reform programmes in the northern counties. On 1 October, the crown commissioners arrived in Louth to fulfil Henry and Cromwell's orders, but they were attacked by an angry mob. What was a protest was now a full rebellion, later called the Pilgrimage of Grace. Lincoln was occupied, and the rebels demanded an end to dissolution, Cromwell's resignation and the dismissal of the newly appointed heretical bishops. Henry, however, was unmoved, and the rebellion petered out on 19 October.

Although the Louth rebellion was a bit of a damp squib, it inspired a more serious rebellion in Yorkshire by Robert Aske, a gentleman farmer who gathered 30,000 men, engaged the crown forces and forced Henry to consider the rebels' demands. He did, or pretended to, and Aske eventually disbanded his forces. The government reacted swiftly by arresting and executing the ringleaders in early 1537, and the rebellion was finally at an end.

Ramsgate Hotel (☎ 602179; 15 Ramsgate; s/d from £20/30) A less spectacular option – the Ramsgate has pretty, comfortable rooms and is very central.

Getting There & Away

Louth is 23 miles northeast of Lincoln, from where there are buses every couple of hours (£3.50, 45 minutes).

AROUND LOUTH
Saltfleetby-Theddlethorpe National Nature Reserve

Ten miles east of Louth along the B1200, which meanders its way through the Fens,

is one of the most attractive **nature reserves** (☎ 01507-338611) in this part of the country. Spread over 5 miles of sand dunes and fresh- and saltwater marsh, it is best appreciated in early summer, when the stunning marsh orchids are in full bloom. In spring and autumn, migratory wildfowl flock to the reserve. Crisscrossing the whole area are dozens of trails, which help to keep your feet dry as you negotiate the myriad lagoons.

You'll need your own transport to get here. At the end of the B1200, take a right on to the A1031 and, about three-quarters of a mile further on, follow the signs for the nature reserve.

Yorkshire

Yorkshire folk are only half-joking when they talk about living in God's Own Country. Heaven-blessed or not, Yorkshire has a sense of 'national' pride comparable only to that found in Scotland or Wales – but not anywhere else in England. And it's not all just wishful thinking either, for Yorkshire was indeed a nation once, and while the Viking-governed Danelaw of the 9th century may be but the stuff of dusty annals, the sense of self that its history engenders has given Yorkshire a confident homogeneity that belies the fact it is actually four separate counties – South Yorkshire, West Yorkshire, North Yorkshire and the East Riding of Yorkshire.

Topographers and administrators may quibble, but compass points matter far less than the place they're south, west, north or east *from*, at least in the minds of the people themselves. Maybe it's the landscape of dark moors and rocky outcrops, or the background of generations struggling to earn a living from the land or the factories, but whatever, Yorkshire folk shoot from the hip and never sit on the fence. Whether it's football, foreign wars, beer or just life in general, things are either great or terrible. There's no in-between.

Against this human story, the Yorkshire landscape is a magnificent backdrop, containing two of England's best national parks, beautiful countryside and a spectacular coastline. The cities, too, attract their share of visitors, with their museums, galleries, pubs and bars. If you make it to Yorkshire, consider yourself lucky; isn't it God's favourite place?

YORKSHIRE

HIGHLIGHTS

- Going medieval in **York's** (p521) winding streets, awe-inspiring minster and fabulous museums
- Strolling down green valleys or hiking over high moors in the **Yorkshire Dales** (p510)
- Shopping, eating, drinking and dancing, then shopping some more in **Leeds** (p500)
- Explore weather-beaten **Whitby** (p543): a favourite with seadogs, sun-lovers and lackeys of the Prince of Darkness
- Riding steam trains on the **Settle–Carlisle Line** (p514)
- Going underground at the **National Coal Mining Museum for England** (p507) near Wakefield

★ Whitby

★ Yorkshire Dales NP

★ Settle

★ York

★ Leeds

★ National Coal Mining Museum for England

■ POPULATION: 4,964,833	■ AREA: 5958 SQ MILES

Information

Yorkshire Tourist Board (☎ 01904-707070; www .yorkshirevisitor.com; 312 Tadcaster Rd, York YO24 1GS) has plenty of general leaflets and brochures. For more detailed information, contact the local Tourist Information Centres (TICs) listed throughout this chapter.

Activities

Within Yorkshire are high peaks, wild hills, tranquil valleys, farmland, moorland and a stupendous coastline. With this fantastic selection, not surprisingly, it's a great place for outdoor activities.

CYCLING

Cycling is a great way to see Yorkshire; there's a vast network of country lanes, although the most scenic areas are also attractive to car drivers, so even some minor roads can be busy at weekends. Options include:

North York Moors Off-road riders can avail themselves of the networks of bridleways, former railways and disused mining tracks now turned over to two-wheel use.

Whitby to Scarborough A traffic-free route that includes a disused railway line, and is an effortless way to tour this rugged coastline.

White Rose Cycle Route A 120-mile cruise from Hull to York to Middlesbrough, via the rolling Yorkshire Wolds and the dramatic edge of the North York Moors, and a traffic-free section on the old railway between Selby and York. It is part of the National Cycle Network (p81).

Yorkshire Dales Great cycling in the quieter areas in the north around Swaledale and Wensleydale, and the west around Dentdale. The areas just outside the park, like Nidderdale, are also good. Also an excellent network of old 'drove roads' (formerly used for driving cattle to market) which wind across lonely hillsides, and tie in neatly with the narrow country lanes in the valley bottoms.

WALKING

For shorter walks and rambles, the best area is the **Yorkshire Dales**, with a great selection of hard and easy walks through scenic valleys or over wild hilltops, with even a few peaks thrown in for good measure. The **Yorkshire Wolds** hold hidden delights, while the quiet valleys and dramatic coasts of the **North York Moors** also have many good opportunities, although the broad ridges of the high moors can be a bit featureless and less attractive for keen walkers.

For general information get hold of the *Walk Yorkshire* brochure from TICs or see www.walkyorkshire.com. All TICs stock a

mountain of leaflets (free or up to £1.50) on local walks, and sell more detailed guidebooks and maps. At train stations and TICs, it's worth looking out for leaflets produced by companies such as Northern Spirit, detailing walks from train stations. Some tie in with train times, so you can walk one way and ride back.

Here's a list of some popular long-distance walks:

Cleveland Way A venerable moor-and-coast classic; details in the North York Moors section (p538).

Coast to Coast Walk England's No 1 walk, 190 miles across northern England eastwards from the Lake District, crosses the Yorkshire Dales and North York Moors. Doing just the Yorkshire sections would take a week to 10 days and offers some of the finest walking of its kind in England.

Dales Way Charming and not-too-strenuous amble from the Yorkshire Dales to the Lake District (p510).

Pennine Way The Yorkshire section of England's most famous walk starts on day two and runs for over 100 miles, via Hebden Bridge, Malham, Horton-in-Ribblesdale and Hawes, passing near Haworth and Skipton.

Wolds Way Beautiful but oft-overlooked walk that winds through the most scenic part of eastern Yorkshire (p517).

Getting There & Around

Yorkshire covers a large part of northern England, and a vast range of landscapes. From the Pennine Hills on the western side of the region (separating Yorkshire from age-old rival Lancashire), you can travel through the green valleys of the Yorkshire Dales, across the plains of the Vale of York and the rolling hills of the North York Moors and Yorkshire Wolds, to finally end at the dramatic east coast.

The major north–south transport routes – the M1 and A1 motorways and the main London to Edinburgh railway line – run through the middle of Yorkshire following the flat lands between the Pennines and the Moors, and serving the cities of Sheffield, Leeds and York.

Yorkshire's main gateway cities by road and rail are Sheffield in the far south, Leeds for the west and York for the centre and north. If you're coming by sea from northern Europe, Hull (in the East Riding) is the region's main port. More specific details for each area are given under Getting There & Away in the separate sections throughout this chapter. For inquiries, the national **Traveline** (☎ 0870 608 2608) covers buses and trains all over Yorkshire.

YORKSHIRE

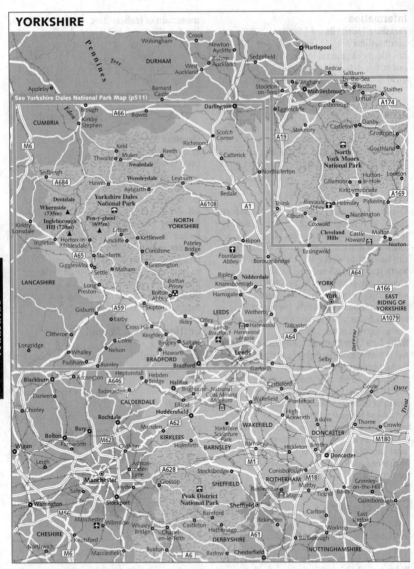

YORKSHIRE

BOAT

Full details on passenger ferries to Hull from northern Europe are given in the main Transport chapter (see p963).

BUS

Long-distance buses and coaches run by **National Express** (☎ 08705 808080) regularly service most cities and large towns in Yorkshire from London, the south of England, the Midlands and Scotland. More details are given under Getting There & Away in the individual town and city sections.

Bus transport around Yorkshire is frequent and efficient, especially between major towns. Services are more sporadic in the

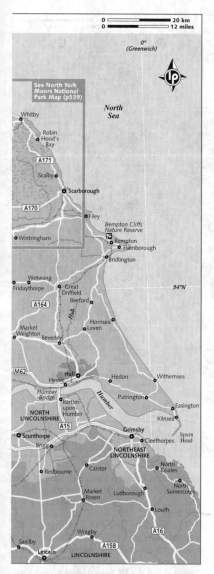

where you might change to reach other places in Yorkshire. There are also direct services between the major towns and cities of Yorkshire and other northern cities like Manchester and Newcastle. One of England's most famous and scenic railways is the Settle–Carlisle Line (SCL), which crosses the Yorkshire Dales via a spectacular series of tunnels and viaducts. Trains start/end in Leeds, and Carlisle is a good stop on the way to Scotland. Call or check out **National Rail Enquiries** (☎ 08457 484950; www .nationalrail.co.uk) for timetable details.

SOUTH YORKSHIRE

For the most part, South Yorkshire is all about Sheffield, the city that for much of its history was all about steel, especially the kind you use to poke food with. For hundreds of years, the 'Sheffield Steel' stamp on your cutlery was a mark of distinction. The steel industry was fuelled by coal, and thankfully there was plenty of it to go around outside of Sheffield.

Sure, a bunch of closed down mills and pits aren't in themselves all that attractive, but what cash flow they generated was spent on some pretty fine monuments, most notable in the grand civic buildings that make up Sheffield's city centre. Furthermore, a host of museums has grown up around the abandoned steel mills and coal pits that preserve the Industrial Age without having to relive it.

SHEFFIELD
☎ 0114 / pop 640,720
For most Brits, Sheffield is synonymous with steel, snooker and *The Full Monty*. A little bit of a snafu, really, considering that the steel industry is virtually dead; snooker is a game for people who believe that ciggies and lager *do* have a part to play in sport; and *The Full Monty,* a feel-good movie sensation about unemployed steelworkers (and, we presume, snooker fans) who turned to stripping to raise some cash, has long since gone to DVD.

Thankfully for Sheffield, the city has moved on. Since the late 1990s, the city has worked hard to reinvent itself. Smart hotels and galleries are springing up, the whole centre is revelling in a major facelift,

national parks but still perfectly adequate for reaching most places – particularly in the summer months (June to September).

TRAIN
The main line between London and Edinburgh runs through Yorkshire with at least 10 services per day, via York and Doncaster –

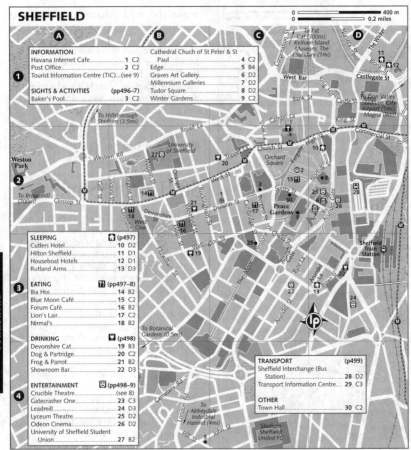

SHEFFIELD

INFORMATION	
Havana Internet Cafe	1 C2
Post Office	2 C2
Tourist Information Centre (TIC)...(see 9)	
SIGHTS & ACTIVITIES	**(pp496–7)**
Baker's Pool	3 C2
Cathedral Chuch of St Peter & St Paul	4 C2
Edge	5 B4
Graves Art Gallery	6 D2
Millennium Galleries	7 D2
Tudor Square	8 D2
Winter Gardens	9 C2

SLEEPING	(p497)
Cutlers Hotel	10 D2
Hilton Sheffield	11 D1
Houseboat Hotels	12 D1
Rutland Arms	13 D3

EATING	(pp497–8)
Bia Hoi	14 B2
Blue Moon Café	15 C2
Forum Café	16 B2
Lion's Lair	17 C2
Nirmal's	18 B2

DRINKING	(p498)
Devonshire Cat	19 B3
Dog & Partridge	20 C2
Frog & Parrot	21 B2
Showroom Bar	22 D3

ENTERTAINMENT	(pp498–9)
Crucible Theatre	(see 8)
Gatecrasher One	23 C3
Leadmill	24 D3
Lyceum Theatre	25 D2
Odeon Cinema	26 D2
University of Sheffield Student Union	27 B2

TRANSPORT	(p499)
Sheffield Interchange (Bus Station)	28 D2
Transport Information Centre	29 C3

OTHER	
Town Hall	30 C2

and several new attractions based on the industrial past are well worth a visit. On the entertainment side, there's a buzz that hasn't been seen for a long while, powered in no small way by an exuberant and ever-growing student population. Sheffield is also a very handy getaway for the Peak District National Park, which brushes up against its western outskirts.

Orientation & Information

Sheffield's bus and train stations are separated from the city centre by a wall of high-rise buildings so ugly that turning around becomes a real option. Don't. Beyond them, however, are the city's most interesting bits, a central area around Church St, Tudor Sq,

Fargate and Barker's Pool. Just west of here Division and Devonshire Sts have hip clothes and record shops, popular restaurants and trendy bars.

The handiest spot for all e-things is **Havana Internet Cafe** (☎ 249 5453; 32 Division St; per 30 mins £1; ☎ 10am-6pm). The **post office** (Norfolk Row; ⌚ 8.30am-5.30pm Mon-Fri, 8.30am-3pm Sat) is just off Fargate, and the **TIC** (www.sheffieldcity.co.uk; Winter Gardens; ⌚ 9.30am-4pm Mon-Sat) has no permanent office, just a temporary desk, but all the usual info.

Sights & Activities

Pride of place goes to the **Winter Gardens**, a wonderfully ambitious space with glass roof, exotic plants, soaring wood-clad arches –

and the tourist information desk. The 21st-century architecture contrasts sharply with the Victorian **town hall** next door, and is further enhanced by the nearby **Peace Gardens** – complete with fountains, sculptures and lawns of lunching office workers whenever there's a bit of sun.

Sheffield's cultural revival is spearheaded by the **Millennium Galleries** (☎ 278 2600; Arundel Gate; www.sheffieldgalleries.org.uk; admission free, special exhibitions £4; ☺ 10am-5pm Mon-Sat, 11am-5pm Sun). Displays cover Sheffield steel and metal-working, contemporary art, craft and design, and an eclectic collection established and inspired by Victorian artist, writer, critic and philosopher John Ruskin.

Nearby, **Graves Art Gallery** (☎ 278 2600; Surrey St; admission free; ☺ 10am-5pm Mon-Sat) has a neat and accessible display of British and European modern art, plus works from the temporarily closed Mappin Gallery (which is scheduled to reopen at the end of 2005).

The **cathedral** on Church St has wonderful stained glass (ancient and modern), a memorial to the crew of the HMS *Sheffield* lost during the Falklands conflict and the grave of the earl of Shrewsbury, famous for being the jailer of Mary Queen of Scots and husband to Bess of Harwick (see p434).

Sheffield's prodigious industrial heritage is the subject of the excellent **Kelham Island Museum** (☎ 272 2106; Alma St; www.simt.co.uk; adult/child £3.50/2; ☺ 10am-4pm Mon-Thu, 11am-4.45pm Sun). The most impressive display is the 12,000-horsepower steam engine (the size of a house) that is powered up twice a day.

For a view of steel from an earlier era, go to **Abbeydale Industrial Hamlet** (☎ 236 7731; adult/child £3/1.50; ☺ 10am-4pm Mon-Thu, 11am-4.45pm Sun mid-Apr–Oct). It's 4 miles southwest of the centre on the A621 (towards the Peak District) and well worth a stop. In the days before factories, metalworking was a cottage industry, just like wool or cotton. These rare (and restored) houses and machines take you right back to that era.

Sleeping

Most of the central options cater primarily to the business traveller, which makes for cheaper weekend rates; there are, alas, no budget options in the city centre.

Houseboat Hotels (☎ 232 6556; www.houseboathotels.com; Victoria Quays, Wharfe St; d/q from £65/85) For a little watery luxury, kick off your shoes

and relax on board your very own house-boat, which comes with its own self-catering kitchen and patio area. Available for groups of two or four only, guests are also entitled to use the gym facilities across the road at the Hilton.

Cutlers Hotel (☎ 273 9939; www.cutlershotel.co.uk; George St; s £38-52, d £52-62) Don't judge a book by its gaudy, 1970s cover: Cutlers may look naff from outside, but inside it's a pretty tidy hotel with comfortable rooms – and the most central option in town for the price.

Rutland Arms (☎ 272 9003; fax 273 1425; 86 Brown St; s/d from £24/37) A centrally located, fine traditional pub with a number of rooms upstairs, some of them with en suite: they're clean and neat but pretty darn small.

Hilton Sheffield (☎ 252 5500; www.hilton.co.uk; Victoria Quay; r £110) Pretty much what you would expect from one of the world's best-known hotel chains: a top-class business hotel with all the facilities, including rooms that have made the name Hilton a byword for standardised luxury.

Eating

For a wide range of city centre options, you can't go wrong on Division St, Devonshire St, West St and Glossop Rd. There are cafés, takeaways, pubs and bars doing food, and a wide range of restaurants.

BUDGET

Forum Café (☎ 272 0569; 127 Devonshire St; lunch about £5; ☺ lunch & dinner Mon-Sat) Open and airy, with coffees, snacks, newspapers, art on the wall and customers who wander in from the vaguely alternative Forum Shopping Centre next door. In the evening, it's more bar-like, with lower lights and louder music.

Blue Moon Café (☎ 276 3443; 2 St James St; snacks £1-3, lunches £3-5; ☺ 7am-8pm Mon-Sat) Serves up rather tasty vegetarian creations, soups and other good-for-you dishes – all served with the ubiquitous salad – in a relaxed and pleasant atmosphere.

MID-RANGE

Bia Hoi (☎ 279 9250; 1 Mappin St; mains £4-8; ☺ noon-7pm Mon-Sat) Under the watchful gaze of a pretty big Buddha, Bia Hoi serves up excellent Vietnamese and Thai dishes; a lunch thrill is the Siam Market menu, an all-you-can-eat smorgasbord of noodles and rice dishes for only £3.95.

YORKSHIRE

Nirmal's (☎ 272 4054; 189 Glossop Rd; mains £5-8; ⓥ lunch & dinner) Gujarati cuisine is the speciality at Sheffield's best Indian restaurant. Its enduring popularity means that in order to get a table, you should call ahead and book one.

TOP END
Lion's Lair (☎ 263 4264; 31 Burgess St; mains about £12; ⓥ lunch & dinner Mon-Sat, noon-5pm Sun) Guinea fowl and tenderloin of springbok are hardly the stuff of pub grub, but this traditional bar – once a rocker's hangout – was given the once-over and is now one of the city's smartest eateries.

Drinking
The nice thing about the city's numerous traditional pubs is that they're popular with everyone, not just pensioners with questionable drinking habits. The best place to start your search is the area around Division and West Sts. Virtually every bar does pub grub until about 7pm.

Fat Cat (☎ 249 4801; 23 Alma St) One of Sheffield's finest pubs, the Fat Cat serves a wide range of real ales (some brewed on the premises) in a wonderfully unreconstructed interior. There are three bars (one bar is non smoking), there's good pub grub, a roaring fire in winter and – in the men's toilets – a fascinating exhibit on local sanitation. It's next door to the Kelham Island Museum.

Frog & Parrot (☎ 272 1280; Division St) The Frog & Parrot pub is home to the world's strongest beer, the 12%-strong 'Roger & Out', and unsuspecting ale-heads saunter in looking to down the equivalent of a pint of fortified wine. Which is precisely the reason why this place only serves this particular brew in half-pint glasses – so that you have more than a 50/50 chance of walking out under your own steam. This no-frills and popular

---

establishment also serves a range of less challenging beers.

Dog & Partridge (☎ 249 0888; 55 Trippett La) A no-nonsense Irish pub with a warren of cosy rooms, a fireplace to warm those places beer won't get to and traditional music in the evenings. It's a little bit of the Auld Sod in Sheffield, and a welcome bit it is too.

Devonshire Cat (☎ 279 6700; 49 Wellington St) A beer-lover's haven, this modern bar looks a bit bland, but one look at the wide selection of top-notch beers from around England and the world will explain its enduring popularity.

Showroom Bar (☎ 249 5479; 7 Paternoster Row) Originally aimed at film fans, this terrific bar with its arty, hip clientele is one of the best night-time destinations in town. The ambience is good, and so is the food, but the service is horribly slow. Out of term-time the slothful moonlighting students go home and real bar-staff pour the drinks.

Entertainment
Sheffield has a good selection of nightclubs, a couple of top-notch theatres and venues that attract big names in music – both classical and popular. The weekly *Sheffield Telegraph* (75p, every Friday) is your key to unlocking Sheffield's entertainment scene.

NIGHTCLUBS
Gatecrasher One (☎ 279 6777; 112 Arundel St; admission £4-6) Sheffield's premier nightclub is the flagship for the renowned Gatecrasher crew; uplifting trance, house, pop and charty R&B sounds bellow out of the fabulous sound system.

Leadmill (☎ 275 4500; www.leadmill.co.uk; 6-7 Leadmill Rd) Virtually every band to have appeared in the *New Musical Express* (NME) since the late 1970s has rocked the stage here and today's brooding breed keep the tradition very much alive; the rocker fan base has had to play nice and share its favourite venue with a number of club nights, the best of which is Saturday night's Sonic Boom, a post-gig funk and Motown get-down.

Boardwalk (☎ 279 9090; www.theboardwalklive.co.uk; 39 Snig Hill) This is an institution, and excellent for live music; local bands, old rockers, up-and-coming stars, world music, the obscure, the novel and the downright weird – they all play here. No real music fan should miss checking what's on.

> ### TOP FIVE PUBS FOR A PROPER PINT
>
> - **Fat Cat** (above; Sheffield)
> - **Duck & Drake** (p504; Leeds)
> - **Ye Olde Black Boy** (p519; Hull)
> - **Ye Olde Starre** (p429; York)
> - **Star Inn** (p540; Harome near Helmsley)

THE REWARDS OF A MISSPENT YOUTH

Snooker – that really difficult game that makes pool look a cinch – doesn't quite generate the same interest as it used to in the late 1980s and early '90s, but April's World Championship has proved to be a stubborn exception. The BBC shows virtually every frame of snooker's top tournament, but TV doesn't capture the thrill of actually sitting in the audience at Sheffield's Crucible Theatre and watching the players do their thing live. Tickets for the championships are available from the theatre **box office** (☎ 249 6000).

University of Sheffield Student Union (☎ 222 8500; Western Bank) A varied and generally good schedule of rock gigs and club nights – including appearances by some pretty classy DJ names – make this a good spot to spend a night, not to mention the cheap lager.

THEATRE & CINEMA

The Crucible and Lyceum theatres on Tudor Sq share the same **box office** (☎ 249 6000). Both are home to excellent regional drama, and the Crucible's respected resident director draws in the big names; the Crucible is also home to the annual snooker world championships (see the boxed text, above).

Showroom Cinema (☎ 275 7727; Paternoster Row) is the largest independent cinema in England, with a great mix of art-house, off-beat and not-quite-mainstream films on four screens. For everything else, there's the **Odeon** (☎ 272 3981; Arundel Gate).

Getting There & Away

For all travel-related info in Sheffield and South Yorkshire, call the **Regional Transport Information Centre** (☎ 01709-515151).

BUS

The bus station – called the Interchange – is just east of the centre, about 100m north of the train station. National Express services link Sheffield with most major centres in the north; there are frequent buses linking Sheffield with the Peak District via Leeds (£4.50, 1¼ hours, hourly) and London (£14.50, four hours, eight daily).

TRAIN

Sheffield is served by trains from all directions: Leeds (£6.60, 30 minutes, hourly); London St Pancras (£52, 2½ hours, around 10 daily) via Derby or Nottingham; Manchester airport (£15.40, 70 minutes); Manchester Piccadilly (£11.40, one hour); and York (£12.20, 80 minutes).

Getting Around

Buses run every 10 minutes during the day (Monday to Saturday). Sheffield also boasts a modern Supertram that trundles through the city centre.

For a day of sightseeing, your best bet is a South Yorkshire Peak **Explorer pass** (£6.25), valid for one day on all of the buses, trams and trains of South Yorkshire and north Derbyshire. Buy passes on your first bus, or at the helpful **Regional Transport Information Centre** (☎ 01709-51515; ☯ 9am-5pm Mon-Sat) just off Pinstone St.

WEST YORKSHIRE

A reputation for being hard-bitten is not easily shaken round these parts, but West Yorkshire does have another face, one that is gentler and far more self-aware, although it simply won't do in this no-nonsense, down-to-earth part of the world to suggest that local folk didn't eat nails for breakfast. It's a confusing and intriguing dichotomy.

Take Leeds and Bradford. Only 9 miles apart (but grown so big that they more or less blend into one massive urban sprawl), they are as different as chalk and cheese. Whereas the latter plods along its dour, industrious path without paying too much heed to how others view it, Leeds has spent the last 10 years at the urban beauticians, styling and grooming itself so as to look its absolute best. And it worked: in 2003 Leeds was voted the Best City in the UK by a national poll.

Beyond the cities, the bleak moorland and deep valleys dotted with Victorian mill towns and villages have long since been abandoned by the wool and cloth industries that gave them life, but they retain a brooding romanticism that continues to fascinate: hardly surprising considering it was these very landscapes that were so vividly evoked by West Yorkshire's most renowned literary exports, the Brontë sisters.

Activities

CYCLING

West Yorkshire isn't great cycling country; many roads are too urban in flavour, and the hills are darned steep, too. The **National Cycle Network** (see boxed text, p81) in West Yorkshire includes the short but traffic-free Leeds to Shipley route, which mostly follows a canal-side path (passing Saltaire, covered in this section), with plans to extend to Bradford by 2005.

WALKING

The valleys and moors of West Yorkshire make good walking country, although the South Pennines (as this area is called) is wedged between the Peak District and the Yorkshire Dales, and has to defer to these areas in terms of sheer quality. The TICs all have leaflets and guidebooks on local walks, or see the main sections on the towns mentioned below, for more ideas. Hebden Bridge and especially Haworth make ideal bases for circular walks, with several long and short options.

The **Haworth to Hebden Bridge Path** is a popular trail that passes through quiet farmland and scenic wooded valleys.

The Pennine Way (p78), England's longest trail, follows the watershed through the area, and some good walks are possible following it for just a day or two.

Getting There & Around

The Metro is West Yorkshire's highly efficient train and bus network, centred on Leeds and Bradford – which are also the main gateways to the county. For transport details call **Metroline** (☎ 0113-245 7676; www.wymetro.com) or the national **Traveline** (☎ 0870 608 2608). MetroRover passes (£5) are good for travel on buses and trains after 9.30am on weekdays and all day at weekends. There's a thicket of additional Rovers covering buses and/or trains (see p971), plus heaps of useful Metro maps and timetables, all available at TICs.

LEEDS

☎ 0113 / pop 443,247

Leeds is an almost perfect reflection of the contemporary British zeitgeist. A child of the New Urban Revolution – that force that overhauls and redesigns punch-drunk industrial cities and rebrands them as the 'new somewhere else of somewhere.' So welcome to the Knightsbridge of the North, a shopping mecca whose counter is just getting longer. From cutting edge couture to contemporary cuisine, Leeds will hand it to you in a stylishly designed bag or serve it on a fancy plate. The city is all about appearance, and in parts it looks damn good, none more so than in the stunning Victorian arcades and upstanding edifices that give the city centre a real architectural gravitas.

Once pulsing with textile manufacturing and trade, this one-time driving industrial force is now pretty much dead, with memorials scattered over the city. Contemporary Leeds is the biggest financial centre in the country outside London, and, on a converse tip, has one of the biggest nightlife scenes. Many bars have late licences, lending the whole proceedings a relaxed flavour. Some legendary club nights have been honing their brand of hedonism for more than a decade, while new venues and versions pop up every time you blink.

Orientation

Most of the action takes place in the city centre, between Boar Lane to the south and The Headrow – the city's main drag – to the north. Briggate, which runs north–south between the two, is the focus of most of the shopping, while the best nightlife is concentrated in the warren of small streets at the western end of Boar Lane. In the last few years there has been a substantial waterfront development along both the River Aire and the Leeds–Liverpool Canal. It's best to explore the city centre on foot.

Information

Gateway to Yorkshire TIC (☎ 242 5242; www.leeds.gov .uk; The Arcade; ☺ 9am-5.30pm Mon-Sat, 10am-4pm Sun) In the train station.

Internet Exchange (☎ 242 1093; 29 Boar Lane; per 30 mins £1; ☺ 9.30am-8pm Mon-Fri, 10am-7pm Sat, 11am-6pm Sun) Near the train station.

Leeds General Infirmary (☎ 243 2799) West of Calverley St in the city centre.

Post office (City Sq; ☺ 9am-5.30pm Mon-Sat)

Waterstone's (☎ 244 4588; 97 Albion St) Has a good selection of maps.

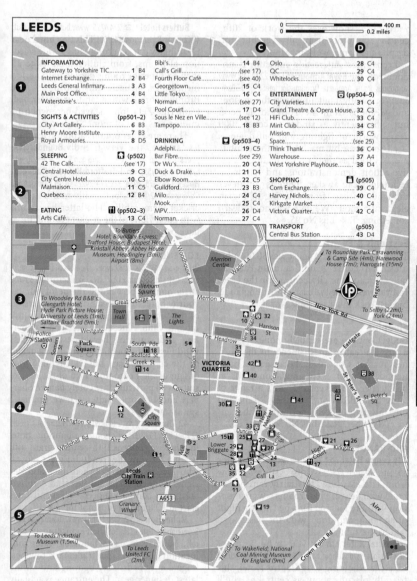

LEEDS

INFORMATION	Bibi's...............................**14** B4	Oslo.................................**28** C4
Gateway to Yorkshire TIC......**1** B4	Call's Grill.......................(see 17)	QC....................................**29** C4
Internet Exchange..............**2** B4	Fourth Floor Café.............(see 17)	Whitelocks.......................**30** C4
Leeds General Infirmary........**3** A3	Georgetown.....................**15** C4	
Main Post Office................**4** B4	Little Tokyo......................**16** C4	**ENTERTAINMENT** ⌕ (pp504–5)
Waterstone's....................**5** B3	Norman............................(see 27)	City Varieties....................**31** C3
	Pool Court........................**17** D4	Grand Theatre & Opera House..**32** C3
SIGHTS & ACTIVITIES (pp501–2)	Sous le Nez en Ville..........(see 12)	HiFi Club...........................**33** C4
City Art Gallery...................**6** B3	Tampopo...........................**18** B3	Mint Club..........................**34** C3
Henry Moore Institute..........**7** B3		Mission.............................**35** C5
Royal Armouries.................**8** D5	**DRINKING** ☐ (pp503–4)	Space................................(see 25)
	Adelphi............................**19** C5	Think Thank......................**36** C4
SLEEPING ☐ (p502)	Bar Fibre..........................(see 29)	Warehouse........................**37** A4
42 The Calls......................(see 17)	Dr Wu's............................**20** C4	West Yorkshire Playhouse....**38** D4
Central Hotel.....................**9** C3	Duck & Drake....................**21** D4	
City Centre Hotel...............**10** C3	Elbow Room......................**22** C5	**SHOPPING** ☐ (p505)
Malmaison........................**11** C5	Guildford..........................**23** B3	Corn Exchange...................**39** C4
Quebecs...........................**12** B4	Milo.................................**24** C4	Harvey Nichols..................**40** C4
	Mook...............................**25** C4	Kirkgate Market.................**41** C4
EATING ☐ (pp502–3)	MPV.................................**26** D4	Victoria Quarter................**42** C4
Arts Café..........................**13** C4	Norman............................**27** C4	
		TRANSPORT (p505)
		Central Bus Station............**43** D4

Sights

Home to a superb collection of 19th- and 20th-century British art, the **City Art Gallery** (☎ 247 8248; www.leeds.gov.uk/artgallery; The Headrow; admission free; ✆ 10am-5pm Mon, Tue, Thu-Sat, 10am-8pm Wed, 1-5pm Sun) is one of northern England's most important galleries. Heavyweights like Constable, Stanley Spencer and Wyndham

Lewis are well represented alongside more recent arrivals like Antony Gormley. Pride of place, however, goes to the outstanding genius of Henry Moore (1898–1986), who graduated from the Leeds School of Art. The adjoining **Henry Moore Institute** (☎ 246 7467; www.henry-moore-fdn.co.uk; admission free; ✆ 10am-5.30pm, 10am-9pm Wed), in a converted Victorian warehouse, showcases the work of 20th-century sculptors from all over but not, despite the name, work by Moore.

Leeds' most interesting museum is undoubtedly the **Royal Armouries** (☎ 220 1940; www .armouries.org.uk; Armouries Dr; admission free; ☼ 10.30am-5pm), originally built to house the armour and weapons from the Tower of London but subsequently expanded to cover 3000 years' worth of fighting and self-defence. It all sounds a bit macho, but the exhibits are as varied as they are fascinating: films, live-action demonstrations and hands-on technology can awaken interests you never thought you had, from jousting to Indian elephant armour. We dare you not to learn something. Take bus No 95.

Festivals & Events

The last weekend in August sees 50,000 plus music fans converge on Bramham Park, 10 miles outside the city centre, for the **Leeds Festival** (www.leedsfestival.com), one of England's biggest rock music extravaganzas.

Sleeping

Budget options are virtually nonexistent in a city that caters unashamedly to the business market. Conversely, because it's a business destination, accommodation tends to be cheaper at weekends. There's a range of fairly basic B&Bs on Woodsley Rd, behind the University of Leeds, northwest of the centre. To get here, take bus No 56, 58 or 60.

MID-RANGE

City Centre Hotel (☎ 242 9019; fax 247 1921; 51 New Briggate; s/d from £29/55) Only a stone's throw from The Headrow, this fairly ramshackle hotel with pea-size bathrooms is a great option if you're looking for a bed after a night of clubbing and don't want the hassle of a taxi to the suburbs.

Central Hotel (☎ 294 1456; fax 294 1551; 35-47 New Briggate; s/d without bath £28/40, with bath £45/50) Like the adjoining City Centre Hotel, this friendly place is about as central as you'll get for the price, but don't expect much: the bathrooms are like Port-A-Loos or airplane toilets. Literally.

Glengarth Hotel (☎ 245 7940; fax 216 8033; 162 Woodsley Rd; s/d from £25/36) A converted family home with a dozen or so tiny rooms that are nevertheless quite comfortable. The breakfast is the best we had in town.

Butlers Hotel (☎ 274 4755; www.butlershotel.co.uk; 40 Cardigan Rd; s/d from £45/60) This fine hotel near Headingley cricket ground has a wide selection of rooms, from cluttered basics to 15 themed superior rooms decked with period furnishings, Jacuzzi baths and one – The Brontë Room – with a fab four-poster bed. Catherine Zeta-Jones stayed here when £1 million was a lot of money to her.

There are other options around Headingley, such as the very friendly **Boundary Express** (☎ /fax 274 7700; 42 Cardigan Rd; d without/with bathroom £42/55) and **Trafford House & Budapest Hotel** (☎ 275 2034; fax 274 2422; 16-18 Cardigan Rd; s/d/tr from £32/49/70), both with rooms full of cricket memorabilia. The latter has rooms with good views of the cricket ground; three have balconies.

TOP END

Quebecs (☎ 244 8989; www.theetoncollection.com; 9 Quebec St; s/d/ste from £125/135/225) Victorian grace at its opulent best is the theme of our favourite hotel in town, a brilliant conversion of the former Victorian Leeds and County Liberal Club. The elaborate wood panelling and stunning heraldic stained-glass windows in the public spaces are matched by the contemporary but equally luxurious design of the bedrooms. Two of the deluxe suites – in particular the cutely named Sherbert and Liquorice suites – have dramatic spiral staircases.

42 The Calls (☎ 244 0099; www.42thecalls.co.uk; 42 The Calls; r £130-375) This snazzy boutique hotel in what was once a 19th-century grain mill is a big hit with the trendy business crowd, who love its sharp, polished lines and designer aesthetic. The smaller studio rooms are pretty compact indeed. Weekend rates start at £99; breakfast is not included.

Malmaison (☎ 398 1000; www.malmaison.com; Sovereign St; d/ste £129/165) Self-consciously stylish, Malmaison has a fabulous waterfront location and all of the trademark touches: huge comfy beds, sexy lighting and all the latest designer gear. The entrance is actually on Swinegate, but Sovereign St just sounds classier.

Eating

In keeping with Leeds' overall rejuvenation, the city's reputation as a culinary centre is growing all the time. You won't have any problems finding good food here.

BUDGET

Arts Café (☎ 243 8243; 42 Call Lane; lunch mains about £5, dinner mains about £8; ☺ lunch & dinner) Local art on the walls and a bohemian vibe throughout make this a popular place for quiet reflection, a chat and a really good cup of coffee to wash down the excellent lunchtime sandwiches.

Norman (☎ 234 3988; 36 Call Lane; mains £5-8; ☺ lunch & dinner) The tasty Japanese noodle menu at one of the city's best bars is the reason to come here before nightfall; this place is as stylish by day as it is popular by night.

Tampopo (☎ 245 1816; 15 South Pde; mains £6-8; ☺ lunch & dinner Mon-Sat, lunch Sun) Masters of the art of conveyor-belt cuisine, Tampopo gets 'em in and out in virtually record time; between coming and going, diners tuck into tantalising noodle and rice dishes from Southeast Asia.

MID-RANGE

Little Tokyo (☎ 243 9090; 24 Central Rd; mains about £10-12; ☺ lunch & dinner Mon-Sat) Fans of genuine Japanese food should go no further than this superb restaurant, which serves a wide array of sushi and sashimi (including half-portions) and Bento box meals – those handy divided trays that serve the Japanese equivalent of a four-course meal.

Georgetown (☎ 245 6677; 24-26 Briggate; mains £8-13; ☺ lunch & dinner) Take a barely converted Victorian watchmaker's shop and turn it into a colonial-style dining room, complete with white linen tablecloths, crystal cut glass and fine bone china. Add a superb Malaysian-style menu and all of a sudden Leeds gets a little bit of Raffles of Singapore c 1930.

Bibi's (☎ 243 0905; 16 Greek St; mains £8-15; ☺ lunch & dinner Mon-Fri, dinner Sat & Sun) One of the city's most popular restaurants, Bibi's serves classic Italian dishes in a questionable setting – too many mirrors and white wicker furniture – but there's no need to argue with the cuisine. Nothing fancy, just good Italian nosh.

Sous le Nez en Ville (☎ 244 0108; Basement, Quebec House, 9 Quebec St; mains £12-18; ☺ lunch & dinner Mon-Sat) The name doesn't make a lot of sense (Under the Nose in Town?) but the expertly presented seafood certainly does at this excellent French restaurant below Quebecs Hotel.

Fourth Floor Café (☎ 204 8000; Harvey Nichols, 107-11 Briggate; mains from £11; ☺ 10am-6pm Mon-Wed & Fri, 9am-10pm Thu & Sat, noon-5pm Sun) A department store with a fancy restaurant? It could only be Harvey Nicks. It's called a café, but don't be fooled: the nosh here is the best of British, even if the portions would only satisfy the models in their catalogue.

TOP END

Two of Leeds' finest restaurants are side by side along The Calls.

Pool Court (☎ 244 4242; 42 The Calls; mains about £18; ☺ lunch & dinner Mon-Thu, dinner Fri & Sat) Leeds' top restaurant is a tiny little room that seats only 35 people (there's more room on the canalside terrace) but it's the only place in town to be blessed by the stars of Michelin. The cuisine is strictly modern British.

Call's Grill (☎ 245 3870; 38 The Calls; steaks £12-20; ☺ dinner Mon-Sat) Although they do a couple of fish dishes and doff a cap to veggies, this place is really all about red meat. Let your heart and wallet do some overtime, because these steaks are divine.

Drinking

The glammed-up hordes of party animals crawl the venues around Boar Lane and Call Lane, where bars are opening all the time. Most bars open till 2am, with an admission charge of £2 to £4, up to £6 at weekends. The more traditional pubs keep regular hours.

BARS

Dr Wu's (☎ 242 7629; 35 Call Lane) Small and chock-full of black leather seats, this grungy bar would slot comfortably into New York's East Village, and don't the punters just know it. The vibe is studied cool and the DJs play a suitable blend of eclectic (but always alternative) sounds.

Mook (☎ 245 9967; Hirst's Yard) Tucked away behind Call Lane, this stylish little bar was drawing in the city's cool kids at the time of writing. Maybe it was the excellent DJs, who play decks that are suspended from the ceiling, or the subdued lighting, which makes everyone that bit more beautiful.

MPV (☎ 243 9486; 5-8 Church St, Kirkgate) This wins our prize for weirdest looking bar in northern England. Four bright red, huge, Portakabins with glass fronts are as eye-catching a design as you'll ever see. Inside, DJs keep the crowd well entertained.

Norman (☎ 234 3988; 36 Call Lane) Lipstick-red seating, crazy-paving mirrors and a ferociously stylish crowd keep this super bar high up on the list of best boozers in town. The weekend DJs – playing mostly a mix of hip-hop, R & B and funk breaks – are uniformly top-notch.

QC (☎ 245 9449; Lower Briggate; ⏱ till 4am Mon-Sat) and **Bar Fibre** (☎ 200888; www.barfibre.com; 168 Lower Briggate) are almost interchangeable chrome-and-glass gay bars, next door to each other; both spill out into the cannily named Queen's Court.

Other tips for a tipple:

Elbow Room (☎ 245 7011; www.elbow-room.co.uk; 64 Call Lane) Pop art, purple pool tables and laid-back music.

Milo (☎ 245 7101; 10 Call Lane) Great bar for eclectic music, from reggae to electronica.

Oslo (☎ 245 7768; Lower Briggate) A trendy bar that is like a cave with a blue backlight.

Velvet (☎ 242 5079; 11-13 Hirst's Yard) Gay bar that can be pretty tough to get into if you're not arm-in-arm with a male model.

PUBS

Duck & Drake (☎ 246 5806; 43 Kirkgate) High ceilings, obligatory pub characters, real ales and regular, free live music – mostly jazz.

Whitelocks (☎ 245 3950; Turk's Head Yard) Great beer and good, old-fashioned décor in a very popular traditional pub dating from 1715. In summer, crowds spill out into the courtyard.

Other recommendations include the **Adelphi** (☎ 245 6377; 3-5 Hunslet Rd), built in 1898 and hardly changed since, and the **Guildford** (☎ 244 9204; 115 The Headrow), an attractive Art Deco classic.

Entertainment

In order to make sense of the ever-evolving scene, get your hands on the monthly *Leeds Guide* (£1.70) or *Absolute Leeds* (£1.50), available in most newsagents.

NIGHTCLUBS

The tremendous Leeds club scene attracts people from miles around. In true northern tradition, people brave the cold wearing next to nothing, even in winter, which is a spectacle in itself. Clubs charge a variety of admission prices, ranging from £3 on a slow weeknight to £10 on Saturday.

HiFi Club (☎ 242 7353; www.thehificlub.co.uk; 2 Central Rd) This intimate club is a good break from the hardcore sounds of four to the

floor: if it's Tamla Motown or the percussive beats of dance-floor jazz that shake your booty, this is the spot for you.

Mint Club (☎ 244 3168; www.themintclubleeds.co .uk; 8 Harrison St) A small club with a big reputation, this usually packed venue generally offers up good house, breakbeats and techno.

Space (☎ 246 1030; Hirsts Yard) White-walled starkly modern venue that specialises in drum 'n' bass, hip-hop and grungy garage; it's incredibly packed at weekends.

Think Thank (☎ 234 0980; 2a Call Lane) The indie '90s are alive and well and rocking the floor at this sweaty little basement club, which throbs to the sounds of everything from the Beastie Boys to the Beatles.

Other danceterias:

Mission (☎ 0870 122 0114; www.clubmission.com; 8-13 Heaton's Ct) A massive new club that redefines the term 'up-for-it'.

Warehouse (☎ 246 8287; 19-21 Somers St) Home to the mixed booty-shaker **Speed Queen** (www.speedqueen .co.uk) featuring an outrageous crowd against a hi-NRG soundtrack.

SPORT

In 2004 the unthinkable happened: **Leeds United Football Club** (☎ 226 1000; www.leedsunited .com; Elland Rd) were relegated from the Premiership amid scandal, poor play and the threat of bankruptcy. But fans remain defiantly optimistic (things surely can't get any worse) and continue to pack the Elland Rd stadium; tickets are now just *slightly* easier to get. Take bus No 51, 52 or 54 from Kirkgate Market.

Since 1890 Headingley has been hosting cricket matches. It is still used for test matches and is the home ground of the **Yorkshire County Cricket Club** (tickets ☎ 278 7394; www.yorkshireccc.org.uk; test match from £25). Take bus No 74 or 75 from Infirmary St.

THEATRE & CINEMA

Culture vultures will find plenty to keep themselves entertained in Leeds.

City Varieties (☎ 243 0808; www.cityvarieties.co.uk; Swan St) This old-fashioned music hall features anything from clairvoyants to country music.

Grand Theatre & Opera House (☎ 222 6222; www.leeds.gov.uk/grandtheatre; 46 New Briggate) Hosts musicals, plays and opera, including performances by acclaimed **Opera North** (☎ 244 5326; www.operanorth.co.uk).

West Yorkshire Playhouse (☎ 213 7700; www .wyplayhouse.com; Quarry Hill Mount) The Playhouse has a sturdy reputation for excellent live drama.

Hyde Park Picture House (☎ 275 2045; www .leedscinema.com; Brudenell Rd) This Edwardian cinema shows a meaty range of art-house and mainstream choices. Take bus No 56 or 63 from the city centre.

Shopping

Leeds' myriad city centre shopping arcades seem to blend into one giant mall. Most of them are unremarkable, but the designer-ridden **Victoria Quarter** (☎ 245 5333) is worth visiting for aesthetic reasons alone. A handful of mosaic-paved, stained-glass roofed Victorian arcades have been beautifully restored (check out the County Arcade). Here, the biggest name is undoubtedly **Harvey Nichols** (☎ 204 8000; 107-11 Briggate), which has its usual selection of upmarket clothes.

A bit closer to earth, the **Kirkgate Market** (☎ 214 5162; ☼ 9am-5pm Mon-Sat, 9am-1pm Wed; open-air market Thu-Tue), once home of Marks, which later joined Spencer, sells fresh produce and cheap goods.

The circular **Corn Exchange** (☎ 234 0363; ☼ 9am-6pm), built in 1865 to house the grain trade, has a wonderful wrought, armadillo-like lid, and is the place to come for one-off clothes, eclectic jewellery or records.

Getting There & Away

AIR

Eight miles north of the city via the A65, **Leeds-Bradford airport** (☎ 250 9696) offers domestic and charter flights, plus international flights to a few major European cities. The Airlink 757 bus operates every 30 minutes between the airport and the bus and train station (£1.80, 40 minutes). A taxi costs about £17.

BUS

National Express (☎ 0870 580 8080; www.national express.com) serves most major cities, including hourly services from London (£17.50, 4½ hours) and Manchester (£7, one hour).

Yorkshire Coastliner (☎ 01653-692556; www.york shirecoastliner.co.uk; coastliner freedom ticket adult £10 per day) has useful services linking Leeds, York, Castle Howard, Goathland and Whitby (Nos 840, 842 and X40), York and Scarborough (Nos 843, 845 and X45).

TRAIN

Leeds City Station has hourly services to/ from London King's Cross (£65.20, 2½ hours), Sheffield (£6.60, 45 minutes), Manchester (£12.10, one hour) and York (£8.10, 30 minutes).

Leeds is also the starting-point for services on the famous Settle–Carlisle line. For more details, see p415.

Getting Around

Metro buses go from the Central Bus Station and on or near City Sq. The various Day Rover passes (see p500) covering trains and/or buses are good for reaching Bradford, Haworth and Hebden Bridge.

AROUND LEEDS

A day out from Leeds opens up a fascinating range of options: stately splendour at Harewood, dust and darkness at the National Coal Mining Museum, or technology and poppadoms at Bradford, to name a few. Places are listed roughly in order of distance from Leeds, first west and north, then south.

Bradford

☎ 01274 / pop 293,717

Only 9 miles west of Leeds but with suburbs so close that they merge into one another, industrial Bradford is Leeds' closest neighbour and distinctly poorer cousin. Or so they will tell you in Leeds. Bradford may not have the same tourist-friendly plumage, but it has a kind of 'ugliness that could not only be tolerated but often enjoyed', according to its favourite cantankerous son, JB Priestley (1894–1984).

Thanks to its role as a major player in the wool trade, Bradford attracted large numbers of Bangladeshis and Pakistanis throughout the 20th century, who – despite occasional racial tensions – have helped reinvigorate the city and give it new energy. A high point of the year is a colourful celebration of Asian music and dance called the Mela, part of the annual Bradford festival which is held at the end of June.

SIGHTS

The top sight during any visit to Bradford is the **National Museum of Photography, Film & Television** (NMPFT; ☎ 202030; www.nmpft.org.uk; admission free, special events & cinemas adult/child £5/3; ☼ 10am-6pm Tue-Sun). It's five exhibit-packed floors tell the story of the recorded visual image from 19th-century cameras and early animation to digital technology and the psychology of advertising. There's lots of hands-on stuff too; you can film yourself in a bedroom scene or play at being a TV newsreader.

The **Colour Museum** (☎ 390955; Providence St; admission £1.50; ☉ 10am-4pm Tue-Sat), oft-overlooked, is a little gem, just a 10-minute walk from the centre. It tells the story of Bradford's wool-dying trade, and has a fascinating section on how our eyes perceive colour, including a display contrasting the visual sense of different species (what's blue to you isn't blue to Fido).

Bradford Industrial Museum (☎ 435900; Moorside Rd, Eccleshill; admission free; ☉ 10am-5pm Tue-Sat, noon-5pm Sun), 3 miles out of the centre, gives a hint of what a Yorkshire textile spinning mill was like at the peak of the Industrial Revolution. Other exhibits include various steam engines (sometimes working), transport from the last 100 years, and a horse-drawn tram to give a quick 'step back in history' round the car park.

EATING
Bradford is famous for its curries, so if you're still here in the evening, don't miss trying one of the city's hundred or so restaurants. A great help in decision making is the **Bradford Curry Guide** (http://website.lineone.net/~bradfordcurryguide) which sorts the rogan josh from the rubbish nosh.

Kashmir (☎ 726513; 27 Morley St; mains £4-5; ☉ evenings to 3am) Bradford's oldest curry house has top tucker, served with no frills or booze (it's BYO). Whatever you do, go for a table upstairs, as the soul-destroying, windowless basement has all the character of a public toilet. It's just around the corner from the NMPFT.

GETTING THERE & AWAY
Bradford is on the Metro train line from Leeds, with very frequent services every day.

Saltaire
A Victorian-era landmark, Saltaire was a model industrial village built in 1851 by philanthropic wool-baron and teetotaller Titus Salt. Overlooking the rows of neat honey-coloured cottages was the then largest factory in the world. Heating, ventilation and good lighting were high on Salt's list of priorities, but there was no way on earth this sober humanitarian was going to give his workers somewhere to indulge in the demon drink, so the town had no pub.

The factory is now **Salt's Mill** (☎ 531163; www.saltsmill.org.uk; admission free; ☉ 10am-6pm), a splendidly bright and airy cathedral-like building where the main draw is a permanent exhibition of work by local boy David Hockney (1937–). There are also shops of books and crafts, and a café.

Saltaire's **TIC** (☎ 774993; www.visitsaltaire.com; 2 Victoria Rd; ☉ 10am-5pm) has maps of the village and runs free hour-long guided walks of the town throughout the year.

Saltaire is 9 miles west of Leeds centre, and 3 miles north of Bradford centre (effectively an outer suburb of Bradford). It's easily reached by Metro rail from both.

Harewood
There's only one reason to stop in Harewood, a tiny hamlet about 7 miles north of Leeds, and that is to visit the great park, sumptuous gardens and mighty edifice of **Harewood House** (☎ 0113-218 1010; www.harewood.org; admission £10, Sun & Bank Hols £11; grounds ☉ 10am-6pm, house 11am-4.30pm Feb–mid-Nov, house & grounds 10am-4pm mid-Nov–Jan). As an outing from Leeds you can easily fill a day here, and if you're heading for Harrogate, stopping off is highly recommended.

A classic example of a stately English pile, the house was built between 1759 and 1772 by the era's designer superstars, a team assembled by John Carr (who designed the exterior). Lancelot 'Capability' Brown laid out the grounds, Thomas Chippendale supplied the furniture (the largest commission he ever received, costing the unheard-of amount of £10,000), Robert Adams designed the interior, and Italy was raided to create an appropriate art collection. The superb terrace was added 100 years later by yet another top name, Sir Charles Barry – he of the Houses of Parliament.

Many locals come to Harewood just to relax or saunter through the grounds, without even thinking of going inside the house. Hours of entertainment can be had in the **Bird Garden**, with many colourful species including penguins (feeding time at 2pm is a highlight), and there's also a boating lake,

WORTH THE TRIP

For close to three centuries, West and South Yorkshire was synonymous with coal production; the collieries shaped and scarred the landscape, while entire villages grew up around the pits, each inhabitant and their descendants destined to spend their working lives underground. The industry came to a shuddering close in the 1980s, but the imprint of coal is still very much in evidence, even if there's only a handful of collieries left. One of these, at Claphouse, is now the **National Coal Mining Museum for England** (☎ 01924-848806; www.ncm.org.uk; Overton, near Wakefield; admission free; ☉ 10am-5pm), a superb testament to the inner workings of the coal mine.

The highlight of a visit is the tour underground; complete with helmet and head-torch you ride in a 'cage' almost 150m down, then follow passages all the way to the coal seam where massive drilling machines now stand idle. Former miners now work as guides, and explain the details – sometimes with a suitably authentic and almost impenetrable mix of local dialect and technical terminology.

Up on top, there are modern audiovisual displays, some fascinating memorabilia, plus exhibits about trade unions, strikes and the wider mining communities – only slightly over-romantic in parts. You can also stroll round the pit-pony stables (with their equine inhabitants also now retired) or the slightly eerie bath-house, totally unchanged since the miners scrubbed off the coal dust and emptied their lockers for the last time. There are also longer nature trails in the surrounding fields and woods.

The museum is about 10 miles south of Leeds, on the A642, which drivers can reach from the M1. By public transport, take a train from Leeds to Wakefield (at least hourly, 15 minutes), and then bus No 232 towards Huddersfield can drop you outside the museum (hourly, 25 minutes).

café and adventure playground. For more activity, there's a network of walking trails around the lake or through the parkland.

From Leeds, use bus No 36 (at least half-hourly Monday to Saturday, hourly on Sunday) which continues to Harrogate. Visitors coming by bus get half-price admission too (so hang on to your ticket). From the main gate, it's a two-mile walk through the grounds to the house and gardens. At busy times there's a free shuttle service.

HEBDEN BRIDGE
☎ 01422 / pop 4086

When the textile industry went south, Hebden Bridge refused to go quietly into the good night. Instead, it raged a bit and then transformed itself into an attractive little tourist trap with a slightly off-centre reputation. Besides the honest-to-God Yorkshire folk that have lived here for years, the town is home to university academics, die-hard hippies and a substantial gay community – all of which explains the inordinate number of craft shops, organic cafés and second-hand bookstores.

The **Hebden Bridge Visitor & Canal Centre** (☎ 843831; Butlers Wharf, New Rd; ☉ 9.30am-5.30pm Mon-Fri, 10.30am-5pm Sat & Sun mid-Mar–mid-Oct, 10am-5pm Mon-Fri, 10.30am-4.15pm Sat & Sun rest of year) has a good stock of maps and leaflets on local walks, including saunters in **Hardcastle Crags**, two unspoilt wooded valleys run by the National Trust (NT), 1½ miles northwest of town off the A6033. There are streams and waterfalls and numerous walking trails, some of which link to the Pennine Way, and another which takes you all the way to Haworth.

Above the town is the much older village of **Heptonstall**, its narrow cobbled street lined with 500-year-old cottages and the ruins of a beautiful 13th-century church. But it is the churchyard of the newer Methodist church that draws the curious visitors, for here is buried the poet Sylvia Plath (1932–63), wife of another famous rhymer, Ted Hughes (1930–98) who was born in these parts.

Sleeping & Eating
High Greenwood Campsite (☎ 842287; tent sites £4.50) Basically just a large, sloping field with a block of facilities in a converted barn, High Greenwood Campsite is about 3 miles northwest of town and can be reached via the lane that runs through Heptonstall. The campsite is just off the footpath between Hebden Bridge and Haworth, near Hardcastle Crags, and the Pennine Way runs nearby too, so it's very popular with walkers.

Mankinholes YHA Hostel (☎ 0870 770 5952; www .yha.org.uk; Todmorden; dm £10.60) A converted 17th-century manor house 4 miles south-west of Hebden Bridge, this hostel has limited facilities (no TV room) but it is very popular with walkers; the Pennine Way is only half a mile from here.

White Lion Hotel (☎ 842197; Bridge Gate; s/d from £28/40) A large 400-year-old coaching inn smack in the middle of town; the rooms in the converted coach house are that little bit more comfortable than the ones in the main house. Downstairs is a popular pub and a pretty good **restaurant** (mains £7-10) with a standard pub grub menu.

Crown Fisheries (Crown St; mains about £4; ⊗ 10am-6.30pm) A terrific chipper that serves up a great supper (fish, chips, bread and butter and tea), and also does takeaways.

Getting There & Away

Hebden Bridge is on the Leeds–Manchester Victoria Metro train line (services about every 30 minutes Monday to Saturday, hourly on Sunday, 45 minutes). Get off at Todmorden for the Mankinholes YHA Hostel.

HAWORTH

⊗ 01535 / pop 6078

Take a handsome village of cobbled streets lined with 18th- and 19th-century dark-stone houses, a quintessential West Yorkshire view of the moors, a bona fide link with the most prodigious literary family in British history and you have Haworth, the home of the Brontë sisters and the country's second-most important literary shrine after Stratford-upon-Avon. Here, in the handsome parsonage behind the church, some of the world's favourite novels were penned, including *Jane Eyre* and *Wuthering Heights*.

Information

The **TIC** (☎ 642329; www.haworth-village.org.uk; 2-4 West Lane; ⊗ 9am-5.30pm Apr-Sep, 9am-5pm Oct-Mar) has an excellent supply of information on

the village, the surrounding area and, of course, the Brontës. Another good source of information is www.brontecountry.co.uk.

Steep, cobbled Main St is lined with cafés, tearooms, pubs and shops selling everything imaginable (and more) bearing the Brontë name. Handy stops might include the **post office** (⊗ 9am-5.30pm Mon-Fri, 9am-12.30pm Sat); **Venables & Bainbridge**, selling used books, including many vintage Brontë volumes; and **Rose & Co Apothecary** (84 Main St), the beautifully restored druggist so favoured by Branwell Brontë.

Sights

Your first stop should be the **Haworth Parish Church** (admission free), a lovely old place of worship, on the site of the 'old' church that the Brontë sisters knew, which was demolished in 1879. In the surrounding churchyard, gravestones are covered in moss, or thrust to one side by growing trees, which gives the whole place a tremendous feeling of age.

Set in a pretty garden overlooking the church and graveyard, the **Brontë Parsonage Museum** (☎ 642323; www.bronte.info; adult/child £4.80/1.50; ⊗ 10am-5.30pm Apr-Sep, 11am-5pm Oct-Mar) is where the Brontë family lived from 1820. Rooms are meticulously furnished and decorated, exactly as they were in the Brontë era, with many personal possessions on display. There's also a neat and informative exhibition, which includes the fascinating miniature books the Brontës wrote as children.

Walking

Haworth is surrounded by the moors of the South Pennines – immediately familiar to Brontë fans – and the TIC has leaflets on local walks to endless Brontë features. A 6½-mile favourite leads to Top Withins, a ruined farm thought to have inspired *Wuthering Heights*, even though a plaque clearly states that the farmhouse bore no resemblance to the one Emily wrote about.

STEAM ENGINES & RAILWAY CHILDREN

Haworth is on the **Keighley & Worth Valley Railway** (KWVR; ☎ 645214; www.kwvr.co.uk; adult/child £7/3.50, adult/child day rover £10/5) – which runs steam and classic diesel engines between Keighley and Oxenhope. It was here, in 1969, that the classic movie *The Railway Children* was shot; Mr Perks was stationmaster at Oakworth, where the Edwardian look has been meticulously maintained. Trains operate around hourly at weekends all year; in holiday periods they run hourly every day.

BAD LUCK BRONTËS

The Rev Patrick Brontë, his wife Maria and six children moved to Haworth Parsonage in 1820. On September 15, 1821, Maria died of cancer, after which her unmarried sister Elizabeth Branwell arrived from Penzance to help raise the children. Three years later, the eldest girl, Maria, was sent home from school on account of ill-health and died in May 1825, aged 11. A few weeks later, her younger sister Elizabeth arrived home sick from the same school and died, aged 10, on June 15. (Years later, Charlotte immortalised the school as the infamous Lowood in *Jane Eyre*.)

The double tragedy led the good reverend to keep his remaining family close to him, and for the next few years the children were home-schooled in a highly creative environment. The children conjured up mythical heroes and countries, and produced miniature home-made books. It was an auspicious start, at least for the three girls, Charlotte, Emily and Anne; the lone boy, Branwell, was more of a painter but he lacked his sisters' drive and discipline. After a short stint as a professional artist, he ended up spending most of his days in the Black Bull pub, drunk and stoned on laudanum obtained across the street at Rose & Co Apothecary. While the three sisters were setting the London literary world alight with the publication of three superb novels – *Jane Eyre*, *Wuthering Heights* and *Agnes Grey* – in one extraordinary year (1847), Branwell was fading quickly, and he died of tuberculosis on 24 September, 1848. The family was devastated, but things quickly got worse. Emily contracted a cold at the funeral that also developed into tuberculosis; she never left the house again and died on December 19. Anne, who had also been sick, was next: Charlotte took her to Scarborough to seek a sea cure but she died on May 28.

The remaining family never recovered. Despite her growing fame, Charlotte struggled with depression and never quite adapted to her high position in literary society. Despite her misgivings, however, she eventually married, but she too died prematurely, in the early stages of pregnancy, on March 31, 1855. All things considered, it's hardly surprising that poor old Patrick Brontë spent the remaining years of his life going increasingly insane.

Other walks can be worked around the Brontë Way, a longer route linking Bradford and Colne via Haworth. Alternatively, the Pennine Way runs west of Haworth and can be followed south to Hebden Bridge (p507). There's also a direct walking route between Haworth and Hebden Bridge, via the scenic valleys of Hardcastle Crags.

Sleeping & Eating

Virtually every second house on Main St does B&B; they're mostly indistinguishable from each other but some are just that little bit cuter. There's little in the way of fine dining in Haworth, but many of the B&Bs also have small cafés that are good for a spot of tourist lunch – mediocre servings of local dishes and safe bets like sandwiches.

Old Registry (☎ 646503; www.oldregistry.com; 2-4 Main St; r £65-80) This is a favourite place in town, a stylishly rustic (or rustically stylish) hotel where each of the carefully themed rooms has a four-poster bed: the Blue Heaven room is just that – at least for fans of Laura Ashley's delphinium blue. We loved the Stage Room, complete with theatrical memorabilia.

Rookery Nook (☎ 643374; 6 Church St; r £12.50-22) Almost attached to the church, this place has spacious rooms with New Age décor though the smaller, budget rooms are pretty cramped. Breakfast (£2.50 to £3.50) is served in the room.

Aitches (☎ 642501; www.aitches.co.uk; 11 West Lane; s/d from £35/50) A classy Victorian stone bungalow with four beautiful rooms, with wrought-iron beds and handsome furnishings.

Weaver's (☎ 643822; 15 West Lane; bar suppers £4-10, 3-course meal £20-25; Tue-Sat) Smart and stylish, with simply the best food in town and a menu featuring local specialities. Get there early and try the tasty two-course 'sampler' menu (£11) at the bar.

Other options:

Apothecary Guest House (☎ 643642; www.theapothecary guesthouse.co.uk; 86 Main St; s/d £20/40) Oak beams and narrow, slanted passageways lead to comfortable, airy rooms – even though some of the chintzy wallpaper is questionable.

Haworth Old Hall (☎ 642709; Sun St; snacks £3, salads £6, mains £6-10) A highly rated inn, with decent food, wine and beer, all served in convivial surroundings. The steak and ale pie is a classic. If you want to linger longer, comfortable doubles cost £50.

Haworth YHA Hostel (☎ 0870 770 5858; www.yha.org
.uk; Longlands Drive, off Lees Lane; dm £11.80; ☺ Feb-Nov,
Fri & Sat only Nov-Jan) A big old house with plenty of
facilities, including a games room, lounge, cycle store and
laundry. It's on the northeastern edge of town.

Getting There & Away

From Leeds, the easiest approach to Haworth
is via Keighley, which is on the Metro train
network. Bus No 500 runs between Keighley and Haworth (six daily, 15 minutes),
and also serves Todmorden and Hebden
Bridge. However, the most interesting way
to get to Haworth from Keighley is via the
KWV Railway (see p508).

YORKSHIRE DALES NATIONAL PARK

A walking and cycling wonderland, the Yorkshire Dales (from the Viking word *dalr*,
meaning 'valleys') is comfortably wedged
in between the Lake District to the west
and the North York Moors to the east. This
marvellous national park is made up of high
hills and moors cut through by rugged
stone walls and spotted with extravagant
houses and the faded, spectral grandeur of
monastic ruins.

It's not just walkers and cyclists who flock
here – car drivers love it too, which makes
for crowded roads, especially on summer
weekends. If you want to avoid this, come
by bus and train and try to get off the
beaten path.

Orientation & Information

The 683-sq-mile Yorkshire Dales National
Park divides into two parts: in the north, two
main valleys run west to east – broad expansive Wensleydale (home of the famous
cheese) and narrow secretive Swaledale. In
the south, the main valleys – Ribblesdale,
Malhamdale, Littondale and Wharfedale – all
run north–south and are the most popular
areas for tourists.

The main Dales gateways are Skipton in
the south and Richmond in the northeast.
Good bases in the park itself include Settle
and Grassington. All have excellent TICs
(some are called park visitors centres), stocking a mountain of local guidebooks and maps,
and providing accommodation details.

To the northwest and west, the towns
of Kirkby Stephen and Kirkby Lonsdale
can also make handy jumping-off points,
although both these spots are outside the
national park boundary, and actually in the
county of Cumbria (despite definite Dales
affiliations).

The *Visitor* newspaper, available from
TICs, lists local events and walks guided by
park rangers, as well as many places to stay
and eat. The official park website at www
.yorkshiredales.org.uk is similarly useful.

Activities

CYCLING

Other than on busy summer weekends, this
is excellent cycling country. Most roads
follow the rivers along the bottom of the
Dales so, although there are still some steep
climbs, there's also plenty on the flat. TICs
stock maps and leaflets with suggested
routes (on-road and off-road) for a day or
longer.

Just one example is the Yorkshire Dales
Cycle Way, an energetic and exhilarating
130-mile loop, taking in the best of the
park. Skipton is a convenient start, from
where you ride up Wharfedale, then steeply
over Floshes Hill to Hawes. From here turn
east along Wensleydale to Aysgarth, then
north over the wild hills to Reeth. The roads
are steep but the scenery is breathtaking.
Follow Swaledale westwards, through remote Keld and down to the market town
of Kirkby Stephen. Then it's south to Sed-
bergh, and up beautiful Dentdale to pop
out at Ribblehead. It's plain sailing now,
through Horton-in-Ribblesdale to Stainforth, one more climb over to Malham, and
finally back to Skipton for tea and medals.

WALKING

The Yorkshire Dales has a vast footpath
network, with options for everything from
easy strolls to challenging hikes; we suggest
a few options throughout this section. Look
out at TICs for leaflets on organised walks
from train stations, notably on the Settle–
Carlisle Line. Serious walkers should equip
themselves with *OS Outdoor Leisure Maps
Nos 2, 10* and *30*, available from TICs.

Two of England's most famous long-
distance routes cross the Dales: the Pennine Way goes through the rugged western half of the park. If you haven't got the

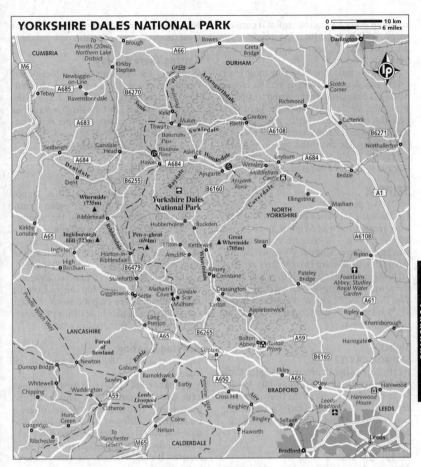

YORKSHIRE DALES NATIONAL PARK

0 ____ 10 km
0 ____ 6 miles

three weeks required to cover all 259 miles, a few days in the Dales, between Malham and Hawes for example, will repay the effort. The Coast to Coast Walk (a 190-mile classic; p78) goes through lovely Swaledale in the northern Dales. Following the route for a few days is highly recommended (see p516 for more information).

Another long-distance possibility is the Dales Way, which begins in Ilkley, follows the River Wharfe through the heart of the Dales, and finishes at Bowness-on-Windermere in the Lake District. If you start at Grassington, it's an easy five-day 60-mile journey. A handy companion guide is *Dales Way* by Arthur Gemmell and Colin Speakman (1996, £4.99), available at most bookshops.

Sleeping

There are many villages in and around the park with a good range of hotels, B&Bs, hostels and campsites. Most rural pubs also do B&B. Walkers and hardy outdoor types can take advantage of camping barns. These are usually owned by farmers, and booking is organised centrally through the **YHA** (☎ 0870 870 8808). For details, TICs have a *Camping Barns in England* leaflet.

Getting There & Around

The main gateway towns of Skipton and Richmond are well served by public transport, and local bus services radiate out from there. Get hold of the very useful *Dales Explorer* timetable from TICs – as well as covering every bus in the region it contains maps, B&B listings, local information and an excellent selection of walks that tie in with bus services.

Going by train, the best and most interesting access to the Dales is via the famous Settle–Carlisle Line (see the boxed text, p514). From the south, trains start in Leeds and pass through Skipton, Settle, and numerous small villages, offering unrivalled access to the hills straight from the station platform. Of course, if you're coming from the north, Carlisle is the place to get on board.

SKIPTON

☎ 01756 / pop 14,313

On the national park's southern edge is the busy market town of Skipton, once known as 'Sheeptown' – there's no guessing what was traded here. Monday, Wednesday, Friday and Saturday are market days on High St, bringing crowds from all over and giving the town something of a festive atmosphere. The **TIC** (☎ 792809; skipton@ytbtic.org.uk; 35 Coach St; 🕑 10am-5pm Mon-Fri, 9am-5pm Sat) is right in the middle of town.

Sights
SKIPTON CASTLE
At the top of the main street, **Skipton Castle** (☎ 792442; High St; admission £4.60; 🕑 10am-6pm Mon-Sat, noon-6pm Sun), is one of the best-preserved medieval castles in England – a fascinating contrast to the ruins you'll see elsewhere – and well worth a visit.

Sleeping & Eating
There's a strip of B&Bs just outside the centre on Keighley Rd. All those between Nos 46 and 57 are worth trying.

Westfield House (☎ 790849; 50 Keighley Rd; s/d from £25/40) The smallish Westfield House is deservedly popular on account of the friendly welcome. The rooms are all adequately comfortable.

Bizzie Lizzies (☎ 793189; 36 Swadford St; mains £5-6; 🕑 lunch & dinner) This modern fish-and-chip restaurant overlooking the canal has won awards for quality, a rare thing for what is essentially deep-fried goodness. There's also an attached takeaway.

Of the pubs, **The Black Horse** (Coach St) is a large place with an outside terrace and meals daily, but our favourite is the **Narrow Boat** (Victoria St), a traditionally styled place

with good beer, friendly service and bar food (no food on weekends).

Getting There & Away
Skipton is the last stop on the Metro network from Leeds (at least hourly, 40 minutes). For heading into the Dales, see the boxed text, p514. For Grassington, take bus No 72 (£4.30, 30 minutes, six per day Monday to Saturday) or No 67 (hourly, Sunday); most go via the train station.

GRASSINGTON

☎ 01756

The perfect base for south Dales jaunts, Grassington's handsome Georgian centre teems with visitors throughout the summer months, soaking up an atmosphere that – despite the odd touch of faux rustication – is as attractive and traditional as you'll find in these parts. It is 6 miles north of Skipton.

The **TIC** (☎ 752774; 🕑 9.30am-5pm daily Apr-Oct, shorter hrs Nov-Mar) is at the big car park on the edge of town. There's a good stock of maps and guides, and a nice little display that puts the surrounding scenery in context.

Sleeping & Eating
There are several B&Bs along and just off Main St.

Devonshire Fell (☎ 718111; www.devonshirefell .co.uk; Burnsall; s/d from £75/115) This one-time gentleman's club for mill owners offers a substantially different aesthetic; here, the style is distinctly contemporary, with beautiful modern furnishings crafted by local experts. It's more like a big city boutique hotel than a rustic country property.

Ashfield House (☎ 752584; www.ashfieldhouse.co .uk; Summers Fold; r per person £38; 🕑 Feb-Nov only) A secluded 17th-century country house behind a walled garden with exposed stone walls, open fireplaces and an all-round cosy feel. It's just off the main square.

Dales Kitchen (☎ 753208; 51 Main St; mains about £5; 🕑 9am-6pm) Classic Yorkshire munchies – rarebits, local sausage and, of course, Wensleydale – in lovely tea rooms in the middle of town.

Getting There & Away
To reach Grassington, see p512. For onward travels the No 72 continues up the valley to the nearby villages of Kettlewell and Buckden.

AROUND GRASSINGTON

North of Grassington, narrow roads lead up the beautiful valley of Wharfedale. Drivers take the road on the west side of the river; if you're cycling, take the quieter east-side option. If you're walking, follow the charming stretch of the Dales Way long-distance footpath through a classic Yorkshire Dales landscape of lush meadows surrounded by dry-stone walls, with traditional field-barns dotting the hillsides.

About 7 and 11 miles respectively from Grassington, the villages of **Kettlewell** and **Buckden** make good places to aim for, between them offering a good choice of campsites, B&Bs, teashops and pubs (all doing food and accommodation).

Check at Grassington TIC about the local buses that trundle up and down Wharfedale daily in the summer months (weekends in winter) – ideal for bringing home weary walkers.

MALHAM
☎ 01729

At the northern end of the quiet and beautiful valley of Malhamdale, this small, traditional village is probably the most visited place in the valley, not only for its charm but also for the natural wonders nearby – all easily reached by foot.

The excellent **TIC** (☎ 830363; malham@ytbtic .co.uk; 🕙 10am-5pm Apr-Oct, Fri-Sun Nov-Mar) has the usual wealth of information, local walks leaflets, maps and guidebooks.

Walking

The 5-mile Malham Landscape Trail (the TIC has details) takes in **Malham Cove**, a huge rock amphitheatre that was once a waterfall to rival Niagara, and **Gordale Scar**, a deep limestone canyon with scenic cascades and the remains of an Iron Age settlement.

For something longer, you can follow various paths eastwards through remote farmland for anything between 6 and 11 miles to reach Grassington, or head west on a great 6-mile hike over the hills to Settle. An even better option is a two-day hike between Grassington and Settle via Malham.

The long-distance Pennine Way passes right through Malham, and you can go north or south for as many days as you like. A day's walk away is Horton-in-Ribblesdale (see p514).

Sleeping & Eating

Malham YHA Hostel (☎ 0870 770 5946; malham@yha .org.uk; dm/d £11.80/42; 🕙 mid-Feb–Nov, Fri & Sat only Dec–mid-Feb) Right in the village centre is this purpose-built hostel; the facilities are top-notch and young children are also well catered for.

Beck Hall (☎ 830332; www.beckhallmalham.com; s/d from £25/50; snacks about £4) This rambling 17th-century country house on the edge of the village is a favourite; of the 11 different rooms, we recommend the Green Room, with its old-style furnishings and four-poster bed. There's a burbling stream flowing through the garden and a nice tearoom.

SETTLE
☎ 01729 / pop 3621

Far too big and bustling to qualify as quaint, Settle does, however, retain enough traditional character in its narrow cobbled streets lined with shops and homely pubs to attract outsiders. The town centres on the large market square that still sees stalls and traders every Tuesday. Access from the main A65 to the east is easy, and there are plenty of accommodation options.

The **TIC** (☎ 825192; settle@ytbtic.co.uk; Town Hall; 🕙 9.30am-5pm) has maps, guidebooks, and an excellent range of local walks leaflets (free).

Sleeping & Eating

Stainforth YHA Hostel (☎ 0870 770 5946; stainforth @yha.org.uk; dm/d £11.80/42) A decent hostel in an old Georgian country house 2 miles north of Settle on the B6479 to Horton-in-Ribblesdale.

Golden Lion Hotel (☎ 822203; www.goldenlion hotel.net; Duke St; s/d £30/54; lunch mains about £6, evening £8-11) This handsome 17th-century coaching inn has 12 warm and comfortable rooms, an old-style pub and a pleasant restaurant that is one of the most popular in town.

Around the square are several cafés, including **The Shambles**, noted for filling fish-and-chip suppers (£5.90) and **Ye Olde Naked Man**, formerly an undertakers and now a bakery with cakes, snacks and ice cream.

Getting There & Away

From the south, trains from Leeds or Skipton to Carlisle (see the boxed text) stop at the station near the town centre; those heading for Morecambe (on the west coast) stop at Giggleswick, about 1½ miles outside town.

THE SETTLE–CARLISLE LINE

The Settle–Carlisle Line (SCL) is one of the greatest rail engineering achievements of the Victorian era and takes passengers across some of the best countryside in northern England. The views from the windows are simply stunning. It was built between 1869 and 1875 after – as legend has it – the chairman of the Midland Railway Company drew a line across the Dales and declared 'that's where I'll have my railway!' He didn't care too much that the mountainsides weren't railway-friendly; *he* wasn't going to handle a blasting cap.

Instead, the job fell to 5000 navvies, 200 of whom died while laying the track.

The Journey

Trains run between Leeds and Carlisle via Settle about eight times a day. The first section of the journey from Leeds is along the Aire Valley, with a stop at **Keighley**, where the Keighley & Worth Valley Railway branches off to Haworth (of Brontë fame, see p509). Next is **Skipton** – gateway to the southern Dales – and then your first sight of proper moors as the train arrives in the attractive market town of **Settle**. The train chugs up the valley beside the River Ribble, through **Horton-in-Ribblesdale**, across the spectacular Ribblehead Viaduct and then plunges through Blea Moor Tunnel, to pop out above Dentdale, where **Dent** station is one of the highest in the country. (Dent village is a couple of miles away down in the valley.) Next stop is **Garsdale Head** (just a few miles west of Hawes), then the train reaches its highest point (356m) at Ais Gill, before leaving the Dales behind and trundling down to **Kirkby Stephen**. The last halts are **Appleby** then **Langwathby,** just northwest of **Penrith** (a jumping-off point for the Lake District), then the train finally pulls into **Carlisle**. What a ride!

The Nuts & Bolts

The entire journey takes two hours and 40 minutes and costs £28 return (from Settle, the return fare to Carlisle is £16.80). Various hop-on hop-off passes for one or three days are also available. Pick up a free SCL timetable – which includes a colour map of the line and brief details about places of interest – from most Yorkshire stations; for more details, contact **National Rail Enquiries** (☎ 08457 484950) or click on to www.settle–carlisle.co.uk or www.settle–carlisle-railway.org.uk.

AROUND SETTLE
Horton-in-Ribblesdale
☎ 01729

A favourite with walkers, cyclists and cavers, the little village of Horton is 5 miles north of Settle. Everything centres on the **Pen-y-ghent Café** (☎ 860333; ⏰ 9am-6pm Mon & Wed-Fri, 8am-6pm Sat & Sun), which serves up filling meals, home-made cakes and pint mugs of tea. The friendly owners sell maps, guidebooks and walking gear, and the café acts as the village **TIC** (horton@ytbtic.co.uk). Walkers on a long hike should avail themselves of the 'safety service', whereby they can register in and out. There's also a **post office shop** for groceries and takeaways.

SLEEPING & EATING

Horton is popular, so your best bet is to book your accommodation in advance.

Golden Lion (☎ 860206; www.goldenlionhotel.co.uk; dm/s/d £8/20/45) Popular with walkers, the Golden Lion is a lively pub with dorms and basic private rooms upstairs, and three public bars downstairs where you can tuck into a bit of grub and wash it down with a pint of hand-pumped ale. They also do evening meals (three-courses £10) and make packed lunches (£5). Breakfast (£5.95) is not included.

Crown Hotel (☎ 860209; www.crown-hotel.co.uk; s/d from £27/55) Another popular rest stop with walkers, the Crown has a variety of basic rooms (with slightly over-the-top floral patterns) and a cosy bar that serves a range of meals.

Other options include: **Dub-Cote Farm Camping Barn** (☎ 860238; www.threepeaksbarn.co.uk; dm £8), a basic-but-lovely 17th-century stone barn half a mile southeast of the village, well equipped with self-catering facilities (BYO sleeping bag and pillow case); the **Knoll** (☎ 860283; s/d £22/40), a neat and efficient house near the village centre; and **Rowe**

House (☎ 860212; s/d from £26/46), a nice homely option on the north side of the village.

The Three Peaks

The landscape north of Settle is dominated by the Three Peaks – Whernside (735m), Ingleborough (723m) and Pen-y-ghent (694m) – and each summit is linked by a long circular route that has been a classic walk for years. The traditional starting point for the route is the Pen-y-ghent Café in Horton-in-Ribblesdale, and walkers try to complete the whole 25-mile route in under 12 hours. Others knock it off in six hours or less. You can also do just a section of the walk – for instance walking from Horton as far as Ribblehead, and returning by train – which is highly recommended.

HAWES

☎ 01969

The best base for exploring the northern Dales is hardly-appealing Hawes, right in the heart of Wensleydale. The busy streets are lined with pretty much everything you'll need, from laundrettes to pottery studios.

The **TIC** (☎ 667450; hawes@ytbtic.co.uk; ☺ 10am-5pm) shares the Old Station building with the **Dales Countryside Museum** (adult/child £3/free), a beautifully presented social history of the area. There's still an old train in the yard, too.

There's also the **Wensleydale Creamery Visitor Centre** (☎ 667664; adult/child £2/1.50; ☺ 9am-5.30pm), devoted to the production of the world-famous powdery-white cheese, but watching guys shovel tons of cheese around is only marginally interesting. You can taste it in the museum and then buy it in the shop, which is free to enter.

About 1½ miles north of town is Hawes' other attraction, **Hardraw Force**, the highest above-ground waterfall in the country. For most of the year it's little more than a trickle on the rocks and not really worth the £1 'toll' you pay at the Green Dragon pub to walk up to it.

Sleeping & Eating

Hawes YHA Hostel (☎ 0870 770 5854; www.yha.org.uk; Town Head; dm £10.60) A modern place on the western edge of town, at the junction of the main A684 (Aysgarth Rd) and B6255.

Cocketts (☎ 667312; www.cocketts.co.uk; Market Pl; d from £60; 2-/3-course meal £14.95/16.95) The most

stylish place in town is a handsome 17th-century stone house with eight delightful rooms decorated in traditional style, two with four-poster beds.

Laburnum House (☎ 667717; www.stayatlaburnumhouse.co.uk; The Holme; s/d from £23/45) A quaint cottage in the centre, with a busy tearoom and terrace downstairs serving tea and scones (£2.50), hearty sandwiches (£3 to £5) and larger meals (£7). The rooms are decorated in various shades of blue.

Green Dragon Inn (☎ 667392; www.greendragoninn.fsnet.co.uk; Hardraw; s/d without breakfast from £18/36, with breakfast £25/43; mains about £5) About 1½ miles north of town is this 'famous' inn where you pay the fee for the nearby waterfall. It's a terrific place, with unspectacular but thoroughly comfortable rooms, home-cooked food, good beer and live bands at weekends.

Bainbridge Ings Caravan & Camp Site (☎ 667354; www.bainbridge-ings.co.uk; car & 2 adults/hikers & cyclists £9/3.50) Pitches are scattered around the edges of stonewalled fields, located around a spacious farmhouse about half a mile east of town. Bottled gas, milk and eggs are sold on site.

There are plenty of pubs, including **The Fountain** (☎ 667206; Market Pl; mains about £6). The traditional **White Hart** (Market Pl; mains about £7) is also good for a pint or a bar meal.

Getting There & Away

Hawes is a public transportation nightmare. From Northallerton, bus Nos 156/157 run to Hawes (four daily Monday to Friday, two hours) via Leyburn, where you can connect with transport to/from Richmond. On Sunday (March to October) there are buses to Hawes from Manchester (No X43) via Skipton and Grassington, and from Leeds (No 803). Between Hawes and the Lake District, bus No 112 runs to/from Kendal (twice daily, 90 minutes), very early in the morning and late in the evening, with a few extra services on some other weekdays. The TIC can advise on other bus services aimed at visitors.

RICHMOND

☎ 01748 / pop 8178

There are two great things about Richmond: it's one of Britain's most charming towns and relatively few people know about it. Cobbled streets and alleyways, lined with

Georgian buildings and old stone cottages, radiate from the large, cobbled market square and give exhilarating glimpses of the surrounding hills and dales. To complete the scene, a massive ruined castle perches high on a rocky outcrop overlooking the town on one side and the rushing River Swale on the other.

Orientation & Information

Richmond is east of the Yorkshire Dales National Park but makes a good gateway for the northern area of the park. Centre of everything is Trinity Church Sq (with market day on Saturday). Just north of here, the **TIC** (☎ 850252; www.richmond.org.uk; Friary Gardens, Victoria Rd; �9.30am-5.30pm Apr-Oct, 9.30am-4.30pm Nov-Mar) has the usual maps and guides, plus several leaflets (around 60p) showing walks in town and the surrounding countryside.

Sights

Top of the pile is the impressive heap that's left of **Richmond Castle** (EH; ☎ 822493; admission £3; ☉ 10am-6pm Apr-Sep, 10am-4pm Oct-Mar), founded in 1070 and one of the first castles in England since Roman times to be built of stone. It's had many uses through the years, including a stint as a prison for conscientious objectors during WWI (there's a small and sobering exhibition about their part in the castle's history). The best part of a visit is the view from the top of the remarkably well-preserved 30m-high tower; you can look down on the market place or over the surrounding hills.

The **Richmondshire Museum** (☎ 825611; Ryder's Wynd; adult/child £1.50/1; ☉ 10.30am-4.30pm Easter-Oct) is a delightful little gem, with very informative staff and local history exhibits including early Yorkshire cave-dweller, James Herriot's surgery, and informative displays on lead mining, which forever altered the Swaledale landscape a century ago.

Activities

West from Richmond walkers can follow paths along the River Swale, upstream and downstream from the town. A longer option is along the north side of Swaledale, following the famous long-distance Coast to Coast route (p78), all the way to Reeth. For a grand day out, take the first bus (£2.20) from Richmond to Reeth then walk back; the TIC has route and bus time details.

Cyclists can also follow Swaledale: as far as Reeth may be enough, while a trip to Keld, then over the high wild moors to Kirkby Stephen is a more serious but very rewarding 33-mile undertaking.

Sleeping

King's Head Hotel (☎ 850220; www.kingsheadrichmond.co.uk; Market Pl; s/d from £69/95) Right on Market Pl, Richmond's fanciest hotel was once described by the painter Turner as 'the finest in Richmondshire'. That was a long time ago. It's still pretty fancy though; each of the traditionally furnished 30 bedrooms have wrought-iron or hardwood beds and plenty of comfort.

Willance House (☎ 824467; www.willancehouse.com; 24 Frenchgate; s/d £30/50) This is an oak-beamed, 17th-century house with four rooms that are small in size but bursting with cutesy character.

There's a batch of pleasant places along Frenchgate, and there are several more on Maison Dieu and Pottergate (the road into town from the east). These include **Pottergate Guesthouse** (☎ 823826; 4 Pottergate), **66 Frenchgate** (☎ 823421; paul@66french.freeserve.co.uk; 66 Frenchgate) and **Emmanuel House** (☎ 823584; 41 Maison Dieu). Singles/doubles cost about £25/40.

SOMETHING SPECIAL

Millgate House (☎ 823571; www.millgatehouse.com; Market Pl; s/d £45/80; (P) (☐)) Behind the unassuming green door and plaque is the unexpected pleasure of one of the nicest guesthouses in England. The owners' exceptional taste is complemented by a range of furnishings from all over the world, which are carefully positioned throughout each of the stunning bedrooms and public areas. While the house itself is wonderful, it is overshadowed by the breathtaking garden at the back, which has views over the River Swale and the Cleveland Hills. In 1995 it won first prize in the RHS National Garden Competition – the plaque was presented by Prince Charles himself. Consequently, the most sought-after room is the Garden Suite, although guests enjoy a fab breakfast within full view of it.

Eating & Drinking

Trinity Church Sq and the surrounding streets have a huge choice of pubs, teashops, cafés and takeaways.

Frenchgate Café (☎ 824949; 29 Frenchgate; lunches about £4, evening mains £7-11; ☺ 10am-10pm Tue-Sun) An all-meals-in-one kind of place, you can tuck into a tidy breakfast in the morning, a large sandwich or pasta dish at lunch and enjoy the delights of their quasi-Continental bistro menu in the evening.

A Taste of Thailand (☎ 829696; 15 King St; mains about £10; ☺ dinner only) Does exactly what it says on the tin. An extensive menu of Thai favourites and a convenient BYO policy.

Surprisingly, despite a vast choice, few of the pubs in Richmond are up to much. After extensive research, the best we found was the **Black Lion Hotel** (☎ 823121; Finkle St; bar food £5, mains in restaurant about £9), with cosy bars, low beams, good beer and food, plus B&B.

Getting There & Away

From Darlington (on the railway between London and Edinburgh) it's easy to reach Richmond on bus No 34 (£4.80, hourly, 30 minutes; four on Sunday). All buses stop in Trinity Church Sq.

SWALEDALE

West of Richmond, the River Swale flows through Swaledale – the quietest and least-visited of the Dales – with a wild and rugged beauty to contrast sharply with the softer, greener places further south. It's hard to imagine, but only a century ago this was a major lead-mining area. When the price of ore fell in the 19th century many people left Swaledale for good. Some went to England's burgeoning industrial cities, and others emigrated – especially to Wisconsin in the USA – leaving Swaledale almost empty, a legacy that remains today, with just a few small lonely villages scattered along its length.

Reeth

In the heart of Swaledale is the village of Reeth – a great base for exploring Swaledale, with shops, cafés and pubs dotted around a large sloping green (Friday is market day). There is a **TIC** (☎ 01748-884059; reeth@ytbtic.co.uk) and many B&B options; one excellent choice is the **Arkleside Hotel** (☎ 01748-884200; www.arklesidehotel.co.uk; s/d from £56/82), made up of a converted row of old cottages just by the green.

To understand Swaledale's fascinating history, the dusty little **Swaledale Folk Museum** (☎ 01748-884373; adult £1; ☺ 10.30am-5pm Easter-Oct) is well worth a look.

EAST RIDING OF YORKSHIRE

The only Yorkshire county to have retained the essence of its Viking name, the East Riding (from Old Danish *Thriding*, or third) was one of three administrative regions created by the conquering Danes in the 9th century – west and north ridings are now West and North Yorkshire.

Dominating the region is the no-nonsense port city of Hull, stolidly seated between the broad horizons of the rivers Humber and Hull; to the north is the market town of Beverley, with lots of 18th-century character and an enormous medieval religious and cultural legacy.

Activities

The Yorkshire Wolds are ideal for gentle walks and cycle tours. Whether you're on two feet or two wheels, the town of Beverley makes a good base, and the northern Wolds can also be easily reached from York.

The area's main long-distance walk is the 80-mile **Wolds Way**. This national trail starts at Hessle, a riverside town 4 miles west of Hull, close to the Humber Bridge, and leads northwards through farmland, hills and quiet villages, to end at the tip of Filey Brigg, a peninsula on the east coast just north of the town of Filey. Billed as 'Yorkshire's best-kept secret', it takes five days, and is an excellent beginners' walk, as the landscape is not high and conditions not too strenuous.

The **Cleveland Way** (p538) also ends at Filey, and for a shorter walk in bracing sea air you can follow the Cleveland Way along a scenic stretch of coast northwards from Filey to Scarborough.

Getting There & Around

Hull is easily reached by rail from Leeds, York, Beverley, Filey and Scarborough, and is also the hub for regional bus services. There is a useful website at www.gettingaround.eastriding.gov.uk.

HULL
☎ 01482 / pop 301,416

Calloused, curmudgeonly Hull is a tough old port, barely affected by the exotic trade that has passed through its docks for centuries. Yet there has been a softening in recent years, if only enough for visitors to experience something other than the unforgiving air of a city that doesn't suffer much of anyone at anytime. Its official name of Kingston-upon-Hull seems like an unnecessary extravagance when plain old Hull will do, and it seems apt that jaundiced, rueful poet Philip Larkin (1922–85) presided over its university library for many years.

Orientation & Information

The Old Town of Hull, which retains a sense of the prosperous Victorian era, is bounded by Ferensway and Freetown Way and the Rivers Humber and Hull. Perched on the waterfront overlooking the Humber is the city's main attraction, a huge aquarium called The Deep. It's all walkable.

Central library (☎ 223344; Albion St) For Internet access.

Post office (57 Jameson St; ☿ 9am-5.30pm Mon-Sat)

TIC (☎ 223559; www.hullcc.gov.uk; 1 Paragon St; ☿ 10am-5pm Mon-Sat, 11am-3pm Sun)

Waterstone's (☎ 580234; 19-21 Jameson St) The best bookshop.

Sights
THE DEEP

The colossal, angled monolith that is **The Deep** (☎ 381000; www.thedeep.co.uk; Tower St; adult/child £6/4; ☿ 10am-6pm) stands at the edge of the port, with great views across the Humber. Inside it's just as dramatic, as echoing commentaries and computer-generated inter-actives run you through the formation of the seas, and onwards. The largest aquarium contains 2.5 million litres of water (and 87 tonnes of salt) and even has a glass lift. To get a good view of the tank's seven different types of sharks, eels, rays and other watery dwellers, it's best (if more pedestrian) to take the stairs, as the lift ride is over no sooner than you start it. And it's rare you see a pod full of people zoom through a tank.

OTHER SIGHTS

Hull has a remarkable collection of city-run museums (☎ 613902; www.hullcc.gov.uk/museums; ☿ 10am-5pm Mon-Sat, 1.30-4.30pm Sun). All share

the same phone number and opening hours and are free unless otherwise stated.

The serene **Ferens Art Gallery** (Queen Victoria Sq), built in 1927, has a decent collection that includes works by Stanley Spencer and Peter Blake.

The dusty-feeling but interesting **Maritime Museum**, in the former dock offices (1871), celebrates Hull's maritime traditions, and includes some daunting whale skeletons.

The well-preserved High St has some eclectic museums. The attractive, Georgian **Wilberforce House** (1639) was the birthplace in 1759 of the antislavery crusader William Wilberforce. It covers the history of slavery and the campaign against it. Behind it is the **Arctic Corsair** (☎ 613902; www.arctic-corsair.co.uk; ☿ 10am-4pm Wed & Fri, 1.30-4pm Sun Easter-Oct); tours demonstrate the hardships of trawling in the Arctic Circle.

The **Streetlife Transport Museum** has recreated 1930s streets, all sorts of historic vehicles to get on and off, and a pleasant garden. The **Hull & East Riding Museum** traces the town's local history from Roman times to the present, with new Anglo-Saxon, medieval and geology galleries.

At the heart of the Old Town, **Holy Trinity Church** (☎ 324835; Market Pl; ☿ 11am-2pm Tue-Fri Oct-Mar, 11am-3pm Mon-Fri, 9.30am-noon Sat Apr-Sep, services Sun year-round) is a magnificent 15th-century building with a striking central tower and a long, tall, unified interior worthy of a cathedral. It features huge areas of windows, built to keep the weight of the walls down as the soil here is unstable.

Moving to some more prosaic architectural treasures, southeast of the church are some famous rare **Art Nouveau gents toilets** (Market Pl) that have been relieving the pressure since 1902. The nearby **King William III Statue** (Market Pl) was erected in 1734 in honour of William of Orange, who besides being king also has the distinction of introducing England to gin, which he brought from his native Holland. The statue's proximity to the toilet is pure coincidence.

Built in 1927, the **Spurn Lightship** is now anchored in the marina. It once provided guidance for ships navigating the notorious Humber estuary.

Walking

The TIC sells a brochure called *The Seven Seas Fish Pavement Trail* (40p), a delightful, historic self-guided tour of the Old Town, following fish shapes embedded in the pavement. Kids love it. Adults might prefer the *Hull Ale Trail* (40p), which needs no explanation.

Sleeping & Eating

Good accommodation options are pretty thin on the ground – most of them are made up of business-oriented hotels and mediocre guesthouses. The TIC will help you to book accommodation for free.

Clyde House Hotel (☎ 214981; anthonysmith@cw com.net; 13 John St; s/d £27/45) Next to leafy Kingston Sq, this is one of the best B&B options near the Old Town. The rooms are nothing fancy, but they are very tidy, as well as comfortable.

Holiday Inn (☎ 0870 400 9043; www.holiday-inn .com; Castle St; r weekday/weekend £120/90) Of the charmless business hotels, the Holiday Inn is the nicest place to stay. It overlooks the marina, and has well-equipped rooms, many with balconies.

Venn (☎ 224004; www.venn.biz; 21 Scale Lane; ✆ Tue-Sat; brasserie mains about £8, 2-/3-course restaurant menu £32/38) Modern British cuisine in all its cool, posh guises hits Hull and – guess what? – sticks nicely. This trendy brasserie serves fancy sandwiches, pizzas and salads, while the more upmarket upstairs restaurant goes to town with dishes like fresh lobster with ravioli of crushed fresh peas and pancetta with a clear tomato and basil jus…gorgeous.

Cerruti (☎ 328501; 10 Nelson St; mains about £12; ✆ Mon-Fri lunch, Mon-Sat dinner) Hull's best Italian restaurant is an attractive place that specialises – unsurprisingly – in seafood.

Entertainment

Come nightfall – especially at weekends – Hull gets raucous and often rowdy. What else did you expect from saltdogs in a seaport? Groups of dangerously under-dressed kids party like tomorrow doesn't matter. If you're that pissed, it wouldn't.

Welly Club (☎ 326131, 221676; 105-7 Beverley Rd; admission free-£5; ✆ till 2am, closed Wed & Sun) Shake a leg to everything from ska to soul, and there's a Saturday residency by home-grown Steve Cobby of local heroes Fila Brazillia.

Ye Olde Black Boy (☎ 326516; 150 High St) A real old-fashioned boozer on a site dating from 1337, this place is smoke-stained and plush-seated in the great English pub tradition.

Hull Truck Theatre (☎ 323638; www.hulltruck.co.uk; Spring St) Home to acclaimed down-to-earth playwright John Godber, this place presents vibrant drama, comedy and Sunday jazz.

Hull New Theatre (☎ 226655; www.hullnewtheatre .co.uk; Kingston Sq) The Hull New is a traditional regional theatre that hosts popular drama, concerts and musicals.

Getting There & Away

The bus station is on Ferensway, just north of the train station. National Express has buses to and from London (£21.50, 5¾ hours, two daily) and Manchester (£12.75, 4¼ hours, one daily). Both National Express and Bus No X46 run frequently to and from York (£6.25, 1¾ hours). Local services also leave from here.

The train station is west of Queen Victoria Sq, in the town centre. Hull has good rail links north and south, and west to York (£13.50, 1¼ hours, hourly) and Leeds (£13.10, one hour, hourly).

The ferry port is 3 miles east of the centre at King George Dock. A bus to/from the train station connects with the ferries.

BEVERLEY
☎ 01482 / pop 29,110

Thoroughly unspoilt Beverley merits far more attention than it has hitherto attracted. Beneath the magnificent medieval minster lies the handsome tangle of the town, literally brimming with exquisite Georgian and Victorian buildings.

Orientation & Information

Beverley is small and easily walked to from either the train or bus stations. There's a large market in the main square on Saturday.

Beverley Bookshop (☎ 0800 616394; 16 Butcher Row)

Library (☎ 885355; Champney Rd; ✆ 9.30am-5pm Mon & Wed, 9.30am-7pm Tue, Thu & Fri, 9am-1pm Sat) Also has a small art gallery with changing exhibitions.

Post office (Register Sq; ✆ 9am-5.30pm Mon-Fri, 9am-12.30pm Sat)

TIC (☎ 391672; beverley@ytbtic.co.uk; 34 Butcher Row; ✆ 9.30am-5.15pm Mon-Fri, 10am-4.45pm Sat, also 10am-2pm Sun Jun-Aug only)

Sights & Attractions

The third church to be built on this site (the first was constructed during the 7th century), the **minster** (☎ 868540; www.beverleyminster.co.uk; admission by donation; ✆ 9am-5.30pm Mon-Sat May-Aug,

9am-5pm Sep-Oct & Mar-Apr, 9am-4pm Nov-Feb, also noon-4pm Sun year-round) dates from 1220, but construction continued for two centuries, spanning the Early English, Decorated and Perpendicular periods. Hailed for its unity of forms, the church has a magnificent Gothic perpendicular west front (1390–1420).

Inside, the nave is strikingly high. Extraordinary medieval faces and demons peer down from every possible vantage point, while expressive stone musicians play silent instruments. Note particularly the 10th-century *fridstol* (Old English for 'peace chair') which gave sanctuary to anyone escaping the law; the fruit- and angel-laden Gothic canopy of the Percy Tomb; the 68 medieval misericords (the largest collection in the country) and the late Norman font (c1170).

There's an interesting display showing the history of the minster and town. Check out the rebuilt treadwheel crane, where workers ground around like hapless hamsters to lift the huge loads necessary to build such medieval structures.

Doomed to play second fiddle to the mother church, **St Mary's** (☎ 865709; admission free; ☼ 9.15am-noon & 1.30-5pm Mon-Fri, 10am-5.30pm Sat & 2-5pm Sun Apr-Sep; 2-4.15pm Oct-Mar) is a glorious church, built in stages between 1120 and 1530. In the North Choir Aisle look out for a carving (c1330) thought to have inspired Lewis Carroll's White Rabbit. The West Front is considered one of England's finest (early 15th century).

Sleeping & Eating

Friary YHA Hostel (☎ 0870 770 5696; Friar's Lane; dm £10.60; ☼ Mon-Sat Easter–end Oct) Here's your chance to stay in a beautiful, restored 14th-century Dominican friary mentioned in Chaucer's *The Canterbury Tales*. This place might just have the best setting in town, only 100m southeast of the minster.

Beverley Arms (☎ 869241; www.regalhotels.co.uk; North Bar Within; s/d from £80/110) Beverley's top spot is a very elegant Georgian coaching house with all the trimmings, although we weren't overly impressed with the faux-old furniture. Make sure to ask for a room in the old building, which has less of an ersatz feel about it.

Eastgate Guest House (☎ 868464; 7 Eastgate; s/d from £27/42, with bathroom £41/53) This relatively central B&B is highly recommended more for its sheer friendliness and relaxed atmosphere than for the floral, simple rooms.

Number One (☎ 862752; www.numberone-bedand breakfast-beverley.co.uk; 1 Woodlands; s/d from £23/38) The Number One comprises three very comfortable rooms in a friendly, welcoming house just west of the town centre.

Cerutti 2 (☎ 866700; Station Sq; mains £9-19; ☼ dinner only Mon-Sat) The only restaurant of note in town is unusually positioned inside the train station. Italian dishes of all kinds are on offer, without the seafood leanings of its sister restaurant in Hull.

White Horse Inn (☎ 861973; 22 Hengate; mains £7-8; ☼ lunch & dinner) Also known as Nellie's, this lovely, dimly lit place has rambling rooms, open fires and tables outside. There's also regular live music and poetry.

Getting There & Away

The train station lies east of the town centre. The bus station is north on Sow Hill.

Bus No X46/X47 links Beverley with York (£3.60, one hour 10 minutes, hourly). There are frequent buses to Hull (Nos 121, 122, 246 and X46/X47, £2.10, 30 minutes).

There are regular trains to and from Scarborough via Filey (£11.10, 1½ hours). Trains to and from Hull (£3.80, 20 minutes) run at least hourly.

NORTH YORKSHIRE

North Yorkshire is the largest and most beautiful of the four Yorkshire counties. The Industrial Revolution never really got a foothold in these parts, keeping the county free of the looming mills and mines that remain elsewhere. Instead, sheep ruled virtually unopposed from the Middle Ages, and the fortunes made in this part of the world were made – literally – on their backs.

North Yorkshire's landscapes are an inviting mix of untouched beauty – best experienced in the county's two magnificent national parks, the Yorkshire Dales (p510) and North York Moors (p538) – and the superb man-made monuments that are a testament to the wealth of the wool trade, from the great houses and rich abbeys to the breathtaking medieval city of York, one of Britain's most visited destinations.

Activities

The best walking and cycling is in the Yorkshire Dales and the North York Moors.

Getting There & Around

The main gateway town is York and a web of buses and trains connect places in North Yorkshire. See the Yorkshire Dales and the North York Moors sections for more specific details. For county-wide information, call the national **Traveline** (☎ 0870 608 2608). There are various Explorer passes, and individual bus and train companies also offer their own saver schemes, so it's always worth asking for advice on the best deal when you buy your ticket.

YORK

☎ 01904 / pop 137,505

York drips with history and heritage and to many visitors it is the epitome of Ye Olde Englishe Towne. It is a city of extraordinary cultural and historical wealth: its medieval spider's web of narrow streets is enclosed by a magnificent circuit of 13th-century walls and, at its heart is the immense, awe-inspiring minster, one of the most beautiful Gothic cathedrals in the world. Medieval charm meets modern savvy, however, and

---

YORK: FROM THE BEGINNING

It seems everybody has wanted a piece of this land at some point in history. In AD 71 the Romans built a fort called Erboracum here, so their troops would have somewhere to sleep after a busy day bashing the local tribes. Over time, a largish civilian settlement grew up around the fort; by the time Constantine the Great was proclaimed emperor here in AD 306 it was a fully-fledged town. After the collapse of the Roman Empire, the town was taken by the Anglo-Saxons who renamed it Eoforwic and made it the capital of the independent kingdom of Northumbria.

In 625 a Roman priest, Paulinus, arrived and converted the king and all his nobles. Two years later, they built the first wooden church; for most of the next century the city was a major centre of learning, attracting students from all over Europe.

The student party lasted until 866, when the next wave of invaders arrived. This time it was those marauding Vikings, who chucked everybody out and gave the town a more tongue-friendly name, Jorvik. It was to be their capital for the next 100 years, and during that time they put a rest to their pillaging ways and turned the city into an important trading port.

Danish rule ended in 954 when King Eadred of Wessex drove out the last Viking ruler and reunited Danelaw with the south, but trouble brewed again in 1066 when King Harold II got his comeuppance at the hands of William the Conqueror at Hastings.

Willie exercised his own brand of tough love in York. After his two wooden castles were captured by an Anglo-Scandinavian army, he torched the whole city (and Durham) and the surrounding countryside so that the rebels knew who was boss – the 'harrying of the north'. The Normans then set about rebuilding the city, including a new minster. From that moment, everything in York was rosy – except for a blip in 1137 when the whole city caught fire – and over the next 300 years it prospered through royal patronage, textiles, trade and the church.

No sooner did the church finally get built, though, than the city went into full recession. In the 15th century Hull took over as the region's main port and the textile industry moved elsewhere. Henry VIII's inability to keep a wife and the ensuing brouhaha with the established church that resulted in the Reformation also hit York pretty hard. However, Henry established a branch of the King's Council here to help govern the north, and this was to contribute to the city's recovery under Elizabeth I and James I.

The council was abolished during Charles I's reign, but the king established his court here during the Civil War, which drew the devastating attentions of the Parliamentarians. They besieged the rabidly pro-monarchist York for three months in 1644, but by a fortuitous accident of history their leader was a local chap called Sir Thomas Fairfax, who prevented his troops from setting York alight, thereby preserving the city and the minster.

Not much happened after that. Throughout the 18th century the city was a fashionable social centre dominated by the aristocracy, who were drawn by its culture and new racecourse. When the railway was built in 1839 thousands of people were employed in the new industries that sprung up around it, such as confectionery. These industries went into decline in the latter half of the 20th century, but by then a new invader was asking for directions at the city gates, armed only with a guidebook.

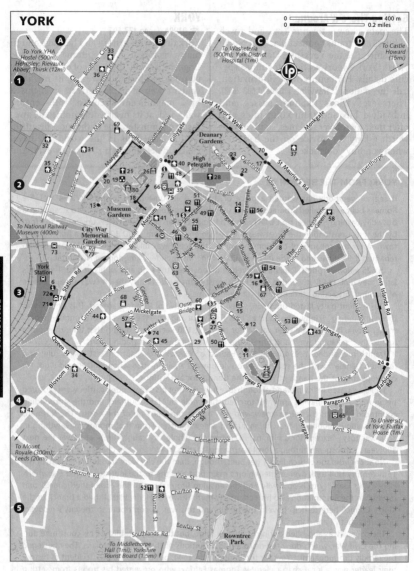

YORK

0 ———— 400 m
0 ———— 0.2 miles

To York YHA
Hostel (500m);
Helmsley; Rievaulx
Abbey; Thirsk (12mi)

To Washeteria
(500m); York District
Hospital (1mi)

To Castle
Howard
(15mi)

Clifton

Booton Cres

Gillygate

Lord Mayor's Walk

Monkgate

Leverthorpe

To National Railway
Museum (400m)

Museum
Gardens

City War
Memorial
Gardens

Deanary
Gardens

High
Petergate

Deangate

Low Petergate

Goodramgate

St Maurice's Rd

Pertholme
Green

York
Station

Leeman Rd

Station Rd

Toft Green

Tanner Row

George Hudson St

Rougier St

Lendal Bridge

Museum St

Blake St

Stonegate

Coney St

New St

Davygate

Parliament St

St Saviourgate

Colliergate

The
Stonebow

Foss

Foss Islands Rd

Micklegate

Trinity La

Priory St

Victor St

Bishophill Senior

Ouse
Bridge

Spurriergate

High
Ousegate

Coppergate

Castlegate

Clifford
St

Piccadilly

Navigation Rd

Walmgate

Queen St

Blossom St

Nunnery La

Cromwell Rd

Skeldergate

Bishopgate

Terry Ave

Tower St

Fishergate

Hope St

Barbican Rd

Paragon St

Kent St

To University
of York; Fairfax
House (1mi)

To Mount
Royale (300m);
Leeds (20mi)

Scarcroft Rd

Clementhorpe

Darnborough St

Vine St

Charlton St

Nunmill St

Bewlay St

Southlands Rd

Rowntree
Park

To Middlethorpe
Hall (1mi); Yorkshire
Tourist Board (1.5mi)

---

tourist-oriented York – with its myriad museums, restaurants, cafés and traditional pubs – is one of the most popular destinations in the whole country.

Orientation

Compact and eminently walkable, York is home to five major landmarks of note: the

wall enclosing the small city centre; the minster at the northern corner; Clifford's Tower at the southern end; the River Ouse that cuts the centre in two; and the train station to the west. Just to avoid the inevitable confusion, remember that round these parts *gate* means street and *bar* means gate.

Information

American Express (☎ 676501; 6 Stonegate; ⏰ 9am-5.30pm Mon-Fri, 9am-5pm Sat) With foreign exchange service.

Borders (☎ 653300; 1-5 Davygate; ⏰ 9am-9pm Mon-Sat, 11am-5pm Sun) Well-stocked bookshop.

Internet Exchange (☎ 638808; 13 Stonegate; per 30 mins £1; ⏰ 9am-7pm Mon-Sat, 11am-6pm Sun)

Post office (22 Lendal; ⏰ 8.30am-5.30pm Mon & Tue, 9am-5.30pm Wed-Sat).

This is York (www.thisisyork.co.uk)

Thomas Cook (☎ 653626; 4 Nessgate) A travel agent offering a full service.

TIC (☎ 621756; www.visityork.org; De Grey Rooms, Exhibition Sq; ⏰ 9am-6pm Mon-Sat, 10am-5pm Sun Apr-Sep, 9am-5pm Mon-Sat, 10am-4pm Sun Oct-Mar) There's another branch at the train station.

York District Hospital (☎ 631313; Wiggington Rd) A mile north of the centre.

Sights
YORK MINSTER

The island's largest medieval cathedral – and easily Yorkshire's most important historic building – is the simply awesome **minster** (☎ 624426; www.yorkminster.org; adult/child £4.50/3, minster & undercroft £6.50/4.50; ⏰ 7am-6pm Mon-Sat, noon-6pm Sun Nov-Mar, to 6.30pm Apr, to 7.30pm May, to 8.30pm Jun-Aug, to 8pm Sep & to 7pm Oct) that dominates the city. Seat of the archbishop of York, the primate of England, it is second in importance only to Canterbury, home of

the primate of *all* England (the two titles were given to settle a debate over whether York or Canterbury was the true centre of the church in England), but that's where Canterbury's superiority ends, for this is without doubt one of Europe's most beautiful Gothic buildings. If this is the only cathedral you visit in Britain, you'll still walk away satisfied.

The first church on the site was a wooden chapel built for Paulinus' baptism of King Edwin on Easter Day 627; its site is marked in the crypt. With deliberate symbolism, the church was built on the site of a Roman basilica, a vast central assembly hall; parts can be seen in the foundations. A stone church was started but fell into disrepair after Edwin's death. St Wilfred built the next church but this was destroyed during William the Conqueror's brutal suppression of the north. The first Norman church was built in stages to 1080; you can see surviving fragments in the foundations and crypt.

The present building, built mainly from 1220 to 1480, manages to represent all the major stages of Gothic architectural development. The transepts were built in the Early English style between 1220 and 1255; the octagonal chapter house was built between 1275 and 1290 in the Decorated style; the nave from 1291 to 1340; and the west towers, west front and central, or lantern, tower were built in the Perpendicular style from 1470 to 1472.

You enter from the south transept, which was badly damaged by fire in 1984 but has now been fully restored. To your right is the 15th-century **choir screen** depicting the 15 kings from William I to Henry VI. Facing you is the magnificent **Five Sisters Window**, with five lancets over 15m high. This is the minster's oldest complete window; most of its tangle of glass dates from around 1250. Just beyond it to the right is the 13th-century **chapter house**, a fine example of the Decorated style. Sinuous stonework surrounds a wonderful uninterrupted space. There are more than 200 expressive carved heads and figures.

Back in the main church, you should notice the unusually wide and tall nave, whose aisles (to the sides) are roofed in stone in contrast to the central roof, which is wood painted to look like stone. On both sides of the nave are painted stone shields of the nobles who met Edward II at a parliament in York. Also note the **dragon's head** projecting from the gallery – it's a crane believed to have been used to lift a font cover. There are several fine **windows** dating from the early 14th century, but the most dominating is the **Great West Window**, from 1338, with beautiful stone tracery.

Beyond the screen and the choir is the **lady chapel** and, behind it, the **high altar**, which is dominated by the huge **Great East Window** (1405). At 23.7m by 9.4m – roughly the size of a tennis court – it is the world's largest medieval stained-glass window and the cathedral's single most important treasure. Needless to say, its epic size matches the epic theme depicted within: the beginning and end of the world as described in Genesis and the Book of Revelations.

The minster's heart is dominated by the awesome **central tower** (adult/child £2.50/1; ✆ 10am-4.30pm Mon-Sat Jan, Feb, Nov & Dec, noon-6pm Mar, 10am-5.30pm Apr, Oct, 10am-6pm May & Sep, 9.30am-6.30pm Jun-Aug, from 12.30pm Sun) which is well worth climbing for the unparalleled views of York. You'll have to tackle a fairly claustrophobic climb of 275 steps and, most probably, a queue of people with cameras in hand. Access to the tower is near the entrance in the south transept, which is dominated by the exquisite **Rose Window** commemorating the union of the royal houses of Lancaster and York, through the marriage of Henry VII and Elizabeth of York, which ended the War of the Roses and began the Tudor dynasty (see p39).

Another set of stairs in the south transept leads down to the **undercroft** (adult/child £3/2, ✆ 10am-4.30pm Mon-Sat Nov-Feb, noon-6pm Mar, 10am-5.30pm Apr & Oct, 10am-6pm May & Sep, 9.30am-6.30pm Jun-Aug, from 12.30pm Sun), where you'll also find the **treasury** and the **crypt**. These should on no account be missed. In 1967 the foundations were excavated when the central tower threatened to collapse; while engineers worked frantically to save the building, archaeologists uncovered Roman and Norman ruins that attest to the site's ancient history – one of the most extraordinary finds is a Roman culvert, still carrying water to the Ouse. The treasury houses 11th-century artefacts, including relics from the graves of medieval archbishops. The crypt contains fragments from the Norman cathedral, including the font showing King Edwin's baptism that also marks the site of Paulinus' original wooden chapel.

AROUND THE MINSTER

Owned by the minster since the 15th century, **St William's College** (✆ 637134; College St) is an attractive half-timbered Tudor building with elegant oriel windows built for the minster's chantry priests.

The **Treasurer's House** (NT; ✆ 624247; Minster Yard; admission £4; ✆ 11am-4.30pm Sat-Thu Apr-Oct) was home to the minster's medieval treasurers. Substantially rebuilt in the 17th and 18th centuries, the 13 rooms house a fine collection of furniture and supply a good insight into 18th-century life. The house is also the setting for one of the city's most enduring ghost stories: during the 1950s, a plumber working in the basement swore he saw a band of Roman soldiers walking *through* the walls; his story remains popular if unproven.

CITY WALLS

You can get onto the walls, built in the 13th century, via steps by **Bootham Bar** (on the site of a Roman gate) and follow them clockwise to **Monk Bar**, a walk offering particularly beautiful views of the minster. There are oodles more access points including those off Station Rd and Monk Bar.

Monk Bar is the best-preserved medieval gate, with a small **Richard III Museum**

(☎ 634191; www.richardiiimuseum.co.uk; admission £2; ☽ 9am-5pm Mar-Oct, 9.30am-4pm Nov-Feb) upstairs. The museum sets out the case of the murdered 'Princes in the Tower' and invites visitors to judge whether their uncle, Richard III, killed them.

Walmgate Bar is England's only city gate with an intact barbican (an extended gateway to ward off uninvited guests), and was built during the reign of Edward III.

MERCHANT ADVENTURERS' HALL
Built between 1357 and 1361, the outstanding **Merchant Adventurers' Hall** (☎ 654818; Fossgate; admission £2; ☽ 9am-5pm Mon-Thu, 9am-3.30pm Fri & Sat, noon-4pm Sun Apr-Sep, 9.30am-3.30pm Mon-Sat Oct-Mar) is one of the most handsome timber-framed buildings in Europe. This stunning building testifies to the power of the medieval guilds, which controlled all foreign trade into and out of York until 1830 – a handy little monopoly.

JORVIK
The much-trumpeted **Jorvik** (☎ 543403; www .vikingjorvik.com; Coppergate; adult/child £7.20/5.10; ☽ 10am-5pm Apr-Oct, 10am-4pm Nov-Mar) sounds terrific: a smells-and-all reconstruction of the original Viking settlement unearthed in this area during excavations in the late 1970s. A 'time-car' transports you 'back in time' and through what the town may have looked like, past groups of fibre-glass figures speaking a language derived from modern Icelandic. It is a bit of fun (for kids at least) but, except for the collection of actual artefacts scattered throughout, not altogether that fascinating. But, considering the crowds that queue up to get in to this museum, what the hell do we know? To cut the queue time considerably, book your tickets online – it only costs £1 more.

If you really want to get stuck into a bit of archaeology, check out the **Archaeological Resource Centre** (ARC; ☎ 654324; St Saviourgate; adult/ child £4.50/4, with Jorvik £10.20/8.10; ☽ 10am-3.30pm Mon-Fri school term, 11am-3pm Mon-Sat school holidays) that is also run by the Jorvik people. It has various programmes that allow for hands-on exploration of archaeology.

CLIFFORD'S TOWER
There's precious little left of York Castle except for this evocative stone **tower** (EH; ☎ 646940; admission £2.50; ☽ 10am-6pm Apr-Jun & Sep, 9.30am-7pm Jul-Aug, 10am-5pm Oct, 10am-4pm Nov-Mar), a highly unusual figure-eight design built into the castle's keep after the original one was destroyed in 1190 during anti-Jewish riots. An angry mob forced 150 Jews to be locked inside the tower, but it wasn't enough, and the hapless victims took their own lives rather than be killed. There's not much to see inside but the views over the city are excellent.

YORK CASTLE MUSEUM
Near Clifford's Tower, this excellent **museum** (☎ 653611; admission £6; ☽ 9.30am-5pm) contains displays of everyday life, with reconstructed domestic interiors, and a less-than-homely prison cell where you can try out the condemned man's bed – in this case Dick Turpin's. There's a bewildering array of evocative everyday objects from the past 400 years, gathered together by a certain Dr Kirk from the 1920s onwards for fear that the items would become obsolete and disappear completely. He wasn't far wrong, which makes this place all the more interesting.

NATIONAL RAILWAY MUSEUM
Most railway museums are the sole preserve of lone men with dog-eared notebooks and grandfathers looking to bond with their grandchildren. While there's no shortage of either here, this **museum** (☎ 621261; www.nrm.org .uk; Leeman Rd; admission free; ☽ 10am-6pm) stands apart on account of its sheer size and incredible collection. Trainspotters and nostalgics will salivate at the massive gathering of engines and carriages from the past, but the attractions for regular folk are the gleaming carriages of the royal trains used by Queen Victoria and Edward VII; the speed-record-breaking *Mallard* (a mighty 2 miles a minute in 1938, still a record for a steam train); and a Series 'O' Japanese bullet train (1964–86), which you can sit in – it is a testament to the speed of technology that the train now appears a tad dated. Just next to it is a **simulator** (£3), which allows you to travel from London to Brighton in real time at supersonic speed – the journey takes four minutes. You can also wander around a vast annexe including the restoration workshops. Allow two hours to do the museum justice.

The museum is slightly out of the way (about 400m west of the train station), so if you don't fancy the walk, you can ride the **road train** (adult/child £1.50/50p; ☾ noon-5pm) that runs every 30 minutes between the minster and the museum.

OTHER SIGHTS

Museum Gardens (☾ dawn-dusk) make a peaceful four-hectare city-centre oasis. Assorted picturesque ruins and buildings include the **Museum Gardens Lodge** (neo-Gothic Revival) dating from 1874 and a 19th-century working **observatory**. The **Multangular Tower** was the western tower of the Roman garrison's defensive wall. The small Roman stones at the bottom have been built up with 13th-century additions.

The classical **Yorkshire Museum** (☎ 629745; adult/child £4/3; ☾ 10am-5pm) has some interesting Roman, Anglo-Saxon, Viking and medieval exhibits, as well as good temporary exhibitions.

The **St Mary's Abbey** (founded 1089) ruins date from 1270 to 1294. The ruined **Gatehall** was its main entrance, providing access from the abbey to the river. The adjacent **Hospitium** dates from the 14th century, although the timber-framed upper storey is a much-restored survivor from the 15th century; it was used as the abbey guesthouse. **St Mary's Lodge** was built around 1470 to provide VIP accommodation.

St Olave's Church (☾ 9am-5pm Mon-Fri) dates from the 15th century, but there has been a church dedicated to Norway's patron saint here since at least 1050.

Adjacent to Museum Gardens on Exhibition Sq is the 19th-century **York City Art Gallery** (☎ 551861; Exhibition Sq; admission free; ☾ 10am-5pm), which includes works by Reynolds, Nash, Boudin and Lowry.

Back inside the walls, the wonky lines inside **Holy Trinity** (☎ 613451; Goodramgate; ☾ 10am-5pm Tue-Sat May-Sep, 10am-4pm Oct-Apr) almost induce seasickness. The church was started in the 13th century and added to over the next 200 years. Rare 17th- to 18th-century box pews surround a two-tier pulpit.

If 18th-century Georgian houses are for you, then a visit to **Fairfax House** (☎ 655543; www.fairfaxhouse.co.uk; Castlegate; adult/child £4.50/1.50; ☾ 11am-5pm Mon-Thu & Sat, 1.30-5pm Sun, guided tours 11am & 2pm Fri late Feb–early Jan) should be on your itinerary. This exquisitely restored property was designed by John Carr (of Harewood House fame; see p506) and features the best

example of rococo stucco work to be found in the north of England.

North of Fairfax House, the quaintly cobbled **Shambles**, complete with overhanging Tudor buildings, hints at what a medieval street might have looked like if it was overrun with people told they have to buy something silly and superfluous and be back on the tour bus in 15 minutes. It takes its name from the Saxon word *shamel*, meaning slaughterhouse.

York Dungeon (☎ 632599; www.thedungeons.com; 12 Clifford St; adult/child £9.95/6.95; ☾ 10.30am-5pm Apr-Sep, 11am-4pm Nov-Jan, 10.30am-4.30pm Oct & Feb-Mar) is a series of exultantly gruesome historical reconstructions. For the especially hardened there's a lovely bit on the plague.

Tours

There's a bewildering array of tours on offer, from historic walking tours to a host of ever-competitive night-time ghost tours – pretty popular in what is reputed to be England's most haunted city.

BUS

York Citysightseeing (☎ 655585; www.city-sightseeing .com; day tickets adult/child £8/3.50) Two hop-on hop-off services calling at all the main sights; buses leave every 15 minutes from Exhibition Sq outside the main TIC.

BOAT

YorkBoat (☎ 628324; www.yorkboat.co.uk; Lendal Bridge; 1hr cruises adult/child £6.50/3.30; ☾ 10.40am, 12.10pm, 1.40pm & 3.10pm Feb-Nov; ghost cruises adult/child £7.50/4; ☾ 6.30pm late Mar–Oct) Runs Ouse cruises from Lendal Bridge which depart King's Staith (behind the fire station) 10 minutes earlier. The obligatory ghost cruise runs nightly in high season from King's Staith.

WALKING

Association of Voluntary Guides (☎ 640780; 10.15am, also 2.15pm Apr-Oct & 6.45pm Jun-Aug) Free two-hour walking tours of the city from Exhibition Sq in front of York City Art Gallery.

Complete York Tour (☎ 706643) A walk around the city and the minster that can be adapted to your preferences. Call for details.

Ghost Hunt of York (☎ 608700; www.ghosthunt.co.uk; adult £4; ☾ 7.30pm) Award-winning and highly entertaining 75-minute tour beginning at the Shambles.

Original Ghost Walk of York (☎ 01759 373090; adult/child £3.50/2.50; ☾ 8pm) Ghouls and ghosts courtesy of a well-established group departing from the King's Arms pub by Ouse Bridge.

Roam'in Tours of York (☎ 07931 668935; www .roamintours.co.uk) History and specialist tours (adult/child £3/1) or you can take its DIY audio tour (£3.50).

Viking Walk (☎ 07796 772001; adult/child £3/2; ⏰ 8.15pm Mon-Sat) Follow the fearsome but friendly Viking Gunhild on a tour of Jorvik. It's a bit of fun. Departures are from Exhibition Sq.

Yorkwalk (☎ 622303; www.yorkwalk.co.uk; adult/child £5/free) Offers a series of two-hour themed walks on an ever-growing list of themes, from the classics – Roman York, the snickelways (alleys) and City Walls – to specialised walks on chocolates and sweets, women in York, secret York and the inevitable graveyard, coffin and plague tour. Walks depart from Museum Gardens Gate on Museum St.

Festivals & Events

For a week in mid-February, York is invaded by Vikings once again as part of the **Jorvik Viking Festival** (☎ 643211; www.viking jorvik.com; Coppergate), which features battle re-enactments, themed walks, markets and other bits of Nordic fun.

Sleeping

Beds are tough to find midsummer, even at the spiked prices of the high season. The TIC's efficient accommodation booking service charges £4, which might be the best four quid you spend in town.

Needless to say, prices go up the closer to the city centre you are. However, there are plenty of decent B&Bs on the streets north and south of Bootham, the northwest continuation of High Petergate; Grosvenor Tce, a handsome street along the railway tracks, is particularly full of them. Southwest of the town centre, there are B&Bs clustered around Scarcroft Rd, Southlands Rd and Bishopthorpe Rd.

BUDGET

York Backpackers (☎ 627720; www.yorkbackpack ers.co.uk; 88-90 Micklegate; dm/d from £13/34) In a Grade I Georgian building that was once home to the High Sheriff of Yorkshire, this large, well-equipped hostel has all the usual facilities as well as Internet access and a residents-only bar that serves cheap beer until 1am.

York Youth Hotel (☎ 625904; www.yorkyouthhotel .demon.co.uk; 11 Bishophill Senior; dm £12-15, s/d £25/44) Offering the cheapest single rooms within the city walls, this is a good option for travellers who are on a budget but still want to stay close to the action.

York YHA Hostel (☎ 0870 770 6102, 0870 770 6103; www.yha.org.uk; Water End, Clifton; dm £17) Once the Rowntree (Quaker confectioners) mansion, this handsome Victorian house in its own grounds is almost entirely self-contained – there's even a bar on the property. Most of the rooms are four-bed dorms. It's about a mile northwest of the TIC; turn left into Bootham, which becomes Clifton (the A19), then left into Water End. There's a riverside footpath from Lendal Bridge, but it's ill lit so avoid it after dark.

Fairfax House (☎ 434784; www.york.ac.uk; 99 Heslington Rd; s £22; ⏰ Jun-Sep only) Part of the University of York, this ivy-clad building offers accommodation in standard, well-equipped rooms, but only outside of term. It is 2 miles southeast of the city. Take bus No 4.

MID-RANGE

Four High Petergate (☎ 658516; www.fourhighpeter gate.co.uk; 4 High Petergate; s/d £50/80) This stunning 18th-century house next to Bootham Bar has been converted into a gorgeous boutique hotel. Indonesian teak furniture, crisp white linen, flat-screen TV and DVD player are standard in all 14 bedrooms, even if the standard singles and doubles are substantially more compact than the superior rooms. Highly recommended for its class and location. The bistro next door is also excellent.

One3Two (☎ 600060; www.one3two.co.uk; 132 The Mount; s/d from £47.50/70; Ⓟ) This is how we would like all B&Bs to be. Five individually designed bedrooms, all with handcrafted teak beds (one has a particularly handsome four-poster), a flat-screen TV and DVD player, elegant old-fashioned bathrooms (but with all the modern amenities) and the kind of breakfast that a French-trained chef might put together. Pure luxury.

Dairy Guesthouse (☎ 639367; www.dairyguest house.co.uk; 3 Scarcroft Rd; s/d £32/50; Ⓟ) A wonderful Victorian home that has retained many of its original features, including pine doors, stained glass, and cast-iron fireplaces, but the real treat is the flower- and plant-filled courtyard, off of which are the cottage-style rooms. The name comes from the time when it served as a town dairy.

23 St Mary's (☎ 622738; www.23stmarys.co.uk; 23 St Mary's; s/d from £34/60; Ⓟ) A smart and stately town house with handsome rooms with en suites; some have hand-painted furniture for

---

SOMETHING SPECIAL

Middlethorpe Hall (☎ 641241; www.middlethorpe.com; Bishopsthorpe Rd; s/d from £109/140; **P**) York's top spot is this breathtaking 17th-century country house set in 20 acres of parkland that was once the home of diarist Lady Mary Wortley Montagu. The rooms are spread between the main house, the restored courtyard buildings and three cottage suites. Although we preferred the grandeur of the rooms in the main house, every room is beautifully decorated with original antiques and oil paintings carefully collected so as to best reflect the period. The magnificent grounds include a white and walled garden and a small lake.

---

that country look, while others are decorated with antiques, lace and a bit of chintz.

Brontë House (☎ 621066; www.bronte-guesthouse .com; 22 Grosvenor Tce; s/d from £34/60) Five wonderful rooms with en suite all decorated completely differently: particularly good is the double with a carved, 19th-century sleigh bed, William Morris wallpaper and assorted bits and bobs from another era.

Bar Convent (☎ 464902; www.bar-convent.org.uk; 17 Blossom St; s/d £37/56) England's oldest working convent (founded in 1686) offers B&B in basic rooms; only a handful have an en suite. Despite the monastic comforts, there's a friendly, welcoming atmosphere about the place.

Other options include:

Alcuin Lodge (☎ 632222; alcuinlodge@aol.com; 15 Sycamore Pl; d from £27) Pretty doubles in a cluttered Victorian house.

Arnot House (☎ 641966; www.arnothouseyork.co.uk; 17 Grosvenor Tce; s/d from £38/62; **P**) Four handsome if unexceptional rooms in a beautifully maintained Victorian house.

Briar Lea Guest House (☎ 635061; www.briarlea.co.uk; 8 Longfield Tce; s/d from £22/40) Clean, simple rooms and a friendly welcome in a house just off Bootham.

City Guesthouse (☎ 622483; www.cityguesthouse.co.uk; 68 Monkgate; s/d from £35/60; **P**) Very tidy house with meticulously arranged furniture & bric-a-brac; vegetarians catered for.

St Denys Hotel (☎ 622207; www.stdenyshotel.co.uk; St Denys Rd; s/d from £45/65) Slightly worn but still comfortable rooms. Good location inside the city walls.

TOP END

Judges Lodging Hotel (☎ 638733; judgeshotel@aol .com; 9 Lendal; s/d from £70/100) An elegant and excellent choice for central accommodation, this fine Georgian mansion has very tasteful rooms – despite one with a Queen Mother theme – in what was once the private home of a county judge.

Mount Royale (☎ 628856; www.mountroyale.co.uk; The Mount; r from £97; **P** **≋**) A grand, William IV–

listed building converted into a superb luxury hotel, complete with a solarium, beauty spa and outdoor heated tub and swimming pool. The rooms in the main house are gorgeous, but the best of the lot are the open-plan garden suites, reached via a corridor of tropical fruit trees and bougainvillea.

Dean Court Hotel (☎ 625082; www.deancourt -york.co.uk; Duncombe Pl; s/d from £90/120) With a commanding position directly across from the minster (you'll only get a church view from the superior rooms), this fine hotel has large, comfortable rooms, although we'd have to put a question mark next to some of the chintzy, pseudo-Georgian décor.

Eating

Eating well in York is not a problem – there are plenty of fine options throughout the centre; many of the city's pubs also do good grub – they're listed in the Drinking section (p529).

BUDGET

Betty's (☎ 659142; St Helen's Sq; sandwiches about £4.50, cream tea £6.50; ☺ 9am-9pm) Afternoon tea, old-school style, in a Yorkshire institution. It's popular, the queues can get pretty long, but it's worth the wait. If you want the full treatment, go after 6pm, when a pianist adds a touch of class.

El Piano (☎ 610676; www.elpiano.co.uk; 15 Grape Lane; mains about £6; ☺ 10am-1am Mon-Sat, noon-midnight Sun) A vegetarian haven, this colourful, Hispanic-style spot has a lovely café downstairs and three themed rooms upstairs: check out the Moroccan room, complete with floor cushions.

Café Concerto (☎ 610478; 21 High Petergate; cakes £2-3, starters £4-6, mains £9.80-12.50; ☺ 10am-10pm) 'Music for your mouth' is the theme of this lovely café facing the minster. The walls are papered with sheet music, but it's the delicious food that makes the most noise – the chicken and avocado sandwich is sensational.

MID-RANGE

Siam House (☎ 624677; 63a Goodramgate; mains £7-10; ☺ lunch & dinner Mon-Sat, dinner only Sun) Delicious, authentic Thai food in about as authentic an atmosphere as you could muster up 6000km from Bangkok. The early bird, three-course special (£10.95) is an absolute steal.

Little Betty's (☎ 622865; 46 Stonegate; afternoon tea £10.25; ☺ 10am-5.30pm) Betty's younger sister is more demure, less frequented, but just as good; you go upstairs and back in time to what feels like the interwar years – it's possible to spot a couple of Agatha Christie look-alikes. The afternoon tea would feed a small village.

Melton's Too (☎ 629222; 25 Walmgate; curries about £9; ☺ lunch & dinner) A very comfortable, booth-lined restaurant that purports to do modern Brit cuisine but actually serves up a terrific Thai green curry, which we highly recommend. It's the slightly scruffier younger brother to Melton's (see below).

Rubicon (☎ 676076; 5 Little Stonegate; mains about £8; ☺ lunch & dinner) When a vegetarian restaurant can attract even the most avid carnivore with a tempting menu of imaginative dishes – why not try the cinnamon couscous and butternut squash with goat's cheese – served in a modern, airy room without ne'er a hippy wall hanging to be seen, it's bound to be a success.

Fiesta Mexicana (☎ 610243; 14 Clifford St; burritos £8.45; ☺ dinner) *Chimichangas, tostadas* and burritos served in a relentlessy happy atmosphere. Students and party groups on the rip add to the fiesta; it's not subtle or subdued, but when is Mexican food ever so?

TOP END

Blue Bicycle (☎ 673990; 34 Fossgate; mains £14-22; ☺ lunch & dinner) Once upon a time, this building was a well-frequented brothel; these days it serves up a different kind of fare to an equally enthusiastic crowd. French food at its finest, served in a romantic, candle-lit room, makes for a top-notch dining experience.

Melton's (☎ 634341; 7 Scarcroft Rd; mains £12-18; ☺ lunch & dinner Tue-Sat, dinner only Mon & lunch only Sun) Foodies come from far and wide to dine in one of Yorkshire's best restaurants. It tends to specialise in fish dishes but doesn't go far wrong with practically everything else,

from Yorkshire beef to the asparagus risotto with pinenuts and herbs. There's an excellent lunch and early dinner set menu (£17).

Rish (☎ 622688; 7 Fossgate; mains £11-20; ☺ lunch & dinner) Hip Brit cuisine – basically traditional classics like Yorkshire fillet steak and bangers and mash given the modern once-over – served in a super-cool, contemporary room that has attracted critical kudos and customers in equal measure.

Drinking

With only a couple of exceptions, the best drinking holes in town are older, traditional pubs. In recent years, the area around Ousegate and Micklegate has gone from moribund to mental, especially at weekends.

Ackhorne (☎ 671421; 9 St Martin's Lane) Tucked away from beery, sloppy Micklegate, this locals' inn is as comfortable as old slippers. Some of the old guys here look like they've morphed with the place.

Black Swan (☎ 686911; Peasholme Green) A classic black-and-white Tudor building where you'll find decent beer, friendly people and live jazz on Sundays. Nice.

Blue Bell (☎ 654904; 53 Fossgate) A tiny, tiny pub with décor dating from 1798 and a surprisingly contemporary crowd (read: lots of young people).

Casa (☎ 639971; 1a Lower Ousegate) This riverside bar with cracking views over the Ouse is our favourite of York's newer additions to the bar scene: it's very modern, with lots of blank white spaces, but not nearly as pretentious as it appears. It does, however, have a strict policy against sportswear.

King's Arms (☎ 659435; King's Staith; lunch about £5) York's best-known pub is a creaky place with a fabulous riverside location – hence its enduring popularity. A perfect spot for a summer's evening.

Ye Olde Starre (☎ 623063; 40 Stonegate) A bit of a tourist trap, but an altogether excellent pub that is popular with locals. It was used as a morgue by the Roundheads, but the atmosphere's improved since then. It has decent ales and a heated outdoor patio overlooked by the minster.

Entertainment

There are a couple of good theatres in York, a fairly interesting cinema, but as far as clubs are concerned, forget it: historic York is best enjoyed without them.

York Theatre Royal (☎ 623568; St Leonard's Pl) Stages well-regarded productions of theatre, opera and dance.

York Barbican Centre (☎ 656688; Barbican Rd) Big-name concerts in a partly pyramidal, modern building.

City Screen (☎ 541144; www.picturehouses.co.uk; 13-17 Coney St) Mainstream and art-house films.

Grand Opera House (☎ 671818; Clifford St) Despite its name this place puts on a wide range of productions.

Shopping

Coney St and its adjoining streets are the hub of York shopping, but the real treat for visitors are the many second-hand and antiquarian bookshops, most of which are clustered in two main areas – Micklegate and Fossgate.

Jack Duncan Books (☎ 641389; 36 Fossgate) Cheap paperbacks and unusual books.

Ken Spellman Booksellers (☎ 624414; 70 Micklegate) This fine shop has been selling rare, antiquarian and second-hand books since 1910.

Worm Holes Bookshop (☎ 620011; www.worm-holes.co .uk; 20 Bootham) Our favourite of York's dusty bookshops, with a decent and far-reaching selection of old and new titles.

Getting There & Away

BUS

The very useful **York Travel Bus Info Centre** (☎ 551400; 20 George Hudson St; ◷ 8.30am-5pm Mon-Fri) has complete schedule information and sells local and regional tickets. All local and regional buses stop along Rougier St, off Station Rd inside the city walls on the western side of Lendal Bridge.

National Express coaches also stop here as well as outside the train station. Tickets can be bought at the TICs. There are services to London (£22, 5¼ hours, four daily), Birmingham (£21.50, three hours, one daily) and Edinburgh (£28.50, 5½ hours, one daily).

CAR & MOTORCYCLE

You won't need a car around the city, but it comes in handy for exploring the surrounding area. Rental options include: **Europcar** (☎ 656161) by platform 1 in the train station which also rents bicycles and stores luggage (£4); **Hertz** (☎ 612586) near platform 3 in the train station; and **Practical Car & Van Rental** (☎ 624848; Tanners Moat) which is good for cheaper deals.

TRAIN

York train station is a stunning masterpiece of Victorian engineering. It also has plenty of arrivals and departures: Birmingham (£38, 2½ hours, hourly); Edinburgh (£38, 2½ hours, hourly); Leeds (£8.10, 50 minutes, hourly); London King's Cross (£49, two hours, hourly); Manchester (£16.10, 1½ hours, six daily); and Scarborough (£9.30, 45 minutes).

Trains also go via Peterborough (£37, 1¾ hours, every 30 minutes), for Cambridge and East Anglia.

Getting Around

The city of York is quite easily walked on foot. You are never really more than 20 minutes from any of the major sights or areas.

BICYCLE

The Bus Info Centre has a useful free map showing York's bike routes. If you are particularly energetic you could pedal out to Castle Howard (15 miles), Helmsley and Rievaulx Abbey (12 miles) and Thirsk (another 12 miles), and then catch a train back to York.

You might also like to do a section of the Trans-Pennine-Trail cycle path from Bishopthorpe in York to Selby (15 miles) along the old railway line. The TICs have maps.

Two rental places are **Bob Trotter** (☎ 622868; 13 Lord Mayor's Walk; rental per day £8), outside Monk Bar; and **Europcar** (☎ 656161; rental per day from £11).

BUS

The local bus service is provided by **First York** (☎ 622992), which sells a **day pass** (£2.20) valid on all of its local buses – although you'll hardly need it if you're sticking close to town. The Bus Info Centre has service details.

CAR & MOTORCYCLE

Be aware that York gets as congested as most English cities in summer, and parking in the centre can be expensive (up to £9 per day), but most guesthouses and hotels have access to parking.

TAXI

Station Taxis (☎ 623332) has a kiosk outside the train station.

AROUND YORK
Castle Howard

Stately homes may be two a penny in England, but you'll have to try pretty damn hard to find one as breathtakingly stunning as **Castle Howard** (☎ 01653-648333; www.castle howard.co.uk; adult/child house & grounds £9.50/6.50, grounds £6.50/4.50; ☷ house 11am-4.30pm, grounds 10am-4.30pm mid-Mar–Oct), a work of supreme theatrical grandeur and audacity set in the rolling Howardian Hills with wandering peacocks on its terraces. This is one of the world's most beautiful buildings, and instantly recognisable for its starring role in *Brideshead Revisited* – which has done its popularity no end of good since the TV series first aired in the early 1980s.

When the earl of Carlisle hired his mate Sir John Vanbrugh in 1699 to design his new home, he was hiring a bloke who had no formal training and was best known as a playwright; luckily Vanbrugh hired Nicholas Hawksmoor, who had worked for Christopher Wren, as his clerk of works – not only would Hawksmoor have a big part to play in the house's design but the two would later do wonders with Blenheim Palace (p338).

If you can, try to visit on a weekday, when it's easier to find the space to appreciate this hedonistic marriage of art, architecture, landscaping and natural beauty. Wandering about the grounds, views open up over the hills, Vanbrugh's playful Temple of the Four Winds and Hawksmoor's stately mausoleum, but the great baroque house with its magnificent central cupola is an irresistible visual magnet. Inside, it is full of treasures, such as the chapel's Pre-Raphaelite stained glass.

Castle Howard is 15 miles northeast of York, 4 miles off the A64. It can be reached by several tours from York. Check with the TIC for up-to-date schedules. Yorkshire Coastliner has a useful bus service that links Leeds, York, Castle Howard, Pickering and Whitby (No 840). A day return from York costs £4.80, while a **Coastliner Freedom ticket** (adult/senior/family £10/7.50/26) is good for unlimited rides all day; buy tickets on the bus.

THIRSK
☎ 01845 / pop 9099

A handsome medieval trading town with tidy, attractive streets and a cobbled central square (Monday and Saturday are market days), Thirsk was made prosperous by its key position on two medieval trading routes: the old drove road between Scotland and York, and the route linking the Yorkshire Dales with the coast. That's all in the past, though: today, the town is all about the legacy of James Herriot, the wry Yorkshire vet adored by millions of fans of *All Creatures Great and Small*.

Thirsk's **TIC** (☎ 522755; thirsk@ytbtic.co.uk; 49 Market Pl; ☷ 10am-5pm Easter-Oct, 11am-4pm Nov-Easter) is on the main square.

Thirsk does a good job as the real-life Darrowby of the books and TV series, and it should, as the real-life Herriot was in fact local vet Alf Wight, whose house and surgery has been dipped in 1940s aspic and turned into the incredibly popular **World of James Herriot** (☎ 524234; www.worldofjamesherriot. org; 23 Kirkgate; admission £4.85; ☷ 10am-6pm Apr-Oct, 11am-4pm Nov-Mar), an excellent museum full of Wight artefacts, a video documentary of his life and a re-creation of the TV show sets. It's all quite well done and you'll be in the company of true fans, many of whom have that look of pilgrimage on their faces.

Almost directly across the street is the less-frequented **Thirsk Museum** (☎ 527707; www.thirskmuseum.org; 14-16 Kirkgate; admission £1.50; ☷ 10am-4pm Mon-Wed, Fri & Sat), which manages to cram a collection of items from Neolithic times to the Herriot era into a tiny house where Thomas Lord (of Lord's Cricket Ground fame) was born in 1755.

Sleeping & Eating

The TIC books B&Bs free of charge and has a handy accommodation list.

Three Tuns Hotel (☎ 523124; www.the-three-tuns -thirsk.co.uk; Market Pl; s/d from £45/65; mains from £6.50) A fairly imposing 18th-century coaching inn best known as having hosted the Wordsworths on their honeymoon in 1802. The bedrooms have changed somewhat since then, and today offer comfortable if unspectacular accommodation.

Getting There & Away

There are frequent daily buses from York (45 minutes).

Thirsk is well served by trains on the line between York and Middlesbrough. However, the train station is a mile west of town and the only way to cover that distance is on foot or by **taxi** (☎ 522473).

AROUND THIRSK
Fountains Abbey & Studley Royal Water Gardens

Sheltered in the secluded valley of the River Skell are two of Yorkshire's most beautiful attractions and an absolute must on your northern itinerary. The strangely obsessive and beautiful formal **Studley Royal water gardens** were built in the 19th century so as to enhance the extensive ruins of the 12th-century **Fountains Abbey** (NT; ☎ 01765-608888; www.fountainsabbey.org.uk; abbey, hall & garden adult £5.50; ☑ 10am-4pm Jan-Mar & Oct-Dec, 10am-6pm Apr-Sep). Together they create a breathtaking picture of pastoral elegance and tranquillity that have made them the most visited of all the National Trust's pay-in properties and Yorkshire's only World Heritage Site.

After falling out with the Benedictines of York in 1132, a band of rebel monks came here to what was then a desolate and unyielding patch of land to found their own monastery. Struggling to make it on their own, they were formally adopted by the Cistercians in 1135: by the middle of the 13th century the new abbey had become the most successful Cistercian venture in the country. It was during this time that most of today's ruins were built, including the church's nave and transepts, outlying buildings and the church's eastern end (the tower was added in the late 15th century).

After the dissolution (p40) the estate was sold into private hands and between 1598 and 1611 Fountains Hall was built with stone from the abbey ruins. The hall and ruins were united with the Studley Royal Estate in 1768.

Studley Royal's main house burnt down in 1946, but the superb landscaping, with its serene artificial lakes, has been barely touched since the 18th century. Studley Royal was owned by John Aislabie (once Chancellor of the Exchequer), who dedicated his life to creating the park after a financial scandal saw him expelled from parliament.

Fountains Abbey is 4 miles west of Ripon off the B6265. The **deer park** (admission free, car park £2) opens during daylight hours. **St Mary's Church** (☑ 1-5pm Apr-Sep) features occasional concerts. There are free one-hour **guided tours** (11am & 2.30pm Apr-Oct & 3.30pm Apr-Sep, garden 2pm Apr-Oct).

Public transport is limited to summer Sunday services.

HARROGATE
☎ 01423 / pop 85,128

This prim and proper old-fashioned resort hit the heights during the Victorian age because of the curative powers of its sulphur water; these days, it is the sweeter-smelling flower shows that attract visitors, but Harrogate has retained much of its nostalgic flavour. Indeed, the pervading feeling is that the town hasn't come all that far since Agatha Christie fled here in 1926 when her marriage broke up.

The town is also close to the eastern edge of Yorkshire Dales National Park, and has many good hotels, B&Bs and restaurants.

THE WHITE MONKS

Founded at Cîteaux in Burgundy in 1098, the Cistercians were hardcore. They rejected the free-lovin', toga-party antics of those wild and crazy Benedictines in favour of an even more rigid and austere form of living: they went to live in the most inhospitable parts of the kingdom and refused to wear underwear. Their habits were made of undyed sheep's wool – hence their nickname – and their diet was barely above starvation level. Nobody complained either, because they were committed to long periods of silence and eight daily services. But with so much time given over to starving themselves in silent prayer, there was no room for work, so they ordained lay brothers who tilled their lands, worked their lead mines and tended their ever-growing flocks of sheep. And so it was that their commitment to a super-disciplined 1st-century Christianity made them powerful and rich – and encouraged other orders like the Augustinians and their old nemesis the Benedictines to follow suit. The Scottish Wars and the Black Death threw an economic spanner in the works though, and they were eventually forced to lease their lands to tenant farmers and live off the proceeds. When Henry VIII went to war with the monasteries in 1536, he used their perceived greed and laziness as partial justification. Surely a case of king pot calling the white kettles black?

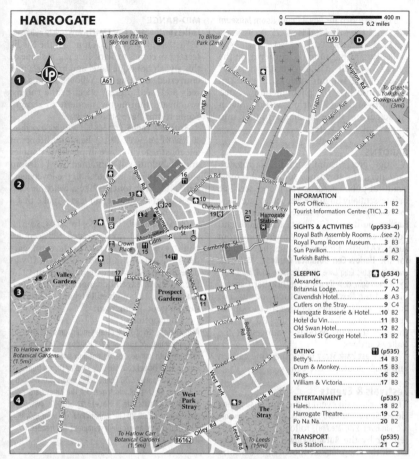

HARROGATE

0 ————— 400 m
0 ————— 0.2 miles

INFORMATION	
Post Office...............................1	B2
Tourist Information Centre (TIC)..2	B2

SIGHTS & ACTIVITIES	(pp533–4)
Royal Bath Assembly Rooms......(see 2)	
Royal Pump Room Museum........3	B3
Sun Pavilion..............................4	A3
Turkish Baths............................5	B2

SLEEPING	(p534)
Alexander................................6	C1
Britannia Lodge........................7	A2
Cavendish Hotel........................8	A3
Cutlers on the Stray...................9	C4
Harrogate Brasserie & Hotel......10	B2
Hotel du Vin...........................11	B3
Old Swan Hotel........................12	B2
Swallow St George Hotel...........13	B2

EATING	(p535)
Betty's...................................14	B3
Drum & Monkey......................15	B3
Kings.....................................16	B2
William & Victoria...................17	B3

ENTERTAINMENT	(p535)
Hales......................................18	B2
Harrogate Theatre....................19	C2
Po Na Na................................20	B2

TRANSPORT	(p535)
Bus Station.............................21	C2

YORKSHIRE

The town's glorious Turkish baths are not to be missed.

Orientation & Information

Harrogate is almost surrounded by gardens including the 80-hectare Stray in the south. The mostly pedestrianised shopping streets, Oxford and Cambridge Sts, are lined with smart shops and the **post office** (11 Cambridge Rd; 9am-5.30pm Mon-Sat).

The **TIC** (☎ 537300; www.harrogate.gov.uk/tourism; Crescent Rd; 9am-6pm Mon-Sat, 10am-1pm Sun Apr-Sep, 9am-5pm Mon-Fri, 9am-4pm Sat Oct-Mar) is in the Royal Baths Assembly Rooms; staff can give information about free historical walking tours offered daily from Easter to October.

Sights & Activities
THE WATERS

Take the plunge into the waters and into the past in the fabulously tiled **Turkish Baths** (☎ 556746; www.harrogate.co.uk/turkishbaths; adult £12; 9am-9pm) in the Royal Baths Assembly Rooms. The mock Moorish facility is gloriously Victorian and offers visitors a range of watery delights – steam rooms, saunas, and so on. A visit should last at least two hours.

There is a complicated schedule of opening hours that are at turns single sex and mixed pairs – contact the baths for more details. You can also prebook a range of reasonably priced massages and other therapies.

The very ornate **Royal Pump Room Museum** (☎ 556188; Crown Pl; adult/child £2/1.25; ⏰ 10am-5pm Mon-Sat, 2-5pm Sun Apr-Oct, 10am-4pm Mon-Sat, 2-4pm Sun Nov-Mar), just around the corner from the baths, was built in 1842 over the most famous of the sulphur springs. It gives an insight into how the phenomenon created the town and the illustrious visitors that it attracted, and there's a chance to tuck into some stinky spa water.

GARDENS

A huge green thumbs-up to Harrogate's gardeners; the town has some of the most beautiful public gardens you'll ever see. The quintessentially English **Valley Gardens** are overlooked by the vast, ornate, glass-domed **Sun Pavilion**, built in 1933. The nearby bandstand houses concerts on Sunday afternoons from June to August. Flower-fanatics should make for the **Harlow Carr Botanical Gardens** (☎ 565418; www.rhs.org.uk; Crag Lane, Beckwithshaw; adult/child £5/1; ⏰ 9.30am-6pm, dusk if earlier), the northern showpiece of the Royal Horticultural Society. The gardens are 1½ miles southwest of town. To get here, take the B6162 Otley Rd or walk through the Pine Woods southwest of the Valley Gardens.

The **West Park Stray** is another fine garden and park, south of the centre.

Festivals & Events

The year's main event is the immense **Spring Flower Show** (☎ 0870 758 3333; www.flowershow.org .uk; admission £10; late Apr), followed in late September by the **Autumn Flower Show** (admission £8). Both take place at the Great Yorkshire Showground.

If fancy shrubs aren't really your thing, there's a lot more fun to be had at the **Great Yorkshire Show** (☎ 541000; www.greatyorkshireshow .org; admission £15), a three-day exhibition staged in mid-July by the Yorkshire Agricultural Society (also held at the showground). It's a real treat, with all manner of farm critters competing for prizes and last year's losers served up in a variety of ways.

Sleeping

BUDGET

Bilton Park (☎ 863121; biltonpark@tcsmail.net; Village Farm, Bilton; tent sites £10; ⏰ Apr-Oct) A convenient campsite 2 miles north of town. Take bus No 201, 203 or 204 from the bus station.

MID-RANGE

Cutlers on the Stray (☎ 524471; www.cutlers-web.co.uk; 19 West Park; d from £80; Ⓟ) A touch of the Mediterranean comes to Yorkshire in the shape of this stylish boutique hotel and brasserie in a converted coaching inn. Yellows, creams and reds are used to great effect in the rooms, which are thoroughly modern in design. Some rooms have Stray views.

Britannia Lodge (☎ 508482; www.britlodge.co.uk; 16 Swan Rd; s/d £50/80; Ⓟ) A beautiful home on a leafy street with three immaculate doubles and a fabulous, self-contained two-bedroom suite (with a real fireplace) on the lovely garden. Nice little touches like a welcome coffee – from a cafetière, no less – make this a very good choice.

Old Swan Hotel (☎ 500055; fax 501154; Swan Rd; s/d from £60/80; Ⓟ) An ivy-coated 18th-century country hotel set in two hectares of gardens – right in the middle of town. It was here that Agatha Christie holed up in 1926; the interiors haven't changed all that much since then. Although still elegant, the rooms need a good going over.

Other options:

Alexander (☎ 503348; thealexander@amserve.net; 88 Franklin Rd; s/d £28/58; Ⓟ) Handsome Victorian mansion with immaculate, unstintingly floral rooms.

Cavendish Hotel (☎ 509637; 3 Valley Dr; s/d from £35/55, four-poster £70) Comfortable rooms with a touch of flounce, the best of which overlook the Valley Gardens.

Harrogate Brasserie & Hotel (☎ 505041; www .brasserie.co.uk; 28-30 Cheltenham Pde; s/d from £52/85) 14 stylish rooms, an excellent restaurant and frequent live jazz.

TOP END

Hotel Du Vin (☎ 856800; www.hotelduvin.com; Prospect Pl; r/ste from £95/145; Ⓟ 🖳) A very stylish boutique hotel to make the other lodgings in town sit up and take notice. Inside the converted town house, standard rooms are spacious and extremely comfortable; each has a trademark huge bed draped in soft Egyptian cotton. The loft suites – with their exposed oak beams, hardwood floors and designer bathrooms – are the nicest rooms we've seen in town. Breakfast (£9.50 to £13.50) is not included.

Swallow St George Hotel (☎ 561431; www.swallow -hotels.com; 1 Ripon Rd; s/d £55/100; Ⓟ 🐾) Big Edwardian building across from the TIC with spacious albeit slightly characterless rooms. There's a health club and indoor pool.

YORKSHIRE

Eating

BUDGET

Betty's (☎ 502746; www.bettysandtaylors.co.uk; 1 Parliament St; mains under £7; ☺ 9am-9pm) A classic tearoom dating from 1919, founded by a Swiss immigrant confectioner. It heaves with scone groupies (tea and scones about £5). A pianist tinkles among the teacups from 6pm.

Harrogate Theatre (Oxford St; sandwiches about £5; ☺ 10am-6pm Mon-Sat) A grand old café that's popular at lunch time.

MID-RANGE

Drum & Monkey (☎ 502650; 5 Montpellier Gardens; mains about £8-11; ☺ lunch & dinner Mon-Sat) Our favourite restaurant in town serves up mouthwatering seafood dishes to an enthusiastic and loyal clientele.

Harrogate Brasserie & Hotel (☎ 505041; 30 Cheltenham Pde; 2-course meal £15; ☺ dinner) There's more than a hint of New Orleans at this friendly, popular brasserie serving up some pretty good French cuisine. Photos of jazz greats adorn the red walls to complement the regular live performances.

William & Victoria (☎ 506883; 6 Cold Bath Rd; mains £8-16; ☺ Mon-Fri lunch, Mon-Sat dinner) A dark and cosy, wood-lined wine bar that serves traditional British food.

Kings (☎ 568600; 24 Kings Rd; starters £5.50, mains about £13; ☺ lunch & dinner Mon-Sat) A light and airy restaurant set in an old Victorian house offering inventive fish dishes and succulent meat options.

Drinking & Entertainment

Hales (☎ 725571; 1-3 Crescent Rd) Have a decent pint of ale or filling pub grub by flickering gaslight at this traditional pub.

Po Na Na (☎ 509758; 2 Kings Rd; free before 11pm; ☺ 10pm-2am Wed-Sat) Harrogate's only half-decent late bar-club, with a none-too outlandish soundtrack of funky stuff, from cheesy '70s disco to contemporary house.

Harrogate Theatre (☎ 502116; www.harrogate theatre.com; Oxford St) Drama, comedy and music staged in Art Deco surroundings.

Getting There & Away

Trains serve Harrogate from Leeds (£5, 50 minutes, about half-hourly) and York (£5, 45 minutes, 10 to 12 daily). National Express bus No 561 runs from Leeds (£2.75, 50 minutes, six daily). Bus No 383 comes from Ripon (£2.75, 25 minutes, four daily).

Bus Nos 36 and 36A also run regularly between Ripon, Harrogate and Leeds. The bus station is just west of the train station.

SCARBOROUGH

☎ 01723 / pop 57,649

A classic English seaside resort, Scarborough first courted popularity in 1620, when it was declared that the waters lapping up against its spectacular white-sand bays were medicinal. Sea-bathing became fashionable for the first time in Britain, and by the mid–18th century it was a successful holiday destination. A construction boom followed, and the seafront saw the addition of a host of elegant Georgian, Victorian and Edwardian buildings.

It sounds very inviting, but once you're on the waterfront the seaside kitsch overwhelms what is left of Scarborough's more genteel side: neon-lit amusement arcades and casinos draw punters away from the donkey rides and tacky souvenir stands. On the plus side, its renowned theatre is the base of England's popular playwright, Alan Ayckbourn, whose plays always premiere here.

Orientation

Modern suburbs sprawl west of the town centre, which is above the old town and the South Bay. The town is on a plateau above the beaches; cliff lifts, steep streets and footpaths provide the links. The Victorian development to the south is separated from the town centre by a steep valley, which has been landscaped and is crossed by high bridges.

The main shopping street, Westborough, has dramatic views of the castle. The North Bay is home to tawdry seashore amusements; the South Bay is more genteel. The old town lies between St Mary's Church, the castle and the Old Harbour.

Information

Complete Computing (☎ 500501; 14 Northway; per 30 mins £1) For your Internet needs.

Laundrette (☎ 375763; 48 North Marine Rd)

Post office (11-15 Aberdeen Walk; ☺ 9am-5.30pm Mon-Fri, 9am-12.30pm Sat)

TIC (☎ 373333; www.discoveryorkshirecoast.com) Valley Bridge Rd (Unit 3, Pavilion House ☺ 9.30am-6pm Apr-Oct, 10am-4.30pm Mon-Sat Nov-Mar) Harbourside (☺ 9.30am-6pm Apr-Oct, 10am-4.30pm Sun Nov-Mar)

Waterstone's (☎ 500414; 97-8 Westborough) For books and magazines.

YORKSHIRE

Sights & Activities

Scarborough is not exclusively about bingo, buckets and burgers – there are a number of sights to distract you from the beach and its goings-on.

Battered **Scarborough Castle** (EH; ☎ 372451; admission £3.20; ☼ 10am-6pm Apr-Sep, 10am-4pm Thu-Mon Nov-Mar) has excellent views across the bays and the town. There's been some kind of fortification here for nearly 2500 years, but the current structure dates from the 12th century. Legend has it that Richard III loved the views so much his ghost just keeps coming back. More corporeal beings can get to it via a 13th-century barbican.

Below the castle is **St Mary's Church** (☎ 500 541; Castle Rd; ☼ 10am-4pm Mon-Fri, 1-4pm Sun May-Sep), dating from 1180 and rebuilt in the 15th and 17th centuries, with some interesting 14th-century chapels. Anne Brontë is buried in the churchyard.

Of all the family-oriented attractions on the bays, the best of the lot is the **Sea Life Centre & Marine Sanctuary** (☎ 376125; www.sealife.co.uk; Scalby Mills; adult/child £7.50/5; ☼ 10am-6pm) overlooking North Bay. Explore Jurassic seas, coral reefs and the world of the octopus with aplomb. The rescue work done with woebegone seals and sea turtles is quite uplifting.

The Pre-Raphaelite, high Victorian interior of **Church of St Martin-on-the-Hill** (☎ 360437; Albion Rd; ☼ 7.30am-5.30pm) was worked on by Burne-Jones, Morris, Maddox Brown and Rossetti.

SCARBOROUGH

```
0                    500 m
0                    0.3 miles
```

INFORMATION
Complete Computing	1 B3
Harbourside Tourist Information Centre	2 C2
Laundrette	3 B2
Post Office	4 B3
Tourist Information Centre (TIC)	5 B3
Waterstone's	6 B3

SIGHTS & ACTIVITIES (pp536-7)
Church of St Martin-on-the-Hill	7 B4
Rotunda Museum	8 B3
Saint Mary's Church	9 C2
Scarborough Castle	10 D2
Sea Life & Marine Sanctuary	11 A1
Secret Spot Surf Shop	12 B3

SLEEPING (p537)
Interludes	13 C2
Red Lea Hotel	14 C4
Royal Hotel	15 C3
Windmill Hotel	16 A3

EATING (p537)
Bonnet	17 B3
Golden Grid	18 C2
Lanterna	19 C2
Secret Spot Surf Shop	20 B3

DRINKING (p538)
Indigo Alley	21 B2
Tap & Spile	22 A4

ENTERTAINMENT (p538)
Stephen Joseph Theatre	23 B3

YORKSHIRE

The **Rotunda Museum** (☎ 374839; Vernon Rd; admission £2.50; ☺ 10am-5pm Tue-Sun Jun-Sep, 11am-4pm Tue, Sat & Sun Oct-May) traces local matters from prehistory to the present, and has changing exhibitions on themes such as the seaside and pirates.

There are some decent waves out in the North Sea and the friendly **Secret Spot Surf Shop** (☎ 500467; www.secretspot.co.uk; 4 Pavilion Tce) can advise on conditions and recommend places for lessons. The shop rents all manner of gear. The best time for waves is September to May.

See p544 for more information about the 20-mile Whitby–Scarborough Coastal Cycle Trail.

Sleeping

If something stays still long enough in town, it'll offer B&B; competition is intense and it's difficult to choose between places. In such a tough market, multi-night stay special offers are two a penny, which means that single night rates are the highest of all.

BUDGET

Scarborough YHA Hostel (☎ 0870 7706022; fax 770 6023; www.yha.org.uk; Burniston Rd; dm £10.25; ☺ Apr-Aug) This simply idyllic hostel in a converted water mill from around 1600 has comfortable four- and six-bed dorms as well as a lounge, self-catering kitchen and laundry. It is 2 miles north of town along the A166 to Whitby. Take bus No 3, 12 or 21.

Scalby Close Caravan Park (☎ 366212; Burniston Rd; tent sites £8-12; ☺ Easter-Oct only) A small park about 2 miles north of town with plenty of pitches for vans and tents as well as five fixed holiday caravans for rent (£63 per night). The park has all the usual facilities. Take bus No 12 or 21.

MID-RANGE

Windmill Hotel (☎ 372735; www.windmill-hotel.co.uk; Mill St; s/d from £35/58; P) A beautifully converted 18th-century mill in the middle of town offers tight-fitting but comfortable doubles around a cobbled courtyard – the upstairs rooms have a small veranda.

Interludes (☎ 360513; www.interludeshotel.co.uk; 32 Princess St; s/d £34/60; P) Owners Ian and Bob have a flair for the theatrical, and have brought it to bear with incredible success on this lovely, gay-friendly Georgian home plastered with old theatrical posters, prints

and other thespian mementos. The individually decorated rooms are given to colourful flights of fancy that can't but put a smile on your face. Children, alas, are not catered for.

Red Lea Hotel (☎ 362431; www.redleahotel.co.uk; Prince of Wales Tce; s/d £45/78; P ☺) An elegant terrace of six Georgian houses makes up this popular choice, which has large rooms rich in velvet drapes, lush carpets and king-size beds. Downstairs is a heated, kidney-shaped swimming pool and, next door, a small leisure centre with sauna, sunbeds and a gym.

TOP END

Wrea Head Country House Hotel (☎ 378211; www .englishrosehotels.co.uk; Barmoor La, Scalby; s/d £75/130) This fabulous country house about 2 miles north of the centre is straight out of *Remains of the Day*. The 20 individually styled bedrooms have canopied, four-poster beds, plush fabrics and delicate furnishings, while the leather couches in the book-cased, wood-heavy lounges seem fit for important discussions over cigars and expensive brandy.

Royal Hotel (☎ 364333; www.englishrosehotels.co .uk; St Nicholas St; s/d from £59/106) Scarborough's most famous hotel has a lavish Regency interior, grand staircase for Shirley Bassey-style entrances, and smart rooms, some with sea views. The perfectly comfortable but characterless rooms just don't compare with the grandeur of the public spaces.

Eating

Lanterna (☎ 363616; 33 Queen St; mains £12-18; ☺ Mon-Sat) Lanterna is a snug Italian spot that specialises in fresh local seafood as well as favourites from the Old Boot; it's the place to go for that special night out in Scarborough.

Golden Grid (☎ 360922; 4 Sandside; cod from £5.50; ☺ lunch & dinner Apr-Oct, to 5pm Nov-Mar) Whoever said fish and chips can't be eaten with dignity and grace has never set foot in the Golden Grid, which has been doling them out since 1883. It's bright and traditional, with starched white tablecloths.

Bonnet (☎ 361033; 38-40 Huntriss Row; mains from £5; café ☺ 9am-5.30pm, restaurant ☺ Fri & Sat dinner) An excellent tearoom, open since 1880, with delicious cakes, a serene courtyard, and adjoining shop selling handmade chocolates.

Entertainment

Indigo Alley (☎ 375823; North Marine Rd) A small and welcoming pub with a good range of beers. There's regular live jazz and blues and Monday theatre in a limpet-sized, curtained-off space.

Tap & Spile (☎ 363837; 94 Falsgrave Rd) A relaxed pub with a few rooms and a good selection of Yorkshire ales.

Stephen Joseph Theatre (☎ 370541; www.sjt .uk.com; Westborough; tickets about £9) Stages a good range of drama. Much-renowned chronicler of middle-class mores, Alan Ayckbourn premieres his plays here.

Getting There & Away

There are reasonably frequent Scarborough & District buses (No 128) along the A170 from Pickering (£4.80, one hour) and Helmsley (£5.50, 1½ hours). The buses leave from Westborough.

There are regular buses, Nos 93 and 93A (via Robin Hood's Bay), from Whitby (£4.80, one hour). No 843 arrives from Leeds (£13.80, one and a half to two hours, eight to 12 daily) via York (£10).

There are regular trains from Hull (£10.40, one hour 20 minutes, hourly), Leeds (£17.20, one hour 20 minutes, six to eight daily) and York (£9.30, 45 minutes, hourly).

Getting Around

Victorian funicular lifts slope up and down Scarborough's steep cliffs to the beach daily from February till the end of October. Local buses leave from the western end of Westborough and outside the train station.

For a taxi call ☎ 361009; £4 should get you to most places in town.

NORTH YORK MOORS NATIONAL PARK

Ridge-top roads across high open moors; rolling whale-back hills cut by deep green valleys hiding farms, villages and the odd castle; a dramatic coastline of sheer cliffs, sheltered bays and long sandy beaches: welcome to the wild and windswept expanse of the North York Moors. Brontë fans should recognise Heathcliff's natural hinterland, and while it is undoubtedly bleak in parts, the region is also glorious in its beauty, never more so than with the vast expanse of heather, which flowers in an explosion of pink and mauve from July to early September. Outside the flowering season, the browns-tending-to-purple on the hills – in vivid contrast to the deep greens of the Dales – give the park its characteristic moody appearance.

Orientation & Information

The park covers 553 sq miles, with hills and steep escarpments forming the northern and western boundaries, and the eastern limit marked by the North Sea coast. The southern border runs roughly parallel to the A170 Thirsk–Scarborough road, and the main gateway towns are Helmsley and Pickering in the south, and Whitby in the northeast – all with good TICs. The national park also runs TICs at Sutton Bank, Danby and Robin Hood's Bay. Although it's outside the park, Scarborough is another good gateway (p535).

The national park produces the very useful *Moors & Coast* visitor guide (50p), available at TICs, hotels etc, with information on things to see and do and an accommodation listing. The park website at www .moors.uk.net is even more comprehensive.

Activities

Several ideas for short walks and rides (from a few hours to all day) are suggested in this section, and TICs stock an excellent range of walking leaflets (around 50p), as well as more comprehensive walking and cycling guidebooks.

CYCLING

Once you've puffed up the escarpment, the North York Moors make fine cycling country, with ideal quiet lanes through the valleys and scenic roads over the hills. There's also a great selection of tracks and former railways for mountain bikes.

WALKING

There are over 1400 miles of walking paths and tracks crisscrossing the moors. The best walking opportunities are along the western escarpment and the cliff tops on the coast. The green and tranquil valleys are also ideal for a spot of relaxed rambling, although, for avid walkers, the broad ridges and rolling high ground of the moors can be a bit featureless after a few hours and for that reason this area is not as popular as the Yorkshire Dales or the Lake District – a plus if you're looking for peace and quiet.

For long-distance walks, the famous **Coast to Coast** route (p78) strides across the park and the **Cleveland Way** covers three sides of the moors' outer rim on its 109-mile, nine-day route from Helmsley to Filey, through a wonderful landscape of escarpments and coastline.

The **Cook Country Walk**, named for explorer Captain Cook, who was born and raised in this area, links several monuments commemorating his life. This 40-mile, three-day route follows the flanks of the Cleveland Hills from Marton (near Middlesbrough), then the superb coast from Staithes south to Whitby.

Sleeping

The national park is ringed with towns and villages, all with a good range of accommodation – although options thin out in the central area. Walkers and outdoor fans can take advantage of the network of camping barns. Most are on farms, with bookings

administered by the **YHA** (☎ 0870 870 8808). For more details TICs have a *Camping Barns in England* leaflet.

Getting There & Around

If you're coming from the south, from York (15 miles outside the park) there are regular buses to Helmsley, Pickering, Scarborough and Whitby.

From the north, head for Middlesbrough, then take the Esk Valley railway line through the northern moors to Whitby, via Grosmont and several other villages which make useful bases. A second line, the North Yorkshire Moors Railway (NYMR), runs through the park from Pickering to Grosmont. Using these two railway lines, much of the moors area is easily accessible for those without wheels.

The highly useful **Moorsbus** (www.moorsbus.net) operates on Sunday from May to October, daily from mid-July to late August or early September, and is ideal for reaching out-of-the-way spots. Pick up a timetable and route map from TICs. A standard Moorsbus day pass costs £2.50, and for £12.50 the pass

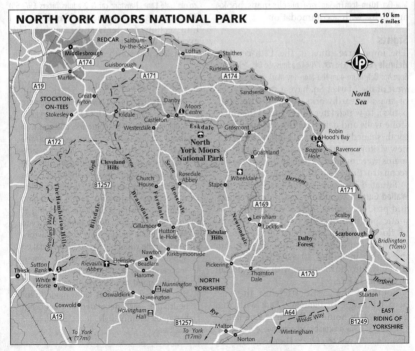

NORTH YORK MOORS NATIONAL PARK

0 _____ 10 km
0 _____ 6 miles

covers you on the Esk Valley and NYMR trains too – a good deal if you plan to really make a day of it. Family tickets and one-off fares for short journeys are also available.

Call the national **Traveline** (☎ 0870 608 2608) for all public bus and train information.

HELMSLEY

☎ 01439 / pop 1559

A classic North Yorkshire market town, Helmsley is a handsome place made up of old houses and historic coaching inns centred on a cobbled square that hosts a market every Friday. Overlooking the lot is a fine Norman castle, and nearby are the superb ruins of Rievaulx Abbey. With several good walks in the area (many taking in historical sights), Helmsley makes a good base for exploring this beautiful southwest corner of the moors.

Orientation & Information

The centre of everything is the Market Pl; all four sides are lined with twee shops, cosy pubs and several cafés. The helpful **TIC** (☎ 770173; www.ryedale.gov.uk; ⊙ 9.30am-5.30pm Mar-Oct, 10am-4pm Fri-Sun Nov-Feb) sells maps, books and helps with accommodation.

Sights

The impressive ruins of the 12th-century **Helmsley Castle** (EH; ☎ 770442; admission £4; ⊙ 10am-6pm Apr-Oct, 10am-4pm Thu-Mon Nov-Mar), just southwest of the Market Sq, have a striking series of massive earthworks (deep ditches and banks), to which later rulers added the thick stone walls and defensive towers – only one tooth-shaped tower survives today. In 2004 a new visitors centre and parts of the castle remains were opened, which include a partial reconstruction of an Elizabethan room.

Situated just outside the castle, **Helmsley Walled Garden** would be just another plant and produce centre, were it not for its dramatic position and its fabulous selection of flowers, fruits and vegetables – some of which are quite rare – not to mention the herbs, including 40 varieties of mint. If you're into horticulture with a historical twist, this is Eden.

South of the castle stretches the superb landscape of **Duncombe Park** with the grand stately home of **Duncombe Park House** (☎ 770213; www.duncombepark.com; house & grounds admission £6.50, park only £2; ⊙ 11am-5.30pm Thu-Sun

late Apr-Oct) at its heart. From the house and formal gardens, wide grassy walkways and terraces lead through woodland to mock-classical temples, while longer walking trails are set out in the parkland – now protected as a nature reserve. The house, ticket office and information centre are 1½ miles south of town, an easy walk through the park. You could easily spend a day here.

Activities

Of the numerous walks in Duncombe Park, the 3½-mile route to Rievaulx Abbey is the real star. The TIC can provide route leaflets, and advise on buses if you don't want to walk both ways. This route is also the overture to the Cleveland Way (see p538).

Sleeping & Eating

Helmsley YHA Hostel (☎ 0870 770 5860; www.yha .org.uk; Carlton Lane; dm £10.60) This purpose-built hostel just outside the centre is a bit like an ordinary suburban home; its location at the start of the Cleveland Way means that it's virtually always full so book in advance.

Wrens of Rydale (☎ 771260; wrensofryedale.fsnet .co.uk; Gale Lane, Nawton; car & 2 adults/hikers £9/7.50) Three acres of pristine parkland divided into sections for tents and caravans. This excellent campsite is located 3 miles east of Helmsley, just south of Beadlam.

SOMETHING SPECIAL

Star Inn (☎ 770397; www.thestaratharome.co .uk; Harome; mains £10-17; r £130-195; ⊙ lunch & dinner Tue-Sat) This thatched cottage pub about 2 miles south of Helmsley just off the A170 is like hitting the rustic-gastro jackpot. In the middle is the kind of pub you could happily get slowly sloshed in, but the only thing to tear you away is the Michelin-starred feast that awaits you in the dining room. Each dish is a delicious rendering of some local favourite with a flight of fancy to make it really special: how about Nawton-bred middle white pig casserole with baked apples, black pudding and sage & Somerset brandy cream? You won't want to leave, and the good news is you don't have to: the adjacent lodge has eight magnificent bedrooms, each decorated in classic but luxurious country style. If we could, we'd live here.

There are a number of old coaching inns on Market Pl that offer B&B, half-decent grub and a pint (or more) of hand-pumped real ale. The **Crown Inn** (☎ 770297; fax 771595; Market Pl; mains £7-10; s/d £36/56) is a homely place that caters to an older, quieter clientele, while **Feathers** (☎ 770275; feathershotel@aol.com; Market Pl; mains about £8; s/d from £42/65) has four-poster beds in some rooms and historical trimmings throughout.

Royal Oak (Market Pl) is the liveliest of the town's pubs, with good beer and bar-meals.

Getting There & Away

All buses stop in the Market Pl. From York to Helmsley, take bus Nos 31, 31A and 31X (£4.70, three per day Monday to Saturday, 1½ hours). Between Helmsley and Scarborough, bus No 128 (£5.70, hourly, 1½ hours; four on Sunday) goes via Pickering.

AROUND HELMSLEY
Rievaulx

The moors' most visited attraction is the famous remains of **Rievaulx Abbey** (EH; ☎ 798228; admission £4; ⊙ 10am-6pm Apr-Sep, 10am-4pm Oct-Mar), about 3 miles west of Helmsley in the small eponymous village. Rievaulx (pronounced ree-voh) is everything a ruin should be: battered enough by the passage of time to give a venerable air, but with enough beautiful stonework, soaring pillars and graceful arches remaining so you can imagine how it looked in its 13th-century heyday.

The site is quite simply idyllic – a secluded, wooded valley overlooking fields and the River Rye – with a view pretty much as it was 900 years ago, when Cistercian monks first arrived. And it seems they enjoyed the scenery just as much as we do today: one abbot, St Aelred, famously described the abbey's surroundings as 'everywhere peace, everywhere serenity'. Perfect for a spot of contemplation. Or a picnic. Or both.

Near the abbey, **Rievaulx Terrace & Temples** (NT; ☎ 798340; admission £3.30; ⊙ 10.30am-6pm Apr-Sep, 10.30am-5pm Oct-Nov) is a section of wooded escarpment once part of extensive Duncombe Park (p540). In the 1750s landscape-gardening fashion favoured a natural or Gothic look, and many aristocrats had mock ruins built in their parks. The Duncombe family went one better, as their lands contained a genuine medieval ruin – Rievaulx Abbey – and the half-mile-long grassy terrace was built, with classical-style temples at each end, so lords and ladies could stroll effortlessly in the 'wilderness' and admire the ruins in the valley below. Today, we can do the same, with views over Ryedale and the Hambleton Hills forming a perfect backdrop.

A visit to these two historic sites makes a great day out from Helmsley, but note that there's no direct access between the abbey and the terrace. Their entrance gates are about a mile apart and easily reached along a lane – steeply uphill if you're going from the abbey to the terrace.

Sutton Bank

Sutton Bank is a dramatically steep escarpment 8 miles west of Helmsley. If you're driving, this may be your entry to the North York Moors. And what an entry. The road climbs steeply up, with magnificent views westwards across to the Pennines and Yorkshire Dales. At the top, there's a **TIC** (☎ 01845-597426; ⊙ 10am-5pm Apr-Oct, 11am-4pm Nov, Dec & Mar, 11am-4pm Sat & Sun Jan & Feb) with exhibitions about the moors, books and maps for sale, and handy leaflets on short walks to nearby viewpoints. If you don't have your own wheels, the Moorsbus service No M3 links Sutton Bank with Helmsley, from where all other parts of the park can be reached.

PICKERING
☎ 01751 / pop 6616

The lively market town of Pickering has its charms – most notably the Norman castle and the fabulous North Yorkshire Moors Railway (see the boxed text, p542), for which Pickering serves as a terminus – but it is too big and bustling to keep you in thrall. It is, however, a handy staging post from which to explore the eastern moors.

The **TIC** (☎ 473791; www.ryedale.gov.uk; The Ropery; ⊙ 9.30am-5.30pm Mon-Sat, 9.30am-4pm Sun Mar-Oct, 10am-4pm Mon-Sat Nov-Feb) has the usual details as well as all NYMR-related info.

Pickering Castle (EH; ☎ 474989; admission £3; ⊙ 10am-6pm Apr-Sep, 10am-4pm Oct-Mar) is a lot like the castles we drew as kids: thick stone outer walls circling the keep, and the lot perched atop a high motte (mound) with great views of the surrounding countryside. Founded by William the Conqueror, it was added to and altered by later kings.

Sleeping & Eating

The White Swan Hotel (☎ 472288; www.white-swan
.co.uk; Market Pl; mains £9-15; s/d from £80/140) The top
spot in town successfully combines a smart
pub, a superb restaurant serving local dishes
with a continental twist and a luxurious little boutique hotel all in one. The stylish
rooms come with DVD players, Penhaligon
toiletries and those wide-head power showers that make you want to stay under them
for hours.

There is a strip of similar B&Bs located
on tree-lined Eastgate (which becomes the
A170 to/from Scarborough). Decent options include **Eden House** (☎ 472289; www.eden-
housebandb.co.uk; 120 Eastgate; s/d £26/52), a pretty
house with cottage-style décor, and flower-

and plant-clad **Rose Folly** (☎ 475067; www.rose
folly.freeserve.co.uk; 112 Eastgate; s/d £25/50), which
has lovely rooms and a beautiful breakfast
conservatory.

There are several cafés and teashops on
Market Pl, and for drinks of another sort
the **Bay Horse** (Market Pl) is a good, no-nonsense
pub.

Getting There & Away

Bus No 128 between Helmsley (40 minutes)
and Scarborough (50 minutes) runs hourly
via Pickering. Yorkshire Coastliner (Nos
840, 842 and X40) ser493vices run to/from
York (£8.70, hourly, 70 minutes).

For train details, see North Yorkshire
Moors Railway, below.

ALL ABOARD PLEASE!

Pickering is the southern terminus of the privately owned **North Yorkshire Moors Railway** (NYMR;
☎ Pickering Station 01751-472508, recorded timetable 01751-473535; www.northyorkshiremoorsrailway.com
or www.nymr.demon.co.uk), which runs for 18 miles through beautiful countryside to the village of
Grosmont. Lovingly restored steam locos pull period carriages, resplendent in polished brass and
bright paintwork, and the railway appeals to train buffs and day-trippers alike. For visitors without
wheels, it's excellent for reaching out-of-the-way spots. Even more useful, Grosmont is also on
the main railway line between Middlesbrough and Whitby, which opens up yet more possibilities
for walking or sightseeing.

Pickering, the railway, and the surrounding countryside can easily absorb a day. At all stations
there's information about waymarked walks, lasting between one and four hours. Generally, there
are four to eight trains daily between April and October. The full journey takes an hour, and tickets
allowing you to get on and get off as much as you like cost £12 (children £5).

From Pickering the line heads northeast through a river valley, and the first stop is **Levisham
station**, 1½ miles west of beautiful Levisham village, which faces Lockton across another steep
valley.

Next along is **Newton Dale**, ideal for walkers heading for the impressive crater-like bowl in
the hills called the Hole of Horcum (or the Devil's Punchbowl); it's a request stop only, so let the
guard know if you want to get off here.

A few miles further is **Goathland**, a picturesque village surrounded by heather-clad moors. It
attracts many visitors because of its status as 'Aidensfield' in the British TV series *Heartbeat*, and
more recently was a set for the *Harry Potter* films. There are several good walks from the station,
including along a pretty trail to Grosmont. If you want to halt for a while, there are several hotel
and B&B options plus a campsite.

At the northern end of the line is the sleepy little village of **Grosmont** (pronounced gro-mont),
although it comes alive when the steam trains pull across the level crossing on the main street.
There are some B&B options here, plus a nice café and a pub doing food, and that's about it.
All change please.

The Nuts & Bolts

You can start your train ride in Pickering, or in Grosmont, which is easily reached from Whitby by
'normal' train along the Esk Valley line (opposite). A grand day out from Pickering combines the
NYMR, the Esk Valley line between Grosmont and Whitby and the bus over the moors between
Whitby and Pickering.

DANBY

☎ 01287

Danby is an isolated stone village deep in the moors at the head of Eskdale, where the surrounding countryside is particularly beautiful. It makes a good base, as the **Moors Centre** (☎ 01439-772737; www.moors.uk.net; ☺ 10am-5pm Apr-Oct, 11am-4pm Nov-Dec & Mar, 11am-4pm Sat & Sun Jan-Feb), the park headquarters, is just half a mile from the village, and has displays, information, a café, an accommodation-booking service and a huge range of local guidebooks, maps and leaflets as well as all the information you'll need on walking routes.

There are several short circular walks from the centre, but first on your list should be Danby Beacon; it's a stiff 2 miles uphill to the northeast, but stunning 360-degree views across the moors sweeten the sweat.

The **Duke of Wellington** (☎ 660351; www.danby-dukeofwellington.co.uk; mains about £7; s/d from £30/60), a fine traditional pub – used as a recruitment centre during the Napoleonic Wars – serves good beer and meals; upstairs there are nine well-appointed rooms.

Getting There & Away

Using the delightful **Esk Valley Railway** (☎ 0845 748 4950; www.eskvalleyrailway.co.uk), access is easy: Whitby (£3) is 20 minutes east; Middlesbrough (£6) is 45 minutes west. There are four departures Monday to Saturday, two on Sunday.

WHITBY

☎ 01947 / pop 13,594

If you're keen for the sea but your interests extend beyond shovels, spades and amusement arcades, Whitby is the place for you. It is the most charming of Northern England's seaside resorts, a handsome maze of narrow, medieval streets leading from a busy fishing harbour packed with colourful boats. Perched above one of the cliffs that hems it all in are the spectacular remains of an ancient abbey. Sure, Whitby has its fair share of seaside paraphernalia, but unlike other resorts, they complement the town's overall aesthetic – in a traditional resort sort of way.

Besides the ordinary sun worshippers and beachcombers that flood the town throughout the summer months, Whitby is popular with fun-loving girls and boys, retirees, hikers, bikers – and even Goths who flock here for two festivals honouring the king of the vampires: Bram Stoker set part of *Dracula* here (see the boxed text p546).

The town was also the birthplace of the famous explorer James Cook, and is the location of arguably the best chipper in the whole island.

Orientation

Whitby is divided in two by the harbour and River Esk estuary. On the east bank (East Cliff) is the older part of town; the newer (19th-century) town grew up on the other side, West Cliff. An intriguing feature of Whitby is that many streets have two names. For example, Abbey Tce and Hudson St are opposite sides of the same street, as are West St and The Esplanade.

Information

Java Café-Bar (Flowergate; per 30 mins £1) Internet access.
Laundrette (72 Church St)
Post office (☺ 8.30am-5.30pm Mon-Sat) Across from the TIC inside the Co-op supermarket.
TIC (☎ 602674; www.discoveryorkshirecoast.com or www.visitwhitby.com; Langborne Rd; ☺ 9.30am-6pm May-Sep, 10am-4.30pm Oct-Apr) A wealth of information on the town and the surrounding moors and coast.

Sights

There are ruins, and then there's **Whitby Abbey** (EH; ☎ 603568; adult £4; ☺ 10am-6pm Apr-Sep, 10am-4pm Thu-Mon Oct-Mar). Dominating the town, in a stunning location, this ancient holy place dates from the 11th to 14th centuries, with huge solid pillars, soaring arches and gaping windows made all the more dramatic with the North Sea sky behind. Nearby, **St Mary's Church** (☺ 10am-5pm Apr-Oct, 10am-4pm Nov-Mar) has an atmospheric interior full of skewed and tilting galleries and box pews. Reach the abbey and the church via the famous 199 steps up the cliff side. Take time out to catch your breath and admire the fantastic view.

Cook-related links are a big deal in Whitby, but the best place to find out about the famous seafarer is at the **Captain Cook Memorial Museum** (☎ 601900; www.cookmuseumwhitby .co.uk; Grape Lane; adult/child £3/2; ☺ 9.45am-5pm Apr-Oct, 11am-3pm Sat & Sun Mar), a house once occupied by the ship-owner to whom Cook was apprenticed. Highlights include Cook's own maps and writings, etchings from the South Seas and a wonderful model of the *Endeavour*, with all the crew and stores laid out for inspection.

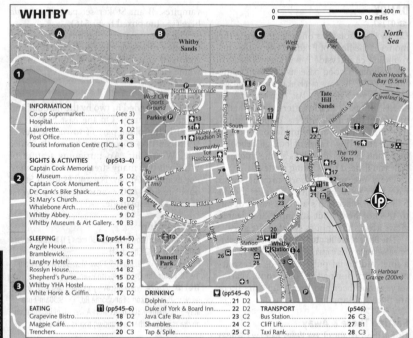

WHITBY

INFORMATION
Co-op Supermarket...............(see 3)
Hospital.............................. **1** C3
Laundrette......................... **2** D2
Post Office......................... **3** C3
Tourist Information Centre (TIC).. **4** C3

SIGHTS & ACTIVITIES (pp543–4)
Captain Cook Memorial
    Museum......................... **5** D2
Captain Cook Monument......... **6** C1
Dr Crank's Bike Shack............ **7** C2
St Mary's Church.................. **8** D2
Whalebone Arch....................(see 6)
Whitby Abbey...................... **9** D2
Whitby Museum & Art Gallery.. **10** B3

SLEEPING (pp544–5)
Argyle House...................... **11** B2
Bramblewick....................... **12** C2
Langley Hotel...................... **13** B1
Rosslyn House..................... **14** B2
Shepherd's Purse................. **15** D2
Whitby YHA Hostel............... **16** D2
White Horse & Griffin............ **17** D2

EATING (pp545–6)
Grapevine Bistro.................. **18** D2
Magpie Café....................... **19** C1
Trenchers.......................... **20** C3

DRINKING (pp545–6)
Dolphin............................ **21** D2
Duke of York & Board Inn........ **22** D2
Java Cafe Bar...................... **23** C2
Shambles.......................... **24** C2
Tap & Spile........................ **25** C3

TRANSPORT (p546)
Bus Station........................ **26** C3
Cliff Lift........................... **27** B1
Taxi Rank.......................... **28** C3

At the top of the cliff near East Tce, the **Captain Cook Monument** shows the great man looking out to sea, usually with a seagull perched on his head. Nearby is the **Whalebone Arch** (it's just that), remembering Whitby's days as a whaling port.

South of here, in a park overlooking the town, is the wonderfully eclectic **Whitby Museum & Art Gallery** (☎ 602908; Pannett Park; adult/child £3/1, art gallery admission free; ☒ 9.30am-5.30pm Mon-Sat, 2-5pm Sun May-Sep, 10am-1pm Tue, 10am-4pm Wed-Sat & 2-4pm Sun Oct-Apr), with fossils, Cook memorabilia, ships in bottles and weird stuff like an amputated hand and an invention for weather forecasting using live leeches. The gallery contains work by the Staithes group of artists.

Activities

Walk up the main road to the new bridge high above the Esk for great views. Or, for something a bit longer, the 5½-mile cliff-top walk south to Robin Hood's Bay is a real treat (allow three hours). Or head north for 11 miles to reach Staithes (five hours). A local bus will get you home again (see p546).

First choice for a bike ride is the excellent 20-mile Whitby to Scarborough Coastal Cycle Trail, which starts a few miles outside town, following the route of an old railway line. It's particularly good for reaching Robin Hood's Bay. Bikes can be hired from **Dr Crank's Bike Shack** (☎ 606661; 20 Skinner St).

Festivals & Events

There's a full programme of festivals throughout the year, when the town is particularly lively. Tops are:

Moor & Coast Festival (www.moorandcoast.co.uk; tickets £30) A traditional folk festival of music, dance and dubious Celtic art over the May Bank Holiday.

Musicport Festival (www.musicport.fsnet.co.uk; £67.50) A weekend-long world music festival in mid-October.

Whitby Gothic Weekends (www.wgw.topmum.co.uk; tickets £35) Goth heaven during the last weekends of April and October; anyone in town not wearing black or false fangs is a weirdo.

Sleeping

Most of the town's B&Bs are concentrated on West Cliff around Hudson St; if a place isn't offering B&B, chances are it's derelict.

Accommodation can be tough to find at festival times; it's wise to book ahead.

BUDGET

Whitby YHA Hostel (☎ 0870 770 6089; www.yha.org.uk; Church La; dm £10.60; ⏰ Apr-Aug, Mon-Sat Sep-Oct, Fri & Sat Nov & Jan-Mar, closed Dec) With an unbeatable position next to the abbey on East Cliff overlooking the town, this hostel doesn't have to try too hard, and it doesn't. You'll have to book well in advance to get your body into one of the basic bunks.

Harbour Grange (☎ 600817; www.whitbybackpackers .co.uk; Spital Bridge; dm £11) Overlooking the harbour, this tidy hostel is conveniently located but has the inconvenience of an 11.30pm curfew; perfect if you're an early-to-bed type, but a pain if you're not.

MID-RANGE

White Horse & Griffin (☎ 604857; www.whitehorse andgriffin.co.uk; 87 Church St; s/d from £35/60) Walk through the suitably olde worlde frontage of this handsome 18th-century coaching inn and discover a boutique hotel with individually designed, super-stylish rooms that have managed to mix the best of tradition (antique panelling, restored period furniture, real flame fires) with the kind of sleek, contemporary lines and modern comforts you'd expect from a top-class guesthouse.

Shepherd's Purse (☎ 820228; www.shepherds purse.co.uk; 95 Church St; s/d from £25/40) This place began life as a beads-and-baubles boutique in 1973, added a wholefood shop and vegetarian restaurant and now offers guesthouse accommodation. The plainer rooms that share a bathroom are perfectly adequate, but we recommend the bedrooms with en suite situated around a lovely courtyard; each has a handsome brass or four-poster bed and nice pine furniture.

Langley Hotel (☎ 604250; www.langleyhotel.com; 16 Royal Cres; s/d £31/60; **P**) The whiff of Victorian splendour may have faded, but the panoramic views from West Cliff are as good as ever. The rooms are tidy and neat, if a little cramped.

Other options include:

Argyle House (☎ 602733; 18 Hudson St; s/d £23/45)

Bramblewick (☎ 604504; www.bramblewick.co.uk; 3 Havelock Pl; s/d £25/48; **P**)

Rosslyn House (☎ 604086; 11 Abbey Tce; s/d £22/45)

Eating & Drinking

For many visitors, Whitby cuisine extends no further than a fish-and-chip supper (served with peas, bread and tea), obtainable most everywhere for between £4 and £5 but preferred at the world's most famous chipper. If you want to keep your cholesterol in check, there are a few other options.

Magpie Café (☎ 602058; 14 Pier Rd; mains £7-10; ⏰ lunch & dinner) The world's best fish and chips, or so the reputation would have it. They are bloody delicious, but the one downer is that the world and his wife knows about this place, and summertime queues can be off-putting.

Trenchers (☎ 603212; New Quay Rd; mains £7-10; ⏰ lunch & dinner) Excellent fish and chips minus the reputation, Trenchers is your best bet if you want to avoid the queues. Don't be put off by the modern look.

Grapevine Bistro (☎ 820275; 2 Grape Lane; tapas about £4-6, mains £7-10; ⏰ lunch & dinner) A highly rated Mediterranean-style place that serves mostly tapas plates but also lays on an evening menu of meat, fish and veggie dishes.

CAPTAIN COOK – WHITBY'S FAMOUS (ADOPTED) SON

Although he wasn't actually born in Whitby, the town has adopted the famous explorer Captain James Cook, and since the first tourists got off the train in Victorian times, local entrepreneurs have mercilessly cashed in on his memory, as endless 'Endeavour Cafés' and 'Captain Cook Chip Shops' testify.

The young James Cook started his apprenticeship in 1746, working on Whitby 'cats' – unique, flat-bottomed ships carrying coal from Newcastle to London. Nine years later he joined the navy, and in 1768 began the first of three great voyages of discovery, during which he reached Australia. Cook returned to Europe with detailed charts, vast notebooks full of etchings and observations, numerous plant and animal samples, and a vast wealth of knowledge garnered from these long journeys. His ships on all three voyages, including the *Endeavour*, were based on the design of 'cats', and in this small but vital way Whitby played a part in world exploration and 18th-century scientific understanding.

WHITBY'S DARK SIDE

The famous story of *Dracula*, inspiration for a thousand lurid movies, was written by Bram Stoker while staying at a B&B in Whitby in 1897. Although most Hollywood versions of the tale concentrate on deepest, darkest Transylvania, much of the original book was set in Whitby, and many sites can still be seen today.

The events are remembered at Whitby's annual Gothic Festival (see Festivals & Events, p544). It's *Rocky Horror* at the seaside – the town is full of people in black, and the atmosphere is fun and relaxed, but quite bizarre.

The TIC sells an excellent *Dracula Trail* leaflet (60p) but a few sites you shouldn't miss include the stone jetty in the harbour, where the Russian boat chartered by Dracula was wrecked as it flew in ahead of the huge storm. You'll need more imagination in the car park in front of the train station; this was once sidings for freight cars, and it's from here that Dracula left Whitby for London in one of his boxes of dirt.

After the town sites, you can climb the same 199 stone steps that the heroine Mina ran up when trying to save her friend Lucy. At the top of the steps is moody St Mary's Church, where Mina first saw Lucy sitting next to a suspicious black being. By that time, of course, it was too late. Cue music. The End.

Shepherd's Purse (☎ 820228; 95 Church St; mains about £6) A veggie place behind a wholefood shop with the same name, with a great range of healthy, interesting snacks and meals, and a very nice courtyard.

Many pubs also serve food, including, of course, fish and chips or crab sandwiches, all for about £5 to £7. A good first choice is the popular **Duke of York** (Church St) at the bottom of the 199 steps, with its classic Whitby atmosphere, while next door the smaller **Board Inn** is another place with views, good beer and seafood. **Dolphin** (Bridge St) has tables inside or out on the pavement, while **Shambles** (Market Pl) is modern and spacious with huge picture windows overlooking the harbour. The **Tap & Spile** (☎ 603937; New Quay Rd) is a straightforward place with good local rock and folk bands.

Getting There & Away

Whitby is 230 miles from London and 45 miles from York.

Bus Nos 93 and 93A run to/from Scarborough (£3.40, one hour, hourly), and to Middlesbrough (about hourly), with fewer services on Sunday. Yorkshire Coastliner (Nos 840 and X40) runs between Whitby and Leeds (£8.60, three hours, seven per day) via Pickering and York.

If you are coming from the north, you can get to Whitby by train by heading along the Esk Valley line from Middlesbrough (£10, 1½ hours, four per day). From the south, it's easier to get a train from York to Scarborough, then a bus from Scarborough to Whitby.

Getting Around

Whitby is a compact place and those 199 steps help burn off the fish and chips. But if you need one, there's a taxi rank near the TIC. The west cliff is also accessible via a **lift** (60p), which perishes the thought of clambering up the steep roads.

AROUND WHITBY
Robin Hood's Bay

Just 5 miles south of Whitby, Robin Hood's Bay has a lot more to do with smugglers than the Sherwood Forest hero, but this picturesque haven is well worth a visit, although like so many places it's very busy on summer weekends.

A single main street called New Rd winds through the old part of town, dropping steeply down from the cliff top to the sea. (There's compulsory parking at the top – don't even think about driving down as there's hardly room to turn at the bottom.) Off New Rd there's a honeycomb of cobbled alleys, secret passages and impossibly small houses. There are giftshops, teashops and a trail of pubs (it might be safer to start from the bottom and work your way up), many with seats outside, so this is an excellent place to just sit and watch the world go by.

Among the pubs, our favourite for ambience is the old **Dolphin**, the **Victoria Hotel** has the best beer and good food, and the **Bay Hotel** is notable for being the end of the famous **Coast to Coast long-distance walk** (p78). Some pubs do B&B and there are several other accommodation options – the TIC in Whitby (p543) can advise.

It's eminently possible to walk or cycle here from Whitby. Also, bus Nos 93 and 93A run hourly between Whitby and Scarborough via Robin Hood's Bay – the bus stop is at the top of the hill, in the new part of town.

Staithes

Tucked beneath high cliffs and running back along the steep banks of a river, the small fishing town of Staithes seems to hide from the modern world, focusing still on its centuries-old battle with the sea. It's a lot less touristy than Robin Hood's Bay: the houses are less prettified, you can see fishermen's jackets drying on lines, and seagulls the size of vultures swoop down the narrow alleys that lead off the main street.

The town's claim to fame is that explorer James Cook worked as a grocer here when a boy. Legend says that fishermen's tales of the high seas, and bad treatment by his master, led him to steal a shilling and run away to Whitby. The rest of the tale is told in great detail in the fascinating and lovingly maintained **Captain Cook & Staithes Heritage Centre** (☎ 01947 841 454; admission £2.50; ☼ 10am-5.30pm), packed to the gunwales with nautical relics.

Staithes is 11 miles from Whitby. To get here, buses on the Whitby-to-Middlesbrough run can drop you at the top of the hill. If you're feeling fit, walking one way and bussing the other makes for a great day out.

Northwest England

CONTENTS

Take one of Europe's most dynamic and pleasant cities. Add the birthplace of the world's best-ever band. Mix in a picture-postcard town where rich layers of history are revealed in multi-tiered architecture. Top it off with the most eye-popping, stomach-churning roller-coaster you've ever been dizzy on. It's life, music, history and pure hedonism. And it's all packed into the relatively tight confines of the northwest.

The northwest was Britain's industrial heartland, which is hardly going to pull the punters. What's really impressive, though, is the fact that the Industrial Revolution was born and raised here into the overwhelming force of capitalism; that the world's first modern city grew up around Manchester's burgeoning mills; and that the endless possibilities of the Age of Reason, that unquenchable optimism that continues to spur contemporary society to greater heights of innovation and advancement, were put through their original paces here. Ancient Rome would have been impressed by the accomplishment.

Perhaps the most compelling aspect of the northwest, however, is how it has embraced the future. The region has wholeheartedly embraced the revolutionary designs and styles of contemporary urban planning, a revolutionary ethos that seeks to combine the best of the past with a new vision, one that takes into account the indomitable desire of people to live well. Come and find out for yourself.

NORTHWEST ENGLAND

HIGHLIGHTS

- Admiring Manchester from the balcony of the **Godlee Observatory** (p553)
- Walking in Roman footsteps around **Chester's city walls** (p563)
- Getting queasy on the rollercoasters at Blackpool's **Pleasure Beach** (p577)
- Exploring the **Isle of Man** (p579) – not just for tax-dodgers and petrol-heads
- The **ferry across the Mersey** (p576): hum the song while enjoying the best views of Liverpool
- Browsing through the **Lady Lever Art Gallery** (p576) in Port Sunlight

- POPULATION: 6,729,800 MILLION
- AREA 5473 SQ MILES

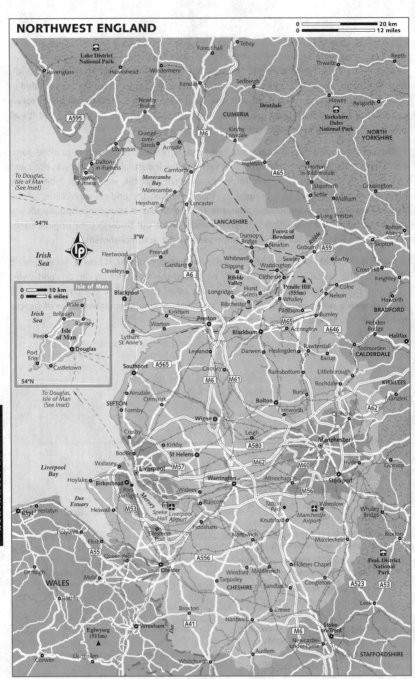

NORTHWEST ENGLAND

0 ____ 20 km
0 ____ 12 miles

Information

Discover England's Northwest (www.visitnorthwest
.com) is the centralised tourist authority that
covers the whole of the northwest.

Getting Around

The towns and cities covered in this chapter
are all within easy reach of each other, and
are well linked by public transport. The two
main cities, Manchester and Liverpool, are
only 34 miles apart and are linked by hourly
bus and train services. Chester is only 18
miles south of Liverpool, but is also easily
accessible from Manchester by train or via
the M56 motorway. Blackpool is 50 miles
to the north of both cities, and is also well
connected. For extensive transport information on Manchester and environs, try **Greater
Manchester Public Transport Authority** (www.gmpte
.com). **Merseytravel** (☎ 236 7676; www.merseytravel.gov
.uk) Takes care of all travel in Merseyside. **National Express** (☎ 08705 808080; www.nationalexpress
.com) runs extensive coach services in the
northwest with Manchester and Liverpool
being major hubs.

MANCHESTER

☎ 0161 / pop 425,000

Manchester is one of Britain's most exciting
and interesting cities, and one of the few
spots on the island that can look London
squarely in the eye and say, 'this is how it's
done, mate'. Sure, it's a little bit of northern
bluster, but it's not that far off the mark.
Here, in the world's first industrial city, a
new revolution is taking place, transforming the birthplace of the Industrial Revolution into a modern metropolis that has
embraced 21st-century style and technology like no other in England. It is surely
indicative of more than just northern one-
upmanship over London and the south that
Manchester looks to Barcelona as its main
rival and inspiration.

To the outsider, Manchester's reputation
is best represented by the almost mythological nightlife that for a brief, crazy time
earned the city the moniker 'Madchester'
and the near-unrivalled success of its biggest
export, the football team and global brand
that is Manchester United. To the insider,
the reputation is merited, but not necessarily for those reasons.

Not only does Manchester have a wealth
of fascinating museums that reflect its
unique role in pioneering developments
of the Industrial Age, but it has managed
to weave the mementos of its past with
forward-looking, ambitious urban development that has already offered us a vision of
what the future holds in store.

HISTORY

Canals and steam-powered cotton mills were
how Manchester was transformed from a
small, disease-infested provincial town into
a very big, disease-infested industrial city. It
all happened in the 1760s, with the construction of the first canal and the invention
of the cotton mill; thereafter Manchester –
and the world – would never be the same
again. When the canal was extended to Liverpool and the open sea in 1776, Manchester –
now dubbed 'Cottonopolis' – kicked into
high gear and took off on the coal-fuelled,
steam-powered gravy train.

There was plenty of gravy to go around,
but the good burghers of 19th-century Manchester made sure that the vast majority of
the city's swollen citizenry (1801, population
90,000; 100 years later, two million) who produced most of it never got their hands on any
of it. Their reward was life in a new kind of
urban settlement, the industrial slum. Working conditions were scarcely better: impossibly long hours, child labour, work-related
accidents and fatalities were commonplace.

The wheels started to come off the train
toward the end of the 19th century. The
USA had begun to flex its industrial muscles
and was taking over a lot of the textile trade;
production in Manchester's mills began to
slow and then stop altogether. By WWII
there was hardly enough cotton produced
in the city to make a tablecloth. The city
was rudely awoken from its economic sleep
in 1996, when an IRA bomb spurred the
authorities into beginning the programme
of urban rejuvenation in evidence today.

ORIENTATION

Shoe power and the excellent Metrolink tram
are the only things you'll need to get around
the compact city centre. All public transportation converges on Piccadilly Gardens,
a few blocks east of the cathedral. Directly
north is the slightly decrepit but totally cool
Northern Quarter. A few blocks southeast

is the Gay Village, centred on Canal St and, just next to it, Chinatown, basically a bunch of restaurants clustered around Portland St.

Southwest of the centre are the Castlefield and Deansgate Locks, a groovy weekend playground for the city's fine young things. Further southwest again – and accessible via Metrolink – are the recently developed Salford Quays, home to the Lowry complex and the Imperial War Museum North. Nearby is Old Trafford football stadium.

INFORMATION
Bookshops
Cornerhouse Bookshop (☎ 200 1514; www.cornerhouse .org/publications; 70 Oxford Rd) Art and film books, specialist magazines and kitschy cards.
Waterstone's Deansgate (☎ 832 1992); St Anne's Sq (☎ 837 3000)

Emergency
Ambulance (☎ 436 3999)
Police station (☎ 872 5050; Bootle St)
Rape Crisis Centre (☎ 273 4500)
Samaritans (☎ 236 8000)

Internet Access
Central Library (☎ 234 1982; St Peter's Sq; ⏱ Net access 1-6pm Mon-Sat; per 30 min £1)
Easy Internet Café (8-10 Exchange St; ⏱ 7.30am-10.50pm Mon-Sat, 9am-10pm Sun)

Internet Resources
City Life (www.citylife.co.uk) Everything you could possibly need to know about how to make the most of the city; the online extension of the excellent weekly mag.

Destination Manchester (www.destination manchester.com)
Manchester City Council (www.manchester.gov.uk) The city's official website.
Manchester Online (www.manchesteronline.co.uk)
Virtual Manchester (www.manchester.com)

Media
The superb *City Life* (£1.50) is published every Wednesday and is the best source of up-to-date listings.

Medical Services
Cameolord Chemist (☎ 236 1445; St Peter's Sq; ⏱ 10am-10pm)
Manchester Royal Infirmary (☎ 276 1234; Oxford Rd)

Post
Post office (Brazennose St; ⏱ 9am-5.30pm Mon-Fri)

Tourist Information
TIC (☎ 234 3157; www.manchester.gov.uk; Town Hall Extension, St Peter's Sq; ⏱ 10am-5.30pm Mon-Sat, 10am-4.30pm Sun) Sells tickets for all sorts of guided walks which operate almost daily year-round and cost adult/child £5/4.

SIGHTS & ACTIVITIES
City Centre
The city's principal administrative centre is the magnificent Victorian Gothic **town hall** (⏱ tours 2pm Sat, Mar-Sep; £4) that dominates Albert Sq. The interior is rich in sculpture and ornate decoration, while the exterior is crowned by an impressive 85m-high tower. You can visit the building on your own, but

---

MANCHESTER IN...

Two Days
Start your visit surrounded by the glorious Victorian trophies of the Industrial Age around Albert Square. Jump onto a Metrolink tram and head south toward Salford Quays and its trio of top attractions, the **Imperial War Museum North** (p556), the **Lowry** (p556) and the **Manchester United Museum** (p556). Pick a restaurant – **Yang Sing** (p559) will do for starters – find a bar and round the night off in a club. The next day, head toward **Castlefield Urban Heritage Park** (p553) before indulging in a spot of retail therapy around the **Millennium Quarter** (p562), breaking up the spendfest with a visit to **Urbis** (p553). Venture east and go alternative in the boutiques and off-beat shops of the **Northern Quarter** (p562).

Four Days
Spread the two-day itinerary out over three days, including a whole day devoted to the Salford Quays; spend more time perusing the city's excellent shopping districts and, if it's a decent enough day, visit the **Godlee Observatory** (p553) before examining the riches of the **Manchester Art Gallery** (p553).

as it's the city's main administrative centre you won't get the same access as you would if you're part of an organised tour, which departs from the TIC.

Just behind it, the elegant, Roman Pantheon lookalike **Central Library** (☎ 234 1900; St Peter's Sq; admission free; ⊗ 10am-8pm Mon-Thu, 10am-6pm Fri & Sat) was built in 1934. It is the country's largest municipal library, with over 20 miles of shelves.

MANCHESTER ART GALLERY

A superb collection of British art and a hefty number of European masters are on display at the city's top **gallery** (☎ 235 8888; Mosley St; admission free; ⊗ 10am-5pm Tue-Sun). The older wing, designed by Charles Barry (of Houses of Parliament fame) in 1834, has an impressive collection that includes 37 Turner watercolours, as well the country's best collection of Pre-Raphaelite art. The new gallery features a permanent collection of 20th-century British art starring Lucien Freud, Francis Bacon, Stanley Spencer, Henry Moore and David Hockney.

JOHN RYLANDS LIBRARY

An easy candidate for top building in town, this marvellous Victorian Gothic **library** (☎ 834 5343; 35 Deansgate) was one hell of a way for the widow Rylands to remember her husband, John. You'll have to wait until the end of 2005 to get inside to admire its breathtaking reading room and its fine collection of early printed books, as it's undergoing a major refurbishment – which includes the addition of a new visitor centre.

URBIS

The stunning glass triangle that is **Urbis** (☎ 907 9099; City Park, Corporation St; admission free; ⊗ 10am-6pm) is a museum about how a city works and – frequently – doesn't work. The walls of the three floors are covered in compelling photographs, interesting statistics and informative timelines, but our favourite parts are the interactive videos, each of which tells stories about real people from radically different backgrounds and how they fare in Manchester. Homelessness, rootlessness and dislocation are major themes of urban living, and Urbis doesn't shy away from encouraging visitors to consider what it's like to sleep on a park bench.

SOMETHING SPECIAL

Maybe it's the vertiginous spiral staircase, but hardly anyone ever visits the fabulous **Godlee Observatory** (☎ 200 4977; fl G, Main Bldg, UMIST, Sackville St; admission free; ⊗ 7-10pm Thu), one of the most interesting places in town. Built in 1902, it is a fully functioning observatory with its original Grubb telescope in place; even the rope and wheels that move the telescope are original. Not only can you glimpse the heavens (if the weather allows), but the views of the city from the balcony are exceptional.

CHETHAM'S LIBRARY & SCHOOL OF MUSIC

Beautiful **Chetham's** (☎ 834 7861; Long Millgate; admission free; ⊗ 9am-12.30pm & 1.30-4pm Mon-Fri) is the city's oldest complete structure (1421). It wouldn't be half as interesting were it not for the fact that during the mid–19th century two of its regular users were Messrs Marx and Engels, whose favourite seats were by the large bay window in the main reading room.

Castlefield Urban Heritage Park

The heart of 19th-century industrial Manchester, a landscape of enormous, weather-stained brick buildings and rusting cast-iron relics of canals, viaducts, bridges, warehouses and market buildings, Castlefield has been successfully transformed into an interesting heritage park. Aside from the huge science museum, the big draw here is the Castlefield Basin. The Bridgewater Canal runs through it; in summertime thousands of people amble about the place and patronise its fine pubs and trendy restaurants. Start at the **visitors centre** (☎ 834 4026; enquiries@castlefield .org.uk; 101 Liverpool Rd; ⊗ 10am-4pm Mon-Fri, noon-4pm Sat & Sun)

MUSEUM OF SCIENCE & INDUSTRY

The city's largest **museum** (☎ 832 1830; Liverpool Rd; admission free; ⊗ 10am-5pm) comprises 2.8 hectares spread over two huge Victorian warehouses and the world's oldest passenger railway terminal. If there's anything you want to know about the Industrial (and post-industrial) Revolution and Manchester's key role in it, you'll find it among the collection of steam engines and locomotives,

NORTHWEST ENGLAND

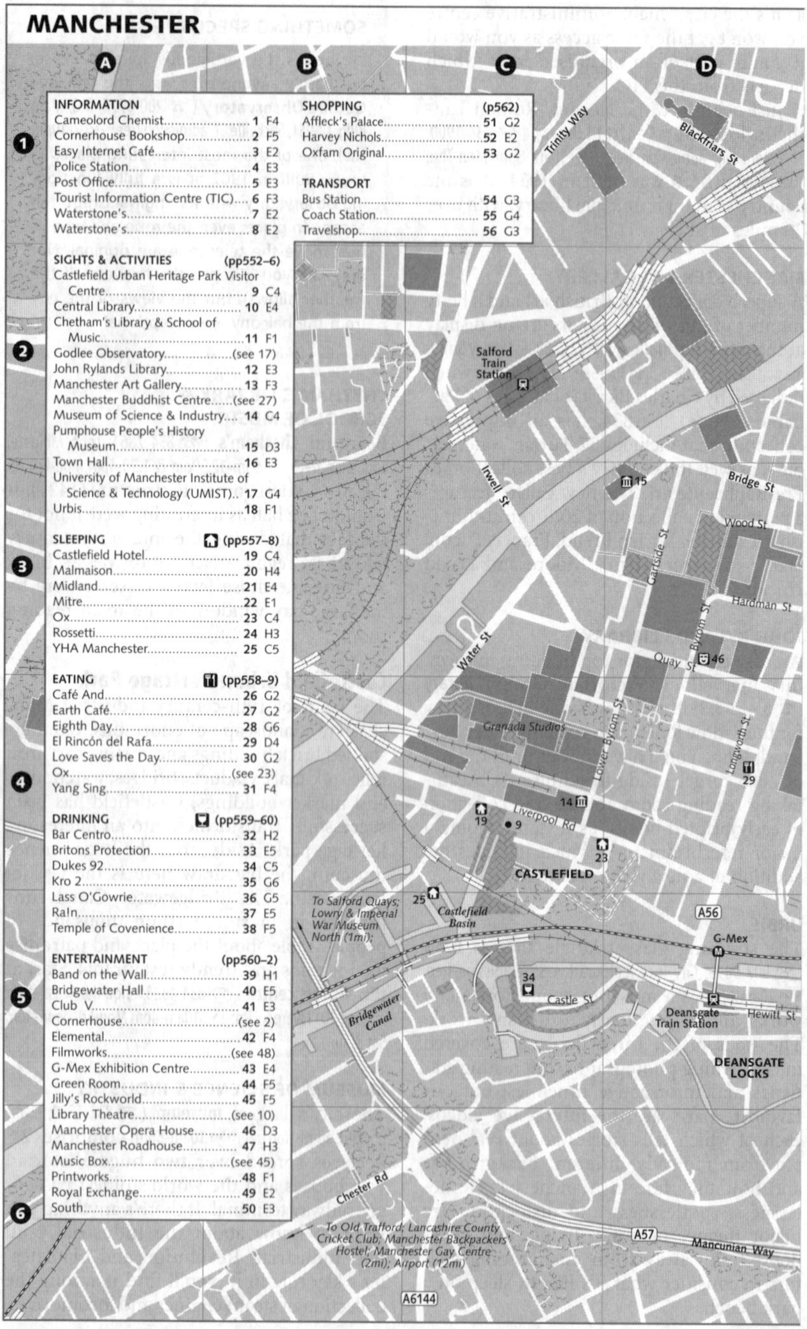

MANCHESTER

Trinty Way

Blackfriars St

Salford
Train
Station

Irwell St

Bridge St

Wood St

Gartside St

Hardman St

Quay St

Byrom St

Water St

Salford Quays;
Lowry & Imperial
War Museum
North (1mi);

Granada Studios

Lower Byrom St

Longworth St

14

19
9

23

Liverpool Rd

CASTLEFIELD

A56

G-Mex

25

Castlefield
Basin

34

Castle St

G-Mex

Deansgate
Train Station

Hewitt St

DEANSGATE
LOCKS

Bridgewater
Canal

Chester Rd

To Old Trafford, Lancashire County
Cricket Club; Manchester Backpackers
Hostel; Manchester Gay Centre
(2mi); Airport (12mi)

Mancunian Way

A57

A6144

NORTHWEST ENGLAND

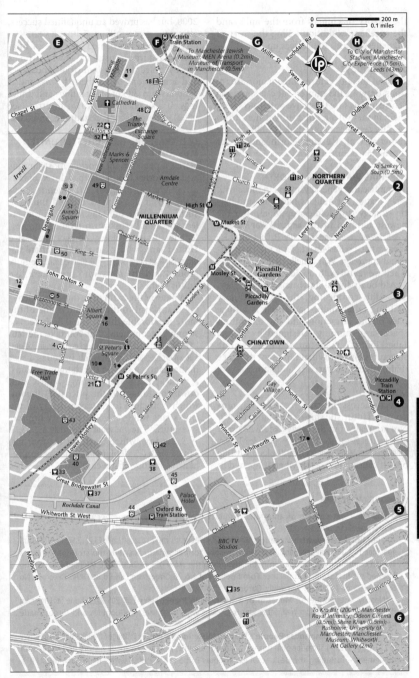

the factory machinery from the mills, and the excellent exhibition telling the story of Manchester from the sewers up.

Salford Quays

West of the city centre, three major attractions draw in the punters, and a shopping centre makes sure they have outlets to spend their money. It's a cinch to get here from the city centre via Metrolink (£1.80); for the Imperial War Museum North and Lowry it's the Harbour City stop.

IMPERIAL WAR MUSEUM NORTH

War museums generally appeal to those with a fascination for military hardware and battle strategy (toy soldiers optional), but the newest addition to the **Imperial War Museum** (☎ 877 9240; www.iwm.org/north; Trafford Wharf Rd; admission free; ☉ 10am-6pm) takes a radically different approach. War is hell, it tells us, but it's a hell we revisit with tragic regularity.

Although the audiovisuals and displays are quite compelling, the extraordinary building (aluminium-clad) itself is a huge part of the attraction and the exhibition spaces are stunning. Designed by Daniel Libeskind, it's made up of three separate structures, or shards that represent the three main theatres of war: air, land and sea.

LOWRY

Directly across the canal from the war museum is a futuristic ship in permanent dock. No, not really, but the **Lowry** (☎ 876 2020; www .thelowry.com; Pier 8, Salford Quays; ☉ 11am-8pm Tue-Fri, 11am-6pm Sun-Mon, 10am-8pm Sat) looks a bit like one. It caused quite a stir when it opened in 2000, but has proved an unqualified success, attracting over a million visitors a year.

The complex is named after one of England's favourite artists, LS Lowry, who is mostly noted for his industrial landscapes and impressions of northern towns, and it contains over 300 of his paintings and drawings. It also encapsulates two theatres (see p562), galleries, shops, restaurants and bars.

OLD TRAFFORD (MANCHESTER UNITED MUSEUM & TOUR)

Here's a paradox: the world's most famous and supported football club, beloved of fans as far apart as Bangkok and Buenos Aires, is the most hated club in England and has a smaller fan base in Manchester than its far less successful cross-town rivals, Manchester City. It's just jealousy, snigger dismissive United fans, who treat the **Old Trafford stadium** (Sir Matt Busby Way; ☉ 9.30am-5pm) like holy ground and the stars who play there like minor deities.

Whatever the truth of it, there's no denying that a visit to the stadium is one of the more memorable things you'll do here. We strongly recommend that you take the **tour** (☎ 868 8631; adult/child £9/6; ☉ every 10min 9.40am-4.30pm except match days), which includes a seat in the stands, a stop in the changing rooms, a peek at the players' lounge and a walk down the tunnel to the pitchside dugout, which is as close to ecstasy as many of the club's fans will ever get. It's pretty impressive stuff. The **museum** (adult/child £5.50/3.75; ☉ 9.30am-5pm), which is part of the tour but can be visited independently, has a comprehensive history of the club.

MORE MUSEUMS

If you can't get enough of annotated exhibits, Manchester has a number of other museums worth checking out.

The **Manchester Jewish Museum** (☎ 834 9879; 190 Cheetham Hill Rd; adult/child £3.25/2.50; ☉ 10.30am-4pm Mon-Thu, 10.30am-5pm Sun), in a Moorish-style former synagogue, tells the story of the city's Jewish community in fascinating detail, including the story of Polish refugee Michael Marks, who opened his first shop with partner Tom Spencer at No 20 Cheetham Hill Rd in 1894. Take bus No 59, 89, 135 or 167 from Piccadilly Gardens.

Nearby, the wonderful **Museum of Transport in Manchester** (☎ 205 2122; Boyle St, Cheetham Hill; adult £3; ☉ 10am-5pm Wed, Sat & Sun) is packed with old buses, fire engines and lorries made in the last 100 years.

The excellent **Pumphouse People's History Museum** (☎ 839 6061; Bridge St; adult/child £1/free, free to all Fri; ☉ 11am-4.30pm Tue-Sun) has well-laid-out exhibits devoted to social history and the labour movement – including the desk at which Thomas Paine (1737–1809) wrote Rights of Man (1791).

MANCHESTER FOR CHILDREN
Urbis (p553) is always full of kids who find
the interactive displays quite engaging, while
Castlefield Urban Heritage Park (p553) is the perfect all-day destination with a host of different activities and exhibits suited to younger
visitors. Here, too, the canalside parks and
walkways are pleasantly distracting. Manchester United's ground **Old Trafford** (opposite) is perennially popular with fans who
are getting younger and younger, while the
Imperial War Museum North (opposite), despite
its sombre themes, is designed to engage the
interest of kids barely into double figures.

City Life Kids (£3.50), available at the TIC
and all bookshops in the city, is a comprehensive guide to virtually every aspect of
family-oriented Manchester.

QUIRKY MANCHESTER
You don't have to work too hard to find
oddity in Manchester: spend enough time
on Piccadilly Circus and you'll know what
we mean. However, for a different (and altogether fabulous) view of the city, climb to
the parapet of the **Godlee Observatory** (p553),
a place virtually nobody ever goes to, a far
cry from the alternative circus that is **Affleck's
Palace** (p562), where in order to go unnoticed
it's best if you look like Marilyn Manson or
a really scruffy Kurt Cobain.

When you're done, you'll have to unwind
with a pint in the **Temple of Convenience** (p560),
a tiny basement pub with a terrific atmosphere located in…a former public toilet.

SLEEPING
Manchester's hotels cater mostly to the
business traveller, but offer a dizzying range
of deals, mostly at weekends, so prices can
fluctuate wildly. We recommend that you
use the TIC's accommodation service (£3)
in order to find the kind of place you want
for the best price. Remember that during
the football season (August to May), rooms
can be almost impossible to find if Manchester United is playing at home.

City Centre
BUDGET
YHA Manchester (☎ 839 9960; www.yha.org.uk; Potato
Wharf; dm £19.50) This purpose-built canalside
hostel is one of the best in the country,
a top-class facility with four- and six-bed
dorms, all with en suite, as well as a host

of good facilities, from a comfortable TV
lounge to a laundry room. It's in the Castlefield area.

MID-RANGE
Castlefield Hotel (☎ 832 7073; www.castlefield-hotel
.co.uk; 3 Liverpool Rd; s/d from £40/56; P ♠) Another
successful warehouse conversion that has resulted in a thoroughly modern business hotel
overlooking the canal basin. It has spacious,
comfortable rooms and excellent amenities,
including a fitness centre and pool that are
free to guests.

Mitre (☎ 834 4128; fax 839 1646; Cathedral Gates; s/d
from £40/70) A stone's throw from the cathedral, this slightly old-fashioned place with
comfortably spartan rooms has found itself
very much in demand over the last few years
as Manchester's chic shopping district has
grown around it.

Ox (☎ 839 7740; www.theox.co.uk; 71 Liverpool Rd;
r £44.95) Not quite your traditional B&B
(breakfast is extra), but an excellent choice
nonetheless; nine oxblood-red rooms with
tidy amenities above a fine gastro-pub (see
p559) in the heart of Castlefield. It's the best
deal in town for the location.

TOP END
Malmaison (☎ 278 1000; www.malmaison.com; Joshua
Hoyle Bldg, Auburn St; r Mon-Fri £129, Sat & Sun £99; ☐)
The Malmaison crowd just doesn't get tired
of picking up designer awards, and this
wonderfully stylish hotel across the street
from the Piccadilly train station is no different. The rooms have all the Malmaison ingredients: huge beds dressed in fine fabrics
and Egyptian cotton, slick art throughout,
and terrific power showers.

Midland (☎ 236 3333; www.themidland.co.uk; Peter
St; d Mon-Fri from £110, Sat & Sun from £80; ☐ ♠)
There could hardly have been a more suitably sumptuous setting for Mr Rolls to shake
hands with Mr Royce than the lobby of this
extraordinary Edwardian hotel just opposite
the G-Mex Exhibition Centre. The luxury
continues through the bars and dining room,
but it all gets a little less dramatic in the bedrooms, which are the height of comfort but
lacking that Edwardian panache. A £12 million refurb is about to get underway.

Rossetti (☎ 247 7744; www.aliashotels.com; 107 Piccadilly St; r from £105; ☐) So long stevedore, hello
Steven Dorff: this converted textile factory
is now one of the city's coolest hotels and

a favourite with showbiz celebs; it's a very stylish blend of original fittings and features with hip art and contemporary design. The loft-style bedrooms feature Moltini designer furniture from Italy, Monsoon showers and stacks of Aqua Sulis toiletries. The super-cool, jeans-wearing staff appear casual, but the service is anything but.

Salford Quays

Lowry (☎ 827 4000; www.rfhotels.com; 50 Dearman's Pl, Chapel Wharf; s/d from £77/125) Simply dripping with designer luxury and five-star comfort, Manchester's top hotel has fabulous rooms with enormous beds, ergonomically designed furniture, walk-in wardrobes and bathrooms finished in Italian porcelain tiles and glass mosaic. You can also soothe yourself with a skin-brightening treatment or an aromatherapy head massage at the health spa.

Other Areas

Manchester Backpackers' Hostel (☎ 865 9296; 64 Cromwell Rd; dm £15) A very pleasant private hostel in Stretford, 2 miles south of the centre, with cooking facilities, a TV lounge and some doubles. It's a cinch to get to and from the centre via the Metrolink (Stretford stop).

GAY & LESBIAN MANCHESTER

The city's gay scene is unsurpassed outside London, and caters to every taste. The useful *Gay & Lesbian Village Guide*, available from the TIC, lists numerous gay bars, clubs, galleries and groups. For other information, check with the **Manchester Gay Centre** (☎ 274 3814; Sydney St, Salford) and the **Lesbian & Gay Foundation** (☎ 235 8035; www.lgf.org.uk; ⏲ 4-10pm). *All Points North* is a good free monthly paper covering the north of England and Scotland. The city's best pink website is www.gaymanchester.co.uk.

At the heart of it all is the Gay Village, centred on Canal St. Here you'll find bars, clubs, restaurants and hotels that cater almost exclusively to the pink pound.

The country's biggest gay and lesbian arts festival, **It's Queer Up North** (IQUP), takes place every two years – the next in spring 2006. **Manchester Pride** kicks off around the end of August each year and attracts over 500,000 people.

University of Manchester/UMIST (☎ 275 2888; www.accommodation.man.ac.uk; Central Accommodations Office, The Precinct Centre, Oxford Rd; dm/d from £9/30; ⏲ Jun-Sep) With over 9000 beds in a variety of rooms, from traditional residence halls to smart, modern flats spread throughout the campuses and suburbs, the university does a roaring summer trade. Call the office (9am to 5pm Monday to Friday) for details and bookings.

EATING

You'd have to go to London to find a bigger choice of cafés and restaurants. The most distinctive restaurant areas are Chinatown, in the city centre, and the southern suburb of Rusholme, on Wilmslow Rd (the extension of Oxford St/Rd), more commonly known as Curry Mile, with a concentration of Indian and Pakistani restaurants unsurpassed in Europe. The Northern Quarter is the place to go for organic hippy shakes and inventive veggie cooking, while the city's fancy restaurants are pretty much spread all over the place. Many bars and pubs also do food; see Drinking, opposite. Below is but a small starter course.

BUDGET

Café And (☎ 834 1136; 74-6 High St; sandwiches £3; ⏲ 9am-7pm Mon-Fri, 10am-7pm Sat, noon-5pm Sun) A trendy café, hip record store, contemporary art gallery and retro furniture shop all in one makes this your one stop for everything you might possibly need in the Northern Quarter. The toasties and wraps are delicious, but it was the excellent organic soups that kept us coming back for more.

Eighth Day (☎ 273 4878; 111 Oxford Rd; mains around £4; ⏲ 9.30am-5pm Mon-Sat) New and most definitely improved after a major clean-up, the students' favourite environment-friendly hang-out sells everything to make you feel good about your place in the world, with everything from fair-trade teas to homeopathic remedies. The vegetarian- and vegan-friendly menu is substantial.

Love Saves the Day (☎ 832 0777; Tib St; house salad £5) The Northern Quarter's most popular café is a New York–style deli, small supermarket and sit-down eatery in one large, airy room. Everybody comes here – from crusties to corporate types – to sit around over a spot of lunch and discuss the day's goings on. A wonderful spot.

SOMETHING FOR THE WEEKEND

A weekend is just about enough time to whet your appetite for Manchester's many delights. After you've checked into somewhere with a little bit of style – the **Rossetti** (p557) has more than enough, while the **Ox** (p557) offers affordable cool – do a little window browsing before grabbing a bite. Pick a bar, any bar, and keep going: there's an unhealthy choice of clubs if you're not that keen on a Saturday-morning start.

Saturday should be about a little sightseeing, and Manchester has something for literally every interest, from art to science and football. Break for dim sum at the fabulous **Yang Sing** (below) and do some more sightseeing, or devote the afternoon to some serious shopping. The evening should be about a meal, a drink and perhaps a concert – from rock to classical. Then another drink and, if you're really up for it, another club.

Saturday night should dictate the pace of Sunday. Brunch, a little browsing and a stroll along the canal bank will deplete the energy of some, while another full day's sightseeing will barely put a dint in others. If you didn't make it to the **Imperial War Museum North** (p556) on Saturday, get there on Sunday.

Earth Café (☎ 834 1996; www.earthcafé.co.uk; 16-20 Turner St; chef's special £5.40; ⊙ 10am-5pm Tue-Sat) Below the Manchester Buddhist Centre, this gourmet vegetarian café is working hard toward becoming the first 100% organic spot in town. The chef's special – a main dish, a side dish and two salad portions – is generally excellent and always filling.

MID-RANGE

El Rincón del Rafa (☎ 839 8819; Longworth St; mains £9-12) Descend the steps into this basement restaurant and find yourself in a little corner of Spain, complete with mouthwatering tapas, bull-fighting posters and the kind of buzz more in keeping with Madrid than Manchester. It's always packed, so book ahead.

Ox (☎ 839 7740; 71 Liverpool Rd; mains £9-12; ⊙ lunch & dinner) Manchester's only gastropub has elevated boozer-dining to a whole new level and earned plenty of kudos in the process. The Brit nouveau cuisine – how's about an oven-roasted T-bone steak with tempura onion rings, beef-steak tomatoes and Portobello mushrooms? – is complemented by an almost exclusively Australian wine list.

Shere Khan (☎ 256 2624; 52 Wilmslow Rd; mains around £7; ⊙ lunch & dinner Sun-Fri) Of the almost impossible selection of curry houses along the Curry Mile, we recommend this place above all others for its plush setting, unfailingly good cuisine, polite and friendly service, and for the fact that its sauces can be found stocked in supermarkets all over the country.

TOP END

Yang Sing (☎ 236 2200; 34 Princess St; lunch mains around £9, dinner mains £16-22; ⊙ lunch & dinner) A serious contender for best Chinese restaurant in England, Yang Sing attracts diners from all over with its exceptional Cantonese cuisine. From a dim sum lunch to a full evening banquet the food is superb, and the waiters will patiently explain the intricacies of each dish to punters who can barely pronounce them.

DRINKING

The current zeitgeist is the trendy café-bar with a wide selection of international beers and plenty of fancy, fruity cocktails, but the city has a boozer for every kind of thirst, from Bailey's to Boddington's. The Northern Quarter is full of trendy bars, while in recent years the Castlefield area has seen a mushrooming of chic watering holes. Otherwise, the area around Deansgate and Albert Sq has a mix of old-style pubs, designer dens and cheesy disco-bars. To make sense of it all, get a copy of the fortnightly *City Life* (£1.50), available just about anywhere.

Bars

Bar Centro (☎ 835 2863; 72-74 Tib St; mains £5-8) A Northern Quarter stalwart, very popular with the bohemian crowd precisely because it doesn't try to be. Great beer, nice staff and a better-than-average bar menu make this one of the choice spots in the area.

Kro Bar (☎ 274 3100; 325 Oxford Rd; sandwiches £2.50, mains £5-8) The ice-cool hand of Scandinavian design is all over this terrific bar in the middle of student-land. A terrific bar menu packs them in at lunch, while night-time DJs keep it going until closing. Its younger brother **Kro 2** (☎ 236 1048; Oxford Rd) is next to the BBC closer to the city, but it's not quite as classy as the original.

Ra!n (☎ 235 6500; 80 Great Bridgewater St) A rival to Dukes 92 (see Pubs) for best outdoor drinking, indoors it's both trendy new-style bar and – downstairs – old-fashioned boozer, so whatever your mood, you'll find the right ambience in this former umbrella factory (there is logic to the name!).

Temple of Convenience (☎ 288 9834; Great Bridgewater St) This tiny basement bar with a capacity of about 30 has a great jukebox and a fine selection of spirits, all crammed into a converted public toilet. Hardly your bog-standard pub.

Pubs

Britons Protection (☎ 236 5895; 50 Great Bridgewater St; mains around £7) Whisky – 200 different kinds of it – is the beverage of choice at this liver-threatening, proper English pub that also does Tudor-style meals (boar, venison and the like). An old-fashioned boozer, no fancy stuff.

Dukes 92 (☎ 839 8646; 2 Castle St) Castlefield's best pub, in converted stables that once belonged to the Duke of Bridgewater, has comfy, deep sofas inside and plenty of seating outside, overlooking Lock 92 of the Rochdale Canal – hence the name. If it's sunny, there's no better spot to enjoy a pint of ale.

Lass O'Gowrie (☎ 273 6932; 36 Charles St; mains around £6) A Victorian classic off Oxford St that brews its own beer in the basement. It's a favourite with students, old-timers and a clique of BBC employees who work just across the street in the Beeb's Manchester HQ. It also provides good-value bar meals.

ENTERTAINMENT
Cinemas

Cornerhouse (☎ 228 2463; www.cornerhouse.org; 70 Oxford St) Your only destination for good arthouse releases; it also has a gallery and a café.

Filmworks (☎ 0870 010 2030; www.thefilmworks.co .uk; Printworks, Exchange Sq) Ultramodern 20-screen complex in the middle of the Printworks centre; there's also an IMAX theatre.

TOP FIVE MANCHESTER ALBUMS

- *Stone Roses* The Stone Roses
- *The Queen is Dead* The Smiths
- *Pills Thrills & Bellyaches* Happy Mondays
- *Permanent* Joy Division
- *Some Friendly* The Charlatans

Odeon (☎ 0870 505 0007; www.odeon.co.uk; 1 Oxford Rd) Chain cinema that shows only mainstream releases on its seven screens.

Live Music
ROCK MUSIC

Band on the Wall (☎ 834 1786; www.bandonthewall .org; 25 Swan St) A top-notch venue that hosts everything from rock to world music, with splashes of jazz, blues and folk thrown in for good measure.

G-Mex Exhibition Centre (☎ 834 2700; Lower Mosley St) A mid-size venue that hosts rock concerts by not-quite-super-successful bands as well as exhibitions and indoor sporting events.

Manchester Roadhouse (☎ 228 1789; www.the roadhouselive.co.uk; 8-10 Newton St) Local bands are put through their paces in front of a generally enthusiastic crowd.

MEN Arena (☎ 950 5000; Great Ducie St) Giant arena that hosts large-scale rock concerts (as well as being the home of the city's ice-hockey and basketball teams).

CLASSICAL MUSIC

Bridgewater Hall (☎ 907 9000; www.bridgewater-hall .co.uk; Lower Mosley St) The world-renowned Hallé Orchestra has its home at this enormous and impressive concert hall, which also hosts a rich and varied programme of other events.

Nightclubs

Having set the standard for how to party in the late 1980s and early 1990s, Manchester's club scene has mellowed substantially since those drug-fuelled halcyon days – even if, paradoxically, there's more choice today. Clubs host a forever-changing mixture of dance nights, so check *City Life* for what's on when you're in town. What follows is but a toe-poke in the vast ocean.

Music Box (☎ 236 9971; www.themusicbox.info; 65 Oxford St; admission £5-12; ✆ Wed-Sat) Deep in the Jilly's Rockworld complex you'll find our favourite club in town and – judging by the queues – just about everyone else's too. They come for the superb monthly club nights, like Mr Scruff's 'Keep it Unreal' and the dirty house of 'Stylus' as well as a host of terrific one-offs.

Sankey's Soap (☎ 661 9085; www.tribalgathering .co.uk; Jersey St, Ancoats; admission free-£10; ⦾ Fri & Sat) With regulars like Danny Tenaglia, Sasha and Layo & Bushwacka in the box, hard-nosed clubbers are in good hands when they trek out to the middle of Ancoats. Techno, breakbeats, tribal and progressive house.

South (831 7756; www.south-club.co.uk; 4A South King St; admission £5-6; ⦾ Fri & Sat) An excellent basement club to kick off the weekend: Friday night is Rock and Roll Bar, featuring

everything from Ibrahim Ferrer to Northern Soul, and Saturday is Disco Rescue – which does exactly what it says.

Other clubs worth checking out include **Elemental** (☎ 236 7227; 69 Oxford St), popular for its mix of commercial and house nights, and **Club V** (☎ 834 9975; 111 Deansgate; admission £5; ⦾ Fri & Sat), a great little basement club that moves to garage beats.

Sport

For most people, Manchester plus sport equals football, and football means Manchester United. That may be true everywhere else (which is why United is covered in the Sights section, p556) but not here – like all good northerners, most Mancunians are

---

THE WAR OF THE ROSES

The War of the Roses was nothing more than a protracted quarrel between two factions, the House of Lancaster (whose symbol was a red rose) and the House of York (represented by a white one), over who should rule England.

It began with the Lancastrian Henry VI (r 1422–61 and 1470–1), who was terrific as a patron of culture and learning, but totally inept as a ruler, and prone to bouts of insanity. During the worst of these he had to hand power over to Richard, Duke of York, who served as protector but acted as king. Henry may have been nutty, but his wife, Margaret of Anjou, was anything but, and in 1460 she put an end to Richard's political ambitions by raising an army to defeat and kill him at the Battle of Wakefield. Round one to Lancaster.

Next it was the turn of Richard's son Edward. In 1461 he avenged his father's defeat by inflicting one of his own on Henry and Margaret, declaring himself Edward IV (r 1461–70 and 1471–83) as a result. One all.

Edward's victory owed much to the political machinations of Richard Neville, Earl of Warwick – appropriately nicknamed 'the kingmaker' – but the throne proved an amnesiac and in time Eddie forgot his friends. In 1470 Warwick jumped ship and sided with the Lancastrians. Edward was exiled and Henry, Margaret and Warwick were all smiles. Half-time and the score was two-one to Lancaster.

Edward came back strongly a year later. He first defeated and killed Warwick at the Battle of Barnet before crushing Henry and Margaret at Tewkesbury. Henry was executed in the Tower of London and Margaret ransomed back to France, where she died in poverty. Just to make sure, Edward also killed their son.

The Yorkists were back in the game, and Edward proved to be a good and popular king. When he died (apparently worn out by his sexual excesses), power passed to his brother Richard, who was to rule as regent until Edward's 12-year-old son came of age. Two months after the king's death, Richard arranged for the 'disappearance' of his nephew and he was crowned Richard III. The Yorkists, however, had scored an own goal, as when rumours of Dickie's dastardly deed became known, he was as popular as a bad smell. In 1485 the Lancastrians, led by the young Henry Tudor, defeated Richard at the Battle of Bosworth, leaving the fallen king to offer his kingdom in exchange for a horse. Final result: victory to Lancaster.

The coronation of Henry VII and his subsequent marriage to Edward IV's daughter Elizabeth put an end to the fighting and ushered in the Tudor dynasty, but it didn't end the rivalry.

They may not be fighting with swords and lances, but one of the great enmities in English football today is that between Lancashire's Manchester United – who wear red – and Yorkshire's Leeds United, who wear all white.

more comfortable supporting the scrappy underdog with the huge heart rather than the well-oiled soccer machine.

MANCHESTER CITY
Manchester's best-loved team is the perennial underachiever, Manchester City. In 2003 the team moved to the spanking-new **City of Manchester stadium** (Sportcity, Rowsley St), where you can enjoy the **Manchester City Experience** (☎ 0870 062 1894; www.mcfc.com; adult/child £7.50/4.50), a tour of the ground, dressing rooms and museum before the inevitable steer into the kit shop. Tours must be booked in advance.

LANCASHIRE COUNTY CRICKET CLUB
Cricket is a big deal here, and the **Lancashire club** (☎ 282 4000; Warwick Rd), founded in 1816 as the Aurora before changing its name in 1864, is one of the most beloved of all England's county teams, despite not having won the county championship since 1930. The really big match in Lancashire's calendar is the Roses match against Yorkshire, but if you're not around for that one, the other games in the county season (admission £10 to £12), which runs throughout the whole summer, are a great day out.

International test matches are also played here occasionally.

Theatre
Green Room (☎ 236 1677; 54 Whitworth St West) The premiere fringe venue in town.

Manchester Opera House (☎ 242 2509; www .manchestertheatres.co.uk; Quay St) West End shows and lavish musicals make up the bulk of the programme.

Library Theatre (☎ 236 7110; Central Library, St Peter's Sq) Old plays and new work in a small theatre beneath the Central Library.

Royal Exchange (☎ 833 9833; St Anne's Sq) Contemporary, interesting plays are standard at this magnificent, modern theatre-in-the-round.

Lowry (☎ 876 2000; www.thelowry.com; Pier 8, Salford Quays) Two theatres – the 1750-capacity Lyric and 460-capacity Quays – host a diverse range of performances, from dance to comedy.

SHOPPING
The huge selection of shops here will send a shopper's pulse into orbit; every taste and budget is catered for.

Millennium Quarter
The area around New Cathedral St, Exchange Sq and the impressive Triangle shopping arcade is the hot new shopping district, full of chichi boutiques and the queen of all department stores, **Harvey Nichols** (☎ 828 8888; 21 New Cathedral St).

Northern Quarter
Rag-trade wholesalers have given way to independent retailers stocking all manner of hip urban apparel, retro fashions and other left-of-centre wear. At the heart of it all is **Affleck's Palace** (Oldham St), a four-storey warehouse jampacked with outlets that Manchester's teenage Goths and the rest of the glumerati have turned into a social day out. The rest of the neighbourhood is full of great shops, including the marvellous **Oxfam Original** (☎ 839 3160; Unit 8, Smithfield Bldg, Oldham St), with terrific retro gear from the 1960s and '70s.

West End
Everything needs a catchy name, so the traditionally upmarket shopping area around St Anne's Sq, King St and Bridge St – full of attractive boutiques for designers both homegrown and international – is now called the West End.

GETTING THERE & AWAY
Air
Manchester airport (☎ 489 3000; www.manchester airport.co.uk) is the largest airport outside London. It is served by 17 locations throughout Britain.

Bus
National Express serves most major cities almost hourly from Chorlton St coach station in the city centre. Destinations include Liverpool (£5.25, 1¼ hours), Leeds (£7, one hour) and London (£19, 4¾ hours).

Train
Manchester Piccadilly is the main station for trains to and from the rest of the country, although Victoria station serves Halifax and Bradford. The two stations are linked by Metrolink. Trains go to Blackpool (£10.45, half-hourly, 1¼ hours), Liverpool Lime St (£10.20, half-hourly, 45 minutes), London (£42, seven daily, three hours) and Newcastle (£36, six daily, three hours).

GETTING AROUND
To/From the Airport
The airport is 12 miles south of the city. A train to or from Victoria Station costs £3.10, a coach £2.70.

Public Transport
The excellent public transportation system can be used with a variety of **Day Saver tickets** (bus £3.30, bus & train £3.80, bus & Metrolink £4.50, train & Metrolink £5, bus, train & Metrolink £6.50). For information about local transport, including night buses, contact the Greater Manchester Public Transportation Authority (GMPTE) **Travelshop** (☎ 228 7811; www.gmpte.com; 9 Portland St, Piccadilly Gardens; ☼ 8am-8pm).

BUS
Centreline bus No 4 provides a free service around the heart of Manchester every 10 minutes. Pick up a route map from the TIC. Most local buses start from Piccadilly Gardens.

METROLINK
There are frequent **Metrolink** (☎ 205 2000; www.metrolink.co.uk) trams between Victoria and Piccadilly train stations and G-Mex (for Castlefield) as well as further afield to Salford Quays. Buy your tickets from the platform machine.

TRAIN
Castlefield is served by Deansgate station with rail links to Piccadilly, Oxford Rd and Salford Crescent stations.

CHESHIRE

Cheshire is a gentle enough place, a mostly agricultural county that is all about farming and a rich Tudor heritage. The genuine black-and-white half-timbered farmhouses shouldn't be confused with the mock-Tudor dream homes owned by the socceratis of Manchester and Liverpool, who once again prove that eight-figure salaries do not necessarily good taste make. For the rest of us, though, Cheshire is really all about Chester.

CHESTER
☎ 01244 / pop 80,120
A slice of Elizabethan England in aspic, Chester is one of the country's most beautiful cities, a compact collection of Tudor buildings (with a bunch of Victorian ones thrown in for good measure) wrapped in an almost intact red sandstone wall that was originally built by the Romans to protect the fortress of Castra Devana.

For much of the Middle Ages Chester was the northwest's most important port, but the gradual silting of the River Dee diminished its importance and by the 18th century it had been overtaken by Liverpool.

These days Chester ekes out a comfortable living as a major retail centre and tourist hotspot: they come, see and shop.

Orientation
Most places of interest are inside the walls, where the Roman street pattern is relatively intact. From the Cross (the stone pillar that marks the town centre), four roads fan out to the four principal gates.

Information
Cheshire Constabulary (☎ 350000; Castle Esplanade)
Chester Royal Infirmary (☎ 365000; St Martin's Way)
Chester Visitors Centre (☎ 351609; Vicar's Lane; ☼ 9.30am-5.30pm Mon-Sat, 10am-4pm Sun May-Oct, 10am-5pm Mon-Sat Nov-Apr)
i-station (☎ 401680; Rufus Ct; Internet access per 30 min £1)
Post office (2 St John St; ☼ 9am-5.30pm Mon-Sat)
TIC (☎ 402111; tis@chestercc.gov.uk; Northgate St; ☼ 9am-5.30pm Mon-Sat, 10am-4pm Sun May-Oct, 10am-5pm Mon-Sat Nov-Apr)

Sights & Activities
CITY WALLS
Perhaps the best way to get a sense of Chester's unique character is to walk the 2-mile circuit along the walls that surround the historic centre. Originally built by the Romans around AD 70, they were altered substantially over the following centuries but have retained their current position since around 1200. The TIC's *Walk Around Chester Walls* leaflet (99p) is an excellent companion guide.

Of the many features along the walls, the most eye-catching is the prominent **Eastgate**, where you can see the most famous clock in England after London's Big Ben, built for Queen Victoria's Diamond Jubilee in 1897.

At the southeastern corner of the walls are the **wishing steps**, added in 1785; local legend claims that if you can run up and down these uneven steps while holding your breath your wish will come true. We question the veracity of this claim because our wish was not a twisted ankle.

Just inside Southgate, known here as **Bridgegate** (as it's at the northern end of the Old Dee Bridge), is the 1664 **Bear & Billet** pub, Chester's oldest timber-framed building and once a tollgate into the city.

On the western side of the walls lies the **Roodee**, Chester's ancient horse-racing track and still one of the country's most beautiful. There are races here during the summer.

THE ROWS

Chester's other great draw is the **Rows**, a series of two-level galleried arcades along the four streets that fan out from the central Cross. The architecture is a handsome mix of Victorian and Tudor (original and mock) buildings that house a fantastic collection of individually owned shops. The origin of the Rows is a little unclear, but it is believed that as the Roman walls slowly crumbled, medieval traders built their shops against the resulting rubble banks, while later arrivals built theirs on top.

OTHER SIGHTS & ACTIVITIES

The **cathedral** (☎ 324756; donation £3; ⏰ 7.30am-6.30pm) was a Benedictine abbey built on the remains of an earlier Saxon church dedicated to St Werburgh. The abbey was closed in 1540 as part of Henry VIII's dissolution

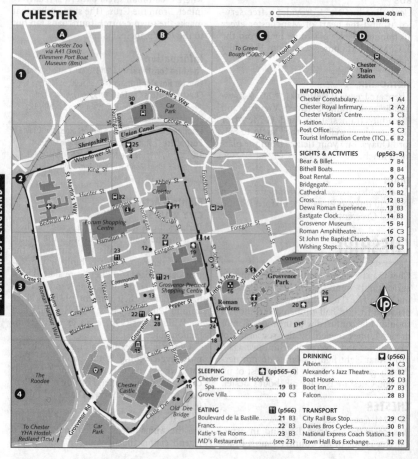

CHESTER

0 ——— 400 m
0 ——— 0.2 miles

INFORMATION
Chester Constabulary	**1** A4
Chester Royal Infirmary	**2** A2
Chester Visitors' Centre	**3** C3
i-station	**4** B2
Post Office	**5** C3
Tourist Information Centre (TIC)	**6** B2

SIGHTS & ACTIVITIES (pp563–5)
Bear & Billet	**7** B4
Bithell Boats	**8** B4
Boat Rental	**9** C3
Bridgegate	**10** B4
Cathedral	**11** B2
Cross	**12** B3
Dewa Roman Experience	**13** B3
Eastgate Clock	**14** B3
Grosvenor Museum	**15** B4
Roman Amphitheatre	**16** C3
St John the Baptist Church	**17** C3
Wishing Steps	**18** C3

SLEEPING (pp565–6)
Chester Grosvenor Hotel & Spa	**19** B3
Grove Villa	**20** C3

EATING (p566)
Boulevard de la Bastille	**21** B3
Francs	**22** B3
Katie's Tea Rooms	**23** B3
MD's Restaurant	(see 23)

DRINKING (p566)
Albion	**24** C3
Alexander's Jazz Theatre	**25** B2
Boat House	**26** D3
Boot Inn	**27** B3
Falcon	**28** B3

TRANSPORT
City Rail Bus Stop	**29** C2
Davies Bros Cycles	**30** B1
National Express Coach Station	**31** B1
Town Hall Bus Exchange	**32** B2

NORTHWEST ENGLAND

frenzy, but was reconsecrated as a cathedral the following year. Although the cathedral itself was given a substantial Victorian facelift, the 12th-century cloister and its surrounding buildings are essentially unaltered and retain much of the structure from the early monastic years.

There are 1¼-hour **guided tours** (adult/child £2.50/1.50; ⏰ 9.30am-4pm Mon-Sat), but they must be booked in advance.

The excellent **Grosvenor Museum** (☎ 402008; Grosvenor St; admission free; ⏰ 10.30am-5pm Mon-Sat, 2-5pm Sun) is the place to go if you want to study Chester's rich and varied history, beginning with a comprehensive collection of Roman tombstones, the largest in the country. At the back of the museum is a preserved Georgian house, complete with kitchen, drawing room, bedroom and bathroom.

The **Dewa Roman Experience** (☎ 343407; Pierpoint Lane; admission £4.20; ⏰ 9am-5pm), just off Bridge St, takes you through a reconstructed Roman street with the aim of showing you what Roman life was like.

The most complete set of genuine Roman remains are opposite the visitors centre, outside the city walls. Here is what's left of the **amphitheatre** (admission free), once an arena that seated 7000 spectators (making it the country's largest), now little more than steps buried in grass.

Adjacent to the amphitheatre is **St John the Baptist Church** (Vicars Lane; ⏰ 9.15am-6pm), built on the site of an older Saxon church in 1075. It started out as a cathedral of Mercia before being rebuilt by the Normans. The eastern end of the church, abandoned in 1581 when St John's became a parish, now lies in peaceful ruin and includes the remains of a Norman choir and medieval chapels.

Steps at the back of the church lead down to the riverside promenade known as the Groves. Here you can hire different kinds of **boats** (⏰ 9am-6pm Apr-Sep; per hr £5-7) with pedals, oars or small engines. This is also the departure point for river cruises (see below).

Tours

The two TICs jointly offer a broad range of walking tours departing from both centres. Each tour lasts between 1½ and two hours.
Ghosthunter Trail (adult/child £3.50/3; ⏰ 7.30pm Thu-Sat Jun-Oct, Sat only Nov-May) The ubiquitous ghost tour, looking for things that go bump in the night.

Pastfinder Tour (adult/child £4/3; ⏰ 10.15am) Covers 2000 years of Chester history
Roman Soldier Patrols (adult/child £4/3; ⏰ 1.45pm Thu-Sat Jun-Aug) This tour of Fortress Deva is led by Caius Julius Quartus; perfect if you've kids in tow.

You can also take a cruise along the Dee; contact **Bithell Boats** (☎ 325394; www.showboatsof chester.co.uk) for details of its 30-minute and hour-long cruises up and down the Dee, including a foray into the gorgeous Eaton Estate, home of the Duke and Duchess of Westminster. All departures are from the riverside along the Groves and cost from £5 to £12.

City Sightseeing Chester (☎ 347452; www.city -sightseeing.com; adult/child £7/2.50, with boat tour £9.50/3.50; ⏰ every 15-30 min Apr-Oct, weekends only Mar) offers open-top bus tours of the city, picking up from the TIC and the visitor centre; the additional river cruise is optional.

Festivals & Events

Held from mid-July to early August, the three -week **Summer Music Festival** (☎ 320700; www .chesterfestivals.co.uk) is a season highlight, featuring performances by all manner of stars both big and small. The **Chester Jazz Festival** (☎ 340005; www.chesterjazz.com; admission free-£8) is a two-week showcase from late August to early September.

Sleeping

If you're visiting between Easter and September, you'd better book early if you want to avoid going over budget or settling for less than you intended. Except for a handful of options – including the city's best – most of the accommodation is outside the city walls but within easy walking distance of the centre. Hoole Rd, a 10- to 15-minute walk from the centre and leading beyond the railway tracks to the M53/M56, is lined with low- to mid-price B&Bs.

BUDGET

Brook St near the train station has a couple of good-value B&Bs from around £20 per person.

Chester YHA Hostel (☎ 0870 770 5762; www.yha .org.uk; 40 Hough Green; dm £14.50) In an elegant Victorian home about a mile from the city centre, you can bed down in a variety of dorms that sleep from two to 10 people. A cafeteria, a kitchen and a shop are on the premises.

MID-RANGE

Grove Villa (☎ 349713; 18 The Groves; s/d from £25/45)
You won't find a more tranquil spot in town than this wonderfully positioned Victorian home overlooking the Dee. The rooms have antique beds and great river views.

Redland (☎ 671024; 64 Hough Green; s/d from £45/70)
The Victorian exterior belies the luxury inside, which is reminiscent of an earlier age. Each of the 13 individually styled (and named) rooms is exquisitely decorated with ornate antiques according to its period; we liked the Jacobean Room with its over-the-top four-poster bed.

TOP END

Green Bough (☎ 326241; www.greenbough.co.uk; 60 Hoole Rd; r from £125) The epitome of the boutique hotel, this exclusive Victorian town house has individually styled rooms that are all dressed in the best Italian fabrics and wall coverings, superb antique furniture and period cast-iron and wooden beds, including a handful of elegant four-posters. Modern touches include plasma-screen TVs, mini-stereos and a range of fancy toiletries.

Chester Grosvenor Hotel & Spa (☎ 324024; www .chestergrosvenor.com; 58 Eastgate St; s/d/ste from £110/ 140/180; P ⊠ 🖵) The best hotel in town with the best location. The huge, sprawling rooms have exquisite period furnishings and modern conveniences such as ISDN lines; the spa (which is open to nonresidents) offers a range of body treatments, including Reiki, Lastone therapy, Indian head massage and four-handed massage.

Eating

There's no shortage of places to eat, but the quality of the fare is often barely above tourist-menu standard. Some pubs do great grub (see right).

Francs (☎ 317952; 14 Cuppin St; mains £8-10; Ⓥ lunch & dinner) A very popular French bistro with a wide-ranging menu of salads, sandwiches and some excellent main courses direct from the French countryside.

Boulevard de la Bastille (Bridge St Row; sandwiches around £3) Our favourite café in town is also one of the most handsome, a very French place on the top tier of the Rows that is perfect for a *café au lait* and *pain au chocolat*.

Katie's Tea Rooms (☎ 400322; 38 Watergate St; tea & scones £3; Ⓥ 9am-5pm Tue-Sat) Stone-walled tea-rooms in a historic building that's the place

---

TOP FIVE PUBS FOR A PINT

- **Philharmonic** (p574; Liverpool)
- **Temple of Convenience** (p560; Manchester)
- **Britons Protection** (p560; Manchester)
- **Albion** (below; Chester)
- **Rover's Return** (p581; Douglas, Isle of Man)

---

to go for a light lunch; after 5pm it turns into **MD's Restaurant** (2 courses £10.50; Ⓥ dinner only Tue-Sat), a continental eatery with a pretty tasty menu.

Drinking

Albion (☎ 340345; 4 Albion St; mains around £8) No children, no music, no chips and no machines or big screens (but plenty of Union Jacks). This 'family-hostile' Edwardian classic is a throwback pub to a time when ale-drinking still had its own *rituals* – another word for ingrained prejudices. Still, this is one of the finest pubs in northwest England precisely because it doggedly refuses to modernise.

Falcon (☎ 314555; Lower Bridge St; mains £4.95) An old-fashioned boozer with a lovely atmosphere; the surprisingly adventurous menu offers up dishes like Jamaican peppered beef or spicy Italian sausage casserole. Great for both a pint and a bite.

Other good pubs include the **Boat House** (The Groves), with great views overlooking the river, and the **Boot Inn** (Eastgate Row), where 14 Roundheads were killed.

Alexander's Jazz Theatre (☎ 340005; Rufus Ct; admission £3-10, free before 10pm) is a combination wine bar, coffee bar and tapas bar.

Getting There & Away

BUS

The National Express bus station is just north of the city inside the ring road. Destinations include Birmingham (£9.50, 2½ hours, four daily), Liverpool (£5.75, one hour, three daily), London (£20, 5½ hours, three daily) and Manchester (£5.25, 1¼ hours, three daily).

For information on local bus services, ring the **Cheshire Bus Line** (☎ 602666). Local buses leave from the **Town Hall Bus Exchange**

(☎ 602666). On Sunday and bank holidays a **Sunday Adventurer ticket** (adult/child £3.50/2.50) gives you unlimited travel in Cheshire.

TRAIN
The train station is a 15-minute walk from the city centre via Foregate St and City Rd, or Brook St. City-Rail Link buses are free for people with rail tickets, and run between the station and Bus Stop A on Frodsham St. Trains go to Liverpool (£3.50, 40 minutes, hourly), London Euston (£46.50, three hours, hourly) and Manchester (£10.20, one hour, hourly).

Getting Around
Much of the city centre is closed to traffic from 10.30am to 4.30pm, so a car is likely to be a hindrance. Anyway, the walled city is easy to walk around and most places of interest are close to the wall.

City buses depart from the **Town Hall Bus Exchange** (☎ 602666).

Davies Bros Cycles (☎ 371341; 5 Delamere St) has mountain bikes for hire at £13 per day.

AROUND CHESTER
The largest of its kind in the country, **Chester Zoo** (☎ 380280; www.chesterzoo.org.uk; adult/child £12/9.50; ☖ 10am-dusk) is about as pleasant a place as caged animals in artificial renditions of their natural habitats could ever expect to live. The zoo is on the A41, 3 miles north of Chester's city centre. Bus Nos 11C and 12C (£2 return, every 15 minutes Monday to Saturday, half-hourly Sunday) run between the town hall and the zoo.

Nearby, on the Shropshire Union Canal about 8 miles north of Chester, is the superb **Ellesmere Port Boat Museum** (☎ 0151-355 5017; www.boatmuseum.org.uk; South Pier Rd; adult/child £5.50/3.70; ☖ 10am-5pm Apr-Oct, 11am-4pm Sat-Wed Nov-Mar), with a large collection of canal boats as well as indoor exhibits. Take Bus No 4 from the Town Hall Bus Exchange in Chester, or it's a 10-minute walk from Ellesmere Port train station.

LIVERPOOL

☎ 0151 / pop 469, 020
Derided and dismissed for decades as a city full of smart-arse scallies who would as soon nick your car as tell you a joke, Liverpool has done a wonderful job of dispelling this largely ridiculous reputation and is eager to arrive as the belle of the ball.

The ball in question takes place in 2008, when the city will be the European Capital of Culture. OK, so 2008 isn't exactly around the corner, but Liverpool is working overtime to get ready. Everywhere you look, handsome old buildings are getting facials and brand new ones are being built – often in place of those plain ugly ones that have scarred the cityscape since the 1960s. The once boarded-up buildings and warehouses of the city centre have been transformed into new shops, cafés and fancy apartments.

To those who'd mock the city for its cultural pretensions, Liverpool will point to life beyond the Beatles – to the city's excellent art galleries and museums, to the fact that it has more listed buildings than any city besides London, to the its varied nightlife, and to the great sense of spirit and togetherness at the core of the Liverpool experience. It's hard to visit and not be affected.

HISTORY
Liverpool grew rich on the back of the triangular trading of slaves for raw materials. From 1700, ships carried cotton goods and hardware from Liverpool to West Africa, where they were exchanged for slaves, who in turn were carried to the West Indies and Virginia, where they were exchanged for sugar, rum, tobacco and raw cotton.

As a great port, the city attracted thousands of immigrants from Ireland and Scotland, and its Celtic influences are still apparent. However, between 1830 and 1930 nine million emigrants – mainly English, Scots and Irish, but also Swedes, Norwegians and Russian Jews – sailed from Liverpool for the New World.

WWII led to a resurgence in Liverpool. Over one million American GIs disembarked here before D-Day and the port was, once again, vital as the western gateway for transatlantic supplies. The arriving GIs brought with them the latest American records, which made Liverpool the first European port of call for the new rhythm and blues that would eventually become rock and roll. Within 20 years, the Mersey beat was *the* sound of British pop and four moptopped Scousers had formed a skiffle band that would become mildly successful.

NORTHWEST ENGLAND

LIVERPOOL

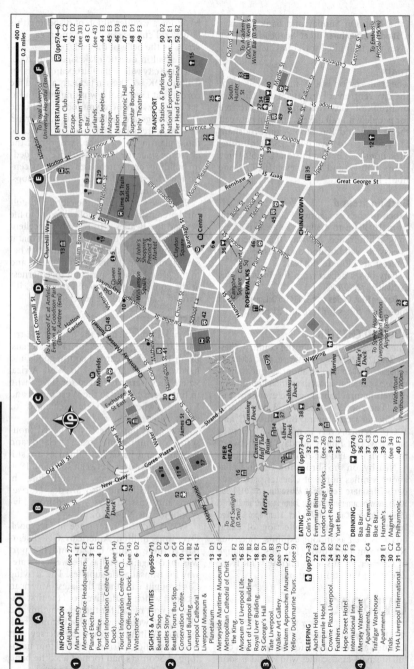

INFORMATION

CaféLatte.net	(see 27)
Mars Pharmacy	1 E1
Merseyside Police Headquarters	2 C3
Planet Electra	3 E1
Post Office	4 D2
Tourist Information Centre (Albert Dock)	(see 14)
Tourist Information Centre (TIC)	5 D1
Tourist Office Albert Dock	(see 14)
Waterstone's	6 D2

SIGHTS & ACTIVITIES (pp569–71)

Beatles Shop	7 D2
Beatles Story	8 C4
Beatles Tours Bus Stop	9 C4
Conservation Centre	10 D2
Cunard Building	11 B2
Liverpool Cathedral	12 E4
Liverpool Museum & Planetarium	13 D1
Merseyside Maritime Museum	14 C3
Metropolitan Cathedral of Christ the King	15 F2
Museum of Liverpool Life	16 B3
Port of Liverpool Building	17 B2
Royal Liver Building	18 B2
St George's Hall	19 D1
Tate Liverpool	20 B3
Walker Art Gallery	21 C2
Western Approaches Museum	21 C2
Yellow Duckmarine Tours	(see 9)

SLEEPING (pp572–3)

Aachen Hotel	22 E2
Campanile Hotel	23 D4
Crowne Plaza Liverpool	24 B2
Feathers	25 F2
Hope Street Hotel	26 F3
International Inn	27 F3
Mersey Waterfront Apartments	28 C4
Trafalgar Warehouse Apartments	29 E1
Trials	30 C2
YHA Liverpool International	31 D4

EATING (pp573–4)

Colin's Bridewell	32 D3
Everyman Bistro	33 F3
London Carriage Works	(see 26)
Magnet Restaurant	34 F3
Yuet Ben	35 E3

DRINKING (p574)

Baa Bar	36 D3
Baby Cream	37 C3
Blue Bar	38 C3
Hannah's	39 E3
Magnet	(see 34)
Philharmonic	40 F3

ENTERTAINMENT (pp574–6)

Cavern Club	41 C2
Escape	42 D2
Everyman Theatre	(see 33)
G-Bar	43 C1
Garlands	44 E3
Heebie Jeebies	45 E3
Masque	46 D3
Nation	47 F3
Philharmonic Hall	48 D1
Superstar Boudoir	49 E3
Unity Theatre	49 F3

TRANSPORT

Bus Station & Parking	50 D2
National Express Coach Station	51 E1
Pier Head Ferry Terminal	52 B2

ORIENTATION
Liverpool is a cinch to get around. The main visitor attractions are Albert Dock, on the waterfront west of the city centre, and the trendy Ropewalks area, south of Hanover St situated just west of the two cathedrals. Lime St Station, the bus station, the Queen Square Centre TIC and the Cavern Quarter, a mecca for Beatles fans, lie just to the north.

The TICs and many of the city's hotels have an excellent tearaway map with all of the city's attractions clearly outlined.

INFORMATION
Bookshops
Waterstone's (☎ 708 6861; 14-16 Bold St)

Emergencies
Merseyside police headquarters (☎ 709 6010; Canning Pl) Opposite Salthouse Dock.

Internet Access
CaféLatte.net (☎ 709 9683; 4 South Hunter St; ☽ 9am-6pm; per 30 min £1)
Planet Electra (☎ 708 0303; 36 London Rd; ☽ 9am-5pm; per 30 min £1)

Internet Resources
Clubs in Liverpool (www.clubsinliverpool.co.uk) Everything you need to know about what goes on when the sun goes down.
Mersey Guide (www.merseyguide.co.uk)
Mersey Partnership (www.merseyside.org.uk) Guide to the greater Mersey area.

Merseyside Today (www.merseysidetoday.co.uk) The city and surrounding area.
TIC (www.visitliverpool.com)

Medical Services
Mars Pharmacy (☎ 709 5271; 68 London Rd) Open until 10pm nightly.
Royal Liverpool University Hospital (☎ 706 2000; Prescot St)

Post
Post office (Ranelagh St; ☽ 9am-5.30pm Mon-Sat)

Tourist Information
The TIC has three city branches. It also has an **accommodation hotline** (☎ 0845 601 1125).
Albert Dock TIC (☎ 0906 680 6886; Merseyside Maritime Museum; ☽ 10am-5pm)
Liverpool John Lennon Airport TIC (☎ 907 1057; Arrivals Hall; ☽ 4am-midnight Apr-Sep, 5am-11pm Oct-Mar)
Queen Square Centre TIC (☎ 0906 680 6886; ☽ 9am-5.30pm Mon-Sat, 10.30am-4.30pm Sun) The main branch.

SIGHTS
The wonderful Albert Dock is the biggest tourist draw and the key to the city's history, but the city centre is where you'll find most of Liverpool's real day-to-day life.

City Centre
ST GEORGE'S HALL
Arguably Liverpool's most impressive building is **St George's Hall** (☎ 707 2391; www.stgeorgeshall.com), built in 1854 and the first European offering of neoclassical architecture.

NORTHWEST ENGLAND

LIVERPOOL IN...

Two Days
Head down to the waterfront and explore the museums of the Albert Dock – the **Tate** (p470), the **Museum of Liverpool Life** (p570) and the **Merseyside Maritime Museum** (p570) – before paying tribute to the Fab Four at the **Beatles Story** (p570). Keep to the Beatles theme and head north toward the **Cavern Quarter** (p571) around Mathew St. Round off your evening with dinner at **London Carriage Works** (p574), a pint at the marvellous **Philharmonic** (p574) and wrap yourself in the crisp white linen sheets of the hip **Hope Street Hotel** (p573). Night hawks can tear it up in the bars and clubs of the hip **Ropewalks** area (p575). The next day, check out the twin delights of the **Liverpool Museum** (p570) and the **Walker Art Gallery** (p570).

Four Days
Follow the two-day itinerary but add in a **Yellow Duckmarine tour** (p572) to experience the docks from the water. Make a couple of pilgrimages to suit your interests: visit **Mendips** (p571) and **20 Forthlin Rd** (p571), the childhood homes of John Lennon and Paul McCartney respectively, now run by the National Trust (NT); or walk on holy ground at **Anfield** (p575), home of Liverpool Football Club.

Curiously, it was built as law courts *and* a concert hall – presumably a judge could hand down a sentence and then relax to a string quartet. It is currently being refurbished and will open in 2005 with a brand-new visitor centre.

WALKER ART GALLERY

Touted as the 'National Gallery of the North', the city's foremost **gallery** (☎ 478 4199; www .liverpoolmuseums.org.uk/walker; William Brown St; admission free; ☉ 10am-5pm Mon-Sat, noon-5pm Sun) is Liverpool's answer to sneering critics who question its cultural credentials in the lead-up to 2008. The history of art from the 14th to the 20th centuries is covered in exquisite detail; strong suits are Pre-Raphaelite art, modern British art and an outstanding collection of sculptures.

LIVERPOOL MUSEUM

Natural history, science and technology are the themes of this sprawling **museum** (☎ 478 4399; www.liverpoolmuseums.org.uk/livmus; William Brown St; admission free; ☉ 10am-5pm Mon-Sat, noon-5pm Sun), where exhibits range from birds of prey to space exploration. There's also a **planetarium** (admission £1). Certain exhibits may be closed when you visit, due to ongoing renovation.

CONSERVATION CENTRE

Ever wonder how art actually gets restored? Find out at this terrific **centre** (☎ 478 4999; www.liverpoolmuseums.org.uk/conservation; Old Haymarket; ☉ 10am-5pm Mon-Sat, noon-5pm Sun) housed in a converted railway-goods depot. Hand-held wands help tell the story, but the real fun is actually attempting a restoration technique with your own hands. Sadly, our trembling paws weren't allowed near anything of value – that was left to the real experts, whose skills are pretty amazing.

WESTERN APPROACHES MUSEUM

The **Combined Headquarters of the Western Approaches** (☎ 227 2008; 1 Rumford St; adult/child £4.75/3.45; ☉ 10.30am-4.30pm Mon-Thu & Sat Mar-Oct), the secret command centre for the Battle of the Atlantic, was abandoned, with virtually everything left intact, when the war ended.

Albert Dock

Liverpool's biggest tourist attraction is Albert Dock, 2¾ hectares of water ringed by enormous cast-iron columns and impressive five-storey warehouses that make up the country's largest group of protected buildings, and now a World Heritage site. Fabulous development has enlivened the dock; here you'll find several outstanding museums and an extension of London's Tate Gallery, as well as fine restaurants and bars.

MERSEYSIDE MARITIME MUSEUM

The story of one of the world's great ports is the theme of this excellent **museum** (☎ 478 4499; admission free; ☉ 10am-5pm) and believe us, it's a graphic and compelling page-turner. The highlight is the Transatlantic Slavery exhibit, which pulls no punches in its portrayal of the shameful trade that made Liverpool rich and left us with the scourge of modern racism. This is heady stuff, and should on no account be missed.

MUSEUM OF LIVERPOOL LIFE

A celebration of Liverpool and its hardy history is on offer at this entertaining **museum** (☎ 478 4080; admission free; ☉ 10am-5pm) that looks at the city in all its guises, from its multiculturalism and trade unionism to its role in the British Army and its unparalleled love of football. Liverpool life was always tough, it tells us, but Scousers have always managed to crack a smile and just keep going. If only real life were that simple.

TATE LIVERPOOL

Touted as the home of modern art in the north, this **gallery** (☎ 702 7400; admission free, special exhibitions adult/child £4/3; ☉ 10am-5.50pm Tue-Sun) features a substantial checklist of 20th-century artists across its four floors as well as touring exhibitions from the mother ship in London's Bankside. But it's all a little sparse, with none of the energy we'd expect from the world-famous Tate.

BEATLES STORY

Liverpool's most popular **museum** (☎ 709 1963; Albert Dock; adult/child £7.95/5.45; ☉ 10am-6pm Mar-Oct, 10am-5pm Nov-Feb) won't illuminate any dark, juicy corners in the turbulent history of the world's most famous foursome – there's ne'er a mention of internal discord, drugs, Yoko Ono or the Frog Song – but there's plenty of genuine memorabilia to keep a Beatles fan happy. The museum is also the departure point for the Magical Mystery and

DOING THE BEATLES TO DEATH

Between March 1961 and August 1963 the Beatles played a staggering 275 gigs in a club on Mathew St called the Cavern, which was essentially a basement with a stage and a sound system. They shared the stage with other local bands who helped define the 'Mersey beat', but it was John, Paul, George and Ringo who emerged into the sunlight of superstardom, unparalleled success and crass marketing.

Forty years later, the club is gone, the band has long since broken up and two of its members are dead, but the phenomenon lives on and is still the biggest tourist magnet in town. The Cavern Quarter – basically a small warren of streets around Mathew St – has been transformed so as to cash in on the band's seemingly unending earning power: the Rubber Soul Oyster Bar, the From Me to You shop and the Lucy in the Sky With Diamonds café should give you an idea of what to expect. If you want to buy some decent memorabilia, check out the **Beatles Shop** (www.thebeatleshop.co.uk; 31 Mathew St), the best of the lot.

True fans will undoubtedly want to visit **Mendips**, the home where John lived with his Aunt Mimi from 1945 to 1963, and **20 Forthlin Rd**, the rather plain terraced home where Paul grew up; you can only do so by prebooked **tour** (☎ 708 8574; adult & child £12; ☯ 10.30am & 11.20am Wed-Sun, Easter-Oct) from Albert Dock; buses depart near the Beatles Story. Visitors to **Speke Hall** (see p577) can also visit both from there.

If you'd rather do it yourself, the TICs also stock the *Discover Lennon's Liverpool* guide and map, and *Robin Jones' Beatles Liverpool*.

Yellow Duckmarine tours (see p572) as well as visits to Mendips and 20 Forthlin Rd (see the boxed text, above).

North of Albert Dock

The area to the north of Albert Dock is known as **Pier Head**, after a stone pier built in the 1760s. This is still the departure point for ferries across the River Mersey (see p576), and was, for millions of migrants, their final contact with European soil.

Today this area is dominated by a trio of Edwardian buildings known as the 'Three Graces', dating from the days when Liverpool's star was still ascending. The southernmost, with the dome mimicking St Paul's Cathedral, is the **Port of Liverpool Building**, completed in 1907. Next to it is the **Cunard Building**, in the style of an Italian palazzo, once HQ to the Cunard Steamship Line. Finally, the **Royal Liver Building** (pronounced lie-ver) was opened in 1911 as the head office of the Royal Liver Friendly Society. It's crowned by Liverpool's symbol, the famous 5.5m copper Liver Bird.

LIVERPOOL FOR CHILDREN

The complex of museums on Albert Dock is extremely popular with kids, especially the **Museum of Liverpool Life** (opposite) and the **Merseyside Maritime Museum** (opposite), which has a couple of boats for kids to mess

about on. The **Yellow Duckmarine tour** (p572) is a sure-fire winner, as is the **Conservation Centre** (opposite), which gets everyone involved in the drama of restoration. Slightly older (and very old) kids – especially those into football – will enjoy the tour of Liverpool FC's **Anfield stadium** (p575) as it means getting your feet on the sacred turf.

QUIRKY LIVERPOOL

When a working public toilet is a tourist attraction, you know you have something special, and the men's loo at the **Philharmonic** (p574) is just that. The **Yellow Duckmarine tour** (p572), an amphibious exploration of Albert Dock, is a bit silly but the guides are hilarious, while the **ferry across the Mersey** (p576) is something special – the tired commuters will give you more than a stare if you sing the song too loudly. The **Grand National Experience** (p575) at Aintree is proof that the English really do love their horses, while the concerts at the **Philharmonic Hall** (p575) often throw up something completely different and avant garde instead of the Beethoven concerto you might expect.

TOURS

The two-hour **Magical Mystery Tour** (☎ 709 3285; all tickets £11.95; ☯ 2.10pm year-round, plus 1.30pm Sat Jul-Aug) takes in all Beatles-related landmarks – their birthplaces, childhood homes, schools and places like Penny Lane and Strawberry Field – before finishing up in the Cavern Club (which isn't the original). Departures are from outside the Beatles Story on Albert Dock.

The **River Explorer Cruise** (☎ 330 1444; adult/child £4.65/2.60; ⊙ hourly 10am-3pm Mon-Fri, 10am-6pm Sat & Sun) lets you do as Gerry & the Pacemakers suggested and 'ferry 'cross the Mersey' on this 50-minute tour, which illuminates the 850-year history of Liverpool as a port. Departures are from Pier Head ferry terminal.

The **Yellow Duckmarine Tour** (☎ 708 7799; adult/child/family £9.95/7.95/29; ⊙ from 11am) takes you to the dock waters in a WWII amphibious vehicle after a quickie tour of the city centre's main points of interest. It's not especially educational, but it is a bit of fun. It leaves from Albert Dock, near the Beatles Story.

FESTIVALS & EVENTS

Africa Oye (www.africaoye.com) A free festival celebrating African music and culture in mid-June.

Aintree Festival (☎ 522 2929; www.aintree.co.uk) A three-day race meet culminating in the world-famous Grand National on the first Saturday in April.

Creamfields (☎ 0208 969 4477; www.creamfields.com) Al fresco dance-fest that brings some of the world's best DJs and dance acts together during the last weekend in August; 2004's headliners were the Chemical Brothers. It takes place at the Old Liverpool airfield in Speke.

Mathew Street Festival (☎ 239 9091; www.mathew streetfestival.com) The world's biggest tribute to the Beatles features six days of music, a convention and a memorabilia auction during the last week of August.

Merseyside International Street Festival (www .brouhaha.uk.com) A three-week extravaganza of world culture beginning in mid-July and featuring indoor and outdoor performances by artists and musicians from pretty much everywhere.

SLEEPING

There's been a small revolution in Liverpool; traditional, don't-try-too-hard B&Bs and bland chain hotels are being challenged by smart, independent boutique hotels and top-class international heavyweights. The result is that if you want even a modicum of character and quality you'll have to pay for it. Beds are tough to find when Liverpool FC is playing at home (it's less of a problem with Everton) and during the Beatles convention in the last week in August.

City Centre
BUDGET
International Inn (☎ 709 8135; www.internationalinn .co.uk; 4 South Hunter St; dm/d £15/36) A superb converted warehouse in the middle of uni-land: heated rooms with en suite and tidy wooden beds and bunks accommodate from two to 10 people. Facilities include a lounge, baggage storage, laundry facilities and 24-hour front desk. The staff are terrific and there's an Internet café next door.

Embassie Hostel (☎ 707 1089; www.embassie.com; 1 Falkner Sq; dm £13.50) Until 1986 this lovely Georgian house was the Venezuelan consulate; it has since been converted into a decent hostel that serves up free tea, coffee and toast at all times. There's also a TV lounge, a games room and a self-catering kitchen.

MID-RANGE
Aachen Hotel (☎ 709 3477; www.aachenhotel.co.uk; 89-91 Mount Pleasant; s/d from £28/46) A perennial favourite is this funky listed house with a mix of rooms, both with en suite and sharing. The décor is strictly late '70s to early '80s – lots of flower patterns and crazy colour schemes – but it's all part of the welcoming, off-beat atmosphere.

Feathers (☎ 709 9655; www.feathers.uk.com; 119-125 Mount Pleasant; s/d from £60/90) A better choice than most of the similarly priced chain hotels is this rambling place, spread across a terrace of Georgian houses close to the Metropolitan Cathedral. The rooms are all uniformly comfortable (except for the wardrobe-sized

---

APARTMENT LUXURY

If you want to live it up in self-catering style, you can opt for a luxury apartment along the waterfront or in the heart of town, which cost between £500 and £750 per week, including gas and electricity.

Trafalgar Warehouse Apartments (☎ 07715 118 419; Trafalgar Warehouse, 17-19 Lord Nelson St) Beautiful converted warehouses with solid wood floors, Jacuzzis and all the trimmings, close to Lime St Station.

Mersey Waterfront Apartments (☎ 487 7440; www.merseywaterfrontapartments.co.uk) Two luxury apartments on King's Dock.

Waterfront Penthouse (☎ 01695 727 877; www.stayinginliverpool.com) One luxury pad on Clippers Quay.

SOMETHING SPECIAL

Hope Street Hotel (☎ 709 3000; www.hopestreethotel.co.uk; 40 Hope St; r/ste from £145/195) The new doyenne of luxurious Liverpool is this boutique hotel in the old London Carriage Works on the city's most fashionable street. The building's original features – heavy wooden beams, cast-iron columns and plenty of exposed brickwork – have been incorporated into a contemporary design inspired by the style of a 16th-century Venetian palazzo. King-sized beds draped in Egyptian cotton, oak floors with under-floor heating, LCD wide-screen TVs (with DVD players) and sleek modern bathrooms replete with a range of REN bath and beauty products are but the most obvious touches of class at this supremely cool address. Breakfast is not included, but can be enjoyed in the fashionable London Carriage Works restaurant on the ground floor (see p574).

---

singles at the top of the building) and all feature nice touches like full-package satellite TV, while the all-you-can-eat buffet breakfast is a welcome morning treat.

TOP END

Trials (☎ 227 1021; www.trialshotel.com; 56 Castle St; s/d £115/130; P ▣) Inside this converted Victorian building are 20 split-level suites primarily aimed at the business traveller, but also a fine option for the luxury-seeker. Jacuzzi baths and broadband Internet are standard. The hotel closed for a major refurb in January 2005 and won't reopen until June; standards (and prices) will undoubtedly go up.

Albert Dock Area
BUDGET

YHA Liverpool International (☎ 0870 770 5924; www.yha.org.uk; 25 Tabley St; dm £19) It looks like an Eastern European apartment complex, but this award-winning hostel, adorned with Beatles memorabilia, is one of the most comfortable in the country. The dorms have en suite and even have heated towel rails, and rates include breakfast.

MID-RANGE

Campanile Hotel (☎ 709 8104; fax 709 8725; cnr Wapping & Chaloner Sts; r £42; P) Functional, motel-style rooms in a purpose-built hotel next to the docks. Great location and perfect for families – children under 12 stay for free.

TOP END

Crowne Plaza Liverpool (☎ 243 8000; www.cpliverpool.com; St Nicholas Pl, Princes Dock, Pier Head; r £115; P ⚐) The paragon of the modern and luxurious business hotel, the Crowne Plaza has a marvellous waterfront location and plenty of facilities, including a health club and swimming pool.

EATING

Liverpool's dining scene is getting better all the time. There are an abundance of choices in Ropewalks, along Hardman and Hope Sts, along Nelson St in the heart of Chinatown or slightly further afield in Lark Lane, near Sefton Park, which is packed with restaurants.

City Centre
BUDGET

Everyman Bistro (☎ 708 9545; 13 Hope St; mains £4-7; ☯ noon-2am Mon-Fri, 11am-2am Sat, 7-10.30pm Sun) Out-of-work actors and other creative types on a budget make this excellent café-restaurant beneath the Everyman Theatre their second home, and with good reason. Great tucker and a terrific atmosphere.

Magnet Restaurant (☎ 709 1998; 41 Hardman St; meals around £6; ☯ 11am-3pm & 5-11pm Mon-Sat, 11am-4pm Sun) Liverpool's answer to a slum-trendy New York diner, complete with red-leather booths, this is the best place in town for a late-night bite, especially if your night is only getting going.

MID-RANGE

Yuet Ben (☎ 709 5772; 1 Upper Duke St; mains £8-12; ☯ 5-11pm Tue-Sun) When it comes to the best Chinese in town, you won't hear too many dissenting voices: Yuet Ben's Beijing cuisine usually comes out tops. The vegetarian banquet could bring round even the most avid carnivore. Try to get a seat by the window and eat in the shadow of Europe's largest Chinese gate.

Keith's Wine Bar (☎ 728 7688; 107 Lark Lane; mains around £5; ☯ 11am-11pm) Friendly, bohemian and mostly vegetarian hangout with a sensational wine cellar that is the favourite resting place of the city's alternative lifestyle crowd.

TOP END

Colin's Bridewell (☎ 707 8003; Campbell Sq; lunch mains £8-9, dinner mains £16; ⊗ noon–11pm) Top-notch British nosh *avec un* continental twist served in a converted police station (the booths are in the old cells); if prison food were this good, the crime rate would soar. It isn't as trendy as some of the city's newer offerings, but it's the insider's choice.

London Carriage Works (☎ 705 2222; 40 Hope St; 2-/3-course meal £22/28; ⊗ 8am-10pm Mon-Sat, 8am-8pm Sun) Paul Askew's award-in-waiting new restaurant is a super-cool reflection of Liverpool's current zeitgeist, A World in One City. Fashionistas, socceristas and the rest of the city's hip brigade share the large, open space that is the dining room – actually more of a bright glass box divided only by a series of sculpted glass shards – and indulge themselves in the marvellous menu with influences from every corner of the world.

DRINKING

A recent survey has put Merseyside at the top of the All-England drinking league. It's official: Scousers love boozing. Health officials may be in despair, but Liverpool has pubs and bars to suit every imaginable taste. Most of the party action takes place in and around Ropewalks, the heart of which is Concert Sq. Unless specified, all the bars included here open until 2am Monday to Saturday, although most have a nominal entry charge after 11pm.

City Centre

Baa Bar (☎ 707 0610; 43-45 Fleet St) The first of Liverpool's style bars has weathered the fierce storm of new rivals with considerable aplomb. Packed virtually every night, it remains one of the city's favourite watering holes; the patio is perfect during the longer summer evenings.

Hannah's (☎ 708 5959; 2 Leece St) One of the top student bars in town. Try to land a table in the outdoor patio, which is covered in the event of rain. Late opening, a friendly, easy-going crowd and some pretty decent music make this place one of the better places to get drunk in.

Magnet (☎ 709 6969; 39 Hardman St) Red leather booths, plenty of velvet and a suitably seedy New York dive atmosphere where Iggy Pop or Tom Waits would feel right at home. The upstairs bar is very cool but totally chilled

out, while downstairs the dancefloor shakes to the best music in town, spun by up-and-comers and supported with guest slots by some of England's most established DJ names. It's two doors down from the eponymous diner (p573).

Philharmonic (☎ 707 2837; 36 Hope St; ⊗ no late opening) This amazing bar, designed by the shipwrights who built the *Lusitania*, is one of the most beautiful in England. The interior is resplendent with etched and stained glass, wrought iron, mosaics and ceramic tiling – and if you think that's good, take a peek inside the marble men's lavatories, the only heritage-listed toilet in the country.

Albert Dock

Blue Bar (☎ 709 7097; Edward Pavilion) You don't need a Premiership contract to guarantee entry anymore, which means that mere mortals can finally enjoy the relaxed ambience of this elegant waterside lounge. So where have all the footballers gone? Downstairs, to the far more glam Baby Blue – a private members' bar.

Baby Cream (☎ 702 5823; Atlantic Pavilion) This super-trendy bar, run by the same crowd that created Liverpool's now-defunct-but-still-legendary Cream nightclub, is gorgeous and pretentious in almost equal measure.

ENTERTAINMENT

There's always something going on in Liverpool – whether it's excellent fringe theatre, a performance by the superb Philharmonic or an all-day rock concert. And then there's the constant backbeat provided by the city's club scene, which pulses and throbs to the wee hours six nights out of seven. For all information, consult the *Liverpool Echo*.

Live Music
ROCK MUSIC
Academy (☎ 794 6868; Liverpool University, 160 Mount Pleasant) This is the best venue to see touring major bands.

Cavern Club (☎ 236 1965; 8-10 Mathew St) 'The world's most famous club' is not the original basement venue where the Fab Four kicked off their careers, but it's a fairly faithful reconstruction. There's usually a good selection of local bands, but look out for the all-day gigs.

CLASSICAL MUSIC
Philharmonic Hall (☎ 709 3789; Hope St) One of Liverpool's most beautiful buildings, the Art Deco Phil is home to the city's main classical orchestra, but it also stages the work of avant-garde musicians such as John Cage and Nick Cave.

Nightclubs
Most of the city's clubs are in Ropewalks, where they compete for customers with a ton of late-night bars; most clubs open at 11pm and turf everyone out by 3am.

Heebie Jeebies (☎ 708 7001; 80-82 Seel St; admission £3-6; ☾ Mon-Sat) Practically every musical style is on offer at this excellent nightclub, from '50s rock and roll to skull-crushing techno. Thursday night's Mixed Bag is especially fun – and free.

Nation (☎ 709 1693; 40 Slater St/Wolstenholme Sq; admission £4-13; ☾ Thu-Sat) Formerly the home of Cream, one of England's most famous club nights, Nation still draws them in – 3000 a night – from everywhere. You can relive a bit of Cream's teeth-shaking energy at the monthly Bugged Out! – the best house and techno night in town.

Masque (☎ 708 8708; 90 Seel St; admission £3-11; ☾ Mon-Sat) This converted theatre is home to our favourite club in town. The fortnightly Saturday Chibuku Shake Shake is one of the best club nights in all of England, led by a mix of superb DJs including Yousef (formerly of Cream) and superstars like Dmitri from Paris and Gilles Peterson. The music ranges from hip-hop to deep house – if you're in town, get in line.

Sport
Liverpool's two football teams – the Reds of Liverpool FC and the blues of Everton – are pretty much the alpha and omega of sporting interest in the city. Yet Liverpool is also home to the Grand National – the world's most famous steeplechase – that is run in the first weekend in April at the Aintree course north of the city (see the boxed text, below).

LIVERPOOL FC
England's most successful football club, **Liverpool FC** (☎ 263 9199; ticket office ☎ 220 2345; www.liverpoolfc.tv; Anfield Rd) epitomises the city's proud identity – even though it hasn't won the league championship since 1990. Virtually unbeatable for much of the 1970s and '80s, the club is looking to a new generation of heroes to fill the packed-but-dusty trophy cabinet.

The club's headquarters is the marvellous Anfield, but plans are in progress to relocate to a new, larger stadium a stone's throw away in Stanley Park before 2008. **Tours** (☎ 260 6677; with museum adult/child £9/5.50; ☾ every couple of hr except match days) of the stadium include the home dressing room, a walk down the famous tunnel and a seat in the dugout, or you can simply pay a visit to the **museum** (adult/child £5/3).

THE GRAND NATIONAL

England loves the gee-gees, but never more so than on the first Saturday in April, when 40-odd ageing stalwarts line up at Aintree to race across 4½ miles and over the most difficult fences in world racing. Since the first running of the Grand National in 1839 – won by the appositely named Lottery – the country has taken the race to heart and there's hardly a household that doesn't tune in, betting slips nervously in hand.

You can book **tickets** (☎ 522 2929; www .aintree.co.uk) for the race, or visit the **Grand National Experience** (☎ 522 2921; adult/child with tour £7/4, without tour £3/2), a visitor centre that includes a race simulator – those jumps are very steep indeed. We recommend the racecourse tour, which takes in the stableyard and the grave of three-time winner Red Rum, the most loved of all Grand National winners.

EVERTON FC
Liverpool's 'other' team are the blues of **Everton FC** (☎ 330 2400, ticket office ☎ 330 2300; www .evertonfc.com; Goodison Park), who may lack their neighbour's pedigree but are their equal in fan passion. **Tours** (☎ 330 2277; adult/child £6.50/4.50; ⊙ 11am & 2pm Sun-Wed & Fri) of Goodison Park run throughout the year except on the Friday before home matches.

Theatre
Most of Liverpool's theatres feature a mix of revues, musicals and stage successes that are easy on the eye and the mind, but there is also more interesting work on offer.

Everyman Theatre (☎ 709 4776; Hope St) This is one of England's most famous repertory theatres and it's an avid supporter of local talent, which has included the likes of Alan Bleasdale.

Unity Theatre (☎ 709 4988; Hope Pl) Fringe theatre for those keen on the unusual and challenging; there's also a great bar on the premises.

GETTING THERE & AWAY
Air
Liverpool John Lennon Airport (☎ 0870 750 8484; www.liverpoolairport.co.uk) serves a variety of destinations including Amsterdam, Barcelona, Dublin and Paris as well as destinations in the UK (Belfast, London and the Isle of Man).

Bus
The **National Express Coach Station** (☎ 0870 580 8080; Norton St) is 300m north of Lime St Station. There are services to and from most major towns, including Manchester (£5.25, hourly, 1¼ hours) and London (£20, seven daily, five to six hours).

Train
Lime St Station has hourly services to almost everywhere, including Chester (£3.50, 40 minutes), London (£55, three hours), Manchester (£10.20, 45 minutes) and Wigan (£6.10, 50 minutes).

GETTING AROUND
To/From the Airport
The airport is 8 miles south of the city centre. **Arriva Airlink** (£1.50; 30 min; ⊙ 6am-11pm) bus Nos 80A and 180 departs from Paradise St Station every 20 minutes and **Airportxpress 500** (£2; 30 min; ⊙ 5.15am-12.15am) buses run

every half-hour from outside Lime St Station. A taxi to the city centre should cost no more than £12.

Boat
The cross-Mersey **ferry** (adult/child £1.10/90p) for Woodside and Seacombe departs from Pier Head Ferry Terminal, next to the Liver Building to the north of Albert Dock.

Car
You won't have much use for a car in Liverpool, and it'll end up costing you plenty in car-park fees. If you must, there are parking meters around the city and a number of open and sheltered car parks. Car break-ins are a major problem, so leave absolutely nothing of value in the car.

Public Transport
Local public transport is coordinated by **Merseytravel** (☎ 236 7676; www.merseytravel.gov.uk). Highly recommended is the **Saveaway Ticket** (adult/child £3.70/1.90), which allows for one day's off-peak travel on all bus, train and ferry services throughout Merseyside. Tickets are available at shops and post offices throughout the city. The **bus station** (Paradise St) is in the centre.

Merseyrail (☎ 702 2071; www.merseyrail.org) is an extensive suburban rail service linking Liverpool with the Greater Merseyside area. There are four stops in the city centre: Lime St, Central (handy for Ropewalks), James St (close to Albert Dock) and Moorfields (for the Western Approaches Museum).

Taxi
Mersey Cabs (☎ 298 2222) operates tourist taxi services and has some cabs adapted for disabled visitors.

AROUND LIVERPOOL

PORT SUNLIGHT
Southwest of Liverpool across the River Mersey on the Wirral Peninsula, Port Sunlight is a picturesque 19th-century village created by the philanthropic Lever family to house workers in its soap factory. The main reason to come here is the wonderful **Lady Lever Art Gallery** (☎ 478 4136; off Greendale Rd; admission free; ⊙ 10am-5pm) where you can see some of the greatest works of the Pre-Raphaelite

Brotherhood, as well as some fine Wedgwood pottery.

Trains run from Liverpool's Lime St station to Port Sunlight.

SPEKE

A marvellous example of a black-and-white half-timbered hall can be visited at **Speke Hall** (NT; ☎ 427 7231; admission £6; ☼ 1-5.30pm Wed-Sun Apr-Oct, 1-4.30pm Sat & Sun Nov-Mar), six miles south of Liverpool in the plain suburb of Speke. It contains several priest's holes where 16th-century Roman Catholic priests could hide when they were forbidden to hold Masses. Any airport bus from Paradise St will drop you within a half mile of the entrance. Speke Hall can also be combined with a National Trust–run, 1½-hour **tour** (☎ 486 4006; with Speke Hall adult/child £12/free) to the childhood homes of both Lennon and McCartney (see the boxed text, p571) – you can book at Speke Hall, at the Beatles Story or at the TICs.

LANCASHIRE

From industry to isolation, Lancashire is the epitome of the northern experience. Besides mighty Manchester – so big that it's administered separately – there's ever-popular Blackpool, the empress of tacky seaside resorts and, further north, the Georgian county town of Lancaster, a handsome and historic example of elegant architecture.

BLACKPOOL

☎ 01253 / pop 142,290

Blackpool attracts more visitors than any other place in Britain outside London, suggesting that tacky does, in fact, work. The point is, though, that Blackpool works not because it's tacky, but because it's more than just tacky: a clever combination of the traditional British-holiday-by-the-sea with high-tech, 21st-century amusements to thrill even the most jaded has ensured that Blackpool will continue to attract its fair share of the sun-holiday crowd. When you consider that the sun is hardly guaranteed in these parts, it's nothing short of a miracle.

Blackpool is famous for its tower, its three piers, its Pleasure Beach and its Illuminations, a successful ploy to extend the brief summer-holiday season. From early

September to early November, 5 miles of the Promenade are illuminated with thousands of electric and neon lights.

Orientation & Information

Blackpool is surprisingly spread out but can still be managed easily without a car – trams run the entire 7-mile length of the seafront Promenade.

There are two TICs in Blackpool; **Clifton St TIC** (☎ 478222; www.visitblackpool.com; 1 Clifton St; ☼ 9am-5pm Mon-Sat) and **North Pier TIC** (☎ 403223; ☼ 9.15am-5pm, 10.15am-4.15pm Sun Apr-Sep).

Pleasure Beach

The main reason for Blackpool's immense popularity is the simply fantastic **Pleasure Beach** (☎ 0870 444 5566; www.blackpoolpleasurebeach .com; admission free; ☼ from 10am Apr–early Nov), a 16-hectare collection of over 145 different rides that attracts 7 million visitors annually. This is the best amusement park you'll find anywhere in Europe. The rides range from the old-style wooden rollercoasters known as 'woodies' to the super-fast, high-tech stomach churners like the Big One, the tallest and fastest roller coaster in Europe.

Rides are divided into categories, and you can buy tickets for individual categories or for a mixture of them all. An unlimited ticket to all rides costs £30 for one day, £45 for two.

There are no set times for closing; it depends how busy they are.

Other Sights

Blackpool's most recognisable landmark is the 150m-high **Blackpool Tower** (☎ 622242; adult/child £12/10; ☼ 10am-11pm Apr-Oct, 10am-6pm Nov-Mar), built in 1894. Inside is a vast entertainment complex that should keep the kids happy, including a Dinosaur Ride, Europe's largest indoor jungle gym and a Moorish circus.

The highlight is the magnificent, rococo **ballroom**, with extraordinary sculptured and gilded plasterwork, murals and chandeliers. Couples still glide across the floor to the melodramatic tones of a huge Wurlitzer organ from 11am to 10pm every day.

Across the road from Pleasure Beach is the **Sandcastle** (☎ 343602; adult/child £7.95/6.50; ☼ from 10am daily May-Oct, Sat & Sun only Nov-Feb), an indoor water complex complete with its own rides.

Near the Central Pier is the state-of-the-art **Sealife Centre** (☎ 622445; New Bonny St; adult/child £7.50/5; ☻ 10am-8pm), which features 8ft sharks and a giant octopus.

Sleeping

With over 2500 hotels, B&Bs and self-catering units, Blackpool knows how to put visitors up for the night. Even with so many places to stay, it is worth booking ahead during the Illuminations. If you want to stay close to the waterfront, prepare for a noisy night; accommodation along Albert and Hornby Rds, 300m from the sea, is quieter. The TIC will assist you in finding a bed.

Big Blue Hotel (☎ 0845 367 3333; www.bigblue hotel.com; Blackpool Pleasure Beach; r from £55; **P**) Cool, minimalist and very much a look into Blackpool's future, this hotel caters to 21st-century demands: smartly kitted-out rooms come with DVD players and computer games, while its location at the southern entrance of Pleasure Beach should ensure that everyone has something to do.

Old Coachhouse (☎ 349195; www.theoldcoachhouse .freeserve.co.uk; 50 Dean St; dinner £20, s/d from £40/70; **P**) A Tudor breath of fresh air is the south shore's oldest building, with 11 handsome rooms; two have four-poster beds and beautiful garden views. A Japanese-style sun deck, a conservatory and an outdoor whirlpool complete the luxury.

Eating

Forget gourmet meals – the Blackpool experience is all about stuffing your face with burgers, hot dogs, doughnuts and fish and chips. Most people eat at their hotels, where roast and three vegetables often costs just £4 a head.

There are a few restaurants around Talbot Sq (near the TIC) on Queen St, Talbot Rd and Clifton St. The most interesting possibility is the Afro-Caribbean **Lagoonda** (☎ 293837; 37 Queen St; mains £9), a friendly, no-nonsense eatery that serves up colourful (and often spicy) dishes with a tropical flavour.

Getting There & Away
BUS

The central coach station is on Talbot Rd, near the town centre. Destinations include Liverpool (£7.25, 1½ hours, one daily), London (£23.50, 6½ hours, five daily) and Manchester (£5.75, 1¾ hours, four daily).

TRAIN

The main train station is Blackpool North, about five blocks east of the North Pier on Talbot Rd. There is a direct service from Manchester (£10.95, 1¼ hours, half-hourly) and Liverpool (£11.60, 1½ hours, seven daily), but most other arrivals change in Preston (£5.05, 30 minutes, half-hourly).

Getting Around

A host of travel-card options for trams and buses ranging from one day to a week are available at the TICs and most newsagents. With more than 14,000 car-parking spaces in Blackpool you'll have no problems parking.

LANCASTER
☎ 01524 / pop 45,950

Although it dates back as far as Roman times, Lancaster's heyday was the 18th century, when it was an important port in the slave trade. The port is much quieter now, but the town's rows of handsome Georgian buildings make this a pleasant stopover on the way to the Ribble Valley.

Information

Post office (85 Market St; ☻ 9am-5.30pm Mon-Fri, 9am-12.30pm Sat)
TIC (☎ 841656; www.visitlancaster.co.uk; 29 Castle Hill; ☻ 9am-5pm Mon-Sat)

Sights

Lancaster's imposing **castle** (☎ 64998; admission £4; ☻ 10am-5pm) was originally built in 1150. Later additions include the **Well Tower** – more commonly known as the Witches' Tower, as it was used to incarcerate the accused of the famous Pendle Witches Trial of 1612 – and the impressive, twin-towered **gatehouse**, both of which were added in the 14th century. Most of what you see today, however, dates from the 18th and 19th centuries, when the castle was substantially reconfigured to suit its new role as a prison, which it retains today. Consequently, visitors can only visit the castle as part of a 45-minute **guided tour** (☻ every 30 min, 10am-4pm).

Immediately next to the castle is the equally fine **priory church** (☎ 65338; admission free; ☻ 9.30am-5pm), which was founded in 1094 but extensively remodelled in the Middle Ages.

The steps between the castle and the church lead you down to the 17th-century **Judges' Lodgings** (☎ 32808; admission £2; ⊙ 10.30am-1pm & 2-5pm Mon-Fri, 2-5pm Sat Jul-Sep, 2-5pm Mon-Sat Oct-Jun), once used by visiting magistrates and now home to a Museum of Furnishings by master builders Gillows of Lancaster (whose work graces the Houses of Parliament) and a Museum of Childhood with memorabilia from the turn of the 20th century.

A couple of other museums complete the picture: the **Maritime Museum** (☎ 64637; St George's Quay; admission £2; ⊙ 11am-5pm Easter-Oct, 12.30-4pm Nov-Easter), in the 18th-century Custom House, recalls the days when Lancaster was a flourishing port at the centre of the slave trade; and the **City Museum** (☎ 64637; Market Sq; admission free; ⊙ 10am-5pm Mon-Sat) has a mixed bag of local historical and archaeological exhibits.

Sleeping & Eating

Swallow King's Arms Hotel (☎ 32451; www.swallow -hotels.com; Market St; mains around £11; s/d £52/77; **P**) Lancaster's top hotel is a period house with modern, comfortable rooms and an all-round businesslike interior. Look out for the beautiful stained-glass windows, one of the only leftovers from the mid–19th century, when Charles Dickens frequented the place. The hotel restaurant is an excellent dining choice.

Otherwise, **Castle Hill House** (☎ 849137; gsutclif@aol.com.uk; 27 St Mary's Pde; s/d £27/42) is a terraced Victorian house right in the middle of town with comfortable, well-furnished rooms, while the **Wagon & Horses** (☎ 846094; 27 St Georges Quay; s/d £30/45) is a pleasant pub next to the Maritime Museum with five comfortable rooms upstairs; only one room has an en suite, but all have river views.

The **Old John of Gaunt** (☎ 32358; 53 Market St; mains around £5-6) is your one-stop shop for traditional pub grub, decent ale and live music.

Getting There & Away

Lancaster is on both the principal west-coast railway line and the Cumbrian Coast Line. Destinations include Carlisle (£19, one hour, hourly), Manchester (£11.05, one hour, hourly) and Morecambe (£1.45, 15 minutes, half-hourly).

ISLE OF MAN

Beloved of tax avoiders and petrol heads, the Isle of Man (*Ellan Vannin* in Manx) is a surprisingly beautiful place and a perfect spot for walking, cycling and driving. It's most famous for its Tourist Trophy (TT) motorcycle races, which add 45,000 to the island's small population every May and June.

Home to the world's oldest continuous parliament, the Isle of Man enjoys special status in Britain, and its annual parliamentary ceremony honours the 1000-year history of the Tynwald (a Scandinavian word meaning 'meeting field'). Unfortunately, Douglas, the capital, is a run-down relic of Victorian tourism with fading B&Bs. The tailless Manx cat and the four-horned Loghtan sheep are unique to the Isle.

Orientation & Information

Only 33 miles long by 13 miles wide, the island is in the middle of the Irish Sea, equidistant from Liverpool, Dublin and Belfast. Ferries arrive at Douglas, the port and main town on the southeast coast. Flights come in to Ronaldsway airport, 10 miles southwest of Douglas. Most of the island's historic sites are operated by **Manx Heritage** (MH; ☎ 648000; www.gov.im/mnh), which offers free admission to National Trust or English Heritage members. Unless otherwise indicated, Manx Heritage sites open 10am to 5pm daily, Easter to October. The **Manx Heritage Pass** (adult/child £10/5) grants you free entry into four of the island's heritage attractions; pick it up at any TIC.

Walking & Cycling

There are plenty of walking trails. Ordnance Survey (OS) Landranger Map 95 (£5.99) covers the whole island, while the free *Walks on the Isle of Man* is available from the TIC in Douglas. The **Millennium Way** is a walking path that runs the length of the island amid some spectacular scenery. The most demanding of all walks is the 90-mile **Raad ny Foillan**, or Road of the Gull, a well-marked path that makes a complete circuit of the island and normally takes approximately five days to complete. Other routes are detailed under the relevant sections following.

There are six designated off-road cycling tracks on the island, each with varying ranges of difficulty.

The island is also home to the **International Cycling Week Festival**, which takes place in mid-July. It's a pretty serious affair, attracting top cyclists from around the world as well as enthusiastic Sunday racers. Check with the TIC in Douglas for details.

Getting There & Away
AIR
Ronaldsway Airport (☎ 01624 821600; Ballasalla) is 10 miles south of Douglas, near Castletown. Buses link the airport with Douglas every 30 minutes between 7am and 11pm; a taxi should cost you no more than £18.

Airline contacts include **British Airways** (☎ 0870 850 9850; www.britishairways.com), who fly from London Gatwick, Luton and Manchester; **Eastern Airways** (☎ 01652-681099; www.easternairways.com) for Leeds-Bradford, Bristol, Birmingham and East Midlands; **Emerald Airways** (☎ 0870 850 5400; www.flyjem.com) flying from Liverpool; **EuroManx Airlines** (☎ 0870 787 7879; www.euromanx.com) for Liverpool and London Stansted, and **Flybe** (☎ 0871 700 0535; www.3flybe.com) who run the London City, Jersey, Bristol and Birmingham routes.

BOAT
Isle of Man Steam Packet (☎ 0870 552 3523; www.steam-packet.com; foot passenger single/return £15/25, car & 2 passengers £199 return) provides a car ferry and

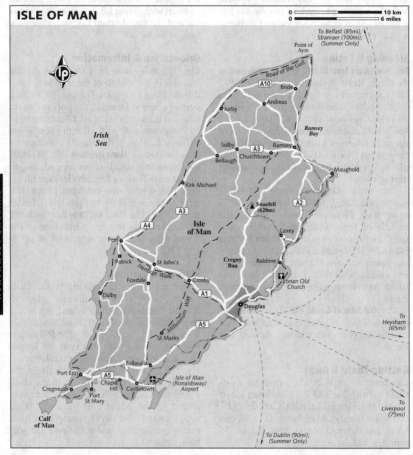

ISLE OF MAN

0 ——— 10 km
0 ——— 6 miles

Irish Sea

To Belfast (85mi);
Stranraer (100mi)
(Summer Only)

Point of Ayre

Road of the Gull

A10 Bride

Jurby
Andreas

Sulby
A3 Ramsey
Bellaugh Churchtown
Ramsey Bay

Maughold

Kirk Michael

A3
▲ Snaefell (620m)
A2

A4
Isle of Man
Laxey

Peel
Patrick St John's
Heritage Walk
Cregny Baa
Baldrine

Foxdale Crosby
Lonan Old Church

Dalby
A1

Millennium Way
Douglas

A5

St Marks

Ballasalla

Port Erin
A5
Cregneash
Chapel Hill Castletown
Isle of Man (Ronaldsway) Airport
Port St Mary

Calf of Man

To Heysham (65mi)

To Liverpool (75mi)

To Dublin (90mi);
(Summer Only)

high-speed catamaran service from Liverpool and Heysham to Douglas.

Getting Around

The island has a comprehensive bus service; the TIC in Douglas has timetables and fare information.

You can hire bicycles from **Eurocycles** (☎ 624909; 8A Victoria Rd; ❍ Mon-Sat) for £12 to £18 per day.

Petrol-heads will love the scenic, sweeping bends that make for some exciting driving – and the fact that outside the town there's no speed limit. Naturally, the most popular drive is along the TT route. Car-hire operators have desks at the airport; they charge from £30 per day.

There are several interesting **rail services** (☎ 663366; ❍ Easter-Sep); discount passes are available:

Douglas–Laxey–Ramsey Electric Tramway (£6 return)
Douglas–Castletown–Port Erin Steam Train (£7 return)
Laxey–Summit Snaefell Mountain Railway (£6 return)

DOUGLAS

☎ 01624 / pop 22,200

All roads lead to Douglas, which is a bit of a shame, as the town isn't all that endearing. Still, it has the best of the island's hotels and restaurants – as well as the bulk of the finance houses frequented so regularly by tax-allergic Brits. The **TIC** (☎ 686766; Sea Terminal Bldg; ❍ 9.15am-7pm daily May-Sep, 9am-5pm daily Apr & Oct, 9am-5.30pm Mon-Fri & 9am-12.30pm Sat Nov-Mar) makes free accommodation bookings.

The **Manx Museum** (MH; admission free; ❍ 10am-5pm Mon-Sat) gives an introduction to everything from the island's prehistoric past to the latest TT race winners.

Sleeping

The seafront promenade is crammed with B&Bs. Unless you booked back in the 1990s, there's little chance of finding accommodation during TT week and the weeks each side of it. The TIC's camping information sheet lists sites all around the island.

Admiral House (☎ 629551; www.admiralhouse.com; Loch Promenade; mains around £8-10, s/d £40/75; P) A warm and elegant guesthouse overlooking the harbour near the ferry port, with 23 spotless modern rooms. Plenty of bright reds and blues feature in the décor, a cheerful alternative to the worn look of a lot of

other seafront B&Bs. In the basement, the smart La Posada is a good Spanish restaurant that does a delicious paella.

Claremont (☎ 698800; www.sleepwellhotels.com; 18-19 Loch Promenade; d/ste £90/125; 🖳 P) The last word in contemporary business style in Douglas, the Claremont has very bright, airy rooms with all the latest gizmos – DVD players, Internet connections and fancy TVs – as well as beautiful limestone bathrooms. The executive rooms have terrific harbour views.

Sefton Hotel (☎ 645500; www.seftonhotel.co.im; Harris Promenade; s/d from £79/96; P 😮) Douglas' best hotel is an upmarket oasis with its own indoor water garden and rooms that range from plain and comfy to elegant and very luxurious – the rooms overlooking the water garden are superb, even better than the ones with sea views. You save up to 10% if you book online.

Eating & Drinking

Spill the Beans (1 Market Hill; snacks around £1.50; ❍ 9.30am-6pm Mon-Sat) The most pleasant coffee shop in Douglas delivers proper caffeine kicks as well as cakes, buns and other sweet snacks.

Tanroagan (☎ 472411; 9 Ridgeway St; mains £9-15; ❍ lunch Mon-Fri, dinner Mon-Sat) The place for all things from the sea, this elegant eatery is the trendiest place in Douglas, serving fresh fish straight off the boats, given the merest of continental twists or just a spell on the hot grill. Reservations are recommended.

There are a few good pubs around, including the popular local hang-out **Tramshunter** (Promenade) and the originally named **Rover's Return** (☎ 676459; 11 Church St) specialising in the local brew Bushy Ales.

AROUND DOUGLAS

You can follow the TT course up and over the mountain or wind around the coast. The mountain route takes you close to the summit of **Snaefell** (621m), the island's highest point. It's an easy walk up to the summit, or you can take the electric tram from Laxey on the coast. The tram stops by the road where **Murray's Motorcycle Museum** (☎ 01624 613328; Bungalow Corner, Mountain Rd; adult/child £3/2; ❍ 10am-5pm May-Oct) displays motorcycles and TT memorabilia.

On the edge of Ramsey is the **Grove Rural Life Museum** (MH; adult/child £3/2). The church in the small village of **Maughold** is on the site of an ancient monastery; a small shelter houses quite a good selection of stone crosses and ancient inscriptions.

Describing the **Laxey Wheel** (MH; adult/child £3/2), built in 1854 to pump water from a mine, as a 'great' wheel is no exaggeration; it measures 22m across and can draw 250 gallons (1140L) of water per minute from a depth of 550m. The wheel-headed cross at **Lonan Old Church** is the island's most impressive early Christian cross.

CASTLETOWN & AROUND

At the island's southern end is Castletown, a quiet harbour town that was originally the capital of the Isle of Man. The town is dominated by the impressive 13th-century **Castle Rushen** (MH; adult/child £4.25/2.25). The flag tower affords fine views of the town and coast. There's also a small **Nautical Museum** (MH; adult/child £3/1.50) displaying, among other things, its pride and joy: *Peggy*, a boat built in 1791 and still housed in its original boathouse. A school dating back to 1570 in **St Mary's church** (MH; admission free) is behind the castle.

Between Castletown and Cregneash, the Iron-Age hillfort at **Chapel Hill** encloses a Viking ship-burial site.

On the southern tip of the island, the **Cregneash Village Folk Museum** (MH; adult/child £3/1.50) recalls traditional Manx rural life. The **Calf of Man**, the small island just off Cregneash, is a bird sanctuary. **Calf Island Cruises** (☎ 832339; adult/child £10/5; ☼ 10.15am, 11.30am & 1.30pm Apr-Oct weather permitting) run between Port Erin and the island.

Port Erin, another Victorian seaside resort, has a small **Railway Museum** (adult/child £1/50p; ☼ 9.30am-5.30pm Apr-Oct) depicting the history of steam railway on the island.

Sleeping

Port Erin has a good range of accommodation, as does Port St Mary, across the headland and linked by steam train.

Aaron House (☎ 835702; aaron_house_iom@yahoo .com; The Promenade, Port St Mary; s/d £30/60) This splendid Victorian-style B&B has fussed over every detail, from the gorgeous brass beds and claw-foot baths to the old-fashioned photographs on the walls – it's like stepping back in time, minus the inconvenience of cold and discomfort. The sea views are simply sensational.

PEEL & AROUND

The west coast's most appealing town, Peel has a fine sandy beach but its real attraction is the 11th-century **Peel Castle** (MH; adult/child £3/1.50), stunningly positioned atop St Patrick's Island and joined to Peel by a causeway.

The excellent **House of Manannan** (MH; adult/child £5/2.50; ☼ year-round) museum uses interactive displays to explain Manx history and its seafaring traditions.

A combined ticket for the castle and museum costs £7.

Three miles east of Peel is **Tynwald Hill** at St John's, where the parliamentary ceremony takes place on 5 July each year.

Sleeping & Eating

Peel has several B&Bs, including the **Fernleigh Hotel** (☎ 842435; Marine Pde; r per person from £22), which has twelve decent bedrooms and includes breakfast in its prices. For a better-than-average bite, head for the **Creek Inn** (☎ 842216; fax 843359; East Quay; mains around £7, r from £33), opposite the House of Manannan, which serves Manx queenies (a small, sweet scallop) and has self-catering rooms.

Cumbria
& The Lakes

Oh there is blessing in this gentle breeze
That blows from the green fields and from the clouds
And from the sky – it beats against my cheek
And seems half-conscious of the joy it gives.

William Wordsworth from The Prelude *(1805)*

Nestled between the Scottish Borders and the English counties of Northumberland, Durham, North Yorkshire and Lancashire, Cumbria is a dramatic, beautiful region. Dotted with cloud-capped hills, plunging valleys, mist-covered tarns and rolling fells, the landscape was shaped during the last Ice Age, when glaciers carved out some of Britain's highest mountains and deepest lakes. Due to its position between Scotland and England, Cumbria has been marked by centuries of conflict between monarchs north and south of the border, and the county is littered with abandoned castles, crumbling keeps and fortified houses. In fact, the area's human history goes back to the earliest periods of Britain's past, demonstrated by the many stone circles and prehistoric monuments scattered throughout the countryside.

Present-day Cumbria is best-known as one of Britain's top hiking destinations: with a huge network of trails, ranging from the sedate to the seriously challenging. But if walking's not your cup of tea, you could take to the lakes aboard a steam-powered gondola, delving into the area's literary heritage around Cockermouth, Hawkshead or Grasmere, or exploring the rich history of towns such as Carlisle and Penrith. William Wordsworth never felt the desire to leave his homeland for long, and it doesn't take much travelling in Cumbria to understand why.

HIGHLIGHTS

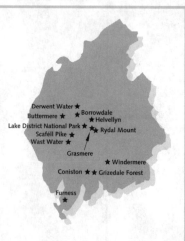

- Taking to the trails in the **Lake District National Park** (p586)
- Cruising the lakes of **Windermere** (p587), **Coniston** (p597) and **Derwent Water** (p586)
- Exploring the valleys of **Buttermere** and **Borrowdale** (p603)
- Admiring the outdoor sculptures of **Grizedale Forest** (p596)
- Following in the footsteps of Wordsworth and co at **Rydal Mount** (p594) and **Grasmere** (p594)
- Surveying the scene from **Helvellyn** (p603) and **Scaféll Pike** (p598)
- Discovering the little-known lake of **Wast Water** (p598)
- Travelling back in time among the ruins of **Furness Abbey** (p604)

Derwent Water ★
Buttermere ★ ★ Borrowdale
★ Helvellyn
Lake District National Park ★ ★★ Rydal Mount
Scaféll Pike ★
Wast Water ★
Grasmere
★ Windermere
Coniston ★ ★ Grizedale Forest
Furness ★

| ▪ POPULATION 487,610 | ▪ AREA: 2629 SQ MILES |

Activities

CYCLING

Cumbria is a good area for cycling, though the steep hills and narrow lanes can be tough going. Keen bikers could consider the waymarked 259-mile circular **Cumbria Cycle Way**. Another possibility is the 140-mile **Sea to Sea Cycle Route** (C2C) from Whitehaven or Workington, through the northern Lake District and North Pennines to Newcastle-upon-Tyne or Sunderland.

WALKING

Cumbria is crisscrossed by stunning footpaths and hiking trails, including the famous 191-mile-long **Coast to Coast**, which cuts west to east through Cumbria towards the Yorkshire Dales and the North Yorkshire Moors. The Cumbrian section, from St Bees to Shap, covers 82 miles and takes five to seven days. A more manageable option is the **Cumbria Way**, a 68-mile, five-day route from Ulverston to Carlisle. Outside the National Park, there are many walks along the often-overlooked Cumbrian coast.

OTHER ACTIVITIES

The Lake District mountains offer top rock climbing, from steep single-pitch routes to longer and less demanding classics that seasoned climbers can tackle solo.

Unsurprisingly, sailing and kayaking are also popular pastimes. Windermere, Derwent Water and Coniston are the top spots.

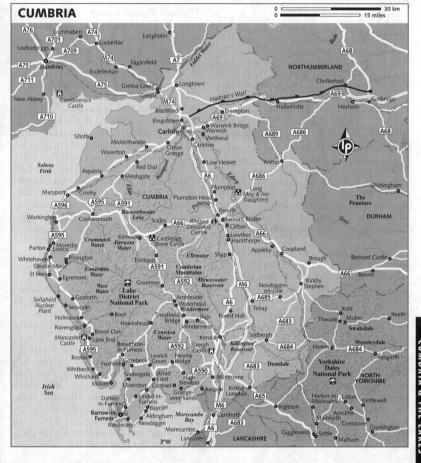

CUMBRIA

Travel Information Centres (TICs) stock a selection of leaflets, maps and guides.

Getting There & Away

There's a direct rail link from Manchester Airport via Preston and Lancaster to Barrow-in-Furness (2½ hours) and Windermere (2¼ hours). Carlisle has several bus services to Keswick. To both Windermere and Carlisle, coaches from London take about 6½ hours, trains 3½ hours.

Getting Around

Traveline (☎ 0870 608 2608; www.traveline-cumbria .co.uk; ⏰ 7am-8pm) provides travel information. TICs stock the free *Getting Around Cumbria* booklet, with timetables for buses, trains and ferries.

BOAT

Windermere, Coniston Water, Ullswater and Derwent Water all offer ferry services, providing time-saving links for walkers. The **Cross-Lakes Shuttle** (☎ 015394-45161) runs shuttle boats and minibuses between Windermere, Esthwaite Water, Grizedale and Coniston Water; cyclists and hikers are welcome. See the Windermere & Bowness (opposite), Coniston (p597) and Keswick (p600) sections for details.

BUS

The main operator is Stagecoach. Its **Explorer ticket** (1/4/7 days £8/18/25), available on the bus, give unlimited travel on services in Cumbria. Other day passes are available for specific areas or for use with First North Western trains.

Stagecoach operates some excellent buses, including No 555/556 (LakesLink) between Lancaster and Carlisle, which stops at all the main towns; No 505 (Coniston Rambler) linking Kendal, Windermere, Ambleside and Coniston; and No 517 (Kirkstone Rambler) between Bowness and Glenridding. The free booklet *Getting Around Cumbria* has comprehensive timetables.

CAR

Avoid bringing a car if you can, to limit congestion and pollution. The bus network is the best way to get around, but you could conceivably use taxis; expect to pay £1.60 to £2 per mile, with a minimum charge of £2.30.

TRAIN

Aside from the Cumbrian Coast Line and the branch line from Oxenholme to Windermere, there are several steam railways, including the Ravenglass & Eskdale Railway (p604) and the Ambleside/Bowness to Haverthwaite Steam Railway (p588).

THE LAKE DISTRICT

I wandered lonely as a cloud
That floats on high o'er dales and hills
When all at once I saw a crowd
A host of dancing daffodils…
William Wordsworth

The Lake District has long been considered one of England's most picturesque areas, and with good reason. The drama and diversity of the Lakeland landscape is unmatched anywhere else in the country – a rich tapestry of jagged mountain ridges, steep-sided valleys, glassy lakes and undulating fells that has bewitched Roman soldiers, Romantic poets and Victorian holidaymakers alike. Despite the increasing demands of mass-scale tourism and heavy industry, especially during the 19th century, the future of the Lakes was ensured when the area became Britain's largest National Park in 1951. Today the Lake District remains one of the most inspiring (and exhilarating) destinations in Britain, a haven for walkers, cyclists, sailors and mountain climbers, as well as less energetic visitors looking to drink in the views, sample a pint or two of local ale or taste some traditional Cumbrian country cooking.

Orientation

The Lake District has a rough star formation, with valleys, ridges and lakes radiating out from the high ground at its centre. The central area is crossed with countless footpaths, but few roads – a hikers' paradise. The main bases are Keswick, a regional centre for climbing and walking, and Windermere, by far the largest and busiest lake. Ambleside and Coniston make less hectic alternatives. Ullswater, Coniston and Derwent Water have a speed restriction of 10mph, and powerboats are banned on Grasmere, Crummock Water and Buttermere. Wast Water is the wildest and least accessible valley.

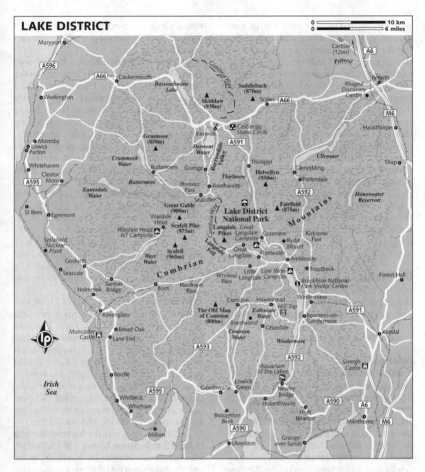

LAKE DISTRICT

Information

The region's TICs stock info on exploring the entire Lake District be it by bus, bike or foot. The Windermere and Keswick branches are excellent; both have free accommodation booking services. The national park runs nine TICs and the main **visitor centre** (☎ 015394-46601; www.lake-district.gov. uk) at Brockhole, near Windermere.

Hostels & Camping Barns

There are almost 30 YHA hostels in the Lakes. The YHA runs an **accommodation booking service** (☎ 015394-31117) and provides shuttle buses linking Ambleside, Butterlip How, Elterwater, Hawkshead, Holly How and Langdale YHAs with Windermere train station. Call **Ambleside YHA** (☎ 015394-32304) or visit www.yhalakedistrict.org.uk.

The Lake District NPA also administers several camping barns, costing around £4 per night; you need all the usual camping gear apart from a tent. Contact **Keswick Information Centre** (☎ 017687-72645) for details.

WINDERMERE & BOWNESS
☎ 015394 / pop 7950

Since the completion of the railway from Kendal in 1847, Lake Windermere, the largest lake in England, has been the first port of call for visitors travelling to the Lake District. It remains the busiest tourist centre within the boundaries of the national park. The twin towns of Bowness and Windermere were established to cater for the large numbers of Victorian tourists who arrived during the late 19th century, and the streets of the upper part of Windermere are still lined with the elegant mansion houses and grand villas in which they stayed. During the summer months, Bowness and the shores of Lake Windermere can seem closer to a seaside resort than a Lakeland beauty spot: boats of all shapes and sizes can be seen gliding across the waters of the lake, and the streets are jammed with souvenir shops, cafés, ice-cream stalls and huge crowds. Thankfully, if you're looking for a spot of peace and tranquillity, the lake itself is never far away – cruise vessels chug out across the water throughout the summer, or if you prefer travelling under your own steam, rowing dinghies and motorboats are easily available for hire.

Orientation

It's 1½ miles downhill from Windermere station to Bowness Pier. Buses and coaches leave from outside the train station. Bowness has the nicest places to eat and is the livelier place to be in the evening.

Information

Brockhole National Park Visitor Centre (☎ 46601; www.lake-district.gov.uk; ☯ 10am-5pm late Mar-Oct) Flagship visitors centre 3 miles north of Windermere on the A591.

Post office (21 Crescent Rd; ☯ 9am-5.30pm Mon-Sat)

TIC Bowness Bay Information Centre (☎ 42895; bownesstic@lake-district.gov.uk; Glebe Rd; ☯ 9.30am-5.30pm Easter-Oct, 10am-4pm Fri-Sun Nov-Mar); Windermere (☎ 46499; windermeretic@southlakeland.gov.uk; Victoria St; ☯ 9am-6pm Apr-Jun & Sep-Oct, 9am-7.30pm Jul & Aug, 9am-5pm Nov-Mar; Internet access per 10min £1) Provides a free accommodation-booking service.

Sights & Activities

The **Windermere Steamboat Museum** (☎ 45565; www.steamboat.co.uk; Rayrigg Rd; adult £3.50; ☯ 10am-5pm mid-Mar–Nov) houses a collection of steam and motor boats, including the world's oldest mechanically powered vessel, and *Esperance*, which Arthur Ransome imagined as Captain Flint's houseboat in *Swallows and Amazons*. The museum also offers trips on a small steam launch (adult £5).

The **World of Beatrix Potter** (☎ 88444; www.hop-skip-jump.com; Crag Brow; adult/child £3.90/2.90; ☯ 10am-5.30pm Apr-Sep, 10am-4.30pm Oct-Mar) has lots of models reconstructing episodes from Potter's tales. A meandering path leads to the real focus – the shop – where you can Potterise your life.

Blackwell Arts & Crafts House (☎ 46139; www.blackwell.org.uk; adult £4.75; ☯ 10am-5pm Apr-Oct, 10am-4pm Feb-Mar, Nov-Dec), 1½ miles south of Bowness, is an impressive 19th-century mansion designed by Mackay Hugh Baillie Scott. It remains one of the finest surviving examples of the Arts & Crafts movement, distinguished by its simple, elegant architecture and sense of space. Most impressive is the White Drawing Room, which looks out across the gleaming lake.

Aquarium of the Lakes (☎ 015395-30153; www.aquariumofthelakes.co.uk; Lakeside, Newby Bridge; adult £5.95; ☯ 9am-6pm Apr-Oct, 9am-5pm Nov-Mar), at the lake's southern end, recreates over 30 freshwater habitats including an underwater tunnel through Windermere's lakebed, complete with pike, arctic char and diving ducks. The best way to arrive is by boat from Bowness or Ambleside (see below).

Windermere Lake Cruises (☎ 015395-31188; www.windermere-lakecruises.co.uk) has a mix of new and old cruisers plying the lake from Bowness Pier. Regular boats run to Ambleside (adult single/return £4.50/6.65), Lakeside (adult single/return £4.60/6.85) and Ferry House (adult single/return £1.60/2.80) for Hawkshead and Hill Top. A Freedom of the Lake ticket allows unlimited cruises for 24 hours (£12). Forty-five-minute evening cruises are also available (adult £5, May to October).

Joint tickets tie in with the **Ambleside/Bowness to Haverthwaite Steam Railway** (☎ 015395-31594; return from Bowness/Ambleside £10.95/14.90; ☯ Apr-Oct) and the **Aquarium of the Lakes** (return ferry & aquarium £11.75 from Bowness, £15.70 from Ambleside).

Motorboat hire costs around £15 per hour for two adults. Rowing boats are £3 an hour.

Sleeping

BUDGET

Windermere YHA Hostel (☎ 43543; windermere@yha.org.uk; Bridge Lane, Troutbeck; dm £11.25; ☯ mid-Feb–Nov, weekends Nov–mid-Feb) This large hostel offers great lake views, 2 miles from the station. Take the A591 to Ambleside and turn right up Bridge Lane at Troutbeck Bridge. Bus Nos 555 and 559 run past Troutbeck Bridge.

Lake District Backpackers Lodge (☎ 46374; www.lakedistrictbackpackers.co.uk; High St; dm/d £12.50/30;

🖥️) A tiny, basic hostel with small dorms in a converted slate-roofed house.

Brendan Chase (☎ 45638; brendanchase@aol.com; 1 & 3 College Rd; s £30, d from £35; ☒) From the floral furniture in the lounge to the HP sauce on the breakfast tables, this Edwardian guesthouse is absolutely everything a budget British B&B should be. The rooms offer few surprises, but the location is ideal for Windermere.

Park Cliffe campsite (☎ 31344; www.parkcliffe .co.uk; Birks Rd; tent sites £12-15.20) This is a fine wooded campsite with all mod cons, a bar and restaurant. It's midway between Windermere and Newby Bridge, off the A592; bus No 618 passes the turn-off, about half a mile away.

MID-RANGE

Applegarth Hotel (☎ 43206; www.applegarthhotel .co.uk; College Rd; s £35, d from £54; P ☒) Without doubt one of the finest residences in Windermere town, this detached house has many original Victorian features including bay windows, a wood-panelled lobby, 18 elegant bedrooms and the odd stained-glass window. Highly recommended.

Archway (☎ 45613; www.communiken.com/archway; 13 College Rd; s/d from £35/40; ☒) Plain, tasteful rooms in a Victorian terrace house, tucked away down a quiet side street away from the hustle and bustle of upper Windermere. Ask for one of the upper rooms with fell views.

Denehurst (☎ 44710; www.denehurst-guesthouse .co.uk; 40 Queens Dr; d £50-80; P ☒) The quaint

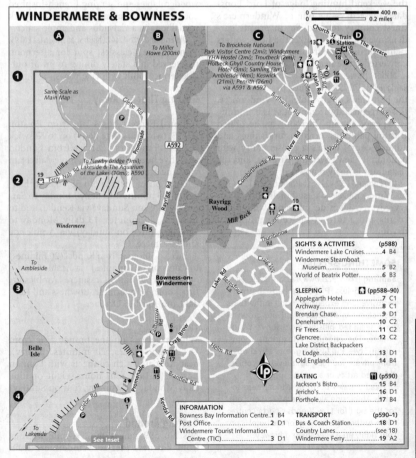

WINDERMERE & BOWNESS

0 — 400 m
0 — 0.2 miles

Same Scale as Main Map

To Miller Howe (200m)

To Brockhole National Park Visitor Centre (2mi); Windermere YHA Hostel (2mi); Troutbeck (2mi); Holbeck Ghyll Country House Hotel (3mi); Samling (3mi); Ambleside (4mi); Keswick (21mi); Penrith (26mi) via A591 & A592

Church St
Train Station
The Terrace
Station Prec

To Newby Bridge (9mi); Lakeside & The Aquarium of the Lakes (10mi); A590

Windermere

To Ambleside

Rayrigg Wood

Mill Beck

Bowness-on-Windermere

Belle Isle

To Lakeside

See Inset

SIGHTS & ACTIVITIES (p588)
Windermere Lake Cruises........4 B4
Windermere Steamboat
  Museum........................5 B2
World of Beatrix Potter........6 B3

SLEEPING 🏠 (pp588–90)
Applegarth Hotel..................7 C1
Archway..............................8 C1
Brendan Chase......................9 D1
Denehurst..........................10 C2
Fir Trees..........................11 C2
Glencree...........................12 C2
Lake District Backpackers
  Lodge..........................13 D1
Old England........................14 B4

EATING 🍴 (p590)
Jackson's Bistro..................15 B4
Jericho's..........................16 D1
Porthole...........................17 B4

INFORMATION
Bowness Bay Information Centre..1 B4
Post Office..........................2 D1
Windermere Tourist Information
  Centre (TIC).......................3 D1

TRANSPORT (p590–1)
Bus & Coach Station................18 D1
Country Lanes...................(see 18)
Windermere Ferry...................19 A2

CUMBRIA & THE LAKES

rooms of this traditional Lakeland house are full of character; some offer wrought-iron bedsteads and oak-beamed attic ceilings. On the breakfast menu are eggs Benedict, French toast and American waffles.

The area around Queens Dr and Lake Rd is full of B&Bs, including **Glencree** (☎ 45822; www.glencreelakes.co.uk; d £40-60; P ✕), a handsome riverside Victorian house, and **Fir Trees** (☎ 42272; www.fir-trees.com; Lake Rd; d £46-84; P ✕), another welcoming Victorian residence further downhill towards Bowness.

TOP END

Holbeck Ghyll Country House Hotel (☎ 32375; www.holbeckghyll.com; Holbeck Lane; s £155, d from £110 per person) This country manor house was once the weekend hunting lodge of Lord Lonsdale; these days it's one of Windermere's finest country retreats. Set in private gardens overlooking the lake, the house offers richly furnished bedrooms, with more in a converted lodge nearby.

Miller Howe (☎ 42536; www.millerhowe.com; Rayrigg Rd; d £170-250) Reckoned by some to have the best views of any hotel in Windermere, this gorgeous Edwardian house is brimming with period charm. The rooms are decorated with oil paintings, original furnishings and antique china; there's a conservatory with panoramic views over the gardens, and the restaurant is justly renowned.

Old England (☎ 42444; Church St; d £120-150) One of Windermere's oldest hotels, this is an ivy-covered lakeside mansion with plush rooms and a turn-of-the-century England flavour.

SOMETHING SPECIAL

Samling (☎ 31922; www.thesamling.com; Dove Nest; d £175-405; P ✕) Perhaps the most exclusive (and expensive) hotel in the Lake District, set in 67 acres of private grounds on a secluded hillside high above Windermere. The effortlessly luxurious rooms scream style and taste – guests can choose from private lounges, split-level balconies, A-framed attics or a private lodge.

Head 2 miles north of Windermere towards Ambleside along the A591. Look out for the sign for Low Woods Sports centre; 300m further, the turning for the hotel is on your right, up a very steep driveway.

Eating

Jericho's (☎ 42522; Birch St; mains from £16; ☽ dinner Tue-Sun) Nouveau cuisine hits the Lakes at this upmarket restaurant, run by a former head chef at Miller Howe. Choose from pan-seared turbot, wild mushroom risotto or Scotch beef fillet, delicately layered on huge plates.

Porthole (☎ 42793; 2 Ash St; mains £11-25; ☽ dinner Wed-Mon) A much-loved restaurant run by the same family for many years, offering classic Italian dishes and seafood in an intimate nautical-themed dining room. Look out for the ship's lantern above the doorway.

Jackson's Bistro (☎ 46264; St Martin's Pl; mains £9-16, 3-course meal £12.95; ☽ dinner) A popular bistro, simply furnished with booths and wooden tables and serving French-inspired cooking such as Barbary duck breast or pork medallions in a Calvados and apple sauce.

Old England (☎ 42444; Church St; afternoon tea £10.95) Windermere's classiest spot for afternoon tea, served in a stately dining room or outside terrace, both with lake views.

Getting There & Away

BUS

National Express buses run from Preston (£9.25, two hours, one daily) on to Keswick (£7.25, 45 minutes). Service from London (£27, five hours 40 minutes, three daily) run via Lancaster and Kendal.

Local buses include No 555/556 to Lancaster (45 minutes, 13 daily Monday to Saturday, three on Sunday) via Kendal, and to Keswick (50 minutes, 13 daily Monday to Saturday, three on Sunday) via Ambleside and Grasmere.

Bus No 505 goes from Kendal (20 minutes) to Coniston (40 minutes) via Ambleside.

Bus No 599 links Grasmere, Ambleside, Brockhole, Windermere, Bowness and Kendal from April to October.

TRAIN

Windermere is on the branch line from Oxenholme (£3.25, 20 minutes, hourly), near Kendal, which connects with London Euston (£61.80, four hours, eight or nine daily Monday to Saturday, four on Sunday) to Glasgow.

Getting Around

Bus No 599 makes the 1½-mile journey from Bowness Pier to Windermere train station about every half-hour. You can call a taxi on ☎ 46664.

KENDAL

☎ 01539 / pop 28,030

Kendal is known to most as the home of Kendal Mintcake – the high-energy snack made from sugar and peppermint oil that sustained Sir Edmund Hillary and Tensing Norgay on their ascent of Everest in 1953. Pre–mint cake, Kendal was founded by Norman barons, has been a market town since 1189, and was a wool and weaving centre from the Middle Ages to the 18th century ('misbegotten knaves in Kendal-green' appear in Shakespeare's *Henry IV Part I*). Its main attractions nowadays are its intriguing museums, an exceptional art gallery and a funky theatre and cinema complex.

Information

Dot Café (☎ 740313; 9.30am-5.30pm; Internet access per 10min/hr £1/5) On the first floor of Westmorland Shopping Centre.

Kendal Launderette (☎ 733754; Blackhall Rd; 8am-6pm Mon-Fri, 8am-5pm Sat & Sun)

Library (☎ 773520; Stricklandgate; 9.30am-5.30pm Mon & Tue, 9.30am-7pm Wed & Fri, 9.30am-1pm Thu, 9am-4pm Sat; Internet access per 30min £1)

Post office (75 Stricklandgate; 9am-5.30pm Mon-Fri, 9am-12.30pm Sat)

TIC (☎ 725758; www.kendaltown.org; Highgate; 9am-5pm Mon-Sat Nov-Easter, & 10am-4pm Sun Easter-Oct) Inside the town hall.

Sights & Activities

Kendal Museum (☎ 721374; www.kendalmuseum .org.uk; Station Rd; adult £3; 10.30am-5.30pm Mon-Sat Apr-Oct, 10.30am-4pm Mon-Sat Nov-Mar), housed in a former wool warehouse, displays local archaeological finds, explores the history of Kendal Castle and has a fine natural history section filled with butterflies, insects and stuffed animals. Alfred Wainwright, of *Pictorial Guide* fame, was honorary curator from 1945 to 1974 and his office and some possessions are still on show.

The **Museum of Lakeland Life** (☎ 722464; www.lakelandmuseum.org.uk; adult £3.50; 10.30am-5pm Mon-Sat Apr-Oct, 10.30am-4pm Mon-Sat Nov-Mar) is opposite the Abbot Hall Art Gallery. This atmospheric museum retraces the region's past using replica buildings and exhibits on local industries such as spinning, mining and bobbin-making. One intriguing room

recreates the study of Arthur Ransome, author of *Swallows and Amazons*.

Across the courtyard, the grand **Abbot Hall Art Gallery** (☎ 722464; www.abbothall.org.uk; adult £4.75; 10.30am-5pm Mon-Sat Apr-Oct, 10.30am-4pm Mon-Sat Nov-Mar) has a surprisingly rich collection, especially strong on watercolour landscapes and the work of local artists such as Daniel Gardner and George Romney. The gallery has links with the Tate, so it often has some superb temporary exhibitions.

It's worth clambering up to the ruins of the 13th-century **Kendal Castle**, east of the river, once owned by the family of Katherine Parr (Henry VIII's last wife), and to **Castle Howe** – the remains of a Norman motte and bailey – to the west. At the lower end of town, the 12th-century **parish church** boasts five impressive aisles and several family chapels.

Kendal Climbing Wall (☎ 721766; www.kendalwall .co.uk; Mint Bridge Rd; adult £6) has a huge indoor wall and offers courses for all levels.

Sleeping

BUDGET

Kendal YHA (☎ 0870 770 5893; kendal@yha.org.uk; 118 Highgate; dm £14.90; Mar-Aug & Dec-Jan, phone ahead at other times;) Housed in part of the 19th-century brewery building, this hostel is a little cramped, but offers pool tables and Internet access.

MID-RANGE

Lakeland Natural Vegetarian Guest House (☎ 73 3011; Low Slack, Queens Rd; www.lakelandnatural.co.uk; s/d/f £39/66/89;) A gorgeous detached Victorian house surrounded by landscaped gardens, linked with the Waterside Wholefoods café. The rooms are smart and simply furnished and the best offer sweeping views over town. The vegetarian breakfast includes Californian muffins and homemade muesli.

Highgate Hotel (☎ 724229; www.highgatehotel.co .uk; 128 Highgate; s/d £35/54;) Near the centre of town, this 18th-century townhouse once belonged to the town doctor and now combines period character with all the mod cons (TV, hairdryers and en-suite bathrooms). A small patio and garden area are available for guest use.

Heaves Hotel (☎ 560396; www.heaveshotel.co.uk; Heaves; s/d from £33/58;) A few miles south of Kendal, near Sizergh Castle, this wonderful family mansion is set in 10 acres of formal gardens and offers a taste of Cumbrian country living. Many of the rooms have four-poster beds and there's a grand hallway, elegant lounge, and even a billiard room.

Other B&B options include **Headlands Hotel** (☎ 732464; 53 Milnthorpe Rd; s/d from £30/50; ✗), the pick of several standard guesthouses clustered along Milnthorpe Rd, and **Martindales** (☎ 724028; 9/11 Sandes Ave; s/d £30/50; ✗), a small, unassuming guesthouse near the train station with chintzy rooms and floral carpets to match.

Eating
RESTAURANTS
Green Room & Vats Bar (☺ from 10am Mon-Sat) Attached to the Brewery (see opposite), serving drinks and café food (salads, wraps, pizza and pasta £4 to £8) by day and a more sophisticated menu by night.

Castle Dairy (☎ 730334; 26 Wildman St; 3 courses £19.95; ☺ lunch & dinner Tue-Sat, lunch Sun) Housed within the rough stone walls of the oldest house in Kendal, this homely restaurant specialises in regional country cooking: game pâté, poached egg florentine, braised venison and *coq au vin* are the order of the day.

Chang Thai Restaurant (☎ 720387; 54 Stramongate; mains £7-12; ☺ dinner Tue-Sun) An excellent Thai restaurant catering for Kendal's spicier side, with a varied menu based around regional curries, seafood and vegetarian dishes.

Paulo Gianni's (☎ 736581; 21a Stramongate; mains £6-8; ☺ lunch & dinner) A popular Italian restaurant, usually packed with office workers during happy hours (noon to 2pm and 5.30pm to 6pm) when pizza and pasta dishes are half price. There's a smart café-bar next door.

CAFÉS
Waterside Wholefoods (☎ 729743; Kent View, Waterside; lunches £4-8; ☺ 8.30am-4.30pm Mon-Sat) Come here for great vegetarian food served by the river, with a selection of sandwiches, chillis, soups and quiches and a mouth-watering range of homemade cakes and organic teas to follow.

1657 Chocolate House (☎ 740702; www.thechocolatehouse.co.uk; 54 Branthwaite Brow) For all things chocolatey, this Kendal institution is hard to beat. Upstairs the frilly café sells cakes, teas and endless varieties of hot chocolate; downstairs, there's a homemade chocolate shop

where you can pick up those all-important bars of mintcake.

Drinking
There are lots of pubs in Kendal where you can down a few local ales – try the rambling **Burgundy's Wine Bar** (Lowther St), the traditional **Olde Fleece** (Highgate) or the **Ring O' Bells** (Kirkland Ave), which stands on consecrated ground.

For more contemporary drinking, **Mint** (☎ 734473; 48-50 Highgate) boasts steel fittings and stone flagstones, and turns into a popular nightclub at weekends. Light meals and free Internet access are available, too.

Entertainment
Once a brewery that supplied much of Westmorland's beer, the excellent **Brewery** (☎ 725133; Highgate; www.breweryarts.co.uk) complex is now the focus of Kendal's arts scene with two cinemas, a theatre and regular programmes of film, dance and live music.

Getting There & Around
BUS
Useful buses include the No 106/107 from Kendal to Penrith (1¼ hours, eight daily Monday to Saturday) and No 505/505S from Windermere, Ambleside, Hawkshead and Coniston (two daily). No 555/556 stops at Kendal, Windermere, Ambleside, Grasmere and Keswick (five to 10 daily).

TRAIN
Kendal train station is on the branch line to Windermere (£2.80, 15 minutes) from Oxenholme. It's 2 miles south of town, with regular trains from Carlisle (£13, one hour) and London Euston (£61.80, four hours).

AROUND KENDAL
Three miles south of Kendal is **Sizergh Castle** (☎ 560070; castle & gardens adult £5.50, gardens only £3; ☺ gardens 12.30-5.30pm, castle 1.30-5.30pm Sun-Thu Apr-Oct), centred around a 14th-century *pele* tower (fortified dwelling). Much of the interior is Elizabethan including some carved chimney pieces and the wood panelling of the Inlaid Chamber, sold to London's Victoria & Albert Museum during hard times and returned after 100 years.

Two miles further south is **Levens Hall** (☎ 560321; www.levenshall.co.uk; bus No 555/556; house & garden £7.50, gardens only £5.80; ☺ gardens 10am-5pm, house noon-5pm Sun-Thu Apr–mid-Oct), which is another impressive Elizabethan manor built around a 14th-century *pele* tower. The house has some great paintings, Jacobean furniture and an unusual leather-panelled dining room. The topiary garden (designed in 1694) could have come straight from *Alice in Wonderland*.

AMBLESIDE
☎ 015394 / pop 3070

Ringed by hills and craggy peaks, Ambleside is one of the Lake District's main walking and climbing bases. Its narrow cobbled streets are packed with B&Bs, teashops, quaint restaurants and rugged walkers taking a day's break from the fells, and though little of the old market town remains, the fine Victorian mansions and grey stone town houses are crammed with Lakeland character. If you're planning on heading for the hills, Ambleside makes an excellent base camp.

Information
Laundromat (☎ 32231; Kelsick Rd; 10am-6pm)
Library (☎ 32507; Kelsick Rd; 10am-5pm Mon, Wed & Thu, 10am-7pm Tue & Fri; Internet access per hr £2)
Post office (☎ 33267; Market Pl; 9am-5pm Mon-Fri, 9am-12.30pm Sat)
TIC (☎ 32582; www.amblesideonline.co.uk; Market Cross; 9am-5pm)

Sights & Activities
The **Armitt Museum** (☎ 31212; www.armitt.com; Rydal Rd; adult £2.50; 10am-5pm) explores Keswick's history and has some interesting stuff on Lake luminaries, including John Ruskin and Beatrix Potter (though her early botanical drawings are strictly for the completist).

The TIC has heaps of walks information. The **Loughrigg circuit** is 7 miles from the Rydal Rd car park to Grasmere Lake and back via woods, farmland and steep hills. For a shorter 2-mile walk, head for the Stockghyll Force waterfall, east of Ambleside. You can return to Ambleside through farmland or continue to Troutbeck, returning via Jenkyn's Crag, a rocky outcrop offering superb views of Windermere – a 7-mile round trip.

Ambleside is on the **Windermere Lake Cruises** route (p588).

Sleeping
BUDGET
Ambleside Backpackers (☎ 32340; www.englishlakes backpackers.co.uk; dm £13.50; P X 🖳) Good inde-

pendent hostel with 72 beds in a converted cottage. If the dorms seem crammed, head for the wood-floored lounge and spacious dining room.

Ambleside YHA Hostel (☎ 0870 770 5672; amble side@yha.org.uk; Windermere Rd; dm £14.40; P X 🖳) A mile south of Ambleside, this huge lakeside house is one of the YHA's flagship hostels. The doubles are understandably popular – book well ahead.

Low Wray (☎ 32810; www.lowwraycampsite.co.uk; tent sites £10-14.50; Easter-Oct) An NT campsite 3 miles south of Ambleside on the western shore of Windermere. Catch bus No 505 and ask to be dropped off as near as possible to Low Wray, then it's a 1-mile walk.

MID-RANGE
Church St and Compston Rd are packed with mid-range B&Bs.

Compston House Hotel (☎ 32305; www.compston house.co.uk; Compston Rd; d from £48; X) Ambleside's self-styled American B&B, where all the rooms are named after American states and decorated accordingly (think sunny Florida and maritime Maine). You can even order a stack of homemade pancakes for breakfast, complete with maple syrup.

Lakes Lodge (☎ 33240; www.lakeslodge.co.uk; Lake Rd; s/d £30/45-60; X 🖳) This unusual option offers a more modern B&B experience: laminate floors, purple-and-cream dining tables and sleek, understated bedrooms equipped with funky beds and DVD players.

Old Vicarage (☎ 33364; www.theoldvicarage.co.uk; Vicarage Rd; d £65-70; P X) No prizes for guessing who this ivy-clad Victorian house used to belong to; these days it's a lovely B&B surrounded by private gardens near Rothay Park. The chintzy wallpaper and frilly curtains are a touch old-fashioned, but it's still a comfortable choice.

TOP FIVE COUNTRY HOTELS

- **Langdale Chase** (p594; Ambleside)
- **Old Dungeon Ghyll Hotel** (p597; Langdale Pikes)
- **Samling** (p590; Windermere)
- **Bridge Hotel** (p603; Buttermore)
- **Holbeck Ghyll** Country House Hotel (p590; Windermere)

Other recommendations:

3 Cambridge Villas (☎ 32307; www.3cambridgevillas .co.uk; Church St; s/d £20/45) Central town house with just a modicum of flounce.

Melrose Hotel (☎ 32500; www.melrose-guesthouse.co .uk; Church St; s/d from £25/50) Pleasant, spacious rooms in a terraced house.

TOP END

Langdale Chase (☎ 32201; www.langdalechase.co.uk; d £130-188) A magnificent 19th-century lake-side mansion, embellished by crenellated turrets and stone verandas, once used as the setting for Alfred Hitchcock's *The Paradine Case*. Oak-panelled rooms, grand mahogany staircases, gorgeous rooms and a private boathouse are just the start.

Grey Friar Lodge Hotel (☎ 33158; www.cumbria -hotels.com; Clappersgate; d £56-116; P ✕) A charming, ivy-covered Victorian house in private gardens near the River Brathay, near Ambleside in Clappersgate. The rambling rooms are filled with antiques and bric-a-brac, and most have four-poster beds and river views.

Eating & Drinking

Lucy's on a Plate (☎ 31191; www.lucysofambleside.co.uk; Church St; mains £7-14; ☯ 10am-9pm) Lucy's started out as a specialist grocery and has now expanded into this charismatic café-restaurant, furnished with rough wooden tables and old church chairs. Choose from the bistro-style menu or a blackboard of daily specials.

Lucy 4 (☎ 34666; 2 St Mary's Lane; tapas £4-8; ☯ dinner) Lucy's latest venture is this laid-back wine bar and tapas restaurant. The twin levels are divided between smoking and nonsmoking areas.

Zeffirelli's Wholefood Pizzeria (☎ 33845; Compston Rd; pizza £5.50-7.45; ☯ lunch & dinner) Offers great pizzas served in a dimly lit dining room or a buzzy garden-room café. Zeffirelli's also runs the cinema next door; the 'Double Feature' menu includes cinema tickets and a two-course meal.

Glass House (☎ 32137; Rydal Rd; ☯ lunch & dinner) This swish Mediterranean and British restaurant is housed in a three-storey conversion of a 16th-century watermill, with millwheels, cogs and machinery left intact.

Other recommendations:

Golden Rule (☎ 32257; Smithy Brow) Popular pub with walkers, away from the tourist buzz.

Pippins (☎ 31338; 10 Lake Rd) Reliable café serving full English breakfasts, jacket potatoes and sandwiches.

Royal Oak (☎ 33382; Market Pl) Lively pub with outside tables, attracting a younger crowd.

Shopping

Compston Rd has enough equipment shops to launch an assault on Everest, with branches of **Rohan** (☎ 32946), **Hawkshead** (☎ 35255) and the **YHA Adventure Shop** (☎ 34284). The **Climber's Shop** (☎ 32297) hires out boots and other equipment.

Getting There & Around

Bus No 555 (and No 599 from April to October) regularly travels from Grasmere (20 minutes), to Windermere (15 minutes) and Kendal (45 minutes).

From April to October, No 505 runs from Coniston (35 minutes, 11 daily Monday to Saturday, six on Sunday), and from Kendal (30 minutes, twice daily Monday to Saturday, once on Sunday) via Windermere.

Bike Treks (☎ 31505; Compston Rd; half/full-day £10/14) hires out bicycles.

AROUND AMBLESIDE
Rydal Mount

William Wordsworth lived at **Rydal Mount** (☎ 33002; www.rydalmount.co.uk; adult £4.50, gardens only £2; ☯ 9.30am-5pm Mar-Oct, 10am-4pm Wed-Mon Nov-Feb) from 1813 to 1850. Set in a hectare of gardens (largely designed by Wordsworth, with terraces and a summerhouse in which to compose), the house is still owned by the poet's descendants. In contrast to the pokey charm of Dove Cottage, Rydal Mount feels like a family home; exhibits include Wordsworth's pen, ink stand and picnic box, and a portrait of the poet by the American artist Henry Inman. On the top floor, you can wander around Wordsworth's study, and below the house you'll find **Dora's Field**, planted with daffodils in memory of the poet's beloved daughter, who died of tuberculosis.

The house is located 1½ miles northwest of Ambleside, just off the A591. Bus No 555 (and No 599 from April to October) – between Grasmere, Ambleside, Windermere and Kendal – stops at the end of the drive.

GRASMERE
☎ 015394 / pop 2700

Ringed by woods, fells and meadows, the slate-stone village of Grasmere is one of the most alluring in the Lakes. Though the village streets are crammed with tourists in summer, the quiet lake itself is undisturbed by motorboats, and there are countless walks leading into the countryside and woods nearby. For many years Grasmere was Wordsworth's adopted home; Dove Cottage and Rydal Mount are both nearby, ensuring a steady flow of poetry pilgrims. Wordsworth is buried under the yew trees of St Oswald's churchyard with his wife Mary and beloved sister Dorothy; nearby is the grave of Coleridge's son, Hartley.

The **TIC** (☎ 35245; Red Bank Rd; ⏰ 9.30am-5.30pm daily Mar-Oct, 10am-3.30pm Sat & Sun Nov-Feb) has some great walking leaflets and can help with finding local accommodation.

Sights
Dove Cottage (☎ 35544; www.wordsworth.org.uk; adult £5.95; ⏰ 9.30am-5.30pm), just off the A591 on the outskirts of Grasmere, is where Wordsworth wrote many of his greatest poems. The white-walled, rose-covered cottage was once a pub and the higgledy-piggledy ceilings, slate floors and roaring fireplaces are enormously atmospheric. Entrance is managed by timed tickets to avoid overcrowding, and an entertaining half-hour guided tour is included in the admission price.

Next door, the **Wordsworth Museum** (admission included with Dove Cottage) houses fascinating letters, journals and manuscripts by Wordsworth and his illustrious friends.

Sleeping
BUDGET
Butterlip How YHA Hostel (☎ 0870 770 5836; grasmere @yha.org.uk; dm £11.90) North of the village, off Easedale Rd, this converted house set in private gardens makes a good base for exploring Grasmere and the lake.

Thorney How YHA Hostel (contact Butterlip How; dm £10.60; ⏰ Apr-Oct) For more seclusion, head for this remote farmhouse, 15 minutes uphill from Grasmere.

Grasmere Hostel (☎ 35055; www.grasmerehostel .co.uk; Broadrayne Farm; dm £14.50) An excellent independent hostel inside a former farmhouse, offering dorms and rooms with en suite, and a Nordic sauna. It's a mile north along the A591; bus No 555 stops at the end of the road on request.

MID-RANGE & TOP END
How Foot Lodge (☎ 35366; www.howfoot.co.uk; Town End; d £52-60; P ✗) Near Dove Cottage, this

stately Victorian villa, owned by the Wordsworth Trust, offers wonderfully plain rooms with views over the garden towards Grasmere Lake.

Beck Allans (☎ 35563; www.beckallans.com; College St; d £52-73; P ✗) Though recently built, this handsome house resembles a much older Lakeland property. Accommodation is divided between smart rooms, self-catering apartments and a charming wood-panelled 'showman's wagon' in the garden.

White Moss House (☎ 35295; www.whitemoss.com; Rydal Water; d £144-188, cottage £99pp; P ✗) Tucked away on the road between Grasmere and Windermere, this much-admired hotel occupies an elegant house that once belonged to Wordsworth. There are five rooms in the main house, filled with trinkets and antiques, and two further bedrooms in a detached cottage.

Other recommendations:
Grasmere Hotel (☎ 35277; www.grasmerehotel.co.uk; Broadgate; d £70-100; P ✗) Flouncy, expensive rooms in an imposing mansion alongside the River Rothay.

Harwood Hotel (☎ 35248; www.harwoodhotel.co.uk; Red Lion Sq; d from £59; P ✗) Sweet rooms (some with lacy four-poster beds) above Harwood's Deli.

Riversdale (☎ 35619; www.riversdalegrasmere.co.uk; White Bridge; d £54-70; P ✗) Simple B&B in a stone cottage on the edge of Grasmere village.

Eating
Dove Cottage Tea Rooms & Restaurant (☎ 35268; mains £9-13; ⏰ tearooms 11am-5pm, restaurant dinner Tue-Sat) A quaint, oak-beamed café-restaurant furnished with dried flowers and wooden tables, serving light lunches and cakes by day and a Mediterranean-flavoured menu in the evening.

Sara's Bistro (☎ 35266; 2 Broadgate; mains £10-12; ⏰ lunch & dinner Tue-Sun) This cheery bistro serves 'chubbie' sandwiches (£3.50 to £4.50) and baguettes, burgers and salads at lunchtime, and more sophisticated dishes like poached salmon and oven-baked chicken after 6pm.

Sarah Nelson's Gingerbread Shop (☎ 35428; www .grasmeregingerbread.co.uk; Church Stile; ⏰ 9.15am-5.30pm Mon-Sat) One of Grasmere's most famous establishments, this minuscule cake shop has been trading in the old village schoolhouse since 1854. Follow your nose as you leave the churchyard.

Travellers Rest Inn (☎ 35604; www.lakedistrictinns .co.uk; mains from £8; d from £74; P ✗) A much-refurbished 16th-century coaching inn on the edge of Grasmere village, with great pub food and comfortable rooms. The only drawback is the A591 running past its door.

Getting There & Away

Bus No 555 runs from Ambleside to Grasmere (20 minutes), stopping at Rydal church and outside Dove Cottage. The seasonal No 599 runs from Kendal via Bowness (one hour, four daily April to October).

HAWKSHEAD

☎ 015394 / pop 1703

With its quaint whitewashed buildings, cobblestone streets and countryside setting, the village of Hawkshead is so picturesque it could have been constructed for the benefit of sightseers. Parking is provided on the outskirts of the village, so it's almost traffic-free.

The **TIC** (☎ 36525; hawksheadtic@lake-district.gov .uk; 🕑 9.30am-5.30pm Apr-Oct, 9.30am-6pm Jul & Aug, 10am-3.30pm Fri, Sat & Sun Nov-Mar) is beside the main car park.

The **Hawkshead Grammar School** (adult £1; 🕑 10am-12.30pm & 1.30-5pm Mon-Sat, 1-5pm Sun Apr-Sep, 1-4.30pm Oct), across Main St from the TIC, was founded in 1585. Unused since 1909, the schoolhouse is set out much as it was when its most famous pupil, William Wordsworth, attended (1779–87) – you can still see the desk on which the young poet painstakingly carved his name.

The **Beatrix Potter Gallery** (NT; ☎ 36355; Red Lion Sq; adult £3; 🕑 10.30am-4.30pm Sat-Wed Apr-Oct) houses the original watercolours from Potter's books in the former offices of her husband, solicitor William Heelis. Entry is by timed ticket.

Sleeping & Eating

Croft Camping & Caravanning (☎ 36374; www.hawk shead-croft.com; North Lonsdale Rd; tent sites £12-14.25; 🕑 mid-Mar–mid-Nov) A pleasant, grassy campsite just east of the town centre.

Hawkshead YHA Hostel (☎ 0870 770 5856; hawks head@yha.org.uk; dm £11.60; 🖳) A mile south on the road to Newby Bridge, this fine Regency building overlooks Esthwaite Water. Bus No 505/506 passes here and stops in Hawkshead village.

Ann Tyson's Cottage (☎ 36405; www.anntysons.co .uk; Wordsworth St; s/d from £27.50/55; 🗶) A delightful cob-walled cottage just off the main square, covered with colourful hanging baskets in summer. Wordsworth boarded here while attending school in Hawkshead, and all the rooms retain their traditional character.

Ivy House Hotel (☎ 36204; www.ivyhousehotel.com; Main St; d £102-106; 🅿 🗶) A superior B&B with a touch of Kensington elegance – plush sofas and antique rugs in the sitting room, wooden four-poster beds in the bedrooms upstairs. The main house has six rooms and there are five more in the Mere Lodge behind.

The village pubs offer good food and accommodation, including the flower-fronted **Queens Head** (☎ 36271; www.queensheadhawkshead .co.uk; Main St; s/d from £46.50/60; 🗶) and the old **Kings Arms** (☎ 36372; www.kingsarmshawkshead.co.uk; The Square; s/d from £38/66).

Minstrels Gallery (☎ 36423; The Square; lunches £4-8) Dating from the 15th century, this gorgeous little teashop is the top place in the village for light lunches and sticky treats.

Getting There & Away

Hawkshead is linked with Windermere, Ambleside and Coniston by bus No 505 (April to October). The **Cross-Lakes Shuttle** (☎ 015394-45161; No 525) climbs to Hilltop (10 minutes, 10 daily July to September, weekends only April to June and November) before connecting with Windermere cruise boats to Bowness.

AROUND HAWKSHEAD
Grizedale Forest

Stretching across the hills between Coniston Water and Esthwaite Water is Grizedale Forest, a dense woodland whose name derives from the Old Norse for wild boar. Since 1977 artists have been fashioning outdoor sculptures in the forest. There are now more than 90 scattered through the park, including a wooden xylophone, a wave of carved ferns and a huge 'man of the forest'. The **Grizedale Visitors Centre** (☎ 01229-860010; www.grizedale.org; 🕑 10am-5pm Easter-Oct, 11am-4pm Nov-Easter) provides information on trails and sells a guide (£3) to the forest sculptures.

The **Cross-Lakes Shuttle** (☎ 015394-45161; bus No 525) runs from Hawkshead to Grizedale (ten daily July to September, weekends only April to June and November).

Hill Top

Beatrix Potter wrote many of her best-known stories in this picture-postcard **farmhouse** (NT; ☎ 36269; adult £4.50; 🕑 10.30am-4.30pm Sat-Wed

Apr-Oct) in the quiet village of Near Sawrey. Keep your eyes peeled during your visit – many of the buildings and furnishings found their way into her illustrations. Tickets are sold for set times; expect long queues during school holidays.

The house is 2 miles south of Hawkshead; bus No 505 (15 minutes, hourly) travels through the village, or you can catch the Cross Lakes Shuttle (£2.20 from Hawkshead, four daily).

CONISTON
☎ 015394 / pop 1867

Above Coniston Water, with its gliding steam yachts and quiet boats, looms the craggy, pock-marked peak known as the Old Man of Coniston (801m). The nearby village grew up around the copper mining industry; these days, there are just a few sleepy streets with two fine pubs and some tourist shops, making Coniston an excellent place for relaxing by the quiet lakeside.

Coniston is best known for the world-record speed attempts made on the lake by Sir Malcolm Campbell and his son, Donald, between the 1930s and 1960s. Donald was killed during an attempt at a record in 1967, when his jet-boat *Bluebird* flipped at 320mph. The boat and its pilot were recovered in 2001; Campbell was buried in the cemetery near St Andrew's church.

Information
Summitreks (☎ 41212; www.summitreks.co.uk; 14 Yewdale Rd) Arranges outdoor activities and hires out walking gear, as well as bikes/kayaks/canoes (£14/15/20 per day).
TIC (☎ 41533; conistontic@lake-district.gov.uk; Coniston Car & Coach Park; ⊙ 9.30am-5.30pm Easter-Oct, 10am-3.30pm Sat & Sun Nov-Easter)
Village Pantry (☎ 41155; Yewtree Rd; Internet access per 30min £2)

Sights & Activities
The **Ruskin Museum** (☎ 41164; adult £3.50; ⊙ 10am-5.30pm) explores Coniston's history, touching on copper mining, Arthur Ransome and the Campbell story. It's also an excellent introduction to John Ruskin, the great Victorian art critic and social campaigner, who bought the nearby house of **Brantwood** (☎ 41396; www .brantwood.org.uk; adult £5.50; ⊙ 11am-5.30pm mid-Mar–mid-Nov, 11am-4.30pm Wed-Sun mid-Nov–mid-Mar) in 1871 and spent the next twenty years expanding and modifying it. The end result is

undoubtedly the finest country estate in the Lake District, incorporating the lavish mansion and 250 acres of landscaped gardens, pastures and woodland. To see Brantwood at its best, it's essential to arrive by boat.

Rescued from dereliction by the NT, the steam yacht **Gondola** (☎ 63850; adult £5.50; five daily Apr-Oct) was first launched on Coniston Water in 1859. The luxurious saloons are refurbished and the boat runs like clockwork between Brantwood and Coniston Pier.

The modern **Coniston Launch** (☎ 36216; www .conistonlaunch.co.uk; north/south lake cruise £4/6) offers cruises on the lake in both directions. The North Lake boat calls at four jetties including Brantwood; the South Lake cruise sails to Lake Bank at the lake's southern end.

Sleeping
Coniston Hall Campsite (☎ 41223; tent sites £8-15; ⊙ Easter-Oct) A lovely lakeside campsite, a mile south of town.

Holly How YHA Hostel (☎ 0870 779 5770; conist onhh@yha.org.uk; Far End; dm £11.80; ⊙ mid-Jun–Nov) A converted slate house set in private grounds near the village, with reasonable dorms and a few double rooms.

Coppermines YHA Hostel (☎ 0870 770 5772; dm £10.60; ⊙ daily Apr-Sep, Tue-Sat Sep-Oct) The former mine manager's house now makes a great hiking hostel, located in a spectacular mountainside setting. Be warned – the access road is very rough.

SOMETHING SPECIAL

Old Dungeon Ghyll Hotel (☎ 37272; www.odg .co.uk; s £41, d from £82; P ✗) Nestled at the base of the Langdale Pikes, this famous old establishment is perhaps the Lake District's quintessential hotel. It's a classic Lakeland inn decked out with antique furniture, period features, solid wood doors and faded carpets; the snug, traditional rooms are endearingly old-fashioned, and though not all have an en suite, the inspirational fell views can't be bettered anywhere else in the Lakes. The real heart of the hotel is in the Walker's Bar, with its roaring fire, white cob walls and hearty welcome after a long day's hike. There are many more luxurious hotels, but none of them can match the Old Dungeon Ghyll for charm and character.

CUMBRIA & THE LAKES

Beech Tree Vegetarian Guest House (☎ 41717; Yewtree Rd; s/d from £30/40; P ✕) A dedicated vegetarian guesthouse with its own tree-shaded garden, located in the old town vicarage. Some of the vibrant rooms share a bathroom; others have private showers.

Oaklands (☎ 41245; www.oaklandsconiston.co.uk; Yewdale Rd; s/d £25/45-50; P ✕) Across the road, this slate-walled private house has a homely family feel, with pastel-coloured rooms and bouncy pocket-sprung beds.

Eating

Black Bull (☎ 41335; Yewdale Rd) This creaky, whitewashed free house is the town's oldest pub and the home of the Coniston Brewing company, which makes its own Bluebird beer.

Bluebird Café (☎ 41649; Lake Rd; lunches £4-6; ✉ breakfast & lunch) Delicious open sandwiches, jacket potatoes and cakes are served in this lakeside café. The outside terrace is usually packed on sunny summer days.

Sun Hotel (☎ 41248; www.thesunconiston.com; mains £8.50-16; s/d from £35/70; P ✕) This gabled turn-of-the-century establishment is the most atmospheric inn in Coniston, just uphill from the village. There's an oak-beamed bar, a conservatory restaurant, and lots of photos of the Bluebird expedition – Donald Campbell had his headquarters here during his fateful campaign.

Getting There & Around

From April to October, bus No 505 runs from Windermere (50 minutes, eight daily Monday to Saturday, six on Sunday) via Ambleside; it also runs from Kendal (one hour 10 minutes, two daily Monday to Saturday).

WASDALE
☎ 019467

Hemmed in by some of the country's highest peaks (including Scaféll Pike and Great Gable), and surrounded by gravel-strewn walls of scree, the wild lake of Wast Water is the deepest lake in the Lake District (79m) and one of the least-visited. It's much harder to get to than the other lakes, it's reached via the Hardknott Pass or from the coast.

Wast Water YHA Hostel (☎ 0870 770 6082; wastwater@yha.org.uk; Wasdale Hall; dm £10.60; ✉ daily Apr-Aug, Thu-Mon Feb-Mar & Sep-Oct, Fri & Sat Nov-Feb) A

19th-century Gothic mansion on the lakeshore, 4 miles south of Wasdale Head.

Wasdale Head Campsite (NT; ☎ 26220; www.wasdalecampsite.org.uk; tent sites £10) A National Trust campsite offering peace and solitude beneath the Scaféll Range.

Wasdale Head Inn (☎ 019467-26229; www.wasdale.com; d £48-98; P ✕) An atmospheric hiker's inn huddled beneath the surrounding mountains near the shore of Wast Water, and an old favourite with hill-goers. Despite its rustic appearance, the hotel is warm, welcoming and very comfortable. Its modern rooms have en suites and there's a wood-panelled resident's lounge, a rustic restaurant and a classic hiker's bar serving the inn's home-brewed beer.

The **Barn Door Shop** (☎ 26384) sells guides and maps and oversees the useful Wasdale website (www.wasdaleweb.com). A short walk away is the tiny parish church; its cemetery is sprinkled with memorials to mountain walkers.

The only public transport to Wast Water is the **Wasdale Taxibus** (☎ 019467-25308), which runs between Gosforth and Wasdale Head on Thursday, Saturday and Sunday – phone to book a seat.

BIZARRE ENGLAND

The Bridge Inn at Stanton Bridge near Wasdale hosts the World's Biggest Liar Competition every November in honour of Will Ritson, first landlord of the Wasdale Head Inn, who used to regale his customers with extravagant folklore. Alternatively, you could head for the World Gurning Competition, held in mid-September in Egremont, near St Bees. To gurn is to pull an ugly face; the challenge is believed to stem from the 12th century, when the lord of the manor handed out sour crab apples to his workers. Local-born Anne Wood won the trophy 24 years running until she was finally beaten in 2001.

COCKERMOUTH
☎ 01900 / pop 7450

Just outside the Lake District National Park, Cockermouth rarely receives as many visitors as the better-known Lakeland towns further south, despite some fine Georgian architecture and a clutch of intriguing museums (including Wordsworth's boyhood home). Consequently, the town makes a good base for exploring the northern reaches of the national park, especially the valleys of Buttermere and Borrowdale.

Information

Library (☎ 325990; Main St; 9.15am-7pm Mon & Wed, 9.15am-5pm Tue & Fri, 9.15am-12.30pm Thu, 9.15am-1pm Sat; Internet access per 30min £1) You'll need to book for Internet access.

Post office (South St; 8am-6pm Mon-Sat) Inside the Lowther Went shopping centre.

TIC (☎ 822634; email@cockermouth-tic.fsnet.co.uk; 9.30am-4.30pm Mon-Sat Apr-Jun & Oct, 9.30am-4pm Jan-Mar, Nov & Dec, 9.30am-5pm & 10am-2pm Sun Jul-Sep) Inside the town hall.

Sights

Wordsworth House (NT; ☎ 824805; Main St; adult £3.50; 11am-4.30pm Mon-Fri Apr-Oct, plus Sat Jun-Aug), was the birthplace and early home of William Wordsworth and his sister Dorothy. Built in 1745 and now operated by the National Trust, the house contains some intriguing Wordsworth memorabilia and original furniture.

Jenning's Brewery (☎ 821011; www.jenningsbrewery.co.uk; adult £4.50) has been churning out traditional ales since 1874. The hour-long factory tours include the chance to sample several brews: choose from traditional Cumberland Ale, Cocker Hoop or the fantastically named Sneck Lifter.

Cumberland Toy & Model Museum (☎ 827606; www.toymuseum.co.uk; Banks Ct; adult £3; 10am-5pm Mar-Oct, 10am-4pm Feb & Nov) houses a cornucopia of dusty dollhouses, train sets and Meccano models guaranteed to delight big and little kids alike.

Castlegate House Gallery (☎ 822149; www.castlegatehouse.co.uk; 10.30am-5pm Mon-Wed, 10.30am-5pm Fri & Sat, 2-5pm Sun), opposite **Cockermouth Castle**, exhibits local artists' work in Georgian surroundings and modern sculpture in its walled garden. The castle itself dates from the 12th century and is now a private residence.

Just outside town is the **Lakeland Sheep & Wool Centre** (☎ 822673; www.sheep-woolcentre.co.uk; Egremont Rd; adult £4; 9.30am-5.30pm, 4 shows Sun-Thu Mar-Nov), which houses the Western Lake District Visitor Centre and puts on daily sheep-themed shows, including shearing, shepherding and dog-handling.

Sleeping

BUDGET

Cockermouth YHA Hostel (☎ 0870 770 5768; cockermouth@yha.org.uk; Double Mills; dm £9.50; Apr-Oct) This 26-bed hostel occupies a 17th-century water mill on the southern edge of town. From Main St follow Station St, then turn left into Fern Bank Rd; the hostel is down a track off Fern Bank Rd.

Rose Cottage (☎ 822189; www.rosecottageguest.co.uk; s/d £35/50) Several flowery rooms in a pretty cottage B&B just outside town.

Simple, good-value B&B options include the **Rook** (☎ 828496; www.therookguesthouse.gbr.cc; 9 Castlegate; s £20, d from £32), a restored 17th-century townhouse with plain, snug rooms, and **Strathearn Guest House** (☎ 826749; www.smoothhound.co.uk/hotels/castlegate; 6 Castlegate; d from £40), which has old-fashioned accommodation in another period house across the road.

MID-RANGE & TOP END

Croft House (☎ 827533; www.croft-guesthouse.com; 6/8 Challoner St; s/d £32/47-50; P ⊠) This lovingly converted Georgian house is the best B&B in town. The rooms are in a modern metropolitan style, with contemporary furniture, and there's a daily changing breakfast menu including fruit salad and Spanish omelettes.

Allerdale Court (☎ 823654; www.allerdalecourthotel.co.uk; Market Pl; s/d from £45/70; P ⊠) In the heart of old Cockermouth, this cosy, traditional hotel offers a selection of rooms, the best of which have corner baths and four-poster beds, and two in-house restaurants: a relaxed Italian (mains £6 to £14) and a formal British dining room (set menu £18.95).

Eating & Drinking

Quince & Medlar (☎ 823579; 13 Castlegate; www.quinceandmedlar.co.uk; mains from £12.65; dinner Tue-Sat) If national awards and glowing reviews are anything to go by, this is probably the best vegetarian restaurant in England. Tuck into a sumptuous red-onion tart or a timbale of broad beans and butternut squash in one of the wood-panelled dining rooms.

Cockatoo Restaurant (☎ 826205; 16 Market Pl; mains £11-15; lunch Wed-Mon, dinner Mon & Wed-Sat) Once a bog-standard fish-fry, the Cockatoo has recently been transformed into a modern bistro serving regional recipes and locally caught seafood – and the takeaway still does the best fish and chips for miles around.

Over the Top (☎ 827016; 36 Kirkgate; ☺ lunch & dinner Wed-Sat) A tiny café furnished with wooden dressers and mismatched tables, usually crammed with a local crowd.

Bitter End (☎ 828993; Kirkgate) This welcoming pub is Cumbria's smallest brewery and serves a selection of excellent homemade ales and good lunch-time grub.

Getting There & Away

Bus No 600 travels to and from Carlisle (one hour, eight daily Monday to Saturday). Nos X5 and X4 between Workington, Keswick and Penrith also stop at Cockermouth (15 daily Monday to Saturday, six on Sunday).

KESWICK

☎ 017687 / pop 4990

Keswick is the Lake District's busy northern centre, a blue-slate market town jostling with B&Bs, pubs, cream-tea outlets and outdoor shops. The town is situated near the shores of Derwent Water, a glassy arc surrounded by fells and dense woodland, studded with five forested islands that could have fallen straight from the pages of *Swallows and Amazons*. Keswick was a centre of the graphite-mining industry in the 16th century; today it's an important walking base, with access to the Cumbria Way and countless trails criss-crossing the surrounding hills.

Information

Keswick Launderette (☎ 75448; Main St; ☺ 7.30am-7pm)

Post office (☎ 72269; 48 Main St; ☺ 9am-5.30pm Mon-Fri, 9am-12.30pm Sat)

TIC (☎ 72645; www.keswick.org; Moot Hall, Market Pl; ☺ 9.30am-5.30pm Apr-Oct, 9.30am-4.30pm Nov-Mar)

U-Compute (☎ 72269; 48 Main St; ☺ 9am-5.30pm; Internet access per hr £2.99) Above the post office.

Sights

People flock to the **Pencil Museum** (☎ 73626; www.pencils.co.uk; Southy Works; adult £2.50; ☺ 9.30am-4pm) to pay homage to the humble pencil, which was first mass-produced in Keswick – attractions include a mine reconstruction, pencil sculptures and the dubious draw of the world's largest pencil.

The classically Victorian **Museum & Art Gallery** (☎ 73263; Station Rd; adult £1; ☺ 10am-4pm Apr-Oct) displays original manuscripts from Wordsworth, Ruskin, Southey and Sir Hugh Walpole, and some fascinating archaeological and natural history exhibits housed in old-fashioned glass cases.

Cars of the Stars Motor Museum (☎ 73757; www.carsofthestars.com; Standish St; adult £4; ☺ 10am-5pm) is a must-see for car junkies. Its fleet of celebrity vehicles includes Chitty Chitty Bang Bang, Herbie the Love Bug, a Batmobile, KITT from *Knightrider* and the Delorean from *Back to the Future*.

Activities

Keswick Climbing Wall & Activity Centre (☎ 72000; www.keswickclimbingwall.co.uk; ☺ 10am-9pm), behind the Pencil Museum, organises outdoor activities including canoeing, abseiling, rock climbing and cycling.

George Fisher (☎ 72178; 2 Borrowdale Rd) is an outdoor-equipment shop with gear for hire.

BOAT TRIPS

The **Keswick Launch Company** (☎ 72263; www.keswick-launch.co.uk; Mar-Nov) calls at seven landing stages around the lake: Ashness Gate, Lodore Falls, High Brandlehow, Low Brandlehow, Hawse End, Nichol End and back to Keswick. Boats leave every half-hour, clockwise and anticlockwise (adult return £5.70, 50 minutes); single fares are also available. The service operates six to eight times daily from December to mid-March. There's also an evening cruise at 7.30pm in summer, which includes a free glass of wine (one hour, adult £6.20, May to September).

Kayaks, windsurfers, rowboats and motorboats are available from **Nichol End Marine** (☎ 73082; Nichol End).

WORTH THE TRIP

A mile east of Keswick stands **Castlerigg Stone Circle**, a mysterious loop of 48 stones believed to be between 3000 and 4000 years old, set on a hilltop surrounded by a brooding amphitheatre of mountains. The purpose of the circle is uncertain (current opinion is divided between a Bronze Age meeting place and a celestial timepiece), but one thing's for certain – those prehistoric builders certainly knew a good site when they saw one. The views in all directions are truly breathtaking.

The TIC has a good leaflet (50p) outlining a 4-mile circular walk from the centre of Keswick.

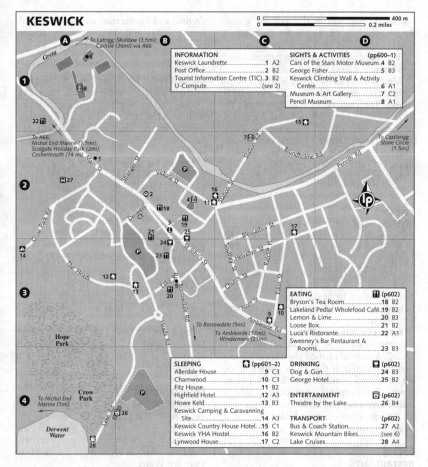

KESWICK

WALKING

Keswick's youth hostels make useful bases for local hikes. Walkers could consider climbing to Skiddaw House YHA Hostel and Caldbeck along the Cumbria Way, or catching the launch to the lake's southern end (see Boat Trips, left) and walking up Borrowdale.

Sleeping

BUDGET

Keswick YHA Hostel (☎ 0870 770 5894; Keswick@yha .org.uk; Station Rd; dm £11; ✕ 🖳) A fine 91-bed hostel in a refurbished wool mill beside the river. The small dorms are very pleasant and some have balconies overlooking Fitz Park. Bike hire is also available.

Local campsites include **Scotgate Holiday Park** (☎ 78343; www.scotgateholidaypark.co.uk; adult/ car £4/2), 2 miles from town (take bus No X5), and **Keswick Camping & Caravanning Club Site** (☎ 72392; Crow Park Rd; tent sites from £15.35) near the lake.

MID-RANGE

Fitz House (☎ 74488; www.fitzhouse.co.uk; 47 Brundholme Tce; d from £40) A splendid B&B in a period town house overlooking Fitz Park, with four rooms and a holiday flat. There's a gorgeous patio and a plant-filled conservatory, complete with fridge, glasses and corkscrew for an early-evening tipple.

Howe Keld (☎ 72417; www.howekeld.co.uk; 5-7 The Heads; s/d £33-35/46-70; 🅿 ✕) Fifteen bright rooms are available in this popular guest-house, which is renowned for its banquet breakfast (choices include air-cured bacon, homemade granola, Canadian pancakes and vegetarian rissoles).

Almost every house along Southey, Blencathra, Helvellyn and Eskin Sts offers B&B rooms. Top choices include **Charnwood** (☎ 74111; 6 Eskin St; d from £48), a listed Victorian residence with stencilled bedrooms; slate-fronted **Lynwood House** (☎ 72398; www.lynwoodhouse.net; 35 Helvellyn St; d from £42); and **Allerdale House** (☎ 73891; 1 Eskin St; d from £40), a stone-walled town house covered in climbing roses.

TOP END
Highfield Hotel (☎ 72508; www.highfieldkeswick.co.uk; The Heads; d with dinner from £100; P ✕) The pick of the Victorian mansions along The Heads, with an impressive array of period features (turrets, bay windows, a grand veranda and even a converted chapel). The best rooms are front facing and have small balconies, with gorgeous views all the way to the lake.

Keswick Country House Hotel (☎ 0845-458-4333; www.thekeswickhotel.co.uk; Station Rd; s/d from £104/124; P ✕) A taste of turn-of-the-century grandeur is on offer at this huge, ornate hotel, set in formal grounds a little way out of town. The steepled, brick-built façade is impressive enough; inside you'll discover an elegant lounge, lavish bedrooms and a beautiful conservatory.

Eating
RESTAURANTS
Lemon & Lime (☎ 73088; 31 Lake Rd; mains £6-14; ✆ lunch & dinner) A new restaurant with a mix of international dishes (fajitas, Cajun red snapper, Thai green curry and Malaysian spicy noodles) served in the relaxed, light-filled dining room.

Luca's Ristorante (☎ 74621; High Hill; starters £3-7.50, mains £8-18; ✆ dinner Tue-Sun) An upmarket Italian restaurant housed in a former school-house, offering classic dishes and more unusual fare (monkfish and salmon skewers, or spinach and ricotta *rotolo*).

Loose Box (☎ 772083; Kings Arms Courtyard; mains £5-6) A good choice for generous, authentic pizzas, attached to the Kings Arms Hotel.

Sweeney's Bar Restaurant & Rooms (☎ 772990; 18-20 Lake Rd; mains £7-12) A recently renovated English and Mediterranean restaurant with leather sofas and contemporary cuisine; pleasant rooms are available upstairs.

CAFÉS
Lakeland Pedlar Wholefood Café (☎ 74492; www.lakelandpedlar.co.uk; Hendersons Yard; mains £5-8; ✆ 9am-5pm) An outstanding vegetarian café with wooden tables and a great Tex-Mex/organic menu. The veggie breakfasts and fair-trade coffee are the perfect way to start to the day.

Bryson's Tea Room (☎ 72257; 42 Main St; meals £6; ✆ Apr-Dec, Mon-Sat Jan-Mar) One of the best-known bakeries in the Lakes now offers an upstairs café serving salads, cakes and light lunches. Try the fruit cake and homemade florentines.

Drinking
George Hotel (☎ 72076; 3 St John's St) This white-washed pub (the oldest in Keswick) was once at the heart of a lucrative racket smuggling pencil materials; nowadays it's a terrific place to hide away a hearty pub lunch.

Dog & Gun (☎ 73463; 2 Lake Rd; mains around £6) Low-ceilinged and flagstone-floored, this town pub is another good spot for a pint of local ale.

Entertainment
Theatre by the Lake (☎ 74411; www.theatrebythelake.com; Lakeside) The Lake District's only repertory theatre company stages new and classic drama in its impressive purpose-built building, which is located on the shores of Derwent Water.

Getting There & Away
BUS
No 555/556 (the LakesLink) connects Keswick with Ambleside (40 minutes), Windermere (50 minutes) and Kendal (1½ hours) at least 10 times daily Monday to Saturday.

The X4/X5 travels from Penrith to Workington via Keswick (14 daily Monday to Saturday, six on Sunday).

Getting Around
Bikes can be hired from **Keswick Mountain Bikes** (☎ 75202; 1 Daleston Ct) and **Keswick Climbing Wall & Activity Centre** (☎ 72000; www.keswickclimbingwall.co.uk) for £15 per day.

For taxis, call **Davies Taxis** (☎ 72676), **Keswick Taxis** (☎ 75585) or **Skiddaw Taxis** (☎ 75600).

BORROWDALE & BUTTERMERE VALLEYS
☎ 017687

Ringed by wooded hills, emerald valleys and granite outcrops, and dotted with little villages and isolated farmhouses, Borrowdale and Buttermere are arguably the most beautiful valleys in the Lake District. With thrilling access to mighty peaks and low-level jaunts, both valley's are a walker's dream, especially during the summer; but the valleys are at their best in autumn, when the oaks and yew trees blaze with colour and the holiday crowds have left for home.

Borrowdale

The valley of Borrowdale stretches for 6 miles from the northern end of Derwent Water to Honister Pass. The valley's stunning position beside Derwent Water and its proximity to Scaféll, Scaféll Pike and Great Gable make it popular with walkers.

The **Derwentwater YHA Hostel** (☎ 0870 770 5792; derwentwater@yha.org.uk; Barrow House; dm £11.80; ☒ Feb-Nov, weekends Nov-Jan) Two miles from Keswick in an extraordinary setting overlooking the lake, this grand manor house was built in the early 19th century; features include extensive grounds and a man-made waterfall.

Borrowdale Hotel (☎ 77224; www.borrowdale hotel.co.uk; d £70-105; P ☒) Three miles from Keswick along the B5289, this impressive stone-fronted hotel occupies a wonderful position backed by woods and rocky peaks. The smart, wallpapered bedrooms all have good views and huge beds – the superior rooms are regal and worth the extra cost.

Around Borrowdale

A couple of miles south of Borrowdale is the small village of **Grange-in-Borrowdale**. Nearby, the valley winds into the jagged ravine known as the **Jaws of Borrowdale**, a famous hiking spot with world-renowned views, especially from the 985-foot **Castle Crag**.

Buttermere

Beyond the tiny village of Seatoller and over the windswept Honister Pass (one of the region's richest slate-mining areas), the main road plummets into the beautiful valley of Buttermere. The road skirts around the edge of Buttermere Lake before reaching beautiful Buttermere village, 4 miles from

Honister and 9 miles from Keswick. From Buttermere, the B5289 cuts north along the eastern shore of Crummock Water.

Buttermere YHA Hostel (☎ 0870 770 5736; buttermere@yha.org.uk; dm £11.60) is a beautiful 70-bed slate house overlooking Buttermere Lake, with views of Red Pike and High Stile.

Fish Hotel (☎ 70253; www.fish-hotel.co.uk; 2-night minimum d £124; P ☒) is an old-fashioned hotel that was once the home of the famous 'Maid of Buttermere', an 18th-century beauty whose admirers included Wordsworth and Coleridge. These days the Maid may have gone but there are still pleasant rooms, good beer and a roaring fire.

Bridge Hotel (☎ 70252; www.bridge-hotel.com; d £126-150 incl dinner; P ☒) offers luxurious accommodation, right in the centre of Buttermere village, with a choice of standard rooms and lavish suites, complete with hill-view balconies and antique furniture.

GETTING THERE & AWAY

Bus No 77/77A services the Buttermere valley four times daily, Easter to October, departing from Keswick bus station.

ULLSWATER & AROUND
☎ 017684

Encircled by trees, patchwork fields and solid stonewalled villages, the silvery curve of Ullswater stretches for 7½ miles between Pooley Bridge and Glenridding and Patterdale to the south. Despite being the second-largest lake, it's much less visited than Windermere and Derwent Water, though in summer it can get crowded along the western edge.

Seven miles south from Pooley Bridge, the riverside town of Glenridding is the busiest of the villages near Ullswater. Helvellyn (949m), the second-highest peak in the Lakes, looms up nearby, and Glenridding makes a great base for tackling the summit. The nearby village of Patterdale, with its wind-worn slate and white houses, is also worth exploring.

Ullswater Information Centre (☎ 82414; glen riddingtic@lake-district.gov.uk; Beckside car park; ☒ 9am-6pm Apr-Oct, 9.30am-3.30pm Fri-Sun Nov-Mar) is a mine of information on local walks.

Ullswater 'Steamers' (☎ 82229; www.ullswater-steamers.co.uk; adult return £6.70-9.30) chug across the lake from Pooley Bridge to Glenridding via Howtown. Steamboats started plying the lake in 1859 but the current vessels, *Lady*

(in operation since 1887) and *Raven* (since 1889), have been converted to conventional power.

The remote **Helvellyn YHA Hostel** (☎ 0870 770 5862; helvellyn@yha.org.uk; Greenside; dm £10.60; ☺ Jul-Aug, phone ahead at other times), 1½ miles from Glenridding, is mainly popular with walkers setting out for Helvellyn. The rough road makes vehicle access tricky.

Completely refurbished in 2001, the old Lakeland-stone **Inn on the Lake** (☎ 82444; www.inn onthelakeullswater.co.uk; s/d £65/118-170) offers a se-lection of modernised rooms, ranging from richly decorated doubles to palatial four-poster suites; lake-view rooms are, unsur-prisingly, the most expensive.

Decent food and beer are served at the **Traveller's Rest** (☎ 82298; mains £6-10), a down-to-earth pub popular with folk from the campsite nearby.

Getting There & Around
Bus No 108 runs from Penrith to Patterdale, calling in at Pooley Bridge and Glenridding (six daily Monday to Saturday). Bus No 517 runs from Bowness Pier to Glenridding (three daily late-July to August, weekends only end-March to July).

CUMBRIAN COAST

It's not the most conventionally beautiful shoreline in Britain, but the rugged Cum-brian coast has a wild grandeur all its own. To the south is the broad, sandy sweep of Morecambe Bay, with interesting sights in the surrounding countryside, including Cartmel Priory, the ruins of Furness Abbey and the bustling town of Ulverston.

Getting Around
The Cumbrian Coast railway line loops 120 miles from Carlisle to Lancaster (both on the main line between London and Glas-gow). Trains run hourly and a single ticket costs £19. Phone ☎ 08457 484950 for full details. At Ravenglass you can change for the narrow-gauge **Ravenglass & Eskdale Railway** (☎ 01229-717171; www.ravenglass-railway.co.uk; adult £8.20), affectionately known as *La'al Ratty*, and originally built in 1875 to carry iron ore. The miniature trains chug along a beautiful 7-mile track into Eskdale and the foothills of the Lake District mountains.

CARTMEL PRIORY
The magnificent 12th century **priory** (☎ 36261; ☺ 9am-5.30pm May-Oct, 9am-3.30pm Nov-Apr) escaped demolition during the dissolution of the monasteries thanks to its status as a par-ish church. Although much of the original glass was destroyed, the 45-foot-high 15th-century **east window** remains glorious and on sunny days the church fills with intense light. The carved choir stalls date from 1440 and the church houses many ornate tombs. Look out for the skulls and hourglasses carved in the floor – 17th- and 18th-century remind-ers of mortality.

FURNESS ABBEY
The rose-coloured ruins of **Furness Abbey** (EH; ☎ 823420; adult £3; ☺ 10am-6pm Apr-Sep, 10am-5pm Oct, 10am-4pm Wed-Sun Nov-Mar) are hidden away in the 'Vale of Deadly Nightshade', 1½ miles north of Barrow-in-Furness. Founded in the 12th century, Furness became one of the most powerful Cistercian abbeys in the north of England, but in 1537 it became one of the first victims of the dissolution. Part of the north and south transepts and the grand bell tower are still standing and the atmospheric ruins are scattered with carved arches and elegant vaulting, hinting at the abbey's former grandeur. An audio guide is included in the admission price.

Bus Nos 6 and 6A from Ulverston to Barrow-in-Furness pass by the abbey on a regular basis.

RAVENGLASS & AROUND
It's quite difficult to imagine the tiny vil-lage of Ravenglass, a quiet cluster of sea-side houses, 27 miles north of Barrow, as an important Roman port. The Romans were drawn to its sheltered harbour, but all that remains of their substantial fort are the walls of a 4th-century **bath house**, half a mile from the train station down a signposted track.

The main attraction in Ravenglass is the much-loved narrow-gauge **Ravenglass & Esk-dale Railway** (☎ 01229-717171; www.ravenglass-railway .co.uk; adult £8.20), affectionately known as *La'al Ratty*, and originally built in 1875 to carry iron ore. The miniature trains chug along a beautiful 7-mile track into Eskdale and the foothills of the Lake District mountains. There's an interesting **museum** at the station, as well as the **Ratty Arms**, a family-friendly pub with good grub. A Wainwright booklet called *Walks from Ratty* (£1.50) is available from the railway.

A mile south of Ravenglass is **Muncaster Castle** (☎ 01229-717614; www.muncaster.co.uk; gardens adult £6, castle adult/child £2.50/1.50; ⏰ gardens 10.30am-6pm, castle noon-5pm Sun-Fri), a grand crenellated castle dating from the 14th century and rebuilt in the 19th. Audio tours explore the castle's history and hauntings, and the huge grounds include an owl centre and an impressive maze.

The controversial **Sellafield Nuclear Power Plant**, a huge local employer, is 5 miles north of Ravenglass. There is a curiously popular **visitors centre** (☎ 019467-27027; www.sellafield.com; admission free; ⏰ 10am-6pm Apr-Oct, 10am-4pm Nov-Mar) which houses Sparking Reaction, a huge-scale interactive exhibition created by the Science Museum in London.

Accommodation is almost nonexistent in Ravenglass. The most interesting place to stay locally is the former **Coachman's Quarters** (☎ 01229-717614; s/d £35/50-60; Ⓟ), in the grounds of Muncaster Castle, which have been converted to provide spacious, comfortable double rooms.

Ravenglass is on the Cumbrian Coast Line, with frequent links north and south along the coast. Bus No 6 from Whitehaven stops at Ravenglass and terminates at Muncaster (70 minutes, five daily). Bus X6 travels the same route on Sunday (four daily).

NORTH & EAST CUMBRIA

Though the dramatic landscapes of the central Lakes are undoubtedly Cumbria's main attraction, the rest of the county – dotted with small rural towns, wild moorland and wind-battered farms – is also well worth exploring, as is the county's only city, Carlisle, best known for its impressive castle and red-sandstone cathedral. South of Carlisle is the old market town of Penrith, which stands at the northern end of the lush Eden Valley.

CARLISLE

☎ 01228 / pop 71,780

The solid redbrick town of Carlisle has been in the frontline of England's defences for the last thousand years. Sacked by the Picts, razed by the Vikings, battered by the Scots and terrorised by the Border Reivers, its stormy location near the Scottish border has left it with a wealth of historical sights including the massive sandstone castle and the remnants of the old town walls, as well as Cumbria's only cathedral. Nowadays a small student population and the lively after-dark scene keep old Carlisle young at heart – but looking out from the castle ramparts or Hadrian's Wall nearby, it's not hard to imagine the bloodiness of bygone days.

History

A Celtic camp or *caer* (preserved in the name of Carlisle) provided an early military station for the Romans. After the construction of Hadrian's Wall, Carlisle became the Romans' administrative centre in the northwest. Following centuries of intermittent conflict between Picts, Saxons and Viking raiders, the Normans seized Carlisle from the Scots in 1092 and William Rufus began construction of the castle and town walls.

The English continued to develop Carlisle as a military stronghold throughout the Middle Ages, constructing the city walls, citadels and the great gates. During the Civil War, Royalist Carlisle was an important strategic base; the city was eventually taken, battered and starving, by the Roundhead Scottish army after a nine-month siege.

Peace only came to Carlisle with the Restoration. The city's future as an industrial centre was sealed with the arrival of the railways and the first cotton mills during the Industrial Revolution.

Orientation

From the M6, the main routes into town are London Rd and Warwick Rd. The train station is south of the city centre, a 10-minute walk from Town Hall Sq (also known as Greenmarket) and the TIC. The bus station is on Lonsdale St, about 250m east. Most of the town's B&Bs are dotted along Victoria Pl and Warwick Rd.

Information

@Cybercafé (☎ 512308; www.atcybercafe.co.uk; 8-10 Devonshire St; ⏰ 8am-10pm Mon-Sat, 10am-10pm Sun; per hr £3) Internet access.
Cumberland Infirmary (☎ 523444; Newtown Rd) Half a mile west of the city centre.

Ottakar's (☎ 542300; 66 Scotch St; ☼ 9am-5.30pm Mon-Sat, noon-4pm Sun) Large chain bookshop stocking new titles and local books.

Police station (☎ 528191) Just north of Town Hall Sq off Scotch St.

Post office (20-34 Warwick Rd)

TIC (☎ 625600; http://historic-carlisle.org.uk; Greenmarket; ☼ 9.30am-5pm Mon-Sat Mar-Jun & Sep-Oct, 9.30am-5.30pm Mon-Sat Jul, 9.30am-6pm Mon-Sat Aug, 10.30am-4.30pm Sun Easter-Aug, 10am-4pm Mon-Sat Nov-Feb)

Sights & Activities
CARLISLE CASTLE

English Heritage's brooding, rust-red **Carlisle Castle** (EH; ☎ 591922; adult £3.80; ☼ 9.30am-6pm Apr-Sep, 10am-4pm Oct-Mar) was built on the site of Celtic and Roman fortresses. The Norman

keep was built in 1092 by William Rufus; Mary Queen of Scots was briefly imprisoned here in 1568 after losing the Scottish throne. A maze of passages and chambers winds around the castle. The castle also houses the **Kings Own Royal Border Regiment Museum**, which tells you all you'd ever want to know about Cumbria's Infantry Regiment. There are daily castle tours (adult/child £1.50/50p, April to September).

CARLISLE CATHEDRAL

The city's red sandstone **cathedral** (☎ 548151; donation £2; ☼ 7.30am-6.15pm Mon-Sat, 7.45am-5pm Sun) was originally constructed as a priory church in 1122. During the 1644-45 siege by Parliamentarian troops, two-thirds of the nave

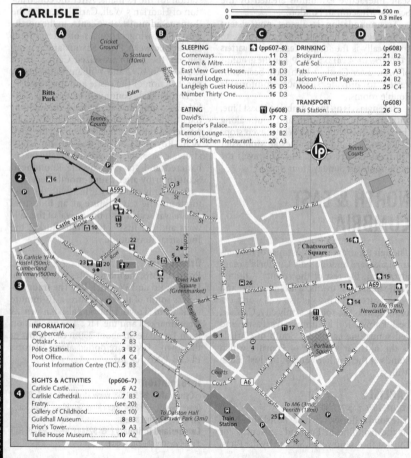

CARLISLE

INFORMATION	
@Cybercafé	1 C3
Ottakar's	2 B3
Police Station	3 B2
Post Office	4 C4
Tourist Information Centre (TIC)	5 B3

SIGHTS & ACTIVITIES	(pp606–7)
Carlisle Castle	6 A2
Carlisle Cathedral	7 B3
Fratry	(see 20)
Gallery of Childhood	(see 10)
Guildhall Museum	8 B3
Prior's Tower	9 A3
Tullie House Museum	10 A2

SLEEPING	(pp607–8)
Cornerways	11 D3
Crown & Mitre	12 B3
East View Guest House	13 D3
Howard Lodge	14 D3
Langleigh Guest House	15 D3
Number Thirty One	16 D3

EATING	(p608)
David's	17 C3
Emperor's Palace	18 D3
Lemon Lounge	19 B2
Prior's Kitchen Restaurant	20 A3

DRINKING	(p608)
Brickyard	21 B2
Café Sol	22 B3
Fats	23 A3
Jackson's/Front Page	24 B2
Mood	25 C4

TRANSPORT	(p608)
Bus Station	26 C3

was torn down to help repair the city wall and castle. Serious restoration didn't begin until 1853 but a surprising amount survives, including the east window and part of the original Norman nave.

Among the notable features are the 15th-century misericords, the very fine 14th-century east window, the lovely Brougham Triptych in the north transept and some ornate choir carvings.

Surrounding the cathedral are other priory relics including the 16th-century **Fratry** (monks dining room; see p608) and the **Prior's Tower**.

TULLIE HOUSE MUSEUM

This excellent **museum** (☎ 534781; Castle St; www .tulliehouse.co.uk; adult £5.20; ☼ 10am-5pm Mon-Sat, noon-5pm Sun Apr-Oct, 10am-4pm Mon-Sat, noon-4pm Sun Nov-Mar) brings Carlisle's history to life. Highlights include a reconstruction of Hadrian's Wall, a lively audiovisual display on the **Border Reivers** (see boxed text, below) and the Whispering Wall, a glass wall that plays local stories through miniature speakers.

Outside, there's a rotunda with great views of Carlisle Castle (which can be reached by an underground walkway from the museum) and a beautifully preserved Georgian town house containing the museum's **gallery of childhood**.

THE BORDER REIVERS

From the Middle Ages to the mid-16th century, the Scottish Borders (known as the Debatable Lands) were terrorised by the Reivers, feuding families who fought and robbed the English, the Scots and each other, and struck fear into the hearts of the local populace. For the Reivers sheep rustling, looting, pillaging, highway robbery and homestead burning became a way of life. Northern Cumbria, Northumberland and the Scottish Borders are littered with small castles, keeps and *peles*, designed to offer some protection against the Reivers' attacks.

It wasn't until James VI of Scotland succeeded Elizabeth I of England and united the two countries that order was finally reasserted. The Reivers are responsible for giving the words 'blackmail' and 'bereaved' to the English language.

GUILDHALL MUSEUM

This small **museum** (☎ 532781; Greenmarket; ☼ noon-4.30pm Tue-Sun Apr-Oct; admission free) houses a modest local-history collection. The most interesting exhibit is the building itself – constructed in about 1405 and later occupied by the trade guilds, it's now the last medieval structure in Carlisle.

Sleeping
BUDGET

Cornerways (☎ 521733; www.cornerwaysguesthouse.co .uk; 107 Warwick Rd; s/d from £20/40; P ☒) A listed Victorian town house on the corner of Warwick Rd and Hartington Pl, offering plain rooms and decorative bedspreads.

East View Guest House (☎ 522112; 110 Warwick Rd; s £25, d from £45; P ☒) On the other side of the road from Cornerways, this simple, no-frills B&B makes a good-value base near the city centre. The nicest rooms here are the larger doubles set back from the main road.

Carlisle YHA Hostel (☎ 0870 770 5752; dee.carruth ers@unn.ac.uk; Bridge Lane; dm £14.50; ☼ Jul-Sep) Housed in the Old Brewery Residences (university halls), next to the castle; open only during the university's summer holidays.

MID-RANGE

Howard Lodge (☎ 529842; pat90howardlodge@aol .com; 90 Warwick Rd; s/d/tr from £25/36/45; P ☒) Another redbrick townhouse along Warwick Rd, offering chintzy comfort, pastel-shaded rooms and some attractive period features including Victorian fireplaces and original cornicing.

Langleigh Guest House (☎ 530440; www.langleigh house.co.uk; 6 Howard Pl; s/d £26/47.50; P ☒) The pick of the mid-range B&Bs around Warwick Rd, arranged over several floors and impeccably restored in Victorian style with ornate furniture, mirrors, tiled fireplaces and tasteful prints.

TOP END

Number Thirty One (☎ 597080; www.number31.free servers.com; 31 Howard Pl; s/d from £60/85; P ☒) Half upmarket B&B, half hotel, this award-winning town house offers three luxurious bedrooms decorated in a quirky style (Mediterranean tones, pastel blues or Oriental baroque). From the bubbling fish tank in the kitchen to the lavishly decorated dining room, this is one B&B that simply oozes class.

Crown & Mitre (☎ 525491; www.crownandmitre-hotel-carlisle.com; English St; s/tw from £79/90; P ✗ ⑤) The oldest, grandest hotel in town, housed in a splendid red-brick Edwardian building on the main square. The highlight is the impressive lobby backed by the original staircase and stained-glass windows, but the plush, modern rooms are very respectable too.

Eating

Emperor's Palace (☎ 402976; Warwick Rd; mains from £8; ☯ dinner Tue-Sun) A top-notch Chinese restaurant; takeaway is available, but discerning diners choose to eat in the main dining room surrounded by gilt Buddhas and Chinese screens.

David's (☎ 523578; 62 Warwick Rd; mains £10-18; ☯ lunch & dinner Tue-Sat) Refined, modern British cuisine served in a smart, converted townhouse, with a menu ranging from sautéed venison to roast cod in Parma ham.

Lemon Lounge (☎ 546363; 18 Fisher St; set menu £18; ☯ lunch & dinner Tue-Sat) Tucked down an alleyway near the cathedral, this lively Mediterranean-flavoured bistro serves light meals and good coffee either in the snug dining room or a walled courtyard.

Prior's Kitchen Restaurant (☎ 543251; lunches £4-6; ☯ 9.45am-3pm or 4pm Mon-Sat) Carlisle's most unusual dining experience can be found beside the cathedral in the Fratry (monks dining room), where you'll find light lunches and afternoon tea served in a vaulted cellar.

Drinking

Café Sol (☎ 522211; 31 Castle St; ☯ 9.30am-6pm Mon-Wed, 9.30am-11pm Thu, 9.30am-midnight Fri & Sat) Near the cathedral, this funky café is decorated with Warhol-style prints and opens late at weekends. Sandwiches and coffee are served by day, beer and cocktails by night.

Jackson's/Front Page (☎ 596868; 4-8 Fisher St) This dingy bar/club is a Carlisle institution and runs nights featuring anything from drum'n'bass to blues and karaoke.

Brickyard (☎ 512220; 14 Fisher St) Housed in the former Memorial Hall, this is the best venue in town for gigs and live music.

Fats (☎ 511774; 48 Abbey St; ☯ 11am-11pm) A funky, open-plan bar and one of the city's top nightspots, boasting exposed stone walls, slate floors, plush sofas and a smooth, urban ambience.

Mood (☎ 520383; www.mood.uk.com; 70 Botchergate; ☯ 11am-2am Mon-Sat, noon-12.30am Sun) Carlisle's contribution to the designer-bar genre. Is it so named because of the lurid purple-and-orange décor, or because of the staff's demeanour? Who cares – it's open till late.

Getting There & Away
BUS
Carlisle is one of Cumbria's main transport hubs. Direct buses run by National Express include London (£28.50, seven hours, three or four daily; other services travel via Preston and Birmingham), Glasgow (from £14.50, two hours, 10 daily), Manchester (£20.50, three hours, three to five daily) and Bristol (£50.50, nine hours, one direct overnight service).

Local buses include No 555/556 (the LakesLink; 3¾ hours, three daily), which passes via Keswick, Grasmere, Ambleside, Windermere and Kendal on its way to Carlisle from Lancaster; No 104 (40 minutes, 13 daily Monday to Saturday, nine on Sunday), which links Carlisle with Penrith; and AD122 (the Hadrian's Wall bus; six daily late May to late September); which connects Hexham and Carlisle in summer.

TRAIN
Regular trains run from London Euston (£72.80, four hours, nine to 11 daily).

Carlisle is the terminus for the following five scenic railways (phone ☎ 08457 484950 for timetable details and information on Day Ranger passes):

Cumbrian Coast Line Follows the coastline to Lancaster (£19, 3½ hours), with views over the Irish Sea.

Glasgow–Carlisle Line The main route to Glasgow passes through spectacular Scottish landscape – the ScotRail route is the most scenic (£27, 1½ hours).

Lakes Line Branches off the main north–south line at Oxenholme near Kendal for Windermere (£15.50, 70 minutes).

Settle–Carlisle Line Cuts southeast across the Yorkshire Dales (£13.40, 1½ hours).

Tyne Valley Line Follows Hadrian's Wall to Newcastle-upon-Tyne (£11.20, 1½ hours).

Getting Around
Call **Radio Taxis** (☎ 527575), **Citadel Station Taxis** (☎ 523971) or **County Cabs** (☎ 596789).

PENRITH
☎ 01768 / pop 14,480
Like many of the towns on the fringes of the Lakes, stout, rosy-bricked Penrith has retained much of its traditional character as a

market town and shopping centre. Many of the shops have their original façades and the streets are lined with craft stores, bakeries and traditional grocers, as well as countless places to buy country clothing and hiking equipment. There's a Tuesday market in the central square. Penrith makes a good base for exploring the Eden Valley, the eastern lakes and the North Pennines.

Information

Library (☎ 242100; St Andrew's Churchyard; ◷ Mon-Sat)
Map Room (☎ 891900; 4 Middlegate; ◷ 9.30am-5pm Mon-Fri, 9am-5pm Sat) Good for local maps and books.
TIC (☎ 867466; pen.tic@eden.gov.uk; Middlegate; ◷ 9.30am-5pm Mon-Sat, 1-4.45pm Sun) Information about the Eden Valley and accommodation booking service.

Sights

The plundered ruins of **Penrith Castle** (◷ 7.30am-9pm Easter-Oct, 7.30am-4.30pm Oct-Easter) are opposite the station. The 14th-century castle was built to resist Scottish raids, one of which razed the town in 1345. The castle was later expanded by Richard, Duke of Gloucester (better known as Richard III), but fell into disrepair in the 16th century.

Legend maintains that several worn, rounded stones in the cemetery at **St Andrew's Church** belong to an Arthurian giant's grave. In fact, the pillars are the remains of Celtic crosses.

The **Penrith Museum** (☎ 867466; admission free), inside the TIC, has some small displays on the town's history.

Sleeping

Glendale Guest House (☎ 862579; www.glendaleguesthouse.com; 4 Portland Pl; s/d £36/55; ✗) One of several friendly and accommodating B&Bs on Portland Place, offering pastel rooms and flowery bedspreads in a typically Victorian house. The huge breakfast includes Cumberland sausage, muesli and fresh fruit salad.

George Hotel (☎ 862696; www.georgehotelpenrith .co.uk; Devonshire St; s/d from £49/86) The wood-panelled lobby and dining rooms of Penrith's oldest hotel are filled with comfortable armchairs and faded photos; the comfy bedrooms share the same old-world atmosphere.

Beckfoot Country House (☎ 713241; www.beckfoot .co.uk; nr Helton; s £38, d from £76; ◷ Mar-Dec; P ✗) Five miles south of Penrith, near the small village of Helton, this cosy manor house is set in peaceful wooded gardens with views over the fells. Rooms are spacious and plainly furnished and there's a paddock behind the house for the owner's Shetland ponies.

Eating

Costas Tapas Bar & Restaurant (☎ 895550; 9 Queen St; tapas from £4.50; ◷ Tue-Sun) A lively, splendidly tacky Spanish-themed bar, with waiting staff in full flamenco gear and huge portions of tapas.

Ruhm Gallery & Café (☎ 867453; www.ruhmgallery .plus.com; 15 Victoria Rd; lunches £4-8; ◷ 9am-5pm Mon-Sat, 10am-4pm Sun) A light, relaxed place to sip your morning coffee, it also does good sandwiches and *paninis* and houses a small gallery of local artwork.

Gianni's Pizzeria (☎ 891791; 11 Market Sq; mains £5-8; ◷ Mon-Sat) Tucked away just off Market Sq, this is one of several decent Italian restaurants in Penrith. The rustic dining room is usually packed at weekends. Main dishes include chicken and seafood, as well as generous helpings of pizza and pasta.

Getting There & Away
BUS

The bus station is northeast of the centre, off Sandgate. Bus No 104 runs between Penrith and Carlisle (£4.50, 45 minutes, 16 daily Monday to Saturday, nine on Sunday).

Bus No X4/X5 connects Penrith to the Lakes and the Cumbrian coast hourly Monday to Saturday and six times on Sunday, calling at Keswick and Cockermouth before terminating at Workington.

TRAIN

Penrith has frequent connections to Carlisle (£5.90, 20 minutes, hourly) and Lancaster (£10.60, 50 to 60 minutes, hourly).

AROUND PENRITH
Rheged Discovery Centre

Housed in the largest grass-covered building in Europe, **Rheged** (☎ 01768-686000; www.rheged .com; 1 film or attraction adult/child £5.50/3.90; ◷ 10am-6pm) is cunningly disguised as a Lakeland hill, 2 miles west of Penrith. Built on a former quarry and rubbish site, the centre houses an IMAX cinema and the Helly Hansen National Mountaineering Exhibition.

The frequent No X4/X5 bus between Penrith and Workington stops at the centre.

Northeast England

Northeast England has never toed the constrictive line of England's peculiar version of civilised living. Here, you won't find tidy country lanes lined with perfectly trimmed hedges or cute punting streams. Instead, this isolated corner offers a vast countryside shaped by furious elements and an equally fearsome history. This is a region of extremes, from the wind-lashed wilderness of Northumberland National Park to the dark, brooding North Pennines and the savage, white-sand stretches of coastline.

Equally extreme is the human drama that has played out against this breathtaking backdrop. Since prehistory, humans have struggled to tame the landscape, but it took the indomitable Romans to really have a go; their legacy is the magnificent Hadrian's Wall, which served as their empire's northern frontier for nearly 300 years. The Normans, later arrivals, weren't to be outdone: they built more castles than anywhere else in the country and, in Durham, erected a cathedral that ranks among the finest in the world. Yet as magnificent as these constructions are, they merely serve to reinforce the impression that the landscape hasn't changed all that much since the whole region was part of the ancient kingdom of Northumbria.

A closer look, however, reveals some fresh scars. For nearly 700 years coal was the lifeblood of the northeast, and when the seams were sealed in the late 1980s the rusting hulk of an industrial age was left behind as well as the communities that grew up in mining's lingering shadow. They have gone to great lengths to shake off the coal dust; none more so than in the region's biggest city, Newcastle, which has transformed itself into one of the most dynamic urban centres in Britain.

HIGHLIGHTS

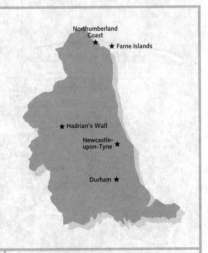

- Gettin' doon in toon with a bottle of dog – aka taking on **Newcastle's wild nightlife** (p619)
- Walking the Roman walk along magnificent **Hadrian's Wall** (p626)
- Castle-spotting along the blustery white-sand beaches of **Northumberland** (p631)
- Fending off bird-shit attacks on **Farne Islands** (p632), covered with puffins, gannets and seals
- Going Norman in **Durham** (p621), a spectacular World Heritage Site

■ POPULATION: 2,515,442	■ AREA: 3320 SQ MILES

Orientation & Information

The Pennine Hills are the dominant geological feature of Northeast England. The hills form a north–south spine that separates the region from Cumbria and Lancashire in the west and they are also the source of major rivers such as the Tees and the Tyne.

All the significant transportation routes are east of this spine, from Durham northwards to Newcastle and Edinburgh. Newcastle is also an important ferry port for Scandinavia. For more information, travellers can log on to the northeast region website at www.thenortheast.com. This is a useful resource.

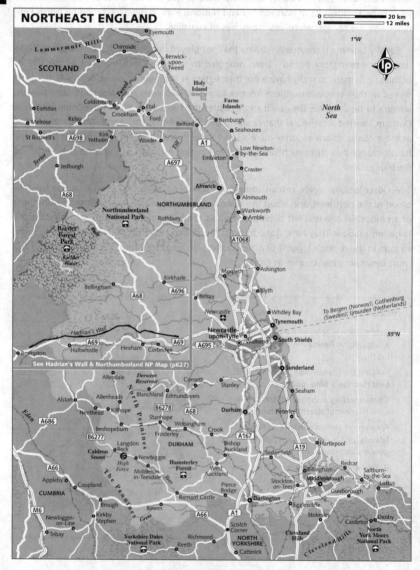

NORTHEAST ENGLAND

Activities

The Pennines' rugged moors and stunning Northumberland coast make for some top-class walking and cycling. If you're out in the open be prepared for wind and rain at any time of year, but when the sun shines, you can't go far wrong. More details on walking and cycling are given in the Outdoor Activities chapter, and suggestions for shorter routes are given throughout this chapter. Regional tourism websites all contain walking and cycling information, and Tourist Information Centres (TICs) all stock leaflets (free) plus maps and guides (usually £1 to £5) covering walking, cycling and other activities.

CYCLING

The **Coast & Castles Cycle Route** is remains a favourite option with cyclists, running south–north along the glorious Northumberland coast between Newcastle and Berwick-upon-Tweed before swinging inland into Scotland to finish at Edinburgh (this route is part of the National Cycle Network; see the boxed text, p81). The coast is exposed, though, so you should check the weather and try to time your ride so that the wind is behind you.

Another possibility is the 140-mile **Sea to Sea Cycle Route** (known as the C2C), which runs across northern England from Whitehaven or Workington on the Cumbria coast, through the northern part of the Lake District, and then over the wild hills of the North Pennines to finish at Newcastle. Five days is needed to complete the route, which is best done west to east to take advantage of the prevailing winds. The C2C is aimed at road bikes, but there are several optional off-road sections along the way.

WALKING

If you like to walk in quiet and fairly remote areas, the North Pennines and the Cheviots further north are the best in England. Long routes through this area include the famous Pennine Way, which keeps mainly to the high ground as it crosses the region between the Yorkshire Dales and the Scottish border, but also goes through sections of river valley and some tedious patches of plantation. The whole route is over 250 miles, but the 70-mile section between

Bowes and Hadrian's Wall would be a fine four-day taster.

Elsewhere in the area, the great Roman ruin of **Hadrian's Wall** is an ideal focus for walkers. There's an enormous variety of easy loops taking in forts and other historical highlights. A long-distance route from end to end is under development, with several sections already open, providing good options for anything from one to four days.

The Northumberland coastline has seemingly endless miles of open beaches, and little in the way of resort towns (the frequently misty weather has seen to that), so walkers can often enjoy this wild, windswept shore in virtual solitude. One of the finest walks is between the villages of Craster and Bamburgh via Dunstanburgh, which includes two of the area's most spectacular castles.

Getting There & Around

See p620 for details of air and sea routes to and from Newcastle.

BUS

Bus transport around the region can be difficult, particularly around the more remote parts of Northumbria in the west. Call ☎ 0870 608 2608 for information on connections, timetables and prices.

Several one-day Explorer tickets are available; always ask if one might be appropriate. The **Explorer North East** (adult/child £5.75/4.75), available on buses, covers Berwick down to Scarborough and allows unlimited travel for one day, as well as numerous admission discounts.

TRAIN

The main lines run north to Edinburgh via Durham, Newcastle and Berwick, and west to Carlisle roughly following Hadrian's Wall. Travelling to or from the south, it may be necessary to make connections at Leeds. Phone ☎ 0845 748 4950 for all train inquiries.

There are numerous Rover tickets for single-day travel and longer periods, so ask if one might be worthwhile. For example, the **North Country Rover** (adult/child £61.50/30.75) allows unlimited travel throughout the north (not including Northumberland) any four days out of eight.

NEWCASTLE-UPON-TYNE

☎ 0191 / pop 189,870

If ever there was evidence needed of the miraculous powers of urban regeneration, look no further than Newcastle. Raised and subsequently abandoned by coal and steel, the city has worked hard to cast off the yoke of industrial wasteland and has matured into a town of some grace and culture. The grand 19th-century streets that swoop elegantly down to the river have been buffed and polished and are now as beautiful as any you will see during your island travels. Along the riverfront itself – home to Newcastle's most recognisable feature, the eclectic array of seven bridges that span the Tyne – the pace of development continues unabated.

For most visitors, however, the real draw are the Geordies themselves: proud, positive and blessed (or cursed) with an ability to party unmatched virtually anywhere else in Europe. The city's nightlife is conducted on an epic, irresponsible scale, which has made it Britain's hen-and-stag capital.

ORIENTATION

The River Tyne marks the boundary between Newcastle to the north and Gateshead to the south; it's also one of the focal points for visitors to the city. Frankly, there's very little to keep you in Gateshead,

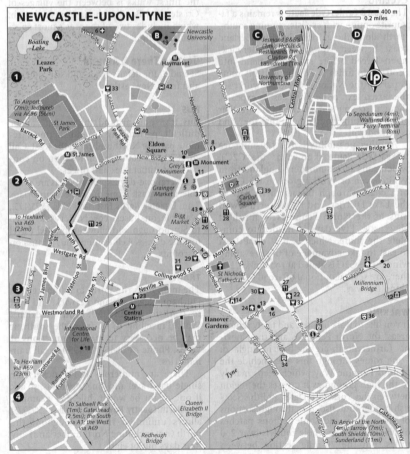

because even the sights on the south bank of the river are more easily accessible by bridge from the northern side. North from the river is Newcastle's attractive Victorian centre, which the tourist authorities insist on calling Grainger Town, although the name elicits shrugs of uncertainty from locals. Jesmond is north of the city centre, and easily reached by bus or with the excellent Metro underground system.

Central Station (train) is south of the city centre. The coach station is on Gallowgate, while local and regional buses leave from Eldon Square and Haymarket bus stations.

Maps

The Ordnance Survey's Mini-Map (£1.50) is a handy foldaway pocket map of Newcastle, but not Gateshead. The **Newcastle Map Centre** (☎ 261 5622; www.newtraveller.com; 1st fl, 55 Grey St) supplies copious amounts of maps and guides.

INFORMATION
Bookshops
Blackwell's Bookshop (☎ 232 6421; 141 Percy St)
Waterstone's (☎ 261 6140; 104 Grey St) There's another branch of this bookshop near Monument Metro, but this one is housed in a lovely building.

Emergency
Police station (☎ 214 6555; cnr Pilgrim & Market Sts)

Internet Access
Internet Exchange (☎ 230 1280; 26-30 Market St) In the same gallery as the TIC, close to Monument Metro.

Laundry
Clayton Road Laundrette (☎ 281 5055; 4 Clayton Rd, Jesmond)

Medical Services
Newcastle General Hospital (☎ 273 8811; Westgate Rd, off Queen Victoria Rd) A mile northwest of the city centre.

Money
Thomas Cook (☎ 219 8000; 6 Northumberland St) Just north of Monument; has a bureau de change.

Post
Main post office (35 Mosley St; ◷ 9am-5.30pm Mon-Fri, 9am-12.30pm Sat) In the city centre.

Tourist Information
Gateshead Quays Visitors Centre (☎ 477 5380; St Mary's Church; ◷ 10am-4pm Sat & Sun)
TIC (☎ 277 8000, booking service ☎ 277 8042; www .newcastle.gov.uk; 132 Grainger St; ◷ 9.30am-5.30pm Mon-Wed, Fri & Sat, 9.30am-7.30pm Thu year-round, plus 10am-4pm Sun Jun-Sep) There's also a convenient TIC at the train station (☎ 277 8000), and a desk at the airport (☎ 214 4422)

SIGHTS
Tyne Quays
Newcastle's most recognisable attractions are the seven bridges that span the Tyne and some of the striking buildings that line it. Along Quayside a handsome boardwalk makes for a pleasant stroll during the day but really comes to life at night, when the bars, clubs and restaurants that line it are full to bursting. A really great way to experience the river and its sights is by cruise (see p617).

BALTIC – THE CENTRE FOR CONTEMPORARY ART
Once a huge, dirty, yellow grainstore overlooking the Tyne, **Baltic** (☎ 478 1810; www.balticmill .com; admission free; ◷ 10am-7pm Mon-Wed, Fri & Sat, 10am-10pm Thu, 10am-5pm Sun) is now a huge, dirty,

yellow art gallery to rival London's Tate Modern. Unlike the Tate, there are no permanent exhibitions here, but the constantly rotating shows feature the work and installations of some of contemporary art's biggest showstoppers. The complex has artists-in-residence, a performance space, a cinema, a bar, a spectacular rooftop restaurant (you'll need to book) and a ground-floor restaurant with riverside tables. There's also a viewing box for a fine Tyne vista.

TYNE BRIDGES

The most famous view in Newcastle is the cluster of Tyne bridges, and the most famous of these is the **Tyne Bridge** (1925–8), built at about the same time as (and very reminiscent of) Australia's Sydney Harbour Bridge. The quaint little **Swing Bridge** pivots in the middle to let ships through. Nearby, **High Level Bridge**, designed by Robert Stephenson, was the world's first road-and-railway bridge (1849). The most recent addition is the multiple-award-winning **Millennium Bridge** (aka Blinking Bridge; 2002), which opens like an eyelid to let ships pass.

OTHER SIGHTS

The Tyne's northern bank was the hub of commercial Newcastle in the 16th century. On Sandhill is **Bessie Surtee's House** (☎ 269 1227; 41-4 Sandhill; admission free; ⊙ 10am-4pm Mon-Fri). Run by English Heritage (EH), it's actually a combination of two 16th- and 17th-century merchant houses – all dark wood and sloping angles. Three rooms are open to the public. The daughter of a wealthy banker, feisty Bessie annoyed Daddy by falling in love with John Scott (1751–1838), a pauper. They eloped to Scotland but it all ended in smiles because John went on to become Lord Chancellor.

Just across the street is the rounded **Guildhall**, built in 1658.

City Centre

Newcastle's Victorian centre, a compact area bordered roughly by Grainger St to the west and Pilgrim St to the east, is supremely elegant and one of the most compelling examples of urban rejuvenation in the entire country. At the heart of it is Grey St, which is lined with fine classical buildings and is one of England's most handsome streets.

NEWCASTLE IN...

Two Days

Kick off your visit along the quayside, taking in the **Tyne bridges** (p615) and the remaining bits of 17th-century Newcastle, **Bessie Surtees' House** (left), before crossing the Millennium Bridge and going to **Baltic** (p615). Wander back across and head toward the elegant Victorian centre, where you should pop into the **Laing Art Gallery** (below) and the **Life Science Centre** (below). Stop off in **Blake's Coffee House** (p618) for a pick-me-up. Work your way up to the **Trent House Soul Bar** (boxed text, p619) and find that song you love but haven't heard in years on the incredible jukebox. And just keep going; everyone else does, so why shouldn't you?

The next day, if your head can take it, take the bus south through Gateshead to the **Angel of the North statue** (p621).

LIFE SCIENCE CENTRE

This excellent **science village** (☎ 243 8210; www .centre-for-life.co.uk; Scotswood Rd; adult £6.95; ⊙ 10am-6pm Mon-Sat, 11am-6pm Sun), part of the sober-minded International Centre for Life (a complex of institutes devoted to the study of genetic science), is one of the more interesting attractions in town. Through a series of hands-on exhibits and the latest technology, you (or your kids) can discover the amazing secrets of life. The highlight is the Crazy Motion Ride, a motion simulator that, among other things, lets you 'feel' what it's like to score a goal at St James' Park and bungee jump from the Tyne Bridge. There's lots of thought-provoking arcade-style games, and if the information sometimes gets lost on the way, never mind, kids will love it.

LAING ART GALLERY

The exceptional collection at the **Laing** (☎ 232 7734; www.twmuseums.org.uk; New Bridge St; admission free; ⊙ 10am-5pm Mon-Sat, 2-5pm Sun) includes works by Kitaj, Frank Auerbach and Henry Moore, and an important collection of paintings by John Martin (1789–1854), a Northumberland-born artist.

Outside the gallery is Thomas Heatherwick's famous **Blue Carpet** (2002) public square, with shimmering blue tiles made from crushed glass and resin.

DISCOVERY MUSEUM

The rick history of Newcastle is uncovered through a fascinating series of exhibits at this excellent **museum** (☎ 232 6789; www.tw museums.org.uk; Blandford Sq; admission free; ⏰ 10am-5pm Mon-Sat, 2-5pm Sun). The exhibits, spread housed in the former Co-Operative Whole-sale Society building, surround the mightily impressive 30m-long *Turbinia*, the fastest ship in the world in 1897. The different sections are all worth a look; our favourites were the self-explanatory Story of the Tyne and the interactive Science Maze, both breath life into subjects that many of us snoozed through in school.

CASTLE GARTH KEEP

The 'New Castle' that gave its name to the city has been largely swallowed up by the railway station, leaving only the square Norman **keep** (adult/child £1.50/50p; ⏰ 9.30am-5.30pm Apr-Sep, 9.30am-4.30pm Oct-Mar) as one of the few remaining fragments. It has a fine chevron-covered chapel and great views across the Tyne bridges from its rooftop.

NEWCASTLE FOR CHILDREN

While Newcastle is generally friendly, this doesn't necessarily mean child-friendly. The city is not overendowed with things for kids to do and places for them to let loose in.

Two main exceptions are the **Life Science Centre** (opposite) and the **Discovery Centre** (above), which should entertain kids for the better part of a whole day.

QUIRKY NEWCASTLE

Take in the David Lynch vibe at **Blackie Boy** (p619), where it's not all it appears to be. Pop your coins into the world's best jukebox at the **Trent House Soul Bar** (boxed text, p619) for the stomping sound of Northern Soul and pretend that Britney Spears never released a record. Take a rowing boat onto the lake at **Leazes Park** – watch out for those fishing rods. Cross one of the **Tyne bridges** (opposite) on foot. Avoid the crumpled-up teenagers and pools of vomit on the **Tuxedo Royale** (p620) – a night on the Boat is a must for all comers to Newcastle's nightlife.

TOURS

The TIC has a wide range of hour-long **walking tours** (adult/child £3/2) running through-out the year, all departing from the main TIC. Some require advance booking; check with the TIC for details.

The best tours are the three-hour sight-seeing cruises run by **River Tyne Cruises** (☎ 296 6740/1; www.tyneleisureline.co.uk; adult/child £11/6; 2pm Sun May–early Sep) from Quayside pier (near Millennium Bridge, opposite Baltic).

SLEEPING

Most visitors come to work or party, which means they're getting up really early or going to bed really late. The city centre's broad range of characterless business hotels, where prices tumble at weekends, generally fit the bill on both counts. The one factor, though, is price: you won't find a room in the centre for anything less than £60 to £70. If you're looking for cheaper, you'll have to go north, to the handsome suburb of Jes-mond, where the forces of gentrification and student power fight it out for territory.

City Centre

With only one exception, the closer you get to the river, the more you'll pay.

MID-RANGE

Premier Lodge (☎ 0870 990 6530; www.premierlodge .com; Quayside; r from £28) With a superb location in the old Exchange Building, this budget chain is right in the heart of the action. If you're here for the party, you shouldn't care that your room has about as much flavour as day-old chewing gum – if all goes according to plan, you won't be spending much time here anyway!

TOP END

Malmaison (☎ 245 5000; www.malmaison.com; Quay-side; d/ste Mon-Thu from £129/165, Fri-Sun from £99/140; 🅿 🖳) The affectedly stylish Malmaison touch has been applied to this former ware-house with considerable success, although they could pull the brake on the quasi-poetic publicity. Big beds, sleek lighting and designer furniture flesh out the Rooms of Many Pillows.

Royal Station (☎ 232 0781; www.royalstationhotel .com; Neville St; s/d £75/90) The epitome of the elegant Victorian railway hotel, this 19th-century classic, with its grand staircase and £25,000 chandelier, was in the midst of a much-needed refurb throughout most of 2004, which aims to bring the fairly basic rooms up to contemporary scratch.

Waterside Hotel (☎ 230 0111; www.waterside hotel.com; 48-52 Sandhill, Quayside; s/d Mon-Thu from £64/78, Fri-Sun from £50/68) The rooms are small, but they're among the most elegant in town: lavish furnishings and velvet drapes in a heritage-listed building. Excellent location.

Jesmond

The bulk of Newcastle's budget and mid-range accommodation is concentrated in the northeastern suburb of Jesmond, mainly on Osborne Rd. There are literally dozens of hotels and B&Bs along this street; below we recommend our favourites.

Catch the Metro to Jesmond or West Jesmond, or bus No 80 near Central Station, or No 30, 30B, 31B or 36 from Westgate Rd.

BUDGET
Newcastle YHA Hostel (☎ 0870 770 5972; www.yha .org.uk; 107 Jesmond Rd; dm £11.80; ☒ daily Feb-Nov, Fri-Sun Dec & Jan) A nice, rambling place with small dorms that are generally full, so book in advance. It's close to the Jesmond Metro stop.

MID-RANGE
Gresham Hotel (☎ 281 6325; www.gresham-hotel.com; 92 Osborne Rd; s/d from £45/68) Plenty of colours light up the rooms at this lovely hotel attached to the trendy Bar Bacca; it's extremely popular with weekend visitors who swear by the attentive-but-informal service.

Whites Hotel (☎ 281 5126; www.whiteshotel.com; 38-42 Osborne Rd; s/d £39/69) First impressions don't promise a great deal – the public areas are a bit tatty – but don't let that put you off; the bedrooms at this fine hotel are all uniformly modern and the service is first rate.

TOP END
New Northumbria Hotel (☎ 281 4961; www.newnorth umbria.co.uk; 61-9 Osborne Rd; s/d Mon-Thu from £75/85, Fri-Sun £55/80; ℗ ▣) Jesmond's top spot is a newish boutique hotel with all the trimmings, including huge rooms with designer furniture, big beds and fancy showers with those oversized heads that deliver water like a sandblaster.

EATING

Like the rest of the city, the dining scene is on the up. Although the town abounds with crappy fast-food outlets and dodgy Chinese and Indian restaurants, there are a growing number of truly excellent restaurants serv-ing a range of cuisines from pretty much everywhere. Many restaurants offer cut-rate early-bird specials and lunch deals.

City Centre
BUDGET
Blake's Coffee House (☎ 261 5463; 53 Grey St; breakfast £2-2.50, sandwiches £2; ☒ 9am-6pm) There is nowhere better than this high-ceilinged café for a Sunday-morning cure on any day of the week. It's friendly, relaxed and serves up the biggest selection of coffees in town, from the gentle push of a Colombian blend to the toxic shove of Old Brown Java. We love it.

MID-RANGE
Blackfriars Café (☎ 261 5945; Friar St; mains £9-13; ☒ dinner Tue-Sat, lunch Tue-Sun) England's oldest purpose-built dining hall was the 12th-century refectory of the Dominican Black Friars, now a superb restaurant with an international menu ranging from Welsh rarebit to Thai beef. Thankfully, not one stone of this grand place has been changed.

Paradiso Café Bar (☎ 221 1240; 1 Market Lane; mains £7-11; ☒ lunch & dinner Mon-Sat, to 7pm Sun) Hidden away in a small alley off Pilgrim St is one of the city's most popular spots. Good food, a mellow atmosphere and a fabulous little balcony for alfresco action keeps this place full almost all the time.

TOP END
Café 21 (☎ 222 0755; 19-21 Queen St; mains £13-17; ☒ lunch & dinner Mon-Sat) Simple but hardly plain, this elegant restaurant, all white table-

---

GAY & LESBIAN NEWCASTLE

Newcastle's pretty vibrant gay scene is outgrowing the 'Pink Triangle' formed by Waterloo, Neville and Collingwood Sts and now stretches as far south as Scotswood Rd. There are plenty of gay bars in the area and one outstanding nightclub.

Powerhouse Nightclub (☎ 261 4507; Times Sq), Newcastle's brashest queer nightclub, recently moved to the International Centre for Life where the décor is reminiscent of an Adam Ant video – flashing lights, video screens and lots of suggestive posing. Its presence in what is a family-oriented attraction is indicative that the gay scene has finally arrived.

cloths and smart seating, offers new interpretations of England's culinary backbone: pork and cabbage, liver and onions and a sensational Angus beef and chips.

Jesmond
There are plenty of dining options in Jesmond, but only one standout.

Pizzeria Francesca (☎ 281 6586; 134 Manor House Rd; mains £4-11.30) This is how Italian restaurants should be: chaotic, noisy, friendly, packed cheek to jowl and absolutely worth making the effort for. Excitable, happy waiters and huge portions of pizza and pasta keep them queuing at the door – get in line and wait because you can't book in advance.

DRINKING
There are few places in England that pursue the art of the bevvy with the same untrammelled fervour as Newcastle. The brash and brazen tend to make for the bars around Bigg Market in short sleeves and short skirts, no matter what the weather is like. The slightly more sophisticated punters gravitate for the cooler bars along Quayside and Mosley St, while the traditional ale merchants have a handful of spit 'n' sawdust pubs to choose from.

We daren't even begin to list the pubs and bars in town, but here's a handful to start with. Get a bottle of dog and get doon.

Bars
Revolution (☎ 261 5774; Collingwood Chambers) This spectacularly successful chain has an outrageously lavish address in Newcastle, complete with marble-pillared interior and a suitably trendy crowd.

Thirty 3i8ht (☎ 261 6463; 38 Lombard St; mains £6-9) A stunning bar featuring big egg-capsule seating and a room dotted with cigarlike tables dominated by a plasma screen. Suitably refined food is served and there are regular DJs.

Pubs
Blackie Boy (11 Groat Market) At first glance, this darkened old boozer looks like any old pub. Look closer. The overly red lighting. The single bookcase. The large leather armchair that is rarely occupied. The signage on the toilets: 'Dick' and 'Fanny'. This place could have featured in *Twin Peaks*, which is why it's so damn popular with everyone.

> **SOMETHING SPECIAL**
>
> **Trent House Soul Bar** (☎ 261 2154; 1-2 Leazes Lane) The wall has a simple message: 'Drink Beer. Be Sincere'. This simply unique place is the best bar in town because it is all about an ethos rather than a look. Totally relaxed and utterly devoid of pretentiousness, it is an old-school boozer that out-cools every other bar because it isn't trying to. And because it has the best jukebox in all of England – you could spend years listening to the extraordinary collection of songs it contains. It is run by the same folks behind the superb **World Headquarters** (see p620).

Crown Posada (31 The Side) An unspoilt, real-ale pub that is a favourite with the more seasoned drinker.

ENTERTAINMENT
Are you up for it? You'd better be: Newcastle's nightlife doesn't mess about. There's nightlife beyond the club scene – you'll just have to wade through a sea of staggering, glassy-eyed clubbers to get to it. For current listings pick up the monthly *North Guide* (£1.60) for good regional information, and the *Crack* (free) at the TIC or bookshops. Club admissions range from £3 to £12.

Live Music
Sage Gateshead (☎ 443 4666; www.thesagegateshead .org; Gateshead Quays) Gateshead's once-forlorn riverside now boasts the Norman Foster–designed glass-and-chrome curves of the Sage Gateshead, which looks like a gigantic bottle lying on its side. When it's finished (sometime toward the end of 2004 or early 2005), it will be the home of the Northern Sinfonia as well as the main northeastern showcase for all other kinds of music, from popular to folk.

Nightclubs
Baja Beach Club (☎ 477 6205; Hillgate Quay) The cheesiest of all cheesy nightclubs, 'Badgers' (as it's known) has palm trees, surfing stuff, barmaids in bikinis and Top-40 slamming tunes for an over-enthusiastic crowd of hormonal, drunken revellers who will inevitably regret that snog against the pillar but right now couldn't care less.

Foundation (☎ 261 8985; 57-9 Melbourne St) Warehouse-style club with a massive sound system, fantastic lighting rig and regular guest slots for heavyweight DJs from all over. If you want a night of hardcore clubbing, this is the place for you.

Tuxedo Royale (☎ 477 8899; Hillgate Quay) A rite of passage for all Geordies, 'the Boat' is like dancing on the cross-Channel ferry. It's cheesy, sloppy and full of drunken teenagers holding down vomit while spinning on the revolving dance floor. Sounds crap, but still packed.

World Headquarters (☎ 261 7007; www.trent house.com; Curtis Mayfield House, Carliol Sq) Dedicated to the genius of black music in all its guises (funk, rare groove, dance-floor jazz, northern soul, genuine R&B, lush disco, proper house and reggae) this fabulous club is strictly for true believers, and judging from the numbers, there are thousands of them.

Sport
Newcastle United Football Club (☎ 201 8400; official site www.nufc.co.uk, unofficial site www.nufc.com; St James' Park, Strawberry Pl) is more than a football team: it's the collective expression of Geordie hope and pride and the release for decades of economic, social and sporting frustration. Its fabulous ground, **St James' Park** (box office ☎ 261 1571) is always packed. Match tickets go on public sale about two weeks before a game or you can try the stadium on the day, but there's no chance for big matches, such as those against archrivals Sunderland.

Theatre
Theatre Royal (☎ 232 2061; www.theatre-royal-new castle.co.uk; 100 Grey St) is the winter home of the Royal Shakespeare Company. It is full of Victorian splendour and has an excellent programme of drama.

GETTING THERE & AWAY
Air
Newcastle International Airport (☎ 286 0966; www .newcastleairport.com) is 7 miles north of the city off the A696. It has direct services to Aberdeen, London, Cardiff, Dublin, Belfast, Oslo, Amsterdam, Paris, Prague, Brussels and a number of destinations in Spain.

Boat
Norway's **Fjord Line** (☎ 296 1313; www.fjordline.co.uk) operates ferries between Newcastle, Stavan-ger and Bergen. **DFDS Seaways** (☎ 0870 533 3000; www.dfdsseaways.co.uk) operates ferries to Newcastle from Kristiansand in Norway, the Swedish port of Gothenburg and the Dutch port of Ijmuiden, near Amsterdam. For online ferry bookings, check out www .newcastleferry.co.uk.

Bus
National Express buses arrive and depart from the Gallowgate coach station. Destinations include Edinburgh (£14, 2¾ hours, three to five daily), London (£25, seven hours, six daily) and York (£11.25, 2½ hours, five daily). For Berwick-upon-Tweed (£4.50, two hours, five daily) take bus No 505, 515 or 525 from Haymarket bus station.

Local and regional buses leave from Haymarket or Eldon Square bus stations. For local buses around the northeast, don't forget the excellent-value Explorer North East ticket, valid on most services for £5.50.

Train
Newcastle is on the main rail line between London and Edinburgh. Services go to Alnmouth (for connections to Alnwick; £5.80, 20 minutes, four daily), Berwick (£11.80, 45 minutes, every two hours), Edinburgh (£35.50, 1½ hours, half-hourly), London King's Cross (£88, three hours, half-hourly) and York (£17, 45 minutes, every 20 minutes).

There's also the scenic Tyne Valley Line (see p628) west to Carlisle.

GETTING AROUND
To/From the Airport & Ferry Terminal
The airport is linked to town by the **Metro** (£2.20; 20min; every 15min).

Bus No 327 (£3.20) links the ferry (at Tyne Commission Quay), Central Station and Jesmond Rd. It leaves the train station 2½ hours and 1¼ hours before each sailing.

There's a taxi rank at the terminal; it costs £14 to the city centre.

Car
Driving around Newcastle isn't fun thanks to the web of roads, bridges and one-way systems, but there are plenty of car parks.

Public Transport
There's a large bus network but the best means of getting around is the excellent underground Metro, with fares from 55p.

There are also several saver passes. The TIC can supply you with route plans for the bus and Metro networks.

The **DaySaver** (£4, after 9am £3.20) gives unlimited Metro travel for one day, and the **DayRover** (adult/child £4.20/2.10) gives unlimited travel on all modes of transport in the Tyne & Wear county for one day.

Taxi
On weekend nights taxis can be rare; try **Noda Taxis** (☎ 222 1888), which has a kiosk outside the entrance to Central Station.

AROUND NEWCASTLE

ANGEL OF THE NORTH
The world's most frequently viewed work of art is this extraordinary 200-tonne, rust-coloured human frame with wings (aka the Gateshead Flasher) towering over the A1 (M) about 5 miles south of Newcastle – if you're driving, you just can't miss it. It's Antony Gormley's most successful work and the country's largest sculpture at 20m high, with a wingspan wider than a Boeing 767. Bus Nos 723 and 724 from Eldon Square and Nos 21, 21A and 21B from Pilgrim St will take you there.

SEGEDUNUM
The last stronghold of Hadrian's Wall was the fort of **Segedunum** (☎ 295 5757; www.twmuseums .org.uk; adult £3.50; ☉ 10am-5pm Apr-Oct, 10am-3.30pm Nov-Mar), 4 miles east of Newcastle at Wallsend. Beneath the 35m tower (climb it for terrific views) is an absorbing site that includes a reconstructed Roman bathhouse (with steaming pools and frescoes) and a fascinating museum that gives visitors a picture of life during Roman times.

Take the Metro to Wallsend.

COUNTY DURHAM

The image of County Durham as a pastoral retreat, full of peaceful villages and unspoilt market towns dotted throughout the lonely, rabbit-inhabited North Pennines is slowly returning after a 300-year-long hiatus. For much of that time up to the mid-1980s, the county was given over almost entirely to coal mining, which created plenty of jobs but didn't do the county's rich medieval past any favours. A brutal and dangerous business, mining was the lifeblood of entire communities, and its sudden death in 1984 at the stroke of a Conservative pen has left some purposeless towns and countryside punctuated with the relics of an industry slowly being reclaimed by nature. At the heart of it all, however, is the county's exquisite capital, one of England's most visited towns and an absolute must on your northern itinerary.

Durham's had a turbulent history, though it pales in comparison with its troublesome northern neighbour. To keep the Scots and local Saxon tribes quiet, William the Conqueror created the title of prince bishop in 1081 and gave them vice-regal power over an area known as the Palatinate of Durham, which became almost a separate country. It raised its own armies, collected taxes and administered a separate legal system that – incredibly – wasn't fully incorporated into the greater English structure until 1971.

Getting Around
The Explorer North East ticket (see opposite) is valid on many services in the county.

DURHAM
☎ 0191 / pop 42,940
Durham is small, posh and exquisite. Its joys are apparent as soon as you get off the train, for crammed onto a hilltop peninsula in a bend of the River Wear is Britain's most beautiful Romanesque cathedral, a masterpiece of Norman architecture that simply doesn't fail to impress. Just in front of it is the enormous castle that for centuries was home to the prince bishops. Surrounding both is a cobweb of cobbled streets that are usually full of upper-crust students as Durham is also a posh university town. The university may not have the wizened prestige of Oxbridge – it was only founded in 1832 – but its terrific academic reputation and competitive rowing team make the disappointment of not getting into Oxford or Cambridge that bit easier to bear.

Once you've visited the cathedral, there's little else to do save walk the cobbled streets and find new spots from which to view Durham's main attraction. Visitors can opt to visit as a day trip from Newcastle, which is recommended unless you plan to do some in-depth exploration of the surrounding county, in which case you could do far worse than base yourself here.

Orientation

Market Pl, the TIC, castle and cathedral are all on the peninsula surrounded by the River Wear. The train and bus stations are to the west on the other side of the river. Using the cathedral as your landmark, you can't really go wrong. The main sites are within easy walking distance of each other.

Information

Post office (Silver St; ☺ 9am-5.30pm Mon-Sat)
Public library (Millenium Pl; ☺ 9.30am-5pm Mon-Sat)
The only place in town to check email.

Thomas Cook (☎ 382 6600; 24-5 Market Pl) Near the post office.
TIC (☎ 384 3720; www.durhamtourism.co.uk; 2 Millennium Pl; ☺ 9.30am-5.30pm Mon-Sat, 10am-4pm Sun)
In the Gala complex, which includes a theatre and cinema.
Waterstone's (☎ 383 1488; 69 Sadler St) A good selection of books.

Sights

DURHAM CATHEDRAL

Britain's most magnificent Romanesque structure will not disappoint, not unless you take Nathaniel Hawthorne's gushing, OTT hyberbole at face value: 'I never saw so lovely and magnificent a scene, nor (being content with this) do I care to see better.' Let's not go nuts here. No building is *that*

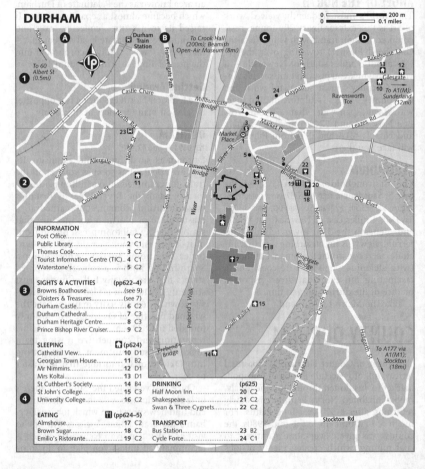

DURHAM

0 —————— 200 m
0 —————— 0.1 miles

INFORMATION
Post Office	**1** C2
Public Library	**2** C1
Thomas Cook	**3** C2
Tourist Information Centre (TIC)	**4** C1
Waterstone's	**5** C2

SIGHTS & ACTIVITIES (pp622-4)
Browns Boathouse	(see 9)
Cloisters & Treasures	(see 7)
Durham Castle	**6** C2
Durham Cathedral	**7** C3
Durham Heritage Centre	**8** C3
Prince Bishop River Cruiser	**9** C2

SLEEPING 🏠 (p624)
Cathedral View	**10** D1
Georgian Town House	**11** B2
Mr Nimmins	**12** D1
Mrs Koltai	**13** D1
St Cuthbert's Society	**14** B4
St John's College	**15** C3
University College	**16** C2

EATING 🍴 (pp624-5)
Almshouse	**17** C2
Brown Sugar	**18** C2
Emilio's Ristorante	**19** C2

DRINKING (p625)
Half Moon Inn	**20** C2
Shakespeare	**21** C2
Swan & Three Cygnets	**22** C2

TRANSPORT
Bus Station	**23** B2
Cycle Force	**24** C1

beautiful, but this definitive Anglo-Norman Romanesque structure is still pretty amazing. We would definitely put it in our 'top churches in Britain' list – as do many others including Unesco, which declared it a World Heritage Site in 1986.

The **cathedral** (☎ 386 4266; www.durhamcathedral .co.uk; donation requested; ⏰ 9.30am-8pm daily mid-Jun–Sep; 9.30am-6.15pm Mon-Sat, 12.30-5pm Sun Oct–mid-Jun, private prayer only 7.30am-9.30am Mon-Sat, 7.45am-12.30pm Sun year-round) is vast and has a pretty fortified look because although it may have been built to pay tribute to God and to house the holy bones of St Cuthbert, it also needed to withstand any potential attack by the pesky Scots and Northumberland tribes who weren't too thrilled by the arrival of the Normans a few years before.

The interior is spectacular. The superb nave is dominated by massive, powerful piers carved in geometric designs. Durham was the first European cathedral to be roofed with stone-ribbed vaulting, which upheld the heavy stone roof and made it possible to build pointed transverse arches, the first in Britain and a great architectural achievement. The central tower dates from 1262, but was damaged in a fire caused by lightning in 1429. It rebuilt entirely in 1470. The western towers were added in 1217–26.

Built in 1175 and renovated 300 years later, the **Galilee Chapel** is one of the most beautiful parts. The northern side's paintings are rare surviving examples of 12th-century wall painting and are thought to feature St Cuthbert and St Oswald. The chapel also contains the Venerable Bede's tomb. Bede was an 8th-century Northumbrian monk, a great historian and polymath whose work *The Ecclesiastical History of the English People* is still the prime source of information on the development of early Christian Britain. Among other things, he introduced the numbering of years from the birth of Jesus.

The Bishop's Throne, built over the tomb of Bishop Thomas Hatfield, dates from the mid–14th century. The high altar is separated from St Cuthbert's tomb by the beautiful stone Neville Screen, made around 1372–80. Until the Reformation the screen included 107 statues of saints.

The cathedral has worthwhile **guided tours** (adult/child £3.50/free; call for times). Evensong is at 5.15pm Tuesday to Saturday (Evening Prayer on Monday) and 3.30pm on Sunday.

The **tower** (adult/child £2.50/1.50; ⏰ 10am-4pm Mon-Sat Mar-Nov, 10am-3pm Dec-Feb) has 325 steps, at the top of which is a splendid view.

Cloisters

The cathedral's monastic buildings are centred on the cloisters, which were rebuilt in 1828. The west door to the cloisters is famous for its 12th-century ironwork. On the western side is a **monastic dormitory** (adult/child 80p/20p; ⏰ 10am-3.30pm Mon-Sat, 12.30pm-3.15pm Sun only Apr-Sep), now a library of 30,000 books and displaying Anglo-Saxon carved stones, with a vaulted undercroft that houses the Treasures and restaurant. A new addition is an **audiovisual display** (adult/child £1/30p; ⏰ 10am-3pm Mon-Sat Apr-Nov) on the building of the cathedral and the life of St Cuthbert.

The Treasures

The **treasures** (adult/student/child £2.50/2/70p; ⏰ 10am-4.30pm Mon-Sat, 2pm-4.30pm Sun) refer to the relics of St Cuthbert, but besides his cross and his coffin there is very little here that is related to the saint. The collection is made up mostly of religious paraphernalia from later centuries.

DURHAM CASTLE

Built as a standard motte-and-bailey fort in 1072, **Durham Castle** (☎ 374 3800; adult £3.50; ⏰ tours only on the hr 10am-12.30pm & 2-4pm Jun-Oct, 2-4pm Mon, Wed, Sat & Sun Nov-May) was the prince bishops' home until 1837, when it became the first college of the new university. It remains a university hall.

The castle has been much altered over the centuries, as each successive prince bishop sought to put his particular imprimatur on the place, but comprehensive restoration and reconstruction were necessary anyway, because the castle is built of soft stone on soft ground. Highlights of the 45-minute tour include the groaning 17th-century Black Staircase, the 16th-century chapel and the beautifully preserved Norman chapel (1080).

OTHER SIGHTS

Near the cathedral, in what was the St Mary le Bow Church, is the **Durham Heritage Centre** (☎ 386 8719; St Mary le Bow, North Bailey; adult/child £1.20/50p; ⏰ 11am-4.30pm Jul-Sep, from 2pm Jun, Sat & Sun Apr, May & Oct), with a pretty crowded collection of displays on Durham's history from the Middle Ages to mining. It's all suitably grim, especially the reconstructed prison cells.

Crook Hall (☎ 384 8028; www.crookhallgardens.co.uk; Sidegate; adult/child £3.80/3; ⏰ 1-5pm Fri-Mon Easter, Sun May & Sep, Sun-Fri Jun-Aug) is a medieval hall with 1.6 hectares of charming small gardens, about half a mile north of the city centre.

Activities

BOATING

The **Prince Bishop River Cruiser** (☎ 386 9525; Elvet Bridge; adult £4; ⏰ 2pm & 3pm Jun-Sep) offers one-hour cruises.

You can hire a rowing boat from **Browns Boathouse** (☎ 386 3779; per hr per person £3) below Elvet Bridge.

WALKS

There are superb views back to the cathedral and castle from the riverbanks; walk around the bend between Elvet and Framwellgate Bridges, or hire a boat at Elvet Bridge.

Guided walks (adult/child £3/free; ⏰ 2pm Wed, Sat & Sun May-Sep; 1½ hrs) leave from Millennium Pl – contact the TIC for details. **Ghost walks** (☎ 386 1500; adult/child £3/1; ⏰ 6.30pm Mon Jun-Sep, 8.30pm Jul & Aug; 1½ hrs) also drift around town.

Sleeping

The ace in the deck for Durham's hostellers is a cathedral view. Considering that the cathedral is the dominant building in town and visible from most everywhere, it's quality, not quantity, that is the real clincher. The TIC makes local bookings free of charge, which is a good thing considering that Durham is always busy with visitors: graduation week in late June results in accommodation gridlock.

Cathedral View (☎ 386 9566; www.cathedralview .com; 212 Gilesgate; s/d £50/70) This plain-fronted Georgian house has no sign, but inside it does exactly what it says on the tin. Six large rooms decorated with lots of cushions, co-ordinated bed linen and window dressings make up the numbers, but it's the three at the back that are worth the fuss; the views of the cathedral are superb. A small breakfast terrace with the same splendid vista is an added touch of real class.

Georgian Town House (☎/fax 386 8070; 10-11 Crossgate; s/d from £55/70) A listed building smack in the middle of town, this B&B has large, airy rooms decorated in the true spirit of

Laura Ashley: elaborate stencilling, plenty of pillows and fancy window dressings. It's close to the cathedral, so the rooms facing it have great views. There is also a small garden with flowers and a rockery.

60 Albert St (☎ 386 0608; www.sixtyalbertstreet .co.uk; s/d from £45/70; P) This tiny place has only three rooms – each stylishly restored with painted, cast-iron beds – which makes for truly attentive, individual service. The breakfast room is a Victorian showcase, with original antiques, polished wood floors and a beautiful fireplace.

A couple of small, similarly priced B&Bs on Gilesgate may not offer much in the way of décor, size or cathedral view, but are worth a try if you're stuck:

Mr Nimmins (☎ 384 6485; www.nimmins.co.uk; 14 Giles-gate; s/d £20/40)

Mrs Koltai (☎ 386 2026; 10 Gilesgate; s/d £20/38)

Eating

Cheap eats aren't a problem in Durham thanks to the students, but quality is a little thin on the ground. Some pubs do good bar food (see Drinking, opposite).

Almshouse (☎ 386 1054; Palace Green; dishes £3-7; ⏰ 9am-5pm) Serves satisfying, imaginative snacks (how about spicy beef with red-bean casserole and rice?) served in a genuine 17th-century house right on Palace Green. It's a shame about the interior, which has been restored to look like any old museum café.

Brown Sugar (☎ 454 2242; New Elvet; dishes £5-7; ⏰ 7.30am-11pm Mon-Sat, 9am-10.30pm Sun) This trendy coffee shop-cum-bar is a favourite with university students, who fold into the oversized leather couches, nibble on a ciabatta sandwich (no ordinary bread here, mate) and talk about how much study they should be doing. A perfect hang-out.

Emilio's Ristorante (☎ 384 0096; 96 Elvet Bridge; pizza or pasta from £6.95; ⏰ lunch Mon-Sat, dinner daily) Durham's top spot for pizza, pasta and other Italian staples has a wonderful location overlooking the Wear. Try the *malfatti al forno*, a kind of oven-baked ravioli filled with ricotta cheese and spinach.

Drinking

Durham may be a big student town, but most of them seem to take the whole study thing really seriously, because the nightlife here isn't as boisterous as you might expect from a university town. There is, however, a fistful of lovely old bars. The TIC has a bi-monthly *What's On* guide.

Half Moon Inn (New Elvet) Sports fans love this old-style bar for its devotion to the mixed pleasures of Sky Sports; we like it for its wonderful whiskies and ales. There's a summer beer garden if you want to avoid the whoops and hollers of the armchair jocks.

Shakespeare (63 Saddler St) As authentic a traditional bar as you're likely to find in these parts, this is the perfect local's boozer, complete with nicotine-stained walls, cosy snugs and a small corner TV to show the racing. Students and silent locals drink shoulder to shoulder.

Swan & Three Cygnets (☎ 384 0242; Elvet Bridge; mains around £8) A high-ceilinged riverside pub with courtyard tables overlooking the river. It also serves some pretty good bar food, usually fancy versions of standard bar fare like bangers and mash.

TOP FIVE PUBS FOR A PINT

■ **Trent House Soul Bar** (p619; Newcastle)

■ **Shakespeare** (above; Durham)

■ **Old Well Inn** (p626; Barnard Castle)

■ **Ye Old Cross** (p632; Alnwick)

■ **Ship** (p634; Holy Island)

Getting There & Away
BUS

The bus station is on North Rd. All National Express buses arrive here, while Bus No 352 links Newcastle and Blackpool via Durham, Barnard Castle, Raby Castle and Kirkby Stephen. Destinations include Edinburgh (£20, four hours, one daily), Leeds (£18.50, 2½ hours, three daily), London (£25, 6½ hours, four daily) and Newcastle (£2.25, 30 minutes, three daily).

TRAIN

There are services at least hourly to Edinburgh (£37.50, two hours), London (£88, three hours), Newcastle (£4.10 single, 20 minutes) and York (£17, one hour).

Getting Around

Pratt's Taxis (☎ 386 0700) charges a minimum of about £2.20. **Cycle Force** (☎ 384 0319; 29 Claypath) charges £16/8.50 per full/half day for mountain-bike hire.

AROUND DURHAM
Beamish Open-Air Museum

A great day out for visitors of all ages, **Beamish** (☎ 0191-370 4000; www.beamish.org.uk; adult Nov-Mar £4, Apr-Oct £14; ⏰ 10am-5pm Apr-Oct, 10am-4pm Tue-Thu, Sat & Sun Nov-Mar, last entry 3pm year-round) is a museum that offers a fabulous warts-and-all portrait of industrial life in the northeast during the 19th and 20th centuries.

You can go underground, explore mine heads, a working farm, a school, a dentist and a pub, and marvel at how every cramped pit cottage seemed to find room for a piano. Don't miss a ride behind an 1815 Steam Elephant locomotive or a replica of Stephenson's Locomotion No 1.

Allow at least three hours to do the place justice. Many elements (such as the railway) aren't open in the winter – call for details.

Beamish is about 8 miles northwest of Durham; it's signposted from the A1(M) – take the A691 west at junction 63. Bus Nos 709 from Newcastle (50 minutes, hourly) and 720 from Durham (30 minutes, hourly) run to the museum.

BARNARD CASTLE
☎ 01833 / pop 6720

The locals call it Barney, which hardly describes this wonderful market town packed with atmospheric pubs and antique shops, all beneath the splendid ruins of a daunting castle and, on the outskirts, an extraordinary French chateau.

The **TIC** (☎ 690909; tourism@teesdale.gov.uk; Woodleigh, Flatts Rd; ⏱ 9.30am-5.30pm Easter-Oct, 11am-4pm Mon-Sat Nov-Mar) handles visitor inquiries.

Sights

Once one of the largest castles in the whole country, **Barnard Castle** (☎ 638212; adult £2.50; ⏱ 10am-6pm Easter-Sep, 10am-5pm Oct, 10am-1pm & 2-4pm Wed-Sun Nov-Mar) was partly dismantled during the 16th century, but its huge bulk, on a cliff above the Tees, still manages to cover more than two very impressive hectares. Founded by Guy de Bailleul and rebuilt around 1150, its occupants spent their time suppressing the locals and fighting off the Scots – on their off days they sat around enjoying the wonderful views of the river.

The 19th-century industrialist and art fanatic John Bowes didn't do things by halves, so when he commissioned a new museum to show off his terrific collection, the result was an extraordinary, Louvre-inspired French chateau 1½ miles west of town. Opened in 1892, the **Bowes Museum** (☎ 690606; www.bowesmuseum.org.uk; adult/student/child £6/5/free; ⏱ 11am-5pm) could give the V&A a run for its money, with lavish furniture and paintings by Canaletto, El Greco and Goya. The museum's most beloved exhibit, however, is the marvellous mechanical silver swan, operated at 12.30pm and 3.30pm.

Sleeping & Eating

Greta House (☎ 631193; 89 Galgate; s/d £35/50) This lovely Victorian home has little touches that show that extra bit of class – fluffy bathrobes, face cloths and posh toiletries. What really did it for us, though, was the stay-in service: a tray of lovely home-made sandwiches and a superb cheeseboard to nibble at from the comfort of bed.

Marwood House (☎ 637493; www.kilgarriff.demon .co.uk; 98 Galgate; s/d £27/48) Another handsome Victorian property with tastefully appointed rooms (the owner's tapestries feature in the décor and her home-made biscuits sit on a tray), but the standout feature is the small fitness room in the basement, complete with a sauna that fits up to four people.

Old Well Inn (☎ 690130; www.oldwellinn.co.uk; 21 The Bank; s/d from £48/60) You won't find larger bedrooms in town than at this old coaching inn, which makes it an excellent option for families – it even takes pets. It has a reputation for excellent, filling pub grub, although the service is somewhat lacklustre at times.

Getting There & Away

Bus No 352 runs daily between Newcastle and Blackpool via Durham, Bishop Auckland, Barnard Castle, Raby Castle and Kirkby Stephen.

AROUND BARNARD CASTLE

The ransacked, spectral ruins of **Egglestone Abbey** (⏱ dawn-dusk), dating from the 1190s, overlook a lovely bend of the Tees. You can envisage the abbey's one-time grandeur despite the gaunt remains. They're a pleasant 1-mile walk south of Barnard Castle.

About 7 miles northeast of town is the sprawling, romantic **Raby Castle** (☎ 660202; www.rabycastle.com; adult £7; ⏱ castle 1-5pm, grounds 11am-5.30pm Sun-Fri Jun-Aug, Wed & Sun May & Sep), a stronghold of the Neville family until it did some ill-judged plotting against the Crown in 1569 (the Rising of the North). Most of the interior dates from the 18th and 19th centuries, but the exterior remains true to the original design, built around a courtyard and surrounded by a moat. There are beautiful formal gardens and a deer park. Bus Nos 8 and 352 zip between Barnard Castle and Raby (20 minutes, eight daily).

NORTH PENNINES

The western half of Durham county consists of fertile, rocky dales that run into the North Pennines. The Rivers Tees and Wear cut through the landscape, creating Teesdale to the south and Weardale to the north. Both are marked by ancient quarries and mines – industries that date back to Roman times. The wilds of the North Pennines, which only peter out just before Hadrian's Wall, are also home to the picturesque Derwent and Allen valleys, north of Weardale.

HADRIAN'S WALL

Hadrian's Wall is proof that the Romans really knew how to take on a big job – the biggest in fact, for this 73-mile wall across the narrow neck of the island, from Solway Firth in the west almost to the mouth of the

Tyne in the east, was Rome's single greatest engineering project. It was built to keep 'us' (Romans, subdued Anglo-Saxons) in and 'them' (hairy barbarians from Scotland) out. It's really a kind of reverse compliment to the Scots. Or so the story goes.

Truth is, the Emperor Hadrian didn't just order the wall built because he was afraid of northern invasion; a concentrated attack at any single point in the wall would have breached it. It was meant to mark the final border of the Roman Empire, as if to say that it would extend no further – another compliment to the Scots? By drawing a physical boundary, the Romans were also tightening their grip on the population to the south – for the first time in history, pass-

ports were issued to citizens of the empire which would mark them out not just as citizens but, more importantly, as taxpayers.

Whatever the history, whys and wherefores, building it was a logistical nightmare. Begun in AD 122, it took six years, oodles of workers and as much invention and ingenuity as local masons could muster. The section from Newcastle to the River Irthing was built of stone, and turf blocks of roughly 3m thick and 4.5m high were used on the section to Solway. A 3m-deep, 9m-wide ditch and mound were excavated immediately in front (except where there were natural defences). Every Roman mile (1.62 miles; even in measurement the Romans outdid us) there was a gateway guarded by a small

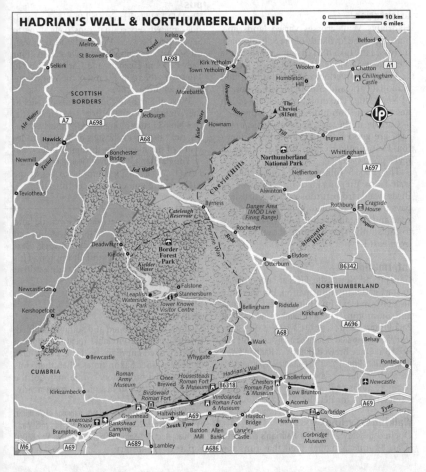

HADRIAN'S WALL & NORTHUMBERLAND NP

fort (milecastle) and between each milecastle were two observation turrets. Milecastles are numbered right across the country, starting with Milecastle 0 at Wallsend and ending with Milecastle 80 at Bowness-on-Solway. Between each were a series of turrets, tagged alphabetically, so Milecastle 37 (a good one; see p630) was followed by Turret 37A, Turret 37B and then Milecastle 38.

A series of forts (that may predate the wall) were built as bases some distance south and 16 actually lay astride it. The prime remaining forts on the wall are Cilurnum (Chesters), Vercovicium (Housesteads) and Banna (Birdoswald). The best forts behind the wall are Corstopitum, at Corbridge, and Vindolanda, north of Bardon Mill.

Orientation

Hadrian's Wall crosses varied landscape. Starting in the lowlands of the Solway coast, it crosses the lush hills east of Carlisle to the bleak, windy ridge of basalt rock known as Whin Sill overlooking Northumberland National Park, and ends in the urban sprawl of Newcastle. The most spectacular section lies between Brampton and Corbridge.

Carlisle, in the west, and Newcastle, in the east, are good starting points, but Brampton, Haltwhistle, Hexham and Corbridge all make good bases.

The B6318 follows the course of the wall from the outskirts of Newcastle to Birdoswald; from Birdoswald to Carlisle it pays to have a detailed map. The main A69 road and the railway line follow 3 or 4 miles to the south. This section follows the wall from east to west.

Information

Carlisle and Newcastle TICs are good places to start gathering information, but there are also TICs in Hexham, Haltwhistle, Corbridge and Brampton. The **Northumberland National Park Visitors Centre** (☎ 01434-344396; ⏰ 9.30am-5pm Mar-May, Sep & Oct, 9.30am-6pm Jun-Aug) is off the B6318 at Once Brewed. There's a **Hadrian's Wall information line** (☎ 01434-322002; www.hadrians-wall.org) too. May sees a spring festival, with lots of re-creations of Roman life along the wall (contact TICs for details).

Walking & Cycling

Opened in May 2003, the **Hadrian's Wall Path** is an 84-mile National Trail that runs the length of the wall from Wallsend in the east to Bowness-on-Solway in the west. The entire route should take about seven days, giving plenty of time to explore the rich archaeological heritage along the way. Anthony Burton's *Hadrian's Wall Path – National Trail Guide* (£12.99), available at most bookshops and TICs in the region, is good for history, archaeology and the like, while the recently published *Essential Guide to Hadrian's Wall Path National Trail* (£3.50) is a top guide to everyday facilities and services along the walk. If you're planning to cycle along it, TICs sell the *Hadrian's Wall Country Cycle Map* (£3).

Getting There & Around

BUS

The AD 122 Hadrian's Wall Bus is a hail-and-ride, guided service that runs daily, June to September, between Wallsend and Bowness-on-Solway via Haltwhistle train station (four daily between Hexham and Carlisle). Bus No 185 covers the route the rest of the year (Monday to Saturday only).

West of Hexham the wall runs parallel to the A69, between Carlisle and Newcastle. Bus No 685 runs along the A69 hourly, passing near the youth hostels and 2 to 3 miles south of the main sites throughout the year.

The **Hadrian's Wall Rover** (adult/child 1-day £6/4, 3-day £10/6) is available from the driver or the TICs, where you can also get timetables.

TRAIN

The railway line between Newcastle and Carlisle (Tyne Valley Line) has stations at Corbridge, Hexham, Haydon Bridge, Bardon Mill, Haltwhistle and Brampton. This service runs daily, but not all trains stop at all stations.

CORBRIDGE

☎ 01434 / pop 2800

Mellow, old-fashioned and suitably cobbled, Corbridge has a enviable location above a green-banked curve in the Tyne. Folks have lived here since Saxon times when there was a substantial monastery, while many of the buildings feature stones nicked from nearby Corstopitum.

The **TIC** (☎ 632815; www.thisiscorbridge.co.uk; Hill St; ⏰ 10am-1pm & 2-6pm Mon-Sat, 1-5pm Sun mid-May–Sep, 10am-1pm & 2-5pm Mon-Sat Easter–mid-May & Oct) is part of the library.

Corbridge Roman Site & Museum
What's left of the Roman garrison town of **Corstopitum** (EH; ☎ 632349; adult £3.50; ⊗ 10am-6pm Apr-Sep, to 4pm Oct, 10am-4pm Sat & Sun Nov-Mar) lies about a half a mile west of Market Pl on Dere St, once the main road from York to Scotland. It is the oldest fortified site in the area, predating the wall itself by some 40 years, when it was used by troops launching retaliation raids into Scotland. Most of what you see here, though, dates from around AD 200, when the fort had developed into a civilian settlement and was the main base along the wall.

Sleeping & Eating
Angel Inn (☎ 632119; www.theangelofcorbridge.co.uk; Main St; mains £12-16, s/d from £49/74) The fanciest place in town is this 17th-century inn that has been given a modern, stylish makeover. The restaurant is superb, with delicate renditions of classic meat (roast rack of lamb, beef medallions) and fish dishes (pan-seared sea bass) winning plenty of kudos as far afield as Newcastle.

Town Barns (☎ 633345; off Trinity Tce; s/d £36/52; ⊗ Apr-Oct) Romantic novelist Catherine Cookson used to own this handsome, spacious house with an appropriately sweeping staircase. The rooms are decorated in classic country-house style, with plenty of pillows and old wooden furniture.

Valley Restaurant (☎ 633434; Station Rd; mains £5.50-14; ⊗ dinner Mon-Sat) This fine Indian restaurant in a lovely building above the station supplies a unique service as well as delicious food. A group of 10 or more diners from Newcastle can catch the train to Corbridge accompanied by a waiter, who will supply snacks and phone ahead to have the meal ready when the train arrives!

Getting There & Away
Bus No 685 between Newcastle and Carlisle comes via Corbridge, as does the half-hourly bus No 602 from Newcastle to Hexham, where you can connect with the Hadrian's Wall bus AD 122. Corbridge is also on the Newcastle–Carlisle railway line.

HEXHAM
☎ 01434 / pop 10,690
The busiest of all the wall towns between Newcastle and Carlisle, Hexham is the perfect spot to stock up and replenish; banks, restaurants and a bunch of high-street shops line the streets that are interlinked by cobbled alleyways. The TIC (☎ 652220; www.hadrians wallcountry.org; Wentworth Car Park; ⊗ 9am-6pm Mon-Sat, 10am-5pm Sun mid-May–Oct, 10am-5pm Mon-Sat Oct–mid-May) is northeast of the town centre.

Sights
Stately **Hexham Abbey** (☎ 602031; ⊗ 9.30am-7pm May-Sep, 9.30am-5pm Oct-Apr) is a marvellous example of early English architecture. Inside, look out for the Saxon crypt, the only surviving element of St Wilifrid's Church, built with inscribed stones from Corstopitum in 674.

The **Old Gaol**, completed in 1333 as England's first purpose-built prison, is the setting for the **Border History Museum** (☎ 652349; adult £2; ⊗ 10am-4.30pm Apr-Oct, Mon, Tue & Sat Oct–mid-Nov). The history of the Border Reivers is retold along with tales of the punishments handed out in the prison.

Sleeping & Eating
Acomb YHA Hostel (☎ 0870 770 5664; www.yha.org.uk; Main St; dm £8.20; ⊗ Apr-Nov) Simple accommodation – basic bunks and functional bathrooms – in a converted stable on the edge of Acomb village, 2½ miles north of Hexham and 2 miles south of the wall. Hexham can be reached by bus (Nos 745 and 880, frequently) or train.

West Close House (☎ 603307; Hextol Tce; s/d from £20/40) This immaculate 1920s house, in a leafy cul-de-sac off Allendale Rd (the B6305) and surrounded by a beautiful garden, is highly recommended for sheer friendliness and comfort.

There are several bakeries on Fore St, and if you turn left into the quaintly named Priestpopple near the bus station, you'll find a selection of restaurants.

For sheer atmosphere, you just can't beat **Dipton Mill** (☎ 606577; Dipton Mill Rd; mains £5-8), a superb country pub 2 miles out on the road to Blanchland, among woodland and by a river. It offers sought-after ploughman's lunches and real ale.

Getting There & Away
Bus No 685 between Newcastle and Carlisle comes through Hexham hourly. The AD 122 and the winter-service No 185 connect with other towns along the wall, and the town is on the Newcastle–Carlisle railway line (hourly).

CHESTERS ROMAN FORT & MUSEUM

The best-preserved remains of a Roman cavalry fort in England are at **Chesters** (EH; ☎ 01434-681379; adult £3.50; ☯ 9.30am-6pm Apr-Sep, 10am-4pm Oct-Mar), set among idyllic green woods and meadows. They include part of a bridge (complex and beautifully constructed) across the River North Tyne, an extraordinary bathhouse and an underfloor heating system. The museum has a large collection of Roman sculpture. Take bus No 682 from Hexham.

HALTWHISTLE

☎ 01434 / pop 3810

The subdued market town of Haltwhistle, basically one long street just north of the A69, claims to be the centre of Britain. Tough to argue, but the residents of Dunsop Bridge, 71 miles south of here, do just that. Whatever the truth of it, Haltwhistle makes a good stop if you want to get some cash and load up on groceries or provisions. Thursday is market day.

The **TIC** (☎ 322002; ☯ 9.30am-1pm & 2-5.30pm Mon-Sat, 1-5pm Sun May-Sep, 9.30am-noon & 1-3.30pm Mon-Tue & Thu-Sat Oct-Apr) is in the train station.

Ashcroft (☎ 320213; www.ashcroftguesthouse.co.uk; Lanty's Lonnen; s/d from £28/56) is a fine Edwardian home surrounded by manicured lawns and gardens, from which there are stunning views (which can also be enjoyed from the breakfast room). The owners like their flowers so much they decorated most of the house accordingly. Highly recommended.

Bus No 685 comes from Newcastle (1½ hours) and Carlisle (45 minutes) 12 times daily. Hadrian's Wall bus No AD 122 (four daily June to early September) or No 185 (October to May) connect Haltwhistle with other places along the wall. Bus No 681 heads south to Alston (55 minutes, three daily Monday to Saturday). The town is also on the Newcastle–Carlisle railway line (hourly).

AROUND HALTWHISTLE

Vindolanda Roman Fort & Museum

The extensive site of **Vindolanda** (☎ 01434-344277; www.vindolanda.com; adult £3.90, with Roman Army Museum £5.60; ☯ 10am-6pm Apr-Sep, 10am-5pm Feb-Mar & Oct-Nov) offers a fascinating glimpse into the daily life of a Roman garrison town. The time-capsule museum displays leather sandals, signature Roman toothbrush-flourish helmet decorations, and countless writing tablets such as a student's marked work ('sloppy'), and a parent's note with a present of socks and underpants (things haven't changed – in this climate you can never have too many).

The museum is just one part of this large, extensively excavated site, which includes impressive parts of the fort and town (excavations continue) and reconstructed turrets and temple.

It's 1½ miles north of Bardon Mill between the A69 and B6318 and a mile from Once Brewed.

Housesteads Roman Fort & Museum

The wall's most dramatic site – and the best-preserved Roman fort in the whole country – is at **Housesteads** (EH; ☎ 01434-344363; adult £3.50; ☯ 10am-6pm Apr-Sep, 10am- 4pm Oct-Mar). From here, high on a ridge and covering 2 hectares, you can survey the moors of Northumberland National Park and the snaking wall, with a sense of awe at the landscape and the aura of the Roman lookouts.

The substantial foundations bring fort life alive. The remains include an impressive hospital, granaries with a ventilation system, and barrack blocks. Most memorable are the spectacularly situated communal, flushable latrines, which summon up Romans at their most mundane.

Housesteads is 2½ miles north of Bardon Mill on the B6318, and about 3 miles from Once Brewed. It's popular, so avoid summer weekends and visit late in the day when the site is quiet and indescribably eerie.

Other Sights

One mile northwest of Greenhead close to Walltown Crags, the kid-pleasing **Roman Army Museum** (☎ 016977-47485; adult/child £3.50/2.50, with Vindolanda £6.50/4.30; ☯ 10am-6pm Apr-Sep, 10am-5pm Feb-Mar & Oct-Nov) provides lots of colourful background detail to wall life, such as how far soldiers had to march per day and whether they could marry.

On a minor road off the B6318, about 3 miles west of Greenhead, is what's left of the **Birdoswald Roman Fort** (EH; ☎ 016977-47602; adult £3; ☯ 10am-5.30pm Mar-Oct), on an escarpment overlooking the beautiful Irthing Gorge. A fine stretch of wall stretches from here to Harrow Scar Milecastle. About half a mile away, across the impressive river footbridge, is another good bit of wall, ending in two turrets and the meticulous structure of the **Willowford Bridge abutment**.

About 3 miles further west along the A69, just across the border in Cumbria, are the peaceful raspberry-coloured ruins of **Lanercost Priory** (EH; ☎ 016977-3030; adult £2.50; ☻ 10am-6pm Apr-Sep, 10am-4pm Thu-Mon Oct), founded in 1166 by Augustinian canons. Ransacked several times, it became a private house after the dissolution, and a priory church was created from the Early English nave. The church has some beautiful Pre-Raphaelite stained glass. The AD 122 bus can drop you at the gate.

Sleeping

Once Brewed YHA Hostel (☎ 0870 770 5980; www.yha .org.uk; Military Rd; Bardon Mill; dm £11.80; ☻ Mar-Oct, Tue-Sat Nov-Feb) A modern and well-equipped hostel central for visiting both Housesteads Fort, 3 miles away, and Vindolanda, 1 mile away. Bus No 685 (from Hexham or Haltwhistle train stations) will drop you at Henshaw, 2 miles south, or you could leave the train at Bardon Mill 2½ miles southeast. The Hadrian's Wall bus drops you at the door June to September.

Greenhead YHA Hostel (☎ 016977-47401; www .yha.org.uk; dm £10.60; ☻ Jul-Aug, call to check other times) A converted Methodist chapel by a trickling stream and a pleasant garden, 3 miles west of Haltwhistle. The hostel is served by bus No AD 122 or 685.

Holmhead Guest House (☎ 016977-47402; www .bandbhadrianswall.com; Thirlwall Castle Farm, Greenhead; dm/s/d £9/41/62) Four fairly compact rooms in a lovely remote old cottage; most of the space is taken up by the big beds. All the rooms have a shower rather than a bath. A barn was recently converted into a large dorm room, perfect for budget walkers and cyclists. Half a mile north of Greenhead.

NORTHUMBERLAND

England's last frontier isn't quite undiscovered, but it feels that way, thanks to the fact that much of the rugged, stunning interior is protected by the confines of a sparsely populated national park. Throughout the region are castles and fortified buildings known as *peles,* testament to its ferocious history as the battleground between north and south, beginning in the days of the

Anglo-Saxon kingdom of Northumbria and only really ending during the 18th century. Nowadays the folks are a largely domesticated bunch, which can hardly be said of the landscapes, which remain as wild as ever.

Getting Around

The great *Northumberland Public Transport Guide* (£1.50) is available from local TICs. Transport options are good, with a train line running along the coast from Newcastle to Berwick and on to Edinburgh.

ALNWICK

☎ 01665 / pop 7770

Northumberland's historic ducal town (pronounced 'Annick') has a genteel grace about it more common in tidy little counties like Berkshire or Surrey. The maze of narrow cobbled streets beneath the imposing shadow of the ubiquitous castle is so pleasant that in 2003 *Country Life* voted it the best place to live in England.

The castle is on the northern side of town and overlooks the River Aln. The **TIC** (☎ 510665; www.alnwick.gov.uk; 2 The Shambles; ☻ 9am-5pm Mon-Sat, 10am-4pm Sun) is by the market place, in a handsome building that was once a butcher's shop.

There has been a market in Alnwick for over 800 years. Market days are Thursday and Saturday, with a Farmers' Market on the last Friday of the month.

Alnwick Castle

The imposing **Alnwick Castle** (☎ 510777; www .alnwickcastle.com; adult/child £7.50/free; ☻ 11am-5pm Apr-Oct), ancestral home of the Duke of Northumberland and a favourite set for filmmakers, has changed little since the 14th century. The interior is sumptuous and extravagant; the six rooms open to the public – state rooms, dining room, guard chamber and library – have an incredible display of Italian paintings, including Titian's *Ecce Homo* and many Canalettos. Magnificent carving decorates the rooms, completed by the Florentine-trained Alnwick school.

The castle is set in parklands designed by Lancelot 'Capability' Brown. The woodland walk offers some great aspects of the castle. Or for a view looking up the River Aln, take the B1340 towards the coast.

Sleeping

White Swan Hotel (☎ 602109; fax 510400; Bondgate Within; s/d from £65/110; **P**)) Alnwick's top address is this 300-year-old coaching inn right in the heart of town. Its rooms are all of a pretty good standard, but this spot stands out for its dining room, which has elaborate original panelling, ceiling and stained-glass windows filched from the *Olympic*, sister ship to the *Titanic*.

A row of handsome Georgian houses along Bondgate Without house several worthwhile options that all charge around £25 per person, including **Lindisfarne Guest House** (☎ 603430; 6 Bondgate Without) and the **Teapot** (☎ 604473; 8 Bondgate Without), which has the largest teapot collection in town.

Eating & Drinking

A number of atmospheric pubs do a good line in grub. The **Market Tavern** (☎ 602759; 7 Fenkle St; stottie £5), near Market Square, is the place to go for a traditional giant beef stottie (bread roll), while **Ye Old Cross** (☎ 602735; Narrowgate; mains around £6) is good for a drink and is known as 'Bottles', after the dusty bottles in the window: 150 years ago the owner collapsed and died while trying to move them and no-one's dared to try since.

Getting There & Away

There are regular buses from Newcastle (Nos 501, 505 and 518, one hour, 28 per day Monday to Saturday, 18 on Sunday). Bus No 518 has 10 to 14 daily services to the attractive towns of Warkworth (25 minutes) and Alnmouth (15 minutes), which has the nearest train station. Bus Nos 505 and 525 come from Berwick (45 minutes, 13 daily Monday to Saturday). The **Arriva Day Pass** (£4.10) is good value.

WARKWORTH

☎ 01665 / pop 1642

Biscuit-coloured Warkworth is little more than a cluster of houses around a loop in the River Coquet, but it makes for an impressive sight, especially if you arrive on the A1068 from Alnwick, when the village unfolds before you to reveal the craggy ruin of the enormous 14th-century castle.

A 'worm-eaten hold of ragged stone', **Warkworth Castle** (EH; ☎ 711423; adult £3; ◷ 10am-6pm Apr-Sep, 10am-4pm Oct, Sat-Mon only Nov-Mar) features in Shakespeare's *Henry IV* Parts I and

II and will not disappoint modern visitors. Yes, it is still pretty worm-eaten and ragged, but it crowns an imposing site, high above the gentle, twisting river.

Tiny, mystical, 14th-century **Warkworth Hermitage** (EH; adult £2; ◷ 11am-5pm Wed & Sun Apr-Sep), carved into the rock, is a few hundred yards upriver. Follow the signs along the path, then take possibly the world's shortest ferry ride. It's a lovely stretch of water and there is **rowing boat hire** (adult/child per 45min £2.50/2; ◷ Sat & Sun May-Sep).

The **Sun Hotel** (☎ 711259; www.rytonpark-sun .co.uk; 6 Castle Tce; mains s/d from £49/75) has 14 huge, country bedrooms above a cosy bar and an elegant restaurant that serves local dishes given the French treatment. There are great views of both castle and river.

In the village centre, **Greenhouse** (☎ 712322; 21 Dial Pl; mains £6.95-13; ◷ lunch & dinner Mon & Wed-Sat, lunch only Sun) is a café-bistro that serves great coffee, cakes and more substantial fish and meat dishes on large pine tables.

Bus No 518 links Newcastle (1½ hours, hourly), Warkworth, Alnmouth and Alnwick. There's a train station on the main east-coast line, about 1½ miles west of town.

FARNE ISLANDS

One of England's most incredible sea-bird colonies is on the **Farne Islands** (NT; ☎ 01665-720651; adult £4.80, £3.80 Apr & Aug-Sep; ◷ 10.30am-6pm Apr & Aug-Sep, Inner Farne also 1.30-5pm May-Jul, Staple also 10.30am-1.30pm May-Jul), a rocky archipelago about 3 miles offshore from the undistinguished fishing village of Seahouses. Visit during breeding season (roughly May to July), when you can see feeding chicks of 20 species of sea bird, including puffins, kittiwakes, arctic terns, eider ducks, cormorants and gulls. This is an extraordinary experience, for there are few places in the world where you can get so close to nesting sea birds. The islands are also home to England's only colony of grey seals.

To protect the islands from environmental damage, the National Trust (NT) has made only two accessible to the public, Inner Farne and Staple Island. Inner Farne is the more interesting of the two, as it is also the site of a tiny chapel (1370, restored 1848) to the memory of St Cuthbert, who lived here for a spell and died here in 687.

Near the Seahouses harbour are a **TIC** (☎ 01655-720884; Seafield Rd; ◷ 10am-5pm Apr-Oct)

and a **National Trust Shop** (☎ 01665-721099; 16 Main St; ☻ 10am-5pm Apr-Oct) for all information on the island.

Getting There & Away

There are various tours, from 1½-hour cruises to all-day specials, and they get going from 10am April to October. Crossings can be rough and may be impossible in bad weather. Some of the boats have no proper cabin, so make sure you've got warm, waterproof clothing if there's a chance of rain. Also recommended is an old hat – those birds sure can ruin a head of hair!

Of the operators from the dock in Seahouses, **Billy Shiel** (☎ 01665-720308; www.farne -islands.com; 3hr tour adult/child £10/8, all-day tour with landing £20/15) is recommended.

BAMBURGH
☎ 01668 / pop 442

Bamburgh is all about the castle, a massive, imposing structure high up on a basalt crag and visible for miles around. The village itself – a tidy fist of houses around a pleasant green – isn't half bad, but it's really just about the castle, a solid contender for England's best.

Bamburgh Castle (☎ 214515; www.bamburghcastle .com; adult/child £5/2; ☻ 11am-5pm Apr-Oct) is built around a powerful Norman keep and played a key role in the border wars. It was restored in the 19th century by the great industrialist Lord Armstrong (p636), who also turned his passion to Cragside. The great halls within are still home to the Armstrong family. It's just inland from long stretches of empty white-sand beach, ideal for blustery walks.

Sleeping & Eating

Bamburgh Hall (☎ 214230; cresswell@farming.co.uk; r £60) This magnificent farmhouse built in 1697 has only one room, but we highly recommend it for the sheer pleasure of the views right down to the sea, and the huge breakfast, served in the very dining room that the Jacobite officers met during the rebellion of 1715.

Victoria Hotel (☎ 214431; www.victoriahotel.net; Front St; mains around £12, s/d £52.50/95) Overlooking the village green is this handsome hotel with bedrooms decorated with quality antiques and – in the superior rooms – handcrafted four-posters. Here you'll also find the best restaurant in town, with a surprisingly adventurous menu where, for instance, chorizo is preferred over Cumberland sausage.

Greenhouse (☎ 214513; www.thegreenhouseguest house.co.uk; 5-6 Front St; s/d from £26/52) With four large, modern rooms with power showers and a mix of views (rooms 1 and 2 overlooking the front are best), this is a decent option, although they are loath to sell a room as a single during the summer.

The **Copper Kettle** is the place to be for tea and you can stock up for a picnic at the **Pantry**.

Getting There & Away

Bus No 501 runs from Newcastle (£4.20, 2¼ hours, two daily Monday to Saturday, one Sunday) stopping at Alnwick and Seahouses. Bus Nos 401 and 501 from Alnwick (£3.70, four to six daily) take one hour.

HOLY ISLAND (LINDISFARNE)
☎ 01289 / pop 179

Holy Island has an almost unearthly quality to it. Fiercely desolate and isolated, it is accessible via a narrow, glinting causeway that only appears at low tide, and has hardly changed since a band of monks lived here until the 9th century. When they left, thanks to the unwelcome attentions of marauding Vikings, they carried with them the illuminated *Lindisfarne Gospels* (now in the British Library in London) and the miraculously preserved body of St Cuthbert, who lived here for a couple of years but preferred the hermit's life on Inner Farne. A priory was reestablished in the 11th century but didn't survive the dissolution in 1537.

The island's peculiar isolation is best appreciated mid-week or preferably out of season, but whatever you do, pay attention to the crossing-time information, available at TICs and on noticeboards throughout the area. Every year there are a handful of go-it-alone fools who are caught midway by the incoming tide and have to abandon their cars.

Sights

Lindisfarne Priory (EH; ☎ 389200; adult £3.50; ☻ 10am-6pm Apr-Oct, 10am-4pm Nov-Mar, Sat & Sun only Nov-Jan) consists of elaborate red-and-grey ruins and the later 13th-century St Mary the Virgin Church. The museum next to these displays the remains of the first monastery and tells the story of the monastic community before and after dissolution.

Twenty pages of the luminescent *Lindisfarne Gospels* are on view electronically at the **Lindisfarne Heritage Centre** (☎ 389004; Marygate; adult/child £2.50/free; ☯ 10am-5pm), which also has displays on the locality.

Half a mile from the village stands the tiny, storybook **Lindisfarne Castle** (NT; ☎ 389244; adult £4; ☯ noon-3pm Apr-Oct), built in 1550 and extended and converted by Sir Edwin Lutyens from 1902 to 1910 for Mr Hudson, the owner of *Country Life* magazine. Its opening times may be extended depending on the tide. A **shuttle bus** (☎ 389236) runs here from the car park.

Sleeping & Eating

It's possible to stay on the island, but you'll need to book in advance.

Open Gate (☎ 389222; theopengate@theopengate .ndo.co.uk; Marygate; s/d £32/54) This spacious Elizabethan stone farmhouse with comfortable rooms caters primarily to those looking for a contemplative experience. There is a small chapel in the basement and a room full of books on Celtic spirituality, and there are organised retreats throughout the year.

Ship (☎ 389311; Marygate; s/d/t from £46/60/80) Three exceptionally comfortable rooms – one has a four-poster – above an 18th-century public house known here as the Tavern. There's good local seafood in the bar.

Getting There & Around

Holy Island can be reached by bus No 477 from Berwick (Wednesday and Saturday only, Monday to Saturday July and August). People taking cars across are requested to park in one of the sign-posted car parks (£4 per day). The sea covers the causeway and cuts the island off from the mainland for about five hours each day. Tide times are listed at TICs, in local papers and each side of the crossing.

BERWICK-UPON-TWEED
☎ 01289 / pop 12,870

England's northernmost city is a salt-crusted fortress town that has the dubious honour of being the most fought-over settlement in Europe, trading hands between the Scots and English a total of 14 times. Although English in name, Berwick's massive ramparts and insular folk give off a vibe that suggests the town really belongs to no-one but itself.

The **TIC** (☎ 330733; www.berwick-upon-tweed.gov.uk; 106 Marygate; ☯ 10am-6pm Easter-Jun, 10am-5pm Jul-Sep, 10am-4pm Mon-Sat Oct-Easter) is helpful. Access the Internet at **Berwick Backpackers** (☎ 331481; 56-8 Bridge St).

Sights & Activities

Berwick's superb **city walls** (EH; admission free) are the town's best attraction. They were begun in 1558 to reinforce an earlier set built during the reign of Edward II. They represented the most state-of-the-art military technology of the day and were designed both to house artillery (in arrowhead-shaped bastions) and to withstand it (the walls are low and massively thick, but it's still a long way to fall).

You can walk almost the entire length of the walls, a circuit of about a mile. It's a must, with wonderful, wide-open views. The TIC has a brochure (40p) describing the main sights.

Recommended are one-hour **guided walks** (adult/child £3/free; ☯ 10am, 11.15am, 12.30pm & 2pm Mon-Fri Apr-Oct) starting from the TIC.

Sleeping & Eating

There are plenty of B&Bs around the town, most of which offer fairly basic but comfortable rooms; the TIC can assist in finding one.

Berwick Backpackers (☎ 331481; www.berwick -backpackers.co.uk; 56-8 Bridge St; dm/s/d £10/14/32) This excellent hostel, basically a series of rooms in the outhouses of a Georgian home around a central courtyard, has one large comfortable dorm, a single and two doubles, all with en suite. It also has Internet access. Highly recommended.

SOMETHING SPECIAL

Coach House (☎ 01890-820293; www.coach housecrookham.com; Crookham; dinner £19.50, r £27-58) This exquisite guesthouse spread about a 17th-century cottage, an old smithy and other outbuildings is one of the finest in the area. There is a wide variety of rooms, from the more traditional (with rare chestnut beams and country-style furniture) to more contemporary layouts flavoured with Mediterranean and even Indian touches. The food, beginning with the superb organic breakfast, is absolutely delicious and the equal of any restaurant around.

No 1 Sallyport (☎ 308827; www.1sallyport-bedand
breakfast.com; Bridge St; r £70-90) Three superb
rooms make this the top choice in town.
The Master Suite is a country-style Georgian classic complete with a wood-burning
stove; the Manhattan Loft, crammed into
the attic, makes the most of the confined
space; but the real treat is the Smugglers'
Suite, with a separate sitting-room complete with widescreen TV, DVD players
and plenty of space to lounge around in.

Café 52 (☎ 306796; 50-52 Bridge St; mains £4-7;
🕙 9am-10pm Mon-Sat) Next door to the hostel,
this fine little café with a tasty bistro-style
menu is a local pioneer of café culture; it's
the only place in town where you can sit
around over a cup of good coffee.

Getting There & Away
BUS
Berwick has good links into the Scottish
Borders; there are buses west to Coldstream,
Kelso and Galashiels. Bus Nos 505, 515 and
525 go to Newcastle (2¼ hours, five daily)
via Alnwick. Bus No 253 goes to Edinburgh
(two hours, six daily Monday to Saturday,
two Sunday) via Dunbar.

TRAIN
Berwick is almost exactly halfway between
Edinburgh (£13.10, 50 minutes) and Newcastle (£13.10, 50 minutes) on the main
east-coast London–Edinburgh line. Half-
hourly trains between Edinburgh and Newcastle stop in Berwick.

Getting Around
The town centre is compact and walkable; if
you're feeling lazy try **Berwick Taxis** (☎ 307771).
Tweed Bicycles (☎ 331476; 17a Bridge St) hires out
mountain bikes for £17 a day.

NORTHUMBERLAND NATIONAL PARK

The lonely, grand landscape of Northumberland National Park is surely England's
last great wilderness, 398 sq miles of natural
wonderland that is home to a mere 2000
people. The challenging landscape is dotted with prehistoric remains and fortified
houses – the thick-walled *peles* that were
the only solid buildings constructed here

until the mid–18th century – while the finest sections of Hadrian's Wall run along the
park's southern edge.

Orientation & Information
The park runs from Hadrian's Wall in the
south, takes in the Simonside Hills in the
east and runs into the Cheviot Hills along
the Scottish border. There are few roads.

For information, contact the **Northumberland National Park** (☎ 01434-605555; www.nnpa.org
.uk; Eastburn, South Park, Hexham). Visitors centres
are in most of the park's towns and villages;
they all handle accommodation bookings.

Walking & Cycling
The most spectacular stretch of **Hadrian's
Wall Path** (p628) is probably between Sew-
ingshields and Greenhead in the south of
the park.

There are many fine walks into the Cheviots, frequently passing by prehistoric
remnants; contact TICs for information.

Though at times strenuous, cycling in the
park is a pleasure; the roads are good and
the traffic is light in this part of Northumberland. There's off-road cycling in Border
Forest Park.

Getting There & Around
Public-transport options are limited, aside
from buses on the A69. See the Hadrian's
Wall section (p628) for access to the south.
Bus No 808 (55 minutes, two daily Mon-
day to Saturday) runs between Otterburn
and Newcastle. Postbus No 815 and bus
No 880 (45 minutes, eight daily Monday to
Saturday, three on Sunday) runs between
Hexham and Bellingham. National Express
No 383 (three hours, one daily, £19) goes
from Newcastle to Edinburgh via Otter-
burn, Byrness (by request), Jedburgh, Mel-
rose and Galashiels.

BELLINGHAM
☎ 01434 / pop 1164
The small, remote village of Bellingham
(bellin-jum) is a pleasant enough spot on
the banks of the Tyne, surrounded by beautiful, deserted countryside on all sides. It is
an excellent base from which to kick off
your exploration of the park.

The **TIC** (☎ 220616; Main St; 🕙 9.30am-1pm &
2-5pm Mon-Sat, 1-5pm Sun Apr-Oct, 2-5pm Mon-Sat Nov-
Mar) handles visitor inquiries.

There's not a lot to see here save the 12th-century **St Cuthbert's Church**, unique because it retains its original stone roof, and **Cuddy's Well**, outside the churchyard wall, which is alleged to have healing powers on account of its blessing by the saint.

The **Hareshaw Linn Walk** passes through a wooded valley and over six bridges, leading to a 9m-high waterfall 2½ miles north of Bellingham (*linn* is an Old English name for waterfall).

Sleeping & Eating

Bellingham's on the Pennine Way; book ahead for accommodation in summer. Most of the B&Bs are clustered around the village green.

Bellingham YHA Hostel (☎ 0870 770 5694; www .yha.org.uk; Woodburn Rd; dm £9.30; ☺ Tue-Sat mid-Apr–Oct, daily Jul & Aug) A cedarwood cabin with spartan facilities on the edge of the village, the hostel is almost always busy, so be sure to book in advance. There are showers, a cycle store and a self-catering kitchen on the premises.

Lyndale Guest House (☎ 220361; www.lyndaleguest house.co.uk; r per person from £20) The bedrooms in this pleasant family home just off the village green are modern and extremely tidy; it's a bit like visiting a really neat relative.

Pub grub is about the extent of the village's dining; recommended are the **Black Bull** (☎ 220226; Main St) and the **Rose & Crown** (☎ 220202; West View, Manchester Sq).

ROTHBURY

☎ 01669 / pop 1960

Once a prosperous Victorian resort, Rothbury is now a pretty, restful market town on the River Coquet that makes a convenient base for the Cheviots.

There's a **TIC and visitors centre** (☎ 620887; Church St; ☺ 10am-5pm Apr-Oct, 10am-6pm Jun-Aug).

The biggest draw in the immediate vicinity is **Cragside House, Garden and Estate** (NT; ☎ 620333; admission to all £8, estate & garden £5.50; house ☺ 1-5.30pm Tue-Sun Apr-Sep, 1-4.30pm Oct, estate & garden ☺ 10.30am-7pm & 11am-4pm Wed-Sun Nov-Dec), the quite incredible country retreat of the first Lord Armstrong. In the 1880s the house had hot and cold running water, as well as a telephone and alarm system, and was the first in the world to be lit by electricity (generated through hydropower).

The Victorian mansion and gardens are well worth exploring. The latter are huge and remarkably varied, from lakes and moors to one of the world's largest rock gardens. Visit in May to see myriad rhododendrons.

The estate is 1 mile north of town on the B6341; there is no public transport to the front gates from Rothbury – try **Rothbury Motors** (☎ 620516) if you need a taxi.

High St is a good place to look for accommodation.

Equipped with beamed ceilings, stone fireplaces and canopied four-poster beds, **Katerina's Guest House** (☎ 602334; Sun Bldgs, High St; www.katerinasguesthouse.co.uk; s/d from £36/50) is one of the nicer options in town, even though the rooms are a little small.

Other similarly priced options include **Alexander House** (☎ 621463; s/d £30/45) and the **Haven** (☎ 620577; Back Crofts; s/d £27/50), on top of a hill.

Food options are limited to pub grub. For takeaway you could try the **Rothbury Bakery** (High St) for pies and sandwiches or **Tully's** (High St) for flapjacks.

Bus No 416 from Morpeth (30 minutes) leaves every two hours Monday to Saturday and three times on Sunday.

Wales

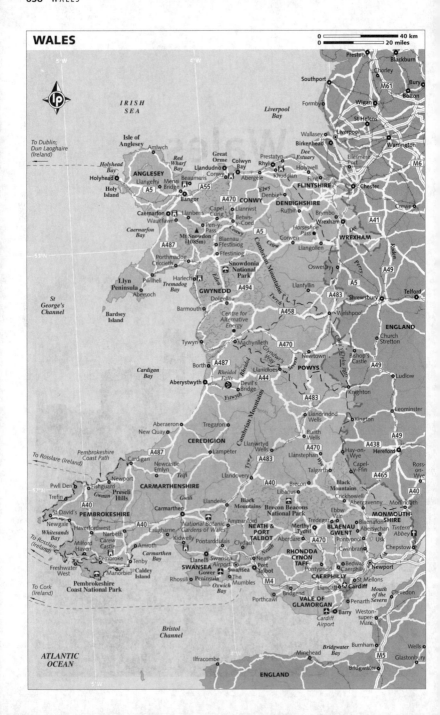

Cardiff
(Caerdydd)

CONTENTS

Cardiff
(Caerdydd)

Cardiff, the capital of Wales, is a fashionable city, where a strong youth culture and firm political identity mix with sports madness and Saturday nights that, for some, are hard to remember. It may be smaller than places such as London and Manchester, but the concentration of modern and historic sights, international restaurants, slick bars and a zinging music scene makes it less overwhelming, just as imaginative and friendlier.

Made a city in only 1905 and a capital in 1955, Cardiff is surging back from drastic decline caused by the collapse of the coal industry. Millennial projects include the monster Millennium Stadium, one of the biggest in Europe, and so dead centre as to paralyse the city on match days. A mile down on the waterfront, the docks have been converted into Cardiff Bay, which is home to two buildings of national pride – the National Assembly, which gives the Welsh their first part-independent voice, and the Wales Millennium Centre, a magnificent performance centre and home to the Welsh National Opera.

Older architectural treats include the grand City Hall and neighbouring National Museum & Gallery of Wales, which are part of the elegant Civic Centre buildings. But best of the lot is Cardiff Castle, the rebuilt fantasy of the fabulously rich 19th-century Marquis of Bute, Cardiff's King of Coal, who fitted out the rooms so he could indulge his dream of living like a medieval prince.

HIGHLIGHTS

- Exploring the castles in and around Cardiff: **Cardiff** (p642), **Caerphilly** (p654) and **Castell Coch** (p653)
- Visiting **Llandaff Cathedral** (p646) – a stunning place of worship in lovely surrounds
- Catching a match, or at least the tour, at **Millennium Stadium** (p642)
- Seeing great art at the **National Museum & Gallery of Wales** (p642)
- Boating on the lake on **Cardiff Bay** (p643) and dining while viewing its glittering harbour
- Relaxing in the spa at **St David's Hotel & Spa** (p648), with floor-to-ceiling windows overlooking Cardiff Bay

Caerphilly ★
Castell Coch ★
Cardiff ★
★
Cardiff Bay

- TELEPHONE CODE: 029
- POPULATION: 327,706

HISTORY
The city began as a Roman fort in AD 75, and the name Cardiff probably derives from Caer Tâf (Taff Fort) or Caer Didi (Didius's Fort, referring to the Roman general Aulus Didius). In 1093 (after the Norman Conquest) Robert Fitzhamon built himself a castle here, which still stands within the modern grounds of Cardiff Castle, and a town grew around it. Welsh uprisings against the Normans in 1183, and again in 1404 led by Owain Glendŵr, inflicted major damage on the town, and for 400 years it failed to thrive.

The settlement took off during the 19th-century iron-making and coal-mining boom, expertly steered by the aristocratic Bute family of Scotland, who inherited Cardiff Castle and lands in the 18th century. The wealth created by their ownership of the city docks and the valley coalfields allowed them to endow the city with fine buildings and to rebuild the castle as a family home. In 1905 Cardiff was designated a city.

In 1913, Cardiff became the world's largest coal port, and the third marquis of Bute became one of the richest men in the world. The population boomed, and a multiethnic, music-loving, working-class community grew up in dockside Butetown.

But hard times came after WWI, followed by the 1930s Depression. During WWII the city was heavily bombed and soon after the coal industry was nationalised. As a result, in 1947, the Butes donated their castle and lands to the city and quit town.

Cardiff became the Welsh capital in 1955, but with coal mining dead the docks were, too, until 1987, when a project began to convert the docks into a waterfront area for culture and leisure. With the addition of a trio of millennial city institutions the Welsh capital now progresses with more confidence.

ORIENTATION
The castle and walls on the northern side of the centre are a good orientation point. Just south of them the Millennium Stadium soars beside the River Taff. East of the stadium is the compact shopping and restaurant zone, and the TIC. The central bus and train stations lie south of the centre, off the lower end of St Mary St, the main vehicular road north–south through the city.

Bute Park extends northwest behind the castle. The elegant Civic Centre, including the National Museum & Gallery of Wales, City Hall and Law Courts, are east of the park, northeast of the castle.

The Cardiff Bay waterfront lies 1 mile southeast of the centre through Butetown.

See p653 for details on getting to/from the airport.

INFORMATION
Bookshops
Oriel (Map p644; High St) For Welsh-language books.
Waterstone's (Map p644; 2a The Hayes & 18-20 Hill's St) Two branches of this well-stocked bookshop.

Emergency
Police station (Map p644; ☎ 2022 2111; King Edward VII Ave) Near Alexandra Gardens.

Internet Access
Cardiff Central Library (Map p644; ☎ 2087 1600; Frederick St; access free; ⏰ 9.30am-6pm Mon-Wed & Fri, 9am-7pm Thu, 9am-5.30pm Sat) Offers Internet access; booking is compulsory.

CARDIFF IN...

One day
Immerse yourself in spectacular neo-Gothic at **Cardiff Castle** (p642) in the morning, then take a walk in **Bute Park** (p642). Have a picnic or eat in central Cardiff – you can nose round the Victorian shopping **arcades** (p652). In the afternoon, head for the **National Museum & Gallery of Wales** (p642). In the evening go to **Cardiff Bay** (p643) for waterside dining, then head back for live music at **Clwb Ifor Bach** (p651).

Two days
Use the One Day itinerary, but dine in the centre in the evening, then on day two, go out to **Llandaff Cathedral** (p646), continuing to **Castell Coch** (p653) and **Caerphilly** (p654). On the second evening, head to **Cardiff Bay** (p543) and its array of fine international restaurants.

Medical Services

Pharmacies rotate late opening hours.

Boots (Map p644; ☎ 2023 1291; 36 Queen St; ☷ 10am-7pm Mon & Fri, 10am-10pm Tue, 10am-9pm Wed & Thu, 10am-6pm Sat, 11am-5pm Sun)

University Hospital of Wales: Heath Park (☎ 2074 7747) Two miles north of the Civic Centre.

Money

All major UK banks (with ATMs and currency desks) are on Queen St and/or St Mary St and High St.

Post

Main post office (Map p644; The Hayes)

Tourist Information

Tourist Information Centre (TIC; Map p644; ☎ 2022 7281; www.visitcardiff.info; The Hayes; ☷ 10am-6pm Mon-Sat, 10am-4pm Sun) Books accommodation and provides information on sights and events in the city and around Wales. Also has Internet access (£1.50 per 20 minutes); bookings are not necessary.

SIGHTS & ACTIVITIES
Cardiff Castle

Entertaining history and outstanding Victorian interior design make **Cardiff Castle** (Map p644; ☎ 2087 8100; www.cardiffcastle.com; Castle St; adult/child grounds only £3/1.90, with castle tour £6/3.70; ☷ 9.30am-6pm Mar-Oct, 9.30am-5pm Nov-Feb) the city's top attraction.

To the right of the entrance are parts of a 3rd-century-AD Roman fort that guarded the River Taff ford. Ahead is the motte and bailey of the 12th-century Norman castle, with great views from the top. And to the left of the entrance are the neo-Gothic Victorian main buildings, the reconstructed castle home of the Butes of Scotland, where the romantic medieval décor is the highlight of the visit.

Here, knights adorn fireplaces, a banqueting hall is complete with a minstrel gallery, and the Bute children's nursery walls are painted with fairytales. The castle is the fantasy of the third marquis of Bute, whose wealth came from family mineral rights in the valleys above the city and from the docks built by his father. The castle work was executed by his talented designer William Burges, completed between 1868 and 1881.

Bute Park & Parkland Corridor

Verdant Bute Park, originally part of the castle estate, stretches northwest following the Taff River away from the castle and centre and is much loved by Cardiff folk. The park is bounded on Castle St, beside the castle, by the **animal wall**, where stone creatures – a pelican, racoons and seals – paw and perch on the parapet.

A good way to explore the parkland, which continues upriver 7 miles via Sophia Gardens and Pontcanna Fields as far as Castell Coch, is to use the Taff Trail walking/cycling route. Hire a bicycle from **Cardiff Caravan Park** (☎ 2039 8362; Pontcanna Fields).

National Museum & Gallery of Wales

The only stuffiness in Wales' charming premier **museum** (Map p644; ☎ 2039 7951; www.nmgw.ac.uk; Gorsedd Gardens Rd; admission free; ☷ 10am-5pm Tue-Sun; wheelchair access) is a little taxidermy. The world-class art collection is a must-see for adults, and the exhibits on natural history and evolution are a wow for kids. Allow a day to see all the treasures, and a half-day to enjoy highlights.

The museum lies northeast of the castle in the Civic Centre, a grid of white stone neoclassical buildings erected during Cardiff's 'black gold' boomtime. Beside the museum is City Hall, the seat of the council, and beside that the Law Courts.

The museum's animal attractions include the 9m-long skeleton of a humpback whale and the world's largest turtle (2.9m by 2.7m). With volcanic eruptions and footage of the country's soaring landscape, the Evolution of Wales exhibit rollicks through 4600 million years.

The national art collection shows the progression from medieval to contemporary art and includes the largest impressionist collection outside Paris. Here you'll see masterpieces by Sandro Botticelli and El Greco, Claude Monet, Camille Pissaro, Paul Cézanne, Henri Matisse and Pierre-Auguste Renoir, David Hockney and also works by Rachel Whiteread.

Welsh artists hold their own, with works by Richard Wilson, and Gwen and Augustus John, including the latter's beguilingly angelic portrait of Dylan Thomas.

Millennium Stadium

The boldness of plonking Cardiff's answer to the Coliseum dead in the city centre has paid off. The gleaming 72,500-seat, three-tiered **Millennium Stadium** (Map p644; ☎ tours

2082 2228; box office 0870 558 2582; www.cardiff-stadium.
co.uk; tours £5; ⏰ 10am-6pm Mon-Sat, 10am-5pm Sun
& bank holidays; wheelchair access) towers over the
streets and the Taff riverside. Its mission
is to serve a sport- and music-mad nation with international rugby and football
matches as well as major gigs such as Robbie Williams and the Manic Street Preachers. Attendance at international matches
has increased dramatically since its completion in 1999 for the Rugby World Cup.
Fans flood in and out of Cardiff with each
event, bringing pride, passion and cheer,
and swaggers and staggers to the pubs and
clubs.

A 45-minute tour, for which you must
book in advance, gives a close-up look at
the stadium. It starts from Entrance 3,
Westgate St, on the city side.

Cardiff Bay

Making a visit to Cardiff's **waterfront** (Map
see right) resembles a trip to the seaside in
the 21st century, and on sunny days, when
the bay reflects the blue sky, the waterfront
is a relaxing place to visit. There is a choice
of lightweight pleasures, such as picking
your flavour at the ice-cream parlour, taking a cruise or sitting in a luxury spa with
the best view in Britain. Then there are
always the art and culture spaces, a public show about the National Assembly for
Wales, which legislates from here, and a
terrific all-ages science centre. On the dockside huddles a flotilla of tempting bars and
restaurants, ranging from the trendy to the
family-friendly.

The story of **Cardiff Bay** starts in the 1880s
when coal was mined in vast quantities
from the nearby hills and exported from
the city docks. After WWII demand for coal
slumped, leading to decline and stagnation
on the quayside and in the local community.
The modern solution was to construct a
1.1km-long **tidal barrage** at the mouth of
the Rivers Taff and Ely, which flooded
their tidal mudflats and created a permanent 495-acre freshwater lake with 13km
of waterfront. Pieces are constantly being
added in the development jigsaw, and in
10 years time the waterfront could look
different again.

The bay lies 1 mile southeast of the city
centre, and is connected by train, bus and
boat (see p646).

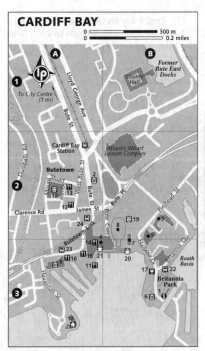

INFORMATION	
Cardiff Bay Visitor Centre	1 B3

SIGHTS & ACTIVITIES	(pp642–5)
Butetown History & Arts Centre	2 A2
Crickhowell House (temporary home for National Assembly of Wales)	3 B2
Mermaid Quay	4 A3
National Assembly for Wales (permanent building)	5 B2
Norwegian Church	6 B3
Pierhead Building	7 B3
Roald Dahl Plass	8 B2
Techniquest	9 A3

SLEEPING	(pp648–9)
St David's Hotel & Spa	10 A3

EATING	(pp649–50)
Bosphorus	11 A3
Caribbean Restaurant	12 A2
City Canteen & Bar	13 A2
Izakaya	14 A3
Scallops	15 A3
Tides	(see 10)
Woods	16 A3

DRINKING	(pp650–1)
Glee Club	(see 4)
Waterguard	17 B3

ENTERTAINMENT	(pp651–2)
Coal Exchange	18 A2
Wales Millennium Centre	19 B2

TRANSPORT	
Bay Island Voyages	20 B3
Cardiff Bay Cruises	21 A3
Guide Friday Tourbus Stop	22 B3
Guide Friday Tourbus Stop	23 A3
Guide Friday Tourbus Stop	24 A2
Waterbus	(see 4)

The **Cardiff Bay Visitor Centre** (☎ 2046 3833; 🕑 9.30am-5pm Mon-Fri, 10.30am-5pm Sat & Sun) is in 'the tube' and displays a model of the bay area.

The city side of the bay, **Mermaid Quay** (www.mermaidquay.co.uk), is the heart of waterfront eating, drinking and shopping. Beside it lies an oval boardwalk, **Roald Dahl Plass**, an open-air venue during the Cardiff Festival (p647) and other events.

Two eminent national bodies reside in Cardiff Bay. The National Assembly for Wales (see the boxed text, p646) has been temporarily housed in plain Crickhowell House while its grand new home next door, the glass-sided, wavy-roofed Richard Rogers' building has been constructed (due

to open in September 2005). Beside the new building, the landmark redbrick **Pierhead Building** houses the **Assembly information centre** (☎ 2089 8200; Pierhead St; admission free; 🕑 9.30am-4.30pm Mon-Thu, 10am-4.30pm Fri, 10.30am-4.30pm Sat & Sun), which explains the devolved body's democratic function.

Inland from the bay looms the jewel in Wales' cultural crown, the spectacular **Wales Millennium Centre** (☎ 2040 2000; www.wmc .org.uk), an international multimedia centre that opened in 2004. It has two theatres and is home to seven companies, headed by the Welsh National Opera. The gleaming gold-roofed structure has mauve slate panelling and was designed by Welsh architect Jonathan Adam.

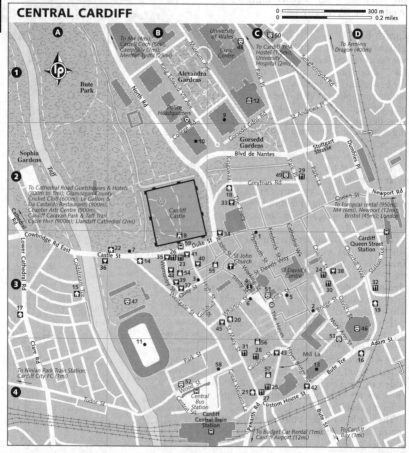

From most points around the bay you can see the little white **Norwegian Church** (☎ 2045 4899; Harbour Dr; admission free; ⏰ 9am-5pm), one of the few remaining historic dockside buildings. Constructed by the Norwegian Seamen's Mission in 1869 it was moved 200m to the waterfront during redevelopment. Author Roald Dahl was christened here and served as president of the preservation trust. The church is now an arts centre with a lovely café (p650).

TECHNIQUEST

Eureka – physics is fun! Cardiff's top children's entertainment is at the science and discovery centre **Techniquest** (☎ 2047 5475; www .techniquest.org; Stuart St; adult/child £6.75/4.65; ⏰ 9.30am-4.30pm Mon-Fri, 9.30am-5pm school holidays, 10.30am-5pm Sat & Sun). Little ones are helplessly absorbed, and adults too are sucked in by the 160 hands-on demonstrations. Visitors can explore whirlwinds, puzzle over balls that hang in mid-air and stargaze to their heart's content in the planetarium. Worth every micrometre.

BUTETOWN

The streets of dockside Victorian **Butetown** (Map p643), inland from the bay, are lined with grand architecture, some restored, most of it dilapidated. This was the heart of the world's coal trade, and home to a lively working-class community of folk from around the world. The quarter used to be known as Tiger Bay and had a repu-

---

BOATING

Catch a waterbus to the city and back, cruise across the bay, or take a high-speed trip out to the English Channel.

■ **Bay Island Voyages** (☎ 01445 420692; www.bayisland.co.uk) Book a high-speed blast through the barrage lock gates (£12, one hour), or to Flatholm and Steepholm Islands (£20, two hours).

■ **Cardiff Bay Cruises** (☎ 2047 2004; www .cardiffbaycruises.com) Half-hour bay cruises (£3, every 20 minutes).

■ **Waterbus** (☎ 07940 142409; www.cardiff cats.com; hop-on/-off trip £5) Plies between Mermaid Quay, the barrage and the city (Taff Landing).

---

tation for being rough and having a superb jazz scene!

The **Butetown History & Arts Centre** (☎ 2025 7657; www.bhac.org; 4 Dock Chambers, Bute St; admission free; ⏰ 10am-5pm Tue-Fri, 11am-4.30pm Sat & Sun) records the ordinary lives of Butetown folk in photo albums (eg from the 1950s youth club) and books, but leaves you yearning to know the full story of the docks' rise and fall.

The **Coal Exchange** (Map p643; ☎ 2049 4917; www.coalexchange.co.uk), in the centre of Mount Stuart Sq, was where the international coal price was once set, and is now a public venue. Peek inside the elaborately wood-carved hall, if you can.

THE NATIONAL ASSEMBLY FOR WALES

The devolved National Assembly, established in 1999, is working hard to justify itself. The low turnout in the 2003 elections (38%) is used by nationalist reformers to prove the need for more powers, while opponents of devolution *per se* say the 60-member body is a flop.

Since inauguration, the Assembly has implemented several popular measures, such as the abolition of school league tables and the introduction of free milk for children under seven. But for many Welsh people, the fact that the central government in Westminster, London, still sets Wales' budget, taxation, foreign policy and defence leaves the Assembly permanently yoked.

From the ruling Labour group's point of view, the 2003 vote weakened nationalism and empowered them to further the traditional Labour social policies under its leader and First Minister, Rhodri Morgan. The 2007 elections are the next test of the people's opinion of their partial independence. Full independence from the UK, meanwhile, appears as distant as ever.

Plenary (full) sessions take place in public and are broadcast. From late September 2005 the Assembly should be housed in a dedicated new **building** (☎ 2089 8477; www.wales.gov.uk) on the waterfront at Cardiff Bay.

GETTING THERE & AWAY

Walk 1 mile south from the city centre down Bute St, or take bus No 6 or 8 from the central bus station (every 15 minutes), No 7 from Hayes Bridge Rd (every 30 minutes) or No 35 from St Mary St (every 15 minutes).

Shuttle trains run from Queen St (not Cardiff Central) station to Cardiff Bay station (three minutes, every 15 minutes), from which it's a quarter-mile walk to the bay.

For details about the Waterbus (city to Mermaid Quay) see p645.

Llandaff Cathedral

A tall and slender exterior, lovely light-filled interior and notable 19th- and 20th-century artworks make **Llandaff Cathedral** (☎ 2056 4554; www.llandaffcathedral.org.uk; Cathedral Rd; admission free) worth the 2-mile trip northwest of the centre to view.

Dating from 1107, the cathedral marks the oldest see in Wales. It crumbled over the centuries and by the 18th century was in need of major attention. Largely restored in the 19th century, repair work was again needed to fix bomb damage after WWII. The towers sum up the building's disturbed history; one was built in the 15th century, the other in the 19th.

Inside, huge plain glass windows provide striking clarity of light. In the centre a striking concrete arch bears the organ and Sir Jacob Epstein's great aluminium sculpture *Christ in Majesty*. In the St Illtyd chapel is a triptych by Dante Gabriel Rossetti, while around the cathedral are stained-glass windows by the Pre-Raphaelite brotherhood (William Morris, Sir Edward Burne-Jones and Ford Madox Brown), along with other artworks of the period.

Bus Nos 24, 25, 33, 60 and 62 (15 minutes, every 10 to 15 minutes) run along Cathedral Rd to and from Llandaff.

WALKING TOUR

WALK FACTS
Distance 1 mile
Duration 1 hour

This tour is a meander around the city centre, taking in the major sights.

Start outside **Cardiff Castle gatehouse (1)**, then head east, examining the extraordinarily animated castle wall – William Burges' idea, but built after his death by his assistant. Originally by the castle's south gate, the animals were moved here after WWI. Then turn right down **Womanby St**, which is lined with warehouses. 'Womanby' has Viking roots and possibly means 'the strangers' quarter' or 'quarter of the keeper of the hounds'. On your right you'll be unable to miss the overgrown spaceship looming over you – **Millennium Stadium (2**; p642).

Take a left down Quay St, then right down High St. Cross over and walk east through the **Central Market (3)**. This glass and cast-iron shed has been flogging food and useful bits since 1891. There's an old market office and clock tower in the centre. You'll come out on **Trinity St**. Across the road is the **Old**

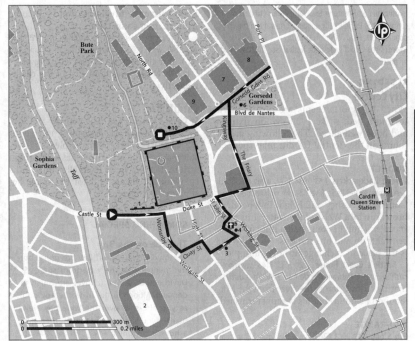

Library (4), for a time the Cardiff's Centre for Visual Arts – unfortunately, potential visitor numbers were vastly overestimated and the plug was pulled a year after it opened. The south façade features figures representing calligraphy, literature, printing, rhetoric and study. The motto *'Ny bydd ddoeth ny ddarlleno'* means 'he will not be wise who will not read'. Skirt round this, taking note of its message, and then head up **Working St** towards the castle. You'll pass graceful **St John's Church (5)**. When you reach the junction with **Queen St**, go right, then left into **The Friary**. At the end you'll reach the junction with **Boulevard de Nantes** (one of Cardiff's twin towns) and **Gorsedd Gardens (6)**. Looming over the gardens are the splendid **City Hall (7)**, the **National Museum & Gallery of Wales (8**; p642) and the **Law Courts (9)**. Cross North Rd to enter **Bute Park (10**; p642).

CARDIFF FOR CHILDREN

A manageable, friendly city, Cardiff's child-friendly sights include **Techniquest** (p645) at Cardiff Bay, and the **National Museum & Gallery of Wales** (p642) for great big animals that can't

get you. A grounds-only ticket at **Cardiff Castle** (p642) allows them to see the peacocks and climb the Norman tower for terrific views.

You can cruise around **Cardiff Bay** or take a high-speed trip out to the **islands** (p645), or lose them in **Bute Park** (p642). The best day trips outside the city are to the immense **Caerphilly Castle**, with its leaning tower (p654) and the **Museum of Welsh Life** (p654).

TOURS

Cardiff Bay Tours (☎ 2070 7882; www.cardiffbaytours .co.uk) Guides accompany you on the Waterbus, coach or road-train around the bay to the barrage.
Guide Friday (☎ 2038 4291; www.guidefriday.com) Hop-on/-off service on an open-top bus, with 11 stops, departing from outside the castle. It leaves daily (April to October only) every 20 to 60 minutes and costs £7. A nonstop tour takes 50 minutes.
John May (☎ 2081 1603) Walks of 1½ hours (£5) guided by a local historian. Sites include the Civic Centre and castle grounds.

FESTIVALS & EVENTS

Cardiff Festival (☎ 2087 2087; www.cardiff-festival .com) The highlight of the city calendar. The month-long midsummer bash features the Welsh Proms (10 days of concerts at St David's Hall), comedy, carnival and the very popular Celtic Food & Drink Festival.

Mardi Gras Cardiff's gay-pride festival (see the boxed text on p650).

SLEEPING
City Centre

When big sports events are on, it's hard to find a bed, so keep an eye on fixtures and book well ahead. The following are all found on the Central Cardiff map (p644).

BUDGET

Cardiff Backpackers (☎ 2034 5577; www.cardiffback packer.com; 98 Neville St, Riverside, dm with light breakfast from £16; 🖳) A slick and bright independent hostel run by a Welsh globetrotter, this great traveller's hub lies only half a mile from the central train and bus stations. Its funky bar is the place to exchange tips over a tipple.

Austin's Guest House (☎ 2037 7148; www.hotel cardiff.com; 11 Coldstream Tce; s/d from £20/35) Austin's may be central (across the river from the Millennium Stadium) but it's cheaply furnished.

MID-RANGE

Big Sleep (☎ 2063 6363; www.thebigsleephotel.com; Bute Tce; r from £55) Highly styled, a bit bashed, good value and central, this 'design B&B' occupies a tall ex-office block. The big rooms are saturated in bright colours – yup, wall-to-wall turquoise – and there's a big Continental breakfast.

West Lodge (☎ /fax 2034 4896; Castle St; s/d from £49.50/65) Stay in a restored medieval gatehouse with interested hosts, instant privacy from the outside world and your name on the sole double-bedroom door.

Sandringham (☎ 2023 2161; www.sandringham -hotel.com; 21 St Mary St; s £30-70, d £40-85) This is a well-established hotel right on the main drag (meaning noise and crowds on Friday and Saturday nights).

Central, efficient hotel chains include **Ibis** (☎ 2064 9250; www.ibishotel.com; Churchill Way; s/d £47/52; 🖳) and **Travelodge** (☎ 0870 191 1723; www.travelodge.co.uk; St Mary St; r from £60).

TOP END

Angel (☎ 2064 9200; www.paramount-hotels.co.uk /angel; Castle St; s/d from £70/80; 🖳 🖳) A large Victorian hotel built at the same time as the nearby castle, the 100-room Angel has a grand entrance hall but remains informal.

Rooms have the fireplaces of old but come with Internet connections.

Other options are the **Holiday Inn** (☎ 0870 400 8140; www.holiday-inn.com; Castle St; r from £105; 🖳) and the **Hilton** (☎ 2064 6300; Kingsway; d £110-160; 🖳 🖳), west and east of the castle, respectively.

Cardiff Bay

St David's Hotel & Spa (Map p643; ☎ 2045 4045; www.thestdavidshotel.com; Havannah St; r from £120; 🖳 🖳 🖳) This exceptionally pleasant five-star place on the waterfront has a 38m-high atrium, big-sky views from all rooms and a spa with a dedicated lift for be-robed, be-slippered pamperees.

SOMETHING SPECIAL

The Spa on the Bay

The mudflats of Cardiff Bay are gone, but the mudpacks at the waterfront spa of St David's Hotel & Spa (above) are much in demand. Mooch in the hydrotherapy pool as you bird-spot over the wide bay view, blanket yourself in fluffy towels, then take a holistic treatment – say, an algae wrap. A day starts from £95, which includes use of the pool, sauna, gym, robes and lunch. For a surreal break from the outside world, it can't be beaten.

Cathedral Rd Area & Cathays

Among the tasteful Victorian town houses of leafy Cathedral Rd, lying parallel west of Bute Park and a 10 to 15 minutes' walk from the centre, is a dozen mid-range places to stay. Cardiff YHA Hostel is the exception: it's in Cathays.

BUDGET

Cardiff Caravan Park (☎ 2039 8362; Pontcanna Fields; tent per adult £4.10) Book in advance at this neat and peaceful parkland site, 1½ mile north of the city centre. It has plenty of grassed area for camping and is a good base from which to explore Cardiff's parkland corridor (see p642).

Cardiff YHA (☎ 0870 770 5750; 2 Wedal Rd, Roath Park; dm with breakfast £14.90) This is a modern, well-appointed hostel but there are no private rooms. You'll find it in Cathays, the student area north of the centre. Take bus No 28, 29 or 29B from the Central station.

Cardiff University (University of Wales; ☎ 2087 4702; www.cardiff.ac.uk; s with shared bathroom/en suite £16/ 19.50) Over 3000 single student-rooms, many just 15 minutes' walk from the city centre, become available from June to September.

MID-RANGE

Town House (☎ 2023 9399; www.thetownhousecardiff .co.uk; 70 Cathedral Rd; s/d with en suite from £45/55; 🖳) The brass-knockered Town House is a Cathedral Rd favourite, and good value for two people. Most rooms are large, and each has a phone and Internet connection (charged at hotel rates).

Annedd Lon (☎ 2022 3349; 157 Cathedral Rd; s/d from £30/50; ✗) It's a comfortable town house of patterned duvet-covers and flouncy trim. Breakfast is served on Portmeirion crockery, right down to the salt and pepper pots.

Lincoln House Hotel (☎ 2039 5558; 118 Cathedral Rd, s/d from £48/75) The only hotel on the road offering 24-hour reception-desk service and a licensed bar has splendid Victorian features, which include the tiled doorway and hall, carved banisters and grand bedroom fireplaces.

Also consider gay-friendly **Courtfield Hotel** (☎ 2022 7701; www.courtfieldhotel.co.uk; 101 Cathedral Rd; s £25, s/d with en suite £45/55); **Church Hotel** (☎ 2034 0881; 126 Cathedral Rd; s/d from £25/45); and the four-star B&B **Beaufort Guest House** (☎ 2023 7003; www.beauforthousecardiff.co.uk; 65 Cathedral Rd; s/d from £45/59), with restored period décor.

EATING

Eating out in Cardiff is a treat, with a broad choice of good, lively restaurants.

City Centre, Cathedral Rd Area & Cathays

All the following places are found on the Central Cardiff map (p644).

BUDGET

Crockertons (☎ 2022 0088; Caroline St; breakfast £3-4.50; ✓ 7am-7pm Mon-Sat, 11am-4pm Sun) Sample the latest breakfasts, juices and snacks in this smart eco-foodie café, which uses local Welsh ingredients where possible. It's open-sided in warm weather.

Capsule (☎ 2038 2882; 48 Charles St; pizzas £5-9; ✓ 10am-6pm Mon & Tue, 10am-10pm Wed-Sat, noon-5pm Sun) Spin a designer pizza at this razor-hip café-restaurant that's located in a small gallery of contemporary art, where simply

parking in one of its Italian Perspex chairs makes you trendy.

In Castle Arcade are two characterful cafés: **Celtic Cauldron** (☎ 2038 7185; 47 Castle Arcade; mains £4-5; ✓ 9.30-4pm) serving wholefood and Welsh cuisine, and tiny **Café Minuet** (☎ 2034 1794; 42 Castle Arcade; mains £5-8; ✓ 11am-5pm Mon-Sat), with an opera-loving Italian chef.

MID-RANGE

Porto's (☎ 2022 0060; 40 St Mary St; mains £12.50; ✓ lunch Tue-Sat, dinner daily) An established Portuguese restaurant specialising in traditional fish dishes and *espetadas* (char-grilled kebabs), with a full wine list. Dinner is served in wood-furnished rooms, and the toe-tapping, finger-snapping Gypsy Kings rule.

Metropolis Bar & Restaurant (☎ 2034 4300; 60 Charles St; mains from £8; ✓ lunch & dinner Mon-Sat) Drink exotic vodkas downstairs and eat imaginative dishes such as sweet potato rosti upstairs at this relaxed, stylish joint that's popular with the 20- and 30-something in-crowd and hen parties. See also p651.

Le Monde (☎ 2038 7376; 60 St Mary St; ✓ lunch & dinner Mon-Sat), **Champers** (☎ 2037 3363; 61 St Mary St; ✓ lunch & dinner to midnight Mon-Sat) and **La Brasserie** (☎ 2023 4134; 60 St Mary St; ✓ lunch & dinner to midnight Mon-Sat, lunch Sun) are a trio of restaurants, each serving succulent fresh fish and meat (eg lemon sole, Scottish beef) in Spanish style, that is, raw from the counter display (mains around £12). The décors vary; Champers and La Brasserie are like pubs, while Le Monde has a clubbier atmosphere.

Casablanca (☎ 2064 1441; 3 Mill Lane; mains £10-16; ✓ lunch & dinner Tue-Sun) This cosy Moroccan eatery offers delicious meze.

Thai House (☎ 2038 7404; 3-5 Guildford Cres; mains £8-11; ✓ lunch & dinner Mon-Sat) The top place for Thai food, served by smiley, silk-swathed waiters.

Other options around Cathedral Rd and Cathays:

Armless Dragon (☎ 2038 2357; 97 Wyeverne Rd; mains £10.50-17; ✓ lunch & dinner Tue-Sat) Offers contemporary Welsh cuisine, northeast of the centre.

Da Castaldo (☎ 2022 1905; 5 Romilly Cres; 3-course meal £17; ✓ lunch & dinner Tue-Sat) A modern Italian restaurant.

TOP END

Razzi (☎ 2064 6300; Hilton Hotel, Kingsway; Sun lunch £19.50, 2-/3-course dinner £22/25; ✓ breakfast, lunch & dinner) This unpretentious restaurant at the

CARDIFF (CAERDYDD)

Hilton is very popular for Sunday lunch, and serves luxurious ingredients such as Gressingham duck from the à la carte menu.

Le Gallois (☎ 2034 1264; 6-10 Romilly Cres; lunch £18, 2-/3-course dinner £30/35; ❥ lunch & dinner Tue-Sat) Give Welsh produce the French treatment and the result is delicacies such as tian of Pembrokeshire crab (cooked in a tian dish of Provence). For more French-Welsh treats, head to Le Gallois in the Cathedral Rd area.

Da Venditto (☎ 2023 0781; 7-8 Park Pl; 3- course meal £32.50; ❥ lunch & dinner Tue-Sat) This elegant, award-winning Italian restaurant, in the centre of town, is very much for grown-ups.

Cardiff Bay

Cardiff's waterfront eateries mostly have contemporary interiors and upmarket cuisine.

BUDGET

Norwegian Church (☎ 2045 4899; Harbour Dr; ❥ 9am-5pm) Changed from a place of worship into an arts centre with a café, the church's wood-lined dining room now serves yummy cakes, waffles and light lunches.

For a Butetown original, head for **Caribbean Restaurant** (☎ 2025 2102; 14 West Bute St; mains from £5.50; ❥ dinner 5-11pm Tue-Thu, 5pm-1am Fri & Sat, 5-9.30pm Sun). For a Butetown newbie, go to the contrastingly flash **City Canteen & Bar** (☎ 2033 1020; 1-2 Mt Stuart Sq; mains £5-6; ❥ lunch & dinner Mon-Fri).

MID-RANGE

Woods (☎ 2049 2400; Pilotage Bldg; mains £10-18; ❥ lunch & dinner Mon-Sat, lunch Sun; wheelchair access) Converted from the dockside building once occupied by the pilots who guided in ships, this classy yet mellow restaurant serves well-priced contemporary dishes. Or you can have chef-prepared fish and chips for a tenner.

Scallops (☎ 2049 7495; Mermaid Quay; mains £10-17; ❥ lunch & dinner) If the idea of tilapia, char-grilled tuna, crayfish or oysters grabs your attention, go to the seafood specialist, Scallops. Dishes are served in a bright beechwood dining room where the glass walls open in summer.

Izakaya (☎ 2049 2939; www.izakaya-japanese-tavern .com; Mermaid Quay; dishes £2-8; ❥ lunch & dinner) Here's a fine Japanese restaurant that provides an oasis of Eastern courtesy and calm. Sit at bamboo booths or large sunken tables (slippers provided) and choose from the large menu of dishes.

Bosphorus (☎ 2048 7477; Mermaid Quay; mains £9-18) Serving tasty Turkish meze and meaty main courses, Bosphorus sits, somewhat exotically, on its own terraced pier.

TOP END

Tides (☎ 2031 3018; St David's Hotel & Spa; 2-/3-course dinner £27.50/35; ❥ lunch & dinner) A young, new chef has made vast improvements to the menus at the St David's Hotel restaurant, a calm, unadorned place with a classic bay view and terrace seating for balmy days.

DRINKING

Saint Mary St becomes one mass drinking scene on Saturday night. The crowds concentrate on the chain booze-halls but individual bars and great pubs still thrive. For a fresher ambience, drink at Cardiff Bay.

Unless indicated, all these venues are found on the Central Cardiff map (p644).

GAY & LESBIAN CARDIFF

Cardiff has Wales' largest and most relaxed gay and lesbian scene (see www.gaycardiff.co.uk). The biggest event is **Mardi Gras** (www.cardiffmardigras.co.uk), held in late August or early September. The city has one notably gay-friendly B&B, the Courtfield Hotel (p649).

The centre of Cardiff's all-inclusive gay nightlife is Charles St. All of the following appear on the Central Cardiff map (p644). Here you'll find **Club X** (☎ 2025 8838; www.clubxcardiff.com; No 35; admission £5; ❥ 10pm-4am Sat), playing mixed music from chart to hard house. Across the road is **Exit Bar** (☎ 2064 0102; No 48; admission £1.50 after 9.30pm; ❥ 6pm-2am), at its best on Friday and Saturday nights. The new kid on the block is the twice-monthly **Club Saviour** (Hayes Bridge Rd; admission £5; ❥ 10pm-4am), held at the Welsh National Ice Rink, and getting rave reviews. The two gay pubs are the **Golden Cross** (☎ 2039 4556; 283 Hayes Bridge Rd; ❥ to 1am Thu-Sat), a content, jolly Victorian pub, and, in Mill Lane, **King's Cross** (☎ 2064 9891; ❥ to 1am Wed-Sat), which has an unfussed atmosphere.

Sugar (☎ 2034 3433; 23 Womanby St; ☼ to 2am Mon-Sat) One of Cardiff's coolest spots, this converted warehouse serves beers and cocktails with DJs playing hip-hop to electro to Nu jazz from Thursday to Saturday. The 2nd and 3rd floors are members-only.

Metropolis Bar & Restaurant (☎ 2034 4300; 60 Charles St) A sophisticated 21st-century pub, this is small but has lots of standing room and good music. Friendly staff mix exotic vodkas, including the house special, containing strawberry purée and champagne. See also p649.

Café Bar Europa (☎ 2066 7776; 25 Castle St; ☼ to 11pm Wed-Sat) A café by day, and bar four nights a week, with DJs and live jazz, easy little Europa is somewhere to enjoy a drink rather than collapse into one.

Recommended pubs:

Callaghans (☎ 2034 7247; Castle St) Live Irish music in the basement of the Holiday Inn.

City Arms (☎ 2022 5258; Quay St; ☼ to 2am Thu-Sat) Late nights, no pretensions.

Goat Major (☎ 2038 3380; cnr Castle & High Sts) Famous old-fashioned Brains brewery-pub, opposite the castle.

Waterguard (Map p643; ☎ 2049 9034; Britannia Park) Contemporary boozer on Cardiff Bay.

ENTERTAINMENT

Cardiff's monthly what's-on magazine is *Buzz*, available at the TIC and bars. Unless indicated, these venues are found on the Central Cardiff map (p644).

Cinemas

Chapter Arts Centre (☎ 2030 4400; www.chapter.org; Market Rd, Canton) Two screens showing arthouse films.

Ster Century (☎ 0870 767 2676; Millennium Plaza, Wood St) Fourteen screens.

UGC (☎ 0870 907 0739; Mary Ann St) Fifteen screens.

Live Music

Cardiff's cutting-edge fashion, culture and friendliness fuse into a scoring live music scene.

Clwb Ifor Bach (☎ 2023 2199; www.clwb.net; 11 Womanby St; admission £3-12; ☼ to 2am Tue & Wed, to btwn 2.30am & 4am Thu-Sat) Cardiff's long-time Welsh indie music venue, where Catatonia and Super Furry Animals got their early breaks, has something on nightly over three floors, from upcoming Welsh bands to DJs performing for a laid-back audience.

Toucan Club (☎ 2037 2212; www.toucanclub.co.uk; 95 St Mary St; admission £3-10; ☼ to 2am) A rated independent venue for live music and DJs playing anything from tribal house to hippy funk. Tuesday is open-mike night for new singer/songwriters, and Sunday sees acoustic chill-out sessions.

St David's Hall (☎ 2087 8444; www.stdavidshall cardiff.co.uk; The Hayes) Engage nightly with the finest pop, world and classical music.

Other notable venues:

Barfly (☎ 2066 7658; www.barflyclub.com; Kingsway; admission from £2; ☼ to 2am) Credible basement joint.

Cardiff International Arena (☎ 2022 4488; Mary Ann St) Big mainstream venue.

Cardiff University Students Union (☎ 2078 1458; Park Pl) Good, bad and ugly bands.

Norwegian Church Arts Centre (Map p643; ☎ 2045 4899) Has class and great acoustics.

Wales Millennium Centre (Map p643; ☎ 2040 2000; www.wmc.org.uk; admission £5-35) Performances in its

---

CARDIFF SWELLS TO THE RHYTHM

A Lonely Planet reader from Wales points out, 'All Welsh people don't sing, it's only 79%'. So those few who don't actually sing obviously like to listen, for Cardiff has a packed live music scene of both rocking Welsh bands and stars of the international rock and classical world.

On the history front, every Welsh Rock fan knows that the now-defunct Catatonia got its break at Clwb Ifor Bach (where Saturday night is Welsh night; see above), and that the Manic Street Preachers played to a packed Millennium Stadium (p642) on Millennium Eve. Cardiff sees performances from Welsh bands Super Furry Animals, Zabrinski, Texas Radio Band and singer-songwriter Amy Wadge. Others to have trod the capital's boards include mumbling Bob Dylan (in 2004), and Engelbert Humperdinck, bluesey Bonnie Raitt and Pop Idol Will Young.

As for singers for whom every night is acoustic night, they either live here or visit regularly. The Welsh National Opera now goes to work at the new Wales Millennium Centre (above), while Dame Kiri de Kanawa features at the Welsh Proms. Had enough of quivering vocal chords? Then get down to the lovely waterfront Norwegian Church Arts Centre (above) to enjoy stimulating performances such as early viola music, perhaps?

inaugural year (2005) include dance and circus performances and the Welsh National Opera's *The Magic Flute*.

Nightclubs

Wanna dance? Try:

Bar Cuba (☎ 2039 7967; The Friary; ☽ to 2am Mon-Sat) Salsa classes on Tuesday, Latin house and party tunes the rest of the week.

Emporium (☎ 2066 4577; 8-10 High St; admission £5-10; ☽ to 4am Thu-Sat) One of the city's biggest clubs.

Sport

Cardiff is a city of sport. Join the fans:

Cardiff City Football Club (tickets ☎ 0845 345 1400; Ninian Park, Sloper Rd)

Cardiff Rugby Football Club (tickets ☎ 2030 2030; Cardiff Arms Park, north of Millennium Stadium)

Glamorgan County Cricket Club (tickets ☎ 2040 9380; Sophia Gardens)

Millennium Stadium (p642)

Theatre

Chapter Arts Centre (☎ 2030 4400; Market Rd, Canton) Cardiff's imaginative alternative stage.

New Theatre (☎ 2087 8889; Park Pl) Restored Edwardian playhouse.

Sherman Theatre (☎ 2064 6900; Senghennydd Rd, Cathays) Shows new drama and comedy.

Two chain comedy venues are **Jongleurs** (☎ 0870 787 0707; Millennium Plaza, Wood St) and **Glee Club** (Map p643; ☎ 0870 241 5093; Mermaid Quay, Cardiff Bay).

GETTING THERE & AWAY

Air

Cardiff airport (☎ 01446-711111; www.cardiffairport online.com), 12 miles southwest of the centre, has daily direct flights to destinations in the UK and Continental Europe with **Air Wales** (☎ 0870 777 3131; www.airwales.co.uk), **bmibaby** (☎ 0870 264 2229; www.bmibaby.com) and **KLM** (☎ 0870 507 4074; www.klmuk.co.uk).

Bus

All local and regional bus companies use the central bus station. For details of fares and timetables, contact **Traveline** (☎ 0870 608 2608).

Arriva Cymru Trawscambria (cross-Wales) bus No 701 Cardiff–Aberystwyth (£11.10, four hours, twice daily) travels via Swansea and Carmarthen, and **First** Shuttle bus No 100 (£5.50, one hour, hourly) travels from Cardiff to Swansea.

Services on **National Express** (☎ 0870 580 8080; www.nationalexpress.com) to/from Cardiff include Birmingham (£19, 2½ hours, four daily), Bristol (£6, 1¼ hours, three daily) and London (£17, 3¼ hours, every two hours).

There is also a Flightlink bus No 201 to/from Heathrow (£32 return, 3½ hours, 11 daily) and Gatwick (£35.50, 4½ hours).

Car & Motorcycle

To get to central Cardiff from the M4 motorway: from the east take junction 29/A48, from the west take junction 32/A470.

Car rental companies are **Budget** (☎ 2072 7499) and **Europcar** (☎ 2049 8978). Prices start from around £30 daily and £140 weekly, and include unlimited mileage.

Train

For details of fares and timetables contact **National Rail Enquiries** (☎ 08457 484950).

Direct services run to/from Birmingham (£21, 2¼ hours, hourly), London Paddington (£40, 2¼ hours, half-hourly), Manchester

---

ARCADES WITH ATMOSPHERE

Window-shopping in one of Cardiff's ornate, intimate Victorian arcades can easily lead to a flash purchase. On sunny days the rays slant through the glazed roofs as you gaze at unique artefacts often unobtainable elsewhere.

The balconied **Castle Arcade** is the most romantic, and hosts browsable **Cardiff Music** (CDs and sheet music of all types; No 31-33), **Cardiff Violins** (including blue models; No 19-23) and pretty, hippy rock shop **Crystals** (No 15). Fashion-focused **High St Arcade** features the cool shoes of **Buzz & Co** (No 13) and clothing from the 1960s and '70s at **Hobo's** (No 26). In polished **Royal Arcade** you'll find aromatic, sausage-hung **Wally's Delicatessen** (No 42), and vintage clothing in **Drop Dead Budgie** (No 10–12). **Wyndham Arcade** is grubbier than the others but has the **Bear Shop** tobacconist (No 14), which supplies cigars, pipes and Jamaican gold by the gram. **Rebel Rebel** (No 31) sells punk dog-collars and Giant African Snail kits, while **Cardiff's Comic Guru Presents** (No 22) is the place for graphic novels.

(£40, 3¼ hours, hourly) and Swansea (£8, 50 minutes, hourly).

Port-side connections (with ferries to Ireland) include: Fishguard, change at Swansea (£14.50, 2½ hours, daily); Holyhead, change at Crewe (£53, six hours, two hourly); and Pembroke Dock, change at Swansea (£14.50, 3½ hours, two daily).

Cardiff is well connected by **Valley Lines** (☎ 2044 9944; www.arrivatrainswales.com) trains to the Llynfi, Rhondda, Cynon, Taff and Rhymney Valleys, which depart from Cardiff Central and Queen St stations.

GETTING AROUND
To/From the Airport

Bus No X91 runs a service between the airport and the central bus station (£3, 30 minutes, hourly). A train service runs between the new Rhoose/Cardiff Airport station (bus link to the airport) and Cardiff Central station (20 minutes, hourly). A taxi to/from the central bus station costs about £16.

Bicycle

The Taff Trail walking/cycle route runs through Cardiff. For bike hire, see p642.

Public Transport

Get a free map and guide to Cardiff's bus and train services from the TIC or the Cardiff Bus office.

Cardiff Bus (☎ 2066 6444; www.cardiffbus.com; St David's House Travel Shop) has an office in the Travel Shop, located just opposite the central bus and train stations. Its services run all over town; present the exact change or a travel pass.

A local City Rider pass (£3.30/11.60 daily/weekly) is valid for travel on buses around Cardiff and Penarth. A regional Network Rider pass (£5/16.60 daily/weekly) covers Cardiff, Penarth, Castell Coch and Caerphilly. Buy passes on the bus or at the Travel Shop.

Local train stations are Cardiff Central, Queen St, Llandaff, Ninian Park and Cardiff Bay (p652). Valley Lines trains (p653) are a good way to reach Caerphilly Castle, Penarth and Rhondda Heritage Park.

Taxi

On the street, flag a black-and-white cab, or for bookings, try **Capital Cars** (☎ 2077 7777).

AROUND CARDIFF

To the south of Cardiff lies the Bristol Channel, and to the north are hills and valleys that are home to fine castles and examples of industrial heritage.

CASTELL COCH

Hidden high in beechwoods, **Castell Coch** (CADW; ☎ 2081 0101; adult £3; 9.30am-5pm Apr, May & Oct, 9.30am-6pm Jun-Sep, 9.30am-4pm Mon-Sat, 11am-4pm Sun Nov-Mar) is a Victorian fantasy rebuilt on the foundations of a real fortress. Decorated and furnished in convincing medieval style, it was the second collaboration of the third marquis of Bute and designer William Burges, in tandem with their work at Cardiff Castle. The highlight is the fabulous drawing room, decorated with detailed mouldings and images from *Aesop's Fables*.

From Cardiff Central station take bus No 26 (hourly Monday to Saturday, two-hourly Sunday) or 132 (half-hourly Monday to Saturday, hourly Sunday) to Tongwynlais for a steep 10-minute walk. Bus 26A (five daily Monday to Friday) runs direct to Castell Coch.

Bus No 26 continues to Caerphilly, for a two-castle day trip.

CAERPHILLY CASTLE

One of Wales' largest castles, massive **Caerphilly Castle** (CADW; ☎ 2088 3143; adult £3; 9.30am-5pm Apr, May & Oct, 9.30am-6pm Jun-Sep, 9.30am-4pm Mon-Sat, 11am-4pm Sun Nov-Mar) is good fun to explore. Built in the 13th century, it has three moats, six portcullises and five defensive doorways. But the best bit is a broken tower that leans further than Pisa's (but the result of subsidence, not assault).

From Cardiff Central station take a Valley Lines train (hourly Monday to Saturday, three on Sunday). To combine a trip to Caerphilly with a visit to Castell Coch on bus No 26, see p653.

MUSEUM OF WELSH LIFE

The backbone of the child-friendly, open-air **Museum of Welsh Life** (☎ 2057 3500; St Fagan's; admission free; 10am-5pm) is a collection of 30 salvaged original buildings showing how people used to live and work. See a school, a steam-powered woollen mill and a complete row of iron-workers' cottages from

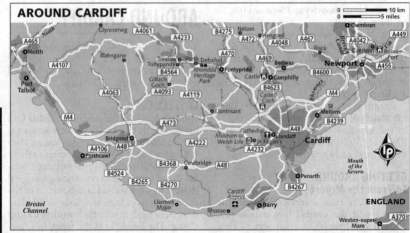

Merthyr Tydfil. Craftspeople work in several buildings, using traditional methods to make items such as clogs and barrels.

The setting is a 100-acre parkland in the grounds of St Fagan's Castle, a 16th-century manor house, 4 miles west of Cardiff. Allow at least half a day for your visit.

From Cardiff Central station/Cathedral Rd take bus No 32 (20 minutes).

PENARTH

Quaint seaside Penarth lies to the south of Cardiff Bay and is the place for a brisk walk out to the Victorian pier. A block east of the train station is the redbrick **Turner House Gallery** (☎ 2070 8870; Plymouth Rd; admission free; ✆ 11am-5pm Wed-Sun), which mounts good changing art exhibitions. From May to October the historic *PS Waverley* departs from Penarth pier on day and evening **cruises** (☎ 0845 130 4647; www.waverleyexcursions.co.uk; 2hr/full day £14/37). It also goes to ports on the North Devon coast.

Take the train from Cardiff Central station (10 minutes, every 20 minutes) or bus No 89, 92, 93 or 94 (20 minutes, every 15 minutes).

RHONDDA HERITAGE PARK

The experience and importance of mining in Wales is demonstrated well in the former Lewis Merthyr colliery in the **Rhondda Valley** (☎ 01443-682036; www.rhonddaheritagepark.com; adult £5.60; ✆ 10am-6pm Apr-Sep, 10am-6pm Tue-Sun Oct-Mar). With ex-miners as guides, the main attraction here is a simulation in which you 'descend' to the coalface, where the sound effects are explosively loud.

The park lies 10 miles northwest of Cardiff, between Pontypridd and Porth. To get here, take a train from Cardiff Central station to Trehafod (40 minutes, half-hourly, five on Sunday). By bus, take Stagecoach No 132 from Cardiff Central (one hour, at least hourly).

CAERLEON ROMAN FORTRESS

The Romans picked sites that were both strategic and eminently habitable. For 200 years, they occupied Isca Silurium on the lush banks of the River Usk, which became a 50-acre township and their most important Welsh base. For relaxation, the 6000 elite soldiers visited the **amphitheatre** (open site), of which evocative mounds remain, and the **baths** (CADW; ☎ 01633-422518; adult £2.50; ✆ 9.30am-5pm daily, noon-5pm Sun Nov-Mar). Near the baths, the **Roman Legionary Museum** (☎ 01633-423134; admission free; ✆ 10am-5pm Mon-Sat, 2-5pm Sun) offers a look at what life was like for Roman soldiers, with finds from jewellery to children's teeth.

The fortress lies 4 miles northeast of Newport. Newport Transport bus Nos 2 and 7 run from Newport bus station to the museum. Newport lies 12 miles east of Cardiff; take the mainline train (15 minutes, at least four hourly).

South Wales

South Wales' first claim to fame has rarely been its natural beauty, more the politics of industrial decline and political struggle. The region, stretching 100 miles from the poetic Wye Valley on the English border to the rugged Atlantic coast of Pembrokeshire, encapsulates the story of the Welsh, from their Celtic origins, through medieval conquest, industrial boom and bust, and recent resurgence as a nation within the UK. But wherever you go, you are never far from fine landscapes, whether recovering or never touched, and the further west you venture, the more remote, good-looking and Welsh the region becomes.

Lying central and to the east, a jaunt from the border, are the capital Cardiff and second city Swansea. Between them lie the steep coal valleys, where relics from the heyday of mining are preserved. Head on away from England and a purer nationality emerges. Across the country the Welsh language is on the rise, but by Carmarthen you are in a region where the language never left the streets and cafés in the first place.

Continue towards the Welsh land's end and you run into the wave-whipped Pembrokeshire Coast National Park, where cliffs and beaches chase each other around the shoreline for almost 200 miles, interrupted only by the occasional pretty village or town. These places include the tasteful resort Tenby on the sheltered, Anglicised south coast, holy St David's on the end, and quaint little Newport on the more rugged north coast, where residents promote Welsh language and crafts, and walkers enjoy arguably the finest coastal vistas in Britain.

HIGHLIGHTS

- Paddling in a kayak down the lovely **Wye River** (p659)
- Admiring the romantic ruins of **Tintern Abbey** (p659)
- Feeling Wales' industrial past first-hand down the **Big Pit** coal mine (p662)
- Surfing, swimming and paddling at glorious Rhossili Bay on the **Gower Peninsula** (p667)
- Enjoying the contemporary landscaping of the **National Botanic Garden** (p669)
- Walking – or hanging by your fingertips – on the ravaged cliffs of **Pembrokeshire** (p670)

- POPULATION 1,741,443
- AREA: 2911 SQ MILES

Activities

There are rich opportunities for outdoor activities across South Wales. These ideas are expanded on in Outdoor Activities (p74) and Directory (p945), with short local walks often suggested throughout this chapter. Tourist Information Centres (TICs) are a good source of maps and guides.

CYCLING

The greening industrial valleys in the south-east are blessed with a wealth of quiet canal towpaths and rail trails, and several forest parks. For longer touring, the **Lôn Las Cymru**, the south–north cross-Wales route, has two southern spurs, one from Cardiff heading up the Taff Vale and crossing the Brecon Beacons, the other running from Chepstow up the lovely Vale of Usk to Abergavenny.

An excellent way to get the feel of South Wales' changing landscape is to ride the **Celtic Trail**, which runs the width of the country from Chepstow to Pembrokeshire.

Mountain bikers get a treat at the dedicated venue of **Afan Argoed Forest Park**, north-east of Swansea. In Pembrokeshire, you can also spin the knobblies in the Preseli Hills on the north coast.

WALKING

One of the best-known long-distance routes is the **Offa's Dyke Path**, which traces the line of English-Welsh border between Chepstow in South Wales and Prestatyn on the north coast. Based around the line of the great embankment built in the 8th century by Offa, king of Mercia, the walk runs through verdant, often remote, hilly landscapes for a total of 177 miles. The hike is challenging and rewarding.

In the south the border follows the valley of the River Wye, also the focus of the **Wye Valley Walk**, a 136-mile riverside trail from Plynlimon in Mid Wales to Chepstow. Offa's Dyke is remote in places and a rewarding challenge; the Wye Valley Walk is easier than the Offa's Dyke Path and is simply beautiful.

However, the main attraction for long-distance walkers is the **Pembrokeshire Coast Path**, a 186-mile clifftop extravaganza between Amroth near Tenby in the south and Poppit Sands near Cardigan in the north. To walk the whole path takes about two weeks, but sections are also perfect for shorter day or weekend circuits.

OTHER ACTIVITIES

The River Wye is one of Britain's finest **canoeing** rivers; Monmouth makes a well-equipped starting point. For perfect sea canoeing, Pembrokeshire has stunning scenery and professional outfits that can instruct and equip you.

Regarding **rock climbing**, once again Pembrokeshire is the main attraction, with thousands of top-quality sea-cliff routes. Here are also beach and mountain **pony trekking**, especially in the Preseli Hills; **surfing**, notably at Newgale and Whitesands Bay near St David's; **sea fishing** and exhilarating **coasteering**.

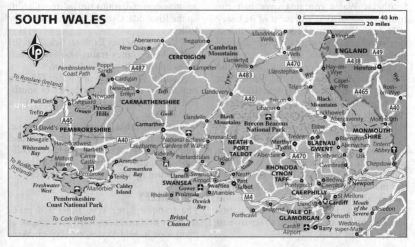

SOUTH WALES

Getting There & Around

The all-Wales *Bus, Rail and Tourist Map & Guide*, available at TICs in the area, is very useful. For details of fares and timetables contact **Traveline** (☎ 0870 608 2608) and **National Rail Enquiries** (☎ 08457 484950).

Train and bus services from England to South Wales and the cities of Newport, Cardiff and Swansea are fast and frequent. The further west you venture, beyond Carmarthen into Pembrokeshire, the less frequent the public transport.

The South Wales main-line railway runs east–west to/from Bristol in England via Cardiff to Swansea, continuing on the West Wales line via Carmarthen to three west coast branches – Fishguard, Pembroke Dock (both ports for Ireland) and Milford Haven. The famously scenic Heart of Wales line runs between Swansea and Shrewsbury (see the boxed text, p688).

The Trawscambria coach No 701 runs daily to/from Cardiff, Swansea and Carmarthen. National Express runs a daily service to/from Bristol and Pembrokeshire.

The **Freedom of South Wales Flexi-Rover** (☎ 0870 900 0777) allows three days of train travel and seven days of bus travel, all within seven days, for £35/30 peak/off-peak (call for dates), as well as discounts at popular sights. Buy it at bus and train stations and TICs.

SOUTHEAST WALES

Southeast Wales contains over half the country's population and most of its heavy industry. However, beyond the urban sprawl are broad swathes of lovely uplands sprinkled with historic sites.

Forming the border with England, the Wye Valley runs between the old market town of Monmouth and the dramatic castle at Chepstow, enhanced by the impressive riverbank ruins of Tintern Abbey around halfway between the two.

The valleys of Taff, Rhymney and Rhondda, from which Wales once supplied the world with coal and iron, fan out north from Cardiff. Overlooked until recently by the majority of visitors, it's a recovering industrial landscape, which at Blaenafon has been awarded World Heritage status. The area makes an intriguing alternative to regular tourist trails.

Poet and writer Dylan Thomas grew up in Swansea. The town is also the gateway to the wildly beautiful Gower Peninsula, with its great sandy beaches and superb cliff scenery.

Activities

Southeast Wales is hilly and verdant, and very good for exploring on foot or by bicycle. The Wye Valley and the Gower Peninsula are two beautiful places for walking, with the additional chance to canoe on the Wye and surf off the Gower. Two of the long-distance trails, the **Wye Valley Walk** and **Offa's Dyke Path**, begin in Chepstow and hike northward up the English border (for both see p659).

Two national cycle trails pass through the region. The north–south **Lôn Las Cymru** splits in the south into two routes, serving Cardiff and Chepstow. The **Celtic Trail** runs east–west, from Chepstow via Swansea (continuing to Pembrokeshire).

You find excellent mountain biking northeast of Swansea (see p665) at the Afan Argoed Forest Park.

Getting There & Around

Bus and train services are good in southeast Wales.

For information about the South Wales main-line railway see below. The Cardiff–Manchester service runs via Abergavenny and Shrewsbury, the Severnside service runs between Cardiff and Gloucester (for Birmingham connections). **Valley Lines** (www .arrivatrainswales.co.uk) trains run to/from Cardiff up the Rhondda, Cynon, Taff and Rhymney Valleys.

A Valley Lines Day Explorer ticket (£6.50) covers Valley Lines trains and Stagecoach buses up the valleys from Cardiff.

A South Wales Network Rider (£5) is a run-around day ticket for buses in southeast Wales, for those services other than First Cymru.

First Cymru has a First Rider day ticket (£5.50) that covers its buses in south and west Wales. It's not valid on the fast Cardiff–Swansea Shuttle. Enquiries for First Cymru are handled by **Traveline** (☎ 0870 608 2608).

WYE VALLEY

The tranquil River Wye flows 154 miles from its mountainous northerly source at Plynlimon in Mid-Wales, via Hay-on-Wye, to Chepstow where it joins the River Severn. The beautiful 16-mile stretch between Monmouth and Chepstow runs through a steep-sided wooded vale and is best explored on foot.

Bus No 69 serves the valley between Chepstow and Monmouth via Tintern daily (50 minutes, every two hours, four on Sunday).

Activities

The **Wye Valley Walk** is a 136-mile riverside trail from Hafren Forest in Plynlimon to Chepstow. For a route map, information and accommodation guidance, look for *The Wye Valley Walk Official Guide* (£7.95). *Discover the Wye Valley on Foot and by Bus* (30p) lists public transport details. *Walks in the Wye Valley* (£4.50) is a further collection of rambles, with some local history. These are stocked by the TICs in Chepstow and Monmouth.

The **Offa's Dyke Path** national trail zig-zags the length of the Welsh-English border. At the southern end it follows the eastern side of the Wye Valley, but is no match for the more beautiful Wye Valley Walk.

The Wye is one of Britain's finest **canoeing** rivers. Outfits that organise guided river trips are listed under Hay-on-Wye (see p699) and Monmouth. The TICs in Monmouth and Chepstow stock *The Canoeist's Guide to the River Wye* (£5).

Bicycle Beano (☎ 01982-560471; www.bicycle -beano.co.uk) organises popular vegetarian cycling holidays in the Wye Valley.

Tintern Abbey

One of the most beautiful ruins in the country, the soaring walls and gaping arched windows of this 14th-century Cistercian abbey (CADW; ☎ 01291-689251; adult £3; ☾ 9.30am-5pm Apr, May & Oct, 9.30-6pm Jun-Sep, 9.30am-4pm Mon-Sat & 11am-4pm Nov-Mar) on the River Wye were depicted by JMW Turner and lauded by William Wordsworth.

A Cistercian house, it was founded in 1131 by Walter de Clare, and the present building dates largely from the 14th century. The abbey functioned until the Dissolution in 1536–40, and a remarkable amount survives compared with other religious sites destroyed at this time.

Due to the abbey's fame, riverside Tintern village is lively with visitors. Should

you like to sit undisturbed to reflect on the atmosphere, it is better to visit towards the end of the day.

One mile upstream, at the Old Station, the **TIC** (☎ 01291-689566) is charmingly housed in old railway carriages. For nice local rambles, pick up a copy of *Popular Walks Around Tintern* (£2.95) here.

The bus ride along the Wye Valley to Tintern is quite scenic. Take Nos 65 and 69 (every two hours, four on Sunday) from Chepstow (15 minutes) and Monmouth (35 minutes).

Monmouth (Trefynwy)
☎ 01600 / pop 8547

Lying at the head of the dramatic Lower Wye Valley, Monmouth is an obvious base for exploring the area on foot or by paddle.

Once the county town of former Monmouthshire, the settlement has switched countries over the centuries and is, for the foreseeable future, fixed in Wales. However, it behaves in a completely English way. Monmouth's modicum of charm is found in the Georgian streets at the top of town.

The **TIC** (☎ 713899; Agincourt Sq) is beneath the portico of the 1724 Shire Hall in central Agincourt Sq. From here Monnow St descends to the Monnow Bridge. Above the square, short Church St is lined with antique and gift shops and eateries.

SIGHTS & ACTIVITIES

The medieval **Monnow Bridge** is Britain's only complete late-13th-century fortified crossing, and was belatedly pedestrianised in 2004.

Monmouth Museum & Local History Centre (☎ 710630; Priory St; admission free; ☾ 10am-1pm & 2-5pm Mon-Sat, 2-5pm Sun) houses a collection of memorabilia relating to Admiral Horatio Nelson, who visited en route to the Pembroke shipyards.

Monmouth Canoe & Activity Centre (☎ 713461; Castle Yard) runs trips on the Wye by canoe (per half-day/full day/week £20/25/150) and kayak (£14/17/98), as well as climbing and caving trips.

SLEEPING & EATING

Monnow Bridge Caravan & Camping (☎ 714004; Drybridge St; 2-person tent sites £7.50) On the riverside, near the Morrow Bridge.

Bob's Restaurant & B&B (☎ 712600; Church St; s/d with en suite £30/50; mains £5-18; ☾ lunch & dinner)

This buzzy place carries a recommendation for palate and pillow. Upstairs, the well-decorated rooms are secluded from the chatter- and laughter-filled restaurant below, which has a long and rich menu of local venison and lamb, Cornish fish and vegetarian dishes.

Two other acceptable B&Bs:

Ebberley Guest House (☎ 713602; 23 St James St; s/d £22/44) A quarter-mile from the TIC.

Verdi Bosco (☎ 710500; 65 Wonastow Rd; s/d £22/38) One double room with en suite, three-quarters of a mile from the TIC.

GETTING THERE & AWAY

Bus services include Nos 65 and 69 along the Wye Valley to/from Chepstow via Tintern (50 minutes, every two hours Monday to Saturday, four on Sunday); No 60 to/from Newport (one hour, every two hours Monday to Saturday, three on Sunday); and No 83 to/from Abergavenny (40 minutes, about every two hours Monday to Saturday, four on Sunday).

Raglan Castle

Built as a rich man's home as well as a fortress, the large and once-stylish **Raglan Castle** (CADW; ☎ 01291-690228; adult £2.75; 9.30am-5pm Apr, May & Oct, 9.30am-6pm Jun-Sep, 9.30am-4pm Mon-Sat & 11am-4pm Sun Nov-Mar) is the finest late-medieval castle-palace in Britain. The dusky-pink stone ruins are decorated with flourishes, and heraldic fireplaces hang halfway up walls whose floors were lost long ago.

Work began in 1435 under Sir William ap Thomas who commissioned the moated, hexagonal Great Tower. His son William Herbert, earl of Pembroke, created a lavish palace, including formal state apartments. The castle succeeded on domestic and military levels; it endured one of the longest sieges of the Civil War, but was wrecked soon afterwards and abandoned.

Raglan Castle lies 7 miles west of Monmouth on the A40 Abergavenny road. Bus No 60 runs from Monmouth to Raglan village (20 minutes, every two hours Monday to Saturday, three on Sunday), then it's a five-minute walk.

CHEPSTOW (CAS GWENT)

☎ 01291 / pop 14,195

The historic old border town of Chepstow at the bottom end of the Lower Wye Valley is a pleasant place to spend the afternoon. The great castle is the main attraction, but the riverside setting and medieval streets add interest and atmosphere.

In medieval times the town earned groats aplenty as a timber and wine port lying in a sheltered location just upriver from the turbulent Severn. The story is told at the worthy little town museum.

Chepstow is the start/finish point for the Wye Valley Walk and Offa's Dyke Path, and is very accessible from England (via the M48 over the original Severn Bridge). In addition to the town sights, it makes a good base for exploring the area; Tintern Abbey lies 5 miles north.

Orientation & Information

Entering Chepstow from the A48, go left on Moor St and head downhill to proceed beneath the Gate House in the Port Wall and descend sloping High, Middle and Bridge Sts to the bottom for the castle, TIC and River Wye.

The **TIC** (☎ 623772; 10am-5.30pm Easter-Oct, 9.30am-noon & 1.30-3.30pm Oct-Easter) is in the castle car park.

Sights

Chepstow Castle (CADW; ☎ 624065; adult £3; 9.30am-5pm Apr, May & Oct, 9.30am-6pm Jun-Sep, 9.30am-4pm Mon-Sat & 11am-4pm Sun Nov-Mar) is a large and superb riverside fortress (far bigger than it appears from the car park), best viewed from the opposite English riverbank. Built in 1067, three years after the Normans invaded England, it is one of the oldest castles in the country and one of the first built of stone. Its purpose was to defend a critical river crossing – and awe the locals.

The fortress remained in military service for over 500 years up to the Civil War. The structure reveals prime examples of the evolution of medieval military architecture.

Chepstow Museum (☎ 625981; Bridge St; admission free; 10.30am-5pm Mon-Sat & 2-5.30pm Sun Jul-Sep, 11am-5pm Mon-Sat & 2-5pm Sun Oct-Jun) has historic prints and drawings of the castle and Wye Valley through the ages. It also has displays on Chepstow's social history, including a freaky early electric hair-drying stand.

Running through town are sections of 13th-century **Port Wall** (Customs Wall), built more to control entry into Chepstow in its mercantile heyday than for defence.

Sleeping, Eating & Drinking

First Hurdle (☎ 622189; 9 Upper Church St; s/d £35/50) This is a comfy, tastefully modernised B&B, about quarter mile up from the TIC.

Afon Gwy Hotel (☎ 620158; 28 Bridge St; s/d £37/49; mains £11-16; ⊗ dinner) The Afon Gwy has a good riverside location and menu, but the décor and terrace need a lift.

Two traditional town hotels are **Castle View Hotel** (☎ 620349; Bridge St; s/d with continental breakfast from £50/71), with a nice guest garden, and the 1610 **George Hotel** (☎ 625363; Moor St; s/d from £70), first above the Gate House.

There are two good places to eat on the old riverfront, round the corner from the TIC.

Wye Knot (☎ 622929; The Back; 2-/3-course meal £17/20; ⊗ Sun lunch & dinner, lunch daily Jul-Aug) This is a recommended contemporary restaurant, with an imaginative menu using all meats, fish and veg.

Boat Inn (☎ 628192; The Back; mains around £14; ⊗ lunch & dinner) Chepstow's popular pub-restaurant has a notable wine list, fish specialities and a relaxed atmosphere, abetted by vodka mixes and pitchers.

Getting There & Away

Services include the National Express coach No 509 to/from London (£17, 2½ hours, every two hours Monday to Saturday, three on Sunday) and Cardiff (£4.25, 50 minutes). Other bus services include No X14 to/from Bristol (£5.75, 50 minutes, hourly) and No 69 to/from Monmouth via Tintern (£3.95, 50 minutes, two hourly Monday to Saturday, four on Sunday).

Trains run direct to/from Cardiff (£5.40, 40 minutes, at least every two hours) and Gloucester (£5.50, 30 minutes, hourly, at least every two hours).

THE VALLEYS

At the height of the industrial revolution in the 18th and 19th centuries, the upland valleys north of Cardiff employed a quarter of a million men in iron and coal production.

Today, the heavy industry is all but gone, and this is a greening landscape peppered with industrial heritage sites. Ten years ago tourism overlooked the area. Nowadays, the valleys make a curious branch of the visitor trail, one that presents a different face of

SOUTH WALES

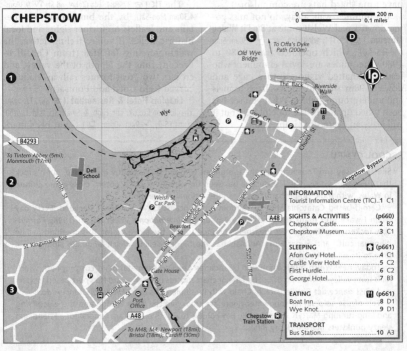

CHEPSTOW

0		200 m
0		0.1 miles

INFORMATION
Tourist Information Centre (TIC)..1 C1

SIGHTS & ACTIVITIES (p660)
Chepstow Castle.......................2 B2
Chepstow Museum....................3 C1

SLEEPING (p661)
Afon Gwy Hotel.......................4 C1
Castle View Hotel.....................5 C2
First Hurdle..............................6 C2
George Hotel............................7 B3

EATING (p661)
Boat Inn..................................8 D1
Wye Knot................................9 D1

TRANSPORT
Bus Station.............................10 A3

British folk history than that of pretty cottages and cream teas.

Blaenafon

☎ 01495 / pop 5626

In 2000 Blaenafon, plus a sizable area of the surrounding upland, which is riddled with remnants from the early days of iron-making, was made a Unesco World Heritage Site.

When constructed in 1789, the **ironworks** (CADW; ☎ 792615; adult £2; ⏰ 9.30am-4.30pm Mon-Fri, 10am-5pm Sat, 10am-4.30pm Sun Apr-Oct, guided tours only Nov-Mar) were the largest and most advanced in the world. The necessary minerals could be extracted locally using labour and transport created for the purpose. In the works you can observe the ground-breaking iron-making process, from charging the three gargantuan furnaces to casting the molten iron. Restoration is exceedingly slow, because the valleys are not over endowed with dollars. The tourist facilities are rudimentary, but staff at the on-site **TIC** (☎ 792615; www.blaenavontic.com) will show you around if they have time (hard hats are compulsory).

Ten minutes' walk away, do not miss going down a real Welsh mine at **Big Pit Mining Museum** (☎ 790311; admission free; ⏰ 9.30am-5pm mid-Feb–Nov), which operated from 1880 to 1980. The guides are jovial ex-miners who lead hard-hatted visitors into a cage and down a 90m shaft to the coalface tunnels and underground stables. What you see has been tidied up and is fine for children, but it will leave an everlasting impression.

Blaenafon is 15 miles north of the city of Newport; buses between the two are Nos 30 (40 minutes, hourly Monday to Saturday) and No 23 (hourly on Sunday), and X24 (55 minutes, every 15 minutes Monday to Saturday).

The town lies a scenic 8-mile drive southeast from Abergavenny (p695) – the journey is very awkward by public transport.

Merthyr Tydfil

☎ 01685 / pop 35,488

Working town Merthyr Tydfil, at the head of Taff Valley, was once the epicentre of iron manufacture, and you can find several minor sites of industry-related heritage here.

The area's story is told at the museum at superb **Cyfarthfa Castle** (☎ 723112; admission free; ⏰ 10am-5.30pm Apr-Sep, 10am-4pm Tue-Fri & noon-4pm Sat & Sun Oct-Mar), home of the ironworks-owning Crawshay family. By contrast, **Joseph Parry's Cottage** (☎ 723112; 4 Chapel Row; admission free; ⏰ 2-5pm Thu-Sun Apr-Oct, by appointment with Cyfarthfa Castle museum Oct-Mar) is one of a line of tiny workers' cottages. Birthplace of the composer, it is furnished as it was in the 1840s.

The **TIC** (☎ 379884; 14a Glebeland St; ⏰ 9.30am-4.30pm Mon-Sat), by the bus station, has details and leaflets on further sights and local historic walks. If you're feeling active, the walking/cycling **Taff Trail** (from Cardiff to Brecon) runs the length of the valley, and crosses two great former railway viaducts, curved Cefn Coed and Pontsarn.

Chaplins Hotel & Restaurant (☎ 387272; www.chaplinshotel.co.uk; cnr High & Swan Sts; s/d £45/60; mains £5-7; ⏰ 9am-10pm; 💻) Great beds mark

---

COOL CYMRU

Shirley Bassey and Tom Jones are the evergreens who put Wales on the music map, but it's rock that rules these days. The last decade has seen the emergence of a potent cross-genre culture in Wales, with indie guitar bands gaining international recognition.

Cardiff-based Catatonia shot to stardom after vocalist Cerys Matthews declared 'Every day when I wake up I thank the Lord I'm Welsh' on the *International Velvet* album (1998). Formidable rockers the Manic Street Preachers continue to rule the airwaves for 30-somethings, while bilingual cult band Super Furry Animals has the biggest-selling Welsh-language album of all time to its name, *Mwng*.

Today, new Welsh music knows no boundaries. Leading Nu-metal band Lostprophets, which hails from valley town Pontypridd, had major chart success in 2004, as did Newport-based rappers and class dance act Goldie Lookin' Chain with its single *Guns don't kill people, rappers do*.

Top of the solo singer-songwriter genre are smoky-voiced Amy Wadge and the electrifying and long-running Martyn Joseph, while newcomers to watch out for are Funeral for a Friend and sleazy punksters Martini Henry Rifles.

this friendly, modern, central hotel, whose hostess caters particularly for solo women travellers, and walkers and cyclists. The 1930s-theme café-bar serves proper coffee, and the well-priced dinner menu is a beef-lasagne regular with vegetarian options.

Maes y Coed (☎ 722246; Park Tce; s/d £23/38, with en suite £30/42) Above the top end of the high street, this is a large, plain place.

Hobo Backpackers (☎ 01495-718422; www.hobo -backpackers.co.uk; Morgan St, Tredegar; dm £12) An independent hostel in central Tredegar (7 miles east of Merthyr, 10 miles west of Blaenafon), this has large cheerful dorms, a new fitted kitchen and hosts who specialise in mountain biking (see p690).

Bus Nos X4 and X40 run to/from Cardiff and Merthyr (50 minutes, every 15 minutes Monday to Saturday). The Beacons Bus runs on summer Sundays (see p692).

SWANSEA (ABERTAWE)
☎ 01792 / pop 270,506

Sitting on broad Swansea Bay at the mouth of the River Tawe (hence its Welsh name), lively Swansea is the second-largest city in Wales and the gateway to the lovely, beach-rich Gower Peninsula.

Dylan Thomas grew up here and called it an 'ugly lovely town'. With some post-war architectural exceptions, those days are thankfully largely history. Swansea is energetic, and has a wide choice of international restaurants and a pulsing weekend bar scene. A handful of good city attractions is focused on the still dockland quarter – a great contrast to the shop-crazy centre. The city lies at the eastern end of a 5-mile promenade (ideal for walking and cycling) around Swansea Bay to Mumbles

Head and the much prettier seaside resort of Oystermouth, called Mumbles.

During the Industrial Revolution, Swansea expanded dramatically to become 'Copperopolis', the epicentre of the global copper-smelting trade. By the 20th century, heavy industry in the town had declined, but still made it a worthy target for the Luftwaffe (German Air Force), which devastated the centre in 1941.

Orientation & Information
From Swansea train station a half-mile walk southwest leads along High St and the Kingsway into the city centre. The central TIC and bus station are off West Way. Ferries arriving from Cork disembark across the Tawe to the east. Swansea University lies 2 miles west of the centre along the seafront. There's also a TIC at Mumbles, 5 miles west around Swansea Bay.

INTERNET ACCESS
Central Library (☎ 516757; Alexandra Rd; access free; ☺ 9am-7pm Mon-Wed & Fri, 9am-5pm Thu & Sat) Booking advisable.
YMCA (☎ 652032; 1 The Kingsway; ☺ 9am-4pm Mon-Fri; per hr £2) Booking not necessary.

LAUNDRY
Lendart Laundrette (91 Bryn-y-Mor Rd)

MEDICAL SERVICES
Morriston Hospital (☎ 702222) Accident & emergency department, 5 miles north of centre.

MONEY
Banks with ATMs dot the streets between The Kingsway and The Quadrant shopping centre.

DYLAN THOMAS IN SWANSEA
'If I had been born and brought up in an igloo and lived on whales, not in it...it would have been extremely unlikely I become a writer' wrote Dylan Thomas in 1952, a year before his death at age 39. Wales' most popular 20th-century poet achieved worldwide renown for his wit and wisdom, his best-known work being the rhythmic, comic radio-play of affectionate characters – *Under Milk Wood* (see p669).

Dylan Thomas' birthplace and home at 5 Cwmdonkin Drive in Uplands has remained unchanged since he wrote two-thirds of his poetry there. View it by arrangement with the Dylan Thomas Centre (above).

Thomas-themed booklets are available from the TIC and the Centre, which also sells recordings of his work. There's also a Dylan trail (see www.dylanthomas.org), plus the annual Dylan Thomas Festival (p665), during which you may catch a performance of *Under Milk Wood*.

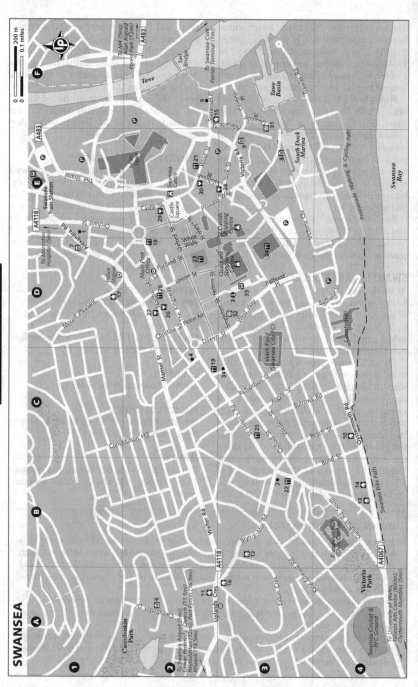

SWANSEA

200 m
0.1 miles

To M4 (5mi);
Afan Argoed
Forest Park (12mi)

To Swansea–Cork
Ferries Terminal (1mi)

Salt
Bridge

Tawe

Tawe
Basin

South Dock
Marina

Swansea Bay

Promenade Walking & Cycling Path

County Hill

Swansea
Train Station

The Strand

Swansea Castle

St Davids
Shopping
Centre

Quadrant
Shopping
Centre

Main Post
Office

Police
Station

Mount Pleasant

Constitution Hill

Vetch Field
(Swansea City FC)

Swansea Bike Path

Brangwyn Hall
Civic Centre

Victoria
Park

Swansea Cricket &
RFC Ground

To Swansea Airport (5mi);
Gower Peninsula: Oxwich (11.5mi);
Reynoldston (12mi); Port Eynon (16.5mi);
Rhossili (18.5mi)

To Morriston
Hospital (5mi)

To University of Wales;
Clyne Gardens (1.5mi); Mumbles (5mi);
Oystermouth Mumbles (5mi)

POST
Main post office (The Kingsway)

TOURIST INFORMATION
Central TIC (☎ 468321; www.visitswanseabay.com; Plymouth St; ☻ 9.30am-5.30pm Mon-Sat year-round, plus 10am-4pm Sun Jun-Sep) Books accommodation.
Mumbles TIC (☎ 361302; ☻ various hrs Easter-Oct) Books accommodation on the Gower Peninsula.

Sights
MARITIME QUARTER
Swansea's old city-side docks have been converted into a smart **maritime quarter**, which is nice to stroll around and features several sights.

This is home to the new **National Waterfront Museum** (☎ 459640; www.waterfrontmuseum .co.uk; admission free; ☻ 10am-5pm), which tells the story of the intense industrialisation of Wales and its effect on the Welsh people, from 1750 through to today. Here is how the coal was won, how the trade unions developed in response and how industrialisation affected the environment. Swansea's copper-processing role is included as part of the national tale.

The absorbing **Dylan Thomas Centre** (National Literature Centre for Wales; ☎ 463980; ☻ 10.30am-4.30pm Tue-Sun), off Somerset Pl, has a good exhibition devoted to the enjoyable work, tempestuous life and early death of the poet. A little second-hand bookshop-café increases a visit's appeal.

The best exhibit in the utterly charming **Swansea Museum** (☎ 653763; Victoria Rd; admission free; ☻ 10am-5pm Tue-Sun) is its very venerable host, the mummy of Hor the Egyptian priest in his low-lit cabinet with video-story. Elsewhere, curios and changing exhibitions provoke glee amid the ho-hum shards of ancient crockery.

GLYNN VIVIAN ART GALLERY
This marble-floored **gallery** (☎ 655006; Alexandra Rd; admission free; ☻ 10am-5pm Tue-Sun) is a principal provincial showcase for Welsh and international art, with work by those such as Gwen and Augustus John as well as masters such as Lucien Pissaro. It also displays Swansea china, European ceramics and clocks.

MUMBLES
The pretty, lively seaside town of Oystermouth, better known as **Mumbles** (after the French mariners' name for the headland's bosomy rocks, *mamelles*) has a pier, a popular ice-cream parlour and the Mumbles Mile (p667).

The extensive ruin of medieval **Oystermouth Castle** (adult £1.50; ☻ 11am-5pm Apr-Sep), in the heart of the village, offers fine views over Swansea Bay.

A 1-mile trek over the headland leads to the fine sandy beaches of **Langland** and **Caswell Bays**.

Cycling
Swansea lies on the east–west Celtic Trail cycle route, which runs from the marina around **Swansea Bay** beachfront to Mumbles. Hire bikes at **Swansea Cycle Centre** (☎ 410710; Wyndham St; per hr/half-day/full-day £3/8/14).

Mountain bikers head for the top-quality purpose-built trails at steep-sided **Afan Argoed Forest Park** (☎ 01639-850564; www.mbwales.com), 12 miles northeast of Swansea off the A4107 (M4 J40).

Festivals & Events
Escape into the Park and **Rock the Park** (www.escape group.com) Two-day dance and rock event in August at Singleton Park near the university.
Dylan Thomas Festival (☎ 463980; www.dylanthomas festival.org) Held every 27 October to 9 November (Thomas'

dates of birth and death), it includes poetry readings and talks around town.

Swansea Festival (www.swanseafestival.co.uk) Classical concerts, drama and exhibitions in October.

Sleeping

Windsor Lodge (☎ 642158; Mount Pleasant; s/d weekday £65/75, weekend £50/65) The nicest place to stay in the city centre, Windsor Lodge is a sedately decorated 18th-century building that's full of retained character and has an excellent restaurant serving mod-Welsh dishes.

The university neighbourhood of Uplands, a mile west of the centre, has a clutch of well-run guesthouses.

Cefn Bryn Guest House (☎ 466687; www.cefnbryn.net; 6 Uplands Cres; s/d from £30/60) Modernised in Millennial chocolate and beige, friendly Cefn Bryn offers big rooms and a separate smoking area.

Crescent (☎ 466814; www.crescentguesthouse.co.uk; 132 Eaton Cres; s/d from £31/50; ✗) Crescent is friendly and well cared for.

White House (☎ 473856; www.thewhitehousehotel.co.uk; 4 Nyanza Tce; s/d £38/66; 💻) This welcoming, well-run, gay-friendly place continues to come up in the world.

SOMETHING SPECIAL

Morgans (☎ 484848; www.morganshotel.co.uk; Somerset Pl; d £100-250; ✗ 👶) This is the five-star hotel of local entrepreneur Martin Morgan, created from the elaborate 1902 Port Authority building, with a stained-glass cupola, wood panelling, subtly designed bedrooms and a canopied courtyard.

Oystermouth Rd, the seafront road that heads westward to Mumbles, has a strip of guesthouses of greatly varying standard. The following are safe bets for comfort and cleanliness.

Bayswater Hotel (☎ 655301; bayswater@supanet.com; No 322; s/d £23/36; ✗) A rare seafront nonsmoking joint.

Devon View (☎ 462008; reception@devonview.co.uk; No 394; s/d £25/50, with en suite £35/70) Fanciest guesthouse on the seafront.

Leonardo's (☎ 470163; www.leonardosguesthouse.co.uk; No 380; s/d from £22/40) Mediterranean themed.

Lyndale (☎ 653882; No 324; s/d £25/40) A worthy neighbour to the Bayswater.

Out at Mumbles several places are handy for beaches and nightlife:

Coast House (☎ 368702; thecoasthouse@aol.com; 708 Mumbles Rd; s/d £30/50) You get great bay views and friendly staff here, in the heart of the action.

Hillcrest House Hotel (☎ 363700; www.hillcresthousehotel.com; 1 Higher Lane; s/d £65/85) Has an excellent restaurant and themed rooms – from Scottish to safari – with leafy outlooks.

Eating

Dining out in Swansea is richly varied and often excellent.

Garuda (☎ 653388; 18 St Helen's Rd; mains £8-11; 🕐 dinner Tue-Sat; ✗) Fuggy with Far Eastern aromas and progressive Swansea youth, Garuda is a bonny Indonesian restaurant. Bring your own wine.

Lounge (☎ 479183; 8 Wind St; mains £7-11; 🕐 noon-10pm Mon-Thu, noon-7pm Fri & Sat, noon-4pm Sun; ✗) The civilised place to eat (and drink) on Wind St, this stylishly converted banking hall serves quality contemporary favourites – but note it switches to drinks-only on Friday and Saturday evenings.

Didier & Stephanie's (☎ 655603; 56 St Helen's Rd; mains around £12; 🕐 lunch & dinner Tue-Sat) This French fixture, one of the best in town, sticks by what it knows best. Try snails, duck with shallots, and walnut meringue with pistachio cream.

Cafe Mambo (☎ 456620; 46 The Kingsway; mains from £9; 🕐 lunch & dinner Mon-Sat) Latin joint Mambo is the funkiest café in town, where spicy chicken, fish dishes and fajitas are devoured to the beat.

Castellamare (☎ 369408; Bracelet Bay; mains around £10; 🕐 lunch & dinner Mon-Fri, noon-10pm Sat & Sun) On its own, out on rugged Mumbles Head, this jolly, romantic restaurant is the place to tuck into fish specialities from a long list of dishes.

Other recommendations:

Govinda's (☎ 468469; 8 Craddock St; mains around £5; 🕐 lunch Sun-Thu, noon-6pm Fri & Sat) Vegan-vegetarian café.

Miah's (☎ 466244; St Helen's Rd; mains £5-9; 🕐 lunch & dinner to midnight Mon-Sat, noon-midnight Sun) A great Indian restaurant in a vaulted former church!

Topo Gigio (☎ 467888; 55 St Helen's Rd; pasta around £5; 🕐 lunch Fri, dinner Tue-Sat) An established Italian eatery.

It's also a treat to buy Welsh lamb and delicacies, including laverbread (seaweed) and cockles from Swansea Bay, in covered **Swansea Market** (⊗ Mon-Sat). Tesco has a mega-market near the bus station.

Drinking
You'd think folk spent the week lost in the desert given the amount they soak up at weekends in Wind St. And there *are* gems here amid the usual alcopop suspects.

No Sign Bar (☎ 465300; 56 Wind St; mains £6-7.50; ⊗ lunch & dinner) A wine bar in a historic building, the No Sign serves good food and tapas.

Indigo (☎ 463466; Salubrious Pl) The hippest bar in town – Indigo has loud beats and a cool vibe.

On Mumbles Rd in Oystermouth the famous Mumbles Mile remains a rite of passage for students. This marathon pub crawl requires the downing of a pint in each of 11 pubs from the White Rose to the Pier.

Entertainment
Buzz magazine (free from the TIC or bars) has club and live music listings.

LIVE MUSIC
Monkey Café Bar (☎ 480822; www.monkeycafé.co.uk; 13 Castle St; admission up to £5; ⊗ 7pm-2am Mon-Sat, 7pm-midnight Sun) This central two-storey live venue is a funky independent place that's popular with students. Musicians and DJs play all genres: jazz, punk, reggae and heavy metal. There's a restaurant, too.

NIGHTCLUBS
Crobar (☎ 477929; 1 Northampton Lane; adult £2-3.50; ⊗ 9pm-3am Fri & Sat, 9pm-1am Sun) Designer club with DJs playing hip-hop, dancehall and dirty house.

Escape (☎ 652854; Northampton Lane; adult £6-12; ⊗ 10pm-3am Thu-Sat) This headlining house/garage club features well-known DJs, and won a 2004 poll for hosting the best dance night in Wales.

THEATRE
Swansea Grand Theatre (☎ 475715; Singleton St) The town's main theatre hosts everything from pantomime to ballet.

Dylan Thomas Theatre (☎ 473238; Gloucester Pl) A favourite place for performances of Thomas' works.

Taliesin Arts Centre (☎ 296883; Singleton Park) At the university campus, 2 miles west of

the city centre on Mumbles Rd, this venue presents music, theatre, dance and film.

Getting There & Away
AIR
Air Wales (☎ 0870 777 3131; www.airwales.com) flies from **Swansea airport** (☎ 204063), 6 miles west of the centre, to Amsterdam, Dublin and London City, and from May to September to Jersey.

BOAT
Swansea Cork Ferries (☎ 456116; www.swanseacork ferries.com) sails to/from Cork (Ireland) four to six times weekly from mid-March to January. The high-season return fare for foot passengers is £64; weekend return car and five passengers is £209. Call for special offers. The terminal lies a mile east of the centre.

BUS
The First Swansea–Cardiff Shuttle bus No 100 (£5.50, one hour) departs hourly Monday to Saturday, and every two hours on Sunday. Beacons Bus No B2 runs into the Brecon Beacons National Park on Sunday and bank holidays from June to August.

TRAIN
Trains from Swansea head to Cardiff (£8, 50 minutes, hourly) and London Paddington (£44, three hours, hourly), and to Fishguard (£8.60, 1½ hours, twice daily Monday to Saturday, one Sunday), connecting with ferries to Ireland.

Swansea is the southern terminus for the famously scenic Heart of Wales line (via Llanelli to Shrewsbury; see the boxed text, p688).

Getting Around
A First Swansea Bay ticket (daily/weekly £3.10/12.50) covers bus travel in and around Swansea, and also the Gower Peninsula and a way up the Swansea Valley. Buy it on the bus.

If you'd prefer to hire a car, try **Avis** (☎ 460939) and **Europcar** (☎ 750526).

For a taxi, call **Yellow Cabs** (☎ 644446).

GOWER PENINSULA
☎ 01792
A short distance from Swansea – and a world apart – the 15-mile-long Gower Peninsula has vast sandy beaches, wild uplands and

ruined castles. Neither walkers, surfers nor holiday-makers can resist this lovely little corner of Wales.

Being so accessible, Gower beaches get very crowded on summer weekends and throughout the months of July and August, when parking can be a problem. For details of beaches, sights and tracks, the *Gower & Swansea Bay Visitors' Map* (£2.75) is useful. Walkers might like *Gower Walks* (£3.50). Use Swansea's **TIC** (☎ 468321) for information and brochures, as well as accommodation options.

Twenty-six miles of Gower coastline are owned by the National Trust (NT), which has a well-stocked **visitors centre** (☎ 390707; Rhossili; ⏲ 10.30am-5.30pm mid-Mar–Oct, 11am-4pm Wed-Sun Nov & Dec, 11am-4pm Sat & Sun Jan–mid-March).

On the south coast, sandy **Oxwich Bay** neighbours reedy Oxwich Nature Reserve. Further west is the family-magnet beach of **Port Eynon**.

At the tip of the peninsula the village of Rhossili looks north along 3-mile long, Atlantic-facing **Rhossili Bay**, the best beach on the Gower (see Surfing, p668). Access and facilities lie at the northern end at **Llangennith**.

From Rhossili village you can walk across the tidal causeway to the rocky, wave-blasted headland of **Worm's Head** (from the Old English *wurm*, meaning dragon) but only for a two-hour period at low tide – and no kidding. A sea-bird colony on the Outer Head includes razorbills, guillemots, kittiwakes, fulmars, puffins and oystercatchers, while seals often bob in the swell.

The wild central uplands of **Cefn Bryn** (185m) reveal glorious 360-degree views of the Gower. Above the village of **Reynoldston**, an immense 25-ton quartz boulder is the fallen capstone of a Neolithic burial chamber known as **Arthur's Stone**.

Surfing

Rhossili Bay has some of Britain's most consistently good surf. For tuition try the **Surf School** (☎ 386426; www.wsfsurfschool.co.uk; 2hr class £20) at Llangennith.

Surfers also head for Rotherslade and Langland Bays and Caswell Bay, near Mumbles. **Gower Surfing Development** (☎ 360370; half-day £30) does beginner courses at Caswell Bay and Llangennith. For daily local surf conditions call **Surfline** (☎ 0901 603 1603).

Sleeping

The Gower Peninsula is surprisingly light on B&B accommodation.

At Oxwich, the hamlet on Oxwich Bay, try the friendly **Frog's Hop** (☎ 391522; s £25-30, d £60-70), and the dependable **Woodside Guest House** (☎ 390791; s/d £51/68), which are both near the beach. **Oxwich Camping Park** (☎ 390777; 2-person tent sites £12; ⏲ Easter-Aug) is 12 minutes' walk from the waves.

At the busier beachside village of Port Eynon, go to **Highmead** (☎ 390300; www.highmeadgower.co.uk; s/d £27/55) for a B&B with a great view and footpath to the beach. **Port Eynon YHA Hostel** (☎ 0870 770 5998; dm £12.50; ⏲ daily Easter–early Nov, with 48hr notice Nov-Easter) occupies an old lifeboat house above the sweeping beach.

Rhossili, an exposed hamlet with a scattering of houses, has only one place on offer – the **Worm's Head Hotel** (☎ 390512; s/d from £45/£70), where the standard falls short of the wonderful location and views.

For a B&B in Llangennith, try **College House** (☎ 386214; s/d £30/46), a lovely place decorated with sculpture and paintings. On the dunes directly behind the beach is the surfers' favourite of **Hillend Caravan & Camping Park** (☎ 386204; 2-person tent sites from £10; ⏲ Easter-Sep), which has a shop and café. Pitches go on a first-come first-served basis.

Inland up the moors at sheep-grazed Reynoldston, **King Arthur Hotel** (☎ 390775; d £60-80; mains around £7) is a relaxed traditional pub with log fires, where you can get sound grub and rooms with en suite.

Getting There & Around

Buses run from Swansea station to Gower destinations every hour or two (less services on Sunday). Bus Nos 18, 18A and 48 serve Oxwich, Port Eynon, Reynoldston and Rhossili. For Llangennith take bus Nos 16 and 16C (Monday to Saturday), and Nos 48 and 49 on Sunday.

A First Swansea Bay ticket (daily/weekly £3.10/12.50) covers bus travel in Swansea and around the Gower. Buy it on the bus.

CARMARTHEN (CAERFYRDDIN)

☎ 01267 / pop 14,648

Carmarthenshire's comfortable county town, the mythical birthplace of Merlin the Magician, is more Welsh than Swansea or Cardiff – you will hear the language spoken

SOUTH WALES

here. It is also close to the magnificent National Botanic Garden and to Dylan Thomas' haunt at Laugharne. The **TIC** (☎ 231557; 113 Lammas St) is in the centre of town.

Bus No X11 runs to Carmarthen from Swansea (£4.20, 1½ hours, half-hourly); and No 322 from Haverfordwest (£3.85, one hour, at least three times daily). Sunday services vary from limited to nonexistent.

Beacons Bus (☎ 01873 853254) No 1 links Carmarthen with Brecon, via the National Botanic Garden, on Sunday from June to August (four). TrawsCambria coach No 701 (Cardiff to Aberystwyth and North Wales) stops daily in Carmarthen, as does National Express coach No 508 or 528 (Haverfordwest to Swansea).

Trains to Carmarthen run from Swansea (45 minutes, hourly, daily) and Cardiff (£11, two hours, six daily).

AROUND CARMARTHEN
National Botanic Garden (Gardd Fotaneg Genedlaethol)

Whether your fingers are green or plain pink, don't miss this contemporary botanical delight where gardening comes up to date and children are heartily in fashion. Plants are displayed in and around beautiful modern buildings and landscaping, built with tact and imagination onto the former Georgian estate of Middleton Hall. One treat is a recessed rivulet that runs 200m down the central Broadwalk into a fountain. Another is the large replanted double-walled garden that originally grew food for the estate. The centrepiece is the 100m-wide Great Glasshouse sunk into the hilltop, where a Mediterranean climate nurtures endangered plants from the South African Cape and Australia, among others.

Children's attractions include a maize maze, willow dens – and racing leaves down that rivulet.

The **botanic garden** (☎ 01558-667148; www .gardenofwales.org.uk; adult £7; ☉ 10am-6pm Easter-Oct, 10am-4.30pm Nov-Easter) lies 7 miles east of Carmarthen, 1½ miles north of the A48 on the B4310.

To reach the garden by public transport, take bus No 166 from Carmarthen (18 minutes, three daily Monday to Saturday). Beacons Bus No 1 runs four times daily from Carmarthen on Sunday and bank holidays from June to August. A taxi from

Carmarthen costs around £10; try **Chris Cars** (☎ 01267 234438).

LAUGHARNE (LACHARN)
☎ 01994 / pop 2940

Whatever your devotion to Dylan Thomas, anyone can enjoy the short walk from the centre of this pretty castle-town along the broad Taff Estuary to the house where Thomas produced some of his finest work.

You can also visit the remains of a 12th-century **castle** (CADW; ☎ 427906; adult £2.75; ☉ 10am-5pm end Mar-end Sep), where Thomas worked in the summerhouse, while his simple grave lies in St Martin's churchyard.

The town is the likely model for the palingrammatic (meaning 'say it backwards') town of Llareggub, the setting for Thomas' best-known piece, *Under Milk Wood* (1954). The spelling was altered after his death to the more delicate Llaregyb.

Dylan Thomas Boathouse

Built with great charm against the cliff overlooking a tiny in-filled harbour, the **boathouse** (☎ 427420; adult £3; ☉ 10am-5pm May-Oct, 10.30am-3pm Nov-Apr) is five minutes' walk from town, either on the waterside Dylan-themed path from beneath the castle or down a leafy lane. Thomas spent the last four years of his life here with his wife, Caitlin, and the house is preserved as a shrine with photographs, manuscripts and recordings of the poet reading from his own works. Above the boathouse, you can look through the window of the wooden garage – 'The Shack', Thomas called it – where he wrote *Under Milk Wood*. From the terrace tearoom of the house you can survey his 'heron priested shore'.

Sleeping & Eating

Laugharne has lately pole-vaulted upmarket.

Dylan's Guesthouse (☎ 07970-680007; www.celtic -retreats.com; d from £85) With estuary views and Jacuzzis in the best rooms, this is no place for roughing it.

Brown's Hotel (☎ 427320; King St) This is the pub where Thomas drank, and it has plans to reinstate its rooms to a high standard. Actor Neil Morrissey, star of the hit UK TV show *Men Behaving Badly*, has a stake in the revamp, as he has at the trendy New Three Mariners coffee-house bar on the next block down.

Stable Door Wine Bar & Brasserie (☎ 427777; Market Lane; mains £13; 🕑 dinner Thu-Sat) Sip fine wines and dine on excellent dishes in a lovely stone building with a conservatory and garden, and occasional live music.

Getting There & Away
Bus No 222 runs to Laugharne from Carmarthen (30 minutes, two-hourly Monday to Saturday, three on Sunday).

PEMBROKESHIRE COAST NATIONAL PARK

Rugged seascapes famous for their beauty, beaches and wildlife make a visit to the Pembrokeshire Coast National Park a trip you'd be mad to miss. The park occupies the outer limits of southwest Wales, a region that, as a whole, is proudly considered by the inhabitants to be West Wales.

Virtually all County Pembrokeshire's 180-mile coastline is included in the national park, and also the offshore islands, the inshore Daugleddau estuary and stretches of moorland in the Preseli Hills.

The main attraction is the beaches, including many surfing strands, while the 186-mile-long clifftop Pembrokeshire Coast Path is a classic walking trail – try to hike at least a part of it. And no-one should miss St David's, where the superb, secreted cathedral marks Wales' holiest place.

Boats make frequent Easter to October trips to view the huge sea-bird colonies on the islands of Skomer, Skokholm and Grassholm, just off the southern headland of St Brides Bay. Grey seals breed on Skomer and on Ramsey Island, off the northerly headland. From promontories on the north coast you may also spot resident bottlenose dolphins and harbour porpoises, as well as migrating dolphins and Minke whales.

Pembrokeshire is the birthplace of coasteering – an adventurous sport-for-all (see the boxed text, p672), while horse riding, along the beaches and inland, is also popular. In places, the cycle touring is also outstanding.

The park's only upland area is the Preseli Hills on the north coast. Grassy, rounded

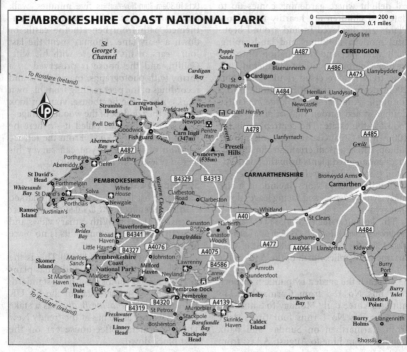

PEMBROKESHIRE COAST NATIONAL PARK

hills, peaking at Foel Cwmcerwyn (535m), are topped by cairns (stone mounds) and rich in prehistoric remains.

Holiday-making plays a large role in Pembrokeshire's identity, particularly along the south coast, which is also known as 'Little England'. Many guesthouses are run by incomers – and more than 50 castles here were built by the Anglo-Norman invaders. The rugged north coast is more Welsh and has a delightfully remote shoreline accessible down dead-end roads and along the coast path.

Orientation & Information

The **park** (www.pembrokeshirecoast.org.uk) consists of four parts: the coastline east of Fishguard to Cardigan and inland to the Preseli Hills; the coastline west of Fishguard around south to Milford Haven; the inland stretches of the Milford Haven waterway; and the coastline around the southern Pembroke peninsula. Incongruous oil terminals – which need deep-water docks for the tankers – along the industrial estuary of Milford Haven disqualify this waterway from the national park.

There are about a dozen TICs in the area, the biggest being at St David's. On arrival, pick up a free copy of *Coast to Coast*, the excellent park visitor newspaper, with day-by-day events and activities, plus contact details for walks, cycle trips, pony treks, island cruises, canoe trips and minibus tours.

For the local weather forecast call **Weathercall** (☎ 0906 850 0414).

Activities

ACTIVITY CENTRES

Two trustworthy Pembrokeshire activity centres between them organise coasteering, sea kayaking, mountain biking, surfing, hiking and climbing.

Preseli Venture (☎ 01348-837709; www.preseli venture.com; half-/full-day £39/78) This adult-only adventure centre lies on the north coast off the A487 between Abermawr Bay and Mathry. The comfortable B&B lodge has a bar and serves decent food.

TYF Adventure (Twr-y-Felin; ☎ 01437-721611, toll-free 0800 132 588; www.tyf.com; 1 High St, St David's; half-day coasteering/half-day other activities £40/36) TYF takes children and offers its own comfortable hotel as an accommodation option. Book by phone or through its shops at St David's and Tenby.

BOAT TRIPS

Pembrokeshire's wealth of sea life is best viewed from one of the boats – little, big or jet-powered – that ply their way around the islands. Skomer, Skokholm and Grassholm lie off the southerly headland of St Brides Bay, while Ramsey Island is off northerly St David's peninsula. Boats also visit Caldey Island from Tenby.

Charges vary, but expect to pay in the region of £18 for a trip. For more information see the sections on St Brides Bay (p676) and St David's (p679), and read the *Coast to Coast* tourist newspaper, free from TICs.

CYCLING

Cycling on the coast path is prohibited, but the lanes and 320 miles of bridleways provide cyclists with many a rolling view of Pembrokeshire.

The highlight of the Celtic Trail national cycle route is the coastal section between Broad Haven near Haverfordwest, St David's and Fishguard. Obtain details from **Sustrans** (☎ 0845 113 0065). For more on Sustrans and the National Cycle Network see the boxed text, p81.For easy mountain biking head to Canaston Woods near Narberth, and for upland tough-stuff, to the bridleways of the Preseli Hills behind Newport (use Ordance Survey Landranger 1:50,000 map 145). Newport Bike Hire (p682) supplies bikes and routes for the north coast and Preseli Hills.

Maps and leaflets of other interesting Pembrokeshire cycle routes are stocked at TICs.

PONY TREKKING & HORSE RIDING

This is an ideal area for riding – either along the beaches, across open moorland or high up in the Preseli Hills – and there are a dozen stables in or near the park; see the free *Coast to Coast* newspaper (in TICs) for listings.

SEA SPORTS

Pembrokeshire has reasonable **surfing** backed by splendid coastal scenery. You will find good breaks and vehicle access at Freshwater West and Newgale, and at Whitesands Bay, near St David's, which is popular with everybody.

You can hire or buy equipment and take lessons with several outfits; try fully mobile

Outer Reef (☎ 01646-680070; www.outerreefsurfschool .com), which moves around following the best conditions; **West Wales Wind, Surf & Sailing** (☎ 01646-636642; www.surfdale.co.uk), which teaches at Newgale, among others; and **Whitesands Surf School** (☎ 01437-720433; www.whitesandssurf school.co.uk; High St), based at Ma Sime's Surf Hut (see map p578) in St David's, surfing at nearby Whitesands Bay.

Reliable activity centres in north Pembrokeshire offer **coasteering** trips, either as dedicated sessions or as part of residential multi-activity programmes include TYF Adventure (p671) at St David's, and Preseli Venture (p671), near Fishguard.

For equipment and tuition in **windsurfing, dinghy sailing** and **canoeing**, again try **West Wales Wind, Surf & Sailing** (☎ 01646-636642; www .surfdale.co.uk) based at Dale. For canoeing try also TYF Adventure and Preseli Venture (for both see p671).

To **scuba dive** down and enjoy Pembrokeshire's rich aquatic life and visit wrecks in the area, go to experienced, fully equipped **West Wales Diving Centre** (☎ 01437-781457; www .westwalesdivers.co.uk; Hasguard Cross), based near Little Haven. It also offers a choice of B&B or bunk accommodation.

Newgale on St Brides Bay has one of the best beaches in Wales for **fishing**.

WALKING

The 186-mile clifftop **Pembrokeshire Coast Path** hugs the shoreline between Amroth on the south coast and Poppit Sands near Cardigan on the north coast. En route lie tiny fishing villages, great sandy bays and desolate landscapes. The persistent rise and fall of the cliffs stiffens the challenge beyond the distance covered. Fifteen days is a good estimate for the total distance, but most people

do shorter sections. Suggested sections for good walks include Dale to Martin's Haven near Marloes, and Solva to Whitesands Bay on St David's peninsula.

Recommended is the detailed *Pembrokeshire Coast Path* by Brian John (£12.99). Ten leaflets (40p each) break the path into sections, plus offer circular walks using those sections. These and literature for other walks are stocked by TICs en route. From the park website (www.pembrokeshirecoast .org.uk) you can also download route maps for 90 walks.

Accommodation is never far off-route and youth hostels are often spaced a day's hike apart, but book ahead between Easter and September. *Coast Path Accommodation* (£2.50), from TICs, carries a full list of options, including places that accept pets.

The route is covered by two Ordnance Survey *Explorer* OL 1:25,000 maps: No 35 (North Pembrokeshire) and No 36 (South Pembrokeshire).

Pembrokeshire Coastal Bus Services (eg the Puffin Shuttle) run the coast daily from June to September, giving access to coastpath sections and circular walks (see p673). The timetable leaflet also lists suggestions for combined bus/walks on the coast path.

Sleeping

B&Bs and hotels exist throughout the park, especially around the well-developed south coast (www.visitpembrokeshire.co.uk). There are 10 YHA hostels: at Manorbier (p674), Lawrenny, Marloes Sands (p676), Broad Haven (p676), Penycwm (p676), St David's (p679), Trefin (p680), Pwll Deri (p680), Trefdraeth (Newport; p682) and Poppit Sands (p683). Fishguard has the Hamilton Backpackers (p682).

COASTEERING & SEA KAYAKING

More or less invented on the Pembrokeshire coast, coasteering is essentially rock climbing with the sea splashing at your heels. Being fairly demanding and quite risky, you need to be suitably equipped, reasonably fit and a capable swimmer, and have a qualified leader with a good knowledge of the coastline, water and weather conditions. See the boxed text, p83 for more details.

The Pembrokeshire coast is also one of the UK's finest playgrounds for sea kayaking, with powerful tidal currents creating huge standing waves between the coast and offshore islands. Paddling here is also a great experience for beginners and nature lovers, for you get the best view of the beautiful cliffscapes (rock stacks, caves and idyllic bays) and wildlife (porpoises and birds) from the water – with no engine roar or fuel fumes.

Getting There & Around

The West Wales main-line railway runs direct services from Swansea (connections for Cardiff and London Paddington) to three branch lines, terminating at Fishguard (ferry for Ireland, £8.60, two hours, two daily), Milford Haven (£8.60, two hours, every two hours Monday to Saturday, four on Sunday) and Pembroke Dock (ferry for Ireland, £8.50, two hours, six daily Monday to Saturday, two on Sunday). A National Express coach runs from London to Haverfordwest (£23.50, seven hours, three times daily).

Once in Pembrokeshire, use buses to get around rather than trains. Note: Sunday services are limited, more so from October to April. The West Wales Rover (£5) is a one-day run-around ticket valid for most buses in Carmarthenshire, Pembrokeshire and Ceredigion, and can be bought on the bus. For details of the multiday runaround Freedom of South Wales Flexi-Rover ticket, which includes trains, see p658.

Daily from May to September (three days weekly October to April) hail-and-ride buses (the Puffin Shuttle, Strumble Shuttle and others) ply the coast path roads, picking up and setting down at any safe point. The useful free timetable of Pembrokeshire Coastal Bus Services, which includes coast path walk mileages and suggestions for combined bus/walks, is available from **Pembrokeshire County Council** (☎ 01437 775227), TICs and accommodation en route. Timetables are also published in the free *Coast to Coast* newspaper.

TENBY (DINBYCH Y PYSGOD)

☎ 01834 / pop 4934

Charming, prosperous party-resort Tenby, located on a rocky promontory surrounded at low tide by golden sands, is the epicentre of the south coast holiday culture. The image of its sheltered harbour and lifeboat slipway overlooked by pastel Georgian town houses is a Pembrokeshire badge. The old town features attractive architecture, steep streets and curious nooks, plus a 500m section of town wall, and the place is popular with well-heeled weekend tourists and sore-heeled coast path walkers.

The castle on the promontory was built by the Normans, and the town was fortified in the 13th century after unsuccessful attempts at recapture by the Welsh. By the 19th century warring was forgotten and Tenby was all the rage with Victorians enjoying new-fashioned holidays by the sea.

Orientation & Information

The town's main landmark is the headland of Castle Hill, site of the Norman stronghold. On the north side is the harbour and North Beach. On the southern side is tiny Castle Sands, then long South Beach. The **train station** (Warren St) is on the western side of town, at the bottom of the street. The **bus station** (Upper Park Rd) is one block south of Warren St.

The **TIC** (☎ 842404; tenbytic@pembrokeshire.gov.uk; The Croft; 🕑 10am-5.30pm (may close Sun) Jun–mid-Jul, 10am-8pm mid-Jul–Aug, 10am-5.30pm Sep, 10am-5pm Oct, 10am-4pm Nov-Easter, 10am-5pm Easter-May) may move offices (to Upper Park St beside the bus stop) during 2005, but at the time of research this was unconfirmed.

Sights & Activities

Tenby's top trip is the 20-minute boat ride from the harbour to **Caldey Island** (☎ 844453; www.caldey-island.co.uk; adult £8; 🕑 10am-3pm Mon-Sat May-Sep), the home of Cistercian monks, plus grey seals and Wales' largest cormorant colony. There are twice-daily guided tours of the monastery and lovely walks around the island, with good views from the south-side lighthouse. Boats depart (every 20 minutes) from the quay at high tide and Castle Sands at low tide. Buy tickets at the harbour kiosk.

The handsomely restored 15th-century **Tudor Merchant's House** (NT; ☎ 842279; Quay Hill; adult £2; 🕑 10am-5pm Apr-Sep, 10am-3pm Oct), furnished according to the time, is worth a visit. The remains of early frescoes are visible on interior walls.

Other sights include the **castle ruins** and, within them, the **Tenby Museum & Art Gallery** (☎ 842809; Castle Hill; adult £2; 🕑 10am-5pm Easter-Dec, 10am-5pm Mon-Fri Jan-Easter), which tells Tenby's story and displays paintings of surrounding landscapes, and portraits by Augustus and Gwen John.

Guided walks of Tenby's historical sites are run by **Town Trails** (☎ 845841; walks £3.75; 🕑 Mon-Sat Jun-Sep & holidays), with themes such as ghosts, poets and painters.

Sleeping

Every second house in parts of Tenby seems to be a B&B or hotel. Meanwhile, the nearest YHA hostel is about 6 miles west at Manorbier (p674).

Gwynne House (☎ 843450; Bridge St; d £50) The best address on the harbour and a fabulous restoration that allows the house's original elegance to shine through – and provides relief from Tenby's otherwise flouncy style – makes Gwynne House a recommendation.

Boulston Cottage (☎ 843289; 29 Trafalgar Rd; s £16-36, d £36-50) Run by a cheerful Italian-Spanish couple, this is close to the bus stop.

Myrtle House (☎ 842508; St Mary's St; d £48-60; ☒) Has bright, flowery rooms, and is close to Castle Sands and South Beach.

Fourcroft Hotel (☎ 842886; www.fourcroft-hotel .co.uk; The Croft; s £39-59, d £78-118; ☒) Great views, an outdoor pool and a garden overlooking North Beach are a treat for guests.

There are more well-kept Victorian places above South Beach:

Augustus House (☎ 843677; South Cliff Gardens; d £50; ☒)

Clement Dale (☎ 843165; South Cliff Gardens; d £50; ☒)

Meadow Farm (☎ 844829; per person on foot £5; ☯ Easter-Sep) A simple camping ground with showers, on the coast path five minutes' walk north of town.

Eating

Tenby's more-tempting eateries boast modern menus and plenty of fresh fish. The larger hotels open their restaurants (expect standard menus) to nonguests.

Plantagenet House Restaurant (☎ 842350; Quay Hill; mains £14-20) The town's top diner has menus of irresistible length, quality and variety, including *healthy* children's dishes (£5), home-made bread and pâtés and more seafood than you can shake a hook at. You can also view its 12th-century Flemish chimney-hearth.

Bay Tree (☎ 843516; Tudor Sq; mains around £9) Enjoy contemporary and traditional Welsh dishes at this bistro.

Pam Pam (☎ 842946; Tudor Sq; mains £11) This rather civilised pub-style restaurant serves seafood, pasta and steaks.

The Reef (☎ 845258; St Julian's St; mains £7-12) A calm Mediterranean-style bistro-restaurant with imaginative seafood and pasta.

Drinking & Entertainment

The cheerful and smoky **Normandie Inn** (☎ 842227; Upper Frog St) puts on live bands playing folk and rock almost daily in summer. Youth hangs out at the **Three Mariners** (☎ 842834; St George's St).

Getting There & Away

The easiest way from Swansea/Carmarthen to Tenby is by direct train (£8.50/£5.45, 1½ hours/40 minutes, six daily Monday to Saturday, three on Sunday), continuing to Pembroke/Pembroke Dock. There's also National Express coach No 508 (40 minutes, twice daily).

From Haverfordwest to Tenby take bus No 349 or 381 (one to 1½ hours, hourly). No 349 runs via Pembroke (40 minutes).

MANORBIER
☎ 01834

'In all the broad lands of Wales, Manorbier is the best place by far,' wrote Wales' great medieval scribe Giraldus Cambrensis – Gerald of Wales – in the 12th century – well, he was born in what was then the new castle! The village certainly is an attractive, secluded place, in a spot 800m above a fine surfing beach on a wild stretch of coastline.

The tumbledown 12th-century **castle** (adult £3.50; ☯ 10.30am-5.30pm Easter-Sep), 200m below the village, houses a collection of bizarre rejects from Madame Tussaud's waxworks in London.

Castlemead Hotel (☎ 871358; www.castlemead hotel.com; d £80) is elegant and unpompous. The **Castle Inn** (☎ 871268; snacks around £3) is a solid old pub in the village. **Manorbier YHA Hostel** (☎ 0870 770 5954; manorbier@yha.org.uk; dm £11.80; ☯ with 48hr notice Mar-Oct) is in an impressively lonely spot 200m from sandy Skrinkle Haven, 1 mile east of Manorbier village.

Bus No 349 runs daily to Manorbier from Haverfordwest (one hour, hourly) and Pembroke (20 minutes), and from Tenby (20 minutes).

PEMBROKE (PENFRO)
☎ 01646 / pop 7214

A medieval town layout and mighty castle guarding a tributary off Milford Haven make little Pembroke worth an afternoon visit. With a fraction of Tenby's visitor numbers, the atmosphere is Welsh and the B&Bs good value.

The castle, one of the most important Norman fortresses in Wales, has a tidal moat, and was home to the early Tudors. **Pembroke TIC** (☎ 622388; Commons Rd; ☯ 10am-5pm Easter-Oct) is south of and below the castle. It stocks the *Town Trail* walking guide, featuring a dozen buildings of interest.

Pembroke Dock, serving ferries for Rosslare (Ireland), is a separate town 2 miles west of Pembroke. Within the Irish Ferries terminal, its hours coinciding with arrivals and departures, is another TIC (☎ 01646-622753; ☉ 10.30am-2.30pm Easter-Sep).

Pembroke Castle

Within the massive walls of the castle (☎ 681510; adult £3; ☉ 9.30am-6pm Apr-Sep, 10am-5pm Mar & Oct, 10am-4pm Nov-Feb), the entertainment includes climbing 100 spiral steps inside the keep for a glorious view (closed in very windy conditions), descending the rough stairway to dank Wogan's Cavern – a massive natural cave with a watergate – and exploring the passages that run between the towers.

The stronghold was built in the 12th and 13th centuries, and 'Strongbow' Richard FitzGilbert, earl of Pembroke, made it his base during the Irish conquest. A plaque marks the 1456 birthplace of Henry, the first Tudor king and father to Henry VIII, the monarch who formalised the union of England and Wales. During the Civil War, the fortress resisted Oliver Cromwell for 48 days until, it is said, he discovered and blocked the water source.

Sleeping & Eating

Beech House (☎ 683740; 78 Main St; s/d £16/32) The friendly seen-everything hostess, with her eye for the disorganised traveller and a passion for wisteria, is a boost to an immediately appealing Georgian villa, which has a fine period lounge.

Woodbine (☎ 686338; 84 Main St; s/d £20/40) Three doors along from Beech House, this sister villa has lighter, more-contemporary furnishings and linen, and a designer dining room.

High Noon Guest House (☎ 683736; www .highnoon.co.uk; Lower Lamphey Rd; s/d £19.50/45) A friendly place (although getting a little worn) that's keen on walkers and cyclists.

Old Kings Arms Hotel (☎ 683611; www.oldkingsarms hotel.co.uk; Main St; s/d £35/55) This friendly, traditional town hotel has a good nonsmoking restaurant (sample mackerel with oatmeal and rhubarb for £11) and great bar food.

Ferry Inn (☎ 682947; mains around £10) This waterside pub, sited where the old Pembroke ferry has been superseded by the soaring Cleddau Bridge, has a palatable mixed menu of pub grub and fish specials. To get

here, head 2 miles north of the town, and go left at the roundabout at the top of the road *just* before the bridge.

Getting There & Away

Bus No 349 calls at Pembroke (and Pembroke Dock) en route between Haverfordwest (40 minutes) and Tenby (40 minutes) hourly Monday to Saturday. On Sunday No 359 runs four times (50 minutes).

Pembroke is on a train branch line from Whitland via Tenby (20 minutes, six daily), which terminates at Pembroke Dock.

Irish Ferries (☎ 0870 517 1717; www.irishferries .com) runs two ferries a day to Rosslare (Ireland) from Pembroke Dock (four hours).

AROUND PEMBROKE

Looming romantically over the glassy River Carew, Carew Castle and its restored tidal mill (☎ 651782; castle £1.90, castle & mill £2.80; ☉ 10am-5pm Easter-Oct) exude historic atmosphere. The 1-mile circular walk around the castle, mill, causeway and bridge is recommended.

The original 12th-century fortification was converted to a manor in Elizabethan times and abandoned in 1690. The Elizabethan tidal mill has a causeway that once trapped the incoming tide in a great pond, then released the waters through sluice gates that turned the millwheels. For 400 years to 1937, the three-storey building ground corn for the castle estate and community.

A tall 11th-century Celtic cross stands by the road near the castle entrance. Opposite, the Carew Inn (☎ 01646-651267; www.carewinn.co.uk; mains £12) now serves top fare – swordfish, seafood, ostrich – within a spruce pubby atmosphere.

The site lies 4 miles east of Pembroke. Bus No 361 runs from Pembroke Dock (not Pembroke) to the Carew cross (10 minutes, four daily Monday to Saturday, not Sunday).

HAVERFORDWEST (HWLFFORDD)

☎ 01437 / pop 13,367

Haverfordwest is a bustling no-nonsense place, with examples of Georgian architecture, but little of the prettiness of other Pembrokeshire towns. It is the transport hub for north Pembrokeshire.

A fortified Flemish settlement was founded here in the 12th century and a castle built about the same time. The former river port was kept busy until the railway arrived in the mid-19th century. These days the castle and riverside priory ruins are fairly plain. The small **Castle Museum & Art Gallery** (☎ 763087; adult £1) is in the outer ward of the castle. The **TIC** (☎ 763110; Old Bridge St) is near the bus station.

Sleeping & Eating

College Guest House (☎ 763710; 93 Hill St; s/d from £30/45) This guesthouse has rooms with en suite and is found up through the old town.

County Hotel (☎ /fax 762144; Salutation Sq; s/d £45/65) The town hotel offers traditional comfort.

The George's (☎ 766683; 24 Market St; mains around £6) A restaurant and coffee-bar up in the old town. As well as the regular dishes, George's offers a mouthwatering six-course fish extravaganza (£25).

Getting There & Away

Bus services from Haverfordwest fan out all over Pembrokeshire. Sunday services are almost nonexistent.

Bus No 412 runs hourly from Cardigan (1½ hours, not on Sunday) via Fishguard and No 411 serves St David's (45 minutes, hourly Monday to Saturday, two on Sunday) and some of these continue to Fishguard.

National Express runs a service from London to Haverfordwest (£23.50, seven hours, three times daily).

Trains run five times a day between Haverfordwest and Swansea (£8.60, 1¾ hours), with connections to Cardiff and London.

ST BRIDES BAY (BAE SAIN FFRAID)

Broad, beautiful St Brides Bay has the best beaches in Wales, and can absorb crowds of holiday-makers in the summer. **Little Haven** is a pretty little village above a fine beach, **Broad Haven** is the liveliest resort and glorious **Newgale** beach is the biggest strand, a honeypot for swimmers and surfers.

The bay lies at the western end of the 'landsker', the invisible boundary running from west to east between the Welsh parts of Pembrokeshire to the north and the anglicised south.

Surfing, Windsurfing & Sailing

In Broad Haven, **Haven Sports** (☎ 01646-680070; www.havensports.co.uk) rents out surfing equipment and offers lessons. For details of other teaching outfits – Outer Reef and West Wales Wind, Surf & Sailing – see p671.

Sleeping

Villages around the bay are packed with mid-range B&Bs. There are also numerous camping grounds, and most farmers are happy to let you use a field for a couple of pounds – ask first.

Newgale Campsite (☎ 01437-710253; tent site per person £4; ☽ Easter-Sep) Camp virtually on the beach here. A café, pub and shop are nearby.

Druidston Hotel (☎ 01437-781221; www.druidstone .co.uk; s/d from £35/70; bar meals around £8) Set high above Druidston Haven, this cosy hotel has a cellar bar and good food.

YHA hostels are well sited for beaches and the coast path:

Broad Haven (☎ 01437-781688; broadhaven@yha.org .uk; dm £11.80; ☽ with 48hr notice Mar-Oct) Panoramic bay views.

Marloes Sands (☎ 01646-636667, for bookings more than 7 days in advance ☎ 01629-592708; reservations@yha .org.uk; dm £8.20; ☽ Apr-Sep). One and a quarter miles from the departure point for trips to Skomer.

Penycwm (☎ 01437-721940; penycwm@yha.org.uk; dm £13.40; ☽ Apr-Oct, 48hr notice Nov-Mar) Five-star hostel 2 miles from beach.

Getting There & Away

The coast path and Marloes, Dale, Broad Haven, Druidston and Newgale are served by the three-daily summertime Puffin Shuttle (p672).

The area is also served by regular bus from Haverfordwest (not on Sunday). For Dale and Marloes take No 315 or 316 (one hour, three daily Monday to Saturday). Broad Haven is the terminus of bus No 311 (20 minutes, five daily Monday to Saturday). Newgale and Penycwm are stops on the route of No 411, which runs hourly Monday to Saturday between Haverfordwest (25 minutes), St David's (40 minutes), and, less frequently, Fishguard (one hour).

SKOMER, SKOKHOLM & GRASSHOLM ISLANDS

These islands, lying off the bay's southern headland, are a marine nature reserve populated by immense sea-bird colonies that are busiest from April to mid-August. Grey seals with pups loll on the beaches during autumn, and porpoises and dolphins pop up in the waves. Cruisers and jet-boats visit from Easter to October, both during the day and in the evenings (when the Manx shearwaters gather to make their nocturnal landing). For further information, consult the *Coast to Coast* newspaper, available at TICs.

Skomer is the largest and easiest island to reach, and home to over half a million breeding sea birds, including puffins, guillemots, razorbills, fulmars, cormorants, shags, and the burrow-breeding Manx shearwater – together Skomer and Skokholm have the largest colony in the world, 160,000 strong. About 150 grey seal pups are born here annually, and porpoise and dolphin sightings are common.

To visit Skomer, the *Dale Princess* cruiser offers daily landing trips (departing at 10am, 11am and noon, returning from 3pm) and round-island trips (departing at 1pm Sunday and Tuesday to Thursday; 10.30am, 11.30am 1pm and 2.30pm Monday). Boats depart from Martin's Haven near Marloes; contact **Dale Sailing** (☎ 01646-601636, www.pembrokeshire islands.co.uk; trips £7, landing fee £6).

Skokholm to the south is known as the habitat for some 35,000 Manx shearwaters and puffins. Accommodation is available on the island; book through the **Wildlife Trust South & West Wales** (☎ 01239-621600).

Lying 11 miles offshore, the smallest island, **Grassholm**, has the second-largest gannet colony in the northern hemisphere – 33,000 pairs. Landing on Grassholm is not permitted, but the fast, exciting Dale Sea Safari, on a rigid inflatable boat (RIB), makes round-island trips (11.30am, 4.30pm and 6.30pm daily), departing from Dale. The Grassholm Gannetry trip runs daily at 2pm, while more expensive evening and specialist trips are also offered through **Dale Sailing** (☎ 0800-028 4090; www.dale-sea-safari.co.uk; trip £20; Brunel Quay, Neyland).

A nightly shearwater watch boat-trip, plus dolphin and porpoise watches, are organised by **Shearwater Safaris** (☎ 01437-781569; www .boatrides.co.uk), departing from Neyland Yacht Haven (near the Cleddau Bridge). It also runs trips around Skomer and Grassholm.

ST DAVID'S (TY-DDEWI)

☎ 01437 / pop 1800

There's something special about St David's that crowds of summer visitors cannot

extinguish. The magic was recognised by Welsh patron saint Dewi Sant, who chose to establish the first monastic community here (a short walk from where he was born) in the 6th century. The cathedral, which preserves his relics in a casket, is a magnificent sight, and if you visit only one religious place in Wales, make it this.

Although little more than a big village, the cathedral earns St David's the title of 'city'. As the original architects intended, you don't see the building itself until you're on top of it. The cathedral was concealed in a stream-fed hollow below what is now the square, in the vain hope of fooling passing Norse raiders.

Information

A combined **National Park Visitors Centre & TIC** (☎ 720392; enquiries@stdavids.pembrokeshirecoast.org .uk; ☺ 9.30am-5.30pm Easter-Oct, 10am-4pm Nov-Easter) is at the top of town, and stocks tourist information on accommodation, and national park literature.

Sights
ST DAVID'S CATHEDRAL
This is the holiest place in Wales – Pope Calixtus II declared in 1124 that two pilgrimages to St David's equalled one to Rome and three equalled one pilgrimage to the holy city of Jerusalem itself; the **cathedral** (☎ 720691; admission by donation £1) has received a stream of pilgrims and visitors ever since. The main grey granite building was constructed in the late 12th century on a site where a church had existed for 600 years. The bishops added chapels and other modifications between the 12th and 16th centuries. In the meantime, Norse pirates ransacked it at least seven times.

The atmosphere inside is one of great antiquity. The floor slopes sharply and the pillars keel drunkenly following a 1248 earthquake. The Norman nave's superb Irish oak ceiling was carved in the 16th century. The equally richly carved choir in the centre of the cross is illuminated from the tower above. The patron saint's shrine (wrecked during the Reformation) is in the northern choir aisle; his relics are kept behind the altar.

Tours of the cathedral (£3) are held at 2.30pm on Monday, Tuesday, Thursday and Friday and take 1½ hours.

BISHOP'S PALACE

Try not to bypass the ruins next to the cathedral of **Bishop's Palace** (CADW; ☎ 720517; adult £2.50; ⌚ 9.30am-5pm Easter-May, 9.30am-6pm Jun-Sep, 9.30am-5pm Oct, 9.30am-4pm Mon-Sat & 11am-4pm Sun Nov-Mar), an elaborate testament to the wealth and influence of the medieval church in this region. Its final imposing form, including the arcades on the parapet, is mostly due to Henry de Gower, bishop from 1327 to 1348.

The palace is a wonderful setting for open-air theatre during the Arts Festival in the summer (see p679).

ST NON'S BAY

St David's alleged birthplace is three-quarters of a mile south of the cathedral on the coast, beside the bay that now bears his mother's name. A spring at the site is attended by pilgrims and believed to have curative powers. Here also are the ruins of the 13th-century **St Non's Chapel**, also a modern chapel and a building used as a retreat.

BEACHES

Two miles northwest of St David's lies westfacing **Whitesands Bay** (Porth Mawr). One of the best surfing beaches, it is usually crowded in summer. The beach at **Porthmelgan**, 15 minutes' walk northwest further around the coast path, is smaller and more secluded.

RAMSEY ISLAND

Just off St David's Head, Ramsey Island has a colony of Atlantic grey seals, thousands of nesting sea birds, porpoise and dolphin appearances and spectacular sea caves.

A range of boat trips covering island landings, cave tours, jet-boating on the Bitches standing waves and whale and dolphin watches are organised by several companies with booking offices in St David's (see details also in the *Coast to Coast* newspaper):

Aquaphobia (Ramsey Powerboats; ☎ 720471, after hr 721648) Operates round-Ramsey tours (£17.50) and others, including evening trips to see shearwaters (£20). Booking office in the grounds of the Grove Hotel, opposite the TIC.

Thousand Islands Expeditions (☎ 721721/721686; www.thousandislands.co.uk; Cross Sq) Round-Ramsey trips (£18) with a landing (three or six hours, guided walks, £14), and evening puffin and shearwater watches (£25). Booking office at the head of the lane, The Pebbles, from the main square to the cathedral.

Voyages of Discovery (☎ 721911; www.ramseyisland .co.uk; 1 High St) Sails to Ramsey (£18), the North Bishops puffin islands (£25) and does whale- and dolphin-spotting trips (£50). Booking office in the main square, opposite Lloyds bank.

Activities

WALKING & CYCLING

The TIC stocks leaflets on walks. The nearest section of coast path lies a mile south of St David's, down lanes and/or footpaths to Porthclais, St Non's Bay or Caerfai Bay (all about a mile apart). The path around St David's peninsula between Solva, St Justinian and Whitesands Bay is a longer trek, served by two youth hostels – St David's and Penycwm.

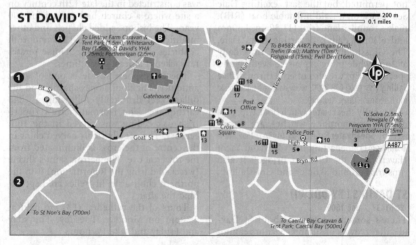

St David's is the most westerly point on the Celtic Trail cycle route (see p671).

WATER SPORTS
Whitesands Bay is a popular place to surf. Whitesands Surf School, operating out of **Ma Sime's Surf Hut** (☎ 720433; High St, St David's) gives lessons here.

TYF Adventure (☎ 01437-721611 in St David's, toll-free 0800 132 588) runs coasteering, sea kayaking, climbing and surfing trips.

Festivals & Events
St David's Cathedral Festival (☎ 720271; festival@st davidscathedral.org.uk) The oak ceiling of St David's Cathedral provides fine acoustics for this festival, which features classical music for 1½ weeks, culminating at the spring bank holiday weekend in late May.

Arts Festival Held during the first two weeks of August, and presents an energetic intro to Shakespeare (set in the magnificent Bishop's Palace), as well as prose and poetry readings.

Sleeping
BUDGET
Caerfai Farm Campsite (☎ 720548; www.caerfai .co.uk; tent sites per person from £5; ☉ Jun-Sep) Here's a tent and motor-home site on an organic dairy farm with a shop and fantastic sea views. It's only three-quarters of a mile south of St David's, 400m from the beach.

Lleithyr Farm Caravan & Tent Park (☎ 720245; www.whitesands-stdavids.co.uk; 2 people & tent £6.50; ☉ Easter-Oct) A short mile from Whitesands Bay, this has a good setting, with spacious fields holding a mixture of caravans (some permanent) and tents.

St David's YHA Hostel (☎ 0870 770 6042; stdavids@yha .org; Llaethdy; dm £9.30; ☉ Wed-Sun Apr–mid-Jul, daily mid-Jul–Sep, Wed-Sun Sep-Oct, with 48hr notice Nov-Feb) Near Whitesands Bay, 1¾ miles northwest of St David's, is a basic, self-catering farmhouse hostel. There's no public transport to the hostel, but the walk is enjoyable. Call for variations to opening times.

Pen Albro Guesthouse (☎ 721865; 18 Goat St; s/d £18/36) A simple, respectable place with a

shared bathroom, around the block from the cathedral.

MID-RANGE
Alandale (☎ 720404; www.stdavids.co.uk/guesthouse /alandale.htm; 43 Nun St; s/d £30/60) Although in the heart of the 'city', the rear view from Alandale, a spick town house, overlooks the green wilds of the peninsula. All the rooms have new en suites – but any shot-putter who does squeeze into the single room bathroom isn't coming out again in a hurry.

Bryn Awel (☎ 720082; 45 High St; s/d low season £25/42, d high season £48) At the top end of town near the TIC, Bryn Awel has cheerful rooms with en suite, and a welcoming hostess who serves up organic ingredients (whenever possible) for breakfast.

The Square (☎ 720333; Cross Sq; s/d from £40/60) Above a 21st-century rustic café (all stripped wood and granite floors), again in the 'city' centre, this is a civilised, contemporary place with nice bathrooms.

TOP END
Old Cross Hotel (☎ 720387; Cross Sq; s/d from £82/100) This conventional, plain but cheerful town hotel is a favourite with the silver-haired surfer brigade.

Eating & Drinking
Pebbles Yard Gallery & Espresso Bar (☎ 720122; The Pebbles) Nice décor above an arty-crafty gallery, a cute patio, fancy coffee and fresh-juice presses unfortunately don't make up for the occasionally very slow service here.

Denvers (☎ 721722; 18 High St; lunches around £5) St David's young outdoor adventure-seekers and the regular holiday-makers come to this daytime café on the main street for good cheap eats, real coffee, and breakfasts.

Cartref (☎ 720422; Cross Sq; snacks around £3, mains around £8; ☉ lunch & dinner) A rambling restaurant serving simple food in a comfortable setting.

Cox's (☎ 720491; 22 High St; mains £14; ☉ dinner Tue-Sat) With the most varied menu in town,

SOUTH WALES

Cox's serves both Welsh beef and Thai sea-food curry, along with pastas and vegetarian choices, surrounded by a cheerful budget décor.

Lawton's (☎ 729220; 16 Nun St; mains £17; ◷ dinner Tue-Sun) Lawton's joins Morgan's Brasserie (following) as St David's classy contemporary eateries. The menu is fish-rich and stars Ramsey Sound lobster (£25) alongside modern classics such as spinach and goats' cheese tart. With an eye on the holiday crowd, children are welcome.

Morgan's Brasserie (☎ 720508; 20 Nun St; mains £15; ◷ dinner Thu-Sat) This well-established restaurant has an inventive menu fusing fish, fashion and Welsh cuisine: mullet with laverbread sauce, for example, or cod with Boursin (garlicky cheese) mash.

Farmer's Arms (Goat St) Busy and relaxed, this is *the* pub.

Getting There & Around

Bus No 411 runs Monday to Saturday from Haverfordwest (45 minutes, hourly Monday to Saturday, two on Sunday) and Fishguard (50 minutes, every two hours).

St David's is served by the summertime buses, the Puffin Shuttle, Celtic Coaster and Strumble Shuttle (see p673), stopping at coast path access points and villages.

To prevent St David's clogging up with traffic, drivers are encouraged to use the free park-and-ride **shuttle bus** (◷ every 15min Apr-Aug); parking is signed at the entrance to town.

AROUND ST DAVID'S

The glorious north coast of St David's peninsula to Fishguard is cove-riddled, rugged and remote, a contrast to the well-settled south. It is among the highlights of the Pembrokeshire Coast Path.

The summertime Strumble Shuttle bus (see p673) serves points along the coast path between St David's and Fishguard.

One nice stop along the coast path is the cove village of **Porthgain**, which has a sheltered harbour and two attractive places to eat and drink. A pint of beer tastes great on the terrace of the child-friendly 250-year-old **Sloop Inn** (☎ 01437-831449; mains £12) but the menu, albeit broad and interesting, would be fairer if it were priced a few pounds cheaper.

The atmospheric, converted **Shed** (☎ 01348-831518; ◷ tearoom 10am-5pm, bistro for dinner) is a tearoom by day (try a baguette with local strong-tasting Llangloffan cheese), and a bistro and wine bar by night.

Around Porthgain and nearby Trefin are several places to stay.

Awel Mor (☎ 01348-837865; www.stdavids.co.uk /guesthouse/awelmor.htm; Penparc; d £60; ✗) This well-kept modern guesthouse has great views.

Court House (☎ 01348-837292; 33 Ffordd y Felin; d £40-50; ✗) Stay in a 200-year-old cottage five minutes off the coast path.

Caerhafod Lodge (☎ 01348-837859; www.caerhafod .co.uk; dm £12) Much liked by readers, this well-equipped hostel lies 1 mile in from the coast path at Caerhafod (1 mile west of Trefin).

This coastline has two YHA hostels:

Pwll Deri (☎ 0870 770 6004; dm £9.30; ◷ Thu-Mon Mar-Oct, daily Jul-Sep, call for precise dates) Atop a 100m cliff, and orientated precisely for coastal sunsets.

Trefin (☎ 0870 770 6074; reservations@yha.org.uk; dm £9.30; ◷ early-Apr–early-Sep) In the Trefin village schoolhouse.

FISHGUARD (ABERGWAUN)

☎ 01348 / pop 3193

Don't dismiss Fishguard as just a ferry port. This inviting little harbourside-and-clifftop town lies on the coast path between the promontories of Strumble Head and Dinas Head, at the mouth of the attractive Gwaun Valley below the western Preseli Hills.

From the centre of town the main road plummets eastward to the picturesque original harbour of Lower Fishguard the setting for the 1971 film of *Under Milk Wood* starring Richard Burton and Elizabeth Taylor.

Ferries to Ireland sail from the neighbouring town of Goodwick (Fishguard Harbour) in the next bay northwest.

Two hundred years ago Fishguard was the improbable setting for the last invasion of Britain. In February 1797 a motley bunch of 1400 French mercenaries and convicts landed nearby with the intention of marching to Liverpool and diverting English troops, thereby allowing another French force to conquer Ireland. However, the invaders stumbled across stocks of Portuguese wine and, disarmed by its potency, were rounded up by the locals. Their surrender was signed in the Royal Oak Inn in the centre of town, which still pulls a good pint.

In 1997 the bicentenary of this event was commemorated by a magnificent 30m **tapestry** telling the story of the invasion. It is planned for this to be on permanent display in the **town hall** (site of the town TIC) from early 2006.

Orientation & Information

The train station (Fishguard Harbour) and ferry port (for Stena Line ferries to Rosslare, Ireland) are at Goodwick, about a 20-minute walk northwest down the hill from central Fishguard.

The town **TIC** (☎ 873484; Market Sq; ⊙ 10am-5pm Easter-May, 10am-5.30pm Jun-Sep, 10am-4pm Mon-Sat Oct-Easter) shares a building with the town hall, which lies on the central roundabout. A second portside **TIC** (☎ 872037; ⊙ 10am-6pm Easter-Oct, 10am-4pm Nov-Easter; Internet per 30min £2), with a Internet café, is inside the Ocean Lab building just near the ferry terminal at Goodwick.

Walking

The TICs stock literature on walks covering Dinas Head (the knobbly coastal promontory 5 miles northeast) and the Preseli Hills, as well as the leaflet (No 2, Newport to Strumble Head, 40p) on the local coast-path section. You can use the summertime tourist buses, the Celtic Coaster, Strumble Shuttle and Poppit Rocket (see p673 for details), for travel to points west and east on the coast path, to walk sections or all the way back.

Sleeping

Fishguard Bay Caravan & Camping Park (☎ 811415; www.fishguardbay.com; 2-person tent site from £8; ⊙ Mar-Dec) Camp on a headland 2 miles east of Fishguard, on the coast path.

Manor Town House (☎ /fax 873260; Main St; s/d £35/54, d with sea view £60) The nicest place in Fishguard. This Georgian town house has lovely big rooms, a cute garden and antique furnishings in the lounge and basement dining room, where the hostess serves guests excellent food (dinner from £21).

Morawel Guesthouse (☎ 873366; Glyn y Mel Rd; Lower Fishguard; s/d £30/50) Morawel's asset is its location down by the old harbour, a pint's throw from the Ship Inn (p682). All rooms have their own fresh, white bathroom.

Avon House (☎ 874476; 76 High St; s £18, d without/with en suite £36/40) This is a modest, friendly place.

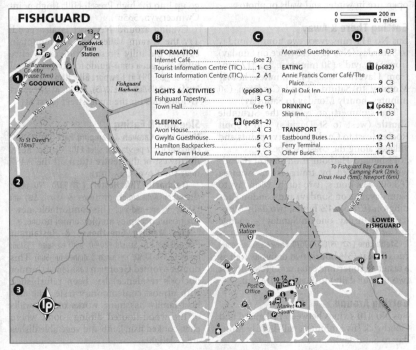

FISHGUARD

INFORMATION	
Internet Café	(see 2)
Tourist Information Centre (TIC)	1 C3
Tourist Information Centre (TIC)	2 A1

SIGHTS & ACTIVITIES	(pp680–1)
Fishguard Tapestry	3 C3
Town Hall	(see 1)

SLEEPING	(pp681–2)
Avon House	4 C3
Gwylfa Guesthouse	5 A1
Hamilton Backpackers	6 C3
Manor Town House	7 C3

Morawel Guesthouse	8 D3

EATING	(p682)
Annie Francis Corner Café/The Plaice	9 C3
Royal Oak Inn	10 C3

DRINKING	(p682)
Ship Inn	11 D3

TRANSPORT	
Eastbound Buses	12 C3
Ferry Terminal	13 A1
Other Buses	14 A1

SOUTH WALES

Hamilton Backpackers (☎ 874797; www.hamilton backpackers.co.uk; 21 Hamilton St; dm/r £13/16) A new kitchen now greets visitors at the friendly, central, comfy and slightly time-worn backpacker hostel.

In Goodwick, only five minutes' walk from the ferry terminal you get great views from **Gwylfa Guesthouse** (☎ 873730; Goodwick Sq; s/d £20/36). A mile northwest up over the hill, friendly **Brynawel Country House** (☎ /fax 874155; Llanwnda; s/d £23.50/47) is conveniently near the coast path.

Eating & Drinking

Annie Francis Corner Café/The Plaice (☎ 874649; Market Sq; mains around £11; ☽ dinner Tue-Sat Jul-Oct) A bakery and café by day, on summer evenings this converts into a fresh-fish diner serving mackerel, sea bass and crab. Bookings are recommended.

Royal Oak Inn (☎ 872514; Market Sq; mains around £8) Full of invasion memorabilia (see p680), the Royal Oak serves good pub platters (mostly fish) and hosts occasional live music.

Ship Inn (Newport Rd) This snug little old boozer, down on the old harbour, has an open fire in winter and walls of photos.

Getting There & Away

Bus No 411 runs every two hours Monday to Saturday (Nos 411/412 twice on Sunday) from St David's (50 minutes). No 412 runs from Haverfordwest (45 minutes, hourly Monday to Saturday) and Cardigan (50 minutes, hourly Monday to Saturday).

The summertime buses, the Strumble Shuttle (west to St David's) and Poppit Rocket (east to Cardigan), serve points and villages along the coast (see p673).

Fishguard Harbour train station (Goodwick) is served by trains from Swansea (£8.60, 1½ hours, two daily Monday to Saturday, one on Sunday) and London Paddington (£78.50, 4½ hours, two daily Monday to Saturday, one on Sunday) – change at Cardiff.

Stena Line (☎ 0870 570 7070; www.stenaline.co.uk) runs a boat (3½ hours, two daily) as well as a faster summertime catamaran (two hours, two to four daily) to Rosslare, Ireland.

Getting Around

Bus No 410 swings between Fishguard and Goodwick (five minutes, half-hourly Monday to Saturday).

NEWPORT (TREFDRAETH)
☎ 01239 / pop 1120

This small, pretty and firmly Welsh community – half the residents speak the language despite the tide of holiday-makers – lies on the mouth of the River Nevern in Newport Bay, overlooked by the rocky outcrop of **Carn Ingli** (347m).

Newport makes a lovely base for enjoying the pleasures of sea and upland. The coast path runs through town, and the Preseli Hills lie 6 miles inland. Be sure not to muddle the village with the city of Newport.

Parrog Beach, north of town, is dwarfed by Newport Sands (Traeth Mawr) across the river.

The **TIC** (☎ 820912; info@newporttic.fsnet.co.uk; Bank Cottages, Long St; ☽ 9.45am-5.30pm Easter-Oct) is seasonal.

Walking & Cycling

The **Siop Lyfrau/Bookshop** (☎ 820401; Market St) stocks plenty of literature on walks and history. You can walk the town trail, along the coast path, up Carn Ingli, through the picturesque Gwaun Valley (Cwm Gwaun) and go up into the high Preseli Hills (high point Cwmcerwyn, 535m).

Cycling around Newport is also good. Try the Gwaun Valley and, for mountain biking, the hilly Preseli bridleways. Hire bikes and get a map-guide for five easy local routes (£5.99) at **Newport Bike Hire** (☎ 820773; East St; per half-/full-day £10/15), based at Newport Wholefoods on the main street (East St).

Sleeping & Eating

Morawelon Caravan & Camping Park (☎ 820565; Parrog Beach; 2-person tent sites £10) Camp here, northwest of the centre (turn off the A487 near the Royal Oak Inn).

Trefdraeth YHA Hostel (☎ 0870 770 6072; reservations@yha.org.uk; cnr Lower & Mary's Sts; dm £11.80; ☽ Apr–mid-Sep) This comfortable, newish hostel occupies an old school house.

Llys Meddyg Guesthouse & Restaurant (☎ 820008; East St; s/d £30/50, with en suite £35/56; mains £12.50-17.50; ☽ lunch & dinner Tue-Sun) This double-fronted Georgian residence (former doctor's residence) has been refurbished with utmost contemporary taste. The arty host-family has hung works on the walls of the wood-floored dining room, where chef-cooked fish, lamb and vegetable dishes are a delight.

Cnapan (☎ 820575; East St; s/d £42/70; mains £14; ☽ lunch & dinner Wed-Mon, no lunch Sun) This popular, highly civilised guesthouse and homely restaurant has charming hosts and airy rooms. You can dine in the garden on warm days.

Soar Hill (☎ 820506; www.soarhill.com; Cilgwyn Rd; s/d £33/56) This is a four-star bluestone-built former smallholding, a 15-minute walk up the hill southeast out of town. The hostess gives lifts to and from the coast path.

Café Fleur (☎ 820131; Market St; ☽ 10.30am-5pm Tue-Sat, dinner Fri & Sat Jul-Sep) A café serving panini (£3.75), waffles (£2) and galettes (£4.75) by day, Café Fleur also opens late for themed (Thai, Italian etc) dinners during the high holiday season.

Getting There & Away

Bus No 412 runs hourly through Newport between Fishguard (15 minutes) and Cardigan (30 minutes), daily Monday to Saturday with two on Sunday.

AROUND NEWPORT
Nevern

The overgrown castle and old **Church of St Brynach** make this hamlet, 2 miles east of Newport, a curious little excursion. St Brynach was a 5th-century Irish holy man who lived in a hut on Carn Ingli, above Newport.

An alley of ancient yew trees leads to the church door through an evocative churchyard, which dates from the 6th century and contains a tall Celtic cross from the 10th and 11th centuries. Inside the church the Maglocunus Stone is considered to be from the 5th century and bears an inscription in *ogham* (an ancient Celtic script) and Latin.

Castell Henllys

A visit to this **castle** (☎ 891319; adult £2.80; ☽ 10am-5pm Apr-Oct) is an intriguing afternoon out for adults and, if mixed with an activity (mostly from May to August, call for details), excellent for children. Ongoing archaeological digs have enabled a faithful reconstruction of an important Iron Age settlement *in situ*. Roundhouses and outbuildings sit on the original foundations looking much as they did then. Craft demonstrations and costumed staff enliven the site. It's 4 miles east of Newport along the A487. Bus No 412 Fishguard–Newport–Cardigan stops at Melina Rd, three-quarters of a mile south.

Pentre Ifan

A little imagination helps validate what (if on foot) is a long hike up the hill to 5500-year-old Pentre Ifan, one of Wales' best-preserved Neolithic *cromlechs* (burial chambers). A huddle of stones turns out to be a delicate arrangement with a great capstone balanced on the pinpoint of upright slabs. This is the skeleton of what was once a huge enclosed earthen mound, the soil blown and washed away by the immense passage of time.

Situated 2 miles south of Nevern, Pentre Ifan is accessible by the hourly bus No 412 from Newport (ask the driver to put you down at the stop for Pentre Ifan), followed by a 2½-mile walk up signposted lanes.

CARDIGAN (ABERTEIFI)
☎ 01239 / pop 4082

Although Cardigan lies in the county of Ceredigion it appears in this Pembrokeshire Coast National Park section, as it's the closest town to the northern end of the coast path. The big walk begins at Poppit Sands to the northwest. The town itself, near the mouth of the River Teifi, is rather mundane.

It wasn't always so, and may not be for much longer. About 900 years ago the castle hosted the first competitive eisteddfod (see the Eisteddfodau for All boxed text, p713), held by Lord Rhys ap Gruffydd in 1176 to select his court musicians. Today, works at the castle are picking up pace, following its appearance on UK TV's *Restoration* programme, with the intention of being fully open to visitors in the future.

The **Heritage Centre** (☎ 614404), in a restored granary by the town bridge, retells Cardigan's history, and has a café.

The **TIC** (☎ 613230; cardigantic@ ceredigion.gov .uk; ☽ 10am-6pm Jul & Aug, 10am-5pm Mon-Sat Sep-Jun) shares the lobby of **Theatr Mwldan** (☎ 621200), the modern town theatre and cinema.

Sleeping & Eating

Brongwyn Caravan & Camping Park (☎ 613644; 2-person tent sites per person £8.50) This park lies 3 miles northeast off the A487 at Penparc.

Poppit Sands YHA Hostel (☎ 0870 770 5996; poppit@yha.org.uk; dm £11.80) Overlooks Cardigan Bay four miles northwest of town, near the start/finish of the Pembrokeshire Coast Path. Bus No 405 serves Poppit Sands, setting down in the car park (15 minutes, five daily, none Sunday) half a mile away.

SOUTH WALES

Brynhyfryd Guest House (☎ 612861; Gwbert Rd; s/d from £19/42) Comfortable and scientifically clean, Brynhyfryd also has friendly hosts.

Highbury (☎ 613403; Pendre; s/d £17.50/35, with en suite £25/44) A large, plain place that's very close to the centre.

Teifi Blu (The Boat; ☎ 621444; mains around £10; ⊗ 11am-11pm) Cardigan's best place to eat occupies a converted Danish fishing trawler that's tethered to the quayside below the town. On the menu are Mediterranean, tapas, fresh seafood and local produce, and the décor is the boat's varnished wooden frame.

Getting There & Away

Bus services include No 412 hourly to/from Haverfordwest (1½ hours) and Fishguard (50 minutes); No 460 or 461 hourly to/from Carmarthen (1½ hours, seven daily Monday to Saturday, three on Sunday). Bus No 405, the summertime Poppit Rocket, runs to/from Fishguard (three times daily May to September).

Mid Wales

The majority of visitors to Mid Wales head for the grass-tufted mountains of the Brecon Beacons National Park, an area rich in soaring landscapes and views. Yet carry on north and you find continuous undisturbed uplands; a mixture of verdant rolling hills, plunging dales and sheep-dotted farmland strewn with hamlets. This is Wales at its most rural, where three out of five people speak the mother tongue.

Along the undulating Marches, the once heavily-disputed borderlands with England, lie little towns with individualist charms such as Hay-on-Wye with its second-hand book stores, Knighton with its Spaceguard Centre and Welshpool with Powis Castle. However, these eastern parts can be indistinguishable from England, as the region changed hands so frequently in medieval times. The long-distance walking trail, Offa's Dyke Path, roughly follows the north-south border and gives an insider view of this land.

Aberystwyth, the only place of size on the west coast, is a lively town with the twin functions of university seat and seaside resort. Machynlleth, Wales' 'first capital', is an attractive old market town and a good base for exploring the Cambrian Mountains and coast. Nearby is the Centre for Alternative Technology, which provides the inspiration and teaching for a green way of life in the hope that visitors take a little away with them.

Puffs of steam spurt from trains on the unforgettable Vale of Rheidol narrow-gauge railway, but for the best window seat on Mid Wales, take a trip on the famous Heart of Wales line.

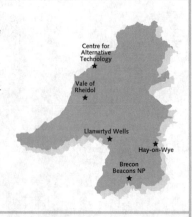

HIGHLIGHTS

- Gazing out of the train window on the **Heart of Wales** line (p688)
- Discovering the light and landscape of the **Brecon Beacons** (p689) on foot or by bike
- Worming your way through the piles of second-hand books at **Hay-on-Wye** (p698)
- Participating in the bizarre events at **Llanwrtyd Wells** (p701)
- Going green and sustainable at the **Centre for Alternative Technology** (p704)
- Chugging on the vintage railway up the **Vale of Rheidol** (p706) to visit the **Devil's Bridge & Falls** (p708)

- POPULATION: 201,728 | - AREA: 2696 SQ MILES

Orientation & Information

The Mid Wales region runs west from the Welsh–English border to Cardigan Bay on the coast, from and including the Brecon Beacons in the south to the start of Snowdonia in the north.

It includes just two counties: Powys and Ceredigion. The former was created in the 1974 reorganisation of Welsh local government from Brecknockshire, Radnorshire and Montgomeryshire, while Cardiganshire maintained its boundaries but reverted to its ancient name Ceredigion.

Activities

The principal area for outdoor adventure is without doubt the Brecon Beacons, but

Mid Wales does have more to offer. Regional tourism websites contain walking and cycling information, and Tourist Information Centres (TICs) stock leaflets, plus maps and guides (usually £1 to £5) that cover walking, cycling and other activities.

CYCLING

With a minimal population and fine hillscapes, Mid Wales is a top cycle-touring destination – as long as your legs can deal with the gradients. The **Lôn Las Cymru** touring route runs the length of Wales from south to north. It crosses the Brecon Beacons and continues via Builth Wells, Rhayader and Llanidloes to Machynlleth, with a higher mountain-bike option between Builth Wells

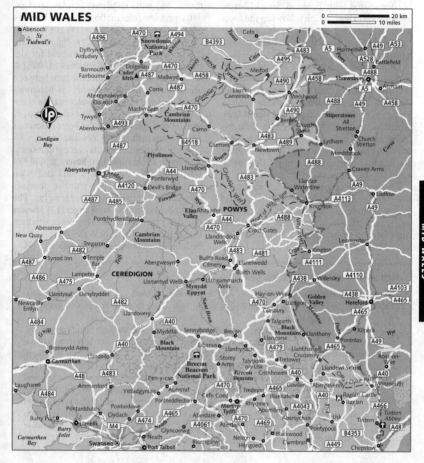

MID WALES

and Machynlleth. Cross-border tours into England also work well.

When it comes to off-roading, **Llanwrtyd Wells** is an excellent mountain-biking hub, and a base for all manner of mad muddy events, both competitive and social. The **Brecon Beacons National Park** is another great place to wear out knobbly tyres, using Brecon or Abergavenny as bases. Good off-road routes are also found near **Machynlleth** and in the **Plynlimon** range, inland from Aberystwyth; you can hire bikes in all above-named towns.

WALKING

Long-distance walking trails in Mid Wales include **Offa's Dyke Path** along the ancient border shared with England, and 132-mile long **Glyndŵr's Way**, which follows in the footsteps of the 15th-century Welsh freedom fighter through fabulously wild and remote countryside.

Other areas for day walks include the high ranges of the ever-popular **Brecon Beacons** and the neighbouring (and usually quieter) **Black Mountain** (singular), **Black Mountains** (plural, and a quite different place) and **Fforest Fawr**, which all fall inside the Brecon Beacons National Park boundary. Brecon town is the most obvious base, with good facilities. Other starting points are Abergavenny, Crickhowell and Hay-on-Wye.

Further north, good bases for exploring the wild and often deserted hills of Mid Wales include Llanwrtyd Wells, Knighton and Machynlleth (also within easy striking distance of Snowdonia National Park; see p716).

OTHER ACTIVITIES

The Brecon Beacons is a major **horse-riding** and **pony-trekking** area, particularly around the Black Mountains, and is also noted for its **hang-gliding** conditions. The rivers are perfect for **canoeing**, with Hay-on-Wye a good base for instruction or equipment hire.

Getting Around

The absence of a direct north-south road slows hilly Mid Wales down. The A470 is the closest you get to a highway between the Brecon Beacons and Snowdonia, and what it loses in speed, it makes up for in looks.

A useful publication is the *Wales Bus, Rail and Tourist Map & Guide* from the Wales Tourist Board. There are buses between towns, but with restricted Sunday services. TICs provide information, as does **Traveline** (☎ 0870 608 2608; www.traveline.org.uk). For travel in Powys, see p701, and for Ceredigion, see p705.

Trains are few and far between; for details contact **National Rail Enquiries** (☎ 08457 48 49 50). The Cambrian Main Line runs between Shrewsbury and Aberystwyth via Machynlleth. Combine travel and watching the scenery on the Heart of Wales line (see the boxed text, below), which skirts the Brecon Beacons and crosses lush Mid Wales diagonally.

Multijourney tickets may save you money. The **North & Mid Wales Flexi-Rover** (☎ 0870 9000 777) is valid for three days' bus and train travel in seven days (£30), and also provides discounted admission to historic sights. The North & Mid Wales Day Ranger (£20) covers one day's travel for train services in this area (other than the Heart of Wales line), and can be bought on the train or at stations.

MID WALES FROM A WINDOW SEAT

The **Heart of Wales line** (☎ 01597-822053; www.heart-of-wales.co.uk) offers a wonderful rolling view of Mid Wales. Described fondly by Bill Bryson as the 'little train', its survival was long fought for by train buffs and local passengers.

The single-carriage shunter travels diagonally across central Wales through beautiful river valleys and green-bathed hills. En route between Swansea on the south coast and Shrewsbury in the English borderlands you travel through six tunnels, over two great viaducts, and stop at a dozen spa and market towns and quaint rural halts. The highlight of the line lies between Llandeilo, Llanwrtyd Wells and Llandrindod Wells, where the train pulls up the Sugar Loaf mountain and rolls across the graceful Cynghordy Viaduct, whose arches shelter a chapel. The full 120-mile, 3¾-hour trip breaks down easily into shorter sections, such as Swansea–Llandrindod Wells (return £11.80, 2¼ hours), Llandeilo–Llandrindod Wells (return £6.90, 1¼ hours) and Llandovery–Knighton (return £8.60, 1½ hours). There are three trains Monday to Saturday, two on summer Sundays and one on winter ones.

BRECON BEACONS

BRECON BEACONS NATIONAL PARK

The summits and ridges of the Brecon Beacons soar in great green and black waves above the surrounding landscape, overlooking farmland to the north and surpassing the ridges of the industrial valleys to the south. Covered mostly with grassy moorland, with only occasional outbreaks of rock, they have a more serene and amenable character than the Snowdonian peaks to the north, yet the blasts of wind and views from the summits yield the same exhilaration.

Around their skirts are hill farms that produce some of the Wales' finest lamb (if that is your wont) and at their base nestles a handful of feature towns and villages that are well accustomed to visitors in search of both an outdoor adventure and a good pint or meal.

The further west you go in the park (Parc Cenedlaethol Bannau Brycheiniog) the more you hear the Welsh tongue spoken.

Walkers may have all areas and angles of the Brecon Beacons nailed, but the region is also excellent for all manner of upland pursuits. This is perfect pony-trekking country. You can go rock-climbing, mountain-biking, gliding or hang-gliding. Lôn Las Cymru, the Welsh National cycle route, traverses north-south. Two long-distance walks within the boundary are Offa's Dyke Path along the eastern border, and the Taff

Trail south from Brecon. You can rent canoes or narrowboats on the Monmouthshire & Brecon Canal and, on the southern side, cavers descend among the deepest holes in Britain. At the park's northern limit you can even turn over an old leaf at Hay-on-Wye, the town of books.

The park runs a mere 15 miles north to south and 45 miles west to east, but embraces four mountain ranges of old red sandstone. The name is derived from the central and highest range of the quartet: the Brecon Beacons themselves, the highpoint of which is Pen-y-Fan (886m). South is Fforest Fawr (Great Forest) whose tumbling streams join the River Neath to empty into Swansea Bay. To the west you find the quieter Black Mountain range peaking at Fan Brycheiniog (802m), and to the east, and easily muddled, the popular Black Mountains (plural) and Waun Fach (811m).

The best base towns are Brecon and Abergavenny, and Hay-on-Wye has a wide range of accommodation. The closest train stations are Abergavenny and Merthyr Tydfil. The Monmouthshire & Brecon Canal follows the valley of the River Usk from Brecon via Abergavenny down to the coast.

Lying 30 miles from the M4 Severn Bridge into England, the park is a few hours' drive from London and the south of Wales.

Information

The park websites are www.breconbeacons .org and www.visitbreconbeacons.com. The

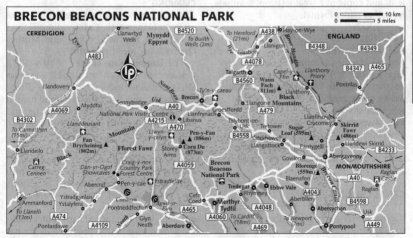

BRECON BEACONS NATIONAL PARK

0 — 10 km
0 — 5 miles

National Park Visitor Centre (See Map p693; Mountain Centre, Libanus; ☎ 01874-623366; ☯ 9.30am-5pm Mon-Fri, 9.30am-5.30pm Sat & Sun Mar-Jun & Sep-Oct, 9.30am-6pm daily Jul-Aug, 9.30am-4.30pm Nov-Feb) lies in open countryside near the village of Libanus, 5 miles southwest of Brecon off the A470. Trails from the centre, an award-winning tearoom and fine views of Pen-y-Fan and Corn Du (873m), make it a much-visited place in summer.

There are four national park information centres:

Abergavenny (☎ 01873-853254; ☯ 9.30am-5.30pm daily Easter-Oct) South of the Black Mountains, has seasonal opening hours and shares space with the town TIC.

Brecon (☎ 01874-622795; ☯ 9.30am-5.30pm daily Easter-Oct, 9.30am-4.30pm Nov-Easter) North of the Brecon Beacons, shares space with the town TIC (p694).

Craig-y-Nos country park (☎ 01639-730395; ☯ 10am-5pm Mon-Fri, 10am-6pm Sat & Sun Mar-Apr & Sep-Oct, 10am-6pm daily May-Aug, 10am-4pm Mon-Fri & 10am-4.30pm Sat & Sun Nov-Feb) In the Upper Swansea Valley between Black Mountain and Fforest Fawr.

Llandovery (☎ 01550-720693; ☯ 10am-1pm & 1.45pm-5.30pm Easter–late-Oct, to 4pm late-Oct–Easter) North of Black Mountain.

The *Brecon Beacons National Park Welcome!* is a very helpful free booklet of activities and places to go. It is available at all information centres.

The centres stock maps and leaflets on activities, including the park walking booklet. Ordnance Survey Explorer OL 1:25,000 maps covering the national park are excellent, and come in a weatherproof laminate as well as paper format.

Activities
ACTIVITY CENTRES
For separate or combined adventures try:

Bikes & Hikes (☎ 01874-610071; www.bikesandhikes .co.uk; activity days from £25) Climbing, caving, mountain walking, gorge scrambling and navigation, also hostel accommodation in Brecon (see p694).

Black Mountain Activities (☎ 01497-847897; www.blackmountain.co.uk; Three Cocks; per half/full day £37.50/49.50) Gorge walking, white-water kayaking, caving, climbing and mountain-biking. Also arranges accommodation.

CANAL CRUISING
At Brecon the 33-mile Monmouthshire & Brecon Canal starts. From there, it makes its way down the valley of the River Usk to Abergavenny, continuing to Pontypool. There are just six locks throughout, and one 22-mile section which is lock-free.

Take a 2½-hour pleasure trip from Brecon (starting outside the Theatr Brycheiniog) with **Dragonfly Cruises** (☎ 07831-685222; www.dragonfly -cruises.co.uk; trips £6; ☯ noon &/or 3pm 2-5 days a week Easter-Oct); call for day-by-day timetable.

Hire a narrowboat for self-piloting from **Cambrian Cruisers** (☎ 01874-665315; www.cambrian cruisers.co.uk; Ty Newydd, Pencelli; from £523 for 3 nights), southeast of Brecon. Or take a motorboat for a spin from **Brecon Boats** (☎ 01874-676401; Travellers Rest Inn, Talybont-on-Usk; per half/full day £40/50).

CAVING & SHOWCAVES
Limestone cave systems beneath the Beacons have some of the longest and deepest holes in Britain. They lie mainly to the south in the Upper Swansea Valley and in the Llangattock hillside above Crickhowell. The TICs have books and leaflets about them, but unless you are an experienced spelunker, you should go on an organised trip with an activity centre (see above).

The magnificent **Dan-yr-Ogof showcaves** (☎ 01639-730284; adult £9; ☯ 10am-3pm Easter-Oct) were discovered in 1912 and feature three separate caves where the stalagmites are augmented by a sound-and-light show. An open-air dinosaur park, Iron Age Farm and shire horses attract the families. The showcaves lie 16 miles south of Brecon, off the A4067 north of Abercraf.

CLIMBING
Climbing sites in the park are limited, generally to Llangattock, Craig-y-dinas (Dinas Rock), near Pontneddfechan, and Morlais Quarry, near Merthyr Tydfil.

The **Llangorse Rope Centre** (☎ 01874-658272; www.activityuk.com; Gilfach Farm, Llangorse; 2-hr session £14) is a fabulous indoor and outdoor climbing centre with a 2km aerial track and natural and faux rock faces suitable for children and adults, beginner and experienced climbers.

CYCLING
The 77-mile Taff Trail runs between Cardiff and Brecon. The mountain section, from Merthyr Tydfil to Talybont-on-Usk, crosses the heart of the park climbing to 450m.

Mountain-biking in the national park is excellent, with 15 easy and hard routes documented on map-leaflets produced by the national park. Guided mountain-biking around the southern Beacons is organised by **Hobo Backpackers Mountain Biking** (☎ 01495-718422; www.hobo-backpackers.co.uk), which offers packages from its hostel in Tredegar (see p663).

Bike hire in Brecon and Abergavenny:

Bicycle Beano (☎ 01982-560471; www.bicycle-beano .co.uk) organises a cycle-touring weekend that includes the Black Mountains and Hay-on-Wye, with vegetarian catering.

Bikes & Hikes (☎ 01874- 610071; www.bikesandhikes .co.uk; per half/full day £13/16) Based at the Brecon hostel of the same name (see p694), it delivers bikes in the locality, guides rides and provides routes.

Bi-Ped Cycles (☎ 01874-622296; Free St; per half/full day £10/14) In Brecon.

Brecon Cycle Centre (☎ 01874-622651; www.brecon cycles.com; Ship St; per half/full day £10/15) Supplies route maps.

Gateway Cycles (☎ 01873-858519; per half/full day £7.50/15) In Abergavenny, for Black Mountains riding.

From June to August, on Sunday and bank holidays, the national park runs the **Beacons Bike Bus** (☎ 01873-853254; www.breconbeacons.org). No B1 hauls a trailer from Cardiff to Brecon, continuing to Talybont, and back (all-day ticket £5.50, plus per bike £2, one service, two hours 10 minutes).

GLIDING
Great ridge and wave soaring make the park a destination for gliding fans. Trial lessons and flights are available at the **Black Mountains Gliding Club** (☎ 01874-711463), near Talgarth.

PONY-TREKKING & HORSE RIDING
The open hillsides are ideal pony-trekking country, particularly in the area around the Black Mountains.

Cantref Riding Centre (☎ 01874-665223; Upper Cantref Farm, Cantref; per hr £9, per half/full day £15/25) Up the slopes south of Brecon.

Grange Pony-Trekking Centre (☎ 01873-890215; www.grangetrekking.co.uk; per hr £12, per half/full day £17/27) At lovely Capel-y-Ffin in the heart of the Black Mountains.

Llangorse Riding Centre (☎ 01874-658272; Gil-fach Farm, Llangorse; beginners/experienced 1hr from £12/15.50) One mile east of Llangorse Lake, and run in partnership with the climbing rope-centre (see p690).

WALKING
The choice of walks in the park is infinite, ranging from a strenuous mountain hike to a gentle stroll along the canal towpath. A

large number of walks are detailed in leaflets and booklets in the information centres (see p689), and the park runs guided walks.

Before setting out on a mountain hike check the weather forecast. Take waterproof clothing even if it's sunny and warm when you start. Carry food but don't share it with sheep and ponies, as they become attracted to cars on the roads and cause accidents.

For information of Beacons Bus services around the park see p692.

Pen-y-Fan & Corn Du
The park's classic and heavily overused summit walk is to the ridgeline peaks of Pen-y-Fan or Corn Du. The walk starts at the car park at the Storey Arms (no longer a pub) on the A470 Merthyr–Brecon road. Park staff call the trail 'the motorway' and urge walkers to choose alternatives, such as the return trip from the Llwyn-y-celyn YHA hostel (three hours) or Brecon (five to six hours). These and other walks are covered in the park leaflet *Walks in the Brecon Area*.

Easier walking is found in a glacial amphitheatre due north of Corn Du around the small lake with the wonderful name of Llyn Cwm Llwch (khlin coom khlooch).

Taff Trail
This runs 77 miles, up from Cardiff to Brecon, largely on canal towpaths and disused railway lines, the most scenic section lying in the national park (see also Cycling, p690).

Canal Walks
The easiest walks in the park follow the towpath of the Monmouthshire & Brecon Canal along the fine valley of the River Usk. Most walkers do the 20-mile Abergavenny–Brecon section, or you can tackle the full 33-mile length between Brecon and Pontypool.

Around Abergavenny
Sugar Loaf (595m), Blorenge (559m) and Skirrid Fawr (486m) are three fine hills in the southeast of the park near Abergavenny, all described in walking literature available at the town's TIC and national park centre.

Black Mountains
Some of the best views from the Offa's Dyke Path extend from the exposed 17-mile ridgeline of the Black Mountains (the

park's eastern region) between Pandy and Hay-on-Wye, above the Vale of Ewyas (see p698).

A less strenuous alternative along the valley bottom follows the River Honddu (hon-thee) from Llanfihangel Crucorney in the south of this range. Two walking leaflets for the northern and southern parts of this area are stocked in the TICs.

Fforest Fawr & Waterfall Walks

This area has a wide variety of scenery, with the Ystradfellte YHA hostel (see below) one handy place to stay.

To the north are mountain walks in terrain similar to the Brecon Beacons. The wooded south is famous for its waterfalls in the verdant, steep-sided gorges of the Hepste, Mellte and Nedd Fechan Rivers. The finest is 8m-high **Sgwd-yr-Eira** (Waterfall of the Snow) on the Hepste, where you can actually walk behind the torrent. This and others lie quite close together on short walks going between Ystradfellte and Pontneddfechan.

Find details in the national park map leaflet *Waterside Places* (£1) at TICs.

Black Mountain

This, the western section of the park, features the wildest and least-visited walking country. The highest point, Fan Brycheiniog, can be reached from Llanddeusant YHA hostel (see below) or via a path off the side road just north of the Dan-yr-Ogof Showcaves (p690).

Sleeping

A fair choice of B&Bs and hotels is found around the national park, with some very fine guesthouses in Abergavenny and Hay-on-Wye, at either end of the Black Mountains. At the top of the tree are the Angel Hotel (p697) in Abergavenny and the Bear Hotel (p695) at Crickhowell.

There are five YHA hostels within the national park:

Brecon (see also p694; Ty'n-y-caeau; ☎ 0870 770 5718; brecon@yha.org.uk; dm £10.60; ☉ daily Mar-Oct, Fri-Sun Nov-Feb) Large former country house, 2½ miles east of Brecon.

Capel-y-Ffin (see also p698; ☎ 0870 770 5748; dm £9.30; ☉ daily Apr-Aug, with 48hr notice Feb-Mar & Sep-Nov) Remote ex-hill farm, 8 miles south of Hay-on-Wye amid the Black Mountains.

Llanddeusant (☎ 0870 770 5930; dm £9.30; ☉ with 48hr notice year-round) A real get-away-from-it-all hostel, below the western Black Mountain.

Llwyn-y-celyn (☎ 0870 770 5936; llwynycelyn@yha.org .uk; dm £10.60; ☉ daily Apr-Aug, Fri & Sat Feb-Mar & Nov, Thu-Mon Sep-Oct) Directly below the central Beacons, by the A470 Merthyr Tydfil–Brecon road.

Ystradfellte (☎ 0870 770 6106; dm £9.30; ☉ with 48hr notice Mar-Sep) In the southern waterfall and caving region of Fforest Fawr.

There are also a dozen independent bunkhouses in the area, but as many cater primarily for groups it is best to book in advance, especially for summer weekends. Contact TICs for a full list or go to www.hostels.com.

With the permission of the farmer or landowner, it may be possible to camp almost anywhere in the park, but not on National Trust (NT) land. TICs list camping grounds in the leaflet *Camping on Farms* (25p).

Getting There & Around

It takes three to four hours to drive to the Brecon Beacons from London, via Newport and the A4042 to Abergavenny.

Regular bus services to the national park towns are good, but few run on Sunday.

Bus No X3 (£4.50, 1½ hours, about hourly) travels from Cardiff to Abergavenny; X4 (£4.50, 1½ hours, half-hourly) runs from Abergavenny to Cardiff via Merthyr Tydfil. Bus No 39 (£4.50, 45 minutes, eight daily) runs between Hay-on-Wye and Brecon; No 63 (£4.50, 1½ hours, three daily) travels between Swansea to Brecon; and No 43 (£4.50, 1½ hours, five daily Monday to Friday) runs from Cardiff to Brecon, but only from Merthyr Tydfil on Saturday and Sunday. For more information on bus services contact **Traveline** (☎ 0870 608 2608).

On Sundays and bank holidays, during June and August, the park runs the **Beacons Bus** (☎ 01873-853254; www.breconbeacons.org; day ticket £5.50), with nine routes (one to three a day), mostly running into and back out of the park.

These include No **1** to/from Carmarthen, the National Botanic Garden & Brecon; No B1 to/from Cardiff, Merthyr Tydfil & Brecon; No B2 to/from Swansea, Craig-y-Nos country park & Brecon; No B5 to/from Bristol, Abergavenny & Brecon; No B6 runs a circuit from Brecon to Brecon Mountain Railway; No B8 to/from Abergavenny &

Brecon; No B9 (Offa's Dyke Circular) circuit from Hay-on-Wye to Llanthony Priory; and No 40 to/from Hereford, Hay-on-Wye & Brecon. These are subject to change annually – call to confirm.

The leaflet *Beacons Bus* has timetables and also dates of park-guided walks into which you can link.

The only train services available are to Cardiff–Merthyr Tydfil (55 minutes, hourly) and to Newport–Abergavenny (25 minutes, hourly).

BRECON
☎ 01874 / pop 7901

The handsome little stone-built town of Brecon (Aberhonddu) is the hub of the national park and has accommodation to suit all budgets. It lies on the old coach road between London and the West Coast of Wales, and where the Honddu River flows into the Usk.

The cathedral and close make a sedate retreat supplemented by a nice café-restaurant, and the Brecknock Museum & Art Gallery is a treasure. Brecon also hosts an internationally renowned jazz festival.

The open-site remains of an Iron Age hill fort lie atop Pen-y-crug 2 miles northwest of the town centre, and those of Brecon Gaer Roman Fort, 3 miles west. In Norman times, the local Welsh chieftain was overthrown by a Norman lord, Bernard de Newmarch, who built the town's castle and church (which later became a cathedral).

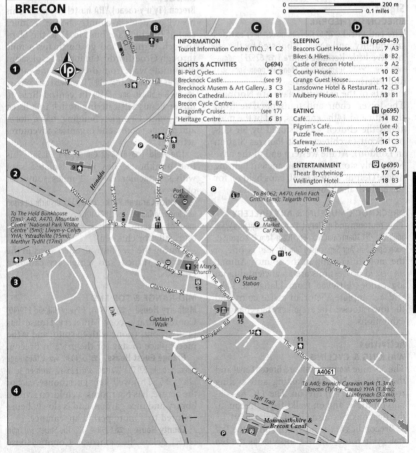

BRECON

0 — 200 m
0 — 0.1 miles

INFORMATION
Tourist Information Centre (TIC).. **1** C2

SIGHTS & ACTIVITIES (p694)
Bi-Ped Cycles.............................**2** C3
Brecknock Castle....................(see 9)
Brecknock Musem & Art Gallery.. **3** C3
Brecon Cathedral.....................**4** B1
Brecon Cycle Centre................**5** B2
Dragonfly Cruises...................(see 17)
Heritage Centre......................**6** B1

SLEEPING (pp694–5)
Beacons Guest House.................**7** A3
Bikes & Hikes..........................**8** B2
Castle of Brecon Hotel..............**9** A2
County House...........................**10** B2
Grange Guest House.................**11** C4
Lansdowne Hotel & Restaurant.. **12** C3
Mulberry House.......................**13** B1

EATING (p695)
Café......................................**14** B2
Pilgrim's Café........................(see 4)
Puzzle Tree...........................**15** C3
Safeway................................**16** C3
Tipple 'n' Tiffin....................(see 17)

ENTERTAINMENT (p695)
Theatr Brycheiniog.................**17** C4
Wellington Hotel....................**18** B3

MID WALES

Orientation & Information

Being small, everything in Brecon lies within walking distance. Most long-distance buses leave from and arrive at The Bulwark in the centre. However, there is no train station. B&Bs are found in two groups: around The Watton road eastward, and over the bridge in Llanfaes.

The **TIC** (☎ 622485; brectic@powys.gov.uk, www.tourismpowys.gov.uk; 🕑 9.30am-5.30pm) is in the Cattle Market car park above Safeway supermarket. The **National Park Information Centre** (☎ 623156; 🕑 9.30am-5.30pm Easter-Oct, 9.30am-4.30pm Nov-Easter) shares the same building. Distinct from this is the official National Park Visitor Centre, which lies five miles southwest of Brecon at Libanus (see p689)

Sights

BRECON CATHEDRAL

The cathedral (☎ 623857; admission free) exudes tranquillity, and a visit is boosted by the attractive little **Heritage Centre** (☎ 625222; admission free; 🕑 10.30am-4.30pm Mon-Sat, noon-3pm Sun) and Pilgrims Café (p695).

Parts of the cathedral nave are Norman. The tower, choir and transepts date from the 13th and 14th centuries, and in the mid-1860s the church was restored by Sir Gilbert Scott (architect of St Pancras Station in London). At the western end of the nave is the only stone cresset (an ancient lighting device) left in Wales; its 30 cups held oil for the cathedral's lamps.

BRECKNOCK MUSEUM & ART GALLERY

This **museum and gallery** (☎ 624121; Captain's Walk; adult £1; 🕑 10am-5pm Mon-Fri, 10am-1pm & 2-5pm Sat, noon-5pm Sun Apr-Sep, closed Sun Oct-Mar) is one of the more interesting in the county. Among its prized possessions are an ancient dugout log canoe retrieved from Llangorse Lake and a complete Victorian assize court and the town stocks. The art gallery has changing exhibitions.

Activities

WALKING & CYCLING

The 33-mile **Monmouthshire & Brecon Canal** and the 77-mile **Taff Trail** walking and cycling route both start in Brecon. The TIC has details on these, and on walks from Brecon up the Beacons. See also Canal Walks p691.

Brecon lies at the northern end of the **Taff Trail** cycle route, which continues as the **Lôn Las Cymru** north via Builth Wells. It is also a centre for excellent national park mountain-biking (see p690).

Festivals & Events

For one weekend in mid-August, colourful awnings and flags transform the monochrome, stone town for the renowned annual **Brecon Jazz Festival**, one of Europe's leading gatherings. Past headline acts have included artists such as Courtney Pine and Sonny Rollins, while George Melly is a regular. For details contact the festival office at the **Theatr Brycheiniog** (☎ 611622; www.breconjazz .co.uk; Canal Rd) by the canal terminus.

Sleeping

BUDGET

Brecon (Ty'n-y-caeau) YHA hostel (see p692) This hostel occupies a country house, 2 miles east of Brecon. Take bus No 21 to the Llanfrynach turning, and go north for a mile through Groesffordd. On foot it's a pleasant 40-minute walk from Brecon via the canal.

Bikes & Hikes (☎ 610071; www.bikesandhikes.co .uk; 10 The Struet; dm £12.50) In central Brecon, this spacious self-catering hostel, in a listed once-grand Georgian building, has a dorm and private rooms, and organises adventure-activities.

The Held (☎ 624646; Cantref; dm £10.50) This fine bunkhouse lies in an isolated spot with spectacular views, 2 miles southeast of Brecon.

Brynich Caravan Park (☎ 623325; Brynich; 2-person tent low/mid/high season £8/9/10) Located 1½ miles east of Brecon, this has excellent facilities, especially for children.

During the jazz festival, open areas in the town are turned into temporary camping grounds.

MID-RANGE & TOP END

Mulberry House (☎ 624461; 3 Priory Hill; s/d £19/40) Contemporary, cosy Mulberry House has pretty rooms (none with en suite) and is the nicest place to stay for the price in Brecon.

Grange Guest House (☎ 624038; www.thegrange -brecon.co.uk; 22 The Watton; s/d £25/40, with en suite £28/46; ⊠) This well-kept guesthouse, east of the centre, has big rooms, a children's video library and nice garden, and is slowly being restored to a more period appearance.

County House (☎ 625844; 100 The Struet; s/d from £30/60) Below the cathedral, County House is an elegantly upmarket Georgian judge's residence with a walled riverside garden.

Lansdowne Hotel & Restaurant (☎ 623321; 39 The Watton; s/d £37.50/55; mains £9-15) This nicely creaky and unostentatious Georgian town hotel is done in original colours, and has a reliable restaurant serving fish and grills.

Beacons Guest House (☎ 623339; beacons@brecon .co.uk; 16 Bridge St; s/d £30/40, with en suite £35/52; mains £10-14; ☷ dinner Tue-Sat) An informal B&B, this has large, floral rooms with fireplaces. Guests feel the benefit of the restaurant: the breakfast menu sometimes includes salmon and a cheese platter.

Castle of Brecon Hotel (☎ 624611; Castle Sq; s /d £59-79/69-99) The top perch in town, now run by Best Western, this Victorian building was constructed onto the modest remains of the Norman Brecknock castle and has mountain views.

Felin Fach Griffin (☎ 620111; www.eatdrinksleep .ltd.uk; s/d from £67.50/92.50) Three miles north of Brecon, off the A470, this has stylish rooms above a pub with thrillingly good food.

Eating & Drinking

The Café (☎ 611191; 39 High St; snacks £3-4) A bright and buzzing café with white floorboards and cool paintings, this serves tasty snacks, coffee and delicious cakes.

Pilgrim's Café (☎ 610610; dishes £5-6; ☷ 10am-5pm Mon-Fri, 11am-4pm Sun) In the cathedral close, beside a lavender garden, this airy place does teas and uses local produce in its simple daytime dishes.

Puzzle Tree (☎ 610005; The Watton; mains £6-16; ☷ lunch & dinner) Brecon finally has a trendy drinking and dining hall in the bright, high-ceilinged Puzzle Tree, opposite the museum. Eat tagliatelle and vegetarian dishes here all week.

Tipple 'n' Tiffin (☎ 611866; Theatr Brycheiniog; mains £6-8; ☷ lunch & dinner Mon-Sat) Friendly, trendy, reasonably priced and nicely placed, the restaurant at the Theatr Brycheiniog (below) is decorated with bright colours and beech-wood furnishings.

Felin Fach Griffin (see p694; starters £5-8, mains £14-16) One of the new breed of contemporary country pubs, restored beams are set off by modern pictures hung on terracotta walls, while local ingredients are cooked in superb, light style.

A Safeway supermarket is near the Cattle Market car park.

Entertainment

Canal-side **Theatr Brycheiniog** (☎ 611622; www .theatrbrycheiniog.co.uk; Canal Rd) is the town's drama and music venue, also with an exhibition centre and the Tipple 'n' Tiffin restaurant (above). The bar at the **Wellington Hotel** (The Bulwark) has live jazz some evenings.

Getting There & Away

Bus services to Brecon are good: No 21 to/from Abergavenny (£4.50, one hour, every two hours); Nos 39 and 40 to/from Hereford via Hay-on-Wye (£4.50, 55 minutes, six daily Monday to Saturday, two on Sunday); and No 63 to/from Swansea (£4.50, 1¼ hours, three daily, none on Sunday).

National Express (☎ 0870 580 8080) run buses to/from London (five hours, daily), with a change at Cardiff (£3.50, 1¼ hours).

Most **Beacons Bus** (☎ 01873-853254) and Bike Bus services stop in Brecon (see p692).

For a cab, call **Brecon Taxis** (☎ 623444).

CRICKHOWELL

☎ 01873 / pop 2000

This prosperous little town lies on the A40 high road between Brecon and Abergavenny, at the point where an arched 17th-century stone bridge crosses the rushing River Usk to the village of Llangattock. The **TIC** (☎ 812105; cricktic@powys.gov.uk; Beaufort St; ☷ 9.30am-1pm 1.30-5pm Mon-Sat, 9am-1pm & 1.30-4pm Sun Easter-Oct) is on the main road.

Bear Hotel (☎ 810408; www.bearhotel.co.uk; Beaufort St; s/d from £57/75; mains £6-15) This classy and cheerfully hospitable old-world coaching inn has an award-winning restaurant (see the boxed text on p697).

Two B&Bs on the high road are the gorgeous John Nash–designed house **Tŷ Gwyn** (☎ 811625; s/d £40/55), and the straightforward **Greenhill Villas** (☎ 811177; 2 Greenhill Villas, Beaufort St; s/d £30/40), where the facilities are shared.

Riverside Caravan Park (☎ 810397; New Rd; 2-person tent sites £9) A small, well-appointed camping ground by the bridge.

ABERGAVENNY

☎ 01873 / pop 14,055

The thriving town of Abergavenny lies in the Vale of Usk surrounded by the eastern peaks of the Brecon Beacons National Park. This lush area, famous for its beauty and produce, has nurtured the growth of an outstanding cuisine scene (see the boxed text on p697).

MID WALES

WORTH THE TRIP

The historic **Tretower Court & Castle** (Cadw; ☎ 01874-730279; adult £2.50; ☉ 10am-5pm Apr-Oct) has a lovely Vale of Usk setting in Tretower village, off the A40, 3 miles northwest of Crickhowell.

The handsome 15th-century stone-built court shows the transition from gloomy castle (see the neighbouring 13th-century tower) to comfortable, fortified house. The wooden balcony in the enclosed courtyard is warmed by the sun and sheltered from the wind: a charming place to embroider tapestry or practise swordwork. The 8m-long hall – not too big, not too small – has a vaulted timber ceiling, where you can imagine the feasting and flirting on high days and holy days. Slightly unkempt rose bushes fill the walled garden with scent and colour, and the twittering antics of the seasonal house-martins and swallows, who zoom in and out of the empty windows and around the rafters, add to the charm.

The house was for centuries the home of the Vaughan family, whose best-known member was the metaphysical poet Henry (1622–95), a fact perfectly in tune with Tretower's romantic atmosphere.

The vale's hills, the natural attraction, also make Abergavenny a good base for walking and outdoor pursuits. The Blaenafon World Heritage site (p662) lies within easy striking distance, 8 miles southwest, up over the head of the valley.

Information

The **TIC** (☎ 857588; ☉ 10am-5.30pm Easter-Oct, 10am-4pm Nov-Easter) is in the same building as the seasonal **National Park Visitor Centre** (☎ 853254; ☉ 9:30am-5.30pm Easter-Oct).

The main post office is on Castle St. Go online at the **library** (☎ 735980; Victoria St; free Internet; ☉ closed Wed & Sun) and **Celtic Computer Systems** (☎ 858111; 39 Cross St; per half hr £2.50).

Sights

Modest-looking **St Mary's church** is worth a stop even on a sunny day for its exceptional treasury of oak, stone and alabaster tombs, and carved Jesse Tree, which shows the family lineage of Jesus. There's a free brochure, and a volunteer warden can answer questions. Make a donation if you can.

Abergavenny Castle overlooks the River Usk meadows and was the scene of Norman treachery in 1175 when William de Braose invited the local Welsh prince, Seisyll ap Dyfnwal, and his knights to dinner – and slaughtered them. In 1645 after several sieges, Royalist forces destroyed the castle beyond any use other than scrambling. However, the keep was restored by the Victorians and now houses the small **Abergavenny Museum** (☎ 854282; admission free; ☉ 11am-1pm & 2-5pm Mon-Sat, 2-5pm Sun Mar-Oct, to 4pm Mon-Sat only in winter), which features curios

such as an 1830s teaset and replica set of medieval armour.

Activities

Abergavenny is well placed for canal and hill walks, mountain sports and cycle touring.

Walks up Sugar Loaf, Blorenge and Skirrid Fawr, which surround Abergavenny, are rewarded with fine views. The walks are detailed in *Walks from Abergavenny* (£2) available from the TIC.

The **Monmouthshire & Brecon Canal** passes just near Llanfoist, southwest of town. Walk the towpath, or hire a boat from **Beacon Park Boats** (☎ 858277; per day £65).

The area is good for family and touring **cycling**, also for testing **mountain-biking** in the big Black Mountains to the north. Ride the canal towpath 20 miles to Brecon, or follow the disused railway line. The 32-mile **Four Castles** route (free leaflet from the TIC) is a hilly, signposted road tour. Hire bikes and get route information at **Gateway Cycles** (☎ 01873-858519) in town and **PedalAway** (☎ 830219; www.hopyardcottages.co.uk; Hopyard Farm, Govilon; mountain bikes £17, tourers £12), 3 miles east of Abergavenny.

Sleeping

BUDGET

Pyscodlyn Farm Caravan & Camping Site (☎ 853271; Llanwenarth Citra; 2-person tent sites £10) Two miles west off the A40, this grassy site lies near the River Usk.

Blacksheep Backpackers (☎ 859125; www.black sheepbackpackers.co.uk; 24 Station Rd; dm £12, private r with en suite £14, both with breakfast; ☐) This independent hostel, opposite the train station, is attached to a busy pub. Self-catering facilities are basic, and the upper-floor dorms a lot fresher than the basement.

Smithy's Bunkhouse (☎ 853432; www.smithys bunkhouse.com; Lower House Farm; dm £9.50) This bunkhouse, 2½ miles north of town in Pantygelli, has comfortable dorms. You can bring your own food or eat at the Crown Inn, opposite. Taxis from Abergavenny cost around £4.50.

The nearest YHA hostel is at Capel-y-Ffin (p698), 15 miles north up the Vale of Ewyas.

MID-RANGE & TOP END

Highfield House (☎ 852371; www.highfieldaberga venny.co.uk; 6 Belmont Rd; s/d £35/55) A handsome, well-kept Victorian villa above town, this has a capacious guest lounge, three en-suite rooms named after local castles, and engaging hosts. The host cooks tasty dinners by arrangement.

Aenon House (☎ 858708; www.aenonhouse.co.uk; 34 Peny-y-pound Rd; s/d from £20/40) A fine walled garden, careful furnishing, pretty rooms and an attentive hostess (who runs the show just for the satisfaction) make Aenon House an Abergavenny favourite. There are no en-suite rooms, but you can have sole use of a bathroom.

Park Guest House (☎ 853715; 36 Hereford Rd; s/d £20/35, with en suite £30/45; ✗) This is a small but comfortable, homely place 10 minutes' walk north of the centre.

Angel Hotel (☎ 857121; 15 Cross St; s/d £60/85) Newly restored in contemporary style (with white bathrooms and slatted blinds), the traditional high-street town hotel, the Angel, is once again the smartest place to sleep and eat (see p698).

Eating

The Vale of Usk is renowned for Welsh cuisine using local venison, lamb and beef,

---

TOP FIVE PLACES TO EAT UP THE USK

The combination of fertile conditions, pride in local produce, and proximity to well-to-do parts of England has made the Vale of Usk area famous for food and the restaurants that cook and serve it. Here is a selection of five outstanding examples:

Bell at Skenfrith (☎ 01600-750235; www.skenfrith.com; d £95-170; mains £12-18) Topping the list for informality, taste and location is this restaurant, 12 miles east of Abergavenny. The character and innlike atmosphere of the 1690 building and former pub lives on in low ceilings and polished-wood floors. The dinner menu is excellent, with a children's organic-food choice and irresistible desserts, and quiet Skenfrith itself adds to the appeal, with a babbling river, ruined medieval fortress and wood-towered church.

Gliffaes Hotel (☎ 01874-730371; www.gliffaeshotel.com; d £75-180; 3-course dinner £30) Long established, and starring a high terrace overlooking its own meadows to the Usk, the Gliffaes, 4 miles west of Crickhowell, is a strapping 1883 Victorian mansion that lies a carriage-drive away from mainstream valley life. The restaurant offers a more conventional modern menu than other restaurants in the region and likes to source 75% of its fresh produce from within 25 miles of the hotel.

Walnut Tree Inn (☎ 01873-852797; www.thewalnuttreeinn.com; Llandewi Skirrid; mains £9-17) There's something of a story behind the Walnut Tree Inn, 3 miles northwest of Abergavenny on the B4521. A Vale of Usk original, the legendary founder Franco Taruschio retired recently, so the restaurant, which is essentially a top-notch Italian in the Welsh countryside, is working on a second-generation identity. Expect delicacies from the nearby smokery and plenty of high-class pasta and meats.

The Foxhunter (☎ 01873-881101; Nantyderry; mains £17-19) Off the road from Abergavenny to Newport, The Foxhunter has a chef who has worked for Marco Pierre White. The cooking is fresh, seasonal and adventurous, and you eat from wooden tables on slate floors before log-burning stoves.

Bear Hotel (see also p695; ☎ 01873-810408; www.bearhotel.co.uk; mains £6-15) Set directly on the Vale of Usk high road in Crickhowell, the Bear has a long and well-loved high-class menu with a variety of delights such as crab dishes and beef and Guinness pie. The hostelry has an air of traditional warmth in harmony with the 21st century rather than at odds with it.

MID WALES

cheese, honey and wines as ingredients. You can enjoy the bounty at a selection of country pubs and restaurants throughout the valley area (see the boxed text, p697), while Abergavenny itself has a regular selection of decent eateries.

Luigi's (☎ 855103; 10 Cross St; mains £6-7; ❤ to 8pm) Garlicky aromas pump out onto the main street from this lively pizza, pasta and toasties café.

Malthouse (☎ 859960; mains £8; ❤ noon-9.30pm Tue-Sat) Here's a funky restaurant with a basement feel, young cheery staff and a modern menu with a Mediterranean twist. Find it behind the Market Hall.

Angel Hotel (see p697; bar & courtyard dishes £6-16, à la carte mains £11-17) For a delicious meal in smart surroundings eat in the bar, the sheltered courtyard or the restaurant at the revitalised Angel.

Getting There & Around

Bus services (Monday to Saturday only) include No X4 to/from Cardiff via Merthyr Tydfil (£4.50, 2¼ hours, half-hourly), No 21 to/from Brecon (£4.50, one hour, six daily) and No 83 to/from Monmouth via Raglan (£4.50, 40 minutes, six daily).

From June to August on Sunday and bank holidays the Beacons Bus serves Abergavenny (see p692).

The train station is a 10-minute walk from the bus station and TIC. Trains run about every hour (less often on Sunday) from Cardiff (40 minutes) via Newport (25 minutes).

For taxis, try **Lewis Taxis** (☎ 854140).

AROUND ABERGAVENNY
Vale of Ewyas (Llanthony Valley)

Offa's Dyke Path runs atop the windblown eastern ridge of this lovely isolated vale. Down below, beside the babbling River Honddu, are the ruins of the 13th-century Augustinian priory church and the monastic buildings of **Llanthony Priory** (Cadw). A superb walk climbs from the car park to the bare ridge above.

The atmospheric **Abbey Hotel** (☎ 890487; s/d Sun-Thu £35/60, d Fri & Sat only £135) is built into the surviving abbey buildings. Having a drink at the vaulted crypt bar is a memorable experience.

Capel-y-Ffin YHA hostel (see p692; ☎ 0870 770 5748) is a simple walkers' hostel a mile north of Capel-y-Ffin village. The 8-mile hike along

Offa's Dyke Path to Hay-on-Wye is recommended, and you can book through the hostel for the adjacent Grange Pony-Trekking Centre (see p691).

On summer Sundays the Beacons Bus runs between Hay and Llanthony Priory (see p692).

HAY-ON-WYE
☎ 01497 / pop 1400

Hay-on-Wye (Y Gelli) is famous for books. Not a few rows of cosseted medieval manuscripts, but hundreds of thousands of volumes covering 2000 subjects in 40 second-hand bookshops. A day spent browsing miles of shelves with the scent of stale paper in the nostrils is mind-warping. You can admire first editions in shiny cabinets, find colleagues' remaindered publications, and eat and drink well among an informed, genteel crowd.

Hay is also famous for book people, first and foremost Richard Booth, the colourful chap whose vision turned the town into the used-book capital of the world. This was prompted by his own vast shop, which he established in the 1960s with stock from institutions and country houses that were shedding their libraries at the time.

Since 1988 the town has hosted an influential Festival of Literature every May/June.

Situated below the Black Mountains, it also makes an excellent base for country pursuits that contrast with bookish ones. Canoe on the lovely River Wye below town, or walk Offa's Dyke Path or the Wye Valley Walk.

Although generally packed with English-folk, Hay is settled in Wales – the border runs 300m northeast of the town centre.

Orientation & Information

Hay's slightly disorientating little centre contains the castle, most of the bookshops, and café-restaurants.

The **TIC** (☎ 820144; Oxford Rd; ❤ 10am-5pm Easter-Oct, 11am-1pm & 2-4pm Oct-Easter), beside the main car park and bus stop, stocks a free listing of the bookshops. There's Internet access at the **library** (Chancery Lane; free Internet) and the TIC (per hour £3).

Bookshops

There are something like 40 second-hand bookshops in Hay, containing hundreds of thousands of books. As you can guess, quantity tends to rule over quality.

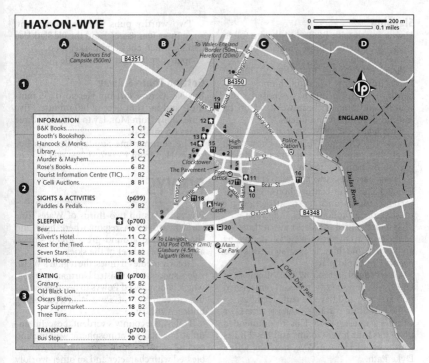

HAY-ON-WYE

Here's a sweet, sleuthy sample:

B & K Books (☎ 820386; Newport St) The world's finest collection on apiculture (bee-keeping).

Booth's Bookshop (☎ 820322; 44 Lion St) 400,000 tomes covering all subjects.

Hancock & Monks (☎ 821784; 15 Broad St) Music books, sheet music and scores.

Murder & Mayhem (☎ 821613; 5 Lion St) Detective fiction, crime and horror.

Rose's Books (☎ 820013; 14 Broad St) Rare children's and illustrated books.

There is also regular sales at **Y Gelli Auctions** (☎ 821179; Broad St).

Activities

Walking includes the historic town walk, local countryside circuits and hikes into the Black Mountains. The TIC stocks route literature.

For **canoeing** down the River Wye, hire craft and get a lift back from **Paddles & Pedals** (☎ 820604; Castle St; kayak per half/full day £10/15), based in town, or from **Wye Valley Canoe Centre** (☎ 847213; Glasbury; per half/full day £10/17.50), whose boathouse lies four miles southwest of Hay.

One mile past Glasbury at Three Cocks is Black Mountain Activities (see p690).

Festivals & Events

The week-long **Hay Festival of Literature** (box office ☎ 821299; www.hayfestival.com; 25 Lion St), every May/June, is a popular, entertaining and thoughtful affair.

Dozens of readings, lectures, concerts and workshops attract hundreds of educated folk. In festival week Hay's population swells 50-fold and bed space is rarer than a hen's tooth.

In 2004 the headliners included such names as adventurers Joe Simpson (*Touching the Void*) and Ranulph Fiennes, and ex-Python and medieval scholar Terry Jones. Comedians Dylan Moran (*Black Books*) and evergreen Ken Dodd also gave performances, while campaigning journalist John Pilger debated propaganda and campaigning rocker Bob Geldof did dads and debt.

A children's festival, **Hay Fever**, runs in conjunction with the grown-up one, for two-year-olds and upward.

MID WALES

Sleeping

Hay is awash with B&Bs, but they're full to capacity at festival time. Single rooms are always limited.

Bear (☎ 821302; Bear St; s/d £24/58; ✖) One of Hay's finest, this beautiful, homely 16th-century coaching inn has exposed stone walling and smooth beamwork set off by tasteful decoration and linens.

Tinto House (☎ 820590; Broad St; d from £50) A wonderful Georgian place to stay, with lovely big rooms and a spectacular flower garden overlooking the Wye.

Seven Stars (see below; ☎ 820886; 11 Broad St; d £60; 🏊) This 16th-century house has comfortable rooms and a rare attraction for these parts: an indoor pool and sauna.

Rest for the Tired (☎ 820550; www.restforthetired .co.uk; 6 Broad St; s/d with en suite £30/45) Marked by an 80-year-old bicycle tyre sign, this is a friendly little old place.

Kilvert's Hotel (see below; ☎ 821042; High Town; s/d £70/90) All rooms at this pleasant refurbished pub are cosy and have en suite facilities.

Old Post Office (☎ 820008; Llanigon; s from £25, d without/with en suite £40/60) This recommended place has four lovely rooms and lies 2 miles southwest of Hay-on-Wye, near the Offa's Dyke Path.

Radnors End Campsite (☎ 820780; per person £4) It's 500m from the Hay Bridge over the Wye on the road to Clyro. The nearest YHA hostel is Capel-y-Ffin, 8 miles south (see p698).

Eating

Eating out in Hay is tasty and tasteful.

The Granary (☎ 820790; Broad St; mains £8; 🕙 9am-9pm during school holidays & the festival, 9am-5.30pm rest of the year) Laura Ashley table cloths and herby smells fill this well-established wholefood café-diner, serving cakes, juice *pressés* (a blend of fruits, flowers and spices with sparkling water, £2), buckwheat and walnut roast (£8) and much more.

Oscars Bistro (☎ 821193; High Town; mains £7.50; 🕙 10.30am-4.30pm) This popular, woody daytime café serves hot dishes (including vegetarian) and filled baguettes.

Kilvert's Hotel (see above; 821042; High Town; lunches £5, mains £12) Eat at bar tables in this relaxed, modern inn where the menu features quail and lamb as well as pizza and pasta.

Seven Stars (see above; mains £12) On the dinner menu is the Stars burger – 0.5lb of Welsh black beef.

Two worthy pubs include the ancient, snug **Three Tuns** (Broad St) and the **Old Black Lion** (Lion St), which cooks upmarket food.

Spar supermarket is on Castle St.

Getting There & Away

Bus No 39 runs to/from Hereford (55 minutes) and to/from Brecon (40 minutes) five times daily from Monday to Saturday, three times on Sunday.

The summertime-Sundays Beacons Bus serves Hay from Hereford (see p692).

POWYS

Powys makes up two-thirds of Wales' fine rural heartland, a region where light and shade tumble around great green slopes, and red kites wheel in the skies.

In early medieval times, the region's Welsh rulers successfully resisted Norman invasion, which later allowed Powys to become part of the larger region of 'Pura Wallia', meaning under Welsh rule.

Today, the county's verdant, peaceful undulations make it atmospheric walking and cycling country. Some of the little towns are blessed with character and an other-worldly atmosphere. Among a small grab of significant attractions, don't miss grand Powis Castle near Welshpool or the stimulating Centre for Alternative Technology near Machynlleth.

Orientation & Information

Powys is located in the country's heart. From the undulating English border it runs west to Ceredigion, and from the Brecon Beacons it runs north to the border with Snowdonia.

The county was created in 1974 by combining southern Brecknockshire, central Radnorshire and northern Montgomeryshire. The northern part is often still referred to as Montgomeryshire.

Activities

CYCLING

Powys has several centres for cycling, particularly mountain biking. Llanwrtyd Wells (p701), Machynlleth (p703) and Nant-yr-Arian (p706) all have easy-to-hard local bike routes, with route-maps available at the tourist information centres.

WALKING

Two national trails run through Powys: **Offa's Dyke Path** (see also p657) and **Glyndŵr's Way**.

Glyndŵr's Way is a 135-mile, eight- to 10-day national trail contained within Powys and based on sites related to Owain Glyndŵr, the Welsh warrior-statesman who led the rebellion against English rule in the early 15th century. The trail draws a great chevron through beautiful countryside between easterly Knighton and Welshpool (both towns also lie on Offa's Dyke Path) via westerly Machynlleth. Powys County Council produces a free information pack on it, including maps and an accommodation listing.

For details on both walks, contact the **Offa's Dyke Centre** (☎ 01547-528753; oda@offasdyke.demon.co.uk) in Knighton.

Getting There & Around

Public transport is limited so advance planning is advisable. The Powys Travel Guide contains mapping and information on buses and trains. Get it from TICs and the **Powys County Council** (☎ 0845 607 6060).

The trains services are sparse but scenic. They include the Cambrian Main Line (Shrewsbury–Aberystwyth), which connects with the Cambrian Coaster at Machynlleth and continues on to Pwllheli. The Heart of Wales line (Shrewsbury–Swansea; see p688) runs across Powys and Mid Wales.

LLANWRTYD WELLS

☎ 01591 / pop 601

Llanwrtyd Wells (khlan-oor-tid) is the wackiest place in Mid Wales, courtesy of a calendar of madcap events organised by playful citizens.

Fine countryside around the old spa town is excellent for riding, walking and cycling – and crazy variations thereof, many involving real ale (see the boxed text 'Get Wacky in Llanwrtyd', p702). Despite being the smallest town in the UK (from the days when to be a town you had to have a charter, a market, a mayor and a corporation) and devoid of sights, Llanwrtyd's in-tune **TIC** (☎ 610666; llanwrtyd-wells.powys.org.uk; Irfon Tce; ⏰ 10am-1pm & 2-5pm) is open year-round supporting these activities. The **library** (☎ 610657; ⏰ 10am-1pm & 2-4.30pm Tue, to 7pm Thu, 10am-1pm Sat) has free Internet access – but watch those short opening times.

With the Cambrian Mountains to the northwest and Mynydd Eppynt to the southeast, the town is in the heart of red kite country (see the boxed text below). Llanwrtyd is also a stop on the handsome Heart of Wales line (see the boxed text on p688)

For cycle routes and bikes, go to **Cycles Irfon** (☎ 610710; www.cyclesirfon.co.uk; Beulah Rd; per half/full day £10/15). For mountain-biking breaks and event participation, contact the **Red Kite Mountain Bike Centre** (☎ 610236) at the **Neuadd**

KITE COUNTRY

In the remote heart of Wales, once you've learned to identify the red kite, your eye persistently scans the skies for its 2m wing-span and aerial acrobatics.

The striking chestnut-coloured kite was once the most abundant bird of prey throughout Britain, but with the expansion in agriculture in the 16th century it was declared vermin and hunted without mercy. By the 19th century, the kite was on the verge of extinction, gone from England and Scotland and down to a few pairs in the Tywi and Cothi Valleys of Wales.

So a hundred years ago, a group of landowners and communities launched their own protection programme, one that has become the longest-running scheme for any bird in the world. There are now hundreds of breeding pairs throughout Wales, their survival supported by an ecotourism scheme that invites visitors to spot the bird in the open skies and to visit regular feeding sites.

The action is centred on the town of Rhayader and its surrounding area. The main feeding centre is **Gigrin Farm** (adult £2.50; ⏰ 3pm Easter-Oct, 2pm Nov-Easter), just outside Rhayader. Feeding also takes place at Nant-yr-Arian Forest Visitor Centre, east of Aberystwyth, and Tregaron Museum, north of Lampeter. You are also virtually guaranteed sightings at the following watching centres: the Elan Valley Visitor Centre, near Rhayader; Gilfach Farm, north of Rhayader; and the Ynyshir RSPB Reserve, near Machynlleth.

For more information contact the **Rhayader Tourist Information Office** (☎ 01597-810591).

GET WACKY IN LLANWRTYD

There's fun afoot, a-wheel or a-pub year-round in Llanwrtyd Wells.

- **Saturnalia Beer Festival** (January) Winter festivities with the Romans, includes a Real Ale Ramble for walkers and Real Ale Wobble for mountain bikers with free beer at each checkpoint.

- **Man vs Horse Marathon** (May–June) A 22-mile cross-country race with a prize purse that rises by £1000 every year a man fails to beat the horse (currently £24,000).

- **World Mountain Bike Bog Snorkelling Championships** (July) Competitors wearing wetsuits and snorkels cycle two lengths of a 55m trench dug in a nearby bog, surfacing twice to navigate.

- **World Bog Snorkelling Championships** (August Bank Holiday) This time it's the swimmers' turn to cover two lengths of the bog.

- **Real Ale Wobble & Ramble** (November) Held in conjunction with the Mid Wales Beer Festival, all mountain-bike rides and walks feature free beer at checkpoints.

Schedules are subject to revision, so confirm with the TIC or organisers **Green Events Ltd** (☎ 01591-610666).

Arms (☎ 610236; www.neuaddarmshotel.co.uk; The Square; s/d £30/50), the town hotel that organises walks, cycle rides and pony-trekking and is often a focus of the special events. Pony trekkers head for **Ffos Farm** (☎ 610371; Ffos Rd; per 1hr/2hr £13/£26).

Drovers Rest (☎ 610264; The Square; s/d £25/45; 3-course dinner £25) This gourmet restaurant also has fine accommodation. A devotedly prepared menu is packed with seafood delivered fresh from Swansea several times a week.

Stonecroft Hostel (☎ 610327; www.stonecroft.co.uk; Dol-y-coed Rd; 1-6 bed r £14) This is a good independent hostel. Neighbouring sister-act the **Stonecroft Inn** (☎ 610332; mains £7) serves tasty, well-priced food, such as game pie, and has live music on Saturday night.

LLANDRINDOD WELLS
☎ 01597 / pop 5024

Boomtime hit spa-town Llandrindod Wells in the Victorian era when ladies and gentle-men arrived by train in droves to take the waters. The architecture of the era survives in grand hotels, houses and ironwork, and every August the townsfolk don bustles and wing collars for the week-long **Victorian Festival**. You can still take a drink directly from the **chalybeate spring** ('chalybeate' refers to the iron salts) in historic Rock Park.

The **TIC** (☎ 822600; www.visit-llandrindod.co.uk; Temple St) is in the Old Town Hall, Memorial Gardens.

Housed in an Art Nouveau motorcar showroom near the centre, the **National Cycle Exhibition** (☎ 825531; www.cyclemuseum.org.uk; adult £2.50; ☒ 10am-4pm daily Easter-Oct, call for days Nov-Feb) tells the fascinating story of bikes through the ages.

Llandrindod lies on the wonderful Heart of Wales line (see the boxed text on p688).

KNIGHTON
☎ 01547 / pop 2743

Knighton (Tref-y-Clawdd) is an amiable little stone-built border town and walking hub which lies midway along Offa's Dyke Path at the terminus of Glyndŵr's Way. Here you'll find the **Offa's Dyke Centre & TIC** (☎ 528753; oda@offasdyke.demon.co.uk; West St; ☒ 9am-5.30pm Easter-Oct, 9am-5pm Mon-Fri Nov-Apr).

Knighton also offers extraterrestrial fun and fascination at the hill-top **Spaceguard Centre** (☎ 01547-520247; www.spaceguarduk.com; Llanshay Lane; adult £5), an observatory 2 miles south of town. The centre owners specialise in tracking NEOs, near-Earth objects (comets and asteroids), and assessing their threat to the planet, meanwhile organising public planetarium shows and daytime telescopic stargazing.

Fleece House (☎ 520168; Market St; s £28-31, d £46-62; ☒) A tastefully decorated, quality B&B in the heart of town.

Knighton is a halt on the scenic Heart of Wales line (see the boxed text; p688).

WELSHPOOL
☎ 01938 / pop 5539

Reasons to visit agreeable little Welshpool include a trip to splendid Powis Castle and a ride on the scenic narrow-gauge railway.

The **TIC** (☎ 552043; ☒ 9.30am-5pm Easter-Oct, 9.30am-5pm Nov-Easter) is in the Spar car park: from the main cross-roads (traffic lights) in the old town centre, go along Church St for 200m – it's on the right.

Sights

Magnificent **Powis Castle & Garden** (NT; ☎ 551929; www.powiscastle@nationaltrust.org.uk; castle & garden £8.50, garden only £5.80; ☺ castle 1-4pm Thu-Mon Mar & Oct, 1-5pm Thu-Mon Apr-Sep, garden 11am-6pm same days as castle) overhangs a world-renowned steeply terraced garden of great clipped yews that shelter rare plants. The red-sandstone fortress dates to 1200, but was furnished and adapted by generations of Herberts and Clives. Indian treasures are on display in the integral **Clive Museum**. The castle is 1 mile south of Welshpool.

Charming vintage **Welshpool & Llanfair Railway** (☎ 810441; www.wllr.org.uk; return trip £9.50; ☺ most days Jun-Aug, most Sat & Sun Mar-Apr, Sep-Oct & Dec) opened for business in 1902, closed in 1956 and was reopened by enthusiasts in 1960. It runs for 8 miles from Raven Square above town to Llanfair Caereinion. Phone for a timetable.

The **Andrew Logan Museum of Sculpture** (☎ 01686-640689; adult £2; ☺ noon-6pm Easter weekend, Sat-Mon May, Thu-Mon Jun-Aug, noon-5pm Sat & Sun Sep, noon-4pm Sat & Sun Oct) is a gallery of the contemporary artist's own dazzling spangly work. It lies, incongruously, in rural little Berriew, 5 miles south of Welshpool.

Getting There & Away

Bus No 10 comes from Shrewsbury (45 minutes, about every two hours Monday to Saturday) as does **National Express** (☎ 0870 580 8080) coach No 97 (30 minutes, daily). National Express coach No 420 stops daily en route from London (£25, seven hours) via Birmingham, continuing to Aberystwyth (£10.25, two hours)

Welshpool is on the Cambrian Main Line between Shrewsbury (25 minutes) and Aberystwyth (£8, 1½ hours), with services about every two hours (fewer on Sunday).

MACHYNLLETH

☎ 01654 / pop 2147

Machynlleth (ma-*hun*-khleth) is a small and upbeat town set amid hills near the head of the Dovey (Dyfi) Valley. To the north rises the mountain massif of Cader Idris (893m), located in the south of Snowdonia National Park (for details see p716).

The town is referred to as the ancient capital of Wales, as it was here in 1404 that rebel-hero Owain Glyndŵr is said to have established the country's first parliament.

More recently it has become a capital for the green movement, driven by the nearby Centre for Alternative Technology (CAT), where the folks have spent 30 years creating methods for sustainable living.

The **TIC** (☎ 702401; Maengwyn St; ☺ 9.30am-5pm Mon-Sat, 9.30am-4pm Sun Apr-Sep) is next to the Owain Glyndŵr Parliament House (below). Get free Internet access opposite at the **library** (☎ 702322; Maengwyn St; ☺ 9.30am-1pm & 2-5pm Tue & Wed, to 7pm Mon & Fri, 9.30am-1pm Sat).

Sights

Do not leave the area without visiting the Centre for Alternative Technology (CAT; see the boxed text on p704), 3 miles north of town.

The late-medieval slate **Owain Glyndŵr Parliament House** (☎ 702827; adult £1; ☺ 11am-3pm Mon-Tue & Thu-Sat, 10am-3pm Wed Easter-Sep), in the main street, actually post-dates Glyndŵr's original venue, but probably resembles it closely. Displays explain Glyndŵr's fight for Welsh independence, but really the place is rather low key.

An extraordinary museum that combines entertainment and education and is good for children, **Celtica** (☎ 702702; www.celticawales.com; Y Plas, Aberystwyth Rd; adult £5; ☺ 10am-6pm) pays tribute to the Celts' defining role in culture and history. The centrepiece is a theatrical but evocative one-hour spectacular about the history and beliefs of Welsh ancestry. Conventional exhibits cover tribes across Europe – and tea-time in the museum's café is a pleasure.

A combined art gallery and converted chapel have grown to become the **Museum of Modern Art for Wales** (MOMA; ☎ 703355; www.momawales.org.uk; Heol Penrallt; ☺ 10am-4pm Mon-Sat). The whitewashed art space displays permanent and changing exhibitions of Welsh work, while the handsome, galleried **Tabernacle chapel** is now a 400-seat auditorium that boasts recording-standard acoustics. It is the scene of August's impressive week-long **Gŵyl Machynlleth Festival** of classical music.

Activities

This region of mountains and valleys is excellent for both major **hikes** and easy ambles. The nearest track for the ascent of Cader Idris is also the most strenuous and direct (see p728): starting from Minffordd, a bus ride

---

THE CENTRE FOR ALTERNATIVE TECHNOLOGY

While the rest of the globe consumes as fast as it can, rescue work continues at the reassuringly sane and stimulating **Centre for Alternative Technology** (CAT; ☎ 705950; www.cat.org.uk; adult £7.20; ✆ 10am-5pm Easter-Oct but 9.30am-6pm mid-Jul-Aug, 10am-4pm Oct-Easter), 3 miles north of Machynlleth.

No-one leaves without being inspired to change the way they live – even just a little – whether it's deciding to insulate the loft with wool (of course!) or crumpling newspaper into compost heaps for happy worms. The CAT is a virtually self-sufficient cooperative where over 50 exhibits demonstrate how wind, water and solar power provide food, heating and telecommunications.

The visit starts with a green theme ride up the side of what is an old quarry in a water-balanced cable-car. A drum beneath the top car fills with stored rainwater, and is then drawn down while the bottom car is pulled up. Other ingenious exhibits abound: a solar-powered telephone, a compost toilet, organic suburban gardening, and a self-heating eco-shop. There's a great licensed organic-wholefood restaurant, and the centre is good for children, who come face to face with a giant mole and can hit the adventure playground – but still may not chase the chickens.

The CAT lies on the A487 road to Dolgellau, part of the Lôn Las Cymru cross-Wales cycle route – cyclists get 10% off admission. Buses run from Machynlleth half-hourly (Nos 32, X32 and 35), with fewer services on Sunday.

---

seven miles north. A booklet (£3.95) available at the TIC details 15 gentle local routes.

The area is also a centre for **mountain biking**. For route information and bike hire, go to **The Holey Trail** (☎ 700411; per half/full day £14/18) and outdoor shop **Greenstiles** (☎ 703543; per half/full day £12/16), both on Maengwyn St. For cycle tourers, the cross-Wales Lôn Las Cymru route passes through town and across the striking Millennium Bridge over the River Dyfi en route for the CAT.

Sleeping

Pendre Guest House (☎ 702088; Maengwyn St; d £50) Stay in a listed 1770 stone-built house that emulates the exterior style of the Parliament House down the road, but has a habitable and elegant Georgian interior.

Maenllwyd (☎ 702928; Newtown Rd; s/d £30/48) This pleasant place, all of its rooms with an en suite, can serve a vegetarian breakfast and has good views from the back.

Wynnstay Hotel (☎ 702941; www.wynnstay-hotel .com; Maengwyn St; s/d £50/80) This warm and thriving traditional coaching inn is full of life in the evenings when the bar and excellent restaurant rev up.

Plas Llwyngwern (☎ 703970; Pantperthog; s £18, d without/with en suite £36/40) Set just 250m from the CAT, this 18th-century house is both wonderful and welcoming. It boasts huge rooms and great views set in vast grounds.

Corris YHA hostel (☎ 0870 770 5778; dm £10.60; ✆ Feb-Oct, call for other months) Situated in the mountain village of Corris, 5 miles up the valley north of Machynlleth, this converted schoolhouse has a 'green' warden who plugs eco-efficiency and ecotourism. The Minffordd trailhead for Cader Idris is a 3-mile walk or bus ride north.

For camping, **Gwerniago Farm** (☎ 791227; Pennal; per 2-person tent sites £6) is a tent-only site, 3 miles west on the A493. **Llwyngwern Farm** (☎ 702492; Corris; per 2-person tent sites £8) is near the CAT.

Eating & Drinking

Quarry Wholefood Café (☎ 702624; Maengwyn St; dishes around £4) This cheerful, pine-clad, baby-friendly place is run by the CAT, so it serves delicious vegetarian and organic food plus Fair Trade tea and coffee. It could, however, update its décor and menu – where are the funky coffees and salads available at other in-tune cafés in Wales?

Wynnstay Hotel (☎ 702941; Maengwyn St; mains £10; ✆ lunch & dinner) With its handsome, spacious stone-floored dining room, cheerful staff, top menus for bar lunches as well as dinner specials that use local meats in imaginative sauces, eg lamb cous-cous with date gravy, the Wynnstay is the essential diner. Especially now there's a separate pizzeria out the back, serving, among others, the

Wynnstay pizza topped with Preseli cheese and cured local ham (£6.50).

The **Skinners Arms** (Penrallt St; mains around £7) and **White Lion** (Pentrehedyn St; mains from £6) are both popular pubs with good grub.

Try the small **Blasau Deli** (Penrallt St) for local cheeses, and also organic chocs and ices.

Getting There & Away

Machynlleth is on the Cambrian Main Line railway (Shrewsbury–Aberystwyth). Services run from Shrewsbury (£11, one hour, every two hours, three on Sunday), and Aberystwyth (30 minutes, every two hours, four on Sunday).

Bus Nos 32 and X32 arrive from Aberystwyth (45 minutes) and Dolgellau (40 minutes) seven times daily Monday to Saturday, twice on Sunday.

CEREDIGION

In the Mid Wales coastal region, County Ceredigion has retained a staunchly Welsh character ever since the Normans tried but failed to subdue it in the 11th century. Echoing this, Welsh is the first language of three out of every five inhabitants.

Aberystwyth, which is the county capital, is a vivacious university town and seaside resort – and it's also the place to pick up one of the best steam-train journeys in Wales.

Getting Around

In addition to the useful nationwide Wales Bus, Rail and Tourist Map & Guide, a public transport map and guide for Ceredigion is available from TICs or by calling **Ceredigion County Council** (☎ 01970-633555). For transport timetables and fares by phone, call **Traveline** (☎ 0870 608 2608).

The county's only main-line railway service runs to Aberystwyth via Welshpool and Machynlleth from Shrewsbury (connecting at Machynlleth with the Cambrian Coaster for stations to Pwllheli).

Ceredigion is covered by two Rover tickets. For train and bus travel valid for three days' travel out of seven, the North and Mid Wales Flexi-Rover (£30) covers that region. For one day's train travel only, use the North & Mid Wales Day Ranger (£20, not valid Saturdays in July and August). Buy them on the buses or at train stations.

ABERYSTWYTH

☎ 01970 / pop 15,935

Aberystwyth's 6500 students bring modern vivacity to this Victorian seaside resort, not to mention a big appetite. For its size, the historic university town has an impressive number of cafés, restaurants, pubs and venues, giving this outpost on the wild Mid-Welsh coastline a cosmopolitan outlook.

Historically, the town was founded by Edward I, whose 13th-century fortress was captured by Owain Glyndŵr in 1404, and finally

---

WELSH MYTHS

Tales of fairies, enchantment, King Arthur and Merlin have been passed down in Wales for centuries, inspired by ancient peoples, battles and wild landscape.

As early as the 9th century a collection of tales of mystery and heroism appeared as the *Historia Britonum*. But the best images come from the 14th-century *The Mabinogion*, with its occasionally terrifying tales of Celtic magic.

Many legends concern floods and submerged cities. The most famous is that of Cardigan Bay off Mid Wales. Seithenyn, keeper of the dykes that kept out the sea, got drunk one night and forgot to shut the sluice gates. The land and 16 cities were inundated with water, and to this day it is alleged you can hear the toll of sunken church bells.

King Arthur appears frequently, especially in *The Mabinogion*. Historians reckon he was a 5th- or 6th-century cavalry leader who led the Britons against Saxon invaders. He was then romanticised into a king of magic deeds, followed by a band of heroes and with wise magician Merlin for counsel. On Mt Snowdon he slew Rita Gawr, a giant who killed kings. And as for Avalon, where the dying Arthur was taken by Merlin, that might be saintly Bardsey Island off the Llyn Peninsula.

The world of Welsh myths is richly imaginative. For more see Robin Gwyndaf's detailed bilingual *Chwedlau Gwerin Cymru: Welsh Folk Tales*.

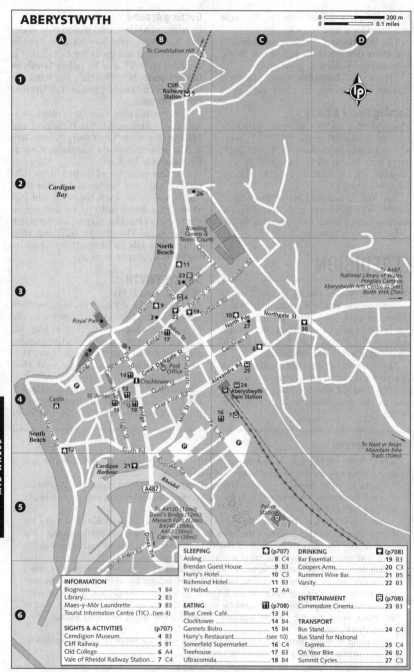

ABERYSTWYTH

0 — 200 m
0 — 0.1 miles

To Constitution Hill

Cliff Railway Station □5

Cardigan Bay

Bowling Greens & Tennis Courts

North Beach

To A487; National Library of Wales; Penglais Campus; Aberystwyth Arts Centre (0.5mi); Borth YHA (7mi)

□26

⌂11
23 □
3 ●
□4
⌂9
2 ●
Marine Tce
Terrace Rd
Bath St
Portland St
Queen's Rd
Loveden Rd
Portland Rd
Northgate St
□20
22
□19
10 ⌂
North Pde
27
Cambrian Pl
8 ⌂
Royal Pier
Eastgate St
Baker St
17
New St
King St
@1
Castle St
Great Darkgate St
Post Office
Chalybeate St
Queen St
Alexandra Rd
□25
24
Aberystwyth Train Station
Castle
⌂
St James Sq
14 ⌂
⌂ Clocktower
13
15
18
Pier St
Bridge St
High St
Grays Inn Rd
Mill St
16
7 ⌂
Park Ave
South Marine Tce
South Beach
⌂12
South Rd
Cardigan Harbour
21 ⌂
Riverside Tce
Rheidol
A487
To A4120 (12mi); Devil's Bridge (12mi); Mynach Falls (12mi); B4340 (38mi); A487 (38mi); Cardigan (38mi)
Dinas Tce
Pen yr angor Rd
Police Station
To Nant yr Arian Mountain-bike Trails (10mi)

MID WALES

INFORMATION
Biognosis.................................**1** B4
Library....................................**2** B3
Maes-y-Môr Laundrette..............**3** B3
Tourist Information Centre (TIC)..(see 4)

SIGHTS & ACTIVITIES   (p707)
Ceredigion Museum...................**4** B3
Cliff Railway............................**5** B1
Old College.............................**6** A4
Vale of Rheidol Railway Station...**7** C4

SLEEPING   ⌂ (p707)
Aisling...................................**8** C4
Brendan Guest House..................**9** B3
Harry's Hotel...........................**10** C3
Richmond Hotel........................**11** B3
Yr Hafod................................**12** A4

EATING   ⍾ (p708)
Blue Creek Café........................**13** B4
Clocktower..............................**14** B4
Gannets Bistro.........................**15** B4
Harry's Restaurant....................(see 10)
Somerfield Supermarket..............**16** C4
Treehouse...............................**17** B3
Ultracomida.............................**18** B4

DRINKING   ♥ (p708)
Bar Essential...........................**19** B3
Coopers Arms..........................**20** C3
Rummers Wine Bar.....................**21** B5
Varsity..................................**22** B3

ENTERTAINMENT   ☺ (p708)
Commodore Cinema....................**23** B3

TRANSPORT
Bus Stand..............................**24** C4
Bus Stand for National Express......................................**25** C4
On Your Bike...........................**26** B2
Summit Cycles.........................**27** C3

destroyed by Oliver Cromwell in 1649. An unassuming backdrop for crazy golf by day, the castle is attractively floodlit at night.

With the arrival of the railway in 1864, Aberystwyth transformed into a fashionable resort and, in 1872, was chosen as the site of the first college of the University of Wales. In 1907 the town became the home of the National Library of Wales, now with a dedicated visitors centre.

The busy, well-stocked TIC (☎ /fax 612125; cnr Terrace Rd & Bath St; ☻ 10am-5pm Mon-Sat Sep-Jun, 10am-6pm daily Jun–early Sep) is a block in from the seafront, and shares a building with the county museum.

You can log on at the library (☎ 617464; Corporation St; free internet) and Biognosis (☎ 636953; Pier St; per hr £3). The Maes-y-Môr Laundrette (Bath St) is near the TIC.

Sights

Aberystwyth's top visitor attraction is the lovingly restored Vale of Rheidol Steam Railway (☎ 625819; www.rheidolrailway.co.uk; adult return trip £11.50), which starts beside the main-line station. From here the vintage narrow-gauge train takes a very leisurely hour to puff 12 miles up to Devil's Bridge, an attraction in itself (see p708). The line opened in 1902 to transport lead and timber, and the Great Western Railway engines date from 1923. The shortest full-line return trip is three hours – don't miss the last train back! Trains run at least twice daily from the end of May to the beginning of September, and fewer days at other times. Ring, or visit the website for a full timetable.

From the far end of North Beach, trains depart every few minutes on the 100-year-old electric Cliff Railway (☎ 617642; www.aberystwythcliffrailway.co.uk; return trip £1.75; ☻ 10am-5.30pm Easter-Oct, 10am-6.30pm Jul-Aug). They run to the top of Constitution Hill (148m). The headland offers good views over the bay and north to Snowdonia, and the chance to play with a hill-top camera obscura, a simple optical instrument from which you can peek virtually into houses below.

The Ceredigion Museum (☎ 633088; Terrace Rd; admission free; ☻ 10am-5pm Mon-Sat), in the former Coliseum theatre and cinema, next to the TIC, has a wonderfully spacious interior, complete with stage. Entertaining exhibits cover Aberystwyth's history – from auditorium pianos to hand-knitted woolly knickers.

Overlooking the town, the National Library of Wales (☎ 623800; www.llgc.org.uk; ☻ 9.30am-6pm Mon-Fri, 9.30am-5pm Sat) houses the Welsh nation's literary treasures in a stately white building. Changing exhibitions of art, photography and artefacts, plus items from the library's collection are held here. In its care is the oldest manuscript in the Welsh language, the 12th-century Black Book of Carmarthen, also the personal papers of famous Welsh men and women, for example, of early 20th-century prime minister David Lloyd George.

The imposing stone-built Old College, on the seafront near Royal Pier, was designed as a hotel but never opened. Instead, the University of Wales was founded in the building in 1872.

Activities

For cycling, the easy, largely car-free Rheidol Trail runs 18km from the seafront up the pretty Rheidol Valley. Ten miles east of Aberystwyth, in the hilly inland region of Plynlimon, you find dedicated mountain-bike trails at Nant yr Arian. Hire family and mountain bikes from On Your Bike (☎ 626996; Queen's Rd; per half/full day from £6/10) and Summit Cycles (☎ 626061; 65 North Pde; per half/full day £14/18), which runs a bike drop-off service.

Sleeping

Yr Hafod (☎ 617579; 1 South Marine Tce; s/d £24/48, d with en suite £58) Enjoy open-sea views and friendly service at this good, plain place on the South Beach seafront.

Harry's Hotel (see p708; ☎ 612647; www.harrys aberystwyth.com; 44 North Pde; s/d £35/60, with en suite £40/80) This is a refurbished, mazelike hotel on the main central drag, with cheery, comfortable rooms – but it's really all about the restaurant…

Aisling (☎ 626980; 21 Alexandra Rd; s/d £26/48) Here's an acceptable no-frills place near the station, where you share bathrooms.

Brendan Guest House (☎ 612252; Marine Tce; s/d £24/48, with en suite £26/52) The main guesthouse on the North Beach, the hospitable Brendan has comfortable 20th-century décor.

Richmond Hotel (☎ 612201; 44-45 Marine Tce; s/d £55/60) The smart place on the North Beach, this is popular with traditional resort-lovers.

Borth YHA hostel (☎ 0870 770 5708; borth@yha .org.uk; dm £10.60; ☻ with 48hr notice Mar-Oct) Stay in a beachfront house in exposed little Borth, 7 miles north.

MID WALES

Eating

Ultracomida (☎ 625400; 3 Bridge St; snacks £3; ☺ 10am-6pm Mon-Fri, 9am-5pm Sat) A new café specialising in Spanish, French and Welsh delicacies (cheeses and chorizo) with which to fill your panini, you can takeaway or sit-in at Ultracomida.

Blue Creek Café (Princess St) This chic little coffee bar is an ideal place to peruse design magazines over a stimulating brew.

Harry's Restaurant (see p706; mains around £14; ☺ Mon-Sat) Harry's has been trendily refurbished, with shining cutlery and high-backed leather chairs, and has sincere hosts. The Continental-influenced à la carte and set menus match the high-quality of the décor, with mountain lamb rubbing shanks with guinea fowl and monkfish.

Clocktower (☎ 626269; Pier St; mains £10; ☺ 10am-4pm daily, dinner Thu-Sat) A popular café-restaurant, you can sit outside beside the tower when the weather's fine, for daytime hoagies (a long Italian sandwich roll) and tortilla wraps, and for evening meals that run from pizza and pasta (£5) to interesting veggie, chicken, pork and salmon plates.

Other temptations include:

Gannets Bistro (☎ 617164; 7 St James Sq; mains £10) Hearty dinners of fresh fish and more.

Treehouse (☎ 615791; 14 Baker St) Chow down at this organic café.

The Somerfield supermarket is beside the train station.

Drinking & Entertainment

Bar Essential (☎ 623318; Portland St) This popular, lively Welsh pub is not so cool, but is a popular launchpad for a weekend night.

Varsity (☎ 615234; Portland St) This place is student-friendly and has a high space-to-tables ratio but not so much character.

Rummers Wine Bar (Bridge St) Right by the bridge, Rummers has DJs and live Welsh bands Thursday to Saturday.

Coopers Arms (☎ 624050; Northgate St) At the bottom of the hill from the university, this is a popular Welsh venue with frequent live music.

Aberystwyth Arts Centre (☎ 623232; Penglais Rd) Based at the university, the town's main arts venue presents film, drama, dance and music programmes, which can be booked at the TIC.

Commodore Cinema (☎ 612421; Bath St) See the current releases here.

Getting There & Away

The No 420 **National Express** (☎ 0870 580 8080) bus to/from London (£25, eight hours) runs daily.

Other bus services include the No **X32** (£4.95, three hours, about two-hourly Monday to Saturday, two on Sunday) to/from Bangor and Carmarthen (£8, two hours, twice daily) for connections to Swansea and Cardiff. The No **701** (£4.95, 1¼ hours, every two hours Monday to Saturday, two on Sunday) runs to/from Dolgellau via Machynlleth, and the No **551** (£5.50, two hours, hourly Monday to Saturday, two on Sunday) travels to/from Cardigan, with a change at Synod Inn.

Aberystwyth is the terminus of the Cambrian Main Line. Trains run from Shrewsbury (£14.70, 1¾ hours, every two hours, four on Sunday). For connections with the Cambrian Coaster line (northwards to Snowdonia: Barmouth, Porthmadog and Pwllheli) change at Machynlleth.

AROUND ABERYSTWYTH
Devil's Bridge & Falls

For a memorable day trip from Aberystwyth take a ride on the Vale of Rheidol Steam Railway (p706) to the waterfalls at Devil's Bridge (Pontarfynach).

Below this hamlet 12 miles inland, the Rivers Mynach and Rheidol tumble together off the Plynlimon (Pumlumon) Hills down a deep, wooded gorge. Just above the rivers' confluence the Rheidol drops 90m in a series of spectacular **waterfalls** viewed from a steep and narrow woodland path (adult £2.50). Spanning the Mynach, **Devil's Bridge** is itself a famous crossing-point where three bridges are stacked above each other. The lowest was supposedly built by the Knights Templar before 1188, the middle one in 1753 and the uppermost road-bridge in recent times. The viewing platform (adult £1) is a 10-minute round-trip on foot.

Like the terrain, the charges are steep, but unfortunately unavoidable – you can't see anything otherwise. Access to the paths to the falls and bridge viewpoint is from the road bridge itself above.

A sleeping option in the direction of Aberystwyth is the hospitable and tidy **Mount Pleasant Guest House** (☎ 01970-890219; d £44, breakfast £4), about 300m west down the A4120 from the Falls.

North Wales

North Wales is the long-time heartland of Welsh nationalism, having led a prolonged campaign for the survival of the musical and literary culture, and fiercely resisted the obliteration of the Welsh language by English. When you hear Welsh spoken in the trendiest bar on the Llŷn Peninsula, you know it is here to stay.

The region is blessed with extremes of rocky mountain summits and fabulous long sandy beaches, attracting walkers, cyclists and family holidaymakers.

The mountain-lover's big draw is Snowdonia National Park, which stars the highest peak in Wales and England and dozens of other accessible summits. As well as rugged uplands, plunging valleys and great estuaries, the park contains man-made fascinations in the vintage mountain steam-trains, which include the Ffestiniog Railway, and in the magical Portmeirion, the fantasy Italianate village in a lovely setting.

Stretching out along the west and north coasts are the great tidal strands, and towns that offer a mix of outstanding castle fortresses such as Caernarfon and Conwy and resort attractions such as Llandudno and Barmouth.

Off the mainland northwest lies the fertile Isle of Anglesey, with its concentration of ancient sites, the interesting little town of Beaumaris and the ferry port Holyhead. Pointing west out to the Atlantic is the wilder and less-visited Llŷn Peninsula, with its beaches and rocky character.

Over to the east lie the grand house of Erddig near Wrexham and jolly Llangollen with its fine waterside dining.

HIGHLIGHTS

- Mock-defending the castles of **Harlech** (p727), **Conwy** (p733), **Caernarfon** (p736) and **Beaumaris** (p738)

- Riding the vintage **Welsh Highland Railway** (p736) and **Ffestiniog Railway** (p725)

- Hiking to the summit of one of **Snowdonia's peaks** (p719)

- Visiting the other-worldly creation that is the village of **Portmeirion** (p726)

- Cycling or ambling along the gleaming **Mawddach Estuary** (p729)

- Making the boat trip over the sound to saintly **Bardsey Island** (p739)

■ POPULATION: 663,397

■ AREA: 2382 SQ MILES

Orientation & Information

Snowdonia National Park occupies much of the western and midwestern part of North Wales, extending virtually from the north coast almost as far south as Machynlleth. Anglesey lies offshore to the northwest and the Llŷn Peninsula points west out to sea.

Tourist Information Centres (TICs) are found in all the well-visited towns, and are particularly well stocked and informed in the park and main coastal resorts.

Gwynedd, the most northwesterly county, is the most traditionally minded and heavily Welsh-speaking corner of Wales, where 70% of people use the mother tongue.

Activities

For outdoor activities the Snowdonia National Park rules. This section provides a few ideas; more information is given throughout this chapter. TICs all stock leaflets plus maps and guides covering walking, cycling and other activities.

ACTIVITY CENTRES

Several outfits organise mountain sports from a half-day to weekends and longer:

Pathfinder Activities (☎ 07781-121820; www.path findersnowdonia.co.uk) Based near Pwllheli, it does guided walking, climbing and kayaking year-round.

Plas-y-Nant (☎ 01286-650227; www.plasynant.com; Betws Garmon) Near Caernarfon, this activity hostel offers accommodation alongside a range of adventure sports. See also its partner outfit, Snowdon Lodge (p726) at Tremadog.

Surf-Lines (☎ 01286-879001; www.adventureshop@ surf-lines.co.uk) Offers water sports (canoeing, kayaking and coasteering), as well as climbing, mountain-biking and walking.

CYCLING

Mountainscapes and old railway lines make Snowdonia and its neighbouring regions excellent destinations for mountain-biking and cycling – with national-standard options for those at the fitter end of the scale.

The **Lôn Las Cymru**, the south-north Wales touring route, offers two options in the south of Snowdonia National Park, between Machynlleth and Porthmadog, before continuing via the Menai Bridge to the Isle of Anglesey and Holyhead. One highlight is the dedicated cycle path across the causeway into Porthmadog.

For gentle car-free riding, scenic former railway lines can be found in the sea-level

Mawddach Trail, near Dolgellau and sprouting from **Caernarfon**, in the north. North Wales also boasts a leading mountain-bike venue, **Coed-y-Brenin Forest Park**, north of Dolgellau, with a network of signposted tracks ranging from easy to hard.

There's also dedicated off-roading near Betws-y-Coed in the **Gwydyr Forest Park** and in **Beddgelert Forest**, west of the Snowdon massif.

WALKING

The north-coast seaside town of Prestatyn is the end of the **Offa's Dyke Path**, a long-distance route along the Wales–England border. The final three days of the route, from Chirk Castle via Llandegla and Bodfari, show off the varied scenery of this northeastern corner of the region.

For day walks, **Mt Snowdon** (1085m), as the highest peak in Wales, is a natural draw with at least six different paths up to the summit. Those on the southern side are harder but offer the most drama. Serious walkers also head for the neighbouring ranges: the fractured, spiky landscape of Tryfan and the Glyders; the smoother tops of the Carnedau; or the less-frequented areas south around the Moelwyns or Cader Idris. Good base towns in the north include Llanberis, Betws-y-Coed and Beddgelert (the last two are also good hubs for low-level walks). In the south of the region, Dolgellau is a recommended base, and another gateway is the town of Machynlleth (p703).

If the weather is bad on the tops of Snowdonia, walkers can head for the coast. The **Llŷn Peninsula** and **Isle of Anglesey** may have sunshine while the high peaks brood under cloud or rain.

OTHER ACTIVITIES

Thanks to the reliable water of the River Dee, **Llangollen** is a **canoeing** centre (as well as walking and cycling base), where local activity centres arrange instruction and equipment. You can also do **white-water canoeing** and **rafting** at **Canolfan Tryweryn**, near Bala. Canoe instruction and many more activities are also available at the **Plas y Brenin** centre at Capel Curig in the north.

Getting There & Around

Useful publications include the *Wales Bus Rail and Tourist Map & Guide* from the

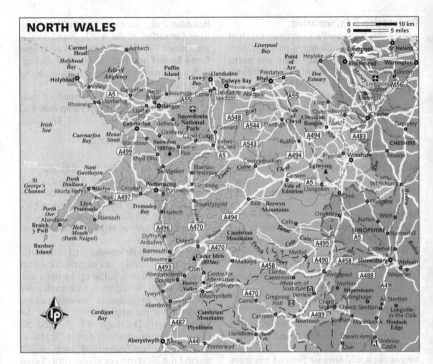

NORTH WALES

Wales Tourist Board and the *Gwynedd Public Transport Map & Timetables* from TICs, park offices and the Gwynedd county **transport unit** (☎ 01286-679535). For Anglesey bus and train timetables, call ☎ 01248-752459, for County Wrexham timetables ☎ 01978-266166. County Conwy timetables are available from Conwy TICs. For individual fares and timetable information contact **Traveline** (☎ 0870 608 2608; www.traveline.org.uk).

Train services to North Wales are good – for more information contact **National Rail Inquiries** (☎ 0845 748 4950) – and include the North Wales Coast line from Chester via Llandudno Junction, Conwy and Bangor to the ferry terminal at Holyhead, and the Cambrian Coaster line from Machynlleth (connections to Birmingham) via Barmouth and Porthmadog to Pwllheli. The Conwy Valley line runs from Llandudno via Betws-y-Coed to Blaenau Ffestiniog, where the narrow-gauge Ffestiniog Railway forms a different kind of train link to Porthmadog.

Multijourney tickets may save you money. The North & Mid Wales Flexi-Rover (£30) is valid for three days' bus and train travel (including on the vintage Ffestiniog Railway) in seven days, and also provides discounted admission to historic sights (call ☎ 0870 900 0777 for details). The North & Mid Wales Day Ranger (£20) covers one day's travel for most train services in this area, and can be bought on the train or at stations. The Gwynedd Red Rover (£4.95) is valid for bus journeys within the county (south, central and northwest Snowdonia and the Llŷn Peninsula), also on some services in northeast Snowdonia, to Betws-y-Coed and Llandudno; buy it from the driver.

NORTHEASTERN WALES

Heading west from England, the north-facing coastline may be lined with so-so beach resorts, but inland the hills set the pulse racing in anticipation of Snowdonia's mountain treats.

Well worth a visit en route are the stately home of Erddig, near Wrexham, and the lively riverbank town of Llangollen, home of the annual International Eisteddfod and a great base for adventure sport.

For travel details see Getting There & Away for the towns (below and p714).

WREXHAM

☎ 01978 / pop 63,084

The main reason for coming to the ordinary town of Wrexham is to visit nearby Erddig, a magnificent, stately 18th-century home and country park.

The **TIC** (☎ 292015; www.borderlands.co.uk; Lambpit St) is open year-round, but is closed on Sunday.

Sights

Inhabited by the Yorke family until 1973, **Erddig** (National Trust; ☎ 355314; adult £7; ☺ house noon-5pm Sat-Wed Easter-Sep, noon-4pm Oct, garden 11am-6pm Sat-Wed Easter-Jun & Sep, 10am-6pm Jul & Aug, 11am-4pm Nov–mid-Dec) provides a rare insight into the 'upstairs-downstairs' relationship between the upper class and servants in Britain. The Yorkes lived here for more than 200 years and were known for the respect with which they treated their staff. Upstairs is a fine collection of furniture, including an impressive state bed,

and original Chinese wallpaper. Downstairs are photographs of servants through the ages and interesting old household devices.

Due to Erddig's popularity, timed admission tickets may be issued. The house lies 2 miles south of Wrexham, off the A525 road to Whitchurch.

Sleeping

Convenient for a trip to Erddig is the comfortable **Grove Guest House** (☎ 354288; 36 Chester Rd; s/d from £22/40).

Getting There & Away

The No 420 **National Express** (☎ 0870 580 8080) bus runs to/from London daily (£23, 5½ hours) and Birmingham via Shrewsbury.

There are other bus services to/from Wrexham such as the No 1 to/from Chester (40 minutes, every 10 minutes, hourly on Sunday) and Nos 555, X5 & 5A to/from Llangollen (30 minutes, every 15 minutes, hourly on Sunday).

Wrexham is on the Chester–Birmingham train line, with services from Chester (15 minutes, about hourly) and Birmingham (£15.20, 1½ hours, every two hours).

EISTEDDFODAU FOR ALL

The **National Eisteddfod** (ey-*steth*-vot, plural eisteddfodau ey-*steth*-vuh-dye) is a celebration of Welsh culture and has become Europe's largest festival of competitive music-making and poetry. Descended from ancient bardic tournaments, where the prize was a post at court, it was reintroduced as a passionate focus of Welsh culture in the 19th century. At the annual event nowadays, over 150,000 visitors attend performances by up to 6000 competitors.

Proceedings are in Welsh, though nonspeakers need not be put off. Audiences include Americans fascinated by their Welsh ancestry, and fringe events feature Welsh bands and artists, which lends a bit of a Glastonbury/Woodstock atmosphere. Held during the first week of August, the venue swings annually between north and south Wales: in 2005 it's in the North Wales district of Eryri; in 2006 in Swansea (for details www.eisteddfod.org.uk).

Children have their own festival, the **Urdd Eisteddfod** (☎ 01970-613100). *Urdd* (irth) is Welsh for youth. The event is held every May at different venues (2005 Wales Millennium Centre, Cardiff). Up to 15,000 performers qualify through a series of local and regional eisteddfodau. Most self-respecting young adults, however, head for the fringe events at the main festival.

Wales' devotion to music and poetry extends way beyond its borders. The colourful **International Eisteddfod** (inquiries ☎ 01978-862000) is held every July at a splendid permanent venue in Llangollen and turns the town into a global village. Established after WWII to promote international harmony, the event attracts 2500 participants from over 40 countries as diverse as Kurdistan and Nigeria. In addition to daily folk music and singing and dancing competitions, gala concerts feature international stars. In 2004 Michael Ball and Aled Jones got top billing. A simultaneous and growing **Fringe Festival** (inquiries ☎ 860030) also takes place with talks, poetry and music.

LLANGOLLEN

☎ 01978 / pop 2930

Jolly little Llangollen straddles the frisky River Dee in the steep-sided Vale of Llangollen, and is well known as the venue of the International Eisteddfod held every July.

The town is also good for coffee-drinking and river-watching, shopping for antiques, and relaxing steam-train or horse-drawn canal-boat trips – it's worth at least a long afternoon. You can also add an evening to sample good dining. The ruined medieval Valle Crucis Abbey lies nearby and there are grand walks round the local heights, while a number of water-sport and activity centres have grown up around the Dee's reliable rapids and the mountain setting.

Engineer Thomas Telford, the Scottish 'Colossus of Roads', dragged the town head on into the 19th century by routing both the London–Holyhead (A5) road and the Llangollen Canal through it. Two miles up the canal is the scenic weir at the Horseshoe Falls, while down the canal is a Telford *meisterwerk*, the soaring Pontcysyllte Aqueduct.

Orientation & Information

Llangollen is small enough to walk around in five minutes. The **TIC** (☎ 860828; www.nwt .co.uk; Castle St; ⊙ 9.30am-5.30pm) is in the old chapel. Internet access is available at the **library** (☎ 869600; Internet free) upstairs. Booking is advisable.

Sights

Intriguing **Plas Newydd** (☎ 861314; adult £3; ⊙ 10am-5pm Easter-Oct) was the home of the Ladies of Llangollen, Lady Eleanor Butler and Sarah Ponsonby (see the boxed text p716). In their own words, the women were 'seized with the oak-carving mania' and transformed the house using a bizarre combination of Gothic and Tudor romantic styles in stained-glass windows and wood panels. They also created formal gardens.

The house lies 400m uphill southeast of the town centre. Last entry is at 4.15pm. Don't confuse it with the National Trust stately home of the same name on Anglesey.

Llangollen Steam Railway (☎ 860979; www.llan gollen-railway.co.uk; return trip £8; ⊙ daily Easter-Oct, most Sat & Sun year-round, closed Jan) puffs along a 7-mile line via Berwyn and the Horseshoe Falls to Glyndyfrdwy and Carrog. The TIC has timetables.

Every day horse-drawn narrowboat **canal trips** (☎ 860702) depart regularly from Llangollen Wharf, just up from the town bridge. Choose from a 45-minute trip (£4) and a two-hour return cruise to Telford's outstanding 38m-high Pontcysyllte Aqueduct (£7.50).

St Collen's Parish Church (Church St; ⊙ 2-6pm Mon-Fri mid-May–Sep) has an exquisite carved oak roof and a memorial to the Ladies of Llangollen, who lie in the graveyard.

The ruin atop the conical hill above the town is the 16th-century **Castell Dinas Brân**. The walk up from the town is exhilarating and the views are fantastic.

The atmospheric, well-tended 13th- and 14th-century ruins of **Valle Crucis Abbey** (Cadw; ☎ 860326; adult £2, admission free Easter-Sep; ⊙ 10am-5pm Easter-Sep, 10am-4pm Oct-Easter) occupy a beautiful setting, 1.5 miles northwest of the town on the A542 to Ruthin.

A mile out on the same road, you pass the small **Llangollen Motor Museum** (☎ 860324; adult £2.50; ⊙ 10am-5pm Tue-Sun Easter-Oct, open by arrangement Nov-Easter) with over 30 vehicles on display dating between 1910 and 1970.

Activities

Walk along the vale on the canal towpath to the weir at Horseshoe Falls or climb to Castell Dinas Brân (the TIC stocks walking literature). Bryn Hughes of **Ceiriog Country Holidays** (☎ 01691-718398; www.walestrails.com) leads guided walks and tours of the area.

For water sports (white-water rafting, canoeing) and other adventure activities (rock-climbing, gorge-walking, mountain-biking and others), either as solo activities or as a multi-activity break, contact the following:

Adventure Activity Solutions (☎ 845009; www .adventure-solutions.co.uk; per half day £60) Also kiting and archery.

JJ Canoeing & Rafting (☎ 860763; www.jjraftcanoe .com; Berwyn Rd; 2hr rafting £32) A mile west of town, it specialises in canoeing and water sports, with a bunkhouse and café on site (see p715).

Llangollen Bike Hire (☎ 860605; www.northwales bikehire.co.uk; 23 Castle St; per hr/full day £3/16) Mountain-biking specialists (canal and mountain routes supplied).

Pro Adventure (☎ 861912; 23 Castle St; per half day £35) Also runs survival courses.

Festivals & Events

Llangollen is the permanent venue of the **International Eisteddfod** (as opposed to the Na-

LLANGOLLEN

tional Eisteddfod; see the boxed text, p713), which annually attracts over 2500 participants in a celebration of global song and dance.

Sleeping

Accommodation around Eisteddfod time in July goes early; book in advance.

Cornerstones (☎ 861569; 15 Bridge St; s/d from £35/55; ✗) This 16th-century house has gorgeous antique-furnished rooms, sloping floorboards and oak beams.

Gales (☎ 860089; 18 Bridge St; s/d Mon-Thu £50/60, Fri-Sun £40/50; ✗) Near the bridge, attached to the best place to eat in town, Gales's rooms retain a simple, original 18th-century character with updated furnishings.

Plas Tegid (☎ 861013; Abbey Rd; d from £20) Come here for a warm welcome and simple, good-value rooms.

Greenbank (☎ 861835; Victoria Sq; s/d £26.50/44) A central Victorian town coaching inn with views of Castell Dinas Brân, Greenbank has an attractive restaurant, too.

Canoe Inn (☎ 860763; www.jjraftcanoe.com; Mile End Mill, Berwyn Rd; dm without/with en suite £12/14, r £17.50) A budget riverside bunkhouse run by JJ Canoeing & Rafting (p714).

Llangollen YHA Hostel (☎ 0870 770 5932; llangollen@yha.org.uk; dm £10.60) Another budget option, this is a former Victorian manor-house hostel, 1.5 miles east of the town centre. Staff can help you plan activities, thanks to their connections with activity centres.

THE LADIES OF LLANGOLLEN

Lady Eleanor Butler and the Honourable Sarah Ponsonby, the Ladies of Llangollen, lived in Plas Newydd from 1780 to 1829 with their maid Mary Carryl. They fell in love in Ireland, where their aristocratic Anglo-Irish families discouraged the relationship, and in a bid to live together, the women eloped to Wales disguised as men. They set up home in Llangollen and devoted themselves to 'friendship, celibacy and the knitting of stockings'.

Their relationship was well known and respected, and the ladies received visits from many national and literary figures of the day, including the Duke of Wellington and William Wordsworth, who penned the words 'sisters in love, a love allowed to climb, even on this earth above the reach of time'.

Their friendship with their maid Mary was also close. Having managed to buy the freehold to Plas Newydd, she bequeathed it to them after her death. Lady Eleanor died in 1829, Sarah Ponsonby two years later. They are buried at St Collen's Parish Church in the centre of Llangollen.

Camp at **Eirianfa Camping Ground** (☎ 860919; Berwyn Rd; 2-person tent sites £8), 1 mile west of Llangollen, and **Wern Isaf Farm** (☎ 860632; 2-person tent sites £8), across the river and to the east.

Eating

Gales Wine & Food Bar (☎ 860089; 18 Bridge St; mains £10; ☼ lunch & dinner Mon-Sat) Irresistible Gales has bulging lunch and dinner menus, offering both staple and imaginative dishes, and a good wine list, served by happy staff.

Corn Mill (☎ 869555; Dee Lane; mains £10; ☼ noon-9.30pm) The beautifully converted Corn Mill has beechwood flooring and cable-wired staircasing. Sitting on the over-river deck, eating from the contemporary menu (fancy bream fillets and spinach frittata?) while enjoying the sound of rushing water is an unexpectedly good Welsh experience.

Fouzi's (lunches £6) Head to this trendy daytime place by the bridge for coffee, panini and crêpes.

James Bailey (Castle St) This delicatessen near the TIC does Welsh oggies (meat, potato and onion pasties).

Drinking & Entertainment

Sun Inn (☎ 860233; Regent St) Great atmosphere and live music on most nights, plus an open fire in winter and excellent ales.

Wynnstay Arms (Bridge St) Another good place for a bevvy.

Getting There & Away

National Express (☎ 0870 580 8080) coach No 420 runs daily to/from Wrexham (30 minutes) and London (£23, five hours) via Birmingham and Shrewsbury.

Bus Nos 5A, 555 and X5 run daily to/from Wrexham (30 minutes, every 15 minutes, hourly on Sunday). No 94 does the same journey seven times daily Monday to Saturday, four times on Sunday. Transport west into Snowdonia is quite limited; No 19 runs to Betws-y-Coed (one hour; every two hours Monday to Saturday) and Llandudno, and No 94 continues to Bala, Dolgellau and Barmouth.

The nearest main-line train station (the steam train doesn't count) is Ruabon on the Shrewsbury–Chester line; Shrewsbury to Ruabon (30 minutes, at least every two hours). A taxi from Ruabon costs about £6. Call **Premier Cars** (☎ 861999).

AROUND LLANGOLLEN
Chirk Castle

This **castle** (NT; ☎ 01691-777701; adult £6; ☼ noon-5pm Wed-Sun Easter-Sep, noon-4pm Oct) is a magnificently preserved Marcher fortress built in 1310 and still inhabited. In 1595 the Myddelton family moved in and adapted it for a more draught-proof and elegant lifestyle. The castle lies 8 miles southeast of Llangollen, 2 miles west of Chirk village, and has fine views over the English borderlands.

SNOWDONIA NATIONAL PARK

In a country overflowing with uplands, Snowdonia National Park (Parc Cenedlaethol Eryri) lords it over the rest, with the highest mountains and steepest valleys of any region in Wales. Dive into the rocky clefts and scramble up the slopes, armed with walking boots, mountain sportsgear or just a widening pair of eyes for guaranteed excitement. The sea is so close that it is simple for visitors to shift in pace between the challenging terrain and the relaxing sandy beaches.

Mount Snowdon at 1085m is the highest piece of rock in Wales and England. No world-beater in elevation, it still strikes a noble pose at the head of a precipitous horseshoe of peaks. Scaling the summit, on foot or by mountain railway, is the goal of a great number of visitors – the park was designated in 1951 as much to prevent the peak from being loved to death as from

being neglected or built upon. Don't miss plenty more mountain hiking around what is an extensive region, from the neighbouring ranges of the Carneddau and Glyders to Cader Idris above Dolgellau in the south. The climbing, white-water rafting, mountain biking and pony trekking are also excellent.

The surrounding coastline features the World Heritage–listed chain of wonderful medieval castles at Caernarfon, Harlech, Conwy, and Beaumaris, each attached to a town of some charm.

Hard-won mineral treasures – copper, gold and slate – buried deep in the mountains permitted the inhabitants a tough living through the ages. Several mines have been reinvented as visitor attractions, along with

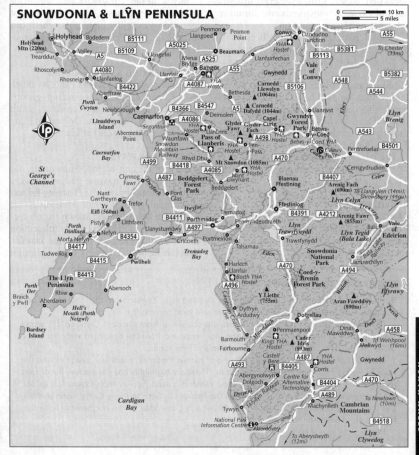

SNOWDONIA & LLŶN PENINSULA

NORTH WALES

vintage railways like the Ffestiniog and Welsh Highland lines, which once hauled the booty down to the sea. The area's high rainfall (pack your waterproof, or buy one here!) is cannily exploited by hydroelectric power stations, and Electric Mountain at Llanberis is one massive underground scheme you can see for yourself.

Orientation & Information

Although the focus is on Snowdon, the park extends 35 miles east-west and a full 50 miles north-south down to Mid Wales.

At your first TIC or park office pick up a copy of *Eryri/Snowdonia*, the free annual visitor newspaper, which is packed with information on the park plus activities and organised walks. Visit www.eryri-npa.gov .uk and www.visitsnowdonia.com for more information.

Helpful park information offices combined with local TICs, are open year-round at Betws-y-Coed and Dolgellau, and seasonally at Aberdovey, Beddgelert, Blaenau Ffestiniog and Harlech. TICs in other towns, both within the park boundary and just beyond, also carry park maps and information. TICs are at Llanberis (open year-round, though not daily in winter), Barmouth, Tywyn, Porthmadog and Machynlleth.

The park's 24-hour weather number is ☎ 09068-500449 (premium rate). Most TICs display weather forecasts.

Activities

CANOEING & WHITE-WATER RAFTING

The **National Whitewater Centre – Canolfan Tryweryn** (p730), near Bala, operates on year-round, white-water rapids.

CYCLING

Dedicated mountain-bike venues with sign-posted graded routes include top spot **Coed-y-Brenin Forest Park** (p728), **Gwydyr Forest Park** (p723) and **Beddgelert Forest Park** (p722). See www.mbwales.com for trail information.

For safety and environmental reasons, a voluntary daytime summertime ban operates on Mt Snowdon on three (otherwise perfectly legal) bridleways, 10am to 5pm daily June to September. You get a better balance of riding at the previously mentioned sites anyway.

Where it follows two alternative routes through the park, the cross-Wales **Lôn Las Cymru** cycle touring trail is particularly hill, but gorgeous.

Bicycle Beano (☎ 01982-560471; www.bicycle -beano.co.uk) organises a week-long tour of Snowdonian cycling highlights, which can include the Llŷn Peninsula, with vegetarian catering.

PONY TREKKING & HORSE RIDING

The **Snowdonia Riding Stables** (☎ 01286-650342; per hr £15, half day £33) takes riding groups through fine scenery at Waunfawr, south of Caernarfon. See also the Dolbadarn Pony Trekking Centre (p720) at Llanberis.

VINTAGE RAILWAYS

A former mining region, Snowdonia has several vintage narrow-gauge railways that run steam trains: the **Ffestiniog Railway** (Porthmadog to Blaenau Ffestiniog; see p725), the **Welsh Highland Railway** (north section Caernarfon to Rhyd Ddu, south section out of Porthmadog; see p725), the **Snowdon Mountain Railway** (Llanberis to the summit;

SNOWDONIA SCENIC TREATS

North Wales is a wonderful place to stand in awe and sigh. Admission to the landscape is permanently free, but you do need plenty of that rare local commodity: clear skies.

Catch one of these big-picture mountain and sea views: from Criccieth Castle (p739) across Tremadog Bay to Harlech Castle (p727) and vice versa, and from the Beaumaris waterfront (see p738) on Anglesey over the waves to the mainland mountains.

Close-ups of the rocky slopes from the grid of narrow mountain roads and passes around the main Snowdon massif are also worth savouring. These are highlights: the Caernarfon–Beddgelert road (A4085), a trip largely duplicated by the Welsh Highland Railway from Caernarfon (p736); the Beddgelert to Pen-y-Gwryd road (A498); the Pass of Llanberis to Pen-y-Gwryd again (A4086); and the craggy section of A5 through the Glyder and Carneddau ranges northeast of Snowdon from south of Bethesda to Capel Curig.

Happy sighs and skies…

see p720) and the **Talyllyn Railway** (Tywyn to Abergynolwyn; see p728). Shorter lines include the **Llanberis Lake Railway** (see p720), the **Fairbourne & Barmouth Railway** and the **Bala Lake Railway**.

WALKING

Mt Snowdon is the main destination for walkers (see the boxed text, below), and Llanberis is the largest nearby base. However, mountain and ridge walks on other slightly lower ranges around the park can be as good and less crowded. In the north try the rugged Glyders (northeast of Snowdon), the domed Carneddau (northeast of the Glyders), the Moelwyns (south of Snowdon) and Moel Hebog and the Nantlle Ridge (southwest of Snowdon). For gentler forest and river trots head for Betws-y-Coed.

In the south, a well-used ascent of Cader Idris (southwest above Dolgellau) is a fine day's walk. Here are also the Arans (northeast of Dolgellau, southwest of Bala), the lesser-known Arenigs (west of Bala) and the challenging Rhinog Ridge (east of Harlech).

Park information centres and some TICs stock useful brochures on the main routes up Snowdon (six) and Cader Idris (three), and a collection of independent route books. Some walks graded easy may still go near steep slopes or over scrambling terrain. Accidents happen, usually on the way down. On average there are 70 serious incidents annually, and 10 people die. If in doubt about your abilities, consider a national park guided walk; ask at TICs or see the *Eryri/ Snowdonia* newspaper.

Be prepared to deal with hostile weather on the tops at any time of year, even on days that start out clear and sunny. Carry warm and waterproof clothing, also food, the appropriate large-scale OS map and a compass. Call for weather information (☎ 09068-500449) before setting out.

Sleeping

Snowdonia has a plentiful supply of accommodation in towns, villages and outlying farmhouses. Betws-y-Coed, Llanberis and Dolgellau have the highest number of mid-range B&Bs and hotels. Budget bed-seekers can use a combination of YHA and independent hostels: see town entries for Bala, Bangor, Beddgelert, Betws-y-Coed, Capel Curig, Caernarfon, Dolgellau, Harlech, Llanberis and Porthmadog.

Mt Snowdon has four YHA hostels:

Llanberis (p721; ☎ 0870 770 5928; llanberis@yha .org.uk), **Snowdon Ranger** (p722; ☎ 0870 770 6038; snowdon@yha.org.uk), **Pen-y-Pass** (p721; ☎ 0870 770 5990; penypass@yha.org.uk) and **Bryn Gwynant** (p722; ☎ 0870 770 5732; bryngwynant@yha.org.uk).

Getting There & Around

For information on buses, trains and multi-ride tickets covering Snowdonia, see p711.

Bus connections between regional towns are adequate (but very limited on Sunday).

SNOWDON UNDER YOUR OWN STEAM

Although half a million people do it annually, the hike to the 1085m summit of Mt Snowdon is still amazing. Lording it over a horseshoe of ridges and other peaks, the summit offers stupendous views on a clear day, and even on overcast ones the clouds may part to give teasing glimpses of the landscape beneath your feet.

Ignore the train option (see the Snowdon Mountain Railway, p720) and you can choose one of six main routes to the top. The easiest and least interesting is the **Llanberis Path** (five hours), which runs beside the railway track. The shortest and, in winter, the safest is the **Snowdon Ranger Path** (five hours), starting from the Snowdon Ranger YHA hostel near Beddgelert. Elsewhere, routes from Pen-y-Pass have the advantage of starting height (but limited car parking at a cost): the **Pyg Track** (5½ hours) is more interesting but involves scrambling, while the **Miner's Track** (five hours) starts gently and steepens. The undemanding **Rhyd Ddu Path** (five hours) approaches from the west, while the most challenging route is the **Watkin Path** from the south, with an ascent of over 1000m from Nantgwynant.

For variations on these walks see the Snowdonia chapter of Lonely Planet's *Walking in Britain*. The Snowdon Sherpa buses (see p719) stop at all the trailheads, and there are also options for accommodation near them all.

NORTH WALES

For Mt Snowdon's mountain towns and trailheads, catch the liveried buses of **Snowdon Sherpa** (☎ 01286-870880), which operates a network that includes Beddgelert, Betws-y-Coed, Capel Curig, Llanberis, Pen-y-Pass, and the surrounding towns of Bethesda, Caernarfon, Llandudno, Llanrwst and Porthmadog. Buses run every hour or two (fewer on Sunday), typically from about May to September. Timetables are available from TICs.

For more information, contact **Traveline** (☎ 0870 608 2608; www.traveline.org.uk).

For details on the multiride tickets that cover park, see p711.

LLANBERIS
☎ 01286 / pop 1842
Cheerful Llanberis is the base town for Mt Snowdon, and a magnet for all manner of climbers and walkers from alpinists to daytrippers. The Snowdon Mountain Railway starts its puffing ascent here and the two town lakes, Llyn Padarn and Llyn Peris, provide water sports and country walks, all within a valley enclosed by immense slate and rock slopes. Welsh is spoken all around this area.

Originally built to house workers in the nearby Dinorwig slate quarry, Llanberis is home to both the Welsh Slate Museum and Electric Mountain, an enlightened, underground hydroelectric power station, which has a worthwhile guided tour.

Accommodation fills up in July and August, for Llanberis is an easy place to linger and walk your legs off.

Orientation & Information
Llanberis is bypassed by the A4086, which also separates the village from the two lakes. Almost all the places to stay and eat are strung out along the High St – you can't get lost. The **TIC** (☎ 870765; llanberis.tic@gwynedd.gov.uk; High St; 9.30am-5.30pm daily Easter-Oct, 11am-4pm Wed & Fri-Sun Nov-Easter) is opposite the post office. For Internet access, see Pete's Eats (p721).

Sights
Fancy letting the train take the strain to the top of Mt Snowdon? Then Britain's only public rack-and-pinion railway, **Snowdon Mountain Railway** (☎ 0870 458 0033; www.snowdonrailway.co.uk; return £20, ascent only £14; up to half-hourly 9am-5pm Easter-Oct), is for you. Since 1896 it has been making the 5-mile, one-hour, 900m climb from Llanberis to the summit station, where hunkers a grim, incongruous 1930s café (due to be sensitively replaced over the coming years). Schedules are weather-dependent and summertime queues can be long. 9am departures in September and October cost half price depending on numbers.

The **Electric Mountain** (☎ 870636; tour £6; 10.30am-4.30pm Wed-Sun Feb-Mar & Nov-Dec, daily Apr-May & Sep-Oct, 9.30am-5.30pm Jun-Aug) is a sparky name for the extraordinary rapid-response, pumped-storage Dinorwig power station. Built deep inside Elidir Mountain, the station uses energy in times of surplus to pump water 600m up from Llyn Peris to the Marchlyn reservoir. When the British switch on the kettle during the break in *Coronation Street*, the water can be released to surge down underground turbines for instant power and tea. The visitors centre (on the far side of the bypass from the town) has free exhibits, and the guided underground bus tour is worth the money.

Vast slate mountains provide the backdrop to the **Welsh Slate Museum** (☎ 870630; www.nmgw; admission free; 10am-5pm Easter-Oct, 10am-4pm Sun-Fri Nov-Easter) in the old Dinorwig quarry beside Llyn Padarn. You can visit the old workshops, see the largest working waterwheel in Britain and attend demonstrations by skilled workmen as they split and dress slate for tiles.

The **Llanberis Lake Steam Railway** (☎ 870549; return trip £6; 11am-4pm daily Jul-Aug, most days Mar-Jun & Sep-Oct) runs the length of Llyn Padarn to Llanberis and back. The 5-mile return-trip takes one hour.

It's a pleasant walk to the small ruin of **Dolbadarn Castle** (Cadw; open site), built in the 13th century to guard Llanberis Pass and sited at the southeastern pass end of the town.

Activities
Llanberis-based outfits that organise adventures on and around Snowdon include **Dolbadarn Pony Trekking Centre** (☎ 870277), which operates from Dolbadarn Hotel (p721) and charges £15 per hour, and **Energy Cycles** (☎ 871892; per half/full day £12/20) has local route information and hires out all-purpose bikes. **High Trek Snowdonia** (☎ 871232; www.hightrek.co.uk) offers guided walking, rock-climbing and scrambling for individuals and groups. **Padarn Watersports Centre** (☎ 870556;

Llyn Padarn) organises kayaking, canoeing, raft building, rock-climbing, abseiling and walks up Mt Snowdon.

Sleeping

BUDGET

Cae Gwyn Camp Site (☎ 870718; per person £3.50) You'll find this site 2 miles southeast of Llanberis, up at Nant Peris.

Snowdon House (☎ 870284; 3 Gwastadnant; tent sites £3.50, dm from £7.50) Situated at Nant Peris, 3 miles southeast of Llanberis en route to Pen-y-Pass, this has a bunkhouse, camping sites and a house to let.

Llanberis YHA Hostel (☎ 0870 770 5928; llanberis@yha.org.uk; dm £11.80; ☒ daily Easter-Oct, with 48hr notice Mar, Sep & Oct) Originally a quarry manager's dwelling, this hostel has views over the slate quarry and three en-suite double rooms in addition to the dorms. It lies half a mile southwest of the town.

Jesse James Bunkhouse (☎ 870521; Penisarwaun; dm from £9) Three miles north of town on the Bangor road, this is a popular walkers' base with a range of accommodation. Bring a sleeping bag and food. JJ is a mountain guide.

Pete's Eats (dm/2-bed r £12/30) Above the café (right) is an eight-bed mixed dorm and two twin rooms sharing a large self-catering lounge. Breakfast (in the café) costs extra.

Heights Hotel (☎ 871179; 74 High St; dm without/with breakfast £14/19, s/d with en suite £25/50) The Heights is a lively place to stay, with a youthful buzz and a popular bar with live music. Rooms are plain and spacious with good views.

MID-RANGE

Beech Bank Guest House (☎ 870414; 2 High St; s/d £17.50/35) Three blocks west of the TIC and overlooking Llyn Padarn, this large Victorian dwelling has friendly staff and a good-value B&B.

Alpine Lodge Hotel (☎ 870294; 1 High St; d from £50) Next door to Beech Bank is a similarly grand house with a range of rooms with en suite and lake views.

Bron-y-graig (☎ 872073; Capel Coch Rd; s/d high season £32/56) Here's a friendly and refined four-star B&B in a former chapel-minister's house with a splendid terraced front garden. Find it 150m off High St (turn at the Spar supermarket). Credit cards are not accepted.

Pen-y-Gwryd (☎ 870211; s/d £28/56, with en suite £34/68) This lovely historic mountaineers'

hotel was used by the 1953 Everest team as a training base – their signatures adorn the ceiling. Residents sit round a single table for the evening meal, and bar food is also available. It lies 7 miles southeast, a mile beyond the Llanberis Pass.

Dolbadarn Hotel (☎ 870277; High St; s/d £20/40) and **Padarn Lake Hotel** (☎ 870260; High St; s/d £36/60) are a pair of conventional mid-range places near the centre with restaurants and bars.

TOP END

Royal Victoria Hotel (☎ 870253; www.royal-victoria -hotel.co.uk; s/d £55/110) Near the Snowdon Mountain Railway station, the Royal is the top roost in town with a first-rate restaurant.

Eating

Pete's Eats (☎ 870117; 40 High St; mains around £5; ☒ 8am-8pm, 8am-9pm Jul & Aug; ☐) The hiker's café, steamy Pete's is crowded with craggy types swapping experiences over generous portions of food before and after their exertions. Try the Big Jim mixed grill (£9.20) if you dare. Upstairs is a free mountain map and book library, and there is also Internet access (5p per minute, minimum 50p) and showers (£2). For accommodation, see left.

Y Bistro (☎ 871278; 45 High St; mains £14; ☒ dinner Tue-Sat) This is the classy place to splash out on Welsh ingredients with a French twist, and creative dishes such as wild board and black pudding.

Y Caban (☎ 870434; High St; mains from £6; ☒ lunch & dinner) This demi-trendy café-bistro at the station end of town serves satisfying meat and vegetarian meals and specials from breakfast time until 9.30pm.

Vaynol Arms (☎ 870284; Nant Peris; mains from £7) A cosy climbers' drinking hole, 2 miles southeast towards the pass, the Vaynol Arms serves meals to suit all pockets; it also has real ales – and real fires.

Heights Hotel (☎ 871179) Another climbers' haunt – its pub has its own climbing wall (see left).

Getting There & Away

Bus Nos 85 and 86 run to/from Bangor (45 minutes, half-hourly Monday to Saturday, fewer on Sunday). Bus No 88 runs to/from Caernarfon (25 minutes, twice hourly, hourly on Sunday); a few services continue to Nant

Peris. The Snowdon Sherpa bus No S1 to/ from the Snowdon trailhead at Pen-y-Pass (20 minutes) departs mostly hourly, including Sunday.

BEDDGELERT
☎ 01766

Lying in the heart of the mountains, pretty Beddgelert makes a lovely base for walkers and sportsfolk. The beautiful Pass of Aberglaslyn is a short walk below, the Snowdon massif looms to the northeast, and no-one should pass the shop Glaslyn Ices without trying one of its 23 home-made flavours (including Turkish Delight).

The town's name, meaning 'Gelert's Grave', refers to one of the best-known Welsh legends, that of Prince Llywelyn's faithful dog, killed by his master in the belief the dog had savaged his baby son. The truth emerged too late that Gelert had fought and killed a wolf attacking the baby.

The village has a **TIC** (☎ 890615; ☺ 9.30am-12.30pm & 1.30-5.30pm Easter-Oct, 9.30am-5.30pm Jul & Aug, 9.30am-4.30pm Fri-Sun Nov-Easter) on the road heading out south.

Sights & Activities
A mile east of the village is the **Sygun Copper Mine** (☎ 510100; fwww.syguncoppermine.co.uk; adult £7.95; ☺ 10am-6pm Easter-Oct, 10.30am-4pm Nov-Easter). Mined since Roman times, this is now a worthy, child-friendly draw complete with underground tour and gold panning.

A popular local **walk** follows the old Welsh Highland Railway track-bed down the Pass of Aberglaslyn. In preparation for the railway's restoration (see p725), the Fisherman's Path diverts around three closed tunnels. When the river is high, you need to exercise caution in places.

Beddgelert Forest, 2 miles north on the A4085 Caernarfon road, has off-road cycling for all levels. **Beics Beddgelert** (☎ 890434; per 2hr/4hr £8/£12) rents bikes and will supply route information.

Sleeping & Eating
Plas Colwyn (☎ 890458; s/d from £20/40) In the centre of the village, Plas Colwyn also offers Welsh food in its restaurant.

Plas Tan y Graig (☎ 890310; www.plastanygraig .co.uk; s/d from £40/50) This nicely upgraded Victorian guesthouse has en-suite rooms and a licensed bar-lounge.

Two YHA hostels and a camping ground serve Snowdon summiteers.

Beddgelert Forest Campsite (☎ 890288; 2-person tent sites £6.80-10.20) Large and well-equipped, a mile north of town on the Caernarfon road, 1.5 miles from a pick-up point for the Rhyd Ddu Path.

Bryn Gwynant (☎ 0870 770 5732; bryngwynant@yha .org.uk; dm £10.60; ☺ daily mid-Feb-Oct) Near the steep Watkin Path trailhead, 4 miles east on the A498.

Snowdon Ranger (☎ 0870 770 6038; snowdon@yha .org.uk; dm £10.60; ☺ daily Apr-Aug) For the steady Snowdon Ranger Path, 5 miles north on the Caernarfon road. Call for detailed opening times.

Beddgelert Tearooms & Bistro (☎ 890543; s/d £25/42; mains around £14; ☺ dinner) This small traditional inn is a café by day and a very good restaurant by night, which offers local meat and fowl including Anglesey pheasant. Rooms, some with exposed flagstone walls, are attractive.

Getting There & Away
Snowdon Sherpa buses include Bus No 24, which runs to/from Caernarfon (79 minutes), continuing to Pen-y-Pass, every two hours Monday to Saturday (fewer on Sunday). Bus Nos 97 and 97A run to/from Porthmadog (30 minutes), and Capel Curig and Betws-y-Coed (one hour), at least every two hours (fewer on Sunday).

CAPEL CURIG
☎ 01690

Muddy boots are no problem in little Capel Curig, one of the park's oldest village resorts at the top of the Vale of Llugwy, below the Carneddau and Moelwyn Ranges. One reason is **Plas y Brenin – the National Mountain Centre** (☎ 720214; www.pyb.co.uk; bunkhouse £6, s/d £20/40). This large, busy centre offers courses, including one-day tasters, in hill-walking, rock-climbing and kayaking, and there's a bar, climbing wall and dry ski-slope at the base, plus a B&B and bunkhouse.

Capel Curig YHA Hostel (☎ 0870 770 5746; capelcurig@yha.org.uk; dm £14.40; ☺ daily mid-Feb–Oct, Fri & Sat Nov–mid-Feb) Enjoy this hostel's looming views to the Snowdon Horseshoe from its location in the village. **Bron Eryri Guest House** (☎ 720240; www.eryriguesthouse.fsnet.co.uk; s/d from £30/50) Bed down in this pretty Victorian house with cosy rooms and good views.

Bryn Tyrch Hotel (☎ 720223; s/d £39/52, with en suite £41/59; lunches £6, dinner mains £9) Capel boasts a great restaurant in this lovely little stone-built hotel, where a good wine list complements a delicious contemporary menu.

Hikers and climbers drink at the bar at the Bryn Tyrch Hotel, in the back bar (built into the rock face) at **Cobdens Hotel** (☎ 720243), and also at Plas y Brenin centre.

The Snowdon Sherpa S3 stops here en route between Bethesda and Pen-y-Pass. Other bus services are as for Betws-y-Coed (below).

BETWS-Y-COED
☎ 01690 / pop 2034

Betws-y-Coed (betoos-y-*koyd*) is a scenic and prosperous tourist village in the wooded Vale of Llugwy, which fills up with visitors at holiday times. The name means 'chapel in the wood' after the 14th-century village church, and is usually shortened to Betws.

Lying 12 miles northeast of Mt Snowdon, Betws makes a good base for walking in the main mountains if you have transport, or for walks and cycling in the hills and forests nearby. On dismal Snowdonia days it's a good place to go shopping for maps, books and waterproof clothing.

Orientation & Information
The village stretches along narrow riverside Holyhead Rd, with all amenities on or just off it.

The **National Park Information Centre & TIC** (☎ 710426; ☾ 9.30am-5.30pm Easter-Oct, 9.30am-4.30pm & closed for lunch Nov-Easter) is in the Royal Oak Stables near the train station.

Activities
There are numerous long **walks** in the surrounding area, as well as the short walk to Swallow Falls (below). The 28-sq-mile Gwydyr Forest, to the northwest of Betws, is full of trails and sights. The *Gwydyr Forest Guide* costs £2 at the TIC and contains nine graded walks.

Gwydyr is also a venue for **mountain-biking** (see www.mbwales.com). Hire bikes and get route information at **Beics Betws** (☎ 710829; per half/full day £14/18), at the top of the steep little road that leads off the main Holyhead Rd up behind the post office.

In good weather while the energetic go walking or cycling, local day-trippers **picnic**

on the boulders of the gushing River Llugwy at the midtown Pont-y-pair Bridge.

Pony trekking in the Gwydyr Forest is organised by **Ty Coch Farm** (☎ 760248; Penmachno; per hr £14), 6 miles south of Betws. Ride for an hour or tackle the popular to-the-pub-and-back ride (around four hours; £31).

Near Betws is **Swallow Falls** (adult £1), 2 miles west, off the A5. Approach the falls along a fine riverside path starting at Pont-y-pair Bridge. **Conwy Falls** (adult £1) is 2 miles south off the A5.

Sleeping
Betws is rolling in accommodation, much of it on the narrow and at-times busy A5 through-road in and beyond town.

Riverside Camping & Caravan Site (☎ 710310; Old Church Rd; per person £5) This lies on the river, 200m beyond the train station.

Betws-y-Coed YHA Hostel (☎ 710796; dm £11.80; ☾ daily) This youth hostel, attached to the Swallow Falls Hotel complex opposite the entrance to Swallow Falls, is a functional place that fills a gap in the accommodation market but has few charms – except the adjacent hotel bar with pub grub – and isn't for lengthy stays. Find it on the A5, 2 miles west of Betws.

Tandinas (☎ 710635; s/d with en suite from £32/48) In the woods half a mile west this B&B has panoramic views of the vale. To get here, cross the mid-town Pont-y-pair Bridge, go left and continue.

Garth Dderwen (☎ 710491; www.garth-dderwen .co.uk; d from £46; ✗) This refreshed Victorian villa, up from the main drag, is friendly and easy on the mood.

The Courthouse (Henllys; ☎ 720534; d £60-70) It's fascinating to stay in this converted 1867 town courthouse and police station, where features identifying its former functions appear in unexpected places throughout: a solid door with a little sliding window in it, and vaulted courthouse roofing in converted bedrooms. The riverbank garden is an ideal place to enjoy a summer martini, and guests from around the world have contributed to the collection of police helmets that hangs above the bar.

Over the midtown Pont-y-pair bridge, town life calms down. Cross and go right for **Bryn Avon** (☎ 710403; s/d £35/52; ✗) and **Swn y Dwr** (☎ 710648; s/d from £35/50; ✗). Go up left to the modern **Tyn y Bryn** (☎ 710273; s/d from

£28/42; ⊠), which has a lovely large garden, and **Summer Hill** (☎ 710306; s/d £22/37, with en suite £25/46; ⊠), with cottagey furnishings.

Eating

The choice of daytime cafés is large, but considering Betws's size, interesting dining is limited. If you have transport, you may like to head to the Bryn Tyrch Hotel restaurant (p722) in Capel Curig.

Cross Keys (☎ 710334; Holyhead Rd; mains £8; ☜ lunch & dinner) This reliable pub-hotel has a regular selection such as Welsh lamb chops and curry of the day, plus good desserts, and a cosy bar.

Conventional restaurants at hotels **Plas Dderwen** (☎ 710388; Holyhead Rd) and **Fairhaven** (☎ 710307; Holyhead Rd) have long menus, at least with lots of fresh fish (mains £8 to £14).

Getting There & Away

Lying midway along the scenic Conwy Valley line, the train is the best way to reach Betws-y-Coed. Train services run direct to/from Llandudno (40 minutes) and Blaenau Ffestiniog (30 minutes), five times daily (three on Sunday).

Snowdon Sherpa bus services include the No S2 to/from Llanrwst (10 times daily, once a day to/from Llandudno) via Betws-y-Coed to/from Pen-y-Pass (seven times on Sunday). The No S3 runs to/from Bethesda and Capel Curig via Betws-y-Coed, and to/from Pen-y-Pass (twice daily, none on Sunday). The No 97 & 97A runs to/from Porthmadog (55 minutes, three daily, none on Sunday) via Beddgelert and Capel Curig.

BLAENAU FFESTINIOG

☎ 01766 / pop 3961

Lying in the heart of Snowdonia yet excluded from the national park, Blaenau (blay-nye) Ffestiniog is an infamous slate-mining town overshadowed by staggering mountains of slag waste.

This dramatic contrast of working 'Snowdonia' encircled by picture-postcard Snowdonia makes it an intriguing place. Blaenau also has two good local attractions: the Ffestiniog Railway, which terminates here and is perhaps the best in Wales, and the Llechwedd Slate Caverns.

Formerly the centre of the slate-mining industry that sustained North Wales during the 19th century, Blaenau was responsible for roofing much of England. The slag heaps exist because for every ton of usable slate extracted, nine tons of rubble are created. Perched on the mountainside the town looks OK in sunshine – enhanced in early summer by rhododendron blooming on the slag – but in rain it is not a place for depressives.

The Ffestiniog Railway (p725) is a scenic 13.5-mile steam railway that once carried the slate from Blaenau to the seaport.

The **TIC** (☎ 830360; Church St) is a friendly, modern place with a good stock of books and maps.

Sights

Formed from old mine-workings, the **Llechwedd Slate Caverns** (☎ 830306; adult £8.25; ☜ 10am-6pm) offers two tours: the 25-minute Deep Mine tour, including a descent on the UK's steepest passenger railway (1:1.8, that's 1.8m across for every metre up or down), and the Miner's Tramway tour through an 1846 network of level tunnels and huge caverns.

Find it 1 mile north of the town centre up the A470 Betwys-y-Coed road.

Sleeping & Eating

Afallon (☎ 830468; Manod Rd; s/d £17.50/35) A spotless place a short mile southeast of the train station along the A470 Ffestiniog road.

Isallt (☎ 832488; Church St; s/d £20/40) Right next to the train station, this is a friendly, straightforward B&B, which also runs a daytime café.

Cae Du (☎ 830847; s/d £24/48; 3-course dinner £12) Lying just outside town, this lone mountainside B&B is friendly and has glorious views. Walkers like it – footpaths lead directly to nearby peaks. You can have dinner by arrangement. Find it signed 1.5 miles south of Blaenau centre, off the A470 Ffestiniog road, up a single-track lane where you must open and shut gates at the railway crossing.

Queens Hotel (☎ 830055; Church St; s/d from £45/60; dishes £6) The historic central town hotel serves light meals.

Getting There & Away

Bus services include the No 1 to/from Caernarfon (1¼ hours, hourly Monday to Saturday, fewer on Sunday) via Porthmadog (30 minutes). The No 35 runs to/from Dolgellau (50 minutes, six daily Monday to

Saturday), and the No 38 travels to/from Barmouth (65 minutes, at least four daily Monday to Saturday) via Harlech.

Blaenau Ffestiniog is the terminus for the narrow-gauge Ffestiniog Railway from Porthmadog (see below), although the bus takes half the time, and for the modern-day Conwy Valley line to/from Llandudno (£5.20, 70 minutes, at least five daily, three on Sunday in summer, fill-in bus in winter) via Betws-y-Coed (30 minutes).

PORTHMADOG

☎ 01766 / pop 3008

People come to Porthmadog for two main reasons – to ride the scenic vintage Ffestiniog Railway, and to visit the nearby fantasy village of Portmeirion.

At the mouth of the tranquil Glaslyn Estuary, the town also provides a classic view of Mt Snowdon. Enjoy the vista from the Cob, a mile-long estuary causeway, which is five minutes' walk from the centre and also carries the vintage railway. Mix in the marina, trendy artefact shops, a fine nearby beach and the town's location on the Cambrian Coaster railway line – and slightly down-at-heel Porthmadog is a hit.

The town grew around the 19th-century harbour built by William Alexander Madocks to handle slate from the mountain mines. Slate quarrying was once the main employment of the town, and continues today to a minor degree.

Next to the Ffestiniog Railway station at the end of the Cob is a TIC (☎ 512981; porthmadog .tic@gwynedd.gov.uk; High St; 9.30am-5.30pm Easter-Jul & Sep-Oct, 9.30am-6pm Aug, 10am-5pm Thu-Tue Nov-Easter). Porthmadog's full-sized train station (Cambrian Coaster line) lies at the far western end of town.

KK Cycles (☎ 512310; 141 High St; per day £9) can recommend cycling routes around the Glaslyn estuary and further afield. Hire mountain bikes (per half/full day £7.50/12.50) from Snowdon Lodge (p726) in Tremadog.

Beautiful long Blackrock Sands, one of North Wales' best beaches, lies 2 miles west of town on the Morfa Brychan road.

Ffestiniog Railway & Welsh Highland Railway

Vintage engines and carriages date back to 1860 on the other-worldly 13.5-mile, narrow-gauge Ffestiniog Railway (☎ 516073; www .festrail.co.uk; halfway/full return trip £8.50/14). The line was built between 1832 and 1836 to haul slate down from the mines of Blaenau Ffestiniog to the port at Porthmadog.

Trains run two to eight times daily from Easter to October, with limited March and November services. For a cheaper ticket (£11), depart on the first or last trains (booking is advisable).

At the western end of town (near the main-line station) you can ride another piece of railway history, albeit a short one for the time being, a 1.75-mile section of the former Welsh Highland Railway (☎ 513402; www .whr.co.uk; return trip £3.70). This is the southern end of the spectacular line that once ran

---

WELSH STEAM RAILWAYS RIDE AGAIN

Wales' narrow-gauge lines are survivors from an industrial heyday of mining and quarrying. Most use steam and diesel engines, often travelling over terrain that defied standard-gauge trains. Many travel through glorious scenery, so their reincarnations are worth riding even if you're no rail buff.

The invention of the steam engine and the rapid spread of the railway transformed 19th-century Britain, but 20th-century industrial decline and road building left many lines defunct. The infamous Beeching report of 1963 closed dozens of rural links and stations, and five years later British Rail fired up its last steam engine.

Enthusiasts couldn't let their passion die, however, and a preservation movement gathered pace. They bought old locomotives, rolling stock, disused lines and stations and restored them – financing their labours of love by offering rides, often with the help of the people who'd previously worked the line.

Nine restored lines around Wales form a group called Great Little Trains of Wales (inquiries Talyllyn Railway ☎ 01654-710472), which offers a Narrow-gauge Wanderer pass (£55), valid on the trains for nine consecutive days.

22 miles northward through the mountains via the Pass of Aberglaslyn and Beddgelert to Caernarfon, and is gradually being reinstated in full. The more substantial northerly section between Caernarfon and Rhyd Ddu is already up and running (see p736).

Sleeping & Eating

Tyddyn Llwyn Hotel (☎ camping 512205, hotel 513903; Morfa Bychan Rd; 2-person tent sites £11, s/d £35/60) Camp or stay in comfortable accommodation here, a half mile along Borth Rd in open countryside. Rooms have an en suite.

Snowdon Lodge (☎ 515354; www.snowdonlodge .co.uk; Church St; dm/d with light breakfast £13/35; 🖳) A mile north of Porthmadog in little Tremadog, the 1888 birthplace of TE Lawrence (Lawrence of Arabia) is now a leading, oft-buzzing Snowdonia hostel. Breakfast is taken in what transforms into the pleasant daytime **Cafe Lawrence** (🕑 11am-5pm Fri-Sun Easter-Oct). There are also a bar and serviceable self-catering kitchen.

Yr Hen Fecws (☎ 514625; www.yrhenfecws.com; 16 Lombard St; s/d £45/55; mains from £8; 🗶) The tasteful place in town to eat and sleep, this stylishly restored stone cottage has exposed-stone walling in its spotlit bedrooms. Enjoy fresh fish, home-made pie and good vegetarian choices in its bistro.

Grapevine (☎ 514230; 152 High St; mains around £9.50; 🕑 7.30am-9pm) A welcoming all-day place that serves vegetarian and baguette breakfasts, pasta lunches, and chicken and steak dinners.

For good beer and pub food try the **Australia** (High St) and, 1 mile north in Tremadog, the **Golden Fleece**.

Getting There & Away

Porthmadog is a hub for this part of Wales.

BUS

National Express (☎ 0870 580 8080) coach No 545 passes through daily from London via Chester and Caernarfon, continuing to Pwllheli. It stops near Snowdon Lodge.

Other bus services are the Snowdon Sherpa Nos 97 and 97A to/from Betws-y-Coed (55 minutes, three daily, none on Sunday) via Beddgelert, Pen-y-Gwryd (for Pen-y-Pass) and Capel Curig. The No 1 travels to/from Blaenau Ffestiniog (30 minutes) and Caernarfon (40 minutes), hourly, fewer on Sunday. Bus No 3 runs to/from Pwllheli (£1.85, 35 minutes, every half hour, six on Sunday), while Bus No X32 runs (five daily, two on Sunday) to/from Dolgellau and Aberystwyth (£5, two hours 20 minutes), and Bangor (£4, one hour).

TRAIN

Porthmadog lies on the scenic Cambrian Coaster line, with trains from Machynlleth (£8, 1¾ hours) and Pwllheli (20 minutes) every two or three hours (fewer on Saturday and Sunday). For vintage trains to Blaenau Ffestiniog, see p725.

AROUND PORTHMADOG
Portmeirion

Portmeirion is a **seaside village** (☎ 01766-770000; www.portmeirion-village.com; adult £5.70; 🕑 9.30am-5.30pm) with a magical twist.

Welsh architect Sir Clough Williams-Ellis spent the years 1926 to 1976 planning and creating his vision of a perfect village in a perfectly romantic place. Portmeirion is thus an otherworldly collection of 50 Italianate buildings, several saved from destruction elsewhere, set on dinky streets around a piazza above a beautiful, broad tidal estuary.

If the pastels and proportions are not to everyone's personal taste, the delightful location and sense of utopian pursuit may be.

Over time Portmeirion has inspired novels, films and the Beatles, and Noel Coward wrote *Blithe Spirit* here. Many people know it as the set for the 1960s cult TV series *The Prisoner*, and fans are still drawn to the annual convention in March. The village was the set for an episode of *Dr Who*, and George Harrison chose it for his 50th-birthday celebrations.

Accommodation is available in village cottages as well as at the **Hotel Portmeirion** (☎ 01766-770000; www.portmeirion-village.com; village d £135, hotel d from £155). **Castell Deudraeth** (☎ 01766-772400; d £155-240), a Victorian mansion that's also part of the village, has a bar and informal grill, and contemporary rooms.

Portmeirion lies 1.75 miles east of Porthmadog across the Cob, then a mile south off the main road. Bus No 98 runs directly to the site twice daily but late afternoons only. More buses and Ffestiniog Railway trains run to the village of Minffordd, from where it's a 1-mile walk.

HARLECH

☎ 01766 / pop 000

Harlech Castle is the most dramatic fortress in Edward I's 13th-century 'iron ring'. The glowering defence overlooks Tremadog Bay from the top of what was a sea cliff when it was constructed. Only the Snowdonia mountains to the north match its majesty.

The weeny hill town, which shares the castle outcrop, offers tea with glorious views, arty gift shops (courtesy of visitor bucks through the ages) and city-standard dining out.

Further exploration along the coastline reveals tempting sandy beaches such as Shell Island, 3 miles south (only accessible at low tide via a causeway) near Llanbedr.

There's a TIC (☎ 780658; High St; ⏲ 9.30am-5.30pm Easter-Oct) above the castle. For train travellers, the station lies on the plain below, meaning a steep 15-minute climb to the castle.

Harlech Castle

You can have a good run-around defending the towers of the **castle** (Cadw; ☎ 780552; adult £3; ⏲ 9.30am-5pm Apr-May & Oct, 9.30am-6pm Jun-Sep, 9.30am-4pm Mon-Sat & 11am-4pm Sun Nov-Mar), which together with the fortresses at Caernarfon, Conwy and Beaumaris is a World Heritage Site. Up to 950 craftsmen from all over Britain were mobilised by the brilliant military architect Master James of St George for its construction (1283–89) following Edward I's final conquest of the Welsh forces.

The fortress's great natural defence is the seaward cliff-face. When it was built, ships could sail supplies right to the base. The landward side is defended by the twin-towered **Great Gatehouse**, with three portcullises, arrow slits and murder holes (portals for boiling fluids). The body of the castle is rectangular with concentric walls; a lower outer wall and a massive internal curtain wall braced by four imposing drum towers.

Sleeping & Eating

Llanbedr YHA Hostel (Harlech YHA; ☎ 0870 770 5926; llanbedr@yha.org.uk; dm £10.60; ⏲ daily Easter-Oct) This hostel lies 3 miles south, well-placed for the coast.

Byrdir House (☎ 780316; www.byrdir.com; High St; s with en suite £34.50, d without/with en suite £45/65) Handsome, spacious white-painted Byrdir House has been tastefully and elegantly modernised.

Castle Cottage (☎ 780479; www.castlecottage harlech.co.uk; s/d from £35/76; 3-course dinner £26) A step from the castle, this is a well-run guesthouse with fine rooms and a sound restaurant (with dinner reductions for guests).

Cemlyn Restaurant & Tearoom (☎ 780425; High St; s/d from £45/60; 2-/3-course dinners £21.50/23.50) Balancing classy food with friendly informality throughout the hungry day, the Cemlyn offers top tea and cake, light meals (Welsh rarebit £4), and tempting dinners featuring, for example, goose, lemon sole and aduki bean casserole. Overnight guests in the airy en-suite rooms get use of the deck and lounge. Room 1 has the best view.

Plas Café (☎ 780204; High St; mains around £7) Enjoy tea with one of the best views in Wales, looking out from an elegant Victorian conservatory and terraced lawn. Meals are served all day.

Getting There & Away

From Harlech bus No 38 runs to/from Barmouth (30 minutes, hourly, none on Sunday) and to/from Blaenau Ffestiniog (30 minutes, 10 times daily, four direct, six change at Oakley Arms to No 1).

Trains on the scenic Cambrian Coaster line (about every two hours) run to/from Machynlleth (£6.90, 1¼ hours) and Porthmadog (30 minutes).

BARMOUTH (ABERMAW)

☎ 01341 / pop 2251

Barmouth is a jolly and, in summer, a bustling family seaside resort. Sandy beaches extend north for miles from the town's seaward side, while around the corner heading inland is one of Wales' finest water and mountainscapes, the beautiful Mawddach (mow-thach) Estuary.

The TIC (☎ 280787; barmouth.tic@gwynedd.gov.uk; Station Rd; ⏲ Mar-Nov), inside the train station, sells leaflets on local walks.

Sights & Activities

Cross the mouth of the estuary on a wooden railway viaduct (with footpath) and walk or cycle the atmospheric **Mawddach Trail** (see p729). Alternatively, climb up steep alleys to the cliffs of **Dinas Oleu** (265m) above, where the popular Panorama Walk has outstanding views to the estuary.

Ferries cross the estuary to the sandy isthmus, Penrhyn Point, and there meet the narrow-gauge **Fairbourne & Barmouth Steam Railway** (☎ 250362; ferry return trip £2.50, train £6.40; ✹ Easter-Sep), which puffs from here 2 miles along the seafront to anonymous Fairbourne village.

The classic **Three Peaks Yacht Race** (inquiries ☎ 280298; www.threepeaksyachtrace.co.uk) sets off from Barmouth every June.

Sleeping & Eating

Wavecrest Hotel (☎ 280330; 8 Marine Pde; s/d from £29/50) Wavecrest is one of the better seaview B&Bs that line Marine Parade, across the tracks from the train station.

Dros-y-Dwr (☎ 280284; www.drosydwr.freeserve .co.uk; 6 Porkington Place; s/d from £30/42) A cut above most guesthouses, this has big, plain rooms, stripped wooden floors and sea views.

Llwyndu Farmhouse (☎ 280144; d from £74; 2-course dinner from £20) On the hillside 2 miles north of town on the A496, this 16th-century house has impressive rooms that overlook the sea. A candlelit restaurant serves good evening food.

Bae Abermaw Hotel (☎ 280550; www.abermaw .com; Panorama Hill; s/d from £94/138) This great granite Victorian building with an open-plan contemporary interior sets off estuary views with aplomb.

Two town restaurants draw the cognoscenti: **Inglenook** (☎ 280807; Harbour Lane; mains around £8) is a quality seafood house, while the cosy **Bistro** (☎ 281009; Church St; mains £6-12) has an international menu.

Getting There & Away

Bus No 38 to/from Blaenau Ffestiniog (65 minutes, at least four daily Monday to Saturday) goes via Harlech. Bus No 94 to/from Wrexham via Llangollen, Bala and Dolgellau (£2, 25 minutes) runs seven times daily (four on Sunday).

Trains on the scenic Cambrian Coaster line run to/from Machynlleth (55 minutes) and Porthmadog (45 minutes) every two or three hours (three on Sunday).

TYWYN & AROUND
☎ 01654

Tywyn is best known as the base of the steam-driven **Talyllyn Railway** (☎ 01654-710472; return trip £10; ✹ mostly daily Easter-Oct). This puffs inland for 7 miles to just past the village of Abergynolwyn, where it once served slate quarries. The line was the inspiration for *Thomas the Tank Engine*, the children's stories by the Rev W Awdry, one of the line's first volunteer guards in the 1950s. A small **railway museum** exhibits some narrow-gauge locomotives, and there's a **TIC** (☎ 01654-710070; High St).

The scenic B4405 road from Tywyn to Dolgellau passes Abergynolwyn, where you can then turn to head 3 miles north to the tumbledown remains of the 13th-century **Castell y Bere** (Cadw; open site) in the Dysynni Valley. Unusual for being a Welsh construction, it was built in 1222 by Llywelyn the Great, but seized by the Normans and abandoned soon after. Walk 300m northeast down the road to the quaint 12th-century **St Michael's Church** and graveyard. Note the leper's window, through which, in less salubrious times, sufferers could observe the sacraments.

DOLGELLAU
☎ 01341 / pop 2407

Set amid hills, Dolgellau (doll-*geth*-lie) is a true Welsh market town of stoic stone buildings, grocery shops selling local cheese, and people clomping about in walking boots. The town is big on the hiking and mountain-bike scenes, with Cader Idris (893m) to the south, one of Snowdonia's headline peaks, and the honeypot mountain-biking trails of Coed-y-Brenin Forest Park to the north. Gentler cycling along the scenic Mawddach Estuary nearby is also popular.

The town owes much of its handsome if unornamented looks to the wealth generated by the wool industry in the 19th century. Indeed, it has over 200 listed buildings, the highest concentration in Wales.

The **TIC** (☎ 422888; tic@dolgellau@hotmail.com; Eldon Sq; ✹ 9.30am-5.30pm daily Easter-Sep, 9.30am-4pm Thu-Mon Oct-Easter) is in the central square. Upstairs is a permanent **exhibition** (admission free) on the area's Quaker heritage. The radical religious community established itself here in the 17th century.

The town's July festival, the **Sesiwn Fawr Dolgellau** (☎ /fax 423355; www.sesiwnfawr.com), is one of Wales' best. For three days the sounds of Welsh folk music and ale appreciation emanate from the recreation ground by the River Wnion.

Activities
CYCLING

For cruisy scenic riding you can't beat the **Mawddach Trail**, which heads southwest from Dolgellau. The town itself is also on a junction of the north-south Lôn Las Cymru cross-Wales cycle touring route. **Coed-y-Brenin Forest Park** (inquiries ☎ 01341-440666; www.mbwales.com), 8 miles north along the A470, is one of the UK's gnarliest mountain-biking destinations, with 70 miles of signposted trails graded beginner to expert. No-one in the café notices if you're filthy, and there's a bike wash and cycle-parts shop.

Hire mountain bikes in Dolgellau at **Greenstiles Bike Shop** (☎ 423332; per half/full day £12/18) and **Dragon Bikes & Kites** (☎ 423008; Smithfield St; per day £13).

WALKING

The beautiful **Mawddach Trail** nearby is a converted railway line that runs for 7.5 miles along the southern side of the Mawddach Estuary to Barmouth. It is accessible from the car park beside the town bridge. There's also the 2-mile **Torrent Walk** along a shaded ravine that was the private path for 'ladies and guests' of the Caerywch Estate. Reach the walk by heading east along the A470; it's signposted off the B4416 road to Brithdir.

The TIC stocks three leaflets (40p each) on the paths up **Cader Idris**. Carry clothing for cold and wet weather even if it's fine as you start out. The standard route is a five-hour-return hike up the 'Dolgellau' or Ty Nant Path (southeast from Ty Nant Farm on the A493). The longest and easiest route is the Tywyn or Llanfihangel y Pennant Path (10 miles, six hours), northeast from the terminus of the Talyllyn Railway (p728) at Abergynolwyn. The shortest and steepest is the Minffordd Path (six miles, five hours), northwest from just below the Minffordd Hotel on the A487 road to Machynlleth.

OTHER ACTIVITIES

Abergwynant Farm & Pony Trekking Centre (☎ 422377; per hr from £10), on the estuary 3.5 miles southwest of town on the A493, offers daily **pony treks** through forests and along the foothills of Cader Idris. Here you can also go **fishing** for trout and salmon on the River Gwynant for £2 a day.

Sleeping

According to legend, anyone who spends the night atop Cader Idris will awake mad or a poet. Luckily, the area has a wide range of alternative accommodation.

Tan-y-Fron (☎ 422638; Arran Rd; 2-person tent sites £12, d £38/50) Stay at the campsite or do B&B at the attached country house with a pretty garden, 500m east of town.

Kings YHA Hostel (☎ 0870 770 5900; kings@yha.org.uk; dm £10.60; ☺ daily Apr-Sep, Fri & Sat Mar & Oct) Lying in a creekside position en route to Cader Idris, Kings is a fine base for exploring the area, and is self-catering only. Go west along the A493, the southern side of the estuary; it's signed after 3.5 miles. From Dolgellau take bus No 28, get off at the Abergwynant Trekking Centre, and walk 1 mile up the lane.

Staylittle B&B (☎ 422355; Peny-y-cefn Rd; s/d £20/38) A nicely simple place, Staylittle – don't be put off by the name – offers plain rooms and home-made jam at breakfast. Cross the bridge, go left and climb for 250m.

Ivy House (☎ 422535; Finsbury Sq; s/d from £35/42) This is a regular, central Georgian style town house.

Aber Cottage (☎ 422460; Smithfield St; s/d £35/55; 5-course dinner £27.50; ☒) An exceptional hostess underpins the culture of homely cheer at this gorgeous cottage B&B (with tearoom and restaurant, see below). It is hard to overpraise the décor and hospitality. Guests who have checked-out can even return at the end of their day's activity for a shower (£3) before setting out for home.

Tyddn Mawr (☎ 422331; Islawrdref, Cader Rd; s/d £40/56) Another outstanding B&B, Tyddn Mawr is here for its open mountainside location directly below the crags and peak of Cader Idris; the summit path runs near to the farm. Rooms are huge and come with an en suite, and the mountain peace (on a calm day) is wondrous. Find it along a lane (signed initially Tywyn) 2.5 miles southwest of the town centre.

Eating

Aber Cottage Tearoom & Restaurant (see left; ☎ 422 460; Smithfield St; 5-course dinner £27.50; ☒) Heavenly cakes and fine cooking mark out homely Aber Cottage. Daytime soup-seekers have a choice of 10 warming home-made broths (£3.50), and evening diners can enjoy fresh local produce, and dishes such as chicken in Marsala (£14).

Dylanwad Da (☎ 422870; 2 Smithfield St; mains £14; ☺ 10am-4pm & dinner Tue-Sat) This modern restaurant and coffee house brings city cuisine to Dolgellau, offering Welsh and international dishes in a contemporary interior.

NORTH WALES

Y Sospan (☎ 423174; Queen's Sq; mains £7-14) A popular all-day café and quality restaurant near the TIC.

Self-caterers can indulge in scrummy Welsh nosh at the Popty R Dref deli, off Eldon Square, and stock up on basics at the **Spar** (Smithfield St).

Getting There & Away

Bus Nos 32 and X32 run to/from Machynlleth (including the Centre for Alternative Technology) eight times daily, twice on Sunday. The No X32 runs five times daily to/from Aberystwyth, and Bangor via Caernarfon. Bus No 94 travels to/from Barmouth (£2, 25 minutes, seven daily, four on Sunday), as well as Bala, Llangollen and Wrexham.

BALA

☎ 01678 / pop 1980

Bala is a small market town at the tip of Llyn Tegid (Bala Lake), Wales' largest natural lake. Water sports are the town's main draw; they're played out on the lake's placid waters and at river rapids out of town at the unique National Whitewater Centre.

The **TIC** (☎ 521021; Pensarn Rd; ⏱ 10am-5.30pm Easter-Oct, 10am-4pm Fri-Mon) is in the lakeside leisure centre 500m southwest of the town centre.

Activities

The **Bala Adventure & Water Sports Centre** (☎ 521 059; www.balawatersports.com; Foreshore, Pensarn Rd) offers introductory sessions (half/full day £33/55) in windsurfing, sailing, canoeing, white-water rafting, mountain-biking, rock-climbing and abseiling. It's near the TIC.

National Whitewater Centre – Canolfan Tryweryn (☎ 521083; www.ukrafting.co.uk; rafting from £20) lies 3.5 miles northwest of Bala on a 1.5-mile stretch of the River Treweryn. Class-IV white-water tumbles here year-round, dependent on releases from the Llyn Celyn reservoir above. Book at least two days in advance, and check the water levels with the centre before you travel.

The **Bala Lake Steam Railway** (☎ 540666; return trip £6.70; ⏱ 4 trips daily Easter-Sep) runs the 4.5-mile length of the lake down the southern bank to Llanuwchllyn. Vintage locos depart from a little station, half a mile south of town off the B4391, for a 1.5-hour return trip.

Cycling around Bala allows you to explore the lakeside, quiet lanes and challenging forestry tracks. Hire bikes and get route details at **Bala Bike Shop** (RH Roberts; ☎ 520252; High St; per half/full day £7.50/12.50).

Sleeping & Eating

Pen-y-bont Touring & Camping Park (☎ 520549; Llangynog Rd; 2-person tent sites £10; ⏱ Apr-Oct) Pitch a tent close to the lake a mile south off the B4391.

Cynwyd YHA Hostel (☎ 01490-412814; The Old Mill, Cynwyd; dm £8.50; ⏱ Easter-Sep) A simple self-catering hostel, it's located 10 miles northeast of town near Corwen, below the Berwyn Mountains.

Bala Backpackers (☎ 521700; www.bala-backpackers.co.uk; 32 Tegid St; dm £10; ✄) This bright, new hostel packs in the beds, has Internet access, snack-making facilities and offers breakfast for £3 extra.

Traian (☎ 520059; 95 Tegid St; s/d £20/40) Clean and friendly, this does basic B&B.

Plas-yn-Dre (☎ 521256; High St; 3-course dinner £16) Bite into a Welsh-influenced menu of lamb and trout dishes, plus regulars such as lasagne, in Plas-yn-Dre's elegant old dining room.

Getting There & Away

Bus No 94 passes through Bala seven times daily (four on Sunday), en route between Barmouth (one hour) and Dolgellau (35 minutes), continuing to Llangollen.

LLANDUDNO

☎ 01492 / pop 14,872

Developed as an upmarket Victorian destination, Llandudno, which lies just outside Snowdonia National Park, is the largest seaside resort in Wales. It boasts a handsome mile-long seafront of regal hotels, seethes with holiday-makers in summer and attracts a steady stream of pensioners year-round.

Its position straddles the low-lying neck – with sweeping beaches each side – of a spectacular 2-mile-long limestone headland, the Great Orme (207m). With its tramway, cable car and superb views over to Snowdonia's peaks, this natural feature is the town's most absorbing attraction.

In 1861 the Liddell family, whose daughter was Lewis Carroll's model for *Alice in Wonderland*, summered in the house that is now the St Tudno Hotel. They later built their own house, now the Gogarth Abbey Hotel.

Orientation & Information

To the northeast lies the grand promenade along North Shore Beach, to the southwest stretches Conwy Bay and West Shore Beach. Mostyn St, parallel to the seafront, is the main shopping street, where branches of all main banks can be found, and also the stop for regional buses. The train station lies 400m back from the promenade

There's a **TIC** (☎ 876413; 1-2 Chapel St; ☙ 9am-5.30pm Easter-Oct, 9.30am-5pm Mon-Sat Nov-Easter). For Internet access head to the **library** (☎ 574010; Mostyn St; admission free) or **Cyber Skills** (☎ 874627; 50 Madoc St; per ½hr £2.50; ☙ Mon-Sat).

Bubbles Laundrette (25 Brookes St) opens daily.

Sights & Activities

There's little clue from town as to the joys of the **Great Orme** headland: superb 360-degree views, Neolithic sites and an encyclopaedic collection of flowers, butterflies and seabirds. The headland is a designated **country park** (inquiries ☎ 874151) and Site of Special Scientific Interest. The leaflet *Discovering the Great Orme* costs 75p from the TIC.

Ascend the slopes in a 1902 tramcar on the **Great Orme Tramway** (☎ 876749; one way/return £3/4; ☙ 10am-6pm Easter-Oct), which leaves every 20 minutes from the top of Church Walks, or by **cable car** (☎ 877205; one-way/return £4.95/5.50), which departs subject to the weather, from Happy Valley above the pier. At the top is a visitors centre with picnic tables, a café and leaflets on the natural history.

The elegant 1877 Victorian **pier** extends 670m into the sea, and was once chiefly an embarkation point for Isle of Man steamers.

Guide Friday (☎ 879133; full trip £5; ☙ May-Sep) does hop-on/hop-off **sightseeing trips** that combine Llandudno and Conwy. Buses leave from the pier half-hourly and make 11 stops.

Take a peek at North Wales' top contemporary art venue, the **Mostyn Gallery** (☎ 879 201; 12 Vaughan St; admission free; ☙ 11am-6pm Mon-Sat), which has changing exhibitions that are usually rewarding. **Llandudno Museum** (☎ 876517; 17-19 Gloddaeth St; adult £1.50; ☙ 10.30am-1pm & 2-5pm Tue-Sat, 2.15-5pm Sun Easter-Oct; 1.30-4.30pm Tue-Sat Nov-Easter) displays a number of local history artefacts and *objets d'art*.

Alice in Wonderland Centre (☎ 860082; 3 Trinity Sq; adult £2.95; ☙ 10am-5pm daily Easter-Oct, 10am-5pm Mon-Sat Nov-Easter) recreates scenes from the Lewis Carroll book, and is somewhere to take children on a rainy day.

A popular excursion from Llandudno is to spectacular **Bodnant Garden** (p733).

Sleeping

Llandudno boasts 400 hotels and guesthouses, so finding a bed is rarely a problem. There are no camping facilities in the area but there is a new hostel.

Llandudno Hostel (☎ 877430; www.hostelworld .com; 14 Charlton St; dm without/with en suite & breakfast £13/15) This comfy renovated five-storey hostel has family rooms but there is no self-catering.

Hawarden Villa Hotel (☎ 860447; 27 Chapel St; s/d £20/40) A welcoming, modest place near the TIC.

Abbey Lodge (☎ 878042; 14 Abbey Rd; s/d from £65/70) Stay in a modern, high-grade guesthouse in a lovingly restored 1870 home with bathtubs and a pretty garden.

Lighthouse (☎ 876819; www.lighthouse-llandudno .co.uk; Marine Dr; ste from £77/135) Head to bed in

---

SOMETHING SPECIAL

It sounds ordinary, a place on the seafront where you can have a sandwich or a bowl of chips, wearing your (albeit clean) shorts or jeans. But **Osborne House** (☎ 860330; www.osbornehouse .com; 17 North Pde) is not an ordinary 'café-grill'. It is a most beautiful town-house hotel that welcomes anyone who steps off the promenade with an interior that gives Victoriana a good name. Black walls, drapes and columns set off polished floors, twinkling chandeliers and marble fireplaces. Whatever you choose – morning coffee, lunch or tea – try to get a seat beside the bar at the high-top table, which is marble and dreamily skylit (natural skylighting is also a feature of the rest of the dining area). The atmosphere is casual given the room prices (see 732), and there's no formal dress code. The sandwich menu starts from £3.50, Welsh afternoon tea including bara brith (traditional fruitcake, literally 'speckled bread') is £6 and a lunchtime bite of crayfish tails £5.50. As the evening light fades from the sky, the candles are lit for dinner and the à la carte menu comes into its own.

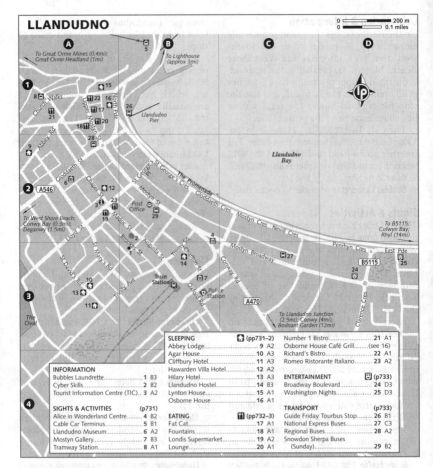

LLANDUDNO

SLEEPING	⌂ (pp731–2)
Abbey Lodge	9 A2
Agar House	10 A3
Cliffbury Hotel	11 A3
Hawarden Villa Hotel	12 A2
Hilary Hotel	13 A3
Llandudno Hostel	14 B3
Lynton House	15 A1
Osborne House	16 A1

EATING	🍴 (pp732–3)
Fat Cat	17 A1
Fountains	18 A3
Londis Supermarket	19 A2
Lounge	20 A1

INFORMATION	
Bubbles Laundrette	1 B3
Cyber Skills	2 B2
Tourist Information Centre (TIC)	3 A2

SIGHTS & ACTIVITIES	(p731)
Alice in Wonderland Centre	4 B2
Cable Car Terminus	5 B1
Llandudno Museum	6 A2
Mostyn Gallery	7 B3
Tramway Station	8 A1

Number 1 Bistro	21 A1
Osborne House Café Grill	(see 16)
Richard's Bistro	22 A1
Romeo Ristorante Italiano	23 A2

ENTERTAINMENT	🎭 (p733)
Broadway Boulevard	24 D3
Washington Nights	25 D3

TRANSPORT	(p733)
Guide Friday Tourbus Stop	26 B1
National Express Buses	27 C3
Regional Buses	28 B2
Snowdon Sherpa Buses (Sunday)	29 B2

luxurious rooms in the converted former lighthouse (in use until 1985) on a 100m-high cliff edge at the end of the Great Orme promontory.

Osborne House (see right; ☎ 860330; www.osborne house.com; 17 North Pde; ste from £135; 🏊) This fabulously decorated seafront town-house hotel has suites only, with a sea view. Guests have use of the swimming pools of nearby sister hotel the Empire.

St David's Rd features several B&Bs worth considering:

Agar House (☎ 875572; www.agarhouse.co.uk; No 17; s/d from £27/46)

Cliffbury Hotel (☎ 877224; www.cliffburyhotel.co.uk; No 34; s/d £24/48)

Hilary Hotel (☎ 875623; kjbooony@tiscali.co.uk; No 32; s/d £25/42)

Eating & Drinking

Osborne House Café Grill (see left; lunches £3.50-9, mains £8.50-15; 🕙 10.30am-10pm, 10.30am-9pm Sun) Classy lunch and dinner with skylighting for all. See also the boxed text, p731.

Romeo Ristorante Italiano (☎ 877777; 25 Lloyd St; meals £7-14) The time-honoured place for pizza and pasta (from £7), and grills (around £14).

Two foodie bistros are upmarket **Richard's** (☎ 875315; 7 Church Walks; 3-course dinner £25; 🕙 dinner Tue-Sat) and cosy, woody **Number 1** (☎ 875424; Old Rd; mains £15; 🕙 dinner Mon-Sat).

Head for Upper Mostyn St for trendy café-bars that serve contemporary platters (£2 to £7) with a good pint, or just a pint on its own.

Fat Cat (☎ 871844; 149 Upper Mostyn St) Real ale and good burgers.

Fountains (☎ 875600; 114 Upper Mostyn St) A high ceiling and outdoor seating.

Lounge (☎ 876120; 143 Upper Mostyn St) The newest designer venue.

There's a Londis minimarket on the junction near the TIC.

Entertainment

Llandudno is full of party people. Clubbers head to **Broadway Boulevard** (☎ 879614; Mostyn Broadway), and over-21s to the Buzz Club upstairs at **Washington Nights** (☎ 877974; East Pde).

Getting There & Away

BUS

National Express (☎ 0870 580 8080) bus No 545 passes through Llandudno daily to/from London (£24, eight hours) via Birmingham and Chester, and to/from Pwllheli (£6, two hours) via Bangor.

Other bus services are Nos 5 & 5X to/from Caernarfon (1½ hours) and Bangor (one hour) via Conwy and Llandudno Junction (hourly, fewer on Sunday). The No 19 travels to/from Conwy (20 minutes) via the railway interchange of Llandudno Junction (twice hourly Monday to Saturday, hourly Sunday). The No 9 runs to/from Llandudno Junction (12 minutes, twice hourly Mon-Sat, none on Sunday), while the Snowdon Sherpa No S2 runs to Pen-y-Pass trailhead for Mt Snowdon via Betws-y-Coed (30 minutes) and Capel Curig (once on Sunday).

TRAIN

Llandudno is well served by trains, including the Conwy Valley line, which runs to/from Blaenau Ffestiniog (£5.20, 70 minutes) via Betws-y-Coed (£3.80, 40 minutes) five times daily Monday to Saturday, three on Sunday.

Hourly direct services run to/from Manchester (£18.60, 2½ hours) via Chester.

For places on the London–Holyhead line such as London Euston (£55, four hours, three daily), change at Llandudno Junction, a short ride from Llandudno (eight minutes, at least half-hourly) or take the No 19 bus.

CONWY

☎ 01492 / pop 3847

Walled castle town Conwy guards the estuary of the River Conwy, just outside

the Snowdonia National Park and is one of Britain's best-surviving medieval settlements. Most folk enjoy a dramatic entrance, arriving at the castle gateway over one of three jostling bridges: the modern road crossing, Thomas Telford's 1826 suspension coaching bridge (now pedestrianised) or Robert Stephenson's 1848 steel railway span.

The **TIC** (☎ 592248; ☯ 9.30am-6pm Jun-Sep, 9.30am-5pm Easter-May & Oct, 9.30am-4pm Mon-Sat & 11am-4pm Sun Nov-Easter) is in the Conwy Castle gift shop in the car park next to the castle. There's free Internet access at the **library** (☎ 596242), but booking is advisable.

Sights

CONWY CASTLE & TOWN WALL

Built in just five years (1282–87) by Edward I following his conquest of Gwynedd, **Conwy Castle** (Cadw; ☎ 592358; adult £3.75; ☯ 9.30am-5pm Apr-May & Oct, 9.30am-6pm Jun-Sep, 9.30am-4pm Mon-Sat & 11am-4pm Sun Nov-Easter) is one of Wales' greatest fortresses and a World Heritage Site.

Forming the exterior, eight massive drum towers punctuate soaring curtain walls with battlements. The inner area is divided into two wards by a massive crosswall. In one ward sits the now roofless great hall (where you can imagine the gatherings), and desirable royal apartments were created in the towers. The views across the estuary and to the peaks of Snowdonia – when it's not veiled in cloud – are exhilarating.

Conwy folk sleep well knowing they are defended by a 0.75-mile-long **town wall**, built simultaneously with the castle. It boasts 22 towers and three original gateways, and you can walk along most of it.

OTHER SIGHTS

Conwy features two fascinating historic houses close together in the centre of town.

Tall, whitewashed **Plas Mawr** (Cadw; ☎ 580167; High St; adult £4.50; ☯ 9.30am-5pm Apr-May & Sep, 9.30am-6pm Jun-Aug, 9.30am-4pm Oct), built in 1585, is one of Britain's finest surviving Elizabethan town houses, its height and elegance an indication of the owner's status. The interior plasterwork is eye-popping, and the admission price includes a helpful autoguide tour.

Two centuries older, the timber-and-plaster **Aberconwy House** (NT; ☎ 592246; Castle St; adult £2.40; ☯ 11am-5pm Wed-Mon Easter-Oct) is a

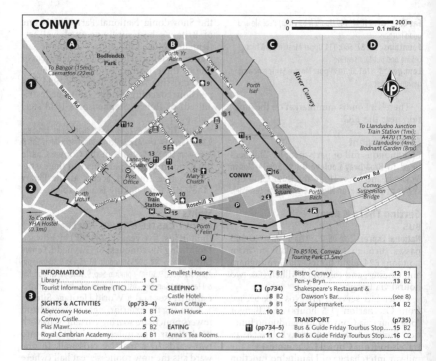

CONWY

INFORMATION		Smallest House...........................**7** B1	Bistro Conwy............................**12** B1
Library..............................**1** C1			Pen-y-Bryn.............................**13** B2
Tourist Informaton Centre (TIC)........**2** C2	**SLEEPING** ⬆ (p734)	Shakespeare's Restaurant &
	Castle Hotel.............................**8** B2	Dawson's Bar...........................(see 8)
SIGHTS & ACTIVITIES (pp733-4)	Swan Cottage...........................**9** B1	Spar Supermarket.....................**14** B2
Aberconwy House.....................**3** B1	Town House............................**10** B2	
Conwy Castle...........................**4** C2		**TRANSPORT** (p735)
Plas Mawr................................**5** B2	**EATING** 🍴 (pp734-5)	Bus & Guide Friday Tourbus Stop.....**15** B2
Royal Cambrian Academy.............**6** B1	Anna's Tea Rooms....................**11** C2	Bus & Guide Friday Tourbus Stop....**16** C2

restored 14th-century wealthy merchant's house with period furnishings, explained by a good audiovisual show.

Behind Plas Mawr, the exhibitions at the modern **Royal Cambrian Academy** (☎ 593413; Crown Lane; ◷ 11am-5pm Tue-Sat, 1-4.30pm Sun), a premier Welsh arts institution, are always worth viewing, and admission is often free.

The small riverside **quay** makes a pleasant walk when it's sunny. A minuscule dwelling near here claims to be the UK's **Smallest House** (adult 75p), where there's correspondingly little to see for your pennies.

The **Guide Friday** hop-on/hop-off sightseeing bus trips, which combine Conwy and Llandudno (see p731), stop beside the train station and at Castle Sq.

A popular excursion is to spectacular **Bodnant Garden** (NT; ☎ 650460; adult £5.50; ◷ 10am-5pm Easter-Oct), 7 miles south off the A470 in the Vale of Conwy. Attractions include great Italianate terraces, formal lawns and a 55m tunnel of yellow laburnum blooms (mid-May to early-June). Bus No 25 from Llandudno passes by hourly. From Conwy, board at Llandudno Junction.

Sleeping

Conwy Touring Park (☎ 592856; 2-person tent sites summer £9) You can camp here, 1.5 miles south of Conwy on the B5106.

Conwy YHA Hostel (☎ 0870 770 5774; conwy@yha .org.uk; Sychnant Pass Rd; dm £13.40; ◷ daily mid-Feb-Nov, most Sat & Sun Dec-mid-Feb) A 10-minute walk from the centre, this is modern and the dorms have shower rooms.

Swan Cottage (☎ 596840; swan.cottage@virgin.net; 18 Berry St; d from £36) The back bedrooms of this small and stuffy cottage on the town through-road have an estuary view.

Town House (☎ 596454; 18 Rosehill St; s £30, d £45-50) Nicely furnished and with nice hosts, the Town House is a comfortable place near the castle.

Castle Hotel (☎ 582800; www.castlewales.co.uk; High St; s/d from £69/95) This historic coach house has characterful rooms (one with a great four-poster bed from 1570) plus good bar food and a restaurant.

Eating

Bistro Conwy (☎ 596326; Chapel St; mains £14) A secluded position hard against the town wall, with a courtyard, adds to this contemporary restaurant's charm. A sample of its temptations is salmon with Welsh mead (£13.50).

Shakespeare's Restaurant & Dawson's Bar (☎ 582800; www.castlewales.co.uk; High St; bar dishes £5-9, restaurant mains £17) Enjoy contemporary eating in an elegantly updated interior at this hotel restaurant and bar located in the Castle Hotel (p734). Between them, the bar and restaurant offer everything from daytime sandwiches, through fajitas to a grand dinnertime list of fresh fish and Welsh meats and cheeses.

And don't miss **Anna's Tearooms** (Castle St), above the Conwy Outdoor Shop, and the small and traditional **Pen-y-bryn** (28 High St).

The Spar supermarket is on High St.

Getting There & Away

Bus services to/from Conwy include Nos 5 and 5X hourly (fewer on Sunday) to/from Caernarfon (70 minutes) via Bangor, continuing to Llandudno Junction and Llandudno; No 19 twice hourly (hourly Sunday) to/from Llandudno (20 minutes) via the railway interchange of Llandudno Junction; and No 27 to/from Llandudno Junction (nine minutes, hourly).

Conwy train station lies on the London–Holyhead line: the train to/from London Euston (£59, four hours, five daily Monday to Saturday, once Sunday) changes at Crewe.

BANGOR

☎ 01248 / pop 15,280

Bangor is pleasantly located within striking distance of Snowdonia National Park on a ridge overlooking the handsome Menai Strait, and is the last stop before the historic bridges to the Isle of Anglesey. The little city springs into action during term-time when students from the 6500-strong body of the University of Wales study and chill with equal dedication.

The central **TIC** (☎ 352786; www.nwt.co.uk; Deiniol Rd; ☯ 10am-1pm & 1.30-5pm Mon-Sat Easter-Oct) is near the cathedral.

Most of **St Deiniol's cathedral**, small, proud and lopsided, is the result of 19th-century restoration. Its treasure is the evocative 500-year-old, carved-oak Mostyn Christ. The Victorian **pier** (adult 25p) stretches 450m out into the Menai Strait and the views are worth a quick stroll.

Sleeping & Eating

Bangor YHA Hostel (☎ 0870 770 5686; bangor@yha.org .uk; Tan-y-bryn; dm £11.80; ☯ daily Apr-Sep, Tue-Sat Oct-Mar) Lying half a mile from the town centre this has views of Penrhyn Castle.

Y Garreg Wen (☎ 353836; 8 Deiniol Rd; s/d £14.50/29) Friendly hospitality awaits at this good-value B&B offering that rarity, single rooms near the station.

Fat Cat Cafe Bar (☎ 370445; 161 High St; mains around £8; ☯ 10am-11pm Mon-Wed, 10am-12pm Thu-Sat, 10am-10.30pm Sun) Students and the rest like to chow down and drink amid Fat Cat's stylish ambience and outdoor seating.

Java (☎ 361652; High St; mains £2.50-12) Funky and laid-back, this place plays good music and serves wonderful international dishes.

Getting There & Away
BUS

The **National Express** (☎ 0870 580 8080) coach No 545 runs daily to/from London (£26, 8½ hours) via Birmingham. Another bus service is the No 1 to/from Porthmadog (1¼ hours) via Caernarfon. All services are less frequent on Sunday. Bus Nos 5 & 5X run to/from Caernarfon (30 minutes) and Llandudno (£3.20, one hour), three hourly. Bus Nos 85 & 86 travel to/from Llanberis (45 minutes, half-hourly, fewer on Sunday), while No X32 travels to/from Aberystwyth (3½ hours, five daily)

TRAIN

Trains operate to/from Chester (£13.20, 70 minutes, hourly) and London Euston (£58.20, four hours, three daily direct). For more options change at Crewe.

AROUND BANGOR
Penrhyn Castle

Superbly sited **Penrhyn Castle** (NT; ☎ 01248-353084; adult/child £7/3.50; ☯ noon-5pm Wed-Mon Apr-Oct, 11am-5pm Wed-Mon Jul & Aug) is a fabulous 19th-century fantasy dwelling. It was built in neo-Norman style between 1820 and 1845 by Thomas Hopper for the Pennant family, who made their fortune in Jamaican sugar and Welsh slate. Extraordinary possessions include a one-ton slate bed made for Queen Victoria and an outstanding collection of paintings. The elaborate interior includes carvings and much Norman-style furniture. Penrhyn, 2 miles east of Bangor's centre, overlooks the sea.

CAERNARFON

☎ 01286

Who can deny getting a buzz from exploring the battlements and spiral staircases of mighty Caernarfon Castle? Guarding the River Seiont on the Menai Strait below the Snowdonia mountains, it was the final flourish in the 'iron ring' Edward I built to rule the Welsh, and nowadays has World Heritage listing.

To consolidate his power, Edward made his son the first Prince of Wales and installed him in the castle. But Caernarfon is a Welsh nationalist heartland, and 600 years later, in 1911, in a bid to involve the British crown more closely with his own constituency, prime minister and Welshman David Lloyd George incurred the ire of local people when he transferred the investiture ceremony for the heir to the British throne to Caernarfon castle. At investiture of Charles, the current Prince of Wales, in 1969, there was an attempt to blow up his train.

Long before all of this, the Romans established the great fort of Segontium above town, at a site now open to the public.

Orientation & Information

The castle is the focus of the town centre on the river beside a large car park. The town walls enclose a small area four streets wide and two deep.

The **TIC** (☎ 672232; caernarfon.tic@gwynedd.gov.uk; Castle St; ⏰ 9.30am-5.30pm Easter-Oct, 10am-4.30pm Mon-Sat Nov-Easter) is opposite the castle entrance.

Free Internet access is available at the **library** (☎ 675944; Pavilion Rd).

Sights & Activities

Caernarfon Castle (Cadw; ☎ 677617; adult £4.50; ⏰ 9.30am-5pm Easter-May & Oct, 9.30am-6pm Jun-Sep, 9.30am-4pm Mon-Sat, 11am-4pm Sun Nov-Mar) is Edward I's most impressive fortress. Stupendously strong, it was built between 1283 and 1301 with polygonal towers and colour-banded masonry modelled on the 5th-century walls of Constantinople. In 1404, 28 men withstood siege by Owain Glyndŵr's army, and during the 17th-century Civil War it was besieged three times without success.

The castle was designed as a seat of government rule and a royal palace. Living quarters with glass windows were fitted in the towers, of which the Eagle Tower is the finest. In the Queen's Tower (named after

Edward's wife Eleanor) is a lively museum of the Royal Welch Fusiliers, Wales' longest-serving infantry regiment.

The atmospheric neighbouring medieval **walled town** features the best eating and drinking holes (but you can't walk the walls).

You can visit a small **Maritime Museum** (Victoria Dock; ⏰ noon-4pm May-Aug) and take pleasure-boat trips in the *Queen of the Sea* (☎ 672772; ⏰ late-May–Oct), which runs 40-minute tours of the lovely Menai Strait from Slate Quay beside the castle.

For a taste of wild mountain scenery, and a unique way to reach Snowdon's skirts for walking or cycling, ride the vintage narrow-gauge **Welsh Highland Railway** (☎ 677018; 3hr return trip £14) on a 12-mile stretch between Caernarfon and Rhyd Ddu. A converted wagon also carries bicycles. The station is on St Helen's Rd, 300m upriver from the castle. The line should eventually be reinstated all the way through the mountains to Porthmadog, where a shorter stretch is also open (see p725).

Substantial foundations of the Roman fort of **Segontium** (Cadw; ☎ 675625; admission free; ⏰ grounds 10.30am-4.30pm, museum 12.30-4.30pm Tue-Sun), a significant garrison on the limit of the Roman Empire, lie just under a mile southeast of the castle. The fort was built for about 1000 men and was occupied for around 300 years from AD 77. A small museum supplies the information needed to appreciate the site.

Two cruisy **walking** and **cycling** trails leave Caernarfon in opposite directions along old railway lines: the scenic 4.5-mile **Lôn Las Menai** along the strait towards Bangor, and the 12-mile **Lôn Eifion** south to Bryncir. The TIC has a map-leaflet, and you can hire bike from **Beics Menai** (☎ 676804; Slate Quay; per 2/4hr £8/10).

Sleeping

Cadnant Valley Camping & Caravan Park (☎ 673196; Llanberis Rd; 2-person tent sites around £12; ⏰ Easter-Oct) This is the local place to camp.

Totters (☎ 672963; www.applemaps.co.uk/totters; 2 High St; dm/r with breakfast £12/14.50) A top hostel, Totters, beside a gateway in the town wall to the sea, is large and light above ground in the dorms and lounge. Then you eat breakfast in the stone-walled basement, where folk have been doing the same thing for 600 years! Clean, cheerful and smoothly-run, with ample burners for self-caterers, it's just cool.

Bryn Hyfryd (☎ 673840; www.brynhyfryd-caernarfon
.co.uk; St David's Rd; s/d £25/50) This handsome
Victorian terraced house has views over
the strait and friendly hosts.

Black Boy Inn (☎ 673604; Northgate St; s/d
£25/40, with en suite £35/55) Stay in a very old,
very friendly pub where rooms have been
crammed with grand furnishings.

Caer Menai (☎ 672612; www.caermenai.co.uk; 15
Church St; d £52-55) Sited in a quiet side street in
a capacious Georgian town house set against
the town wall, Caer Menai has fine newly
decorated en-suite rooms, of which No 7
has the best view – skimming the medieval
masonry to the Menai Strait.

Eating

Molly's (☎ 673238; Hole in the Wall St; mains around
£12; ☺ lunch & dinner) Enjoy an adventurous
chef's menu in this tasteful little wooden
diner, where fresh fish plays a leading role.

Stone's Bistro (☎ 671152; Hole in the Wall St;
mains around £10; ☺ dinner Tue-Sat) A few doors
along, Stone's is another sincere option,
with meaty mains and intriguing vegetarian
choices, such as potato and banana bake.

Caffi Maes (4 Castle Sq; ☺ 9.30am-5.30pm) Time
for tea at this snug place with yummy cakes
and hot toasties.

Getting There & Away

There are no main-line train services to
Caernarfon, but buses are plentiful, including the Snowdon Sherpa bus No S4 to/from
Pen-y-Pas via Snowdon Ranger YHA hostel
and Beddgelert (30 minutes, hourly). Other
services include the No 1 to/from Porthmadog (40 minutes, about hourly) and Bangor
(20 minutes, six daily); other services run
on Sunday less frequently. Bus Nos 5 and
5X run to/from Bangor (30 minutes) and
Llandudno (1½ hours) hourly (fewer on
Sunday). The No X32 runs to/from Bangor
(20 minutes) and Aberystwyth (three hours)
five times daily, while No 88 runs to/from
Llanberis (twice-hourly, hourly on Sunday)

ISLE OF ANGLESEY
(YNYS MÔN)

Anglesey's low-lying and verdant nature
provides a mellow contrast to rugged
mainland Snowdonia, a mild shock perhaps

to anyone who's arrived that way (less so for
visitors off the ferries from Ireland). Indeed,
one attraction is the long full-height views
of Snowdon's peaks. Another is sections
of characterful coastline.

North Wales draws much of its wheat and
cattle from Anglesey. This fertility probably
played a role in attracting a considerable
ancient population, one which over time
bequeathed Wales' greatest concentration
of ancient sites. Anglesey was also a holy
place to the Celts. It was the last outpost
to be conquered by the Romans – and is
often referred to as Mam Cymru, Mother
of Wales.

Even if most travellers belt straight to the
port of Holyhead, they head across one of
the pair of historic bridges over the Menai
Strait. Thomas Telford's 1826 crossing,
the first permanent link, is 174m long
with a 30m high central span that allowed
the passage of tall ships. In 1850 Robert
Stephenson built the **Britannia Bridge** to carry
the newly-laid railway line. This now bears
most of the road traffic too.

Dotted mostly around the coast, the
ancient remains number around 20 and run
down the ages from prehistoric to Roman
and early Christian times. TICs stock a useful
free map leaflet *Historic Anglesey* with their
details. Neolithic burial mound **Bryn Celli
Ddhu** probably gets top billing (find it 600m
from the car park on the A4080 west of Plas
Newydd, two miles west of Llanfair PG).

LLANFAIRPWLLGWYNGYLLGOGERYCH-
WYRNDROBWLLLLANTYSILIOGOGOGOCH

This nondescript village on the railway line
to Holyhead was given the longest name of
any place in Britain in the 19th century as a
tourist wheeze. The 58 letters are generally
shortened to Llanfair PG or Llanfairpwll,
and mean 'St Mary's Church in the hollow
of the White Hazel near a rapid whirlpool
and the Church of St Tysilio near the Red
Cave'. The **TIC** (☎ 01248-713177) is in the knitwear shop next to the train station.

PLAS NEWYDD

One of North Wales' most elegant stately
homes (NT; ☎ 01248-714795; adult £5; ☺ house noon-
5pm Sat-Wed, gardens 11am-5.30pm Sat-Wed Easter-Oct),
this 18th-century Gothic masterpiece was
designed for the marquis of Anglesey, a cavalry commander at the Battle of Waterloo.

NORTH WALES

Don't confuse it with the Ladies of Llangollen's Plas Newydd. Sited overlooking the Menai Strait it has fabulous views of Snowdonia, while the house contains a celebrated room-sized *trompe l'oeil* dreamscape of Mt Snowdon by Rex Whistler. Plas Newydd is 1.5 miles south of Llanfair PG train station.

BEAUMARIS
☎ 01248 / pop 1513

Beaumaris is a historic coastal town with an outstanding castle just outside the Menai Strait. A centre for boat trips and water sports, the views from the shore over to Snowdonia are sweeping.

Sights & Activities

Beaumaris Castle (Cadw; ☎ 810361; adult £3; ☽ 9.30am-5pm Easter-May & Oct daily, 9.30am-6pm Jun-Sep daily, 9.30am-4pm Mon-Sat & 11am-4pm Sun Nov-Easter), a World Heritage Site, belongs to the 'iron ring' that Edward I built to rule the Welsh. It was constructed by brilliant military architect James of St George between 1295 and 1298 on a flat shoreline site that allowed a symmetrical design. Money ran out before fortifications reached full height – the result being a castle of greater charm than menace. Technically progressive, the moat and concentric 'walls within walls' layout created four lines of defence. Attackers faced 14 other obstacles, including gateway murder holes for boiling liquids.

Allow two hours to visit the historic buildings of local law and order, the **Beaumaris Courthouse & Gaol** (Cadw; ☎ 810921; adult £4; ☽ 10.30am-5pm Easter-Sep). The courthouse is nearly 400 years old, and the forbidding gaol contains the last-surviving treadwheel in Britain (for hard-labour prisoners).

Operators run summer **cruises** from Beaumaris pier to Puffin Island to see seals and puffins, or along the Menai Strait. **Starida Sea Services** (☎ 810746) runs (weather-dependent) one-hour cruises, (adult £5, six daily Easter to October) from a kiosk on the pier.

Sleeping & Eating

Kingsbridge Caravan & Camping Park (☎ 490636; Llanfaes; per person tent sites from £3.50) Convenient to the town is this camping ground, 1.5 miles north on the B5109 towards Llangoed.

Mountfield (☎ 810380; offseason s/d from £35/60) On the far side of the castle from town, this handsome and well-preserved 1930s villa has an uninterrupted view to the mainland mountains.

Ye Olde Bulls Head Inn (☎ 810329; Castle St; s/d with en suite £62/89) Modernised with flair, the old town inn dates back to 1472 and boasts both Charles Dickens and Samuel Johnson as past guests.

Getting There & Away

Bus Nos 53, 57 and 58 run to/from Bangor (30 minutes, hourly Monday to Saturday, every two hours Sunday).

HOLYHEAD (CAERGYBI) & HOLY ISLAND
☎ 01407 / pop 11,237

A major departure point for ferries to Ireland, Holyhead, on Holy Island, is a workaday town with few distractions – chiefly the functional harbourfront and a fine arts centre – but fine coastal surrounds.

The **TIC** (☎ 762622; ☽ 8.30am-6pm), in Terminal 1 at the ferry port near the train station, stocks free leaflets on cycle routes and circular walks around Anglesey.

Ucheldre Centre (☎ 763361; Ucheldre Ave; ☽ 10am-5pm Mon-Sat, 2-5pm Sun) is a progressive arts centre in a converted chapel, which shows films and hosts live music and drama.

Exposure to the Irish Sea has created a coastline of rugged cliffs and beaches around Holy Island. West of town rises **Holyhead Mountain** (220m). At its western base, signposted from town, is **South Stack lighthouse**, open to all visitors who can tackle the 400-step descent to the offshore rock. **Trearddur Bay**, 2.5 miles south of Holyhead, is Anglesey's main water-sports centre and has a sheltered sandy beach.

Sleeping & Eating

Tyn Rhôs Camping Site (☎ 860369; Ravenspoint Rd; 2-person tent sites £8.50) This is at Trearddur Bay, 2.5 miles south.

Outdoor Alternative (☎ 860469; Cerrig-yr-adar; dm £12.75) Five miles south of Holyhead above the sandy cove of Rhoscolyn Bay, this recommended contemporary residential (and sea kayaking) centre has dorms and camp sites.

B&Bs in Holyhead are accustomed to late arrivals off the ferry.

Ferry Lodge Guest House (☎ 765276; 89 Newry St; s/d £35/45) With spotless en-suite rooms, this welcomes walkers and cyclists.

NORTH WALES

Yr Hendre (☎ 762929; www.yr-hendre.co.uk; Porth-y-Felin Rd; s/d £30/55) A very smart guesthouse on a green, this has plush, tasteful rooms and good outlooks.

Ucheldre Kitchen (☎ 763361; Ucheldre Ave; mains £5; ☺ 10am-5pm Mon-Sat, 2-5pm Sun) Attached to the Ucheldre Centre (p738), this café offers well-priced lunch dishes such as vegetable quiche as well as all-day standards such as jacket potatoes.

Getting There & Away

Both **Irish Ferries** (☎ 0870 517 1717) and **Stena Line** (☎ 0870 570 7070) run ferries from Holyhead to Ireland (see p963). From Bangor the quickest way to Holyhead is by train: from Chester via both Llandudno Junction (55 minutes) and Bangor (30 minutes) about hourly.

Bus No 4 runs frequently to/from Bangor (1½ hours, half-hourly Monday to Saturday) and bus No 44 runs from Bangor every two hours on Sunday.

LLŶN PENINSULA

There's something irresistible about peninsulas, in the way they suggest wilderness and isolation. The Llŷn (pronounced khlee'en) provides both. It also remains a proud stronghold of Welsh language and nationalism. At 24 miles long, once you pass beyond the main towns of Criccieth and Pwllheli (the railway terminus), the 'pointing arm' of Wales has a windswept coastline and several good beaches: anglicised **Abersoch** seven miles west of Pwllheli; empty four-mile-long, surf-lover's **Hell's Mouth** (Porth Neigwl) three miles further on; and also at the whitewashed village of **Aberdaron** near the tip, where you can catch a boat to

Bardsey Island (see the boxed text, below). On the north coast, the sandy semi-circular bay at **Porth Dinllaen** near Morfa Nefyn is a sheltered water sports centre.

For buses see Pwllheli (p740). Drivers and cyclists can explore with the OS 1:50,000 map No 123 (on sale at TICs). Beyond Pwllhelli, the only **TIC** (☎ 01758-712929; ☺ 10am-noon early-Jan–Mar & Nov–mid-Dec, 10am-2pm Mar-Easter & Sep-Oct, 10am-5pm Easter-Aug) is at Abersoch.

CRICCIETH

☎ 01766 / pop 1826

Criccieth's small cliff-top castle has stony beaches to either side and a sweeping dress-circle view of Tremadog Bay – on a clear day you can wave at Harlech Castle on the far side. The genteel coastal resort attached makes a pleasant halt en route to the Llŷn. The nearest TIC is in Pwllheli (p740).

Criccieth Castle (Cadw; ☎ 522227; adult £2.75; ☺ 10am-4.30pm Easter-Jun, 10am-5.30pm Jun-Sep, open site Nov-Easter) pre-dates Edward I's post-conquest defences by 40 years. The castle was originally constructed by native Welsh prince Llywelyn the Great in 1239, but was overrun in 1283 by Edward I's forces who probably added the distinctive twin-towered gatehouse. A hundred years later, in 1404, Owain Glyndŵr recovered the fortress for the Welsh, and destroyed it beyond further military use.

Sleeping & Eating

Budget Accommodation (☎ 523098; 11 Marine Terrace; bed £11.50; ☺ May-Sep) An unusual independent hostel, this is a regular seafront house with only private bedrooms, and comfortable and relaxed for it. Continental breakfast is £1.50, but note that the kitchen is equipped only for snacks and microwave cooking.

OVER THE SEA TO BARDSEY

Two-mile-long Bardsey Island (Ynys Enlli), off the tip of the peninsula, once known as the Isle of 20,000 Saints, was an important early Christian site. At a time when journeys to Italy were long and perilous, three pilgrimages to Bardsey across the treacherous Sound equalled one to Rome. More likely the 20,000 were pilgrims rather than saints.

The **Bardsey Island Trust** (☎ 01758-760667; www.bardsey.org; return trip £28) organises ferries to the island twice daily June to August (weather permitting) from Porth Meudwy (1.5 miles west of Aberdaron) and Pwllheli. The trip takes 15 minutes. You have four hours on the island to see 6th-century carved stones, 13th-century abbey tower ruins and a significant colony of Manx shearwaters.

Seaspray (☎ 522373; 4 Marine Tce; s/d £25/50) This is a good one in a line of tall terraced seafront guesthouses with bay windows.

Lion Hotel (☎ 522460; s/d £40/68) On the town green, this traditional hotel has rooms with views of the town's castle and sea.

Criccieth has two good restaurants, both on the High St through-road.

Granvilles (☎ 522506; mains £12; ☽ lunch & dinner Thu-Tue) Has a good wine list and menu that sometimes stars Cardigan Bay sea bass. Booking is necessary.

Tiffins (☎ 522165; mains £12; ☽ lunch Wed-Mon, dinner daily) A slightly simpler place than Granvilles, serving delicious, varied meals.

Getting There & Away

Criccieth is on the Cambrian Coaster train line between Porthmadog (eight minutes, about every two hours, three on Sunday) and Pwllheli.

PWLLHELI

☎ 01758 / pop 3861

The only sizeable place on the peninsula, lively seaside Pwllheli (poolth-*heh*-lee) is known for its Welshness: Plaid Cymru, the nationalist party, was formed here in 1925. It is also the end of the Cambrian Coaster railway line.

There are a modern marina and pleasant walking on South Beach promenade (just under a mile from the centre), and good clothing and gift shops around the high street, but little else.

The **TIC** (☎ 613000; pwllheli.tic@gwynedd.gov.uk; ☽ 9am-5pm Easter-Oct, 10.30am-4.30pm Mon-Wed & Fri & Sat Nov-Easter), opposite the train station, is well-stocked with information on the peninsula.

Sleeping & Eating

Bank Place (☎ 612103; 29 Stryd Fawr; s/d around £20/32) Two blocks north of the TIC, this is a simple and acceptable B&B.

Rhosydd (☎ 612956; 6 Glan Cymerau; s/d from £18/36; ☒) Also worth a try is this B&B, which features wheelchair access, three blocks southwest of the central square.

ESI Café Bar (☎ 701321; Station Sq; lunch £4-8, mains £12; ☽ 11am-11pm, food to 9pm) This café-bar, beside the TIC, is a gob-smackingly hip place, where you lounge in brown leather chairs to drink fashionable coffee, eat light platters of whitebait or pâté, or have a full dinner of, say, monkfish or Welsh lamb.

Getting There & Away

Buses to the east include No 3 to Porthmadog (£1.85, 35 minutes, every half-hour, six on Sunday) and No 12 to Caernarfon (£2, 45 minutes, hourly, fewer on Sunday). Buses heading west along the Llŷn Peninsula are Bus No 8 to Nefyn (£1.50, 15 minutes, about hourly, four on Sunday), Nos 17 and 17B to Aberdaron (£2.20, 40 minutes, every two hours, none on Sunday) and No 18 to Abersoch (£1.20, 25 minutes, about hourly, four on Sunday).

The Cambrian Coaster travels to Pwllheli from Machynlleth via Porthmadog (£2.80, 20 minutes) every two or three hours Monday to Friday (fewer on weekends).

Scotland

GRANT DIXON

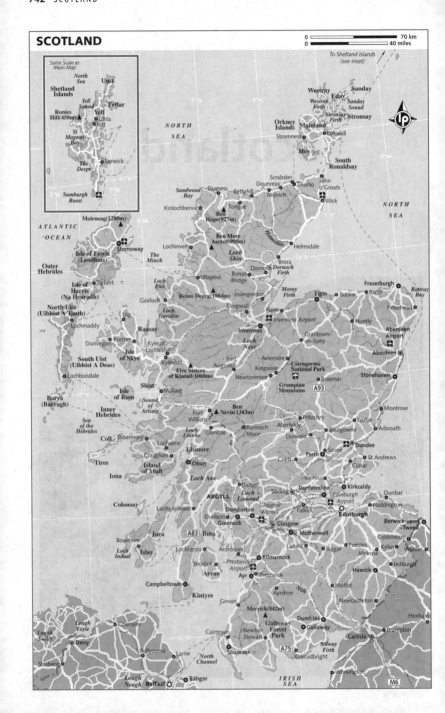

SCOTLAND

0 ——— 70 km
0 ——— 40 miles

Shetland Islands (inset)
Same Scale as Main Map

North Sea
Unst
Shetland Islands
Yell Sound
Fetlar
Ronies Hill(450m)▲
Yell
Uyea
Toft
St Magnus Bay
The Deeps
Lerwick
60°N
Sumburgh Roost
2°W 1°W

Westray
Sanday
Westray Firth
Eday
Sanday Sound
Stronsay Firth
Stronsay
Orkney Islands
Mainland
Stromness
Kirkwall
Hoy
South Ronaldsay

NORTH SEA

Moirneag(1280m)▲

ATLANTIC OCEAN

Isle of Lewis (Leodhais)
Stornoway
The Minch

Outer Hebrides

Isle of Harris (Na Hearadh)
Tarbert

North Uist (Uibhist A Tuath)
Lochmaddy

Uig
Raasay
Dunvegan
Portree

South Uist (Uibhist A Deas)
Isle of Skye
Lochboisdale

Sleat
Kyle of Lochalsh
Kyleakin
Five Sisters of Kintail(1068m)▲

Barra (Barragh)

Isle of Rum
Sound of Arisaig

Inner Hebrides
Sea of the Hebrides

Coll
Tobermory
Lochaline
Lismore

Tiree
Craignure
Island of Mull
Oban

Iona

Colonsay

Sandwood Bay
Durness
Bettyhill
Kinlochbervie
Ben Hope(927m)▲
Tongue
Melvich
Kinlochbervie
Ben More Assynt(998m)▲
Lochinver
Loch Shin
Helmsdale
Helmsdale
Brora
Ullapool
Dornoch
Dornoch Firth
Loch Ewe
Bonar Bridge
Gairloch
Beinn Dearg(1084m)▲
Invergordon
Moray Firth
Elgin
Buckie
Banff
Loch Torridon
Dingwall
Nairn
Inverness Airport
Huntly
Inverness
Grantown-on-Spey
Loch Ness
Fort Augustus
Aviemore
Kingussie
Cairngorms National Park
Aberdeen Airport
Aberdeen
Newtonmore
Braemar
Stonehaven
Grampian Mountains
A93

Dunreay
Scrabster
Thurso
John o'Groats
Wick

NORTH SEA

Fraserburgh
Rattray Bay
Peterhead

Mallaig
Ben Nevis(1343m)▲
Fort William
Glencoe
Rannoch Moor
Aberfeldy
Pitlochry
Forfar
Arbroath
Loch Linnhe
Dunkeld
Blairgowrie
Montrose

Loch Awe
Crieff
Scone
Dundee
Perth
St Andrews
Cupar

Tarbet
Loch Lomond
Kinross
Kirkcaldy
Dunbar
Stirling
Dunfermline
ARGYLL
Lochgilphead
Dumbarton
Glasgow Airport
Falkirk
Edinburgh Airport
Edinburgh
Haddington
Dunoon
Glasgow
Berwick-upon-Tweed
Greenock
Motherwell
Bowmore
Jura
Bute
Lanark
Biggar
Peebles
Kelso
Wooler
Loch Indaal
Islay
Lochranza
Ardrossan
Kilmarnock
Coldstream
Melrose
Brodick
Prestwick Airport
Jedburgh
Arran
Ayr
Prestwick
Hawick
Campbeltown
Kintyre
Ayrshire
Moffat
Newcastleton
Hexham
Girvan
Nith
Merrick(842m)▲
Galloway Forest Park
Dumfries
Brampton
Cairnryan
Newton Stewart
Galloway
Solway Firth
Carlisle
Stranraer
A75
Kirkcudbright
North Channel
Workington
M6

Lough Foyle
Coleraine
Lough Swilly
Derry
Ballymena
Larne
Strabane
Lough Neagh
Belfast
Bangor
IRISH SEA

Edinburgh

Scotland's capital has a magic that seldom fails to captivate visitors. Modern sophistication melds with staunch tradition from both ends of the social spectrum to create a unique whole, built in noble stone in the most spectacular of settings. It is no exaggeration to describe it as one of the most lovable, and livable, cities on the planet.

The joy of Edinburgh (pronounced *ed*-inbra) is its size. While it possesses all the facilities of a major metropolis, there's no hours spent crossing town to get to the latest nightlife hotspot, or wandering about with a street directory. Exploring the city on foot is a delight, and is always punctuated by views: the majestic castle clinging to its volcanic crag, Arthur's Seat like a chunk of the Highlands dropped into town, or the glimmering Firth of Forth.

Occupying the ridge below the castle, the Old Town, riddled with alleys and vaults, contrasts with the orderly Georgian elegance of the New Town. It's no surprise that Unesco has slapped a World Heritage order on both.

Glaswegians like to deride Edinburgh as not being 'the real Scotland', but the number of visitors beguiled by its charms, and a high student population, dispel any myth of Edinburgh being conservative and reserved. However, Edinburgh has its gritty side too; the social deprivation displayed in the film *Trainspotting* still exists in certain areas.

Edinburgh's spirit soars every August with a number of festivals including the Edinburgh Fringe. The city reveals an amazing number of venues at this time and hundreds of thousands of visitors enjoy its varied concentration of great pubs and restaurants.

HIGHLIGHTS

- Cracking into some seafood in **Leith** (p763), the port that's gone upmarket but still has a mariner's soul

- Seeing the fantastic **Edinburgh Castle** (p749) from as many different angles as you can and standing proud atop its battlements with a soldier stance

- Chilling your bones with an evening **walk** (p759) through Edinburgh's dark and desperate history

- Agonising over which of Broughton St's excellent **pubs** (p765) you'd take to a desert island with you

- Unravelling the mysteries of the Green Man at **Rosslyn Chapel** (p770), a Templar conundrum in stone

- Debating the avant-garde architecture of the spanking new **Scottish Parliament building** (p753)

- TELEPHONE CODE: 0131
- POPULATION: 430,000

HISTORY

Edinburgh began to grow in the 11th century when markets developed at the foot of the fortress, and from 1124 King David I held court at the castle and founded the abbey at Holyrood. The first effective town wall was constructed around 1450 and circled the Old Town and the area around Grassmarket. This restricted, defensible zone became a medieval Manhattan, forcing its densely packed inhabitants to build tenements that soared to 12 storeys.

The city played an important role in the Reformation, led by the firebrand John Knox, but later, when James VI of Scotland succeeded to the English crown in 1603, he moved the court to London. Edinburgh's importance waned, to be further reduced by the Act of Union in 1707.

Nonetheless, cultural and intellectual life flourished; during the Scottish Enlightenment (about 1740–1830) Edinburgh became known as 'a hotbed of genius'. In the second half of the 18th century a new city was created across the ravine to the north, and the population soon exploded. A new ring of crescents and circuses was built south of New Town, and grey Victorian terraces sprang up. In the 20th century the poor that occupied the Old Town were moved into new housing estates further out, estates that now experience severe social problems.

A history of separatist feelings meant Scottish devolution was always on the cards. After a successful referendum held by the newly elected Labour Party in 1997, the first Scottish parliament since 1707 was convened in Edinburgh, a capital once more, on 12 May 1999. Under the leadership of Donald Dewar (1937–2000), who became the First Minister, the Labour Party formed a government in coalition with the Liberal Democrats. The Scottish National Party (SNP), with about 30% of the vote, became the second-largest party and de facto opposition, its biggest political success. Jack McConnell is currently First Minister and presided as the Queen opened the new Scottish Parliament building in October 2004.

EDINBURGH IN...

Two Days

With a full Scottish breakfast from your quarters on board, make your way to the **Old Town** (p749) and wander slowly up the **Royal Mile** (p752) to the **castle** (p749), hopefully beating the tour buses there. Walk back down the Mile, lunch-bound, and turn right on to George IV Bridge. If you're hungry, **Maison Bleue** (p763) is just around the corner; for something lighter, the **Elephant House** (p762) will trumpet a welcome. Satisfied, continue down the Mile to check out **Holyroodhouse** (p753) and the controversial new **Scottish Parliament** (p753). In the evening, scare yourself with a guided walk by **Mercat Tours** (p759), then duck across North Bridge for a late dinner at **Howie's** (p764). If, afterwards, you've got a thirst to be slaked, the **bars of Broughton St** (p765) are but five minutes' walk.

The next morning, banish any lingering whisky from your breath with the clean air of an ascent of **Arthur's Seat** (p754). Next, satisfy those retail urges by patrolling **Princes St** (p768), stopping at the **Great Grog Wine Bar** (p766) for refreshment, if it's a nice day. Then head down to Leith – see the **royal yacht Britannia** (p757), and hit the **Shore** (p765) for an aperitif before seafood at **Fishers** (p762).

Four Days

Your third morning could be spent – depending on the weather – at either the **Royal Botanic Gardens** (p757) or in the newly refurbished **Royal Scottish Academy** (p756). From here, lunch in cobbled **Stockbridge** (p763) isn't too far away. An afternoon stroll up **Calton Hill** (p756) beckons, but then, so does the beer garden at **Pear Tree House** (p765), and the good-value eateries nearby might tip the balance in favour of the latter!

On the fourth day, fan of *The Da Vinci Code* or not, head to **Rosslyn Chapel** (p770), most enigmatic of buildings, and top off your stay with a sumptuous dinner at the **Atrium** (p763), one of the city's finest restaurants.

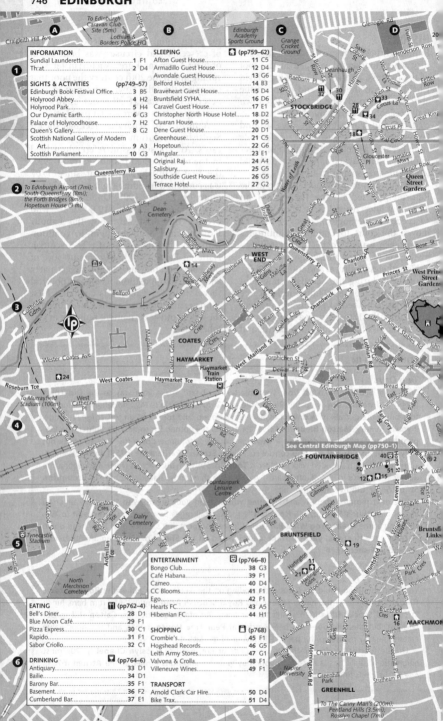

INFORMATION
Sundial Launderette................1 F1
Th:at..2 D4

SIGHTS & ACTIVITIES (pp749–57)
Edinburgh Book Festival Office....3 B5
Holyrood Abbey........................4 H2
Holyrood Park..........................5 H4
Our Dynamic Earth....................6 G3
Palace of Holyroodhouse............7 H2
Queen's Gallery........................8 G2
Scottish National Gallery of Modern
Art..9 A3
Scottish Parliament..................10 G3

SLEEPING (pp759–62)
Afton Guest House....................11 C5
Armadillo Guest House..............12 D4
Avondale Guest House..............13 G6
Belford Hostel..........................14 B3
Braveheart Guest House............15 D4
Bruntsfield SYHA......................16 D6
Caravel Guest House..................17 E1
Christopher North House Hotel....18 D2
Clauran House..........................19 D5
Dene Guest House....................20 D1
Greenhouse..............................21 C5
Hopetoun................................22 G6
Mingalar..................................23 E1
Original Raj..............................24 A4
Salisbury..................................25 G5
Southside Guest House..............26 G5
Terrace Hotel............................27 G2

EATING (pp762–4)
Bell's Diner..............................28 D1
Blue Moon Café........................29 F1
Pizza Express............................30 C1
Rapido....................................31 F1
Sabor Criollo............................32 C1

DRINKING (pp764–6)
Antiquary................................33 D1
Bailie......................................34 D1
Barony Bar................................35 F1
Basement................................36 F2
Cumberland Bar........................37 E1

ENTERTAINMENT (pp766–8)
Bongo Club..............................38 G3
Café Habana............................39 F1
Cameo....................................40 D4
CC Blooms................................41 F1
Ego..42 F1
Hearts FC................................43 A5
Hibernian FC............................44 H1

SHOPPING (p768)
Crombie's................................45 D4
Hogshead Records....................46 G5
Leith Army Stores......................47 G1
Valvona & Crolla......................48 F1
Villeneuve Wines......................49 F1

TRANSPORT
Arnold Clark Car Hire................50 D4
Bike Trax..................................51 D4

ORIENTATION

The biggest landmark is the rocky peak of Arthur's Seat, southeast of the centre. The Old and New Towns are separated by Princes St Gardens, with the castle dominating both of them.

Edinburgh's main shopping street, Princes St, runs along the northern side of the gardens. At the garden's eastern end, Calton Hill is crowned by several monuments. The Royal Mile (Lawnmarket, High St and Canongate) is the parallel equivalent in the Old Town.

See p769 for details on getting to/from the airport.

Maps

Lonely Planet publishes the Edinburgh City Map (£3.99), which has a complete index of streets and sights. Another useful, portable map with street index is the Collins Central Edinburgh Street Atlas (£2.99), available at most bookshops and Tourist Information Centres (TICs).

INFORMATION
Bookshops

Blackwell's (Map pp750-1; ☎ 622 8222; www.blackwell.co.uk; 53 South Bridge; ☼ daily)

Ottakar's (Map pp750-1; ☎ 225 4495; www.ottakars.co.uk; 57 George St; ☼ daily)

Waterstone's (Map pp750-1; ☎ 226 2666; www.waterstones.co.uk; 128 Princes St; ☼ daily) The largest of Edinburgh's three branches.

Emergency

Dial ☎ 999 or ☎ 112 for police, ambulance, fire brigade or coastguard.

Internet Access

As well as the places listed here, most hostels have a terminal, as do several cafés and libraries, and the tourist information centre.

EasyInternet Café (Map pp750-1; ☎ 220 3580; 58 Rose St; per hr around £1.60; ☼ 7am-10pm Mon-Sat, 9am-10pm Sun) Giant place – no unaccompanied minors allowed.

e-corner (Map pp750-1; ☎ 558 7858; Platform 1, Waverley Station; per hr £3; ☼ 8am-9pm) In the train station concourse.

Internet Café (Map pp750-1; ☎ 226 5400; 98 West Bow; per hr £2; ☼ 10am-11pm)

Th:at (Map pp746-7; ☎ 0870 770 4121; 1a Brougham St; per hr £2; ☼ 8.30am-10pm)

Internet Resources

City of Edinburgh Council (www.edinburgh.gov.uk) Has an events guide.

Edinburgh Guide (www.edinburghguide.com) Theatre, film and events listings, plus a directory of useful links.

Laundry

Most of the backpacker hostels have a good-value laundry service. Otherwise, try **Sundial Launderette** (Map pp746-7; ☎ 556 2743; 7 East London St; ☼ 8am-7pm Mon-Fri, 8am-4pm Sat, 10am-2pm Sun)

Left Luggage

There are left-luggage facilities at Edinburgh Airport (£3 per 24 hours) and Waverley train station (£4.50 per 24 hours). There are also handy lockers in the concourse at the bus station (£3 to £5 per 24 hours depending on size).

Libraries

Central Library (Map pp750-1; ☎ 242 8000; George IV Bridge; ☼ 10am-8pm Mon-Thu, 10am-5pm Fri, 9am-1pm Sat) Several specialist sections, a large reference collection, and free Internet access.

Medical Services

Royal Infirmary (☎ 536 1000; Little France, Old Dalkeith Rd) There's a 24-hour emergency service at this recently moved infirmary, 2½ miles southeast of the Royal Commonwealth Pool.

Money

There are numerous banks with ATMs throughout the city, particularly around St Andrew Sq and George St. There's a bureau de change in the Edinburgh & Scotland Information Centre (see Tourist Information, below), but post offices, banks or **Amex** (Map pp750-1; ☎ 718 2501; 139 Princes St) have better rates.

Post

Main post office (Map pp750-1; ☎ 0845 722 3344; St James Centre, Leith St)

Tourist Information

Edinburgh & Scotland Information Centre (ESIC; Map pp750-1; ☎ 0845 225 5121; www.edinburgh.org; 3 Princes St; ☼ 9am-5pm Mon-Wed, 9am-6pm Thu-Sat, 10am-5pm Sun Oct-Apr; 9am-7pm Mon-Sat, 10am-7pm Sun May-Sep, closes at 8pm in Jul & Aug; wheelchair access) Edinburgh's main information centre. You will queue. Internet access at £3 per hour; bureau de change; accommodation booking.

Old Town Information Centre (Map pp750-1; Tron Kirk, High St; ⊗ 10am-5.30pm Apr-Oct, noon-5pm Nov-Mar) Information on tours and walking routes in the Old Town.
Tourist Information Desk (Edinburgh Airport; ⊗ 6.30am-10.30pm) Near international arrivals.

Travel Agencies

STA Travel (Map pp750-1; ☎ 226 7747; www.statravel .co.uk; 27 Forrest Rd; ⊗ Mon-Sat)
Student Flights (Map pp750-1; ☎ 226 6868; www .studentflights.co.uk; 53 Forrest Rd; ⊗ Mon-Sat)

SIGHTS

Most of Edinburgh's visitor attractions are concentrated in a fairly small area: the Old Town, whose focus is the Royal Mile (a cobbled street that runs downhill from the castle to Holyroodhouse); and, north of here across a deep gully, the New Town, with its elegant and well-ordered streets.

The Old Town
EDINBURGH CASTLE

Perched high on an extinct black volcano, **Edinburgh Castle** (Map pp750-1; ☎ 225 9846; HS; Castle Hill; adult/child £9.50/2; ⊗ 9.30am-6pm Apr-Oct, 9.30am-5pm Nov-Mar; wheelchair access) couldn't be more dominant; it towers over Scotland's capital and leaves an indelible impression at first sight. It constantly reminds visitors and residents of its presence, both because it's visible from nearly every part of the city, and also because the One o'Clock Gun booms out from its battlements at lunch time. Although muscular and eminently defensible, it's very much an iron fist in a velvet glove: viewed from the New Town its large windows and dressed façades appear more those of a mansion than a fortress. This impression is dispelled immediately upon entry as you file through the gateway in its thick wall!

The castle is the reason that Edinburgh exists. Such a commanding and inaccessible location was fortified from prehistoric times and became a vital strategic point in the struggles between Scotland and the 'auld enemy' south of the border. Captured by the English during the Wars of Independence (1174–1356), the castle was destroyed by the Scots as part of Robert the Bruce's scorched earth policies in 1313 and wasn't rebuilt until 1371 (by David II). Little of this work survives, however, as the castle was strengthened and renovated in the 16th, 17th and 18th centuries.

Before visiting the castle itself, it's worth wandering around the streets below – follow Castle Tce, which descends from the Royal Mile by the Hub Festival office – to fully appreciate its situation. Three sides of glacier-scoured basalt drop almost vertically from the walls, which exude invulnerability. In fact, the castle was taken several times and often changed hands between the Scots and

---

THE STONE OF DESTINY

Alleged to have accompanied the Scots in all their mythical journeys, the original Stone of Destiny (the Fatal Stone) was a carved block of sandstone brought to Scotland by missionaries from Ireland. In AD 838 it was eventually placed in the abbey at Scone, a couple of miles north of Perth, where for the next four and a half centuries Scottish monarchs were invested upon it.

Stolen by Edward I in 1296, this venerable talisman was incorporated into the Coronation Chair, used by all English (and later British) monarchs, in London's Westminster Abbey. That is, until a plucky band of Scottish students re-abducted the Stone on Christmas Day 1950 and smuggled it back to Scotland, dropping and breaking it on the way (it was patched up by a stonemason).

King George VI was 'sorely troubled about the loss' but three months later, the Stone turned up on the altar of the ruined Arbroath Abbey. Before the public was aware that the Stone had even been found, it was back in London. No charges were brought, and Ian Hamilton – who led this jolly caper and later became a prominent QC – published his story in *The Taking of the Stone of Destiny*.

In 1996 the sandstone block was returned to Scotland, but it now resides in Edinburgh Castle rather than at the site of the abbey in Scone.

Many Scots, however, hold that the original stone is safely hidden somewhere in Scotland and that Edward I was fobbed off with an imitation. This is possibly true – descriptions of the original stone state that it was decorated with intricate carvings. But given that Scottish nationalism is running high, this powerful symbol of Scotland would surely have been brought out by now.

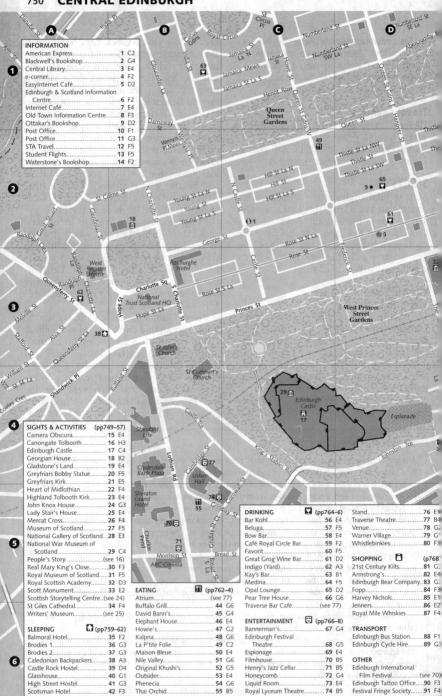

INFORMATION

American Express	1	C2
Blackwell's Bookshop	2	G4
Central Library	3	E4
e-corner	4	F2
EasyInternet Café	5	D2
Edinburgh & Scotland Information Centre	6	F2
Internet Café	7	E4
Old Town Information Centre	8	F3
Ottakar's Bookshop	9	D2
Post Office	10	F1
Post Office	11	G3
STA Travel	12	F5
Student Flights	13	F5
Waterstone's Bookshop	14	F2

SIGHTS & ACTIVITIES (pp749–57)

Camera Obscura	15	E4
Canongate Tolbooth	16	H3
Edinburgh Castle	17	C4
Georgian House	18	B2
Gladstone's Land	19	E4
Greyfriars Bobby Statue	20	F5
Greyfriars Kirk	21	E5
Heart of Midlothian	22	F4
Highland Tolbooth Kirk	23	E4
John Knox House	24	G3
Lady Stair's House	25	E4
Mercat Cross	26	F4
Museum of Scotland	27	F5
National Gallery of Scotland	28	E3
National War Museum of Scotland	29	C4
People's Story	(see 16)	
Real Mary King's Close	30	F3
Royal Museum of Scotland	31	F5
Royal Scottish Academy	32	D3
Scott Monument	33	E2
Scottish Storytelling Centre	(see 24)	
St Giles Cathedral	34	F4
Writers' Museum	(see 25)	

SLEEPING (pp759–62)

Balmoral Hotel	35	E2
Brodies	36	G3
Brodies 2	37	G3
Caledonian Backpackers	38	A3
Castle Rock Hostel	39	D4
Glasshouse	40	G1
High Street Hostel	41	F4
Scotsman Hotel	42	F3
Witchery by the Castle	43	E4

EATING (pp762–4)

Atrium	(see 77)	
Buffalo Grill	44	G6
David Bann's	45	G4
Elephant House	46	E4
Howie's	47	G2
Kalpna	48	G6
La P'tite Folie	49	C2
Maison Bleue	50	E4
Nile Valley	51	G6
Original Khushi's	52	G5
Outsider	53	E4
Phenecia	54	G6
Thai Orchid	55	B5
Witchery by the Castle	(see 43)	

DRINKING (pp764–6)

Bar Kohl	56	E4
Beluga	57	F5
Bow Bar	58	E4
Café Royal Circle Bar	59	F2
Favorit	60	F5
Great Grog Wine Bar	61	D2
Indigo (Yard)	62	A3
Kay's Bar	63	B1
Medina	64	F5
Opal Lounge	65	D2
Pear Tree House	66	G6
Traverse Bar Café	(see 77)	

ENTERTAINMENT (pp766–8)

Bannerman's	67	G4
Edinburgh Festival Theatre	68	G5
Espionage	69	E4
Filmhouse	70	B5
Henry's Jazz Cellar	71	B5
Honeycomb	72	G4
Liquid Room	73	E4
Royal Lyceum Theatre	74	B5
Royal Oak	75	G4

Stand	76	E1
Traverse Theatre	77	B4
Venue	78	G2
Warner Village	79	G?
Whistlebinkies	80	F3

SHOPPING (p768)

21st Century Kilts	81	G3
Armstrong's	82	E4
Edinburgh Bear Company	83	G3
Fopp	84	F3
Harvey Nichols	85	E1
Jenners	86	E2
Royal Mile Whiskies	87	F4

TRANSPORT

Edinburgh Bus Station	88	F1
Edinburgh Cycle Hire	89	G3

OTHER

Edinburgh International Film Festival	(see 70)	
Edinburgh Tattoo Office	90	F3
Festival Fringe Society	91	F4
The Hub	(see 23)	

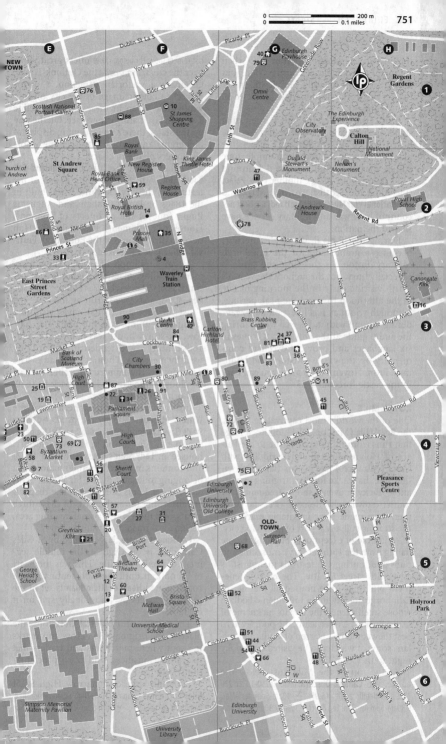

the English. It last saw action in 1745 when Bonnie Prince Charlie's army tried, but failed, to breach its walls, but it's still in active service as the headquarters of the Royal Scots regiment.

Inside the castle, the most interesting sights include: the **Stone of Destiny** (see the boxed text, p749); **St Margaret's Chapel** (the oldest building in Edinburgh), a simple stone edifice probably built by David I around 1130 in memory of his mother; the **Palace** (including the Scottish crown jewels); and the **National War Museum of Scotland**, a good account of how war and military service have shaped the nation.

During the Festival, the castle forecourt becomes a grandstand for the Edinburgh Military Tattoo. At this time the castle is especially busy, but throughout the year it's worth visiting early in the morning or late in the afternoon to avoid the peak periods. Although you may feel like a plonker wandering around with it, it's well worth hiring the audio guide at the entrance: it comes in six languages and provides excellent commentary on the castle's history and buildings. From November to May, you can park in the castle forecourt (£3).

ROYAL MILE

One of the world's most captivating streets, the **Royal Mile** (Map pp750-1) follows a ridge that runs from Edinburgh Castle to the Palace of Holyroodhouse and is riddled with *closes* (entrances) and *wynds* (lanes) on either side that make for an intriguing exploration. Tacky souvenir shops, frequented by tourist crowds who descend over the summer, have made their inevitable mark, but the street is still a real part of a thriving city. It's a jumble of exceptional buildings (some dating from the 15th century), museums and pubs and, during the festivals in August, is alive with street theatre. The elegant tenement buildings once housed all manner of Edinburgh society in an unhygienic bedlam whose smell earned the city its nickname of 'Auld Reekie'. Underneath, the poor lived as best they could in a warren of vaults and cellars, some of which can be visited on spooky night tours (see p759).

At the top of the Mile, just below the castle, the **Camera Obscura** (Map pp750-1; ☎ 226 3709; Castlehill; adult £5.95; ☺ 10am-5pm Nov-Mar, 9.30am-6pm Apr-Jun, Sep & Oct, 9.30am-7.30pm Jul & Aug,

last camera show 1hr before close) offers great views over the city from *inside* the Outlook Tower. Originally a Victorian attraction, a mirror projects a colour image of the city on to a white table. Even in these days of satellite TV, it's a fascinating experience. On the way up the stairs, there's an intriguing display of holograms and optical illusions: the whole visit offers plenty of charm.

Further down the hill, the **Highland Tolbooth Kirk** with its 73m spire, is one of the features of the city's skyline. It was built in the 1840s by James Graham and Augustus Pugin (one of the architects of London's Houses of Parliament). It contains the Hub ticket centre – home of the Edinburgh Festival office (see the boxed text, p759).

A typical example of an Old Town tenement building, **Gladstone's Land** (Map pp750-1; ☎ 226 5856; 477 Lawnmarket; adult £3.50; ☺ 10am-5pm Mon-Sat, 2-5pm Sun Apr-Oct), run by the National Trust for Scotland (NTS), gives visitors a fascinating glimpse of the past. The narrow, six-storey house was built in the mid-16th century and extended around 1617 by wealthy merchant Thomas Gledstanes. The best room is the Painted Chamber with its fabulous painted roof, dating back to 1620, and ornate oak furniture.

Just by here in an atmospheric close, the **Writers' Museum** (Map pp750-1; ☎ 529 4901; Lady Stair's Close, Lawnmarket; admission free; ☺ 10am-5pm Mon-Sat, plus 2-5pm Sun during Edinburgh Festival) is housed in **Lady Stair's House** (built in 1622) and contains manuscripts and memorabilia belonging to Robert Burns, Sir Walter Scott and Robert Louis Stevenson. The displays are absorbing for enthusiasts of these three greats, and there's also a small reading area, designed to make you want to linger.

Parliament Square, largely filled by St Giles Cathedral, is on High St, the middle segment of the Royal Mile. This was the heart of Edinburgh until the 18th century, and a cobblestoned **Heart of Midlothian** is set in the ground. Passers-by traditionally spit on it for luck.

The 19th-century **Mercat Cross** took the place of the original 1365 cross and marks the spot where merchants and traders met to transact business, and royal proclamations were read.

Looming large over narrow High St, **St Giles Cathedral** (Map pp750-1; High St; admission free, donations encouraged; ☺ 9am-5pm Mon-Sat, 1-5pm Sun

Oct-Apr; 9am-7pm Mon-Fri, 1-7pm Sun May-Sep) has giant stained-glass windows providing a kaleidoscope of colour (even on a dull day) and rows of hexagonal columns and crowning arches crisscrossing their way along the length of the building.

Inside is a **statue of John Knox**, minister from 1559 to 1572; he preached his uncompromising Calvinist message and launched the Scottish Reformation from here. The new austerity this ushered in led to changes in the building's interior – decorations, altars and the relics of St Giles were thrown into the Nor Loch, the disgusting lake-cum-cesspit that once fostered disease in the place where Princes Street Gardens and Waverley Station now stand.

The **Real Mary King's Close** (Map pp750-1; ☎ 0870 243 0160; 2 Warriston's Close; adult/child £7/5; ☸ 10am-9pm Apr-Oct, 10am-4pm Nov-Mar) is one way to penetrate the underground world beneath the Old Town. The spooky visit brings to life the sorts of people that may have dwelt here, both rich and poor, who tell stories of their lives. The grimmest is from a man whose job was burying plague victims.

Dating from 1490, **John Knox House** (Map pp750-1; ☎ 556 9579; www.scottishstorytellingcentre .co.uk; 43 High St) is the oldest surviving tenement in Edinburgh. The outside staircase, overhanging upper floors and crow-stepped gables are typical of a 15th-century town house. John Knox is thought to have occupied the 2nd floor from 1561 to 1572. The labyrinthine interior reveals the original walls, fireplaces, painted ceiling and an interesting display on his life, but at time of research was closed until mid-2005, when it will re-open as part of the **Scottish Storytelling Centre**.

The Mile continues below High St as Canongate. A fine example of 16th-century architecture, **Canongate Tolbooth** (Map pp750-1; ☎ 529 4057; 163 Canongate; admission free; ☸ 10am-5pm Mon-Sat, plus 2-5pm Sun Aug) has picturesque turrets and a projecting clock. It served in turn as a collection point for tolls, a council house, a courtroom and a jail. It now houses an absorbing museum, the **People's Story**, relating the story of the life, work and pastimes of ordinary Edinburgh folk from the late-18th century to the present.

SCOTTISH PARLIAMENT

On 9 October 2004, the newest building in the Old Town was opened. The **Scottish Parliament** (Map pp746-7; ☎ 348 5000; www.scottish .parliament.uk; Holyrood Rd; admission free; ☸ 10am-6pm Mon-Fri Apr-Oct, 10am-4pm Mon-Fri Nov-Mar, 10am-4pm Sat & Sun year-round, plus 9am-7pm on days when Parliament is in session, normally Tue-Thu Sep-Jun; wheelchair access) was meant to have been a triumphant symbol of devolution but turned into a shabby political scandal (see the boxed text, p754). However, now that it's finally open, it has won great praise for its architecture: the original design, by the late Enric Miralles, sought to take advantage of the dramatic panorama of Arthur's Seat rising starkly above. The interior is beautifully light and fluid, and it is to be hoped that the inspiring vistas provoke some sort of feelings of humility in the sitting members. Entry is by guided tour; it's advisable to book ahead.

PALACE OF HOLYROODHOUSE & HOLYROOD ABBEY

Developed from a guesthouse attached to medieval Holyrood Abbey, the **Palace of Holyroodhouse** (Map pp746-7; ☎ 556 1096; £11 incl Queen's Gallery, £8 without; ☸ 9.30am-6pm Apr-Oct, 9.30am-4.30pm Nov-Mar) is the monarch's official residence in Scotland, so access to it is very restricted.

Highlights include the royal apartments, with intricately carved plaster ceilings, floor-to-ceiling tapestries and mythological paintings; the King's Bed Chamber is a particularly good example. The modern **Queen's Gallery** (Map pp746-7), suitably blue in colour, hosts changing exhibitions of artwork from the extensive royal collection.

The **abbey** (Map pp746-7), founded by David I in 1128, was probably named after a fragment of the cross (*rood* is an old word for cross) said to have belonged to his mother St Margaret. Most of the surviving ruins date from the 12th and 13th centuries, although a doorway in the far southeastern corner survives from the original Norman church.

James IV extended the abbey guesthouse in 1501; the oldest surviving section of the building, the northwestern tower, was built in 1529 as a royal apartment. Mary, Queen of Scots spent 16 eventful years living in the tower. During this time she married Darnley (in the abbey) and Bothwell (in what is now the Picture Gallery), and this is where she debated with John

Knox and witnessed the murder of her secretary Rizzio. (This man, from Piedmont, had much influence with the queen, and it was rumoured that the two were lovers. He was stabbed 57 times in front of a heavily pregnant Mary by her husband and a group of Protestant nobles.)

This older part of the palace is by far the most interesting, with the dim lighting adding to its sense of skulduggery. There's a certain fascination in following in Mary's footsteps and seeing the room where Rizzio was cut down.

The complex sometimes closes for State functions or when the Queen is in residence, usually in mid-May and mid-June to early July (follow the link Art & Residences from www.royal.gov.uk).

HOLYROOD PARK & ARTHUR'S SEAT

Edinburgh is blessed with having a wilderness on its doorstep. Holyrood Park (Map pp746–7) covers 260 hectares of varied landscape, including mountains, moorland, lochs and fields, and contains some rare plants and insects. The highest point is the 251m-high extinct volcano, Arthur's Seat.

You can circumnavigate the park by car or bike and it has several excellent walks – see the boxed text, p755.

OUR DYNAMIC EARTH

Looking like a giant white crustacean from the outside, this modern, interactive **museum** (Map pp746-7; ☎ 550 7800; www.dynamicearth.co.uk; Holyrood Rd; adult/child £8.95/5.45; ☽ 10am-5pm Apr-Jun, Sep & Oct, 10am-6pm Jul & Aug, 10am-5pm Wed-Sun Nov-Mar; wheelchair access) sits in the shadow of the brooding Salisbury Crags. Younger kids will love the extravaganza of special effects, which recreate and explore the planet's history from the Big Bang to the present day, although there's somewhat more emphasis on style than substance.

South of the Royal Mile
THE GRASSMARKET & AROUND

The Grassmarket, dominated by the looming castle, is a touristy pocket of restaurants and pubs, the latter particularly rowdy at weekends. Beneath this boisterous façade, however, lies a seamy past. This was the main place for public executions and over 100 hanged Covenanters are commemorated with a cross at the eastern end. The notorious murderers William Burke and William Hare operated from a now-vanished close off the western end. In around 1827 they enticed at least 18 victims here, suffocated them and sold the bodies to Edinburgh's medical schools.

THE HOLYROOD FIASCO

One thing that they won't tell you much about on a visit to the Scottish Parliament – but you'll be able to get almost any Scot to vent a strong opinion on – is the scandal of its construction. Once devolution was confirmed, plans were quickly underway to construct a suitable parliament building. The Holyrood site was chosen, and designs were submitted for what was envisaged as a flagship project, garlanded with many noble-sounding democratic phrases.

The winning design was by Catalan architect Enric Miralles, whose vision was deemed to fall within the budgetary scope. Initial projections had been around the £40 million mark: this figure was soon adjusted upwards, but nobody could have envisaged the shambles that was to ensue.

After Donald Dewar was elected First Minister in May 1999 he estimated the final cost would be more in the region of £109 million, but within a year this had doubled, and construction finally started in June 2000. Management of the project was bungled throughout, and it scarcely helped that both Miralles and Dewar passed away within months of the foundation stone being laid.

Ongoing delays coupled with the complete absence of anyone willing to accept ultimate responsibility for the project led to costs spiralling yet again. When the building finally opened in October 2004, the new democracy had footed a bill of in excess of £430 million. An inquiry, the Fraser report, commissioned by Parliament after massive public and media pressure, was severely critical of 'blurred lines of communication' but failed to lay the blame directly at any particular door. Previously, George Reid, presiding officer, had publicly apologised to the nation on behalf of the Scottish Parliament. By the time what *Scotsman* columnist Bill Jamieson described as a 'Pimp's Pavilion' opened, some Scots had completely lost interest in the issue, faith shaken by the whole sordid affair.

The Grassmarket can be approached from George IV Bridge via **Victoria St**, an unusual two-tiered street clinging to the ridge below the Royal Mile. The **Cowgate** runs parallel to the Royal Mile off the eastern end of Grassmarket, under the George IV and South Bridges, and is a tunnel of nightlife and alleyways. A major fire in December 2002 destroyed a substantial section of its southern side; the site has yet to be redeveloped.

GREYFRIARS KIRK & KIRKYARD

At the bottom of a stone canyon made up of tenements, churches, volcanic cliffs and the castle, Greyfriars Kirkyard is one of Edinburgh's most evocative spots – a peaceful oasis dotted with memorials surrounded a dramatic skyline.

The **church** (Map pp750-1) was built over a Franciscan friary and opened for worship in 1620. The National Covenant was signed here in 1638, affirming the independence of the Scottish Church from Charles I's attempts to reintroduce episcopacy. Many of those who signed were executed and, in 1679, 1200 Covenanters were held prisoner in terrible conditions in an enclosure in the yard.

More heartwarmingly, the churchyard holds the remains of **Greyfriars Bobby** (Map pp750-1), a Skye terrier who, from 1858 to 1872, maintained a vigil over his master's grave; during his 14-year mission he was fed and cared for by locals. His story, immortalised in a novel by Eleanor Atkinson, was later turned into a Disney film. Tour groups congregate on the street outside, around an underwhelmingly tiny statue of the faithful hound.

ROYAL MUSEUM OF SCOTLAND & MUSEUM OF SCOTLAND

These two **museums** (Map pp750-1; ☎ 247 4219; www.nms.ac.uk; Chambers St; admission free; ☑ 10am-5pm Mon & Wed-Sat, 10am-8pm Tue, noon-5pm Sun; wheelchair access) make a very good couple.

The Royal Museum of Scotland, with its bright, airy sun-roofed hall, is a Victorian building housing a comprehensive collection covering the natural world; archaeology; Chinese, Islamic and European decorative art; and even technology. Next door, the beautifully integrated, modern, sandstone Museum of Scotland explores the history of Scotland in chronological order, starting with the country's earliest history in the basement and finishing with the most recent on the top floor.

The New Town

The 18th century New Town runs along a parallel ridge to the Old Town, separated from it by a valley taken up by Princes Street Gardens. Its stately order contrasts starkly to the tangled confusion of the Old Town.

It was born out of the upper classes' desire to create healthier and more fitting quarters as the city staggered under a burgeoning population. The stability introduced by the 1707 Act of Union made this dream a reality; Nor Loch, at the northern foot of Castle Rock, was drained and the North Bridge was constructed.

The New Town grew rapidly and continued to sprout squares, circuses, parks and terraces; some of its finest neoclassical architecture was designed by Robert Adam.

ARTHUR'S SEAT IN A FLASH

The short hike up Arthur's Seat is the best walk around the city. In summer you'll see the silhouettes of many ant-like figures trudging up Edinburgh's peak for superb views. The relatively easy walk to the summit takes about 45 minutes. From the Palace of Holyroodhouse make your way to Queen's Dr, cross the road and walk up the footpath that angles left up the hill. When you reach the top of a rise, turn left on a rough path (the main footpath leads to the valley of Hunter's Bog) and walk along the foot of the crags. Keep to the higher left fork that ascends steeply up steps to a saddle. Turn right and climb the final short ascent to the summit of Arthur's Seat (251m). It gets windy up here, but the views make it all worthwhile, and you'll return to town ruddy-faced, clean-lunged, and feeling like you've spent a week hillwalking!

Descend easterly to the road at Dunsapie Loch – turn right here and walk to Duddingston Loch. Pop into the nearby **Sheep Heid Inn** (☎ 656 6951; 43 The Causeway, Duddingston), perhaps the oldest pub in Edinburgh with a licence dating back to 1360, for some well-deserved refreshments and then walk back to Holyrood by following the Radical Rd along the foot of Salisbury Crags.

CALTON HILL

Hovering above Edinburgh's stately skyline, **Calton Hill** rises 100m above the eastern end of Princes St and is strewn with grandiose Athenian-style memorials mostly dating from the first half of the 19th century. A walk around the summit affords tremendous views of Edinburgh, taking in the entire panorama from Holyrood Park to the Firth of Forth.

PRINCES ST

Princes St is a spectacular retail thoroughfare with exquisite views across the gardens to the castle and the jumble of striking façades that line the Old Town.

About midway down Princes St, the massive Gothic spire of the **Scott Monument** (Map pp750-1; ☎ 529 4068; adult £2.50; ♥ 9am-6pm Mon-Sat & 10am-6pm Sun Apr-Sep, 9am-3pm Mon-Sat & 10am-3pm Sun Oct-Mar), built by public subscription after Sir Walter Scott's death in 1832, testifies to a popularity largely inspired by his role in rebuilding pride in Scottish identity. You enter this somewhat gloomy edifice via Princes St Gardens and climb 287 steps up a narrow winding staircase. From the top there are good views of the city.

Princes Street Gardens, home of a colourful Christmas market (the mulled wine is a godsend!) and ice rink in December, are cut by **The Mound** – a huge pile of earth dumped during the construction of the New Town, which provides a road link between the Old and New Towns.

ROYAL SCOTTISH ACADEMY & NATIONAL GALLERY OF SCOTLAND

The Grecian-style **Royal Scottish Academy** (RSA; Map pp750-1; ☎ 225 6671; www.royalscottishacademy .org; The Mound; admission times & charges depend on exhibitions; wheelchair access), built in 1826, has recently created more than a few red faces among those responsible for the Scottish Parliament debacle. An ambitious refurbishment program culminated, in August 2004, with the triumphant opening – on time, on budget, and half funded by public donation – of a sleek underground exhibition space and shopping precinct linking the noble building to its neighbour, the National Gallery. The results are excellent: a huge modern facility (worthy of showcasing the best of international art) that enhances the neo-Doric lines of the original building.

The opening exhibition, of Titian and other Venetian Renaissance artists, whetted the appetite for what should evolve into Scotland's premier gallery. The Academy also remains devoted to its original purpose, which is to exhibit Scottish art (usually of a very high standard) by RSA members.

The **National Gallery of Scotland** (Map pp750-1; ☎ 624 6200; www.nationalgalleries.org; The Mound; admission free; ♥ 10am-5pm Fri-Wed, 10am-7pm Thu; wheelchair access), behind the RSA, is another imposing neoclassical building. It houses an important collection of European art in opulent halls. There are paintings by masters from the Renaissance to the Impressionists, but, considering where you are, the Scottish artists – especially William MacTaggart – deserve plenty of your time.

GEORGE ST & CHARLOTTE SQUARE

George St was originally envisaged as the main thoroughfare of the residential New Town. It's now home to highly successful Scottish financial institutions. It runs from St Andrew Sq (home of Harvey Nichols and the bus station) in the east to Charlotte Sq in the west.

The latter was designed in 1791 by Robert Adam and is regarded as the jewel of the New Town. On the northern side of the square is a Georgian masterpiece, Bute House at No 6, the official residence of Scotland's First Minister.

Next door, the **Georgian House** (NTS; Map pp750-1; ☎ 225 2160; 7 Charlotte Sq; adult £5; ♥ 10am-5pm Apr-Oct, 11am-3pm Nov, Dec & Mar) has been beautifully restored and refurnished to show how Edinburgh's elite lived at the end of the 18th century, when the New Town was first settled. A 35-minute video brings it all to life.

SCOTTISH NATIONAL GALLERY OF MODERN ART

Just beyond Edinburgh's West End, the western extension of the New Town, is this bright, modern **gallery** (Map pp746-7; ☎ 624 6200; www.nationalgalleries.org; 75 Belford Rd; admission free; ♥ 10am-5pm Fri-Wed, 10am-7pm Thu), housed in an impressive classical building surrounded by a sculpture park. The collection concentrates on 20th-century art, with works by Henri Matisse, Pablo Picasso, René Magritte and Henry Moore among others. Most space is given to Scottish painters and it's small enough not to overwhelm. To get here, take bus No 13 from George St.

Northern Edinburgh

The New Town's Georgian architecture extends north to **Stockbridge**, one of the most pleasant suburbs to wander through – it's quite trendy but has retained a village-like charm that gives it a distinct, vibrant identity. There are plenty of shops, restaurants and pubs here.

North of Stockbridge, the lovely **Royal Botanic Gardens** (☎ 552 7171; 20a Inverleith Row; admission free, for glasshouses £3.50; ☯ 10am-dusk; wheelchair access) is in a beautiful spot, and the 70 landscaped acres are well worth a stroll for their exotic plants, colourful rhododendrons and views of Edinburgh's skyline. Bus Nos 8, 23, 27 and 37 pass the gardens.

LEITH

Flamboyant Leith is Edinburgh's main port, although it remained an independent burgh until the 1920s. It's still among Britain's busiest ports but in the 1960s and '70s it fell into a sad state – abandoned to council housing and frequented by drug dealers. A recent revival means that it's now home to many of the city's best pubs and restaurants.

Parts of this neighbourhood are still a little rough but it's a distinctive, colourful corner of Edinburgh. The prettiest area is around The Shore.

The royal yacht **Britannia** (☎ 555 5566; Ocean Dr, Leith; adult £8.50; ☯ 9.30am-4.30pm Apr-Sep, 10am-3.30pm Oct-Mar; wheelchair access), moored by the new Ocean Terminal shopping complex, was used for royal travels abroad from 1953 until its decommissioning in 1997. This monument to 1950s style and décor offers an intriguing insight into remarkably simple royal tastes. Thermometers maintaining bathroom temperatures and windbreaks designed to prevent a sudden gust revealing royal undies are some of the idiosyncrasies built into the design. Exploration is via self-guided multilingual tour.

Frequent buses, including No 11 from St Andrew Sq, will whisk you down to Leith. A bus for *Britannia* leaves regularly from Waverley Bridge outside the train station.

ACTIVITIES

Edinburgh has several spots to escape the city bustle on foot or two wheels. An obvi-

---

TOP FIVE ATTRACTIONS FOR THE YOUNG & RESTLESS

- **Real Mary King's Close** (p753) Explore Edinburgh's dark underground.

- **Camera Obscura** (p752) Fun and games with optical illusions.

- **Our Dynamic Earth** (p754) A plethora of special effects and activities.

- **Holyrood Park** (p754) Burn energy and feed the swans in the city's own little Highlands.

- **Rapido** (p763) If they want fish and chips, better make it the city's best!

---

ous choice is Holyrood Park, where walkers can ascend **Arthur's Seat** for spectacular views; a road runs right around the base of the volcano for an easy break right by the Royal Mile. From the southern side of the park, a cycleway follows an old railway 5 miles east to the coastal town of Musselburgh. See the boxed text on p755 for details.

It's possible to walk or cycle along the serene wooded riverbanks of the **Water of Leith**, which runs from the Pentland Hills 20 miles down to the city centre, and on to Leith. There are access points and signposts throughout its length: one of the best short walks is from Stockbridge to historic Dean Village, once a milling community, where the waterway is spanned by a Thomas Telford bridge.

WALKING TOUR

Edinburgh's Old Town spreads down the Royal Mile to the east of the castle and southwards to the Grassmarket and Greyfriars. This walk explores a few of the Old Town's many interesting nooks and crannies, and involves a fair bit of climbing up and down steep stairs and closes.

Begin on the **Castle Esplanade (1)**, which provides a grandstand view southwards over the Grassmarket; the prominent quadrangular building with all the turrets is George Heriot's School, which you'll be passing later on. Head towards Castlehill and the start of the Royal Mile. The 17th-century house on the right, above the steps of North Castle Wynd, is known as **Cannonball House (2)** because of the iron ball lodged in the wall (look between, and slightly below, the two largest windows). It was not fired in anger, but instead marks the gravitation height to which water would flow naturally from the city's first piped water supply.

The low, rectangular building across the street (now a touristy tartan-weaving mill) was originally the reservoir that held the Old Town's water supply. On its western wall is the **Witches Well (3)**, where a modern bronze fountain commemorates around 4000 people (mostly women) who were burnt or strangled in Edinburgh between 1479 and 1722 on suspicion of witchcraft.

Go past the reservoir and turn left down Ramsay Lane, and take a look at **Ramsay Garden (4)** – one of the most desirable addresses in Edinburgh – where late-19th-century apartments were built around the nucleus of the octagonal Ramsay Lodge, once home

WALK FACTS

Distance 1½ miles
Duration 1–2 hours

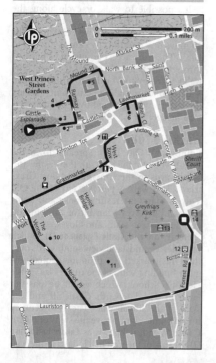

to poet Allan Ramsay. The cobbled street continues around to the right below student residences, to the twin towers of the **New College (5)** – home to Edinburgh University's Faculty of Divinity. Nip into the courtyard to see the **statue of John Knox** (p753).

Just past New College, turn right and climb up the stairs into Milne's Court, a student residence that houses the public entrance to what was once the temporary home of the Scottish Parliament. Exit into the Lawnmarket, cross the street (bearing slightly left) and duck into **Riddell's Court (6)** at No 322–8, a typical Old Town close. You'll find yourself in a small courtyard, but the house in front of you, built in 1590, was originally the edge of the street (the building you just walked under was added in 1726 – check the inscription in the doorway on the right). The arch (with the inscription 'VIVENDO DISCIMUS', 'we live and learn') leads into the original 16th-century courtyard.

Go back into the street, turn right, and then right again down Fisher's Close, which ejects you onto the delightful Victoria Tce, strung above the cobbled curve of shop-lined Victoria St. Wander right, enjoying the view – **Maxie's Bistro (7)**, located at the far end of the terrace, is a great place to stop for a rest and a drink – then descend the stairs at the foot of Upper Bow and continue downhill to the Grassmarket (p754). At the eastern end, outside Maggie Dickson's pub, is the **Covenanters' Monument (8)**; if you're feeling peckish, there are several good places to eat and a couple of good pubs – Robert Burns once stayed at the **White Hart Inn (9)**.

At the west end of the Grassmarket, turn left up the flight of stairs known as the Vennel. At the top of the steps on the left you'll find the **Flodden Wall (10)**. Follow its extension, the Telfer Wall, to Lauriston Pl and turn left along the impressive façade of **George Heriot's School (11)**. Note that this is the back of the building – the front was designed to face the castle and impress the inhabitants of the Grassmarket.

Turn left again at Forrest Rd, and if it's a Sunday afternoon pop into **Sandy Bell's (12)** for a pint and some Scottish folk music. Finish off your walk with a stroll through **Greyfriars Kirkyard (13**; p755) or a visit to the **Museum of Scotland (14**; p755).

TOURS

The long-established **Mercat Tours** (☎ 557 6464; www.mercattours.com) is one of several offering walking tours and has a wide range, including trips into Edinburgh's excavated underground closes and vaults, which have been the site of many reported supernatural phenomena. Tour times are displayed on the Royal Mile near St Giles Cathedral, and start from the Mercat Cross.

The highly recommended three-hour **Adrian's City Cycle Tour** (☎ 07966 447206; www.edinburghcycletour.com; tour adult £15), on bicycle, runs twice daily at 10am and 2.30pm and takes three hours.

The 5-mile trip takes you to all parts of the city centre, and Adrian provides an entertaining commentary at the stops along the way.

It's £15 (£10 for students and backpackers). The tours leave from the Abbey Sanctuary bookshop by the gates of Holyroodhouse at the bottom of the Royal Mile. Phone ahead to make sure there are bikes available.

Open-topped buses depart from Waverley Bridge, outside the train station, and offer traditional hop-on, hop-off tours of the main sights. **City Sightseeing Edinburgh** (☎ 220 0770; www.edinburghtour.com) charges £8.50, and runs four slightly different routes under a variety of names.

SLEEPING

Edinburgh has masses of accommodation but the city still fills up quickly over the New Year, at Easter, between mid-May and mid-September (particularly while the festivals

---

FESTIVAL FRENZY & FREEBIES

Activity in the 'festival city' peaks during August, when a smorgasbord of culture is up for grabs. It's a terrific time to be in Edinburgh, but booking accommodation months ahead is strongly advised.

The three-week **Edinburgh International Festival** is the world's largest, most important arts festival, with the best performers playing to capacity audiences. Prebooking is strongly recommended and prices are generally reasonable. The programme, published in March, is available from the Edinburgh Festival office, also known as the **Hub** (Map pp750-1; ☎ 473 2000; www.eif.co.uk; Highland Tolbooth Kirk, Castlehill; ⏰ 10am-5pm Mon-Sat) and contains discount vouchers. Alternatively, half-price tickets are sold on the day of some performances at the Hub, and 50 tickets for each event are on sale for £5 an hour before the performance at the venue itself.

The less formal but equally entertaining **Edinburgh Festival Fringe**, running at roughly the same time, is an extravaganza of would-be stars and avant-garde performance. Possibly the largest such event in the world (over 1000 different shows in 2004), the repertoire is eclectic and booking is also advised. Most tickets cost £5 to £10; during the first two days the box office holds a two-for-one ticket frenzy and the *Scotsman* newspaper offers two-for-one vouchers every day in its Festival Guide. If that's still out of your price range, there are around 100 completely free shows, a month of street theatre on the Royal Mile and Fringe Sunday – with free performances in marquees in The Meadows. Programmes and tickets are available, from June, from the **Festival Fringe Society** (Map pp750-1; ☎ 226 0000; www.edfringe.com; 180 High St).

Several other festivals and events take place in August, including the hugely popular **Edinburgh Military Tattoo**, a lavish event of regimental posturing on the Esplanade of Edinburgh Castle. Contact the **Tattoo Office** (Map pp750-1; ☎ 225 1188; www.edinburgh-tattoo.co.uk; 33 Market St) for tickets.

The 10-day **Edinburgh Jazz & Blues Festival** (☎ 668 2019; www.jazzmusic.co.uk) attracts top musicians from around the world. The two-week **Edinburgh International Film Festival** (Map pp750-1; ☎ 623 8030; www.edfilmfest.org.uk; 88 Lothian Rd) is the world's oldest film festival. Authors and literary enthusiasts gather in Charlotte Sq for the **Edinburgh Book Festival** (☎ 228 5444; www.edbookfest.co.uk; 137 Dundee St), which also runs for two weeks.

Hogmanay (www.edinburghshogmanay.org), the Scottish celebration of the New Year, is another major fixture in Edinburgh's festival calendar, with a massive street party on Princes St, spectacular fireworks from the castle and events in various venues around town. You have to reserve your pass for Princes St in advance: this was formerly free but now costs £2.50. Check the website for details of the telephone hotline.

EDINBURGH

are in full swing) or when there's a major event in the sporting calendar. Book in advance if possible or use the ESIC's booking service (p748). Prices here do not reflect the increases that usually apply during the Edinburgh Festival.

The Old Town & South of the Royal Mile
BUDGET

Brodies 2 (Map pp750-1; ☎ 556 2223; www.brodies hostels.co.uk; 93 High St; dm £10.50-21.90, d from £45; ✗ ▢) This friendly hostel right on the Royal Mile is a step up from some of the grungier backpacker places around. Good value except in summer, it has dorm beds with a bit of fight in them and very smart doubles with either attached or shared bathrooms. There's free Internet access among facilities that are stylish and modern.

High Street Hostel (Map pp750-1; ☎ 557 3984; www.scotlands-top-hostels.com; 8 Blackfriars St; dm £12-13.50; ✗ ▢) This long-established, well-equipped hostel is consistently very busy due to its great location just off the Royal Mile. The dorms are large enough although can be a little stuffy, and there are good facilities, including a pool table, video lounge, and bike rental; the kitchen, however, is very simple. The hostel has a reputation as a party place.

Brodies 1 (Map pp750-1; ☎ 556 6770; www.brodies hostels.co.uk; 12 High St; dm £10.50-16.50; ✗ ▢) The original Brodies is small and a good choice. The 17th-century building is a cosy wooden-beamed delight and the common area sociable. The dorms are classy, with original design and quality mattresses. The kitchen is good, and there's laundry facilities.

Other recommendations:
Bruntsfield SYHA (Map pp746-7; ☎ 0870 004 1114; www.syha.org.uk; 7 Bruntsfield Cres; dm £16; ✗ ▢) Excellent location by park, fine facilities, 24-hour access, and a quiet friendly atmosphere.
Castle Rock Hostel (Map pp750-1; ☎ 225 9666; www .scotlands-top-hostels.com; 15 Johnston Tce; dm £12-13.50, d £40-45; ✗ ▢) Terrific position in the shadow of the looming castle. Receives good feedback from travellers.

MID-RANGE

There's a high concentration of B&Bs along Newington Rd, and also in Bruntsfield.

Southside Guest House (Map pp746-7; ☎ 668 4422; www.southsideguesthouse.co.uk; 8 Newington Rd; s/d from £42/64; ✗) You'll find no porcelain spaniels or families of ducks on the walls here, for this

excellent southside option has transcended the B&B category and feels more like a stylish modern boutique hotel. Decorated with a light and unfailingly tasteful touch, it features distinct and beautiful rooms with DVD and wooden floors. The wholefood café downstairs ensures that, for once, there's proper coffee at breakfast time!

Greenhouse (Map pp746-7; ☎ 622 7634; www.green house-edinburgh.com; 14 Hartington Gardens; r per person £30-40; ✗) This quiet guesthouse will appeal to vegetarians and vegans: even the shampoo and soaps in the bathrooms are free of animal products. The rooms are homely and have huge windows. Best of all, though, is the inventive and massive breakfast menu: you could stay a fortnight here and not sample all its delights!

Cluaran House (Map pp746-7; ☎ 221 0047; www .cluaran-house-edinburgh.co.uk; 47 Leamington Tce; s/d from £40/70; ✗) This sensitively restored town house is a stylish pad, all colour, comfort and elegance, lightened by cheery Gallic inscription painted on the walls. It has excellent period features and wooden floorboards throughout; the rooms are lovely, particularly number 3, which has big bay windows.

Afton Guest House (Map pp746-7; ☎ 229 1019; www.afton-g-house.co.uk; 1 Hartington Gardens; r per person £18-30; ✗) This bright clean spot has plush carpeted rooms, some of which are large enough to include a mini-lounge suite and still have plenty of space. It's considerably cheaper than its neighbours and accommodates single travellers.

Salisbury (Map pp746-7; ☎ 667 1264; www.salis buryguesthouse.co.uk; 45 Salisbury Rd; s/d from £30/50; ✗) This semidetached sandstone guesthouse is 10 minutes south of the centre by bus in Newington. It's a classy, genteel Georgian place with fluted columns beside its entrance. The rooms, if a little small, ooze warmth and serenity and most peer out onto the lovely back garden.

Other recommendations:
Armadillo Guest House (Map pp746-7; ☎ 229 6457; 12 Gilmore Pl; r per person £15-30) Good value and gay-friendly.
Avondale Guest House (Map pp746-7; ☎ 667 6779; 10 South Gray St; s/d from £25/45; P ✗) Welcoming, traditional pad in a quiet neighbourhood.
Braveheart Guest House (Map pp746-7; ☎ 221 9192; www.braveheartguesthouse.co.uk; 26 Gilmore Pl; s £20-25, d £50-60; P ✗) Set on a street with many B&B options, this one wins regular plaudits from readers.

Hopetoun (Map pp746-7; ☎ 667 7691; www.hopetoun
.com; 15 Mayfield Rd; r per person £20-45; ✗) Informal
and hospitable, with two large, homely rooms that have a
modern touch.

TOP END

Scotsman Hotel (Map pp750-1; ☎ 556 5565; www
.thescotsmanhotel.com; North Bridge; r from £200; P ✗
🖳 🕱) Until recently the HQ of Edinburgh's
main newspaper, this superbly situated hotel
is an exciting place to stay. Much of the interior has been left alone: the rooms are all
distinct, according to their different functions when in the hands of the fourth estate.
All are utterly comfortable, with amazing
facilities, including a computer terminal and
DVD player; there's also an on-site health
club. The bar is called 399, for that is how
many malts it stocks.

Witchery by the Castle (Map pp750-1; ☎ 225 5613;
www.thewitchery.com; 352 Castlehill; ste from £250) Right
below the castle are some of the most opu-
lent, over-the-top suites you could possibly
imagine. Above and opposite the famous
Witchery restaurant (p763), these little pleasure palaces are done out in lavish Gothic
style, with four-posters, antiques and suits
of armour. All seven suites are very different,
and could come from the fantasies of a mad
count. Just the spot for a honeymoon.

The New Town & Northern Edinburgh

BUDGET

Belford Hostel (Map pp746-7; ☎ 225 6209; www.hoppo
.com; 6 Douglas Gardens; dm £12-18; ✗ 🖳) Housed
in an atmospheric converted church in the
West End, this hostel is very cheerful – the
bar, complete with pool table, sees to that.
There are good facilities and no curfew; the
dorms range from four to 10 beds and there
are also doubles and twins. From September
to May, the hostel offers an excellent weekly
rate of £50, so it's a good option if you plan
to find short-term work here.

Edinburgh Caravan Club Site (☎ 312 6874; www
.caravanclub.co.uk; 35 Marine Dr; tent sites £3.50-5, plus per
person £3.80-5) This campsite is five miles from
the centre in the suburbs of Edinburgh. It's
in a nice position, overlooking the Firth of
Forth, and has excellent facilities. Although
geared primarily for caravans, there are
plenty of tent sites. It's essential to book
during summer, when no cars are allowed
in the tent area. Take bus no 8A from
Broughton St.

Another recommendation:

Caledonian Backpackers (Map pp750-1; ☎ 476 7224;
www.caledonianbackpackers.com; 3 Queensferry St; dm
£11-16, d £34-36; ✗ 🖳) Good hostel ambitious to raise
the bar in terms of backpacker accommodation, and right
by Princes St.

MID-RANGE

Mingalar (Map pp746-7; ☎ 556 7000; www.criper.com;
2 East Claremont St; s/d from £27/45; P ✗ 🖳) The
name means 'welcome' in Burmese, and
this is truly a place where you'll feel right at
home. The charming, erudite hosts encourage guests to treat the house as their own:
there's a kitchenette and computer available,
and the rooms have been beautifully refurbished to highlight the elegant Georgian
lines of the house. Breakfast is a cheerful
affair and well above average: in short, this
is one of Edinburgh's best value B&Bs.

Ardmor House (☎ 554 4944; www.ardmorhouse.com;
74 Pilrig St; s/d from £45/64; ✗) It's through staying in places like this that you realize that
'effortless style' is an oxymoron. What the
charming host here has created is a light and
enticingly chic abode that no doubt took a
hell of a lot of work to create! It's described
as 'gay owned, straight friendly' and with
décor that is beautifully detailed yet not
fussy, this is a great place to stay for all.

Caravel Guest House (Map pp746-7; ☎ 556 4444;
www.caravelhouse.co.uk; 30 London St; r per person £20-
30; ✗) Right by the rich vein of pubs and
restaurants that is Broughton St, the Caravel is an excellent choice. The comfortable
rooms have a charmingly old-fashioned
style to them, the hospitality is impeccable, and there's a great Moroccan restaurant
downstairs.

Christopher North House Hotel (Map pp746-7;
☎ 225 2720; www.christophernorth.co.uk; 6 Gloucester Pl;
s/d from £68/90; ✗) This small, elegant, boutique
hotel is handy for everything in Stockbridge.
Once the home of a writer and philosopher,
it's intimate, and decorated plushly, with
striped wallpaper and embroidered bedcovers. A touch of old Vienna class is added
by the Austrian-themed café-bar.

Other recommendations:

Dene Guest House (Map pp746-7; ☎ 556 2700; www
.deneguesthouse.com; 7 Eyre Pl; s/d from £20/40; ✗) The
cheaper rooms here can be a bit cramped but it's a friendly,
accommodating place.

Original Raj (Map pp746-7; ☎ 346 1333; www.raj
empire.com; 6 West Coates; r £60-90; P ✗) South Asian

splendour: colourful Indian cotton decorates the beds, while you can tuck into samosas for breakfast (but no kedgeree!).
Terrace Hotel (Map pp746–7; ☎ 556 3423; www.terrace hotel.co.uk; 37 Royal Tce; s/d from £31/45; ✕) Best of several on this street with good value terraced elegance.

TOP END
Balmoral Hotel (Map pp750–1; ☎ 556 2414; www .thebalmoralhotel.com; 1 Princes St; s/d from £195/225; P ✕ ☎) Edinburgh's most famous hotel stands stocky as a castle at the corner of Princes St and North Bridge. Some rooms have wonderful views, although the interior ones can be a little claustrophobic. However, the standard of facilities and service is first class. Famous heads to hit the pillows include Kylie Minogue; there are regular promotional deals listed on its website.

Glasshouse (Map pp750–1; ☎ 525 8200; www.theeton collection.com; 2 Greenside Pl; r from £175; P ✕) One of Edinburgh's newest hotels is in a slightly bizarre position, straddling the ugly Omni cinema and shopping precinct and the beautiful façade of a 19th-century church. The rooms, however, are all class, with floorboards and floor-to-ceiling windows. The bathrooms feature equally stylish modern design.

EATING

There are good-value restaurants scattered all around the city. For cheap eats, the best areas are where the student population is high – especially near the university around Nicolson St, but you can also take advantage of the fact that most Edinburgh restaurants offer a very cheap set menu at lunch time. Two of the best zones for evening dining are Stockbridge and around the Shore in Leith.

The Old Town & South of the Royal Mile
BUDGET
Elephant House (Map pp750–1; ☎ 220 5355; 21 George IV Bridge; snacks £3–5; ☷ 8am-11pm Mon-Fri, 9am-11pm Sat & Sun; ✕ 💻) You couldn't really ask for more from a café. As well as great coffee and tea, and delicious baguettes and pastries, there are big sociable tables, castle views, newspapers, cheapish bottles of wine, Internet access (£2 per hour) and elephants in all shapes and sizes. No wonder this is where JK Rowling penned much of the first Harry Potter novel.

Original Khushi's (Map pp750–1; ☎ 667 0888; 26 Potterrow; mains £4–8; ☷ noon-11pm Mon-Sat, 5-11pm Sun; ✕ 💻) This Edinburgh curry institution is well into its sixth decade but has recently moved into sleek new premises, all big windows and polished floorboards. Happily, the food, with the carefully marinated meat oozing with spicy flavours, is as good as ever, and priced ever so fairly. There's no liquor licence, but it's BYOB (bring your own bottle) with no corkage charge.

Nile Valley (Map pp750–1; ☎ 667 8200; 6 Chapel St; lunch £4.95, wraps £2–3, mains £6–10; ☷ lunch & dinner Mon-Sat) This relaxed and expansive Sudanese restaurant is one of the city's budget bargains. Whether you opt for a takeaway wrap in fresh pitta-style bread, the cheap-as-chips lunch menu (*foul*, a delicious broad bean dish, is a must), or the wider evening selection, you'll be amazed by the rich, powerful flavours on offer. It's BYOB with no corkage, too!

Another recommendation:
Kalpna (Map pp750–1; ☎ 667 9890; 2 St Patrick's Sq; mains £4–8; ☷ lunch Mon-Sat, dinner Mon-Sun; ✕) Well into its third decade, this Indian vegetarian restaurant is a firm favourite.

MID-RANGE
Outsider (Map pp750–1; ☎ 226 3131; 15 George IV Bridge; dishes £6–10; ☷ noon-11pm; ✕ ; wheelchair access) Rarely do places tamper with the restaurant paradigm, so this chic but easy-going eatery is a very pleasant surprise. There are no starters, and most of the dishes are designed for sharing. The ultrafriendly staff will guide you through the menu, which includes such sections as 'soupy stir-fries' (the chorizo and chickpea one is a must) and 'CHL splits'. The wine list takes the mickey out of the genre, and the overall experience is at once classy but enlivening.

Maison Bleue (Map pp750-1; ☎ 226 1900; 36 Victoria St; meals £8-16, set lunch or pretheatre £15; ☺ lunch & dinner; ✗) This lovable restaurant offers an innovative menu in the form of 'Bouchees (mouthfuls), Bouchees Doubles or Brochettes (skewers)'. The menu combines French with North African and Asian flavours, all in a cheerful atmosphere. The light lunch deal of three bouchees is the best value – quality dishes in dainty portions. Try the mouthwatering goats' cheese or the filling Lebanese platter.

David Bann's (Map pp750-1; ☎ 556 5888; 56 St Mary's St; mains £9-11; ☺ 11am-10pm Sun-Thu, 11am-midnight Fri & Sat; ✗) This stylish spot is proof that vegetarian restaurants don't have to come with a built-in Bob Marley soundtrack. The exquisite creations include light bar meals as well as suave and modish restaurant dining. Main courses such as spicy kofta balls or a delicate but very filling risotto will satisfy even the most ardent carnivore. Many vegan options are available, too.

Thai Orchid (Map pp750-1; ☎ 228 4438; 44 Grindlay St; mains £6-11; ☺ lunch & dinner Mon-Sat; ✗) This intimate green restaurant is especially handy for the West End theatres and will make sure you're served fast if there's a show to catch. Although you wouldn't want to discuss state secrets at the closely packed tables, the warm welcome and consistently reliable Thai food make this a winner.

Other recommendations:

Buffalo Grill (Map pp750-1; ☎ 667 7427; 12 Chapel St; set lunch £9, mains £8-15; ☺ lunch & dinner Mon-Fri, dinner only Sat & Sun) Juicy steaks are served at this popular BYOB restaurant.

Phenecia (Map pp750-1; ☎ 662 4493; 55 West Nicolson St; set lunch £4.95, mains £6-12; ☺ lunch & dinner Mon-Sat) Vast range of Mediterranean delicacies, ideal for sharing. Friendly and heaps of vegetarian choice.

TOP END

Atrium (Map pp750-1; ☎ 228 8882; 10 Cambridge St; set lunch/dinner £13.50/25, mains £18-22; ☺ lunch & dinner Mon-Fri, dinner Sat; ✗; wheelchair access) Considered by many to be Edinburgh's best restaurant, Atrium sits above the Traverse Theatre in the West End. It's lofty reputation is built on solid foundations, with a consistent quality of produce, presentation and snoot-free service that make dining here a joy. The menu is short but memorable, with the breast of duck especially succulent; the intimate, soothing décor caps what is all-round excellence.

SOMETHING SPECIAL

If the castle and the spooky streets of the old town have got you in the mood for a bit of lavish historical fantasy, you couldn't do better than dinner at **Witchery by the Castle** (Map pp750-1; ☎ 225 5613; 352 Castlehill; set lunch £9.95, mains £13-28; ☺ lunch & dinner). Just down from the castle, the sumptuous furnishings of this Edinburgh classic keep visitors streaming in. There are two dining areas, the lower of which, the Secret Garden, is light and airy, while the higher is more theatrically Gothic. The food matches the surroundings, with oysters, fillet steaks and smoked salmon prominent. The best-value way to appreciate the ambience is at lunch time (the same price is offered in the early evening and late at night).

The New Town & Northern Edinburgh

BUDGET

Blue Moon Café (Map pp746-7; ☎ 557 0911; 36 Broughton St; light meals £4-8; ☺ 11am-10pm Mon-Thu, 10am-10pm Fri-Sun; ✗) This local institution has for years been a focal point for the area's gay scene but gives a warm welcome to everyone. It is deservedly popular, dishing up veggie meals, sensational burgers and knockout all-day breakfasts on the weekend, with a bloody mary first on the menu.

Pizza Express (Map pp746-7; ☎ 332 7229; 1 Deanhaugh St, Stockbridge; pizzas £6-10; ☺ 11.30am-11pm; ✗) Yes, it's a chain, but it's a chain that chooses excellent locations for its restaurants – and this branch, by the Water of Leith in Stockbridge, is the best. On a sunny day – or, more realistically, a nonrainy day – you can't beat sitting on the terrace by the river and munching the good-quality pizza with a bottle of white wine close at hand.

Rapido (Map pp746-7; ☎ 556 2041; 77 Broughton St; takeaways £2-5; ☺ 11.30am-2pm, 4.30pm-late) One of Edinburgh's best takeaways, and handily situated for closing time at the many pubs on this street. It's a chip shop with class – where else could you get a peppered turkey-steak supper? – and also serves tasty baked potatoes, pizzas and wraps.

MID-RANGE

Fishers (☎ 554 5666; 1 The Shore, Leith; mains £13-16; ☺ noon-10.30pm) This cosy bistro sits in a 17th-century signal tower on the Leith Shore. The delight of it is that it has the cheery atmosphere of a pub combined with the superb seafood of the classiest restaurant. Simple options like mussels in white wine sauce or fish cakes take on new dimensions here, while the seafood platter at £15.95 renders a starter completely unnecessary. Chirpy service adds to the appeal.

Howie's (Map pp750-1; ☎ 556 5766; 29 Waterloo Pl; 2-course lunch/dinner £8.75/15.95; ⓨ lunch & dinner; ⊠) The most attractive branch of this popular Edinburgh institution, this is a large light space in what was once a chapel. To fully appreciate the interior, and profit from the view, go for a table on the raised dais. The constantly changing menu always features interesting takes on Scottish produce, and is excellent value for the quality. It's BYOB (£3), but as the charming staff will inform you, the wines here are well priced and drinkable.

Loon Fung (☎ 556 1781; 2 Warriston Pl; mains £7-12; ⓨ noon-11.30pm Mon-Fri, 2-11.30pm Sat & Sun; ⊠; wheelchair access) Edinburgh foodies always nod sagely when this Cantonese restaurant is brought into the conversation. It has a very solid reputation and deservedly so, because its Cantonese food is authentic and varied, a mile away from the hunks of freeze-dried meat swimming in sauce that sometimes passes for Chinese food in these parts. Try the steamed dim sum, which are particularly delicate and tasty. It's worth booking ahead to get an upstairs table. Follow Broughton St or Dundas St north through their various name changes; the restaurant is on a roundabout where the two meet.

La P'tite Folie (Map pp750-1; ☎ 225 7983; 61 Frederick St; set lunch £6.95, mains £10-13; ⓨ lunch & dinner)

There's a very authentic French bistro–feel to this happy little place. Its retro décor of memorabilia and an engagingly flustered feel make it an inviting stop, as does the fine presentation and quality of the dishes, which include good-quality steak, duck and fish, as well as an extensive wine list. Its set lunch is such good value that you ought to wear a balaclava.

Other recommendations:

Bell's Diner (Map pp746-7; ☎ 225 8116; 7 St Stephen St; burgers from £7; ⓨ dinner Sun-Fri, noon-10.30pm Sat) Best burgers in Edinburgh. Book ahead.

Sabor Criollo (Map pp746-7; ☎ 332 3322; 36 Deanhaugh St; mains £6-9; ⓨ lunch & dinner Tue-Sun) South American specialities in a relaxed basement eatery.

TOP END

Restaurant Martin Wishart (☎ 553 3557; 54 The Shore; set lunch £18.50, mains £23-26; ⓨ lunch & dinner Tue-Fri, dinner Sat; ⊠; wheelchair access) You know that once restaurants start bearing the chef's name, you're in rarified culinary air. A fairly modest and sober dining area in Leith showcases the work of Edinburgh's first Michelin-starred kitchen. The menu changes regularly but features game, fish, and meat always prepared with exquisitely delicate sauces; the wine list is a suitable consort.

DRINKING

Edinburgh has got the full range when it comes to having a 'wee swallie'. From lavishly panelled locals to slinky shooter bars, and from decadent dockside havens to shaggy student speakeasies: the choice is yours! Happy hunting grounds for pubs and bars include Broughton St, the university area, Stockbridge and Leith.

SCOTLAND'S NATIONAL DISH

Most foreigners balk at the idea of chopped lungs, heart and liver all mixed with oatmeal, and boiled in a sheep's stomach. Scotland's national dish, however, is best enjoyed with an absence of delicate sensibilities and an accompanying dose of whisky, under which circumstances it tastes surprisingly good.

Haggis should be served with *tatties* and *neeps* (mashed potatoes and turnips).

It's central to the celebrations of 25 January in honour of Scotland's national poet, Robert Burns. On Burns Night a piper announces the arrival of the haggis and Burns' poem *Address to a Haggis* is recited to this 'Great chieftain o' the puddin-race'. The bulging stomach is then lanced with a *dirk* (dagger) to reveal the steaming offal within.

Vegetarians (and quite a few carnivores, no doubt) will be relieved to know that veggie haggis is available in plenty of Scotland's restaurants.

SOMETHING SPECIAL

So, you're in Edinburgh and you're looking for the 'typical' Scottish pub to escape from the strengthening drizzle. Cue the **Barony Bar** (Map pp746-7; ☎ 557 0546; 81 Broughton St). 'If pubs had a Platonic form, the Barony would be it.' That quote, from a longtime local, about sums up this enchanting spot. Newspapers, warming pub grub, plenty of worn wooden tables, and always a rock-solid bunch of folk complement the real ales and cold lager perfectly. It's one of the city's best.

The Old Town & South of the Royal Mile

Traverse Bar Café (Map pp750-1; ☎ 228 5383; 10 Cambridge St) Lurking low and large under the Traverse Theatre in the West End, this is an excellent choice unless you've got tickets to a show: you might not want to leave. With art exhibitions on the walls, a host of good draught beer choices and an atmosphere that subtly winds up from casual chat to buzzy preclub, it's a fine place.

Bow Bar (Map pp750-1; ☎ 226 7667; 80 West Bow, Victoria St) A gloriously traditional little boozer that fights its corner staunchly among more raucous newcomers, this bar is one of Edinburgh's best places to learn about whisky. With well over 100 malts in stock, bar staff happy to explain their nuances, and real ales to accompany them, it's the sort of place you pray will never change.

Pear Tree House (Map pp750-1; ☎ 667 7533; 38 West Nicolson St) In the heart of the student zone, this boisterous pub boasts one of Edinburgh's few beer gardens, with plenty of wooden tables in an enclosed courtyard; perfect for a long summer evening. But the interior, with its island bar, is also comfortable, and there are board games and comfy seats for inclement weather.

Canny Man's (☎ 447 1484; 239 Morningside Rd) Although it's a fair trek on a bus from the heart of town, this unique pub is well worth it. Opened in the 19th century, it seems to have changed little, and feels more like a rambling, eccentric house, with little drinking nooks and a beer garden; it's festooned top to bottom with flowers without and antiques within. There's a subdued, genteel atmosphere: a better first port of call than last.

Other recommendations:

Bar Kohl (Map pp750-1; ☎ 225 6936; 54 George IV Bridge) Smooth modern preclubbing; 300 different types of vodka awaiting your personal attention!

Beluga (Map pp750-1; ☎ 624 4545; 30a Chambers St) Vast and sleek downstairs bar, classy and popular.

Favorit (Map pp750-1; ☎ 220 6880; 19 Teviot Pl) Quiet spot for a late night chat. Serves food until 2.30am.

Medina (Map pp750-1; ☎ 225 6313; 45 Lothian St) Cosy underground student fave; the ultimate spot for a drunken canoodle, with its Moroccan cushions and secluded seating areas.

The New Town & Northern Edinburgh

Basement (Map pp746-7; ☎ 557 0097; 10a Broughton St) This cheerful underground spot is another Broughton St classic. It's impossible not to relax here, whether you're sitting at the quirky bulldozer tables, chowing down on the decent Tex-Mex grub, or sitting at the bar chatting with the chirpy folk in loud Hawaiian shirts who pull the pints.

Cumberland Bar (Map pp746-7; ☎ 558 3134; 1 Cumberland St) This exceptionally cosy New Town pub pours close to the best pint in Edinburgh. The great range of real ales are well cared for, and the lager comes out frothy and colder than the norm. Add the homely wooden interior, small beer garden, and yarning mix of people, and it's a gem.

Kay's (Map pp750-1; ☎ 225 1858; 39 Jamaica St West) Tucked away in a seldom-trodden backstreet, this bar can be tricky to find but is worth the effort. Formerly a wine merchant's, and still decorated with the tools of that trade, there's not a gimmick in sight – no music, just real ales, malt whiskies, an old-style publican and honest stews.

The Pond (☎ 467 3825; 2 Bath Rd, Leith) A bit out of the way, in the unfashionable part of Leith, this bar is a temple to German beer and an extremely convivial spot. With retro furniture, including a highly unusual hanging chair, fish tanks, a curious beer garden, and a Generation X crowd, it rekindles faith lost through being in too many chain pubs. The beer is served perfectly in chilled glasses.

Café Royal Circle Bar (Map pp750-1; ☎ 556 1884; 19 West Register St) Nestled on a wee alley off Princes St, this is a remarkably beautiful pub. Decorated in sumptuous style, all carved wood and polished brass, it has tiled panels of famous Scots on the wall, a gorgeous ceiling, and a classic island bar. But it remains a very convivial and open place – there's not a hint of snootiness in the air.

Great Grog Wine Bar (Map pp750-1; ☎ 225 1616; 83 Rose St) Most of Rose St's many pubs are unremarkable, so this upbeat spot is very welcome. The name says it all: there's a big choice of wines, comfortable modern furniture and, in summer, a great outdoor terrace to watch the people passing by. Be warned: you'll feel foolish if you order a glass and then end up staying longer and drinking more than what a bottle would have cost.

Bailie (Map pp746-7; ☎ 225 4673; 2 St Stephen St; ⊙ food served 11am-9pm Mon-Sat, 12.30-9pm Sun) Stockbridge likes to think of itself as a somewhat exclusive village, and the Bailie is the village pub. Warm and enchantingly cosy, it is the hub of the community and always buzzes with chat, as the elders debate local matters over a pint of Guinness and bright young things plan social engagements. It also serves high-quality bar meals. Just don't mention the 's' word (suburb!).

Other recommendations:

Antiquary (Map pp746-7; ☎ 225 2858; 72 St Stephen St) Another character-laden Stockbridge boozer, this basement bar has chrome salespeople shaking their heads in dismay.

Indigo (Yard) (Map pp750-1; ☎ 220 5603; 7 Charlotte Lane) Stylish but inclusive with a covered (patio) and very good (food).

Opal Lounge (Map pp750-1; ☎ 226 2275; 51a George St) Stylish and well-dressed bar in the business district. Open until 3am.

Port o'Leith (☎ 554 3568; 58 Constitution St, Leith) A Leith classic from before it became trendy: nautical, happy, volatile, community-minded, authentic, unique.

Shore (☎ 553 5080; 3 The Shore, Leith) Tiny bar enlarged by smoke and mirrors. Warm, cosy and romantic, with candlelit tables.

Waterfront (☎ 554 7427; 1c Dock Pl, Leith) Dark and atmospheric Leith wine bar with conservatory and terrace; check out the scent dispenser in the gents' loos!

ENTERTAINMENT

For full coverage buy *The List* (£2.20), a fortnightly magazine with listings for theatre, cinema, clubs, and also kids' events.

Cinemas

Cameo (Map pp746-7; ☎ 228 4141; 38 Home St) Arthouse and mainstream films.

Filmhouse (Map pp750-1; ☎ 228 2688; 88 Lothian Rd) Edinburgh's best cinema, showing arthouse, classic and foreign films.

Warner Village (Map pp750-1; ☎ 0870 240 6020; Greenside Pl) Big releases.

Gay & Lesbian Venues

Edinburgh has a lively gay scene, much of it concentrated in the 'pink triangle' around Greenside Pl and the top of Broughton St. The venues here are both gay- and lesbian-friendly. The Blue Moon Café (see p763) is a good spot to meet people quietly, and here you can browse through the handy *Scotsgay* magazine.

Café Habana (Map pp746-7; ☎ 558 1270; 22 Greenside Pl; ⊙ 1.30pm-1am) This razzle-dazzle place positively gleams with glam, and is a popular preclub venue. Set on two levels, it's got charmingly out-of-fashion furniture and super-friendly staff. Normally a fairly quiet spot for a drink and a chat, it gets hot and lively at weekends with dance hits and cheap drinks.

CC Blooms (Map pp746-7; ☎ 556 9331; 23 Greenside Pl; ⊙ 10.30pm-3am) Still the daddy of the Edinburgh gay scene, CC's heaves nightly with a happy sweaty throng. The music varies from frenetic dance to disco classics. Free admission means it can get very crowded.

Live Music

Henry's Jazz Cellar (Map pp750-1; ☎ 538 7385; 8 Morrison St; ⊙ Tue-Sun until 3am) This is the place to come to see jazz the way it's meant to be seen; in a small, dark, smoky basement. There's live music six nights a week, and it's usually of very high quality. Entry tends to be £5 or more, but it's worth it for the atmosphere.

Bannerman's (Map pp750-1; ☎ 556 3254; 212 Cowgate) Tucked below the Royal Mile, this dark and atmospheric double-sided bar is a place to come to sip a pint away from the tourist frenzy. There's live music nearly every night, which tends to be up-and-coming local rock bands who entertain a youngish crowd.

Royal Oak (Map pp750-1; ☎ 557 2976; 1 Infirmary St) Proudly traditional, this tiny pub is a friendly spot where folk musicians gather. There's no standing on ceremony; everybody talks to everybody else; there are regular impromptu jam sessions and, downstairs, a larger space where live bands play.

Whistlebinkies (Map pp750-1; ☎ 557 5114; 4 South Bridge) In a prime position just off the Royal Mile, this refurbished late-night drinking den can get impossibly crowded at weekends. It's

CAPITAL GIGS *Bryan McRitchie*

There are nights of live music in Edinburgh that will stay with you forever. Especially during the festival, the city becomes a different entity – a thriving hub of culture and passion that would grace any live music experience. With such a mixture of nationalities vibrantly colouring the atmosphere, it unfortunately highlights Edinburgh's main problem during the rest of the year. There is a reserved nature to the local populace that can turn the most exciting, enthralling performance into a reasonably pleasant night's entertainment. Maybe it's a lack of passion, unreasonable expectations or maybe people are more interested about being seen at the 'right' gigs rather than appreciating the quality of the music on offer. Whatever the reason, don't expect to be blown away by the local crowds' reception, whoever the artist may be. If you are lucky enough to experience a night of pure musical appreciation and enjoyment, treasure it, for you never know how long you will have to wait for the next one.

There are gigs on offer every night and there is no end of local, national and international artists and promoters trying to encourage a more passionate climate for live music. The tide is beginning to turn and, for such a popular capital, it's about time.

Even with these difficulties Edinburgh continues to produce a very high quality of local artists. Ballboy is plying a fine line in intelligently crafted paeans wrapped in a strong pop sensibility, while X-Tigers takes a heavier, more jagged approach, combining melody with a surging intensity and charisma. Degrassi leaks angularity and melody with a hardcore subtlety that comes enjoyably close to implosion, while the combination of break beats, dirty blues and traditional folk combine to make Mystery Juice an exceptional and original live experience.

From across the Firth of Forth in Fife, James Yorkston and the Athletes peddles a beautifully restrained nu-folk vibe, which is both consuming and hypnotic. In a similar aesthetic but with a more psychedelic trajectory, Lone Pigeon treads a delicate path through fragile tales of life.

There is a lot of talent hiding in the dark cellars and clubs of Edinburgh; it's about time these artists were given the reception they deserve.

Bryan McRitchie is an Edinburgh-based singer and musician.

still a fun place for a pint, though, with its atmospheric little vaults tucked under South Bridge, and there's decent live music nightly before things get too packed.

Nightclubs

Edinburgh offers a variety of venues with club nights ranging from seriously cool to pure cheese. Note that many club nights occur monthly, in the same venue. Covers range from £3 to £12 and most venues stay open until 3am.

Ego (Map pp746-7; ☎ 478 7434; 14 Picardy Pl; ☼ nightly) This is a glamorous venue just around the corner from Broughton St, where you can wiggle to wild electronic jazz or boogie to dazzling disco. There's something different on nearly every night: one of the most popular is Vegas, a 'sleazy listening' swing night, where everyone looks the part. It's held monthly on Saturday.

Venue (Map pp750-1; ☎ 557 3073; 17-21 Calton Rd; ☼ Thu-Sun) Just by the back entrance to the train station are these three floors of dark, sweaty dancing. 3D on Friday is particularly good value, for there is a different type of music on each floor. This venue is also the new home of Joy, Edinburgh's longest running gay club night, monthly on a Saturday.

Honeycomb (Map pp750-1; ☎ 530 5540; 15 Niddry St) Honeycomb is a serious den of dance. In the old vaults under South Bridge, it is a dark and delicious venue with plenty of space to shake the tush. Many of its nights are top-quality house, but Manga (which usually happens monthly on Fridays) is widely considered Scotland's best drum'n'bass night. It's often free midweek – Motherfunk is gratis every Tuesday.

Other recommendations:

Bongo Club (Map pp746-7; ☎ 558 7604; 37 Holyrood Rd; ☼ nightly) A varied and always interesting bag, particularly strong on dub, funk and hip-hop.

Espionage (Map pp750-1; ☎ 477 7007; 4 India Bldgs, Victoria St; ☼ 7pm-3am) Free entry to this massive boisterous and unsubtle bar-club. Get here early, or queue.

Liquid Room (Map pp750-1; ☎ 225 2564; 9c Victoria St; ☼ Tue-Sun) Top acts, mostly house, but Evol is an excellent indie night on Friday.

Sport

Though neither has looked like challenging the dominance of the Glasgow giants in recent times, Edinburgh's football clubs are strongly supported. **Hibernian** (Map pp746-7; ☎ 661 2159; www.hibs.co.uk; Easter Rd Stadium, Albion Pl), the pride of Leith and known as Hibs or the Hibees, traditionally draws its support from the city's Catholic community, while **Hearts** (Map pp746-7; ☎ 200 7201; www.heartsfc.co.uk; Tynecastle Stadium, Gorgie Rd), nicknamed the Jambos, represents the other side.

Edinburgh heaves during the season of rugby internationals. The Six Nations tournament runs from January to March, and Edinburgh's home games are played at **Murrayfield Stadium** (☎ 346 5000; www.sru.org.uk; 112 Roseburn St), west of Haymarket. It can be difficult to get accommodation over these weekends.

Theatre

Edinburgh has more than its fair share of theatres, mostly because of the frantic festival activity.

Edinburgh Festival Theatre (Map pp750-1; ☎ 529 6000; 13-29 Nicolson St) Everything from ballet to folk music from around the world, and also the city's main venue for opera and dance.

Royal Lyceum Theatre (Map pp750-1; ☎ 248 4848; 30 Grindlay St) High quality drama, concerts and ballet.

Stand (Map pp750-1; ☎ 558 7272; 5 York Pl; ☯ nightly) Atmospheric comedy venue with shows every night.

Traverse Theatre (Map pp750-1; ☎ 228 1404; 10 Cambridge St) Top-class venue staging an exciting programme of drama and dance.

SHOPPING

Princes St is the main shopping thoroughfare, with dozens of major high-street names. The recently opened Ocean Terminal in Leith also draws shoppers to its wide selection of large stores. For more-quirky shopping, hit Cockburn St and Victoria St in the Old Town, or Stockbridge, particularly St Stephen St.

Clothing

21st Century Kilts (Map pp750-1; ☎ 557 0256; 555 Castlehill) This outlet succeeds in bringing tartan into the new millennium, with fashion superseding tradition.

Armstrongs (Map pp750-1; ☎ 220 5557; 83 The Grassmarket) You'll find an excellent selection of second-hand retro clothing here. There is another branch at 64 Clerk St.

Leith Army Stores (Map pp746-7; ☎ 556 2337; 7 Brunswick Pl, Leith Walk) This is a cracking outlet for bargain outdoor gear and army surplus clothing.

Department Stores

Harvey Nichols (Map pp750-1; ☎ 524 8388; 30 St Andrew Sq) This new kid on the block opened to wide acclaim. It stocks a wide designer range.

Jenners (Map pp750-1; ☎ 225 2442; 48 Princes St) An Edinburgh institution, opened in 1838. Stocked with gifts, a wide range of clothing and much more in a gorgeous old building.

Other Shops

Royal Mile Whiskies (Map pp750-1; ☎ 225 3383; 379 High St) Although packed with tourists, this shop has a great selection, but not always at the sharpest prices.

Villeneuve Wines (Map pp746-7; ☎ 558 8441; 49a Broughton St) Edinburgh's best independent wine retailer, with a great Lebanese range.

Fopp (Map pp750-1; ☎ 220 0133; 55 Cockburn St) A cheap record shop that is an Edinburgh success story, and now taking on the big boys.

Hogshead Records (Map pp746-7; ☎ 667 5274; 62 South Clerk St) Strong on rock and alternative sounds.

Edinburgh Bear Company (Map pp750-1; ☎ 557 9564; 46 High St) For all your teddy-bear requirements!

Crombie's (Map pp746-7; ☎ 557 0111; 97 Broughton St) Famous nationwide for its fine sausages and meats.

Valvona & Crolla (Map pp746-7; ☎ 556 6066; 19 Elm Row) Historic and cavernous Italian deli. Quality superb, prices to match.

GETTING THERE & AWAY
Air

Edinburgh airport (☎ 344 3213), 7 miles west of the city in Turnhouse, has services to other cities in the UK, Ireland and Continental Europe. The main airlines servicing the city are **British Airways** (☎ 0845 773 3377; www.ba.com), **British Midland** (☎ 0870 600 6868; www.flybmi.com) and **EasyJet** (☎ 0870 600 0000; www.easyjet.com). These airlines have domestic services from London, Bristol and Manchester, among others, and British Midland, British Airways and their subsidiaries offer flights to many other Scottish destinations such as Shetland, Inverness, Stornoway and Orkney.

Bus

Edinburgh's brand new bus station (Map pp750-1) is on the eastern side of St Andrew Sq. There are frequent daily links to/from many cities in England and Wales with **National Express** (☎ 0870 580 8080; www .nationalexpress.com) and **Scottish Citylink** (☎ 0870 550 5050; www.citylink.co.uk), the main operators. Bus fares from London are competitive. At the time of writing, **Silver Choice** (☎ 01355 249 499; www.silverchoicetravel.co.uk) offers the cheapest deal (from £24 return, 9½ hours). This service departs 10pm daily from London's Victoria Coach Station and 9.30pm from Edinburgh, involving a transfer at Hamilton. The service is popular so you'll need to book.

National Express runs the same route (from £33 return, 9½ hours, up to four daily). There are also services to Newcastle (£14, 2¾ hours, three to five daily) and York (£28.50, 5¾ hours, one daily).

Scottish Citylink buses connect Edinburgh with all of Scotland's major cities and towns, including **Aberdeen** (£16.40, 3¼ hours, hourly); **Dundee** (£8.60, two hours, hourly); **Fort William** (£19, four hours, three daily); **Glasgow** (£4, 1¼ hours, every 15 to 20 minutes); **Inverness** (£15.90, four hours, hourly); **Perth** (£6.10, 1¼ hours, one to two hourly); **Portree, Isle of Skye** (£28.70, eight hours, two a day) and **Stirling** (£4, one hour, hourly).

The **Motorvator** (☎ 01698 870 768) competes on the Glasgow run, offering a slightly cheaper fare. It goes half-hourly Monday to Saturday and hourly on Sunday (1¼ hours).

Car & Motorcycle

The main approaches to Edinburgh can clog up very quickly at rush hour, so it's worth timing your arrival and departure to avoid these periods.

Train

The main train station is Waverley in the heart of the city, although most trains also stop at Haymarket station, which is convenient for the West End.

There are very frequent daily trains from London's King's Cross. Apart from Apex fares (which must be booked seven days in advance), tickets are expensive.

ScotRail has two northern lines from Edinburgh: one cuts north across the Grampians to Inverness (£32.90, 3½ hours, six to nine daily) and on to Thurso; the other follows the coast north around to Aberdeen (£32.90, 2½ hours, hourly or more frequently) and on to Inverness. There are trains every 15 to 30 minutes to Glasgow (£9, 50 minutes).

For more details and general information, phone ☎ 0845 748 4950.

GETTING AROUND
To/From the Airport

Between 5am and midnight, frequent LRT Airlink buses run from Waverley Bridge near the train station to the airport, taking 35 minutes and costing £3.30/5 one way/ return. A taxi costs around £15 one way.

Bicycle

Although there are plenty of steep hills to negotiate, Edinburgh is ideal for cycling (as nothing is more than half an hour away), the traffic is fairly tolerable and scenic Holyrood Park is close by. There are plenty of cycle lanes on the major streets.

Edinburgh Cycle Hire (Map pp750-1; ☎ 556 5560; 29 Blackfriars St; ☼ 10am-6pm), just off the Royal Mile, hires out mountain and hybrid bikes for £10 for a half-day, £15 for 24 hours, or £70 per week. **Bike Trax** (Map pp746-7; ☎ 228 6333; www.biketrax.co.uk; 11 Lochrin Pl; ☼ Mon-Sat Sep-Jun, daily Jul & Aug), off Home St near Tollcross, is equally helpful and charges the same rates as Edinburgh Cycle Hire.

Car & Motorcycle

In addition to the big national operators, who have offices both in town and at the airport, the ESIC has details of reputable local car-rental companies. **Arnold Clark** (Map pp746-7; ☎ 0845 607 4500; 13 Lochrin Pl) is one who has rates starting at £19/95 per day/week.

Driving in Edinburgh is fairly straightforward, but the city is famed for the vigilance and ruthlessness of its army of parking inspectors, so be sure to observe regulations.

Public Transport

The two main companies, **Lothian** (☎ 555 6363) and **First Edinburgh** (☎ 663 9233), provide frequent, cheap services. You buy tickets when you board buses and for Lothian services you need exact change. For most short trips, the fare is 80p. A Day Saver ticket (£2.50, or £2 after 9.30am Monday to Friday, all day at weekends), available from bus drivers when you board, covers a whole day's travel. After midnight there are special night buses (£2). The free *Edinburgh Travelmap* is useful – it shows bus routes around the city and is available from the TIC, or contact **Traveline** (☎ 0870 608 2608; www.travelinescotland.com).

Taxi
There are numerous central taxi ranks; costs are reasonable and £5 to £6 gets you almost anywhere around the centre. Local companies include **Central Radio Taxis** (☎ 229 2468) and **City Cabs** (☎ 228 1211). Both companies have wheelchair-accessible vehicles.

AROUND EDINBURGH

SOUTH QUEENSFERRY & INCHCOLM
Eight miles west of Edinburgh, South Queensferry lies on the southern bank of the Firth of Forth. Deriving its name from the frequent crossings made by St Margaret in the 12th century to commute between her palaces in Edinburgh and Dunfermline, South Queensferry's bridges have negated the need for boats. The magnificent Forth Rail Bridge is one of the finest Victorian engineering achievements. Completed in 1890 after seven years' work and the deaths of 58 men, it's over a mile long; the adjacent Forth Road Bridge is a graceful suspension bridge.

Offshore, tiny Inchcolm Island (only 800m long) houses Scotland's best-preserved assemblage of monastic buildings, including a medieval **abbey** (☎ 01383 823332; adult £3; ☼ 9.30am-6.30pm Apr-Oct), which was founded for Augustinian priors in 1123, and is run by Historic Scotland (HS). During the 14th century, the English attacked the abbey repeatedly, necessitating a redesign in the 15th century. The cloisters that remain are from this period, but the remarkably preserved octagonal chapterhouse, with its stone roof, in the well-tended grounds has survived from the 13th century.

The **Maid of the Forth** (☎ 0131-331 4857; www .maidoftheforth.co.uk) leaves from Hawes Pier and cruises under the bridges to the Island.

Weather permitting, there are daily sailings from July to September (weekends only from April to June and October) and tickets cost £11.50 (which includes entry to the abbey).

Frequent trains run from Edinburgh to South Queensferry's Dalmeny station (15 minutes). There are also numerous buses, including First Edinburgh bus No 88, westbound from Princes St.

Hopetoun House
Two miles west of South Queensferry, **Hopetoun House** (☎ 0131-331 2451; www.hopetounhouse .com; adult £6.50; ☼ 10am-5.30pm Apr-Sep; wheelchair access), one of Scotland's finest stately homes, has a superb location amid 100 acres of stunning landscaped grounds beside the Firth of Forth. There are two parts: the older built between 1699 and 1702 to Sir William Bruce's plans and dominated by a splendid stairwell, the newer designed between 1720 and 1750 by William Adam and his sons, Robert and John. The rooms have splendid furnishings and a considerable number of art treasures.

ROSSLYN CHAPEL
Recently thrust into the limelight by the bestselling thriller *The Da Vinci Code* (visits have increased exponentially), this **chapel** (☎ 0131-440 2159; adult/child £5/free; ☼ 10am-5pm Mon-Sat, noon-4.45pm Sun), about 7 miles south of Edinburgh in the village of Roslin, is steeped in beauty and symbolism and is one of Scotland's most unique and ornate churches. Built in 1446 by William St Clair, Rosslyn is particularly renowned for its magnificent carvings. These include biblical figures, examples of the pagan 'Green Man', and flowers, vines and imagery of plants apparently from America, which predate Columbus' arrival in that continent by 100 years! With its wealth of Templar and Masonic connections, it's no wonder it's been central to many occult theories; some believe that the Holy Grail is buried in chambers beneath the chapel. Major restoration is ongoing, and the chapel now lives under a large steel awning, but its awe-inspiring and mysterious interior still leaves the head churning. First bus No 62 leaves hourly from Edinburgh bus station.

Southern Scotland

SOUTHERN SCOTLAND

Historic sites, great walking and cycling, and energised Glasgow are just some of the wealth of things to appreciate among the verdant hills of Southern Scotland. They can all be enjoyed with a degree of freedom, for they lack the 'must-see' cachet of destinations further north, and are less crowded.

Historically, the most frequent tourists to the region were raiding English armies; the grim borderland fortifications saw skirmishing aplenty, and most were taken and retaken several times. One of the attractions for the soldiers was the loot to be had in the Borders, where large prosperous abbeys bossed agricultural communities. All were regularly ransacked before their destruction in the Reformation; today their ruins, linked by cycling and walking paths, are among Scotland's most atmospheric historic sites.

The west of the region is hillier, and has some extensive forest cover in between bustling market towns. The hills cascade down to sandy stretches of coastline blessed with Scotland's best weather. This is the land of Robert Burns, Scotland's best-loved poet, whose varied verse reflects his earthy attitudes and active social life. Arran, visible offshore, offers great cycling, walking, and scenery.

Another major drawcard, New Lanark is a fascinating reconstructed mill community on the banks of the bubbly River Clyde. The region's main attraction, however, is better known. The Clyde descends from here to Glasgow, a city built on shipyards that was once one of the Empire's foremost industrial powerhouses. It's Scotland's biggest city and a fascinatingly vital place, riding a wave of urban renewal that has brought it back among Europe's elite. A visit is an unforgettable experience.

HIGHLIGHTS

- Tactfully talking football in one of **Glasgow's** (p787) earthy pubs or fashion in its glitzy style bars

- Dining in style in **Merchant City** (p778), where tobacco barons once ruled the roost

- Hiking or cycling between the noble ruins of the **Border Abbeys** (p795)

- Marvelling at the radical social reform instituted in the mill community of **New Lanark** (p793)

- Blowing away the cobwebs on the healthy, accessible and beautiful **Isle of Arran** (p809)

- Browsing the numerous second-hand bookshops of **Wigtown** (p805)

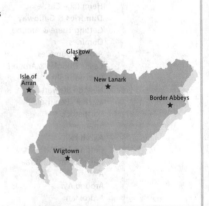

- POPULATION: 2,701,580

- AREA: 7464 SQ MILES

History

This region was traditionally a dubious borderland between the Scots and their chief tormentors, and for centuries was basically lawless, as local chiefs sought to augment their power by doing dirty deals with one side or the other. The Border abbeys set up in the 12th century succeeded in maintaining order for a period, but were soon reduced to ruins by rampaging English raiding parties, a pattern that continued right up until the union in 1707.

Activities

Many outdoor enthusiasts in Scotland head straight for the northwest, but Southern Scotland has plenty to offer, with a large number of walking and cycling routes. A summary is given in the Outdoor Activities chapter (p75), and suggestions for shorter routes are given throughout this chapter.

Several long-distance **walking/cycling routes** originate in Glasgow, and many form part of the constantly expanding National Cycle Network and follow off-road routes for most of the way. The Tourist Information Centre (TIC) in Glasgow (p778) has a range of maps and leaflets detailing these routes, many of which start from Bell's Bridge by the Scottish Exhibition & Conference Centre (SECC), beside the river.

The **Glasgow to Loch Lomond Route** traverses residential and industrial areas following disused train lines and towpaths. The route actually extends all the way to Inverness, from Balloch via Aberfoyle to link with the Glen Ogle Trail, Killin, Pitlochry and Aviemore.

The **Glasgow to Irvine/Ardrossan and West Kilbride Cycle Way** runs via Paisley, then off-road as far as Glengarnock. From there to Kilwinning it follows minor roads, then the route is partly off-road to Ardrossan from which ferries leave for the Isle of Arran.

The **Glasgow to Edinburgh** route has now opened. It partly follows the Clyde Walkway and a disused railway line.

The long-distance footpath, the **West Highland Way**, begins in Milngavie, 8 miles north of Glasgow, and runs for 95 miles to Fort William.

One of Scotland's great long-distance walks, the challenging **Southern Upland Way** runs for 212 miles and stretches from coast to coast across southern Scotland. It's far better walked west to east, as the prevailing winds are westerlies; starting at Portpatrick, and finishing at Cockburnspath in East Lothian. There are several tough stretches with sturdy hills to be climbed, but the sheer variety of landscape traversed makes it memorable. For more information, check out the excellent website www.southernuplandway.com.

Getting Around

Glasgow is an obvious transport hub, and bus services are good throughout the region. Train services are more limited. Other stations of interest include Berwick-upon-Tweed (in Northumberland on the English side of the border, but the natural jumping-off point for the Tweed Valley) on the main east-coast line; at Dumfries on the main west-coast line; and at Stranraer and Ayr, which are linked to Glasgow.

GLASGOW

☎ 0141 / pop 629,500

Urban renewal is a buzzword these days, and Glasgow has embraced the concept with enormous vigour. That, however, won't surprise anyone who has been to the place: few cities in Britain have the contagious energy that you'll find bubbling away on its streets and in its justifiably famous pubs and bars. Glasgow is a highlight of any trip to Scotland.

Once synonymous with bleak poverty and grim desperation, the city of Glasgow has managed to turn things around to the point that, for many, it is now almost a byword for style and chic. Gone are the rusting relics of a moribund shipbuilding industry, to be replaced by absorbing attractions on the Clyde that celebrate that very heritage.

Scotland's largest city also has a wealth of longer-established attractions that command the visitor's attention, none more so than its cathedral, a Gothic beauty that survived the Reformation largely intact. The famous Burrell Collection is a whimsical assemblage of art set in magnificent parkland, while the Glasgow School of Art is the finest achievement of Charles Rennie Mackintosh, a belatedly recognised architectural genius whose work graces several corners of the city.

Glasgow is not all architectural perfection, though. A sublime Victorian town house overshadowed by a 1950s concrete eyesore can be seen as part of Glasgow's chaotic charm, but the towering housing schemes in the city's suburbs reflect ongoing social problems and levels of deprivation seldom seen in 21st century Western Europe.

Traditionally, Glaswegians have sought solace in drink, and the city's amazing collection of spots for a pint is unrivalled north of London. With their dark wood and no-nonsense approach, traditional pubs entice a visit, while an ever-increasing selection of style bars embrace sophistication without losing the unpretentious gregariousness that is the ace of Glasgow's many drawcards.

HISTORY

Glasgow grew around the cathedral founded by St Kertigan, later to become St Mungo, in the 6th century. Unfortunately, with the exception of the cathedral, virtually nothing of the medieval city remains. It was swept away by the energetic people of a new age – the age of capitalism, the Industrial Revolution and the British Empire.

In the 18th century, much of the tobacco trade between Europe and the USA was routed through Glasgow and provided a great source of wealth. Even after the tobacco trade declined in the 19th century, the city continued to prosper as a centre of textile manufacturing, shipbuilding and the coal and steel industries. The outward appearance

SOUTHERN SCOTLAND

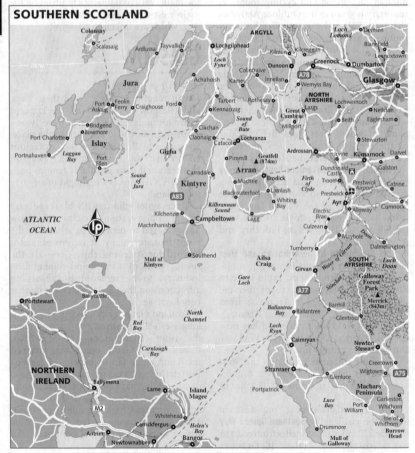

of prosperity, however, was tempered by the dire working conditions in the factories.

In the first half of the 20th century, Glasgow was the centre of Britain's munitions industry, supplying arms and ships for the two world wars, in the second of which the city was carpet-bombed. In the postwar years, however, the port and heavy industries began to dwindle and by the early 1970s, the city seemed doomed. Unlike Edinburgh, working-class Glasgow had few alternatives when recession hit and the city became synonymous with unemployment, economic depression and urban violence, centred on high-rise housing schemes such as the infamous Gorbals. The urban development programmes of recent times

have renewed confidence, but behind the optimism the standard of living remains low compared with the rest of Britain and life continues to be tough for many. Lifting the living standard for all the city's inhabitants will likely be a long and slow process.

ORIENTATION

Glasgow's tourist sights are spread over a wide area. The city centre is built on a grid system north of the River Clyde. The two train stations, bus station and the TIC are all within a couple of blocks of George Square, the main city square. Running east-west along a ridge in the northern part of the city, Sauchiehall St (first syllable pronounced soch as in loch) has a pedestrian mall

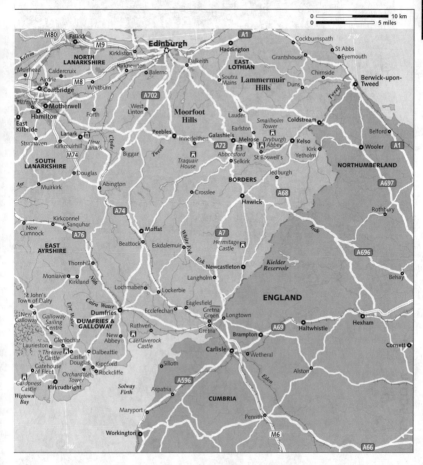

GLASGOW

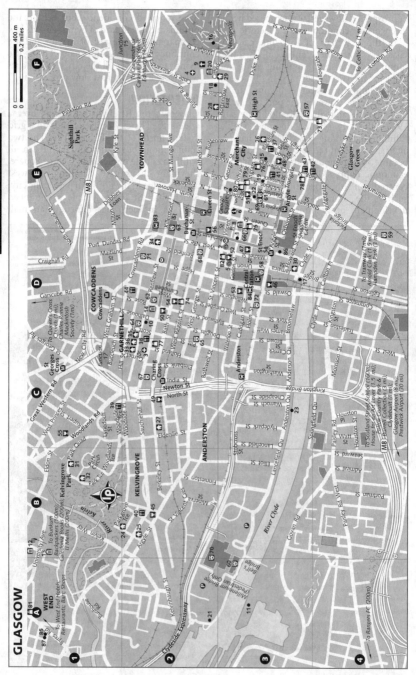

with numerous shops at its eastern end. Merchant City is the commercial district, east of George Square, and a focus for trendy eating and drinking. The West End, divided from the centre by the M8 motorway, is a similarly buzzy nightlife zone, with a more student-driven feel. Motorways bore through the bleak suburbs and the airport lies 8 miles west of the centre.

Maps
The *A-Z Premier Street Map* (£4.75) is a clear fold-out map of Glasgow and suburbs that includes a street index. It's widely available in bookshops and newsagents.

INFORMATION
Bookshops
Borders (☎ 222 7700; 98 Buchanan St) Wide range of Scottish literature, good travel section, and a café.

Emergency
Dial ☎ 999 or ☎ 112 for police, ambulance, fire brigade or coastguard.

Internet Access
EasyInternet Café (☎ 222 2364; 57 St Vincent St; per hr about £1.50; ⊙ 7am-10.45pm) Under-18s need an adult companion to enter.

Hillhead Library (☎ 339 7223; 348 Byres Rd; free; ⊙ 10am-8pm Mon-Tue, 10am-5pm Wed, noon-8pm Thu, 9am-5pm Fri-Sat) Free access, but book ahead.
Th:at (☎ 222 2227; 8 Renfield St; per hr £1.80 or day pass £3; ⊙ 10am-10pm) Near Central Station and does a decent cup of coffee.

Internet Resources
Glasgow Galleries (www.glasgowgalleries.co.uk)
Glasgow Museums (www.glasgowmuseums.com)
Greater Glasgow & Clyde Valley Tourist Board (www.seeglasgow.com)

Laundry
Havelock Laundry (☎ 339 1499; 10 Havelock Rd) Just off Byres Rd.

Medical Services
Glasgow Dental Hospital (☎ 211 9600; 378 Sauchiehall St) Dental emergencies.
Glasgow Royal Infirmary (☎ 211 4000; 84 Castle St) Medical emergencies and outpatients facilities.

Money
The post office offers the most competitive rates on exchange of US dollars and euros. There's a bureau de change at the TIC and at both airports. There are many banks with ATMs around the centre and at the airports.

Post

Main Post Office (47 St Vincent St; ⏰ 8.30am-5.45pm Mon-Fri, 9am-5.30pm Sat)

Tourist Information

TIC (www.seeglasgow.com) Central (☎ 204 4400; 11 George Sq; ⏰ 9am-6pm Mon-Sat Oct-May, 9am-7pm Mon-Sat Jun & Sep, 9am-8pm Mon-Sat Jul & Aug, Sun 10am-6pm year-round); Glasgow Airport (☎ 848 4440; ⏰ 7.30am-5pm) The central TIC is crisp and competent, and will book accommodation for a £2 charge.

SIGHTS
City Centre

A walking tour (see p782) covers most of the following sights. Two buildings designed by CR Mackintosh – the Glasgow School of Art (p781) and the Scotland School Church (p781) – are also in the area.

GEORGE SQUARE

The TIC is here, just south of Queen St train station and a good starting point for getting to know the city. This large open space is dignified by statues of famous folk from Glasgow and the surrounding area, including Robert Burns, James Watt, Sir John Moore, and, atop a column, Sir Walter Scott. A pair of charismatic lions guard the war memorial and get chatted to by people weaving their way home at the weekend.

The grand **City Chambers** (☎ 287 4018; George Sq; wheelchair access), the seat of local government, was built in the 1880s at the high point of the city's prosperity. The interior is even more extravagant than the exterior, and the chambers have sometimes been used as a movie location to represent the Kremlin or the Vatican. There are free 45-minute tours at 10.30am and 2.30pm Monday to Friday; these are worthwhile for the sheer opulence on show.

MERCHANT CITY

The beating heart of the Glasgow's boom years can be found south and east of the City Chambers, in **Merchant City**, a planned 18th-century civic expansion. The 'Tobacco Lords' were entrepreneurs who profited from lucrative transatlantic trade routes, importing tobacco, rum, and sugar. The noble civic and private buildings they erected have recently found renewal as stylish apartments as well as some of Glasgow's best bars and restaurants.

The contemporary paintings and sculpture inside the **Gallery of Modern Art** (☎ 229 1996; www.glasgowmuseums.com; Queen St; admission free; ⏰ 10am-5pm Mon-Wed & Sat, 10am-8pm Thu, 11am-5pm Fri & Sun; wheelchair access) presents a marked contrast with the building itself. It's particularly geared for kids, with plenty of activities; this light-hearted approach seems to have rubbed off on the local community, for the horseback statue of the Duke of Wellington outside the building always wears a traffic cone on his head, despite the fact the council removes it on a daily basis!

Designed by renowned Scottish architect Robert Adam in 1791 to house the trades guild; the interior of the **Trades Hall** (☎ 552 2418; 85 Glassford St; adult £3.50; ⏰ 10am-5pm Mon-Fri, 10am-2pm Sat, noon-5pm Sun Apr-Oct, noon-5pm Sun Nov-Mar; wheelchair access) features sumptuous wooden panelling.

GLASGOW CATHEDRAL

The dark and imposing interior of **Glasgow Cathedral** (☎ 552 6891; admission free; ⏰ 9.30am-6pm Mon-Sat, 1-5pm Sun Apr-Sep, 9.30am-4pm Mon-Sat, 1-4pm Sun Oct-Mar; wheelchair access), run by Historic Scotland (HS) conjures up medieval might. The cathedral is a shining example of Gothic architecture and the only mainland Scottish cathedral to survive the Reformation. Most of the current building dates from the 15th century (only the western towers were destroyed) for the city's trade guilds fought to save the structure, which then became the principal Protestant church.

Much of the cathedral's stained glass is modern, but the older glasswork includes extraordinarily detailed miniature panels in the Blacadder aisle and in the lower church.

This place has been hallowed ground for over 1500 years. The site was blessed for Christian burial in 397 by St Ninian. The first building was consecrated in 1136, in the presence of King David I, but it burned in 1197 and was rebuilt as the lower church.

The **lower church** is the most interesting part; its forest of pillars creates a powerful atmosphere around the altar that sits on St Mungo's tomb, the focus of a famous medieval pilgrimage.

Behind the cathedral, the crumbling tombs of the city's rich and famous crowd the renovated **Necropolis**. An atmospheric and mildly gothic stroll up the hill rewards you with good city views.

TIDE IS TURNING FOR THE CLYDE

As most Glaswegians are acutely aware, Glasgow built the Clyde and the Clyde built Glasgow, the union giving the city its 19th-century tag as the second city of the Empire.

Recently Glasgow has been returning to its roots. There has been a major campaign to rejuvenate the riverfront and celebrate the city's unique industrial heritage. Although in the centre of town, the riverbank is still a little grim and soulless, some intriguing drawcards can be found a 20-minute walk to the west.

Clyde Attractions

Scotland's flagship millennium project, the fascinating, ultramodern **Glasgow Science Centre** (☎ 420 5000; 50 Pacific Quay; Science Mall £6.95, IMAX £6.95, combined ticket £9.95, Planetarium supplement £2; ☽ 10am-6pm; wheelchair access) is made up of two cosmic-looking buildings. It will keep the kids entertained for hours (and it's not bad fun for adults too!). The centre consists of an IMAX theatre and an interactive science mall; a bounty of discovery for young, inquisitive minds. Take First bus No 30 from Union St to the Scottish Exhibition & Conference Centre (SECC), and cross the bridge.

Just across the Clyde from the Science Centre, via pedestrianised Millennium Bridge, is the **Tall Ship** (☎ 222 2513; www.thetallship.com; Stobcross Rd; adult £4.50, one child per adult free; ☽ 10am-5pm Mar-Oct, 10am-4pm Nov-Feb), one of five sailing ships built on the Clyde still afloat. The *Glenlee* was launched in December 1896 and eventually purchased by the Clyde Maritime Trust and restored. The sheer size of this three-masted ship is impressive and inside are displays about her history, restoration and life on board in the early 20th century.

Inside the nearby old **Pumphouse**, now a visitors centre, is an exhibit on the man-made history of the river, which involved the amazing dredging work carried out to enable the big ships to sail into Glasgow. Evidence of the old shipyards still prevail here, in foundations of a swing bridge, trolley tracks and old warehouses.

Further away from the centre, it's easy to see why **Clydebuilt** (☎ 886 1013; Kings Inch Rd; adult £3.50; ☽ 10am-6pm Mon-Thu & Sat, 11am-5pm Sun; wheelchair access) is such a popular museum. It's a superb collection of model ships, industrial displays and narrative vividly painting the history of the Clyde – its fate inextricably linked with Glasgow and its people. There's a three-screen, audiovisual display on the decline of the Clyde's shipyards. Outside you can board *Kyles*, an 1872 vessel typical of that churned out around here and a perfect place to contemplate the now-defunct cornerstone of Glasgow's industrial heritage.

Walking the Clyde

It's possible to walk 9 miles of the Clyde through Glasgow, although parts of the route can be rather desolate and fairly gloomy. An outstanding section lies between the Victoria Bridge and the SECC, taking in 150 years of bridge engineering and a chunk of Glasgow's shipbuilding heritage.

The Clyde Walkway is in the process of being continued right through to the Falls of Clyde (p794) in Lanark and should be about 40 miles long when completed.

Getting Around on the Clyde

The **Pride o' the Clyde** (☎ 07711 250 969; Central Station Bridge), a brilliant way to travel, is a waterbus linking Glasgow city centre with the Braehead Shopping Centre, home of the Clydebuilt museum. There are five to six sailings a day each way and the 30-minute journey costs £3/5 for a one-way/return trip. It's a great way to see the regeneration taking place along the Clyde and avoid the city congestion.

Waverley (☎ 0845 130 4647; www.waverleyexcursions.co.uk; Anderston Quay), the world's last ocean-going paddle steamer (built in 1947), cruises the Firth of Clyde from April to September; its website details days of departure. It serves several towns and islands of Bute, Great Cumbrae and Arran, as well as other coastal areas in the UK. Tickets cost between £6 and £30, depending on your destination.

It takes about 15 minutes to walk to the cathedral from George Square, but numerous buses pass by: Nos 11, 12, 38, 42 and 56.

ST MUNGO MUSEUM OF RELIGIOUS LIFE & ART

A heartwarming achievement in this hotbed of sectarianism, this **museum** (☎ 553 2557; www .glasgowmuseums.com; 2 Castle St; admission free; ⏰ 10am-5pm Mon-Thu & Sat, 11am-5pm Fri & Sun; wheelchair access) in the cathedral forecourt is a daring attempt to capture the world's main religions in an artistic nutshell, while presenting the similarities and differences in how they approach common themes such as birth, marriage, and death.

The attraction is twofold. First is the impressive art, which smudges the lines between religion and culture, and second the opportunity to delve into different faiths, displayed without false sentimentality or 'love thy neighbour' preaching. It's a simple concept, and a valuable one.

The building may look like a restored antiquity, but is in fact a £6.5 million reconstruction of the bishop's palace that once stood here, and only dates from the early 1990s. There are three **galleries** representing religion as art, religious life and, on the top floor, religion in Scotland. In the main gallery, Dali's powerful and moody *Christ of St John of the Cross* hangs among Hindu and Islamic works. Outside, you'll find a Zen Buddhist garden.

PROVAND'S LORDSHIP

Across the road from St Mungo's Museum, **Provand's Lordship** (☎ 552 8819; www.glasgow museums.com; 3 Castle St; admission free; ⏰ 10am-5pm Mon-Thu & Sat, 11am-5pm Fri & Sun) is the oldest house in Glasgow. Provand's Lordship is a rare example of 15th-century domestic Scottish architecture in the city, built in 1471 as a manse for the chaplain of St Nicholas Hospital. Particularly interesting to explore, the ceilings and doorways are low and the rooms are decked out with staunch oak furniture and period artefacts; one room is a reconstruction of the living space of an early 16th-century chaplain. The building's best feature is its authentic feel – if you ignore the tacky, imitation-stone linoleum covering the ground floor. There is a 'mediaeval' garden out the back as well.

MCLELLAN GALLERIES

During the long-term refurbishment of the Kelvingrove Art Gallery & Museum, scheduled to re-open in 2006, some of the art from the fine collection is housed in the **McLellan Galleries** (☎ 565 4137; www .glasgowmuseums.com; 270 Sauchiehall St; admission free; ⏰ 10am-5pm Mon-Thu & Sat, 11am-5pm Fri & Sun; wheelchair access). Highlights include Rembrandt's *Man in Armour*, and some other fine Flemish canvases, as well as examples of the Glasgow Style and pre- and post-Renaissance Italian art.

West End

The West End is Glasgow's other 'centre', where you'll find the university, an imposing array of restaurants and bars, shops, Mackintosh's Queen's Cross Church (p781) and the extensive Kelvingrove Park.

HUNTERIAN MUSEUM & ART GALLERY

Part of the university, and now housed in two separate buildings on either side of University Ave, the **Hunterian Museum** (☎ 330 4221; University Ave; www.hunterian.gla.ac.uk; admission free; ⏰ 9.30am-5pm Mon-Sat) was opened in 1807 as Scotland's first public museum. It houses the collection of William Hunter (1718–83), famous physician, medical teacher and one-time student of the university. It comprises a disparate collection of artefacts including a medieval coin collection, fossils and minerals, dinosaur eggs, Romano-British stone slabs and carvings, and some of Captain Cook's curios from his voyages to the South Seas. The West African carvings incorporating the arrival of Europeans are fascinating.

From the medieval cloisters of the museum, head to the nearby modern concrete building housing the **Hunterian Art Gallery** (☎ 330 5431; www.hunterian.gla.ac.uk; 82 Hillhead St; admission free; ⏰ 9.30am-5pm Mon-Sat; wheelchair access). The Scottish colourists (Peploe, JD Fergusson, Cadell) are well represented, and include McTaggart's Impressionistic Scottish landscapes and a gem by Thomas Millie Dow. The **Mackintosh House** is also part of the gallery. Set up as a reconstruction of the architect's demolished Glasgow home, the style is quite startling even today. You ascend from the gallery's gloomy ground floor into the cool, white austere drawing room. There's something otherworldly about the mannered style of

Scottish Parliament (p753),
Edinburgh, Scotland

View of Edinburgh Castle (p749), Edinburgh,
Scotland

Royal Oak (p766), Edinburgh,
Scotland

Port of Leith (p757), Edinburgh, Scotland

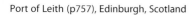

NICOLA WELLS

Boats moored, Isle of Iona (p829), Scotland

Statue of Robert the Bruce near Stirling Castle (p831), Stirling, Scotland

MARTIN MOOS

GRAEME CORNWALLIS

Lochranza Castle (p810), Isle of Arran, Scotland

Melrose Abbey (p796), Melrose, Scotland

GLENN BEAN

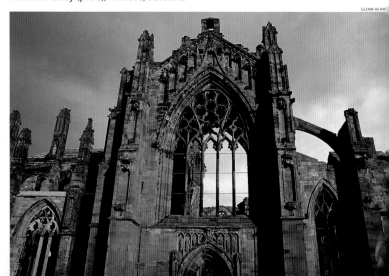

the beaten silver panels, the long-backed chairs and the surface decorations echoing Celtic manuscript illuminations.

Bus Nos 44 and 44A pass this way from the city centre (Hope St); it's also just a short walk from Hillhead underground station.

Outside Glasgow
BURRELL COLLECTION

Arguably, Glasgow's top attraction, the **Burrell Collection** (☎ 287 2550; Pollok Country Park, Pollokshaws Rd; admission free, parking £1; ☻ 10am-5pm Mon-Thu & Sat, 11am-5pm Fri & Sun; wheelchair access), was amassed by wealthy industrialist Sir William Burrell (accent the first syllable) before it was donated to the city. The building, 3 miles south of the centre, was a result of a design competition in 1971; from the outside it seems somewhat of a hybrid, but the spectacular interior provides a fitting setting for its exhibits and European stained glass. Floor-to-ceiling windows admit a flood of natural light, and the trees and landscape outside enhance the effect created by the exhibits. Many of the doorways between galleries are stunning carved portals purloined from Spanish and Italian churches. This idiosyncratic collection includes everything from Chinese porcelain and medieval furniture to paintings by Boudin and Cézanne and sculpture. It isn't so big as to be overwhelming, and the stamp of the collector creates an intriguing coherence.

Most visitors will find a favourite part of this museum, but the exquisite tapestry galleries are outstanding. Intricate stories are woven into staggering, wall-size pieces dating from the 13th century; the massive *Triumph of the Virgin* exemplifies the complexity in nature and theme of this medium, drawing on crusader tales to recreate the Holy Land (though none too accurately in the case of the camels).

In springtime, it's worth making a full day of your trip here and spending some time wandering in the beautiful park, studded with flowers. Once part of the estates of Pollok House (see following), the grounds have numerous enticing picnic spots; if you're not heading further north, here's the place to see shaggy Highland cattle, as well as heavy horses.

There are guided tours of the gallery (free) at 10.30am and 2pm. Numerous buses pass the gates (including Nos 45, 47, 48 and 57 from Union St) and there's a twice-hourly bus service between the gallery and the gates (a pleasant 10-minute walk).

POLLOK HOUSE

It's possible to visit the National Trust of Scotland's (NTS) **Pollok House**, (☎ 616 6410; Pollok Country Park, Pollokshaws Rd; admission £6; ☻ 10am-5pm), a sumptuous Edwardian mansion brim-full of period furniture and with walls heavy with paintings. The servants' quarters alone give an idea of how the British aristocracy once lived.

Mackintosh Buildings

Glasgow has some superb Art Nouveau buildings designed by the Scottish architect

---

THE GENIUS OF CHARLES RENNIE MACKINTOSH

The quirky, linear and geometric designs of this famous Scottish architect and designer have had almost as much influence on the city as have Gaudí's on Barcelona. Many of the buildings Mackintosh designed in Glasgow are now open to the public, and you'll see his tall, thin, Art Nouveau typeface repeatedly reproduced.

Born in 1868, he studied at the Glasgow School of Art. In 1896, when he was aged 27, his design won a competition for the School of Art's new building on Renfrew St. The first part was opened in 1899 and is considered to be the earliest example of Art Nouveau in Britain, and Mackintosh's supreme architectural achievement. This building demonstrates his skill in combining function and style. Also a furniture designer and decorative artist, he went on to design many more buildings.

Although Mackintosh's genius was quickly recognised on the Continent (he contributed to a number of exhibitions in France, Germany and Austria), he didn't receive the same encouragement in Scotland. His architectural career here lasted only until 1914 when he moved to England to concentrate on furniture design. He died in 1928, but it was only in the last decades of the 20th century that Mackintosh's genius became widely recognised.

and designer, Charles Rennie Mackintosh (CRM). From February to November there are weekend tours of these buildings (once or twice a month); the cost is £285/482 for one/two people, including dinner, bed and breakfast for two nights, lunches, coach, guide and admission to the Mackintosh buildings. Contact the **Charles Rennie Mackintosh Society** (CRM Society; ☎ 946 6600; www.crmsociety.com) in the Queen's Cross Church for details.

GLASGOW SCHOOL OF ART

Widely recognised as Mackintosh's greatest building, the **Glasgow School of Art** (☎ 353 4526; 167 Renfrew St) still houses the educational institution. It's hard not to be impressed by the thoroughness of the design – the architect's pencil seems to have shaped everything inside and outside the building. The interior design is austere, with simple colour combinations (often just black and cream) and those uncomfortable-looking, high-backed chairs for which he is famous. The building was named as one of the world's 100 greatest artistic achievements of the 20th century by the BBC.

Entry is by guided tour only (£5) at 11am and 2pm Monday to Friday, 10.30am and 11.30am Saturday from October to March (six daily 10.30am to 2.30pm from April to September). Parts of the school may be closed to visitors if they're in use.

QUEEN'S CROSS CHURCH

Now the headquarters of the CRM Society, **Queen's Cross Church** (☎ 946 6600; 870 Garscube Rd; adult/child £2/free; ☼ 10am-5pm Mon-Fri year-round, 2-5pm Sun Mar-Oct), on the corner of Maryhill Rd north of the centre, is the only one of Mackintosh's church designs to be built (1896); and has stunning window tracery and relief carvings. It's the simplicity of the design that makes it so inspiring. There's an information centre, a small display and a gift shop.

OTHER MACKINTOSHIANA

The **Scotland Street School** (☎ 287 0500; 225 Scotland St; admission free; ☼ 10am-5pm Mon-Thu & Sat, 11am-5pm Fri & Sun; wheelchair access), an impressive Mackintosh building dominated by two glass-stair towers, is now a museum of education from Victorian times to WWII; it may sound dull but it's actually fascinating.

Although designed in 1901 as an entry in a competition run by a German magazine,

the **House for an Art Lover** (☎ 353 4770; Bellahouston Park, 10 Drumbreck Rd; adult £3.50; ☼ 10am-4pm Mon-Wed, 10am-1pm Thu-Sun Apr-Sep, 10am-1pm Sat & Sun Oct-Mar, call for weekday admission times), 1½ miles south of the river, was only completed in 1996. It's part of the Glasgow School of Art and has permanent Mackintosh displays. Its rooms are stunning for their light and elegance.

The principal rooms from Mackintosh's house have been reconstructed as the Mackintosh House at the Hunterian Art Gallery (see p780).

ACTIVITIES

There are numerous green spaces within the city. **Pollok Country Park** surrounds the Burrell Collection with many woodland trails. Nearer the centre, the **Kelvin Walkway** follows the River Kelvin through Kelvingrove Park, the Botanic Gardens and on to Dawsholm Park. Also there is a walk along the Clyde (p779). Several long-distance walking/cycling routes originate in Glasgow (see p773).

WALKING TOUR

Start your walk on busy pedestrianised Buchanan St, just outside Borders bookshop. Heading east from here along Exchange St, you pass through the ornamental **entrance gateway (1)** to Merchant City.

If you were a 19th century industrialist, the Royal Exchange directly ahead of you might well have been your destination, but this stately colonnaded neoclassical building is now the **Gallery of Modern Art (2**; p778).

The horseback statue of the Duke of Wellington is facing down Ingram St, which you should follow for a couple of blocks. Continue southwards down Glassford St past **Trades Hall (3**; p778).

Turn left onto Wilson St, where the bulky **Sheriff Court (4)** fills a whole block. It was built in 1842 as Glasgow's town hall and merchants' house; it's currently undergoing major renovation. Continue eastwards past Ingram Square, another warehouse development, to **Merchant Square (5)**, a covered courtyard that was once the city's fruit market but now bustles with cafés and bars. Across the road is **Blackfriars (6**; p787), one of the city's most relaxed pubs; grab a window seat and see what's going on. Refreshment on board, continue along Bell St, a continu-

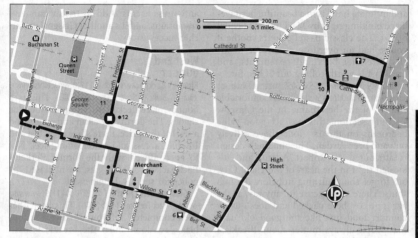

WALK FACTS

Distance 2.5 miles
Duration 1–3 hours

ation of Wilson St, and emerge onto High St. Take a left and follow the street uphill to **Glasgow Cathedral** (**7**; p778).

Behind the cathedral, wind your way up through the noble tombs of the **Necropolis (8)** with rewarding city views, before heading back down and taking in the **St Mungo Museum of Religious Life and Art** (**9**; p778) and **Provand's Lordship** (**10**; p778).

Then follow busy Cathedral St back towards the centre, passing the buildings of the University of Strathclyde as you go. A left down North Frederick St and you'll reach **George Square** (**11**; p778) with its statues of famous Glaswegians and the monumental **City Chambers** (**12**; p778).

TOURS

There are two open-top bus tours of Glasgow offering commentary and following a similar city route. Both start on George Square outside the TIC and offer a hop-on, hop-off service. **City Sightseeing** (☎ 204 0444) run similar buses in many world cities, while **Classic Glasgow Tour** (☎ 636 3190) is run by First, the urban bus company. There are also **taxi tours** (☎ 429 7070) of the city available; costing £25/45 per vehicle for a one-/two-hour trip. All cabs are wheelchair accessible.

SLEEPING

Finding decent options in July and August can be difficult – for a B&B, arrive reasonably early and use the TIC's booking service. Beware of 'backpacker accommodation' advertised at train/bus stations – listings often amount to nothing more than a scam where backpackers find themselves sleeping in filthy shared flats because the nonexistent hostel is being 'renovated'.

City Centre
BUDGET
Campus Village (☎ 548 4381; r per person £16, 6-bed flat per person weekly £54, B&B with en suite s/d £32/45.50; ☷ mid-Jun–Sep; **P** ✗) During summer, the University of Strathclyde, off Cathedral St and opposite Glasgow Cathedral, offers accommodation in shared, single-sex, self-catering flats on a weekly basis or good-value B&B with 24-hour access.

Euro Hostel (☎ 222 2828; www.euro-hostels.co.uk; 318 Clyde St; dm £13.75, s/tw £29/37; ✗ ▯; wheelchair access) This is a hulking giant in a former hall of residence near Central Station. There's a very institutional feel to the place, but the bunks are comfortable enough, and there's a bar and 24-hour reception. Dorm rates are fine, but you'll get much better value elsewhere for singles and twins. Continental breakfast included.

MID-RANGE
The Old Schoolhouse (☎ 332 7600; oschoolh@hotmail .com; 194 Renfrew St; s/d from £35/52; ✗) This small

and intimate hotel is in a beautiful heritage-listed building right by Mackintosh's School of Art. The classic pastel colours soothe if you've had an overdose of chrome in the city's trendier bars and restaurants, and breakfast is worth rolling out of bed for.

Babbity Bowster (☎ 552 5055; babbitybowster@go fornet.co.uk; 16 Blackfriars St; s/d £35/50) Comfortable winner of the best name in the Glasgow sleeping section, this has six good-value bedrooms on the 1st floor above a lively pub and beer garden. The building's design is attributed to Robert Adam, and it's located right in the heart of Merchant City, but forget about turning in before the pub shuts. There's no excuse to, anyway, as the bar is atmosphere-packed and does quality comfort food just like the good old days that people always mutter about. Breakfast is not included.

Cathedral House Hotel (☎ 552 3519; fax 552 2444; www.cathedralhousehotel.com; 28 Cathedral Sq; s/d £55/85; P ✗) Charmingly, this is a small urban version of some of the ornate turreted baronial castles that speckle the highlands. Right by the cathedral, it offers rooms decorated with an artistic eye, as well as a restaurant serving well-regarded Scottish cuisine.

Hampton Court Hotel (☎ 332 6623; www.hampton court.activehotels.com; 230 Renfrew St; s/d from £25/40) A stone's throw from the School of Art, this place is bright, clean, and offers very solid value. Some of the upbeat rooms have en suites; there's more light at the front of the building, but there's also a primary school opposite… Don't be even a minute late to breakfast or you'll go hungry!

Victorian House (☎ 332 0129; thevictorian@uk online.co.uk; 212 Renfrew St; s/d £32/46, with en suite £39/56; ✗) This is another fine option on a street that bristles with hotels. Run by the same management as the Old Schoolhouse, it's similarly decorated if not quite as charming, but is plenty comfortable and has more rooms.

TOP END

Langs Hotel (☎ 333 1500; www.langshotels.co.uk; 2 Port Dundas Pl; s/d £100/110; ✗ ; wheelchair access) This towering place right next to the bus station has taken the style-bar concept and made a hotel of it. With an on-site spa centre, the emphasis is on relaxation, and the rooms, with CD player, Playstation, massive beds and artful colour schemes, are powerful anti-stress agents. Add in trendy bars and restaurants, and it's another Glasgow urban-chic success story.

West End
BUDGET

Blue Sky Backpackers (☎ 221 1710; www.blueskyhostel .com; 65 Berkeley St; dm £8, d £30; 🖵) This is a bouncy place decked out in optimistic blue shades. The dorms are clean and comfy and a steal at this price; there's free breakfast and Internet access and a welcoming feel. Not to be confused with the former Berkeley Backpackers, which has been closed by police for serious dodginess.

Glasgow SYHA Hostel (☎ 0870 004 1119; www.syha .org.uk; 7 Park Tce; dm £14; ✗ 🖵) This hostel has been completely refurbished after a serious blaze, so don't burn the breakfast toast. Located in a charming town house on a hill above Kelvingrove Park, this is one of Scotland's best official hostels, with 24-hour access; excellent facilities and a big-city buzz about the place. From Central Station, take bus No 44 and get off at the first stop on Woodlands Rd.

Glasgow Backpackers Hostel (☎ 332 9099; www .scotlands-top-hostels.com; 17 Park Tce; dm £10.50, tw £24; 🕒 Jul-Sep; ✗) This is a spacious summer-only hostel in a University of Glasgow residence on a quiet West End street. The rooms, unlike in term time, are clean and well-kept; it's very popular and has free tea and coffee.

Bunkum Backpackers (☎ 581 4481; www.bunkum glasgow.co.uk; 26 Hillhead St; dm £12, tw £32; P ✗) In a noble old house on a quiet street, this hostel has very spacious dorms as well as a large kitchen and laundry facilities. Not a party place – there's a wee hint of temperance in the air – but the proximity of the West End's restaurants and bars make this a great base. Keep your eyes on the street numbers, for it's not well signposted.

MID-RANGE

Alamo Guest House (☎ 339 2395; 46 Gray St; www .alamoguesthouse.com; s/d from £22/40) A fascinating place that is lent much character by a variety of furnishings, from exquisite Victorian wooden dressers and wardrobes to obscure Eastern European heraldic mouldings. The charismatic owners will make you very welcome and will chart you a gastronomic path through the West End that could take you a fortnight! Top value.

SOMETHING SPECIAL

Seeking the relaxed comfort of a country hotel, but with the buzz of Glasgow's West End a few minutes' stroll away? Head for **Kirklee Hotel** (☎ 334 5555; 11 Kensington Gate; www.kirkleehotel.co.uk; s/d £55/72; ✗) While handy for Byres Rd, this is a little oasis of peace. Set in an attractive row of sandstone terraces and with a lovingly tended garden, it's an intimate place decorated with an eclectic range of artwork and run by solicitous hosts. And not to worry about looking your best for strained introductions and forced conversation over morning cereal: breakfast is brought to your room!

Belhaven Hotel (☎ 339 3222; www.belhavenhotel .com; 15 Belhaven Tce; s/d £40/65; ✗ ; wheelchair access) A quiet and stately hotel that yet is perfectly situated for raiding expeditions on the restaurants of the West End. The décor is light and elegant, synching well with the plaster mouldings of the original design. The front rooms have huge windows, and there's a lounge with cane furniture and Kingfisher lager on tap. It's just off Great Western Rd.

Argyll Hotel (☎ 337 3313; www.argyllhotelglasgow .co.uk; 973 Sauchiehall St; s/d £58/72; P ✗ 🖳) This hotel is designed to resemble a Highland shooting lodge, but the tartan carpet and hunting pictures stop short of the tacky and, backed by an impeccable welcome, carry plenty of charm. This old town house preserves some elegant cornicing in its high-ceilinged rooms, the pricier of which come with four-poster beds. The same management run the slightly cheaper Angus Hotel across the road.

TOP END

One Devonshire Gardens (☎ 339 2001; www.onedevon shiregardens.com; 1 Devonshire Gardens; s/d from £135/185; P ✗) Just off Great Western Rd, this is the city's classic five-star hotel, and where major celebrities stay when in town. A far cry from your Hiltons, this establishment oozes class and taste, occupying a row of terraced houses with the relaxed confidence of a landed laird. The rooms vary in size and equipment, but all are luxurious, with beds designed for a long lie-in. The hotel's Room Glasgow restaurant is also excellent.

Outside Glasgow

Craigendmuir Caravan Park (☎ 779 4159; Campsie View; 2-person pitches £10) Four miles northeast of the city, this camping option is a 15-minute walk from Stepps station (on the Cumbernauld rail line from Queen St station) and accommodates cars and tents in comfort, with a fine range of facilities.

EATING

The main concentrations of restaurants, of which Glasgow has a full complement, are in Merchant City, and off Byres Rd in the West End. Many offer a two- or three-course lunch special for as little as £4.50. Similarly, many places offer a 'pretheatre' evening menu for diners arriving before 7pm. Bear in mind that many of the pubs listed on p787 also do cheap and filling pub meals.

City Centre

BUDGET

Bargo (☎ 553 4771; 80 Albion St; mains £5-8; ⏱ noon-6.45pm; wheelchair access) This bar captures modern 'girder chic' without sacrificing comfort. The high space with its barcode-patterned chairs and large windows staring out at Merchant City becomes a trendy bar in the evenings, but is a bargain lunch spot. A cheerful mixture of Mediterranean and Tex-Mex dishes are on offer for a song – try the mussels or the excellent tuna steak with mango salsa – and wash it down with a bottle of ultracheap wine.

Centre for Contemporary Arts (☎ 332 7959; 350 Sauchiehall St; light meals £3-8; ⏱ 11am-9.30pm Tue-Sat, 11am-4pm Sun; ✗ ; wheelchair access) This centre for the performing arts has a very cool atrium bar/café that attracts all manner of unhurried folk. The glass roof adds atmosphere, whether it's filtering sunlight or (more often) reverberating with raindrops; the menu offers quality Mediterranean-style snacks and light meals through the day, and selected main courses by night (the fish is especially good here).

Mono (☎ 553 2400; 12 Kings Ct; mains £5-7; ⏱ noon-10pm; ✗ ; wheelchair access) Without a doubt this is Glasgow's best destination for vegetarian (in fact, vegan) food. A one-stop shop for books, music, and organic ales, the food here is wholesome but warming and hearty; the atmosphere relaxed and without prejudice. And the scrumptious desserts will have dairy farmers shaking their heads in dismay.

SOMETHING SPECIAL

Everyone knows that some of the world's best Indian food can be eaten in Britain; the tricky bit is finding quality amid so much mediocrity. But Glaswegians know that the cosy **Wee Curry Shop** (☎ 353 0777; 7 Buccleuch St; mains £5-8; ❤ lunch & dinner Mon-Sat; ✗) punches well above its size; it has developed a stellar reputation for serving up some of the best curry you're likely to find north of Bradford. The strong, fresh flavours will renew the faith of those tested by too many mediocre *tikka masalas* over the years, and the lunch special at £4.75 will make you think it's your birthday. There's a new **branch** (☎ 357 5280; 23 Ashton Lane) above Jinty McGinty's pub; booking ahead for either is essential.

MID-RANGE

Mao (☎ 564 5161; 84 Brunswick St; mains £7-9; ❤ noon-11pm; ✗ ; wheelchair access) This is the archetypal Asian fusion restaurant, with bright, effective service cheering diners behind the Warhol portraits of the Chairman on the windows. The menu is helpful and accessible, there are plenty of vegetarian choices, and the quality and presentation confidently high. The range of Asian beers, including the excellent Chinese Tsingtao, make up for the poor but pricy wine list.

Trattoria Gia (☎ 552 7411; 17 King St; mains £7-13, set lunch £8.50; ❤ lunch Tue-Sat, dinner Tue-Sun; wheelchair access) This is the image of what should appear in a picture dictionary after the word 'trattoria'. Checked tablecloths, expansive hosts, rich fragrances of garlic and tomato and a happy atmosphere combine to make this a very pleasurable experience. The quality of the Italian food is a large step up from the norm, too, with succulent seafood dishes adding weight to pasta and pizza prepared with plenty of flair.

Café Gandolfi (☎ 552 6813; 64 Albion St; mains £7-10; ❤ 9am-11.30pm Mon-Sat; noon-11.30pm Sun; ✗) Aging gracefully, this establishment has seen trendy bars and restaurants come and go around it for many years, and still remains a firm favourite. Once part of the old cheese market in Merchant City, this beautifully furnished bistro offers top-notch Scottish fare, managing to keep hearty textures while banishing stodge. Downstairs is a cheaper bar

menu, which offers equally enticing food in a more contemporary space.

West End
BUDGET
Beanscene (☎ 334 6776; Cresswell Lane; sandwiches £3.70; ❤ 8am-11pm Mon-Sat, 10am-11pm Sun; ✗ ; wheelchair access) Although there are a few branches of this café across the city, it is a far cry from the institutionalised mediocrity of the larger coffee chains. There's a lively student pulse in this friendly West End branch, where you sit at low wooden tables on sinfully comfortable sofas. There's a fine range of sandwiches and sweet snacks, and often live music in the evenings. And the black stuff gets the caffeine addict's thumbs-up.

MID-RANGE
Konaki (☎ 342 4010; 920 Sauchiehall St; mains £6-8; ❤ lunch Mon-Sat, dinner daily; wheelchair access) Bringing a touch of sunshine to Sauchiehall St, this is a friendly and unpretentious Greek restaurant offering exceptional value. The starters (£2 to £4) are a particular highlight of the authentic menu – in fact, ordering a whole lot of them to share is the most enjoyable way to eat here. There are several Greek wines to accompany your meal, and you can't miss the rare chance of knocking back a traditional coffee and ouzo at the end of it.

Stravaigin II (☎ 334 7165; 8 Ruthven Lane; mains £10-17; ❤ noon-11pm; ✗ ; wheelchair access) A buzzy modern place that is one of two eateries run by the son of the chef at the Ubiquitous Chip (local restaurant critics never tire of the 'off the old block' puns). With an intimate feel and 1st-class service, the prices charged seem very reasonable, particularly as the leap-of-faith fusions of diverse world flavours tend to work very well indeed.

TOP END
Cook's Room (☎ 353 0707; 13 Woodside Tce; mains £15-20; ❤ lunch & dinner Mon-Sat; ✗) This is that rarest of beasts: a high-class gourmet dining experience without a hint of pretentiousness. This quiet basement space is decked out with lovely wooden furniture (including some church pews) and characterised by relaxed and personal service. The menu is short and changes regularly, but always features exquisitely prepared and intriguingly textured dishes, Scottish in character but drawing confidently from other cuisines.

Ubiquitous Chip (☎ 334 5007; 12 Ashton Lane; set lunch/dinner £21.80/32.80; 😋 lunch & dinner; wheelchair access) Named to poke fun at Scotland's perceived lack of culinary sophistication, this has been one of Glasgow's best restaurants for many years. A francophile finesse enhances dishes of select Scottish ingredients; plates of Perth woodpigeon, Finnan haddie, or Ayrshire lamb will take your palate around the country. An extensive (if far from cheap) wine list and plenty of whiskies round off a memorable experience. Above, Upstairs at the Chip provides cheaper, bistro-style food with a similarly advanced set of principles. There are also bar meals at the atmospheric upstairs pub, while the cute 'Wee Pub' down the side alley also offers plenty of drinking pleasure.

DRINKING

Glaswegians spend a frightening percentage of their income on bevvy, which is why (or perhaps because) some of Scotland's best nightlife is found in the din and sometimes roar of the city's pubs and bars. Glasgow is famous for the 'style bar', a fashion-conscious move away from the traditional wood and sawdust boozer. Happily, most of these venues, no matter how much they paid the designers, are still unpretentious and welcoming places. Merchant City is the trendy spot for a drink, with any number of different concept-bars, while the West End has reliable spots off Byres Rd, where all manner of folk mingle happily.

City Centre

Horse Shoe (☎ 229 5711; 17 Drury Lane) Although famed as having the longest continuous bar in the UK, the real highlight of this unpretentious local is the fine selection of cheap lagers and real ales. One of the city's legendary pubs, its cheap lunches have been a workers' staple for years – just £3.20 gets you soup, a main course, and a dessert, served upstairs or at the back of the main bar.

Arches (☎ 565 1000; 253 Argyle St) It's one-stop culture fix. As well as an avant-garde theatre and nightclub, this venue under Central Station has a downstairs bar whose intimate tables belie the cavernous space it's in. All sorts of people drop by for a drink, which is why it's one of the city's best bars.

Brunswick Cellars (☎ 311 1820; 239 Sauchiehall St) Easy to miss, with a narrow entrance next to

Oddbins on Sauchiehall St, this is probably not the place to take the mother-in-law. It's an underground den that throbs with grungy character and has plenty of cheap drink offers and live music. Stash yourself in one of the claustrophobic seating spaces and you'll quickly lose all awareness of time.

Bar 10 (☎ 572 1448; 10 Mitchell St) This was the place that moved the goalposts in the early '90s, converting a warehouse into Glasgow's first style bar. While fickle fashion followers have moved on, it remains something of a drinking icon, and is a relaxed spot hidden in an alley in the heart of the city.

Blackfriars (☎ 552 5294; 36 Bell St) One of the least self-conscious of the bars in Merchant City, this is a soothing spot for a drink, particularly if you can nab a seat looking out over the street corner, busy with Glasgow folk walking about their business. There are always enticing real ales on tap, and usually plenty of punters up for a chat.

Spy Bar (☎ 221 7711; 153 Bath St) Once Glasgow's trendiest spot, this basement hang-out still has a certain cachet as a place to be seen. Don't let that put you off, though, for the drinks are priced fairly and the staff would serve Worzel Gummidge with a cheery smile. Designed with a light hand, the bar has comfy booths and video screens projecting arty collages. Arrive early if you want a seat, for by the time the DJs get going at night, it's usually packed.

Other recommendations:

Bon Accord (☎ 248 4427; 153 North St) Glasgow's temple to real ale boasts a lip-smacking line of Scottish and English beers.

Corinthian (☎ 552 1101; 191 Ingram St; 😋 until 3am) A venue with many facets and an awesome domed bar, formerly a courtroom.

Pivo Pivo (☎ 564 8100; 15 Waterloo St) An amazing array of bottled lagers from every continent (we found names cropping up from long-forgotten foreign hangovers).

Waxy O'Connor's (☎ 354 5154; 44 West George St) This lager labyrinth could be an Escher sketch and is a cut above most Irish theme pubs.

West End

Jinty McGinty's (☎ 339 0747; 23 Ashton Lane) This is a boozer that is almost authentically Irish enough to avoid the moniker 'Irish pub'. It's a very jovial place, usually packed to the rafters and spilling out on to the lane. There's live folk music most nights, and cosy little booths where you can sip a pint of black while perusing the biographies of Irish writers on the walls.

Uisge Beatha (☎ 564 1596; 232-246 Woodlands Rd) This is a top place and an antidote to style bars. A quirky mish-mash of animal heads and portraits of depressed nobility, it's patrolled by Andy Capp–like characters during the day and a mixed bag of punters at night. The name is Gaelic for whisky (literally 'water of life') of which it sells more than a hundred varieties.

Vodka Wódka (☎ 341 0669; 31 Ashton Lane) This good-humoured and trendy place mainly dedicates itself to the spirit it is named for. There are many varieties, including a fearsome Polish 80 per-center that will make or break your night. DJs play daily, but even better is the small vodka garden out the back, perfect for a cool mixed drink on a long summer evening.

Other recommendations:

54 Below (☎ 357 5454; 3 Kelvingrove St) Stylish, with strategically low lighting and chilled music, but relaxed and unpretentious. A tempting preclub destination.

Tennents (☎ 341 1024; 191 Byres Rd) A venerable joint that is well into its second century of supplying thirsty Westenders with well-tended real ales.

ENTERTAINMENT

The *List* (£2.20) is an invaluable fortnightly events guide available at newsagents and bookshops and detailing nightclubs, cinema screenings, plays and concerts for both Glasgow and Edinburgh.

Cinemas

Glasgow Film Theatre (☎ 332 8128; 12 Rose St; www.gft.org.uk; adult £4-5) This is the city's best cinema for those who like looking beyond the mainstream. A classic arthouse venue, with a great selection of international independent film, and frequent screenings themed on a particular genre or director.

Odeon City Centre (☎ 332 3413; 56 Renfield St; adult £3-5.25) Very much your standard modern multiplex, showing recent big releases on nine giant screens, near the Buchanan Street bus station.

Grosvenor (☎ 339 8444; Ashton Lane; adult £3.50-6.50) This well-loved cinema has recently re-opened to popular acclaim. It's a Glasgow favourite, as it's situated right in the heart of West End restaurant and publand, perfect for dissecting the movie over a meal or a drink afterwards.

Gay & Lesbian Venues

Glasgow has a lively and welcoming gay and lesbian scene, with most of the action to be found in the Merchant City area. Both gays and lesbians are welcome at each venue listed here, though the Waterloo is mostly frequented by men.

Waterloo Bar (☎ 229 5890; 306 Argyle St) This traditional pub on the corner of Wellington St, is Scotland's oldest gay bar. It's a good place to meet people of all ages, has a large group of friendly regulars, and couldn't be less sceney.

Polo Lounge (☎ 553 1221; 84 Wilson St) A splendiferous bar decorated in plush style with heavy curtains and horsehair armchairs. The opulent surrounds contrast with the laid-back atmosphere, although things get more heated in the downstairs dance pits.

Delmonica's (☎ 552 4803; 69 Virginia St) This spot is a well-established funhouse with cheap drink deals and well-loved pop hits merging into dance music as the evening progresses. A favourite haunt for those on the prowl, it's the place to come if you're looking for company.

Live Music

Glasgow has Scotland's best live music scene (see the boxed text, p789). As well as the venues listed below, several of the bars and clubs listed (p787 and p789) have frequent live acts: these include Brunswick Cellars, Jinty McGinty's, and the Cathouse.

King Tut's Wah Wah Hut (☎ 221 5279; www .kingtuts.co.uk; 272a St Vincent St; ☒ Mon-Sat & Sun if there's a gig on) A legend in its own gig time, this great venue has live music nearly every night of the week, covering a whole range of stuff from indie rock to hip-hop. Certain events are ticketed and will sell out, so check availability beforehand.

Nice 'n' Sleazy (☎ 333 0900; www.nicensleazy.com; 421 Sauchiehall St) Some may feel that the '70s décor at this relaxed bar and venue strays way beyond the comfortable into the kitsch, but perhaps that's part of its considerable appeal. The music covers all tastes, although rock predominates. When the house is full, which it often is, the atmosphere is fantastic.

Barrowland (☎ 552 4601; www.glasgow-barrowland .com; 244 Gallowgate) With a name spoken with affection and some reverence in the rock scene, this is one of the city's biggest and oldest venues and certainly its most enchanting. An old-time dancehall, it's got a movie-set feel to it and has great acoustics and an anything-goes vibe.

Scottish Exhibition & Conference Centre (SECC; ☎ 0870 040 4000; www.secc.co.uk; Finnieston Quay) On the Clyde River, this and its adjoining armadillo-shaped **Clyde Auditorium** (same contact details) cater for the big acts to hit the city. The acoustics are better in the auditorium than the hangar-like SECC, but tickets don't come cheap for either.

Nightclubs

The club scene is huge and continually changing. Glaswegians usually hit the clubs after the pubs have closed, so many clubs offer a discounted admission and cheaper drinks before 11pm. Most also give student discounts. Entry to most clubs is between £3 and £5, although places often offer free passes around nearby bars. Most clubs close around 3am or 4am. Club nights tend to change venues regularly, so always check the *List*.

Arches (☎ 565 1000; www.thearches.co.uk; 253 Argyle St; admission £8-13; ☼ Fri-Sun) One of the city's largest and most popular clubs and one that reliably pulls top DJs from all over Britain and Europe. There's something on most Friday, Saturday, and Sunday nights, whether it's The Funk Room, a must for funk and hip-hop freaks; Colours, with cutting-edge dance; or any of a wide variety of monthly events. It's also one of the city's best bars (p787).

Glasgow School of Art (☎ 332 0691; 167 Renfrew St; admission £5-8; ☼ Tue-Sun). Not just a student zone, but a destination for those in the know. There's always something interesting on, particularly drum and bass, but on Saturdays it's time for Freakmenoovers, a mecca for hip-hop north of the border.

Cathouse (☎ 248 6606; 15 Union St; admission £4; ☼ Thu-Sat) A three-floor twilight zone for rock, metal, indie, goth, industrial and EBM fans. There's a mixture of well-worn leather and trendy darkwave teens; it's atmospheric,

SCOTLAND'S LIVE MUSIC CAPITAL *Bryan McRitchie*

Year after year, touring artists and travellers alike name Glasgow as one of their favourite cities in the world to enjoy live music.

As much of Glasgow's character is encapsulated within the soul and humour of its inhabitants, the main reason for the city's musical success lies within its audience and the musical community it has bred and nurtured for years. Glaswegians laugh together, cry together and sing together, and it is their passion and intensity, coupled with an almost intrinsic understanding and love of music, that makes the live-music experience in Glasgow unique.

With such a strong musical heritage it is inevitable that Glasgow and its surrounding communities consistently introduce a string of potent acts to an enthusiastic audience.

Originally from Ireland but now adopted Glaswegians, Snow Patrol brings a subtle, poetic beauty to their barbed-wire and cotton-wool alternative guitar pop. In a similar vein Odeon Beatclub, the latest pretenders to Glasgow's live-music crown, are currently cresting on their wave of guitar-propelled melodic snapshots on modern-day life. In the process they are building a persuasive live reputation and a considerable fanbase, as are Sneak Attack Tigers with their heavier assault. Intertwining lush arrangements, delicate instrumentation and battered guitars, the Delgados bounce between male and female vocal leads as they generate an encompassing sonic landscape full of cinematic swells and tainted prose. Biffy Clyro, Aereogramme and Terra Diablo all serve up interestingly distinct slices of Glaswegian rock. Sons and Daughters blend blues, country and folk with intense passion and anger while Viva Stereo dabble in electro guitar noise beat confusion.

On any given night you may find your breath taken by a wave of voices as the audience spontaneously harmonises with an artist on a chorus, a song or even, on special nights, an entire show. Maybe it's the spine-tingling, hear-a-pin-drop silence that the audience respectfully affords an artist as they perform a quiet, acoustic or delicate piece. Whatever the occasion, the band or the venue, Glasgow is, by proxy of its inhabitants, a music city, an intricate web of emotions and poetry, passion and melody, and most of all honesty and soul.

Bryan McRitchie is an Edinburgh-based singer and musician.

SOUTHERN SCOTLAND

central, and has pleasingly cheap drinks. Only £1 entry before 11pm.

MAS (☎ 221 7080; 29 Royal Exchange Sq; admission £3-8; ☺ Thu-Tue) This spot has some of the city's best hard-house rocking the packed and sweaty crowd, a reputation for a party vibe and quality DJs. Sunday nights here are a long-time Glasgow classic for those who just won't lie down and take Monday on the chin.

Sport

Scottish football is dominated by the 'Old Firm', Celtic and Rangers, whose rivalry often involves burying the hatchet…right where it hurts (see the boxed text, below). Scotland play their international matches at **Hampden Park** (☎ 620 4000; www.hampdenpark .co.uk), a stadium that also holds a moderately interesting football museum. Hampden Park is 3 miles south of the centre.

Theatre

Theatre Royal (☎ 332 9000; www.theatreroyalglasgow .com; 282 Hope St; wheelchair access) This venue is the city's major performance space for opera – the Scottish Opera is based here – and ballet. Cheap standby tickets are available for some performances: ask at the box office.

Tramway (☎ 330 3501; www.tramway.org; 25 Albert Dr; wheelchair access) The Tramway is a cutting-edge space for contemporary theatre, per-forming arts and exhibitions. A typical week here might see performances from a Japanese group playing traditional stringed instruments, an Estonian radio choir, and a sharp piece of local postmodern theatre.

Glasgow Royal Concert Hall (☎ 353 8000; www .grch.com; 2 Sauchiehall St; wheelchair access) A feast of classical music is performed in this huge venue, but it goes further than that. Big-name rock stars often play here, and every January there's a festival of Celtic music. Check the website for what's coming up.

Citizens' Theatre (☎ 429 0022; 119 Gorbals St; tickets £6-15) This elegant Victorian theatre is one of the most highly regarded in Scotland. It consistently turns out high-quality performances, whether they be old favourites given new life, or new Scottish plays on their debut run.

Centre for Contemporary Arts (☎ 332 7521; 350 Sauchiehall St) The centre showcases the visual and performing arts, including exhibitions, forums, and cinema. It also has a very cool bar/café (p785) and is very much a place to be seen for the young and arty.

SHOPPING

Bristling with retail outlets, Glasgow is one of the UK's premier shopping destinations outside of London. The city centre is the place to head for high-street and international fashion chains, while quirkier

---

THE OLD FIRM

The historical turbulence between Catholics and Protestants in Scotland is reflected in the passionate support for the 'Old Firm', Glasgow and Scotland's two biggest football clubs. **Rangers** (☎ 0870 600 1972; www.rangers.co.uk; Ibrox Stadium, 150 Edmiston Dr) play in dark blue and have a predominantly Protestant fan base, while **Celtic** (seltic; ☎ 551 8653; www.celticfc.co.uk; Celtic Park, Parkhead), play in green and white hoops and have been traditionally Catholic. When the two play each other, there's absolutely no love lost: violence is common, both on and off the pitch.

It can be difficult for an outsider to understand the emotions these clubs engender in Scotland; it's as if all the hardships and emotions of day-to-day life, as well as the divisions of history get channelled into this one issue. The troubles in neighbouring Northern Ireland have also played their part. Neil Lennon, an Irish Protestant playing for Celtic, received death threats for his 'betrayal' of the Protestant cause, while poor old Mo Johnston, the first Catholic to play for Rangers in half a century when he joined them in the late 1980s, was hated by both sets of supporters!

Both clubs have been criticised heavily for not doing more to dissuade fans from open chanting of violent sectarian songs at matches, but their managements are aware of the fanatical levels of support both the clubs enjoy and unwilling to build bridges – after all, rivalry and hatred mean plenty of bums on seats at games.

On the pitch, the two clubs have completely dominated Scottish football throughout the league's existence. Rangers managed a run of nine championships in a row in the 1990s, but in recent times Celtic have been more dominant, and reached the UEFA Cup Final in 2003.

independent shops cluster along Great Western and Byres Rds in the West End.

For high fashion, you might want to check out places such as **Versace** (☎ 552 6510) in the stylish **Italian Centre** (John St). Alternatively, **Designer Exchange** (☎ 221 6898; 3 Royal Exchange Ct), just off Royal Exchange Square, stocks cheaper samples and resale designer labels. Trendy traders litter Sauchiehall, Argyle, and Buchanan Sts' pedestrian malls. **Dr Jives** (☎ 552 5451; 111 Candleriggs) stock a more cutting-edge, streetwise range.

You can't go past the flea market every weekend at the **Barras** (☎ 552 7258; London Rd), but for more traditional Scottish fashion, **Geoffrey (Tailor) Kiltmaker** (☎ 331 2388; 309 Sauchiehall St) is the place to head to take some tartan home.

Contemporary art from Scotland and the rest of the UK can be found at **Glasgow Print Studio** (☎ 552 0704; 25 King St) and **Compass Gallery** (☎ 221 6370; 178 West Regent St). **Glasgow Style** (☎ 552 8391; Hutcheson's Hall, 158 Ingram St) has excellent, locally crafted furniture, ceramics and jewellery.

In the West End, you could spend plenty of time browsing diverse shops such as **OneWorld** (☎ 357 1567; 100 Byres Rd), which stocks an eclectic range of arty gifts from around the globe, all of them fair-traded; **Fopp** (☎ 357 0774; 358 Byres Rd), a cheap independent Scottish record outlet; or the musty **Caledonia Books** (☎ 334 9663; 483 Great Western Rd), a treasure-trove of rare tomes.

And if you're a consumer looking for something consumable, you're not short of choice either. **Heart Buchanan** (☎ 334 7626; 380 Byres Rd), as well as being an intimate deli with the highest-quality Mediterranean produce, also prepare gourmet pre-ordered meals to take away. Picnics wouldn't be the same without nearby **IJ Mellis** (☎ 334 6845; 492 Great Western Rd), a branch of the country's premier cheesemonger, while **Peckham's** (☎ 347 1454; 124 Byres Rd) is a reliable source of fine foods and Scottish beers. In the centre, hit **Robert Graham & Co** (☎ 221 6588; 71 St Vincent St) for an excellent selection of malt whiskies and cigars.

GETTING THERE & AWAY

Air

Eight miles west of the city near Paisley, **Glasgow Airport** (☎ 887 1111) handles domestic traffic and international flights, including some direct transatlantic routes. It's the main airport for most of the Scottish islands. Glasgow Prestwick airport, 30 miles southwest of Glasgow is used by the budget carrier Ryanair.

EasyJet (☎ 0870 600 0000; www.easyjet.com) flies to and from Glasgow Airport to several British destinations including London Stansted (from £18 one-way, 1¼ hours, five daily), and also to Amsterdam (from £23 one-way, 1¾ hours, one daily)

Ryanair (☎ 0870 156 9569; www.ryanair.com) flies from Prestwick to London Stansted (from £12 one-way, 1¼ hours, six daily) and European destinations including Dublin (from £13 one-way, 45 minutes, about four flights daily) and Paris (from £22 one-way, 1½ hours, up to four daily).

British Airways (☎ 0870 850 9850; www.british airways.com) and its subsidiaries service many mainland and island destinations from Glasgow, including Stornoway (from £93 return; one hour; two daily) and Sumburgh in the Shetland Islands (from £151 return, 2½ hours; two daily).

Bus

Long-distance buses arrive and depart from **Buchanan bus station**. Bus fares from London are competitive. **Silver Choice** (☎ 01355 249 499; www.silverchoicetravel.co.uk) currently offers the cheapest deal (from £24 return; 8½ hours; departs 10am and 10pm daily from London's Victoria Coach Station and Glasgow). The service is popular so you'll need to book.

National Express (☎ 08705 80 80 80; www.national express.com) runs the same route (from £33 return, 8½ hours, up to four daily). There are also direct buses from Heathrow airport (one nightly at 11.05pm).

National Express also runs services to/ from Birmingham (from £33 return, six to eight hours, four daily), Manchester (from £22 return, five hours, five to six daily), Newcastle (from £22.50 return, four hours, one daily) and York (from £26.50 return, seven hours, one daily).

Citylink has buses to most major towns in Scotland. There are buses to Edinburgh (£4, 1¼ hours) every 15 to 20 minutes). There are also frequent buses daily to the following: Stirling (£4, 45 minutes), Perth (£6.50, 1½ hours), Inverness (£15.90, four hours) and Aberdeen (£16.40, 3½ hours). Heading up the west coast, there are buses to Oban (£12.20, three hours, two to three daily), Fort William (£13, three hours, four daily) and Portree on Skye (£22, 6½ hours, three daily). For Northern Ireland there are buses to Stranraer (£10, 2½ hours, two daily), where there are connecting ferries to Belfast (£20 single from Glasgow).

The **Motorvator** (☎ 01698 870 768) competes on the Edinburgh run, offering a slightly cheaper fare. It goes half-hourly Monday to Saturday and hourly on Sundays (1¼ hours).

Walkers should check out **First** (☎ 423 6600) which runs buses roughly hourly to Milngavie (30 minutes), the starting point of the West Highland Way.

Car

There are numerous car-rental companies; the big names have offices at the airport. **Arnold Clark** (☎ 0845 607 4500; 43 Allison St) is a Scottish operator with a good reputation and has rates starting at £19/95 per day/week. **Clarkson** (☎ 771 3990; www.clarksonofglasgow .com; 89 Byres Rd) have several city locations and offer similar rates.

Train

Glasgow has two train stations. Generally, Central Station serves southern Scotland, England and Wales, and Queen St serves the north and east. There are buses every 10 minutes between the two (50p or free with a through train ticket), or it's a 10-minute walk.

There are direct trains from London's King's Cross and Euston stations; they're not cheap, but they're much quicker (£86, 5½ hours, 10 direct daily) and more comfortable than the bus. You can get much cheaper fares if you book in advance.

First ScotRail (☎ 08457 484950; www.firstscotrail .com) operates the West Highland line north to Oban (£15.60, three hours, up to three daily) and Fort William (£18.70, 3¾ hours, two or three daily) and direct links to Dundee (£21.60, 1½ hours, hourly), Aberdeen (£32.90, 2½ hours, hourly) and Edinburgh (£9, 50 minutes, half hourly). Trains to Inverness (£32.90, 3½ hours, 11 daily) sometimes require a change in Aberdeen.

GETTING AROUND
To/From the Airport

There are bus services between Glasgow International Airport and Buchanan bus station (£3.30/5 single/return, 25 minutes, every 15 minutes daily). A taxi costs £15 to £20 to the centre. You can get to and from Prestwick by both bus (1½ hours; hourly) or train (50 minutes; every half hour). The last bus leaves Prestwick at 9.58pm; the last train at 11.08pm.

Bicycle

Just off the southern end of Byres Rd, **West End Cycles** (☎ 357 1344; 16 Chancellor St; ☽ Mon-Sat 10am-5.45pm) rents out 24-speed mountain bikes for £15/85 per day/week.

Car

The city centre's complex, one-way system, dead-end streets and restricted parking make driving an unattractive proposition, though street parking is easier in the West End. The presence of the motorway (M8) makes getting around easier only if you don't miss your turn-off, otherwise you could find yourself several miles out of the centre before you reach the first exit.

Public Transport

At the **St Enoch Square Travel Centre** (☎ 226 4826; ☽ 8.30am-5.30pm Mon-Sat), in the centre of St Enoch Square, the staff provide information on all transport in the Glasgow region. Here you can get a copy of the complicated but useful *Glasgow Mapmate* (£1), which shows all local bus routes run by First. You can buy tickets when you board local buses, but on most you must have exact change. For most trips in the city, fares are 80p. A day ticket is good value (£2.20 after 9.30am). After midnight there are limited night buses from George Square.

The circular Underground line serves 15 stations in the city's centre, west and south of the city (£1). A Discovery Ticket (£1.70) gives unlimited travel after 9.30am on the system for a day. The Roundabout Glasgow ticket (£4) includes travel on suburban trains. You'll see signs at some train stations for 'Low Level Trains', these are part of the suburban network, not the Underground.

Taxi

There's no shortage of taxis and you can hail them from the street. If you order a taxi from **Glasgow-Wide Taxis** (☎ 429 7070) by phone you can pay by credit card. All cabs are wheelchair-accessible.

LANARKSHIRE

The growth of Glasgow has made a satellite conglomeration of the towns of East Kilbride, Hamilton, Motherwell, Coatbridge, and Airdrie. The greatest attraction here is the birthplace museum of David Livingstone in Blantyre. A little further afield, however, the Clyde Valley scores its way through the centre of the shire in an exuberant tangle of foliage, wildlife, and waterfalls. On the riverbank is the World Heritage Site of New Lanark, a fascinating renovation of a 19th century cotton mill and the houses of the workers who ran it. The pioneering manager of the mill blazed a trail with all sorts of social initiatives for the labourers in a Utopian experiment that had far-reaching consequences in later decades.

BLANTYRE

☎ 01698 / pop 17,300

The birthplace of David Livingstone was founded as a cotton mill in the late 18th century. That zealous and pious doctor, missionary, and explorer was raised in a one-room tenement and worked in the mill by day from the age of 10, going to the local school at night. Amazingly for a time in which most mill workers were barely able to write their names, he managed to get himself into university to study medicine. He wouldn't recognise his hometown now, as it has become a rather depressing dormitory suburb of Glasgow. The house where he was born, however, has been preserved as an excellent museum.

The **David Livingstone Centre** (NTS; ☎ 823140; 165 Station Rd; adult £3.50; ☼ 10am-5pm Mon-Sat, 12.30-5pm Sun Apr-Christmas; wheelchair access) tells the story of his life from his early days in Blantyre to the 30 years he spent in Africa, where he named the Victoria Falls on one of his numerous journeys. It's a good display and brings to life the incredible hardships of his missionary existence, his battles against slavery, and his famous meeting with Stanley. There's a child-friendly African wildlife feature, and the grassy park that the museum is set in makes a perfect picnic spot, despite a rather alarming sculpture of a lion attack.

Buses stop on Main St, but it's best to come to Blantyre by train from the low-level platforms at Glasgow Central (20 minutes,

twice hourly). Head straight down the hill from the station to reach the museum.

LANARK & NEW LANARK

☎ 01555 / pop 8250

Below the market town of Lanark, famous in modern Scotland as the home of rally driver Colin McRae, is the World Heritage Site of New Lanark – an intriguing collection of restored mill buildings and warehouses in an attractive gorge by the River Clyde.

Once the largest cotton-spinning complex in Britain, it was better known for the pioneering social experiments of Robert Owen, who managed the mill from 1800. He provided his workers with housing, a cooperative store (the inspiration for the modern cooperative movement), the world's first nursery school for children, a school with adult-education classes, a sick-pay fund for workers and a social centre he called the New Institute for the Formation of Character. You'll need at least half a day to explore this large site; there's plenty to see.

Orientation & Information

The helpful **TIC** (☎ 661661; Horsemarket, Ladyacre Rd; ☼ 10am-12.30pm & 1-5pm Mon-Sat year-round & Sun Easter-Sep) is in Lanark, right by the adjacent bus and train stations. New Lanark is a mile downhill from here.

Sights

The best way to get the feel of New Lanark is to wander round the outside of this impressive place. What once must have been a thriving, noisy, grimy industrial village, pumping out enough cotton to wrap the planet, is now a peaceful oasis with only the swishing of trees and relentless roar of the River Clyde to be heard.

At the **visitors centre** (☎ 661345; www.newlanark .org; adult £5.95; ☼ 11am-5pm; most sections wheelchair access) you need to purchase a ticket to enter the main attractions. These include the **New Millennium Experience**, an innovative high-tech ride to New Lanark's past and possible future. The kids will love it, as it's reminiscent of a fun-park ride, although it may be a little feel-good for some tastes. The visit continues to the din of a huge working spinning mule, producing woollen yarn – the only fabric to be made here since the mills closed in 1968.

There is Robert Owen's **home** and also his **school** where you can see exhibitions on 'saving New Lanark', as well as the **Annie McLeod Experience** – a high-tech, audiovisual where the spirit of a 10-year-old mill girl describes life here in 1820.

After you've seen New Lanark you can then walk up to the **Falls of Clyde** through the beautiful nature reserve. Before you go, drop into the **Falls of Clyde Wildlife Centre** (☎ 665262; fallsofclyde@swt.org.uk; admission free; ◷ 11am-5pm Mar-Dec, noon-4pm Jan & Feb) by the river in New Lanark. There are wildlife and conservation exhibitions and you can organise bat walks (£2.50) or badger watching (£5) here. The riverside path takes you 2½ miles to the beautiful **Cora Linn** (waterfalls that inspired both Turner and Wordsworth). The Clyde is enchanting here, bubbling joyously over the rocks; it seems a different river from its sterner incarnation in Glasgow.

Sleeping

New Lanark Mill Hotel (☎ 667200; hotel@newlanark .org; s/d with en suite from £64.50/99, cottages per night from £44.50; P ✗) Right in the heart of the mill complex, this efficient hotel is an excellent conversion from one of the original buildings. There are smart and welcoming rooms or self-catering accommodation in nearby cottages.

New Lanark SYHA Hostel (☎ 0870 004 1143; www .syha.org.uk; Wee Row; dm adult/child £11.50/9; ◷ Mar-Oct; ✗ ▭) This hostel has a cracking location in an old mill building by the River Clyde. It's really atmospheric to be lodged within the restored mill complex although the place itself has a slightly puritanical feel. There are tidy four-bed dorms with en suites and one twin room.

Mrs Shirley Buchanan (☎ 661002; 5 Hardacres; r per person £18) This place offers high comfort without too many frills. It's good value.

Eating & Drinking

La Vigna (☎ 664320; 40 Wellgate; mains £10-17; ◷ lunch & dinner Mon-Sat, dinner Sun) This well-established local favourite is a great spot, seemingly plucked from some bygone age with its quietly efficient service and, charmingly, a separate menu for ladies – without prices! The food is distinctly Italian, albeit using sound Scottish venison, beef, and fish – there are also vegetarian options. The set-price lunch is fine value at £12.95.

Crown Tavern (☎ 664639; 17 Hope St; mains £6-12, bar meals £5; restaurant ◷ dinner daily). Tucked away

off the main street, this agreeable pub is a highly regarded place that does good bar meals. Better still is its restaurant, which offers plentiful portions of pasta, seafood, and vegetarian dishes in the evenings.

New Lanark Mill Hotel (☎ 667200; hotel@newlanark .org; New Lanark; two-course dinner £18.50, bar meals £3-8, ◷ bar meals 11am-9.30pm Sun-Thu, 11am-6pm Fri & Sat, restaurant dinner daily; ✗ ; wheelchair access) It's the best place to eat in New Lanark. The relaxed, family-friendly bar serves decent meals, such as braised chunks of steak in a rich sauce with mash. Upstairs, and only open for dinner, the Mill restaurant serves classier fare with a great view over the bubbly river below. The focus is on Scottish meat and fish, but there's a very tasty hot pot stewed in heather ale as a vegetarian option.

Getting There & Around

Lanark is 25 miles southeast of Glasgow and easily visited on a day-trip from that city. Trains (55 minutes, hourly) run from Glasgow Central's low-level platforms. There are also express buses from Glasgow (one hour, hourly Monday to Saturday).

The 20-minute walk down the valley to New Lanark is worth it for the views, but Stuart's Coaches run hourly from the train station. Returning to Lanark, the last bus leaves New Lanark at 4.42pm (6.50pm Sunday).

SCOTTISH BORDERS

Scotland's turbulent historical relationship with England is nowhere better brought to life than in the Borders, scene of countless betrayals, heroics and brutalities over the centuries. Far from being the desolate battleground of which its name might conjure images, it's enchantingly beautiful, with innumerable shades of the tufted green creating an artist's palette of the tufted hills and dappled woodland of the region. Folk in Edinburgh and the north of England are well-aware of its charms, but it's comparatively little-visited from further afield.

This is the land of Sir Walter Scott, and although the man could have romanticised a can of baked beans, he got it spot-on when lyrically describing the beauties of his home patch. Divided by the tinkling River Tweed, the Borders is one of the most appealing places in the country to cycle, and there are a great number of waymarked routes.

The region's small well-groomed towns make excellent places to stay and boast, among other enticements, the ruins of several majestic abbeys. Small *burghs* supported large, prosperous monastic communities from the 12th century onwards. The wealth of these made them fat tethered goats for the English armies during the Border wars and the abbeys were destroyed and rebuilt numerous times.

Activities

The Borders Tourist Board has a number of brochures, including *Cycling, Walking* and *Fishing* in the Scottish Borders. Walking possibilities include the challenging coast-to-coast **Southern Upland Way, St Cuthbert's Way** and the recently created **Borders Abbeys Way**, which will eventually link all the great border abbeys of Kelso, Jedburgh, Melrose and Dryburgh in a 65-mile circuit, with separate routes for walkers and cyclists. The cycle route is complete, and, at time of writing, the hiking route was complete from Kelso to Melrose via Jedburgh, Hawick, and Selkirk.

For cyclists there are also a range of trails in the Tweed Valley and Glentress Forest Park, well marked and detailed in brochures available from TICs in the region, as well as the **Border Loop**, a signposted 250-mile circuit right around the Borders.

Getting Around

There's a good network of local buses, although they are comparatively expensive. **First** (☎ 0870 872 7271) operates between the border towns and connects the larger towns with Edinburgh as well as Berwick-upon-Tweed. **National Express** (☎ 08705 808080; www .nationalexpress.com) services between Edinburgh and Newcastle/Leeds stop in Jedburgh and Galashiels.

Useful local bus companies serving border towns include **Munro's of Jedburgh** (☎ 01835-862253) and **Buskers** (☎ 01896-755808, Galashiels).

First has Rover tickets allowing a day/week (£6.45/28) of unlimited travel around the Scottish Borders.

PEEBLES

☎ 01721 / pop 8100

Peebles doesn't have any great attractions, yet it's the kind of town you could happily spend a few days in. It's a good base for exploring the area and is in a delightful spot, set among rolling wooded hills on the banks of the River Tweed. There are plenty of shops and little intriguing squares and streets between the High St and the river: the place is made for strolling.

The extremely helpful **TIC** (☎ 0870 608 0404; peebles@scot-borders.co.uk; High St; daily Apr-Oct, Mon-Sat Nov-Mar) has bundles of information.

Sights & Activities

The gorgeous **riverside walk** along the Tweed has plenty of grassed areas ideal for a picnic and there's a children's playground (near the main road bridge). You could even walk to **Neidpath Castle** (☎ 720333; adult £3; 10.30am-5pm Wed-Sat, 12.30-5pm Sun May-Sep), a 14th-century tower house perched on a bluff above the River Tweed about 1 mile west of town.

Poke your head inside **Tweeddale Museum & Art Gallery** (☎ 724820; High St; admission free; 10am-1pm & 2-5pm). It's mainly given over to the written word and famous border sons such as Sir Walter Scott. There's also a 'museum' of a Victorian museum.

Sleeping & Eating

Cross Keys Hotel (☎ 724222; Northgate; s/d with en suite £32/56, mains £6-13; P) Formerly a coaching inn, this 17th-century place maintains a tradition of fine hospitality. The well-appointed rooms vary markedly in size; the lounge bar has an excellent array of real ales, a beer garden, and filling bar meals, while the brasserie offers succulent treats instead of mangers full of hay.

Cringletie House (☎ 725750; www.cringletie.com; s/d £95/115, lunch £8-20, 3-course dinner £34; P) Situated about 2½ miles north of Peebles on the A703, this hotel calls itself a house, but that's being coy, it's a mansion! A very comfortable baronial mansion in fact, set in lovely grounds with an excellent gourmet restaurant; just the place to enjoy some luxurious Borders hospitality.

Sunflower Restaurant (☎ 722420; 4 Bridgegate; lunch £12.90, dinner mains £15-20; lunch daily, dinner Wed-Sat; ; wheelchair access) If a restaurant in the Borders can lure punters from Edinburgh down for dinner, you know it must be good. It's relaxed and friendly, but presents local produce of the highest order in the evenings: the pheasant is exceptional, but there are options for vegetarians too.

Getting There & Away

The bus stop is beside the post office on Eastgate. First bus No 62 runs to/from Edinburgh (one hour, every half-hour) and to Galashiels (45 minutes, hourly) and Melrose (one hour, hourly).

AROUND PEEBLES
Traquair House

Without doubt one of Britain's great noble residences, historic **Traquair House** (☎ 01896-830323; www.traquair.co.uk; adult £5.75; ☉ noon-5pm Apr-May & Sep, 10.30am-5.30pm Jun-Aug, 11am-4pm Oct), though others may be more aesthetically pleasing, has a powerful, ethereal beauty – and exploring it is like time travelling. It's believed parts were constructed long before the first official record of its existence in 1107. The massive tower house was gradually expanded over the next 500 years, but has remained virtually unchanged since 1642.

Since the 15th century, the house has belonged to various branches of the Stuart family, whose unwavering Catholicism and loyalty to the Stuart cause is largely why development ceased when it did. One of the most fascinating features is the concealed room where priests secretly lived and gave Mass – up to the passing of the 1829 Catholic Emancipation Act. Other beautiful timeworn rooms hold fascinating relics, including the cradle Mary Queen of Scots used for her son, James VI.

There are many more recent attractions, including a maze and adventure playground to keep younger ones happy, and a brewery to engage the over-18s. You can even stay here (£90/150 for a single/double), with three elegant rooms, complete with delicate colour scheme and canopied beds to make you feel like you're in one of those classic British films; these have to be prebooked. The house is set in beautiful parkland, and there are many woodland walks and secluded picnic spots.

The house is 1½ miles south of Innerleithen, about 6 miles southeast of Peebles. Bus C1 departs from Peebles at 10.15am for Traquair daily and returns at 2.50pm.

SELKIRK
☎ 01750 / pop 5740

While the noisy throb of machinery no doubt once filled the river valleys below Selkirk, a prosperous mill town in the early 19th century, today it sits placidly

and prettily atop its steep ridge. Miscreant millworkers who got on the wrong side of the law would have come face to face in court with Sir Walter Scott, who was sheriff here for three decades.

The **TIC** (☎ 0870 608 0404; Halliwell's House; ☉ daily Apr-Oct) is off Market Place. **Sir Walter Scott's Courtroom** (☎ 720096; Market Pl; admission free; ☉ 10am-4pm Mon-Fri, 10am-2pm Sat Apr-Sep, also 10am-2pm Sun May-Aug, 1-4pm Mon-Sat Oct) details Scott's period of laying down the law as well as displaying his life and writings; there's also a great account of the courageous explorer Mungo Park's search for the River Niger.

County Hotel (☎ 721233; www.countyhotelselkirk .co.uk; Market Square; s/d from £32.50/55, bar meals around £7; ☉ lunch & dinner; P ✗) is a former coaching inn that has well-refurbished rooms with couches and a high level of comfort. It's popular with golfers, not least for its upmarket and highly satisfying bar meals.

First Edinburgh bus Nos 73 and 95 run half-hourly Monday to Friday (hourly on Saturday) to Galashiels and Edinburgh (1½ hours). Bus No 72 links Selkirk and Melrose (hourly, three on Sunday, 20 minutes).

MELROSE
☎ 01896 / pop 1650

Tiny, charming Melrose is a genteel village running on the well-greased wheels of tourism. This little enclave is a complete contrast to overbearing Galashiels, whose urban sprawl laps at its western edges. Sitting at the feet of the three heather-covered Eildon Hills, Melrose entices walkers and cyclists. It has a classic market square, some attractive parks and its most famous resident, one of the great abbey ruins, where the heart of Robert the Bruce was buried after numerous posthumous adventures.

Information

The commendably cheerful and helpful **TIC** (☎ 0870 608 0404; Abbey House; ☉ Mon-Sat Nov-Mar, daily Apr-Oct), across from Melrose Abbey, has a lovely front garden and stacks of information on the Borders region as well as other parts of Scotland and even (whisper it) England.

Sights & Activities
MELROSE ABBEY

Perhaps the most interesting of all the great border abbeys, **Melrose Abbey** (HS; ☎ 822562; adult £3.50; ☉ 9.30am-6.30pm Apr-Sep, 9.30am-4.30pm

Mon-Sat, 2-4.30pm Sun Oct-Mar; wheelchair access) was repeatedly destroyed by the English in the 14th century. Rebuilt in the 15th century in a surprisingly ornate style for the Cistercian order, it was never completed, and by the time the Reformation came around there were just 15 monks in the formerly thriving community. The remaining broken shell is pure Gothic and the ruins are famous for their decorative stonework. Sir Walter Scott loved strolling around here.

The abbey was founded by King David I in 1136 for Cistercian monks from Rievaulx in Yorkshire, and was rebuilt by Robert the Bruce. After that king's death, his heart was sealed in a casket and, according to his wishes, borne by the Black Douglas into battle against the Moors in the Spanish Reconquista. It was recovered despite Douglas' death and defeat there and brought back here for solemn interment.

WALKING & CYCLING
There are attractive walks in the surrounding Eildon Hills, and the coast-to-coast **Southern Upland Way** and the **Tweed Cycleway** pass through Melrose. **St Cuthbert's Way** begins at the abbey. See Activities (p796) for details of the **Border Abbeys Way**.

Sleeping
Twelve of Melrose (☎ 822122; www.twelveofmelrose .com; 12 High St; s/d £50/65; P X) This eye-opening new B&B in the heart of town has all the feel of a French boutique hotel but at a very reasonable price. While the three rooms are beautifully wallpapered and fitted and have excellent bathrooms as well as DVD players, it's the small touches that will seduce you: cashmere hot-water bottles, a glass of wine to welcome you, and fabulous breakfasts.

Eildon House (☎ 820196; www.eildonhouse.co.uk; Huntly Ave; s/d from £30/60; P X) This beautifully renovated Victorian house is one of Melrose's most hospitable options. While all three rooms are welcoming, it's worth paying a little extra to secure the front room, a huge space with super moulded cornicing and a gleaming en suite. The easygoing hosts will do their utmost to make your stay a happy one; they even print weather forecasts on the morning breakfast menu! To get there, turn off the main road opposite the parish church by the rugby field.

Melrose SYHA Hostel (☎ 0870 004 1141; www .syha.org.uk; dm £12.50; ☉ Mar-Oct; P X ▣) This large Georgian mansion on the edge of town makes a great first impression with its fine symmetrical staircase. Spick and span dorms are complemented by Internet access, a large garden and BBQ area. Not a party house, this hostel is mainly used by walkers looking to turn in early. From Market Square, follow the signposts for the A68; if you're walking, there's a quicker path signposted alongside the abbey.

Other recommendations:
Braidwood (☎ 822488; www.braidwoodmelrose.co.uk; Buccleuch St; s/d from £25/£46; X) Very near the abbey, with high-quality facilities and a warm welcome.
Burt's Hotel (☎ 822285; www.burtshotel.co.uk; Market Sq; s/d £54/98; P) Retains period charm and offers indulgent, luxury accommodation.
Millars Hotel (☎ 822645; www.millarshotel.co.uk; Market Sq; s/d from £50/85) Friendly central hostelry: rooms to the back of the hotel are particularly cosy and quiet.

Eating
All of Melrose's pubs offer excellent food, including vegetarian options.

Marmions Brasserie (☎ 822245; Buccleuch St; mains £7-15; ☉ 9am-6pm & 6.30-10pm; X) Near the abbey, the atmospheric, oak-panelled Marmions Brasserie gives much pleasure to lunchers with dishes such as its duck cassoulet, but turns up the quality (and price) even more at dinner time, when gastronomic delights such as roast quail and braised lamb make their appearance on the menu.

Russell's Restaurant (☎ 822335; Market Sq; meals £5-7; ☉ 9.30am- 4.30pm Mon-Thu, 9.30am-5pm Fri & Sat, noon-5pm Sun; X) This tearoom/restaurant is a favourite Melrose meeting point and sits on the fine line between classy and twee. There's a large range of snacks as well as more substantial lunches; the coffee here is pretty decent too.

Getting There & Away
Both First and Munro's of Jedburgh provide frequent bus links to nearby Galashiels, Kelso and Jedburgh, as well as Edinburgh (£4.50, two hours, hourly), although you can save some time by catching a bus to Galashiels and hopping on an express service there. Bus No 62 runs to Peebles (£3.75, 1¼ hours, hourly).

SOUTHERN SCOTLAND

AROUND MELROSE
Dryburgh Abbey
The most beautiful and intact Border abbey is Dryburgh, partly because the neighbouring town of Dryburgh no longer exists (another victim of the wars), and partly because it's in a lovely, sheltered valley by the River Tweed; accompanied only by a symphony of birdsong. **Dryburgh Abbey** (HS; ☎ 01835-822381; adult £3; ⊙ 9.30am-6.30pm Apr-Sep, 9.30am-4.30pm Mon-Sat, 2-4.30pm Sun Oct-Mar; wheelchair access) conjures up images of 12th-century, monastic life more successfully than its counterparts in nearby towns. Dating from about 1150, it belonged to the Premonstratensians, a religious order founded in France. The pink-hued stone ruins were chosen as the burial place for Sir Walter Scott. Pack a picnic as there are some beautiful grassy spots.

The abbey is 5 miles southeast of Melrose on the B6404, which passes famous **Scott's View** overlooking the valley.

Abbotsford House
Fans of Sir Walter Scott should drop by his former residence, **Abbotsford House** (☎ 01896-752043; adult £4.50; ⊙ 9.30am-5.30pm Mon-Sat, 2-5pm Sun mid-Mar-Oct, 9.30am-5pm Sun Jun-Sep). Probably drawing inspiration from the surrounding 'wild' countryside, which contrasts sharply with the symmetrical manicured gardens, he created an extraordinary collection of works. These are on display and many other personal possessions litter his mansion.

The house is about 2 miles west of Melrose between the River Tweed and B6360. Frequent buses run between Galashiels

and Melrose; alight at the Tweedbank roundabout and follow the signposts (it's a 15-minute walk).

KELSO
☎ 01573 / pop 5100
The prosperous regional town of Kelso is centred on a broad square flanked by Georgian buildings and surrounded by narrow cobbled streets. While it lacks the quaint charm of some of the Borders settlements, its lively daytime buzz is refreshing evidence of life beyond tourism.

Information
The **TIC** (☎ 0870 608 0404; kelso@scot-borders.co.uk; Town House, The Square; ⊙ Mon-Sat Nov-Mar, daily Apr-Oct) is on the main plaza and has limited information on the region.

Kelso Library (☎ 223171; Bowmont St; ⊙ Mon-Sat) offers free Internet access.

Sights
KELSO ABBEY
Reduced to ruins by English raids in the 16th century, picturesque **Kelso Abbey** (HS; admission free; ⊙ 9.30am-6pm Mon-Sat, 2-6pm Sun Apr-Sep, 9.30am-4pm Mon-Sat, 2-4pm Sun Oct-Dec; wheelchair access) was once one of the richest monasteries in southern Scotland. It was built by Tironensians, an order founded at Tiron in Picardy, and brought to the Scottish Borders around 1113 by King David I. The abbey precincts have an undeniably romantic appeal and preserve some fine architectural fragments, while the nearby octagonal **Old Parish Church** (⊙ 10am-4pm Mon-Fri May-Sep), built in 1773, is intriguing.

SIR WALTER SCOTT

Sir Walter Scott (1771–1832) is one of Scotland's greatest literary sons. Born in Edinburgh, he moved to his uncle's farm at Sandyknowe (p800) in the Borders as a child. It was here, rambling around the countryside, that he gained a passion for historical ballads and Scottish heroes. After studying in Edinburgh he bought Abbotsford (above), a country house in the Borders.

Scott wrote a number of successful ballads. *The Lay of the Last Minstrel* (1805) was an early critical success; further works earning him an international reputation included *The Lady of the Lake* (1810), set around Loch Katrine and the Trossachs. He later turned his hand to novels and virtually invented the historical genre. *Waverley* (1814), which dealt with the 1745 Jacobite rebellion, set the classical pattern of the historical novel. Other works included *Guy Mannering* (1815) and *Rob Roy* (1817).

Later in life Scott wrote obsessively to stave off bankruptcy as a result of a crisis in a printing business in which he was a partner. His works virtually single-handedly revived interest in Scottish history and legend in the early 19th century. TICs stock a *Sir Walter Scott Trail* booklet taking you to many places associated with his life in the Borders.

FLOORS CASTLE

Grandiose **Floors Castle** (☎ 223333; adult £5.75; ⏰ 10am-4.30pm Easter-Oct), Scotland's largest inhabited house, overlooks the Tweed about a mile northwest of Kelso. Built by William Adam in the 1720s, the original Georgian simplicity was 'improved' during the 1840s with the addition of rather ridiculous battlements and turrets.

Inside, keep an eye out for the vivid colours of the 17th-century Flemish tapestries in the drawing room and the intricate oak carvings in the ornate ballroom. Palatial windows unfurl a ribbon of green countryside extending well beyond the estate. While the real owners are the Dukes of Roxburghe, this was Tarzan's ancestral home in the film *Greystoke*.

Activities

WALKING & CYCLING

The **Pennine Way**, which starts its long journey at Edale in the Peak District, ends at Kirk Yetholm, 6 miles southeast of Kelso, where most walkers celebrate with a drink at the Border Inn and stay at the hostel there.

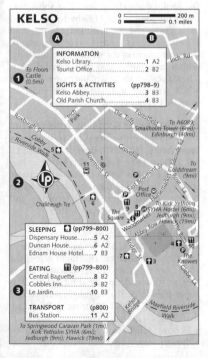

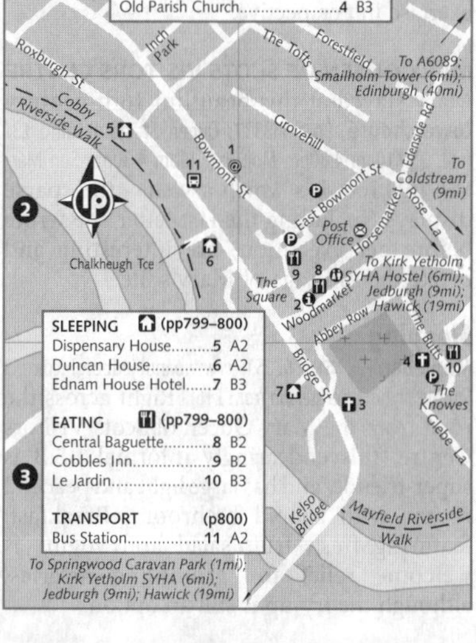
KELSO
0 200 m
0 0.1 miles
INFORMATION
Kelso Library....1 A2
Tourist Office....2 B2
SIGHTS & ACTIVITIES (pp798–9)
Kelso Abbey....3 B3
Old Parish Church....4 B3
SLEEPING (pp799–800)
Dispensary House....5 A2
Duncan House....6 A2
Ednam House Hotel....7 B3
EATING (pp799–800)
Central Baguette....8 B2
Cobbles Inn....9 B2
Le Jardin....10 B3
TRANSPORT (p800)
Bus Station....11 A2
To Floors Castle (0.5mi)
Inch Rd
Roxburgh St
Cobby Riverside Walk
Inch Park
The Tofts
Forestfield
To A6089; Smailholm Tower (6mi); Edinburgh (40mi)
Grovehill
Bowmont St
East Bowmont St
Edenside Rd
To Coldstream (9mi)
Rose La
Post Office
Horsemarket
To Kirk Yetholm SYHA Hostel (6mi); Jedburgh (9mi); Hawick (19mi)
Chalkheugh Tce
The Square
Woodmarket
Abbey Row
The Butts
Bridge St
The Knowes
Glebe La
Kelso Bridge
Mayfield Riverside Walk
To Springwood Caravan Park (1mi); Kirk Yetholm SYHA (6mi); Jedburgh (9mi); Hawick (19mi)

There is also the new **Borders Abbeys Way**, which will link the area's great abbeys in a 65-mile circuit, one for hikers and one for cyclists. The cycle route is complete, and, at time of writing, the southern loop of the hiking route was complete from Kelso to Melrose. The TIC has free leaflets with map and description of the routes, as well as another detailing other cycling trails around the town.

Less-ambitious walkers can take the riverside path to Floors Castle, signposted off Roxburgh St, just off the Square.

Sleeping & Eating

Kelso is good on accommodation but limited at dinner time.

Dispensary House (☎ 228738; 106 Roxburgh St; s/d £30/56; ⊠) Halfway between the centre and Floors Castle, this riverside choice is set in a solid stone house dating from the 18th century that was once the town hospital. It has wonderful views, sumptuous rooms (one with a four-poster bed) and clipped accents; both rooms have huge en suites.

Ednam House Hotel (☎ 224168; www.ednamhouse.com; Bridge St; s/d from £66.50/89; 2-course dinner £18; ⏰ lunch & dinner; Ⓟ) The town's most luxurious option is idyllically set on the riverbank near the abbey. The place has quite a sporting feel to it – don't be surprised if conversations in the lounge centre mainly on trout flies and greenside bunkers – but it's very cosy and has an excellent restaurant open to the public. The welcome to the room is excellent, with a wee drink and fresh fruit.

Kirk Yetholm SYHA Hostel (☎ 0870 004 1132; dm £10; ⏰ Apr-Sep; Ⓟ ⊠) This hostel 6 miles southeast of Kelso is always full of exhausted walkers glowing with a sense of happy achievement, for it's at the end of the Pennine Way walking route. It's fairly simple as hostels go and is set in a slightly forbidding Georgian mansion, but the atmosphere is great, although if you're not a hiker you might feel a wee bit left out! Bus No 81 runs to/from Kelso up to seven times daily from Monday to Saturday.

Central Baguette (☎ 228853; 52 The Square; baguettes from £1.25; ⏰ 8.30am-2.30pm Mon-Sat) Very near the tourist office, this cheery little operation dishes up delicious, imaginative baguettes that range from brie and cranberry to Thai chicken. It's perfect for an impromptu picnic or an angler's lunch.

Other recommendations:

Cobbles Inn (☎ 223548; 7 Bowmont St; mains £7-10; ❍ lunch & dinner) Pub meals that are a cut above the average in size, choice, and quality.

Duncan House (☎ 225682; www.tweedbreaks.co.uk; 2 Chalkheugh Tce; s/d £35/56; **P** ✕) Great base, especially for anglers, overlooking a tempting stretch of the Tweed.

Le Jardin (☎ 228288; 5a The Knowes; mains £4-6; ❍ 10am-4.30pm Mon-Sat; ✕) A snug little café tucked away behind the abbey with vegetarian choices.

Springwood Caravan Park (☎ 224596; admin@springwood.biz; tent pitches £12; ❍ Mar-Oct; wheelchair access) You won't be lonely here, as this well-equipped site is quite a big operation.

Getting There & Away

Munro's of Jedburgh run regular buses to Edinburgh, some involving a connection (£5.50; two hours, five to eight daily). There are also very frequent departures for Jedburgh (25 minutes, 10 Monday to Saturday, five on Sunday) and Galashiels via Melrose (55 minutes, hourly).

Swan's Coaches has frequent buses from Berwick-upon-Tweed to Kelso (one hour, five daily Monday to Saturday; two on Sunday).

AROUND KELSO
Smailholm Tower

One of the most evocative sights in the borders, **Smailholm Tower** (HS; ☎ 01573-460365; adult £2.20; ❍ 9.30am-6.30pm daily Apr-Sep, 9.30am-4.30pm Sat, 2-4.30pm Sun Oct-Mar) is perched on a rocky knoll with a panoramic view from the top. The narrow stone tower brings the bloody uncertainties of the Borders alive; inside is a rather sparse costume figure exhibition and tapestries portraying characters from a Sir Walter Scott work.

The nearby farm, **Sandyknowe**, was owned by Scott's grandfather. Scott's imagination was fired by the ballads and stories he heard here as a child, and by the ruined tower of his ancestors. You pass through the farmyard to get to the tower.

The tower is 6 miles west of Kelso, a mile south of Smailholm village on the B6397.

JEDBURGH

☎ 01835 / pop 4090

While once a favourite target of cross-border raiders, the historic town of Jedburgh now attracts a more placid species of southern visitor, wielding not swords but cameras and credit cards. Deservedly one of the most popular of the border towns, it's a compact oasis, where many old buildings and *wynds* (narrow alleys) have been intelligently restored, inviting exploration by foot. It's constantly busy with domestic tourists, but wander into some of the pretty side streets and you won't hear a pin drop!

The large, efficient **TIC** (☎ 0870 608 0404; www.scot-borders.co.uk; Murray's Green; ❍ daily Apr-Oct, Mon-Sat Nov-Mar) has a bureau de change and runs excellent guided walks of the town at 6pm Monday, Wednesday, and Friday from April to October (£2). The **library** (Castlegate; ❍ Mon-Fri), just up the hill from Marketplace, has free Internet access.

Sights
JEDBURGH ABBEY

Dominating the town skyline like a battle-scarred but proud warrior, magnificent **Jedburgh Abbey** (HS; ☎ 863925; adult £3.50; ❍ 9.30am-6.30pm Apr-Sep, 9.30am-4.30pm Mon-Sat, 2-4.30pm Sun Oct-Mar; wheelchair access with notice) is an atmospheric ruin. The red sandstone remains are roofless but intact and the jutting ribs bring similar understanding and simple wonder as does the form of a skeleton leaf. The abbey was originally founded in 1138 by King David I as a priory for Augustinian canons, and efforts are being made to recreate some of the atmosphere of the monastic community, with a herb garden and audiovisual display. The staircase at the end of the nave is slippery when wet, but worth it for the view, an exercise in perspective.

MARY QUEEN OF SCOTS VISITORS CENTRE

Mary stayed at this beautiful 16th-century **tower house** (☎ 863331; Queen St; adult/child £3/free; ❍ 10am-4.30pm Mon-Sat, 11am-4.30pm Sun Mar-Nov) in 1566. It's worth a visit – the sparse displays (including the last letter she wrote before her execution) are interesting and evoke the sad saga of Mary's life.

Sleeping

Maplebank (☎ 862051; www.bandbjedburgh.com; 3 Smiths Wynd; r per person from £16). Right across the road from the Mary Queen of Scots Visitors Centre, this endearingly informal B&B is super-friendly and has large light and peaceful rooms with shared bathroom. Breakfast, featuring fresh fruit salad and yogurt is welcome relief for grumbling arteries, although the fry-up is still an option.

Glenfriars House (☎ 862000; www.edenroad.demon .co.uk;Friarsgate;s/d£30/50; **P**) Classy in a run-down kind of way, this elegant Georgian mansion has stupendous views and endearingly ramshackle decadence with its four-poster beds and spacious rooms. It's on a narrow road parallel to and above High St.

Other recommendations:

Craigowen Guest House (☎ 862604; 30 High St; s/d £25/40; ✗) Under new management, with refurbished rooms in a central location.

Reiver's Rest (☎ 864977; www.reiversrest.co.uk; 91 Bongate St; s/d £20/40; **P** ✗) Only one room, but what a room, with a big double bed and a sauna!

Eating

Nightjar (☎ 862552; 1 Abbey Close; mains £8-10; ☺ dinner Tue-Sat; ✗) On the road up to the castle, this classy and intimate little bistro brings a welcome cosmopolitan sophistication to the tearoom-plagued Borders. While fine Scottish dishes are present, the thought of global delights such as rice noodles, halloumi cheese, and calf's liver stewed in marsala will have you pacing anxiously in the late afternoon like an alcoholic before opening time.

Cookie Jar (37 High St; breakfast £4.50, meals £3-6; ☺ 10am-5pm) This colourful café has a bright little dining area, just perfect for a coffee and snack. The freshly prepared sandwiches, rolls and sweetie treaties are too tempting for most mortals. Grab a window seat, they're good for a bout of people watching.

Getting There & Away

Jedburgh has good bus connections around the Borders, with frequent buses to Melrose, Kelso, Peebles, Selkirk, and Galashiels run by Munro's of Jedburgh. The same company also runs to Edinburgh (£5.60, two hours, eight daily Monday to Saturday, five on Sunday). First Edinburgh also covers some of these routes.

HERMITAGE CASTLE

The 'guardhouse of the bloodiest valley in Britain', **Hermitage Castle** (HS; ☎ 01387-770244; adult £2.20; ☺ 9.30am-6.30pm Apr-Sep, 9.30am-4.30pm Oct & Nov) embodies the brutal history of the Scottish Borders. Desolate yet all undaunted with its massive squared stone walls, it looks more like a lair for orc raiding parties than a home for Scottish nobility, and is one of the bleakest and most stirring of Scottish ruins.

Strategically crucial, it was the scene of many a dark deed and dirty deal with the English invaders, all of which rebounded heavily on the perfidious Scottish lord in question. Here, in 1338, Sir William Douglas imprisoned his enemy Sir Alexander Ramsay and deliberately starved him to death. Mary Queen of Scots famously visited the wounded tenant of the castle, Lord Bothwell, in 1566. Fortified, he recovered to (probably) murder her husband, marry her himself, then abandon her months later and flee into exile.

There's ongoing repair work which means there's little to see inside, but it's the exterior view that you come for. Bring some lunch and munch it on the grass in the lee of the utterly imposing walls.

The castle is 12 miles south of Hawick on the B6357, and 5½ miles northeast of Newcastleton, a mile off the B6339. Buses from Hawick go as far as Newcastleton.

DUMFRIES & GALLOWAY

The southwest portion of Scotland is usually bypassed by tourists, which makes it a very inviting destination for some, particularly in summer when other parts of the country can be crowded. And what summers they have here: mild and sunny is the norm, an un-Scottish phenomenon that has allowed the development of some famous gardens.

The attractions in the region are many. Just outside the town of Dumfries, superb Caerlaverock Castle is one of the most beautifully situated castles in the country; further west Kirkcudbright, at the head of a natural harbour, is a lovely place to wander through – the restored High St has attracted many artistic endeavours. Book fanatics will relish the tiny town of Wigtown on the Machars peninsula, bristling with nearly 30 bookshops full of new and second-hand titles on every subject under the sun. Beyond there you can explore Whithorn Cathedral and Priory, the remains of a mission predating St Columba on Iona by over 150 years.

Stranraer in the far west is a ferry port for Northern Ireland. Nearby, nostalgic Portpatrick sits on a rugged stretch of coast on the Galloway peninsula and has a pretty harbour and some great places to stay.

SOUTHERN SCOTLAND

Getting There & Around

Eurolines (☎ 0870 514 3219) operates bus services between London and Belfast, via Birmingham, Manchester, Dumfries, the towns along the A75, and Stranraer.

Local bus operators cover the region comprehensively. The principal operators are **McEwan's** (☎ 01387-256533) and **Stagecoach Western** (☎ 01387-260383).

Two train lines from Carlisle to Glasgow cross the region, via Dumfries and Moffat respectively. The line from Glasgow to Stranraer runs via Ayr.

DUMFRIES

☎ 01387 / pop 31,000

The surprisingly large town of Dumfries is known as the Queen of the South. The town is built on the bubbly River Nith, which is crossed by beautiful red sandstone bridges. The grassy areas on the riverbank make this the most pleasant area of town; there are also several important Burns-related museums and a pub that he used to frequent.

Information

The **TIC** (☎ 253862; 64 Whitesands; ☺ daily Apr-mid Oct, Mon-Sat mid Oct-Mar) is opposite the car park by the river and has stacks of information on the whole region.

If you want to check your emails, the **library** (☎ 253820; Catherine St; ☺ Mon-Sat) has a good free Internet system.

Burnsiana

The **Robert Burns Centre** (☎ 264808; Mill Rd; admission free, audiovisual £1.55; ☺ 10am-8pm Mon-Sat, 2-5pm Sun Apr-Sep, 10am-1pm & 2-5pm Tue-Sat Oct-Mar) is an award-winning museum located in an old mill on the banks of the River Nith across from the TIC. It relates the story of Burns and Dumfries in the 1790s. The audiovisual display replicates the exhibition's content.

Red-sandstone **Burns House** (☎ 255297; Burns St; admission free; ☺ 10am-5pm Mon-Sat, 2-5pm Sun Apr-Sep, 10am-1pm & 2-5pm Tue-Sat Oct-Mar) is a place of pilgrimage for Burns enthusiasts. Here the poet spent the last years of his life and there are some interesting relics, original letters and manuscripts. Look out for his signature

---

ROBERT BURNS

Best remembered for penning *Auld Lang Syne*, Robert Burns (1759–96) is Scotland's most famous poet, and a popular hero whose birthday (25 January) is celebrated as **Burns Night** by Scots around the world.

Burns was born in 1759 in Alloway. Although his mother was illiterate and his parents poor farmers, they sent him to the local school where he soon showed an aptitude for literature and a fondness for the folk song. He began to write his own songs and satires, some of which he distributed privately. When the problems of his arduous farming life were compounded by the threat of prosecution from the father of Jean Armour, with whom he'd had an affair, he decided to emigrate to Jamaica. He gave up his share of the family farm and published his poems to raise money for the journey.

The poems were so well reviewed in Edinburgh that Burns decided to remain in Scotland and devote himself to writing. He went to Edinburgh in 1787 to publish a second edition, but the financial rewards were insufficient to live on and he had to take a job as a customs officer in Dumfriesshire. He contributed many songs to collections published by Johnson & Thomson in Edinburgh, and a third edition of his poems was published in 1793. To give an idea of the prodigious writings of the man, Robert Burns composed more than 28,000 lines of verse over 22 years. He died in Dumfries in 1796, aged 37, after a heart attack. He had eventually married Jean Armour, with whom he had nine children; she even took in a couple of his illegitimate ones, sighing 'Our Robbie should have had twa wives'.

While some dispute Burns' claim to true literary genius, he was certainly an accomplished poet and songwriter, and has been compared to Chaucer for his verse tale *Tam o'Shanter*. Burns wrote in Lallans, lowland Scots that isn't very accessible to the foreigner. Perhaps this is part of his appeal. He was also very much a man of the people, satirising the upper classes and the church for their hypocrisy.

The Burns connection in Southern Scotland is milked for all it's worth and TICs have a Burns Heritage Trail leaflet leading you to every place that can claim some link with the bard.

scratched into a small upstairs window. Nearby, Burns' **mausoleum** is in the graveyard at St Michael's Kirk. Back in the centre at the top of High St is a **statue** of the bard.

Sleeping
Fulwood Hotel (☎ 252262; 30 Lovers Walk; s/d from £30/50; ☒) Very close to the train station, the Fulwood is one of several decent options in this quiet area. The rooms have modern furnishings and lots of natural light, and the friendly owner is particularly partial to antipodean guests.

Torbay Lodge (☎ 253922; www.torbaylodge.co.uk; 31 Lovers Walk; s/d £25/50; ℗ ☒) This guesthouse has elegant rooms decorated in a light, flowery style. It's particularly good value for singles, and features a very acceptable breakfast with fresh seasonal fruit available.

Eating & Drinking
Hullabaloo (☎ 259679; Mill Rd; mains £8-12; ☺ lunch daily & dinner Tue-Sat; ☒) This smart modern restaurant at the Robert Burns Centre is easily Dumfries' most adventurous place to eat. Lighter lunchtime fare includes delicious soups and sandwiches, while full-blown dinner mains feature creative salads, tender steaks, and a range of good-value seafood dishes.

Globe Inn (☎ 252335; 56 High St; bar meals £4-6) This long traditional pub is down a narrow *wynd* off the main shopping street. Reputedly Burns' favourite watering hole and scene of one of his numerous seductions, it has no-nonsense pub grub and outdoor seating in summer. The only gripe is that there's probably a couple of pictures too many of the local hero!

Getting There & Away
BUS
Eurolines bus Nos 920 and 921 run twice daily between London and Belfast via Dumfries and Stranraer. Dumfries to Carlisle costs £6 and takes an hour. Citylink connects Dumfries with Glasgow (£7.40, two hours, three daily, two on Sunday).

Local buses run regularly to Kirkcudbright (1¼ hours, at least hourly Monday to Saturday, six on Sunday) and towns along the A75 to Stranraer (£5.40, two hours, six daily Monday to Saturday, three on Sunday). The quickest way to get to Edinburgh is to take the Citylink service to Moffat and connect there.

TRAIN
There are trains to Carlisle (£6.80, 35 minutes, at least hourly Monday to Saturday, five on Sunday), and direct to Glasgow (£10.30, 1¾ hours, eight daily, two on Sunday).

AROUND DUMFRIES
Caerlaverock Castle
The ruins of **Caerlaverock Castle** (HS; ☎ 01387-770244; by Glencaple; adult £4; ☺ 9.30am-6.30pm Apr-Sep, 9.30am-4.30pm Oct-Mar; wheelchair access), on a stretch of the Solway coast, are among the loveliest. Surrounded by a moat, lawns and stands of trees, the unusual pink-hued, triangular, stone castle looks impregnable – but it fell several times. The present castle dates from the late 13th century. Inside, there's an extraordinary Scottish Renaissance façade to apartments built 1634. The castle is 8 miles southeast of Dumfries on the B725. Monday to Saturday, Stagecoach Western bus No 371 runs nine times a day (twice Sunday) to the castle from Dumfries.

Ruthwell Cross
A couple of miles beyond Caerlaverock, in the hamlet of Ruthwell, the **church** (☎ 01387-870249; admission free by calling keyholder) holds one of Europe's most important early Christian monuments. The six-metre high Ruthwell Cross is carved top to bottom in New Testament scenes and is inscribed with a poem, *The Dream of the Rood*, written in a Saxon runic alphabet and is considered one of the earliest examples of English language literature. The cross was built in the mid 7th century in a gesture of defiance against the Roman church's increasing control.

CASTLE DOUGLAS & AROUND
☎ 01556 / pop 3700
Castle Douglas attracts a lot of daytrippers, but hasn't been 'spruced up' for tourism – it's an open, well-cared-for former cotton town. There are some remarkably beautiful areas close to the centre such as the small **Carlingwark Loch**.

The helpful **TIC** (☎ 502611; King St; ☺ Apr-Sep) is in a small park.

Threave Castle
About 3 miles west of town off the A75 is **Threave Castle** (HS; ☎ 07711-223101; admission incl ferry £2.50; ☺ 9.30am-6.30pm Apr-Sep), an impressively bleak tower on a small island in the middle

of the lovely River Dee. It's only a shell, but a romantic ruin nonetheless. Built in the late 14th century by the cheerfully named Archibald the Grim, it became a principal stronghold for the Douglases.

It's a 10-minute steep walk from the car park to pick up the ferry (a small open boat) across to the island.

Sleeping & Eating

Douglas Arms Hotel (☎ 502231; www.douglasarmshotel.co.uk; King St; s/d £40/72; **P** ☒) Right in the middle of town on the gunbarrel-straight main street, this sturdy white hotel was originally a coaching inn. These days modern conveniences and comforts sustain the weary traveller, not least of which is the cosy bar with fine food and real ales.

Designs (179 King St; light meals £3-6; ☼ 9.30am-5.30pm Mon-Sat; ☒) With an innovative gallery of contemporary art upstairs and a light, appealing café below, this makes a good stop for lunch. It's at its best on a sunny afternoon, when you can sit out in the enclosed garden and snack on fresh, tasty sandwiches or a range of diet-busting cakes.

Getting There & Around

MacEwan's bus No 501 between Dumfries and Kirkcudbright stops in Castle Douglas hourly. The **Castle Douglas Cycle Centre** (☎ 504 542; 11 Church St) hires mountain bikes for £10 per 24 hours, a good option if you're planning a castle visit.

KIRKCUDBRIGHT

☎ 01557 / pop 3400

Kirkcudbright (pronounced kir-*koo*-bree), with its dignified streets of 17th- and 18th-century merchants' houses and appealing harbour, is the ideal base for exploring the beautiful south coast. This delightful open-plan town has one of the most perfectly restored High Streets imaginable. It has a reputation as an artists' colony, although most of the painting getting done seems to be touching up the perfect façades.

The **TIC** (☎ 330494; kirkcudbright@dgtb.visitscotland.com; Harbour Sq; ☼ daily Mar-Nov, Mon-Fri Dec-Feb) has plenty of useful information about the surrounding area.

Sights & Activities

Kirkcudbright is a great town for a wander and it won't be long before you stumble across its charming sights. **MacLellan's Castle** (HS; ☎ 331856; adult £2.20; ☼ 9.30am-6.30pm Apr-Sep), near the harbour, was built in 1577. Inside look for the 'lairds' lug', a 16th-century hidey hole designed for the laird to eavesdrop on his guests. Nearby, the 17th-century **Broughton House** (NTS; ☎ 330437; 12 High St; adult £2; ☼ Apr-Oct) was once the home of EJ Hornel, a painter of the early 20th-century 'Glasgow Boys' movement. The house (due to reopen after renovation in mid 2005) features many of his works and a beautiful Japanese garden.

Sleeping & Eating

The guesthouses on High St tend to be more expensive than those in nearby streets.

Gladstone House (☎ 331734; 48 High St; s/d £39/60; ☒) Set in the loveliest bit of the town, this is a very noble Georgian house with a charming façade of irregular stone. The interior is just as gorgeous, with three elegant rooms with en suite and an upmarket feel. It's the perfect just-so pad to enjoy this dapper little town.

Royal Hotel (☎ 331213; www.theroyalhotel.net; St Cuthbert St; s/d £30/53; bar meals £5-8; ☼ food served all day) This large, gracious old pub dominates the town's main crossroads. It offers spacious, comfortable rooms that satisfy without enthralling. It's a good place to take the kids, with several family rooms and a child-friendly bar that serves excellent food at reasonable prices.

Auld Alliance (☎ 330569; 5 Castle St; mains £9-16; ☼ dinner daily & lunch Sun; open Apr-Oct) This is the best place to eat in town set in a striking black-and-white building. Its name refers to the political alliance between Scotland and France, but here alludes to its combination of local fresh produce (such as small scallops known as queenies) and French cooking and wine. Booking is advised.

Other recommendations:

Parkview (☎ 330056; 22 Millburn St; s/d £19/34) Small, blue, friendly and warm guesthouse.

Silvercraigs Caravan & Camping Site (☎ 330123; Silvercraigs Rd; pitches from £8.70) A brilliant spot overlooking the town.

Getting There & Away

There are regular local buses to/from Dumfries (1¼ hours, at least hourly Monday to Saturday, six on Sunday). In the other direction buses go to Stranraer (1½ hours, four daily Monday to Saturday, two on Sunday).

NEWTON STEWART

☎ 01671 / pop 3600

On the banks of the sparkling River Cree, Newton Stewart is at the heart of some beautiful countryside; it's popular with hikers and anglers. The **TIC** (☎ 402431; Dashwood Sq; ☉ Apr-Oct) is off the top of High St.

Most accommodation is in Minnigaff, a village just across the bridge. The **Minnigaff SYHA** (☎ 0870 004 1142; dm £10; ☉ Apr-Sep; **P** ☒) is well equipped in a former school that will bring back memories of grazed knees in playground games. **Flowerbank Guest House** (☎ 402629; Millcroft Rd; www.flowerbankgh.com; r per person £20-27; **P** ☒) is an 18th-century house set in a magnificent, landscaped garden that stretches down to the banks of the River Cree.

Newton Stewart is served by regular buses running between Stranraer (45 minutes, five daily Monday to Saturday, three on Sunday) and Dumfries (1½ hours, six daily from Monday to Saturday, three on Sunday). The town is also a starting point for frequent buses south to Wigtown and Whithorn.

MACHARS PENINSULA

South of Newtown Stewart, the Galloway Hills give way to the serene pastures of the Machars peninsula, which is ideal for walking and cycling. The south has many early Christian sites and the 25-mile **Pilgrims Way**.

From Newtown Stewart, bus No 415 runs 10 to 14 times daily Monday to Saturday (five only on Sunday) to the peninsula's towns and villages.

Wigtown

☎ 01988 / pop 990

Wigtown is a huge success story. Economically run down for many years, the town's revival began in 1998 when it became Scotland's 'National Book Town'. Today, nearly 30 bookshops offer the widest selection of books in Scotland and book enthusiasts the opportunity to get lost here for days! Check out www.wigtown-booktown.co.uk for more information.

The **Book Corner** (☎ 402010; 2 High St; www .mccormicknicholson.co.uk/book-cnr-wigtown1.htm; ☉ daily May-Oct, Mon-Sat Nov-Apr) is one place to go if you're serious about book hunting. There's a fantastic selection of new and second-hand titles. **Glaisnock House** (☎ 402249; www .glaisnockhouse.co.uk; 20 South Main St; s/d £23/46; ☉ lunch & dinner Tue-Sun; **P** ☒), in the town centre, has

a range of excellent rooms (most have an en suite) with plush furnishings. It also has a licensed restaurant with a three-course evening meal costing a very reasonable £12. **Reading Lasses Bookshop Café** (☎ 403266; 17 South Main St; www.reading-lasses.com; ☉ 10am-5pm Mon-Sat year-round, noon-5pm Sun May-Oct) provides good caffeine to prolong your reading time and is also a bookshop specialising in women's studies. Snacks here, including local cheeses, chutneys and oatcakes (£4.50), are worth tucking into.

Whithorn

☎ 01988 / pop 870

Whithorn has a wide, appealing High St virtually closed at both ends; it was designed originally to enclose a medieval market. Economic woes mean there are few facilities in town, but it's worth visiting because of its fascinating history.

In 397, while the Romans were still in Britain, St Ninian established the first Christian mission beyond Hadrian's Wall in Whithorn (predating St Columba on Iona by 166 years). The extensive ruins of Whithorn Priory, built to house St Ninian's remains and once the focus of an important medieval pilgrimage, are now the centre point for the **Whithorn Story Visitors Centre** (HS; ☎ 500508; 45 George St; adult £2.70; ☉ 10.30am-5pm Apr-Oct). There's also an audiovisual display and a museum that houses the Latinus Stone (c 450), reputedly Scotland's oldest Christian artefact.

Isle of Whithorn

☎ 01988 / pop 400

The Isle of Whithorn (once an island but now part of a peninsula) is a small, raggedy fishing village with an attractive harbour and colourful houses. **St Ninian's Chapel**, probably built for pilgrims who landed nearby, is sited on an evocative, rocky headland.

Steam Packet Inn Hotel (☎ 500334; www .steampacketinn.com; Harbour Row; r per person £25-35; mains £4-7), on the quayside, is a recommended, popular pub that has real ales, scrumptious bar meals and comfortable lodging.

PORTPATRICK

☎ 01776 / pop 590

Portpatrick is a charming port town on a rugged stretch of coast on the Galloway peninsula. Until the mid-19th century it was the main port for Northern Ireland. It's now a coastguard station, a quiet family-oriented resort and the starting point for the **Southern Upland Way** (see p773).

There are lots of places to stay on North Crescent, which curves around the harbour. **Knowe Guest House** (☎ 810441; www.theknowe.co.uk; 1 North Cres; s/d with en suite from £30/42; ✗) has all the comforts of home and five rooms that offer great views over the pretty wee harbour. Tysties Coffee Shop is also on the premises.

For a real dose of luxury, head 3 miles southeast to **Knockinaam Lodge** (☎ 810471; www .knockinaamlodge.com; dinner, B&B per person from £115; ☿ dinner; P ✗), a former hunting lodge on a little sandy bay. It's where Churchill plotted the endgame of WWII – you can stay in his suite – and it's a very romantic place to get away from it all. The excellent French-style cuisine is backed up by a great range of wines and single malts.

Local bus No 367 runs to Stranraer hourly Monday to Saturday (three times on Sunday).

STRANRAER
☎ 01776 / pop 10,850

Stranraer is more pleasant than the average ferry port, although it's a little on the scrappy side. There's no reason to stay unless you're catching or coming off a ferry, or you need a base to explore some of the beautiful Galloway peninsula.

Information

The **TIC** (☎ 702595; stranraer@dgtb.visitscotland.com; 28 Harbour St; ☿ daily Apr-Oct, Mon-Sat Nov-Mar) is friendly and carries all the ferry timetables. Internet access is free at the **Stranraer Library** (☎ 707400; North Strand St; ☿ Mon-Sat), just near the TIC.

Sleeping & Eating

Jan Da Mar Guest House (☎ 706194; www.jandamar .co.uk; 1 Ivy Pl, London Rd; s/d from £18/32) This long-standing favourite is one of the most welcoming B&Bs you could hope to encounter. The large, light rooms are a bargain, there's a great lounge with books and board games, and the well-travelled owners, with whom you'll immediately be on first-name terms, are an absolute delight. As well as English they speak German, Dutch, French and Spanish (in that order!).

Balyett Farm Hostel and B&B (☎ 703395; balyett@btopenworld.com; Cairnryan Rd; dm £10, s/d from £25/36; P ✗ 🖳) This peaceful option is a mile north of town on the A77, but never fear: the accommodating owners will pick you up from the ferry or train station. The hostel section accommodates six people and has a kitchen/living area, shower and toilet. The B&B is at the nearby ivy-covered farmhouse and has sparkling, clean rooms and a homely feel.

L'Aperitif (☎ 702991; London Rd; mains £6-12; ☿ lunch & dinner) Although the location is fairly unprepossessing, this is comfortably the best restaurant in town. Despite the name, there's a fairly Italian touch to the menu, which impresses with both its length and quality. The seafood is especially tasty here; if you eat before 7pm you can nab three courses for a bargain £12.50.

Getting There & Away
BOAT

There are two alternatives from Stranraer to reach Northern Ireland: **P&O** (☎ 0870 242 4777; www.poirishsea.com) ferries from Cairnryan

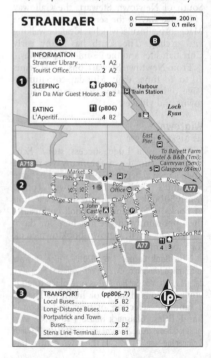

STRANRAER

INFORMATION		
Stranraer Library	1	A2
Tourist Office	2	A2

SLEEPING	🏠	(p806)
Jan Da Mar Guest House	3	B2

EATING	🍴	(p806)
L'Aperitif	4	B2

TRANSPORT		(pp806–7)
Local Buses	5	B2
Long-Distance Buses	6	B2
Portpatrick and Town Buses	7	B2
Stena Line Terminal	8	B1

to Larne (Northern Ireland); and **Stena Line** (☎ 0870 570 7070; www.stenaline.com) ferries from Stranraer to Belfast.

The Cairnryan to Larne service is used mainly by motorists and hauliers. Cairnryan is 5 miles north of Stranraer, on the northern side of Loch Ryan. Bus No 358 runs there frequently.

BUS
Eurolines buses head to London via Dumfries, Manchester, and Birmingham.

Citylink is the best bus service to Glasgow (£10, 2½ hours, two daily): it meets the ferries from Belfast. There are also local buses to Kirkcudbright (1½ hours, four daily Monday to Saturday, two on Sunday) and towns on the A75 eg Newton Stewart (45 minutes, five daily Monday to Saturday, three on Sunday) and Dumfries (£5.40, two hours, six daily Monday to Saturday, three on Sunday).

TRAIN
The train station is on the ferry pier. There are regular services to/from Glasgow (£15.60, 2½ hours, seven daily Monday to Saturday, three on Sunday), although only some are direct.

AYRSHIRE

The Ayrshire coast is a sunny stretch of spectacular beaches backed by rich farmland and world-famous golf courses. This setting inspired Robert Adam to create Culzean castle, one of the finest stately homes in the country. It's also the birthplace of the famous poet Robert Burns with enough here to satisfy his most-fanatic admirers. The delightful island of Arran is easily accessible, varied and scenic, and great for walkers and cyclists.

Getting Around
Stagecoach West Scotland (☎ 01292-613500) is the main operator on the mainland and on Arran, where there are also post buses run by **Royal Mail** (☎ 01463-256200) whizzing around the island. Ferries to here and Great Cumbrae are run by **CalMac** (☎ 0870 565 0000; www.calmac.co.uk).

ISLE OF GREAT CUMBRAE
☎ 01475 / pop 1430
The island of Great Cumbrae is only 4 miles long, but it's called 'great' because it's bigger

than the privately owned Little Cumbrae island just south. It's an ideal daytrip from Glasgow; walking or cycling is the best way to explore the hilly terrain.

Millport is the main town and windsurfing is a popular activity off its sandy beaches. You'll find the **TIC** (☎ 01292-678100; 28 Stuart St; ☼ Apr-Sep) on the waterfront. The town holds a couple of interesting records: just down from the tourist office, at 50 Stuart St, is the world's narrowest house; the façade measure just 119 centimetres across! Millport also boasts Europe's smallest cathedral, **The Cathedral of the Isles** (☎ 530353; College St; admission free; ☼ daily), and the interesting **Robertson Museum & Aquarium** (☎ 530581; adult £1.50; ☼ Mon-Sat Jun-Sep, Mon-Fri Oct-May) on the edge of town towards the ferry pier. Less charmingly, Great Cumbrae is also home to the Hunterston nuclear plant. Although one of the two reactors is already decommissioned, and the second due to be retired shortly, chances are another will be built to help reduce Britain's greenhouse gas emissions.

There are few accommodation choices if you plan to stay, but **Cir Mhor** (☎ 530723; 35 West Bay Rd, Millport; d or tw £36; P ✗) is a comfortable if unexciting B&B overlooking the water with a couple of clean and tidy rooms that share a bathroom and a garden.

A CalMac ferry links the town of Largs on the mainland with Great Cumbrae (passenger/car £3.95/17.25 return, 10 minutes, frequent). Island buses meet the ferries for the short journey to Millport. Largs has frequent bus and train connections to Glasgow.

Several places in Millport hire out bikes, including **Mapes** (☎ 530444; 3 Guildford St; ☼ daily), which charges £4 for a half day.

AYR
☎ 01292 / pop 46,400
Ayr is a large, bustling town and a convenient base for a tour of Burns territory. The town's long sandy beach has made it a popular family seaside resort since Victorian times, and the world championship golf courses of Turnberry and Troon are within easy reach. There are many fine Georgian and Victorian buildings, although some areas of town are showing signs of neglect. It's also known for its racecourse – the top course in Scotland, with more racing days than any other in Britain.

SOUTHERN SCOTLAND

Information
Carnegie Library (☎ 618492; 12 Main St; ☯ 10am-7.30pm Mon, Tue, Thu & Fri, 10am-5pm Wed & Sat) Free Internet access.

TIC (☎ 678100; 12 Sandgate; info@ayrshire-arran.com; ☯ 9am-5pm Mon-Sat year-round, 10am-5pm Sun Jul & Aug)

Sights
Apart from the **beach**, attractions in Ayr are mainly Burns-related. The bard was baptised in the **Auld Kirk** (old church) off High St. Several of his poems are set in Ayr. In his *Twa Brigs*, Ayr's old and new bridges argue with one another. The **Auld Brig**, near the bottom of High St, was built in 1491 and spans the river just down from the church.

Sleeping
Neighbouring Alloway, birthplace of Robert Burns, has a couple of luxurious accommodation options, too (right).

No 26 The Crescent (☎ 287329; 26 Bellevue Cres; www.26crescent.freeserve.co.uk; s/d £40/56; ✖) This elegant Victorian terrace sits in a quiet street and offers a genuine welcome. The rooms boast some lovely wooden furniture as well as period features such as fireplaces – one even has a four-poster bed – and the owner is very knowledgeable about Scotland and can help you plan an itinerary.

Richmond Guest House (☎ 265153; www.richmond-guest-house.co.uk; 38 Park Circus; s/d from £30/50) One of several good choices on this peaceful crescent, this place has beautiful, big rooms with sweeping bay windows, leather furniture and high ceilings. It's cosy and plush, and several of the rooms are suitable for families.

Eglinton Guest House (☎ 264623; 23 Eglinton Tce; s/d from £19/38) This Georgian property is in a quiet area with a range of rooms. The owners offer competitive rates, giving you the choice to go without breakfast (£5 cheaper), a welcome concession to consumer choice!

Other recommendations:

Heads of Ayr Caravan Park (☎ 442269; Dunure Rd; pitches from £8) Great location. From Ayr take the A719 south; it's about 5 miles away.

Lochinver (☎ 265086; 32 Park Circus; r per person from £21; P ✖) Family-run place, slightly cheaper than others in the area.

Eating & Drinking
Fouters (☎ 261391; 2a Academy St; mains £7-13; ☯ lunch & dinner Tue-Sat; ✖) This long-established Ayr cellar restaurant opposite the town hall is

under new owners but remains a top place to eat. Although their own assertion that it's the 'best restaurant in central Scotland' won't win prizes for either humility or geography, there's no arguing with the quality of the local produce: the lamb with ratatouille and red-wine sauce is particularly flavoursome.

Tam o'Shanter (230 High St; mains £5-7) Named for the Burns poem about a pissed farmer on his way home from the pub, the Tam is Ayr's best traditional boozer, and has a great thatched roof and cosy, gracefully ageing feel. As you'd expect, Burnsiana festoons the walls, but it doesn't live off that: the pub meals next door are cheap, wholesome, and filling.

Hunny Pot (☎ 263239; 35 Beresford Tce; light meals £3-6; ☯ 9am-10pm Mon-Sat, 10.30am-9pm Sun) This Winnie-the-Pooh–themed coffee shop and licensed restaurant is cutesy, likeable, busy and competently staffed. It serves a range of open sandwiches, salads and more-substantial meals.

Getting There & Away
The main bus operator is Stagecoach Western; its X77 service goes to Glasgow (one hour, hourly). There are also services to Stranraer (£6, 1¾ hours, four to nine daily). There are frequent trains from Glasgow Central to Ayr (50 minutes, half-hourly) and some trains continue south to Stranraer (£10.40, 1½ hours from Ayr, seven daily).

AROUND AYR
Alloway
☎ 01292

The pretty village of Alloway, on the southern outskirts of Ayr, should be on the itinerary of every Robert Burns fan – he was born here on 25 January 1759. The sights are within easy walking distance of each other and come under the umbrella title of **Burns National Heritage Park** (☎ 443700; www.burnsheritagepark.com; admission to all sites £5; ☯ 9.30am-5.30pm Apr-Oct, 10am-5pm Nov-Mar).

Burns Cottage & Museum (stand-alone admission £3) stands by the main road from Ayr. Born in the little box bed in this cramped thatched cottage, Burns' first seven years of life are detailed in an audiovisual here. A fascinating museum of Burnsiana next to the cottage, exhibits some fabulous artwork as well as many of his songs and letters.

From here you can visit the ruins of **Alloway Auld Kirk**, the setting for the witches' dance in *Tam o'Shanter*. Burns' father, William Burnes (his son dropped the 'e') is buried in the kirkyard.

The nearby **Tam o' Shanter Experience** has a clever audiovisual display of the famous poem, although an understanding of Burns' 18th-century lowland Scots dialect would greatly enhance appreciation.

Alloway has two excellent accommodation options. **Brig O'Doon House Hotel** (☎ 442466; www.costleyhotels.co.uk; s/d from £85/120; dinner mains £10-17) is a grand place with a good reputation for food, while the **Ivy House** (☎ 442336; www .theivyhouse.uk.com; s/d from £90/110; P ⊠), off the road to Ayr, is a small, luxurious hotel with a fine restaurant and a BBQ patio.

Alloway is 3 miles south of Ayr. Stagecoach Western bus No 57 runs (hourly 8.45am to 6pm Monday to Saturday) between Alloway and Ayr.

Electric Brae

On the A719 (9 miles south of Ayr), a beautiful stretch of road overlooking the Firth of Clyde is named the Electric Brae. All sorts of theories abound for why cars appear to roll up the slope, and go backwards when they should be going downhill, but the truth doesn't concern ley lines, electromagnetic forces, or faerie folk; it's just an extraordinary powerful optical illusion. Locals are used to tourists experimenting, so put the hazards on, take the handbrake off, and prepare to be amazed!

Culzean Castle

The Scottish National Trust's flagship property, magnificent **Culzean** (cul-lane; ☎ 01655-884455; admission park & castle £9, park only £5; ✆ castle 10.30am-5pm Apr-Oct, park 9.30am-sunset year-round; wheelchair access), is one of the most impressive of Scotland's great stately homes. The entrance to the castle is a converted viaduct and on approach the architectural masterpiece appears like a mirage, floating into view.

Designed by Robert Adam, who was encouraged to exercise his romantic genius in its design, this 18th-century mansion is perched dramatically on the edge of the cliffs. Robert Adam was the most influential architect of his time, renowned for his meticulous attention to detail and the elegant classical embellishments with which he decorated his ceilings and fireplaces. The

beautiful oval staircase here is regarded as one of his finest achievements.

On the 1st floor, the opulence of the circular saloon contrasts violently with the views of the wild sea below. Lord Cassillis' bedroom is said to be haunted by a lady in green, mourning for a lost baby.

Culzean is 12 miles south of Ayr; bus No 58 or 60 from Ayr (30 minutes, 11 daily Monday to Saturday) pass the park gates, from where it's a 20-minute walk through the grounds to the castle.

ARDROSSAN
☎ 01294 / pop 11,000

The only reason for coming here is to catch a CalMac ferry to Arran. Trains leave Glasgow Central (55 minutes, five daily) to connect with ferries (see the Isle of Arran, p812). If you need a B&B, try **Edenmore Guest House** (☎ 462306; 47 Parkhouse Rd; r per person £18-25; P) on the main A78 road at the south end of town. You'll get a genuine welcome from the host, if not from the barking dogs!

ISLE OF ARRAN
☎ 01770 / pop 5060

While many tourists pass Arran by, with minds firmly focused on more northerly isles, it has long been a favourite weekend or day-trip destination for Scots, particularly from Glasgow. Arran is exceptionally beautiful, and short-term visitors should scribble Arran into their quick-fire itinerary – the variations in Scotland's dramatic landscape can all be experienced on this one small island.

It's a particular favourite with walkers and cyclists, who can take it easy along the gentle coastal roads, or head for the mountainous interior. At weekends, the convivial local pubs hum with the chatter of satisfied hikers, with flushed faces and bodies no doubt relieved to have been spared the rigours of the Glasgow clubbing scene. Head for the north, where the scenery is wilder, and the bucket and spade brigade in the south seem far away.

Orientation & Information

The ferry from Ardrossan docks at Brodick, the island's main town. A road runs right around the island – there are also a few that cut across the hilly interior. To the south of Brodick, Lamlash is actually the capital and, like Whiting Bay further south, a popular seaside resort. From the pretty village of Lochranza in the north there's a nonwinter ferry link to Claonaig on the Kintyre peninsula.

The TIC (☎ 303774; ☼ 9am-7.30pm Mon-Sat, 10am-5pm Sun Jun-Sep, 9am-5pm Mon-Thu, 9am-7.30pm Fri, 9am-5pm Sat Oct-May) is near Brodick pier. There's also tourist information available on the ferry in high season. Brodick has two banks with ATMs, car- and bike-hire facilities, and a Co-op supermarket, where you can also access the Internet. Other places to get online on the island include the Kildonan Hotel (p812) and the Catacol Bay Hotel (p812).

Sights & Activities
BRODICK & AROUND
Most visitors arrive in **Brodick**, the pulsing metropolis (well, not quite!) of the island, and congregate along the coastal road to admire the town's long curving bay.

Two and a half miles north of town, **Brodick Castle** (NTS; ☎ 302202; castle & gardens/gardens £8/4; ☼ castle 11am-5pm Apr-Oct, gardens 10am-sunset year-round) is wallpapered with prized deer heads, but boasts a stunning formal dining room,

ISLE OF ARRAN

with peculiar table furnishings among other salons. Only a small portion of the still-inhabited castle is open to visitors, and the extensive grounds, now a country park with various trails among the rhododendrons, justify the steep entry fee.

THE NORTH
Heading to the very north, on the island's main road, visitors weave through lush glens bordered by some of Arran's towering mountain splendour. Look out for seals on your way! **Lochranza** is a village in a small bay at the north of the island. It's the island's most picturesque and peaceful settlement. On a promontory stand the ruins of the 13th-century **Lochranza Castle** (HS; admission free, ☼ if closed, ask in shop for keyholder). Also in Lochranza is **Isle of Arran Distillers** (☎ 830264; tours adult/child £3.50/free; ☼ 10am-5pm Apr-Oct, tours on the hr) where you can go on an innovative tour of this modern distillery.

THE SOUTH
On the western side of the island are the **Machrie Moor Stone Circles** – with six rings of stone circles dating from the 2nd millennium BC.

In the southern part of the island the road drops into little wooded valleys, and it's particularly lovely around **Lagg**. At **Kildonan** there are a string of rocky beaches and the ruins of an ivy-clad castle.

North of Whiting Bay is **Lamlash**, an upmarket resort in a gorgeous setting, strung out along the beachfront. There are wooded hills to the south and across the bay, **Holy Island**, which is owned by Tibetan Buddhists whose **Peace Centre** (☎ 013873-73232; www .holyisland.org) accepts guests and runs retreats, though it does allow day visits. There's a **ferry** (☎ 600349) every 15 minutes (£9 return, eight daily May to September). The walk to the highest point (314m) of the island takes two to three hours return from the pier.

WALKING & CYCLING
The walk up **Goatfell** (874m) takes up to eight hours return, starting/finishing in Brodick. If the weather is good, there are superb views from the summit to Ben Lomond and the coast of Northern Ireland. It can, however, be very cold and windy. Make sure you have the appropriate maps (available at the TIC), waterproof gear and a compass.

The 50-mile circuit on the coastal road is popular with cyclists and has few serious hills – more in the south than north.

Sleeping

It's advisable to book, especially at weekends, even outside the busy summer months.

BRODICK
Mid-Range

You get a better feel for the island if you get out into the smaller villages, although Brodick does have numerous places to stay.

Glencloy Farm Guesthouse (☎ 302351; www.smooth hound.co.uk/hotels/glencloy; Glencloy Rd; s/d £35/46, with bathroom £45/60; P ✗) This relaxed and friendly B&B just outside Brodick packs warmth in its welcome and is charmingly down to earth. The colourful rooms all have a VCR, and you can watch videos from the hosts' large collection. There are bikes to borrow, fresh eggs from the chickens in the garden, and plans for peacocks!

Rosaburn Lodge (☎ /fax 302383; r per person £28-32; P ✗ ; wheelchair access) This recommended little place is a haven of quiet and light – the friendly hosts allege there are 45 windows in the house. The rooms are spotless and look out on the gardens, which run down to the River Rosa. There's also a suite (£70 to £80) which is closer to an apartment than a bedroom. You'll find Rosaburn on the main road, on the northern edge of Brodick.

Belvedere Guest House (☎ 302397; www.vision -unlimited.co.uk; Alma Rd; s/d from £20/40; P ✗) This peaceful B&B is in a pleasant spot above the bustle of Shore Rd. It's worth paying the extra cost of a room looking out at the view across the bay. The four-course dinners with plenty of vegetarian choices for £25 have earned high accolades, and it also offers holistic healing and de-stressing packages.

Top End

Kilmichael Country House Hotel (☎ 302219; www .kilmichael.com; Glen Cloy; s £95, d £120-190; P ✗) Arran's oldest building houses the island's best hotel, 2½ miles west of Brodick Pier. It's intimate and very tasteful and stylish, with many East Asian prints that impart elegance with a light hand. There are rooms both in the main house and the old stables; all are excellent, with huge bathrooms and some with four-poster beds. There's also a high-quality four-course dinner available for £35.

LOCHRANZA

This quiet village is one of the island's best places to stay.

Budget

Lochranza SYHA Hostel (☎ 0870 004 1140; www.syha .org.uk; dm £11; ✉ Mar-Oct; P ✗) The most hospitable and relaxed of places, this hostel has a fine setting in the north of the island. Dorms are clean and spacious, and there's plenty of information on walking and cycling routes.

Lochranza Golf, Caravan & Camping (☎ 830273; Lochranza; per tent/person £2.60/3.70; ✉ Apr-Oct; P) It's on a picturesque spot, but look out for wayward golf balls!

Mid Range

Castlekirk (☎ 830202; r per person from £20; ✉ Mar-Nov) This marvellous-looking B&B, housed in a converted 19th-century church, is an excellent choice. Opposite the castle, it has congenial folk, comfortable rooms, and a fine collection of local Scottish art, including a magnificent carved eagle.

Lochranza Hotel (☎ /fax 830223; www.lochranza .co.uk; s/d £42/72; P ✗) The focus of the village, being the only place you can get an evening meal, this bastion of Arran hospitality has comfortable if slightly overpriced rooms decked out in pink. The showers are pleasingly powerful, and the front rooms have fantastic views over the bay.

Other recommendations:

Apple Lodge (☎ /fax 830229; d or tw £66; P ✗) Upmarket B&B. Not by the bay, but makes up for it with elegantly furnished rooms and lounge.

Croftbank (☎ 830201; s/d from £22/40; ✗) A wee guesthouse with two snug attic rooms that look out over the castle and the bay.

KILDONAN & WHITING BAY
Budget

Seal Shore Camping (☎ 820320; Kildonan; per person £5; P) This friendly spot has a decent grassed area on the seafront at the southern end of the island. It's breezy, but that means no midges! There's a laundry, a pool table, and it's right next to the Kildonan Hotel, which does bar meals. Open all year, but ring ahead in winter.

Whiting Bay SYHA (☎ 0870 004 1158; www.syha .org.uk; dm £11; ✉ Apr-Oct; P ✗) A tad plainer than its cousin hostel in the north. It's at the western end of the Whiting Bay strip.

Mid Range

Kildonan Hotel (☎ 820207; www.kildonanhotel.com; d from £75; **P** ✗ ▢) This hotel has one of the best settings imaginable, looking out over the water with seals basking on the rocks outside. The new rooms are furnished with a certain Scandinavian feel, and the beds are comfortable indeed. There's good food to be had here too, and transfers to and from the ferry.

Eating

Creelers (☎ 302810; Duchess Ct; mains £12-17; ✆ lunch & dinner Tue-Sun; ✗) Near Brodick Castle, this highly decorated (think medals not frills) seafood restaurant is the island's best eatery. Creations such as their scallop and monkfish Provencale are the reason for this, added to the fact that only the freshest produce from Arran and the Western Isles is used. Their smokehouse next door sells produce over the counter.

Catacol Bay Hotel (☎ 830231; Catacol; bar meals £6-8; ✆ noon-10pm; ▢) Situated on a lonely bay a mile from Lochranza, this eccentric and lovable pub is one of the island's best spots for a pint, particularly if cask ales are your thing. It's also a spot to eat, with no-frills bar meals in generous portions. There's a famous Sunday buffet from noon to 4pm for £8.95 and tables outside to enjoy the view.

Isle of Arran Distillers Restaurant (☎ 830264; Lochranza; mains £8-13; ✆ 10am-5pm; ✗) Set in the distillery itself, this is the best restaurant in the north of the island and an attractive lunching spot. Arran's specialities, including

salmon, game and cheese, are used in inventive and elegant taste sensations. Skip the baguettes and go straight to the mains.

Other recommendations:

Kildonan Hotel (☎ 820207; Kildonan; mains £6-8; ✆ noon-9pm; ▢) Big portions and friendly service in a pub with polished wooden floors and seals on the rocks.

Lochranza Hotel (☎ 830223; Lochranza; mains £6-11; ✆ lunch & dinner) Only place in town for an evening meal, with decent, solid, Scottish pub food and plenty of malts behind the bar.

Getting There & Away

CalMac runs a daily car ferry between Ardrossan and Brodick (person/car £8.25/44 return, 55 minutes, four to six daily). It also operates a service between Claonaig on the Kintyre peninsula and Lochranza from late March to late October (person/car £7.35/33.50 return, 30 minutes, seven to nine daily).

Getting Around

The island is easy to get around thanks to the efficient bus system. Buses mainly run from Brodick to Blackwaterfoot, some anticlockwise around the island via Corrie and Lochranza (45 minutes, four to six daily) and some clockwise via Lamlash and Whiting Bay (30 minutes, four to twelve daily). An Arran Rural Rover gives a day's travel on buses for £3.50 (buy on board).

In Brodick, several places hire bikes including the **Boathouse** (☎ 302868; The Beach), with mountain bikes from £11/35 per day/week.

GARETH MCCORMACK

Fishing boats moored, Ullapool (p900), Scotland

Shepherd's cottage near Durness (p898),
Scotland

GRAEME CORNWALLIS

GRANT DIXON

Viking runic carvings, Maes
Howe (p923), Stenness,
Scotland

Cuillin Hills (p908), Isle of Skye, Scotland

DAVID TIPLING

Skara Brae (p924), Scotland

GARETH MCCORMACK

Am Basteir and Sgurr a'Fhionn Choire, Cuillin Hills (p908), Isle of Skye, Scotland

GRAEME CORNWALLIS

Loch Broom, Ullapool (p900), Scotland

GRANT DIS

Central Scotland

Stretching across the narrow waist of the country, and including its broad eastern shoulder, central Scotland covers a whole gamut of terrain, from the grim peaks of the southern Highlands to the quiet agricultural coastlines of Fife and the Grampian coast. Not so much a distinct region as a buffer between north and south, the region is crammed full of attractions, whether you're captivated by castles, inspired by islands, hung-up on hiking or wowed by whisky.

As you trudge up and down the wooden hillscapes of the Trossachs, you may wonder if you'll ever see flat land again, yet a bare 60 miles east will see you choosing which course to play at St Andrews, home of the world's most infuriating sport. In the east you can investigate Scotland's industrial and maritime powerhouses of Dundee and Aberdeen, while on the other side of the region, the one-road island of Jura has more deer than humans and seems a lifetime away from anywhere.

While there are several spots that visitors have sought for generations – Stirling's noble castle, lavish Scone Palace, romantic Loch Lomond, or the sacred and magical island of Iona – there's opportunity aplenty here to explore little-known corners of Scotland. The island of Islay enchants with its hospitality and distilleries, while Kilmartin is the cradle of modern Scotland. The valley of Glen Lyon was viewed by the ancients as a gateway to the spirit land and retains a marvellously otherworldly ambience, while the vertiginous harbour hamlet of Pennan seems to defy the very sea that laps at its doorsteps.

HIGHLIGHTS

- Delving into the secrets of **Glen Lyon** (p852), Scotland's most gorgeous hidden valley
- Weaving your way between tours of the seven working distilleries of **Islay** (p821)
- Pacing the turf of sacred **Iona** (p829), burial place of dozens of Scottish kings including Macbeth
- Blocking the gate at **Stirling Castle** (p831): hold it and you hold the country
- Exploring Dundee's industrial past at the fascinating **Verdant Works** (p864) museum
- Coming up the eighteenth at **St Andrews' Old Course** (p841), the crowd's cheers ringing in your mind

- POPULATION 1,585,620
- AREA: 10,480 SQ MILES

Activities
CYCLING

Long-distance touring routes (established as part of the National Cycle Network – see Spreading the Net, p81) in Central Scotland include the northern section of the 214-mile **Lochs & Glens Cycle Route**. It starts in Glasgow, and winds its way through the region's heart via Loch Ness and Pitlochry to Inverness, and includes some wonderful traffic-free sections. The first part of the route between Glasgow and Loch Lomond is especially popular.

For shorter rides, the western part of central Scotland offers the islands of **Islay**, **Jura** and **Mull** – all ideally explored by bike for a day or longer. If you don't have your own wheels, bikes can be hired on Mull or Islay.

If you're after something longer, a great cycling tour of **central Scotland's islands** might start with a circuit, or half-circuit, of the Isle of Arran (p809). From here, take a ferry to the Kintyre Peninsula and loop down to Campbeltown. Take a ferry to Islay and Jura, before returning to the mainland, reaching the port of Oban and taking another ferry to Mull. If you still have time, another ferry from Mull takes you back to the mainland at Kilchoan, from where you can reach Mallaig.

In the southeast part of this region, **Fife** takes cycling very seriously, and the local tourist authority has produced several maps and leaflets detailing cycle routes in this area. There are only a few steep hills here, and the country roads are fairly quiet.

WALKING

One of Britain's most-trodden and best-known long-distance walks, the **West Highland Way**, runs through the western part of the region. It starts just outside Glasgow and covers 95 miles (150km) of path and track through the mountains and glens, via Loch Lomond and Rannoch Moor, to finish at Fort William with fine views of Ben Nevis. Most walkers do the route in a week – this time-span is another reason for its popularity.

Many areas crossed by the West Highland Way make fine walking destinations in their own right. For example, overlooking Loch Lomond is the mountain of Ben Lomond, which is most easily reached from Rowardennan on the east shore of the loch.

One of the most challenging islands to walk is Jura, whose centre is dominated by the rugged Paps.

The central part of the region is dominated by the Grampian and Cairngorm mountain ranges. These high and wild areas tend to be favoured by serious walkers, but there are opportunities for easier strolls and rambles too. Good bases include the highland settlements of Pitlochry and Braemar.

Getting Around
BOAT

Ferries to the Hebridean islands off the west coast are mostly run by Caledonian Mac-Brayne, or **CalMac** (☎ 08705 650000; www.calmac.co.uk). Most routes depart from Oban. If you plan to island hop, you'll save money by planning your trip in advance and buying one of CalMac's Island Hopscotch tickets. A popular route leaves from Ardrossan and includes the ferry to Arran, on to the Kintyre peninsula and thence to Islay, returning to Oban. This costs £22.25 for passengers and £115 for a vehicle – a saving of over 20%.

There are also Island Rover Passes covering the whole system. These are available for eight/15 consecutive days and are great value, costing £47.50/69 for passengers and £228/341 for vehicles. Bicycles travel free on this pass, but you'll need to book your car space on the busier routes.

BUS

Scottish Citylink (☎ 0870 550 5050; www.citylink.co.uk) links the main towns in the area and Perth is a major hub for its services. Bus transport around the northeast coast is reasonable – **Stagecoach Bluebird** (☎ 01224-212266; www.stagecoachbus.com) is the main operator of local services. **Postbuses** (☎ 01246-546329; www.postbus.royalmail.com) serve remote communities, charging on average £2 to £5 for single journeys.

TRAIN

There are three north-south lines, connected by a fourth running northeast from Glasgow to Aberdeen via Dundee. These include the West Highland line, Britain's most spectacular rail journey, running from Glasgow to Fort William and Mallaig. East-west travel usually involves backtracking to Glasgow.

The Central Scotland Rover pass allows unlimited travel for three days in a seven-day period on First ScotRail trains between Edinburgh and Glasgow and the Fife and Stirling areas. It costs £29 and is available from all train stations.

CENTRAL SCOTLAND

CENTRAL SCOTLAND

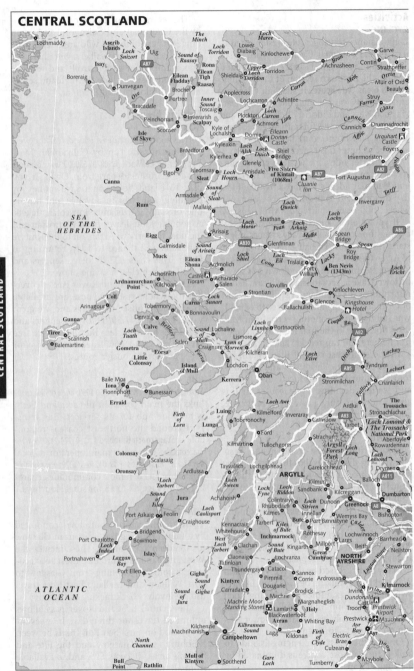

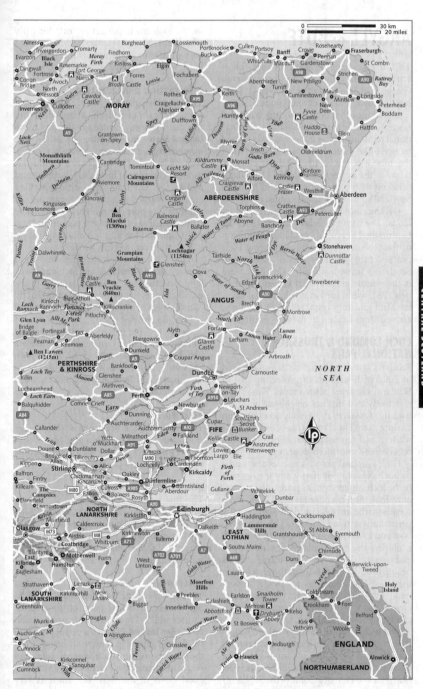

ARGYLL & BUTE

This diverse western region is chock-full of attractions. In easy striking distance from Glasgow, it is an accessible jewel in Scotland's crown and deservedly popular.

It includes the 'bonnie bonnie banks' of Loch Lomond, part of Scotland's first national park; further west the coast is lacerated by fjord-like sea lochs whose surfaces reflect the mood of the weather. Kilmartin Glen, home to the ancient kingdom of Dalriada, is bristling with prehistoric sites and home to Scotland's most enthusiastic museum.

Off the coast is an array of fascinating islands. The names of Islay's malts – Ardbeg, Laphroaig, Lagavulin – read like a pantheon of the whisky world; while exploring their peaty depths you'll be treated to some of Scotland's finest hospitality. Opposite, Jura is the remote getaway that Orwell chose to pen *1984*, while, further north, are spectacular Mull and tiny Iona, where St Columba arrived from Ireland in the 6th century.

LOCH LOMOND & TROSSACHS NATIONAL PARK

Scotland's first national park was created in 2002 with the aim of protecting two of Scotland's heaviest-visited areas. The park is effectively two distinct neighbouring areas, with the Trossachs most easily accessed from Stirling (see The Trossachs, p836) and the western half centred on giant Loch Lomond, on Glasgow's northern doorstep.

Loch Lomond plays a close second-fiddle to Loch Ness in popularity and a large part of the loch suffers from its proximity to Glasgow. In summer, a huge influx of visitors descends on the busy A82 and the southern tip, particularly around Balloch. This is motorboat and jet ski season and you'd be better off exploring the more isolated, less-developed east coast. The drive to Rowardennan is beautiful and after this town the area, which the West Highland Way follows, is seldom tread by tourists. Alternatively, the whole area is more sedate in early spring, which can be a good time to visit.

The loch, the largest single inland waterway in Britain, was formed by the action of glaciers, and lay at the junction of the three ancient Scottish kingdoms of Strathclyde, Dalriada and Pictland. Some of the 37 islands

in the loch made perfect retreats for early Christians. The missionary St Mirrin spent some time on Inchmurrin, the largest island, which is named after him.

Information & Orientation

The wedge-shaped loch runs 22 miles north from the town of Balloch, where you'll find the main gateway centre for the park. **Loch Lomond Shores Visitors Centre** (☎ 0845 345 4978; www.lochlomond-trossachs.org; ☼ 9am-7pm Apr-Sep, 10am-5pm Oct-Mar; ▣ ; wheelchair access) is a hideous modern complex of high-class shopping and audiovisual entertainment with a parking area the size of a small European nation. Although its purpose is highly questionable (surely the idea of a national park must be to get people outdoors) it has all the necessary information on the park itself.

The loch straddles the Highland fault line separating lowland and highland Scotland, and the most dramatic scenery in the north changes distinctly as you move south. Standing guard over the loch is Ben Lomond (974m) on the east coast.

As well as the gateway centre, there are Tourist Information Centres (TICs) in **Balloch** (☎ 0870 720 0607; Balloch Rd; ☼ Apr-Oct); **Drymen** (☎ 0870 720 0611; ☼ May-Sep), in the library on the square; and **Tarbet** (☎ 0870 720 0623; Main St; ☼ Apr-mid Oct).

Activities

The national park organises a whole range of summer activities, from guided walks to archery displays. Ask for a current schedule from information centres.

BOAT TRIPS

The main centre for boat trips is Balloch, where, among others, **Sweeney's Cruises** (☎ 01389-752376; www.sweeney.uk.com) offers a wide range of trips from £5.30 an hour. There's a 2½-hour cruise (£8) to the village of Luss, allowing 30 minutes ashore.

WALKING & CYCLING

The big walk is the **West Highland Way** (p815) but it's easy to access parts of the trail for shorter walks. From Rowardennan you can tackle **Ben Lomond** (974m), a popular five- to six- hour round trip. The route begins from the car park by the Rowardennan Hotel, and you can return via Ptarmigan (731m) for good views of the loch. The route is very popular so consider doing it in reverse (ie ascend via Ptarmigan) to avoid the crowds.

A couple of fulfilling woodland walks leave from the village of Balmaha on the eastern shore of the loch. The **Millennium Forest Path** is a 40-minute introduction to the tree and plant life of the area, with gentle information on species. A longer stroll is the three-hour ascent of **Conic Hill**, which rewards with fantastic views along the loch.

The main cycle route is the **Glasgow, Loch Lomond & Killin Cycle Way**, which reaches the loch at Balloch. Most of the route is set back to the east of the loch, through the Queen Elizabeth Forest Park. In summer, stick to the quieter, older roads beside the A82.

Sleeping & Eating

There are numerous B&Bs, centred on Luss, Balloch, Inverbeg, and Tarbet.

Loch Lomond SYHA Hostel (☎ 0870 004 1136; www .syha.org.uk; Arden; dm £14; ☺ Mar-Oct; P ☒ ☐) This hostel, set in beautiful grounds 2 miles north of Balloch, is an awesome place to stay. An imposing, and reputedly haunted, mansion with luxurious dorms and bathrooms, it has more of a five-star than backpacker feel and is one of Scotland's most impressive budget accommodations. You'll need to book well ahead in summer.

Drover's Inn (☎ 01301-704234; Inverarnan; r per person from £23, bar meals £6-9; P ; wheelchair access) This historic inn at the northern end of the loch shouldn't be missed. It has smoke-blackened walls, bare wooden floors and wee drams served by barmen in kilts, as well as tables outside. If you've an aversion to moth-eaten stuffed animals, close your eyes when you enter. There's regular live music, and there are faded but characterful rooms upstairs, and more modern rooms in an annexe.

Oak Tree Inn (☎ 01360-870357; www.oak-tree -inn.co.uk; Balmaha; s/d £45/64; P ☒) This warm and welcoming spot on the east side of the loch has colourful and comfortable en-suite rooms as well as two bunk rooms with four beds. Its welcoming, child-friendly restaurant serves comfort food in big portions for weary walkers.

Other recommendations include:

Cashel Caravan & Camping Site (☎ 01360-870234; Rowardennan; pitches from £8; ☺ late Mar-Oct) Popular and well-positioned on the eastern shore.

Rowardennan SYHA Hostel (☎ 0870 004 1148; www .syha.org.uk; Rowardennan, near Drymen; dm £12;

☺ Mar-Oct; P ☒) On the east edge of the loch; the perfect base for climbing Ben Lomond.

Getting There & Away

Citylink buses link Glasgow with Balloch (40 minutes, nine daily) and continue up the west coast to Luss (55 minutes) and Tarbet (65 minutes); some bus services continue to Ardlui (1¼ hours).

There are two railway lines. From Glasgow, one serves Balloch (35 minutes, half hourly); the other line is the West Highland Line to Oban and Fort William (two to five daily), which follows the loch from Tarbet to Ardlui.

INVERARAY

☎ 01499 / pop 510

Blinding white-washed buildings (consider sunglasses), entertaining local attractions and a stunning spot on the shores of Loch Fyne ensure Inveraray is a tourist magnet (best visited out of season). While you probably won't stay here long, you shouldn't miss it if you're in the area.

Inveraray is a fine example of a planned town, built by the Duke of Argyll when he revamped his castle in the 18th century. The **TIC** (☎ 0870 720 0616; Front St; ☺ year round) is beside the spectacularly beautiful loch.

Inveraray Castle

Half a mile north of the town, **Inveraray Castle** (☎ 302203; www.inveraray-castle.com; adult £5.90; ☺ 10am-5.45pm Mon-Thu & Sat, 1-5.45pm Sun Apr-May & Oct, 10am-5.45pm Mon-Sat, 1-5.45pm Sun Jun-Sep) has been the seat of the chiefs of Clan Campbell, the dukes of Argyll, since the 15th century. The current 18th-century building includes whimsical turrets and fake battlements. Inside is the armoury hall, whose walls are patterned with over 1000 pole arms, dirks and Lochaber axes, many of which were stuck into Catholics during the Jacobite rebellions. The dining and drawing rooms have ornate ceilings and there's a collection of porcelain.

Inveraray Jail

The Georgian courthouse and **jail** (☎ 302381; Church Sq; adult £5.75; ☺ 9.30am-6pm Apr-Oct, 10am-5pm Nov-Mar) is an award-winning, interactive tourist attraction. You can sit in on a trial, try out a cell and discover the harsh torture meted out to unfortunate souls in the 16th and 17th centuries, or the many that were transported to Australia in the 19th century for minor crimes such as stealing a loaf of bread. The attention to detail (such as a life-size inmate squatting on a 19th-century toilet) more than compensates for the sometimes tedious commentary.

Sleeping & Eating

Argyll Hotel (☎ 302466; www.the-argyll-hotel.co.uk; Front St; s/d from £50/59, bar meals £5-9; **P**) This stately white building overlooks the loch and was built in 1750. Although it was recently acquired by the Best Western chain, they haven't managed to ruin it yet; it still has plenty of character, an air of elegance, couches in the bar that you'll never get out of, and good service. Book a day in advance for the best rates.

Inveraray SYHA Hotel (☎ 0870 004 1125; www.syha .org.uk; Dalmally Rd; dm £11; ☼ Apr-Sep; **P** ✗) Located in an hospitable, modern bungalow, this is a handy and sociable little spot. To get here, head through the arched gateway on the loch front; this used to be an elegant avenue of trees separating the Duke's lands from the village.

Loch Fyne Oyster Bar (☎ 600236; Cairndow; mains £8-20; ☼ 9am-8pm; wheelchair access) Although now encompassing a couple of dozen restaurants throughout the UK, this started as a humble oyster bar – here, 6 miles north of Inveraray on the A83. It recently hit the headlines as MPs Gordon Brown and John Prescott met here for a spot of political intriguing; they knew what they were doing, as the seafood is excellent and served in an unpretentious manner. Cheaper fish and other food are sold in the attached shop.

Getting There & Away

From Glasgow, Citylink buses travel to Inveraray (£7.60, 1¾ hours, five to six daily). There are also buses between Inveraray and Oban (one hour, two to three daily). Buses arrive and depart from the loch shore.

KILMARTIN GLEN

☎ 01546 / pop 490

Exploration of this magical glen is like treading in the footprints of the past. Mid-Argyll is the cradle of modern Scotland and Kilmartin is the heart of one of Scotland's most concentrated areas of prehistoric sites. Burial cairns, stone circles and hill forts litter the countryside (within a 6-mile radius of Kilmartin town there are 25 sites with standing stones and over 100 rock carvings). Irish invaders founded Dalriada and formed the kingdom of Alba here, which eventually united a large part of Scotland.

Sights

The **Museum of Ancient Culture** (☎ 510278; Kilmartin; adult £4.50; ☼ 10am-5.30pm; wheelchair access) is a fascinating centre for archaeology and landscape interpretation with artefacts from the sites, reconstructions, interactive displays and guided tours. There's an excellent selection of books and souvenirs in the shop, too, and a fine café. It's one of Scotland's best museums but at time of research was threatened with closure due to lack of any public funding. If you find it closed, it's a real black

---

SCOTLAND'S BIRTHPLACE

The oldest monuments in Kilmartin Glen date from around 5000 years ago and comprise a linear cemetery of **burial cairns**, running south of Kilmartin village for 1½ miles. There are also two stone circles at **Temple Wood**, ¾ mile southwest of Kilmartin. Although not much remains now, the stones are in a surreal setting surrounded by farmland. Four miles north of Lochgilphead, at **Achnabreck**, elaborate cup-and-ring designs cut into rock faces resemble ripples caused by a pebble breaking the surface of a pond. The site has been described as 'one of the most extensive early rock carvings in Britain' and has outstanding views over Loch Fyne.

The hill fort of **Dunadd**, 4 miles north of Lochgilphead, was the royal residence of the first kings of Dalriada, and was probably where the Stone of Destiny, used in the investiture ceremony, was located. The faint rock carvings – an ogham inscription (ancient script), a wild boar and two footprints – were probably used in some kind of inauguration ceremony. The fort overlooks farmland and the boggy plain that is now the **Moine Mhor Nature Reserve**. Clamber to the top of the fort and you'll gaze upon the same countryside as the ancient kings did, thousands of years ago. Be careful when it's wet – it gets slippery.

mark for the Scottish government's commitment to its own heritage.

In Kilmartin **churchyard** beside the museum there are some 10th-century Celtic crosses as well as some medieval masonry (in the form of 700-year-old gravestones).

Sleeping & Eating

Dunchraigaig House (☎ 605209; dunchraig@aol.com; A86; s/d from £25/44; P ☒) Just a couple of miles south of Kilmartin on the main road, this B&B is situated right near the Temple Wood standing stones. The rooms are bright, modern and spotless, and the home decorated with care and character.

Kilmartin Hotel (☎ 510250; www.kilmartin-hotel .com; Kilmartin; s/d from £32/50, bar meals £6-12; P) The whitewashed village hotel has cramped rooms, some with en suite, but is a popular place with a restaurant and small, atmospheric pub, with a good selection of real ales and malts. The bar gets crowded when rowdy local farmer meetings take over.

Getting There & Away

The Lochgilphead to Oban bus stops at Kilmartin (15 minutes, one daily Monday to Saturday), as does the return bus from Oban (1¼ hours).

KINTYRE PENINSULA

Almost an island, the Kintyre Peninsula has only a narrow strand connecting it to the wooded hills of Knapdale at Tarbert. Magnus Barefoot the Viking, who was allowed to claim any island he circumnavigated, made his men drag their longship across this strand to validate his claim.

Tarbert, in the peninsula's north, is the gateway to Kintyre and a busy fishing village. The **TIC** (☎ 0870 720 0624; Harbour St; Internet per hr £3; Apr-Oct; ▢) has Internet access. Above the town is a small, crumbling **castle** built by Robert the Bruce.

There are CalMac ferries to terminals at **Kennacraig** (☎ 01880-730253) for Port Askaig and Port Ellen (person/car £13.20/71 return, two hours) on Islay, and at Claonaig for Lochranza (per person/car £7.35/33.50 return, 30 minutes, seven to nine daily, late March to late October) on the north of Arran.

Isle of Gigha

From Tayinloan on the west coast, there are ferries (person/car £5.15/19.30 return, 20 minutes, six to 10 daily on the hour) to the **Isle of Gigha** (*ghee*-a; www.isle-of-gigha.co.uk), a flat island 7 miles long by about 1 mile wide. Recently bought from its original owner by the residents themselves, it's known for its sandy beaches and the subtropical **Achamore Gardens** (adult £2; 9am-dusk). The **Gigha Hotel** (☎ 01583-505254; www.isle-of-gigha.co.uk; s/d £47.50/79; P ☒) has a good restaurant and lively bar.

Campbeltown

☎ 01586 / pop 5150

About 10 miles north of Campbeltown rolling farmland drops suddenly into the thudding waves of the Atlantic and the coast is punctuated by rocky beaches. Reminiscent of the Isle of Skye, the sun dances coyly behind ever passing clouds with the light dramatically changing the landscape, dominated by miles of stone-fencing crawling its way over hills and pastureland.

Noted for its cheeses and whiskies, Campbeltown was in its prime in the late-19th century, now it feels like a long way from anywhere else. Nevertheless the town is impressively situated around a small loch surrounded by hills. The **TIC** (☎ 552056; McKinnon House, The Pier; year-round) is a friendly place where you'll probably get to hear some town gossip. There were once dozens of distilleries here – and the Campbeltown style is considered just as distinct as, say, Speyside – but now there are just two. You can visit **Springbank** (☎ 552085; Longrow; adult £3; Mon-Fri at 2pm by arrangement), one of the most respected and traditional of producers, who, despite being a small-scale, personal operation, do their own malting and bottling. Beyond Campbeltown, a narrow, winding road leads to the **Mull of Kintyre**, popularised by Paul McCartney's song of the same name – and the mist does indeed roll in.

Campbeltown is linked by Citylink buses to Glasgow (£13.10, 4½ hours, three daily).

ISLE OF ISLAY

☎ 01496 / pop 3460 / elevation 76m

The friendliest of islands, Islay is the home of several of the world's best whiskies. If that doesn't tempt you, then the birdlife, fine seafood, and leaping dolphins might. Although not as scenic as the more visited islands, Islay (*eye*-lah) is one of the most appealing destinations on the west coast; life here revolves around the distilleries, of which there are seven active, with another defunct, and one soon to open. Many of them are legendary for their peatiness and their names reverberate on the tongue like a pantheon of Celtic deities. Remember the golden rule of travel around the island – a wave to passers-by is mandatory and yet another small delight of this enchanting place. You're much better visiting the island during the week, as most of the distilleries shut at weekends. The **Islay Festival of Malt & Music** in early June is a wonderful time to visit, but you'll need to book accommodation months in advance.

Orientation

There are two ferry terminals, both served from Kennacraig on Kintyre. Port Askaig stares across at mountainous Jura from the east of Islay, while in the south is the larger Port Ellen, with three distilleries nearby. Across Loch Indaal is the attractive village of Port Charlotte.

Information

McTaggart Community CyberCafe (30 Mansfield Pl, Port Ellen; per hr £1; ⏰ 11am-10pm Mon-Sat, noon-9pm Sun) Several computers and cheap snacks.

TIC (☎ 810254; The Square, Bowmore; ⏰ 9.30am-5.30pm Mon-Sat, 2-5pm Sun Apr-Aug, 10am-5pm Mon-Sat Sep-Oct, noon-4pm Mon-Fri Nov-Mar) Welcoming.

Sights & Activities

Seven **whisky distilleries** welcome visitors for guided tours. Most tours cost £2 to £3 and some are by appointment only. All are closed on Sunday, and only two – Bowmore and Bruichladdich – are open on Saturday. Many of Islay's whisky's have a distinctive peaty taste; a quality more acute at the southerly distilleries of Ardbeg, Lagavulin and Laphroaig. By far the most charming to visit are Ardbeg and, particularly, **Bruichladdich** (brookladdie; ☎ 850221; Bruichladdich, nr Port Charlotte; tour £3; ⏰ tours 10.30am, 11.30am, 2.30pm Mon-Fri, 10.30am & 2.30pm Sat). Triumphantly re-opened in 2001 by master distiller Jim McEwan and partners, it is one of Scotland's few distilleries to be independently owned. The enthusiasm here is palpable, and the refusal to compromise on quality is evident in their award-winning whiskies, which are fresh and light-bodied. If you're going to visit any distillery in Scotland, make this the one. To get there, take a Port Charlotte-bound bus and jump off when you see the distinctive

turquoise gates. Drivers be warned, the complimentary dram(s) are generous.

Nearby in Port Charlotte, there's Bronze Age relics, an illicit still, memorabilia and countless human stories relating Islay's long history at the quirky **Museum of Islay Life** (☎ 850358; Port Charlotte; adult £2.50; ⏰ 10am-5pm Mon-Sat, 2-5pm Sun Easter-Oct, call for winter opening).

Islay was an early focus for Christianity. The exceptional 8th-century **Kildalton Cross** at Kildalton Chapel, 8 miles northeast of Port Ellen, is one of Scotland's few remaining Celtic high crosses.

In the capital, Bowmore, the **Round Church** was built in 1767 in this unusual shape to ensure the devil had no corners to hide in.

Over 250 recorded bird species make Islay wonderful for **bird-watching**. It's an important wintering ground for white-fronted and barnacle geese, who outnumber the Ileachs 10 to one; local farms are hard hit when the squadrons land.

Sleeping & Eating

Harbour Inn (☎ 810330; www.harbour-inn.com; Bowmore; s/d £65/95; mains £15-20; ⏰ lunch & dinner; ✗) An absolute star on both the sleeping and eating fronts, this hospitable and courteous hotel overlooks Loch Indaal. Its rooms, which must be booked in advance (no single rates available over summer) are newly done out in light wooden furniture and are large and supremely comfortable. The restaurant showcases the very best of local game and seafood – the scallops are sensational – beautifully presented and served. Sip a whisky in the cane-furnished lounge while your food is prepared.

Distillery House (☎ 850495; mamak@btInternet .com; Port Charlotte; per person £20; ✗) The former Lochindaal distillery is now a B&B run by charming and unassuming locals who provide comfortable, lived-in rooms and cheery service. Happily, they also make cracking marmalade, jams, and oatcakes, so you can't go wrong. It's opposite the SYHA hostel.

Glenmachrie Guesthouse (☎ 302560; www.glen machrie.com; s/d £53/76; P ✗) This peaceful and friendly farmhouse is located 4 miles north of Port Ellen, near the island's tiny airport. A great hideaway at any time of year, it's especially appealing to birdwatchers in the autumn, when flocks of geese descend. The owners know bucketloads about the island, and put on fabulous dinners for an extra

£27 – they use fresh local produce and can be vegetarian on request.

Lambeth (☎ 810597; lambethguesthouse@scali.co.uk; Jamieson St, Bowmore; B&B per person £22; ✗) Staying at these simple, good-value lodging, you'll realise why the island has such a reputation for hospitality. It really feels like you're staying with friends. Rooms are cosy, with shared bath, although it's planned to make them en suite soonish. They do an excellent two-course dinner for guests here for £7.50.

Croft Kitchen (☎ 850230; Port Charlotte; mains £11-15; ☺ 10am-8.30pm Thu-Tue Apr-Oct; ✗) This casual and offbeat bistro serves delicious seafood for dinner in the summer months and also does snacks during the day. There are several vegetarian options and reserving a table is essential. One of the best bets is the mixed seafood platter (£14.50). It's opposite the Museum of Islay Life.

Other recommendations:

Islay SYHA Hostel (☎ 0870 004 1128; www.syha.org.uk; Port Charlotte; dm £11.50; ☺ Mar-Sep; ✗) Clean but slightly gruff.

Lochside Hotel (☎ 810244; 19 Shore St, Bowmore) Every serious whisky drinker should pop their nose into the bar here; there are around 400 malts on offer, with all sorts of rare bottlings.

Port Charlotte Hotel (☎ 850360; Port Charlotte; mains £12-17; ✗) The restaurant here serves classy Scottish cuisine, and the cosy bar is the way forward if you fancy a malt.

Getting There & Away

British Airways (☎ 0870 850 9850; www.britishairways.com) operates one to three flights per day from Glasgow to Islay (from £100 return, 40 minutes).

CalMac has a ferry from Kennacraig to Port Ellen and another to Port Askaig (both person/car £13.20/71 return, 2½ hours). They operate daily but on Sunday there is a ferry to Port Ellen only. Citylink buses from Glasgow connect with the ferry at Kennacraig. In summer there is a ferry between Port Askaig and Colonsay (person/car £4.10/21.20, 1¼ hours) and on to Oban.

Getting Around

Islay Coaches (☎ 840273) and postbuses operate frequent services from Monday to Saturday (plus one Sunday service April to October) between Port Ellen, Bowmore and Port Askaig.

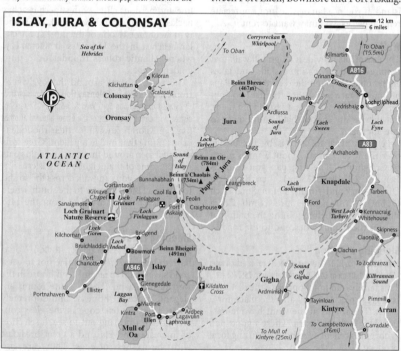

ISLAY, JURA & COLONSAY

You'll probably need a taxi if you're doing serious distillery investigation – call **Lamont** (☎ 07899-756159), a larger-than-life character who clocks up 45,000 miles a year on this tiny island.

Islay's size makes it ideal to explore by bike and **Bowmore post office** (☎ 810366; ☖ 9am-1pm Mon-Sat) hires out mountain bikes for £10 per day.

ISLE OF JURA
☎ 01496 / pop 200 / elevation 132m

The island where George Orwell wrote *1984* has a far higher population of deer than of people, who are outnumbered more than 30 to one. Almost treeless, it looms over the eastern end of Islay with fascinating menace. It's a walkers' paradise, with a wild landscape dominated by the island's stark, brooding peaks, the Paps of Jura (named for their breast-like shape). If you're not a hiker, there is little else to do, apart from visiting the **Isle of Jura Distillery** (☎ 820240; tours by appointment) in Craighouse, the island's only village. Orwell stayed in a cottage, **Barnhill** (☖ 01786-850274; per week from £450; sleeps 8), at the far north of the island. If you're a fan or, like him, appreciate remote places, you may want to rent it.

Walking
The **Paps of Jura** provide a tough hill walk that requires good navigational skills and takes eight hours, although the record for the Paps of Jura fell race is just three hours! Look out for adders – the island is infested with them, but they're shy snakes that'll move away as you approach.

A good place to start is by the bridge over the River Corran, about 3 miles north of Craighouse. The first pap you reach is Beinn a' Chaolais (734m), then Beinn an Oir (784m) and finally Beinn Shiantaich (755m). Most people also climb Corra Bheinn (569m) before joining the path that crosses the island to descend to the road.

Sleeping & Eating
Jura Hotel (☎ 820243; www.jurahotel.co.uk; Craighouse; s/d without bathroom £47/70, with bathroom £55/86; **P**) This family-run hotel opposite the distillery is a great place to stay and *the* place for a drink. The rooms at the front have fantastic views, but cost extra. There's good pub grub and excellent evening meals using local produce.

Gwen Boardman (☎ 820379; 7 Woodside, Craighouse; d £34-38; ☒) Just up the hill from the distillery, it's not exactly the picture-perfect island cottage, being part of a row of concrete terraces, but the two comfortable rooms – a family and a twin – are value for money.

Getting There & Away
The only access to Jura is via Islay. A small car ferry shuttles the five minutes between Port Askaig and Feolin (person/car day return £2.40/10.80) roughly hourly from Monday to Saturday, with six services on Sunday. The last ferry back from Jura is 4.45pm Monday to Saturday, and 6.10pm Sunday. A **bus service** (☎ 820314) runs three to five times a day from the ferry to Craighouse and to the north of the island. It meets some ferries, but some journeys are request only, so call the day before.

ISLE OF COLONSAY
☎ 01951 / pop 110

Remote Colonsay is that island paradise you've always dreamed about. Unspoilt, lush green fields bordered by a rocky coastline and perilous cliffs, with superb beaches backed by machair and woodland. The island is in fact home to one of the most spectacular beaches in the Hebrides at **Kiloran Bay**, where Atlantic rollers thunder onto pure golden sands.

It's worth a stroll around the lovely subtropical gardens of **Colonsay House** (admission free; ☖ walled garden noon-5pm Wed & 3-5pm Fri Easter-Sep, discreet wandering in the rest of the estate allowed at other times), in Kiloran, known for their rhododendrons. Bring that midge repellent! Grey seals are often seen around the coast and wild goats inhabit some of the neighbouring islets.

At low tide you can walk across the strand to the small **Isle of Oronsay**, to the south, where the ruins of the priory date from the 14th century.

Sleeping & Eating
Seaview (☎ 200315; s/d £36/60; **P** ☒) You'd have to be a serious insomniac not to get a good sleep in this peaceful croft house in the west of the island. The en-suite rooms are elegant, peaceful, homely, and supremely quiet. There's a telescope in the glass conservatory for peering out to sea, a selection of interesting novels, and a great breakfast with the freshest of eggs. There are also

apartments for weekly rent. To get there; head straight ahead from the ferry and keep going; this road runs around the island, and after three miles, you'll see Seaview signposted on the right.

Keeper's Backpackers Lodge (☎ 200312; dm/tw £10/£28; P ✗) On the edge of the ground of Colonsay House in a former gamekeeper's lodge near Loch Fada in Kiloran, this bunkhouse has a 30-minute walk from the ferry. The kitchen is well equipped and they hire out bikes for £5 per day.

Isle of Colonsay Hotel (☎ 200316; www.colonsay .org.uk; Scalasaig; per person £40-65; restaurant mains £15-19; ⏰ ring ahead for winter opening) A 500m walk straight ahead from the ferry, the island's main hostelry is a plush 18th-century place with well-appointed rooms, some with lovely views and four-poster beds. Their bistro serves bar meals and the more upmarket restaurant serves excellent Scottish cuisine, including a formidable 'Braveheart' sirloin topped with haggis and mustard.

Getting There & Away
CalMac has ferries to Scalasaig from: Oban (person/car £10.90/53, 2¼ hours) daily except Tuesday April-October and thrice weekly November-March; Islay's Port Askaig (person/car £4.10/21.20, 1¼ hours) on Wednesday; and from Kennacraig on the Kintyre Peninsula (person/car £10.90/53, 3½ hours) on Wednesday. Additional sailings operate Saturday from late June to late August.

OBAN
☎ 01631 / pop 8120 / elevation 64m
Oban is a peaceful waterfront town on a delightful bay with sweeping views…out of season. In summer it's hectic, reflecting the popularity of the nearby islands. The town itself, although mildly interesting, relies on its importance as a major connection point with the Inner and Outer Hebrides for its thriving trade. It's the biggest town in the area but it's easy to get around on foot. Atop the hill is **McCaig's Folly**, a curious Victorian recreation of the Colosseum!

Orientation
Facing west and running along the shore of Oban Bay, the town of Oban looks out towards the islands. The ferry terminal is at the southern end of town, next to the train station. North of here, the town is centred on George St, which runs north-south along the harbour. Most of the accommodation is at the northern end of town.

Information
Fancy That (☎ 562996; 13 George St; Internet per 15 min £1.25)
TIC (☎ 563122; info@oban.org.uk; Argyll Sq; ⏰ daily) Helpful, busy, and very well-stocked.

Sights & Activities
To see just how the golden nectar is made **Oban Distillery** (☎ 572004; Stafford St; tours £4; ⏰ Mon-Fri Jan-Mar & Nov, Mon-Sat Apr-Jun & Oct, daily Jul-Sep), in the heart of town, has been producing Oban single malt whisky since 1794.

It's a pleasant 20-minute walk north from the SYHA hostel along the coast to **Dunollie Castle**, built by the MacDougalls of Lorne in the 15th century. It's open all the time and very much a ruin. You could continue along this road to the beach at **Ganavan Sands**, 2.5 miles from Oban.

A TIC leaflet lists regional **bike rides**. They include a 7-mile Gallanach circular tour, a 16-mile route to Seil Island, and routes to Connel, Glenlonan and Kilmore.

Sleeping
You should book your rooms in advance if you're here between June and September. Beware the northern end of George St, where many of the B&Bs charge outrageous prices for substandard rooms.

BUDGET
Oban Backpackers Lodge (☎ 562107; www.scotlands -top-hostels.com; Breadalbane St; dm £12; ⏰ Mar-Oct, ring for winter opening; ✗ 🖥) This big, colourful, clean place has a great vibe and is creatively decorated with cartoon characters and a big painted map on the wall. Facilities are great, with a large kitchen, a pool table and a sociable and very comfy front lounge. Breakfast is available for £1.90.

Jeremy Inglis Hostel (☎ 565065; 21 Airds Cres; dm £7.50, s/d from £11/22) This unusual place is Oban's budget bargain. The homely rooms feel more like a B&B than a hostel and are adorned with flowers and cuddly toys. A continental breakfast is included, which features the friendly, helpful owner's delicious homemade jam. If there's no one at the hostel try its office (McTavish's) across the square from the TIC.

Oban Caravan & Camping Park (☎ 562425; www
.obancaravanpark.com; Gallanachmore Farm; pitches £9-10;
❧ Apr-Oct) Right by the sea, 2½ miles south
of Oban towards Gallanach, this campsite is
in a tranquil spot and has a duckpond that's
a hit with youngsters. A bus service from
the train station stops right outside.

MID-RANGE

There are plenty of B&Bs on Breadalbane St,
and more expensive, sea-facing ones along
Corran Esplanade at the north end of town.

Kilchrenan House (☎ 562663; www.kilchrenanhouse
.co.uk; r per person £30-39; ❧ Feb-Nov; Ⓟ ✗) This
luscious property has elegant décor and a
warm, friendly feel. Most of the thoughtfully
furnished rooms have great views out over
the water, but room Nos 5 and 9 are the
best – No 5 has a huge freestanding bathtub,
perfect for soaking weary bones. Porridge
and kippers for breakfast!

Maridon Guest House (☎ 562670; maridonhse@aol
.com; Dunuaran Rd; s/d £25/44; ✗) Very handy for
the ferry terminal, this chunky house is unmissable with its sky-blue façade. Its seven
large rooms are comfortable, with soft carpets, large wooden beds, and good bathrooms. Some have views over the water and
the owners are tripping over themselves to
look after you.

Palace Hotel (☎ 562294; www.thepalacehotel.active
hotels.com; George St; r per person £20-29) Right in
the heart of town, the old-fashioned Palace
Hotel isn't for those that love their modern
conveniences; it's more about worn armchairs and clinking pipes. What it's got going
for it, though, is the engagingly welcoming
management, its position, price, and views
from the front rooms.

Sandvilla Guesthouse (☎ 562803; www.holidayoban
.co.uk; Breadalbane St; r per person from £20; Ⓟ ✗)
One of the best options on this street, this
efficiently run guesthouse has five good-
sized en-suite rooms. They are modern and
clean, with new carpets, beds, and wooden
furniture and, for once, a decent TV.

Another recommendations is:

Invercloy Guest House (☎ 562058; www.invercloy.co
.uk; Ardconnel Tce; r per person £19-26; Ⓟ ✗) Crisp
white linen and grand views of the CalMac ferry chugging
across the harbour.

TOP END

Manor House (☎ 562087; www.manorhouseoban.com;
Gallanach Rd; dinner, B&B per person from £59) This
delightful small hotel is located south round
the bay, in an 18th century building originally built by the Duke of Argyll to house his
widowed mother. The rooms are decorated
in sumptuous period style, and the salon
and dining rooms are particularly luxurious.
Dinner, included in the price, is a gourmet four-course affair; the restaurant is also
open to the public.

Eating & Drinking

Oban has many fine seafood restaurants
but is short on appealing pubs.

Shellfish kiosk (Queens Park Pl; plates from £2-5;
❧ 11am-7pm) This simple stall overlooking the
harbour in the centre of town produces simple, sublime, seafood straight off the boats.
Prices are incredibly reasonable: scallops
lightly seared in lemon butter and served
with brown bread would put many a pricey
restaurant to shame and cost just £4.95.

Reservation (☎ 563542; 108 George St; mains lunch
£4-8, dinner £8-12; ❧ lunch & dinner) This candlelit
main-street restaurant has a native American theme and makes an atmospheric dinner spot. There are appetising vegetarian
choices such as blue cheese and spinach
croquettes, good-value seafood and game
dishes and very personable service. Best of
all is the offbeat wine-list, with fine offerings from little-known wine nations such
as Uruguay and Moldova.

Julie's (☎ 565952; 37 Stafford St; light meals £4-7;
❧ 10am-5pm Mon-Sat; ✗) Opposite the distillery, this cheerfully scatty tearoom serves up
sandwiches and light meals (try the tasty
smoked salmon), coffees, and toothsome
treacle scones. There's also ice cream, and
tables outside in case of good weather.

Studio (☎ 562030; Craigard Rd; 3 course dinner £14.75;
❧ dinner) A local institution, this place de-
serves its good reputation. When it's full it
can veer to the crowded end of the intimate
scale, but the down-to-earth service is a delight. The food is of quality without pretensions to gourmet status: good, solid Scottish
seafood or roast meats. You're often better
off à la carte than with the set menu.

Oban Inn (☎ 562484; Stafford St) Dating from
1790, this pub overlooks the harbour by
the North Pier. It's a lively spot with a traditional bar and an admirable range of single
malts. There are basic bar meals available,
and it's the best spot in town for a good
chinwag with the locals.

Other recommendations:

Ee.Usk (☎ 565666; North Pier; mains lunch £6-10, dinner £10-17; 🕑 lunch & dinner; ✗ ; wheelchair access) Bright & breezy modern seafood in a great harbourside location.

Gallery (☎ 564641; Gibraltar St; mains lunch £4-7, dinner £9-13; 🕑 lunch & dinner; ✗) Warmly lit and cosy, with great sea bass.

Nevis Bakery (☎ 562262; 12 Stevenson St; 🕑 8am-5.30pm Mon-Sat; snacks £0.80-2, light meals £2-4) Delicious scotch pies and hearty fry-ups.

Oban Chocolate Company (☎ 566099; 9 Craigard Rd) Turn back ye sinners! Luscious hot chocolate and goodies made on-site.

Getting There & Away

BOAT

Numerous CalMac boats link Oban with the Inner and Outer Hebrides. In winter ferries run less often. There are also ferry services to Barra and South Uist (person/car £20.20/74, five/seven hours respectively, five to seven times weekly); Coll (person/car £12.30/72, 2¾ hours, five weekly); Colonsay (person/car £10.90/53, 2¼ hours, three to five weekly); Mull (person/car £3.85/34.50, 45 minutes, five to six daily); and Tiree (person/car £12.30/72, four hours, daily).

BUS

Citylink runs buses to Oban from Glasgow (£12.20, three hours, two to three daily), Inveraray (one hour, two to three daily) and Fort William (£7.80, 1½ hours, four daily Monday to Saturday).

TRAIN

From Glasgow you could opt for a **First Scot Rail** (☎ 08457 48 49 50; www.firstscotrail.com) train to Oban (£15.60, three hours, up to three daily), which is at the end of a scenic branch line that leaves the West Highland line at Crianlarich.

Getting Around

Oban Cycles (☎ 566996; 29 Lochside St; 🕑 Mon-Sat) rents out mountain bikes for £15 per 24 hours.

ISLE OF MULL

pop 2700 / elevation 271m

The darling of the Southern Hebrides, Mull pulsates with its annual tourist injection, which courses through the soggy island every summer. It's not difficult to see why. Easily accessed from the mainland, Mull is an environmental playground with jaw-dropping mountain scenery and a lush, sprawling interior. Offshore is the spiritual magnet that is the holy Isle of Iona, while the main town, Tobermory, has lately experienced a boom of its own: it gets a huge dose of toddler tourism as it's the place where the kids' hit show *Balamory* is filmed.

Orientation & Information

Two-thirds of Mull's population live in Tobermory, in the north. Most visitors to the island arrive in Craignure, on the eastern coast.

There are TICs located at **Craignure** (☎ 08707-200610; 🕑 year-round), opposite the quay, and at **Tobermory** (☎ 0870 720 0625; Main St; 🕑 Apr-Oct). Internet access is available at the SYHA hostel and Spar supermarket in Tobermory.

Sights & Activities

There's little to keep you in Craignure, except to catch the **Mull Rail** (☎ 01680-812494; www .mullrail.co.uk; adult return £4) narrow-gauge, miniature steam train that takes passengers 1½ miles south to **Torosay Castle** (☎ 01680-812421; adult £5; 🕑 10.30am-5pm Apr-Oct). This rambling Victorian mansion in the Scottish Baronial style is set in a beautiful garden. 'Take your time but not our spoons' advises the sign, and you're left to wander at will.

Two miles further on, **Duart Castle** (☎ 812309; www.duartcastle.com; £4.50, 🕑 10.30am-5.30pm Apr–mid -Oct) is the ancestral seat of the Maclean clan and sits in a spectacular position on a rocky outcrop overlooking the Sound of Mull. Mostly dating from the 17th century, a 20th-century restoration removed some of its character, but you can still see the dungeons and appreciate the turbulent history of the castle and the clan who inhabited it.

Mull's capital is **Tobermory**, a sparkling little fishing port in the island's north. The brightly painted houses strung out along a sheltered bay surrounded by wooded hills, make this one of the prettiest villages in Scotland.

The **Marine Discovery Centre** (☎ 01688-302620; 28 Main St; admission free; 🕑 10am-5pm Mon-Fri & 11am-4pm Sun Apr-Oct, 11am-5pm Mon-Fri Nov-Mar) is a research centre that has informative displays on the local marine population. They can organise whale and dolphin spotting trips.

You can walk up **Ben More** (966m), the highest peak on Mull, which has spectacular views across to the surrounding islands

CENTRAL SCOTLAND

when the weather is clear. A trail leads up the mountain from Loch na Keal, by the bridge on the B8035, about 8 miles southwest of Salen. Allow six hours for the return trip.

Sleeping & Eating

TOBERMORY

Tobermory SYHA Hostel (☎ 0870 004 1151; www .syha.org.uk; Main St; dm £11.50; ✆ Mar-Oct; ✗) Set on the waterfront in a cheerful red building, this hostel is highly popular with backpackers and must be booked in advance in summer. It's got an excellent kitchen and spotless, if somewhat austere dorms.

Failte Guest House (☎ 01688-302495; www.failte guesthouse.co.uk; Main St; s/d from £25/48; ✗) This guesthouse has gorgeous rooms, dazzling bathrooms and 'what a great view' windows, in a primo spot overlooking the bay. The house is yet another of the perfect façades along the front, and looks like it could be made of Lego. The best rooms are the upstairs ones, with sloping attic ceilings.

Highland Cottage (☎ 01688-302030; www.highland cottage.co.uk; Breadalbane St; d/tw from £110; 4-course dinner £31.50; ✆ Apr-mid Oct, call for winter opening; P ✗ ;

wheelchair access) A luxurious and intimate small hotel a street back from the harbour in the centre of town. The rooms, named after islands, are small and stylish, with video and CD player; more upmarket rooms have four-poster beds. The restaurant is of the highest class, offering sumptuous Scottish feasts, and is open to the public. Book ahead.

Mishnish Hotel (☎ 01688-302009; Main St; mains £6-12; ✆ lunch & dinner) This fine traditional Scottish pub has survived the deluge of gambling machines afflicting so many of Scotland's watering holes. Behind the bright yellow façade, and amid a healthy mix of locals and tourists, you can burrow into a nook or cranny, toast by the open fireplace or lounge in a booth. Large pub meals are good value and there's often live music and a disco on Saturday nights.

Other recommendations:

34 Main St (☎ 01688-302530; 34 Main St; s/d £10/20; ✗) Two neat and cosy attic rooms, at bargain room-only rates. Why don't more places do this?

Back Brae (☎ 302422; Back Brae; mains £8-14; ✆ dinner; ✗) Snug and atmospheric old restaurant with great Scottish seafood and steaks.

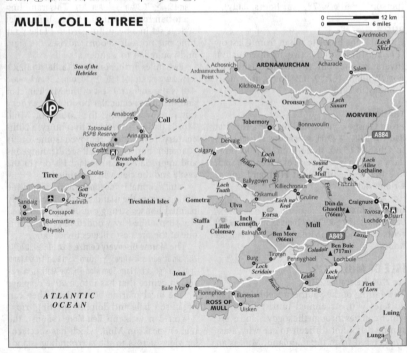

MULL, COLL & TIREE

DERVAIG

Achnadrish House (☎ 01688-400388; achnadrish@hot mail.com; Dervaig Rd; s £30-40, d £50-70; **P**) Two miles out of Dervaig, heading towards Tobermory, this romantic, luxury hideaway offers great value. Set in a 17th-century shooting lodge and surrounded by a lovely grassy garden, it's run by a kindly couple who spoil their guests rotten, with chocolate and home-made shortbread, and there's a lounge with comfy sofas to sink into.

CRAIGNURE

Shieling Holidays (☎ 01680-812496; www.shielingholi days.co.uk; Craignure; dm £9, cottage tent £24; ☑ late Mar-Oct; **P**) A 10 minute walk from the ferry, this large and well-equipped campsite runs a whole lot of activities, including seal-spotting trips. They hire bikes and offer a variety of accommodation, including unique 'cottage tents', with beds, furniture, heating, and simple kitchen. There's a two-night minimum for them; some are en suite.

Getting There & Away

CalMac ferries go from Oban to Craignure (person/car £6.60/46.50 return, 45 minutes, up to six daily). The shortest crossing links Fishnish, 6 miles northwest of Craignure, with Lochaline (person/car £4.05/17.70 return, 15 minutes, at least hourly) on the Morvern Peninsula. From Tobermory a service runs to Kilchoan on the Ardnamurchan Peninsula (person/car £3.70/18.50, 35 minutes, seven daily Monday to Saturday, plus five Sunday June to August).

Getting Around

Bowman's Coaches (☎ 01680-812313) is the main bus operator with connections to the villages from the ferry ports, including a useful Craignure to Tobermory service (£4/6 single/return; one hour, up to six daily Monday to Saturday, twice on Sunday). This route is also run by an express minibus, the **Mull Shuttle** (☎ 01688-302343, £3.50/5.50; meets every ferry). There's also a bus connecting Craignure to Fionnphort (£6/9; 1¼ hours, up to four times daily Monday to Saturday, and once on Sunday) for the island of Iona.

Cycling is a good way to get around and you can rent bikes from a number of places. In Tobermory try **Brown's Hardware Shop** (☎ 01688-302020; Main St); mountain bikes are £13 per day.

ISLE OF IONA

☎ 01681 / pop 130

From the moment you hit Iona's sandy shores you'll probably notice a difference about this island. A harmonious, almost reverent aura pervades the place. Iona is indeed special – but the crowds that pile off the tour buses make it difficult to appreciate. It's best to stay overnight. After things have quietened down a little, you can walk to the top of the hill or look around the ancient graveyard where 48 of Scotland's early kings, including Macbeth, are buried.

Run by Historic Scotland (HS), **Iona Abbey** (☎ 700512; adult £3.30; ☑ 9.30am-6.30pm Apr-Sep, 9.30am-4.30pm Oct-Mar; wheelchair access) is the focus of the island and contains some of the most outstanding examples of stone carvings in Britain. A replica of the astounding St John's Cross stands just outside St Columba's shrine – the original massive 8th-century work is in the **Infirmary Museum** along with many other fine examples of early Christian and medieval carved stones. The spectacular nave, dominated by high stone arches and wooden beams, is a highlight of the abbey – sitting outside is a bench with 'Be Still' etched into the woodwork, summarising the mood nicely.

St Columba landed on Iona from Ireland in 563 before setting out to convert Scotland. He established Iona's monastery, where the *Book of Kells* – the prize attraction of Dublin's Trinity College – is believed to have been transcribed. The book was taken to Kells in Ireland when Viking raids drove the monks from Iona.

The monks returned and the monastery prospered until its destruction during the Reformation. The ruins were given to the Church of Scotland in 1899, and by 1910, priests who established the **Iona Community** had reconstructed the abbey. It's still a flourishing spiritual community holding regular courses and retreats.

Iona Hostel (☎ 700781; www.ionahostel.co.uk; dm £15; **P** ✗), at the far northern end of the island, is sparkling clean and well equipped with 21 comfortably functional rooms, an open fireplace in the common area and terrific views. The staff are friendly, and it's quiet and cosy; the price includes a simple breakfast.

Shore Cottage (☎ 700744; www.shorecottage.co .uk; s/d £30/54; **P** ✗) is a gleaming new B&B

with a cheery welcome and upbeat rooms with bright blue beds and modern en-suite bathrooms. It's a short walk south of the ferry pier.

For sustenance or refreshment, head for the **Argyll Hotel** (☎ 700334; mains £8-14; ❤ 12.30-2pm, 7-8.30pm Feb-Nov), not quite your typical island restaurant, for it's got an admirably ecological outlook. The vegies are home-grown, the eggs are free-range, and even the tasty lamb and beef are from animals that led a fulfilled life. Portions are generous, and there's plenty of vegetarian/vegan choice.

From Fionnphort on the southwestern extremity of Mull a CalMac passenger ferry brings you to Iona (£3.60 return, five minutes, frequent).

ISLE OF STAFFA

This uninhabited island off Mull is truly a magnificent sight, and once there you'll understand why it inspired Mendelssohn to compose *Hebridean Overture*. It forms the eastern end of that geological phenomenon (made up of massive, hexagonal basalt pillars) which begins in Northern Ireland where it's known as the Giant's Causeway. Here the pillars are called the Colonnade and form a series of cathedral-like caverns including **Fingal's Cave**, which pushes out of the sea like a grand pipe organ. You can walk into the cave via a causeway if the sea is calm. Staffa is also visited by a sizeable **puffin colony**. The TICs on Mull book tickets for boat trips (£15, three hours), most of which leave from Fionnphort.

ISLE OF COLL

☎ 01879 / pop 160
This windswept, sleepy little island, 7 miles west of Mull, isn't packed with visitor sites, but for many people that's the attraction. Ringed by sandy beaches, the island is an important refuge for the corncrake, which visits in summer; you can find out about it at the small RSPB post at Totronald. Nearby, Breachacha Castles are two fortified tower houses built by the Maclean Clan.

For accommodation the **Coll Hotel** (☎ 230334; www.collhotel.co.uk; Arinagour; r per person £30-50, mains lunch £5-9, dinner £8-16; P ✗), Coll's only water-ing hole, has tidy rooms with great views and a restaurant serving first-rate seafood.

CalMac ferries run to Coll from Oban (per person/car £12.30/72, 2¾ hours) on Monday, Tuesday, Wednesday, Friday and Saturday, and continue to Tiree.

ISLE OF TIREE

☎ 01879 / pop 770
A low-lying island with some beautiful, sandy beaches, Tiree has one of the best sun-shine records in Britain – there's nowhere for the clouds to get trapped. That's the good news. The bad news is, like Coll, the island is subject to howling Atlantic gales. The canny island, however, has turned this to its ad-vantage. It's the **windsurfing** capital of Scot-land and is even referred to as 'the Hawaii of the north'... perhaps not, but there are competitions during the Tiree Wave Classic each October. Call **Wild Diamond Windsurfing** (☎ 220399; www.tireewindsurfing.com) for informa-tion; they also run windsurfing and kitesurf-ing courses.

For accommodation try **Kirkapol House** (☎ 220729; www.kirkapoltiree.co.uk; Gott Bay; s/d £28/52; P ✗), a converted 19th-century church, and the best place on the island. Dinner is also available here.

British Airways flies from Glasgow to **Tiree airport** (☎ 220309) for around £100 return. CalMac ferries from Oban (per person/car £12.30/72; four hours, one daily) arrive via Coll, and on Thursdays via Barra.

STIRLING REGION

The city of Stirling and its surrounding area looms large in Scottish history and Scots hearts for, with its pivotal position between the Lowlands and Highlands, it has seen the bravest of deeds against the repressive Eng-lish. William Wallace, portrayed in the film *Braveheart*, pursued his freedom struggle in these lands and is commemorated by a gi-gantic monument, which overlooks Ban-nockburn, where Robert the Bruce achieved Scotland's greatest military triumph.

Stirling itself boasts one of the country's finest castles, and has an atmospheric old town, while another well-preserved fortress, Doune, lies nearby and will be familiar to fans of Monty Python. Northwest of here, the Trossachs is a region of stunning natural beauty and a top destination for walkers and cyclists, especially since it recently became, along with the Loch Lomond region, Scot-land's first ever national park. This was the home of yet another legendary Scot, Rob Roy, whose deeds, although somewhat less glittering than those of the freedom fighters, have earned him a Robin Hood–like position in history.

ACTIVITIES

The West Highland Way cuts along the western region from Glasgow to Fort William (see p815). There are numerous other walks in the area. Collins *Walk Loch Lomond & the Trossachs* (£5.99) is a useful guidebook available from TICs.

The **Glasgow, Loch Lomond & Killin Cycle Way** crosses the region from the centre of Glasgow via Balloch on the southern tip of Loch Lomond, Aberfoyle and Callander (in the Trossachs), Loch Earn, Killin and Loch Tay. There are detours through Queen Elizabeth Forest Park and around Loch Katrine. It's a good route for walkers as well as cyclists because it follows forest trails, old train routes and canal towpaths. A brochure showing the route is available from TICs.

GETTING AROUND

First (☎ 01324-613777; www.firstgroup.com) is the main bus operator. Stirling town is the rail hub, but the lines only skirt the region, so you'll be relying on buses if you don't have your own transport.

STIRLING

☎ 01786 / pop 32,700 / elevation 47m

It's no coincidence that strategically vital Stirling, which dominates Scotland's narrow waist, was the location for two of Scotland's most crucial independence battles, involving William Wallace, of *Braveheart* fame, and Robert the Bruce. Its castle is what draws visitors; perched on a crag at the top of the town, it's one of the country's finest medieval fortresses. Staring at it across a couple of miles of open country is the brooding Wallace monument, a Victorian-era creation to honour the giant freedom fighter.

While much of modern Stirling is a fairly banal urban centre, nestled in the streets below the castle are many buildings that bear witness to the town's centuries at the forefront of Scottish power, and wandering the cobbled streets is a real pleasure, especially as the city boasts a couple of old pubs of huge character and charm to quench your thirst at along the way.

Information

Esquires (☎ 443356; Thistles Shopping Centre; per hr £2.50) Internet access.
Library (Corn Exchange Rd; ⊙ 9.30am-5.30pm Mon, Wed, Fri & Sat, 9.30am-7pm Tue & Thu) Free Internet.
Royal Burgh of Stirling Visitors Centre Just below the castle entrance.
TIC (☎ 0870 720 0620; stirlingtic@aillst.ossian.net; 41 Dumbarton Rd; ⊙ Mon-Sat Oct-May, daily Jun-Sep) Very short on courtesy when we visited.

Sights
STIRLING CASTLE

Hold Stirling and you control the country. This simple strategy has ensured that a **castle** (HS; ☎ 450000; combined Stirling Castle & Argyll's Lodging per adult/child £8/2, good audio tour extra £2; ⊙ 9.30am-6.30pm Apr-Sep, 9.30am-5pm Oct-Mar; mostly wheelchair access) has existed here since prehistoric times. Commanding superb views, you cannot help drawing parallels with Edinburgh castle – but many find Stirling more atmospheric. The location, architecture and historical significance combine to make it one of the grandest of all Scottish castles. This means it draws plenty of visitors, so it's advisable to visit in the afternoon; many tourists come on day trips from Edinburgh or Glasgow, so you may have the castle to yourself by about 4pm.

The current building dates from the late-14th to the 16th century, when it was a residence of the Stuart monarchs. The spectacular palace was constructed by French masons in the reign of James V. In the Great Kitchens, there is an excellent depiction of 16th-century food preparation – apparently only men used to work in the kitchen.

This is one of Scotland's most prized attractions and money has been poured into the castle's continuing programme of improvements, which will culminate in the recreation of the king and queen's chambers in the time of James V, with ornate tapestries and furnishings. The **visitors centre**, just below, has useful audiovisual introductions to the castle's history and architecture.

Last entry to the castle is an hour before close. There's a car park next to the castle (£2).

Complete with turrets, the spectacular **Argyll's Lodging** – by the castle at the top of Castle Wynd – is the most impressive 17th-century town house in Scotland. It's the former home of William Alexander, an earl

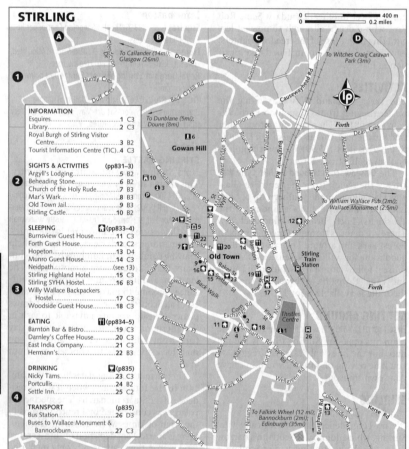

STIRLING

INFORMATION	
Esquires	1 C3
Library	2 C3
Royal Burgh of Stirling Visitor	
Centre	3 B2
Tourist Information Centre (TIC)	4 C3

SIGHTS & ACTIVITIES	(pp831–3)
Argyll's Lodging	5 B2
Beheading Stone	6 B2
Church of the Holy Rude	7 B3
Mar's Wark	8 B3
Old Town Jail	9 B3
Stirling Castle	10 B2

SLEEPING	(pp833–4)
Burnsview Guest House	11 C3
Forth Guest House	12 C2
Hopeton	13 D4
Munro Guest House	14 C3
Neidpath	(see 13)
Stirling Highland Hotel	15 C3
Stirling SYHA Hostel	16 B3
Willy Wallace Backpackers	
Hostel	17 C3
Woodside Guest House	18 C3

EATING	(pp834–5)
Barnton Bar & Bistro	19 C3
Darnley's Coffee House	20 C3
East India Company	21 C3
Hermann's	22 B3

DRINKING	(p835)
Nicky Tams	23 C3
Portcullis	24 B2
Settle Inn	25 C2

TRANSPORT	(p835)
Bus Station	26 D3
Buses to Wallace Monument &	
Bannockburn	27 C3

of Stirling and noted literary figure. It has been tastefully restored to give an insight into lavish 17th-century aristocratic life.

OLD TOWN

Below the castle, the old town has a remarkably different feel to modern Stirling, its cobblestone streets packed with fine examples of 15th- to 17th-century architecture.

Stirling has the best **town wall** in Scotland; built around 1547 it can be followed on the **Back Walk**. The walk follows the line of the wall from Dumbarton Rd (near the TIC) to the castle, and then continues round Castle Rock and back to the Old Town. There are great views from the path, and you could make a short detour to Gowan Hill to see

the **Beheading Stone**, now encased in iron bars to keep ritual axe murderers away. **Mar's Wark**, on Castle Wynd at the head of the Old Town, is the remaining ornate façade of a Renaissance-style town house commissioned in 1569 by the wealthy Earl of Mar, Regent of Scotland during James VI's minority.

The **Church of the Holy Rude** (St John St; admission free; 11am-4pm May-Sep) is a little further down Castle Wynd and has been the town's parish church for 500 years. James VI was crowned here in 1567. The nave and tower date from 1456 and the church features one of the few surviving medieval open-timber roofs.

Old Town Jail (450050; St John St; adult £5.50; 9.30am-6pm Apr-Sep, 9.30am-5pm Oct & Mar, 9.30am-4pm Nov-Feb; wheelchair access) is something of a

WORTH THE TRIP

Scotland's canals were once vital avenues for the transportation of goods but were quickly replaced by the railways and left to fall into dereliction. A recent project restored two of the most important canals, the Union and the Forth & Clyde. With a difference in level of 115 feet, the two were once linked by an arduous series of 11 locks, but the construction of the unique **Falkirk Wheel** has changed all that. Its rotating arms literally scoop boats up and lift them to the higher waterway; it's an engineering marvel that makes a compelling visit.

When you visit the **Wheel** (☎ 08700 500 208; Lime Rd, near Falkirk; www.thefalkirkwheel.co.uk; £8, parking £2; ☒ 9.30am-6.30pm Apr-Oct, 9am-5pm Nov-Mar; wheelchair access to visitors centre only) you will be taken in a small boat, which leaves half-hourly from the visitors centre and, reaching the wheel, get lifted up to the Union Canal before being gently brought back down to the Forth & Clyde again in the wheel's other arm. The ascent takes about 15 minutes.

Falkirk is 10 miles southeast of Stirling, and the Wheel is just off the A803 a mile west of town; it's well signposted. There are regular trains from Stirling, Edinburgh, and Glasgow to Falkirk High station. Cross the carpark to Drossie St and head downhill until you hit Gartcows Rd. Turn left into it; from here, local bus No 3 will take you to the wheel.

tourist trap but it will definitely be a hit with kids, as actors in costume portray the hardships of prison life in an entertaining and innovative style.

NATIONAL WALLACE MONUMENT

Two miles north of Stirling is Scotland's towering Victorian Gothic **monument to Sir William Wallace** (☎ 472140; www.nationalwallacemonument.com; adult £6; ☒ 10am-5pm Mar-May & Oct, 10am-6pm Jun, 9.30am-6.30pm Jul & Aug, 9.30am-5pm Sep, 10.30am-4pm Nov-Feb), who was hung, drawn and quartered by the English in 1305 and was portrayed by Mel Gibson in the film *Braveheart*. The view of seven battlegrounds – one of them at Stirling Bridge where Wallace defeated the English in 1297 – from the top is as breathtaking as the climb. The monument contains interesting displays including a parade of other Scottish heroes and Wallace's mighty two-handed sword. Clearly the man was no weakling.

Local bus Nos 62 and 63 run from Murray Pl in Stirling to the visitors' centre, from where frequent shuttle buses (50p) run up the hill to the monument itself. Otherwise, it's about a half-hour walk from the centre of Stirling.

BANNOCKBURN

On 24 June 1314 the greatest victory in Scotland's struggle to remain independent from the English took place at the Battle of Bannockburn. Robert the Bruce overcame superior numbers and sent Edward II's English force running for their lives.

At the **Bannockburn Heritage Centre** (☎ 812664; adult £3.50; ☒ 10am-5.30pm Easter-Oct, 10.30am-4pm Nov-24 Dec & Feb-Easter; wheelchair access), run by the Nation Trust for Scotland (NTS), the story is told in a simple and eloquent exhibition, including an audiovisual display. There is also a handy timeline of events. Outside is the Borestone site, said to be Robert the Bruce's command post before the battle. His grim-looking statue is also here, dressed in full battle gear and mounted on a charger.

The site is 2 miles south of Stirling and never closes; the last audiovisual show at the Heritage Centre is half an hour before closing. You can reach the site on bus No 51 from Murray Pl in the centre of Stirling.

Tours

From May to early October **City Sightseeing** (☎ 446611; www.citysightseeingstirling.co.uk) has an open-top, hop-on, hop-off bus tour hourly from the castle through the city to the Wallace Monument; there are two buses every hour. A day ticket costs £6.

Sleeping

BUDGET

Witches Craig Caravan & Camping Park (☎ 474947; www.witchescraig.co.uk; Blairlogie; tent pitch £10.50-12.50; ☒ Apr-Oct) This site is in a brilliant spot right at the foot of the Ochil Hills, which are begging to be walked! The facilities are clean, the welcome friendly, and it's just 3 miles east of Stirling, just after the turnoff to the Wallace Monument by the A91.

CENTRAL SCOTLAND

Willy Wallace Backpackers Hostel (☎ 446773; www.willywallacehostel.com; 77 Murray Pl; dm £12, tw & d £26-30; ✗ ☐) This highly convenient central hostel is friendly, spacious, and sociable. The dormitories are large and light, there's free tea and coffee, a good kitchen, and 24-hour access. Other amenities include a laundry service and Sass, the exuberant hostel dog. The helpful folk here will make an onward booking for you free of charge.

Stirling SYHA Hostel (☎ 473442; www.syha.org.uk; St John St; dm £13.50; ℗ ✗ ☐ ; wheelchair access) In a perfect location on the way up to the castle in the old town, this hostel is concealed by the façade of an 18th-century church. Once inside, however, it's clean, efficient, and modern. It's often described by travellers as the best SYHA hostel they've seen. The dorms are small but well equipped, there's a handful of twins with single beds, and there's access until 2am.

MID-RANGE

Stirling has heaps of B&B accommodation. There are several on Linden Ave, close to the bus station; the road to the National Wallace Monument is also rich hunting ground.

Forth Guest House (☎ 471020; www.forthguesthouse.freeserve.co.uk; 23 Forth Pl; s/d from £20/45; ✗) You can't miss this small Georgian terrace just over the bridge near the train station: its façade and front garden are a riot of blooming flowers possibly visible from orbit. The rooms are ultracommodious and furnished with style but no frippery. Bathrooms are modern, and the top floor rooms with their sloping ceilings are especially lovable. There's easy parking outside, an important consideration in Stirling.

Munro Guest House (☎ 472685; www.munroguesthouse.co.uk; 14 Princes St; s/d £28/40, with en suite £30/44; ✗) This snug B&B is very handy for train and bus station and, although right in the centre of town, is on a quiet side street. The rooms are small but sinfully comfortable, with big beds to stretch out on. The breakfast is another thing that keeps people coming back.

Woodside Guest House (☎ 475470; 4 Back Walk footpath, off Dumbarton Rd; s/d with shower from £20/32; ✗) This striking building right across from the TIC offers very well-priced accommodation in a location where higher rates could have been expected. The rooms are peaceful, and management is friendly if a little

eccentric. The showers and the breakfasts are nothing special, but that can be forgiven at this price.

Burns View Guest House (☎ 451002; m.watt@totalise.co.uk; 1 Albert Pl; d £36-44; ✗) This small B&B has three en-suite rooms and will appeal to those who don't plan to roll in pissed from the pub at three in the morning. Definitely not for party animals, it's run with sobriety by thoughtful owners who enjoy hosting discerning guests.

Other recommendations:

Hopeton (☎ 473418; 28 Linden Ave; s/d £20/36; ℗ ✗)

Neidpath (☎ 469017; 24 Linden Ave; s/d from £30/42; ℗ ✗)

TOP END

Stirling Highland Hotel (☎ 272727; www.paramount-hotels.co.uk; Spittal St; r from £126; ℗ ✗ ☐ ☎) The town's smartest hotel is a sympathetic refurbishment of the old high school. Although the public areas still feel a little institutional, the rooms are of the highest comfort, and the facilities, which include pool, spa, gym, sauna, and squash courts, are a rarity for a city centre hotel in these parts. Check the website for special offers before booking.

Eating

East India Company (☎ 471330; 7 Viewfield Pl; mains £5-9; ☽ dinner) Despite an unprepossessing façade, this basement Indian restaurant is one of the best spots in Scotland for a curry. Sumptuously decorated to resemble a ship's stateroom, with portraits of tea-barons on the wall to conjure images of the days of the clippers, the restaurant offers exquisite dishes from all parts of India. There's a buffet dinner available, but you're better off going à la carte, and savouring the unspeakably toothsome flavours.

Hermann's (☎ 450632; 58 Broad St; starters £3-6, mains £12-16; ☽ lunch & dinner; ✗) This quiet Scottish-Austrian restaurant is one of Stirling's more elegant choices. Focus on the solid wooden tables or the bright back conservatory rather than the tartan carpet or misplaced wildlife photos, and enjoy anything from Cullen skink or venison stew to schnitzel and spätzle. There's always a tempting vegetarian option, and you can accompany your meal with Austrian wines, which are little-known but of pleasing and delicate quality.

Darnley's Coffee House (☎ 474468; 18 Bow St; snacks under £5; ☽ 10am-6pm; ✗) Housed in one of Stirling's most historic buildings, this is a longtime favourite for a pit-stop as you visit the sights. While espresso fans will query the lack of a machine, there's plenty of cosy atmosphere and a range of healthy snacks.

Barnton Bar & Bistro (☎ 461698; 312 Barnton St; lunch £4-6; ☽ 10am-late) Opposite the main post office, this popular student hangout serves an all-day breakfast that would not leave Pavarotti complaining (£4.95) and scrumptious baguettes as well as a range of typical lunches. It's also not a bad spot for a beer or two of an evening.

Drinking

Settle Inn (☎ 474609; St Mary's Wynd) Stirling's oldest pub is a gem. The cheery staff go beyond the call to make both visitors and locals feel at home, and there's always an interesting guest ale on tap. There are plenty of atmospheric nooks to settle down with a whisky against the winter chills too. Vies with the castle as the best place to spend a couple of hours in Stirling.

Portcullis (☎ 472290; Castle Wynd) This gracious old pub is another fine drinking option. With an atmospheric beer garden, this stonebuilt former primary school serves good ales and malts and has a cosy buzz inside on winter evenings. Food is served until 9pm, but you may need an hour or so to get through the massive portions.

Other recommendations:

Nicky Tams (29 Baker St) Small and convivial pub with frequent live music upstairs and a resident ghost.

William Wallace (Causewayhead Roundabout, below National Wallace Monument) Fine tartan-bedecked thirstquencher after climbing the monument. Dedicated corner for Old Farts.

Getting There & Away

BUS

Citylink services are available to and from Aberdeen (£15.90, three hours, hourly including some indirect); Dundee (£7.60, 1½ hours, half-hourly); Edinburgh (£4, one hour, hourly, also operated by First); Fort William (£14.60, 2¾ hours, one direct daily, other services via Glasgow); Glasgow (£4, 45 minutes, hourly); and Perth (£4.70, 50 minutes, half-hourly).

TRAIN

Half-hourly services run to Edinburgh (£5.50, 50 minutes) and Glasgow (£5.70,

40 minutes). There are hourly services to Perth (£8.30, 30 minutes), Dundee (£12.70, 50 minutes) and Aberdeen (£31.20, two hours).

AROUND STIRLING
Dunblane

☎ 01786 / pop 7900 / elevation 87m

Dunblane, 5 miles northwest of Stirling, is a small, pretty town with a couple of good attractions. It is difficult not to associate the town with the horrific massacre that took place in the primary school in 1996. For visitor information, contact the **TIC** (☎ 824428; Stirling Rd; ☽ May–mid-Sep).

Dunblane Cathedral (HS; ☎ 823388; admission free; ☽ 9.30am-6.30pm Mon-Sat, 1-6.30pm Sun Apr-Sep, 9.30am- 4.30pm Mon-Sat, 2-4.30pm Sun Oct-Mar) is the main attraction and it's well worth a detour. The simple, elegant, sandstone building is a superb example of the Gothic style. A standing stone commemorates the slain children, while there's also a 10th century carved Celtic stone at the head of the nave.

First runs frequent buses to Dunblane from Stirling. Trains to Dunblane run every 15 to 30 minutes from Stirling.

Doune

☎ 01786 / pop 1635 / elevation 58m

Doune is a quiet if slightly twee rural town, but was once the capital of the ancient kingdom of Menteith and later became a famous centre for the manufacture of sporrans and pistols.

Doune Castle (HS; ☎ 841742; adult £3; ☽ 9.30am-6.30pm Apr-Oct, 9.30am-4pm Nov-Mar) is one of the best-preserved 14th-century castles in Scotland, having remained largely unchanged since it was built for the Duke of Albany. It was a favourite royal hunting lodge, but was also of great strategic importance because it controlled the route between the Lowlands and Highlands. Mary Queen of Scots stayed here, as did Bonnie Prince Charlie – the first as a guest, the second as a prisoner. There are great views from the castle walls and the lofty gatehouse is impressive, rising nearly 30m. Many visitors come for the Monty Python connection: the castle featured in the *Holy Grail*.

Doune is 8 miles northwest of Stirling. First buses connect to Stirling (30 minutes) roughly hourly from Monday to Saturday, less frequently on Sunday.

THE TROSSACHS

A region of outstanding natural beauty, the Trossachs first gained popularity as a tourist destination in the early 19th century, when curious visitors came from all over Britain drawn by the romantic prose of Sir Walter Scott's *Lady of the Lake,* inspired by Loch Katrine, and *Rob Roy,* about the bravado and derring-do of the region's most famous son.

A transition zone between the Lowlands and the Highlands, it's an area of forested hills and achingly beautiful lakes that offer great cycling and hiking within fairly easy reach of Glasgow and Edinburgh. While the name originally referred to the narrow glen between Loch Katrine and Loch Achray, it now describes a wider scenic area whose variety of wildlife and delicate environment led to it becoming part of Scotland's first national park. Created in 2002, Loch Lomond & the Trossachs National Park (see p818) straddles the shires of Argyll and Stirling and protects a zone that was in danger of being harmed by excessive tourist development.

In summer the region can be overburdened with coach tours, but many of these are daytrippers, so peaceful long evenings gazing at the reflections in the nearest loch are still possible.

Aberfoyle & Around

☎ 01877 / pop 575 / elevation 87m

Crawling with visitors most weekends, Aberfoyle, is a hit with domestic coach tourists and best avoided by everyone else, unless you're using it as a base from which to explore the beautiful Trossachs.

Aberfoyle is on the eastern edge of the Queen Elizabeth Forest Park, which stretches right across to the hills beside Loch Lomond. Visit the barn-sized **TIC** (☎ 0870 720 0604; Main St; 10am-5pm daily Apr-Oct, 10am-4pm Sat & Sun Nov-Mar) for information. It also has Internet for £1.80 per 15 minutes.

Four miles east off the A81 is one of Scotland's two lakes (as opposed to its lochs), **Lake Menteith**. The substantial ruins of **Inchmahome Priory** (HS; ☎ 385294; adult £3.50; 9.30am-6.30pm Apr-Sep), where Mary Queen of Scots was kept safe as a child during Henry VIII's 'Rough Wooing' (when Henry attacked Stirling to force Mary Queen of Scots to marry his son in order to unite the kingdoms), are on Inchmahome Island. A ferry, included in the admission price, takes visitors from the village to the Augustinian priory.

On a hill, about half a mile north of Aberfoyle, on the A821, is the **Queen Elizabeth Forest Park Visitors Centre** (☎ 382258; parking fee £1; 10am-6pm Mar-24 Dec), which has audiovisual displays and information about the many walks and cycle routes in and around the park. It's worth visiting for the views.

WALKING & CYCLING

Waymarked trails start from the visitors centre on a hill above the town.

An excellent 20-mile circular cycle route links with the **ferry** (☎ 376316) at Loch Katrine.

ROB ROY

Tourist literature in The Trossachs doesn't let you forget that this is Rob Roy country. Robert MacGregor (1671–1734) was the wild leader of the wildest of Scotland's clans, Clan Gregor. Roy is an anglicisation of the Gaelic 'ruadh' (red): he was nicknamed for his ginger locks. Although he claimed direct descent from a 10th-century king of the Scots and rights to the lands the clan occupied, these estates stood between powerful neighbours who had the MacGregors outlawed, hence their sobriquet 'Children of the Mist'. Adopting another surname, Rob became a prosperous livestock trader, before a dodgy deal led to a warrant for his arrest.

A legendary swordsman, the fugitive from justice then became notorious for his daring raids into the Lowlands to carry off cattle and sheep. He was forever hiding from potential captors; he was twice imprisoned, but escaped dramatically on both occasions. He finally turned himself in, and received his liberty and a pardon from the king. He lies buried in the churchyard at Balquhidder, by Loch Voil (see the boxed text, p838); his uncompromising epitaph reads 'MacGregor despite them'. Much like Robin Hood, the life of this bandit has been glorified over the years, largely due to Sir Walter Scott's novel and the 1995 film. He has a reputation as a champion of the poor and is viewed fondly by Scots, who see his life as a symbol of the long struggle of the common folk against the inequable ownership of vast tracts of the country by landed aristocrats.

From Aberfoyle, join the Glasgow, Loch Lomond & Killin Cycle Way (see p831) on the forest trail, or take the A821 over Duke's Pass. Following the southern shore of Loch Achray, you reach the pier on Loch Katrine. The ferry should drop you at Stronachlachar (£4.50) on the western shore: it sails at 11am daily except Wednesday; note that afternoon sailings don't stop here. From Stronachlachar, follow the B829 via Loch Ard to Aberfoyle.

SLEEPING & EATING
Altskeith (☎ 387266; www.altskeith.com; Loch Ard Rd; s/d £48/66; **P** ✕) This country hotel on the shores of stunning Loch Ard is one of the Trossachs' most tempting places to stay. An 18th-century house with history has been lovingly renovated by the engagingly bouncy host, who is full of advice on how to best enjoy your stay. The rooms have big wooden beds, perfect for lolling in to admire the views of the loch; downstairs is an eminently comfortable lounge and bar. The hotel is 3½ miles west of Aberfoyle on the B829.

Forth Inn (☎ 382372; Main St; bar meals £5-6; ✕ food served all day; **P** ✕) In the middle of the village, this busy pub is the best spot around for a drink and for value-packed pub grub. It's often full of coach parties during the day, but if you head on down in the evening you'll find a much more enjoyable local atmosphere. Don't worry if you have one too many, as there are rooms upstairs, which, although a tad overpriced, are modern and comfortable with plenty of natural light and bathrooms where everything works.

GETTING THERE & AWAY
First buses connect Aberfoyle to Stirling (one hour, up to four daily). For details of the useful bus service, Trossachs Trundler, see p838.

Callander
☎ 01877 / pop 2750 / elevation 130m
Callander has been pulling in the tourists for over 150 years, especially domestic daytrippers from Glasgow and Stirling who flock to the town on weekends, clogging the main street with traffic. It's a good base to explore the surrounding area and not a bad spot to just stroll about.

The crowded still but helpful **Rob Roy & Trossachs Visitors Centre** (☎ 0870 720 0628; info@callander.visitscotland.com; Ancaster Sq; ✕ daily Mar-Dec, Sat & Sun Jan-Feb) is also the TIC. A Rob Roy audiovisual (£3.25) gives some insight into the famous man.

DOT Computing (☎ 331571; 50 Main St; per hr £4; ✕ 10am-9pm Mon-Sat, 1-9pm Sun) has Internet access.

SLEEPING
Callander seems to have more B&Bs than private homes. There are some great places to stay for all budgets.

Trossachs Backpackers (☎ 331200; www.scottish-hostel.com; dm £13.50, self-catering f per person £16; **P** ✕ 🖳 ; wheelchair access) This purpose-built property is in a beautifully isolated spot a mile from town. The dorms are excellent, very spacious with four or six beds and have their own bathroom. Rates include continental breakfast, and there's a helpful, easy-going atmosphere. A new lounge has big windows looking out across the countryside, and there's on-site cycle hire and plenty of advice on potential routes. To get there, take Bridge St off Main St, then turn right onto Invertrossachs Rd and follow it for a mile.

Roman Camp Hotel (☎ 330003; www.roman-camp-hotel.co.uk; s/d from £75/125; **P** ✕ ; wheelchair access) Beautifully located by the river, this mansion is named for a presumed Roman ruin in the neighbouring field. A typical country house, its endearing features include a lounge with blazing fire, as well as a library with a tiny secret chapel. There are three grades of room; the standards are certainly luxurious, but the superior ones are even more appealing, with period furniture, armchairs, and a fireplace. The restaurant is open to the public and very highly rated (dinner £39).

Arden House (☎ 330235; www.ardenhouse.org.uk; Bracklinn Rd; s/d £35/60; ✕ Apr-Oct; **P** ✕) Very close to the centre, but well away from cars and crowds, this guesthouse is a wonderful place for grown-ups (no kids under 14 allowed) and was used as the setting for the TV series *Doctor Finlay's Casebook*. The rooms, named for characters in the show, are decorated with faultless taste and include a suite with great views. The hosts are solicitous and enjoy a conversation.

Other recommendations include:
Abbotsford Lodge (☎ 330066; Stirling Rd; s/d from £22/43; **P**) Comfy rooms with or without bathroom, and a relaxed welcome.

SOMETHING SPECIAL

The village of Balquhidder (bal-whidder), 11 miles northwest of Callander, is famous as being the final resting place of Rob Roy, who is buried with his wife and two sons in the small churchyard. No less a drawcard is the sublime and romantic hotel **Monachyle Mhor** (☎ 01877-384622; www.monachylemhor .com; s/d from £55/95; Feb-Dec; P). A working farm with exceptional hospitality, it overlooks two lochs and is utterly relaxing. The rooms have plenty of character and furniture you wish could fit in your suitcase but the highlight is the fine food, based around game, served up in the restaurant. Reservations are, not surprisingly, essential.

Buses from Callander that are bound for Killin will drop you off at the Kings House Hotel, 9 miles north of Callander on the A84. Balquhidder is 2 miles west of here, but you'll have to walk. The Monachyle Mhor is just beyond the village.

East Mains House (☎ 330535; www.eastmainshouse .net; Bridgend; s/d from £24/44; P) A Georgian house set in large garden, with en-suite rooms, and sociable lounge.

EATING & DRINKING

Callander Meadows (☎ 330181; 24 Main St; mains £9-11; lunch & dinner Wed-Sun, daily Jun-Aug;) Run by chefs who formerly plied their trade at famous Gleneagles, this is a sophisticated restaurant with price that are surprisingly reasonable: if you have lunch here for six quid, you'll feel like Rob Roy after a successful cattle raid. The menu is mainly Scottish, and the dishes are prepared with flair and presented with style. Upstairs there are three rooms (from £46 to £54) elegantly kitted out with dark-varnished furnishings and striped wallpaper. One of the rooms has a four-poster bed and all are colourful in the most stylish way.

Lade Inn (☎ 330152; Kilmahog). A mile north of town, this sociable local is the sort of appealing and inviting place that leaves you wondering where your afternoon went to. It's child-friendly, does decent bar meals (£4 to £8), and serves a good pint of ale, sometimes home-brewed. There's live music at weekends.

GETTING THERE & AWAY

First and Morrison's buses from Stirling (45 minutes) run hourly from Monday to Saturday and less frequently on Sunday.

There is also a Citylink bus between Edinburgh (£9.10, 1¾ hours, one daily) and Fort William (£13.30, 2¼ hours, one daily), stopping in Callander.

The vintage **Trossachs Trundler** (☎ 01786-442707) is a useful bus service that does a circuit including Callander, Aberfoyle, Port of Menteith and Loch Katrine. The bus operates eight times daily (except Wednesday), June to September; the full trip around the Trossachs takes 1½ hours and costs £5. The service is wheelchair accessible. Alternatively, postbus No 24 does the same circuit twice daily Monday to Friday (once on Saturday) via Port of Menteith and Brig o'Turk.

GETTING AROUND

Based at Trossachs Backpackers, the **Wheels Cycling Centre** (☎ 331100; www.scottish-cycling.com) hires out bikes for £7.50/12.50 per half-/full day.

Loch Katrine

The rugged area around this beautiful loch, 6 miles north of Aberfoyle and 10 miles west of Callander, is the heart of the Trossachs. From late March to late October, **SS Sir Walter Scott** (☎ 01877-376316; www.lochkatrine.com) sails Loch Katrine from Trossachs Pier at the eastern tip of the loch. The morning journey leaves at 11am daily except Wednesday and stops on the other side at Stronachlachar before returning (£6.90 return); two daily afternoon cruises just do a circuit (£5.90).

KILLIN

☎ 01567 / pop 670 / elevation 183m

Roaring through the centre of this little village are the frothy **Falls of Dochart**. The canny locals have made the best of their unusual water feature, pulling in many a passing tourist coach. Killin is in the northeastern corner of Stirlingshire and is a handy base for exploration of the mighty mountains and glens.

The helpful, informative **TIC** (☎ 0870 720 0627; Main St; daily Mar-Oct, Sat & Sun Feb) is in the Breadalbane Folklore Centre.

Walking & Cycling

Five miles northeast of Killin and rising above Loch Tay is Ben Lawers (1214m; see

Ben Lawers – a Classic Route, p853). There's a NTS visitors centre and trails lead to the summit.

Killin is at the northern end of the cycle way from Glasgow (see p831).

Sleeping & Eating

Falls of Dochart Inn (☎ 820270; www.thefallsinn.co.uk; s/d £30/60; mains £7-10; ☺ bar food all day; **P**) Overlooking the falls across the bridge from town, this old coaching inn oozes character. The en-suite rooms have been renovated but still have a fair dollop of historical flavour (try and get one with falls view), while downstairs the bar is equipped for rain, hail, or shine, with outdoor tables and a crackling log fire in the cosy interior. The bar food is pretty good, and there's a restaurant menu in the evenings, too.

Killin SYHA Hostel (☎ 0870 004 1131; www.syha.org .uk; dm £11; ☺ Mar-Oct; ✗) This popular hangout for walkers is a friendly spot with a good kitchen, efficient drying room, and clean dorms. It's situated in a lovely Victorian mansion at the northern end of the village about a mile from the centre on the main road.

Getting There & Away

First operates a service from Stirling via Callander (£4.75, 1¾ hours, twice daily Monday to Friday, one on Saturday). There is also a postbus service (No 202) between Aberfeldy and Killin (1½ hours, Monday to Saturday).

Killin is on the Citylink bus route linking Perth (£4.30, 1¼ hours) and Oban (£7.90, 1½ hours); there are two buses each way on Friday-Monday only. Daily buses to Fort William and Edinburgh stop at the service station on the main road four miles south of town.

FIFE

This proud little county, a tongue of land between the Firths of Forth and Tay, was home to generations of Scottish monarchs and still likes to style itself 'The Kingdom of Fife'. Also a centre for early Scottish Christianity, it has many attractions for the visitor.

Not least of these is St Andrews, dominated by its university, the most ancient in Scotland. It has a wealth of stately buildings

and, as the birthplace and headquarters of golf, draws professionals and keen slashers alike to take on the Old Course and its famously blustery conditions.

While much of Fife's southern coast has become a depressing sprawl of suburbia, home of Edinburgh commuters, once you leave these behind you reach the enchanting corner of the East Neuk, dotted with fishing villages where you can munch on fresh local crabs while gazing across the Firth of Forth. In the west, the dignified village of Culross is an incredibly well-preserved 17th-century burgh.

Despite integration with the rest of Scotland, Fife has held onto its unique Lowland identity. Many people enter 'the kingdom' via the Forth Rd or Tay Rd bridges – perhaps crossing these enormous gateways adds to the sense of arriving somewhere different. Certainly the laidback and serene nature of the region is immediately apparent; rolling, tumbling, lush farmland dominates the countryside.

GETTING AROUND

Fife Council produces a useful transport map, *Getting Around Fife*, available from TICs, bus and train stations and has a **Public Transport Information Line** (☎ 01592-416060). **Stagecoach** (☎ 01334-474238; www.stagecoachbus .com) is the main bus operator.

If you're driving from the Forth Rd Bridge to St Andrews, a slower but much more scenic route than the M90/A91 is along the signposted Fife Coastal Tourist Route, although you're better off joining it at Leven rather than trawling through a succession of dormitory suburbs of Edinburgh around Kirkcaldy.

ST ANDREWS

☎ 01334 / pop 14,200 / elevation 33m

The name of Fife's major attraction conjures up two things: golf and Prince William. The former, as it is the sport's spiritual home and headquarters of its governing body, the latter because the man who calls the head of state 'Granny' is an undergraduate at the university, which is Scotland's oldest.

The Old Course, the world's most famous, has a striking seaside location at the western end of town. Although it's difficult to get a game (see the boxed text, p841), it's still a thrilling experience to stroll the hallowed turf. Even if you're not into belting little white balls with a stick, it's worth making tracks to St Andrews anyway, as it boasts an impressive concoction of medieval ruins and idyllic coastal scenery. Sometimes, however, it can feel like the least Scottish of places, with six thousand university students and staff from all over Britain in what, although technically a city, is a very small place.

The golf and the generally wealthy student population have made St Andrews, at least on the surface, an affluent sort of place. It's said by some that the dollar sign was invented at the university here; whether true or not, there's certainly not a lot to make the shoestring traveller smile. St Andrews

is a place to forget the budget, stroll the picturesque streets, and enjoy the startling quality of the local restaurants.

History

It's believed St Andrews was founded by the Greek monk St Regulus in the 4th century. He brought important relics from Greece, including some of the bones of St Andrew, who became Scotland's patron saint.

The town soon grew into a major pilgrimage centre for the shrine of the saint and developed into an ecclesiastical centre. Scotland's first university was founded here in 1410.

Although golf was being played here by the 15th century, the Old Course dates

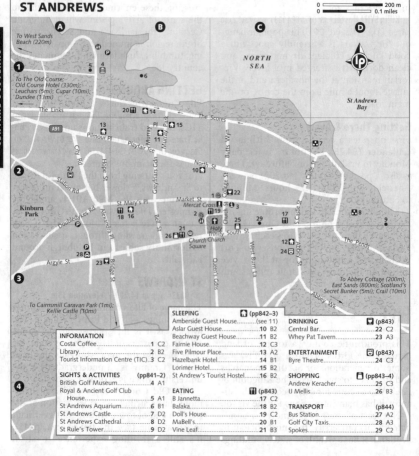

ST ANDREWS

| 0 | 200 m |
| 0 | 0.1 miles |

NORTH SEA

St Andrews Bay

To West Sands Beach (220m)

To The Old Course; Old Course Hotel (330m); Leuchars (5mi); Cupar (10mi); Dundee (13mi)

The Links
The Scores
A91
Pilmour Pl
Playfair Tce
City Rd
Sutton Rd
Hope St
Murray Pl
Murray Park
Greyfriars Gdns
North St
Butts Wynd
College St
The Scores

Kinburn Park
Doubledykes Rd
Alexandra Pl
St Mary's Pl
Bell St
Market St
Mercat Cross
Church St
Holy Trinity Church
Church Square
South St
West Burn La
N Castle St
S Castle St
Abbey St
The Pends
Abbey Wk

Argyle St
Bridge St
Queen's Gdns

To Cairnsmill Caravan Park (1mi); Kellie Castle (10mi)

To Abbey Cottage (200m); East Sands (800m); Scotland's Secret Bunker (5mi); Crail (10mi)

SLEEPING ⌂ (pp842–3)	
Amberside Guest House...........(see 11)	
Aslar Guest House.................10 B2	
Beachway Guest House...........11 B2	
Fairnie House......................12 C3	
Five Pilmour Place................13 A2	
Hazelbank Hotel...................14 B1	
Lorimer Hotel......................15 B2	
St Andrew's Tourist Hostel......16 B2	

DRINKING 🍺 (p843)	
Central Bar.........................22 C2	
Whey Pat Tavern..................23 A3	

| ENTERTAINMENT 🎭 (p843) | |
| Byre Theatre.......................24 C3 | |

SHOPPING 🛍 (pp843–4)	
Andrew Keracher..................25 C3	
IJ Mellis............................26 B3	

INFORMATION	
Costa Coffee.......................1 C2	
Library..............................2 B2	
Tourist Information Centre (TIC)..3 C2	

SIGHTS & ACTIVITIES (pp841–2)	
British Golf Museum................4 A1	
Royal & Ancient Golf Club House...5 A1	
St Andrews Aquarium..............6 B1	
St Andrews Castle..................7 D2	
St Andrews Cathedral..............8 D2	
St Rule's Tower.....................9 D2	

EATING 🍴 (p843)	
B Jannetta.........................17 C2	
Balaka..............................18 B2	
Doll's House.......................19 C2	
MaBell's...........................20 B1	
Vine Leaf..........................21 B3	

TRANSPORT (p844)	
Bus Station........................27 A2	
Golf City Taxis.....................28 A3	
Spokes.............................29 C2	

from the following century. The Royal & Ancient Golf Club was founded in 1754 and the imposing clubhouse was built a hundred years later.

Orientation & Information

St Andrews preserves its medieval plan of parallel streets with small closes leading off them. The most important parts of the old town lie east of the bus station. The university buildings are integrated into the central part of the town. There's a small harbour near the cathedral and two sandy beaches.

Useful businesses:

Costa Coffee (Market St; per hr £3; ☺ 8am-6pm Mon-Sat, 10am-6pm Sun) Internet access.

St Andrews Library (☎ 412685; Church Square; ☺ 9.30am-5pm Mon, Fri, Sat, 9.30am-7pm Tue-Thu) Free Internet access.

TIC (☎ 472021; www.standrews.com; standrewstic@kftb .ossian.net; 70 Market St; ☺ Mon-Sat Oct-Mar, daily Apr-Sep) Mountains of information about Fife.

Sights

ST ANDREWS CATHEDRAL

The ruins of St Andrews' once mighty **cathedral** (HS; ☎ 472563; cathedral & castle £4, cathedral only £2.50; ☺ 9.30am-6.30pm Apr-Sep, 9.30am-4.30pm Oct-Mar) have been described as 'the greatest achievement in Scottish medieval architecture'. It was once the largest and one of the most magnificent cathedrals in the country, and it's possible to get a sense of its immensity from the remaining but ruined western end.

Although it was founded in 1160, it was not consecrated until 1318. It stood as the focus of this important pilgrimage centre until 1559, when it was pillaged during the Reformation.

St Andrews' alleged bones lay under the high altar; until the cathedral was built, they had been enshrined in the nearby Church of St Regulus (St Rule). All that remains is **St Rule's Tower**, well worth the climb for the view across St Andrews and a great place for taking photographs. In the same area are parts of the ruined 13th-century **priory**. The visitors centre includes the calefactory, the only room where the monks could warm themselves by a fire. There's also a **museum** with a collection of Celtic crosses and gravestones found on the site. There's an entry fee for access to the museum and St Rule's Tower, but the ruins you can absorb freely.

ST ANDREWS CASTLE

With dramatic coastline views, **St Andrews castle** (HS; ☎ 477196; cathedral & castle £4, castle only

---

PLAYING THE OLD COURSE

Golf has been played at St Andrews since the 15th century and by 1457 was apparently so popular that James II had to place a ban on it because it was interfering with his troops' archery practice. Everyone knows that St Andrews is the home of golf, but few people realise that anyone can play on the Old Course, the world's most famous golf course. Although it lies beside the exclusive, all-male (female bartenders and waiters are, unsurprisingly, allowed) Royal & Ancient Golf Club, the Old Course is a public course and is not owned by the club.

Getting a tee-off time is something of a lottery. Unless you book months in advance, the only chance you have of playing here is by entering a ballot at the **caddie office** (☎ 466666) before 2pm on the day before you wish to play. Be warned that applications by ballot are normally heavily oversubscribed, and green fees are a mere £110. There's no play allowed on Sunday. If your number doesn't come up, there are five other public courses in the area, none with quite the cachet of the Old Course but all of them significantly cheaper. Their fees are: New £55, Jubilee £50, Eden £30, Strathtyrum £20 and Balgove £10. If you play on a windy day expect those scores to balloon: Nick Faldo famously stated that when it blows here, 'even the seagulls walk'.

Advance bookings for the Old Course can be made by letter, telephone, or online to the **Reservations Office, St Andrews Links Trust** (☎ 01334-466666; www.standrews.org.uk; Pilmour House, St Andrews, Fife KY16 9SF). You must reserve before 30 Jun the year before you wish to play. It's advisable to book at least a year in advance and you must present a handicap certificate from your club.

The trust runs frequent guided walks of the Old Course; these take half an hour (£1) and will take you to famous landmarks like the Swilcan Bridge and the Road Hole bunker. Call the number above for times, which vary according to events on the course.

£3; 9.30am-6.30pm Apr-Sep, 9.30am-4.30pm Oct-Mar), round from the cathedral, is mainly in ruins, but the site itself is evocative. The most interesting thing to see is the complex of **siege tunnels**, said to be the best surviving example of castle siege engineering in Europe. You can walk along the damp, mossy tunnels, lit by electric lights – but be warned, it helps if you're short!

Given St Andrews' ecclesiastical beginnings, it's no surprise to learn that the castle was founded around 1200 as the fortified home of the bishop. In the 1450s the young king James II often stayed here. After the execution of Protestant reformers in 1545, other reformers retaliated by murdering Cardinal Beaton and taking over the castle. The cardinal's body was hung from a window in the Fore Tower before being tossed into the bottle-shaped dungeon. The reformers then spent almost a year holed up in the castle, during which they dug the siege tunnels.

THE SCORES

From the castle, the Scores follows the coast west. At the west end is **St Andrews Aquarium** (474786; www.standrewsaquarium.co.uk; adult £5.85; 10am-6pm Apr-Oct, call for winter opening; wheelchair access), where, bizarrely, you can snack on fish and chips in the café after your visit.

Nearby, the **British Golf Museum** (460046; www.britishgolfmuseum.co.uk; Bruce Embankment; adult £4; 9.30am-5.30pm Apr–mid-Oct, reduced hrs winter; wheelchair access, carers free) is a must for all obsessed golfers. It's an interesting, modern museum with audiovisual displays and touch screens, as well as plenty of golfing memorabilia.

Opposite the museum is the **Royal & Ancient Golf Club house**. Outside the club is the **Old Course**, which you can stroll on in the evenings, and beside it stretch the sands of the beach made famous by the film *Chariots of Fire*.

Sleeping

Accommodation in St Andrews is overpriced, but there's a wide choice, except during summer when things fill up quickly. The biggest concentration of B&Bs is on Murray Park, off the Scores.

BUDGET

St Andrews Tourist Hostel (479911; fax 479988; St Marys Pl; dm £12-16;) The town's only hostel fills up quickly, and should be reserved ahead. Close to the bus station, it has bright, clean, and spacious dorms with high ceilings, a big TV lounge, kitchen and laundry service. There's 24 hour access and a friendly buzz.

Cairnsmill Caravan Park (473604; www.ukparks .co.uk/cairnsmill; Largo Rd; 2-person pitches £12; Apr-Oct;) One mile south of St Andrews, off the A915, this superbly equipped campsite is on a crest with brilliant views of town. There's not much space between sites – they pack 'em in, but with a pool, snooker room and bar, who's complaining?

MID-RANGE

Abbey Cottage (473727; coull@lineone.net; Abbey Walk; d £46-50;) Set in a large rambling garden on the edge of town, this kindly place is quirky and engaging. It feels like you're staying on a farm rather than in town, what with fresh eggs for breakfast, tasty porridge, and a doocot (dovecote) outside. The three rooms are comfy, but even better is the relaxed and humorous atmosphere. The owner is a photographer, and stunning wildlife shots decorate the round breakfast room.

Fairnie House (474094; www.fairniehouse.free serve.co.uk; 10 Abbey St; s/d from £28/42) This congenial B&B is ideally located in the centre and has one attractive double and two twin rooms with colourful carpets and solid wooden beds. The owner is an animal lover – there's even a pet jackdaw – and you'll feel at ease mighty quickly. The communal dining room also encourages conversation.

Aslar Guest House (473460; www.aslar.com; 120 North St; s/d from £36/72;) This is an elegant Georgian terraced house with sumptuous rooms: they are large, stylishly fitted-out in light wood, and have satellite TV and DVD player. There's a real feeling of relaxed luxury without fussiness, and the hosts are enchanting. You'll need to book well ahead.

Hazelbank Hotel (472466; www.hazelbank.com; 28 the Scores; d from £70;) This hotel offers the best value accommodation along the Scores. Family-run, the place is characterised by a genuine welcome and exceptional personal service. The best rooms are those at the front; they cost a little more but are worth every penny for their super views along the beach and out to sea.

Lorimer House (476599; www.lorimerhouse .com; 19 Murray Park; per person £25-40;) This Victorian terrace is one of several good B&Bs

on this street and has a narrow staircase and small rooms which are a bit cluttered but comfortable nevertheless. The family rooms are much more spacious and the top-floor room has good views.

Other recommendations include:

Amberside Guest House (☎ 474644; 4 Murray Park; s/d from £30/50)

Beachway Guest House (☎ 473319; 6 Murray Park; s/d £30/50) Much better inside than out. Vegemite for breakfast!

Top End

Five Pilmour Place (☎ 478665; www.5pilmourplace .com; 5 Pilmour Pl; s/d from £50/100; ✗ ⬚) This intimate newly opened guesthouse very close to the Old Course is one of the town's best places to stay. Much thought has gone in to creating a contemporary space that doesn't compromise on either style or comfort. Unobtrusively decorated with curious artefacts, it's run with class seldom seen in larger establishments. The rooms, with luscious duvets on the king-sized beds, plasma-screen TV, CD and DVD player, invoke such languor that you're in danger of missing the gourmet breakfast.

Old Course Hotel (☎ 474371; www.oldcoursehotel .co.uk; r from £269; P ✗) This imposing hotel is where the top players bed down when the British Open is in town. A vast, luxurious establishment right by the golf course and the western end of town, it has its own championship course, resident golf pros, a spa, and a team of therapists and beauticians. Often cheaper deals are advertised on their website.

Eating & Drinking

Doll's House (☎ 477422; 3 Church Sq; mains £10-18; ☯ lunch & dinner; ✗) Kitted out like the bedroom of a Victorian child with dark wood furniture and rocking horses, this offers a highly enjoyable lunching or dining experience. Apart from the atmospheric space and outdoor terrace, the cuisine is a class act, with inventive flair applied to traditional Scottish and European dishes served in generous portions. The set meals are brilliant value: just £6.95 for a two course lunch, or £11.95 for dinner before 7pm.

Balaka (☎ 474825; 3 Alexandra Pl; starters £3-4, mains £7-14; ☯ lunch & dinner Mon-Sat; ✗) This Bangladeshi restaurant comes highly recommended for its curries, which are seasoned with herbs grown in its own plot of land. Sean Connery

has got his accent round the menu here; he can't fail to have been impressed by the remarkably good-natured service. The £6.95 lunch deal is worthwhile.

B Jannetta (☎ 473285; 31 South St; 2-dip cone from £1.50; ✗) This is a St Andrews institution, which offers 52 varieties of ice cream. On a hot weekend there's a constant stream of people outside the place feverishly licking delicious cones before they become puddles. The most popular flavour? Vanilla. The weirdest? Irn Bru!

Central Bar (☎ 478296; 77 Market St) Right in the heart of things, this bar is also something of an institution, although the polished wood sometimes creaks under the weight of hundreds of frustrated would-be golfers waiting for the rain to clear. There's always a wide range of Scottish beers, including a few guest selections.

MaBells (☎ 472622; 40 the Scores; bar meals £5-9; ☯ noon-9pm Sun-Thu, noon-8pm Fri & Sat) This basement bar below the St Andrews Golf Hotel is a trendy hangout for the university crowd and a somewhat brainless preclub venue at weekends. Better is the wide range of excellent bar food, which draws everyone from hungry golfers debating missed putts to students flirting over piles of textbooks.

Other recommendations include:

Vine Leaf (☎ 477497; 131 South St; 2-course dinner £19.95; ☯ dinner Tue-Sun; ✗) Gourmet seafood, game and vegetarian dishes in a refined atmosphere.

Whey Pat Tavern (☎ 477740; 1 Bridge St, cnr Argyle St) An old-fashioned convivial pub with bar stools and comfy bench seating. It has a range of ales on tap and is a good place to escape the crowds.

Entertainment

Check the local *What's On* guide, available from the TIC, for current events. You could also check their website, www.standrews .com.

Byre Theatre (☎ 475000; www.byretheatre.com; Abbey St) Originally housed in a cowshed, hence the name, St Andrews main theatre now resides in a smart new building that cleverly takes advantage of natural light. As well as the performances, it's got a very pleasant café and bar.

Shopping

There are heaps of charity shops in St Andrews, thronged with students looking for fashion bargains.

Andrew Keracher (☎ 472541; 73 South St) Widely regarded as Scotland's finest fishmonger.

IJ Mellis (☎ 471410; 149 South St) A wealth of cheeses that you can smell halfway down the street.

Getting There & Away

Stagecoach has a bus service from Edinburgh to St Andrews (£5.50, two hours, hourly). Some of these can be booked extra cheaply over the Internet at www.megabus.com. There are also buses to Glasgow (£5.80; 2½ hours, hourly), Stirling (£5.20; two hours, six to seven Monday to Saturday) and Dundee (30 minutes, half hourly).

The nearest train station to St Andrews is Leuchars (*lew*-kars), 5 miles away. It's on the coastal line, servicing Edinburgh (£8.90, one hour, hourly), Dundee, Aberdeen and Inverness. Bus Nos 94, 96 and 99 connect the station with St Andrews very frequently.

Getting Around

To park in the centre of town you need a voucher, bought from the TIC or various shops in town. Parking police are vigilant.

A taxi from the train station at Leuchars to the town centre costs around £8 with **Golf City Taxis** (☎ 477788).

Spokes (☎ 477835; 77 South St; ◯ 9am-5.30pm Mon-Sat) hires out hybrids and mountain bikes from £10.50 per day.

AROUND ST ANDREWS
Kellie Castle

A magnificent example of Lowland Scottish domestic architecture, **Kellie Castle** (NTS: ☎ 01333-720271; castle/grounds only £5/2; ◯ 1-5pm Easter weekend & Jun-Sep, garden & grounds ◯ 9.30am-dusk year-round) has creaky floors, crooked little doorways and some marvellous works of art, which give it an air of authenticity. It's set in a beautiful garden and many rooms contain superb plasterwork, the Vine room is the most exquisite. The original part of the building dates from 1360 and was enlarged to its present dimensions around 1606.

Kellie Castle is 3 miles northwest of Pittenweem on the B9171. Stagecoach Fife bus Nos 61A and 61B from St Andrews pass the castle gates five times daily from Monday to Saturday.

Scotland's Secret Bunker

A compelling and fascinating relic of the Cold War, **Scotland's Secret Bunker** (☎ 01333-310301; www.secretbunker.co.uk; adult £7.20; ◯ 10am-6pm Apr-Oct, last admission 5pm; 🖳) is by the B9131 about 5 miles south of St Andrews. It was earmarked to be one of Britain's underground command and control centres and a home for Scots leaders in the event of nuclear war. Hidden 30 metres underground and surrounded by reinforced concrete are the austere operation rooms, communication centre and dormitories. It's very authentic and uses original artefacts of the period, which make for an absorbing exploration.

If the spine-tingling atmosphere isn't enough, a harrowing film called *The War Game*, which was banned by the BBC, gives a horrifying account of the realities of a nuclear war. It's graphic and definitely not for kids, but highlights the madness of the era. The Scottish Campaign for Nuclear Disarmament (CND) has an exhibition, bringing home the realities of Britain's current nuclear Trident policy. There's also an underground café and free Internet access.

Stagecoach Fife bus No 61A runs hourly (from Monday to Saturday) between St Andrews and Anstruther, and can drop you at a crossroads close to the bunker.

EAST NEUK
☎ 01333

South of St Andrews, the section of the southern Fife coast that stretches from Leven east to the point at Fife Ness is known as East Neuk. There are picturesque fishing villages and some good coastal walks in the area.

Crail
pop 1700

Pretty wee Crail has a much photographed harbour surrounded by stone cottages with red-tiled roofs. You can buy lobster and crabs from a kiosk at the harbour. Just to the east is a large grassed area with seating, the perfect place to munch on your shellfish while admiring the view across to the Isle of May.

See the small and friendly **TIC** (☎ 450869; 62 Marketgait; ◯ 10am-1pm & 2-5pm Mon-Sat, noon-5pm Sun Apr-Sep) for information. The village's history and involvement with the fishing industry is outlined in the **Crail Museum** (☎ 450869; admission free; ◯ Easter & Jun-Sep), in the same building.

Caiplie House (☎ 450564; www.caipliehouse.com; 53 High St North; r with/without en suite £55/45; ✗), in the village centre, has large rooms with big soft beds perfect for flopping down after a day's touring, walking, or golfing, a lounge with chessboard, and a pretty dining room where breakfast is served: dinners can also be arranged. The top floor room has a sea view.

Crail is located 10 miles southeast of St Andrews. Stagecoach bus No 95 connects them hourly.

Anstruther
pop 3440

This is a bubbly fishing village with lots of twisting streets, interesting wynds and knick-knack shops lining Rodger and High Sts. Walking about is definitely the best way to absorb the atmosphere of the place, starting at the harbour, once one of Scotland's busiest ports.

The **TIC** (☎ 311073; Harbourhead; ☽ Apr-mid Oct) is by the harbour and is extremely helpful and efficient.

Drop into the **Scottish Fisheries Museum** (☎ 310628; adult/child £4.50/free; ☽ 10am-4.30pm Mon-Sat, noon-4.30pm Sun Oct-Mar, 10am-5.30pm Mon-Sat, 11am-5pm Sun Apr-Sep; wheelchair access), beside the TIC. Displays include a typical fishing family's cottage and the history of Anstruther's once important herring and whaling industries.

From the harbour you can take a four- to five-hour excursion aboard the **May Princess** (☎ 310103; www.isleofmayferry.com; adult £15; Sat-Thu May-Oct) to the Isle of May, a nature reserve; sailing times depend on the tide (check the website) and the crossing takes just under an hour. You might well spot dolphins on the way across; once there the cliffs are packed with breeding kittiwakes, razorbills, guillemots, shags and puffins from May to July. Inland are the remains of **St Adrian's Chapel**, a 12th-century monastery.

SLEEPING & EATING

Spindrift (☎ 310573; www.thespindrift.co.uk; Pittenweem Rd; s/d £41/62; ℗ ✗) One of the best-value guesthouses in Fife, this former sea-captain's house is a good place to spoil yourself. No detail of generous hospitality is lacking here; there are even teddy bears to welcome you to the en-suite rooms, one of which is decked out like a ship's cabin with views out to sea. There's a bar/lounge with a good selection of Scottish beers, and the exceptionally friendly hosts do a generous breakfast, including porridge which has been voted the best in the Kingdom.

Gaberlunzie House (☎ 312337; 18 High St; s/d £25/40) This snug 16th-century cottage is next to the best pub in town and offers likeably informal accommodation. The rooms are en suite and some can be a little noisy from the road outside. The intriguing name is an old Scottish word for a wandering beggar, but don't worry, that's not what the hosts think of their guests…

Cellar Restaurant (☎ 310378; 24 East Green; 3 course set-dinner £30; ☽ lunch Wed-Sun, dinner Mon-Sat; ✗) Tucked away behind the museum, this is famous for its variety of seafood. It's heavily booked in summer; if you get a table, adorn it with local crab, lobster, or the excellent marinated herring.

Dreel Tavern (☎ 310727; 16 High St; bar meals £5-11; ☽ lunch & dinner) This atmospheric traditional pub appeals for its low ceilings and bright and breezy staff. There's appetising food served and several real ales on tap, including the brilliantly-named 'Bitter and Twisted', a Stirlingshire-brewed beer oozing with fresh hoppy flavour.

Other recommendations:
Anstruther Fish Bar (42 Shore St; ☽ 11.30am-10pm) Pricy at £6.20 for a haddock supper, but Prince William's favourite chip shop redefines the genre.

Seafood Restaurant (☎ 730327; 16 West End, St Monans; ☽ lunch & dinner; ✗) Swish seafood winner on the harbour in St Monans, four miles west. The Dover sole is a star.

GETTING THERE & AWAY

The hourly Stagecoach bus No 95 runs daily from Leven (45 minutes) to Anstruther and on to St Andrews (45 minutes) via Crail.

FALKLAND

☎ 01337 / pop 1180 / elevation 130m

Below the soft ridges of the Lomond Hills in the centre of Fife is the charming village of Falkland. Rising majestically out of the town centre and dominating the skyline is the outstanding 16th-century **Falkland Palace** (NTS; ☎ 857397; adult £7; ☽ 10am-6pm Mon-Sat, 1-5pm Sun Mar-Oct, last admission an hr before closing), a country residence of the Stuart monarchs. Mary Queen of Scots is said to have spent the happiest days of her life 'playing the country girl in the woods and parks' at Falkland.

French and Scottish craftspeople were employed to create this masterpiece of Scottish Gothic architecture, built between 1501 and 1541 to replace a castle dating from the 12th century. The chapel, which has a beautiful painted ceiling, and the king's bedchamber have both been restored. Don't miss the prodigious 17th-century Flemish hunting tapestries in the hall.

Outside in the ample gardens, one feature of an ancient royal leisure-centre still exists: the oldest royal tennis court in Britain, built in 1539 for James V, is in the grounds and still in use.

Sleeping & Eating

Burgh Lodge (☎ 857710; www.burghlodge.co.uk; Back Wynd; dm £12, tw £24, r 4-/5-person £44/56; P ☒ 🖳 ; wheelchair access) An excellent budget choice, this sparklingly refurbished hostel has terrific views of the Lomond Hills and enthusiastic management. The rooms are bright as a new pin; there are dorm beds as well as twin and family rooms available. Guests have use of a modern kitchen and laundry service; this is as upmarket as hostel accommodation gets.

Hunting Lodge (☎ 857226; www.s-h-systems.co.uk/hotels/huntinglodge.html; High St; s/d £25/40, with en suite £40/55; P) This cosy little inn opposite the palace dates back to 1607 and oozes character and unstuffy local charm. It's a great place for a pint at any time of day, and has the added benefit of homely upstairs rooms, with or without bathroom.

Getting There & Away

Eleven miles north of Falkland is Kirkcaldy. Stagecoach buses arrive roughly every two hours to/from Perth (one hour) and Cupar (30 minutes), from where you can connect to St Andrews, from Monday to Saturday.

ROSYTH FERRIES

Rosyth, 3 miles south of unappealing Dunfermline, is home to a ferry-link with mainland Europe, namely Zeebrugge in Belgium (see p966 for further details of this service). From Edinburgh, Stagecoach bus X2 runs to Rosyth (35 minutes) and connects with the ferries. There are frequent local services from Dunfermline, and buses to the train station at nearby Inverkeithing connect with rail services to Edinburgh, Perth, and Inverness.

CULROSS
☎ 01383 / pop 540

An enchanting little town, Culross (*cooross*) is the best-preserved example of a 17th-century Scottish burgh and the NTS owns 20 of the buildings, including the palace. Small, red-tiled, whitewashed buildings line the cobbled streets and the winding Back Causeway to the Abbey is embellished with whimsical street-front stone cottages.

As the birthplace of St Mungo, Glasgow's patron saint, Culross was an important religious centre from the 6th century. The burgh developed as a trading centre under the business-like laird George Bruce (a descendant of Robert the Bruce), whose mining techniques involved digging long tunnels under the sea to reach coal. Vigorous trade resulted between Culross and the Forth ports and Holland, enabling Bruce to build and complete the palace by 1611. When a storm flooded the tunnels and min-

WORTH THE TRIP

The unattractive sprawl of Dunfermline conceals an excellent historical attraction, easily accessed on a day-trip from Edinburgh, Stirling or St Andrews. In a commanding but sheltered spot, **Dunfermline Abbey** (HS; ☎ 01383-739026; adult £2.50; ⏰ 9.30am-6.30pm Apr-Sep, 9.30am-4.30pm Mon-Wed & Sat, 9.30am-12.30pm Thu, 2-4.30pm Sun Oct-Mar) was built by David I in the 12th century as a Benedictine monastery. It grew into a major religious centre, eclipsing the island of Iona (off Mull) as the favourite royal burial ground. Many monarchs are buried here, including Robert the Bruce, under the pulpit. The area you can explore is the wonderful Norman nave with ornate columns and superb stained-glass windows. Note the picture of Robert the Bruce standing over the devil (England perhaps?).

Next to the abbey are the ruins of **Dunfermline Palace** (admission included in abbey ticket) rebuilt from the abbey guesthouse in the 16th century for James VI, whose son, the ill-fated Charles I, was born here in 1600.

There are frequent buses to Edinburgh (40 minutes), Stirling (1¼ hours) and St Andrews (1¼ hours). There are also regular trains from Edinburgh (30 minutes).

ing became impossible the town switched to making linen and shoes.

You can visit **Culross Palace** (☎ 880359; adult £5; ✆ noon-5pm Easter-Sep), more a large house than a palace, which features decorative, painted woodwork and an interior largely unchanged since the early 17th century, as well as a recreated formal garden from the era. The **Town House** and the **Study** (included in palace ticket), also early 17th century, are open to the public, but the other NTS properties can only be viewed from the outside.

On the hill is the grand, ruined **Culross Abbey** (HS; admission free; ✆ 9.30am-7pm Mon-Sat, 2-7pm Sun Apr-Sep, 9.30am-4pm Mon-Sat, 2-4pm Sun Oct-Mar), founded by the Cistercians in 1217; the choir of the abbey church is now the parish church.

Culross is 12 miles west of the Forth Rd Bridge, off the A985. Stagecoach bus No 14/14A runs between Stirling (one hour, hourly) and Dunfermline (20 minutes, hourly), via Culross.

PERTHSHIRE & KINROSS

The joys of Perthshire are many and varied; it's a region crammed full of attractions and has a magical quality to it, especially on a summer evening. You never know what's around the next corner: another stunning lake perhaps, or a picture-perfect Scottish village?

The main town, Perth, is an excellent little place, quiet, but with an outstanding attraction in the lavish country mansion that is Scone Palace. Further north, another sumptuous residence in Blair Castle stands near the touristy town of Pitlochry.

It's more remote western Perthshire that really gets pulses racing, though. The enchanting valley of Glen Lyon winds its way to a dead end west of the village of Fortingall, birthplace of Pontius Pilate. Stunning Loch Tay is nearby; the river Tay runs east from here towards Dunkeld, which has an outstanding cathedral, among the most beautifully situated in the country.

Scenically, Perthshire and Kinross contain in miniature as many variations in terrain as Scotland itself, from the bleak expanse of Rannoch Moor in the west to the rich farmland of the Carse of Gowrie between Perth and Dundee.

GETTING AROUND

The A9, Scotland's busiest road, cuts across the centre of this region through Perth and Pitlochry. It's the fast route into the Highlands and to Inverness, and very busy.

Perth & Kinross Council produce a useful public transport map that's available at all TICS in the area; it shows all services in the region. **Stagecoach** (☎ 01738-629339; www.stage coachbus.com) and **Strathtay Scottish** (☎ 01382-228345) run local services.

Trains run alongside the A9, destined for Aviemore and Inverness. The other main line connects Perth with Stirling (in the south) and Dundee and Arbroath (in the east).

PERTH

☎ 01738 / pop 43,500 / elevation 22m

Elegantly perched on the banks of the Tay, Scotland's longest river, Perth is a noble old town that was once the country's capital. On its outskirts, Scone Palace, a country house of staggering luxury, is built alongside the mound where Scotland's kings were once crowned. It's a must-see, but the city itself is a bustling, liveable place enriched by stately architecture, fine galleries, spacious parks, and a few cracking pubs and restaurants. It's a beautiful place, but happily not one that dolls itself up to flirt coyly with tourists, which just adds to its considerable appeal. It's an important regional hub and is within easy striking distance of Edinburgh and Glasgow.

Information

AK Bell Library (York Pl) Free Internet access.
Gig@Bytes (☎ 451580; 5 St Paul's Sq; per hr £5; ✆ 10am-6.30pm Mon-Sat, noon-5pm Sun) Internet access.
Laundry Shop (50 George St)
Perth Royal Infirmary (☎ 623311; Taymount Tce)
TIC (☎ 450 600; ✆ 9am-5pm Mon-Fri, 10am-3pm Sat Nov-Mar, 9am-6pm Mon-Sat, 10am-5pm Sun Apr-Jun, 9am-7pm Mon-Sat, 9.30am-6pm Sun Jul-Sep, 9am-5pm Mon-Sat, 10am-5pm Sun Oct) Will furnish you with a map of Perth and well-prepared information sheets.

Sights
SCONE PALACE

So thanks to all at once and to each one,
Whom we invite to see us crowned at Scone.

Macbeth

Decadent **Scone Palace** (skoon; ☎ 552300; www
.scone-palace.co.uk; adult £6.75; ⏰ 9.30am-5.30pm Apr-
Oct, last admission 5pm; partial wheelchair access), 2
miles north of Perth, was built in 1580 on a
site intrinsic to Scottish history. Here in 838,
Kenneth MacAlpin became the first king of
a united Scotland and brought the Stone of
Destiny, on which all Scottish kings were
ceremonially invested, to Moot Hill. In 1296
Edward I of England carted the talisman off
to Westminster Abbey. It remained there for
700 years before being returned to Scotland,
when it went to Edinburgh Castle rather
than Scone. See The Stone of Destiny, p749
for details.

A visit here doesn't really conjure up
hoary days of bearded warrior kings swear-
ing oaths in the mist, however, as Scone is
a 19th century mansion of the highest level
of luxury. The interior of the palace is a
gallery of fine French furniture, including
Marie Antoinette's writing table, numerous
clocks, and a needlework hanging by Mary
Queen of Scots. There's porcelain galore
and antique Chinese vases, and the walls
are festooned with regal portraits of aristocrats. Even the cornices, ceilings and walls
are exquisite (the drawing room's wallpaper
is silk!). The Murray family, Earls of Mansfield, have owned the palace for almost 400
years and still host family functions in their
sumptuous abode.

Outside, the resident peacocks unfold
their splendid plumage in the magnificent
grounds, which incorporate pine arbour with
some magnificent trees, a butterfly garden,
and a maze to keep the kids happy. Moot
Hill, where the old kings were crowned, is
topped by a chapel and faces the palace.

From the centre of Perth, cross the bridge,
turn left, and keep bearing left until you
reach the gates of the estate (15 to 20 minutes). From here, it's another half-mile
or so to the palace. Stagecoach bus No 3,
and Strathtay bus No 58 stop at the gates
roughly hourly; the tourist office will give
you a complete timetable.

ST JOHN'S KIRK

One block south of High St, this redoubta-
ble stone **church** (admission free; ⏰ 10am-4pm Mon-
Sat, 10am-1pm Sun May-Sep, before services during the rest

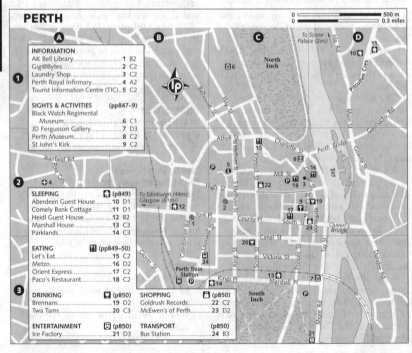

PERTH

INFORMATION	
AK Bell Library	1 B2
Gig@Bytes	2 C2
Laundry Shop	3 C2
Perth Royal Infirmary	4 A2
Tourist Information Centre (TIC)	5 C2

SIGHTS & ACTIVITIES	(pp847–9)
Black Watch Regimental Museum	6 C1
JD Fergusson Gallery	7 D3
Perth Museum	8 C2
St John's Kirk	9 C2

SLEEPING	(p849)
Aberdeen Guest House	10 D1
Comely Bank Cottage	11 D1
Heidl Guest House	12 B2
Marshall House	13 C3
Parklands	14 C3

EATING	(pp849–50)
Let's Eat	15 C2
Metzo	16 C2
Orient Express	17 C2
Paco's Restaurant	18 C2

DRINKING	(p850)
Brennans	19 D2
Twa Tams	20 C3

SHOPPING	(p850)
Goldrush Records	22 C2
McEwen's of Perth	23 D2

ENTERTAINMENT	(p850)
Ice Factory	21 D3

TRANSPORT	(p850)
Bus Station	24 B3

To Scone Palace (2mi)

North Inch

To Edinburgh (44mi); Glasgow (61mi)

Perth Train Station

South Inch

Queen's Bridge

of the year) dates from the 15th century, although the site was first consecrated in 1126 and serves as an impressive reminder of the Reformation in Scotland. In 1559 John Knox preached a powerful sermon here, inciting a frenzied destruction of Scone abbey and other religious sites. Perth used to be known as St John's Town after this church; the football team here is still called St Johnstone.

PERTH MUSEUM

The city's main **museum** (☎ 632488; cnr George & Charlotte Sts; admission free; ☺ Mon-Sat 10am-5pm year-round & also 1-4.30pm Sun early Jun-late Sep; wheelchair access) is worth a stroll through for the elegant neo-classical interior alone. There's a varied shower of exhibits, ranging from portraits of dour lairds to some good local social history. A geological room provides more entertainment for the young, while there are often excellent temporary exhibitions.

JD FERGUSSON GALLERY

Within the original Perth waterworks building, aptly titled the Round House, this **gallery** (☎ 441944; cnr Marshall Pl & Tay St; admission free; ☺ 10am-5pm Mon-Sat) has the most extensive collection of work by notable Scottish Colourist and Perthshire local JD Fergusson. At time of writing it was closed for renovation, but should be open by early 2005.

BLACK WATCH REGIMENTAL MUSEUM

Housed in a mansion on the edge of North Inch, this **museum** (☎ 0131 310 8530; admission by donation, £3.50 recommended; ☺ 10am-3.30pm Mon-Fri Oct-Apr, 10am-4.30pm Mon-Sat May-Sep) honours Scotland's foremost regiment. Formed in 1725 to combat rural banditry, the Black Watch have fought in numerous campaigns, re-created here with paintings, memorabilia, anecdotes, and countless medals. There's little attempt at historical perspective: there's justifiable pride in the regiment's role in the gruelling trench warfare of WWI, where it suffered nearly 30,000 casualties, but no hint of sheepishness about less glorious colonial engagements, such as against the 'Fuzzy Wuzzies' of Sudan. Most recently, the Black Watch have been engaged in Basra, Iraq, now sporting combat trousers instead of the traditional kilts. At the time of research the regiment's future was in doubt as the government looked at ways to streamline the British Army.

Sleeping

Most of the accommodation is across the river, especially along Pitcullen Cres, which is exclusively devoted to B&Bs. There is currently no hostel accommodation in Perth.

Comely Bank Cottage (☎ 631118; www.comely bankcottage.co.uk; 19 Pitcullen Cres; s/d £28/46; [P] [X]) This is one of the best B&Bs on this stretch, a beautifully kept family home offering large and commodious rooms with spacious en suite. The hospitable owner will make you feel very welcome.

Parklands (☎ 622451; www.theparklandshotel.com; 2 St Leonard's Bank; s/d from £69/89; [P] [X] [💻]) This is a delightful place overlooking the verdant expanse of South Inch. While the rooms conserve the character of this beautiful building, formerly the residence of the town's mayors, they also offer modern conveniences such as CD and DVD players and wireless broadband Internet. The rooms are all different in size and price, but all offer a high degree of comfort. The restaurant has a fine reputation and a terrace to lap up the Perthshire sun.

Aberdeen Guest House (☎ 633183; www.smooth hound.co.uk/hotels/aberdeenguesthouse; 13 Pitcullen Cres; s/d from £20/40) Despite being on a principal road, this B&B offers a cosy retreat from its flower-bedecked window boxes to its well-furnished, spacious rooms. Breakfasts are worth getting up for, and the host thoughtful and considerate.

Heidl Guest House (☎ 635031; www.heidl.co.uk; 43 York Pl; s/d £22/38; [P]) The Heidl stands out with its green painted façade and is quite a bargain. The rooms are light and have good-sized beds, and even the one facing the busy road isn't too noisy. Shared bathrooms (there's also one en suite) are very clean and the owners are helpful.

Another recommendation is:

Marshall House (☎ 442886; gallagher@marshall-guest -house.freeserve-co.uk; 6 Marshall Pl; s/d £30/40; [P] [X]) Excellent location right opposite the parklands of South Inch.

Eating

Metzo (☎ 626016; 33 George St; mains £10-13; ☺ lunch & dinner Mon-Sat, dinner Sun; [X] ; wheelchair access) This is a zippy modern eatery whose light contemporary interior – shaved floorboards, abstract art, and large windows – buzzes with chatter. There's substance to the style; enticing daily specials enhance a French bistro-style menu bursting with confident flavours and served with effortless charm.

Orient Express (☎ 633334; 47 South St; main dishes £5-10; ☽ lunch & dinner; ☒ , wheelchair access) This eatery has changed character a few times recently but is now a tastefully decorated and quietly stylish Turkish restaurant – there are certainly no tourist board posters up here. The fresh and lively dishes come with warm bread and include a humus feisty with garlic, yoghurt-smothered Iskender kebabs and more delights. A shot of raki makes the perfect digestive. There's a daily lunch special for £4.95.

Let's Eat (☎ 643377; 79 Kinnoul St; mains £10-13; ☽ lunch & dinner; ☒) This place has built a very solid reputation on the back of its charmingly unpretentious name and toothsome Scottish dishes, prepared with a dash of Mediterranean flair. It's a Perth favourite for a celebratory meal out, so make sure you get a booking made at weekends, although the happy staff will do their level best to fit you in.

Paco's Restaurant (☎ 622290; 3 Mill St; mains £6-12; ☽ lunch & dinner) A well-loved local eating spot, Paco's is popular for its outdoor seating and wide-ranging menu. Whatever you fancy, you'll probably find it here – steaks, seafood, pizza, pasta, and Mexican all feature, including plenty of vegetarian choice. The portions are generous and the quality unspectacular but reliable.

Drinking

Twa Tams (☎ 634500; 79 Scott St) This place is comfortably Perth's best pub. There's something on nearly every night; the joint has a sound reputation for attracting talented young bands to town, and it's a great spot to see live music. There's also, crucially, a walled beer garden which is where to be when the sun is shining, enjoying a pint and a pub lunch.

Brennans (38 St John's St, ☽ Mon-Sat) Recently re-opened after refurbishment, this old favourite happily preserves its warren-like appeal. There's regular live music and a cheery throng of locals – at the back there's even a 'Cuban' bar with salsa going loud and late at weekends.

Entertainment

Ice Factory (Shore Rd; ☽ Thu-Sat) Widely known as one of Scotland's best nightclubs outside of Glasgow and Edinburgh, this is near the harbour in the south of town. Built around an open courtyard, high-jinks in the paddling pool are the norm as people take a break from the dancefloor. High-profile Scottish house DJs often appear and, true to its name, it's a pretty cool place.

Shopping

McEwen's of Perth (☎ 623444; 56 St John's St) This venerable old department store is famous throughout Scotland and sells distinguished and upmarket clothing.

Goldrush Records (☎ 629730; 9 Kinnoull St) A down-to-earth spot that has a well-priced range of second-hand and new CDs, as well as some vinyl.

Getting There & Away

Citylink operates one or two buses every hour to/from Aberdeen (£12.70, 2½ hours); Dundee (35 minutes); Edinburgh (£6.10, 1¼ hours); Glasgow (£6.50, 1½ hours); and Inverness (£11.30, 2½ hours, at least three daily).

Trains run to Edinburgh £10.30, 1½ hours, two hourly) and Glasgow (Queen St; £10.30, one hour, at least hourly Monday to Saturday, two-hourly Sunday).

PERTH TO AVIEMORE

There are several major sights strung out along the A9, which becomes a scenic treat after Pitlochry – it's the main route north to Aviemore in the Highlands.

Dunkeld & Birnam

☎ 01350 / pop 1000 / elevation 78m
Dunkeld is a pretty town with quirky shops, some great nearby walks and one of the best attractions in the region.

The smiling staff at **Dunkeld TIC** (☎ 727688; The Cross; ☽ daily) offer a friendly welcome and plenty of information.

Dunkeld Cathedral (HS; ☎ 0131 668 6800; High St; admission free; ☽ 9.30am-6.30pm Mon-Sat, 2-6.30pm Sun Apr-Sep, 9.30am-4pm Mon-Sat, 2-4pm Sun Oct-Mar; wheelchair access) has one of Scotland's most beautiful settings. Situated between open grassland which drops into the River Tay on one side, and rolling hills on the other, it will make you linger. Half the cathedral is still in use as a church – the rest is in ruins, and you can explore it all. Completed in 1350, the choir is the original church's oldest part. The 15th-century tower is also still standing and contains a small

---

SOMETHING SPECIAL

If you fancy a touch of ultimate highland luxury, you couldn't do better than beetle up the A9 a couple of miles past Dunkeld, and turn left down the B898, for after 4½ miles, you'll come to **Kinnaird Estate** (☎ 01796-482440; www.kinnairdestate.com; dinner, B&B r from £275; **P** 🖳 ; wheelchair access). This creeper-covered Edwardian mansion surrounded by quiet green lawns has nine lavishly furnished rooms that are more like suites, with plush carpet, sofas, and teddy bears. The service is faultless and the dinners, included in the price, showcase the finest Scottish produce complemented by a long wine list. It's fairly formal, with no kids under 12 allowed, and jacket and tie required for men in the restaurant, but it's one of Britain's classiest and most memorable hotels.

---

museum. The cathedral was damaged during the Reformation and burnt in the battle of Dunkeld in 1689.

A collection of **artisan's houses** restored by the NTS line High and Cathedral Sts; most have plaques with a brief history of their origins. Across Telford Bridge is **Birnam**, made famous by Shakespeare's *Macbeth*. There's plenty left of Birnam Wood, which has several walking and cycling trails detailed by the TIC; there's also a small **Beatrix Potter Park** (the author spent childhood holidays in the area).

Citylink buses from Glasgow/Edinburgh (£8.90, two hours, at least three daily) to Inverness stop at the Birnam train station just outside Birnam. Frequent Stagecoach buses head to Perth (20 minutes) and Pitlochry (20 minutes, Monday to Saturday).

Trains depart for Edinburgh (£10.30, 1½ hours, five daily Monday to Saturday, one on Sunday), Glasgow (£10.30, 1½ hours, two direct daily), and Inverness (£17.30, 2 hours, three to seven daily).

Pitlochry

☎ 01796 / pop 2564 / elevation 147m

Teeming with visitors and tourbuses, Pitlochry is rapidly losing the Highland charm it once possessed. It can be a good base for more-appealing destinations nearby, however, and you're assured of solace at one

of Scotland's best pubs, a 20-minute walk from the main street.

Edradour (☎ 472095; www.edradour.co.uk; tours free; 🕑 daily Mar-Oct, Mon-Sat Nov-mid Dec), proudly Scotland's smallest distillery, is 2½ miles east of Pitlochry.

The efficient **TIC** (☎ 472215; 22 Atholl Rd; 🕑 daily Apr-Oct, Mon-Sat Nov-Mar) has a currency exchange facility. It sells a brochure, *Pitlochry Walks*, detailing several medium-length walks in the surrounding countryside. **Computer Services Centre** (67 Atholl Rd; per hr from £3.60) has Internet connections upstairs.

SLEEPING & EATING

Pitlochry is packed with places to stay, but anything central tends to be pricey.

Moulin Hotel (☎ 472196; Moulin; mains £6-9; 🕑 food served 11am-9.30pm) A mile away but a world apart, this atmospheric little inn was trading centuries before the tartan tack came to Pitlochry. With its romantic low ceilings, ageing wood and booth seating, it's a great spot to escape the crowds for a drink and a meal. The Highland comfort food is excellent, particularly the haggis, or the venison stew, and you can accompany it with the hotel's home-brewed ales: the smooth, reddish Atholl Ale is particularly good. The best way to get here is to walk: it's a pretty uphill stroll through green fields, and an easy roll down the hill with mind and body satisfied.

Pitlochry Backpackers Hotel (☎ 470044; www.scotlands-top-hostels.com; 134 Atholl Rd; dm £11-12, tw & d £27-36; **P** 🗶 🖳) Right in the thick of things, this excellent, sociable hostel is in a nice old building with great views over the main drag. The dorms are comfortable enough, and there are nice cosy doubles available too, with shared bathroom. Breakfast, laundry, and bike hire are all available.

Derrybeg Guest House (☎ 472070; www.derrybeg.co.uk; 18 Lower Oakfield; r per person £20-28; **P** 🗶) This well-established choice is set in two adjacent stone buildings with a large garden. The en-suite rooms have big windows and are decorated with discriminating good cheer. There are great views, and discounts for longer stays, including self-catering apartments. A four-course dinner here is a recommendable experience for £16.50.

Atholl Villa (☎ 473820; www.athollvilla.co.uk; 29 Atholl Rd; r per person from £20; **P** 🗶 ; wheelchair access) Right opposite the tourist office, this attractive stone house appeals with its large lawn and flowery garden, a great spot to sit on a sunny day. Inside it's bright and cheery. One of the rooms is exceptionally spacious, and there's a pleasant conservatory lounge. No children.

Other recommendations:

Knockendarroch Hotel (☎ 473473; www.knockendarroch.co.uk; Higher Oakfield; s/d dinner & B&B £90/138; **P**) Lavish Highland hospitality, classy but friendly, with dinners fit for Pavarotti.

McKay's Hotel (☎ 473888; 138 Atholl Rd; mains £6-11; ☺ lunch & dinner, snacks all day) Good bar favourites: try the tuna steak or the chargrilled salmon.

Pitlochry SYHA Hostel (☎ 0870 004 1145; www.syha.org.uk; Knockard Rd; dm £12; ☺ Mar-Oct; **P** 🗙 🖳) Overlooks the town centre and has great views.

GETTING THERE & AWAY

Buses operated by Citylink run roughly every hour and connect Pitlochry to Inverness (£9.10, two hours), Perth (40 minutes), Edinburgh (£9, two hours) and Glasgow (£9, 2¼ hours).

Pitlochry is on the main rail line from Perth (30 minutes, nine daily Monday to Saturday, four on Sunday) to Inverness.

Blair Castle

One of the most popular tourist attractions in Scotland, **Blair Castle** (☎ 01796-481207; www.blair-castle.co.uk; adult £6.70; ☺ 10am-6pm Apr-Oct, last admission 4.30pm, call for winter opening) and the 28,000 hectares it sits on, is the seat of the Duke of Atholl. Outside this impressive, white castle, set beneath forested slopes above the River Garry, there's a parade of the Atholl Highlanders every May – the only (legal) private army in Britain.

The original tower was built in 1269, but the castle has undergone significant remodelling since then. Thirty rooms are open to the public and they present a wonderful picture of upper-class Highland life from the 16th century to the late-20th century. The dining room is sumptuous – check out the 9-pint wine glasses – and the ballroom is a vaulted chamber that's a virtual stag cemetery.

The current duke is a distant relative (in every sense of the word – he lives in South Africa) to the 10th duke, who died a bachelor in 1996. He visits the castle every May to review the Atholl Highlanders. Blair Castle meanwhile is held in trust, controlled by the 10th duke's sister, who still lives in a wing of the castle.

Blair Castle is 7 miles north of Pitlochry, and a mile from the village of Blair Atholl. Local buses run to Blair Atholl four to six times daily, and a couple go direct to the castle. There's a train station but few trains stop here.

WEST PERTHSHIRE

This remote area of Perthshire is a jewel in Central Scotland's crown. It's difficult to reach via public transport – buses are usually once-a-day postal services – however, these fabulous hills and lochs are well worth making an effort to see, and Glen Lyon is perhaps Scotland's most beautiful valley.

The closest **TIC** (☎ 01887-820276; the Square; ☺ daily Apr-Oct, Mon-Sat Nov-Mar) in the village of **Aberfeldy**, the gateway to the region. Stagecoach runs buses to Aberfeldy from Perth (1¼ hours, hourly Monday to Saturday) and from Pitlochry (45 minutes, 10 daily Monday to Saturday, three on Sunday).

Loch Tay & Kenmore

☎ 01887 / elevation 476m

The bulk of mighty **Ben Lawers** (1214m) looms above Loch Tay and is part of a National Nature Reserve that includes the nearby Tarmachan range. There's a **Ben Lawers visitors centre** (☎ 01567 820397; admission £1; ☺ 10.30am-5pm Apr-Sep), 5 miles east of Killin, off the A827, which sells the *Ben Lawers Nature Trail* booklet, describing the area's flora and fauna.

The wealthy village of **Kenmore** lies at the eastern end of Loch Tay. It's a small but pretty place dominated by a church and clock tower and the striking archway of the privately owned Taymouth Castle. Don't forget the camera, it's the perfect place for some happy snaps. On the loch just across from town (10 minutes' walk) is a picturesque reconstructed **crannog**, an ancient form of house built on stilts in the water for defensive purposes.

Kenmore Hotel (☎ 830205, www.kenmorehotel.com; s/d from £59/88; **P** 🗙 ; wheelchair access) is the reason to stop here. It's an historic inn (founded 1572) and has a lovely beer garden by the riverbank. In the bar, cosy with its roaring fire, look out for the verses written on the chimney piece by Robert Burns in 1787 – it's a romantic description of the countryside. The rooms, many of which have bay windows overlooking the River

BEN LAWERS – A CLASSIC ROUTE

The trek up Ben Lawers starts at the visitors centre and is one of the best walks in the area. The trip to the top and back can take up to five hours and you need wet weather gear, water and food. Take the nature trail that heads northeast. After the boardwalk protecting a bog, cross a stile, then fork left and ascend along a burn (to the right). At the next rise, fork right and cross the burn. A few minutes' later ignore the nature trail's right turn and continue ascending parallel to the burn's left bank for just over half a mile. Leave the protected zone by another stile and steeply ascend Beinn Ghlas' shoulder. Reaching a couple of large rocks, ignore a northbound footpath and continue zigzagging uphill. The rest of the ascent is a straightforward succession of three false summits. The last and steepest section alternates between erosion sculpted rock and a meticulously crafted cobbled trail. Views of the North Sea, and Atlantic, are outstanding on a clear day.

Tay, have been modernised without losing their character.

There are regular buses from Aberfeldy to Kenmore (20 minutes).

FORTINGALL

West of Aberfeldy, the pretty village of Fortingall is at the turn-off to Glen Lyon. Tranquil and picturesque, it has 19th-century thatched cottages, and is famous, curiously, as the possible birthplace of Pontius Pilate and for its ancient yew tree.

Fortingall Hotel (☎ 830367; www.fortingall.com; s/d £42.50/85; ☺ mid Mar-Oct; P ✗) is the place to come for a bit of solitude and is a great base for walks. The rooms look out over the green meadows and have beds that say 'sleep in me', complete with canopies. There's a restaurant and bar, only open to guests. Part of the hotel dates from 1300.

GLEN LYON

The longest enclosed glen in Scotland runs for some 34 unforgettable miles of rickety stone bridges, Victorian lodges, Caledonian pine forest and sheer peaks (splashed with red and orange heather) poking through swirling clouds. It becomes wilder and more uninhabited as it snakes its way west toward Loch Lyon and is proof that hidden treasures still exist in Scotland. The ancients believed it to be a gateway to faerie land, and even the most skeptical of people will be entranced by the valley's magic.

From Fortingall, a narrow road winds its way up the glen – another road from the Ben Lawers visitors centre crosses the hills and reaches the glen halfway in, at Bridge of Balgie. No caravans are allowed on these roads, but if you're keen and you've the time,

cycling through Glen Lyon is a wonderful way to experience this special place.

There's little in the way of attractions in the valley – the majestic and lonely scenery is the reason to be here, but at **Glenlyon Arts and Crafts**, next to the post office at Bridge of Balgie, a selection of fine handmade pieces are on sale, including some beautiful works carved from yew and elm.

Invervar Lodge (☎ 01887 877206; 5 miles from Fortingall; r per person £25-40; P ✗), despite being an old highland hunting lodge, is strictly a tartan-free zone. It would be difficult to imagine a better base for walking, or more relaxed and welcoming hosts, who have renovated the house to offer more space and light without compromising the original design. The bedrooms are utterly lovable, with wrought-iron beds; some have fireplaces. At time of writing accommodation was on a self-catering basis, but the owners plan to offer meals; in the meantime, guests have use of a large modern kitchen. The place is exceptionally child-friendly, and if the family fancy sleeping out, there are even tepees for rent nearby.

The only public transport in the glen is Postbus No 211, which leaves Aberfeldy at 9am, Monday to Saturday, returning from Glen Lyon post office at 1.25pm.

ABERDEENSHIRE & MORAY

The shoulder of Scotland juts out defiantly into the North Sea, which has traditionally provided a living in the form of fishing. With fish stocks dwindling, however, the discovery of oil gave a crucial boost to the region, particularly Aberdeen, which is now a prosperous, bustling city thanks to the giant offshore rigs.

Inland, the hard, wind-whipped coast gives way to a more peaceful agricultural zone, studded with dozens of whisky distilleries, concentrated in the Speyside area. Some of the giants of malt whisky can be found here and the happy tippler could spend weeks just tasting drams!

West of Aberdeen, the beautiful Dee Valley runs through woodlands, which harbour the Queen's residence of Balmoral Castle, to Braemar, a popular base for mountain walking and handy for the ski-slopes of Glenshee. It's this diversity that is the real appeal of this corner of the country.

ABERDEEN

☎ 01224 / pop 184,800 / elevation 36m

Scotland's third-largest settlement's moniker of 'The Granite City' may conjure up images of a dour, funless sort of town, but nothing could be further from the truth. It's a vibrant prosperous place driven by the offshore riches of the North Sea gas and oil reserves and has some excellent, boisterous nightlife.

The whole city is indeed built of granite – even the roads are paved with the stuff – and on a sunny day every building glints cheerfully as the sun reflects off the spangling of mica particles. When it rains, as it likes to do in these parts, it can be a little less inspiring!

Aberdeen has some great museums and galleries, including, fittingly for a place which seems to have its back to the Highlands and its face out to sea, a maritime museum. Nearby, the bustling fish market opens at dawn as it has done for centuries.

The soft Aberdonian tones mingle here with the accents of transient multinational oilworkers and a large student population from around the country, ensuring that the inviting pubs, roaring clubs and decent restaurants are always busy.

History

Aberdeen was a prosperous North Sea trading and fishing port centuries before oil was considered a valuable commodity. After the townspeople supported Robert the Bruce against the English at the Battle of Bannockburn in 1314, the king rewarded the town with land for which he had previously received rent. The money was diverted into the Common Good Fund, to be spent on town amenities, as it still is today.

Since the 1970s, Aberdeen has become the main onshore service port for one of the largest oilfields in the world; its harbour is Britain's second busiest in terms of ship movement. Unemployment rates, once among the highest in the country, dropped dramatically, but have since fluctuated with the rise and fall of the price of oil.

Orientation

Aberdeen is built on a ridge that runs east-west between the River Dee and River Don. Union St, the main commercial street, follows the line of the ridge. The bus and train stations are next to each other, off Guild St, south of Union St. The ferry quay is east of the bus and train stations, off Market St.

Old Aberdeen and the university are north of Union St. To the east lies a couple of miles of clean, sandy beach.

Information

Aberdeen Royal Infirmary (☎ 681818; Foresterhill) Northeast of the centre, Aberdeen's major hospital has a 24hr accident & emergency unit.

Central Library (☎ 652500; Rosemount Viaduct; 🕒 9am-8pm Mon-Thu, 9am-5pm Fri & Sat) Free Internet access; sessions limited to 30 minutes.

Ottakar's (☎ 592440; 3 Union Bridge; 🕒 daily) Central bookshop.

Soul & Spice Café (☎ 645200; 15 Belmont St; per hr £2; 🕒 10am-late) Friendly Internet café.

TIC (☎ 288828; 23 Union St; 🕒 9am-5.30pm Mon-Sat mid-Sep–mid-Jun, 9am-7pm Mon-Sat, 10am-4pm Sun mid-Jun–mid-Sep)

Sights

MARITIME MUSEUM

Partly set in the oldest building in the city, the **Maritime Museum** (☎ 337700; Shiprow; admission free; 🕒 10am-5pm Mon-Sat, noon-3pm Sun; wheelchair access) has lots of interactive displays, statistics on humanity's impact on the ocean (frightening), and bags of information on life aboard an oil rig. There's even a translation of the mysterious BBC shipping forecast.

Sections on shipbuilding and technological maritime advances over the centuries recall the days when speedy Aberdeen clippers competed on the tea runs from India

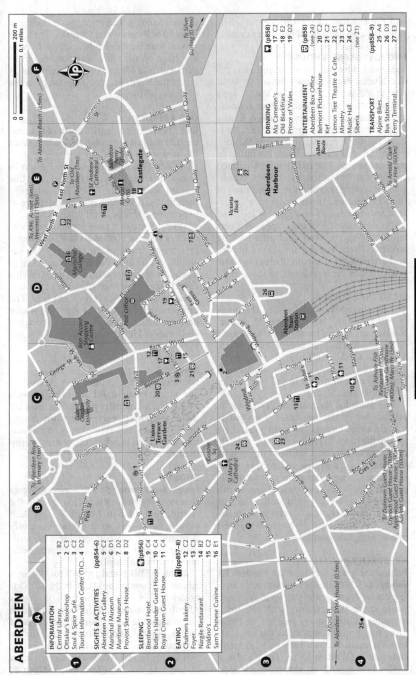

ABERDEEN

0   200 m
0   0.1 miles

CENTRAL SCOTLAND

and the Far East in the 19th century. The museum also has a good basement café.

PROVOST SKENE'S HOUSE

Surrounded by ugly concrete and glass office blocks, **Provost Skene's House** (☎ 641086; Broad St; admission free; ✆ 10am-5pm Mon-Sat, 1-4pm Sun) is a late medieval, turreted town house near Marischal College, occupied in the 17th century by the provost (the Scots equivalent of a mayor) Sir George Skene.

Typical of its kind, the house has intimate, panelled rooms. The 1622 tempera-painted ceiling, with its Catholic symbolism, is unusual for having survived the depredation of the Reformation. It has undergone extensive restoration and is a gem of its time, featuring earnest looking angels, St Peter with crowing cockerels, and grim-looking soldiers. There is also a small local history and archaeology museum, including some grisly human remains found in the area.

MARISCHAL COLLEGE

The 5th Earl Marischal founded this huge building in 1593, which currently accommodates the science faculty of the University of Aberdeen. The present building is of late Victorian Gothic, and is made peculiar by the use of granite. It's actually the second-largest granite structure in the world, after El Escorial near Madrid.

The **Marischal Museum** (☎ 274301; Broad St; admission free; ✆ 10am-5pm Mon-Fri, 2-5pm Sun) is straight ahead through the main quadrangle and up the stairs. In one room, there's a lively depiction of northeast Scotland through its famous people, customs, architecture, trade and myths. The other gallery is set up as an anthropological overview of the world, incorporating objects from vastly different cultures. Both rooms are arranged thematically, the latter with Polynesian wooden masks alongside gasmasks and so on.

ABERDEEN ART GALLERY

Behind the grand façade of the **Aberdeen Art Gallery** (☎ 523700; Schoolhill; admission free; ✆ 10am-5pm Mon-Sat, 2-5pm Sun; wheelchair access) is a cool, white space that exhibits both the work of young contemporary painters and also more traditional works, including an excellent Victorian Scottish section, with many canvases by William Dyce. There's also a Rodin bronze and an extensive selection

of watercolours and etchings, including a handful of Picassos and Chagalls. There are several Joan Eardley landscapes; she lived in a cottage on the cliffs near Stonehaven in the 1950s and 60s and painted tempestuous oils of the North Sea and poignant portraits of slum children.

OLD ABERDEEN

Old Aberdeen is a district north of the centre. The name is somewhat misleading, since the area south around the harbour is actually older; Old Aberdeen is called Alton in Gaelic, meaning village by the pool, and this was anglicised to Old Town. The university buildings and St Machar's Cathedral are at the centre of this peaceful urban oasis.

With its massive twin towers, the 15th-century **St Machar's Cathedral** (☎ 485988; Chanonry; ✆ 9am-5pm), is one of the country's few examples of a fortified cathedral. According to legend, St Machar was ordered to establish a church where the river takes the shape of a bishop's crook, which it does just here. The cathedral is best known for its impressive heraldic ceiling, dating from 1520, which has 48 shields of kings, nobles, archbishops and bishops.

Sleeping

Southwest of the centre, Bon Accord St and Great Western Rd are bristling with B&Bs. The oil industry means that there are many temporary workers in town during the week; it's easier finding accommodation at weekends, when many hotels drop their rates.

BUDGET

Adelphi Guest House (☎ 583078; www.adelphiguest house.com; 8 Whinhill Rd; s/d from £20/35; ✗) On the continuation of Bon Accord St, this B&B offers quiet rooms, some overlooking leafy parkland. All are comfortable and well-equipped, with cable TV and big firm beds; most rooms are en suite.

Aberdeen SYHA Hostel (☎ 0870 004 1100; www .syha.org.uk; 8 Queen's Rd; dm £13.50; **P** ✗ 🖳) This hostel a mile west of the train station is Aberdeen through and through, housed in a sturdy granite town house. There are good facilities including laundry service; beds are in small, clean dormitories, and there are two family rooms. Walk west along Union St and take the right fork along Albyn Pl until you reach a roundabout; Queen's Rd continues on the western side.

MID-RANGE

Butler's Islander Guest House (☎ 212411; www .butlersguesthouse.com; 122 Crown St; s/d from £26/46; ✗ ▢) This welcoming spot is handy for both the centre and transport options. The rooms are cosy, most with small en-suite bathrooms, and there's free Internet access for guests. Best of all is the charismatic breakfast menu, which features Aberdeen brose, a fortifying blend of porridge, whisky and honey that is guaranteed to send you out to see the sights in a good mood.

Dunrovin Guest House (☎ 586081; 168 Bon Accord St; www.dunrovinguesthouse.co.uk; s/d £25/37, with en suite £30/46; Ⓟ ✗) An excellent choice in the area; this friendly granite home has good rooms with great natural light and shiny modern en suites. The triple room, with lots of space, is particularly good for families.

Applewood Guest House (☎ 580617; 154 Bon Accord St; s/d £25/40; Ⓟ ✗) This bright and chirpy B&B is somewhat Tardis-like, with far more rooms and space than appears possible from outside. The rooms, some en suite, are mostly large and all are clean as a whistle and comfortably appointed.

Royal Crown Guest House (☎ 586461; www.royal crown.co.uk; 111 Crown St; s/d from £25/40; Ⓟ ✗) Just five minutes' walk from the train station, this popular spot has eight small but well-furnished rooms. It's very handy for the centre, and a veggie breakfast is provided if requested.

Other recommendations:

Brentwood Hotel (☎ 595440; www.brentwood-hotel.co .uk; 101 Crown St; s/d £77/87, weekends £37/54; Ⓟ ✗) Substantial weekend discounts and a good bar below.

Crynoch Guest House (☎ 582743; crynoch@btInternet .com; 164 Bon Accord St; B&B s/d from £24/48; Ⓟ ✗) Friendly spot with some en-suite rooms. Crynoch means 'thistle' in Gaelic;

Kildonan Guest House (☎ 316115; 410 Great Western Rd; s/d from £25/40; Ⓟ ✗) Light, bright rooms and efficiently run. There's a terrific family room upstairs.

TOP END

Marcliffe (☎ 861000; www.marcliffe.com; North Deeside Rd; s/d from £115/130; Ⓟ ✗ ; wheelchair access) Aberdeen's most luxurious accommodation is to be found at the end of a winding driveway in 10 acres of parkland. The rooms combine antique furniture and country-house

comfort with stylish modern bathrooms; the restaurant offers fine Scottish produce with a massive wine list. You can fish on the river Dee within the grounds. Packages including dinner are available – check the website for weekend deals.

Eating

Silver Darling (☎ 576229; Pocra Quay; mains £16-19; ☽ lunch Mon-Fri, dinner Mon-Sat; ✗) Beautifully situated at the southern end of the Beach Esplanade overlooking the port entrance, this restaurant is named after the herring which used to drive the economy in these parts. With the location and name, you'd be well-advised to order seafood, which is renowned and sublime.

Foyer (☎ 582277; Trinity Church, 82a Crown St; lunch £6, mains £9-14; ☽ 9.30pm-11.30pm Tue-Wed, 9.30pm-midnight Thu-Sat; ✗ ; wheelchair access) Set in a converted church, this light contemporary gallery-restaurant funds an enterprise which assists homeless youth. At lunch you can chow down on old favourites like toad-in-the-hole but in the evenings more-creative combinations come out, such as blue cheese soufflé, one of many vegetarian choices.

Nargile Restaurant (☎ 636093; 77 Skene St; mains £8-13; ☽ lunch & dinner until 10.30pm Mon-Sat) This is a highly regarded Aberdeen institution and one of the best Turkish restaurants in the country. Modern décor and fine dining complement carefully prepared meals like melt-in-the-mouth kebabs and *tavuk saltasi* (chargrilled chicken in honey and mustard sauce). The £9.95 pretheatre dinner is a bargain.

Ashvale Fish Restaurant (☎ 596981; 46 Great Western Rd; mains £5-9; ☽ 11.45am-11pm; ✗) This popular fish and chip restaurant and takeaway has a wide-reaching fame. A great place for the family, with plenty to eat and do for kids, it serves all types of battered seafood and sizzling steaks. If you finish the 'Ashvale Whale', a mighty portion of cod and chips, you get a certificate and a free one next time.

Sam's Chinese Cuisine (☎ 626233; 13 King St; mains £8-13; ☽ lunch & dinner; ✗) This smart restaurant, also known as Hua Zhong Xin, is a hop away from Union St and a big jump in class and imagination above the average Highland Chinese takeaway. The menu is well set-out and includes intriguing choices. The Peking duck is lusciously textured, the nonkfish stir-fries are exquisite, while the volcanic' king prawns will have you grabbing for your glass in a hurry. Service is slow, but that's because the dishes are freshly prepared.

Other recommendations:

Chalmers Bakery (14 Back Wynd; takeaways £1-3; 7.30am-5pm Mon-Sat;) Quality bakery that also does tasty cheap eats.

Lemon Tree Theatre & Cafe (☎ 642230; 5 West North St; mains £4-6.50; noon-3pm Wed-Sun), theatre (see right) café serving excellent coffee, meals (like scrumptious tortilla wraps with exotic fillings) and cakes.

Poldino's (☎ 647777; 7 Little Belmont St; pastas £6-9, other mains £12-18; lunch & dinner Mon-Sat) Long time Italian favourite; the pricy seafood mains are more memorable than the pasta.

Drinking

There are numerous style bars on and around Belmont St; a new one seems to be opening every day.

Prince of Wales (☎ 640597; 7 St Nicholas Lane) Aberdeen's best-known pub is in an insignificant alley off Union street. Boasting a counter that stretches to the horizon, gnarled wooden floorboards, and a buzz of soft Aberdonian accents well lubricated by a range of guest beers, it's a haven of good cheer and a Scottish pub par excellence.

Ma Cameron's (☎ 644487; 6 Little Belmont St) The city's oldest pub is much larger than it looks and was established when Bastilles were being stormed and American wars of independence fought. Despite numerous refits and cheap drink promos, it remains a low-ceilinged sort of a place and is still a good spot for a dram.

Old Blackfriars (☎ 581922; 52 Castlegate) The most intimate of the inner city pubs, this is a great traditional bar with low roofs, timber interior and a warren-like layout. It also does excellent bar meals.

Entertainment

To find out about current listings check *What's on in Aberdeen,* available from the TIC, or the bimonthly *Aberdeen Arts & Recreation Listings.* You can book tickets for most plays and concerts at the **Aberdeen Box Office** (☎ 641122; Union St) by the Music Hall.

CINEMAS

Belmont Picturehouse (☎ 343534; 49 Belmont St) Superbly located for a post-movie debrief over a gin and tonic, this cinema shows new releases, arthouse classics, and themed series of films. Essential.

NIGHTCLUBS

Belmont St is the place to go for preclub action; check the noticeboards in One-Up Records at number 17 for upcoming club nights.

Ministry (☎ 211661; 16 Dee St; cover £3-8) Like many of Aberdeen's restaurant, pubs, and clubs, this is housed in a former church – have the people lost their faith? It attracts a youngish, studenty crowd and usually showcases good DJs on Friday, Saturday, and Sunday nights.

Kef (☎ 684000; 9 Belmont St; admission around £5) One of the city's most popular venues, with decadent cushions backing a Moorish harem design concept. Echoes of the Middle East are less prominent around the lager-soaked bar and the decks, from which a range of high-quality sounds emanate. Upstairs is **Siberia**, a cool vodka bar with a conservatory space – perfect for relaxing before hitting the club.

THEATRE & MUSIC

Music Hall (☎ 632080; Union St) Right in the heart of town, this is the main venue for classical music concerts. Adjacent is a box office where you can book tickets for many events in Aberdeen.

Lemon Tree Theatre & Cafe (☎ 642230; 5 West North St) The Lemon Tree usually has an interesting programme of dance, music or drama. It hosts festivals and often has rock, jazz and folk bands playing.

Getting There & Away

AIR

Seven miles northwest of the city centre, **Aberdeen airport** (☎ 722331), known as Dyce, has numerous domestic flights, including Orkney and Shetland, and a few European flights. Bus No 27 runs there from Union St regularly (35 minutes).

BOAT

The passenger terminal is a short walk east of the train and bus stations. **NorthLink Ferries** (☎ 0845 600 0449; www.northlinkferries.co.uk) runs car ferries from Aberdeen to Lerwick (passenger £19.25 to £29.50, car and driver £100 to £135, cabins extra, 12 to 15 hours, daily) on the Shetland Islands, some via Kirkwall (passenger £14.75 to £22.50, car and driver £73 to £102.50, six hours, three to four weekly) on the Orkney Islands.

BUS
Citylink runs to Dundee (£9, two hours, more than hourly), Edinburgh (£16.40, 3¼ hours, hourly), Glasgow (£16.40, 3½ hours, hourly), Perth (£12.70, 2½ hours, hourly) and Stirling (£15.90, three hours, hourly including some indirect). Stagecoach runs to Inverness (£10.50, 3¾ hours, hourly).

TRAIN
Destinations served from Aberdeen by rail include Edinburgh (£32.90, 2½ hours, hourly or more frequently), Glasgow (£32.90, 2½ hours, hourly), Dundee (£19.10, 1¼ hours, two hourly), Inverness (£19.90, 2¼ hours, five to 10 daily) and Stirling (£31.20, two hours).

Getting Around
BICYCLE
Mountain bikes can be rented from **Alpine Bikes** (☎ 211455; 64 Holburn St; ☿ daily). It charges £15 per day during the week and £30 for the weekend (Friday evening to Monday morning).

BUS
The two principal local operators are **First Aberdeen** (☎ 650065) and **Stagecoach Bluebird** (☎ 212266). First Aberdeen has a free leaflet detailing services and routes. The most useful services are First Aberdeen bus Nos 18, 19 and 24 from Union St to Great Western Rd, No 27 from the bus station to the SYHA Hostel, and No 20 for Old Aberdeen.

CAR
There are several car-rental companies in Aberdeen. **Arnold Clark** (☎ 249159; Girdleness Rd) has competitive rates starting at £18 per day for a small car.

DEESIDE & DONSIDE
This region is home to some outstanding natural beauty. The moderate heights around areas such as Braemar, in upper Deeside, are terrific for walking. If you're a Royal enthusiast, the Queen's Scottish residence is here at Balmoral; if not don't worry, there are more fanciful examples

of Scottish baronial architecture here than anywhere else in Scotland. The TICs have information on a Castle Trail, but you will need your own wheels.

The River Dee, flowing through the southern part of this area, has its source in the Cairngorm Mountains, to the west. The River Don follows a shorter, almost parallel, course.

Balmoral Castle
This **castle** (☎ 01339-742534; www.balmoralcastle .com; adult/child £5/1, 50p parking; ☿ 10am-5pm Easter-Jul; wheelchair access) was built for Queen Victoria in 1855 as a private residence for the royal family. If you're a royal fanatic, you'll love Balmoral, if not then it is difficult to justify the entry fee to see lots of photos of smiling royals, a few pieces of art, some stuffed animals and the odd piece of history about the various Highland regiments. The grounds themselves, by the River Dee, are lovely for a stroll. Only a small part of the castle is open, the rest is closed to the prying eyes of the public.

Balmoral is just off the A93 (where there's a TIC) near the village of Crathie and can be reached on buses running between Aberdeen and Braemar (see p860).

Braemar & Around
☎ 01339 / pop 410 / elevation 312m

Braemar, surrounded by mountains, has long been a visitors' favourite and a base for walking or skiing at nearby Glenshee. Although it gets busy with coach parties, it still makes a good stop; it's at its best in the evenings when, breathing the fresh mountain air, urbanites tend to wonder why they live in a city. Five miles west of Braemar is the tiny settlement of Inverey: numerous mountain **walks** start from here, including the adventurous **Lairig Ghru walk** – 21 miles over the pass to Aviemore.

The **TIC** (☎ 741600; The Mews, Mar Rd; ☿ daily) has lots of useful information on walks in the area. On the first Saturday in September, Braemar is invaded by 20,000 people, including the royal family, for the **Braemar Gathering** (Highland Games); bookings during this period are essential.

SIGHTS & ACTIVITIES
North of the village, turreted **Braemar Castle** (☎ 741219; adult £4; ☿ 10am-5pm Apr-Oct; wheelchair

access) dates from 1628, and was a garrison post after the 1745 Jacobite Rebellion.

An easy walk from Braemar is up **Creag Choinnich** (538m), a hill to the east above the A93. There are route markers and the walk takes about 1½ hours. For a longer walk (three hours) and superb views of the Cairngorms, climb **Morrone** (859m), the mountain south of Braemar. Another fine place for leisurely hiking is around the Falls of Linn, beyond Inverey.

SLEEPING
Rucksacks (☎ 41517; 15 Mar Rd; dm with/without linen £9/7; ✕ ▣) This highly recommended spot is the ultimate walkers' hostel. It's warm, clean, hugely welcoming and boasts many creature comforts such as a barbecue, communal kitchen, duvets on the bunk beds, laundry service, Internet terminal, and even a sauna! Even if you're not staying here, you can use the Net (during the day) or put on a load of washing – nothing is too much trouble for the delightful owner.

Craiglea (☎ 741641; www.craigleabraemar.com; Hillside Dr; s/d from £30/44; ✕) This homely, family-run guesthouse has fine large rooms painted in bright colours, including one that boasts a luxury bathtub. They can arrange evening meals or packed lunches for walkers, and the breakfast is very good.

Other recommendations:
Braemar Lodge (☎ 741627; www.braemarlodge.co.uk; Glenshee Rd; s/d £25/50, dm £10, weekly self-catering log cabins £300-400; ℗ ✕) Classy, restored shooting lodge on the outskirts of the town with a range of good-value accommodation.
Inverey SYHA Hostel (☎ 0870 004 1126; www.syha.org.uk; dm £9.50; ☉ May-Sep) Basic walkers' digs in a beautiful, isolated spot. A mile beyond Inverey.
St Margarets (☎ 741697; 13 School Rd; tw from £36; ✕) Only one room, the 'Sunflower Suite': grab it if you can. Enchanting owner doesn't charge extra for singles.

EATING
Most of the places to eat in Braemar are the pubs and hotels, which serve generally uninspiring bar meals until about 8pm. There is nowhere to eat or drink in Inverey.

The Gathering Place (☎ 741234; Invercauld Rd; mains £10-13; ☉ dinner Tue-Sun; ✕) This modern bistro on the riverbank is a welcome addition indeed to the culinary scene. With contemporary Scottish flavours having been given a Mediterranean shake-up, tasty

creations such as rabbit cassoulet or haggis filo parcels are the pleasing result, and are complemented by a good range of wines and welcoming service.

GETTING THERE & AWAY
Stagecoach Bluebird bus No 201 from Aberdeen to Braemar (£6.80, 2¼ hours, hourly daily, two-hourly on Sunday) travels along the Dee valley. Postbus No 072 leaves Braemar daily Monday to Saturday for Inverey, the SYHA Hostel, and the Linn of Dee.

Glenshee
☎ 01250
The route along the A93, through Glenshee, is one of the most spectacular drives in the country. Meandering burns and stark soaring peaks, splotched with glaring snow, dwarf open-mouthed drivers. It's surprising there aren't more accidents along this road!

This local **resort** (☎ 01339-741320; www.ski-glenshee.co.uk) is Britain's major ski resort, but average facilities and unreliable snowcover leave it a long way short of world-class. There are 38 pistes and the chairlift can whisk you up to the top of The Cairwell (933m).

As well as the accommodation centres of Braemar and Blairgowrie, there are places to stay in Spittal of Glenshee, 6 miles south of the resort. **Spittal of Glenshee Hotel** (☎ 885215; spittalglenshee@aol.com; dm £15, r per person £18-32; ℗ ✕) is a very 'Scottish experience' – it's a friendly ski-style lodge with a big bar serving massive portions. There's a bunkhouse, and all rates include breakfast. It's a good base for walking too, and you can take a companion – the hotel dog!

Dalmunzie House (☎ 885224; www.dalmunzie.com; Glenshee; s/d from £50/70, 3 course dinner £26; ℗ ; wheelchair access) is a grand property situated in a glen among bare hills, 1¼ miles north of Spittal on a side road. There's great walking on the vast estate as well as the highest golf course in Britain. Inside, it's all roaring fires, leather armchairs, wood panelling, and, in some of the rooms, posh four-poster beds.

There is a Strathtay Scottish service from Perth to Blairgowrie (50 minutes, about six daily). The only service from Blairgowrie to the Glenshee area is the once daily Monday to Saturday postbus to Spittal of Glenshee.

SPEYSIDE

The inland road between Aberdeen and Inverness skirts the Spey Valley, a fertile zone which harbours a frightening number of whisky distilleries, including most of the famous names in the pantheon of Scottish malts. The Speyside style tends toward the rich, sweet, and nutty, and they are many people's favourite tipple. The region is best explored by car, but the **Speyside Way** is a footpath that follows a disused rail line from the Cairngorms to the coast at Spey Bay, passing through utterly tranquil riverside scenery and not a few distilleries.

Dufftown

☎ 01340 / pop 1450 / elevation 249m

'Rome may be built on seven hills, but Dufftown's built on seven stills' claim locals. It's a good base for the area, with seven operational distilleries in town. It was founded only in 1817 by James Duff, 4th Earl of Fife. The **TIC** (☎ 820501; 9a The Square; ☽ Mon-Sat Easter-Oct, Mon-Sun Jul & Aug) is in the clock tower.

North of town is the **Glenfiddich Distillery Visitors Centre** (☎ 820373; www.glenfiddich.com; admission free; ☽ 9.30am-4.30pm Mon-Fri mid Oct-Easter, 9.30am-4.30pm Mon-Sat, noon-4.30pm Sun Easter-mid Oct). Visitors are guided through the process of distilling, and can also see whisky being bottled – the only Highland distillery where this is done on the premises. Your free dram really is free.

The **Fife Arms Hotel** (☎ 820220; www.fifearms dufftown.co.uk; 2 The Square; s/d £27/44; **P**; wheelchair access) is right across from the TIC. It's a down-to-earth and unpretentious place with extremely welcoming owners. The motel-style rooms are colourful and comfortable, and the bar serves such unlikely fare as ostrich steaks amid more-familiar options. **La Faisanderie** (☎ 821273; the Square; set lunch/dinner £11.80/22.50; ☽ dinner Wed-Mon, lunch Thu-Mon) is a great place to eat, run by a respected local chef. The interior is decorated in French auberge-style with a cheerful mural and pheasants hiding in every corner. The menu, which features plenty of game, won't disappoint and is excellent value for the quality on offer.

Stagecoach Bluebird links Dufftown to Elgin (50 minutes, hourly). Enthusiasts run a heritage railway between Keith and Dufftown; services operate three times a day over summer weekends.

Around Dufftown

The Fiddich river runs northwest from Dufftown three miles before joining the Spey at Craigellachie; a couple of miles northwest of here is the **Macallan distillery** (☎ 01340-872280; www.themacallan.com; ☽ 11am-3pm Mon-Fri Nov-Mar, 9.30am-5pm Mon-Sat Apr-Oct). This highly rated sherry-casked malt is one of Scotland's finest, particularly in its sublime 18-, 25-, and 30-year-old incarnations. The fine tour is free and includes a dram.

Two miles southwest of Craigellachie, the charming village of Aberlour is on the Speyside way. The home of Walkers, whose sinfully buttery shortbread is seen around the world, it boasts a fine local pub next to the old station. The **Mash Tun** (☎ 01340-881771; 7 Broomfield Sq) is built of reassuringly solid stone and has a great line-up of real ales, plenty of local whisky, and filling bar meals. Hourly buses link Dufftown, Craigellachie, and Aberlour, but there's also a scenic four-mile footpath clearly waymarked.

GRAMPIAN COAST

The Grampians meet the sea at Stonehaven, home to spectacular Dunnottar Castle. Continuing north around the coast from Aberdeen, there are long stretches of sand and, on the north coast, some magical fishing villages – such as Pennan, where the film *Local Hero* was shot.

Pennan & Around

☎ 01261 / pop 22

The tiny harbour hamlet of Pennan, built at the base of steep cliffs, is one of the gems of this part of Scotland's coast. The single street of houses in this former fishing settlement seems completely at the mercy of the grey sea; it's an unforgettable location that was immortalised in the mouse-that-roared British classic *Local Hero*.

The village's red phonebox featured prominently in the film, as did the pub, the cosy **Pennan Inn** (☎ 561201; r per person from £24, mains £6-10). The beating heart of this community, it has cramped but atmospheric little rooms and a convivial bar, particularly memorable if the weather turns harsh and the wind and rain drum at the windows.

The nearby village of **Crovie** (crivvy) is similarly atmospheric, as is the larger settlement of Gardenstown, which rolls down a cliffside. These towns were never just fishing ports; their remoteness meant that they were ideal for smugglers' intrigues, and became important harbours for the movement of illicitly distilled whisky.

Stagecoach Bluebird buses run north from Aberdeen to Fraserburgh (£5.10, 1½ hours, at least hourly). Onward buses running from Fraserburgh to Banff stop at the junctions to these villages, from where it's a short but steep downhill walk.

Banff & Macduff

☎ 01261 / pop 3990 (combined) / elevation 37m (Macduff)

A popular seaside resort, the twin towns of Banff and Macduff are separated by Banff Bridge. Banff is a fairly attractive little town and nearby Macduff is a busy fishing port. The **TIC** (☎ 812419; High St, Banff; ☒ Mon-Sat Apr-Oct, Mon-Sun Jul & Aug) has plenty of brochures about the area and is helpful.

Duff House (☎ 818181; adult £4.50; ☒ 11am-5pm Apr-Oct, 11am-4pm Thu-Sun Nov-Mar), in Banff upstream from the bridge and across from the TIC, is an impressive Georgian baroque mansion designed by William Adam. Completed in 1749, it's been a hotel, hospital and POW camp and is now an art gallery housing a collection of paintings from the National Gallery of Scotland. The House hosts regular live performances including theatre and dance; call to find out what's on.

Stagecoach Bluebird runs buses from Aberdeen and Elgin (one hour, hourly) to Banff and Macduff.

Elgin

☎ 01343 / pop 20,800 / elevation 21m

At the heart of Moray, Elgin has been the provincial capital since the 13th century.

One of the country's sunniest towns, Elgin is a sedate, genteel sort of place, albeit one without a great deal going on. The friendly, helpful **TIC** (☎ 542666; 17 High St; ☒ daily Apr-Oct, Mon-Sat Nov-Mar) dishes out an abundance of leaflets.

Elgin Cathedral (HS; ☎ 547171; adult £3; ☒ 9.30am-6.30pm Apr-Sep, 9.30am-4.30pm Mon-Wed & Sat, 2-4.30pm Sun Oct-Mar) is made of soft sandstone and is undergoing constant restoration, though it must have been magnificent once. It's known as the 'lantern of the north', and was consecrated in 1224. In 1390 it was burnt down by the infamous Wolf of Badenoch (see The Wolf of Badenoch, below) It was rebuilt, but ruined once more in the Reformation.

A few minutes' walk from the centre of the town, **Carrick House** (☎ 569321; 13 South Guildry St; s/d from £24/36; ☒) is a noble Georgian house with rooms kept clean and proper and a log fire in the lounge.

Hourly services along the coast by Stagecoach Bluebird run to Banff and Macduff (one hour), south to Dufftown (50 minutes), west to Inverness (one hour), and southeast to Aberdeen (£8.50, two hours). Trains run four to 10 times daily from Elgin to Aberdeen and Inverness.

Stonehaven

☎ 01569 / pop 9580

A pretty, low-key seaside resort, Stonehaven is nestled around a bay with some good walks and one of the most spectacularly situated castles in the country. The **TIC** (☎ 762806; 66 Allardice St; ☒ 10am-7pm Mon-Sat, 1-6pm Sun) is very helpful.

The most pleasant way to reach **Dunnottar Castle** (☎ 762173; adult £3.50; ☒ 9am-6pm Mon-Sat,

---

THE WOLF OF BADENOCH

Of all the hard figures of medieval Scotland, few inspired as much terror as Alexander Stewart, Earl of Buchan (1343–1405), illegitimate son of the king and better known as the Wolf of Badenoch. A cruel landowner with a number of castles in the Strathspey region, he was not a man to get on the wrong side of, as the Bishop of Moray found out in 1390. When the earl ditched his wife in favour of his mistress, the bishop excommunicated him. The monk that bore the message of excommunication was thrown headfirst into a well, and the infuriated Wolf, accompanied by a band of 'wild and wicked Highland men', embarked on an orgy of destruction, burning first Forres, then Elgin, to the ground, destroying the cathedral and nearby Pluscarden Abbey in the process. Amazingly, he still managed to be buried in Dunkeld cathedral! Legend says his death came on a dark, stormy night. The Devil came calling on a black horse and challenged the Wolf to a game of chess. The Wolf lost, and the devil took his life (and soul) as his prize.

2-5pm Sun Easter-Oct, 9am-dusk Mon-Fri Nov-Mar), is on foot; it's about a fifteen minute walk from the harbour. The castle ruins are sensational, spread out across a grassy promontory rising 45m above the sea – as dramatic a film set as any director could wish for. It was last used for Zeffirelli's *Hamlet*, starring Mel Gibson. The original fortress was built in the 9th century; the keep is the most substantial remnant, but the restored Drawing Room is more interesting.

An appealing place to stay is **Twentyfour-shorehead** (☎ 767750; twentyfourshorehead@btopen world.com; 24 Shorehead; s/d £40/50; ✗). Right on the harbour in a 300-year-old former co-operage; it's a hugely relaxing spot renovated with taste and flair. The bright rooms have big bay windows looking over the water, where you can spot birds and seals using the binoculars thoughtfully provided.

Nearby, **Marine Hotel** (☎ 762155; 9 Shorehead; mains £8-10; ☾ lunch & dinner) is a real-ale pub which overlooks the harbour and has a 1970's jukebox in the backroom of the public bar. Excellent meals are freshly prepared, and the menu changes regularly, although fresh seafood is always present.

Buses regularly stop in Stonehaven travelling between Dundee (£7.30, 1½ hours, hourly) and Aberdeen (45 minutes, at least hourly), as do trains following the same route.

DUNDEE & ANGUS

Often bypassed by visitors, this attractive region of peaceful glens running down to the sea has traditionally been more concerned with making a living than prettifying itself for tourism. It makes an appealing destination for precisely this reason.

The city of Dundee, dealt a body blow with the collapse of its traditional industries of jute and whaling, is achieving notable success with its programme of urban renewal. While it's still far from an attractive place, it has several excellent modern attractions and cultural centres, including the superb Verdant Works jute museum.

Angus was an important part of the Pictish kingdom in the 7th and 8th centuries; it's also famous for harbouring Glamis castle, childhood home of the Queen Mother, and where the bloody deeds of *Macbeth* are

set. Arbroath is one of several appealing seaside towns, dignified by a majestic ruined abbey, and home to one of Scotland's greatest culinary achievements, the smokie.

GETTING AROUND
Strathtay Scottish (☎ 01382-228054; www.strathtay buses.com) is the main bus operator between Dundee and places in Angus. Trains run east along the scenic coastline from Dundee to Arbroath and Montrose.

DUNDEE
☎ 01382 / pop 154,700 / elevation 75m
Scotland's fourth-largest city has always been quick to adapt. Legend says that one day, when a cargo of bitter oranges was left to rot onboard a ship, an enterprising grandmother took them home, boiled them up, and produced the first batch of marmalade. Jam was one of the three Js that drove the city's economy for many decades. The other two were journalism, in the form of the *Desperate Dan* and *Beano* comics, and the jute industry. Dan himself stands proud in the city's main square, while the rise and fall of jute is explained in one of Britain's most enthralling museums, Verdant Works.

Severe urban poverty in the wake of the collapse of the jute industry gave the city a grim reputation, and poor civic planning left Dundee with a series of ugly architectural eyesores that still scar the town, but things are now ambitiously moving forward. Waterfront redevelopment is slowly taking advantage of the city's beautiful position on the Firth of Tay, while the newly opened museum Sensation is one of the nation's best for kids. Broughty Ferry, a few miles east, has always been where Dundonians, the most open and welcoming of folk, head at weekends to stroll on the beach or nestle down with a pint and a pub lunch. A fashionable destination Dundee isn't – yet – but anyone interested in urban renewal or authentic Scottish cities will find plenty here.

History
In the 19th century, Dundee was a major player in the shipbuilding and railway engineering industries. Linen and wool gave way to jute and, since whale oil was used in the production of jute, whaling developed

alongside. At one time there were as many as 41,000 people employed in the textile industry, and as the jute workers became redundant, tough economic times led to the city developing a reputation as one of the most 'red' in Britain. Winston Churchill, who was once MP for Dundee, described speaking to 'an audience of lions with Communist teeth'. The city was also important in the suffragette movement.

Orientation

Most people approach the city from the Tay Rd Bridge or along the A90 from Perth; both routes take you into the centre. Four miles east of Dundee is Broughty Ferry, Dundee's seaside resort, and a good base.

Information

Dundee City Library (Wellgate Shopping Centre; ☺ 9.30am-9pm Mon-Fri, 9.30am-5pm) Free Internet access.
TIC (☎ 527527; enquires@angusanddundee.co.uk; 21 Castle St; ☺ 9am-5pm Mon-Sat Oct-May, 9am-6pm Mon-Sat, noon-4pm Sun Jun-Sep) Very helpful. Internet access £1 for 15 minutes.

Sights
VERDANT WORKS

One of Britain's best museums, **Verdant Works** (☎ 225282; www.verdantworks.com; West Henderson's Wynd; adult £5.95, £10.95 combined ticket with Discovery Point; ☺ 10am-6pm Mon-Sat, 11am-6pm Sun Easter-Oct, 10-30am-4.30pm Wed-Sat, 11am-4.30pm Sun Nov-Easter; wheelchair access) brings the history of Dundee's jute industry to life. The museum is housed

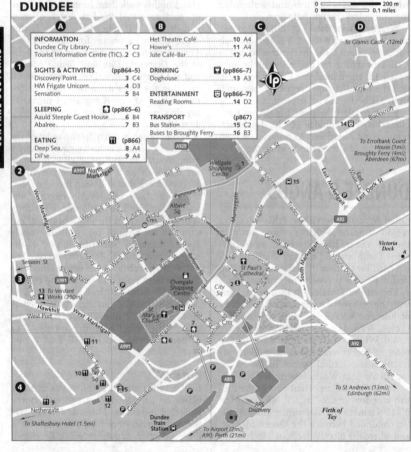

DUNDEE

0 — 200 m
0 — 0.1 miles

| INFORMATION | |
| Dundee City Library..................1 C2 |
| Tourist Information Centre (TIC)..2 C3 |

| SIGHTS & ACTIVITIES (pp864–5) | |
| Discovery Point...........................3 C4 |
| HM Frigate Unicorn.....................4 D3 |
| Sensation....................................5 B4 |

| SLEEPING 🛏 (pp865–6) | |
| Aauld Steeple Guest House...........6 B4 |
| Abalree......................................7 B3 |

| EATING 🍴 (p866) | |
| Deep Sea....................................8 A4 |
| Dil'se...9 A4 |

| Het Theatre Café.......................10 A4 |
| Howie's....................................11 A4 |
| Jute Café-Bar............................12 A4 |

| DRINKING 🍷 (pp866–7) | |
| Doghouse.................................13 A3 |

| ENTERTAINMENT 🎭 (pp866–7) | |
| Reading Rooms.........................14 D2 |

| TRANSPORT (p867) | |
| Bus Station...............................15 C2 |
| Buses to Broughty Ferry...........16 B3 |

To Glamis Castle (12mi)
To Errolbank Guest House (1mi); Broughty Ferry (4mi); Aberdeen (67mi)
To Verdant Works (250m)
To St Andrews (13mi); Edinburgh (62mi)
To Shaftesbury Hotel (1.5mi)
To Airport (2mi); A90; Perth (21mi)

Victoria Dock
RRS Discovery
Firth of Tay
Dundee Train Station
Tay Rd Bridge

CENTRAL SCOTLAND

in a restored jute mill; your visit begins with a charismatic guided tour, with plenty of atmosphere given by recorded voices with impenetrable Dundonian accents. The whole process of jute making is explained, and staff demonstrate the working of the production line with functioning machines. There's a display of social history that gives the visit so much more meaning than just jute; the museum as a whole makes powerful statements about the rise and fall of heavy industry and its effect on the ordinary population. There's plenty here to keep the kids entertained as well, and the enthusiasm and humour of the staff make it a memorable experience.

DISCOVERY POINT

It's worth checking out **Discovery Point** (☎ 201 245; www.rrsdiscovery.com; adult £6.25, combined ticket with Verdant Works £10.95; ◷ 10am-6pm Mon-Sat, 11am-6pm Sun Apr-Oct, 10am-5pm Mon-Sat, 11am-5pm Sun Nov-Mar), centred on Captain Scott's famous polar expedition vessel, *Discovery*, which was constructed here in 1900 with a hull more than half a metre thick to survive the Antarctic pack ice. Scott sailed for the Antarctic in 1901 and, in a not uneventful voyage, spent two winters trapped in the ice as the endeavour ended in disaster.

There are some excellent displays on Antarctic exploration and Scott's expedition, and you can then go on board the ship, moored in dry-dock, to see the cabins used by Scott and his crew.

HM FRIGATE UNICORN

Constructed in 1824, the **Unicorn** (☎ 200893; www.frigateunicorn.org; adult £3.50; ◷ 10am-5pm Apr-Oct, noon-4pm Wed-Fri, 10am-4pm Sat & Sun Nov-Mar) is the oldest British-built warship still afloat – perhaps that's because it never saw action.

Wandering around the frigate's four decks gives an excellent impression of what it must have been like for the 300-strong crew to live in such cramped conditions. The entry price includes a guided tour. The *Unicorn* is berthed in Victoria Dock, east of the Tay Rd Bridge. Plans are afoot to take it out of the water into a dry-dock facility in order to ensure its preservation.

SENSATION

The latest attraction in Dundee's impressive reinvention of itself is a modern **museum**

(☎ 228800; www.sensation.org.uk; Greenmarket; adult/child £6.50/4.50; ◷ 10am-5pm; ♿ wheelchair access) designed for the young and the energetic. One of the country's best family attractions, it's an ideal place for kids, tired perhaps of art galleries and noble buildings, to reclaim the holiday. As the name suggests, the place is designed interactively, with dozens of hands-on attractions in five halls based on each of the senses. A giant head gives you the chance to slide down the nostril; elsewhere you can experience zero-gravity in a gyroscope (be prepared to queue) or explore the innards of a leaf.

BROUGHTY FERRY

This pleasant suburb, known to locals simply as 'The Ferry', is 4 miles east of Dundee. There's a long, sandy beach and a number of good places to eat and drink – some have great views across the Firth of Tay to Fife.

Broughty Castle Museum (☎ 436916; HS; Castle Green; admission free; ◷ 10am-4pm Mon-Sat, 12.30-4pm Sun Apr-Sep, 10am-4pm Tue-Sat, 12.30-4pm Sun Oct-Mar) is a reconstructed 16th-century tower guarding the entrance to the Firth of Tay. It has a good display on Dundee's whaling industry and great views.

The easiest way to get to Broughty Ferry is to take bus No 40, 75, 76, or 80 from Nethergate.

Sleeping

Broughty Ferry has several good options; Monifieth Rd is a good place to hunt down B&Bs.

BUDGET

Abalree (☎ 223867; fax 229239; 20 Union St; s/d from £15/30) This excellent budget guesthouse is run enthusiastically by genial, died-in-the-wool Dundonians who love a chat. Right in the city centre, the building's dark staircase gives no clue of the colourful and comfortable rooms with TV inside. Shared bathrooms are small but clean, and there's 24-hour access.

Aauld Steeple Guest House (☎ 200302; 94 Nethergate; s/d from £21/36; ✗) Another very central option and one that provides excellent lodging. The double rooms are particularly spacious and some overlook St Marys Church. The only problem can be noise from the pissed and disorderly outside on the street at weekends.

MID-RANGE

Ashley House (☎ 776109; www.ashley-house.com; 15 Monifieth Rd, Broughty Ferry; s/d £30/45; P ✗) This is a fine place indeed, run by thoughtful hosts who make their guests very comfortable. All the four rooms are a little different; a couple have a VCR, one has a very ornate bathroom, but all are bright and have top-notch beds. You can easily walk from here to the centre of Broughty Ferry – along Brook St.

Errolbank Guest House (☎/fax 462118; 9 Dalgleish Rd; s/d from £26/46; P ✗) This quiet family home is a mile east of the centre in a quiet leafy street. It's a friendly, peaceful, hideaway with easy bus access to and from the centre and Broughty Ferry. Some rooms have a view of the firth, and are decorated with flowery cheeriness. The breakfasts have been praised too. No credit cards are accepted.

Other recommendations:

Marlee Guest House (☎ 779435; 3 Norrie St, Broughty Ferry; s/d £30/45; ✗) Just off Monifieth Rd, this has clean and bright lavishly furnished rooms in the Ferry.

Shaftesbury Hotel (☎ 669216; www.shaftesbury-hotel .co.uk; 1 Hyndford St; s/d from £51/68; ✗ ; wheelchair access) Former jute baron's mansion that preserves much period character.

Eating

Dil'se (☎ 221501; 99 Perth Rd; mains £7-14; ☽ lunch & dinner; ✗ ; wheelchair access) This newly-risen star on the Dundee eating scene is a Bangladeshi restaurant that has already won the Good Curry Guide's award for best restaurant in Scotland. It's a large, glass-fronted spot as innovative in its modern lines as its mouth-watering menu. Old favourites such as perfectly marinated chicken tikka are irresistibly flavoursome, while innovations such as Mas Bangla, which is an unexpected take on Scottish salmon, are equally unforgettable.

Howie's (☎ 200399; 25 South Tay St; 2 course lunch/dinner £8.75/15.95; ☽ lunch & dinner; ✗ ; wheelchair access) The relaxed contemporary elegance and sharply-priced fine dining of this group of restaurants has made them a reliable favourite in Edinburgh. The formula works here too, with two floors of sleek polished floorboards, plenty of choice on the set menu, and even four luxurious rooms with various weekend packages available.

Het Theatre Café (☎ 206699; Tay Square; mains £7-11; ☽ café 10am-late Mon-Sat, restaurant lunch & dinner Mon-Sat; ✗ ; wheelchair access) A chic arty hangout at the Dundee Rep Theatre, this is a European-style café, bar and restaurant and a great place for a caffeine hit, a snack, or a fuller meal – there are many vegetarian options available.

Jute Café-Bar (☎ 606220; Dundee Contemporary Arts Centre, Nethergate; mains £7-13; ☽ 10.30am-9.30pm; ✗ ; wheelchair access) This sexy little café is yet more evidence that Dundee's dour reputation is being firmly consigned to the past. There are some inventive dishes here such as tuna and roast chilli wraps and honey glazed spicy pork skewers; it's a good spot for people watching and is embraced by young and old alike.

Deep Sea (☎ 224449, 81 Nethergate; take-away £3.50; ☽ 9.30am-6.30pm Mon-Sat; ✗) It's a curious feature of Scotland that many of its best fish-and-chip shops are run by Italian families. The jovial Tuscan Dundonians here fry up an excellent cod supper, which you can eat here or take away. Portions are generous; the only pity is that it closes in the evenings, although, seeing the bedlam at other chip shops after pub closing, you can only really applaud their wisdom.

Visocchi's (☎ 779297; 40 Gray St, Broughty Ferry; pasta & pizza £6-10; ☽ breakfast, lunch & dinner Tue-Sun; ✗) This ice-cream shop and café is an institution in the Ferry. It's all things to all people, whether you're after a tasty vanilla cone to lick on the beach, a quick pizza before a night on the town, or a seriously strong double espresso the morning after.

Drinking & Entertainment

Some of the best spots for a few pints are in Broughty Ferry. In Dundee, the Jute Café-Bar and Het Theatre Café listed in Eating are also relaxed places to sip a glass of something.

Doghouse (☎ 227080; 13 Brown St) This big, tall, barn of a bar, Dundee's alternative HQ and best venue for live music, has recently triumphantly re-opened. Dark, spacious, and atmospheric, there's live music – mostly rock – on every weekend, and well-attended comedy nights on Mondays. There are pool tables, a long bar, good crack (conversation), and also a few tables outdoors. Never has being in the doghouse been such a pleasure.

Fisherman's Tavern (☎ 775941; 12 Fort St, Broughty Ferry) This community pub serves good cask ales and is a terrific little nook and cranny pub. Once you order a drink you won't want to leave. There's also a beer garden, scene of a rowdy and thoroughly enjoyable **beer festival** every June, the proceeds of which go to the local lifeboat association.

Ship Inn (☎ 779176; 121 Fisher St, Broughty Ferry) Located on the seafront, this cabin-style wooden pub is small, intimate, and full of nautical fittings. They do fine bar meals; it's very cosy, and you can look out across the Firth of Tay, and see the local lifeboats launching for drills or rescues.

Reading Rooms (☎ 0790 535 3301; www.thereading rooms.co.uk; 57 Blackscroft; 🕑 3pm-2.30am Wed-Sun) Some of Scotland's best club nights take place in this innovative venue, as well as regular live music. You can hear everything from big band and jazz to punk and the latest electronic sounds. There's a pleasant beer garden, and free breakdance lessons on Wednesday evenings.

Shopping

While the city centre has the usual mega-malls, Broughty Ferry and Perth Rd have a few quirkier options.

Izta (☎ 737666; 29 Gray St, Broughty Ferry) This enchantingly offbeat shop is a perfect spot to find a gift for someone who won't appreciate a tartan tea-towel. There's high quality furniture, silver jewellery, mirrors, and curiosities, many with a Mexican flavour.

Getting There & Away

If you're driving over the Tay Rd Bridge from Fife, it's toll-free in that direction only; leaving Dundee it costs 80p (arrogant folk from other cities sneer that it's the only reason why anyone lives there!).

AIR

The **airport** (☎ 643242; Riverside Dr) is roughly 1½ miles west of the centre; daily flights head to London City Airport (p169) with **ScotAirways** (☎ 0870 606 0707; www.scotairways.co.uk).

BUS

There are Citylink services to/from Edinburgh (£8.60, two hours, hourly), Glasgow (£9, 2¼ hours, hourly), Perth (£4, 35 minutes, half-hourly) and Aberdeen (£9, two hours, more than hourly).

TRAIN

There is no shortage of services from Edinburgh (£16.40, 1¼ hours, one or two hourly)

and Glasgow (£21.60, 1½ hours, at least hourly). Trains for Aberdeen (£19.10, 1¼ hours, two hourly) run via Arbroath and Stonehaven.

AROUND DUNDEE
Glamis Castle

Looking every bit a Scottish castle, with turrets and battlements, **Glamis Castle** (glarms; ☎ 01307-840393; castle & grounds £6.80, grounds only £3.50; 🕑 10am-6pm Apr-Oct, last admission 4.30pm, ring for winter opening; wheelchair access to grounds only, free) was the legendary setting for Shakespeare's *Macbeth*.

The Grampians and an extensive park provide a spectacular backdrop for this family home of the Earls of Strathmore and Kinghorne. The daughter of one of the earls, Elizabeth Bowes-Lyon, better known as the Queen Mother, grew up here.

The only way to see the inside of the castle is by taking one of the tours (every 15 minutes). Guides make a real effort to make the tours interesting for children also; the tours take about 50 minutes. The most impressive room is the drawing room, with its arched plasterwork ceiling, while the frescoes on the roof of the chapel (apparently its haunted) are magnificent. There's a display of armour and weaponry in the crypt (also haunted).

The castle is 12 miles north of Dundee in the village of Glamis. There are Strathtay Scottish buses from Dundee (35 minutes, one to three daily) to the castle itself, and a couple more that stop in the adjacent village. The Dundee TIC has a leaflet on reaching the castle by bus.

ARBROATH
☎ 01241 / pop 22,800

Arbroath is a thriving little resort town riding nicely off the back of the tourist dollar. It's the source of the famous Arbroath smokie (smoked haddock): they are exquisitely flavoured – you can't leave town without trying one! The town also takes great pride in its football team, world record holders from the day in 1885 when they beat hapless Bon Accord 36-0! The **TIC** (☎ 872609; Market Pl; 🕑 daily Jun-Aug, Mon-Sat Sep-May) is worth visiting.

The town was established as a fishing port in the 12th century, and the settlement grew up around **Arbroath Abbey** (HS; ☎ 878756;

adult £3.30; ⏱ 9.30am-6.30pm Apr-Oct, 9.30am-4.30pm Oct-Mar; almost complete wheelchair access). King William the Lion, who is buried here, founded the abbey in 1178. It was at the abbey that Robert the Bruce signed Scotland's famous declaration of independence from England in 1320, which contained the oft-quoted words: 'It is in truth not for glory, nor riches, nor honours that we are fighting, but for freedom'. Closed following the Dissolution, the fortified abbey fell into ruin but enough survives to make this a very impressive sight. The **visitors centre** next door outlines the turbulent history of the abbey, as well as providing a good virtual tour of how it might have looked in its prime. It makes a laudable effort to provide accessible information for kids too.

Scurdy Guesthouse (☎ 872417; 33 Marketgate; s/d from £20/32) is awash with flowers and has homely good-sized rooms and benevolent owners. There's the option of shared bathrooms or en-suite rooms. It's handy to the centre of town and near the tourist office.

The **Old Brewhouse** (☎ 879945; 3 High St; mains £5-9, ⏱ lunch & dinner) is a pub right on the harbour wall, a perfect place to try a smokie, which are very tasty here. There's cosy indoor seating, tables outside for a sunny day, and the addictive Orkney Dark Island on tap.

Strathtay Scottish has buses from Dundee (45 minutes, frequent), as does Citylink from Edinburgh/Glasgow. However, the scenic trip along the coast from Dundee (20 minutes, up to three an hour) makes the train journey worthwhile.

Highlands & Northern Islands

Everything you ever imagined about Scotland can be found here, in the vast wilderness that is the Highlands and northern islands. The epic, brutal majesty of nature will etch itself on your mind; it is a place to which you'll always feel a pull to return. Soaring peaks and bleak moorland, clean air and straight talking; you are a lifetime away from the stresses of urban life here in Britain's far north.

The space here is exhilarating, but also melancholy, if you reflect on the brutal evictions of the Highland Clearances. Broken stone speaks of shattered communities that once eked out a living here from the harsh terrain. Harsh, but beautiful beyond description, this area leaves the visitor dumbstruck as vista after vista unfolds, of rockfaces sliding down to dark lochs, of stern castles, of sun, mists, heather, and a coastline gouged out by the last Ice Age.

While the north and west Highlands have a titanic profile of mountains and cliffs, the windswept, treeless Orkneys and Shetlands have a different appeal with a raw, bare beauty, intriguing Viking origins and cracking hospitality.

The whole region is a place visitors have an irresistible urge to interact with; through a windscreen is not enough to fully appreciate the tangible spirit of the place. The spongy spring of ground underfoot, the exfoliating wind, the glow of a well-earned malt, even the bite of the pesky midge; these are what keep people returning to this magical zone.

HIGHLIGHTS

- Sending your brain into overload with the scenic majesty of the coasts around **Durness** (p898)

- Pondering Viking graffiti and Stone-Age architecture at **Skara Brae** (p924) and **Maes Howe** (p923)

- Hiking the imposing and jagged **Cuillin Hills** (p908) on Skye

- De-stressing with the marvellous beachside remoteness of the **Baile-na-Cille** (p913) hotel

- Diving the wrecks of the German High Seas Fleet at **Scapa Flow** (p923)

- Watching a ferry chugging up the sound into beautiful **Ullapool** (p900)

- POPULATION: 276,649

- AREA: 12,041 SQ MILES

Activities

For outdoor-lovers, and walkers especially, heaven is the highlands of Scotland. You can come here for 50 years and still find a 'new' peak or footpath, so for occasional visitors this section can only hope to provide a few essential pointers. More information is given in the main Activities chapter located near the start of this book, and suggestions for shorter routes are given throughout this chapter. Regional TICs stock free leaflets plus maps and guides covering walking, cycling and other activities.

CYCLING

There are few roads in northern Scotland, but almost every one is a joy to cycle – they wind through glorious scenery, and are frequently light on traffic, although distances between towns (or any settlements at all) can be long. The northern section of the 214-mile **Lochs & Glens Cycle Route**, starts in Glasgow and winds its way through the heart of the region via Loch Ness and Pitlochry to end in Inverness. The **Aberdeen to John o'Groats Cycle Route** leads inland across the Aberdeenshire Peninsula, via Inverness, before aiming north for the extreme northeast point on the British mainland, and continuing on through Orkney and Shetland as well. On the other side of the region, if you set aside a couple of weeks, and had fair weather, one of the most rewarding (and possibly hardest) rides available follows the stunning roads of the west coast through Kyle of Lochalsh, Kinlochewe, Gairloch, Ullapool and Inchnadamph – and possibly all the way to Cape Wrath.

And finally, the islands – Skye is a wonderful destination, and is the most easily reached island in this region. The cycling tour of central Scotland's islands outlined under Activities in the Central Scotland chapter could be continued from here by riding the quiet roads between Kilchoan and Mallaig (OK, the final stretch from Lochailort isn't quiet), and then taking the ferry over to Skye.

If you wanted to go even further, ferries from Skye sail to the Outer Hebrides, where an end-to-end tour of this island chain is a popular cycling option. The only disadvantage with heading this way is that you may often be facing the wind (it usually comes from the southwest, and has the whole of the Atlantic to get up speed), so doing this tour in reverse is another option, sailing from Oban to Barra or South Uist, heading 10 miles north to Harris and Lewis, and then going by ferry back to Skye and the mainland. There are bike-rental outfits on Skye, Lewis, Barra and South Uist.

WALKING

Long-distance walking possibilities in this region include the **Great Glen Way**, a 70-mile jaunt from Fort William to Inverness along the Great Glen – a massive geological fault which almost divides the northwest Highlands from the rest of Scotland, and the **West Highland Way** which runs from Fort William south towards Glasgow (p880). If you don't want to go the whole distance, Glencoe (21 miles) makes a good place to aim for and it is a fine area in its own right for mountain walking. A more leisurely, and very beautiful, route is the **Speyside Way** (p875), which follows one of Scotland's best-loved rivers from the Cairngorm foothills to the coast.

For day walks, areas include the Cairngorm range, with Aviemore making a good base. There are short and low-level walks in two large forest estates nearby – Rothiemurchus and Glen More – and some very serious high-level walks on the mountain summits. In the southwest of this region, Fort William is the place to head if you fancy **climbing** Britain's highest peak, Ben Nevis, and numerous other summits – although conditions here can be very serious, so you need to be fully prepared with appropriate equipment. There are also pleasant and far less strenuous walks along Glen Nevis.

North of Fort William, the area inland from the west coast is packed with what are undoubtedly the finest mountains in Britain. This is often remote, serious country (no signposts, often no paths) but if you know what you're doing, it's unbeatable, with endless square miles to yourself, and views so clear on some days that the Outer Hebrides seem a mere hop away. Areas to head for include Glen Shiel, the mountains of Torridon, and the peaks of the far northwest such as Suilven and Quinag.

Off the west coast, of all the Scottish islands, Skye offers some of the finest walking. Further west again, North Harris is

HIGHLANDS & NORTHERN ISLANDS

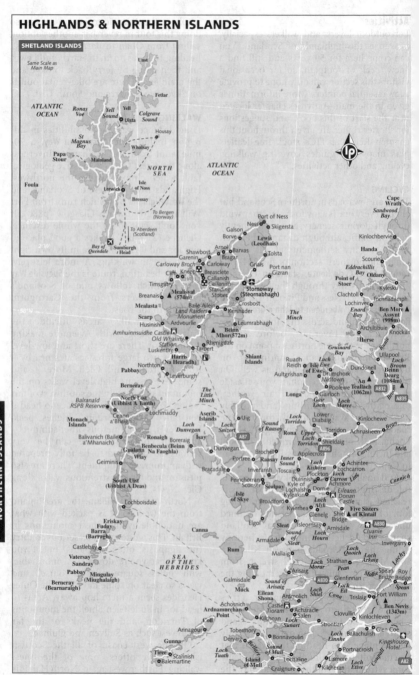

SHETLAND ISLANDS

Same Scale as
Main Map

*ATLANTIC
OCEAN*

Unst

Fetlar

*Ronas
Voe*

Yell
Sound

Yell

Colgrave
Sound

Uista

*St
Magnus
Bay*

Housay

Papa
Stour

Mainland

Whalsay

*NORTH
SEA*

Foula

Lerwick

Isle
of Noss

Bressay

To Bergen
(Norway)

To Aberdeen
(Scotland)

Bay of
Quendale

Sumburgh
Head

2° W

*ATLANTIC
OCEAN*

Cape
Wrath

*Sandwood
Bay*

Kinlochbervie

Handa

Scourie

*Eddrachillis
Bay*

Oldany

Point of
Stoer

Kylesku

Clachtoll

Inchnadamph

Lochinver

Ben More
Assynt
(998m)

*Enard
Bay*

Archiltibuie

Knockan

Horse

Ullapool

Loch
Broom

Port of Ness

Ness

Skigersta

Galson

Lewis
(Leodhais)

Borve

Shawbost

Arnol

Barvas

Bragar

Garenin

Tolsta

Grias

Carloway Broch

Carloway

Port nan
Gizran

Cliff

Knepp

Breasclete

Callanish

Timsgatry

Callanish
Standing
Stones

Stornoway
(Steornabhagh)

Breanais

Mealisval
(574m)

Mealasta

Baile Ailein

Crosbost

Scarp

Land Raiders
Monument

Kershader

*The
Minch*

Husinish

Ardvourlie

Leumrabhagh

Amhuinnsuidhe Castle

Beinn
Mhor(572m)

Luskentire

Old Whaling
Station

Rhenigdale

Harris
(Na Hearadh)

Tarbert

*Shiant
Islands*

Northton

Pabbay

Leverburgh

Berneray

*The
Little
Minch*

Balranald
RSPB Reserve

North Uist
(Uibhist A Tuath)

Ceann
a'Bhaigh

Lochmaddy

Monach
Islands

Borerlay

Ronaigh

Isay

Balivanich (Baile
a'Mhanaich)

Gualann

Benbecula (Beinn
Na Faoghla)

Geirinis

Wiay

South Uist
(Uibhist A Deas)

Lochboisdale

Eriskay

Fuday

Barra
(Barraigh)

Castlebay

Vatersay

Sandray

Pabbay

Mingulay
(Miughalaigh)

Berneray
(Bearnaraigh)

*Gruinard
Bay*

Ruadh
Reidh

Loch
Ewe

Isle
of Ewe

Dundonell

Aultgrishan

Drumchork

Midtown

An
Teallach
(1084m)

Beinn
Dearg

Poolewe

Longa

Gair
Loch

Lower
Diabaig

Loch
Maree

Kinlochewe

Achnasheen

Uig

Rona

Upper
Loch
Torridon

Torridon

Shieldaig

Loch
Snizort

Sound
of Raasay

Lower
Loch
Torridon

Aserib
Islands

Loch
Dunvegan

Applecross

Dunvegan

Brochel

Loch
Kishorn

Loch
Carron

Bochcarron

Achintee

Portree

Raasay

Inner
Sound

Plockton

Carron

Duirinish

Achmore

Bracadale

Inverarish

Toscaig

Kyle of
Lochalsh

Dornie

Eilean
Donan
Castle

Peinchorran

Sconser

Seatpay

Kyleakin

Isle
of Skye

Broadford

Loch
Alsh

Kylerhea

Five Sisters
of Kintail

Shiel
Bridge

Isleornsay

Glenelg

Elgol

Sleat

Loch
Hourn

Amisdale

Cluanie
Inn

Sound
of
Sleat

Invergarry

Canna

Armadale

Loch
Quoich

Loch
Arkaig

Strathan

Rum

Mallaig

Loch
Morar

Pean

Spean
Bridge

Roy
Bridge

*SEA
OF THE
HEBRIDES*

Eigg

Arisaig

Glenfinnan

Loch
Eil

Cona

Trislaig

Fort William

Galmisdale

Sound
of
Arisaig

Loch
Shiel

Muck

Eilean
Shona

Clovullin

Ben Nevis
(1343m)

Achosnich

Ardnamurchan
Point

Castle
Tioram

Ardmolich

Acharacle

Salen

Strontian

Kinlochleven

Coll

Arinagour

Kilchoan

Loch
Sunart

Glen Coe

Kingshouse
Hotel

Gunna

Dervaig

Tobermory

Bonnavoulin

Loch
Linnhe

Ballachulish

Portnacroish

Tiree

Scarinish

Balemartine

Loch
Tuath

Sound
of Mull

Lochaline

Island
of Mull

Lismore

Loch
Etive

Craignure

Kilcheran

A82

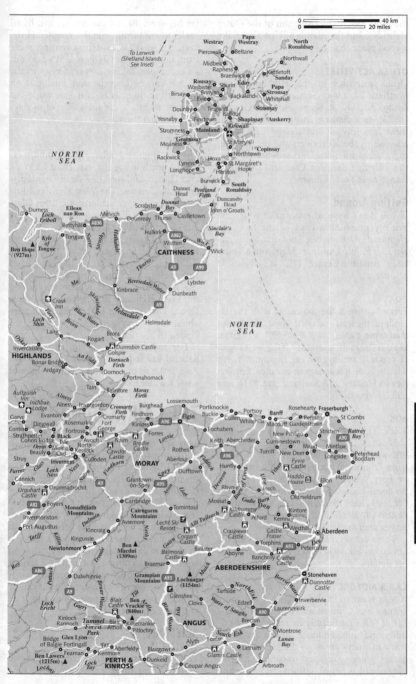

the most mountainous region of the Outer Hebrides, and the islands of Uist also make a good place to aim for.

OTHER ACTIVITIES

Other activities in the Highlands and northern Islands of Scotland include **scuba diving**, notably at Scapa Flow in Orkney (p923); **rock climbing** and mountaineering, most famously on and around Ben Nevis; and fishing, both on rivers and the sea. The main areas for **skiing** and **snowboarding** are the Cairngorms, Glen Coe, and the Nevis Range near Fort William.

Getting Around

If you don't have wheels, make your first priority grabbing a copy of the free *The Highlands, Orkney, Shetland and the Western Isles Public Transport Map* from a Tourist Information Centre (TIC). It's a valuable resource.

BOAT

Ferries connect the mainland with the islands off the west and north coasts. **Caledonian MacBrayne** (CalMac; ☎ 0870 565 0000; www.calmac .co.uk) is the main operator off the west coast. If you're travelling by car in summer, it's wise to book a few days in advance. For ferries to Orkney and Shetland, see p916 and p932, respectively.

BUS

Wick, Thurso, Ullapool and Kyle of Lochalsh can all be reached by **Citylink** (☎ 0870 550 5050; www.citylink.co.uk) bus from Inverness, or from Edinburgh and Glasgow via Inverness or Fort William. Another major operator on local routes is **Rapsons/Highland Country** (☎ 01463-710555; www.rapsons.co.uk). The **Royal Mail Postbus** (☎ 0845 774 0740; www.postbus.royalmail.com) serves many remote communities.

There are several bus services specifically aimed at backpackers; see Transport (p963) for details.

CAR & MOTORCYCLE

If you want to explore some of the more remote areas you should consider hiring a car; it will significantly increase your flexibility and independence. Roads are single track in many areas, so duck into passing places when you spot oncoming traffic. Plan ahead as petrol stations can be few and

far between. Rental-car outlets are listed under towns throughout this chapter. However, it's worth considering renting a car from Edinburgh or Glasgow as it works out a bit cheaper. Taking cars on ferries to the islands can be an expensive business; on the further-flung islands it can work out cheaper to hire a car for a couple of days once you get there.

TRAIN

The two Highland railway lines from Inverness – north along the east coast to Wick and Thurso, and west to Kyle of Lochalsh – are justly famous. The West Highland line also follows a spectacular route from Glasgow to Fort William and Mallaig (for the Isle of Skye and the Small Isles).

ScotRail's Highland Rover ticket gives four days of unlimited travel to be used within eight days (£59) on the lines from Inverness to Wick and Thurso, Kyle of Lochalsh, Aberdeen and Aviemore; and on the West Highland line between Glasgow, Oban, Fort William and Mallaig; enquire about local ferry and bus travel also included in the ticket.

For rail information, you can call the **National Rail Enquiries** (☎ 08457 48 49 50; www .nationalrail.co.uk) or check ScotRail's website at www.scotrail.co.uk.

THE CAIRNGORMS

This spectacular pocket of Scotland is an outdoor paradise encompassing Britain's second-highest mountain range, which towers over forests of regenerating native Caledonian pine and a broad valley cut by the sparkling River Spey. It presents a different aspect throughout the year; walkers and bird-watchers pace the forest paths in spring and summer, hoping for a glimpse of the rare capercaillie or osprey, while in winter things crank up at Britain's largest ski resort. Throughout, the proud Cairngorm peaks overlook proceedings; it can be difficult to tell where these mountains end and the clouds begin.

AVIEMORE

☎ 01479 / pop 2397

Touristy Aviemore is the main access town for the Cairngorm range. Aspiring to become a Highland Chamonix, the settlement has fallen well short of the mark, and its crass architectural follies have made the town ugly rather than swanky. Fortunately, the outstanding natural beauty of the surrounding area and the plethora of activities on offer mean you shouldn't need to spend much time in town anyway! If you're using public transport, it does make a convenient base; if you're with wheels, head for other spots.

Orientation & Information

Aviemore is just off the A9 bypass. Grampian Rd is a frenzy of tourist tack so you can hardly get lost. The train station, banks and eateries are on this road. The Cairngorms skiing and hiking area is 8 miles southeast of Aviemore at the end of the Ski Rd (B970/A951), which runs through two large forest estates: Rothiemurchus and Glen More.

The busy **TIC** (☎ 0870 050 4000; Grampian Rd; ☺ daily Apr-Oct, closed Sun Nov-Mar), was, at the time of research, about to make a new home in the Aviemore Shopping Centre next to the train station in the heart of town. It has a bureau de change and sells many Ordnance Survey (OS) maps of the area, as well as books on walking in the Cairngorms.

There's a cluster of ATMs just outside Tesco supermarket on Grampian Rd. Many outdoor equipment shops along Grampian Rd organise hire and ski lessons. Try **Ellis Brigham** (☎ 810175; 9 Grampian Rd), near the train station. The cheapest of several places to get online is the **Old Bridge Hotel** (Dalfaber Rd; per hr £2) on the other side of the tracks.

Activities
ACTIVITY CENTRES

Glenmore Lodge (☎ 861256; www.glenmorelodge .co.uk; Loch Morlich) is a seriously impressive centre for training courses in almost any snow, rock, or water-based activity you care to name. It offers levels of professionalism many outfits only dream of; most courses last three to five days, although there are some one-day sessions. The lodge offers excellent accommodation (see p876).

FISHING

Pull on the waders, choose your favourite fly and ready the frypan – this is fishing

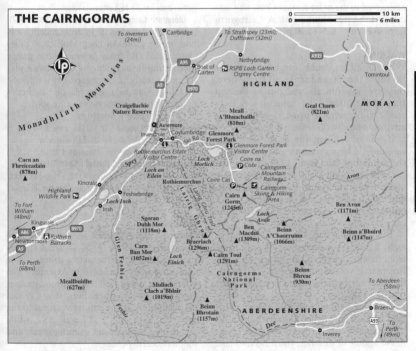

country. The TIC has information on beats and permits for the River Spey and various lochs. Local shops, such as **Speyside Sports** (☎ 810656; 1 Station Sq), sell fishing permits (local rivers/lochs £25/15). Less demanding, the **Rothiemurchus Fishery** (☎ 810703; Rothiemurchus Estate) has stocked lochs, rod hire and tuition available. You might even spot an osprey plucking a trout from the water.

SKIING

With 28 runs **CairnGorm Mountain** (☎ 861261; www.cairngormmountain.com) is Britain's largest ski area. The snow, as elsewhere in Scotland, is notoriously unreliable, but if there's a good fall has blanketed the area, and the sun happens to be burning through the clouds, you'll be in a unique position to drink in the beauty of this country; the skiing isn't half bad either. The season runs from December until the snow melts, which can be at the end of April.

The ski area is about 9 miles southeast of Aviemore. Ski tows and the controversial Cairngorm Mountain Railway funicular start from the main Coire Cas car park, and are connected to the more distant Coire na Ciste car park by free shuttle bus. A Cairngorm day ticket costs £25/15.50 per adult/child.

WALKING

Whereas hikers could formerly catch the ski-lift to the top and strike off from there, they are now not allowed out of the top funicular station. The funicular railway was a controversial project, opposed by environmentalists (see boxed text, p877).

If you're looking for a half-day hike (around 4½ hours return), you can walk to the summit of **Cairn Gorm** (1245m) from the car park at the end of the Ski Rd. From there you can continue south to walk to **Ben Macdui** (1309m – Britain's second-highest peak), but this can take eight to 10 hours from the car park, and it's a serious walk.

The **Lairig Ghru trail**, which can take up to eight hours, is a demanding 24-mile route from Aviemore over the Lairig Ghru Pass to Braemar. If you're not doing the full route, it's still worth hiking the six-hour return trip up to the pass.

These are serious walks, and, with Scotland's weather being notoriously changeable, it's imperative to go properly equipped. Even in the middle of summer, you'll need to take

plenty of sustenance and liquids, as well as a good map, a compass, and windproof jacket. Always ask about conditions before heading out. In winter these walks are not to be attempted without serious equipment and experience of snowy conditions.

A more sedate, and extremely beautiful walk, the **Speyside Way** is a waymarked trail that follows the River Spey from Aviemore to the coast at Spey Bay, passing through whisky country and running along a former railway line.

Sleeping
BUDGET

There are several hostels and bunkhouses in Aviemore and along the Ski Rd.

Aviemore SYHA Hostel (☎ 0870 004 1104; www .syha.org.uk; 25 Grampian Rd; dm £13; wheelchair access; P ☒ 💻) Near the start of the Ski Rd at the southern end of town, this spacious and facility-packed hostel has all the skier or walker could ask for: drying room, pool table, Internet, and no sardining in the dorms. There are plenty of rooms suitable for families, and the 2am curfew is very generous by SYHA standards.

Glenmore Camping & Caravan Park (☎ 861271; Loch Morlich; tent sites from £8) In an excellent location on the shores of Loch Morlich, 6 miles along the Ski Rd from Aviemore, this grassy green campsite has plenty of open space, picnic tables, and the Cairngorms as a majestic backdrop. Can be midge-plagued if there's no breeze but it's otherwise a fine spot.

Other recommendations:

Aviemore Bunkhouse (☎ 811181; www.aviemore -bunkhouse.com; Dalfaber Rd; dm £12; wheelchair access; P ☒ 💻) Spanking-new independent hostel.

Cairngorm Lodge SYHA Hostel (☎ 0870 004 1137; www.syha.org.uk; Loch Morlich; dm £12; 🕑 mid-Dec–Oct; P ☒ 💻) Six miles from Aviemore along the Ski Rd; you should pre-book.

MID-RANGE

Glenmore Lodge (☎ 861256; www.glenmorelodge.org .uk; Loch Morlich; s/d £30/40; P ☒ 💻 ☎) A serious training centre for the active-minded, this excellent facility 6 miles from Aviemore also offers crisp, quality B&B accommodation at an amazingly low price. Even if you're not enrolled on a course, you have access to the gym, climbing wall, and kayak pool, while a convivial bar provides evening meals and mountaineering chat.

Ardlogie Guest House (☎ 810747; www.aviemore
.co.uk/ardlogie; Dalfaber Rd; s/d from £25/40; ℗ ✗)
Behind the train station, this is a welcoming spot with a pretty garden. It's very quiet,
with just the cheerful puffing of the odd
steam train to be heard, and offers plenty
of extra value, as guests get free use of the
facilities at the Dalfaber Golf and Country
Club, including Jacuzzi, gym and sauna.

Ravenscraig Guest House (☎ 810278; www.avie
moreonline.com; Grampian Rd; s £20-26, d £40-52; ℗ ✗)
A cut above many of the main road options
in Aviemore, this recommended B&B has
refurbished en-suite rooms, some with views
of the mountains. Breakfast is plentiful, includes a vegetarian option, and is served in
an appealing glassed-in patio.

Other recommendations:

Cairngorm Hotel (☎ 810233; www.cairngorm.com;
Grampian Rd; s/d £31.50/63; ℗ ▣) Several antlers
classier than most of the Aviemore strip.
MacKenzie's Highland Inn (☎ 810672;
mackhotel@aol.com; 125 Grampian Rd; r £50; ℗ ✗) A
good one for families: a bit tacky and very child friendly.

TOP END
Corrour House Hotel (☎ 810220; www.corrourhousehotel
.co.uk; Inverdruie; per person from £50; ℗ closed Nov;
℗ ✗) Just a mile from Aviemore off Ski
Rd, this boutique hotel is decorated in opulent country style. A grassy strip offers views
of the Lairig Ghru Pass, and early risers may
spot deer grazing outside the breakfast room
windows. A five-course dinner is available to
guests and public for £27.50.

Eating & Drinking
Aviemore has no shortage of eateries, but
few are particularly inviting.

Old Bridge Inn (☎ 811137; 23 Dalfaber Rd; mains £9-
13; ℗ lunch & dinner; ▣) Tucked away across the
railway line (follow the footpath underneath,
or take the turn-off from the Ski Rd), this is
an atmospheric old inn that feels miles away
from the tasteless tack on the main drag. As
well as being the town's best pub, a range
of fine Scottish cuisine is served in the rear
restaurant, including a great sirloin steak.

Café Mambo (☎ 811670; Grampian Rd; mains £5-9;
℗ 9am-11pm daily, food served noon-8.30pm Sun-Thu &
noon-7.30pm Fri & Sat) While elsewhere this spot
would be laughably try-hard, here it almost
seems a haven of normalcy. With a colourful
interior, espresso machine and good-value
range of Tex-Mex and burgers, it appeals as a
daytime destination as much as at night.

Other recommendations:

Coffee Corner (☎ 810564; Grampian Rd; snacks £2-4;
℗ 9am-5pm) On the main strip, serving tasty toasted
sandwiches and soups.
Hamblett's (☎ 810300; 72 Grampian Rd; mains £7-12;
℗ 11.30am-10pm; ✗) Quality meals with a pleasing
wholefood orientation; several vegetarian choices on offer.

Getting There & Away
BUS
Citylink buses travel to Edinburgh (£14.10,
3¼ hours, hourly), Glasgow (£14.10, 3½
hours, hourly), Inverness (45 minutes, 12 to
15 daily), Newtonmore/Kingussie (25 minutes, five to seven daily) and Pitlochry (1¼
hours, hourly).

TRAIN
There are direct train services to Glasgow/
Edinburgh (£31.90, three hours, five to nine
daily) and Inverness (£7.70, 45 minutes, four
to eight daily).

CRANKING UP CONSERVATION IN THE CAIRNGORMS

It's a sad fact that, although the Cairngorm region is one of Scotland's most precious wildernesses,
short-term money-making has traditionally taken the front seat over environmental or social
concerns. The architectural disaster that is Aviemore, and the controversial ski-slope funicular
that was literally railroaded over loud protests from conservation lobbies, are ample evidence
of this, but things seem to have taken a turn for the better. After much political to-ing and fro-
ing that resulted in the original proposed area being halved, the Cairngorms National Park was
officially opened on 1 September 2003.

At 1400 sq miles, it is the UK's largest national park, and encompasses the whole mountain
range as far east as Ballater in the Dee Valley. As well as harbouring a significant population of
fauna, including rare bird species such as the osprey, the capercaillie, and the golden eagle, its
regenerated Caledonian forest and high-altitude sub-Arctic vegetation are of particular ecological
value and make the region a paradise for walkers and cyclists.

Getting Around

Highland Country services link Aviemore and Cairngorm (20 minutes, three to eight daily).

Bothy Bikes (☎ 811111; Ski Rd, Inverdruie; ☺ 9am-5.30pm), a mile from Aviemore up the Ski Rd, is one of several operators that hire bikes, but is unquestionably the best for its enthusiasm and professionalism. A bike costs £15 for a day, and comes with free and in-depth advice on planning the best possible route!

The **Strathspey Steam Railway** (☎ 01479-810725; www.strathspeyrailway.co.uk) operates between Aviemore, Boat of Garten and Broomhill from March to October and around Christmas.

AROUND AVIEMORE
Rothiemurchus Estate

The **Rothiemurchus Estate Visitor Centre** (☎ 812 345; www.rothiemurchus.net; Ski Rd, Inverdruie; ☺ 9.30am-5.30pm) is a mile from Aviemore. Pick up the free *Activities, Maps & Walks* brochure and the basic footpath maps.

The vast estate, owned by a single family, has free access to 50 miles of footpaths, including some particularly attractive trails through the Caledonian pine forests and around enchanting Loch an Eilein with its island ruin. Visitors can also opt for ranger-guided walks, Land Rover tours, and fishing for rainbow trout at the estate's fish farm or in the River Spey.

Glenmore Forest Park

Around Loch Morlich, 6 miles from Aviemore, the Ski Rd passes through 2000 hectares of pine and spruce that make up Glenmore Forest Park.

The **visitors centre** (☎ 861220), near steely-grey Loch Morlich, has a small exhibition on forests and sells the *Glen More Forest Guide Map*, detailing local walks, which include the three-hour return ascent of Meall a'Bhuachaillie that looms over the loch.

The popular **Loch Morlich Watersports Centre** (☎ 861221; ☺ May-Oct) is a great spot for kids of all ages to learn basic sailing, windsurfing, and canoeing in placid if chilly water off a pretty artificial beach.

Kincraig & Around

Kincraig, 7 miles southwest of Aviemore, is close to some great attractions. The **Highland Wildlife Park** (☎ 01540-651270; www.highlandwild lifepark.org; adult £8; ☺ 10am-7pm Apr-Oct, 10am-4pm

Nov-Mar), about 1½ miles south of the village, features a drive-through reserve. Inside are animals that once roamed wild around this country, including mighty horned ruminants such as the shaggy European bison, who always strangely seem to resemble an acquaintance, stately red deer and the elegantly coiffeured Przewalski's horses. No car, no problem – you'll get driven around by one of the friendly staff.

Glen Feshie, a lovely, tranquil glen is big-sky country and extends south into the Cairngorms. **Glen Feshie Hostel** (☎ 01540-651323; glen feshiehostel@totalise.co.uk; dm £9.50; P ✗), about 5 miles from Kincraig, is a friendly, independent, cosy bothy popular with hikers. Rates include bed linen and a steaming bowl of porridge to start the day. It's at the end of the road into the glen and you can self-cater or let your hosts do the cooking.

There are Citylink and Highland Country buses connecting Kincraig and Aviemore (six to eight buses daily).

Boat of Garten

Near Carrbridge, Boat of Garten is known as the Osprey Village because these rare birds of prey nest at the **RSPB Loch Garten Osprey Centre** (☎ 01479-831476; Grianan Tulloch; adult £2.50; ☺ 10am-6pm Apr-Aug; wheelchair access) in Abernethy Forest Reserve. You can watch them from a state-of-the-art hide equipped with telescopes, video monitoring, and gossip about their recent mating activity; they migrate here from West Africa annually and volunteers guard the site throughout the nesting season to deter egg collectors. The centre is signposted about 2 miles from the village.

The best way to get to Boat of Garten is on the Strathspey Steam Railway. It runs at least five times daily from Aviemore – a 3rd-class ticket costs £9 return.

KINGUSSIE & NEWTONMORE
☎ 01540 / pop 2392

These sleepy one-street villages located on the edge of rust-red heather-clad hills and flourishing woodland are separated by just a couple of miles of fields. This peaceful co-existence counts for nothing on the shinty field, however, when sticks and teeth fly in an effort to gain the upper hand in this tough relative of hurling. Off the grass, the villages are best known as the home of Scotland's fine Highland Folk Museum, with a section in each of the two settlements. The Kingussie one also serves as a **TIC** (☎ 661297; Duke St; ◷ Mon-Sat Apr-Oct).

Sights

The **Highland Folk Museum** (☎ 661307; www.high landfolk.com) is divided into two distinct sections, one in each village. The **Kingussie Museum** (Duke St; adult £2.50, joint 2-day ticket £6; ◷ 9.30am-5.30pm Mon-Sat Apr-Aug, Mon-Fri Sep & Oct; wheelchair access) has a large collection of relics of Highland life, as well as a reconstructed smokehouse and watermill. The **Newton-more Museum** (Kingussie Rd; adult £5, joint 2-day ticket £6; ◷ 10.30am-5.30pm Apr-Aug, 11am-4.30pm Sep, 11am-4.30pm Mon-Fri Oct; wheelchair access) is a huge outdoor complex that includes a whole blackhouse village built using traditional methods, and a working farm. During summer, both sites have frequent demonstrations of traditional crafts, and the whole ensemble is a refreshing and unromanticised look at Highland life as it once was.

Walking

The **Monadhliath Mountains**, northwest of Kingussie, attract fewer hikers than the nearby Cairngorms, and makes an ideal destination for walkers seeking peace and solitude. However, during the deer-stalking season (August to October), you'll need to check with the TIC before setting out.

Sleeping & Eating

Newtonmore Hostel (☎ 673360; www.highlandhostel .co.uk; Main St, Newtonmore; dm £10; P ✗) This is the walker's hostel *par excellence*, with a warm welcome, laundry and drying room, and clean no-frills bothy-style option. It's in a modern, cosy wooden building with a fine kitchen and relaxing lounge area with plenty of board games and local information. It's relaxed and you can hire bikes if you stay here.

The Hermitage (☎ 662137; thehermitage-scotland .com; Spey St, Kingussie; s/d from £21/42; P ✗) This lovely, quaint old residence is all sophistication and style, although without any fussiness. There's a big garden and a cosy guest lounge with a log fire, and it's just by the Highland Folk Museum.

Homewood Lodge (☎ 661507; www.homewood -lodge-kingussie.co.uk; Newtonmore Rd, Kingussie; s/d £22/44; P ✗) On the southern outskirts of Kingussie, this exceptionally welcoming home offers super value. Set well above the main road, it's a quiet spot whose lounge and some bedrooms offer vast perspectives through sparklingly clean windows over fields to the Cairngorms beyond. All of the renovated bedrooms have an en suite and are thoughtfully designed with soothing colour schemes.

The Cross (☎ 661166; www.thecross.co.uk; Tweed Mill Brae, Ardbroilach Rd, Kingussie; DB&B per person £80-110, 2-course dinner £28.50; ◷ Tue-Sat mid-Feb–Dec; P ✗) One of the Highlands' top hotel-restaurants, this converted mill has quirkily shaped bedrooms that offer a taste of Scotland without tartan or antlers; the best look over the river but all offer high comfort. And comfort is all you'll be looking for after one of the superb five-course dinners, all complemented by a long and passionate wine list, which includes many fine dessert 'stickies'.

The Glen (☎ 673203; Main St, Newtonmore; mains £5-9; ◷ food served noon-9pm; ✗) There's good reason that actors from *Monarch of the Glen* like to dine here after a hard day on the set: it does the best pub food in the area, but at distinctly unceleb prices. There's a huge range of daily specials, and the choices range from creamy fisherman's pie to fiery Thai curries, all served with warm-hearted cheer.

Getting There & Away

Kingussie and Newtonmore are on the main Edinburgh/Glasgow to Inverness route; there are Citylink bus services to Aviemore (25 minutes, five to seven daily) and Inverness (one hour, six to eight Monday to Saturday, three on Sunday).

There are trains, more stopping in Kingussie than Newtonmore, to Edinburgh (£31.90, 2¾ hours, nine Monday to Saturday, four on Sunday) and Inverness (£7.70, one hour, eight Monday to Saturday, four on Sunday).

THE GREAT GLEN

The Great Glen is a spectacular line of loch-filled cavities stretching from Inverness to Fort William. It's one of the world's major geological fault lines, created by intense geothermal activity over 400 million years ago. It contains Britain's deepest freshwater lake, Loch Ness. The dramatic origins of this route are evident in the often vast and humbling backdrops of lochs Linnhe, Lochy, Oich and Ness, all of which are linked by the

Caledonian Canal. Historically, this area has also been an important communication (and invasion) route.

Activities

The 80-mile **Great Glen Cycle Route** via Fort Augustus follows canal towpaths and gravel tracks through forests to avoid busy roads where possible. The *Cycling in the Forest* leaflet, available from TICs and the Forestry Commission, provides details.

The **Great Glen Way** is a 70-mile walk, via Drumnadrochit and Fort Augustus, which opened in April 2002. It's an excellent opportunity to absorb the beauty of the glen's lochs and mountains, and Nessie-hunters will be able to explore the banks of Loch Ness in fine detail. The route takes four days, but those short on time can utilise some of the sections as day walks. Walking towards Fort William affords the best views.

Both the Great Glen Cycle Route and Great Glen Way run between Fort William and Inverness – note that some sections are shared between walkers and cyclists.

FORT WILLIAM & AROUND

☎ 01397 / pop 9902

Sitting on the banks of a loch, and backed by the magnificent bulk of Ben Nevis, Fort William has the potential to be an appealing Highland town. Unfortunately, it's nothing of the sort; the town is separated from the water by an insensitively placed bypass and the main business seems to be flogging tourist tack. If you're into walking and climbing, it makes a very handy HQ. As well as being the end point of the West Highland Way, it's the base camp for an assault on Ben Nevis, Britain's highest mountain at 1343m. The peak overlooks the magical valley of Glen Nevis, which begins near the northern end of the town and extends west below the slopes of Ben Nevis. The valley and the mountains are popular with serious hikers and climbers but are easily accessed by amateurs as well.

Orientation & Information

Fort William meanders along the edge of Loch Linnhe for several miles but has a fairly compact centre. The main street is pedestrianised and stocked with gift shops – it's a pleasant stroll that, like the town itself, isn't going to take up valuable disc space in your long-term memory.

Glen Nevis (Ionad Nibheis) Visitor Centre (☎ 705922; ☺ Easter–mid-Oct) Two miles southeast along the glen from town.

Library (High St; ☺ 10am-8pm Mon & Thu, 10am-6pm Tue & Fri, 10am-1pm Wed & Sat) Free Internet access.

TIC (☎ 0845 225 5121; fortwilliam@host.co.uk; Cameron Sq; ☺ 9am-7pm Mon-Sat, 10am-4pm Sun Easter-Aug, 9am-6pm Mon-Sat, 10am-2pm Sun Sep-Oct, 10am-5pm Mon-Sat Nov-Easter; 🖳)

Sights & Activities

WEST HIGHLAND MUSEUM

Just next to the TIC, this **museum** (☎ 702169; Cameron Sq; adult £3; ☺ 10am-4pm Mon-Sat Oct-May, 10am-5pm Jun-Sep, 2-5pm Sun Jul & Aug) is ideal for anyone with a yen to see Bonnie Prince Charlie as an umbrella stand. It's also good for history buffs, with exhibits on the Highlands' military, archaeological, artistic and even musical past. The eclectic showcase is a refreshing change from the usual focus on war and social hierarchy.

WALKING

The most obvious hike, up **Ben Nevis**, should not be undertaken lightly. The weather at the top is more often bad (with thick mist). Be prepared for the worst, even if it's sunny when you set off. Bring warm clothes, a detailed map, food and something to drink.

The path begins in Glen Nevis, either from the car park by Achintee Farm (on the northern side of the river and reached by the road through Claggan), or from the SYHA hostel on the road up the glen. These two trails join after less than a mile, then follow the Red Burn before zigzagging up to the summit and the ruins of the old observatory. It can take three to five hours to reach the top and 2½ to four hours to get down again.

There are pleasant (far less strenuous) walks along Glen Nevis through the gorge at the eastern end to beautiful **Steall Meadows**. You could also walk part of the **West Highland Way** from Fort William to Kinlochleven via Glen Nevis (14 miles) or even to Glencoe (21 miles to the junction with the A82).

The **Great Glen Way** begins and ends at the Old Fort in Fort William. You could do the Fort William to Gairlochy section of the walk (21 miles return) in just a day. It's a lovely scenic path overlooking the River Lochy, with views to Ben Nevis. You'll pass **Neptune's Staircase**, a spectacular flight of five lochs at Banavie.

Sleeping

Fort William has numerous B&Bs, hostels and hotels, but they fill up quickly in summer; booking ahead is wise.

BUDGET

Mrs Chisholm (☎ 705548; 5 Grange Rd; rm per person £12.50-17; ☒) A little gem of a B&B, this unsigned spot has just two rooms with shared bathroom, with great views over the loch. The double is especially appealing, with plenty of space to stretch out. You'll get the most warm-hearted and genuine welcome and the best-value stay in this part of Scotland.

Farr Cottage (☎ 772315; www.farrcottage.com; Corpach; dm/tw £12/30; P ☒ ☐) This excellent hostel is in a pleasant village by the Caledonian Canal just over 3 miles from Fort William and easily accessed on bus No 45 from Middle St. It has everything a budget traveller desires: friendly and energetic owners who organise all sorts of activities, two kitchens, videos, books, and satellite TV. The dorms are clean and new-looking, there's a licensed bar, and a relaxed welcoming feel.

Fort William Backpackers (☎ 700711; www.scotlands-top-hostels.com; Alma Rd; dm £13; ☒ ☐) This sociable hostel is handy for the train and bus stations and pulses with a mixture of backpackers and hikers, the latter often setting out when the former are going to bed. It's engagingly relaxed and welcoming, and the communal kitchen and lounge areas are excellent.

Other recommendations:

Glen Nevis Caravan & Camping Park (☎ 702191; www.glen-nevis.co.uk; Glen Nevis; tent sites £7.30-10.70; ☺ mid-Mar–Oct) In 30 hectares of lush green space at the foot of Ben Nevis, with good facilities.

Glen Nevis SYHA Hostel (☎ 0870 004 1120; www.syha .org.uk; Glen Nevis; dm £13; P ☒ ☐) A bit school camp in style, but the start of the path up Ben Nevis is outside its front door.

MID-RANGE

The B&Bs in and around Fassifern Rd are closest to the train and bus stations. Achintore Rd, which runs south by the loch, is packed with mostly generic B&Bs, but a few stand out.

St Andrew's Guesthouse (☎ 703038; www.fort william-accommodation.co.uk; Fassifern Rd; r per person £18-25;

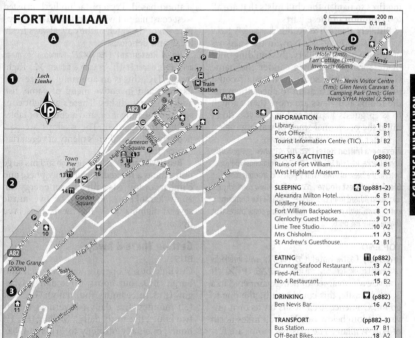

FORT WILLIAM

0   200 m
0   0.1 mi

INFORMATION	
Library.................................1	B1
Post Office...........................2	B1
Tourist Information Centre (TIC)........3	B2

SIGHTS & ACTIVITIES	(p880)
Ruins of Fort William............4	B1
West Highland Museum...........5	B2

SLEEPING	(pp881–2)
Alexandra Milton Hotel.............6	B1
Distillery House....................7	D1
Fort William Backpackers..........8	C1
Glenlochy Guest House.............9	D1
Lime Tree Studio....................10	A2
Mrs Chisholm......................11	A3
St Andrew's Guesthouse..........12	B1

EATING	(p882)
Crannog Seafood Restaurant..........13	A2
Fired-Art..........................14	A2
No.4 Restaurant....................15	B2

DRINKING	(p882)
Ben Nevis Bar......................16	A2

TRANSPORT	(pp882–3)
Bus Station.........................17	B1
Off-Beat Bikes......................18	A2

(⊙Jan-Oct; P ⌧) The best of the B&Bs on this stretch, this former schoolhouse and headmaster's quarters is something special. A stone's throw from the main street, it offers tranquillity, great views, large rooms, stained glass, and a touch of class above and beyond the norm in this town.

Lime Tree Studio (☎ 701806; www.limetreestudio .co.uk; Achintore Rd; s/d from £25/45; P ⌧) This excellent place is art gallery and B&B, and is adorned with atmospheric scenes of lonely, evocative Scotland painted here. Although on one of the town's principal roundabouts, you don't really hear the traffic; perhaps the bright and breezy rooms take your mind elsewhere. It's a great place for solo travellers, with good-value single rooms.

The Grange (☎ 705516; www.thegrange-scotland .co.uk; Grange Rd; d/tw £76-96; ⊙Mar-Nov; P ⌧) This place calls itself a B&B but is really a boutique hotel. Overlooking the loch from its own luxuriant grounds, it has four rooms dignified by chaises longues, Victorian free-standing baths, and other antique furniture. The hosts add countless little extras to make your stay a memorable one, including blazing fires to banish the chill mists that are all too common in these parts.

Distillery House (☎ 700103; disthouse@aol.com; North Rd; s/d £45/70; P ⌧) Now in the shadows of the Ben Nevis distillery, this building once made spirits of its own, under the name Glenlochy. While some of the staff could probably do with a dram to cheer them up, the rooms and views are more than enough to keep guests happy, as long as you don't mind the occasional smell of wafting malt.

Other recommendations:

Alexandra Milton Hotel (☎ 702241; www.miltonhotels .com; The Parade; s/d £45/90; P ⌧) Traditional Highland hotel in the heart of town, with stylish and spacious rooms.

Glenlochy Guest House (☎ 702909; www.glenlochy.co .uk; North Rd; s/d from £25/40; P ⌧) At the northern end of town, with rooms that would shame some places that charge twice the price.

TOP END

Inverlochy Castle Hotel (☎ 702177; www.inverlochy castlehotel.co.uk; Torlundy; s/d from £205/290; P ⌧) If you've ever dreamed of being pampered in a Scottish castle, this could well be the one to go for. Opulence itself, it sits on its own private fiefdom below Ben Nevis, 3 miles north of Fort William. The massive rooms are furnished with a formal but colourful elegance

and the beds often bear the weight of minor and major public figures. The guest areas are adorned with hunting trophies and log fires, the carefully tended grounds include a stocked trout loch, and the restaurant is of the highest order. Reservations are essential.

Eating & Drinking

There's some good eating to be done here, but there are also plenty of places that feed on tourists like a cruising whale on plankton.

Fired-Art (☎ 705005; 147 High St; snacks £1-4; ⊙11am-4pm Sun & Mon, 10am-5.30pm Tue-Sat; ⌧ ⌨) On those days when you can't even see the mountains, let alone climb them, it's reassuring to know that such a great café exists in Fort William. Up front it's sophistication over good espressos or tasty soups and sandwiches, while up the back it's like a relaxed art class, for you can paint your own pottery here, with advice from the cheery staff that's helpful but not intrusive.

Crannog Seafood Restaurant (☎ 705589; Town Pier; mains £13-18; lunch & dinner; ⌧) Fort William's finest restaurant is right on the loch and serves exquisite taste sensations, mostly seafood-based. Try a pistachio herb-crusted west coast halibut with risotto and pink peppercorn or the catch of the day, always fresh, local, and delicious.

No. 4 Restaurant (☎ 704222; Cameron Sq; mains lunch £5-8, dinner £8-17; ⊙lunch & dinner; ⌧) Right by the TIC, this is an appealing choice with its fresh and inventive menu of game, fish and vegetarian dishes. There's a bright conservatory seating area, and a couple of tables in the small garden. The scallops are particularly tasty, but there's plenty of vegetarian choice, too.

Ben Nevis Bar (☎ 702295; 105 High St) This large pub exudes a relaxed, jovial atmosphere and climbers or tourists with leftover energy can enjoy karaoke on Tuesday or live music several nights a week. Bar meals are served upstairs.

Getting There & Away

BUS

Citylink buses operate services to Edinburgh (£19, four hours, three daily); Glasgow (£13, three hours, four daily); Glen Coe (30 minutes, five daily); Inverness (£8.40, two hours, five to six daily); Mallaig (£4, 1½ hours, one daily Monday to Friday); Oban (£7.80, 1½ hours, four daily Monday to

Saturday); and Portree (£16.40, three hours, three direct daily).

TRAIN
There are trains from Glasgow to Fort William (£18.70, 3¾ hours, two or three daily) and from Mallaig (£7.80, 1½ hours, three or four daily). An overnight train connects Fort William and London Euston (£70 in a seat, £115 with a bed, 13¼ hours), but you'll miss the wonderful views.

Getting Around
Highland Country buses operate 11 services Monday to Saturday, and four on Sunday from June to September, between the bus station and the Glen Nevis SYHA Hostel. Buses to Corpach run every 20 to 25 minutes, except on Sunday when they're hourly.

Off-Beat Bikes (☎ 704008; www.offbeatbikes.co.uk; 117 High St) supplies mountain bikes for £10/15 per half/full day.

GLEN COE
Scotland's most famous glen is a pure microcosm of the magnificent Highlands. Heathered ranges, waterfalls, rivers and staggering mountains reign in this changeable and untamed domain. A lonely road winds its way through the centre of this landscape, mil-lions of years in the making. Three massive, brooding spurs, known as the Three Sisters dominate the south, while the tip of Aonach Eagach ridge, at 900m, peers into the valley below in the north. Walkers of all abilities challenge themselves with the variety of spectacular hikes. Less-energetic visitors can still experience this wilderness, while bunking down in some excellent accommodation.

Glen Coe was written into the history books in 1692 when the MacDonalds were murdered by the Campbells in what became known as the Glen Coe Massacre.

Walking
This is serious walking country and you'll need maps, warm clothes, food and water. The **Glen Coe Visitor Centre** (p884) stocks lots of useful information.

A great six- to seven-hour hike leads through the Lost Valley, a hidden mountain sanctuary, to the top of **Bidean nam Bian** (1141m).

Aonach Eagach, the glen's northern wall, is said to be the best ridge walk on the Scottish mainland, but it's difficult in places and you need a good head for heights. Some parts could almost be graded a rock climb. It's best done from east to west, and there's a path up the hillside north of Allt-na-Reigh

---

THE GLEN COE MASSACRE
The brutal murders that took place here in 1692 were particularly shameful, perpetrated as they were by one Highland clan on another (with whom they were lodging as guests).

In an attempt to quash remaining Jacobite loyalties among the Highland clans, William III had ordered that all chiefs take an oath of loyalty to him by the end of the year (1691). Maclain, the elderly chief of the MacDonalds of Glen Coe, was late in setting out to fulfil the king's demand, and going first to Fort William rather than Inverary made him later still. He thus missed the deadline.

The Secretary of State for Scotland, Sir John Dalrymple, declared that the MacDonalds should be punished as an example to other Highland clans, some of whom had not bothered to even take the oath. A company of 120 soldiers, mainly of the Campbell clan, was sent to the glen. Since their leader was related by marriage to Maclain, the troops were billeted in MacDonald homes. It was a long-standing tradition for clans to provide hospitality to passing travellers.

After they'd been guests for 12 days, the order came for the soldiers to put to death all Mac-Donalds under the age of 70. Some Campbells alerted the MacDonalds to their intended fate, while others turned on their hosts at 5am on 13 February, shooting Maclain and 37 other men, women and children. Some died before they knew what was happening, while 300 others fled into the snow, where some died of exposure.

The ruthless brutality of the incident caused a public uproar and after an inquiry several years later, Dalrymple lost his job. There's a monument to Maclain in Glen Coe village and members of the MacDonald clan still gather here on 13 February each year. The Clachaig Inn (p884) even has a plate on the door saying 'No hawkers or Campbells'!

and down from Sgor nam Fiannaidh towards Loch Achtriochtan. The more direct gully that leads to Clachaig Inn isn't a safe way down. It takes seven to eight hours.

Glen Coe Village

☎ 01855 / pop 334

Sixteen miles south of Fort William on the A82, this small village sits at the entrance to the glen by Loch Leven and is dignified by the soaring mountains around it. The small thatched **Glen Coe Folk Museum** (☎ 811664; adult/child £2/free; ☺ 10am-5.30pm Mon-Sat May-Sep) houses a historical collection, including military memorabilia and costumes.

About 1½ miles from the village along the road into the glen is the excellent **Glen Coe Visitor Centre** (NTS; ☎ 811307; Invergan; adult £3.50; ☺ daily Mar-Oct, Fri-Mon Nov-Feb; wheelchair access). A modern facility with an ecotourism bent, the centre provides information on the geological, environmental and cultural history of Glen Coe via interactive, audiovisual and hi-tech displays. The story of the Glen Coe Massacre in all its gory detail is also told.

SLEEPING & EATING

Glen Coe SYHA Hostel (☎ 0870 004 1122; www.syha .org.uk; dm £12; P X 🖳) A walk of a couple of miles from the village on the northern side of the River Coe, this hostel is a little institutional but well-equipped, popular for walkers, and not far from the Clachaig Inn.

Clachaig Inn (☎ 811252; www.clachaig.com; s/d from £38/76, bar meals £4-10; P X) This welcoming historic inn, 2½ miles southeast of Glen Coe village, is what any walker dreams of at the end of a hard day. The colourful, comfortable rooms aren't the half of it, for there are two cosy and convivial bars with real ales, good food, bike hire, a papier mâché stag's head, and a terrace with awe-inspiring views of the mountainscape around.

Other recommendations:

Inchconnal (☎ 811958; Glen Coe village; d/tw £36-40; P X) Best option in Glen Coe itself. Value-packed attic rooms in flowery stone cottage.

Red Squirrel Campsite (☎ 811256; tent sites per person £5.50) Plenty of tree cover, lawns and secluded spots on the road on the northern bank of the Coe.

GETTING THERE & AWAY

Highland Country and Citylink buses operate buses between Fort William and Glen Coe (30 minutes, five daily Monday to Saturday), the latter also operates to/from Glasgow (£11.60, 2½ hours, four daily).

Kinlochleven

☎ 01855 / pop 897

At North Ballachulish you can take the beautiful side road running up Loch Leven to Kinlochleven. As well as the excellent walking hereabouts, **Ice Factor** (☎ 831100; www.ice -factor.co.uk; ☺ 9am-10pm) is a fine modern facility with indoor ice-climbing and rock-climbing walls as well as instruction in all aspects of mountaineering.

The West Highland Way passes through town and walkers often stay overnight here. The excellent **Blackwater Hostel** (☎ 831253; www .blackwaterhostel.co.uk; Lab Rd; dm £11; X) has small, spotless dorms that come with en suite and TV; you can camp here, too. **Kings House Hotel** (☎ 851259; www.kingy.com; s/d from £24/48; P X) is one of Scotland's oldest established inns and this popular hotel sits solitary and reverent at the eastern end of the glen, dwarfed by the route's magnificent peaks. Walkers conquering the West Highland Way fuel up on the reputable haggis, neeps and tatties here (accompanied by liquid refreshments, of course).

Glen Coe Ski Centre

About 1½ miles east from Kings House Hotel, on the other side of the A82, is the car park and base station for this ski centre, where commercial skiing in Scotland first started in 1956.

The **chair lift** (☎ 851226; www.glencoemountain .com; ☺ year-round) is the easiest way to get to the dramatic 640m-high viewpoint and several good walks.

FORT AUGUSTUS

☎ 01320 / pop 508

In a previous life, Fort Augustus was the headquarters for General Wade's military road-building operations in the 18th century. Today, it is a neat and picturesque package of a town, thriving on tourists who come to soak up the scenic environment at the head of Loch Ness.

Life and activity hums around the Caledonian Canal, and while the streets are teeming by day, early evening seems to induce people into a relaxed lull. Even hardened travellers will succumb to sunset on the grassy slopes by the water, but only until they are lured in to the canalside pubs by food, beverages and music.

The **TIC** (☎ 366367; ⊙ 10am-5pm Apr-Oct), in the central car park, charges £3 for local accommodation bookings. There's Internet access a few doors up at **Neuk Internet Café & Restaurant** (☎ 366208; per hour £6; ⊙ 10am-8pm).

Sights & Activities

At Fort Augustus, boats using the **Caledonian Canal** are raised and lowered 12m by five locks. It's worth watching, and the pleasant promenade is an ideal vantage point to observe, soak up some sun or compare accents with fellow tourists. The promontory between the canal and the River Oich affords a fine view over Loch Ness. Tiny **Cherry Island**, on the Inverness side of Fort Augustus, was originally a *crannog*, or artificial island settlement.

The fort itself was built between 1729 and 1742, then occupied by Benedictines in 1876, who founded an **abbey**, which is now, controversially, to be developed into luxury flats.

The **Royal Scot** (☎ 366277; www.cruiselochness .com; cruises £7.50; hourly departures 10am-4pm Mar-Nov) offers Loch Ness cruises with 'the most hi-tech sonar on the loch', so you might catch a glimpse of Nessie.

Sleeping & Eating

Morag's Lodge (☎ 366289; moragslodge@hotmail .com; Bunnoich Brae; dm/d £12.50/30; wheelchair access; P ✕ ▯) This clean, colourful hostel is very well run and all that a backpacker could wish for, set in a quiet location, with views over the wooded hills around. The cheery dorms are named after Scottish films, there's a cheap buffet dinner available, a massive kitchen, and a sociable bar. You'll find it off the main road in the northern part of town.

Nia-Roo Lodge (☎ 366783; www.niaroo.com; Fort William Rd; s/d from £20/40; P ✕) Decorated with plush red carpets and with a large range of rooms with light mauve walls, this is one of the town's best B&Bs. Grab a room at the back if you can; they are quieter and look over hills rather than the road. The name doesn't refer to marsupials: it's the Scots for 'our own' written backwards!

The best places to eat are the atmospheric pubs along the canal. **The Lock Inn** (☎ 366302; mains £7-9; ⊙ lunch & dinner; ✕) is a cosy local with a small Scottish menu, including

choices such as salmon, Orkney herring, and sometimes fresh local langousines. **The Bothy** (☎ 366736; mains £8-15; ⊙ food served 11am-10pm; ✕) isn't quite as enticing for a drink, but wins on food by a short half-head, with a range of delicious evening specials such as Barbary duck bolstering an all-day bar menu.

Getting There & Away

Citylink buses operate services to Fort William (£7.80, one hour, five to six daily) and Inverness (£7.60, one hour, five to six daily).

LOCH NESS

Shrouded in myth, exploited by legend and spectacularly scenic, steely-blue Loch Ness stretches 23 miles from Fort Augustus at its southern end, nearly as far as Inverness. It's the biggest body of fresh water in Britain, and its deep, dark, bitterly cold waters have been extensively explored for Nessie, the elusive Loch Ness monster. While visitors still crowd the shores, hoping for a glimpse, even the most ardent Nessie-hunters have become disillusioned in recent years.

Along the northwestern shore runs the congested A82, while the more tranquil and extremely picturesque B862 follows the southeastern shore. A complete circuit of the loch is about 70 miles, and you'll have the best views travelling anticlockwise.

Drumnadrochit

☎ 01456 / pop 813

Seized by monster madness, tacky and bulging with gift shops, Nessie fever reaches a crescendo in Drumnadrochit with two ferociously competitive monster exhibitions snaffling up passing tourist pounds. If only the beastie knew all the fuss it was causing in this town, which should be avoided in summer when the annual Nessie frenzy is at its peak. Ironically, the town isn't actually even on the lake; the road ducks inland slightly at this point.

The friendly **TIC** (☎ 459076; A82; ⊙ year-round) shells out leaflets on the area.

LOCH NESS 2000

Traditionally, two rival exhibitions have competed for the tourist pound here, pasting on names such as 'original' and 'official' willy-nilly to try and gain some sort of authenticity. The better of the two has now seen the light, and transformed itself into an excellent multilingual display. **Loch Ness 2000** (☎ 450573; www.loch-ness-scotland.com; adult £5.95; ☺ 9am-8pm; wheelchair access) is focussed more on explaining the Nessie phenomenon than perpetuating its existence and has an intriguing history of the loch, its mythology, sightings, and recent scientific investigations through a series of audiovisual displays. It's impressive, but it still couldn't resist making you fight through a phalanx of stuffed green Nessies in the shop on the way out.

URQUHART CASTLE
Due to its sublime location overlooking Loch Ness, **Urquhart Castle** (HS; ☎ 450551; adult/child £6/1.20; ☺ 9.30am-6.30pm Apr-Sep, 9.30am-4.30pm Oct-Mar, phone for extended hours Jul & Aug; wheelchair access) sees its fair share of tour buses. Although it is brilliantly positioned, and atmospheric with its green lawns and lochside site, it's slightly overpriced considering that it's mostly in ruins.

The castle was repeatedly sacked, damaged and rebuilt over the centuries, but the unfortunate inhabitants of the Great Glen were also regularly pillaged and robbed in the process. It was finally blown up in 1692 to prevent Jacobites using it and its remains perch dramatically on the edge of the loch.

An audiovisual display in the visitors centre tells more of the history of the castle, and has a collection of artefacts and a café.

The castle is a couple of miles southeast of Drumnadrochit. Buses running between Fort William and Inverness will stop outside both ways.

SLEEPING & EATING
Loch Ness Backpackers Lodge (☎ 450807; www.lochness-backpackers.com; East Lewiston; dm £10.50, d & tw £27; P ✗) This good-value hostel is three-quarters of a mile from Drumnadrochit. It's a friendly place with clean six-bed dorms, small but bright doubles and twins, a family room and a large barbecue area. It's colourful, cheerful, and recommended. To get here take the A82 towards Fort William and turn left when you see the sign for Loch Ness Inn, just before the bridge.

Drumbuie Farm (☎ 450634; drumbuie@amserve.net; r per person £23-27; P ✗) On the right just before you enter Drumnadrochit from Inverness, this farmhouse is a dose of tranquility from monster-mania. The bright frilly rooms are tidy and welcoming, and there are great views over fields down to the loch from the breakfast room.

Drumnadrochit Hotel (☎ 450218; www.loch-ness-scotland.com; s £35-45, d £59-79, dinner £11-13; ☺ lunch

---

NESSIE
There's a tale of St Columba meeting 'Nessie' (the Loch Ness Monster) in the 6th century, but the craze really developed after 1933, when the A82 road was completed along the northern banks of the loch.

The classic photograph of a dinosaurlike creature's long neck emerging from the water was taken in 1934, from which time the monster hunt gathered pace. After decades of speculation, interest peaked again during the 1960s, and a (despairingly unsuccessful) vigil by the loch was mounted in 1962. Inconclusive evidence did not deter die-hard spotters, who founded a Loch Ness Monster Fan Club, poring over the 1000 or so 'sightings' by the year 2000.

In recent years sonar hunts, underwater cameras and computer studies have resulted in disappointment for the true believers; the general conclusion has been that there is insufficient aquatic life to actually sustain even one sizeable reptile. One interesting observation was of the underwater currents in the loch. Caused by temperature fluctuations beneath the surface, currents running against the surface flow can carry objects with them, making a tree trunk, for example, appear to be swimming vigorously upstream. The number of sightings of large creatures, however, is significant; it has been suggested that sturgeon, who occasionally swim up Scottish rivers to breed, might have been responsible for the confusion, what with their enormous bulk and unusual head.

None of which is good news for the Nessie industry, which is having to pedal ever harder to make a go of it. Nevertheless, asking around in the pubs hereabouts, there's always one story or another. 'Old Jock's been fishing this loch for 40 years, but he swears the other day he saw something big. Were nae a fish, he said'. So keep your camera handy just in case!

& dinner; (P) (X)) Dominating the centre of the village, this hotel leaves it up to the individual to decide whether it's ugly or interesting. It's better inside; the rooms are unremarkable but well-equipped, and the restaurant light and attractive, with a smell of new wood and big panes of glass looking towards the loch. It's noted for its fine cuisine and child-friendliness (the turkey Nessies are popular!) and has very obliging service.

GETTING THERE & AWAY

Citylink has bus services along Loch Ness between Fort William (£8.40, 1½ hours, five to six daily) and Inverness (30 minutes, seven to eight daily), which goes via Drumnadrochit.

INVERNESS

☎ 01463 / pop 40,949

The fast-growing city of Inverness is the main settlement in the Highland region and both gateway and hub of the area. On the Moray Firth, at the northern end of the Great Glen, it boasts a striking location without having a massive number of visitor attractions. With its easy transport connections to both the western and northern regions, it's almost inevitable that you'll pass through here at some point. If your time is limited, it's also a spot to book a whistle-stop tour: a day in the Orkneys, for example.

When you arrive in town, throw the luggage down on the bed and head straight down to the river for a stroll; you'll surely

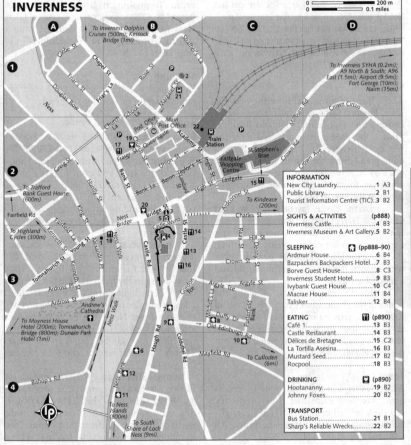

INVERNESS

INFORMATION	
New City Laundry	1 A3
Public Library	2 B1
Tourist Information Centre (TIC)	3 B2

SIGHTS & ACTIVITIES	(p888)
Inverness Castle	4 B3
Inverness Museum & Art Gallery	5 B2

SLEEPING	(pp888–90)
Ardmuir House	6 B4
Bazpackers Backpackers Hotel	7 B3
Borve Guest House	8 C3
Inverness Student Hotel	9 B3
Ivybank Guest House	10 C4
Macrae House	11 B4
Talisker	12 B4

EATING	(p890)
Café 1	13 B3
Castle Restaurant	14 B3
Délices de Bretagne	15 C2
La Tortilla Asesina	16 B3
Mustard Seed	17 B2
Rocpool	18 B3

DRINKING	(p890)
Hootananny	19 B2
Johnny Foxes	20 B2

TRANSPORT	
Bus Station	21 B1
Sharp's Reliable Wrecks	22 B2

HIGHLANDS &
NORTHERN ISLANDS

appreciate it! If you've got a spare day, head out on a boat into the Moray Firth in search of dolphins.

Inverness knows how to look after its tourists, the lifeblood of its economy. While quality pubs and restaurants are few, the places you find are invariably friendly, and make you realise why this is considered one of Britain's best cities for quality of life.

Information

Main Post Office (Queensgate; ☼ daily) Has a currency exchange.

New City Laundry (☎ 242507; 15 Young St; ☼ daily) Coin-op launderette with Internet access.

Public library (☎ 236463; Margaret St; ☼ Mon-Sat) Free Internet access.

TIC (☎ 234353; inverness@host.co.uk; Castle Wynd; ☼ 9am-5pm Mon-Fri, 10am-4pm Sat Nov-May, 9am-6pm Mon-Sat, 10am-4pm Sun Jun & Jul, 9am-7pm Mon-Sat, 9.30am-4pm Sun Aug, 9am-5pm Mon-Sat, 10am-2pm Sun Sep & Oct) Currency exchange, accommodation booking, and CalMac ferry office. It also books tickets for tours and has Internet access for £2.50 per hour.

Sights

At the heart of town, and towering over the river, **Inverness Castle** is a much more recent construction than most Highland fortifications – the present rose-coloured structure was built between 1837 and 1847. It's still quite grand from the outside, and is a fine place to be at sunset, but that's as much as you'll get to see, as the building currently serves as the Sheriff's Court.

Nearby the castle, **Inverness Museum & Art Gallery** (☎ 237114; Castle Wynd; admission free; ☼ 9am-5pm Mon-Sat) is hardly earth shattering, but it is a good way to amuse on a rainy afternoon. It contains wildlife dioramas, period rooms with historical weapons, Pictish stones and a modest art gallery.

The town's real joy is a stroll along the banks of the shallow but extremely beautiful River Ness, crossed by various footbridges. If you continue along the riverside for about ½ a mile south of the centre, you'll come to the **Ness Islands**, an alluring picnic spot.

Tours

As well as trips in the immediate Inverness area, travellers with little time or money can explore further-flung parts of the Highlands using various customised tours. All are bookable at the TIC.

BUS TOURS

Open-top, hop-on, hop-off bus tours of Inverness centre and also of Cawdor Castle, Fort George, and the Culloden battlefield are run by **City Sightseeing** (☎ 224000; ☼ Easter & late May-Sep). A day ticket on the city tour costs £5, on the Culloden tour £8.50. The same company also runs trips to the Cairngorms (£25).

John o'Groats Ferries (☎ 01955-611353; www.jog ferry.co.uk) runs day trips from June to early September to the Orkney Islands (£45), while **Puffin Express** (☎ 717181; www.puffinexpress .co.uk) runs a wider range of recommended summer day-trips to the Orkneys, Skye, Lewis, and other destinations.

CRUISES

From Tomnahurich Bridge, the **Jacobite Queen** (☎ 233999; www.jacobite.co.uk) cruises Loch Ness from £8/6 per adult/child. A return trip to Urquhart Castle, including admission, costs £12/8.

Sleeping

In the peak season, either prebook your accommodation or start looking early.

BUDGET

Bazpackers Backpackers Hotel (☎ 717663; bazmail@ btopenworld.com; 4 Culduthel Rd; dm £11, tw £28; ☒ ☐) A likeable budget pad with some top panoramas of the river and cathedral, this small sociable place has several comfortable nooks, including a garden with barbecue, lounge with log-fire and books, and clean comfortable dorms. The 24-hour access will please the stopouts.

Inverness Student Hotel (☎ 236556; www.scotlands -top-hostels.com; 8 Culduthel Rd; dm £11-12; ☐ ☒ ☐) Just beyond the castle, this friendly spot looks a bit grubby from outside but actually boasts clean light dorms, a small kitchen, and a grungy lounge with hard-to-beat views over the River Ness. The beds are named after whiskies: if you're the early-to-bed type this may not be your cup of cocoa. There's a laundry service, and bike hire for £12 per day.

Inverness SYHA Hostel (☎ 231771; www.syha.org .uk; Victoria Dr; dm & tw per person £13.50; wheelchair access; ☐ ☒ ☐) One of the SYHA's flagships, this very popular spot 15 minutes' walk north of the centre is deservedly popular for its modern and comfortable facilities. There are some doubles and twins with en suite, and a gleaming space-age kitchen. Booking is essential in summer.

MID-RANGE
There are heaps of B&Bs in town; a plethora of pricier options line the riverbank, while Old Edinburgh Rd and Ardconnel St are cheaper hunting grounds.

Kindeace (☎ 241041; www.kindeace.co.uk; 9 Lovat Rd; s/d £22/44; ✗) In one of Inverness' many elegant Victorian houses, this B&B is decorated with much more flair and imagination than most. The walls are hung with an intriguing variety of art from around the world and the welcome is genuine if a little scatty. The home-baked bread for breakfast is delicious.

Ivybank Guest House (☎ 232796; www.ivybank guesthouse.com; 28 Old Edinburgh Rd; s/d from £25/50; P ✗) This magnificent Heritage-listed home is highly recommended. Lovingly restored, it features all sorts of elegant fittings and sometimes seems more like a country castle than an urban residence. There's a sumptuous mahogany staircase and rooms bursting with elegance and character. There's a large tree-filled garden, too.

Macrae House (☎ 243658; joycemacrae@hotmail .com; 24 Ness Bank; s/d from £30/46; P ✗) This great spot has a charmingly cheerful owner who, unlike some others on this stretch, doesn't believe that a riverside location warrants doubling the tariff. The rooms, all of which have en suite or private bathroom, are enticingly homely, and those that don't look over the Ness overlook the carefully kept garden.

Ardmuir House (☎ 231151; www.ardmuir.com; 16 Ness Bank; s/d from £35/58; ☺ Mar-Oct; P ✗) A family-run, Georgian place, with a 1970s retro feel that probably isn't intentional but is hard to dislike. The rooms are flowery and comfortable – those overlooking the river cost a bit extra, but for the views of the cathedral, are worth shelling out for.

Moyness House Hotel (☎ 233836; www.moyness .co.uk; 6 Bruce Gardens; s/d from £33/66; P ✗) Just off the A82 to the west of the River Ness, this very upmarket Victorian villa has a walled garden pretty as a picture and rooms that have plenty of period style without being fussy. It's very peaceful and you feel as if you could be in a country lodge.

Other recommendations:

Borve Guest House (☎ 234738; www.theborve.com; 9 Old Edinburgh Rd; s/d from £25/48; P ✗) Sizeable, good-looking rooms a short walk from the centre.

Talisker (☎ 236221; 25 Ness Bank; s/d £40/60; P ✗) Friendly and conscientious spot by the fast-flowing Ness.

Trafford Bank Guest House (☎ 241414; www.trafford bankguesthouse.co.uk; 96 Fairfield Rd; s/d £55/75; P ✗) Plenty of welcoming touches such as fresh flowers and fruit in this upmarket former bishops' house.

TOP END
Dunain Park Hotel (☎ 230512; www.dunainparkhotel .co.uk; Dunain Park; r per person from £79; P ✗ ☺) A mile southwest of the centre on the A82, this country pile bristles with elegance. For a stylish stay by the Highlands' capital, you

---

FROLICKING ON THE FIRTH

Wedging its way into the Highlands from the North Sea, the Moray Firth is a favoured stomping ground for wild salmon. This happy punter draws a variety of agile fishers into the estuary, the most enigmatic being the 130-plus bottlenose dolphins, whose thick, insular layer of blubber distinguishes them from their south-sea cousins. Their sociable antics have earned them celebrity status and the area a trade in tour groups.

Unfortunately, research has revealed a 6% decline in dolphin numbers every year, due largely to the adverse effects of the burgeoning human population along the coast. In response, the Whale and Dolphin Conservation Society (WDCS) has launched a diligent campaign to increase awareness and impose strict guidelines for dolphin-watching cruises.

If you're looking for a dolphin fix, two WDCS-approved operators are **Inverness Dolphin Cruises** (☎ 01463-717900; adult/child £10/7.50; 5 to 6 daily departures; ☺ Mar-Oct) in Inverness, or **Dolphin Ecosse** (☎ 01381-600323; www.dolphinecosse.co.uk; ages 4 and up £20; 2½ hr) in Cromarty. You're most likely to see a platinum body slice through the water around Kessock Bridge, Chanonry Point or Spey Bay, but the dolphins aren't in cahoots with the boats, so sightings often come down to luck. The commentaries are excellent, however, and you may also spot ospreys, minke whales, seals and porpoises.

couldn't do better. It has so few rooms that you feel like a guest and not a number.

Eating & Drinking

Mustard Seed (☎ 220220; 16 Fraser St; 2-course lunch £5.95, mains £9-14; ☿ lunch & dinner; wheelchair access; ☒) Despite having long been regarded as the town's favourite spot for a special meal, there's nothing pretentious about this restaurant, with its lofty two-level interior and towering wine-filled bar. The flowery balcony is a delight when the weather plays fair, but the Mediterranean-influenced gourmet cuisine appeals wherever you're sitting and showcases the best of Highland and island produce.

Délices de Bretagne (☎ 712422; 6 Stephen's Brae; light meals £4-7; ☿ 9am-5pm Mon-Sat, 10am-5pm Sun; ☒) The best spot in town for a cup of coffee, this intimate French café entices all-comers with its Art-Nouveau prints, gourmet filled croissants, and tasty salads. Better yet is the mulled wine – guaranteed to banish those drizzle and sleet blues.

La Tortilla Asesina (☎ 709809; 99 Castle St; tapas £2-5; ☿ 10.30am-1am) The Hispanophile owners of this cosy spot have combed Spain for recipes and produce and have succeeded in creating the most authentic tapas bar in Scotland. It's perfect for sharing a range of flavours with friends, or grabbing a beer and a late bite after the pub closes.

Rocpool (☎ 717274; 1 Ness Walk; 2-course lunch £7.95, mains £12-18; ☿ lunch & dinner; ☒) This sophisticated eatery, with its *de rigueur* misspelled name, offers a range of mouth-watering choices on its polished wooden floorboards just across the bridge from the heart of town. From toothsome snack-sized portions of southern European creations to the elaborate main dishes, there's quality all the way, and plenty of vegetarian choice, too.

Hootananny (☎ 233651; 67 Church St) An extraordinary place in a former bank building, this three-floored bar is all things to all men and women. The charismatic downstairs bar has live ceilidh and folk bands nightly and serves simple Scottish meals all day, while the 2nd floor has livelier rock and blues bands from Wednesday to Sunday. Meanwhile, the cosy and intimate upstairs bar has stand-up comedians at weekends, taking the piss out of punters who are a mite too comfy on the yielding sofas.

Johnny Foxes (☎ 236577; cnr Bridge & Bank Sts) Not a bad spot for a quiet pint and a pub lunch during the day, this Irish theme pub becomes unashamedly brash and loud on weekend nights, when the punters pack the place to the rafters. The music is hardly traditional Scottish, but it is where people go if they feel like a Highland fling.

Other recommendations:

Café 1 (☎ 226200; 75 Castle St; mains £8-15; ☿ lunch & dinner Mon-Sat; ☒) Classy modern spot opposite the castle, serving dainty portions on candlelit tables.

Castle Restaurant (☎ 230925; 41 Castle St; mains £4-6; ☿ 8am-8.30pm) A traditional café that prides itself on plain, plentiful food at low prices.

Getting There & Away

AIR

Nine miles east of town at Dalcross, **Inverness airport** (☎ 01667-464000) offers flights to Edinburgh, Glasgow, Stornoway and other centres, as well as London Luton with **easyJet** (☎ 0870 600 0000).

BUS

Buses to Aberdeen (£10.50, 3¾ hours, hourly) are run by Stagecoach Bluebird. **National Express** (☎ 0870 580 8080; www.nationalexpress .com) operates buses to/from London (£37.50, 13½ hours, one to three daily). **Citylink** runs buses to/from Edinburgh (£15.90, four hours, hourly); Fort William (£8.40, two hours, five to six daily); Glasgow (£15.90, four hours, hourly); Portree (£14, 3¼ hours, two to three buses daily); Thurso (£11.65, 3½ hours, four or five daily); and Ullapool (£7.30, 1¼ hours, two daily from Monday to Saturday).

The Citylink buses to Ullapool and Thurso connect with ferries to Stornoway and Orkney respectively.

The Orkney Bus is a bus-ferry-bus service between Inverness and Kirkwall, via John o'Groats (see Getting There & Away, p918).

TRAIN

There are direct trains to Aberdeen (£19.90, 2¼ hours, five to 10 daily), Edinburgh (£32.90, 3¼ hours, hourly), Glasgow (£32.90, 3½ hours, 11 daily, including some services changing in Aberdeen), London (£70 to £115, 8½ to 11½ hours, two daily) and Thurso (£13, 3½ hours, one to two daily).

The line to Kyle of Lochalsh (£14.60, 2½ hours, four daily Monday to Saturday, two on Sundays) is one of the great scenic journeys in Britain.

Getting Around
TO/FROM THE AIRPORT
The twice-daily airport bus connects with Stornoway and London flights (£2.50, 20 minutes). A taxi costs about £12.

BICYCLE
There are great cycling opportunities out of Inverness and several rental outlets including **Highland Cycles** (☎ 234789; 16a Telford St), which rents out bikes for £12 for 24 hours.

BUS
There are some interesting side trips to be made from Inverness, and **Rapsons/Highland Country** (☎ 710555) operates bus services to places including Nairn, Forres, the Culloden battlefield and Cawdor. The Tourist Trail Day Explorer offers unlimited travel on buses to Inverness, Nairn, Culloden, Cawdor Castle, and Fort George and costs a bargain £5.

CAR
The TIC's free *Visitor Guide* includes a handy section on car hire. As well as the big boys there's **Sharp's Reliable Wrecks** (☎ 236684; 1st fl, Highland Rail House, Station Sq), an excellent set-up where the cars are much better than the name implies and rates start from £23 per day.

AROUND INVERNESS
Unless otherwise stated Highland Country buses service the sights mentioned in this section.

Culloden
The Battle of Culloden in 1746, the last battle fought on British soil, saw the defeat of Bonnie Prince Charlie and the slaughter of over 1200 Highlanders in a 68-minute rout.

The sombre 49-hectare moor where the conflict took place has scarcely changed. The site, with its many markers and memorials, is always open and provides a reflective place to wander, soaking up the trauma of this fearsome battle.

The duke of Cumberland won the label 'Butcher Cumberland' for his brutal treatment of the defeated Scottish forces. The battle sounded the death knell of the old clan system, and the merciless Highland Clearances soon followed as the old loyalties were cast aside for material gain.

The **visitors centre** (NTS; ☎ 01463-790607; adult £5; ⊗ 9am-6pm daily Apr-Oct, 9am-7pm Jul & Aug, 11am-4pm Nov, Dec, Feb & Mar, closed Jan) isn't great value for money but presents some background information on the battle and provides good audioguides to the site. There are also guided tours (£3) which are presented with plenty of tourist-friendly enthusiasm and take about an hour.

Culloden is situated about 6 miles east of Inverness.

Cawdor
Cawdor Castle (☎ 01667-404401; www.cawdorcastle .com; adult £6.50; ⊗ 10am-5.30pm May–mid-Oct), 14th-century home of the Thanes of Cawdor, was reputedly the castle of Shakespeare's Macbeth and the location of Duncan's murder. The central tower dates from the 14th century, but the wings are 17th-century additions. The castle is still inhabited, and opulently furnished. The explanatory boards in each room reveal an unexpected humorist at work.

Cawdor Tavern (☎ 01667-404777; bar meals £5-9) in the nearby village is worth a stop, although deciding what to drink can be difficult as it stocks over 100 varieties of whisky. There's also reasonable pub grub, with most specials under £8, and live music at weekends.

Fort George
Covering much of the headland here, **Fort George** (HS; ☎ 01667-462777; adult £6; ⊗ 9.30am-6.30pm Apr-Sep, 9.30am-4.30pm Mon-Sat, 2-4.30pm Sun Oct-Mar; wheelchair access) is a virtually unaltered 18th-century artillery fortification – one of the best examples of its kind in Europe. It was completed in 1769 as a base for George II's army and is still a barracks. The mile-plus walk around the ramparts offers fine views out to sea – where there's a good chance of spotting dolphins – and back to the Great Glen. Given its size, you'll need several hours to look around; the visitors centre dishes out a map.

It's off the A96 about 11 miles northeast of Inverness.

Black Isle & Cromarty
Actually a peninsula rather than an island, Black Isle can be reached from Inverness by a short cut across the **Kessock Bridge**.

In Rosemarkie, the **Groam House Museum** (☎ 01381-620961; admission free; ✆ daily May-Sep, 2-4pm Sat & Sun Oct-Apr) has a superb collection of Pictish stones incised with designs as well as a gazetteer of Pictish sites, which speckle this part of the coast. Donations are encouraged.

In the Cromarty Firth, you are likely to see the huge insectlike offshore oil rigs, which were built at Nigg before being towed out to the North Sea.

The attractive village of Cromarty is at the peninsula's northeastern end. **Cromarty Courthouse** (☎ 01381-600418; Church St; adult £3.50; ✆ 10am-5pm Apr-Oct, noon-4pm Nov-Dec & Mar) details the town's history with contemporary references. It's very engaging and the kids will love the talking mannequins, especially the oddball aristocrat Sir Thomas Urquhart, a direct descendant of Adam and Eve according to his own family tree.

Several places offer a roof for the night, including **Mrs Robertson** (☎ 01381-600488; 7 Church St; r per person £16), in a lovable old house, who also hires out bikes (£5 per day).

Rapsons Highland Country runs buses from Inverness to Rosemarkie (30 minutes, roughly hourly Monday to Saturday, three on Sunday). Most (although none on Sunday) continue onto Cromarty (55 minutes). A Black Isle Day Explorer allows unlimited travel for £5.

Brodie Castle

Set in 70 hectares of parkland, **Brodie Castle** (NTS; ☎ 01309-641371; adult £5; ✆ 11am-5.30pm Mon-Sat, 1.30-5.30pm Sun Apr-Sep) has several highlights, including an early 19th-century library, which has over 6000 dusty, peeling books. There are some wonderful clocks, and a 17th-century dining room with wildly extravagant mythological carvings in the plaster ceiling, although you'd swear it was woodcarving. Best of all, you may get to chat with the current, ageing laird who dons a National Trust badge and sometimes mingles with visitors.

The Brodies have lived here since 1160, but the present structure was built in 1567, with many extensions being added over the years.

The castle is 8 miles east of the small town of Nairn. Stagecoach Bluebird runs to Brodie from Inverness (45 minutes, hourly), via Culloden.

EAST COAST

The east coast is where the real desolation of the Highlands begins to unfold – both in scenery and atmosphere. The road traverses the Cromarty and Dornoch Firths and heads north along wild and pristine coastline; the northern segment, Caithness, has a proud Viking heritage that persists in its place names. With an interior dominated by the vast and mournful Sutherland mountain range, the only interruptions en route are the small and pleasant towns moored precariously on the coast's edge.

Getting Around

The region is well served by buses, and trains follow the coast up to Wick then across to Thurso. **Citylink** (☎ 0870 550 5050) runs regular bus services from Inverness to Wick, stopping at most towns on the A9 and A99 along the way, before taking the short cut inland to Thurso. **Rapson Highland Country** (☎ 01463-222244) operates buses from Wick to Thurso, via the coast and John o'Groats.

TAIN & AROUND

Tain, graced by noble sandstone buildings, is Scotland's oldest royal burgh. **Tain Through Time** (☎ 01862-894089; Tower St; adult £3.50; ✆ 10am-5pm Mon-Sat Apr-Oct) is a heritage centre set in three buildings which describes the ancient burgh as a place of pilgrimage; admission includes an audio tour of the town. Drop by the excellent **Glenmorangie Distillery** (☎ 01862-892477; www.glenmorangie.com; ✆ 9am-5pm Mon-Fri & 10am-4pm Sat Jun-Aug, last tour 90min before close), which produces fine Highland malt; tours are £2.50.

The A9 crosses Dornoch Firth. Alternatively, from Ardgay at the head of Dornoch Firth, a small road leads 10 miles up Strathcarron to **Croick**, the scene of notorious evictions during the 1845 Highland Clearances. Refugee crofters from Glencalvie scratched their tragic messages on the eastern windows of Croick Church.

Another detour from Ardgay along the Kyle of Sutherland leads after 4½ miles to Carbisdale Castle (the last castle to be built in Scotland, dating from 1917), which now houses the extraordinary **Carbisdale Castle SYHA Hostel** (☎ 0870 004 1109; www.syha.org.uk; Culrain; dm £13.50; ✆ Mar-Oct; Ⓟ ☒ 🖳). Good enough to house the exiled Norwegian royal family, this opulent place is a unique hostelling experience, with grand salons, art and statuary for days, great views, wooden grounds, and a top-floor ghost. Booking is advised, as it's a popular group destination. The sweeping **Bonar Bridge** then crosses the head of the firth to rejoin the A9 just before Dornoch.

DORNOCH & AROUND
☎ 01862 / pop 1206

It's difficult to believe that Scotland's last executed witch perished in a vat of boiling tar in Dornoch in 1722, because today this gorgeous village is a picture of serenity. This symphony in sandstone bewitches visitors with flowers, greenery and affable locals at every turn; nearby are some superb stretches of beach. Dornoch was catapulted into the headlines in 2000 when Madonna married Guy Ritchie at nearby Skibo Castle but seems to have recovered from the inundation of journalists and star-seekers.

The **TIC** (☎ 810916; 9.30am-5.30pm Mon-Sat, 10am-5pm Sun Apr-Oct, 10am-5pm Tue-Sat Nov-Mar) is in the main square. It hires bikes for £12 a day and has Internet access. If it's shut, you can get information at the old town jail, opposite.

Dornoch Cathedral is endearingly built of rough stone and has a simple and powerfully beautiful interior with a criss-cross of light streaming through adjacent stained-glass windows. It was originally destroyed in 1570 during a clan feud and wasn't completely rebuilt until 1835-7.

Dornoch has several campsites and plenty of B&Bs.

Dornoch Castle (☎ 810216; www.dornochcastlehotel .com; Castle St; chalet £60-80, castle r £110-140; wheelchair access; P) This is a great spot in a 16th-century former bishop's palace, right opposite the cathedral and offering a variety of rooms. The chalet rooms in the garden are pleasant if unremarkable, while the castle itself has rooms furnished in grand style. Check the website for off-season specials and weekend deals.

Trevose Guest House (☎ 810269; trevose@amserve .net; Cathedral Sq; s/d from £21/42; Mar-Sep;) This guesthouse lacks nothing in location; it's right by the cathedral too, and vibrant in season with a riot of rose bushes in the garden.

> **SOMETHING SPECIAL**
>
> Seven miles north of Dornoch, the A839 heads inland towards Lairg and Loch Shin. The hamlet of Rogart boasts a unique form of backpacker accommodation. **Sleeperzzz .com** (☎ 01408-641343; www.sleeperzzz.com; Rogart Station; dm £10; Mar-Oct;) is set in two lovingly restored railway carriages parked up in a siding at the train station. The compartments have been converted into two-person dorms; each carriage also has a kitchenette and a tiny lounge. The delightful owners let guests use bikes free of charge; for meals, the local pub is a sterling place just a minute away. You can reach here by train on the Inverness–Wick line, and you'll save a pound for doing so!

Eagle Hotel (☎ 810008; Castle St; meals £6-10) A top little boozer, complete with eccentric ornamentation and man-sized meals.

Citylink has bus services to/from Inverness (£6.50, 1¼ hours, four to five daily) and Thurso (£9.85, 2¼ hours, four to five daily), stopping at Dornoch's square.

Dunrobin Castle
Heading north from Dornoch, the road passes **Dunrobin Castle** (☎ 01408-633177; adult £6.60; 10.30am-5.30pm Mon-Sat, noon-5.30pm Jul & Aug, 10.30am-4.30pm Apr-Jun & Sep–mid-Oct), a mile north of Golspie at the end of a film-set driveway. It's the largest house in the Highlands (187 rooms) and dates back to around 1275. The towers and turrets outside weave a fairytale-esque atmosphere, belied by the memory of the cruel Duke of Sutherland, who cleared 15,000 people from the North of Scotland during his residence here.

Displayed are numerous wildlife trophies and animal skins, betraying the family's taste for hunting, and innumerable gifts from farm tenants (the ones who were left, obviously). Falconry demonstrations are given three times a day in the formal gardens. Nearby, a museum offers an eclectic mix of archaeological finds, natural-history exhibits, more big-game trophies and an excellent collection of Pictish stones found in Sutherland.

CAITHNESS
The northeast corner of Scotland, Caithness, is a memorable and distinct region.

HIGHLANDS & NORTHERN ISLANDS

It bristles with the remains of prehistoric settlements and traces of the Vikings, who long held sway over this area. Inland is a lonely and evocative bogland, a haven for birds, while on the coast green swathes drop abruptly to the sea, with harbours nestling at the bottom of the cliffs that flourished on the back of the herring trade.

Helmsdale
☎ 01431 / pop 771

Helmsdale is a pretty and petite village surrounded by some stunning, undulating coastline and the River Helmsdale – one of the best salmon rivers in the Highlands. Tourist information can be had in the friendly **Strath Ullie shop** (☎ 821402; Shore St) by the pretty harbour. The worthwhile **Timespan Heritage Centre** (☎ 821327; Dunrobin St; adult £4; ⊙ 9.30am-5pm Mon-Sat & 2-5pm Sun Easter-Oct) has details of the 1869 Strath of Kildonan gold rush, art exhibitions, and a model of Dame Barbara Cartland, the late queen of pulp-romance novels.

There are several B&Bs in town, but you can't beat the location of the **Customs House** (☎ 821648; Shore St; s/d from £16/32), a welcoming spot with a pretty little front yard and rooms with plush quilts and great views. It's great value. Simpler beds are up for grabs at **Helmsdale SYHA Hostel** (☎ 0870 004 1124; www .syha.org.uk; dm £9.50; ⊙ May-Sep; ✖). It's pretty basic but good for groups, with large 12-bed dorms and a cavernous dining hall.

Cartland holidayed in Helmsdale for over 60 years and Nancy Sinclair, former proprietor of **La Mirage** (☎ 821625; 7 Dunrobin St; snacks £1.50-3, mains £6-13; ⊙ noon-8.45pm) designed her restaurant in homage to the Dame. The restaurant oozes pink kitsch; a drawcard in itself. There's a price war of comic proportions with the **Bunillidh** (☎ 821457; 2 Dunrobin St; snacks £1.50-3, mains £6-13; ⊙ noon-8.45pm) opposite; great options for fish done either cheap or classy.

Helmsdale to Wick

This route boasts several Celtic sites. From Latheron, follow the A9 to Achavanich,

---

THE HIGHLAND CLEARANCES & CROFTING

The vast spaces of the Highlands are a wilderness that's one of Europe's least populated zones. This wasn't always the case, however; crumbling stone cottages in small clutches throughout even the most deserted areas are mute witnesses to one of the darkest and most heartless episodes of Scottish history: the Highland Clearances.

The traditional way of life in the Highlands was of simple farming on land which was effectively controlled by the local clan chief. In exchange for an annual tithe, and occasional conscription of able-bodied men for clan military service, these farmers were left to pursue the lifestyle they had led for centuries.

In the wake of Culloden, however, king George II banned private armies, and new land laws were introduced that made the clan chiefs actual owners of their traditional lands, often vast tracts of territory. Heads addled by the prospect of vast riches, these lairds decided that sheep were more profitable than agriculture, and proceeded to evict tens of thousands of farmers from their lands. The Clearances forced these desperate folk to emigrate – to the Americas or the Southern Hemisphere – or head for the cities in the hope of finding work. Those who chose to pursue farming were marginalised into whatever narrow or barren bits of land they could subsist on; this became known as crofting. It was always precarious, as rights were granted on a year-by-year basis, so at any moment a crofter could lose not only the farm but also the house they had built on it.

When the economic depression of the late-19th century hit, many couldn't pay their rent. This time, however, they resisted expulsion, instead forming the Highland Land Reform Association and their own political party. Their resistance led to several of their demands being acceded to by the government, including security of tenure, fair rents and eventually the supply of land for new crofts.

Crofters are now protected by more laws, and a recent decree gives them the absolute right to purchase the land that they farm. At the end of November 2004, a law came into effect abolishing all remaining aspects of the feudal system, but Scotland is perhaps still struggling with the loss of community and population the brutality of the Clearances caused.

wedged between Loch Rangag and Loch Stemster, then double back on the road to Lybster to the 40 or so **Achavanich Standing Stones**.

Just beyond Lybster, a turn-off leads to the **Grey Cairns of Camster**, 5 miles north of the A99. Dating from between 4000 BC and 2500 BC, the burial chambers are hidden in long, low mounds rising from an evocatively desolate stretch of moor. You can enter the main chamber but you must crawl into the well-preserved Round Cairn.

The **Hill o'Many Stanes**, just beyond the Camster turn-off, is a curious, fan-shaped arrangement of 22 rows of small stones probably dating from around 2000 BC. Nearer to Wick at Ulbster, the **Cairn o'Get** is 400 metres off the A99, and then a 2-mile walk. Steps lead down to a small, picturesque harbour, directly opposite the Cairn o'Get.

Wick

☎ 01955 / pop 7333

Not the prettiest of places, gritty Wick is a little down-at-heel, but was once the world's largest herring fishing port; the collapse of the market for the 'silver darlings' after WWII signed a death warrant for the town's industry, and Wick hasn't yet recovered.

Wick is a transport gateway town for the surrounding area. **British Airways** (☎ 0845 773 3377; www.ba.com) flies to Wick from Aberdeen, Edinburgh and Orkney. Citylink runs four to five buses daily to/from Thurso (40 minutes) and Inverness (£11.65, three hours). Highland Country runs a service from Wick to John o'Groats (one hour, four daily Monday to Saturday) for those wanting to jump on the passenger ferry to Orkney. Trains service Wick from Inverness (£13, four hours, two or three daily).

John o'Groats

☎ 01955 / pop 579

If John was a person, he'd be a second-hand car salesman or a gerrymandering politician. How else to explain the seedy tourist trap that has grown around the lie that it's the most northerly place in Britain? It's not – that title goes to Dunnet Head further west. The only reason to come here is to catch a passenger ferry to Orkney – while waiting for it to leave, amuse yourself at the various enterprising individuals staggering into the car park, having completed the 874-mile trek from Land's End in Cornwall with all manner of unlikely companions: a fridge, a team of oxen, and a ball 'n' chain have all been done.

The **TIC** (☎ 611373; 9am-6pm Easter-Oct) is beside the car park.

Highland Country runs services to/from Thurso (one hour, five daily Monday to Saturday).

See p916 for details of the passenger ferry to Orkney, and the car ferry 3 miles west of here in Gills Bay.

Dunnet Head

A stretch of narrow road across a bog takes you to the most northerly point on the British mainland, the dramatic Dunnet Head. The head is marked by a lighthouse (built by Robert Stevenson, grandfather of Robert Louis Stevenson) that dates from 1832. The tricky Pentland Firth, the strait between Orkney and the mainland, stretches from Duncansby Head to Dunnet Head.

Dunnet Head B&B (☎ 01847-851774; www.dunnet head.co.uk; s/d £23/42; Easter-Sep; P) offers sound and welcoming B&B accommodation and can arrange evening meals.

NORTH & WEST COAST

The isolated north and northwest coastline is an absolute visual feast. Fjordlike inlets, pristine beaches, soaring mountains, and mirrorlike lochs festooned with waterlilies leave an indelible imprint on the visitor's mind. The landscapes here have mood and personality, and beware of traversing them too quickly, or you'll end up in hospital with a severe case of scenic overload!

The primal landscape shelters the odd small village and town, where people seem bonded by remoteness and natural beauty. This is perhaps the most memorable corner of an unforgettable country, and one that visitors return to again and again.

After descending past the awesome mountainscape of the Assynt, the road emerges at the charming harbour village of Ullapool, a perfect place to rest up and absorb what you have seen. Heading further south again can come as a rude shock as you encounter main roads, traffic, and tour buses!

Banks and petrol stations are few and far between, so check your funds and fuel before setting out.

Getting Around

Public transport in the northwest is very patchy. Getting to Thurso or Kyle of Lochalsh by bus or train is easy, but it can be difficult to follow the coast between these places. Bus services are infrequent, and on a Sunday you'll go nowhere at all. Postbuses and Highland Country services run along the north coast. The alternative is to come north from Inverness via Lairg. There are trains daily to Lairg, from where Postbus No 104 and 105 run north to Durness. There are frequent Highland Country and Citylink buses between Inverness and Ullapool.

Off the main routes, renting a car is a better option. Hitching is widely practised, and as easy as you'll ever find it.

THURSO & SCRABSTER

☎ 01847 / pop 7737

The most northerly town on the British mainland, Thurso is a quiet place with a riverbank, a pretty town beach and not a great deal else. Although it lacks a charismatic Highland pub, it's a handy overnight stop if you're heading west or on the way to Orkney,

and has some good accommodation choices and down-to-earth people keen for a chat.

The nearby coast has arguably the best, most regular surf in Britain. There's an excellent right-hand reef break on the eastern side of town, directly in front of Lord Caithness' castle, and another shallow reef break 5 miles west at Brimms Ness. The water can chill you to the bone though, so make sure you're fully kitted out. For more on surfing see p83.

Ferries cross from the port of Scrabster, on the outskirts of Thurso, to Orkney.

Information

Computer Game Centre (☎ 894510; 33 High St; per hr £2; ⊙ 10.30am-8pm Mon-Sat, noon-4pm Sun) Internet access amid the rat-tat-tat of automatic gunfire.

Library (Davidsons Lane; ⊙ Mon-Sat) Free Internet access.

TIC (☎ 892371; Riverside Rd; ⊙ Mon-Sat Apr & May, daily Jun-Oct) By the river.

Sleeping

Sandra's Backpackers Hostel (☎ 894575; www .sandras-backpackers.ukf.net; 24 Princes St; dm/d £10/28; wheelchair access with notice; ☒ ☐) This superbly

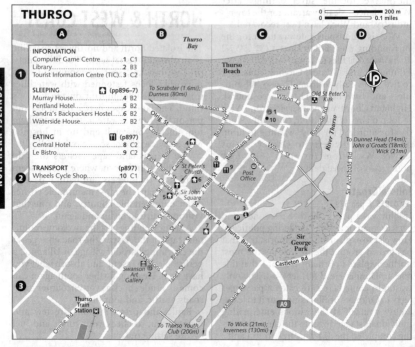

THURSO

0 —————— 200 m
0 —————— 0.1 miles

INFORMATION
Computer Game Centre............1 C1
Library.................................2 B3
Tourist Information Centre (TIC)..3 C2

SLEEPING (pp896–7)
Murray House..........................4 B2
Pentland Hotel.........................5 B2
Sandra's Backpackers Hostel......6 B2
Waterside House.......................7 B2

EATING (p897)
Central Hotel...........................8 C2
Le Bistro................................9 C2

TRANSPORT (p897)
Wheels Cycle Shop...................10 C1

Thurso Bay

Thurso Beach

To Scrabster (1.6mi);
Durness (80mi)

Shore St
Wilson La
Old St Peter's
Kirk

Swanson St

Olrig St

Cowie La

Beach

Rotterdam St

Wilson St

Grove La

Riverside Rd

River Thurso

To Dunnet Head (14mi);
John o'Groats (18mi);
Wick (21mi)

Sir Archibald Rd

East Church St
West Church St

Campbell St

Traill St

Manson's La

Post Office

St Peter's Church

Sir John's Square

St George St

Thurso Bridge

Sir George Park

Castleton Rd

Barrock St
Paterson's La

Princes St

Riddell La

Brabster St
Janet St

Davidsons La

Swanson Art Gallery

Thurso Train Station

Lovers' La

Ormlie Rd

Millbank Rd

A9

To Thurso Youth Club (200m)

To Wick (21mi);
Inverness (130mi)

refurbished hostel above the local chippie is one of the Highlands' best backpacker options. The word 'budget' here applies to the guests, not the management, which provides dozens of little features to make your stay comfortable, such as individual reading lamps in the luxurious en-suite dorms, polished wood floors, a great kitchen, cheap bike-hire, and a free continental breakfast. It's also a good place to garner information about the region, about which the owner is passionate.

Waterside House (☎ 894751; www.watersidehouse .info; 3 Janet St; r per person £15-20; ✗) Opposite the river, this well-priced B&B is a lot more spacious than it appears from outside. The rooms are uncluttered and very tastefully decorated in cool blue colours; some have an en suite, but the shared bathrooms are blindingly clean too. Breakfast is a tasty affair, with the welcome option of bacon-and-egg rolls as an alternative to the weighty fry-up.

Murray House (☎ 895759; www.murrayhousebb .com; 1 Campbell St; s £25, d £40-60; **P**) Extra effort goes into guests' comfort at this well-run setup; you'll be well looked-after. The big, carpeted, en-suite, flowery rooms have wooden beds in lovely dark wood; there's also a fine lounge with video and board games.

Other recommendations:

Pentland Hotel (☎ 893202; www.pentlandhotel.co.uk; Princes St; s/d £41/75; ✗) Refurbished hotel with an upmarket bar and pleasing, if unexciting, rooms.

Thurso Youth Club (☎ 892964; Millbank Rd; dm £9; ☾ Jul & Aug; **P** ✗ ▣) Summer-only hostel with excellent facilities, including pool table, and large cheery dorms.

Eating & Drinking

Le Bistro (☎ 893737; 12 Traill St; mains £8-10; ☾ 10am-8.30pm Tue-Sat, 5-8.30pm Mon; ✗) An intimate bistro serving top-quality nosh, from coffee and snacks to ambitious main meals that combine local and international flavours. It's a much better option in the evenings than during the day, when try-hards regard it as something of a place to be seen.

Central Hotel (☎ 893129; Traill St; bar meals £3-7; ☾ lunch & dinner) A recent refit means the downstairs bar is somewhat more soulless than in yesteryear, but upstairs remains a good spot to overlook the throbbing heart of Thurso. It's decorated with a quirky assemblage of flying machines hanging from a pink ceiling; the adjacent restaurant area is child-friendly and serves filling bar meals.

Getting There & Away

Citylink runs buses from Inverness (£11.65, 3½ hours, four or five daily) to Thurso, via Wick. Highland Country operates a service to Wick (45 minutes, hourly) and also to John o'Groats (one hour, five daily Monday to Saturday).

There are train services from Inverness (£13, 3½ hours, two to three daily), but space for bicycles is limited so book ahead.

Getting Around

It's a 2-mile walk from Thurso train station to the ferry port at Scrabster, or there are buses from Olrig St (80p). **Wheels Cycle Shop** (☎ 896124; 35 High St) rents out mountain bikes from £8 per day.

WEST FROM THURSO

Outside Thurso's town limits, the landscape returns to the vast, spectacular and occasionally dramatic, revealing the true grandeur of the north coast. Eighty winding coastal miles carry you from Thurso to Durness. On the coast 10 miles west of Thurso, at **Dounreay**, is a nuclear power station that was the first in the world to supply mains electricity. It's now decommissioned, but still employs some 3000 people charged with ensuring a safe shutdown, which will take until 2047. The **visitors centre** (☎ 01847-802572; admission free; ☾ 10am-4pm Apr-Oct) pumps out propaganda about the benefits of nuclear power. Just before Melvich, the A897 leads 14 miles south into the Flow Country to the **RSPB Forsinard Peatlands Visitor Centre** (☎ 01641-571225; ☾ Apr-Oct), which provides details on the surrounding 8000-hectare nature reserve; terrific for bird-watchers.

Bettyhill is a crofting community named after Elizabeth, countess of Sutherland, who evicted her tenants from Strathnaver to make way for more profitable sheep, then resettled the tenants here. The **TIC** (☎ 01641-521342; ☾ Mon-Sat Apr-Oct & Sun Jun-Aug), by the main road, has a small café in the same building. **Strathnaver Museum** (☎ 01641-521418; adult £1.90; ☾ 10am-1pm & 2-5pm Mon-Sat Apr-Oct), in an old church a stone's throw away, tells the sad story of the Strathnaver Clearances. There's an 8th-century Pictish cross in the graveyard behind the museum.

The wonderful beach at **Coldbackie** is overlooked by the Watch Hill viewpoint. Only 2 miles further on is **Tongue**, overlooked by the gaunt 14th-century ruins of Castle Varrich. It's a great little place; the **Tongue Hotel** (☎ 01847-611206; www.tonguehotel.co.uk; s/d from £45/70; restaurant mains £9-15, bar meals £5-7; ⊙ Apr-Oct, restaurant lunch & dinner; P ✕) is an all-in-one, offering plush rooms in a former hunting-lodge, high-quality restaurant meals such as venison stew, great views, and a dark den of a downstairs bar with cheap snacks and a pool table. Down by the causeway, **Tongue SYHA** (☎ 0870 004 1153; www.syha.org.uk; dm £10.50; ⊙ Apr-Sep; P ✕) is more austere, but has recently refurbished facilities and a spectacular location right by the **Kyle of Tongue** (a *kyle* is a strait).

From Tongue it's 30 miles to Durness – you can either take the causeway across the Kyle of Tongue or the beautiful old road that climbs up to the head of the kyle. The road crosses a desolate moor to the northern end of **Loch Hope**. Beyond Loch Hope, **Heilam** has stunning views out over **Loch Eriboll**, Britain's deepest sea inlet.

DURNESS
☎ 01971 / pop 353

The scattered village of Durness is strung out along sea cliffs, which rise from a series of pristine beaches. It's a magical spot revealing some of the best of the northern coastline, and makes a great base for exploring the area.

The bend-over-backwards **TIC** (☎ 511259; ⊙ 10am-5pm Easter-Sep, 10am-1.30pm Oct-Easter) has plenty of information on the surrounding area.

Sights

There is a path down to gaping **Smoo Cave**, which is a mile east of the TIC. The vast cave entrance stands at the end of an inlet, or *geo*, and after heavy rain a river cascades through its roof and then flows out to sea. At low tide you can walk into the cave; **tours** (☎ 511704; per person £3; ⊙ 11am-4pm Apr-May, 10am-5pm Jun-Sep) will take you further into its depths. Durness has several beautiful **beaches**, including Rispond to the east, Sargo Sands below town, and Balnakeil to the west; the sea offers some superb scuba-diving sites complete with wrecks, caves, seals and whales. At **Balnakeil**, which is less than a mile beyond Durness, a ramshackle craft village occupies what was once a early-warning radar station. A walk along

the beach to the north leads to **Faraid Head**, where you can see puffin colonies in early summer.

Sleeping & Eating

Sango Sands Caravan Park (☎ 511262; tent sites per person £4.25; ⊙ Apr-Oct) You couldn't imagine a better location for a campsite, with great grassy areas on the edge of cliffs descending to two lovely sand beaches. Facilities are pretty good, although management can be surly.

Lazy Crofter Bunkhouse (☎ 511209; www.durness hostel.com; dm £9; ✕) The Lazy Crofter is an excellent, relaxed hostel where guests are left to their own devices. It has neat, tartan, snug-as-a-bug bunks and great facilities, including laundry, drying room, kitchen and lounge. Check in at Mackay's Hotel next door.

Mackay's Hotel (☎ 511202; www.visitmackays.com; s/d from £45/90; ⊙ Mar-Oct; P ✕) This classy yet intimate hotel has only six rooms and was recently refurbished. It sports wooden floorboards and furniture, big, inviting beds and a relaxed minimalist feel. The restaurant is highly recommended too, but best of all is the heartfelt Highland welcome.

Loch Croispol Bookshop (☎ 511777; 17c Balnakeil Craft Village; light meals £3-6; ⊙ 10am-5.30pm Mon-Sat, 10am-4pm Sun; wheelchair access; ✕) Located a mile west of Durness in the intriguing craft village, the friendly Loch Croispol Bookshop is a great place for when it's pouring with rain, for you can sit here browsing books, drinking coffee, and trying the delicious snacks and lunches, with plenty of vegetarian choices.

Getting There & Away

Postbus operates a service between Durness to Tongue (1½ hours, one daily Monday to Saturday) and on to Lairg, where you can connect with trains. Tim Dearman Coaches runs during summer only from Inverness via Ullapool; see Getting There & Away (p890) for details.

DURNESS TO ULLAPOOL

It may only be 69 miles from Durness to Ullapool, but with plenty of side trips and stunning diversions to be made along the way, you could spend a week making the journey. The scenery on this stretch is as epic as the *Bhagavad Gita* and *The Lord of the Rings* rolled into one.

Cape Wrath

The most northwesterly point of the mainland, Cape Wrath is crowned by a lighthouse (dating from 1827) and stands close to the seabird colonies on Clo Mor Cliffs, the mainland's highest sea cliffs. Getting to Cape Wrath involves a **ferry ride** (☎ 01971-511376) from Keoldale across the Kyle of Durness (£4 return) and a connecting **minibus** (☎ 01971-511287) for the 11 miles to the cape (£6.50 return). Services operate one to four times daily from April to September, weather permitting.

South of Cape Wrath, **Sandwood Bay** boasts one of Britain's most isolated beaches. It's about 4½ miles north of the end of a track from Blairmore (approach from Kinlochbervie), or you could walk south from the cape (allow eight hours) and onto Blairmore.

Handa Island & Scourie

Boats (☎ 01971-502347; £7 return) go out regularly to Handa Island's important seabird sanctuary from Tarbet, Monday to Saturday from April to September. You may see skuas and puffins, as well as seals. There are great views to the **Old Man of Stoer** (p899) across Eddrachillis Bay. Scourie is a pretty crofting community in an excellent area for fishing.

REMOTE BUT REWARDING

As you travel along the coasts of northern Scotland it's sometimes easy to forget the interior Highlands, even though their presence is always so visible. Only a few roads, some single-track, provide access to this bleak but inspiring high country.

From June to September, just south of Lairg, at the southern end of Loch Shin, you can watch salmon leaping the **Falls of Shin** on their way upstream. From Lairg, single-track roads run north to Tongue, northwest to Laxford Bridge (between Durness and Kylesku) and west to Ledmore (between Kylesku and Ullapool). The Tongue road, the A836, **Ben Klibreck** (721m) and **Ben Loyal** (764m). Just west of Ben Loyal lies **Ben Hope** (927m), at the head of Loch Hope.

There are buses from Tain to Lairg, run by McLeod's coaches, while you can also get there by train from Inverness. Postbus services connect Lairg to the northwest coast; see Getting Around under North & West Coast (p896).

Kylesku & Loch Glencoul

Cruises on steely-blue Loch Glencoul pass treacherous-looking mountains, seal colonies, a soaring golden eagle if you're in luck, and the 213m-drop of **Eas a'Chual Aulin**, Britain's highest waterfall. In summer **Statesman Cruises** (☎ 01971-502345) runs two-hour trips at 11am and 3pm Sunday to Thursday (2pm Friday) from Kylesku Old Ferry Pier costing £12.50. While you wait, you can have a pint and a snack or meal in the **Kylesku Hotel** (☎ 01971-502231; s/d from £45/70; bar meals £8-11, 2-course dinners £21.95; ✆ Mar-Oct; P ✗) overlooking the pier. It's a hospitable place which does fine seafood and has comfortable if unremarkable rooms. It may be under new management soon, so phone to confirm opening and prices.

Old Man of Stoer

It's about a 30-mile detour off the main A894 out and back to the Point of Stoer and the Rhu Stoer Lighthouse (1870). Along the coast road be prepared for single-car-width roads, blind bends and summits…and sheep. The rewards are spectacular views, pretty villages and excellent beaches. From the lighthouse, it's a good one-hour cliff walk to the Old Man of Stoer, a spectacular sea stack (a tower of rock rising from the sea). There are more good beaches between Stoer and Lochinver, as well as a hostel. **Achmelvich Beach SYHA Hostel** (☎ 0870 004 1102; www.syha.org.uk; Achmelvich; dm £10.50; ✆ Apr-Sep; P ✗) is in an unforgettable location by a beautiful stretch of white sand. It's a place to relax and forget about the rest of the world. Facilities are simple; the nearest shop is 4 miles south in Lochinver. The Lochinver–Drumbeg postbus will drop you 1½ mile away.

Lochinver & Around

☎ 01571 / pop 650

Some stunning country surrounds this busy little fishing port. The **TIC** (☎ 844330; Main St; ✆ 10am-5pm Apr-Oct) organises fishing permits and has an interesting visitors centre relating the history of the Assynt region. The **Hills of Assynt**, near Lochinver, are popular with walkers and include the peaks Ben More Assynt (998m), Canisp (846m), Quinag (808m) and Suilven (731m).

There are several B&Bs in town, but the most memorable place to stay is **The Albannach Hotel** (☎ 844407; www.thealbannach.co.uk; DB&B per person from £100; ☉ Mar-Nov; P ✕). With stunning water views and spacious, relaxing rooms, you couldn't ask for more, except, perhaps, the finest of Scottish gourmet cooking using organic and free-range produce! Five-course dinners cost £40 for nonresidents. Cheaper but admirable food is available at the **Riverside Bistro** (☎ 844356; Main St; meals £4-10; ✕), which has an outstanding ensemble of inventive food made with local produce. There are lots of vegetarian choices, and its pies are culinary heaven.

Knockan, Inverpolly & Around

About 3 miles south of Knockan (known for its weird rock formations – older geological layers on top of younger layers), there are geological and nature trails and a Scottish National Heritage **interpretation centre** (☎ 01854-613418), beside Inverpolly National Nature Reserve. The reserve has many glacial lochs and the three peaks of Cul Beag (769m), Cul Mor (849m) and Stac Pollaidh (613m).

Boat trips (☎ 01854-622200) operate to the Summer Isles from the crofting village of **Achiltibuie**, reached by a circuitous route around Loch Lurgainn (head west off the A835 at Drumrunie). There are two departures daily, Monday to Saturday and trips cost £15, or £20 for an all-day cruise.

ULLAPOOL

☎ 01854 / pop 1308

Ullapool's harbour-side façade is postcard perfect and, on a sunny day, its surrounding rocky slopes are mirrored in the glassy veneer of its bay. The tops of the retreating hills surrounding the bay trap feathery wisps of cloud in transit to inland areas.

It's a busy place in summer, as it's the main access point for the Outer Hebrides; a ferry runs from here to Stornoway. Feel sorry for the people who just rush through, as they are missing one of the most alluring towns in Scotland. There are few attractions, but piles of accommodation, a magical setting, great seafood and a couple of good pubs.

Information

Royal Bank of Scotland (Ladysmith St) Has ATM.
TIC (☎ 612135; ullapool@host.co.uk; Argyle St; ☉ daily Jun-Sep, Mon-Sat Apr-May & Oct, Mon-Fri Nov-Mar) Dishes out information.
Ullapool Bookshop (☎ 612356; Quay St) Lots of books on Scottish topics and maps of the area.

Ullapool Library (☎ 612543; Mill St; ☉ Mon-Fri) Free Internet access.

Sights & Activities

Set in a converted church built by Thomas Telford, the **Ullapool Museum** (☎ 612987; 7 West Argyle St; adult £3; ☉ 10am-5pm Mon-Sat Apr-Oct, 10am-4pm Sat Nov-Mar; wheelchair access) relates the history of Loch Broom through interactive displays and other exhibits.

In July and August, **CalMac** (www.calmac .co.uk) runs day trips to the islands of Lewis and Harris; these can be remarkably good value. Inquire at the CalMac office on the harbour or check its website. The **Summer Queen** (☎ 612472; www.summerqueen.co.uk; Ullapool Pier) runs four-hour cruises of the Summer Isles leaving at 10am from April to September.

Sleeping

There are lots of B&Bs and guesthouses along Seaforth Rd and Pulteney St, and on Argyle St near the Quay St junction.

Scotpackers/West House Hostel (☎ 613126; www.scotpackers-hostels.co.uk; West Argyle St; dm £11-12; ✕ 🖳) A rambling colourful house, this hostel has laid-back management and good common areas. The four- to six-bed dorms are airy and all have and en suite; the kitchen is large, with all the kit. Not far from the hostel are double rooms in a crofter's house (£15 per person).

Ptarmigan B&B (☎ 612232; North Rd; r per person from £18; P ✕) This gloriously unassuming place a mile from the centre boasts million-dollar views of the loch. You can enjoy them from the comfy quarters – both the larger en-suite rooms or the ones with private bathroom are good value – but especially dallying over morning coffee, as the charming host does everything right at the breakfast table.

Brae Guest House (☎ 612421; Shore St; s/d from £23/46; ☉ May-Sep; P ✕) You can't beat the location of this whitewashed house right on the waterfront. It's a top spot to stay; the endearing owner has been in the B&B business for nigh on half a century, so she knows a thing or two about making guests comfortable!

Woodlands (☎ 612701; www.ullapoolbandb.com; 1a Pulteney St; d & tw £34-38; ☉ Easter–mid-Dec; P ✕) Run by a cheery couple who make their own marmalade, jams and bread and even smoke their own fish, this good-value choice has two

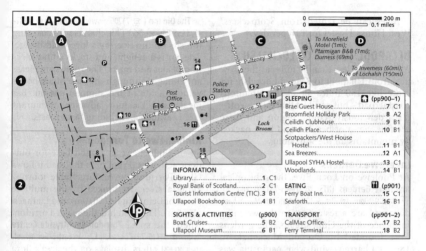

comfortable rooms that share a bathroom. Tuck into possibly the best breakfast in town here; you can also get a tasty packed lunch if you're heading for the hills.

Ceilidh Place (☎ 612103; www.theceilidhplace.com; 14 West Argyle St; r per person £45-65; P 🖳) This enchanting nook-and-cranny hotel exudes warmth, class, and character. All the rooms are different, but all have intriguing art, wood-lined fittings, and, enchantingly, hot-water-bottles. Best of all is the guest lounge, a sumptuous space packed with sofas and chaises-longues; it's a very special room to relax in with a whisky.

Ceilidh Clubhouse (West Lane; per person £15) Opposite Ceilidh Place, this has upmarket bunkhouse accommodation with great showers. You don't share the rooms with strangers, so booking is advisable.

Other recommendations:

Broomfield Holiday Park (☎ 612664; www.broom fieldhp.fsnet.co.uk; tent sites £5-9; ☺ May-Oct) Great location with grassy lochside pitches and a stone's throw from the heart of town. Take midge repellent.

Sea Breezes (☎ 612148; 2 West Tce; s/d £25/40; ✕) Engaging, personal, relaxed, with great views from the double room.

Ullapool SYHA Hostel (☎ 0870 004 1156; www.syha.org .uk; Shore St; dm £11.50; ☺ Mar-Oct; ✕ 🖳) Right on the harbour-side, welcoming and clean. Try to grab a room with harbour views.

Eating & Drinking

Ferry Boat Inn (☎ 612366; www.ferryboat-inn.com; Shore St; 2-/3-course dinner £18.25/21.50; ☺ bar meals all day plus dinner 6.30-9pm) This cosy waterfront pub, known locally as the FBI, is the town's best watering hole, with a delightfully inviting bar area. It also puts a creative spin on traditional (and nontraditional: try the ostrich in tarragon sauce!) fare making for a delectable menu. There's also good barfood of the scampi and chips variety for £5 to £7.

The Seaforth (☎ 612122; cnr Quay & Shore Sts; meals downstairs £5-10, bistro mains £8-18; ☺ food served noon-10pm; ✕) This big brash pub in the heart of town is often packed with people, who flock here for the excellent fish and chips or pints of cockles on offer. There are outdoor tables with midge buster, but if you want to get away from the crowded chaos, head upstairs to the quieter bistro, which lets you enjoy the view and the meal in peace.

Morefield Motel (☎ 612161; North Rd; dishes £7-10) This motel serves some outstanding local seafood, including langoustine, salmon, swordfish and lobster, in its lounge bar. It has a deservedly fine reputation and is popular with locals and tourists alike. The Seafood Rendezvous for two should only be attempted if you've been fasting. The motel is off the A835, a mile north of the harbour (follow Mill St).

Getting There & Around

Citylink has bus services from Inverness (£7.30, 1½ hours, two daily Monday to Saturday) to Ullapool linking in with the ferry to Stornoway on Lewis.

Bikes can be rented from Scotpackers/ West House Hostel for £10 per day.

ULLAPOOL TO KYLE OF LOCHALSH

Although it's less than 50 miles as the crow flies from Ullapool to Kyle of Lochalsh, it's more like 150 miles along the circuitous coastal road – but don't let that put you off – it's a deliciously remote region and there are fine views of beaches and bays backed by mountains all the way along.

Inverewe Gardens

At Poolewe on Loch Ewe, the subtropical **Inverewe Gardens** (NTS; ☎ 01445-781200; adult £7; ⏰ 9am-9.30pm Apr-Oct, 9.30am-4pm Nov-Mar; wheelchair access) are a testament to the warming influence of the Gulf Stream. The gardens were founded by Osgood Mackenzie in 1862 – a barren, windswept peninsula was gradually transformed into a luxuriant, colourful, 26-hectare garden. There's a pleasant cafeteria-style restaurant selling soup and sandwiches.

Gairloch

☎ 01445 / pop 1056

Gairloch is a peaceful group of villages stretched out around the inner end of a loch. In summer, tourism hits this place big time and there are plenty of places to stay. The surrounding area is known for its sandy beaches and good fishing, while walkers use the town as a base. The **TIC** (☎ 712130; ⏰ Mon-Sat Easter-Oct), in the car park in Auchtercairn, has a bureau de change. **Gairloch Heritage Museum** (☎ 712287; Auchtercairn; adult £3; ⏰ 10am-5pm Mon-Sat Apr-Sep, 10am-1.30pm Mon-Fri Oct) tells of life in the western Highlands, complete with a typical crofting cottage.

From April to October, the **Spirit of Skye** (☎ 712777; www.overtheseatoskye.com) runs twice a day from Gairloch to Portree on Skye. It's a comfortable, passenger-only boat; a one-way fare is £10, and takes 90 minutes.

Rua Reidh Lighthouse (☎ 771263; www.scotland-info.co.uk/rr-house.htm; dm £9.50, d £26-36; P ✗) By far the most interesting place to stay in the area, this lighthouse is evocatively situated at the end of the road, 13 miles from Gairloch by Melvaig. There's a wide choice of rooms, from dorms to family rooms, with or without bathroom. Evening meals available on request. It's an excellent place, giving guests a taste of a lighthouse-keeper's life.

The Old Inn (☎ 712006; www.theoldinn.co.uk; s £32-45, d £55-84; P ✗) This characterful coaching inn sits on the river by a lovely old bridge. The bar is a delight, and stocks a fine selection of ales and malts. The rooms are pleasant enough, although they are much better value outside of the summer season. Bar meals as well as more advanced restaurant fare is available, including tasty roasts.

Kinlochewe to Torridon

Small Kinlochewe is a good base for outdoor activities. From here the road follows Glen Torridon, an unforgettable journey along a river overlooked by the multiple peaks of Beinn Eighe (1010m) and Liathach (1055m). The road hits the sea at Torridon, where the small **Torridon Countryside Centre** (NTS; ☎ 01445-791221; adult £2; ⏰ Easter-Sep; wheelchair access) offers displays on the area's flora and fauna, including a short audiovisual display and, in another building down the road, a Deer Museum.

Loch Torridon Country House Hotel (☎ 791242; www.lochtorridonhotel.com; standard s £62-107, standard d £99-148; ⏰ Feb-Dec; wheelchair access; P ✗ ▢) This lavish Victorian shooting lodge has an awe-inspiring position looking across the loch to three peaks, with Liathach looming impossibly large opposite. Even the standard rooms are pretty special, but if you plump for one of the pricier Master rooms, you'll feel like you're living the last days of Rome.

SOMETHING SPECIAL

A long side trip abandons the A896 to the remote Applecross Peninsula. The easier route follows the coast road, but you can also cross the Bealach na Ba, the highest mountain pass in Britain at 627m, with a series of hairpin bends and ever more majestic views.

In the small village of Applecross is a place to really forget about the rest of the world. The **Applecross Inn** (☎ 01520-744262; www.applecross.uk.com; Shore St; s/d from £32.50/50; bar meals £7-11, dinner mains £10-20; P ✗) is a longstanding family-run favourite, with excellent bar meals, hearty dinners, and well-priced rooms with great views across the sea to Skye.

A postbus runs daily Monday to Saturday from Torridon to Applecross.

There's great walking to be done, and the friendly staff can organize any number of activities on land or water for you. The adjacent **Ben Damph Lodges** (☎ 791242; ☽ Easter–early Nov; s/d £45/64) occupies the former stables and has motel-style rooms which share the great location but lack the luxury. It's all new and clean, and there's a friendly bar serving lunches and dinners.

Plockton

☎ 01599 / pop 378

Plockton is so idyllic it could be designed by Hollywood, but there's nothing fake about the grandeur and beauty of this set. Maybe that's why the popular TV series *Hamish Macbeth* was filmed here. There's something Hawaii-esque about the view over the harbour – the small, protected bay is dotted with mini islands and surrounded by rocky mountains carpeted in greenery. The main street of this delightful town is lined with palms and whitewashed houses, each with a seagull perched on its chimney-stack gazing out to sea.

Calum's Seal Trips (☎ 544306; adult £5) runs seal-watching cruises – there are swarms of seals just outside the harbour and the trip comes with an excellent and informative commentary.

SLEEPING & EATING

Plockton Station Bunkhouse (☎ 544235; mickcoe @btlnternet.com; dm £10; Ⓟ ☒) This cosy, modern hostel by the train station gets lots of light in the comfortable, well-equipped common areas upstairs and has a good kitchen-lounge. Despite the fact that the owners also run a B&B called 'Nessun Dorma' (nobody shall sleep), you get a very good night's kip in the pinewood bunks.

The Shieling (☎ 544282; www.lochalsh.net/shieling; r per person £24; ☽ Easter-Oct; ☒) This hedge-girt B&B has a thatched blackhouse in the garden. Right by the sea on a headland overlooking the harbour, the place has personality and two carpeted rooms with views and big beds easy on the eye and firm on the back.

The Manse (☎ 544442; www.painting-in-plockton .com; Innes St; r per person £26-31; ☒) This guesthouse is delightfully decadent. A place to spoil yourself, it proudly claims to be the most expensive B&B in town! One double has a four-poster bed and a huge black-and-white tiled bathroom with free-standing

bathtub. The guesthouse doubles as an art gallery, with walls bright with the owner's works; she also runs painting courses.

Plockton Hotel (☎ 544274; www.plocktonhotel.co .uk; Harbour St; s/d £55/90; ☒) On the waterfront, the dark façade of this hotel signals a place of various pleasures. When the sun shines, you can't beat a seat in the harbour-side beer garden, but in times of drizzle, you can sit inside and crack your way into local prawns and crab of a quality that transcends normal pub food. The rooms live up to the standard too; ample in size, with vast beds and unforgettable views. Cheaper pads are available in an attached cottage.

GETTING THERE & AWAY

Plockton is 6 miles north of Kyle of Lochalsh. The two are connected by a postbus that runs once daily Monday to Saturday, and by trains (15 minutes, four daily Monday to Saturday, two on Sunday).

KYLE OF LOCHALSH

☎ 01599 / pop 739

Spare a thought for poor Kyle of Lochalsh. Formerly the main ferry port to cross to Skye, it has now been rendered redundant by the Skye Bridge. There's no reason to stay; you'd be better off going on to Skye or heading to nearby Plockton.

The **TIC** (☎ 534276; ☽ Apr-Oct) is beside the seafront car park.

Kyle can be reached by bus from Inverness (£11.40, two hours, two daily), and by direct Citylink buses from Glasgow (£20, five to six hours, three daily), which continue on to Skye.

The 82-mile train ride between Inverness and Kyle of Lochalsh (£14.60, 2½ hours, four daily Monday to Saturday, two on Sundays) is one of Scotland's most scenic.

AROUND KYLE OF LOCHALSH
Eilean Donan Castle

Photogenically sited at the entrance to Loch Duich, **Eilean Donan Castle** (☎ 01599-555202; www .eileandonancastle.com; adult £4.50; ☽ 10am-5.30pm Apr-Oct) is one of Scotland's most evocative castles, and must be in millions of photo albums. It's very much a re-creation inside with an excellent introductory exhibition. Look out for the photos of scenes from the movie *Highlander* filmed here. There's also a sword used at the Battle of Culloden in 1746.

The castle was ruined in a Jacobite uprising in 1719 and not rebuilt until 1932.

ROAD TO THE ISLES

The indescribably spectacular, 46-mile 'Road to the Isles' (the A830) runs from Fort William via Glenfinnan to Arisaig and Mallaig and is redolent with Bonnie Prince Charlie associations.

At Glenfinnan, you'll find the **Glenfinnan Monument** (NTS; ☎ 01397-722250) erected in 1815 to commemorate the clansmen who died in the Jacobite cause. The **visitors centre** (adult£2; ☼ daily Apr-Oct; wheelchair access) recounts the story of the 1745 uprising that started here and ended nearby 14 months later when the prince fled to France. A lookout tower offers fine views over Loch Shiel.

From the pier at **Arisaig**, the **Sheerwater** (☎ 01687-450224; www.arisaig.co.uk) runs day trips for foot passengers to the islands of Rum, Eigg and Muck from May to September. The return fares are £15 to Eigg and Muck, and £19 to Rhum; trips last three to seven hours. From Arisaig, the road winds around attractive bays, and some of the country's most beautiful beaches known as the **Silver Sands of Morar**. Morar village is at the entrance to **Loch Morar**, Britain's deepest body of fresh water. It's said to contain its own monster, named Morag, giving hope to disillusioned Nessie hunters.

MALLAIG
☎ 01687 / pop 797

Travellers to the Isle of Skye, or the Small Isles may find themselves overnighting in the bustling fishing village of Mallaig. There's a **TIC** (☎ 462170; ☼ year-round).

Sheena's Backpackers Lodge (☎ 462764; Harbour View; dm £11; ☒) This is a popular, friendly spot in the centre, with a good vibe and a café with garden.

Anchorage (☎ 462454; anchoragemallaig@btopenworld.com; Gillies Park; r per person £16-25; ☒) A decent B&B with en-suite rooms near the ferry terminal.

Shiel Buses (☎ 01967-431272) runs to/from Fort William (1½ hours, one daily Monday to Friday).

The beautiful West Highland railway line operates between Fort William and Mallaig (£7.80, 1¼ hours, four daily) with connections from Glasgow. From early June to early October, the **Jacobite steam train** (☎ 01463-239026; www.steamtrain.info) runs from Fort William to Mallaig (£19 single, two hours, one service daily Monday to Friday, plus Sunday in August).

CalMac operates ferries from Mallaig to Armadale on Skye (person/car £3.05/16.90 single, 25 minutes, eight to nine Monday to Saturday, plus Sunday mid-May to mid-September).

ISLE OF SKYE

Redolent with romance, Skye is the largest of Scotland's islands, and one of its most beautiful. An ethereal light squeezes through the clouds and bathes the rugged splendour that reaches sublime levels with the striking Cuillin Hills that thrust skywards in the south.

It's a spot for everyone, with walkers plotting their assaults on a dozen Munros, and less energetic visitors cruising the island's castles or sheltering from the drizzle in some of the inviting Skye watering holes. For drizzle there often is: Skye's name comes from an old Norse word for 'cloud' and residents, many of whom speak Gaelic, will tell you that if you're not wet already, you will be soon!

Of course, all this splendour, and the ease of access, mean that you won't have the island to yourself: it's Scotland's most visited offshore destination. Reserving accommodation is a must in the height of summer and you may fancy heading off on some of the smaller roads to explore corners that tour buses don't reach.

Getting There & Away

The obvious way to arrive is via the bridge from Kyle of Lochalsh (£5.70 toll each way), but there are still various ways to travel 'over the sea to Skye'. CalMac operates ferries from mainland Mallaig to Armadale (person/car £3.05/16.90 single, 25 minutes, eight to nine Monday to Saturday, plus Sundays mid-May to mid-Sep).

There's also the six-car **Skye Ferry** (☎ 01599-511302; www.skyeferry.co.uk) from Glenelg to Kylerhea, about 4 miles southeast of Kyleakin (person/car and four passengers £1/7, 10 minutes, frequent Easter to October, no Sunday service before late May), or the passenger-only ferry from Gairloch (see p902). From April to October the *Spirit of*

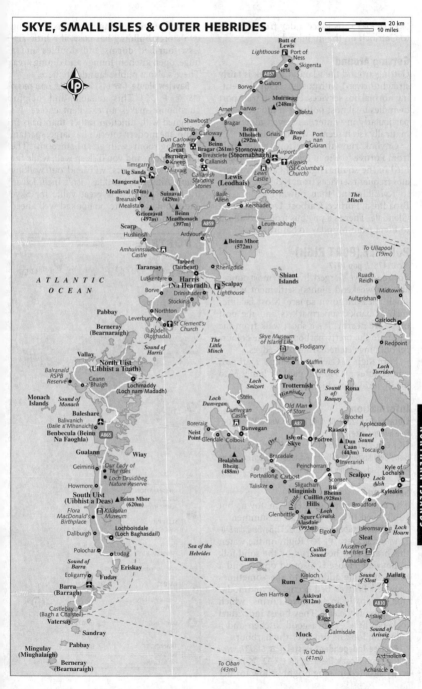

SKYE, SMALL ISLES & OUTER HEBRIDES

0 —————— 20 km
0 —————— 10 miles

Butt of
Lewis
Lighthouse ● Port of
Ness
A857 ● Ness ● Skigersta
Borve ● Galson

Muirneag
(248m) ▲
Arnol ● Barvas ● Tolsta
Shawbost
Garenin ● Bragar
Dun Carloway ● Carloway   Beinn
Broch ● Beinn   Mholach
Great   Bragar (261m) ● Stornoway   (292m) ▲   Griais   *Broad*   Port
Bernera ● Breasclete (Steòrnabhagh) ●   *Bay*   nan
Kneep   Callanish   Airport   Giùran
Timsgarry ● Miavaig   *Callanish*   Lews   ● Aignish
Uig Sands ●   *Standing*   Lewis   Castle   (St Columba's
Mangersta ●   *Stones*   (Leodhais)   Church)
Mealisval (574m) ▲   Suinaval   Baile   Crosbost
Breanais ●   (429m) ▲   Ailean   *The*
Mealista ●   Kershader   *Minch*
Griomaval   Beinn
(497m) ▲   Meadhonach   Leumrabhagh
Scarp   (397m) ▲   A859
Hushinish   *To Ullapool*
Amhuinnsuidhe ●   ▲ Beinn Mhor   *(19mi)*
Castle   (572m)
Taransay   Ruadh
Tarbert   Rhenigdale   Reidh
(Tairbeart) ●   Midtown
ATLANTIC   Luskentyre ● Harris   Shiant   Aultgrishan
OCEAN   (Na Hearadh) ● Scalpay   Islands
Borve ● Drinishader ● *Lighthouse*   Gairloch
Stockinish
Pabbay   Northton
Leverburgh ● St Clement's   *To*
Berneray   Rodel ● Church   *Little*   Redpoint
(Bearnaraigh)   (Roghadal)   *Minch*   *Loch*
Valley   *Sound of*   *Torridon*
North Uist   *Harris*   Skye Museum
(Uibhist a Tuath)   of Island Life
Balranald   Quiraing ● Flodigarry
RSPB   Ceann ●   Staffin
Reserve   a'Bhaigh   Uig ● *Kilt Rock*
Monach   *Sound of*   Lochmaddy   Trotternish   Rona
Islands   *Monach*   (Loch nam Madadh)   *Loch*   *Hinnisdal*   *Sound*
Baleshare   *Snizort*   *of*   Brochel
Balivanich   Stein   Old Man   *Raasay*
Benbecula (Beinn   (Baile a'Mhanaich)   *Loch*   Dunvegan   of Storr   Applecross
Na Faoghla)   A865   *Dunvegan*   Castle   Raasay
Gualann   Wiay   Boreraig ●   ● Dunvegan   Isle of ● Portree   Inner
Geirinis   Our Lady of   Neist   Ose   Skye   A87   Dun   Sound
The Isles   Point ● Glendale ● Colbost   ▲ Caan   Toscaig
Howmore ●   Loch Druidibeg   Bracadale   (443m)   Inverarish
Nature Reserve   Healabhal   Peinchorran   Kyle of
South Uist   Bheag   Portnalong ● Carbost   Lochalsh
(Uibhist a Deas) ▲ Beinn Mhor   (488m)   Sligachan   Sconser   Scalpay   *Loch*
(620m)   Talisker   Minginish   Blà   *Alsh*
Flora   ● Kildonan   Bheinn   Kyleakin
MacDonald's   Museum   Cuillin ▲   Broadford
Birthplace   Glenbrittle   Hills   *Loch*
Daliburgh   Sgurr   Coruisk   Isleornsay ● *Loch*
Lochboisdale   Alasdair   Elgol   *Hourn*
(Loch Baghasdail)   (993m)   Museum of   Sleat
Polochar ●   *Sea of the*   *Cuillin*   the Isles
Ludag   *Hebrides*   *Sound*   Armadale
Sound of   Eriskay   Canna   *Sound*
Barra   Kinloch ●   *of Sleat* ● Mallaig
Eoligarry ●   Fuday   Rum   A830
Barra   Glen Harris ● ▲ Askival   Cleadale   Arisaig
(Barragh)   (812m)   *Sound*
Castlebay   Eigg   *of*
(Bagh a Chaisteil) ●   Muck ● Galmisdale   *Arisaig*
Vatersay   *To Oban*   Ardmolich ●
Mingulay   Pabbay   *(41mi)*
(Miughalaigh)   Berneray   *To Oban*   Acharacle ●
(Bearnaraigh)   *(43mi)*

**HIGHLANDS &
NORTHERN ISLANDS**

Skye (p902) runs twice a day from Portree to Gairloch on the mainland.

Getting Around

Getting around the island midweek is fairly straightforward, with postbuses supplementing normal bus services. However, transport dwindles to almost nothing at the weekend, particularly in winter, and even more dramatically (so it seems) when it rains.

Citylink runs three or four buses daily from Portree to Uig in the north and Broadford in the south. Highland Country operates frequent services from Kyle of Lochalsh to Kyleakin and then onward services to Broadford, Portree, Carbost, Dunvegan and Glendale. There's a postbus from Broadford to Elgol from Monday to Saturday.

PORTREE (PORT RIGH)

☎ 01478 / pop 1917

Portree is Skye's largest, liveliest (most noticeable on weekend nights) settlement with a small, pleasant town square. Most facilities such as banks, supermarkets and the post office are nearby. It's a short walk from the centre to the pretty harbour and the colourful buildings etched around its edges.

Port Righ is Gaelic for King's Harbour, named after a 1540 call paid by James V to pacify local clan chieftains.

Information

Library (☎ 612697; Bayfield Rd; ⏰ Mon & Wed-Sat) Free Internet access.

TIC (☎ 612137; Bayfield Rd; ⏰ Mon-Sat Oct-Easter, daily Easter-Sep) Just south of Bridge Rd. It does foreign exchange, and there's also Internet access (£1 for 20 minutes).

Sleeping

There are numerous B&Bs in town, but you'll need to reserve ahead in summer.

Bayfield Backpackers (☎ 612231; Bayfield; dm £10-12; wheelchair access; P 🗶) Right on the water, this brand-new hostel run by the solid folk at Bayview House is a sound option and a most welcome addition to the sometimes crowded Portree bed scene. Accommodation is mostly in four-bed dorms, which are rigorously clean. They boast individual lockers; there's also a good kitchen and a verandah looking out over the harbour.

Portree Independent Hostel (☎ 613737; www .portreehostel.f9.co.uk; The Green; dm £11-12; 🗶) Centrally situated in a big bright yellow former

post office on the main road, this rambling two-storey building has cosy, if a little airless, four-bed dorms and doubles and a huge, open kitchen, lounge and dining area. There's also a public laundrette here.

Bayview House (☎ 613340; Bayfield; r per person £15-20; P 🗶) This reliable and helpful guesthouse makes an excellent choice. It's designed with function rather than frills in mind; the modern interior has large, spartan, sparkling rooms with great bathrooms. The beds are firm and you'll sleep well, while the owners, keen hikers, will lend out walking maps. Although breakfast isn't included in the rates, Bayview is great value for Skye and should therefore be booked well ahead in summer.

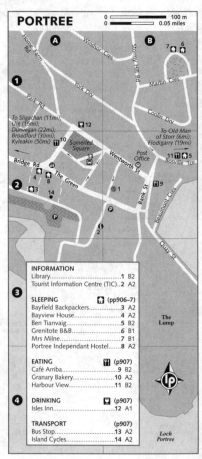

INFORMATION	
Library.................................1 B2	
Tourist Information Centre (TIC)..2 A2	

SLEEPING	🏠 (pp906-7)
Bayfield Backpackers.................3 A2	
Bayview House.........................4 A2	
Ben Tianvaig............................5 A2	
Grenitote B&B..........................6 B1	
Mrs Milne...............................7 B1	
Portree Independant Hostel......8 A2	

EATING	🍴 (p907)
Café Arriba..............................9 B2	
Granary Bakery.......................10 A2	
Harbour View.........................11 B2	

DRINKING	🍺 (p907)
Isles Inn.................................12 A1	

TRANSPORT	(p907)
Bus Stop................................13 A2	
Island Cycles.........................14 A2	

Ben Tianavaig (☎ 612152; 5 Bosville Tce; r £55-60; Ⓟ ☒ 🖥) Overlooking the harbour, this refurbished guesthouse is the sort of place that'll have you pleading with your boss to let you extend your holiday. The rooms are large and light, and named after Australian cities. The ones with views are a little pricier but well worth the extra outlay. Best of all is the relaxed and genuine welcome from charming people who make the effort to get to know their guests.

Other recommendations:

Grenitote B&B (☎ 612808; e.a.matheson@amserve .net; 9 Martin Cres; s/d £25/40) Warm welcome in a quiet residential area uphill from the centre.

Mrs Milne (☎ 612552; 8 Martin Cres; r per person £18-22) Quiet and peaceful with stylish and very commodious rooms.

Eating & Drinking

Most of the hotels around Somerled Sq do good pub food; have a wander and check the menus.

Granary Bakery (☎ 612873; Somerled Sq; light meals £1-3; ☾ 9am-6pm Mon-Sat) This busy bakery churns out great-value snacks such as pies, pasties and delicious, fresh rolls. Most of the town seems to buy their lunch here and it's not difficult to see why.

Café Arriba (☎ 611830; Quay Brae; breakfast £3.95, mains £5-10; ☾ 7am-10pm; ☒) This new kid on the block has attracted a loyal local following as well as pulling in visitors. It does a hearty breakfast, decent coffee, and has well-priced comfort-food main meals. There's plenty of vegetarian choice.

Harbour View (☎ 612069; 7 Bosville Tce; mains £12-18; ☾ lunch & dinner; ☒) This is a good, upmarket choice for lovers of food from the deep (ocean that is, not fryer). The seafood chowder is a soup that bursts with flavour, while the monkfish with ginger and honey or the freshest of langoustines won't be forgotten in a hurry either.

Isles Inn (☎ 612129; Somerled Sq; bar meals £5-8, dinner mains £9-12; ☾ food served noon-9pm) This cheery pub is the most fun in town, with an old-style themed interior, roaring fire, and a summer crowd spilling out onto the square outside. The bar meals, with the usual suspects, and the dinner menu, which is of the steak and salmon variety, are consistently good.

Getting There & Away

Somerled Square is the Portree bus stop. Citylink runs to/from Inverness (£14, 3¼ hours, two to three buses daily), Glasgow (£22, 6½ hours, three daily) via Fort William and Edinburgh (£28.70, eight hours, two daily).

Getting Around

Island Cycles (☎ 613121; www.isbuc.co.uk; The Green; ☾ 9am-5pm Mon-Sat) hires out bikes for £12 for 24 hours or £10 for a day hire.

KYLEAKIN (CAOL ACAIN)

☎ 01599 / pop 380

Even more than Kyle of Lochalsh, Kyleakin had the carpet pulled from under its feet by the opening of the Skye Bridge, but it's a pleasant waterside town, popular with backpackers and bus tours. It can be a good place to find accommodation if the island is heavily booked up.

Dun Caan Hostel (☎ 534087; www.skyerover.co.uk; Pier Rd; dm £10-12) One of four hostels in Kyleakin, this is the only independent one, and quieter than the ones on the backpacker bus circuit. It's run by a couple who take pride in it and in welcoming guests welcome. Everything exudes cosiness, from the wood-fitted kitchen to the snug lounge and dorms. It has a great position overlooking the harbour with views from every room, and the owners can hire bikes, advise on sightseeing and walking, or even take you on an island tour.

Mrs MacRae (☎ 534197; 17 Kyleside; r per person £15-18; ☒) This B&B just has two rooms: a single and a double, but they are both kick-ass and have magical views over Loch Alsh. They share a sparkling-clean bathroom and you'll be treated to a healthy dose of genuine Highland hospitality. A bargain.

ARMADALE (ARMADAL)

☎ 01471 / pop 9063

If you arrive on Skye by boat from Mallaig you'll wind up in remote Armadale. **Armadale Castle** was built in various stages by the MacDonald clan between 1790 and 1815. Only ruins remain, but the grounds contain magnificent gardens and the excellent **Museum of the Isles** (☎ 844305; adult £4.80; ☾ 9.30am-5.30pm Apr-Oct, call for winter opening hr; wheelchair access). This engrossing exhibition is like a walk-through encyclopaedia, relating the history of the Western Isles from the Norse raids and settlement, to the disintegration of Gaelic culture and Scottish emigration. There is a number of new marked walking trails in the woodlands here; if you just want to stroll, there are access points off the main road which don't require paying the admission for the castle gardens.

Armadale SYHA Hostel (☎ 844260; www.syha.org .uk; dm £10.50; ☼ Apr-Sep; P ✗) This simple hostel is reminiscent of a rustic ski lodge. The kitchen and common room have great views over the water and it's just 350m from the ferry terminal.

Eight miles from Armadale, in the arty harbour hamlet of Isleornsay is **Hotel Eilean Iarmain** (☎ 833332; www.eilean-iarmain.co.uk; r per person £45-63; P ✗), a gloriously traditional small hotel decorated in Victorian style, all fireplaces, antique furniture and chintz. The rooms are all different and have their own character, as does the bar, which serves posh bar nosh, and the restaurant, which has a fine reputation for its seafood and service.

BROADFORD (AN T-ATH LEATHANN)
☎ 01471 / pop 1237

Broadford is a useful service centre with lots of accommodation, but not much character: it straggles along the main road in an attempt to milk pounds out of passing tourists. The **TIC** (☎ 822361; ☼ daily Apr-Oct) is near the large Esso petrol station.

Broadford SYHA Hostel (☎ 822442; www.syha .org.uk; dm £12; ☼ Mar-Oct; P ✗ 🖵) A modern place in a quiet spot with a great outlook and good facilities. It also has neat doubles.

LimeStone Cottage (☎ 822142; www.limestone cottage.co.uk; 4 Lime Park; r per person £22-30; ✗) A delightful, ivy-covered, traditional stone cottage offering friendly service and beautiful rooms – particularly the cosy top-floor ones with sloping ceiling – with views over the water.

You can hire a bike from **Fairwinds Cycle Hire** (☎ 822270), near the Broadford Hotel – the big place on the main road through town – for £7 per day.

CUILLIN HILLS & MINGINISH PENINSULA
☎ 01478

The varied and imposing rocky Cuillin Hills, west of Broadford, command both respect and wonder from those beneath. Keen walkers and climbers challenge themselves on the rugged beauty of the Black Cuillin ridge – considered by many to be the most visually impressive mountain range in the British Isles. This is no walk in the park, however,

Sgurr Alasdair, at 993m, is the highest point and to completely traverse the Black Cuillin ridge requires two days, some serious mountain climbing and proper equipment.

The crossroads at **Sligachan** (Sligeachan) is a popular jumping-off point for Cuillin climbers. It's a spectacular spot dwarfed by the mighty hills. Here you'll find the large, cheery, and child-friendly **Sligachan Hotel** (☎ 650204; www.sligachan.co.uk; dm £10, s/d £50/70; bar meals £5-10, mains £10-16; wheelchair access; P ✗ 🖵), which has everything a weary climber or rainbound traveller could require. There's a jovial, barnlike bar with heaps of malts and real ales as well as filling bar meals served until 11pm. There's also a more formal restaurant, and, if you want to stay, there are classy if faded rooms, and a bunkhouse. There's also a basic campsite (☎ 07786-435294; tent sites per person £4; ☼ Easter-Oct), opposite the hotel.

At Carbost's **Talisker Distillery** (☎ 614308; ☼ 9.30am-5pm Mon-Sat Easter-Oct, 2-5pm Mon-Fri Nov-Easter) you can sample this excellent sweetish, peaty, and powerful single malt, once favoured by Robert Louis Stevenson, when you take the tipple tour (£4), which focuses more on the joys of mass-production than the qualities of whisky. Three miles further on, **Skyewalker Independent Hostel** (☎ 640250; http://freespace.virgin.net/skyewalker.hostel; Fiscavaig Rd, Portnalong; dm £8; wheelchair access; P ✗) is at a former school and has excellent facilities, with wooden bunks and a lounge where many a Munro-bagging tale is told.

NORTHWEST SKYE
☎ 01470

On the western side of the Waternish Peninsula, **Dunvegan Castle** (☎ 521206; adult £6.50; ☼ 10am-5.30pm Apr-Oct, 11am-4pm Nov-Mar) dates back to the 13th century, although it was restored in Romantic style in the mid-19th century. The 14th-century pictures of St Kilda, Britain's far-flung western outpost, are fascinating. To really get your money's worth from the steep admission fee, however, you need to make time to enjoy the vast and lovely gardens.

If you're staying in Dunvegan try **Tables Hotel** (☎ 521404; www.tables-hotel.co.uk; s £25-48, d £52-76; P ✗), a friendly, family-run place with a conservatory and garden with great views across the loch.

Five miles from Dunvegan, on the road to Glendale, the **Three Chimneys** (☎ 511258;

www.threechimneys.co.uk; 2-course lunch £17.50, 3-course dinner £42; ⓨ lunch Mon-Sat, dinner daily) is one of Scotland's best restaurants. Romantically set in a whitewashed crofter's cottage, it presents the finest of seafood, including local scallops and oysters, prepared with delicate sauces that subtly enhance the flavours. There are also unspeakably toothsome steak and game dishes. Classy but very expensive rooms are available next door to sleep it all off.

From Monday to Saturday, there are three to five bus services from Portree to Dunvegan Castle. Postbuses also run this route.

TROTTERNISH PENINSULA
☎ 01470

North of Portree, Skye's coastal scenery is at its most magical in the Trotternish Peninsula. Look out in particular for the rocky spike of the **Old Man of Storr**, the spectacular **Kilt Rock** and the ruins of **Duntulm Castle**. Whatever the weather it is difficult not to be blown away by the savage beauty of this place.

The tiny hamlet of **Flodigarry** (Flodaigearraidh) has a couple of excellent places to stay. The **Flodigarry Country House Hotel** (☎ 552203; www .flodigarry.co.uk; r main house/cottage per person from £65/54; ⓨ food served noon-9.30pm; wheelchair access; Ⓟ ⊠) is a highlight of Skye hostelry. The main house rooms have massive soft beds with period furniture; the superior ones have great views. The adjacent cottage is the former (restored) home of Flora MacDonald. There's also a conservatory restaurant, a more formal dining room, and a pub curiously decorated with inscriptions from the Alhambra. The place is in a magnificent location, surrounded by woods and lawns, but it's a favourite lunch stop for tour parties, and the pub is lively every night, so if you're looking for a quiet retreat this ain't the one.

Dun Flodigarry Hostel (☎ 552212; hostel.flodigarry@ btInternet.com; dm/tw £10/22; wheelchair access; Ⓟ ⊠ 🖳) About 100m from Flodigarry Country House Hotel, the Dun has stupendous views, a huge dining area and clean, old rooms – it's a great place to stay and caters for families. You can camp on the lawn outside.

At the northern end of the peninsula at Kilmuir (Cille Mhoire), the **Skye Museum of Island Life** (☎ 552206; adult £2; ⓨ 9.30am-5pm Mon-Sat Apr-Oct) re-creates crofting life in a series of thatched cottages overlooking marvellous scenery.

Up the hill from the museum in the Kilmuir cemetery is **Flora MacDonald's grave**. Flora became famous for helping Bonnie Prince Charlie escape following his defeat at the Battle of Culloden in 1746. She dressed him up in drag to play her maid as they escaped over the sea to Skye. She was imprisoned in the Tower of London for a year for her pains.

Uig (Uige)
From whichever direction you come into Uig, the startling picture-perfect harbour, enclosed by steep hills, rarely fails to impress – particularly if the CalMac ferry is chugging across the bay.

Ard-Na-Mara (☎ 542281; www.isleofskyebandb.co.uk; 11 Idrigill; r per person £19-25; Ⓟ) This is an intimate family-run B&B has a great position with sea views. It's very hospitable and populated by some amazingly large and affectionate borzoi dogs. All the rooms have an en suite, and there's a good four-bed room for travelling groups. No children under 12 are permitted. If coming from the ferry, turn left past the pub at the end of the pier.

Uig Hotel (☎ 542205; www.uighotel.com; s/d £35/58) This stately old coaching inn has fine views over the bay. It's under new management, a hospitable couple who have added a brace of Highland cattle to the permanent residents list. The rooms are dazzlingly clean, and most boast views over the bay. The cuisine includes such atypical specialities as crocodile with scallops, and springbok fillet! Good value.

The Pub at the Pier (☎ 542212; The Pier; mains £8-10) The pub does standard, filling meals, but there's terrific 180-degree views over the harbour, a terrace outside to watch the ferry come and go, and it serves real Isle of Skye ale from the brewery next door.

From Uig pier, CalMac has ferry services to Lochmaddy on North Uist (person/car £9.15/44 single, 1¾ hours, one or two daily) and to Tarbert on Harris (person/car £9.15/44 single, 1½ hours, one or two daily Monday to Saturday).

ISLE OF RAASAY
☎ 01478 / pop 194

There are great walks on this long, narrow, rugged island off Skye's northeast coast. Forest Enterprise publishes a free leaflet with suggested walks and forest trails. There's no petrol on Raasay (Rathatsair).

Raasay SYHA Hostel (☎ 0870 004 1146; www.syha
.org.uk; dm £9.50; ✆ mid-May–Aug) Just north of
Inverarish, it overlooks Skye and is a basic
place in a great setting.

CalMac operates ferries from Sconser
on Skye (between Portree and Broadford)
to Inverarish on Raasay (person/car return
£4.45/17.95, 15 minutes, nine to 11 Monday
to Saturday).

OUTER HEBRIDES

The Outer Hebridean islands are Scotland's wild frontier, an outpost shielding
the mainland from the full force of the
Atlantic. Also called the Western Isles, or
Na h-Eileanan an Iar in Gaelic, these are
isolated, windswept, treeless places, very romantic and quite distinct from other parts
of the country.

Named by the Vikings, whose word
havbredey translates to 'islands at the edge
of the earth', these islands subsist on fishing, weaving, and crofting; the distinctive
horned Hebridean sheep have right of way
on the roads around here. Scottish Gaelic
is a working language here: signposts put
the Gaelic first, and almost half of Gaelic-
speaking Scots live on these islands.

Religion is deeply imbedded, particularly
on the Protestant islands of Lewis, Harris,
and North Uist. Everything is shut on a Sunday as locals dress in their Sabbath best for
a day of churchgoing, contemplation, and
bible-reading. This is part of the islands'
charm: the Hebrides are a destination for
people looking to change down a gear and
appreciate a bit of raw nature.

Outside the semibustle of Stornoway,
life exists mostly in small villages compiled
of crumbling ruinous stone cottages interspersed with fresh, squat concrete bunga-
lows; until relatively recently the main unit
of housing was the blackhouse, a primitive
cottage with dry stone walls and a thatched
roof built around a peat hearth.

The landscapes can be mournful, but
they're also striking. Treeless, moorland
plateaus envelop much of the terrain, as do
wide horizons of sky and water, dazzling
white beaches, azure bays and stony hills.
Stoic mountains and sprawling lochs also
take their place in the Hebrides, teeming
with a diversity of wildflowers and birdlife.

Defiant archaeological sites, including some
of Britain's finest Neolithic standing stones,
have survived thousands of years of Atlantic
wind assaults, and signal a history shrouded
in myth.

Orientation & Information

The Outer Hebrides consists of over 200 islands running in a 130-mile arc from north
to south, shielding the northwest coast of
Scotland. Lewis and Harris are actually one
island with a border of high hills between
them. Stornoway, on Lewis, is the largest
town in the Outer Hebrides, with a reasonable range of facilities.

North Uist, Benbecula and South Uist are
joined by bridge and causeway. Benbecula
has a large army and air force base.

There are TICs in every ferry port. Those
in Stornoway and Tarbert open year-round
(the others open early April to mid-October)
and remain open late for ferry arrivals.

Getting There & Away

AIR

British Airways/Loganair (☎ 0845 779 9977; www
.ba.com), **BMI** (☎ 0870 607 0555; www.flybmi.com) and
Highland Airways (☎ 0845 450 2245; www.highland
airways.co.uk) fly to the islands, and there are
airports at Stornoway, on Lewis, and on
Benbecula and Barra. The main airport, 4
miles east of Stornoway, is served by daily
flights from Edinburgh, Glasgow and Inverness (Sunday flights started in 2002, despite heavy church opposition). There are
also flights to Benbecula and Barra from
Glasgow from Monday to Saturday.

BOAT

CalMac (www.calmac.co.uk) runs comfortable
passenger and car ferries from Ullapool to
Stornoway on Lewis (person/car £14.05/69
single, 2¾ hours, two daily Monday to
Saturday, three daily Wednesday and Friday July & August); from Uig, on the Isle
of Skye, to Tarbert on Harris (person/car
£9.15/44 single, 1½ hours, one or two daily
Monday to Saturday) and to Lochmaddy on
North Uist (person/car £9.15/44 single, 1¾
hours, one or two daily).

From Oban, ferries go to Castlebay on
Barra (person/car £20.20/74, five hours) and
onto Lochboisdale on South Uist (person/
car £25.95/108, 6¾ hours). The timetables
are complicated and, especially from July to

September, car space can fill up fast. Advance booking is essential, although foot and bicycle passengers should have no problems.

There are 12 different Island Hopscotch fares for set routes in the Outer Hebrides, offering worthwhile savings (check the CalMac website for details).

Getting Around

The *Skye and Western Isles Travel Guide,* from TICs for £1, lists all current air, bus and ferry services. Visitors without their own transport should anticipate a fair amount of hitching and walking. Flights by **BA** (☎ 0845 773 3377; www.ba.com) partners link the islands of Barra, Benbecula and Lewis. At Barra the planes land on the beach at Cockle Strand, so timetables depend on tides. Ferries run between Leverburgh on Harris and Berneray on North Uist and between Lochboisdale on South Uist and Castlebay on Barra.

There are limited bus services and none on Sunday.

BICYCLE

Cycling north to south is quite popular, but allow at least a week for the trip. The main problems are difficult weather, strong winds (you hear stories of people cycling downhill and freewheeling uphill) and sheep that believe they have the right of way.

Bikes are available for hire from **Alex Dan's Cycle Centre** (☎ 01851-704025; 67 Kenneth St, Stornoway, Lewis); **Barra Cycle Hire** (☎ 01871-810284; 29 St Brendan's Rd, Castlebay, Barra); and **Rothan Cycles** (☎ 01870-620283; 9 Howmore, South Uist). Booking is advisable.

CAR & MOTORCYCLE

Most roads are single-track – sheep wandering onto them pose the main hazard. Petrol stations are far apart, expensive and usually closed on Sunday.

Cars can be hired from around £20 per day from **Mackinnon Self Drive** (☎ 01851-702984; 18 Inaclete Rd, Stornoway, Lewis); **Gaeltech Car Hire** (☎ 01859-520460; Grimisdale Guest House, Leverburgh, Harris); and **Laing Motors** (☎ 01878-700267; Lochboisdale, South Uist).

LEWIS (LEODHAIS)

☎ 01851 / pop 18,489

Lewis is the northern part of the northernmost of the Hebridean islands. Its ethereal, remote landscape is dominated in the low, flat northern half by the vast Black Moor, peat moorland peppered with numerous, small, freshwater lochs. The coastal fringes have some arable land and are surprisingly densely populated, although not particularly attractive. Peat cutting is a serious business here, providing many islanders with their prime source of fuel. In summer, visitors will see piles of it drying in the sun beside long, freshly cut turf trenches running through the moorland.

The Sabbath is strictly observed; people devote the day to worship and contemplation. While it can be frustrating if your time is limited that nearly everything is shut (restaurants and hotels are about the only things open) it can be satisfying to just go with the flow, stroll about, and let the stress peel away.

Stornoway (Steornabhagh)

pop 8569

Stornoway is the bustling 'capital' of the Outer Hebrides and the only real town in the archipelago. It's a surprisingly busy little place with cars and people swamping the centre during the day. Set on a beautiful natural harbour, it may not blow your socks off, but it does makes a pleasant introduction to this remote corner of the country. Make sure you try some black pudding while you're here; it's Britain's best and absolutely delicious!

Stornoway is the Outer Hebrides' administrative and commercial centre, and the base for the Western Isles Council (Comhairle nan Eilean), a hospital and the islands' Gaelic TV and radio stations. There's an airport and a ferry link with Ullapool (see p901).

ORIENTATION & INFORMATION

Stornoway is on the east coast and compact enough to make exploring on foot easy. The ferry docks at the CalMac terminal on the foreshore; the bus station is next door.

Library (19 Cromwell St; 🕐 10am-5pm Mon-Sat) Free Internet access.

Western Isles Tourist Board TIC (☎ 703088; www.witb.co.uk; 26 Cromwell St; 🕐 Mon-Sat) Open later for ferry arrivals.

SIGHTS

The small **Museum nan Eilean** (☎ 709266; Francis St; admission free; 🕐 10am-5.30pm Mon-Sat Apr-Sep, 10am-5pm Tue-Fri, 10am-1pm Sat Oct-Mar) should be the first stop on every visitor's itinerary. It's an excellent attempt to string together a loose history of the Outer Hebrides. Traditional island life is explored, as are the changes inflicted by progress and technology.

SLEEPING

Laxdale Holiday Park (☎ 703234; www.laxdaleholiday park.com; 6 Laxdale Lane; tent sites £4.50-6, dm £10-11; ☺ campsite Apr-Oct, bunkhouse year-round; **P** ✗) North of town, 1½ miles off the A857, this small friendly site has trees, good grassy areas for camping and is convenient to town. There's also a good bunkhouse with a modern, colourful feel.

Fair Haven Hostel (☎ 701869; www.hebrideansurf .co.uk; 28 Francis St; dm/d £10/30; ✗ 🖵) This relaxed backpackers is well-equipped and run by friendly folk who organise surfing trips and bike hire. A bit of sardining goes on in the dorms, but there's a lounge with videos, and a laundry service.

Royal Hotel (☎ 702109; www.calahotels.com; Cromwell St; s/d £58/89; **P** ✗) The Royal is a solid and welcoming option on Stornoway's main street. The clean rooms vary in size and are designed to satisfy rather than thrill, but there's good service and two bars, one dark wood and traditional, one sleek and modern.

Kildun (☎ 703247; kildun@bushInternet.com; 14 Goathill Rd; s/d from £18/36; **P** ✗) This delightfully peaceful B&B is a 10-minute walk uphill from the centre. Don't bother asking for a front-door key – they don't need things like that around here, but make sure you try the local black pudding at breakfast – you'll be hooked.

Other recommendations:

Park Guest House (☎ 702485; 30 James St; r per person without/with en suite £21/29; ✗) Beautiful Victorian building with stepped gables. It also does high-class seafood in the restaurant.

Thorlee Guesthouse (☎ 703250; cnr Cromwell & South Beach; s/d £15/30) Bargain accommodation with warm, spacious rooms overlooking the harbour.

EATING & DRINKING

Thai Café (☎ 701811; 27 Church St; mains £5-7; ☺ lunch & dinner Mon-Sat; ✗) An unremarkable exterior belies a superb little restaurant run by real Thais. The dishes burst with flavour, and, if you believe you can judge a Thai place on its *pad thai* noodles, this is a standout. There's no license, but you can bring your own bottle for 50p corkage.

Digby Chick (☎ 700026; 28 Point St; mains £13-17; ☺ lunch & dinner Mon-Sat; ✗) A touch of elegance has come to Stornoway dining with the opening of this cool contemporary space. Seafood is treated with a delicate and confident touch, and other combinations are imaginative, colourful and successful. You can eat three courses for £13.95 between 5.30pm and 6.30pm.

HS-1 (☎ 702109; Cromwell St; mains £5-8; ☺ noon-9pm Mon-Sat, 5-9pm Sun) This bright and cheerful young eatery has proved a hit with Stornoway's young and fashionable. It does a fairly staple line in Tex-Mex, with tasty fajitas, juicy steaks, and cheaper snacks such as tortilla wraps. On Sunday you have to book, and need to eat to have a drink.

Other recommendations:

Stornoway Balti House (☎ 706116; 24 South Beach St; main dishes £5-8; ☺ lunch & dinner daily) Delectable Indian food.

The Heb (South Beach St; ☺ Fri & Sat night) The young folks' answer to the Free Church. Cheesy nightclub packing them in on Friday (until 2am) and Saturday (midnight) nights.

GETTING THERE & AWAY

Buses run from Stornoway to Tarbert (one hour, five daily Monday to Saturday) and Leverburgh (£3.90, two hours, five daily Monday to Saturday).

Maclennan Coaches (☎ 702114) run a circular route from Stornoway to Callanish, Carloway, and Arnol; the timetable means you've got time to visit one or two in a day. An all-day ticket costs £5.

Arnol Blackhouse Museum

This **museum** (HS; ☎ 710395; adult £3; ☺ 9.30am-6.30pm Mon-Sat Apr-Sep, 9.30am-4.30pm Mon-Sat Oct-Mar), about 2 miles west of Barvas off the A858, is very impressive. Built in 1885, the blackhouse, a combined byre, barn and home, was inhabited until 1964 and now offers a rare insight into the old crofting way of life, particularly if the peat fire is smouldering away inside. With no chimney, the fireplace was never allowed to go out (understandable considering the icy climate). There's also a whitehouse here, with mortared walls rather than dry stone.

Carloway (Carlabagh) & Garenin (Gearrannan)

Carloway looks across a beautiful loch to the southern mountains and contains the defiantly perched **Dun Carloway Broch**, a well-preserved, 2000-year-old dry-stone defensive tower. It's amazing how effectively this building still shelters from howling Atlantic gales. If you get the place to yourself, you're likely to get an eerie feel inside as you crawl through the little entrance ways. Nearby is the **Doune Broch Centre** (☎ 643338; admission free; 10am-5pm Mon-Sat late May–early Sep) with a fascinating interpretative display.

At nearby Garenin, the **Gearrannan Blackhouse Village** sits on the verge of a dramatic Atlantic shelf above a small stony beach. The village is actually nine restored thatched-roof blackhouses and marvellously picturesque. In the **blackhouse** (admission free; 10am-5pm Mon-Sat; wheelchair access) closest to the entrance is a small display on the village's history and restoration, and a café serving cheap snacks.

Another of the blackhouses is the **Garenin Crofters' Hostel** (www.gatliff.org.uk; dm £8), which is both basic and wonderfully atmospheric. It's far bigger inside than you'd imagine, and is especially warm and snug when the wind is whistling outside.

Callanish (Calanais)

Callanish is 12 miles west of Stornoway and home to the **Callanish Standing Stones** (HS; daily), which form one of the most complete stone circles in Britain. Their wild and secluded setting, on a promontory overlooking Loch Roag, makes it easier to appreciate their ancient mystique, and almost alien aura, without distraction. Built about 4000 years ago, this stone circle predates the pyramids by 1000 years. Its stubborn survival, the mystery of its construction, its impressive scale and undeniable beauty have an intimidating effect. You may find yourself glancing skywards and pondering that burning question – what was it for?

The **Calanais Visitor Centre** (☎ 621422; admission free; 10am-7pm Mon-Sat Apr-Sep, 10am-4pm Oct-Mar) is a tour de force of discreet design. Inside is a **small exhibition** (adult £1.75), which through interactive exhibits, photos and an audio-visual display, speculates about the purpose and construction of the stones.

Mealista (Mealasta) & Around

The road to Mealista (the B8011 southwest of Callanish, signposted to Uig) takes you through the most remote parts of Lewis.

Follow the road around towards **Breanais** for some truly wonderful white-sand beaches, although the surf can make swimming treacherous. The famous 12th-century walrus-ivory Lewis chess pieces were discovered in the sand dunes here in 1831; of the 78 pieces, 67 wound up in the British Museum in London.

With one of the most utopian situations imaginable, **Baile-na-Cille** (☎ 672242; randjgollin@compuserve.com; Timsgarry; r per person £39, dinner £24; mid-Mar–mid-Sep; P X) is one of Britain's best hotels for a remote, beautiful, and relaxing stay. It overlooks a startling stretch of white beach, one of many in the area, and has a variety of charmingly converted rooms. The delight is the atmosphere: informal, child- and dog-friendly, and helpful; the owners will bend over backwards to accommodate families, with cheaper bunk accommodation and separate meals for children. Dinner is a communal affair, with fine home-cooking. Unforgettable.

HARRIS (NA HEARADH)

☎ 01859 / pop 1984

Harris is the scenic jewel in the Outer Hebridean crown, combining mountains, pristine, Caribbean-like beaches, expanses of *machair* (grass and wildflower-covered sand dunes) and weird rocky hills and coastline.

North Harris is actually the forbidding mountainous southern tip of Lewis – the Clisham (An Cliseam) is the highest point at 799m. South Harris, across the land bridge at Tarbert, is less mountainous but has a fascinating variety of landscapes and snow-white beaches.

Harris is famous for Harris Tweed, high-quality woollen cloth still hand-woven in islanders' homes. Tarbert TIC can tell you about weavers and workshops you can visit.

Tarbert (Tairbeart)

pop 1338

Tarbert is a village port midway between North and South Harris with ferry connections to Uig on the Isle of Skye. It's serene and pretty, enjoying a spectacular location on a narrow land-bridge between two lochs, and overshadowed by mountains.

The **TIC** (☎ 502011; Pier Rd; Mon-Sat) is signposted up the hill and stays open late for ferry arrivals. Tarbert has basic facilities: a petrol station, an ATM at the TIC and two general stores. The **Harris Tweed Shop** (☎ 502493; Main St) stocks a wide range of books on the islands, and some good-value woollen hats.

Rockview Bunkhouse (☎ 502081; Main St; dm £10) Its cramped dorms are a bit cell-like but it has good facilities. If you enjoy the communal-living vibe then this is your utopia. Ask at the post office if nobody's about.

Skyeview (☎ 502095; 1 Scott Rd; r per person from £20; ☺ Apr-Oct; P ☒) Up the hill behind the Harris Hotel, this tranquil little place has two great rooms and genuine, generous hosts. You can just about see Skye if the weather's kind, and the delicious home-made marmalade beats those awful plastic sachets hands down!

Harris Hotel (☎ 502154; www.harrishotel.com; r per person from £45, 3-course dinner £24; ☺ lunch & dinner; P ☒) The town's best choice has a long history of fine Hebridean hospitality. The rooms are furnished in colourful modern style; there are good off-season specials. There's a conservatory lounge and a gorgeous dining room where absolutely massive portions of quality local lamb, for one, are dished out. For cheaper nosh, the **Isle of Harris Inn** (☎ 502566; bar meals £5-8; ☺ Mon-Sat) next door does big bar meals in a relaxed family setting.

Harris Coaches operates buses running to/from Leverburgh (50 minutes, four to five daily Monday to Saturday) and Stornoway (one hour, five daily Monday to Saturday).

For ferries to Uig on Skye, see Getting There & Away, p910.

South Harris

If you don't think Britain has real beaches, wait until you see South Harris. The A859 wraps around the west coast and is backed by rolling *machair* and mountains, with views across to North Harris and to off-shore islands. Azure waters give way to shallow turquoise, and lap lazily against achingly tempting sandy shores. The best beach here is Luskentyre; if the sun is shining it looks like paradise!

The east, or Bays, coast is a strange, rocky moonscape, studded with small ponds and still dotted with numerous crofts. It's difficult to imagine how anyone could have survived in such an inhospitable environment – but they did, and still do.

There were grand plans for **Leverburgh** (An t-Ob) to become a major fishing port in the early 20th century, but the fishing

boom never came and now it's a quiet little place passed through by travellers on their way to and from the Uists.

Am Bothan (☎ 520251; www.ambothan.com; dm £13; wheelchair access; ☒) In a quirky, wooden house, this is superbly equipped hostel with a peat fire, cosy furniture, and small, neat dorms with duvets and comfy mattresses. The porch is great for morning coffee; you can also hire bikes here.

Sorrel Cottage (☎ 520319; sorrel.cottage@virgin.net; 2 Glen; r per person £20-25; P) If you're after a guesthouse check out this cottage, on the way into town from Tarbert, with terrific little attic rooms. You can save a fiver by opting for room-only, or go the whole hog and try a generous home-cooked dinner. There are bikes for hire too.

A ferry goes from Leverburgh to the Isle of Berneray (person/car £5.20/23.70, 1¼ hours, three to four Monday to Saturday), which is connected by causeway to North Uist.

Three miles east at **Rodel** (Roghadal) stands the remarkable **St Clement's Church** (HS; admission free), built between the 1520s and 1550s, only to be abandoned in 1560 after the Reformation. Inside the echoing hall there's the fascinating tomb of Alexander MacLeod, the man responsible for the initial construction, and some fine stone carvings.

NORTH UIST (UIBHIST A TUATH)
☎ 01876 / pop 1657

North Uist, half-drowned by small lochs, is noted for its fishing but also has some magnificent beaches on the western side and great views north to the mountains of Harris. For bird-watchers this is an earthly paradise, with huge populations of migrant waders – oystercatchers, lapwings, curlews and redshanks – at every turn. The landscape is less mountainous and less wild than Harris but it has a sleepy, subtle appeal.

Car ferries for Leverburgh, on South Harris, leave from **Berneray**, connected to North Uist by a causeway.

Lochmaddy (Loch nam Madadh)
There isn't much to keep you in tiny Lochmaddy, but it's the first town you hit after arriving on the Berneray ferry. A Bank of Scotland ATM enables you to cash up for the couple of stores, petrol station, post office and pub. The **TIC** (☎ 500321; ☺ Mon-Sat Apr-Oct) also opens for late ferry arrivals.

The **Taigh Chearsabhagh Museum** (☎ 500293; adult £1; ☻ 10am-5pm Mon-Sat Feb-Dec) is a converted 18th-century inn and Lochmaddy's main culture fix, with two galleries and a museum that accommodates changing exhibitions. The café serves good soup and sandwiches.

Uist Outdoor Centre (☎ 500480; www.uistoutdoorcentre.co.uk; dm £11; wheelchair access) This is a place for active types and has clean, four-bed dorms and offers a range of half- and full-day adventures, including abseiling, kayaking and diving.

Old Court House (☎ 500358; r per person £23-25; P ✗) A gorgeous Georgian stone building and a charming place to stay. The rooms have every facility and go quickly. It's good value for singles.

Lochmaddy Hotel (☎ 500331; www.lochmaddyhotel.co.uk; r per person £35-45; mains around £7-10; P) is the only hotel in town. Some of the stylish and traditional rooms upstairs overlook the harbour, while the appealing bar below is a constant blend of anglers, locals and tourists. Good pub nosh, including seafood, venison and king-sized steaks, is served here.

Balranald RSPB Reserve

At this reserve, 18 miles west of Lochmaddy off the A865, you can watch the migrant waders or the rare red-necked phalarope and listen for corncrakes. There's a **visitors centre** (☎ 510372; ☻ Apr-Sep) with a resident warden.

BENBECULA (BEINN NA FAOGHLA)
☎ 01870 / pop 1249

Squeezed between North Uist and South Uist and connected to them by causeways, Benbecula is a low-lying island that's almost as much water as land. The army's Hebrides Rocket Range takes up most of the west coast and **Balivanich** (Baile a'Mhanaich), a commercial centre servicing the troops, is probably the only reason for a visit. Here you'll find services such as a bunkhouse, ATM, post office, and supermarket.

SOUTH UIST (UIBHIST A DEAS)
☎ 01878 / pop 1951

South Uist is the second-largest island in the Outer Hebrides and rewards those who explore beyond the main north–south road (A865). Once again, it lacks the drama of Harris, but there's an expansiveness that

has its own magic. The west coast is low, with *machair* backing an almost continuous sandy beach, while the east coast is quite hilly, with **Beinn Mhor** reaching 620m, and cut by four large sea lochs.

As you drive south from Benbecula, watch out for the granite statue of **Our Lady of the Isles** standing on the slopes of Ben Rueval, a sign that you've reached the Catholic southern Hebrides.

Lochboisdale (Loch Baghasdail)

The ferry port of Lochboisdale in the southeast is the island's largest settlement, although you'll likely be muttering 'grim' and 'bleak' rather than running to the postcard shop. The **TIC** (☎ 700286; ☻ Easter–mid-Oct) also opens for late ferry arrivals. There is a branch of the Royal Bank of Scotland with an ATM here and petrol pumps.

Lochside Cottage (☎ 700472; B&B per person £20) lives up to its name; if it's raining you could just about cast a line out of the beautiful conservatory lounge! There are two appealing rooms and friendly owners who'll pick you up from the ferry.

Lochboisdale Hotel (☎ 700332; www.lochboisdale.com; s/d £51/76, bar meals £8-12; P) This hotel, above the ferry terminal, is old-fashioned with bright, sea-facing rooms. There are filling bar meals served in the pub.

There are CalMac ferries between Lochboisdale and Castlebay on Barra (person/car £5.75/33.50, 1½ hours). Ferries sail roughly every second day, with additional summer services. Check schedules for exact times.

Howmore (Tobha Mor)

This attractive coastal village in the northwest, with its thatched cottages and ruined medieval chapels, was the burial site of the Clan Ranald chiefs.

About 6 miles south of Howmore, the excellent **Kildonan museum** (☎ 710343; adult £1.50; ☻ 10am-5pm Mon-Sat & 2-5pm Sun Easter-Oct) details crofting life using artefacts and an absorbing black-and-white photography exhibition. There are also many local accounts of harsh Hebridean life.

Tobha Mor Crofters' Hostel (www.gatliff.org.uk; dm £8) is in the village. To get to it, take the turn-off from the A865 to Tobha Mor – the basic stone-cottage is by the church at the road's end. Motorists should be wary of the uneven driveway.

The South

The southern tip of the island looks across to the islands of Eriskay and Barra. A causeway links Ludag on South Uist to Eriskay, and there's a CalMac ferry between Eriskay and Ardmhor on Barra (person/car £5.50/16.25, 40 minutes, four to five daily).

BARRA (BARRAIGH)

☎ 01871 / pop 1172

Barra is a tiny island, just 12 miles in circumference and ideal for exploring on foot. With beautiful beaches, *machair*, hills, Neolithic remains and a strong sense of community, it could be said to encapsulate the Outer Hebridean experience.

Castlebay (Bagh a Chaisteil) in the south is the largest village. There's a **TIC** (☎ 810 336; Main St; ☼ Apr-Oct). The village gets its name from **Kisimul Castle** (HS; ☎ 810313; adult £3.30; ☼ 9.30am-6.30pm Apr-Oct), which was built by the MacNeil clan in the 12th century and gifted to Historic Scotland in 2000 for an annual rental of £1 plus a bottle of whisky.

Dunard Hostel (☎ 810443; www.isleofbarrahostel .com; dm/tw & d £10/28; ✗) A friendly, family-run hostel with 12 beds. It's just a five-minute walk from the ferry and it organises sea-kayaking tours. It's very relaxed and homely.

Faire Mhaoldonaich (☎ 810441; www.fairemhaol donaich.com; r per person £20-23; ☼ Apr-Oct; P ✗), Just 1½ miles from the pier in Nask, this has very comfortable rooms with great views over Castlebay and a pleasant sun lounge for guests.

CalMac ferries operate from Castlebay to Lochboisdale – see Lochboisdale (p915) for details. For details on the ferry between Oban and Castlebay, see Getting There & Away on p910.

ORKNEY ISLANDS

Lying only a few miles off the north coast of the mainland, the Orkneys have a magic to them that is difficult to pin down. The archipelago consists of 70 islands, of which only 16 are inhabited; these fertile green lands, stripped of trees by the howling winds, form a sort of oasis in the wild Atlantic. The climate, warmed by the Gulf Stream, is surprisingly moderate, with April and May being the driest months.

Part of the islands' appeal is the feeling of walking in ancient footsteps. There are over 1000 identified prehistoric sites dotting the Orkneys, including the staggering village of Skara Brae, complete with stone-age DIY shelving and Ikea bed units. Standing stones are another powerful message from the past, as is the huge chambered cairn of Maes Howe. This latter is adorned with runes – graffiti from treasure-seeking Vikings – and indeed the whole of the archipelago is imbued with the legacy of those intriguing Norse folk. They bossed these islands for centuries; you can read of some of their deeds in the *Orkneyinga Saga*.

Kirkwall and Stromness, both on the largest island (known as Mainland), are the two main towns and both have considerable appeal; Kirkwall with its market-town bustle, and Stromness with its grey stone streets telling tales of both joys and hardships of island life. Here, and all over the islands, you'll find inviting drinking holes in which to experience Orcadian hospitality, legendary for its openness and warmth.

Orkney is also popular with bird-watchers, and the Royal Society for the Protection of Birds (RSPB) runs several reserves. The clear waters around the islands also attract divers, and the melancholy wrecks off Scapa Flow offers one of the most interesting dive sites in Europe.

GETTING THERE & AWAY

AIR

There are flights to Kirkwall airport on **BA/Loganair** (☎ 0870 850 9850; www.ba.com) daily from Aberdeen, Edinburgh, Glasgow, Inverness and the Shetlands, with connections to London. If your dates are flexible, buy the tickets online, as you can easily see which days still have cheaper fares available. The cheapest return tickets cost around £165 from London and £108 from Inverness.

BOAT & BUS

Drivers should book these crossings well in advance in summer, although, even if it's fully booked, there's always a chance of turning up a couple of hours before and squeezing on if there's extra space.

Pentland Ferries (☎ 01856-831226; www.pentland ferries.co.uk) operates a ferry between Gill's Bay, three miles west of John o'Groats, and St Margaret's Hope on Orkney (person/car

ORKNEY ISLANDS

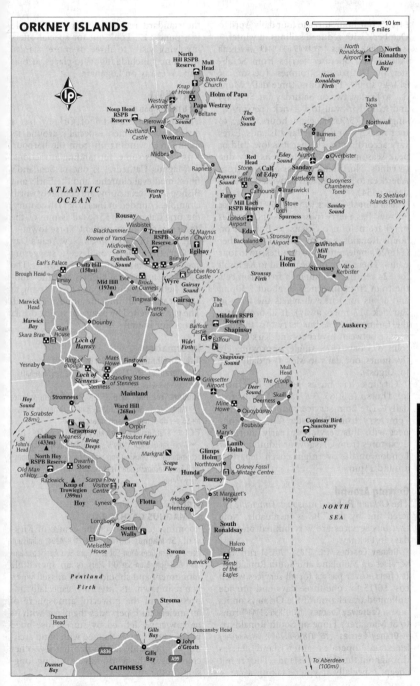

0 ——— 10 km
0 ——— 5 miles

North Hill RSPB Reserve
Mull Head
St Boniface Church
Knap of Howar
Holm of Papa
Westray Airport
Papa Westray
Beltane
Noup Head RSPB Reserve
Pierowall
Papa Sound
Noltland Castle
Westray
Midbea
Rapness
Westray Firth

North Ronaldsay Airport
North Ronaldsay
Linklet Bay
North Ronaldsay Firth
Tafts Ness
Scar
Butness
Northwall
Sanday Airport
Overbister
Sanday
Kettletoft
Quoyness Chambered Tomb

Red Head
Stone of Setter
Calf of Eday
Eday Sound
Rapness Sound
Faray
Calfsound
Braeswick
Mill Loch RSPB Reserve
Loth
Stove
Spurness
Sanday Sound

To Shetland Islands (90mi)

ATLANTIC OCEAN

Rousay
Wasbister
Blackhammer
Knowe of Yarso
Trumland RSPB Reserve
Sourin
St Magnus Church
London Airport
Backaland
Eday
Stronsay Airport
Whitehall
Mill Bay
Stronsay
Vat o Kerbister
Linga Holm
Stronsay Firth

Midhowe Cairn
Egilsay
Brinyan
Eynhallow Sound
Earl's Palace
Costa Hill (150m)
Birsay
Brough Head
Mid Hill (193m)
Evie
Broch of Gurness
Tingwall
Taversoe Tuick
Cubbie Roo's Castle
Wyre
Gairsay Sound
Gairsay
The Galt
Mildam RSPB Reserve

Marwick Head
Marwick Bay
Skara Brae
Skaill House
Dounby
Loch of Harray
Maes Howe
Finstown
Balfour Castle
Balfour
Shapinsay
Wide Firth
Shapinsay Sound

Yesnaby
Ring of Brodgar
Loch of Stenness
Standing Stones of Stenness
Stenness
Mainland
Ward Hill (268m)
Orphir
Kirkwall
Grimsetter Airport
Deer Sound
Mull Head
The Gloup
Skaill
Deerness
Mine Howe
Quoybrurray
Foubister

Hoy Sound
Stromness
To Scrabster (28mi)
Graemsay
Cuilags (433m)
Moaness
Bring Deeps
Houton Ferry Terminal
Markgraf
Scapa Flow
Glimps Holm
Northtown
St Mary's
Lamb Holm
Orkney Fossil & Vintage Centre
Copinsay Bird Sanctuary
Copinsay
Auskerry

St John's Head
North Hoy RSPB Reserve
Old Man of Hoy
Rackwick
Dwarfie Stone
Knap of Trowiegien (399m)
Scarpa Flow Visitor Centre
Fara
Hunda
Burray
Hoxa
Herston
St Margaret's Hope
Hoy
Lyness
Flotta
NORTH SEA

Longhope
South Walls
Melsetter House
Swona
South Ronaldsay
Halcro Head
Burwick
Tomb of the Eagles

Pentland Firth

Stroma

Dunnet Head
Gills Bay
Duncansby Head
John o'Groats
Gills Bay
A836
A99
Dunnet Bay
CAITHNESS
To Aberdeen (100mi)

£10/25, one hour, three to four daily April to October), with reduced sailings in winter.

Northlink Ferries (☎ 0845 600 0449; www.north linkferries.co.uk) operates ferries from Scrabster, by Thurso, to Stromness (person/car £14/43 single, 1½ hours, three daily Monday to Friday, two on Saturday and Sunday) and from Kirkwall to Lerwick (person/car single £17.75/73.75, eight hours, three to four weekly) on the Shetland Islands. Fares vary according to whether it is low, mid or peak season and travel durations vary due to winds. NorthLink Ferries also sail from Aberdeen to Kirkwall and Lerwick (see Aberdeen, p854).

John o'Groats Ferries (☎ 01955-611353; www.jog ferry.co.uk) has a ferry (passengers and bicycles only) from John o'Groats to Burwick on South Ronaldsay from May to September (£16/26 single/return, 40 minutes, up to four daily). There is an off-peak deal to Kirkwall for £24 return. In Thurso, a free bus meets the train from Inverness at about 2.50pm, and a bus for Kirkwall meets the ferry in Burwick (17 miles away). It also operates the Orkney Bus, a bus-ferry-bus through service between Inverness and Kirkwall via John o'Groats (£28 single, approximately five hours, one daily in May, two daily June to August).

Citylink has buses leaving Inverness for Thurso (£11.65, 3½ hours, four or five daily). The 2pm service connects with the 7pm ferry from Scrabster. You can connect with this service on early morning departures from Glasgow or Edinburgh, or London on the overnight coach departing around 11pm.

Getting Around

The *Orkney Public Transport Timetable* offered free by the TIC is invaluable. Note that bus services are very limited on Sundays in Orkney.

Orkney Coaches (☎ 01856 870555) run bus services on Mainland and South Ronaldsay. It offers Rover passes for all services which cost £6/15 for one/three days and provide unlimited travel around the Orkneys on its buses. **Causeway Coaches** (☎ 01856-831444) runs to St Margaret's Hope on South Ronaldsay.

Orkney Ferries (☎ 01856-872044; www.orkney ferries.co.uk) operates inter-island ferries throughout the Orkney Islands. They're not cheap, especially if you're taking a car –

the standard return fare for your vehicle is around £17. Look out for special offers involving visits to three or more islands, which may include flights to places such as Papa Westray on Loganair.

KIRKWALL

☎ 01856 / pop 6206

The busy little capital of Orkney has a distinctive character, especially around its main street winding up from the harbour. Kirkwall has some outstanding attractions: St Magnus Cathedral is one of Scotland's finest medieval churches and the Earl's and Bishop's Palace, nearby, are definitely worth a ramble. Founded in the early 11th century, the original part of Kirkwall is one of the best examples of an ancient Norse town.

If you're in Kirkwall on New Year's Day or Christmas Day, you'll see a staggering spectacle, a crazy ball game known as The Ba'. Two teams, the Uppies and the Doonies, fight their way through town, trying to get a leather ball into the opposition goal. The game, fuelled by plenty of strong drink, can go for hours!

Information

Kirkwall Library (Junction Rd) Free Internet access.
Launderama (☎ 872982; 47 Albert St; ☯ Mon-Sat) Service washes for £6.
Support Training (☎ 873582; 2 West Tankerness Lane; ☯ 8am-9.30pm Mon-Fri, 10am-5pm Sat) Internet access for £6 per hour, half price on Saturday.
TIC (☎ 872856; www.visitorkney.com; 6 Broad St; ☯ Mon-Sat Oct-Apr, daily May-Sep) Bureau de change, accommodation booking and a good range of publications on Orkney; recommended is *Walks in Orkney* (£5.99) by Mary Welsh.

Sights
ST MAGNUS CATHEDRAL

Looming genially over the centre of Kirkwall, **St Magnus Cathedral** (☎ 874894; admission free; ☯ 9am-6pm Mon-Sat & 2-6pm Sun Apr-Sep, 9am-1pm & 2-5pm Mon-Sat Oct-Mar) is an incredible monument and should not be missed when you're in town. Its interior is especially impressive and the powerful atmosphere of an ancient faith pervades the place, with its narrow nave defined by sturdy rose-hued pillars and its aisles flanked with blind arching. It's probably fair to say that few other churches in the world have a Viking longship on the altar.

KIRKWALL

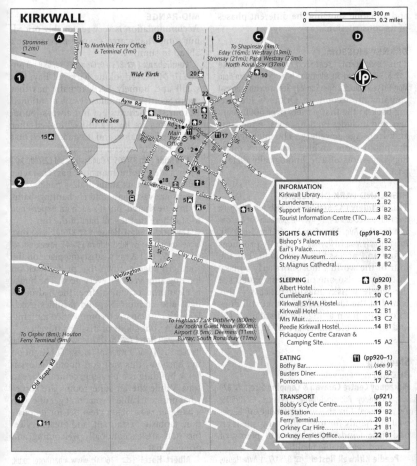

| 0 | | 300 m |
| 0 | | 0.2 miles |

INFORMATION

Kirkwall Library	**1** B2
Launderama	**2** B2
Support Training	**3** B2
Tourist Information Centre (TIC)	**4** B2

SIGHTS & ACTIVITIES (pp918-20)

Bishop's Palace	**5** B2
Earl's Palace	**6** B2
Orkney Museum	**7** B2
St Magnus Cathedral	**8** B2

SLEEPING (p920)

Albert Hotel	**9** B1
Cumliebank	**10** C1
Kirkwall SYHA Hostel	**11** A4
Kirkwall Hotel	**12** B1
Mrs Muir	**13** C2
Peedie Kirkwall Hostel	**14** B1
Pickaquoy Centre Caravan & Camping Site	**15** A2

EATING (pp920-1)

Bothy Bar	(see 9)
Busters Diner	**16** B2
Pomona	**17** C2

TRANSPORT (p921)

Bobby's Cycle Centre	**18** B2
Bus Station	**19** B2
Ferry Terminal	**20** B1
Orkney Car Hire	**21** B1
Orkney Ferries Office	**22** B1

Earl Rognvald Kolsson commissioned the cathedral in 1137 in the name of his uncle, Magnus Erlendsson, who was betrayed and killed by his cousin during a squabble over control of Orkney. The result of 300 years of construction and alteration, it includes Romanesque, transitional and Gothic styles.

The bones of Magnus are interred in one of the pillars in the cathedral. Other memorials include a statue of John Rae, the Arctic explorer, rifle at side, and the bell from HMS *Royal Oak*, sunk in WWII losing 833 of its crewmembers.

There are tours of the upper levels of the cathedral during summer, twice a day on Tuesday and Thursday. They cost £5 and take around 40 minutes.

EARL'S PALACE & BISHOP'S PALACE

Near the cathedral, and on opposite sides of the street, these two ruined **palaces** (☎ 871918; adult £2.20; ⏰ 9.30am-6.30pm Apr-Sep) are worth poking around. The Earl's Palace was once known as the finest example of Renaissance architecture in Scotland. It's the better of the two buildings, with many of its lower rooms still intact. One room contains an interesting history of its builder, Earl Patrick Stewart, who was executed in Edinburgh for treason. He started construction about 1600 but ran out of money and it was never completed.

The Bishop's Palace was built in the mid-12th century to provide comfortable lodgings for Bishop William the Old. There's a good view of the cathedral from the tower, and a plaque showing the different phases of its construction.

ORKNEY MUSEUM

This excellent, restored **merchant's house** (☎ 873191; Broad St; admission free; ☯ 10.30am-5pm Mon-Sat year-round, 2-5pm Sun May-Sep; wheelchair access) contains an account of Orkney's life dating back to the first settlers over 5000 years ago, and includes Pictish stones, 'bone' pins and Iron-Age jewellery. The highlight is the photo-room archive downstairs offering snap-shots of a technologically distant past.

HIGHLAND PARK DISTILLERY

This **distillery** (☎ 874619; www.highlandpark.co.uk; Holm Rd; guided tour £4; ☯ 10am-5pm Mon-Sat & noon-5pm Sun May-Aug, 10am-5pm Mon-Fri Apr, Sep & Oct, 2pm tour only Mon-Fri Nov-Mar) not only produces a fine and accessible single malt, but the tour of the world's most northerly whisky distillery is also one of the best. You'll see the whole whisky-making process – this is one of the few distilleries that still does its own barley malting. The distillery's 18- and 25-year-old malts are of the highest class.

Sleeping

BUDGET

Pickaquoy Centre Caravan & Camping Site (☎ 879 900; Pickaquoy Rd; small/large tent sites £3.70/5.75; ☯ year-round) On the western edge of Kirkwall but handy for town, this campsite is an odd little windswept place with plenty of grass and reasonable facilities.

Peedie Kirkwall Hostel (☎ 875477; 1 Ayre House, Ayre Rd; dm £10; ✗) This is a compact and clean independent hostel on the waterfront, with small dorms but plenty of space to stretch out in the bunks.

Kirkwall SYHA Hostel (☎ 0870 004 1133; www.syha .org.uk; Old Scapa Rd; dm £11; ☯ Apr-Sep; P ✗ 💻) In one of Orkney's ugliest buildings, this hostel is a 20-minute walk from the harbour on the edge of town backing on to green fields. Although it has a good kitchen and sociable dining area and comfortable bunks, it loses marks for its prisonlike feel, and potentially long walk to the bathroom. There are no power points in the dorms, not really good enough in these days of mobile phones. However, it's rarely full, and there's no curfew.

MID-RANGE

Accommodation is very reasonably priced, but somewhat scarce – you'll need to book ahead in summer.

Cumliebank (☎ 873160; Cromwell Rd; B&B per person £17; ✗) Overlooking Kirkwall Bay, this small and homely B&B actually has that warm Scottish hospitality always mentioned in tourist brochures but not always found. The rooms are large and well looked-after and excellent value, and it's guaranteed that you'll want to extend your stay.

Mrs Muir (☎ 874805; 2 Dundas Cres; s/d £25/40; ✗) This stately mini-mansion has character shining out of its stained-glass panels. The rooms are vast, light, and enchanting; bathrooms are shared, but it's such an experience to stay here that it's all part of the fun.

Lav'rockha Guest House (☎ 876103; lavrockha@ orkney.com; Inganess Rd; s/d from £30/44; wheelchair access; P ✗ 💻) A very satisfying place on the southern edge of town that prides itself on looking after visitors' every need. The house is clean and ornament-free, the bedrooms light and comfortable, and facilities excellent. It's particularly recommended for families with young kids or disabled travellers.

Kirkwall Hotel (☎ 872232; www.kirkwallhotel.com; Harbour St; s/d £46/70; wheelchair access; 💻) Right on the harbour, this vast and noble Victorian brick building is a pleasing, central place to stay. While the en-suite rooms are somewhat unremarkable if you don't get one with a harbour view, it's a great bet for its position, fantastic restaurant, and great service: the staff are exceptionally welcoming and professional.

Albert Hotel (☎ 876000; www.alberthotel.co.uk; Mounthoolie Lane; s/d £50/81; wheelchair access; ✗ 💻) Whether you stay here or not, you'll probably end up here at some point in one of its bars or restaurant; convenient and welcoming, it's a great spot. The rooms aren't going to win design awards but they are well-equipped and have big comfy beds.

Eating & Drinking

There are several places to eat around Bridge St, near the harbour.

Pomona (☎ 872325; Albert St; snacks £1-3; ☯ 10am-5pm) This is an honest no-frills greasy-spoon café of a type that was once an institution but is now in danger of extinction in many parts of Britain. Whether you're in for tea and toast, a sandwich, or the big all-day breakfast, you're guaranteed a kind welcome and a generous word. It's also one of the only spots in town for a coffee on Sunday morning, although everybody seems to need one after Saturday night.

Busters (☎ 876717; 1 Mounthoolie Lane; meals £4-7; ☺ 4.30-10pm Mon-Fri, noon-10pm Sat, 12.30-7.30pm Sun; ☒) This popular spot is a tribute to the American diner, with its red checked tablecloths and ketchup bottles primed for use. There's good food on offer, such as burgers, Tex-Mex, and pizzas. It's licensed and also a sure hit with kids. Takeaways are available.

Albert Hotel (☎ 876000; Mounthoolie Lane; bar meals £5-9, mains £12-16; ☺ lunch & dinner; ☒) The Albert Hotel is a great place for food. Both its bars do well-above-average appetising meals with plenty of invention. Stables, the more formal restaurant, offers intimacy and high-quality seafood – try the local crab. There's also an extensive wine list.

Kirkwall Hotel (☎ 872232; www.kirkwallhotel.com; Harbour St; mains £9-15; ☺ lunch & dinner; ☒) The restaurant in the grand old Kirkwall is reckoned by most locals to be the capital's best. Although the menu offers juicy steaks and some vegetarian dishes, the seafood is the highlight, and comes exquisitely presented and prepared with sauces that bring out, rather than subdue, the flavours of the sea.

Bothy Bar (☎ 876000; Mounthoolie Lane) Kirkwall's best bar is part of the Albert Hotel, and throbs with happy conversation. All sorts mix here: it's a dark, convivial sort of place with a good jukebox and cosy tables which opens until 1am at weekends. Matchmakers is another bar in the same building, but its atmosphere is quieter and more hotel-like.

Getting There & Away

The **airport** (☎ 872494) is 2½ miles from the town centre. See Getting There & Away (p916) for flight information. For flights and ferries to the northern islands, see the individual islands.

From the bus station, Orkney Coaches runs to Evie (45 minutes, up to seven daily Monday to Friday, four on Saturday); Orphir & Houton (30 minutes, six daily Monday to Friday, three on Saturday); Stromness (40 minutes, 13 daily Monday to Friday, seven on Saturday, four on Sunday); and Tingwall (35 minutes, up to seven daily Monday to Friday, three on Saturday).

Causeway Coaches travels to St Margaret's Hope (30 minutes, four daily Monday to Friday, three on Saturday) on South Ronaldsay.

From June to early September, Orkney Coaches runs two daily buses from Kirkwall to Stromness via the Standing Stones at Stenness, the Ring of Brodgar, and Skara Brae.

Getting Around

There are several car-rental places such as **Orkney Car Hire** (☎ 872866; www.orkneycarhire.co.uk; Junction Rd), where rates are from about £34 per day, all-inclusive. **Bobby's Cycle Centre** (☎ 875777; Tankerness Lane) rents out mountain bikes from £8 per day.

WEST & NORTH MAINLAND
Stromness
☎ 01856 / pop 1609

The rambling, winding streets flanking the port of Stromness have changed little since the 18th century and the flagstone-paved main street, interspersed with rivulets of wee alleys, curves down to the waterfront, amid attractive stone cottages. Guesthouses, pubs and eateries interrupt traditional trade along the main street, where cars and pedestrians move at the same pace. As a place to stay, many visitors prefer Stromness to Kirkwall.

The **TIC** (☎ 850716; ☺ 8am-4.30pm Apr-Oct, 1-3pm Mon-Fri Nov-Mar) is in the ferry terminal and stays open later when ferries dock. There's free Internet access at **Stromness Library** (Hellihole Rd; ☺ afternoons Mon-Sat & also Sat morning).

SIGHTS

The main attraction of Stromness is pacing its sinuous main street and watching boats come and go in the harbour. However, the superb **Stromness Museum** (☎ 850025; 52 Alfred St; adult £2.50; ☺ 10am-5pm Apr-Oct) has an extraordinary collection of bits and bobs representing the town's rich maritime heritage, including exhibits on whaling and the scuttled German High Seas fleet.

SLEEPING

Point of Ness Caravan & Camping Site (☎ 873535; tent sites £3.70-5.80) This well-positioned campsite overlooks the bay from its breezy situation on a headland south of the centre. It's well-maintained and reasonably equipped and cutely circled by a small picket fence.

Stromness SYHA Hostel (☎ 0870 004 1150; www
.syha.org.uk; Hellihole Rd; dm £10.50; ☺ May-Sep; Ⓟ ☒)
Recently renovated, this hostel at the southern end of town is about a 10-minute stroll
from the ferry terminal. It's clean and well
kitted-out, but there's a certain rule-bound
joylessness about the place, which may deter
those who plan to spend more time in pubs
than on walking trails.

Mrs M Spence (☎ 850949; 45 John St; B&B s/d
£20/40; ☒) Despite the somewhat grim appearance of the houses on this street above
the harbour, this is a welcoming and cheerful B&B with decent upstairs rooms and a
host who likes to see her guests tucking in
to the full Scottish at breakfast time.

Miller's House & Harbour Side Guest House
(☎ 851969; millershouse@orkney.com; 13 John St; s/d
£28/45; ☒) These two renovated historic
houses are very close to the ferry in central
Stromness. Sleeping gets done in the Harbour
Side, where the en-suite rooms are tastefully
decorated. You have breakfast nearby in
the Miller's House, one of Stromness' oldest homes, with wooden floors and furniture
and a very generous spread indeed.

Stromness Hotel (☎ 850298; www.stromnesshotel
.com; Victoria St; s/d from £40/80; Ⓟ ☒) This towering
stone hotel dominates the centre of town
in traditionally grand fashion. The décor
is plush and doesn't seem to have been
touched much since the days a tug on the
bell pull would summon a servant; all part
of its charm, as are the super views from the
giant windows.

Other recommendations:

Brown's Hostel (☎ 850661; 45 Victoria St; dm £10;
☒) Small, central, and popular hostel that can be a bit
claustrophobic.

Ferry Inn (☎ 850280; www.ferryinn.com; John St; s/d
£32/54; ☒) Right on the harbour with tidy en-suite rooms
and some basic but simple options in a nearby annexe.

EATING & DRINKING

Ferry Inn (☎ 850280; John St; mains £6-15; ☺ lunch
& dinner daily; ☒) The town's best boozer is
also an excellent and convivial spot to eat.
Decorated like a boat, with walls plastered
with naval charts, it's exactly what a portside
pub should be. The food comes out in huge
portions, and includes value-packed daily
specials as well as mouth-watering and inventive meat and seafood dishes. For a pint
try Orkney Dark Island or Red McGregor,
two of the local brews.

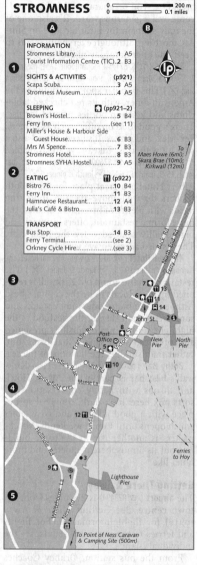

STROMNESS

0 ————— 200 m
0 ————— 0.1 miles

INFORMATION
Stromness Library.............................1 A5
Tourist Information Centre (TIC)...2 B3

SIGHTS & ACTIVITIES   (p921)
Scapa Scuba......................................3 A5
Stromness Museum...........................4 A5

SLEEPING ☖   (pp921–2)
Brown's Hostel..................................5 B4
Ferry Inn.....................................(see 11)
Miller's House & Harbour Side
   Guest House...................................6 B3
Mrs M Spence....................................7 B3
Stromness Hotel................................8 B3
Stromness SYHA Hostel....................9 A5

EATING 🍴   (p922)
Bistro 76...10 B4
Ferry Inn...11 B3
Hamnavoe Restaurant.....................12 A4
Julia's Café & Bistro........................13 B3

TRANSPORT
Bus Stop..14 B3
Ferry Terminal...........................(see 2)
Orkney Cycle Hire......................(see 3)

To
Maes Howe (6mi);
Skara Brae (10mi);
Kirkwall (12mi)

Ferries
to Hoy

To Point of Ness Caravan
& Camping Site (500m)

Julia's Café & Bistro (☎ 850904; 20 Ferry Rd; mains
lunch £4-9, dinner £10-13; ☺ café all day & dinner Wed-Sun;
☒) Busy but friendly, this conservatory-style
café looks over to the ferry terminal and has
creative café fare eg melts and enticing vegetarian concoctions. In the evenings things get
a little more formal, with high-quality plates
and an intimate candlelit ambience.

Bistro 76 (☎ 851803; 76 Victoria St; mains £10-15; ☺ noon-11pm, dinner 5-11pm) Underneath the Orca Hotel, Bistro 76 is an intimate cellar restaurant with a stand-out menu that will entice most palates through the door. There is also no-frills takeaway fare available here, and a simple daily special that is good, cheap and filling, and which is served between 5pm and 8pm.

Hamnavoe Restaurant (☎ 850606; 35 Graham Place; mains £11-15; ☺ dinner Wed-Sun Apr-Sep; ☒) Taking itself more seriously than most in town, the Hamnavoe offers gourmet cuisine in an elegant dining room. Local Orkney produce is used in creatively designed dishes, with an emphasis on seafood, which has a high reputation.

GETTING THERE & AWAY
Orkney Coaches runs to Kirkwall (40 minutes, 13 daily Monday to Friday, seven on Saturday, four on Sunday) and Birsay (25 minutes, one on Monday and Thursday). From May to September, there are three to four daily buses to Skara Brae (20 minutes).

For details on ferries to/from Scrabster and Lerwick see Getting There & Away (p933). For ferry services to/from Aberdeen see p854. For boats to Hoy, see p926.

GETTING AROUND
You can rent a bike from £6 per day at **Orkney Cycle Hire** (☎ 850255; 54 Dundas St).

Stenness
This village is little more than a petrol station, a few houses and a hotel. A mile east, however, are some of the most extraordinary prehistoric monuments on Orkney. It's easy to get here by bus as the road between Stromness and Kirkwall passes through here.

MAES HOWE
Egypt has the pyramids, Scotland has Maes Howe. Constructed nearly 5000 years ago, **Maes Howe** (☎ 01856-761606; adult £3; ☺ tours every 45 min 9.45am-5.15pm Apr-Sep, 9.45am-3.45pm Mon-Sat, 2.15-3.45pm Sun Oct-Mar) is the finest chambered tomb in Western Europe. A long stone passage leads into a chamber in the centre of an

---

SCAPA FLOW WRECKS

The wrecks that litter these clear waters make Scapa Flow the best diving location in Europe. Enclosed by Mainland, Hoy and South Ronaldsay, this is one of the world's largest natural harbours and has been used by vessels as diverse as King Haakon's Viking ships in the 13th century and the NATO fleet of today.

It was from Scapa Flow that the British Home Fleet sailed to meet the German High Seas Fleet at the Battle of Jutland on 31 May 1916. After the war, 74 German ships were interned in Scapa. Conditions for the German sailors were poor and there were several mutinies as negotiations for the fate of the ships dragged on. When the terms of the armistice were agreed on 6 May 1919 with the announcement of a severely reduced German navy, Admiral von Reuter, who was in charge of the German fleet in Scapa Flow, decided to take matters into his own hands. On 21 June, a secret signal was passed from ship to ship and the British watched incredulously as every German ship began to sink. Fifty-two of them went to the bottom, with the rest left aground in shallow water.

Most of the ships were salvaged, but seven vessels remain to attract divers. There are three battleships – the *König*, the *Kronprinz Wilhelm* and the *Markgraf* – all of which are all over 25,000 tonnes. The first two were subjected to blasting for scrap metal, but the Markgraf is undamaged and considered one of the best dives in the area. Four light cruisers (4400 to 5600 tonnes) – the *Karlsruhe*, *Dresden*, *Brummer* and *Köln* – are particularly interesting as they lie on their sides and are very accessible to divers. The *Karlsruhe*, although severely damaged, is only 9m below the surface. Its twisted superstructure has now become a huge metal reef encrusted with diverse sea life.

As well as the German wrecks, numerous other ships litter the Scapa Flow seabed. If you're interested in diving in Scapa Flow, try the PADI-affiliated **Scapa Scuba** (see map p922; ☎ 01856-851218; www.scapascuba.co.uk; 13 Ness Rd, Stromness) which offers tuition and trips, as do many other operators. If you're not a diver, you can experience the wrecks with **Roving Eye Boat Trips** (☎ 01856-811309; www.rovingeye.co.uk; Orphir), which explores the wrecks with a diving robot that transmits video footage to the comfort of the boat. The three-hour trips are terrific and cost £25.

earth-covered mound, which is over 6.7m high and 35m across. The size of the local sandstone slabs used, and the skill with which they were laid, is mind-boggling.

During the winter solstice, Maes Howe takes on Indiana Jones–type qualities as blood-red sunsets align themselves with the passage, striking a cairn entrance at the rear of the chamber with alarming precision.

In the 12th century Vikings returning from the Crusades broke into the tomb searching for treasure. They found none, but left a wonderfully earthy collection of graffiti, carved in runes on the walls. Some of it's pretty basic of the 'Thorni bedded Helgi' and the 'Ottarfila-was-ere' variety. There are also more intricate carvings of mythical beasts.

Entry is by an excellent guided tour (lasting 20 minutes) filling your mind with both awe and questions about this astonishing place.

Get your ticket in Tormiston Mill, on the other side of the road from Maes Howe, where there's a café, gift shop and small exhibition. In summer, it's worth ringing a few hours ahead to book the tour time that suits you.

STANDING STONES OF STENNESS
Near Maes Howe stand only four of the original 12 mighty boulders that once formed a **ring** (HS; admission free; ⏰ 24 hr). Fenced off from the world outside, just like the sheep in the next field, the stones are impressive for their sheer size (one is over 5m high) and, of course, age – they were erected around 2500 BC.

RING OF BRODGAR
About a mile along the road from Stenness towards Skara Brae is a wide circle of **standing stones** (HS; admission free; ⏰ 24 hr), some over 5m tall. Twenty-five of the original 50 stones are still standing above the heather. It's an impressive sight and a powerful place. These old stones, raised skywards 4500 years ago, still attract the forces of nature – on 5 June 1980, one was struck by lightning.

Skara Brae
Idyllically situated by a sandy bay 8 miles north of Stromness, **Skara Brae** (HS; ☎ 01856-841815; adult/child £5/1.30; ⏰ 9.30am-6.30pm Apr-Sep, 9.30am-4.30pm Oct-Mar; wheelchair access) is northern

Europe's best-preserved prehistoric village. Predating the pyramids of Giza as well as Stonehenge, it is staggeringly complete: even the stone furniture – beds, boxes and dressers – has survived the 4500 years since a community last lived and breathed here. This is largely due to the wind, which rapidly buried the buildings in sand once they were deserted, where they remained until 1850, when a severe storm ripped the top off the dunes, exposing the first unsuspected stones.

There's an excellent interactive exhibition and short video, arming visitors with facts and theory and enhancing the impact of the site. It's also worth buying the guidebook, which gives a guided tour involving eight viewpoints. Before heading for the site itself, inspect the reconstruction of a typical house, which brings the excavation brilliantly to life.

Your ticket is also valid for **Skaill House**, an early 17th-century mansion inhabited by William Watt, the founder of the village.

Private transport is the best way to get here, but from May to September there are three to four buses daily to and from Stromness.

POO BREW
So you like a bit of the *odd* Scottish brew and you're looking for something that packs a bit of wallop? Good news: After discovering what is believed to be a 5000-year-old brewery within Skara Brae, scientists at the 2002 Orkney Science Fair meticulously recreated a stone-age beer, spicing it up with…cow dung. Samplers claimed it was a potent brew, not to be served in pint mugs.

Although the poo brew is not yet in mass production, perhaps you should check your next pint in Orkney for whiffy qualities.

Birsay
The small village of Birsay, once the most important settlement on Orkney, is 8 miles north of Skara Brae and in its centre stand the ruins of the **Earl's Palace** (HS; admission free; ⏰ 24 hrs). The palace was built in the 16th century by the despotic Robert Stewart, scourge of the Orkney peasants. Today, it's an atmospheric spot, with walls of honey-coloured stone slowly crumbling among green lawns.

When the tide is low, you can walk out to the **Brough of Birsay** (HS; ☎ 01856-841815; adult £1.80; ☻ 9.30am-6.30pm mid-Jun–Sep), three quarters of a mile from the Earl's Palace. It's the ruins of a Norse settlement built around the 12th-century St Peter's Church. A number of long houses are among the relics.

You couldn't do better on Orkney than spend a night or three at **Linkshouse** (☎ 01856-721221; www.ewaf.co.uk; The Palace, Birsay; s/d £30/50; P X). Once a summering spot for Kirkwall and Stromness gentry, this well-kept stone house looks over bright green grass to the sea, a vista best appreciated from the 'loo with a view' in the double room. There's a cosy lounge and an enchanting little gazebo to relax with a book, but best of all is the kind and gentle hospitality, which includes fantastic breakfasts with home-made sausages and inventive vegetarian choices such as sweetcorn pancakes.

Evie

Signposted from Evie is the **Broch of Gurness** (☎ 01856-751414; adult £3; ☻ 9.30am-6.30pm Apr-Sep) which, built around 100 BC, is the best example of a fortified stone tower to be found in Orkney. Surrounding it are the shells of houses, discernable by the hearths in the centre of each. In later times it was used as a Viking burial site: not all were sent out to sea in blazing longships. The small visitors centre helps unravel the mysteries of this ancient culture.

Eviedale Campsite & Bothy (☎ 01856-751270; colin.richardson@orkney.com; small/large tent sites £4/7, dm £5, self-catering cottages per week from £230; ☻ Apr-Sep) has a good grassy area for camping with picnic tables, and a very basic bothy with four beds but no showers. Next door is self-catering accommodation in excellent renovated farm cottages, furnished in country style. If no-one's about, ask at the dairy farm just up the road and opposite the campsite.

Woodwick House (☎ 01856-751330; www.woodwick house.co.uk; Woodwick Bay; s/d from £32/56; P X), accessed from a road near the Tingwall ferry dock, is a country-house hotel with plenty of stately décor but few pretensions. The uncluttered rooms are large, and there are extensive gardens with glimpses of the sea. It's a fair way from the eat streets of London or New York, so just as well the dinners are home-cooked gourmet affairs that leave you sated and happy for £24 a head.

EAST MAINLAND, BURRAY & SOUTH RONALDSAY

After a German U-boat sneaked into Scapa Flow and sank the battleship HMS *Royal Oak* in 1939, Sir Winston Churchill ordered better protection for the naval base. Using concrete blocks and old ships, the channels between some of the islands around Scapa Flow were blocked. The **Churchill Barriers**, as they're known, now link the islands of Lamb Holm, Glimps Holm, Burray and South Ronaldsay to Mainland. There are good sandy beaches by Barrier Nos 3 and 4.

East Mainland is mainly agricultural. On the far-eastern shore a mile north of Skaill (at the end of the Deerness Rd), is the **Gloup**, a spectacular natural arch and sea cave, and further north, the **Brough of Deerness**, a Norse or Pictish monastic complex. There are large colonies of nesting seabirds at Mull Head.

On the island of Lamb Holm, the **Italian Chapel** (☎ 01856-781268; admission free; ☻ 9am-10pm Apr-Sep, 9am-4.30pm Oct-Mar) is all that remains of a prisoner of war (POW) camp that housed the Italian prisoners who worked on the Churchill Barriers. They built the remarkable chapel in their spare time, using two Nissen huts, scrap metal and their considerable artistic and decorative skills. It's a moving testament to faith and cooperation, and a useful lesson in management skills: the British commanding officer of the prison camp supported and facilitated the project.

A visit is recommended to the **Tomb of the Eagles** (☎ 01856-831339; Liddle Farm, Isbister; adult £3.50; ☻ 9.30am-6pm Apr-Oct, 10am-noon Nov-Mar), located on the southern tip of South Ronaldsay. The 5000-year-old burial chamber was discovered by local farmers, who now run an excellent guided tour, which includes a hands-on examination of remains and an entertaining visit to the burial chamber. A number of sea eagle claws and bones were found within the tomb, which perhaps indicates that the group revered the bird as a totem; other tombs on the island have revealed remains of different animals. However, here, as in archaeological sites around the world, some of the theories aired are leaps ahead of the evidence!

The main village on South Ronaldsay is **St Margaret's Hope**, named after Margaret, the Maid of Norway, who was to have married Edward II of England but is thought to have died here in 1290 on her way to the wedding. It's a beautiful little stone-built place, and makes a tranquil place to stay. It's also the terminus for the cheaper of the two mainland car ferries.

Sleeping & Eating

The **Creel** (☎ 01856-831311; www.thecreel.co.uk; Front Rd; mains £17.80, s/d £55/80; ☺ Apr–mid-Oct, dinner only; restaurant wheelchair access; ✗) As one of Scotland's highest-rated seafood restaurants, this isn't the place to turn up to on a whim: booking well in advance is essential. With smart but unfussy modern décor of slate floor and wooden tables, the place lets the food do the talking, and it does. Hand-dived wild scallops are perhaps the highlight of the varying menu, but the flavours are consistently excellent, right down to the home-made bannocks, a traditional Orkney barley bread. There are also first-class rooms, some with panoramic views of the small harbour.

Backpackers Hostel (☎ 01856-831205; Back Rd, St Margaret's Hope; dm £11) This lovely stone cottage is run by the neighbouring Murray Arms Hotel. There's a good dorm, as well as a single, twins, and a triple. The kitchen and lounge are excellent, but with a terraced café and bar meals available in the same complex, self-caterers will be sorely tempted to stay.

Ankersted (☎ 01856-731217; ankersted@tinyworld .co.uk; Burray; r per person £19; ℗ ✗) This likeable little place has modern rooms with private bathroom that offer top value. The B&B overlooks Watersound Bay and Barrier No 4, and there's an upstairs guest lounge, which is the best spot to appreciate the view.

Getting There & Away

Causeway Coaches operates buses between Kirkwall and St Margaret's Hope (30 minutes, four daily Monday to Friday, three on Saturday). Orkney Coaches runs the Kirkwall–Burwick service (50 minutes) which connects with the ferries. For ferry information see Getting There & Away, p916.

HOY

☎ 01856 / pop 392

The second largest of Orkney's islands got the lion's share of this archipelago's scenic beauty. Shallow turquoise bays lace the perimeter, while peat and moorland cover the highest hills in Orkney (the name Hoy means High Island).

Whether on foot or in wheels, access to the dramatic landscape and spectacular cliff scenery will tempt hands to cameras. **St John's Head** (346m), on the west coast, is one of the highest vertical cliffs in Britain. The celebrated **Old Man of Hoy**, a 137m-high sea stack off the northwest coast, is the island's best-known sight. The finest scenery is in the north of the island, a large part of which forms the **North Hoy RSPB Reserve**.

There are some excellent walks around the island, the most popular being to the edge of the cliffs opposite the Old Man of Hoy. Allow about seven hours for the return trip from Moaness Pier on the east coast where the ferries dock. Alternatively, you can walk to the Old Man from Rackwick, a village on the west coast overlooking a secluded bay with sheer cliffs arising on either side. There's a hostel here from where the three-hour return walk to the Old Man begins.

The car ferry from Mainland arrives at Lyness, which was an important naval base during both the World Wars, when the British Grand Fleet was based in Scapa Flow. Here, the **Scapa Flow Visitor Centre** (☎ 791300; admission by donation; ☺ 9am-4.30pm Mon-Fri, 10am-4pm Sun May-Sep) is well worth a visit. It's a fascinating naval museum incorporating a photographic display in an old pumphouse. Most interesting is the account of the sinking of the German High Seas Fleet after WWI; there's also a cheerful little café.

Sleeping & Eating

Rackwick SYHA Hostel (☎ 873535; www.syha.org .uk; Rackwick; dm £7.70; ☺ early Mar–late Sep; ℗ ✗) One of two simple SYHA hostels on Hoy (the other is in Moaness), this is a snug, clean place popular with walkers. In easy striking distance of the Old Man himself, it's a place where you'll need your own sleeping bag and supplies. The warden will come around to collect your dosh in the evening.

Stoneyquoy Farm (☎ 791234; www.visithoy.com; r per person £20; ℗ ✗ ▣) This is the place to come if you prefer great views and generous hospitality to rules and flowery wallpaper. A working farm (3 miles from Lyness towards Longhope), it's a spot that gets back to the original idea of B&B, where you actually feel welcomed into a real home. The rooms are comfortable, but you won't want to spend much time in them when you can ramble in the fields or chat over coffee with your fellow guests or the delightful hosts, who also run day tours of the island. Phone ahead, as they may be moving to nearby Upper Settir; the experience, which includes a memorable breakfast, is guaranteed not to change. Tasty evening meals are also available.

St John's Manse (☎ 791240; btwn Lyness & Longhope; s/d £25/50; **P** ✖ 🖳) This recommended guesthouse is a real place to relax. If you're not relaxing in the garden with its beautifully manicured rockery, you may be dozing in your excellent bedroom to the sound of lapping waves. The hosts are thoughtful and knowledgeable about the island and have furnished the place elegantly in noble wooden furniture.

Stromabank Hotel (☎ 701494; Longhope; bar meals £6-9; ✕ lunch Sat & Sun, dinner Fri-Wed) Set in the hills behind Longhope, this is one of Hoy's few spots for a pie and a pint. The bar and location are atmospheric, and there's little competition, so the boss can be as grumpy as he sees fit. The food's pretty good though!

Getting There & Away

A **passenger ferry** (☎ 01856-850624) operates between Stromness and Moaness Pier (person/bicycle £2.90/0.60 single, 30 minutes, two to five daily May to September). There's a reduced schedule from October to April.

Orkney Ferries (☎ 01856-811397) also sails to Hoy (Lyness and Longhope) and the island of Flotta from Houton on Mainland (person/car £5.80/17.50 return, three to six daily). The more limited Sunday service runs from May to late September. Flotta and Houton are 20 minutes and 35 minutes from Lyness, respectively.

NORTHERN ISLANDS

The group of windswept islands north of Mainland provides a refuge for migrating birds and a nesting ground for seabirds; there are several RSPB reserves. Some of the islands are also rich in archaeological sites. However, the beautiful scenery, with wonderful white-sand beaches and lime-green to azure seas, is the main attraction.

The TICs in both Kirkwall and Stromness have a useful brochure, *The Islands of Orkney*, which includes maps and details of these islands. Note that the pronunciation of the 'ay' ending of each island name is 'ee' (eg Shapinsay is pronounced Shapinsee).

Orkney Ferries operates an efficient ferry service. From Kirkwall you can go on day trips to many of the islands most days of the week, but it's really worth staying for at least a few nights.

Shapinsay
☎ 01856 / pop 300

A short ferry trip from Kirkwall, Shapinsay is a fertile, highly cultivated, low-lying island much favoured as a basking spot by both common and grey seals. **Balfour Castle** (☎ 711282; www.balfourcastle.com; adult £17), built in the Scottish Baronial-style, is the most impressive sight and is now a hotel. There are tours of the castle on Sunday at 2.15pm, May to September, which must be booked in advance. The admission price includes entry into the castle, a generous serve of tea and scones, and a return ferry ticket. You can also stay at Balfour Castle (DB&B per person from £85), which has grand, old-fashioned, Victorian rooms with the added attraction that you are, of course, spending the night in a castle.

Girnigoe (☎ 711256; Girnigoe; s/d £25/40; **P** ✖), at the opposite end of the island from the ferry terminal, is an excellent place to fetch up for a night or two. The rooms are simply furnished but with a very homely touch, and have electric blankets for those chilly nights. Even better is the cooking, with generous breakfasts, including local kippers for those who fancy it, and dinner on request that is an absolute bargain at £12.

Orkney Ferries operates a ferry from Kirkwall (person/car £5.80/17.50 return, 25 minutes, five to six daily May to September). There are limited services in winter.

Rousay
☎ 01856 / pop 267

This wild and windswept hilly island lying close to Mainland's northeast is known (more by tourist brochures than locals admittedly) as 'the Egypt of the North'. It is incredibly well endowed in archaeological sites, including several elaborate burial cairns. It also has the important **Trumland RSPB Reserve** and three lochs with good trout fishing.

Heading west from the ferry pier, you'll strike a rich vein of ruins: the impressive burial mound of **Taversoe Tuick**, built on two levels, and the cairns of **Yarso** and **Blackhammer**.

Holding the remains of 25 people and dating from the 3rd millennium BC, the 'Great Ship of Death', as **Midhowe Cairn** is called, is the longest chambered cairn in Orkney. Its about 5½ miles west of the pier and a steep walk downhill. Nearby, **Midhowe Broch** is the best example of these prehistoric fortresses in Orkney.

The walk from Midhowe Cairn to Westness Farm is only a mile, but spans some 5000 years of Orkney history, taking you past Viking and Pictish burial sites, prehistoric brochs and knowes (burial mounds), and several noble ruins from the 16th to 19th centuries. The leaflet *Westness Walk*, available from TICs on Mainland and usually in the Pier pub by the ferry, describes the route in detail.

SLEEPING & EATING

Trumland Farm (☎ 821252; Trumland Farm; tent sites £3 per person; dm £8, bedding £2 extra; P ✗) This farm, just half a mile west of the ferry, has a self-contained hostel with great views, an excellent kitchen, and two comfortable but cramped six-bed dorms. You can pitch tents on the grass outside and use the hostel facilities, and bike hire is also available from the cordial owners.

Ervadale (☎ 821351; r per person from £20; P ✗) Set on the side of a heathery hill and, like most places on the island, has stress-beating views over the grass and water. The en-suite room is large and comfortable, and guests have access to a lounge with videos for when the weather closes in.

Pier Restaurant (☎ 821359; meals £5-7; ☷ 11am-9pm Mon-Sat) This restaurant, by the ferry pier, is an ideal spot for homely bar meals, a coffee or whisky while waiting for the ferry, or a chat and a game of pool after a long day's walking. There's also Internet access.

GETTING THERE & AWAY

A small **car ferry** (☎ 751360) connects Tingwall (Mainland) with Brinyan on Rousay (person/car £5.80/17.50 return, 30 minutes, five to six daily) and the other nearby islands of Egilsay and Wyre.

GETTING AROUND

Good bikes can be rented for £7 per day from Trumland Farm. The island's one road makes a pleasant, slightly hilly, circuit of about 14 miles.

Egilsay & Wyre

These two small islands lie 1½ miles east of Rousay. On Egilsay, a **cenotaph** marks the spot where Earl Magnus was murdered in 1116. After his martyrdom, pilgrims flocked to the island and St Magnus Kirk, now roofless, was built. Today, much of the island is an **RSPB reserve**.

Wyre is even smaller than Egilsay. In the mid-12th century it was the domain of the Viking baron Kolbein Hruga ('Cubbie Roo'). The ruins of his **castle** and St Mary's Chapel can be visited for free. Seal sightings at the beach on Wyre's western sliver are virtually guaranteed.

These two islands are reached on the Rousay-Tingwall ferry (see Rousay, previous). Booking the ferry is mandatory for the return journey.

Stronsay

☎ 01857 / pop 358

Low-lying Stronsay attracts walkers and cyclists for its lack of serious inclines, and beautiful landscapes over its four curving bays. It's also a good spot to observe wildlife, with plenty of portly seals basking on the rocks, and a healthy population of migratory birds. There are good coastal walks and, in the east, the **Vat o'Kirbister** is the best example of a *gloup* (natural arch) in Orkney.

Stronsay Fishmart (☎ 616386; Whitehall; dm £10; ✗) This 10-bed hostel, in Stronsay's old herring station, is clean, no-frills and well-run but lacking homely touches; linen is a pricey £3 extra and there's a café on-site. It's right next to the ferry dock.

Stronsay Hotel (☎ 616213; www.stronsayhotel .com; Whitehall; s/d from £25/50; wheelchair access; P ✗) The Stronsay Hotel has immaculate refurbished rooms, with recommended pub grub in the stay-for-another bar, with the seafood particularly succulent. Walkers will be satisfied by the packed lunches on offer, too.

Flights from Kirkwall (£31 one-way, 10 to 30 minutes, two daily Monday to Saturday) are operated by BA/Loganair.

Orkney Ferries links Stronsay with Kirkwall (person/car £11.60/26.20 return, 1½ hours, two daily) and Eday (passenger/car £5.80/13.10 return, 35 minutes, one Monday, Wednesday, Thursday, Friday and Saturday).

Eday

☎ 01857 / pop 121

Northwest of Stronsay and only 8 miles long, Eday has a hilly centre and cultivated fields around its coast. Occupied for at least the last 5000 years, Eday has numerous chambered cairns, and also one of Orkney's most impressively located standing stones, the **Stone of Setter**.

Eday's favourite yarn concerns the pirate John Gow, who made a dog's breakfast of a raiding expedition on the local laird's mansion, Carrick House, in 1725. After running his ship aground, his men got pissed at the local and he ended up hanged dockside in London for his efforts.

It's worth getting hold of the *Eday Heritage Walk* leaflet, which details an interesting four-hour ramble from the Eday shop near the ferry pier to the sandstone **Red Head** in the island's north.

Eday SYHA Hostel (☎ 622206; www.syha.org.uk; London Bay; dm £8; ☺ Apr-Sep; P ✗) The Eday SYHA Hostel is a simple place set in a renovated wooden building that is halfway between a church hall and a barracks. The facilities are minimal; you'll need your own sleeping bag. The site is 4 miles north of the ferry on the Bay of London at the waist of the island.

Skaill (☎ 622271; Skaill; DB&B per person £32; ☺ closed Apr-mid May; P ✗) A warm, friendly and comfortable working sheep farm at Skaill, near the church. Mrs Cockram's meals are also good and there's plenty of bird-watching advice freely offered.

BA/Loganair flies from Kirkwall (£31 one-way, 30 minutes, two flights every Wednesday only) to London airport – that's London in Eday. The ferry service from Kirkwall sails via Stronsay (return passenger/car £11.60/26.20, 1½ hours, two daily). There's also a link between Sanday and Eday.

Sanday

☎ 01857 / pop 478

This island is aptly named, for the best **beaches** in Orkney are here – dazzling white sand of the sort you'd expect in the Caribbean. The island is 12 miles long and almost entirely flat, apart from the cliffs at **Spurness**. There are several archaeological sites, the most impressive being the **Quoyness Chambered Tomb**, similar to Maes Howe, dating from the 3rd millennium BC.

Quivals Rest (☎ 841700; www.quivals.co.uk; Quivals; s/d from £17/28; P ✗ 🖳) A great place for an active family, this all-in-one B&B offers a multitude of things such as bike hire, car hire, and canoeing. They'll pick you up from the ferry, and there's a small on-site craft and book shop.

BA/Loganair flies from Kirkwall (£31 one-way, 20 minutes, two Monday to Saturday) to Sanday and Westray. Orkney Ferries operates a service between Kirkwall and Sanday (person/car £11.60/26.20 return, 1½ hours, two daily, May to mid-September). There's also a link to Eday.

Westray

☎ 01857 / pop 563

Remote but well-loved by those who visit, Westray is perhaps the most interesting of the Northern Isles, with its varied attractions that include fertile farmland, prehistoric sites, some sandy beaches, impressive cliff scenery and the ruins of the 6th-century **Noltland Castle** (a fortified Z-plan house). It's also famous for the **Noup Head RSPB Reserve**, in the northwest, which attracts tens of thousands of breeding seabirds each year, including a sizeable posse of puffins.

In the north, **Pierowall**, the main village and one of the best natural harbours in Orkney, was once an important Viking base. Ferries from Kirkwall dock at Rapness, about 7 miles south of Pierowall.

SLEEPING & EATING

The Barn (☎ 677214; www.thebarnwestray.com; Chalmersquoy; tent sites £3, dm £11.75; wheelchair access; P ✗) This attractive and intimate hostel is one of the Orkneys' best. With a cosy TV lounge, bike hire, plenty of facilities and local advice, and clean comfortable dorms, you'd be forgiven for forgetting that you were in budget accommodation.

Bis Geos Hostel (☎ 677420; www.bis-geos.co.uk; Bis Geos; dm £10; ☺ Apr-Oct; P ✗ 🖳) This renovated farmhouse is another spectacularly good hostel, and boasts some tremendous views over the sea. It's about 2 miles west of Pierowall, and has a well-equipped kitchen. The owners also run some self-catering cottages and hire bikes.

Pierowall Hotel (☎ 677472; pierowall.hotel@btopenworld.com; r per person £20-38; P) Without the grand old architecture of some of the island hotels, this central gathering place is nevertheless a classic in its own meal-times. Famed for its high-quality fish and chips, it's also a convivial local and has reasonable B&B accommodation.

GETTING THERE & AWAY
For information on flights see Sanday, p929. Orkney Ferries link Kirkwall with Rapness on Westray (person/car £11.60/26.20 return, 1½ hours, two daily) and Papa Westray.

Papa Westray
☎ 01857 / pop 65
This exquisitely peaceful island, known simply as Papay ('papee'), is just 4 miles long and a mile wide. Nevertheless, the island attracts plenty of superlatives – Europe's oldest domestic building is the **Knap of Howar** (built about 5500 years ago), the world's shortest scheduled flight is the two-minute hop across Papa Sound from Westray, and the largest colony of Arctic terns in Europe is at **North Hill**. Papa Westray was also the cradle of Christianity in Orkney – the restored **St Boniface Kirk** was founded in the 8th century and impresses visitors with its fine restored 12th-century stonework and ancient emanations.

At Beltane, just over a mile north from the ferry, **Beltane Guest House** (☎ 644267; papaybeltane2@hotmail.com; dm £10, s/d £27/50; ✗) is an excellent hostel-cum-hotel and the best place to stay on the island. There are clean and comfortable dorms, as well as simple but spanking new and more than adequate en-suite rooms. There are sizeable lunches and dinners on offer, using local beef, seafood, lamb, and vegetables. There's also a shop here.

Flying to the island of Papa Westray (£15, 15 minutes, two daily Monday to Saturday) or North Ronaldsay (£15, 25 minutes, two daily except for three on Wednesday and one on Sunday) from Kirkwall is an amazing deal compared to other flights in Orkney – about twice the distance for half the price.

There's a private passenger-only **ferry** (☎ 677216) from Pierowall on Westray to Papa Westray (£5.40, 25 minutes, three to six daily) operating from May to September. Orkney Ferries also has a service from Kirkwall (person/car £11.60/26.20 return, two hours, one on Tuesday and Friday).

North Ronaldsay
☎ 01857 / pop 70
Pity the poor sheep on this remote, windswept island – they're kept off the rich farmland by a wall and forced to feed mostly on seaweed, which is said to give their meat a unique flavour.

North Ronaldsay is only 3 miles long, 1 mile wide and almost completely flat. The island is an important stopover point for migratory birds.

Observatory Guest House (☎ 633200; www.nrbo .f2s.com; dm £10, s/d £31/51; P ✗ 🖳) This guesthouse in the southwest offers excellent solar and wind-powered accommodation on a working croft. It's especially designed for bird-watchers, for whom various activities can be organised. There are dorm rooms as well as en-suite twins and doubles; dinner is available for an extra £9.

See Papa Westray (left) for details of flights. Orkney Ferries operates a service from Kirkwall (person/car £11.60/26.20 return, 2¾ hours, one on Friday only, plus every second Sunday from late May to August).

SHETLAND ISLANDS

Lovers of wild and desolate places should make a beeline for the Shetlands, way out in the North Sea. The nearest mainland town is Bergen in Norway, and the place sometimes seems to have more in common with Norse lands than British ones. There's a distinct Scandinavian lilt to the local accent, and walking down streets named King Haakon or St Olaf recalls the fact that the Shetlands were under Norse rule until 1469 when they were gifted to Scotland as part of a Danish princess' dowry.

Their remote location is belied by the activity and charisma of Lerwick, the capital, causing you to forget the hundred plus oceanic miles between you and mainland Scotland. Once outside the humming capital, however, the isolation sweeps you off your feet, as frequent thundering gales snarl across the raw landscape, which is virtually treeless.

The archipelago consists of more than 100 islands, only 15 of which are inhabited. The largest island – rather inaccurately named Mainland – houses, as well as Lerwick, the international airport at Sumburgh

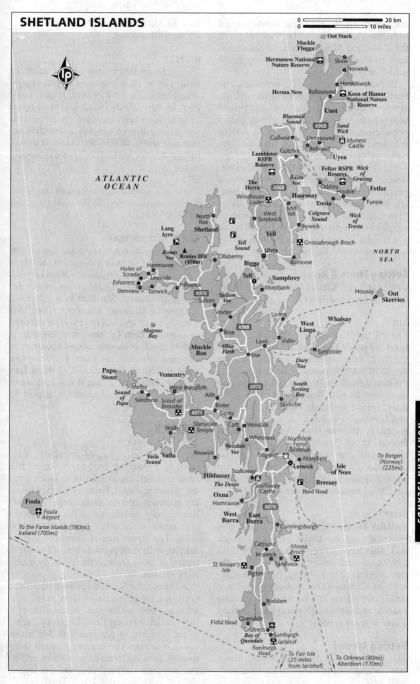

SHETLAND ISLANDS

0 ——— 20 km
0 ——— 10 miles

ATLANTIC OCEAN

Out Stack

Muckle Flugga

Hermaness National Nature Reserve

Skaw
Norwick

Haroldswick

Herma Ness
Baltasound
Keen of Hamar National Nature Reserve

Unst

Bluemull Sound

A968

Sand Wick

Cullivoe
Uyeasound
Muness Castle
Gutcher
Belmont

Uyea

Lumbister RSPB Reserve

Feltar RSPB Reserve
Oddsta
Houbie
Wick of Gruting

The Herra
A968

Basta Voe

Hascosay

Tresta
Fetlar
Funzie

Windhouse Lodge

West Sandwick
Mid Yell

Colgrave Sound
Aywick
Wick of Tresta

North Roe
Shetland

Yell Sound

Yell

Ulsta

Grossabrough Broch

NORTH SEA

Lang Ayre

Ronas Voe
Hamnavoe
Ronies Hill (450m)
Ollaberrry

Bigga

Burravoe

Holes of Scrada
Leascole
Eshaness
Stenness
Tanwick
Hillswick

Toft
Samphrey

Mossbank

Housay
Out Skerries

Sullom

Sullom Voe

Voxter

Lunna

West Linga

Whalsay

St Magnus Bay

Brae

A968

Muckle Roe

Olna Firth
Voe
Laxo
Vidlin

Symbister

Dury Voe

Papa Stour

Vementry

West Burrafirth
Aith

South Nesting Bay

Skellister

Melby
Sandness
Scord of Brouster

Sound of Papa

A971
Bixter
Tresta

Foula
Foula Airport

*To the Faroe Islands (180mi);
Iceland (700mi)*

Walls

Stanydale Temple
Cott
Weisdale
Whiteness

A970

Reawick

Weisdale Voe

Northlink Ferry Terminal

Tingwall
Maryfield
Isle of Noss

Vaila

Vaila Sound

Hildassay

Scalloway
Lerwick

The Deeps

Oxna
Hamnavoe

Scalloway Castle
Bressay
Bard Head

West Burra
East Burra

A970

Cunningsburgh

To Bergen (Norway) (225mi)

Catpund

Mousa Broch

Hoswick
Sandwick

St Ninian's Isle
Bigton

Boddam

Fitful Head
Quendale

Bay of Quendale
Grutness
Sumburgh
Jarlshof
Sumburgh Head

To Fair Isle (25 miles from Jarlshof)

To Orkneys (80mi); Aberdeen (170mi)

and two of Shetland's finest archaeological sites, the stony ruins of Jarlshof village in the south, and Mousa Broch, off the south-western coast – Scotland's most complete Iron-Age tower.

Hundreds of species of birds reside along Shetland's coastline (check out the website at www.wildlife.shetland.co.uk) and people converge to see the 250,000-strong puffin population, as well as the teeming seabird colonies, which breathe life into the fore-boding cliffs.

Shetland is the base for the North Sea oil-fields. Oil has brought a certain amount of prosperity to the islands: visitors will ben-efit from some impressively located places to stay, including *böds*, an excellent series of simple hostels (www.camping-bods.com); you'll usually need a sleeping bag, stove, and coins to feed the electric meter.

Getting There & Away

Unlike Orkney, Shetland is expensive to get to from mainland Britain.

AIR

The oil industry ensures that air connec-tions are good. The main airport is at Sum-burgh, 25 miles south of Lerwick. **BA/Logan Air** (☎ 01595-840246; www.ba.com) operates flights to/from Aberdeen (from £165 return, one hour, two to four daily). You can also fly direct from Edinburgh, Glasgow, Inverness and London as well as Oslo in Norway, op-erated by **Widerøe** (www.wideroe.no). **Highland Airways** (☎ 0845 450 2245; www.highlandairways.co.uk) also runs flights from Inverness. BA/Loga-nair also operates a low-flying turboprop aircraft between Orkney and Shetland (from £85.20, 40 minutes, one daily).

BOAT

Northlink Ferries (☎ 01856-851144; www.northlink ferries.co.uk) runs car ferries between Lerwick and Aberdeen (passenger single £19.25 to £29.50, car and driver £100 to £135 single, cabins extra, 12 to 15 hours, daily) via Kirk-wall; see Getting There & Away (p916). For details of the ferry link between the Shetland Islands and Bergen (Norway) see Getting There & Away (p966).

Getting Around

The invaluable *Shetland Transport Time-table*, available from the TIC and the airport, lists all local connections and costs £1 – a sound investment.

BICYCLE

If it's fine, cycling on the islands' excellent roads can be an exhilarating way to experi-ence Shetland's stark beauty. It can, how-ever, be very windy (wind speeds of up to 194mph have been recorded!) and shelter is scarce. Eric Brown upstairs at **Grantfield Ga-rage** (see map p933; ☎ 01595-692709; North Rd, Lerwick), hires out bikes for £7.50/45 per day/week.

BUS

There are several bus operators available; for information on all their services call ☎ 01595-694100.

CAR & MOTORCYCLE

Shetland's wide roads seem like motorways after driving Orkney's narrower, winding lanes. There are car rental offices in Lerwick and at the airport where prices are similar across the board. **Star Rent-A-Car** (☎ 692075; 22 Commercial Rd, Lerwick, & Sumburgh airport) is a friendly outfit and will have you on the road in minutes. **Bolts Car Hire** (☎ 01595-693636; 26 North Rd, Lerwick) is another sound operator; its cheapest vehicles cost around £56 for two days, including insurance. Call **Allied Taxis** (☎ 01595-690069) for a cab; it will cost about £35 travelling from Sumburgh airport to Lerwick.

LERWICK

☎ 01595 / pop 6830

Lerwick, the only place of any size in Shet-land, is a buzzing harbour town with a lively feel, defying its relative isolation from the rest of Scotland. Grand Victorian hous-ing abounds and its main shopping street is mercifully mostly free of the chain stores that make every other British town look alike. The street names themselves are a delight, with such gems as Pirate Lane and, typical of the Scandinavian feel of the place, King Haakon St.

Although the Shetland Islands have been occupied for several thousand years, Ler-wick was only established in the 17th cen-tury. Dutch herring fleets began to shelter in the harbour, in preference to Scalloway, which was then the capital. A small com-munity grew up to trade with them and by the late-19th century this was the largest

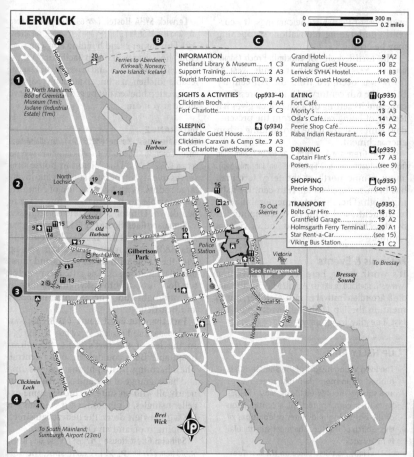

LERWICK

herring town in northern Europe. Today, it's the main port of entry into the Shetlands and transit point to the North Sea oil rigs and a great place to hang about and watch the boats come and go.

Information
Shetland Library (☎ 693868; Lower Hillhead; 10am-7pm Mon, Wed & Fri, 10am-5pm Tue, Thu & Sat) Free Internet access.

Support Training (☎ 695026; 6a Mounthooly St; 9am-1pm & 2-5pm Mon-Fri) Internet access at £2 per hour.

TIC (☎ 693434; www.visitshetland.com; Market Cross; 8am-6pm Mon-Fri, 8am-4pm Sat & Sun Apr-Oct, 9am-5pm Mon-Fri Nov-Mar) Bureau de change and excellent range of books, maps and brochures.

Sights & Activities
Above the town, there are good views of Lerwick's ferries chugging across the harbour, and the island of Bressay from the battlements of **Fort Charlotte** (admission free; 9.30am-dusk), although there's not much to see in the fort itself. It was built in 1653 by troops from the Cromwellian fleet. It now provides the headquarters for the Territorial Army.

Drop into **Shetland Museum** (☎ 695057; www .shetland-museum.org.uk; Lower Hillhead; admission free; 10am-7pm Mon, Wed & Fri, 10am-5pm Tue, Thu & Sat) for an introduction to the island's 5000-year history. Inside are terrific exhibits on Shetland's fishing heritage, along with medieval pottery, grisly human remains and fine examples of Pictish stone carvings. It's currently undergoing renovation, so opening may be erratic.

The fortified site of **Clickimin Broch** (admission free; ☼ 24 hr), about half a mile west of town, was occupied from the 7th century BC to the 6th century AD. It's impressively large and its setting on a small loch gives it a feeling of being removed from the present-day – unusual given the surrounding urban encroachment.

Böd of Gremista Museum (☎ 695057; admission free; ☼ 10am-1pm & 2-5pm Wed-Sun Jun–mid-Sep), about a mile north of the ferry terminal, has been restored as an 18th-century fishing booth. There's a lot of memorabilia and an authentic feel to the place, compounded by the chatty old salt who shows visitors around.

Festivals & Events

It's worth being here for the **Folk Festival** (www.sffs.shetland.co.uk) in April/May, or the **Fiddle & Accordion Festival** in mid-October, not to mention the Up Helly Aa knees-up on the last Tuesday in January.

UP HELLY AA!!!

The long Viking history of the Shetlands has rubbed off in more than just street names and square-shouldered locals. Most villages have their own fire festival, a continuation of the old Viking midwinter celebrations of the rebirth of the sun. The most spectacular is in Lerwick.

Up Helly Aa takes place on the last Tuesday in January. Squads of 'guizers' dress in Viking costume and march through the streets with blazing torches, dragging a replica longship, which they then surround and burn, bellowing out Viking songs from behind bushy beards.

Sleeping

BUDGET

Clickimin Caravan & Camp Site (☎ 741000; Lochside; tent sites £6.20; ☼ May-Sep; P ☺) Well-equipped, small, and tidy, this campsite is located near the broch of the same name near the loch. A path behind the complex takes you up into the hills for fine views over Lerwick. Adjacent is a large sports facility, which includes a swimming pool.

Lerwick SYHA Hostel (☎ 692114; www.syha.org.uk; King Harald St; dm £11; ☼ Apr-Sep; wheelchair access; ☒) This rather grand building houses a spacious hostel with modern facilities. With a shop, laundry, café and a small but serviceable kitchen, it's understandably popular and is often booked out by groups, so reserve ahead if you can.

MID-RANGE

Carradale Guest House (☎ 692251; carradale@bush internet.com; 36 King Harald St; r without/with en suite per person £22/25; ☒) This Victorian house preserves plenty of period style in its lovely large rooms. With a concoction of comforts and amiable hosts, it makes a fine place to bed down. Dinner is available on request.

Kumalang Guest House (☎ 695731; kumalang@aol.com; 89 St Olaf St; s/d from £24/40) The rooms in this B&B are guaranteed to cheer you up with their colourful duvet covers and miss-breakfast mattresses. The attic room on the top floor is best, with a skylight beaming in the midnight sun. The welcome is cheery and heartfelt.

Fort Charlotte Guest House (☎ 692140; www.fortcharlotte.co.uk; 1 Charlotte St; s/d from £20/45; ☒) In the lee of the fort's walls, this ultra-hospitable B&B couldn't be more central. The charming hosts put their guests first and have a range of fine and cheerful rooms, nearly all with en suite, including some excellent singles. Grab Room 4 if you can – it has a great view down the pedestrian street, a sloping roof, and an Oriental theme.

Solheim Guest House (☎ 695275; 34 King Harald St; s/d from £22/40; P ☒) A cosy spot, the Solheim offers a genuine welcome and a filling breakfast. The rooms, which are mostly en-suite, have plenty of facilities and seem larger than they are. Dinner available on request.

Grand Hotel (☎ 695788; www.kgqhotels.co.uk; 24 Commercial St; s/d £65/90; ☼ year-round except 1st 2 weeks of Jan; P) This imposing Victorian hotel certainly lives up to its name, with plush varnished staircases that recall the pre-aviation days when ports were the centres of the international world. There's a warm feel to both décor and service, and the rooms have plenty of character, especially those with sea views. There's a babysitting service, a good restaurant and the island's only nightclub, open on Friday nights and charmingly named Posers.

Eating & Drinking

In recent years the eating options in Lerwick have improved immensely although, like the islands themselves, prices can seem closer to Norway than Scotland.

Peerie Shop Café (☎ 692817; Esplanade; light meals from £3; ☺ 9am-6pm Mon-Sat; ✗) With its trim, industrial décor and sociable outdoor terrace, this café is as close as Lerwick comes to stylish. There are soups, sandwiches, a great carrot cake and proper strong espressos.

Raba (☎ 695585; 26 Commercial Rd; mains £6-9; ☺ midday-midnight Sat & Sun) Although the décor is a bit suspect, with token Indian knick-knacks and dodgy wallpaper, this restaurant does an excellent and well-priced selection of curries. On Sunday there's an all-day buffet. Takeaway is also available.

Fort Café (☎ 693125; 2 Commercial Rd; fish & chips £2.50-3.50) Unusually for a fishing port, Lerwick lacks a decent seafood restaurant. This fish bar is the next best thing though, with excellent haddock suppers with chunky chips. Although there's a small dining area, if the evening's fine, take 'em down to the harbour and watch the boats bobbing on the water.

Monty's (☎ 696555; 5 Mounthooly St; lunch mains £5-8, dinner mains £10-16; ☺ lunch Tue-Sat, dinner Mon-Sat; ✗) This intimate bistro is Lerwick's classiest option and a comfortable space indeed with its stone walls and floorboards imparting a cosy feel. There's a small menu that focuses on Scottish produce, with a fair amount of imagination used in certain ensembles. Lunch is better value than dinner.

Osla's Café (☎ 696005; 88 Commercial St; meals £5-11; ☺ noon-8pm Mon-Sat, & Sun Jun-Aug; ✗) This sparky little joint serves scrumptious sweet and savoury pancakes and whopping toasted sandwiches; for more substantial fare, head upstairs for pizzas, pastas and steaks.

Captain Flint's (☎ 692249; 2 Commercial Rd; ☺ daily) Comfortably Lerwick's best pub, this upstairs den might deceive you into thinking you're on a ship after a couple of whiskies. It's convivial with a mix of all-comers and has views out over the harbour.

Shopping

Shetland is world-famous for its woollen jerseys, cardigans and sweaters.

Judane (☎ 693724; ☺ 9am-5pm Mon-Fri) A no-frills factory shop on the industrial estate north past the power station, a mile from

town. It sells plain sweaters from £10 and patterned ones from £15.

Peerie Shop (☎ 892817; Esplanade; ☺ 9am-6pm Mon-Sat) One of the island's best souvenir shops, with plenty of woollens, attractive ceramics and innovative knick-knacks and postcards.

Getting There & Away

See Getting There & Away under Shetland Islands (p932) for details on ferries to Orkney and Aberdeen. From the main airport at Sumburgh, **Leask's** (☎ 693162) runs regular buses to meet flights (50 minutes), although you may wait a while on Sunday, when there are only two services.

AROUND LERWICK

Two islands lie across the water from Lerwick: **Bressay** (pronounced Bressah), and beyond it the National Nature Reserve of the **Isle of Noss**, which is well worth visiting to see seabirds nesting on its 180m-high cliffs.

From the dock below Fort Charlotte in Lerwick, there are **ferries** (☎ 07626-980317) to Maryfield on Bressay (person/car £3/6.80, seven minutes, frequent). It's then a 2½-mile walk across the island; some people bring rented bikes from Lerwick.

An inflatable dinghy shuttles between Bressay and the Isle of Noss (£3, 10am to 5pm Tuesday, Wednesday and Friday to Sunday mid-May to August). Check with the TIC before leaving Lerwick as the Noss dinghy doesn't operate in bad weather.

Six miles west of Lerwick, **Scalloway** (Scallowah), the former capital of Shetland, is a busy fishing village with the spooky and largely intact ruins of **Scalloway Castle** (HS; ☎ 01886-841815; admission free; ☺ 9.30am-5pm Mon-Sat, key from Royal Hotel on Sun), built in 1600, rising above the warehouses of the port. The small **Scalloway Museum** (☎ 880675; Main St; admission free; ☺ Mon-Sat May-Sep) nearby is interesting for its displays on the 'Shetland Bus', the boats that the Norwegian resistance operated from Scalloway during WWII. Buses run from Lerwick 11 times daily, Monday to Saturday.

SOUTH MAINLAND
Sandwick & Around
☎ 01950 / pop 800

Opposite the scattered village of Sandwick, where you pass the 60-degree latitude line, is the small isle of Mousa, an RSPB reserve, on which stands the impressive double-walled fortified tower **Mousa Broch**. The best-preserved broch in Britain, it was built between 100 BC and AD 100. There are daily boat trips (£9, 15 minutes), allowing 2½ hours on the island from April to September. Phone **Tom & Cynthia Jamieson** (☎ 01950-431367; www.mousaboattrips.co.uk) in advance for reservations.

There are five to seven buses daily (three on Sunday) between Lerwick and Sandwick.

Sumburgh & Around
☎ 01950

At the southern tip of Mainland, this village is the location of the international airport and **Jarlshof** (HS; ☎ 01667-460232; adult £3.30; ☯ 9.30am-12.30pm & 1.30-6.30pm Apr-Sep), Shetland's most impressive archaeological attraction. This prehistoric and Norse settlement was hidden under the sand until exposed by a gale at the turn of the 20th century. It's a thought-provoking place, mainly in ruins, but with a fascinating intact wheelhouse which has defied time. You should buy the short guide, which interprets the ruins (otherwise a fair bit of imagination is required), from a number of vantage points.

Near Jarlshof you can visit **Sumburgh Head** where large colonies of puffins, kittiwakes, fulmars, guillemots and razorbills nest. It's also not a bad location to spot dolphins and whales. Five miles northwest of Sumburgh is the hamlet of Scousburgh, below which is Shetland's best beach, the gloriously white Scousburgh Sands. You can camp here by permission from the landowner (☎ 460742).

Sumburgh Hotel (☎ 460201; www.sumburgh-hotel .zetnet.co.uk; s/d from £45/60; [P]) This is a large pub and hotel right by Jarlshof and very handy for the airport. The bar meals vary in quality, but the daily specials are usually plentiful and tasty. It organises loads of activities, including fishing, cycling and pony-trekking.

To get here from Lerwick take the airport bus (50 minutes, five daily Monday to Saturday, two on Sunday) and get off at the second-last stop.

NORTH MAINLAND
The red, basalt lava cliffs of Eshaness, in the Mainland's northwest, form some of the most impressively wild coastal scenery in Scotland. Howling Atlantic gales whip the ocean into a whitecap frenzy, before smashing into the base of the cliffs, carving them into weird formations. When the winds subside, this is good walking country. **Johnnie Notions Camping Böd** (☎ 08701 999 440; dm £5; ☯ Apr-Sep) at nearby Hamnavoe offers very basic dorm accommodation in a small stone cottage with large bunks but no electricity. Book at the Lerwick TIC or by phone.

The **Tangwick haa Museum** (☎ 01806-503389; admission free; ☯ 1-5pm Mon-Fri, 11am-7pm Sat & Sun May-Sep) captures a sense of the community here, mainly through its wonderful collection of ancient black-and-white photos.

Buses from Lerwick (three Monday to Friday, two on Saturday) run as far as Hillswick, 7 miles from Eshaness. A mile short of here, signalled by a puffin signpost, you'll strike **Almara** (☎ 01806-503261; www.almara.shetland.co.uk; s/d £22/44; [P] [✗]). You'll be hard-pressed to find a better B&B in Scotland. The rooms are fantastic – one has a reclinable massage bed, another a private bathroom with honeymoon-style Jacuzzi – but the welcome is even more memorable. You'll feel completely at home and appreciated, whether chatting over breakfast in the wooden conservatory with views to kill for, or strumming a guitar in the spacious lounge. Ask about the Italian bubble-bath disaster!

The **Booth Vegetarian Restaurant & Café** (☎ 01806-503348; ☯ May-Sep) serves vegetarian food in a hippy crofters house. Incredibly, there's no bill – you're asked to put a donation in a box, all of which gets donated to the local wildlife sanctuary.

Near Brae, 11 miles back along the Lerwick road, **Busta House Hotel** (☎ 01806-522506; www.bustahouse.com; s/d £75/100; [P] [✗]), is a luxurious, genteel country-house hotel, visible for miles with its step gables and whitewashed walls. The renovated rooms are a little bland but undeniably comfortable, and there's a fine restaurant, which offers four-course dinners for £30.

YELL & UNST
☎ 01957 / pop 720

Yell is a desolate, heather-covered peat moor, but there are some good coastal and hill walks. **Windhouse Lodge** (☎ 0870 199 9440, 702231; dm £5; ☯ Apr-Sep) is a charming stonebuilt *böd* in the centre of the island below the haunted ruins of **Windhouse**. Book at the Lerwick TIC and take plenty of 50p coins to operate the electricity and hot-water meter.

Pinewood (☎ 702427; South Aywick; s/d £22/44; P X) has the comforts of home in a laid-back house overlooking the islands of Fetlar, Unst and Skerries. Dinner can be arranged with advance notice, and there's a shop next door.

Unst is the northernmost part of Britain. Fittingly, its northernmost point is a wonderfully wild and windy nature reserve, **Hermaness**, where you can sit on the cliffs, commune with the puffins and gaze across the sea into the Arctic Circle. Robert Louis Stevenson wrote *Treasure Island* while living on Unst – his uncle built the lighthouse on **Muckle Flugga**, a rock near Hermaness. There are several accommodation options, among them the excellent **Gardiesfauld Hostel** (☎ 755240; www.gardiesfauld.shetland.co.uk; 2 East Rd, Uyeasound; dm £10; ☺ Apr-Sep; wheelchair access; P X) which has modern facilities, a lounge, campsite, and bikes for rent.

Yell and Unst are connected with Mainland by small car **ferries** (☎ 722259) operating between Toft and Ulsta (car and driver/passenger £6.80/3, 20 minutes, frequent) as well as Gutcher and Belmont (car and driver/passenger £3.40/1.50, 10 minutes, frequent).

OTHER ISLANDS

Fetlar, where there's an RSPB reserve, is connected to the islands of Yell and Unst (car and driver/passenger £6.80/3, 25 minutes,

six to eight daily) by regular **ferries** (☎ 01957-722259).

West of Shetland is **Foula**, a windy island supporting a community of 40 people, 1500 sheep and 500,000 seabirds amid dramatic cliff scenery. It's reached by twice-weekly ferries from Walls (person/car single £2.60/12, two hours), and planes from Tingwall (£25 single, 15 minutes, four weekly)

Fair Isle is Britain's most remote, inhabited island. It's known for its patterned knitwear, still produced here in the island's cooperative; it's also a bird-watcher's paradise. Twenty-four miles from Sumburgh and only 3 miles by 1½ miles in size, it was given to the NTS in 1954. The **Fair Isle Lodge & Bird Observatory** (☎ 01595-760258; www.fairislebirdobs .co.uk; dm £30, s/d £42/74; P X) offers full-board accommodation with guided bird walks included. Locals also offer rooms with meals; try the peaceful **Mrs Coull** (☎ 01595-760248; kathleen .coull@lineone.net; B&B per person £22-24; P X) in a great old building in Schoolton.

From Tingwall, BA/Loganair operates flights to Fair Isle (from £28 single, 25 minutes, twice on Monday, Wednesday, Friday year-round and on Saturday May to September). A day return-trip allows about seven hours on the island. Ferries sail from Grutness (near Sumburgh) with the odd one from Lerwick to Fair Isle (person/car single £2.60/12, three hours, one on Tuesday and Saturday year-round and Thursday from May to September). Book with **JW Stout** (☎ 01595-760222).

The Channel Islands

CONTENTS

Jersey	941
Guernsey	942
Herm	943
Alderney	943
Sark	944

Just 7½ miles from France, the Channel Islands are an odd little corner of Britain, an ideal spot for a holiday from a holiday. There's a vaguely tropical feel here, which meshes nicely with the nexus of English and French culture and the storied background of the place. White, sandy beaches, rugged coastal walks and an embarrassment of flowers make the islands a relaxing place to visit; at the same time, the rich political and military history adds interest for history buffs. Best of all, the islands are just French enough to seem exotic and foodie-friendly, but not so much as to intimidate Francophobes.

Though British, the Bailiwicks of Jersey and Guernsey are administered locally; the latter includes Alderney, Sark and Herm. Jersey and Guernsey, the largest and most accessible islands, specialise in excellent seafood and easy coastal walks and are primarily the fresh-scrubbed holiday realm of pensioners and families with young children. The three smaller islands, each attractively frozen at a different point in time, are more remote and sparsely populated, with distinct landscapes and atmospheres.

The Channel Islands have low tax rates and no VAT. They print their own currency; it's exchangeable on a par with the British pound, but you can't use it in the rest of the UK. Similarly, posting mail from the islands requires local stamps.

HIGHLIGHTS

- Cycling the unlit night-time paths around fiercely rustic **Sark** (p944)
- Exploring the footpaths that wander up, down and all around the jagged coast of **Guernsey** (p942)
- Pretending you're an exiled writer – a really wealthy, eccentric one – at **Victor Hugo's house** (p942)
- Taking a holiday from your holiday by walking the circumference of tranquil **Herm** (p943)
- Enjoying a bird-watching boat trip around the wild island of **Alderney** (p943)
- Redefining your expectations at the progressive **Jersey Zoo** (p941)

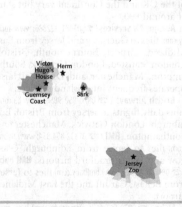

- POPULATION 162,000
- AREA: 120 SQ MILES

THE CHANNEL ISLANDS

History

Once part of the continental mainland, the land masses that are now the Channel Islands separated following the Ice Age. Evidence of Neolithic settlements has been found, and the Romans used the islands as trading posts. Strategically important because of their location, they are thronged with military souvenirs from various eras.

Until 1066 the islands were part of Normandy; they became part of the English kingdom when William of Normandy (aka 'William the Conqueror') was crowned the king of England. They were used as sparring grounds until 1483, when England and France agreed that the territory would remain neutral in the event of war. Then, in 1939, this happy-go-lucky resort suddenly found itself the only British soil to be occupied by German forces during WWII. This harsh period of Channel Islands history is well represented in various sights, including the many German fortifications still remaining.

Transport

GETTING THERE & AWAY
Air

Jersey and Guernsey are the main points of entry; Jersey's airport is larger and busier than Guernsey. There is no passport control between the UK, the Republic of Ireland and the Channel Islands.

Return-trip fares to the islands from London on the following airlines range from £49 to £300. Fares from other parts of the UK and the Continent vary but start at around £90.

Aurigny Air Services (☎ 01481-822886; www.aurigny.com) flies to Guernsey and Jersey from East Midlands airport, Bournemouth, Bristol, London Stansted, London Gatwick, Southampton, Manchester and Dinard. It also operates frequent inter-island services.

British Airways (☎ 0870 850 9850; www.ba.com) runs daily flights to Jersey from Bristol, Edinburgh, London Gatwick, Manchester and Southampton. **BMI** (☎ 01332 854 854; www.flybmi.com) flies to Jersey from Edinburgh, Glasgow and Leeds Bradford airports. **BMI baby** (☎ 0870 264 2229; www.bmibaby.com) flies to Jersey from Belfast, Cardiff and the East Midlands airport.

Flybe (☎ 0870 567 6676; www.flybe.com) has frequent routes between Jersey/Guernsey and

CHANNEL ISLANDS

English Channel
Alderney
St Anne
Cherbourg
St Peter Port-Weymouth
Weymouth-St Helier
FRANCE
Guernsey
Herm
St Peter Port
Sark
Carteret
Jersey
St Helier
Passage de la Déroute
Les Minquiers
Îles Chausey
St Malo-Portsmouth
Golfe de St Malo
Baie du Mont St Michel
St Malo

Belfast, Birmingham, Dublin, Edinburgh, Exeter, Glasgow, Isle of Man, London and Southampton. **rockhopper** (☎ 01481-824567; www.rockhopper.aero) operates flights from Bournemouth and frequent inter-island services.

Boat

Condor Ferries (☎ 0845 122 2000; www.condorferries.co.uk) runs daily fast ferries to/from Poole and Weymouth. Return fares between the UK and the islands start at £54 for a foot passenger, £249 for a car and driver. There's also a slow daily ferry from Portsmouth to Guernsey (6½ hours there, 13 hours back) and Jersey (10 hours) – the fares are about the same.

Condor has daily fast ferries to St Malo in France from Guernsey (1¾ hrs, return foot passenger £25, car and two adults £95). Prices are about the same for the return fast-ferry service between Guernsey and Jersey (one hour).

Emeraude (☎ 01481-711414 in Guernsey, 01534-766566 in Jersey; www.emeraude.co.uk; day trips passenger £29, car & driver from £99) also runs ferry services between Jersey and St Malo in France.

JERSEY

☎ 01534 / pop 90,502

The busy capital of Jersey, St Helier, is part vacationland and part high-rolling financial district. Suit-clad guys in shades buzz around in convertibles while, mere feet away, families relax in swimsuits on the beach. Later, everyone meets up to eat in the same fine restaurants. A recommended base is St Aubin, to the southwest, an attractive little string of seafood restaurants fronting a harbour village. The north coast of the island is wilder and more remote, good for walking and cycling.

Orientation & Information

Covering 45 sq miles, the island is roughly rectangular in shape; St Helier is on the south coast.

Jersey Tourism (☎ 500700; www.jersey.com; Liberation Sq, St Helier; ⏰ 8.30am-5.30pm Mon-Fri & 9am-1pm Sat Oct-Apr, 8.30am-5.30pm Mon-Fri & 9am-1pm Sat & Sun Apr-Jun, 8.30am-7pm daily Jun-Oct) is opposite the bus station, a short walk from the ferry terminal.

iPoint (☎ 731 287; ipointfunland@hotmail.com; 25-26 The Esplanade, St Helier; ⏰ 8am-10pm daily; 1hr £3) is an internet cafe in an amusement park.

Sights

Far removed from the cooped-up misery of many zoos, **Jersey Zoo** (☎ 860000; www.durrell .org; Les Augres Manor, Trinity; adult/child £9.95/7.25; ⏰ 9.30am-6pm Apr-Oct, 10am-5pm Nov-Mar; P) is an inspiring place. Founded by writer and naturalist Gerald Durrell, it emphasises the conservation of endangered species. The arrangements allow the inhabitants a remarkable amount of freedom, with monkeys and lemurs roaming a natural wooded environment. The centre breeds endangered animals, releasing them back into the wild, and trains worldwide representatives so they can continue the conservation work. Talks given by enthusiastic keepers are recommended. To get here, take bus No 3A, 3B or 23.

Hulking high up above the small port of Gorey, **Mont Orgueil Castle** (☎ 853292; www.jersey heritagetrust.org; adult/child £5.10/free; ⏰ 10am-6pm daily Apr-Oct, 10am-dusk Mon-Fri Nov-Mar) is the finest of the island's many coastal castles. Although the original construction dates from the 13th century, it was added to over a period of 400 years.

Elizabeth Castle (☎ 723971; St Aubin's Bay; adult/child £5.10/free; ⏰ 10am-6pm Apr-Oct) is worth a visit by virtue of its splendid location, accessible on foot over the causeway or by ferry at high tide.

Captive Island (☎ 860808; www.jerseywartunnels .com; adult £8; ⏰ 9.30am-5.30pm daily Feb-mid-Nov, Sat & Sun mid-Nov-Dec) is an exhibition about the occupation housed in the eerie surroundings of a German underground hospital (built around a network of tunnels hacked out from 1941 to 1945 by slave labourers). Some of the rooms are set up as wards and treatment rooms, while other parts of the chilling tunnels are filled with the sound and flickering light of the compelling exhibition, using film footage and anecdotal accounts to bring Jersey's occupation vividly to life.

Jersey Museum (☎ 633300; The Weighbridge, St Helier; adult/child £5.10/free; ⏰ 10am-5pm Apr-Oct, 10am-4pm Nov-Mar), near the tourist office, has an interesting roundup of the island's history, including carefully restored rooms from an adjoining 19th-century merchant's house (the bedrooms and playroom provide a sharp contrast to the servants' shoeboxes upstairs).

Sleeping & Eating

Jersey Tourism publishes a long list of places to stay and operates a free booking service, **Jerseylink** (☎ 500888). Book ahead in summer.

Longueville Manor (☎ 725501; www.longueville manor.com; Longueville Rd, St Saviour; s/d from £105/210; restaurant mains around £30; P ☒) A stately 13th-century Norman manor house noted for its Michelin-starred restaurant, the Longueville, east of St Helier off the A3, is the island's top hotel. Its opulent rooms, each named after a rose, are decorated with antiques, plush curtains and canopies, and warm, subtle lighting.

Royal Yacht Hotel (☎ 720511; theroyalyacht@mail .com; The Weighbridge, St Helier; r from £45) This hotel, housed in a powder-blue building that almost looks as if it could sail away, claims to be the oldest in St Helier. It's well-located close to Liberation Sq, and its Victorian-with-all-the-modern-fixings rooms have views overlooking the marina.

Old Court House Inn (☎ 746433; St Aubin's Harbour, St Brelade; r £40-240) A fine building dating back to 1450, this hotel has boldly decorated rooms with good views, and there's tasty food available on a lovely flower-laden patio. Excellent food is served in the bistro, the courtyard restaurant and the schooner-shaped Westward Bar, partly made from old ship beams.

Rose Farm Camping (☎ 741231; tent sites from £6.50) This site, in a pretty St Aubin setting, is friendly and also popular with backpackers. To get here, take bus No 14.

Museum Brasserie (☎ 510069; The Weighbridge, St Helier; mains £6-14; ☽ lunch daily, dinner Wed-Sat) This wonderful place attached to the Jersey Museum offers fresh fish and other dishes and spills into a delightful courtyard, with seating among flowerpots and water features.

Suma's (☎ 853291; Gorey Hill, Gorey; mains around £16; ☽ lunch & dinner Mon-Sat, lunch Sun) Small, smart and pale blue, Suma's does Mediterranean-influenced food. There's a little terrace overlooked by Mont Orgueil Castle.

Getting There & Around
Aurigny has daily flights between Jersey and Guernsey (15 minutes) and Alderney (20 minutes). Emeraude and Condor link Jersey and Guernsey as part of their ferry services to mainland destinations (one hour).

Between the airport and St Helier there's a choice of taxi (£8 to £10) or bus (£2, 15 to 45 minutes). Heavy traffic makes car hire potentially unappealing, but it's usually cheap; try **Aardvark/Zebra** (☎ 736556; www .zebrahire.com; 9 Esplanade, St Helier). Hire bikes from **Jersey Cycletours** (☎ 482898; Corbiere Walk, St Aubin).

GUERNSEY
☎ 01481 / pop 65,031
Being in Guernsey is like falling into a giant flowerbox. Everything's in bloom, all year round. Its homey cottages and tropical air encourage a glitz-free version of Caribbean-style relaxation. The capital, St Peter Port, has narrow cobblestone streets winding up and down steep hills to the water's edge. There are a couple of good shopping streets and several upmarket restaurants. Guernsey's chief appeal, though, is at its fringes, where perilous cliffside walking trails reveal dramatic scenery and gentle crescents of beach.

Orientation
Guernsey is two-thirds the size of Jersey, which makes it roughly 9 miles long by 4 miles wide. The Bailiwick of Guernsey includes the smaller islands of Herm (p943), Sark (p944) and Alderney (p943).

Information
Checkers Superstore (☎ 739600; Admiral Park, St Peter Port; ☽ 8.30am-8pm Mon-Thu, 8.30am-9pm Fri, 8am-8pm Sat; Internet access per min 1p) The tourist office has a list of Internet points; this supermarket on the waterfront has new, fast computers.

Guernsey Tourist Board (☎ 723552; www.guernsey touristboard.com; North Plantation, St Peter Port; ☽ 9am-5pm Mon-Fri, 9am-4pm Sat, 9.30am-12.30pm Sun) The helpful tourist office is on the waterfront; there are also information desks at the airport and ferry terminals.

Sights & Activities
Of numerous appealing beaches, **Cobo Bay** is recommended for surfing and northern **Pembroke** for family fun.

St Peter Port is overlooked by sprawling **Castle Cornet** (☎ 721657; adult/child £6/free; ☽ 10am-5pm Apr-Sep), the last Royalist stronghold during the Civil War. It houses several museums, including an enjoyable exhibition on its rollicking history, and covers Guernsey's maritime tradition.

Victor Hugo was exiled from France in 1851 following Napoleon III's coup, living in St Peter Port from 1856 to 1870. His home, **Hauteville House** (☎ 721911; 38 Hauteville; adult/child £5/free, admission by guided tour only; ☽ 10am-noon & 2-5pm Mon-Sat Apr-Jun & Sep, 10am-5pm Mon-Sat Jul & Aug) has been preserved. It's all DIY opulence, with Hugo's larger-than-life personality imprinted on everything: the writer gleefully searched out bric-a-brac and used mundane objects to create all sorts of extraordinary pieces, such as a candelabra made of bobbins. Hugo wrote many towering works in his rooftop glass lookout, including *Les Misérables*.

The **German Military Underground Hospital** (☎ 239100; La Vassalerie Rd, St Andrews; ☽ 2-3pm Sun & Thu Mar & Nov, 2-4pm daily Apr & Oct, 10am-noon & 2-4pm daily May-Jun & Sep, 10am-noon & 2-4.30pm daily Jul-Aug) is the largest underground hospital in the Channel Islands. Like its Jersey counterpart it was built using slave labour, taking 3½ years (although it was in use for only nine months). Unlike the Jersey hospital, this tunnel network has been left a void: it's a frightening, echoing place, with dank walls and vanishing tunnels. The emptiness is a solemn and evocative reminder of the people who worked and died creating the tunnels, as well as the injured soldiers who were brought here. To get here, take bus No 4 or 5.

Far removed from the military, the **Little Chapel** in St Andrews dates from 1914 and is colourfully decorated with local shells and broken pots, giving it a Gaudí-gingerbread concoction effect. The door is always open.

Sleeping

Old Government House Hotel (☎ 724921; www.ogh hotel.com; Ann's Place, St Peter Port; r £70-300; wheelchair access; P ⓦ) The former official residence of the Guernsey governors is a grand hotel with good views of the harbour and the islands of Herm and Sark. The apartmentlike suites are good value. Ask for a room with sea view and balcony.

Le Friquet (☎ 256509; www.lefriquethotel.com; Rue de Friquet, Castel; r from £30; P ✗ ⓦ) For a remote, secret-garden getaway, it's hard to beat Le Friquet, an old restored farmhouse towards the middle of the island with a sculpted garden, duck pond, picnic tables on the lawn and renowned Sunday dinners at the Falcon Carvery Restaurant. Bus schedules are limited, but the hotel offers car hire from £10 a day.

Eating

Le Frégate (☎ 724624; St Peter Port; mains around £12) Considered Guernsey's top restaurant, this fine French restaurant offers formal dining in a country house hotel with panoramic harbour views.

Yacht Inn (☎ 715488; South Esplanade, St Peter Port; pub snacks from £3) At the other end of the spectrum is this lively pub, one of many places around the port catering to the nautical set; it serves good pub grub and gets crowded during sporting events.

Choet Tea Rooms (☎ 246129; Choet Bay, Vale; cakes from £1) A traditional beach café with outdoor tables, this is the place for home-made cakes as well as typical seaside fare such as crab salads.

Getting There & Around

For information on getting to Guernsey by air or boat, see p940.

From the airport to St Peter Port there's a choice of taxi (£9, 15 minutes) or bus (£1, 20 minutes). The information desk at the airport has a handy local bus timetable and map. **Value Rent-a-Car** (☎ 243547; www.value.guern sey.net) has outlets at the airport and harbour.

Quay Cycle Hire (☎ 714146; New Jetty, St Peter Port) rents bicycles; for faster wheels, hire a motorcycle at **Millard & Co** (☎ 720777; www.millards .org; St Peter Port).

HERM

☎ 01481 / pop 97

A 20-minute boat trip from Guernsey, Herm is a tiny, pretty island of white beaches and flower-strewn hills. It's a wheel-free zone: no cars, motorcycles or even bicycles are allowed. Walking its circumference is an extremely pleasant way to spend a couple of hours.

The island has been overseen by the Hayworth family for more than 50 years, but previous occupants included a Prussian count, who tried to establish a wallaby population there, and Compton MacKenzie, author of *Whiskey Galore*, who eventually fled the 'haunted' island.

Sleeping & Eating

Accommodation is booked through the island's **administration office** (☎ 722377; www .herm-island.com).

White House Hotel (☎ 722159; fax 710066; www .herm-island.com; r per person from £67) Upmarket and fairly formal, the White House appeals to a sedate crowd, with its tranquil garden overlooking the bay and rooms with superb views. The adjoining Ship Restaurant has a pretty terrace and decent pub menu (mains from £6).

Mermaid Tavern (☎ 710170; mains from £5) Next to the White House, this pub has a more vivacious atmosphere and serves tasty food in a large, noisy courtyard.

The island also has two beach kiosks.

Getting There & Away

Travel Trident (☎ 721379) runs ferries to Herm from Guernsey (adult £8, 20 minutes, 6 to 8 times daily).

ALDERNEY

☎ 01481 / pop 2400

Alderney is the third largest of the Channel Islands – and still just 3.5 miles by 1.5 miles at its widest point. Home to a relatively isolated community – no ferries serve the island, which puts off day-trippers – Alderney is a charming, friendly place where everyone seems to know each other. The airport even provides a box of knitting to occupy you while you wait for your flight!

A good time to visit is the first week in August, when the carnival and mayhem of the Alderney Week festivities takes place (but book ahead).

Orientation & Information

Most of the population lives in St Anne, a village-sized capital with cobbled streets, less than a mile from the airport.

Alderney Tourism (☎ 823737) shares an office with Alderney Wildlife Trust.

Sights & Activities

Alderney Wildlife Trust (☎ 823737; www.alderney.gov .gg; Victoria St, St Anne; ☺ 10am-noon), the smallest of its kind, has information and guided walks on Alderney's wildlife, including the winsome blonde hedgehog and passing gannets and puffins. The latter may be observed on the recommended two-hour boat trips around the island (around £12); tickets are sold at **Alderney Gift Box** (☎ 823532) or **McAllister's Fish Shop** (☎ 823666), both on Victoria St.

St Anne has a small, friendly **museum** (☎ 823222; ☺ 10am-noon daily & 2-4pm Mon-Fri Apr-Oct) with local history exhibits and relics of the occupation.

Sleeping

Essex Lodge (☎ 823557; Longis Bay; r per person from £35-45) This is a classy guesthouse in a remote location overlooking a little bay; you'll need your own transport if you stay here.

Rose & Crown Hotel (☎ 823414; roseandcrown@al derney.ws; Le Huret; s/d from £40-55) A pub dating from the 18th century in the heart of St Anne, the Rose & Crown has comfortable rooms, good food and an off-license with a carefully curated selection of 500-plus wines, neatly filling all your basic holiday needs at once.

Eating & Drinking

Albert House (☎ 822243; Victoria St; mains around £7) This impressive building, with deep-red walls and big paintings, is a fine focus for the main street – a friendly pub serving top-notch food.

First & Last (☎ 823162; Harbourside; starters £4-6.50; ☺ Tue-Sat, lunch Sun) A local favourite, this homey place has blue-and-white checked tablecloths and a fishy theme that complements its mean bouillabaisse.

Old Barn Restaurant (☎ 822537; Longis Bay; mains £12) Next door to Essex Lodge, this place serves food made with its own organically grown produce.

Getting There & Around

For information on flights to Alderney from Guernsey, Jersey or mainland UK see p940.

Central Cars (☎ 822971; 23 Victoria St, St Anne) rents cars and minimokes (light jeeps), while **Peddle Power** (☎ 822286; Les Rocquettes, St Anne) offers bike hire. For a taxi, call ☎ 823760.

SARK

☎ 01481 / pop 580

Sark is best known as Europe's only remaining feudal state. The seigneur, Michael Beaumont, rules through a constitution dating back to Elizabethan times and contains many anachronisms; eg only the seigneur may keep pigeons. The island is traffic-free; there's no street lighting, and the only engines are attached to tractors. Cycling the dark paths at night is magical – but bring a torch.

Numerous tracks around the coastal cliffs lead to interesting formations such as the Venus Pool, a rock pool visible at low tide. The tourist office has maps and information on walks.

Orientation & Information

Three miles by 1.5 miles, with a beautiful, 30-mile jagged coastline, the island is divided into Sark and Little Sark, which are linked by the isthmus La Coupee.

Sark Tourism (☎ 832345; www.sark.info) is near the ferry dock.

Sleeping & Eating

La Sablonnerie (☎ 832061; fax 832408; r per person £30-85; starters £6-8, mains £12, snacks £4) This hotel on Little Sark is a fine converted farmhouse amid lush gardens, with rustic-yet-grand rooms and a good restaurant and tea garden.

La Moinerie (☎ 832089; r per person £28-38; mains around £10) A traditional Sark stone farmhouse with pretty rooms, this hotel complex set in a wooded valley has a lovely low-beamed bar and restaurant serving huge portions of delicious fresh fish, caught by the owner.

Getting There & Around

Isle of Sark Shipping (☎ 724059; www.sarkshipping .guernsey.net; one-way/day return £14.50/21) is based on Guernsey and offers daily sailings from St Peter Port. **Condor** (☎ 0845 122 2000; www.con dorferries.co.uk) and **Emeraude** (☎ 01534-766566) run day trips from Jersey (both around £37, 45 minutes).

Tractor-pulled luggage carriers meet the ferries; horse-drawn carriages are another transport option. **Avenue Cycle Hire** (☎ 832102; The Avenue) rents bikes.

Directory

Countrywide practical information is given in this Britain Directory. For details on specific areas, flip to the relevant regional chapter.

ACCOMMODATION

Accommodation in Britain is as varied as the sights you visit, and whatever your budget, it's likely to be your main expense. The wide choice – from hip hotels to basic barns, tiny cottages to grand castles – is all part of the attraction, and we make numerous recommendations throughout this book. To help you choose, most Sleeping sections are divided into three per-person price bands: budget (under £20); mid-range (£20 to £50); and top end (over £50).

To save you phoning loads of places or walking the streets, most Tourist Information Centres (TICs) will book accommodation for you. In England and Wales they charge a 10% fee, which is *usually* subtracted from the accommodation price. In Scotland, TICs charge 10% plus around £2 for this service. Most TICs also participate in the Book-A-Bed-Ahead (BABA) scheme, arranging accommodation for the next two nights anywhere in Britain. The charge is around £3 plus the usual 10% deposit.

B&Bs & Guesthouses

The B&B ('bed and breakfast') is a great British institution. Basically you get a room in somebody's house, and at smaller places you'll really feel part of the family. Larger B&Bs may have four or five rooms, and more facilities. 'Guesthouse' is sometimes just another name for a B&B, although they can be larger, with higher rates.

In country areas, your B&B might be in a village or isolated farm; in cities it's usually a suburban house. Wherever, facilities usually reflect price: for around £15 per person you get a simple bedroom and share the bathroom. For around £25 you get extras such as TV or 'hospitality tray' (kettle, cups, tea, coffee), and a private bathroom – either down the hall, or en suite.

B&B prices are usually quoted per person, but based on two people sharing a room. Solo travellers have to search for single rooms, and pay a 20% to 50% premium. Some B&Bs simply won't take single people (unless you pay the full double-room price), especially in summer.

Here are some more B&B tips:

- Advance reservations are always preferred, and are essential during popular periods
- B&Bs that aren't listed with the local tourist board are nearly always cheaper
- If you're on a flexible itinerary, or haven't booked ahead, places with spare rooms hang up a 'Vacancies' sign
- Many B&Bs are nonsmoking, or only allow smoking in the lounge
- If a B&B is full, owners may recommend another place nearby (possibly a private

house taking occasional guests, not in tourist listings)

■ Rates may rise at busy times, and differ from those quoted in this book

■ In cities, some B&Bs are for long-term residents or people on welfare; they don't take passing tourists

■ Most B&Bs cater for walkers and cyclists, but some don't; let them know if you'll be turning up with dirty boots or wheels

■ Some places reduce rates for longer stays (two or three nights); others require a minimum two nights at weekends

■ Most B&Bs serve enormous breakfasts; some also offer packed lunches (around £3) and evening meals (around £10)

■ If you're in a hurry, B&Bs may give a discount for not having breakfast, but this is unusual. Bed-only rates are more common at ferry ports.

■ When booking, check where your B&B actually is. In country areas, postal addresses include the nearest town, which may be 20 miles away! For those on foot, some B&B owners will pick you up by car for a small charge.

Bunkhouses & Camping Barns

A bunkhouse is a simple place to stay, handy for walkers or anyone on a budget in the countryside. They usually have stoves and basic showers, but you provide your sleeping bag, and possibly cooking gear. Most charge £7.50 to £10 per person per night.

Camping barns are even simpler: they're usually converted farm buildings, providing shelter for walkers in country areas. They have sleeping platforms, a cooking area, and basic toilets outside. Take everything you'd need to camp except the tent. Charges are around £4 per person.

Camping

The opportunities for camping in Britain are numerous – great if you're on a tight budget, or simply enjoy fresh air and the great outdoors. In rural areas, camping grounds (called campsites in Britain) range from farmers' fields with a tap and a basic toilet costing around £2 per night, to smarter affairs with hot showers and many other facilities charging £5 or more.

Homestays

Instead of using B&Bs or hotels, another option is to stay at a private house. There's a network of homeowners across Britain with a room or two available for paying guests. It can be a great way to meet locals under their own roof, although many deals are aimed at overseas students staying for several months, while other 'homestays' are effectively exclusive self-catering accommodation. Rates range from £20 per person per night in sub-

---

ACCOMMODATION CONTACTS

An excellent first stop is **Stilwell's** (www.stilwell.co.uk), a massive user-friendly database of accommodation for independent tourists, including holiday cottages, B&Bs, hotels, campsites and hostels. Stillwell's is not a booking agency – once you've found what you want, you deal with the cottage or B&B owner direct – so you don't pay any extra agency fees.

Recommended guidebooks include the annually published *Good Hotel Guide* and the *Which? Good Bed & Breakfast Guide*; both are genuinely independent (hotels have to be good, they can't pay to get in). Back on the web, agencies include **Bed & Breakfast Nationwide** (www.bedandbreakfastnationwide.com) and **Hoseasons Country Cottages** (☎ 01502-502588; www.hoseasons.co.uk). For a great selection of good-value exclusive B&Bs in London, see www.uptownres.co.uk.

For details on hostels contact the **YHA** (☎ 0870 770 8868, 01629-592700; www.yha.org.uk) or **SYHA** (☎ 08701 553255; www.syha.org.uk). The YHA website also covers camping barns. **Independent Backpackers Hostels Scotland** (www.hostel-scotland.co.uk) produces an invaluable free leaflet (available at TICs and hostels) listing over 120 places to stay. The **Independent Hostel Guide** (www.independenthostelguide.co.uk) lists hundreds of hostels all across Britain and beyond, and is by far the best site available. It's also available in book form (£4.95) at hostels or from the website.

If you're planning to camp extensively, it's well worth joining the **Camping & Caravanning Club** (☎ 024-7669 4995; www.campingandcaravanningclub.co.uk), which owns over 90 campsites and lists thousands more in the excellent and invaluable *Big Sites Book* (free to members). Annual membership costs £29 and includes discounted rates on club sites and various other services.

urban houses, up to £100 or more for luxurious options such as manors surrounded by beautiful countryside or castles overlooking the sea. For more ideas see www.homestays.co.uk, www.homestayfinder.com and www.uniquehomestays.com.

Hostels

There are two types of hostel in Britain – those run by the Youth Hostels Association of England & Wales (YHA) and Scottish Youth Hostels Association (SYHA), and independent hostels. There are hostels in rural areas, towns and cities, and they're aimed at all types of traveller – whether you're a backpacker, a long-distance cyclist or touring by car. And you don't have to be young or single to use them.

INDEPENDENT HOSTELS

Britain's independent hostels and backpacker hostels offer a great welcome. In rural areas, some are little more than simple bunkhouses (charging around £5), while others are almost up to B&B standard, charging £15 or more.

In cities, backpackers hostels are perfect for young budget travellers from around the world. Most are open 24/7, with a lively atmosphere, good range of rooms (doubles or dorms), bar, café, Internet and laundry. Prices are around £15 for a dorm bed, or £20 to £35 for a bed in a private room.

YHA & SYHA HOSTELS

Youth hostels once had an austere image, but today they're a great option for budget travellers. Some are purpose-built, others in cottages or grand country houses. (Carbisdale Castle – p893 – in Scotland is one of the finest hostels we know – more like a hotel or art gallery.) Facilities include: showers, lounge, gear-drying room, small dorms and equipped self-catering kitchen. Many hostels also have four-person family rooms, some with private bathroom. Long rows of beds and queues for cold showers are a thing of the past.

Charges vary; small hostels cost around £10, larger hostels with more facilities cost up to about £19. SYHA hostels in Edinburgh and Glasgow cost around £15, and London's excellent YHA hostels cost around £25. Meals (optional) cost about £4 for breakfasts and packed lunches, and around £6 for three-course dinners.

> ### HOSTEL CHARGES
>
> Throughout this book, we list adult prices for staying at YHA and SYHA hostels. Under-18s pay about 75% of adult rates at YHA hostels, and about 85% at SYHA hostels.

If you're a member of the YHA, SYHA or another Hostelling International (HI) organisation, rates are cheaper by £1 to £2 per night. To join the YHA costs £14 per year; the SYHA is £6. Under-18s get half price.

Hostels have complicated opening times and days, especially in country areas out of tourist season, so check these before turning up. Smaller rural hostels may close between 10am and 5pm. The YHA and SYHA publish annual guides listing all their hostels, including details of opening times, services and how to get there.

Reservations are usually possible, and you can often pay in advance by credit card.

Hotels

A hotel in Britain can be a simple place with a few rooms or a huge affair with fancy facilities, grand staircases, acres of grounds and the requisite row of stag-heads on the wall. Charges vary as much as quality and atmosphere, with singles/doubles costing from £30/40 to £100/150 or beyond. More money doesn't always mean a better hotel: whatever your budget, some are excellent value while others overcharge. Throughout this book, we guide you to the best choices.

Chain hotels along motorways depend on business trade, so offer discount weekend rates and often a flat charge (eg £40 for a twin-bed room and private bathroom). In London and other British cities travellers can find similar hotels – motorway-style in the centre of town – which can be very good value, although many of them are a tad lacking in atmosphere. Look out for new arrival EasyHotels, with no-frills airline-style rates and rooms, which may possibly revolutionise the bargain-accommodation scene in Britain.

Pubs & Inns

As well as selling drinks, many pubs and inns offer B&B, particularly in country areas. Staying in a pub can be good fun – you're automatically at the centre of the

> **REACH FOR THE STARS**
>
> Most accommodation in Britain is registered with a tourist board, and hotels are awarded stars according to their standards. But more stars don't necessarily make a place any better for independent-minded traveller who can see beyond floral wallpaper and a choice of shampoo sachets in the shower. Many hotels and B&Bs with one or two stars are owner-managed, and guests are made to feel especially welcome. Conversely, some five-star places have loads of facilities, but can feel a bit fussy and impersonal.
>
> During the research for this book we stayed at a great farmhouse B&B, which in the eyes of the local tourist board deserved only two stars, apparently because the walls weren't painted (they were beautiful natural stone) and because there was no coffee tray (even though there were just two guestrooms, and high-quality espresso available in the kitchen at the drop of a hat).
>
> Some small hotels and B&Bs, exasperated by narrow-minded ratings inspectors (not to mention the cost of being registered), have opted out completely. This means if you see a place with no stars or diamonds on your travels around Britain, it doesn't necessarily mean it's bad. It also means that if you use official accommodation lists as your only source, you might miss out on a real gem.

community – although accommodation varies enormously, from stylish suites to threadbare rooms aimed at (and last used by) 1950s commercial salesmen. Expect to pay around £15 per person at the cheap end, around £30 for something better. A major advantage for solo travellers is that pubs are more likely to have single rooms.

If a pub does B&B, it normally does meals – served in the bar, or in a smarter restaurant. Breakfast may also be served in the bar next morning; not always enhanced by the smell of stale beer and ashtrays

Self-Catering & Rental Accommodation

If you want to slow down and get to know a place better, renting for a week or two can be ideal. Choose from neat town apartments, quaint old houses or converted farms (although always called 'cottages'), all with bedrooms, bathroom, lounge and equipped kitchen.

At busy times (especially July and August) you'll need to book ahead, and cottages for four people cost from around £200 to £300 per week. At quieter times, £150 to £180 is more usual, and you may be able to rent for a long weekend.

University Accommodation

Many universities offer student accommodation to visitors during July and August vacations. You usually get a functional single bedroom with private bathroom, and self-catering flats are also available. Prices range from £10 to £30 per person.

ACTIVITIES

This section covers a selection of organised activities which you might tie in with your travels around Britain. The two most popular outdoor activities, walking and cycling, are covered in the Outdoor Activities chapter, along with some information on rock-climbing and surfing. For ideas on organised activity holidays see p969.

Canoeing & Kayaking

Britain has numerous rivers, lakes and canals, as well as a fabulous coastline, with great opportunities for canoeing and kayaking. Of the two disciplines, kayaks (enclosed boats) are far more popular in Britain than Canadian-style canoes, although the term 'canoeing' generally covers both.

If you're a beginner, or just need to hire a boat, there are outdoor centres all over which rent equipment and arrange courses. Local TICs are your best bet for first inquiries, and we mention several centres in this book. It's always best to seek local advice first, as rivers are private and can only be used by canoeists at certain times of year, while offshore it's essential to know about tides and currents. (There are fatalities each year as ill-prepared paddlers are swept out to sea.)

The main governing body is the **British Canoe Union** (www.bcu.org.uk). In Wales, contact the **Welsh Canoeing Association** (www.welsh-canoeing .org.uk) and in Scotland the **Scottish Canoe Association** (www.scot-canoe.org). These sites list local clubs, places to canoe, instruction and hire centres, regulations, guidebooks etc.

SOMETHING DIFFERENT FOR THE WEEKEND?

Britain has a huge choice of hotels and cottages, but if you thirst for even more variety, contact the **Landmark Trust** (☎ 01628-825925; www.landmarktrust.org.uk), an architectural charity that rents historic buildings; your options include medieval castles, Napoleonic forts and 18th-century follies.

Another option is **Distinctly Different** (www.distinctlydifferent.co.uk), specialising in unusual, bizarre or even vaguely risqué accommodation. Can't sleep at night? How about a former funeral parlour? Need to spice up your romance? Then go for the converted brothel or the 'proudly phallic' lighthouse. Feeling brave? We have just the haunted inn for you, sir.

Back safely down to earth with the final option: the **National Trust** (NT; www.nationaltrust.org .uk) has over 300 holiday cottages and 80 B&Bs, many on NT-owned working farms or the land of stately homes owned or run by the Trust.

Beginners might start with Britain's network of canals; along with other inland waterways, there's 2000 miles of safe canoeing here. For river touring, classics include the Thames, the lower Wye, the upper Severn, the Avon, the Trent, the Forth and the Spey. Lakes where canoeing is permitted include Windermere, Coniston and Derwentwater in Cumbria, and Loch Lomond and Loch Ness in Scotland. If you want white water, head for Llangollen or Bala in Wales, or the rivers Nith and Orchy in Scotland. In England, you can sample the artificially created but always reliable rapids at Holme Pierrepont, near Nottingham.

Then there's the coast, whether you want to surf, rock-hop or enjoy gentle smooth-water touring. The western side of Britain offers endless opportunities, with open stretches, numerous islands and sheltered bays, plus inlets, lochs and estuaries which penetrate deep inland. In England, go for Devon and Cornwall. In Wales you can't beat dreamy Pembrokeshire, which offers some of the finest conditions in Britain. In North Wales, white-water river and sea canoeing are available at the training centres of Plas y Brenin and Plas Menai.

For sea touring in northwest Scotland, the islands of the Inner Hebrides, such as Mull and Jura, are relatively sheltered, with hundreds of deserted lochs and wild shores if you've got a yen for exploration. The Outer Hebrides are much more serious, especially on the west-facing side, but are still a venue for world-class adventures.

Fishing

Fishing is enormously popular in Britain, but it's highly regulated. Many prime stretches of river are privately owned with exclusive fishing rights. There's a fishing club on the idyllic trout-filled River Itchen in Hampshire where it's rumoured even Prince Charles had to join the waiting list.

Having said that, there are some rivers that can be freely fished, although everyone needs a licence. These cost from £3 per day to £60 for the season, and are available from post offices in England and Wales or from the website of the **Environment Agency** (www .environment-agency.gov.uk/fish).

The fishing-licence situation in Scotland is more complicated, as you may need separate permits for different rivers. They can be very costly. For more details, check the website of the **Scottish Federation for Coarse Angling** (www.sfca.co.uk).

When travelling, the best place to cast around for information is a local TIC. Ask about local clubs or places offering fishing for a day or two, such as stocked lochs and reservoirs (some with rod hire and tuition available), or hotels with their own fishing lakes or access for guests to private stretches of river.

If you're interested in fishing at sea rather than on rivers, boats (with skipper, and often with tackle) can be hired for the day or a few hours at most seaside resorts around the country; the website of the **National Federation of Sea Anglers** (www.nfsa.org.uk) is a good place for information.

Golf

Britain, and particularly Scotland, is the home of golf, with around 2000 private and public golf courses in Britain, and 500 in Scotland alone. (There are, in fact, more golf courses per capita in Scotland than any other country in the world. See p839 for more background on this royal and ancient game.)

Some exclusive private clubs admit only golfers who have a handicap certificate from their own club, but most welcome visitors (and charge around £40). Public courses run by town or city councils are open to anyone, and cost from around £10 (more at weekends). Top-end hotels may have arrangements with nearby courses which get you reduced fees or guaranteed tee-off times. If you need to hire, a set of golf clubs costs £5 to £10 per round.

For serious information, the **English Golf Union** (☎ 01526-354500; www.englishgolfunion.org) can, among other things, provide a list of affiliated clubs. The **Welsh Golfing Union** (☎ 01633-430830; www.welshgolf.org) is similar. The **Scottish Golf Union** (☎ 01382-549500; www.scottishgolf.com) is much more useful as it also has lots of detail aimed specifically at visitors.

A fine place to start for overseas golfers is the **Golf Club of Great Britain** (☎ 020-8390 3113; www.golfclubgb.co.uk); this friendly organisation can advise on where to play, and arranges regular tournaments.

Hang Gliding & Paragliding

There's a relatively small but thriving hang gliding and (especially) paragliding scene in Britain, with a good selection of varied flying sites. Before doing anything, contact the **British Hang Gliding & Paragliding Association** (www.bhpa.co.uk) for details on clubs and training schools. If you have your own gear, it's also essential to check local regulations regarding access, as nearly all land is privately owned in Britain, and launching or landing in the wrong place can cause big problems.

English regions for flying include the Peak District, Yorkshire Dales and Lake District. The Long Mynd, near Shrewsbury, is particularly renowned. In Wales the most popular flying area is around Abergavenny, with access to the nearby Black Mountains and Brecon Beacons. In Scotland, the main site in the Glasgow/Edinburgh area is Tinto Hill, south of Glasgow. Further north, Glen Coe and Aonach Mhor (near Fort William) have good potential in northerly winds, and as both are ski areas in winter there are handy cable cars to transport you up to the launch site!

Horse Riding & Pony Trekking

There's a theory that humans are genetically programmed to absorb the world at walking pace. It's all to do with our nomadic ancestors, apparently. Add the extra height, and seeing Britain from horseback is a highly recommended way to go.

Across the country, riding centres cater to all levels of proficiency, especially in national parks and other rural areas. Generally, pony trekking is aimed at novice riders. If you're more experienced in equestrian matters, most centres have horses available.

Many riding centres advertise in national-park newspapers (available free from hotels and TICs). A half-day pony trek costs around £15, a full day £20 to £30. Serious riders pay higher rates for superior mounts. The **British Horse Society** (☎ 0870 120 2244; www.bhs.org.uk) publishes *Where to Ride*, which lists riding centres throughout the UK.

Areas where riding can easily be arranged include Dartmoor, Exmoor, the New Forest, South Downs, North York Moors, South and North Pennines, Yorkshire Dales, Cheviot Hills, Brecon Beacons, the Cambrian Mountains of mid-Wales, and the Galloway Hills in Scotland. Established long-distance horse-riding routes include the South Downs Way in southeast England and the Pennine Bridleway through Derbyshire and Yorkshire.

Sailing & Windsurfing

Britain has a nautical heritage and sailing is a very popular pastime – in everything from tiny dinghies to oceangoing yachts. In recent years there's been a massive surge in windsurfing too. Your first port of call for any sailing or windsurfing matter should be the **Royal Yachting Association** (☎ 0845 345 0400; www.rya.org.uk). This organisation can provide all the details you need about training centres where you can learn the ropes, improve your skills or simply charter a boat for pleasure.

As well as lakes and reservoirs, there's a good choice of coastal sailing centres eg Norfolk and Suffolk, the Solent (between Southampton and the Isle of Wight), southeast England (including Brighton, Eastbourne and Dover), Devon and Cornwall, and the Channel Islands. In Wales, places include the Gower Peninsula and Pembrokeshire. In Scotland, head for the Firth of Forth near Edinburgh, the area north of Largs (west of Glasgow), or Inverness.

Skiing & Snowboarding

Surely no-one comes to Britain to ski or board, what with the Alps just a short hop away? But yes, there's a ski scene in Scotland, based around a handful of resorts complete with lifts, runs, equipment hire and even an *aprés* atmosphere in the evening. OK, the runs are far less extensive than anything you'll find in Switzerland, the weather is less reliable, and snowfalls are just not what they used to be (global warning is real, folks!), but on a sunny day, after a good dump of the white stuff, a day or two on the slopes here can be very pleasant indeed.

The high season is January to March/April, and the biggest ski centre is Cairngorm (Aviemore is the nearest town with a skibus to the slopes). Other resorts include Glenshee, south of Cairngorm, and the Lecht, north of Cairngorm. Near Fort William, the Nevis Range offers the highest ski runs. Your final option is Glen Coe, about 30 miles from Fort William.

It's easy to hire skis, boards, lessons and clothing when you arrive at the resort. Adult lift passes cost £15 to £20 per day, or £65 to £70 for a five-day pass (photo required). In a group, ski lessons cost £15 to £24 for a day, and £60 to £75 for five days. Cheaper all-inclusive packages are also available.

VisitScotland (☎ 0845 225 5121; www.visitscotland .com) has a detailed *Ski Scotland* brochure and dedicated ski webpages, with details on resorts, accommodation, tour operators, hotel packages and so on.

Away from the slopes and paraphernalia, Scotland also offers Nordic (cross-country) skiing, and there are even a few places in northern England and North Wales where you can hire cross-country skis for those occasional days when there's enough snow on the Pennines or the Carneddau.

BUSINESS HOURS

Most offices (government and private sector) and businesses operate from 9am to 5pm Monday to Friday.

Most shops are open from 9am to between 5pm and 6pm from Monday to Saturday, and many are open from 10am to 11am to 4pm on Sunday. In smaller towns and country areas, shops usually close at weekends, and for lunch (1pm to 2pm), and maybe on Wednesday or Thursday afternoon too.

Post offices operate from 9am to between 5pm and 6pm, Monday to Friday, and larger branches open 9am to 1pm or 9am to 5pm on Saturdays too.

Most banks are open 9.30am to 5pm Monday to Friday (smaller branches may shut at 4pm) and larger bank branches also open Saturday morning 9.30am to 1pm.

London and large cities have convenience stores that are open 24/7. At the other end of the scale, in the Outer Hebrides some locals adhere strictly to the Scriptures, so on Sunday the shops are shut, the pubs are closed, the ferries don't run, and even the public toilets are padlocked.

When you're sightseeing, large museums and major places of interest are usually open every day. Some smaller places open just five or six days per week, usually including Saturday and Sunday, but may close on Monday and/or Tuesday. Much depends on the time of year – places will open daily in high season, but maybe just at weekends (or they will keep shorter hours) in quieter periods.

Restaurants open either for lunch (about noon to 3pm) and dinner (about 7pm to 10pm in smaller towns, up to 11pm or midnight in cities), or they might open for lunch *or* dinner. Restaurants are usually open every day of the week, although some close on Sunday evening, or all day Monday.

The opening hours of cafés and teashops also vary according to location. In towns and cities, cafés may open from 7am, providing breakfast for commuters, but close mid-afternoon. Others stay open until 5pm or 6pm. In country areas, cafés and teashops open for lunch, and may keep going until 7pm, catering for post-stately-home tourists or hikers down from the hill.

In winter in country areas, café/restaurant hours are cut back, while some places close completely from October to Easter.

Pubs in towns and country areas usually open daily from 11am to 11pm, although some shut 3pm to 6pm. In cities, some pubs enjoy longer hours, or have been reclassified as clubs – so the fun keeps going until 2am or later.

Throughout this book, many restaurants and cafés are listed and reviewed, and we indicate if they're open for lunch or dinner or both, but precise opening times and days are given only if they differ markedly from the pattern outlined here.

CHILDREN

Travelling with children is a great excuse if you secretly yearn to visit railway museums or ride the scariest rollercoaster in the country. And all sorts of other activities for children are offered by national parks and resort towns, especially during the school holidays (see p956 for holiday dates). Local TICs are a great source of information on kid-friendly attractions. To help you further we've included sections such as 'Manchester for Children' in all the big-city sections.

For sleeping options, some hotels welcome kids (with their parents) and provide cots, toys and baby-sitting services, while others prefer to maintain an adult atmosphere, so check this in advance. Likewise restaurants: some will have crayons and highchairs, and not mind if the menu lands on the floor; others firmly say 'no children after 6pm'. Under-18s are banned from pubs and bars, unless they're specifically 'family-friendly' (and many are, especially those serving food).

On the sticky topic of dealing with nappies (diapers) while travelling, most museums and historical attractions usually have very good baby-changing facilities (cue old joke: I swapped mine for a nice souvenir), as do department stores. Elsewhere, you'll find facilities in motorway service stations and city-centre toilets – although the latter can sometimes be a bit on the grimy side.

Breastfeeding in public can still raise eyebrows, but if done modestly is usually considered OK. For more advice see www .babygoes2.com – packed with tips, advice and encouragement for parents on the move.

CLIMATE CHARTS

Britain's changeable weather is discussed on p13. These charts give the figures:

CUSTOMS

The UK has a two-tier customs system: one for goods bought in another European Union (EU) country where duties and taxes have already been paid, the other for goods bought duty-free outside the EU. Here we have a summary of the rules; for more details and information see www.hmce.gov .uk or look under Customs Allowances on www.visitbritain.com.

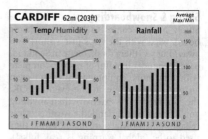

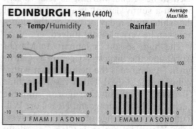

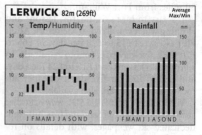

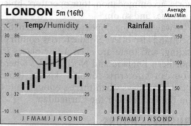

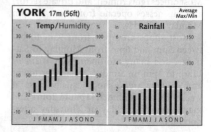

Duty Free

If you bring duty-free goods from outside the EU, the limits include 200 cigarettes, 2L of still wine, plus 1L of spirits or another 2L of wine, 60cc of perfume, and other duty-free goods (including beer) to the value of £145.

Tax & Duty Paid

There is no limit to the goods you can bring from *within* the EU (if taxes have been paid), but customs officials use the following guidelines to distinguish personal use from commercial imports: 3000 cigarettes, 200 cigars, 10L of spirits, 20L of fortified wine, 90L of wine and 110L of beer. Still enough to have one hell of a party.

DANGERS & ANNOYANCES
Crime

Britain is a remarkably safe country, considering the wealth disparities you'll see in many areas, but crime is not unknown in London and other cities, so you should take care – especially at night. When travelling by tube, tram or suburban train choose a carriage containing lots of other people. It's also best to avoid deserted tube stations at night; a bus or taxi can be a safer choice.

Pickpockets and snatchers operate in crowded public places, so money and important documents are best kept out of sight and out of reach, rather than in a daypack or shoulder-bag.

In large hotels, don't leave valuables lying around; put them in your bag, or use the room safe if there is one. There's no harm doing the same at city B&Bs too; in rural areas there's much less risk. In hostels with shared dorms, keep your stuff packed away, and carry valuables with you. Many hostels provide lockers, but you need your own padlock.

If you're driving, remove luggage from the car when parking overnight in cities and towns. The same applies even in some apparently safe rural locations. While you're out walking in the countryside, someone may be walking off with your belongings. Where possible, look for secure parking areas near TICs.

Midges

The millions of tiny biting insects called midges which take to the air on cool windless evenings are not a danger, but they're

---

SATURDAY NIGHT HEAVER

In cities and towns, the sight of bleary-eyed lads desperately ordering four pints of beer 15 minutes before closing time may be a sign of trouble ahead; Britain's archaic pub laws mean groups of liquored-up 'lager louts' are all tossed onto the streets shortly after 11pm, so brawls are not unknown. Recent liberalisation of the rules (allowing pubs to stay open longer, or reclassify as 'clubs' – with the same result) may ease the pressure, but does nothing for the splattered evidence of too much ale and vindaloo which decorates the pavements next morning. The solution: keep a low profile on Saturday night, give drunken yobs a wide berth – and watch where you step.

---

very annoying if you're camping between June and August, especially in northern England, and most notoriously in Scotland. If you're staying in hostels or B&Bs they're no problem, but the gardens of country pubs can be a bit 'midgey' around sunset. Ways to counter the attack include wearing light-coloured clothing and using midge repellents (available in pharmacies and outdoor stores – those without DDT include Moziguard and Swamp Gel).

Minicabs

In large cities, avoid unlicensed minicabs unless you know where you're going. Tricks include driving round in circles, then charging an enormous fare. Use a metered taxi, or phone a reputable minicab company and get an upfront quote for the ride.

DISABLED TRAVELLERS

If you happen to be in a wheelchair, use crutches, or just find moving about a bit tricky, you won't have many problems in Britain. All new buildings have wheelchair access, and hotels in grand old country houses often have ramps and other facilities added. Smaller B&Bs and guesthouses are often harder to adapt, so you'll have less choice here. In cities, new buses have low floors for easy access, as do many long-distance trains. If they don't, just have a word with station staff, and they'll be happy to help.

At TICs in Scotland, you can pick up a comprehensive booklet called *Accessible*

Scotland, detailing all the accommodation and attractions that are wheelchair accessible. There's similar countrywide information at www.visitbritain.com. Other useful organisations, publications and websites:

All Go Here (www.allgohere.com)

Disability UK (www.disabilityuk.com) Includes details of shopmobility schemes.

Good Access Guide (www.goodaccessguide.co.uk)

Holiday Care Service (☎ 0845 124 9971, 020-8760 0072; www.holidaycare.org.uk) Publisher of numerous booklets on UK travel.

Royal Association for Disability & Rehabilitation (RADAR; ☎ 020-7250 3222; www.radar.org.uk) Published titles include *Holidays in Britain & Ireland*.

Tripscope (☎ 0845 758 5641, 0117-939 7782; www.tripscope.org.uk)

ELECTRICITY

The standard voltage throughout Britain is 230 to 240V. Plugs have three square pins.

EMBASSIES & CONSULATES
British Embassies Abroad

Below is a selection of British embassies, consulates and high commissions (collectively know as 'diplomatic missions') abroad. For a complete list, see the website of the **Foreign & Commonwealth Office** (www.fco.gov.uk), which also lists foreign embassies in the UK.

Australia (☎ 02-6270 6666; www.uk.emb.gov.au; Commonwealth Ave, Yarralumla, Canberra, ACT 2600)

Canada (☎ 613-237 1530; www.britainincanada.org; 80 Elgin St, Ottawa, Ontario K1P 5K7)

France (☎ 01 44 51 31 00; www.amb-grandebretagne.fr; 35 rue du Faubourg Saint Honoré, 75383 Paris Cedex 8)

Germany (☎ 030-204 570; www.britischebotschaft.de; Wilhelmstrasse 70, 10117 Berlin)

Ireland (☎ 01-205 3700; www.britishembassy.ie; 29 Merrion Rd, Ballsbridge, Dublin 4)

Japan (☎ 03-5211 1100; www.uknow.or.jp; 1 Ichiban-cho, Chiyoda-ku, Tokyo 102-8381)

Netherlands (☎ 070-427 0427; www.britain.nl; Lange Voorhout 10, 2514 ED The Hague)

New Zealand (☎ 04-924 2888; www.britain.org.nz; 44 Hill St, Wellington 1)

USA (☎ 202-588 6500; www.britainusa.com; 3100 Massachusetts Ave NW, Washington, DC 20008)

Embassies in Britain

A selection of embassies, consulates and high commissions in London is given below. Some countries also have representation in Edinburgh and Cardiff (although these defer to London HQ in most instances

relating to tourists). Remember – your embassy won't be much help if you're in trouble for committing a crime locally. Even as a foreigner, you are bound by the laws of Britain.

Australia (☎ 020-7379 4334; www.australia.org.uk; Strand, WC2B 4LA)

Canada (☎ 020-7258 6600; www.canada.org.uk; 1 Grosvenor Sq, W1X 0AB)

France (☎ 020-7073 1000; www.ambafrance.org.uk; 58 Knightsbridge, SW1 7JT)

Germany (☎ 020-7824 1300; www.german-embassy.org.uk; 23 Belgrave Sq, SW1X 8PX)

Ireland (☎ 020-7235 2171; 17 Grosvenor Pl, SW1X 7HR)

Japan (☎ 020-7465 6500; www.uk.emb-japan.go.jp; 101 Piccadilly, W1J 7JT)

Netherlands (☎ 020-7590 3200; www.netherlands-embassy.org.uk; 38 Hyde Park Gate, SW7 5DP)

New Zealand (☎ 020-7930 8422; www.nzembassy.com/uk; 80 Haymarket, SW1Y 4TQ)

USA (☎ 020-7499 9000; www.usembassy.org.uk; 24 Grosvenor Sq, W1A 1AE)

FESTIVALS & EVENTS

Countless festivals and events are held in Britain, and below is a selection of biggies that are worth tying in with your travels. In addition, towns and villages have smaller festivals or annual fairs, and many of these are listed in the regional chapters.

January

New Year Celebrations (January 1, city centres nationwide) Get drunk, make resolutions and kiss strangers as the bells chime midnight.

February

Jorvik Viking Festival (York) Horned helmets galore, plus mock invaders and Viking longship races.

March

University Boat Race (London) Traditional rowing contest on the River Thames, between Oxford and Cambridge University teams.

Crufts Dog Show (Birmingham) Highlight of the canine year. Top dogs abound.

April

Grand National (First Saturday in April, Aintree, Liverpool) The most famous horse race of them all, with notoriously high jumps.

May

FA Cup Final (early May, Cardiff or Wembley) Gripping end to a venerable football tournament.

Brighton Festival (Brighton) Lively and innovative three-week arts feast.

Chelsea Flower Show (late May, London) Blooming marvellous.

Bath International Music Festival (Mid-May to early June, Bath) Top-class classical music and opera, plus jazz and world music, with art-full Fringe attached.

Glyndebourne (end of May to August, Lewes, Sussex) World-class opera in country-house gardens.

June

Beating Retreat (early June, London) Military bands march down Whitehall.

Derby Week (early June, Epsom, Surrey) Horse-racing and people-watching.

Trooping the Colour (mid-June, London) Whitehall again; bearskins and pageantry for the Queen's birthday parade.

Royal Ascot (mid-June, Ascot, Berkshire) More horse-racing, more people-watching, plus outrageous hats.

Royal Highland Show (late June, Edinburgh) Scotland's national display piece with big-horned cattle, cabers, bagpipes, kilts – the lot.

Glastonbury Festival (late June, Pilton, Somerset) Huge open-air musical happening, with hippy roots.

Royal Regatta (late June/early July, Henley-on-Thames, Oxfordshire) Premier rowing and social event. No hippies here.

Mardi Gras Pride in the Park (June/July, London) Loud and proud, one of Europe's largest gay and lesbian festivals.

Wimbledon – Lawn Tennis Championships (late June to early July, London) Two weeks of rapid-fire returns.

July

Hampton Court Palace International Flower Show (early July, London) Does exactly what it says on the tin.

Royal Welsh Show (mid-July, Builth Wells) National agricultural and cultural gathering.

T in the Park (Glasgow) Open-air pop, rock and dance music. Scotland's answer to Glastonbury.

Sesiwn Fawr (Dolgellau) Three-day rock, folk and beer bash in Mid Wales. Fast-growing and free.

International Eisteddfod (Llangollen) Lively mix of cultures from Wales and far beyond.

Cowes Week (late July, Isle of Wight) Yachting spectacular.

International Flying Display (late July, Farnborough, Surrey) World's largest aeroplane show.

York Early Music Festival (late July, York) Medieval choirs and concerts.

Womad (late July, Reading, Berkshire) Global gathering of world and roots music.

August

Royal National Eisteddfod (early August, alternates between South and North Wales: 2005 Snowdonia, 2006 Swansea) The ancient bardic tradition continues; a festival

of Welsh language, music and literature at its most powerful and inspirational.

Military Tattoo (Edinburgh) Three weeks of pageantry and soldierly displays.

Edinburgh International Arts Festival (Edinburgh) World-class arts gathering, overshadowed only by its own Fringe.

Notting Hill Carnival (late August, London) Spectacular multicultural feast, Caribbean style.

Reading Festival (late August, Reading, Berkshire) Three-day open-air rock, pop and dance extravaganza.

Leeds Festival (late August, Leeds, Yorkshire) The Reading of the North, and just as good.

September

Braemar Gathering (first Saturday in September, Braemar, Deeside) With over 20,000 people, including the Royals, 'gathering' is an understatement for this famous Highland knees-up.

October

Horse of the Year Show (Birmingham) Top show-jumping event. No long faces.

November

Guy Fawkes Day (5 November, nationwide) Bonfires and fireworks around the country.

December

New Year Celebrations (31 December, city centres nationwide) That's another year gone! So see it out in style. The biggest crowds are in London's Trafalgar Square, but Edinburgh's Hogmanay party tops the list for atmosphere. Then get ready for midnight – see January.

FOOD

For a flavour of Britain's cuisine, see the main Food & Drink chapter. For a real taste, visit some of the restaurants we recommend throughout this book. Most Eating sections are divided into three per-meal price bands: Budget (under £10); Mid-Range (£10 to £20); Top End (over £20).

GAY & LESBIAN TRAVELLERS

Britain is a generally tolerant place for gays and lesbians. Certainly it's possible for people to acknowledge their homosexuality in ways that would have been unthinkable 20 years ago. That said, there remain pockets of hostility. You only need read the *Mail* or *Telegraph* to realise the limits of tolerance.

London, Glasgow, Manchester, Cardiff and Brighton have flourishing gay scenes, and in other sizable cities (and even some small towns such as Hebden Bridge in Yorkshire) you'll find communities not entirely in the closet. For more details see the specific Gay & Lesbian boxed texts throughout this book.

For information, listings and contacts see monthly magazines (and websites) *Gay Times* (www.gaytimes.co.uk) and *Diva* (www.divamag.co.uk). Another useful source of information is the **Lesbian & Gay Switchboard** (☎ 020-7837 7324; www.llgs.org.uk).

HERITAGE ORGANISATIONS

If you plan to visit historic sights, membership of Britain's historical or conservation organisations gives you free entry to properties, reciprocal arrangements with other heritage organisations, maps, information handbooks and so on. The main organisations are: National Trust (NT), and its partner organisation National Trust for Scotland (NTS); English Heritage (EH) and its related organisations Historic Scotland (HS), and Cadw, the Welsh historic monuments agency. You can join at the first site you visit. If you are a member of a similar organisation in your own country, this may get you free or discounted entry at sites in Britain. We have included the relevant acronym (NT, EH etc) in the information after every property listed in this book.

Cadw (☎ 029-2050 0200; www.cadw.wales.gov.uk) Manages sites in Wales (the name means 'to keep'). Membership costs adults £28 per year, 16 to 20 years £18 and children £14. Family membership costs £53 or £35 for a single-parent family. Cadw members are also eligible for half-price admission to EH and HS sites.

English Heritage (☎ 0870 333 1181; www.english -heritage.org.uk) A state-funded organisation, responsible for the upkeep of numerous historic sites. Some are free, while others cost £1.50 to £6. Annual membership costs £34 per adult, £58 per couple (£38 for senior couples). Alternatively, an Overseas Visitors Pass for 7/14 days (£15/19) allows free admission to most EH sites, and half-price for HS and Cadw sites.

Historic Scotland (☎ 0131-668 8999; www.historic -scotland.gov.uk) Manages more than 330 historic sites, and goes to great lengths to make things engaging and interesting for kids and adults, as well as accessible for less able visitors. A year's membership costs £32 for adults (£61 family), giving free admission to HS sites and half-price admission to EH and Cadw properties. 'Explorer' passes cost £15 for three days in five, £22 for seven days in 14, £25 for 10 days in 30. Students and seniors get 25% discount on passes.

National Trust (☎ 0870 458 4000; www.nationaltrust .org.uk) Protects hundreds of historic buildings (normally around £5 to enter) plus vast tracts of land with scenic importance in England and Wales. Membership costs £36 per year (£16.50 for under-26s, and £50 to £65 for families). Alternatively, a NT touring pass gives free admission to NT and NTS properties for 7/14-day periods (£16/20); families and couples get cheaper rates.

National Trust for Scotland (☎ 0131-243 9300; www.nts.org.uk) Cares for over 100 properties and around 75,000 hectares of countryside. A year's membership costs £33 (£12/25/54 for under-25/senior/family)

Great British Heritage Pass

This pass gives you access to almost 600 historic and heritage properties run by the bodies listed above, and many privately owned sites in England, Wales, Scotland and Northern Ireland. A four-day pass costs £28, seven days £39, 15 days £52, and one month is £70. It's available overseas from VisitBritain offices (or online at www.visitbritain.com /heritagepass), from travel agencies overseas specialising in Britain, and from larger TICs throughout Britain. It can only be purchased by non-Brits though (show your passport).

National Trust Grading System

The National Trust divides each site into grade bands to give added guidance on their significance. Those identified as being of a sufficiently high level of interest to merit a national designation, including those considered to be of exceptional historic interest, are designated Grade II. Sites of international importance are classified as grade I.

HISTORIC PROPERTY PRICES

Nearly all properties under the charge of NT, EH, NTS, HS and Cadw charge half-price for children, so only adult admission fees are quoted in this book.

HOLIDAYS
Public Holidays

In Britain, most businesses and banks close on public holidays (hence the quaint term 'bank holiday'). In Scotland, bank holidays are just for the banks, and many businesses stay open. Instead, Scottish towns normally have a spring and autumn holiday, but the dates vary from town to town.

Holidays (for the whole of Britain, unless specified):
New Year's Day 1 January
Good Friday March/April
Easter Monday (Except Scotland) March/April
May Day First Monday in May
Spring Bank Holiday Last Monday in May
Summer Bank Holiday (Scotland) First Monday in August
Summer Bank Holiday (England & Wales) Last Monday in August
Christmas Day 25 December
Boxing Day 26 December

In Scotland, 2 January is also a holiday – so everyone can recover from Hogmanay. Across Britain, if a public holiday falls on a weekend, the nearest Monday is usually taken instead. Some small museums and places of interest close on public holidays, but larger attractions specifically gear up, and this is their busiest time, although nearly everything closes on Christmas Day. Generally speaking, if a place closes on Sunday, it'll probably be shut on bank holidays as well.

School Holidays
The main school holidays are generally as follows:
Easter Holiday The week before and week after Easter
Summer Holiday Third week of July to first week of September
Christmas Holiday Mid-December to first week of January

There are three week-long 'half-term' school holidays – usually late February to early March and late May and late October. At school-holiday times, especially in the summer, roads and resorts get busy, and prices go up.

INSURANCE
Travel insurance is highly recommended for all overseas visitors to Britain. Car insurance is covered on p968.

INTERNET ACCESS
Places with Internet access are common in Britain, but they're not on every corner. We've listed Internet cafés where they exist in the cities described in this book, and in the bigger cities access costs around £1 per hour. Out in the sticks you can pay up to £5 per hour. Public libraries often have free access, but only for 30-minute slots. If you're planning to use your laptop to get online, your own connection cable may not fit in British sockets – although adaptors are easy to buy at electrical stores in airports or city centres.

LEGAL AGE

The age of consent in England is 16 (gay and straight). You can also get married at 16 (with permission from parents), but you'll have to wait two years for the toast – only over-18s can buy alcohol. Over-16s may buy cigarettes, so you can have a celebratory smoke instead.

You usually have to be 18 to enter a pub or bar, although the rules are different if you have a meal. Some bars and clubs are over-21 only, so you won't see many high-chairs – although a lot of school uniforms may be in evidence.

LEGAL MATTERS
Driving Crimes & Transport Fines
Drink-driving is a serious offence. For more information, and details of speed limits and parking rules, see p968. On buses and trains (including the London Underground), people without a valid ticket for their journey may be fined on the spot.

Drugs
Illegal drugs are widely available, especially in clubs. All the usual dangers apply, and deaths associated with ecstasy are not uncommon – to the apparent delight of shrill tabloid newspapers. The government reclassified cannabis in 2002: possession remains a criminal offence, but the punishment for carrying a small amount is usually a warning. Dealers face far stiffer penalties, as do people caught with any other 'recreational' drugs.

MAPS
For a map of the whole country, a road atlas is handy – especially if you're travelling by car. The main publishers are Ordnance Survey (OS) and Automobile Association (AA), with atlases in all sizes and scales. If you plan to use minor roads, you'll need a scale of about 1:200,000 (3 miles to 1 inch). Most atlases cost £7 to £10 and are updated annually, which means old editions are sold off every January – look for bargains at motorway service stations.

For more detail, OS *Landrangers* (scale 1:50,000) are ideal for walking and cycling. OS *Explorer* maps (1:25,000) are even better for walking in lowland areas, but can sometimes be hard to read in complex mountain landscapes. Your best choice here is the excellent series by **Harvey Maps** (www.harveymaps .co.uk), covering mountain areas and national parks, plus routes for hikers and bikers.

MONEY

The currency of Britain is the pound sterling. Coins include 5p, 10p, 20p, 50p, £1 and £2. Notes (bills) come in £5, £10, £20 and £50 denominations. Scotland has £1 notes too. Foreign currencies are not accepted if you're buying goods and services, except for a few places in southern England which take euros.

In England and Wales, notes are issued by the Bank of England, and in Scotland by Clydesdale Bank, Bank of Scotland and Royal Bank of Scotland. All are legal tender on both sides of the border, but if you have any problems getting them accepted, ask a bank to swap them.

A guide to exchange rates is given on the inside front cover, and some pointers on costs are given on p13.

ATMs

Debit or credit cards are perfect companions – the best invention for travellers since the backpack. You can use them to withdraw cash from ATMs ('cash machines') – which are easy to find in cities and even small towns. But ATMs aren't fail-safe, and it's a major headache if your only card gets swallowed, so take a back-up.

Credit & Debit Cards

Visa, MasterCard and American Express (Amex) credit and debit cards are widely accepted in Britain, and are good for larger hotels, flights, long-distance travel, car hire etc. Most shops take cards, but other small businesses such as pubs or B&Bs often only take cash or cheque.

Moneychangers

Finding somewhere to change your money (cash, travellers cheques) into pounds is never a problem in cities, where banks and bureaus compete for business. Be careful using bureaus: some have poor rates

or outrageous commissions. You can also change money at some post offices – handy in country areas. When collecting your pounds, avoid £50 notes, many traders won't take them because fakes circulate.

Taxes & Refunds

Value-added tax (VAT) is a 17.5% sales tax on most goods and services. Non-EU residents who leave the EU within three months of making the purchase may claim a refund. Shops advertise 'Tax-Free Shopping' in their window if they participate in what's officially known as the Retail Export Scheme. The minimum purchase is usually around £75. You must show ID and ask for the VAT refund form, part of which must be completed by the retailer – who'll also explain exactly how you get your money back (usually by having it refunded to your credit card) and any administration charges they make.

Tipping & Bargaining

In restaurants you're expected to leave a tip of around 10%, unless the service was unsatisfactory. (It might be already added to your bill but you still don't have to pay if the food or service was bad.) The same might apply at smarter cafés and teashops.

Taxi drivers expect tips (about 10%, or rounded up to the nearest pound), especially in London. It's less usual to tip minicab drivers. Toilet attendants (if you see them loitering) may get tipped around 50p.

In pubs, when ordering drinks or food at the bar, tips are not expected – although if you order a big round, especially towards the end of the evening, saying 'and one for yourself' will endear you to the staff. In pubs that double as restaurants, if you order food at the table, and your meal is brought to you, then a tip may be appropriate – if the food and service have been good, of course.

In shops, bargaining is rare to the point of nonexistence, although it is occasionally encountered at markets. Having said that, it's fine to ask if there are 'student discounts' or 'tourist discounts' on items such as theatre tickets, books, sports gear or electrical items. It's surprising how many places will give you 10% off.

Travellers Cheques

Travellers cheques (TCs) offer protection from theft, but they're not used much in

Britain since credit cards and ATMs became the method of choice for most travellers. If you prefer TCs, note that they are rarely accepted for purchases (except at large hotels), so for cash you need to go to a bank or bureau anyway.

POST

Although queues in main post offices can be long, the Royal Mail delivers a good service. In 2005 within the UK, first-class letters cost 28p and usually takes one day; 2nd-class (21p) up to three days. Airmail costs are 27p to EU countries, 47p for other European countries, and 47p for Americas or Australasia (up to 10g). Rates go up every year. More details on all prices see www.royalmail.com

RADIO & TV
Radio

The British Broadcasting Corporation (BBC) is a venerable institution, with several channels dominating the airwaves. Foreigners are amazed that public service radio can produce such a range of professional, innovative, up-to-date and stimulating programmes. All this – and without adverts too!

Music station BBC Radio 1 (98.8MHz FM) plays everything from syrupy pop to underground garage, with a predominantly young audience and some truly inane presenters. When you're too old for this, turn to BBC Radio 2 (88 to 92MHz FM); it plays favourites from the 1960s to today, plus country, jazz and world music, with a few presenters who also got too old for Radio 1.

BBC Radio 3 (91.3 MHz FM) plays predominantly classical music, but also goes into roots and world, while media gem BBC Radio 4 (93.5MHz FM, 198kHz LW) offers news, comment, analysis, current affairs, drama and humour. Radio 5 Live (693kHz MW), aka 'Radio Bloke', provides a mix of sport and talk.

Once you cross the borders, BBC Radio Scotland takes over from Radio 4's frequency, while BBC Radio Wales offers daily news and features, and BBC Radio Cymru transmits the same in Welsh.

Alongside the BBC are many commercial broadcasters. Every city has at least one music station, while national channels include pop-orientated Virgin Radio (1215Hz MW) and pleasantly nonhighbrow classical specialist Classic FM (100-102MHz FM).

TV

Turning to TV, Britain produces some of the world's best programming, with the BBC once again leading the way, although with competition from cable and satellite some shows tend to be dumbed down as ratings are chased.

There are five free-to-air TV channels (called 'terrestrial' to distinguish from cable and satellite). BBC1 and BBC2 are publicly funded and don't carry advertising; ITV, Channel 4 and Channel 5 are commercial stations. Of these, BBC2 and Channel 4 generally have the most interesting programming. Several channels have variations in Wales and Scotland and in the English regions. Additionally, Scottish TV (STV) carries Gaelic-speaking programmes while Wales has Welsh-speaking S4C (Siannel 4 Cymru – Channel 4 Wales).

TELEPHONE

Britain's famous red phone boxes can still be seen in city streets, although soul-less glass cubicles are more common these days. Public phones accept coins, and usually credit cards. Minimum charge is 20p for local calls. To save hunting for change, prepaid British Telecom (BT) Phonecard Plus cards (£3, £5, £10 or £20) are widely available from post offices and newsagents.

Codes or numbers starting with ☎ 0500 or ☎ 0800 are free-phone; ☎ 0845 is local-call rate; ☎ 0870 is national-call rate; ☎ 0891 or ☎ 0906 is premium rate, and the cost should be specified by the organisation that you're phoning (usually in their advertising literature). Codes for mobile phones (cell phones) usually start with ☎ 07 – dearer than calling a landline.

Local & National Calls

Local calls (within 35 miles) are cheaper than national calls. All calls are cheaper 6pm to 8am Monday to Friday, and midnight Friday to midnight Sunday. From private phones, rates vary between telecom providers. From BT public phones the weekday rate is about 5p per minute; evenings and weekends it's about 1p per minute.

For the operator call ☎ 100. For directory inquiries, several agencies compete for your business, and charge from 10p to 40p; numbers include ☎ 118 500, ☎ 118 192, ☎ 118 118 and ☎ 118 811.

International Calls

To call outside the UK dial ☎ 00, then the country code, the area code (you usually drop the initial zero) and the number. For country codes, see the inside front cover of this book. Direct-dialled calls to most overseas countries can be made from public phones, and it's usually cheaper 8pm to 8am Monday to Friday and at weekends. You can undercut BT international rates with a phone card (usually £10 or £20) usable on any phone by dialling an access number then a PIN (you don't insert it into the machine). There are dozens of cards, usually available from city newsagents – with rates of various companies often vividly displayed.

To make reverse-charge (collect) calls, dial ☎ 155 for the international operator. It's an expensive option, but what the hell – the other person is paying!

To call Britain from abroad, dial your country's international access code, then 44 (the UK country code), then the area code (dropping the first 0), and the phone number.

Mobile Phones

Over 80% of Britons own a mobile phone, and can tell their loved ones they're 'on the train', while the terse medium of text (SMS) is a national passion – with a billion messages sent each month. For visitors too, a mobile phone can be very handy, but the UK system (GSM 900/1800) is compatible only with Europe and Australia, not with North America or Japan (although phones that work globally are increasingly common).

Even if a phone registered overseas works in the UK, a call to someone just up the road will be routed internationally, and charged accordingly. An option is to buy a local SIM card (around £30), which includes a UK number, and use that in your own handset (as long as your phone isn't locked by your home network). A second option is a pay-as-you-go phone (from around £50), which comes with its own number. To stay in credit, you simply buy 'top-up' cards at newsagents or service stations.

TIME

Wherever you are in the world, time is measured in relation to Greenwich Mean Time (GMT) – or Universal Time Coordinated (UTC), as it's more accurately called – so a highlight for many visitors to London is a trip to Greenwich, and its famous line dividing the western and eastern hemispheres.

To give you an idea, if it is noon in London, it is 4am on the same day in San Francisco, 7am in New York, and 10pm in Sydney. British summer time (BST) is Britain's daylight saving; one hour ahead of GMT from late March to late October.

TOURIST INFORMATION

Before leaving home, check the comprehensive and wide-ranging website of **VisitBritain** (www.visitbritain.com) or the more specific sites: www.visitengland.com, www.visitscotland .com and www.visitwales.com. Between them they cover all angles of national tourism, with links to numerous other sites. Details of local and regional websites and tourist organisations are also given at the start of each main chapter throughout this book.

Tourist Offices Abroad

VisitBritain's main overseas offices are listed below. Those with an office address can deal with walk-in visitors. For the others it's phone or email only. As well as information, they can help with discount travel cards, often available only if you book before arrival in Britain.

Australia (☎ 02-9021 4400; www.visitbritain.com/au; 15 Blue St, North Sydney, NSW 2060)
Canada (☎ 1 888 847 4885; www.visitbritain.com/ca)
France (☎ 01 58 36 50 50; www.visitbritain.com/vb3-fr-fr)
Germany (☎ 01801-46 86 42; www.visitbritain.com/de; Hackescher Markt 1, 10178 Berlin)
Ireland (☎ 01-670 8000; www.visitbritain.com/ie; 18-19 College Green, Dublin 2)
Japan (☎ 03-5562 2550; www.visitbritain.com/jp; 1F Akasaka Twin Tower, Minato-ku, Tokyo 107-0052)
Netherlands (☎ 020-689 0002; www.visitbritain.com/nl)
New Zealand (☎ 0800 700741; www.visitbritain.com/nz)
USA (☎ 800 462 2748; www.travelbritain.org; 551 Fifth Ave, New York, NY 10176)

Local Tourist Offices

Every British city and town has an official Tourist Information Centre (TIC), with incredibly friendly staff, free leaflets, books and maps for sale, and loads of advice on places to go and things to see in the local area. Some TICs are run by national parks and often have small exhibitions about the area.

Most TICs keep regular business hours, while in popular tourist areas they open daily year-round. Smaller TICs close from October to March.

In some places, you'll also see Visitor Information Points – usually just a leaflet dispenser in a local shop or post office. This is handy for gathering information on nearby attractions and services, but the staff usually do not provide additional details (they're running the shop!). Confusingly titled Visitor Information Centres are usually privately owned booking agencies – for local self-catering cottages or similar. You can often pick up leaflets here, but the staff rarely provide additional (or independent) tourism information.

VISAS

If you're a European Economic Area (EEA) national, you don't need a visa, and may live and work in Britain freely. Citizens of Australia, Canada, New Zealand, South Africa and the USA are given 'leave to enter' Britain at their point of arrival for up to six months, but are prohibited from working. (If you intend to seek work, see p962.)

British immigration authorities are tough, and if they suspect you're coming to Britain for more than a holiday, you may need to prove that you have funds to support yourself, or details of hotels and tours booked, or personal letters from people you'll be visiting. Having a return ticket helps, too.

Visa and entry regulations are always subject to change, so it's vital to check with your local British embassy before leaving home. For more information check www.ukvisas.gov.uk or www.ind.homeoffice.gov.uk.

Visa Extensions

Tourist visas can only be extended in clear emergencies (eg an accident) otherwise you will have to leave the UK (perhaps going to Ireland or France) and apply for a fresh one, although this tactic will arouse suspicion after the second or third go. To extend (or attempt to extend) your stay, contact the **Home Office Immigration & Nationality Directorate** (☎ 0870 606 7766; www.ind.homeoffice.gov.uk) before your existing visa expires.

WEIGHTS & MEASURES

Britain is in transition when it comes to weights and measures, as it has been for the last 20 years – and will be for 20 more. Most people still use 'imperial' units of inches,

---

TRACE THE ANCESTORS

If you're a visitor with ancestors who once lived in Britain, your trip could be a good chance to learn more. You may even discover long-lost relatives. These guidelines will get you started.

Start at the **Family Records Centre** (☎ 0870 243 7788; www.familyrecords.gov.uk; 1 Myddelton St, London EC1R 1UW). This helpful department of the Public Records Office is used to ancestor-hunters and has publications (available by post) outlining the process. You'll need a passport as ID to see original records. Documents referring to individuals are closed for 100 years to safeguard confidentiality.

The **Association of Genealogists & Researchers in Archives** (www.agra.org.uk) lists professional researchers, who (for a fee) can search for ancestors or living relatives on your behalf.

---

feet, yards and miles, although on maps mountain heights are given in metres only.

For weight, many people use pounds and ounces, even though since January 2000 goods in shops must be measured in kilograms. And nobody knows their weight in pounds (like Americans) or kilograms (like the rest of the world); Brits weigh themselves in stones, an archaic unit of 14 pounds.

When it comes to volume, things are even worse: most liquids are sold in litres or halflitres, except milk and beer, which come in pints. Garages sell petrol priced in pence per litre, but measure car performance in miles per gallon. Great, isn't it? And just to make it really interesting, British gallons are not quite the same size as American gallons (and quarts are a different kettle of fish, too).

In this book we have reflected this wacky system of mixed measurements. Heights are given in metres (m), and distances in miles. For conversion tables, see the inside front cover.

WOMEN TRAVELLERS

The occasional wolf-whistle or groper on the London Underground aside, solo women will find attitudes in Britain fairly enlightened. There's nothing to stop women going into pubs alone, for example – although you may feel conspicuous. Restaurants may

DIRECTORY

assume you're waiting for a date unless you specify a table for one, but once you've clarified, it's no big deal.

The contraceptive pill is available free on prescription in Britain, as is the morning-after pill (also on sale at chemists). Condoms are often sold in women's toilets as well as men's. Most big towns have a Well Woman Clinic that can advise on general health issues; find its address in the local phone book.

Safety is not a major issue, although commonsense caution should be observed in big cities, especially at night. Hitching is always unwise. Most cities and towns have a Rape Crisis centre, where information or counselling is free and confidential; see www.rapecrisis.org.uk.

WORK

Nationals of most European countries don't need a permit to work in Britain, but everyone else does. If this is the main purpose of your visit, you must be sponsored by a British company. For more details see Visas (p961).

If you're a Commonwealth citizen with a UK-born parent, a Certificate of Entitle-ment to the Right of Abode allows you to live and work in Britain free of immigration control. If a grandparent was born in the UK you may be eligible for an Ancestry Employment Certificate allowing full-time work for up to four years.

Commonwealth citizens without UK ancestry under 31 can take temporary work, but need a Working Holiday Entry Certificate – which must be obtained in advance, and is valid for four years. You're not allowed to engage in business, pursue a career (evidently serving in bars doesn't count) or work as an athlete or entertainer. Au pair placements are generally permitted.

Full-time students from the USA can get six-month work permits; the **British Universities North America Club** (☎ 020-7251 3472; www .bunac.org) can provide advice and assistance. For more advice, www.workingholiday guru.com is a handy site aimed mainly at Australians coming to Europe. Other good sources include www.gumtree.com and www.tntmagazine.com – the latter connected to weekly *TNT Magazine*, available free in London.

Transport

CONTENTS

GETTING THERE & AWAY

London is an international transport hub, so you can easily find long-haul flights to Britain from just about anywhere in the world. On shorter flights to/from Ireland and mainland Europe, the recent emergence of budget (or 'no-frills' airlines, as they're often called in Britain) has increased competition – and reduced fares – considerably.

Your other main option between Britain and mainland Europe is ferry, either port-to-port or combined with a long-distance bus trip – although journeys can be long and savings not huge compared to budget airfares. International trains are much more comfortable, and the Channel Tunnel allows direct services between Britain, France and Belgium.

Travelling between England, Scotland and Wales is easy. The bus and train systems are fully integrated and in most cases you won't even know you've crossed the border. Passports are not required (although some Scots and Welsh may think otherwise!)

AIR
Airports & Airlines

London's Heathrow and Gatwick are the two main airports for international flights, though some transatlantic planes zip direct to regional airports such as Birmingham,

Edinburgh, Glasgow and Manchester. All these airports are also served by numerous scheduled and charter flights to/from Continental Europe and Ireland; other airports include Luton and Stanstead (both near London), Aberdeen, Bristol, East Midlands, Edinburgh, Glasgow, Newcastle, Nottingham, Southampton and many more, including the new neatly tagged Robin Hood Doncaster Sheffield Airport – destined to be a major northern entrepot.

HEATHROW

Some 15 miles west of central London, **Heathrow** (LHR; ☎ 0870 000 0123; www.baa.com/main/airports/heathrow) is the world's busiest international airport. Heathrow has four terminals, with a fifth under construction and a sixth mooted. Make sure you know which terminal your flight is departing from, because airlines and flights can shift around the airport.

Heathrow can feel chaotic and crowded so allow yourself plenty of time to get lost in the labyrinth of shops, bars and restaurants. Each terminal has competitive currency-exchange facilities, information counters and accommodation desks.

For inquiries and flight information phone ☎ 0870 000 0123. There is no booking fee at the London Underground **Hotel**

Reservation Service (☎ 020-8564 8808), which can help book rooms near the airport, although the service on the arrivals floor charges £5.

There are **left-luggage facilities** at Terminal 1 (☎ 020-8745 5301), Terminal 2 (☎ 020-8745 4599), Terminal 3 (☎ 020-8759 3344) and Terminal 4 (☎ 020-8745 7460). They open from 5am to 11pm, and charge £3.50 for up to six hours, or £4 per day. All can forward baggage.

GATWICK

Smaller, better-organised **Gatwick** (LGW; ☎ 0870 000 2468; www.baa.com/main/airports/gatwick) is 30 miles south of central London. North and South Terminals are connected by monorail (which takes two minutes). Charters, scheduled airlines and no-frills carrier EasyJet fly from Gatwick.

Most of the world's major airlines have services to/from Britain, including the following (with their UK contact/reservation numbers):

Aer Lingus (☎ 0845 084 4444; www.aerlingus.com)
Air Canada (☎ 0871 220 1111; www.aircanada.ca)
Air France (☎ 0845 359 1000; www.airfrance.com)
Air New Zealand (☎ 0800 028 4149; www.airnewzealand.co.nz)
Alitalia (☎ 0870 544 8259; www.alitalia.com)
American Airlines (☎ 08457 789 789; www.americanairlines.com)
British Airways (☎ 0870 850 9850; www.ba.com)
British Midland (☎ 08706 070 555; www.flybmi.com)
Cathay Pacific (☎ 020-8834 8888; www.cathaypacific.com)
Continental Airlines (☎ 01293-776464; www.continental.com)
Delta Air Lines (☎ 0800 414767; www.delta.com)
El Al Israel Airlines (☎ 020-7957 4100; www.elal.co.il)
Emirates Airlines (☎ 0870 243 2222; www.emirates.com)
Iberia (☎ 0845 850 9000; www.iberia.com)
KLM-Royal Dutch Airlines (☎ 0870 507 4074; www.klm.com)
Lufthansa (☎ 08708 377 747; www.lufthansa.com)
Qantas Airways (☎ 08457 747 767; www.qantas.com.au)
Scandinavian Airlines (SAS) (☎ 020-8990 7159; www.scandinavian.net)
Singapore Airlines (☎ 0870 608 8886; www.singaporeair.com)
South African Airways (☎ 0870 747 1111; www.flysaa.com)
United Airlines (☎ 08458 444 777; www.united.com)
Virgin Atlantic (☎ 0870 380 2007; www.virgin-atlantic.com)

Budget airlines flying between Britain and other European countries can offer real bargains.

Main players:

EasyJet (☎ 0870 600 0000; www.easyjet.com)
Ryanair (☎ 0871 246 0000; www.ryanair.com)
Virgin Express (☎ 0870 730 1134; www.virgin-express.com)

To save trawling several sites, services such as www.skyscanner.com, www.whichbudget.com and www.lowcostairlines.org have information on many scheduled budget airlines. Fares vary according to demand, and are best bought online. The only downside is that some flights land at minor airports a considerable distance from the centre of the city they claim to serve.

Charter flights are another option. You can buy seat-only deals on the planes that carry tourists between, for example, Britain and numerous Mediterranean resorts. Contact high street travel agencies, or specialist websites such as www.flightline.co.uk and www.cheapflights.co.uk.

Tickets

You can buy your airline ticket from a travel agent (in person, by phone, or on the Internet), or direct from the airline (the best deals are often available online only). Whichever, it always pays to shop around. Internet travel agents such as www.travelocity.com and www.expedia.com work well if you're doing a straightforward trip, but for anything slightly complex there's no substitute for a real live travel agent who knows about options, special deals and so on.

The best place to start your search for agents or airlines is the travel section of a weekend newspaper. Look over the advertisements, phone a few numbers, check a few websites, build up an idea of possibilities, and then take it from there. Remember, you usually get what you pay for: cheaper flights may leave at unsociable hours or include

> **DEPARTURE TAX**
>
> Flights within the UK, and from the UK to EU destinations, attract a £10 departure tax. For other international flights from the UK you pay £20. This is usually included in the ticket price.

several stopovers. For quick and comfortable journeys, you have to fork out more cash.

From Australia & New Zealand

To Britain from Australasia is a very popular route, with a wide range of fares from around A$1500 to A$3000 return. From New Zealand it is often best to go via Australia. Round-the-world (RTW) tickets can sometimes work out cheaper than a straightforward return. Major agencies:

AUSTRALIA
Flight Centre (☎ 13 31 33 Australia-wide; www.flight centre.com.au)
STA Travel (☎ 1300 733 035 Australia-wide; www.sta travel.com.au)

NEW ZEALAND
Flight Centre (☎ 0800 243544; www.flightcentre.co.nz)
STA Travel (☎ 0508 782 872; www.sta.travel.co.nz)

From Canada & USA

The Atlantic hop between Britain and North America is the world's busiest transcontinental route, and competition means a continuous price war. Return fares from the east coast to London range from US$300 to US$600. From the west coast, fares are about US$100 higher. Major agencies:

CANADA
Flight Centre (☎ 1888-967 5355; www.flightcentre.ca)
Travel CUTS (☎ 866 246 9762; www.travelcuts.com)

USA
Flight Centre (☎ 1866-WORLD 51; www.flightcentre.us)
STA Travel (☎ 800 781 4040; www.statravel.com)

LAND
Bus & Coach

You can easily get between Britain and numerous cities in Ireland or mainland Europe via long-distance bus (usually called 'coach' in Britain). The international bus network **Eurolines** (www.eurolines.com) connects a huge number of destinations; the website has links to operators in each country, and gives contact details of local offices. In Britain, you can book Eurolines tickets on the phone or at the website of **National Express** (☎ 08705 808080; www.nationalexpress.com), and at many travel agencies.

Bus or coach travel may be slower and less comfortable than going by train, but it's

usually cheaper, especially if you're under 25 or over 60. Some sample single fares (and approximate journey times) are: Amsterdam to London €50 (10 hours); Barcelona €125 (24 hours); Dublin €30 (12 hours). Frequent special offers can bring these fares down, but it's still worth checking the budget airlines. You may pay a similar price and save a large chunk of journey time.

Train
CHANNEL TUNNEL SERVICES

The Channel Tunnel makes direct train travel between Britain and continental Europe a fast and enjoyable option. High-speed **Eurostar** (☎ 08705 186 186; www.eurostar.com) passenger services hurtle at least 10 times daily between London and Paris (three hours), and London and Brussels (2½ hours), via Ashford and Calais. A new high-speed rail link on the British side will be complete in 2007 and slice another 30 minutes off the journey.

You can buy Eurostar tickets from travel agencies, major train stations or direct from Eurostar. The normal single fare between London and Paris/Brussels is £149, but advance deals can drop to around £100 return, or less. Seniors and under-25s get reductions. Bicycles must be in a bike bag.

The other alternative is the **Eurotunnel** (☎ 0870 353535; www.eurotunnel.com). You drive to the coast (Folkestone in Britain, Calais in France), drive onto a train, get transported through the tunnel, and drive off at the other end. The trains run about four times hourly from 6am to 10pm, then hourly. Loading and unloading is one hour; the journey takes 35 minutes. You can book in advance direct to Eurotunnel or pay on the spot (cash or credit card). A car (and passengers) costs around £200 return, but there are often cheaper promotional fares.

TRAIN & FERRY CONNECTIONS

As well as Eurostar, many 'normal' trains run between Britain and mainland Europe. You buy a direct ticket, but get off the train at the port, walk onto a ferry, then get another train on the other side. Routes include: Amsterdam to London (via Hook of Holland and Harwich); Brussels to London (via Ostende and Dover); Paris to London (via Calais and Dover). Single fares are

TRANSPORT

about £50, but cheaper deals are usually available.

Travelling between Ireland and Britain, the main train-ferry-train route is Dublin to London, via Dun-Laoghaire and Holyhead. From southern Ireland, ferries sail between Rosslare and Fishguard or Pembroke (Wales), with train connections on either side.

SEA

The main ferry routes between Britain, Ireland and mainland Europe include Holyhead to Dun-Laoghaire (Ireland), Dover to Calais (France), Dover to Ostende (Belgium), Harwich to Hook of Holland (Netherlands) and Hamburg (Germany), Hull to Zeebrugge (Belgium) and Rotterdam (Netherlands), Portsmouth to Santander and Bilbao (Spain), Newcastle to Bergen (Norway) and Gothenberg (Sweden), Rosyth, near Edinburgh, to Zeebrugge, Lerwick, Shetland to Bergen (Norway), but there are many more.

Stiff competition from Eurotunnel and budget airlines has forced ferry operators to offer constant discounted fares, although options vary massively according to time of day or year. The best cross-channel bargains are return fares – often much cheaper than two singles; sometimes cheaper than *one* single! If you're a foot passenger, or cycling, you've got more flexibility. If you're driving a car, planning ahead is worthwhile: as well as the usual variants (time of year etc), fares depend on the size of car and the number of passengers. On longer ferry trips, the fare might include a cabin.

Main ferry operators (and their UK contact numbers) include:

Brittany Ferries (☎ 08703 665 333; www.brittany -ferries.com)
Fjord Line (☎ 0191-296 1313; www.fjordline.co.uk)
Hoverspeed (☎ 0870 240 8070; www.hoverspeed.co.uk)
Irish Ferries (☎ 08705 171717; www.irishferries.com)
P&O Ferries (☎ 08705 202020; www.poferries.com)
Speedferries (☎ 01304-203000; www.speedferries.com)
Stena Line (☎ 08705 707070; www.stenaline.com)
Superfast Ferries (☎ 0870 234 0870; www.superfast .com)

Another option is www.ferrybooker.com – an online agency covering all sea ferry routes, plus Eurotunnel.

GETTING AROUND

For getting around Britain by public transport, your main options are train and bus. Services between major towns and cities are generally good, although expensive compared to other European countries. Delays are frequent too, especially on the rail network, but these tend to afflict commuters rather than visitors: So your journey from London to Bath runs 30 minutes late. What's the problem? You're on holiday!

As long as you have time, with a mix of train, coach, local bus, the odd taxi, walking and occasionally hiring a bike, you can get almost anywhere. You'll certainly see more of the countryside than you might slogging along grey motorways, in the serene knowledge that you're doing less environmental damage. Having said that, in some rural areas the bus services can be patchy, so a car can often be handy for reaching out-of-the-way spots.

Public Transport Information (www.pti.org.uk) is a very useful website covering services nationwide (although some areas are better represented than others) with numerous links to help plan your journey.

AIR

Britain's domestic air companies include British Airways, British Midland, EasyJet and Ryanair, but flights are rarely necessary for tourists. If you're in a mad rush you might consider a flight between London and Glasgow or Edinburgh, but express trains often compare favourably with planes once airport down-time is factored in. On price, you might get a bargain airfare, but with advance planning trains can be cheaper.

BICYCLE

Britain is a compact country, and getting around by bicycle is perfectly feasible – and a great way to really see the country – if you've got time to spare. For more ideas see p79.

BUS & COACH

If you're on a tight budget, long-distance buses are nearly always the cheapest way to get around the country, when compared to flights and trains, although they're also the slowest (sometimes by a considerable margin). Shorter bus trips around cities or rural areas are covered in the Local Transport section (p969).

In Britain, long-distance express buses are called coaches, and in many towns there are separate bus and coach stations. Make sure you go to the right place!

National Express (☎ 08705 808080; www.national express.com) is the main operator, with a wide network and frequent services between main centres. **Scottish Citylink** (☎ 08705 505050; www.city link.co.uk), part of the National Express group, is Scotland's leading coach company. Some sample single fares; London to York £22, London to Cardiff £17, London to Edinburgh £29. Special offer 'fun fares' can be as low as £1.

Also offering fares from £1 is **Megabus** (www .megabus.com) a budget airline-style service between about 20 main destinations around the country. Go at a quiet time, book early, and your ticket will be very cheap. Book later, for a busy time and… you get the picture. Along the same lines is the recently launched **EasyBus** (www.easybus.co.uk).

There are many smaller regional operators across the country, several forming part of the Stagecoach, Arriva or First networks.

Bus Passes & Discounts

Bus passes for touring the whole country include the National Express Brit Xplorer, offering unlimited travel for seven days (£70), 14 days (£120) and 28 days (£190). You don't need to book journeys in advance

---

ALL THE FUN OF THE FARES

On coaches and especially trains, passengers are frequently faced with a bewildering array of ticket types and prices. Throughout this book we give the price for single tickets (unless otherwise specified) bought on the day you travel, outside peak times ie outside 7am to 9.30am and 4pm to 6pm on weekdays, and about 4pm to 8pm on Friday and Sunday evenings. If you plan your itinerary at least three days ahead, and buy your tickets in advance, you'll make considerable savings on the prices we quote in this book. If you're buying return fares, note that they can be anything from double the single price to only very slightly more (for example, a London to York 'saver' single train fare is £65; a 'saver' return is £66).

---

with this pass; if the coach has a spare seat – you can take it. This deal is only available to non-Brits though. (Local bus passes are covered under Local Transport, p969.)

National Express also offers Discount Coachcards to full-time students, under-26s and people over 50. Proof and a passport photo are required. Cards cost £10, and get you 25% to 50% off standard adult fares. Families and disabled travellers also get discounts.

Information

For information on bus travel around Britain, contact the national **Traveline** (☎ 0870 608 2608; www.traveline.org.uk). By phone, you get transferred automatically to an advisor in the region you're phoning from; for details on another part of the country you may have to be transferred to another assistant. Once you're on the spot, double-check at a Tourist Information Centre (TIC) before planning your day's activities around a bus that you later find out only runs on Thursdays after a full moon.

CAR & MOTORCYCLE

Travelling by private car or motorbike, you can be independent and flexible, and reach remote places. For solo budget travellers a downside of car travel is the expense, and in cities you'll need superhuman skills to negotiate heaving traffic, plus deep pockets for parking charges. But if there's two or more, car travel can sometimes work out cheaper than public transport.

Motorways and main A-roads are dual carriageways and zip you from one end of the country to another. Lesser A-roads, B-roads and minor roads are much more scenic and fun – especially in northern England – winding through the countryside from village to village; ideal for car or motorcycle touring. You can't travel fast, but you won't care.

Petrol costs around 80p per litre. Diesel is slightly cheaper. Note also that fuel prices rise the further you get away from regional centres.

Motoring Organisations

Large motoring organisations include the **Automobile Association** (☎ 0870 600 0371; www.theaa .com) and the **Royal Automobile Club** (☎ customer services 08705 722 722, membership services 08007 317 090; www.rac.co.uk); annual membership starts at around £40, including 24-hour breakdown assistance. A greener alternative is the **Environmental Transport Association** (☎ 01932-828882; www.eta.co.uk); it provides all the usual services (breakdown assistance, roadside rescue, vehicle inspections etc) but doesn't campaign for more roads.

Parking

Britain is small, and people love their cars, so there's often not enough parking space to go round – especially in urban areas or popular national parks. Many cities have short-stay and long-stay car parks; the latter are cheaper though maybe less convenient. You either pay an attendant at the car park gate or get a ticket to stick inside your car. In some Scottish towns you have to get a disc or permit (usually available from local shops or newsagents) to display what time you arrived in the parking spot. In major towns and cities all over Britain 'park and ride' systems allow you to park in a satellite car park and then ride to the centre on the regular buses provided for an all-in-one price.

Yellow lines (single or double) along the edge of the road indicate restrictions. Find the nearby sign that spells out when you can and can't park. In London and other big cities, traffic wardens operate with efficiency; if you park on the yellow lines at the wrong time, your car will be clamped or towed away, and it'll cost you £100 or more to get driving again. In some cities there are also red lines, which mean no stopping at all. Ever.

Purchase

If you're planning a long tour around Britain you may want to buy a vehicle. You can find a banger for £300, and a reasonable car for around £1000. If you want a camper van, expect to pay at least £2000 for something reliable, although for a decent second-hand vehicle you'll be looking closer to £10,000. For more prices, pick up *Autotrader* magazine, or look at www.autotrader.co.uk.

To be on the road, all cars require:

- a Ministry of Transport (MOT) safety certificate, valid for one year
- third-party insurance – shop around, but expect to pay at least £300
- a registration form ('log book') signed by both the buyer and seller
- a 'tax disc' – £88/160 for six months/one year (less for engines under 1100cc).

It saves loads of hassle to buy a vehicle with a valid MOT certificate and tax disc; both remain with the car through change of ownership. Third-party insurance goes with the driver rather than the car, so you'll still have to arrange this.

Rental

Compared to many countries (especially the USA) rental rates are expensive in Britain; you should expect to pay around £250 per week for a small car (unlimited mileage). Rates rise at busy times, and drop at quiet times (especially at EasyRentacar, where you also get better rates for advance reservations, and special offers can drop to £3 per day).

Some main players:

Avis (☎ 08700 100 287; www.avis.co.uk)
Budget (☎ 08701 565656; www.budget.co.uk)
EasyRentacar (☎ 0906 333 3333; www.easycar.com)
Europcar (☎ 0870 607 5000; www.europcar.co.uk)
Hertz (☎ 0870 844 8844; www.hertz.co.uk)
National (☎ 0870 400 4502; www.nationalcar.co.uk)
Sixt (☎ 01246-506776; www.e-sixt.co.uk)
Thrifty (☎ 01494-751600; www.thrifty.co.uk)

Many international websites have separate pages for customers in different countries, and the price to hire a car in Britain on, say, the USA pages can be cheaper or more expensive than the same car on the Australia pages (or, indeed, on the UK pages). The moral is – you have to surf a lot of sites to find the best deals.

Your other alternative is to use an Internet search engine to locate small local car rental companies in Britain who can undercut the big boys. Generally those in cities are cheaper than those in rural areas. See under Getting Around in the main city sections for more details. Or see a rental broker site such as **United Kingdom Car Hire** (www.uk-carhire.net).

Road Rules

A foreign driving licence is valid in Britain for up to 12 months. If you plan to bring a car from Europe, it's illegal to drive without (at least) third-party insurance. Some other important rules:

- drive on the left (!)
- wear fitted seat belts in cars
- wear crash helmets on motorcycles
- give way to your right at junctions and roundabouts

- always use the left-side lane on motorways and dual-carriageways, unless overtaking (although so many people ignore this rule, you might think it wasn't law)
- don't use a mobile phone while driving unless it's fully hands-free (another rule frequently flouted).

Speed limits are 30mph (48km/h) in built-up areas, 60mph (96km/h) on main roads, and 70mph (112km/h) on motorways and dual carriageways. Drinking and driving is taken very seriously: you're allowed a blood-alcohol level of 80mg/100mL (0.8mg/mL) and campaigners want it reduced to 50mg/100mL (0.5mg/mL).

All drivers should read the *Highway Code*. It's often stocked by TICs, and available online at www.roads.dft.gov.uk/roadsafety (and, incidentally, often around number seven in national nonfiction best-seller tables).

HITCHING

Hitching is not as common as it used to be in Britain. Travellers should understand that they're taking a small but potentially serious risk, and we don't recommend it. If you decide to go by thumb, note that it's illegal to hitch on motorways; you must use approach roads or service stations.

However, as is the case with so many other things, it's all different in remote rural areas such as Mid Wales or northwest Scotland, where hitching is a part of getting around – especially if you're a hiker. On some Scottish islands, local drivers may stop and offer you a lift without you even asking.

LOCAL TRANSPORT
Bus

British cities usually have good local public transport systems, although buses are often run by a confusing number of companies. The larger cities have suburban 'overground' and underground rail services, and several cities (such as Manchester and Sheffield) have modern tram systems too. For on-the-spot information, more details are given in the city sections throughout this book. For even more information, head to TICs.

For shorter trips in rural areas popular with tourists (especially national parks) there are frequent bus services Easter to September. Elsewhere in the countryside, bus timetables are designed to serve schools and industry,

so there can be few midday and weekend services, or buses may link local villages to a market town on only one day each week.

BUS PASSES

If you're taking a few local bus rides in a single day of energetic sight-seeing, ask about local bus passes (with names like Day Rover, Wayfarer or Explorer), which are cheaper than buying individual tickets. If you plan to linger longer in one area, three-day passes are a great bargain. Often they can be bought on your first bus, and may include local rail services. Specific passes are mentioned in the regional chapters throughout this book, and it's always worth asking ticket clerks or bus drivers about your options.

Postbus

A postbus is a van on usual mail service that also carries passengers. They operate in rural areas (and some of the most scenic and remote parts of the country), and are especially useful for walkers and backpackers. For information and timetables contact **Royal Mail Postbus** (☎ 08457 740 740; www.postbus.royalmail.com).

Taxi

There are two main sorts of taxi: the famous black cabs (some carry advertising livery in other colours these days) which have meters and can be hailed in the street, and minicabs which can only be called by phone. In London and other big cities, taxis cost £2 to £3 per mile. In rural areas, it's about half this, which means when it's Sunday and you find that the next bus out of the charming town you've just hiked to is on Monday, a taxi can get keep you moving. If you call **National Cabline** (☎ 0800 123444) from a landline phone, the service will pinpoint your location and transfer you to an approved local company.

Ferries

Local ferries, from the mainland to the Isle of Wight or the Scottish islands for example, are covered in the relevant sections in the regional chapters.

TOURS & ACTIVITY HOLIDAYS

If time is limited or you prefer to travel in a group, a tour is a great way to get around, especially if it's combined with an activity. This section suggests some Britain-wide tours and holidays, while local choices are listed in the relevant chapters. Many national parks organise activity days or weekends – concentrating on wildlife and outdoor stuff like landscape painting or dry-stone walling. For more information inquire at local TICs or see suggestions on www.visitbritain.com.

Acorn Activities (☎ 08707 405055; www.acornactivities .co.uk) Themed tours and day-trips from abseiling to yachting, via cycling, silver-smithing and much more.

Backpacker Co (☎ 020-8896 6070; www.backpacker.co .uk) Day trips to classic British sporting events, and tours further afield.

Beics Eryri (☎ 01286-676637; www.beicseryri.clara.net) Welsh cycle tour specialists with tours and custom-made itineraries.

Black Prince Holidays (☎ 01527-575115; www.black prince.com) Canal boats for hire, traditional on the outside, modern on the inside, from bases across Britain, for three days, a week or more.

British Trust for Conservation Volunteers (☎ 01302-572244; www.btcv.org) Environmental working holidays, for weekends or longer.

Bus Wales (☎ 01446-774652; www.buswalestours.com) Good-humoured trips round the mountains, castles and sights of Wales – plus the chance to learn the basics of the Welsh language.

Bushwakkers (☎ 01874-636552; www.bushwakkers.co .uk) Relaxed company offering minibus tours to Wales, with horse-riding and canoeing optional, and partying obligatory.

Classique Tours (☎ 0141-889 4050; www.classiquetours .co.uk) Well-established company offering tours of Scotland's Highlands and Islands, including the Hebrides and the wilder northwest region, in lovingly refurbished historic coaches, staying at country hotels and inns.

Contiki (☎ 020-8290 6422; www.contiki.com) Fun-packed bus tours of Britain.

Contours (☎ 017684-80451; www.contours.co.uk) Self-guided walking tours on long-distance paths. Routes, accommodation and baggage transfer is all arranged; you travel when and as fast as you like.

Country Lanes (☎ 01425-655022; www.countrylanes.co .uk) Guided and self-guided cycling and walking tours throughout Britain.

Dragon Tours (☎ 01874-658124; www.dragonbackpacker tours.co.uk) Individually focussed tours of Wales, from 'all-over explorer' to 'beach and mountains special' led by a Welsh historian with a passion for his country, ancient and modern.

Heart of Scotland (☎ 0131-558 8855; www.heartof scotlandtours.co.uk) An excellent choice of day-tours from Edinburgh, to lochs, castles and battlefields and more.

Macbackpackers (☎ 0131-558 9900; www.macback packers.com) Minibus tours across Scotland, from one day to a week or longer, staying in great hostels; plus a hop-on/hop-off backpacker bus service.

Rabbie's Trail Burners (☎ 0131-226 3133; www.rabbies .com) Impressive range of short and long tours around Scotland, plus self-drive tours, city breaks, accommodation booking and online souvenir shop!

Radical Travel Network, Haggis Adventures (☎ 0131-557 9393; www.radicaltravel.com, www.haggis adventures.com) Highly rated tours throughout England, Wales and Scotland, aimed squarely at the young, fun and budget-conscious.

Road Trip (☎ 0845 200 6791; www.roadtrip.co.uk) Wide range of minibus tours through Britain, ideal for backpackers, for one, three or five days, with optional activities.

Rough Tracks (☎ 07000-560 749; www.rough-tracks.co .uk) Specialists in off-road and on-road cycling tours – with a group or tailor-made – in England, Wales, and beyond.

Shaggy Sheep (☎ 01267-281202; www.shaggysheep .com) Light-hearted, unhurried, tailored tours of Wales' high spots, with an option for activities and your choice of accommodation.

SYHA (☎ 08701 553255; www.syha.org.uk) The Scottish Youth Hostel Association offers an excellent range of good-value tours and activity holidays, including canoeing, mountain-biking, pony trekking and mountain walking, in various parts of Scotland.

Walkabout Scotland (☎ 0131-661 7168; www.walk aboutscotland.com) Edinburgh-based walking specialists, with strolls, hikes and treks across Scotland, for the day, the weekend or longer, for all levels of fitness and experience.

YHA (☎ 0870 770 8868; www.yha.org.uk) Massive range of walking tours. Guided or self-guided, group or independent, long-distance paths to weekend rambles, and activity holidays (caving, climbing, horse riding, mountain-biking, kayaking and countless others) for people of all ages, plus active family breaks – including paint-ball weekends to work out all those issues.

TRAIN

For long-distance travel around Britain, trains are generally faster and more comfortable than coaches, but they can be more expensive, although with discount tickets they can be competitive – and often take you through beautiful countryside. Train services are run by about 20 different operating companies (for example, First Great Western runs from London to Bath, GNER covers the East Coast line), while track and stations are run by Network Rail. For passengers this system can be confusing, but information and ticket-buying services are increasingly centralised.

Your first stop for timetable and fare information should be **National Rail Enquiries** (☎ 08457 484950, 020-7278 5240; www.nationalrail .co.uk). By phone, once you've checked times and fares, you then have to contact the relevant train operator to actually buy the ticket (for the cheaper advance-purchase tickets), or you can buy on the spot at stations (but advance purchase discount tickets are not always available here). The National Rail Enquiries website has direct links to the individual operators and to two centralised ticketing services (www.thetrainline.com and www.Qjump.co.uk) and also has special offers, plus real-time links to station departure boards, so you see if your train is on time (or not).

Classes

There are two classes of rail travel: first and standard (often called 2nd class). First class costs around 50% more than standard class and, except on very crowded trains, is not really worth it. At the weekend, however, some operators offer upgrades from standard to 1st class for an additional fee of around £10 (up to £15 for long journeys). Sometimes it's worth shelling out the extra if you suddenly find yourself on a busy train, fighting for breathing space, let alone sitting space. (Note: you pay on the train itself.)

Costs & Reservations

For short journeys (under about 50 miles), it's easiest to buy tickets on the spot at train stations. You won't save much by buying in advance. You may get a choice of express or stopping service – the latter is obviously slower, but can be cheaper, and may take you through charming countryside or grotty suburbs.

For longer journeys, on-the-spot fares are always available, but cheaper if bought three days before travel (and even cheaper with more notice). Advance purchase gets you a reserved seat, too. The cheapest fares apply to a specific train service though, and may be nonrefundable, so if you miss your train, you'll have to buy another ticket. Some tickets are more expensive to buy, but allow you to change times for around £5, thus allowing a bit more flexibility.

If you have to change trains, or use two or more train operators, you still buy one ticket – valid for the whole of your journey. The main railcards are also accepted by all operators.

If you buy by phone or website, you can have the ticket posted to you (UK only), or collect it at the originating station on the day of travel, either at the ticket desk (get there with time to spare, as queues can be long) or via automatic machines.

For short or long trips, fares are usually cheaper outside 'peak' travel times (ie not when everyone else is trying to get to or from work). It's worth avoiding Friday and Sunday too, as fares are higher on these busy days.

BIKES ON TRAINS

Bicycles can be taken on most long-distance train journeys for about £3, but space limitations and ridiculously complicated booking regulations often makes this difficult, especially if you have to change trains. It really is like the train operators don't want customers, and this impression was confirmed in mid-2004 when a PR manager of a large train company was quoted as saying 'I can never understand why people choose to carry one form of transport on another.' Not only did this display a worrying lack of knowledge (the answer is because many commuters like to ride from home to the station, take the train, then ride station-to-work), it also showed appalling short-sightedness. It also indicates why Britain is still years away from achieving an integrated transport policy.

Despite the hoops and barriers, with persistence you can usually get yourself (and your bike) where you want to be. Start with **National Rail Enquiries** (☎ 08457 484950; www.nationalrail.co.uk) and have a big cup of coffee or stress-reliever handy.

A bit of good news: Although bikes are rarely allowed on busy commuter services (hence many savvy cyclists have switched to folding bikes), on local trains outside peak times and on any shorter trip in rural areas there's generally much less trouble; bikes can be taken free of charge on a first-come-first-served basis. Even so, there may be space limits.

And a final warning: when railways are being repaired, cancelled trains are replaced by buses – and they won't take bikes.

Following are the main fare types. The varying prices of London to York tickets are given by way of example.

Apex Must be bought at least seven days in advance. Valid for one month and requires a fixed return date. Limited seats are available, so you must book well ahead to get this fare. (London–York single/return £37/38.)

Cheap Day Single/Return Available on the spot. Valid only on the specified day, but has some restrictions (eg no travel before 9.30am).

Day Return Valid any time on the day specified. Cheaper than an open return.

Open Single/Return Available on the spot. Any train. No restrictions. Valid for a month. (London–York single/return £69/138.)

Saver Single/Return Available on the spot. Return valid for one month. More restrictions (eg no peak travel, morning and evening). (London–York single/return £65/66.)

SuperAdvance Must be bought before 6pm on day before travel, but only a limited number of seats available, so can sell out. Buy further ahead if possible. Valid for one month, but you must fix your return journey date. (London–York single/return £49/50.)

SuperSaver Available on the spot. Cheaper than saver, but even more restrictions (eg no peak or weekend travel).

Children under five travel free; those aged between five and 15 pay half-price, except on tickets already heavily discounted.

Railcards

If staying in Britain for a while, railcards cost £20 (valid for a year, available from major stations) and get you 33% discounts on most train fares. On the Family and Network cards, children get 60%, and the fee is easily repaid in a couple of journeys. Proof of age and a passport photo may be required. For details see www.railcard.co.uk.

Disabled Person's Railcard Costs £14. Cannot be bought at stations, but you can get an application form there, or from www.nationalrail.co.uk. Call ☎ 0191-281 8103 for more details.

Family Railcard Covers up to four adults and four children travelling together.

Network Card If you're concentrating on southeast England (eg London to Dover, Weymouth, Cambridge or Oxford), this card covers up to four adults travelling together outside peak times.

Senior Railcard For anyone over 60.

Young Person's Railcard You must be between 16 and 25, or a full-time UK student.

Train Passes

Local train passes usually cover rail networks around a city (many include bus travel too), and are mentioned throughout this book.

For country-wide travel, BritRail passes are good value, but only for visitors from overseas and *cannot be bought in Britain*. They must be bought in your country of origin from a specialist travel agent. There are many BritRail variants, each available in three different versions: for England only; for the whole of Britain (England, Wales and Scotland); for the UK and Ireland. Below is an outline of the main options, quoting adult prices. Children's passes are usually half price (or free with some adult passes), and seniors get discounts too. For about 30% extra you can upgrade to 1st class. Other deals include a rail pass combined with the use of a hire car, or travel in Britain combined with one Eurostar journey.

BRITRAIL CONSECUTIVE

Unlimited travel on all trains in Britain for 4, 8, 15, 22 or 30 days, for US$189/269/400/500/600. Anyone getting their money's worth out of the last pass should earn some sort of endurance award.

BRITRAIL FLEXIPASS

These passes mean you don't have to get on a train every day to get full value. Your options are four day's unlimited travel in Britain within a 60-day period for US$239, eight in 60 for US$345, or 15 in 60 for US$520.

ALL LINE ROVERS

If you don't (or can't) buy a BritRail pass, an All Line Rover gives unlimited travel anywhere on the national rail network (£338/515 for seven/14 days), and can be purchased in Britain, by anyone.

INTERNATIONAL PASSES

Eurail passes are not accepted in Britain, and InterRail passes are only valid if bought in another mainland European country.

Health

CONTENTS

Britain is a healthy place to travel, and the National Health Service (NHS) provides an excellent service, free at the point of delivery, which, although Brits may complain, is better than most other countries can offer. Across the country, hygiene standards are high (despite what your nose tells you on a crowded tube train) and there are no unusual diseases to worry about. Your biggest risks will be from overdoing some activities – physical, chemical or other.

BEFORE YOU GO

No immunisations are mandatory for a visit to Britain.

European Economic Area (EEA) nationals can obtain free emergency treatment in Britain on presentation of an E111 form, validated in their home country. Reciprocal arrangements between the UK and some other countries around the world (including Australia) allows their citizens to receive free emergency medical treatment and subsidised dental care at British hospitals, and with general practitioners (GPs) and dentists. For more details see the 'overseas visitors' section on the Department of Heath website: www.dh.gov.uk.

Regardless of nationality, anyone will receive free emergency treatment at accident and emergency departments of NHS hospitals. Travel insurance, however, is advisable, as it offers greater flexibility over where and how you're treated, and covers expenses for emergency repatriation.

Pharmacists can advise on minor ailments such as sore throats and earache. In large cities, there's always one pharmacy (chemist) open 24 hours.

Internet resources

Lonely Planet's website (www.lonelyplanet .com) has links to the World Health Organi-

zation (WHO) and the US Centers for Disease Control & Prevention. Other good sites include the following:

www.ageconcern.org.uk Advice on travel for the elderly.
www.mariestopes.org.uk Women's health and contraception.
www.mdtravelhealth.com Worldwide travel health recommendations, updated daily.
www.who.int/ith WHO publication *International Travel and Health* available.

IN TRANSIT
Deep Vein Thrombosis (DVT)

DVT refers to blood clots that form in the legs during plane flights, chiefly because of prolonged immobility. The longer the flight, the greater the risk. The chief symptom is swelling of, or pain in, the foot, ankle or calf. When a blood clot travels to the lungs, it may cause chest pain and breathing difficulties.

To prevent DVT on extended flights, you should walk around the cabin, exercise your leg muscles by periodically contracting them while sitting, drink plenty of fluids and avoid alcohol.

Jet Lag

To avoid jet lag (common when you're crossing more than five time zones), try drinking plenty of nonalcoholic fluids and eating light meals. Upon arrival, get exposure to natural sunlight and readjust your schedule (for meals, sleep and so on) as soon as possible.

IN BRITAIN
Hypothermia

If the body loses heat faster than it can produce it hypothermia occurs. If you are walking in winter, especially in Scotland or other mountainous areas, it is surprisingly easy to

---

NATIONAL HEALTH WEBSITES

If you're visiting Britain from overseas, it's a good idea to consult your government's travel health website before departure. These include the following:

Australia (www.dfat.gov.au/travel/)
Canada (www.travelhealth.gc.ca)
USA (www.cdc.gov/travel/)

get dangerously cold due to a combination of wind, wet clothing, fatigue and hunger, even if the air temperature is above freezing. Adequate clothing, food and drink (and a 'space blanket' or 'bivvy bag' for emergencies) are essential. Make sure you wear the appropriate gear if you are surfing or windsurfing as the water can be very cold.

Symptoms of hypothermia are exhaustion, numb skin (particularly toes and fingers), shivering, blue or grey pallor, slurred speech, irrational or violent behaviour, lethargy, stumbling, dizzy spells, muscle cramps and violent bursts of energy. Irrationality may take the form of sufferers claiming they're warm and trying to take off their clothes.

To treat mild hypothermia, first get the sufferer out of the wind and/or rain, remove their clothing if it's wet and replace it with dry, warm clothing. Give them hot liquids – not alcohol – and some high-energy, easily digestible food. Do not rub victims; instead, allow them to slowly warm themselves. The recognition and treatment of mild hypothermia is the only way to prevent severe hypothermia, which is a critical condition.

Sunburn

In summertime in Britain, even when there's cloud cover, it's possible to get sunburnt surprisingly quickly – especially if you're on water. Use sunscreen, wear a hat and cover up with a shirt and trousers.

Water

The tap water in Britain is always safe unless there is a sign to the contrary (eg on trains). Do not drink straight from streams in the countryside – you never know what's upstream.

Women's Health

Emotional stress, exhaustion and travelling through time zones can contribute to an upset in the menstrual pattern. If using oral contraceptives, remember some antibiotics, diarrhoea and vomiting can stop them from working.

If you're already pregnant, travel is usually possible, but you should always consult your doctor. The most risky times for travel are the first 12 weeks of pregnancy and after 30 weeks.

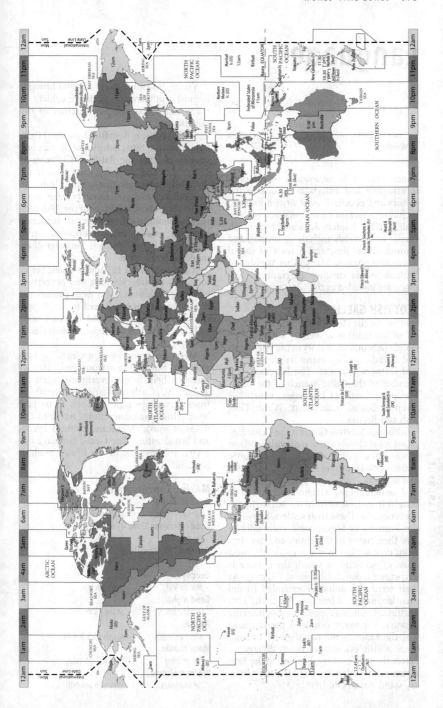

Language

CONTENTS

Lonely Planet's *British Phrasebook* offers an informative and entertaining look at the history and peculiarities of British English, including a section on regional accents and dialects. The chapters dedicated to Scottish Gaelic and Welsh include grammar and pronunciation tips, and a feast of useful words and phrases. Many other Welsh and Scottish words (mainly geographical features) are included in the Glossary on p978.

SCOTTISH GAELIC

Scottish Gaelic (*Gàidhlig*, pronounced 'gallic' in Scotland) is spoken by about 80,000 people in Scotland, mainly in the Highlands and islands, and by many native speakers and learners overseas. The language is a member of the Celtic branch of the Indo-European family of languages, which has given us Gaelic, Irish, Manx, Welsh, Cornish and Breton.

Although Scottish Gaelic is the Celtic language most closely associated with Scotland it was quite a latecomer to those shores. Other Celtic languages in the form of Pictish and Brittonic had existed prior to the arrival and settlement by Gaelic-speaking Celts (Gaels) from Ireland from the 4th to the 6th centuries AD. These Irish settlers, known to the Romans as Scotti, were eventually to give their name to the entire country. Initially they settled in the area on the west coast of Scotland in which their name is perpetuated, Earra Ghaidheal (Argyll). As their territorial influence extended so did their language and from the 9th to the 11th centuries Gaelic was spoken throughout the country. For many centuries the language was the same as the language of Ireland; there is little evidence of much divergence before the 13th century. Even up to the 18th century the bards adhered to the strict literary standards of Old Irish.

Viking invasions from AD 800 brought linguistic influences, which are evident in many of the coastal place names of the Highlands.

Gaelic culture flourished in the Highlands until the 18th century and the Jacobite rebellions. After the Battle of Culloden in 1746 many Gaelic speakers were forced off their ancestral lands; this 'ethnic cleansing' by landlords and governments culminated in the Highland Clearances of the 19th century. Although still studied at academic level, the spoken language declined, being regarded as a mere 'peasant' language of no modern significance.

It was only in the 1970s that Gaelic began to make a comeback with a new generation of young enthusiasts who were determined that it should not be allowed to die. People from all over Scotland, and indeed worldwide, are beginning to appreciate their Gaelic heritage.

After two centuries of decline, the language is now being encouraged through financial help from government agencies and the EU. Gaelic education is flourishing from playgroups right through to tertiary level. This renaissance flows out into the fields of music, literature, cultural events and broadcasting. The Gaelic language has a vital role to play in the life of modern Scotland.

Making Conversation

Good morning.
   Madainn mhath.   mating vah
Good afternoon/Good evening.
   Feasgar math.   feskur mah
Goodbye. (lit: Blessings go with you)
   Beannachd leat.   byan·nukhk laht
Goodbye. (The same with you)
   Mar sin leat.   mar shin laht
Good night.
   Oidhche mhath.   ai·khuh vah
Please.
   Mas e do thoil e.   ma·she duh hol eh
Many thanks.
   Móran taing.   moe·ran tah·eeng
You're welcome.
   'Se do bheatha.   shey duh veh·huh

What's your name?

Dé an t-ainm a tha ort?   jen ta·nam a horsht?

I'm ...

Is mise ...   smee·shuh ...

Good health/Cheers!

Slàinte mhath!   slaan·chuh vah!

WELSH

The Welsh language belongs to the Celtic branch of the Indo-European language family. Closely related to Breton and Cornish, and more distantly to Irish, Scottish and Manx, it is the strongest Celtic language both in terms of numbers of speakers (over 500,000) and place in society. It was once spoken throughout the island of Britain south of a line between modern Glasgow and Edinburgh, but was gradually pushed westwards by the invading Angles and Saxons following the retreat of the Roman legions in the 5th century. Several thousand Welsh speakers also live in the Welsh colony in Patagonia. Its earliest literature was written towards the end of the 6th century in what is now southern Scotland, when court poets Taliesin and Aneurin pioneered a literary tradition which continued for some 14 centuries.

By the early modern period, Welsh had lost its status as an official language. The Acts of Union with England (1536 and 1542) deprived the language of all administrative functions. However, translations of the Book of Common Prayer (1567) and the Bible (1588) into Welsh gave the language a limited public function again. Up until the industrial revolution, most Welsh people spoke only Welsh, and some 50% still spoke Welsh in 1900. Thereafter the language retreated more rapidly, so that by 1961, only 26% were Welsh-speaking and there was general alarm that the language would totally disappear.

The Saunders Lewis BBC radio lecture, *Tynged yr Iaith tuhng-ed uhrr yaith,* 'The Fate of the Language' in 1962 led to the creation of *Cymdeithas yr Iaith Gymraeg kuhm-day-thas uhrr yaith guhm-raig,* a protest movement in support of the language. It was spearheaded by university students and inspired by pop singers like Dafydd Iwan, and succeeded through campaigns of civil disobedience in winning equal recognition for Welsh in one domain of society

after another. Recent figures would suggest that the decline has been halted. The language has reasserted its position in the educational system, with the Welsh-language TV channel S4C since 1983, and in recent years with the resurgence of Welsh as a badge of national identity, particularly among the young.

Wales is famous for having the longest place name in the world – Llanfairpwllgwyngyllgogerychwyrndrobwllllantysiliogogogoch (hlan·vairr·poohl·gwin·gihl·gogerr·uh·khwirrn·dro·boohl·hlan·tuh·sil·ee·ohgo·go·gokh) – which, translated, means 'St Mary's Church in the hollow of the White Hazel near a rapid whirlpool and the Church of St Tysilio near the Red Cave'. This can be tricky to say after a pint or three of Brains!

Making Conversation

Good morning.

Bore da.   bo·rre dah

Good afternoon.

Prynhawn da.   pruhn·hown dah

Good night.

Nos da.   nohs da

Hello.

Sut mae.   sit mai

Goodbye.

Hwyl fawr.   hueyl vowrr

Thanks.

Diolch.   dee·olkh

What's your name?

Beth yw eich enw chi?   beth yu whch en·oo khee?

Cheers!

Iechyd da!   yekh·id dah!

How much?

Faint?   vaint?

Also available from Lonely Planet:
British Phrasebook

Glossary

abbey – a monastery of monks or nuns or the buildings they used

agister – someone paid to care for stock

aisle – passageway or open space along either side of a church's nave

aka – also known as

almshouse – accommodation offered to the aged or needy

ambulatory – processional aisle at the eastern end of a cathedral, behind the altar

apse – semicircular or rectangular area for clergy, traditionally at eastern end of church

BABA – Book-A-Bed-Ahead scheme

bailey – outermost wall of a castle

bairn – baby (northern England)

banger – old, cheap car

bangers – sausages

bap – bun

baptistry – separate area of a church used for baptisms

bar – gate (York, and some other northern cities)

barbican – an extended gateway in a castle designed to make entry difficult for unwanted guests

barrel vault – semicircular arched roof

beck – stream (northern England)

bent – not altogether legal

bevvied – drunk

bevvy – a drink (originally from northern England)

bill – restaurant check

billion – the British billion is a million million (unlike the American billion – a thousand million)

biscuit – cookie

bitter – beer

black pudding – a type of sausage made from dried blood and other ingredients

blatherskite – boastful or talkative person (northern England)

bloke – man

bodge job – poor-quality repair

bonnet (of car) – hood

boot (of car) – trunk

boss – covering for the meeting point of the ribs in a vaulted roof

bothy – hut or mountain shelter (Scotland)

brass – memorial common in medieval churches consisting of a brass plate set into the floor or a tomb

bridleway – path that can be used by walkers, horse riders and cyclists

broch – defensive tower (Scotland)

Brummie – a native of Birmingham

bum – backside (not tramp, layabout etc)

bus – local bus; see also *coach*

buttress – vertical support for a wall; see *flying buttress*

BYO – bring your own

C&CC – Camping & Caravanning Club

caff – cheap café

cairn – pile of stones marking path, junction or peak

campanile – free-standing belfry or bell tower

canny – good, great, wise (northern England)

capital – head of column

cenotaph – a tomblike monument, memorial to person/s whose remains lie elsewhere

chancel – eastern end of the church, usually reserved for choir and clergy

chantry – chapel established by a donor for use in their name after death

chapel – small, more private shrine or area of worship off the main body of the church

chapel of ease – chapel built for those who lived too far away from the parish church

chapterhouse – building in a cathedral close where the dean meets with the chapter, the clergy who run the cathedral

cheers – goodbye; thanks; also a drinking toast

chemist – pharmacist

chevet – chapels radiating out in a semicircular sweep

chine – valleylike fissure leading to the sea (southern England)

chips – deep-fried potato pieces, fries

choir – area in the church where the choir is seated

circus – a junction of several streets, usually circular

clerestory – also clearstory; a wall of windows above the triforium in a church

cloister – covered walkway linking the church with adjacent monastic buildings

close – buildings grouped around a cathedral, also known as the precincts

clunch – chalk (used in connection with chalk walls in building)

coach – long-distance bus

coaching inn – inn along a stagecoach route at which horses were changed in the days before trains and motor transport

coasteering – adventurous activity which involves making your way around a rocky coastline by climbing, scrambling, jumping or swimming

cob – mixture of mud and straw for building

collegiate – church with a chapter of canons and prebendaries, but not a cathedral

corbel – stone or wooden projection from a wall supporting a beam or arch

cot – crib
couchette – sleeping berth in a train or ferry
courgette – zucchini
courts – courtyards
crack – good conversation (originally from Ireland)
cream tea – a cup of tea and a scone with jam and thick cream
crisps – potato chips
croft – plot of land with adjoining house worked by the occupiers
crossing – intersection of the nave and transepts in a church

dear – expensive
DIY – do-it-yourself, as in handyman shop
dolmen – chartered tomb
donkey engine – small (sometimes portable) engine to drive machinery
dosh – money, wealth
dough – money
downs – rolling upland, characterised by lack of trees
dram – whisky measure
duvet – doona

EH – English Heritage
en-suite room – a hotel room with private attached bathroom (ie shower, basin and toilet)
Essex – derogatory adjective, as in Essex girl, meaning tarty, and identified with '80s consumerism
EU – European Union
evensong – daily evening service (Church of England)

fag – cigarette; also a boring task
fagged – exhausted
fanny – female genitals, not backside
fell race – tough running race through hills or moors
fen – drained or marshy low-lying flat land
fiver – five-pound note
flat – apartment
flip-flops – thongs
flying buttress – supporting buttress in the form of one side of an open arch
font – basin used for baptisms, usually towards the western end of a church, often in a separate baptistry
footpath – sidewalk
frater – common room or dining area in a medieval monastery

gaffer – boss or foreman
gate – street (York, and some other northern cities)
gen – information
ginnel – alleyway (Yorkshire)
graft – work (not corruption)
grand – one thousand
greasy spoon – cheap café
grockle – tourist

gutted – very disappointed
guv, guvner – from governor, a respectful term of address for owner or boss; can be used ironically

hammered – drunk
hart – deer
hire – rent
hosepipe – garden hose
hotel – accommodation with food and bar, not always open to passing trade
Huguenots – French Protestants

inn – pub with accommodation

jam – jelly
jelly – jello
jumper – sweater

kippers – salted and smoked fish, traditionally herring
kirk – church

lady chapel – chapel, usually at the eastern end of a cathedral, dedicated to the Virgin Mary
lager lout – see yob
lancet – pointed window in Early English style
lass – young woman (northern England)
ley – clearing
lierne vault – a vault containing many tertiary ribs
lift – elevator
lock – part of a canal or river that can be closed off and the water levels changed to raise or lower boats
lolly – money; also candy on a stick (possibly frozen)
lorry – truck
love – term of address, not necessarily to someone likeable

machair – grass- and wildflower-covered sand dunes
mad – insane, not angry
manky – low quality
Martello tower – small, circular tower used for coastal defence
mate – a friend of any gender, or term of address, usually between males
midge – a mosquito-like insect
minster – a church connected to a monastery
misericord – hinged choir seat with a bracket (often elaborately carved) that can be leant against
motorway – freeway
motte – mound on which a castle was built

naff – inferior, in poor taste
nappies – diapers
nave – main body of the church at the western end, where the congregation gathers
neeps – turnips

NT – National Trust
NYMR – North Yorkshire Moors Railway

oast house – building containing a kiln for drying hops
off-license ('offie') – carry-out alcoholic drinks shop
OS – Ordnance Survey
owlers – smugglers

pargeting – decorative stucco plasterwork
pee ('p') – pence
pete – fortified houses
pimms – a popular English spirit mixed with lemonade, mint and fresh fruit drunk by the pitcher in summer
pint – beer (as in 'let me buy you a pint')
piscina – basin for priests to wash their hands
pissed – drunk (not angry)
pissed off – angry
pitch – playing field
ponce – ostentatious or effeminate male; also to borrow (usually permanently)
pop – fizzy drink (northern England)
postbus – minibus that follows postal delivery routes, carrying mail and passengers
presbytery – eastern area of the chancel beyond the choir, where the clergy operate
priory – religious house governed by a prior, inferior to an abbey
provost – mayor
pulpit – raised box where priest gives sermons
punter – customer

queue – line
quid – pound
quire – medieval term for choir

ramble – a short easy walk
rebud – a heraldic device suggesting the name of its owner
refectory – monastic dining room
reiver – warrior (northern England)
reredos – literally 'behind the back'; backdrop to an altar
return ticket – round-trip ticket
roll-up – roll-your-own cigarette
rood – archaic word for cross (in churches)
rood screen – a screen carrying a rood or crucifix, which separated the nave from the chancel
RSPB – Royal Society for the Protection of Birds
RSPCA – Royal Society for the Prevention of Cruelty to Animals
rubber – eraser
rubbish bin – garbage can
rugger – rugby

sacked – fired
sambo, sarnie – sandwich

sarsen – a sandstone boulder, a geological remnant, usually found in chalky areas (sometimes used in Neolithic constructions, eg Stonehenge, Avebury)
sett – tartan pattern
shag – have sex; also a tough or tiring task
shagged – tired
sheila-na-gig – a Celtic fertility symbol of a woman with exaggerated genitalia, often seen carved in stone on churches and castles. Rare in England, found mainly in The Marches, along border with Wales
shout – to buy a group of people drinks, usually reciprocated
shut – partially covered passage
single ticket – one-way ticket
sixth-form college – further education college
Sloane Ranger – wealthy, superficial, but well-connected young person
snicket – alleyway (York)
snog – long, drawn-out kiss (not just a peck on the cheek)
spondulicks – money
squint – angled opening in a wall or pillar to allow a view of a church's altar
SSSI – Site of Special Scientific Interest
stone – unit of weight equivalent to 14lb or 6.35kg
subway – underpass (for pedestrians)
sweet – candy

ta – thanks
tatties – potatoes
thwaite – clearing in a forest (northern England)
TIC – Tourist Information Centre
ton – one hundred (slang)
tor – Celtic word describing a pointed hill
torch – flashlight
Tory – Conservative (political party)
towpath – a path running beside a river or canal, where horses once towed barges
trainers – tennis shoes or sneakers
transepts – north-south projections from a church's nave, often added at a later date and giving the whole church a cruciform cross-shaped plan
traveller – nomadic person (traditional and new-age hippy types)
triforium – internal wall passage above a church's arcade and below the clerestory; behind it is the 'blind' space above the side aisle
tron – public weighbridge
tube – London's underground railway
twit – a foolish (sometimes annoying) person
twitcher – obsessive birdwatcher
twitten – passage, small lane

undercroft – vaulted underground room or cellar
underground – London's underground railway (subway)

VAT – value-added tax, levied on most goods and services, currently 17.5%

vault – roof with arched ribs, usually in a decorative pattern

verderer – officer upholding law and order in the royal forests

vestry – robing room, where the parson keeps his robes and puts them on

wanker – a stupid/worthless person (offensive slang)

wide boy – ostentatious go-getter, usually on the make

wolds – open, rolling countryside

yob – hooligan

ziggurat – rectangular temple tower or tiered mound

Behind the Scenes

THIS BOOK

This is the 6th edition of Lonely Planet's *Great Britain* guide. The 1st edition was written by Richard Everest, Tony Wheeler and Bryn Thomas; the 2nd edition was updated by Bryn Thomas, Sean Sheehan and Pat Yale. The 3rd edition was written by Bryn Thomas, Tom Smallman and Pat Yale; the 4th edition was updated by Ryan ver Berkmoes, Lou Callan, Nick Ray, Fionn Davenport, Neal Bedford, Oda O'Carroll and Tom Smallman; the 5th edition was updated by David Else, Abigail Hole, Alan Murphy, Fionn Davenport, Martin Hughes, Nicky Crowther and Paul Bloomfield.

David Else coordinated this edition, and wrote the front and end matter; Etain O'Carroll covered The Marches and Oxfordshire, Gloucestershire & The Cotswolds, and part of the Southwest England chapter; Fionn Davenport did the Northeast and Northwest and Yorkshire; Becky Ohlsen took care of Eastern England, the Midlands and the Channel Islands; Oliver Berry updated Cumbria and part of Southwest England; Martin Hughes tackled London; Sam Martin researched the Southeast Coast and the Home Counties; Andy Symington covered Scotland; and Nicky Crowther topped it all off with Wales.

The Health chapter was adapted from material written by Dr Caroline Evans. Neil Wilson's text was used for Edinburgh's walking tour and Abigail Hole wrote the walking tour for Cardiff.

THANKS from the Authors

David Else Massive appreciation to my wife Corinne, who kept me topped up with coffee and checked

through all my chapters, making sure they were ready for those wonderful eagle-eyed Lonely Planet editors. Thanks also to co-authors Andy, Etain, Becky, Olly, Fionn, Martin and Nicky for their advice and input on this project, and to the various arts, music, sport and literature specialists who helped me get my facts straight: Heather Dickson, Lydia Cook, Roy Thompson, Sarah Johnstone, John Else, Kate Whateley, Tom Hall and Tom Parkinson. And finally, thanks to Alan Murphy and Amanda Canning at Lonely Planet's London office for editorial guidance and soothing lager beers along the way.

Oliver Berry Special thanks go once again to Susie Berry, for love, listening and long-distance phone calls; to the staff of Britain's tourist offices, especially the ladies of Whitehaven; to the characters I met along the way; to Trevellas for long afternoons and late-night fires; to WW and SC for shining a light; and to the Hobo, my constant travelling companion. Thanks also to my Lonely Planet partners Alan Murphy, who gave me the chance to write about my favourite places, and David Else, who kept the show on the road.

Nicky Crowther Nicky would like to thank the charming B&B ladies, youth hostel wardens and good cooks of Wales for easing the burden of her research, also the folks at home who watched the flocks by night.

Fionn Davenport England is a terrific country, full of friendly, helpful people who made my job a hell of a lot easier. If you met me along the way

---

THE LONELY PLANET STORY

The story begins with a classic travel adventure: Tony and Maureen Wheeler's 1972 journey across Europe and Asia to Australia. There was no useful information about the overland trail then, so Tony and Maureen published the first Lonely Planet guidebook to meet a growing need.

From a kitchen table, Lonely Planet has grown to become the largest independent travel publisher in the world, with offices in Melbourne (Australia), Oakland (USA) and London (UK). Today Lonely Planet guidebooks cover the globe. There is an ever-growing list of books and information in a variety of media. Some things haven't changed. The main aim is still to make it possible for adventurous travellers to get out there – to explore and better understand the world.

At Lonely Planet we believe travellers can make a positive contribution to the countries they visit – if they respect their host communities and spend their money wisely. Every year 5% of company profit is donated to charities around the world.

and succumbed to my pestering ways, I hope you remember me and my gratitude for your guidance. Pestering is a travel writer's lot, it seems, and the staff at LP bore the brunt of much of it, not least Alan Murphy, Amanda Canning et al. Thanks guys and let's do it again sometime. Thanks to Laura Fraser, without whom England just isn't the same. Finally, big thanks to my occasional travel mate and constant soul mate, Libby McCormack, who made even the greyest day seem sunny.

Martin Hughes Thanks to Kirsti, Jeremy, Jane, Sean, Ardal, Melanie, Amanda, Emma, Marco, Gianfranco and Zola. Also, big thanks to Amanda, Fiona and Tom in the London office, for their time, effort and expertise.

Sam Martin Big, big, big thanks to Rob and Holly Burr, whose generous spirit and tiny London flat made this trip possible. Cheers to Phil and his car (but not his driving). Best to Richard in Broadstairs (Good luck in Thailand!), the two Virginia commune dwellers and everyone else who selflessly offered tips and guidance for a Texan in England. Biggest thanks of all go to Denise for all her hard work – I couldn't have done it without you – and to the mighty Ford, whose charm and curiosity sparked many a conversation on the road.

Etain O'Carroll Huge thanks to all the patient staff at TICs around my area for answering endless questions and queries, and special thanks to staff in Ironbridge Gorge, Tetbury and Porlock for giving me so much time. Sincere thanks also to Julian Owen, music editor at *Venue Magazine* for his boxed text on the Bristol Music Scene, and to Glyn Whiting in Pembridge for the local lowdown. Thanks also to Adrian Southgate, Pauline Rogers, Ian Sinclair, Frances Rogers and Peter and Sheila Baseby for suggestions on additions to the text and as always, giant thanks to Mark for getting me through what seemed like an endless mountain of paper.

Becky Ohlsen Thanks to David Else, Alan Murphy and Amanda Canning at LP, Matt McNally in Norwich, Anne and Richard Symonds and Phil Jones in Castleton, Zach Hull & Patrick Leyshock of the Sang-Froid Riding Club, Pete Wild, Steve Aylett, John Graham, and everyone in all the tourist offices, museums and pubs who gave me such great travel tips.

Andy Symington Andy sends many thanks to all the people who furnished him with information and help along the road, particularly in TICs. He would also specifically like to give thanks for the generous hospitality of Martin Leonard, Riika Åkerlind, Colin Bell & Amy Allanson, David and Juliette Paton and Jim Walker, for the thirst of many more Scottish friends, and for the support and company of my parents. And lastly, gratitude aplenty to Begoña García de León, for shared whiskies and much more.

CREDITS

The sixth edition of *Great Britain* was commissioned and developed in Lonely Planet's London office by Amanda Canning and Alan Murphy (and many thanks to Imogen Franks). Rachel Imeson and Glenn van der Knijff managed this project, while Andrea Baster, Craig Kilburn and Gina Tsarouhas were the coordinating editors, assisted by an editorial cast of thousands: Sally Hassell, Nancy Ianni, Kate James, Evan Jones, Thalia Kalkipsakis, Joanne Newell, Elizabeth Swan, Katrina Webb and Simon Williamson. Joelene Kowalski coordinated cartography with help from Jovan Djukanovic, Jacqueline Nguyen, Simon Tillema, Chris Thomas, Amanda Sierp and Julie Sheridan. Indra Kilfolye coordinated layout with assistance from Adam Bextream, Jim Hsu, Laura Jane, David Kemp, Jacqui Saunders and Wibowo Rusli.

THANKS from Lonely Planet
Many thanks to the travellers who used the last edition and wrote to us with helpful hints, useful advice and interesting anecdotes:

A Z Abrahams, Oscar Abrahamsson, Palmer Acheson, Jeff Adams, Karen Adamson, Maarten Adelmeijer, Graeme Aitken, Altan Akat, Mils & Kirsten Ake-Anderson, Eddie Alaszewski, Bruno Alazard, Knut Albert Solem, Brooke Aldrich, Kelly Alexander, Greg Alford, Peter H Allan, Trevor Allcott, Graydon Allen, Jennifer Allore, Richard Althoff, Kate Amos, Dick Anderson, Nils Andreas Thommesen, Lynn Andrews, David Antonsen, Elwin Arens, Kaare Arkteg, M & J Armstrong, Chris Arundel, John Astley, Newell Augur, Collette Awberry-Beck, Barbara Axon **B** Don Bacon, Michael Baker, Pam Baker, Bruce Baldey, Vickie Barnes, Lisa Barresi, Bonnie Baskin, G A Battrun, Philip Baum, Leigh Baumann, NP Baykov, Jane Becker, Sarah Bekessy, Carmen Bekker, Graeme Bell, Jinapon & Richard Bell, A Justin Bell, Sarah Bellamy, Michele Beltrame, Jennifer Bennett, David Benson, Maxine Beresford, Linda Berg, Beth Bergen, AH Berry, Jason Berry, Heather Beswick, Mary Bickmore, Michael Bidinger, Roger Bielec, Lisette Billard, L Birnie, Emma H Black, M Blackie, Philip Bladon, James Blakley, J Bly, Marilyn & John Boatman, Bert Bodecker, Anthea Boden, Barbara Bodenschatz, Billie Bonevski, Bernd B Bongartz, Leslie Boot, ID Booth, Shannon Boothman, Dirk Borowski, Sally Bothroyd, David Bounds, James Boyd, The Boyles, Andy Bradshaw, Michael Brant, Barry & Rosmary Breed, EM Bremmer, Alasdair Brooks, Louise & Stephen Broughton, Chris Brown, Hannah Brown, Joanna Brown,

Melanie Brown, Rosemary Brown, Ron Browne, M Ter Brugge, Mike Brycefound, Julian Bryers, Klaus Bryn, Ian Buchanan, KA Burnett, Laura Burr, Elvira Burster, Nicholas Burton, Dana Byerley **C** Sonia Cairns, Fran Callinan, Christopher Calvert, Joe Campbell, Liam Campbell, Lisa Cantonwine, Helen Cardrick, Gary & Jessie Carlson, Fo Carmichael-Jones, James Carr, Alex Castrodale, Maxine Caws, Simon Chambers, Jane Chandler, Hortensia Chang, Wilma Chappill, Ted Charlton, Jonathan Chatfield, Michelle Chee, Simon Chegg, Fei Chiao Liao, Ian Chivas, Lynn R Chong, Mette Christiansen, Amanda Christie, Melissa Christie, Goldie Church, JM Cimelli, Tim Clack, Alan Clark, M & M Clark, Fiona Clarke, Patrice Clausse, James Cocks, Bill Coker, Sandy Colburn, Daniel & Marie Cole, Robyne & Bob Collings, Gez Collins, Tracey Collins, Margaret Combs, Belinda Coombs, Dee Cooper, WB Cooper, David Cope, Nicola Coppola, Jodie Cordell, Christian Corkin, Rose Corney, Dominic Coughlin, Daniel Cox, Tony Craggs, Sallt Craiborne, Jean Craig, Karen Crawford, Graham Crews, C Croke, Bob Cromwell, Mike Crook, Stephen Cross, Joseph Cultice, Pam Currie, Rebecca Cutri-Kohart **D** H Daddona, Mark Daker, Martin Dammann, Pam Davidson, Tamsin Davidson, Jean Davidson Sinclair, Norma Davies, Richard Davies, Kara Davis, Sue Davis, Keith Dawson, Chris Day, Mary De Ruyter, Antoine De Vermouthier, Simone De Wet, Ron Deacon, Dawn Dean, Andre Delfos, Garry Denke, Kate Dennis, Robin DeWan, Nicky Dewey, Julieanne & Stephen Dimitrios, Anne Dolan, Amanda Donovan, S Dorn, Dennis Dorney, Eliane Dosker, Gina Doubleday, Marie & Stewart Dougan, Jennifer Doyle, B Doyle, Peter Draper, Eve Drimmie, Leanne Drummond, Michael Dudley, Barbara Dunn, Phil Dunnington, Helen Dupplaw, Anneli Dyall, Julie Dyer **E** Alison East, Ashley Eastwood, Mark Edebone, Sally Edwards, Robert Egg, Wendy & Tom Ellingham, Tiffany Ellis, Toby Ellison, Kalvin Embling, Hanne Espolin Johnson, Wayne Evan **F** Emmanuel Fankhauser, Gunda Feddersen, Karen, Sarah Feigh, Graybeal, Chris Ferguson, Gregory Fields, Maggie Fifoot, Sue Findlay, Beth Ann Finlay, Jody Finver, Jack FitzSimons, FB Fogarty, Belinda Fogg, Karen & Roberta For, John Forde, Terry Forkwit, Paola Formenti, Dell Forrester, James Forrester, Carol Forsyth, Louise Foster, S Fotini, Emma Foulger, Meg Francis, John Franklin, Melissa Freeland, Heidrun Fritsch, Patricia & Richard Fryett, Johnathan Fuller, Peter Fulop, Mr & Mrs Fyvie **G** Scott Gaeckle, Janice Gahan,

Peter Gainsford, Fran Gale, Oscar Gallego, Rachelle Garland, Paul Garrett, Valerie Garrett, Mark Gaskell, Alma & Joe Gaskill, Cindy Geyer, Chris Gibb, Scott Gilmore, Nicole Glaser, Christian Glockner, Andrew Gnoza, David Godley, Kirsten & Arron Goodwin, Mathew Gore, Ruth Goreham, Louise Gorrie, Denise Gow, S Graham, Meahan Grande, Katie Grant, Matthew Gream, John Green, Paul Greening, Debbie Greenstreet, Edith Gregoire, D Greiling, E Griffiths, Mike Griffiths, Bjorn Olav Gruner Kvam, Cath Gurlick, Sarah Guy **H** Andrew Haas, Ursula Haas, Jo Ann & Mark Haendel, Pam Hainsworth, Samantha Halewood, Paul Hallam, Denis Halliwell, Honey Halpern, Nigel Hamilton, Britta Hammersley, Charis Hammond, Kym Hammond, Andy Hancock, Julie Handley, Graham Hannaford, Lina Harbinson, Cecilia Harlitz, Charles Harmer, Wendy & Mike Harper, C Harris, Peter Harry, Karen Hart, Peter Hart, Stephen Harvey, Jenny Harwood, Sue Hawley, Phillipa Hay, Mavis & Doug Haynes, Helen Hazelwood, Allan Henderson, Pauline Henderson, Jim Hendrickson, Alex Hendry, Stacey Henerey, Mike Hergert, John Hesketh, D Higbre, Denise Highton, Indra Hildebrandt, Colin Hill, N Hill, Cheng Hin Saw, Charlotte Hindle, Gloria Hiscock, Ted Hiscock, Babs Hodgin, Fiona Hodson, Marieke Hohnen, Judith Holbrook, J R Holder, Amanda Holland, Liz Holman, Becky Holmes, Mark Holmes, Natalie Holmes, Janita Holt, S P Holt, R Honeyman, Mark Houlder, Jan Howard Finder, KB Hubbard, Alvin T. Hudec, Mark Hudson, David Hugh Smith, Christine Hughes, Victoria Hughes, Nick Humphrey, Jill & Rod Hunter, Mike Huntington, Carol Hutton, Heather Hutton, James Hyde, Christiane Hyde Citron, **I** Suzanne Ingram Armstrong, Takayoshi Ito **J** Colin Jack, Marcia Jackson, Paul Jackson, Stephan Jacobi, Marian Jago, Barbara James, Diana James, Jennifer Jameson, Tanya Janzen, Jill Jarvis, Simon Jason, Willan T Jenkins, Ann Johns, A Johnston, MD Jones, Rob Jones, Leah Judd, Muijel Juittio, AV Julian **K** Uli Kaiser, Noa Kamrat, Jerry & Irene Katz, Robert Kavash, Robert & Ellen Kavash, LR Keane, Dr John Kennedy, Yvonne & Peter Kerr, Hans-Dieter Kerstholt, Roslyn Kinett, MJ Kinrade, Christine Kirton, Tony Kirwood, Kathy Kitao, Sue Kitchin, Cato Kjavvik, Meaghan Kombol, Ivana Kotalova, Brian Kovacsi, Simon Kretschmer, Pavlina Krzovski, H Kuivenhoven **L** DJ Lake, Jackie Lake, Rich Lamuru, Donna Lancaster, Kristine Lang, Monica Lanier, Lucie LaPlante, Kylie Lawrence, Heather Lawson, Gareth Lawton, Cecilia Leishman,

SEND US YOUR FEEDBACK

We love to hear from travellers – your comments keep us on our toes and help make our books better. Our well-travelled team reads every word on what you loved or loathed about this book. Although we cannot reply individually to postal submissions, we always guarantee that your feedback goes straight to the appropriate authors, in time for the next edition. Each person who sends us information is thanked in the next edition – and the most useful submissions are rewarded with a free book.

To send us your updates – and find out about Lonely Planet events, newsletters and travel news – visit our award-winning website: **www.lonelyplanet.com/feedback**.

Note: We may edit, reproduce and incorporate your comments in Lonely Planet products such as guidebooks, websites and digital products, so let us know if you don't want your comments reproduced or your name acknowledged. For a copy of our privacy policy visit www.lonelyplanet .com/privacy.

Cherie LeLievre, Peter Lemtis, Jamie Leveille, Gaye & Andrew Leverton, Jenny Leviston, Felicia Lim, Sharon Lim, Mike Lima, Jodi Lipson, Simon Lock, Edgar Locke, JP Logan, Peter Lommer Kristensen, Alison Longley, Peggy Longley, R Loomes, Sheila & John Lough, MJ Louis, Tammara Lowdell, Derek Luce, Jodie Lugton, Charlotte Luongo, Clare Lynam **M** Trine & Bruce MacAdam, Chris MacCarthy, Shelley MacGregor, Kristina Macku, Hilda MacLean, Ofra Magidor, Robyn Mainsbridge, Lawrence Manion, Mitzi & Pete Margetts, John Markham, PD & SY Markham, KL Marsden, Brent Marshall, James Marshall, Tony & Elaine Martin, Tanya Martion, Ron Matson, Pat Matsumoto, Jory F Mattison, Ira Matuschke, Glen Mauchline, Sandra Mayo, Paula Mazzocato, Jamie McBride, Frank McCready, Sarah McDonald, Kenneth Mcfarlane, Tim McFarlane, Paul McGirr, Richard & Jane McGowan, Sharon McGrath, Ross McGregor, V McHugh, Than McIntosh, Luke McKean, Brendan McKenzie, Catherine Mclean, Donny McLean, Iain McPherson, Tim McVicar, Helen McWilliam, Katie Mecke, Caroline Mecklem, John Meehan, Pete & Deb Meigs, Jihn & Jillian Meredith, Margart Micheben, D & O Middleton, O. Middleton, Joan Midgley-Wood, Jo Miklosi, Kathleen Millea, Craig Miller, Langdon Miller, Martin Miller, Rod Miller, Edward Mills, Ann Mione, Brenda Miskie, Paul Mitchell, Keith Moody, Matt Moore, Susan Moore, Audrey Moran, Bethan Morgan, Dan Morris, Deidre Morrow, Trish Morrow, Kay Mould, PH Mountford, Kathryn Mumell, David Murray, Sarah Musts **N** Anand Narasimhan, Toni Nash, Scott Neilson, Margaret Netcaffe, Jeff Newcomer, Jennifer Ngai, Stuart B Nicol, Stewart Nicolson, John & Anne Nield, Dorothy Nielsen, Mil Niepold, Reeves Novak, Nards & Chona Novicio, Richard Nunns **O** Robin Oakes, R Oakes-Garnett, Pam & Gordon Oates, Tim Oliver Eynck, Rebecca O'Meara, Levon Ounanian **P** Esteli Padila, John Palgan, Chris Parker, Linton Parker, Simone Parkinson, Deborah Pascoe, Kevin Paszalek, Carolina Patane, Maisa Patel, S Patel, Jimmy Patrick Haffenrichter, Leigh Patterson, Shalom S Paul, Mike Pavasovic, Kim Pavlak, Mr & Mrs Pearce, Robert Pearl, John Peck, George Peckham, Paul Pederson, John Pender, Robin Percy, Monica & Rok Perkavac, Kate & Bob Perrett, Geraldine Perriam, Jim Peter, Kay Peter, Cathrin Petersen, Katriu Petzer, Karen Phillips, Alison Pickard, Lance Pierce, Janine Pike, Tomaz Pintar, MN Plant, Martin Platt, William Plummer, Susan Pogue, NC Pollack, Elizabeth Poole, R Porter, Stephen Porter, Claire Potgieter, Dee Poujade, Melissa Powell, Thomas G Power, Robin Preece, Jason Prisley, Heather Pruiksma, Joan Pryse, Stefan Punkenhofer, Ivone Purnami **Q** VI Quarmby, Betty Quast **R** Mark Rainsley, Karlmarx Rajangam, J Ramano, M Ramsay, L Rapke, Megan Rapp, Karl Raven, Daniel Reedman, R Rees, William Reeves, Valerie Reichel Moberg, Paula Reid, Steve Reid, Deen Reilly, Timothy Reilly, Thorsten Reiss, DeeDee Remington, Silke Remmel, Anja Renner, Peter Richardson, Craig Richmond, Jo Rider, Mark Ridgwell, Barry Rigby, Evan Roberts, Gareth Roberts, Gillian M Roberts, James Roberts, Kate Robertson, Alicia Robinson, Bernie Robinson, Trish Robson, Raul Rodriguez, Stan Rolfe, Eva Romano, Belinda Romers, W Rosenboom, Rebecca Ross, Jules & Dr Rossman, Ian David Row, Judith Rowell, Amber Rowland, Ed Rozmiarek, Winfried Ruger, Claire Ruscoe, Francis M Russell, Roz Russell, Michelle Ryan, Kim Ryder, Andy Ryland **S** Marcin Sadurski, Marie-Louise Sahraoui, Maria & Colin Sanders, Jeff Sandvig, Peter Sarrett, Tracy Savage, Jo Sawyer, Mark Schiefelbein, Martin Schirra, Biancha Schmitt, Peter Schoch, Bernhard Schoene, Deborah Schubert, Katherine Scott, Nichola Scott, Lucy Scott Brown, Marre Sebastian, Hubert Segain, Michael Seidenbusch, Michele Seigerman, B Van Selm, Steve Senkiw, Sam Sesame, Laura Shanner, Deepak Sharma, A Shepherd, Ruth Sherwin, Laura Shevchenko, Phyl Shimeld, Mark Shuttleworth, Mary Siddall, Rachel Sides, Harvinder Sidhu, Delphine Sifflet, Margie & Lloyd Simes, Pete Simonson, Colette Sinclair, Antonio Skliris, Alex Sky, Michael Slattery, Sue Slogrove, Marnie Smedley, A Smith, Ceri Smith, Dale Smith, Jason Smith, Jean Smith, Judy Smith, Penny Smith, RA Smith, Ray Smith, Sally Smith, Paul Smitz, Timothy So, Vaclav Sochor, Jeremy Speechley, Gary Spinks, Jackie & Jason Staines, Andrew Stark, Emily Stead, Helen Stephen, A Stevens, Rupert Stewart, WG Stockman, Charlotte Stockwell, Kathryn Stokes, Mark Stone, Tina Storm Nielsen, Vanessa Stubbs, Elaine Sutton, Ray Swenson, Thor & Mary Swope, Dorothy E Synnot **T** Terence Tam, Mohit Tandon, Emanuela Tasinto, Simon Taskunas, GF Taylor, Mike Taylor, Peter Taylor, Michael Teague, AR Teesdale, Sandra Tegtmeier, Malla Tennila, Amish Thakkar, Jean Thio, Carol A Thomas, Elizabeth Thomas, James Thomas, Melissa Thomas, Nigel Thomas, Paula Thomas, P & J Thompson, Peter B Thompson, J Thorburn, Christine Tiscareno, Carmel Tobin, Andrea Todd, Robert Torensen-Davies, Heike Trauschies, Yvonne Trevaskis, Chris Truax, Colin Tucker, Lisa Tyndall, Bruce & Beryl Tyrie **U** Masumi Ubukata, Susan Udin, Susanne Ueberhuber **V** Wendy Valois, Rene Van Eijk, Randall Van Someren, Jerry Varner, Sabrina A Varsi, B Vazda, Suzanne Veletta, Hans Von Tour, Sterling Vorus **W** Simon Wake, Richard Walker, Shane Walker, Sue Walker, R Wallis, Maurice Walmsley, Heather Walsh, Alan & Liz Walter, S Walton, Barry Ward, PR Ward, Rosie Ward, Phil Waring, Louis Warwick, RJ Washington, VA Waters, Elaine Weatherston, Genevieve Webb, Julie Webb, Sally Webb, Adrian Wedgewood, Sandra L Wehrley, Sally Weigand, Ulrike Weiss, Linda Weissenburger, Bernard Wellings, Sandra Wells, Kevin Wenlock, W L West III, Richard Wheatley, John & Deborah Wheaton, Judy Whitby, Lisa Elaine White, Stephen Whittaker, Dennis Whittle, Elizabeth Wilder, Kathy Wilhelm, Rod Willard, Kathleen A Williams, Russell Williams, DR Williamson, Ian Willis, Brad Wilson, Diarmuid Wilson, Dom Wilson, Paul Wilson, Royce Wilson, Sandra Winter, Barbara Wolf, Jennifer Wolfersberger, Yvonne Wolff, C Tim Wood, Laura Wood, Margaret Wood, Tim Wood, David Woodhouse, Priscilla Woodward, John Wren, Stewart Wright **Y** Melissa Yap, Elinor Yeo, JM Yeo, Rod York, Caroline Yorke, Andrew Young, Jason Young, Paul Young **Z** Peter Zender, Susan Zimmerman & Morris Zwi.

ACKNOWLEDGMENTS
Many thanks to the following for the use of their content:
Globe on back cover © Mountain High Maps 1993 Digital Wisdom, Inc.; London Underground Map © 2005 London Transport Museum

ACKNOWLEDGMENTS

Index

INDEX

INDEX

INDEX

000 Map pages
000 Location of colour photographs

INDEX

INDEX

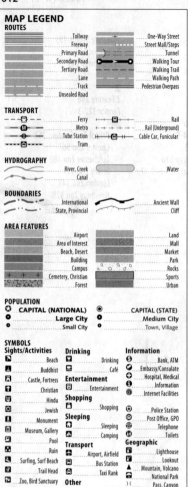

MAP LEGEND
ROUTES

Tollway
Freeway
Primary Road
Secondary Road
Tertiary Road
Lane
Track
Unsealed Road

One-Way Street
Street Mall/Steps
Tunnel
Walking Tour
Walking Trail
Walking Path
Pedestrian Overpass

TRANSPORT

Ferry
Metro
Tube Station
Tram

Rail
Rail (Underground)
Cable Car, Funicular

HYDROGRAPHY

River, Creek
Canal

Water

BOUNDARIES

International
State, Provincial

Ancient Wall
Cliff

AREA FEATURES

Airport
Area of Interest
Beach, Desert
Building
Campus
Cemetery, Christian
Forest

Land
Mall
Market
Park
Rocks
Sports
Urban

POPULATION

⦿ **CAPITAL (NATIONAL)**
● **Large City**
○ Small City

◉ CAPITAL (STATE)
● Medium City
○ Town, Village

SYMBOLS

Sights/Activities
Beach
Buddhist
Castle, Fortress
Christian
Hindu
Jewish
Monument
Museum, Gallery
Pool
Ruin
Surfing, Surf Beach
Trail Head
Zoo, Bird Sanctuary

Eating
Eating

Drinking
Drinking
Café

Entertainment
Entertainment

Shopping
Shopping

Sleeping
Sleeping
Camping

Transport
Airport, Airfield
Bus Station
Taxi Rank

Other
● Other Site
Parking Area

Information
Bank, ATM
Embassy/Consulate
Hospital, Medical
Information
Internet Facilities
Police Station
Post Office, GPO
Telephone
Toilets

Geographic
Lighthouse
Lookout
Mountain, Volcano
National Park
Pass, Canyon
River Flow
Waterfall

LONELY PLANET OFFICES

Australia
Head Office
Locked Bag 1, Footscray, Victoria 3011
☎ 03 8379 8000, fax 03 8379 8111
talk2us@lonelyplanet.com.au

USA
150 Linden St, Oakland, CA 94607
☎ 510 893 8555, toll free 800 275 8555
fax 510 893 8572, info@lonelyplanet.com

UK
72–82 Rosebery Ave,
Clerkenwell, London EC1R 4RW
☎ 020 7841 9000, fax 020 7841 9001
go@lonelyplanet.co.uk

Published by Lonely Planet Publications Pty Ltd
ABN 36 005 607 983

© Lonely Planet 2005

© photographers as indicated 2005

Cover photographs by Lonely Planet Images: South Bank Lion, Charlotte Hindle (front); the Black Cuillin reflected in the waters of a small lochan, Isle of Skye, Gareth McCormack (back). Many of the images in this guide are available for licensing from Lonely Planet Images: www.lonelyplanetimages.com

All rights reserved. No part of this publication may be copied, stored in a retrieval system, or transmitted in any form by any means, electronic, mechanical, recording or otherwise, except brief extracts for the purpose of review, and no part of this publication may be sold or hired, without the written permission of the publisher.

Printed through Colorcraft Ltd, Hong Kong.
Printed in China

Lonely Planet and the Lonely Planet logo are trademarks of Lonely Planet and are registered in the US Patent and Trademark Office and in other countries.

Lonely Planet does not allow its name or logo to be appropriated by commercial establishments, such as retailers, restaurants or hotels. Please let us know of any misuses: www.lonelyplanet.com/ip